REGULATIONS

Title 12
Banks and Banking

Parts 300 to 499

Revised as of January 1, 2012

Containing a codification of documents
of general applicability and future effect

As of January 1, 2012

Published by the Office of the Federal Register
National Archives and Records Administration
as Special Edition of the Federal Register

Table of Contents

	Page
Explanation	v

Title 12:

Chapter III—Federal Deposit Insurance Corporation	3
Chapter IV—Export-Import Bank of the United States	1025

Finding Aids:

Table of CFR Titles and Chapters	1083
Alphabetical List of Agencies Appearing in the CFR	1103
List of CFR Sections Affected	1113

Cite this Code: CFR

To cite the regulations in this volume use title, part and section number. Thus, 12 CFR 303.0 refers to title 12, part 303, section 0.

Explanation

The Code of Federal Regulations is a codification of the general and permanent rules published in the Federal Register by the Executive departments and agencies of the Federal Government. The Code is divided into 50 titles which represent broad areas subject to Federal regulation. Each title is divided into chapters which usually bear the name of the issuing agency. Each chapter is further subdivided into parts covering specific regulatory areas.

Each volume of the Code is revised at least once each calendar year and issued on a quarterly basis approximately as follows:

Title 1 through Title 16..as of January 1
Title 17 through Title 27..as of April 1
Title 28 through Title 41..as of July 1
Title 42 through Title 50..as of October 1

The appropriate revision date is printed on the cover of each volume.

LEGAL STATUS

The contents of the Federal Register are required to be judicially noticed (44 U.S.C. 1507). The Code of Federal Regulations is prima facie evidence of the text of the original documents (44 U.S.C. 1510).

HOW TO USE THE CODE OF FEDERAL REGULATIONS

The Code of Federal Regulations is kept up to date by the individual issues of the Federal Register. These two publications must be used together to determine the latest version of any given rule.

To determine whether a Code volume has been amended since its revision date (in this case, January 1, 2012), consult the "List of CFR Sections Affected (LSA)," which is issued monthly, and the "Cumulative List of Parts Affected," which appears in the Reader Aids section of the daily Federal Register. These two lists will identify the Federal Register page number of the latest amendment of any given rule.

EFFECTIVE AND EXPIRATION DATES

Each volume of the Code contains amendments published in the Federal Register since the last revision of that volume of the Code. Source citations for the regulations are referred to by volume number and page number of the Federal Register and date of publication. Publication dates and effective dates are usually not the same and care must be exercised by the user in determining the actual effective date. In instances where the effective date is beyond the cut-off date for the Code a note has been inserted to reflect the future effective date. In those instances where a regulation published in the Federal Register states a date certain for expiration, an appropriate note will be inserted following the text.

OMB CONTROL NUMBERS

The Paperwork Reduction Act of 1980 (Pub. L. 96-511) requires Federal agencies to display an OMB control number with their information collection request.

Many agencies have begun publishing numerous OMB control numbers as amendments to existing regulations in the CFR. These OMB numbers are placed as close as possible to the applicable recordkeeping or reporting requirements.

OBSOLETE PROVISIONS

Provisions that become obsolete before the revision date stated on the cover of each volume are not carried. Code users may find the text of provisions in effect on a given date in the past by using the appropriate numerical list of sections affected. For the period before April 1, 2001, consult either the List of CFR Sections Affected, 1949–1963, 1964–1972, 1973–1985, or 1986–2000, published in eleven separate volumes. For the period beginning April 1, 2001, a "List of CFR Sections Affected" is published at the end of each CFR volume.

"[RESERVED]" TERMINOLOGY

The term "[Reserved]" is used as a place holder within the Code of Federal Regulations. An agency may add regulatory information at a "[Reserved]" location at any time. Occasionally "[Reserved]" is used editorially to indicate that a portion of the CFR was left vacant and not accidentally dropped due to a printing or computer error.

INCORPORATION BY REFERENCE

What is incorporation by reference? Incorporation by reference was established by statute and allows Federal agencies to meet the requirement to publish regulations in the Federal Register by referring to materials already published elsewhere. For an incorporation to be valid, the Director of the Federal Register must approve it. The legal effect of incorporation by reference is that the material is treated as if it were published in full in the Federal Register (5 U.S.C. 552(a)). This material, like any other properly issued regulation, has the force of law.

What is a proper incorporation by reference? The Director of the Federal Register will approve an incorporation by reference only when the requirements of 1 CFR part 51 are met. Some of the elements on which approval is based are:

(a) The incorporation will substantially reduce the volume of material published in the Federal Register.

(b) The matter incorporated is in fact available to the extent necessary to afford fairness and uniformity in the administrative process.

(c) The incorporating document is drafted and submitted for publication in accordance with 1 CFR part 51.

What if the material incorporated by reference cannot be found? If you have any problem locating or obtaining a copy of material listed as an approved incorporation by reference, please contact the agency that issued the regulation containing that incorporation. If, after contacting the agency, you find the material is not available, please notify the Director of the Federal Register, National Archives and Records Administration, 8601 Adelphi Road, College Park, MD 20740-6001, or call 202-741-6010.

CFR INDEXES AND TABULAR GUIDES

A subject index to the Code of Federal Regulations is contained in a separate volume, revised annually as of January 1, entitled CFR INDEX AND FINDING AIDS. This volume contains the Parallel Table of Authorities and Rules. A list of CFR titles, chapters, subchapters, and parts and an alphabetical list of agencies publishing in the CFR are also included in this volume.

An index to the text of "Title 3—The President" is carried within that volume.

The Federal Register Index is issued monthly in cumulative form. This index is based on a consolidation of the "Contents" entries in the daily Federal Register.

A List of CFR Sections Affected (LSA) is published monthly, keyed to the revision dates of the 50 CFR titles.

REPUBLICATION OF MATERIAL

There are no restrictions on the republication of material appearing in the Code of Federal Regulations.

INQUIRIES

For a legal interpretation or explanation of any regulation in this volume, contact the issuing agency. The issuing agency's name appears at the top of odd-numbered pages.

For inquiries concerning CFR reference assistance, call 202-741-6000 or write to the Director, Office of the Federal Register, National Archives and Records Administration, 8601 Adelphi Road, College Park, MD 20740-6001 or e-mail fedreg.info@nara.gov.

THIS TITLE

Title 12—BANKS AND BANKING is composed of eight vol volumes are arranged in the following order: Parts 1– 299, 300–499, 500–599, part 600–899, and 900–end. The first 1–199 is comprised of chapter I—Comptroller of the Curr Treasury. The second, third and fourth volumes containi prised of chapter II—Federal Reserve System. The fifth 300–499 is comprised of chapter III—Federal Deposit Ins chapter IV—Export-Import Bank of the United States. taining parts 500–599 is comprised of chapter V—Office of partment of the Treasury. The seventh volume containi prised of chapter VI—Farm Credit Administration, chapt Union Administration, chapter VIII—Federal Financing B containing part 900–end is comprised of chapter IX—Fe Board, chapter XI—Federal Financial Institutions Exami XIV—Farm Credit System Insurance Corporation, chapt the Treasury, chapter XVII—Office of Federal Housing En partment of Housing and Urban Development and chapter velopment Financial Institutions Fund, Department of t tents of these volumes represent all of the current regu this title of the CFR as of January 1, 2012.

For this volume, Michele Bugenhagen was Chief Editor Regulations publication program is under the direction of sisted by Ann Worley.

Title 12—Banks and Banking

(This book contains parts 300 to 499)

	Part
CHAPTER III—Federal Deposit Insurance Corporation	303
CHAPTER IV—Export-Import Bank of the United States	400

CHAPTER III—FEDERAL DEPOSIT INSURANCE CORPORATION

SUBCHAPTER A—PROCEDURE AND RULES OF PRACTICE

Part		Page
300–302	[Reserved]	
303	Filing procedures	5
304	Forms, instructions, and reports	48
305–306	[Reserved]	
307	Certification of assumption of deposits and notification of changes of insured status	49
308	Rules of practice and procedure	51
309	Disclosure of information	134
310	Privacy Act regulations	148
311	Rules governing public observation of meetings of the Corporation's Board of Directors	153
312	[Reserved]	
313	Procedures for corporate debt collection	158

SUBCHAPTER B—REGULATIONS AND STATEMENTS OF GENERAL POLICY

323	Appraisals	177
324	[Reserved]	
325	Capital maintenance	181
326	Minimum security devices and procedures and Bank Secrecy Act compliance	287
327	Assessments	289
328	Advertisement of membership	338
329	[Reserved]	
330	Deposit insurance coverage	341
331	[Reserved]	
332	Privacy of consumer financial information	358
333	Extension of corporate powers	385
334	Fair credit reporting	387
335	Securities of nonmember insured banks	420
336	FDIC employees	428
337	Unsafe and unsound banking practices	433
338	Fair housing	439
339	Loans in areas having special flood hazards	442

Part		Page
340	Restrictions on sale of assets by the Federal Deposit Insurance Corporation	446
341	Registration of securities transfer agents	449
342	[Reserved]	
343	Consumer protection in sales of insurance	451
344	Recordkeeping and confirmation requirements for securities transactions	455
345	Community reinvestment	463
346	Disclosure and reporting of CRA-related agreements	484
347	International banking	496
348	Management official interlocks	520
349	Retail foreign exchange transactions	524
350	Disclosure of financial and other information by FDIC-insured State nonmember banks	539
351	[Reserved]	
352	Nondiscrimination on the basis of disability	541
353	Suspicious activity reports	545
357	Determination of economically depressed regions	547
359	Golden parachute and indemnification payments	548
360	Resolution and receivership rules	555
361	Minority and Women Outreach Program contracting	595
362	Activities of insured State banks and insured savings associations	596
363	Annual independent audits and reporting requirements	619
364	Standards for safety and soundness	646
365	Real estate lending standards	655
366	Minimum standards of integrity and fitness for an FDIC contractor	667
367	Suspension and exclusion of contractor and termination of contracts	671
368	Government securities sales practices	680
369	Prohibition against use of interstate branches primarily for deposit production	683
370	Temporary liquidity guarantee program	685
371	Recordkeeping requirements for qualified financial contracts	703
380	Orderly liquidation authority	707
381	Resolution plans	722
390	Regulations transferred from the Office of Thrift Supervision	733
391	Former Office of Thrift Supervision regulations	986

SUBCHAPTER A—PROCEDURE AND RULES OF PRACTICE

PARTS 300-302 [RESERVED]

PART 303—FILING PROCEDURES

Sec.
303.0 Scope.

Subpart A—Rules of General Applicability

303.1 Scope.
303.2 Definitions.
303.3 General filing procedures.
303.4 Computation of time.
303.5 Effect of Community Reinvestment Act performance on filings.
303.6 Investigations and examinations.
303.7 Public notice requirements.
303.8 Public access to filing.
303.9 Comments.
303.10 Hearings and other meetings.
303.11 Decisions.
303.12 Waivers.
303.13 [Reserved]
303.14 Being "engaged in the business of receiving deposits other than trust funds."
303.15 Certain limited liability companies deemed incorporated under State law.
303.16–303.19 [Reserved]

Subpart B—Deposit Insurance

303.20 Scope.
303.21 Filing procedures.
303.22 Processing.
303.23 Public notice requirements.
303.24 Application for deposit insurance for an interim institution.
303.25 Continuation of deposit insurance upon withdrawing from membership in the Federal Reserve System.
303.26–303.39 [Reserved]

Subpart C—Establishment and Relocation of Domestic Branches and Offices

303.40 Scope.
303.41 Definitions.
303.42 Filing procedures.
303.43 Processing.
303.44 Public notice requirements.
303.45 Special provisions.
303.46 Financial education programs that include the provision of bank products and services.
303.47–303.59 [Reserved]

Subpart D—Merger Transactions

303.60 Scope.
303.61 Definitions.
303.62 Transactions requiring prior approval.
303.63 Filing procedures.
303.64 Processing.
303.65 Public notice requirements.
303.66–303.79 [Reserved]

Subpart E—Change in Bank Control

303.80 Scope.
303.81 Definitions.
303.82 Transactions requiring prior notice.
303.83 Transactions not requiring prior notice.
303.84 Filing procedures.
303.85 Processing.
303.86 Public notice requirements.
303.87–303.99 [Reserved]

Subpart F—Change of Director or Senior Executive Officer

303.100 Scope.
303.101 Definitions.
303.102 Filing procedures and waiver of prior notice.
303.103 Processing.
303.104–303.119 [Reserved]

Subpart G—Activities of Insured State Banks

303.120 Scope.
303.121 Filing procedures.
303.122 Processing.
303.123–303.139 [Reserved]

Subpart H—Activities of Insured Savings Associations

303.140 Scope.
303.141 Filing procedures.
303.142 Processing.
303.143–303.159 [Reserved]

Subpart I—Mutual-to-Stock Conversions

303.160 Scope.
303.161 Filing procedures.
303.162 Waiver from compliance.
303.163 Processing.
303.164–303.179 [Reserved]

Subpart J—International Banking

303.180 Scope.
303.181 Definitions.
303.182 Establishing, moving or closing a foreign branch of a state nonmember bank; § 347.103.
303.183 Investment by insured state nonmember banks in foreign organizations; § 347.108.
303.184 Moving an insured branch of a foreign bank.
303.185 Merger transactions involving foreign banks or foreign organizations.

§ 303.0

303.186 Exemptions from insurance requirement for a state branch of a foreign bank; § 347.206.
303.187 Approval for an insured state branch of a foreign bank to conduct activities not permissible for federal branches; § 347.213
303.188–303.199 [Reserved]

Subpart K—Prompt Corrective Action

303.200 Scope.
303.201 Filing procedures.
303.202 Processing.
303.203 Applications for capital distribution.
303.204 Applicationsfor acquisitions, branching, and new lines of business.
303.205 Applications for bonuses and increased compensation for senior executive officers.
303.206 Application for payment of principal or interest on subordinated debt.
303.207 Restricted activities for critically undercapitalized institutions.
303.208–303.219 [Reserved]

Subpart L—Section 19 of the FDI Act (Consent to Service of Persons Convicted of Certain Criminal Offenses)

303.220 Scope.
303.221 Filing procedures.
303.222 Service at another insured depository institution.
303.223 Applicant's right to hearing following denial.
303.224–303.239 [Reserved]

Subpart M—Other Filings

303.240 General.
303.241 Reduce or retire capital stock or capital debt instruments.
303.242 Exercise of trust powers.
303.243 Brokered deposit waivers.
303.244 Golden parachute and severance plan payments.
303.245 Waiver of liability for commonly controlled depository institutions.
303.246 Conversion with diminution of capital.
303.247 Continue or resume status as an insured institution following termination under section 8 of the FDI Act.
303.248 Truth in Lending Act—Relief from reimbursement.
303.2490 Management official interlocks.
303.250 Modification of conditions.
303.251 Extension of time.
303.252–303.259 [Reserved]

Subpart N [Reserved]

AUTHORITY: 12 U.S.C. 378, 1464, 1813, 1815, 1817, 1818, 1819 (Seventh and Tenth), 1820, 1823, 1828, 1831a, 1831e, 1831o, 1831p-1, 1831w, 1835a, 1843(1), 3104, 3105, 3108, 3207; 15 U.S.C. 1601–1607.

SOURCE: 67 FR 79247, Dec. 27, 2002, unless otherwise noted.

§ 303.0 Scope.

(a) This part describes the procedures to be followed by both the FDIC and applicants with respect to applications, requests, or notices (filings) required to be filed by statute or regulation. Additional details concerning processing are explained in related FDIC statements of policy.

(b) Additional application procedures may be found in the following FDIC regulations:

(1) 12 CFR part 327—Assessments (Request for review of assessment risk classification);

(2) 12 CFR part 328—Advertisement of Membership (Application for temporary waiver of advertising requirements);

(3) 12 CFR part 345—Community Reinvestment (CRA strategic plans and requests for designation as a wholesale or limited purpose institution);

Subpart A—Rules of General Applicability

§ 303.1 Scope.

Subpart A prescribes the general procedures for submitting filings to the FDIC which are required by statute or regulation. This subpart also prescribes the procedures to be followed by the FDIC, applicants and interested parties during the process of considering a filing, including public notice and comment. This subpart explains the availability of expedited processing for eligible depository institutions (defined in § 303.2(r)). Certain terms used throughout this part are also defined in this subpart.

§ 303.2 Definitions.

Except as modified or otherwise defined in this part, terms used in this part that are defined in the Federal Deposit Insurance Act (12 U.S.C. 1811 et seq.) have the meanings provided in the Federal Deposit Insurance Act. Additional definitions of terms used in this part are as follows:

(a) *Act* or *FDI Act* means the Federal Deposit Insurance Act (12 U.S.C. 1811 *et seq.*).

(b) *Adjusted part 325 total assets* means adjusted 12 CFR part 325 total assets as calculated and reflected in the FDIC's Report of Examination.

(c) *Adverse comment* means any objection, protest, or other adverse written statement submitted by an interested party relative to a filing. The term adverse comment shall not include any comment concerning the Community Reinvestment Act (CRA), fair lending, consumer protection, or civil rights that the appropriate regional director or designee determines to be frivolous (for example, raising issues between the commenter and the applicant that have been resolved). The term adverse comment also shall not include any other comment that the appropriate regional director or designee determines to be frivolous (for example, a non-substantive comment submitted primarily as a means of delaying action on the filing).

(d) *Amended order to pay* means an order to forfeit and pay civil money penalties, the amount of which has been changed from that assessed in the original notice of assessment of civil money penalties.

(e) *Applicant* means a person or entity that submits a filing to the FDIC.

(f) *Application* means a submission requesting FDIC approval to engage in various corporate activities and transactions.

(g) *Appropriate FDIC region* and *appropriate regional director* mean, respectively, the FDIC region and the FDIC regional director which the FDIC designates as follows:

(1) When an institution or proposed institution that is the subject of a filing or administrative action is not and will not be part of a group of related institutions, the appropriate FDIC region for the institution and any individual associated with the institution is the FDIC region in which the institution or proposed institution is or will be located, and the appropriate regional director is the regional director for that region; or

(2) When an institution or proposed institution that is the subject of a filing or administrative action is or will be part of a group of related institutions, the appropriate FDIC region for the institution and any individual associated with the institution is the FDIC region in which the group's major policy and decision makers are located, or any other region the FDIC designates on a case-by-case basis, and the appropriate regional director is the regional director for that region.

(h) *Associate director* means any associate director of the Division of Supervision and Consumer Protection (DSC) or, in the event such title become obsolete, any official of equivalent authority within the division.

(i) *Book capital* means total equity capital which is comprised of perpetual preferred stock, common stock, surplus, undivided profits and capital reserves, as those items are defined in the instructions of the Federal Financial Institutions Examination Council (FFIEC) for the preparation of Consolidated Reports of Condition and Income for insured banks.

(j) *Comment* means any written statement of fact or opinion submitted by an interested party relative to a filing.

(k) *Corporation* or *FDIC* means the Federal Deposit Insurance Corporation.

(l) *CRA protest* means any adverse comment from the public related to a pending filing which raises a negative issue relative to the Community Reinvestment Act (CRA) (12 U.S.C. 2901 *et seq.*), whether or not it is labeled a protest and whether or not a hearing is requested.

(m) *Deputy director* means the deputy director of the Division of Supervision and Consumer Protection (DSC) or, in the event such title become obsolete, any official of equivalent or higher authority within the division.

(n) *Deputy regional director* means any deputy regional director of the Division of Supervision and Consumer Protection (DSC) or, in the event such title become obsolete, any official of equivalent authority within the same FDIC region of DSC.

(o) *Appropriate FDIC office* means the office designated by the appropriate regional director or designee.

(p) *DSC* means the Division of Supervision and Consumer Protection or, in the event the Division of Supervision

§ 303.2

and Consumer Protection is reorganized, such successor division.

(q) *Director* means the Director of the Division of Supervision and Consumer Protection (DSC) or, in the event such title become obsolete, any official of equivalent or higher authority within the division.

(r) *Eligible depository institution* means a depository institution that meets the following criteria:

(1) Received an FDIC-assigned composite rating of 1 or 2 under the Uniform Financial Institutions Rating System (UFIRS) as a result of its most recent federal or state examination;

(2) Received a satisfactory or better Community Reinvestment Act (CRA) rating from its primary federal regulator at its most recent examination, if the depository institution is subject to examination under part 345 of this chapter;

(3) Received a compliance rating of 1 or 2 from its primary federal regulator at its most recent examination;

(4) Is well-capitalized as defined in the appropriate capital regulation and guidance of the institution's primary federal regulator; and

(5) Is not subject to a cease and desist order, consent order, prompt corrective action directive, written agreement, memorandum of understanding, or other administrative agreement with its primary federal regulator or chartering authority.

(s) *Filing* means an application, notice or request submitted to the FDIC under this part.

(t) *General Counsel* means the head of the Legal Division of the FDIC or any official within the Legal Division exercising equivalent authority for purposes of this part.

(u) *Insider* means a person who is or is proposed to be a director, officer, organizer, or incorporator of an applicant; a shareholder who directly or indirectly controls 10 percent or more of any class of the applicant's outstanding voting stock; or the associates or interests of any such person.

(v) *Institution-affiliated party* shall have the same meaning as provided in section 3(u) of the Act (12 U.S.C. 1813(u)).

(w) *NEPA* means the National Environmental Policy Act of 1969 (42 U.S.C. 4321 *et seq.*).

(x) *NHPA* means the National Historic Preservation Act of 1966 (16 U.S.C. 470 *et seq.*).

(y) *Notice* means a submission notifying the FDIC that a depository institution intends to engage in or has commenced certain corporate activities or transactions.

(z) *Notice to primary regulator* means the notice described in section 8(a)(2)(A) of the Act concerning termination of deposit insurance (12 U.S.C. 1818(a)(2)(A)).

(aa) *Regional counsel* means a regional counsel of the Legal Division or, in the event the title becomes obsolete, any official of equivalent authority within the Legal Division.

(bb) *Regional director* means any regional director in the Division of Supervision and Consumer Protection (DSC), or in the event such title become obsolete, any official of equivalent authority within the division.

(cc) [Reserved]

(dd) *Standard conditions* means the conditions that the FDIC may impose as a routine matter when approving a filing, whether or not the applicant has agreed to their inclusion. The following conditions, or variations thereof, are standard conditions:

(1) That the applicant has obtained all necessary and final approvals from the appropriate federal or state authority or other appropriate authority;

(2) That if the transaction does not take effect within a specified time period, or unless, in the meantime, a request for an extension of time has been approved, the consent granted shall expire at the end of the specified time period;

(3) That until the conditional commitment of the FDIC becomes effective, the FDIC retains the right to alter, suspend or withdraw its commitment should any interim development be deemed to warrant such action; and

(4) In the case of a merger transaction (as defined in ¶ 303.61(a) of this part), including a corporate reorganization, that the proposed transaction not be consummated before the 30th calendar day (or shorter time period as may be prescribed by the FDIC with

the concurrence of the Attorney General) after the date of the order approving the merger transaction.

(ee) *Tier 1 capital* shall have the same meaning as provided in ¶ 325.2(v) of this chapter (12 CFR 325.2(v)).

(ff) *Total assets* shall have the same meaning as provided in ¶ 325.2(x) of this chapter (12 CFR 325.2(x)).

[67 FR 79247, Dec. 27, 2002, as amended at 68 FR 50459, Aug. 21, 2003]

§ 303.3 General filing procedures.

Unless stated otherwise, filings should be submitted to the appropriate FDIC office. Forms and instructions for submitting filings may be obtained from any FDIC regional director. If no form is prescribed, the filing should be in writing; be signed by the applicant or a duly authorized agent; and contain a concise statement of the action requested. For specific filing and content requirements, consult the appropriate subparts of this part. The FDIC may require the applicant to submit additional information.

§ 303.4 Computation of time.

For purposes of this part, and except as otherwise specifically provided, the FDIC begins computing the relevant period on the day after an event occurs (e.g., the day after a substantially complete filing is received by the FDIC or the day after publication begins) through the last day of the relevant period. When the last day is a Saturday, Sunday or federal holiday, the period runs until the end of the next business day.

[67 FR 79247, Dec. 27, 2002, as amended at 68 FR 50459, Aug. 21, 2003]

§ 303.5 Effect of Community Reinvestment Act performance on filings.

Among other factors, the FDIC takes into account the record of performance under the Community Reinvestment Act (CRA) of each applicant in considering a filing for approval of:

(a) The establishment of a domestic branch;

(b) The relocation of the bank's main office or a domestic branch;

(c) The relocation of an insured branch of a foreign bank;

(d) A transaction subject to the Bank Merger Act; and

(e) Deposit insurance.

§ 303.6 Investigations and examinations.

The FDIC may examine or investigate and evaluate facts related to any filing under this chapter to the extent necessary to reach an informed decision and take any action necessary or appropriate under the circumstances.

§ 303.7 Public notice requirements.

(a) *General.* The public must be provided with prior notice of a filing to establish a domestic branch, relocate a domestic branch or the main office, relocate an insured branch of a foreign bank, engage in a merger transaction, initiate a change of control transaction, or request deposit insurance. The public has the right to comment on, or to protest, these types of proposed transactions during the relevant comment period. In order to fully apprise the public of this right, an applicant shall publish a public notice of its filing in a newspaper of general circulation. For specific publication requirements, consult subparts B (Deposit Insurance), C (Branches and Relocations), D (Merger Transactions), E (Change in Bank Control), and J (International Banking) of this part.

(b) *Confirmation of publication.* The applicant shall mail or otherwise deliver a copy of the newspaper notice to the appropriate FDIC office as part of its filing, or, if a copy is not available at the time of filing, promptly after publication.

(c) *Content of notice.* (1) The public notice referred to in paragraph (a) of this section shall consist of the following:

(i) *Name and address of the applicant(s).* In the case of an application for deposit insurance for a de novo bank, include the names of all organizers or incorporators. In the case of an application to establish a branch, include the location of the proposed branch or, in the case of an application to relocate a branch or main office, include the current and proposed address of the office. In the case of a merger application, include the names of all parties to the transaction. In the case of a notice

§ 303.8

of acquisition of control, include the name(s) of the acquiring parties. In the case of an application to relocate an insured branch of a foreign bank, include the current and proposed address of the branch.

(ii) Type of filing being made;

(iii) Name of the depository institution(s) that is the subject matter of the filing;

(iv) That the public may submit comments to the appropriate FDIC regional director;

(v) The address of the appropriate FDIC office where comments may be sent (the same location where the filing will be made);

(vi) The closing date of the public comment period as specified in the appropriate subpart; and

(vii) That the nonconfidential portions of the application are on file in the appropriate FDIC office and are available for public inspection during regular business hours; photocopies of the nonconfidential portion of the application file will be made available upon request.

(2) The requirements of paragraphs (c)(1)(iv) through (vii) of this section may be satisfied through use of the following notice:

Any person wishing to comment on this application may file his or her comments in writing with the regional director of the Federal Deposit Insurance Corporation at the appropriate FDIC office [insert address of office] not later than [insert closing date of the public comment period specified in the appropriate subpart of part 303]. The nonconfidential portions of the application are on file at the appropriate FDIC office and are available for public inspection during regular business hours. Photocopies of the nonconfidential portion of the application file will be made available upon request.

(d) *Multiple transactions.* The FDIC may consider more than one transaction, or a series of transactions, to be a single filing for purposes of the publication requirements of this section. When publishing a single public notice for multiple transactions, the applicant shall explain in the public notice how the transactions are related. The closing date of the comment period shall be the closing date of the longest public comment period that applies to any of the related transactions.

(e) *Joint public notices.* For a transaction subject to public notice requirements by the FDIC and another federal or state banking authority, the FDIC will accept publication of a single joint notice containing all the information required by both the FDIC and the other federal agency or state banking authority, provided that the notice states that comments must be submitted to the appropriate FDIC office and, if applicable, the other federal or state banking authority.

(f) Where public notice is required, the FDIC may determine on a case-by-case basis that unusual circumstances surrounding a particular filing warrant modification of the publication requirements.

§ 303.8 Public access to filing.

(a) *General.* For filings subject to a public notice requirement, any person may inspect or request a copy of the non-confidential portions of a filing (the public file) until 180 days following final disposition of a filing. Following the 180-day period, non-confidential portions of an application file will be made available in accordance with ' 303.8(c). The public file generally consists of portions of the filing, supporting data, supplementary information, and comments submitted by interested persons (if any) to the extent that the documents have not been afforded confidential treatment. To view or request photocopies of the public file, an oral or written request should be submitted to the appropriate FDIC office. The public file will be produced for review not more than one business day after receipt by the appropriate FDIC office of the request (either written or oral) to see the file. The FDIC may impose a fee for photocopying in accordance with § 309.5(f) of this chapter at the rates the FDIC publishes annually in the FEDERAL REGISTER.

(b) *Confidential treatment.* (1) The applicant may request that specific information be treated as confidential. The following information generally is considered confidential:

(i) Personal information, the release of which would constitute a clearly unwarranted invasion of privacy;

(ii) Commercial or financial information, the disclosure of which could result in substantial competitive harm to the submitter; and

(iii) Information, the disclosure of which could seriously affect the financial condition of any depository institution.

(2) If an applicant requests confidential treatment for information that the FDIC does not consider to be confidential, the FDIC may include that information in the public file after notifying the applicant. On its own initiative, the FDIC may determine that certain information should be treated as confidential and withhold that information from the public file.

(c) *FOIA requests*. A written request for information withheld from the public file, or copies of the public file following closure of the file 180 days after final disposition, should be submitted pursuant to the Freedom of Information Act (5 U.S.C. 552) and part 309 of this chapter to the FDIC, Attn: FOIA/Privacy Group, Legal Division, 550 17th Street, NW., Washington, DC 20429.

§ 303.9 Comments.

(a) *Submission of comments*. For filings subject to a public notice requirement, any person may submit comments to the appropriate FDIC regional director during the comment period.

(b) *Comment period*—(1) *General*. Consult appropriate subparts of this part for the comment period applicable to a particular filing.

(2) *Extension*. The FDIC may extend or reopen the comment period if:

(i) The applicant fails to file all required information on a timely basis to permit review by the public or makes a request for confidential treatment not granted by the FDIC that delays the public availability of that information;

(ii) Any person requesting an extension of time satisfactorily demonstrates to the FDIC that additional time is necessary to develop factual information that the FDIC determines may materially affect the application; or

(iii) The FDIC determines that other good cause exists.

(3) *Solicitation of comments*. Whenever appropriate, the appropriate regional director may solicit comments from any person or institution which might have an interest in or be affected by the pending filing.

(4) *Applicant response*. The FDIC will provide copies of all comments received to the applicant and may give the applicant an opportunity to respond.

§ 303.10 Hearings and other meetings.

(a) *Matters covered*. This section covers hearings and other proceedings in connection with filings and determinations for or by:

(1) Deposit insurance by a proposed new depository institution or operating non-insured institution;

(2) An insured state nonmember bank to establish a domestic branch or to relocate a main office or domestic branch;

(3) Relocation of an insured branch of a foreign bank;

(4)(i) Merger transaction which requires the FDIC's prior approval under the Bank Merger Act (12 U.S.C. 1828(c));

(ii) Except as otherwise expressly provided, the provisions of this § 303.10 shall not be applicable to any proposed merger transaction which the FDIC Board of Directors determines must be acted upon immediately to prevent the probable failure of one of the institutions involved, or must be handled with expeditious action due to an existing emergency condition, as permitted by the Bank Merger Act (12 U.S.C. 1828(c)(6));

(5) Nullification of a decision on a filing; and

(6) Any other purpose or matter which the FDIC Board of Directors in its sole discretion deems appropriate.

(b) *Hearing requests*. (1) Any person may submit a written request for a hearing on a filing:

(i) To the appropriate regional director before the end of the comment period; or

(ii) To the appropriate regional director, pursuant to a notice to nullify a decision on a filing issued pursuant to § 303.11(g)(2)(i) or (ii).

(2) The request must describe the nature of the issues or facts to be presented and the reasons why written submissions would be insufficient to make an adequate presentation of those issues or facts to the FDIC. A

§ 303.10

person requesting a hearing shall simultaneously submit a copy of the request to the applicant.

(c) *Action on a hearing request.* The appropriate regional director, after consultation with the Legal Division, may grant or deny a request for a hearing and may limit the issues that he or she deems relevant or material. The FDIC generally grants a hearing request only if it determines that written submissions would be insufficient or that a hearing otherwise would be in the public interest.

(d) *Denial of a hearing request.* If the appropriate regional director, after consultation with the Legal Division, denies a hearing request, he or she shall notify the person requesting the hearing of the reason for the denial. A decision to deny a hearing request shall be a final agency determination and is not appealable.

(e) *FDIC procedures prior to the hearing*—(1) *Notice of hearing.* The FDIC shall issue a notice of hearing if it grants a request for a hearing or orders a hearing because it is in the public interest. The notice of hearing shall state the subject and date of the filing, the time and place of the hearing, and the issues to be addressed. The FDIC shall send a copy of the notice of hearing to the applicant, to the person requesting the hearing, and to anyone else requesting a copy.

(2) The presiding officer shall be the regional director or designee or such other person as may be named by the Board or the Director. The presiding officer is responsible for conducting the hearing and determining all procedural questions not governed by this section.

(f) *Participation in the hearing.* Any person who wishes to appear (participant) shall notify the appropriate regional director of his or her intent to participate in the hearing no later than 10 days from the date that the FDIC issues the Notice of Hearing. At least 5 days before the hearing, each participant shall submit to the appropriate regional director, as well as to the applicant and any other person as required by the FDIC, the names of witnesses, a statement describing the proposed testimony of each witness, and one copy of each exhibit the participant intends to present.

(g) *Transcripts.* The FDIC shall arrange for a hearing transcript. The person requesting the hearing and the applicant each shall bear the cost of one copy of the transcript for his or her use unless such cost is waived by the presiding officer and incurred by the FDIC.

(h) *Conduct of the hearing*—(1) *Presentations.* Subject to the rulings of the presiding officer, the applicant and participants may make opening and closing statements and present and examine witnesses, material, and data.

(2) *Information submitted.* Any person presenting material shall furnish one copy to the FDIC, one copy to the applicant, and one copy to each participant.

(3) *Laws not applicable to hearings.* The Administrative Procedure Act (5 U.S.C. 551 *et seq.*), the Federal Rules of Evidence (28 U.S.C. Appendix), the Federal Rules of Civil Procedure (28 U.S.C. Rule 1 *et seq.*), and the FDIC's Rules of Practice and Procedure (12 CFR part 308) do not govern hearings under this § 303.10.

(i) *Closing the hearing record.* At the applicant's or any participant's request, or at the FDIC's discretion, the FDIC may keep the hearing record open for up to 10 days following the FDIC's receipt of the transcript. The FDIC shall resume processing the filing after the record closes.

(j) *Disposition and notice thereof.* The presiding officer shall make a recommendation to the FDIC within 20 days following the date the hearing and record on the proceeding are closed. The FDIC shall notify the applicant and all participants of the final disposition of a filing and shall provide a statement of the reasons for the final disposition.

(k) *Computation of time.* In computing periods of time under this section, the provisions of § 308.12 of the FDIC's Rules of Practice and Procedure (12 CFR 308.12) shall apply.

(l) *Informal proceedings.* The FDIC may arrange for an informal proceeding with an applicant and other interested parties in connection with a filing, either upon receipt of a written request for such a meeting made during the comment period, or upon the FDIC's own initiative. No later than 10 days prior to an informal proceeding, the appropriate regional director shall notify the applicant and each person who requested a hearing or oral presentation of the date, time, and place of the proceeding. The proceeding may assume any form, including a meeting with FDIC representatives at which participants will be asked to present their views orally. The regional director may hold separate meetings with each of the participants.

(m) *Authority retained by FDIC Board of Directors to modify procedures.* The FDIC Board of Directors may delegate authority by resolution on a case-by-case basis to the presiding officer to adopt different procedures in individual matters and on such terms and conditions as the Board of Directors determines in its discretion. The resolution shall be made available for public inspection and copying in the Office of the General Counsel, Executive Secretary Section under the Freedom of Information Act (5 U.S.C. 552(a)(2)).

§ 303.11 Decisions.

(a) *General procedures.* The FDIC may approve, conditionally approve, deny, or not object to a filing after appropriate review and consideration of the record. The FDIC will promptly notify the applicant and any person who makes a written request of the final disposition of a filing. If the FDIC denies a filing, the FDIC will immediately notify the applicant in writing of the reasons for the denial.

(b) *Authority retained by FDIC Board of Directors to modify procedures.* In acting on any filing under this part, the FDIC Board of Directors may by resolution adopt procedures which differ from those contained in this part when it deems it necessary or in the public interest to do so. The resolution shall be made available for public inspection and copying in the Office of the General Counsel, Executive Secretary Section under the Freedom of Information Act (5 U.S.C. 552(a)(2)).

(c) *Expedited processing.* (1) A filing submitted by an eligible depository institution as defined in § 303.2(r) will receive expedited processing as specified in the appropriate subparts of this part unless the FDIC determines to remove the filing from expedited processing for any of the reasons set forth in paragraph (c)(2) of this section. Except for filings made pursuant to subpart J (International Banking), expedited processing will not be available for any filing that the appropriate regional director does not have delegated authority to approve.

(2) *Removal of filing from expedited processing.* The FDIC may remove a filing from expedited processing at any time prior to final disposition if:

(i) For filings subject to public notice under § 303.7, an adverse comment is received that warrants additional investigation or review;

(ii) For filings subject to evaluation of CRA performance under § 303.5, a CRA protest is received that warrants additional investigation or review, or the appropriate regional director determines that the filing presents a significant CRA or compliance concern;

(iii) For any filing, the appropriate regional director determines that the filing presents a significant supervisory concern, or raises a significant legal or policy issue; or

(iv) For any filing, the appropriate regional director determines that other good cause exists for removal.

(3) For purposes of this section, a significant CRA concern includes, but is not limited to, a determination by the appropriate regional director that, although a depository institution may have an institution-wide rating of satisfactory or better, a depository institution's CRA rating is less than satisfactory in a state or multi-state metropolitan statistical area, or a depository institution's CRA performance is less than satisfactory in a metropolitan statistical area as defined in 12 CFR 345.12 (MSA) or in the non-MSA portion of a state in which it seeks to expand through approval of an application for a deposit facility as defined in 12 U.S.C. 2902(3).

(4) If the FDIC determines that it is necessary to remove a filing from expedited processing pursuant to paragraph (c)(2) of this section, the FDIC promptly will provide the applicant with a written explanation

(d) *Multiple transactions.* If the FDIC is considering related transactions,

§ 303.11

some or all of which have been granted expedited processing, then the longest processing time for any of the related transactions shall govern for purposes of approval.

(e) *Abandonment of filing.* A filing must contain all information set forth in the applicable subpart of this part. To the extent necessary to evaluate a filing, the FDIC may require an applicant to provide additional information. If information requested by the FDIC is not provided within the time period specified by the agency, the FDIC may deem the filing abandoned and shall provide written notification to the applicant and any interested parties that submitted comments to the FDIC that the file has been closed.

(f) *Appeals and requests for reconsideration*—(1) *General.* Appeal procedures for a denial of a change in bank control (subpart E), change in senior executive officer or board of directors (subpart F) or denial of an application pursuant to section 19 of the FDI Act (subpart L) are contained in 12 CFR part 308, subparts D, L, and M, respectively. For all other filings covered by this chapter for which appeal procedures are not provided by regulation or other written guidance, the procedures specified in paragraphs (f) (2) and (3) of this section shall apply. A decision to deny a request for a hearing is a final agency determination and is not appealable.

(2) *Filing procedures.* Within 15 days of receipt of notice from the FDIC that its filing has been denied, any applicant may file a request for reconsideration with the appropriate regional director.

(3) *Content of filing.* A request for reconsideration must contain the following information:

(i) A resolution of the board of directors of the applicant authorizing filing of the request if the applicant is a corporation, or a letter signed by the individual(s) filing the request if the applicant is not a corporation;

(ii) Relevant, substantive information that for good cause was not previously set forth in the filing; and

(iii) Specific reasons why the FDIC should reconsider its prior decision.

(4)–(5) [Reserved]

(6) *Processing.* The FDIC will notify the applicant whether reconsideration will be granted or denied within 15 days of receipt of a request for reconsideration. If a request for reconsideration is granted pursuant to § 303.11(f), the FDIC will notify the applicant of the final agency decision on such filing within 60 days of its receipt of the request for reconsideration.

(g) *Nullification, withdrawal, revocation, amendment, and suspension of decisions on filings*—(1) *Grounds for action.* Except as otherwise provided by law or regulation, the FDIC may nullify, withdraw, revoke, amend or suspend a decision on a filing if it becomes aware at anytime:

(i) Of any material misrepresentation or omission related to the filing or of any material change in circumstance that occurred prior to the consummation of the transaction or commencement of the activity authorized by the decision on the filing; or

(ii) That the decision on the filing is contrary to law or regulation or was granted due to clerical or administrative error.

(iii) Any person responsible for a material misrepresentation or omission in a filing or supporting materials may be subject to an enforcement action and other penalties, including criminal penalties provided in Title 18 of the United States Code.

(2) *Notice of intent and temporary order.* (i) Except as provided in § 303.11(g)(2)(ii), before taking action under this § 303.11(g), the FDIC shall issue and serve on an applicant written notice of its intent to take such action. A notice of intent to act on a filing shall include:

(A) The reasons for the proposed action; and

(B) The date by which the applicant may file a written response with the FDIC.

(ii) The FDIC may issue a temporary order on a decision on a filing without providing an applicant a prior notice of intent if the FDIC determines that:

(A) It is necessary to reevaluate the impact of a change in circumstance prior to the consummation of the transaction or commencement of the activity authorized by the decision on the filing; or

Federal Deposit Insurance Corporation § 303.14

(B) The activity authorized by the filing may pose a threat to the interests of the depository institution's depositors or may threaten to impair public confidence in the depository institution.

(iii) A temporary order shall provide the applicant with an opportunity to make a written response in accordance with § 303.11(g)(3) of this section.

(3) *Response to notice of intent or temporary order.* An applicant may file a written response to a notice of intent or a temporary order within 15 days from the date of service of the notice or temporary order. The written response should include:

(i) An explanation of why the proposed action or temporary order is not warranted; and

(ii)(A) Any other relevant information, mitigation circumstance, documentation, or other evidence in support of the applicant's position. An applicant may also request a hearing under § 303.10.

(B) Failure by an applicant to file a written response with the FDIC to a notice of intent or a temporary order within the specified time period, shall constitute a waiver of the opportunity to respond and shall constitute consent to a final order under this paragraph (g). The FDIC shall consider any such response, if filed in a timely manner, within 30 days of receiving the response.

(4) *Effective date.* All orders issued pursuant to this section shall become effective immediately upon issuance unless otherwise stated therein.

[67 FR 79247, Dec. 27, 2002, as amended at 68 FR 50459, Aug. 21, 2003]

§ 303.12 Waivers.

(a) The Board of Directors, of the FDIC (Board) may, for good cause and to the extent permitted by statute, waiver the applicability of any provision of this chapter.

(b) The provisions of this chapter may be suspended, revoked, amended or waived for good cause shown, in whole or in part, at any time by the Board, subject to the provisions of the Administrative Procedure Act and the provisions of this chapter. Any provision of the rules may be waived by the Board on its own motion or on petition if good cause thereof is shown.

[68 FR 50459, Aug. 21, 2003]

§ 303.13 [Reserved]

§ 303.14 Being "engaged in the business of receiving deposits other than trust funds."

(a) Except as provided in paragraphs (b), (c), and (d) of this section, a depository institution shall be "engaged in the business of receiving deposits other than trust funds" only if it maintains one or more non-trust deposit accounts in the minimum aggregate amount of $500,000.

(b) An applicant for federal deposit insurance under section 5 of the FDI Act, 12 U.S.C. 1815(a), shall be deemed to be "engaged in the business of receiving deposits other than trust funds" from the date that the FDIC approves deposit insurance for the institution until one year after it opens for business.

(c) Any depository institution that fails to satisfy the minimum deposit standard specified in paragraph (a) of this section as of two consecutive call report dates (*i.e.*, March 31st, June 30th, September 30th, and December 31st) shall be subject to a determination by the FDIC that the institution is not "engaged in the business of receiving deposits other than trust funds" and to termination of its insured status under section 8(p) of the FDI Act, 12 U.S.C. 1818(p). For purposes of this paragraph, the first three call report dates after the institution opens for business are excluded.

(d) Notwithstanding any failure by an insured depository institution to satisfy the minimum deposit standard in paragraph (a) of this section, the institution shall continue to be "engaged in the business of receiving deposits other than trust funds" for purposes of section 3 of the FDI Act until the institution's insured status is terminated by the FDIC pursuant to a proceeding under section 8(a) or section 8(p) of the FDI Act. 12 U.S.C. 1818(a) or 1818(p).

§ 303.15 Certain limited liability companies deemed incorporated under State law.

(a) For purposes of the definition of "State bank" in 12 U.S.C. 1813(a)(2) and this Chapter, a banking institution that is chartered as a limited liability company (LLC) under the law of any State is deemed to be "incorporated" under the law of the State, if

(1) The institution is not subject to automatic termination, dissolution, or suspension upon the happening of some event (including, e.g., the death, disability, bankruptcy, expulsion, or withdrawal of an owner of the institution), other than the passage of time;

(2) The exclusive authority to manage the institution is vested in a board of managers or directors that is elected or appointed by the owners, and that operates in substantially the same manner as, and has substantially the same rights, powers, privileges, duties, responsibilities, as a board of directors of a bank chartered as a corporation in the State;

(3) Neither State law, nor the institution's operating agreement, bylaws, or other organizational documents provide that an owner of the institution is liable for the debts, liabilities, and obligations of the institution in excess of the amount of the owner's investment; and

(4) Neither State law, nor the institution's operating agreement, bylaws, or other organizational documents require the consent of any other owner of the institution in order for an owner to transfer an ownership interest in the institution, including voting rights.

(b) For purposes of the Federal Deposit Insurance Act and this Chapter,

(1) Each of the terms "stockholder" and "shareholder" includes an owner of any interest in a bank chartered as an LLC, including a member or participant;

(2) The term "director" includes a manager or director of a bank chartered as an LLC, or other person who has, with respect to such a bank, authority substantially similar to that of a director of a corporation;

(3) The term "officer" includes an officer of a bank chartered as an LLC, or other person who has, with respect to such a bank, authority substantially similar to that of an officer of a corporation; and

(4) Each of the terms "voting stock," "voting shares," and "voting securities" includes ownership interests in a bank chartered as an LLC, as well as any certificates or other evidence of such ownership interests.

[68 FR 7308, Feb. 13, 2003]

§§ 303.16–303.19 [Reserved]

Subpart B—Deposit Insurance

§ 303.20 Scope.

This subpart sets forth the procedures for applying for deposit insurance for a proposed depository institution or an operating noninsured depository institution under section 5 of the FDI Act (12 U.S.C. 1815). It also sets forth the procedures for requesting continuation of deposit insurance for a state-chartered bank withdrawing from membership in the Federal Reserve System and for interim institutions chartered to facilitate a merger transaction. Each bank that results from the conversion of a Federal savings association into multiple banks pursuant to section 5(i)(5) of the Home Owners' Loan Act, 12 U.S.C. 1464(i)(5), is treated as a proposed depository institution or a de novo institution, as appropriate, for purposes of this subpart.

[67 FR 79247, Dec. 27, 2002, as amended at 73 FR 2145, Jan. 14, 2008]

§ 303.21 Filing procedures.

(a) Applications for deposit insurance shall be filed with the appropriate FDIC office. The relevant application forms and instructions for applying for deposit insurance for an existing or proposed depository institution may be obtained from any FDIC regional director.

(b) An application for deposit insurance for an interim depository institution shall be filed and processed in accordance with the procedures set forth in § 303.24, subject to the provisions of § 303.62(b)(2) regarding deposit insurance for interim institutions. An interim institution is defined as a state-

Federal Deposit Insurance Corporation § 303.24

or federally-chartered depository institution that does not operate independently but exists solely as a vehicle to accomplish a merger transaction.

(c) A request for continuation of deposit insurance upon withdrawing from membership in the Federal Reserve System shall be in letter form and shall provide the information prescribed in § 303.25.

§ 303.22 Processing.

(a) *Expedited processing for proposed institutions.* (1) An application for deposit insurance for a proposed institution which will be a subsidiary of an eligible depository institution as defined in § 303.2(r) or an eligible holding company will be acknowledged in writing by the FDIC and will receive expedited processing unless the applicant is notified in writing to the contrary and provided with the basis for that decision. An eligible holding company is defined as a bank or thrift holding company that has consolidated assets of at least $150 million or more; a BOPEC rating of at least "2" for bank holding companies or an above average or "A" rating for thrift holding companies; and at least 75 percent of its consolidated depository institution assets comprised of eligible depository institutions. The FDIC may remove an application from expedited processing for any of the reasons set forth in § 303.11(c)(2).

(2) Under expedited processing, the FDIC will take action on an application within 60 days of receipt of a substantially complete application or 5 days after the expiration of the comment period described in § 303.23, whichever is later. Final action may be withheld until the FDIC has assurance that permission to organize the proposed institution will be granted by the chartering authority. Notwithstanding paragraph (a)(1) of this section, if the FDIC does not act within the expedited processing period, it does not constitute an automatic or default approval.

(b) *Standard processing.* For those applications that are not processed pursuant to the expedited procedures, the FDIC will provide the applicant with written notification of the final action when the decision is rendered.

[67 FR 79247, Dec. 27, 2002, as amended at 68 FR 50459, Aug. 21, 2003]

§ 303.23 Public notice requirements.

(a) *De novo institutions and operating noninsured institutions.* The applicant shall publish a notice as prescribed in § 303.7 in a newspaper of general circulation in the community in which the main office of the depository institution is or will be located. Notice shall be published as close as practicable to, but no sooner than five days before, the date the application is mailed or delivered to the appropriate FDIC office. Comments by interested parties must be received by the appropriate regional director within 30 days following the date of publication, unless the comment period has been extended or reopened in accordance with § 303.9(b)(2).

(b) *Exceptions to public notice requirements.* No publication shall be required in connection with the granting of insurance to a new depository institution established pursuant to the resolution of a depository institution in default, or to an interim depository institution formed solely to facilitate a merger transaction, or for a request for continuation of federal deposit insurance by a state-chartered bank withdrawing from membership in the Federal Reserve System.

§ 303.24 Application for deposit insurance for an interim institution.

(a) *Application required.* Subject to § 303.62(b)(2), a deposit insurance application is required for a state-chartered interim institution if the related merger transaction is subject to approval by a federal banking agency other than the FDIC. A separate application for deposit insurance for an interim institution is not required in connection with any merger requiring FDIC approval pursuant to subpart D of this part.

(b) *Content of separate application.* A letter application for deposit insurance for an interim institution, accompanied by a copy of the related merger

§ 303.25

application, shall be filed with the appropriate FDIC office. The letter application shall briefly describe the transaction and contain a statement that deposit insurance is being requested for an interim institution that does not operate independently but exists solely as a vehicle to accomplish a merger transaction which will be reviewed by a federal banking agency other than the FDIC.

(c) *Processing.* An application for deposit insurance for an interim depository institution will be acknowledged in writing by the FDIC. Final action will be taken within 21 days after receipt of a substantially complete application, unless the applicant is notified in writing that additional review is warranted. If the FDIC does not act within the expedited processing period, it does not constitute an automatic or default approval.

§ 303.25 Continuation of deposit insurance upon withdrawing from membership in the Federal Reserve System.

(a) *Content of application.* To continue its insured status upon withdrawal from membership in the Federal Reserve System, a state-chartered bank shall submit a letter application to the appropriate FDIC office. A complete application shall consist of the following information:

(1) A copy of the letter, and any attachments thereto, sent to the appropriate Federal Reserve Bank setting forth the bank's intention to terminate its membership;

(2) A copy of the letter from the Federal Reserve Bank acknowledging the bank's notice to terminate membership;

(3) A statement regarding any anticipated changes in the bank's general business plan during the next 12-month period; and

(4)(i) A statement by the bank's management that there are no outstanding or proposed corrective programs or supervisory agreements with the Federal Reserve System.

(ii) If such programs or agreements exist, a statement by the applicant that its Board of Directors is willing to enter into similar programs or agreements with the FDIC which would become effective upon withdrawal from the Federal Reserve System.

(b) *Processing.* An application for deposit insurance under this section will be acknowledged in writing by the FDIC. The FDIC shall notify the applicant, within 15 days of receipt of a substantially complete application, either that federal deposit insurance will continue upon termination of membership in the Federal Reserve System or that additional review is warranted and the applicant will be notified, in writing, of the FDIC's final decision regarding continuation of deposit insurance. If the FDIC does not act within the expedited processing period, it does not constitute an automatic or default approval.

§§ 303.26–303.39 [Reserved]

Subpart C—Establishment and Relocation of Domestic Branches and Offices

§ 303.40 Scope.

(a) *General.* This subpart sets forth the application requirements and procedures for insured state nonmember banks to establish a branch, relocate a branch or main office, and retain existing branches after the interstate relocation of the main office subject to the approval by the FDIC pursuant to sections 13(f), 13(k), 18(d) and 44 of the FDI Act.

(b) *Merger transaction.* Applications for approval of the acquisition and establishment of branches in connection with a merger transaction under section 18(c) of the FDI Act (12 U.S.C. 1828(c)), are processed in accordance with subpart D (Merger Transactions) of this part.

(c) *Insured branches of foreign banks and foreign branches of domestic banks.* Applications regarding insured branches of foreign banks and foreign branches of domestic banks are processed in accordance with subpart J (International Banking) of this part.

(d) *Interstate acquisition of individual branch.* Applications requesting approval of the interstate acquisition of an individual branch or branches located in a state other than the applicant's home state without the acquisition of the whole bank are treated as

Federal Deposit Insurance Corporation § 303.42

interstate bank merger transactions under section 44 of the FDI Act (12 U.S.C. 1831a(u)), and are processed in accordance with subpart D (Merger Transactions) of this part.

§ 303.41 Definitions.

For purposes of this subpart:

(a) *Branch*, except as provided in this paragraph, includes any branch bank, branch office, additional office, or any branch place of business located in any State of the United States or in any territory of the United States, Puerto Rico, Guam, American Samoa, the Trust Territory of the Pacific Islands, the Virgin Islands, and the Northern Mariana Islands at which deposits are received or checks paid or money lent. A branch does not include an automated teller machine, an automated loan machine, a remote service unit, or a facility described in section 303.46. The term branch also includes the following:

(1) A *messenger service* that is operated by a bank or its affiliate that picks up and delivers items relating to transactions in which deposits are received or checks paid or money lent. A messenger service established and operated by a non-affiliated third party generally does not constitute a branch for purposes of this subpart. Banks contracting with third parties to provide messenger services should consult with the FDIC to determine if the messenger service constitutes a branch.

(2) A *mobile branch*, other than a messenger service, that does not have a single, permanent site and uses a vehicle that travels to various locations to enable the public to conduct banking business. A mobile branch may serve defined locations on a regular schedule or may serve a defined area at varying times and locations.

(3) A *temporary branch* that operates for a limited period of time not to exceed one year as a public service, such as during an emergency or disaster situation.

(4) A *seasonal branch* that operates at various periodically recurring intervals, such as during state and local fairs, college registration periods, and other similar occasions.

(b) *Branch relocation* means a move within the same immediate neighborhood of the existing branch that does not substantially affect the nature of the business of the branch or the customers of the branch. Moving a branch to a location outside its immediate neighborhood is considered the closing of an existing branch and the establishment of a new branch. Closing of a branch is covered in the FDIC Statement of Policy Concerning Branch Closing Notices and Policies. 1 FDIC Law, Regulations, Related Acts 5391; see § 309.4 (a) and (b) of this chapter for availability.

(c) *De novo branch* means a branch of a bank which is established by the bank as a branch and does not become a branch of such bank as a result of:

(1) The acquisition by the bank of an insured depository institution or a branch of an insured depository institution; or

(2) The conversion, merger, or consolidation of any such institution or branch.

(d) *Home state* means the state by which the bank is chartered.

(e) *Host state* means a state, other than the home state of the bank, in which the bank maintains, or seeks to establish and maintain, a branch.

[67 FR 79247, Dec. 27, 2002, as amended at 73 FR 35338, June 23, 2008; 73 FR 55432, Sept. 25, 2008]

§ 303.42 Filing procedures.

(a) *General.* An applicant shall submit an application to the appropriate FDIC office on the date the notice required by § 303.44 is published, or within 5 days after the date of the last required publication.

(b) *Content of filing.* A complete letter application shall include the following information:

(1) A statement of intent to establish a branch, or to relocate the main office or a branch;

(2) The exact location of the proposed site including the street address. With regard to messenger services, specify the geographic area in which the services will be available. With regard to a mobile branch specify the community or communities in which the vehicle will operate and the manner in which it will be used;

(3) Details concerning any involvement in the proposal by an insider of

§ 303.43

the bank as defined in § 303.2(u), including any financial arrangements relating to fees, the acquisition of property, leasing of property, and construction contracts;

(4) A statement on the impact of the proposal on the human environment, including, information on compliance with local zoning laws and regulations and the effect on traffic patterns for purposes of complying with the applicable provisions of the NEPA and the FDIC Statement of Policy on NEPA (1 FDIC Law, Regulations, Related Acts 5185; see § 309.4 (a) and (b) of this chapter for availability);

(5) A statement as to whether or not the site is eligible for inclusion in the National Register of Historic Places for purposes of complying with applicable provisions of the NHPA and the FDIC Statement of Policy on NHPA (1 FDIC Law, Regulations, Related Acts 5175; see § 309.4 (a) and (b) of this chapter for availability) including documentation of consultation with the State Historic Preservation Officer, as appropriate;

(6) Comments on any changes in services to be offered, the community to be served, or any other effect the proposal may have on the applicant's compliance with the CRA;

(7) A copy of each newspaper publication required by § 303.44 of this subpart, the name and address of the newspaper, and date of the publication;

(8) When an application is submitted to relocate the main office of the applicant from one state to another, a statement of the applicant's intent regarding retention of branches in the state where the main office exists prior to relocation.

(c) *Undercapitalized institutions.* Applications to establish a branch by applicants subject to section 38 of the FDI Act (12 U.S.C. 1831o) also should provide the information required by § 303.204. Applications pursuant to sections 38 and 18(d) of the FDI Act (12 U.S.C. 1831o and 1828(d)) may be filed concurrently or as a single application.

(d) *Additional information.* The FDIC may request additional information to complete processing.

§ 303.43 Processing.

(a) *Expedited processing for eligible depository institutions.* An application filed under this subpart by an eligible depository institution as defined in § 303.2(r) will be acknowledged in writing by the FDIC and will receive expedited processing, unless the applicant is notified in writing to the contrary and provided with the basis for that decision. The FDIC may remove an application from expedited processing for any of the reasons set forth in § 303.11(c)(2). Absent such removal, an application processed under expedited processing will be deemed approved on the latest of the following:

(1) The 21st day after receipt by the FDIC of a substantially complete filing;

(2) The 5th day after expiration of the comment period described in § 303.44; or

(3) In the case of an application to establish and operate a de novo branch in a state that is not the applicant's home state and in which the applicant does not maintain a branch, the 5th day after the FDIC receives confirmation from the host state that the applicant has both complied with the filing requirements of the host state and submitted a copy of the application with the FDIC to the host state bank supervisor.

(b) *Standard processing.* For those applications which are not processed pursuant to the expedited procedures, the FDIC will provide the applicant with written notification of the final action when the decision is rendered.

§ 303.44 Public notice requirements.

(a) *Newspaper publications.* For applications to establish or relocate a branch, a notice as described in § 303.7(c) shall be published once in a newspaper of general circulation. For applications to relocate a main office, notice shall be published at least once each week on the same day for two consecutive weeks. The required publication shall be made in the following communities:

(1) *To establish a branch.* In the community in which the main office is located and in the communities to be served by the branch (including messenger services and mobile branches).

(2) *To relocate a main office.* In the community in which the main office is

Federal Deposit Insurance Corporation § 303.61

currently located and in the community to which it is proposed the main office will relocate.

(3) *To relocate a branch.* In the community in which the branch is located.

(b) *Public comments.* Comments by interested parties must be received by the appropriate regional director within 15 days after the date of the last newspaper publication required by paragraph (a) of this section, unless the comment period has been extended or reopened in accordance with §303.9(b)(2).

(c) *Lobby notices.* In the case of applications to relocate a main office or a branch, a copy of the required newspaper publication shall be posted in the public lobby of the office to be relocated for at least 15 days beginning on the date of the last published notice required by paragraph (a) of this section.

§ 303.45 Special provisions.

(a) *Emergency or disaster events.* (1) In the case of an emergency or disaster at a main office or a branch which requires that an office be immediately relocated to a temporary location, applicants shall notify the appropriate FDIC office within 3 days of such temporary relocation.

(2) Within 10 days of the temporary relocation resulting from an emergency or disaster, the bank shall submit a written application to the appropriate FDIC office, that identifies the nature of the emergency or disaster, specifies the location of the temporary branch, and provides an estimate of the duration the bank plans to operate the temporary branch.

(3) As part of the review process, the FDIC will determine on a case by case basis whether additional information is necessary and may waive public notice requirements.

(b) *Redesignation of main office and existing branch.* In cases where an applicant desires to redesignate its main office as a branch and redesignate an existing branch as the main office, a single application shall be submitted. The FDIC may waive the public notice requirements in instances where an application presents no significant or novel policy, supervisory, CRA, compliance or legal concerns. A waiver will be granted only to a redesignation within the applicant's home state.

(c) *Expiration of approval.* Approval of an application expires if within 18 months after the approval date a branch has not commenced business or a relocation has not been completed.

§ 303.46 Financial education programs that include the provision of bank products and services.

No branch application or prior approval is required in order for a state nonmember bank to participate in one or more financial education programs that involve receiving deposits, paying withdrawals, or lending money if:

(a) Such service or services are provided on school premises, or a facility used by the school;

(b) Such service or services are provided at the discretion of the school;

(c) The principal purpose of each program is financial education. For example, the principal purpose of a program would be considered to be financial education if the program is designed to teach students the principles of personal financial management, banking operations, or the benefits of saving for the future, and is not designed for the purpose of profit-making; and

(d) Each program is conducted in a manner that is consistent with safe and sound banking practices and complies with applicable law.

[73 FR 35338, June 23, 2008]

§§ 303.47–303.59 [Reserved]

Subpart D—Merger Transactions

§ 303.60 Scope.

This subpart sets forth the application requirements and procedures for transactions subject to FDIC approval under the Bank Merger Act, section 18(c) of the FDI Act (12 U.S.C. 1828(c)). Additional guidance is contained in the FDIC "Statement of Policy on Bank Merger Transactions" (1 FDIC Law, Regulations, Related Acts 5145; see §309.4(a) and (b) of this chapter for availability).

§ 303.61 Definitions.

For purposes of this subpart:

(a) *Merger transaction* includes any transaction:

21

§ 303.62

(1) In which an insured depository institution merges or consolidates with any other insured depository institution or, either directly or indirectly, acquires the assets of, or assumes liability to pay any deposits made in, any other insured depository institution; or

(2) In which an insured depository institution merges or consolidates with any noninsured bank or institution or assumes liability to pay any deposits made in, or similar liabilities of, any noninsured bank or institution, or in which an insured depository institution transfers assets to any noninsured bank or institution in consideration of the assumption of any portion of the deposits made in the insured depository institution.

(b) *Corporate reorganization* means a merger transaction that involves solely an insured depository institution and one or more of its affiliates.

(c) *Interim merger transaction* means a merger transaction (other than a purchase and assumption transaction) between an operating depository institution and a newly-formed depository institution or corporation that will not operate independently and that exists solely for the purpose of facilitating a corporate reorganization.

(d) *Resulting institution* refers to the acquiring, assuming or resulting institution in a merger transaction.

[67 FR 79247, Dec. 27, 2002, as amended at 71 FR 20526, Apr. 21, 2006; 73 FR 2145, Jan. 14, 2008]

§ 303.62 Transactions requiring prior approval.

(a) *Merger transactions.* The following merger transactions require the prior written approval of the FDIC under this subpart:

(1) Any merger transaction, including any corporate reorganization, interim merger transaction, or optional conversion, in which the resulting institution is to be an insured state nonmember bank; and

(2) Any merger transaction, including any corporate reorganization or interim merger transaction, that involves an uninsured bank or institution.

(b) *Related provisions.* Transactions covered by this subpart also may be subject to other provisions or application requirements, including the following:

(1) *Interstate merger transactions.* Merger transactions between insured banks that are chartered in different states are subject to the provisions of section 44 of the FDI Act (12 U.S.C. 1831u). In the case of a merger transaction that consists of the acquisition by an out of state bank of a branch without acquisition of the bank, the branch is treated for section 44 purposes as a bank whose home state is the state in which the branch is located.

(2) *Deposit insurance.* An application for deposit insurance will be required in connection with a merger transaction between a state-chartered interim institution and an insured depository institution if the related merger application is being acted upon by a federal banking agency other than the FDIC. If the FDIC is the federal banking agency responsible for acting on the related merger application, a separate application for deposit insurance is not necessary. Procedures for applying for deposit insurance are set forth in subpart B of this part. An application for deposit insurance will not be required in connection with a merger transaction (other than a purchase and assumption transaction) of a federally-chartered interim institution and an insured institution, even if the resulting institution is to operate under the charter of the federal interim institution.

(3) *Branch closings.* Branch closings in connection with a merger transaction are subject to the notice requirements of section 42 of the FDI Act (12 U.S.C. 1831r–1), including requirements for notice to customers. These requirements are addressed in the "Interagency Policy Statement Concerning Branch Closings Notices and Policies" (1 FDIC Law, Regulations, Related Acts (FDIC) 5391; see § 309.4(a) and (b) of this chapter for availability.)

(4) *Undercapitalized institutions.* Applications for a merger transaction by applicants subject to section 38 of the FDI Act (12 U.S.C. 1831o) should also provide the information required by § 303.204. Applications pursuant to sections 38 and 18(c) of the FDI Act (12

Federal Deposit Insurance Corporation § 303.64

U.S.C, 1831*o* and 1828(c)) may be filed concurrently or as a single application.

(5) *Certification of assumption of deposit liability.* An insured depository institution assuming deposit liabilities of another insured institution must provide certification of assumption of deposit liability to the FDIC in accordance with 12 CFR part 307.

[67 FR 79247, Dec. 27, 2002, as amended at 71 FR 20526, Apr. 21, 2006]

§ 303.63 Filing procedures.

(a) *General.* Applications required under this subpart shall be filed with the appropriate FDIC office. The appropriate forms and instructions may be obtained upon request from any FDIC regional director.

(b) *Merger transactions.* Applications for approval of merger transactions shall be accompanied by copies of all agreements or proposed agreements relating to the merger transaction and any other information requested by the FDIC.

(c) *Interim merger transactions.* Applications for approval of interim merger transactions and any related deposit insurance applications shall be made by filing the forms and other documents required by paragraphs (a) and (b) of this section and such other information as may be required by the FDIC for consideration of the request for deposit insurance.

[67 FR 79247, Dec. 27, 2002, as amended at 73 FR 2145, Jan. 14, 2008]

§ 303.64 Processing.

(a) *Expedited processing for eligible depository institutions*—(1) *General.* An application filed under this subpart by an eligible depository institution as defined in § 303.2(r) and which meets the additional criteria in paragraph (a)(4) of this section will be acknowledged by the FDIC in writing and will receive expedited processing, unless the applicant is notified in writing to the contrary and provided with the basis for that decision. The FDIC may remove an application from expedited processing for any of the reasons set forth in § 303.11(c)(2).

(2) Under expedited processing, the FDIC will take action on an application by the date that is the latest of:

(i) 45 days after the date of the FDIC's receipt of a substantially complete merger application; or

(ii) 10 days after the date of the last notice publication required under § 303.65 of this subpart; or

(iii) 5 days after receipt of the Attorney General's report on the competitive factors involved in the proposed transaction; or

(iv) For an interstate merger transaction subject to the provisions of section 44 of the FDI Act (12 U.S.C. 1831u), 5 days after the FDIC receives confirmation from the host state (as defined in § 303.41(e)) that the applicant has both complied with the filing requirements of the host state and submitted a copy of the FDIC merger application to the host state's bank supervisor.

(3) Notwithstanding paragraph (a)(1) of this section, if the FDIC does not act within the expedited processing period, it does not constitute an automatic or default approval.

(4) *Criteria.* The FDIC will process an application using expedited procedures if:

(i) Immediately following the merger transaction, the resulting institution will be "well-capitalized" pursuant to subpart B of part 325 of this chapter (12 CFR part 325); and

(ii)(A) All parties to the merger transaction are eligible depository institutions as defined in § 303.2(r); or

(B) The acquiring party is an eligible depository institution as defined in § 303.2(r) and the amount of the total assets to be transferred does not exceed an amount equal to 10 percent of the acquiring institution's total assets as reported in its report of condition for the quarter immediately preceding the filing of the merger application.

(b) *Standard processing.* For those applications not processed pursuant to the expedited procedures, the FDIC will provide the applicant with written notification of the final action taken by the FDIC on the application when the decision is rendered.

§ 303.65 Public notice requirements.

(a) *General.* Except as provided in paragraph (b) of this section, an applicant for approval of a merger transaction must publish notice of the proposed transaction on at least three occasions at approximately equal intervals in a newspaper of general circulation in the community or communities where the main offices of the merging institutions are located or, if there is no such newspaper in the community, then in the newspaper of general circulation published nearest thereto.

(1) *First publication.* The first publication of the notice should be as close as practicable to the date on which the application is filed with the FDIC, but no more than 5 days prior to the filing date.

(2) *Last publication.* The last publication of the notice shall be on the 25th day after the first publication or, if the newspaper does not publish on the 25th day, on the newspaper's publication date that is closest to the 25th day.

(b) *Exceptions*—(1) *Emergency requiring expeditious action.* If the FDIC determines that an emergency exists requiring expeditious action, notice shall be published twice. The first notice shall be published as soon as possible after the FDIC notifies the applicant of such determination. The second notice shall be published on the 7th day after the first publication or, if the newspaper does not publish on the 7th day, on the newspaper's publication date that is closest to the 7th day.

(2) *Probable failure.* If the FDIC determines that it must act immediately to prevent the probable failure of one of the institutions involved in a proposed merger transaction, publication is not required.

(c) *Content of notice*—(1) *General.* The notice shall conform to the public notice requirements set forth in § 303.7.

(2) *Branches.* If it is contemplated that the resulting institution will operate offices of the other institution(s) as branches, the following statement shall be included in the notice required in § 303.7(b):

It is contemplated that all offices of the above-named institutions will continue to be operated (with the exception of [insert identity and location of each office that will not be operated]).

(3) *Emergency requiring expeditious action.* If the FDIC determines that an emergency exists requiring expeditious action, the notice shall specify as the closing date of the public comment period the date that is the 10th day after the date of the first publication.

(d) *Public comments.* Comments must be received by the appropriate FDIC office within 30 days after the first publication of the notice, unless the comment period has been extended or reopened in accordance with § 303.9(b)(2). If the FDIC has determined that an emergency exists requiring expeditious action, comments must be received by the appropriate FDIC office within 10 days after the first publication.

§§ 303.66–303.79 [Reserved]

Subpart E—Change in Bank Control

§ 303.80 Scope.

This subpart sets forth the procedures for submitting a notice to acquire control of an insured state nonmember bank or a parent company of an insured state nonmember bank pursuant to the Change in Bank Control Act of 1978, section 7(j) of the FDI Act (12 U.S.C. 1817(j)).

[68 FR 50459, Aug. 21, 2003]

§ 303.81 Definitions.

For purposes of this subpart:

(a) *Acquisition* includes a purchase, assignment, transfer, pledge or other disposition of voting shares, or an increase in percentage ownership resulting from a redemption of voting shares of an insured state nonmember bank or a parent company.

(b) *Acting in concert* means knowing participation in a joint activity or parallel action towards a common goal of acquiring control of an insured state nonmember bank or a parent company, whether or not pursuant to an express agreement.

(c) *Control* means the power, directly or indirectly, to direct the management or policies of an insured bank or a parent company or to vote 25 percent or more of any class of voting shares of an insured bank or a parent company.

Federal Deposit Insurance Corporation

(d) *Parent Company* means any company that controls, directly or indirectly, an insured state nonmember bank.

(e) *Person* means an individual, corporation, partnership, trust, association, joint venture, pool, syndicate, sole proprietorship, unincorporated organization, and any other form of entity; and a voting trust, voting agreement, and any group of persons acting in concert.

[68 FR 50459, Aug. 21, 2003]

§ 303.82 Transactions requiring prior notice.

(a) *Prior notice requirement.* Any person acting directly or indirectly, or through or in concert with one or more persons, shall give the FDIC 60 days prior written notice, as specified in § 303.84, before acquiring control of an insured state nonmember bank or any parent company, unless the acquisition is exempt under § 303.83.

(b) *Acquisition requiring prior notice*—(1) *Acquisition of control.* The acquisition of control, unless exempted, requires prior notice to the FDIC.

(2) *Rebuttable presumption of control.* The FDIC presumes that an acquisition of voting shares of an insured state nonmember bank or a parent company constitutes the acquisition of the power to direct the management or policies of an insured bank or a parent company requiring prior notice to the FDIC, if, immediately after the transaction, the acquiring person (or persons acting in concert) will own, control, or hold with power to vote 10 percent or more of any class of voting shares of the institution, and if:

(i) The institution has registered shares under section 12 of the Securities Exchange Act of 1934 (15 U.S.C. 78l); or

(ii) No other person will own, control or hold the power to vote a greater percentage of that class of voting shares immediately after the transaction. If two or more persons, not acting in concert, each propose to acquire simultaneously equal percentages of 10 percent or more of a class of voting shares of an insured state nonmember bank or a parent company, each such person shall file prior notice with the FDIC.

§ 303.83

(c) *Acquisition of loans in default.* The FDIC presumes an acquisition of a loan in default that is secured by voting shares of an insured state nonmember bank or a parent company to be an acquisition of the underlying shares for purposes of this section.

(d) *Other transactions.* Acquisitions other than those set forth in paragraph (b)(2) of this section resulting in a person's control of less than 25 percent of a class of voting shares of an insured state nonmember bank or a parent company are not deemed by the FDIC to constitute control for purposes of the Change in Bank Control Act.

(e) *Rebuttal of presumptions.* Prior notice to the FDIC is not required for any acquisition of voting shares under the presumption of control set forth in this section, if the FDIC finds that the acquisition will not result in control. The FDIC will afford any person seeking to rebut a presumption in this section an opportunity to present views in writing or, if appropriate, orally before its designated representatives at an informal meeting.

[67 FR 79247, Dec. 27, 2002, as amended at 68 FR 50460, Aug. 21, 2003]

§ 303.83 Transactions not requiring prior notice.

(a) *Exempt transactions.* The following transactions do not require notice to the FDIC under this subpart:

(1) The acquisiition of additional voting shares of an insured state nonmember bank or a parent company by a person who:

(i) Held the power to vote 25 percent or more of any class of voting shares of the institution continuously since the later of March 9, 1979, or the date that the institution commenced business as an insured state nonmember bank or a parent company; or

(ii) Is presumed, under § 303.82(b)(2), to have controlled the institution continuously since March 9, 1979, if the aggregate amount of voting shares held does not exceed 25 percent or more of any class of voting shares of the institution or, in other cases, where the FDIC determines that the person has controlled the institution continuously since March 9, 1979;

(2) The acquisition of additional shares of a class of voting shares of an

§ 303.84

insured state nonmember bank or a parent company by any person (or persons acting in concert) who has lawfully acquired and maintained control of the institution (for purposes of § 303.82) after complying with the procedures of the Change in Bank Control Act to acquire voting shares of the institution under this subpart;

(3) Acquisitions of voting shares subject to approval under section 3 of the Bank Holding Company Act (12 U.S.C. 1842(a)), section 18(c) of the FDI Act (12 U.S.C. 1828(c)), or section 10 of the Home Owners' Loan Act (12 U.S.C. 1467a);

(4) Transactions exempt under the Bank Holding Company Act: foreclosures by institutional lenders, fiduciary acquisitions by banks, and increases of majority holdings by bank holding companies described in sections 2(a)(5), 3(a)(A), or 3(a)(B) respectively of the Bank Holding Company Act (12 U.S.C. 1841(a)(5), 1842(a)(A), and 1842(a)(B));

(5) A customary one-time proxy solicitation;

(6) The receipt of voting shares of an insured state nonmember bank or a parent company through a pro rata stock dividend;

(7) The acquisition of voting shares in a foreign bank, which has an insured branch or branches in the United States. (This exemption does not extend to the reports and information required under paragraphs 9, 10, and 12 of the Change in Bank Control Act of 1978 (12 U.S.C. 1817(j)(9), (10), and (12)) and;

(8) The acquisition of voting shares of a depository institution holding company that either the Board of Governors of the Federal Reserve System or the Office of Thrift Supervision reviews pursuant to the Change in Bank Control Act (12 U.S.C. 1817(j)).

(b) *Prior notice exemption.* (1) The following acquisitions of voting shares of an insured state nonmember bank or a parent company, which otherwise would require prior notice under this subpart, are not subject to the prior notice requirements if the acquiring person notifies the appropriate FDIC office within 90 calendar days after the acquisition and provides any relevant information requested by the FDIC:

(i) The acquisition of voting shares through inheritance;

(ii) The acquisition of voting shares as a bona fide gift; or

(iii) The acquisition of voting shares in satisfaction of a debt previously contracted in good faith, except that the acquirer of a defaulted loan secured by a controlling amount of a state nonmember bank's voting securities or a parent company's voting securities shall file a notice before the loan is acquired.

(2) The following acquisitions of voting shares of an insured state nonmember bank or a parent company, which otherwise would require prior notice under this subpart, are not subject to the prior notice requirements if the acquiring person notifies the appropriate FDIC office within 90 calendar days after receiving notice of the acquisition and provides any relevant information requested by the FDIC.

(i) A percentage increase in ownership of voting shares resulting from a redemption of voting shares by the issuing bank or a parent company; or

(ii) The sale of shares by any shareholder that is not within the control of a person resulting in that person becoming the largest shareholder.

(3) Nothing in paragraph (b)(1) of this section limits the authority of the FDIC to disapprove a notice pursuant to § 303.85(c).

[67 FR 79247, Dec. 27, 2002, as amended at 68 FR 50460, Aug. 21, 2003]

§ 303.84 Filing procedures.

(a) *Filing notice.* (1) A notice required under this subpart shall be filed with the appropriate FDIC office and shall contain all the information required by paragraph 6 of the Change in Bank Control Act, section 7 (j) of the FDI Act, (12 U.S.C. 1817(j)(6)), or prescribed in the designated interagency form which may be obtained from any FDIC regional director.

(2) The FDIC may waive any of the informational requirements of the notice if the FDIC determines that it is in the public interest.

(3) A notificant shall notify the appropriate FDIC office immediately of any material changes in a notice submitted to the FDIC, including changes in financial or other conditions.

Federal Deposit Insurance Corporation §303.86

(4) When the acquiring person is an individual, or group of individuals acting in concert, the requirement to provide personal financial data may be satisfied by a current statement of assets and liabilities and an income summary, as required in the designated interagency form, together with a statement of any material changes since the date of the statement or summary. The FDIC may require additional information if appropriate.

(b) *Other laws.* Nothing in this subpart shall affect any obligation which the acquiring person(s) may have to comply with the federal securities laws or other laws.

§303.85 Processing.

(a) *Acceptance of notice, additional information.* The FDIC shall notify the person or persons submitting a notice under this subpart in writing of the date the notice is accepted as substantially complete. The FDIC may request additional information at any time.

(b) *Commencement of the 60-day notice period: consummation of acquisition.* (1) The 60-day notice period specified in §303.82 shall commerce on the day after the date of acceptance of a substantially complete notice by the appropriate regional director. The notificant(s) may consummate the proposed acquisition after the expiration of the 60-day notice period, unless the FDIC disapproves the proposed acquisition or extends the notice period.

(c) *Disapproval of acquisition of control.* Subpart D of 12 CFR part 308 sets forth the rules of practice and procedure for a notice of disapproval.

[67 FR 79247, Dec. 27, 2002, as amended at 68 FR 50460, Aug. 21, 2003]

§303.86 Public notice requirements.

(a) *Publication*—(1) *Newspaper announcement.* Any person(s) filing a notice under this subpart shall publish an announcement soliciting public comment on the proposed acquisition. The announcement shall be published in a newspaper of general circulation in the community in which the home office of the state nonmember bank to be acquired is located. The announcement shall be published as close as is practicable to the date the notice is filed with the appropriate FDIC office, but in no event more than 10 calendar days before or after the filing date.

(2) *Contents of newspaper announcement.* The newspaper announcement shall conform to the public notice requirements set forth in §303.7.

(b) *Delay of publication.* The FDIC may permit delay in the publication required by this section if the FDIC determines, for good cause, that it is in the public interest to grant such a delay. Requests for delay of publication may be submitted to the appropriate FDIC office.

(c) *Shortening or waiving public comment period, waiving publications; acting before close of public comment period.* The FDIC may shorten the public comment period to a period of not less than 10 days, or waive the public comment or newspaper publication requirements of paragraph (a) of this section, or act on a notice before the expiration of a public comment period, if it determines in writing either that an emergency exists or that disclosure of the notice, solicitation of public comment, or delay until expiration of the public comment period would seriously threaten the safety and soundness of the bank to be acquired.

(d) *Consideration of public comments.* In acting upon a notice filed under this subpart, the FDIC shall consider all public comments received in writing within 20 days following the required newspaper publication or, if the FDIC has shortened the public comment period pursuant to paragraph (c) of this section, within such shorter period.

(e) *Publication if filing is subsequent to acquisition of control.* (1) Whenever a notice of a proposed acquisition of control is not filed in accordance with the Change in Bank Control Act and these regulations, the acquiring person(s) shall, within 10 days of being so directed by the FDIC, publish an announcement of the acquisition of control in a newspaper of general circulation in the community in which the home office of the state nonmember bank to be acquired is located.

(2) The newspaper announcement shall contain the name(s) of the acquiror(s), the name of the depository institution involved, and the date of

the acquisition of the stock. The announcement shall also contain a statement indicating that the FDIC is currently reviewing the acquisition of control. The announcement also shall state that any person wishing to comment on the change in control may do so by submitting written comments to the appropriate regional director of the FDIC (give address of appropriate FDIC office) within 20 days following the required newspaper publication.

[67 FR 79247, Dec. 27, 2002, as amended at 68 FR 50461, Aug. 21, 2003]

§§ 303.87–303.99 [Reserved]

Subpart F—Change of Director or Senior Executive Officer

§ 303.100 Scope.

This subpart sets forth the circumstances under which an insured state nonmember bank must notify the FDIC of a change in any member of its board of directors or any senior executive officer and the procedures for filing such notice. This subpart implements section 32 of the FDI Act (12 U.S.C. 1831i).

§ 303.101 Definitions.

For purposes of this subpart:

(a) *Director* means a person who serves on the board of directors or board of trustees of an insured state nonmember bank, except that this term does not include an advisory director who:

(1) Is not elected by the shareholders;

(2) Is not authorized to vote on any matters before the board of directors or board of trustees or any committee thereof;

(3) Solely provides general policy advice to the board of directors or board of trustees and any committee thereof; and

(4) Has not been identified by the FDIC as a person who performs the functions of a director for purposes of this subpart.

(b) *Senior executive officer* means a person who holds the title of president, chief executive officer, chief operating officer, chief managing official (in an insured state branch of a foreign bank), chief financial officer, chief lending officer, or chief investment officer, or, without regard to title, salary, or compensation, performs the function of one or more of these positions. *Senior executive officer* also includes any other person identified by the FDIC, whether or not hired as an employee, with significant influence over, or who participates in, major policymaking decisions of the insured state nonmember bank.

(c) *Troubled condition* means any insured state nonmember bank that:

(1) Has a composite rating, as determined in its most recent report of examination, of 4 or 5 under the Uniform Financial Institutions Rating System (UFIRS), or in the case of an insured state branch of a foreign bank, an equivalent rating; or

(2) Is subject to a proceeding initiated by the FDIC for termination or suspension of deposit insurance; or

(3) Is subject to a cease-and-desist order or written agreement issued by either the FDIC or the appropriate state banking authority that requires action to improve the financial condition of the bank or is subject to a proceeding initiated by the FDIC or state authority which contemplates the issuance of an order that requires action to improve the financial condition of the bank, unless otherwise informed in writing by the FDIC; or

(4) Is informed in writing by the FDIC that it is in troubled condition for purposes of the requirements of this subpart on the basis of the bank's most recent report of condition or report of examination, or other information available to the FDIC.

§ 303.102 Filing procedures and waiver of prior notice.

(a) *Insured state nonmember banks.* An insured state nonmember bank shall give the FDIC written notice, as specified in paragraph (c)(1) of this section, at least 30 days prior to adding or replacing any member of its board of directors, employing any person as a senior executive officer of the bank, or changing the responsibilities of any senior executive officer so that the person would assume a different senior executive officer position, if:

(1) The bank is not in compliance with all minimum capital requirements applicable to the bank as determined on the basis of the bank's most

Federal Deposit Insurance Corporation § 303.103

recent report of condition or report of examination;

(2) The bank is in troubled condition; or

(3) The FDIC determines, in connection with its review of a capital restoration plan required under section 38(e)(2) of the FDI Act (12 U.S.C. 1831o(e)(2)) or otherwise, that such notice is appropriate.

(b) *Insured branches of foreign banks.* In the case of the addition of a member of the board of directors or a change in senior executive officer in a foreign bank having an insured state branch, the notice requirement shall not apply to such additions and changes in the foreign bank parent, but only to changes in senior executive officers in the state branch.

(c) *Waiver of prior notice*—(1) *Waiver requests.* The FDIC may permit an individual, upon petition by the bank to the appropriate FDIC office, to serve as a senior executive officer or director before filing the notice required under this subpart if the FDIC finds that:

(i) Delay would threaten the safety or soundness of the bank;

(ii) Delay would not be in the public interest; or

(iii) Other extraordinary circumstances exist that justify waiver of prior notice.

(2) *Automatic waiver.* In the case of the election of a new director not proposed by management at a meeting of the shareholders of an insured state nonmember bank, the prior 30-day notice is automatically waived and the individual immediately may begin serving, provided that a complete notice is filed with the appropriate FDIC office within two business days after the individual's election.

(3) *Effect on disapproval authority.* A waiver shall not affect the authority of the FDIC to disapprove a notice within 30 days after a waiver is granted under paragraph (c)(1) of this section or the election of an individual who has filed a notice and is serving pursuant to an automatic waiver under paragraph (c)(2) of this section.

(d)(1) *Content of filing.* The notice required by paragraph (a) of this section shall be filed with the appropriate FDIC office and shall contain information pertaining to the competence, experience, character, or integrity of the individual with respect to whom the notice is submitted, as prescribed in the designated interagency form which is available from any FDIC regional director. The FDIC may require additional information.

(2) *Modification.* The FDIC may modify or accept other information in place of the requirements of paragraph (d)(1) of this section for a notice filed under this subpart.

§ 303.103 **Processing.**

(a) *Processing.* The 30-day notice period specified in § 303.102(a) shall begin on the date substantially all information required to be submitted by the notificant pursuant to § 303.102(c)(1) is received by the appropriate FDIC office. The FDIC shall notify the bank submitting the notice of the date on which the notice is accepted for processing and of the date on which the 30-day notice period will expire. If processing cannot be completed within 30 days, the notificant will be advised in writing, prior to expiration of the 30-day period, of the reason for the delay in processing and of the additional time period, not to exceed 60 days, in which processing will be completed.

(b) *Commencement of service*—(1) *At expiration of period.* A proposed director or senior executive officer may begin service after the end of the 30-day period or any other additional period as provided under paragraph (a) of this section, unless the FDIC disapproves the notice before the end of the period.

(2) *Prior to expiration of period.* A proposed director or senior executive officer may begin service before the end of the 30-day period or any additional time period as provided under paragraph (a) of this section, if the FDIC notifies the bank and the individual in writing of the FDIC's intention not to disapprove the notice.

(c) *Notice of disapproval.* The FDIC may disapprove a notice filed under § 303.102 if the FDIC finds that the competence, experience, character, or integrity of the individual with respect to whom the notice is submitted indicates that it would not be in the best interests of the depositors of the bank or in the best interests of the public to permit the individual to be employed

§§ 303.104–303.119

by, or associated with, the bank. Subpart L of 12 CFR part 308 sets forth the rules of practice and procedure for a notice of disapproval.

§§ 303.104–303.119 [Reserved]

Subpart G—Activities of Insured State Banks

§ 303.120 Scope.

This subpart sets forth procedures for complying with notice and application requirements contained in subpart A of part 362 of this chapter, governing insured state banks and their subsidiaries engaging in activities which are not permissible for national banks and their subsidiaries. This subpart sets forth procedures for complying with notice and application requirements contained in subpart B of part 362 of this chapter, governing certain activities of insured state nonmember banks, their subsidiaries, and certain affiliates. This subpart also sets forth procedures for complying with the notice requirements contained in subpart E of part 362 of this chapter, governing subsidiaries of insured state nonmember banks engaging in financial activities.

§ 303.121 Filing procedures.

(a) *Where to file.* A notice or application required by subpart A, subpart B, or subpart E of part 362 of this chapter shall be submitted in writing to the appropriate FDIC office.

(b) *Contents of filing.* A complete letter notice or letter application shall include the following information:

(1) *Filings generally.* (i) A brief description of the activity and the manner in which it will be conducted;

(ii) The amount of the bank's existing or proposed direct or indirect investment in the activity as well as calculations sufficient to indicate compliance with any specific capital ratio or investment percentage limitation detailed in subpart A, B, or E of part 362 of this chapter;

(iii) A copy of the bank's business plan regarding the conduct of the activity;

(iv) A citation to the state statutory or regulatory authority for the conduct of the activity;

(v) A copy of the order or other document from the appropriate regulatory authority granting approval for the bank to conduct the activity if such approval is necessary and has already been granted;

(vi) A brief description of the bank's policy and practice with regard to any anticipated involvement in the activity by a director, executive office or principal shareholder of the bank or any related interest of such a person; and

(vii) A description of the bank's expertise in the activity.

(2) [Reserved]

(3) *Copy of application or notice filed with another agency.* If an insured state bank has filed an application or notice with another federal or state regulatory authority which contains all of the information required by paragraph (b) (1) of this section, the insured state bank may submit a copy to the FDIC in lieu of a separate filing.

(4) *Additional information.* The FDIC may request additional information to complete processing.

§ 303.122 Processing.

(a) *Expedited processing.* A notice filed by an insured state bank seeking to commence or continue an activity under § 362.3(a)(2)(iii)(A)(2), § 362.4(b)(3)(i), or § 362.4(b)(5) of this chapter will be acknowledged in writing by the FDIC and will receive expedited processing, unless the applicant is notified in writing to the contrary and provided a basis for that decision. The FDIC may remove the notice from expedited processing for any of the reasons set forth in § 303.11(c)(2). Absent such removal, a notice processed under expedited processing is deemed approved 30 days after receipt of a complete notice by the FDIC (subject to extension for an additional 15 days upon written notice to the bank) or on such earlier date authorized by the FDIC in writing.

(b) *Standard processing for applications and notices that have been removed from expedited processing.* For an application filed by an insured state bank seeking to commence or continue an activity under § 362.3(a)(2)(iii)(A)(2), § 362.3(b)(2)(i), § 362.3(b)(2)(ii)(A), § 362.3(b)(2)(ii)(C), § 362.4(b)(1),

Federal Deposit Insurance Corporation

§ 362.4(b)(4), § 362.5(b)(2), or § 362.8(b) or seeking a waiver or modification under § 362.18(e) or § 362.18(g)(3) of this chapter or for notices which are not processed pursuant to the expedited processing procedures, the FDIC will provide the insured State bank with written notification of the final action as soon as the decision is rendered. The FDIC will normally review and act in such cases within 60 days after receipt of a completed application or notice (subject to extension for an additional 30 days upon written notice to the bank), but failure of the FDIC to act prior to the expiration of these periods does not constitute approval.

§§ 303.123–303.139 [Reserved]

Subpart H—Activities of Insured Savings Associations

§ 303.140 Scope.

This subpart sets forth procedures for complying with the notice and application requirements contained in subpart C of part 362 of this chapter, governing insured state savings associations and their service corporations engaging in activities which are not permissible for federal savings associations and their service corporations. This subpart also sets forth procedures for complying with the notice requirements contained in subpart D of part 362 of this chapter, governing insured savings associations which establish or engage in new activities through a subsidiary.

§ 303.141 Filing procedures.

(a) *Where to file.* All applications and notices required by subpart C or subpart D of part 362 of this chapter are to be in writing and filed with the appropriate FDIC office.

(b) *Contents of filing*—(1) *Filings generally.* A complete letter notice or letter application shall include the following information:

(i) A brief description of the activity and the manner in which it will be conducted;

(ii) The amount of the association's existing or proposed direct or indirect investment in the activity as well as calculations sufficient to indicate compliance with any specific capital ratio or investment percentage limitation

§ 303.142

detailed in subpart C or D of part 362 of this chapter;

(iii) A copy of the association's business plan regarding the conduct of the activity;

(iv) A citation to the state statutory or regulatory authority for the conduct of the activity;

(v) A copy of the order or other document from the appropriate regulatory authority granting approval for the association to conduct the activity if such approval is necessary and has already been granted;

(vi) A brief description of the association's policy and practice with regard to any anticipated involvement in the activity by a director, executive officer or principal shareholder of the association or any related interest of such a person; and

(vii) A description of the association's expertise in the activity.

(2) [Reserved]

(3) *Copy of application or notice filed with another agency.* If an insured savings association has filed an application or notice with another federal or state regulatory authority which contains all of the information required by paragraph (b)(1) of this section, the insured state bank may submit a copy to the FDIC in lieu of a separate filing.

(4) *Additional information.* The FDIC may request additional information to complete processing.

§ 303.142 Processing.

(a) *Expedited processing.* A notice filed by an insured state savings association seeking to commence or continue an activity under § 362.11(b)(2)(ii) of this chapter will be acknowledged in writing by the FDIC and will receive expedited processing, unless the applicant is notified in writing to the contrary and provided a basis for that decision. The FDIC may remove the notice from expedited processing for any of the reasons set forth in § 303.11(c)(2). Absent such removal, a notice processed under expedited processing is deemed approved 30 days after receipt of a complete notice by the FDIC (subject to extension for an additional 15 days upon written notice to the bank) or on such earlier date authorized by the FDIC in writing.

§§ 303.143–303.159

(b) *Standard processing for applications and notices that have been removed from expedited processing.* For an application filed by an insured state savings association seeking to commence or continue an activity under § 362.11(a)(2)(ii), § 362.11(b)(2)(i), § 362.12(b)(1) of this chapter or for notices which are not processed pursuant to the expedited processing procedures, the FDIC will provide the insured state savings association with written notification of the final action as soon as the decision is rendered. The FDIC will normally review and act in such cases within 60 days after receipt of a completed application or notice (subject to extension for an additional 30 days upon written notice to the bank), but failure of the FDIC to act prior to the expiration of these periods does not constitute approval.

(c) *Notices of activities in excess of an amount permissible for a federal savings association; subsidiary notices.* Receipt of a notice filed by an insured state savings association as required by § 362.11(b)(3) or § 362.15 of this chapter will be acknowledged in writing by the FDIC. The notice will be reviewed at the appropriate FDIC office, which will take such action as it deems necessary and appropriate.

§§ 303.143–303.159 [Reserved]

Subpart I—Mutual-To-Stock Conversions

§ 303.160 Scope.

This subpart sets forth the notice requirements and procedures for the conversion of an insured mutual state-chartered savings bank to the stock form of ownership. The substantive requirements governing such conversions are contained in § 333.4 of this chapter.

§ 303.161 Filing procedures.

(a) *Prior notice required.* In addition to complying with the substantive requirements in § 333.4 of this chapter, an insured state-chartered mutually owned savings bank that proposes to convert from mutual to stock form shall file with the FDIC a notice of intent to convert to stock form.

(b) *General.* (1) A notice required under this subpart shall be filed in letter form with the appropriate FDIC office at the same time as required conversion application materials are filed with the institution's state regulator.

(2) An insured mutual savings bank chartered by a state that does not require the filing of a conversion application shall file a notice in letter form with the appropriate FDIC office as soon as practicable after adoption of its plan of conversion.

(c) *Content of notice.* The notice shall provide a description of the proposed conversion and include all materials that have been filed with any state or federal banking regulator and any state or federal securities regulator. At a minimum, the notice shall include, as applicable, copies of:

(1) The plan of conversion, with specific information concerning the record date used for determining eligible depositors and the subscription offering priority established in connection with any proposed stock offering;

(2) Certified board resolutions relating to the conversion;

(3) A business plan, including a detailed discussion of how the capital acquired in the conversion will be used, expected earnings for at least a three-year period following the conversion, and a justification for any proposed stock repurchases;

(4) The charter and bylaws of the converted institution;

(5) The bylaws and operating plans of any other entities formed in connection with the conversion transaction, such as a holding company or charitable foundation;

(6) A full appraisal report, prepared by an independent appraiser, of the value of the converting institution and the pricing of the stock to be sold in the conversion transaction;

(7) Detailed descriptions of any proposed management or employee stock benefit plans or employment agreements and a discussion of the rationale for the level of benefits proposed, individually and by participant group;

(8) Indemnification agreements;

(9) A preliminary proxy statement and sample proxy;

(10) Offering circular(s) and order form;

(11) All contracts or agreements relating to solicitation, underwriting,

Federal Deposit Insurance Corporation

market-making, or listing of conversion stock and any agreements among members of a group regarding the purchase of unsubscribed shares;

(12) A tax opinion concerning the federal income tax consequences of the proposed conversion;

(13) Consents from experts to use their opinions as part of the notice; and

(14) An estimate of conversion-related expenses.

(d) *Additional information.* The FDIC, in its discretion, may request any additional information it deems necessary to evaluate the proposed conversion. The institution proposing to convert from mutual to stock form shall promptly provide such information to the FDIC.

(e) *Acceptance of notice.* The 60-day notice period specified in § 303.163 shall commence on the date of receipt of a substantially complete notice. The FDIC shall notify the institution proposing to convert in writing of the date the notice is accepted.

(f) *Related applications.* Related applications that require FDIC action may include:

(1) Applications for deposit insurance, as required by subpart B of this part; and

(2) Applications for consent to merge, as required by subpart D of this part.

§ 303.162 Waiver from compliance.

(a) *General.* An institution proposing to convert from mutual to stock form may file with the appropriate FDIC office a letter requesting waiver of compliance with this subpart or § 333.4 of this chapter:

(1) When compliance with any provision of this section or § 333.4 of this chapter would be inconsistent or in conflict with applicable state law, or

(2) For any other good cause shown.

(b) *Content of filing.* In making a request for waiver under paragraph (a) of this section, the institution shall demonstrate that the requested waiver, if granted, would not result in any effects that would be detrimental to the safety and soundness of the institution, entail a breach of fiduciary duty on part of the institution's management or otherwise be detrimental or inequitable to the institution, its depositors, any other insured depository institution(s), the Deposit Insurance Fund, or to the public interest.

[67 FR 79247, Dec. 27, 2002, as amended at 71 FR 20526, Apr. 21, 2006]

§ 303.163 Processing.

(a) *General considerations.* The FDIC shall review the notice and other materials submitted by the institution proposing to convert from mutual to stock form, specifically considering the following factors:

(1) The proposed use of the proceeds from the sale of stock, as set forth in the business plan;

(2) The adequacy of the disclosure materials;

(3) The participation of depositors in approving the transaction;

(4) The form of the proxy statement required for the vote of the depositors/members on the conversion;

(5) Any proposed increased compensation and other remuneration (including stock grants, stock option rights and other similar benefits) to be granted to officers and directors/trustees of the bank in connection with the conversion;

(6) The adequacy and independence of the appraisal of the value of the mutual savings bank for purposes of determining the price of the shares of stock to be sold;

(7) The process by which the bank's trustees approved the appraisal, the pricing of the stock, and the proposed compensation arrangements for insiders;

(8) The nature and apportionment of stock subscription rights; and

(9) The bank's plans to fulfill its commitment to serving the convenience and needs of its community.

(b) *Additional considerations.* (1) In reviewing the notice and other materials submitted under this subpart, the FDIC will take into account the extent to which the proposed conversion transaction conforms with the various provisions of the mutual-to-stock conversion regulations of the Office of Thrift Supervision (OTS) (12 CFR part 563b), as currently in effect at the time the notice is submitted. Any non-conformity with those provisions will be closely reviewed.

§§ 303.164–303.179

(2) Conformity with the OTS requirements will not be sufficient for FDIC regulatory purposes if the FDIC determines that the proposed conversion transaction would pose a risk to the bank's safety or soundness, violate any law or regulation, or present a breach of fiduciary duty.

(c) *Notice period.* (1) The period in which the FDIC may object to the proposed conversion transaction shall be the later of:

(i) 60 days after receipt of a substantially complete notice of proposed conversion; or

(ii) 20 days after the last applicable state or other federal regulator has approved the proposed conversion.

(2) The FDIC may, in its discretion, extend the initial 60-day period for up to an additional 60 days by providing written notice to the institution.

(d) *Letter of non-objection.* If the FDIC determines, in its discretion, that the proposed conversion transaction would not pose a risk to the institution's safety or soundness, violate any law or regulation, or present a breach of fiduciary duty, then the FDIC shall issue to the institution proposing to convert a letter of non-objection to the proposed conversion.

(e) *Letter of objection.* If the FDIC determines, in its discretion, that the proposed conversion transaction poses a risk to the institution's safety or soundness, violates any law or regulation, or presents a breach of fiduciary duty, then the FDIC shall issue a letter to the institution stating its objection(s) to the proposed conversion and advising the institution not to consummate the proposed conversion until such letter is rescinded. A copy of the letter of objection shall be furnished to the institution's primary state regulator and any other state or federal banking regulator and state or federal securities regulator involved in the conversion.

(f) *Consummation of the conversion.* (1) An institution may consummate the proposed conversion upon either:

(i) The receipt of a letter of non-objection; or

(ii) The expiration of the notice period.

(2) If a letter of objection is issued, then the institution shall not consummate the proposed conversion until the FDIC rescinds such letter.

§§ 303.164–303.179 [Reserved]

Subpart J—International Banking

§ 303.180 Scope.

This subpart sets forth procedures for complying with application requirements relating to the foreign activities of insured state nonmember banks, U.S. activities of insured branches of foreign banks, and certain foreign mergers of insured depository institutions.

§ 303.181 Definitions.

For the purposes of this subpart, the following additional definitions apply:

(a) *Board of Governors* means the Board of Governors of the Federal Reserve System.

(b) *Comptroller* means the Office of the Comptroller of the Currency.

(c) *Eligible insured branch.* An insured branch will be treated as an eligible depository institution within the meaning of § 303.2(r) if the insured branch:

(1) Received an FDIC-assigned composite ROCA supervisory rating (which rates risk management, operational controls, compliance, and asset quality) of 1 or 2 as a result of its most recent federal or state examination, and the FDIC, Comptroller, or Board of Governors have not expressed concern about the condition or operations of the foreign banking organization or the support it offers the branch;

(2) Received a satisfactory or better Community Reinvestment Act (CRA) rating from its primary federal regulator at its most recent examination, if the depository institution is subject to examination under part 345 of this chapter;

(3) Received a compliance rating of 1 or 2 from its primary federal regulator at its most recent examination;

(4) Is well-capitalized as defined in subpart B of part 325 of this chapter; and

(5) Is not subject to a cease and desist order, consent order, prompt corrective action directive, written agreement, memorandum of understanding, or other administrative agreement with any U.S. bank regulatory authority.

Federal Deposit Insurance Corporation § 303.182

(d) *Federal branch* means a federal branch of a foreign bank as defined by § 347.202 of this chapter.

(e) *Foreign bank* means a foreign bank as defined by § 347.202 of this chapter.

(f) *Foreign branch* means a foreign branch of an insured state nonmember bank as defined by § 347.102 of this chapter.

(g) *Foreign organization* means a foreign organization as defined by § 347.102 of this chapter.

(h) *Insured branch* means an insured branch of a foreign bank as defined by § 347.202 of this chapter.

(i) *Noninsured branch* means a noninsured branch of a foreign bank as defined by § 347.202 of this chapter.

(j) *State branch* means a state branch of a foreign bank as defined by § 347.202 of this chapter.

§ 303.182 Establishing, moving or closing a foreign branch of an insured state nonmember bank.

(a) Notice procedures for general consent. Notice in the form of a letter from an eligible depository institution establishing or relocating a foreign branch pursuant to § 347.117(a) of this chapter must be provided to the appropriate FDIC office no later than 30 days after taking such action. The notice must include the location of the foreign branch, including a street address, and a statement that the foreign branch has not been located on a site on the World Heritage List or on the foreign country's equivalent of the National Register of Historic Places (National Register), in accordance with section 402 of the National Historic Preservation Act Amendments of 1980 (NHPA Amendments Act) (16 U.S.C. 470a-2). The FDIC will provide written acknowledgment of receipt of the notice.

(b) Filing procedures for other branch establishments—(1) Where to file. An applicant seeking to establish a foreign branch other than under § 347.117(a) of this chapter shall submit an application to the appropriate FDIC office.

(2) Content of filing. A complete letter application must include the following information:

(i) The exact location of the proposed foreign branch, including the street address, and a statement whether the foreign branch will be located on a site on the World Heritage List or on the foreign country's equivalent of the National Register, in accordance with section 402 of the NHPA Amendments Act;

(ii) Details concerning any involvement in the proposal by an insider of the applicant, as defined in § 303.2(u) of this part, including any financial arrangements relating to fees, the acquisition of property, leasing of property, and construction contracts;

(iii) A brief description of the applicant's business plan with respect to the foreign branch; and

(iv) A brief description of the proposed activities of the branch and, to the extent any of the proposed activities are not authorized by § 347.115 of this chapter, the applicant's reasons why they should be approved.

(3) Additional information. The FDIC may request additional information to complete processing.

(c) Processing—(1) Expedited processing for eligible depository institutions. An application filed under § 347.118(a) of this chapter by an eligible depository institution as defined in § 303.2(r) of this part seeking to establish a foreign branch by expedited processing will be acknowledged in writing by the FDIC and will receive expedited processing, unless the applicant is notified in writing to the contrary and provided with the basis for that decision. The FDIC may remove the application from expedited processing for any of the reasons set forth in § 303.11(c)(2) of this part. Absent such removal, an application processed under expedited processing is deemed approved 45 days after receipt of a substantially complete application by the FDIC, or on such earlier date authorized by the FDIC in writing.

(2) Standard processing. For those applications that are not processed pursuant to the expedited procedures, the FDIC will provide the applicant with written notification of the final action when the decision is rendered.

(d) Closing. Notices of branch closing under § 347.121 of this chapter, in the form of a letter including the name, location, and date of closing of the closed

§ 303.183

branch, shall be filed with the appropriate FDIC office no later than 30 days after the branch is closed.

[70 FR 17558, Apr. 6, 2005]

§ 303.183 Investment by insured state nonmember banks in foreign organization.

(a) *Notice procedures for general consent.* Notice in the form of a letter from an eligible depository institution making direct or indirect investments in a foreign organization pursuant to § 347.117(b) of this chapter shall be provided to the appropriate FDIC office no later than 30 days after taking such action. The FDIC will provide written acknowledgment of receipt of the notice.

(b) *Filing procedures for other investments*—(1) *Where to file.* An applicant seeking to make a foreign investment other than under § 347.117(b) of this chapter shall submit an application to the appropriate FDIC office.

(2) *Content of filing.* A complete application shall include the following information:

(i) Basic information about the terms of the proposed transaction, the amount of the investment in the foreign organization and the proportion of its ownership to be acquired;

(ii) Basic information about the foreign organization, its financial position and income, including any available balance sheet and income statement for the prior year, or financial projections for a new foreign organization;

(iii) A listing of all shareholders known to hold ten percent or more of any class of the foreign organization's stock or other evidence of ownership, and the amount held by each;

(iv) A brief description of the applicant's business plan with respect to the foreign organization;

(v) A brief description of any business or activities which the foreign organization will conduct directly or indirectly in the United States, and to the extent such activities are not authorized by subpart A of part 347, the applicant's reasons why they should be approved;

(vi) A brief description of the foreign organization's activities, and to the extent such activities are not authorized by subpart A of part 347, the appli-

cant's reasons why they should be approved; and

(vii) If the applicant seeks approval to engage in underwriting or dealing activities, a description of the applicant's plans and procedures to address all relevant risks.

(3) *Additional information.* The FDIC may request additional information to complete processing.

(c) *Processing*—(1) Expedited processing for eligible depository institutions. An application filed under § 347.118(b) of this chapter by an eligible depository institution as defined in § 303.2(r) of this part seeking to make direct or indirect investments in a foreign organization will be acknowledged in writing by the FDIC and will receive expedited processing, unless the applicant is notified in writing to the contrary and provided with the basis for that decision. The FDIC may remove the application from expedited processing for any of the reasons set forth in § 303.11(c)(2) of this part. Absent such removal, an application processed under expedited processing is deemed approved 45 days after receipt of a substantially complete application by the FDIC, or on such earlier date authorized by the FDIC in writing.

(2) *Standard processing.* For those applications which are not processed pursuant to the expedited procedures, the FDIC will provide the applicant with written notification of the final action when the decision is rendered.

(d) *Divestiture.* If an insured state nonmember bank holding 50 percent or more of the voting equity interests of a foreign organization or otherwise controlling the foreign organization divests itself of such ownership or control, the insured state nonmember bank shall file a notice in the form of a letter, including the name, location, and date of divestiture of the foreign organization, with the appropriate FDIC office no later than 30 days after the divestiture.

[67 FR 79247, Dec. 27, 2002, as amended at 70 FR 17558, Apr. 6, 2005]

§ 303.184 Moving an insured branch of a foreign bank.

(a) *Filing procedures*—(1) *Where and when to file.* An application by an insured branch of a foreign bank seeking

Federal Deposit Insurance Corporation § 303.184

the FDIC's consent to move from one location to another, as required by section 18(d)(1) of the FDI Act (12 U.S.C. 1828(d)(1)), shall be submitted in writing to the appropriate FDIC office on the date the notice required by paragraph (c) of this section is published, or within 5 days after the date of the last required publication.

(2) *Content of filing.* A complete letter application shall include the following information:

(i) The exact location of the proposed site, including the street address;

(ii) Details concerning any involvement in the proposal by an insider of the applicant, as defined in § 303.2(u), including any financial arrangements relating to fees, the acquisition of property, leasing of property, and construction contracts;

(iii) A statement of the impact of the proposal on the human environment, including information on compliance with local zoning laws and regulations and the effect on traffic patterns, for purposes of complying with the applicable provisions of the NEPA, and the FDIC "Statement of Policy on NEPA" (1 FDIC Law, Regulations, Related Acts 5185; see § 309.4(a) and (b) of this chapter for availability).

(iv) A statement as to whether or not the site is eligible for inclusion in the National Register of Historic Places for purposes of complying with the applicable provisions of the NHPA, and the FDIC AStatement of Policy on NHPA" (1 FDIC Law, Regulations, Related Acts 5175; see § 309.4(a) and (b) of this chapter for availability), including documentation of consultation with the State Historic Preservation Officer, as appropriate.

(v) Comments on any changes in services to be offered, the community to be served, or any other effect the proposal may have on the applicant's compliance with the CRA; and

(vi) A copy of the newspaper publication required by paragraph (c) of this section, as well as the name and address of the newspaper and the date of the publication.

(3) *Comptroller's application.* If the applicant is filing an application with the Comptroller which contains the information required by paragraph (a)(2) of this section, the applicant may submit a copy to the FDIC in lieu of a separate application.

(4) *Additional information.* The FDIC may request additional information to complete processing.

(b) Processing—(1) *Expedited processing for eligible insured branches.* An application filed by an eligible insured branch as defined in § 303.181(c) of this part will be acknowledged in writing by the FDIC and will receive expedited processing if the applicant is proposing to move within the same state, unless the applicant is notified to the contrary and provided with the basis for that decision. The FDIC may remove an application from expedited processing for any of the reasons set forth in § 303.11(c)(2) of this part. Absent such removal, an application processed under expedited processing will be deemed approved on the latest of the following:

(i) The 21st day after the FDIC's receipt of a substantially complete application; or

(ii) The 5th day after expiration of the comment period described in paragraph (c) of this section.

(2) *Standard processing.* For those applications that are not processed pursuant to the expedited procedures, the FDIC will provide the applicant with written notification of the final action as soon as the decision is rendered.

(c) *Publication requirement and comment period*—(1) *Newspaper publications.* The applicant shall publish a notice of its proposal to move from one location to another, as described in § 303.7(b), in a newspaper of general circulation in the community in which the insured branch is located prior to its being moved and in the community to which it is to be moved. The notice shall include the insured branch's current and proposed addresses.

(2) *Public comments.* All public comments must be received by the appropriate regional director within 15 days after the date of the last newspaper publication required by paragraph (c)(1) of this section, unless the comment period has been extended or reopened in accordance with § 303.9(b)(2).

(3) *Lobby notices.* If the insured branch has a public lobby, a copy of the newspaper publication shall be posted in the public lobby for at least 15 days

§ 303.185

beginning on the date of the publication required by paragraph (c)(1) of this section.

(d) *Other approval criteria.* (1) The FDIC may approve an application under this section if the criteria in paragraphs (d)(1)(i) through (d)(1)(vi) of this section is satisfied.

(i) The factors set forth in section 6 of the FDI Act (12 U.S.C. 1816) have been considered and favorably resolved;

(ii) The applicant is at least adequately capitalized as defined in subpart B of part 325 of this chapter;

(iii) Any financial arrangements which have been made in connection with the proposed relocation and which involve the applicant's directors, officers, major shareholders, or their interests are fair and reasonable in comparison to similar arrangements that could have been made with independent third parties;

(iv) Compliance with the CRA, the NEPA, the NHPA and any applicable related regulations, including 12 CFR part 345, has been considered and favorably resolved;

(v) No CRA protest as defined in §303.2(l) has been filed which remains unresolved or, where such a protest has been filed and remains unresolved, the Director or designee concurs that approval is consistent with the purposes of the CRA and the applicant agrees in writing to any conditions imposed regarding the CRA; and

(vi) The applicant agrees in writing to comply with any conditions imposed by the FDIC, other than the standard conditions defined in §303.2(dd) which may be imposed without the applicant's written consent.

(e) *Relocation of insured branch from one state to another.* If the foreign bank proposes to relocate an insured state branch to a state that is outside the state where the branch is presently located, in addition to meeting the approval criteria contained in paragraph (d) of this section, the foreign bank must:

(i) Comply with any applicable state laws or regulations of the states affected by the proposed relocation; and

(ii) Obtain any required regulatory approvals from the appropriate state licensing authority of the state to which the insured branch proposes to relocate before relocating the existing branch operations and surrendering its existing license to the appropriate state licensing authority of the state from which the branch is relocating.

[67 FR 79247, Dec. 27, 2002, as amended at 70 FR 17559, Apr. 6, 2005]

§ 303.185 **Merger transactions involving foreign banks or foreign organizations.**

(a) *Merger transactions involving an insured branch of a foreign bank.* Merger transactions requiring the FDIC's prior approval as set forth in §303.62 include any merger transaction in which the resulting institution is an insured branch of a foreign bank which is not a federal branch, or any merger transaction which involves any insured branch and any uninsured institution. In such cases:

(1) References to an eligible depository institution in subpart D of this part include an eligible insured branch as defined in §303.181;

(2) The definition of a corporate reorganization in §303.61(b) includes a merger transaction between an insured branch and other branches, agencies, or subsidiaries in the United States of the same foreign bank; and

(3) For the purposes of §303.62(b)(1) on interstate mergers, a merger transaction involving an insured branch is one involving the acquisition of a branch of an insured bank without the acquisition of the bank for purposes of section 44 of the FDI Act (12 U.S.C. 1831u) only when the merger transaction involves fewer than all the insured branches of the same foreign bank in the same state.

(b) *Certain merger transactions with foreign organizations outside any State.* Merger transactions requiring the FDIC's prior approval as set forth in §303.62 include any merger transaction in which an insured depository institution becomes directly liable for obligations which will, after the merger transaction, be treated as deposits under section 3(l)(5)(A)(i)–(ii) of the FDI Act (12 U.S.C. 1813(l)(5)(A)(i)–(ii)), as a result of a merger or consolidation with a foreign organization or an assumption of liabilities of a foreign organization.

Federal Deposit Insurance Corporation § 303.187

§ 303.186 Exemptions from insurance requirements for a state branch of a foreign bank.

(a) *Filing procedures*—(1) *Where to file.* An application by a foreign bank for consent to operate as a noninsured state branch, as permitted by § 347.215(b) of this chapter, shall be submitted in writing to the appropriate FDIC office.

(2) *Content of filing.* A complete letter application shall include the following information:

(i) The kinds of deposit activities in which the state branch proposes to engage;

(ii) The expected source of deposits;

(iii) The manner in which deposits will be solicited;

(iv) How the activity will maintain or improve the availability of credit to all sectors of the United States economy, including the international trade finance sector;

(v) That the activity will not give the foreign bank an unfair competitive advantage over United States banking organizations; and

(vi) A resolution by the applicant's board of directors, or evidence of approval by senior management if a resolution is not required pursuant to the applicant's organizational documents, authorizing the filing of the application.

(3) *Additional information.* The FDIC may request additional information to complete processing.

(4) *Processing.* The FDIC will provide the applicant with written notification of the final action taken.

[67 FR 79247, Dec. 27, 2002, as amended at 70 FR 17559, Apr. 6, 2005]

§ 303.187 Approval for an insured state branch of a foreign bank to conduct activities not permissible for federal branches.

(a) *Filing procedures*—(1) *Where to file.* An application by an insured state branch seeking approval to conduct activities not permissible for a federal branch, as required by § 347.212(a) of this chapter, shall be submitted in writing to the appropriate FDIC office.

(2) *Content of filing.* A complete letter application shall include the following information:

(i) A brief description of the activity, including the manner in which it will be conducted and an estimate of the expected dollar volume associated with the activity;

(ii) An analysis of the impact of the proposed activity on the condition of the United States operations of the foreign bank in general and of the branch in particular, including a copy of the feasibility study, management plan, financial projections, business plan, or similar document concerning the conduct of the activity;

(iii) A resolution by the applicant's board of directors, or evidence of approval by senior management if a resolution is not required pursuant to the applicant's organizational documents, authorizing the filing of the application;

(iv) A statement by the applicant of whether it is in compliance with sections 347.209 and 347.210 of this chapter;

(v) A statement by the applicant that it has complied with all requirements of the Board of Governors concerning applications to conduct the activity in question and the status of each such application, including a copy of the Board of Governors' disposition of such application, if applicable; and

(vi) A statement of why the activity will pose no significant risk to the Deposit Insurance Fund.

(3) *Board of Governors application.* If the application to the Board of Governors contains the information required by paragraph (a) of this section, the applicant may submit a copy to the FDIC in lieu of a separate letter application.

(4) *Additional information.* The FDIC may request additional information to complete processing.

(b) *Divestiture or cessation*—(1) *Where to file.* Divestiture plans necessitated by a change in law or other authority, as required by § 347.212(e) of this chapter, shall be submitted in writing to the appropriate FDIC office.

(2) *Content of filing.* A complete letter application shall include the following information:

(i) A detailed description of the manner in which the applicant proposes to divest itself of or cease the activity in question; and

§§ 303.188–303.199

(ii) A projected timetable describing how long the divestiture or cessation is expected to take.

(3) *Additional information.* The FDIC may request additional information to complete processing.

[67 FR 79247, Dec. 27, 2002, as amended at 70 FR 17559, Apr. 6, 2005; 71 FR 20526, Apr. 21, 2006]

§§ 303.188–303.199 [Reserved]

Subpart K—Prompt Corrective Action

§ 303.200 Scope.

(a) *General.* (1) This subpart covers applications filed pursuant to section 38 of the FDI Act (12 U.S.C. 1831*o*), which requires insured depository institutions that are not adequately capitalized to receive approval prior to engaging in certain activities. Section 38 restricts or prohibits certain activities and requires an insured depository institution to submit a capital restoration plan when it becomes undercapitalized. The restrictions and prohibitions become more severe as an institution's capital level declines.

(2) Definitions of the capital categories referenced in this Prompt Corrective Action subpart may be found in subpart B of part 325 of this chapter, § 325.103(b) for state nonmember banks and § 325.103(c) for insured branches of foreign banks.

(b) *Institutions covered.* Restrictions and prohibitions contained in subpart B of part 325 of this chapter apply primarily to insured state nonmember banks and insured branches of foreign banks, as well as to directors and senior executive officers of those institutions. Portions of subpart B of part 325 of this chapter also apply to all insured depository institutions that are deemed to be critically undercapitalized.

§ 303.201 Filing procedures.

Applications shall be filed with the appropriate FDIC office. The application shall contain the information specified in each respective section of this subpart, and shall be in letter form as prescribed in § 303.3. Additional information may be requested by the FDIC. Such letter shall be signed by the president, senior officer or a duly authorized agent of the insured depository institution and be accompanied by a certified copy of a resolution adopted by the institution's board of directors or trustees authorizing the application.

§ 303.202 Processing.

The FDIC will provide the applicant with a subsequent written notification of the final action taken as soon as the decision is rendered.

§ 303.203 Applications for capital distributions.

(a) *Scope.* An insured state nonmember bank and any insured branch of a foreign bank shall submit an application for capital distribution if, after having made a capital distribution, the institution would be undercapitalized, significantly undercapitalized, or critically undercapitalized.

(b) *Content of filing.* An application to repurchase, redeem, retire or otherwise acquire shares or ownership interests of the insured depository institution shall describe the proposal, the shares or obligations which are the subject thereof, and the additional shares or obligations of the institution which will be issued in at least an amount equivalent to the distribution. The application also shall explain how the proposal will reduce the institution's financial obligations or otherwise improve its financial condition. If the proposed action also requires an application under section 18(i) of the FDI Act (12 U.S.C. 1828(i)) as implemented by § 303.241 of this part regarding prior consent to retire capital, such application should be filed concurrently with, or made a part of, the application filed pursuant to section 38 of the FDI Act (12 U.S.C. 1831*o*).

§ 303.204 Applications for acquisitions, branching, and new lines of business.

(a) *Scope.* (1) Any insured state nonmember bank and any insured branch of a foreign bank which is undercapitalized or significantly undercapitalized, and any insured depository institution which is critically undercapitalized, shall submit an application to engage in acquisitions, branching or new lines of business.

Federal Deposit Insurance Corporation § 303.207

(2) A new line of business will include any new activity exercised which, although it may be permissible, has not been exercised by the institution.

(b) *Content of filing.* Applications shall describe the proposal, state the date the institution's capital restoration plan was accepted by its primary federal regulator, describe the institution's status in implementing the plan, and explain how the proposed action is consistent with and will further the achievement of the plan or otherwise further the purposes of section 38 of the FDI Act. If the FDIC is not the applicant's primary federal regulator, the application also should state whether approval has been requested from the applicant's primary federal regulator, the date of such request and the disposition of the request, if any. If the proposed action also requires applications pursuant to section 18 (c) or (d) of the FDI Act (mergers and branches) (12 U.S.C. 1828 (c) or (d)), such applications should be filed concurrently with, or made a part of, the application filed pursuant to section 38 of the FDI Act (12 U.S.C. 1831o).

§ 303.205 Applications for bonuses and increased compensation for senior executive officers.

(a) *Scope.* Any insured state nonmember bank or insured branch of a foreign bank that is significantly or critically undercapitalized, or any insured state nonmember bank or any insured branch of a foreign bank that is undercapitalized and which has failed to submit or implement in any material respect an acceptable capital restoration plan, shall submit an application to pay a bonus or increase compensation for any senior executive officer.

(b) *Content of filing.* Applications shall list each proposed bonus or increase in compensation, and for the latter shall identify compensation for each of the twelve calendar months preceding the calendar month in which the institution became undercapitalized. Applications also shall state the date the institution's capital restoration plan was accepted by the FDIC, and describe any progress made in implementing the plan.

§ 303.206 Application for payment of principal or interest on subordinated debt.

(a) *Scope.* Any critically undercapitalized insured depository institution shall submit an application to pay principal or interest on subordinated debt.

(b) *Content of filing.* Applications shall describe the proposed payment and provide an explanation of action taken under section 38(h)(3)(A)(ii) of the FDI Act (action other than receivership or conservatorship). The application also shall explain how such payments would further the purposes of section 38 of the FDI Act (12 U.S.C. 1831o). Existing approvals pursuant to requests filed under section 18(i)(1) of the FDI Act (12 U.S.C. 1828(i)(1)) (capital stock reductions or retirements) shall not be deemed to be the permission needed pursuant to section 38.

§ 303.207 Restricted activities for critically undercapitalized institutions.

(a) *Scope.* Any critically undercapitalized insured depository institution shall submit an application to engage in certain restricted activities.

(b) *Content of filing.* Applications to engage in any of the following activities, as set forth in sections 38(i)(2) (A) through (G) of the FDI Act, shall describe the proposed activity and explain how the activity would further the purposes of section 38 of the FDI Act (12 U.S.C. 1831o):

(1) Enter into any material transaction other than in the usual course of business including any action with respect to which the institution is required to provide notice to the appropriate federal banking agency. Materiality will be determined on a case-by-case basis;

(2) Extend credit for any highly leveraged transaction (as defined in part 325 of this chapter);

(3) Amend the institution's charter or bylaws, except to the extent necessary to carry out any other requirement of any law, regulation, or order;

(4) Make any material change in accounting methods;

(5) Engage in any covered transaction (as defined in section 23A(b) of the Federal Reserve Act (12 U.S.C. 371c(b));

§§ 303.208–303.219   12 CFR Ch. III (1–1–12 Edition)

(6) Pay excessive compensation or bonuses. Part 364 of this chapter provides guidance for determining excessive compensation; or

(7) Pay interest on new or renewed liabilities at a rate that would increase the institution's weighted average cost of funds to a level significantly exceeding the prevailing rates of interest on insured deposits in the institution's normal market area. Section 337.6 of this chapter (Brokered deposits) provides guidance for defining the relevant terms of this provision; however this provision does not supersede the general prohibitions contained in § 337.6.

§§ 303.208–303.219 [Reserved]

Subpart L—Section 19 of the FDI Act (Consent to Service of Persons Convicted of Certain Criminal Offenses)

§ 303.220 Scope.

This subpart covers applications under section 19 of the FDI Act (12 U.S.C. 1829). Pursuant to section 19, any person who has been convicted of any criminal offense involving dishonesty, breach of trust, or money laundering, or has agreed to enter into a pretrial diversion or similar program in connection with a prosecution for such offense, may not become, or continue as, an institution-affiliated party of an insured depository institution; own or control, directly or indirectly, any insured depository institution; or otherwise participate, directly or indirectly, in the conduct of the affairs of any insured depository institution without the prior written consent of the FDIC.

§ 303.221 Filing procedures.

(a) *Where to file.* An application under section 19 of the FDI Act shall be filed with the appropriate FDIC office.

(b) *Contents of filing.* Application forms may be obtained from any FDIC regional director. The FDIC may require additional information beyond that sought in the form, as warranted, in individual cases.

§ 303.222 Service at another insured depository institution.

In the case of a person who has already been approved by the FDIC under this subpart or section 19 of the FDI Act in connection with a particular insured depository institution, such person may not become an institution affiliated party, or own or control directly or indirectly another insured depository institution, or participate in the conduct of the affairs of another insured depository institution, without the prior written consent of the FDIC.

§ 303.223 Applicant's right to hearing following denial.

An applicant may request a hearing following a denial of an application in accordance with the provisions of part 308 of this chapter.

§§ 303.224–303.239 [Reserved]

Subpart M—Other Filings

§ 303.240 General.

This subpart sets forth the filing procedures to be followed when seeking the FDIC's consent to engage in certain activities or accomplish other matters as specified in the individual sections contained herein. For those matters covered by this subpart that also have substantive FDIC regulations or related statements of policy, references to the relevant regulations or statements of policy are contained in the specific sections.

§ 303.241 Reduce or retire capital stock or capital debt instruments.

(a) *Scope.* This section contains the procedures to be followed by an insured state nonmember bank to seek the prior approval of the FDIC to reduce the amount or retire any part of its common or preferred stock, or to retire any part of its capital notes or debentures pursuant to section 18(i)(1) of the Act (12 U.S.C. 1828(i)(1)).

(b) *Where to file.* Applicants shall submit a letter application to the appropriate FDIC office.

(c) *Content of filing.* The application shall contain the following:

(1) The type and amount of the proposed change to the capital structure and the reason for the change;

Federal Deposit Insurance Corporation § 303.242

(2) A schedule detailing the present and proposed capital structure;

(3) The time period that the proposal will encompass;

(4) If the proposal involves a series of transactions affecting Tier 1 capital components which will be consummated over a period of time which shall not exceed twelve months, the application shall certify that the insured depository institution will maintain itself as a well-capitalized institution as defined in part 325 of this chapter, both before and after each of the proposed transactions;

(5) If the proposal involves the repurchase of capital instruments, the amount of the repurchase price and the basis for establishing the fair market value of the repurchase price;

(6) A statement that the proposal will be available to all holders of a particular class of outstanding capital instruments on an equal basis, and if not, the details of any restrictions; and

(7) The date that the applicant's board of directors approved the proposal.

(d) *Additional information.* The FDIC may request additional information at any time during processing of the application.

(e) *Undercapitalized institutions.* Procedures regarding applications by an undercapitalized insured depository institution to retire capital stock or capital debt instruments pursuant to section 38 of the FDI Act (12 U.S.C. 1831o) are set forth in subpart K (Prompt Corrective Action), § 303.203. Applications pursuant to sections 38 and 18(i) may be filed concurrently, or as a single application.

(f) *Expedited processing for eligible depository institutions.* An application filed under this section by an eligible depository institution as defined in § 303.2(r) will be acknowledged in writing by the FDIC and will receive expedited processing, unless the applicant is notified in writing to the contrary and provided with the basis for that decision. The FDIC may remove an application from expedited processing for any of the reasons set forth in § 303.11(c)(2). Absent such removal, an application processed under expedited processing will be deemed approved 20 days after the FDIC's receipt of a substantially complete application.

(g) *Standard processing.* For those applications that are not processed pursuant to expedited procedures, the FDIC will provide the applicant with written notification of the final action as soon as the decision is rendered.

§ 303.242 Exercise of trust powers.

(a) *Scope.* This section contains the procedures to be followed by a state nonmember bank to seek the FDIC's prior consent to exercise trust powers. The FDIC's prior consent to exercise trust powers is not required in the following circumstances:

(1) Where a state nonmember bank received authority to exercise trust powers from its chartering authority prior to December 1, 1950; or

(2) Where an insured depository institution continues to conduct trust activities pursuant to authority granted by its chartering authority subsequent to a charter conversion or withdrawal from membership in the Federal Reserve System.

(b) *Where to file.* Applicants shall submit to the appropriate FDIC office a completed form, "Application for Consent To Exercise Trust Powers". This form may be obtained from any FDIC regional director.

(c) *Content of filing.* The filing shall consist of the completed trust application form.

(d) *Additional information.* The FDIC may request additional information at any time during processing of the filing.

(e) *Expedited processing for eligible depository institutions.* An application filed under this section by an eligible depository institution as defined in § 303.2(r) will be acknowledged in writing by the FDIC and will receive expedited processing, unless the applicant is notified in writing to the contrary and provided with the basis for that decision. The FDIC may remove an application from expedited processing for any of the reasons set forth in § 303.11(c)(2). Absent such removal, an application processed under expedited procedures will be deemed approved 30 days after the FDIC's receipt of a substantially complete application.

§ 303.243

(f) *Standard processing.* For those applications that are not processed pursuant to the expedited procedures, the FDIC will provide the applicant with written notification of the final action when the decision is rendered.

§ 303.243 Brokered deposit waivers.

(a) *Scope.* Pursuant to section 29 of the FDI Act (12 U.S.C. 1831f) and part 337 of this chapter, an adequately capitalized insured depository institution may not accept, renew or roll over any brokered deposits unless it has obtained a waiver from the FDIC. A well-capitalized insured depository institution may accept brokered deposits without a waiver, and an undercapitalized insured depository institution may not accept, renew or roll over any brokered deposits under any circumstances. This section contains the procedures to be followed to file with the FDIC for a brokered deposit waiver. The FDIC will provide notice to the depository institution's appropriate federal banking agency and any state regulatory agency, as appropriate, that a request for a waiver has been filed and will consult with such agency or agencies, prior to taking action on the institution's request for a waiver. Prior notice and/or consultation shall not be required in any particular case if the FDIC determines that the circumstances require it to take action without giving such notice and opportunity for consultation.

(b) *Where to file.* Applicants shall submit a letter application to the appropriate FDIC office.

(c) *Content of filing.* The application shall contain the following:

(1) The time period for which the waiver is requested;

(2) A statement of the policy governing the use of brokered deposits in the institution's overall funding and liquidity management program;

(3) The volume, rates and maturities of the brokered deposits held currently and anticipated during the waiver period sought, including any internal limits placed on the terms, solicitation and use of brokered deposits;

(4) How brokered deposits are costed and compared to other funding alternatives and how they are used in the institution's lending and investment activities, including a detailed discussion of asset growth plans;

(5) Procedures and practices used to solicit brokered deposits, including an identification of the principal sources of such deposits;

(6) Management systems overseeing the solicitation, acceptance and use of brokered deposits;

(7) A recent consolidated financial statement with balance sheet and income statements; and

(8) The reasons the institution believes its acceptance, renewal or rollover of brokered deposits would pose no undue risk.

(d) *Additional information.* The FDIC may request additional information at any time during processing of the application.

(e) *Expedited processing for eligible depository institutions.* An application filed under this section by an eligible depository institution as defined in this paragraph will be acknowledged in writing by the FDIC and will receive expedited processing, unless the applicant is notified in writing to the contrary and provided with the basis for that decision. For the purpose of this section, an applicant will be deemed an eligible depository institution if it satisfies all of the criteria contained in § 303.2(r) except that the applicant may be adequately capitalized rather than well-capitalized. The FDIC may remove an application from expedited processing for any of the reasons set forth in § 303.11(c)(2). Absent such removal, an application processed under expedited procedures will be deemed approved 21 days after the FDIC's receipt of a substantially complete application.

(f) *Standard processing.* For those filings which are not processed pursuant to the expedited procedures, the FDIC will provide the applicant with written notification of the final action as soon as the decision is rendered.

(g) *Conditions for approval.* A waiver issued pursuant to this section shall:

(1) Be for a fixed period, generally no longer than two years, but may be extended upon refiling; and

(2) May be revoked by the FDIC at any time by written notice to the institution.

Federal Deposit Insurance Corporation § 303.245

§ 303.244 Golden parachute and severance plan payments.

(a) *Scope.* Pursuant to section 18(k) of the FDI Act (12 U.S.C. 1828(k)) and part 359 of this chapter, an insured depository institution or depository institution holding company may not make golden parachute payments or excess nondiscriminatory severance plan payments unless the depository institution or holding company obtains permission to make such payments in accordance with the rules contained in part 359 of this chapter. This section contains the procedures to file for the FDIC's consent when such consent is necessary under part 359 of this chapter.

(1) *Golden parachute payments.* A troubled insured depository institution or a troubled depository institution holding company is prohibited from making golden parachute payments (as defined in § 359.1(f)(1) of this chapter) unless it obtains the consent of the appropriate federal banking agency and the written concurrence of the FDIC. Therefore, in the case of golden parachute payments, the procedures in this section apply to all troubled insured depository institutions and troubled depository institution holding companies.

(2) *Excess nondiscriminatory severance plan payments.* In the case of excess nondiscriminatory severance plan payments as provided by § 359.1(f)(2)(v) of this chapter, the FDIC's consent is necessary for state nonmember banks that meet the criteria set forth in § 359.1(f)(1)(ii) of this chapter. In addition, the FDIC's consent is required for all insured depository institutions or depository institution holding companies that meet the same criteria and seek to make payments in excess of the 12-month amount specified in § 359.1(f)(2)(v).

(b) *Where to file.* Applicants shall submit a letter application to the appropriate FDIC regional director.

(c) *Content of filing.* The application shall contain the following:

(1) The reasons why the applicant seeks to make the payment;

(2) An identification of the institution-affiliated party who will receive the payment;

(3) A copy of any contract or agreement regarding the subject matter of the filing;

(4) The cost of the proposed payment and its impact on the institution's capital and earnings;

(5) The reasons why the consent to the payment should be granted; and

(6) Certification and documentation as to each of the points cited in § 359.4(a)(4).

(d) *Additional information.* The FDIC may request additional information at any time during processing of the filing.

(e) *Processing.* The FDIC will provide the applicant with a subsequent written notification of the final action taken as soon as the decision is rendered.

[67 FR 79247, Dec. 27, 2002, as amended at 68 FR 50461, Aug. 21, 2003]

§ 303.245 Waiver of liability for commonly controlled depository institutions.

(a) *Scope.* Section 5(e) of the FDI Act (12 U.S.C. 1815(e)) creates liability for commonly controlled insured depository institutions for losses incurred or anticipated to be incurred by the FDIC in connection with the default of a commonly controlled insured depository institution or any assistance provided by the FDIC to any commonly controlled insured depository institution in danger of default. In addition to certain statutory exceptions and exclusions contained in sections 5(e)(6), (7) and (8), the FDI Act also permits the FDIC, in its discretion, to exempt any insured depository institution from this liability if it determines that such exemption is in the best interests of the Deposit Insurance Fund. This section describes procedures to request a conditional waiver of liability pursuant to section 5 of the FDI Act (12 U.S.C. 1815(e)(5)(A)).

(b) *Definition.* Conditional waiver of liability means an exemption from liability pursuant to section 5(e) of the FDI Act (12 U.S.C. 1815(e)) subject to terms and conditions.

(c) *Where to file.* Applicants shall submit a letter application to the appropriate FDIC office.

(d) *Content of filing.* The application shall contain the following information:

(1) The basis for requesting a waiver;

§ 303.246

(2) The existence of any significant events (e.g., change in control, capital injection, etc.) that may have an impact upon the applicant and/or any potentially liable institution;

(3) Current, and if applicable, pro forma financial information regarding the applicant and potentially liable institution(s); and

(4) The benefits to the appropriate FDIC insurance fund resulting from the waiver and any related events.

(e) *Additional information.* The FDIC may request additional information at any time during the processing of the filing.

(f) *Processing.* The FDIC will provide the applicant with written notification of the final action as soon as the decision is rendered.

(g) *Failure to comply with terms of conditional waiver.* In the event a conditional waiver of liability is issued, failure to comply with the terms specified therein may result in the termination of the conditional waiver of liability. The FDIC reserves the right to revoke the conditional waiver of liability after giving the applicant written notice of such revocation and a reasonable opportunity to be heard on the matter pursuant to § 303.10.

[67 FR 79247, Dec. 27, 2002, as amended at 71 FR 20526, Apr. 21, 2006]

§ 303.246 Conversion with diminution of capital.

(a) *Scope.* This section contains the procedures to be followed by an insured federal depository institution seeking the prior written consent of the FDIC pursuant to section 18(i)(2) of the FDI Act (12 U.S.C. 1828(i)(2)) to convert from an insured federal depository institution to an insured state nonmember bank (except a District bank) where the capital stock or surplus of the resulting bank will be less than the capital stock or surplus, respectively, of the converting institution at the time of the shareholders' meeting approving such conversion.

(b) *Where to file.* Applicants shall submit a letter application to the appropriate FDIC office.

(c) *Content of filing.* The application shall contain the following information:

(1) A description of the proposed transaction;

(2) A schedule detailing the present and proposed capital structure; and

(3) A copy of any documents submitted to the state chartering authority with respect to the charter conversion.

(d) *Additional information.* The FDIC may request additional information at any time during the processing.

(e) *Processing.* The FDIC will provide the applicant with written notification of the final action when the decision is rendered.

[67 FR 79247, Dec. 27, 2002. Redesignated at 71 FR 20526, Apr. 21, 2006]

§ 303.247 Continue or resume status as an insured institution following termination under section 8 of the FDI Act.

(a) *Scope.* This section relates to an application by a depository institution whose insured status has been terminated under section 8 of the FDI Act (12 U.S.C. 1818) for permission to continue or resume its status as an insured depository institution. This section covers institutions whose deposit insurance continues in effect for any purpose or for any length of time under the terms of an FDIC order terminating deposit insurance, but does not cover operating non-insured depository institutions which were previously insured by the FDIC, or any non-insured, non-operating depository institution whose charter has not been surrendered or revoked.

(b) *Where to file.* Applicants shall submit a letter application to the appropriate FDIC office.

(c) *Content of filing.* The filing shall contain the following information:

(1) A complete statement of the action requested, all relevant facts, and the reason for such requested action; and

(2) A certified copy of the resolution of the depository institution's board of directors authorizing submission of the filing.

(d) *Additional information.* The FDIC may request additional information at any time during processing of the filing.

(e) *Processing.* The FDIC will provide the applicant with written notification

Federal Deposit Insurance Corporation § 303.250

of the final action as soon as the decision is rendered.

[67 FR 79247, Dec. 27, 2002. Redesignated at 71 FR 20526, Apr. 21, 2006]

§ 303.248 Truth in Lending Act—Relief from reimbursement.

(a) *Scope.* This section applies to requests for relief from reimbursement pursuant to the Truth in Lending Act (15 U.S.C. 1601 et seq.) and Regulation Z (12 CFR part 226). Related delegations of authority are also set forth.

(b) *Procedures to be followed in filing initial requests for relief.* Requests for relief from reimbursement shall be filed with the appropriate FDIC office or within 60 days after receipt of the compliance report of examination containing the request to conduct a file search and make restitution to affected customers. The filing shall contain a complete and concise statement of the action requested, all relevant facts, the reasons and analysis relied upon as the basis for such requested action, and all supporting documentation.

(c) *Additional information.* The FDIC may request additional information at any time during processing of any such requests.

(d) *Processing.* The FDIC will acknowledge receipt of the request for reconsideration and provide the applicant with written notification of its determination within 60 days of its receipt of the request for reconsideration.

(e) *Procedures to be followed in filing requests for reconsideration.* Within 15 days of receipt of written notice that its request for relief has been denied, the requestor may petition the appropriate FDIC office for reconsideration of such request in accordance with the procedures set forth in § 303.11(f).

[67 FR 79247, Dec. 27, 2002. Redesignated at 71 FR 20526, Apr. 21, 2006]

§ 303.249 Management official interlocks.

(a) *Scope.* This section contains the procedures to be followed by an insured state nonmember bank to seek the approval of FDIC to establish an interlock pursuant to the Depository Institutions Management Interlocks Act (12 U.S.C. 3207), section 13 of the FDI Act (12 U.S.C. 1823(k)) and part 348 of this chapter (12 CFR part 348).

(b) *Where to file.* Applicants shall submit a letter application to the appropriate FDIC office.

(c) *Content of filing.* The application shall contain the following:

(1) A description of the proposed interlock;

(2) A statement of reason as to why the interlock will not result in a monopoly or a substantial lessening of competition; and

(3) If the applicant is seeking an exemption set forth in § 348.5 or 348.6 of this chapter, a description of the particular exemption which is being requested and a statement of reasons as to why the exemption is applicable.

(d) *Additional information.* The FDIC may request additional information at any time during processing of the filing.

(e) *Processing.* The FDIC will provide the applicant with written notification of the final action when the decision is rendered.

[67 FR 79247, Dec. 27, 2002. Redesignated at 71 FR 20526, Apr. 21, 2006]

§ 303.250 Modification of conditions.

(a) *Scope.* This section contains the procedures to be followed by an insured depository institution to seek the prior consent of the FDIC to modify the requirement of a prior approval of a filing issued by the FDIC.

(b) *Where to file.* Applicants should submit a letter application to the appropriate FDIC regional director.

(c) *Content of filing.* The application should contain the following information:

(1) A description of the original approved application;

(2) A description of the modification requested; and

(3) The reason for the request.

(d) *Additional information.* The FDIC may request additional information at any time during processing of the filing.

(e) *Processing.* The FDIC will provide the applicant with a written notification of the final action as soon as the decision is rendered.

[67 FR 79247, Dec. 27. Redesignated at 71 FR 20526, Apr. 21, 2006]

§ 303.251 Extension of time.

(a) *Scope.* This section contains the procedures to be followed by an insured depository institution to seek the prior consent of the FDIC for additional time to fulfill a condition required in an approval of a filing issued by the FDIC or to consummate a transaction which was the subject of an approval by the FDIC.

(b) *Where to file.* Applicants shall submit a letter application to the appropriate FDIC office.

(c) *Content of filing.* The application shall contain the following information:

(1) A description of the original approved application;

(2) Identification of the original time limitation;

(3) The additional time period requested; and

(4) The reason for the request.

(d) *Additional information.* The FDIC may request additional information at any time during processing of the filing.

(e) *Processing.* The FDIC will provide the applicant with written notification of the final action as soon as the decision is rendered.

[67 FR 79247, Dec. 27. Redesignated at 71 FR 20526, Apr. 21, 2006]

§§ 303.252–303.259 [Reserved]

PART 304—FORMS, INSTRUCTIONS, AND REPORTS

Sec.
304.1 Purpose.
304.2 Where to obtain forms and instructions.
304.3 Reports.

AUTHORITY: 5 U.S.C. 552; 12 U.S.C. 1817, 1831, 1867.

SOURCE: 67 FR 18793, Apr. 17, 2002, unless otherwise noted.

§ 304.1 Purpose.

Part 304 informs the public where it may obtain forms and instructions for reports, applications, and other submittals used by the FDIC, and also describes certain forms that are not described elsewhere in FDIC regulations.

§ 304.2 Where to obtain forms and instructions.

Forms and instructions used in connection with applications, reports, and other submittals used by the FDIC can be obtained by contacting the FDIC Public Information Center (801 17th Street, NW., Washington, DC 20434; telephone: 800–276–6003 or 202–416–6940), except as noted below in § 304.3. In addition, many forms and instructions can be obtained from FDIC regional offices. A list of FDIC regional offices can be obtained from the FDIC Public Information Center or found at the FDIC's web site at *http://www.fdic.gov,* or in the directory of FDIC Law, Regulations and Related Acts published by the FDIC.

§ 304.3 Reports.

(a) Consolidated Reports of Condition and Income, Forms FFIEC 031 and 041. Pursuant to section 7(a) of the Federal Deposit Insurance Act (12 U.S.C. 1817(a)), every national bank, state member bank, and insured state nonmember bank is required to file Consolidated Reports of Condition and Income (also known as the Call Report) in accordance with the instructions for these reports. All assets and liabilities, including contingent assets and liabilities, must be reported in, or otherwise taken into account in the preparation of, the Call Report. The FDIC uses Call Report data to calculate deposit insurance assessments and monitor the condition, performance, and risk profile of individual banks and the banking industry. Reporting banks must also submit annually such information on small business and small farm lending as the FDIC may need to assess the availability of credit to these sectors of the economy. The report forms and instructions can be obtained from the Division of Supervision and Consumer Protection (DSC), FDIC, Washington, DC 20429.

(Approved by the Office of Management and Budget under control number 3064–0052)

(b) Report of Assets and Liabilities of U.S. Branches and Agencies of Foreign Banks, Form FFIEC 002. Pursuant to section 7(a) of the Federal Deposit Insurance Act (12 U.S.C. 1817(a)), every insured U.S. branch of a foreign bank is

Federal Deposit Insurance Corporation

§ 307.1

required to file a Report of Assets and Liabilities of U.S. Branches and Agencies of Foreign Banks in accordance with the instructions for the report. All assets and liabilities, including contingent assets and liabilities, must be reported in, or otherwise taken into account in the preparation of the report. The FDIC uses the reported data to calculate deposit insurance assessments and monitor the condition, performance, and risk profile of individual insured branches and the banking industry. Insured branches must also submit annually such information on small business and small farm lending as the FDIC may need to assess the availability of credit to these sectors of the economy. Because the Board of Governors of the Federal Reserve System collects and processes this report on behalf of the FDIC, the report forms and instructions can be obtained from Federal Reserve District Banks or through the web site of the Federal Financial Institutions Examination Council, *http://www.ffiec.gov/*.

(Approved by the Office of Management and Budget under control number 7100-0032)

(c) *Summary of Deposits, Form FDIC 8020/05.* Form 8020/05 is a report on the amount of deposits for each authorized office of an insured bank with branches; unit banks do not report. Reports as of June 30 of each year must be submitted no later than the immediately succeeding July 31. The report forms and the instructions for completing the reports will be furnished to all such banks by, or may be obtained upon request from, the Division of Supervision and Consumer Protection (DSC), FDIC, 550 17th Street, NW., Washington, DC 20429.

(Approved by the Office of Management and Budget under control number 3064-0061)

(d) *Notification of Performance of Bank Services, Form FDIC 6120/06.* Pursuant to Section 7 of the Bank Service Company Act (12 U.S.C. 1867), as amended, FDIC supervised banks must notify the agency about the existence of a service relationship within thirty days after the making of the contract or the performance of the service, whichever occurs first. Form FDIC 6120/06 may be used to satisfy the notice requirement. The form contains identification, location and contact information for the bank, the servicer, and a description of the services provided. In lieu of the form, notification may be provided by letter. Either the form or the letter containing the notice information must be submitted to the regional director—Division of Supervision and Consumer Protection (DSC) of the region in which the bank's main office is located.

(Approved by the Office of Management and Budget under control number 3064-0029)

PARTS 305-306 [RESERVED]

PART 307—CERTIFICATION OF ASSUMPTION OF DEPOSITS AND NOTIFICATION OF CHANGES OF INSURED STATUS

Sec.
307.1 Scope and purpose.
307.2 Certification of assumption of deposit liabilities.
307.3 Notice to depositors when insured status is voluntarily terminated and deposits are not assumed.
APPENDIX A TO PART 307—TRANSFERRING INSTITUTION LETTERHEAD
APPENDIX B TO PART 307—INSTITUTION LETTERHEAD

AUTHORITY: 12 U.S.C. 1818(a)(6); 1818(q); and 1819(a) [Tenth].

SOURCE: 71 FR 8791, Feb. 21, 2006, unless otherwise noted.

§ 307.1 Scope and purpose.

(a) *Scope.* This Part applies to all insured depository institutions, as defined in section 3(c)(2) of the Federal Deposit Insurance Act (FDI Act) (12 U.S.C. 1813(c)(2)).

(b) *Purpose.* This Part sets forth the rules governing:

(1) The time and manner for providing certification to the FDIC regarding the assumption of all of the deposit liabilities of an insured depository institution by one or more insured depository institutions; and

(2) The notification that an insured depository institution shall provide its depositors when a depository institution's insured status is being voluntarily terminated without its deposits being assumed by one or more insured depository institutions.

§ 307.2 Certification of assumption of deposit liabilities.

(a) *When certification is required.* Whenever all of the deposit liabilities of an insured depository institution are assumed by one or more insured depository institutions by merger, consolidation, other statutory assumption, or by contract, the transferring insured depository institution, or its legal successor, shall provide an accurate written certification to the FDIC that its deposit liabilities have been assumed. No certification shall be required when deposit liabilities are assumed by an operating insured depository institution from an insured depository institution in default, as defined in section 3(x)(1) of the FDI Act (12 U.S.C. 1813(x)(1)), and that has been placed under FDIC receivership.

(b) *Certification requirements.* The certification required by paragraph (a) of this section shall be provided on official letterhead of the transferring insured depository institution or its legal successor, signed by a duly authorized official, and state the date the assumption took effect. The certification shall indicate the date on which the transferring institution's authority to engage in banking has terminated or will terminate as well as the method of termination (e.g., whether by the surrender of its charter, by the cancellation of its charter or license to conduct a banking business, or otherwise). The certification may follow the form contained in Appendix A of this part. In a merger or consolidation where there is only one surviving entity which is the legal successor to both the transferring and assuming institutions, the surviving entity shall provide any required certification.

(c) *Filing.* The certification required by paragraph (a) of this section shall be provided within 30 calendar days after the assumption takes effect, and shall be submitted to the appropriate Regional Director of the FDIC's Division of Supervision and Consumer Protection, as defined in 12 CFR 303.2(g).

(d) *Evidence of assumption.* The receipt by the FDIC of an accurate certification for a total assumption as required by paragraphs (a), (b) and (c) of this section shall constitute satisfactory evidence of such deposit assumption, as required by section 8(q) of the FDI Act (12 U.S.C. 1818(q)), and the insured status of the transferring institution shall terminate on the date of the receipt of the certification. In appropriate circumstances, the FDIC, in its sole discretion, may require additional information, or may consider other evidence of a deposit assumption to constitute satisfactory evidence of such assumption for purposes of section 8(q).

(e) *Issuance of an order.* The Executive Secretary, upon request from the Director of the Division of Supervision and Consumer Protection and with the concurrence of the General Counsel, or their respective designees, shall issue an order terminating the insured status of the transferring insured depository institution as of the date of receipt by the FDIC of satisfactory evidence of such assumption, pursuant to section 8(q) of the FDI Act and this regulation. Generally, no order shall be issued, under this paragraph, and insured status shall be cancelled by operation of law:

(1) If the charter of the transferring institution has been cancelled, revoked, rescinded, or otherwise terminated by operation of applicable state or federal statutes or regulations, or by action of the chartering authority for the transferring institution essentially contemporaneously, that is, generally within five business days after all deposits have been assumed; or

(2) If the transferring institution is an insured depository institution in default and for which the FDIC has been appointed receiver.

§ 307.3 Notice to depositors when insured status is voluntarily terminated and deposits are not assumed.

(a) *Notice required.* An insured depository institution that has obtained authority from the FDIC to terminate its insured status under sections 8(a), 8(p) or 18(i)(3) of the FDI Act without its deposit liabilities being assumed by one or more insured depository institutions shall provide to each of its depositors, at the depositor's last known address of record on the books of the institution, prior written notification of the date the institution's insured status shall terminate.

Federal Deposit Insurance Corporation

(b) *Prior approval of notice.* The insured depository institution shall provide the appropriate Regional Director of the FDIC's Division of Supervision and Consumer Protection, as defined in 12 CFR 303.2(g), a copy of the proposed notice for approval. After being approved, the notice shall be provided to depositors by the insured depository institution at the time and in the manner specified by the appropriate Regional Director.

(c) *Form of notice.* The notice to depositors required by paragraph (a) of this section shall be provided on the official letterhead of the insured depository institution, shall bear the signature of a duly authorized officer, and, unless otherwise specified by the appropriate Regional Director, may follow the form of the notice contained in Appendix B of this part.

(d) *Other requirements possible.* The FDIC may require the insured depository institution to take such other actions as the FDIC considers necessary and appropriate for the protection of depositors.

APPENDIX A TO PART 307—TRANSFERRING INSTITUTION LETTERHEAD

[Date]

[Name and Address of appropriate FDIC Regional Director]

SUBJECT: *Certification of Total Assumption of Deposits*

This certification is being provided pursuant to 12 U.S.C. 1818(q) and 12 CFR 307.2. On [state the date the deposit assumption took effect], [state the name of the depository institution assuming the deposit liabilities] assumed all of the deposits of [state the name and location of the transferring institution whose deposits were assumed]. [If applicable, state the date and method by which the transferring institution's authority to engage in banking was or will be terminated.] Please contact the undersigned, at [telephone number], if additional information is needed.

Sincerely,

By:

[Name and Title of Authorized Representative]

APPENDIX B TO PART 307—INSTITUTION LETTERHEAD

[Date]

[Name and Address of Depositor]

SUBJECT: *Notice to Depositor of Voluntary Termination of Insured Status*

The insured status of [name of insured depository institution], under the provisions of the Federal Deposit Insurance Act, will terminate as of the close of business on [state the date] ("termination date"). Insured deposits in the [name of insured depository institution] on the termination date, less all withdrawals from such deposits made subsequent to that date, will continue to be insured by the Federal Deposit Insurance Corporation, to the extent provided by law, until [state the date]. The Federal Deposit Insurance Corporation will not insure any new deposits or additions to existing deposits made by you after the termination date.

This Notice is being provided pursuant to 12 CFR 307.3.

Please contact [name of institution official in charge of depositor inquiries], at [name and address of insured depository institution] if additional information is needed regarding this Notice or the insured status of your account(s).

Sincerely,

By:

[Name and Title of Authorized Representative]

PART 308—RULES OF PRACTICE AND PROCEDURE

Subpart A—Uniform Rules of Practice and Procedure

Sec.
308.1 Scope.
308.2 Rules of construction.
308.3 Definitions.
308.4 Authority of Board of Directors.
308.5 Authority of the administrative law judge.
308.6 Appearance and practice in adjudicatory proceedings.
308.7 Good faith certification.
308.8 Conflicts of interest.
308.9 Ex parte communications.
308.10 Filing of papers.
308.11 Service of papers.
308.12 Construction of time limits.
308.13 Change of time limits.
308.14 Witness fees and expenses.
308.15 Opportunity for informal settlement.
308.16 FDIC's right to conduct examination.
308.17 Collateral attacks on adjudicatory proceeding.
308.18 Commencement of proceeding and contents of notice.
308.19 Answer.
308.20 Amended pleadings.
308.21 Failure to appear.
308.22 Consolidation and severance of actions.
308.23 Motions.
308.24 Scope of document discovery.

Pt. 308 12 CFR Ch. III (1-1-12 Edition)

308.25 Request for document discovery from parties.
308.26 Document subpoenas to nonparties.
308.27 Deposition of witness unavailable for hearing.
308.28 Interlocutory review.
308.29 Summary disposition.
308.30 Partial summary disposition.
308.31 Scheduling and prehearing conferences.
308.32 Prehearing submissions.
308.33 Public hearings.
308.34 Hearing subpoenas.
308.35 Conduct of hearings.
308.36 Evidence.
308.37 Post-hearing filings.
308.38 Recommended decision and filing of record.
308.39 Exceptions to recommended decision.
308.40 Review by Board of Directors.
308.41 Stays pending judicial review.

Subpart B—General Rules of Procedure

308.101 Scope of Local Rules.
308.102 Authority of Board of Directors and Executive Secretary.
308.103 Appointment of administrative law judge.
308.104 Filings with the Board of Directors.
308.105 Custodian of the record.
308.106 Written testimony in lieu of oral hearing.
308.107 Document discovery.

Subpart C—Rules of Practice Before the FDIC and Standards of Conduct

308.108 Sanctions.
308.109 Suspension and disbarment.

Subpart D—Rules and Procedures Applicable to Proceedings Relating to Disapproval of Acquisition of Control

308.110 Scope.
308.111 Grounds for disapproval.
308.112 Notice of disapproval.
308.113 Answer to notice of disapproval.
308.114 Burden of proof.

Subpart E—Rules and Procedures Applicable to Proceedings Relating to Assessment of Civil Penalties for Willful Violations of the Change in Bank Control Act

308.115 Scope.
308.116 Assessment of penalties.
308.117 Effective date of, and payment under, an order to pay.
308.118 Collection of penalties.

Subpart F—Rules and Procedures Applicable to Proceedings for Involuntary Termination of Insured Status

308.119 Scope.

308.120 Grounds for termination of insurance.
308.121 Notification to primary regulator.
308.122 Notice of intent to terminate.
308.123 Notice to depositors.
308.124 Involuntary termination of insured status for failure to receive deposits.
308.125 Temporary suspension of deposit insurance.
308.126 Special supervisory associations.

Subpart G—Rules and Procedures Applicable to Proceedings Relating to Cease-and-Desist Orders

308.127 Scope.
308.128 Grounds for cease-and-desist orders.
308.129 Notice to state supervisory authority.
308.130 Effective date of order and service on bank.
308.131 Temporary cease-and-desist order.

Subpart H—Rules and Procedures Applicable to Proceedings Relating to Assessment and Collection of Civil Money Penalties for Violation of Cease-and-Desist Orders and of Certain Federal Statutes, Including Call Report Penalties

308.132 Assessment of penalties.
308.133 Effective date of, and payment under, an order to pay.

Subpart I—Rules and Procedures for Imposition of Sanctions Upon Municipal Securities Dealers or Persons Associated With Them and Clearing Agencies or Transfer Agents

308.134 Scope.
308.135 Grounds for imposition of sanctions.
308.136 Notice to and consultation with the Securities and Exchange Commission.
308.137 Effective date of order imposing sanctions.

Subpart J—Rules and Procedures Relating to Exemption Proceedings Under Section 12(h) of the Securities Exchange Act of 1934

308.138 Scope.
308.139 Application for exemption.
308.140 Newspaper notice.
308.141 Notice of hearing.
308.142 Hearing.
308.143 Decision of Board of Directors.

Subpart K—Procedures Applicable to Investigations Pursuant to Section 10(c) of the FDIA

308.144 Scope.
308.145 Conduct of investigation.

# Federal Deposit Insurance Corporation	Pt. 308

308.146 Powers of person conducting investigation.
308.147 Investigations confidential.
308.148 Rights of witnesses.
308.149 Service of subpoena.
308.150 Transcripts.

Subpart L—Procedures and Standards Applicable to a Notice of Change in Senior Executive Officer or Director Pursuant to Section 32 of the FDIA

308.151 Scope.
308.152 Grounds for disapproval of notice.
308.153 Procedures where notice of disapproval issues pursuant to § 303.103(c) of this chapter.
308.154 Decision on review.
308.155 Hearing.

Subpart M—Procedures and Standards Applicable to an Application Pursuant to Section 19 of the FDIA

308.156 Scope.
308.157 Relevant considerations.
308.158 Filing papers and effective date.
308.159 Denial of applications.
308.160 Hearings.

Subpart N—Rules and Procedures Applicable to Proceedings Relating to Suspension, Removal, and Prohibition Where a Felony Is Charged

308.161 Scope.
308.162 Relevant considerations.
308.163 Notice of suspension or prohibition, and orders of removal or prohibition.
308.164 Hearings.

Subpart O—Liability of Commonly Controlled Depository Institutions

308.165 Scope.
308.166 Grounds for assessment of liability.
308.167 Notice of assessment of liability.
308.168 Effective date of and payment under an order to pay.

Subpart P—Rules and Procedures Relating to the Recovery of Attorney Fees and Other Expenses

308.169 Scope.
308.170 Filing, content, and service of documents.
308.171 Responses to application.
308.172 Eligibility of applicants.
308.173 Prevailing party.
308.174 Standards for awards.
308.175 Measure of awards.
308.176 Application for awards.
308.177 Statement of net worth.
308.178 Statement of fees and expenses.
308.179 Settlement negotiations.
308.180 Further proceedings.

308.181 Recommended decision.
308.182 Board of Directors action.
308.183 Payment of awards.

Subpart Q—Issuance and Review of Orders Pursuant to the Prompt Corrective Action Provisions of the Federal Deposit Insurance Act

308.200 Scope.
308.201 Directives to take prompt corrective action.
308.202 Procedures for reclassifying a bank based on criteria other than capital.
308.203 Order to dismiss a director or senior executive officer.
308.204 Enforcement of directives.

Subpart R—Submission and Review of Safety and Soundness Compliance Plans and Issuance of Orders To Correct Safety and Soundness Deficiencies

308.300 Scope.
308.301 Purpose.
308.302 Determination and notification of failure to meet a safety and soundness standard and request for compliance plan.
308.303 Filing of safety and soundness compliance plan.
308.304 Issuance of orders to correct deficiencies and to take or refrain from taking other actions.
308.305 Enforcement of orders.

Subpart S—Applications for a Stay or Review of Actions of Bank Clearing Agencies

308.400 Scope.
308.401 Applications for stays of disciplinary sanctions or summary suspensions by a bank clearing agency.
308.402 Applications for review of final disciplinary sanctions, denials of participation, or prohibitions or limitations of access to services imposed by bank clearing agencies.

Subpart T—Program Fraud Civil Remedies and Procedures

308.500 Basis, purpose, and scope.
308.501 Definitions.
308.502 Basis for civil penalties and assessments.
308.503 Investigations.
308.504 Review by the reviewing official.
308.505 Prerequisites for issuing a complaint.
308.506 Complaint.
308.507 Service of complaint.
308.508 Answer.
308.509 Default upon failure to file an answer.

§ 308.1

308.510 Referral of complaint and answer to the ALJ.
308.511 Notice of hearing.
308.512 Parties to the hearing.
308.513 Separation of functions.
308.514 Ex parte contacts.
308.515 Disqualification of reviewing official or ALJ.
308.516 Rights of parties.
308.517 Authority of the ALJ.
308.518 Prehearing conferences.
308.519 Disclosure of documents.
308.520 Discovery.
308.521 Exchange of witness lists, statements, and exhibits.
308.522 Subpoenas for attendance at hearing.
308.523 Protective order.
308.524 Witness fees.
308.525 Form, filing, and service of papers.
308.526 Computation of time.
308.527 Motions.
308.528 Sanctions.
308.529 The hearing and burden of proof.
308.530 Determining the amount of penalties and assessments.
308.531 Location of hearing.
308.532 Witnesses.
308.533 Evidence.
308.534 The record.
308.535 Post-hearing briefs.
308.536 Initial decision.
308.537 Reconsideration of initial decision.
308.538 Appeal to the Board of Directors.
308.539 Stays ordered by the Department of Justice.
308.540 Stay pending appeal.
308.541 Judicial review.
308.542 Collection of civil penalties and assessments.
308.543 Right to administrative offset.
308.544 Deposit in Treasury of United States.
308.545 Compromise or settlement.
308.546 Limitations.

Subpart U—Removal, Suspension, and Debarment of Accountants From Performing Audit Services

308.600 Scope.
308.601 Definitions.
308.602 Removal, suspension, or debarment.
308.603 Automatic removal, suspension, and debarment.
308.604 Notice of removal, suspension, or debarment.
308.605 Application for reinstatement.

AUTHORITY: 5 U.S.C. 504, 554–557; 12 U.S.C. 93(b), 164, 505, 1815(e), 1817, 1818, 1820, 1828, 1829, 1829b, 1831i, 1831m(g)(4), 1831o, 1831p–1, 1832(c), 1884(b), 1972, 3102, 3108(a), 3349, 3909, 4717, 15 U.S.C. 78(h) and (i), 78o–4(c), 78o–5, 78q–1, 78s, 78u, 78u–2, 78u–3, and 78w, 6801(b), 6805(b)(1); 28 U.S.C. 2461 note; 31 U.S.C. 330, 5321; 42 U.S.C. 4012a; Sec. 3100(s), Pub. L. 104–134, 110 Stat. 1321–358; and Pub. L. 109–351.

SOURCE: 56 FR 37975, Aug. 9, 1991, unless otherwise noted.

Subpart A—Uniform Rules of Practice and Procedure

§ 308.1 Scope.

This subpart prescribes rules of practice and procedure applicable to adjudicatory proceedings as to which hearings on the record are provided for by the following statutory provisions:

(a) Cease-and-desist proceedings under section 8(b) of the Federal Deposit Insurance Act ("FDIA") (12 U.S.C. 1818(b));

(b) Removal and prohibition proceedings under section 8(e) of the FDIA (12 U.S.C. 1818(e));

(c) Change-in-control proceedings under section 7(j)(4) of the FDIA (12 U.S.C. 1817(j)(4)) to determine whether the Federal Deposit Insurance Corporation ("FDIC"), should issue an order to approve or disapprove a person's proposed acquisition of an institution and/or institution holding company;

(d) Proceedings under section 15C(c)(2) of the Securities Exchange Act of 1934 ("Exchange Act") (15 U.S.C. 78o–5), to impose sanctions upon any government securities broker or dealer or upon any person associated or seeking to become associated with a government securities broker or dealer for which the FDIC is the appropriate regulatory agency;

(e) Assessment of civil money penalties by the FDIC against institutions, institution-affiliated parties, and certain other persons for which it is the appropriate regulatory agency for any violation of:

(1) Sections 22(h) and 23 of the Federal Reserve Act ("FRA"), or any regulation issued thereunder, and certain unsafe or unsound practices or breaches of fiduciary duty, pursuant to 12 U.S.C. 1828(j);

(2) Section 106(b) of the Bank Holding Company Act Amendments of 1970 ("BHCA Amendments of 1970"), and certain unsafe or unsound practices or breaches of fiduciary duty, pursuant to 12 U.S.C. 1972(2)(F);

(3) Any provision of the Change in Bank Control Act of 1978, as amended (the "CBCA"), or any regulation or order issued thereunder, and certain

unsafe or unsound practices, or breaches of fiduciary duty, pursuant to 12 U.S.C. 1817(j)(16);

(4) Section 7(a)(1) of the FDIA, pursuant to 12 U.S.C. 1817(a)(1);

(5) Any provision of the International Lending Supervision Act of 1983 ("ILSA"), or any rule, regulation or order issued thereunder, pursuant to 12 U.S.C. 3909;

(6) Any provision of the International Banking Act of 1978 ("IBA"), or any rule, regulation or order issued thereunder, pursuant to 12 U.S.C. 3108;

(7) Certain provisions of the Exchange Act, pursuant to section 21B of the Exchange Act (15 U.S.C. 78u–2);

(8) Section 1120 of the Financial Institutions Reform, Recovery, and Enforcement Act of 1989 ("FIRREA") (12 U.S.C. 3349), or any order or regulation issued thereunder;

(9) The terms of any final or temporary order issued under section 8 of the FDIA or of any written agreement executed by the FDIC, the terms of any condition imposed in writing by the FDIC in connection with the grant of an application or request, certain unsafe or unsound practices or breaches of fiduciary duty, or any law or regulation not otherwise provided herein pursuant to 12 U.S.C. 1818(i)(2);

(10) Any provision of law referenced in section 102(f) of the Flood Disaster Protection Act of 1973 (42 U.S.C. 4012a(f)) or any order or regulation issued thereunder; and

(11) Any provision of law referenced in 31 U.S.C. 5321 or any order or regulation issued thereunder;

(f) Remedial action under section 102(g) of the Flood Disaster Protection Act of 1973 (42 U.S.C. 4012a(g));

(g) Proceedings under section 10(k) of the FDIA (12 U.S.C. 1820(k)) to impose penalties for violations of the post-employment restrictions under that subsection; and

(h) This subpart also applies to all other adjudications required by statute to be determined on the record after opportunity for an agency hearing, unless otherwise specifically provided for in the Local Rules.

[56 FR 37975, Aug. 9, 1991, as amended at 61 FR 20347, May 6, 1996; 70 FR 69639, Nov. 17, 2005]

§ 308.2 Rules of construction.

For purposes of this subpart:

(a) Any term in the singular includes the plural, and the plural includes the singular, if such use would be appropriate;

(b) Any use of a masculine, feminine, or neuter gender encompasses all three, if such use would be appropriate;

(c) The term *counsel* includes a nonattorney representative; and

(d) Unless the context requires otherwise, a party's counsel of record, if any, may, on behalf of that party, take any action required to be taken by the party.

§ 308.3 Definitions.

For purposes of this subpart, unless explicitly stated to the contrary:

(a) *Administrative law judge* means one who presides at an administrative hearing under authority set forth at 5 U.S.C. 556.

(b) *Adjudicatory proceeding* means a proceeding conducted pursuant to these rules and leading to the formulation of a final order other than a regulation.

(c) *Board of Directors* or *Board* means the Board of Directors of the Federal Deposit Insurance Corporation or its designee.

(d) *Decisional employee* means any member of the Federal Deposit Insurance Corporation's or administrative law judge's staff who has not engaged in an investigative or prosecutorial role in a proceeding and who may assist the Board of Directors or the administrative law judge, respectively, in preparing orders, recommended decisions, decisions, and other documents under the Uniform Rules.

(e) *Designee* of the Board of Directors means officers or officials of the Federal Deposit Insurance Corporation acting pursuant to authority delegated by the Board of Directors as provided in 12 CFR part 303 of this chapter or by specific resolution of the Board of Directors.

(f) *Enforcement Counsel* means any individual who files a notice of appearance as counsel on behalf of the FDIC in an adjudicatory proceeding.

§ 308.4

(g) *Executive Secretary* means the Executive Secretary of the Federal Deposit Insurance Corporation or his or her designee.

(h) *FDIC* means the Federal Deposit Insurance Corporation.

(i) *Final order* means an order issued by the FDIC with or without the consent of the affected institution or the institution-affiliated party, that has become final, without regard to the pendency of any petition for reconsideration or review.

(j) *Institution* includes:

(1) Any bank as that term is defined in section 3(a) of the FDIA (12 U.S.C. 1813(a));

(2) Any bank holding company or any subsidiary (other than a bank) of a bank holding company as those terms are defined in the BHCA (12 U.S.C. 1841 et seq.);

(3) Any savings association as that term is defined in section 3(b) of the FDIA (12 U.S.C. 1813(b)), any savings and loan holding company or any subsidiary thereof (other than a bank) as those terms are defined in section 10(a) of the HOLA (12 U.S.C. 1467(a));

(4) Any organization operating under section 25 of the FRA (12 U.S.C. 601 et seq.);

(5) Any foreign bank or company to which section 8 of the IBA (12 U.S.C. 3106), applies or any subsidiary (other than a bank) thereof; and

(6) Any federal agency as that term is defined in section 1(b) of the IBA (12 U.S.C. 3101(5)).

(k) *Institution-affiliated party* means any institution-affiliated party as that term is defined in section 3(u) of the FDIA (12 U.S.C. 1813(u)).

(l) *Local Rules* means those rules promulgated by the FDIC in those subparts of this part other than subpart A.

(m) *Office of Financial Institution Adjudication* ("OFIA") means the executive body charged with overseeing the administration of administrative enforcement proceedings of the Office of the Comptroller of the Currency ("OCC"), the Board of Governors of the Federal Reserve Board ("FRB"), the FDIC, the Office of Thrift Supervision ("OTS") and the National Credit Union Administration ("NCUA").

(n) *Party* means the FDIC and any person named as a party in any notice.

(o) *Person* means an individual, sole proprietor, partnership, corporation, unincorporated association, trust, joint venture, pool, syndicate, agency or other entity or organization, including an institution as defined in paragraph (j) of this section.

(p) *Respondent* means any party other than the FDIC.

(q) *Uniform Rules* means those rules in subpart A of this part that pertain to the types of formal administrative enforcement actions set forth at § 308.01 and as specified in subparts B through P of this part.

(r) *Violation* includes any action (alone or with another or others) for or toward causing, bringing about, participating in, counseling, or aiding or abetting a violation.

§ 308.4 Authority of Board of Directors.

The Board of Directors may, at any time during the pendency of a proceeding, perform, direct the performance of, or waive performance of, any act which could be done or ordered by the administrative law judge.

§ 308.5 Authority of the administrative law judge.

(a) *General rule.* All proceedings governed by this part shall be conducted in accordance with the provisions of chapter 5 of title 5 of the United States Code. The administrative law judge shall have all powers necessary to conduct a proceeding in a fair and impartial manner and to avoid unnecessary delay.

(b) *Powers.* The administrative law judge shall have all powers necessary to conduct the proceeding in accordance with paragraph (a) of this section, including the following powers:

(1) To administer oaths and affirmations;

(2) To issue subpoenas, subpoenas duces tecum, and protective orders, as authorized by this part, and to quash or modify any such subpoenas and orders;

(3) To receive relevant evidence and to rule upon the admission of evidence and offers of proof;

(4) To take or cause depositions to be taken as authorized by this subpart;

(5) To regulate the course of the hearing and the conduct of the parties and their counsel;

(6) To hold scheduling and/or prehearing conferences as set forth in § 308.31;

(7) To consider and rule upon all procedural and other motions appropriate in an adjudicatory proceeding, provided that only the Board of Directors shall have the power to grant any motion to dismiss the proceeding or to decide any other motion that results in a final determination of the merits of the proceeding;

(8) To prepare and present to the Board of Directors a recommended decision as provided herein;

(9) To recuse himself or herself by motion made by a party or on his or her own motion;

(10) To establish time, place and manner limitations on the attendance of the public and the media for any public hearing; and

(11) To do all other things necessary and appropriate to discharge the duties of a presiding officer.

§ 308.6 Appearance and practice in adjudicatory proceedings.

(a) *Appearance before the FDIC or an administrative law judge*—(1) *By attorneys.* Any member in good standing of the bar of the highest court of any state, commonwealth, possession, territory of the United States, or the District of Columbia may represent others before the FDIC if such attorney is not currently suspended or debarred from practice before the FDIC.

(2) *By non-attorneys.* An individual may appear on his or her own behalf; a member of a partnership may represent the partnership; a duly authorized officer, director, or employee of any government unit, agency, institution, corporation or authority may represent that unit, agency, institution, corporation or authority if such officer; director, or employee is not currently suspended or debarred from practice before the FDIC.

(3) *Notice of appearance.* Any individual acting as counsel on behalf of a party, including the FDIC, shall file a notice of appearance with OFIA at or before the time that individual submits papers or otherwise appears on behalf of a party in the adjudicatory proceeding. The notice of appearance must include a written declaration that the individual is currently qualified as provided in paragraph (a)(1) or (a)(2) of this section and is authorized to represent the particular party. By filing a notice of appearance on behalf of a party in an adjudicatory proceeding, the counsel agrees and represents that he or she is authorized to accept service on behalf of the represented party and that, in the event of withdrawal from representation, he or she will, if required by the administrative law judge, continue to accept service until new counsel has filed a notice of appearance or until the represented party indicates that he or she will proceed on a *pro se* basis.

(b) *Sanctions.* Dilatory, obstructionist, egregious, contemptuous or contumacious conduct at any phase of any adjudicatory proceeding may be grounds for exclusion or suspension of counsel from the proceeding.

[56 FR 37975, Aug. 9, 1991, as amended at 61 FR 20347, May 6, 1996]

§ 308.7 Good faith certification.

(a) *General requirement.* Every filing or submission of record following the issuance of a notice shall be signed by at least one counsel of record in his or her individual name and shall state that counsel's address and telephone number. A party who acts as his or her own counsel shall sign his or her individual name and state his or her address and telephone number on every filing or submission of record.

(b) *Effect of signature.* (1) The signature of counsel or a party shall constitute a certification that: The counsel or party has read the filing or submission of record; to the best of his or her knowledge, information, and belief formed after reasonable inquiry, the filing or submission of record is well-grounded in fact and is warranted by existing law or a good faith argument for the extension, modification, or reversal of existing law; and the filing or submission of record is not made for any improper purpose, such as to harass or to cause unnecessary delay or needless increase in the cost of litigation.

§ 308.8

(2) If a filing or submission of record is not signed, the administrative law judge shall strike the filing or submission of record, unless it is signed promptly after the omission is called to the attention of the pleader or movant.

(c) *Effect of making oral motion or argument.* The act of making any oral motion or oral argument by any counsel or party constitutes a certification that to the best of his or her knowledge, information, and belief formed after reasonable inquiry, his or her statements are well-grounded in fact and are warranted by existing law or a good faith argument for the extension, modification, or reversal of existing law, and are not made for any improper purpose, such as to harass or to cause unnecessary delay or needless increase in the cost of litigation.

§ 308.8 Conflicts of interest.

(a) *Conflict of interest in representation.* No person shall appear as counsel for another person in an adjudicatory proceeding if it reasonably appears that such representation may be materially limited by that counsel's responsibilities to a third person or by the counsel's own interests. The administrative law judge may take corrective measures at any stage of a proceeding to cure a conflict of interest in representation, including the issuance of an order limiting the scope of representation or disqualifying an individual from appearing in a representative capacity for the duration of the proceeding.

(b) *Certification and waiver.* If any person appearing as counsel represents two or more parties to an adjudicatory proceeding or also represents a nonparty on a matter relevant to an issue in the proceeding, counsel must certify in writing at the time of filing the notice of appearance required by § 308.6(a):

(1) That the counsel has personally and fully discussed the possibility of conflicts of interest with each such party and non-party; and

(2) That each such party and nonparty waives any right it might otherwise have had to assert any known conflicts of interest or to assert any non-material conflicts of interest during the course of the proceeding.

[56 FR 37975, Aug. 9, 1991, as amended at 61 FR 20347, May 6, 1996]

§ 308.9 Ex parte communications.

(a) *Definition*—(1) *Ex parte communication* means any material oral or written communication relevant to the merits of an adjudicatory proceeding that was neither on the record nor on reasonable prior notice to all parties that takes place between:

(i) An interested person outside the FDIC (including such person's counsel); and

(ii) The administrative law judge handling that proceeding, the Board of Directors, or a decisional employee.

(2) *Exception.* A request for status of the proceeding does not constitute an ex parte communication.

(b) *Prohibition of ex parte communications.* From the time the notice is issued by the FDIC until the date that the Board of Directors issues its final decision pursuant to § 308.40(c):

(1) No interested person outside the FDIC shall make or knowingly cause to be made an ex parte communication to any member of the Board of Directors, the administrative law judge, or a decisional employee; and

(2) No member of the Board of Directors, no administrative law judge, or decisional employee shall make or knowingly cause to be made to any interested person outside the FDIC any ex parte communication.

(c) *Procedure upon occurrence of ex parte communication.* If an ex parte communication is received by the administrative law judge, any member of the Board of Directors or other person identified in paragraph (a) of this section, that person shall cause all such written communications (or, if the communication is oral, a memorandum stating the substance of the communication) to be placed on the record of the proceeding and served on all parties. All other parties to the proceeding shall have an opportunity, within ten days of receipt of service of the ex parte communication, to file responses thereto and to recommend any sanctions that they believe to be appropriate under the circumstances. The administrative law judge or the Board

Federal Deposit Insurance Corporation § 308.11

of Directors shall then determine whether any action should be taken concerning the ex parte communication in accordance with paragraph (d) of this section.

(d) *Sanctions.* Any party or his or her counsel who makes a prohibited ex parte communication, or who encourages or solicits another to make any such communication, may be subject to any appropriate sanction or sanctions imposed by the Board of Directors or the administrative law judge including, but not limited to, exclusion from the proceedings and an adverse ruling on the issue which is the subject of the prohibited communication.

(e) *Separation of functions.* Except to the extent required for the disposition of ex parte matters as authorized by law, the administrative law judge may not consult a person or party on any matter relevant to the merits of the adjudication, unless on notice and opportunity for all parties to participate. An employee or agent engaged in the performance of investigative or prosecuting functions for the FDIC in a case may not, in that or a factually related case, participate or advise in the decision, recommended decision, or agency review of the recommended decision under § 308.40 except as witness or counsel in public proceedings.

[56 FR 37975, Aug. 9, 1991, as amended at 60 FR 24762, May 10, 1995]

§ 308.10 Filing of papers.

(a) *Filing.* Any papers required to be filed, excluding documents produced in response to a discovery request pursuant to §§ 308.25 and 308.26, shall be filed with the OFIA, except as otherwise provided.

(b) *Manner of filing.* Unless otherwise specified by the Board of Directors or the administrative law judge, filing may be accomplished by:

(1) Personal service;

(2) Delivering the papers to a reliable commercial courier service, overnight delivery service, or to the U.S. Post Office for Express Mail delivery;

(3) Mailing the papers by first class, registered, or certified mail; or

(4) Transmission by electronic media, only if expressly authorized, and upon any conditions specified, by the Board of Directors or the administrative law judge. All papers filed by electronic media shall also concurrently be filed in accordance with paragraph (c) of this section.

(c) *Formal requirements as to papers filed*—(1) *Form.* All papers filed must set forth the name, address, and telephone number of the counsel or party making the filing and must be accompanied by a certification setting forth when and how service has been made on all other parties. All papers filed must be double-spaced and printed or typewritten on 8½×11 inch paper, and must be clear and legible.

(2) *Signature.* All papers must be dated and signed as provided in § 308.7.

(3) *Caption.* All papers filed must include at the head thereof, or on a title page, the name of the FDIC and of the filing party, the title and docket number of the proceeding, and the subject of the particular paper.

(4) *Number of copies.* Unless otherwise specified by the Board of Directors, or the administrative law judge, an original and one copy of all documents and papers shall be filed, except that only one copy of transcripts of testimony and exhibits shall be filed.

§ 308.11 Service of papers.

(a) *By the parties.* Except as otherwise provided, a party filing papers shall serve a copy upon the counsel of record for all other parties to the proceeding so represented, and upon any party not so represented.

(b) *Method of service.* Except as provided in paragraphs (c)(2) and (d) of this section, a serving party shall use one or more of the following methods of service:

(1) Personal service;

(2) Delivering the papers to a reliable commercial courier service, overnight delivery service, or to the U.S. Post Office for Express Mail delivery;

(3) Mailing the papers by first class, registered, or certified mail; or

(4) Transmission by electronic media, only if the parties mutually agree. Any papers served by electronic media shall also concurrently be served in accordance with the requirements of § 308.10(c).

(c) *By the Board of Directors.* (1) All papers required to be served by the

§ 308.12

Board of Directors or the administrative law judge upon a party who has appeared in the proceeding in accordance with § 308.6, shall be served by any means specified in paragraph (b) of this section.

(2) If a party has not appeared in the proceeding in accordance with § 308.6, the Board of Directors or the administrative law judge shall make service by any of the following methods:

(i) By personal service;

(ii) If the person to be served is an individual, by delivery to a person of suitable age and discretion at the physical location where the individual resides or works;

(iii) If the person to be served is a corporation or other association, by delivery to an officer, managing or general agent, or to any other agent authorized by appointment or by law to receive service and, if the agent is one authorized by statute to receive service and the statute so requires, by also mailing a copy to the party;

(iv) By registered or certified mail addressed to the party's last known address; or

(v) By any other method reasonably calculated to give actual notice.

(d) *Subpoenas.* Service of a subpoena may be made:

(1) By personal service;

(2) If the person to be served is an individual, by delivery to a person of suitable age and discretion at the physical location where the individual resides or works;

(3) By delivery to an agent which, in the case of a corporation or other association, is delivery to an officer, managing or general agent, or to any other agent authorized by appointment or by law to receive service and, if the agent is one authorized by statute to receive service and the statute so requires, by also mailing a copy to the party;

(4) By registered or certified mail addressed to the person's last known address; or

(5) In such other manner as is reasonably calculated to give actual notice.

(e) *Area of service.* Service in any state, territory, possession of the United States, or the District of Columbia, on any person or company doing business in any state, territory, possession of the United States, or the District of Columbia, or on any person as otherwise provided by law, is effective without regard to the place where the hearing is held, provided that if service is made on a foreign bank in connection with an action or proceeding involving one or more of its branches or agencies located in any state, territory, possession of the United States, or the District of Columbia, service shall be made on at least one branch or agency so involved.

[56 FR 37975, Aug. 9, 1991, as amended at 61 FR 20347, May 6, 1996]

§ 308.12   Construction of time limits.

(a) *General rule.* In computing any period of time prescribed by this subpart, the date of the act or event that commences the designated period of time is not included. The last day so computed is included unless it is a Saturday, Sunday, or Federal holiday. When the last day is a Saturday, Sunday, or Federal holiday, the period runs until the end of the next day that is not a Saturday, Sunday, or Federal holiday. Intermediate Saturdays, Sundays, and Federal holidays are included in the computation of time. However, when the time period within which an act is to be performed is ten days or less, not including any additional time allowed for in paragraph (c) of this section, intermediate Saturdays, Sundays, and Federal holidays are not included.

(b) *When papers are deemed to be filed or served.* (1) Filing and service are deemed to be effective:

(i) In the case of personal service or same day commercial courier delivery, upon actual service;

(ii) In the case of overnight commercial delivery service, U.S. Express Mail delivery, or first class, registered, or certified mail, upon deposit in or delivery to an appropriate point of collection;

(iii) In the case of transmission by electronic media, as specified by the authority receiving the filing, in the case of filing, and as agreed among the parties, in the case of service.

(2) The effective filing and service dates specified in paragraph (b) (1) of this section may be modified by the Board of Directors or administrative law judge in the case of filing or by

Federal Deposit Insurance Corporation § 308.18

agreement of the parties in the case of service.

(c) *Calculation of time for service and filing of responsive papers.* Whenever a time limit is measured by a prescribed period from the service of any notice or paper, the applicable time limits are calculated as follows:

(1) If service is made by first class, registered, or certified mail, add three calendar days to the prescribed period;

(2) If service is made by express mail or overnight delivery service, add one calendar day to the prescribed period; or

(3) If service is made by electronic media transmission, add one calendar day to the prescribed period, unless otherwise determined by the Board of Directors or the administrative law judge in the case of filing, or by agreement among the parties in the case of service.

[56 FR 37975, Aug. 9, 1991, as amended at 61 FR 20348, May 6, 1996]

§ 308.13 Change of time limits.

Except as otherwise provided by law, the administrative law judge may, for good cause shown, extend the time limits prescribed by the Uniform Rules or by any notice or order issued in the proceedings. After the referral of the case to the Board of Directors pursuant to § 308.38, the Board of Directors may grant extensions of the time limits for good cause shown. Extensions may be granted at the motion of a party or of the Board of Directors after notice and opportunity to respond is afforded all non-moving parties, or on the administrative law judge's own motion.

§ 308.14 Witness fees and expenses.

Witnesses subpoenaed for testimony or depositions shall be paid the same fees for attendance and mileage as are paid in the United States district courts in proceedings in which the United States is a party, provided that, in the case of a discovery subpoena addressed to a party, no witness fees or mileage need be paid. Fees for witnesses shall be tendered in advance by the party requesting the subpoena, except that fees and mileage need not be tendered in advance where the FDIC is the party requesting the subpoena. The FDIC shall not be required to pay any fees to, or expenses of, any witness not subpoenaed by the FDIC.

§ 308.15 Opportunity for informal settlement.

Any respondent may, at any time in the proceeding, unilaterally submit to Enforcement Counsel written offers or proposals for settlement of a proceeding, without prejudice to the rights of any of the parties. No such offer or proposal shall be made to any FDIC representative other than Enforcement Counsel. Submission of a written settlement offer does not provide a basis for adjourning or otherwise delaying all or any portion of a proceeding under this part. No settlement offer or proposal, or any subsequent negotiation or resolution, is admissible as evidence in any proceeding.

§ 308.16 FDIC's right to conduct examination.

Nothing contained in this subpart limits in any manner the right of the FDIC to conduct any examination, inspection, or visitation of any institution or institution-affiliated party, or the right of the FDIC to conduct or continue any form of investigation authorized by law.

§ 308.17 Collateral attacks on adjudicatory proceeding.

If an interlocutory appeal or collateral attack is brought in any court concerning all or any part of an adjudicatory proceeding, the challenged adjudicatory proceeding shall continue without regard to the pendency of that court proceeding. No default or other failure to act as directed in the adjudicatory proceeding within the times prescribed in this subpart shall be excused based on the pendency before any court of any interlocutory appeal or collateral attack.

§ 308.18 Commencement of proceeding and contents of notice.

(a) *Commencement of proceeding.* (1)(i) Except for change-in-control proceedings under section 7(j)(4) of the FDIA (12 U.S.C. 1817(j)(4)), a proceeding governed by this subpart is commenced by issuance of a notice by the FDIC.

§ 308.19

(ii) The notice must be served by the Executive Secretary upon the respondent and given to any other appropriate financial institution supervisory authority where required by law.

(iii) The notice must be filed with the OFIA.

(2) Change-in-control proceedings under section 7(j)(4) of the FDIA (12 U.S.C. 1817(j)(4)) commence with the issuance of an order by the FDIC.

(b) *Contents of notice.* The notice must set forth:

(1) The legal authority for the proceeding and for the FDIC's jurisdiction over the proceeding;

(2) A statement of the matters of fact or law showing that the FDIC is entitled to relief;

(3) A proposed order or prayer for an order granting the requested relief;

(4) The time, place, and nature of the hearing as required by law or regulation;

(5) The time within which to file an answer as required by law or regulation;

(6) The time within which to request a hearing as required by law or regulation; and

(7) That the answer and/or request for a hearing shall be filed with OFIA.

§ 308.19 Answer.

(a) *When.* Within 20 days of service of the notice, respondent shall file an answer as designated in the notice. In a civil money penalty proceeding, respondent shall also file a request for a hearing within 20 days of service of the notice.

(b) *Content of answer.* An answer must specifically respond to each paragraph or allegation of fact contained in the notice and must admit, deny, or state that the party lacks sufficient information to admit or deny each allegation of fact. A statement of lack of information has the effect of a denial. Denials must fairly meet the substance of each allegation of fact denied; general denials are not permitted. When a respondent denies part of an allegation, that part must be denied and the remainder specifically admitted. Any allegation of fact in the notice which is not denied in the answer must be deemed admitted for purposes of the proceeding. A respondent is not required to respond to the portion of a notice that constitutes the prayer for relief or proposed order. The answer must set forth affirmative defenses, if any, asserted by the respondent.

(c) *Default*—(1) *Effect of failure to answer.* Failure of a respondent to file an answer required by this section within the time provided constitutes a waiver of his or her right to appear and contest the allegations in the notice. If no timely answer is filed, Enforcement Counsel may file a motion for entry of an order of default. Upon a finding that no good cause has been shown for the failure to file a timely answer, the administrative law judge shall file with the Board of Directors a recommended decision containing the findings and the relief sought in the notice. Any final order issued by the Board of Directors based upon a respondent's failure to answer is deemed to be an order issued upon consent.

(2) *Effect of failure to request a hearing in civil money penalty proceedings.* If respondent fails to request a hearing as required by law within the time provided, the notice of assessment constitutes a final and unappealable order.

§ 308.20 Amended pleadings.

(a) *Amendments.* The notice or answer may be amended or supplemented at any stage of the proceeding. The respondent must answer an amended notice within the time remaining for the respondent's answer to the original notice, or within ten days after service of the amended notice, whichever period is longer, unless the Board of Directors or administrative law judge orders otherwise for good cause.

(b) *Amendments to conform to the evidence.* When issues not raised in the notice or answer are tried at the hearing by express or implied consent of the parties, they will be treated in all respects as if they had been raised in the notice or answer, and no formal amendments are required. If evidence is objected to at the hearing on the ground that it is not within the issues raised by the notice or answer, the administrative law judge may admit the evidence when admission is likely to assist in adjudicating the merits of the action and the objecting party fails to satisfy the administrative law judge

Federal Deposit Insurance Corporation

that the admission of such evidence would unfairly prejudice that party's action or defense upon the merits. The administrative law judge may grant a continuance to enable the objecting party to meet such evidence.

[61 FR 20348, May 6, 1996]

§ 308.21 Failure to appear.

Failure of a respondent to appear in person at the hearing or by a duly authorized counsel constitutes a waiver of respondent's right to a hearing and is deemed an admission of the facts as alleged and consent to the relief sought in the notice. Without further proceedings or notice to the respondent, the administrative law judge shall file with the Board of Directors a recommended decision containing the findings and the relief sought in the notice.

§ 308.22 Consolidation and severance of actions.

(a) *Consolidation.* (1) On the motion of any party, or on the administrative law judge's own motion, the administrative law judge may consolidate, for some or all purposes, any two or more proceedings, if each such proceeding involves or arises out of the same transaction, occurrence or series of transactions or occurrences, or involves at least one common respondent or a material common question of law or fact, unless such consolidation would cause unreasonable delay or injustice.

(2) In the event of consolidation under paragraph (a)(1) of this section, appropriate adjustment to the prehearing schedule must be made to avoid unnecessary expense, inconvenience, or delay.

(b) *Severance.* The administrative law judge may, upon the motion of any party, sever the proceeding for separate resolution of the matter as to any respondent only if the administrative law judge finds that:

(1) Undue prejudice or injustice to the moving party would result from not severing the proceeding; and

(2) Such undue prejudice or injustice would outweigh the interests of judicial economy and expedition in the complete and final resolution of the proceeding.

§ 308.23 Motions.

(a) *In writing.* (1) Except as otherwise provided herein, an application or request for an order or ruling must be made by written motion.

(2) All written motions must state with particularity the relief sought and must be accompanied by a proposed order.

(3) No oral argument may be held on written motions except as otherwise directed by the administrative law judge. Written memoranda, briefs, affidavits or other relevant material or documents may be filed in support of or in opposition to a motion.

(b) *Oral motions.* A motion may be made orally on the record unless the administrative law judge directs that such motion be reduced to writing.

(c) *Filing of motions.* Motions must be filed with the administrative law judge, except that following the filing of the recommended decision, motions must be filed with the Executive Secretary for disposition by the Board of Directors.

(d) *Responses.* (1) Except as otherwise provided herein, within ten days after service of any written motion, or within such other period of time as may be established by the administrative law judge or the Executive Secretary, any party may file a written response to a motion. The administrative law judge shall not rule on any oral or written motion before each party has had an opportunity to file a response.

(2) The failure of a party to oppose a written motion or an oral motion made on the record is deemed a consent by that party to the entry of an order substantially in the form of the order accompanying the motion.

(e) *Dilatory motions.* Frivolous, dilatory or repetitive motions are prohibited. The filing of such motions may form the basis for sanctions.

(f) *Dispositive motions.* Dispositive motions are governed by §§ 308.29 and 308.30.

§ 308.24 Scope of document discovery.

(a) *Limits on discovery.* (1) Subject to the limitations set out in paragraphs (b), (c), and (d) of this section, a party to a proceeding under this subpart may obtain document discovery by serving

§ 308.25

a written request to produce documents. For purposes of a request to produce documents, the term "documents" may be defined to include drawings, graphs, charts, photographs, recordings, data stored in electronic form, and other data compilations from which information can be obtained, or translated, if necessary, by the parties through detection devices into reasonably usable form, as well as written material of all kinds.

(2) Discovery by use of deposition is governed by subpart I of this part.

(3) Discovery by use of interrogatories is not permitted.

(b) *Relevance.* A party may obtain document discovery regarding any matter, not privileged, that has material relevance to the merits of the pending action. Any request to produce documents that calls for irrelevant material, that is unreasonable, oppressive, excessive in scope, unduly burdensome, or repetitive of previous requests, or that seeks to obtain privileged documents will be denied or modified. A request is unreasonable, oppressive, excessive in scope or unduly burdensome if, among other things, it fails to include justifiable limitations on the time period covered and the geographic locations to be searched, the time provided to respond in the request is inadequate, or the request calls for copies of documents to be delivered to the requesting party and fails to include the requestor's written agreement to pay in advance for the copying, in accordance with § 308.25.

(c) *Privileged matter.* Privileged documents are not discoverable. Privileges include the attorney-client privilege, work-product privilege, any government's or government agency's deliberative-process privilege, and any other privileges the Constitution, any applicable act of Congress, or the principles of common law provide.

(d) *Time limits.* All discovery, including all responses to discovery requests, shall be completed at least 20 days prior to the date scheduled for the commencement of the hearing. No exceptions to this time limit shall be permitted, unless the administrative law judge finds on the record that good cause exists for waiving the requirements of this paragraph.

[56 FR 37975, Aug. 9, 1991, as amended at 61 FR 20348, May 6, 1996]

§ 308.25 Request for document discovery from parties.

(a) *General rule.* Any party may serve on any other party a request to produce for inspection any discoverable documents that are in the possession, custody, or control of the party upon whom the request is served. The request must identify the documents to be produced either by individual item or by category, and must describe each item and category with reasonable particularity. Documents must be produced as they are kept in the usual course of business or must be organized to correspond with the categories in the request.

(b) *Production or copying.* The request must specify a reasonable time, place, and manner for production and performing any related acts. In lieu of inspecting the documents, the requesting party may specify that all or some of the responsive documents be copied and the copies delivered to the requesting party. If copying of fewer than 250 pages is requested, the party to whom the request is addressed shall bear the cost of copying and shipping charges. If a party requests 250 pages or more of copying, the requesting party shall pay for the copying and shipping charges. Copying charges are the current per-page copying rate imposed by 12 CFR part 310 implementing the Freedom of Information Act (5 U.S.C. 552). The party to whom the request is addressed may require payment in advance before producing the documents.

(c) *Obligation to update responses.* A party who has responded to a discovery request with a response that was complete when made is not required to supplement the response to include documents thereafter acquired, unless the responding party learns that:

(1) The response was materially incorrect when made; or

(2) The response, though correct when made, is no longer true and a failure to amend the response is, in substance, a knowing concealment.

Federal Deposit Insurance Corporation § 308.26

(d) *Motions to limit discovery.* (1) Any party that objects to a discovery request may, within ten days of being served with such request, file a motion in accordance with the provisions of § 308.23 to strike or otherwise limit the request. If an objection is made to only a portion of an item or category in a request, the portion objected to shall be specified. Any objections not made in accordance with this paragraph and § 308.23 are waived.

(2) The party who served the request that is the subject of a motion to strike or limit may file a written response within five days of service of the motion. No other party may file a response.

(e) *Privilege.* At the time other documents are produced, the producing party must reasonably identify all documents withheld on the grounds of privilege and must produce a statement of the basis for the assertion of privilege. When similar documents that are protected by deliberative process, attorney-work-product, or attorney-client privilege are voluminous, these documents may be identified by category instead of by individual document. The administrative law judge retains discretion to determine when the identification by category is insufficient.

(f) *Motions to compel production.* (1) If a party withholds any documents as privileged or fails to comply fully with a discovery request, the requesting party may, within ten days of the assertion of privilege or of the time the failure to comply becomes known to the requesting party, file a motion in accordance with the provisions of § 308.23 for the issuance of a subpoena compelling production.

(2) The party who asserted the privilege or failed to comply with the request may file a written response to a motion to compel within five days of service of the motion. No other party may file a response.

(g) *Ruling on motions.* After the time for filing responses pursuant to this section has expired, the administrative law judge shall rule promptly on all motions filed pursuant to this section. If the administrative law judge determines that a discovery request, or any of its terms, calls for irrelevant material, is unreasonable, oppressive, excessive in scope, unduly burdensome, or repetitive of previous requests, or seeks to obtain privileged documents, he or she may deny or modify the request, and may issue appropriate protective orders, upon such conditions as justice may require. The pendency of a motion to strike or limit discovery or to compel production is not a basis for staying or continuing the proceeding, unless otherwise ordered by the administrative law judge. Notwithstanding any other provision in this part, the administrative law judge may not release, or order a party to produce, documents withheld on grounds of privilege if the party has stated to the administrative law judge its intention to file a timely motion for interlocutory review of the administrative law judge's order to produce the documents, and until the motion for interlocutory review has been decided.

(h) *Enforcing discovery subpoenas.* If the administrative law judge issues a subpoena compelling production of documents by a party, the subpoenaing party may, in the event of noncompliance and to the extent authorized by applicable law, apply to any appropriate United States district court for an order requiring compliance with the subpoena. A party's right to seek court enforcement of a subpoena shall not in any manner limit the sanctions that may be imposed by the administrative law judge against a party who fails to produce subpoenaed documents.

[56 FR 37975, Aug. 9, 1991, as amended at 61 FR 20348, May 6, 1996]

§ 308.26 Document subpoenas to nonparties.

(a) *General rules.* (1) Any party may apply to the administrative law judge for the issuance of a document discovery subpoena addressed to any person who is not a party to the proceeding. The application must contain a proposed document subpoena and a brief statement showing the general relevance and reasonableness of the scope of documents sought. The subpoenaing party shall specify a reasonable time, place, and manner for making production in response to the document subpoena.

§ 308.27

(2) A party shall only apply for a document subpoena under this section within the time period during which such party could serve a discovery request under § 308.24(d). The party obtaining the document subpoena is responsible for serving it on the subpoenaed person and for serving copies on all parties. Document subpoenas may be served in any state, territory, or possession of the United States, the District of Columbia, or as otherwise provided by law.

(3) The administrative law judge shall promptly issue any document subpoena requested pursuant to this section. If the administrative law judge determines that the application does not set forth a valid basis for the issuance of the subpoena, or that any of its terms are unreasonable, oppressive, excessive in scope, or unduly burdensome, he or she may refuse to issue the subpoena or may issue it in a modified form upon such conditions as may be consistent with the Uniform Rules.

(b) *Motion to quash or modify.* (1) Any person to whom a document subpoena is directed may file a motion to quash or modify such subpoena, accompanied by a statement of the basis for quashing or modifying the subpoena. The movant shall serve the motion on all parties, and any party may respond to such motion within ten days of service of the motion.

(2) Any motion to quash or modify a document subpoena must be filed on the same basis, including the assertion of privilege, upon which a party could object to a discovery request under § 308.25(d), and during the same time limits during which such an objection could be filed.

(c) *Enforcing document subpoenas.* If a subpoenaed person fails to comply with any subpoena issued pursuant to this section or any order of the administrative law judge which directs compliance with all or any portion of a document subpoena, the subpoenaing party or any other aggrieved party may, to the extent authorized by applicable law, apply to an appropriate United States district court for an order requiring compliance with so much of the document subpoena as the administrative law judge has not quashed or modified. A party's right to seek court enforcement of a document subpoena shall in no way limit the sanctions that may be imposed by the administrative law judge on a party who induces a failure to comply with subpoenas issued under this section.

§ 308.27 **Deposition of witness unavailable for hearing.**

(a) *General rules.* (1) If a witness will not be available for the hearing, a party desiring to preserve that witness' testimony for the record may apply in accordance with the procedures set forth in paragraph (a)(2) of this section, to the administrative law judge for the issuance of a subpoena, including a subpoena duces tecum, requiring the attendance of the witness at a deposition. The administrative law judge may issue a deposition subpoena under this section upon showing that:

(i) The witness will be unable to attend or may be prevented from attending the hearing because of age, sickness or infirmity, or will otherwise be unavailable;

(ii) The witness' unavailability was not procured or caused by the subpoenaing party;

(iii) The testimony is reasonably expected to be material; and

(iv) Taking the deposition will not result in any undue burden to any other party and will not cause undue delay of the proceeding.

(2) The application must contain a proposed deposition subpoena and a brief statement of the reasons for the issuance of the subpoena. The subpoena must name the witness whose deposition is to be taken and specify the time and place for taking the deposition. A deposition subpoena may require the witness to be deposed at any place within the country in which that witness resides or has a regular place of employment or such other convenient place as the administrative law judge shall fix.

(3) Any requested subpoena that sets forth a valid basis for its issuance must be promptly issued, unless the administrative law judge on his or her own motion, requires a written response or requires attendance at a conference concerning whether the requested subpoena should be issued.

Federal Deposit Insurance Corporation §308.28

(4) The party obtaining a deposition subpoena is responsible for serving it on the witness and for serving copies on all parties. Unless the administrative law judge orders otherwise, no deposition under this section shall be taken on fewer than ten days' notice to the witness and all parties. Deposition subpoenas may be served in any state, territory, possession of the United States, or the District of Columbia, on any person or company doing business in any state, territory, possession of the United States, or the District of Columbia, or as otherwise permitted by law.

(b) *Objections to deposition subpoenas.* (1) The witness and any party who has not had an opportunity to oppose a deposition subpoena issued under this section may file a motion with the administrative law judge to quash or modify the subpoena prior to the time for compliance specified in the subpoena, but not more than ten days after service of the subpoena.

(2) A statement of the basis for the motion to quash or modify a subpoena issued under this section must accompany the motion. The motion must be served on all parties.

(c) *Procedure upon deposition.* (1) Each witness testifying pursuant to a deposition subpoena must be duly sworn, and each party shall have the right to examine the witness. Objections to questions or documents must be in short form, stating the grounds for the objection. Failure to object to questions or documents is not deemed a waiver except where the ground for the objection might have been avoided if the objection had been timely presented. All questions, answers, and objections must be recorded.

(2) Any party may move before the administrative law judge for an order compelling the witness to answer any questions the witness has refused to answer or submit any evidence the witness has refused to submit during the deposition.

(3) The deposition must be subscribed by the witness, unless the parties and the witness, by stipulation, have waived the signing, or the witness is ill, cannot be found, or has refused to sign. If the deposition is not subscribed by the witness, the court reporter taking the deposition shall certify that the transcript is a true and complete transcript of the deposition.

(d) *Enforcing subpoenas.* If a subpoenaed person fails to comply with any order of the administrative law judge which directs compliance with all or any portion of a deposition subpoena under paragraph (b) or (c)(3) of this section, the subpoenaing party or other aggrieved party may, to the extent authorized by applicable law, apply to an appropriate United States district court for an order requiring compliance with the portions of the subpoena that the administrative law judge has ordered enforced. A party's right to seek court enforcement of a deposition subpoena in no way limits the sanctions that may be imposed by the administrative law judge on a party who fails to comply with, or procures a failure to comply with, a subpoena issued under this section.

§ 308.28 **Interlocutory review.**

(a) *General rule.* The Board of Directors may review a ruling of the administrative law judge prior to the certification of the record to the Board of Directors only in accordance with the procedures set forth in this section and § 308.23.

(b) *Scope of review.* The Board of Directors may exercise interlocutory review of a ruling of, the administrative law judge if the Board of Directors finds that:

(1) The ruling involves a controlling question of law or policy as to which substantial grounds exist for a difference of opinion;

(2) Immediate review of the ruling may materially advance the ultimate termination of the proceeding;

(3) Subsequent modification of the ruling at the conclusion of the proceeding would be an inadequate remedy; or

(4) Subsequent modification of the ruling would cause unusual delay or expense.

(c) *Procedure.* Any request for interlocutory review shall be filed by a party with the administrative law judge within ten days of his or her ruling and shall otherwise comply with § 308.23. Any party may file a response to a request for interlocutory review in accordance with § 308.23(d). Upon the expiration of the time for filing all responses, the administrative law judge shall refer the matter to the Board of Directors for final disposition.

(d) *Suspension of proceeding.* Neither a request for interlocutory review nor any disposition of such a request by the Board of Directors under this section suspends or stays the proceeding unless otherwise ordered by the administrative law judge or the Board of Directors.

§ 308.29 Summary disposition.

(a) *In general.* The administrative law judge shall recommend that the Board of Directors issue a final order granting a motion for summary disposition if the undisputed pleaded facts, admissions, affidavits, stipulations, documentary evidence, matters as to which official notice may be taken, and any other evidentiary materials properly submitted in connection with a motion for summary disposition show that:

(1) There is no genuine issue as to any material fact; and

(2) The moving party is entitled to a decision in its favor as a matter of law.

(b) *Filing of motions and responses.* (1) Any party who believes that there is no genuine issue of material fact to be determined and that he or she is entitled to a decision as a matter of law may move at any time for summary disposition in its favor of all or any part of the proceeding. Any party, within 20 days after service of such a motion, or within such time period as allowed by the administrative law judge, may file a response to such motion.

(2) A motion for summary disposition must be accompanied by a statement of the material facts as to which the moving party contends there is no genuine issue. Such motion must be supported by documentary evidence, which may take the form of admissions in pleadings, stipulations, depositions, investigatory depositions, transcripts, affidavits and any other evidentiary materials that the moving party contends support his or her position. The motion must also be accompanied by a brief containing the points and authorities in support of the contention of the moving party. Any party opposing a motion for summary disposition must file a statement setting forth those material facts as to which he or she contends a genuine dispute exists. Such opposition must be supported by evidence of the same type as that submitted with the motion for summary disposition and a brief containing the points and authorities in support of the contention that summary disposition would be inappropriate.

(c) *Hearing on motion.* At the request of any party or on his or her own motion, the administrative law judge may hear oral argument on the motion for summary disposition.

(d) *Decision on motion.* Following receipt of a motion for summary disposition and all responses thereto, the administrative law judge shall determine whether the moving party is entitled to summary disposition. If the administrative law judge determines that summary disposition is warranted, the administrative law judge shall submit a recommended decision to that effect to the Board of Directors. If the administrative law judge finds that no party is entitled to summary disposition, he or she shall make a ruling denying the motion.

§ 308.30 Partial summary disposition.

If the administrative law judge determines that a party is entitled to summary disposition as to certain claims only, he or she shall defer submitting a recommended decision as to those claims. A hearing on the remaining issues must be ordered. Those claims for which the administrative law judge has determined that summary disposition is warranted will be addressed in the recommended decision filed at the conclusion of the hearing.

§ 308.31 Scheduling and prehearing conferences.

(a) *Scheduling conference.* Within 30 days of service of the notice or order commencing a proceeding or such other time as parties may agree, the administrative law judge shall direct counsel for all parties to meet with him or her in person at a specified time and place prior to the hearing or to confer by telephone for the purpose of scheduling the course and conduct of the proceeding. This meeting or telephone

Federal Deposit Insurance Corporation § 308.34

conference is called a "scheduling conference." The identification of potential witnesses, the time for and manner of discovery, and the exchange of any prehearing materials including witness lists, statements of issues, stipulations, exhibits and any other materials may also be determined at the scheduling conference.

(b) *Prehearing conferences.* The administrative law judge may, in addition to the scheduling conference, on his or her own motion or at the request of any party, direct counsel for the parties to meet with him or her (in person or by telephone) at a prehearing conference to address any or all of the following:

(1) Simplification and clarification of the issues;

(2) Stipulations, admissions of fact, and the contents, authenticity and admissibility into evidence of documents;

(3) Matters of which official notice may be taken;

(4) Limitation of the number of witnesses;

(5) Summary disposition of any or all issues;

(6) Resolution of discovery issues or disputes;

(7) Amendments to pleadings; and

(8) Such other matters as may aid in the orderly disposition of the proceeding.

(c) *Transcript.* The administrative law judge, in his or her discretion, may require that a scheduling or prehearing conference be recorded by a court reporter. A transcript of the conference and any materials filed, including orders, becomes part of the record of the proceeding. A party may obtain a copy of the transcript at his or her expense.

(d) *Scheduling or prehearing orders.* At or within a reasonable time following the conclusion of the scheduling conference or any prehearing conference, the administrative law judge shall serve on each party an order setting forth any agreements reached and any procedural determinations made.

§ 308.32 Prehearing submissions.

(a) Within the time set by the administrative law judge, but in no case later than 14 days before the start of the hearing, each party shall serve on every other party, his or her:

(1) Prehearing statement;

(2) Final list of witnesses to be called to testify at the hearing, including name and address of each witness and a short summary of the expected testimony of each witness;

(3) List of the exhibits to be introduced at the hearing along with a copy of each exhibit; and

(4) Stipulations of fact, if any.

(b) Effect of failure to comply. No witness may testify and no exhibits may be introduced at the hearing if such witness or exhibit is not listed in the prehearing submissions pursuant to paragraph (a) of this section, except for good cause shown.

§ 308.33 Public hearings.

(a) *General rule.* All hearings shall be open to the public, unless the FDIC, in its discretion, determines that holding an open hearing would be contrary to the public interest. Within 20 days of service of the notice or, in the case of change-in-control proceedings under section 7(j)(4) of the FDIA (12 U.S.C. 1817(j)(4)), within 20 days from service of the hearing order, any respondent may file with the Executive Secretary a request for a private hearing, and any party may file a reply to such a request. A party must serve on the administrative law judge a copy of any request or reply the party files with the Executive Secretary. The form of, and procedure for, these requests and replies are governed by § 308.23. A party's failure to file a request or a reply constitutes a waiver of any objections regarding whether the hearing will be public or private.

(b) *Filing document under seal.* Enforcement Counsel, in his or her discretion, may file any document or part of a document under seal if disclosure of the document would be contrary to the public interest. The administrative law judge shall take all appropriate steps to preserve the confidentiality of such documents or parts thereof, including closing portions of the hearing to the public.

[56 FR 37975, Aug. 9, 1991, as amended at 61 FR 20349, May 6, 1996]

§ 308.34 Hearing subpoenas.

(a) *Issuance.* (1) Upon application of a party showing general relevance and

§ 308.35

reasonableness of scope of the testimony or other evidence sought, the administrative law judge may issue a subpoena or a subpoena *duces tecum* requiring the attendance of a witness at the hearing or the production of documentary or physical evidence at the hearing. The application for a hearing subpoena must also contain a proposed subpoena specifying the attendance of a witness or the production of evidence from any state, territory, or possession of the United States, the District of Columbia, or as otherwise provided by law at any designated place where the hearing is being conducted. The party making the application shall serve a copy of the application and the proposed subpoena on every other party.

(2) A party may apply for a hearing subpoena at any time before the commencement of a hearing. During a hearing, a party may make an application for a subpoena orally on the record before the administrative law judge.

(3) The administrative law judge shall promptly issue any hearing subpoena requested pursuant to this section. If the administrative law judge determines that the application does not set forth a valid basis for the issuance of the subpoena, or that any of its terms are unreasonable, oppressive, excessive in scope, or unduly burdensome, he or she may refuse to issue the subpoena or may issue it in a modified form upon any conditions consistent with this subpart. Upon issuance by the administrative law judge, the party making the application shall serve the subpoena on the person named in the subpoena and on each party.

(b) *Motion to quash or modify.* (1) Any person to whom a hearing subpoena is directed or any party may file a motion to quash or modify the subpoena, accompanied by a statement of the basis for quashing or modifying the subpoena. The movant must serve the motion on each party and on the person named in the subpoena. Any party may respond to the motion within ten days of service of the motion.

(2) Any motion to quash or modify a hearing subpoena must be filed prior to the time specified in the subpoena for compliance, but not more than ten days after the date of service of the subpoena upon the movant.

(c) *Enforcing subpoenas.* If a subpoenaed person fails to comply with any subpoena issued pursuant to this section or any order of the administrative law judge which directs compliance with all or any portion of a document subpoena, the subpoenaing party or any other aggrieved party may seek enforcement of the subpoena pursuant to § 308.26(c).

[56 FR 37975, Aug. 9, 1991, as amended at 61 FR 20349, May 6, 1996]

§ 308.35 Conduct of hearings.

(a) *General rules.* (1) Hearings shall be conducted so as to provide a fair and expeditious presentation of the relevant disputed issues. Each party has the right to present its case or defense by oral and documentary evidence and to conduct such cross examination as may be required for full disclosure of the facts.

(2) *Order of hearing.* Enforcement Counsel shall present its case-in-chief first, unless otherwise ordered by the administrative law judge, or unless otherwise expressly specified by law or regulation. Enforcement Counsel shall be the first party to present an opening statement and a closing statement, and may make a rebuttal statement after the respondent's closing statement. If there are multiple respondents, respondents may agree among themselves as to their order of presentation of their cases, but if they do not agree the administrative law judge shall fix the order.

(3) *Examination of witnesses.* Only one counsel for each party may conduct an examination of a witness, except that in the case of extensive direct examination, the administrative law judge may permit more than one counsel for the party presenting the witness to conduct the examination. A party may have one counsel conduct the direct examination and another counsel conduct re-direct examination of a witness, or may have one counsel conduct the cross examination of a witness and another counsel conduct the re-cross examination of a witness.

(4) *Stipulations.* Unless the administrative law judge directs otherwise, all stipulations of fact and law previously

Federal Deposit Insurance Corporation § 308.36

agreed upon by the parties, and all documents, the admissibility of which have been previously stipulated, will be admitted into evidence upon commencement of the hearing.

(b) *Transcript.* The hearing must be recorded and transcribed. The reporter will make the transcript available to any party upon payment by that party to the reporter of the cost of the transcript. The administrative law judge may order the record corrected, either upon motion to correct, upon stipulation of the parties, or following notice to the parties upon the administrative law judge's own motion.

[56 FR 37975, Aug. 9, 1991, as amended at 61 FR 20349, May 6, 1996]

§ 308.36 Evidence.

(a) *Admissibility.* (1) Except as is otherwise set forth in this section, relevant, material, and reliable evidence that is not unduly repetitive is admissible to the fullest extent authorized by the Administrative Procedure Act and other applicable law.

(2) Evidence that would be admissible under the Federal Rules of Evidence is admissible in a proceeding conducted pursuant to this subpart.

(3) Evidence that would be inadmissible under the Federal Rules of Evidence may not be deemed or ruled to be inadmissible in a proceeding conducted pursuant to this subpart if such evidence is relevant, material, reliable and not unduly repetitive.

(b) *Official notice.* (1) Official notice may be taken of any material fact which may be judicially noticed by a United States district court and any material information in the official public records of any Federal or state government agency.

(2) All matters officially noticed by the administrative law judge or Board of Directors shall appear on the record.

(3) If official notice is requested or taken of any material fact, the parties, upon timely request, shall be afforded an opportunity to object.

(c) *Documents.* (1) A duplicate copy of a document is admissible to the same extent as the original, unless a genuine issue is raised as to whether the copy is in some material respect not a true and legible copy of the original.

(2) Subject to the requirements of paragraph (a) of this section, any document, including a report of examination, supervisory activity, inspection or visitation, prepared by an appropriate Federal financial institution regulatory agency or state regulatory agency, is admissible either with or without a sponsoring witness.

(3) Witnesses may use existing or newly created charts, exhibits, calendars, calculations, outlines or other graphic material to summarize, illustrate, or simplify the presentation of testimony. Such materials may, subject to the administrative law judge's discretion, be used with or without being admitted into evidence.

(d) *Objections.* (1) Objections to the admissibility of evidence must be timely made and rulings on all objections must appear on the record.

(2) When an objection to a question or line of questioning propounded to a witness is sustained, the examining counsel may make a specific proffer on the record of what he or she expected to prove by the expected testimony of the witness, either by representation of counsel or by direct interrogation of the witness.

(3) The administrative law judge shall retain rejected exhibits, adequately marked for identification, for the record, and transmit such exhibits to the Board of Directors.

(4) Failure to object to admission of evidence or to any ruling constitutes a waiver of the objection.

(e) *Stipulations.* The parties may stipulate as to any relevant matters of fact or the authentication of any relevant documents. Such stipulations must be received in evidence at a hearing, and are binding on the parties with respect to the matters therein stipulated.

(f) *Depositions of unavailable witnesses.* (1) If a witness is unavailable to testify at a hearing, and that witness has testified in a deposition to which all parties in a proceeding had notice and an opportunity to participate, a party may offer as evidence all or any part of the transcript of the deposition, including deposition exhibits, if any.

(2) Such deposition transcript is admissible to the same extent that testimony would have been admissible had that person testified at the hearing,

§ 308.37

provided that if a witness refused to answer proper questions during the depositions, the administrative law judge may, on that basis, limit the admissibility of the deposition in any manner that justice requires.

(3) Only those portions of a deposition received in evidence at the hearing constitute a part of the record.

§ 308.37 Post-hearing filings.

(a) *Proposed findings and conclusions and supporting briefs.* (1) Using the same method of service for each party, the administrative law judge shall serve notice upon each party, that the certified transcript, together with all hearing exhibits and exhibits introduced but not admitted into evidence at the hearing, has been filed. Any party may file with the administrative law judge proposed findings of fact, proposed conclusions of law, and a proposed order within 30 days following service of this notice by the administrative law judge or within such longer period as may be ordered by the administrative law judge.

(2) Proposed findings and conclusions must be supported by citation to any relevant authorities and by page references to any relevant portions of the record. A post-hearing brief may be filed in support of proposed findings and conclusions, either as part of the same document or in a separate document. Any party who fails to file timely with the administrative law judge any proposed finding or conclusion is deemed to have waived the right to raise in any subsequent filing or submission any issue not addressed in such party's proposed finding or conclusion.

(b) *Reply briefs.* Reply briefs may be filed within 15 days after the date on which the parties' proposed findings, conclusions, and order are due. Reply briefs must be strictly limited to responding to new matters, issues, or arguments raised in another party's papers. A party who has not filed proposed findings of fact and conclusions of law or a post-hearing brief may not file a reply brief.

(c) *Simultaneous filing required.* The administrative law judge shall not order the filing by any party of any brief or reply brief in advance of the other party's filing of its brief.

[56 FR 37975, Aug. 9, 1991, as amended at 61 FR 20349, May 6, 1996]

§ 308.38 Recommended decision and filing of record.

(a) *Filing of recommended decision and record.* Within 45 days after expiration of the time allowed for filing reply briefs under § 308.37(b), the administrative law judge shall file with and certify to the Executive Secretary, for decision, the record of the proceeding. The record must include the administrative law judge's recommended decision, recommended findings of fact, recommended conclusions of law, and proposed order; all prehearing and hearing transcripts, exhibits, and rulings; and the motions, briefs, memoranda, and other supporting papers filed in connection with the hearing. The administrative law judge shall serve upon each party the recommended decision, findings, conclusions, and proposed order.

(b) *Filing of index.* At the same time the administrative law judge files with and certifies to the Executive Secretary for final determination the record of the proceeding, the administrative law judge shall furnish to the Executive Secretary a certified index of the entire record of the proceeding. The certified index shall include, at a minimum, an entry for each paper, document or motion filed with the administrative law judge in the proceeding, the date of the filing, and the identity of the filer. The certified index shall also include an exhibit index containing, at a minimum, an entry consisting of exhibit number and title or description for: Each exhibit introduced and admitted into evidence at the hearing; each exhibit introduced but not admitted into evidence at the hearing; each exhibit introduced and admitted into evidence after the completion of the hearing; and each exhibit introduced but not admitted into evidence after the completion of the hearing.

[61 FR 20350, May 6, 1996]

§ 308.39 Exceptions to recommended decision.

(a) *Filing exceptions.* Within 30 days after service of the recommended decision, findings, conclusions, and proposed order under § 308.38, a party may file with the Executive Secretary written exceptions to the administrative law judge's recommended decision, findings, conclusions or proposed order, to the admission or exclusion of evidence, or to the failure of the administrative law judge to make a ruling proposed by a party. A supporting brief may be filed at the time the exceptions are filed, either as part of the same document or in a separate document.

(b) *Effect of failure to file or raise exceptions.* (1) Failure of a party to file exceptions to those matters specified in paragraph (a) of this section within the time prescribed is deemed a waiver of objection thereto.

(2) No exception need be considered by the Board of Directors if the party taking exception had an opportunity to raise the same objection, issue, or argument before the administrative law judge and failed to do so.

(c) *Contents.* (1) All exceptions and briefs in support of such exceptions must be confined to the particular matters in, or omissions from, the administrative law judge's recommendations to which that party takes exception.

(2) All exceptions and briefs in support of exceptions must set forth page or paragraph references to the specific parts of the administrative law judge's recommendations to which exception is taken, the page or paragraph references to those portions of the record relied upon to support each exception, and the legal authority relied upon to support each exception.

§ 308.40 Review by Board of Directors.

(a) *Notice of submission to Board of Directors.* When the Executive Secretary determines that the record in the proceeding is complete, the Executive Secretary shall serve notice upon the parties that the proceeding has been submitted to the Board of Directors for final decision.

(b) *Oral argument before the Board of Directors.* Upon the initiative of the Board of Directors or on the written request of any party filed with the Executive Secretary within the time for filing exceptions, the Board of Directors may order and hear oral argument on the recommended findings, conclusions, decision, and order of the administrative law judge. A written request by a party must show good cause for oral argument and state reasons why arguments cannot be presented adequately in writing. A denial of a request for oral argument may be set forth in the Board of Directors' final decision. Oral argument before the Board of Directors must be on the record.

(c) *Final decision.* (1) Decisional employees may advise and assist the Board of Directors in the consideration and disposition of the case. The final decision of the Board of Directors will be based upon review of the entire record of the proceeding, except that the Board of Directors may limit the issues to be reviewed to those findings and conclusions to which opposing arguments or exceptions have been filed by the parties.

(2) The Board of Directors shall render a final decision within 90 days after notification of the parties that the case has been submitted for final decision, or 90 days after oral argument, whichever is later, unless the Board of Directors orders that the action or any aspect thereof be remanded to the administrative law judge for further proceedings. Copies of the final decision and order of the Board of Directors shall be served upon each party to the proceeding, upon other persons required by statute, and, if directed by the Board of Directors or required by statute, upon any appropriate state or Federal supervisory authority.

§ 308.41 Stays pending judicial review.

The commencement of proceedings for judicial review of a final decision and order of the FDIC may not, unless specifically ordered by the Board of Directors or a reviewing court, operate as a stay of any order issued by the FDIC. The Board of Directors may, in its discretion, and on such terms as it finds just, stay the effectiveness of all or any part of its order pending a final decision on a petition for review of that order.

§ 308.101

Subpart B—General Rules of Procedure

§ 308.101 Scope of Local Rules.

(a) Subparts B and C of the Local Rules prescribe rules of practice and procedure to be followed in the administrative enforcement proceedings initiated by the FDIC as set forth in § 308.01 of the Uniform Rules.

(b) Except as otherwise specifically provided, the Uniform Rules and subpart B of the Local Rules shall not apply to subparts D through T of the Local Rules.

(c) Subpart C of the Local Rules shall apply to any administrative proceeding initiated by the FDIC.

[56 FR 37975, Aug. 9, 1991, as amended at 64 FR 62100, Nov. 16, 1999; 66 FR 9189, Feb. 7, 2001]

§ 308.102 Authority of Board of Directors and Executive Secretary.

(a) *The Board of Directors.* (1) The Board of Directors may, at any time during the pendency of a proceeding, perform, direct the performance of, or waive performance of, any act which could be done or ordered by the Executive Secretary.

(2) Nothing contained in this part 308 shall be construed to limit the power of the Board of Directors granted by applicable statutes or regulations.

(b) *The Executive Secretary.* (1) When no administrative law judge has jurisdiction over a proceeding, the Executive Secretary may act in place of, and with the same authority as, an administrative law judge, except that the Executive Secretary may not hear a case on the merits or make a recommended decision on the merits to the Board of Directors.

(2) Pursuant to authority delegated by the Board of Directors, the Executive Secretary and Assistant Executive Secretary, upon the advice and recommendation of the Deputy General Counsel for Litigation or, in his absence, the Assistant General Counsel, Trial Litigation Section, may issue rulings in proceedings under sections 7(j), 8, 18(j), 19, 32 and 38 of the FDIA (12 USC 1817(j), 1818, 1828(j), 1829, 1831i and 1831o concerning:

(i) Denials of requests for private hearing;

(ii) Interlocutory appeals;

(iii) Stays pending judicial review;

(iv) Reopenings of the record and/or remands of the record to the ALJ;

(v) Supplementation of the evidence in the record;

(vi) All remands from the courts of appeals not involving substantive issues;

(vii) Extensions of stays of orders terminating deposit insurance; and

(viii) All matters, including final decisions, in proceedings under section 8(g) of the FDIA (12 U.S.C. 1818(g)).

[56 FR 37975, Aug. 9, 1991, as amended at 64 FR 62100, Nov. 16, 1999; 67 FR 71071, Nov. 29, 2002]

§ 308.103 Appointment of administrative law judge.

(a) *Appointment.* Unless otherwise directed by the Board of Directors or as otherwise provided in the Local Rules, a hearing within the scope of this part 308 shall be held before an administrative law judge of the Office of Financial Institution Adjudication ("OFIA").

(b) *Procedures.* (1) The Executive Secretary shall promptly after issuance of the notice refer the matter to the OFIA which shall secure the appointment of an administrative law judge to hear the proceeding.

(2) OFIA shall advise the parties, in writing, that an administrative law judge has been appointed.

§ 308.104 Filings with the Board of Directors.

(a) *General rule.* All materials required to be filed with or referred to the Board of Directors in any proceedings under this part 308 shall be filed with the Executive Secretary, Federal Deposit Insurance Corporation, 550 17th Street, NW., Washington, DC 20429.

(b) *Scope.* Filings to be made with the Executive Secretary include pleadings and motions filed during the proceeding; the record filed by the administrative law judge after the issuance of a recommended decision; the recommended decision filed by the administrative law judge following a motion for summary disposition; referrals by the administrative law judge of motions for interlocutory review; motions and responses to motions filed by the parties after the record has been certified to the Board of Directors; exceptions and requests for oral argument; and any other papers required to be filed with the Board of Directors under this part 308.

§ 308.105 Custodian of the record.

The Executive Secretary is the official custodian of the record when no administrative law judge has jurisdiction over the proceeding. As the official custodian, the Executive Secretary shall maintain the official record of all papers filed in each proceeding.

§ 308.106 Written testimony in lieu of oral hearing.

(a) *General rule.* (1) At any time more than fifteen days before the hearing is to commence, on the motion of any party or on his or her own motion, the administrative law judge may order that the parties present part or all of their case-in-chief and, if ordered, their rebuttal, in the form of exhibits and written statements sworn to by the witness offering such statements as evidence, provided that if any party objects, the administrative law judge shall not require such a format if that format would violate the objecting party's right under the Administrative Procedure Act, or other applicable law, or would otherwise unfairly prejudice that party.

(2) Any such order shall provide that each party shall, upon request, have the same right of oral cross-examination (or redirect examination) as would exist had the witness testified orally rather than through a written statement. Such order shall also provide that any party has a right to call any hostile witness or adverse party to testify orally.

(b) *Scheduling of submission of written testimony.* (1) If written direct testimony and exhibits are ordered under paragraph (a) of this section, the administrative law judge shall require that it be filed within the time period for commencement of the hearing, and the hearing shall be deemed to have commenced on the day such testimony is due.

(2) Absent good cause shown, written rebuttal, if any, shall be submitted and the oral portion of the hearing begun within 30 days of the date set for filing written direct testimony.

(3) The administrative law judge shall direct, unless good cause requires otherwise, that—

(i) All parties shall simultaneously file any exhibits and written direct testimony required under paragraph (b)(1) of this section; and

(ii) All parties shall simultaneously file any exhibits and written rebuttal required under paragraph (b)(2) of this section.

(c) *Failure to comply with order to file written testimony.* (1) The failure of any party to comply with an order to file written testimony or exhibits at the time and in the manner required under this section shall be deemed a waiver of that party's right to present any evidence, except testimony of a previously identified adverse party or hostile witness. Failure to file written testimony or exhibits is, however, not a waiver of that party's right of cross-examination or a waiver of the right to present rebuttal evidence that was not required to be submitted in written form.

(2) Late filings of papers under this section may be allowed and accepted only upon good cause shown.

§ 308.107 Document discovery.

(a) Parties to proceedings set forth at § 308.01 of the Uniform Rules and as provided in the Local Rules may obtain discovery only through the production of documents. No other form of discovery shall be allowed.

(b) Any questioning at a deposition of a person producing documents pursuant to a document subpoena shall be strictly limited to the identification of documents produced by that person and a reasonable examination to determine whether the subpoenaed person made an adequate search for, and has produced, all subpoenaed documents.

Subpart C—Rules of Practice Before the FDIC and Standards of Conduct

§ 308.108 Sanctions.

(a) *General rule.* Appropriate sanctions may be imposed when any counsel or party has acted, or failed to act, in a manner required by applicable

§ 308.109

statute, regulations, or order, and that act or failure to act:

(1) Constitutes contemptuous conduct;

(2) Has in a material way injured or prejudiced some other party in terms of substantive injury, incurring additional expenses including attorney's fees, prejudicial delay, or otherwise;

(3) Is a clear and unexcused violation of an applicable statute, regulation, or order; or

(4) Has unduly delayed the proceeding.

(b) *Sanctions.* Sanctions which may be imposed include any one or more of the following:

(1) Issuing an order against the party;

(2) Rejecting or striking any testimony or documentary evidence offered, or other papers filed, by the party;

(3) Precluding the party from contesting specific issues or findings;

(4) Precluding the party from offering certain evidence or from challenging or contesting certain evidence offered by another party;

(5) Precluding the party from making a late filing or conditioning a late filing on any terms that are just; and

(6) Assessing reasonable expenses, including attorney's fees, incurred by any other party as a result of the improper action or failure to act.

(c) *Limits on dismissal as a sanction.* No recommendation of dismissal shall be made by the administrative law judge or granted by the Board of Directors based on the failure to hold a hearing within the time period called for in this part 308, or on the failure of an administrative law judge to render a recommended decision within the time period called for in this part 308, absent a finding:

(1) That the delay resulted solely or principally from the conduct of the FDIC enforcement counsel;

(2) That the conduct of the FDIC enforcement counsel is unexcused;

(3) That the moving respondent took all reasonable steps to oppose and prevent the subject delay;

(4) That the moving respondent has been materially prejudiced or injured; and

(5) That no lesser or different sanction is adequate.

(d) *Procedure for imposition of sanctions.* (1) The administrative law judge, upon the request of any party, or on his or her own motion, may impose sanctions in accordance with this section, provided that the administrative law judge may only recommend to the Board of Directors the sanction of entering a final order determining the case on the merits.

(2) No sanction, other than refusing to accept late papers, authorized by this section shall be imposed without prior notice to all parties and an opportunity for any counsel or party against whom sanctions would be imposed to be heard. Such opportunity to be heard may be on such notice, and the response may be in such form, as the administrative law judge directs. The opportunity to be heard may be limited to an opportunity to respond orally immediately after the act or inaction covered by this section is noted by the administrative law judge.

(3) Requests for the imposition of sanctions by any party, and the imposition of sanctions, shall be treated for interlocutory review purposes in the same manner as any other ruling by the administrative law judge.

(4) *Section not exclusive.* Nothing in this section shall be read as precluding the administrative law judge or the Board of Directors from taking any other action, or imposing any restriction or sanction, authorized by applicable statute or regulation.

§ 308.109 **Suspension and disbarment.**

(a) *Discretionary suspension and disbarment.* (1) The Board of Directors may suspend or revoke the privilege of any counsel to appear or practice before the FDIC if, after notice of and opportunity for hearing in the matter, that counsel is found by the Board of Directors:

(i) Not to possess the requisite qualifications to represent others;

(ii) To be seriously lacking in character or integrity or to have engaged in material unethical or improper professional conduct;

(iii) To have engaged in, or aided and abetted, a material and knowing violation of the FDIA; or

Federal Deposit Insurance Corporation § 308.109

(iv) To have engaged in contemptuous conduct before the FDIC. Suspension or revocation on the grounds set forth in paragraphs (a)(1) (ii), (iii), and (iv) of this section shall only be ordered upon a further finding that the counsel's conduct or character was sufficiently egregious as to justify suspension or revocation.

(2) Unless otherwise ordered by the Board of Directors, an application for reinstatement by a person suspended or disbarred under paragraph (a)(1) of this section may be made in writing at any time more than three years after the effective date of the suspension or disbarment and, thereafter, at any time more than one year after the person's most recent application for reinstatement. The suspension or disbarment shall continue until the applicant has been reinstated by the Board of Directors for good cause shown or until, in the case of a suspension, the suspension period has expired. An applicant for reinstatement under this provision may, in the Board of Directors' sole discretion, be afforded a hearing.

(b) *Mandatory suspension and disbarment.* (1) Any counsel who has been and remains suspended or disbarred by a court of the United States or of any state, territory, district, commonwealth, or possession; or any person who has been and remains suspended or barred from practice before the OCC, Board of Governors, the OTS, the NCUA, the Securities and Exchange Commission, or the Commodity Futures Trading Commission; or any person who has been convicted of a felony, or of a misdemeanor involving moral turpitude, within the last ten years, shall be suspended automatically from appearing or practicing before the FDIC. A disbarment, suspension, or conviction within the meaning of this paragraph (b) shall be deemed to have occurred when the disbarring, suspending, or convicting agency or tribunal enters its judgment or order, regardless of whether an appeal is pending or could be taken, and includes a judgment or an order on a plea of nolo contendere or on consent, regardless of whether a violation is admitted in the consent.

(2) Any person appearing or practicing before the FDIC who is the subject of an order, judgment, decree, or finding of the types set forth in paragraph (b)(1) of this section shall promptly file with the Executive Secretary a copy thereof, together with any related opinion or statement of the agency or tribunal involved. Failure to file any such paper shall not impair the operation of any other provision of this section.

(3) A suspension or disbarment under paragraph (b)(1) of this section from practice before the FDIC shall continue until the applicant has been reinstated by the Board of Directors for good cause shown, provided that any person suspended or disbarred under paragraph (b)(1) of this section shall be automatically reinstated by the Executive Secretary, upon appropriate application, if all the grounds for suspension or disbarment under paragraph (b)(1) of this section are subsequently removed by a reversal of the conviction (or the passage of time since the conviction) or termination of the underlying suspension or disbarment. An application for reinstatement on any other grounds by any person suspended or disbarred under paragraph (b)(1) of this section may be filed no sooner than one year after the suspension or disbarment, and thereafter, a new request for reinstatement may be made no sooner than one year after the counsel's most recent reinstatement application. The application must comply with the requirements of § 303.3 of this chapter. An applicant for reinstatement under this provision may, in the Board of Directors' sole discretion, be afforded a hearing.

(c) *Hearings under this section.* Hearings conducted under this section shall be conducted in substantially the same manner as other hearings under the Uniform Rules, provided that in proceedings to terminate an existing FDIC suspension or disbarment order, the person seeking the termination of the order shall bear the burden of going forward with an application and with the burden of proving the grounds supporting the application, and that the Board of Directors may, in its sole discretion, direct that any proceeding to terminate an existing suspension or disbarment by the FDIC be limited to written submissions.

§ 308.110

(d) *Summary suspension for contemptuous conduct.* A finding by the administrative law judge of contemptuous conduct during the course of any proceeding shall be grounds for summary suspension by the administrative law judge of a counsel or other representative from any further participation in that proceeding for the duration of that proceeding.

(e) *Practice defined.* Unless the Board of Directors orders otherwise, for the purposes of this section, practicing before the FDIC includes, but is not limited to, transacting any business with the FDIC as counsel or agent for any other person and the preparation of any statement, opinion, or other paper by a counsel, which statement, opinion, or paper is filed with the FDIC in any registration statement, notification, application, report, or other document, with the consent of such counsel.

[56 FR 37975, Aug. 9, 1991, as amended at 64 FR 62100, Nov. 16, 1999; 68 FR 48270, Aug. 13, 2003]

Subpart D—Rules and Procedures Applicable to Proceedings Relating to Disapproval of Acquisition of Control

§ 308.110 Scope.

Except as specifically indicated in this subpart, the rules and procedures in this subpart, subpart B of the Local Rules, and the Uniform Rules shall apply to proceedings in connection with the disapproval by the Board of Directors or its designee of a proposed acquisition of control of an insured nonmember bank.

§ 308.111 Grounds for disapproval.

The following are grounds for disapproval of a proposed acquisition of control of an insured nonmember bank:

(a) The proposed acquisition of control would result in a monopoly or would be in furtherance of any combination or conspiracy to monopolize or attempt to monopolize the banking business in any part of the United States;

(b) The effect of the proposed acquisition of control in any section of the United States may be to substantially lessen competition or to tend to create a monopoly or would in any other manner be in restraint of trade, and the anticompetitive effects of the proposed acquisition of control are not clearly outweighed in the public interest by the probable effect of the transaction in meeting the convenience and needs of the community to be served;

(c) Either the financial condition of any acquiring person or the future prospects of the institution might jeopardize the financial stability of the bank or prejudice the interest of the depositors of the bank.

(d) The competence, experience, or integrity of any acquiring person or of any of the proposed management personnel indicates that it would not be in the interest of the depositors of the bank, or in the interest of the public, to permit such person to control the bank;

(e) Any acquiring person neglects, fails, or refuses to furnish to the FDIC all the information required by the FDIC; or

(f) The FDIC determines that the proposed acquisition would result in an adverse effect on the Deposit Insurance Fund.

[56 FR 37975, Aug. 9, 1991, as amended at 71 FR 20526, Apr. 21, 2006; 73 FR 2145, Jan. 14, 2008]

§ 308.112 Notice of disapproval.

(a) *General rule.* (1) Within three days of the decision by the Board of Directors or its designee to disapprove a proposed acquisition of control of an insured nonmember bank, a written notice of disapproval shall be mailed by first class mail to, or otherwise served upon, the party seeking acquire control.

(2) The notice of disapproval shall:

(i) Contain a statement of the basis for the disapproval; and

(ii) Indicate that a hearing may be requested by filing a written request with the Executive Secretary within ten days after service of the notice of disapproval; and if a hearing is requested, that an answer to the notice of disapproval, as required by § 308.113, must be filed within 20 days after service of the notice of disapproval.

(b) *Waiver of hearing.* Failure to request a hearing pursuant to this section shall constitute a waiver of the

Federal Deposit Insurance Corporation § 308.116

opportunity for a hearing and the notice of disapproval shall constitute a final and unappealable order.

(c) Section 308.18(b) of the Uniform Rules shall not apply to the content of the Notice of Disapproval.

§ 308.113 Answer to notice of disapproval.

(a) *Contents.* (1) An answer to the notice of disapproval of a proposed acquisition of control shall be filed within 20 days after service of the notice of disapproval and shall specifically deny those portions of the notice of disapproval which are disputed. Those portions of the notice of disapproval which are not specifically denied are deemed admitted by the applicant.

(2) Any hearing under this subpart shall be limited to those parts of the notice of disapproval that are specifically denied.

(b) *Failure to answer.* Failure of a respondent to file an answer required by this section within the time provided constitutes a waiver of his or her right to appear and contest the allegations in the notice of disapproval. If no timely answer is filed, Enforcement Counsel may file a motion for entry of an order of default. Upon a finding that no good cause has been shown for the failure to file a timely answer, the administrative law judge shall file a recommended decision containing the findings and relief sought in the notice. A final order issued by the Board of Directors based upon a respondent's failure to answer is deemed to be an order issued upon consent.

§ 308.114 Burden of proof.

The ultimate burden of proof shall be upon the person proposing to acquire a depository institution. The burden of going forward with a *prima facie* case shall be upon the FDIC.

Subpart E—Rules and Procedures Applicable to Proceedings Relating to Assessment of Civil Penalties for Willful Violations of the Change in Bank Control Act

§ 308.115 Scope.

The rules and procedures of this subpart, subpart B of the Local Rules and the Uniform Rules shall apply to proceedings to assess civil penalties against any person for willful violation of the Change in Bank Control Act of 1978 (12 U.S.C. 1817(j)), or any regulation or order issued pursuant thereto, in connection with the affairs of an insured nonmember bank.

§ 308.116 Assessment of penalties.

(a) *In general.* The civil money penalty shall be assessed upon the service of a Notice of Assessment which shall become final and unappealable unless the respondent requests a hearing pursuant to § 308.19(c)(2).

(b) *Amount.* (1) Any person who violates any provision of the Change in Bank Control Act or any rule, regulation, or order issued by the FDIC pursuant thereto, shall forfeit and pay a civil money penalty of not more than $5,000 for each day the violation continues.

(2) Any person who violates any provision of the Change in Bank Control Act or any rule, regulation, or order issued by the FDIC pursuant thereto; or recklessly engages in any unsafe or unsound practice in conducting the affairs of a depository institution; or breaches any fiduciary duty; which violation, practice or breach is part of a pattern of misconduct; or causes or is likely to cause more than a minimal loss to such institution; or results in pecuniary gain or other benefit to such person, shall forfeit and pay a civil money penalty of not more than $25,000 for each day such violation, practice or breach continues.

(3) Any person who knowingly violates any provision of the Change in Bank Control Act or any rule, regulation, or order issued by the FDIC pursuant thereto; or engages in any unsafe or unsound practice in conducting the affairs of a depository institution; or

§ 308.117

breaches any fiduciary duty; and knowingly or recklessly causes a substantial loss to such institution or a substantial pecuniary gain or other benefit to such institution or a substantial pecuniary gain or other benefit to such person by reason of such violation, practice or breach, shall forfeit and pay a civil money penalty not to exceed:

(i) In the case of a person other than a depository institution—$1,000,000 per day for each day the violation, practice or breach continues; or

(ii) In the case of a depository institution—an amount not to exceed the lesser of $1,000,000 or one percent of the total assets of such institution for each day the violation, practice or breach continues.

(4) *Adjustment of civil money penalties by the rate of inflation pursuant to section 31001(s) of the Debt Collection Improvement Act.* After December 31, 2008:

(i) Any person who engages in a violation as set forth in paragraph (b)(1) of this section shall forfeit and pay a civil money penalty of not more than $7,500 for each day the violation continues.

(ii) Any person who engages in a violation, unsafe or unsound practice or breach of fiduciary duty, as set forth in paragraph (b)(2) of this section, shall forfeit and pay a civil money penalty of not more than $37,500 for each day such violation, practice or breach continues.

(iii) Any person who knowingly engages in a violation, unsafe or unsound practice or breach of fiduciary duty, as set forth in paragraph (b)(3) of this section, shall forfeit and pay a civil money penalty not to exceed:

(A) In the case of a person other than a depository institution—$1,375,000 per day for each day the violation, practice or breach continues; or

(B) In the case of a depository institution—an amount not to exceed the lesser of $1,375,000 or one percent of the total assets of such institution for each day the violation, practice or breach continues.

(c) *Mitigating factors.* In assessing the amount of the penalty, the Board of Directors or its designee shall consider the gravity of the violation, the history of previous violations, respondent's financial resources, good faith, and any other matters as justice may require.

(d) *Failure to answer.* Failure of a respondent to file an answer required by this section within the time provided constitutes a waiver of his or her right to appear and contest the allegations in the notice of disapproval. If no timely answer is filed, Enforcement Counsel may file a motion for entry of an order of default. Upon a finding that no good cause has been shown for the failure to file a timely answer, the administrative law judge shall file a recommended decision containing the findings and relief sought in the notice. A final order issued by the Board of Directors based upon a respondent's failure to answer is deemed to be an order issued upon consent.

[56 FR 37975, Aug. 9, 1991, as amended at 61 FR 57990, Nov. 12, 1996; 65 FR 64887, Oct. 31, 2000; 69 FR 61305, Oct. 18, 2004; 73 FR 73157, Dec. 2, 2008]

§ 308.117 **Effective date of, and payment under, an order to pay.**

If the respondent both requests a hearing and serves an answer, civil penalties assessed pursuant to this subpart are due and payable 60 days after an order to pay, issued after the hearing or upon default, is served upon the respondent, unless the order provides for a different period of payment. Civil penalties assessed pursuant to an order to pay issued upon consent are due and payable within the time specified therein.

§ 308.118 **Collection of penalties.**

The FDIC may collect any civil penalty assessed pursuant to this subpart by agreement with the respondent, or the FDIC may bring an action against the respondent to recover the penalty amount in the appropriate United States district court. All penalties collected under this section shall be paid over to the Treasury of the United States.

Subpart F—Rules and Procedures Applicable to Proceedings for Involuntary Termination of Insured Status

§ 308.119 **Scope.**

(a) *Involuntary termination of insurance pursuant to section 8(a) of the*

Federal Deposit Insurance Corporation § 308.121

FDIA. The rules and procedures in this subpart, subpart B of the Local Rules and the Uniform Rules shall apply to proceedings in connection with the involuntary termination of the insured status of an insured bank depository institution or an insured branch of a foreign bank pursuant to section 8(a) of the FDIA (12 U.S.C. 1818(a)), except that the Uniform Rules and subpart B of the Local Rules shall not apply to the temporary suspension of insurance pursuant to section 8(a)(8) of the FDIA (12 U.S.C. 1818(a)(8)).

(b) *Involuntary termination of insurance pursuant to section 8(p) of the Act.* The rules and procedures in § 308.124 of this subpart F shall apply to proceedings in connection with the involuntary termination of the insured status of an insured depository institution or an insured branch of a foreign bank pursuant to section 8(p) of the FDIA (12 U.S.C. 1818(p)). The Uniform Rules shall not apply to proceedings under section 8(p) of the FDIA.

§ 308.120 Grounds for termination of insurance.

(a) *General rule.* The following are grounds for involuntary termination of insurance pursuant to section 8(a) of the FDIA:

(1) An insured depository institution or its directors or trustees have engaged or are engaging in unsafe or unsound practices in conducting the business of such depository institution;

(2) An insured depository institution is in an unsafe or unsound condition such that it should not continue operations as an insured depository institution; or

(3) An insured depository institution or its directors or trustees have violated an applicable law, rule, regulation, order, condition imposed in writing by the FDIC in connection with the granting of any application or other request by the insured depository institution or have violated any written agreement entered into between the insured depository institution and the FDIC.

(b) *Extraterritorial acts of foreign banks.* An act or practice committed outside the United States by a foreign bank or its directors or trustees which would otherwise be a ground for termination of insured status under this section shall be a ground for termination if the Board of Directors finds:

(1) The act or practice has been, is, or is likely to be a cause of, or carried on in connection with or in furtherance of, an act or practice committed within any state, territory, or possession of the United States or the District of Columbia that, in and of itself, would be an appropriate basis for action by the FDIC; or

(2) The act or practice committed outside the United States, if proven, would adversely affect the insurance risk of the FDIC.

(c) *Failure of foreign bank to secure removal of personnel.* The failure of a foreign bank to comply with any order of removal or prohibition issued by the Board of Directors or the failure of any person associated with a foreign bank to appear promptly as a party to a proceeding pursuant to section 8(e) of the FDIA (12 U.S.C. 1818(e)), shall be a ground for termination of insurance of deposits in any branch of the bank.

§ 308.121 Notification to primary regulator.

(a) *Service of notification.* (1) Upon a determination by the Board of Directors or its designee pursuant to § 308.120 of an unsafe or unsound practice or condition or of a violation, a notification shall be served upon the appropriate Federal banking agency of the insured depository institution, or the State banking supervisor if the FDIC is the appropriate Federal banking agency.

The notification shall be served not less than 30 days before the Notice of Intent to Terminate Insured Status required by section 8(a)(2)(B) of the FDIA (12 U.S.C. 1818(a)(2)(B)), and § 308.122, except that this period for notification may be reduced or eliminated with the agreement of the appropriate Federal banking agency.

(2) *Appropriate Federal banking agency* shall have the meaning given that term in section 3(q) of the FDIA (12 U.S.C. 1813(q)), and shall be the OCC in the case of a national bank, a District bank or an insured Federal branch of a foreign bank; the FDIC in the case of an insured nonmember bank, including an insured State branch of a foreign

§ 308.122

bank; the Board of Governors in the case of a state member bank; or the OTS in the case of an insured Federal or state savings association.

(3) In the case of a state nonmember bank, insured Federal branch of a foreign bank, or state member bank, in addition to service of the notification upon the appropriate Federal banking agency, a copy of the notification shall be sent to the appropriate State banking supervisor.

(4) In instances in which a Temporary Order Suspending Insurance is issued pursuant to section 8(a)(8) of the FDIA (12 U.S.C. 1818(a)(8)), the notification may be served concurrently with such order.

(b) *Contents of notification.* The notification shall contain the FDIC's determination, and the facts and circumstances upon which such determination is based, for the purpose of securing correction of such practice, condition, or violation.

§ 308.122 Notice of intent to terminate.

(a) If, after serving the notification under § 308.121, the Board of Directors determines that any unsafe or unsound practices, condition, or violation, specified in the notification, requires the termination of the insured status of the insured depository institution, the Board of Directors or its designee, if it determines to proceed further, shall cause to be served upon the insured depository institution a notice of its intention to terminate insured status not less than 30 days after service of the notification, unless a shorter time period has been agreed upon by the appropriate Federal banking agency.

(b) The Board of Directors or its designee shall cause a copy of the notice to be sent to the appropriate Federal banking agency and to the appropriate state banking supervisor, if any.

§ 308.123 Notice to depositors.

If the Board of Directors enters an order terminating the insured status of an insured depository institution or branch, the insured depository institution shall, on the day that order becomes final, or on such other day as that order prescribes, mail a notification of termination of insured status to each depositor at the depositor's last address of record on the books of the insured depository institution or branch. The insured depository institution shall also publish the notification in two issues of a local newspaper of general circulation and shall furnish the FDIC with proof of such publications. The notification to depositors shall include information provided in substantially the following form:

Notice

(Date)_____.

1. The status of the _____, as an (insured depository institution) (insured branch) under the provisions of the Federal Deposit Insurance Act, will terminate as of the close of business on the _____ day of_____, 19___.

2. Any deposits made by you after that date, either new deposits or additions to existing deposits, will not be insured by the Federal Deposit Insurance Corporation.

3. Insured deposits in the (depository institution) (branch) on the _____ day of_____, 19___, will continue to be insured, as provided by Federal Deposit Insurance Act, for *2 years* after the close of business on the _____ day of _____, 19___. Provided, however, that any withdrawals after the close of business on the _____ day of _____, 19___, will reduce the insurance coverage by the amount of such withdrawals.

_____
(Name of (depository institution or branch)

_____
(Address)

The notification may include any additional information the depository institution deems advisable, provided that the information required by this section shall be set forth in a conspicuous manner on the first page of the notification.

§ 308.124 Involuntary termination of insured status for failure to receive deposits.

(a) *Notice to show cause.* When the Board of Directors or its designee has evidence that an insured depository institution is not engaged in the business of receiving deposits, other than trust funds, the Board of Directors or its designee shall give written notice of this evidence to the depository institution and shall direct the depository institution to show cause why its insured status should not be terminated under the provisions of section 8(p) of the FDIA (12 U.S.C. 1818(p)). The insured depository institution shall have 30 days after receipt of the notice, or such

Federal Deposit Insurance Corporation § 308.125

longer period as is prescribed in the notice, to submit affidavits, other written proof, and any legal arguments that it is engaged in the business of receiving deposits other than trust funds.

(b) *Notice of termination date.* If, upon consideration of the affidavits, other written proof, and legal arguments, the Board of Directors determines that the depository institution is not engaged in the business of receiving deposits, other than trust funds, the finding shall be conclusive and the Board of Directors shall notify the depository institution that its insured status will terminate at the expiration of the first full semiannual assessment period following issuance of that notification.

(c) *Notification to depositors of termination of insured status.* Within the time specified by the Board of Directors and prior to the date of termination of its insured status, the depository institution shall mail a notification of termination of insured status to each depositor at the depositor's last address of record on the books of the depository institution. The depository institution shall also publish the notification in two issues of a local newspaper of general circulation and shall furnish the FDIC with proof of such publications. The notification to depositors shall include information provided in substantially the following form:

Notice

(Date)_____.
The status of the _____, as an (insured depository institution) (insured branch) under the Federal Deposit Insurance Act, will terminate on the _____ day of_____, 19___, and its deposits will thereupon cease to be insured.

_____
(Name of depository institution or branch)

_____
(Address)

The notification may include any additional information the depository institution deems advisable, provided that the information required by this section shall be set forth in a conspicuous manner on the first page of the notification.

§ 308.125 **Temporary suspension of deposit insurance.**

(a) If, while an action is pending under section 8(a)(2) of the FDIA (12 U.S.C. 1818(a)(2)), the Board of Directors, after consultation with the appropriate Federal banking agency, finds that an insured depository institution (other than a special supervisory association to which § 308.126 of this subpart applies) has no tangible capital under the capital guidelines or regulations of the appropriate Federal banking agency, the Board of Directors may issue a Temporary Order Suspending Deposit Insurance, pending completion of the proceedings under section 8(a)(2) of the FDIA (12 U.S.C. 1818(a)(2)).

(b) The temporary order shall be served upon the insured institution and a copy sent to the appropriate Federal banking agency and to the appropriate State banking supervisor.

(c) The temporary order shall become effective ten days from the date of service upon the insured depository institution. Unless set aside, limited, or suspended in proceedings under section 8(a)(8)(D) of the FDIA (12 U.S.C. 1818(a)(8)(D)), the temporary order shall remain effective and enforceable until an order terminating the insured status of the institution is entered by the Board of Directors and becomes final, or the Board of Directors dismisses the proceedings.

(d) *Notification to depositors of suspension of insured status.* Within the time specified by the Board of Directors and prior to the suspension of insured status, the depository institution shall mail a notification of suspension of insured status to each depositor at the depositor's last address of record on the books of the depository institution. The depository institution shall also publish the notification in two issues of a local newspaper of general circulation and shall furnish the FDIC with proof of such publications. The notification to depositors shall include information provided in substantially the following form:

Notice

(Date)_____.
1. The status of the _____, as an (insured depository institution) (insured branch) under the provisions of the Federal Deposit Insurance Act, will be suspended as of the close of business on the _____ day of _____, 19___, pending the completion of administrative proceedings under section 8(a) of the Federal Deposit Insurance Act.

§ 308.126

2. Any deposits made by you after that date, either new deposits or additions to existing deposits, will not be insured by the Federal Deposit Insurance Corporation.

3. Insured deposits in the (depository institution) (branch) on the _____ day of _____, 19____, will continue to be insured for _____ after the close of business on the _____ day of _____, 19____. Provided, however, that any withdrawals after the close of business on the _____ day of _____, 19____, will reduce the insurance coverage by the amount of such withdrawals.

_____
(Name of depository institution or branch)

_____
(Address)

The notification may include any additional information the depository institution deems advisable, provided that the information required by this section shall be set forth in a conspicuous manner on the first page of the notification.

§ 308.126 Special supervisory associations.

If the Board of Directors finds that a savings association is a special supervisory association under the provisions of section 8(a)(8)(B) of the FDIA (12 U.S.C. 1818(a)(8)(B)) for purposes of temporary suspension of insured status, the Board of Directors shall serve upon the association its findings with regard to the determination that the capital of the association, as computed using applicable accounting standards, has suffered a material decline; that such association or its directors or officers, is engaging in an unsafe or unsound practice in conducting the business of the association; that such association is in an unsafe or unsound condition to continue operating as an insured association; or that such association or its directors or officers, has violated any law, rule, regulation, order, condition imposed in writing by any Federal banking agency, or any written agreement, or that the association failed to enter into a capital improvement plan acceptable to the Corporation prior to January, 1990.

Subpart G—Rules and Procedures Applicable to Proceedings Relating to Cease-and-Desist Orders

§ 308.127 Scope.

(a) *Cease-and-desist proceedings under sections 8 and 50 of the FDIA.* The rules and procedures of this subpart, subpart B of the Local Rules and the Uniform Rules shall apply to proceedings to order an insured nonmember bank or an institution-affiliated party to cease and desist from practices and violations described in section 8(b) of the FDIA, 12 U.S.C. 1818(b), and section 50 of the FDIA, 12 U.S.C. 1831aa.

(b) *Proceedings under the Securities Exchange Act of 1934.* (1) The rules and procedures of this subpart, subpart B of the Local Rules and the Uniform Rules shall apply to proceedings by the Board of Directors to order a municipal securities dealer to cease and desist from any violation of law or regulation specified in section 15B(c)(5) of the Securities Exchange Act, as amended (15 U.S.C. 78o–4(c)(5)) where the municipal securities dealer is an insured nonmember bank or a subsidiary thereof.

(2) The rules and procedures of this subpart, subpart B of the Local Rules and the Uniform Rules shall apply to proceedings by the Board of Directors to order a clearing agency or transfer agent to cease and desist from failure to comply with the applicable provisions of section 17, 17A and 19 of the Securities Exchange Act of 1934, as amended (15 U.S.C. 78q, 78q–1, 78s), and the applicable rules and regulations thereunder, where the clearing agency or transfer agent is an insured nonmember bank or a subsidiary thereof.

[56 FR 37975, Aug. 9, 1991, as amended at 64 FR 62100, Nov. 16, 1999; 72 FR 67235, Nov. 28, 2007]

§ 308.128 Grounds for cease-and-desist orders.

(a) *General rule.* The Board of Directors or its designee may issue and have served upon any insured nonmember bank or an institution-affiliated party a notice, as set forth in § 308.18 of the Uniform Rules for practices and violations as described in § 308.127.

Federal Deposit Insurance Corporation

§ 308.131

(b) *Extraterritorial acts of foreign banks.* An act, violation or practice committed outside the United States by a foreign bank or an institution-affiliated party that would otherwise be a ground for issuing a cease-and-desist order under paragraph (a) of this section or a temporary cease-and-desist order under § 308.131 of this subpart, shall be a ground for an order if the Board of Directors or its designee finds that:

(1) The act, violation or practice has been, is, or is likely to be a cause of, or carried on in connection with or in furtherance of, an act, violation or practice committed within any state, territory, or possession of the United States or the District of Columbia which act, violation or practice, in and of itself, would be an appropriate basis for action by the FDIC; or

(2) The act, violation or practice, if proven, would adversely affect the insurance risk of the FDIC.

§ 308.129 Notice to state supervisory authority.

The Board of Directors or its designee shall give the appropriate state supervisory authority notification of its intent to institute a proceeding pursuant to subpart G of this part, and the grounds thereof. Any proceedings shall be conducted according to subpart G of this part, unless, within the time period specified in such notification, the state supervisory authority has effected satisfactory corrective action. No insured institution or other party who is the subject of any notice or order issued by the FDIC under this section shall have standing to raise the requirements of this subpart as grounds for attacking the validity of any such notice or order.

§ 308.130 Effective date of order and service on bank.

(a) *Effective date.* A cease-and-desist order issued by the Board of Directors after a hearing, and a cease-and-desist order issued based upon a default, shall become effective at the expiration of 30 days after the service of the order upon the bank or its official. A cease-and-desist order issued upon consent shall become effective at the time specified therein. All cease-and-desist orders shall remain effective and enforceable, except to the extent they are stayed, modified, terminated, or set aside by the Board of Directors or its designee or by a reviewing court.

(b) *Service on banks.* In cases where the bank is not the respondent, the cease-and-desist order shall also be served upon the bank.

§ 308.131 Temporary cease-and-desist order.

(a) *Issuance.* (1) When the Board of Directors or its designee determines that the violation, or the unsafe or unsound practice, as specified in the notice, or the continuation thereof, is likely to cause insolvency or significant dissipation of assets or earnings of the bank, or is likely to weaken the condition of the bank or otherwise prejudice the interests of its depositors prior to the completion of the proceedings under section 8(b) of the FDIA (12 U.S.C. 1818(b)) and § 308.128 of this subpart, the Board of Directors or its designee may issue a temporary order requiring the bank or an institution-affiliated party to immediately cease and desist from any such violation, practice or to take affirmative action to prevent such insolvency, dissipation, condition or prejudice pending completion of the proceedings under section 8(b) of the FDIA (12 U.S.C. 1818(b)).

(2) When the Board of Directors or its designee issues a Notice of charges pursuant to 12 U.S.C. 1818(b)(1) which specifies on the basis of particular facts and circumstances that a bank's books and records are so incomplete or inaccurate that the FDIC is unable, through the normal supervisory process, to determine the financial condition of the bank or the details or purpose of any transaction or transactions that may have a material effect on the financial condition of the bank, then the Board of Directors or its designee may issue a temporary order requiring:

(i) The cessation of any activity or practice which gave rise, whether in whole or in part, to the incomplete or inaccurate state of the books or records; or

(ii) Affirmative action to restore such books or records to a complete

§ 308.132

and accurate state, until the completion of the proceedings under section 8(b) of the FDIA (12 U.S.C. 1818(b)).

(3) The temporary order shall be served upon the bank or the institution-affiliated party named therein and shall also be served upon the bank in the case where the temporary order applies only to an institution-affiliated party.

(b) *Effective date.* A temporary order shall become effective when served upon the bank or the institution-affiliated party. Unless the temporary order is set aside, limited, or suspended by a court in proceedings authorized under section 8(c)(2) of the FDIA (12 U.S.C. 1818(c)(2)), the temporary order shall remain effective and enforceable pending completion of administrative proceedings pursuant to section 8(b) of the FDIA (12 U.S.C. 1818(b)) and entry of an order which has become final, or with respect to paragraph (a)(2) of this section the FDIC determines by examination or otherwise that the bank's books and records are accurate and reflect the financial condition of the bank.

(c) *Uniform Rules do not apply.* The Uniform Rules and subpart B of the Local Rules shall not apply to the issuance of temporary orders under this section.

Subpart H—Rules and Procedures Applicable to Proceedings Relating to Assessment and Collection of Civil Money Penalties for Violation of Cease-and-Desist Orders and of Certain Federal Statutes, Including Call Report Penalties

§ 308.132 Assessment of penalties.

(a) *Scope.* The rules and procedures of this subpart, subpart B of the Local Rules, and the Uniform Rules shall apply to proceedings to assess and collect civil money penalties, including civil money penalties for violation of section 7(a) of the FDIA (12 U.S.C. 1817(a)).

(b) *Relevant considerations.* In determining the amount of the civil penalty to be assessed, the Board of Directors or its designee shall consider the financial resources and good faith of the bank or official, the gravity of the violation, the history of previous violations, and any such other matters as justice may require.

(c) *Amount.* (1) The Board of Directors or its designee may assess civil money penalties pursuant to section 8(i) of the FDIA (12 U.S.C. 1818(i)), and § 308.01(e)(1) of the Uniform Rules.

(2) The Board of Directors or its designee may assess civil money penalties pursuant to section 7(a) of the FDIA (12 U.S.C. 1817(a)) as follows:

(i) *Late filing—Tier One penalties.* In cases in which a bank fails to make or publish its Report of Condition and Income (Call Report) within the appropriate time periods, a civil money penalty of not more than $2,200 per day may be assessed where the bank maintains procedures in place reasonably adapted to avoid inadvertent error and the late filing occurred unintentionally and as a result of such error; or the bank inadvertently transmitted a Call Report which is minimally late. Pursuant to the Debt Collection Improvement Act of 1996, for violations of paragraph (c)(2)(i) which occur after December 31, 2008, the following maximum Tier One penalty amounts contained in paragraphs (c)(2)(i)(A) and (B) of this section shall apply for each day that the violation continues.

(A) *First offense.* Generally, in such cases, the amount assessed shall be $330 per day for each of the first 15 days for which the failure continues, and $660 per day for each subsequent day the failure continues, beginning on the sixteenth day. For banks with less than $25,000,000 in assets, the amount assessed shall be the greater of $110 per day or 1/1000th of the bank's total assets (1/10th of a basis point) for each of the first 15 days for which the failure continues, and $220 or 1/500th of the bank's total assets, 1/5 of a basis point) for each subsequent day the failure continues, beginning on the sixteenth day.

(B) *Subsequent offenses.* Where the bank has been delinquent in making or publishing its Call Report within the preceding five quarters, the amount assessed for the most current failure shall generally be $550 per day for each of the first 15 days for which the failure continues, and $1,100 per day for each subsequent day the failure continues, beginning on the sixteenth day. For

Federal Deposit Insurance Corporation § 308.132

banks with less than $25,000,000 in assets, those amounts, respectively, shall be ⅟₅₀₀th of the bank's total assets and ⅟₂₅₀th of the bank's total assets.

(C) *Mitigating factors.* The amounts set forth in paragraph (c)(2)(i)(A) of this section may be reduced based upon the factors set forth in paragraph (b) of this section.

(D) *Lengthy or repeated violations.* The amounts set forth in this paragraph (c)(2)(i) will be assessed on a case-by-case basis where the amount of time of the bank's delinquency is lengthy or the bank has been delinquent repeatedly in making or publishing its Call Reports.

(E) *Waiver.* Absent extraordinary circumstances outside the control of the bank, penalties assessed for late filing shall not be waived.

(ii) *Late filing—Tier Two penalties.* Where a bank fails to make or publish its Call Report within the appropriate time period, the Board of Directors or its designee may assess a civil money penalty of not more than $20,000 per day for each day the failure continues. Pursuant to the Debt Collection Improvement Act of 1996, for violations which occur after December 31, 2008, the maximum Tier Two penalty amount will increase to $32,000 per day for each day the failure continues.

(iii) *False or misleading reports or information*—(A) *Tier One penalties.* In cases in which a bank submits or publishes any false or misleading Call Report or information, the Board of Directors or its designee may assess a civil money penalty of not more than $2,200 per day for each day the information is not corrected, where the bank maintains procedures in place reasonably adapted to avoid inadvertent error and the violation occurred unintentionally and as a result of such error; or the bank inadvertently transmits a Call Report or information which is false or misleading.

(B) *Tier Two penalties.* Where a bank submits or publishes any false or misleading Call Report or other information, the Board of Directors or its designee may assess a civil money penalty of not more than $20,000 per day for each day the information is not corrected. Pursuant to the Debt Collection Improvement Act of 1996, for violations which occur after December 31, 2008, the maximum Tier Two penalty amount will increase to $32,000 per day for each day the information is not corrected.

(C) *Tier Three penalties.* Where a bank knowingly or with reckless disregard for the accuracy of any Call Report or information submits or publishes any false or misleading Call Report or other information, the Board of Directors or its designee may assess a civil money penalty of not more than the lesser of $1,375,000 or 1 percent of the bank's total assets per day for each day the information is not corrected. Pursuant to the Debt Collection Improvement Act of 1996, for violations which occur after December 31, 2008, the maximum Tier Three penalty amount will increase to the lesser of $1,250,000 per day or 1 percent of the bank's total assets per day for each day the information is not corrected.

(D) *Mitigating factors.* The amounts set forth in this paragraph (c)(2) may be reduced based upon the factors set forth in paragraph (b) of this section.

(3) *Adjustment of civil money penalties by the rate of inflation pursuant to section 31001(s) of the Debt Collection Improvement Act.* Pursuant to section 31001(s) of the Debt Collection Improvement Act, for violations which occur after December 31, 2008, the Board of Directors or its designee may assess civil money penalties in the maximum amounts as follows:

(i) *Civil money penalties assessed pursuant to section 8(i)(2) of the FDIA.* Tier One civil money penalties may be assessed pursuant to section 8(i)(2)(A) of the FDIA (12 U.S.C. 1818(i)(2)(A)) in an amount not to exceed $7,500 for each day during which the violation continues. Tier Two civil money penalties may be assessed pursuant to section 8(i)(2)(B) of the FDIA (12 U.S.C. 1818(i)(2)(B)) in an amount not to exceed $37,500 for each day during which the violation, practice or breach continues. Tier Three civil money penalties may be assessed pursuant to section 8(i)(2)(C)(12 U.S.C. 1818(i)(2)(C)) in an amount not to exceed, in the case of any person other than an insured depository institution $1,375,000 or, in the

§ 308.132

case of any insured depository institution, an amount not to exceed the lesser of $1,375,000 or 1 percent of the total assets of such institution for each day during which the violation, practice, or breach continues.

(A) Civil money penalties may be assessed pursuant to section 8(i)(2) of the FDIA in the amounts set forth in this paragraph (c)(3)(i) for violations of various consumer laws, including, the Home Mortgage Disclosure Act (12 U.S.C. 2804 et seq. and 12 CFR 203.6), the Expedited Funds Availability Act (12 U.S.C. 4001 et seq.), the Truth in Savings Act (12 U.S.C. 4301 et seq.), the Real Estate Settlement Procedures Act (12 U.S.C. 2601 et seq. and 12 CFR part 3500), the Truth in Lending Act (15 U.S.C. 1601 et seq.), the Fair Credit Reporting Act (15 U.S.C. 1681 et seq.), the Equal Credit Opportunity Act (15 U.S.C. 1691 et seq.), the Fair Debt Collection Practices Act (15 U.S.C. 1692 et seq.), the Electronic Funds Transfer Act (15 U.S.C. 1693 et seq.) and the Fair Housing Act (42 U.S.C. 3601 et seq.) in the amounts set forth in paragraphs (c)(3)(i) through (c)(3)(iii) of this section.

(ii) *Civil money penalties assessed pursuant to section 7(c) of the FDIA for late filing or the submission false or misleading certified statements.* Tier One civil money penalties may be assessed pursuant to section 7(c)(4)(A) of the FDIA (12 U.S.C. 1817(c)(4)(A)) in an amount not to exceed 2,200 for each day during which the failure to file continues or the false or misleading information is not corrected. Tier Two civil money penalties may be assessed pursuant to section 7(c)(4)(B) of the FDIA (12 U.S.C. 1817(c)(4)(B)) in an amount not to exceed $32,000 for each day during which the failure to file continues or the false or misleading information is not corrected. Tier Three civil money penalties may be assessed pursuant to section 7(c)(4)(C) in an amount not to exceed the lesser of $1,375,000 or 1 percent of the total assets of the institution for each day during which the failure to file continues or the false or misleading information is not corrected.

(iii) *Civil money penalties assessed pursuant to section 10(e)(4) of the FDIA for refusal to allow examination or to provide required information during an examination.* Pursuant to section 10(e)(4) of the FDIA (12 U.S.C. 1820(e)(4)), civil money penalties may be assessed against any affiliate of an insured depository institution which refuses to permit a duly-appointed examiner to conduct an examination or to provide information during the course of an examination as set forth in section 20(b) of the FDIA (12 U.S.C. 1820(b)), in an amount not to exceed $7,500 for each day the refusal continues.

(iv) *Civil money penalties assessed pursuant to section 18(a)(3) of the FDIA for incorrect display of insurance logo.* Pursuant to section 18(a)(3) of the FDIA (12 U.S.C. 1828(a)(3)), civil money penalties may be assessed against an insured depository institution which fails to correctly display its insurance logo pursuant to that section, in an amount not to exceed $110 for each day the violation continues.

(v) *Civil money penalties assessed pursuant to section 18(h) of the FDI Act for failure to timely pay assessment*—(A) *In General.*Subject to paragraph (c)(3)(v)(C) of this section, any insured depository institution which fails or refuses to pay any assessment shall be subject to a penalty in an amount of not more than 1 percent of the amount of the assessment due for each day that such violation continues.

(B) *Exception In Case Of Dispute.*Paragraph (A) of this section shall not apply if—

(*1*) The failure to pay an assessment is due to a dispute between the insured depository institution and the Corporation over the amount of such assessment; and

(*2*) The insured depository institution deposits security satisfactory to the Corporation for payment upon final determination of the issue.

(C) *Special Rule For Small Assessment Amounts.*If the amount of the assessment which an insured depository institution fails or refuses to pay is less than $10,000 at the time of such failure or refusal, the amount of any penalty to which such institution is subject under paragraph (A) of this section shall not exceed $100 for each day that such violation continues.

Federal Deposit Insurance Corporation § 308.132

(D) *Authority To Modify Or Remit Penalty.*;The Corporation, in the sole discretion of the Corporation, may compromise, modify or remit any penalty which the Corporation may assess or has already assessed under paragraph (c)(3)(v)(A) of this section upon a finding that good cause prevented the timely payment of an assessment.

(vi) *Civil money penalties assessed pursuant to section 19b(j) of the FDIA for recordkeeping violations.* Pursuant to section 19b(j) of the FDIA (12 U.S.C. 1829b(j)), civil money penalties may be assessed against an insured depository institution and any director, officer or employee thereof who wilfully or through gross negligence violates or causes a violation of the recordkeeping requirements of that section or its implementing regulations in an amount not to exceed $16,000 per violation.

(vii) *Civil fine pursuant to 12 U.S.C. 1832(c) for violation of provisions forbidding interest-bearing demand deposit accounts.* Pursuant to 12 U.S.C. 1832(c), any depository institution which violates the prohibition on deposit or withdrawal from interest-bearing accounts via negotiable or transferable instruments payable to third parties shall be subject to a fine of $1,100 per violation.

(viii) *Civil penalties for violations of security measure requirements under 12 U.S.C. 1884.* Pursuant to 12 U.S.C. 1884, an institution which violates a rule establishing minimum security requirements as set forth in 12 U.S.C. 1882, shall be subject to a civil penalty not to exceed $110 for each day of the violation.

(ix) *Civil money penalties assessed pursuant to the Bank Holding Company Act of 1970 for prohibited tying arrangements.* Pursuant to the Bank Holding Company Act of 1970, Tier One civil money penalties may be assessed pursuant to 12 U.S.C. 1972(2)(F)(i) in an amount not to exceed $7,500 for each day during which the violation continues. Tier Two civil money penalties may be assessed pursuant to 12 U.S.C. 1972(2)(F)(ii) in an amount not to exceed $37,500 for each day during which the violation, practice or breach continues. Tier Three civil money penalties may be assessed pursuant to 12 U.S.C. 1972(2)(F)(iii) in an amount not to exceed, in the case of any person other than an insured depository institution $1,375,000 for each day during which the violation, practice, or breach continues or, in the case of any insured depository institution, an amount not to exceed the lesser of $1,375,000 or 1 percent of the total assets of such institution for each day during which the violation, practice, or breach continues.

(x) *Civil money penalties assessed pursuant to the International Banking Act of 1978.* Pursuant to the International Banking Act of 1978 (IBA) (12 U.S.C. 3108(b)), civil money penalties may be assessed for failure to comply with the requirements of the IBA pursuant to section 8(i)(2) of the FDIA (12 U.S.C. 1818(i)(2)), in the amounts set forth in paragraph (c)(3)(i) of this section.

(xi) *Civil money penalties assessed for appraisal violations.* Pursuant to 12 U.S.C. 3349(b), where a financial institution seeks, obtains, or gives any other thing of value in exchange for the performance of an appraisal by a person that the institution knows is not a state certified or licensed appraiser in connection with a federally related transaction, a civil money penalty may be assessed pursuant to section 8(i)(2) of the FDIA (12 U.S.C. 1818(i)(2)) in the amounts set forth in paragraph (c)(3)(i) of this section.

(xii) *Civil money penalties assessed pursuant to International Lending Supervision Act.* Pursuant to the International Lending Supervision Act (ILSA) (12 U.S.C. 3909(d)), the CMP that may be assessed against any banking institution or any officer, director, employee, agent or other person participating in the conduct of the affairs of such banking institution is amount not to exceed $1,100 for each day a violation of the ILSA or any rule, regulation or order issued pursuant to ILSA continues.

(xiii) *Civil money penalties assessed for violations of the Community Development Banking and Financial Institution Act.* Pursuant to the Community Development Banking and Financial Institution Act (Community Development Banking Act) (12 U.S.C. 4717(b)) a civil money penalty may be assessed for violations of the Community Development Banking Act pursuant to section 8(i)(2)

§ 308.133

of the FDIA (12 U.S.C. 1818(i)(2)), in the amounts set forth in paragraph (c)(3)(i) of this section.

(xiv) *Civil money penalties assessed for violations of the Securities Exchange Act of 1934.* Pursuant to section 21B of the Securities Exchange Act of 1934 (Exchange Act) (15 U.S.C. 78u–2), civil money penalties may be assessed for violations of certain provisions of the Exchange Act, where such penalties are in the public interest. Tier One civil money penalties may be assessed pursuant to 15 U.S.C. 78u–2(b)(1) in an amount not to exceed $7,500 for a natural person or $70,000 for any other person for violations set forth in 15 U.S.C. 78u–2(a). Tier Two civil money penalties may be assessed pursuant to 15 U.S.C. 78u–2(b)(2) in an amount not to exceed—for each violation set forth in 15 U.S.C. 78u–2(a)—$70,000 for a natural person or $350,000 for any other person if the act or omission involved fraud, deceit, manipulation, or deliberate or reckless disregard of a regulatory requirement. Tier Three civil money penalties may be assessed pursuant to 15 U.S.C. 78u–2(b)(3) for each violation set forth in 15 U.S.C. 78u–2(a), in an amount not to exceed $140,000 for a natural person or $675,000 for any other person, if the act or omission involved fraud, deceit, manipulation, or deliberate or reckless disregard of a regulatory requirement; and such act or omission directly or indirectly resulted in substantial losses, or created a significant risk of substantial losses to other persons or resulted in substantial pecuniary gain to the person who committed the act or omission.

(xv) Civil money penalties assessed for false claims and statements pursuant to the Program Fraud Civil Remedies Act. Pursuant to the Program Fraud Civil Remedies Act (31 U.S.C. 3802), civil money penalties of not more than $7,500 per claim or statement may be assessed for violations involving false claims and statements.

(xvi) *Civil money penalties assessed for violations of the Flood Disaster Protection Act.* Pursuant to the Flood Disaster Protection Act (FDPA)(42 U.S.C. 4012a(f)), civil money penalties may be assessed against any regulated lending institution that engages in a pattern or practice of violations of the FDPA in an amount not to exceed $385 per violation, and not to exceed a total of $135,000 annually.

(xvii) *Civil money penalties assessed for violation of one-year restriction on Federal examiners of financial institutions.* Pursuant to section 10(k) of the Federal Deposit Insurance Act (12 U.S.C. 1820(k)), the Board of Directors or its designee may assess a civil money penalty of up to $250,000 against any covered former Federal examiner of a financial institution who, in violation of section 1820(k) and within the one-year period following termination of government service as an employee, serves as an officer, director, or consultant of a financial or depository institution, a holding company, or of any other entity listed in section 10(k), without the written waiver or permission by the appropriate Federal banking agency or authority under section 1820(k)(5). Pursuant to the Debt Collection Improvement Act of 1996, for any violation of section 10(k) which occurs after December 31, 2008, the maximum penalty amount will increase to $275,000.

[56 FR 37975, Aug. 9, 1991, as amended at 61 FR 57991, Nov. 12, 1996; 64 FR 62100, Nov. 16, 1999; 65 FR 64887, Oct. 31, 2000; 66 FR 9189, Feb. 7, 2001; 69 FR 61305, Oct. 18, 2004; 71 FR 65713, Nov. 9, 2006; 73 FR 73157, Dec. 2, 2008]

§ 308.133 Effective date of, and payment under, an order to pay.

(a) *Effective date.* (1) Unless otherwise provided in the Notice, except in situations covered by paragraph (a)(2) of this section, civil penalties assessed pursuant to this subpart are due and payable 60 days after the Notice is served upon the respondent.

(2) If the respondent both requests a hearing and serves an answer, civil penalties assessed pursuant to this subpart are due and payable 60 days after an order to pay, issued after the hearing or upon default, is served upon the respondent, unless the order provides for a different period of payment. Civil penalties assessed pursuant to an order to pay issued upon consent are due and payable within the time specified therein.

(b) *Payment.* All penalties collected under this section shall be paid over to the Treasury of the United States.

Federal Deposit Insurance Corporation § 308.136

Subpart I—Rules and Procedures for Imposition of Sanctions Upon Municipal Securities Dealers or Persons Associated With Them and Clearing Agencies or Transfer Agents

§ 308.134 Scope.

The rules and procedures in this subpart, subpart B of the Local Rules and the Uniform Rules shall apply to proceedings by the Board of Directors or its designee:

(a) To censure, limit the activities of, suspend, or revoke the registration of, any municipal securities dealer for which the FDIC is the appropriate regulatory agency;

(b) To censure, suspend, or bar from being associated with such a municipal securities dealer, any person associated with such a municipal securities dealer; and

(c) To deny registration, to censure limit the activities of, suspend, or revoke the registration of, any transfer agent or clearing agency for which the FDIC is the appropriate regulatory agency. This subpart and the Uniform Rules shall not apply to proceedings to postpone or suspend registration of a transfer agent or clearing agency pending final determination of denial or revocation of registration.

§ 308.135 Grounds for imposition of sanctions.

(a) *Action under section 15(b)(4) of the Exchange Act.* The Board of Directors or its designee may issue and have served upon any municipal securities dealer for which the FDIC is the appropriate regulatory agency, or any person associated or seeking to become associated with a municipal securities dealer for which the FDIC is the appropriate regulatory agency, a written notice of its intention to censure, limit the activities or functions or operations of, suspend, or revoke the registration of, such municipal securities dealer, or to censure, suspend, or bar the person from being associated with the municipal securities dealer, when the Board of Directors or its designee determines:

(1) That such municipal securities dealer or such person

(i) Has committed any prohibited act or omitted any required act specified in subparagraph (A), (D), or (E) of section 15(b)(4) of the Exchange Act, as amended (15 U.S.C. 78o);

(ii) Has been convicted of any offense specified in section 15(b)(4)(B) of the Exchange Act within ten years of commencement of proceedings under this subpart; or

(iii) Is enjoined from any act, conduct, or practice specified in section 15(b)(4)(C) of the Exchange Act; and

(2) That it is in the public interest to impose any of the sanctions set forth in paragraph (a) of this section.

(b) *Action under sections 17 and 17A of the Exchange Act.* The Board of Directors or its designee may issue, and have served upon any transfer agent or clearing agency for which the FDIC is the appropriate regulatory agency, a written Notice of its intention to deny registration to, censure, place limitations on the activities or function or operations of, suspend, or revoke the registration of, the transfer agent or clearing agency, when the Board of Directors or its designee determines:

(1) That the transfer agent or clearing agency has willfully violated, or is unable to comply with, any applicable provision of section 17 or 17A of the Exchange Act, as amended, or any applicable rule or regulation issued pursuant thereto; and

(2) That it is in the public interest to impose any of the sanctions set forth in paragraph (b) of this section.

§ 308.136 Notice to and consultation with the Securities and Exchange Commission.

Before initiating any proceedings under § 308.135, the FDIC shall:

(a) Notify the Securities and Exchange Commission of the identity of the municipal securities dealer or associated person against whom proceedings are to be initiated, and the nature of and basis for the proposed action; and

(b) Consult with the Commission concerning the effect of the proposed action on the protection of investors and the possibility of coordinating the action with any proceeding by the Commission against the municipal securities dealer or associated person.

§ 308.137 Effective date of order imposing sanctions.

An order issued by the Board of Directors after a hearing or an order issued upon default shall become effective at the expiration of 30 days after the service of the order, except that an order of censure, denial, or revocation of registration is effective when served. An order issued upon consent shall become effective at the time specified therein. All orders shall remain effective and enforceable except to the extent they are stayed, modified, terminated, or set aside by the Board of Directors, its designee, or a reviewing court, provided that orders of suspension shall continue in effect no longer than 12 months.

Subpart J—Rules and Procedures Relating to Exemption Proceedings Under Section 12(h) of the Securities Exchange Act of 1934

§ 308.138 Scope.

The rules and procedures of this subpart J shall apply to proceedings by the Board of Directors or its designee to exempt, in whole or in part, an issuer of securities from the provisions of sections 12(g), 13, 14(a), 14(c), 14(d), or 14(f) of the Exchange Act, as amended (15 U.S.C. 78l, 78m, 78n (a), (c) (d) or (f)), or to exempt an officer or a director or beneficial owner of securities of such an issuer from the provisions of section 16 of the Exchange Act (15 U.S.C. 78p).

§ 308.139 Application for exemption.

Any interested person may file a written application for an exemption under this subpart with the Executive Secretary, Federal Deposit Insurance Corporation, 550 17th Street NW., Washington, DC 20429. The application shall specify the exemption sought and the reason therefor, and shall include a statement indicating why the exemption would be consistent with the public interest or the protection of investors.

§ 308.140 Newspaper notice.

(a) *General rule.* If the Board of Directors or its designee, in its sole discretion, decides to further consider an application for exemption, there shall be served upon the applicant instructions to publish one notification in a newspaper of general circulation in the community where the main office of the issuer is located. The applicant shall furnish proof of such publication to the Executive Secretary or such other person as may be directed in the instructions.

(b) *Contents.* The notification shall contain the name and address of the issuer and the name and title of the applicant, the exemption sought, a statement that a hearing will be held, and a statement that within 30 days of publication of the newspaper notice, interested persons may submit to the FDIC written comments on the application for exemption and a written request for an opportunity to be heard. The address of the FDIC must appear in the notice.

§ 308.141 Notice of hearing.

Within ten days after expiration of the period for receipt of comments pursuant to § 308.140, the Executive Secretary shall serve upon the applicant and any person who has requested an opportunity to be heard written notification indicating the place and time of the hearing. The hearing shall be held not later than 30 days after service of the notification of hearing. The notification shall contain the name and address of the presiding officer designated by the Executive Secretary and a statement of the matters to be considered.

§ 308.142 Hearing.

(a) *Proceedings are informal.* Formal rules of evidence, the adjudicative procedures of the APA (5 U.S.C. 554–557), the Uniform Rules and § 308.108 of subpart B of the Local Rules shall not apply to hearings under this subpart.

(b) *Hearing Procedure.* (1) Parties to the hearing may appear personally or through counsel and shall have the right to introduce relevant and material documents and to make an oral statement.

(2) There shall be no discovery in proceeding under this subpart J.

(3) The presiding officer shall have discretion to permit presentation of

Federal Deposit Insurance Corporation §308.146

witnesses within specified time limits, provided that a list of witnesses is furnished to the presiding officer prior to the hearing. Witnesses shall be sworn, unless otherwise directed by the presiding officer. The presiding officer may ask questions of any witness and each party may cross-examine any witness presented by an opposing party.

(4) The proceedings shall be on the record and the transcript shall be promptly submitted to the Board of Directors. The presiding officer shall make recommendations to the Board of Directors, unless the Board of Directors, in its sole discretion, directs otherwise.

§ 308.143 Decision of Board of Directors.

Following submission of the hearing transcript to the Board of Directors, the Board of Directors may grant the exemption where it determines, by reason of the number of public investors, the amount of trading interest in the securities, the nature and extent of the issuer's activities, the issuer's income or assets, or otherwise, that the exemption is consistent with the public interest or the protection of investors. Any exemption shall be set forth in an order specifying the terms of the exemption, the person to whom it is granted, and the period for which it is granted. A copy of the order shall be served upon each party to the proceeding.

Subpart K—Procedures Applicable to Investigations Pursuant to Section 10(c) of the FDIA

§ 308.144 Scope.

The procedures of this subpart shall be followed when an investigation is instituted and conducted in connection with any open or failed insured depository institution, any institutions making application to become insured depository institutions, and affiliates thereof, or with other types of investigations to determine compliance with applicable law and regulations, pursuant to section 10(c) of the FDIA (12 U.S.C. 1820(c)). The Uniform Rules and subpart B of the Local Rules shall not apply to investigations under this subpart.

§ 308.145 Conduct of investigation.

An investigation conducted pursuant to section 10(c) of the FDIA shall be initiated only upon issuance of an order by the Board of Directors; or by the General Counsel, the Director of the Division of Supervision and Consumer Protection (DSC), the Director of the Division of Depositor and Asset Services, or their respective designees as set forth at § 303.272 of this chapter. The order shall indicate the purpose of the investigation and designate FDIC's representative(s) to direct the conduct of the investigation. Upon application and for good cause shown, the persons who issue the order of investigation may limit, quash, modify, or withdraw it. Upon the conclusion of the investigation, an order of termination of the investigation shall be issued by the persons issuing the order of investigation.

[56 FR 37975, Aug. 9, 1991, as amended at 60 FR 31384, June 15, 1995; 64 FR 62100, Nov. 16, 1999]

§ 308.146 Powers of person conducting investigation.

The person designated to conduct a section 10(c) investigation shall have the power, among other things, to administer oaths and affirmations, to take and preserve testimony under oath, to issue subpoenas and subpoenas duces tecum and to apply for their enforcement to the United States District Court for the judicial district or the United States court in any territory in which the main office of the bank, institution, or affiliate is located or in which the witness resides or conducts business. The person conducting the investigation may obtain the assistance of counsel or others from both within and outside the FDIC. The persons who issue the order of investigation may limit, quash, or modify any subpoena or subpoena duces tecum, upon application and for good cause shown. The person conducting an investigation may report to the Board of Directors any instance where any attorney has been guilty of contemptuous conduct. The Board of Directors, upon motion of the person conducting the investigation, or on its own motion, may make a finding of contempt and may then summarily suspend,

§ 308.147

without a hearing, any attorney representing a witness from further participation in the investigation.

§ 308.147 Investigations confidential.

Investigations conducted pursuant to section 10(c) shall be confidential. Information and documents obtained by the FDIC in the course of such investigations shall not be disclosed, except as provided in part 309 of this chapter and as otherwise required by law.

§ 308.148 Rights of witnesses.

In an investigation pursuant to section 10(c):

(a) Any person compelled or requested to furnish testimony, documentary evidence, or other information, shall upon request be shown and provided with a copy of the order initiating the proceeding;

(b) Any person compelled or requested to provide testimony as a witness or to furnish documentary evidence may be represented by a counsel who meets the requirements of § 308.6 of the Uniform Rules. That counsel may be present and may:

(1) Advise the witness before, during, and after such testimony;

(2) Briefly question the witness at the conclusion of such testimony for clarification purposes; and

(3) Make summary notes during such testimony solely for the use and benefit of the witness;

(c) All persons testifying shall be sequestered. Such persons and their counsel shall not be present during the testimony of any other person, unless permitted in the discretion of the person conducting the investigation;

(d) In cases of a perceived or actual conflict of interest arising out of an attorney's or law firm's representation of multiple witnesses, the person conducting the investigation may require the attorney to comply with the provisions of § 308.8 of the Uniform Rules; and

(e) Witness fees shall be paid in accordance with § 308.14 of the Uniform Rules.

[56 FR 37975, Aug. 9, 1991, as amended at 64 FR 62100, Nov. 16, 1999]

§ 308.149 Service of subpoena.

Service of a subpoena shall be accomplished in accordance with § 308.11 of the Uniform Rules.

§ 308.150 Transcripts.

(a) *General rule.* Transcripts of testimony, if any, in an investigation pursuant to section 10(c) shall be recorded by an official reporter, or by any other person or means designated by the person conducting the investigation. A witness may, solely for the use and benefit of the witness, obtain a copy of the transcript of his or her testimony at the conclusion of the investigation or, at the discretion of the person conducting the investigation, at an earlier time, provided the transcript is available. The witness requesting a copy of his or her testimony shall bear the cost thereof.

(b) *Subscription by witness.* The transcript of testimony shall be subscribed by the witness, unless the person conducting the investigation and the witness, by stipulation, have waived the signing, or the witness is ill, cannot be found, or has refused to sign. If the transcript of the testimony is not subscribed by the witness, the official reporter taking the testimony shall certify that the transcript is a true and complete transcript of the testimony.

Subpart L—Procedures and Standards Applicable to a Notice of Change in Senior Executive Officer or Director Pursuant to Section 32 of the FDIA

§ 308.151 Scope.

The rules and procedures set forth in this subpart shall apply to the notice filed by a state nonmember bank pursuant to section 32 of the FDIA (12 U.S.C. 1831i) and § 303.102 of this chapter for the consent of the FDIC to add or replace an individual on the Board of Directors, or to employ any individual as a senior executive officer, or change the responsibilities of any individual to a position of senior executive officer where:

(a) The bank is not in compliance with all minimum capital requirements applicable to it as determined

Federal Deposit Insurance Corporation

§ 308.155

by the FDIC on the basis of such institution's most recent report of condition or report of examination or inspection;

(b) The bank is in a troubled condition as defined in § 303.101(c) of this chapter; or

(c) The FDIC determines, in connection with the review of a capital restoration plan required under section 38(e)(2) of the FDIA (12 U.S.C. 1831o(e)(2)) or otherwise, that such prior notice is appropriate.

[64 FR 62100, Nov. 16, 1999]

§ 308.152 Grounds for disapproval of notice.

The Board of Directors or its designee may issue a notice of disapproval with respect to a notice submitted by a state nonmember bank pursuant to section 32 of the FDIA (12 U.S.C. 1831i) where:

(a) The competence, experience, character, or integrity of the individual with respect to whom such notice is submitted indicates that it would not be in the best interests of the depositors of the state nonmember bank to permit the individual to be employed by or associated with such bank; or

(b) The competence, experience, character, or integrity of the individual with respect to whom such notice is submitted indicates that it would not be in the best interests of the public to permit the individual to be employed by, or associated with, the state nonmember bank.

[56 FR 37975, Aug. 9, 1991, as amended at 64 FR 62101, Nov. 16, 1999]

§ 308.153 Procedures where notice of disapproval issues pursuant to § 303.103(c) of this chapter.

(a) The Notice of Disapproval shall be served upon the insured state nonmember bank and the candidate for director or senior executive officer. The Notice of Disapproval shall:

(1) Summarize or cite the relevant considerations specified in § 308.152;

(2) Inform the individual and the bank that a request for review of the disapproval may be filed within fifteen days of receipt of the Notice of Disapproval; and

(3) Specify that additional information, if any, must be contained in the request for review.

(b) The request for review must be filed at the appropriate regional office.

(c) The request for review must be in writing and should:

(1) Specify the reasons why the FDIC should reconsider its disapproval; and

(2) Set forth relevant, substantive and material documents, if any, that for good cause were not previously set forth in the notice required to be filed pursuant to section 32 of the FDIA (12 U.S.C. 1831i).

[56 FR 37975, Aug. 9, 1991, as amended at 64 FR 62101, Nov. 16, 1999]

§ 308.154 Decision on review.

(a) Within 30 days of receipt of the request for review, the Board of Directors or its designee, shall notify the bank and/or the individual filing the reconsideration (hereafter "petitioner") of the FDIC's decision on review.

(b) If the decision is to grant the review and approve the notice, the bank and the individual involved shall be so notified.

(c) A denial of the request for review pursuant to section 32 of the FDIA shall:

(1) Inform the petitioner that a written request for a hearing, stating the relief desired and the grounds therefore, may be filed with the Executive Secretary within 15 days after the receipt of the denial; and

(2) Summarize or cite the relevant considerations specified in § 308.152.

(d) If a decision is not rendered within 30 days, the petitioner may file a request for a hearing within fifteen days from the date of expiration.

§ 308.155 Hearing.

(a) *Hearing dates.* The Executive Secretary shall order a hearing to be commenced within 30 days after receipt of a request for a hearing filed pursuant to § 308.154. Upon request of the petitioner or the FDIC, the presiding officer or the Executive Secretary may order a later hearing date.

(b) *Burden of proof.* The ultimate burden of proof shall be upon the candidate for director or senior executive officer. The burden of going forward

§ 308.155

with a *prima facie* case shall be upon the FDIC.

(c) *Hearing procedure.* (1) The hearing shall be held in Washington, DC or at another designated place, before a presiding officer designated by the Executive Secretary.

(2) The provisions of §§ 308.6 through 308.12, 308.16, and 308.21 of the Uniform Rules and §§ 308.101 through 308.102, and 308.104 through 308.106 of subpart B of the Local Rules shall apply to hearings held pursuant to this subpart.

(3) The petitioner may appear at the hearing and shall have the right to introduce relevant and material documents and make an oral presentation. Members of the FDIC enforcement staff may attend the hearing and participate as representatives of the FDIC enforcement staff.

(4) There shall be no discovery in proceedings under this subpart.

(5) At the discretion of the presiding officer, witnesses may be presented within specified time limits, provided that a list of witnesses is furnished to the presiding officer and to all other parties prior to the hearing. Witnesses shall be sworn, unless otherwise directed by the presiding officer. The presiding officer may ask questions of any witness. Each party shall have the opportunity to cross-examine any witness presented by an opposing party. The transcript of the proceedings shall be furnished, upon request and payment of the cost thereof, to the petitioner afforded the hearing.

(6) In the course of or in connection with any hearing under paragraph (c) of this section the presiding officer shall have the power to administer oaths and affirmations, to take or cause to be taken depositions of unavailable witnesses, and to issue, revoke, quash, or modify subpoenas and subpoenas duces tecum. Where the presentation of witnesses is permitted, the presiding officer may require the attendance of witnesses from any state, territory, or other place subject to the jurisdiction of the United States at any location where the proceeding is being conducted. Witness fees shall be paid in accordance with § 308.14 of the Uniform Rules.

(7) Upon the request of the applicant afforded the hearing, or the members of the FDIC enforcement staff, the record shall remain open for five business days following the hearing for the parties to make additional submissions to the record.

(8) The presiding officer shall make recommendations to the Board of Directors or its designee, where possible, within fifteen days after the last day for the parties to submit additions to the record.

(9) The presiding officer shall forward his or her recommendation to the Executive Secretary who shall promptly certify the entire record, including the recommendation to the Board of Directors or its designee. The Executive Secretary's certification shall close the record.

(d) *Written submissions in lieu of hearing.* The petitioner may in writing waive a hearing and elect to have the matter determined on the basis of written submissions.

(e) *Failure to request or appear at hearing.* Failure to request a hearing shall constitute a waiver of the opportunity for a hearing. Failure to appear at a hearing in person or through an authorized representative shall constitute a waiver of hearing. If a hearing is waived, the order shall be final and unappealable, and shall remain in full force and effect.

(f) *Decision by Board of Directors or its designee.* Within 45 days following the Executive Secretary's certification of the record to the Board of Directors or its designee, the Board of Directors or its designee shall notify the affected individual whether the denial of the notice will be continued, terminated, or otherwise modified. The notification shall state the basis for any decision of the Board of Directors or its designee that is adverse to the petitioner. The Board of Directors or its designee shall promptly rescind or modify the denial where the decision is favorable to the petitioner.

[56 FR 37975, Aug. 9, 1991, as amended at 64 FR 62101, Nov. 16, 1999]

Federal Deposit Insurance Corporation

Subpart M—Procedures and Standards Applicable to an Application Pursuant to Section 19 of the FDIA

§ 308.156 Scope.

The rules and procedures set forth in this subpart shall apply to an application filed pursuant to section 19 of the FDIA (12 U.S.C. 1829) by an insured depository institution and/or an individual, who has been convicted of any criminal offense involving dishonesty or a breach of trust or money laundering or who has agreed to enter into a pretrial diversion or similar program in connection with the prosecution of such offense, to seek the prior written consent of the FDIC to become or continue as an institution-affiliated party with respect to an insured depository institution; to own or control directly or indirectly an insured depository institution; or to participate directly or indirectly in any manner in the conduct of the affairs of an insured depository institution.

[56 FR 37975, Aug. 9, 1991, as amended at 64 FR 62101, Nov. 16, 1999; 64 FR 72913, Dec. 29, 1999]

§ 308.157 Relevant considerations.

(a) In proceedings under § 308.156 on an application to become or continue as an institution-affiliated party with respect to an insured depository institution; to own or control directly or indirectly an insured depository institution; or to participate directly or indirectly in any manner in the conduct of the affairs of an insured depository institution, the following shall be considered:

(1) Whether the conviction or entry into a pretrial diversion or similar program is for a criminal offense involving dishonesty or breach of trust or money laundering;

(2) Whether participation directly or indirectly by the person in any manner in the conduct of the affairs of the insured depository institution constitutes a threat to the safety or soundness of the insured depository institution or the interests of its depositors, or threatens to impair public confidence in the insured depository institution;

(3) Evidence of the applicant's rehabilitation;

(4) The position to be held by the applicant;

(5) The amount of influence and control the applicant will be able to exercise over the affairs and operations of the insured depository institution;

(6) The ability of the management at the insured depository institution to supervise and control the activities of the applicant;

(7) The level of ownership which the applicant will have at the insured depository institution;

(8) Applicable fidelity bond coverage for the applicant; and

(9) Additional factors in the specific case that appear relevant.

(b) The question of whether a person, who was convicted of a crime or who agreed to enter a pretrial diversion or similar program, was guilty of that crime shall not be at issue in a proceeding under this subpart.

[56 FR 37975, Aug. 9, 1991, as amended at 64 FR 62101, Nov. 16, 1999]

§ 308.158 Filing papers and effective date.

(a) *Filing with the regional office.* Applications pursuant to section 19 shall be filed by in the appropriate regional office. Unless a waiver has been granted pursuant to paragraph (c) of this section, only an insured depository institution may file an application. Persons meeting the de minimis criteria set forth in the FDIC's Statement of Policy on Section 19 of the FDIA (63 FR 66177 (1998)) need not file an application.

(b) *Effective date.* An application pursuant to section 19 may be made in writing at any time more than one year after the issuance of a decision denying an application pursuant to section 19. The removal and/or prohibition pursuant to section 19 shall continue until the individual has been reinstated by the Board of Directors or its designee for good cause shown.

(c) *Waiver applications.* If an institution does not file an application regarding an individual, the individual may file a request for a waiver of the

§ 308.159

institution filing requirement for section 19 of the FDIA. Such a waiver application shall be filed with the appropriate regional office and shall set forth substantial good cause why the application should be granted. The Director of the Division of Supervision and Consumer Protection (DSC) and, where confirmed in writing by the director, a deputy director or an associate director may grant or deny applications requesting waivers of the institution filing requirement. The authority delegated under this section shall be exercised only upon the concurrent certification of the General Counsel or his designee that the action to be taken is not inconsistent with section 19 of the FDIA.

[64 FR 62101, Nov. 16, 1999]

§ 308.159 Denial of applications.

A denial of an application pursuant to section 19 shall:

(a) Inform the applicant that a written request for a hearing, stating the relief desired and the grounds therefor and any supporting evidence, may be filed with the Executive Secretary within 60 days after the denial; and

(b) Summarize or cite the relevant considerations specified in § 308.157 of this subpart.

§ 308.160 Hearings.

(a) *Hearing dates.* The Executive Secretary shall order a hearing to be commenced within 60 days after receipt of a request for hearing on an application filed pursuant to § 308.159. Upon the request of the applicant or FDIC enforcement counsel, the presiding officer or the Executive Secretary may order a later hearing date.

(b) *Burden of proof.* The ultimate burden of proof shall be upon the person proposing to become or continue as an institution-affiliated party with respect to an insured depository institution; to own or control directly or indirectly an insured depository institution; or to participate directly or indirectly in any manner in the conduct of the affairs of an insured depository institution. The burden of going forward with a *prima facie* case shall be upon the FDIC.

(c) *Hearing procedure.* (1) The hearing shall be held in Washington, DC, or at another designated place, before a presiding officer designated by the Executive Secretary.

(2) The provisions of §§ 308.6 through 308.12, 308.16, and 308.21 of the Uniform Rules and §§ 308.101 through 308.102 and 308.104 through 308.106 of subpart B of the Local Rules shall apply to hearings held pursuant to this subpart.

(3) The applicant may appear at the hearing and shall have the right to introduce relevant and material documents and oral argument. Members of the FDIC enforcement staff may attend the hearing and participate as a party.

(4) There shall be no discovery in proceedings under this subpart.

(5) At the discretion of the presiding officer, witnesses may be presented within specified time limits, provided that a list of witnesses is furnished to the presiding officer and to all other parties prior to the hearing. Witnesses shall be sworn, unless otherwise directed by the presiding officer. The presiding officer may ask questions of any witness. Each party shall have the opportunity to cross-examine any witness presented by an opposing party. The transcript of the proceedings shall be furnished, upon request and payment of the cost thereof, to the applicant afforded the hearing.

(6) In the course of or in connection with any hearing under this subsection, the presiding officer shall have the power to administer oaths and affirmations, to take or cause to be taken depositions of unavailable witnesses, and to issue, revoke, quash, or modify subpoenas and subpoenas duces tecum. Where the presentation of witnesses is permitted, the presiding officer may require the attendance of witnesses from any state, territory, or other place subject to the jurisdiction of the United States at any location where the proceeding is being conducted. Witness fees shall be paid in accordance with § 308.14 of the Uniform Rules.

(7) Upon the request of the applicant afforded the hearing, or FDIC enforcement staff, the record shall remain open for five business days following the hearing for the parties to make additional submissions to the record.

Federal Deposit Insurance Corporation § 308.162

(8) The presiding officer shall make recommendations to the Board of Directors, where possible, within 20 days after the last day for the parties to submit additions to the record.

(9) The presiding officer shall forward his or her recommendation to the Executive Secretary who shall promptly certify the entire record, including the recommendation to the Board of Directors or its designee. The Executive Secretary's certification shall close the record.

(d) *Written submissions in lieu of hearing.* The applicant or the bank may in writing waive a hearing and elect to have the matter determined on the basis of written submissions.

(e) *Failure to request or appear at hearing.* Failure to request a hearing shall constitute a waiver of the opportunity for a hearing. Failure to appear at a hearing in person or through an authorized representative shall constitute a waiver of hearing. If a hearing is waived, the person shall remain barred under section 19.

(f) *Decision by Board of Directors or its designee.* Within 60 days following the Executive Secretary's certification of the record to the Board of Directors or its designee, the Board of Directors or its designee shall notify the affected person whether the person shall remain barred under section 19. The notification shall state the basis for any decision of the Board of Directors or its designee that is adverse to the applicant.

[56 FR 37975, Aug. 9, 1991, as amended at 64 FR 62101, Nov. 16, 1999]

Subpart N—Rules and Procedures Applicable to Proceedings Relating to Suspension, Removal, and Prohibition Where a Felony Is Charged

SOURCE: 72 FR 67235, Nov. 28, 2007, unless otherwise noted.

§ 308.161 Scope.

The rules and procedures set forth in this subpart shall apply to the following:

(a) Proceedings to suspend an institution-affiliated party of an insured state nonmember bank, or to prohibit such party from further participation in the conduct of the affairs of any depository institution, if continued service or participation by such party posed, poses, or may pose a threat to the interests of the depositors of, or threatened, threatens, or may threaten to impair public confidence in, any relevant depository institution (as defined at section 1818(g)(1)(E) of Title 12), where the individual is the subject of any state or federal information, indictment, or complaint, involving the commission of, or participation in:

(1) A crime involving dishonesty or breach of trust punishable by imprisonment exceeding one year under state or federal law; or

(2) A criminal violation of section 1956, 1957, or 1960 of Title 18 or section 5322 or 5324 of Title 31.

(b) Proceedings to remove from office or to prohibit an institution-affiliated party from further participation in the conduct of the affairs of any depository institution without the consent of the Board of Directors or its designee where:

(1) A judgment of conviction or an agreement to enter a pre-trial diversion or other similar program has been entered against such party in connection with a crime described in paragraph (a)(1) of this section that is not subject to further appellate review, if continued service or participation by such party posed, poses, or may pose a threat to the interests of the depositors of, or threatened, threatens, or may threaten to impair public confidence in, any relevant depository institution (as defined at section 1818(g)(1)(E) of Title 12); or

(2) A judgment of conviction or an agreement to enter a pre-trial diversion or other similar program has been entered against such party in connection with a crime described in paragraph (a)(2) of this section.

§ 308.162 Relevant considerations.

(a)(1) In proceedings under § 308.161(a) and (b) for a notice of suspension or prohibition, or a removal or prohibition order, the following shall be considered:

(i) Whether the alleged offense is a crime which is punishable by imprisonment for a term exceeding one year under state or federal law and which involves dishonesty or breach of trust; and

(ii) Whether the alleged offense is a criminal violation of section 1956, 1957, or 1960 of Title 18 or section 5322 or 5324 of Title 31; and

(iii) Whether continued service or participation by the institution-affiliated party posed, poses, or may pose a threat to the interests of the depositors of, or threatened, threatens, or may threaten to impair public confidence in, any relevant depository institution (as defined at section 1818(g)(1)(E) of Title 12).

(b) The question of whether an institution-affiliated party is guilty of the subject crime shall not be tried or considered in a proceeding under this subpart.

§ 308.163 Notice of suspension or prohibition, and orders of removal or prohibition.

(a) *Notice of suspension or prohibition.*

(1) The Board of Directors or its designee may suspend or prohibit from further participation in the conduct of the affairs of any depository institution an institution-affiliated party by written notice of suspension or prohibition upon a determination by the Board of Directors or its designee that the grounds for such suspension or prohibition exist. The written notice of suspension or prohibition shall be served upon the institution-affiliated party and any depository institution that the subject of the action is affiliated with at the time the notice is issued.

(2) The suspension or prohibition shall be effective immediately upon service on the institution-affiliated party, and shall remain in effect until final disposition of the information, indictment, complaint, or until it is terminated by the Board of Directors or its designee under the provisions of § 308.164 or otherwise.

(b) *Order of removal or prohibition.*

(1) The Board of Directors or its designee may issue an order removing or prohibiting from further participation in the conduct of the affairs of any depository institution an institution-affiliated party, when a final judgment of conviction not subject to further appellate review is entered against the institution-affiliated party for a crime referred to in § 308.161(a)(1) and continued service or participation by such party posed, poses, or may pose a threat to the interests of the depositors of, or threatened, threatens, or may threaten to impair public confidence in, any relevant depository institution (as defined at section 1818(g)(1)(E) of Title 12).

(2) An order of removal or prohibition shall be entered if a judgment of conviction is entered against the institution-affiliated party for a crime described in § 308.161(a)(2).

(c) The notice of suspension or prohibition or the order of removal or prohibition shall:

(1) Inform the institution-affiliated party that a written request for a hearing, stating the relief desired and grounds therefore, and any supporting evidence, may be filed with the Executive Secretary within 30 days after receipt of the written notice or order; and

(2) Summarize or cite to the relevant considerations specified in § 308.162 of this subpart.

§ 308.164 Hearings.

(a) *Hearing dates.* The Executive Secretary shall order a hearing to be commenced within 30 days after receipt of a request for hearing filed pursuant to § 308.163. Upon the request of the institution-affiliated party, the presiding officer or the Executive Secretary may order a later hearing date.

(b) *Hearing procedure.* (1) The hearing shall be held in Washington, DC, or at another designated place, before a presiding officer designated by the Executive Secretary.

(2) The provisions of §§ 308.6 through 308.12, 308.16, and 308.21 of the Uniform Rules and §§ 308.101 through 308.102 and 308.104 through 308.106 of subpart B of the Local Rules shall apply to hearings held pursuant to this subpart.

(3) The institution-affiliated party may appear at the hearing and shall have the right to introduce relevant and material documents and oral argument. Members of the FDIC enforcement staff may attend the hearing and participate as representatives of the FDIC enforcement staff.

Federal Deposit Insurance Corporation § 308.166

(4) There shall be no discovery in proceedings under this subpart.

(5) At the discretion of the presiding officer, witnesses may be presented within specified time limits, provided that a list of witnesses is furnished to the presiding officer and to all other parties prior to the hearing. Witnesses shall be sworn, unless otherwise directed by the presiding officer. The presiding officer may ask questions of any witness. Each party shall have the opportunity to cross-examine any witness presented by an opposing party. The transcript of the proceedings shall be furnished, upon request and payment of the cost thereof, to the institution-affiliated party afforded the hearing.

(6) In the course of or in connection with any hearing under paragraph (b) of this section, the presiding officer shall have the power to administer oaths and affirmations, to take or cause to be taken depositions of unavailable witnesses, and to issue, revoke, quash, or modify subpoenas and subpoenas duces tecum. Where the presentation of witnesses is permitted, the presiding officer may require the attendance of witnesses from any state, territory, or other place subject to the jurisdiction of the United States at any location where the proceeding is being conducted. Witness fees shall be paid in accordance with § 308.14 of the Uniform Rules.

(7) Upon the request of the institution-affiliated party afforded the hearing, or the members of the FDIC enforcement staff, the record shall remain open for five business days following the hearing for the parties to make additional submissions to the record.

(8) The presiding officer shall make recommendations to the Board of Directors, where possible, within 10 days after the last day for the parties to submit additions to the record.

(9) The presiding officer shall forward his or her recommendation to the Executive Secretary who shall promptly certify the entire record, including the recommendation to the Board of Directors. The Executive Secretary's certification shall close the record.

(c) *Written submissions in lieu of hearing.* The institution-affiliated party may in writing waive a hearing and elect to have the matter determined on the basis of written submissions.

(d) *Failure to request or appear at hearing.* Failure to request a hearing shall constitute a waiver of the opportunity for a hearing. Failure to appear at a hearing in person or through an authorized representative shall constitute a waiver of hearing. If a hearing is waived, the order shall be final and unappealable, and shall remain in full force and effect pursuant to § 308.163.

(e) *Decision by Board of Directors or its designee.* Within 60 days following the Executive Secretary's certification of the record to the Board of Directors or its designee, the Board of Directors or its designee shall notify the institution-affiliated party whether the notice of suspension or prohibition or the order of removal or prohibition will be continued, terminated, or otherwise modified. The notification shall state the basis for any decision of the Board of Directors or its designee that is adverse to the institution-affiliated party. The Board of Directors or its designee shall promptly rescind or modify a notice of suspension or prohibition or an order of removal or prohibition where the decision is favorable to the institution-affiliated party.

Subpart O—Liability of Commonly Controlled Depository Institutions

§ 308.165 Scope.

The rules and procedures in this subpart, subpart B of the Local Rules and the Uniform Rules shall apply to proceedings in connection with the assessment of cross-guaranty liability against commonly controlled depository institutions.

§ 308.166 Grounds for assessment of liability.

Any insured depository institution shall be liable for any loss incurred or reasonably anticipated to be incurred by the corporation, subsequent to August 9, 1989, in connection with the default of a commonly controlled insured depository institution, or any loss incurred or reasonably anticipated to be incurred in connection with any assistance provided by the Corporation to any commonly controlled depository institution in danger of default.

§ 308.167

§ 308.167 Notice of assessment of liability.

(a) The amount of liability shall be assessed upon service of a Notice of Assessment of Liability upon the liable depository institution, within two years of the date the Corporation incurred the loss.

(b) *Contents of Notice.* (1) The Notice of Assessment of Liability shall set forth:

(i) The basis for the FDIC's jurisdiction over the proceeding;

(ii) A statement of the Corporation's good faith estimate of the amount of loss it has incurred or anticipates incurring;

(iii) A statement of the method by which the estimated loss was calculated;

(iv) A proposed order directing payment by the liable institution of the FDIC's estimated amount of loss, and the schedule under which the payment will be due;

(v) In cases involving more than one liable institution, the estimated amount of each institution's share of the liability.

(2) The Notice of Assessment of Liability shall advise the liable institution(s):

(i) That an answer must be filed within 20 days after service of the Notice;

(ii) That, if a hearing is requested, a request for a hearing must be filed within 20 days after service of the Notice;

(iii) That if a hearing is requested, such hearing will be held within the judicial district in which the liable institution is found, or, in cases involving more than one liable institution, within a judicial district in which at least one liable institution is found;

(iv) That, unless the administrative law judge sets a different date, the hearing will commence 120 days after service of the Notice of Assessment of Liability; and

(v) That failure to request a hearing shall render the Notice of Assessment a final and unappealable order.

§ 308.168 Effective date of and payment under an order to pay.

(a) Unless otherwise provided in the Notice of Assessment of Liability, payment of the assessment shall be due on or before the 21st day after service of the Assessment of Liability, under the terms of the schedule for payment set forth therein.

(b) All payments collected shall be paid to the Corporation.

(c) Failure to request a hearing as prescribed herein shall render the order to pay final and unappealable.

Subpart P—Rules and Procedures Relating to the Recovery of Attorney Fees and Other Expenses

§ 308.169 Scope.

This subpart, and the Equal Access to Justice Act (5 U.S.C. 504), which it implements, apply to adversary adjudications before the FDIC. The types of adjudication covered by this subpart are those listed in § 308.01 of the Uniform Rules. The Uniform Rules and subpart B of the Local Rules apply to any proceedings to recover fees and expenses under this subpart.

§ 308.170 Filing, content, and service of documents.

(a) *Time to file.* An application and any other pleading or document related to the application shall be filed with the Executive Secretary within 30 days after service of the final order of the Board of Directors in disposition of the proceeding whenever:

(1) The applicant seeks an award pursuant to 5 U.S.C. 504(a)(1) as the prevailing party in the adversary adjudication or in a discrete significant substantive portion of the proceeding; or

(2) The applicant, in an adversary adjudication arising from an action to enforce compliance with a statutory or regulatory requirement, asserts pursuant to 5 U.S.C. 504(a)(4) that the demand by the FDIC is substantially in excess of the decision of the administrative law judge and is unreasonable when compared with such decision under the facts and circumstances of the case.

(b) *Content.* The application and related documents shall conform to the requirements of § 308.10(b) and (c) of the Uniform Rules.

Federal Deposit Insurance Corporation § 308.172

(c) *Service.* The application and related documents shall be served on all parties to the adversary adjudication in accordance with § 308.11 of the Uniform Rules, except that statements of net worth shall be served only on counsel for the FDIC.

(d) Upon receipt of an application, the Executive Secretary shall refer the matter to the administrative law judge who heard the underlying adversary proceeding, provided that if the original administrative law judge is unavailable, or the Executive Secretary determines, in his or her sole discretion, that there is cause to refer the matter to a different administrative law judge, the matter shall be referred to a different administrative law judge.

[56 FR 37975, Aug. 9, 1991, as amended at 64 FR 62102, Nov. 16, 1999]

§ 308.171 Responses to application.

(a) *By FDIC.* (1) Within 20 days after service of an application, counsel for the FDIC may file with the Executive Secretary and serve on all parties an answer to the application. Unless counsel for the FDIC requests and is granted an extension of time for filing or files a statement of intent to negotiate under § 308.179 of this subpart, failure to file an answer within the 20-day period will be treated as a consent to the award requested.

(2) The answer shall explain in detail any objections to the award requested and identify the facts relied on in support of the FDIC's position. If the answer is based on any alleged facts not already in the record of the proceeding, the answer shall include either supporting affidavits or a request for further proceedings under § 308.180.

(b) *Reply to answer.* The applicant may file a reply with regard to an application filed pursuant to 5 U.S.C. 504 (a)(1), if the FDIC has addressed in its answer any of the following issues: that the position of the FDIC was substantially justified, that the applicant unduly protracted the proceedings, or that special circumstances make an award unjust. The applicant may file a reply with regard to an application filed pursuant to 5 U.S.C. 504 (a)(4), if the FDIC has addressed in its answer any of the following issues: that the applicant has committed a willful violation of law or otherwise acted in bad faith, that the FDIC's demand is reasonable when compared to the decision of the administrative law judge or that special circumstances make an award unjust. The reply shall be filed within 15 days after service of the answer. If the reply is based on any alleged facts not already in the record of the proceeding, the reply shall include either supporting affidavits or a request for further proceedings under § 308.180.

(c) *By other parties.* Any party to the adversary adjudication, other than the applicant and the FDIC, may file comments on an application within 20 days after service of the application. If the applicant is entitled to file a reply to the FDIC's answer under paragraph (b) of this section, another party may file comments on the answer within 15 days after service of the answer. A commenting party may not participate in any further proceedings on the application unless the administrative law judge determines that the public interest requires such participation in order to permit additional exploration of matters raised in the comments.

(d) *Additional response.* Additional filings in the nature of pleadings may be submitted only by leave of the administrative law judge.

[56 FR 37975, Aug. 9, 1991, as amended at 64 FR 62102, Nov. 16, 1999]

§ 308.172 Eligibility of applicants.

(a) *General rule.* To be eligible for an award under this subpart, an applicant must have been named or admitted as a party to the proceeding. In addition, the applicant must show that it meets all other conditions of eligibility set out in paragraph (b) of this section.

(b) *Types of eligible applicant.* The types of eligible applicant are:

(1) An individual with a net worth of not more than $2,000,000 at the time the adversary adjudication was initiated; or

(2) Any owner of an unincorporated business, or any partnership, corporation, associations, unit of local government or organization, the net worth of which did not exceed $7,000,000 and which did not have more than 500 employees at the time the adversary adjudication was initiated.

§ 308.173

(3) For purposes of an application filed pursuant to 5 U.S.C. 504(a)(4), a small entity as defined in 5 U.S.C. 601.

(c) *Factors to be considered.* In determining the types of eligible applicants:

(1) An applicant who owns an unincorporated business shall be considered as an *individual* rather than a *sole owner of an unincorporated business* if the issues on which he or she prevails are related to personal interests rather than to business interests.

(2) An applicant's net worth includes the value of any assets disposed of for the purpose of meeting an eligibility standard and excludes the value of any obligations incurred for this purpose. Transfers of assets or obligations incurred for less than reasonably equivalent value will be presumed to have been made for this purpose.

(3) The net worth of a bank shall be established by the net worth information reported in conformity with applicable instructions and guidelines on the bank's Consolidated Report of Condition and Income filed for the last reporting date before the initiation of the adversary adjudication.

(4) The employees of an applicant include all those persons who were regularly providing services for remuneration for the applicant, under its direction and control, on the date the adversary adjudication was initiated. Part-time employees are included as though they were full-time employees.

(5) The net worth and number of employees of the applicant and all of its affiliates shall be aggregated to determine eligibility. The aggregated net worth shall be adjusted if necessary to avoid counting the net worth of any entity twice. As used in this subpart, *affiliates* are individuals, corporations, and entities that directly or indirectly or acting through one or more entities control a majority of the voting shares of the applicant; and corporations and entities of which the applicant directly or indirectly owns or controls a majority of the voting shares. The Board of Directors may, however, on the recommendation of the administrative law judge, or otherwise, determine that such aggregation with regard to one or more of the applicant's affiliates would be unjust and contrary to the purposes of this subpart in light of the actual relationship between the affiliated entities. In such a case the net worth and employees of the relevant affiliate or affiliates will not be aggregated with those of the applicant. In addition, the Board of Directors may determine that financial relationships of the applicant other than those described in this paragraph constitute special circumstances that would make an award unjust.

(6) An applicant that participates in a proceeding primarily on behalf of one or more other persons or entities that would be ineligible is not itself eligible for an award.

[56 FR 37975, Aug. 9, 1991, as amended at 64 FR 62102, Nov. 16, 1999]

§ 308.173 Prevailing party.

(a) *General rule.* An eligible applicant who, following an adversary adjudication has gained victory on the merits in the proceeding is a "prevailing party". An eligible applicant may be a "prevailing party" if a settlement of the proceeding was effected on terms favorable to it or if the proceeding against it has been dismissed. In appropriate situations an applicant may also have prevailed if the outcome of the proceeding has substantially vindicated the applicant's position on the significant substantive matters at issue, even though the applicant has not totally avoided adverse final action.

(b) *Segregation of costs.* When a proceeding has presented a number of discrete substantive issues, an applicant may have prevailed even though all the issues were not resolved in its favor. If such an applicant is deemed to have prevailed, any award shall be based on the fees and expenses incurred in connection with the discrete significant substantive issue or issues on which the applicant's position has been upheld. If such segregation of costs is not practicable, the award may be based on a fair proration of those fees and expenses incurred in the entire proceeding which would be recoverable under § 308.175 if proration were not performed, whether separate or prorated treatment is appropriate, and the appropriate proration percentage, shall be determined on the facts of the particular case. Attention shall be given to the significance and nature of the respective issues and their separability and interrelationship.

§ 308.174 Standards for awards.

(a) For applications filed pursuant to 5 U.S.C. 504(a)(1), a prevailing applicant may receive an award for fees and expenses unless the position of the FDIC during the proceeding was substantially justified or special circumstances make the award unjust. An award will be reduced or denied if the applicant has unduly or unreasonably protracted the proceedings. Awards for fees and expenses incurred before the date on which the adversary adjudication was initiated are allowable if their incurrence was necessary to prepare for the proceeding.

(b) For applications filed pursuant to 5 U.S.C. 504(a)(4), an applicant may receive an award unless the demand by the FDIC was reasonable when compared with the decision of the administrative law judge, the applicant has committed a willful violation of law or otherwise acted in bad faith, or special circumstances make an award unjust.

[64 FR 62102, Nov. 16, 1999]

§ 308.175 Measure of awards.

(a) *General rule.* Awards will be based on rates customarily charged by persons engaged in the business of acting as attorneys, agents, and expert witnesses, even if the services were made available without charge or at a reduced rate, provided that no award under this subpart for the fee of an attorney or agent may exceed $125 per hour. No award to compensate an expert witness may exceed the highest rate at which the FDIC pays expert witnesses. An award may include the reasonable expenses of the attorney, agent, or expert witness as a separate item, if the attorney, agent, or expert witness ordinarily charges clients separately for such expenses. Fees and expenses awarded under 5 U.S.C. 504(a)(4) related to defending against an excessive demand shall be paid only as a consequence of appropriations paid in advance.

(b) *Determination of reasonableness of fees.* In determining the reasonableness of the fee sought for an attorney, agent, or expert witness, the administrative law judge shall consider the following:

(1) If the attorney, agent, or expert witness is in private practice, his or her customary fee for like services, or, if he or she is an employee of the applicant, the fully allocated cost of the services;

(2) The prevailing rate for similar services in the community in which the attorney, agent, or expert witness ordinarily performs services;

(3) The time actually spent in the representation of the applicant;

(4) The time reasonably spent in light of the difficulty or complexity of the issues in the proceeding; and

(5) Such other factors as may bear on the value of the services provided.

(c) *Awards for studies.* The reasonable cost of any study, analysis, test, project, or similar matter prepared on behalf of an applicant may be awarded to the extent that the charge for the service does not exceed the prevailing rate payable for similar services, and the study or other matter was necessary for preparation of the applicant's case and not otherwise required by law or sound business or financial practice.

[56 FR 37975, Aug. 9, 1991, as amended at 64 FR 62102, Nov. 16, 1999]

§ 308.176 Application for awards.

(a) *Contents.* An application for an award of fees and expenses under this subpart shall contain:

(1) The name of the applicant and an identification of the proceeding;

(2) For applications filed pursuant to 5 U.S.C. 504(a)(1), a showing that the applicant has prevailed, and an identification of each issue with regard to which the applicant believes that the position of the FDIC in the proceeding was not substantially justified;

(3) For applications filed pursuant to 5 U.S.C. 504(a)(4), a showing that the demand by the FDIC is substantially in excess of the decision of the administrative law judge and is unreasonable when compared with such decision under the facts and circumstances of the case;

(4) A statement of the amount of fees and expenses for which an award is sought;

§ 308.177

(5) For applications filed pursuant to 5 U.S.C. 504(a)(4), a statement of the amount of fees and expenses which constitute appropriations paid in advance;

(6) If the applicant is not an individual, a statement of the number of its employees on the date the proceeding was initiated;

(7) A description of any affiliated individuals or entities, as defined in § 308.172(c)(5), or a statement that none exist;

(8) A declaration that the applicant, together with any affiliates, had a net worth not more than the ceiling established for it by § 308.172(b) as of the date the proceeding was initiated;

(9) For applications filed pursuant to 5 U.S.C. 504(a)(1), a statement whether the applicant is a small entity as defined in 5 U.S.C. 601; and

(10) Any other matters that the applicant wishes the FDIC to consider in determining whether and in what amount an award should be made.

(b) *Verification.* The application shall be signed by the applicant or an authorized officer or attorney of the applicant. It shall also contain or be accompanied by a written verification under oath or under penalty of perjury that the information provided in the application and supporting documents is true and correct.

[56 FR 37975, Aug. 9, 1991, as amended at 64 FR 62102, Nov. 16, 1999]

§ 308.177 Statement of net worth.

(a) *General rule.* A statement of net worth must be filed with the application for an award of fees. The statement shall reflect the net worth of the applicant and all affiliates of the applicant.

(b) *Contents.* (1) The statement of net worth may be in any form convenient to the applicant which fully discloses all the assets and liabilities of the applicant and all the assets and liabilities of its affiliates, as of the time of the initiation of the adversary adjudication. Unaudited financial statements are acceptable unless the administrative law judge or the Board of Directors otherwise requires. Financial statements or reports to a Federal or state agency, prepared before the initiation of the adversary adjudication for other purposes, and accurate as of a date not more than three months prior to the initiation of the proceeding, are acceptable in establishing net worth as of the time of the initiation of the proceeding, unless the administrative law judge or the Board of Directors otherwise requires.

(2) In the case of applicants or affiliates that are not banks, net worth shall be considered for the purposes of this subpart to be the excess of total assets over total liabilities, as of the date the underlying proceeding was initiated, except as adjusted under § 308.172(c)(2). Assets and liabilities of individuals shall include those beneficially owned within the meaning of the FDIC's rules and regulations.

(3) If the applicant or any of its affiliates is a bank, the portion of the statement of net worth which relates to the bank shall consist of a copy of the bank's last Consolidated Report of Condition and Income filed before the initiation of the adversary adjudication. In all cases the administrative law judge or the Board of Directors may call for additional information needed to establish the applicant's net worth as of the initiation of the proceeding. Except as adjusted by additional information that was called for under the preceding sentence, net worth shall be considered for the purposes of this subpart to be the total equity capital (or, in the case of mutual savings banks, the total surplus accounts) as reported, in conformity with applicable instructions and guidelines, on the bank's Consolidated Report of Condition and Income filed for the last reporting date before the initiation of the proceeding.

(c) *Statement confidential.* Unless otherwise ordered by the Board of Directors or required by law, the statement of net worth shall be for the confidential use of counsel for the FDIC, the Board of Directors, and the administrative law judge.

§ 308.178 Statement of fees and expenses.

The application shall be accompanied by a statement fully documenting the fees and expenses for which an award is sought. A separate itemized statement shall be submitted for each professional firm or individual whose services are covered by the application,

Federal Deposit Insurance Corporation § 308.183

showing the hours spent in work in connection with the proceeding by each individual, a description of the specific services performed, the rate at which each fee has been computed, any expenses for which reimbursement is sought, the total amount claimed, and the total amount paid or payable by the applicant or by any other person or entity for the services performed. The administrative law judge or the Board of Directors may require the applicant to provide vouchers, receipts, or other substantiation for any expenses claimed.

§ 308.179 Settlement negotiations.

If counsel for the FDIC and the applicant believe that the issues in a fee application can be settled, they may jointly file with the Executive Secretary with a copy to the administrative law judge a statement of their intent to negotiate a settlement. The filing of this statement shall extend the time for filing an answer under § 308.171 for an additional 30 days, and further extensions may be granted by the administrative law judge upon the joint request of counsel for the FDIC and the applicant.

[56 FR 37975, Aug. 9, 1991, as amended at 64 FR 62102, Nov. 16, 1999]

§ 308.180 Further proceedings.

(a) *General rule.* Ordinarily, the determination of a recommended award will be made by the administrative law judge on the basis of the written record. However, on request of either the applicant or the FDIC, or on his or her own initiative, the administrative law judge may order further proceedings such as an informal conference, oral argument, additional written submissions, or an evidentiary hearing. Such further proceedings will be held only when necessary for full and fair resolution of the issues arising from the application and will be conducted promptly and expeditiously.

(b) *Request for further proceedings.* A request for further proceedings under this section shall specifically identify the information sought or the issues in dispute and shall explain why additional proceedings are necessary.

(c) *Hearing.* Ordinarily, the administrative law judge shall hold an oral evidentiary hearing only on disputed issues of material fact which cannot be adequately resolved through written submissions.

§ 308.181 Recommended decision.

The administrative law judge shall file with the Executive Secretary a recommended decision on the fee application not later than 90 days after the filing of the application or 30 days after the conclusion of the hearing, whichever is later. The recommended decision shall include written proposed findings and conclusions on the applicant's eligibility and its status as a prevailing party and an explanation of the reasons for any difference between the amount requested and the amount of the recommended award. The recommended decision shall also include, if at issue, proposed findings on whether the FDIC's position was substantially justified, whether the applicant unduly protracted the proceedings, or whether special circumstances make an award unjust. The administrative law judge shall file the record of the proceeding on the fee application and, at the same time, serve upon each party a copy of the recommended decision, findings, conclusions, and proposed order.

§ 308.182 Board of Directors action.

(a) *Exceptions to recommended decision.* Within 20 days after service of the recommended decision, findings, conclusions, and proposed order, the applicant or counsel for the FDIC may file with the Executive Secretary written exceptions thereto. A supporting brief may also be filed.

(b) *Decision of Board of Directors.* The Board of Directors shall render its decision within 60 days after the matter is submitted to it by the Executive Secretary. The Executive Secretary shall furnish copies of the decision and order of the Board of Directors to the parties. Judicial review of the decision and order may be obtained as provided in 5 U.S.C. 504(c)(2).

§ 308.183 Payment of awards.

An applicant seeking payment of an award made by the Board of Directors shall submit to the Executive Secretary a statement that the applicant will not seek judicial review of the decision and order or that the time for seeking further review has passed and no further review has been sought. The FDIC will pay the amount awarded within 30 days after receiving the applicant's statement, unless judicial review of the award or of the underlying decision of the adversary adjudication has been sought by the applicant or any other party to the proceeding.

Subpart Q—Issuance and Review of Orders Pursuant to the Prompt Corrective Action Provisions of the Federal Deposit Insurance Act

SOURCE: 57 FR 44897, Sept. 29, 1992, unless otherwise noted.

§ 308.200 Scope.

The rules and procedures set forth in this subpart apply to banks, insured branches of foreign banks and senior executive officers and directors of banks that are subject to the provisions of section 38 of the Federal Deposit Insurance Act (section 38) (12 U.S.C. 1831o) and subpart B of part 325 of this chapter.

[57 FR 44897, Sept. 29, 1992; 57 FR 48426, Oct. 23, 1992]

§ 308.201 Directives to take prompt corrective action.

(a) *Notice of intent to issue directive*—(1) *In general.* The FDIC shall provide an undercapitalized, significantly undercapitalized, or critically undercapitalized bank prior written notice of the FDIC's intention to issue a directive requiring such bank to take actions or to follow proscriptions described in section 38 that are within the FDIC's discretion to require or impose under section 38 of the FDI Act, including sections 38 (e)(5), (f)(2), (f)(3), or (f)(5). The bank shall have such time to respond to a proposed directive as provided by the FDIC under paragraph (c) of this section.

(2) *Immediate issuance of final directive.* If the FDIC finds it necessary in order to carry out the purposes of section 38 of the FDI Act, the FDIC may, without providing the notice prescribed in paragraph (a)(1) of this section, issue a directive requiring a bank immediately to take actions or to follow proscriptions described in section 38 that are within the FDIC's discretion to require or impose under section 38 of the FDI Act, including section 38 (e)(5), (f)(2), (f)(3), or (f)(5). A bank that is subject to such an immediately effective directive may submit a written appeal of the directive to the FDIC. Such an appeal must be received by the FDIC within 14 calendar days of the issuance of the directive, unless the FDIC permits a longer period. The FDIC shall consider any such appeal, if filed in a timely matter, within 60 days of receiving the appeal. During such period of review, the directive shall remain in effect unless the FDIC, in its sole discretion, stays the effectiveness of the directive.

(b) *Contents of notice.* A notice of intention to issue a directive shall include:

(1) A statement of the bank's capital measures and capital levels;

(2) A description of the restrictions, prohibitions or affirmative actions that the FDIC proposes to impose or require;

(3) The proposed date when such restrictions or prohibitions would be effective or the proposed date for completion of such affirmative actions; and

(4) The date by which the bank subject to the directive may file with the FDIC a written response to the notice.

(c) *Response to notice*—(1) *Time for response.* A bank may file a written response to a notice of intent to issue a directive within the time period set by the FDIC. The date shall be at least 14 calendar days from the date of the notice unless the FDIC determines that a shorter period is appropriate in light of the financial condition of the bank or other relevant circumstances.

(2) *Content of response.* The response should include:

(i) An explanation why the action proposed by the FDIC is not an appropriate exercise of discretion under section 38;

(ii) Any recommended modification of the proposed directive; and

(iii) Any other relevant information, mitigating circumstances, documentation, or other evidence in support of

Federal Deposit Insurance Corporation § 308.202

the position of the bank regarding the proposed directive.

(d) *FDIC consideration of response.* After considering the response, the FDIC may:

(1) Issue the directive as proposed or in modified form;

(2) Determine not to issue the directive and so notify the bank; or

(3) Seek additional information or clarification of the response from the bank or any other relevant source.

(e) *Failure to file response.* Failure by a bank to file with the FDIC, within the specified time period, a written response to a proposed directive shall constitute a waiver of the opportunity to respond and shall constitute consent to the issuance of the directive.

(f) *Request for modification or rescission of directive.* Any bank that is subject to a directive under this subpart may, upon a change in circumstances, request in writing that the FDIC reconsider the terms of the directive, and may propose that the directive be rescinded or modified. Unless otherwise ordered by the FDIC, the directive shall continue in place while such request is pending before the FDIC.

§ 308.202 Procedures for reclassifying a bank based on criteria other than capital.

(a) *Reclassification based on unsafe or unsound condition or practice*—(1) *Issuance of notice of proposed reclassification*—(i) *Grounds for reclassification.* (A) Pursuant to § 325.103(d) of this chapter, the FDIC may reclassify a well capitalized bank as adequately capitalized or subject an adequately capitalized or undercapitalized institution to the supervisory actions applicable to the next lower capital category if:

(*1*) The FDIC determines that the bank is in unsafe or unsound condition; or

(*2*) The FDIC, pursuant to section 8(b)(8) of the FDI Act (12 U.S.C. 1818(b)(8)), deems the bank to be engaged in an unsafe or unsound practice and not to have corrected the deficiency.

(B) Any action pursuant to this paragraph (a)(1)(i) shall hereinafter be referred to as *reclassification*.

(ii) *Prior notice to institution.* Prior to taking action pursuant to § 325.103(d) of this chapter, the FDIC shall issue and serve on the bank a written notice of the FDIC's intention to reclassify the bank.

(2) *Contents of notice.* A notice of intention to reclassify a bank based on unsafe or unsound condition shall include:

(i) A statement of the bank's capital measures and capital levels and the category to which the bank would be reclassified;

(ii) The reasons for reclassification of the bank;

(iii) The date by which the bank subject to the notice of reclassification may file with the FDIC a written appeal of the proposed reclassification and a request for a hearing, which shall be at least 14 calendar days from the date of service of the notice unless the FDIC determines that a shorter period is appropriate in light of the financial condition of the bank or other relevant circumstances.

(3) *Response to notice of proposed reclassification.* A bank may file a written response to a notice of proposed reclassification within the time period set by the FDIC. The response should include:

(i) An explanation of why the bank is not in an unsafe or unsound condition or otherwise should not be reclassified; and

(ii) Any other relevant information, mitigating circumstances, documentation, or other evidence in support of the position of the bank regarding the reclassification.

(4) *Failure to file response.* Failure by a bank to file, within the specified time period, a written response with the FDIC to a notice of proposed reclassification shall constitute a waiver of the opportunity to respond and shall constitute consent to the reclassification.

(5) *Request for hearing and presentation of oral testimony or witnesses.* The response may include a request for an informal hearing before the FDIC under this section. If the bank desires to present oral testimony or witnesses at the hearing, the bank shall include a request to do so with the request for an informal hearing. A request to present oral testimony or witnesses shall specify the names of the witnesses and the

§ 308.203

general nature of their expected testimony. Failure to request a hearing shall constitute a waiver of any right to a hearing, and failure to request the opportunity to present oral testimony or witnesses shall constitute a waiver of any right to present oral testimony or witnesses.

(6) *Order for informal hearing.* Upon receipt of a timely written request that includes a request for a hearing, the FDIC shall issue an order directing an informal hearing to commence no later than 30 days after receipt of the request, unless the bank requests a later date. The hearing shall be held in Washington, DC or at such other place as may be designated by the FDIC, before a presiding officer(s) designated by the FDIC to conduct the hearing.

(7) *Hearing procedures.* (i) The bank shall have the right to introduce relevant written materials and to present oral argument at the hearing. The bank may introduce oral testimony and present witnesses only if expressly authorized by the FDIC or the presiding officer(s). Neither the provisions of the Administrative Procedure Act (5 U.S.C. 554–557) governing adjudications required by statute to be determined on the record nor the Uniform Rules of Practice and Procedure in this part apply to an informal hearing under this section unless the FDIC orders that such procedures shall apply.

(ii) The informal hearing shall be recorded, and a transcript shall be furnished to the bank upon request and payment of the cost thereof. Witnesses need not be sworn, unless specifically requested by a party or the presiding officer(s). The presiding officer(s) may ask questions of any witness.

(iii) The presiding officer(s) may order that the hearing be continued for a reasonable period (normally five business days) following completion of oral testimony or argument to allow additional written submissions to the hearing record.

(8) *Recommendation of presiding officers.* Within 20 calendar days following the date the hearing and the record on the proceeding are closed, the presiding officer(s) shall make a recommendation to the FDIC on the reclassification.

(9) *Time for decision.* Not later than 60 calendar days after the date the record is closed or the date of the response in a case where no hearing was requested, the FDIC will decide whether to reclassify the bank and notify the bank of the FDIC's decision.

(b) *Request for rescission of reclassification.* Any bank that has been reclassified under this section, may, upon a change in circumstances, request in writing that the FDIC reconsider the reclassification, and may propose that the reclassification be rescinded and that any directives issued in connection with the reclassification be modified, rescinded, or removed. Unless otherwise ordered by the FDIC, the bank shall remain subject to the reclassification and to any directives issued in connection with that reclassification while such request is pending before the FDIC.

§ 308.203 Order to dismiss a director or senior executive officer.

(a) *Service of notice.* When the FDIC issues and serves a directive on a bank pursuant to § 308.201 of this part requiring the bank to dismiss from office any director or senior executive officer under § 38(f)(2)(F)(ii) of the FDI Act, the FDIC shall also serve a copy of the directive, or the relevant portions of the directive where appropriate, upon the person to be dismissed.

(b) *Response to directive*—(1) *Request for reinstatement.* A director or senior executive officer who has been served with a directive under paragraph (a) of this section (Respondent) may file a written request for reinstatement. The request for reinstatement shall be filed within 10 calendar days of the receipt of the directive by the Respondent, unless further time is allowed by the FDIC at the request of the Respondent.

(2) *Contents of request; informal hearing.* The request for reinstatement shall include reasons why the Respondent should be reinstated, and may include a request for an informal hearing before the FDIC under this section. If the Respondent desires to present oral testimony or witnesses at the hearing, the Respondent shall include a request to do so with the request for an informal hearing. The request to present

Federal Deposit Insurance Corporation § 308.204

oral testimony or witnesses shall specify the names of the witnesses and the general nature of their expected testimony. Failure to request a hearing shall constitute a waiver of any right to a hearing and failure to request the opportunity to present oral testimony or witnesses shall constitute a waiver of any right or opportunity to present oral testimony or witnesses.

(3) *Effective date.* Unless otherwise ordered by the FDIC, the dismissal shall remain in effect while a request for reinstatement is pending.

(c) *Order for informal hearing.* Upon receipt of a timely written request from a Respondent for an informal hearing on the portion of a directive requiring a bank to dismiss from office any director or senior executive officer, the FDIC shall issue an order directing an informal hearing to commence no later than 30 days after receipt of the request, unless the Respondent requests a later date. The hearing shall be held in Washington, DC, or at such other place as may be designated by the FDIC, before a presiding officer(s) designated by the FDIC to conduct the hearing.

(d) *Hearing procedures.* (1) A Respondent may appear at the hearing personally or through counsel. A Respondent shall have the right to introduce relevant written materials and to present oral argument. A Respondent may introduce oral testimony and present witnesses only if expressly authorized by the FDIC or the presiding officer(s). Neither the provisions of the Administrative Procedure Act governing adjudications required by statute to be determined on the record nor the Uniform Rules of Practice and Procedure in this part apply to an informal hearing under this section unless the FDIC orders that such procedures shall apply.

(2) The informal hearing shall be recorded, and a transcript shall be furnished to the Respondent upon request and payment of the cost thereof. Witnesses need not be sworn, unless specifically requested by a party or the presiding officer(s). The presiding officer(s) may ask questions of any witness.

(3) The presiding officer(s) may order that the hearing be continued for a reasonable period (normally five business days) following completion of oral testimony or argument to allow additional written submissions to the hearing record.

(e) *Standard for review.* A Respondent shall bear the burden of demonstrating that his or her continued employment by or service with the bank would materially strengthen the bank's ability:

(1) To become adequately capitalized, to the extent that the directive was issued as a result of the bank's capital level or failure to submit or implement a capital restoration plan; and

(2) To correct the unsafe or unsound condition or unsafe or unsound practice, to the extent that the directive was issued as a result of classification of the bank based on supervisory criteria other than capital, pursuant to section 38(g) of the FDI Act.

(f) *Recommendation of presiding officers.* Within 20 calendar days following the date the hearing and the record on the proceeding are closed, the presiding officer(s) shall make a recommendation to the FDIC concerning the Respondent's request for reinstatement with the bank.

(g) *Time for decision.* Not later than 60 calendar days after the date the record is closed or the date of the response in a case where no hearing was requested, the FDIC shall grant or deny the request for reinstatement and notify the Respondent of the FDIC's decision. If the FDIC denies the request for reinstatement, the FDIC shall set forth in the notification the reasons for the FDIC's action.

§ 308.204 Enforcement of directives.

(a) *Judicial remedies.* Whenever a bank fails to comply with a directive issued under section 38, the FDIC may seek enforcement of the directive in the appropriate United States district court pursuant to section 8(i)(1) of the FDI Act (12 U.S.C. 1818(i)(1)).

(b) *Administrative remedies*—(1) *Failure to comply with directive.* Pursuant to section 8(i)(2)(A) of the FDI Act, the FDIC may assess a civil money penalty against any bank that violates or otherwise fails to comply with any final directive issued under section 38 and against any institution-affiliated party

§ 308.300

who participates in such violation or noncompliance.

(2) *Failure to implement capital restoration plan.* The failure of a bank to implement a capital restoration plan required under section 38, or subpart B of part 325 of this chapter, or the failure of a company having control of a bank to fulfill a guarantee of a capital restoration plan made pursuant to section 38(e)(2) of the FDI Act shall subject the bank to the assessment of civil money penalties pursuant to section 8(i)(2)(A) of the FDI Act.

(c) *Other enforcement action.* In addition to the actions described in paragraphs (a) and (b) of this section, the FDIC may seek enforcement of the provisions of section 38 or subpart B of part 325 of this chapter through any other judicial or administrative proceeding authorized by law.

[57 FR 44897, Sept. 29, 1992; 57 FR 48426, Oct. 23, 1992]

Subpart R—Submission and Review of Safety and Soundness Compliance Plans and Issuance of Orders To Correct Safety and Soundness Deficiencies

SOURCE: 60 FR 35684, July 10, 1995, unless otherwise noted.

§ 308.300 Scope.

The rules and procedures set forth in this subpart apply to insured state nonmember banks and to state-licensed insured branches of foreign banks, that are subject to the provisions of section 39 of the Federal Deposit Insurance Act (section 39) (12 U.S.C. 1831p–1).

§ 308.301 Purpose.

Section 39 of the FDI Act requires the FDIC to establish safety and soundness standards. Pursuant to section 39, a bank may be required to submit a compliance plan if it is not in compliance with a safety and soundness standard established by guideline under section 39(a) or (b). An enforceable order under section 8 of the FDI Act may be issued if, after being notified that it is in violation of a safety and soundness standard established under section 39, the bank fails to submit an acceptable compliance plan or fails in any material respect to implement an accepted plan. This subpart establishes procedures for requiring submission of a compliance plan and issuing an enforceable order pursuant to section 39.

§ 308.302 Determination and notification of failure to meet a safety and soundness standard and request for compliance plan.

(a) *Determination.* The FDIC may, based upon an examination, inspection or any other information that becomes available to the FDIC, determine that a bank has failed to satisfy the safety and soundness standards set out in part 364 of this chapter and in the Interagency Guidelines Establishing Standards for Safety and Soundness in appendix A and the Interagency Guidelines Establishing Standards for Safeguarding Customer Information in appendix B to part 364 of this chapter.

(b) *Request for compliance plan.* If the FDIC determines that a bank has failed a safety and soundness standard pursuant to paragraph (a) of this section, the FDIC may request, by letter or through a report of examination, the submission of a compliance plan and the bank shall be deemed to have notice of the request three days after mailing of the letter by the FDIC or delivery of the report of examination.

[60 FR 35684, July 10, 1995, as amended at 66 FR 8638, Feb. 1, 2001]

§ 308.303 Filing of safety and soundness compliance plan.

(a) *Schedule for filing compliance plan*—(1) *In general.* A bank shall file a written safety and soundness compliance plan with the FDIC within 30 days of receiving a request for a compliance plan pursuant to § 308.302(b), unless the FDIC notifies the bank in writing that the plan is to be filed within a different period.

(2) *Other plans.* If a bank is obligated to file, or is currently operating under, a capital restoration plan submitted pursuant to section 38 of the FDI Act (12 U.S.C. 1831o), a cease-and-desist order entered into pursuant to section 8 of the FDI Act, a formal or informal agreement, or a response to a report of examination or report of inspection, it

may, with the permission of the FDIC, submit a compliance plan under this section as part of that plan, order, agreement, or response, subject to the deadline provided in paragraph (a)(1) of this section.

(b) *Contents of plan.* The compliance plan shall include a description of the steps the bank will take to correct the deficiency and the time within which those steps will be taken.

(c) *Review of safety and soundness compliance plans.* Within 30 days after receiving a safety and soundness compliance plan under this subpart, the FDIC shall provide written notice to the bank of whether the plan has been approved or seek additional information from the bank regarding the plan. The FDIC may extend the time within which notice regarding approval of a plan will be provided.

(d) *Failure to submit or implement a compliance plan*—(1) *Supervisory actions.* If a bank fails to submit an acceptable plan within the time specified by the FDIC or fails in any material respect to implement a compliance plan, then the FDIC shall, by order, require the bank to correct the deficiency and may take further actions provided in section 39(e)(2)(B). Pursuant to section 39(e)(3), the FDIC may be required to take certain actions if the bank commenced operations or experienced a change in control within the previous 24-month period, or the bank experienced extraordinary growth during the previous 18-month period.

(2) *Extraordinary growth.* For purposes of paragraph (d)(1) of this section, extraordinary growth means an increase in assets of more than 7.5 percent during any quarter within the 18-month period preceding the issuance of a request for submission of a compliance plan, by a bank that is not well capitalized for purposes of section 38 of the FDI Act. For purposes of calculating an increase in assets, assets acquired through merger or acquisition approved pursuant to the Bank Merger Act (12 U.S.C. 1828(c)) will be excluded.

(e) *Amendment of compliance plan.* A bank that has filed an approved compliance plan may, after prior written notice to and approval by the FDIC, amend the plan to reflect a change in circumstance. Until such time as a proposed amendment has been approved, the bank shall implement the compliance plan as previously approved.

§ 308.304 **Issuance of orders to correct deficiencies and to take or refrain from taking other actions.**

(a) *Notice of intent to issue order*—(1) *In general.* The FDIC shall provide a bank prior written notice of the FDIC's intention to issue an order requiring the bank to correct a safety and soundness deficiency or to take or refrain from taking other actions pursuant to section 39 of the FDI Act. The bank shall have such time to respond to a proposed order as provided by the FDIC under paragraph (c) of this section.

(2) *Immediate issuance of final order.* If the FDIC finds it necessary in order to carry out the purposes of section 39 of the FDI Act, the FDIC may, without providing the notice prescribed in paragraph (a)(1) of this section, issue an order requiring a bank immediately to take actions to correct a safety and soundness deficiency or take or refrain from taking other actions pursuant to section 39. A bank that is subject to such an immediately effective order may submit a written appeal of the order to the FDIC. Such an appeal must be received by the FDIC within 14 calendar days of the issuance of the order, unless the FDIC permits a longer period. The FDIC shall consider any such appeal, if filed in a timely matter, within 60 days of receiving the appeal. During such period of review, the order shall remain in effect unless the FDIC, in its sole discretion, stays the effectiveness of the order.

(b) *Contents of notice.* A notice of intent to issue an order shall include:

(1) A statement of the safety and soundness deficiency or deficiencies that have been identified at the bank;

(2) A description of any restrictions, prohibitions, or affirmative actions that the FDIC proposes to impose or require;

(3) The proposed date when such restrictions or prohibitions would be effective or the proposed date for completion of any required action; and

(4) The date by which the bank subject to the order may file with the FDIC a written response to the notice.

§ 308.305

(c) *Response to notice*—(1) *Time for response.* A bank may file a written response to a notice of intent to issue an order within the time period set by the FDIC. Such a response must be received by the FDIC within 14 calendar days from the date of the notice unless the FDIC determines that a different period is appropriate in light of the safety and soundness of the bank or other relevant circumstances.

(2) *Contents of response.* The response should include:

(i) An explanation why the action proposed by the FDIC is not an appropriate exercise of discretion under section 39;

(ii) Any recommended modification of the proposed order; and

(iii) Any other relevant information, mitigating circumstances, documentation, or other evidence in support of the position of the bank regarding the proposed order.

(d) *Agency consideration of response.* After considering the response, the FDIC may:

(1) Issue the order as proposed or in modified form;

(2) Determine not to issue the order and so notify the bank; or

(3) Seek additional information or clarification of the response from the bank, or any other relevant source.

(e) *Failure to file response.* Failure by a bank to file with the FDIC, within the specified time period, a written response to a proposed order shall constitute a waiver of the opportunity to respond and shall constitute consent to the issuance of the order.

(f) *Request for modification or rescission of order.* Any bank that is subject to an order under this subpart may, upon a change in circumstances, request in writing that the FDIC reconsider the terms of the order, and may propose that the order be rescinded or modified. Unless otherwise ordered by the FDIC, the order shall continue in place while such request is pending before the FDIC.

§ 308.305 Enforcement of orders.

(a) *Judicial remedies.* Whenever a bank fails to comply with an order issued under section 39, the FDIC may seek enforcement of the order in the appropriate United States district court pursuant to section 8(i)(1) of the FDI Act.

(b) *Failure to comply with order.* Pursuant to section 8(i)(2)(A) of the FDI Act, the FDIC may assess a civil money penalty against any bank that violates or otherwise fails to comply with any final order issued under section 39 and against any institution-affiliated party who participates in such violation or noncompliance.

(c) *Other enforcement action.* In addition to the actions described in paragraphs (a) and (b) of this section, the FDIC may seek enforcement of the provisions of section 39 or this part through any other judicial or administrative proceeding authorized by law.

Subpart S—Applications for a Stay or Review of Actions of Bank Clearing Agencies

SOURCE: 61 FR 48403, Sept. 11, 1996, unless otherwise noted.

§ 308.400 Scope.

This subpart is issued by the Corporation pursuant to sections 17A(b)(3)(g), 17A(b)(5)(C), 19 and 23 of the Securities Exchange Act of 1934 (Exchange Act), as amended (15 U.S.C. 78q–1 (b)(3)(g), (b)(5)(C), 78s, 78w). It applies to applications by banks insured by the Corporation (other than members of the Federal Reserve System) for a stay or review of certain actions by clearing agencies registered under the Exchange Act, for which the Securities and Exchange Commission (Commission) is not the appropriate regulatory agency under section 3(a)(34)(B) of the Exchange Act (bank clearing agencies).

§ 308.401 Applications for stays of disciplinary sanctions or summary suspensions by a bank clearing agency.

Applications to the Corporation for a stay of disciplinary action imposed by registered clearing agencies pursuant to section 17(b)(3)(G) of the Exchange Act, or summary suspension or limitation or prohibition of access under section 17(b)(5)(C) of the Exchange Act shall be made according to the rules adopted by the Commission (17 CFR 240.19d–2). References to the "Commission" in 17 CFR 240.19d–2 are deemed to refer to the "Corporation."

Federal Deposit Insurance Corporation § 308.501

§ 308.402 Applications for review of final disciplinary sanctions, denials of participation, or prohibitions or limitations of access to services imposed by bank clearing agencies.

Proceedings on an application to the Corporation under section 19(d)(2) of the Exchange Act for review of any final disciplinary sanctions, denials of participation, or prohibitions or limitations of access to services imposed by bank clearing agencies shall be conducted according to the procedures set forth in rules adopted by the Commission (17 CFR 240.19d-3). References to the "Commission" in 17 CFR 240.19d-3 are deemed to refer to the "Corporation."

Subpart T—Program Fraud Civil Remedies and Procedures

SOURCE: 66 FR 9189, Feb. 7, 2001, unless otherwise noted.

§ 308.500 Basis, purpose, and scope.

(a) *Basis.* This subpart implements the Program Fraud Civil Remedies Act, Pub. L. 99-509, sections 6101-6104, 100 Stat. 1874 (October 21, 1986), codified at 31 U.S.C. 3801-3812, (PFCRA) and made applicable to the Federal Deposit Insurance Corporation (FDIC) by section 23 of the Resolution Trust Corporation Completion Act (Pub. L. 103-204, 107 Stat. 2369). 31 U.S.C. 3809 of the statute requires each Authority head to promulgate regulations necessary to implement the provisions of the statute.

(b) *Purpose.* This subpart:

(1) Establishes administrative procedures for imposing civil penalties and assessments against persons who make, submit, or present or cause to be made, submitted, or presented false, fictitious, or fraudulent claims or written statements to the FDIC or to its agents; and

(2) Specifies the hearing and appeal rights of persons subject to allegations of liability for such penalties and assessments.

(c) *Scope.* This subpart applies only to persons who make, submit, or present or cause to be made, submitted, or presented false, fictitious, or fraudulent claims or written statements to the FDIC or to its agents acting on behalf of the FDIC in connection with FDIC employment matters, FDIC contracting activities, and the FDIC Asset Purchaser Certification Program. It does not apply to false claims or statements made in connection with programs (other than as set forth in the preceding sentence) related to the FDIC's regulatory, supervision, enforcement, insurance, receivership or liquidation responsibilities. The FDIC is restricting the scope of applicability of this subpart because other civil and administrative remedies are adequate to redress fraud in the areas not covered.

§ 308.501 Definitions.

For purposes of this subpart:

(a) *Administrative Law Judge (ALJ)* means the presiding officer appointed by the Office of Financial Institution Adjudication pursuant to 12 U.S.C. 1818 note and 5 U.S.C. 3105.

(b) *Authority* means the Federal Deposit Insurance Corporation (FDIC).

(c) *Authority head* or *Board* means the Board of Directors of the FDIC, which is herein designated by the Chairman of the FDIC to serve as head of the FDIC for PFCRA matters.

(d) *Benefit* means, in the context of "statement" as defined in 31 U.S.C. 3801(a)(9), any financial assistance received from the FDIC that amounts to $150,000 or less. The term does not include the FDIC's deposit insurance program.

(e) *Claim* means any request, demand, or submission:

(1) Made to the FDIC for property, services, or money (including money representing grants, loans, insurance, or benefits);

(2) Made to a recipient of property, services, or money from the FDIC or to a party to a contract with the FDIC;

(i) For property or services if the United States:

(A) Provided such property or services;

(B) Provided any portion of the funds for the purchase of such property or services; or

(C) Will reimburse such recipient or party for the purchase of such property or services;

(ii) For the payment of money (including money representing grants,

§ 308.502

loans, insurance, or benefits) if the United States:

(A) Provided any portion of the money requested or demanded; or

(B) Will reimburse such recipient or party for any portion of the money paid on such request or demand; or

(3) Made to the FDIC that has the effect of decreasing an obligation to pay or account for property, services, or money.

(f) *Complaint* means the administrative complaint served by the reviewing official on the defendant under § 308.506 of this subpart.

(g) *Corporation* means the Federal Deposit Insurance Corporation.

(h) *Defendant* means any person alleged in a complaint under § 308.506 of this subpart to be liable for a civil penalty or assessment under § 308.502 of this subpart.

(i) *Government* means the United States Government.

(j) *Individual* means a natural person.

(k) *Initial decision* means the written decision of the ALJ required by § 308.509 or § 308.536 of this subpart, and includes a revised initial decision issued following a remand or a motion for consideration.

(l) *Investigating official* means the Inspector General of the FDIC, or an officer or employee of the Inspector General designated by the Inspector General. The investigating official must serve in a position that has a rate of basic pay under the pay scale utilized by the FDIC that is equal to or greater than 120 percent of the minimum rate of basic pay for grade 15 under the federal government's General Schedule.

(m) *Knows or has reason to know*, means that a person, with respect to a claim or statement:

(1) Has actual knowledge that the claim or statement is false, fictitious, or fraudulent;

(2) Acts in deliberate ignorance of the truth or falsity of the claim or statement; or

(3) Acts in reckless disregard of the truth or falsity of the claim or statement.

(n) *Makes*, wherever it appears, includes the terms "presents", "submits", and "causes to be made, presented, or submitted." As the context requires, "making" or "made" likewise includes the corresponding forms of such terms.

(o) *Person* means any individual, partnership, corporation, association, or private organization, and includes the plural of that term.

(p) *Representative* means an attorney, who is a member in good standing of the bar of any state, territory, or possession of the United States or of the District of Columbia or the Commonwealth of Puerto Rico, and designated by a party in writing.

(q) *Reviewing official* means the General Counsel of the FDIC or his designee who is:

(1) Not subject to supervision by, or required to report to, the investigating official;

(2) Not employed in the organizational unit of the FDIC in which the investigating official is employed; and

(3) Serving in a position that has a rate of basic pay under the pay scale utilized by the FDIC that is equal to or greater than 120 percent of the minimum rate of basic pay for grade 15 under the federal government's General Schedule.

(r) *Statement* means any representation, certification, affirmation, document, record, or accounting or bookkeeping entry made:

(1) With respect to a claim or to obtain the approval or payment of a claim (including relating to eligibility to make a claim); or

(2) With respect to (including relating to eligibility for):

(i) A contract with, or a bid or proposal for a contract with; or

(ii) A grant, loan, or benefit received, directly or indirectly, from the FDIC, or any state, political subdivision of a state, or other party, if the United States government provides any portion of the money or property under such contract or for such grant, loan, or benefit, or if the government will reimburse such state, political subdivision, or party for any portion of the money or property under such contract or for such grant, loan, or benefit.

§ 308.502 Basis for civil penalties and assessments.

(a) *Claims.* (1) A person who makes a false, fictitious, or fraudulent claim to the FDIC is subject to a civil penalty of

Federal Deposit Insurance Corporation § 308.502

up to $5,000 per claim. A claim is false, fictitious, or fraudulent if the person making the claim knows, or has reason to know, that:

(i) The claim is false, fictitious, or fraudulent; or

(ii) The claim includes, or is supported by, a written statement that asserts a material fact which is false, fictitious or fraudulent; or

(iii) The claim includes, or is supported by, a written statement that:

(A) Omits a material fact; and

(B) Is false, fictitious, or fraudulent as a result of that omission; and

(C) Is a statement in which the person making the statement has a duty to include the material fact; or

(iv) The claim seeks payment for providing property or services that the person has not provided as claimed.

(2) Each voucher, invoice, claim form, or other individual request or demand for property, services, or money constitutes a separate claim.

(3) A claim will be considered made to the FDIC, recipient, or party when the claim is actually made to an agent, fiscal intermediary, or other entity, including any state or political subdivision thereof, acting for or on behalf of the FDIC, recipient, or party.

(4) Each claim for property, services, or money that constitutes any one of the elements in paragraph (a)(1) of this section is subject to a civil penalty regardless of whether the property, services, or money is actually delivered or paid.

(5) If the FDIC has made any payment (including transferred property or provided services) on a claim, a person subject to a civil penalty under paragraph (a)(1) of this section will also be subject to an assessment of not more than twice the amount of such claim (or portion of the claim) that is determined to constitute a false, fictitious, or fraudulent claim under paragraph (a)(1) of this section. The assessment will be in lieu of damages sustained by the FDIC because of the claims.

(6) The amount of any penalty assessed under paragraph (a)(1) of this section will be adjusted for inflation in accordance with § 308.132(c)(3)(xv) of this part.

(7) The penalty specified in paragraph (a)(1) of this section is in addition to any other remedy allowable by law.

(b) *Statements.* (1) A person who submits to the FDIC a false, fictitious or fraudulent statement is subject to a civil penalty of up to $5,000 per statement. A statement is false, fictitious or fraudulent if the person submitting the statement to the FDIC knows, or has reason to know, that:

(i) The statement asserts a material fact which is false, fictitious, or fraudulent; or

(ii) The statement omits a material fact that the person making the statement has a duty to include in the statement; and

(iii) The statement contains or is accompanied by an express certification or affirmation of the truthfulness and accuracy of the contents of the statement.

(2) Each written representation, certification, or affirmation constitutes a separate statement.

(3) A statement will be considered made to the FDIC when the statement is actually made to an agent, fiscal intermediary, or other entity, including any state or political subdivision thereof, acting for or on behalf of the FDIC.

(4) The amount of any penalty assessed under paragraph (a)(1) of this section will be adjusted for inflation in accordance with § 308.132(c)(3)(xv) of this part.

(5) The penalty specified in paragraph (a)(1) of this section is in addition to any other remedy allowable by law.

(c) *Failure to file declaration/certification.* Where, as a prerequisite to conducting business with the FDIC, a person is required by law to file one or more declarations and/or certifications, and the person intentionally fails to file such declaration/certification, the person will be subject to the civil penalties as prescribed by this subpart.

(d) *Intent.* No proof of specific intent to defraud is required to establish liability under this section.

(e) *Liability.* (1) In any case in which it is determined that more than one person is liable for making a claim or statement under this section, each such person may be held jointly and

§ 308.503

severally liable for a civil penalty under this section.

(2) In any case in which it is determined that more than one person is liable for making a claim under this section on which the FDIC has made payment (including transferred property or provided services), an assessment may be imposed against any such person or jointly and severally against any combination of such persons.

§ 308.503 Investigations.

(a) If an investigating official concludes that a subpoena pursuant to the authority conferred by 31 U.S.C. 3804(a) is warranted:

(1) The subpoena will identify the person to whom it is addressed and the authority under which the subpoena is issued and will identify the records or documents sought;

(2) The investigating official may designate a person to act on his or her behalf to receive the documents sought; and

(3) The person receiving such subpoena will be required to provide the investigating official or the person designated to receive the documents a certification that the documents sought have been produced, or that such documents are not available, and the reasons therefor, or that such documents, suitably identified, have been withheld based upon the assertion of an identified privilege.

(b) If the investigating official concludes that an action under the PFCRA may be warranted, the investigating official will submit a report containing the findings and conclusions of such investigation to the reviewing official.

(c) Nothing in this section will preclude or limit an investigating official's discretion to refer allegations directly to the United States Department of Justice (DOJ) for suit under the False Claims Act (31 U.S.C. 3729 *et seq.*) or other civil relief, or to preclude or limit the investigating official's discretion to defer or postpone a report or referral to the reviewing official to avoid interference with a criminal investigation or prosecution.

(d) Nothing in this section modifies any responsibility of an investigating official to report violations of criminal law to the Attorney General.

§ 308.504 Review by the reviewing official.

(a) If, based on the report of the investigating official under § 308.503(b) of this subpart, the reviewing official determines that there is adequate evidence to believe that a person is liable under § 308.502 of this subpart, the reviewing official will transmit to the Attorney General a written notice of the reviewing official's intention to issue a complaint under § 308.506 of this subpart.

(b) Such notice will include:

(1) A statement of the reviewing official's reasons for issuing a complaint;

(2) A statement specifying the evidence that supports the allegations of liability;

(3) A description of the claims or statements upon which the allegations of liability are based;

(4) An estimate of the amount of money or the value of property, services, or other benefits requested or demanded in violation of § 308.502 of this subpart;

(5) A statement of any exculpatory or mitigating circumstances that may relate to the claims or statements known by the reviewing official or the investigating official; and

(6) A statement that there is a reasonable prospect of collecting an appropriate amount of penalties and assessments. Such a statement may be based upon information then known, or upon an absence of any information indicating that the person may be unable to pay such amount.

§ 308.505 Prerequisites for issuing a complaint.

(a) The reviewing official may issue a complaint under § 308.506 of this subpart only if:

(1) The DOJ approves the issuance of a complaint in a written statement described in 31 U.S.C. 3803(b)(1); and

(2) In the case of allegations of liability under § 308.502(a) of this subpart with respect to a claim (or a group of related claims submitted at the same time as defined in paragraph (b) of this section) the reviewing official determines that the amount of money or the value of property or services demanded or requested does not exceed $150,000.

118

Federal Deposit Insurance Corporation § 308.508

(b) For the purposes of this section, a group of related claims submitted at the same time will include only those claims arising from the same transaction (e.g., grant, loan, application, or contract) that are submitted simultaneously as part of a single request, demand, or submission.

(c) Nothing in this section will be construed to limit the reviewing official's authority to join in a single complaint against a person claims that are unrelated or were not submitted simultaneously, regardless of the amount of money, or the value of property or services, demanded or requested.

§ 308.506 Complaint.

(a) On or after the date the DOJ approves the issuance of a complaint in accordance with 31 U.S.C. 3803(b)(1), the reviewing official may serve a complaint on the defendant, as provided in § 308.507 of this subpart.

(b) The complaint will state:

(1) The allegations of liability against the defendant, including the statutory basis for liability, or identification of the claims or statements that are the basis for the alleged liability, and the reasons why liability allegedly arises from such claims or statements;

(2) The maximum amount of penalties and assessments for which the defendant may be held liable;

(3) Instructions for filing an answer and to request a hearing, including a specific statement of the defendant's right to request a hearing by filing an answer and to be represented by a representative; and

(4) That failure to file an answer within 30 days of service of the complaint will result in the imposition of the maximum amount of penalties and assessments without right to appeal, as provided in § 308.509 of this subpart.

(c) At the same time the reviewing official serves the complaint, he or she will provide the defendant with a copy of this subpart.

§ 308.507 Service of complaint.

(a) Service of a complaint will be made by certified or registered mail or by delivery in any manner authorized by rule 4(c) of the Federal Rules of Civil Procedure (28 U.S.C. App.). Service is complete upon receipt.

(b) Proof of service, stating the name and address of the person on whom the complaint was served, and the manner and date of service, may be made by:

(1) Affidavit of the individual serving the complaint by delivery;

(2) A United States Postal Service return receipt card acknowledging receipt; or

(3) Written acknowledgment of receipt by the defendant or his or her representative.

§ 308.508 Answer.

(a) The defendant may request a hearing by filing an answer with the reviewing official within 30 days of service of the complaint. An answer will be deemed to be a request for hearing.

(b) In the answer, the defendant:

(1) Must admit or deny each of the allegations of liability made in the complaint;

(2) Must state any defense on which the defendant intends to rely;

(3) May state any reasons why the defendant contends that the penalties and assessments should be less than the statutory maximum; and

(4) Must state the name, address, and telephone number of the person authorized by the defendant to act as defendant's representative, if any.

(c) If the defendant is unable to file an answer meeting the requirements of paragraph (b) of this section within the time provided:

(1) The defendant may, before the expiration of 30 days from service of the complaint, file with the reviewing official a general answer denying liability and requesting a hearing, and a request for an extension of time within which to file an answer meeting the requirements of paragraph (b) of this section.

(2) The reviewing official will file promptly with the ALJ the complaint, the general answer denying liability, and the request for an extension of time as provided in § 308.510 of this subpart.

(3) For good cause shown, the ALJ may grant the defendant up to 30 additional days within which to file an answer meeting the requirements of paragraph (b) of this section.

§ 308.509 Default upon failure to file an answer.

(a) If the defendant does not file an answer within the time prescribed in § 308.508(a) of this subpart, the reviewing official may refer the complaint to the ALJ.

(b) Upon the referral of the complaint, the ALJ will promptly serve on defendant in the manner prescribed in § 308.507 of this subpart, a notice that an initial decision will be issued under this section.

(c) If the defendant fails to answer, the ALJ will assume the facts alleged in the complaint to be true, and, if such facts establish liability under § 308.502 of this subpart, the ALJ will issue an initial decision imposing the maximum amount of penalties and assessments allowed under the statute.

(d) Except as otherwise provided in this section, by failing to file a timely answer, the defendant waives any right to further review of the penalties and assessments imposed under paragraph (c) of this section, and the initial decision will become final and binding upon the parties 30 days after it is issued.

(e) If, before such an initial decision becomes final, the defendant files a motion with the ALJ seeking to reopen on the grounds that extraordinary circumstances prevented the defendant from filing an answer, the initial decision will be stayed pending the ALJ's decision on the motion.

(f) If, in the motion to reopen under paragraph (e) of this section, the defendant can demonstrate extraordinary circumstances excusing the failure to file a timely answer, the ALJ will withdraw the initial decision in paragraph (c) of this section, if such a decision has been issued, and will grant the defendant an opportunity to answer the complaint.

(g) A decision of the ALJ denying a defendant's motion to reopen under paragraph (e) of this section is not subject to reconsideration under § 308.537 of this subpart.

(h) The decision denying the motion to reopen under paragraph (e) of this section may be appealed by the defendant to the Board by filing a notice of appeal with the Board within 15 days after the ALJ denies the motion. The timely filing of a notice of appeal will stay the initial decision until the Board decides the issue.

(i) If the defendant files a timely notice of appeal with the Board, the ALJ will forward the record of the proceeding to the Board.

(j) The Board will decide whether extraordinary circumstances excuse the defendant's failure to file a timely answer based solely on the record before the ALJ.

(k) If the Board decides that extraordinary circumstances excuse the defendant's failure to file a timely answer, the Board will remand the case to the ALJ with instructions to grant the defendant an opportunity to answer.

(l) If the Board decides that the defendant's failure to file a timely answer is not excused, the Board will reinstate the initial decision of the ALJ, which will become final and binding upon the parties 30 days after the Board issues such decision.

§ 308.510 Referral of complaint and answer to the ALJ.

Upon receipt of an answer, the reviewing official will file the complaint and answer with the ALJ. The reviewing official will include the name, address, and telephone number of a representative of the Corporation.

§ 308.511 Notice of hearing.

(a) When the ALJ receives the complaint and answer, the ALJ will promptly serve a notice of hearing upon the defendant in the manner prescribed by § 308.507 of this subpart. At the same time, the ALJ will send a copy of such notice to the representative of the Corporation.

(b) The notice will include:

(1) The tentative time, date, and place, and the nature of the hearing;

(2) The legal authority and jurisdiction under which the hearing is to be held;

(3) The matters of fact and law to be asserted;

(4) A description of the procedures for the conduct of the hearing;

(5) The name, address, and telephone number of the representative of the Corporation and of the defendant, if any; and

Federal Deposit Insurance Corporation § 308.516

(6) Other matters as the ALJ deems appropriate.

§ 308.512 Parties to the hearing.

(a) The parties to the hearing will be the defendant and the Corporation.

(b) Pursuant to the False Claims Act (31 U.S.C. 3730(c)(5)), a private plaintiff under the False Claims Act may participate in these proceedings to the extent authorized by the provisions of that Act.

§ 308.513 Separation of functions.

(a) The investigating official, the reviewing official, and any employee or agent of the FDIC who takes part in investigating, preparing, or presenting a particular case may not, in such case or a factually related case:

(1) Participate in the hearing as the ALJ;

(2) Participate or advise in the initial decision or the review of the initial decision by the Board, except as a witness or a representative in public proceedings; or

(3) Make the collection of penalties and assessments under 31 U.S.C. 3806.

(b) The ALJ will not be responsible to, or subject to the supervision or direction of, the investigating official or the reviewing official.

(c) Except as provided in paragraph (a) of this section, the representative for the FDIC will be an attorney employed in the FDIC's Legal Division; however, the representative of the FDIC may not participate or advise in the review of the initial decision by the Board.

§ 308.514 Ex parte contacts.

No party or person (except employees of the ALJ's office) will communicate in any way with the ALJ on any matter at issue in a case, unless on notice and opportunity for all parties to participate. This provision does not prohibit a person or party from inquiring about the status of a case or asking routine questions concerning administrative functions or procedures.

§ 308.515 Disqualification of reviewing official or ALJ.

(a) A reviewing official or ALJ in a particular case may disqualify himself or herself at any time.

(b) A party may file with the ALJ a motion for disqualification of a reviewing official or an ALJ. An affidavit alleging conflict of interest or other reason for disqualification must accompany the motion.

(c) Such motion and affidavit must be filed promptly upon the party's discovery of reasons requiring disqualification, or such objections will be deemed waived.

(d) Such affidavit must state specific facts that support the party's belief that personal bias or other reason for disqualification exists and the time and circumstances of the party's discovery of such facts. The representative of record must certify that the affidavit is made in good faith and this certification must accompany the affidavit.

(e) Upon the filing of such a motion and affidavit, the ALJ will proceed no further in the case until he or she resolves the matter of disqualification in accordance with paragraph (f) of this section.

(f)(1) If the ALJ determines that a reviewing official is disqualified, the ALJ will dismiss the complaint without prejudice.

(2) If the ALJ disqualifies himself or herself, the case will be reassigned promptly to another ALJ.

(3) If the ALJ denies a motion to disqualify, the Board may determine the matter only as part of the Board's review of the initial decision upon appeal, if any.

§ 308.516 Rights of parties.

Except as otherwise limited by this subpart, all parties may:

(a) Be accompanied, represented, and advised by a representative;

(b) Participate in any conference held by the ALJ;

(c) Conduct discovery;

(d) Agree to stipulations of fact or law which will be made part of the record;

(e) Present evidence relevant to the issues at the hearing;

(f) Present and cross-examine witnesses;

(g) Present oral arguments at the hearing as permitted by the ALJ; and

§ 308.517

(h) Submit written briefs and proposed findings of fact and conclusions of law.

§ 308.517 Authority of the ALJ.

(a) The ALJ will conduct a fair and impartial hearing, avoid delay, maintain order, and assure that a record of the proceeding is made.

(b) The ALJ has the authority to:

(1) Set and change the date, time, and place of the hearing upon reasonable notice to the parties;

(2) Continue or recess the hearing in whole or in part for a reasonable period of time;

(3) Hold conferences to identify or simplify the issues, or to consider other matters that may aid in the expeditious disposition of the proceeding;

(4) Administer oaths and affirmations;

(5) Issue subpoenas requiring the attendance of witnesses and the production of documents at depositions or at hearings;

(6) Rule on motions and other procedural matters;

(7) Regulate the scope and timing of discovery;

(8) Regulate the course of the hearing and the conduct of representatives and parties;

(9) Examine witnesses;

(10) Receive, rule on, exclude, or limit evidence;

(11) Upon motion of a party, take official notice of facts, decide cases, in whole or in part, by summary judgment where there is no disputed issue of material fact;

(12) Conduct any conference, argument, or hearing on motions in person or by telephone; and

(13) Exercise such other authority as is necessary to carry out the responsibilities of the ALJ under this subpart.

(c) The ALJ does not have the authority to make any determinations regarding the validity of federal statutes or regulations or of directives, rules, resolutions, policies, orders or other such general pronouncements issued by the Corporation.

§ 308.518 Prehearing conferences.

(a) The ALJ may schedule prehearing conferences as appropriate.

(b) Upon the motion of any party, the ALJ will schedule at least one prehearing conference at a reasonable time in advance of the hearing.

(c) The ALJ may use prehearing conferences to discuss the following:

(1) Simplification of the issues;

(2) The necessity or desirability of amendments to the pleading, including the need for a more definite statement;

(3) Stipulations and admissions of fact as to the contents and authenticity of documents;

(4) Whether the parties can agree to submission of the case on a stipulated record;

(5) Whether a party chooses (subject to the objection of other parties) to waive appearance at an oral hearing and to submit only documentary evidence and written argument;

(6) Limitation of the number of witnesses;

(7) Scheduling dates for the exchange of witness lists and of proposed exhibits;

(8) Discovery;

(9) The time, date, and place for the hearing; and

(10) Such other matters as may tend to expedite the fair and just disposition of the proceedings.

(d) The ALJ may issue an order containing all matters agreed upon by the parties or ordered by the ALJ at a prehearing conference.

§ 308.519 Disclosure of documents.

(a) Upon written request to the reviewing official, the defendant may review any relevant and material documents, transcripts, records, and other materials that relate to the allegations set out in the complaint and upon which the findings and conclusions of the investigating official under § 308.503(b) of this subpart are based, unless such documents are subject to a privilege under federal law. Upon payment of fees for duplication, the defendant may obtain copies of such documents.

(b) Upon written request to the reviewing official, the defendant also may obtain a copy of all exculpatory information in the possession of the reviewing official or investigating official relating to the allegations in the complaint, even if it is contained in a

Federal Deposit Insurance Corporation § 308.521

document that would otherwise be privileged. If the document would otherwise be privileged, only that portion containing exculpatory information must be disclosed.

(c) The notice sent to the Attorney General from the reviewing official as described in § 308.504 of this subpart is not discoverable under any circumstances.

(d) The defendant may file a motion to compel disclosure of the documents subject to the provisions of this section. Such a motion may only be filed with the ALJ following the filing of an answer pursuant to § 308.508 of this subpart.

§ 308.520 Discovery.

(a) The following types of discovery are authorized:

(1) Requests for production of documents for inspection and copying;

(2) Requests for admission of the authenticity of any relevant document or of the truth of any relevant fact;

(3) Written interrogatories; and

(4) Depositions.

(b) For the purpose of this section and §§ 308.521 and 308.522 of this subpart, the term *documents* includes information, documents, reports, answers, records, accounts, papers, and other data or documentary evidence. Nothing contained in this subpart will be interpreted to require the creation of a document.

(c) Unless mutually agreed to by the parties, discovery is available only as ordered by the ALJ. The ALJ will regulate the timing of discovery.

(d) *Motions for discovery.* (1) A party seeking discovery may file a motion with the ALJ and a copy of the requested discovery, or in the case of depositions, a summary of the scope of the proposed deposition, must accompany such motions.

(2) Within 10 days of service, a party may file an opposition to the motion and/or a motion for protective order as provided in § 308.523 of this subpart.

(3) The ALJ may grant a motion for discovery only if he or she finds that the discovery sought:

(i) Is necessary for the expeditious, fair, and reasonable consideration of the issues;

(ii) Is not unduly costly or burdensome;

(iii) Will not unduly delay the proceeding; and

(iv) Does not seek privileged information.

(4) The burden of showing that discovery should be allowed is on the party seeking discovery.

(5) The ALJ may grant discovery subject to a protective order under § 308.523 of this subpart.

(e) *Dispositions.* (1) If a motion for deposition is granted, the ALJ will issue a subpoena for the deponent, which may require the deponent to produce documents. The subpoena will specify the time, date, and place at which the deposition will be held.

(2) The party seeking to depose must serve the subpoena in the manner prescribed in § 308.507 of this subpart.

(3) The deponent may file with the ALJ a motion to quash the subpoena or a motion for a protective order within 10 days of service.

(4) The party seeking to depose must provide for the taking of a verbatim transcript of the deposition, and must make the transcript available to all other parties for inspection and copying.

(f) Each party must bear its own costs of discovery.

§ 308.521 Exchange of witness lists, statements, and exhibits.

(a) At least 15 days before the hearing or at such other time as may be ordered by the ALJ, the parties must exchange witness lists, copies of prior statements of proposed witnesses, and copies of proposed hearing exhibits, including copies of any written statements that the party intends to offer in lieu of live testimony in accordance with § 308.532(b) of this subpart. At the time such documents are exchanged, any party that intends to rely on the transcript of deposition testimony in lieu of live testimony at the hearing, if permitted by the ALJ, must provide each party with a copy of the specific pages of the transcript it intends to introduce into evidence.

(b) If a party objects, the ALJ will not admit into evidence the testimony of any witness whose name does not appear on the witness list or any exhibit

§ 308.522

not provided to the opposing party as provided in paragraph (a) of this section unless the ALJ finds good cause for the failure or that there is no prejudice to the objecting party.

(c) Unless another party objects within the time set by the ALJ, documents exchanged in accordance with paragraph (a) of this section will be deemed to be authentic for the purpose of admissibility at the hearing.

§ 308.522 Subpoenas for attendance at hearing.

(a) A party wishing to procure the appearance and testimony of any individual at the hearing may request that the ALJ issue a subpoena.

(b) A subpoena requiring the attendance and testimony of an individual may also require the individual to produce documents at the hearing.

(c) A party seeking a subpoena must file a written request not less than 15 days before the date fixed for the hearing unless otherwise allowed by the ALJ for good cause shown. Such request must specify any documents to be produced and must designate the witnesses and describe the address and location thereof with sufficient particularity to permit such witnesses to be found.

(d) The subpoena must specify the time, date, and place at which the witness is to appear and any documents the witness is to produce.

(e) The party seeking the subpoena must serve it in the manner prescribed in § 308.507 of this subpart. A subpoena on a party or upon an individual under the control of a party may be served by first class mail.

(f) A party or the individual to whom the subpoena is directed may file with the ALJ a motion to quash the subpoena within 10 days after service or on or before the time specified in the subpoena for compliance if it is less than 10 days after service.

§ 308.523 Protective order.

(a) A party or a prospective witness or deponent may file a motion for a protective order with respect to discovery sought by an opposing party or with respect to the hearing, seeking to limit the availability or disclosure of evidence.

(b) In issuing a protective order, the ALJ may make any order which justice requires to protect a party or person from annoyance, embarrassment, oppression, or undue burden or expense, including one or more of the following:

(1) That the discovery will not be conducted;

(2) That the discovery will be conducted only on specified terms and conditions, including a designation of the time or place;

(3) That the discovery will be conducted only through a method of discovery other than that requested;

(4) That certain matters not be inquired into, or that the scope of discovery be limited to certain matters;

(5) That discovery be conducted with no one present except persons designated by the ALJ;

(6) That the contents of discovery or evidence be sealed or otherwise kept confidential;

(7) That a deposition after being sealed be opened only by order of the ALJ;

(8) That a trade secret or other confidential research, development, commercial information, or facts pertaining to any criminal investigation, proceeding, or other administrative investigation not be disclosed or be disclosed only in a designated way; or

(9) That the parties simultaneously file specified documents or information enclosed in sealed envelopes to be opened as directed by the ALJ.

§ 308.524 Witness fees.

The party requesting a subpoena must pay the cost of the fees and mileage of any witness subpoenaed in the amounts that would be payable to a witness in a proceeding in United States District Court. A check for witness fees and mileage must accompany the subpoena when served, except that when a subpoena is issued on behalf of the FDIC, a check for witness fees and mileage need not accompany the subpoena.

§ 308.525 Form, filing, and service of papers.

(a) *Form.* (1) Documents filed with the ALJ must include an original and two copies.

Federal Deposit Insurance Corporation § 308.528

(2) Every pleading and paper filed in the proceeding must contain a caption setting forth the title of the action, the case number assigned by the ALJ, and a designation of the paper (e.g., motion to quash subpoena).

(3) Every pleading and paper must be signed by, and must contain the address and telephone number of the party or the person on whose behalf the paper was filed, or his or her representative.

(4) Papers are considered filed when they are mailed by certified or registered mail. Date of mailing may be established by a certificate from the party or its representative or by proof that the document was sent by certified or registered mail.

(b) *Service.* A party filing a document with the ALJ must, at the time of filing, serve a copy of such document on every other party. Service upon any party of any document other than those required to be served as prescribed in § 308.507 of this subpart must be made by delivering a copy or by placing a copy of the document in the United States mail, postage prepaid, and addressed to the party's last known address. When a party is represented by a representative, service must be made upon such representative in lieu of the actual party. The ALJ may authorize facsimile transmission as an acceptable form of service.

(c) *Proof of service.* A certificate by the individual serving the document by personal delivery or by mail, setting forth the manner of service, will be proof of service.

§ 308.526 Computation of time.

(a) In computing any period of time under this subpart or in an order issued thereunder, the time begins with the day following the act, event, or default, and includes the last day of the period, unless it is a Saturday, Sunday, or legal holiday observed by the federal government, in which event it includes the next business day.

(b) When the period of time allowed is less than 7 days, intermediate Saturdays, Sundays, and legal holidays observed by the federal government will be excluded from the computation.

(c) Where a document has been served or issued by placing it in the mail, an additional 5 days will be added to the time permitted for any response.

§ 308.527 Motions.

(a) Any application to the ALJ for an order or ruling must be by motion. Motions must state the relief sought, the authority relied upon, and the facts alleged, and must be filed with the ALJ and served on all other parties. Motions may include, without limitation, motions for summary judgment.

(b) Except for motions made during a prehearing conference or at the hearing, all motions must be in writing. The ALJ may require that oral motions be reduced to writing.

(c) Within 15 days after a written motion is served, or any other time as may be fixed by the ALJ, any party may file a response to such motion.

(d) The ALJ may not grant a written motion before the time for filing responses thereto has expired, except upon consent of the parties or following a hearing on the motion, but may overrule or deny such motion without awaiting a response.

(e) The ALJ will make a reasonable effort to dispose of all outstanding motions prior to the beginning of the hearing.

§ 308.528 Sanctions.

(a) The ALJ may sanction a person, including any party or representative for:

(1) Failing to comply with an order, rule, or procedure governing the proceeding;

(2) Failing to prosecute or defend an action; or

(3) Engaging in other misconduct that interferes with the speedy, orderly, or fair conduct of the hearing.

(b) Any such sanction, including but not limited to, those listed in paragraphs (c), (d), and (e) of this section, must reasonably relate to the severity and nature of the failure or misconduct.

(c) When a party fails to comply with an order, including an order for taking a deposition, the production of evidence within the party's control, or a request for admission, the ALJ may:

(1) Draw an inference in favor of the requesting party with regard to the information sought;

§ 308.529

(2) In the case of requests for admission, deem each matter of which an admission is requested to be admitted;

(3) Prohibit the party failing to comply with such order from introducing evidence concerning, or otherwise relying upon, testimony relating to the information sought; and

(4) Strike any part of the related pleading or other submissions of the party failing to comply with such request.

(d) If a party fails to prosecute or defend an action under this subpart commenced by service of a notice of hearing, the ALJ may dismiss the action or may issue an initial decision imposing penalties and assessments.

(e) The ALJ may refuse to consider any motion, request, response, brief, or other document which is not filed in a timely fashion.

§ 308.529 The hearing and burden of proof.

(a) The ALJ will conduct a hearing on the record in order to determine whether the defendant is liable for a civil penalty or assessment under § 308.502 of this subpart, and, if so, the appropriate amount of any such civil penalty or assessment considering any aggravating or mitigating factors.

(b) The FDIC must prove defendant's liability and any aggravating factors by a preponderance of the evidence.

(c) The defendant must prove any affirmative defenses and any mitigating factors by a preponderance of the evidence.

(d) The hearing will be open to the public unless otherwise ordered by the ALJ for good cause shown.

§ 308.530 Determining the amount of penalties and assessments.

(a) In determining an appropriate amount of civil penalties and assessments, the ALJ and the Board, upon appeal, should evaluate any circumstances that mitigate or aggravate the violation and should articulate in their opinions the reasons that support the penalties and assessments they impose. Because of the intangible costs of fraud, the expense of investigating such conduct, and the need to deter others who might be similarly tempted, ordinarily double damages and a significant civil penalty should be imposed.

(b) Although not exhaustive, the following factors are among those that may influence the ALJ and the Board in determining the amount of penalties and assessments to impose with respect to the misconduct (*i.e.*, the false, fictitious, or fraudulent claims or statement) charged in the complaint:

(1) The number of false, fictitious, or fraudulent claims or statements;

(2) The time period over which such claims or statements were made;

(3) The degree of the defendant's culpability with respect to the misconduct;

(4) The amount of money or the value of the property, services, or benefit falsely claimed;

(5) The value of the government's actual loss as a result of the misconduct, including foreseeable consequential damages and the costs of investigation;

(6) The relationship of the amount imposed as civil penalties to the amount of the government's loss;

(7) The potential or actual impact of the misconduct upon national defense, public health or safety, or public confidence in the management of government programs and operations, including particularly the impact on the intended beneficiaries of such programs;

(8) Whether the defendant has engaged in a pattern of the same or similar misconduct;

(9) Whether the defendant attempted to conceal the misconduct;

(10) The degree to which the defendant has involved others in the misconduct or in concealing it;

(11) Where the misconduct of employees or agents is imputed to the defendant, the extent to which the defendant's practices fostered or attempted to preclude such misconduct;

(12) Whether the defendant cooperated in or obstructed an investigation of the misconduct;

(13) Whether the defendant assisted in identifying and prosecuting other wrongdoers;

(14) The complexity of the program or transaction, and the degree of the defendant's sophistication with respect to it, including the extent of the defendant's prior participation in the program or in a similar transaction;

Federal Deposit Insurance Corporation § 308.533

(15) Whether the defendant has been found, in any criminal, civil, or administrative proceeding to have engaged in similar misconduct or to have dealt dishonestly with the Government of the United States or of a state, directly or indirectly; and

(16) The need to deter the defendant and others from engaging in the same or similar misconduct.

(c) Nothing in this section will be construed to limit the ALJ or the Board from considering any other factors that in any given case may mitigate or aggravate the offense for which penalties and assessments are imposed.

(d) Civil money penalties that are assessed pursuant to this subpart are subject to adjustment on a four-year basis to account for inflation as required by section 4 of the Federal Civil Penalties Inflation Adjustment Act of 1990, as amended (codified at 28 U.S.C. 2461, note) (*see also* 12 CFR 308.132(c)(3)(xv)).

§ 308.531 Location of hearing.

(a) The hearing may be held:

(1) In any judicial district of the United States in which the defendant resides or transacts business;

(2) In any judicial district of the United States in which the claim or statement at issue was made; or

(3) In such other place as may be agreed upon by the defendant and the ALJ.

(b) Each party will have the opportunity to present argument with respect to the location of the hearing.

(c) The hearing will be held at the place and at the time ordered by the ALJ.

§ 308.532 Witnesses.

(a) Except as provided in paragraph (b) of this section, testimony at the hearing will be given orally by witnesses under oath or affirmation.

(b) At the discretion of the ALJ, testimony may be admitted in the form of a written statement or deposition. The party offering a written statement must provide all other parties with a copy of the written statement along with the last known address of the witness. Sufficient time must be allowed for other parties to subpoena the witness for cross-examination at the hearing. Prior written statements and deposition transcripts of witnesses identified to testify at the hearing must be exchanged as provided in § 308.521(a) of this subpart.

(c) The ALJ will exercise reasonable control over the mode and order of interrogating witnesses and presenting evidence so as to:

(1) Make the interrogation and presentation effective for the ascertainment of the truth;

(2) Avoid needless consumption of time; and

(3) Protect witnesses from harassment or undue embarrassment.

(d) The ALJ will permit the parties to conduct such cross-examination as may be required for a full and true disclosure of the facts.

(e) At the discretion of the ALJ, a witness may be cross-examined on matters relevant to the proceeding without regard to the scope of his or her direct examination. To the extent permitted by the ALJ, cross-examination on matters outside the scope of direct examination will be conducted in the manner of direct examination and may proceed by leading questions only if the witness is a hostile witness, an adverse party, or a witness identified with an adverse party.

(f) Upon motion of any party, the ALJ will order witnesses excluded so that they cannot hear the testimony of other witnesses. This rule does not authorize exclusion of:

(1) A party who is an individual;

(2) In the case of a party that is not an individual, an officer or employee of the party appearing for the entity pro se or designated by the party's representative; or

(3) An individual whose presence is shown by a party to be essential to the presentation of its case, including an individual employed by the Corporation engaged in assisting the representative for the Corporation.

§ 308.533 Evidence.

(a) The ALJ will determine the admissibility of evidence.

(b) Except as provided in this subpart, the ALJ will not be bound by the Federal Rules of Evidence (28 U.S.C. App.). However, the ALJ may apply the

Federal Rules of Evidence where appropriate, e.g., to exclude unreliable evidence.

(c) The ALJ will exclude irrelevant and immaterial evidence.

(d) Although relevant, evidence may be excluded if its probative value is substantially outweighed by the danger of unfair prejudice, confusion of the issues, or by considerations of undue delay or needless presentation of cumulative evidence.

(e) Although relevant, evidence may be excluded if it is privileged under federal law.

(f) Evidence concerning offers of compromise or settlement will be inadmissible to the extent provided in rule 408 of the Federal Rules of Evidence.

(g) The ALJ will permit the parties to introduce rebuttal witnesses and evidence.

(h) All documents and other evidence offered or taken for the record must be open to examination by all parties, unless otherwise ordered by the ALJ pursuant to § 308.523 of this subpart.

§ 308.534 The record.

(a) The hearing will be recorded by audio or videotape and transcribed. Transcripts may be obtained following the hearing from the ALJ at a cost not to exceed the actual cost of duplication.

(b) The transcript of testimony, exhibits, and other evidence admitted at the hearing, and all papers and requests filed in the proceeding constitute the record for the decision by the ALJ and the Board.

(c) The record may be inspected and copied (upon payment of a reasonable fee) by anyone, unless otherwise ordered by the ALJ pursuant to § 308.523 of this subpart.

§ 308.535 Post-hearing briefs.

The ALJ may require the parties to file post-hearing briefs. In any event, any party may file a post-hearing brief. The ALJ will fix the time for filing such briefs, not to exceed 60 days from the date the parties receive the transcript of the hearing or, if applicable, the stipulated record. Such briefs may be accompanied by proposed findings of fact and conclusions of law. The ALJ may permit the parties to file reply briefs.

§ 308.536 Initial decision.

(a) The ALJ will issue an initial decision based only on the record, which will contain findings of fact, conclusions of law, and the amount of any penalties and assessments imposed.

(b) The findings of fact will include a finding on each of the following issues:

(1) Whether the claims or statements identified in the complaint, or any portions of such claims or statements, violate § 308.502 of this subpart; and

(2) If the person is liable for penalties or assessments, the appropriate amount of any such penalties or assessments considering any mitigating or aggravating factors that he or she finds in the case, such as those described in § 308.530 of this subpart.

(c) The ALJ will promptly serve the initial decision on all parties within 90 days after the time for submission of post-hearing briefs and reply briefs (if permitted) has expired. The ALJ will at the same time serve all parties with a statement describing the right of any defendant determined to be liable for a civil penalty or assessment to file a motion for reconsideration with the ALJ or a notice of appeal with the Board. If the ALJ fails to meet the deadline contained in this paragraph, he or she will notify the parties of the reason for the delay and will set a new deadline.

(d) Unless the initial decision of the ALJ is timely appealed to the Board, or a motion for reconsideration of the initial decision is timely filed, the initial decision will constitute the final decision of the Board and will be final and binding on the parties 30 days after it is issued by the ALJ.

§ 308.537 Reconsideration of initial decision.

(a) Except as provided in paragraph (d) of this section, any party may file a motion for reconsideration of the initial decision within 20 days of receipt of the initial decision. If service is made by mail, receipt will be presumed to be 5 days from the date of mailing in the absence of proof to the contrary.

(b) Every motion for reconsideration must set forth the matters claimed to

Federal Deposit Insurance Corporation § 308.539

have been erroneously decided and the nature of the alleged errors. The motion must be accompanied by a supporting brief.

(c) Responses to the motions will be allowed only upon order of the ALJ.

(d) No party may file a motion for reconsideration of an initial decision that has been revised in response to a previous motion for reconsideration.

(e) The ALJ may dispose of a motion for reconsideration by denying it or by issuing a revised initial decision.

(f) If the ALJ denies a motion for reconsideration, the initial decision will constitute the final decision of the FDIC and will be final and binding on all parties 30 days after the ALJ denies the motion, unless the final decision is timely appealed to the Board in accordance with § 308.538 of this subpart.

(g) If the ALJ issues a revised initial decision, that decision will constitute the final decision of the FDIC and will be final and binding on the parties 30 days after it is issued, unless it is timely appealed to the Board in accordance with § 308.538 of this subpart.

§ 308.538 Appeal to the Board of Directors.

(a) Any defendant who has filed a timely answer and who is determined in an initial decision to be liable for a civil penalty or assessment may appeal such decision to the Board by filing a notice of appeal with the Board in accordance with this section.

(b)(1) No notice of appeal may be filed until the time period for filing a motion for reconsideration under § 308.537 of this subpart has expired.

(2) If a motion for reconsideration is timely filed, a notice of appeal must be filed within 30 days after the ALJ denies the motion or issues a revised initial decision, whichever applies.

(3) If no motion for reconsideration is timely filed, a notice of appeal must be filed within 30 days after the ALJ issues the initial decision.

(4) The Board may extend the initial 30-day period for an additional 30 days if the defendant files with the Board a request for an extension within the initial 30-day period and shows good cause.

(c) If the defendant files a timely notice of appeal with the Board, the ALJ will forward the record of the proceeding to the Board.

(d) A notice of appeal will be accompanied by a written brief specifying exceptions to the initial decision and reasons supporting the exceptions.

(e) The representative for the Corporation may file a brief in opposition to exceptions within 30 days of receiving the notice of appeal and accompanying brief.

(f) There is no right to appear personally before the Board.

(g) There is no right to appeal any interlocutory ruling by the ALJ.

(h) In reviewing the initial decision, the Board will not consider any objection that was not raised before the ALJ unless a demonstration is made of extraordinary circumstances causing the failure to raise the objection.

(i) If any party demonstrates to the satisfaction of the Board that additional evidence not presented at such hearing is material and that there were reasonable grounds for the failure to present such evidence at such hearing, the Board will remand the matter to the ALJ for consideration of such additional evidence.

(j) The Board may affirm, reduce, reverse, compromise, remand, or settle any penalty or assessment determined by the ALJ in any initial decision.

(k) The Board will promptly serve each party to the appeal with a copy of the decision of the Board and a statement describing the right of any person determined to be liable for a penalty or an assessment to seek judicial review.

(l) Unless a petition for review is filed as provided in 31 U.S.C. 3805 after a defendant has exhausted all administrative remedies under this subpart and within 60 days after the date on which the Board serves the defendant with a copy of the Board's decision, a determination that a defendant is liable under § 308.502 of this subpart is final and is not subject to judicial review.

§ 308.539 Stays ordered by the Department of Justice.

If at any time the Attorney General or an Assistant Attorney General designated by the Attorney General transmits to the Board a written finding

§ 308.540

that continuation of the administrative process described in this subpart with respect to a claim or statement may adversely affect any pending or potential criminal or civil action related to such claim or statement, the Board will stay the process immediately. The Board may order the process resumed only upon receipt of the written authorization of the Attorney General.

§ 308.540 Stay pending appeal.

(a) An initial decision is stayed automatically pending disposition of a motion for reconsideration or of an appeal to the Board.

(b) No administrative stay is available following a final decision of the Board.

§ 308.541 Judicial review.

Section 3805 of Title 31, United States Code, authorizes judicial review by an appropriate United States District Court of a final decision of the Board imposing penalties or assessments under this subpart and specifies the procedures for such review.

§ 308.542 Collection of civil penalties and assessments.

Sections 3806 and 3808(b) of Title 31, United States Code, authorize actions for collection of civil penalties and assessments imposed under this subpart and specify the procedures for such actions.

§ 308.543 Right to administrative offset.

The amount of any penalty or assessment which has become final, or for which a judgment has been entered under § 308.541 or § 308.542 of this subpart, or any amount agreed upon in a compromise or settlement under § 308.545 of this subpart, may be collected by administrative offset under 31 U.S.C. 3716, except that an administrative offset may not be made under this section against a refund of an overpayment of federal taxes, then or later owing by the United States to the defendant.

§ 308.544 Deposit in Treasury of United States.

All amounts collected pursuant to this subpart will be deposited as miscellaneous receipts in the Treasury of the United States, except as provided in 31 U.S.C. 3806(g).

§ 308.545 Compromise or settlement.

(a) Parties may make offers of compromise or settlement at any time.

(b) The reviewing official has the exclusive authority to compromise or settle a case under this subpart at any time after the date on which the reviewing official is permitted to issue a complaint and before the date on which the ALJ issues an initial decision.

(c) The Board has exclusive authority to compromise or settle a case under this subpart any time after the date on which the ALJ issues an initial decision, except during the pendency of any review under § 308.541 of this subpart or during the pendency of any action to collect penalties and assessments under § 308.542 of this subpart.

(d) The Attorney General has exclusive authority to compromise or settle a case under this subpart during the pendency of any review under § 308.541 of this subpart or of any action to recover penalties and assessments under 31 U.S.C. 3806.

(e) The investigating official may recommend settlement terms to the reviewing official, the Board, or the Attorney General, as appropriate. The reviewing official may recommend settlement terms to the Board, or the Attorney General, as appropriate.

(f) Any compromise or settlement must be in writing.

§ 308.546 Limitations.

(a) The notice of hearing with respect to a claim or statement will be served in the manner specified in § 308.507 of this subpart within 6 years after the date on which such claim or statement is made.

(b) If the defendant fails to file a timely answer, service of notice under § 308.509(b) of this subpart will be deemed a notice of a hearing for purposes of this section.

(c) The statute of limitations may be extended by agreement of the parties.

Federal Deposit Insurance Corporation § 308.602

Subpart U—Removal, Suspension, and Debarment of Accountants From Performing Audit Services

SOURCE: 68 FR 48270, Aug. 13, 2003, unless otherwise noted.

§ 308.600 Scope.

This subpart, which implements section 36(g)(4) of the FDIA (12 U.S.C. 1831m(g)(4)), provides rules and procedures for the removal, suspension, or debarment of independent public accountants and accounting firms from performing independent audit and attestation services required by section 36 of the FDIA (12 U.S.C. 1831m) for insured depository institutions for which the FDIC is the appropriate Federal banking agency.

§ 308.601 Definitions.

As used in this subpart, the following terms shall have the meaning given below unless the context requires otherwise:

(a) *Accounting firm* means a corporation, proprietorship, partnership, or other business firm providing audit services.

(b) *Audit services* means any service required to be performed by an independent public accountant by section 36 of the FDIA and 12 CFR part 363, including attestation services.

(c) *Independent public accountant* (accountant) means any individual who performs or participates in providing audit services.

§ 308.602 Removal, suspension, or debarment.

(a) *Good cause for removal, suspension, or debarment*—(1) *Individuals.* The Board of Directors may remove, suspend, or debar an independent public accountant under section 36 of the FDIA from performing audit services for insured depository institutions for which the FDIC is the appropriate Federal banking agency if, after service of a notice of intention and opportunity for hearing in the matter, the Board of Directors finds that the accountant:

(i) Lacks the requisite qualifications to perform audit services;

(ii) Has knowingly or recklessly engaged in conduct that results in a violation of applicable professional standards, including those standards and conflicts of interest provisions applicable to accountants through the Sarbanes-Oxley Act of 2002 (Pub. L. 107-204, 116 Stat. 745 (2002)) (Sarbanes-Oxley Act) and developed by the Public Company Accounting Oversight Board and the Securities and Exchange Commission;

(iii) Has engaged in negligent conduct in the form of:

(A) A single instance of highly unreasonable conduct that results in a violation of applicable professional standards in circumstances in which an accountant knows, or should know, that heightened scrutiny is warranted; or

(B) Repeated instances of unreasonable conduct, each resulting in a violation of applicable professional standards, that indicate a lack of competence to perform audit services;

(iv) Has knowingly or recklessly given false or misleading information, or knowingly or recklessly participated in any way in the giving of false or misleading information, to the FDIC or any officer or employee of the FDIC;

(v) Has engaged in, or aided and abetted, a material and knowing or reckless violation of any provision of the Federal banking or securities laws or the rules and regulations thereunder, or any other law;

(vi) Has been removed, suspended, or debarred from practice before any Federal or state agency regulating the banking, insurance, or securities industries, other than by an action listed in § 308.603, on grounds relevant to the provision of audit services; or

(vii) Is suspended or debarred for cause from practice as an accountant by any duly constituted licensing authority of any state, possession, commonwealth, or the District of Columbia.

(2) *Accounting firms.* If the Board of Directors determines that there is good cause for the removal, suspension, or debarment of a member or employee of an accounting firm under paragraph (a)(1) of this section, the Board of Directors also may remove, suspend, or debar such firm or one or more offices of such firm. In considering whether to

131

§ 308.602

remove, suspend, or debar an accounting firm or an office thereof, and the term of any sanction against an accounting firm under this section, the Board of Directors may consider, for example:

(i) The gravity, scope, or repetition of the act or failure to act that constitutes good cause for the removal, suspension, or debarment;

(ii) The adequacy of, and adherence to, applicable policies, practices, or procedures for the accounting firm's conduct of its business and the performance of audit services;

(iii) The selection, training, supervision, and conduct of members or employees of the accounting firm involved in the performance of audit services;

(iv) The extent to which managing partners or senior officers of the accounting firm have participated, directly, or indirectly through oversight or review, in the act or failure to act; and

(v) The extent to which the accounting firm has, since the occurrence of the act or failure to act, implemented corrective internal controls to prevent its recurrence.

(3) *Limited scope orders.* An order of removal, suspension (including an immediate suspension), or debarment may, at the discretion of the Board of Directors, be made applicable to a limited number of insured depository institutions for which the FDIC is the appropriate Federal banking agency.

(4) *Remedies not exclusive.* The remedies provided in this subpart are in addition to any other remedies the FDIC may have under any other applicable provision of law, rule, or regulation.

(b) *Proceedings to remove, suspend or debar*—(1) *Initiation of formal removal, suspension, or debarment proceedings.* The Board of Directors may initiate a proceeding to remove, suspend, or debar an accountant or accounting firm from performing audit services by issuing a written notice of intention to take such action that names the individual or firm as a respondent and describes the nature of the conduct that constitutes good cause for such action.

(2) *Hearings under paragraph (b) of this section.* An accountant or firm named as a respondent in the notice issued under paragraph (b)(1) of this section

12 CFR Ch. III (1–1–12 Edition)

may request a hearing on the allegations contained in the notice. Hearings conducted under this paragraph shall be conducted in the same manner as other hearings under the Uniform Rules of Practice and Procedure (12 CFR part 308, subpart A) (Uniform Rules).

(c) *Immediate suspension from performing audit services*—(1) *In general.* If the Board of Directors serves a written notice of intention to remove, suspend, or debar an accountant or accounting firm from performing audit services, the Board of Directors may, with due regard for the public interest and without a preliminary hearing, immediately suspend such accountant or firm from performing audit services for insured depository institutions for which the FDIC is the appropriate Federal banking agency if the Board of Directors:

(i) Has a reasonable basis to believe that the accountant or accounting firm has engaged in conduct (specified in the notice served upon the accountant or accounting firm under paragraph (b)(1) of this section) that would constitute grounds for removal, suspension, or debarment under paragraph (a) of this section;

(ii) Determines that immediate suspension is necessary to avoid immediate harm to an insured depository institution or its depositors or to the depository system as a whole; and

(iii) Serves such respondent with written notice of the immediate suspension.

(2) *Procedures.* An immediate suspension notice issued under this paragraph will become effective upon service. Such suspension will remain in effect until the date the Board of Directors dismisses the charges contained in the notice of intention, or the effective date of a final order of removal, suspension, or debarment issued by the Board of Directors to the respondent.

(3) *Petition to stay.* Any accountant or accounting firm immediately suspended from performing audit services in accordance with paragraph (c)(1) of this section may, within 10 calendar days after service of the notice of immediate suspension, file a petition with the Executive Secretary for a stay of

such immediate suspension. If no petition is filed within 10 calendar days, the immediate suspension shall remain in effect.

(4) *Hearing on petition.* Upon receipt of a stay petition, the Executive Secretary will designate a presiding officer who will fix a place and time (not more than 10 calendar days after receipt of the petition, unless extended at the request of petitioner) at which the immediately suspended party may appear, personally or through counsel, to submit written materials and oral argument. Any FDIC employee engaged in investigative or prosecuting functions for the FDIC in a case may not, in that or a factually related case, serve as a presiding officer or participate or advise in the decision of the presiding officer or of the FDIC, except as witness or counsel in the proceeding. In the sole discretion of the presiding officer, upon a specific showing of compelling need, oral testimony of witnesses also may be presented. Enforcement counsel may represent the agency at the hearing. In hearings held pursuant to this paragraph there shall be no discovery, and the provisions of §§ 308.6 through 308.12, § 308.16, and § 308.21 of the Uniform Rules will apply.

(5) *Decision on petition.* Within 30 calendar days after the hearing, the presiding officer will issue a decision. The presiding officer will grant a stay upon a demonstration that a substantial likelihood exists of the respondent's success on the issues raised by the notice of intention and that, absent such relief, the respondent will suffer immediate and irreparable injury, loss, or damage. In the absence of such a demonstration, the presiding officer will notify the parties that the immediate suspension will be continued pending the completion of the administrative proceedings pursuant to the notice of intention. The presiding officer will serve a copy of the decision on, and simultaneously certify the record to, the Executive Secretary.

(6) *Review of presiding officer's decision.* The parties may seek review of the presiding officer's decision by filing a petition for review with the Executive Secretary within 10 calendar days after service of the decision. Replies must be filed within 10 calendar days after the petition filing date. Upon receipt of a petition for review and any reply, the Executive Secretary will promptly certify the entire record to the Board of Directors. Within 60 calendar days of the Executive Secretary's certification, the Board of Directors will issue an order notifying the affected party whether or not the immediate suspension should be continued or reinstated. The order will state the basis of the Board's decision.

§ 308.603 Automatic removal, suspension, and debarment.

(a) An independent public accountant or accounting firm may not perform audit services for insured depository institutions for which the FDIC is the appropriate Federal banking agency if the accountant or firm:

(1) Is subject to a final order of removal, suspension, or debarment (other than a limited scope order) issued by the Board of Governors of the Federal Reserve System, the Office of the Comptroller of the Currency, or the Office of Thrift Supervision under section 36 of the FDIA;

(2) Is subject to a temporary suspension or permanent revocation of registration or a temporary or permanent suspension or bar from further association with any registered public accounting firm issued by the Public Company Accounting Oversight Board or the Securities and Exchange Commission under sections 105(c)(4)(A) or (B) of the Sarbanes-Oxley Act (15 U.S.C. 7215(c)(4)(A) or (B)); or

(3) Is subject to an order of suspension or denial of the privilege of appearing or practicing before the Securities and Exchange Commission.

(b) Upon written request, the FDIC, for good cause shown, may grant written permission to such accountant or firm to perform audit services for insured depository institutions for which the FDIC is the appropriate Federal banking agency. The written request must comply with the requirements of § 303.3 of this chapter.

§ 308.604 Notice of removal, suspension, or debarment.

(a) *Notice to the public.* Upon the issuance of a final order for removal,

§ 308.605

suspension, or debarment of an independent public accountant or accounting firm from providing audit services, the FDIC will make the order publicly available and provide notice of the order to the other Federal banking agencies.

(b) *Notice to the FDIC by accountants and firms.* An accountant or accounting firm that provides audit services to any insured depository institution for which the FDIC is the appropriate Federal banking agency must provide the FDIC with written notice of:

(1) any currently effective order or other action described in §§ 308.602(a)(1)(vi) through (a)(1)(vii) or §§ 308.603(a)(2) through (a)(3); and

(2) any currently effective action by the Public Company Accounting Oversight Board under sections 105(c)(4)(C) or (G) of the Sarbanes-Oxley Act (15 U.S.C. 7215(c)(4)(C) or (G)).

(c) *Timing and place of notice.* Written notice required by this paragraph shall be given no later than 15 calendar days following the effective date of an order or action, or 15 calendar days before an accountant or accounting firm accepts an engagement to provide audit services, whichever date is earlier. The written notice must be filed by the independent public accountant or accounting firm with the FDIC, Accounting and Securities Disclosure Section, 550 17th Street, NW., Washington, DC 20429.

[68 FR 48270, Aug. 13, 2003, as amended at 74 FR 32245, July 7, 2009; 74 FR 35745, July 20, 2009]

§ 308.605 Application for reinstatement.

(a) *Form of petition.* Unless otherwise ordered by the Board of Directors, an application for reinstatement by an independent public accountant, an accounting firm, or an office of a firm that was removed, suspended, or debarred under § 308.602 may be made in writing at any time. The application must comply with the requirements of § 303.3 of this chapter.

(b) *Procedure.* An applicant for reinstatement under this section may, in the sole discretion of the Board of Directors, be afforded a hearing. In reinstatement proceedings, the person seeking reinstatement shall bear the burden of going forward with an application and proving the grounds asserted in support of the application, and the Board of Directors may, in its sole discretion, direct that any reinstatement proceeding be limited to written submissions. The removal, suspension, or debarment shall continue until the Board of Directors, for good cause shown, has reinstated the applicant or until the suspension period has expired. The filing of an application for reinstatement will not stay the effectiveness of the removal, suspension, or debarment of an accountant or firm.

PART 309—DISCLOSURE OF INFORMATION

Sec.
309.1 Purpose and scope.
309.2 Definitions.
309.3 Federal Register publication.
309.4 Publicly available records.
309.5 Procedures for requesting records.
309.6 Disclosure of exempt records.
309.7 Service of process.

AUTHORITY: 5 U.S.C. 552; 12 U.S.C. 1819 "Seventh" and "Tenth."

SOURCE: 60 FR 61465, Nov. 30, 1995, unless otherwise noted.

§ 309.1 **Purpose and scope.**

This part sets forth the basic policies of the Federal Deposit Insurance Corporation regarding information it maintains and the procedures for obtaining access to such information, including disclosure of information transferred to Federal Deposit Insurance Corporation from the Office of Thrift Supervision pursuant to section 312 and 323 of the Dodd-Frank Wall Street Reform and Consumer Protection Act, Public Law 111-203. Section 309.2 sets forth definitions applicable to this part 309. Section 309.3 describes the types of information and documents typically published in the FEDERAL REGISTER. Section 309.4 explains how to access public records maintained on the Federal Deposit Insurance Corporation's World Wide Web page and in the Federal Deposit Insurance Corporation's Public Information Center or "PIC," and describes the categories of records generally found there. Section 309.5 implements the Freedom of Information Act (5 U.S.C.

Federal Deposit Insurance Corporation

§ 309.3

552). Section 309.6 authorizes the discretionary disclosure of exempt records under certain limited circumstances. Section 309.7 outlines procedures for serving a subpoena or other legal process to obtain information maintained by the FDIC.

[76 FR 35965, June 21, 2011]

§ 309.2 Definitions.

For purposes of this part:

(a) The term *depository institution*, as used in § 309.6, includes depository institutions that have applied to the Corporation for federal deposit insurance, closed depository institutions, presently operating federally insured depository institutions, foreign banks, branches of foreign banks, and all affiliates of any of the foregoing.

(b) The terms *Corporation* or *FDIC* mean the Federal Deposit Insurance Corporation.

(c) The words *disclose* or *disclosure*, as used in § 309.6, mean to give access to a record, whether by producing the written record or by oral discussion of its contents. Where the Corporation employee authorized to release Corporation documents makes a determination that furnishing copies of the documents is necessary, the words *disclose* or *disclosure* include the furnishing of copies of documents or records. In addition, *disclose* or *disclosure* as used in § 309.6 is synonymous with the term *transfer* as used in the Right to Financial Privacy Act of 1978 (12 U.S.C. 3401 et seq.).

(d) The term *examination* includes, but is not limited to, formal and informal investigations of irregularities involving suspected violations of federal or state civil or criminal laws, or unsafe and unsound practices as well as such other investigations as may be conducted pursuant to law.

(e) The term *record* includes records, files, documents, reports, correspondence, books, and accounts, or any portion thereof, in any form the FDIC regularly maintains them.

(f) The term *report of examination* includes, but is not limited to, examination reports resulting from examinations of depository institutions conducted jointly by Corporation examiners and state banking authority examiners or other federal financial institution examiners, as well as reports resulting from examinations conducted solely by Corporation examiners. The term also includes compliance examination reports.

(g) The term *customer financial records*, as used in § 309.6, means an original of, a copy of, or information known to have been derived from, any record held by a depository institution pertaining to a customer's relationship with the depository institution but does not include any record that contains information not identified with or identifiable as being derived from the financial records of a particular customer. The term *customer* as used in § 309.6 refers to individuals or partnerships of five or fewer persons.

(h) The term *Director of the Division having primary authority* includes Deputies to the Chairman and directors of FDIC Divisions and Offices that create, maintain custody, or otherwise have primary responsibility for the handling of FDIC records or information.

[60 FR 61465, Nov. 30, 1995, as amended at 63 FR 16404, Apr. 3, 1998]

§ 309.3 Federal Register publication.

The FDIC publishes the following information in the FEDERAL REGISTER for the guidance of the public:

(a) Descriptions of its central and field organization and the established places at which, the officers from whom, and the methods whereby, the public may secure information, make submittals or requests, or obtain decisions;

(b) Statements of the general course and method by which its functions are channeled and determined, including the nature and requirements of all formal and informal procedures available;

(c) Rules of procedure, descriptions of forms available or the places at which forms may be obtained, and instructions as to the scope and contents of all papers, reports or examinations;

(d) Substantive rules of general applicability adopted as authorized by law, and statements of general policy or interpretations of general applicability formulated and adopted by the FDIC;

(e) Every amendment, revision or repeal of the foregoing; and

§ 309.4

(f) General notices of proposed rulemaking.

§ 309.4 Publicly available records.

(a) *Records available on the FDIC's World Wide Web page*—(1) *Discretionary release of documents.* The FDIC encourages the public to explore the wealth of resources available on the FDIC's World Wide Web page, located at: *http://www.fdic.gov.* The FDIC has elected to publish a broad range of materials on its World Wide Web page, including consumer guides; financial and statistical information of interest to the banking industry; and information concerning the FDIC's responsibilities and structure.

(2) *Documents required to be made available via computer telecommunications.* (i) The following types of documents created on or after November 1, 1996, and required to be made available through computer telecommunications, may be found on the FDIC's World Wide Web page located at: *http://www.fdic.gov:*

(A) Final opinions, including concurring and dissenting opinions, as well as final orders and written agreements, made in the adjudication of cases;

(B) Statements of policy and interpretations adopted by the Board of Directors that are not published in the FEDERAL REGISTER;

(C) Administrative staff manuals and instructions to staff that affect the public;

(D) Copies of all records released to any person under § 309.5 that, because of the nature of their subject matter, the FDIC has determined are likely to be the subject of subsequent requests;

(E) A general index of the records referred to in paragraph (a)(2)(i)(D) of this section.

(ii) To the extent permitted by law, the FDIC may delete identifying details when it makes available or publishes a final opinion, final order, statement of policy, interpretation or staff manual or instruction. If redaction is necessary, the FDIC will, to the extent technically feasible, indicate the amount of material deleted at the place in the record where such deletion is made unless that indication in and of itself will jeopardize the purpose for the redaction.

(b) *Public Information Center.* The FDIC maintains a Public Information Center or "PIC" that contains Corporate records that the Freedom of Information Act requires be made available for regular inspection and copying, as well as any records or information the FDIC, in its discretion, has regularly made available to the public. The PIC has extensive materials of interest to the public, including many Reports, Summaries and Manuals used or published by the Corporation that are made available, by appointment, for inspection and copying. The PIC is open from 9:00 AM to 4:00 PM, Monday through Friday, excepting federal holidays. It is located at 3501 North Fairfax Drive, Room E-1005, Arlington, VA 22226. The PIC may be reached during business hours by calling 1-(877) 275-3342 or 1-(703) 562-2000.

(c) *Applicable fees.* (i) If applicable, fees for furnishing records under this section are as set forth in § 309.5(f) except that all categories of requesters shall be charged duplication costs.

(ii) Information on the FDIC's World Wide Web page is available to the public without charge. If, however, information available on the FDIC's World Wide Web page is provided pursuant to a Freedom of Information Act request processed under § 309.5, then fees apply and will be assessed pursuant to § 309.5(f).

[63 FR 16404, Apr. 3, 1998, as amended at 76 FR 35965, June 21, 2011]

§ 309.5 Procedures for requesting records.

(a) *Definitions.* For purposes of this section:

(1) *Commercial use request* means a request from or on behalf of a requester who seeks records for a use or purpose that furthers the commercial, trade, or profit interests of the requester or the person on whose behalf the request is made. In determining whether a request falls within this category, the FDIC will determine the use to which a requester will put the records requested and seek additional information as it deems necessary.

(2) *Direct costs* means those expenditures the FDIC actually incurs in searching for, duplicating, and, in the

Federal Deposit Insurance Corporation § 309.5

case of commercial requesters, reviewing records in response to a request for records.

(3) *Duplication* means the process of making a copy of a record necessary to respond to a request for *records* or for inspection of original records that contain exempt material or that cannot otherwise be directly inspected. Such copies can take the form of paper copy, microfilm, audiovisual records, or machine readable records (e.g., magnetic tape or computer disk).

(4) *Educational institution* means a preschool, a public or private elementary or secondary school, an institution of undergraduate or graduate higher education, an institution of professional education, and an institution of vocational education, which operates a program or programs of scholarly research.

(5) *Noncommercial scientific institution* means an institution that is not operated on a commercial basis as that term is defined in paragraph (a)(1) of this section, and which is operated solely for the purpose of conducting scientific research, the results of which are not intended to promote any particular product or industry.

(6) *Representative of the news media* means any person primarily engaged in gathering news for, or a free-lance journalist who can demonstrate a reasonable expectation of having his or her work product published or broadcast by, an entity that is organized and operated to publish or broadcast news to the public. The term news means information that is about current events or that would be of current interest to the general public.

(7) *Review* means the process of examining records located in response to a request for records to determine whether any portion of any record is permitted to be withheld as exempt information. It includes processing any record for disclosure, e.g., doing all that is necessary to excise them or otherwise prepare them for release.

(8) *Search* includes all time spent looking for material that is responsive to a request, including page-by-page or line-by-line identification of material within records. Searches may be done manually and/or by computer using existing programming.

(b) *Making a request for records.* (1) The request shall be submitted in writing to the Freedom of Information Act/Privacy Act Group ("FOIA/PA Group"), Legal Division :

(i) By completing the online request form located on the FDIC's World Wide Web page, found at: *http://www.fdic.gov;*

(ii) By facsimile clearly marked Freedom of Information Act Request to the FOIA/PA Group: (703) 562-2797; or

(iii) By sending a letter to: Federal Deposit Insurance Corporation, Attn: FOIA/PA Group, 550 17th Street, NW., Washington, DC 20429.

(2) The request shall contain the following information:

(i) The name and address of the requester, an electronic mail address, if available, and the telephone number at which the requester may be reached during normal business hours;

(ii) Whether the requester is an educational institution, noncommercial scientific institution, or news media representative;

(iii) A statement agreeing to pay the applicable fees, or a statement identifying a maximum fee that is acceptable to the requester, or a request for a waiver or reduction of fees that satisfies paragraph (f)(1)(x) of this section; and

(iv) The preferred form and format of any responsive information requested, if other than paper copies.

(3) A request for identifiable records shall reasonably describe the records in a way that enables the FDIC's staff to identify and produce the records with reasonable effort and without unduly burdening or significantly interfering with any of the FDIC's operations.

(c) *Defective requests.* The FDIC need not accept or process a request that does not reasonably describe the records requested or that does not otherwise comply with the requirements of this part. The FDIC may return a defective request, specifying the deficiency. The requester may submit a corrected request, which will be treated as a new request.

(d) *Processing requests*—(1) *Receipt of requests.* Upon receipt of any request that satisfies paragraph (b) of this section, the FOIA/PA Group, Legal Division shall assign the request to the appropriate processing track pursuant to

§ 309.5

this section. The date of receipt for any request, including one that is addressed incorrectly or that is referred by another agency, is the date the FOIA/PA Group actually receives the request.

(2) *Multitrack processing.* (i) The FDIC provides different levels of processing for categories of requests under this part. Requests for records that are readily identifiable by the FOIA/PA Group, and that have already been cleared for public release may qualify for fast-track processing. All other requests shall be handled under normal processing procedures, unless expedited processing has been granted pursuant to paragraph (d)(3) of this section.

(ii) The FDIC will make the determination whether a request qualifies for fast-track processing. A requester may contact the FOIA/PA Group to learn whether a particular request has been assigned to fast-track processing. If the request has not qualified for fast-track processing, the requester will be given an opportunity to refine the request in order to qualify for fast-track processing. Changes made to requests to obtain faster processing must be in writing.

(3) *Expedited processing.* (i) Where a person requesting expedited access to records has demonstrated a compelling need for the records, or where the FDIC has determined to expedite the response, the FDIC shall process the request as soon as practicable. To show a compelling need for expedited processing, the requester shall provide a statement demonstrating that:

(A) The failure to obtain the records on an expedited basis could reasonably be expected to pose an imminent threat to the life or physical safety of an individual; or

(B) The requester can establish that they are primarily engaged in information dissemination as their main professional occupation or activity, and there is urgency to inform the public of the government activity involved in the request; and

(C) The requester's statement must be certified to be true and correct to the best of the person's knowledge and belief and explain in detail the basis for requesting expedited processing.

(ii) The formality of the certification required to obtain expedited treatment may be waived by the FDIC as a matter of administrative discretion.

(4) A requester seeking expedited processing will be notified whether expedited processing has been granted within ten (10) working days of the receipt of the request. If the request for expedited processing is denied, the requester may file an appeal pursuant to the procedures set forth in paragraph (h) of this section, and the FDIC shall respond to the appeal within ten (10) working days after receipt of the appeal.

(5) *Priority of responses.* Consistent with sound administrative process the FDIC processes requests in the order they are received in the separate processing tracks. However, in the agency's discretion, or upon a court order in a matter to which the FDIC is a party, a particular request may be processed out of turn.

(6) *Notification.* (i) The time for response to requests will be twenty (20) working days except:

(A) In the case of expedited treatment under paragraph (d)(3) of this section;

(B) Where the running of such time is suspended for the calculation of a cost estimate for the requester if the FDIC determines that the processing of the request may exceed the requester's maximum fee provision or if the charges are likely to exceed $250 as provided for in paragraph (f)(1)(v) of this section;

(C) Where the running of such time is suspended for the payment of fees pursuant to the paragraphs (d)(6)(i)(B) and (f)(1) of this section; or

(D) In unusual circumstances, as defined in 5 U.S.C. 552(a)(6)(B) and further described in paragraph (d)(6)(iii) of this section.

(ii) In unusual circumstances as referred to in paragraph (d)(6)(i)(D) of this section, the time limit may be extended for a period of:

(A) Ten (10) working days as provided by written notice to the requester, setting forth the reasons for the extension and the date on which a determination is expected to be dispatched; or

(B) Such alternative time period as agreed to by the requester or as reasonably determined by the FDIC when the

Federal Deposit Insurance Corporation

§ 309.5

FDIC notifies the requester that the request cannot be processed in the specified time limit.

(iii) Unusual circumstances may arise when:

(A) The records are in facilities, such as field offices or storage centers, that are not located at the FDIC's Washington office;

(B) The records requested are voluminous or are not in close proximity to one another; or

(C) There is a need to consult with another agency or among two or more components of the FDIC having a substantial interest in the determination.

(7) *Response to request.* In response to a request that satisfies the requirements of paragraph (b) of this section, a search shall be conducted of records maintained by the FDIC in existence on the date of receipt of the request, and a review made of any responsive information located. The FDIC shall notify the requester of:

(i) The FDIC's determination of the request;

(ii) The reasons for the determination;

(iii) If the response is a denial of an initial request or if any information is withheld, the FDIC will advise the requester in writing:

(A) If the denial is in part or in whole;

(B) The name and title of each person responsible for the denial (when other than the person signing the notification);

(C) The exemptions relied on for the denial; and

(D) The right of the requester to appeal the denial to the FDIC's General Counsel within 30 business days following receipt of the notification, as specified in paragraph (h) of this section.

(e) *Providing responsive records.* (1) Copies of requested records shall be sent to the requester by regular U.S. mail to the address indicated in the request, unless the requester elects to take delivery of the documents at the FDIC or makes other acceptable arrangements, or the FDIC deems it appropriate to send the documents by another means.

(2) The FDIC shall provide a copy of the record in any form or format requested if the record is readily reproducible by the FDIC in that form or format, but the FDIC need not provide more than one copy of any record to a requester.

(3) By arrangement with the requester, the FDIC may elect to send the responsive records electronically if a substantial portion of the request is in electronic format. If the information requested is made pursuant to the Privacy Act of 1974, 5 U.S.C. 552a, it will not be sent by electronic means unless reasonable security measures can be provided.

(f) *Fees*—(1) *General rules.* (i) Persons requesting records of the FDIC shall be charged for the direct costs of search, duplication, and review as set forth in paragraphs (f)(2) and (f)(3) of this section, unless such costs are less than the FDIC's cost of processing the requester's remittance.

(ii) Requesters will be charged for search and review costs even if responsive records are not located or, if located, are determined to be exempt from disclosure.

(iii) Multiple requests seeking similar or related records from the same requester or group of requesters will be aggregated for the purposes of this section.

(iv) If the FDIC determines that the estimated costs of search, duplication, or review of requested records will exceed the dollar amount specified in the request, or if no dollar amount is specified, the FDIC will advise the requester of the estimated costs (if greater than the FDIC's cost of processing the requester's remittance). The requester must agree in writing to pay the costs of search, duplication, and review prior to the FDIC initiating any records search.

(v) If the FDIC estimates that its search, duplication, and review costs will exceed $250.00, the requester must pay an amount equal to 20 percent of the estimated costs prior to the FDIC initiating any records search.

(vi) The FDIC shall ordinarily collect all applicable fees under the final invoice before releasing copies of requested records to the requester.

(vii) The FDIC may require any requester who has previously failed to pay the charges under this section

§ 309.5

within 30 calendar days of mailing of the invoice to pay in advance the total estimated costs of search, duplication, and review. The FDIC may also require a requester who has any charges outstanding in excess of 30 calendar days following mailing of the invoice to pay the full amount due, or demonstrate that the fee has been paid in full, prior to the FDIC initiating any additional records search.

(viii) The FDIC may begin assessing interest charges on unpaid bills on the 31st day following the day on which the invoice was sent. Interest will be at the rate prescribed in section 3717 of title 31 of the United States Code and will accrue from the date of the invoice.

(ix) The time limit for the FDIC to respond to a request will not begin to run until the FDIC has received the requester's written agreement under paragraph (f)(1)(iv) of this section, and advance payment under paragraph (f)(1) (v) or (vii) of this section, or payment of outstanding charges under paragraph (f)(1)(vii) or (viii) of this section.

(x) As part of the initial request, a requester may ask that the FDIC waive or reduce fees if disclosure of the records is in the public interest because it is likely to contribute significantly to public understanding of the operations or activities of the government and is not primarily in the commercial interest of the requester. Determinations as to a waiver or reduction of fees will be made by the FOIA/PA Group, Legal Division (or designee) and the requester will be notified in writing of his/her determination. A determination not to grant a request for a waiver or reduction of fees under this paragraph may be appealed to the FDIC's General Counsel (or designee) pursuant to the procedure set forth in paragraph (h) of this section.

(2) *Chargeable fees by category of requester.* (i) Commercial use requesters shall be charged search, duplication and review costs.

(ii) Educational institutions, noncommercial scientific institutions and news media representatives shall be charged duplication costs, except for the first 100 pages.

(iii) Requesters not described in paragraph (f)(2) (i) or (ii) of this section shall be charged the full reasonable direct cost of search and duplication, except for the first two hours of search time and first 100 pages of duplication.

(3) *Fee schedule.* The dollar amount of fees which the FDIC may charge to records requesters will be established by the Chief Financial Officer of the FDIC (or designee). The FDIC may charge fees that recoup the full allowable direct costs it incurs. Fees are subject to change as costs change.

(i) *Manual searches for records.* The FDIC will charge for manual searches for records at the basic rate of pay of the employee making the search plus 16 percent to cover employee benefit costs. Where a single class of personnel (e.g., all clerical, all professional, or all executive) is used exclusively, the FDIC, at its discretion, may establish and charge an average rate for the range of grades typically involved.

(ii) *Computer searches for records.* The fee for searches of computerized records is the actual direct cost of the search, including computer time, computer runs, and the operator's time apportioned to the search. The fee for a computer printout is the actual cost. The fees for computer supplies are the actual costs. The FDIC may, at its discretion, establish and charge a fee for computer searches based upon a reasonable FDIC-wide average rate for central processing unit operating costs and the operator's basic rate of pay plus 16 percent to cover employee benefit costs.

(iii) *Duplication of records.* (A) The per-page fee for paper copy reproduction of documents is the average FDIC-wide cost based upon the reasonable direct costs of making such copies.

(B) For other methods of reproduction or duplication, the FDIC will charge the actual direct costs of reproducing or duplicating the documents.

(iv) *Review of records.* The FDIC will charge commercial use requesters for the review of records at the time of processing the initial request to determine whether they are exempt from mandatory disclosure at the basic rate of pay of the employee making the search plus 16 percent to cover employee benefit costs. Where a single class of personnel (e.g., all clerical, all professional, or all executive) is used

Federal Deposit Insurance Corporation § 309.5

exclusively, the FDIC, at its discretion, may establish and charge an average rate for the range of grades typically involved. The FDIC will not charge at the administrative appeal level for review of an exemption already applied. When records or portions of records are withheld in full under an exemption which is subsequently determined not to apply, the FDIC may charge for a subsequent review to determine the applicability of other exemptions not previously considered.

(v) *Other services.* Complying with requests for special services, other than a readily produced electronic form or format, is at the FDIC's discretion. The FDIC may recover the full costs of providing such services to the requester.

(4) *Publication of fee schedule and effective date of changes.* (i) The fee schedule is made available on the FDIC's World Wide Web page, found at *http://www.fdic.gov.*

(ii) The fee schedule will be set forth in the "Notice of Federal Deposit Insurance Corporation Records Fees" issued in December of each year or in such "Interim Notice of Federal Deposit Insurance Corporation Records Fees" as may be issued. Copies of such notices may be obtained at no charge from the Federal Deposit Insurance Corporation, FOIA/PA Group, 550 17th Street NW., Washington, DC 20429, and are available on the FDIC's World Wide Web page as noted in paragraph (f)(4)(i) of this section.

(iii) The fees implemented in the December or Interim Notice will be effective 30 days after issuance.

(5) *Use of contractors.* The FDIC may contract with independent contractors to locate, reproduce, and/or disseminate records; provided, however, that the FDIC has determined that the ultimate cost to the requester will be no greater than it would be if the FDIC performed these tasks itself. In no case will the FDIC contract out responsibilities which the Freedom of Information Act (FOIA) (5 U.S.C. 552) provides that the FDIC alone may discharge, such as determining the applicability of an exemption or whether to waive or reduce fees.

(g) *Exempt information.* A request for records may be denied if the requested record contains information which falls into one or more of the following categories.[1] If the requested record contains both exempt and nonexempt information, the nonexempt portions which may reasonably be segregated from the exempt portions will be released to the requester. If redaction is necessary, the FDIC will, to the extent technically feasible, indicate the amount of material deleted at the place in the record where such deletion is made unless that indication in and of itself will jeopardize the purpose for the redaction. The categories of exempt records are as follows:

(1) Records that are specifically authorized under criteria established by an Executive Order to be kept secret in the interest of national defense or foreign policy and are in fact properly classified pursuant to such Executive Order;

(2) Records related solely to the internal personnel rules and practices of the FDIC;

(3) Records specifically exempted from disclosure by statute, provided that such statute:

(i) Requires that the matters be withheld from the public in such a manner as to leave no discretion on the issue; or

(ii) Establishes particular criteria for withholding or refers to particular types of matters to be withheld;

(4) Trade secrets and commercial or financial information obtained from a person that is privileged or confidential;

(5) Interagency or intra-agency memoranda or letters that would not be available by law to a private party in litigation with the FDIC;

(6) Personnel, medical, and similar files (including financial files) the disclosure of which would constitute a clearly unwarranted invasion of personal privacy;

---

[1] Classification of a record as exempt from disclosure under the provisions of this paragraph (g) shall not be construed as authority to withhold the record if it is otherwise subject to disclosure under the Privacy Act of 1974 (5 U.S.C. 552a) or other federal statute, any applicable regulation of FDIC or any other federal agency having jurisdiction thereof, or any directive or order of any court of competent jurisdiction.

(7) Records compiled for law enforcement purposes, but only to the extent that the production of such law enforcement records:

(i) Could reasonably be expected to interfere with enforcement proceedings;

(ii) Would deprive a person of a right to a fair trial or an impartial adjudication;

(iii) Could reasonably be expected to constitute an unwarranted invasion of personal privacy;

(iv) Could reasonably be expected to disclose the identity of a confidential source, including a state, local, or foreign agency or authority or any private institution which furnished records on a confidential basis;

(v) Would disclose techniques and procedures for law enforcement investigations or prosecutions, or would disclose guidelines for law enforcement investigations or prosecutions if such disclosure could reasonably be expected to risk circumvention of the law; or

(vi) Could reasonably be expected to endanger the life or physical safety of any individual;

(8) Records that are contained in or related to examination, operating, or condition reports prepared by, on behalf of, or for the use of the FDIC or any agency responsible for the regulation or supervision of financial institutions; or

(9) geological and geophysical information and data, including maps, concerning wells.

(h) *Appeals.* (1) Appeals should be addressed to the Federal Deposit Insurance Corporation, Attn: FOIA/PA Group, FDIC, 550 17th Street, NW., Washington, DC 20429.

(2) A person whose initial request for records under this section, or whose request for a waiver of fees under paragraph (f)(1)(x) of this section, has been denied, either in part or in whole, has the right to appeal the denial to the FDIC's General Counsel (or designee) within 30 business days after receipt of notification of the denial. Appeals of denials of initial requests or for a waiver of fees must be in writing and include any additional information relevant to consideration of the appeal.

(3) Except in the case of an appeal for expedited treatment under paragraph (d)(3) of this section, the FDIC will notify the appellant in writing within 20 business days after receipt of the appeal and will state:

(i) Whether it is granted or denied in whole or in part;

(ii) The name and title of each person responsible for the denial (if other than the person signing the notification);

(iii) The exemptions relied upon for the denial in the case of initial requests for records; and

(iv) The right to judicial review of the denial under the FOIA.

(4) If a requester is appealing for denial of expedited treatment, the FDIC will notify the appellant within 10 business days after receipt of the appeal of the FDIC's disposition.

(5) Complete payment of any outstanding fee invoice will be required before an appeal is processed.

(i) *Records of another agency.* If a requested record is the property of another federal agency or department, and that agency or department, either in writing or by regulation, expressly retains ownership of such record, upon receipt of a request for the record the FDIC will promptly inform the requester of this ownership and immediately shall forward the request to the proprietary agency or department either for processing in accordance with the latter's regulations or for guidance with respect to disposition.

[63 FR 16404, Apr. 3, 1998, as amended at 67 FR 71071, Nov. 29, 2002; 76 FR 35965, June 21, 2011; 76 FR 63818, Oct. 14, 2011]

§ 309.6 Disclosure of exempt records.

(a) *Disclosure prohibited.* Except as provided in paragraph (b) of this section or by 12 CFR part 310,[2] no person shall disclose or permit the disclosure of any exempt records, or information contained therein, to any persons other than those officers, directors, employees, or agents of the Corporation who have a need for such records in the performance of their official duties. In any

---

[2] The procedures for disclosing records under the Privacy Act are separately set forth in 12 CFR part 310.

Federal Deposit Insurance Corporation § 309.6

instance in which any person has possession, custody or control of FDIC exempt records or information contained therein, all copies of such records shall remain the property of the Corporation and under no circumstances shall any person, entity or agency disclose or make public in any manner the exempt records or information without written authorization from the Director of the Corporation's Division having primary authority over the records or information as provided in this section.

(b) *Disclosure authorized.* Exempt records or information of the Corporation may be disclosed only in accordance with the conditions and requirements set forth in this paragraph (b). Requests for discretionary disclosure of exempt records or information pursuant to this paragraph (b) may be submitted directly to the Division having primary authority over the exempt records or information or to the FOIA/PA Group for forwarding to the appropriate Division having primary authority over the records sought. Such administrative request must clearly state that it seeks discretionary disclosure of exempt records, clearly identify the records sought, provide sufficient information for the Corporation to evaluate whether there is good cause for disclosure, and meet all other conditions set forth in paragraph (b)(1) through (10) of this section. Information regarding the appropriate FDIC Division having primary authority over a particular record or records may be obtained from the FOIA/PA Group. Authority to disclose or authorize disclosure of exempt records of the Corporation is delegated as follows:

(1) *Disclosure to depository institutions.* The Director of the Corporation's Division having primary authority over the exempt records, or designee, may disclose to any director or authorized officer, employee or agent of any depository institution, information contained in, or copies of, exempt records pertaining to that depository institution.

(2) *Disclosure to state banking agencies.* The Director of the Corporation's Division having primary authority over the exempt records, or designee, may in his or her discretion and for good cause, disclose to any authorized officer or employee of any state banking or securities department or agency, copies of any exempt records to the extent the records pertain to a state-chartered depository institution supervised by the agency or authority, or where the exempt records are requested in writing for a legitimate depository institution supervisory or regulatory purpose.

(3) *Disclosure to federal financial institutions supervisory agencies and certain other agencies.* The Director of the Corporation's Division having primary authority over the exempt records, or designee, may in his or her discretion and for good cause, disclose to any authorized officer or employee of any federal financial institution supervisory agency including the Comptroller of the Currency, the Board of Governors of the Federal Reserve System, Bureau of Consumer Financial Protection, the Financial Stability Oversight Council, the Securities and Exchange Commission, the National Credit Union Administration, or any other agency included in section 1101(7) of the Right to Financial Privacy Act of 1978 (12 U.S.C. 3401 *et seq.*) (RFPA), any exempt records for a legitimate depository institution supervisory or regulatory purpose. The Director, or designee, may in his or her discretion and for good cause, disclose exempt records, including customer financial records, to certain other federal agencies as referenced in section 1113 of the RFPA for the purposes and to the extent permitted therein, or to any foreign bank regulatory or supervisory authority as provided, and to the extent permitted, by section 206 of the Federal Deposit Insurance Corporation Improvement Act of 1991 (12 U.S.C. 3109). Finally, the Director, or designee, may in his or her discretion and for good cause, disclose reports of examination or other confidential supervisory information concerning any depository institution or other entity examined by the Corporation under authority of Federal law to: Any other Federal or State agency or authority with supervisory or regulatory authority over the depository institution or other entity; any officer, director, or receiver of such depository institution or entity; and any other person that the Corporation determines to be appropriate.

§ 309.6

(4) *Disclosure to prosecuting or investigatory agencies or authorities.* (i) Reports of Apparent Crime pertaining to suspected violations of law, which may contain customer financial records, may be disclosed to federal or state prosecuting or investigatory authorities without giving notice to the customer, as permitted in the relevant exceptions of the RFPA.

(ii) The Director of the Corporation's Division having primary authority over the exempt records, or designee, may disclose to the proper federal or state prosecuting or investigatory authorities, or to any authorized officer or employee of such authority, copies of exempt records pertaining to irregularities discovered in depository institutions which are believed to constitute violations of any federal or state civil or criminal law, or unsafe or unsound banking practices, provided that customer financial records may be disclosed without giving notice to the customer, only as permitted by the relevant exceptions of the RFPA. Unless such disclosure is initiated by the FDIC, customer financial records shall be disclosed only in response to a written request which:

(A) Is signed by an authorized official of the agency making the request;

(B) Identifies the record or records to which access is requested; and

(C) Gives the reasons for the request.

(iii) When notice to the customer is required to be given under the RFPA, the Director of the Corporation's Division having primary authority over the exempt records, or designee, may disclose customer financial records to any federal or state prosecuting or investigatory agency or authority, provided, that:

(A) The General Counsel, or designee, has determined that disclosure is authorized or required by law; or

(B) Disclosure is pursuant to a written request that indicates the information is relevant to a legitimate law enforcement inquiry within the jurisdiction of the requesting agency and:

(1) The Director of the Corporation's Division having primary authority over the exempt records, or designee,

certifies pursuant to section 1112(a)[3] of the RFPA that the records are believed relevant to a legitimate law enforcement inquiry within the jurisdiction of the receiving agency; and

(2) A copy of such certification and the notice required by section 1112(b)[4] of the RFPA is sent within fourteen days of the disclosure to the customer whose records are disclosed.[5]

(5) *Disclosure to servicers and serviced institutions.* The Director of the Corporation's Division having primary authority over the exempt records, or designee, may disclose copies of any exempt record related to a depository institution data center, service corporation, or any other data center that provides data processing or related services to an insured institution (hereinafter referred to as "data center") to:

(i) The examined data center;

(ii) Any insured institution that receives data processing or related services from the examined data center;

(iii) Any state agency or authority which exercises general supervision over an institution serviced by the examined data center; and

---

[3] The form of certification generally is as follows. Additional information may be added:

Pursuant to section 1112(a) of the Right to Financial Privacy Act of 1978 (12 U.S.C. 3412), I, _____ [name and appropriate title] hereby certify that the financial records described below were transferred to (agency or department) in the belief that they were relevant to a legitimate law enforcement inquiry, within the jurisdiction of the receiving agency.

[4] The form of notice generally is as follows. Additional information may be added:

Dear Mr./Ms. _____:

Copies of, or information contained in, your financial records lawfully in the possession of the Federal Deposit Insurance Corporation have been furnished to (agency or department) pursuant to the Right to Financial Privacy Act of 1978 for the following purpose: _____. If you believe that this transfer has not been made to further a legitimate law enforcement inquiry, you may have legal rights under the Right to Financial Privacy Act of 1978 or the Privacy Act of 1974.

[5] Whenever the Corporation is subject to a court-ordered delay of the customer notice, the notice shall be sent immediately upon the expiration of the court-ordered delay.

Federal Deposit Insurance Corporation § 309.6

(iv) Any federal financial institution supervisory agency which exercises general supervision over an institution serviced by the examined data center. The federal supervisory agency may disclose any such examination report received from the Corporation to an insured institution over which it exercises general supervision and which is serviced by the examined data center.

(6) *Disclosure to third parties.* (i) Except as otherwise provided in paragraphs (c) (1) through (5) of this section, the Director of the Corporation's Division having primary authority over the exempt records, or designee, may in his or her discretion and for good cause, disclose copies of any exempt records to any third party where requested to do so in writing. Any such written request shall:

(A) Specify, with reasonable particularity, the record or records to which access is requested; and

(B) Give the reasons for the request.

(ii) Either prior to or at the time of any disclosure, the Director or designee shall require such terms and conditions as he deems necessary to protect the confidential nature of the record, the financial integrity of any depository institution to which the record relates, and the legitimate privacy interests of any individual named in such records.

(7) *Authorization for disclosure by depository institutions or other third parties.* (i) The Director of the Corporation's Division having primary authority over the exempt records, or designee, may, in his or her discretion and for good cause, authorize any director, officer, employee, or agent of a depository institution to disclose copies of any exempt record in his custody to anyone who is not a director, officer or employee of the depository institution. Such authorization must be in response to a written request from the party seeking the record or from management of the depository institution to which the report or record pertains. Any such request shall specify, with reasonable particularity, the record sought, the party's interest therein, and the party's relationship to the depository institution to which the record relates.

(ii) The Director of the Corporation's Division having primary authority over the exempt records, or designee, may, in his or her discretion and for good cause, authorize any third party, including a federal or state agency, that has received a copy of a Corporation exempt record, to disclose such exempt record to another party or agency. Such authorization must be in response to a written request from the party that has custody of the copy of the exempt record. Any such request shall specify the record sought to be disclosed and the reasons why disclosure is necessary.

(iii) Any subsidiary depository institution of a bank holding company or a savings and loan holding company may reproduce and furnish a copy of any report of examination of the subsidiary depository institution to the parent holding company without prior approval of the Director of the Division having primary authority over the exempt records and any depository institution may reproduce and furnish a copy of any report of examination of the disclosing depository institution to a majority shareholder if the following conditions are met:

(A) The parent holding company or shareholder owns in excess of 50% of the voting stock of the depository institution or subsidiary depository institution;

(B) The board of directors of the depository institution or subsidiary depository institution at least annually by resolution authorizes the reproduction and furnishing of reports of examination (the resolution shall specifically name the shareholder or parent holding company, state the address to which the reports are to be sent, and indicate that all reports furnished pursuant to the resolution remain the property of the Federal Deposit Insurance Corporation and are not to be disclosed or made public in any manner without the prior written approval of the Director of the Corporation's Division having primary authority over the exempt records as provided in paragraph (b) of this section;

(C) A copy of the resolution authorizing disclosure of the reports is sent to the shareholder or parent holding company; and

§ 309.6

(D) The minutes of the board of directors of the depository institution or subsidiary depository institution for the meeting immediately following disclosure of a report state:

(*1*) That disclosure was made;
(*2*) The date of the report which was disclosed;
(*3*) To whom the report was sent; and
(*4*) The date the report was disclosed.

(iv) With respect to any disclosure that is authorized under this paragraph (b)(7), the Director of the Corporation's Division having primary authority over the exempt records, or designee, shall only permit disclosure of records upon determining that good cause exists. If the exempt record contains information derived from depository institution customer financial records, disclosure is to be authorized only upon the condition that the requesting party and the party releasing the records comply with any applicable provision of the RFPA. Before authorizing the disclosure, the Director (or designee) may require that both the party having custody of a copy of a Corporation exempt record and the party seeking access to the record agree to such limitations as the Director (or designee) deems necessary to protect the confidential nature of the record, the financial integrity of any depository institution to which the record relates and the legitimate privacy interests of any persons named in such record.

(8) *Disclosure by General Counsel.* (i) The Corporation's General Counsel, or designee, may disclose or authorize the disclosure of any exempt record in response to a valid judicial subpoena, court order, or other legal process, and authorize any current or former officer, director, employee, agent of the Corporation, or third party, to appear and testify regarding an exempt record or any information obtained in the performance of such person's official duties, at any administrative or judicial hearing or proceeding where such person has been served with a valid subpoena, court order, or other legal process requiring him or her to testify. The General Counsel shall consider the relevancy of such exempt records or testimony to the litigation, and the interests of justice, in determining whether to disclose such records or testimony. Third parties seeking disclosure of exempt records or testimony in litigation to which the FDIC is not a party shall submit a request for discretionary disclosure directly to the General Counsel.[6] Such request shall specify the information sought with reasonable particularity and shall be accompanied by a statement with supporting documentation showing in detail the relevance of such exempt information to the litigation, justifying good cause for disclosure, and a commitment to be bound by a protective order. Failure to exhaust such administrative request prior to service of a subpoena or other legal process may, in the General Counsel's discretion, serve as a basis for objection to such subpoena or legal process. Customer financial records may not be disclosed to any federal agency that is not a federal financial supervisory agency pursuant to this paragraph unless notice to the customer and certification as required by the RFPA have been given except where disclosure is subject to the relevant exceptions set forth in the RFPA.

(ii) The General Counsel, or designee, may in his or her discretion and for good cause, disclose or authorize disclosure of any exempt record or testimony by a current or former officer, director, employee, agent of the Corporation, or third party, sought in connection with any civil or criminal hearing, proceeding or investigation without the service of a judicial subpoena, or other legal process requiring such disclosure or testimony, if he or she determines that the records or testimony are relevant to the hearing, proceeding or investigation and that disclosure is in the best interests of justice and not otherwise prohibited by Federal statute. Customer financial records shall not be disclosed to any federal agency

---

[6] This administrative requirement does not apply to subpoenas, court orders or other legal process issued for records of depository institutions held by the FDIC as Receiver or Conservator. Subpoenas, court orders or other legal process issued for such records will be processed in accordance with State and Federal law, regulations, rules and privileges applicable to FDIC as Receiver or Conservator.

pursuant to this paragraph that is not a federal financial supervisory agency, unless the records are sought under the Federal Rules of Civil Procedure (28 U.S.C. appendix) or the Federal Rules of Criminal Procedure (18 U.S.C. appendix) or comparable rules of other courts and in connection with litigation to which the receiving federal agency, employee, officer, director, or agent, and the customer are parties, or disclosure is otherwise subject to the relevant exceptions in the RFPA. Where the General Counsel or designee authorizes a current or former officer, director, employee or agent of the Corporation to testify or disclose exempt records pursuant to this paragraph (b)(8), he or she may, in his or her discretion, limit the authorization to so much of the record or testimony as is relevant to the issues at such hearing, proceeding or investigation, and he or she shall give authorization only upon fulfillment of such conditions as he or she deems necessary and practicable to protect the confidential nature of such records or testimony.

(9) *Authorization for disclosure by the Chairman of the Corporation's Board of Directors.* Except where expressly prohibited by law, the Chairman of the Corporation's Board of Directors may in his or her discretion, authorize the disclosure of any Corporation records. Except where disclosure is required by law, the Chairman may direct any current or former officer, director, employee or agent of the Corporation to refuse to disclose any record or to give testimony if the Chairman determines, in his or her discretion, that refusal to permit such disclosure is in the public interest.

(10) *Limitations on disclosure.* All steps practicable shall be taken to protect the confidentiality of exempt records and information. Any disclosure permitted by paragraph (b) of this section is discretionary and nothing in paragraph (b) of this section shall be construed as requiring the disclosure of information. Further, nothing in paragraph (b) of this section shall be construed as restricting, in any manner, the authority of the Board of Directors, the Chairman of the Board of Directors, the Director of the Corporation's Division having primary authority over the exempt records, the Corporation's General Counsel, or their designees, or any other Corporation Division or Office head, in their discretion and in light of the facts and circumstances attendant in any given case, to require conditions upon and to limit the form, manner, and extent of any disclosure permitted by this section. Wherever practicable, disclosure of exempt records shall be made pursuant to a protective order and redacted to exclude all irrelevant or non-responsive exempt information.

[60 FR 61465, Nov. 30, 1995, as amended at 63 FR 16408, Apr. 3, 1998; 67 FR 71071, Nov. 29, 2002; 73 FR 2146, Jan. 14, 2008; 76 FR 35965, June 21, 2011]

§ 309.7 Service of process.

(a) *Service.* Any subpoena or other legal process to obtain information maintained by the FDIC shall be duly issued by a court having jurisdiction over the FDIC, and served upon either the Executive Secretary (or designee), FDIC, 550 17th Street, NW., Washington, DC 20429, or the Regional Director or Regional Manager of the FDIC region where the legal action from which the subpoena or process was issued is pending. A list of the FDIC's regional offices is available from the Office of Public Affairs, FDIC, 550 17th Street, NW., Washington, DC 20429 (telephone 202–898–6996). Where the FDIC is named as a party, service of process shall be made pursuant to the Federal Rules of Civil Procedure, and upon the Executive Secretary (or designee), FDIC, 550 17th Street NW., Washington, DC 20429, or upon the agent designated to receive service of process in the state, territory, or jurisdiction in which any insured depository institution is located. Identification of the designated agent in the state, territory, or jurisdiction may be obtained from the Executive Secretary or from the Office of the General Counsel, FDIC, 550 17th Street NW., Washington, DC 20429. The Executive Secretary (or designee), Regional Director or designated agent shall immediately forward any subpoena, court order or legal process to the General Counsel. The Corporation may require the payment of fees, in accordance with the fee schedule referred to in § 309.5(c)(3), prior to the release of any records requested pursuant to any subpoena or other legal process.

(b) *Notification by person served.* If any current or former officer, director, employee or agent of the Corporation, or any other person who has custody of records belonging to the FDIC, is served with a subpoena, court order, or other process requiring that person's attendance as a witness concerning any matter related to official duties, or the production of any exempt record of the Corporation, such person shall promptly advise the General Counsel of such service, of the testimony and records described in the subpoena, and of all relevant facts which may be of assistance to the General Counsel in determining whether the individual in question should be authorized to testify or the records should be produced. Such person should also inform the court or tribunal which issued the process and the attorney for the party upon whose application the process was issued, if known, of the substance of this section.

(c) *Appearance by person served.* Absent the written authorization of the Corporation's General Counsel, or designee, to disclose the requested information, any current or former officer, director, employee, or agent of the Corporation, and any other person having custody of records of the Corporation, who is required to respond to a subpoena or other legal process, shall attend at the time and place therein specified and respectfully decline to produce any such record or give any testimony with respect thereto, basing such refusal on this section.

[60 FR 61465, Nov. 30, 1995, as amended at 67 FR 71071, Nov. 29, 2002]

PART 310—PRIVACY ACT REGULATIONS

Sec.
310.1 Purpose and scope.
310.2 Definitions.
310.3 Procedures for requests pertaining to individual records in a system of records.
310.4 Times, places, and requirements for identification of individuals making requests.
310.5 Disclosure of requested information to individuals.
310.6 Special procedures: Medical records.
310.7 Request for amendment of record.
310.8 Agency review of request for amendment of record.
310.9 Appeal of adverse initial agency determination on access or amendment.
310.10 Disclosure of record to person other than the individual to whom it pertains.
310.11 Fees.
310.12 Penalties.
310.13 Exemptions.

AUTHORITY: 5 U.S.C. 552a.

SOURCE: 40 FR 46274, Oct. 6, 1975, unless otherwise noted.

§ 310.1 Purpose and scope.

The purpose of this part is to establish regulations implementing the Privacy Act of 1974, 5 U.S.C. 552a. These regulations delineate the procedures that an individual must follow in exercising his or her access or amendment rights under the Privacy Act to records maintained by the Corporation in systems of records, including information transferred to Federal Deposit Insurance Corporation from the Office of Thrift Supervision pursuant to sections 312 and 323 of the Dodd-Frank Wall Street Reform and Consumer Protection Act, Public Law 111–203.

[76 FR 35965, June 21, 2011]

§ 310.2 Definitions.

For purposes of this part:

(a) The term *Corporation* means the Federal Deposit Insurance Corporation;

(b) The term *individual* means a natural person who is either a citizen of the United States or an alien lawfully admitted for permanent residence;

(c) The term *maintain* includes maintain, collect, use, disseminate, or control;

(d) The term *record* means any item, collection or grouping of information about an individual that contains his/her name, or the identifying number, symbol, or other identifying particular assigned to the individual;

(e) The term *system of records* means a group of any records under the control of the Corporation from which information is retrieved by the name of the individual or some identifying number, symbol or other identifying particular assigned to the individual;

(f) The term *designated system of records* means a system of records which has been listed and summarized

Federal Deposit Insurance Corporation § 310.4

in the FEDERAL REGISTER pursuant to the requirements of 5 U.S.C. 552a(e);

(g) The term *routine use* means, with respect to disclosure of a record, the use of such record for a purpose which is compatible with the purpose for which it was created;

(h) The terms *amend* or *amendment* mean any correction, addition to or deletion from a record; and

(i) The term *system manager* means the agency official responsible for a designated system of records, as denominated in the FEDERAL REGISTER publication of "Systems of Records Maintained by the Federal Deposit Insurance Corporation."

[40 FR 46274, Oct. 6, 1975, as amended at 42 FR 6796, Feb. 4, 1977]

§ 310.3 Procedures for requests pertaining to individual records in a system of records.

(a) Any present or former employee of the Corporation seeking access to, or amendment of, his/her official personnel records maintained by the Corporation shall submit his/her request in such manner as is prescribed by the United States Office of Personnel Management in part 297 of its rules and regulations (5 CFR part 297). For access to, or amendment of, other government-wide records systems maintained by the Corporation, the procedures prescribed in the respective FEDERAL REGISTER Privacy Act system notice shall be followed.

(b) Requests by individuals for access to records pertaining to them and maintained within one of the Corporation's designated systems of records should be submitted in writing to the Federal Deposit Insurance Corporation, Attn: FOIA/PA Group, 550 17th Street, NW., Washington, DC 20429. Each such request should contain a reasonable description of the records sought, the system or systems in which such record may be contained, and any additional identifying information, as specified in the Corporation's FEDERAL REGISTER "Notice of Systems of Records" for that particular system, copies of which are available upon request from the FOIA/PA Group.

[40 FR 46274, Oct. 6, 1975, as amended at 42 FR 6796, Feb. 4, 1977; 61 FR 43419, Aug. 23, 1996; 67 FR 71071, Nov. 29, 2002; 76 FR 35965, June 21, 2011]

§ 310.4 Times, places, and requirements for identification of individuals making requests.

(a) Individuals may request access to records pertaining to themselves by submitting a written request as provided in § 310.3 of these regulations, or by appearing in person on weekdays, other than official holidays, at the Federal Deposit Insurance Corporation, Attn: FOIA/PA Group, 550 17th Street, NW., Washington, DC 20429, between the hours of 8:30 a.m. and 5 p.m.

(b) Individuals appearing in person at the Corporation seeking access to or amendment of their records shall present two forms of reasonable identification, such as employment identification cards, driver's licenses, or other identification cards or documents typically used for identification purposes.

(c) Except for records that must be publicly disclosed pursuant to the Freedom of Information Act, 5 U.S.C. 552, where the Corporation determines it to be necessary for the individual's protection, a certification of a duly commissioned notary public, of any state or territory, attesting to the requesting individual's identity, or an unsworn declaration subscribed to as true under the penalty of perjury under the laws of the United States of America, at the election of the individual, may be required before a written request seeking access to or amendment of a record will be honored. The Corporation may also require that individuals provide minimal identifying data such as full name, date and place of birth, or other personal information necessary to ensure proper identity before processing requests for records.

[40 FR 46274, Oct. 6, 1975, as amended at 42 FR 6796, Feb. 4, 1977; 61 FR 43419, Aug. 23, 1996; 67 FR 71071, Nov. 29, 2002; 76 FR 35966, June 21, 2011]

§ 310.5 Disclosure of requested information to individuals.

(a) Except to the extent that Corporation records pertaining to an individual:

(1) Are exempt from disclosure under §§ 310.6 and 310.13 of this part, or

(2) Were compiled in reasonable anticipation of a civil action or proceeding, the Corporation will make such records available upon request for purposes of inspection and copying by the individual (after proper identity verification as provided in § 310.4) and, upon the individual's request and written authorization, by another person of the individual's own choosing.

(b) The FOIA/PA Group will notify, in writing, the individual making a request, whenever practicable within ten business days following receipt of the request, whether any specified designated system of records maintained by the Corporation contains a record pertaining to the individual. Where such a record does exist, the FOIA/PA Group also will inform the individual of the system manager's decision whether to grant or deny the request for access. In the event existing records are determined not to be disclosable, the notification will inform the individual of the reasons for which disclosure will not be made and will provide a description of the individual's right to appeal the denial, as more fully set forth in § 310.9. Where access is to be granted, the notification will specify the procedures for verifying the individual's identity, as set forth in § 310.4.

(c) Individuals will be granted access to records disclosable under this part 310 as soon as is practicable. The FOIA/PA Group will give written notification of a reasonable period within which individuals may inspect disclosable records pertaining to themselves at the offices of the FOIA/PA Group during normal business hours. Alternatively, individuals granted access to records under this part may request that copies of such records be forwarded to them. Fees for copying such records will be assessed as provided in § 310.11.

[40 FR 46274, Oct. 6, 1975, as amended at 42 FR 6796, Feb. 4, 1977; 67 FR 71071, Nov. 29, 2002]

§ 310.6 Special procedures: Medical records.

Medical records shall be disclosed on request to the individuals to whom they pertain, except, if in the judgment of the Corporation, the transmission of the medical information directly to the requesting individual could have an adverse effect upon such individual. In the event medical information is withheld from a requesting individual due to any possible adverse effect such information may have upon the individual, the Corporation shall transmit such information to a medical doctor named by the requesting individual for release of the patient.

[40 FR 46274, Oct. 6, 1975, as amended at 61 FR 43420, Aug. 23, 1996]

§ 310.7 Request for amendment of record.

The Corporation will maintain all records it uses in making any determination about any individual with such accuracy, relevance, timeliness and completeness as is reasonably necessary to assure fairness to the individual in the determination. An individual may request that the Corporation amend any portion of a record pertaining to that individual which the Corporation maintains in a designated system of records. Such a request should be submitted in writing to the Federal Deposit Insurance Corporation, Attn: FOIA/PA Group, 550 17th Street, NW., Washington, DC 20429 and should contain the individual's reason for requesting the amendment and a description of the record (including the name of the appropriate designated system and category thereof) sufficient to enable the Corporation to identify the particular record or portion thereof with respect to which amendment is sought.

[76 FR 35966, June 21, 2011]

§ 310.8 Agency review of request for amendment of record.

(a) Requests by individuals for the amendment of records will be acknowledged by the FOIA/PA Group, and referred to the system manager of the system of records in which the record is contained for determination, within ten business days following receipt of

Federal Deposit Insurance Corporation

such requests. Promptly thereafter, the FOIA/PA Group will notify the individual of the system manager's decision to grant or deny the request to amend.

(b) If the system manager denies a request to amend a record, the notification of such denial shall contain the reason for the denial and a description of the individual's right to appeal the denial as more fully set forth in § 310.9.

[40 FR 46274, Oct. 6, 1975, as amended at 42 FR 6796, Feb. 4, 1977; 67 FR 71071, Nov. 29, 2002; 76 FR 35966, June 21, 2011]

§ 310.9 Appeal of adverse initial agency determination on access or amendment.

(a) A system manager's denial of an individual's request for access to or amendment of a record pertaining to him/her may be appealed in writing to the Corporation's General Counsel (or designee) within 30 business days following receipt of notification of the denial. Such an appeal should be addressed to the Federal Deposit Insurance Corporation, Attn: FOIA/PA Group, 550 17th Street, NW., Washington, DC 20429, and contain all the information specified in § 310.3 or for initial requests to amend in § 310.7, as well as any other additional information the individual deems relevant for the consideration by the General Counsel (or designee) of the appeal.

(b) The General Counsel (or designee) will normally make a final determination with respect to an appeal made under this part within 30 business days following receipt by the Office of the Executive Secretary of the appeal. The General Counsel (or designee) may, however, extend this 30-day time period for good cause. Where such an extension is required, the individual making the appeal will be notified of the reason for the extension and the expected date upon which a final decision will be given.

(c) If the General Counsel (or designee) affirms the initial denial of a request for access or to amend, he or she will inform the individual affected of the decision, the reason therefor, and the right of judicial review of the decision. In addition, as pertains to a request for amendment, the individual may at that point submit to the Corporation a concise statement setting forth his or her reasons for disagreeing with the Corporation's refusal to amend.

(d) Any statement of disagreement with the Corporation's refusal to amend, filed with the Corporation by an individual pursuant to § 310.9(c), will be included in the disclosure of any records under the authority of § 310.10(b). The Corporation may in its discretion also include a copy of a concise statement of its reasons for not making the requested amendment.

(e) The General Counsel (or designee) may on his or her own motion refer an appeal to the Board of Directors for a determination, and the Board of Directors on its own motion may consider an appeal.

[52 FR 34290, Sept. 10, 1987, as amended at 61 FR 43420, Aug. 23, 1996; 67 FR 71071, Nov. 29, 2002; 76 FR 35966, June 21, 2011]

§ 310.10 Disclosure of record to person other than the individual to whom it pertains.

(a) Except as provided in paragraph (b) of this section, the Corporation will not disclose any record contained in a designated system of records to any person or agency except with the prior written consent of the individual to whom the record pertains.

(b) The restrictions on disclosure in paragraph (a) of this section do not apply to any of the following disclosures:

(1) To those officers and employees of the Corporation who have a need for the record in the performance of their duties;

(2) Which is required under the Freedom of Information Act (5 U.S.C. 552);

(3) For a routine use listed with respect to a designated system of records;

(4) To the Bureau of the Census for purposes of planning or carrying out a census or survey or related activity pursuant to the provisions of title 13 U.S.C.;

(5) To a recipient who has provided the Corporation with advance adequate written assurance that the record will be used solely as a statistical research or reporting record, and the record is

§ 310.11

to be transferred in a form that is not individually identifiable;

(6) To the National Archives and Records Administration as a record which has sufficient historical or other value to warrant its continued preservation by the United States Government, or for evaluation by the Archivist of the United States or his or her designee to determine whether the record has such value;

(7) To another agency or to an instrumentality of any governmental jurisdiction within or under the control of the United States for a civil or criminal law enforcement activity if the activity is authorized by law, and if the head of the agency or instrumentality has made a written request to the Corporation specifying the particular portion desired and the law enforcement activity for which the record is sought;

(8) To a person pursuant to a showing of compelling circumstances affecting the health or safety of an individual if, upon such disclosure, notification is transmitted to the last known address of such individual;

(9) To either House of Congress, or, to the extent of matter within its jurisdiction, any committee or subcommittee thereof, any joint committee of Congress or subcommittee of any such joint committee;

(10) To the Comptroller General, or any of his or her authorized representatives, in the course of the performance of the duties of the General Accounting Office;

(11) Pursuant to the order of a court of competent jurisdiction.

(12) To a consumer reporting agency in accordance with section 3711(f) of Title 31.

(c) The Corporation will adhere to the following procedures in the case of disclosure of any record pursuant to the authority of paragraphs (b)(3) through (b)(12) of this section.

(1) The Corporation will keep a record of the date, nature and purpose of each such disclosure, as well as the name and address of the person or agency to whom such disclosure is made; and

(2) The Corporation will retain and, with the exception of disclosures made pursuant to paragraph (b)(7) of this section, make available to the individual named in the record for the greater of five years or the life of the record all material compiled under paragraph (d)(1) of this section with respect to disclosure of such record.

(d) Whenever a record which has been disclosed by the Corporation under authority of paragraph (b) of this section is, within a reasonable amount of time after such disclosure, either amended by the Corporation or the subject of a statement of disagreement, the Corporation will transmit such additional information to any person or agency to whom the record was disclosed, if such disclosure was subject to the accounting requirements of paragraph (c)(1) of this section.

[40 FR 46274, Oct. 6, 1975, as amended at 61 FR 43420, Aug. 23, 1996]

§ 310.11 Fees.

The Corporation, upon a request for records disclosable pursuant to the Privacy Act of 1974 (5 U.S.C. 552a), shall charge a fee of $0.10 per page for duplicating, except as follows:

(a) If the Corporation determines that it can grant access to a record only by providing a copy of the record, no fee will be charged for providing the first copy of the record or any portion thereof;

(b) Whenever the aggregate fees computed under this section do not exceed $10 for any one request, the fee will be deemed waived by the Corporation; or

(c) Whenever the Corporation determines that a reduction or waiver is warranted, it may reduce or waive any fees imposed for furnishing requested information pursuant to this section.

[40 FR 46274, Oct. 6, 1975, as amended at 61 FR 43420, Aug. 23, 1996]

§ 310.12 Penalties.

Subsection (i)(3) of the Privacy Act of 1974 (5 U.S.C. 552a(i)(3)) imposes criminal penalties for obtaining Corporation records on individuals under false pretenses. The subsection provides as follows:

Any person who knowingly and willfully requests or obtains any record concerning an individual from an agency under false pretenses shall be guilty of a misdemeanor and fined not more than $5,000.

Federal Deposit Insurance Corporation

§ 311.2

§ 310.13 Exemptions.

The following systems of records are exempt from §§ 310.3 through 310.9 and § 310.10(c)(2) of these rules:

(a) Investigatory material compiled for law enforcement purposes in the following systems of records is exempt from §§ 310.3 through 310.9 and § 310.10(c)(2) of these rules;

Provided, however, That if any individual is denied any right, privilege, or benefit to which he/she would otherwise be entitled under Federal law, or for which he/she would otherwise be eligible, as a result of the maintenance of such material, such material shall be disclosed to such individual, except to the extent that the disclosure of such material would reveal the identity of a source who furnished information to the Government under an express promise that the identity of the source would be held in confidence, or, prior to September 27, 1975, under an implied promise that the identity of the source would be held in confidence:

30–64–0002—Financial institutions investigative and enforcement records system.

30–64–0010—Investigative files and records.

(b) Investigatory material compiled solely for the purpose of determining suitability, eligibility, or qualifications for Corporation employment to the extent that disclosure of such material would reveal the identity of a source who furnished information to the Corporation under an express promise that the identity of the source would be held in confidence, or, prior to September 27, 1975, under an implied promise that the identity of the source would be held in confidence, in the following systems of records, is exempt from §§ 310.3 through 310.9 and § 310.10(c)(2) of these rules:

30–64–0001—Attorney-legal intern applicant system.

30–64–0010—Investigative files and records.

(c) Testing or examination material used solely to determine or assess individual qualifications for appointment or promotion in the Corporation's service, the disclosure of which would compromise the objectivity or fairness of the testing, evaluation, or examination process in the following system of records, is exempt from §§ 310.3 through 310.9 and § 310.10(c)(2) of these rules:

30–64–0009—Examiner training and education records.

[42 FR 6797, Feb. 4, 1977, as amended at 42 FR 33720, July 1, 1977; 54 FR 38507, Sept. 19, 1989; 61 FR 43420, Aug. 23, 1996]

PART 311—RULES GOVERNING PUBLIC OBSERVATION OF MEETINGS OF THE CORPORATION'S BOARD OF DIRECTORS

Sec.
311.1 Purpose.
311.2 Definitions.
311.3 Meetings.
311.4 Procedures for announcing meetings.
311.5 Regular procedure for closing meetings.
311.6 Expedited procedure for announcing and closing certain meetings.
311.7 General Counsel certification.
311.8 Transcripts and minutes of meetings.

AUTHORITY: 5 U.S.C. 552b and 12 U.S.C. 1819.

SOURCE: 42 FR 14675, Mar. 16, 1977, unless otherwise noted.

§ 311.1 Purpose.

This part implements the policy of the "Government in the Sunshine Act", section 552b of title 5 U.S.C., which is to provide the public with as much information as possible regarding the decision making process of certain Federal agencies, including the Federal Deposit Insurance Corporation, while preserving the rights of individuals and the ability of the agency to carry out its responsibilities.

§ 311.2 Definitions.

For purposes of this part:

(a) *Board* means Board of Directors of the Federal Deposit Insurance Corporation and includes any subdivision of the Board authorized to act on behalf of the Corporation.

(b) *Meeting* means the deliberations (including those conducted by conference telephone call, or by any other method) of at least three members where such deliberations determine or result in the joint conduct or disposition of agency business but does not include:

(1) Deliberations to determine whether meetings will be open or closed or

§ 311.3

whether information pertaining to closed meetings will be withheld;

(2) Informal background discussions among Board members and staff which clarify issues and expose varying views;

(3) Decision-making by circulating written material to individual Board members;

(4) Sessions with individuals from outside the Corporation where Board members listen to a presentation and may elicit additional information.

(c) *Member* means a member of the Board.

(d) *Open to public observation* and *open to the public* mean that individuals may witness the meeting, but not participate in the deliberations. The meeting may be recorded, photographed, or otherwise reproduced if the reproduction does not disturb the meeting.

(e) *Public announcement* and *publicly announce* mean making reasonable effort under the particular circumstances of each case to fully inform the public. This may include posting notice on the Corporation's public notice bulletin board maintained in the lobby of its offices located at 550 17th Street, NW., Washington, DC 20429, issuing a press release and employing other methods of notification that may be desirable in a particular situation.

[42 FR 14675, Mar. 16, 1977, as amended at 42 FR 59494, Nov. 18, 1977; 54 FR 38965, Sept. 22, 1989; 61 FR 38357, July 24, 1996]

§ 311.3 Meetings.

(a) *Open meetings.* Except as provided in paragraph (b) of this section, every portion of every meeting of the Corporation's Board will be open to public observation. Board members will not jointly conduct or dispose of Corporation business other than in accordance with this part.

(b) *When meetings may be closed and announcements and disclosures withheld.* Except where the Board finds that the public interest requires otherwise, a meeting or portion thereof may be closed, and announcements and disclosure pertaining thereto may be withheld when the Board determines that such meeting or portion of the meeting or the disclosure of such information is likely to:

(1) Disclose matters that are: (i) Specifically authorized under criteria established by an Executive order to be kept secret in the interests of national defense or foreign policy and (ii) in fact properly classified pursuant to such Executive order;

(2) Relate solely to the internal personnel rules and practices of the Corporation;

(3) Disclose matters specifically exempted from disclosure by statute (other than the Freedom of Information Act, 5 U.S.C. 552): *Provided,* That such statute: (i) Requires that the matters be withheld from the public in such a manner as to leave no discretion on the issue, or (ii) establishes particular types of matters to be withheld;

(4) Disclose trade secrets and commercial or financial information obtained from a person and privileged or confidential;

(5) Involve accusing any person of a crime, or formally censuring any person;

(6) Disclose information of a personal nature where disclosure would constitute a clearly unwarranted invasion of personal privacy;

(7) Disclose investigatory records compiled for law enforcement purposes, or information which if written would be contained in such records, but only to the extent that the production of such records or information would: (i) Interfere with enforcement proceedings, (ii) deprive a person of a right to a fair trial or an impartial adjudication, (iii) constitute an unwarranted invasion of personal privacy, (iv) disclose the identity of a confidential source, (v) disclose investigative techniques and procedures, or (vi) endanger the life or physical safety of law enforcement personnel;

(8) Disclose information contained in or related to examination, operating, or condition reports prepared by, on behalf of, or for the use of the Corporation or any other agency responsible for the supervision of financial institutions;

(9) Disclose information the premature disclosure of which would be likely to:

(i)(A) Lead to significant financial speculation in currencies, securities, or commodities, or

(B) Significantly endanger the stability of any financial institution; or

Federal Deposit Insurance Corporation §311.5

(ii) Significantly frustrate implementation of a proposed Corporation action, except that this paragraph (b)(9)(ii) shall not apply in any instance where the Corporation has already disclosed to the public the content or nature of its proposed action, or where the Corporation is required by law to make such disclosure on its own initiative prior to taking final action on such proposal; or

(10) Specifically concern the Corporation's issuance of a subpoena, or the Corporation's participation in a civil action or proceeding, an action in a foreign court or international tribunal, or an arbitration, or the initiation, conduct, or disposition by the Corporation of a particular case of formal agency adjudication pursuant to the procedures in 5 U.S.C. 554 or otherwise involving a determination on the record after opportunity for a hearing.

§311.4 Procedures for announcing meetings.

(a) *Scope.* Except to the extent that such announcements are exempt from disclosure under §311.3(b), announcements relating to open meetings, and meetings closed under the regular closing procedures of §311.5, will be made in the manner set forth in this section.

(b) *Time and content of announcement.* The Corporation will make public announcement at least seven days before the meeting of the time, place, and subject matter of the meeting, whether it is to be open or closed to the public, and the name and telephone number of the official designated by the Corporation to respond to requests for information about the meeting. This announcement will be made unless a majority of the Board determines by a recorded vote that Corporation business requires that a meeting be called on lesser notice. In such cases, the Corporation will make public announcement of the time, place, and subject matter of the meeting, and whether it is open or closed to the public, at the earliest practicable time, which may be later than the commencement of the meeting.

(c) *Changing time or place of meeting.* The time or place of a meeting may be changed following the public announcement required by paragraph (b) of this section only if the Corporation publicly announces the change at the earliest practicable time, which may be later than the commencement of the meeting.

(d) *Changing subject matter or nature of meeting.* The subject matter of a meeting, or the determination to open or close a meeting or a portion of a meeting, may be changed following the public announcement only if:

(1) A majority of the entire Board determines by recorded vote that agency business so requires and that no earlier announcement of the change was possible; and,

(2) The Corporation publicly announces the change and the vote of each member upon such change at the earliest practicable time, which may be later than the commencement of the meeting.

(e) *Publication of announcements in Federal Register.* Immediately following each public announcement under this section, such announcement will be submitted for publication in the FEDERAL REGISTER by the Executive Secretary.

[42 FR 14675, Mar. 16, 1977, as amended at 67 FR 71071, Nov. 29, 2002]

§311.5 Regular procedure for closing meetings.

(a) *Scope.* Unless §311.6 is applicable, the procedures for closing meetings will be those set forth in this section.

(b) *Procedure.* (1) A decision to close a meeting or portion of a meeting will be taken only when a majority of the entire Board votes to take such action. In deciding whether to close a meeting or portion of a meeting, the Board will consider whether the public interest requires an open meeting. A separate vote of the Board will be taken with respect to each meeting which is proposed to be closed in whole or in part to the public. A single vote may be taken with respect to a series of meetings which are proposed to be closed in whole or in part to the public, or with respect to any information concerning such series of meetings, so long as each meeting in the series involves the same particular matters and is scheduled to be held no more than thirty days after the initial meeting in the series. The

§ 311.6

vote of each Board member will be recorded and no proxies will be allowed.

(2) Any individual whose interests may be directly affected may request that the Corporation close any portion of a meeting for any of the reasons referred to in paragraph (b) (5), (6), or (b)(7) of § 311.3. Requests should be directed to the Executive Secretary, Federal Deposit Insurance Corporation, 550 17th Street, NW., Washington, DC 20429. After receiving notice that an individual desires a portion of a meeting to be closed, the Board, upon request of any one of its members, will vote by recorded vote whether to close the relevant portion of the meeting. This procedure will apply even if the individual's request is made subsequent to the announcement of a decision to hold an open meeting.

(3) The Corporation's General Counsel will make the public certification required by § 311.7.

(4) Within 1 day after any vote taken pursuant to paragraphs (b)(1) or (2) of this section, the Corporation will make publicly available a written copy of the vote, reflecting the vote of each Board member. Except to the extent that such information is exempt from disclosure, if a meeting or portion of a meeting is to be closed to the public, the Corporation will make publicly available within 1 day after the required vote a full written explanation of its action, together with a list of all persons expected to attend the meeting and their affiliation.

(5) The Corporation will publicly announce the time, place, and subject matter of the meeting, with determinations as to open and closed portions, in the manner and within the time limits prescribed in § 311.4.

[42 FR 14675, Mar. 16, 1977; 42 FR 16616, Mar. 29, 1977, as amended at 42 FR 59494, Nov. 18, 1977; 67 FR 71071, Nov. 29, 2002]

§ 311.6 Expedited procedure for announcing and closing certain meetings.

(a) *Scope.* Since a majority of its meetings may properly be closed pursuant to paragraph (b)(4), (8), (9)(i), or (b)(10) of § 311.3, subsection (d)(4) of the Government in the Sunshine Act (5 U.S.C. 552b) allows the Corporation to use expedited procedures in closing meetings under these four subparagraphs. Absent a compelling public interest to the contrary, meetings or portions of meetings that can be expected to be closed using these procedures include, but are not limited to: Administrative enforcement proceedings under section 8 of the Federal Deposit Insurance Act (12 U.S.C. 1818); appointment of the Corporation as conservator of a depository institution, or as receiver, liquidator or liquidating agent of a closed depository institution or a depository institution in danger of closing; and certain management and liquidation activities pursuant to such appointments; possible financial assistance by the Corporation under section 13 of the Federal Deposit Insurance Act (12 U.S.C. 1823); certain depository institution applications including applications to establish or move branches, applications to merge, and applications for insurance; and investigatory activity under section 10(c) of the Federal Deposit Insurance Act (12 U.S.C. 1820(c)). In announcing and closing meetings or portions of meetings under this section, the following procedures will be observed.

(b) *Announcement.* Except to the extent that such information is exempt from disclosure under the provisions of § 311.3(b) the Corporation will make public announcement of the time, place and subject matter of the meeting and of each portion thereof at the earliest practicable time. This announcement will be published in the FEDERAL REGISTER if publication can be effected at least 1 day prior to the scheduled date of the meeting.

(c) *Procedure for closing.* (1) The Corporation's General Counsel will make the public certification required by § 311.7.

(2) At the beginning of a meeting or portion of a meeting to be closed under this section, a recorded vote of the Board will be taken. The Board will determine by its vote whether to proceed with the closing. If a majority of the entire Board votes to close, the meeting will be closed to public observation. Even though a meeting or portion thereof could properly be closed under this section, a majority of the entire Board may find that the public interest

Federal Deposit Insurance Corporation §311.8

requires an open session and vote, reflecting the vote of each Board member, will be made available to the public.

[42 FR 14675, Mar. 16, 1977; 42 FR 16616, Mar. 29, 1977, as amended at 54 FR 38965, Sept. 22, 1989]

§311.7 General Counsel certification.

For every meeting or portion thereof closed under §311.5 or §311.6, the Corporation's General Counsel will publicly certify that, in the opinion of such General Counsel, the meeting may be closed to the public and will state each relevant exemptive provision. In the absence of the General Counsel, the next ranking official in the Legal Division may perform the certification. If the General Counsel and such next ranking official in the Legal Division are both absent, the official in the Legal Division who is then next in rank may provide the required certification. A copy of this certification, together with a statement from the presiding officer of the meeting setting forth the time and place of the meeting, and the persons present, will be retained in the Board's permanent files.

[42 FR 14675, Mar. 16, 1977, as amended at 61 FR 38357, July 24, 1996]

§311.8 Transcripts and minutes of meetings.

(a) *When required.* The Corporation will maintain a complete transcript, identifying each speaker, to record fully the proceedings of each meeting or portion of a meeting closed to the public, except that in the case of a meeting or portions of a meeting closed to the public pursuant to paragraph (b)(8), (9)(i), or (10) of §311.3, the Corporation may, in lieu of a transcript, maintain a set of minutes.

(b) *Content of minutes.* If minutes are maintained, they will fully and clearly describe all matters discussed and will provide a full and accurate summary of any actions taken, and the reasons for taking such action. Minutes will also include a description of each of the views expressed by each person in attendance on any item and the record of any roll call vote, reflecting the vote of each member. All documents considered in connection with any action will be identified in the minutes.

(c) *Available material.* The Corporation will maintain a complete verbatim copy of the transcript or minutes of each meeting or portion of a meeting closed to the public for a period of at least 2 years after the meeting, or until 1 year after the conclusion of any proceeding with respect to which the meeting or portion was held, whichever occurs later. The Corporation will make promptly available to the public the transcript, identifying each speaker, or minutes of items on the agenda or testimony of any witness received at the closed meeting except that in cases where the Privacy Act of 1974 (5 U.S.C. 552a) does not apply, the Corporation may withhold information exempt from disclosure under §311.3(b). For the convenience of members of the public who may be unable to attend open meetings of the Board, the Corporation will maintain for at least 2 years a set of minutes of each meeting of the Board or portion thereof open to public observation.

(d) *Procedures for inspecting or copying available material.* (1) An individual may inspect materials made available under paragraph (c) of this section at the offices of the Executive Secretary, Federal Deposit Insurance Corporation, 550 17th Street, NW., Washington, DC 20429, during normal business hours. If the individual desires a copy of such material, the Corporation will furnish copies at a cost of 10 cents per page. Whenever the Corporation determines that in the public interest a reduction or waiver is warranted, it may reduce or waive any fees imposed under this section.

(2) An individual may also submit a written request for transcripts or minutes, reasonably identifying the records sought, to the Executive Secretary, Federal Deposit Insurance Corporation, 550 17th Street, NW., Washington, DC 20429.

(e) *Procedures for obtaining documents identified in minutes.* Copies of documents identified in minutes or considered by the Board in connection with any action identified in the minutes may be made available to the public upon request, to the extent permitted by the Freedom of Information Act,

Pt. 313

under the provisions of 12 CFR part 309, Disclosure of Information.

[42 FR 14675, Mar. 16, 1977, as amended at 61 FR 38357, July 24, 1996; 67 FR 71071, Nov. 29, 2002]

PART 312 [RESERVED]

PART 313—PROCEDURES FOR CORPORATE DEBT COLLECTION

Subpart A—Scope, Purpose, Definitions and Delegations of Authority

Sec.
313.1 Scope.
313.2 Purpose.
313.3 Definitions.
313.4 Delegations of authority.
313.5–313.19 [Reserved]

Subpart B—Administrative Offset

313.20 Applicability and scope.
313.21 Definitions.
313.22 Collection.
313.23 Offset prior to completion of procedures.
313.24 Omission of procedures.
313.25 Debtor's rights.
313.26 Interest.
313.27 Refunds.
313.28 No requirement for duplicate notice.
313.29 Requests for offset to other federal agencies.
313.30 Requests for offset from other federal agencies.
313.31–313.39 [Reserved]

Subpart C—Salary Offset

313.40 Scope.
313.41 Notice requirement where FDIC is creditor agency.
313.42 Procedures to request a hearing.
313.43 Failure to timely submit request for hearing.
313.44 Procedure for hearing.
313.45 Certification of debt by FDIC as creditor agency.
313.46 Notice of salary offset where FDIC is the paying agency.
313.47 Voluntary repayment agreements as alternative to salary offset where the FDIC is the creditor agency.
313.48 Special review of repayment agreement or salary offset due to changed circumstances.
313.49 Coordinating salary offset with other agencies.
313.50 Interest, penalties, and administrative costs.
313.51 Refunds.
313.52 Request from a creditor agency for services of a hearing official.

313.53 Non-waiver of rights by payments.
313.54 Exception to due process procedures.
313.55 Salary adjustments.
313.56–313.79 [Reserved]

Subpart D—Administrative Wage Garnishment

313.80 Scope and purpose.
313.81 Notice.
313.82 Debtor's rights.
313.83 Form of hearing.
313.84 Effect of timely request.
313.85 Failure to timely request a hearing.
313.86 Hearing official.
313.87 Procedure.
313.88 Format of hearing.
313.89 Date of decision.
313.90 Content of decision.
313.91 Finality of agency action.
313.92 Failure to appear.
313.93 Wage garnishment order.
313.94 Certification by employer.
313.95 Amounts withheld.
313.96 Exclusions from garnishment.
313.97 Financial hardship.
313.98 Ending garnishment.
313.99 Prohibited actions by employer.
313.100 Refunds.
313.101 Right of action.
313.102–313.119 [Reserved]

Subpart E—Tax Refund Offset

313.120 Scope.
313.121 Definitions.
313.122 Notification of debt to FMS.
313.123 Certification and referral of debt.
313.124 Pre-offset notice and consideration of evidence.
313.125 No requirement for duplicate notice.
313.126 Referral of past-due, legally enforceable debt.
313.127 Correcting and updating referral.
313.128 Disposition of amounts collected.
313.129–313.139 [Reserved]

Subpart F—Civil Service Retirement and Disability Fund Offset

313.140 Future benefits.
313.141 Notification to OPM.
313.142 Request for administrative offset.
313.143 Cancellation of deduction.
313.144–313.159 [Reserved]

Subpart G—Mandatory Centralized Administrative Offset

313.160 Treasury notification.
313.161 Certification of debt.
313.162 Compliance with 31 CFR part 285.
313.163 Notification of debts of 180 days or less.
313.164–313.180 [Reserved]

Federal Deposit Insurance Corporation

§ 313.3

AUTHORITY: 12 U.S.C. 1819(a); 5 U.S.C. 5514; Pub. L. 104–143; 110 Stat. 1321 (31 U.S.C. 3701, 3711, 3716).

SOURCE: 67 FR 48527, July 25, 2002, unless otherwise noted.

Subpart A—Scope, Purpose, Definitions and Delegations of Authority

§ 313.1 Scope.

This part establishes FDIC procedures for the collection of certain debts owed to the United States.

(a) This part applies to collections by the FDIC from:

(1) Federal employees who are indebted to the FDIC;

(2) Employees of the FDIC who are indebted to other agencies; and

(3) Other persons, organizations, or entities that are indebted to the FDIC, except those excluded in paragraph (b)(3) of this section.

(b) This part does not apply:

(1) To debts or claims arising under the Internal Revenue Code of 1986 (Title 26, U.S. Code), the Social Security Act (42 U.S.C. 301 et seq.), or the tariff laws of the United States;

(2) To a situation to which the Contract Disputes Act (41 U.S.C. 601 et seq.) applies; or

(3) In any case where collection of a debt is explicitly provided for or prohibited by another statute.

(c) This part applies only to:

(1) Debts owed to and payments made by the FDIC acting in its corporate capacity, that is, in connection with employee matters such as travel-related claims and erroneous overpayments, contracting activities involving corporate operations, debts related to requests to the FDIC for documents under the Freedom of Information Act (FOIA), or where a request for an offset is received by the FDIC from another federal agency; and

(2) Criminal restitution debt owed to the FDIC in either its corporate capacity or its receivership capacity.

(3) With the exception of criminal restitution debt noted in paragraph (c)(2) of this section, this part does not apply to debts owed to or payments made by the FDIC in connection with the FDIC's liquidation, supervision, enforcement, or insurance responsibilities, nor does it limit or affect the FDIC's authority with respect to debts and/or claims pursuant to 12 U.S.C. 1819(a) and 1820(a).

(d) Nothing in this part 313 precludes the compromise, suspension, or termination of collection actions, where appropriate, under: standards implementing the Debt Collection Improvement Act (DCIA) (31 U.S.C. 3711 et seq.), the Federal Claims Collection Standards (FCCS) (31 CFR chapter IX and parts 900 through 904); or any other applicable law.

[67 FR 48527, July 25, 2002, as amended at 71 FR 75661, Dec. 18, 2006]

§ 313.2 Purpose.

(a) The purpose of this part is to implement federal statutes and regulatory standards authorizing the FDIC to collect debts owed to the United States. This part is consistent with the following federal statutes and regulations:

(1) DCIA at 31 U.S.C. 3711 (collection and compromise of claims); section 3716 (administrative offset), section 3717 (interest and penalty on claims), and section 3718 (contracts for collection services);

(2) 5 U.S.C. 5514 (salary offset);

(3) 5 U.S.C. 5584 (waiver of claims for overpayment);

(4) 31 CFR chapter IX and parts 900 through 904 (Federal Claims Collection Standards);

(5) 5 CFR part 550, subpart K (salary offset);

(6) 31 U.S.C. 3720D, 31 CFR 285.11 (administrative wage garnishment);

(7) 26 U.S.C. 6402(d), 31 U.S.C. 3720A and 31 CFR 285.2 (tax refund offset); and

(8) 5 CFR 831.1801 through 1808 (U. S. Office of Personnel Management (OPM) offset).

(b) Collectively, these statutes and regulations prescribe the manner in which federal agencies should proceed to establish the existence and validity of debts owed to the federal government and describe the remedies available to agencies to offset valid debts.

§ 313.3 Definitions.

Except where the context clearly indicates otherwise or where the term is defined elsewhere in this subpart, the

159

§ 313.3

following definitions shall apply to this subpart.

(a) *Agency* means a department, agency, court, court administrative office, or instrumentality in the executive, judicial, or legislative branch of government, including government corporations.

(b) *Board* means the Board of Directors of the FDIC.

(c) *Centralized administrative offset* means the mandatory referral to the Secretary of the Treasury by a creditor agency of a past due debt which is more than 180 days delinquent, for the purpose of collection under the Treasury's centralized offset program.

(d) *Certification* means a written statement transmitted from a creditor agency to a paying agency for purposes of administrative or salary offset, to FMS for offset or to the Secretary of the Treasury for centralized administrative offset. The certification confirms the existence and amount of the debt and verifies that required procedural protections have been afforded the debtor. Where the debtor requests a hearing on a claimed debt, the decision by a hearing official or administrative law judge constitutes a certification.

(e) *Chairman* means the Chairman of the FDIC.

(f) *Compromise* means the settlement or forgiveness of a debt under 31 U.S.C. 3711, in accordance with standards set forth in the FCCS and applicable federal law.

(g) *Creditor agency* means an agency of the federal government to which the debt is owed, or a debt collection center when acting on behalf of a creditor agency to collect a debt.

(h) *Debt* means an amount owed to the United States from loans insured or guaranteed by the United States and all other amounts due the United States from fees, leases, rents, royalties, services, sales of real or personal property, overpayments, penalties, damages, interest, restitution, fines and forfeitures, and all other similar sources. For purposes of this part, a debt owed to the FDIC constitutes a debt owed to the United States.

(i) *Debt collection center* means the Department of the Treasury or other government agency or division designated by the Secretary of the Treasury with authority to collect debts on behalf of creditor agencies in accordance with 31 U.S.C. 3711(g).

(j) *Director* means the Director of the Division of Finance (DOF), the Director of the Division of Administration (DOA), or the Director of the Division of Resolutions and Receiverships (DRR), as applicable, or the applicable Director's delegate.

(k) *Disposable pay* means that part of current adjusted basic pay, special pay, incentive pay, retired pay, retainer pay, and, in the case of an employee not entitled to adjusted basic pay, other authorized pay, remaining for each pay period after the deduction of any amount required by law to be withheld. The FDIC shall allow the following deductions in determining the amount of disposable pay that is subject to salary offset:

(1) Federal employment taxes;

(2) Federal, state, or local income taxes to the extent authorized or required by law, but no greater than would be the case if the employee claimed all dependents to which he or she is entitled and such additional amounts for which the employee presents evidence of a tax obligation supporting the additional withholding;

(3) Medicare deductions;

(4) Health insurance premiums;

(5) Normal retirement contributions, including employee contributions to the Thrift Savings Plan or the FDIC 401(k) Plan;

(6) Normal life insurance premiums (e.g., Serviceman's Group Life Insurance and "Basic Life" Federal Employee's Group Life Insurance premiums), not including amounts deducted for supplementary coverage;

(7) Amounts mandatorily withheld for the United States Soldiers' and Airmen's Home;

(8) Fines and forfeiture ordered by a court-martial or by a commanding officer.

(l) *Division of Administration* (DOA) means the Division of Administration of the FDIC.

(m) *Division of Finance* (DOF) means the Division of Finance of the FDIC.

(n) *Division of Resolutions and Receiverships (DRR)* means the Division of Resolutions and Receiverships of the FDIC.

Federal Deposit Insurance Corporation § 313.20

(o) *Federal Claims Collection Standards* (FCCS) means standards published at 31 CFR chapter IX and parts 900 through 904.

(p) *Garnishment* means the process of withholding amounts from the disposable pay of a person employed outside the federal government, and the paying of those amounts to a creditor in satisfaction of a withholding order.

(q) *Hearing official* means an administrative law judge or other individual authorized to conduct a hearing and issue a final decision in response to a debtor's request for hearing. A hearing official may not be under the supervision or control of the Chairman or FDIC Board when the FDIC is the creditor agency.

(r) *Notice of Intent to Offset or Notice of Intent* means a written notice from a creditor agency to an employee, organization, entity, or restitution debtor that claims a debt and informs the debtor that the creditor agency intends to collect the debt by administrative offset. The notice also informs the debtor of certain procedural rights with respect to the claimed debt and offset.

(s) *Notice of Salary Offset* means a written notice from a paying agency to its employee informing the employee that salary offset to collect a debt due to the creditor agency will begin at the next officially established pay interval. The paying agency transmits this notice to its employee after receiving a certification from the creditor agency.

(t) *Paying agency* means the agency of the federal government that employs the individual who owes a debt to an agency of the federal government. The same agency may be both the creditor agency and the paying agency.

(u) *Salary offset* means an administrative offset to collect a debt under 5 U.S.C. 5514 by deduction(s) at one or more officially established pay intervals from the current pay account of an employee without his or her consent.

(v) *Waiver* means the cancellation, remission, forgiveness or non-recovery of a debt allegedly owed by an employee to an agency, as authorized or required by 5 U.S.C. 5584 or any other law.

(w) *Withholding order* means any order for withholding or garnishment of pay issued by an agency, or judicial or administrative body. For purposes of administrative wage garnishment, the terms "wage garnishment order" and "garnishment order" have the same meaning as "withholding order."

[67 FR 48527, July 25, 2002, as amended at 71 FR 75661, Dec. 18, 2006]

§ 313.4 Delegations of authority.

Authority to conduct the following activities to collect debt, other than criminal restitution debt, on behalf of the FDIC in its corporate capacity is delegated to the Director of DOA or Director of DOF, as applicable; and authority to collect criminal restitution debt on behalf of the FDIC in either its receivership or corporate capacity is delegated to the Director of DRR; or to the applicable Director's delegate; to:

(a) Initiate and carry out the debt collection process on behalf of the FDIC, in accordance with the FCCS;

(b) Accept or reject compromise offers and suspend or terminate collection actions to the full extent of the FDIC's legal authority under 12 U.S.C. 1819(a) and 1820(a), 31 U.S.C. 3711(a)(2), and any other applicable statute or regulation, provided, however, that no such claim shall be compromised or collection action terminated, except upon the concurrence of the FDIC General Counsel or his or her designee;

(c) Report to consumer reporting agencies certain data pertaining to delinquent debts, where appropriate;

(d) Use administrative offset procedures, including salary offset, to collect debts; and

(e) Take any other action necessary to promptly and effectively collect debts owed to the United States in accordance with the policies contained herein and as otherwise provided by law.

[67 FR 48527, July 25, 2002, as amended at 71 FR 75661, Dec. 18, 2006]

§§ 313.5–313.19 [Reserved]

Subpart B—Administrative Offset

§ 313.20 Applicability and scope.

The provisions of this subpart apply to the collection of debts owed to the

§ 313.21

United States arising from transactions with the FDIC. Administrative offset is authorized under the DCIA. This subpart is consistent with the FCCS on administrative offset issued by the Department of Justice.

§ 313.21 Definitions.

(a) *Administrative offset* means withholding funds payable by the United States to, or held by the United States for, a person to satisfy a debt.

(b) *Person* includes a natural person or persons, profit or nonprofit corporation, partnership, association, trust, estate, consortium, or other entity which is capable of owing a debt to the United States Government except that agencies of the United States, or any state or local government shall be excluded.

§ 313.22 Collection.

(a) The Director may collect a claim from a person by administrative offset of monies payable by the Government only after:

(1) Providing the debtor with due process required under this part; and

(2) Providing the paying agency with written certification that the debtor owes the debt in the amount stated and that the FDIC, as creditor agency, has complied with this part.

(b) Prior to initiating collection by administrative offset, the Director should determine that the proposed offset is within the scope of this remedy, as set forth in 31 CFR 901.3(a). Administrative offset under 31 U.S.C. 3716 may not be used to collect debts more than 10 years after the federal government's right to collect the debt first accrued, except as otherwise provided by law. In addition, administrative offset may not be used when a statute explicitly prohibits its use to collect the claim or type of claim involved.

(c) Unless otherwise provided, debts or payments not subject to administrative offset under 31 U.S.C. 3716 may be collected by administrative offset under common law, or any other applicable statutory authority.

§ 313.23 Offset prior to completion of procedures.

The FDIC may collect a debt by administrative offset prior to the completion of the procedures described in § 313.25, if:

(a) Failure to offset a payment would substantially prejudice the FDIC's ability to collect the debt; and

(b) The time before the payment is to be made does not reasonably permit completion of the procedures described in § 313.25. Such prior offsetting shall be followed promptly by the completion of the procedures described in § 313.25.

§ 313.24 Omission of procedures.

The FDIC shall not be required to follow the procedures described in § 313.25 where:

(a) The offset is in the nature of a recoupment (*i.e.*, the FDIC may offset a payment due to the debtor when both the payment due to the debtor and the debt owed to the FDIC arose from the same transaction); or

(b) The debt arises under a contract as set forth in *Cecile Industries, Inc.* v. *Cheney*, 995 F.2d 1052 (Fed. Cir. 1993), which provides that procedural protections under administrative offset do not supplant or restrict established procedures for contractual offsets accommodated by the Contracts Disputes Act; or

(c) In the case of non-centralized administrative offsets, the FDIC first learns of the existence of a debt due when there would be insufficient time to afford the debtor due process under these procedures before the paying agency makes payment to the debtor; in such cases, the Director shall give the debtor notice and an opportunity for review as soon as practical and shall refund any money ultimately found not to be due to the U.S. Government.

§ 313.25 Debtor's rights.

Unless the procedures described in § 313.23 are used, prior to collecting any claim by administrative offset or referring such claim to another agency for collection through administrative offset, the Director shall provide the debtor with the following:

(a) Written notification of the nature and amount of the claim, the intention of the Director to collect the claim through administrative offset, and a statement of the rights of the debtor under this paragraph;

Federal Deposit Insurance Corporation § 313.30

(b) An opportunity to inspect and copy the records of the FDIC with respect to the claim, unless such records are exempt from disclosure;

(c) An opportunity to have the FDIC's determination of indebtedness reviewed by the Director:

(1) Any request by the debtor for such review shall be in writing and shall be submitted to the FDIC within 30 calendar days of the date of the notice of the offset. The Director may waive the time limit for requesting review for good cause shown by the debtor;

(2) Upon acceptance of a request for review by the debtor, the FDIC shall provide the debtor with a reasonable opportunity for an oral hearing when the determination turns on an issue of credibility or veracity, or the Director determines that the question of the indebtedness cannot be resolved by review of the documentary evidence alone. Unless otherwise required by law, an oral hearing under this section is not required to be a formal evidentiary hearing, although the Director shall document all significant matters discussed at the hearing. In cases where an oral hearing is not required by this section, the Director shall make his determination based on a documentary hearing consisting of a review of the written record; and

(d) An opportunity to enter into a written agreement for the voluntary repayment of the amount of the claim at the discretion of the Director.

§ 313.26 Interest.

Pursuant to 31 U.S.C. 3717, the FDIC shall assess interest, penalties and administrative costs on debts owed to the United States. The FDIC is authorized to assess interest and related charges on debts that are not subject to 31 U.S.C. 3717 to the extent authorized under the common law or other applicable statutory authority.

§ 313.27 Refunds.

Amounts recovered by administrative offset but later found not to be owed to the Government shall be promptly refunded. Unless required by law or contract, such refunds shall not bear interest.

§ 313.28 No requirement for duplicate notice.

Where the Director has previously given a debtor any of the required notice and review opportunities with respect to a particular debt, the Director is not required to duplicate such notice and review opportunities prior to initiating administrative offset.

§ 313.29 Requests for offset to other federal agencies.

The Director may request that a debt owed to the FDIC be administratively offset against funds due and payable to a debtor by another federal agency. In requesting administrative offset, the FDIC, as the creditor agency, will certify in writing to the federal agency holding funds payable to the debtor:

(a) That the debtor owes the debt;

(b) The amount and basis of the debt; and

(c) That the FDIC has complied with the requirements of its own administrative offset regulations and the applicable provisions of 31 U.S.C. 3716 with respect to providing the debtor with due process, unless otherwise provided.

§ 313.30 Requests for offset from other federal agencies.

Any federal agency may request that funds due and payable to its debtor by the FDIC be administratively offset by the FDIC in order to collect a debt owed to such agency by the debtor. The FDIC shall initiate the requested offset only upon:

(a) Receipt of written certification from the creditor agency stating:

(1) That the debtor owes the debt;

(2) The amount and basis of the debt; and

(3) That the agency has complied with its own administrative offset regulations and with the applicable provisions of 31 CFR 901.3, including providing any required hearing or review.

(b) A determination by the creditor agency that collection by offset against funds payable by the FDIC would be in the best interest of the United States and that such offset would not otherwise be contrary to law.

§§ 313.31–313.39 [Reserved]

Subpart C—Salary Offset

§ 313.40 Scope.

These salary offset regulations are issued in compliance with 5 U.S.C. 5514 and 5 CFR part 550, subpart K, and apply to the collection of debts owed by employees of the FDIC or other federal agencies. These salary offset procedures do not apply where an employee consents to the recovery of a debt from his current pay account. These procedures do not apply to debts arising under the Internal Revenue Code, the tariff laws of the United States or to any case where collection of a debt by salary offset is explicitly provided for or prohibited by another statute (e.g., travel advances under 5 U.S.C. 5705 and employee training expenses under 5 U.S.C. 4108). These procedures do not preclude an employee from requesting waiver of an erroneous payment under 5 U.S.C. 5584, or in any way questioning the amount or validity of a debt, in the manner specified by law or these agency regulations. This section also does not preclude an employee from requesting waiver of the collection of a debt under any other applicable statutory authority. When possible, salary offset through centralized administrative offset procedures should be attempted before seeking salary offset from a paying agency different than the creditor agency.

§ 313.41 Notice requirement where FDIC is creditor agency.

Where the FDIC seeks salary offset under 5 U.S.C. 5514 as the creditor agency, the FDIC shall first provide the employee with a written Notice of Intent to Offset at least 30 calendar days before salary offset is to commence. The Notice of Intent to Offset shall include the following information and statements:

(a) That the Director has determined that a debt is owed to the FDIC and intends to collect the debt by means of deduction from the employee's current disposable pay account until the debt and all accumulated interest is paid in full or otherwise resolved;

(b) The amount of the debt and the factual basis for the debt;

(c) A salary offset schedule stating the frequency and amount of each deduction, stated as a fixed dollar amount or percentage of disposable pay (not to exceed 15%);

(d) That in lieu of salary offset, the employee may propose a voluntary repayment plan to satisfy the debt on terms acceptable to the FDIC, which must be documented in writing, signed by the employee and the Director or the Director's designee, and documented in the FDIC's files;

(e) The FDIC's policy concerning interest, penalties, and administrative costs, and a statement that such assessments must be made, unless excused in accordance with the FCCS;

(f) That the employee has the right to inspect and copy FDIC records not exempt from disclosure relating to the debt claimed, or to receive copies of such records if the employee or the employee's representative is unable personally to inspect the records, due to geographical or other constraints:

(1) That such requests must be made in writing, and identify by name and address the Director or other designated individual to whom the request should be sent; and

(2) That upon receipt of such a request, the Director or the Director's designee shall notify the employee of the time and location where the records may be inspected and copied;

(g) That the employee has a right to request a hearing regarding the existence and amount of the debt claimed or the salary offset schedule proposed by the FDIC, provided that the employee files a request for such a hearing with the FDIC in accordance with § 313.42 that such a hearing will be conducted by an impartial official who is an administrative law judge or other hearing official not under the supervision or control of the Board;

(h) The procedure and deadline for requesting a hearing, including the name, address, and telephone number of the Director or other designated individual to whom a request for hearing must be sent;

(i) That a request for hearing must be received by the FDIC on or before the 30th calendar day following receipt of the Notice of Intent, and that filing of

Federal Deposit Insurance Corporation

§ 313.44

a request for hearing will stay the collection proceedings;

(j) That the FDIC will initiate salary offset procedures not less than 30 days from the date of the employee's receipt of the Notice of Intent to Offset, unless the employee files a timely request for a hearing;

(k) That if a hearing is held, the administrative law judge or other hearing official will issue a decision at the earliest practical date, but not later than 60 days after the filing of the request for the hearing, unless the employee requests a delay in the proceedings which is granted by the hearing official;

(l) That any knowingly false or frivolous statements, representations, or evidence may subject the employee to:

(1) Disciplinary procedures appropriate under 5 U.S.C. chapter 75, 5 CFR part 752, or any other applicable statutes or regulations;

(2) Penalties under the False Claims Act, 31 U.S.C. 3729 through 3731, or under any other applicable statutory authority; or

(3) Criminal penalties under 18 U.S.C. 286, 287, 1001, and 1002 or under any other applicable statutory authority;

(m) That the employee also has the right to request waiver of overpayment pursuant to 5 U.S.C. 5584, and may exercise any other rights and remedies available under statutes or regulations governing the program for which the collection is being made; and

(n) That amounts paid on or deducted from debts that are later waived or found not to be owed to the United States will be promptly refunded to the employee, unless there are applicable contractual or statutory provisions to the contrary.

§ 313.42 Procedures to request a hearing.

(a) To request a hearing, an employee must send a written request to the Director. The request must be received by the Director within 30 calendar days after the employee's receipt of the Notice of Intent.

(b) The request must be signed by the employee and must fully identify and explain with reasonable specificity all the facts, evidence, and witnesses, if any, that the employee believes support his or her position. The request for hearing must state whether the employee is requesting an oral or documentary hearing. If an oral hearing is requested, the request shall explain why the matter cannot be resolved by a review of documentary evidence alone.

§ 313.43 Failure to timely submit request for hearing.

If the Director does not receive an employee's request for hearing within the 30-day period set forth in § 313.42(a), the employee shall not be entitled to a hearing. However, the Director may accept an untimely request for hearing if the employee can show that the delay was the result of circumstances beyond his or her control or that he or she failed to receive actual notice of the filing deadline.

§ 313.44 Procedure for hearing.

(a) *Obtaining the services of a hearing official.* When the FDIC is the creditor agency and the debtor is an FDIC employee, the FDIC shall designate an administrative law judge or contact any agent of another agency designated in appendix A to 5 CFR part 581 to arrange for a hearing official. When the FDIC is the creditor agency and the debtor is not an FDIC employee (*i.e.*, the debtor is employed by another federal agency, also known as the paying agency), and the FDIC cannot provide a prompt and appropriate hearing before an administrative law judge or a hearing official furnished pursuant to a lawful arrangement, the FDIC may contact an agent of the paying agency designated in appendix A to 5 CFR part 581 to arrange for a hearing official. The paying agency must cooperate with the FDIC to provide a hearing official, as required by the FCCS.

(b) *Notice and format of hearing*—(1) *Notice.* The hearing official shall determine whether the hearing shall be oral or documentary and shall notify the employee of the form of the hearing. If the hearing will be oral, the notice shall set forth the date, time, and location of the hearing, which must be held within 30 calendar days after the request is received, unless the employee requests that the hearing be delayed. If the hearing will be documentary, the

§ 313.45

employee shall be notified to submit evidence and written arguments in support of his or her case to the hearing official within 30 calendar days.

(2) *Oral hearing.* The hearing official may grant a request for an oral hearing if he or she determines that the issues raised by the employee cannot be resolved by review of documentary evidence alone (e.g., where credibility or veracity are at issue). An oral hearing is not required to be an adversarial adjudication, and the hearing official is not required to apply rules of evidence. Witnesses who testify in oral hearings shall do so under oath or affirmation. Oral hearings may take the form of, but are not limited to:

(i) Informal conferences with the hearing official in which the employee and agency representative are given full opportunity to present evidence, witnesses, and argument;

(ii) Informal meetings in which the hearing examiner interviews the employee; or

(iii) Formal written submissions followed by an opportunity for oral presentation.

(3) *Documentary hearing.* If the hearing official determines that an oral hearing is not necessary, he or she shall decide the issues raised by the employee based upon a review of the written record.

(4) *Record.* The hearing official shall maintain a summary record of any hearing conducted under this section.

(c) *Rescheduling of the hearing date.* The hearing official shall reschedule a hearing if requested to do so by both parties, who shall be given reasonable notice of the time and place of this new hearing.

(d) *Failure to appear.* In the absence of good cause, an employee who fails to appear at a hearing shall be deemed, for the purpose of this subpart, to admit the existence and amount of the debt as described in the Notice of Intent. If the representative of the creditor agency fails to appear, the hearing official shall proceed with the hearing as scheduled, and issue a decision based upon the oral testimony presented and the documentation submitted by both parties.

(e) *Date of decision.* The hearing official shall issue a written decision based upon the evidence and information developed at the hearing, as soon as practicable after the hearing, but not later than 60 calendar days after the date on which the request for hearing was received by the FDIC, unless the hearing was delayed at the request of the employee. In the event of such a delay, the 60-day decision period shall be extended by the number of days by which the hearing was postponed. The decision of the hearing official shall be final.

(f) *Content of decision.* The written decision shall include:

(1) A summary of the facts concerning the origin, nature, and amount of the debt;

(2) The hearing official's findings, analysis, and conclusions; and

(3) The terms of the repayment schedule, if applicable.

(g) *Official certification of debt.* The hearing official's decision shall constitute an official certification regarding the existence and amount of the debt for purposes of executing salary offset under 5 U.S.C. 5514. Where the FDIC is the creditor agency but not the current paying agency, the FDIC may make a certification regarding the existence and amount of the debt owed to the FDIC, based on the hearing official's certification. The FDIC may make this certification to: the Secretary of the Treasury so that Treasury may offset the employee's current pay account by means of centralized administrative offset (5 CFR 550.1108); or to the current paying agency (5 CFR 550.1109). If the hearing official determines that a debt may not be collected through salary offset but the FDIC as the creditor agency determines that the debt is still valid, the FDIC may seek collection of the debt through other means, including administrative offset of other federal payments or litigation.

§ 313.45 **Certification of debt by FDIC as creditor agency.**

The Director may also issue a certification of the debt where there has not been a hearing, if the employee has admitted the debt, or failed to contest the existence and amount of the debt in a timely manner (e.g., by failing to

Federal Deposit Insurance Corporation § 313.48

request a hearing). The certification shall be in writing and shall state:

(a) The amount and basis of the debt owed by the employee;

(b) The date the FDIC's right to collect the debt first accrued;

(c) That the FDIC's debt collection regulations have been approved by OPM pursuant to 5 CFR part 550, subpart K;

(d) If the collection is to be made by lump-sum payment, the amount and date such payment will be collected;

(e) If the collection is to be made in installments through salary offset, the number of installments to be collected, the amount of each installment, and the date of the first installment, if a date other than the next officially established pay period; and

(f) The date the employee was notified of the debt, the action(s) taken pursuant to the FDIC's regulations, and the dates such actions were taken.

§ 313.46 Notice of salary offset where FDIC is the paying agency.

(a) Upon issuance of a proper certification by the Director for debts owed to the FDIC, or upon receipt of a proper certification from a creditor agency, the Director shall send the employee a written notice of salary offset. Such notice shall advise the employee:

(1) That certification has been issued by the Director or received from another creditor agency;

(2) Of the amount of the debt and of the deductions to be made; and

(3) Of the initiation of salary offset at the next officially established pay interval or as otherwise provided for in the certification.

(b) Where appropriate, the Director shall provide a copy of the notice to the creditor agency and advise such agency of the dollar amount to be offset and the pay period when the offset will begin.

§ 313.47 Voluntary repayment agreements as alternative to salary offset where the FDIC is the creditor agency.

(a) In response to a Notice of Intent, an employee may propose to voluntarily repay the debt through scheduled voluntary payments, in lieu of salary offset. An employee who wishes to repay a debt in this manner shall submit to the Director a written agreement proposing a repayment schedule. This proposal must be received by the Director within 30 calendar days after receipt of the Notice of Intent.

(b) The Director shall notify the employee whether the employee's proposed voluntary repayment agreement is acceptable. It is within the discretion of the Director whether to accept or reject the debtor's proposal, or whether to propose to the debtor a modification of the proposed repayment agreement:

(1) If the Director decides that the proposed repayment agreement is unacceptable, he or she shall notify the employee and the employee shall have 30 calendar days from the date he or she received notice of the decision in which to file a request for a hearing on the proposed repayment agreement, as provided in § 313.42; or

(2) If the Director decides that the proposed repayment agreement is acceptable or the debtor agrees to a modification proposed by the Director, the agreement shall be put in writing and signed by both the employee and the Director.

§ 313.48 Special review of repayment agreement or salary offset due to changed circumstances.

(a) An employee subject to a voluntary repayment agreement or salary offset payable to the FDIC as creditor agency may request a special review by the Director of the amount of the salary offset or voluntary repayment, based on materially changed circumstances, including, but not limited to, catastrophic illness, divorce, death, or disability. A request for special review may be made at any time.

(b) In support of a request for special review, the employee shall submit to the Director a detailed statement and supporting documents for the employee, his or her spouse, and dependents indicating:

(1) Income from all sources;

(2) Assets;

(3) Liabilities;

(4) Number of dependents;

(5) Monthly expenses for food, housing, clothing, and transportation;

(6) Medical expenses; and

(7) Exceptional expenses, if any.

(c) The employee shall also file an alternative proposed offset or payment schedule and a statement, with supporting documents, showing why the current salary offset or payments result in extreme financial hardship to the employee.

(d) The Director shall evaluate the statement and supporting documents and determine whether the original salary offset or repayment schedule imposes extreme financial hardship on the employee, for example, by preventing the employee from meeting essential subsistence expenses such as food, housing, clothing, transportation, and medical care. The Director shall notify the employee in writing within 30 calendar days of his or her determination.

(e) If the special review results in a revised salary offset or repayment schedule, the Director shall provide a new certification to the paying agency.

§ 313.49 Coordinating salary offset with other agencies.

(a) *Responsibility of the FDIC as the creditor agency.* Upon completion of the procedures established in § 313.40 through § 313.45, the Director shall take the following actions:

(1) Submit a debt claim to the paying agency, containing the information described in paragraphs (a)(2) and (a)(3) of this section, together with the certification of debt or an installment agreement (or other instruction regarding the payment schedule, if applicable).

(2) If the collection must be made in installments, inform the paying agency of the amount or percentage of disposable pay to be collected in each installment. The Director may also inform the paying agency of the commencement date and number of installments to be paid, if a date other than the next officially established pay period is required.

(3) Unless the employee has consented to the salary offset in writing or has signed a statement acknowledging receipt of the required procedures and the written consent or statement is forwarded to the paying agency, the Director must also advise the paying agency of the actions the FDIC has taken under 5 U.S.C. 5514 and state the dates such action was taken.

(4) If the employee is in the process of separating from employment, the Director shall submit the debt claim to the employee's paying agency for collection by lump-sum deduction from the employee's final check. The paying agency shall certify the total amount of its collection and furnish a copy of the certification to the FDIC and to the employee.

(5) If the employee is already separated and all payments due from his or her former paying agency have been paid, the Director may, unless otherwise prohibited, request that money due and payable to the employee from the federal government, including payments from the Civil Service Retirement and Disability Fund (5 CFR 831.1801), be administratively offset to collect the debt.

(6) In the event an employee transfers to another paying agency, the Director shall not repeat the procedures described in § 313.40 through § 313.45 in order to resume collecting the debt. Instead, the FDIC shall review the debt upon receiving the former paying agency's notice of the employee's transfer and shall ensure that collection is resumed by the new paying agency. The FDIC must submit a properly certified claim to the new paying agency before collection can be resumed.

(b) *Responsibility of the FDIC as the paying agency*—(1) *Complete claim.* When the FDIC receives a properly certified claim from a creditor agency, the employee shall be given written notice of the certification, the date salary offset will begin, and the amount of the periodic deductions. The FDIC shall schedule deductions to begin at the next officially established pay interval or as otherwise provided for in the certification.

(2) *Incomplete claim.* When the FDIC receives an incomplete certification of debt from a creditor agency, the FDIC shall return the debt claim with notice that procedures under 5 U.S.C. 5514 and 5 CFR 550.1104 must be followed and that a properly certified debt claim must be received before action will be taken to collect from the employee's current pay account.

Federal Deposit Insurance Corporation

§ 313.54

(3) *Review.* The FDIC is not authorized to review the merits of the creditor agency's determination with respect to the amount or validity of the debt certified by the creditor agency.

(4) *Employees who transfer from one paying agency to another agency.* If, after the creditor agency has submitted the debt claim to the FDIC, the employee transfers to a different paying agency before the debt is collected in full, the FDIC must certify the total amount collected on the debt. One copy of the certification shall be furnished to the employee, and one copy shall be sent to the creditor agency along with notice of the employee's transfer. If the FDIC is aware that the employee is entitled to payments from the Civil Service Retirement and Disability Fund, or other similar payments, it must provide written notification to the agency responsible for making such payments that the debtor owes a debt (including the amount) and that the requirements set forth herein and in the OPM's regulation (5 CFR part 550, subpart K) have been fully met.

§ 313.50 Interest, penalties, and administrative costs.

Where the FDIC is the creditor agency, it shall assess interest, penalties, and administrative costs pursuant to 31 U.S.C. 3717 and 31 CFR parts 900 through 904.

§ 313.51 Refunds.

(a) Where the FDIC is the creditor agency, it shall promptly refund any amount deducted under the authority of 5 U.S.C. 5514 when the debt is compromised or otherwise found not to be owing to the United States, or when an administrative or judicial order directs the FDIC to make a refund.

(b) Unless required by law or contract, such refunds shall not bear interest.

§ 313.52 Request from a creditor agency for services of a hearing official.

(a) The FDIC may provide a hearing official upon request of the creditor agency when the debtor is employed by the FDIC and the creditor agency cannot provide a prompt and appropriate hearing before a hearing official furnished pursuant to another lawful arrangement.

(b) The FDIC may provide a hearing official upon request of a creditor agency when the debtor works for the creditor agency and that agency cannot arrange for a hearing official.

(c) The Director shall arrange for qualified personnel to serve as hearing officials.

(d) Services rendered under paragraph (a) of this section shall be provided on a fully reimbursable basis pursuant to 31 U.S.C. 1535.

§ 313.53 Non-waiver of rights by payments.

A debtor's payment, whether voluntary or involuntary, of all or any portion of a debt being collected pursuant to this section shall not be construed as a waiver of any rights that the debtor may have under any statute, regulation, or contract except as otherwise provided by law or contract.

§ 313.54 Exception to due process procedures.

(a) The procedures set forth in this subpart shall not apply to routine intra-agency salary adjustments of pay, including the following:

(1) Any adjustment to pay arising out of an employee's election of coverage or a change in coverage under a federal benefits program requiring periodic deductions from pay, if the amount to be recovered was accumulated over four pay periods or less;

(2) A routine adjustment of pay that is made to correct an overpayment attributable to clerical or administrative errors or delays in processing pay documents, if the overpayment occurred within the four pay periods preceding the adjustment and, at the time of such adjustment or as soon thereafter as is practical, the individual is provided written notice of the nature and amount of the adjustment and the point of contact for contesting such adjustment; or

(3) Any adjustment to collect a debt amount to $50 or less, if, at the time of such adjustment, or as soon thereafter as is practical, the individual is provided written notice of the nature and amount of the adjustment and the

§ 313.55

point of contact for contesting such adjustment.

(b) The procedure for notice to the employee and collection of such adjustments is set forth in § 313.55.

§ 313.55 Salary adjustments.

Any negative adjustment to pay arising out of an employee's election of coverage, or a change in coverage, under a federal benefits program requiring periodic deductions from pay shall not be considered collection of a "debt" for the purposes of this section if the amount to be recovered was accumulated over four pay periods or less. In such cases, the FDIC shall not apply this subpart C, but will provide a clear and concise statement in the employee's earnings statement advising the employee of the previous overpayment at the time the adjustment is made.

§§ 313.56–313.79 [Reserved]

Subpart D—Administrative Wage Garnishment

§ 313.80 Scope and purpose.

(a) These administrative wage garnishment regulations are issued in compliance with 31 U.S.C. 3720D and 31 CFR 285.11(f). The subpart provides procedures for the FDIC to collect money from a debtor's disposable pay by means of administrative wage garnishment. The receipt of payments pursuant to this subpart does not preclude the FDIC from pursuing other debt collection remedies, including the offset of federal payments. The FDIC may pursue such debt collection remedies separately or in conjunction with administrative wage garnishment. This subpart does not apply to the collection of delinquent debts from the wages of federal employees from their federal employment. Federal pay is subject to the federal salary offset procedures set forth in 5 U.S.C. 5514 and other applicable laws.

§ 313.81 Notice.

At least 30 days before the initiation of garnishment proceedings, the Director will send, by first class mail to the debtor's last known address, a written notice informing the debtor of:

(a) The nature and amount of the debt;

(b) The FDIC's intention to initiate proceedings to collect the debt through deductions from the debtor's pay until the debt and all accumulated interest penalties and administrative costs are paid in full;

(c) An explanation of the debtor's rights as set forth in § 313.82(c); and

(d) The time frame within which the debtor may exercise these rights. The FDIC shall retain a stamped copy of the notice indicating the date the notice was mailed.

§ 313.82 Debtor's rights.

The FDIC shall afford the debtor the opportunity:

(a) To inspect and copy records related to the debt;

(b) To enter into a written repayment agreement with the FDIC, under terms agreeable to the FDIC; and

(c) To the extent that a debt owed has not been established by judicial or administrative order, to request a hearing concerning the existence or amount of the debt or the terms of the repayment schedule. With respect to debts established by a judicial or administrative order, a debtor may request a hearing concerning the payment or other discharge of the debt. The debtor is not entitled to a hearing concerning the terms of the proposed repayment schedule if these terms have been established by written agreement.

§ 313.83 Form of hearing.

(a) If the debtor submits a timely written request for a hearing as provided in § 313.82(c), the FDIC will afford the debtor a hearing, which at the FDIC's option may be oral or written. The FDIC will provide the debtor with a reasonable opportunity for an oral hearing when the Director determines that the issues in dispute cannot be resolved by review of the documentary evidence, for example, when the validity of the claim turns on the issue of credibility or veracity.

(b) If the FDIC determines that an oral hearing is appropriate, the time and location of the hearing shall be established by the FDIC. An oral hearing may, at the debtor's option, be conducted either in person or by telephone

Federal Deposit Insurance Corporation

conference. All travel expenses incurred by the debtor in connection with an in-person hearing will be borne by the debtor. All telephonic charges incurred during the hearing will be the responsibility of the agency.

(c) In cases when it is determined that an oral hearing is not required by this section, the FDIC will accord the debtor a "paper hearing," that is, the FDIC will decide the issues in dispute based upon a review of the written record.

§ 313.84 Effect of timely request.

If the FDIC receives a debtor's written request for hearing within 15 business days of the date the FDIC mailed its notice of intent to seek garnishment, the FDIC shall not issue a withholding order until the debtor has been provided the requested hearing, and a decision in accordance with § 313.88 and § 313.89 has been rendered.

§ 313.85 Failure to timely request a hearing.

If the FDIC receives a debtor's written request for hearing after 15 business days of the date the FDIC mailed its notice of intent to seek garnishment, the FDIC shall provide a hearing to the debtor. However, the FDIC will not delay issuance of a withholding order unless it determines that the untimely filing of the request was caused by factors over which the debtor had no control, or the FDIC receives information that the FDIC believes justifies a delay or cancellation of the withholding order.

§ 313.86 Hearing official.

A hearing official may be any qualified individual, as determined by the FDIC, including an administrative law judge.

§ 313.87 Procedure.

After the debtor requests a hearing, the hearing official shall notify the debtor of:

(a) The date and time of a telephonic hearing;

(b) The date, time, and location of an in-person oral hearing; or

(c) The deadline for the submission of evidence for a written hearing.

§ 313.88 Format of hearing.

The FDIC will have the burden of proof to establish the existence or amount of the debt. Thereafter, if the debtor disputes the existence or amount of the debt, the debtor must prove by a preponderance of the evidence that no debt exists, or that the amount of the debt is incorrect. In addition, the debtor may present evidence that the terms of the repayment schedule are unlawful, would cause a financial hardship to the debtor, or that collection of the debt may not be pursued due to operation of law. The hearing official shall maintain a record of any hearing held under this section. Hearings are not required to be formal, and evidence may be offered without regard to formal rules of evidence. Witnesses who testify in oral hearings shall do so under oath or affirmation.

§ 313.89 Date of decision.

The hearing official shall issue a written opinion stating his or her decision as soon as practicable, but not later than sixty (60) days after the date on which the request for such hearing was received by the FDIC. If the FDIC is unable to provide the debtor with a hearing and decision within sixty (60) days after the receipt of the request for such hearing:

(a) The FDIC may not issue a withholding order until the hearing is held and a decision rendered; or

(b) If the FDIC had previously issued a withholding order to the debtor's employer, the withholding order will be suspended beginning on the 61st day after the date the FDIC received the hearing request and continuing until a hearing is held and a decision is rendered.

§ 313.90 Content of decision.

The written decision shall include:

(a) A summary of the facts presented;

(b) The hearing official's findings, analysis and conclusions; and

(c) The terms of any repayment schedule, if applicable.

§ 313.91 Finality of agency action.

Unless the FDIC on its own initiative orders review of a decision by a hearing official pursuant to 17 CFR 201.431(c), a decision by a hearing official shall become the final decision of the FDIC for the purpose of judicial review under the Administrative Procedure Act.

§ 313.92 Failure to appear.

In the absence of good cause shown, a debtor who fails to appear at a scheduled hearing will be deemed as not having timely filed a request for a hearing.

§ 313.93 Wage garnishment order.

(a) Unless the FDIC receives information that it believes justifies a delay or cancellation of the withholding order, the FDIC will send by first class mail a withholding order to the debtor's employer within 30 days after the debtor fails to make a timely request for a hearing (i.e., within 15 business days after the mailing of the notice of the FDIC's intent to seek garnishment) or, if a timely request for a hearing is made by the debtor, within 30 days after a decision to issue a withholding order becomes final.

(b) The withholding order sent to the employer will be in the form prescribed by the Secretary of the Treasury, on the FDIC's letterhead, and signed by the head of the agency or delegate. The order will contain all information necessary for the employer to comply with the withholding order, including the debtor's name, address, and social security number, as well as instructions for withholding and information as to where payments should be sent.

(c) The FDIC will keep a stamped copy of the order indicating the date it was mailed.

§ 313.94 Certification by employer.

Along with the withholding order, the FDIC will send to the employer a certification in a form prescribed by the Secretary of the Treasury. The employer shall complete and return the certification to the FDIC within the time frame prescribed in the instructions to the form. The certification will address matters such as information about the debtor's employment status and disposable pay available for withholding.

§ 313.95 Amounts withheld.

(a) Upon receipt of the garnishment order issued under this section, the employer shall deduct from all disposable pay paid to the debtor during each pay period the amount of garnishment described in paragraphs (b) through (d) of this section.

(b) Subject to the provisions of paragraphs (c) and (d) of this section, the amount of garnishment shall be the lesser of:

(1) The amount indicated on the garnishment order up to 15% of the debtor's disposable pay; or

(2) The amount set forth in 15 U.S.C. 1673(a)(2). The amount set forth at 15 U.S.C. 1673(a)(2) is the amount by which the debtor's disposable pay exceeds an amount equivalent to thirty times the minimum wage. See 29 CFR 870.10.

(c) When a debtor's pay is subject to withholding orders with priority, the following shall apply:

(1) Unless otherwise provided by federal law, withholding orders issued under this section shall be paid in the amounts set forth under paragraph (b) of this section and shall have priority over other withholding orders which are served later in time. However, withholding orders for family support shall have priority over withholding orders issued under this section.

(2) If amounts are being withheld from a debtor's pay pursuant to a withholding order served on an employer before a withholding order issued pursuant to this section, or if a withholding order for family support is served on an employer at any time, the amounts withheld pursuant to the withholding order issued under this section shall be the lesser of:

(i) The amount calculated under paragraph (b) of this section; or

(ii) An amount equal to 25% of the debtor's disposable pay less the amount(s) withheld under the withholding order(s) with priority.

(3) If a debtor owes more than one debt to the FDIC, the FDIC may issue multiple withholding orders. The total amount garnished from the debtor's pay for such orders will not exceed the amount set forth in paragraph (b) of this section.

(d) An amount greater than that set forth in paragraphs (b) and (c) of this section may be withheld upon the written consent of the debtor.

Federal Deposit Insurance Corporation § 313.101

(e) The employer shall promptly pay to the FDIC all amounts withheld in accordance with the withholding order issued pursuant to this section.

(f) An employer shall not be required to vary its normal pay and disbursement cycles in order to comply with the withholding order.

(g) Any assignment or allotment by the employee of the employee's earnings shall be void to the extent it interferes with or prohibits execution of the withholding order under this section, except for any assignment or allotment made pursuant to a family support judgment or order.

(h) The employer shall withhold the appropriate amount from the debtor's wages for each pay period until the employer receives notification from the FDIC to discontinue wage withholding. The garnishment order shall indicate a reasonable period of time within which the employer is required to commence wage withholding.

§ 313.96 Exclusions from garnishment.

The FDIC will not garnish the wages of a debtor it knows has been involuntarily separated from employment until the debtor has been re-employed continuously for at least 12 months. The debtor has the burden of informing the FDIC of the circumstances surrounding an involuntary separation from employment.

§ 313.97 Financial hardship.

(a) A debtor whose wages are subject to a wage withholding order under this section, may, at any time, request a review by the FDIC of the amount garnished, based on materially changed circumstances such as disability, divorce, or catastrophic illness which result in financial hardship.

(b) A debtor requesting a review under this section shall submit the basis for claiming that the current amount of garnishment results in a financial hardship to the debtor, along with supporting documentation.

(c) If a financial hardship is found, the FDIC will downwardly adjust, by an amount and for a period of time agreeable to the FDIC, the amount garnished to reflect the debtor's financial condition. The FDIC will notify the employer of any adjustments to the amounts to be withheld.

§ 313.98 Ending garnishment.

(a) Once the FDIC has fully recovered the amounts owed by the debtor, including interest, penalties, and administrative costs consistent with the FCCS, the FDIC will send the debtor's employer notification to discontinue wage withholding.

(b) At least annually, the FDIC will review its debtors' accounts to ensure that garnishment has been terminated for accounts that have been paid in full.

§ 313.99 Prohibited actions by employer.

The DCIA prohibits an employer from discharging, refusing to employ, or taking disciplinary action against the debtor due to the issuance of a withholding order under this subpart.

§ 313.100 Refunds.

(a) If a hearing official determines that a debt is not legally due and owing to the United States, the FDIC shall promptly refund any amount collected by means of administrative wage garnishment.

(b) Unless required by federal law or contract, refunds under this section shall not bear interest.

§ 313.101 Right of action.

The FDIC may sue any employer for any amount that the employer fails to withhold from wages owed and payable to its employee in accordance with this subpart. However, a suit will not be filed before the termination of the collection action involving a particular debtor, unless earlier filing is necessary to avoid expiration of any applicable statute of limitations. For purposes of this subpart, "termination of the collection action" occurs when the agency has terminated collection action in accordance with the FCCS (31 CFR 903.1 through 903.5) or other applicable standards. In any event, termination of the collection action will have been deemed to occur if the FDIC has not received any payments to satisfy the debt from the particular debtor

§§ 313.102–313.119

whose wages were subject to garnishment, in whole or in part, for a period of one (1) year.

§§ 313.102–313.119 [Reserved]

Subpart E—Tax Refund Offset

§ 313.120 Scope.

The provisions of 26 U.S.C. 6402(d) and 31 U.S.C. 3720A authorize the Secretary of the Treasury to offset a delinquent debt owed to the United States Government from the tax refund due a taxpayer when other collection efforts have failed to recover the amount due. In addition, the FDIC is authorized to collect debts by means of administrative offset under 31 U.S.C. 3716 and, as part of the debt collection process, to notify the Financial Management Service (FMS), a bureau of the Department of the Treasury, of the amount of such debt for collection by tax refund offset.

§ 313.121 Definitions.

For purposes of this subpart E:

(a) *Debt* or *claim* means an amount of money, funds or property which has been determined by the FDIC to be due to the United States from any person, organization, or entity, except another federal agency.

(b) *Debtor* means a person who owes a debt or a claim. The term "person" includes any individual, organization or entity, except another federal agency.

(c) *Tax refund offset* means withholding or reducing a tax refund payment by an amount necessary to satisfy a debt owed by the payee(s) of a tax refund payment.

(d) *Tax refund payment* means any overpayment of federal taxes to be refunded to the person making the overpayment after the Internal Revenue Service (IRS) makes the appropriate credits.

§ 313.122 Notification of debt to FMS.

The FDIC shall notify FMS of the amount of any past due, legally enforceable non-tax debt owed to it by a person, for the purpose of collecting such debt by tax refund offset. Notification and referral to FMS of such debts does not preclude FDIC's use of any other debt collection procedures, such as wage garnishment, either separately or in conjunction with tax refund offset.

§ 313.123 Certification and referral of debt.

When the FDIC refers a past-due, legally enforceable debt to FMS for tax refund offset, it will certify to FMS that:

(a) The debt is past due and legally enforceable in the amount submitted to FMS and that the FDIC will ensure that collections are properly credited to the debt;

(b) Except in the case of a judgment debt or as otherwise allowed by law, the debt is referred for offset within ten years after the FDIC's right of action accrues;

(c) The FDIC has made reasonable efforts to obtain payment of the debt, in that it has:

(1) Submitted the debt to FMS for collection by administrative offset and complied with the provisions of 31 U.S.C. 3716(a) and related regulations;

(2) Notified, or has made a reasonable attempt to notify, the debtor that the debt is past-due, and unless repaid within 60 days after the date of the notice, will be referred to FMS for tax refund offset;

(3) Given the debtor at least 60 days to present evidence that all or part of the debt is not past-due or legally enforceable, considered any evidence presented by the debtor, and determined that the debt is past-due and legally enforceable; and

(4) Provided the debtor with an opportunity to make a written agreement to repay the debt; and

(d) The debt is at least $25.

§ 313.124 Pre-offset notice and consideration of evidence.

(a) For purposes of § 313.123(c)(2), the FDIC has made a reasonable effort to notify the debtor if it uses the current address information contained in its records related to the debt. The FDIC may, but is not required to, obtain address information from the IRS pursuant to 26 U.S.C. 6103(m)(2), (4), (5).

(b) For purposes of § 313.123(c)(3), if evidence presented by a debtor is considered by an agent of the FDIC, or

Federal Deposit Insurance Corporation

other entities or persons acting on behalf of the FDIC, the debtor must be accorded at least 30 days from the date the agent or other entity or person determines that all or part of the debt is past-due and legally enforceable to request review by an officer or employee of the FDIC of any unresolved dispute. The FDIC must then notify the debtor of its decision.

§ 313.125 No requirement for duplicate notice.

Where the director has previously given a debtor any of the required notice and review opportunities with respect to a particular debt, the Director is not required to duplicate such notice and review opportunities prior to initiating tax refund offset.

[71 FR 75661, Dec. 18, 2006]

§ 313.126 Referral of past-due, legally enforceable debt.

The FDIC shall submit past-due, legally enforceable debt information for tax refund offset to FMS, as prescribed by FMS. For each debt, the FDIC will include the following information:

(a) The name and taxpayer identification number (as defined in 26 U.S.C. 6109) of the debtor;

(b) The amount of the past-due and legally enforceable debt;

(c) The date on which the debt became past-due; and

(d) The designation of FDIC as the agency referring the debt.

[67 FR 48527, July 25, 2002. Redesignated at 71 FR 75661, Dec. 18, 2006]

§ 313.127 Correcting and updating referral.

If, after referring a past-due legally enforceable debt to FMS as provided in § 313.125, the FDIC determines that an error has been made with respect to the information transmitted to FMS, or if the FDIC receives a payment or credits a payment to the account of the debtor referred to FMS for offset, or if the debt amount is otherwise incorrect, the FDIC shall promptly notify FMS and make the appropriate correction of the FDIC's records. FDIC will provide certification as required under § 313.123 for any increases to amounts owed. In the event FMS rejects an FDIC certification for failure to comply with § 323.123, the FDIC may resubmit the debt with a corrected certification.

[67 FR 48527, July 25, 2002. Redesignated at 71 FR 75661, Dec. 18, 2006]

§ 313.128 Disposition of amounts collected.

FMS will transmit amounts collected for past-due, legally enforceable debts, less fees charged under this section, to the FDIC's account. The FDIC will reimburse FMS and the IRS for the cost of administering the tax refund offset program. FMS will deduct the fees from amounts collected prior to disposition and transmit a portion of the fees deducted to reimburse the IRS for its share of the cost of administering the tax refund offset program. To the extent allowed by law, the FDIC may add the offset fees to the debt.

[67 FR 48527, July 25, 2002. Redesignated at 71 FR 75661, Dec. 18, 2006]

§§ 313.129–313.139 [Reserved]

Subpart F—Civil Service Retirement and Disability Fund Offset

§ 313.140 Future benefits.

Unless otherwise prohibited by law, the FDIC may request that a debtor's anticipated or future benefit payments under the Civil Service Retirement and Disability Fund (Fund) be administratively offset in accordance with regulations at 5 CFR 831.1801 through 831.1808.

§ 313.141 Notification to OPM.

When making a request for administrative offset under § 313.140, the FDIC shall provide OPM with a written certification that:

(a) The debtor owes the FDIC a debt, including the amount of the debt;

(b) The FDIC has complied with the applicable statutes, regulations, and procedures of OPM; and

(c) The FDIC has complied with the requirements of 31 CFR parts 900 through 904, including any required hearing or review.

§ 313.142 Request for administrative offset.

The Director shall request administrative offset under § 313.140, as soon as practical after completion of the applicable procedures in order to help ensure that offset be initiated prior to expiration of the applicable statute of limitations. At such time as the debtor makes a claim for payments from the Fund, if at least a year has elapsed since the offset request was originally made, the debtor shall be permitted to offer a satisfactory repayment plan in lieu of offset upon establishing that changed financial circumstances would render the offset unjust.

§ 313.143 Cancellation of deduction.

If the FDIC collects part or all of the debt by other means before deductions are made or completed pursuant to § 313.140, the FDIC shall act promptly to modify or terminate its request for such offset.

Subpart G—Mandatory Centralized Administrative Offset

§ 313.160 Treasury notification.

(a) In accordance with 31 U.S.C. 3716, the FDIC as a creditor agency must notify the Secretary of the Treasury of all debts that are delinquent (over 180 days past due), as defined in the FCCS, to enable the Secretary to seek collection by centralized administrative offset. This includes debts the FDIC seeks to recover from the pay account of an employee of another agency by means of salary offset.

(b) For purposes of centralized administrative offset, a claim or debt is not delinquent if:

(1) It is in litigation or foreclosure;
(2) It will be disposed of under an asset sale program within one year after becoming eligible for sale;
(3) It has been referred to a private collection contractor for collection;
(4) It has been referred to a debt collection center;
(5) It will be collected under internal offset, if such offset is sufficient to collect the claim within three years after the date the debt or claim is first delinquent; and
(6) It is within a specific class of claims or debts which the Secretary of the Treasury has determined to be exempt, at the request of an agency.

§ 313.161 Certification of debt.

Prior to referring a delinquent debt to the Secretary of the Treasury, the Director must have complied with the requirements of 5 U.S.C. 5514, and 5 CFR part 550, subpart K, governing salary offset, and the FDIC regulations. The Director shall certify, in a form acceptable to the Secretary, that:

(a) The debt is past due and legally enforceable; and
(b) The FDIC has complied with all due process requirements under 31 U.S.C. 3716 and the FDIC's administrative offset regulations.

§ 313.162 Compliance with 31 CFR part 285.

The Director shall also comply with applicable procedures for referring a delinquent debt for purposes of centralized offset which are set forth at 31 CFR part 285 and the FCCS.

§ 313.163 Notification of debts of 180 days or less.

The Director, in his discretion, may also notify the Secretary of the Treasury of debts that have been delinquent for 180 days or less, including debts the FDIC seeks to recover by means of salary offset.

§§ 313.164–313.180 [Reserved]

SUBCHAPTER B—REGULATIONS AND STATEMENTS OF GENERAL POLICY

PART 323—APPRAISALS

Sec.
323.1 Authority, purpose, and scope.
323.2 Definitions.
323.3 Appraisals required; transactions requiring a State certified or licensed appraiser.
323.4 Minimum appraisal standards.
323.5 Appraiser independence.
323.6 Professional association membership; competency.
323.7 Enforcement.

AUTHORITY: 12 U.S.C. 1818, 1819 ["Seventh" and "Tenth"], and 3331–3352.

SOURCE: 55 FR 33888, Aug. 20, 1990, unless otherwise noted.

§ 323.1 Authority, purpose, and scope.

(a) *Authority.* This part is issued under 12 U.S.C. 1818, 1819 ["Seventh" and "Tenth"] and title XI of the Financial Institutions Reform, Recovery, and Enforcement Act of 1989 ("FIRREA") (Pub. L. 101–73, 103 Stat. 183, 12 U.S.C. 3331 *et seq.* (1989)).

(b) *Purpose and scope.* (1) Title XI provides protection for federal financial and public policy interests in real estate related transactions by requiring real estate appraisals used in connection with federally related transactions to be performed in writing, in accordance with uniform standards, by appraisers whose competency has been demonstrated and whose professional conduct will be subject to effective supervision. This part implements the requirements of title XI and applies to all federally related transactions entered into by the FDIC or by institutions regulated by the FDIC (*regulated institutions*).

(2) This part: (i) Identifies which real estate-related financial transactions require the services of an appraiser;

(ii) Prescribes which categories of federally related transactions shall be appraised by a State certified appraiser and which by a State licensed appraiser; and

(iii) Prescribes minimum standards for the performance of real estate appraisals in connection with federally related transactions under the jurisdiction of the FDIC.

§ 323.2 Definitions.

(a) *Appraisal* means a written statement independently and impartially prepared by a qualified appraiser setting forth an opinion as to the market value of an adequately described property as of a specific date(s), supported by the presentation and analysis of relevant market information.

(b) *Appraisal Foundation* means the Appraisal Foundation established on November 30, 1987, as a not-for-profit corporation under the laws of Illinois.

(c) *Appraisal Subcommittee* means the Appraisal Subcommittee of the Federal Financial Institutions Examination Council.

(d) *Business loan* means a loan or extension of credit to any corporation, general or limited partnership, business trust, joint venture, pool, syndicate, sole proprietorship, or other business entity.

(e) *Complex 1-to-4 family residential property appraisal* means one in which the property to be appraised, the form of ownership, or market conditions are atypical.

(f) *Federally related transaction* means any real estate-related financial transactions entered into after the effective date hereof that:

(1) The FDIC or any regulated institution engages in or contracts for; and

(2) Requires the services of an appraiser.

(g) *Market value* means the most probable price which a property should bring in a competitive and open market under all conditions requisite to a fair sale, the buyer and seller each acting prudently and knowledgeably, and assuming the price is not affected by undue stimulus. Implicit in this definition is the consummation of a sale as of a specified date and the passing of title from seller to buyer under conditions whereby:

(1) Buyer and seller are typically motivated;

§ 323.3

(2) Both parties are well informed or well advised, and acting in what they consider their own best interests;

(3) A reasonable time is allowed for exposure in the open market;

(4) Payment is made in terms of cash in U.S. dollars or in terms of financial arrangements comparable thereto; and

(5) The price represents the normal consideration for the property sold unaffected by special or creative financing or sales concessions granted by anyone associated with the sale.

(h) *Real estate* or *real property* means an identified parcel or tract of land, with improvements, and includes easements, rights of way, undivided or future interests and similar rights in a tract of land, but does not include mineral rights, timber rights, growing crops, water rights and similar interests severable from the land when the transaction does not involve the associated parcel or tract of land.

(i) *Real estate-related financial transaction* means any transaction involving:

(1) The sale, lease, purchase, investment in or exchange of real property, including interests in property, or the financing thereof; or

(2) The refinancing of real property or interests in real property; or

(3) The use of real property or interests in property as security for a loan or investment, including mortgage-backed securities.

(j) *State certified appraiser* means any individual who has satisfied the requirements for certification in a State or territory whose criteria for certification as a real estate appraiser currently meet the minimum criteria for certification issued by the Appraiser Qualifications Board of the Appraisal Foundation. No individual shall be a State certified appraiser unless such individual has achieved a passing grade upon a suitable examination administered by a State or territory that is consistent with and equivalent to the Uniform State Certification Examination issued or endorsed by the Appraiser Qualifications Board. In addition, the Appraisal Subcommittee must not have issued a finding that the policies, practices, or procedures of a State or territory are inconsistent with title XI of FIRREA. The FDIC may, from time to time, impose additional qualification criteria for certified appraisers performing appraisals in connection with federally related transactions within its jurisdiction.

(k) *State licensed appraiser* means any individual who has satisfied the requirements for licensing in a State or territory where the licensing procedures comply with title XI of FIRREA and where the Appraisal Subcommittee has not issued a finding that the policies, practices, or procedures of the State or territory are inconsistent with title XI. The FDIC may, from time to time, impose additional qualification criteria for licensed appraisers performing appraisals in connection with federally related transactions within its jurisdiction.

(l) *Tract development* means a project of five units or more that is constructed or is to be constructed as a single development.

(m) *Transaction value* means: (1) For loans or other extensions of credit, the amount of the loan or extension of credit;

(2) For sales, leases, purchases, and investments in or exchanges of real property, the market value of the real property interest involved; and

(3) For the pooling of loans or interests in real property for resale or purchase, the amount of the loan or market value of the real property calculated with respect to each such loan or interest in real property.

[55 FR 33888, Aug. 20, 1990, as amended at 57 FR 9049, Mar. 16, 1992; 59 FR 29501, June 7, 1994]

§ 323.3 Appraisals required; transactions requiring a State certified or licensed appraiser.

(a) *Appraisals required.* An appraisal performed by a State certified or licensed appraiser is required for all real estate-related financial transactions except those in which:

(1) The transaction value is $250,000 or less;

(2) A lien on real estate has been taken as collateral in an abundance of caution;

(3) The transaction is not secured by real estate;

Federal Deposit Insurance Corporation § 323.3

(4) A lien on real estate has been taken for purposes other than the real estate's value;

(5) The transaction is a business loan that:

(i) Has a transaction value of $1 million or less; and

(ii) Is not dependent on the sale of, or rental income derived from, real estate as the primary source of repayment;

(6) A lease of real estate is entered into, unless the lease is the economic equivalent of a purchase or sale of the leased real estate;

(7) The transaction involves an existing extension of credit at the lending institution, provided that:

(i) There has been no obvious and material change in market conditions or physical aspects of the property that threatens the adequacy of the institution's real estate collateral protection after the transaction, even with the advancement of new monies; or

(ii) There is no advancement of new monies, other than funds necessary to cover reasonable closing costs;

(8) The transaction involves the purchase, sale, investment in, exchange of, or extension of credit secured by, a loan or interest in a loan, pooled loans, or interests in real property, including mortgaged-backed securities, and each loan or interest in a loan, pooled loan, or real property interest met FDIC regulatory requirements for appraisals at the time of origination;

(9) The transaction is wholly or partially insured or guaranteed by a United States government agency or United States government sponsored agency;

(10) The transaction either:

(i) Qualifies for sale to a United States government agency or United States government sponsored agency; or

(ii) Involves a residential real estate transaction in which the appraisal conforms to the Federal National Mortgage Association or Federal Home Loan Mortgage Corporation appraisal standards applicable to that category of real estate;

(11) The regulated institution is acting in a fiduciary capacity and is not required to obtain an appraisal under other law; or

(12) The FDIC determines that the services of an appraiser are not necessary in order to protect Federal financial and public policy interests in real estate-related financial transactions or to protect the safety and soundness of the institution.

(b) *Evaluations required.* For a transaction that does not require the services of a State certified or licensed appraiser under paragraph (a)(1), (a)(5) or (a)(7) of this section, the institution shall obtain an appropriate evaluation of real property collateral that is consistent with safe and sound banking practices.

(c) *Appraisals to address safety and soundness concerns.* The FDIC reserves the right to require an appraisal under this part whenever the agency believes it is necessary to address safety and soundness concerns.

(d) *Transactions requiring a State certified appraiser*—(1) *All transactions of $1,000,000 or more.* All federally related transactions having a transaction value of $1,000,000 or more shall require an appraisal prepared by a State certified appraiser.

(2) *Nonresidential transactions of $250,000 or more.* All federally related transactions having a transaction value of $250,000 or more, other than those involving appraisals of 1-to-4 family residential properties, shall require an appraisal prepared by a State certified appraiser.

(3) *Complex residential transactions of $250,000 or more.* All complex 1-to-4 family residential property appraisals rendered in connection with federally related transactions shall require a State certified appraiser if the transaction value is $250,000 or more. A regulated institution may presume that appraisals of 1-to-4 family residential properties are not complex, unless the institution has readily available information that a given appraisal will be complex. The regulated institution shall be responsible for making the final determination of whether the appraisal is complex. If during the course of the appraisal a licensed appraiser identifies factors that would result in the property, form of ownership, or market conditions being considered atypical, then either:

(i) The regulated institution may ask the licensed appraiser to complete the appraisal and have a certified appraiser approve and co-sign the appraisal; or

(ii) The institution may engage a certified appraiser to complete the appraisal.

(e) *Transactions requiring either a State certified or licensed appraiser.* All appraisals for federally related transactions not requiring the services of a State certified appraiser shall be prepared by either a State certified appraiser or a State licensed appraiser.

(f) *Effective date.* Regulated institutions are required to use state certified or licensed appraisers as set forth in this section no later than December 31, 1992, unless otherwise required by law.

[55 FR 33888, Aug. 20, 1990, as amended at 57 FR 9050, Mar. 16, 1992; 59 FR 29501, June 7, 1994]

§ 323.4 Minimum appraisal standards.

For federally related transactions, all appraisals shall, at a minimum:

(a) Conform to generally accepted appraisal standards as evidenced by the Uniform Standards of Professional Appraisal Practice (USPAP) promulgated by the Appraisal Standards Board of the Appraisal Foundation, 1029 Vermont Ave., NW., Washington, DC 20005, unless principles of safe and sound banking require compliance with stricter standards;

(b) Be written and contain sufficient information and analysis to support the institution's decision to engage in the transaction;

(c) Analyze and report appropriate deductions and discounts for proposed construction or renovation, partially leased buildings, non-market lease terms, and tract developments with unsold units;

(d) Be based upon the definition of market value as set forth in this part; and

(e) Be performed by State licensed or certified appraisers in accordance with requirements set forth in this part.

[59 FR 29502, June 7, 1994]

§ 323.5 Appraiser independence.

(a) *Staff appraisers.* If an appraisal is prepared by a staff appraiser, that appraiser must be independent of the lending, investment, and collection functions and not involved, except as an appraiser, in the federally related transaction, and have no direct or indirect interest, financial or otherwise, in the property. If the only qualified persons available to perform an appraisal are involved in the lending, investment, or collection functions of the regulated institution, the regulated institution shall take appropriate steps to ensure that the appraisers exercise independent judgment and that the appraisal is adequate. Such steps include, but are not limited to, prohibiting an individual from performing appraisals in connection with federally related transactions in which the appraiser is otherwise involved and prohibiting directors and officers from participating in any vote or approval involving assets on which they performed an appraisal.

(b) *Fee appraisers.* (1) If an appraisal is prepared by a fee appraiser, the appraiser shall be engaged directly by the regulated institution or its agent, and have no direct or indirect interest, financial or otherwise, in the property or the transaction.

(2) A regulated institution also may accept an appraisal that was prepared by an appraiser engaged directly by another financial services institution, if:

(i) The appraiser has no direct or indirect interest, financial or otherwise, in the property or the transaction; and

(ii) The regulated institution determines that the appraisal conforms to the requirements of this part and is otherwise acceptable.

[55 FR 33888, Aug. 20, 1990, as amended by 59 FR 29502, June 7, 1994]

§ 323.6 Professional association membership; competency.

(a) *Membership in appraisal organizations.* A State certified appraiser or a State licensed appraiser may not be excluded from consideration for an assignment for a federally related transaction solely by virtue of membership or lack of membership in any particular appraisal organization.

(b) *Competency.* All staff and fee appraisers performing appraisals in connection with federally related transactions must be State certified or licensed, as appropriate. However, a

Federal Deposit Insurance Corporation

State certified or licensed appraiser may not be considered competent solely by virtue of being certified or licensed. Any determination of competency shall be based upon the individual's experience and educational background as they relate to the particular appraisal assignment for which he or she is being considered.

§ 323.7 Enforcement.

Institutions and institution-affiliated parties, including staff appraisers and fee appraisers, may be subject to removal and/or prohibition orders, cease and desist orders, and the imposition of civil money penalties pursuant to the Federal Deposit Insurance Act, 12 U.S.C. 1811 *et seq.*, as amended, or other applicable law.

PART 324 [RESERVED]

PART 325—CAPITAL MAINTENANCE

Subpart A—Minimum Capital Requirements

Sec.
325.1 Scope.
325.2 Definitions.
325.3 Minimum leverage capital requirement.
325.4 Inadequate capital as an unsafe or unsound practice or condition.
325.5 Miscellaneous.
325.6 Issuance of directives.

Subpart B—Prompt Corrective Action

325.101 Authority, purpose, scope, other supervisory authority, and disclosure of capital categories.
325.102 Notice of capital category.
325.103 Capital measures and capital category definitions.
325.104 Capital restoration plans.
325.105 Mandatory and discretionary supervisory actions under section 38.
APPENDIX A TO PART 325—STATEMENT OF POLICY ON RISK-BASED CAPITAL
APPENDIX B TO PART 325—STATEMENT OF POLICY ON CAPITAL ADEQUACY
APPENDIX C TO PART 325—RISK-BASED CAPITAL FOR STATE NON-MEMBER BANKS: MARKET RISK
APPENDIX D TO PART 325—CAPITAL ADEQUACY GUIDELINES FOR BANKS: INTERNAL-RATINGS-BASED AND ADVANCED MEASUREMENT APPROACHES

AUTHORITY: 12 U.S.C. 1815(a), 1815(b), 1816, 1818(a), 1818(b), 1818(c), 1818(t), 1819(Tenth), 1828(c), 1828(d), 1828(i), 1828(n), 1828(o), 1831o, 1835, 3907, 3909, 4808; Pub. L. 102–233, 105 Stat. 1761, 1789, 1790 (12 U.S.C. 1831n note); Pub. L. 102–242, 105 Stat. 2355, as amended by Pub. L. 103–325, 108 Stat. 2160, 2233 (12 U.S.C. 1828 note); Pub. L. 102–242, 105 Stat. 2236, 2386, as amended by Pub. L. 102–550, 106 Stat. 3672, 4089 (12 U.S.C. 1828 note).

Subpart A—Minimum Capital Requirements

§ 325.1 Scope.

The provisions of this subpart A apply to those circumstances for which the Federal Deposit Insurance Act or this chapter requires an evaluation of the adequacy of an insured depository institution's capital structure. The FDIC is required to evaluate capital before approving various applications by insured depository institutions. The FDIC also must evaluate capital, as an essential component, in determining the safety and soundness of state nonmember banks it insures and supervises and in determining whether depository institutions are in an unsafe or unsound condition. This subpart A establishes the criteria and standards the FDIC will use in calculating the minimum leverage capital requirement and in determining capital adequacy. In addition, appendix A to this subpart sets forth the FDIC's risk-based capital policy statement and appendix B to this subpart includes a statement of policy on capital adequacy that provides interpretational guidance as to how this subpart will be administered and enforced. In accordance with subpart B of part 325, the FDIC also must evaluate an institution's capital for purposes of determining whether the institution is subject to the prompt corrective action provisions set forth in section 38 of the Federal Deposit Insurance Act (12 U.S.C. 1831o).

[58 FR 8219, Feb. 12, 1993]

§ 325.2 Definitions.

(a) *Allowance for loan and lease losses* means those general valuation allowances that have been established through charges against earnings to absorb losses on loans and lease financing receivables. Allowances for loan and lease losses exclude allocated

§ 325.2

transfer risk reserves established pursuant to 12 U.S.C. 3904 and specific reserves created against identified losses.

(b) *Assets classified loss* means:

(1) When measured as of the date of examination of an insured depository institution, those assets that have been determined by an evaluation made by a state or federal examiner as of that date to be a loss; and

(2) When measured as of any other date, those assets:

(i) That have been determined—

(A) By an evaluation made by a state or federal examiner at the most recent examination of an insured depository institution to be a loss; or

(B) By evaluations made by the insured depository institution since its most recent examination to be a loss; and

(ii) That have not been charged off from the insured depository institution's books or collected.

(c) *Bank* means an FDIC-insured, state-chartered commercial or savings bank that is not a member of the Federal Reserve System and for which the FDIC is the appropriate federal banking agency pursuant to section 3(q) of the FDI Act (12 U.S.C. 1813(q)).

(d) *Common stockholders' equity* means the sum of common stock and related surplus, undivided profits, disclosed capital reserves that represent a segregation of undivided profits, and foreign currency translation adjustments, less net unrealized holding losses on available-for-sale equity securities with readily determinable fair values.

(e)(1) *Control* has the same meaning assigned to it in section 2 of the Bank Holding Company Act (12 U.S.C. 1841), and the term *controlled* shall be construed consistently with the term *control.*

(2) *Exclusion for fiduciary ownership.* No insured depository institution or company controls another insured depository institution or company by virtue of its ownership or control of shares in a fiduciary capacity. Shares shall not be deemed to have been acquired in a fiduciary capacity if the acquiring insured depository institution or company has sole discretionary authority to exercise voting rights with respect thereto.

(3) *Exclusion for debts previously contracted.* No insured depository institution or company controls another insured depository institution or company by virtue of its ownership or control of shares acquired in securing or collecting a debt previously contracted in good faith, until two years after the date of acquisition. The two-year period may be extended at the discretion of the appropriate federal banking agency for up to three one-year periods.

(f) *Controlling person* means any person having control of an insured depository institution and any company controlled by that person.

(g)(1) *Credit-enhancing interest-only strip* means an on-balance sheet asset that, in form or in substance:

(i) Represents the contractual right to receive some or all of the interest due on transferred assets; and

(ii) Exposes the bank to credit risk directly or indirectly associated with the transferred assets that exceeds a pro rata share of the bank's claim on the assets, whether through subordination provisions or other credit enhancement techniques.

(2) *Reservation of authority.* In determining whether a particular interest cash flow functions, directly or indirectly, as a credit-enhancing interest-only strip, the FDIC will consider the economic substance of the transaction. The FDIC, through the Director of Supervision, or other designated FDIC official reserves the right to identify other interest cash flows or related assets as credit-enhancing interest-only strips.

(h) *Face amount* means the notional principal, or face value, amount of an off-balance sheet item; the amortized cost of an asset not held for trading purposes; and the fair value of a trading asset.

(i)(1) *Highly leveraged transaction* means an extension of credit to or investment in a business by an insured depository institution where the financing transaction involves a buyout, acquisition, or recapitalization of an existing business and one of the following criteria is met:

(i) The transaction results in a liabilities-to-assets leverage ratio higher than 75 percent; or

Federal Deposit Insurance Corporation § 325.2

(ii) The transaction at least doubles the subject company's liabilities and results in a liabilities-to-assets leverage ratio higher than 50 percent; or

(iii) The transaction is designated an HLT by a syndication agent or a federal bank regulator.

(2) Notwithstanding paragraph (g)(1) of this section, loans and exposures to any obligor in which the total financing package, including all obligations held by all participants is $20 million or more, or such lower level as the FDIC may establish by order on a case-by-case basis, will be excluded from this definition.

(j) *Identified losses* means:

(1) When measured as of the date of examination of an insured depository institution, those items that have been determined by an evaluation made by a state or federal examiner as of that date to be chargeable against income, capital and/or general valuation allowances such as the allowance for loan and lease losses (examples of identified losses would be assets classified loss, off-balance sheet items classified loss, any provision expenses that are necessary for the institution to record in order to replenish its general valuation allowances to an adequate level, liabilities not shown on the institution's books, estimated losses in contingent liabilities, and differences in accounts which represent shortages); and

(2) When measured as of any other date, those items:

(i) That have been determined—

(A) By an evaluation made by a state or federal examiner at the most recent examination of an insured depository institution to be chargeable against income, capital and/or general valuation allowances; or

(B) By evaluations made by the insured depository institution since its most recent examination to be chargeable against income, capital and/or general valuation allowances; and

(ii) For which the appropriate accounting entries to recognize the loss have not yet been made on the insured depository institution's books nor has the item been collected or otherwise settled.

(k) *Insured depository institution* means any depository institution (except for a foreign bank having an insured branch) the deposits of which are insured in accordance with the provisions of the Federal Deposit Insurance Act (12 U.S.C. 1811 *et seq.*)

(l) *Intangible assets* means those assets that are required to be reported as intangible assets in a banking institution's "Reports of Condition and Income" (Call Report) or in a savings association's "Thrift Financial Report."

(m) *Leverage ratio* means the ratio of Tier 1 capital to total assets, as calculated under this part.

(n) *Management fee* means any payment of money or provision of any other thing of value to a company or individual for the provision of management services or advice to the bank or related overhead expenses, including payments related to supervisory, executive, managerial, or policymaking functions, other than compensation to an individual in the individual's capacity as an officer or employee of the bank.

(o) *Minority interests in consolidated subsidiaries* means minority interests in equity capital accounts of those subsidiaries that have been consolidated for the purpose of computing regulatory capital under this part, except that minority interests which fail to provide meaningful capital support are excluded from this definition.

(p) *Mortgage servicing assets* means those assets (net of any related valuation allowances) that result from contracts to service loans secured by real estate (that have been securitized or are owned by others) for which the benefits of servicing are expected to more than adequately compensate the servicer for performing the servicing. For purposes of determining regulatory capital under this part, mortgage servicing assets will be recognized only to the extent that the assets meet the conditions, limitations, and restrictions described in § 325.5 (f).

(q) *Noncumulative perpetual preferred stock* means perpetual preferred stock (and related surplus) where the issuer has the option to waive payment of dividends and where the dividends so waived do not accumulate to future periods nor do they represent a contingent claim on the issuer. Preferred stock issues where the dividend is reset periodically based, in whole or in part,

§ 325.2

upon the bank's current credit standing, including but not limited to, auction rate, money market and remarketable preferred stock, are excluded from this definition of noncumulative perpetual preferred stock, regardless of whether the dividends are cumulative or noncumulative.

(r) *Perpetual preferred stock* means a preferred stock that does not have a maturity date, that cannot be redeemed at the option of the holder, and that has no other provisions that will require future redemption of the issue. It includes those issues of preferred stock that automatically convert into common stock at a stated date. It excludes those issues, the rate on which increases, or can increase, in such a manner that would effectively require the issuer to redeem the issue.

(s) *Risk-weighted assets* means total risk-weighted assets, as calculated in accordance with the FDIC's Statement of Policy on Risk-Based Capital (appendix A to part 325).

(t) *Savings association* means any federally-chartered savings association, any state-chartered savings association, and any corporation (other than a bank) that the Board of Directors of the FDIC and the Director of the Office of Thrift Supervision jointly determine to be operating in substantially the same manner as a savings association.

(u) *Tangible equity* means the amount of core capital elements as defined in Section I.A.1. of the FDIC's Statement of Policy on Risk-Based Capital (appendix A to this Part 325), plus the amount of outstanding cumulative perpetual preferred stock (including related surplus), minus all intangible assets except mortgage servicing assets to the extent that the FDIC determines pursuant to § 325.5(f) of this part that mortgage servicing assets may be included in calculating the bank's Tier 1 capital.

(v) *Tier 1 capital* or *core capital* means the sum of common stockholders' equity, noncumulative perpetual preferred stock (including any related surplus), and minority interests in consolidated subsidiaries, minus all intangible assets (other than mortgage servicing assets, nonmortgage servicing assets, and purchased credit card relationships eligible for inclusion in core capital pursuant to § 325.5(f)), minus credit-enhancing interest-only strips that are not eligible for inclusion in core capital pursuant to § 325.5(f), minus deferred tax assets in excess of the limit set forth in § 325.5(g), minus identified losses (to the extent that Tier 1 capital would have been reduced if the appropriate accounting entries to reflect the identified losses had been recorded on the insured depository institution's books), minus investments in financial subsidiaries subject to 12 CFR part 362, subpart E, and minus the amount of the total adjusted carrying value of nonfinancial equity investments that is subject to a deduction from Tier 1 capital as set forth in section II.B.(6) of appendix A to this part.

(w) *Tier 1 risk-based capital ratio* means the ratio of Tier 1 capital to risk-weighted assets, as calculated in accordance with the FDIC's Statement of Policy on Risk-Based Capital (appendix A to part 325).

(x) *Total assets* means the average of total assets required to be included in a banking institution's "Reports of Condition and Income" (Call Report) or, for savings associations, the consolidated total assets required to be included in the "Thrift Financial Report," as these reports may from time to time be revised, as of the most recent report date (and after making any necessary subsidiary adjustments for state nonmember banks as described in §§ 325.5(c) and 325.5(d) of this part), minus intangible assets (other than mortgage servicing assets, nonmortgage servicing assets, and purchased credit card relationships eligible for inclusion in core capital pursuant to § 325.5(f)), minus credit-enhancing interest-only strips that are not eligible for inclusion in core capital pursuant to § 325.5(f), minus deferred tax assets in excess of the limit set forth in § 325.5(g), minus assets classified loss and any other assets that are deducted in determining Tier 1 capital, and minus the amount of the total adjusted carrying value of nonfinancial equity investments that is subject to a deduction from Tier 1 capital as set forth in section II.B.(6) of appendix A to this part. For banking institutions, the average of total assets is found in the

Federal Deposit Insurance Corporation § 325.3

Call Report schedule of quarterly averages. For savings associations, the consolidated total assets figure is found in Schedule CSC of the Thrift Financial Report.

(y) *Total risk-based capital ratio* means the ratio of qualifying total capital to risk-weighted assets, as calculated in accordance with the FDIC's Statement of Policy on Risk-Based Capital (appendix A to part 325).

(z) *Written agreement* means an agreement in writing executed by authorized representatives entered into with the FDIC by an insured depository institution which is enforceable by an action under section 8(a) and/or section 8(b) of the Federal Deposit Insurance Act (12 U.S.C. 1818 (a), (b)).

[56 FR 10160, Mar. 11, 1991, as amended at 57 FR 44899, Sept. 29, 1992; 58 FR 6368, 6369, Jan. 28, 1993; 58 FR 8219, Feb. 12, 1993; 58 FR 60103, Nov. 15, 1993; 59 FR 66666, Dec. 28, 1994; 60 FR 8187, Feb. 13, 1995; 60 FR 39232, Aug. 1, 1995; 63 FR 42677, Aug. 10, 1998; 66 FR 59652; Nov. 29, 2001; 67 FR 3804, Jan. 25, 2002]

§ 325.3 Minimum leverage capital requirement.

(a) *General.* Banks must maintain at least the minimum leverage capital requirement set forth in this section. The capital standards in this part are the minimum acceptable for banks whose overall financial condition is fundamentally sound, which are well-managed and which have no material or significant financial weaknesses. Thus, the FDIC is not precluded from requiring an institution to maintain a higher capital level based on the institution's particular risk profile. Where the FDIC determines that the financial history or condition, managerial resources and/or the future earnings prospects of a bank are not adequate, or where a bank has sizable off-balance sheet or funding risks, significant risks from concentrations of credit or nontraditional activities, excessive interest rate risk exposure, or a significant volume of assets classified substandard, doubtful or loss or otherwise criticized, the FDIC will take these other factors into account in analyzing the bank's capital adequacy and may determine that the minimum amount of capital for that bank is greater than the minimum standards stated in this section. These same criteria will apply to any insured depository institution making an application to the FDIC that requires the FDIC to consider the adequacy of the institution's capital structure.

(b) *Minimum leverage capital requirement.* (1) The minimum leverage capital requirement for a bank (or an insured depository institution making application to the FDIC) shall consist of a ratio of Tier 1 capital to total assets of not less than 3 percent if the FDIC determines that the institution is not anticipating or experiencing significant growth and has well-diversified risk, including no undue interest rate risk exposure, excellent asset quality, high liquidity, good earnings and in general is considered a strong banking organization, rated composite 1 under the Uniform Financial Institutions Rating System (the CAMELS rating system) established by the Federal Financial Institutions Examination Council.

(2) For all but the most highly-rated institutions meeting the conditions set forth in paragraph (b)(1) of this section, the minimum leverage capital requirement for a bank (or for an insured depository institution making an application to the FDIC) shall consist of a ratio of Tier 1 capital to total assets of not less than 4 percent.

(c) *Insured depository institutions with less than the minimum leverage capital requirement.* (1) A bank (or an insured depository institution making an application to the FDIC) operating with less than the minimum leverage capital requirement does not have adequate capital and therefore has inadequate financial resources.

(2) Any insured depository institution operating with an inadequate capital structure, and therefore inadequate financial resources, will not receive approval for an application requiring the FDIC to consider the adequacy of its capital structure or its financial resources.

(3) As required under § 325.104(a)(1) of this part, a bank must file a written capital restoration plan with the appropriate FDIC regional director within 45 days of the date that the bank receives notice or is deemed to have notice that the bank is undercapitalized, significantly undercapitalized or critically undercapitalized, unless the FDIC

§ 325.4

notifies the bank in writing that the plan is to be filed within a different period.

(4) In any merger, acquisition or other type of business combination where the FDIC must give its approval, where it is required to consider the adequacy of the financial resources of the existing and proposed institutions, and where the resulting entity is either insured by the FDIC or not otherwise federally insured, approval will not be granted when the resulting entity does not meet the minimum leverage capital requirement.

(d) *Exceptions.* Notwithstanding the provisions of paragraphs (a), (b) and (c) of this section:

(1) The FDIC, in its discretion, may approve an application pursuant to the Federal Deposit Insurance Act where it is required to consider the adequacy of capital if it finds that such approval must be taken to prevent the closing of a depository institution or to facilitate the acquisition of a closed depository institution, or, when severe financial conditions exist which threaten the stability of an insured depository institution or of a significant number of depository institutions insured by the FDIC or of insured depository institutions possessing significant financial resources, such action is taken to lessen the risk to the FDIC posed by an insured depository institution under such threat of instability.

(2) The FDIC, in its discretion, may approve an application pursuant to the Federal Deposit Insurance Act where it is required to consider the adequacy of capital or the financial resources of the insured depository institution where it finds that the applicant has committed to and is in compliance with a reasonable plan to meet its minimum leverage capital requirements within a reasonable period of time.

(Approved by the Office of Management and Budget under control number 3064–0075 for use through December 31, 1993)

[56 FR 10162, Mar. 11, 1991, as amended at 58 FR 8219, Feb. 12, 1993; 59 FR 64564, Dec. 15, 1994; 60 FR 45609, Aug. 31, 1995; 62 FR 55493, Oct. 24, 1997; 64 FR 10200, Mar. 2, 1999; 66 FR 59652, Nov. 29, 2001]

§ 325.4 Inadequate capital as an unsafe or unsound practice or condition.

(a) *General.* As a condition of federal deposit insurance, all insured depository institutions must remain in a safe and sound condition.

(b) *Unsafe or unsound practice.* Any bank which has less than its minimum leverage capital requirement is deemed to be engaged in an unsafe or unsound practice pursuant to section 8(b)(1) and/or 8(c) of the Federal Deposit Insurance Act (12 U.S.C. 1818(b)(1) and/or 1818(c)). Except that such a bank which has entered into and is in compliance with a written agreement with the FDIC or has submitted to the FDIC and is in compliance with a plan approved by the FDIC to increase its Tier 1 leverage capital ratio to such level as the FDIC deems appropriate and to take such other action as may be necessary for the bank to be operated so as not to be engaged in such an unsafe or unsound practice will not be deemed to be engaged in an unsafe or unsound practice pursuant to section 8(b)(1) and/or 8(c) of the Federal Deposit Insurance Act (12 U.S.C. 1818(b)(1) and/or 1818(c)) on account of its capital ratios. The FDIC is not precluded from taking section 8(b)(1), section 8(c) or any other enforcement action against a bank with capital above the minimum requirement if the specific circumstances deem such action to be appropriate. Under the conditions set forth in section 8(t) of the Federal Deposit Insurance Act (12 U.S.C. 1818(t)), the FDIC also may take section 8(b)(1) and/or 8(c) enforcement action against any savings association that is deemed to be engaged in an unsafe or unsound practice on account of its inadequate capital structure.

(c) *Unsafe or unsound condition.* Any insured depository institution with a ratio of Tier 1 capital to total assets that is less than two percent is deemed to be operating in an unsafe or unsound condition pursuant to section 8(a) of the Federal Deposit Insurance Act (12 U.S.C. 1818(a)).

(1) A bank with a ratio of Tier 1 capital to total assets of less than two percent which has entered into and is in compliance with a written agreement with the FDIC (or any other insured depository institution with a ratio of

Federal Deposit Insurance Corporation § 325.5

Tier 1 capital to total assets of less than two percent which has entered into and is in compliance with a written agreement with its primary federal regulator and to which agreement the FDIC is a party) to increase its Tier 1 leverage capital ratio to such level as the FDIC deems appropriate and to take such other action as may be necessary for the insured depository institution to be operated in a safe and sound manner, will not be subject to a proceeding by the FDIC pursuant to 12 U.S.C. 1818(a) on account of its capital ratios.

(2) An insured depository institution with a ratio of Tier 1 capital to total assets that is equal to or greater than two percent may be operating in an unsafe or unsound condition. The FDIC is not precluded from bringing an action pursuant to 12 U.S.C. 1818(a) where an insured depository institution has a ratio of Tier 1 capital to total assets that is equal to or greater than two percent.

[56 FR 10162, Mar. 11, 1991]

§ 325.5 Miscellaneous.

(a) *Intangible assets.* Any intangible assets that were explicitly approved by the FDIC as part of the bank's regulatory capital on a specific case basis will be included in capital under the terms and conditions that were approved by the FDIC, provided that the intangible asset is being amortized over a period not to exceed 15 years or its estimated useful life, whichever is shorter. However, pursuant to section 18(n) of the Federal Deposit Insurance Act (12 U.S.C. 1828(n)), an unidentifiable intangible asset such as goodwill, if acquired after April 12, 1989, cannot be included in calculating regulatory capital under this part.

(b) *Reservation of authority.* Notwithstanding the definition of *Tier 1 capital* in § 325.2(t) of this subpart and the risk-based capital definitions of Tier 1 and Tier 2 capital in appendix A to this subpart, the Director of the Division of Supervision and Consumer Protection (DSC) may, if the Director finds a newly developed or modified capital instrument or a particular balance sheet entry or account to be the functional equivalent of a component of Tier 1 or Tier 2 capital, permit one or more insured depository institutions to include all or a portion of such instrument, entry, or account as Tier 1 or Tier 2 capital, permanently, or on a temporary basis, for purposes of this part. Similarly, the Director of the Division of Supervision and Consumer Protection (DSC) may, if the Director finds that a particular Tier 1 or Tier 2 capital component or balance sheet entry or account has characteristics or terms that diminish its contribution to an insured depository institution's ability to absorb losses, require the deduction of all or a portion of such component, entry, or account from Tier 1 or Tier 2 capital.

(c) *Securities subsidiary.* For purposes of this part, any securities subsidiary subject to 12 CFR 337.4 shall not be consolidated with its bank parent and any investment therein shall be deducted from the bank parent's Tier 1 capital and total assets.

(d) *Depository institution subsidiary.* Any domestic depository institution subsidiary that is not consolidated in the "Reports of Condition and Income" (Call Report) of its insured parent bank shall be consolidated with the insured parent bank for purposes of this part. The financial statements of the subsidiary that are to be used for this consolidation must be prepared in the same manner as the "Reports of Condition and Income" (Call Report). A domestic depository institution subsidiary of a savings association shall be consolidated for purposes of this part if such consolidation also is required pursuant to the capital requirements of the association's primary federal regulator.

(e) *Restrictions relating to capital components.* To qualify as Tier 1 capital under this part or Tier 1 or Tier 2 capital under appendix A to this part, a capital instrument must not contain or be subject to any conditions, covenants, terms, restrictions, or provisions that are inconsistent with safe and sound banking practices. A condition, covenant, term, restriction, or provision is inconsistent with safe and sound banking practices if it:

(1) Unduly interferes with the ability of the issuer to conduct normal banking operations;

§ 325.5

(2) Results in significantly higher dividends or interest payments in the event of deterioration in the financial condition of the issuer;

(3) Impairs the ability of the issuer to comply with statutory or regulatory requirements regarding the disposition of assets or incurrence of additional debt; or

(4) Limits the ability of the FDIC or a similar regulatory authority to take any necessary action to resolve a problem bank or failing bank situation.

Other conditions and covenants that are not expressly listed in paragraphs (e)(1) through (e)(4) of this section also may be inconsistent with safe and sound banking practices.

(f) *Treatment of mortgage servicing assets, purchased credit card relationships, nonmortgage servicing assets, and credit-enhancing interest-only strips.* For purposes of determining Tier 1 capital under this part, mortgage servicing assets, purchased credit card relationships, nonmortgage servicing assets, and credit-enhancing interest-only strips will be deducted from assets and from common stockholders' equity to the extent that these items do not meet the conditions, limitations, and restrictions described in this section. Banks may elect to deduct disallowed servicing assets and disallowed credit-enhancing interest-only strips on a basis that is net of a proportional amount of any associated deferred tax liability recorded on the balance sheet. Any deferred tax liability netted in this manner cannot also be netted against deferred tax assets when determining the amount of deferred tax assets that are dependent upon future taxable income and calculating the maximum allowable amount of these assets under paragraph (g) of this section.

(1) *Valuation.* The fair value of mortgage servicing assets, purchased credit card relationships, nonmortgage servicing assets, and credit-enhancing interest-only strips shall be estimated at least quarterly. The quarterly fair value estimate shall include adjustments for any significant changes in the original valuation assumptions, including changes in prepayment estimates or attrition rates. The FDIC in its discretion may require independent fair value estimates on a case-by-case basis where it is deemed appropriate for safety and soundness purposes.

(2) *Fair value limitation.* For purposes of calculating Tier 1 capital under this part (but not for financial statement purposes), the balance sheet assets for mortgage servicing assets, purchased credit card relationships, and nonmortgage servicing assets will each be reduced to an amount equal to the lesser of:

(i) 90 percent of the fair value of these assets, determined in accordance with paragraph (f)(1) of this section; or

(ii) 100 percent of the remaining unamortized book value of these assets (net of any related valuation allowances), determined in accordance with the instructions for the preparation of the "Reports of Income and Condition" (Call Reports).

(3) *Tier 1 capital limitations.* (i) The maximum allowable amount of mortgage servicing assets, purchased credit card relationships, and nonmortgage servicing assets in the aggregate will be limited to the lesser of:

(A) 100 percent of the amount of Tier 1 capital that exists before the deduction of any disallowed mortgage servicing assets, any disallowed purchased credit card relationships, any disallowed nonmortgage servicing assets, any disallowed credit-enhancing interest-only strips, any disallowed deferred tax assets, and any nonfinancial equity investments; or

(B) The sum of the amounts of mortgage servicing assets, purchased credit card relationships, and nonmortgage servicing assets, determined in accordance with paragraph (f)(2) of this section.

(ii) The maximum allowable amount of credit-enhancing interest-only strips, whether purchased or retained, will be limited to the lesser of:

(A) 25 percent of the amount of Tier 1 capital that exists before the deduction of any disallowed mortgage servicing assets, any disallowed purchased credit card relationships, any disallowed nonmortgage servicing assets, any disallowed credit-enhancing interest-only strips, any disallowed deferred tax assets, and any nonfinancial equity investments; or

Federal Deposit Insurance Corporation § 325.5

(B) The sum of the face amounts of all credit-enhancing interest-only strips.

(4) *Tier 1 capital sublimit.* In addition to the aggregate limitation on mortgage servicing assets, purchased credit card relationships, and nonmortgage servicing assets set forth in paragraph (f)(3) of this section, a sublimit will apply to purchased credit card relationships and nonmortgage servicing assets. The maximum allowable amount of the aggregate of purchased credit card relationships and nonmortgage servicing assets will be limited to the lesser of:

(i) 25 percent of the amount of Tier 1 capital that exists before the deduction of any disallowed mortgage servicing assets, any disallowed purchased credit card relationships, any disallowed nonmortgage servicing assets, any disallowed credit-enhancing interest-only strips, any disallowed deferred tax assets, and any nonfinancial equity investments; or

(ii) The sum of the amounts of purchased credit card relationships and nonmortgage servicing assets determined in accordance with paragraph (f)(2) of this section.

(g) *Treatment of deferred tax assets.* For purposes of calculating Tier 1 capital under this part (but not for financial statement purposes), deferred tax assets are subject to the conditions, limitations, and restrictions described in this section.

(1) *Deferred tax assets that are dependent upon future taxable income.* These assets are:

(i) Deferred tax assets arising from deductible temporary differences that exceed the amount of taxes previously paid that could be recovered through loss carrybacks if existing temporary differences (both deductible and taxable and regardless of where the related deferred tax effects are reported on the balance sheet) fully reverse at the calendar quarter-end date; and

(ii) Deferred tax assets arising from operating loss and tax credit carryforwards.

(2) *Tier 1 capital limitations.* (i) The maximum allowable amount of deferred tax assets that are dependent upon future taxable income, net of any valuation allowance for deferred tax assets, will be limited to the lesser of:

(A) The amount of deferred tax assets that are dependent upon future taxable income that is expected to be realized within one year of the calendar quarter-end date, based on projected future taxable income for that year; or

(B) 10 percent of the amount of Tier 1 capital that exists before the deduction of any disallowed mortgage servicing assets, any disallowed nonmortgage servicing assets, any disallowed purchased credit card relationships, any disallowed credit-enhancing interest-only strips, any disallowed deferred tax assets, and any nonfinancial equity investments.

(ii) For purposes of this limitation, all existing temporary differences should be assumed to fully reverse at the calendar quarter-end date. The recorded amount of deferred tax assets that are dependent upon future taxable income, net of any valuation allowance for deferred tax assets, in excess of this limitation will be deducted from assets and from equity capital for purposes of determining Tier 1 capital under this part. The amount of deferred tax assets that can be realized from taxes paid in prior carryback years and from the reversal of existing taxable temporary differences generally would not be deducted from assets and from equity capital. However, notwithstanding the first three sentences in this paragraph, the amount of carryback potential that may be considered in calculating the amount of deferred tax assets that a member of a consolidated group (for tax purposes) may include in Tier 1 capital may not exceed the amount which the member could reasonably expect to have refunded by its parent.

(3) *Projected future taxable income.* Projected future taxable income should not include net operating loss carryforwards to be used within one year of the most recent calendar quarter-end date or the amount of existing temporary differences expected to reverse within that year. Projected future taxable income should include the estimated effect of tax planning strategies that are expected to be implemented to realize tax carryforwards that will otherwise expire during that

§ 325.6

year. Future taxable income projections for the current fiscal year (adjusted for any significant changes that have occurred or are expected to occur) may be used when applying the capital limit at an interim calendar quarter-end date rather then preparing a new projection each quarter.

(4) *Unrealized holding gains and losses on available-for-sale debt securities.* The deferred tax effects of any unrealized holding gains and losses on available-for-sale debt securities may be excluded from the determination of the amount of deferred tax assets that are dependent upon future taxable income and the calculation of the maximum allowable amount of such assets. If these deferred tax effects are excluded, this treatment must be followed consistently over time.

(5) *Goodwill and other intangible assets.* This paragraph (g)(5) provides the capital treatment for intangible assets acquired in a nontaxable business combination, and goodwill acquired in a taxable business combination.

(i) *Intangible assets acquired in nontaxable purchase business combinations.* A deferred tax liability that is specifically related to an intangible asset (other than mortgage servicing assets, nonmortgage servicing assets, and purchased credit card relationships) acquired in a nontaxable purchase business combination may be netted against this intangible asset. Only the net amount of this intangible asset must be deducted from Tier 1 capital.

(ii) *Goodwill acquired in a taxable purchase business combination.* A deferred tax liability that is specifically related to goodwill acquired in a taxable purchase business combination may be netted against this goodwill. Only the net amount of this goodwill must be deducted from Tier 1 capital.

(iii) *Treatment of a netted deferred tax liability.* When a deferred tax liability is netted in accordance with paragraph (g)(5)(i) or (ii) of this section, the taxable temporary difference that gives rise to this deferred tax liability must be excluded from existing taxable temporary differences when determining the amount of deferred tax assets that are dependent upon future taxable income and calculating the maximum allowable amount of such assets.

(iv) *Valuation.* The FDIC in its discretion may require independent fair value estimates for goodwill and other intangible assets on a case-by-case basis where it is deemed appropriate for safety and soundness purposes.

[56 FR 10163, Mar. 11, 1991, as amended at 57 FR 7047, Mar. 4, 1992; 58 FR 6369, Jan. 28, 1993; 58 FR 8219, Feb. 12, 1993; 60 FR 8187, Feb. 13, 1995; 60 FR 39232, Aug. 1, 1995; 63 FR 42677, Aug. 10, 1998; 66 FR 59652, Nov. 29, 2001; 65 FR 3804, Jan. 25, 2002; 73 FR 79606, Dec. 30, 2008]

§ 325.6 Issuance of directives.

(a) *General.* A directive is a final order issued to a bank that fails to maintain capital at or above the minimum leverage capital requirement as set forth in §§ 325.3 and 325.4. A directive issued pursuant to this section, including a plan submitted under a directive, is enforceable in the same manner and to the same extent as a final cease-and-desist order issued under 12 U.S.C. 1818(b).

(b) *Issuance of directives.* If a bank is operating with less than the minimum leverage capital requirement established by this regulation, the Board of Directors, or its designee(s), may issue and serve upon any insured state nonmember bank a directive requiring the bank to restore its capital to the minimum leverage capital requirement within a specified time period. The directive may require the bank to submit to the appropriate FDIC regional director, or other specified official, for review and approval, a plan describing the means and timing by which the bank shall achieve the minimum leverage capital requirement. After the FDIC has approved the plan, the bank may be required under the terms of the directive to adhere to and monitor compliance with the plan. The directive may be issued during the course of an examination of the bank, or at any other time that the FDIC deems appropriate, if the bank is found to be operating with less than the minimum leverage capital requirement.

(c) *Notice and opportunity to respond to issuance of a directive.* (1) If the FDIC makes an initial determination that a directive should be issued to a bank pursuant to paragraph (b) of this section, the FDIC, through the appropriate designated official(s), shall serve written notification upon the bank of its intent to issue a directive. The notice shall include the current Tier 1 leverage capital ratio, the basis upon which said ratio was calculated, the proposed capital injection, the proposed date for achieving the minimum leverage capital requirement and any other relevant information concerning the decision to issue a directive. When deemed appropriate, specific requirements of a proposed plan for meeting the minimum leverage capital requirement may be included in the notice.

(2) Within 14 days of receipt of notification, the bank may file with the appropriate designated FDIC official(s) a written response, explaining why the directive should not be issued, seeking modification of its terms, or other appropriate relief. The bank's response shall include any information, mitigating circumstances, documentation or other relevant evidence which supports its position, and may include a plan for attaining the minimum leverage capital requirement.

(3) After considering the bank's response, the appropriate designated FDIC official(s) shall serve upon the bank a written determination addressing the bank's response and setting forth the FDIC's findings and conclusions in support of any decision to issue or not to issue a directive. The directive may be issued as originally proposed or in modified form. The directive may order the bank to:

(i) Achieve the minimum leverage capital requirement established by this regulation by a certain date;

(ii) Submit for approval and adhere to a plan for achieving the minimum leverage capital requirement;

(iii) Take other action as is necessary to achieve the minimum leverage capital requirement; or

(iv) A combination of the above actions.

If a directive is to be issued, it may be served upon the bank along with the final determination.

(4) Any bank, upon a change in circumstances, may request the FDIC to reconsider the terms of a directive and may propose changes in the plan under which it is operating to meet the minimum leverage capital requirement. The directive and plan continue in effect while such request is pending before the FDIC.

(5) All papers filed with the FDIC must be postmarked or received by the appropriate designated FDIC official(s) within the prescribed time limit for filing.

(6) Failure by the bank to file a written response to notification of intent to issue a directive within the specified time period shall constitute consent to the issuance of such directive.

(d) *Enforcement of a directive.* (1) Whenever a bank fails to follow the directive or to submit or adhere to its capital adequacy plan, the FDIC may seek enforcement of the directive in the appropriate United States district court, pursuant to 12 U.S.C. 3907(b)(2)(B)(ii), in the same manner and to the same extent as if the directive were a final cease-and-desist order. In addition to enforcement of the directive, the FDIC may seek assessment of civil money penalties for violation of the directive against any bank, any officer, director, employee, agent, or other person participating in the conduct of the affairs of the bank, pursuant to 12 U.S.C. 3909(d).

(2) The directive may be issued separately, in conjunction with, or in addition to, any other enforcement mechanisms available to the FDIC, including cease-and-desist orders, orders of correction, the approval or denial of applications, or any other actions authorized by law. In addition to addressing a bank's minimum leverage capital requirement, the capital directive may also address minimum risk-based capital requirements that are to be maintained and calculated in accordance with appendix A to this part.

[56 FR 10164, Mar. 11, 1991]

Subpart B—Prompt Corrective Action

SOURCE: 57 FR 44900, Sept. 29, 1992, unless otherwise noted.

§ 325.101 Authority, purpose, scope, other supervisory authority, and disclosure of capital categories.

(a) *Authority.* This subpart is issued by the FDIC pursuant to section 38

§ 325.102

(section 38) of the Federal Deposit Insurance Act (FDI Act), as added by section 131 of the Federal Deposit Insurance Corporation Improvement Act of 1991 (Pub. L. 102–242, 105 Stat. 2236 (1991)) (12 U.S.C. 1831o).

(b) *Purpose.* Section 38 of the FDI Act establishes a framework of supervisory actions for insured depository institutions that are not adequately capitalized. The principal purpose of this subpart is to define, for FDIC-insured state-chartered nonmember banks, the capital measures and capital levels, and for insured branches of foreign banks, comparable asset-based measures and levels, that are used for determining the supervisory actions authorized under section 38 of the FDI Act. This subpart also establishes procedures for submission and review of capital restoration plans and for issuance and review of directives and orders pursuant to section 38.

(c) *Scope.* This subpart implements the provisions of section 38 of the FDI Act as they apply to FDIC-insured state-chartered nonmember banks and insured branches of foreign banks for which the FDIC is the appropriate Federal banking agency. Certain of these provisions also apply to officers, directors and employees of those insured institutions. In addition, certain provisions of this subpart apply to all insured depository institutions that are deemed critically undercapitalized.

(d) *Other supervisory authority.* Neither section 38 nor this subpart in any way limits the authority of the FDIC under any other provision of law to take supervisory actions to address unsafe or unsound practices, deficient capital levels, violations of law, unsafe or unsound conditions, or other practices. Action under section 38 of the FDI Act and this subpart may be taken independently of, in conjunction with, or in addition to any other enforcement action available to the FDIC, including issuance of cease and desist orders, capital directives, approval or denial of applications or notices, assessment of civil money penalties, or any other actions authorized by law.

(e) *Disclosure of capital categories.* The assignment of a bank or insured branch under this subpart within a particular capital category is for purposes of implementing and applying the provisions of section 38. Unless permitted by the FDIC or otherwise required by law, no bank may state in any advertisement or promotional material its capital category under this subpart or that the FDIC or any other federal banking agency has assigned the bank to a particular capital category.

§ 325.102 Notice of capital category.

(a) *Effective date of determination of capital category.* A bank shall be deemed to be within a given capital category for purposes of section 38 of the FDI Act and this subpart as of the date the bank is notified of, or is deemed to have notice of, its capital category, pursuant to paragraph (b) of this section.

(b) *Notice of capital category.* A bank shall be deemed to have been notified of its capital levels and its capital category as of the most recent date:

(1) A Consolidated Report of Condition and Income (Call Report) is required to be filed with the FDIC;

(2) A final report of examination is delivered to the bank; or

(3) Written notice is provided by the FDIC to the bank of its capital category for purposes of section 38 of the FDI Act and this subpart or that the bank's capital category has changed as provided in § 325.103(d).

(c) *Adjustments to reported capital levels and capital category*—(1) *Notice of adjustment by bank.* A bank shall provide the appropriate FDIC regional director with written notice that an adjustment to the bank's capital category may have occurred no later than 15 calendar days following the date that any material event has occurred that would cause the bank to be placed in a lower capital category from the category assigned to the bank for purposes of section 38 and this subpart on the basis of the bank's most recent Call Report or report of examination.

(2) *Determination by the FDIC to change capital category.* After receiving notice pursuant to paragraph (c)(1) of this section, the FDIC shall determine whether to change the capital category of the bank and shall notify the bank of the FDIC's determination.

§ 325.103 Capital measures and capital category definitions.

(a) *Capital measures.* For purposes of section 38 and this subpart, the relevant capital measures shall be:

(1) The total risk-based capital ratio;

(2) The Tier 1 risk-based capital ratio; and

(3) The leverage ratio.

(b) *Capital categories.* For purposes of section 38 and this subpart, a bank shall be deemed to be:

(1) *Well capitalized* if the bank:

(i) Has a total risk-based capital ratio of 10.0 percent or greater; and

(ii) Has a Tier 1 risk-based capital ratio of 6.0 percent or greater; and

(iii) Has a leverage ratio of 5.0 percent or greater; and

(iv) Is not subject to any written agreement, order, capital directive, or prompt corrective action directive issued by the FDIC pursuant to section 8 of the FDI Act (12 U.S.C. 1818), the International Lending Supervision Act of 1983 (12 U.S.C. 3907), or section 38 of the FDI Act (12 U.S.C. 1831o), or any regulation thereunder, to meet and maintain a specific capital level for any capital measure.

(2) *Adequately capitalized* if the bank:

(i) Has a total risk-based capital ratio of 8.0 percent or greater; and

(ii) Has a Tier 1 risk-based capital ratio of 4.0 percent or greater; and

(iii) Has:

(A) A leverage ratio of 4.0 percent or greater; or

(B) A leverage ratio of 3.0 percent or greater if the bank is rated composite 1 under the CAMELS rating system in the most recent examination of the bank and is not experiencing or anticipating significant growth; and

(iv) Does not meet the definition of a *well capitalized* bank.

(3) *Undercapitalized* if the bank:

(i) Has a total risk-based capital ratio that is less than 8.0 percent; or

(ii) Has a Tier 1 risk-based capital ratio that is less than 4.0 percent; or

(iii)(A) Except as provided in paragraph (b)(3)(iii)(B) of this section, has a leverage ratio that is less than 4.0 percent; or

(B) Has a leverage ratio that is less than 3.0 percent if the bank is rated composite 1 under the CAMELS rating system in the most recent examination of the bank and is not experiencing or anticipating significant growth.

(4) *Significantly undercapitalized* if the bank has:

(i) A total risk-based capital ratio that is less than 6.0 percent; or

(ii) A Tier 1 risk-based capital ratio that is less than 3.0 percent; or

(iii) A leverage ratio that is less than 3.0 percent.

(5) *Critically undercapitalized* if the insured depository institution has a ratio of tangible equity to total assets that is equal to or less than 2.0 percent.

(c) Capital categories for insured branches of foreign banks. For purposes of the provisions of section 38 and this subpart, an insured branch of a foreign bank shall be deemed to be:

(1) Well capitalized if the insured branch:

(i) Maintains the pledge of assets required under § 347.209 of this chapter; and

(ii) Maintains the eligible assets prescribed under § 347.210 of this chapter at 108 percent or more of the preceding quarter's average book value of the insured branch's third-party liabilities; and

(iii) Has not received written notification from:

(A) The OCC to increase its capital equivalency deposit pursuant to 12 CFR 28.15(b), or to comply with asset maintenance requirements pursuant to 12 CFR 28.20; or

(B) The FDIC to pledge additional assets pursuant to § 347.209 of this chapter or to maintain a higher ratio of eligible assets pursuant to § 347.210 of this chapter.

(2) Adequately capitalized if the insured branch:

(i) Maintains the pledge of assets required under § 347.209 of this chapter; and

(ii) Maintains the eligible assets prescribed under § 347.210 of this chapter at 106 percent or more of the preceding quarter's average book value of the insured branch's third-party liabilities; and

(iii) Does not meet the definition of a well capitalized insured branch.

(3) Undercapitalized if the insured branch:

§ 325.104

(i) Fails to maintain the pledge of assets required under § 347.209 of this chapter; or

(ii) Fails to maintain the eligible assets prescribed under § 347.210 of this chapter at 106 percent or more of the preceding quarter's average book value of the insured branch's third-party liabilities.

(4) *Significantly undercapitalized* if it fails to maintain the eligible assets prescribed under § 347.210 of this chapter at 104 percent or more of the preceding quarter's average book value of the insured branch's third-party liabilities.

(5) *Critically undercapitalized* if it fails to maintain the eligible assets prescribed under § 347.210 of this chapter at 102 percent or more of the preceding quarter's average book value of the insured branch's third-party liabilities.

(d) *Reclassifications based on supervisory criteria other than capital.* The FDIC may reclassify a well capitalized bank as adequately capitalized and may require an adequately capitalized bank or an undercapitalized bank to comply with certain mandatory or discretionary supervisory actions as if the bank were in the next lower capital category (except that the FDIC may not reclassify a significantly undercapitalized bank as critically undercapitalized) (each of these actions are hereinafter referred to generally as "reclassifications") in the following circumstances:

(1) *Unsafe or unsound condition.* The FDIC has determined, after notice and opportunity for hearing pursuant to § 308.202(a) of this chapter, that the bank is in unsafe or unsound condition; or

(2) *Unsafe or unsound practice.* The FDIC has determined, after notice and opportunity for hearing pursuant to § 308.202(a) of this chapter, that, in the most recent examination of the bank, the bank received and has not corrected a less-than-satisfactory rating for any of the categories of asset quality, management, earnings, or liquidity.

[57 FR 44900, Sept. 29, 1992, as amended at 63 FR 17074, Apr. 8, 1998; 66 FR 59653, Nov. 29, 2001; 70 FR 17559, Apr. 6, 2005]

§ 325.104 Capital restoration plans.

(a) *Schedule for filing plan*—(1) *In general.* A bank shall file a written capital restoration plan with the appropriate FDIC regional director within 45 days of the date that the bank receives notice or is deemed to have notice that the bank is undercapitalized, significantly undercapitalized, or critically undercapitalized, unless the FDIC notifies the bank in writing that the plan is to be filed within a different period. An adequately capitalized bank that has been required pursuant to § 325.103(d) of this subpart to comply with supervisory actions as if the bank were undercapitalized is not required to submit a capital restoration plan solely by virtue of the reclassification.

(2) *Additional capital restoration plans.* Notwithstanding paragraph (a)(1) of this section, a bank that has already submitted and is operating under a capital restoration plan approved under section 38 and this subpart is not required to submit an additional capital restoration plan based on a revised calculation of its capital measures or a reclassification of the institution under § 325.103 unless the FDIC notifies the bank that it must submit a new or revised capital plan. A bank that is notified that it must submit a new or revised capital restoration plan shall file the plan in writing with the appropriate FDIC regional director within 45 days of receiving such notice, unless the FDIC notifies the bank in writing that the plan must be filed within a different period.

(b) *Contents of plan.* All financial data submitted in connection with a capital restoration plan shall be prepared in accordance with the instructions provided on the Call Report, unless the FDIC instructs otherwise. The capital restoration plan shall include all of the information required to be filed under section 38(e)(2) of the FDI Act. A bank that is required to submit a capital restoration plan as a result of a reclassification of the bank pursuant to § 325.103(d) of this subpart shall include a description of the steps the bank will take to correct the unsafe or unsound condition or practice. No plan shall be

Federal Deposit Insurance Corporation § 325.104

accepted unless it includes any performance guarantee described in section 38(e)(2)(C) of the FDI Act by each company that controls the bank.

(c) *Review of capital restoration plans.* Within 60 days after receiving a capital restoration plan under this subpart, the FDIC shall provide written notice to the bank of whether the plan has been approved. The FDIC may extend the time within which notice regarding approval of a plan shall be provided.

(d) *Disapproval of capital plan.* If a capital restoration plan is not approved by the FDIC, the bank shall submit a revised capital restoration plan within the time specified by the FDIC. Upon receiving notice that its capital restoration plan has not been approved, any undercapitalized bank (as defined in § 325.103(b) of this subpart) shall be subject to all of the provisions of section 38 and this subpart applicable to significantly undercapitalized institutions. These provisions shall be applicable until such time as a new or revised capital restoration plan submitted by the bank has been approved by the FDIC.

(e) *Failure to submit capital restoration plan.* A bank that is undercapitalized (as defined in § 325.103(b) of this subpart) and that fails to submit a written capital restoration plan within the period provided in this section shall, upon the expiration of that period, be subject to all of the provisions of section 38 and this subpart applicable to significantly undercapitalized institutions.

(f) *Failure to implement capital restoration plan.* Any undercapitalized bank that fails in any material respect to implement a capital restoration plan shall be subject to all of the provisions of section 38 and this subpart applicable to significantly undercapitalized institutions.

(g) *Amendment of capital restoration plan.* A bank that has filed an approved capital restoration plan may, after prior written notice to and approval by the FDIC, amend the plan to reflect a change in circumstance. Until such time as a proposed amendment has been approved, the bank shall implement the capital restoration plan as approved prior to the proposed amendment.

(h) *Performance guarantee by companies that control a bank*—(1) *Limitation on liability*—(i) *Amount limitation.* The aggregate liability under the guarantee provided under section 38 and this subpart for all companies that control a specific bank that is required to submit a capital restoration plan under this subpart shall be limited to the lesser of:

(A) An amount equal to 5.0 percent of the bank's total assets at the time the bank was notified or deemed to have notice that the bank was undercapitalized; or

(B) The amount necessary to restore the relevant capital measures of the bank to the levels required for the bank to be classified as adequately capitalized, as those capital measures and levels are defined at the time that the bank initially fails to comply with a capital restoration plan under this subpart.

(ii) *Limit on duration.* The guarantee and limit of liability under section 38 and this subpart shall expire after the FDIC notifies the bank that it has remained adequately capitalized for each of four consecutive calendar quarters. The expiration or fulfillment by a company of a guarantee of a capital restoration plan shall not limit the liability of the company under any guarantee required or provided in connection with any capital restoration plan filed by the same bank after expiration of the first guarantee.

(iii) *Collection on guarantee.* Each company that controls a given bank shall be jointly and severally liable for the guarantee for such bank as required under section 38 and this subpart, and the FDIC may require and collect payment of the full amount of that guarantee from any or all of the companies issuing the guarantee.

(2) *Failure to provide guarantee.* In the event that a bank that is controlled by any company submits a capital restoration plan that does not contain the guarantee required under section 38(e)(2) of the FDI Act, the bank shall, upon submission of the plan, be subject to the provisions of section 38 and this subpart that are applicable to banks that have not submitted an acceptable capital restoration plan.

(3) *Failure to perform guarantee.* Failure by any company that controls a bank to perform fully its guarantee of any capital plan shall constitute a material failure to implement the plan for purposes of section 38(f) of the FDI Act. Upon such failure, the bank shall be subject to the provisions of section 38 and this subpart that are applicable to banks that have failed in a material respect to implement a capital restoration plan.

§ 325.105 **Mandatory and discretionary supervisory actions under section 38.**

(a) *Mandatory supervisory actions*—(1) *Provisions applicable to all banks.* All banks are subject to the restrictions contained in section 38(d) of the FDI Act on payment of capital distributions and management fees.

(2) *Provisions applicable to undercapitalized, significantly undercapitalized, and critically undercapitalized banks.* Immediately upon receiving notice or being deemed to have notice, as provided in § 325.102 of this subpart, that the bank is undercapitalized, significantly undercapitalized, or critically undercapitalized, the bank shall become subject to the provisions of section 38 of the FDI Act:

(i) Restricting payment of capital distributions and management fees (section 38(d));

(ii) Requiring that the FDIC monitor the condition of the bank (section 38(e)(1));

(iii) Requiring submission of a capital restoration plan within the schedule established in this subpart (section 38(e)(2));

(iv) Restricting the growth of the bank's assets (section 38(e)(3)); and

(v) Requiring prior approval of certain expansion proposals (section 38(e)(4)).

(3) *Additional provisions applicable to significantly undercapitalized, and critically undercapitalized banks.* In addition to the provisions of section 38 of the FDI Act described in paragraph (a)(2) of this section, immediately upon receiving notice or being deemed to have notice, as provided in § 325.102 of this subpart, that the bank is significantly undercapitalized, or critically undercapitalized, or that the bank is subject to the provisions applicable to institutions that are significantly undercapitalized because the bank failed to submit or implement in any material respect an acceptable capital restoration plan, the bank shall become subject to the provisions of section 38 of the FDI Act that restrict compensation paid to senior executive officers of the institution (section 38(f)(4)).

(4) *Additional provisions applicable to critically undercapitalized institutions.* (i) In addition to the provisions of section 38 of the FDI Act described in paragraphs (a)(2) and (a)(3) of this section, immediately upon receiving notice or being deemed to have notice, as provided in § 325.102 of this subpart, that the insured depository institution is critically undercapitalized, the institution is prohibited from doing any of the following without the FDIC's prior written approval:

(A) Entering into any material transaction other than in the usual course of business, including any investment, expansion, acquisition, sale of assets, or other similar action with respect to which the depository institution is required to provide notice to the appropriate Federal banking agency;

(B) Extending credit for any highly leveraged transaction;

(C) Amending the institution's charter or bylaws, except to the extent necessary to carry out any other requirement of any law, regulation, or order;

(D) Making any material change in accounting methods;

(E) Engaging in any covered transaction (as defined in section 23A(b) of the Federal Reserve Act (12 U.S.C. 371c(b));

(F) Paying excessive compensation or bonuses;

(G) Paying interest on new or renewed liabilities at a rate that would increase the institution's weighted average cost of funds to a level significantly exceeding the prevailing rates of interest on insured deposits in the institution's normal market areas; and

(H) Making any principal or interest payment on subordinated debt beginning 60 days after becoming critically undercapitalized except that this restriction shall not apply, until July 15, 1996, with respect to any subordinated debt outstanding on July 15, 1991, and not extended or otherwise renegotiated after July 15, 1991.

(ii) In addition, the FDIC may further restrict the activities of any critically undercapitalized institution to carry out the purposes of section 38 of the FDI Act.

(5) *Exception for certain savings associations.* The restrictions in paragraph (a)(4) of this section shall not apply, before July 1, 1994, to any insured savings association if:

(i) The savings association had submitted a plan meeting the requirements of section 5(t)(6)(A)(ii) of the Home Owners' Loan Act (12 U.S.C. 1464(t)(6)(A)(ii)) prior to December 19, 1991;

(ii) The Director of OTS had accepted the plan prior to December 19, 1991; and

(iii) The savings association remains in compliance with the plan or is operating under a written agreement with the appropriate federal banking agency.

(b) *Discretionary supervisory actions.* In taking any action under section 38 that is within the FDIC's discretion to take in connection with:

(1) An insured depository institution that is deemed to be undercapitalized, significantly undercapitalized, or critically undercapitalized, or has been reclassified as undercapitalized, or significantly undercapitalized; or

(2) An officer or director of such institution, the FDIC shall follow the procedures for issuing directives under §§ 308.201 and 308.203 of this chapter, unless otherwise provided in section 38 or this subpart.

APPENDIX A TO PART 325—STATEMENT OF POLICY ON RISK-BASED CAPITAL

Capital adequacy is one of the critical factors that the FDIC is required to analyze when taking action on various types of applications and when conducting supervisory activities related to the safety and soundness of individual banks and the banking system. In view of this, the FDIC's Board of Directors has adopted part 325 of its regulations, which sets forth (1) minimum standards of capital adequacy for insured state nonmember banks and (2) standards for determining when an insured bank is in an unsafe or unsound condition by reason of the amount of its capital.

This capital maintenance regulation was designed to establish, in conjunction with other Federal bank regulatory agencies, uniform capital standards for all federally-regulated banking organizations, regardless of size. The uniform capital standards were based on ratios of capital to total assets. While those leverage ratios have served as a useful tool for assessing capital adequacy, the FDIC believes there is a need for a capital measure that is more explicitly and systematically sensitive to the risk profiles of individual banks. As a result, the FDIC's Board of Directors has adopted this Statement of Policy on Risk-Based Capital to supplement the part 325 regulation. This statement of policy does not replace or eliminate the existing part 325 capital-to-total assets leverage ratios.

The framework set forth in this statement of policy consists of (1) a definition of capital for risk-based capital purposes, and (2) a system for calculating risk-weighted assets by assigning assets and off balance sheet items to broad risk categories. A bank's risk-based capital ratio is calculated by dividing its qualifying total capital base (the numerator of the ratio) by its risk-weighted assets (the denominator).[1] Table I outlines the definition of capital and provides a general explanation of how the risk-based capital ratio is calculated, Table II summarizes the risk weights and risk categories, and Table III sets forth the credit conversation factors for off-balance sheet items. Additional explanations of the capital definitions, the risk-weighted asset calculations, and the minimum risk-based capital ratio guidelines are provided in Sections I, II and III of this statement of policy.

In addition, when certain banks that engage in trading activities calculate their risk-based capital ratio under this appendix A, they must also refer to appendix C of this part, which incorporates capital charges for certain market risks into the risk-based capital ratio. When calculating their risk-based capital ratio under this appendix A, such banks are required to refer to appendix C of this part for supplemental rules to determine qualifying and excess capital, calculate risk-weighted assets, calculate market risk equivalent assets and add them to risk-weighted assets, and calculate risk-based capital ratios as adjusted for market risk.

This statement of policy applies to all *FDIC-insured state-chartered banks* (excluding insured branches of foreign banks) that are *not* members of the Federal Reserve System, hereafter referred to as *state nonmember banks*, regardless of size, and to all circumstances in which the FDIC is required to

---

[1] Period-end amounts, rather than average balances, normally will be used when calculating risk-based capital ratios. However, on a case-by-case basis, ratios based on average balances may also be required if supervisory concerns render it appropriate.

evaluate the capital of a banking organization. Therefore, the risk-based capital framework set forth in this statement of policy will be used in the examination and supervisory process as well as in the analysis of applications that the FDIC is required to act upon.

The risk-based capital ratio focuses principally on broad categories of credit risk, however, the ratio does not take account of many other factors that can affect a bank's financial condition. These factors include overall interest rate risk exposure, liquidity, funding and market risks; the quality and level of earnings; investment, loan portfolio, and other concentrations of credit risk, certain risks arising from nontraditional activities; the quality of loans and investments; the effectiveness of loan and investment policies; and management's overall ability to monitor and control financial and operating risks, including the risk presented by concentrations of credit and nontraditional activities. In addition to evaluating capital ratios, an overall assessment of capital adequacy must take account of each of these other factors, including, in particular, the level and severity of problem and adversely classified assets as well as a bank's interest rate risk as measured by the bank's exposure to declines in the economic value of its capital due to changes in interest rates. For this reason, the final supervisory judgment on a bank's capital adequacy may differ significantly from the conclusions that might be drawn solely from the absolute level of the bank's risk-based capital ratio.

In light of these other considerations, banks generally are expected to operate above the minimum risk-based capital ratio. Banks contemplating significant expansion plans, as well as those institutions with high or inordinate levels of risk, should hold capital commensurate with the level and nature of the risks to which they are exposed.

I. DEFINITION OF CAPITAL FOR THE RISK-BASED CAPITAL RATIO

A bank's qualifying total capital base consists of two types of capital elements: *core capital elements* (Tier 1) and *supplementary capital elements* (Tier 2). To qualify as an element of Tier 1 or Tier 2 capital, a capital instrument should not contain or be subject to any conditions, covenants, terms, restrictions, or provisions that are inconsistent with safe and sound banking practices.

A. The Components of Qualifying Capital (see Table I)

1. *Core capital elements (Tier 1) consists of:*
i. Common stockholders' equity capital (includes common stock and related surplus, undivided profits, disclosed capital reserves that represent a segregation of undivided profits, and foreign currency translation adjustments, less net unrealized holding losses on available-for-sale equity securities with readily determinable fair values);
ii. Noncumulative perpetual preferred stock,[2] including any related surplus; and
iii. Minority interests in the equity capital accounts of consolidated subsidiaries.

(a) At least 50 percent of the qualifying total capital base should consist of Tier 1 capital. Core (Tier 1) capital is defined as the sum of core capital elements minus all intangible assets (other than mortgage servicing assets, nonmortgage servicing assets and purchased credit card relationships eligible for inclusion in core capital pursuant to §325.5(f)),[3] minus credit-enhancing interest-only strips that are not eligible for inclusion in core capital pursuant to §325.5(f), minus any disallowed deferred tax assets, and minus any amount of nonfinancial equity investments required to be deducted pursuant to section II.B.(6) of this Appendix.

(b) Although nonvoting common stock, noncumulative perpetual preferred stock, and minority interests in the equity capital accounts of consolidated subsidiaries are normally included in Tier 1 capital, voting common stockholders' equity generally will be expected to be the dominant form of Tier 1 capital. Thus, banks should avoid undue reliance on nonvoting equity, preferred stock and minority interests.

(c) Although minority interests in consolidated subsidiaries are generally included in regulatory capital, exceptions to this general rule will be made if the minority interests fail to provide meaningful capital support to the consolidated bank. Such a situation could arise if the minority interests are entitled to a preferred claim on essentially low risk assets of the subsidiary. Similarly, although credit-enhancing interest-only strips and intangible assets in the form of mortgage servicing assets, nonmortgage servicing assets and purchased credit card relationships are generally recognized for risk-based capital purposes, the deduction of part or all of the credit-enhancing interest-only strips, mortgage servicing assets, nonmortgage servicing assets and purchased credit card

---

[2] Preferred stock issues where the dividend is reset periodically based, in whole or in part, upon the bank's current credit standing, including but not limited to, auction rate, money market or remarketable preferred stock, are assigned to Tier 2 capital, regardless of whether the dividends are cumultive or noncumulative.

[3] An exception is allowed for intangible assets that are explicitly approved by the FDIC as part of the bank's regulatory capital on a specific case basis. These intangibles will be included in capital for risk-based capital purposes under the terms and conditions that are specifically approved by the FDIC.

Federal Deposit Insurance Corporation

relationships may be required if the carrying amounts of these assets are excessive in relation to their market value or the level of the bank's capital accounts. Credit-enhancing interest-only strips, mortgage servicing assets, nonmortgage servicing assets, purchased credit card relationships and deferred tax assets that do not meet the conditions, limitations and restrictions described in § 325.5(f) and (g) of this part will not be recognized for risk-based capital purposes.

(d) Minority interests in small business investment companies, investment funds that hold nonfinancial equity investments (as defined in section II.B.(6)(ii) of this appendix A), and subsidiaries that are engaged in nonfinancial activities are not included in the bank's Tier 1 or total capital base if the bank's interest in the company or fund is held under one of the legal authorities listed in section II.B.(6)(ii) of this appendix A.

2. *Supplementary capital elements (Tier 2)* consist of:

i. Allowance for loan and lease losses, up to a maximum of 1.25 percent of risk-weighted assets;

ii. Cumulative perpetual preferred stock, long-term preferred stock (original maturity of at least 20 years), and any related surplus;

iii. Perpetual preferred stock (and any related surplus) where the dividend is reset periodically based, in whole or part, on the bank's current credit standing, regardless of whether the dividends are cumulative or noncumulative;

iv. Hybrid capital instruments, including mandatory convertible debt securities;

v. Term subordinated debt and intermediate-term preferred stock (original average maturity of five years or more) and any related surplus; and

vi. Net unrealized holding gains on equity securities (subject to the limitations discussed in paragraph I.A.2.(f) of this section).

The maximum amount of Tier 2 capital that may be recognized for risk-based capital purposes is limited to 100 percent of Tier 1 capital (after any deductions for disallowed intangibles and disallowed deferred tax assets). In addition, the combined amount of term subordinated debt and intermediate-term preferred stock that may be treated as part of Tier 2 capital for risk-based capital purposes is limited to 50 percent of Tier 1 capital. Amounts in excess of these limits may be issued but are not included in the calculation of the risk-based capital ratio.

(a) *Allowance for loan and lease losses.* Allowances for loan and lease losses are reserves that have been established through a charge against earnings to absorb future losses on loans or lease financing receivables. Allowances for loan and lease losses exclude *allocated transfer risk reserves,*[4] and reserves created against identified losses.

This risk-based capital framework provides a phasedown during the transition period of the extent to which the allowance for loan and lease losses may be included in an institution's capital base. By year-end 1990, the allowance for loan and lease losses, as an element of supplementary capital, may constitute no more than 1.5 percent of risk-weighted assets and, by year-end 1992, no more than 1.25 percent of risk-weighted assets.[5]

(b) *Preferred stock.* Perpetual preferred stock is defined as preferred stock that does not have a maturity date, that cannot be redeemed at the option of the holder, and that has no other provisions that will require future redemption of the issue. Long-term preferred stock includes limited-life preferred stock with an original maturity of 20 years or more, provided that the stock cannot be redeemed at the option of the holder prior to maturity, except with the prior approval of the FDIC.

Cumulative perpetual preferred stock and long-term preferred stock qualify for inclusion in supplementary capital provided that the instruments can absorb losses while the issuer operates as a going concern (a fundamental characteristic of equity capital) and provided the issuer has the option to defer payment of dividends on these instruments. Given these conditions, and the perpetual or long-term nature of the intruments, there is no limit on the amount of these preferred stock instruments that may be included with Tier 2 capital.

Noncumulative perpetual preferred stock where the dividend is reset periodically based, in whole or in part, on the bank's current credit standing, including auction rate, money market, or remarketable preferred stock, are also assigned to Tier 2 capital without limit, provided the above conditions are met.

---

[4] Allocated transfer risk reserves are reserves that have been established in accordance with section 905(a) of the International Lending Supervision Act of 1983 against certain assets whose value has been found by the U.S. supervisory authorities to have been significantly impaired by protracted transfer risk problems.

[5] The amount of the allowance for loan and lease losses that may be included as a supplementary capital element is based on a percentage of gross risk-weighted assets. A bank may deduct reserves for loan and lease losses that are in excess of the amount permitted to be included in capital, as well as allocated transfer risk reserves, from gross risk-weighted assets when computing the denominator of the risk-based capital ratio.

(c) *Hybrid capital instruments.* Hybrid capital instruments include instruments that have certain characteristics of both debt and equity. In order to be included as supplementary capital elements, these instruments should meet the following criteria:

(1) The instrument should be unsecured, subordinated to the claims of depositors and general creditors, and fully paid-up.

(2) The instrument should not be redeemable at the option of the holder prior to maturity, except with the prior approval of the FDIC. This requirement implies that holders of such instruments may not accelerate the payment of principal except in the event of bankruptcy, insolvency, or reorganization.

(3) The instrument should be available to participate in losses while the issuer is operating as a going concern. (Term subordinated debt would not meet this requirement.) To satisfy this requirement, the instrument should convert to common or perpetual preferred stock in the event that the sum of the undivided profits and capital surplus accounts of the issuer results in a negative balance.

(4) The instrument should provide the option for the issuer to defer principal and interest payments if: (a) The issuer does not report a profit in the preceding annual period, defined as combined profits (*i.e.*, net income) for the most recent four quarters, *and* (b) the issuer eliminates cash dividends on its common and preferred stock.

Mandatory convertible debt securities, which are subordinated debt instruments that require the issuer to convert such instruments into common or perpetual preferred stock by a date at or before the maturity of the debt instruments, will qualify as hybrid capital instruments provided the maturity of these instruments is 12 years or less and the instruments meet the criteria set forth below for "term subordinated debt." There is no limit on the amount of hybrid capital instruments that may be included within Tier 2 capital.

(d) *Term subordinated debt and intermediate-term preferred stock.* The aggregate amount of term subordinated debt (excluding mandatory convertible debt securities) and intermediate-term preferred stock (including any related surplus) that may be treated as Tier 2 capital for risk-based capital purposes is limited to 50 percent of Tier 1 capital. Term subordinated debt and intermediate-term preferred stock should have an original average maturity of at least five years to qualify as supplementary capital and should not be redeemable at the option of the holder prior to maturity, except with the prior approval of the FDIC. For state nonmember banks, a *term subordinated debt* instrument is an obligation other than a deposit obligation that:

(1) Bears on its face, in boldface type, the following: This obligation is not a deposit and is not insured by the Federal Deposit Insurance Corporation;

(2)(i) Has a maturity of at least five years; or

(ii) In the case of an obligation or issue that provides for scheduled repayments of principal, has an average maturity of at least five years; provided that the Director of the Division of Supervision and Consumer Protection (DSC) may permit the issuance of an obligation or issue with a shorter maturity or average maturity if the Director has determined that exigent circumstances require the issuance of such obligation or issue; provided further that the provisions of this paragraph I.A.2.(d)(2) shall not apply to mandatory convertible debt obligations or issues;

(3) States express that the obligation:

(i) Is subordinated and junior in right of payment to the issuing bank's obligations to its depositors and to the bank's other obligations to its general and secured creditors; and

(ii) Is ineligible as collateral for a loan by the issuing bank;

(4) Is unsecured;

(5) States expressly that the issuing bank may not retire any part of its obligation without the prior written consent of the FDIC or other primary federal regulator; and

(6) Includes, if the obligation is issued to a depository institution, a specific waiver of the right of offset by the lending depository institution.

Subordinated debt obligations issued prior to December 2, 1987 that satisfied the definition of the term "subordinated note and debenture" that was in effect prior to that date also will be deemed to be term subordinated debt for risk-based capital purposes. An optional redemption ("call") provision in a subordinated debt instrument that is exercisable by the issuing bank in less than five years will not be deemed to constitute a maturity of less than five years, provided that the obligation otherwise has a stated contractual maturity of at least five years; the call is exercisable solely at the discretion or option of the issuing bank, and not at the discretion or option of the holder of the obligation; and the call is exercisable only with the express prior written consent of the FDIC under 12 U.S.C. 1828(i)(1) at the time early redemption or retirement is sought, and such consent has not been given in advance at the time of issuance of the obligation. Optional redemption provisions will be accorded similar treatment when determining the perpetual nature and/or maturity of preferred stock and other capital instruments.

(e) *Discount of limited-life supplementary capital instruments.* As a limited-life capital instrument approaches maturity, the instrument begins to take on charcteristics of a short-term obligation and becomes less like

Federal Deposit Insurance Corporation

a component of capital. Therefore, for risk-based capital purposes, the outstanding amount of term subordinated debt and limited-life preferred stock eligible for inclusion in capital will be adjusted downward, or discounted, as the instruments approach maturity. Each limited-life capital instrument will be discounted by reducing the outstanding amount of the capital instrument eligible for inclusion as supplementary capital by a fifth of the original amount (less redemptions) each year during the instrument's last five years before maturity. Such instruments, therefore, will have no capital value when they have a remaining maturity of less than a year.

(f) *Unrealized gains on equity securities and unrealized gains (losses) on other assets.* Up to 45 percent of pretax net unrealized holding gains (that is, the excess, if any, of the fair value over historical cost) on available-for-sale equity securities with readily determinable fair values may be included in supplementary capital. However, the FDIC may exclude all or a portion of these unrealized gains from Tier 2 capital if the FDIC determines that the equity securities are not prudently valued. Unrealized gains (losses) on other types of assets, such as bank premises and available-for-sale debt securities, are not included in supplementary capital, but the FDIC may take these unrealized gains (losses) into account as additional factors when assessing a bank's overall capital adequacy.

B. Deductions from Capital and Other Adjustments

Certain assets are deducted from a bank's capital base for the purpose of calculating the numerator of the risk-based capital ratio.[6] These assets include:

(1) All *intangible assets* other than mortgage servicing assets, nonmortgage servicing assets and purchased credit card relationships.[7] These disallowed intangibles are deducted from the core capital (Tier 1) elements.

(2) Investments in *unconsolidated* banking and finance subsidiaries.[8] This includes any equity or debt capital investments in banking or finance subsidiaries if the subsidiaries are not consolidated for regulatory capital requirements.[9] Generally, these investments include equity and debt capital securities

---

[6] Any assets deducted from capital when computing the numerator of the risk-based capital ratio will also be excluded from risk-weighted assets when computing the denominator of the ratio.

[7] In addition to mortgage servicing assets, nonmortgage servicing assets and purchased credit card relationships, certain other intangibles may be allowed if explicitly approved by the FDIC as part of the bank's regulatory capital on a specific case basis. In evaluating whether other types of intangibles should be recognized for regulatory capital purposes on a specific case basis, the FDIC will accord special attention to the general characteristics of the intangibles, including: (1) The separability of the intangible asset and the ability to sell it separate and apart from the bank or the bulk of the bank's assets, (2) the certainty that a readily identifiable stream of cash flows associated with the intangible asset can hold its value notwithstanding the future prospects of the bank, and (3) the existence of a market of sufficient depth to provide liquidity for the intangible asset.

[8] For risk-based capital purposes, these subsidiaries are generally defined as any company that is primarily engaged in banking or finance and in which the bank, either directly or indirectly, owns more than 50 percent of the outstanding voting stock but does not consolidate the company for regulatory capital purposes. In addition to investments in unconsolidated banking and finance subsidiaries, the FDIC may, on a case-by-case basis, deduct investments in associated companies or joint ventures, which are generally defined as any companies in which the bank, either directly or indirectly, owns 20 to 50 percent of the outstanding voting stock. Alternatively, the FDIC may, in certain cases, apply an appropriate risk-weighted capital charge against a bank's proportionate interest in the assets of associated companies and joint ventures. The definitions for subsidiaries, associated companies and joint ventures are contained in the instructions for the preparation of the Consolidated Reports of Condition and Income.

[9] Consolidation requirements for regulatory capital purposes generally follow the consolidation requirements set forth in the instructions for preparation of the consolidated Reports of Condition and Income. However, although investments in subsidiaries representing majority ownership in another Federally-insured depository institution are not consolidated for purposes of the consolidated Reports of Condition and Income that are filed by the parent bank, they are generally consolidated for purposes of determining FDIC regulatory capital requirements. Therefore, investments in these depository institution subsidiaries generally will not be deducted for risk-based capital purposes; rather, assets and liabilities of such subsidiaries will be consolidated with those of the parent bank when calculating the risk-based capital ratio. In addition, although securities subsidiaries established pursuant to 12 CFR 337.4 are consolidated for Report of Condition and Income purposes, they are not consolidated for regulatory capital purposes.

and any other instruments or commitments that are deemed to be capital of the subsidiary. These investments are deducted from the bank's total (Tier 1 plus Tier 2) capital base.

(3) Investments in *securities subsidiaries* established pursuant to 12 CFR 337.4. The FDIC may also consider deducting investments in other subsidiaries, either on a case-by-case basis or, as with securities subsidiaries, based on the general characteristics or functional nature of the subsidiaries.

(4) *Reciprocal holdings* of capital instruments of banks that represent intentional cross-holdings by the banks. These holdings are deducted from the bank's total capital base.

(5) *Deferred tax assets* in excess of the limit set forth in § 325.5(g). These disallowed deferred tax assets are deducted from the core capital (Tier 1) elements.

On a case-by-case basis, and in conjunction with supervisory examinations, other deductions from capital may also be required, including any adjustments deemed appropriate for assets classified as loss.

II. PROCEDURES FOR COMPUTING RISK-WEIGHTED ASSETS

A. General Procedures

1. Under the risk-based capital framework, a bank's balance sheet assets and credit equivalent amounts of off-balance sheet items are assigned to one of four broad risk categories according to the obligor or, if relevent, the guarantor or the nature of the collateral. The aggregate dollar amount in each category is then multiplied by the risk weight assigned to that category. The resulting weighted values from each of the four risk categories are added together and this sum is the *risk-weighted assets* total that, as adjusted.[10] comprises the denominator of the risk-based capital ratio.

2. The risk-weighted amounts for all off-balance sheet items are determined by a two-step process. First, the notional principal, or face value, amount of each off-balance sheet item generally is multiplied by a credit conversion factor to arrive at a balance sheet *credit equivalent amount*. Second, the credit equivalent amount generally is assigned to the appropriate risk category, like any balance sheet asset, according to the obligor or, if relevant, the guarantor or the nature of the collateral.

3. The Director of the Division of Supervision and Consumer Protection (DSC) may, on a case-by-case basis, determine the appropriate risk weight for any asset or credit equivalent amount that does not fit wholly within one of the risk categories set forth in this Appendix A or that imposes risks on a bank that are not commensurate with the risk weight otherwise specified in this Appendix A for the asset or credit equivalent amount. In addition, the Director of the Division of Supervision and Consumer Protection (DSC) may, on a case-by-case basis, determine the appropriate credit conversion factor for any off-balance sheet item that does not fit wholly within one of the credit conversion factors set forth in this Appendix A or that imposes risks on a bank that are not commensurate with the credit conversion factor otherwise specified in this Appendix A for the off-balance sheet item. In making such a determination, the Director of the Division of Supervision and Consumer Protection (DSC) will consider the similarity of the asset or off-balance sheet item to assets or off-balance sheet items explicitly treated in sections II.B and II.C of this appendix A, as well as other relevant factors.

4. The Director of the Division of Supervision and Consumer Protection (DSC) may, on a case-by-case basis, determine that the regulatory capital treatment for an exposure or other relationship to an entity that is not subject to consolidation on the balance sheet is not commensurate with the risk of the exposure and the relationship of the bank to the entity. In making this determination, the Director of DSC may require the bank to treat the entity as if it were consolidated on the balance sheet of the bank for risk-based capital purposes and calculate the appropriate risk-based capital ratios accordingly.

5. Optional Transition Provisions Related to the Implementation of Consolidation Requirements Under FAS 167

Section II.A.5 of this appendix provides optional transition provisions for a State nonmember bank that is required for financial and regulatory reporting purposes, as a result of its implementation of Statement of Financial Accounting Standards No. 167, *Amendments to FASB Interpretation No. 46(R)* (FAS 167), to consolidate certain variable interest entities (VIEs) as defined under United States generally accepted accounting principles (GAAP). These transition provisions apply through the end of the fourth quarter following the date of a bank's implementation of FAS 167 (implementation date).

i. *Exclusion period.*

(a) *Exclusion of risk-weighted assets for the first and second quarters.* For the first two quarters after the implementation date (exclusion period), including for the two calendar quarter-end regulatory report dates within those quarters, a bank may exclude from risk-weighted assets:

(1) Subject to the limitations in paragraph iii. of this section II.A.5, assets held by a

---

[10] Any asset deducted from a bank's capital accounts when computing the numerator of the risk-based capital ratio will also be excluded from risk-weighted assets when calculating the denominator for the ratio.

Federal Deposit Insurance Corporation

VIE, provided that the following conditions are met:

(i) The VIE existed prior to the implementation date,

(ii) The bank did not consolidate the VIE on its balance sheet for calendar quarter-end regulatory report dates prior to the implementation date,

(iii) The bank must consolidate the VIE on its balance sheet beginning as of the implementation date as a result of its implementation of FAS 167, and

(iv) The bank excludes all assets held by VIEs described in paragraphs i.(a)(1)(i) through (iii) of this section II.A.5; and

(2) Subject to the limitations in paragraph iii. of this section II.A.5, assets held by a VIE that is a consolidated asset-backed commercial paper (ABCP) program, provided that the following conditions are met:

(i) The bank is the sponsor of the ABCP program,

(ii) Prior to the implementation date, the bank consolidated the VIE onto its balance sheet under GAAP and excluded the VIE's assets from the bank's risk-weighted assets, and

(iii) The bank chooses to exclude all assets held by ABCP program VIEs described in paragraphs i.(a)(2)(i) and (ii) of this section II.A.5.

(b) *Risk-weighted assets during exclusion period.* During the exclusion period, including the two calendar quarter-end regulatory report dates within the exclusion period, a bank adopting the optional provisions of this paragraph i. of this section II.A.5 must calculate risk-weighted assets for its contractual exposures to the VIEs referenced in paragraph i.(a) of this section II.A.5 on the implementation date and include this calculated amount in its risk-weighted assets. Such contractual exposures may include direct-credit substitutes, recourse obligations, residual interests, liquidity facilities, and loans.

(c) *Inclusion of ALLL in Tier 2 capital for the first and second quarters.* During the exclusion period, including for the two calendar quarter-end regulatory report dates within the exclusion period, a bank that excludes VIE assets from risk-weighted assets pursuant to paragraph i.(a) of this section II.A.5 may include in Tier 2 capital the full amount of the allowance for loan and lease losses (ALLL) calculated as of the implementation date that is attributable to the assets it excludes pursuant to paragraph i.(a) of this section II.A.5 (inclusion amount). The amount of ALLL includable in Tier 2 capital in accordance with this paragraph shall not be subject to the limitations set forth in paragraph i. of section I.A.2.

ii. *Phase-in period.*

(a) *Exclusion amount.* For purposes of this paragraph ii. of this section II.A.5, exclusion amount is defined as the amount of risk-weighted assets excluded in paragraph i.(a) of this section II.A.5 as of the implementation date.

(b) *Risk-weighted assets for the third and fourth quarters.* A bank that excludes assets of consolidated VIEs from risk-weighted assets pursuant to paragraph i.(a) of this section II.A.5 may, for the third and fourth quarters after the implementation date (phase-in period), including for the two calendar quarter-end regulatory report dates within those quarters, exclude from risk-weighted assets 50 percent of the exclusion amount, provided that the bank may not include in risk-weighted assets pursuant to this paragraph an amount less than the aggregate risk-weighted assets calculated pursuant to paragraph i.(b) of this section II.A.5.

(c) *Inclusion of ALLL in Tier 2 capital for the third and fourth quarters.* A bank that excludes assets of consolidated VIEs from risk-weighted assets pursuant to paragraph ii.(b) of this section II.A.5 may, for the phase-in period, include in Tier 2 capital 50 percent of the inclusion amount it included in Tier 2 capital during the exclusion period, notwithstanding the limit on including ALLL in Tier 2 capital in paragraph i. of section I.A.2.

iii. *Implicit recourse limitation.* Notwithstanding any other provision in this section II.A.5, assets held by a VIE to which the bank has provided recourse through credit enhancement beyond any contractual obligation to support assets it has sold may not be excluded from risk-weighted assets.

B. Other Considerations

1. *Indirect Holdings of Assets.* Some of the assets on a bank's balance sheet may represent an indirect holding of a pool of assets; for example, mutual funds. An investment in shares of a mutual fund whose portfolio consists solely of various securities or money market instruments that, if held separately, would be assigned to different risk categories, generally is assigned to the risk category appropriate to the highest risk-weighted asset that the fund is permitted to hold in accordance with the stated investment objectives set forth in its prospectus. The bank may, at its option, assign the investment on a pro rata basis to different risk categories according to the investment limits in the fund's prospectus, but in no case will indirect holdings through shares in any mutual fund be assigned to a risk weight less than 20 percent. If the bank chooses to assign its investment on a pro rata basis, and the sum of the investment limits in the fund's prospectus exceeds 100 percent, the bank must assign risk weights in descending order. If, in order to maintain a necessary degree of short-term liquidity, a fund is permitted to hold an insignificant amount of its assets in short-term, highly liquid securities of superior credit quality that do not qualify for a preferential risk weight, such securities will

generally be disregarded in determining the risk category to which the bank's holdings in the overall fund should be assigned. The prudent use of hedging instruments by a mutual fund to reduce the risk of its assets will not increase the risk weighting of the mutual fund investment. For example, the use of hedging instruments by a mutual fund to reduce the interest rate risk of its government bond portfolio will not increase the risk weight of that fund above the 20 percent category. Nonetheless, if the fund engages in any activities that appear speculative in nature or has any other characteristics that are inconsistent with the preferential risk weighting assigned to the fund's assets, holdings in the fund will be assigned to the 100 percent risk category.

2. *Collateral.* In determining risk weights of various assets, the only forms of collateral that are formally recognized by the risk-based capital framework are cash on deposit in the lending bank; securities issued or guaranteed by the central governments of the OECD-based group of countries,[11] U.S. Government agencies, or U.S. Government-sponsored agencies; and securities issued or guaranteed by multilateral lending institutions or regional development banks. Claims fully secured by such collateral are assigned to the 20 percent risk category. The extent to which these securities are recognized as collateral for risk-based capital purposes is determined by their current market value. If a claim is partially secured, the portion of the claim that is not covered by the collateral is assigned to the risk category appropriate to the obligor or, if relevant, the guarantor.

3. *Guarantees.* Guarantees of the OECD and non-OECD central governments, U.S. Government agencies, U.S. Government-sponsored agencies, state and local governments of the OECD-based group of countries, multilateral lending institutions and regional development banks, U.S. depository institutions, foreign banks, and qualifying OECD-based securities firms are also recognized. If a claim is partially guaranteed, the portion of the claim that is not fully covered by the guarantee is assigned to the risk category appropriate to the obligor or, if relevant, the collateral.

4. *Maturity.* Maturity is generally not a factor in assigning items to risk categories with the exceptions of claims on non-OECD banks, commitments, and interest rate and foreign exchange rate related contracts. Except for commitments, short-term is defined as one year or less *remaining* maturity and long-term is defined as over one year *remaining* maturity. In the case of commitments, short-term is defined as one year or less *original* maturity and long-term is defined as over one year original maturity.[12]

5. *Recourse, Direct Credit Substitutes, Residual Interests and Mortgage- and Asset-Backed Securities.* For purposes of this section II.B.5 of this appendix A, the following definitions will apply.

a. *Definitions*—(1) *Credit derivative* means a contract that allows one party (the "protection purchaser") to transfer the credit risk of an asset or off-balance sheet credit exposure to another party (the "protection provider"). The value of a credit derivative is dependent, at least in part, on the credit performance of the "reference asset."

(2) *Credit-enhancing interest only strip* is defined in § 325.2(g).

(3) *Credit-enhancing representations and warranties* means representations and warranties that are made or assumed in connection with a transfer of assets (including loan servicing assets) and that obligate the bank to protect investors from losses arising from credit risk in the assets transferred or the loans serviced. Credit-enhancing representations and warranties include promises to protect a party from losses resulting from the default or nonperformance of another party or from an insufficiency in the value of the collateral. Credit-enhancing representations and warranties do not include:

---

[11] The OECD-based group of countries comprises all full members of the Organization for Economic Cooperation and Development (OECD) regardless of entry date, as well as countries that have concluded special lending arrangements with the International Monetary Fund (IMF) associated with the IMF's General Arrangements to Borrow, but excludes any country that has rescheduled its external sovereign debt within the previous five years. As of November 1995, the OECD included the following countries: Australia, Austria, Belgium, Canada, Denmark, Finland, France, Germany, Greece, Iceland, Ireland, Italy, Japan, Luxembourg, Mexico, the Netherlands, New Zealand, Norway, Portugal, Spain, Sweden, Switzerland, Turkey, the United Kingdom, and the United States; and Saudi Arabia had concluded special lending arrangements with the IMF associated with the IMF's General Arrangements to Borrow. A rescheduling of external sovereign debt generally would include any renegotiation of terms arising from a country's inability or unwillingness to meet its external debt service obligations, but generally would not include renegotiations of debt in the normal course of business, such as a renegotiation to allow the borrower to take advantage of a decline in interest rates or other change in market conditions.

[12] Through year-end 1992, remaining rather than original maturity may be used for determining term to maturity for commitments.

Federal Deposit Insurance Corporation

(i) Early default clauses and similar warranties that permit the return of, or premium refund clauses covering, 1–4 family residential first mortgage loans that qualify for a 50 percent risk weight for a period not to exceed 120 days from the date of transfer. These warranties may cover only those loans that were originated within 1 year of the date of transfer;

(ii) Premium refund clauses that cover assets guaranteed, in whole or in part, by the U.S. Government, a U.S. Government agency or a government-sponsored enterprise, provided the premium refund clauses are for a period not to exceed 120 days from the date of transfer; or

(iii) Warranties that permit the return of assets in instances of misrepresentation, fraud or incomplete documentation.

(4) *Direct credit substitute* means an arrangement in which a bank assumes, in form or in substance, credit risk associated with an on- or off-balance sheet credit exposure that was not previously owned by the bank (third-party asset) and the risk assumed by the bank exceeds the pro rata share of the bank's interest in the third-party asset. If the bank has no claim on the third-party asset, then the bank's assumption of any credit risk with respect to the third party asset is a direct credit substitute. Direct credit substitutes include, but are not limited to:

(i) Financial standby letters of credit, which includes any letter of credit or similar arrangement, however named or described, that support financial claims on a third party that exceed a bank's *pro rata* share of losses in the financial claim;

(ii) Guarantees, surety arrangements, credit derivatives, and similar instruments backing financial claims;

(iii) Purchased subordinated interests or securities that absorb more than their *pro rata* share of credit losses from the underlying assets;

(iv) Credit derivative contracts under which the bank assumes more than its *pro rata* share of credit risk on a third party asset or exposure;

(v) Loans or lines of credit that provide credit enhancement for the financial obligations of an account party;

(vi) Purchased loan servicing assets if the servicer:

(A) Is responsible for credit losses with the loans being serviced,

(B) Is responsible for making servicer cash advances (unless the advances are not direct credit substitutes because they meet the conditions specified in section II.B.5(a)(9) of this Appendix A), or

(C) Makes or assumes credit-enhancing representations and warranties with respect to the loans serviced;

(vii) Clean-up calls on third party assets. Clean-up calls that are exercisable at the option of the bank (as servicer or as an affiliate of the servicer) when the pool balance is 10 percent or less of the original pool balance are not direct credit substitutes; and

(viii) Liquidity facilities that provide liquidity support to ABCP (other than eligible ABCP liquidity facilities).

(5) *Eligible ABCP liquidity facility* means a liquidity facility supporting ABCP, in form or in substance, that is subject to an asset quality test at the time of draw that precludes funding against assets that are 90 days or more past due or in default. In addition, if the assets that an eligible ABCP liquidity facility is required to fund against are externally rated assets or exposures at the inception of the facility, the facility can be used to fund only those assets or exposures that are externally rated investment grade at the time of funding. Notwithstanding the eligibility requirements set forth in the two preceding sentences, a liquidity facility will be considered an eligible ABCP liquidity facility if the assets that are funded under the liquidity facility and which do not meet the eligibility requirements are guaranteed, either conditionally or unconditionally, by the U.S. government or its agencies, or by the central government of an OECD country.

(6) *Externally rated* means that an instrument or obligation has received a credit rating from a nationally recognized statistical rating organization.

(7) *Face amount* means the notional principal, or face value, amount of an off-balance sheet item; the amortized cost of an asset not held for trading purposes; and the fair value of a trading asset.

(8) *Financial asset* means cash or other monetary instrument, evidence of debt, evidence of an ownership interest in an entity, or a contract that conveys a right to receive or exchange cash or another financial instrument from another party.

(9) *Financial standby letter of credit* means a letter of credit or similar arrangement that represents an irrevocable obligation to a third-party beneficiary:

(i) To receive money borrowed by, or advanced to, or advanced to, or for the account of, a second party (the account party), or

(ii) To make payment on behalf of the account party, in the event that the account party fails to fulfill its obligation to the beneficiary.

(10) *Liquidity facility* means a legally binding commitment to provide liquidity support to ABCP by lending to, or purchasing assets from, any structure, program, or conduit in the event that funds are required to repay maturing ABCP.

(11) *Mortgage servicer cash advance* means funds that a residential mortgage servicer advances to ensure an uninterrupted flow of payments, including advances made to cover foreclosure costs or other expenses to facilitate the timely collection of the loan. A

mortgage servicer cash advance is not a recourse obligation or a direct credit substitute if:

(i) The mortgage servicer is entitled to full reimbursement and this right is not subordinated to other claims on the cash flows from the underlying asset pool; or

(ii) For any one loan, the servicer's obligation to make nonreimbursable advances is contractually limited to an insignificant amount of the outstanding principal of that loan.

(12) *Nationally recognized statistical rating organization (NRSRO)* means an entity recognized by the Division of Market Regulation of the Securities and Exchange Commission (or any successor Division) (Commission) as a nationally recognized statistical rating organization for various purposes, including the Commission's uniform net capital requirements for brokers and dealers (17 CFR 240.15c3–1).

(13) *Recourse* means an arrangement in which a bank retains, in form or in substance, of any credit risk directly or indirectly associated with an asset it has sold (in accordance with generally accepted accounting principles) that exceeds a *pro rata* share of the bank's claim on the asset. If a bank has no claim on an asset it has sold, then the retention of any credit risk is recourse. A recourse obligation typically arises when an institution transfers assets in a sale and retains an obligation to repurchase the assets or absorb losses due to a default of principal or interest or any other deficiency in the performance of the underlying obligor or some other party. Recourse may exist implicitly where a bank provides credit enhancement beyond any contractual obligation to support assets it has sold. The following are examples of recourse arrangements:

(i) Credit-enhancing representations and warranties made on the transferred assets;

(ii) Loan servicing assets retained pursuant to an agreement under which the bank:

(A) Is responsible for losses associated with the loans being serviced, or

(B) Is responsible for making mortgage servicer cash advances (unless the advances are not a recourse obligation because they meet the conditions specified in section II.B.5(a)(11) of this Appendix A);

(iii) Retained subordinated interests that absorb more than their *pro rata* share of losses from the underlying assets;

(iv) Assets sold under an agreement to repurchase, if the assets are not already included on the balance sheet;

(v) Loan strips sold without contractual recourse where the maturity of the transferred portion of the loan is shorter than the maturity of the commitment under which the loan is drawn;

(vi) Credit derivative contracts under which the bank retains more than its pro rata share of credit risk on transferred assets;

(vii) Clean-up calls at inception that are greater than 10 percent of the balance of the original pool of transferred loans. Clean-up calls that are 10 percent or less of the original pool balance that are exercisable at the option of the bank are not recourse arrangements; and

(viii.) Liquidity facilities that provide liquidity support to ABCP (other than eligible ABCP liquidity facilities).

(14) *Residual interest* means any on-balance sheet asset that represents an interest (including a beneficial interest) created by a transfer that qualifies as a sale (in accordance with generally accepted accounting principles (GAAP)) of financial assets, whether through a securitization or otherwise, and that exposes a bank to credit risk directly or indirectly associated with the transferred assets that exceeds a *pro rata* share of the bank's claim on the assets, whether through subordination provisions or other credit enhancement techniques. Residual interests generally include credit-enhancing I/Os, spread accounts, cash collateral accounts, retained subordinated interests, other forms of over-collateralization, and similar assets that function as a credit enhancement. Residual interests further include those exposures that, in substance, cause the bank to retain the credit risk of an asset or exposure that had qualified as a residual interest before it was sold. Residual interests generally do not include interests purchased from a third party, except that purchased credit-enhancing I/Os are residual interests for purposes of the risk-based capital treatment in this appendix.

(15) *Risk participation* means a participation in which the originating party remains liable to the beneficiary for the full amount of an obligation (*e.g.*, a direct credit substitute) notwithstanding that another party has acquired a participation in that obligation.

(16) *Securitization* means the pooling and repackaging by a special purpose entity of assets or other credit exposures into securities that can be sold to investors. Securitization includes transactions that create stratified credit risk positions whose performance is dependent upon an underlying pool of credit exposures, including loans and commitments.

(17) *Sponsor* means a bank that establishes an ABCP program; approves the sellers permitted to participate in the program; approves the asset pools to be purchased by the program; or administers the ABCP program by monitoring the assets, arranging for debt placement, compiling monthly reports, or ensuring compliance with the program documents and with the program's credit and investment policy.

(18) *Structured finance program* means a program where receivable interests and asset-

Federal Deposit Insurance Corporation Pt. 325, App. A

backed securities issued by multiple participants are purchased by a special purpose entity that repackages those exposures into securities that can be sold to investors. Structured finance programs allocate credit risks, generally, between the participants and credit enhancement provided to the program.

(19) *Traded position* means a position that is externally rated and is retained, assumed or issued in connection with a securitization, where there is a reasonable expectation that, in the near future, the rating will be relied upon by unaffiliated investors to purchase the position; or an unaffiliated third party to enter into a transaction involving the position, such as a purchase, loan, or repurchase agreement.

(b) *Credit equivalent amounts and risk weights of recourse obligations and direct credit substitutes*—(1) *General rule for determining the credit-equivalent amount.* Except as otherwise provided, the credit-equivalent amount for a recourse obligation or direct credit substitute is the full amount of the credit-enhanced assets for which the bank directly or indirectly retains or assumes credit risk multiplied by a 100% conversion factor. Thus, a bank that extends a partial direct credit substitute, *e.g.*, a financial standby letter of credit that absorbs the first 10 percent of loss on a transaction, must maintain capital against the full amount of the assets being supported.

(2) *Risk-weight factor.* To determine the bank's risk-weighted assets for an off-balance sheet recourse obligation or a direct credit substitute, the credit equivalent amount is assigned to the risk category appropriate to the obligor in the underlying transaction, after considering any associated guarantees or collateral. For a direct credit substitute that is an on-balance sheet asset, *e.g.*, a purchased subordinated security, a bank must calculate risk-weighted assets using the amount of the direct credit substitute and the full amount of the assets it supports, *i.e.*, all the more senior positions in the structure. The treatment covered in this paragraph (b) is subject to the low-level exposure rule provided in section II.B.5(h)(1) of this appendix A.

(c) *Credit equivalent amount and risk weight of participations in, and syndications of, direct credit substitutes.* Subject to the low-level exposure rule provided in section II.B.5(h)(1) of this appendix A, the credit equivalent amount for a participation interest in, or syndication of, a direct credit substitute (excluding purchased credit-enhancing interest-only strips) is calculated and risk weighted as follows:

(1) *Treatment for direct credit substitutes for which a bank has conveyed a risk participation.* In the case of a direct credit substitute in which a bank has conveyed a risk participation, the full amount of the assets that are supported by the direct credit substitute is converted to a credit equivalent amount using a 100% conversion factor. However, the *pro rata* share of the credit equivalent amount that has been conveyed through a risk participation is then assigned to whichever risk-weight category is lower: the risk-weight category appropriate to the obligor in the underlying transaction, after considering any associated guarantees or collateral, or the risk-weight category appropriate to the party acquiring the participation. The *pro rata* share of the credit equivalent amount that has not been participated out is assigned to the risk-weight category appropriate to the obligor, guarantor, or collateral. For example, the *pro rata* share of the full amount of the assets supported, in whole or in part, by a direct credit substitute conveyed as a risk participation to a U.S. domestic depository institution or an OECD bank is assigned to the 20 percent risk category.[13]

(2) *Treatment for direct credit substitutes in which the bank has acquired a risk participation.* In the case of a direct credit substitute in which the bank has acquired a risk participation, the acquiring bank's *pro rata* share of the direct credit substitute is multiplied by the full amount of the assets that are supported by the direct credit substitute and converted using a 100% credit conversion factor. The resulting credit equivalent amount is then assigned to the risk-weight category appropriate to the obligor in the underlying transaction, after considering any associated guarantees or collateral.

(3) *Treatment for direct credit substitutes related to syndications.* In the case of a direct credit substitute that takes the form of a syndication where each party is obligated only for its *pro rata* share of the risk and there is no recourse to the originating entity, each bank's credit equivalent amount will be calculated by multiplying only its pro rata share of the assets supported by the direct credit substitute by a 100% conversion factor. The resulting credit equivalent amount is then assigned to the risk-weight category appropriate to the obligor in the underlying transaction, after considering any associated guarantees or collateral.

(d) *Externally rated positions: credit-equivalent amounts and risk weights.*—(1) *Traded positions.* With respect to a recourse obligation, direct credit substitute, residual interest (other than a credit-enhancing interest-only strip) or mortgage- or asset-backed security that is a "traded position" and that has received an external rating on a long-term position that is one grade below investment grade or better or a short-term position that

---

[13] A risk participation with a remaining maturity of one year or less that is conveyed to a non-OECD bank is also assigned to the 20 percent risk category.

207

is investment grade, the bank may multiply the face amount of the position by the appropriate risk weight, determined in accordance with Table A or B of this appendix A, as appropriate.[14] If a traded position receives more than one external rating, the lowest rating will apply.

TABLE A

Long-term rating category	Examples	Risk weight (In percent)
Highest or second highest investment grade	AAA, AA	20
Third highest investment grade	A	50
Lowest investment grade	BBB	100
One category below investment grade	BB	200

TABLE B

Short-term rating category	Examples	Risk weight (In percent)
Highest investment grade	A–1, P–1	20
Second highest investment grade	A–2, P–2	50
Lowest investment grade	A–3, P–3	100

(2) *Non-traded positions.* A recourse obligation, direct credit substitute, residual interest (but not a credit-enhancing interest-only strip) or mortgage- or asset-backed security extended in connection with a securitization that is not a "traded position" may be assigned a risk weight in accordance with section II.B.5(d)(1) of this appendix A if:

(i) It has been externally rated by more than one NRSRO;

(ii) It has received an external rating on a long-term position that is one category below investment grade or better or a short-term position that is investment grade by all NRSROs providing a rating;

(iii) The ratings are publicly available; and

(iv) The ratings are based on the same criteria used to rate traded positions. If the ratings are different, the lowest rating will determine the risk category to which the recourse obligation, direct credit substitute, residual interest, or mortgage- or asset-backed security will be assigned.

(e) *Senior positions not externally rated.* For a recourse obligation, direct credit substitute, residual interest or mortgage- or asset-backed security that is not externally rated but is senior in all features to a traded position (including collateralization and maturity), a bank may apply a risk weight to the face amount of the senior position in accordance with section II.B.5(d)(1) of this appendix A, based upon the risk weight of the traded position, subject to any current or prospective supervisory guidance and the bank satisfying the FDIC that this treatment is appropriate. This section will apply only if the traded position provides substantial credit support for the entire life of the unrated position.

(f) *Residual interests*—(1) *Concentration limit on credit-enhancing interest-only strips.* In addition to the capital requirement provided by section II.B.5(f)(2) of this appendix A, a bank must deduct from Tier 1 capital the face amount of all credit-enhancing interest-only strips in excess of 25 percent of Tier 1 capital in accordance with §325.5(f)(3).

(2) *Credit-enhancing interest-only strip capital requirement.* After applying the concentration limit to credit-enhancing interest-only strips in accordance with §325.5(f)(3), a bank must maintain risk-based capital for a credit-enhancing interest-only strip, equal to the remaining face amount of the credit-enhancing interest-only strip (net of the remaining proportional amount of any existing associated deferred tax liability recorded on the balance sheet), even if the amount of risk-based capital required to be maintained exceeds the full risk-based capital requirement for the assets transferred. Transactions that, in substance, result in the retention of credit risk associated with a transferred credit-enhancing interest-only strip will be treated as if the credit-enhancing interest-only strip was retained by the bank and not transferred.

(3) *Other residual interests capital requirement.* Except as otherwise provided in section II.B.5(d) or (e) of this appendix A, a bank must maintain risk-based capital for a residual interest (excluding a credit-enhancing interest-only strip) equal to the face amount of the residual interest (net of any existing associated deferred tax liability recorded on

---

[14] Stripped mortgage-backed securities and similar instruments, such as interest-only strips that are not credit-enhancing and principal-only strips, must be assigned to the 100% risk category.

Federal Deposit Insurance Corporation

Pt. 325, App. A

the balance sheet), even if the amount of risk-based capital required to be maintained exceeds the full risk-based capital requirement for the assets transferred. Transactions that, in substance, result in the retention of credit risk associated with a transferred residual interest will be treated as if the residual interest was retained by the bank and not transferred.

(4) *Residual interests and other recourse obligations.* Where the aggregate capital requirement for residual interests (including credit-enhancing interest-only strips) and recourse obligations arising from the same transfer of assets exceed the full risk-based capital requirement for assets transferred, a bank must maintain risk-based capital equal to the greater of the risk-based capital requirement for the residual interest as calculated under sections II.B.5(f)(2) through (3) of this appendix A or the full risk-based capital requirement for the assets transferred.

(g) *Positions that are not rated by an NRSRO.* A bank's position (other than a residual interest) in a securitization or structured finance program that is not rated by an NRSRO may be risk-weighted based on the bank's determination of the credit rating of the position, as specified in Table C of this appendix A, multiplied by the face amount of the position. In order to qualify for this treatment, the bank's system for determining the credit rating of the position must meet one of the three alternative standards set out in section II.B.5(g)(1) through (3) of this appendix A.

TABLE C

Rating category	Examples	Risk Weight (In percent)
Investment grade	BBB or better	100
One category below investment grade	BB	200

(1) *Internal risk rating used for asset-backed programs.* A bank extends a direct credit substitute (but not a purchased credit-enhancing interest-only strip) to an asset-backed commercial paper program sponsored by the bank and the bank is able to demonstrate to the satisfaction of the FDIC, prior to relying upon its use, that the bank's internal credit risk rating system is adequate. Adequate internal credit risk rating systems usually contain the following criteria:[15]

(i) The internal credit risk rating system is an integral part of the bank's risk management system that explicitly incorporates the full range of risks arising from a bank's participation in securitization activities;

(ii) Internal credit ratings are linked to measurable outcomes, such as the probability that the position will experience any loss, the position's expected loss given default, and the degree of variance in losses given default on that position;

(iii) The internal credit risk rating system must separately consider the risk associated with the underlying loans or borrowers, and the risk associated with the structure of a particular securitization transaction;

(iv) The internal credit risk rating system identifies gradations of risk among "pass" assets and other risk positions;

(v) The internal credit risk rating system must have clear, explicit criteria (including for subjective factors), that are used to classify assets into each internal risk grade;

(vi) The bank must have independent credit risk management or loan review personnel assigning or reviewing the credit risk ratings;

(vii) An internal audit procedure should periodically verify that internal risk ratings are assigned in accordance with the bank's established criteria;

(viii) The bank must monitor the performance of the internal credit risk ratings assigned to nonrated, nontraded direct credit substitutes over time to determine the appropriateness of the initial credit risk rating assignment and adjust individual credit risk ratings, or the overall internal credit risk ratings system, as needed; and

(ix) The internal credit risk rating system must make credit risk rating assumptions that are consistent with, or more conservative than, the credit risk rating assumptions and methodologies of NRSROs.

(2) *Program Ratings.* A bank extends a direct credit substitute or retains a recourse obligation (but not a residual interest) in connection with a structured finance program and an NRSRO has reviewed the terms of the program and stated a rating for positions associated with the program. If the program has options for different combinations of assets, standards, internal credit enhancements and other relevant factors, and the NRSRO specifies ranges of rating categories to them, the bank may apply the rating category applicable to the option that corresponds to the bank's position. In order to rely on a program rating, the bank must demonstrate to the FDIC's satisfaction that

---

[15] The adequacy of a bank's use of its internal credit risk rating system must be demonstrated to the FDIC considering the criteria listed in this section and the size and complexity of the credit exposures assumed by the bank.

the credit risk rating assigned to the program meets the same standards generally used by NRSROs for rating traded positions. The bank must also demonstrate to the FDIC's satisfaction that the criteria underlying the NRSRO's assignment of ratings for the program are satisfied for the particular position issued by the bank. If a bank participates in a securitization sponsored by another party, the FDIC may authorize the bank to use this approach based on a program rating obtained by the sponsor of the program.

(3) *Computer Program.* A bank is using an acceptable credit assessment computer program that has been developed by an NRSRO to determine the rating of a direct credit substitute or recourse obligation (but not a residual interest) extended in connection with a structured finance program. In order to rely on the rating determined by the computer program, the bank must demonstrate to the FDIC's satisfaction that ratings under the program correspond credibly and reliably with the ratings of traded positions. The bank must also demonstrate to the FDIC's satisfaction the credibility of the program in financial markets, the reliability of the program in assessing credit risk, the applicability of the program to the bank's position, and the proper implementation of the program.

(h) *Limitations on risk-based capital requirements*—(1) *Low-level exposure rule.* If the maximum exposure to loss retained or assumed by a bank in connection with a recourse obligation, a direct credit substitute, or a residual interest is less than the effective risk-based capital requirement for the credit-enhanced assets, the risk-based capital required under this appendix A is limited to the bank's maximum contractual exposure, less any recourse liability account established in accordance with generally accepted accounting principles. This limitation does not apply when a bank provides credit enhancement beyond any contractual obligation to support assets it has sold.

(2) *Mortgage-related securities or participation certificates retained in a mortgage loan swap.* If a bank holds a mortgage-related security or a participation certificate as a result of a mortgage loan swap with recourse, capital is required to support the recourse obligation plus the percentage of the mortgage-related security or participation certificate that is not covered by the recourse obligation. The total amount of capital required for the on-balance sheet asset and the recourse obligation, however, is limited to the capital requirement for the underlying loans, calculated as if the bank continued to hold these loans as an on-balance sheet asset.

(3) *Related on-balance sheet assets.* If a recourse obligation or direct credit substitute also appears as a balance sheet asset, the asset is risk-weighted only under this section II.B.5 of this appendix A, except in the case of loan servicing assets and similar arrangements with embedded recourse obligations or direct credit substitutes. In that case, the on-balance sheet servicing assets and the related recourse obligations or direct credit substitutes must both be separately risk weighted and incorporated into the risk based capital calculation.

(i) *Alternative Capital Calculation for Small Business Obligations*—(1) *Definitions.* For purposes of this section II.B. 5(i):

(i) *Qualified bank* means a bank that:

(A) Is well capitalized as defined in §325.103(b)(1) without applying the capital treatment described in this section II.B.5(i), or

(B) Is adequately capitalized as defined in §325.103(b)(2) without applying the capital treatment described in this section II.B.5(i) and has received written permission by order of the FDIC to apply the capital treatment described in this section II.B.5(i).

(iii) *Small business* means a business that meets the criteria for a small business concern established by the Small Business Administration in 13 CFR part 121 pursuant to 15 U.S.C. 632.

(2) *Capital and reserve requirements.* Notwithstanding the risk-based capital treatment outlined in any other paragraph (other than paragraph (i) of this section II.B.5), with respect to a transfer with recourse of a small business loan or a lease to a small business of personal property that is a sale under generally accepted accounting principles, and for which the bank establishes and maintains a non-capital reserve under generally accepted accounting principles sufficient to meet the reasonable estimated liability of the bank under the recourse arrangement; a qualified bank may elect to include only the face amount of its recourse in its risk-weighted assets for purposes of calculating the bank's risk-based capital ratio.

(3) *Limit on aggregate amount of recourse.* The total outstanding amount of recourse retained by a qualified bank with respect to transfers of small business loans and leases to small businesses of personal property and included in the risk-weighted assets of the bank as described in section II.B.5(i)(2) of this appendix A may not exceed 15 percent of the bank's total risk-based capital, unless the FDIC specifies a greater amount by order.

(4) *Bank that ceases to be qualified or that exceeds aggregate limit.* If a bank ceases to be a qualified bank or exceeds the aggregate limit in section II.B.5(i)(3) of this appendix A, the bank may continue to apply the capital treatment described in section II.B.5(i)(2) of this appendix A to transfers of small business loans and leases to small businesses of personal property that occurred when the

Federal Deposit Insurance Corporation

bank was qualified and did not exceed the limit.

(5) *Prompt correction action not affected.* (i) A bank shall compute its capital without regard to this section II.B.5(i) for purposes of prompt corrective action (12 U.S.C. 1831o) unless the bank is a well capitalized bank (without applying the capital treatment described in this section II.B.5(i)) and, after applying the capital treatment described in this section II.B.5(i), the bank would be well capitalized.

(ii) A bank shall compute its capital without regard to this section II.B.5(i) for purposes of 12 U.S.C. 1831o(g) regardless of the bank's capital level.

(6) *Nonfinancial equity investments.* (i) General. A bank must deduct from its Tier 1 capital the sum of the appropriate percentage (as determined below) of the adjusted carrying value of all nonfinancial equity investments held by the bank or by its direct or indirect subsidiaries. For purposes of this section II.B.(6), investments held by a bank include all investments held directly or indirectly by the bank or any of its subsidiaries.

(ii) *Scope of nonfinancial equity investments.* A nonfinancial equity investment means any equity investment held by the bank in a nonfinancial company: through a small business investment company (SBIC) under section 302(b) of the Small Business Investment Act of 1958 (15 U.S.C. 682(b));[16] under the portfolio investment provisions of Regulation K issued by the Board of Governors of the Federal Reserve System (12 CFR 211.8(c)(3)); or under section 24 of the Federal Deposit Insurance Act (12 U.S.C. 1831a), other than an investment held in accordance with section 24(f) of that Act.[17] A nonfinancial company is an entity that engages in any activity that has not been determined to be permissible for the bank to conduct directly, or to be financial in nature or incidental to financial activities under section 4(k) of the Bank Holding Company Act (12 U.S.C. 1843(k)).

(iii) *Amount of deduction from core capital.* (A) The bank must deduct from its Tier 1 capital the sum of the appropriate percentages, as set forth in the table following this paragraph, of the adjusted carrying value of all nonfinancial equity investments held by the bank. The amount of the percentage deduction increases as the aggregate amount of nonfinancial equity investments held by the bank increases as a percentage of the bank's Tier 1 capital.

DEDUCTION FOR NONFINANCIAL EQUITY INVESTMENTS

Aggregate adjusted carrying value of all nonfinancial equity investments held directly or indirectly by the bank (as a percentage of the Tier 1 capital of the bank)[1]	Deduction from Tier 1 Capital (as a percentage of the adjusted carrying value of the investment)
Less than 15 percent	8 percent.
15 percent to 24.99 percent	12 percent.
25 percent and above	25 percent.

[1] For purposes of calculating the adjusted carrying value of nonfinancial equity investments as a percentage of Tier 1 capital, Tier 1 capital is defined as the sum of core capital elements net of goodwill and net of all identifiable intangible assets other than mortgage servicing assets, nonmortgage servicing assets and purchased credit card relationships, but prior to the deduction for any disallowed mortgage servicing assets, any disallowed nonmortgage servicing assets, any disallowed purchased credit card relationships, any disallowed credit-enhancing interest-only strips (both purchased and retained), any disallowed deferred tax assets, and any nonfinancial equity investments.

(B) These deductions are applied on a marginal basis to the portions of the adjusted carrying value of nonfinancial equity investments that fall within the specified ranges of the parent bank's Tier 1 capital. For example, if the adjusted carrying value of all nonfinancial equity investments held by a bank equals 20 percent of the Tier 1 capital of the bank, then the amount of the deduction would be 8 percent of the adjusted carrying value of all investments up to 15 percent of the bank's Tier 1 capital, and 12 percent of the adjusted carrying value of all investments in excess of 15 percent of the bank's Tier 1 capital.

(C) The total adjusted carrying value of any nonfinancial equity investment that is subject to deduction under this paragraph is excluded from the bank's risk-weighted assets for purposes of computing the denominator of the bank's risk-based capital ratio

---

[16] An equity investment made under section 302(b) of the Small Business Investment Act of 1958 in a SBIC that is not consolidated with the bank is treated as a nonfinancial equity investment.

[17] The Board of Directors of the FDIC, acting directly, may, in exceptional cases and after a review of the proposed activity, permit a lower capital deduction for investments approved by the Board of Directors under section 24 of the FDI Act so long as the bank's investments under section 24 and SBIC investments represent, in the aggregate, less than 15 percent of the Tier 1 capital of the bank. The FDIC reserves the authority to impose higher capital charges on any investment where appropriate.

and from total assets for purposes of calculating the denominator of the leverage ratio.[18]

(D) This Appendix establishes *minimum* risk-based capital ratios and banks are at all times expected to maintain capital commensurate with the level and nature of the risks to which they are exposed. The risk to a bank from nonfinancial equity investments increases with its concentration in such investments and strong capital levels above the minimum requirements are particularly important when a bank has a high degree of concentration in nonfinancial equity investments (*e.g.*, in excess of 50 percent of Tier 1 capital). The FDIC intends to monitor banks and apply heightened supervision to equity investment activities as appropriate, including where the bank has a high degree of concentration in nonfinancial equity investments, to ensure that each bank maintains capital levels that are appropriate in light of its equity investment activities. The FDIC also reserves authority to impose a higher capital charge in any case where the circumstances, such as the level of risk of the particular investment or portfolio of investments, the risk management systems of the bank, or other information, indicate that a higher minimum capital requirement is appropriate.

(iv) *SBIC investments.* (A) No deduction is required for nonfinancial equity investments that are held by a bank through one or more SBICs that are consolidated with the bank or in one or more SBICs that are not consolidated with the bank to the extent that all such investments, in the aggregate, do not exceed 15 percent of the bank's Tier 1 capital. Any nonfinancial equity investment that is held through an SBIC or in an SBIC and that is not required to be deducted from Tier 1 capital under this section II.B.(6)(iv) will be assigned a 100 percent risk-weight and included in the bank's consolidated risk-weighted assets.[19]

(B) To the extent the adjusted carrying value of all nonfinancial equity investments that a bank holds through one or more SBICs that are consolidated with the bank or in one or more SBICs that are not consolidated with the bank exceeds, in the aggregate, 15 percent of the bank's Tier 1 capital, the appropriate percentage of such amounts (as set forth in the table in section II.B.(6)(iii)(A)) must be deducted from the bank's common stockholders' equity in determining the bank's Tier 1 capital. In addition, the aggregate adjusted carrying value of all nonfinancial equity investments held by a bank through a consolidated SBIC and in a non-consolidated SBIC (including any investments for which no deduction is required) must be included in determining, for purposes of the table in section II.B.(6)(iii)(A), the total amount of nonfinancial equity investments held by the bank in relation to its Tier 1 capital.

(v) *Transition provisions.* No deduction under this section II.B.(6) is required to be made with respect to the adjusted carrying value of any nonfinancial equity investment (or portion of such an investment) that was made by the bank prior to March 13, 2000, or that was made by the bank after such date pursuant to a binding written commitment[20] entered into prior to March 13, 2000, provided that in either case the bank has continuously held the investment since the relevant

---

[18] For example, if 8 percent of the adjusted carrying value of a nonfinancial equity investment is deducted from Tier 1 capital, the entire adjusted carrying value of the investment will be excluded from both risk-weighted assets and total assets in calculating the respective denominators for the risk-based capital and leverage ratios.

[19] If a bank has an investment in a SBIC that is consolidated for accounting purposes but that is not wholly owned by the bank, the adjusted carrying value of the bank's nonfinancial equity investments through the SBIC is equal to the bank's proportionate share of the adjusted carrying value of the SBIC's investments in nonfinancial companies. The remainder of the SBIC's adjusted carrying value (*i.e.*, the minority interest holders' proportionate share) is excluded from the risk-weighted assets of the bank. If a bank has an investment in a SBIC that is not consolidated for accounting purposes and has current information that identifies the percentage of the SBIC's assets that are equity investments in nonfinancial companies, the bank may reduce the adjusted carrying value of its investment in the SBIC proportionately to reflect the percentage of the adjusted carrying value of the SBIC's assets that are not equity investments in nonfinancial companies. If a bank reduces the adjusted carrying value of its investment in a non-consolidated SBIC to reflect financial investments of the SBIC, the amount of the adjustment will be risk weighted at 100 percent and included in the bank's risk-weighted assets.

[20] A "binding written commitment" means a legally binding written agreement that requires the bank to acquire shares or other equity of the company, or make a capital contribution to the company, under terms and conditions set forth in the agreement. Options, warrants, and other agreements that give a bank the right to acquire equity or make an investment, but do not require the bank to take such actions, are not considered a binding written commitment for purposes of this section II.B.(6)(v).

investment date.[21] For purposes of this section II.B.(6)(v) a nonfinancial equity investment made prior to March 13, 2000, includes any shares or other interests received by the bank through a stock split or stock dividend on an investment made prior to March 13, 2000, provided the bank provides no consideration for the shares or interests received and the transaction does not materially increase the bank's proportional interest in the company. The exercise on or after March 13, 2000, of options or warrants acquired prior to March 13, 2000, is *not* considered to be an investment made prior to March 13, 2000, if the bank provides any consideration for the shares or interests received upon exercise of the options or warrants. Any nonfinancial equity investment (or portion thereof) that is not required to be deducted from Tier 1 capital under this section II.B.(6)(v) must be included in determining the total amount of nonfinancial equity investments held by the bank in relation to its Tier 1 capital for purposes of the table in section II.B.(6)(iii)(A). In addition, any nonfinancial equity investment (or portion thereof) that is not required to be deducted from Tier 1 capital under this section II.B.(6)(v) will be assigned a 100-percent risk weight and included in the bank's consolidated risk-weighted assets.

(vi) *Adjusted carrying value.* (A) For purposes of this section II.B.(6), the "adjusted carrying value" of investments is the aggregate value at which the investments are carried on the balance sheet of the bank reduced by any unrealized gains on those investments that are reflected in such carrying value but excluded from the bank's Tier 1 capital and associated deferred tax liabilities. For example, for equity investments held as available-for-sale (AFS), the adjusted carrying value of the investments would be the aggregate carrying value of those investments (as reflected on the consolidated balance sheet of the bank) less any unrealized gains on those investments that are included in other comprehensive income and not reflected in Tier 1 capital, and associated deferred tax liabilities.[22]

(B) As discussed above with respect to consolidated SBICs, some equity investments may be in companies that are consolidated for accounting purposes. For investments in a nonfinancial company that is consolidated for accounting purposes under generally accepted accounting principles, the bank's adjusted carrying value of the investment is determined under the equity method of accounting (net of any intangibles associated with the investment that are deducted from the bank's core capital in accordance with section I.A.(1) of this appendix A). Even though the assets of the nonfinancial company are consolidated for accounting purposes, these assets (as well as the credit equivalent amounts of the company's off-balance sheet items) should be excluded from the bank's risk-weighted assets for regulatory capital purposes.

(vii) *Equity investments.* For purposes of this section II.B.(6), an equity investment means any equity instrument (including common stock, preferred stock, partnership interests, interests in limited liability companies, trust certificates and warrants and call options that give the holder the right to purchase an equity instrument), any equity feature of a debt instrument (such as a warrant or call option), and any debt instrument that is convertible into equity where the instrument or feature is held under one of the legal authorities listed in section II.B.(6)(ii) of this appendix A. An investment in any other instrument (including subordinated debt) may be treated as an equity investment if, in the judgment of the FDIC, the instrument is the functional equivalent of equity or exposes the bank to essentially the same risks as an equity instrument.

6. *Asset-backed commercial paper programs.* a. An asset-backed commercial paper (ABCP) program means a program that primarily issues externally rated commercial paper backed by assets or other exposures held in a bankruptcy-remote, special purpose entity.

b. If a bank has multiple overlapping exposures (such as a program-wide credit enhancement and multiple pool-specific liquidity facilities) to an ABCP program that is

---

[21] For example, if a bank made an equity investment in 100 shares of a nonfinancial company prior to March 13, 2000, the adjusted carrying value of that investment would not be subject to a deduction under this section II.B.(6). However, if the bank made any additional equity investment in the company after March 13, 2000, such as by purchasing additional shares of the company (including through the exercise of options or warrants acquired before or after March 13, 2000) or by making a capital contribution to the company and such investment was not made pursuant to a binding written commitment entered into before March 13, 2000, the adjusted carrying value of the additional investment would be subject to a deduction under this section II.B.(6). In addition, if the bank sold and repurchased, after March 13, 2000, 40 shares of the company, the adjusted carrying value of those 40 shares would be subject to a deduction under this section II.B.(6).

[22] Unrealized gains on available-for-sale equity investments may be included in Tier 2 capital to the extent permitted under section I.A.(2)(f) of this appendix A. In addition, the net unrealized losses on available-for-sale equity investments are deducted from Tier 1 capital in accordance with section I.A.(1) of this appendix A.

Pt. 325, App. A

not consolidated for risk-based capital purposes, the bank is not required to hold capital under duplicative risk-based capital requirements under this appendix against the overlapping position. Instead, the bank should apply to the overlapping position the applicable risk-based capital treatment that results in the highest capital charge.

C. *Risk Weights for Balance Sheet Assets (see Table II)*

The risk based capital framework contains five risk weight categories—0 percent, 20 percent, 50 percent, 100 percent, and 200 percent. In general, if a particular item can be placed in more than one risk category, it is assigned to the category that has the lowest risk weight. An explanation of the components of each category follows:

Category 1—Zero Percent Risk Weight. a. This category includes cash (domestic and foreign) owned and held in all offices of the bank or in transit; balances due from Federal Reserve Banks and central banks in other OECD countries; the portions of local currency claims on or unconditionally guaranteed by non-OECD central governments to the extent that the bank has liabilities booked in that currency; and gold bullion held in the bank's own vaults or in another bank's vaults on an allocated basis, to the extent it is offset by gold bullion liabilities.[23]

b. The zero percent risk category also includes direct claims[24] (including securities, loans, and leases) on, and the portions of claims that are unconditionally guaranteed by, OECD central governments[25] and U.S.

---

[23] All other bullion holdings are to be assigned to the 100 percent risk weight category.

[24] For purposes of determining the appropriate risk weights for this risk-based capital framework, the terms *claims* and *securities* refer to loans or other *debt* obligations of the entity on whom the claim is held. Investments in the form of stock or equity holdings in commercial or financial firms are generally assigned to the 100 percent risk category.

[25] A central government is defined to include departments and ministries, including the central bank, of the central government. The U.S. central bank includes the 12 Federal Reserve Banks. The definition of central government does not include state, provincial or local governments or commercial enterprises owned by the central government. In addition, it does not include local government entities or commercial enterprises whose obligations are guaranteed by the central government. OECD central governments are defined as central governments of the OECD-based group of countries. Non-OECD central governments are defined as central

12 CFR Ch. III (1-1-12 Edition)

Government agencies.[26] Federal Reserve Bank stock also is included in this category.

c. This category also includes claims on, and claims guaranteed by, qualifying securities firms incorporated in the United States or other members of the OECD-based group of countries that are collateralized by cash on deposit in the lending bank or by securities issued or guaranteed by the United States or OECD central governments (including U.S. government agencies), provided that a positive margin of collateral is required to be maintained on such a claim on a daily basis, taking into account any change in a bank's exposure to the obligor or counterparty under the claim in relation to the market value of the collateral held in support of the claim.

Category 2—20 Percent Risk Weight. a. This category includes short-term claims (including demand deposits) on, and portions of short-term claims that are guaranteed[27] by, U.S. depository institutions[28] and foreign

---

governments of countries that do not belong to the OECD-based group of countries.

[26] For risk-based capital purposes U.S. Government agency is defined as an instrumentality of the U.S. Government whose debt obligations are fully and explicitly guaranteed as to the timely payment of principal and interest by the full faith and credit of the U.S. Government. These agencies include the Government National Mortgage Association (GNMA), the Veterans Administration (VA), the Federal Housing Administration (FHA), the Farmers Home Administration (FHA), the Export-Import Bank (Exim Bank), the Overseas Private Investment Corporation (OPIC), the Commodity Credit Corporation (CCC), and the Small Business Administration (SBA). U.S. Government agencies generally do not directly issue securities to the public; however, a number of U.S. Government agencies, such as GNMA, guarantee securities that are publicly held.

[27] Claims guaranteed by U.S. depository institutions and foreign banks include risk participations in both bankers acceptances and standby letters of credit, as well as participations in commitments, that are *conveyed* to other U.S. depository institutions or foreign banks.

[28] U.S. depository institutions are defined to include branches (foreign and domestic) of federally-insured banks and depository institutions chartered and headquartered in the 50 states of the United States, the District of Columbia, Puerto Rico, and U.S. territories and possessions. The definition encompasses banks, mutual or stock savings banks, savings or building and loan associations, cooperative banks, credit unions, international banking facilities of domestic depository institutions, and U.S.-chartered depository institutions owned by foreigners. However,

214

banks;[29] portions of claims collateralized by cash held in a segregated deposit account of the lending bank; cash items in process of collection, both foreign and domestic; and long-term claims on, and portions of long-term claims guaranteed by, U.S. depository institutions and OECD banks.[30] This category also includes a claim[31] on, or guaranteed by, qualifying securities firms incorporated in the United States or other member of the OECD-based group of countries[32]

---

this definition excludes branches and agencies of foreign banks located in the U.S. and bank holding companies.

[29] Foreign banks are distinguished as either OECD banks or non-OECD banks. OECD banks include banks and their branches (foreign and domestic) organized under the laws of countries (other than the U.S.) that belong to the OECD-based group of countries. Non-OECD banks include banks and their branches (foreign and domestic) organized under the laws of countries that do not belong to the OECD-based group of countries. For risk-based capital purposes, a bank is defined as an institution that engages in the business of banking; is recognized as a bank by the bank supervisory or monetary authorities of the country of its organization or principal banking operations; receives deposits to a substantial extent in the regular course of business; and has the power to accept demand deposits.

[30] Long-term claims on, or guaranteed by, non-OECD banks and all claims on bank holding companies are assigned to the 100 percent risk weight category, as are holdings of bank-issued securities that qualify as capital of the issuing banks for risk-based capital purposes.

[31] Claims on a qualifying securities firm that are instruments the firm, or its parent company, uses to satisfy its applicable capital requirements are not eligible for this risk weight.

[32] With regard to securities firms incorporated in the United States, qualifying securities firms are those securities firms that are broker-dealers registered with the Securities and Exchange Commission (SEC) and are in compliance with the SEC's net capital rule, 17 CFR 240.15c3–1. With regard to securities firms incorporated in any other country in the OECD-based group of countries, qualifying securities firms are those securities firms that a bank is able to demonstrate are subject to consolidated supervision and regulation (covering their direct and indirect subsidiaries, but not necessarily their parent organizations) comparable to that imposed on banks in OECD countries. Such regulation must include risk-based capital requirements comparable to those applied to banks under the Accord on International Convergence of Capital Measurement and Capital

provided that: the qualifying securities firm has a long-term issuer credit rating, or a rating on at least one issue of long-term debt, in one of the three highest investment grade rating categories from a nationally recognized statistical rating organization; or the claim is guaranteed by the firm's parent company and the parent company has such a rating. If ratings are available from more than one rating agency, the lowest rating will be used to determine whether the rating requirement has been met. This category also includes a collateralized claim on a qualifying securities firm in such a country, without regard to satisfaction of the rating standard, provided that the claim arises under a contract that:

(1) Is a reverse repurchase/repurchase agreement or securities lending/borrowing transaction executed using standard industry documentation;

(2) Is collateralized by debt or equity securities that are liquid and readily marketable;

(3) Is marked-to-market daily;

(4) Is subject to a daily margin maintenance requirement under the standardized documentation; and

(5) Can be liquidated, terminated, or accelerated immediately in bankruptcy or similar proceeding, and the security or collateral agreement will not be stayed or avoided, under applicable law of the relevant jurisdiction.[33]

Standards (1988, as amended in 1998) (Basel Accord). Claims on a qualifying securities firm that are instruments the firm, or its parent company, uses to satisfy its applicable capital requirements are not eligible for this risk weight and are generally assigned to at least a 100 percent risk weight. In addition, certain claims on qualifying securities firms are eligible for a zero percent risk weight if the claims are collateralized by cash on deposit in the lending bank or by securities issued or guaranteed by the United States or OECD central governments (including U.S. government agencies), provided that a positive margin of collateral is required to be maintained on such a claim on a daily basis, taking into account any change in a bank's exposure to the obligor or counterparty under the claim in relation to the market value of the collateral held in support of the claim.

[33] For example, a claim is exempt from the automatic stay in bankruptcy in the United States if it arises under a securities contract or a repurchase agreement subject to section 555 or 559 of the Bankruptcy Code, respectively (11 U.S.C. 555 or 559), a qualified financial contract under section 11(e)(8) of the Federal Deposit Insurance Act (12 U.S.C. 1821(e)(8)), or a netting contract between financial institutions under sections 401–407 of

Continued

b. This category also includes claims on, or portions of claims guaranteed by, U.S. Government-*sponsored* agencies;[34] and portions of claims (including repurchase agreements) collateralized by securities issued or guaranteed by OECD central governments, U.S. Government agencies, or U.S. Government-sponsored agencies. Also included in the 20 percent risk category are portions of claims that are conditionally guaranteed by OECD central governments and U.S. Government agencies,[35] as well as portions of local currency claims that are conditionally guaranteed by non-OECD central governments to the extent that the bank has liabilities booked in that currency.

c. General obligation claims on, or portions of claims guaranteed by, the full faith and credit of states or other political subdivisions of the United States or other countries of the OECD-based group are also assigned to this 20 percent risk category.[36] In addition, this category includes claims on the International Bank for Reconstruction and Development (World Bank), International Finance Corporation the Inter-American Development Bank, the Asian Development Bank, the African Development Bank, the European Investment Bank, the European Bank for Reconstruction and Development, the Nordic Investment Bank, and other multilateral lending institutions or regional development institutions in which the U.S. Government is a shareholder or contributing member, as well as portions of claims guaranteed by such organizations or collateralized by their securities.

d. This category also includes recourse obligations, direct credit substitutes, residual interests (other than a credit-enhancing interest-only strip) and asset- or mortgage-backed securities rated in the highest or second highest investment grade category, e.g., AAA, AA, in the case of long-term ratings, or the highest rating category, e.g., A-1, P-1, in the case of short-term ratings.

a. *Category 3—50 Percent Risk Weight.* This category includes loans fully secured by first liens[37] on *one-to-four family residential properties,* provided that such loans have been approved in accordance with prudent underwriting standards, including standards relating to the loan amount as a percent of the appraised value of the property,[38] and provided that the loans are not past due 90 days or more or carried in nonaccrual status.[39] The types of loans that qualify as loans secured by one-to-four family residential properties are listed in the instructions for preparation of the Consolidated Reports of Condition and Income. These properties may be either owner-occupied or rented. In addition, for risk-based capital purposes, loans secured

---

the Federal Deposit Insurance Corporation Improvement Act of 1991 (12 U.S.C. 4401–4407), or the Board's Regulation EE (12 CFR part 231).

[34] For risk-based capital purposes, U.S. Government-sponsored agencies are defined as agencies originally established or chartered by the U.S. Government to serve public purposes specified by the U.S. Congress but whose debt obligations are *not explicitly* guaranteed by the full faith and credit of the U.S. Government. These agencies include the Federal Home Loan Mortgage Corporation (FHLMC), the Federal National Mortgage Association (FNMA), the Farm Credit System, the Federal Home Loan Bank System, and the Student Loan Marketing Association (SLMA). For risk-based capital purposes, claims on U.S. Government-sponsored agencies also include capital stock in a Federal Home Loan Bank that is held as a condition of membership in that Bank.

[35] For risk-based capital purposes, a conditional guarantee is deemed to exist if the validity of the guarantee by the OECD central government or the U.S. Government agency is dependent upon some affirmative action (e.g., servicing requirements on the part of the beneficiary of the guarantee). Portions of claims that are unconditionally guaranteed by OECD central governments or U.S. Government agencies are assigned to the zero percent risk category.

[36] Claims on, or guaranteed by, states or other political subdivisions of countries that do not belong to the OECD-based group of countries are to be placed in the 100 percent risk weight category.

[37] If a bank holds the first and junior lien(s) on a residential property and no other party holds an intervening lien, the transactions are treated as a single loan secured by a first lien for purposes of determining the loan-to-value ratio and assigning a risk weight.

[38] For risk-based capital purposes, the loan-to-value ratio generally is based upon the most current appraised value of the property. The appraisal should be performed in a manner consistent with the Federal banking agencies' real estate appraisal guidelines and with the bank's own appraisal guidelines.

[39] This category would also include a first-lien residential mortgage loan on a one-to-four family property that was appropriately assigned a 50 percent risk weight pursuant to this section immediately prior to modification (on a permanent or trial basis) under the Home Affordable Mortgage Program established by the U.S. Department of Treasury, so long as the loan, as modified, is not 90 days or more past due or in nonaccrual status and meets other applicable criteria for a 50 percent risk weight. In addition, real estate loans that do not meet all of the specified criteria or that are made for the purpose of property development are placed in the 100 percent risk category.

Federal Deposit Insurance Corporation

by one-to-four family residential properties include loans to builders with substantial project equity for the construction of one-to-four family residences that have been presold under firm contracts to purchasers who have obtained firm commitments for permanent qualifying mortgage loans and have made substantial earnest money deposits. Such loans to builders will be considered prudently underwritten only if the bank has obtained sufficient documentation that the buyer of the home intends to purchase the home (i.e., has a legally binding written sales contract) and has the ability to obtain a mortgage loan sufficient to purchase the home (i.e., has a firm written commitment for permanent financing of the home upon completion), provided the following criteria are met:

By order of the Board of Directors.

(1) The purchaser is an individual(s) who intends to occupy the residence and is not a partnership, joint venture, trust, corporation, or any other entity (including an entity acting as a sole proprietorship) that is purchasing one or more of the homes for speculative purposes;

(2) The builder must incur at least the first ten percent of the direct costs (i.e., actual costs of the land, labor, and material) before any drawdown is made under the construction loan and the construction loan may not exceed 80 percent of the sales price of the presold home;

(3) The purchaser has made a substantial "earnest money deposit" of no less than three percent of the sales price of the home and the deposit must be subject to forfeiture if the purchaser terminates the sales contract; and

(4) The earnest money deposit must be held in escrow by the bank financing the builder or by an independent party in a fiduciary capacity and the escrow agreement must provide that, in the event of default arising from the cancellation of the sales contract by the buyer, the escrow funds must first be used to defray any costs incurred by the bank.

b. This category also includes loans fully secured by first liens on multifamily residential properties,[40] provided that:

(1) The loan amount does not exceed 80 percent of the value[41] of the property securing the loan as determined by the most current appraisal or evaluation, whichever may be appropriate (75 percent if the interest rate on the loan changes over the term of the loan);

(2) For the property's most recent fiscal year, the ratio of annual net operating income generated by the property (before payment of any debt service on the loan) to annual debt service on the loan is not less than 120 percent (115 percent if the interest rate on the loan changes over the term of the loan) or, in the case of a property owned by a cooperative housing corporation or nonprofit organization, the property generates sufficient cash flow to provide comparable protection to the bank;

(3) Amortization of principal and interest on the loan occurs over a period of not more than 30 years;

(4) The minimum original maturity for repayment of principal on the loan is not less than seven years;

(5) All principal and interest payments have been made on a timely basis in accordance with the terms of the loan for at least one year before the loan is placed in this category;[42]

(6) The loan is not 90 days or more past due or carried in nonaccrual status; and

(7) The loan has been made in accordance with prudent underwriting standards.

c. This category also includes *revenue* (non-general obligation) bonds or similar obligations, including loans and leases, that are obligations of states or political subdivisions of the United States or other OECD countries, but for which the government entity is committed to repay the debt with revenues from the specific projects financed, rather than from general tax funds (e.g., municipal

---

[40] The types of loans that qualify as loans secured by multifamily residential properties are listed in the instructions for preparation of the Consolidated Reports of Condition and Income. In addition, from the standpoint of the selling bank, when a multifamily residential property loan is sold subject to a *pro rata* loss sharing arrangement which provides for the purchaser of the loan to share in any loss incurred on the loan on a *pro rata* basis with the selling bank, that portion of the loan is not subject to the risk-based capital standards. In connection with sales of multifamily residential property loans in which the purchaser of the loan shares in any loss incurred on the loan with the selling bank on other than a *pro rata* basis, the selling bank must treat these other loss sharing arrangements in accordance with section II.B.5 of this appendix A.

[41] At the origination of a loan to purchase an existing property, the term "value" means the lesser of the actual acquisition cost or the estimate of value set forth in an appraisal or evaluation, whichever may be appropriate.

[42] In the case where the existing owner of a multifamily residential property refinances a loan on that property, all principal and interest payments on the loan being refinanced must have been made on a timely basis in accordance with the terms of that loan for at least the preceding year. The new loan must meet all of the other eligibility criteria in order to qualify for a 50 percent risk weight.

revenue bonds). In addition, the credit equivalent amount of derivative contracts that do not qualify for a lower risk weight are assigned to the 50 percent risk category.

d. This category also includes recourse obligations, direct credit substitutes, residual interests (other than a credit-enhancing interest-only strip) and asset- or mortgage-backed securities rated in the third highest investment grade category, e.g., A, in the case of long-term ratings, or the second highest rating category, e.g., A-2, P-2, in the case of short-term ratings.

Category 4—100 Percent Risk Weight. (a) All assets not included in the categories above in section II.C of this appendix A, except the assets specifically included in the 200 percent category below in section II.C of this appendix A and assets that are otherwise risk weighted in accordance with section II.B.5 of this appendix A, are assigned to this category, which comprises standard risk assets. The bulk of the assets typically found in a loan portfolio would be assigned to the 100 percent category.

(b) This category includes:

(1) Long-term claims on, and the portions of long-term claims that are guaranteed by, non-OECD banks, and all claims on non-OECD central governments that entail some degree of transfer risk;[43]

(2) All claims on foreign and domestic private-sector obligors not included in the categories above in section II.C of this appendix A (including loans to nondepository financial institutions and bank holding companies);

(3) Claims on commercial firms owned by the public sector;

(4) Customer liabilities to the bank on acceptances outstanding involving standard risk claims;[44]

(5) Investments in fixed assets, premises, and other real estate owned;

(6) Common and preferred stock of corporations, including stock acquired for debts previously contracted;

(7) Commercial and consumer loans (except those assigned to lower risk categories due to recognized guarantees or collateral and loans secured by residential property that qualify for a lower risk weight);

(8) Recourse obligations, direct credit substitutes, residual interests (other than a credit-enhancing interest-only strip) and asset-or mortgage-backed securities rated in the lowest investment grade category, e.g., BBB, as well as certain positions (but not residual interests) which the bank rates pursuant to section section II.B.5(g) of this appendix A.;

(9) Industrial-development bonds and similar obligations issued under the auspices of states or political subdivisions of the OECD-based group of countries for the benefit of a private party or enterprise where that party or enterprise, not the government entity, is obligated to pay the principal and interest;

(10) All obligations of states or political subdivisions of countries that do not belong to the OECD-based group; and

(11) Stripped mortgage-backed securities and similar instruments, such as interest-only strips that are not credit-enhancing and principal-only strips.

(12) Claims representing capital of a qualifying securities firm.

(c) The following assets also are assigned a risk weight of 100 percent if they have not already been deducted from capital: investments in unconsolidated companies, joint ventures, or associated companies; instruments that qualify as capital issued by other banks; deferred tax assets; and mortgage servicing assets, nonmortgage servicing assets, and purchased credit card relationships.

(d) Subject to the requirements below, a bank may assign an asset not included in the categories above to the risk weight category applicable under the capital guidelines for bank holding companies (12 CFR part 225, appendix A), provided that all of the following conditions apply:

(1) The bank is not authorized to hold the asset under applicable law other than debt previously contracted or similar authority; and

(2) The risks associated with the asset are substantially similar to the risks of assets that are otherwise assigned to a risk weight category less than 100 percent under this appendix.

Category 5—200 Percent Risk Weight. This category includes:

(a) Externally rated recourse obligations, direct credit substitutes, residual interests (other than a credit-enhancing interest-only strip), and asset- and mortgage-backed securities that are rated one category below the lowest investment grade category, e.g., BB,

---

[43] Such assets include all non-local currency claims on, and the portions of claims that are guaranteed by, non-OECD central governments and those portions of local currency claims on, or guaranteed by, non-OECD central governments that exceed the local currency liabilities held by the bank.

[44] Customer liabilities on acceptances outstanding involving nonstandard risk claims, such as claims on U.S. depository institutions, are assigned to the risk category appropriate to the identity of the obligor or, if relevant, the nature of the collateral or guarantees backing the claims. Portions of acceptances conveyed as risk participations to U.S. depository institutions or foreign banks are assigned to the 20 percent risk category appropriate to short-term claims guaranteed by U.S. depository institutions and foreign banks.

to the extent permitted in section II.B.5.(d) of this appendix A; and

(b) A position (but not a residual interest) in a securitization or structured finance program that is not rated by an NRSRO for which the bank determines that the credit risk is equivalent to one category below investment grade, e.g., BB, to the extent permitted in section II.B.5.(g) of this appendix A.

D. Conversion Factors for Off-Balance Sheet Items (see Table III)

The face amount of an off-balance sheet item is generally incorporated into the risk-weighted assets in two steps. The face amount is first multiplied by a credit conversion factor, except as otherwise specified in section II.B.5 of this appendix A for direct credit substitutes and recourse obligations. The resultant credit equivalent amount is assigned to the appropriate risk category according to the obligor or, if relevant, the guarantor, the nature of any collateral, or external credit ratings.[46]

1. *Items With a 100 Percent Conversion Factor.* (a) Except as otherwise provided in section II.B.5. of this appendix A, the full amount of an asset or transaction supported, in whole or in part, by a direct credit substitute or a recourse obligation. Direct credit substitutes and recourse obligations are defined in section II.B.5. of this appendix A.

(b) Sale and repurchase agreements, if not already included on the balance sheet, and forward agreements. Forward agreements are legally binding contractual obligations to purchase assets with drawdown which is certain at a specified future date. Such obligations include forward purchases, forward forward deposits placed,[47] and partly-paid shares and securities; they do not include commitments to make residential mortgage loans or forward foreign exchange contracts.

(c) Securities lent by a bank are treated in one of two ways, depending upon whether the lender is exposed to risk of loss. If a bank, as agent for a customer, lends the customer's securities and does not indemnify the customer against loss, then the securities transaction is excluded from the risk-based capital calculation. On the other hand, if a bank lends its own securities or, acting as agent for a customer, lends the customer's securities and indemnifies the customer against loss, the transaction is converted at 100 percent and assigned to the risk weight category appropriate to the obligor or, if applicable, to the collateral delivered to the lending bank or the independent custodian acting on the lending bank's behalf.

2. *Items With a 50 Percent Conversion Factor.*

a. Transaction-related contingencies are to be converted at 50 percent. Such contingencies include bid bonds, performance bonds, warranties, and *performance standby letters of credit* related to particular transactions, as well as acquisitions of risk participations in performance standby letters of credits. Performance standby letters of credit (performance bonds) are irrevocable obligations of the bank to pay a third-party beneficiary when a customer (account party) *fails to perform* on some contractual nonfinancial obligation. Thus, performance standby letters of credit represent obligations backing the performance of *nonfinancial* or *commercial* contracts or undertakings. To the extent permitted by law or regulation, performance standby letters of credit include arrangements backing, among other things, subcontractors' and suppliers' performance, labor and materials contracts, and construction bids.

b. The unused portion of *commitments* with an *original* maturity exceeding *one year*, including underwriting commitments and commercial and consumer credit commitments, also are to be converted at 50 percent. Original maturity is defined as the length of time between the date the commitment is issued and the earliest date on which: (1) The bank can at its option, *unconditionally* (without cause) cancel the commitment,[48] and (2) the bank is scheduled to (and as a normal practice actually does) review the facility to determine whether or not it should be extended and, on at least an annual basis, continues to regularly review the facility. Facilities that are unconditionally cancelable (without cause) at any time by the bank are not deemed to be commitments, provided the bank makes a separate credit decision before each drawing under the facility.

c.i. Commitments are defined as any legally binding arrangements that obligate a bank to extend credit in the form of loans or lease financing receivables; to purchase

---

[46] The sufficiency of collateral and guarantees for off-balance-sheet items is determined by the market value of the collateral or the amount of the guarantee in relation to the face amount of the item, except for derivative contracts, for which this determination is generally made in relation to the credit equivalent amount. Collateral and guarantees are subject to the same provisions noted under section II.B of this appendix A.

[47] Forward forward deposits accepted are treated as interest rate contracts.

[48] In the case of home equity or mortgage lines of credit secured by liens on one-to-four family residential properties, a bank is deemed able to unconditionally cancel the commitment if, at its option, it can prohibit additional extensions of credit, reduce the credit line, and terminate the commitment to the full extent permitted by relevant Federal law.

loans, securities, or other assets; or to participate in loans and leases. Commitments also include overdraft facilities, revolving credit, home equity and mortgage lines of credit, eligible ABCP liquidity facilities, and similar transactions. Normally, commitments involve a written contract or agreement and a commitment fee, or some other form of consideration. Commitments are included in weighted-risk assets regardless of whether they contain *material adverse change* clauses or other provisions that are intended to relieve the issuer of its funding obligation under certain conditions. In the case of commitments structured as syndications, where the bank is obligated solely for its *pro rata* share, only the bank's proportional share of the syndicated commitment is taken into account in calculating the risk-based capital ratio.

ii. Banks that are subject to the market risk rules in appendix C to part 325 are required to convert the notional amount of eligible ABCP liquidity facilities, in form or in substance, with an original maturity of over one year that are carried in the trading account at 50 percent to determine the appropriate credit equivalent amount even though those facilities are structured or characterized as derivatives or other trading book assets. Liquidity facilities that support ABCP, in form or in substance, (including those positions to which the market risk rules may not be applied as set forth in section 2(a) of appendix C of this part) that are not eligible ABCP liquidity facilities are to be considered recourse obligations or direct credit substitutes, and assessed the appropriate risk-based capital treatment in accordance with section II.B.5. of this appendix.

d. In the case of commitments structured as syndications where the bank is obligated only for its *pro rata* share, the risk-based capital framework includes only the bank's proportional share of such commitments. Thus, after a commitment has been converted at 50 percent, portions of commitments that have been conveyed to other U.S. depository institutions or OECD banks, but for which the originating bank retains the full obligation to the borrower if the participating bank fails to pay when the commitment is drawn upon, will be assigned to the 20 percent risk category. The acquisition of such a participation in a commitment would be converted at 50 percent and the credit equivalent amount would be assigned to the risk category that is appropriate for the account party obligor or, if relevant, to the nature of the collateral or guarantees.

e. Revolving underwriting facilities (RUFs), note issuance facilities (NIFs), and other similar arrangements also are converted at 50 percent. These are facilities under which a borrower can issue on a revolving basis short-term notes in its own name, but for which the underwriting banks have a legally binding commitment either to purchase any notes the borrower is unable to sell by the rollover date or to advance funds to the borrower.

3. *Items With a 20 Percent Conversion Factor.* Short-term, self-liquidating, trade-related contingencies which arise from the movement of goods are converted at 20 percent. Such contingencies include *commercial letters of credit* and other documentary letters of credit collateralized by the underlying shipments.

4. *Items With a 10 Percent Conversion Factor.* a. Unused portions of eligible ABCP liquidity facilities with an original maturity of one year or less that provide liquidity support to ABCP also are converted at 10 percent.

b. Banks that are subject to the market risk rules in appendix C to part 325 are required to convert the notional amount of eligible ABCP liquidity facilities, in form or in substance, with an original maturity of one year or less that are carried in the trading account at 10 percent to determine the appropriate credit equivalent amount even though those facilities are structured or characterized as derivatives or other trading book assets. Liquidity facilities that provide liquidity support to ABCP, in form or in substance, (including those positions to which the market risk rules may not be applied as set forth in section 2(a) of appendix C of this part) that are not eligible ABCP liquidity facilities are to be considered recourse obligations or direct credit substitutes and assessed the appropriate risk-based capital requirement in accordance with section II.B.5. of this appendix.

5. *Items With a Zero Percent Conversion Factor.* These include unused portions of commitments, with the exception of eligible ABCP liquidity facilities, with an original maturity of one year or less, or which are unconditionally cancelable at any time, provided a separate credit decision is made before each drawing under the facility. Unused portions of *retail credit card lines* and related plans are deemed to be short-term commitments if the bank, in accordance with applicable law, has the unconditional option to cancel the credit line at any time.

E. Derivative Contracts (Interest Rate, Exchange Rate, Commodity (including precious metal) and Equity Derivative Contracts)

1. Credit equivalent amounts are computed for each of the following off-balance-sheet derivative contracts:

(a) Interest Rate Contracts
(i) Single currency interest rate swaps.
(ii) Basis swaps.
(iii) Forward rate agreements.
(iv) Interest rate options purchased (including caps, collars, and floors purchased).
(v) Any other instrument linked to interest rates that gives rise to similar credit risks (including when-issued securities and forward deposits accepted).

(b) Exchange Rate Contracts
(i) Cross-currency interest rate swaps.
(ii) Forward foreign exchange contracts.
(iii) Currency options purchased.
(iv) Any other instrument linked to exchange rates that gives rise to similar credit risks.

(c) Commodity (including precious metal) or Equity Derivative Contracts
(i) Commodity- or equity-linked swaps.
(ii) Commodity- or equity-linked options purchased.
(iii) Forward commodity- or equity-linked contracts.
(iv) Any other instrument linked to commodities or equities that gives rise to similar credit risks.

2. Exchange rate contracts with an original maturity of 14 calendar days or less and derivative contracts traded on exchanges that require daily receipt and payment of cash variation margin may be excluded from the risk-based ratio calculation. Gold contracts are accorded the same treatment as exchange rate contracts except gold contracts with an original maturity of 14 calendar days or less are included in the risk-based calculation. Over-the-counter options purchased are included and treated in the same way as other derivative contracts.

3. *Credit Equivalent Amounts for Derivative Contracts.* (a) The credit equivalent amount of a derivative contract that is not subject to a qualifying bilateral netting contract in accordance with section II.*E*.5. of this appendix A is equal to the sum of:

(i) The current exposure (which is equal to the mark-to-market value,[49] if positive, and is sometimes referred to as the replacement cost) of the contract; and

(ii) An estimate of the potential future credit exposure.

(b) The current exposure is determined by the mark-to-market value of the contract. If the mark-to-market value is positive, then the current exposure is equal to that mark-to-market value. If the mark-to-market value is zero or negative, then the current exposure is zero.

(c) The potential future credit exposure of a contract, including a contract with a negative mark-to-market value, is estimated by multiplying the notional principal amount of the contract by a credit conversion factor. Banks should, subject to examiner review, use the effective rather than the apparent or stated notional amount in this calculation. The credit conversion factors are:

CONVERSION FACTOR MATRIX

Remaining maturity	Interest rate	Exchange rate and gold	Equity	Precious metals, except gold	Other commodities
One year or less	0.0%	1.0%	6.0%	7.0%	10.0%
More than one year to five years	0.5%	5.0%	8.0%	7.0%	12.0%
More than five years	1.5%	7.5%	10.0%	8.0%	15.0%

(d) For contracts that are structured to settle outstanding exposure on specified dates and where the terms are reset such that the market value of the contract is zero on these specified dates, the remaining maturity is equal to the time until the next reset date. For interest rate contracts with remaining maturities of more than one year and that meet these criteria, the conversion factor is subject to a minimum value of 0.5 percent.

(e) For contracts with multiple exchanges of principal, the conversion factors are to be multiplied by the number of remaining payments in the contract. Derivative contracts not explicitly covered by any of the columns of the conversion factor matrix are to be treated as "other commodities."

(f) No potential future exposure is calculated for single currency interest rate swaps in which payments are made based upon two floating rate indices (so called floating/floating or basis swaps); the credit exposure on these contracts is evaluated solely on the basis of their mark-to-market values.

4. *Risk Weights and Avoidance of Double Counting.* (a) Once the credit equivalent amount for a derivative contract, or a group of derivative contracts subject to a qualifying bilateral netting agreement, has been determined, that amount is assigned to the risk category appropriate to the counterparty, or, if relevant, the guarantor or the nature of any collateral. However, the maximum weight that will be applied to the credit equivalent amount of such contracts is 50 percent.

(b) In certain cases, credit exposures arising from the derivative contracts covered by these guidelines may already be reflected, in part, on the balance sheet. To avoid double

---

[49] Mark-to-market values are measured in dollars, regardless of the currency or currencies specified in the contract and should reflect changes in both underlying rates, prices and indices, and counterparty credit quality.

counting such exposures in the assessment of capital adequacy and, perhaps, assigning inappropriate risk weights, counterparty credit exposures arising from the types of instruments covered by these guidelines may need to be excluded from balance sheet assets in calculating a bank's risk-based capital ratio.

(c) The FDIC notes that the conversion factors set forth in section II.E.3. of appendix A, which are based on observed volatilities of the particular types of instruments, are subject to review and modification in light of changing volatilities or market conditions.

(d) Examples of the calculation of credit equivalent amounts for these types of contracts are contained in Table IV of this appendix A.

5. *Netting.* (a) For purposes of this appendix A, netting refers to the offsetting of positive and negative mark-to-market values when determining a current exposure to be used in the calculation of a credit equivalent amount. Any legally enforceable form of bilateral netting (that is, netting with a single counterparty) of derivative contracts is recognized for purposes of calculating the credit equivalent amount provided that:

(i) The netting is accomplished under a written netting contract that creates a single legal obligation, covering all included individual contracts, with the effect that the bank would have a claim or obligation to receive or pay, respectively, only the net amount of the sum of the positive and negative mark-to-market values on included individual contracts in the event that a counterparty, or a counterparty to whom the contract has been validly assigned, fails to perform due to default, bankruptcy, liquidation, or similar circumstances;

(ii) The bank obtains a written and reasoned legal opinion(s) representing that in the event of a legal challenge, including one resulting from default, insolvency, bankruptcy or similar circumstances, the relevant court and administrative authorities would find the bank's exposure to be such a net amount under:

(*1*) The law of the jurisdiction in which the counterparty is chartered or the equivalent location in the case of noncorporate entities and, if a branch of the counterparty is involved, then also under the law of the jurisdiction in which the branch is located;

(*2*) The law that governs the individual contracts covered by the netting contract; and

(*3*) The law that governs the netting contract.

(iii) The bank establishes and maintains procedures to ensure that the legal characteristics of netting contracts are kept under review in the light of possible changes in relevant law; and

(iv) The bank maintains in its file documentation adequate to support the netting of derivative contracts, including a copy of the bilateral netting contract and necessary legal opinions.

(b) A contract containing a walkaway clause is not eligible for netting for purposes of calculating the credit equivalent amount.[50]

(c) By netting individual contracts for the purpose of calculating its credit equivalent amount, a bank represents that it has met the requirements of this appendix A and all the appropriate documents are in the bank's files and available for inspection by the FDIC. Upon determination by the FDIC that a bank's files are inadequate or that a netting contract may not be legally enforceable under any one of the bodies of law described in paragraphs (ii)(1) through (3) of section II.E.5.(a) of this appendix A, underlying individual contracts may be treated as though they were not subject to the netting contract.

(d) The credit equivalent amount of derivative contracts that are subject to a qualifying bilateral netting contract is calculated by adding:

(i) The net current exposure of the netting contract; and

(ii) The sum of the estimates of potential future exposure for all individual contracts subject to the netting contract, adjusted to take into account the effects of the netting contract.[51]

(e) The net current exposure is the sum of all positive and negative mark-to-market values of the individual contracts subject to the netting contract. If the net sum of the mark-to-market values is positive, then the net current exposure is equal to that sum. If the net sum of the mark-to-market values is zero or negative, then the net current exposure is zero.

(f) The effects of the bilateral netting contract on the gross potential future exposure are recognized through application of a formula, resulting in an adjusted add-on amount (A_{net}). The formula, which employs the ratio of net current exposure to gross current exposure (NGR) is expressed as:

$$A_{net} = (0.4 \times A_{gross}) + 0.6(NGR \times A_{gross})$$

---

[50] For purposes of this section, a walkaway clause means a provision in a netting contract that permits a non-defaulting counterparty to make lower payments than it would make otherwise under the contract, or no payment at all, to a defaulter or to the estate of a defaulter, even if a defaulter or the estate of a defaulter is a net creditor under the contract.

[51] For purposes of calculating potential future credit exposure for foreign exchange contracts and other similar contracts in which notional principal is equivalent to cash flows, total notional principal is defined as the net receipts to each party falling due on each value date in each currency.

The effect of this formula is that A_{net} is the weighted average of A_{gross}, and A_{gross} adjusted by the NGR.

(g) The NGR may be calculated in either one of two ways—referred to as the counterparty-by-counterparty approach and the aggregate approach.

(i) Under the counterparty-by-counterparty approach, the NGR is the ratio of the net current exposure of the netting contract to the gross current exposure of the netting contract. The gross current exposure is the sum of the current exposures of all individual contracts subject to the netting contract calculated in accordance with section II.E. of this appendix A.

(ii) Under the aggregate approach, the NGR is the ratio of the sum of all of the net current exposures for qualifying bilateral netting contracts to the sum of all of the gross current exposures for those netting contracts (each gross current exposure is calculated in the same manner as in section II.E.5.(g)(i) of this appendix A). Net negative mark-to-market values to individual counterparties cannot be used to offset net positive current exposures to other counterparties.

(iii) A bank must use consistently either the counterparty-by-counterparty approach or the aggregate approach to calculate the NGR. Regardless of the approach used, the NGR should be applied individually to each qualifying bilateral netting contract to determine the adjusted add-on for that netting contract.

III. MINIMUM RISK-BASED CAPITAL RATIO

Subject to section II.B.5. of this appendix A, banks generally will be expected to meet a minimum ratio of qualifying total capital to risk-weighted assets of 8 percent, of which at least 4 percentage points should be in the form of core capital (Tier 1). Any bank that does not meet the minimum risk-based capital ratio, or whose capital is otherwise considered inadequate, generally will be expected to develop and implement a capital plan for achieving an adequate level of capital, consistent with the provisions of this risk-based capital framework and §325.104, the specific circumstances affecting the individual bank, and the requirements of any related agreements between the bank and the FDIC.

TABLE I—DEFINITION OF QUALIFYING CAPITAL

Components	Minimum requirements
(1) CORE CAPITAL (Tier 1)	Must equal or exceed 4% of weighted-risk assets.
(a) Common stockholders' equity	No limit.[1]
(b) Noncumulative perpetual preferred stock and any related surplus.	No limit.[1]
(c) Minority interest in equity accounts of consolidated	No limit.[1]
(d) Less: All intangible assets other than certain mortgage servicing assets, nonmortgage servicing assets and purchased credit card relationships.	([2]).
(e) Less: Certain credit-enhancing interest-only strips and nonfinancial equity investments required to be deducted from capital.	([3]).
(f) Less: Certain deferred tax assets	([4]).
(2) SUPPLEMENTARY CAPITAL (Tier 2)	Total of tier 2 is limited to 100% of tier 1.[5]
(a) Allowance for loan and lease losses	Limited to 1.25% of weighted-risk assets.[5]
(b) Unrealized gains on certain equity securities.[6]	Limited to 45% of pretax net unrealized gains.[6]
(c) Cumulative perpetual and long-term preferred stock (original maturity of 20 years or more) and any related surplus.	No limit within tier 2; long-term preferred is amortized for capital purposes as it approaches maturity.
(d) Auction rate and similar preferred stock (both cumulative and non-cumulative).	No limit within Tier 2.
(e) Hybrid capital instruments (including mandatory convertible debt securities).	No limit within Tier 2.
(f) Term subordinated debt and intermediate-term preferred stock (original weighted average maturity of five years or more).	Term subordinated debt and intermediate-term preferred stock are limited to 50% of Tier 1[5] and amortized for capital purposes as they approach maturity.
(3) DEDUCTIONS (from sum of tier 1 and tier 2)	
(a) Investments in banking and finance subsidiaries that are not consolidated for regulatory capital purposes	
(b) Intentional, reciprocal cross-holdings of capital securities issued by banks	
(c) Other deductions (such as investment in other subsidiaries or joint ventures) as determined by supervisory authority.	On a case-by-case basis or as a matter of policy after formal consideration of relevant issues.
(4) TOTAL CAPITAL	Must equal or exceed 8% of weighted-risk assets.

[1] No express limits are placed on the amounts of nonvoting common, noncumulative perpetual preferred stock, and minority interests that may be recognized as part of Tier 1 capital. However, voting common stockholders' equity capital generally will be expected to be the dominant form of Tier 1 capital and banks should avoid undue reliance on other Tier 1 capital elements.
[2] The amounts of mortgage servicing assets, nonmortgage servicing assets and purchased credit card relationships that can be recognized for purposes of calculating Tier 1 capital are subject to the limitations set forth in §325.5(f). All deductions are for capital purposes only; deductions would not affect accounting treatment.

[3] The amounts of credit-enhancing interest-only strips that can be recognized for purposes of calculating Tier 1 capital are subject to the limitations set forth in § 325.5(f). The amounts of nonfinancial equity investments that must be deducted for purposes of calculating Tier 1 capital are set forth in section II.B.(6) of appendix A to part 325.
[4] Deferred tax assets are subject to the capital limitations set forth in § 325.5(g).
[5] Amounts in excess of limitations are permitted but do not qualify as capital.
[6] Unrealized gains on equity securities are subject to the capital limitations set forth in paragraph I.A(2)(f) of appendix A to part 325.

CALCULATION OF THE RISK-BASED CAPITAL RATIO

When calculating the risk-based capital ratio under the framework set forth in this statement of policy, qualifying total capital (the numerator) is divided by risk-weighted assets (the denominator). The process of determining the numerator for the ratio is summarized in Table I. The calculation of the denominator is based on the risk weights and conversion factors that are summarized in Tables II and III.

When determining the amount of risk-weighted assets, balance sheet assets are assigned an appropriate risk weight (see Table II) and off-balance sheet items are first converted to a credit equivalent amount (see Table III) and then assigned to one of the risk weight categories set forth in Table II.

The balance sheet assets and the credit equivalent amount of off-balance sheet items are multiplied by the appropriate risk weight percentages and the sum of these risk-weighted amounts is the gross risk-weighted asset figure used in determining the denominator of the risk-based capital ratio. Any items deducted from capital when computing the amount of qualifying capital may also be excluded from risk-weighted assets when calculating the denominator for the risk-based capital ratio.

TABLE II—SUMMARY OF RISK WEIGHTS AND RISK CATEGORIES

Category 1—Zero Percent Risk Weight

(1) Cash (domestic and foreign).
(2) Balances due from Federal Reserve Banks and central banks in other OECD countries.
(3) Direct claims on, and portions of claims unconditionally guaranteed by, the U.S. Treasury, U.S. Government agencies,[1] and central governments in other OECD countries.
(4) Portions of local currency claims on, or unconditionally guaranteed by, non-OECD central governments (including non-OECD central banks), to the extent the bank has liabilities booked in that currency.

(5) Gold bullion held in the bank's own vaults or in another bank's vaults on an allocated basis, to the extent that it is offset by gold bullion liabilities
(6) Federal Reserve Bank stock.
(7) Claims on, or guaranteed by, qualifying securities firms incorporated in the United States or other members of the OECD-based group of countries that are collateralized by cash on deposit in the lending bank or by securities issued or guaranteed by the United States or OECD central governments (including U.S. government agencies), provided that a positive margin of collateral is required to be maintained on such a claim on a daily basis, taking into account any change in a bank's exposure to the obligor or counterparty under the claim in relation to the market value of the collateral held in support of the claim.

Category 2—20 Percent Risk Weight

(1) Cash items in the process of collection.
(2) All claims (long- and short-term) on, and portions of claims (long- and short-term) guaranteed by, U.S. depository institutions and OECD banks.
(3) Short-term (remaining maturity of one year or less) claims on, and portions of short-term claims guaranteed by, non-OECD banks.
(4) Portions of loans and other claims conditionally guaranteed by the U.S. Treasury, U.S. Government agencies,[1] or central governments in other OECD countries and portions of local currency claims conditionally guaranteed by non-OECD central governments to the extent that the bank has liabilities booked in that currency.
(5) Securities and other claims on, and portions of claims guaranteed by, U.S. Government-*sponsored* agencies.[2]
(6) Portions of loans and other claims (including repurchase agreements) collateralized[3] by securities issued or guaranteed by the U.S. Treasury, U.S. Government agencies, U.S. Government-sponsored

---

[1] For the purpose of calculating the risk-based capital ratio, a U.S. Government agency is defined as an instrumentality of the U.S. Government whose obligations are fully and explicitly guaranteed as to the timely repayment of principal and interest by the full faith and credit of the U.S. Government.

[2] For the purpose of calculating the risk-based capital ratio, a U.S. Government-*sponsored* agency is defined as an agency originally established or chartered to serve public purposes specified by the U.S. Congress but whose obligations are not *explicitly* guaranteed by the full faith and credit of the U.S. Government.

[3] Degree of collateralization is determined by current market value.

Federal Deposit Insurance Corporation

agencies or central governments in other OECD countries.

(7) Portions of loans and other claims collateralized[3] by cash on deposit in the lending bank.

(8) General obligation claims on, and portions of claims guaranteed by, the full faith and credit of states or other political subdivisions of OECD countries, including U.S. state and local governments.

(9) Claims on, and portions of claims guaranteed by, official multilateral lending institutions or regional development institutions in which the U.S. Government is a shareholder or a contributing member.

(10) Portions of claims collateralized[3] by securities issued by official multilateral lending institutions or regional development institutions in which the U.S. Government is a shareholder or contributing member.

(11) Investments in shares of mutual funds whose portfolios are permitted to hold only assets that qualify for the zero or 20 percent risk categories.

(12) Recourse obligations, direct credit substitutes, residual interests (other than credit-enhancing interest-only strips) and asset- or mortgage-backed securities rated in either of the two highest investment grade categories, e.g., AAA or AA, in the case of long-term ratings, or the highest rating category, e.g., A-1, P-1, in the case of short-term ratings.

(13) Claims on, and claims guaranteed by, qualifying securities firms incorporated in the United States or other member of the OECD-based group of countries provided that:

a. The qualifying securities firm has a rating in one of the top three investment grade rating categories from a nationally recognized statistical rating organization; or

b. The claim is guaranteed by a qualifying securities firm's parent company with such a rating.

(14) Certain collateralized claims on qualifying securities firms in the United States or other member of the OECD-based group of countries, without regard to satisfaction of the rating standard, provided that the claim arises under a contract that:

a. Is a reverse repurchase/repurchase agreement or securities lending/borrowing transaction executed under standard industry documentation;

b. Is collateralized by liquid and readily marketable debt or equity securities;

c. Is marked to market daily;

d. Is subject to a daily margin maintenance requirement under the standard documentation; and

e. Can be liquidated, terminated, or accelerated immediately in bankruptcy or similar proceeding, and the security or collateral agreement will not be stayed or avoided, under applicable law of the relevant country.

Pt. 325, App. A

Category 3—50 Percent Risk Weight

(1) Loans fully secured by first liens on one-to-four family residential properties (including certain presold residential construction loans), provided that the loans were approved in accordance with prudent underwriting standards and are not past due 90 days or more or carried in nonaccrual status.

(2) Loans fully secured by first liens on multifamily residential properties that have been prudently underwritten and meet specified requirements with respect to loan-to-value ratio, level of annual net operating income to required debt service, maximum amortization period, minimum original maturity, and demonstrated timely repayment performance.

(3) Recourse obligations, direct credit substitutes, residual interests (other than credit-enhancing interest-only strips) and asset- or mortgage-backed securities rated in the third-highest investment grade category, e.g., A, in the case of long-term ratings, or the second highest rating category, e.g., A-2, P-2, in the case of short-term ratings.

(4) Revenue bonds or similar obligations, including loans and leases, that are obligations of U.S. state or political subdivisions of the United States or other OECD countries but for which the government entity is committed to repay the debt only out of revenues from the specific projects financed.

(5) Credit equivalent amounts of interest rate and foreign exchange rate related contracts, except for those assigned to a lower risk category.

Category 4—100 Percent Risk Weight

(1) All other claims on private obligors.

(2) Claims on, or guaranteed by, non-OECD banks with a remaining maturity exceeding one year.

(3) Claims on non-OECD central governments that are not included in item 4 of Category 1 or item 3 of Category 2, and all claims on non-OECD state and local governments.

(4) Obligations issued by U.S. state or local governments or other OECD local governments (including industrial development authorities and similar entities) that are repayable solely by a private party or enterprise.

(5) Premises, plant, and equipment; other fixed assets; and other real estate owned.

(6) Investments in any unconsolidated subsidiaries, joint ventures, or associated companies—if not deducted from capital.

(7) Instruments issued by other banking organizations that qualify as capital.

(8) Claims on commercial firms owned by the U.S. Government or foreign governments.

(9) Recourse obligations, direct credit substitutes, residual interests (other than credit-enhancing interest-only strips) and asset-

or mortgage-backed securities rated in the lowest investment grade category, e.g., BBB, as well as certain positions (but not residual interests) which the bank rates pursuant to section II.B.5(g) of this appendix A.

(10) All other assets, including any intangible assets that are not deducted from capital, and the credit equivalent amounts[4] of off-balance sheet items not assigned to a different risk category.

Category 5—200 Percent Risk Weight.

(1) Externally rated recourse obligations, direct credit substitutes, residual interests (other than credit-enhancing interest-only strips), and asset- and mortgage-backed securities that are rated one category below the lowest investment grade category, e.g., BB, to the extent permitted in section II.B.5(d) of this appendix A; and

(2) A position (but not a residual interest) extended in connection with a securitization or structured financing program that is not rated by an NRSRO for which the bank determines that the credit risk is equivalent to one category below investment grade, e.g., BB, to the extent permitted in section II.B.5.(g) of this appendix A.

[54 FR 11509, Mar. 21, 1989]

EDITORIAL NOTE: For FEDERAL REGISTER citations affecting appendix A to part 325, see the List of CFR Sections Affected, which appears in the Finding Aids section of the printed volume and at *www.fdsys.gov.*

EDITORIAL NOTE: At 76 FR 37629, June 28, 2011, appendix A to part 325 was amended, however, the amendment could not be incorporated due to the inaccurate amendatory instruction. The new footnote 45 could not be added because there was no text for a new 45 to incorporate.

APPENDIX B TO PART 325—STATEMENT OF POLICY ON CAPITAL ADEQUACY

Part 325 of the Federal Deposit Insurance Corporation rules and regulations (12 CFR part 325) sets forth minimum leverage capital requirements for fundamentally sound, well-managed banks having no material or significant financial weaknesses. It also defines capital and sets forth sanctions which will be used against banks which are in violation of the part 325 regulation. This statement of policy on capital adequacy provides some interpretational and definitional guidance as to how this part 325 regulation will be administered and enforced by the FDIC.

---
[4] In general, for each off-balance sheet item, a conversion factor (see Table III) must be applied to determine the "credit equivalent amount" prior to assigning the off-balance sheet item to a risk weight category.

This statement of policy also addresses certain aspects of the FDIC's minimum risk-based capital guidelines that are set forth in appendix A to part 325. This statement of policy does not address the prompt corrective action provisions mandated by the Federal Deposit Insurance Corporation Improvement Act of 1991. However, section 38 of the Federal Deposit Insurance Act and subpart B of part 325 provide guidance on the prompt corrective action provisions, which generally apply to institutions with inadequate levels of capital.

I. ENFORCEMENT OF MINIMUM CAPITAL REQUIREMENTS

Section 325.3(b)(1) specifies that FDIC-supervised, state-chartered nonmember commercial and savings banks (or other insured depository institutions making applications to the FDIC that require the FDIC to consider the adequacy of the institutions' capital structure) must maintain a minimum leverage ratio of Tier 1 (or core) capital to total assets of at least 3 percent; however, this minimum only applies to the most highly-rated banks (i.e., those with a composite CAMELS rating of 1 under the Uniform Financial Institutions Rating System established by the Federal Financial Institutions Examination Council) that are not anticipating or experiencing any significant growth. All other state nonmember banks would need to meet a minimum leverage ratio that is at least 100 to 200 basis points above this minimum. That is, in accordance with § 325.3(b)(2), an absolute minimum leverage ratio of not less than 4 percent must be maintained by those banks that are not highly-rated or that are anticipating or experiencing significant growth.

In addition to the minimum leverage capital standards, section III of appendix A to part 325 indicates that state nonmember banks generally are expected to maintain a minimum risk-based capital ratio of qualifying total capital to risk-weighted assets of 8 percent, with at least one-half of that total capital amount consisting of Tier 1 capital.

State nonmember banks (hereinafter referred to as "banks") operating with leverage capital ratios below the minimums set forth in part 325 will be deemed to have inadequate capital and will be in violation of the part 325 regulation. Furthermore, banks operating with risk-based capital ratios below the minimums set forth in appendix A to part 325 generally will be deemed to have inadequate capital. Banks failing to meet the minimum leverage and/or risk-based capital ratios normally can expect to have any application submitted to the FDIC denied (if such application requires the FDIC to evaluate the adequacy of the institution's capital structure) and also can expect to be subject to the use of capital directives or other formal enforcement action by the FDIC to increase capital.

Capital adequacy in banks which have capital ratios at or above the minimums will be assessed and enforced based on the following factors (these same criteria will apply to any insured depository institutions making applications to the FDIC and to any other circumstances in which the FDIC is requested or required to evaluate the adequacy of a depository institution's capital structure):

A. Banks Which Are Fundamentally Sound and Well-Managed

The minimum leverage capital ratios set forth in §325.3(b)(2) and the minimum risk-based capital ratios set forth in section III of appendix A to part 325 generally will be viewed as the minimum acceptable capital standards for banks whose overall financial condition is fundamentally sound, which are well-managed and which have no material or significant financial weaknesses. While the FDIC will make this determination in each bank based upon its own condition and specific circumstances, this definition will generally apply to those banks evidencing a level of risk which is no greater than that normally associated with a Composite rating of 1 or 2 under the Uniform Financial Institutions Rating System. Banks meeting this definition which are in compliance with the minimum leverage and risk-based capital ratio standards will not generally be required by the FDIC to raise new capital from external sources.

The FDIC does, however, encourage such banks to maintain capital well above the minimums, particularly those institutions that are anticipating or experiencing significant growth, and will carefully evaluate their earnings and growth trends, dividend policies, capital planning procedures and other factors important to the continuous maintenance of adequate capital. Adverse trends or deficiencies in these areas will be subject to criticism at regular examinations and may be an important factor in the FDIC's action on applications submitted by such banks. In addition, the FDIC's consideration of capital adequacy in banks making applications to the FDIC will also fully examine the expected impact of those applications on the bank's ability to maintain its capital adequacy. In all cases, banks should maintain capital commensurate with the level and nature of risks, including the volume and severity of adversely classified assets, to which they are exposed.

B. All Other Banks

Banks not meeting the definition set forth in I.A. of this appendix, that is, banks evidencing a level of risk which is at least as great as that normally associated with a Composite rating of 3, 4, or 5 under the Uniform Financial Institutions Rating System, will be required to maintain capital higher than the minimum regulatory requirement and at a level deemed appropriate in relation to the degree of risk within the institution. These higher capital levels will normally be addressed through memorandums of understanding between the FDIC and the bank or, in cases of more pronounced risk, through the use of formal enforcement actions under section 8 of the Federal Deposit Insurance Act (12 U.S.C. 1818).

C. Capital Requirements of Primary Regulator

Notwithstanding I.A. and B. of this appendix, all banks (or other depository institutions making applications to the FDIC that require the FDIC to consider the adequacy of the institutions' capital structure) will be expected to meet any capital requirements established by their primary state or federal regulator which exceed the minimum capital requirement set forth in the FDIC's part 325 regulation. In addition, the FDIC will, when establishing capital requirements higher than the minimum set forth in the regulation, consult with an institution's primary state or federal regulator.

II. CAPITAL PLANS

Section 325.4(b) specifies that any bank which has less than its minimum leverage capital requirement is deemed to be engaging in an unsafe or unsound banking practice unless it has submitted, and is in compliance with, a plan approved by the FDIC to increase its Tier 1 leverage capital ratio to such level as the FDIC deems appropriate.

As required under §325.104(a)(1) of this part, a bank must file a written capital restoration plan with the appropriate FDIC regional director within 45 days of the date that the bank receives notice or is deemed to have notice that the bank is undercapitalized, significantly undercapitalized or critically undercapitalized, unless the FDIC notifies the bank in writing that the plan is to be filed within a different period. The amount of time allowed to achieve the minimum leverage capital requirement will be evaluated by the FDIC on a case-by-case basis and will depend on a number of factors, including the viability of the bank and whether it is fundamentally sound and well-managed.

Banks evidencing more than normal levels of risk will normally have their minimum capital requirements established in a formal or informal enforcement proceeding. The time frames for meeting these requirements will be set forth in such actions and will generally require some immediate action on the bank's part to meet its minimum capital requirement. The reasonableness of capital plans submitted by depository institutions in connection with applications as provided

Pt. 325, App. B

for in §325.3(d)(2) will be determined in conjunction with the FDIC's consideration of the application.

III. WRITTEN AGREEMENTS

Section 325.4(c) provides that any insured depository institution with a Tier 1 capital to total assets (leverage) ratio of less than 2 percent must enter into and be in compliance with a written agreement with the FDIC (or with its primary federal regulator with FDIC as a party to the agreement) to increase its Tier 1 leverage capital ratio to such level as the FDIC deems appropriate or may be subject to a section 8(a) termination of insurance action by the FDIC. Except in the very rarest of circumstances, the FDIC will require that such agreements contemplate immediate efforts by the depository institution to acquire the required capital.

The guidance in this section III is not intended to preclude the FDIC from taking section 8(a) or other enforcement action against any institution, regardless of its capital level, if the specific circumstances deem such action to be appropriate.

IV. CAPITAL COMPONENTS

Section 325.2 sets forth the definition of Tier 1 capital for the leverage standard as well as the definitions for the various instruments and accounts which are included therein. Although nonvoting common stock, noncumulative perpetual preferred stock, and minority interests in consolidated subsidiaries are normally included in Tier 1 capital, voting common stockholders' equity generally will be expected to be the dominant form of Tier 1 capital. Thus, banks should avoid undue reliance on nonvoting equity, preferred stock and minority interests. The following provides some additional guidance with respect to some of the items that affect the calculation of Tier 1 capital.

A. *Intangible Assets*

The FDIC permits state nonmember banks to record intangible assets on their books and to report the value of such assets in the Consolidated Reports of Condition and Income ("Call Report"). As noted in the instructions for preparation of the Consolidated Reports of Condition and Income (published by the Federal Financial Institutions Examination Council), intangible assets may arise from business combinations accounted for under the purchase method and acquisitions of portions or segments of another institution's business, such as branch offices, mortgage servicing portfolios, and credit card portfolios.

Notwithstanding the authority to report all intangible assets in the Consolidated Reports of Condition and Income, §325.2(v) of the regulation specifies that mortgage servicing assets, nonmortgage servicing assets and purchased credit card relationships are the only intangible assets which will be allowed as Tier 1 capital.[1] The portion of equity capital represented by other types of intangible assets will be deducted from equity capital and assets in the computation of a bank's Tier 1 capital. Certain of these intangible assets may, however, be recognized for regulatory capital purposes if explicitly approved by the Director of the Division of Supervision and Consumer Protection (DSC) as part of the bank's regulatory capital on a specific case basis. These intangibles will be included in regulatory capital under the terms and conditions that are specifically approved by the FDIC.[2]

In certain instances banks may have investments in unconsolidated subsidiaries or joint ventures that have large volumes of intangible assets. In such instances the bank's consolidated statements will reflect an investment in a tangible asset even though such investment will, in fact, be represented by a large volume of intangible assets. In any such situation where this is material,

---

[1] Although intangible assets in the form of mortgage servicing assets, nonmortgage servicing assets and purchased credit card relationships are generally recognized for regulatory capital purposes, the ––deduction of part or all of the mortgage servicing assets, nonmortgage servicing assets and purchased credit card relationships may be required if the carrying amounts of these rights are excessive in relation to their market value or the level of the bank's capital accounts. In this regard, mortgage servicing assets, nonmortgage servicing assets and purchased credit card relationships will be recognized for regulatory capital purposes only to the extent the rights meet the conditions, limitations and restrictions described in §325.5(f).

[2] This specific approval must be received in accordance with §325.5(b). In evaluating whether other types of intangibles should be recognized for regulatory capital purposes, the FDIC will accord special attention to the general characteristics of the intangibles, including: (1) The separability of the intangible asset and the ability to sell it separate and apart from the bank or the bulk of the bank's assets, (2) the certainty that a readily identifiable stream of cash flows associated with the intangible asset can hold its value notwithstanding the future prospects of the bank, and (3) the existence of a market of sufficient depth to provide liquidity for the intangible asset. However, pursuant to section 18(n) of the Federal Deposit Insurance Act (12 U.S.C. 1828(n)), specific approval cannot be given for an unidentifiable intangible asset, such as goodwill, if acquired after April 12, 1989.

the bank's investment in the unconsolidated subsidiary will be divided into a tangible and an intangible portion based on the percentage of intangible assets to total assets in the subsidiary. The intangible portion of the investment will be treated as if it were an intangible asset on the bank's books in the calculation of Tier 1 capital. However, intangible assets in the form of mortgage servicing assets, nonmortgage servicing assets and purchased credit card relationships, including servicing intangibles held by mortgage banking subsidiaries, are subject to the specific criteria set forth in § 325.5(f).

B. Perpetual Preferred Stock

Perpetual preferred stock is defined as preferred stock that does not have a maturity date, that cannot be redeemed at the option of the holder, and that has no other provisions that will require future redemption of the issue. Also, pursuant to section 18(i)(1) of the Federal Deposit Insurance Act (12 U.S.C. 1828(i)(1)), a state nonmember bank cannot, without the prior consent of the FDIC, reduce the amount or retire any part of its perferred stock. (This prior consent is also required for the reduction or retirement of any part of a state nonmember bank's common stock or capital notes and debentures.)

Noncumulative perpetual preferred stock is generally included in Tier 1 capital. Nonetheless, it is possible for banks to issue preferred stock with a dividend rate which escalates to such a high rate that the terms become so onerous as to effectively force the bank to call the issue (for example, an issue with a low initial rate that is scheduled to escalate to much higher rates in subsequent periods). Preferred stock issues with such onerous terms have much the same characteristics as limited life preferred stock in that the bank would be effectively forced to redeem the issue to avoid performance of the onerous terms. Such instruments may be disallowed as Tier 1 capital and, for risk-based capital purposes, would be included in Tier 2 capital only to the extent that the instruments fall within the limitations applicable to intermediate-term preferred stock. Banks which are contemplating issues bearing terms which may be so characterized are encouraged to submit them to the appropriate FDIC regional office for review prior to issuance. Nothing herein shall prohibit banks from issuing floating rate preferred stock issues where the rate is constant in relation to some outside market or index rate. However, noncumulative floating rate instruments where the rate paid is based in some part on the current credit standing of the bank, and all cumulative preferred stock instruments, are excluded from Tier 1 capital. These instruments are included in Tier 2 capital for risk-based capital purposes in accordance with the limitations set forth in appendix A to part 325.

The FDIC will also require that issues of perpetual preferred stock be consistent with safe and sound banking practices. Issues which would unduly enrich insiders or which contain dividend rates or other terms which are inconsistent with safe and sound banking practices will likely be the subject of appropriate supervisory response from the FDIC. Banks contemplating preferred stock issues which may pose safety and soundness concerns are encouraged to submit such issues to the appropriate FDIC regional office for review prior to sale. Pursuant to § 325.5(e), capital instruments that contain or that are subject to any conditions, covenants, terms, restrictions or provisions that are inconsistent with safe and sound banking practices will not qualify as capital under part 325.

C. Other Instruments or Transactions Which Fail To Provide Capital Support

Section 325.5(b) specifies that any capital component or balance sheet entry or account which has characteristics or terms that diminish its contribution to an insured depository institution's ability to absorb losses shall be deducted from capital. An example involves certain types of minority interests in consolidated subsidiaries. Minority interests in consolidated subsidiaries have been included in capital based on the fact that they provide capital support to the risk in the consolidated subsidiaries. Certain transactions have been structured where a bank forms a subsidiary by transferring essentially risk-free or low-risk assets to the subsidiary in exchange for common stock of the subsidiary. The subsidiary then sells preferred stock to third parties.

The preferred stock becomes a minority interest in a consolidated subsidiary but, in effect, represents an essentially risk-free or low-risk investment for the preferred stockholders. This type of minority interest fails to provide any meaningful capital support to the consolidated entity inasmuch as it has a preferred claim on the essentially risk-free or low-risk assets of the subsidiary. In addition, certain minority interests are not substantially equivalent to permanent equity in that the interests must be paid off on specified future dates, or at the option of the holders of the minority interests, or contain other provisions or features that limit the ability of the minority interests to effectively absorb losses. Capital instruments or transactions of this nature which fail to absorb losses or provide meaningful capital support will be deducted from Tier 1 capital.

D. Mandatory Convertible Debt

Mandatory convertible debt securities are subordinated debt instruments that require the issuer to convert such instruments into common or perpetual preferred stock by a date at or before the maturity of the debt instruments. The maturity of these instruments must be 12 years or less and the instruments must also meet the other criteria set forth in appendix A to part 325. Mandatory convertible debt is excluded from Tier 1 capital but, for risk-based capital purposes, is included in Tier 2 capital as a "hybrid capital instrument."

So-called "equity commitment notes," which merely require a bank to sell common or perpetual preferred stock during the life of the subordinated debt obligation, are specifically excluded from the definition of mandatory convertible debt securities and are only included in Tier 2 capital under the risk-based capital framework to the extent that they satisfy the requirements and limitations for "term subordinated debt" set forth in appendix A to part 325.

V. ANALYSIS OF CONSOLIDATED COMPANIES

In determining a bank's compliance with its minimum capital requirements the FDIC will, with two exceptions, generally utilize the bank's consolidated statements as defined in the instructions for the preparation of Consolidated Reports of Condition and Income.

The first exception relates to securities subsidiaries of state nonmember banks which are subject to §337.4 of the FDIC's rules and regulations (12 CFR 337.4). Any subsidiary subject to this section must be a bona fide subsidiary which is adequately capitalized. In addition, §337.4(b)(3) requires that any insured state nonmember bank's investment in such a subsidiary shall not be counted towards the bank's capital. In those instances where the securities subsidiary is consolidated in the bank's Consolidated Report of Condition it will be necessary, for the purpose of calculating the bank's Tier 1 capital, to adjust the Consolidated Report of Condition in such a manner as to reflect the bank's investment in the securities subsidiary on the equity method. In this case, and in those cases where the securities subsidiary has not been consolidated, the investment in the subsidiary will then be deducted from the bank's capital and assets prior to calculation of the bank's Tier 1 capital ratio. (Where deemed appropriate, the FDIC may also consider deducting investments in other subsidiaries, either on a case-by-case basis or, as with securities subsidiaries, based on the general characteristics or functional nature of the subsidiaries.)

The second exception relates to the treatment of subsidiaries of insured banks that are domestic depository institutions such as commercial banks, savings banks, or savings associations. These subsidiaries are not consolidated on a line-by-line basis with the insured bank parent in the bank parent's Consolidated Reports of Condition and Income. Rather, the instructions for these reports provide that bank investments in such depository institution subsidiaries are to be reported on an unconsolidated basis in accordance with the equity method. Since the FDIC believes that the minimum capital requirements should apply to a bank's depository activities in their entirety, regardless of the form that the organization's corporate structure takes, it will be necessary, for the purpose of calculating the bank's Tier 1 leverage and total risk-based capital ratios, to adjust a bank parent's Consolidated Report of Condition to consolidate its domestic depository institution subsidiaries on a line-by-line basis. The financial statements of the subsidiary that are used for this consolidation must be prepared in the same manner as the Consolidated Report of Condition.

The FDIC will, in determining the capital adequacy of a bank which is a member of a bank holding company or chain banking group, consider the degree of leverage and risks undertaken by the parent company or other affiliates. Where the level of risk in a holding company system is no more than normal and the consolidated company is adequately capitalized at all appropriate levels, the FDIC generally will not require additional capital in subsidiary banks under its supervision over and above that which would be required for the subsidiary bank on its own merit. In cases where a holding company or other affiliated banks (or other companies) evidence more than a normal degree of risk (either by virtue of the quality of their assets, the nature of the activities conducted, or other factors) or where the affiliated organizations are inadequately capitalized, the FDIC will consider the potential impact of the additional risk or excess leverage upon an individual bank to determine if such factors will likely result in excessive requirements for dividends, management fees, or other support to the holding company or affiliated organizations which would be detrimental to the bank. Where the excessive risk or leverage in such organizations is determined to be potentially detrimental to the bank's condition or its ability to maintain adequate capital, the FDIC may initiate appropriate supervisory action to limit the bank's ability to support its weaker affiliates and/or require higher than minimum capital ratios in the bank.

VI. APPLICABILITY OF PART 325 TO SAVINGS ASSOCIATIONS

Section 325.3(c) indicates that, where the FDIC is required to evaluate the adequacy of any depository institution's (including any savings association's) capital structure in conjunction with an application filed by the institution, the FDIC will not approve the application if the depository institution does not meet the minimum leverage capital requirement set forth in § 325.3(b).

Also, § 325.4(b) states that, under certain conditions specified in section 8(t) of the Federal Deposit Insurance Act, the FDIC may take section 8(b)(1) and/or 8(c) enforcement action against a savings association that is deemed to be engaged in an unsafe or unsound practice on account of its inadequate capital structure. Section 325.4(c) further specifies that any insured depository institution with a Tier 1 leverage ratio (as defined in part 325) of less than 2 percent is deemed to be operating in an unsafe or unsound condition pursuant to section 8(a) of the Federal Deposit Insurance Act.

In addition, the Office of Thrift Supervision (OTS), as the primary federal regulator of savings associations, has established minimum core capital leverage, tangible capital and risk-based capital requirements for savings associations (12 CFR part 567). In this regard, certain differences exist between the methods used by the OTS to calculate a savings association's capital and the methods set forth by the FDIC in part 325. These differences include, among others, the core capital treatment for investments in subsidiaries and for certain intangible assets.

In determining whether a savings association's application should be approved pursuant to § 325.3(c), or whether an unsafe or unsound practice or condition exists pursuant to §§ 325.4(b) and 325.4(c), the FDIC will consider the extent of the savings association's capital as determined in accordance with part 325. However, the FDIC will also consider the extent to which a savings association is in compliance with (a) the minimum capital requirements set forth by the OTS, (b) any related capital plans for meeting the minimum capital requirements approved by the OTS, and/or (c) any other criteria deemed by the FDIC as appropriate based on the association's specific circumstances.

[56 FR 10166, Mar. 11, 1991, as amended at 58 FR 6369, Jan. 28, 1993; 58 FR 8219, Feb. 12, 1993; 58 FR 60103, Nov. 15, 1993; 60 FR 39232, Aug. 1, 1995; 63 FR 42678, Aug. 10, 1998; 66 FR 59661, Nov. 29, 2001]

APPENDIX C TO PART 325—RISK-BASED CAPITAL FOR STATE NON-MEMBER BANKS: MARKET RISK

Section 1. Purpose, Applicability, Scope, and Effective Date

(a) *Purpose.* The purpose of this appendix is to ensure that banks with significant exposure to market risk maintain adequate capital to support that exposure.[1] This appendix supplements and adjusts the risk-based capital ratio calculations under appendix A of this part with respect to those banks.

(b) *Applicability.* (1) This appendix applies to any insured state nonmember bank whose trading activity[2] (on a worldwide consolidated basis) equals:

(i) 10 percent or more of total assets;[3] or

(ii) $1 billion or more.

(2) The FDIC may additionally apply this appendix to any insured state nonmember bank if the FDIC deems it necessary or appropriate for safe and sound banking practices.

(3) The FDIC may exclude an insured state nonmember bank otherwise meeting the criteria of paragraph (b)(1) of this section from coverage under this appendix if it determines the bank meets such criteria as a consequence of accounting, operational, or similar considerations, and the FDIC deems it consistent with safe and sound banking practices.

(c) *Scope.* The capital requirements of this appendix support market risk associated with a bank's covered positions.

(d) *Effective date.* This appendix is effective as of January 1, 1997. Compliance is not mandatory until January 1, 1998. Subject to supervisory approval, a bank may opt to comply with this appendix as early as January 1, 1997.[4]

Section 2. Definitions

For purposes of this appendix, the following definitions apply:

(a) *Covered positions* means all positions in a bank's trading account, and all foreign exchange[5] and commodity positions, whether or not in the trading account.[6] Positions include on-balance-sheet assets and liabilities

---

[1] This appendix is based on a framework developed jointly by supervisory authorities from the countries represented on the Basle Committee on Banking Supervision and endorsed by the Group of Ten Central Bank Governors. The framework is described in a Basle Committee paper entitled "Amendment to the Capital Accord to Incorporate Market Risks," January 1996. Also see modifications issued in September 1997.

[2] Trading activity means the gross sum of trading assets and liabilities as reported in the bank's most recent quarterly Consolidated Report of Condition and Income (Call Report).

[3] Total assets means quarter-end total assets as reported in the bank's most recent Call Report.

[4] A bank that voluntarily complies with the final rule prior to January 1, 1998, must comply with all of its provisions.

[5] Subject to FDIC review, a bank may exclude structural positions in foreign currencies from its covered positions.

[6] The term trading account is defined in the instructions to the Call Report.

and off-balance-sheet items. Securities subject to repurchase and lending agreements are included as if they are still owned by the lender. Covered positions exclude all positions in a bank's trading account that, in form or in substance, act as liquidity facilities that provide liquidity support to asset-backed commercial paper. Such excluded positions are subject to the risk-based capital requirements set forth in appendix A of this part.

(b) *Market risk* means the risk of loss resulting from movements in market prices. Market risk consists of general market risk and specific risk components.

(1) *General market risk* means changes in the market value of covered positions resulting from broad market movements, such as changes in the general level of interest rates, equity prices, foreign exchange rates, or commodity prices.

(2) *Specific risk* means changes in the market value of specific positions due to factors other than broad market movements and includes event and default risk as well as idiosyncratic variations.

(c) *Tier 1* and *Tier 2 capital* are defined in appendix A of this part.

(d) *Tier 3 capital* is subordinated debt that is unsecured; is fully paid up; has an original maturity of at least two years; is not redeemable before maturity without prior approval by the FDIC; includes a lock-in clause precluding payment of either interest or principal (even at maturity) if the payment would cause the issuing bank's risk-based capital ratio to fall or remain below the minimum required under appendix A of this part; and does not contain and is not covered by any covenants, terms, or restrictions that are inconsistent with safe and sound banking practices.

(e) *Value-at-risk (VAR)* means the estimate of the maximum amount that the value of covered positions could decline during a fixed holding period within a stated confidence level, measured in accordance with section 4 of this appendix.

Section 3. Adjustments to the Risk-Based Capital Ratio Calculations.

(a) *Risk-based capital ratio denominator.* A bank subject to this appendix shall calculate its risk-based capital ratio denominator as follows:

(1) *Adjusted risk-weighted assets.* Calculate adjusted risk-weighted assets, which equals risk-weighted assets (as determined in accordance with appendix A of this part), excluding the risk-weighted amounts of all covered positions (except foreign exchange positions outside the trading account and over-the-counter derivative positions)[7] and

receivables arising from the posting of cash collateral that is associated with securities borrowing transactions to the extent the receivables are collateralized by the market value of the borrowed securities, provided that the following conditions are met:

(i) The transaction is based on securities includable in the trading book that are liquid and readily marketable,

(ii) The transaction is marked to market daily,

(iii) The transaction is subject to daily margin maintenance requirements, and

(iv)(A) The transaction is a securities contract for the purposes of section 555 of the Bankruptcy Code (11 U.S.C. 555), a qualified financial contract for the purposes of section 11(e)(8) of the Federal Deposit Insurance Act (12 U.S.C. 1821(e)(8)), or a netting contract between or among financial institutions for the purposes of sections 401–407 of the Federal Deposit Insurance Corporation Improvement Act of 1991 (12 U.S.C. 4401–4407), or the Board's Regulation EE (12 CFR Part 231); or

(B) If the transaction does not meet the criteria set forth in paragraph (iv)(A) of this section, then either:

(*1*) The bank has conducted sufficient legal review to reach a well-founded conclusion that:

(*i*) The securities borrowing agreement executed in connection with the transaction provides the bank the right to accelerate, terminate, and close-out on a net basis all transactions under the agreement and to liquidate or set off collateral promptly upon an event of counterparty default, including in a bankruptcy, insolvency, or other similar proceeding of the counterparty; and

(*ii*) Under applicable law of the relevant jurisdiction, its rights under the agreement are legal, valid, binding, and enforceable and any exercise of rights under the agreement will not be stayed or avoided; or

(*2*) The transaction is either overnight or unconditionally cancelable at any time by the bank, and the bank has conducted sufficient legal review to reach a well-founded conclusion that:

(*i*) The securities borrowing agreement executed in connection with the transaction provides the bank the right to accelerate, terminate, and close-out on a net basis all transactions under the agreement and to liquidate or set off collateral promptly upon an event of counterparty default; and

(*ii*) Under the law governing the agreement, its rights under the agreement are legal, valid, binding, and enforceable.

(2) *Measure for market risk.* Calculate the measure for market risk, which equals the

---

[7] Foreign-exchange positions outside the trading account and all over-the-counter derivative positions, whether or not in the trading account, must be included in adjusted risk-weighted assets as determined in appendix A of this part.

Federal Deposit Insurance Corporation

sum of the VAR-based capital charge, the specific risk add-on (if any), and the capital charge for de minimis exposures (if any).

(i) *VAR-based capital charge.* The VAR-based capital charge equals the higher of:
 (A) The previous day's VAR measure; or
 (B) The average of the daily VAR measures for each of the preceding 60 business days multiplied by three, except as provided in section 4(e) of this appendix;
(ii) *Specific risk add-on.* The specific risk add-on is calculated in accordance with section 5 of this appendix; and
(iii) *Capital charge for de minimis exposure.* The capital charge for de minimis exposure is calculated in accordance with section 4(a) of this appendix.

(3) *Market risk equivalent assets.* Calculate market risk equivalent assets by multiplying the measure for market risk (as calculated in paragraph (a)(2) of this section) by 12.5.

(4) *Denominator calculation.* Add market risk equivalent assets (as calculated in paragraph (a)(3) of this section) to adjusted risk-weighted assets (as calculated in paragraph (a)(1) of this section). The resulting sum is the bank's risk-based capital ratio denominator.

(b) *Risk-based capital ratio numerator.* A bank subject to this appendix shall calculate its risk-based capital ratio numerator by allocating capital as follows:

(1) *Credit risk allocation.* Allocate Tier 1 and Tier 2 capital equal to 8.0 percent of adjusted risk-weighted assets (as calculated in paragraph (a)(1) of this section).[8]

(2) *Market risk allocation.* Allocate Tier 1, Tier 2, and Tier 3 capital equal to the measure for market risk as calculated in paragraph (a)(2) of this section. The sum of Tier 2 and Tier 3 capital allocated for market risk must not exceed 250 percent of Tier 1 capital allocated for market risk. (This requirement means that Tier 1 capital allocated in this paragraph (b)(2) must equal at least 28.6 percent of the measure for market risk.)

(3) *Restrictions.* (i) The sum of Tier 2 capital (both allocated and excess) and Tier 3 capital (allocated in paragraph (b)(2) of this section) may not exceed 100 percent of Tier 1 capital (both allocated and excess).[9]

(ii) Term subordinated debt (and intermediate-term preferred stock and related surplus) included in Tier 2 capital (both allocated and excess) may not exceed 50 percent of Tier 1 capital (both allocated and excess).

(4) *Numerator calculation.* Add Tier 1 capital (both allocated and excess), Tier 2 capital (both allocated and excess), and Tier 3 capital (allocated under paragraph (b)(2) of this section). The resulting sum is the bank's risk-based capital ratio numerator.

Section 4. Internal Models

(a) *General.* For risk-based capital purposes, a bank subject to this appendix must use its internal model to measure its daily VAR, in accordance with the requirements of this section.[10] The FDIC may permit a bank to use alternative techniques to measure the market risk of de minimis exposures so long as the techniques adequately measure associated market risk.

(b) *Qualitative requirements.* A bank subject to this appendix must have a risk management system that meets the following minimum qualitative requirements:

(1) The bank must have a risk control unit that reports directly to senior management and is independent from business trading units.

(2) The bank's internal risk measurement model must be integrated into the daily management process.

(3) The bank's policies and procedures must identify, and the bank must conduct, appropriate stress tests and backtests.[11] The bank's policies and procedures must identify the procedures to follow in response to the results of such tests.

(4) The bank must conduct independent reviews of its risk measurement and risk management systems at least annually.

(c) *Market risk factors.* The bank's internal model must use risk factors sufficient to measure the market risk inherent in all covered positions. The risk factors must address

---

[8] A bank may not allocate Tier 3 capital to support credit risk (as calculated under appendix A of this part).

[9] Excess Tier 1 capital means Tier 1 capital that has not been allocated in paragraphs (b)(1) and (b)(2) of this section. Excess Tier 2 capital means Tier 2 capital that has not been allocated in paragraph (b)(1) and (b)(2) of this section, subject to the restrictions in paragraph (b)(3) of this section.

[10] A bank's internal model may use any generally accepted measurement techniques, such as variance-covariance models, historical simulations, or Monte Carlo simulations. However, the level of sophistication and accuracy of a bank's internal model must be commensurate with the nature and size of its covered positions. A bank that modifies its existing modeling procedures to comply with the requirements of this appendix for risk-based capital purposes should, nonetheless, continue to use the internal model it considers most appropriate in evaluating risks for other purposes.

[11] Stress tests provide information about the impact of adverse market events on a bank's covered positions. Backtests provide information about the accuracy of an internal model by comparing a bank's daily VAR measures to its corresponding daily trading profits and losses.

interest rate risk,[12] equity price risk, foreign exchange rate risk, and commodity price risk.

(d) *Quantitative requirements.* For regulatory capital purposes, VAR measures must meet the following quantitative requirements:

(1) The VAR measures must be calculated on a daily basis using a 99 percent, one-tailed confidence level with a price shock equivalent to a ten-business day movement in rates and prices. In order to calculate VAR measures based on a ten-day price shock, the bank may either calculate ten-day figures directly or convert VAR figures based on holding periods other than ten days to the equivalent of a ten-day holding period (for instance, by multiplying a one-day VAR measure by the square root of ten).

(2) The VAR measures must be based on an historical observation period (or effective observation period for a bank using a weighting scheme or other similar method) of at least one year. The bank must update data sets at least once every three months or more frequently as market conditions warrant.

(3) The VAR measures must include the risks arising from the non-linear price characteristics of options positions and the sensitivity of the market value of the positions to changes in the volatility of the underlying rates or prices. A bank with a large or complex options portfolio must measure the volatility of options positions by different maturities.

(4) The VAR measures may incorporate empirical correlations within and across risk categories, provided that the bank's process for measuring correlations is sound. In the event that the VAR measures do not incorporate empirical correlations across risk categories, then the bank must add the separate VAR measures for the four major risk categories to determine its aggregate VAR measure.

(e) *Backtesting.* (1) Beginning one year after a bank starts to comply with this appendix, a bank must conduct backtesting by comparing each of its most recent 250 business days' actual net trading profit or loss[13] with the corresponding daily VAR measures generated for internal risk measurement purposes and calibrated to a one-day holding period and a 99 percent, one-tailed confidence level.

(2) Once each quarter, the bank must identify the number of exceptions, that is, the number of business days for which the magnitude of the actual daily net trading loss, if any, exceeds the corresponding daily VAR measure.

(3) A bank must use the multiplication factor indicated in Table 1 of this appendix in determining its capital charge for market risk under section 3(a)(2)(i)(B) of this appendix until it obtains the next quarter's backtesting results, unless the FDIC determines that a different adjustment or other action is appropriate.

TABLE 1—MULTIPLICATION FACTOR BASED ON RESULTS OF BACKTESTING

Number of exceptions	Multiplication factor
4 or fewer	3.00
5	3.40
6	3.50
7	3.65
8	3.75
9	3.85
10 or more	4.00

Section 5. Specific Risk

(a) *Modeled specific risk.* A bank may use its internal model to measure specific risk. If the bank has demonstrated to the FDIC that its internal model measures the specific risk, including event and default risk as well as idiosyncratic variation, of covered debt and equity positions and includes the specific risk measure in the VAR-based capital charge in section 3(a)(2)(i) of this appendix, then the bank has no specific risk add-on for purposes of section 3(a)(2)(ii) of this appendix. The model should explain the historical price variation in the trading portfolio and capture concentration, both magnitude and changes in composition. The model should also be robust to an adverse environment and have been validated through backtesting which assesses whether specific risk is being accurately captured.

(b) *Add-on charge for modeled specific risk.* A bank that incorporates specific risk in its internal model but fails to demonstrate to the FDIC that its internal model adequately measures all aspects of specific risk for covered debt and equity positions, including event and default risk, as provided by section 5(a) of this appendix, must calculate the bank's specific risk add-on for purposes of section 3(a)(2)(ii) of this appendix as follows:

(1) If the model is capable of valid separation of the VAR measure into a specific risk portion and a general market risk portion, then the specific risk add-on is equal to the previous day's specific risk portion.

---

[12] For material exposures in the major currencies and markets, modeling techniques must capture spread risk and must incorporate enough segments of the yield curve—at least six—to capture differences in volatility and less than perfect correlation of rates along the yield curve.

[13] Actual net trading profits and losses typically include such things as realized and unrealized gains and losses on portfolio positions as well as fee income and commissions associated with trading activities.

(2) If the model does not separate the VAR measure into a specific risk portion and a general market risk portion, then the specific risk add-on is the sum of the previous day's VAR measures for subportfolios of covered debt and equity positions.

(c) *Add-on charge if specific risk is not modeled.* If a bank does not model specific risk in accordance with paragraph (a) or (b) of this section, the bank's specific risk add-on charge for purposes of section 3(a)(2)(ii) of this appendix equals the sum of the components for covered debt and equity positions. If a bank models, in accordance with paragraph (a) or (b) of this section, the specific risk of covered debt positions but not covered equity positions (or vice versa), then the bank's specific risk add-on charge for the positions not modeled is the component for covered debt or equity positions as appropriate:

(1) *Covered debt positions.* (i) For purposes of this section 5, covered debt positions means fixed-rate or floating-rate debt instruments located in the trading account and instruments located in the trading account with values that react primarily to changes in interest rates, including certain non-convertible preferred stock, convertible bonds, and instruments subject to repurchase and lending agreements. Also included are derivatives (including written and purchased options) for which the underlying instrument is a covered debt instrument that is subject to a non-zero specific risk capital charge.

(A) For covered debt positions that are derivatives, a bank must risk-weight (as described in paragraph (c)(1)(iii) of this section) the market value of the effective notional amount of the underlying debt instrument or index portfolio. Swaps must be included as the notional position in the underlying debt instrument or index portfolio, with a receiving side treated as a long position and a paying side treated as a short position; and

(B) For covered debt positions that are options, whether long or short, a bank must risk-weight (as described in paragraph (c)(1)(iii) of this section) the market value of the effective notional amount of the underlying debt instrument or index multiplied by the option's delta.

(ii) A bank may net long and short covered debt positions (including derivatives) in identical debt issues or indices.

(iii) A bank must multiply the absolute value of the current market value of each net long or short covered debt position by the appropriate specific risk weighting factor indicated in Table 2 of this appendix. The specific risk capital charge component for covered debt positions is the sum of the weighted values.

TABLE 2—SPECIFIC RISK WEIGHTING FACTORS FOR COVERED DEBT POSITIONS

Category	Remaining maturity (contractual)	Weighting factor (in percent)
Government	N/A	0.00
Qualifying	6 months or less	0.25
	Over 6 months to 24 months.	1.00
	Over 24 months	1.60
Other	N/A	8.00

(A) The *government* category includes all debt instruments of central governments of OECD-based countries [14] including bonds, Treasury bills, and other short-term instruments, as well as local currency instruments of non-OECD central governments to the extent the bank has liabilities booked in that currency.

(B) The *qualifying* category includes debt instruments of U.S. government-sponsored agencies, general obligation debt instruments issued by states and other political subdivisions of OECD-based countries, multilateral development banks, and debt instruments issued by U.S. depository institutions or OECD-banks that do not qualify as capital of the issuing institution.[15] This category also includes other debt instruments, including corporate debt and revenue instruments issued by states and other political subdivisions of OECD countries, that are:

(*1*) Rated investment-grade by at least two nationally recognized credit rating services;

(*2*) Rated investment-grade by one nationally recognized credit rating agency and not rated less than investment-grade by any other credit rating agency; or

(*3*) Unrated, but deemed to be of comparable investment quality by the reporting bank and the issuer has instruments listed on a recognized stock exchange, subject to review by the FDIC.

(C) The *other* category includes debt instruments that are not included in the government or qualifying categories.

(2) *Covered equity positions.* (i) For purposes of this section 5, covered equity positions means equity instruments located in the trading account and instruments located in the trading account with values that react primarily to changes in equity prices, including voting or non-voting common stock, certain convertible bonds, and commitments to buy or sell equity instruments. Also included are derivatives (including written and purchased options) for which the underlying is a covered equity position.

---

[14] Organization for Economic Cooperation and Development (OECD)-based countries is defined in appendix A of this part.

[15] U.S. government-sponsored agencies, multilateral development banks, and OECD banks are defined in appendix A of this part.

(A) For covered equity positions that are derivatives, a bank must risk weight (as described in paragraph (c)(2)(iii) of this section) the market value of the effective notional amount of the underlying equity instrument or equity portfolio. Swaps must be included as the notional position in the underlying equity instrument or index portfolio, with a receiving side treated as a long position and a paying side treated as a short position; and

(B) For covered equity positions that are options, whether long or short, a bank must risk weight (as described in paragraph (c)(2)(iii) of this section) the market value of the effective notional amount of the underlying equity instrument or index multiplied by the option's delta.

(ii) A bank may net long and short covered equity positions (including derivatives) in identical equity issues or equity indices in the same market.[16]

(iii)(A) A bank must multiply the absolute value of the current market value of each net long or short covered equity position by a risk weighting factor of 8.0 percent, or by 4.0 percent if the equity is held in a portfolio that is both liquid and well-diversified.[17] For covered equity positions that are index contracts comprising a well-diversified portfolio of equity instruments, the net long or short position is multiplied by a risk weighting factor of 2.0 percent.

(B) For covered equity positions from the following futures-related arbitrage strategies, a bank may apply a 2.0 percent risk weighting factor to one side (long or short) of each position with the opposite side exempt from charge, subject to review by the FDIC:

(1) Long and short positions in exactly the same index at different dates or in different market centers; or

(2) Long and short positions in index contracts at the same date in different but similar indices.

(C) For futures contracts on broadly-based indices that are matched by offsetting positions in a basket of stocks comprising the index, a bank may apply a 2.0 percent risk weighting factor to the futures and stock basket positions (long and short), provided that such trades are deliberately entered into and separately controlled, and that the basket of stocks comprises at least 90 percent of the capitalization of the index.

(iv) The specific risk capital charge component for covered equity positions is the sum of the weighted values.

[61 FR 47376, Sept. 6, 1996, as amended at 62 FR 68068, Dec. 30, 1997; 64 FR 19038, Apr. 19, 1999; 65 FR 75859, Dec. 5, 2000; 69 FR 44924, July 28, 2004; 71 FR 8937, Feb. 22, 2006]

APPENDIX D TO PART 325—CAPITAL ADEQUACY GUIDELINES FOR BANKS: INTERNAL-RATINGS-BASED AND ADVANCED MEASUREMENT APPROACHES

Part I General Provisions
Section 1 Purpose, Applicability, Reservation of Authority, and Principle of Conservatism
Section 2 Definitions
Section 3 Minimum Risk-Based Capital Requirements
Part II Qualifying Capital
Section 11 Additional Deductions
Section 12 Deductions and Limitations Not Required
Section 13 Eligible Credit Reserves
Part III Qualification
Section 21 Qualification Process
Section 22 Qualification Requirements
Section 23 Ongoing Qualification
Section 24 Merger and Acquisition Transitional Arrangements
Part IV Risk-Weighted Assets for General Credit Risk
Section 31 Mechanics for Calculating Total Wholesale and Retail Risk-Weighted Assets
Section 32 Counterparty Credit Risk of Repo-Style Transactions, Eligible Margin Loans, and OTC Derivative Contracts
Section 33 Guarantees and Credit Derivatives: PD Substitution and LGD Adjustment Approaches
Section 34 Guarantees and Credit Derivatives: Double Default Treatment
Section 35 Risk-Based Capital Requirement for Unsettled Transactions
Part V Risk-Weighted Assets for Securitization Exposures
Section 41 Operational Criteria for Recognizing the Transfer of Risk
Section 42 Risk-Based Capital Requirement for Securitization Exposures
Section 43 Ratings-Based Approach (RBA)

---

[16] A bank may also net positions in depository receipts against an opposite position in the underlying equity or identical equity in different markets, provided that the bank includes the costs of conversion.

[17] A portfolio is liquid and well-diversified if: (1) it is characterized by a limited sensitivity to price changes of any single equity issue or closely related group of equity issues held in the portfolio; (2) the volatility of the portfolio's value is not dominated by the volatility of any individual equity issue or by equity issues from any single industry or economic sector; (3) it contains a large number of individual equity positions, with no single position representing a substantial portion of the portfolio's total market value; and (4) it consists mainly of issues traded on organized exchanges or in well-established over-the-counter markets.

Federal Deposit Insurance Corporation Pt. 325, App. D

Section 44 Internal Assessment Approach (IAA)
Section 45 Supervisory Formula Approach (SFA)
Section 46 Recognition of Credit Risk Mitigants for Securitization Exposures
Section 47 Risk-Based Capital Requirement for Early Amortization Provisions
Part VI Risk-Weighted Assets for Equity Exposures
Section 51 Introduction and Exposure Measurement
Section 52 Simple Risk Weight Approach (SRWA)
Section 53 Internal Models Approach (IMA)
Section 54 Equity Exposures to Investment Funds
Section 55 Equity Derivative Contracts
Part VII Risk-Weighted Assets for Operational Risk
Section 61 Qualification Requirements for Incorporation of Operational Risk Mitigants
Section 62 Mechanics of Risk-Weighted Asset Calculation
Part VIII Disclosure
Section 71 Disclosure Requirements
Part IX Transition Provisions
Section 81 Optional Transition Provisions Related to the Implementation of Consolidation Requirements Under FAS 167

PART I. GENERAL PROVISIONS

Section 1. Purpose, Applicability, Reservation of Authority, and Principle of Conservatism

(a) *Purpose.* This appendix establishes:

(1) Minimum qualifying criteria for banks using bank-specific internal risk measurement and management processes for calculating risk-based capital requirements;

(2) Methodologies for such banks to calculate their risk-based capital requirements; and

(3) Public disclosure requirements for such banks.

(b) *Applicability.* (1) This appendix applies to a bank that:

(i) Has consolidated assets, as reported on the most recent year-end Consolidated Report of Condition and Income (Call Report) equal to $250 billion or more;

(ii) Has consolidated total on-balance sheet foreign exposure at the most recent year-end equal to $10 billion or more (where total on-balance sheet foreign exposure equals total cross-border claims less claims with head office or guarantor located in another country plus redistributed guaranteed amounts to the country of head office or guarantor plus local country claims on local residents plus revaluation gains on foreign exchange and derivative products, calculated in accordance with the Federal Financial Institutions Examination Council (FFIEC) 009 Country Exposure Report);

(iii) Is a subsidiary of a depository institution that uses 12 CFR part 3, appendix C, 12 CFR part 208, appendix F, 12 CFR part 325, appendix D, or 12 CFR part 567, appendix C, to calculate its risk-based capital requirements; or

(iv) Is a subsidiary of a bank holding company that uses 12 CFR part 225, appendix G, to calculate its risk-based capital requirements.

(2) Any bank may elect to use this appendix to calculate its risk-based capital requirements.

(3) A bank that is subject to this appendix must use this appendix unless the FDIC determines in writing that application of this appendix is not appropriate in light of the bank's asset size, level of complexity, risk profile, or scope of operations. In making a determination under this paragraph, the FDIC will apply notice and response procedures in the same manner and to the same extent as the notice and response procedures in 12 CFR 325.6(c).

(c) *Reservation of authority*—(1) *Additional capital in the aggregate.* The FDIC may require a bank to hold an amount of capital greater than otherwise required under this appendix if the FDIC determines that the bank's risk-based capital requirement under this appendix is not commensurate with the bank's credit, market, operational, or other risks. In making a determination under this paragraph, the FDIC will apply notice and response procedures in the same manner and to the same extent as the notice and response procedures in 12 CFR 325.6(c).

(2) *Specific risk-weighted asset amounts.* (i) If the FDIC determines that the risk-weighted asset amount calculated under this appendix by the bank for one or more exposures is not commensurate with the risks associated with those exposures, the FDIC may require the bank to assign a different risk-weighted asset amount to the exposures, to assign different risk parameters to the exposures (if the exposures are wholesale or retail exposures), or to use different model assumptions for the exposures (if relevant), all as specified by the FDIC.

(ii) If the FDIC determines that the risk-weighted asset amount for operational risk produced by the bank under this appendix is not commensurate with the operational risks of the bank, the FDIC may require the bank to assign a different risk-weighted asset amount for operational risk, to change elements of its operational risk analytical framework, including distributional and dependence assumptions, or to make other changes to the bank's operational risk management processes, data and assessment systems, or quantification systems, all as specified by the FDIC.

(3) The FDIC may, on a case-by-case basis, determine that the regulatory capital treatment for an exposure or other relationship to

an entity that is not subject to consolidation on the balance sheet is not commensurate with the risk of the exposure and the relationship of the bank to the entity. In making this determination, the FDIC may require the bank to treat the entity as if it were consolidated on the balance sheet of the bank for risk-based capital purposes and calculate the appropriate risk-based capital ratios accordingly.

(4) *Other supervisory authority.* Nothing in this appendix limits the authority of the FDIC under any other provision of law or regulation to take supervisory or enforcement action, including action to address unsafe or unsound practices or conditions, deficient capital levels, or violations of law.

(d) *Principle of conservatism.* Notwithstanding the requirements of this appendix, a bank may choose not to apply a provision of this appendix to one or more exposures, provided that:

(1) The bank can demonstrate on an ongoing basis to the satisfaction of the FDIC that not applying the provision would, in all circumstances, unambiguously generate a risk-based capital requirement for each such exposure greater than that which would otherwise be required under this appendix;

(2) The bank appropriately manages the risk of each such exposure;

(3) The bank notifies the FDIC in writing prior to applying this principle to each such exposure; and

(4) The exposures to which the bank applies this principle are not, in the aggregate, material to the bank.

Section 2. Definitions

Advanced internal ratings-based (IRB) systems means a bank's internal risk rating and segmentation system; risk parameter quantification system; data management and maintenance system; and control, oversight, and validation system for credit risk of wholesale and retail exposures.

Advanced systems means a bank's advanced IRB systems, operational risk management processes, operational risk data and assessment systems, operational risk quantification systems, and, to the extent the bank uses the following systems, the internal models methodology, double default excessive correlation detection process, IMA for equity exposures, and IAA for securitization exposures to ABCP programs.

Affiliate with respect to a company means any company that controls, is controlled by, or is under common control with, the company.

Applicable external rating means:

(1) With respect to an exposure that has multiple external ratings assigned by NRSROs, the lowest solicited external rating assigned to the exposure by any NRSRO; and

(2) With respect to an exposure that has a single external rating assigned by an NRSRO, the external rating assigned to the exposure by the NRSRO.

Applicable inferred rating means:

(1) With respect to an exposure that has multiple inferred ratings, the lowest inferred rating based on a solicited external rating; and

(2) With respect to an exposure that has a single inferred rating, the inferred rating.

Asset-backed commercial paper (ABCP) program means a program that primarily issues commercial paper that:

(1) Has an external rating; and

(2) Is backed by underlying exposures held in a bankruptcy-remote SPE.

Asset-backed commercial paper (ABCP) program sponsor means a bank that:

(1) Establishes an ABCP program;

(2) Approves the sellers permitted to participate in an ABCP program;

(3) Approves the exposures to be purchased by an ABCP program; or

(4) Administers the ABCP program by monitoring the underlying exposures, underwriting or otherwise arranging for the placement of debt or other obligations issued by the program, compiling monthly reports, or ensuring compliance with the program documents and with the program's credit and investment policy.

Backtesting means the comparison of a bank's internal estimates with actual outcomes during a sample period not used in model development. In this context, backtesting is one form of out-of-sample testing.

Bank holding company is defined in section 2 of the Bank Holding Company Act (12 U.S.C. 1841).

Benchmarking means the comparison of a bank's internal estimates with relevant internal and external data or with estimates based on other estimation techniques.

Business environment and internal control factors means the indicators of a bank's operational risk profile that reflect a current and forward-looking assessment of the bank's underlying business risk factors and internal control environment.

Carrying value means, with respect to an asset, the value of the asset on the balance sheet of the bank, determined in accordance with GAAP.

Clean-up call means a contractual provision that permits an originating bank or servicer to call securitization exposures before their stated maturity or call date. See also *eligible clean-up call.*

Commodity derivative contract means a commodity-linked swap, purchased commodity-linked option, forward commodity-linked contract, or any other instrument linked to commodities that gives rise to similar counterparty credit risks.

Federal Deposit Insurance Corporation — Pt. 325, App. D

Company means a corporation, partnership, limited liability company, depository institution, business trust, special purpose entity, association, or similar organization.

Control. A person or company *controls* a company if it:

(1) Owns, controls, or holds with power to vote 25 percent or more of a class of voting securities of the company; or

(2) Consolidates the company for financial reporting purposes.

Controlled early amortization provision means an early amortization provision that meets all the following conditions:

(1) The originating bank has appropriate policies and procedures to ensure that it has sufficient capital and liquidity available in the event of an early amortization;

(2) Throughout the duration of the securitization (including the early amortization period), there is the same pro rata sharing of interest, principal, expenses, losses, fees, recoveries, and other cash flows from the underlying exposures based on the originating bank's and the investors' relative shares of the underlying exposures outstanding measured on a consistent monthly basis;

(3) The amortization period is sufficient for at least 90 percent of the total underlying exposures outstanding at the beginning of the early amortization period to be repaid or recognized as in default; and

(4) The schedule for repayment of investor principal is not more rapid than would be allowed by straight-line amortization over an 18-month period.

Credit derivative means a financial contract executed under standard industry credit derivative documentation that allows one party (the protection purchaser) to transfer the credit risk of one or more exposures (reference exposure) to another party (the protection provider). See also *eligible credit derivative.*

Credit-enhancing interest-only strip (CEIO) means an on-balance sheet asset that, in form or in substance:

(1) Represents a contractual right to receive some or all of the interest and no more than a minimal amount of principal due on the underlying exposures of a securitization; and

(2) Exposes the holder to credit risk directly or indirectly associated with the underlying exposures that exceeds a pro rata share of the holder's claim on the underlying exposures, whether through subordination provisions or other credit-enhancement techniques.

Credit-enhancing representations and warranties means representations and warranties that are made or assumed in connection with a transfer of underlying exposures (including loan servicing assets) and that obligate a bank to protect another party from losses arising from the credit risk of the underlying exposures. Credit-enhancing representations and warranties include provisions to protect a party from losses resulting from the default or nonperformance of the obligors of the underlying exposures or from an insufficiency in the value of the collateral backing the underlying exposures. Credit-enhancing representations and warranties do not include:

(1) Early default clauses and similar warranties that permit the return of, or premium refund clauses that cover, first-lien residential mortgage exposures for a period not to exceed 120 days from the date of transfer, provided that the date of transfer is within one year of origination of the residential mortgage exposure;

(2) Premium refund clauses that cover underlying exposures guaranteed, in whole or in part, by the U.S. government, a U.S. government agency, or a U.S. government sponsored enterprise, provided that the clauses are for a period not to exceed 120 days from the date of transfer; or

(3) Warranties that permit the return of underlying exposures in instances of misrepresentation, fraud, or incomplete documentation.

Credit risk mitigant means collateral, a credit derivative, or a guarantee.

Credit-risk-weighted assets means 1.06 multiplied by the sum of:

(1) Total wholesale and retail risk-weighted assets;

(2) Risk-weighted assets for securitization exposures; and

(3) Risk-weighted assets for equity exposures.

Current exposure means, with respect to a netting set, the larger of zero or the market value of a transaction or portfolio of transactions within the netting set that would be lost upon default of the counterparty, assuming no recovery on the value of the transactions. Current exposure is also called replacement cost.

Default—(1) *Retail.* (i) A retail exposure of a bank is in default if:

(A) The exposure is 180 days past due, in the case of a residential mortgage exposure or revolving exposure;

(B) The exposure is 120 days past due, in the case of all other retail exposures; or

(C) The bank has taken a full or partial charge-off, write-down of principal, or material negative fair value adjustment of principal on the exposure for credit-related reasons.

(ii) Notwithstanding paragraph (1)(i) of this definition, for a retail exposure held by a non-U.S. subsidiary of the bank that is subject to an internal ratings-based approach to capital adequacy consistent with the Basel Committee on Banking Supervision's "International Convergence of Capital Measurement and Capital Standards: A Revised Framework" in a non-U.S. jurisdiction, the bank may elect to use the definition of default that is used in that jurisdiction, provided that the bank has obtained prior approval from the FDIC to use the definition of default in that jurisdiction.

(iii) A retail exposure in default remains in default until the bank has reasonable assurance of repayment and performance for all contractual principal and interest payments on the exposure.

(2) *Wholesale.* (i) A bank's wholesale obligor is in default if:

(A) The bank determines that the obligor is unlikely to pay its credit obligations to the bank in full, without recourse by the bank to actions such as realizing collateral (if held); or

(B) The obligor is past due more than 90 days on any material credit obligation(s) to the bank.[1]

(ii) An obligor in default remains in default until the bank has reasonable assurance of repayment and performance for all contractual principal and interest payments on all exposures of the bank to the obligor (other than exposures that have been fully written-down or charged-off).

Dependence means a measure of the association among operational losses across and within units of measure.

Depository institution is defined in section 3 of the Federal Deposit Insurance Act (12 U.S.C. 1813).

Derivative contract means a financial contract whose value is derived from the values of one or more underlying assets, reference rates, or indices of asset values or reference rates. Derivative contracts include interest rate derivative contracts, exchange rate derivative contracts, equity derivative contracts, commodity derivative contracts, credit derivatives, and any other instrument that poses similar counterparty credit risks. Derivative contracts also include unsettled securities, commodities, and foreign exchange transactions with a contractual settlement or delivery lag that is longer than the lesser of the market standard for the particular instrument or five business days.

Early amortization provision means a provision in the documentation governing a securitization that, when triggered, causes investors in the securitization exposures to be repaid before the original stated maturity of the securitization exposures, unless the provision:

(1) Is triggered solely by events not directly related to the performance of the underlying exposures or the originating bank (such as material changes in tax laws or regulations); or

(2) Leaves investors fully exposed to future draws by obligors on the underlying exposures even after the provision is triggered.

Economic downturn conditions means, with respect to an exposure held by the bank, those conditions in which the aggregate default rates for that exposure's wholesale or retail exposure subcategory (or subdivision of such subcategory selected by the bank) in the exposure's national jurisdiction (or subdivision of such jurisdiction selected by the bank) are significantly higher than average.

Effective maturity (M) of a wholesale exposure means:

(1) For wholesale exposures other than repo-style transactions, eligible margin loans, and OTC derivative contracts described in paragraph (2) or (3) of this definition:

(i) The weighted-average remaining maturity (measured in years, whole or fractional) of the expected contractual cash flows from the exposure, using the undiscounted amounts of the cash flows as weights; or

(ii) The nominal remaining maturity (measured in years, whole or fractional) of the exposure.

(2) For repo-style transactions, eligible margin loans, and OTC derivative contracts subject to a qualifying master netting agreement for which the bank does not apply the internal models approach in paragraph (d) of section 32 of this appendix, the weighted-average remaining maturity (measured in years, whole or fractional) of the individual transactions subject to the qualifying master netting agreement, with the weight of each individual transaction set equal to the notional amount of the transaction.

(3) For repo-style transactions, eligible margin loans, and OTC derivative contracts for which the bank applies the internal models approach in paragraph (d) of section 32 of this appendix, the value determined in paragraph (d)(4) of section 32 of this appendix.

Effective notional amount means, for an eligible guarantee or eligible credit derivative, the lesser of the contractual notional amount of the credit risk mitigant and the EAD of the hedged exposure, multiplied by the percentage coverage of the credit risk mitigant. For example, the effective notional amount of an eligible guarantee that covers, on a pro rata basis, 40 percent of any losses on a $100 bond would be $40.

Eligible clean-up call means a clean-up call that:

(1) Is exercisable solely at the discretion of the originating bank or servicer;

(2) Is not structured to avoid allocating losses to securitization exposures held by investors or otherwise structured to provide credit enhancement to the securitization; and

(3)(i) For a traditional securitization, is only exercisable when 10 percent or less of

---

[1] Overdrafts are past due once the obligor has breached an advised limit or been advised of a limit smaller than the current outstanding balance.

Federal Deposit Insurance Corporation

the principal amount of the underlying exposures or securitization exposures (determined as of the inception of the securitization) is outstanding; or

(ii) For a synthetic securitization, is only exercisable when 10 percent or less of the principal amount of the reference portfolio of underlying exposures (determined as of the inception of the securitization) is outstanding.

Eligible credit derivative means a credit derivative in the form of a credit default swap, n^{th}-to-default swap, total return swap, or any other form of credit derivative approved by the FDIC, provided that:

(1) The contract meets the requirements of an eligible guarantee and has been confirmed by the protection purchaser and the protection provider;

(2) Any assignment of the contract has been confirmed by all relevant parties;

(3) If the credit derivative is a credit default swap or n^{th}-to-default swap, the contract includes the following credit events:

(i) Failure to pay any amount due under the terms of the reference exposure, subject to any applicable minimal payment threshold that is consistent with standard market practice and with a grace period that is closely in line with the grace period of the reference exposure; and

(ii) Bankruptcy, insolvency, or inability of the obligor on the reference exposure to pay its debts, or its failure or admission in writing of its inability generally to pay its debts as they become due, and similar events;

(4) The terms and conditions dictating the manner in which the contract is to be settled are incorporated into the contract;

(5) If the contract allows for cash settlement, the contract incorporates a robust valuation process to estimate loss reliably and specifies a reasonable period for obtaining post-credit event valuations of the reference exposure;

(6) If the contract requires the protection purchaser to transfer an exposure to the protection provider at settlement, the terms of at least one of the exposures that is permitted to be transferred under the contract provides that any required consent to transfer may not be unreasonably withheld;

(7) If the credit derivative is a credit default swap or n^{th}-to-default swap, the contract clearly identifies the parties responsible for determining whether a credit event has occurred, specifies that this determination is not the sole responsibility of the protection provider, and gives the protection purchaser the right to notify the protection provider of the occurrence of a credit event; and

(8) If the credit derivative is a total return swap and the bank records net payments received on the swap as net income, the bank records offsetting deterioration in the value of the hedged exposure (either through reductions in fair value or by an addition to reserves).

Pt. 325, App. D

Eligible credit reserves means all general allowances that have been established through a charge against earnings to absorb credit losses associated with on- or off-balance sheet wholesale and retail exposures, including the allowance for loan and lease losses (ALLL) associated with such exposures but excluding allocated transfer risk reserves established pursuant to 12 U.S.C. 3904 and other specific reserves created against recognized losses.

Eligible double default guarantor, with respect to a guarantee or credit derivative obtained by a bank, means:

(1) *U.S.-based entities.* A depository institution, a bank holding company, a savings and loan holding company (as defined in 12 U.S.C. 1467a) provided all or substantially all of the holding company's activities are permissible for a financial holding company under 12 U.S.C. 1843(k), a securities broker or dealer registered with the SEC under the Securities Exchange Act of 1934 (15 U.S.C. 78o *et seq.*), or an insurance company in the business of providing credit protection (such as a monoline bond insurer or re-insurer) that is subject to supervision by a State insurance regulator, if:

(i) At the time the guarantor issued the guarantee or credit derivative or at any time thereafter, the bank assigned a PD to the guarantor's rating grade that was equal to or lower than the PD associated with a long-term external rating in the third-highest investment-grade rating category; and

(ii) The bank currently assigns a PD to the guarantor's rating grade that is equal to or lower than the PD associated with a long-term external rating in the lowest investment-grade rating category; or

(2) *Non-U.S.-based entities.* A foreign bank (as defined in §211.2 of the Federal Reserve Board's Regulation K (12 CFR 211.2)), a non-U.S.-based securities firm, or a non-U.S.-based insurance company in the business of providing credit protection, if:

(i) The bank demonstrates that the guarantor is subject to consolidated supervision and regulation comparable to that imposed on U.S. depository institutions, securities broker-dealers, or insurance companies (as the case may be), or has issued and outstanding an unsecured long-term debt security without credit enhancement that has a long-term applicable external rating of at least investment grade;

(ii) At the time the guarantor issued the guarantee or credit derivative or at any time thereafter, the bank assigned a PD to the guarantor's rating grade that was equal to or lower than the PD associated with a long-term external rating in the third-highest investment-grade rating category; and

(iii) The bank currently assigns a PD to the guarantor's rating grade that is equal to or lower than the PD associated with a long-term external rating in the lowest investment-grade rating category.

Eligible guarantee means a guarantee that:

(1) Is written and unconditional;

(2) Covers all or a pro rata portion of all contractual payments of the obligor on the reference exposure;

(3) Gives the beneficiary a direct claim against the protection provider;

(4) Is not unilaterally cancelable by the protection provider for reasons other than the breach of the contract by the beneficiary;

(5) Is legally enforceable against the protection provider in a jurisdiction where the protection provider has sufficient assets against which a judgment may be attached and enforced;

(6) Requires the protection provider to make payment to the beneficiary on the occurrence of a default (as defined in the guarantee) of the obligor on the reference exposure in a timely manner without the beneficiary first having to take legal actions to pursue the obligor for payment;

(7) Does not increase the beneficiary's cost of credit protection on the guarantee in response to deterioration in the credit quality of the reference exposure; and

(8) Is not provided by an affiliate of the bank, unless the affiliate is an insured depository institution, bank, securities broker or dealer, or insurance company that:

(i) Does not control the bank; and

(ii) Is subject to consolidated supervision and regulation comparable to that imposed on U.S. depository institutions, securities broker-dealers, or insurance companies (as the case may be).

Eligible margin loan means an extension of credit where:

(1) The extension of credit is collateralized exclusively by liquid and readily marketable debt or equity securities, gold, or conforming residential mortgages;

(2) The collateral is marked to market daily, and the transaction is subject to daily margin maintenance requirements;

(3) The extension of credit is conducted under an agreement that provides the bank the right to accelerate and terminate the extension of credit and to liquidate or set off collateral promptly upon an event of default (including upon an event of bankruptcy, insolvency, or similar proceeding) of the counterparty, provided that, in any such case, any exercise of rights under the agreement will not be stayed or avoided under applicable law in the relevant jurisdictions;[2] and

(4) The bank has conducted sufficient legal review to conclude with a well-founded basis (and maintains sufficient written documentation of that legal review) that the agreement meets the requirements of paragraph (3) of this definition and is legal, valid, binding, and enforceable under applicable law in the relevant jurisdictions.

Eligible operational risk offsets means amounts, not to exceed expected operational loss, that:

(1) Are generated by internal business practices to absorb highly predictable and reasonably stable operational losses, including reserves calculated consistent with GAAP; and

(2) Are available to cover expected operational losses with a high degree of certainty over a one-year horizon.

Eligible purchased wholesale exposure means a purchased wholesale exposure that:

(1) The bank or securitization SPE purchased from an unaffiliated seller and did not directly or indirectly originate;

(2) Was generated on an arm's-length basis between the seller and the obligor (intercompany accounts receivable and receivables subject to contra-accounts between firms that buy and sell to each other do not satisfy this criterion);

(3) Provides the bank or securitization SPE with a claim on all proceeds from the exposure or a pro rata interest in the proceeds from the exposure;

(4) Has an M of less than one year; and

(5) When consolidated by obligor, does not represent a concentrated exposure relative to the portfolio of purchased wholesale exposures.

Eligible securitization guarantor means:

(1) A sovereign entity, the Bank for International Settlements, the International Monetary Fund, the European Central Bank, the European Commission, a Federal Home Loan Bank, Federal Agricultural Mortgage Corporation (Farmer Mac), a multilateral development bank, a depository institution, a bank holding company, a savings and loan holding company (as defined in 12 U.S.C. 1467a) provided all or substantially all of the holding company's activities are permissible for a financial holding company under 12 U.S.C. 1843(k), a foreign bank (as defined in §211.2 of the Federal Reserve Board's Regulation K (12 CFR 211.2)), or a securities firm;

---

[2] This requirement is met where all transactions under the agreement are (i) executed under U.S. law and (ii) constitute "securities contracts" under section 555 of the Bankruptcy Code (11 U.S.C. 555), qualified financial contracts under section 11(e)(8) of the Federal Deposit Insurance Act (12 U.S.C. 1821(e)(8)), or netting contracts between or among financial institutions under sections 401–407 of the Federal Deposit Insurance Corporation Improvement Act of 1991 (12 U.S.C. 4401–4407) or the Federal Reserve Board's Regulation EE (12 CFR part 231).

Federal Deposit Insurance Corporation   **Pt. 325, App. D**

(2) Any other entity (other than a securitization SPE) that has issued and outstanding an unsecured long-term debt security without credit enhancement that has a long-term applicable external rating in one of the three highest investment-grade rating categories; or

(3) Any other entity (other than a securitization SPE) that has a PD assigned by the bank that is lower than or equal to the PD associated with a long-term external rating in the third highest investment-grade rating category.

Eligible servicer cash advance facility means a servicer cash advance facility in which:

(1) The servicer is entitled to full reimbursement of advances, except that a servicer may be obligated to make non-reimbursable advances for a particular underlying exposure if any such advance is contractually limited to an insignificant amount of the outstanding principal balance of that exposure;

(2) The servicer's right to reimbursement is senior in right of payment to all other claims on the cash flows from the underlying exposures of the securitization; and

(3) The servicer has no legal obligation to, and does not, make advances to the securitization if the servicer concludes the advances are unlikely to be repaid.

Equity derivative contract means an equity-linked swap, purchased equity-linked option, forward equity-linked contract, or any other instrument linked to equities that gives rise to similar counterparty credit risks.

Equity exposure means:

(1) A security or instrument (whether voting or non-voting) that represents a direct or indirect ownership interest in, and is a residual claim on, the assets and income of a company, unless:

(i) The issuing company is consolidated with the bank under GAAP;

(ii) The bank is required to deduct the ownership interest from tier 1 or tier 2 capital under this appendix;

(iii) The ownership interest incorporates a payment or other similar obligation on the part of the issuing company (such as an obligation to make periodic payments); or

(iv) The ownership interest is a securitization exposure;

(2) A security or instrument that is mandatorily convertible into a security or instrument described in paragraph (1) of this definition;

(3) An option or warrant that is exercisable for a security or instrument described in paragraph (1) of this definition; or

(4) Any other security or instrument (other than a securitization exposure) to the extent the return on the security or instrument is based on the performance of a security or instrument described in paragraph (1) of this definition.

Excess spread for a period means:

(1) Gross finance charge collections and other income received by a securitization SPE (including market interchange fees) over a period minus interest paid to the holders of the securitization exposures, servicing fees, charge-offs, and other senior trust or similar expenses of the SPE over the period; divided by

(2) The principal balance of the underlying exposures at the end of the period.

Exchange rate derivative contract means a cross-currency interest rate swap, forward foreign-exchange contract, currency option purchased, or any other instrument linked to exchange rates that gives rise to similar counterparty credit risks.

Excluded mortgage exposure means any one-to four-family residential pre-sold construction loan for a residence for which the purchase contract is cancelled that would receive a 100 percent risk weight under section 618(a)(2) of the Resolution Trust Corporation Refinancing, Restructuring, and Improvement Act and under 12 CFR part 325, appendix A, section II.C.

Expected credit loss (ECL) means:

(1) For a wholesale exposure to a non-defaulted obligor or segment of non-defaulted retail exposures that is carried at fair value with gains and losses flowing through earnings or that is classified as held-for-sale and is carried at the lower of cost or fair value with losses flowing through earnings, zero.

(2) For all other wholesale exposures to non-defaulted obligors or segments of non-defaulted retail exposures, the product of PD times LGD times EAD for the exposure or segment.

(3) For a wholesale exposure to a defaulted obligor or segment of defaulted retail exposures, the bank's impairment estimate for allowance purposes for the exposure or segment.

(4) Total ECL is the sum of expected credit losses for all wholesale and retail exposures other than exposures for which the bank has applied the double default treatment in section 34 of this appendix.

Expected exposure (EE) means the expected value of the probability distribution of non-negative credit risk exposures to a counterparty at any specified future date before the maturity date of the longest term transaction in the netting set. Any negative market values in the probability distribution of market values to a counterparty at a specified future date are set to zero to convert the probability distribution of market values to the probability distribution of credit risk exposures.

Expected operational loss (EOL) means the expected value of the distribution of potential aggregate operational losses, as generated by the bank's operational risk quantification system using a one-year horizon.

Expected positive exposure (EPE) means the weighted average over time of expected (non-

243

negative) exposures to a counterparty where the weights are the proportion of the time interval that an individual expected exposure represents. When calculating risk-based capital requirements, the average is taken over a one-year horizon.

Exposure at default (EAD). (1) For the on-balance sheet component of a wholesale exposure or segment of retail exposures (other than an OTC derivative contract, or a repo-style transaction or eligible margin loan for which the bank determines EAD under section 32 of this appendix), EAD means:

(i) If the exposure or segment is a security classified as available-for-sale, the bank's carrying value (including net accrued but unpaid interest and fees) for the exposure or segment less any allocated transfer risk reserve for the exposure or segment, less any unrealized gains on the exposure or segment, and plus any unrealized losses on the exposure or segment; or

(ii) If the exposure or segment is not a security classified as available-for-sale, the bank's carrying value (including net accrued but unpaid interest and fees) for the exposure or segment less any allocated transfer risk reserve for the exposure or segment.

(2) For the off-balance sheet component of a wholesale exposure or segment of retail exposures (other than an OTC derivative contract, or a repo-style transaction or eligible margin loan for which the bank determines EAD under section 32 of this appendix) in the form of a loan commitment, line of credit, trade-related letter of credit, or transaction-related contingency, EAD means the bank's best estimate of net additions to the outstanding amount owed the bank, including estimated future additional draws of principal and accrued but unpaid interest and fees, that are likely to occur over a one-year horizon assuming the wholesale exposure or the retail exposures in the segment were to go into default. This estimate of net additions must reflect what would be expected during economic downturn conditions. Trade-related letters of credit are short-term, self-liquidating instruments that are used to finance the movement of goods and are collateralized by the underlying goods. Transaction-related contingencies relate to a particular transaction and include, among other things, performance bonds and performance-based letters of credit.

(3) For the off-balance sheet component of a wholesale exposure or segment of retail exposures (other than an OTC derivative contract, or a repo-style transaction or eligible margin loan for which the bank determines EAD under section 32 of this appendix) in the form of anything other than a loan commitment, line of credit, trade-related letter of credit, or transaction-related contingency, EAD means the notional amount of the exposure or segment.

(4) EAD for OTC derivative contracts is calculated as described in section 32 of this appendix. A bank also may determine EAD for repo-style transactions and eligible margin loans as described in section 32 of this appendix.

(5) For wholesale or retail exposures in which only the drawn balance has been securitized, the bank must reflect its share of the exposures' undrawn balances in EAD. Undrawn balances of revolving exposures for which the drawn balances have been securitized must be allocated between the seller's and investors' interests on a pro rata basis, based on the proportions of the seller's and investors' shares of the securitized drawn balances.

Exposure category means any of the wholesale, retail, securitization, or equity exposure categories.

External operational loss event data means, with respect to a bank, gross operational loss amounts, dates, recoveries, and relevant causal information for operational loss events occurring at organizations other than the bank.

External rating means a credit rating that is assigned by an NRSRO to an exposure, provided:

(1) The credit rating fully reflects the entire amount of credit risk with regard to all payments owed to the holder of the exposure. If a holder is owed principal and interest on an exposure, the credit rating must fully reflect the credit risk associated with timely repayment of principal and interest. If a holder is owed only principal on an exposure, the credit rating must fully reflect only the credit risk associated with timely repayment of principal; and

(2) The credit rating is published in an accessible form and is or will be included in the transition matrices made publicly available by the NRSRO that summarize the historical performance of positions rated by the NRSRO.

Financial collateral means collateral:

(1) In the form of:

(i) Cash on deposit with the bank (including cash held for the bank by a third-party custodian or trustee);

(ii) Gold bullion;

(iii) Long-term debt securities that have an applicable external rating of one category below investment grade or higher;

(iv) Short-term debt instruments that have an applicable external rating of at least investment grade;

(v) Equity securities that are publicly traded;

(vi) Convertible bonds that are publicly traded;

(vii) Money market mutual fund shares and other mutual fund shares if a price for the shares is publicly quoted daily; or

(viii) Conforming residential mortgages; and

(2) In which the bank has a perfected, first priority security interest or, outside of the United States, the legal equivalent thereof (with the exception of cash on deposit and notwithstanding the prior security interest of any custodial agent).

GAAP means generally accepted accounting principles as used in the United States.

Gain-on-sale means an increase in the equity capital (as reported on Schedule RC of the Call Report) of a bank that results from a securitization (other than an increase in equity capital that results from the bank's receipt of cash in connection with the securitization).

Guarantee means a financial guarantee, letter of credit, insurance, or other similar financial instrument (other than a credit derivative) that allows one party (beneficiary) to transfer the credit risk of one or more specific exposures (reference exposure) to another party (protection provider). See also *eligible guarantee.*

High volatility commercial real estate (HVCRE) exposure means a credit facility that finances or has financed the acquisition, development, or construction (ADC) of real property, unless the facility finances:

(1) One- to four-family residential properties; or

(2) Commercial real estate projects in which:

(i) The loan-to-value ratio is less than or equal to the applicable maximum supervisory loan-to-value ratio in the FDIC's real estate lending standards at 12 CFR part 365, appendix A.

(ii) The borrower has contributed capital to the project in the form of cash or unencumbered readily marketable assets (or has paid development expenses out-of-pocket) of at least 15 percent of the real estate's appraised "as completed" value; and

(iii) The borrower contributed the amount of capital required by paragraph (2)(ii) of this definition before the bank advances funds under the credit facility, and the capital contributed by the borrower, or internally generated by the project, is contractually required to remain in the project throughout the life of the project. The life of a project concludes only when the credit facility is converted to permanent financing or is sold or paid in full. Permanent financing may be provided by the bank that provided the ADC facility as long as the permanent financing is subject to the bank's underwriting criteria for long-term mortgage loans.

Inferred rating. A securitization exposure has an *inferred rating* equal to the external rating referenced in paragraph (2)(i) of this definition if:

(1) The securitization exposure does not have an external rating; and

(2) Another securitization exposure issued by the same issuer and secured by the same underlying exposures:

(i) Has an external rating;

(ii) Is subordinated in all respects to the unrated securitization exposure;

(iii) Does not benefit from any credit enhancement that is not available to the unrated securitization exposure; and

(iv) Has an effective remaining maturity that is equal to or longer than that of the unrated securitization exposure.

Interest rate derivative contract means a single-currency interest rate swap, basis swap, forward rate agreement, purchased interest rate option, when-issued securities, or any other instrument linked to interest rates that gives rise to similar counterparty credit risks.

Internal operational loss event data means, with respect to a bank, gross operational loss amounts, dates, recoveries, and relevant causal information for operational loss events occurring at the bank.

Investing bank means, with respect to a securitization, a bank that assumes the credit risk of a securitization exposure (other than an originating bank of the securitization). In the typical synthetic securitization, the investing bank sells credit protection on a pool of underlying exposures to the originating bank.

Investment fund means a company:

(1) All or substantially all of the assets of which are financial assets; and

(2) That has no material liabilities.

Investors' interest EAD means, with respect to a securitization, the EAD of the underlying exposures multiplied by the ratio of:

(1) The total amount of securitization exposures issued by the securitization SPE to investors; divided by

(2) The outstanding principal amount of underlying exposures.

Loss given default (LGD) means:

(1) For a wholesale exposure, the greatest of:

(i) Zero;

(ii) The bank's empirically based best estimate of the long-run default-weighted average economic loss, per dollar of EAD, the bank would expect to incur if the obligor (or a typical obligor in the loss severity grade assigned by the bank to the exposure) were to default within a one-year horizon over a mix of economic conditions, including economic downturn conditions; or

(iii) The bank's empirically based best estimate of the economic loss, per dollar of EAD, the bank would expect to incur if the obligor (or a typical obligor in the loss severity grade assigned by the bank to the exposure) were to default within a one-year horizon during economic downturn conditions.

(2) For a segment of retail exposures, the greatest of:

(i) Zero;

(ii) The bank's empirically based best estimate of the long-run default-weighted average economic loss, per dollar of EAD, the bank would expect to incur if the exposures in the segment were to default within a one-year horizon over a mix of economic conditions, including economic downturn conditions; or

(iii) The bank's empirically based best estimate of the economic loss, per dollar of EAD, the bank would expect to incur if the exposures in the segment were to default within a one-year horizon during economic downturn conditions.

(3) The economic loss on an exposure in the event of default is all material credit-related losses on the exposure (including accrued but unpaid interest or fees, losses on the sale of collateral, direct workout costs, and an appropriate allocation of indirect workout costs). Where positive or negative cash flows on a wholesale exposure to a defaulted obligor or a defaulted retail exposure (including proceeds from the sale of collateral, workout costs, additional extensions of credit to facilitate repayment of the exposure, and draw-downs of unused credit lines) occur after the date of default, the economic loss must reflect the net present value of cash flows as of the default date using a discount rate appropriate to the risk of the defaulted exposure.

Main index means the Standard & Poor's 500 Index, the FTSE All-World Index, and any other index for which the bank can demonstrate to the satisfaction of the FDIC that the equities represented in the index have comparable liquidity, depth of market, and size of bid-ask spreads as equities in the Standard & Poor's 500 Index and FTSE All-World Index.

Multilateral development bank means the International Bank for Reconstruction and Development, the International Finance Corporation, the Inter-American Development Bank, the Asian Development Bank, the African Development Bank, the European Bank for Reconstruction and Development, the European Investment Bank, the European Investment Fund, the Nordic Investment Bank, the Caribbean Development Bank, the Islamic Development Bank, the Council of Europe Development Bank, and any other multilateral lending institution or regional development bank in which the U.S. government is a shareholder or contributing member or which the FDIC determines poses comparable credit risk.

Nationally recognized statistical rating organization (NRSRO) means an entity registered with the SEC as a nationally recognized statistical rating organization under section 15E of the Securities Exchange Act of 1934 (15 U.S.C. 78o-7).

Netting set means a group of transactions with a single counterparty that are subject to a qualifying master netting agreement or qualifying cross-product master netting agreement. For purposes of the internal models methodology in paragraph (d) of section 32 of this appendix, each transaction that is not subject to such a master netting agreement is its own netting set.

N^{th}-*to-default credit derivative* means a credit derivative that provides credit protection only for the nth-defaulting reference exposure in a group of reference exposures.

Obligor means the legal entity or natural person contractually obligated on a wholesale exposure, except that a bank may treat the following exposures as having separate obligors:

(1) Exposures to the same legal entity or natural person denominated in different currencies;

(2)(i) An income-producing real estate exposure for which all or substantially all of the repayment of the exposure is reliant on the cash flows of the real estate serving as collateral for the exposure; the bank, in economic substance, does not have recourse to the borrower beyond the real estate collateral; and no cross-default or cross-acceleration clauses are in place other than clauses obtained solely out of an abundance of caution; and

(ii) Other credit exposures to the same legal entity or natural person; and

(3)(i) A wholesale exposure authorized under section 364 of the U.S. Bankruptcy Code (11 U.S.C. 364) to a legal entity or natural person who is a debtor-in-possession for purposes of Chapter 11 of the Bankruptcy Code; and

(ii) Other credit exposures to the same legal entity or natural person.

Operational loss means a loss (excluding insurance or tax effects) resulting from an operational loss event. Operational loss includes all expenses associated with an operational loss event except for opportunity costs, forgone revenue, and costs related to risk management and control enhancements implemented to prevent future operational losses.

Operational loss event means an event that results in loss and is associated with any of the following seven operational loss event type categories:

(1) Internal fraud, which means the operational loss event type category that comprises operational losses resulting from an act involving at least one internal party of a type intended to defraud, misappropriate property, or circumvent regulations, the law, or company policy, excluding diversity- and discrimination-type events.

(2) External fraud, which means the operational loss event type category that comprises operational losses resulting from an act by a third party of a type intended to defraud, misappropriate property, or circumvent the law. Retail credit card losses arising from non-contractual, third-party

Federal Deposit Insurance Corporation

initiated fraud (for example, identity theft) are external fraud operational losses. All other third-party initiated credit losses are to be treated as credit risk losses.

(3) Employment practices and workplace safety, which means the operational loss event type category that comprises operational losses resulting from an act inconsistent with employment, health, or safety laws or agreements, payment of personal injury claims, or payment arising from diversity- and discrimination-type events.

(4) Clients, products, and business practices, which means the operational loss event type category that comprises operational losses resulting from the nature or design of a product or from an unintentional or negligent failure to meet a professional obligation to specific clients (including fiduciary and suitability requirements).

(5) Damage to physical assets, which means the operational loss event type category that comprises operational losses resulting from the loss of or damage to physical assets from natural disaster or other events.

(6) Business disruption and system failures, which means the operational loss event type category that comprises operational losses resulting from disruption of business or system failures.

(7) Execution, delivery, and process management, which means the operational loss event type category that comprises operational losses resulting from failed transaction processing or process management or losses arising from relations with trade counterparties and vendors.

Operational risk means the risk of loss resulting from inadequate or failed internal processes, people, and systems or from external events (including legal risk but excluding strategic and reputational risk).

Operational risk exposure means the 99.9th percentile of the distribution of potential aggregate operational losses, as generated by the bank's operational risk quantification system over a one-year horizon (and not incorporating eligible operational risk offsets or qualifying operational risk mitigants).

Originating bank, with respect to a securitization, means a bank that:

(1) Directly or indirectly originated or securitized the underlying exposures included in the securitization; or

(2) Serves as an ABCP program sponsor to the securitization.

Other retail exposure means an exposure (other than a securitization exposure, an equity exposure, a residential mortgage exposure, an excluded mortgage exposure, a qualifying revolving exposure, or the residual value portion of a lease exposure) that is managed as part of a segment of exposures with homogeneous risk characteristics, not on an individual-exposure basis, and is either:

(1) An exposure to an individual for non-business purposes; or

(2) An exposure to an individual or company for business purposes if the bank's consolidated business credit exposure to the individual or company is $1 million or less.

Over-the-counter (OTC) derivative contract means a derivative contract that is not traded on an exchange that requires the daily receipt and payment of cash-variation margin.

Probability of default (PD) means:

(1) For a wholesale exposure to a non-defaulted obligor, the bank's empirically based best estimate of the long-run average one-year default rate for the rating grade assigned by the bank to the obligor, capturing the average default experience for obligors in the rating grade over a mix of economic conditions (including economic downturn conditions) sufficient to provide a reasonable estimate of the average one-year default rate over the economic cycle for the rating grade.

(2) For a segment of non-defaulted retail exposures, the bank's empirically based best estimate of the long-run average one-year default rate for the exposures in the segment, capturing the average default experience for exposures in the segment over a mix of economic conditions (including economic downturn conditions) sufficient to provide a reasonable estimate of the average one-year default rate over the economic cycle for the segment and adjusted upward as appropriate for segments for which seasoning effects are material. For purposes of this definition, a segment for which seasoning effects are material is a segment where there is a material relationship between the time since origination of exposures within the segment and the bank's best estimate of the long-run average one-year default rate for the exposures in the segment.

(3) For a wholesale exposure to a defaulted obligor or segment of defaulted retail exposures, 100 percent.

Protection amount (P) means, with respect to an exposure hedged by an eligible guarantee or eligible credit derivative, the effective notional amount of the guarantee or credit derivative, reduced to reflect any currency mismatch, maturity mismatch, or lack of restructuring coverage (as provided in section 33 of this appendix).

Publicly traded means traded on:

(1) Any exchange registered with the SEC as a national securities exchange under section 6 of the Securities Exchange Act of 1934 (15 U.S.C. 78f); or

(2) Any non-U.S.-based securities exchange that:

(i) Is registered with, or approved by, a national securities regulatory authority; and

(ii) Provides a liquid, two-way market for the instrument in question, meaning that there are enough independent bona fide offers to buy and sell so that a sales price reasonably related to the last sales price or current bona fide competitive bid and offer quotations can be determined promptly and a trade can be settled at such a price within five business days.

Qualifying central counterparty means a counterparty (for example, a clearinghouse) that:

(1) Facilitates trades between counterparties in one or more financial markets by either guaranteeing trades or novating contracts;

(2) Requires all participants in its arrangements to be fully collateralized on a daily basis; and

(3) The bank demonstrates to the satisfaction of the FDIC is in sound financial condition and is subject to effective oversight by a national supervisory authority.

Qualifying cross-product master netting agreement means a qualifying master netting agreement that provides for termination and close-out netting across multiple types of financial transactions or qualifying master netting agreements in the event of a counterparty's default, provided that:

(1) The underlying financial transactions are OTC derivative contracts, eligible margin loans, or repo-style transactions; and

(2) The bank obtains a written legal opinion verifying the validity and enforceability of the agreement under applicable law of the relevant jurisdictions if the counterparty fails to perform upon an event of default, including upon an event of bankruptcy, insolvency, or similar proceeding.

Qualifying master netting agreement means any written, legally enforceable bilateral agreement, provided that:

(1) The agreement creates a single legal obligation for all individual transactions covered by the agreement upon an event of default, including bankruptcy, insolvency, or similar proceeding, of the counterparty;

(2) The agreement provides the bank the right to accelerate, terminate, and close-out on a net basis all transactions under the agreement and to liquidate or set off collateral promptly upon an event of default, including upon an event of bankruptcy, insolvency, or similar proceeding, of the counterparty, provided that, in any such case, any exercise of rights under the agreement will not be stayed or avoided under applicable law in the relevant jurisdictions; and

(3) The bank has conducted sufficient legal review to conclude with a well-founded basis (and maintains sufficient written documentation of that legal review) that:

(i) The agreement meets the requirements of paragraph (2) of this definition; and

(ii) In the event of a legal challenge (including one resulting from default or from bankruptcy, insolvency, or similar proceeding) the relevant court and administrative authorities would find the agreement to be legal, valid, binding, and enforceable under the law of the relevant jurisdictions;

(4) The bank establishes and maintains procedures to monitor possible changes in relevant law and to ensure that the agreement continues to satisfy the requirements of this definition; and

(5) The agreement does not contain a walkaway clause (that is, a provision that permits a non-defaulting counterparty to make a lower payment than it would make otherwise under the agreement, or no payment at all, to a defaulter or the estate of a defaulter, even if the defaulter or the estate of the defaulter is a net creditor under the agreement).

Qualifying revolving exposure (QRE) means an exposure (other than a securitization exposure or equity exposure) to an individual that is managed as part of a segment of exposures with homogeneous risk characteristics, not on an individual-exposure basis, and:

(1) Is revolving (that is, the amount outstanding fluctuates, determined largely by the borrower's decision to borrow and repay, up to a pre-established maximum amount);

(2) Is unsecured and unconditionally cancelable by the bank to the fullest extent permitted by Federal law; and

(3) Has a maximum exposure amount (drawn plus undrawn) of up to $100,000.

Repo-style transaction means a repurchase or reverse repurchase transaction, or a securities borrowing or securities lending transaction, including a transaction in which the bank acts as agent for a customer and indemnifies the customer against loss, provided that:

(1) The transaction is based solely on liquid and readily marketable securities, cash, gold, or conforming residential mortgages;

(2) The transaction is marked-to-market daily and subject to daily margin maintenance requirements;

(3)(i) The transaction is a "securities contract" or "repurchase agreement" under section 555 or 559, respectively, of the Bankruptcy Code (11 U.S.C. 555 or 559), a qualified financial contract under section 11(e)(8) of the Federal Deposit Insurance Act (12 U.S.C. 1821(e)(8)), or a netting contract between or among financial institutions under sections 401–407 of the Federal Deposit Insurance Corporation Improvement Act of 1991 (12 U.S.C. 4401–4407) or the Federal Reserve Board's Regulation EE (12 CFR part 231); or

(ii) If the transaction does not meet the criteria set forth in paragraph (3)(i) of this definition, then either:

(A) The transaction is executed under an agreement that provides the bank the right to accelerate, terminate, and close-out the transaction on a net basis and to liquidate or set off collateral promptly upon an event of default (including upon an event of bankruptcy, insolvency, or similar proceeding) of the counterparty, provided that, in any such case, any exercise of rights under the agreement will not be stayed or avoided under applicable law in the relevant jurisdictions; or

(B) The transaction is:

(*1*) Either overnight or unconditionally cancelable at any time by the bank; and

(*2*) Executed under an agreement that provides the bank the right to accelerate, terminate, and close-out the transaction on a net basis and to liquidate or set off collateral promptly upon an event of counterparty default; and

(*4*) The bank has conducted sufficient legal review to conclude with a well-founded basis (and maintains sufficient written documentation of that legal review) that the agreement meets the requirements of paragraph (3) of this definition and is legal, valid, binding, and enforceable under applicable law in the relevant jurisdictions.

Residential mortgage exposure means an exposure (other than a securitization exposure, equity exposure, or excluded mortgage exposure) that is managed as part of a segment of exposures with homogeneous risk characteristics, not on an individual-exposure basis, and is:

(1) An exposure that is primarily secured by a first or subsequent lien on one- to four-family residential property; or

(2) An exposure with an original and outstanding amount of $1 million or less that is primarily secured by a first or subsequent lien on residential property that is not one to four family.

Retail exposure means a residential mortgage exposure, a qualifying revolving exposure, or an other retail exposure.

Retail exposure subcategory means the residential mortgage exposure, qualifying revolving exposure, or other retail exposure subcategory.

Risk parameter means a variable used in determining risk-based capital requirements for wholesale and retail exposures, specifically probability of default (PD), loss given default (LGD), exposure at default (EAD), or effective maturity (M).

Scenario analysis means a systematic process of obtaining expert opinions from business managers and risk management experts to derive reasoned assessments of the likelihood and loss impact of plausible high-severity operational losses. Scenario analysis may include the well-reasoned evaluation and use of external operational loss event data, adjusted as appropriate to ensure relevance to a bank's operational risk profile and control structure.

SEC means the U.S. Securities and Exchange Commission.

Securitization means a traditional securitization or a synthetic securitization.

Securitization exposure means an on-balance sheet or off-balance sheet credit exposure that arises from a traditional or synthetic securitization (including credit-enhancing representations and warranties).

Securitization special purpose entity (securitization SPE) means a corporation, trust, or other entity organized for the specific purpose of holding underlying exposures of a securitization, the activities of which are limited to those appropriate to accomplish this purpose, and the structure of which is intended to isolate the underlying exposures held by the entity from the credit risk of the seller of the underlying exposures to the entity.

Senior securitization exposure means a securitization exposure that has a first priority claim on the cash flows from the underlying exposures. When determining whether a securitization exposure has a first priority claim on the cash flows from the underlying exposures, a bank is not required to consider amounts due under interest rate or currency derivative contracts, fees due, or other similar payments. Both the most senior commercial paper issued by an ABCP program and a liquidity facility that supports the ABCP program may be senior securitization exposures if the liquidity facility provider's right to reimbursement of the drawn amounts is senior to all claims on the cash flows from the underlying exposures except amounts due under interest rate or currency derivative contracts, fees due, or other similar payments.

Servicer cash advance facility means a facility under which the servicer of the underlying exposures of a securitization may advance cash to ensure an uninterrupted flow of payments to investors in the securitization, including advances made to cover foreclosure costs or other expenses to facilitate the timely collection of the underlying exposures. See also *eligible servicer cash advance facility*.

Sovereign entity means a central government (including the U.S. government) or an agency, department, ministry, or central bank of a central government.

Sovereign exposure means:

(1) A direct exposure to a sovereign entity; or

(2) An exposure directly and unconditionally backed by the full faith and credit of a sovereign entity.

Subsidiary means, with respect to a company, a company controlled by that company.

Synthetic securitization means a transaction in which:

(1) All or a portion of the credit risk of one or more underlying exposures is transferred to one or more third parties through the use of one or more credit derivatives or guarantees (other than a guarantee that transfers

only the credit risk of an individual retail exposure);

(2) The credit risk associated with the underlying exposures has been separated into at least two tranches reflecting different levels of seniority;

(3) Performance of the securitization exposures depends upon the performance of the underlying exposures; and

(4) All or substantially all of the underlying exposures are financial exposures (such as loans, commitments, credit derivatives, guarantees, receivables, asset-backed securities, mortgage-backed securities, other debt securities, or equity securities).

Tier 1 capital is defined in 12 CFR part 325, appendix A, as modified in part II of this appendix.

Tier 2 capital is defined in 12 CFR part 325, appendix A, as modified in part II of this appendix.

Total qualifying capital means the sum of tier 1 capital and tier 2 capital, after all deductions required in this appendix.

Total risk-weighted assets means:

(1) The sum of:

(i) Credit risk-weighted assets; and

(ii) Risk-weighted assets for operational risk; minus

(2) Excess eligible credit reserves not included in tier 2 capital.

Total wholesale and retail risk-weighted assets means the sum of risk-weighted assets for wholesale exposures to non-defaulted obligors and segments of non-defaulted retail exposures; risk-weighted assets for wholesale exposures to defaulted obligors and segments of defaulted retail exposures; risk-weighted assets for assets not defined by an exposure category; and risk-weighted assets for nonmaterial portfolios of exposures (all as determined in section 31 of this appendix) and risk-weighted assets for unsettled transactions (as determined in section 35 of this appendix) minus the amounts deducted from capital pursuant to 12 CFR part 325, appendix A (excluding those deductions reversed in section 12 of this appendix).

Traditional securitization means a transaction in which:

(1) All or a portion of the credit risk of one or more underlying exposures is transferred to one or more third parties other than through the use of credit derivatives or guarantees;

(2) The credit risk associated with the underlying exposures has been separated into at least two tranches reflecting different levels of seniority;

(3) Performance of the securitization exposures depends upon the performance of the underlying exposures;

(4) All or substantially all of the underlying exposures are financial exposures (such as loans, commitments, credit derivatives, guarantees, receivables, asset-backed securities, mortgage-backed securities, other debt securities, or equity securities);

(5) The underlying exposures are not owned by an operating company;

(6) The underlying exposures are not owned by a small business investment company described in section 302 of the Small Business Investment Act of 1958 (15 U.S.C. 682); and

(7) The underlying exposures are not owned by a firm an investment in which qualifies as a community development investment under 12 U.S.C. 24(Eleventh).

(8) The FDIC may determine that a transaction in which the underlying exposures are owned by an investment firm that exercises substantially unfettered control over the size and composition of its assets, liabilities, and off-balance sheet exposures is not a traditional securitization based on the transaction's leverage, risk profile, or economic substance.

(9) The FDIC may deem a transaction that meets the definition of a traditional securitization, notwithstanding paragraph (5), (6), or (7) of this definition, to be a traditional securitization based on the transaction's leverage, risk profile, or economic substance.

Tranche means all securitization exposures associated with a securitization that have the same seniority level.

Underlying exposures means one or more exposures that have been securitized in a securitization transaction.

Unexpected operational loss (UOL) means the difference between the bank's operational risk exposure and the bank's expected operational loss.

Unit of measure means the level (for example, organizational unit or operational loss event type) at which the bank's operational risk quantification system generates a separate distribution of potential operational losses.

Value-at-Risk (VaR) means the estimate of the maximum amount that the value of one or more exposures could decline due to market price or rate movements during a fixed holding period within a stated confidence interval.

Wholesale exposure means a credit exposure to a company, natural person, sovereign entity, or governmental entity (other than a securitization exposure, retail exposure, excluded mortgage exposure, or equity exposure). Examples of a wholesale exposure include:

(1) A non-tranched guarantee issued by a bank on behalf of a company;

(2) A repo-style transaction entered into by a bank with a company and any other transaction in which a bank posts collateral to a company and faces counterparty credit risk;

(3) An exposure that a bank treats as a covered position under 12 CFR part 325, appendix C for which there is a counterparty credit risk capital requirement;

Federal Deposit Insurance Corporation

Pt. 325, App. D

(4) A sale of corporate loans by a bank to a third party in which the bank retains full recourse;

(5) An OTC derivative contract entered into by a bank with a company;

(6) An exposure to an individual that is not managed by a bank as part of a segment of exposures with homogeneous risk characteristics; and

(7) A commercial lease.

Wholesale exposure subcategory means the HVCRE or non-HVCRE wholesale exposure subcategory.

Section 3. Minimum Risk-Based Capital Requirements

(a)(1) Except as modified by paragraph (c) of this section or by section 23 of this appendix, each bank must meet a minimum:

(i) Total risk-based capital ratio of 8.0 percent; and

(ii) Tier 1 risk-based capital ratio of 4.0 percent.

(2) A bank's total risk-based capital ratio is the lower of:

(i) Its total qualifying capital to total risk-weighted assets, and

(ii) Its total risk-based capital ratio as calculated under appendix A of this part.

(3) A bank's tier 1 risk-based capital ratio is the lower of:

(i) Its tier 1 capital to total risk-weighted assets, and

(ii) Its tier 1 risk-based capital ratio as calculated under appendix A of this part.

(b) Each bank must hold capital commensurate with the level and nature of all risks to which the bank is exposed.

(c) When a bank subject to appendix C of this part calculates its risk-based capital requirements under this appendix, the bank must also refer to appendix C of this part for supplemental rules to calculate risk-based capital requirements adjusted for market risk.

PART II. QUALIFYING CAPITAL

Section 11. Additional Deductions

(a) *General.* A bank that uses this appendix must make the same deductions from its tier 1 capital and tier 2 capital required in 12 CFR part 325, appendix A, except that:

(1) A bank is not required to deduct certain equity investments and CEIOs (as provided in section 12 of this appendix); and

(2) A bank also must make the deductions from capital required by paragraphs (b) and (c) of this section.

(b) *Deductions from tier 1 capital.* A bank must deduct from tier 1 capital any gain-on-sale associated with a securitization exposure as provided in paragraph (a) of section 41 and paragraphs (a)(1), (c), (g)(1), and (h)(1) of section 42 of this appendix.

(c) *Deductions from tier 1 and tier 2 capital.* A bank must deduct the exposures specified in paragraphs (c)(1) through (c)(7) in this section 50 percent from tier 1 capital and 50 percent from tier 2 capital. If the amount deductible from tier 2 capital exceeds the bank's actual tier 2 capital, however, the bank must deduct the excess from tier 1 capital.

(1) *Credit-enhancing interest-only strips (CEIOs).* In accordance with paragraphs (a)(1) and (c) of section 42 of this appendix, any CEIO that does not constitute gain-on-sale.

(2) *Non-qualifying securitization exposures.* In accordance with paragraphs (a)(4) and (c) of section 42 of this appendix, any securitization exposure that does not qualify for the Ratings-Based Approach, the Internal Assessment Approach, or the Supervisory Formula Approach under sections 43, 44, and 45 of this appendix, respectively.

(3) *Securitizations of non-IRB exposures.* In accordance with paragraphs (c) and (g)(4) of section 42 of this appendix, certain exposures to a securitization any underlying exposure of which is not a wholesale exposure, retail exposure, securitization exposure, or equity exposure.

(4) *Low-rated securitization exposures.* In accordance with section 43 and paragraph (c) of section 42 of this appendix, any securitization exposure that qualifies for and must be deducted under the Ratings-Based Approach.

(5) *High-risk securitization exposures subject to the Supervisory Formula Approach.* In accordance with paragraphs (b) and (c) of section 45 of this appendix and paragraph (c) of section 42 of this appendix, certain high-risk securitization exposures (or portions thereof) that qualify for the Supervisory Formula Approach.

(6) *Eligible credit reserves shortfall.* In accordance with paragraph (a)(1) of section 13 of this appendix, any eligible credit reserves shortfall.

(7) *Certain failed capital markets transactions.* In accordance with paragraph (e)(3) of section 35 of this appendix, the bank's exposure on certain failed capital markets transactions.

Section 12. Deductions and Limitations Not Required

(a) *Deduction of CEIOs.* A bank is not required to make the deductions from capital for CEIOs in 12 CFR part 325, appendix A, section II.B.5.

(b) *Deduction for certain equity investments.* A bank is not required to make the deductions from capital for nonfinancial equity investments in 12 CFR part 325, appendix A, section II.B.

Section 13. Eligible Credit Reserves

(a) *Comparison of eligible credit reserves to expected credit losses*—(1) *Shortfall of eligible* credit reserves. If a bank's eligible credit reserves are less than the bank's total expected credit losses, the bank must deduct the shortfall amount 50 percent from tier 1 capital and 50 percent from tier 2 capital. If the amount deductible from tier 2 capital exceeds the bank's actual tier 2 capital, the bank must deduct the excess amount from tier 1 capital.

(2) *Excess eligible credit reserves.* If a bank's eligible credit reserves exceed the bank's total expected credit losses, the bank may include the excess amount in tier 2 capital to the extent that the excess amount does not exceed 0.6 percent of the bank's credit-risk-weighted assets.

(b) *Treatment of allowance for loan and lease losses.* Regardless of any provision in 12 CFR part 325, appendix A, the ALLL is included in tier 2 capital only to the extent provided in paragraph (a)(2) of this section and in section 24 of this appendix.

PART III. QUALIFICATION

Section 21. Qualification Process

(a) *Timing.* (1) A bank that is described in paragraph (b)(1) of section 1 of this appendix must adopt a written implementation plan no later than six months after the later of April 1, 2008, or the date the bank meets a criterion in that section. The implementation plan must incorporate an explicit first floor period start date no later than 36 months after the later of April 1, 2008, or the date the bank meets at least one criterion under paragraph (b)(1) of section 1 of this appendix. The FDIC may extend the first floor period start date.

(2) A bank that elects to be subject to this appendix under paragraph (b)(2) of section 1 of this appendix must adopt a written implementation plan.

(b) *Implementation plan.* (1) The bank's implementation plan must address in detail how the bank complies, or plans to comply, with the qualification requirements in section 22 of this appendix. The bank also must maintain a comprehensive and sound planning and governance process to oversee the implementation efforts described in the plan. At a minimum, the plan must:

(i) Comprehensively address the qualification requirements in section 22 of this appendix for the bank and each consolidated subsidiary (U.S. and foreign-based) of the bank with respect to all portfolios and exposures of the bank and each of its consolidated subsidiaries;

(ii) Justify and support any proposed temporary or permanent exclusion of business lines, portfolios, or exposures from application of the advanced approaches in this appendix (which business lines, portfolios, and exposures must be, in the aggregate, immaterial to the bank);

(iii) Include the bank's self-assessment of:

(A) The bank's current status in meeting the qualification requirements in section 22 of this appendix; and

(B) The consistency of the bank's current practices with the FDIC's supervisory guidance on the qualification requirements;

(iv) Based on the bank's self-assessment, identify and describe the areas in which the bank proposes to undertake additional work to comply with the qualification requirements in section 22 of this appendix or to improve the consistency of the bank's current practices with the FDIC's supervisory guidance on the qualification requirements (gap analysis);

(v) Describe what specific actions the bank will take to address the areas identified in the gap analysis required by paragraph (b)(1)(iv) of this section;

(vi) Identify objective, measurable milestones, including delivery dates and a date when the bank's implementation of the methodologies described in this appendix will be fully operational;

(vii) Describe resources that have been budgeted and are available to implement the plan; and

(viii) Receive approval of the bank's board of directors.

(2) The bank must submit the implementation plan, together with a copy of the minutes of the board of directors' approval, to the FDIC at least 60 days before the bank proposes to begin its parallel run, unless the FDIC waives prior notice.

(c) *Parallel run.* Before determining its risk-based capital requirements under this appendix and following adoption of the implementation plan, the bank must conduct a satisfactory parallel run. A satisfactory parallel run is a period of no less than four consecutive calendar quarters during which the bank complies with the qualification requirements in section 22 of this appendix to the satisfaction of the FDIC. During the parallel run, the bank must report to the FDIC on a calendar quarterly basis its risk-based capital ratios using 12 CFR part 325, appendix A and the risk-based capital requirements described in this appendix. During this period, the bank is subject to 12 CFR part 325, appendix A.

(d) *Approval to calculate risk-based capital requirements under this appendix.* The FDIC will notify the bank of the date that the bank may begin its first floor period if the FDIC determines that:

(1) The bank fully complies with all the qualification requirements in section 22 of this appendix;

(2) The bank has conducted a satisfactory parallel run under paragraph (c) of this section; and

(3) The bank has an adequate process to ensure ongoing compliance with the qualification requirements in section 22 of this appendix.

Federal Deposit Insurance Corporation
Pt. 325, App. D

Section 22. Qualification Requirements

(a) *Process and systems requirements.* (1) A bank must have a rigorous process for assessing its overall capital adequacy in relation to its risk profile and a comprehensive strategy for maintaining an appropriate level of capital.

(2) The systems and processes used by a bank for risk-based capital purposes under this appendix must be consistent with the bank's internal risk management processes and management information reporting systems.

(3) Each bank must have an appropriate infrastructure with risk measurement and management processes that meet the qualification requirements of this section and are appropriate given the bank's size and level of complexity. Regardless of whether the systems and models that generate the risk parameters necessary for calculating a bank's risk-based capital requirements are located at any affiliate of the bank, the bank itself must ensure that the risk parameters and reference data used to determine its risk-based capital requirements are representative of its own credit risk and operational risk exposures.

(b) *Risk rating and segmentation systems for wholesale and retail exposures.* (1) A bank must have an internal risk rating and segmentation system that accurately and reliably differentiates among degrees of credit risk for the bank's wholesale and retail exposures.

(2) For wholesale exposures:

(i) A bank must have an internal risk rating system that accurately and reliably assigns each obligor to a single rating grade (reflecting the obligor's likelihood of default). A bank may elect, however, not to assign to a rating grade an obligor to whom the bank extends credit based solely on the financial strength of a guarantor, provided that all of the bank's exposures to the obligor are fully covered by eligible guarantees, the bank applies the PD substitution approach in paragraph (c)(1) of section 33 of this appendix to all exposures to that obligor, and the bank immediately assigns the obligor to a rating grade if a guarantee can no longer be recognized under this appendix. The bank's wholesale obligor rating system must have at least seven discrete rating grades for non-defaulted obligors and at least one rating grade for defaulted obligors.

(ii) Unless the bank has chosen to directly assign LGD estimates to each wholesale exposure, the bank must have an internal risk rating system that accurately and reliably assigns each wholesale exposure to a loss severity rating grade (reflecting the bank's estimate of the LGD of the exposure). A bank employing loss severity rating grades must have a sufficiently granular loss severity grading system to avoid grouping together exposures with widely ranging LGDs.

(3) For retail exposures, a bank must have an internal system that groups retail exposures into the appropriate retail exposure subcategory, groups the retail exposures in each retail exposure subcategory into separate segments with homogeneous risk characteristics, and assigns accurate and reliable PD and LGD estimates for each segment on a consistent basis. The bank's system must identify and group in separate segments by subcategories exposures identified in paragraphs (c)(2)(ii) and (iii) of section 31 of this appendix.

(4) The bank's internal risk rating policy for wholesale exposures must describe the bank's rating philosophy (that is, must describe how wholesale obligor rating assignments are affected by the bank's choice of the range of economic, business, and industry conditions that are considered in the obligor rating process).

(5) The bank's internal risk rating system for wholesale exposures must provide for the review and update (as appropriate) of each obligor rating and (if applicable) each loss severity rating whenever the bank receives new material information, but no less frequently than annually. The bank's retail exposure segmentation system must provide for the review and update (as appropriate) of assignments of retail exposures to segments whenever the bank receives new material information, but generally no less frequently than quarterly.

(c) *Quantification of risk parameters for wholesale and retail exposures.* (1) The bank must have a comprehensive risk parameter quantification process that produces accurate, timely, and reliable estimates of the risk parameters for the bank's wholesale and retail exposures.

(2) Data used to estimate the risk parameters must be relevant to the bank's actual wholesale and retail exposures, and of sufficient quality to support the determination of risk-based capital requirements for the exposures.

(3) The bank's risk parameter quantification process must produce appropriately conservative risk parameter estimates where the bank has limited relevant data, and any adjustments that are part of the quantification process must not result in a pattern of bias toward lower risk parameter estimates.

(4) The bank's risk parameter estimation process should not rely on the possibility of U.S. government financial assistance, except for the financial assistance that the U.S. government has a legally binding commitment to provide.

(5) Where the bank's quantifications of LGD directly or indirectly incorporate estimates of the effectiveness of its credit risk management practices in reducing its exposure to troubled obligors prior to default, the

253

bank must support such estimates with empirical analysis showing that the estimates are consistent with its historical experience in dealing with such exposures during economic downturn conditions.

(6) PD estimates for wholesale obligors and retail segments must be based on at least five years of default data. LGD estimates for wholesale exposures must be based on at least seven years of loss severity data, and LGD estimates for retail segments must be based on at least five years of loss severity data. EAD estimates for wholesale exposures must be based on at least seven years of exposure amount data, and EAD estimates for retail segments must be based on at least five years of exposure amount data.

(7) Default, loss severity, and exposure amount data must include periods of economic downturn conditions, or the bank must adjust its estimates of risk parameters to compensate for the lack of data from periods of economic downturn conditions.

(8) The bank's PD, LGD, and EAD estimates must be based on the definition of default in this appendix.

(9) The bank must review and update (as appropriate) its risk parameters and its risk parameter quantification process at least annually.

(10) The bank must at least annually conduct a comprehensive review and analysis of reference data to determine relevance of reference data to the bank's exposures, quality of reference data to support PD, LGD, and EAD estimates, and consistency of reference data to the definition of default contained in this appendix.

(d) *Counterparty credit risk model.* A bank must obtain the prior written approval of the FDIC under section 32 of this appendix to use the internal models methodology for counterparty credit risk.

(e) *Double default treatment.* A bank must obtain the prior written approval of the FDIC under section 34 of this appendix to use the double default treatment.

(f) *Securitization exposures.* A bank must obtain the prior written approval of the FDIC under section 44 of this appendix to use the Internal Assessment Approach for securitization exposures to ABCP programs.

(g) *Equity exposures model.* A bank must obtain the prior written approval of the FDIC under section 53 of this appendix to use the Internal Models Approach for equity exposures.

(h) *Operational risk*—(1) *Operational risk management processes.* A bank must:

(i) Have an operational risk management function that:

(A) Is independent of business line management; and

(B) Is responsible for designing, implementing, and overseeing the bank's operational risk data and assessment systems, operational risk quantification systems, and related processes;

(ii) Have and document a process (which must capture business environment and internal control factors affecting the bank's operational risk profile) to identify, measure, monitor, and control operational risk in bank products, activities, processes, and systems; and

(iii) Report operational risk exposures, operational loss events, and other relevant operational risk information to business unit management, senior management, and the board of directors (or a designated committee of the board).

(2) *Operational risk data and assessment systems.* A bank must have operational risk data and assessment systems that capture operational risks to which the bank is exposed. The bank's operational risk data and assessment systems must:

(i) Be structured in a manner consistent with the bank's current business activities, risk profile, technological processes, and risk management processes; and

(ii) Include credible, transparent, systematic, and verifiable processes that incorporate the following elements on an ongoing basis:

(A) *Internal operational loss event data.* The bank must have a systematic process for capturing and using internal operational loss event data in its operational risk data and assessment systems.

(*1*) The bank's operational risk data and assessment systems must include a historical observation period of at least five years for internal operational loss event data (or such shorter period approved by the FDIC to address transitional situations, such as integrating a new business line).

(*2*) The bank must be able to map its internal operational loss event data into the seven operational loss event type categories.

(*3*) The bank may refrain from collecting internal operational loss event data for individual operational losses below established dollar threshold amounts if the bank can demonstrate to the satisfaction of the FDIC that the thresholds are reasonable, do not exclude important internal operational loss event data, and permit the bank to capture substantially all the dollar value of the bank's operational losses.

(B) *External operational loss event data.* The bank must have a systematic process for determining its methodologies for incorporating external operational loss event data into its operational risk data and assessment systems.

(C) *Scenario analysis.* The bank must have a systematic process for determining its methodologies for incorporating scenario analysis into its operational risk data and assessment systems.

Federal Deposit Insurance Corporation

(D) *Business environment and internal control factors.* The bank must incorporate business environment and internal control factors into its operational risk data and assessment systems. The bank must also periodically compare the results of its prior business environment and internal control factor assessments against its actual operational losses incurred in the intervening period.

(3) *Operational risk quantification systems.* (i) The bank's operational risk quantification systems:

(A) Must generate estimates of the bank's operational risk exposure using its operational risk data and assessment systems;

(B) Must employ a unit of measure that is appropriate for the bank's range of business activities and the variety of operational loss events to which it is exposed, and that does not combine business activities or operational loss events with demonstrably different risk profiles within the same loss distribution;

(C) Must include a credible, transparent, systematic, and verifiable approach for weighting each of the four elements, described in paragraph (h)(2)(ii) of this section, that a bank is required to incorporate into its operational risk data and assessment systems;

(D) May use internal estimates of dependence among operational losses across and within units of measure if the bank can demonstrate to the satisfaction of the FDIC that its process for estimating dependence is sound, robust to a variety of scenarios, and implemented with integrity, and allows for the uncertainty surrounding the estimates. If the bank has not made such a demonstration, it must sum operational risk exposure estimates across units of measure to calculate its total operational risk exposure; and

(E) Must be reviewed and updated (as appropriate) whenever the bank becomes aware of information that may have a material effect on the bank's estimate of operational risk exposure, but the review and update must occur no less frequently than annually.

(ii) With the prior written approval of the FDIC, a bank may generate an estimate of its operational risk exposure using an alternative approach to that specified in paragraph (h)(3)(i) of this section. A bank proposing to use such an alternative operational risk quantification system must submit a proposal to the FDIC. In determining whether to approve a bank's proposal to use an alternative operational risk quantification system, the FDIC will consider the following principles:

(A) Use of the alternative operational risk quantification system will be allowed only on an exception basis, considering the size, complexity, and risk profile of the bank;

(B) The bank must demonstrate that its estimate of its operational risk exposure generated under the alternative operational risk quantification system is appropriate and can be supported empirically; and

(C) A bank must not use an allocation of operational risk capital requirements that includes entities other than depository institutions or the benefits of diversification across entities.

(i) *Data management and maintenance.* (1) A bank must have data management and maintenance systems that adequately support all aspects of its advanced systems and the timely and accurate reporting of risk-based capital requirements.

(2) A bank must retain data using an electronic format that allows timely retrieval of data for analysis, validation, reporting, and disclosure purposes.

(3) A bank must retain sufficient data elements related to key risk drivers to permit adequate monitoring, validation, and refinement of its advanced systems.

(j) *Control, oversight, and validation mechanisms.* (1) The bank's senior management must ensure that all components of the bank's advanced systems function effectively and comply with the qualification requirements in this section.

(2) The bank's board of directors (or a designated committee of the board) must at least annually review the effectiveness of, and approve, the bank's advanced systems.

(3) A bank must have an effective system of controls and oversight that:

(i) Ensures ongoing compliance with the qualification requirements in this section;

(ii) Maintains the integrity, reliability, and accuracy of the bank's advanced systems; and

(iii) Includes adequate governance and project management processes.

(4) The bank must validate, on an ongoing basis, its advanced systems. The bank's validation process must be independent of the advanced systems' development, implementation, and operation, or the validation process must be subjected to an independent review of its adequacy and effectiveness. Validation must include:

(i) An evaluation of the conceptual soundness of (including developmental evidence supporting) the advanced systems;

(ii) An ongoing monitoring process that includes verification of processes and benchmarking; and

(iii) An outcomes analysis process that includes back-testing.

(5) The bank must have an internal audit function independent of business-line management that at least annually assesses the effectiveness of the controls supporting the bank's advanced systems and reports its findings to the bank's board of directors (or a committee thereof).

(6) The bank must periodically stress test its advanced systems. The stress testing

must include a consideration of how economic cycles, especially downturns, affect risk-based capital requirements (including migration across rating grades and segments and the credit risk mitigation benefits of double default treatment).

(k) *Documentation.* The bank must adequately document all material aspects of its advanced systems.

Section 23. Ongoing Qualification

(a) *Changes to advanced systems.* A bank must meet all the qualification requirements in section 22 of this appendix on an ongoing basis. A bank must notify the FDIC when the bank makes any change to an advanced system that would result in a material change in the bank's risk-weighted asset amount for an exposure type, or when the bank makes any significant change to its modeling assumptions.

(b) *Failure to comply with qualification requirements.* (1) If the FDIC determines that a bank that uses this appendix and has conducted a satisfactory parallel run fails to comply with the qualification requirements in section 22 of this appendix, the FDIC will notify the bank in writing of the bank's failure to comply.

(2) The bank must establish and submit a plan satisfactory to the FDIC to return to compliance with the qualification requirements.

(3) In addition, if the FDIC determines that the bank's risk-based capital requirements are not commensurate with the bank's credit, market, operational, or other risks, the FDIC may require such a bank to calculate its risk-based capital requirements:

(i) Under 12 CFR part 325, appendix A; or

(ii) Under this appendix with any modifications provided by the FDIC.

Section 24. Merger and Acquisition Transitional Arrangements

(a) *Mergers and acquisitions of companies without advanced systems.* If a bank merges with or acquires a company that does not calculate its risk-based capital requirements using advanced systems, the bank may use 12 CFR part 325, appendix A to determine the risk-weighted asset amounts for, and deductions from capital associated with, the merged or acquired company's exposures for up to 24 months after the calendar quarter during which the merger or acquisition consummates. The FDIC may extend this transition period for up to an additional 12 months. Within 90 days of consummating the merger or acquisition, the bank must submit to the FDIC an implementation plan for using its advanced systems for the acquired company. During the period when 12 CFR part 325, appendix A apply to the merged or acquired company, any ALLL, net of allocated transfer risk reserves established pursuant to 12 U.S.C. 3904, associated with the merged or acquired company's exposures may be included in the acquiring bank's tier 2 capital up to 1.25 percent of the acquired company's risk-weighted assets. All general allowances of the merged or acquired company must be excluded from the bank's eligible credit reserves. In addition, the risk-weighted assets of the merged or acquired company are not included in the bank's credit-risk-weighted assets but are included in total risk-weighted assets. If a bank relies on this paragraph, the bank must disclose publicly the amounts of risk-weighted assets and qualifying capital calculated under this appendix for the acquiring bank and under 12 CFR part 325, appendix A for the acquired company.

(b) *Mergers and acquisitions of companies with advanced systems*—(1) If a bank merges with or acquires a company that calculates its risk-based capital requirements using advanced systems, the bank may use the acquired company's advanced systems to determine the risk-weighted asset amounts for, and deductions from capital associated with, the merged or acquired company's exposures for up to 24 months after the calendar quarter during which the acquisition or merger consummates. The FDIC may extend this transition period for up to an additional 12 months. Within 90 days of consummating the merger or acquisition, the bank must submit to the FDIC an implementation plan for using its advanced systems for the merged or acquired company.

(2) If the acquiring bank is not subject to the advanced approaches in this appendix at the time of acquisition or merger, during the period when 12 CFR part 325, appendix A apply to the acquiring bank, the ALLL associated with the exposures of the merged or acquired company may not be directly included in tier 2 capital. Rather, any excess eligible credit reserves associated with the merged or acquired company's exposures may be included in the bank's tier 2 capital up to 0.6 percent of the credit-risk-weighted assets associated with those exposures.

PART IV. RISK-WEIGHTED ASSETS FOR GENERAL CREDIT RISK

Section 31. Mechanics for Calculating Total Wholesale and Retail Risk-Weighted Assets

(a) *Overview.* A bank must calculate its total wholesale and retail risk-weighted asset amount in four distinct phases:

(1) Phase 1—categorization of exposures;

(2) Phase 2—assignment of wholesale obligors and exposures to rating grades and segmentation of retail exposures;

(3) Phase 3—assignment of risk parameters to wholesale exposures and segments of retail exposures; and

(4) Phase 4—calculation of risk-weighted asset amounts.

Federal Deposit Insurance Corporation

Pt. 325, App. D

(b) *Phase 1—Categorization.* The bank must determine which of its exposures are wholesale exposures, retail exposures, securitization exposures, or equity exposures. The bank must categorize each retail exposure as a residential mortgage exposure, a QRE, or an other retail exposure. The bank must identify which wholesale exposures are HVCRE exposures, sovereign exposures, OTC derivative contracts, repo-style transactions, eligible margin loans, eligible purchased wholesale exposures, unsettled transactions to which section 35 of this appendix applies, and eligible guarantees or eligible credit derivatives that are used as credit risk mitigants. The bank must identify any on-balance sheet asset that does not meet the definition of a wholesale, retail, equity, or securitization exposure, as well as any nonmaterial portfolio of exposures described in paragraph (e)(4) of this section.

(c) *Phase 2—Assignment of wholesale obligors and exposures to rating grades and retail exposures to segments*—(1) *Assignment of wholesale obligors and exposures to rating grades.* (i) The bank must assign each obligor of a wholesale exposure to a single obligor rating grade and must assign each wholesale exposure to which it does not directly assign an LGD estimate to a loss severity rating grade.

(ii) The bank must identify which of its wholesale obligors are in default.

(2) *Segmentation of retail exposures.* (i) The bank must group the retail exposures in each retail subcategory into segments that have homogeneous risk characteristics.

(ii) The bank must identify which of its retail exposures are in default. The bank must segment defaulted retail exposures separately from non-defaulted retail exposures.

(iii) If the bank determines the EAD for eligible margin loans using the approach in paragraph (b) of section 32 of this appendix, the bank must identify which of its retail exposures are eligible margin loans for which the bank uses this EAD approach and must segment such eligible margin loans separately from other retail exposures.

(3) *Eligible purchased wholesale exposures.* A bank may group its eligible purchased wholesale exposures into segments that have homogeneous risk characteristics. A bank must use the wholesale exposure formula in Table 2 in this section to determine the risk-based capital requirement for each segment of eligible purchased wholesale exposures.

(d) *Phase 3—Assignment of risk parameters to wholesale exposures and segments of retail exposures*—(1) *Quantification process.* Subject to the limitations in this paragraph (d), the bank must:

(i) Associate a PD with each wholesale obligor rating grade;

(ii) Associate an LGD with each wholesale loss severity rating grade or assign an LGD to each wholesale exposure;

(iii) Assign an EAD and M to each wholesale exposure; and

(iv) Assign a PD, LGD, and EAD to each segment of retail exposures.

(2) *Floor on PD assignment.* The PD for each wholesale obligor or retail segment may not be less than 0.03 percent, except for exposures to or directly and unconditionally guaranteed by a sovereign entity, the Bank for International Settlements, the International Monetary Fund, the European Commission, the European Central Bank, or a multilateral development bank, to which the bank assigns a rating grade associated with a PD of less than 0.03 percent.

(3) *Floor on LGD estimation.* The LGD for each segment of residential mortgage exposures (other than segments of residential mortgage exposures for which all or substantially all of the principal of each exposure is directly and unconditionally guaranteed by the full faith and credit of a sovereign entity) may not be less than 10 percent.

(4) *Eligible purchased wholesale exposures.* A bank must assign a PD, LGD, EAD, and M to each segment of eligible purchased wholesale exposures. If the bank can estimate ECL (but not PD or LGD) for a segment of eligible purchased wholesale exposures, the bank must assume that the LGD of the segment equals 100 percent and that the PD of the segment equals ECL divided by EAD. The estimated ECL must be calculated for the exposures without regard to any assumption of recourse or guarantees from the seller or other parties.

(5) *Credit risk mitigation—credit derivatives, guarantees, and collateral.* (i) A bank may take into account the risk reducing effects of eligible guarantees and eligible credit derivatives in support of a wholesale exposure by applying the PD substitution or LGD adjustment treatment to the exposure as provided in section 33 of this appendix or, if applicable, applying double default treatment to the exposure as provided in section 34 of this appendix. A bank may decide separately for each wholesale exposure that qualifies for the double default treatment under section 34 of this appendix whether to apply the double default treatment or to use the PD substitution or LGD adjustment treatment without recognizing double default effects.

(ii) A bank may take into account the risk reducing effects of guarantees and credit derivatives in support of retail exposures in a segment when quantifying the PD and LGD of the segment.

(iii) Except as provided in paragraph (d)(6) of this section, a bank may take into account the risk reducing effects of collateral in support of a wholesale exposure when quantifying the LGD of the exposure and may take into account the risk reducing effects of collateral in support of retail exposures when quantifying the PD and LGD of the segment.

(6) *EAD for OTC derivative contracts, repo-style transactions, and eligible margin loans.* (i) A bank must calculate its EAD for an OTC derivative contract as provided in paragraphs (c) and (d) of section 32 of this appendix. A bank may take into account the risk-reducing effects of financial collateral in support of a repo-style transaction or eligible margin loan and of any collateral in support of a repo-style transaction that is included in the bank's VaR-based measure under 12 CFR part 325, appendix C through an adjustment to EAD as provided in paragraphs (b) and (d) of section 32 of this appendix. A bank that takes collateral into account through such an adjustment to EAD under section 32 of this appendix may not reflect such collateral in LGD.

(ii) A bank may attribute an EAD of zero to:

(A) Derivative contracts that are publicly traded on an exchange that requires the daily receipt and payment of cash-variation margin;

(B) Derivative contracts and repo-style transactions that are outstanding with a qualifying central counterparty (but not for those transactions that a qualifying central counterparty has rejected); and

(C) Credit risk exposures to a qualifying central counterparty in the form of clearing deposits and posted collateral that arise from transactions described in paragraph (d)(6)(ii)(B) of this section.

(7) *Effective maturity.* An exposure's M must be no greater than five years and no less than one year, except that an exposure's M must be no less than one day if the exposure has an original maturity of less than one year and is not part of a bank's ongoing financing of the obligor. An exposure is not part of a bank's ongoing financing of the obligor if the bank:

(i) Has a legal and practical ability not to renew or roll over the exposure in the event of credit deterioration of the obligor;

(ii) Makes an independent credit decision at the inception of the exposure and at every renewal or roll over; and

(iii) Has no substantial commercial incentive to continue its credit relationship with the obligor in the event of credit deterioration of the obligor.

(e) *Phase 4—Calculation of risk-weighted assets*—(1) *Non-defaulted exposures.* (i) A bank must calculate the dollar risk-based capital requirement for each of its wholesale exposures to a non-defaulted obligor (except eligible guarantees and eligible credit derivatives that hedge another wholesale exposure and exposures to which the bank applies the double default treatment in section 34 of this appendix) and segments of non-defaulted retail exposures by inserting the assigned risk parameters for the wholesale obligor and exposure or retail segment into the appropriate risk-based capital formula specified in Table 2 and multiplying the output of the formula (K) by the EAD of the exposure or segment. Alternatively, a bank may apply a 300 percent risk weight to the EAD of an eligible margin loan if the bank is not able to meet the agencies' requirements for estimation of PD and LGD for the margin loan.

Table 2 – IRB Risk-Based Capital Formulas for Wholesale Exposures to Non-Defaulted Obligors and Segments of Non-Defaulted Retail Exposures[1]

Retail	Capital Requirement (K) Non-Defaulted Exposures	$K = \left[LGD \times N\left(\dfrac{N^{-1}(PD) + \sqrt{R} \times N^{-1}(0.999)}{\sqrt{1-R}} \right) - (LGD \times PD) \right]$	
	Correlation Factor (R)	For residential mortgage exposures: $R = 0.15$	
		For qualifying revolving exposures: $R = 0.04$	
		For other retail exposures: $R = 0.03 + 0.13 \times e^{-35 \times PD}$	
Wholesale	Capital Requirement (K) Non-Defaulted Exposures	$K = \left[LGD \times N\left(\dfrac{N^{-1}(PD) + \sqrt{R} \times N^{-1}(0.999)}{\sqrt{1-R}} \right) - (LGD \times PD) \right] \times \left(\dfrac{1 + (M - 2.5) \times b}{1 - 1.5 \times b} \right)$	
	Correlation Factor (R)	For HVCRE exposures: $R = 0.12 + 0.18 \times e^{-50 \times PD}$	
		For wholesale exposures other than HVCRE exposures: $R = 0.12 + 0.12 \times e^{-50 \times PD}$	
	Maturity Adjustment (b)	$b = (0.11852 - 0.05478 \times \ln(PD))^2$	

[1] $N(.)$ means the cumulative distribution function for a standard normal random variable. $N^{-1}(.)$ means the inverse cumulative distribution function for a standard normal random variable. The symbol e refers to the base of the natural logarithms, and the function $\ln(.)$ refers to the natural logarithm of the expression within parentheses. The formulas apply when PD is greater than zero. If PD equals zero, the capital requirement K is set equal to zero.

(ii) The sum of all the dollar risk-based capital requirements for each wholesale exposure to a non-defaulted obligor and segment of non-defaulted retail exposures calculated in paragraph (e)(1)(i) of this section and in paragraph (e) of section 34 of this appendix equals the total dollar risk-based capital requirement for those exposures and segments.

(iii) The aggregate risk-weighted asset amount for wholesale exposures to non-defaulted obligors and segments of non-defaulted retail exposures equals the total dollar risk-based capital requirement calculated in paragraph (e)(1)(ii) of this section multiplied by 12.5.

(2) *Wholesale exposures to defaulted obligors and segments of defaulted retail exposures.* (i) The dollar risk-based capital requirement for each wholesale exposure to a defaulted obligor equals 0.08 multiplied by the EAD of the exposure.

(ii) The dollar risk-based capital requirement for a segment of defaulted retail exposures equals 0.08 multiplied by the EAD of the segment.

(iii) The sum of all the dollar risk-based capital requirements for each wholesale exposure to a defaulted obligor calculated in paragraph (e)(2)(i) of this section plus the dollar risk-based capital requirements for each segment of defaulted retail exposures calculated in paragraph (e)(2)(ii) of this section equals the total dollar risk-based capital requirement for those exposures and segments.

(iv) The aggregate risk-weighted asset amount for wholesale exposures to defaulted obligors and segments of defaulted retail exposures equals the total dollar risk-based capital requirement calculated in paragraph (e)(2)(iii) of this section multiplied by 12.5.

(3) *Assets not included in a defined exposure category.* (i) A bank may assign a risk-weighted asset amount of zero to cash owned and held in all offices of the bank or in transit and for gold bullion held in the bank's own vaults, or held in another bank's vaults on an allocated basis, to the extent the gold bullion assets are offset by gold bullion liabilities.

(ii) The risk-weighted asset amount for the residual value of a retail lease exposure equals such residual value.

(iii) The risk-weighted asset amount for any other on-balance-sheet asset that does not meet the definition of a wholesale, retail, securitization, or equity exposure equals the carrying value of the asset.

(4) *Non-material portfolios of exposures.* The risk-weighted asset amount of a portfolio of exposures for which the bank has demonstrated to the FDIC's satisfaction that the portfolio (when combined with all other portfolios of exposures that the bank seeks to treat under this paragraph) is not material to the bank is the sum of the carrying values of on-balance sheet exposures plus the notional amounts of off-balance sheet exposures in the portfolio. For purposes of this paragraph (e)(4), the notional amount of an OTC derivative contract that is not a credit derivative is the EAD of the derivative as calculated in section 32 of this appendix.

Section 32. Counterparty Credit Risk of Repo-Style Transactions, Eligible Margin Loans, and OTC Derivative Contracts

(a) *In General.* (1) This section describes two methodologies—a collateral haircut approach and an internal models methodology—that a bank may use instead of an LGD estimation methodology to recognize the benefits of financial collateral in mitigating the counterparty credit risk of repo-style transactions, eligible margin loans, collateralized OTC derivative contracts, and single product netting sets of such transactions and to recognize the benefits of any collateral in mitigating the counterparty credit risk of repo-style transactions that are included in a bank's VaR-based measure under 12 CFR part 325, appendix C. A third methodology, the simple VaR methodology, is available for single product netting sets of repo-style transactions and eligible margin loans.

(2) This section also describes the methodology for calculating EAD for an OTC derivative contract or a set of OTC derivative contracts subject to a qualifying master netting agreement. A bank also may use the internal models methodology to estimate EAD for qualifying cross-product master netting agreements.

(3) A bank may only use the standard supervisory haircut approach with a minimum 10-business-day holding period to recognize in EAD the benefits of conforming residential mortgage collateral that secures repo-style transactions (other than repo-style transactions included in the bank's VaR-based measure under 12 CFR part 325, appendix C), eligible margin loans, and OTC derivative contracts.

(4) A bank may use any combination of the three methodologies for collateral recognition; however, it must use the same methodology for similar exposures.

(b) *EAD for eligible margin loans and repo-style transactions*—(1) *General.* A bank may recognize the credit risk mitigation benefits of financial collateral that secures an eligible margin loan, repo-style transaction, or single-product netting set of such transactions by factoring the collateral into its LGD estimates for the exposure. Alternatively, a bank may estimate an unsecured LGD for the exposure, as well as for any repo-style transaction that is included in the bank's VaR-based measure under 12 CFR part 325, appendix C, and determine the EAD of the exposure using:

(i) The collateral haircut approach described in paragraph (b)(2) of this section;

(ii) For netting sets only, the simple VaR methodology described in paragraph (b)(3) of this section; or

(iii) The internal models methodology described in paragraph (d) of this section.

(2) *Collateral haircut approach*—(i) *EAD equation.* A bank may determine EAD for an eligible margin loan, repo-style transaction, or netting set by setting EAD equal to max $\{0, [(\Sigma E - \Sigma C) + \Sigma(Es \times Hs) + \Sigma(Efx \times Hfx)]\}$, where:

(A) ΣE equals the value of the exposure (the sum of the current market values of all instruments, gold, and cash the bank has lent, sold subject to repurchase, or posted as collateral to the counterparty under the transaction (or netting set));

(B) ΣC equals the value of the collateral (the sum of the current market values of all instruments, gold, and cash the bank has borrowed, purchased subject to resale, or taken as collateral from the counterparty under the transaction (or netting set));

(C) Es equals the absolute value of the net position in a given instrument or in gold (where the net position in a given instrument or in gold equals the sum of the current market values of the instrument or gold the bank has lent, sold subject to repurchase, or posted as collateral to the counterparty minus the sum of the current

Federal Deposit Insurance Corporation

market values of that same instrument or gold the bank has borrowed, purchased subject to resale, or taken as collateral from the counterparty);

(D) Hs equals the market price volatility haircut appropriate to the instrument or gold referenced in Es;

(E) Efx equals the absolute value of the net position of instruments and cash in a currency that is different from the settlement currency (where the net position in a given currency equals the sum of the current market values of any instruments or cash in the currency the bank has lent, sold subject to repurchase, or posted as collateral to the counterparty minus the sum of the current market values of any instruments or cash in the currency the bank has borrowed, purchased subject to resale, or taken as collateral from the counterparty); and

(F) Hfx equals the haircut appropriate to the mismatch between the currency referenced in Efx and the settlement currency.

(ii) *Standard supervisory haircuts.* (A) Under the standard supervisory haircuts approach:

(*1*) A bank must use the haircuts for market price volatility (Hs) in Table 3, as adjusted in certain circumstances as provided in paragraph (b)(2)(ii)(A)(*3*) and (*4*) of this section;

TABLE 3—STANDARD SUPERVISORY MARKET PRICE VOLATILITY HAIRCUTS [1]

Applicable external rating grade category for debt securities	Residual maturity for debt securities	Issuers exempt from the 3 basis point floor	Other issuers
Two highest investment-grade rating categories for long-term ratings/highest investment-grade rating category for short-term ratings.	≤ 1 year >1 year, ≤ 5 years > 5 years	0.005 0.02 0.04	0.01 0.04 0.08
Two lowest investment-grade rating categories for both short- and long-term ratings.	≤ 1 year > 1 year, ≤ 5 years > 5 years	0.01 0.03 0.06	0.02 0.06 0.12
One rating category below investment grade	All	0.15	0.25
Main index equities (including convertible bonds) and gold		0.15	
Other publicly traded equities (including convertible bonds), conforming residential mortgages, and nonfinancial collateral.		0.25	
Mutual funds		Highest haircut applicable to any security in which the fund can invest.	
Cash on deposit with the bank (including a certificate of deposit issued by the bank) ...		0	

[1] The market price volatility haircuts in Table 3 are based on a ten-business-day holding period.

(*2*) For currency mismatches, a bank must use a haircut for foreign exchange rate volatility (Hfx) of 8 percent, as adjusted in certain circumstances as provided in paragraph (b)(2)(ii)(A)(*3*) and (*4*) of this section.

(*3*) For repo-style transactions, a bank may multiply the supervisory haircuts provided in paragraphs (b)(2)(ii)(A)(*1*) and (*2*) of this section by the square root of ½ (which equals 0.707107).

(*4*) A bank must adjust the supervisory haircuts upward on the basis of a holding period longer than ten business days (for eligible margin loans) or five business days (for repo-style transactions) where and as appropriate to take into account the illiquidity of an instrument.

(iii) *Own internal estimates for haircuts.* With the prior written approval of the FDIC, a bank may calculate haircuts (Hs and Hfx) using its own internal estimates of the volatilities of market prices and foreign exchange rates.

(A) To receive FDIC approval to use its own internal estimates, a bank must satisfy the following minimum quantitative standards:

(*1*) A bank must use a 99th percentile one-tailed confidence interval.

(*2*) The minimum holding period for a repo-style transaction is five business days and for an eligible margin loan is ten business days. When a bank calculates an own-estimates haircut on a T_N-day holding period, which is different from the minimum holding period for the transaction type, the applicable haircut (H_M) is calculated using the following square root of time formula:

$$H_M = H_N \sqrt{\frac{T_M}{T_N}}, \text{ where}$$

(i) T_M equals 5 for repo-style transactions and 10 for eligible margin loans;

(ii) T_N equals the holding period used by the bank to derive H_N; and

(iii) H_N equals the haircut based on the holding period T_N.

(3) A bank must adjust holding periods upwards where and as appropriate to take into account the illiquidity of an instrument.

(4) The historical observation period must be at least one year.

(5) A bank must update its data sets and recompute haircuts no less frequently than quarterly and must also reassess data sets and haircuts whenever market prices change materially.

(B) With respect to debt securities that have an applicable external rating of investment grade, a bank may calculate haircuts for categories of securities. For a category of securities, the bank must calculate the haircut on the basis of internal volatility estimates for securities in that category that are representative of the securities in that category that the bank has lent, sold subject to repurchase, posted as collateral, borrowed, purchased subject to resale, or taken as collateral. In determining relevant categories, the bank must at a minimum take into account:

(1) The type of issuer of the security;

(2) The applicable external rating of the security;

(3) The maturity of the security; and

(4) The interest rate sensitivity of the security.

(C) With respect to debt securities that have an applicable external rating of below investment grade and equity securities, a bank must calculate a separate haircut for each individual security.

(D) Where an exposure or collateral (whether in the form of cash or securities) is denominated in a currency that differs from the settlement currency, the bank must calculate a separate currency mismatch haircut for its net position in each mismatched currency based on estimated volatilities of foreign exchange rates between the mismatched currency and the settlement currency.

(E) A bank's own estimates of market price and foreign exchange rate volatilities may not take into account the correlations among securities and foreign exchange rates on either the exposure or collateral side of a transaction (or netting set) or the correlations among securities and foreign exchange rates between the exposure and collateral sides of the transaction (or netting set).

(3) *Simple VaR methodology.* With the prior written approval of the FDIC, a bank may estimate EAD for a netting set using a VaR model that meets the requirements in paragraph (b)(3)(iii) of this section. In such event, the bank must set EAD equal to max {0, [(ΣE—ΣC) + PFE]}, where:

(i) ΣE equals the value of the exposure (the sum of the current market values of all instruments, gold, and cash the bank has lent, sold subject to repurchase, or posted as collateral to the counterparty under the netting set);

(ii) ΣC equals the value of the collateral (the sum of the current market values of all instruments, gold, and cash the bank has borrowed, purchased subject to resale, or taken as collateral from the counterparty under the netting set); and

(iii) PFE (potential future exposure) equals the bank's empirically based best estimate of the 99th percentile, one-tailed confidence interval for an increase in the value of (ΣE—ΣC) over a five-business-day holding period for repo-style transactions or over a ten-business-day holding period for eligible margin loans using a minimum one-year historical observation period of price data representing the instruments that the bank has lent, sold subject to repurchase, posted as collateral, borrowed, purchased subject to resale, or taken as collateral. The bank must validate its VaR model, including by establishing and maintaining a rigorous and regular back-testing regime.

(c) *EAD for OTC derivative contracts.* (1) A bank must determine the EAD for an OTC derivative contract that is not subject to a qualifying master netting agreement using the current exposure methodology in paragraph (c)(5) of this section or using the internal models methodology described in paragraph (d) of this section.

(2) A bank must determine the EAD for multiple OTC derivative contracts that are subject to a qualifying master netting agreement using the current exposure methodology in paragraph (c)(6) of this section or using the internal models methodology described in paragraph (d) of this section.

(3) *Counterparty credit risk for credit derivatives.* Notwithstanding the above, (i) A bank that purchases a credit derivative that is recognized under section 33 or 34 of this appendix as a credit risk mitigant for an exposure that is not a covered position under 12 CFR part 325, appendix C need not compute a separate counterparty credit risk capital requirement under this section so long as the bank does so consistently for all such credit derivatives and either includes all or excludes all such credit derivatives that are subject to a master netting agreement from any measure used to determine counterparty credit risk exposure to all relevant counterparties for risk-based capital purposes.

(ii) A bank that is the protection provider in a credit derivative must treat the credit derivative as a wholesale exposure to the reference obligor and need not compute a counterparty credit risk capital requirement for the credit derivative under this section, so long as it does so consistently for all such credit derivatives and either includes all or excludes all such credit derivatives that are subject to a master netting agreement from any measure used to determine counterparty credit risk exposure to all relevant counterparties for risk-based capital purposes (unless the bank is treating the credit derivative as a covered position under 12 CFR part 325, appendix C, in which case the bank must compute a supplemental counterparty credit risk capital requirement under this section).

(4) *Counterparty credit risk for equity derivatives.* A bank must treat an equity derivative contract as an equity exposure and compute a risk-weighted asset amount for the equity derivative contract under part VI (unless the bank is treating the contract as a covered position under 12 CFR part 325, appendix C). In addition, if the bank is treating the contract as a covered position under 12 CFR part 325, appendix C and in certain other cases described in section 55 of this appendix, the bank must also calculate a risk-based capital requirement for the counterparty credit risk of an equity derivative contract under this part.

(5) *Single OTC derivative contract.* Except as modified by paragraph (c)(7) of this section, the EAD for a single OTC derivative contract that is not subject to a qualifying master netting agreement is equal to the sum of the bank's current credit exposure and potential future credit exposure (PFE) on the derivative contract.

(i) *Current credit exposure.* The current credit exposure for a single OTC derivative contract is the greater of the mark-to-market value of the derivative contract or zero.

(ii) *PFE.* The PFE for a single OTC derivative contract, including an OTC derivative contract with a negative mark-to-market value, is calculated by multiplying the notional principal amount of the derivative contract by the appropriate conversion factor in Table 4. For purposes of calculating either the PFE under this paragraph or the gross PFE under paragraph (c)(6) of this section for exchange rate contracts and other similar contracts in which the notional principal amount is equivalent to the cash flows, notional principal amount is the net receipts to each party falling due on each value date in each currency. For any OTC derivative contract that does not fall within one of the specified categories in Table 4, the PFE must be calculated using the "other" conversion factors. A bank must use an OTC derivative contract's effective notional principal amount (that is, its apparent or stated notional principal amount multiplied by any multiplier in the OTC derivative contract) rather than its apparent or stated notional principal amount in calculating PFE. PFE of the protection provider of a credit derivative is capped at the net present value of the amount of unpaid premiums.

TABLE 4—CONVERSION FACTOR MATRIX FOR OTC DERIVATIVE CONTRACTS [1]

Remaining maturity [2]	Interest rate	Foreign exchange rate and gold	Credit (investment-grade reference obligor) [3]	Credit (non-investment-grade reference obligor)	Equity	Precious metals (except gold)	Other
One year or less	0.00	0.01	0.05	0.10	0.06	0.07	0.10
Over one to five years	0.005	0.05	0.05	0.10	0.08	0.07	0.12
Over five years	0.015	0.075	0.05	0.10	0.10	0.08	0.15

[1] For an OTC derivative contract with multiple exchanges of principal, the conversion factor is multiplied by the number of remaining payments in the derivative contract.
[2] For an OTC derivative contract that is structured such that on specified dates any outstanding exposure is settled and the terms are reset so that the market value of the contract is zero, the remaining maturity equals the time until the next reset date. For an interest rate derivative contract with a remaining maturity of greater than one year that meets these criteria, the minimum conversion factor is 0.005.
[3] A bank must use the column labeled "Credit (investment-grade reference obligor)" for a credit derivative whose reference obligor has an outstanding unsecured long-term debt security without credit enhancement that has a long-term applicable external rating of at least investment grade. A bank must use the column labeled "Credit (non-investment-grade reference obligor)" for all other credit derivatives.

(6) *Multiple OTC derivative contracts subject to a qualifying master netting agreement.* Except as modified by paragraph (c)(7) of this section, the EAD for multiple OTC derivative contracts subject to a qualifying master netting agreement is equal to the sum of the net current credit exposure and the adjusted sum of the PFE exposure for all OTC derivative contracts subject to the qualifying master netting agreement.

(i) *Net current credit exposure.* The net current credit exposure is the greater of:

(A) The net sum of all positive and negative mark-to-market values of the individual OTC derivative contracts subject to the qualifying master netting agreement; or

(B) zero.

(ii) *Adjusted sum of the PFE.* The adjusted sum of the PFE, Anet, is calculated as Anet = (0.4×Agross)+(0.6×NGR×Agross), where:

(A) Agross = the gross PFE (that is, the sum of the PFE amounts (as determined under paragraph (c)(5)(ii) of this section) for each individual OTC derivative contract subject to the qualifying master netting agreement); and

(B) NGR = the net to gross ratio (that is, the ratio of the net current credit exposure to the gross current credit exposure). In calculating the NGR, the gross current credit exposure equals the sum of the positive current credit exposures (as determined under paragraph (c)(5)(i) of this section) of all individual OTC derivative contracts subject to the qualifying master netting agreement.

(7) *Collateralized OTC derivative contracts.* A bank may recognize the credit risk mitigation benefits of financial collateral that secures an OTC derivative contract or single-product netting set of OTC derivatives by factoring the collateral into its LGD estimates for the contract or netting set. Alternatively, a bank may recognize the credit risk mitigation benefits of financial collateral that secures such a contract or netting set that is marked to market on a daily basis and subject to a daily margin maintenance requirement by estimating an unsecured LGD for the contract or netting set and adjusting the EAD calculated under paragraph (c)(5) or (c)(6) of this section using the collateral haircut approach in paragraph (b)(2) of this section. The bank must substitute the EAD calculated under paragraph (c)(5) or (c)(6) of this section for ΣE in the equation in paragraph (b)(2)(i) of this section and must use a ten-business-day minimum holding period ($T_M = 10$).

(d) *Internal models methodology.* (1) With prior written approval from the FDIC, a bank may use the internal models methodology in this paragraph (d) to determine EAD for counterparty credit risk for OTC derivative contracts (collateralized or uncollateralized) and single-product netting sets thereof, for eligible margin loans and single-product netting sets thereof, and for repo-style transactions and single-product netting sets thereof. A bank that uses the internal models methodology for a particular transaction type (OTC derivative contracts, eligible margin loans, or repo-style transactions) must use the internal models methodology for all transactions of that transaction type. A bank may choose to use the internal models methodology for one or two of these three types of exposures and not the other types. A bank may also use the internal models methodology for OTC derivative contracts, eligible margin loans, and repo-style transactions subject to a qualifying cross-product netting agreement if:

(i) The bank effectively integrates the risk mitigating effects of cross-product netting into its risk management and other information technology systems; and

(ii) The bank obtains the prior written approval of the FDIC. A bank that uses the internal models methodology for a transaction type must receive approval from the FDIC to cease using the methodology for that transaction type or to make a material change to its internal model.

(2) Under the internal models methodology, a bank uses an internal model to estimate the expected exposure (EE) for a netting set and then calculates EAD based on that EE.

(i) The bank must use its internal model's probability distribution for changes in the market value of a netting set that are attributable to changes in market variables to determine EE.

(ii) Under the internal models methodology, EAD = α x effective EPE, or, subject to FDIC approval as provided in paragraph (d)(7), a more conservative measure of EAD.

(A) $\text{EffectiveEPE}_{t_k} = \sum_{k=1}^{n} \text{EffectiveEE}_{t_k} \times \Delta t_k$

(that is, effective EPE is the time-weighted average of effective EE where the weights are the proportion that an individual effective EE represents in a one-year time interval) where:

(*1*) Effective EE_{t_k} = max (Effective $\text{EE}_{t_{k-1}}$, EE_{t_k}) (that is, for a specific date$_{t_k}$, effective EE is the greater of EE at that date or the effective EE at the previous date); and

(*2*) t_k represents the kth future time period in the model and there are n time periods represented in the model over the first year; and

(B) $\alpha = 1.4$ except as provided in paragraph (d)(6), or when the FDIC has determined that the bank must set α higher based on the bank's specific characteristics of counterparty credit risk.

(iii) A bank may include financial collateral currently posted by the counterparty as collateral (but may not include other forms of collateral) when calculating EE.

(iv) If a bank hedges some or all of the counterparty credit risk associated with a netting set using an eligible credit derivative, the bank may take the reduction in exposure to the counterparty into account when estimating EE. If the bank recognizes this reduction in exposure to the counterparty in its estimate of EE, it must also use its internal model to estimate a separate EAD for the bank's exposure to the protection provider of the credit derivative.

(3) To obtain FDIC approval to calculate the distributions of exposures upon which the EAD calculation is based, the bank must demonstrate to the satisfaction of the FDIC that it has been using for at least one year an internal model that broadly meets the following minimum standards, with which the bank must maintain compliance:

(i) The model must have the systems capability to estimate the expected exposure to the counterparty on a daily basis (but is not expected to estimate or report expected exposure on a daily basis).

(ii) The model must estimate expected exposure at enough future dates to reflect accurately all the future cash flows of contracts in the netting set.

(iii) The model must account for the possible non-normality of the exposure distribution, where appropriate.

(iv) The bank must measure, monitor, and control current counterparty exposure and the exposure to the counterparty over the whole life of all contracts in the netting set.

(v) The bank must be able to measure and manage current exposures gross and net of collateral held, where appropriate. The bank must estimate expected exposures for OTC derivative contracts both with and without the effect of collateral agreements.

(vi) The bank must have procedures to identify, monitor, and control specific wrong-way risk throughout the life of an exposure. Wrong-way risk in this context is the risk that future exposure to a counterparty will be high when the counterparty's probability of default is also high.

(vii) The model must use current market data to compute current exposures. When estimating model parameters based on historical data, at least three years of historical data that cover a wide range of economic conditions must be used and must be updated quarterly or more frequently if market conditions warrant. The bank should consider using model parameters based on forward-looking measures, where appropriate.

(viii) A bank must subject its internal model to an initial validation and annual model review process. The model review should consider whether the inputs and risk factors, as well as the model outputs, are appropriate.

(4) *Maturity.* (i) If the remaining maturity of the exposure or the longest-dated contract in the netting set is greater than one year, the bank must set M for the exposure or netting set equal to the lower of five years or M(EPE),[3] where:

$$\text{(A)} \quad M(EPE) = 1 + \frac{\sum\limits_{t_k > 1\, year}^{maturity} EE_k \times \Delta t_k \times df_k}{\sum\limits_{k=1}^{t_k \leq 1\, year} effectiveEE_k \times \Delta t_k \times df_k}$$

(B) df_k is the risk-free discount factor for future time period t_k; and

(C) $\Delta t_k = t_k - t_{k-1}$.

(ii) If the remaining maturity of the exposure or the longest-dated contract in the netting set is one year or less, the bank must set M for the exposure or netting set equal to one year, except as provided in paragraph (d)(7) of section 31 of this appendix.

(5) *Collateral agreements.* A bank may capture the effect on EAD of a collateral agreement that requires receipt of collateral when exposure to the counterparty increases but may not capture the effect on EAD of a collateral agreement that requires receipt of collateral when counterparty credit quality deteriorates. For this purpose, a collateral agreement means a legal contract that specifies the time when, and circumstances under which, the counterparty is required to pledge collateral to the bank for a single financial contract or for all financial contracts in a netting set and confers upon the bank a perfected, first priority security interest (notwithstanding the prior security interest of any custodial agent), or the legal equivalent thereof, in the collateral posted by the counterparty under the agreement. This security interest must provide the bank with a right to close out the financial positions and liquidate the collateral upon an event of default of, or failure to perform by, counterparty under the collateral agreement. A contract would not satisfy this requirement if the bank's exercise of rights under the agreement may be stayed or avoided under applicable law in the relevant jurisdictions. Two methods are available to capture the effect of a collateral agreement:

(i) With prior written approval from the FDIC, a bank may include the effect of a collateral agreement within its internal model used to calculate EAD. The bank may set EAD equal to the expected exposure at the end of the margin period of risk. The margin period of risk means, with respect to a netting set subject to a collateral agreement, the time period from the most recent exchange of collateral with a counterparty until the next required exchange of collateral plus the period of time required to sell and realize the proceeds of the least liquid collateral that can be delivered under the terms of the collateral agreement and, where

---

[3] Alternatively, a bank that uses an internal model to calculate a one-sided credit valuation adjustment may use the effective credit duration estimated by the model as M(EPE) in place of the formula in paragraph (d)(4).

applicable, the period of time required to re-hedge the resulting market risk, upon the default of the counterparty. The minimum margin period of risk is five business days for repo-style transactions and ten business days for other transactions when liquid financial collateral is posted under a daily margin maintenance requirement. This period should be extended to cover any additional time between margin calls; any potential closeout difficulties; any delays in selling collateral, particularly if the collateral is illiquid; and any impediments to prompt re-hedging of any market risk.

(ii) A bank that can model EPE without collateral agreements but cannot achieve the higher level of modeling sophistication to model EPE with collateral agreements can set effective EPE for a collateralized netting set equal to the lesser of:

(A) The threshold, defined as the exposure amount at which the counterparty is required to post collateral under the collateral agreement, if the threshold is positive, plus an add-on that reflects the potential increase in exposure of the netting set over the margin period of risk. The add-on is computed as the expected increase in the netting set's exposure beginning from current exposure of zero over the margin period of risk. The margin period of risk must be at least five business days for netting sets consisting only of repo-style transactions subject to daily remargining and daily marking-to-market, and ten business days for all other netting sets; or

(B) Effective EPE without a collateral agreement.

(6) *Own estimate of alpha.* With prior written approval of the FDIC, a bank may calculate alpha as the ratio of economic capital from a full simulation of counterparty exposure across counterparties that incorporates a joint simulation of market and credit risk factors (numerator) and economic capital based on EPE (denominator), subject to a floor of 1.2. For purposes of this calculation, economic capital is the unexpected losses for all counterparty credit risks measured at a 99.9 percent confidence level over a one-year horizon. To receive approval, the bank must meet the following minimum standards to the satisfaction of the FDIC:

(i) The bank's own estimate of alpha must capture in the numerator the effects of:

(A) The material sources of stochastic dependency of distributions of market values of transactions or portfolios of transactions across counterparties;

(B) Volatilities and correlations of market risk factors used in the joint simulation, which must be related to the credit risk factor used in the simulation to reflect potential increases in volatility or correlation in an economic downturn, where appropriate; and

(C) The granularity of exposures (that is, the effect of a concentration in the proportion of each counterparty's exposure that is driven by a particular risk factor).

(ii) The bank must assess the potential model uncertainty in its estimates of alpha.

(iii) The bank must calculate the numerator and denominator of alpha in a consistent fashion with respect to modeling methodology, parameter specifications, and portfolio composition.

(iv) The bank must review and adjust as appropriate its estimates of the numerator and denominator of alpha on at least a quarterly basis and more frequently when the composition of the portfolio varies over time.

(7) *Other measures of counterparty exposure.* With prior written approval of the FDIC, a bank may set EAD equal to a measure of counterparty credit risk exposure, such as peak EAD, that is more conservative than an alpha of 1.4 (or higher under the terms of paragraph (d)(2)(ii)(B) of this section) times EPE for every counterparty whose EAD will be measured under the alternative measure of counterparty exposure. The bank must demonstrate the conservatism of the measure of counterparty credit risk exposure used for EAD. For material portfolios of new OTC derivative products, the bank may assume that the current exposure methodology in paragraphs (c)(5) and (c)(6) of this section meets the conservatism requirement of this paragraph for a period not to exceed 180 days. For immaterial portfolios of OTC derivative contracts, the bank generally may assume that the current exposure methodology in paragraphs (c)(5) and (c)(6) of this section meets the conservatism requirement of this paragraph.

Section 33. Guarantees and Credit Derivatives: PD Substitution and LGD Adjustment Approaches

(a) *Scope.* (1) This section applies to wholesale exposures for which:

(i) Credit risk is fully covered by an eligible guarantee or eligible credit derivative; or

(ii) Credit risk is covered on a pro rata basis (that is, on a basis in which the bank and the protection provider share losses proportionately) by an eligible guarantee or eligible credit derivative.

(2) Wholesale exposures on which there is a tranching of credit risk (reflecting at least two different levels of seniority) are securitization exposures subject to the securitization framework in part V.

(3) A bank may elect to recognize the credit risk mitigation benefits of an eligible guarantee or eligible credit derivative covering an exposure described in paragraph (a)(1) of this section by using the PD substitution approach or the LGD adjustment approach in paragraph (c) of this section or, if the transaction qualifies, using the double

Federal Deposit Insurance Corporation

default treatment in section 34 of this appendix. A bank's PD and LGD for the hedged exposure may not be lower than the PD and LGD floors described in paragraphs (d)(2) and (d)(3) of section 31 of this appendix.

(4) If multiple eligible guarantees or eligible credit derivatives cover a single exposure described in paragraph (a)(1) of this section, a bank may treat the hedged exposure as multiple separate exposures each covered by a single eligible guarantee or eligible credit derivative and may calculate a separate risk-based capital requirement for each separate exposure as described in paragraph (a)(3) of this section.

(5) If a single eligible guarantee or eligible credit derivative covers multiple hedged wholesale exposures described in paragraph (a)(1) of this section, a bank must treat each hedged exposure as covered by a separate eligible guarantee or eligible credit derivative and must calculate a separate risk-based capital requirement for each exposure as described in paragraph (a)(3) of this section.

(6) A bank must use the same risk parameters for calculating ECL as it uses for calculating the risk-based capital requirement for the exposure.

(b) *Rules of recognition.* (1) A bank may only recognize the credit risk mitigation benefits of eligible guarantees and eligible credit derivatives.

(2) A bank may only recognize the credit risk mitigation benefits of an eligible credit derivative to hedge an exposure that is different from the credit derivative's reference exposure used for determining the derivative's cash settlement value, deliverable obligation, or occurrence of a credit event if:

(i) The reference exposure ranks pari passu (that is, equally) with or is junior to the hedged exposure; and

(ii) The reference exposure and the hedged exposure are exposures to the same legal entity, and legally enforceable cross-default or cross-acceleration clauses are in place to assure payments under the credit derivative are triggered when the obligor fails to pay under the terms of the hedged exposure.

(c) *Risk parameters for hedged exposures*—(1) *PD substitution approach*—(i) *Full coverage.* If an eligible guarantee or eligible credit derivative meets the conditions in paragraphs (a) and (b) of this section and the protection amount (P) of the guarantee or credit derivative is greater than or equal to the EAD of the hedged exposure, a bank may recognize the guarantee or credit derivative in determining the bank's risk-based capital requirement for the hedged exposure by substituting the PD associated with the rating grade of the protection provider for the PD associated with the rating grade of the obligor in the risk-based capital formula applicable to the guarantee or credit derivative in Table 2 and using the appropriate LGD as described in paragraph (c)(1)(iii) of this section.

Pt. 325, App. D

If the bank determines that full substitution of the protection provider's PD leads to an inappropriate degree of risk mitigation, the bank may substitute a higher PD than that of the protection provider.

(ii) *Partial coverage.* If an eligible guarantee or eligible credit derivative meets the conditions in paragraphs (a) and (b) of this section and the protection amount (P) of the guarantee or credit derivative is less than the EAD of the hedged exposure, the bank must treat the hedged exposure as two separate exposures (protected and unprotected) in order to recognize the credit risk mitigation benefit of the guarantee or credit derivative.

(A) The bank must calculate its risk-based capital requirement for the protected exposure under section 31 of this appendix, where PD is the protection provider's PD, LGD is determined under paragraph (c)(1)(iii) of this section, and EAD is P. If the bank determines that full substitution leads to an inappropriate degree of risk mitigation, the bank may use a higher PD than that of the protection provider.

(B) The bank must calculate its risk-based capital requirement for the unprotected exposure under section 31 of this appendix, where PD is the obligor's PD, LGD is the hedged exposure's LGD (not adjusted to reflect the guarantee or credit derivative), and EAD is the EAD of the original hedged exposure minus P.

(C) The treatment in this paragraph (c)(1)(ii) is applicable when the credit risk of a wholesale exposure is covered on a partial pro rata basis or when an adjustment is made to the effective notional amount of the guarantee or credit derivative under paragraph (d), (e), or (f) of this section.

(iii) *LGD of hedged exposures.* The LGD of a hedged exposure under the PD substitution approach is equal to:

(A) The lower of the LGD of the hedged exposure (not adjusted to reflect the guarantee or credit derivative) and the LGD of the guarantee or credit derivative, if the guarantee or credit derivative provides the bank with the option to receive immediate payout upon triggering the protection; or

(B) The LGD of the guarantee or credit derivative, if the guarantee or credit derivative does not provide the bank with the option to receive immediate payout upon triggering the protection.

(2) *LGD adjustment approach*—(i) *Full coverage.* If an eligible guarantee or eligible credit derivative meets the conditions in paragraphs (a) and (b) of this section and the protection amount (P) of the guarantee or credit derivative is greater than or equal to the EAD of the hedged exposure, the bank's risk-based capital requirement for the hedged exposure is the greater of:

(A) The risk-based capital requirement for the exposure as calculated under section 31 of this appendix, with the LGD of the exposure adjusted to reflect the guarantee or credit derivative; or

(B) The risk-based capital requirement for a direct exposure to the protection provider as calculated under section 31 of this appendix, using the PD for the protection provider, the LGD for the guarantee or credit derivative, and an EAD equal to the EAD of the hedged exposure.

(ii) *Partial coverage.* If an eligible guarantee or eligible credit derivative meets the conditions in paragraphs (a) and (b) of this section and the protection amount (P) of the guarantee or credit derivative is less than the EAD of the hedged exposure, the bank must treat the hedged exposure as two separate exposures (protected and unprotected) in order to recognize the credit risk mitigation benefit of the guarantee or credit derivative.

(A) The bank's risk-based capital requirement for the protected exposure would be the greater of:

(*1*) The risk-based capital requirement for the protected exposure as calculated under section 31 of this appendix, with the LGD of the exposure adjusted to reflect the guarantee or credit derivative and EAD set equal to P; or

(*2*) The risk-based capital requirement for a direct exposure to the guarantor as calculated under section 31 of this appendix, using the PD for the protection provider, the LGD for the guarantee or credit derivative, and an EAD set equal to P.

(B) The bank must calculate its risk-based capital requirement for the unprotected exposure under section 31 of this appendix, where PD is the obligor's PD, LGD is the hedged exposure's LGD (not adjusted to reflect the guarantee or credit derivative), and EAD is the EAD of the original hedged exposure minus P.

(3) *M of hedged exposures.* The M of the hedged exposure is the same as the M of the exposure if it were unhedged.

(d) *Maturity mismatch.* (1) A bank that recognizes an eligible guarantee or eligible credit derivative in determining its risk-based capital requirement for a hedged exposure must adjust the effective notional amount of the credit risk mitigant to reflect any maturity mismatch between the hedged exposure and the credit risk mitigant.

(2) A maturity mismatch occurs when the residual maturity of a credit risk mitigant is less than that of the hedged exposure(s).

(3) The residual maturity of a hedged exposure is the longest possible remaining time before the obligor is scheduled to fulfill its obligation on the exposure. If a credit risk mitigant has embedded options that may reduce its term, the bank (protection purchaser) must use the shortest possible residual maturity for the credit risk mitigant. If a call is at the discretion of the protection provider, the residual maturity of the credit risk mitigant is at the first call date. If the call is at the discretion of the bank (protection purchaser), but the terms of the arrangement at origination of the credit risk mitigant contain a positive incentive for the bank to call the transaction before contractual maturity, the remaining time to the first call date is the residual maturity of the credit risk mitigant. For example, where there is a step-up in cost in conjunction with a call feature or where the effective cost of protection increases over time even if credit quality remains the same or improves, the residual maturity of the credit risk mitigant will be the remaining time to the first call.

(4) A credit risk mitigant with a maturity mismatch may be recognized only if its original maturity is greater than or equal to one year and its residual maturity is greater than three months.

(5) When a maturity mismatch exists, the bank must apply the following adjustment to the effective notional amount of the credit risk mitigant: $Pm = E \times (t - 0.25)/(T - 0.25)$, where:

(i) Pm = effective notional amount of the credit risk mitigant, adjusted for maturity mismatch;

(ii) E = effective notional amount of the credit risk mitigant;

(iii) t = the lesser of T or the residual maturity of the credit risk mitigant, expressed in years; and

(iv) T = the lesser of five or the residual maturity of the hedged exposure, expressed in years.

(e) *Credit derivatives without restructuring as a credit event.* If a bank recognizes an eligible credit derivative that does not include as a credit event a restructuring of the hedged exposure involving forgiveness or postponement of principal, interest, or fees that results in a credit loss event (that is, a charge-off, specific provision, or other similar debit to the profit and loss account), the bank must apply the following adjustment to the effective notional amount of the credit derivative: $Pr = Pm \times 0.60$, where:

(1) Pr = effective notional amount of the credit risk mitigant, adjusted for lack of restructuring event (and maturity mismatch, if applicable); and

(2) Pm = effective notional amount of the credit risk mitigant adjusted for maturity mismatch (if applicable).

(f) *Currency mismatch.* (1) If a bank recognizes an eligible guarantee or eligible credit derivative that is denominated in a currency different from that in which the hedged exposure is denominated, the bank must apply the following formula to the effective notional amount of the guarantee or credit derivative: $Pc = Pr \times (1 - H_{FX})$, where:

(i) Pc = effective notional amount of the credit risk mitigant, adjusted for currency mismatch (and maturity mismatch and lack of restructuring event, if applicable);

(ii) Pr = effective notional amount of the credit risk mitigant (adjusted for maturity mismatch and lack of restructuring event, if applicable); and

(iii) H_{FX} = haircut appropriate for the currency mismatch between the credit risk mitigant and the hedged exposure.

(2) A bank must set H_{FX} equal to 8 percent unless it qualifies for the use of and uses its own internal estimates of foreign exchange volatility based on a ten-business-day holding period and daily marking-to-market and remargining. A bank qualifies for the use of its own internal estimates of foreign exchange volatility if it qualifies for:

(i) The own-estimates haircuts in paragraph (b)(2)(iii) of section 32 of this appendix;

(ii) The simple VaR methodology in paragraph (b)(3) of section 32 of this appendix; or

(iii) The internal models methodology in paragraph (d) of section 32 of this appendix.

(3) A bank must adjust H_{FX} calculated in paragraph (f)(2) of this section upward if the bank revalues the guarantee or credit derivative less frequently than once every ten business days using the square root of time formula provided in paragraph (b)(2)(iii)(A)(2) of section 32 of this appendix.

Section 34. Guarantees and Credit Derivatives: Double Default Treatment

(a) *Eligibility and operational criteria for double default treatment.* A bank may recognize the credit risk mitigation benefits of a guarantee or credit derivative covering an exposure described in paragraph (a)(1) of section 33 of this appendix by applying the double default treatment in this section if all the following criteria are satisfied.

(1) The hedged exposure is fully covered or covered on a pro rata basis by:

(i) An eligible guarantee issued by an eligible double default guarantor; or

(ii) An eligible credit derivative that meets the requirements of paragraph (b)(2) of section 33 of this appendix and is issued by an eligible double default guarantor.

(2) The guarantee or credit derivative is:

(i) An uncollateralized guarantee or uncollateralized credit derivative (for example, a credit default swap) that provides protection with respect to a single reference obligor; or

(ii) An nth-to-default credit derivative (subject to the requirements of paragraph (m) of section 42 of this appendix).

(3) The hedged exposure is a wholesale exposure (other than a sovereign exposure).

(4) The obligor of the hedged exposure is not:

(i) An eligible double default guarantor or an affiliate of an eligible double default guarantor; or

(ii) An affiliate of the guarantor.

(5) The bank does not recognize any credit risk mitigation benefits of the guarantee or credit derivative for the hedged exposure other than through application of the double default treatment as provided in this section.

(6) The bank has implemented a process (which has received the prior, written approval of the FDIC) to detect excessive correlation between the creditworthiness of the obligor of the hedged exposure and the protection provider. If excessive correlation is present, the bank may not use the double default treatment for the hedged exposure.

(b) *Full coverage.* If the transaction meets the criteria in paragraph (a) of this section and the protection amount (P) of the guarantee or credit derivative is at least equal to the EAD of the hedged exposure, the bank may determine its risk-weighted asset amount for the hedged exposure under paragraph (e) of this section.

(c) *Partial coverage.* If the transaction meets the criteria in paragraph (a) of this section and the protection amount (P) of the guarantee or credit derivative is less than the EAD of the hedged exposure, the bank must treat the hedged exposure as two separate exposures (protected and unprotected) in order to recognize double default treatment on the protected portion of the exposure.

(1) For the protected exposure, the bank must set EAD equal to P and calculate its risk-weighted asset amount as provided in paragraph (e) of this section.

(2) For the unprotected exposure, the bank must set EAD equal to the EAD of the original exposure minus P and then calculate its risk-weighted asset amount as provided in section 31 of this appendix.

(d) *Mismatches.* For any hedged exposure to which a bank applies double default treatment, the bank must make applicable adjustments to the protection amount as required in paragraphs (d), (e), and (f) of section 33 of this appendix.

(e) *The double default dollar risk-based capital requirement.* The dollar risk-based capital requirement for a hedged exposure to which a bank has applied double default treatment is K_{DD} multiplied by the EAD of the exposure. K_{DD} is calculated according to the following formula: $K_{DD} = K_o \times (0.15 + 160 \times PD_g)$,

Where:

(1)

$$K_O = LGD_g \times \left[N\left(\frac{N^{-1}(PD_o) + N^{-1}(0.999)\sqrt{\rho_{os}}}{\sqrt{1-\rho_{os}}} \right) - PD_o \right] \times \left[\frac{1+(M-2.5)\times b}{1-1.5\times b} \right]$$

(2) PD_g = PD of the protection provider.

(3) PD_o = PD of the obligor of the hedged exposure.

(4) LGD_g = (i) The lower of the LGD of the hedged exposure (not adjusted to reflect the guarantee or credit derivative) and the LGD of the guarantee or credit derivative, if the guarantee or credit derivative provides the bank with the option to receive immediate payout on triggering the protection; or

(ii) The LGD of the guarantee or credit derivative, if the guarantee or credit derivative does not provide the bank with the option to receive immediate payout on triggering the protection.

(5) ρ_{os} (asset value correlation of the obligor) is calculated according to the appropriate formula for (R) provided in Table 2 in section 31 of this appendix, with PD equal to PD_o.

(6) b (maturity adjustment coefficient) is calculated according to the formula for b provided in Table 2 in section 31 of this appendix, with PD equal to the lesser of PD_o and PD_g.

(7) M (maturity) is the effective maturity of the guarantee or credit derivative, which may not be less than one year or greater than five years.

Section 35. Risk-Based Capital Requirement for Unsettled Transactions

(a) *Definitions.* For purposes of this section:

(1) *Delivery-versus-payment (DvP) transaction* means a securities or commodities transaction in which the buyer is obligated to make payment only if the seller has made delivery of the securities or commodities and the seller is obligated to deliver the securities or commodities only if the buyer has made payment.

(2) *Payment-versus-payment (PvP) transaction* means a foreign exchange transaction in which each counterparty is obligated to make a final transfer of one or more currencies only if the other counterparty has made a final transfer of one or more currencies.

(3) *Normal settlement period.* A transaction has a *normal settlement period* if the contractual settlement period for the transaction is equal to or less than the market standard for the instrument underlying the transaction and equal to or less than five business days.

(4) *Positive current exposure.* The positive current exposure of a bank for a transaction is the difference between the transaction value at the agreed settlement price and the current market price of the transaction, if the difference results in a credit exposure of the bank to the counterparty.

(b) *Scope.* This section applies to all transactions involving securities, foreign exchange instruments, and commodities that have a risk of delayed settlement or delivery. This section does not apply to:

(1) Transactions accepted by a qualifying central counterparty that are subject to daily marking-to-market and daily receipt and payment of variation margin;

(2) Repo-style transactions, including unsettled repo-style transactions (which are addressed in sections 31 and 32 of this appendix);

(3) One-way cash payments on OTC derivative contracts (which are addressed in sections 31 and 32 of this appendix); or

(4) Transactions with a contractual settlement period that is longer than the normal settlement period (which are treated as OTC derivative contracts and addressed in sections 31 and 32 of this appendix).

(c) *System-wide failures.* In the case of a system-wide failure of a settlement or clearing system, the FDIC may waive risk-based capital requirements for unsettled and failed transactions until the situation is rectified.

(d) *Delivery-versus-payment (DvP) and payment-versus-payment (PvP) transactions.* A bank must hold risk-based capital against any DvP or PvP transaction with a normal settlement period if the bank's counterparty has not made delivery or payment within five business days after the settlement date. The bank must determine its risk-weighted asset amount for such a transaction by multiplying the positive current exposure of the transaction for the bank by the appropriate risk weight in Table 5.

TABLE 5—RISK WEIGHTS FOR UNSETTLED DvP AND PvP TRANSACTIONS

Number of business days after contractual settlement date	Risk weight to be applied to positive current exposure (percent)
From 5 to 15	100
From 16 to 30	625
From 31 to 45	937.5
46 or more	1,250

(e) *Non-DvP/non-PvP (non-delivery-versus-payment/non-payment-versus-payment) transactions.* (1) A bank must hold risk-based capital against any non-DvP/non-PvP transaction with a normal settlement period if

Federal Deposit Insurance Corporation

the bank has delivered cash, securities, commodities, or currencies to its counterparty but has not received its corresponding deliverables by the end of the same business day. The bank must continue to hold risk-based capital against the transaction until the bank has received its corresponding deliverables.

(2) From the business day after the bank has made its delivery until five business days after the counterparty delivery is due, the bank must calculate its risk-based capital requirement for the transaction by treating the current market value of the deliverables owed to the bank as a wholesale exposure.

(i) A bank may assign an obligor rating to a counterparty for which it is not otherwise required under this appendix to assign an obligor rating on the basis of the applicable external rating of any outstanding unsecured long-term debt security without credit enhancement issued by the counterparty.

(ii) A bank may use a 45 percent LGD for the transaction rather than estimating LGD for the transaction provided the bank uses the 45 percent LGD for all transactions described in paragraphs (e)(1) and (e)(2) of this section.

(iii) A bank may use a 100 percent risk weight for the transaction provided the bank uses this risk weight for all transactions described in paragraphs (e)(1) and (e)(2) of this section.

(3) If the bank has not received its deliverables by the fifth business day after the counterparty delivery was due, the bank must deduct the current market value of the deliverables owed to the bank 50 percent from tier 1 capital and 50 percent from tier 2 capital.

(f) *Total risk-weighted assets for unsettled transactions.* Total risk-weighted assets for unsettled transactions is the sum of the risk-weighted asset amounts of all DvP, PvP, and non-DvP/non-PvP transactions.

PART V. RISK-WEIGHTED ASSETS FOR SECURITIZATION EXPOSURES

Section 41. Operational Criteria for Recognizing the Transfer of Risk

(a) *Operational criteria for traditional securitizations.* A bank that transfers exposures it has originated or purchased to a securitization SPE or other third party in connection with a traditional securitization may exclude the exposures from the calculation of its risk-weighted assets only if each of the conditions in this paragraph (a) is satisfied. A bank that meets these conditions must hold risk-based capital against any securitization exposures it retains in connection with the securitization. A bank that fails to meet these conditions must hold risk-based capital against the transferred exposures as if they had not been securitized and must deduct from tier 1 capital any after-tax gain-on-sale resulting from the transaction. The conditions are:

(1) The transfer is considered a sale under GAAP;

(2) The bank has transferred to third parties credit risk associated with the underlying exposures; and

(3) Any clean-up calls relating to the securitization are eligible clean-up calls.

(b) *Operational criteria for synthetic securitizations.* For synthetic securitizations, a bank may recognize for risk-based capital purposes the use of a credit risk mitigant to hedge underlying exposures only if each of the conditions in this paragraph (b) is satisfied. A bank that fails to meet these conditions must hold risk-based capital against the underlying exposures as if they had not been synthetically securitized. The conditions are:

(1) The credit risk mitigant is financial collateral, an eligible credit derivative from an eligible securitization guarantor or an eligible guarantee from an eligible securitization guarantor;

(2) The bank transfers credit risk associated with the underlying exposures to third parties, and the terms and conditions in the credit risk mitigants employed do not include provisions that:

(i) Allow for the termination of the credit protection due to deterioration in the credit quality of the underlying exposures;

(ii) Require the bank to alter or replace the underlying exposures to improve the credit quality of the pool of underlying exposures;

(iii) Increase the bank's cost of credit protection in response to deterioration in the credit quality of the underlying exposures;

(iv) Increase the yield payable to parties other than the bank in response to a deterioration in the credit quality of the underlying exposures; or

(v) Provide for increases in a retained first loss position or credit enhancement provided by the bank after the inception of the securitization;

(3) The bank obtains a well-reasoned opinion from legal counsel that confirms the enforceability of the credit risk mitigant in all relevant jurisdictions; and

(4) Any clean-up calls relating to the securitization are eligible clean-up calls.

Section 42. Risk-Based Capital Requirement for Securitization Exposures

(a) *Hierarchy of approaches.* Except as provided elsewhere in this section:

(1) A bank must deduct from tier 1 capital any after-tax gain-on-sale resulting from a securitization and must deduct from total capital in accordance with paragraph (c) of this section the portion of any CEIO that does not constitute gain-on-sale.

(2) If a securitization exposure does not require deduction under paragraph (a)(1) of

this section and qualifies for the Ratings-Based Approach in section 43 of this appendix, a bank must apply the Ratings-Based Approach to the exposure.

(3) If a securitization exposure does not require deduction under paragraph (a)(1) of this section and does not qualify for the Ratings-Based Approach, the bank may either apply the Internal Assessment Approach in section 44 of this appendix to the exposure (if the bank, the exposure, and the relevant ABCP program qualify for the Internal Assessment Approach) or the Supervisory Formula Approach in section 45 of this appendix to the exposure (if the bank and the exposure qualify for the Supervisory Formula Approach).

(4) If a securitization exposure does not require deduction under paragraph (a)(1) of this section and does not qualify for the Ratings-Based Approach, the Internal Assessment Approach, or the Supervisory Formula Approach, the bank must deduct the exposure from total capital in accordance with paragraph (c) of this section.

(5) If a securitization exposure is an OTC derivative contract (other than a credit derivative) that has a first priority claim on the cash flows from the underlying exposures (notwithstanding amounts due under interest rate or currency derivative contracts, fees due, or other similar payments), with approval of the FDIC, a bank may choose to set the risk-weighted asset amount of the exposure equal to the amount of the exposure as determined in paragraph (e) of this section rather than apply the hierarchy of approaches described in paragraphs (a)(1) through (4) of this section.

(b) *Total risk-weighted assets for securitization exposures.* A bank's total risk-weighted assets for securitization exposures is equal to the sum of its risk-weighted assets calculated using the Ratings-Based Approach in section 43 of this appendix, the Internal Assessment Approach in section 44 of this appendix, and the Supervisory Formula Approach in section 45 of this appendix, and its risk-weighted assets amount for early amortization provisions calculated in section 47 of this appendix.

(c) *Deductions.* (1) If a bank must deduct a securitization exposure from total capital, the bank must take the deduction 50 percent from tier 1 capital and 50 percent from tier 2 capital. If the amount deductible from tier 2 capital exceeds the bank's tier 2 capital, the bank must deduct the excess from tier 1 capital.

(2) A bank may calculate any deduction from tier 1 capital and tier 2 capital for a securitization exposure net of any deferred tax liabilities associated with the securitization exposure.

(d) *Maximum risk-based capital requirement.* Regardless of any other provisions of this part, unless one or more underlying exposures does not meet the definition of a wholesale, retail, securitization, or equity exposure, the total risk-based capital requirement for all securitization exposures held by a single bank associated with a single securitization (including any risk-based capital requirements that relate to an early amortization provision of the securitization but excluding any risk-based capital requirements that relate to the bank's gain-on-sale or CEIOs associated with the securitization) may not exceed the sum of:

(1) The bank's total risk-based capital requirement for the underlying exposures as if the bank directly held the underlying exposures; and

(2) The total ECL of the underlying exposures.

(e) *Amount of a securitization exposure.* (1) The amount of an on-balance sheet securitization exposure that is not a repo-style transaction, eligible margin loan, or OTC derivative contract (other than a credit derivative) is:

(i) The bank's carrying value minus any unrealized gains and plus any unrealized losses on the exposure, if the exposure is a security classified as available-for-sale; or

(ii) The bank's carrying value, if the exposure is not a security classified as available-for-sale.

(2) The amount of an off-balance sheet securitization exposure that is not an OTC derivative contract (other than a credit derivative) is the notional amount of the exposure. For an off-balance-sheet securitization exposure to an ABCP program, such as a liquidity facility, the notional amount may be reduced to the maximum potential amount that the bank could be required to fund given the ABCP program's current underlying assets (calculated without regard to the current credit quality of those assets).

(3) The amount of a securitization exposure that is a repo-style transaction, eligible margin loan, or OTC derivative contract (other than a credit derivative) is the EAD of the exposure as calculated in section 32 of this appendix.

(f) *Overlapping exposures.* If a bank has multiple securitization exposures that provide duplicative coverage of the underlying exposures of a securitization (such as when a bank provides a program-wide credit enhancement and multiple pool-specific liquidity facilities to an ABCP program), the bank is not required to hold duplicative risk-based capital against the overlapping position. Instead, the bank may apply to the overlapping position the applicable risk-based capital treatment that results in the highest risk-based capital requirement.

(g) *Securitizations of non-IRB exposures.* If a bank has a securitization exposure where any underlying exposure is not a wholesale exposure, retail exposure, securitization exposure, or equity exposure, the bank must:

Federal Deposit Insurance Corporation

(1) If the bank is an originating bank, deduct from tier 1 capital any after-tax gain-on-sale resulting from the securitization and deduct from total capital in accordance with paragraph (c) of this section the portion of any CEIO that does not constitute gain-on-sale;

(2) If the securitization exposure does not require deduction under paragraph (g)(1), apply the RBA in section 43 of this appendix to the securitization exposure if the exposure qualifies for the RBA;

(3) If the securitization exposure does not require deduction under paragraph (g)(1) and does not qualify for the RBA, apply the IAA in section 44 of this appendix to the exposure (if the bank, the exposure, and the relevant ABCP program qualify for the IAA); and

(4) If the securitization exposure does not require deduction under paragraph (g)(1) and does not qualify for the RBA or the IAA, deduct the exposure from total capital in accordance with paragraph (c) of this section.

(h) *Implicit support.* If a bank provides support to a securitization in excess of the bank's contractual obligation to provide credit support to the securitization (implicit support):

(1) The bank must hold regulatory capital against all of the underlying exposures associated with the securitization as if the exposures had not been securitized and must deduct from tier 1 capital any after-tax gain-on-sale resulting from the securitization; and

(2) The bank must disclose publicly:

(i) That it has provided implicit support to the securitization; and

(ii) The regulatory capital impact to the bank of providing such implicit support.

(i) *Eligible servicer cash advance facilities.* Regardless of any other provisions of this part, a bank is not required to hold risk-based capital against the undrawn portion of an eligible servicer cash advance facility.

(j) *Interest-only mortgage-backed securities.* Regardless of any other provisions of this part, the risk weight for a non-credit-enhancing interest-only mortgage-backed security may not be less than 100 percent.

(k) *Small-business loans and leases on personal property transferred with recourse.* (1) Regardless of any other provisions of this appendix, a bank that has transferred small-business loans and leases on personal property (small-business obligations) with recourse must include in risk-weighted assets only the contractual amount of retained recourse if all the following conditions are met:

(i) The transaction is a sale under GAAP.

(ii) The bank establishes and maintains, pursuant to GAAP, a non-capital reserve sufficient to meet the bank's reasonably estimated liability under the recourse arrangement.

Pt. 325, App. D

(iii) The loans and leases are to businesses that meet the criteria for a small-business concern established by the Small Business Administration under section 3(a) of the Small Business Act (15 U.S.C. 632).

(iv) The bank is well capitalized, as defined in the FDIC's prompt corrective action regulation at 12 CFR part 325, subpart B. For purposes of determining whether a bank is well capitalized for purposes of this paragraph, the bank's capital ratios must be calculated without regard to the capital treatment for transfers of small-business obligations with recourse specified in paragraph (k)(1) of this section. For purposes of determining whether a bank is well capitalized for purposes of this paragraph, the bank's capital ratios must be calculated without regard to the capital treatment for transfers of small-business obligations with recourse specified in paragraph (k)(1) of this section.

(2) The total outstanding amount of recourse retained by a bank on transfers of small-business obligations receiving the capital treatment specified in paragraph (k)(1) of this section cannot exceed 15 percent of the bank's total qualifying capital.

(3) If a bank ceases to be well capitalized or exceeds the 15 percent capital limitation, the preferential capital treatment specified in paragraph (k)(1) of this section will continue to apply to any transfers of small-business obligations with recourse that occurred during the time that the bank was well capitalized and did not exceed the capital limit.

(4) The risk-based capital ratios of the bank must be calculated without regard to the capital treatment for transfers of small-business obligations with recourse specified in paragraph (k)(1) of this section as provided in 12 CFR part 325, appendix A.

(l) N^{th}-*to-default credit derivatives*—(1) *First-to-default credit derivatives*—(i) *Protection purchaser.* A bank that obtains credit protection on a group of underlying exposures through a first-to-default credit derivative must determine its risk-based capital requirement for the underlying exposures as if the bank synthetically securitized the underlying exposure with the lowest risk-based capital requirement and had obtained no credit risk mitigant on the other underlying exposures.

(ii) *Protection provider.* A bank that provides credit protection on a group of underlying exposures through a first-to-default credit derivative must determine its risk-weighted asset amount for the derivative by applying the RBA in section 43 of this appendix (if the derivative qualifies for the RBA) or, if the derivative does not qualify for the RBA, by setting its risk-weighted asset amount for the derivative equal to the product of:

(A) The protection amount of the derivative;

(B) 12.5; and

(C) The sum of the risk-based capital requirements of the individual underlying exposures, up to a maximum of 100 percent.

(2) *Second-or-subsequent-to-default credit derivatives*—(i) *Protection purchaser.* (A) A bank that obtains credit protection on a group of underlying exposures through a nth-to-default credit derivative (other than a first-to-default credit derivative) may recognize the credit risk mitigation benefits of the derivative only if:

(*1*) The bank also has obtained credit protection on the same underlying exposures in the form of first-through-(n-1)-to-default credit derivatives; or

(*2*) If n-1 of the underlying exposures have already defaulted.

(B) If a bank satisfies the requirements of paragraph (m)(2)(i)(A) of this section, the bank must determine its risk-based capital requirement for the underlying exposures as if the bank had only synthetically securitized the underlying exposure with the nth lowest risk-based capital requirement and had obtained no credit risk mitigant on the other underlying exposures.

(ii) *Protection provider.* A bank that provides credit protection on a group of underlying exposures through a nth-to-default credit derivative (other than a first-to-default credit derivative) must determine its risk-weighted asset amount for the derivative by applying the RBA in section 43 of this appendix (if the derivative qualifies for the RBA) or, if the derivative does not qualify for the RBA, by setting its risk-weighted asset amount for the derivative equal to the product of:

(A) The protection amount of the derivative;

(B) 12.5; and

(C) The sum of the risk-based capital requirements of the individual underlying exposures (excluding the n-1 underlying exposures with the lowest risk-based capital requirements), up to a maximum of 100 percent.

Section 43. Ratings-Based Approach (RBA)

(a) *Eligibility requirements for use of the RBA*—(1) *Originating bank.* An originating bank must use the RBA to calculate its risk-based capital requirement for a securitization exposure if the exposure has two or more external ratings or inferred ratings (and may not use the RBA if the exposure has fewer than two external ratings or inferred ratings).

(2) *Investing bank.* An investing bank must use the RBA to calculate its risk-based capital requirement for a securitization exposure if the exposure has one or more external or inferred ratings (and may not use the RBA if the exposure has no external or inferred rating).

(b) *Ratings-based approach.* (1) A bank must determine the risk-weighted asset amount for a securitization exposure by multiplying the amount of the exposure (as defined in paragraph (e) of section 42 of this appendix) by the appropriate risk weight provided in Table 6 and Table 7.

(2) A bank must apply the risk weights in Table 6 when the securitization exposure's applicable external or applicable inferred rating represents a long-term credit rating, and must apply the risk weights in Table 7 when the securitization exposure's applicable external or applicable inferred rating represents a short-term credit rating.

(i) A bank must apply the risk weights in column 1 of Table 6 or Table 7 to the securitization exposure if:

(A) N (as calculated under paragraph (e)(6) of section 45 of this appendix) is six or more (for purposes of this section only, if the notional number of underlying exposures is 25 or more or if all of the underlying exposures are retail exposures, a bank may assume that N is six or more unless the bank knows or has reason to know that N is less than six); and

(B) The securitization exposure is a senior securitization exposure.

(ii) A bank must apply the risk weights in column 3 of Table 6 or Table 7 to the securitization exposure if N is less than six, regardless of the seniority of the securitization exposure.

(iii) Otherwise, a bank must apply the risk weights in column 2 of Table 6 or Table 7.

TABLE 6—LONG-TERM CREDIT RATING RISK WEIGHTS UNDER RBA AND IAA

Applicable external or inferred rating (Illustrative rating example)	Column 1 Risk weights for senior securitization exposures backed by granular pools	Column 2 Risk weights for non-senior securitization exposures backed by granular pools	Column 3 Risk weights for securitization exposures backed by non-granular pools
Highest investment grade (for example, AAA)	7%	12%	20%
Second highest investment grade (for example, AA)	8%	15%	25%
Third-highest investment grade—positive designation (for example, A+)	10%	18%	35%
Third-highest investment grade (for example, A)	12%	20%	
Third-highest investment grade—negative designation (for example, A−)	20%	35%	

Federal Deposit Insurance Corporation
Pt. 325, App. D

TABLE 6—LONG-TERM CREDIT RATING RISK WEIGHTS UNDER RBA AND IAA—Continued

Applicable external or inferred rating (Illustrative rating example)	Column 1 Risk weights for senior securitization exposures backed by granular pools	Column 2 Risk weights for non-senior securitization exposures backed by granular pools	Column 3 Risk weights for securitization exposures backed by non-granular pools
Lowest investment grade—positive designation (for example, BBB+)	35%	50%	
Lowest investment grade (for example, BBB)	60%	75%	
Lowest investment grade—negative designation (for example, BBB−)	100%		
One category below investment grade—positive designation (for example, BB+)	250%		
One category below investment grade (for example, BB)	425%		
One category below investment grade—negative designation (for example, BB−)	650%		
More than one category below investment grade	Deduction from tier 1 and tier 2 capital.		

TABLE 7—SHORT-TERM CREDIT RATING RISK WEIGHTS UNDER RBA AND IAA

Applicable external or inferred rating (Illustrative rating example)	Column 1 Risk weights for senior securitization exposures backed by granular pools	Column 2 Risk weights for non-senior securitization exposures backed by granular pools	Column 3 Risk weights for securitization exposures backed by non-granular pools
Highest investment grade (for example, A1)	7%	12%	20%
Second highest investment grade (for example, A2)	12%	20%	35%
Third highest investment grade (for example, A3)	60%	75%	75%
All other ratings	Deduction from tier 1 and tier 2 capital.		

Section 44. Internal Assessment Approach (IAA)

(a) *Eligibility requirements.* A bank may apply the IAA to calculate the risk-weighted asset amount for a securitization exposure that the bank has to an ABCP program (such as a liquidity facility or credit enhancement) if the bank, the ABCP program, and the exposure qualify for use of the IAA.

(1) *Bank qualification criteria.* A bank qualifies for use of the IAA if the bank has received the prior written approval of the FDIC. To receive such approval, the bank must demonstrate to the FDIC's satisfaction that the bank's internal assessment process meets the following criteria:

(i) The bank's internal credit assessments of securitization exposures must be based on publicly available rating criteria used by an NRSRO.

(ii) The bank's internal credit assessments of securitization exposures used for risk-based capital purposes must be consistent with those used in the bank's internal risk management process, management information reporting systems, and capital adequacy assessment process.

(iii) The bank's internal credit assessment process must have sufficient granularity to identify gradations of risk. Each of the bank's internal credit assessment categories must correspond to an external rating of an NRSRO.

(iv) The bank's internal credit assessment process, particularly the stress test factors for determining credit enhancement requirements, must be at least as conservative as the most conservative of the publicly available rating criteria of the NRSROs that have provided external ratings to the commercial paper issued by the ABCP program.

(A) Where the commercial paper issued by an ABCP program has an external rating from two or more NRSROs and the different NRSROs' benchmark stress factors require different levels of credit enhancement to achieve the same external rating equivalent, the bank must apply the NRSRO stress factor that requires the highest level of credit enhancement.

(B) If any NRSRO that provides an external rating to the ABCP program's commercial paper changes its methodology (including stress factors), the bank must evaluate whether to revise its internal assessment process.

(v) The bank must have an effective system of controls and oversight that ensures compliance with these operational requirements and maintains the integrity and accuracy of the internal credit assessments. The bank must have an internal audit function independent from the ABCP program business line and internal credit assessment process that assesses at least annually whether the controls over the internal credit assessment process function as intended.

(vi) The bank must review and update each internal credit assessment whenever new material information is available, but no less frequently than annually.

(vii) The bank must validate its internal credit assessment process on an ongoing basis and at least annually.

(2) *ABCP-program qualification criteria.* An ABCP program qualifies for use of the IAA if all commercial paper issued by the ABCP program has an external rating.

(3) *Exposure qualification criteria.* A securitization exposure qualifies for use of the IAA if the exposure meets the following criteria:

(i) The bank initially rated the exposure at least the equivalent of investment grade.

(ii) The ABCP program has robust credit and investment guidelines (that is, underwriting standards) for the exposures underlying the securitization exposure.

(iii) The ABCP program performs a detailed credit analysis of the sellers of the exposures underlying the securitization exposure.

(iv) The ABCP program's underwriting policy for the exposures underlying the securitization exposure establishes minimum asset eligibility criteria that include the prohibition of the purchase of assets that are significantly past due or of assets that are defaulted (that is, assets that have been charged off or written down by the seller prior to being placed into the ABCP program or assets that would be charged off or written down under the program's governing contracts), as well as limitations on concentration to individual obligors or geographic areas and the tenor of the assets to be purchased.

(v) The aggregate estimate of loss on the exposures underlying the securitization exposure considers all sources of potential risk, such as credit and dilution risk.

(vi) Where relevant, the ABCP program incorporates structural features into each purchase of exposures underlying the securitization exposure to mitigate potential credit deterioration of the underlying exposures. Such features may include wind-down triggers specific to a pool of underlying exposures.

(b) *Mechanics.* A bank that elects to use the IAA to calculate the risk-based capital requirement for any securitization exposure must use the IAA to calculate the risk-based capital requirements for all securitization exposures that qualify for the IAA approach. Under the IAA, a bank must map its internal assessment of such a securitization exposure to an equivalent external rating from an NRSRO. Under the IAA, a bank must determine the risk-weighted asset amount for such a securitization exposure by multiplying the amount of the exposure (as defined in paragraph (e) of section 42 of this appendix) by the appropriate risk weight in Table 6 and Table 7 in paragraph (b) of section 43 of this appendix.

Section 45. Supervisory Formula Approach (SFA)

(a) *Eligibility requirements.* A bank may use the SFA to determine its risk-based capital requirement for a securitization exposure only if the bank can calculate on an ongoing basis each of the SFA parameters in paragraph (e) of this section.

(b) *Mechanics.* Under the SFA, a securitization exposure incurs a deduction from total capital (as described in paragraph (c) of section 42 of this appendix) and/or an SFA risk-based capital requirement, as determined in paragraph (c) of this section. The risk-weighted asset amount for the securitization exposure equals the SFA risk-based capital requirement for the exposure multiplied by 12.5.

(c) *The SFA risk-based capital requirement.* (1) If K_{IRB} is greater than or equal to L + T, the entire exposure must be deducted from total capital.

(2) If K_{IRB} is less than or equal to L, the exposure's SFA risk-based capital requirement is UE multiplied by TP multiplied by the greater of:

(i) 0.0056 * T; or

(ii) S[L + T] − S[L].

(3) If K_{IRB} is greater than L and less than L + T, the bank must deduct from total capital an amount equal to UE*TP*(K_{IRB} − L), and the exposure's SFA risk-based capital requirement is UE multiplied by TP multiplied by the greater of:

(i) 0.0056 * (T − (K_{IRB} − L)); or

(ii) S[L + T] − S[K_{IRB}].

(d) *The supervisory formula:*

Federal Deposit Insurance Corporation Pt. 325, App. D

$$(1)\ S[Y] = \begin{cases} Y & \text{when } Y \le K_{IRB} \\ K_{IRB} + K[Y] - K[K_{IRB}] + \dfrac{d \cdot K_{IRB}}{20}(1 - e^{\frac{20 \cdot (K_{IRB} - Y)}{K_{IRB}}}) & \text{when } Y > K_{IRB} \end{cases}$$

$$(2)\ K[Y] = (1-h) \cdot \left[(1 - \beta[Y;a,b]) \cdot Y + \beta[Y;a+1,b] \cdot c\right]$$

$$(3)\ h = \left(1 - \frac{K_{IRB}}{EWALGD}\right)^N$$

$$(4)\ a = g \cdot c$$

$$(5)\ b = g \cdot (1-c)$$

$$(6)\ c = \frac{K_{IRB}}{1-h}$$

$$(7)\ g = \frac{(1-c) \cdot c}{f} - 1$$

$$(8)\ f = \frac{v + K_{IRB}^{\,2}}{1-h} - c^2 + \frac{(1 - K_{IRB}) \cdot K_{IRB} - v}{(1-h) \cdot 1000}$$

$$(9)\ v = K_{IRB} \cdot \frac{(EWALGD - K_{IRB}) + .25 \cdot (1 - EWALGD)}{N}$$

$$(10)\ d = 1 - (1-h) \cdot (1 - \beta[K_{IRB};a,b]).$$

(11) In these expressions, β[Y; a, b] refers to the cumulative beta distribution with parameters a and b evaluated at Y. In the case where N = 1 and EWALGD = 100 percent, S[Y] in formula (1) must be calculated with K[Y] set equal to the product of K$_{IRB}$ and Y, and d set equal to 1 − K$_{IRB}$.

(e) *SFA parameters*—(1) *Amount of the underlying exposures (UE).* UE is the EAD of any underlying exposures that are wholesale and retail exposures (including the amount of any funded spread accounts, cash collateral accounts, and other similar funded credit enhancements) plus the amount of any underlying exposures that are securitization exposures (as defined in paragraph (e) of section 42 of this appendix) plus the adjusted carrying value of any underlying exposures that are equity exposures (as defined in paragraph (b) of section 51 of this appendix).

(2) *Tranche percentage (TP).* TP is the ratio of the amount of the bank's securitization

exposure to the amount of the tranche that contains the securitization exposure.

(3) *Capital requirement on underlying exposures (K_{IRB}).* (i) K_{IRB} is the ratio of:

(A) The sum of the risk-based capital requirements for the underlying exposures plus the expected credit losses of the underlying exposures (as determined under this appendix as if the underlying exposures were directly held by the bank); to

(B) UE.

(ii) The calculation of K_{IRB} must reflect the effects of any credit risk mitigant applied to the underlying exposures (either to an individual underlying exposure, to a group of underlying exposures, or to the entire pool of underlying exposures).

(iii) All assets related to the securitization are treated as underlying exposures, including assets in a reserve account (such as a cash collateral account).

(4) *Credit enhancement level (L).* (i) L is the ratio of:

(A) The amount of all securitization exposures subordinated to the tranche that contains the bank's securitization exposure; to

(B) UE.

(ii) A bank must determine L before considering the effects of any tranche-specific credit enhancements.

(iii) Any gain-on-sale or CEIO associated with the securitization may not be included in L.

(iv) Any reserve account funded by accumulated cash flows from the underlying exposures that is subordinated to the tranche that contains the bank's securitization exposure may be included in the numerator and denominator of L to the extent cash has accumulated in the account. Unfunded reserve accounts (that is, reserve accounts that are to be funded from future cash flows from the underlying exposures) may not be included in the calculation of L.

(v) In some cases, the purchase price of receivables will reflect a discount that provides credit enhancement (for example, first loss protection) for all or certain tranches of the securitization. When this arises, L should be calculated inclusive of this discount if the discount provides credit enhancement for the securitization exposure.

(5) *Thickness of tranche (T).* T is the ratio of:

(i) The amount of the tranche that contains the bank's securitization exposure; to

(ii) UE.

(6) *Effective number of exposures (N).* (i) Unless the bank elects to use the formula provided in paragraph (f) of this section,

$$N = \frac{(\sum_i EAD_i)^2}{\sum_i EAD_i^2}$$

where EAD_i represents the EAD associated with the ith instrument in the pool of underlying exposures.

(ii) Multiple exposures to one obligor must be treated as a single underlying exposure.

(iii) In the case of a re-securitization (that is, a securitization in which some or all of the underlying exposures are themselves securitization exposures), the bank must treat each underlying exposure as a single underlying exposure and must not look through to the originally securitized underlying exposures.

(7) *Exposure-weighted average loss given default (EWALGD).* EWALGD is calculated as:

$$EWALGD = \frac{\sum_i LGD_i \cdot EAD_i}{\sum_i EAD_i}$$

where LGD_i represents the average LGD associated with all exposures to the ith obligor. In the case of a re-securitization, an LGD of 100 percent must be assumed for the underlying exposures that are themselves securitization exposures.

(f) *Simplified method for computing N and EWALGD.* (1) If all underlying exposures of a securitization are retail exposures, a bank may apply the SFA using the following simplifications:

(i) h = 0; and

(ii) v = 0.

(2) Under the conditions in paragraphs (f)(3) and (f)(4) of this section, a bank may employ a simplified method for calculating N and EWALGD.

(3) If C_1 is no more than 0.03, a bank may set EWALGD = 0.50 if none of the underlying exposures is a securitization exposure or EWALGD = 1 if one or more of the underlying exposures is a securitization exposure, and may set N equal to the following amount:

$$N = \frac{1}{C_1 C_m + \left(\frac{C_m - C_1}{m-1}\right) \max(1 - mC_1, 0)}$$

Federal Deposit Insurance Corporation

Pt. 325, App. D

where:

(i) C_m is the ratio of the sum of the amounts of the 'm' largest underlying exposures to UE; and

(ii) The level of m is to be selected by the bank.

(4) Alternatively, if only C_1 is available and C_1 is no more than 0.03, the bank may set EWALGD = 0.50 if none of the underlying exposures is a securitization exposure or EWALGD = 1 if one or more of the underlying exposures is a securitization exposure and may set N = 1/C_1.

Section 46. Recognition of Credit Risk Mitigants for Securitization Exposures

(a) *General.* An originating bank that has obtained a credit risk mitigant to hedge its securitization exposure to a synthetic or traditional securitization that satisfies the operational criteria in section 41 of this appendix may recognize the credit risk mitigant, but only as provided in this section. An investing bank that has obtained a credit risk mitigant to hedge a securitization exposure may recognize the credit risk mitigant, but only as provided in this section. A bank that has used the RBA in section 43 of this appendix or the IAA in section 44 of this appendix to calculate its risk-based capital requirement for a securitization exposure whose external or inferred rating (or equivalent internal rating under the IAA) reflects the benefits of a credit risk mitigant provided to the associated securitization or that supports some or all of the underlying exposures may not use the credit risk mitigation rules in this section to further reduce its risk-based capital requirement for the exposure to reflect that credit risk mitigant.

(b) *Collateral*—(1) *Rules of recognition.* A bank may recognize financial collateral in determining the bank's risk-based capital requirement for a securitization exposure (other than a repo-style transaction, an eligible margin loan, or an OTC derivative contract for which the bank has reflected collateral in its determination of exposure amount under section 32 of this appendix) as follows. The bank's risk-based capital requirement for the collateralized securitization exposure is equal to the risk-based capital requirement for the securitization exposure as calculated under the RBA in section 43 of this appendix or under the SFA in section 45 of this appendix multiplied by the ratio of adjusted exposure amount (SE*) to original exposure amount (SE), where:

(i) SE* = max {0, [SE—C x (1 – Hs – Hfx)]};

(ii) SE = the amount of the securitization exposure calculated under paragraph (e) of section 42 of this appendix;

(iii) C = the current market value of the collateral;

(iv) Hs = the haircut appropriate to the collateral type; and

(v) Hfx = the haircut appropriate for any currency mismatch between the collateral and the exposure.

(2) *Mixed collateral.* Where the collateral is a basket of different asset types or a basket of assets denominated in different currencies, the haircut on the basket will be

$$H = \sum_i a_i H_i,$$

where a_i is the current market value of the asset in the basket divided by the current market value of all assets in the basket and H_i is the haircut applicable to that asset.

(3) *Standard supervisory haircuts.* Unless a bank qualifies for use of and uses own-estimates haircuts in paragraph (b)(4) of this section:

(i) A bank must use the collateral type haircuts (Hs) in Table 3;

(ii) A bank must use a currency mismatch haircut (Hfx) of 8 percent if the exposure and the collateral are denominated in different currencies;

(iii) A bank must multiply the supervisory haircuts obtained in paragraphs (b)(3)(i) and (ii) by the square root of 6.5 (which equals 2.549510); and

(iv) A bank must adjust the supervisory haircuts upward on the basis of a holding period longer than 65 business days where and as appropriate to take into account the illiquidity of the collateral.

(4) *Own estimates for haircuts.* With the prior written approval of the FDIC, a bank may calculate haircuts using its own internal estimates of market price volatility and foreign exchange volatility, subject to paragraph (b)(2)(iii) of section 32 of this appendix. The minimum holding period (TM) for securitization exposures is 65 business days.

(c) *Guarantees and credit derivatives*—(1) *Limitations on recognition.* A bank may only recognize an eligible guarantee or eligible credit derivative provided by an eligible securitization guarantor in determining the bank's risk-based capital requirement for a securitization exposure.

(2) *ECL for securitization exposures.* When a bank recognizes an eligible guarantee or eligible credit derivative provided by an eligible securitization guarantor in determining the bank's risk-based capital requirement for a securitization exposure, the bank must also:

(i) Calculate ECL for the protected portion of the exposure using the same risk parameters that it uses for calculating the risk-weighted asset amount of the exposure as described in paragraph (c)(3) of this section; and

(ii) Add the exposure's ECL to the bank's total ECL.

Pt. 325, App. D **12 CFR Ch. III (1-1-12 Edition)**

(3) *Rules of recognition.* A bank may recognize an eligible guarantee or eligible credit derivative provided by an eligible securitization guarantor in determining the bank's risk-based capital requirement for the securitization exposure as follows:

(i) *Full coverage.* If the protection amount of the eligible guarantee or eligible credit derivative equals or exceeds the amount of the securitization exposure, the bank may set the risk-weighted asset amount for the securitization exposure equal to the risk-weighted asset amount for a direct exposure to the eligible securitization guarantor (as determined in the wholesale risk weight function described in section 31 of this appendix), using the bank's PD for the guarantor, the bank's LGD for the guarantee or credit derivative, and an EAD equal to the amount of the securitization exposure (as determined in paragraph (e) of section 42 of this appendix).

(ii) *Partial coverage.* If the protection amount of the eligible guarantee or eligible credit derivative is less than the amount of the securitization exposure, the bank may set the risk-weighted asset amount for the securitization exposure equal to the sum of:

(A) *Covered portion.* The risk-weighted asset amount for a direct exposure to the eligible securitization guarantor (as determined in the wholesale risk weight function described in section 31 of this appendix), using the bank's PD for the guarantor, the bank's LGD for the guarantee or credit derivative, and an EAD equal to the protection amount of the credit risk mitigant; and

(B) *Uncovered portion.* (1) 1.0 minus the ratio of the protection amount of the eligible guarantee or eligible credit derivative to the amount of the securitization exposure); multiplied by

(2) The risk-weighted asset amount for the securitization exposure without the credit risk mitigant (as determined in sections 42–45 of this appendix).

(4) *Mismatches.* The bank must make applicable adjustments to the protection amount as required in paragraphs (d), (e), and (f) of section 33 of this appendix for any hedged securitization exposure and any more senior securitization exposure that benefits from the hedge. In the context of a synthetic securitization, when an eligible guarantee or eligible credit derivative covers multiple hedged exposures that have different residual maturities, the bank must use the longest residual maturity of any of the hedged exposures as the residual maturity of all the hedged exposures.

Section 47. Risk-Based Capital Requirement for Early Amortization Provisions

(a) *General.* (1) An originating bank must hold risk-based capital against the sum of the originating bank's interest and the investors' interest in a securitization that:

(i) Includes one or more underlying exposures in which the borrower is permitted to vary the drawn amount within an agreed limit under a line of credit; and

(ii) Contains an early amortization provision.

(2) For securitizations described in paragraph (a)(1) of this section, an originating bank must calculate the risk-based capital requirement for the originating bank's interest under sections 42–45 of this appendix, and the risk-based capital requirement for the investors' interest under paragraph (b) of this section.

(b) *Risk-weighted asset amount for investors' interest.* The originating bank's risk-weighted asset amount for the investors' interest in the securitization is equal to the product of the following 5 quantities:

(1) The investors' interest EAD;

(2) The appropriate conversion factor in paragraph (c) of this section;

(3) K_{IRB} (as defined in paragraph (e)(3) of section 45 of this appendix);

(4) 12.5; and

(5) The proportion of the underlying exposures in which the borrower is permitted to vary the drawn amount within an agreed limit under a line of credit.

(c) *Conversion factor.* (1)(i) Except as provided in paragraph (c)(2) of this section, to calculate the appropriate conversion factor, a bank must use Table 8 for a securitization that contains a controlled early amortization provision and must use Table 9 for a securitization that contains a non-controlled early amortization provision. In circumstances where a securitization contains a mix of retail and nonretail exposures or a mix of committed and uncommitted exposures, a bank may take a pro rata approach to determining the conversion factor for the securitization's early amortization provision. If a pro rata approach is not feasible, a bank must treat the mixed securitization as a securitization of nonretail exposures if a single underlying exposure is a nonretail exposure and must treat the mixed securitization as a securitization of committed exposures if a single underlying exposure is a committed exposure.

(ii) To find the appropriate conversion factor in the tables, a bank must divide the three-month average annualized excess spread of the securitization by the excess spread trapping point in the securitization structure. In securitizations that do not require excess spread to be trapped, or that specify trapping points based primarily on performance measures other than the three-month average annualized excess spread, the excess spread trapping point is 4.5 percent.

280

Federal Deposit Insurance Corporation

Pt. 325, App. D

TABLE 8—CONTROLLED EARLY AMORTIZATION PROVISIONS

	Uncommitted	Committed
Retail Credit Lines	Three-month average annualized excess spread Conversion Factor (CF). 133.33% of trapping point or more, 0% CF. less than 133.33% to 100% of trapping point, 1% CF. less than 100% to 75% of trapping point, 2% CF. less than 75% to 50% of trapping point, 10% CF. less than 50% to 25% of trapping point, 20% CF. less than 25% of trapping point, 40% CF.	90% CF
Non-retail Credit Lines	90% CF	90% CF

TABLE 9—NON-CONTROLLED EARLY AMORTIZATION PROVISIONS

	Uncommitted	Committed
Retail Credit Lines	Three-month average annualized excess spread Conversion Factor (CF). 133.33% of trapping point or more, 0% CF. less than 133.33% to 100% of trapping point, 5% CF. less than 100% to 75% of trapping point, 15% CF. less than 75% to 50% of trapping point, 50% CF. less than 50% of trapping point, 100% CF.	100% CF
Non-retail Credit Lines	100% CF	100% CF

(2) For a securitization for which all or substantially all of the underlying exposures are residential mortgage exposures, a bank may calculate the appropriate conversion factor using paragraph (c)(1) of this section or may use a conversion factor of 10 percent. If the bank chooses to use a conversion factor of 10 percent, it must use that conversion factor for all securitizations for which all or substantially all of the underlying exposures are residential mortgage exposures.

PART VI. RISK-WEIGHTED ASSETS FOR EQUITY EXPOSURES

Section 51. Introduction and Exposure Measurement

(a) *General.* To calculate its risk-weighted asset amounts for equity exposures that are not equity exposures to investment funds, a bank may apply either the Simple Risk Weight Approach (SRWA) in section 52 of this appendix or, if it qualifies to do so, the Internal Models Approach (IMA) in section 53 of this appendix. A bank must use the look-through approaches in section 54 of this appendix to calculate its risk-weighted asset amounts for equity exposures to investment funds.

(b) *Adjusted carrying value.* For purposes of this part, the adjusted carrying value of an equity exposure is:

(1) For the on-balance sheet component of an equity exposure, the bank's carrying value of the exposure reduced by any unrealized gains on the exposure that are reflected in such carrying value but excluded from the bank's tier 1 and tier 2 capital; and

(2) For the off-balance sheet component of an equity exposure, the effective notional principal amount of the exposure, the size of which is equivalent to a hypothetical on-balance sheet position in the underlying equity instrument that would evidence the same change in fair value (measured in dollars) for a given small change in the price of the underlying equity instrument, minus the adjusted carrying value of the on-balance sheet component of the exposure as calculated in paragraph (b)(1) of this section. For unfunded equity commitments that are unconditional, the effective notional principal amount is the notional amount of the commitment. For unfunded equity commitments that are conditional, the effective notional principal amount is the bank's best estimate of the amount that would be funded under economic downturn conditions.

Section 52. Simple Risk Weight Approach (SRWA)

(a) *General.* Under the SRWA, a bank's aggregate risk-weighted asset amount for its equity exposures is equal to the sum of the risk-weighted asset amounts for each of the bank's individual equity exposures (other than equity exposures to an investment fund) as determined in this section and the risk-weighted asset amounts for each of the bank's individual equity exposures to an investment fund as determined in section 54 of this appendix.

(b) *SRWA computation for individual equity exposures.* A bank must determine the risk-weighted asset amount for an individual equity exposure (other than an equity exposure to an investment fund) by multiplying the adjusted carrying value of the equity exposure or the effective portion and ineffective portion of a hedge pair (as defined in paragraph (c) of this section) by the lowest applicable risk weight in this paragraph (b).

(1) *0 percent risk weight equity exposures.* An equity exposure to an entity whose credit exposures are exempt from the 0.03 percent PD floor in paragraph (d)(2) of section 31 of this appendix is assigned a 0 percent risk weight.

(2) *20 percent risk weight equity exposures.* An equity exposure to a Federal Home Loan Bank or Farmer Mac is assigned a 20 percent risk weight.

(3) *100 percent risk weight equity exposures.* The following equity exposures are assigned a 100 percent risk weight:

(i) *Community development equity exposures.* An equity exposure that qualifies as a community development investment under 12 U.S.C. 24 (Eleventh), excluding equity exposures to an unconsolidated small business investment company and equity exposures held through a consolidated small business investment company described in section 302 of the Small Business Investment Act of 1958 (15 U.S.C. 682).

(ii) *Effective portion of hedge pairs.* The effective portion of a hedge pair.

(iii) *Non-significant equity exposures.* Equity exposures, excluding exposures to an investment firm that would meet the definition of a traditional securitization were it not for the FDIC's application of paragraph (8) of that definition and has greater than immaterial leverage, to the extent that the aggregate adjusted carrying value of the exposures does not exceed 10 percent of the bank's tier 1 capital plus tier 2 capital.

(A) To compute the aggregate adjusted carrying value of a bank's equity exposures for purposes of this paragraph (b)(3)(iii), the bank may exclude equity exposures described in paragraphs (b)(1), (b)(2), (b)(3)(i), and (b)(3)(ii) of this section, the equity exposure in a hedge pair with the smaller adjusted carrying value, and a proportion of each equity exposure to an investment fund equal to the proportion of the assets of the investment fund that are not equity exposures or that meet the criterion of paragraph (b)(3)(i) of this section. If a bank does not know the actual holdings of the investment fund, the bank may calculate the proportion of the assets of the fund that are not equity exposures based on the terms of the prospectus, partnership agreement, or similar contract that defines the fund's permissible investments. If the sum of the investment limits for all exposure classes within the fund exceeds 100 percent, the bank must assume for purposes of this paragraph (b)(3)(iii) that the investment fund invests to the maximum extent possible in equity exposures.

(B) When determining which of a bank's equity exposures qualify for a 100 percent risk weight under this paragraph, a bank first must include equity exposures to unconsolidated small business investment companies or held through consolidated small business investment companies described in section 302 of the Small Business Investment Act of 1958 (15 U.S.C. 682), then must include publicly traded equity exposures (including those held indirectly through investment funds), and then must include non-publicly traded equity exposures (including those held indirectly through investment funds).

(4) *300 percent risk weight equity exposures.* A publicly traded equity exposure (other than an equity exposure described in paragraph (b)(6) of this section and including the ineffective portion of a hedge pair) is assigned a 300 percent risk weight.

(5) *400 percent risk weight equity exposures.* An equity exposure (other than an equity exposure described in paragraph (b)(6) of this section) that is not publicly traded is assigned a 400 percent risk weight.

(6) *600 percent risk weight equity exposures.* An equity exposure to an investment firm that:

(i) Would meet the definition of a traditional securitization were it not for the FDIC's application of paragraph (8) of that definition; and

(ii) Has greater than immaterial leverage is assigned a 600 percent risk weight.

(c) *Hedge transactions*—(1) *Hedge pair.* A hedge pair is two equity exposures that form an effective hedge so long as each equity exposure is publicly traded or has a return that is primarily based on a publicly traded equity exposure.

(2) *Effective hedge.* Two equity exposures form an effective hedge if the exposures either have the same remaining maturity or each has a remaining maturity of at least three months; the hedge relationship is formally documented in a prospective manner (that is, before the bank acquires at least one of the equity exposures); the documentation specifies the measure of effectiveness (E) the bank will use for the hedge relationship throughout the life of the transaction; and the hedge relationship has an E greater than or equal to 0.8. A bank must measure E at least quarterly and must use one of three alternative measures of E:

(i) Under the dollar-offset method of measuring effectiveness, the bank must determine the ratio of value change (RVC). The RVC is the ratio of the cumulative sum of the periodic changes in value of one equity exposure to the cumulative sum of the periodic changes in the value of the other equity exposure. If RVC is positive, the hedge is not effective and E equals 0. If RVC is negative and greater than or equal to −1 (that is, between zero and −1), then E equals the absolute value of RVC. If RVC is negative and less than −1, then E equals 2 plus RVC.

(ii) Under the variability-reduction method of measuring effectiveness:

$$E = 1 - \frac{\sum_{t=1}^{T}(X_t - X_{t-1})^2}{\sum_{t=1}^{T}(A_t - A_{t-1})^2}, \text{ where}$$

(A) $X_t = A_t - B_t$;
(B) A_t = the value at time t of one exposure in a hedge pair; and
(C) B_t = the value at time t of the other exposure in a hedge pair.

(iii) Under the regression method of measuring effectiveness, E equals the coefficient of determination of a regression in which the change in value of one exposure in a hedge pair is the dependent variable and the change in value of the other exposure in a hedge pair is the independent variable. However, if the estimated regression coefficient is positive, then the value of E is zero.

(3) The effective portion of a hedge pair is E multiplied by the greater of the adjusted carrying values of the equity exposures forming a hedge pair.

(4) The ineffective portion of a hedge pair is (1–E) multiplied by the greater of the adjusted carrying values of the equity exposures forming a hedge pair.

Section 53. Internal Models Approach (IMA)

(a) *General.* A bank may calculate its risk-weighted asset amount for equity exposures using the IMA by modeling publicly traded and non-publicly traded equity exposures (in accordance with paragraph (c) of this section) or by modeling only publicly traded equity exposures (in accordance with paragraph (d) of this section).

(b) *Qualifying criteria.* To qualify to use the IMA to calculate risk-based capital requirements for equity exposures, a bank must receive prior written approval from the FDIC. To receive such approval, the bank must demonstrate to the FDIC's satisfaction that the bank meets the following criteria:

(1) The bank must have one or more models that:
(i) Assess the potential decline in value of its modeled equity exposures;
(ii) Are commensurate with the size, complexity, and composition of the bank's modeled equity exposures; and
(iii) Adequately capture both general market risk and idiosyncratic risk.

(2) The bank's model must produce an estimate of potential losses for its modeled equity exposures that is no less than the estimate of potential losses produced by a VaR methodology employing a 99.0 percent, one-tailed confidence interval of the distribution of quarterly returns for a benchmark portfolio of equity exposures comparable to the bank's modeled equity exposures using a long-term sample period.

(3) The number of risk factors and exposures in the sample and the data period used for quantification in the bank's model and benchmarking exercise must be sufficient to provide confidence in the accuracy and robustness of the bank's estimates.

(4) The bank's model and benchmarking process must incorporate data that are relevant in representing the risk profile of the bank's modeled equity exposures, and must include data from at least one equity market cycle containing adverse market movements relevant to the risk profile of the bank's modeled equity exposures. In addition, the bank's benchmarking exercise must be based on daily market prices for the benchmark portfolio. If the bank's model uses a scenario methodology, the bank must demonstrate that the model produces a conservative estimate of potential losses on the bank's modeled equity exposures over a relevant long-term market cycle. If the bank employs risk factor models, the bank must demonstrate through empirical analysis the appropriateness of the risk factors used.

(5) The bank must be able to demonstrate, using theoretical arguments and empirical evidence, that any proxies used in the modeling process are comparable to the bank's modeled equity exposures and that the bank has made appropriate adjustments for differences. The bank must derive any proxies for its modeled equity exposures and benchmark portfolio using historical market data that are relevant to the bank's modeled equity exposures and benchmark portfolio (or, where not, must use appropriately adjusted data), and such proxies must be robust estimates of the risk of the bank's modeled equity exposures.

(c) *Risk-weighted assets calculation for a bank modeling publicly traded and non-publicly traded equity exposures.* If a bank models publicly traded and non-publicly traded equity exposures, the bank's aggregate risk-weighted asset amount for its equity exposures is equal to the sum of:

(1) The risk-weighted asset amount of each equity exposure that qualifies for a 0 percent, 20 percent, or 100 percent risk weight under paragraphs (b)(1) through (b)(3)(i) of section 52 (as determined under section 52 of this appendix) and each equity exposure to

an investment fund (as determined under section 54 of this appendix); and

(2) The greater of:

(i) The estimate of potential losses on the bank's equity exposures (other than equity exposures referenced in paragraph (c)(1) of this section) generated by the bank's internal equity exposure model multiplied by 12.5; or

(ii) The sum of:

(A) 200 percent multiplied by the aggregate adjusted carrying value of the bank's publicly traded equity exposures that do not belong to a hedge pair, do not qualify for a 0 percent, 20 percent, or 100 percent risk weight under paragraphs (b)(1) through (b)(3)(i) of section 52 of this appendix, and are not equity exposures to an investment fund;

(B) 200 percent multiplied by the aggregate ineffective portion of all hedge pairs; and

(C) 300 percent multiplied by the aggregate adjusted carrying value of the bank's equity exposures that are not publicly traded, do not qualify for a 0 percent, 20 percent, or 100 percent risk weight under paragraphs (b)(1) through (b)(3)(i) of section 52 of this appendix, and are not equity exposures to an investment fund.

(d) *Risk-weighted assets calculation for a bank using the IMA only for publicly traded equity exposures.* If a bank models only publicly traded equity exposures, the bank's aggregate risk-weighted asset amount for its equity exposures is equal to the sum of:

(1) The risk-weighted asset amount of each equity exposure that qualifies for a 0 percent, 20 percent, or 100 percent risk weight under paragraphs (b)(1) through (b)(3)(i) of section 52 (as determined under section 52 of this appendix), each equity exposure that qualifies for a 400 percent risk weight under paragraph (b)(5) of section 52 or a 600 percent risk weight under paragraph (b)(6) of section 52 (as determined under section 52 of this appendix), and each equity exposure to an investment fund (as determined under section 54 of this appendix); and

(2) The greater of:

(i) The estimate of potential losses on the bank's equity exposures (other than equity exposures referenced in paragraph (d)(1) of this section) generated by the bank's internal equity exposure model multiplied by 12.5; or

(ii) The sum of:

(A) 200 percent multiplied by the aggregate adjusted carrying value of the bank's publicly traded equity exposures that do not belong to a hedge pair, do not qualify for a 0 percent, 20 percent, or 100 percent risk weight under paragraphs (b)(1) through (b)(3)(i) of section 52 of this appendix, and are not equity exposures to an investment fund; and

(B) 200 percent multiplied by the aggregate ineffective portion of all hedge pairs.

Section 54. Equity Exposures to Investment Funds

(a) *Available approaches.* (1) Unless the exposure meets the requirements for a community development equity exposure in paragraph (b)(3)(i) of section 52 of this appendix, a bank must determine the risk-weighted asset amount of an equity exposure to an investment fund under the Full Look-Through Approach in paragraph (b) of this section, the Simple Modified Look-Through Approach in paragraph (c) of this section, the Alternative Modified Look-Through Approach in paragraph (d) of this section, or, if the investment fund qualifies for the Money Market Fund Approach, the Money Market Fund Approach in paragraph (e) of this section.

(2) The risk-weighted asset amount of an equity exposure to an investment fund that meets the requirements for a community development equity exposure in paragraph (b)(3)(i) of section 52 of this appendix is its adjusted carrying value.

(3) If an equity exposure to an investment fund is part of a hedge pair and the bank does not use the Full Look-Through Approach, the bank may use the ineffective portion of the hedge pair as determined under paragraph (c) of section 52 of this appendix as the adjusted carrying value for the equity exposure to the investment fund. The risk-weighted asset amount of the effective portion of the hedge pair is equal to its adjusted carrying value.

(b) *Full Look-Through Approach.* A bank that is able to calculate a risk-weighted asset amount for its proportional ownership share of each exposure held by the investment fund (as calculated under this appendix as if the proportional ownership share of each exposure were held directly by the bank) may either:

(1) Set the risk-weighted asset amount of the bank's exposure to the fund equal to the product of:

(i) The aggregate risk-weighted asset amounts of the exposures held by the fund as if they were held directly by the bank; and

(ii) The bank's proportional ownership share of the fund; or

(2) Include the bank's proportional ownership share of each exposure held by the fund in the bank's IMA.

(c) *Simple Modified Look-Through Approach.* Under this approach, the risk-weighted asset amount for a bank's equity exposure to an investment fund equals the adjusted carrying value of the equity exposure multiplied by the highest risk weight in Table 10 that applies to any exposure the fund is permitted to hold under its prospectus, partnership agreement, or similar contract that defines the fund's permissible investments (excluding derivative contracts that are used for hedging rather than speculative purposes

Federal Deposit Insurance Corporation

Pt. 325, App. D

and that do not constitute a material portion of the fund's exposures).

TABLE 10—MODIFIED LOOK-THROUGH APPROACHES FOR EQUITY EXPOSURES TO INVESTMENT FUNDS

Risk weight	Exposure class
0 percent	Sovereign exposures with a long-term applicable external rating in the highest investment-grade rating category and sovereign exposures of the United States.
20 percent	Non-sovereign exposures with a long-term applicable external rating in the highest or second-highest investment-grade rating category; exposures with a short-term applicable external rating in the highest investment-grade rating category; and exposures to, or guaranteed by, depository institutions, foreign banks (as defined in 12 CFR 211.2), or securities firms subject to consolidated supervision and regulation comparable to that imposed on U.S. securities broker-dealers that are repo-style transactions or bankers' acceptances.
50 percent	Exposures with a long-term applicable external rating in the third-highest investment-grade rating category or a short-term applicable external rating in the second-highest investment-grade rating category.
100 percent	Exposures with a long-term or short-term applicable external rating in the lowest investment-grade rating category.
200 percent	Exposures with a long-term applicable external rating one rating category below investment grade.
300 percent	Publicly traded equity exposures.
400 percent	Non-publicly traded equity exposures; exposures with a long-term applicable external rating two rating categories or more below investment grade; and exposures without an external rating (excluding publicly traded equity exposures).
1,250 percent	OTC derivative contracts and exposures that must be deducted from regulatory capital or receive a risk weight greater than 400 percent under this appendix.

(d) *Alternative Modified Look-Through Approach.* Under this approach, a bank may assign the adjusted carrying value of an equity exposure to an investment fund on a pro rata basis to different risk weight categories in Table 10 based on the investment limits in the fund's prospectus, partnership agreement, or similar contract that defines the fund's permissible investments. The risk-weighted asset amount for the bank's equity exposure to the investment fund equals the sum of each portion of the adjusted carrying value assigned to an exposure class multiplied by the applicable risk weight. If the sum of the investment limits for exposure classes within the fund exceeds 100 percent, the bank must assume that the fund invests to the maximum extent permitted under its investment limits in the exposure class with the highest risk weight under Table 10, and continues to make investments in order of the exposure class with the next highest risk weight under Table 10 until the maximum total investment level is reached. If more than one exposure class applies to an exposure, the bank must use the highest applicable risk weight. A bank may exclude derivative contracts held by the fund that are used for hedging rather than for speculative purposes and do not constitute a material portion of the fund's exposures.

(e) *Money Market Fund Approach.* The risk-weighted asset amount for a bank's equity exposure to an investment fund that is a money market fund subject to 17 CFR 270.2a–7 and that has an applicable external rating in the highest investment-grade rating category equals the adjusted carrying value of the equity exposure multiplied by 7 percent.

Section 55. Equity Derivative Contracts

Under the IMA, in addition to holding risk-based capital against an equity derivative contract under this part, a bank must hold risk-based capital against the counterparty credit risk in the equity derivative contract by also treating the equity derivative contract as a wholesale exposure and computing a supplemental risk-weighted asset amount for the contract under part IV. Under the SRWA, a bank may choose not to hold risk-based capital against the counterparty credit risk of equity derivative contracts, as long as it does so for all such contracts. Where the equity derivative contracts are subject to a qualified master netting agreement, a bank using the SRWA must either include all or exclude all of the contracts from any measure used to determine counterparty credit risk exposure.

PART VII. RISK-WEIGHTED ASSETS FOR OPERATIONAL RISK

Section 61. Qualification Requirements for Incorporation of Operational Risk Mitigants

(a) *Qualification to use operational risk mitigants.* A bank may adjust its estimate of operational risk exposure to reflect qualifying operational risk mitigants if:

(1) The bank's operational risk quantification system is able to generate an estimate of the bank's operational risk exposure (which does not incorporate qualifying operational risk mitigants) and an estimate of

the bank's operational risk exposure adjusted to incorporate qualifying operational risk mitigants; and

(2) The bank's methodology for incorporating the effects of insurance, if the bank uses insurance as an operational risk mitigant, captures through appropriate discounts to the amount of risk mitigation:

(i) The residual term of the policy, where less than one year;

(ii) The cancellation terms of the policy, where less than one year;

(iii) The policy's timeliness of payment;

(iv) The uncertainty of payment by the provider of the policy; and

(v) Mismatches in coverage between the policy and the hedged operational loss event.

(b) *Qualifying operational risk mitigants.* Qualifying operational risk mitigants are:

(1) Insurance that:

(i) Is provided by an unaffiliated company that has a claims payment ability that is rated in one of the three highest rating categories by a NRSRO;

(ii) Has an initial term of at least one year and a residual term of more than 90 days;

(iii) Has a minimum notice period for cancellation by the provider of 90 days;

(iv) Has no exclusions or limitations based upon regulatory action or for the receiver or liquidator of a failed depository institution; and

(v) Is explicitly mapped to a potential operational loss event; and

(2) Operational risk mitigants other than insurance for which the FDIC has given prior written approval. In evaluating an operational risk mitigant other than insurance, the FDIC will consider whether the operational risk mitigant covers potential operational losses in a manner equivalent to holding regulatory capital.

Section 62. Mechanics of Risk-Weighted Asset Calculation

(a) If a bank does not qualify to use or does not have qualifying operational risk mitigants, the bank's dollar risk-based capital requirement for operational risk is its operational risk exposure minus eligible operational risk offsets (if any).

(b) If a bank qualifies to use operational risk mitigants and has qualifying operational risk mitigants, the bank's dollar risk-based capital requirement for operational risk is the greater of:

(1) The bank's operational risk exposure adjusted for qualifying operational risk mitigants minus eligible operational risk offsets (if any); or

(2) 0.8 multiplied by the difference between:

(i) The bank's operational risk exposure; and

(ii) Eligible operational risk offsets (if any).

(c) The bank's risk-weighted asset amount for operational risk equals the bank's dollar risk-based capital requirement for operational risk determined under paragraph (a) or (b) of this section multiplied by 12.5.

PART VIII. DISCLOSURE

Section 71. Disclosure Requirements

(a) Each bank must publicly disclose each quarter its total and tier 1 risk-based capital ratios and their components (that is, tier 1 capital, tier 2 capital, total qualifying capital, and total risk-weighted assets).[4]

(b) A bank must comply with paragraph (b) of section 71 of appendix G to the Federal Reserve Board's Regulation Y (12 CFR part 225, appendix G) unless it is a consolidated subsidiary of a bank holding company or depository institution that is subject to these requirements.

PART IX. TRANSITION PROVISIONS

Section 81. Optional Transition Provisions Related to the Implementation of Consolidation Requirements Under FAS 167

(a) *Scope, applicability, and purpose.* This section 81 provides optional transition provisions for a State nonmember bank that is required for financial and regulatory reporting purposes, as a result of its implementation of Statement of Financial Accounting Standards No. 167, *Amendments to FASB Interpretation No. 46(R)* (FAS 167), to consolidate certain variable interest entities (VIEs) as defined under GAAP. These transition provisions apply through the end of the fourth quarter following the date of a bank's implementation of FAS 167 (implementation date).

(b) *Exclusion period.*

(1) *Exclusion of risk-weighted assets for the first and second quarters.* For the first two quarters after the implementation date (exclusion period), including for the two calendar quarter-end regulatory report dates within those quarters, a bank may exclude from risk-weighted assets:

(i) Subject to the limitations in paragraph (d) of this section 81, assets held by a VIE, provided that the following conditions are met:

(A) The VIE existed prior to the implementation date,

(B) The bank did not consolidate the VIE on its balance sheet for calendar quarter-end regulatory report dates prior to the implementation date,

---

[4] Other public disclosure requirements continue to apply—for example, Federal securities law and regulatory reporting requirements.

(C) The bank must consolidate the VIE on its balance sheet beginning as of the implementation date as a result of its implementation of FAS 167, and

(D) The bank excludes all assets held by VIEs described in paragraphs (b)(1)(i)(A) through (C) of this section 81; and

(ii) Subject to the limitations in paragraph (d) of this section 81, assets held by a VIE that is a consolidated ABCP program, provided that the following conditions are met:

(A) The bank is the sponsor of the ABCP program,

(B) Prior to the implementation date, the bank consolidated the VIE onto its balance sheet under GAAP and excluded the VIE's assets from the bank's risk-weighted assets, and

(C) The bank chooses to exclude all assets held by ABCP program VIEs described in paragraphs (b)(1)(ii)(A) and (B) of this section 81.

(2) *Risk-weighted assets during exclusion period.* During the exclusion period, including for the two calendar quarter-end regulatory report dates within the exclusion period, a bank adopting the optional provisions in paragraph (b) of this section must calculate risk-weighted assets for its contractual exposures to the VIEs referenced in paragraph (b)(1) of this section 81 on the implementation date and include this calculated amount in risk-weighted assets. Such contractual exposures may include direct-credit substitutes, recourse obligations, residual interests, liquidity facilities, and loans.

(3) *Inclusion of ALLL in Tier 2 capital for the first and second quarters.* During the exclusion period, including for the two calendar quarter-end regulatory report dates within the exclusion period, a bank that excludes VIE assets from risk-weighted assets pursuant to paragraph (b)(1) of this section 81 may include in Tier 2 capital the full amount of the ALLL calculated as of the implementation date that is attributable to the assets it excludes pursuant to paragraph (b)(1) of this section 81 (inclusion amount). The amount of ALLL includable in Tier 2 capital in accordance with this paragraph shall not be subject to the limitations set forth in section 13(a)(2) and (b) of this Appendix.

(c) *Phase-in period.*

(1) *Exclusion amount.* For purposes of this paragraph (c), exclusion amount is defined as the amount of risk-weighted assets excluded in paragraph (b)(1) of this section as of the implementation date.

(2) *Risk-weighted assets for the third and fourth quarters.* A bank that excludes assets of consolidated VIEs from risk-weighted assets pursuant to paragraph (b)(1) of this section may, for the third and fourth quarters after the implementation date (phase-in period), including for the two calendar quarter-end regulatory report dates within those quarters, exclude from risk-weighted assets 50 percent of the exclusion amount, provided that the bank may not include in risk-weighted assets pursuant to this paragraph an amount less than the aggregate risk-weighted assets calculated pursuant to paragraph (b)(2) of this section 81.

(3) *Inclusion of ALLL in Tier 2 capital for the third and fourth quarters.* A bank that excludes assets of consolidated VIEs from risk-weighted assets pursuant to paragraph (c)(2) of this section may, for the phase-in period, include in Tier 2 capital 50 percent of the inclusion amount it included in Tier 2 capital during the exclusion period, notwithstanding the limit on including ALLL in Tier 2 capital in section 13(a)(2) and (b) of this Appendix.

(d) *Implicit recourse limitation.* Notwithstanding any other provision in this section 81, assets held by a VIE to which the bank has provided recourse through credit enhancement beyond any contractual obligation to support assets it has sold may not be excluded from risk-weighted assets.

[72 FR 69396, 69437, Dec. 7, 2007; 73 FR 21690, Apr. 22, 2008; 75 FR 4651, Jan. 28, 2010; 76 FR 37629, June 28, 2011]

PART 326—MINIMUM SECURITY DEVICES AND PROCEDURES AND BANK SECRECY ACT[1] COMPLIANCE

Subpart A—Minimum Security Procedures

Sec.
326.0 Authority, purpose, and scope.
326.1 Definitions.
326.2 Designation of security officer.
326.3 Security program.
326.4 Reports.

Subpart B—Procedures for Monitoring Bank Secrecy Act Compliance

326.8 Bank Secrecy Act compliance.

AUTHORITY: 12 U.S.C. 1813, 1815, 1817, 1818, 1819 (Tenth), 1881–1883; 31 U.S.C. 5311–5314 and 5316–5332.2

Subpart A—Minimum Security Procedures

SOURCE: 56 FR 13581, Apr. 3, 1991, unless otherwise noted.

---

[1] In its original form, subchapter II of chapter 53 of title 31 U.S.C., was part of Pub. L. 91–508 which requires recordkeeping for and reporting of currency transactions by banks and others and is commonly known as the *Bank Secrecy Act.*

§ 326.0 Authority, purpose, and scope.

(a) This part is issued by the Federal Deposit Insurance Corporation ("FDIC") pursuant to section 3 of the Bank Protection Act of 1968 (12 U.S.C. 1882). It applies to insured state banks that are not members of the Federal Reserve System. It requires each bank to adopt appropriate security procedures to discourage robberies, burglaries, and larcenies and to assist in identifying and apprehending persons who commit such acts.

(b) It is the responsibility of the bank's board of directors to comply with this part and ensure that a written security program for the bank's main office and branches is developed and implemented.

(Approved by the Office of Management and Budget under control number 3064-0095)

§ 326.1 Definitions.

For the purposes of this part—

(a) The term *insured nonmember bank* means any bank, including a foreign bank having a branch the deposits of which are insured in accordance with the provisions of the Federal Deposit Insurance Act, which is not a member of the Federal Reserve System. The term does not include any institution chartered or licensed by the Comptroller of the Currency, any District bank, or any savings association.

(b) The term *banking office* includes any branch of an insured nonmember bank, and, in the case of an insured state nonmember bank, it includes the main office of that bank.

(c) The term *branch* for a bank chartered under the laws of any state of the United States includes any branch bank, branch office, branch agency, additional office, or any branch place of business located in any state or territory of the United States, District of Columbia, Puerto Rico, Guam, American Samoa, the Trust Territory of the Pacific Islands, the Northern Mariana Islands or the Virgin Islands at which deposits are received or checks paid or money lent. In the case of a foreign bank, as defined in § 347.202 of this chapter, the term *branch* has the same meaning given in § 347.202 of this chapter.

[56 FR 13581, Apr. 3, 1991, as amended at 63 FR 17075, Apr. 8, 1998]

§ 326.2 Designation of security officer.

Upon the issuance of federal deposit insurance, the board of directors of each insured nonmember bank[2] shall designate a security officer who shall have the authority, subject to the approval of the board of directors, to develop, within a reasonable time, but no later than 180 days, and to administer a written security program for each banking office.

§ 326.3 Security program.

(a) *Contents of security program.* The security program shall:

(1) Establish procedures for opening and closing for business and for the safekeeping of all currency, negotiable securities, and similar valuables at all times;

(2) Establish procedures that will assist in identifying persons committing crimes against the bank and that will preserve evidence that may aid in their identification and prosecution; such procedures may include, but are not limited to:

(i) Retaining a record of any robbery, burglary, or larceny committed against the bank;

(ii) Maintaining a camera that records activity in the banking office; and

(iii) Using identification devices, such as prerecorded serial-numbered bills, or chemical and electronic devices;

(3) Provide for initial and periodic training of officers and employees in their responsibilities under the security program and in proper employee conduct during and after a robbery, burglary or larceny; and

(4) Provide for selecting, testing, operating and maintaining appropriate security devices, as specified in paragraph (b) of this section.

---

[2]The term *board of directors* includes the managing official of an insured branch of a foreign bank for purposes of 12 CFR 326.0–326.4.

Federal Deposit Insurance Corporation

(b) *Security devices.* Each insured nonmember bank shall have, at a minimum, the following security devices:

(1) A means of protecting cash or other liquid assets, such as a vault, safe, or other secure space;

(2) A lighting system for illuminating, during the hours of darkness, the area around the vault, if the vault is visible from outside the banking office;

(3) An alarm system or other appropriate device for promptly notifying the nearest responsible law enforcement officers of an attempted or perpetrated robbery or burglary;

(4) Tamper-resistant locks on exterior doors and exterior windows that may be opened; and

(5) Such other devices as the security officer determines to be appropriate, taking into consideration:

(i) The incidence of crimes against financial institutions in the area;

(ii) The amount of currency or other valuables exposed to robbery, burglary, and larceny;

(iii) The distance of the banking office from the nearest responsible law enforcement officers;

(iv) The cost of the security devices;

(v) Other security measures in effect at the banking office; and

(vi) The physical characteristics of the structure of the banking office and its surroundings.

§ 326.4 Reports.

The security officer for each insured nonmember bank shall report at least annually to the bank's board of directors on the implementation, administration, and effectiveness of the security program.

Subpart B—Procedures for Monitoring Bank Secrecy Act Compliance

§ 326.8 Bank Security Act compliance.

(a) *Purpose.* This subpart is issued to assure that all insured nonmember banks as defined in 12 CFR 326.1 establish and maintain procedures reasonably designed to assure and monitor their compliance with the requirements of subchapter II of chapter 53 of title 31, United States Code, and the implementing regulations promulgated thereunder by the Department of Treasury at 31 CFR chapter X.

(b) *Compliance procedures*—(1) *Program requirement.* Each bank shall develop and provide for the continued administration of a program reasonably designed to assure and monitor compliance with recordkeeping and reporting requirements set forth in subchapter II of chapter 53 of title 31, United States Code, and the implementing regulations issued by the Department of Treasury at 31 CFR chapter X. The compliance program shall be written, approved by the bank's board of directors, and noted in the minutes.

(2) *Customer identification program.* Each bank is subject to the requirements of 31 U.S.C. 5318(l) and the implementing regulation jointly promulgated by the FDIC and the Department of the Treasury at 31 CFR 1020.220.

[76 FR 14793, Mar. 18, 2011]

PART 327—ASSESSMENTS

Subpart A—In General

Sec.
327.1 Purpose and scope.
327.2 Certified statements.
327.3 Payment of assessments.
327.4 Assessment rates.
327.5 Assessment base.
327.6 Mergers and consolidations; other terminations of insurance.
327.7 Payment of interest on assessment underpayments and overpayments.
327.8 Definitions.
327.9 Assessment pricing methods.
327.10 Assessment rate schedules.
327.11 Special assessments.
327.12 Prepayment of quarterly risk-based assessments.
327.15 Emergency special assessments.

APPENDIX A TO SUBPART A—METHOD TO DERIVE PRICING MULTIPLIERS AND UNIFORM AMOUNT
APPENDIX B TO SUBPART A—CONVERSION OF SCORECARD MEASURES INTO SCORE
APPENDIX C TO SUBPART A—CONCENTRATION MEASURES
APPENDIX D TO SUBPART A—DESCRIPTION OF THE LOSS SEVERITY MEASURE

Subpart B—Implementation of One-Time Assessment Credit

327.30 Purpose and scope.
327.31 Definitions.
327.32 Determination of aggregate credit amount.

§ 327.1

327.33 Determination of eligible institution's credit amount.
327.34 Transferability of credits.
327.35 Application of credits.
327.36 Requests for review of credit amount.

Subpart C—Implementation of Dividend Requirements

327.50 Dividends.

AUTHORITY: 12 U.S.C. 1441, 1813, 1815, 1817–19, 1821.

SOURCE: 54 FR 51374, Dec. 15, 1989, unless otherwise noted.

Subpart A—In General

SOURCE: Sections 327.1 through 327.8 appear at 71 FR 69277, Nov. 30, 2006, unless otherwise noted.

§ 327.1 Purpose and scope.

(a) *Scope.* This part 327 applies to any insured depository institution, including any insured branch of a foreign bank.

(b) *Purpose.* (1) Except as specified in paragraph (b)(2) of this section, this part 327 sets forth the rules for:

(i) The time and manner of filing certified statements by insured depository institutions;

(ii) The time and manner of payment of assessments by such institutions;

(iii) The payment of assessments by depository institutions whose insured status has terminated;

(iv) The classification of depository institutions for risk; and

(v) The processes for review of assessments.

(2) Deductions from the assessment base of an insured branch of a foreign bank are stated in subpart B part 347 of this chapter.

§ 327.2 Certified statements.

(a) *Required.* (1) The certified statement shall also be known as the quarterly certified statement invoice. Each insured depository institution shall file and certify its quarterly certified statement invoice in the manner and form set forth in this section.

(2) The quarterly certified statement invoice shall reflect the institution's risk assignment, assessment base, assessment computation, and assessment amount, for each quarterly assessment period.

(b) *Availability and access.* (1) The Corporation shall make available to each insured depository institution via the FDIC's e-business Web site FDIC*connect* a quarterly certified statement invoice each assessment period.

(2) Insured depository institutions shall access their quarterly certified statement invoices via FDIC*connect*, unless the FDIC provides notice to insured depository institutions of a successor system. In the event of a contingency, the FDIC may employ an alternative means of delivering the quarterly certified statement invoices. A quarterly certified statement invoice delivered by any alternative means will be treated as if it had been downloaded from FDIC*connect*.

(3) Institutions that do not have Internet access may request a renewable one-year exemption from the requirement that quarterly certified statement invoices be accessed through FDIC*connect*. Any exemption request must be submitted in writing to the Manager of the Assessments Section.

(4) Each assessment period, the FDIC will provide courtesy e-mail notification to insured depository institutions indicating that new quarterly certified statement invoices are available and may be accessed on FDIC*connect*. E-mail notification will be sent to all individuals with FDIC*connect* access to quarterly certified statement invoices.

(5) E-mail notification may be used by the FDIC to communicate with insured depository institutions regarding quarterly certified statement invoices and other assessment-related matters.

(c) *Review by institution.* The president of each insured depository institution, or such other officer as the institution's president or board of directors or trustees may designate, shall review the information shown on each quarterly certified statement invoice.

(d) *Retention by institution.* If the appropriate officer of the insured depository institution agrees that, to the best of his or her knowledge and belief, the information shown on the quarterly certified statement invoice is true, correct, and complete and in accordance with the Federal Deposit Insurance Act and the regulations issued under it, the institution shall pay the

Federal Deposit Insurance Corporation

§ 327.3

amount specified on the quarterly certified statement invoice and shall retain it in the institution's files for three years as specified in section 7(b)(4) of the Federal Deposit Insurance Act.

(e) *Amendment by institution.* If the appropriate officer of the insured depository institution determines that, to the best of his or her knowledge and belief, the information shown on the quarterly certified statement invoice is not true, correct, and complete and in accordance with the Federal Deposit Insurance Act and the regulations issued under it, the institution shall pay the amount specified on the quarterly certified statement invoice, and may:

(1) Amend its report of condition, or other similar report, to correct any data believed to be inaccurate on the quarterly certified statement invoice; amendments to such reports timely filed under section 7(g) of the Federal Deposit Insurance Act but not permitted to be made by an institution's primary federal regulator may be filed with the FDIC for consideration in determining deposit insurance assessments; or

(2) Amend and sign its quarterly certified statement invoice to correct a calculation believed to be inaccurate and return it to the FDIC by the applicable payment date specified in § 327.3(b)(2).

(f) *Certification.* Data used by the Corporation to complete the quarterly certified statement invoice has been previously attested to by the institution in its reports of condition, or other similar reports, filed with the institution's primary federal regulator. When an insured institution pays the amount shown on the quarterly certified statement invoice and does not correct that invoice as provided in paragraph (e) of this section, the information on that invoice shall be deemed true, correct, complete, and certified for purposes of paragraph (a) of this section and section 7(c) of the Federal Deposit Insurance Act.

(g) *Requests for revision of assessment computation.* (1) The timely filing of an amended report of condition or other similar report under paragraph (e)(1) of this section, or the timely filing of an amended quarterly certified statement invoice under paragraph (e)(2), that will result in a change to deposit insurance assessments owed or paid by an insured depository institution, shall be treated as a timely filed request for revision of computation of quarterly assessment payment under § 327.3(f).

(2) The assessment rate on the quarterly certified statement invoice shall be amended only if it is inconsistent with the assessment risk assignment(s) provided to the institution by the Corporation for the assessment period in question pursuant to § 327.4(a). Agreement with the assessment rate shall not be deemed to constitute agreement with the assessment risk assignment. An institution may request review of an assessment risk assignment it believes to be incorrect pursuant to § 327.4(c).

§ 327.3 Payment of assessments.

(a) *Required*—(1) *In general.* Each insured depository institution shall pay to the Corporation for each assessment period an assessment determined in accordance with this part 327.

(2) *Notice of designated deposit account.* For the purpose of making such payments, each insured depository institution shall designate a deposit account for direct debit by the Corporation. No later than 30 days prior to the next payment date specified in paragraph (b)(2) of this section, each institution shall provide notice to the Corporation via FDIC*connect* of the account designated, including all information and authorizations needed by the Corporation for direct debit of the account. After the initial notice of the designated account, no further notice is required unless the institution designates a different account for assessment debit by the Corporation, in which case the requirements of the preceding sentence apply.

(3) *Transition Rule for Financing Corporation (FICO) Payments.* Quarterly FICO payments shall be collected by the FDIC without interruption during the assessment system transitional period in 2007. All insured depository institutions shall make scheduled quarterly FICO payments on January 2, 2007 (unless prepaid on December 30, 2006),

291

§ 327.3

and March 30, 2007, based upon, respectively, their September 30, 2006, and December 31, 2006 reported assessment bases, which shall be the final assessment bases calculated pursuant to 12 CFR 327.5(a) and (b) (2006). Simultaneous collection of deposit insurance assessments and FICO assessments will resume in June of 2007, based on the March 31, 2007 reported assessment base.

(b) *Assessment payment*—(1) *Quarterly certified statement invoice.* Starting with the first assessment period of 2007, no later than 15 days prior to the payment date specified in paragraph (b)(2) of this section, the Corporation will provide to each insured depository institution a quarterly certified statement invoice showing the amount of the assessment payment due from the institution for the prior quarter (net of credits or dividends, if any), and the computation of that amount. Subject to paragraph (e) of this section, the invoiced amount on the quarterly certified statement invoice shall be the product of the following: the assessment base of the institution for the prior quarter computed in accordance with § 327.5 multiplied by the institution's rate for that prior quarter as assigned to the institution pursuant to §§ 327.4(a) and 327.9.

(2) *Quarterly payment date and manner.* The Corporation will cause the amount stated in the applicable quarterly certified statement invoice to be directly debited on the appropriate payment date from the deposit account designated by the insured depository institution for that purpose, as follows:

(i) In the case of the assessment payment for the quarter that begins on January 1, the payment date is the following June 30;

(ii) In the case of the assessment payment for the quarter that begins on April 1, the payment date is the following September 30;

(iii) In the case of the assessment payment for the quarter that begins on July 1, the payment date is the following December 30; and

(iv) In the case of the assessment payment for the quarter that begins on October 1, the payment date is the following March 30.

(c) *Necessary action, sufficient funding by institution.* Each insured depository institution shall take all actions necessary to allow the Corporation to debit assessments from the insured depository institution's designated deposit account. Each insured depository institution shall, prior to each payment date indicated in paragraph (b)(2) of this section, ensure that funds in an amount at least equal to the amount on the quarterly certified statement invoice are available in the designated account for direct debit by the Corporation. Failure to take any such action or to provide such funding of the account shall be deemed to constitute nonpayment of the assessment. Penalties for failure to timely pay assessments are provided for at 12 CFR 308.132(c)(3)(v).

(d) *Business days.* If a payment date specified in paragraph (b)(2) falls on a date that is not a business day, the applicable date shall be the previous business day.

(e) *Payment adjustments in succeeding quarters.* Quarterly certified statement invoices provided by the Corporation may reflect adjustments, initiated by the Corporation or an institution, resulting from such factors as amendments to prior quarterly reports of condition, retroactive revision of the institution's assessment risk assignment, and revision of the Corporation's assessment computations for prior quarters.

(f) *Request for revision of computation of quarterly assessment payment*—(1) *In general.* An institution may submit a written request for revision of the computation of the institution's quarterly assessment payment as shown on the quarterly certified statement invoice in the following circumstances:

(i) The institution disagrees with the computation of the assessment base as stated on the quarterly certified statement invoice;

(ii) The institution determines that the rate applied by the Corporation is inconsistent with the assessment risk assignment(s) provided to the institution in writing by the Corporation for the assessment period for which the payment is due; or

(iii) The institution believes that the quarterly certified statement invoice

Federal Deposit Insurance Corporation

does not fully or accurately reflect adjustments provided for in paragraph (e) of this section.

(2) *Inapplicability.* This paragraph (f) is not applicable to requests for review of an institution's assessment risk assignment, which are covered by § 327.4(c) of this part.

(3) *Requirements.* Any such request for revision must be submitted within 90 days from the date the computation being challenged appears on the institution's quarterly certified statement invoice. The request for revision shall be submitted to the Manager of the Assessments Section and shall provide documentation sufficient to support the change sought by the institution. If additional information is requested by the Corporation, such information shall be provided by the institution within 21 days of the date of the request for additional information. Any institution submitting a timely request for revision will receive written notice from the Corporation regarding the outcome of its request. Upon completion of a review, the DOF Director (or designee) shall promptly notify the institution in writing of his or her determination of whether revision is warranted. If the institution requesting revision disagrees with that determination, it may appeal to the FDIC's Assessment Appeals Committee. Notice of the procedures applicable to appeals will be included with the written determination.

(g) *Quarterly certified statement invoice unavailable.* Any institution whose quarterly certified statement invoice is unavailable on FDIC*connect* by the fifteenth day of the month in which the payment is due shall promptly notify the Corporation. Failure to provide prompt notice to the Corporation shall not affect the institution's obligation to make full and timely assessment payment. Unless otherwise directed by the Corporation, the institution shall preliminarily pay the amount shown on its quarterly certified statement invoice for the preceding assessment period, subject to subsequent correction.

[54 FR 51374, Dec. 15, 1989, as amended at 74 FR 9550, Mar. 4, 2009]

§ 327.4 **Assessment rates.**

(a) *Assessment risk assignment.* For the purpose of determining the annual assessment rate for insured depository institutions under § 327.9, each insured depository institution will be provided an assessment risk assignment. Notice of an institution's current assessment risk assignment will be provided to the institution with each quarterly certified statement invoice. Adjusted assessment risk assignments for prior periods may also be provided by the Corporation. Notice of the procedures applicable to reviews will be included with the notice of assessment risk assignment provided pursuant to paragraph (a) of this section.

(b) *Payment of assessment at rate assigned.* Institutions shall make timely payment of assessments based on the assessment risk assignment in the notice provided to the institution pursuant to paragraph (a) of this section. Timely payment is required notwithstanding any request for review filed pursuant to paragraph (c) of this section. Assessment risk assignments remain in effect for future assessment periods until changed. If the risk assignment in the notice is subsequently changed, any excess assessment paid by the institution will be credited by the Corporation, with interest, and any additional assessment owed shall be paid by the institution, with interest, in the next assessment payment after such subsequent assignment or change. Interest payable under this paragraph shall be determined in accordance with § 327.7.

(c) *Requests for review.* An institution that believes any assessment risk assignment provided by the Corporation pursuant to paragraph (a) of this section is incorrect and seeks to change it must submit a written request for review of that risk assignment. An institution cannot request review through this process of the CAMELS ratings assigned by its primary federal regulator or challenge the appropriateness of any such rating; each federal regulator has established procedures for that purpose. An institution may also request review of a determination by the FDIC to assess the institution as a large, highly complex, or a small institution (§ 327.9(e)(3)) or a determination by the

§ 327.5

FDIC that the institution is a new institution (§ 327.9(f)(5)). Any request for review must be submitted within 90 days from the date the assessment risk assignment being challenged pursuant to paragraph (a) of this section appears on the institution's quarterly certified statement invoice. The request shall be submitted to the Corporation's Director of the Division of Insurance and Research in Washington, DC, and shall include documentation sufficient to support the change sought by the institution. If additional information is requested by the Corporation, such information shall be provided by the institution within 21 days of the date of the request for additional information. Any institution submitting a timely request for review will receive written notice from the Corporation regarding the outcome of its request. Upon completion of a review, the Director of the Division of Insurance and Research (or designee) or the Director of the Division of Supervision and Consumer Protection (or designee) or any successor divisions, as appropriate, shall promptly notify the institution in writing of his or her determination of whether a change is warranted. If the institution requesting review disagrees with that determination, it may appeal to the FDIC's Assessment Appeals Committee. Notice of the procedures applicable to appeals will be included with the written determination.

(d) *Disclosure restrictions.* The portion of an assessment risk assignment provided to an institution by the Corporation pursuant to paragraph (a) of this section that reflects any supervisory evaluation or confidential information is deemed to be exempt information within the scope of § 309.5(g)(8) of this chapter and, accordingly, is governed by the disclosure restrictions set out at § 309.6 of this chapter.

(e) *Limited use of assessment risk assignment.* Any assessment risk assignment provided to a depository institution under this part 327 is for purposes of implementing and operating the FDIC's risk-based assessment system. Unless permitted by the Corporation or otherwise required by law, no institution may state in any advertisement or promotional material, or in any other public place or manner, the assessment risk assignment provided to it pursuant to this part.

(f) *Effective date for changes to risk assignment.* Changes to an insured institution's risk assignment resulting from a supervisory ratings change become effective as of the date of written notification to the institution by its primary federal regulator or state authority of its supervisory rating (even when the CAMELS component ratings have not been disclosed to the institution), if the FDIC, after taking into account other information that could affect the rating, agrees with the rating. If the FDIC does not agree, the FDIC will notify the institution of the FDIC's supervisory rating; resulting changes to an insured institution's risk assignment become effective as of the date of written notification to the institution by the FDIC.

(g) *Designated Reserve Ratio.* The designated reserve ratio for the Deposit Insurance Fund is 2 percent.

[71 FR 69277, 69326, Nov. 30, 2006, as amended at 75 FR 79293, Dec. 20, 2010; 76 FR 10704, Feb. 25, 2011]

§ 327.5 Assessment base.

(a) *Assessment base for all insured depository institutions.* Except as provided in paragraphs (b), (c), and (d) of this section, the assessment base for an insured depository institution shall equal the average consolidated total assets of the insured depository institution during the assessment period minus the average tangible equity of the insured depository institution during the assessment period.

(1) *Average consolidated total assets defined and calculated.* Average consolidated total assets are defined in the schedule of quarterly averages in the Consolidated Reports of Condition and Income, using either a daily averaging method or a weekly averaging method as described in paragraphs (a)(1)(i) or (ii) of this section. The amounts to be reported as daily averages are the sum of the gross amounts of consolidated total assets for each calendar day during the quarter divided by the number of calendar days in the quarter. The amounts to be reported as weekly averages are the sum of the gross amounts of consolidated total assets for each Wednesday during the quarter divided

Federal Deposit Insurance Corporation § 327.5

by the number of Wednesdays in the quarter. For days that an office of the reporting institution (or any of its subsidiaries or branches) is closed (e.g., Saturdays, Sundays, or holidays), the amounts outstanding from the previous business day will be used. An office is considered closed if there are no transactions posted to the general ledger as of that date. For institutions that begin operating during the calendar quarter, the amounts to be reported as daily averages are the sum of the gross amounts of consolidated total assets for each calendar day the institution was operating during the quarter divided by the number of calendar days the institution was operating during the quarter.

(i) *Institutions that must report average consolidated total assets using a daily averaging method.* All insured depository institutions that report $1 billion or more in quarter-end consolidated total assets on their March 31, 2011 Consolidated Report of Condition and Income or Thrift Financial Report (or successor report), and all institutions that become insured after March 31, 2011, shall report average consolidated total assets as of the close of business for each day of the calendar quarter.

(ii) *Institutions that may report average consolidated total assets using a weekly averaging method.* All insured depository institutions that report less than $1 billion in quarter-end consolidated total assets on their March 31, 2011, Consolidated Report of Condition and Income or Thrift Financial Report may report average consolidated total assets as an average of the balances as of the close of business on each Wednesday during the calendar quarter, or may at any time opt permanently to report average consolidated total assets on a daily basis as set forth in paragraph (a)(1)(i) of this section. Once an institution that reports average consolidated total assets using a weekly average reports average consolidated total assets equal to or greater than $1 billion for two consecutive quarters, it shall permanently report average consolidated total assets using daily averaging starting in the next quarter.

(iii) *Mergers and consolidations.* The average calculation of the assets of the surviving or resulting institution in a merger or consolidation shall include the assets of all the merged or consolidated institutions for the days in the quarter prior to the merger or consolidation, whether reported by the daily or weekly method.

(2) *Average tangible equity defined and calculated.* Tangible equity is defined as Tier 1 capital.

(i) *Calculation of average tangible equity.* Except as provided in paragraph (a)(2)(ii) of this section, average tangible equity shall be calculated using monthly averaging. Monthly averaging means the average of the three month-end balances within the quarter.

(ii) *Alternate calculation of average tangible equity.* Institutions that report less than $1 billion in quarter-end consolidated total assets on their March 31, 2011 Consolidated Reports of Condition and Income or Thrift Financial Reports may report average tangible equity using an end-of-quarter balance or may at any time opt permanently to report average tangible equity using a monthly average balance. An institution that reports average tangible equity using an end-of-quarter balance and reports average daily or weekly consolidated assets of $1 billion or more for two consecutive quarters shall permanently report average tangible equity using monthly averaging starting in the next quarter. Newly insured institutions shall report using monthly averaging.

(iii) *Calculation of average tangible equity for the surviving institution in a merger or consolidation.* For the surviving institution in a merger or consolidation, Tier 1 capital shall be calculated as if the merger occurred on the first day of the quarter in which the merger or consolidation occurred.

(3) *Consolidated subsidiaries*— (i) *Reporting for insured depository institutions with consolidated subsidiaries that are not insured depository institutions.* For insured institutions with consolidated subsidiaries that are not insured depository institutions, assets, including assets eliminated in consolidation, shall be calculated using a daily or weekly averaging method, corresponding to the daily or weekly averaging requirement of the parent institution. The Consolidated Reports of

Condition and Income instructions in effect for the quarter for which data is being reported shall govern calculation of the average amount of subsidiaries' assets, including those assets eliminated in consolidation. An insured depository institution that reports average tangible equity using a monthly averaging method and that has subsidiaries that are not insured depository institutions shall use monthly average reporting for the subsidiaries. The monthly average data for these subsidiaries, however, may be calculated for the current quarter or for the prior quarter consistent with the method used to report average consolidated total assets and in conformity with Consolidated Reports of Condition and Income requirements. Once the method of reporting the subsidiaries' assets and tangible equity is chosen, however (current quarter or prior quarter), insured depository institutions cannot change the reporting method from quarter to quarter. An institution that reports consolidated assets and tangible equity using data for the prior quarter may switch to concurrent reporting on a permanent basis.

(ii) *Reporting for insured depository institutions with consolidated insured depository subsidiaries.* Insured depository institutions that consolidate with other insured depository institutions for financial reporting purposes shall report for the parent and for each subsidiary individually, daily average consolidated total assets or weekly average consolidated total assets, as appropriate under paragraph (a)(1)(i) or (ii) above, and tangible equity, without consolidating their insured depository institution subsidiaries into the calculations. Investments in insured depository institution subsidiaries should be included in total assets using the equity method of accounting.

(b) *Assessment base for banker's banks*—(1) *Bankers bank defined.* A banker's bank for purposes of calculating deposit insurance assessments shall meet the definition of banker's bank as that term is used in 12 U.S.C. 24. Banker's banks that have funds from government capital infusion programs (such as TARP and the Small Business Lending Fund), and stock owned by the FDIC resulting from banks failures, as well as non-bank-owned stock resulting from equity compensation programs, are not thereby excluded from the definition of banker's banks.

(2) *Self-certification.* Institutions that meet the requirements of paragraph (b)(1) of this section shall so certify to that effect each quarter on the Consolidated Reports of Condition and Income or Thrift Financial Report or successor report.

(3) *Assessment base calculation for banker's banks.* A banker's bank shall pay deposit insurance assessments on its assessment base as calculated in paragraph (a) of this section provided that it conducts 50 percent or more of its business with entities other than its parent holding company or entities other than those controlled (control has the same meaning as in section 3(w)(5) of the FDI Act) either directly or indirectly by its parent holding company. The assessment base will exclude the average (daily or weekly depending on how the institution calculates its average consolidated total assets) amount of reserve balances passed through to the Federal Reserve, the average amount of reserve balances held at the Federal Reserve for its own account (including all balances due from the Federal Reserve as described in the instructions to line 4 of Schedule RC–A of the Consolidated Report of Condition and Income as of December 31, 2010), and the average amount of the institution's federal funds sold, but in no case shall the amount excluded exceed the sum of the bank's average amount of total deposits of commercial banks and other depository institutions in the United States and the average amount of its federal funds purchased.

(c) *Assessment base for custodial banks*—(1) *Custodial bank defined.* A custodial bank for purposes of calculating deposit insurance assessments shall be an insured depository institution with previous calendar-year trust assets (fiduciary and custody and safekeeping assets, as described in the instructions to Schedule RC–T of the Consolidated Report of Condition and Income as of December 31, 2010) of at least $50 billion or an insured depository institution that derived more than 50 percent of its

Federal Deposit Insurance Corporation § 327.6

total revenue (interest income plus non-interest income) from trust activity over the previous calendar year.

(2) *Assessment base calculation for custodial banks.* A custodial bank shall pay deposit insurance assessments on its assessment base as calculated in paragraph (a) of this section, but the FDIC will exclude from that assessment base the daily or weekly average (depending on how the bank reports its average consolidated total assets) of all asset types described in the instructions to lines 34, 35, 36, and 37 of Schedule RC–R of the Consolidated Report of Condition and Income as of December 31, 2010 with a Basel risk weighting of 0 percent, regardless of maturity, plus 50 percent of those asset types described in lines 34, 35, 36, and 37 of Schedule RC–R as of December 31, 2010 with a Basel risk weighting of 20 percent regardless of maturity subject to the limitation that the daily or weekly average value of these assets cannot exceed the daily or weekly average value of those deposits classified as transaction accounts in the instructions to Schedule RC–E of the Consolidated Report of Condition and Income as of December 31, 2010, and identified by the institution as being directly linked to a fiduciary or custodial and safekeeping account asset.

(d) *Assessment base for insured branches of foreign banks.* Average consolidated total assets for an insured branch of a foreign bank are defined as total assets of the branch (including net due from related depository institutions) in accordance with the schedule of assets and liabilities in the Report of Assets and Liabilities of U.S. Branches and Agencies of Foreign Banks as of the assessment period for which the assessment is being calculated, but measured using the definition for reporting total assets in the schedule of quarterly averages in the Consolidated Reports of Condition and Income, and calculated using the appropriate daily or weekly averaging method under paragraph (a)(1)(i) or (ii) of this section. Tangible equity for an insured branch of a foreign bank is eligible assets (determined in accordance with § 347.210 of the FDIC's regulations) less the book value of liabilities (exclusive of liabilities due to the foreign bank's head office, other branches, agencies, offices, or wholly owned subsidiaries) calculated on a monthly or end-of-quarter basis, according to the branch's size.

(e) *Newly insured institutions.* A newly insured institution shall pay an assessment for the assessment period during which it became insured. The FDIC will prorate the newly insured institution's assessment amount to reflect the number of days it was insured during the period.

[76 FR 10704, Feb. 25, 2011]

§ 327.6 Mergers and consolidations; other terminations of insurance.

(a) *Final quarterly certified invoice for acquired institution.* An institution that is not the resulting or surviving institution in a merger or consolidation must file a report of condition for every assessment period prior to the assessment period in which the merger or consolidation occurs. The surviving or resulting institution shall be responsible for ensuring that these reports of condition are filed and shall be liable for any unpaid assessments on the part of the institution that is not the resulting or surviving institution.

(b) *Assessment for quarter in which the merger or consolidation occurs.* For an assessment period in which a merger or consolidation occurs, consolidated total assets for the surviving or resulting institution shall include the consolidated total assets of all insured depository institutions that are parties to the merger or consolidation as if the merger or consolidation occurred on the first day of the assessment period. Tier 1 capital shall be reported in the same manner.

(c) *Other termination.* When the insured status of an institution is terminated, and the deposit liabilities of such institution are not assumed by another insured depository institution—

(1) *Payment of assessments; quarterly certified statement invoices.* The depository institution whose insured status is terminating shall continue to file and certify its quarterly certified statement invoice and pay assessments for the assessment period its deposits are insured. Such institution shall not be

§ 327.7

required to certify its quarterly certified statement invoice and pay further assessments after it has paid in full its deposit liabilities and the assessment to the Corporation required to be paid for the assessment period in which its deposit liabilities are paid in full, and after it, under applicable law, goes out of business or transfers all or substantially all of its assets and liabilities to other institutions or otherwise ceases to be obliged to pay subsequent assessments.

(2) *Payment of deposits; certification to Corporation.* When the deposit liabilities of the depository institution have been paid in full, the depository institution shall certify to the Corporation that the deposit liabilities have been paid in full and give the date of the final payment. When the depository institution has unclaimed deposits, the certification shall further state the amount of the unclaimed deposits and the disposition made of the funds to be held to meet the claims. For assessment purposes, the following will be considered as payment of the unclaimed deposits:

(i) The transfer of cash funds in an amount sufficient to pay the unclaimed and unpaid deposits to the public official authorized by law to receive the same; or

(ii) If no law provides for the transfer of funds to a public official, the transfer of cash funds or compensatory assets to an insured depository institution in an amount sufficient to pay the unclaimed and unpaid deposits in consideration for the assumption of the deposit obligations by the insured depository institution.

(3) *Notice to depositors.* (i) The depository institution whose insured status is terminating shall give sufficient advance notice of the intended transfer to the owners of the unclaimed deposits to enable the depositors to obtain their deposits prior to the transfer. The notice shall be mailed to each depositor and shall be published in a local newspaper of general circulation. The notice shall advise the depositors of the liquidation of the depository institution, request them to call for and accept payment of their deposits, and state the disposition to be made of

12 CFR Ch. III (1-1-12 Edition)

their deposits if they fail to promptly claim the deposits.

(ii) If the unclaimed and unpaid deposits are disposed of as provided in paragraph (c)(2)(i) of this section, a certified copy of the public official's receipt issued for the funds shall be furnished to the Corporation.

(iii) If the unclaimed and unpaid deposits are disposed of as provided in paragraph (c)(2)(ii) of this section, an affidavit of the publication and of the mailing of the notice to the depositors, together with a copy of the notice and a certified copy of the contract of assumption, shall be furnished to the Corporation.

(4) *Notice to Corporation.* The depository institution whose insured status is terminating shall advise the Corporation of the date on which it goes out of business or transfers all or substantially all of its assets and liabilities to other institutions or otherwise ceases to be obliged to pay subsequent assessments and the method whereby the termination has been effected.

(d) *Resumption of insured status before insurance of deposits ceases.* If a depository institution whose insured status has been terminated is permitted by the Corporation to continue or resume its status as an insured depository institution before the insurance of its deposits has ceased, the institution will be deemed, for assessment purposes, to continue as an insured depository institution and must thereafter file and certify its quarterly certified statement invoices and pay assessments as though its insured status had not been terminated. The procedure for applying for the continuance or resumption of insured status is set forth in § 303.248 of this chapter.

[76 FR 10706, Feb. 25, 2011]

§ 327.7 Payment of interest on assessment underpayments and overpayments.

(a) *Payment of interest*—(1) *Payment by institutions.* Each insured depository institution shall pay interest to the Corporation on any underpayment of the institution's assessment.

(2) *Payment by Corporation.* The Corporation will pay interest on any overpayment by the institution of its assessment.

Federal Deposit Insurance Corporation § 327.8

(3) *Accrual of interest.* (i) Interest on an amount owed to or by the Corporation for the underpayment or overpayment of an assessment shall accrue interest at the relevant interest rate.

(ii) Interest on an amount specified in paragraph (a)(3)(i) of this section shall begin to accrue on the day following the regular payment date, as provided for in § 327.3(b)(2), for the amount so overpaid or underpaid, provided, however, that interest shall not begin to accrue on any overpayment until the day following the date such overpayment was received by the Corporation. Interest shall continue to accrue through the date on which the overpayment or underpayment (together with any interest thereon) is discharged.

(iii) The relevant interest rate shall be redetermined for each quarterly assessment interval. A quarterly assessment interval begins on the day following a regular payment date, as specified in § 327.3(b)(2), and ends on the immediately following regular payment date.

(b) *Interest rates.* (1) The relevant interest rate for a quarterly assessment interval that includes the month of January, April, July, and October, respectively, is the coupon equivalent yield of the average discount rate set on the 3-month Treasury bill at the last auction held by the United States Treasury Department during the preceding December, March, June, and September, respectively.

(2) The relevant interest rate for a quarterly assessment interval will apply to any amounts overpaid or underpaid on the payment date immediately prior to the beginning of the quarterly assessment interval. The relevant interest rate will also apply to any amounts owed for previous overpayments or underpayments (including any interest thereon) that remain outstanding, after any adjustments to such overpayments or underpayments have been made thereon, at the end of the regular payment date immediately prior to the beginning of the quarterly assessment interval. Interest will be compounded daily.

§ 327.8 Definitions.

For the purpose of this part 327:

(a) *Deposits.* The term *deposit* has the meaning specified in section 3(*l*) of the Federal Deposit Insurance Act.

(b) *Quarterly report of condition.* The term *quarterly report of condition* means a report required to be filed pursuant to section 7(a)(3) of the Federal Deposit Insurance Act.

(c) *Assessment period—In general.* The term *assessment period* means a period beginning on January 1 of any calendar year and ending on March 31 of the same year, or a period beginning on April 1 of any calendar year and ending on June 30 of the same year; or a period beginning on July 1 of any calendar year and ending on September 30 of the same year; or a period beginning on October 1 of any calendar year and ending on December 31 of the same year.

(d) *Acquiring institution.* The term *acquiring institution* means an insured depository institution that assumes some or all of the deposits of another insured depository institution in a terminating transfer.

(e) *Small institution.* An insured depository institution with assets of less than $10 billion as of December 31, 2006, and an insured branch of a foreign institution shall be classified as a small institution. If, after December 31, 2006, an institution classified as large under paragraph (f) of this section (other than an institution classified as large for purposes of § 327.9(e)) reports assets of less than $10 billion in its quarterly reports of condition for four consecutive quarters, the FDIC will reclassify the institution as small beginning the following quarter.

(f) *Large institution.* An institution classified as large for purposes of § 327.9(e) or an insured depository institution with assets of $10 billion or more as of December 31, 2006 (other than an insured branch of a foreign bank or a highly complex institution) shall be classified as a large institution. If, after December 31, 2006, an institution classified as small under paragraph (e) of this section reports assets of $10 billion or more in its quarterly reports of condition for four consecutive quarters, the FDIC will reclassify the institution as large beginning the following quarter.

(g) *Highly complex institution.* (1) A highly complex institution is:

§ 327.8

(i) An insured depository institution (excluding a credit card bank) that has had $50 billion or more in total assets for at least four consecutive quarters that is controlled by a U.S. parent holding company that has had $500 billion or more in total assets for four consecutive quarters, or controlled by one or more intermediate U.S. parent holding companies that are controlled by a U.S. holding company that has had $500 billion or more in assets for four consecutive quarters; or

(ii) A processing bank or trust company.

(2) Control has the same meaning as in section 3(w)(5) of the FDI Act. A U.S. parent holding company is a parent holding company incorporated or organized under the laws of the United States or any State, as the term "State" is defined in section 3(a)(3) of the FDI Act. If, after December 31, 2010, an institution classified as highly complex under paragraph (g)(1)(i) of this section falls below $50 billion in total assets in its quarterly reports of condition for four consecutive quarters, or its parent holding company or companies fall below $500 billion in total assets for four consecutive quarters, the FDIC will reclassify the institution beginning the following quarter. If, after December 31, 2010, an institution classified as highly complex under paragraph (a)(1)(ii) of this section falls below $10 billion in total assets for four consecutive quarters, the FDIC will reclassify the institution beginning the following quarter.

(h) *CAMELS composite and CAMELS component ratings.* The terms *CAMELS composite ratings* and *CAMELS component ratings* shall have the same meaning as in the Uniform Financial Institutions Rating System as published by the Federal Financial Institutions Examination Council.

(i) *ROCA supervisory ratings.* ROCA supervisory ratings rate risk management, operational controls, compliance, and asset quality.

(j) *New depository institution.* A new insured depository institution is a bank or savings association that has been federally insured for less than five years as of the last day of any quarter for which it is being assessed.

(k) *Established depository institution.* An established insured depository institution is a bank or savings association that has been federally insured for at least five years as of the last day of any quarter for which it is being assessed.

(1) *Merger or consolidation involving new and established institution(s).* Subject to paragraphs (k)(2), (3), (4), and (5) of this section and § 327.9(f)(3) and (4), when an established institution merges into or consolidates with a new institution, the resulting institution is a new institution unless:

(i) The assets of the established institution, as reported in its report of condition for the quarter ending immediately before the merger, exceeded the assets of the new institution, as reported in its report of condition for the quarter ending immediately before the merger; and

(ii) Substantially all of the management of the established institution continued as management of the resulting or surviving institution.

(2) *Consolidation involving established institutions.* When established institutions consolidate, the resulting institution is an established institution.

(3) *Grandfather exception.* If a new institution merges into an established institution, and the merger agreement was entered into on or before July 11, 2006, the resulting institution shall be deemed to be an established institution for purposes of this part.

(4) *Subsidiary exception.* Subject to paragraph (k)(5) of this section, a new institution will be considered established if it is a wholly owned subsidiary of:

(i) A company that is a bank holding company under the Bank Holding Company Act of 1956 or a savings and loan holding company under the Home Owners' Loan Act, and:

(A) At least one eligible depository institution (as defined in 12 CFR 303.2(r)) that is owned by the holding company has been chartered as a bank or savings association for at least five years as of the date that the otherwise new institution was established; and

(B) The holding company has a composite rating of at least "2" for bank holding companies or an above average or "A" rating for savings and loan

Federal Deposit Insurance Corporation § 327.9

holding companies and at least 75 percent of its insured depository institution assets are assets of eligible depository institutions, as defined in 12 CFR 303.2(r); or

(ii) An eligible depository institution, as defined in 12 CFR 303.2(r), that has been chartered as a bank or savings association for at least five years as of the date that the otherwise new institution was established.

(5) *Effect of credit union conversion.* In determining whether an insured depository institution is new or established, the FDIC will include any period of time that the institution was a federally insured credit union.

(l) *Risk assignment.* For all small institutions and insured branches of foreign banks, risk assignment includes assignment to Risk Category I, II, III, or IV, and, within Risk Category I, assignment to an assessment rate or rates. For all large institutions and highly complex institutions, risk assignment includes assignment to an assessment rate or rates.

(m) *Unsecured debt*—For purposes of the unsecured debt adjustment as set forth in § 327.9(d)(1) and the depository institution debt adjustment as set forth in § 327.9(d)(2), unsecured debt shall include senior unsecured liabilities and subordinated debt.

(n) *Senior unsecured liability*—For purposes of the unsecured debt adjustment as set forth in § 327.9(d)(1) and the depository institution debt adjustment as set forth in § 327.9(d)(2), senior unsecured liabilities shall be the unsecured portion of other borrowed money as defined in the quarterly report of condition for the reporting period as defined in paragraph (b) of this section, but shall not include any senior unsecured debt that the FDIC has guaranteed under the Temporary Liquidity Guarantee Program, 12 CFR part 370.

(o) *Subordinated debt*—For purposes of the unsecured debt adjustment as set forth in § 327.9(d)(1) and the depository institution debt adjustment as set forth in § 327.9(d)(2), subordinated debt shall be as defined in the quarterly report of condition for the reporting period; however, subordinated debt shall also include limited-life preferred stock as defined in the quarterly report of condition for the reporting period.

(p) *Long-term unsecured debt*—For purposes of the unsecured debt adjustment as set forth in § 327.9(d)(1) and the depository institution debt adjustment as set forth in § 327.9(d)(2), long-term unsecured debt shall be unsecured debt with at least one year remaining until maturity; however, any such debt where the holder of the debt has a redemption option that is exercisable within one year of the reporting date shall not be deemed long-term unsecured debt.

(q) *Reciprocal deposits*—Deposits that an insured depository institution receives through a deposit placement network on a reciprocal basis, such that: (1) for any deposit received, the institution (as agent for depositors) places the same amount with other insured depository institutions through the network; and (2) each member of the network sets the interest rate to be paid on the entire amount of funds it places with other network members.

(r) *Parent holding company*—A parent holding company has the same meaning as "depository institution holding company," as defined in § 3(w) of the FDI Act.

(s) *Processing bank or trust company*—A processing bank or trust company is an institution whose last three years' non-lending interest income, fiduciary revenues, and investment banking fees, combined, exceed 50 percent of total revenues (and its last three years fiduciary revenues are non-zero), and whose total fiduciary assets total $500 billion or more, and whose total assets for at least four consecutive quarters have been $10 billion or more.

(t) *Credit card bank*—A credit card bank is a bank for which credit card receivables plus securitized receivables exceed 50 percent of assets plus securitized receivables.

(u) *Control*—Control has the same meaning as in section 2 of the Bank Holding Company Act of 1956, 12 U.S.C. 1841(a)(2).

[54 FR 51374, Dec. 15, 1989, as amended at 74 FR 9551, Mar. 4, 2009; 76 FR 10707, Feb. 25, 2011]

§ 327.9 Assessment pricing methods.

(a) *Small institutions*—(1) *Risk Categories.* Each small insured depository institution shall be assigned to one of the following four Risk Categories

§ 327.9

based upon the institution's capital evaluation and supervisory evaluation as defined in this section.

(i) *Risk Category I.* Small institutions in Supervisory Group A that are Well Capitalized will be assigned to Risk Category I.

(ii) *Risk Category II.* Small institutions in Supervisory Group A that are Adequately Capitalized, and small institutions in Supervisory Group B that are either Well Capitalized or Adequately Capitalized will be assigned to Risk Category II.

(iii) *Risk Category III.* Small institutions in Supervisory Groups A and B that are Undercapitalized, and small institutions in Supervisory Group C that are Well Capitalized or Adequately Capitalized will be assigned to Risk Category III.

(iv) *Risk Category IV.* Small institutions in Supervisory Group C that are Undercapitalized will be assigned to Risk Category IV.

(2) *Capital evaluations.* Each small institution will receive one of the following three capital evaluations on the basis of data reported in the institution's Consolidated Reports of Condition and Income or Thrift Financial Report (or successor report, as appropriate) dated as of March 31 for the assessment period beginning the preceding January 1; dated as of June 30 for the assessment period beginning the preceding April 1; dated as of September 30 for the assessment period beginning the preceding July 1; and dated as of December 31 for the assessment period beginning the preceding October 1.

(i) *Well Capitalized.* A Well Capitalized institution is one that satisfies each of the following capital ratio standards: Total risk-based ratio, 10.0 percent or greater; Tier 1 risk-based ratio, 6.0 percent or greater; and Tier 1 leverage ratio, 5.0 percent or greater.

(ii) *Adequately Capitalized.* An Adequately Capitalized institution is one that does not satisfy the standards of Well Capitalized under this paragraph but satisfies each of the following capital ratio standards: Total risk-based ratio, 8.0 percent or greater; Tier 1 risk-based ratio, 4.0 percent or greater; and Tier 1 leverage ratio, 4.0 percent or greater.

(iii) *Undercapitalized.* An undercapitalized institution is one that does not qualify as either Well Capitalized or Adequately Capitalized under paragraphs (a)(2)(i) and (ii) of this section.

(3) *Supervisory evaluations.* Each small institution will be assigned to one of three Supervisory Groups based on the Corporation's consideration of supervisory evaluations provided by the institution's primary federal regulator. The supervisory evaluations include the results of examination findings by the primary federal regulator, as well as other information that the primary federal regulator determines to be relevant. In addition, the Corporation will take into consideration such other information (such as state examination findings, as appropriate) as it determines to be relevant to the institution's financial condition and the risk posed to the Deposit Insurance Fund. The three Supervisory Groups are:

(i) *Supervisory Group "A."* This Supervisory Group consists of financially sound institutions with only a few minor weaknesses;

(ii) *Supervisory Group "B."* This Supervisory Group consists of institutions that demonstrate weaknesses which, if not corrected, could result in significant deterioration of the institution and increased risk of loss to the Deposit Insurance Fund; and

(iii) *Supervisory Group "C."* This Supervisory Group consists of institutions that pose a substantial probability of loss to the Deposit Insurance Fund unless effective corrective action is taken.

(4) *Financial ratios method.* A small insured depository institution in Risk Category I shall have its initial base assessment rate determined using the financial ratios method.

(i) Under the financial ratios method, each of six financial ratios and a weighted average of CAMELS component ratings will be multiplied by a corresponding pricing multiplier. The sum of these products will be added to a uniform amount. The resulting sum shall equal the institution's initial base assessment rate; provided, however, that no institution's initial base assessment rate shall be less than the minimum initial base assessment rate

Federal Deposit Insurance Corporation § 327.9

in effect for Risk Category I institutions for that quarter nor greater than the maximum initial base assessment rate in effect for Risk Category I institutions for that quarter. An institution's initial base assessment rate, subject to adjustment pursuant to paragraphs (d)(1), (2), and (3) of this section, as appropriate (resulting in the institution's total base assessment rate, which in no case can be lower than 50 percent of the institution's initial base assessment rate), and adjusted for the actual assessment rates set by the Board under §327.10(f), will equal an institution's assessment rate. The six financial ratios are: Tier 1 Leverage Ratio; Loans past due 30–89 days/gross assets; Nonperforming assets/gross assets; Net loan charge-offs/gross assets; Net income before taxes/risk-weighted assets; and the Adjusted brokered deposit ratio. The ratios are defined in Table A.1 of Appendix A to this subpart. The ratios will be determined for an assessment period based upon information contained in an institution's report of condition filed as of the last day of the assessment period as set out in paragraph (a)(2) of this section. The weighted average of CAMELS component ratings is created by multiplying each component by the following percentages and adding the products: Capital adequacy—25%, Asset quality—20%, Management—25%, Earnings—10%, Liquidity—10%, and Sensitivity to market risk—10%. The following table sets forth the initial values of the pricing multipliers:

Risk measures*	Pricing multipliers**
Tier 1 Leverage Ratio	(0.056)
Loans Past Due 30–89 Days/Gross Assets	0.575
Nonperforming Assets/Gross Assets	1.074
Net Loan Charge-Offs/Gross Assets	1.210
Net Income before Taxes/Risk-Weighted Assets	(0.764)
Adjusted brokered deposit ratio	0.065
Weighted Average CAMELS Component Rating	1.095

*Ratios are expressed as percentages.
**Multipliers are rounded to three decimal places.

(ii) The six financial ratios and the weighted average CAMELS component rating will be multiplied by the respective pricing multiplier, and the products will be summed. To this result will be added the uniform amount. The resulting sum shall equal the institution's initial base assessment rate; provided, however, that no institution's initial base assessment rate shall be less than the minimum initial base assessment rate in effect for Risk Category I institutions for that quarter nor greater than the maximum initial base assessment rate in effect for Risk Category I institutions for that quarter.

(iii) *Uniform amount and pricing multipliers.* Except as adjusted for the actual assessment rates set by the Board under §327.10(f), the uniform amount shall be:

(A) 4.861 whenever the assessment rate schedule set forth in §327.10(a) is in effect;

(B) 2.861 whenever the assessment rate schedule set forth in §327.10(b) is in effect;

(C) 1.861 whenever the assessment rate schedule set forth in §327.10(c) is in effect; or

(D) 0.861 whenever the assessment rate schedule set forth in §327.10(d) is in effect.

(iv) *Implementation of CAMELS rating changes*—(A) *Changes between risk categories.* If, during a quarter, a CAMELS composite rating change occurs that results in a Risk Category I institution moving from Risk Category I to Risk Category II, III or IV, the institution's initial base assessment rate for the portion of the quarter that it was in Risk Category I shall be determined using the supervisory ratings in effect before the change and the financial ratios as of the end of the quarter, subject to adjustment pursuant to paragraphs (d)(1), (2), and (3) of this section, as appropriate, and adjusted for the actual assessment rates set by the Board under §327.10(f). For the portion of the quarter that the institution was not in Risk Category I, the institution's initial base assessment rate, which shall be subject to adjustment pursuant to paragraphs (d)(1), (2), and (3), shall be determined under the assessment schedule for the appropriate Risk Category. If, during a quarter, a CAMELS composite rating change occurs that results in an institution moving from Risk Category II, III or IV to Risk Category I, then the financial ratios method shall apply for the portion of the

§ 327.9

quarter that it was in Risk Category I, subject to adjustment pursuant to paragraphs (d)(1), (2) and (3) of this section, as appropriate, and adjusted for the actual assessment rates set by the Board under § 327.10(f). For the portion of the quarter that the institution was not in Risk Category I, the institution's initial base assessment rate, which shall be subject to adjustment pursuant to paragraphs (d)(1), (2), and (3) of this section shall be determined under the assessment schedule for the appropriate Risk Category.

(B) *Changes within Risk Category I.* If, during a quarter, an institution's CAMELS component ratings change in a way that will change the institution's initial base assessment rate within Risk Category I, the initial base assessment rate for the period before the change shall be determined under the financial ratios method using the CAMELS component ratings in effect before the change, subject to adjustment pursuant to paragraphs (d)(1), (2), and (3) of this section, as appropriate. Beginning on the date of the CAMELS component ratings change, the initial base assessment rate for the remainder of the quarter shall be determined using the CAMELS component ratings in effect after the change, again subject to adjustment pursuant to paragraphs (d)(1), (2), and (3) of this section, as appropriate.

(b) *Large and Highly Complex institutions*—(1) *Assessment scorecard for large institutions (other than highly complex institutions).* (i) A large institution other than a highly complex institution shall have its initial base assessment rate determined using the scorecard for large institutions.

SCORECARD FOR LARGE INSTITUTIONS

	Scorecard measures and components	Measure weights (percent)	Component weights (percent)
P	Performance Score		
P.1	Weighted Average CAMELS Rating	100	30
P.2	Ability to Withstand Asset-Related Stress	....	50
	Tier 1 Leverage Ratio	10	
	Concentration Measure	35	
	Core Earnings/Average Quarter-End Total Assets *	20	
	Credit Quality Measure	35	
P.3	Ability to Withstand Funding-Related Stress	....	20
	Core Deposits/Total Liabilities	60	
	Balance Sheet Liquidity Ratio	40	
L	Loss Severity Score		
L.1	Loss Severity Measure	....	100

*Average of five quarter-end total assets (most recent and four prior quarters)

(ii) The scorecard for large institutions produces two scores: performance score and loss severity score.

(A) *Performance score for large institutions.* The performance score for large institutions is a weighted average of the scores for three measures: the weighted average CAMELS rating score, weighted at 30 percent; the ability to withstand asset-related stress score, weighted at 50 percent; and the ability to withstand funding-related stress score, weighted at 20 percent.

(*1*) *Weighted average CAMELS rating score.* (i) To compute the weighted average CAMELS rating score, a weighted average of an institution's CAMELS component ratings is calculated using the following weights:

CAMELS Component	Weight
C	25%
A	20%
M	25%
E	10%
L	10%
S	10%

(*ii*) A weighted average CAMELS rating converts to a score that ranges from 25 to 100. A weighted average rating of 1 equals a score of 25 and a weighted average of 3.5 or greater equals a score of 100. Weighted average CAMELS ratings between 1 and 3.5 are assigned a score between 25 and 100. The score increases at an increasing rate as the weighted average CAMELS rating increases. Appendix B of this subpart describes the conversion of a weighted average CAMELS rating to a score.

(2) *Ability to withstand asset-related stress score.* (*i*) The ability to withstand asset-related stress score is a weighted average of the scores for four measures: Tier 1 leverage ratio; concentration measure; the ratio of core earnings to average quarter-end total assets; and the credit quality measure. Appendices A and C of this subpart define these measures.

(*ii*) The Tier 1 leverage ratio and the ratio of core earnings to average quarter-end total assets are described in appendix A and the method of calculating the scores is described in appendix C of this subpart.

(*iii*) The score for the concentration measure is the greater of the higher-risk assets to Tier 1 capital and reserves score or the growth-adjusted portfolio concentrations score. Both ratios are described in appendix C.

(*iv*) The score for the credit quality measure is the greater of the criticized and classified items to Tier 1 capital and reserves score or the underperforming assets to Tier 1 capital and reserves score.

(*v*) The following table shows the cutoff values and weights for the measures used to calculate the ability to withstand asset-related stress score. Appendix B of this subpart describes how each measure is converted to a score between 0 and 100 based upon the minimum and maximum cutoff values, where a score of 0 reflects the lowest risk and a score of 100 reflects the highest risk.

CUTOFF VALUES AND WEIGHTS FOR MEASURES TO CALCULATE ABILITY TO WITHSTAND ASSET-RELATED STRESS SCORE

Measures of the ability to withstand asset-related stress	Cutoff values Minimum (percent)	Cutoff values Maximum (percent)	Weights (percent)
Tier 1 Leverage Ratio	6	13	10
Concentration Measure			35
Higher–Risk Assets to Tier 1 Capital and Reserves; or	0	135	
Growth-Adjusted Portfolio Concentrations	4	56	
Core Earnings/Average Quarter-End Total Assets*	0	2	20
Credit Quality Measure			35
Criticized and Classified Items/Tier 1 Capital and Reserves; or	7	100	
Underperforming Assets/Tier 1 Capital and Reserves	2	35	

*Average of five quarter-end total assets (most recent and four prior quarters).

§ 327.9

(vi) The score for each measure in the table in paragraph (b)(1)(ii)(A)(2)(v) is multiplied by its respective weight and the resulting weighted score is summed to arrive at the score for an ability to withstand asset-related stress, which can range from 0 to 100, where a score of 0 reflects the lowest risk and a score of 100 reflects the highest risk.

(3) *Ability to withstand funding-related stress score.* Two measures are used to compute the ability to withstand funding-related stress score: a core deposits to total liabilities ratio, and a balance sheet liquidity ratio. Appendix A of this subpart describes these measures. Appendix B of this subpart describes how these measures are converted to a score between 0 and 100, where a score of 0 reflects the lowest risk and a score of 100 reflects the highest risk. The ability to withstand funding-related stress score is the weighted average of the scores for the two measures. In the following table, cutoff values and weights are used to derive an institution's ability to withstand funding-related stress score:

CUTOFF VALUES AND WEIGHTS TO CALCULATE ABILITY TO WITHSTAND FUNDING-RELATED STRESS SCORE

Measures of the ability to withstand funding-related stress	Cutoff values		Weights (percent)
	Minimum (percent)	Maximum (percent)	
Core Deposits/Total Liabilities	5	87	60
Balance Sheet Liquidity Ratio	7	243	40

(4) *Calculation of Performance Score.* In paragraph (b)(1)(ii)(A)(3), the scores for the weighted average CAMELS rating, the ability to withstand asset-related stress, and the ability to withstand funding-related stress are multiplied by their respective weights (30 percent, 50 percent and 20 percent, respectively) and the results are summed to arrive at the performance score. The performance score cannot be less than 0 or more than 100, where a score of 0 reflects the lowest risk and a score of 100 reflects the highest risk.

(B) *Loss severity score.* The loss severity score is based on a loss severity measure that is described in Appendix D of this subpart. Appendix B also describes how the loss severity measure is converted to a score between 0 and 100. The loss severity score cannot be less than 0 or more than 100, where a score of 0 reflects the lowest risk and a score of 100 reflects the highest risk. Cutoff values for the loss severity measure are:

CUTOFF VALUES TO CALCULATE LOSS SEVERITY SCORE

Measure of loss severity	Cutoff values	
	Minimum (percent)	Maximum (percent)
Loss Severity	0	28

(C) *Total Score.* The performance and loss severity scores are combined to produce a total score. The loss severity score is converted into a loss severity factor that ranges from 0.8 (score of 5 or lower) to 1.2 (score of 85 or higher). Scores at or below the minimum cutoff of 5 receive a loss severity factor of 0.8, and scores at or above the maximum cutoff of 85 receive a loss severity factor of 1.2. The following linear interpolation converts loss severity scores between the cutoffs into a loss severity factor:

(*Loss Severity Factor* = 0.8 + [0.005 * (*Loss Severity Score* − 5)].

The performance score is multiplied by the loss severity factor to produce a total score (total score = performance score * loss severity factor). The total score can be up to 20 percent higher or lower than the performance score but cannot be less than 30 or more than 90. The total score is subject to adjustment, up or down, by a maximum of 15 points, as set forth in paragraph (b)(3) of this section. The resulting total score after adjustment cannot be less than 30 or more than 90.

(D) *Initial base assessment rate.* A large institution with a total score of 30 pays the minimum initial base assessment rate and an institution with a total score of 90 pays the maximum initial

Federal Deposit Insurance Corporation § 327.9

base assessment rate. For total scores between 30 and 90, initial base assessment rates rise at an increasing rate as the total score increases, calculated according to the following formula:

$$Rate = Minimum\ Rate + \left[\left(\left(1.4245 \times \left(\frac{Score}{100}\right)^3\right) - 0.0385\right) \times (Maximum\ Rate - Minimum\ Rate)\right]$$

where Rate is the initial base assessment rate (expressed in basis points), Maximum Rate is the maximum initial base assessment rate then in effect (expressed in basis points), and Minimum Rate is the minimum initial base assessment rate then in effect (expressed in basis points). Initial base assessment rates are subject to adjustment pursuant to paragraphs (b)(3), (d)(1), (d)(2), of this section; large institutions that are not well capitalized or have a CAMELS composite rating of 3, 4 or 5 shall be subject to the adjustment at paragraph (d)(3); these adjustments shall result in the institution's total base assessment rate, which in no case can be lower than 50 percent of the institution's initial base assessment rate.

(2) *Assessment scorecard for highly complex institutions.* (i) A highly complex institution shall have its initial base assessment rate determined using the scorecard for highly complex institutions.

SCORECARD FOR HIGHLY COMPLEX INSTITUTIONS

		Measures and components	Measure weights (percent)	Component weights (percent)
P	....	Performance Score		
P.1	....	Weighted Average CAMELS Rating	100	30
P.2	....	Ability To Withstand Asset-Related Stress		50
		Tier 1 Leverage Ratio	10	
		Concentration Measure	35	
		Core Earnings/Average Quarter-End Total Assets	20	
		Credit Quality Measure and Market Risk Measure	35	
P.3	....	Ability To Withstand Funding-Related Stress		20
		Core Deposits/Total Liabilities	50	
		Balance Sheet Liquidity Ratio	30	
		Average Short-Term Funding/Average Total Assets	20	
L	....	Loss Severity Score		
L.1	....	Loss Severity		100

(ii) The scorecard for highly complex institutions produces two scores: performance and loss severity.

(A) *Performance score for highly complex institutions.* The performance score for highly complex institutions is the weighted average of the scores for three components: weighted average CAMELS rating, weighted at 30 percent; ability to withstand asset-related stress score, weighted at 50 percent; and ability to withstand funding-related stress score, weighted at 20 percent.

(1) *Weighted average CAMELS rating score.* (i) To compute the score for the weighted average CAMELS rating, a weighted average of an institution's CAMELS component ratings is calculated using the following weights:

§ 327.9

CAMELS Component	Weight
C	25%
A	20%
M	25%
E	10%
L	10%
S	10%

(ii) A weighted average CAMELS rating converts to a score that ranges from 25 to 100. A weighted average rating of 1 equals a score of 25 and a weighted average of 3.5 or greater equals a score of 100. Weighted average CAMELS ratings between 1 and 3.5 are assigned a score between 25 and 100. The score increases at an increasing rate as the weighted average CAMELS rating increases. Appendix B of this subpart describes the conversion of a weighted average CAMELS rating to a score.

(2) *Ability to withstand asset-related stress score.* (i) The ability to withstand asset-related stress score is a weighted average of the scores for four measures: Tier 1 leverage ratio; concentration measure; ratio of core earnings to average quarter-end total assets; credit quality measure and market risk measure. Appendix A of this subpart describes these measures.

(ii) The Tier 1 leverage ratio and the ratio of core earnings to average quarter-end total assets are described in appendix A and the method of calculating the scores is described in appendix B of this subpart.

(iii) The score for the concentration measure for highly complex institutions is the greatest of the higher-risk assets to the sum of Tier 1 capital and reserves score, the top 20 counterparty exposure to the sum of Tier 1 capital and reserves score, or the largest counterparty exposure to the sum of Tier 1 capital and reserves score. Each ratio is described in appendix A of this subpart. The method used to convert the concentration measure into a score is described in appendix C of this subpart.

(iv) The credit quality score is the greater of the criticized and classified items to Tier 1 capital and reserves score or the underperforming assets to Tier 1 capital and reserves score. The market risk score is the weighted average of three scores—the trading revenue volatility to Tier 1 capital score, the market risk capital to Tier 1 capital score, and the level 3 trading assets to Tier 1 capital score. All of these ratios are described in appendix A of this subpart and the method of calculating the scores is described in appendix B. Each score is multiplied by its respective weight, and the resulting weighted score is summed to compute the score for the market risk measure. An overall weight of 35 percent is allocated between the scores for the credit quality measure and market risk measure. The allocation depends on the ratio of average trading assets to the sum of average securities, loans and trading assets (trading asset ratio) as follows:

(v) Weight for credit quality score = 35 percent * (1—trading asset ratio); and,

(vi) Weight for market risk score = 35 percent * trading asset ratio.

(vii) Each of the measures used to calculate the ability to withstand asset-related stress score is assigned the following cutoff values and weights:

Federal Deposit Insurance Corporation § 327.9

CUTOFF VALUES AND WEIGHTS FOR MEASURES TO CALCULATE THE ABILITY TO WITHSTAND ASSET-RELATED STRESS SCORE

Measures of the ability to withstand asset-related stress	Cutoff values Minimum (percent)	Cutoff values Maximum (percent)	Market risk measure (percent)	Weights (percent)
Tier 1 Leverage Ratio	6	13		10.
Concentration Measure				35.
Higher Risk Assets/Tier 1 Capital and Reserves;	0	135		
Top 20 Counterparty Exposure/Tier 1 Capital and Reserves; or.	0	125		
Largest Counterparty Exposure/Tier 1 Capital and Reserves.	0	20		
Core Earnings/Average Quarter-end Total Assets	0	2		20.
Credit Quality Measure*				35* (1 − Trading Asset Ratio).
Criticized and Classified Items to Tier 1 Capital and Reserves; or.	7	100		
Underperforming Assets/Tier 1 Capital and Reserves.	2	35		
Market Risk Measure*				35* Trading Asset Ratio.
Trading Revenue Volatility/Tier 1 Capital	0	2	60	
Market Risk Capital/Tier 1 Capital	0	10	20	
Level 3 Trading Assets/Tier 1 Capital	0	35	20	

*Combined, the credit quality measure and the market risk measure are assigned a 35 percent weight. The relative weight of each of the two scores depends on the ratio of average trading assets to the sum of average securities, loans and trading assets (trading asset ratio).

(*viii*) [Reserved]

(*ix*) The score of each measure is multiplied by its respective weight and the resulting weighted score is summed to compute the ability to withstand asset-related stress score, which can range from 0 to 100, where a score of 0 reflects the lowest risk and a score of 100 reflects the highest risk.

(3) *Ability to withstand funding related stress score.* Three measures are used to calculate the score for the ability to withstand funding-related stress: a core deposits to total liabilities ratio, a balance sheet liquidity ratio, and average short-term funding to average total assets ratio. Appendix A of this subpart describes these ratios. Appendix B of this subpart describes how each measure is converted to a score. The ability to withstand funding-related stress score is the weighted average of the scores for the three measures. In the following table, cutoff values and weights are used to derive an institution's ability to withstand funding-related stress score:

CUTOFF VALUES AND WEIGHTS TO CALCULATE ABILITY TO WITHSTAND FUNDING-RELATED STRESS MEASURES

Measures of the ability to withstand funding-related stress	Cutoff values Minimum (percent)	Cutoff values Maximum (percent)	Weights (percent)
Core Deposits/Total Liabilities	5	87	50
Balance Sheet Liquidity Ratio	7	243	30
Average Short-term Funding/Average Total Assets	2	19	20

(4) *Calculation of Performance Score.* The weighted average CAMELS score, the ability to withstand asset-related stress score, and the ability to withstand funding-related stress score are multiplied by their respective weights (30 percent, 50 percent and 20 percent, respectively) and the results are summed to arrive at the performance score, which cannot be less than 0 or more than 100.

(B) *Loss severity score.* The loss severity score is based on a loss severity measure described in appendix D of this subpart. Appendix B of this subpart also describes how the loss severity

§ 327.9

measure is converted to a score between 0 and 100. Cutoff values for the loss severity measure are:

CUTOFF VALUES FOR LOSS SEVERITY MEASURE

Measure of loss severity	Cutoff values	
	Minimum (percent)	Maximum (percent)
Loss Severity	0	28

(C) *Total Score.* The performance and loss severity scores are combined to produce a total score. The loss severity score is converted into a loss severity factor that ranges from 0.8 (score of 5 or lower) to 1.2 (score of 85 or higher). Scores at or below the minimum cutoff of 5 receive a loss severity factor of 0.8, and scores at or above the maximum cutoff of 85 receive a loss severity factor of 1.2. The following linear interpolation converts loss severity scores between the cutoffs into a loss severity factor:

(Loss Severity Factor = 0.8 + [0.005 * (Loss Severity Score − 5)]. The performance score is multiplied by the loss severity factor to produce a total score (total score = performance score * loss severity factor). The total score can be up to 20 percent higher or lower than the performance score but cannot be less than 30 or more than 90. The total score is subject to adjustment, up or down, by a maximum of 15 points, as set forth in paragraph (b)(3) of this section. The resulting total score after adjustment cannot be less than 30 or more than 90.

(D) *Initial base assessment rate.* A highly complex institution with a total score of 30 pays the minimum initial base assessment rate and an institution with a total score of 90 pays the maximum initial base assessment rate. For total scores between 30 and 90, initial base assessment rates rise at an increasing rate as the total score increases, calculated according to the following formula:

$$Rate = Minimum\ Rate + \left[\left(\left(1.4245 \times \left(\frac{Score}{100}\right)^3\right) - 0.0385\right) \times (Maximum\ Rate - Minimum\ Rate)\right]$$

where Rate is the initial base assessment rate (expressed in basis points), Maximum Rate is the maximum initial base assessment rate then in effect (expressed in basis points), and Minimum Rate is the minimum initial base assessment rate then in effect (expressed in basis points). Initial base assessment rates are subject to adjustment pursuant to paragraphs (b)(3), (d)(1), and (d)(2) of this section; highly complex institutions that are not well capitalized or have a CAMELS composite rating of 3, 4 or 5 shall be subject to the adjustment at paragraph (d)(3); these adjustments shall result in the institution's total base assessment rate, which in no case can be lower than 50 percent of the institution's initial base assessment rate.

(3) *Adjustment to total score for large institutions and highly complex institutions.* The total score for large institutions and highly complex institutions is subject to adjustment, up or down, by a maximum of 15 points, based upon significant risk factors that are not adequately captured in the appropriate scorecard. In making such adjustments, the FDIC may consider such information as financial performance and condition information and other market or supervisory information. The FDIC will also consult with an institution's primary federal regulator and, for state chartered institutions, state banking supervisor.

Federal Deposit Insurance Corporation § 327.9

(i) *Prior notice of adjustments*—(A) *Prior notice of upward adjustment.* Prior to making any upward adjustment to an institution's total score because of considerations of additional risk information, the FDIC will formally notify the institution and its primary federal regulator and provide an opportunity to respond. This notification will include the reasons for the adjustment and when the adjustment will take effect.

(B) *Prior notice of downward adjustment.* Prior to making any downward adjustment to an institution's total score because of considerations of additional risk information, the FDIC will formally notify the institution's primary federal regulator and provide an opportunity to respond.

(ii) *Determination whether to adjust upward; effective period of adjustment.* After considering an institution's and the primary federal regulator's responses to the notice, the FDIC will determine whether the adjustment to an institution's total score is warranted, taking into account any revisions to scorecard measures, as well as any actions taken by the institution to address the FDIC's concerns described in the notice. The FDIC will evaluate the need for the adjustment each subsequent assessment period. Except as provided in paragraph (b)(3)(iv) of this section, the amount of adjustment cannot exceed the proposed adjustment amount contained in the initial notice unless additional notice is provided so that the primary federal regulator and the institution may respond.

(iii) *Determination whether to adjust downward; effective period of adjustment.* After considering the primary federal regulator's responses to the notice, the FDIC will determine whether the adjustment to total score is warranted, taking into account any revisions to scorecard measures. Any downward adjustment in an institution's total score will remain in effect for subsequent assessment periods until the FDIC determines that an adjustment is no longer warranted. Downward adjustments will be made without notification to the institution. However, the FDIC will provide advance notice to an institution and its primary federal regulator and give them an opportunity to respond before removing a downward adjustment.

(iv) *Adjustment without notice.* Notwithstanding the notice provisions set forth above, the FDIC may change an institution's total score without advance notice under this paragraph, if the institution's supervisory ratings or the scorecard measures deteriorate.

(c) *Insured branches of foreign banks*—(1) *Risk categories for insured branches of foreign banks.* Insured branches of foreign banks shall be assigned to risk categories as set forth in paragraph (a)(1) of this section.

(2) *Capital evaluations for insured branches of foreign banks.* Each insured branch of a foreign bank will receive one of the following three capital evaluations on the basis of data reported in the institution's Report of Assets and Liabilities of U.S. Branches and Agencies of Foreign Banks dated as of March 31 for the assessment period beginning the preceding January 1; dated as of June 30 for the assessment period beginning the preceding April 1; dated as of September 30 for the assessment period beginning the preceding July 1; and dated as of December 31 for the assessment period beginning the preceding October 1.

(i) *Well Capitalized.* An insured branch of a foreign bank is Well Capitalized if the insured branch:

(A) Maintains the pledge of assets required under § 347.209 of this chapter; and

(B) Maintains the eligible assets prescribed under § 347.210 of this chapter at 108 percent or more of the average book value of the insured branch's third-party liabilities for the quarter ending on the report date specified in paragraph (c)(2) of this section.

(ii) *Adequately Capitalized.* An insured branch of a foreign bank is Adequately Capitalized if the insured branch:

(A) Maintains the pledge of assets required under § 347.209 of this chapter; and

(B) Maintains the eligible assets prescribed under § 347.210 of this chapter at 106 percent or more of the average book value of the insured branch's third-party liabilities for the quarter ending on the report date specified in paragraph (c)(2) of this section; and

§ 327.9   12 CFR Ch. III (1-1-12 Edition)

(C) Does not meet the definition of a Well Capitalized insured branch of a foreign bank.

(iii) *Undercapitalized.* An insured branch of a foreign bank is undercapitalized institution if it does not qualify as either Well Capitalized or Adequately Capitalized under paragraphs (c)(2)(i) and (ii) of this section.

(3) *Supervisory evaluations for insured branches of foreign banks.* Each insured branch of a foreign bank will be assigned to one of three supervisory groups as set forth in paragraph (a)(3) of this section.

(4) *Assessment method for insured branches of foreign banks in Risk Category I.* Insured branches of foreign banks in Risk Category I shall be assessed using the weighted average ROCA component rating.

(i) *Weighted average ROCA component rating.* The weighted average ROCA component rating shall equal the sum of the products that result from multiplying ROCA component ratings by the following percentages: Risk Management—35%, Operational Controls—25%, Compliance—25%, and Asset Quality—15%. The weighted average ROCA rating will be multiplied by 5.076 (which shall be the pricing multiplier). To this result will be added a uniform amount. The resulting sum—the initial base assessment rate—will equal an institution's total base assessment rate; provided, however, that no institution's total base assessment rate will be less than the minimum total base assessment rate in effect for Risk Category I institutions for that quarter nor greater than the maximum total base assessment rate in effect for Risk Category I institutions for that quarter.

(ii) *Uniform amount.* Except as adjusted for the actual assessment rates set by the Board under § 327.10(f), the uniform amount for all insured branches of foreign banks shall be:

(A) −3.127 whenever the assessment rate schedule set forth in § 327.10(a) is in effect;

(B) −5.127 whenever the assessment rate schedule set forth in § 327.10(b) is in effect;

(C) −−6.127 whenever the assessment rate schedule set forth in § 327.10(c) is in effect; or

(D) −7.127 whenever the assessment rate schedule set forth in § 327.10(d) is in effect.

(iii) *Insured branches of foreign banks not subject to certain adjustments.* No insured branch of a foreign bank in any risk category shall be subject to the adjustments in paragraphs (b)(3), (d)(1), or (d)(3) of this section.

(iv) *Implementation of changes between Risk Categories for insured branches of foreign banks.* If, during a quarter, a ROCA rating change occurs that results in an insured branch of a foreign bank moving from Risk Category I to Risk Category II, III or IV, the institution's initial base assessment rate for the portion of the quarter that it was in Risk Category I shall be determined using the weighted average ROCA component rating. For the portion of the quarter that the institution was not in Risk Category I, the institution's initial base assessment rate shall be determined under the assessment schedule for the appropriate Risk Category. If, during a quarter, a ROCA rating change occurs that results in an insured branch of a foreign bank moving from Risk Category II, III or IV to Risk Category I, the institution's assessment rate for the portion of the quarter that it was in Risk Category I shall equal the rate determined as provided using the weighted average ROCA component rating. For the portion of the quarter that the institution was not in Risk Category I, the institution's initial base assessment rate shall be determined under the assessment schedule for the appropriate Risk Category.

(v) *Implementation of changes within Risk Category I for insured branches of foreign banks.* If, during a quarter, an insured branch of a foreign bank remains in Risk Category I, but a ROCA component rating changes that will affect the institution's initial base assessment rate, separate assessment rates for the portion(s) of the quarter before and after the change(s) shall be determined under this paragraph (c)(4) of this section.

(d) *Adjustments*—(1) *Unsecured debt adjustment to initial base assessment rate for all institutions.* All institutions, except new institutions as provided under paragraphs (f)(1) and (2) of this section and insured branches of foreign banks

Federal Deposit Insurance Corporation § 327.9

as provided under paragraph (c)(4)(iii) of this section, shall be subject to an adjustment of assessment rates for unsecured debt. Any unsecured debt adjustment shall be made after any adjustment under paragraph (b)(3) of this section.

(i) *Application of unsecured debt adjustment.* The unsecured debt adjustment shall be determined as the sum of the initial base assessment rate plus 40 basis points; that sum shall be multiplied by the ratio of an insured depository institution's long-term unsecured debt to its assessment base. The amount of the reduction in the assessment rate due to the adjustment is equal to the dollar amount of the adjustment divided by the amount of the assessment base.

(ii) *Limitation*—No unsecured debt adjustment for any institution shall exceed the lesser of 5 basis points or 50 percent of the institution's initial base assessment rate.

(iii) *Applicable quarterly reports of condition*—Unsecured debt adjustment ratios for any given quarter shall be calculated from quarterly reports of condition (Consolidated Reports of Condition and Income and Thrift Financial Reports, or any successor reports to either, as appropriate) filed by each institution as of the last day of the quarter.

(2) *Depository institution debt adjustment to initial base assessment rate for all institutions.* All institutions shall be subject to an adjustment of assessment rates for unsecured debt held that is issued by another depository institution. Any such depository institution debt adjustment shall be made after any adjustment under paragraphs (b)(3) and (d)(1) of this section.

(i) *Application of depository institution debt adjustment.* An insured depository institution shall pay a 50 basis point adjustment on the amount of unsecured debt it holds that was issued by another insured depository institution to the extent that such debt exceeds 3 percent of the institution's Tier 1 capital. The amount of long-term unsecured debt issued by another insured depository institution shall be calculated using the same valuation methodology used to calculate the amount of such debt for reporting on the asset side of the balance sheets.

(ii) *Applicable quarterly reports of condition.* Depository institution debt adjustment ratios for any given quarter shall be calculated from quarterly reports of condition (Consolidated Reports of Condition and Income and Thrift Financial Reports, or any successor reports to either, as appropriate) filed by each institution as of the last day of the quarter.

(3) *Brokered Deposit Adjustment.* All small institutions in Risk Categories II, III, and IV, all large institutions and all highly complex institutions, except large and highly complex institutions (including new large and new highly complex institutions) that are well capitalized and have a CAMELS composite rating of 1 or 2, shall be subject to an assessment rate adjustment for brokered deposits. Any such brokered deposit adjustment shall be made after any adjustment under paragraphs (b)(3), (d)(1), and (d)(2) of this section. The brokered deposit adjustment includes all brokered deposits as defined in Section 29 of the Federal Deposit Insurance Act (12 U.S.C. 1831f), and 12 CFR 337.6, including reciprocal deposits as defined in § 327.8(p), and brokered deposits that consist of balances swept into an insured institution from another institution. The adjustment under this paragraph is limited to those institutions whose ratio of brokered deposits to domestic deposits is greater than 10 percent; asset growth rates do not affect the adjustment. Insured branches of foreign banks are not subject to the brokered deposit adjustment as provided in paragraph (c)(4)(iii) of this section.

(i) *Application of brokered deposit adjustment.* The brokered deposit adjustment shall be determined by multiplying 25 basis points by the ratio of the difference between an insured depository institution's brokered deposits and 10 percent of its domestic deposits to its assessment base.

(ii) *Limitation.* The maximum brokered deposit adjustment will be 10 basis points; the minimum brokered deposit adjustment will be 0.

(iii) *Applicable quarterly reports of condition.* Brokered deposit ratios for any given quarter shall be calculated from

§ 327.9

the quarterly reports of condition (Call Reports and Thrift Financial Reports, or any successor reports to either, as appropriate) filed by each institution as of the last day of the quarter.

(e) *Request to be treated as a large institution*—(1) *Procedure.* Any institution with assets of between $5 billion and $10 billion may request that the FDIC determine its assessment rate as a large institution. The FDIC will consider such a request provided that it has sufficient information to do so. Any such request must be made to the FDIC's Division of Insurance and Research. Any approved change will become effective within one year from the date of the request. If an institution whose request has been granted subsequently reports assets of less than $5 billion in its report of condition for four consecutive quarters, the institution shall be deemed a small institution for assessment purposes.

(2) *Time limit on subsequent request for alternate method.* An institution whose request to be assessed as a large institution is granted by the FDIC shall not be eligible to request that it be assessed as a small institution for a period of three years from the first quarter in which its approved request to be assessed as a large institution became effective. Any request to be assessed as a small institution must be made to the FDIC's Division of Insurance and Research.

(3) An institution that disagrees with the FDIC's determination that it is a large, highly complex, or small institution may request review of that determination pursuant to § 327.4(c).

(f) *New and established institutions and exceptions*—(1) *New small institutions.* A new small Risk Category I institution shall be assessed the Risk Category I maximum initial base assessment rate for the relevant assessment period. No new small institution in any risk category shall be subject to the unsecured debt adjustment as determined under paragraph (d)(1) of this section. All new small institutions in any Risk Category shall be subject to the depository institution debt adjustment as determined under paragraph (d)(2) of this section. All new small institutions in Risk Categories II, III, and IV shall be subject to the brokered deposit adjustment as determined under paragraph (d)(3) of this section.

(2) *New large institutions and new highly complex institutions.* All new large institutions and all new highly complex institutions shall be assessed under the appropriate method provided at paragraph (b)(1) or (2) of this section and subject to the adjustments provided at paragraphs (b)(3), (d)(2), and (d)(3) of this section. No new highly complex or large institutions are entitled to adjustment under paragraph (d)(1) of this section. If a large or highly complex institution has not yet received CAMELS ratings, it will be given a weighted CAMELS rating of 2 for assessment purposes until actual CAMELS ratings are assigned.

(3) *CAMELS ratings for the surviving institution in a merger or consolidation.* When an established institution merges with or consolidates into a new institution, if the FDIC determines the resulting institution to be an established institution under § 327.8(k)(1), its CAMELS ratings for assessment purposes will be based upon the established institution's ratings prior to the merger or consolidation until new ratings become available.

(4) *Rate applicable to institutions subject to subsidiary or credit union exception.* A small Risk Category I institution that is established under § 327.8(k)(4) or (5), but does not have CAMELS component ratings, shall be assessed at 2 basis points above the minimum initial base assessment rate applicable to Risk Category I institutions until it receives CAMELS component ratings. Thereafter, the assessment rate will be determined by annualizing, where appropriate, financial ratios obtained from all quarterly reports of condition that have been filed, until the institution files four quarterly reports of condition. If a large or highly complex institution is considered established under § 327.8(k)(4) or (5), but does not have CAMELS component ratings, it will be given a weighted CAMELS rating of 2 for assessment purposes until actual CAMELS ratings are assigned.

(5) *Request for review.* An institution that disagrees with the FDIC's determination that it is a new institution

Federal Deposit Insurance Corporation § 327.10

may request review of that determination pursuant to § 327.4(c).

(g) *Assessment rates for bridge depository institutions and conservatorships.* Institutions that are bridge depository institutions under 12 U.S.C. 1821(n) and institutions for which the Corporation has been appointed or serves as conservator shall, in all cases, be assessed at the Risk Category I minimum initial base assessment rate, which shall not be subject to adjustment under paragraphs (b)(3), (d)(1), (2) or (3) of this section.

[76 FR 10708, Feb. 25, 2011]

§ 327.10 **Assessment rate schedules.**

(a) *Assessment rate schedules before the reserve ratio of the DIF reaches 1.15 percent*—(1) *Applicability.* The assessment rate schedules in paragraph (a) of this section will cease to be applicable when the reserve ratio of the DIF first reaches 1.15 percent.

(2) *Initial Base Assessment Rate Schedule.* Before the reserve ratio of the DIF reaches 1.15 percent, the initial base assessment rate for an insured depository institution shall be the rate prescribed in the following schedule:

INITIAL BASE ASSESSMENT RATE SCHEDULE BEFORE THE RESERVE RATIO OF THE DIF REACHES 1.15 PERCENT

	Risk category I	Risk category II	Risk category III	Risk category IV	Large and highly complex institutions
Initial base assessment rate	5–9	14	23	35	5–35

*All amounts for all risk categories are in basis points annually. Initial base rates that are not the minimum or maximum rate will vary between these rates.

(i) *Risk Category I Initial Base Assessment Rate Schedule.* The annual initial base assessment rates for all institutions in Risk Category I shall range from 5 to 9 basis points.

(ii) *Risk Category II, III, and IV Initial Base Assessment Rate Schedule.* The annual initial base assessment rates for Risk Categories II, III, and IV shall be 14, 23, and 35 basis points, respectively.

(iii) All institutions in any one risk category, other than Risk Category I, will be charged the same initial base assessment rate, subject to adjustment as appropriate.

(iv) *Large and Highly Complex Institutions Initial Base Assessment Rate Schedule.* The annual initial base assessment rates for all large and highly complex institutions shall range from 5 to 35 basis points.

(3) *Total Base Assessment Rate Schedule after Adjustments.* Before the reserve ratio of the DIF reaches 1.15 percent, the total base assessment rates after adjustments for an insured depository institution shall be as prescribed in the following schedule.

TOTAL BASE ASSESSMENT RATE SCHEDULE (AFTER ADJUSTMENTS)* BEFORE THE RESERVE RATIO OF THE DIF REACHES 1.15 PERCENT**

	Risk category I	Risk category II	Risk category III	Risk category IV	Large and highly complex institutions
Initial base assessment rate	5–9	14	23	35	5–35
Unsecured debt adjustment	(4.5)–0	(5)–0	(5)–0	(5)–0	(5)–0
Brokered deposit adjustment		0–10	0–10	0–10	0–10
Total base assessment rate	2.5–9	9–24	18–33	30–45	2.5–45

*All amounts for all risk categories are in basis points annually. Total base rates that are not the minimum or maximum rate will vary between these rates.
**Total base assessment rates do not include the depository institution debt adjustment.

(i) *Risk Category I Total Base Assessment Rate Schedule.* The annual total base assessment rates for all institutions in Risk Category I shall range from 2.5 to 9 basis points.

(ii) *Risk Category II Total Base Assessment Rate Schedule.* The annual total

§ 327.10

base assessment rates for Risk Category II shall range from 9 to 24 basis points.

(iii) *Risk Category III Total Base Assessment Rate Schedule.* The annual total base assessment rates for Risk Category III shall range from 18 to 33 basis points.

(iv) *Risk Category IV Total Base Assessment Rate Schedule.* The annual total base assessment rates for Risk Category IV shall range from 30 to 45 basis points.

(v) *Large and Highly Complex Institutions Total Base Assessment Rate Schedule.* The annual total base assessment rates for all large and highly complex institutions shall range from 2.5 to 45 basis points.

(b) *Assessment rate schedules once the reserve ratio of the DIF first reaches 1.15 percent, and the reserve ratio for the immediately prior assessment period is less than 2 percent*—(1) *Initial Base Assessment Rate Schedule.* Once the reserve ratio of the DIF first reaches 1.15 percent, and the reserve ratio for the immediately prior assessment period is less than 2 percent, the initial base assessment rate for an insured depository institution shall be the rate prescribed in the following schedule:

INITIAL BASE ASSESSMENT RATE SCHEDULE ONCE THE RESERVE RATIO OF THE DIF REACHES 1.15 PERCENT AND THE RESERVE RATIO FOR THE IMMEDIATELY PRIOR ASSESSMENT PERIOD IS LESS THAN 2 PERCENT

	Risk category I	Risk category II	Risk category III	Risk category IV	Large and highly complex institutions
Initial base assessment rate	3–7	12	19	30	3–30

* All amounts for all risk categories are in basis points annually. Initial base rates that are not the minimum or maximum rate will vary between these rates.

(i) *Risk Category I Initial Base Assessment Rate Schedule.* The annual initial base assessment rates for all institutions in Risk Category I shall range from 3 to 7 basis points.

(ii) *Risk Category II, III, and IV Initial Base Assessment Rate Schedule.* The annual initial base assessment rates for Risk Categories II, III, and IV shall be 12, 19, and 30 basis points, respectively.

(iii) All institutions in any one risk category, other than Risk Category I, will be charged the same initial base assessment rate, subject to adjustment as appropriate.

(iv) *Large and Highly Complex Institutions Initial Base Assessment Rate Schedule.* The annual initial base assessment rates for all large and highly complex institutions shall range from 3 to 30 basis points.

(2) *Total Base Assessment Rate Schedule after Adjustments.* Once the reserve ratio of the DIF first reaches 1.15 percent, and the reserve ratio for the immediately prior assessment period is less than 2 percent, the total base assessment rates after adjustments for an insured depository institution shall be as prescribed in the following schedule.

TOTAL BASE ASSESSMENT RATE SCHEDULE (AFTER ADJUSTMENTS)* ONCE THE RESERVE RATIO OF THE DIF REACHES 1.15 PERCENT AND THE RESERVE RATIO FOR THE IMMEDIATELY PRIOR ASSESSMENT PERIOD IS LESS THAN 2 PERCENT **

	Risk category I	Risk category II	Risk category III	Risk category IV	Large and highly complex institutions
Initial base assessment rate	3–7	12	19	30	3–30
Unsecured debt adjustment	(3.5)–0	(5)–0	(5)–0	(5)–0	(5)–0
Brokered deposit adjustment	....	0–10	0–10	0–10	0–10
Total base assessment rate	1.5–7	7–22	14–29	25–40	1.5–40

* All amounts for all risk categories are in basis points annually. Total base rates that are not the minimum or maximum rate will vary between these rates.
** Total base assessment rates do not include the depository institution debt adjustment.

Federal Deposit Insurance Corporation § 327.10

(i) *Risk Category I Total Base Assessment Rate Schedule.* The annual total base assessment rates for institutions in Risk Category I shall range from 1.5 to 7 basis points.

(ii) *Risk Category II Total Base Assessment Rate Schedule.* The annual total base assessment rates for Risk Category II shall range from 7 to 22 basis points.

(iii) *Risk Category III Total Base Assessment Rate Schedule.* The annual total base assessment rates for Risk Category III shall range from 14 to 29 basis points.

(iv) *Risk Category IV Total Base Assessment Rate Schedule.* The annual total base assessment rates for Risk Category IV shall range from 25 to 40 basis points.

(v) *Large and Highly Complex Institutions Total Base Assessment Rate Schedule.* The annual total base assessment rates for all large and highly complex institutions shall range from 1.5 to 40 basis points.

(c) *Assessment rate schedules if the reserve ratio of the DIF for the prior assessment period is equal to or greater than 2 percent and less than 2.5 percent*—(1) *Initial Base Assessment Rate Schedule.* If the reserve ratio of the DIF for the prior assessment period is equal to or greater than 2 percent and less than 2.5 percent, the initial base assessment rate for an insured depository institution, except as provided in paragraph (e) of this section, shall be the rate prescribed in the following schedule:

INITIAL BASE ASSESSMENT RATE SCHEDULE IF RESERVE RATIO FOR PRIOR ASSESSMENT PERIOD IS EQUAL TO OR GREATER THAN 2 PERCENT BUT LESS THAN 2.5 PERCENT

	Risk category I	Risk category II	Risk category III	Risk category IV	Large and highly complex institutions
Initial base assessment rate	2–6	10	17	28	2–28

*All amounts for all risk categories are in basis points annually. Initial base rates that are not the minimum or maximum rate will vary between these rates.

(i) *Risk Category I Initial Base Assessment Rate Schedule.* The annual initial base assessment rates for all institutions in Risk Category I shall range from 2 to 6 basis points.

(ii) *Risk Category II, III, and IV Initial Base Assessment Rate Schedule.* The annual initial base assessment rates for Risk Categories II, III, and IV shall be 10, 17, and 28 basis points, respectively.

(iii) All institutions in any one risk category, other than Risk Category I, will be charged the same initial base assessment rate, subject to adjustment as appropriate.

(iv) *Large and Highly Complex Institutions Initial Base Assessment Rate Schedule.* The annual initial base assessment rates for all large and highly complex institutions shall range from 2 to 28 basis points.

(2) *Total Base Assessment Rate Schedule after Adjustments.* If the reserve ratio of the DIF for the prior assessment period is equal to or greater than 2 percent and less than 2.5 percent, the total base assessment rates after adjustments for an insured depository institution, except as provided in paragraph (e) of this section, shall be as prescribed in the following schedule.

TOTAL BASE ASSESSMENT RATE SCHEDULE (AFTER ADJUSTMENTS)* IF RESERVE RATIO FOR PRIOR ASSESSMENT PERIOD IS EQUAL TO OR GREATER THAN 2 PERCENT BUT LESS THAN 2.5 PERCENT**

	Risk category I	Risk category II	Risk category III	Risk category IV	Large and highly complex institutions
Initial base assessment rate	2–6	10	17	28	2–38
Unsecured debt adjustment	(3)–0	(5)–0	(5)–0	(5)–0	(5)–0
Brokered deposit adjustment		0–10	0–10	0–10	0–10
Total base assessment rate	1–6	5–20	12–27	23–38	1–38

*All amounts for all risk categories are in basis points annually. Total base rates that are not the minimum or maximum rate will vary between these rates.
**Total base assessment rates do not include the depository institution debt adjustment.

§ 327.10

(i) *Risk Category I Total Base Assessment Rate Schedule.* The annual total base assessment rates for institutions in Risk Category I shall range from 1 to 6 basis points.

(ii) *Risk Category II Total Base Assessment Rate Schedule.* The annual total base assessment rates for Risk Category II shall range from 5 to 20 basis points.

(iii) *Risk Category III Total Base Assessment Rate Schedule.* The annual total base assessment rates for Risk Category III shall range from 12 to 27 basis points.

(iv) *Risk Category IV Total Base Assessment Rate Schedule.* The annual total base assessment rates for Risk Category IV shall range from 23 to 38 basis points.

(v) *Large and Highly Complex Institutions Total Base Assessment Rate Schedule.* The annual total base assessment rates for all large and highly complex institutions shall range from 1 to 38 basis points.

(d) *Assessment rate schedules if the reserve ratio of the DIF for the prior assessment period is greater than 2.5 percent—* (1) *Initial Base Assessment Rate Schedule.* If the reserve ratio of the DIF for the prior assessment period is greater than 2.5 percent, the initial base assessment rate for an insured depository institution, except as provided in paragraph (e) of this section, shall be the rate prescribed in the following schedule:

INITIAL BASE ASSESSMENT RATE SCHEDULE IF RESERVE RATIO FOR PRIOR ASSESSMENT PERIOD IS GREATER THAN OR EQUAL TO 2.5 PERCENT

	Risk category I	Risk category II	Risk category III	Risk category IV	Large and highly complex institutions
Initial base assessment rate	1–5	9	15	25	1–25

* All amounts for all risk categories are in basis points annually. Initial base rates that are not the minimum or maximum rate will vary between these rates.

(i) *Risk Category I Initial Base Assessment Rate Schedule.* The annual initial base assessment rates for all institutions in Risk Category I shall range from 1 to 5 basis points.

(ii) *Risk Category II, III, and IV Initial Base Assessment Rate Schedule.* The annual initial base assessment rates for Risk Categories II, III, and IV shall be 9, 15, and 25 basis points, respectively.

(iii) All institutions in any one risk category, other than Risk Category I, will be charged the same initial base assessment rate, subject to adjustment as appropriate.

(iv) *Large and Highly Complex Institutions Initial Base Assessment Rate Schedule.* The annual initial base assessment rates for all large and highly complex institutions shall range from 1 to 25 basis points.

(2) *Total Base Assessment Rate Schedule after Adjustments.* If the reserve ratio of the DIF for the prior assessment period is greater than 2.5 percent, the total base assessment rates after adjustments for an insured depository institution, except as provided in paragraph (e) of this section, shall be the rate prescribed in the following schedule:

TOTAL BASE ASSESSMENT RATE SCHEDULE (AFTER ADJUSTMENTS) * IF RESERVE RATIO FOR PRIOR ASSESSMENT PERIOD IS GREATER THAN OR EQUAL TO 2.5 PERCENT **

	Risk category I	Risk category II	Risk category III	Risk category IV	Large and highly complex institutions
Initial base assessment rate	1–5	9	15	25	1–25
Unsecured debt adjustment	(2.5)–0	(4.5)–0	(5)–0	(5)–0	(5)–0
Brokered deposit adjustment		0–10	0–10	0–10	0–10
Total Base Assessment Rate	0.5–5	4.5–19	10–25	20–35	0.5–35

* All amounts for all risk categories are in basis points annually. Total base rates that are not the minimum or maximum rate will vary between these rates.
**Total base assessment rates do not include the depository institution debt adjustment.

Federal Deposit Insurance Corporation § 327.11

(i) *Risk Category I Total Base Assessment Rate Schedule.* The annual total base assessment rates for institutions in Risk Category I shall range from 0.5 to 5 basis points.

(ii) *Risk Category II Total Base Assessment Rate Schedule.* The annual total base assessment rates for Risk Category II shall range from 4.5 to 19 basis points.

(iii) *Risk Category III Total Base Assessment Rate Schedule.* The annual total base assessment rates for Risk Category III shall range from 10 to 25 basis points.

(iv) *Risk Category IV Total Base Assessment Rate Schedule.* The annual total base assessment rates for Risk Category IV shall range from 20 to 35 basis points.

(v) *Large and Highly Complex Institutions Total Base Assessment Rate Schedule.* The annual total base assessment rates for all large and highly complex institutions shall range from 0.5 to 35 basis points.

(e) *Assessment Rate Schedules for New Institutions.* New depository institutions, as defined in 327.8(j), shall be subject to the assessment rate schedules as follows:

(1) *Prior to the reserve ratio of the DIF first reaching 1.15 percent after September 30, 2010.* After September 30, 2010, if the reserve ratio of the DIF has not reached 1.15 percent, new institutions shall be subject to the initial and total base assessment rate schedules provided for in paragraph (a) of this section.

(2) *Assessment rate schedules once the DIF reserve ratio first reaches 1.15 percent after September 30, 2010.* After September 30, 2010, once the reserve ratio of the DIF first reaches 1.15 percent, new institutions shall be subject to the initial and total base assessment rate schedules provided for in paragraph (b) of this section, even if the reserve ratio equals or exceeds 2 percent or 2.5 percent.

(f) *Total Base Assessment Rate Schedule adjustments and procedures*—(1) *Board Rate Adjustments.* The Board may increase or decrease the total base assessment rate schedule in paragraphs (a) through (d) of this section up to a maximum increase of 2 basis points or a fraction thereof or a maximum decrease of 2 basis points or a fraction thereof (after aggregating increases and decreases), as the Board deems necessary. Any such adjustment shall apply uniformly to each rate in the total base assessment rate schedule. In no case may such rate adjustments result in a total base assessment rate that is mathematically less than zero or in a total base assessment rate schedule that, at any time, is more than 2 basis points above or below the total base assessment schedule for the Deposit Insurance Fund in effect pursuant to paragraph (b) of this section, nor may any one such adjustment constitute an increase or decrease of more than 2 basis points.

(2) *Amount of revenue.* In setting assessment rates, the Board shall take into consideration the following:

(i) Estimated operating expenses of the Deposit Insurance Fund;

(ii) Case resolution expenditures and income of the Deposit Insurance Fund;

(iii) The projected effects of assessments on the capital and earnings of the institutions paying assessments to the Deposit Insurance Fund;

(iv) The risk factors and other factors taken into account pursuant to 12 U.S.C. 1817(b)(1); and

(v) Any other factors the Board may deem appropriate.

(3) *Adjustment procedure.* Any adjustment adopted by the Board pursuant to this paragraph will be adopted by rulemaking, except that the Corporation may set assessment rates as necessary to manage the reserve ratio, within set parameters not exceeding cumulatively 2 basis points, pursuant to paragraph (f)(1) of this section, without further rulemaking.

(4) *Announcement.* The Board shall announce the assessment schedules and the amount and basis for any adjustment thereto not later than 30 days before the quarterly certified statement invoice date specified in § 327.3(b) of this part for the first assessment period for which the adjustment shall be effective. Once set, rates will remain in effect until changed by the Board.

[76 FR 10717, Feb. 25, 2011]

§ 327.11 Special assessments.

(a) *Special assessment imposed on June 30, 2009.* On June 30, 2009, the FDIC

§ 327.12

shall impose a special assessment on each insured depository institution of 5 basis points based on the institution's total assets less Tier 1 capital as reported on the report of condition for the second assessment period of 2009. The special assessment paid by any institution shall not exceed 10 basis points times the institution's assessment base for the second quarter 2009 risk-based assessment.

(b) *Special assessments after June 30, 2009*—(1) *Authority for additional special assessments.* After June 30, 2009, if the reserve ratio of the Deposit Insurance Fund is estimated to fall to a level that the Board believes would adversely affect public confidence or to a level which shall be close to or below zero at the end of a calendar quarter, a special assessment of up to 5 basis points on total assets less Tier 1 capital as reported on the report of condition for that calendar quarter may be imposed by a vote of the Board on all insured depository institutions. For any institution, the amount of such a special assessment shall not exceed 10 basis points times the institution's assessment base reported as of the date that the special assessment is imposed.

(2) *Termination of authority.* The authority to impose additional special assessments under this paragraph (b) shall terminate on January 1, 2010, but such termination of authority shall not prevent the Corporation from thereafter collecting any special assessment imposed prior to January 1, 2010.

(3) *Estimation process.* For purposes of any special assessment under this paragraph (b), the FDIC shall estimate the reserve ratio of the Deposit Insurance Fund for the applicable calendar quarter end from available data on, or estimates of, insurance fund assessment income, investment income, operating expenses, other revenue and expenses, and loss provisions, including provisions for anticipated failures. The FDIC will assume that estimated insured deposits will increase during the quarter at the average quarterly rate over the previous four quarters.

(4) *Imposition and announcement of special assessments.* Any special assessment under this paragraph (b) shall be imposed on the last day of a calendar quarter and shall be announced by the end of such quarter. As soon as practicable after announcement, the FDIC will have a notice of the special assessment published in the FEDERAL REGISTER.

(c) *Invoicing of any special assessments.* The FDIC shall advise each insured depository institution of the amount and calculation of any special assessment imposed under paragraph (a) or (b) of this section. This information shall be provided at the same time as the institution's quarterly certified statement invoice for the assessment period in which the special assessment was imposed.

(d) *Payment of any special assessment.* Each insured depository institution shall pay to the Corporation any special assessment imposed under paragraph (a) or (b) of this section in compliance with and subject to the provisions of §§ 327.3, 327.6 and 327.7 of subpart A, and the provisions of subpart B. The payment date for any special assessment shall be the date provided in § 327.3(b)(2) for the institution's quarterly certified statement invoice for the calendar quarter in which the special assessment was imposed.

[74 FR 25644, May 29, 2009]

§ 327.12 Prepayment of quarterly risk-based assessments.

(a) *Requirement to prepay assessment.* On December 30, 2009, each insured depository institution shall pay to the FDIC a prepaid assessment, which shall equal its estimated quarterly risk-based assessments aggregated for the fourth quarter of 2009, and all of 2010, 2011, and 2012 (the "prepayment period").

(b) *Calculation of prepaid assessment*— (1) *Prepaid assessment*—(i) *Fourth quarter 2009 and all of 2010.* An institution's prepaid assessment for the fourth quarter of 2009 and for all of 2010 shall be determined by multiplying its prepaid assessment rate as defined in paragraph (b)(2) of this section times the corresponding prepaid assessment base for each quarter as determined pursuant to paragraph (b)(3) of this section.

(ii) *All of 2011 and 2012.* An institution's prepaid assessment for each quarter of 2011 and 2012 shall be determined by multiplying the sum of its prepaid assessment rate as defined in

Federal Deposit Insurance Corporation § 327.12

paragraph (b)(2) of this section, plus .75 basis points (which implements the 3 basis point increase in annual assessment rates adopted by the Board on September 29, 2009), times the corresponding prepaid assessment base for each quarter determined pursuant to paragraph (b)(3) of this section.

(2) *Prepaid assessment rate.* For each quarter of the prepayment period, an institution's prepaid assessment rate shall equal the total base assessment rate that the institution would have paid for the third quarter of 2009 had the institution's CAMELS ratings in effect on September 30, 2009, and, where applicable, long-term debt issuer ratings in effect on September 30, 2009, been in effect for the entire third quarter of 2009.

(3) *Prepaid assessment base.* For each quarter of the prepayment period, an institution's prepaid assessment base shall be calculated by increasing its third quarter 2009 assessment base at an annual rate of 5 percent.

(4) *Finality of prepaid assessment.* The prepaid assessment rate and prepaid assessment base defined in paragraphs (b)(2) and (3) of this section shall be determined based upon data in the FDIC's computer systems as of December 24, 2009. Changes to data underlying an institution's adjusted total base assessment rate or assessment base, whether by amendment to a report of condition or otherwise, received by the FDIC after December 24, 2009, shall not affect an institution's prepaid assessment.

(5) *Prepaid assessment rates for mergers and consolidations.* For mergers and consolidations recorded in the FDIC's computer systems no later than December 24, 2009, the acquired institution's prepaid assessment rate under paragraph (b)(2) of this section shall be the prepaid assessment rate of the acquiring institution.

(c) *Invoicing of prepaid assessment.* The FDIC shall advise each insured depository institution of the amount and calculation of its prepaid assessment at the same time the FDIC provides the institution's quarterly certified statement invoice for the third quarter of 2009. The FDIC will re-invoice through FDICconnect based upon any data changes as provided in paragraph (b)(4) of this section.

(d) *Payment of prepaid assessment.* Each insured depository institution shall pay to the Corporation the amount of its prepaid assessment as required under paragraph (a) of this section in compliance with and subject to the provisions of §§ 327.3 and 327.7 of subpart A.

(1) *Exception to ACH payment.* If an institution's prepaid assessment is greater than $99 million, the institution shall make payment by wire transfer to the FDIC, rather than by funding its designated deposit account for payment via ACH as provided in § 327.3 of subpart A.

(2) *One-time assessment credits.* The FDIC will not apply an institution's one-time assessment credit under subpart B of this part 327 to reduce an institution's prepaid assessment. The FDIC will apply an institution's remaining one-time assessment credits under Part 327 subpart B to its quarterly deposit insurance assessments before applying its prepaid assessments.

(e) *Use of prepaid assessments.* Prepaid assessments shall only be used to offset regular quarterly risk-based deposit insurance assessments payable under this subpart A. The FDIC will begin offsetting regular quarterly risk-based deposit insurance assessments against prepaid assessments on March 30, 2010. The FDIC will continue to make such offsets until the earlier of the exhaustion of the institution's prepaid assessment or June 30, 2013. Any prepaid assessment remaining after collection of the amount due on June 30, 2013, shall be returned to the institution. If the FDIC, in its discretion, determines that its liquidity needs allow, it may return any remaining prepaid assessment to the institution prior to June 30, 2013.

(f) *Transfers.* An insured depository institution may enter into an agreement to transfer, but not pledge, any portion of that institution's prepaid assessment to another insured depository institution, provided that the parties to the agreement notify the FDIC's Division of Finance and submit a written agreement, signed by legal representatives of both institutions. The parties must include documentation stating

§ 327.12

that each representative has the legal authority to bind the institution. The institution transferring its prepaid assessment shall submit the required notice and documentation through FDIC*connect*. That information will be presented by the FDIC through FDIC*connect* to the institution acquiring the prepaid assessments for its acceptance. The adjustment to the amount of the prepaid assessment for each institution involved in the transfer will be made in the next assessment invoice that is sent at least 10 days after the FDIC's receipt of acceptance by the institution acquiring the prepaid assessments.

(g) *Prepaid assessments following a merger.* In the event that an insured depository institution merges with, or consolidates into, another insured depository institution, the surviving or resulting institution will be entitled to use any unused portion of the acquired institution's prepaid assessment not otherwise transferred pursuant to paragraph (f) of this section.

(h) *Disposition in the event of failure or termination of insured status.* In the event of failure of an insured depository institution, any amount of its prepaid assessment remaining (other than any amounts needed to satisfy its assessment obligations not yet offset against the prepaid amount) will be refunded to the institution's receiver. In the event that an insured depository institution's insured status terminates, any amount of its prepaid assessment remaining (other than any amounts needed to satisfy its assessment obligations not yet offset against the prepaid amount) will be refunded to the institution, subject to the provisions of § 327.6 of subpart A.

(i) *Exemptions*—(1) *Exemption without application.* The FDIC, after consultation with an institution's primary federal regulator, will exercise its discretion as supervisor and insurer to exempt an institution from the prepayment requirement under paragraph (a) of this section if the FDIC determines that the prepayment would adversely affect the safety and soundness of that institution. No application is required for this review and the FDIC will notify any affected institution of its exemption by November 23, 2009.

12 CFR Ch. III (1-1-12 Edition)

(2) *Application for exemption.* An institution may also apply to the FDIC for an exemption from the prepayment requirement under paragraph (a) of this section if the prepayment would significantly impair the institution's liquidity, or would otherwise create extraordinary hardship. Written applications for exemption from the prepayment obligation must be submitted to the Director of the Division of Supervision and Consumer Protection on or before December 1, 2009, by electronic mail (*prepaidassessment@fdic.gov*) or fax (202–898–6676). The application must contain a full explanation of the need for the exemption and provide supporting documentation, including current financial statements, cash flow projections, and any other relevant information, including any information the FDIC may request. The FDIC will exercise its discretion in deciding whether to exempt an institution that files an application for exemption. An application shall be deemed denied unless the FDIC notifies an applying institution by December 15, 2009, either that the institution is exempt from the prepaid assessment or the FDIC has postponed determination under paragraph (i)(4) of this section. The FDIC's denial of applications for exemption will be final and not subject to further agency review.

(3) *Application for withdrawal of exemption.* An institution that has received an exemption under paragraph (i)(1) of this section may request that the FDIC withdraw the exemption. Written applications for withdrawal of exemption must be submitted to the Director of the Division of Supervision and Consumer Protection on or before December 1, 2009, by electronic mail (*prepaidassessment@fdic.gov*) or fax (202–898–6676). The application must contain a full explanation of the reasons the exemption is not needed and provide supporting documentation, including current financial statements, cash flow projections, and any other relevant information, including any information the FDIC may request. The FDIC, after consultation with the institution's primary Federal regulator, will exercise its discretion in deciding whether to withdraw the exemption. The FDIC

Federal Deposit Insurance Corporation § 327.15

will notify an institution of its decision to withdraw the exemption by December 15, 2009; that determination will be final and not subject to further agency review. An application shall be deemed denied unless the FDIC notifies an applying institution by December 15, 2009, that the exemption is withdrawn.

(4) *Postponement of determination.* The FDIC may postpone making a determination on any application for exemption filed under paragraph (i)(2) of this section until no later than January 14, 2010. An institution notified by the FDIC of such postponement will not have to pay the prepaid assessment calculated under paragraph (b) of this section on December 30, 2009. If the FDIC denies the application for exemption, the FDIC will notify the institution of the denial and of the date by which the institution must pay the prepaid assessment. The due date for payment of the prepaid assessment after such a denial will be no less than 15 days after the date of the notice of denial.

(5) *Obligation to pay third quarter 2009 assessment.* Any institution exempted from the prepayment requirement or any institution whose application for exemption has been postponed under this section shall pay to the Corporation on December 30, 2009, any amount due for the third quarter of 2009 as shown on the certified statement invoice for that quarter.

[74 FR 59065, Nov. 17, 2009]

§ 327.15 Emergency special assessments.

(a) *Emergency special assessment imposed on June 30, 2009.* On June 30, 2009, the FDIC shall impose an emergency special assessment of 20 basis points on each insured depository institution based on the institution's assessment base calculated pursuant to § 327.5 for the second assessment period of 2009.

(b) *Emergency special assessments after June 30, 2009.* After June 30, 2009, if the reserve ratio of the Deposit Insurance Fund is estimated to fall to a level that that the Board believes would adversely affect public confidence or to a level which shall be close to zero or negative at the end of a calendar quarter, an emergency special assessment of up to 10 basis points may be imposed by a vote of the Board on all insured depository institutions based on each institution's assessment base calculated pursuant to § 327.5 for the corresponding assessment period.

(1) *Estimation process.* For purposes of any emergency special assessment under this paragraph (b), the FDIC shall estimate the reserve ratio of the Deposit Insurance Fund for the applicable calendar quarter end from available data on, or estimates of, insurance fund assessment income, investment income, operating expenses, other revenue and expenses, and loss provisions, including provisions for anticipated failures. The FDIC will assume that estimated insured deposits will increase during the quarter at the average quarterly rate over the previous four quarters.

(2) *Imposition and announcement of emergency special assessments.* Any emergency special assessment under this paragraph (b) shall be on the last day of a calendar quarter and shall be announced by the end of such quarter. As soon as practicable after announcement, the FDIC will have a notice published in the FEDERAL REGISTER of the emergency special assessment.

(c) *Invoicing of any emergency special assessments.* The FDIC shall advise each insured depository institution of the amount and calculation of any emergency special assessment imposed under paragraph (a) or (b) of this section. This information shall be provided at the same time as the institution's quarterly certified statement invoice for the assessment period in which the emergency special assessment was imposed.

(d) *Payment of any emergency special assessment.* Each insured depository institution shall pay to the Corporation any emergency special assessment imposed under paragraph (a) or (b) of this section in compliance with and subject to the provisions of §§ 327.3, 327.6 and 327.7 of subpart A, and the provisions of subpart B. The payment date for any emergency special assessment shall be the date provided in § 327.3(b)(2) for the institution's quarterly certified statement invoice for the calendar quarter in which the emergency special assessment was imposed.

[74 FR 9341, Mar. 3, 2009]

APPENDIX A TO SUBPART A OF PART 327—METHOD TO DERIVE PRICING MULTIPLIERS AND UNIFORM AMOUNT

I. INTRODUCTION

The uniform amount and pricing multipliers are derived from:
- A model (the Statistical Model) that estimates the probability that a Risk Category I institution will be downgraded to a composite CAMELS rating of 3 or worse within one year;
- Minimum and maximum downgrade probability cutoff values, based on data from June 30, 2008, that will determine which small institutions will be charged the minimum and maximum initial base assessment rates applicable to Risk Category I;
- The minimum initial base assessment rate for Risk Category I, equal to 12 basis points, and
- The maximum initial base assessment rate for Risk Category I, which is four basis points higher than the minimum rate.

II. THE STATISTICAL MODEL

The Statistical Model is defined in equations 1 and 3 below.

Equation 1

Downgrade(0,1)$_{i,t}$ = β_0 + β_1 (Tier 1 Leverage Ratio$_T$) + β_2 (Loans past due 30 to 89 days ratio$_{i,t}$) + β_3 (Nonperforming asset ratio$_{i,t}$) + β_4 (Net loan charge-off ratio$_{i,t}$) + β_5 (Net income before taxes ratio$_{i,t}$) + β_6 (Adjusted brokered deposit ratio$_{i,t}$) + β_7 (Weighted average CAMELS component rating$_{i,t}$) where Downgrade(01)$_{i,t}$ (the dependent variable—the event being explained) is the incidence of downgrade from a composite rating of 1 or 2 to a rating of 3 or worse during an on-site examination for an institution i between 3 and 12 months after time t. Time t is the end of a year within the multi-year period over which the model was estimated (as explained below). The dependent variable takes a value of 1 if a downgrade occurs and 0 if it does not.

The explanatory variables (regressors) in the model are six financial ratios and a weighted average of the "C," "A," "M," "E" and "L" component ratings. The six financial ratios included in the model are:
- Tier 1 leverage ratio
- Loans past due 30–89 days/Gross assets
- Nonperforming assets/Gross assets
- Net loan charge-offs/Gross assets
- Net income before taxes/Risk-weighted assets
- Brokered deposits/domestic deposits above the 10 percent threshold, adjusted for the asset growth rate factor

Table A.1 defines these six ratios along with the weighted average of CAMELS component ratings. The adjusted brokered deposit ratio ($B_{i,T}$) is calculated by multiplying the ratio of brokered deposits to domestic deposits above the 10 percent threshold by an asset growth rate factor that ranges from 0 to 1 as shown in Equation 2 below. The asset growth rate factor ($A_{i,T}$) is calculated by subtracting 0.4 from the four-year cumulative gross asset growth rate (expressed as a number rather than as a percentage), adjusted for mergers and acquisitions, and multiplying the remainder by 3⅓. The factor cannot be less than 0 or greater than 1.

Equation 2

$$B_{i,T} = \left(\frac{Brokered\ Deposits_{i,T}}{Domestic\ Deposits_{i,T}} - 0.10 \right) * A_{i,T}$$

$$\text{where } A_{i,T} = \left[\left(\frac{GrossAssets_{i,T} - GrossAssets_{i,T-4}}{GrossAssets_{i,T-4}} - 0.4 \right) * \frac{10}{3} \right], \text{ subject to } 0 \leq A_{i,T} \leq 1 \text{ and } B_{i,T} \geq 0.$$

The component rating for sensitivity to market risk (the "S" rating) is not available for years prior to 1997. As a result, and as described in Table A.1, the Statistical Model is estimated using a weighted average of five component ratings excluding the "S" component. Delinquency and non-accrual data on government guaranteed loans are not available before 1993 for Call Report filers and before the third quarter of 2005 for TFR filers. As a result, and as also described in Table A.1, the Statistical Model is estimated without deducting delinquent or past-due government guaranteed loans from either the loans past due 30–89 days to gross assets ratio or the nonperforming assets to gross assets ratio. Reciprocal deposits are not presently reported in the Call Report or TFR. As a result, and as also described in Table A.1, the Statistical Model is estimated without deducting reciprocal deposits from brokered

Federal Deposit Insurance Corporation
Pt. 327, Subpt. A, App. A

deposits in determining the adjusted brokered deposit ratio.

TABLE A.1—DEFINITIONS OF REGRESSORS

Regressor	Description
Tier 1 Leverage Ratio (%)	Tier 1 capital for Prompt Corrective Action (PCA) divided by adjusted average assets based on the definition for prompt corrective action.
Loans Past Due 30–89 Days/Gross Assets (%)	Total loans and lease financing receivables past due 30 through 89 days and still accruing interest divided by gross assets (gross assets equal total assets plus allowance for loan and lease financing receivable losses and allocated transfer risk).
Nonperforming Assets/Gross Assets (%)	Sum of total loans and lease financing receivables past due 90 or more days and still accruing interest, total nonaccrual loans and lease financing receivables, and other real estate owned divided by gross assets.
Net Loan Charge-Offs/Gross Assets (%)	Total charged-off loans and lease financing receivables debited to the allowance for loan and lease losses less total recoveries credited to the allowance to loan and lease losses for the most recent twelve months divided by gross assets.
Net Income before Taxes/Risk-Weighted Assets (%).	Income before income taxes and extraordinary items and other adjustments for the most recent twelve months divided by risk-weighted assets.
Adjusted brokered deposit ratio (%)	Brokered deposits divided by domestic deposits less 0.10 multiplied by the asset growth rate factor (which is the term $A_{i,T}$ as defined in equation 2 above) that ranges between 0 and 1.
Weighted Average of C, A, M, E and L Component Ratings.	The weighted sum of the "C," "A," "M," "E" and "L" CAMELS components, with weights of 28 percent each for the "C" and "M" components, 22 percent for the "A" component, and 11 percent each for the "E" and "L" components. (For the regression, the "S" component is omitted.)

The financial variable regressors used to estimate the downgrade probabilities are obtained from quarterly reports of condition (Reports of Condition and Income and Thrift Financial Reports). The weighted average of the "C," "A," "M," "E" and "L" component ratings regressor is based on component ratings obtained from the most recent bank examination conducted within 24 months before the date of the report of condition.

The Statistical Model uses ordinary least squares (OLS) regression to estimate downgrade probabilities. The model is estimated with data from a multi-year period (as explained below) for all institutions in Risk Category I, except for institutions established within five years before the date of the report of condition.

The OLS regression estimates coefficients, β_j for a given regressor j and a constant amount, β_0, as specified in equation 1. As shown in equation 3 below, these coefficients are multiplied by values of risk measures at time T, which is the date of the report of condition corresponding to the end of the quarter for which the assessment rate is computed. The sum of the products is then added to the constant amount to produce an estimated probability, d_{iT}, that an institution will be downgraded to 3 or worse within 3 to 12 months from time T.

The risk measures are financial ratios as defined in Table A.1, except that: (1) The loans past due 30 to 89 days ratio and the nonperforming asset ratio are adjusted to exclude the maximum amount recoverable from the U.S. Government, its agencies or government-sponsored agencies, under guarantee or insurance provisions; (2) the weighted sum of six CAMELS component ratings is used, with weights of 25 percent each for the "C" and "M" components, 20 percent for the "A" component, and 10 percent each for the "E," "L," and "S" components; and (3) reciprocal deposits are deducted from brokered deposits in determining the adjusted brokered deposit ratio.

Equation 3

$d_{iT} = \beta_0 + \beta_1$ (Tier 1 Leverage Ratio$_{iT}$) + β_2 (Loans past due 30 to 89 days ratio$_{iT}$) + β_3 (Nonperforming asset ratio$_{iT}$) + β_4 (Net loan charge-off ratio$_{iT}$) + β_5 (Net income before taxes ratio$_{iT}$) + β_6 (Adjusted brokered deposit ratio$_{iT}$) + β_7 (Weighted average CAMELS component rating$_{iT}$)

III. MINIMUM AND MAXIMUM DOWNGRADE PROBABILITY CUTOFF VALUES

The pricing multipliers are also determined by minimum and maximum downgrade probability cutoff values, which will be computed as follows:

• The minimum downgrade probability cutoff value will be the maximum downgrade probability among the twenty-five percent of all small insured institutions in Risk Category I (excluding new institutions) with the lowest estimated downgrade probabilities, computed using values of the risk measures as of June 30, 2008.[1][2] The minimum downgrade probability cutoff value is 0.0182.

• The maximum downgrade probability cutoff value will be the minimum downgrade probability among the fifteen percent of all small insured institutions in Risk Category I (excluding new institutions) with the highest estimated downgrade probabilities, computed using values of the risk measures as of June 30, 2008. The maximum downgrade probability cutoff value is 0.1506.

IV. Derivation of Uniform Amount and Pricing Multipliers

The uniform amount and pricing multipliers used to compute the annual base assessment rate in basis points, P_{iT}, for any such institution i at a given time T will be determined from the Statistical Model, the minimum and maximum downgrade probability cutoff values, and minimum and maximum initial base assessment rates in Risk Category I as follows:

Equation 4

$P_{iT} = \alpha_0 + \alpha_1 * d_{iT}$ subject to $Min \leq P_{iT} \leq Min + 4$

where α_0 and α_1 are a constant term and a scale factor used to convert d_{iT} (the estimated downgrade probability for institution i at a given time T from the Statistical Model) to an assessment rate, respectively, and Min is the minimum initial base assessment rate expressed in basis points. (P_{iT} is expressed as an annual rate, but the actual rate applied in any quarter will be $P_{iT}/4$.) The maximum initial base assessment rate is 4 basis points above the minimum ($Min + 4$)

Solving equation 4 for minimum and maximum initial base assessment rates simultaneously,

$Min = \alpha_0 + \alpha_1 * 0.0182$ and $Min + 4 = \alpha_0 + \alpha_1 * 0.1506$

where 0.0182 is the minimum downgrade probability cutoff value and 0.1506 is the maximum downgrade probability cutoff value, results in values for the constant amount, α_0 and the scale factor, α_1:

Equation 5

$$\alpha_0 = Min - \frac{4 * 0.0182}{(0.1506 - 0.0182)} = Min - 0.550$$

and *Equation 6*

$$\alpha_1 = \frac{4}{(0.1506 - 0.0182)} = 30.211$$

Substituting equations 3, 5 and 6 into equation 4 produces an annual initial base assessment rate for institution i at time T, P_{iT}, in terms of the uniform amount, the pricing multipliers and the ratios and weighted average CAMELS component rating referred to in 12 CFR 327.9(d)(2)(i):

Equation 7

$P_{iT} = [(Min - 0.550) + 30.211* \beta_0] + 30.211 * [\beta_1$ (Tier 1 Leverage Ratio$_T$)] + 30.211 * [β_2 (Loans past due 30 to 89 days ratio$_T$)] + 30.211 * [β_3 (Nonperforming asset ratio$_T$)] + 30.211 * [β_4 (Net loan charge-off ratio$_T$)] + 30.211 * [β_5 (Net income before taxes ratio$_T$)] + 30.211 * [β_6 (Adjusted brokered deposit ratio$_T$)] + 30.211 * [β_7 (Weighted average CAMELS component rating$_T$)]

again subject to $Min \leq P_{iT} \leq Min + 4$

where $(Min - 0.550) + 30.211 * \beta_0$ equals the uniform amount, $30.211 * \beta_j$ is a pricing multiplier for the associated risk measure j, and T is the date of the report of condition corresponding to the end of the quarter for which the assessment rate is computed.

V. Updating the Statistical Model, Uniform Amount, and Pricing Multipliers

The initial Statistical Model is estimated using year-end financial ratios and the weighted average of the "C," "A," "M," "E" and "L" component ratings over the 1988 to 2006 period and downgrade data from the 1989 to 2007 period. The FDIC may, from time to time, but no more frequently than annually, re-estimate the Statistical Model with updated data and publish a new formula for determining initial base assessment rates—equation 7—based on updated uniform

---

[1] As used in this context, a "new institution" means an institution that has been chartered as a bank or thrift for less than five years.

[2] For purposes of calculating the minimum and maximum downgrade probability cutoff values, institutions that have less than $100,000 in domestic deposits are assumed to have no brokered deposits.

Federal Deposit Insurance Corporation

Pt. 327, Subpt. A, App. A

amounts and pricing multipliers. However, the minimum and maximum downgrade probability cutoff values will not change without additional notice-and-comment rulemaking. The period covered by the analysis will be lengthened by one year each year; however, from time to time, the FDIC may drop some earlier years from its analysis.

VI. DESCRIPTION OF SCORECARD MEASURES

Tier 1 Leverage Ratio	Tier 1 capital for Prompt Corrective Action (PCA) divided by adjusted average assets based on the definition for prompt corrective action.
Concentration Measure for Large Insured depository institutions (excluding Highly Complex Institutions).	The concentration score for large institutions is the higher of the following two scores:
(1) Higher-Risk Assets/Tier 1 Capital and Reserves.	Sum of construction and land development (C&D) loans (funded and unfunded), leveraged loans (funded and unfunded), nontraditional mortgages, and subprime consumer loans divided by Tier 1 capital and reserves. See Appendix C for the detailed description of the ratio.
(2) Growth-Adjusted Portfolio Concentrations ...	The measure is calculated in the following steps: (1) Concentration levels (as a ratio to Tier 1 capital and reserves) are calculated for each broad portfolio category: • C&D, • Other commercial real estate loans, • First lien residential mortgages (including non-agency residential mortgage-backed securities), • Closed-end junior liens and home equity lines of credit (HELOCs), • Commercial and industrial loans, • Credit card loans, and • Other consumer loans. (2) Risk weights are assigned to each loan category based on historical loss rates. (3) Concentration levels are multiplied by risk weights and squared to produce a risk-adjusted concentration ratio for each portfolio. (4) Three-year merger-adjusted portfolio growth rates are then scaled to a growth factor of 1 to 1.2 where a 3-year cumulative growth rate of 20 percent or less equals a factor of 1 and a growth rate of 80 percent or greater equals a factor of 1.2. If three years of data are not available, a growth factor of 1 will be assigned. (5) The risk-adjusted concentration ratio for each portfolio is multiplied by the growth factor and resulting values are summed. See Appendix C for the detailed description of the measure.
Concentration Measure for Highly Complex Institutions.	Concentration score for highly complex institutions is the highest of the following three scores:

(1) Higher-Risk Assets/Tier 1 Capital and Reserves.	Sum of C&D loans (funded and unfunded), leveraged loans (funded and unfunded), non-traditional mortgages, and subprime consumer loans divided by Tier 1 capital and reserves. See Appendix C for the detailed description of the measure.
(2) Top 20 Counterparty Exposure/Tier 1 Capital and Reserves.	Sum of the total exposure amount to the largest 20 counterparties (in terms of exposure amount) divided by Tier 1 capital and reserves. Counterparty exposure is equal to the sum of Exposure at Default (EAD) associated with derivatives trading and Securities Financing Transactions (SFTs) and the gross lending exposure (including all unfunded commitments) for each counterparty or borrower at the consolidated entity level.[1]
(3) Largest Counterparty Exposure/Tier 1 Capital and Reserves.	The amount of exposure to the largest counterparty (in terms of exposure amount) divided by Tier 1 capital and reserves. Counterparty exposure is equal to the sum of Exposure at Default (EAD) associated with derivatives trading and Securities Financing Transactions (SFTs) and the gross lending exposure (including all unfunded commitments) for each counterparty or borrower at the consolidated entity level.
Core Earnings/Average Quarter-End Total Assets.	Core earnings are defined as net income less extraordinary items and tax-adjusted realized gains and losses on available-for-sale (AFS) and held-to-maturity (HTM) securities, adjusted for mergers. The ratio takes a four-quarter sum of merger-adjusted core earnings and divides it by an average of five quarter-end total assets (most recent and four prior quarters). If four quarters of data on core earnings are not available, data for quarters that are available will be added and annualized. If five quarters of data on total assets are not available, data for quarters that are available will be averaged.
Credit Quality Measure	The credit quality score is the higher of the following two scores:
(1) Criticized and Classified Items/Tier 1 Capital and Reserves.	Sum of criticized and classified items divided by the sum of Tier 1 capital and reserves. Criticized and classified items include items an institution or its primary federal regulator have graded "Special Mention" or worse and include retail items under Uniform Retail Classification Guidelines, securities, funded and unfunded loans, other real estate owned (ORE), other assets, and marked-to-market counterparty positions, less credit valuation adjustments.[2] Criticized and classified items exclude loans and securities in trading books, and the amount recoverable from the U.S. government, its agencies, or government-sponsored agencies, under guarantee or insurance provisions.

Federal Deposit Insurance Corporation Pt. 327, Subpt. A, App. A

(2) Underperforming Assets/Tier 1 Capital and Reserves.	Sum of loans that are 30 days or more past due and still accruing interest, nonaccrual loans, restructured loans (including restructured 1–4 family loans), and ORE, excluding the maximum amount recoverable from the U.S. government, its agencies, or government-sponsored agencies, under guarantee or insurance provisions, divided by a sum of Tier 1 capital and reserves.
Core Deposits/Total Liabilities	Total domestic deposits excluding brokered deposits and uninsured non-brokered time deposits divided by total liabilities.
Balance Sheet Liquidity Ratio	Sum of cash and balances due from depository institutions, federal funds sold and securities purchased under agreements to resell, and the market value of available for sale and held to maturity agency securities (excludes agency mortgage-backed securities but includes all other agency securities issued by the U.S. Treasury, U.S. government agencies, and U.S. government sponsored enterprises) divided by the sum of federal funds purchased and repurchase agreements, other borrowings (including FHLB) with a remaining maturity of one year or less, 5 percent of insured domestic deposits, and 10 percent of uninsured domestic and foreign deposits.[3]
Potential Losses/Total Domestic Deposits (Loss Severity Measure).	Potential losses to the DIF in the event of failure divided by total domestic deposits. Appendix D describes the calculation of the loss severity measure in detail.
Market Risk Measure for Highly Complex Institutions.	The market risk score is a weighted average of the following three scores:
(1) Trading Revenue Volatility/Tier 1 Capital	Trailing 4-quarter standard deviation of quarterly trading revenue (merger-adjusted) divided by Tier 1 capital.
(2) Market Risk Capital/Tier 1 Capital	Market risk capital divided by Tier 1 capital.[4]
(3) Level 3 Trading Assets/Tier 1 Capital	Level 3 trading assets divided by Tier 1 capital.
Average Short-term Funding/Average Total Assets.	Quarterly average of federal funds purchased and repurchase agreements divided by the quarterly average of total assets as reported on Schedule RC–K of the Call Reports.

[1] EAD and SFTs are defined and described in the compilation issued by the Basel Committee on Banking Supervision in its June 2006 document, "International Convergence of Capital Measurement and Capital Standards." The definitions are described in detail in Annex 4 of the document. Any updates to the Basel II capital treatment of counterparty credit risk would be implemented as they are adopted. http://www.bis.org/publ/bcbs128.pdf.

[2] A marked-to-market counterparty position is equal to the sum of the net marked-to-market derivative exposures for each counterparty. The net marked-to-market derivative exposure equals the sum of all positive marked-to-market exposures net of legally enforceable netting provisions and net of all collateral held under a legally enforceable CSA plus any exposure where excess collateral has been posted to the counterparty. For purposes of the Criticized and Classified Items/Tier 1 Capital and Reserves definition a marked-to-market counterparty position less any credit valuation adjustment can never be less than zero.

[3] Deposit runoff rates for the balance sheet liquidity ratio reflect changes issued by the Basel Committee on Banking Supervision in its December 2010 document, "Basel III: International Framework for liquidity risk measurement, standards, and monitoring," http://www.bis.org/publ/bcbs188.pdf.

[4] Market risk capital is defined in Appendix C of Part 325 of the FDIC Rules and Regulations,. http://www.fdic.gov/regulations/laws/rules/2000-4800.html#fdic2000appendixctopart325.

[74 FR 9557, Mar. 4, 2009, as amended at 76 FR 10720, Feb. 25, 2011; 76 FR 17521, Mar. 30, 2011]

Pt. 327, Subpt. A, App. B

APPENDIX B TO SUBPART A OF PART 327—CONVERSION OF SCORECARD MEASURES INTO SCORE

1. Weighted Average CAMELS Rating

Weighted average CAMELS ratings between 1 and 3.5 are assigned a score between 25 and 100 according to the following equation:

$S = 25 + [(20/3) * (C^2 - 1)]$,

where:
S = the weighted average CAMELS score; and
C = the weighted average CAMELS rating.

2. Other Scorecard Measures

For certain scorecard measures, a lower ratio implies lower risk and a higher ratio implies higher risk. These measures include:
- Concentration measure;
- Credit quality measure;
- Market risk measure;
- Average short-term funding to average total assets ratio; and
- Potential losses to total domestic deposits ratio (loss severity measure).

For those measures, a value between the minimum and maximum cutoff values is converted linearly to a score between 0 and 100, according to the following formula:

$S = (V - \text{Min}) * 100/(\text{Max} - \text{Min})$,

where S is score (rounded to three decimal points), V is the value of the measure, Min is the minimum cutoff value and Max is the maximum cutoff value.

For other scorecard measures, a lower value represents higher risk and a higher value represents lower risk. These measures include:
- Tier 1 leverage ratio;
- Core earnings to average quarter-end total assets ratio;
- Core deposits to total liabilities ratio; and
- Balance sheet liquidity ratio.

For those measures, a value between the minimum and maximum cutoff values is converted linearly to a score between 0 and 100, according to the following formula:

$S = (\text{Max} - V) * 100/(\text{Max} - \text{Min})$,

where S is score (rounded to three decimal points), V is the value of the measure, Max is the maximum cutoff value and Min is the minimum cutoff value.

[76 FR 10720, Feb. 25, 2011]

APPENDIX C TO SUBPART A TO PART 327—CONCENTRATION MEASURES

The concentration score is the higher of the higher-risk assets to Tier 1 capital and reserves score or the growth-adjusted portfolio concentrations score. The concentration score for highly complex institutions is the highest of the higher-risk assets to Tier 1 capital and reserves score, the Top 20 counterparty exposure to Tier 1 capital and reserves score, or the largest counterparty to Tier 1 capital and reserves score. The higher-risk assets to Tier 1 capital and reserve ratio and the growth-adjusted portfolio concentration measure are described below.

A. Higher-Risk Assets/Tier 1 Capital and Reserves

The higher-risk assets to Tier 1 capital and reserves ratio is the sum of the concentrations in each of four risk areas described below and is calculated as:

$$H_i = \sum_{k=1}^{4} \left(\frac{\text{Amount of Exposure}_{i,k}}{\text{Tier 1 Capital} + \text{Reserves}_i} \right)$$

where:
H is institution i's higher-risk concentration measure and
k is a risk area.[1] The four risk areas (k) are defined as:
- Construction and land development loans (funded and unfunded);
- Leveraged loans (funded and unfunded);[2]
- Nontraditional mortgage loans; and
- Subprime consumer loans.[3]

The risk areas are defined according to the interagency guidance for a given product with specific modifications made to minimize reporting discrepancies. The definitions for each risk area are as follows:

1. *Construction and Land Development Loans:* Construction and development loans include construction and land development

---

[1] The high-risk concentration ratio is rounded to two decimal points.
[2] Unfunded amounts include irrevocable and revocable commitments.

[3] Each loan concentration category should include purchased credit impaired loans and should exclude the amount recoverable from the U.S. government, its agencies, or government-sponsored agencies, under guarantee or insurance provisions.

loans outstanding and unfunded commitments.

2. *Leveraged Loans*: Leveraged loans include: (1) All commercial loans (funded and unfunded) with an original amount greater than $1 million that meet any one of the conditions below at either origination or renewal, except real estate loans; (2) securities issued by commercial borrowers that meet any one of the conditions below at either origination or renewal, except securities classified as trading book; and (3) and securitizations that are more than 50 percent collateralized by assets that meet any one of the conditions below at either origination or renewal, except securities classified as trading book.[4][5]

• Loans or securities where borrower's total or senior debt to trailing twelve-month EBITDA[6] (i.e. operating leverage ratio) is greater than 4 or 3 times, respectively. For purposes of this calculation, the only permitted EBITDA adjustments are those adjustments specifically permitted for that borrower in its credit agreement; or

• Loans or securities that are designated as highly leveraged transactions (HLT) by syndication agent.[7]

3. *Nontraditional Mortgage Loans:* Nontraditional mortgage loans includes all residential loan products that allow the borrower to defer repayment of principal or interest and includes all interest-only products, teaser rate mortgages, and negative amortizing mortgages, with the exception of home equity lines of credit (HELOCs) or reverse mortgages.[8][9][10]

For purposes of the higher-risk concentration ratio, nontraditional mortgage loans include securitizations where more than 50 percent of the assets backing the securitization meet one or more of the preceding criteria for nontraditional mortgage loans, with the exception of those securities classified as trading book.

4. *Subprime Loans:* Subprime loans include loans made to borrowers that display one or more of the following credit risk characteristics (excluding subprime loans that are previously included as nontraditional mortgage loans) at origination or upon refinancing, whichever is more recent.

• Two or more 30-day delinquencies in the last 12 months, or one or more 60-day delinquencies in the last 24 months;

• Judgment, foreclosure, repossession, or charge-off in the prior 24 months;

• Bankruptcy in the last 5 years; or

• Debt service-to-income ratio of 50 percent or greater, or otherwise limited ability to cover family living expenses after deducting total monthly debt-service requirements from monthly income.[11]

Subprime loans also include loans identified by an insured depository institution as subprime loans based upon similar borrower characteristics and securitizations where more than 50 percent of assets backing the securitization meet one or more of the preceding criteria for subprime loans, excluding those securities classified as trading book.

B. Growth-Adjusted Portfolio Concentration Measure

The growth-adjusted concentration measure is the sum of the concentration ratio for each of seven portfolios, adjusted for risk weights and growth. The product of the risk weight and the concentration ratio for each portfolio is first squared and then multiplied

---

[4] The following guidelines should be used to determine the "original amount" of a loan:

(1) For loans drawn down under lines of credit or loan commitments, the "original amount" of the loan is the size of the line of credit or loan commitment when the line of credit or loan commitment was most recently approved, extended, or renewed prior to the report date. However, if the amount currently outstanding as of the report date exceeds this size, the "original amount" is the amount currently outstanding on the report date.

(2) For loan participations and syndications, the "original amount" of the loan participation or syndication is the entire amount of the credit originated by the lead lender.

(3) For all other loans, the "original amount" is the total amount of the loan at origination or the amount currently outstanding as of the report date, whichever is larger.

[5] Leveraged loans criteria are consistent with guidance issued by the Office of the Comptroller of the Currency in its Comptroller's Handbook, *http://www.occ.gov/static/publications/handbook/LeveragedLending.pdf*, but do not include all of the criteria in the handbook.

[6] Earnings before interest, taxes, depreciation, and amortization.

[7] *http://www.fdic.gov/news/news/press/2001/pr2801.html.*

[8] For purposes of this rule making, a teaser-rate mortgage loan is defined as a mortgage with a discounted initial rate where the lender offers a lower rate and lower payments for part of the mortgage term.

[9] *http://www.fdic.gov/regulations/laws/federal/2006/06noticeFINAL.html.*

[10] A mortgage loan is no longer considered a nontraditional mortgage once the teaser rate has expired. An interest only loan is no longer considered nontraditional once the loan begins to amortize.

[11] *http://www.fdic.gov/news/news/press/2001/pr0901a.html;* however, the definition in the text above excludes any reference to FICO or other credit bureau scores.

by the growth factor for each. The measure is calculated as:

$$N_i = \sum_{k=1}^{7}\left[w_k * \left(\frac{\text{Amount of exposure}_{i,k}}{\text{Tier 1 Capital} + \text{Reserves}_i}\right)\right]^2 * g_k$$

where:
N is institution *i*'s growth-adjusted portfolio concentration measure;[12]
k is a portfolio;
g is a growth factor for institution i's portfolio k; and,
w is a risk weight for portfolio *k*.

The seven portfolios (k) are defined based on the Call Report/TFR data and they are:
• Construction and land development loans;
• Other commercial real estate loans;
• First-lien residential mortgages and non-agency residential mortgage-backed securities (excludes CMOs, REMICS, CMO and REMIC residuals, and stripped MBS issued by non-U.S. Government issuers for which the collateral consists of MBS issued or guaranteed by U.S. government agencies);
• Closed-end junior liens and home equity lines of credit (HELOCs);
• Commercial and industrial loans;
• Credit card loans; and
• Other consumer loans.[13][14]

The growth factor, g, is based on a three-year merger-adjusted growth rate for a given portfolio; g ranges from 1 to 1.2 where a 20 percent growth rate equals a factor of 1 and an 80 percent growth rate equals a factor of 1.2.[15] For growth rates less than 20 percent, g is 1; for growth rates greater than 80 percent, g is 1.2. For growth rates between 20 percent and 80 percent, the growth factor is calculated as:

$$g_{i,k} = 1 + \left[\frac{1}{3}(G_{i,k} - 0.20)\right]$$

where $G_{i,k} = \frac{V_{i,k,t}}{V_{i,k,t-12}} - 1$, V is the portfolio amount as reported on the Call Report or TFR

The risk weight for each portfolio reflects relative peak loss rates for banks at the 90th percentile during the 1990–2009 period.[16] These loss rates were converted into equivalent risk weights as shown in Table C.1.

---

[12] The growth-adjusted portfolio concentration measure is rounded to two decimal points.

[13] All loan concentrations should include the fair value of purchased credit impaired loans.

[14] Each loan concentration category should exclude the amount of loans recoverable from the U.S. government, its agencies, or government-sponsored agencies, under guarantee or insurance provisions.

[15] The growth factor is rounded to two decimal points.

[16] The risk weights are based on loss rates for each portfolio relative to the loss rate for C&I loans, which is given a risk weight of 1. The peak loss rates were derived as follows. The loss rate for each loan category for each bank with over $5 billion in total assets was calculated for each of the last twenty calendar years (1990–2009). The highest value of the 90th percentile of each loan category over the twenty year period was selected as the peak loss rate.

Federal Deposit Insurance Corporation Pt. 327, Subpt. A, App. D

TABLE C.1—90TH PERCENTILE ANNUAL LOSS RATES FOR 1990–2009 PERIOD AND CORRESPONDING RISK WEIGHTS

Portfolio	Loss rates (90th percentile) (percent)	Risk weights
First-Lien Mortgages	2.3	0.5
Second/Junior Lien Mortgages	4.6	0.9
Commercial and Industrial (C&I) Loans	5.0	1.0
Construction and Development (C&D) Loans	15.0	3.0
Commercial Real Estate Loans, excluding C&D	4.3	0.9
Credit Card Loans	11.8	2.4
Other Consumer Loans	5.9	1.2

[76 FR 10720, Feb. 25, 2011]

APPENDIX D TO SUBPART A OF PART 327—DESCRIPTION OF THE LOSS SEVERITY MEASURE

The loss severity measure applies a standardized set of assumptions to an institution's balance sheet to measure possible losses to the FDIC in the event of an institution's failure. To determine an institution's loss severity rate, the FDIC first applies assumptions about uninsured deposit and other unsecured liability runoff, and growth in insured deposits, to adjust the size and composition of the institution's liabilities. Assets are then reduced to match any reduction in liabilities.[1] The institution's asset values are then further reduced so that the Tier 1 leverage ratio reaches 2 percent.[2] In both cases, assets are adjusted pro rata to preserve the institution's asset composition. Assumptions regarding loss rates at failure for a given asset category and the extent of secured liabilities are then applied to estimated assets and liabilities at failure to determine whether the institution has enough unencumbered assets to cover domestic deposits. Any projected shortfall is divided by current domestic deposits to obtain an end-of-period loss severity ratio. The loss severity measure is an average loss severity ratio for the three most recent quarters of data available.

Runoff and Capital Adjustment Assumptions

Table D.1 contains run-off assumptions.

TABLE D.1—RUNOFF RATE ASSUMPTIONS

Liability type	Runoff rate* (percent)
Insured Deposits	(10)
Uninsured Deposits	58
Foreign Deposits	80
Federal Funds Purchased	100
Repurchase Agreements	75
Trading Liabilities	50
Unsecured Borrowings <= 1 Year	75
Secured Borrowings <= 1 Year	25
Subordinated Debt and Limited Liability Preferred Stock	15

* A negative rate implies growth.

Given the resulting total liabilities after runoff, assets are then reduced pro rata to preserve the relative amount of assets in each of the following asset categories and to achieve a Tier 1 leverage ratio of 2 percent:
- Cash and Interest Bearing Balances;
- Trading Account Assets;
- Federal Funds Sold and Repurchase Agreements;
- Treasury and Agency Securities;
- Municipal Securities;
- Other Securities;
- Construction and Development Loans;
- Nonresidential Real Estate Loans;
- Multifamily Real Estate Loans;

---

[1] In most cases, the model would yield reductions in liabilities and assets prior to failure. Exceptions may occur for institutions primarily funded through insured deposits, which the model assumes to grow prior to failure.

[2] Of course, in reality, runoff and capital declines occur more or less simultaneously as an institution approaches failure. The loss severity measure assumptions simplify this process for ease of modeling.

§ 327.30

- 1–4 Family Closed-End First Liens;
- 1–4 Family Closed-End Junior Liens;
- Revolving Home Equity Loans; and
- Agricultural Real Estate Loans.

Recovery Value of Assets at Failure

Table D.2 shows loss rates applied to each of the asset categories as adjusted above.

TABLE D.2—ASSET LOSS RATE ASSUMPTIONS

Asset category	Loss rate (percent)
Cash and Interest Bearing Balances	0.0
Trading Account Assets	0.0
Federal Funds Sold and Repurchase Agreements	0.0
Treasury and Agency Securities	0.0
Municipal Securities	10.0
Other Securities	15.0
Construction and Development Loans	38.2
Nonresidential Real Estate Loans	17.6
Multifamily Real Estate Loans	10.8
1–4 Family Closed-End First Liens	19.4
1–4 Family Closed-End Junior Liens	41.0
Revolving Home Equity Loans	41.0
Agricultural Real Estate Loans	19.7
Agricultural Loans	11.8
Commercial and Industrial Loans	21.5
Credit Card Loans	18.3
Other Consumer Loans	18.3
All Other Loans	51.0
Other Assets	75.0

Secured Liabilities at Failure

Federal home loan bank advances, secured federal funds purchased and repurchase agreements are assumed to be fully secured.

Foreign deposits are treated as fully secured because of the potential for ring fencing.

Loss Severity Ratio Calculation

The FDIC's loss given failure (LGD) is calculated as:

$$LGD = \frac{InsuredDeposits_{Failure}}{DomesticDeposits_{Failure}} \times \left(DomesticDeposits_{Failure} - RecoveryValueofAssets_{Failure} + SecuredLiabilities_{Failure} \right)$$

An end-of-quarter loss severity ratio is LGD divided by total domestic deposits at quarter-end and the loss severity measure for the scorecard is an average of end-of-period loss severity ratios for three most recent quarters.

[76 FR 10724, Feb. 25, 2011]

Subpart B—Implementation of One-Time Assessment Credit

AUTHORITY: 12 U.S.C. 1817(e)(3).

SOURCE: 71 FR 61383, Oct. 18, 2006, unless otherwise noted.

§ 327.30 Purpose and scope.

(a) *Scope.* This subpart B of part 327 implements the one-time assessment credit required by section 7(e)(3) of the Federal Deposit Insurance Act, 12 U.S.C. 1817(e)(3) and applies to insured depository institutions.

(b) *Purpose.* This subpart B of part 327 sets forth the rules for:

(1) Determination of the aggregate amount of the one-time credit;

(2) Identification of eligible insured depository institutions;

(3) Determination of the amount of each eligible institution's December 31, 1996 assessment base ratio and one-time credit;

(4) Transferability of credit amounts among insured depository institutions;

(5) Application of such credit amounts against assessments; and

(6) An institution's request for review of the FDIC's determination of a credit amount.

Federal Deposit Insurance Corporation

§ 327.31 Definitions.

For purposes of this subpart and subpart C:

(a) The *average assessment rate* for any assessment period means the aggregate assessment charged all insured depository institutions for that period divided by the aggregate assessment base for that period.

(b) *Board* means the Board of Directors of the FDIC.

(c) *De facto rule* means any transaction in which an insured depository institution assumes substantially all of the deposit liabilities and acquires substantially all of the assets of any other insured depository institution at the time of the transaction.

(d) An *eligible insured depository institution:*

(1) Means an insured depository institution that:

(i) Was in existence on December 31, 1996, and paid a deposit insurance assessment before December 31, 1996; or

(ii) Is a successor to an insured depository institution referred to in paragraph (d)(1)(i) of this section; and

(2) does not include an institution if its insured status has terminated as of or after the effective date of this regulation.

(e) *Merger* means any transaction in which an insured depository institution merges or consolidates with any other insured depository institution. Notwithstanding part 303, subpart D, for purposes of this subpart B and subpart C of this part, *merger* does not include transactions in which an insured depository institution either directly or indirectly acquires the assets of, or assumes liability to pay any deposits made in, any other insured depository institution, but there is not a legal merger or consolidation of the two insured depository institutions.

(f) *Resulting institution* refers to the acquiring, assuming, or resulting institution in a merger.

(g) *Successor* means a resulting institution or an insured depository institution that acquired part of another insured depository institution's 1996 assessment base ratio under paragraph 327.33(c) of this subpart under the *de facto* rule.

§ 327.32 Determination of aggregate credit amount.

The aggregate amount of the one-time credit shall equal $4,707,580,238.19.

§ 327.33 Determination of eligible institution's credit amount.

(a) Subject to paragraph (c) of this section, allocation of the one-time credit shall be based on each eligible insured depository institution's 1996 assessment base ratio.

(b) Subject to paragraph (c) of this section, an eligible insured depository institution's 1996 assessment base ratio shall consist of:

(1) Its assessment base as of December 31, 1996 (adjusted as appropriate to reflect the assessment base of December 31, 1996, of all institutions for which it is the successor), as the numerator; and

(2) The combined aggregate assessment bases of all eligible insured depository institutions, including any successor institutions, as of December 31, 1996, as the denominator.

(c) If an insured depository institution is a successor to an eligible insured depository institution under the *de facto* rule, as defined in paragraph 327.31(c) of this subpart, the successor and the eligible insured depository institution will divide the eligible insured depository institution's 1996 assessment base ratio pro rata, based on the deposit liabilities assumed in the transaction. In any subsequent transaction involving an insured depository institution that previously engaged in a transaction to which the *de facto* rule applied, the insured depository institution may not be deemed to have transferred more than its remaining 1996 assessment base ratio. If the transferring institution is no longer an insured depository institution after the transfer, the last successor will acquire the transferring institution's remaining 1996 assessment base ratio.

§ 327.34 Transferability of credits.

(a) Any remaining amount of the one-time assessment credit and the associated 1996 assessment base ratio shall transfer to a successor of an eligible insured depository institution.

(b) Prior to the final determination of its 1996 assessment base and one-

§ 327.35

time assessment credit amount by the FDIC, an eligible insured depository institution may enter into an agreement to transfer any portion of such institution's one-time credit amount and 1996 assessment base ratio to another insured depository institution. The parties to the agreement shall notify the FDIC's Division of Finance and submit a written agreement, signed by legal representatives of both institutions. The parties must include documentation stating that each representative has the legal authority to bind the institution. The adjustment to credit amount and the associated 1996 assessment base ratio shall be made in the next assessment invoice that is sent at least 10 days after the FDIC's receipt of the written agreement.

(c) An eligible insured depository institution may enter into an agreement after the final determination of its 1996 assessment base ratio and one-time credit amount by the FDIC to transfer any portion of such institution's one-time credit amount to another insured depository institution. The parties to the agreement shall notify the FDIC's Division of Finance and submit a written agreement, signed by legal representatives of both institutions. The parties must include documentation stating that each representative has the legal authority to bind the institution. The adjustment to the credit amount shall be made in the next assessment invoice that is sent at least 10 days after the FDIC's receipt of the written agreement.

§ 327.35 Application of credits.

(a) Subject to the limitations in paragraph (b) of this section, the amount of an eligible insured depository institution's one-time credit shall be applied to the maximum extent allowable by law against that institution's quarterly assessment payment under subpart A of this part, until the institution's credit is exhausted.

(b) The following limitations shall apply to the application of the credit against assessment payments.

(1) For assessments that become due for assessment periods beginning in calendar years 2008, 2009, and 2010, the credit may not be applied to more than 90 percent of the quarterly assessment.

(2) For an insured depository institution that exhibits financial, operational, or compliance weaknesses ranging from moderately severe to unsatisfactory, or is not at least adequately capitalized (as defined pursuant to section 38 of the Federal Deposit Insurance Act) at the beginning of an assessment period, the amount of the credit that may be applied against the institution's quarterly assessment for that period shall not exceed the amount that the institution would have been assessed if it had been assessed at the average assessment rate for all insured institutions for that period. The FDIC shall determine the average assessment rate for an assessment period based upon its best estimate of the average rate for the period. The estimate shall be made using the best information available, but shall be made no earlier than 30 days and no later than 20 days prior to the payment due date for the period.

(3) If the FDIC has established a restoration plan pursuant to section 7(b)(3)(E) of the Federal Deposit Insurance Act, the FDIC may elect to restrict the application of credit amounts, in any assessment period, up to the lesser of:

(i) The amount of an insured depository institution's assessment for that period; or

(ii) The amount equal to 3 basis points of the institution's assessment base.

§ 327.36 Requests for review of credit amount.

(a)(1) As soon as practicable after the publication date of this rule, the FDIC shall notify each insured depository institution by FDIC*connect* or mail of its 1996 assessment base ratio and credit amount in a Statement of One-Time Credit ("Statement"), if any. An insured depository institution may submit a request for review of the FDIC's determination of the institution's 1996 assessment base ratio or credit amount as shown on the Statement within 30 days after the effective date of this rule. Such review may be requested if:

(i) The institution disagrees with a determination as to eligibility for the credit that relates to that institution's credit amount;

Federal Deposit Insurance Corporation § 327.36

(ii) The institution disagrees with the calculation of the credit as stated on the Statement; or

(iii) The institution believes that the 1996 assessment base ratio attributed to the institution on the Statement does not fully or accurately reflect its own 1996 assessment base or appropriate adjustments for successors.

(2) If an institution does not submit a timely request for review, that institution is barred from subsequently requesting review of its credit amount, subject to paragraph (e) of this section.

(b)(1) An insured depository institution may submit a request for review of the FDIC's adjustment to the credit amount in a quarterly invoice within 30 days of the date on which the FDIC provides the invoice. Such review may be requested if:

(i) The institution disagrees with the calculation of the credit as stated on the invoice; or

(ii) The institution believes that the 1996 assessment base ratio attributed to the institution due to the adjustment to the invoice does not fully or accurately reflect appropriate adjustments for successors since the last quarterly invoice.

(2) If an institution does not submit a timely request for review, that institution is barred from subsequently requesting review of its credit amount, subject to paragraph (e) of this section.

(c) The request for review shall be submitted to the Division of Finance and shall provide documentation sufficient to support the change sought by the institution. At the time of filing with the FDIC, the requesting institution shall notify, to the extent practicable, any other insured depository institution that would be directly and materially affected by granting the request for review and provide such institution with copies of the request for review, the supporting documentation, and the FDIC's procedures for requests under this subpart. In addition, the FDIC also shall make reasonable efforts, based on its official systems of records, to determine that such institutions have been identified and notified.

(d) During the FDIC's consideration of the request for review, the amount of credit in dispute shall not be available for use by any institution.

(e) Within 30 days of being notified of the filing of the request for review, those institutions identified as potentially affected by the request for review may submit a response to such request, along with any supporting documentation, to the Division of Finance, and shall provide copies to the requesting institution. If an institution that was notified under paragraph (c) does not submit a response to the request for review, that institution may not:

(1) Subsequently dispute the information submitted by other institutions on the transaction(s) at issue in the review process; or

(2) Appeal the decision by the Director of the Division of Finance.

(f) If additional information is requested of the requesting or affected institutions by the FDIC, such information shall be provided by the institution within 21 days of the date of the FDIC's request for additional information.

(g) Any institution submitting a timely request for review will receive a written response from the FDIC's Director of the Division of Finance, (or his or her designee), notifying the requesting and affected institutions of the determination of the Director as to whether the requested change is warranted. Notice of the procedures applicable to appeals under paragraph (h) of this section will be included with the Director's written determination. Whenever feasible, the FDIC will provide the institution with the aforesaid written response the later of:

(1) Within 60 days of receipt by the FDIC of the request for revision;

(2) If additional institutions have been notified by the requesting institution or the FDIC, within 60 days of the date of the last response to the notification; or

(3) If additional information has been requested by the FDIC, within 60 days of receipt of the additional information.

(h) Subject to paragraph (e) of this section, the insured depository institution that requested review under this section, or an insured depository institution materially affected by the Director's determination, that disagrees

§ 327.50

with that determination may appeal to the FDIC's Assessment Appeals Committee on the same grounds as set forth under paragraph (a) of this section. Any such appeal must be submitted within 30 calendar days from the date of the Director's written determination. Notice of the procedures applicable to appeals under this section will be included with the Director's written determination. The decision of the Assessment Appeals Committee shall be the final determination of the FDIC.

(i) Any adjustment to an institution's credits resulting from a determination by the Director of the FDIC's Assessment Appeals Committee shall be reflected in the institution's next assessment invoice. The adjustment to credits shall affect future assessments only and shall not result in a retroactive adjustment of assessment amounts owed for prior periods.

Subpart C—Implementation of Dividend Requirements

AUTHORITY: 12 U.S.C. 1817(e)(2), (4).

SOURCE: 73 FR 73162, Dec. 2, 2008, unless otherwise noted.

§ 327.50 Dividends.

(a) *Suspension of dividends.* The Board will suspend dividends indefinitely whenever the DIF reserve ratio exceeds 1.50 percent at the end of any year.

(b) *Assessment rate schedule if DIF reserve ratio exceeds 1.50 percent.* In lieu of dividends, when the DIF reserve ratio exceeds 1.50 percent, assessment rates shall be determined as set forth in section 327.10, as appropriate.

[76 FR 10725, Feb. 25, 2011]

PART 328—ADVERTISEMENT OF MEMBERSHIP

Sec.
328.0 Scope.
328.1 Official sign.
328.2 Display and procurement of official sign.
328.3 Official advertising statement requirements.
328.4 Prohibition against receiving deposits at same teller station or window as non-insured institution.

AUTHORITY: 12 U.S.C. 1818(a), 1819 (Tenth), 1828(a).

SOURCE: 72 FR 66102, Nov. 13, 2006, unless otherwise noted.

§ 328.0 Scope.

Part 328 describes the official sign of the FDIC and prescribes its use by insured depository institutions. It also prescribes the official advertising statement insured depository institutions must include in their advertisements. For purposes of part 328, the term "insured depository institution" includes insured branches of a foreign depository institution. Part 328 does not apply to non-insured offices or branches of insured depository institutions located in foreign countries.

§ 328.1 Official sign.

(a) The official sign referred to in this part shall be 7″ by 3″ in size, with black lettering and gold background, and of the following design:

Federal Deposit Insurance Corporation § 328.2

(b) The "symbol" of the Corporation, as used in this part, shall be that portion of the official sign consisting of "FDIC" and the two lines of smaller type above and below "FDIC."

[72 FR 66102, Nov. 13, 2006, as amended at 75 FR 49365, Aug. 13, 2010]

§ 328.2 Display and procurement of official sign.

(a) *Display of official sign.* Each insured depository institution shall continuously display the official sign at each station or window where insured deposits are usually and normally received in the depository institution's principal place of business and in all its branches.

(1) *Other locations*—(i) *Within the institution.* In addition to locations where display of the official sign is required under this § 328.2(a), an insured depository institution may display the official sign in other locations at the institution.

(ii) *Other facilities.* An insured depository institution may display the official sign on or at Remote Service Facilities. If an insured depository institution displays the official sign at a Remote Service Facility, and if there are any noninsured institutions that share in the Remote Service Facility, any insured depository institution that displays the official sign must clearly show that the sign refers only to a designated insured depository institution(s). As used in this part, the term "Remote Service Facility" includes any automated teller machine, cash dispensing machine, point-of-sale terminal, or other remote electronic facility where deposits are received.

(2) *Varied signs.* Instead of displaying the official sign, an insured depository institution may display signs that vary from the official sign in size, color, or material at any location where display of the official sign is required or permitted under this § 328.2(a). However, any such varied sign that is displayed in locations where display of the official sign is required under this § 328.2(a) must not be smaller in size than the official sign and must have the same color for the text and symbols.

(3) *Newly insured institutions.* A depository institution shall display the official sign no later than its twenty-first day of operation as an insured depository institution, unless the institution promptly requested the official sign from the Corporation, but did not receive it before that date.

(b) *Procuring official sign.* An insured depository institution may procure the official sign from the Corporation for official use at no charge. Information on obtaining the official sign is posted on the FDIC's internet Web site, *http://www.fdic.gov*. Alternatively, insured depository institutions may, at their expense, procure from commercial suppliers signs that vary from the official sign in size, color, or material. Any insured depository institution which has promptly submitted a written request for an official sign to the Corporation shall not be deemed to have violated

339

§ 328.3

this § 328.2 by failing to display the official sign, unless the insured depository institution fails to display the official sign after receipt thereof.

(c) *Required changes in sign.* The Corporation may require any insured depository institution, upon at least thirty (30) days' written notice, to change the wording of the official sign in a manner deemed necessary for the protection of depositors or others.

§ 328.3 **Official advertising statement requirements.**

(a) *Advertisement defined.* The term "advertisement," as used in this part, shall mean a commercial message, in any medium, that is designed to attract public attention or patronage to a product or business.

(b) *Official advertising statement.* The official advertising statement shall be in substance as follows: "Member of the Federal Deposit Insurance Corporation."

(1) *Optional short title and symbol.* The short title "Member of FDIC" or "Member FDIC," or a reproduction of the symbol of the Corporation (as described in § 328.1(b)), may be used by insured depository institutions at their option as the official advertising statement.

(2) *Size and print.* The official advertising statement shall be of such size and print to be clearly legible. If the symbol of the Corporation is used as the official advertising statement, and the symbol must be reduced to such proportions that the two lines of smaller type above and below "FDIC" are indistinct and illegible, those lines of smaller type may be blocked out or dropped.

(c) *Use of official advertising statement in advertisements*—(1) *General requirement.* Except as provided in § 328.3(d), each insured depository institution shall include the official advertising statement prescribed in § 328.3(b) in all advertisements that either promote deposit products and services or promote non-specific banking products and services offered by the institution. For purposes of this § 328.3, an advertisement promotes non-specific banking products and services if it includes the name of the insured depository institution but does not list or describe particular products or services offered by the institution. An example of such an advertisement would be, "Anytown Bank, offering a full range of banking services."

(2) *Foreign depository institutions.* When a foreign depository institution has both insured and noninsured U.S. branches, the depository institution must also identify which branches are insured and which branches are not insured in all of its advertisements requiring use of the official advertising statement.

(3) *Newly insured institutions.* A depository institution shall include the official advertising statement in its advertisements no later than its twenty-first day of operation as an insured depository institution.

(d) *Types of advertisements which do not require the official advertising statement.* The following types of advertisements do not require use of the official advertising statement:

(1) Statements of condition and reports of condition of an insured depository institution which are required to be published by State or Federal law;

(2) Insured depository institution supplies such as stationery (except when used for circular letters), envelopes, deposit slips, checks, drafts, signature cards, deposit passbooks, certificates of deposit, etc.;

(3) Signs or plates in the insured depository institution offices or attached to the building or buildings in which such offices are located;

(4) Listings in directories;

(5) Advertisements not setting forth the name of the insured depository institution;

(6) Entries in a depository institution directory, provided the name of the insured depository institution is listed on any page in the directory with a symbol or other descriptive matter indicating it is a member of the Federal Deposit Insurance Corporation;

(7) Joint or group advertisements of depository institution services where the names of insured depository institutions and noninsured institutions are listed and form a part of such advertisements;

Federal Deposit Insurance Corporation

(8) Advertisements by radio or television, other than display advertisements, which do not exceed thirty (30) seconds in time;

(9) Advertisements which are of the type or character that make it impractical to include the official advertising statement, including, but not limited to, promotional items such as calendars, matchbooks, pens, pencils, and key chains; and

(10) Advertisements which contain a statement to the effect that the depository institution is a member of the Federal Deposit Insurance Corporation, or that the depository institution is insured by the Federal Deposit Insurance Corporation, or that its deposits or depositors are insured by the Federal Deposit Insurance Corporation to at least $100,000 for each depositor.

(e) *Restrictions on using the official advertising statement when advertising non-deposit products*—(1) *Definitions*—

(i) *Non-deposit product.* As used in this part, the term "non-deposit product" shall include, but is not limited to, insurance products, annuities, mutual funds, and securities. For purposes of this definition, a credit product is not a non-deposit product.

(ii) *Hybrid product.* As used in this part, the term "hybrid product" shall mean a product or service that has both deposit product features and non-deposit product features. A sweep account is an example of a hybrid product.

(2) *Non-deposit product advertisements.* Except as provided in §328.3(e)(4), an insured depository institution shall not include the official advertising statement, or any other statement or symbol which implies or suggests the existence of Federal deposit insurance, in any advertisement relating solely to non-deposit products.

(3) *Hybrid product advertisements.* Except as provided in §328.3(e)(4), an insured depository institution shall not include the official advertising statement, or any other statement or symbol which implies or suggests the existence of federal deposit insurance, in any advertisement relating solely to hybrid products.

(4) *Mixed advertisements.* In advertisements containing information about both insured deposit products and non-deposit products or hybrid products, an insured depository institution shall clearly segregate the official advertising statement or any similar statement from that portion of the advertisement that relates to the non-deposit products.

(f) *Official advertising statement in non-English language.* The non-English equivalent of the official advertising statement may be used in any advertisement, provided that the translation has had the prior written approval of the Corporation.

§ 328.4 Prohibition against receiving deposits at same teller station or window as noninsured institution.

(a) *Prohibition.* An insured depository institution may not receive deposits at any teller station or window where any noninsured institution receives deposits or similar liabilities.

(b) *Exception.* This §328.4 does not apply to deposits received at a Remote Service Facility.

PART 329 [RESERVED]

PART 330—DEPOSIT INSURANCE COVERAGE

Sec.
330.1 Definitions.
330.2 Purpose.
330.3 General principles.
330.4 Continuation of separate deposit insurance after merger of insured depository institutions.
330.5 Recognition of deposit ownership and fiduciary relationships.
330.6 Single ownership accounts.
330.7 Accounts held by an agent, nominee, guardian, custodian or conservator.
330.8 Annuity contract accounts.
330.9 Joint ownership accounts.
330.10 Revocable trust accounts.
330.11 Accounts of a corporation, partnership or unincorporated association.
330.12 Accounts held by a depository institution as the trustee of an irrevocable trust.
330.13 Irrevocable trust accounts.
330.14 Retirement and other employee benefit plan accounts.
330.15 Accounts held by government depositors.
330.16 Noninterest-bearing transaction accounts.
330.101 Premiums.

§ 330.1

AUTHORITY: 12 U.S.C. 1813(l), 1813(m), 1817(i), 1818(q), 1819(Tenth), 1820(f), 1821(a), 1822(c).

SOURCE: 63 FR 25756, May 11, 1998, unless otherwise noted.

§ 330.1 Definitions.

For the purposes of this part:

(a) *Act* means the Federal Deposit Insurance Act (12 U.S.C. 1811 *et seq.*).

(b) *Corporation* means the Federal Deposit Insurance Corporation.

(c) *Default* has the same meaning as provided under section 3(x) of the Act (12 U.S.C. 1813(x)).

(d) *Deposit* has the same meaning as provided under section 3(l) of the Act (12 U.S.C. 1813(l)).

(e) *Deposit account records* means account ledgers, signature cards, certificates of deposit, passbooks, corporate resolutions authorizing accounts in the possession of the insured depository institution and other books and records of the insured depository institution, including records maintained by computer, which relate to the insured depository institution's deposit taking function, but does not mean account statements, deposit slips, items deposited or cancelled checks.

(f) *FDIC* means the Federal Deposit Insurance Corporation.

(g) *Independent activity.* A corporation, partnership or unincorporated association shall be deemed to be engaged in an "independent activity" if the entity is operated primarily for some purpose other than to increase deposit insurance.

(h) *Insured branch* means a branch of a foreign bank any deposits in which are insured in accordance with the provisions of the Act.

(i) *Insured deposit* has the same meaning as that provided under section 3(m)(1) of the Act (12 U.S.C. 1813(m)(1)).

(j) *Insured depository institution* is any depository institution whose deposits are insured pursuant to the Act, including a foreign bank having an insured branch.

(k) *Interest*, with respect to a deposit, means any payment to or for the account of any depositor as compensation for the use of funds constituting a deposit. A bank's absorption of expenses incident to providing a normal banking function or its forbearance from charging a fee in connection with such a service is not considered a payment of interest.

(l) *Natural person* means a human being.

(m) *Non-contingent trust interest* means a trust interest capable of determination without evaluation of contingencies except for those covered by the present worth tables and rules of calculation for their use set forth in § 20.2031–7 of the Federal Estate Tax Regulations (26 CFR 20.2031–7) or any similar present worth or life expectancy tables which may be adopted by the Internal Revenue Service.

(n) *Sole proprietorship* means a form of business in which one person owns all the assets of the business, in contrast to a partnership or corporation.

(o) *Standard maximum deposit insurance amount*, referred to as the "SMDIA" hereafter, means $250,000 adjusted pursuant to subparagraph (F) of section 11(a)(1) of the FDI Act (12 U.S.C. 1821(a)(1)(F)).

(p) *Trust estate* means the determinable and beneficial interest of a beneficiary or principal in trust funds but does not include the beneficial interest of an heir or devisee in a decedent's estate.

(q) *Trust funds* means funds held by an insured depository institution as trustee pursuant to any irrevocable trust established pursuant to any statute or written trust agreement.

(r) *Trust interest* means the interest of a beneficiary in an irrevocable express trust (other than an employee benefit plan) created either by written trust instrument or by statute, but does not include any interest retained by the settlor.

(s) *Noninterest-bearing transaction account* means—

(1) A deposit or account maintained at an insured depository institution—

(i) With respect to which interest is neither accrued nor paid;

(ii) On which the depositor or account holder is permitted to make withdrawals by negotiable or transferable instrument, payment orders of withdrawal, telephone or other electronic media transfers, or other similar items for the purpose of making payments or transfers to third parties or others; and

(iii) On which the insured depository institution does not reserve the right to require advance notice of an intended withdrawal; and

(2) A trust account established by an attorney or law firm on behalf of a client, commonly known as an *Interest on Lawyers Trust Account*, or a functionally equivalent account, as determined by the Corporation.

[63 FR 25756, May 11, 1998, as amended at 71 FR 14631, Mar. 23, 2006; 73 FR 61660, Oct. 17, 2008; 74 FR 47716, Sept. 17, 2009; 75 FR 49365, Aug. 13, 2010; 75 FR 69583, Nov. 15, 2010; 76 FR 4816, Jan. 27, 2011; 76 FR 41395, July 14, 2011]

§ 330.2 Purpose.

The purpose of this part is to clarify the rules and define the terms necessary to afford deposit insurance coverage under the Act and provide rules for the recognition of deposit ownership in various circumstances.

§ 330.3 General principles.

(a) *Ownership rights and capacities.* The insurance coverage provided by the Act and this part is based upon the ownership rights and capacities in which deposit accounts are maintained at insured depository institutions. All deposits in an insured depository institution which are maintained in the same right and capacity (by or for the benefit of a particular depositor or depositors) shall be added together and insured in accordance with this part. Deposits maintained in different rights and capacities, as recognized under this part, shall be insured separately from each other. (Example: Single ownership accounts and joint ownership accounts are insured separately from each other.)

(b) *Deposits maintained in separate insured depository institutions or in separate branches of the same insured depository institution.* Any deposit accounts maintained by a depositor at one insured depository institution are insured separately from, and without regard to, any deposit accounts that the same depositor maintains at any other separately chartered and insured depository institution, even if two or more separately chartered and insured depository institutions are affiliated through common ownership. (Example: Deposits held by the same individual at two different banks owned by the same bank holding company would be insured separately, per bank.)

The deposit accounts of a depositor maintained in the same right and capacity at different branches or offices of the same insured depository institution are not separately insured; rather they shall be added together and insured in accordance with this part.

(c) *Deposits maintained by foreigners and deposits denominated in foreign currency.* The availability of deposit insurance is not limited to citizens and residents of the United States. Any person or entity that maintains deposits in an insured depository institution is entitled to the deposit insurance provided by the Act and this part. In addition, deposits denominated in a foreign currency shall be insured in accordance with this part. Deposit insurance for such deposits shall be determined and paid in the amount of United States dollars that is equivalent in value to the amount of the deposit denominated in the foreign currency as of close of business on the date of default of the insured depository institution. The exchange rates to be used for such conversions are the 12 PM rates (the "noon buying rates for cable transfers") quoted for major currencies by the Federal Reserve Bank of New York on the date of default of the insured depository institution, unless the deposit agreement specifies that some other widely recognized exchange rates are to be used for all purposes under that agreement, in which case, the rates so specified shall be used for such conversions.

(d) *Deposits in insured branches of foreign banks.* Deposits in an insured branch of a foreign bank which are payable by contract in the United States shall be insured in accordance with this part, except that any deposits to the credit of the foreign bank, or any office, branch, agency or any wholly owned subsidiary of the foreign bank, shall not be insured. All deposits held by a depositor in the same right and capacity in more than one insured branch of the same foreign bank shall be added together for the purpose of determining the amount of deposit insurance.

§ 330.3

(e) *Deposits payable solely outside of the United States and certain other locations.* Any obligation of an insured depository institution which is payable solely at an office of such institution located outside the States of the United States, the District of Columbia, Puerto Rico, Guam, the Commonwealth of the Northern Mariana Islands, American Samoa, the Trust Territory of the Pacific Islands, and the Virgin Islands, is not a deposit for the purposes of this part.

(f) *International banking facility deposits.* An "international banking facility time deposit," as defined by the Board of Governors of the Federal Reserve System in Regulation D (12 CFR 204.8(a)(2)), or in any successor regulation, is not a deposit for the purposes of this part.

(g) *Bank investment contracts.* As required by section 11(a)(8) of the Act (12 U.S.C. 1821(a)(8)), any liability arising under any investment contract between any insured depository institution and any employee benefit plan which expressly permits "benefit responsive withdrawals or transfers" (as defined in section 11(a)(8) of the Act) are not insured deposits for purposes of this part. The term "substantial penalty or adjustment" used in section 11(a)(8) of the Act means, in the case of a deposit having an original term which exceeds one year, all interest earned on the amount withdrawn from the date of deposit or for six months, whichever is less; or, in the case of a deposit having an original term of one year or less, all interest earned on the amount withdrawn from the date of deposit or three months, whichever is less.

(h) *Application of state or local law to deposit insurance determinations.* In general, deposit insurance is for the benefit of the owner or owners of funds on deposit. However, while ownership under state law of deposited funds is a necessary condition for deposit insurance, ownership under state law is not sufficient for, or decisive in, determining deposit insurance coverage. Deposit insurance coverage is also a function of the deposit account records of the insured depository institution and of the provisions of this part, which, in the interest of uniform national rules for deposit insurance coverage, are controlling for purposes of determining deposit insurance coverage.

(i) *Determination of the amount of a deposit*—(1) *General rule.* The amount of a deposit is the balance of principal and interest unconditionally credited to the deposit account as of the date of default of the insured depository institution, plus the ascertainable amount of interest to that date, accrued at the contract rate (or the anticipated or announced interest or dividend rate), which the insured depository institution in default would have paid if the deposit had matured on that date and the insured depository institution had not failed. In the absence of any such announced or anticipated interest or dividend rate, the rate for this purpose shall be whatever rate was paid in the immediately preceding payment period.

(2) *Discounted certificates of deposit.* The amount of a certificate of deposit sold by an insured depository institution at a discount from its face value is its original purchase price plus the amount of accrued earnings calculated by compounding interest annually at the rate necessary to increase the original purchase price to the maturity value over the life of the certificate.

(3) *Waiver of minimum requirements.* In the case of a deposit with a fixed payment date, fixed or minimum term, or a qualifying or notice period that has not expired as of such date, interest thereon to the date of closing shall be computed according to the terms of the deposit contract as if interest had been credited and as if the deposit could have been withdrawn on such date without any penalty or reduction in the rate of earnings.

(j) *Continuation of insurance coverage following the death of a deposit owner.* The death of a deposit owner shall not affect the insurance coverage of the deposit for a period of six months following the owner's death unless the deposit account is restructured. The operation of this grace period, however, shall not result in a reduction of coverage. If an account is not restructured within six months after the owner's death, the insurance shall be provided

Federal Deposit Insurance Corporation § 330.5

on the basis of actual ownership in accordance with the provisions of § 330.5(a)(1).

[63 FR 25756, May 11, 1998, as amended at 64 FR 15656, Apr. 1, 1999]

§ 330.4 Continuation of separate deposit insurance after merger of insured depository institutions.

Whenever the liabilities of one or more insured depository institutions for deposits are assumed by another insured depository institution, whether by merger, consolidation, other statutory assumption or contract:

(a) The insured status of the institutions whose liabilities have been assumed terminates on the date of receipt by the FDIC of satisfactory evidence of the assumption; and

(b) The separate insurance of deposits assumed continues for six months from the date the assumption takes effect or, in the case of a time deposit, the earliest maturity date after the six-month period. In the case of time deposits which mature within six months of the date the deposits are assumed and which are renewed at the same dollar amount (either with or without accrued interest having been added to the principal amount) and for the same term as the original deposit, the separate insurance applies to the renewed deposits until the first maturity date after the six-month period. Time deposits that mature within six months of the deposit assumption and that are renewed on any other basis, or that are not renewed and thereby become demand deposits, are separately insured only until the end of the six-month period.

§ 330.5 Recognition of deposit ownership and fiduciary relationships.

(a) *Recognition of deposit ownership*—(1) *Evidence of deposit ownership.* Except as indicated in this paragraph (a)(1) or as provided in § 330.3(j), in determining the amount of insurance available to each depositor, the FDIC shall presume that deposited funds are actually owned in the manner indicated on the deposit account records of the insured depository institution. If the FDIC, in its sole discretion, determines that the deposit account records of the insured depository institution are clear and unambiguous, those records shall be considered binding on the depositor, and the FDIC shall consider no other records on the manner in which the funds are owned. If the deposit account records are ambiguous or unclear on the manner in which the funds are owned, then the FDIC may, in its sole discretion, consider evidence other than the deposit account records of the insured depository institution for the purpose of establishing the manner in which the funds are owned. Despite the general requirements of this paragraph (a)(1), if the FDIC has reason to believe that the insured depository institution's deposit account records misrepresent the actual ownership of deposited funds and such misrepresentation would increase deposit insurance coverage, the FDIC may consider all available evidence and pay claims for insured deposits on the basis of the actual rather than the misrepresented ownership.

(2) *Recognition of deposit ownership in custodial accounts.* In the case of custodial deposits, the interest of each beneficial owner may be determined on a fractional or percentage basis. This may be accomplished in any manner which indicates that where the funds of an owner are commingled with other funds held in a custodial capacity and a portion thereof is placed on deposit in one or more insured depository institutions without allocation, the owner's insured interest in the deposit in any one insured depository institution would represent, at any given time, the same fractional share as his or her share of the total commingled funds.

(b) *Fiduciary relationships*—(1) *Recognition.* The FDIC will recognize a claim for insurance coverage based on a fiduciary relationship only if the relationship is expressly disclosed, by way of specific references, in the "deposit account records" (as defined in § 330.1(e)) of the insured depository institution. Such relationships include, but are not limited to, relationships involving a trustee, agent, nominee, guardian, executor or custodian pursuant to which funds are deposited. The express indication that the account is held in a fiduciary capacity will not be necessary, however, in instances where

§ 330.5

the FDIC determines, in its sole discretion, that the titling of the deposit account and the underlying deposit account records sufficiently indicate the existence of a fiduciary relationship. This exception may apply, for example, where the deposit account title or records indicate that the account is held by an escrow agent, title company or a company whose business is to hold deposits and securities for others.

(2) *Details of fiduciary relationships.* If the deposit account records of an insured depository institution disclose the existence of a relationship which might provide a basis for additional insurance (including the exception provided for in paragraph (b)(1) of this section), the details of the relationship and the interests of other parties in the account must be ascertainable either from the deposit account records of the insured depository institution or from records maintained, in good faith and in the regular course of business, by the depositor or by some person or entity that has undertaken to maintain such records for the depositor.

(3) *Multi-tiered fiduciary relationships.* In deposit accounts where there are multiple levels of fiduciary relationships, there are two methods of satisfying paragraphs (b)(1) and (b)(2) of this section to obtain insurance coverage for the interests of the true beneficial owners of a deposit account.

(i) One method is to:

(A) Expressly indicate, on the deposit account records of the insured depository institution, the existence of each and every level of fiduciary relationships; and

(B) Disclose, at each level, the name(s) and interest(s) of the person(s) on whose behalf the party at that level is acting.

(ii) An alternative method is to:

(A) Expressly indicate, on the deposit account records of the insured depository institution, that there are multiple levels of fiduciary relationships;

(B) Disclose the existence of additional levels of fiduciary relationships in records, maintained in good faith and in the regular course of business, by parties at subsequent levels; and

(C) Disclose, at each of the levels, the name(s) and interest(s) of the person(s) on whose behalf the party at that level is acting. No person or entity in the chain of parties will be permitted to claim that they are acting in a fiduciary capacity for others unless the possible existence of such a relationship is revealed at some previous level in the chain.

(4) *Exceptions*—(i) *Deposits evidenced by negotiable instruments.* If any deposit obligation of an insured depository institution is evidenced by a negotiable certificate of deposit, negotiable draft, negotiable cashier's or officer's check, negotiable certified check, negotiable traveler's check, letter of credit or other negotiable instrument, the FDIC will recognize the owner of such deposit obligation for all purposes of claim for insured deposits to the same extent as if his or her name and interest were disclosed on the records of the insured depository institution; provided, that the instrument was in fact negotiated to such owner prior to the date of default of the insured depository institution. The owner must provide affirmative proof of such negotiation, in a form satisfactory to the FDIC, to substantiate his or her claim. Receipt of a negotiable instrument directly from the insured depository institution in default shall, in no event, be considered a negotiation of said instrument for purposes of this provision.

(ii) *Deposit obligations for payment of items forwarded for collection by depository institution acting as agent.* Where an insured depository institution in default has become obligated for the payment of items forwarded for collection by a depository institution acting solely as agent, the FDIC will recognize the holders of such items for all purposes of claim for insured deposits to the same extent as if their name(s) and interest(s) were disclosed as depositors on the deposit account records of the insured depository institution, when such claim for insured deposits, if otherwise payable, has been established by the execution and delivery of prescribed forms. The FDIC will recognize such depository institution forwarding such items for the holders thereof as agent for such holders for the purpose of making an assignment to the FDIC of their rights against the insured depository institution in default and for

Federal Deposit Insurance Corporation

the purpose of receiving payment on their behalf.

[63 FR 25756, May 11, 1998, as amended at 64 FR 15656, Apr. 1, 1999]

§ 330.6 Single ownership accounts.

(a) *Individual accounts.* Funds owned by a natural person and deposited in one or more deposit accounts in his or her own name shall be added together and insured up to the SMDIA in the aggregate. Exception: Despite the general requirement in this paragraph (a), if more than one natural person has the right to withdraw funds from an individual account (excluding persons who have the right to withdraw by virtue of a Power of Attorney), the account shall be treated as a joint ownership account (although not necessarily a qualifying joint account) and shall be insured in accordance with the provisions of § 330.9, unless the deposit account records clearly indicate, to the satisfaction of the FDIC, that the funds are owned by one individual and that other signatories on the account are merely authorized to withdraw funds on behalf of the owner.

(b) *Sole proprietorship accounts.* Funds owned by a business which is a "sole proprietorship" (as defined in § 330.1(n)) and deposited in one or more deposit accounts in the name of the business shall be treated as the individual account(s) of the person who is the sole proprietor, added to any other individual accounts of that person, and insured up to the SMDIA in the aggregate.

(c) *Single-name accounts containing community property funds.* Community property funds deposited into one or more deposit accounts in the name of one member of a husband-wife community shall be treated as the individual account(s) of the named member, added to any other individual accounts of that person, and insured up to the SMDIA in the aggregate.

(d) *Accounts of a decedent and accounts held by executors or administrators of a decedent's estate.* Funds held in the name of a decedent or in the name of the executor, administrator, or other personal representative of his or her estate and deposited into one or more deposit accounts shall be added together and insured up to the SMDIA in the aggregate; provided, however, that nothing in this paragraph (d) shall affect the operation of § 330.3(j). The deposit insurance provided by this paragraph (d) shall be separate from any insurance coverage provided for the individual deposit accounts of the executor, administrator, other personal representative or the beneficiaries of the estate.

[63 FR 25756, May 11, 1998, as amended at 71 FR 14631, Mar. 23, 2006; 76 FR 41395, July 14, 2011]

§ 330.7 Accounts held by an agent, nominee, guardian, custodian or conservator.

(a) *Agency or nominee accounts.* Funds owned by a principal or principals and deposited into one or more deposit accounts in the name of an agent, custodian or nominee, shall be insured to the same extent as if deposited in the name of the principal(s). When such funds are deposited by an insured depository institution acting as a trustee of an irrevocable trust, the insurance coverage shall be governed by the provisions of § 330.13.

(b) *Guardian, custodian or conservator accounts.* Funds held by a guardian, custodian, or conservator for the benefit of his or her ward, or for the benefit of a minor under the Uniform Gifts to Minors Act, and deposited into one or more accounts in the name of the guardian, custodian or conservator shall, for purposes of this part, be deemed to be agency or nominee accounts and shall be insured in accordance with paragraph (a) of this section.

(c) *Accounts held by fiduciaries on behalf of two or more persons.* Funds held by an agent, nominee, guardian, custodian, conservator or loan servicer, on behalf of two or more persons jointly, shall be treated as a joint ownership account and shall be insured in accordance with the provisions of § 330.9.

(d) *Mortgage servicing accounts.* Accounts maintained by a mortgage servicer, in a custodial or other fiduciary capacity, which are comprised of payments by mortgagors of principal and interest, shall be insured for the cumulative balance paid into the account by the mortgagors, up to the limit of the SMDIA per mortgagor. Accounts maintained by a mortgage

§ 330.8

servicer, in a custodial or other fiduciary capacity, which are comprised of payments by mortgagors of taxes and insurance premiums shall be added together and insured in accordance with paragraph (a) of this section for the ownership interest of each mortgagor in such accounts. This provision is effective as of October 10, 2008, for all existing and future mortgage servicing accounts.

(e) *Custodian accounts for American Indians.* Paragraph (a) of this section shall not apply to any interest an individual American Indian may have in funds deposited by the Bureau of Indian Affairs of the United States Department of the Interior (the "BIA") on behalf of that person pursuant to 25 U.S.C. 162(a), or by any other disbursing agent of the United States on behalf of that person pursuant to similar authority, in an insured depository institution. The interest of each American Indian in all such accounts maintained at the same insured depository institution shall be added together and insured, up to the SMDIA, separately from any other accounts maintained by that person in the same insured depository institution.

[63 FR 25756, May 11, 1998, as amended at 71 FR 14631, Mar. 23, 2006; 73 FR 61660, Oct. 17, 2008; 74 FR 47716, Sept. 17, 2009]

§ 330.8 **Annuity contract accounts.**

(a) Funds held by an insurance company or other corporation in a deposit account for the sole purpose of funding life insurance or annuity contracts and any benefits incidental to such contracts, shall be insured separately in the amount of up to the SMDIA per annuitant, provided that, pursuant to a state statute:

(1) The corporation establishes a separate account for such funds;

(2) The account cannot be charged with the liabilities arising out of any other business of the corporation; and

(3) The account cannot be invaded by other creditors of the corporation in the event that the corporation becomes insolvent and its assets are liquidated.

(b) Such insurance coverage shall be separate from the insurance provided for any other accounts maintained by the corporation or the annuitants at the same insured depository institution.

[63 FR 25756, May 11, 1998, as amended at 71 FR 14631, Mar. 23, 2006]

§ 330.9 **Joint ownership accounts.**

(a) *Separate insurance coverage.* Qualifying joint accounts, whether owned as joint tenants with the right of survivorship, as tenants in common or as tenants by the entirety, shall be insured separately from any individually owned (single ownership) deposit accounts maintained by the co-owners. (Example: If A has a single ownership account and also is a joint owner of a qualifying joint account, A's interest in the joint account would be insured separately from his or her interest in the individual account.) Qualifying joint accounts in the names of both husband and wife which are comprised of community property funds shall be added together and insured up to twice the SMDIA, separately from any funds deposited into accounts bearing their individual names.

(b) *Determination of insurance coverage.* The interests of each co-owner in all qualifying joint accounts shall be added together and the total shall be insured up to the SMDIA. (Example: "A&B" have a qualifying joint account with a balance of $150,000; "A&C" have a qualifying joint account with a balance of $200,000; and "A&B&C" have a qualifying joint account with a balance of $375,000. A's combined ownership interest in all qualifying joint accounts would be $300,000 ($75,000 plus $100,000 plus $125,000); therefore, A's interest would be insured in the amount of $250,000 and uninsured in the amount of $50,000. B's combined ownership interest in all qualifying joint accounts would be $200,000 ($75,000 plus $125,000); therefore, B's interest would be fully insured. C's combined ownership interest in all qualifying joint accounts would be $225,000 ($100,000 plus $125,000); therefore, C's interest would be fully insured.

(c) *Qualifying joint accounts.* (1) A joint deposit account shall be deemed to be a qualifying joint account, for purposes of this section, only if:

(i) All co-owners of the funds in the account are "natural persons" (as defined in § 330.1(l)); and

Federal Deposit Insurance Corporation § 330.10

(ii) Each co-owner has personally signed a deposit account signature card; and

(iii) Each co-owner possesses withdrawal rights on the same basis.

(2) The signature-card requirement of paragraph (c)(1)(ii) of this section shall not apply to certificates of deposit, to any deposit obligation evidenced by a negotiable instrument, or to any account maintained by an agent, nominee, guardian, custodian or conservator on behalf of two or more persons.

(3) All deposit accounts that satisfy the criteria in paragraph (c)(1) of this section, and those accounts that come within the exception provided for in paragraph (c)(2) of this section, shall be deemed to be jointly owned provided that, in accordance with the provisions of § 330.5(a), the FDIC determines that the deposit account records of the insured depository institution are clear and unambiguous as to the ownership of the accounts. If the deposit account records are ambiguous or unclear as to the manner in which the deposit accounts are owned, then the FDIC may, in its sole discretion, consider evidence other than the deposit account records of the insured depository institution for the purpose of establishing the manner in which the funds are owned. The signatures of two or more persons on the deposit account signature card or the names of two or more persons on a certificate of deposit or other deposit instrument shall be conclusive evidence that the account is a joint account (although not necessarily a qualifying joint account) unless the deposit records as a whole are ambiguous and some other evidence indicates, to the satisfaction of the FDIC, that there is a contrary ownership capacity.

(d) *Nonqualifying joint accounts.* A deposit account held in two or more names which is not a qualifying joint account, for purposes of this section, shall be treated as being owned by each named owner, as an individual, corporation, partnership, or unincorporated association, as the case may be, and the actual ownership interest of each individual or entity in such account shall be added to any other single ownership accounts of such individual or other accounts of such entity, and shall be insured in accordance with the provisions of this part governing the insurance of such accounts.

(e) *Determination of interests.* The interests of the co-owners of qualifying joint accounts, held as tenants in common, shall be deemed equal, unless otherwise stated in the depository institution's deposit account records. This section applies regardless of whether the conjunction "and" or "or" is used in the title of a joint deposit account, even when both terms are used, such as in the case of a joint deposit account with three or more co-owners.

[63 FR 25756, May 11, 1998, as amended at 64 FR 15656, Apr. 1, 1999; 64 FR 62102, Nov. 16, 1999; 71 FR 14631, Mar. 23, 2006; 74 FR 47716, Sept. 17, 2009; 76 FR 41395, July 14, 2011]

§ 330.10 Revocable trust accounts.

(a) *General rule.* Except as provided in paragraph (e) of this section, the funds owned by an individual and deposited into one or more accounts with respect to which the owner evidences an intention that upon his or her death the funds shall belong to one or more beneficiaries shall be separately insured (from other types of accounts the owner has at the same insured depository institution) in an amount equal to the total number of different beneficiaries named in the account(s) multiplied by the SMDIA. This section applies to all accounts held in connection with informal and formal testamentary revocable trusts. Such informal trusts are commonly referred to as payable-on-death accounts, in-trust-for accounts or Totten Trust accounts, and such formal trusts are commonly referred to as living trusts or family trusts. (*Example 1:* Account Owner "A" has a living trust account with four different beneficiaries named in the trust. A has no other revocable trust accounts at the same FDIC-insured institution. The maximum insurance coverage would be $1,000,000, determined by multiplying 4 times $250,000 (the number of beneficiaries times the SMDIA). (*Example 2:* Account Owner "A" has a payable-on-death account naming his niece and cousin as beneficiaries, and A also has, at the same FDIC-insured institution, another payable-on-death account naming the

§ 330.10

same niece and a friend as beneficiaries. The maximum coverage available to the account owner would be $750,000. This is because the account owner has named only three *different* beneficiaries in the revocable trust accounts—his niece and cousin in the first, and the same niece and a friend in the second. The naming of the same beneficiary in more than one revocable trust account, whether it be a payable-on-death account or living trust account, does not increase the total coverage amount.) (*Example 3:* Account Owner "A" establishes a living trust account, with a balance of $300,000, naming his two children "B" and "C" as beneficiaries. A also establishes, at the same FDIC-insured institution, a payable-on-death account, with a balance of $300,000, also naming his children B and C as beneficiaries. The maximum coverage available to A is $500,000, determined by multiplying 2 times $250,000 (the number of different beneficiaries times the SMDIA). A is uninsured in the amount of $100,000. This is because all funds that a depositor holds in both living trust accounts and payable-on-death accounts, at the same FDIC-insured institution and naming the same beneficiaries, are aggregated for insurance purposes and insured to the applicable coverage limits.)

(b) *Required intention and naming of beneficiaries.* (1) The required intention in paragraph (a) of this section that upon the owner's death the funds shall belong to one or more beneficiaries must be manifested in the "title" of the account using commonly accepted terms such as, but not limited to, "in trust for," "as trustee for," "payable-on-death to," or any acronym therefor. For purposes of this requirement, "title" includes the electronic deposit account records of the institution. (For example, the FDIC would recognize an account as a revocable trust account even if the title of the account signature card does not designate the account as a revocable trust account as long as the institution's electronic deposit account records identify (through a code or otherwise) the account as a revocable trust account.) The settlor of a revocable trust shall be presumed to own the funds deposited into the account.

(2) For informal revocable trust accounts, the beneficiaries must be specifically named in the deposit account records of the insured depository institution.

(c) *Definition of beneficiary.* For purposes of this section, a beneficiary includes a natural person as well as a charitable organization and other nonprofit entity recognized as such under the Internal Revenue Code of 1986, as amended.

(d) *Interests of beneficiaries outside the definition of beneficiary in this section.* If a beneficiary named in a trust covered by this section does not meet the definition of beneficiary in paragraph (c) of this section, the funds corresponding to that beneficiary shall be treated as the individually owned (single ownership) funds of the owner(s). As such, they shall be aggregated with any other single ownership accounts of such owner(s) and insured up to the SMDIA per owner. (*Example:* Account Owner "A" establishes a payable-on-death account naming a pet as beneficiary with a balance of $100,000. A also has an individual account at the same FDIC-insured institution with a balance of $175,000. Because the pet is not a "beneficiary," the two accounts are aggregated and treated as a single ownership account. As a result, A is insured in the amount of $250,000, but is uninsured for the remaining $25,000.)

(e) *Revocable trust accounts with aggregate balances exceeding five times the SMDIA and naming more than five different beneficiaries.* Notwithstanding the general coverage provisions in paragraph (a) of this section, for funds owned by an individual in one or more revocable trust accounts naming more than five different beneficiaries and whose aggregate balance is more than five times the SMDIA, the maximum revocable trust account coverage for the account owner shall be the greater of either: five times the SMDIA or the aggregate amount of the interests of each different beneficiary named in the trusts, to a limit of the SMDIA per different beneficiary. (*Example 1:* Account Owner "A" has a living trust with a balance of $1 million and names two friends, "B" and "C" as beneficiaries.

Federal Deposit Insurance Corporation § 330.10

At the same FDIC-insured institution, A establishes a payable-on-death account, with a balance of $1 million naming his two cousins, "D" and "E" as beneficiaries. Coverage is determined under the general coverage provisions in paragraph (a) of this section, and not this paragraph (e). This is because all funds that A holds in both living trust accounts and payable-on-death accounts, at the same FDIC-insured institution, are aggregated for insurance purposes. Although A's aggregated balance of $2 million is more than five times the SMDIA, A names only four different beneficiaries, and coverage under this paragraph (e) applies only if there are more than five different beneficiaries. A is insured in the amount of $1 million (4 beneficiaries times the SMDIA), and uninsured for the remaining $1 million.) (*Example 2:* Account Owner "A" has a living trust account with a balance of $1,500,000. Under the terms of the trust, upon A's death, A's three children are each entitled to $125,000, A's friend is entitled to $15,000, and a designated charity is entitled to $175,000. The trust also provides that the remainder of the trust assets shall belong to A's spouse. In this case, because the balance of the account exceeds $1,250,000 (5 times the SMDIA) and there are more than five different beneficiaries named in the trust, the maximum coverage available to A would be the greater of: $1,250,000 or the aggregate of each different beneficiary's interest to a limit of $250,000 per beneficiary. The beneficial interests in the trust for purposes of determining coverage are: $125,000 for each of the children (totaling $375,000), $15,000 for the friend, $175,000 for the charity, and $250,000 for the spouse (because the spouse's $935,000 is subject to the $250,000 per-beneficiary limitation). The aggregate beneficial interests total $815,000. Thus, the maximum coverage afforded to the account owner would be $1,250,000, the greater of $1,250,000 or $815,000.)

(f) *Co-owned revocable trust accounts.* (1) Where an account described in paragraph (a) of this section is established by more than one owner, the respective interest of each account owner (which shall be deemed equal) shall be insured separately, per different beneficiary, up to the SMDIA, subject to the limitation imposed in paragraph (e) of this section. (*Example 1:* A and B, two individuals, establish a payable-on-death account naming their three nieces as beneficiaries. Neither A nor B has any other revocable trust accounts at the same FDIC-insured institution. The maximum coverage afforded to A and B would be $1,500,000, determined by multiplying the number of owners (2) times the SMDIA ($250,000) times the number of different beneficiaries (3). In this example, A would be entitled to revocable trust coverage of $750,000 and B would be entitled to revocable trust coverage of $750,000.) (*Example 2:* A and B, two individuals, establish a payable-on-death account naming their two children, two cousins, and a charity as beneficiaries. The balance in the account is $1,750,000. Neither A nor B has any other revocable trust accounts at the same FDIC-insured institution. The maximum coverage would be determined (under paragraph (a) of this section) by multiplying the number of account owners (2) times the number of different beneficiaries (5) times $250,000, totaling $2,500,000. Because the account balance ($1,750,000) is less than the maximum coverage amount ($2,500,000), the account would be fully insured.) (*Example 3:* A and B, two individuals, establish a living trust account with a balance of $3.75 million. Under the terms of the trust, upon the death of both A and B, each of their three children is entitled to $600,000, B's cousin is entitled to $380,000, A's friend is entitled to $70,000, and the remaining amount ($1,500,000) goes to a charity. Under paragraph (e) of this section, the maximum coverage, as to each co-owned account owner, would be the greater of $1,250,000 or the aggregate amount (as to each co-owner) of the interest of each different beneficiary named in the trust, to a limit of $250,000 per account owner per beneficiary. The beneficial interests in the trust considered for purposes of determining coverage for account owner A are: $750,000 for the children (each child's interest attributable to A, $300,000, is subject to the $250,000-per-beneficiary limitation), $190,000 for the cousin, $35,000 for the friend, and $250,000 for the charity (the charity's

§ 330.11

interest attributable to A, $750,000, is subject to the $250,000 per-beneficiary limitation). As to A, the aggregate amount of the beneficial interests eligible for deposit insurance coverage totals $1,225,000. Thus, the maximum coverage afforded to account co-owner A would be $1,250,000, which is the greater of $1,250,000 or the aggregate of all the beneficial interests attributable to A (limited to $250,000 per beneficiary), which totaled slightly less at $1,225,000. Because B has equal ownership interest in the trust, the same analysis and coverage determination also would apply to B. Thus, of the total account balance of $3.75 million, $2.5 million would be insured and $1.25 million would be uninsured.)

(2) Notwithstanding paragraph (f)(1) of this section, where the owners of a co-owned revocable trust account are themselves the sole beneficiaries of the corresponding trust, the account shall be insured as a joint account under § 330.9 and shall not be insured under the provisions of this section. (*Example:* If A and B establish a payable-on-death account naming themselves as the sole beneficiaries of the account, the account will be insured as a joint account because the account does not satisfy the intent requirement (under paragraph (a) of this section) that the funds in the account belong to the named beneficiaries upon the owners' death. The beneficiaries are in fact the actual owners of the funds during the account owners' lifetimes.)

(g) For deposit accounts held in connection with a living trust that provides for a life-estate interest for designated beneficiaries, the FDIC shall value each such life estate interest as the SMDIA for purposes of determining the insurance coverage available to the account owner under paragraph (e) of this section. (*Example:* Account Owner "A" has a living trust account with a balance of $1,500,000. Under the terms of the trust, A provides a life estate interest for his spouse. Moreover, A's three children are each entitled to $275,000, A's friend is entitled to $15,000, and a designated charity is entitled to $175,000. The trust also provides that the remainder of the trust assets shall belong to A's granddaughter. In this case, because the balance of the account exceeds $1,250,000 ((5) five times the SMDIA) and there are more than five different beneficiaries named in the trust, the maximum coverage available to A would be the greater of: $1,250,000 or the aggregate of each different beneficiary's interest to a limit of $250,000 per beneficiary. The beneficial interests in the trust considered for purposes of determining coverage are: $250,000 for the spouse's life estate, $750,000 for the children (because each child's $275,000 is subject to the $250,000 per-beneficiary limitation), $15,000 for the friend, $175,000 for the charity, and $250,000 for the granddaughter (because the granddaughter's $310,000 remainder is limited by the $250,000 per-beneficiary limitation). The aggregate beneficial interests total $1,440,000. Thus, the maximum coverage afforded to the account owner would be $1,440,000, the greater of $1,250,000 or $1,440,000.)

(h) *Revocable trusts that become irrevocable trusts.* Notwithstanding the provisions in section 330.13 on the insurance coverage of irrevocable trust accounts, if a revocable trust account converts in part or entirely to an irrevocable trust upon the death of one or more of the trust's owners, the trust account shall continue to be insured under the provisions of this section. (*Example:* Assume A and B have a trust account in connection with a living trust, of which they are joint grantors. If upon the death of either A or B the trust transforms into an irrevocable trust as to the deceased grantor's ownership in the trust, the account will continue to be insured under the provisions of this section.)

(i) This section shall apply to all existing and future revocable trust accounts and all existing and future irrevocable trust accounts resulting from formal revocable trust accounts.

[74 FR 47716, Sept. 17, 2009]

§ 330.11 Accounts of a corporation, partnership or unincorporated association.

(a) *Corporate accounts.* (1) The deposit accounts of a corporation engaged in any "independent activity" (as defined in § 330.1(g)) shall be added together and insured up to the SMDIA in the aggregate. If a corporation has divisions or

Federal Deposit Insurance Corporation § 330.12

units which are not separately incorporated, the deposit accounts of those divisions or units shall be added to any other deposit accounts of the corporation. If a corporation maintains deposit accounts in a representative or fiduciary capacity, such accounts shall not be treated as the deposit accounts of the corporation but shall be treated as fiduciary accounts and insured in accordance with the provisions of § 330.7.

(2) Notwithstanding any other provision of this part, any trust or other business arrangement which has filed or is required to file a registration statement with the Securities and Exchange Commission pursuant to section 8 of the Investment Company Act of 1940 (15 U.S.C. 80a–8) or that would be required so to register but for the fact it is not created under the laws of the United States or a state or but for sections 2(b), 3(c)(1), or 6(a)(1) of that act shall be deemed to be a corporation for purposes of determining deposit insurance coverage. An exception to this paragraph (a)(2) shall exist for any trust or other business arrangement established by a state or that is a state agency or state public instrumentality as part of a qualified tuition savings program under section 529 of the Internal Revenue Code (26 U.S.C. 529). A deposit account of such a trust or business arrangement shall not be deemed to be the deposit of a corporation provided that: The funds in the account may be traced to one or more particular investors or participants; and the existence of the trust relationships is disclosed in accordance with the requirements of § 330.5. If these conditions are satisfied, each participant's funds shall be insured as a deposit account of the participant.

(b) *Partnership accounts.* The deposit accounts of a partnership engaged in any "independent activity" (as defined in § 330.1(g)) shall be added together and insured up to the SMDIA in the aggregate. Such insurance coverage shall be separate from any insurance provided for individually owned (single ownership) accounts maintained by the individual partners. A partnership shall be deemed to exist, for purposes of this paragraph, any time there is an association of two or more persons or entities formed to carry on, as co-owners, an unincorporated business for profit.

(c) *Unincorporated association accounts.* The deposit accounts of an unincorporated association engaged in any independent activity shall be added together and insured up to the SMDIA in the aggregate, separately from the accounts of the person(s) or entity(ies) comprising the unincorporated association. An unincorporated association shall be deemed to exist, for purposes of this paragraph, whenever there is an association of two or more persons formed for some religious, educational, charitable, social or other noncommercial purpose.

(d) *Non-qualifying entities.* The deposit accounts of an entity which is not engaged in an "independent activity" (as defined in § 330.1(g)) shall be deemed to be owned by the person or persons owning the corporation or comprising the partnership or unincorporated association, and, for deposit insurance purposes, the interest of each person in such a deposit account shall be added to any other deposit accounts individually owned by that person and insured up to the SMDIA in the aggregate.

[63 FR 25756, May 11, 1998, as amended at 70 FR 33692, June 9, 2005; 70 FR 62059, Oct. 28, 2005; 71 FR 14631, Mar. 23, 2006]

§ 330.12 Accounts held by a depository institution as the trustee of an irrevocable trust.

(a) *Separate insurance coverage.* "Trust funds" (as defined in § 330.1(q)) held by an insured depository institution in its capacity as trustee of an irrevocable trust, whether held in its trust department, held or deposited in any other department of the fiduciary institution, or deposited by the fiduciary institution in another insured depository institution, shall be insured up to the SMDIA for each owner or beneficiary represented. This insurance shall be separate from, and in addition to, the insurance provided for any other deposits of the owners or the beneficiaries.

(b) *Determination of interests.* The insurance for funds held by an insured depository institution in its capacity as trustee of an irrevocable trust shall be determined in accordance with the following provisions:

353

§ 330.13

(1) *Allocated funds of a trust estate.* If trust funds of a particular "trust estate" (as defined in § 330.1(p)) are allocated by the fiduciary and deposited, the insurance with respect to such trust estate shall be determined by ascertaining the amount of its funds allocated, deposited and remaining to the credit of the claimant as fiduciary at the insured depository institution in default.

(2) *Interest of a trust estate in unallocated trust funds.* If funds of a particular trust estate are commingled with funds of other trust estates and deposited by the fiduciary institution in one or more insured depository institutions to the credit of the depository institution as fiduciary, without allocation of specific amounts from a particular trust estate to an account in such institution(s), the percentage interest of that trust estate in the unallocated deposits in any institution in default is the same as that trust estate's percentage interest in the entire commingled investment pool.

(c) *Limitation on applicability.* This section shall not apply to deposits of trust funds belonging to a trust which is classified as a corporation under § 330.11(a)(2).

[63 FR 25756, May 11, 1998, as amended at 71 FR 14631, Mar. 23, 2006; 76 FR 41395, July 14, 2011]

§ 330.13 Irrevocable trust accounts.

(a) *General rule.* Funds representing the "non-contingent trust interest(s)" (as defined in § 330.1(m)) of a beneficiary deposited into one or more deposit accounts established pursuant to one or more irrevocable trust agreements created by the same settlor(s) (grantor(s)) shall be added together and insured up to the SMDIA in the aggregate. Such insurance coverage shall be separate from the coverage provided for other accounts maintained by the settlor(s), trustee(s) or beneficiary(ies) of the irrevocable trust(s) at the same insured depository institution. Each "trust interest" (as defined in § 330.1(r)) in any irrevocable trust established by two or more settlors shall be deemed to be derived from each settlor pro rata to his or her contribution to the trust.

(b) *Treatment of contingent trust interests.* In the case of any trust in which certain trust interests do not qualify as non-contingent trust interests, the funds representing those interests shall be added together and insured up to the SMDIA in the aggregate. Such insurance coverage shall be in addition to the coverage provided for the funds representing non-contingent trust interests which are insured pursuant to paragraph (a) of this section.

(c) *Commingled accounts of bankruptcy trustees.* Whenever a bankruptcy trustee appointed under Title 11 of the United States Code commingles the funds of various bankruptcy estates in the same account at an insured depository institution, the funds of each Title 11 bankruptcy estate will be added together and insured up to the SMDIA, separately from the funds of any other such estate.

[63 FR 25756, May 11, 1998, as amended at 71 FR 14631, Mar. 23, 2006; 76 FR 41395, July 14, 2011]

§ 330.14 Retirement and other employee benefit plan accounts.

(a) "Pass-through" insurance. Any deposits of an employee benefit plan in an insured depository institution shall be insured on a "pass-through" basis, in the amount of up to the SMDIA for the non-contingent interest of each plan participant, provided the rules in § 330.5 are satisfied. Deposits eligible for coverage under paragraph (b)(2) of this section that also are deposits of a employee benefit plan or deposits of an deferred compensation plan described in section 457 of the Internal Revenue Code of 1986 (26 U.S.C. 457) in an insured depository institution shall be insured on a "pass-through" basis in the amount of $250,000 for the non-contingent interest of each plan participant, provided the rules in § 330.5 are satisfied.

(b) *Aggregation*—(1) *Multiple plans.* Funds representing the non-contingent interests of a beneficiary in an employee benefit plan, or eligible deferred compensation plan described in section 457 of the Internal Revenue Code of 1986 (26 U.S.C. 457), which are deposited in one or more deposit accounts shall be aggregated with any other deposited funds representing such interests of the same beneficiary in other employee

Federal Deposit Insurance Corporation § 330.14

benefit plans, or eligible deferred compensation plans described in section 457 of the Internal Revenue Code of 1986, established by the same employer or employee organization.

(2) *Certain retirement accounts.* Deposits in an insured depository institution made in connection with the following types of retirement plans shall be aggregated and insured in the amount of up to $250,000 per participant:

(i) Any individual retirement account described in section 408(a) of the Internal Revenue Code of 1986 (26 U.S.C. 408(a));

(ii) Any eligible deferred compensation plan described in section 457 of the Internal Revenue Code of 1986 (26 U.S.C. 457); and

(iii) Any individual account plan defined in section 3(34) of the Employee Retirement Income Security Act (ERISA) (29 U.S.C. 1002) and any plan described in section 401(d) of the Internal Revenue Code of 1986 (26 U.S.C. 401(d)), to the extent that participants and beneficiaries under such plans have the right to direct the investment of assets held in individual accounts maintained on their behalf by the plans.

(c) *Determination of interests*—(1) *Defined contribution plans.* The value of an employee's non-contingent interest in a defined contribution plan shall be deemed to be the employee's account balance as of the date of default of the insured depository institution, regardless of whether said amount was derived, in whole or in part, from contributions of the employee and/or the employer to the account.

(2) *Defined benefit plans.* The value of an employee's non-contingent interest in a defined benefit plan shall be deemed to be the present value of the employee's interest in the plan, evaluated in accordance with the method of calculation ordinarily used under such plan, as of the date of default of the insured depository institution.

(3) *Amounts taken into account.* For the purposes of applying the rule under paragraph (b)(2) of this section, only the present vested and ascertainable interests of each participant in an employee benefit plan or "457 Plan," excluding any remainder interest created by, or as a result of, the plan, shall be taken into account in determining the amount of deposit insurance accorded to the deposits of the plan.

(d) *Treatment of contingent interests.* In the event that employees' interests in an employee benefit plan are not capable of evaluation in accordance with the provisions of this section, or an account established for any such plan includes amounts for future participants in the plan, payment by the FDIC with respect to all such interests shall not exceed the SMDIA in the aggregate.

(e) *Overfunded pension plan deposits.* Any portion of an employee benefit plan's deposits which is not attributable to the interests of the beneficiaries under the plan shall be deemed attributable to the overfunded portion of the plan's assets and shall be aggregated and insured up to the SMDIA, separately from any other deposits.

(f) *Definitions of "depositor", "employee benefit plan", "employee organization" and "non-contingent interest".* Except as otherwise indicated in this section, for purposes of this section:

(1) The term *depositor* means the person(s) administering or managing an employee benefit plan.

(2) The term *employee benefit plan* has the same meaning given to such term in section 3(3) of the Employee Retirement Income Security Act of 1974 (ERISA) (29 U.S.C. 1002) and includes any plan described in section 401(d) of the Internal Revenue Code of 1986.

(3) The term *employee organization* means any labor union, organization, employee representation committee, association, group, or plan, in which employees participate and which exists for the purpose, in whole or in part, of dealing with employers concerning an employee benefit plan, or other matters incidental to employment relationships; or any employees' beneficiary association organized for the purpose, in whole or in part, of establishing such a plan.

(4) The term *non-contingent interest* means an interest capable of determination without evaluation of contingencies except for those covered by the present worth tables and rules of calculation for their use set forth in § 20.2031-7 of the Federal Estate Tax

355

§ 330.15

Regulations (26 CFR 20.2031–7) or any similar present worth or life expectancy tables as may be published by the Internal Revenue Service.

[63 FR 25756, May 11, 1998, as amended at 64 FR 15657, Apr. 1, 1999; 71 FR 14631, Mar. 23, 2006; 71 FR 53550, Sept. 12, 2006]

§ 330.15 Accounts held by government depositors.

(a) *Extent of insurance coverage*—(1) *Accounts of the United States.* Each official custodian of funds of the United States lawfully depositing such funds in an insured depository institution shall be separately insured in the amount of:

(i) Up to the SMDIA in the aggregate for all time and savings deposits; and

(ii) Up to the SMDIA in the aggregate for all demand deposits.

(2) *Accounts of a state, county, municipality or political subdivision.* (i) Each official custodian of funds of any state of the United States, or any county, municipality, or political subdivision thereof, lawfully depositing such funds in an insured depository institution in the state comprising the public unit or wherein the public unit is located (including any insured depository institution having a branch in said state) shall be separately insured in the amount of:

(A) Up to the SMDIA in the aggregate for all time and savings deposits; and

(B) Up to the SMDIA in the aggregate for all demand deposits.

(ii) In addition, each such official custodian depositing such funds in an insured depository institution outside of the state comprising the public unit or wherein the public unit is located, shall be insured in the amount of up to the SMDIA in the aggregate for all deposits, regardless of whether they are time, savings or demand deposits.

(3) *Accounts of the District of Columbia.* (i) Each official custodian of funds of the District of Columbia lawfully depositing such funds in an insured depository institution in the District of Columbia (including an insured depository institution having a branch in the District of Columbia) shall be separately insured in the amount of:

(A) Up to the SMDIA in the aggregate for all time and savings deposits; and

(B) Up to the SMDIA in the aggregate for all demand deposits.

(ii) In addition, each such official custodian depositing such funds in an insured depository institution outside of the District of Columbia shall be insured in the amount of up to the SMDIA in the aggregate for all deposits, regardless of whether they are time, savings or demand deposits.

(4) *Accounts of the Commonwealth of Puerto Rico and other government possessions and territories.* (i) Each official custodian of funds of the Commonwealth of Puerto Rico, the Virgin Islands, American Samoa, the Trust Territory of the Pacific Islands, Guam, or The Commonwealth of the Northern Mariana Islands, or of any county, municipality, or political subdivision thereof lawfully depositing such funds in an insured depository institution in Puerto Rico, the Virgin Islands, American Samoa, the Trust Territory of the Pacific Islands, Guam, or The Commonwealth of the Northern Mariana Islands, respectively, shall be separately insured in the amount of:

(A) Up to the SMDIA in the aggregate for all time and savings deposits; and

(B) Up to the SMDIA in the aggregate for all demand deposits.

(ii) In addition, each such official custodian depositing such funds in an insured depository institution outside of the commonwealth, possession or territory comprising the public unit or wherein the public unit is located, shall be insured in the amount of up to the SMDIA in the aggregate for all deposits, regardless of whether they are time, savings or demand deposits.

(5) *Accounts of an Indian tribe.* Each official custodian of funds of an Indian tribe (as defined in 25 U.S.C. 1452(c)), including an agency thereof having official custody of tribal funds, lawfully depositing the same in an insured depository institution shall be separately insured in the amount of:

(i) Up to the SMDIA in the aggregate for all time and savings deposits; and

(ii) Up to the SMDIA in the aggregate for all demand deposits.

Federal Deposit Insurance Corporation

§ 330.16

(b) *Rules relating to the "official custodian"*—(1) *Qualifications for an "official custodian"*. In order to qualify as an "official custodian" for the purposes of paragraph (a) of this section, such custodian must have plenary authority, including control, over funds owned by the public unit which the custodian is appointed or elected to serve. Control of public funds includes possession, as well as the authority to establish accounts for such funds in insured depository institutions and to make deposits, withdrawals, and disbursements of such funds.

(2) *Official custodian of the funds of more than one public unit*. For the purposes of paragraph (a) of this section, if the same person is an official custodian of the funds of more than one public unit, he or she shall be separately insured with respect to the funds held by him or her for each such public unit, but shall not be separately insured by virtue of holding different offices in such public unit or, except as provided in paragraph (c) of this section, holding such funds for different purposes.

(3) *Split of authority or control over public unit funds*. If the exercise of authority or control over the funds of a public unit requires action by, or the consent of, two or more officers, employees, or agents of such public unit, then they will be treated as one "official custodian" for the purposes of this section.

(c) *Public bond issues*. Where an officer, agent or employee of a public unit has custody of certain funds which by law or under a bond indenture are required to be set aside to discharge a debt owed to the holders of notes or bonds issued by the public unit, any deposit of such funds in an insured depository institution shall be deemed to be a deposit by a trustee of trust funds of which the noteholders or bondholders are pro rata beneficiaries, and the beneficial interest of each noteholder or bondholder in the deposit shall be separately insured up to the SMDIA.

(d) *Definition of "political subdivision"*. The term "political subdivision" includes drainage, irrigation, navigation, improvement, levee, sanitary, school or power districts, and bridge or port authorities and other special districts created by state statute or compacts between the states. It also includes any subdivision of a public unit mentioned in paragraphs (a)(2), (a)(3) and (a)(4) of this section or any principal department of such public unit:

(1) The creation of which subdivision or department has been expressly authorized by the law of such public unit;

(2) To which some functions of government have been delegated by such law; and

(3) Which is empowered to exercise exclusive control over funds for its exclusive use.

[63 FR 25756, May 11, 1998, as amended at 71 FR 14631, Mar. 23, 2006]

§ 330.16 Noninterest-bearing transaction accounts.

(a) *Separate insurance coverage.* From December 31, 2010, through December 31, 2012, a depositor's funds in a "noninterest-bearing transaction account" (as defined in § 330.1(s)) are fully insured, irrespective of the SMDIA. Such insurance coverage shall be separate from the coverage provided for other accounts maintained at the same insured depository institution.

(b) *Certain swept funds.* Notwithstanding its normal rules and procedures regarding sweep accounts under 12 CFR 360.8, the FDIC will treat funds swept from a noninterest-bearing transaction account to a noninterest-bearing savings deposit account as being in a noninterest-bearing transaction account.

(c) *Disclosure and notice requirements.* (1) By no later than February 28, 2011, each depository institution that offers noninterest-bearing transaction accounts must post prominently the following notice in the lobby of its main office, in each domestic branch and, if it offers Internet deposit services, on its Web site:

NOTICE OF CHANGES IN TEMPORARY FDIC INSURANCE COVERAGE FOR TRANSACTION ACCOUNTS

All funds in a "noninterest-bearing transaction account" are insured in full by the Federal Deposit Insurance Corporation from December 31, 2010, through December 31, 2012. This temporary unlimited coverage is in addition to, and separate from, the coverage of at least $250,000 available to depositors under the FDIC's general deposit insurance rules.

§ 330.101

The term "noninterest-bearing transaction account" includes a traditional checking account or demand deposit account on which the insured depository institution pays no interest. It also includes Interest on Lawyers Trust Accounts ("IOLTAs"). It does not include other accounts, such as traditional checking or demand deposit accounts that may earn interest, NOW accounts, and money-market deposit accounts.

For more information about temporary FDIC insurance coverage of transaction accounts, visit *www.fdic.gov*.

(2) Institutions participating in the FDIC's Transaction Account Guarantee Program on December 31, 2010, must provide a notice by mail to depositors with negotiable order of withdrawal accounts that are protected in full as of that date under the Transaction Account Guarantee Program that, as of January 1, 2011, such accounts no longer will be eligible for unlimited protection. This notice must be provided to such depositors no later than December 31, 2010.

(3) If an institution uses sweep arrangements, modifies the terms of an account, or takes other actions that result in funds no longer being eligible for full coverage under this section, the institution must notify affected customers and clearly advise them, in writing, that such actions will affect their deposit insurance coverage.

[75 FR 69583, Nov. 15, 2010, as amended at 76 FR 4816, Jan. 27, 2011; 76 FR 41395, July 14, 2011]

§ 330.101 Premiums.

This interpretive rule describes certain payments that are not deemed to be "interest" as defined in § 330.1(k).

(a) Premiums, whether in the form of merchandise, credit, or cash, given by a bank to the holder of a deposit will not be regarded as "interest" as defined in § 330.1(k) if:

(1) The premium is given to the depositor only at the time of the opening of a new account or an addition to an existing account;

(2) No more than two premiums per deposit are given in any twelve-month interval; and

(3) The value of the premium (in the case of merchandise, the total cost to the bank, including shipping, warehousing, packaging, and handling costs) does not exceed $10 for a deposit of less than $5,000 or $20 for a deposit of $5,000 or more.

(b) The costs of premiums may not be averaged.

(c) A bank may not solicit funds for deposit on the basis that the bank will divide the funds into several accounts for the purpose of enabling the bank to pay the depositor more than two premiums within a twelve-month interval on the solicited funds.

(d) The bank must retain sufficient information for examiners to determine that the requirements of this section have been satisfied.

(e) Notwithstanding paragraph (a) of this section, any premium that is not, directly or indirectly, related to or dependent on the balance in a demand deposit account and the duration of the account balance shall not be considered the payment of interest on a demand deposit account and shall not be subject to the limitations in paragraph (a) of this section.

[76 FR 41395, July 14, 2011]

PART 331 [RESERVED]

PART 332—PRIVACY OF CONSUMER FINANCIAL INFORMATION

Sec.
332.1 Purpose and scope.
332.2 Model privacy form and examples.
332.3 Definitions.

Subpart A—Privacy and Opt Out Notices

332.4 Initial privacy notice to consumers required.
332.5 Annual privacy notice to customers required.
332.6 Information to be included in privacy notices.
332.7 Form of opt out notice to consumers; opt out methods.
332.8 Revised privacy notices.
332.9 Delivering privacy and opt out notices.

Subpart B—Limits on Disclosures

332.10 Limits on disclosure of nonpublic personal information to nonaffiliated third parties.
332.11 Limits on redisclosure and reuse of information.
332.12 Limits on sharing account number information for marketing purposes.

Federal Deposit Insurance Corporation

Subpart C—Exceptions

332.13 Exception to opt out requirements for service providers and joint marketing.
332.14 Exceptions to notice and opt out requirements for processing and servicing transactions.
332.15 Other exceptions to notice and opt out requirements.

Subpart D—Relation to Other Laws; Effective Date

332.16 Protection of Fair Credit Reporting Act.
332.17 Relation to State laws.
332.18 Effective date; transition rule.
APPENDIX A TO PART 332—MODEL PRIVACY FORM

AUTHORITY: 12 U.S.C. 1819 (Seventh and Tenth); 15 U.S.C. 6801 et seq.

SOURCE: 65 FR 35216, June 1, 2000, unless otherwise noted.

§ 332.1 Purpose and scope.

(a) *Purpose.* This part governs the treatment of nonpublic personal information about consumers by the financial institutions listed in paragraph (b) of this section. This part:

(1) Requires a financial institution to provide notice to customers about its privacy policies and practices;

(2) Describes the conditions under which a financial institution may disclose nonpublic personal information about consumers to nonaffiliated third parties; and

(3) Provides a method for consumers to prevent a financial institution from disclosing that information to most nonaffiliated third parties by "opting out" of that disclosure, subject to the exceptions in §§ 332.13, 332.14, and 332.15.

(b) *Scope.* (1) This part applies only to nonpublic personal information about individuals who obtain financial products or services primarily for personal, family, or household purposes from the institutions listed below. This part does not apply to information about companies or about individuals who obtain financial products or services for business, commercial, or agricultural purposes. This part applies to the United States offices of entities for which the Federal Deposit Insurance Corporation (FDIC) has primary federal supervisory authority. They are referred to in this part as "you." These are: banks insured by the FDIC (other than members of the Federal Reserve System), insured state branches of foreign banks, and certain subsidiaries of such entities.

(2) Nothing in this part modifies, limits, or supersedes the standards governing individually identifiable health information promulgated by the Secretary of Health and Human Services under the authority of sections 262 and 264 of the Health Insurance Portability and Accountability Act of 1996 (42 U.S.C. 1320d–1320d–8).

§ 332.2 Model privacy form and examples.

(a) *Model privacy form.* Use of the model privacy form in appendix A of this part, consistent with the instructions in appendix A, constitutes compliance with the notice content requirements of §§ 332.6 and 332.7 of this part, although use of the model privacy form is not required.

(b) *Examples.* The examples in this part are not exclusive. Compliance with an example, to the extent applicable, constitutes compliance with this part.

[74 FR, 62935, Dec. 1, 2009]

§ 332.3 Definitions.

As used in this part, unless the context requires otherwise:

(a) *Affiliate* means any company that controls, is controlled by, or is under common control with another company.

(b)(1) *Clear and conspicuous* means that a notice is reasonably understandable and designed to call attention to the nature and significance of the information in the notice.

(2) *Examples*—(i) *Reasonably understandable.* You make your notice reasonably understandable if you:

(A) Present the information in the notice in clear, concise sentences, paragraphs, and sections;

(B) Use short explanatory sentences or bullet lists whenever possible;

(C) Use definite, concrete, everyday words and active voice whenever possible;

(D) Avoid multiple negatives;

(E) Avoid legal and highly technical business terminology whenever possible; and

§ 332.3

(F) Avoid explanations that are imprecise and readily subject to different interpretations.

(ii) *Designed to call attention.* You design your notice to call attention to the nature and significance of the information in it if you:

(A) Use a plain-language heading to call attention to the notice;

(B) Use a typeface and type size that are easy to read;

(C) Provide wide margins and ample line spacing;

(D) Use boldface or italics for key words; and

(E) In a form that combines your notice with other information, use distinctive type size, style, and graphic devices, such as shading or sidebars, when you combine your notice with other information.

(iii) *Notices on web sites.* If you provide a notice on a web page, you design your notice to call attention to the nature and significance of the information in it if you use text or visual cues to encourage scrolling down the page if necessary to view the entire notice and ensure that other elements on the web site (such as text, graphics, hyperlinks, or sound) do not distract attention from the notice, and you either:

(A) Place the notice on a screen that consumers frequently access, such as a page on which transactions are conducted; or

(B) Place a link on a screen that consumers frequently access, such as a page on which transactions are conducted, that connects directly to the notice and is labeled appropriately to convey the importance, nature, and relevance of the notice.

(c) *Collect* means to obtain information that you organize or can retrieve by the name of an individual or by identifying number, symbol, or other identifying particular assigned to the individual, irrespective of the source of the underlying information.

(d) *Company* means any corporation, limited liability company, business trust, general or limited partnership, association, or similar organization.

(e)(1) *Consumer* means an individual who obtains or has obtained a financial product or service from you that is to be used primarily for personal, family, or household purposes, or that individual's legal representative.

(2) *Examples*—(i) An individual who applies to you for credit for personal, family, or household purposes is a consumer of a financial service, regardless of whether the credit is extended.

(ii) An individual who provides nonpublic personal information to you in order to obtain a determination about whether he or she may qualify for a loan to be used primarily for personal, family, or household purposes is a consumer of a financial service, regardless of whether the loan is extended.

(iii) An individual who provides nonpublic personal information to you in connection with obtaining or seeking to obtain financial, investment, or economic advisory services is a consumer regardless of whether you establish a continuing advisory relationship.

(iv) If you hold ownership or servicing rights to an individual's loan that is used primarily for personal, family, or household purposes, the individual is your consumer, even if you hold those rights in conjunction with one or more other institutions. (The individual is also a consumer with respect to the other financial institutions involved.) An individual who has a loan in which you have ownership or servicing rights is your consumer, even if you, or another institution with those rights, hire an agent to collect on the loan.

(v) An individual who is a consumer of another financial institution is not your consumer solely because you act as agent for, or provide processing or other services to, that financial institution.

(vi) An individual is not your consumer solely because he or she has designated you as trustee for a trust.

(vii) An individual is not your consumer solely because he or she is a beneficiary of a trust for which you are a trustee.

(viii) An individual is not your consumer solely because he or she is a participant or a beneficiary of an employee benefit plan that you sponsor or for which you act as a trustee or fiduciary.

(f) *Consumer reporting agency* has the same meaning as in section 603(f) of the Fair Credit Reporting Act (15 U.S.C. 1681a(f)).

Federal Deposit Insurance Corporation

§ 332.3

(g) *Control* of a company means:

(1) Ownership, control, or power to vote 25 percent or more of the outstanding shares of any class of voting security of the company, directly or indirectly, or acting through one or more other persons;

(2) Control in any manner over the election of a majority of the directors, trustees, or general partners (or individuals exercising similar functions) of the company; or

(3) The power to exercise, directly or indirectly, a controlling influence over the management or policies of the company, as the FDIC determines.

(h) *Customer* means a consumer who has a customer relationship with you.

(i)(1) *Customer relationship* means a continuing relationship between a consumer and you under which you provide one or more financial products or services to the consumer that are to be used primarily for personal, family, or household purposes.

(2) *Examples*—(i) *Continuing relationship.* A consumer has a continuing relationship with you if the consumer:

(A) Has a deposit or investment account with you;

(B) Obtains a loan from you;

(C) Has a loan for which you own the servicing rights;

(D) Purchases an insurance product from you;

(E) Holds an investment product through you, such as when you act as a custodian for securities or for assets in an Individual Retirement Arrangement;

(F) Enters into an agreement or understanding with you whereby you undertake to arrange or broker a home mortgage loan for the consumer;

(G) Enters into a lease of personal property with you; or

(H) Obtains financial, investment, or economic advisory services from you for a fee.

(ii) *No continuing relationship.* A consumer does not, however, have a continuing relationship with you if:

(A) The consumer obtains a financial product or service only in isolated transactions, such as using your ATM to withdraw cash from an account at another financial institution or purchasing a cashier's check or money order;

(B) You sell the consumer's loan and do not retain the rights to service that loan; or

(C) You sell the consumer airline tickets, travel insurance, or traveler's checks in isolated transactions.

(j) *Federal functional regulator* means:

(1) The Board of Governors of the Federal Reserve System;

(2) The Office of the Comptroller of the Currency;

(3) The Board of Directors of the Federal Deposit Insurance Corporation;

(4) The Director of the Office of Thrift Supervision;

(5) The National Credit Union Administration Board; and

(6) The Securities and Exchange Commission.

(k)(1) *Financial institution* means any institution the business of which is engaging in activities that are financial in nature or incidental to such financial activities as described in section 4(k) of the Bank Holding Company Act of 1956 (12 U.S.C. 1843(k)).

(2) *Financial institution* does not include:

(i) Any person or entity with respect to any financial activity that is subject to the jurisdiction of the Commodity Futures Trading Commission under the Commodity Exchange Act (7 U.S.C. 1 *et seq.*);

(ii) The Federal Agricultural Mortgage Corporation or any entity chartered and operating under the Farm Credit Act of 1971 (12 U.S.C. 2001 *et seq.*); or

(iii) Institutions chartered by Congress specifically to engage in securitizations, secondary market sales (including sales of servicing rights), or similar transactions related to a transaction of a consumer, as long as such institutions do not sell or transfer nonpublic personal information to a nonaffiliated third party.

(l)(1) *Financial product or service* means any product or service that a financial holding company could offer by engaging in an activity that is financial in nature or incidental to such a financial activity under section 4(k) of the Bank Holding Company Act of 1956 (12 U.S.C. 1843(k)).

(2) *Financial service* includes your evaluation or brokerage of information that you collect in connection with a

§ 332.3

request or an application from a consumer for a financial product or service.

(m)(1) *Nonaffiliated third party* means any person except:

(i) Your affiliate; or

(ii) A person employed jointly by you and any company that is not your affiliate (but *nonaffiliated third party* includes the other company that jointly employs the person).

(2) *Nonaffiliated third party* includes any company that is an affiliate solely by virtue of your or your affiliate's direct or indirect ownership or control of the company in conducting merchant banking or investment banking activities of the type described in section 4(k)(4)(H) or insurance company investment activities of the type described in section 4(k)(4)(I) of the Bank Holding Company Act of 1956 (12 U.S.C. 1843(k)(4)(H) and (I)).

(n)(1) *Nonpublic personal information* means:

(i) Personally identifiable financial information; and

(ii) Any list, description, or other grouping of consumers (and publicly available information pertaining to them) that is derived using any personally identifiable financial information that is not publicly available.

(2) *Nonpublic personal information* does not include:

(i) Publicly available information, except as included on a list described in paragraph (n)(1)(ii) of this section; or

(ii) Any list, description, or other grouping of consumers (and publicly available information pertaining to them) that is derived without using any personally identifiable financial information that is not publicly available.

(3) *Examples of lists*—(i) Nonpublic personal information includes any list of individuals' names and street addresses that is derived in whole or in part using personally identifiable financial information that is not publicly available, such as account numbers.

(ii) Nonpublic personal information does not include any list of individuals' names and addresses that contains only publicly available information, is not derived in whole or in part using personally identifiable financial infor-

mation that is not publicly available, and is not disclosed in a manner that indicates that any of the individuals on the list is a consumer of a financial institution.

(o)(1) *Personally identifiable financial information* means any information:

(i) A consumer provides to you to obtain a financial product or service from you;

(ii) About a consumer resulting from any transaction involving a financial product or service between you and a consumer; or

(iii) You otherwise obtain about a consumer in connection with providing a financial product or service to that consumer.

(2) *Examples*—(i) *Information included.* Personally identifiable financial information includes:

(A) Information a consumer provides to you on an application to obtain a loan, credit card, or other financial product or service;

(B) Account balance information, payment history, overdraft history, and credit or debit card purchase information;

(C) The fact that an individual is or has been one of your customers or has obtained a financial product or service from you;

(D) Any information about your consumer if it is disclosed in a manner that indicates that the individual is or has been your consumer;

(E) Any information that a consumer provides to you or that you or your agent otherwise obtain in connection with collecting on a loan or servicing a loan;

(F) Any information you collect through an Internet "cookie" (an information collecting device from a web server); and

(G) Information from a consumer report.

(ii) *Information not included.* Personally identifiable financial information does not include:

(A) A list of names and addresses of customers of an entity that is not a financial institution; and

(B) Information that does not identify a consumer, such as aggregate information or blind data that does not contain personal identifiers such as account numbers, names, or addresses.

Federal Deposit Insurance Corporation § 332.4

(p)(1) *Publicly available information* means any information that you have a reasonable basis to believe is lawfully made available to the general public from:

(i) Federal, State, or local government records;

(ii) Widely distributed media; or

(iii) Disclosures to the general public that are required to be made by Federal, State, or local law.

(2) *Reasonable basis.* You have a reasonable basis to believe that information is lawfully made available to the general public if you have taken steps to determine:

(i) That the information is of the type that is available to the general public; and

(ii) Whether an individual can direct that the information not be made available to the general public and, if so, that your consumer has not done so.

(3) *Examples*—(i) *Government records.* Publicly available information in government records includes information in government real estate records and security interest filings.

(ii) *Widely distributed media.* Publicly available information from widely distributed media includes information from a telephone book, a television or radio program, a newspaper, or a web site that is available to the general public on an unrestricted basis. A web site is not restricted merely because an Internet service provider or a site operator requires a fee or a password, so long as access is available to the general public.

(iii) *Reasonable basis.* (A) You have a reasonable basis to believe that mortgage information is lawfully made available to the general public if you have determined that the information is of the type included on the public record in the jurisdiction where the mortgage would be recorded.

(B) You have a reasonable basis to believe that an individual's telephone number is lawfully made available to the general public if you have located the telephone number in the telephone book or the consumer has informed you that the telephone number is not unlisted.

(q) *You* means:

(1) A bank insured by the FDIC (other than a member of the Federal Reserve System);

(2) An insured state branch of a foreign bank; and

(3) A subsidiary of either such entity except:

(i) A broker or dealer that is registered under the Securities and Exchange Act of 1934 (15 U.S.C. 78a et seq.);

(ii) A registered investment adviser, properly registered by or on behalf of either the Securities Exchange Commission or any State, with respect to its investment advisory activities and its activities incidental to those investment advisory activities;

(iii) An investment company that is registered under the Investment Company Act of 1940 (15 U.S.C. 80a–1 et seq.); or

(iv) An insurance company, with respect to its insurance activities and its activities incidental to those insurance activities, that is subject to supervision by a State insurance regulator.

Subpart A—Privacy and Opt Out Notices

§ 332.4 Initial privacy notice to consumers required.

(a) *Initial notice requirement.* You must provide a clear and conspicuous notice that accurately reflects your privacy policies and practices to:

(1) *Customer.* An individual who becomes your customer, not later than when you establish a customer relationship, except as provided in paragraph (e) of this section; and

(2) *Consumer.* A consumer, before you disclose any nonpublic personal information about the consumer to any nonaffiliated third party, if you make such a disclosure other than as authorized by §§ 332.14 and 332.15.

(b) *When initial notice to a consumer is not required.* You are not required to provide an initial notice to a consumer under paragraph (a) of this section if:

(1) You do not disclose any nonpublic personal information about the consumer to any nonaffiliated third party, other than as authorized by §§ 332.14 and 332.15; and

(2) You do not have a customer relationship with the consumer.

§ 332.4

(c) *When you establish a customer relationship*—(1) *General rule.* You establish a customer relationship when you and the consumer enter into a continuing relationship.

(2) *Special rule for loans.* You establish a customer relationship with a consumer when you originate a loan to the consumer for personal, family, or household purposes. If you subsequently transfer the servicing rights to that loan to another financial institution, the customer relationship transfers with the servicing rights.

(3)(i) *Examples of establishing customer relationship.* You establish a customer relationship when the consumer:

(A) Opens a credit card account with you;

(B) Executes the contract to open a deposit account with you, obtains credit from you, or purchases insurance from you;

(C) Agrees to obtain financial, economic, or investment advisory services from you for a fee; or

(D) Becomes your client for the purpose of your providing credit counseling or tax preparation services.

(ii) *Examples of loan rule.* You establish a customer relationship with a consumer who obtains a loan for personal, family, or household purposes when you:

(A) Originate the loan to the consumer; or

(B) Purchase the servicing rights to the consumer's loan.

(d) *Existing customers.* When an existing customer obtains a new financial product or service from you that is to be used primarily for personal, family, or household purposes, you satisfy the initial notice requirements of paragraph (a) of this section as follows:

(1) You may provide a revised privacy notice, under § 332.8, that covers the customer's new financial product or service; or

(2) If the initial, revised, or annual notice that you most recently provided to that customer was accurate with respect to the new financial product or service, you do not need to provide a new privacy notice under paragraph (a) of this section.

(e) *Exceptions to allow subsequent delivery of notice.* (1) You may provide the initial notice required by paragraph (a)(1) of this section within a reasonable time after you establish a customer relationship if:

(i) Establishing the customer relationship is not at the customer's election; or

(ii) Providing notice not later than when you establish a customer relationship would substantially delay the customer's transaction and the customer agrees to receive the notice at a later time.

(2) *Examples of exceptions*—(i) *Not at customer's election.* Establishing a customer relationship is not at the customer's election if you acquire a customer's deposit liability or the servicing rights to a customer's loan from another financial institution and the customer does not have a choice about your acquisition.

(ii) *Substantial delay of customer's transaction.* Providing notice not later than when you establish a customer relationship would substantially delay the customer's transaction when:

(A) You and the individual agree over the telephone to enter into a customer relationship involving prompt delivery of the financial product or service; or

(B) You establish a customer relationship with an individual under a program authorized by Title IV of the Higher Education Act of 1965 (20 U.S.C. 1070 *et seq.*) or similar student loan programs where loan proceeds are disbursed promptly without prior communication between you and the customer.

(iii) *No substantial delay of customer's transaction.* Providing notice not later than when you establish a customer relationship would not substantially delay the customer's transaction when the relationship is initiated in person at your office or through other means by which the customer may view the notice, such as on a web site.

(f) *Delivery.* When you are required to deliver an initial privacy notice by this section, you must deliver it according to § 332.9. If you use a short-form initial notice for non-customers according to § 332.6(d), you may deliver your privacy notice according to § 332.6(d)(3).

§ 332.5 Annual privacy notice to customers required.

(a)(1) *General rule.* You must provide a clear and conspicuous notice to customers that accurately reflects your privacy policies and practices not less than annually during the continuation of the customer relationship. *Annually* means at least once in any period of 12 consecutive months during which that relationship exists. You may define the 12-consecutive-month period, but you must apply it to the customer on a consistent basis.

(2) *Example.* You provide a notice annually if you define the 12-consecutive-month period as a calendar year and provide the annual notice to the customer once in each calendar year following the calendar year in which you provided the initial notice. For example, if a customer opens an account on any day of year 1, you must provide an annual notice to that customer by December 31 of year 2.

(b)(1) *Termination of customer relationship.* You are not required to provide an annual notice to a former customer.

(2) *Examples.* Your customer becomes a former customer when:

(i) In the case of a deposit account, the account is inactive under your policies;

(ii) In the case of a closed-end loan, the customer pays the loan in full, you charge off the loan, or you sell the loan without retaining servicing rights;

(iii) In the case of a credit card relationship or other open-end credit relationship, you no longer provide any statements or notices to the customer concerning that relationship or you sell the credit card receivables without retaining servicing rights; or

(iv) You have not communicated with the customer about the relationship for a period of 12 consecutive months, other than to provide annual privacy notices or promotional material.

(c) *Special rule for loans.* If you do not have a customer relationship with a consumer under the special rule for loans in § 332.4(c)(2), then you need not provide an annual notice to that consumer under this section.

(d) *Delivery.* When you are required to deliver an annual privacy notice by this section, you must deliver it according to § 332.9.

§ 332.6 Information to be included in privacy notices.

(a) *General rule.* The initial, annual and revised privacy notices that you provide under §§ 332.4, 332.5, and 332.8 must include each of the following items of information, in addition to any other information you wish to provide, that applies to you and to the consumers to whom you send your privacy notice:

(1) The categories of nonpublic personal information that you collect;

(2) The categories of nonpublic personal information that you disclose;

(3) The categories of affiliates and nonaffiliated third parties to whom you disclose nonpublic personal information, other than those parties to whom you disclose information under §§ 332.14 and 332.15;

(4) The categories of nonpublic personal information about your former customers that you disclose and the categories of affiliates and nonaffiliated third parties to whom you disclose nonpublic personal information about your former customers, other than those parties to whom you disclose information under §§ 332.14 and 332.15;

(5) If you disclose nonpublic personal information to a nonaffiliated third party under § 332.13 (and no other exception in § 332.14 or 332.15 applies to that disclosure), a separate statement of the categories of information you disclose and the categories of third parties with whom you have contracted;

(6) An explanation of the consumer's right under § 332.10(a) to opt out of the disclosure of nonpublic personal information to nonaffiliated third parties, including the method(s) by which the consumer may exercise that right at that time;

(7) Any disclosures that you make under section 603(d)(2)(A)(iii) of the Fair Credit Reporting Act (15 U.S.C. 1681a(d)(2)(A)(iii)) (that is, notices regarding the ability to opt out of disclosures of information among affiliates);

(8) Your policies and practices with respect to protecting the confidentiality and security of nonpublic personal information; and

(9) Any disclosure that you make under paragraph (b) of this section.

§ 332.6

(b) *Description of nonaffiliated third parties subject to exceptions.* If you disclose nonpublic personal information to third parties as authorized under §§ 332.14 and 332.15, you are not required to list those exceptions in the initial or annual privacy notices required by §§ 332.4 and 332.5. When describing the categories with respect to those parties, it is sufficient to state that you make disclosures to other nonaffiliated companies:

(1) For your everyday business purposes, such as [*include all that apply*] to process transactions, maintain account(s), respond to court orders and legal investigations, or report to credit bureaus; or

(2) As permitted by law.

(c) *Examples*—(1) *Categories of nonpublic personal information that you collect.* You satisfy the requirement to categorize the nonpublic personal information that you collect if you list the following categories, as applicable:

(i) Information from the consumer;

(ii) Information about the consumer's transactions with you or your affiliates;

(iii) Information about the consumer's transactions with nonaffiliated third parties; and

(iv) Information from a consumer reporting agency.

(2) *Categories of nonpublic personal information you disclose*—(i) You satisfy the requirement to categorize the nonpublic personal information that you disclose if you list the categories described in paragraph (c)(1) of this section, as applicable, and a few examples to illustrate the types of information in each category.

(ii) If you reserve the right to disclose all of the nonpublic personal information about consumers that you collect, you may simply state that fact without describing the categories or examples of the nonpublic personal information you disclose.

(3) *Categories of affiliates and nonaffiliated third parties to whom you disclose.* You satisfy the requirement to categorize the affiliates and nonaffiliated third parties to whom you disclose nonpublic personal information if you list the following categories, as applicable, and a few examples to illustrate the types of third parties in each category.

(i) Financial service providers;

(ii) Non-financial companies; and

(iii) Others.

(4) *Disclosures under exception for service providers and joint marketers.* If you disclose nonpublic personal information under the exception in § 332.13 to a nonaffiliated third party to market products or services that you offer alone or jointly with another financial institution, you satisfy the disclosure requirement of paragraph (a)(5) of this section if you:

(i) List the categories of nonpublic personal information you disclose, using the same categories and examples you used to meet the requirements of paragraph (a)(2) of this section, as applicable; and

(ii) State whether the third party is:

(A) A service provider that performs marketing services on your behalf or on behalf of you and another financial institution; or

(B) A financial institution with whom you have a joint marketing agreement.

(5) *Simplified notices.* If you do not disclose, and do not wish to reserve the right to disclose, nonpublic personal information about customers or former customers to affiliates or nonaffiliated third parties except as authorized under §§ 332.14 and 332.15, you may simply state that fact, in addition to the information you must provide under paragraphs (a)(1), (a)(8), (a)(9), and (b) of this section.

(6) *Confidentiality and security.* You describe your policies and practices with respect to protecting the confidentiality and security of nonpublic personal information if you do both of the following:

(i) Describe in general terms who is authorized to have access to the information; and

(ii) State whether you have security practices and procedures in place to ensure the confidentiality of the information in accordance with your policy. You are not required to describe technical information about the safeguards you use.

(d) *Short-form initial notice with opt out notice for non-customers*—(1) You

Federal Deposit Insurance Corporation §332.7

may satisfy the initial notice requirements in §§ 332.4(a)(2), 332.7(b), and 332.7(c) for a consumer who is not a customer by providing a short-form initial notice at the same time as you deliver an opt out notice as required in § 332.7.

(2) A short-form initial notice must:

(i) Be clear and conspicuous;

(ii) State that your privacy notice is available upon request; and

(iii) Explain a reasonable means by which the consumer may obtain that notice.

(3) You must deliver your short-form initial notice according to § 332.9. You are not required to deliver your privacy notice with your short-form initial notice. You instead may simply provide the consumer a reasonable means to obtain your privacy notice. If a consumer who receives your short-form notice requests your privacy notice, you must deliver your privacy notice according to § 332.9.

(4) *Examples of obtaining privacy notice.* You provide a reasonable means by which a consumer may obtain a copy of your privacy notice if you:

(i) Provide a toll-free telephone number that the consumer may call to request the notice; or

(ii) For a consumer who conducts business in person at your office, maintain copies of the notice on hand that you provide to the consumer immediately upon request.

(e) *Future disclosures.* Your notice may include:

(1) Categories of nonpublic personal information that you reserve the right to disclose in the future, but do not currently disclose; and

(2) Categories of affiliates or nonaffiliated third parties to whom you reserve the right in the future to disclose, but to whom you do not currently disclose, nonpublic personal information.

(f) *Model privacy form.* Pursuant to § 332.2(a) of this part, a model privacy form that meets the notice content requirements of this section is included in appendix A of this part.

[65 FR 35216, June 1, 2000, as amended at 74 FR 62935, Dec. 1, 2009]

§ 332.7 Form of opt out notice to consumers; opt out methods.

(a) (1) *Form of opt out notice.* If you are required to provide an opt out notice under § 332.10(a), you must provide a clear and conspicuous notice to each of your consumers that accurately explains the right to opt out under that section. The notice must state:

(i) That you disclose or reserve the right to disclose nonpublic personal information about your consumer to a nonaffiliated third party;

(ii) That the consumer has the right to opt out of that disclosure; and

(iii) A reasonable means by which the consumer may exercise the opt out right.

(2) *Examples*—(i) *Adequate opt out notice.* You provide adequate notice that the consumer can opt out of the disclosure of nonpublic personal information to a nonaffiliated third party if you:

(A) Identify all of the categories of nonpublic personal information that you disclose or reserve the right to disclose, and all of the categories of nonaffiliated third parties to which you disclose the information, as described in § 332.6(a)(2) and (3), and state that the consumer can opt out of the disclosure of that information; and

(B) Identify the financial products or services that the consumer obtains from you, either singly or jointly, to which the opt out direction would apply.

(ii) *Reasonable opt out means.* You provide a reasonable means to exercise an opt out right if you:

(A) Designate check-off boxes in a prominent position on the relevant forms with the opt out notice;

(B) Include a reply form together with the opt out notice;

(C) Provide an electronic means to opt out, such as a form that can be sent via electronic mail or a process at your web site, if the consumer agrees to the electronic delivery of information; or

(D) Provide a toll-free telephone number that consumers may call to opt out.

(iii) *Unreasonable opt out means.* You *do not* provide a reasonable means of opting out if:

(A) The only means of opting out is for the consumer to write his or her

367

§ 332.7

own letter to exercise that opt out right; or

(B) The only means of opting out as described in any notice subsequent to the initial notice is to use a check-off box that you provide with the initial notice but did not include with the subsequent notice.

(iv) *Specific opt out means.* You may require each consumer to opt out through a specific means, as long as that means is reasonable for that consumer.

(b) *Same form as initial notice permitted.* You may provide the opt out notice together with or on the same written or electronic form as the initial notice you provide in accordance with § 332.4.

(c) *Initial notice required when opt out notice delivered subsequent to initial notice.* If you provide the opt out notice later than required for the initial notice in accordance with § 332.4, you must also include a copy of the initial notice with the opt out notice in writing or, if the consumer agrees, electronically.

(d) *Joint relationships*—(1) If two or more consumers jointly obtain a financial product or service from you, you may provide a single opt out notice. Your opt out notice must explain how you will treat an opt out direction by a joint consumer (as explained in paragraph (d)(5) of this section).

(2) Any of the joint consumers may exercise the right to opt out. You may either:

(i) Treat an opt out direction by a joint consumer as applying to all of the associated joint consumers; or

(ii) Permit each joint consumer to opt out separately.

(3) If you permit each joint consumer to opt out separately, you must permit one of the joint consumers to opt out on behalf of all of the joint consumers.

(4) You may not require *all* joint consumers to opt out before you implement *any* opt out direction.

(5) *Example.* If John and Mary have a joint checking account with you and arrange for you to send statements to John's address, you may do any of the following, but you must explain in your opt out notice which opt out policy you will follow:

(i) Send a single opt out notice to John's address, but you must accept an opt out direction from either John or Mary.

(ii) Treat an opt out direction by either John or Mary as applying to the entire account. If you do so, and John opts out, you may not require Mary to opt out as well before implementing John's opt out direction.

(iii) Permit John and Mary to make different opt out directions. If you do so:

(A) You must permit John and Mary to opt out for each other;

(B) If both opt out, you must permit both to notify you in a single response (such as on a form or through a telephone call); and

(C) If John opts out and Mary does not, you may only disclose nonpublic personal information about Mary, but not about John and not about John and Mary jointly.

(e) *Time to comply with opt out.* You must comply with a consumer's opt out direction as soon as reasonably practicable after you receive it.

(f) *Continuing right to opt out.* A consumer may exercise the right to opt out at any time.

(g) *Duration of consumer's opt out direction*—(1) A consumer's direction to opt out under this section is effective until the consumer revokes it in writing or, if the consumer agrees, electronically.

(2) When a customer relationship terminates, the customer's opt out direction continues to apply to the nonpublic personal information that you collected during or related to that relationship. If the individual subsequently establishes a new customer relationship with you, the opt out direction that applied to the former relationship does not apply to the new relationship.

(h) *Delivery.* When you are required to deliver an opt out notice by this section, you must deliver it according to § 332.9.

(i) *Model privacy form.* Pursuant to § 332.2(a) of this part, a model privacy form that meets the notice content requirements of this section is included in Appendix A of this part.

[65 FR 35216, June 1, 2000, as amended at 74 FR 62936, Dec. 1, 2009]

Federal Deposit Insurance Corporation

§ 332.8 Revised privacy notices.

(a) *General rule.* Except as otherwise authorized in this part, you must not, directly or through any affiliate, disclose any nonpublic personal information about a consumer to a nonaffiliated third party other than as described in the initial notice that you provided to that consumer under § 332.4, unless:

(1) You have provided to the consumer a clear and conspicuous revised notice that accurately describes your policies and practices;

(2) You have provided to the consumer a new opt out notice;

(3) You have given the consumer a reasonable opportunity, before you disclose the information to the nonaffiliated third party, to opt out of the disclosure; and

(4) The consumer does not opt out.

(b) *Examples*—(1) Except as otherwise permitted by §§ 332.13, 332.14, and 332.15, you must provide a revised notice before you:

(i) Disclose a new category of nonpublic personal information to any nonaffiliated third party;

(ii) Disclose nonpublic personal information to a new category of nonaffiliated third party; or

(iii) Disclose nonpublic personal information about a former customer to a nonaffiliated third party, if that former customer has not had the opportunity to exercise an opt out right regarding that disclosure.

(2) A revised notice is not required if you disclose nonpublic personal information to a new nonaffiliated third party that you adequately described in your prior notice.

(c) *Delivery.* When you are required to deliver a revised privacy notice by this section, you must deliver it according to § 332.9.

§ 332.9 Delivering privacy and opt out notices.

(a) *How to provide notices.* You must provide any privacy notices and opt out notices, including short-form initial notices, that this part requires so that each consumer can reasonably be expected to receive actual notice in writing or, if the consumer agrees, electronically.

(b) (1) *Examples of reasonable expectation of actual notice.* You may reasonably expect that a consumer will receive actual notice if you:

(i) Hand-deliver a printed copy of the notice to the consumer;

(ii) Mail a printed copy of the notice to the last known address of the consumer;

(iii) For the consumer who conducts transactions electronically, post the notice on the electronic site and require the consumer to acknowledge receipt of the notice as a necessary step to obtaining a particular financial product or service; or

(iv) For an isolated transaction with the consumer, such as an ATM transaction, post the notice on the ATM screen and require the consumer to acknowledge receipt of the notice as a necessary step to obtaining the particular financial product or service.

(2) *Examples of unreasonable expectation of actual notice.* You may *not*, however, reasonably expect that a consumer will receive actual notice of your privacy policies and practices if you:

(i) Only post a sign in your branch or office or generally publish advertisements of your privacy policies and practices; or

(ii) Send the notice via electronic mail to a consumer who does not obtain a financial product or service from you electronically.

(c) *Annual notices only.* You may reasonably expect that a customer will receive actual notice of your annual privacy notice if:

(1) The customer uses your web site to access financial products and services electronically and agrees to receive notices at the web site, and you post your current privacy notice continuously in a clear and conspicuous manner on the web site; or

(2) The customer has requested that you refrain from sending any information regarding the customer relationship, and your current privacy notice remains available to the customer upon request.

(d) *Oral description of notice insufficient.* You may not provide any notice required by this part solely by orally explaining the notice, either in person or over the telephone.

§ 332.10

(e) *Retention or accessibility of notices for customers*—(1) For customers only, you must provide the initial notice required by § 332.4(a)(1), the annual notice required by § 332.5(a), and the revised notice required by § 332.8 so that the customer can retain them or obtain them later in writing or, if the customer agrees, electronically.

(2) *Examples of retention or accessibility.* You provide a privacy notice to the customer so that the customer can retain it or obtain it later if you:

(i) Hand-deliver a printed copy of the notice to the customer;

(ii) Mail a printed copy of the notice to the last known address of the customer; or

(iii) Make your current privacy notice available on a web site (or a link to another web site) for the customer who obtains a financial product or service electronically and agrees to receive the notice at the web site.

(f) *Joint notice with other financial institutions.* You may provide a joint notice from you and one or more of your affiliates or other financial institutions, as identified in the notice, as long as the notice is accurate with respect to you and the other institutions.

(g) *Joint relationships.* If two or more consumers jointly obtain a financial product or service from you, you may satisfy the initial, annual, and revised notice requirements of §§ 332.4(a), 332.5(a), and 332.8(a), respectively, by providing one notice to those consumers jointly.

Subpart B—Limits on Disclosures

§ 332.10 Limits on disclosure of nonpublic personal information to nonaffiliated third parties.

(a) (1) *Conditions for disclosure.* Except as otherwise authorized in this part, you may not, directly or through any affiliate, disclose any nonpublic personal information about a consumer to a nonaffiliated third party unless:

(i) You have provided to the consumer an initial notice as required under § 332.4;

(ii) You have provided to the consumer an opt out notice as required in § 332.7;

(iii) You have given the consumer a reasonable opportunity, before you disclose the information to the nonaffiliated third party, to opt out of the disclosure; and

(iv) The consumer does not opt out.

(2) *Opt out definition.* Opt out means a direction by the consumer that you not disclose nonpublic personal information about that consumer to a nonaffiliated third party, other than as permitted by §§ 332.13, 332.14, and 332.15.

(3) *Examples of reasonable opportunity to opt out.* You provide a consumer with a reasonable opportunity to opt out if:

(i) *By mail.* You mail the notices required in paragraph (a)(1) of this section to the consumer and allow the consumer to opt out by mailing a form, calling a toll-free telephone number, or any other reasonable means within 30 days from the date you mailed the notices.

(ii) *By electronic means.* A customer opens an on-line account with you and agrees to receive the notices required in paragraph (a)(1) of this section electronically, and you allow the customer to opt out by any reasonable means within 30 days after the date that the customer acknowledges receipt of the notices in conjunction with opening the account.

(iii) *Isolated transaction with consumer.* For an isolated transaction, such as the purchase of a cashier's check by a consumer, you provide the consumer with a reasonable opportunity to opt out if you provide the notices required in paragraph (a)(1) of this section at the time of the transaction and request that the consumer decide, as a necessary part of the transaction, whether to opt out before completing the transaction.

(b) *Application of opt out to all consumers and all nonpublic personal information*—(1) You must comply with this section, regardless of whether you and the consumer have established a customer relationship.

(2) Unless you comply with this section, you may not, directly or through any affiliate, disclose any nonpublic personal information about a consumer that you have collected, regardless of whether you collected it before or after receiving the direction to opt out from the consumer.

(c) *Partial opt out.* You may allow a consumer to select certain nonpublic

Federal Deposit Insurance Corporation § 332.11

personal information or certain nonaffiliated third parties with respect to which the consumer wishes to opt out.

§ 332.11 Limits on redisclosure and reuse of information.

(a)(1) *Information you receive under an exception.* If you receive nonpublic personal information from a nonaffiliated financial institution under an exception in § 332.14 or 332.15 of this part, your disclosure and use of that information is limited as follows:

(i) You may disclose the information to the affiliates of the financial institution from which you received the information;

(ii) You may disclose the information to your affiliates, but your affiliates may, in turn, disclose and use the information only to the extent that you may disclose and use the information; and

(iii) You may disclose and use the information pursuant to an exception in § 332.14 or 332.15 in the ordinary course of business to carry out the activity covered by the exception under which you received the information.

(2) *Example.* If you receive a customer list from a nonaffiliated financial institution in order to provide account processing services under the exception in § 332.14(a), you may disclose that information under any exception in § 332.14 or 332.15 in the ordinary course of business in order to provide those services. For example, you could disclose the information in response to a properly authorized subpoena or to your attorneys, accountants, and auditors. You could not disclose that information to a third party for marketing purposes or use that information for your own marketing purposes.

(b)(1) *Information you receive outside of an exception.* If you receive nonpublic personal information from a nonaffiliated financial institution other than under an exception in § 332.14 or 332.15 of this part, you may disclose the information only:

(i) To the affiliates of the financial institution from which you received the information;

(ii) To your affiliates, but your affiliates may, in turn, disclose the information only to the extent that you can disclose the information; and

(iii) To any other person, if the disclosure would be lawful if made directly to that person by the financial institution from which you received the information.

(2) *Example.* If you obtain a customer list from a nonaffiliated financial institution outside of the exceptions in § 332.14 and 332.15:

(i) You may use that list for your own purposes; and

(ii) You may disclose that list to another nonaffiliated third party only if the financial institution from which you purchased the list could have lawfully disclosed the list to that third party. That is, you may disclose the list in accordance with the privacy policy of the financial institution from which you received the list, as limited by the opt out direction of each consumer whose nonpublic personal information you intend to disclose, and you may disclose the list in accordance with an exception in § 332.14 or 332.15, such as to your attorneys or accountants.

(c) *Information you disclose under an exception.* If you disclose nonpublic personal information to a nonaffiliated third party under an exception in § 332.14 or 332.15 of this part, the third party may disclose and use that information only as follows:

(1) The third party may disclose the information to your affiliates;

(2) The third party may disclose the information to its affiliates, but its affiliates may, in turn, disclose and use the information only to the extent that the third party may disclose and use the information; and

(3) The third party may disclose and use the information pursuant to an exception in § 332.14 or 332.15 in the ordinary course of business to carry out the activity covered by the exception under which it received the information.

(d) *Information you disclose outside of an exception.* If you disclose nonpublic personal information to a nonaffiliated third party other than under an exception in § 332.14 or 332.15 of this part, the third party may disclose the information only:

(1) To your affiliates;

(2) To its affiliates, but its affiliates, in turn, may disclose the information

only to the extent the third party can disclose the information; and

(3) To any other person, if the disclosure would be lawful if you made it directly to that person.

§ 332.12 Limits on sharing account number information for marketing purposes.

(a) *General prohibition on disclosure of account numbers.* You must not, directly or through an affiliate, disclose, other than to a consumer reporting agency, an account number or similar form of access number or access code for a consumer's credit card account, deposit account, or transaction account to any nonaffiliated third party for use in telemarketing, direct mail marketing, or other marketing through electronic mail to the consumer.

(b) *Exceptions.* Paragraph (a) of this section does not apply if you disclose an account number or similar form of access number or access code:

(1) To your agent or service provider solely in order to perform marketing for your own products or services, as long as the agent or service provider is not authorized to directly initiate charges to the account; or

(2) To a participant in a private label credit card program or an affinity or similar program where the participants in the program are identified to the customer when the customer enters into the program.

(c) *Examples*—(1) *Account number.* An account number, or similar form of access number or access code, does not include a number or code in an encrypted form, as long as you do not provide the recipient with a means to decode the number or code.

(2) *Transaction account.* A transaction account is an account other than a deposit account or a credit card account. A transaction account does not include an account to which third parties cannot initiate charges.

Subpart C—Exceptions

§ 332.13 Exception to opt out requirements for service providers and joint marketing.

(a) *General rule.* (1) The opt out requirements in §§ 332.7 and 332.10 do not apply when you provide nonpublic personal information to a nonaffiliated third party to perform services for you or functions on your behalf, if you:

(i) Provide the initial notice in accordance with § 332.4; and

(ii) Enter into a contractual agreement with the third party that prohibits the third party from disclosing or using the information other than to carry out the purposes for which you disclosed the information, including use under an exception in § 332.14 or 332.15 in the ordinary course of business to carry out those purposes.

(2) *Example.* If you disclose nonpublic personal information under this section to a financial institution with which you perform joint marketing, your contractual agreement with that institution meets the requirements of paragraph (a)(1)(ii) of this section if it prohibits the institution from disclosing or using the nonpublic personal information except as necessary to carry out the joint marketing or under an exception in § 332.14 or 332.15 in the ordinary course of business to carry out that joint marketing.

(b) *Service may include joint marketing.* The services a nonaffiliated third party performs for you under paragraph (a) of this section may include marketing of your own products or services or marketing of financial products or services offered pursuant to joint agreements between you and one or more financial institutions.

(c) *Definition of joint agreement.* For purposes of this section, joint agreement means a written contract pursuant to which you and one or more financial institutions jointly offer, endorse, or sponsor a financial product or service.

§ 332.14 Exceptions to notice and opt out requirements for processing and servicing transactions.

(a) *Exceptions for processing transactions at consumer's request.* The requirements for initial notice in § 332.4(a)(2), for the opt out in §§ 332.7 and 332.10 and for service providers and joint marketing in § 332.13 do not apply if you disclose nonpublic personal information as necessary to effect, administer, or enforce a transaction that

Federal Deposit Insurance Corporation § 332.15

a consumer requests or authorizes, or in connection with:

(1) Servicing or processing a financial product or service that a consumer requests or authorizes;

(2) Maintaining or servicing the consumer's account with you, or with another entity as part of a private label credit card program or other extension of credit on behalf of such entity; or

(3) A proposed or actual securitization, secondary market sale (including sales of servicing rights), or similar transaction related to a transaction of the consumer.

(b) *Necessary to effect, administer, or enforce a transaction* means that the disclosure is:

(1) Required, or is one of the lawful or appropriate methods, to enforce your rights or the rights of other persons engaged in carrying out the financial transaction or providing the product or service; or

(2) Required, or is a usual, appropriate or acceptable method:

(i) To carry out the transaction or the product or service business of which the transaction is a part, and record, service, or maintain the consumer's account in the ordinary course of providing the financial service or financial product;

(ii) To administer or service benefits or claims relating to the transaction or the product or service business of which it is a part;

(iii) To provide a confirmation, statement, or other record of the transaction, or information on the status or value of the financial service or financial product to the consumer or the consumer's agent or broker;

(iv) To accrue or recognize incentives or bonuses associated with the transaction that are provided by you or any other party;

(v) To underwrite insurance at the consumer's request or for reinsurance purposes, or for any of the following purposes as they relate to a consumer's insurance: account administration, reporting, investigating, or preventing fraud or material misrepresentation, processing premium payments, processing insurance claims, administering insurance benefits (including utilization review activities), participating in research projects, or as otherwise required or specifically permitted by Federal or State law; or

(vi) In connection with:

(A) The authorization, settlement, billing, processing, clearing, transferring, reconciling or collection of amounts charged, debited, or otherwise paid using a debit, credit, or other payment card, check, or account number, or by other payment means;

(B) The transfer of receivables, accounts, or interests therein; or

(C) The audit of debit, credit, or other payment information.

§ 332.15 Other exceptions to notice and opt out requirements.

(a) *Exceptions to opt out requirements.* The requirements for initial notice in § 332.4(a)(2), for the opt out in §§ 332.7 and 332.10, and for service providers and joint marketing in § 332.13 do not apply when you disclose nonpublic personal information:

(1) With the consent or at the direction of the consumer, provided that the consumer has not revoked the consent or direction;

(2) (i) To protect the confidentiality or security of your records pertaining to the consumer, service, product, or transaction;

(ii) To protect against or prevent actual or potential fraud, unauthorized transactions, claims, or other liability;

(iii) For required institutional risk control or for resolving consumer disputes or inquiries;

(iv) To persons holding a legal or beneficial interest relating to the consumer; or

(v) To persons acting in a fiduciary or representative capacity on behalf of the consumer;

(3) To provide information to insurance rate advisory organizations, guaranty funds or agencies, agencies that are rating you, persons that are assessing your compliance with industry standards, and your attorneys, accountants, and auditors;

(4) To the extent specifically permitted or required under other provisions of law and in accordance with the Right to Financial Privacy Act of 1978 (12 U.S.C. 3401 *et seq.*), to law enforcement agencies (including a federal functional regulator, the Secretary of the Treasury, with respect to 31 U.S.C.

§ 332.16

Chapter 53, Subchapter II (Records and Reports on Monetary Instruments and Transactions) and 12 U.S.C. Chapter 21 (Financial Recordkeeping), a State insurance authority, with respect to any person domiciled in that insurance authority's State that is engaged in providing insurance, and the Federal Trade Commission), self-regulatory organizations, or for an investigation on a matter related to public safety;

(5) (i) To a consumer reporting agency in accordance with the Fair Credit Reporting Act (15 U.S.C. 1681 *et seq.*), or

(ii) From a consumer report reported by a consumer reporting agency;

(6) In connection with a proposed or actual sale, merger, transfer, or exchange of all or a portion of a business or operating unit if the disclosure of nonpublic personal information concerns solely consumers of such business or unit; or

(7) (i) To comply with Federal, State, or local laws, rules and other applicable legal requirements;

(ii) To comply with a properly authorized civil, criminal, or regulatory investigation, or subpoena or summons by Federal, State, or local authorities; or

(iii) To respond to judicial process or government regulatory authorities having jurisdiction over you for examination, compliance, or other purposes as authorized by law.

(b) *Examples of consent and revocation of consent.* (1) A consumer may specifically consent to your disclosure to a nonaffiliated insurance company of the fact that the consumer has applied to you for a mortgage so that the insurance company can offer homeowner's insurance to the consumer.

(2) A consumer may revoke consent by subsequently exercising the right to opt out of future disclosures of nonpublic personal information as permitted under § 332.7(f).

Subpart D—Relation to Other Laws; Effective Date

§ 332.16 Protection of Fair Credit Reporting Act.

Nothing in this part shall be construed to modify, limit, or supersede the operation of the Fair Credit Reporting Act (15 U.S.C. 1681 *et seq.*), and no inference shall be drawn on the basis of the provisions of this part regarding whether information is transaction or experience information under section 603 of that Act.

§ 332.17 Relation to State laws.

(a) *In general.* This part shall not be construed as superseding, altering, or affecting any statute, regulation, order, or interpretation in effect in any State, except to the extent that such State statute, regulation, order, or interpretation is inconsistent with the provisions of this part, and then only to the extent of the inconsistency.

(b) *Greater protection under State law.* For purposes of this section, a State statute, regulation, order, or interpretation is not inconsistent with the provisions of this part if the protection such statute, regulation, order, or interpretation affords any consumer is greater than the protection provided under this part, as determined by the Federal Trade Commission, after consultation with the FDIC, on the Federal Trade Commission's own motion, or upon the petition of any interested party.

§ 332.18 Effective date; transition rule.

(a) *Effective date.* This part is effective November 13, 2000. In order to provide sufficient time for you to establish policies and systems to comply with the requirements of this part, the FDIC has extended the time for compliance with this part until July 1, 2001.

(b)(1) *Notice requirement for consumers who are your customers on the compliance date.* By July 1, 2001, you must have provided an initial notice, as required by § 332.4, to consumers who are your customers on July 1, 2001.

(2) *Example.* You provide an initial notice to consumers who are your customers on July 1, 2001, if, by that date, you have established a system for providing an initial notice to all new customers and have mailed the initial notice to all your existing customers.

(c) *Two-year grandfathering of service agreements.* Until July 1, 2002, a contract that you have entered into with a nonaffiliated third party to perform services for you or functions on your behalf satisfies the provisions of § 332.13(a)(1)(ii) of this part, even if the

Federal Deposit Insurance Corporation

Pt. 332, App. A

contract does not include a requirement that the third party maintain the confidentiality of nonpublic personal information, as long as you entered into the contract on or before July 1, 2000.

APPENDIX A TO PART 332—MODEL PRIVACY FORM

A. The Model Privacy Form

Version 1: Model Form With No Opt-Out.

Rev. [insert date]

FACTS	WHAT DOES [NAME OF FINANCIAL INSTITUTION] DO WITH YOUR PERSONAL INFORMATION?
Why?	Financial companies choose how they share your personal information. Federal law gives consumers the right to limit some but not all sharing. Federal law also requires us to tell you how we collect, share, and protect your personal information. Please read this notice carefully to understand what we do.
What?	The types of personal information we collect and share depend on the product or service you have with us. This information can include: ■ Social Security number and [income] ■ [account balances] and [payment history] ■ [credit history] and [credit scores] When you are *no longer* our customer, we continue to share your information as described in this notice.
How?	All financial companies need to share customers' personal information to run their everyday business. In the section below, we list the reasons financial companies can share their customers' personal information; the reasons [name of financial institution] chooses to share; and whether you can limit this sharing.

Reasons we can share your personal information	Does [name] share?	Can you limit this sharing?
For our everyday business purposes— such as to process your transactions, maintain your account(s), respond to court orders and legal investigations, or report to credit bureaus		
For our marketing purposes— to offer our products and services to you		
For joint marketing with other financial companies		
For our affiliates' everyday business purposes— information about your transactions and experiences		
For our affiliates' everyday business purposes— information about your creditworthiness		
For our affiliates to market to you		
For nonaffiliates to market to you		

Questions?	Call [phone number] or go to [website]

Pt. 332, App. A 12 CFR Ch. III (1-1-12 Edition)

Page 2

Who we are	
Who is providing this notice?	[insert]

What we do	
How does [name of financial institution] protect my personal information?	To protect your personal information from unauthorized access and use, we use security measures that comply with federal law. These measures include computer safeguards and secured files and buildings. [insert]
How does [name of financial institution] collect my personal information?	We collect your personal information, for example, when you ■ [open an account] or [deposit money] ■ [pay your bills] or [apply for a loan] ■ [use your credit or debit card] [We also collect your personal information from other companies.] OR [We also collect your personal information from others, such as credit bureaus, affiliates, or other companies.]
Why can't I limit all sharing?	Federal law gives you the right to limit only ■ sharing for affiliates' everyday business purposes—information about your creditworthiness ■ affiliates from using your information to market to you ■ sharing for nonaffiliates to market to you State laws and individual companies may give you additional rights to limit sharing. [See below for more on your rights under state law.]

Definitions	
Affiliates	Companies related by common ownership or control. They can be financial and nonfinancial companies. ■ [affiliate information]
Nonaffiliates	Companies not related by common ownership or control. They can be financial and nonfinancial companies. ■ [nonaffiliate information]
Joint marketing	A formal agreement between nonaffiliated financial companies that together market financial products or services to you. ■ [joint marketing information]

Other important information	
[insert other important information]	

Federal Deposit Insurance Corporation   **Pt. 332, App. A**

Version 2: Model Form with Opt-Out by Telephone and/or Online.

Rev. [insert date]

FACTS	WHAT DOES [NAME OF FINANCIAL INSTITUTION] DO WITH YOUR PERSONAL INFORMATION?
Why?	Financial companies choose how they share your personal information. Federal law gives consumers the right to limit some but not all sharing. Federal law also requires us to tell you how we collect, share, and protect your personal information. Please read this notice carefully to understand what we do.
What?	The types of personal information we collect and share depend on the product or service you have with us. This information can include: ■ Social Security number and [income] ■ [account balances] and [payment history] ■ [credit history] and [credit scores]
How?	All financial companies need to share customers' personal information to run their everyday business. In the section below, we list the reasons financial companies can share their customers' personal information; the reasons [name of financial institution] chooses to share; and whether you can limit this sharing.

Reasons we can share your personal information	Does share?	Can you limit this sharing?
For our everyday business purposes— such as to process your transactions, maintain your account(s), respond to court orders and legal investigations, or report to credit bureaus		
For our marketing purposes— to offer our products and services to you		
For joint marketing with other financial companies		
For our affiliates' everyday business purposes— information about your transactions and experiences		
For our affiliates' everyday business purposes— information about your creditworthiness		
For our affiliates to market to you		
For nonaffiliates to market to you		

To limit our sharing	■ Call [phone number]—our menu will prompt you through your choice(s) or ■ Visit us online: [website] **Please note:** If you are a *new* customer, we can begin sharing your information [30] days from the date we sent this notice. When you are *no longer* our customer, we continue to share your information as described in this notice. However, you can contact us at any time to limit our sharing.
Questions?	Call [phone number] or go to [website]

Pt. 332, App. A **12 CFR Ch. III (1-1-12 Edition)**

Page 2

Who we are	
Who is providing this notice?	[insert]

What we do	
How does [name of financial institution] protect my personal information?	To protect your personal information from unauthorized access and use, we use security measures that comply with federal law. These measures include computer safeguards and secured files and buildings. [insert]
How does [name of financial institution] collect my personal information?	We collect your personal information, for example, when you ■ [open an account] or [deposit money] ■ [pay your bills] or [apply for a loan] ■ [use your credit or debit card] [We also collect your personal information from other companies.] OR [We also collect your personal information from others, such as credit bureaus, affiliates, or other companies.]
Why can't I limit all sharing?	Federal law gives you the right to limit only ■ sharing for affiliates' everyday business purposes—information about your creditworthiness ■ affiliates from using your information to market to you ■ sharing for nonaffiliates to market to you State laws and individual companies may give you additional rights to limit sharing. [See below for more on your rights under state law.]
What happens when I limit sharing for an account I hold jointly with someone else?	[Your choices will apply to everyone on your account.] OR [Your choices will apply to everyone on your account—unless you tell us otherwise.]

Definitions	
Affiliates	Companies related by common ownership or control. They can be financial and nonfinancial companies. ■ [affiliate information]
Nonaffiliates	Companies not related by common ownership or control. They can be financial and nonfinancial companies. ■ [nonaffiliate information]
Joint marketing	A formal agreement between nonaffiliated financial companies that together market financial products or services to you. ■ [joint marketing information]

Other important information	
[insert other important information]	

Federal Deposit Insurance Corporation — Pt. 332, App. A

Version 3: Model Form with Mail-In Opt-Out Form.

Rev. [insert date]

FACTS	WHAT DOES [NAME OF FINANCIAL INSTITUTION] DO WITH YOUR PERSONAL INFORMATION?
Why?	Financial companies choose how they share your personal information. Federal law gives consumers the right to limit some but not all sharing. Federal law also requires us to tell you how we collect, share, and protect your personal information. Please read this notice carefully to understand what we do.
What?	The types of personal information we collect and share depend on the product or service you have with us. This information can include: • Social Security number and [income] • [account balances] and [payment history] • [credit history] and [credit scores]
How?	All financial companies need to share customers' personal information to run their everyday business. In the section below, we list the reasons financial companies can share their customers' personal information; the reasons [name of financial institution] chooses to share; and whether you can limit this sharing.

Reasons we can share your personal information	Does [name of financial institution] share?	Can you limit this sharing?
For our everyday business purposes— such as to process your transactions, maintain your account(s), respond to court orders and legal investigations, or report to credit bureaus		
For our marketing purposes— to offer our products and services to you		
For joint marketing with other financial companies		
For our affiliates' everyday business purposes— information about your transactions and experiences		
For our affiliates' everyday business purposes— information about your creditworthiness		
For our affiliates to market to you		
For nonaffiliates to market to you		

To limit our sharing	• Call [phone number]—our menu will prompt you through your choice(s) • Visit us online: [website] or • Mail the form below **Please note:** If you are a *new* customer, we can begin sharing your information [30] days from the date we sent this notice. When you are *no longer* our customer, we continue to share your information as described in this notice. However, you can contact us at any time to limit our sharing.
Questions?	Call [phone number] or go to [website]

✂- -

Mail-in Form

Leave Blank OR [If you have a joint account, your choice(s) will apply to everyone on your account unless you mark below. ☐ Apply my choices only to me]	Mark any/all you want to limit: ☐ Do not share information about my creditworthiness with your affiliates for their everyday business purposes. ☐ Do not allow your affiliates to use my personal information to market to me. ☐ Do not share my personal information with nonaffiliates to market their products and services to me.	
	Name **Address** **City, State, Zip**	**Mail to:** [Name of Financial Institution] [Address1] [Address2] [City], [ST] [ZIP]

Page 2

Who we are

Who is providing this notice?	[insert]

What we do

How does [name of financial institution] protect my personal information?	To protect your personal information from unauthorized access and use, we use security measures that comply with federal law. These measures include computer safeguards and secured files and buildings. [insert]
How does [name of financial institution] collect my personal information?	We collect your personal information, for example, when you ■ [open an account] or [deposit money] ■ [pay your bills] or [apply for a loan] ■ [use your credit or debit card] [We also collect your personal information from other companies.] OR [We also collect your personal information from others, such as credit bureaus, affiliates, or other companies.]
Why can't I limit all sharing?	Federal law gives you the right to limit only ■ sharing for affiliates' everyday business purposes—information about your creditworthiness ■ affiliates from using your information to market to you ■ sharing for nonaffiliates to market to you State laws and individual companies may give you additional rights to limit sharing. [See below for more on your rights under state law.]
What happens when I limit sharing for an account I hold jointly with someone else?	[Your choices will apply to everyone on your account.] OR [Your choices will apply to everyone on your account—unless you tell us otherwise.]

Definitions

Affiliates	Companies related by common ownership or control. They can be financial and nonfinancial companies. ■ [affiliate information]
Nonaffiliates	Companies not related by common ownership or control. They can be financial and nonfinancial companies. ■ [nonaffiliate information]
Joint marketing	A formal agreement between nonaffiliated financial companies that together market financial products or services to you. ■ [joint marketing information]

Other important information

[insert other important information]

Federal Deposit Insurance Corporation   Pt. 332, App. A

Version 4. Optional Mail-in Form.

Mail-in Form	
Leave Blank OR [If you have a joint account, your choice(s) will apply to everyone on your account unless you mark below. ☐ Apply my choices only to me]	Mark any/all you want to limit: ☐ Do not share information about my creditworthiness with your affiliates for their everyday business purposes. ☐ Do not allow your affiliates to use my personal information to market to me. ☐ Do not share my personal information with nonaffiliates to market their products and services to me. Name Address City, State, Zip

Mail To: [Name of Financial Institution], [Address 1] [Address 2], [City], [ST] [ZIP]

B. General Instructions

1. How the Model Privacy Form Is Used

(a) The model form may be used, at the option of a financial institution, including a group of financial institutions that use a common privacy notice, to meet the content requirements of the privacy notice and opt-out notice set forth in §§ 332.6 and 332.7 of this part.

(b) The model form is a standardized form, including page layout, content, format, style, pagination, and shading. Institutions seeking to obtain the safe harbor through use of the model form may modify it only as described in these Instructions.

(c) Note that disclosure of certain information, such as assets, income, and information from a consumer reporting agency, may give rise to obligations under the Fair Credit Reporting Act [15 U.S.C. 1681–1681x] (FCRA), such as a requirement to permit a consumer to opt out of disclosures to affiliates or designation as a consumer reporting agency if disclosures are made to nonaffiliated third parties.

(d) The word "customer" may be replaced by the word "member" whenever it appears in the model form, as appropriate.

2. The Contents of the Model Privacy Form

The model form consists of two pages, which may be printed on both sides of a single sheet of paper, or may appear on two separate pages. Where an institution provides a long list of institutions at the end of the model form in accordance with Instruction C.3(a)(1), or provides additional information in accordance with Instruction C.3(c), and such list or additional information exceeds the space available on page two of the model form, such list or additional information may extend to a third page.

(a) *Page One.* The first page consists of the following components:

(1) Date last revised (upper right-hand corner).

(2) Title.

(3) Key frame (Why?, What?, How?).

(4) Disclosure table ("Reasons we can share your personal information").

(5) "To limit our sharing" box, as needed, for the financial institution's opt-out information.

(6) "Questions" box, for customer service contact information.

(7) Mail-in opt-out form, as needed.

(b) *Page Two.* The second page consists of the following components:

(1) Heading (Page 2).

(2) Frequently Asked Questions ("Who we are" and "What we do").

(3) Definitions.

(4) "Other important information" box, as needed.

3. The Format of the Model Privacy Form

The format of the model form may be modified only as described below.

(a) *Easily readable type font.* Financial institutions that use the model form must use an easily readable type font. While a number of factors together produce easily readable type font, institutions are required to use a minimum of 10-point font (unless otherwise expressly permitted in these Instructions) and sufficient spacing between the lines of type.

(b) *Logo.* A financial institution may include a corporate logo on any page of the notice, so long as it does not interfere with the readability of the model form or the space constraints of each page.

(c) *Page size and orientation.* Each page of the model form must be printed on paper in portrait orientation, the size of which must be sufficient to meet the layout and minimum font size requirements, with sufficient white space on the top, bottom, and sides of the content.

(d) *Color.* The model form must be printed on white or light color paper (such as cream) with black or other contrasting ink color. Spot color may be used to achieve visual interest, so long as the color contrast is distinctive and the color does not detract from the readability of the model form. Logos may also be printed in color.

(e) *Languages.* The model form may be translated into languages other than English.

C. Information Required in the Model Privacy Form

The information in the model form may be modified only as described below:

1. Name of the Institution or Group of Affiliated Institutions Providing the Notice

Insert the name of the financial institution providing the notice or a common identity of affiliated institutions jointly providing the notice on the form wherever [name of financial institution] appears.

2. Page One

(a) *Last revised date.* The financial institution must insert in the upper right-hand corner the date on which the notice was last revised. The information shall appear in minimum 8-point font as "rev. [month/year]" using either the name or number of the month, such as "rev. July 2009" or "rev. 7/09".

(b) *General instructions for the "What?" box.*

(1) The bulleted list identifies the types of personal information that the institution collects and shares. All institutions must use the term "Social Security number" in the first bullet.

(2) Institutions must use five (5) of the following terms to complete the bulleted list: income; account balances; payment history; transaction history; transaction or loss history; credit history; credit scores; assets; investment experience; credit-based insurance scores; insurance claim history; medical information; overdraft history; purchase history; account transactions; risk tolerance; medical-related debts; credit card or other debt; mortgage rates and payments; retirement assets; checking account information; employment information; wire transfer instructions.

(c) *General instructions for the disclosure table.* The left column lists reasons for sharing or using personal information. Each reason correlates to a specific legal provision described in paragraph C.2(d) of this Instruction. In the middle column, each institution must provide a "Yes" or "No" response that accurately reflects its information sharing policies and practices with respect to the reason listed on the left. In the right column, each institution must provide in each box one of the following three (3) responses, as applicable, that reflects whether a consumer can limit such sharing: "Yes" if it is required to or voluntarily provides an opt-out; "No" if it does not provide an opt-out; or "We don't share" if it answers "No" in the middle column. Only the sixth row ("For our affiliates to market to you") may be omitted at the option of the institution. *See* paragraph C.2(d)(6) of this Instruction.

(d) *Specific disclosures and corresponding legal provisions.*

(1) *For our everyday business purposes.* This reason incorporates sharing information under §§ 332.14 and 332.15 and with service providers pursuant to § 332.13 of this part other than the purposes specified in paragraphs C.2(d)(2) or C.2(d)(3) of these Instructions.

(2) *For our marketing purposes.* This reason incorporates sharing information with service providers by an institution for its own marketing pursuant to § 332.13 of this part. An institution that shares for this reason may choose to provide an opt-out.

(3) *For joint marketing with other financial companies.* This reason incorporates sharing information under joint marketing agreements between two or more financial institutions and with any service provider used in connection with such agreements pursuant to § 332.13 of this part. An institution that shares for this reason may choose to provide an opt-out.

(4) *For our affiliates' everyday business purposes—information about transactions and experiences.* This reason incorporates sharing information specified in sections 603(d)(2)(A)(i) and (ii) of the FCRA. An institution that shares for this reason may choose to provide an opt-out.

(5) *For our affiliates' everyday business purposes—information about creditworthiness.* This reason incorporates sharing information pursuant to section 603(d)(2)(A)(iii) of the FCRA. An institution that shares for this reason must provide an opt-out.

(6) *For our affiliates to market to you.* This reason incorporates sharing information specified in section 624 of the FCRA. This reason may be omitted from the disclosure table when: The institution does not have affiliates (or does not disclose personal information to its affiliates); the institution's affiliates do not use personal information in a manner that requires an opt-out; or the institution provides the affiliate marketing notice separately. Institutions that include

Federal Deposit Insurance Corporation

Pt. 332, App. A

this reason must provide an opt-out of indefinite duration. An institution that is required to provide an affiliate marketing opt-out, but does not include that opt-out in the model form under this part, must comply with section 624 of the FCRA and 12 CFR part 334, subpart C, with respect to the initial notice and opt-out and any subsequent renewal notice and opt-out. An institution not required to provide an opt-out under this subparagraph may elect to include this reason in the model form.

(7) *For nonaffiliates to market to you.* This reason incorporates sharing described in §§ 332.7 and 332.10(a) of this part. An institution that shares personal information for this reason must provide an opt-out.

(e) *To limit our sharing:* A financial institution must include this section of the model form *only* if it provides an opt-out. The word "choice" may be written in either the singular or plural, as appropriate. Institutions must select one or more of the applicable opt-out methods described: Telephone, such as by a toll-free number; a Web site; or use of a mail-in opt-out form. Institutions may include the words "toll-free" before telephone, as appropriate. An institution that allows consumers to opt out online must provide either a specific Web address that takes consumers directly to the opt-out page or a general Web address that provides a clear and conspicuous direct link to the opt-out page. The opt-out choices made available to the consumer who contacts the institution through these methods must correspond accurately to the "Yes" responses in the third column of the disclosure table. In the part titled "Please note" institutions may insert a number that is 30 or greater in the space marked "[30]." Instructions on voluntary or state privacy law opt-out information are in paragraph C.2(g)(5) of these Instructions.

(f) *Questions box.* Customer service contact information must be inserted as appropriate, where [phone number] or [Web site] appear. Institutions may elect to provide either a phone number, such as a toll-free number, or a Web address, or both. Institutions may include the words "toll-free" before the telephone number, as appropriate.

(g) *Mail-in opt-out form.* Financial institutions must include this mail-in form *only* if they state in the "To limit our sharing" box that consumers can opt out by mail. The mail-in form must provide opt-out options that correspond accurately to the "Yes" responses in the third column in the disclosure table. Institutions that require customers to provide only name and address may omit the section identified as "[account #]." Institutions that require additional or different information, such as a random opt-out number or a truncated account number, to implement an opt-out election should modify the "[account #]" reference accordingly. This includes institutions that require customers with multiple accounts to identify each account to which the opt-out should apply. An institution must enter its opt-out mailing address: In the far right of this form (*see* version 3); or below the form (*see* version 4). The reverse side of the mail-in opt-out form must not include any content of the model form.

(1) *Joint accountholder.* Only institutions that provide their joint accountholders the choice to opt out for only one accountholder, in accordance with paragraph C.3(a)(5) of these Instructions, must include in the far left column of the mail-in form the following statement: "If you have a joint account, your choice(s) will apply to everyone on your account unless you mark below. ☐ Apply my choice(s) only to me." The word "choice" may be written in either the singular or plural, as appropriate. Financial institutions that provide insurance products or services, provide this option, and elect to use the model form may substitute the word "policy" for "account" in this statement. Institutions that do not provide this option may eliminate this left column from the mail-in form.

(2) *FCRA Section 603(d)(2)(A)(iii) opt-out.* If the institution shares personal information pursuant to section 603(d)(2)(A)(iii) of the FCRA, it must include in the mail-in opt-out form the following statement: "☐ Do not share information about my creditworthiness with your affiliates for their everyday business purposes."

(3) *FCRA Section 624 opt-out.* If the institution incorporates section 624 of the FCRA in accord with paragraph C.2(d)(6) of these Instructions, it must include in the mail-in opt-out form the following statement: "☐ Do not allow your affiliates to use my personal information to market to me."

(4) *Nonaffiliate opt-out.* If the financial institution shares personal information pursuant to § 332.10(a) of this part, it must include in the mail-in opt-out form the following statement: "☐ Do not share my personal information with nonaffiliates to market their products and services to me."

(5) *Additional opt-outs.* Financial institutions that use the disclosure table to provide opt-out options beyond those required by Federal law must provide those opt-outs in this section of the model form. A financial institution that chooses to offer an opt-out for its own marketing in the mail-in opt-out form must include one of the two following statements: "☐ Do not share my personal information to market to me." *or* "☐ Do not use my personal information to market to me." A financial institution that chooses to offer an opt-out for joint marketing must include the following statement: "☐ Do not share my personal information with other financial institutions to jointly market to me."

(h) *Barcodes.* A financial institution may elect to include a barcode and/or "tagline" (an internal identifier) in 6-point font at the bottom of page one, as needed for information internal to the institution, so long as these do not interfere with the clarity or text of the form.

3. Page Two

(a) *General Instructions for the Questions.* Certain of the Questions may be customized as follows:

(1) *"Who is providing this notice?"* This question may be omitted where only one financial institution provides the model form and that institution is clearly identified in the title on page one. Two or more financial institutions that jointly provide the model form must use this question to identify themselves as required by §332.9(f) of this part. Where the list of institutions exceeds four (4) lines, the institution must describe in the response to this question the general types of institutions jointly providing the notice and must separately identify those institutions, in minimum 8-point font, directly following the "Other important information" box, or, if that box is not included in the institution's form, directly following the "Definitions." The list may appear in a multi-column format.

(2) *"How does [name of financial institution] protect my personal information?"* The financial institution may only provide additional information pertaining to its safeguards practices following the designated response to this question. Such information may include information about the institution's use of cookies or other measures it uses to safeguard personal information. Institutions are limited to a maximum of 30 additional words.

(3) *"How does [name of financial institution] collect my personal information?"* Institutions must use five (5) of the following terms to complete the bulleted list for this question: Open an account; deposit money; pay your bills; apply for a loan; use your credit or debit card; seek financial or tax advice; apply for insurance; pay insurance premiums; file an insurance claim; seek advice about your investments; buy securities from us; sell securities to us; direct us to buy securities; direct us to sell your securities; make deposits or withdrawals from your account; enter into an investment advisory contract; give us your income information; provide employment information; give us your employment history; tell us about your investment or retirement portfolio; tell us about your investment or retirement earnings; apply for financing; apply for a lease; provide account information; give us your contact information; pay us by check; give us your wage statements; provide your mortgage information; make a wire transfer; tell us who receives the money; tell us where to send the money; show your government-issued ID; show your driver's license; order a commodity futures or option trade. Institutions that collect personal information from their affiliates and/or credit bureaus must include after the bulleted list the following statement: "We also collect your personal information from others, such as credit bureaus, affiliates, or other companies." Institutions that do not collect personal information from their affiliates or credit bureaus but do collect information from other companies must include the following statement instead: "We also collect your personal information from other companies." Only institutions that do not collect any personal information from affiliates, credit bureaus, or other companies can omit both statements.

(4) *"Why can't I limit all sharing?"* Institutions that describe state privacy law provisions in the *"Other important information"* box must use the bracketed sentence: "See below for more on your rights under state law." Other institutions must omit this sentence.

(5) *"What happens when I limit sharing for an account I hold jointly with someone else?"* Only financial institutions that provide opt-out options must use this question. Other institutions must omit this question. Institutions must choose one of the following two statements to respond to this question: "Your choices will apply to everyone on your account." or "Your choices will apply to everyone on your account—unless you tell us otherwise." Financial institutions that provide insurance products or services and elect to use the model form may substitute the word "policy" for "account" in these statements.

(b) *General Instructions for the Definitions.*

The financial institution must customize the space below the responses to the three definitions in this section. This specific information must be in italicized lettering to set off the information from the standardized definitions.

(1) *Affiliates.* As required by §332.6(a)(3) of this part, where [*affiliate information*] appears, the financial institution must:

(i) If it has no affiliates, state: "[*name of financial institution*] *has no affiliates*";

(ii) If it has affiliates but does not share personal information, state: "[*name of financial institution*] *does not share with our affiliates*"; or

(iii) If it shares with its affiliates, state, as applicable: "*Our affiliates include companies with a [common corporate identity of financial institution] name; financial companies such as [insert illustrative list of companies]; nonfinancial companies, such as [insert illustrative list of companies]; and others, such as [insert illustrative list].*"

(2) *Nonaffiliates.* As required by §332.6(c)(3) of this part, where [*nonaffiliate information*] appears, the financial institution must:

Federal Deposit Insurance Corporation § 333.4

(i) If it does not share with nonaffiliated third parties, state: *"[name of financial institution] does not share with nonaffiliates so they can market to you"*; or

(ii) If it shares with nonaffiliated third parties, state, as applicable: *"Nonaffiliates we share with can include [list categories of companies such as mortgage companies, insurance companies, direct marketing companies, and nonprofit organizations]."*

(3) *Joint Marketing.* As required by § 332.13 of this part, where *[joint marketing]* appears, the financial institution must:

(i) If it does not engage in joint marketing, state: *"[name of financial institution] doesn't jointly market"*; or

(ii) If it shares personal information for joint marketing, state, as applicable: *"Our joint marketing partners include [list categories of companies such as credit card companies]."*

(c) *General instructions for the "Other important information" box.* This box is optional. The space provided for information in this box is not limited. Only the following types of information can appear in this box.

(1) State and/or international privacy law information; and/or

(2) Acknowledgment of receipt form.

[74 FR 69236, Dec. 1, 2009]

PART 333—EXTENSION OF CORPORATE POWERS

REGULATIONS

Sec.
333.1 Classification of general character of business.
333.2 Change in general character of business.
333.4 Conversions from mutual to stock form.

INTERPRETATIONS

333.101 Prior consent not required.

AUTHORITY: 12 U.S.C. 1816, 1818, 1819 ("Seventh", "Eighth" and "Tenth"), 1828, 1828(m), 1831p-1(c).

REGULATIONS

§ 333.1 Classification of general character of business.

State nonmember insured banks are divided into five categories for the purpose of classifying their general character or type of business,[2] viz: commercial banks, banks and trust companies, savings banks (including mutual and stock), industrial banks, and cash depositories.

[15 FR 8644, Dec. 6, 1950]

§ 333.2 Change in general character of business.

No State nonmember insured bank (except a District bank) or branch thereof shall hereafter cause or permit any change to be made in the general character or type of business exercised by it after the effective date of this part without the prior written consent of the Corporation.

[15 FR 8644, Dec. 6, 1950]

§ 333.4 Conversions from mutual to stock form.

(a) *Scope.* This section applies to the conversion of insured mutual state savings banks to the stock form of ownership. It supplements the procedural and other requirements for such conversions in subpart I of part 303 of this chapter. This section also applies, to the extent appropriate, to the reorganization of insured mutual state savings banks to the mutual holding company form of ownership. As determined by the Board of Directors of the FDIC on a case-by-case basis, the requirements of paragraphs (d), (e), and (f) of this section do not apply to mutual-to-stock conversions of insured mutual state savings banks whose capital category under § 325.103 of this chapter is "undercapitalized", "significantly undercapitalized" or "critically undercapitalized". As provided in § 303.162 of this chapter, the Board of Directors of the FDIC may grant a waiver in writing from any requirement of this section for good cause shown.

(b) *Definition of Eligible Depositor.* For purposes of this section, *eligible depositors* are depositors holding qualifying deposits at the bank as of a date designated in the bank's plan of conversion that is not less than one year prior to the date of adoption of the plan of conversion by the converting bank's board of directors/trustees.

(c) *Requirements.* In addition to other requirements that may be imposed by the applicable state statutes and regulations and other federal statutes and regulations, including subpart I of part 303 of this chapter, an insured mutual

---
[2] A bank's business may include two or more of the general classifications.

385

state savings bank shall not convert to the stock form of ownership unless the following requirements are satisfied:

(1) Eligible depositors shall have higher subscription rights than employee stock ownership plans;

(2) The proposed conversion shall be approved by a vote of at least a majority of the bank's depositors and, as reasonably determined by the bank's directors or trustees, other stakeholders of the bank who are entitled to vote on the conversion, unless the applicable state law requires a higher percentage, in which case the higher percentage shall be used. Voting may be in person or by proxy; and

(3) Management shall not use proxies executed outside the context of the proposed conversion to satisfy the voting requirement imposed in the previous paragraph.

(d) *Restriction on repurchase of stock.* An insured mutual state savings bank that has converted from the mutual to stock form of ownership may not repurchase its capital stock within one year following the date of its conversion to stock form, except that stock repurchases of no greater than 5% of the bank's outstanding capital stock may be repurchased during this one-year period where compelling and valid business reasons are established, to the satisfaction of the FDIC. Any stock repurchases shall be subject to the requirements of section 18(i)(1) of the Federal Deposit Insurance Act (12 U.S.C. 1828(i)(1)).

(e) *Stock benefit plan limitations.* The FDIC will presume that a stock option plan or management or employee stock benefit plan that does not conform with the applicable percentage limitations of the regulations issued by the Office of Thrift Supervision constitutes excessive insider benefits and thereby evidences a breach of the board of directors' or trustees' fiduciary responsibility. In addition, no converted insured mutual state savings bank shall, for one year from the date of the conversion, implement a stock option plan or management or employee stock benefit plan, other than a tax-qualified employee stock ownership plan, unless each of the following requirements is met:

(1) Each of the plans was fully disclosed in the proxy solicitation and conversion stock offering materials;

(2) All such plans are approved by a majority of the bank's stockholders, or in the case of a recently formed holding company, its stockholders, prior to implementation at a duly called meeting of shareholders, either annual or special, to be held no sooner than six months after the completion of the conversion;

(3) In the case of a savings bank subsidiary of a mutual holding company, all such plans are approved by a majority of stockholders other than its parent mutual holding company prior to implementation at a duly called meeting of shareholders, either annual or special, to be held no sooner than six months following the stock issuance;

(4) For stock option plans, stock options are granted at no lower than the market price at which the stock is trading at the time of grant; and

(5) For management or employee stock benefit plans, no conversion stock is used to fund the plans.

[59 FR 61246, Nov. 30, 1994, as amended at 63 FR 44750, Aug. 20, 1998; 68 FR 50461, Aug. 21, 2003]

INTERPRETATIONS

§ 333.101 Prior consent not required.

(a) The extension by any State nonmember insured bank of its business to include personal, character or installment loans, or the extension by an industrial bank of its business to include the business of a commercial bank, is not a change in the general character or type of business requiring the prior written consent of the Corporation.

(b) An insured State nonmember bank, not exercising trust powers, may act as trustee or custodian of Individual Retirement Accounts established pursuant to the Employee Retirement Income Security Act of 1974 (26 U.S.C. 408), Self-Employed Retirement Plans established pursuant to the Self-Employed Individuals Retirement Act of 1962 (26 U.S.C. 401), Roth Individual Retirement Accounts and Coverdell Education Savings Accounts established pursuant to the Taxpayer Relief Act of 1997 (26 U.S.C. 408A and 530 respectively), Health Savings Accounts

Federal Deposit Insurance Corporation

established pursuant to the Medicare Prescription Drug Improvement, and Modernization Act of 2003 (26 U.S.C. 223), and other similar accounts without the prior written consent of the Corporation provided:

(1) The bank's duties as trustee or custodian are essentially custodial or ministerial in nature,

(2) The bank is required to invest the funds from such plans only

(i) In its own time or savings deposits, or

(ii) In any other assets at the direction of the customer, provided the bank does not exercise any investment discretion or provide any investment advice with respect to such account assets, and

(3) The bank's acceptance of such accounts without trust powers is not contrary to applicable State law.

[41 FR 2375, Jan. 16, 1976, as amended at 50 FR 10754, Mar. 18, 1985; 70 FR 60422, Oct. 18, 2005]

PART 334—FAIR CREDIT REPORTING

Sec.

Subpart A—General Provisions

334.1 Purpose and scope.
334.2 Examples.
334.3 Definitions.

Subparts B [Reserved]

Subpart C—Affiliate Marketing

334.20 Coverage and definitions.
334.21 Affiliate marketing opt-out and exceptions.
334.22 Scope and duration of opt-out.
334.23 Contents of opt-out notice; consolidated and equivalent notices.
334.24 Reasonable opportunity to opt out.
334.25 Reasonable and simple methods of opting out.
334.26 Delivery of opt-out notices.
334.27 Renewal of opt-out.
334.28 Effective date, compliance date, and prospective application.

Subpart D Medical Information

334.30 Obtaining or using medical information in connection with a determination of eligibility for credit.
334.31 Limits on redisclosure of information.
334.32 Sharing medical information with affiliates.

Subpart E—Duties of Furnishers of Information

334.40 Scope.
334.41 Definitions.
334.42 Reasonable policies and procedures concerning the accuracy and integrity of furnished information.
334.43 Direct disputes.

Subparts F–H [Reserved]

Subpart I—Duties of Users of Consumer Reports Regarding Address Discrepancies and Records Disposal

334.80–334.81 [Reserved]
334.82 Duties of users regarding address discrepancies.
334.83 Disposal of consumer information.

Subpart J—Identity Theft Red Flags

334.90 Duties regarding the detection, prevention, and mitigation of identity theft.
334.91 Duties of card issuers regarding changes of address.

APPENDICES A–B TO PART 334 [RESERVED]
APPENDIX C TO PART 334—MODEL FORMS FOR OPT-OUT NOTICES
APPENDIX D TO PART 334 [RESERVED]
APPENDIX E TO PART 334—INTERAGENCY GUIDELINES CONCERNING THE ACCURACY AND INTEGRITY OF INFORMATION FURNISHED TO CONSUMER REPORTING AGENCIES
APPENDICES F–I TO PART 334 [RESERVED]
APPENDIX J TO PART 334—INTERAGENCY GUIDELINES ON IDENTITY THEFT DETECTION, PREVENTION, AND MITIGATION

AUTHORITY: 12 U.S.C. 1818, 1819 (Tenth), and 1831p–1; 15 U.S.C. 1681a, 1681b, 1681c, 1681m, 1681s, 1681s–2, 1681s–3, 1681t, 1681w, 6801 et seq., Pub. L. 108–159, 117 Stat. 1952.

SOURCE: 69 FR 77618, Dec. 28, 2004, unless otherwise noted.

Subpart A—General Provisions

SOURCE: 70 FR 70685, Nov. 22, 2005, unless otherwise noted.

§ 334.1 Purpose and scope.

(a) *Purpose.* The purpose of this part is to implement the Fair Credit Reporting Act. This part generally applies to persons that obtain and use information about consumers to determine the consumer's eligibility for products, services, or employment, share such information among affiliates, and furnish information to consumer reporting agencies.

§ 334.2

(b) *Scope.* Except as otherwise provided in this part, the regulations in this part apply to insured state nonmember banks, insured state licensed branches of foreign banks, and subsidiaries of such entities (except brokers, dealers, persons providing insurance, investment companies, and investment advisers).

[72 FR 62963, Nov. 7, 2007]

§ 334.2 Examples.

The examples in this part are not exclusive. Compliance with an example, to the extent applicable, constitutes compliance with this part. Examples in a paragraph illustrate only the issue described in the paragraph and do not illustrate any other issue that may arise in this part.

§ 334.3 Definitions.

For purposes of this part, unless explicitly stated otherwise:

(a) *Act* means the Fair Credit Reporting Act (15 U.S.C. 1681 *et seq.*).

(b) *Affiliate* means any company that is related by common ownership or common corporate control with another company.

(c) [Reserved]

(d) *Company* means any corporation, limited liability company, business trust, general or limited partnership, association, or similar organization.

(e) *Consumer* means an individual.

(f)–(h) [Reserved]

(i) *Common ownership or common corporate control* means a relationship between two companies under which:

(1) One company has, with respect to the other company:

(i) Ownership, control, or power to vote 25 percent or more of the outstanding shares of any class of voting security of a company, directly or indirectly, or acting through one or more other persons;

(ii) Control in any manner over the election of a majority of the directors, trustees, or general partners (or individuals exercising similar functions) of a company; or

(iii) The power to exercise, directly or indirectly, a controlling influence over the management or policies of a company, as the FDIC determines; or

(2) Any other person has, with respect to both companies, a relationship described in paragraphs (i)(1)(i) through (i)(1)(iii) of this section.

(j) [Reserved]

(k) *Medical information* means:

(1) Information or data, whether oral or recorded, in any form or medium, created by or derived from a health care provider or the consumer, that relates to:

(i) The past, present, or future physical, mental, or behavioral health or condition of an individual;

(ii) The provision of health care to an individual; or

(iii) The payment for the provision of health care to an individual.

(2) The term does not include:

(i) The age or gender of a consumer;

(ii) Demographic information about the consumer, including a consumer's residence address or e-mail address;

(iii) Any other information about a consumer that does not relate to the physical, mental, or behavioral health or condition of a consumer, including the existence or value of any insurance policy; or

(iv) Information that does not identify a specific consumer.

(l) *Person* means any individual, partnership, corporation, trust, estate cooperative, association, government or governmental subdivision or agency, or other entity.

[70 FR 70685, Nov. 22, 2005, as amended at 72 FR 63760, Nov. 9, 2007]

Subparts B [Reserved]

Subpart C—Affiliate Marketing

SOURCE: 72 FR 62963, Nov. 7, 2007, unless otherwise noted.

§ 334.20 Coverage and definitions.

(a) *Coverage.* Subpart C of this part applies to insured state nonmember banks, insured state licensed branches of foreign banks, and subsidiaries of such entities (except brokers, dealers, persons providing insurance, investment companies, and investment advisers).

(b) *Definitions.* For purposes of this subpart:

(1) *Clear and conspicuous.* The term "clear and conspicuous" means reasonably understandable and designed to

call attention to the nature and significance of the information presented.

(2) *Concise.* (i) *In general.* The term "concise" means a reasonably brief expression or statement.

(ii) *Combination with other required disclosures.* A notice required by this subpart may be concise even if it is combined with other disclosures required or authorized by federal or state law.

(3) *Eligibility information.* The term "eligibility information" means any information the communication of which would be a consumer report if the exclusions from the definition of "consumer report" in section 603(d)(2)(A) of the Act did not apply. Eligibility information does not include aggregate or blind data that does not contain personal identifiers such as account numbers, names, or addresses.

(4) *Pre-existing business relationship.* (i) *In general.* The term "pre-existing business relationship" means a relationship between a person, or a person's licensed agent, and a consumer based on—

(A) A financial contract between the person and the consumer which is in force on the date on which the consumer is sent a solicitation covered by this subpart;

(B) The purchase, rental, or lease by the consumer of the person's goods or services, or a financial transaction (including holding an active account or a policy in force or having another continuing relationship) between the consumer and the person, during the 18-month period immediately preceding the date on which the consumer is sent a solicitation covered by this subpart; or

(C) An inquiry or application by the consumer regarding a product or service offered by that person during the three-month period immediately preceding the date on which the consumer is sent a solicitation covered by this subpart.

(ii) *Examples of pre-existing business relationships.* (A) If a consumer has a time deposit account, such as a certificate of deposit, at a depository institution that is currently in force, the depository institution has a pre-existing business relationship with the consumer and can use eligibility information it receives from its affiliates to make solicitations to the consumer about its products or services.

(B) If a consumer obtained a certificate of deposit from a depository institution, but did not renew the certificate at maturity, the depository institution has a pre-existing business relationship with the consumer and can use eligibility information it receives from its affiliates to make solicitations to the consumer about its products or services for 18 months after the date of maturity of the certificate of deposit.

(C) If a consumer obtains a mortgage, the mortgage lender has a pre-existing business relationship with the consumer. If the mortgage lender sells the consumer's entire loan to an investor, the mortgage lender has a pre-existing business relationship with the consumer and can use eligibility information it receives from its affiliates to make solicitations to the consumer about its products or services for 18 months after the date it sells the loan, and the investor has a pre-existing business relationship with the consumer upon purchasing the loan. If, however, the mortgage lender sells a fractional interest in the consumer's loan to an investor but also retains an ownership interest in the loan, the mortgage lender continues to have a pre-existing business relationship with the consumer, but the investor does not have a pre-existing business relationship with the consumer. If the mortgage lender retains ownership of the loan, but sells ownership of the servicing rights to the consumer's loan, the mortgage lender continues to have a pre-existing business relationship with the consumer. The purchaser of the servicing rights also has a pre-existing business relationship with the consumer as of the date it purchases ownership of the servicing rights, but only if it collects payments from or otherwise deals directly with the consumer on a continuing basis.

(D) If a consumer applies to a depository institution for a product or service that it offers, but does not obtain a product or service from or enter into a financial contract or transaction with the institution, the depository institution has a pre-existing business relationship with the consumer and can therefore use eligibility information it receives from an affiliate to make solicitations to the consumer about its products or services for three months after the date of the application.

(E) If a consumer makes a telephone inquiry to a depository institution about its products or services and provides contact information to the institution, but does not obtain a product or service from or enter into a financial contract or transaction with the institution, the depository institution has a pre-existing business relationship with the consumer and can therefore use eligibility information it receives from an affiliate to make solicitations to the consumer about its products or services for three months after the date of the inquiry.

(F) If a consumer makes an inquiry to a depository institution by e-mail about its products or services, but does not obtain a product or service from or enter into a financial contract or transaction with the institution, the depository institution has a pre-existing business relationship with the consumer and can therefore use eligibility information it receives from an affiliate to make solicitations to the consumer about its products or services for three months after the date of the inquiry.

(G) If a consumer has an existing relationship with a depository institution that is part of a group of affiliated companies, makes a telephone call to the centralized call center for the group of affiliated companies to inquire about products or services offered by the insurance affiliate, and provides contact information to the call center, the call constitutes an inquiry to the insurance affiliate that offers those products or services. The insurance affiliate has a pre-existing business relationship with the consumer and can therefore use eligibility information it receives from its affiliated depository institution to make solicitations to the consumer about its products or services for three months after the date of the inquiry.

(iii) *Examples where no pre-existing business relationship is created.* (A) If a consumer makes a telephone call to a centralized call center for a group of affiliated companies to inquire about the consumer's existing account at a depository institution, the call does not constitute an inquiry to any affiliate other than the depository institution that holds the consumer's account and does not establish a pre-existing business relationship between the consumer and any affiliate of the account-holding depository institution.

(B) If a consumer who has a deposit account with a depository institution makes a telephone call to an affiliate of the institution to ask about the affiliate's retail locations and hours, but does not make an inquiry about the affiliate's products or services, the call does not constitute an inquiry and does not establish a pre-existing business relationship between the consumer and the affiliate. Also, the affiliate's capture of the consumer's telephone number does not constitute an inquiry and does not establish a pre-existing business relationship between the consumer and the affiliate.

(C) If a consumer makes a telephone call to a depository institution in response to an advertisement that offers a free promotional item to consumers who call a toll-free number, but the advertisement does not indicate that the depository institution's products or services will be marketed to consumers who call in response, the call does not create a pre-existing business relationship between the consumer and the depository institution because the consumer has not made an inquiry about a product or service offered by the institution, but has merely responded to an offer for a free promotional item.

(5) *Solicitation*—(i) *In general.* The term "solicitation" means the marketing of a product or service initiated by a person to a particular consumer that is—

(A) Based on eligibility information communicated to that person by its affiliate as described in this subpart; and

(B) Intended to encourage the consumer to purchase or obtain such product or service.

(ii) *Exclusion of marketing directed at the general public.* A solicitation does not include marketing communications that are directed at the general

Federal Deposit Insurance Corporation

§ 334.21

public. For example, television, general circulation magazine, and billboard advertisements do not constitute solicitations, even if those communications are intended to encourage consumers to purchase products and services from the person initiating the communications.

(iii) *Examples of solicitations.* A solicitation would include, for example, a telemarketing call, direct mail, e-mail, or other form of marketing communication directed to a particular consumer that is based on eligibility information received from an affiliate.

(6) *You* means a person described in paragraph (a) of this section.

§ 334.21 Affiliate marketing opt-out and exceptions.

(a) *Initial notice and opt-out requirement*—(1) *In general.* You may not use eligibility information about a consumer that you receive from an affiliate to make a solicitation for marketing purposes to the consumer, unless—

(i) It is clearly and conspicuously disclosed to the consumer in writing or, if the consumer agrees, electronically, in a concise notice that you may use eligibility information about that consumer received from an affiliate to make solicitations for marketing purposes to the consumer;

(ii) The consumer is provided a reasonable opportunity and a reasonable and simple method to "opt out," or prohibit you from using eligibility information to make solicitations for marketing purposes to the consumer; and

(iii) The consumer has not opted out.

(2) *Example.* A consumer has a homeowner's insurance policy with an insurance company. The insurance company furnishes eligibility information about the consumer to its affiliated depository institution. Based on that eligibility information, the depository institution wants to make a solicitation to the consumer about its home equity loan products. The depository institution does not have a pre-existing business relationship with the consumer and none of the other exceptions apply. The depository institution is prohibited from using eligibility information received from its insurance affiliate to make solicitations to the consumer about its home equity loan products unless the consumer is given a notice and opportunity to opt out and the consumer does not opt out.

(3) *Affiliates who may provide the notice.* The notice required by this paragraph must be provided:

(i) By an affiliate that has or has previously had a pre-existing business relationship with the consumer; or

(ii) As part of a joint notice from two or more members of an affiliated group of companies, provided that at least one of the affiliates on the joint notice has or has previously had a pre-existing business relationship with the consumer.

(b) *Making solicitations*—(1) *In general.* For purposes of this subpart, you make a solicitation for marketing purposes if—

(i) You receive eligibility information from an affiliate;

(ii) You use that eligibility information to do one or more of the following:

(A) Identify the consumer or type of consumer to receive a solicitation;

(B) Establish criteria used to select the consumer to receive a solicitation; or

(C) Decide which of your products or services to market to the consumer or tailor your solicitation to that consumer; and

(iii) As a result of your use of the eligibility information, the consumer is provided a solicitation.

(2) *Receiving eligibility information from an affiliate, including through a common database.* You may receive eligibility information from an affiliate in various ways, including when the affiliate places that information into a common database that you may access.

(3) *Receipt or use of eligibility information by your service provider.* Except as provided in paragraph (b)(5) of this section, you receive or use an affiliate's eligibility information if a service provider acting on your behalf (whether an affiliate or a nonaffiliated third party) receives or uses that information in the manner described in paragraphs (b)(1)(i) or (b)(1)(ii) of this section. All relevant facts and circumstances will determine whether a person is acting as your service provider when it receives or uses an affiliate's eligibility

§ 334.21

information in connection with marketing your products and services.

(4) *Use by an affiliate of its own eligibility information.* Unless you have used eligibility information that you receive from an affiliate in the manner described in paragraph (b)(1)(ii) of this section, you do not make a solicitation subject to this subpart if your affiliate:

(i) Uses its own eligibility information that it obtained in connection with a pre-existing business relationship it has or had with the consumer to market your products or services to the consumer; or

(ii) Directs its service provider to use the affiliate's own eligibility information that it obtained in connection with a pre-existing business relationship it has or had with the consumer to market your products or services to the consumer, and you do not communicate directly with the service provider regarding that use.

(5) *Use of eligibility information by a service provider*—(i) *In general.* You do not make a solicitation subject to Subpart C of this part if a service provider (including an affiliated or third-party service provider that maintains or accesses a common database that you may access) receives eligibility information from your affiliate that your affiliate obtained in connection with a pre-existing business relationship it has or had with the consumer and uses that eligibility information to market your products or services to the consumer, so long as—

(A) Your affiliate controls access to and use of its eligibility information by the service provider (including the right to establish the specific terms and conditions under which the service provider may use such information to market your products or services);

(B) Your affiliate establishes specific terms and conditions under which the service provider may access and use the affiliate's eligibility information to market your products and services (or those of affiliates generally) to the consumer, such as the identity of the affiliated companies whose products or services may be marketed to the consumer by the service provider, the types of products or services of affiliated companies that may be marketed, and the number of times the consumer

may receive marketing materials, and periodically evaluates the service provider's compliance with those terms and conditions;

(C) Your affiliate requires the service provider to implement reasonable policies and procedures designed to ensure that the service provider uses the affiliate's eligibility information in accordance with the terms and conditions established by the affiliate relating to the marketing of your products or services;

(D) Your affiliate is identified on or with the marketing materials provided to the consumer; and

(E) You do not directly use your affiliate's eligibility information in the manner described in paragraph (b)(1)(ii) of this section.

(ii) *Writing requirements.* (A) The requirements of paragraphs (b)(5)(i)(A) and (C) of this section must be set forth in a written agreement between your affiliate and the service provider; and

(B) The specific terms and conditions established by your affiliate as provided in paragraph (b)(5)(i)(B) of this section must be set forth in writing.

(6) *Examples of making solicitations.* (i) A consumer has a deposit account with a depository institution, which is affiliated with an insurance company. The insurance company receives eligibility information about the consumer from the depository institution. The insurance company uses that eligibility information to identify the consumer to receive a solicitation about insurance products, and, as a result, the insurance company provides a solicitation to the consumer about its insurance products. Pursuant to paragraph (b)(1) of this section, the insurance company has made a solicitation to the consumer.

(ii) The same facts as in the example in paragraph (b)(6)(i) of this section, except that after using the eligibility information to identify the consumer to receive a solicitation about insurance products, the insurance company asks the depository institution to send the solicitation to the consumer and the depository institution does so. Pursuant to paragraph (b)(1) of this section, the insurance company has made a solicitation to the consumer because

Federal Deposit Insurance Corporation § 334.21

it used eligibility information about the consumer that it received from an affiliate to identify the consumer to receive a solicitation about its products or services, and, as a result, a solicitation was provided to the consumer about the insurance company's products.

(iii) The same facts as in the example in paragraph (b)(6)(i) of this section, except that eligibility information about consumers that have deposit accounts with the depository institution is placed into a common database that all members of the affiliated group of companies may independently access and use. Without using the depository institution's eligibility information, the insurance company develops selection criteria and provides those criteria, marketing materials, and related instructions to the depository institution. The depository institution reviews eligibility information about its own consumers using the selection criteria provided by the insurance company to determine which consumers should receive the insurance company's marketing materials and sends marketing materials about the insurance company's products to those consumers. Even though the insurance company has received eligibility information through the common database as provided in paragraph (b)(2) of this section, it did not use that information to identify consumers or establish selection criteria; instead, the depository institution used its own eligibility information. Therefore, pursuant to paragraph (b)(4)(i) of this section, the insurance company has not made a solicitation to the consumer.

(iv) The same facts as in the example in paragraph (b)(6)(iii) of this section, except that the depository institution provides the insurance company's criteria to the depository institution's service provider and directs the service provider to use the depository institution's eligibility information to identify depository institution consumers who meet the criteria and to send the insurance company's marketing materials to those consumers. The insurance company does not communicate directly with the service provider regarding the use of the depository institution's information to market its products to the depository institution's consumers. Pursuant to paragraph (b)(4)(ii) of this section, the insurance company has not made a solicitation to the consumer.

(v) An affiliated group of companies includes a depository institution, an insurance company, and a service provider. Each affiliate in the group places information about its consumers into a common database. The service provider has access to all information in the common database. The depository institution controls access to and use of its eligibility information by the service provider. This control is set forth in a written agreement between the depository institution and the service provider. The written agreement also requires the service provider to establish reasonable policies and procedures designed to ensure that the service provider uses the depository institution's eligibility information in accordance with specific terms and conditions established by the depository institution relating to the marketing of the products and services of all affiliates, including the insurance company. In a separate written communication, the depository institution specifies the terms and conditions under which the service provider may use the depository institution's eligibility information to market the insurance company's products and services to the depository institution's consumers. The specific terms and conditions are: a list of affiliated companies (including the insurance company) whose products or services may be marketed to the depository institution's consumers by the service provider; the specific products or types of products that may be marketed to the depository institution's consumers by the service provider; the categories of eligibility information that may be used by the service provider in marketing products or services to the depository institution's consumers; the types or categories of the depository institution's consumers to whom the service provider may market products or services of depository institution affiliates; the number and/or types of marketing communications that the service provider may send to the depository institution's consumers; and the length of time during which the service provider may market the products or services of the depository institution's affiliates to its consumers. The depository institution periodically evaluates the service provider's compliance with these terms and conditions. The insurance company asks the service provider to market insurance products to certain consumers who have deposit accounts with the depository institution. Without using the depository institution's eligibility information, the insurance company develops selection criteria and provides those criteria, marketing materials, and related instructions to the service provider. The service provider uses the depository institution's eligibility information from the common database to identify the depository institution's consumers to whom insurance products will be marketed. When the insurance company's marketing materials are provided to the identified consumers, the name of the depository institution is displayed on the insurance marketing materials, an introductory letter that accompanies the marketing materials, an account statement that accompanies the marketing materials, or the envelope containing the marketing materials. The requirements of paragraph (b)(5) of this section have been satisfied, and the insurance company has not made a solicitation to the consumer.

(vi) The same facts as in the example in paragraph (b)(6)(v) of this section, except that the terms and conditions permit the service provider to use the depository institution's eligibility information to market the products and services of other affiliates to the depository institution's consumers whenever the service provider deems it appropriate to do so. The service provider uses the depository institution's eligibility information in accordance with the discretion afforded to it by the terms and conditions. Because the terms and conditions are not specific, the requirements of paragraph (b)(5) of this section have not been satisfied.

(c) *Exceptions.* The provisions of this subpart do not apply to you if you use eligibility information that you receive from an affiliate:

(1) To make a solicitation for marketing purposes to a consumer with whom you have a pre-existing business relationship;

(2) To facilitate communications to an individual for whose benefit you provide employee benefit or other services pursuant to a contract with an employer related to and arising out of the current employment relationship or status of the individual as a participant or beneficiary of an employee benefit plan;

(3) To perform services on behalf of an affiliate, except that this subparagraph shall not be construed as permitting you to send solicitations on behalf of an affiliate if the affiliate would not be permitted to send the solicitation as a result of the election of the consumer to opt out under this subpart;

(4) In response to a communication about your products or services initiated by the consumer;

(5) In response to an authorization or request by the consumer to receive solicitations; or

(6) If your compliance with this subpart would prevent you from complying with any provision of State insurance laws pertaining to unfair discrimination in any State in which you are lawfully doing business.

(d) *Examples of exceptions*—(1) *Example of the pre-existing business relationship exception.* A consumer has a deposit account with a depository institution. The consumer also has a relationship with the depository institution's securities affiliate for management of the consumer's securities portfolio. The depository institution receives eligibility information about the consumer from its securities affiliate and uses that information to make a solicitation to the consumer about the depository institution's wealth management services. The depository institution may make this solicitation even if the consumer has not been given a notice and opportunity to opt out because the depository institution has a pre-existing business relationship with the consumer.

(2) *Examples of service provider exception.* (i) A consumer has an insurance policy issued by an insurance company. The insurance company furnishes eligibility information about the consumer to its affiliated depository institution. Based on that eligibility information,

Federal Deposit Insurance Corporation § 334.21

the depository institution wants to make a solicitation to the consumer about its deposit products. The depository institution does not have a pre-existing business relationship with the consumer and none of the other exceptions in paragraph (c) of this section apply. The consumer has been given an opt-out notice and has elected to opt out of receiving such solicitations. The depository institution asks a service provider to send the solicitation to the consumer on its behalf. The service provider may not send the solicitation on behalf of the depository institution because, as a result of the consumer's opt-out election, the depository institution is not permitted to make the solicitation.

(ii) The same facts as in paragraph (d)(2)(i) of this section, except the consumer has been given an opt-out notice, but has not elected to opt out. The depository institution asks a service provider to send the solicitation to the consumer on its behalf. The service provider may send the solicitation on behalf of the depository institution because, as a result of the consumer's not opting out, the depository institution is permitted to make the solicitation.

(3) *Examples of consumer-initiated communications.* (i) A consumer who has a deposit account with a depository institution initiates a communication with the depository institution's credit card affiliate to request information about a credit card. The credit card affiliate may use eligibility information about the consumer it obtains from the depository institution or any other affiliate to make solicitations regarding credit card products in response to the consumer-initiated communication.

(ii) A consumer who has a deposit account with a depository institution contacts the institution to request information about how to save and invest for a child's college education without specifying the type of product in which the consumer may be interested. Information about a range of different products or services offered by the depository institution and one or more affiliates of the institution may be responsive to that communication. Such products or services may include the following: Mutual funds offered by the institution's mutual fund affiliate; section 529 plans offered by the institution, its mutual fund affiliate, or another securities affiliate; or trust services offered by a different financial institution in the affiliated group. Any affiliate offering investment products or services that would be responsive to the consumer's request for information about saving and investing for a child's college education may use eligibility information to make solicitations to the consumer in response to this communication.

(iii) A credit card issuer makes a marketing call to the consumer without using eligibility information received from an affiliate. The issuer leaves a voice-mail message that invites the consumer to call a toll-free number to apply for the issuer's credit card. If the consumer calls the toll-free number to inquire about the credit card, the call is a consumer-initiated communication about a product or service and the credit card issuer may now use eligibility information it receives from its affiliates to make solicitations to the consumer.

(iv) A consumer calls a depository institution to ask about retail locations and hours, but does not request information about products or services. The institution may not use eligibility information it receives from an affiliate to make solicitations to the consumer about its products or services because the consumer-initiated communication does not relate to the depository institution's products or services. Thus, the use of eligibility information received from an affiliate would not be responsive to the communication and the exception does not apply.

(v) A consumer calls a depository institution to ask about retail locations and hours. The customer service representative asks the consumer if there is a particular product or service about which the consumer is seeking information. The consumer responds that the consumer wants to stop in and find out about certificates of deposit. The customer service representative offers to provide that information by telephone and mail additional information and application materials to the consumer. The consumer agrees and provides or confirms contact information for receipt of the materials to be

§ 334.22

mailed. The depository institution may use eligibility information it receives from an affiliate to make solicitations to the consumer about certificates of deposit because such solicitations would respond to the consumer-initiated communication about products or services.

(4) *Examples of consumer authorization or request for solicitations.* (i) A consumer who obtains a mortgage from a mortgage lender authorizes or requests information about homeowner's insurance offered by the mortgage lender's insurance affiliate. Such authorization or request, whether given to the mortgage lender or to the insurance affiliate, would permit the insurance affiliate to use eligibility information about the consumer it obtains from the mortgage lender or any other affiliate to make solicitations to the consumer about homeowner's insurance.

(ii) A consumer completes an online application to apply for a credit card from a credit card issuer. The issuer's online application contains a blank check box that the consumer may check to authorize or request information from the credit card issuer's affiliates. The consumer checks the box. The consumer has authorized or requested solicitations from the card issuer's affiliates.

(iii) A consumer completes an online application to apply for a credit card from a credit card issuer. The issuer's online application contains a pre-selected check box indicating that the consumer authorizes or requests information from the issuer's affiliates. The consumer does not deselect the check box. The consumer has not authorized or requested solicitations from the card issuer's affiliates.

(iv) The terms and conditions of a credit card account agreement contain preprinted boilerplate language stating that by applying to open an account the consumer authorizes or requests to receive solicitations from the credit card issuer's affiliates. The consumer has not authorized or requested solicitations from the card issuer's affiliates.

(e) *Relation to affiliate-sharing notice and opt-out.* Nothing in this subpart limits the responsibility of a person to comply with the notice and opt-out provisions of section 603(d)(2)(A)(iii) of the Act where applicable.

§ 334.22 **Scope and duration of opt-out.**

(a) *Scope of opt-out*—(1) *In general.* Except as otherwise provided in this section, the consumer's election to opt out prohibits any affiliate covered by the opt-out notice from using eligibility information received from another affiliate as described in the notice to make solicitations to the consumer.

(2) *Continuing relationship*—(i) *In general.* If the consumer establishes a continuing relationship with you or your affiliate, an opt-out notice may apply to eligibility information obtained in connection with—

(A) A single continuing relationship or multiple continuing relationships that the consumer establishes with you or your affiliates, including continuing relationships established subsequent to delivery of the opt-out notice, so long as the notice adequately describes the continuing relationships covered by the opt-out; or

(B) Any other transaction between the consumer and you or your affiliates as described in the notice.

(ii) *Examples of continuing relationships.* A consumer has a continuing relationship with you or your affiliate if the consumer—

(A) Opens a deposit or investment account with you or your affiliate;

(B) Obtains a loan for which you or your affiliate owns the servicing rights;

(C) Purchases an insurance product from you or your affiliate;

(D) Holds an investment product through you or your affiliate, such as when you act or your affiliate acts as a custodian for securities or for assets in an individual retirement arrangement;

(E) Enters into an agreement or understanding with you or your affiliate whereby you or your affiliate undertakes to arrange or broker a home mortgage loan for the consumer;

(F) Enters into a lease of personal property with you or your affiliate; or

(G) Obtains financial, investment, or economic advisory services from you or your affiliate for a fee.

(3) *No continuing relationship*—(i) *In general.* If there is no continuing relationship between a consumer and you or your affiliate, and you or your affiliate obtain eligibility information about a consumer in connection with a transaction with the consumer, such as an isolated transaction or a credit application that is denied, an opt-out notice provided to the consumer only applies to eligibility information obtained in connection with that transaction.

(ii) *Examples of isolated transactions.* An isolated transaction occurs if—

(A) The consumer uses your or your affiliate's ATM to withdraw cash from an account at another financial institution; or

(B) You or your affiliate sells the consumer a cashier's check or money order, airline tickets, travel insurance, or traveler's checks in isolated transactions.

(4) *Menu of alternatives.* A consumer may be given the opportunity to choose from a menu of alternatives when electing to prohibit solicitations, such as by electing to prohibit solicitations from certain types of affiliates covered by the opt-out notice but not other types of affiliates covered by the notice, electing to prohibit solicitations based on certain types of eligibility information but not other types of eligibility information, or electing to prohibit solicitations by certain methods of delivery but not other methods of delivery. However, one of the alternatives must allow the consumer to prohibit all solicitations from all of the affiliates that are covered by the notice.

(5) *Special rule for a notice following termination of all continuing relationships*—(i) *In general.* A consumer must be given a new opt-out notice if, after all continuing relationships with you or your affiliate(s) are terminated, the consumer subsequently establishes another continuing relationship with you or your affiliate(s) and the consumer's eligibility information is to be used to make a solicitation. The new opt-out notice must apply, at a minimum, to eligibility information obtained in connection with the new continuing relationship. Consistent with paragraph (b) of this section, the consumer's decision not to opt out after receiving the new opt-out notice would not override a prior opt-out election by the consumer that applies to eligibility information obtained in connection with a terminated relationship, regardless of whether the new opt-out notice applies to eligibility information obtained in connection with the terminated relationship.

(ii) *Example.* A consumer has a checking account with a depository institution that is part of an affiliated group. The consumer closes the checking account. One year after closing the checking account, the consumer opens a savings account with the same depository institution. The consumer must be given a new notice and opportunity to opt out before the depository institution's affiliates may make solicitations to the consumer using eligibility information obtained by the depository institution in connection with the new savings account relationship, regardless of whether the consumer opted out in connection with the checking account.

(b) *Duration of opt-out.* The election of a consumer to opt out must be effective for a period of at least five years (the "opt-out period") beginning when the consumer's opt-out election is received and implemented, unless the consumer subsequently revokes the opt-out in writing or, if the consumer agrees, electronically. An opt-out period of more than five years may be established, including an opt-out period that does not expire unless revoked by the consumer.

(c) *Time of opt-out.* A consumer may opt out at any time.

§ 334.23 **Contents of opt-out notice; consolidated and equivalent notices.**

(a) *Contents of opt-out notice.* (1) *In general.* A notice must be clear, conspicuous, and concise, and must accurately disclose:

(i) The name of the affiliate(s) providing the notice. If the notice is provided jointly by multiple affiliates and each affiliate shares a common name, such as "ABC," then the notice may indicate that it is being provided by multiple companies with the ABC name or multiple companies in the

§ 334.23

ABC group or family of companies, for example, by stating that the notice is provided by "all of the ABC companies," "the ABC banking, credit card, insurance, and securities companies," or by listing the name of each affiliate providing the notice. But if the affiliates providing the joint notice do not all share a common name, then the notice must either separately identify each affiliate by name or identify each of the common names used by those affiliates, for example, by stating that the notice is provided by "all of the ABC and XYZ companies" or by "the ABC banking and credit card companies and the XYZ insurance companies";

(ii) A list of the affiliates or types of affiliates whose use of eligibility information is covered by the notice, which may include companies that become affiliates after the notice is provided to the consumer. If each affiliate covered by the notice shares a common name, such as "ABC," then the notice may indicate that it applies to multiple companies with the ABC name or multiple companies in the ABC group or family of companies, for example, by stating that the notice is provided by "all of the ABC companies," "the ABC banking, credit card, insurance, and securities companies," or by listing the name of each affiliate providing the notice. But if the affiliates covered by the notice do not all share a common name, then the notice must either separately identify each covered affiliate by name or identify each of the common names used by those affiliates, for example, by stating that the notice applies to "all of the ABC and XYZ companies" or to "the ABC banking and credit card companies and the XYZ insurance companies";

(iii) A general description of the types of eligibility information that may be used to make solicitations to the consumer;

(iv) That the consumer may elect to limit the use of eligibility information to make solicitations to the consumer;

(v) That the consumer's election will apply for the specified period of time stated in the notice and, if applicable, that the consumer will be allowed to renew the election once that period expires;

(vi) If the notice is provided to consumers who may have previously opted out, such as if a notice is provided to consumers annually, that the consumer who has chosen to limit solicitations does not need to act again until the consumer receives a renewal notice; and

(vii) A reasonable and simple method for the consumer to opt out.

(2) *Joint relationships.* (i) If two or more consumers jointly obtain a product or service, a single opt-out notice may be provided to the joint consumers. Any of the joint consumers may exercise the right to opt out.

(ii) The opt-out notice must explain how an opt-out direction by a joint consumer will be treated. An opt-out direction by a joint consumer may be treated as applying to all of the associated joint consumers, or each joint consumer may be permitted to opt-out separately. If each joint consumer is permitted to opt out separately, one of the joint consumers must be permitted to opt out on behalf of all of the joint consumers and the joint consumers must be permitted to exercise their separate rights to opt out in a single response.

(iii) It is impermissible to require *all* joint consumers to opt out before implementing *any* opt-out direction.

(3) *Alternative contents.* If the consumer is afforded a broader right to opt out of receiving marketing than is required by this subpart, the requirements of this section may be satisfied by providing the consumer with a clear, conspicuous, and concise notice that accurately discloses the consumer's opt-out rights.

(4) *Model notices.* Model notices are provided in appendix C of this part.

(b) *Coordinated and consolidated notices.* A notice required by this subpart may be coordinated and consolidated with any other notice or disclosure required to be issued under any other provision of law by the entity providing the notice, including but not limited to the notice described in section 603(d)(2)(A)(iii) of the Act and the Gramm-Leach-Bliley Act privacy notice.

(c) *Equivalent notices.* A notice or other disclosure that is equivalent to the notice required by this subpart,

Federal Deposit Insurance Corporation § 334.25

and that is provided to a consumer together with disclosures required by any other provision of law, satisfies the requirements of this section.

§ 334.24 Reasonable opportunity to opt out.

(a) *In general.* You must not use eligibility information about a consumer that you receive from an affiliate to make a solicitation to the consumer about your products or services, unless the consumer is provided a reasonable opportunity to opt out, as required by § 334.21(a)(1)(ii) of this part.

(b) *Examples of a reasonable opportunity to opt out.* The consumer is given a reasonable opportunity to opt out if:

(1) *By mail.* The opt-out notice is mailed to the consumer. The consumer is given 30 days from the date the notice is mailed to elect to opt out by any reasonable means.

(2) *By electronic means.* (i) The opt-out notice is provided electronically to the consumer, such as by posting the notice at an Internet Web site at which the consumer has obtained a product or service. The consumer acknowledges receipt of the electronic notice. The consumer is given 30 days after the date the consumer acknowledges receipt to elect to opt out by any reasonable means.

(ii) The opt-out notice is provided to the consumer by e-mail where the consumer has agreed to receive disclosures by e-mail from the person sending the notice. The consumer is given 30 days after the e-mail is sent to elect to opt out by any reasonable means.

(3) *At the time of an electronic transaction.* The opt-out notice is provided to the consumer at the time of an electronic transaction, such as a transaction conducted on an Internet Web site. The consumer is required to decide, as a necessary part of proceeding with the transaction, whether to opt out before completing the transaction. There is a simple process that the consumer may use to opt out at that time using the same mechanism through which the transaction is conducted.

(4) *At the time of an in-person transaction.* The opt-out notice is provided to the consumer in writing at the time of an in-person transaction. The consumer is required to decide, as a necessary part of proceeding with the transaction, whether to opt out before completing the transaction, and is not permitted to complete the transaction without making a choice. There is a simple process that the consumer may use during the course of the in-person transaction to opt out, such as completing a form that requires consumers to write a "yes" or "no" to indicate their opt-out preference or that requires the consumer to check one of two blank check boxes—one that allows consumers to indicate that they want to opt out and one that allows consumers to indicate that they do not want to opt out.

(5) *By including in a privacy notice.* The opt-out notice is included in a Gramm-Leach-Bliley Act privacy notice. The consumer is allowed to exercise the opt-out within a reasonable period of time and in the same manner as the opt-out under that privacy notice.

§ 334.25 Reasonable and simple methods of opting out.

(a) *In general.* You must not use eligibility information about a consumer that you receive from an affiliate to make a solicitation to the consumer about your products or services, unless the consumer is provided a reasonable and simple method to opt out, as required by § 334.21(a)(1)(ii) of this part.

(b) *Examples.* (1) *Reasonable and simple opt-out methods.* Reasonable and simple methods for exercising the opt-out right include—

(i) Designating a check-off box in a prominent position on the opt-out form;

(ii) Including a reply form and a self-addressed envelope together with the opt-out notice;

(iii) Providing an electronic means to opt out, such as a form that can be electronically mailed or processed at an Internet Web site, if the consumer agrees to the electronic delivery of information;

(iv) Providing a toll-free telephone number that consumers may call to opt out; or

(v) Allowing consumers to exercise all of their opt-out rights described in a consolidated opt-out notice that includes the privacy opt-out under the Gramm-Leach-Bliley Act, 15 U.S.C. 6801 et seq., the affiliate sharing opt-out under the Act, and the affiliate marketing opt-out under the Act, by a single method, such as by calling a single toll-free telephone number.

(2) *Opt-out methods that are not reasonable and simple.* Reasonable and simple methods for exercising an opt-out right *do not* include—

(i) Requiring the consumer to write his or her own letter;

(ii) Requiring the consumer to call or write to obtain a form for opting out, rather than including the form with the opt-out notice;

(iii) Requiring the consumer who receives the opt-out notice in electronic form only, such as through posting at an Internet Web site, to opt out solely by paper mail or by visiting a different Web site without providing a link to that site.

(c) *Specific opt-out means.* Each consumer may be required to opt out through a specific means, as long as that means is reasonable and simple for that consumer.

§ 334.26 Delivery of opt-out notices.

(a) *In general.* The opt-out notice must be provided so that each consumer can reasonably be expected to receive actual notice. For opt-out notices provided electronically, the notice may be provided in compliance with either the electronic disclosure provisions in this subpart or the provisions in section 101 of the Electronic Signatures in Global and National Commerce Act, 15 U.S.C. 7001 et seq.

(b) *Examples of reasonable expectation of actual notice.* A consumer may reasonably be expected to receive actual notice if the affiliate providing the notice:

(1) Hand-delivers a printed copy of the notice to the consumer;

(2) Mails a printed copy of the notice to the last known mailing address of the consumer;

(3) Provides a notice by e-mail to a consumer who has agreed to receive electronic disclosures by e-mail from the affiliate providing the notice; or

(4) Posts the notice on the Internet Web site at which the consumer obtained a product or service electronically and requires the consumer to acknowledge receipt of the notice.

(c) *Examples of no reasonable expectation of actual notice.* A consumer may *not* reasonably be expected to receive actual notice if the affiliate providing the notice:

(1) Only posts the notice on a sign in a branch or office or generally publishes the notice in a newspaper;

(2) Sends the notice via e-mail to a consumer who has not agreed to receive electronic disclosures by e-mail from the affiliate providing the notice; or

(3) Posts the notice on an Internet Web site without requiring the consumer to acknowledge receipt of the notice.

§ 334.27 Renewal of opt-out.

(a) *Renewal notice and opt-out requirement*—(1) *In general.* After the opt-out period expires, you may not make solicitations based on eligibility information you receive from an affiliate to a consumer who previously opted out, unless:

(i) The consumer has been given a renewal notice that complies with the requirements of this section and §§ 334.24 through 334.26 of this part, and a reasonable opportunity and a reasonable and simple method to renew the opt-out, and the consumer does not renew the opt-out; or

(ii) An exception in § 334.21(c) of this part applies.

(2) *Renewal period.* Each opt-out renewal must be effective for a period of at least five years as provided in § 334.22(b) of this part.

(3) *Affiliates who may provide the notice.* The notice required by this paragraph must be provided:

(i) By the affiliate that provided the previous opt-out notice, or its successor; or

(ii) As part of a joint renewal notice from two or more members of an affiliated group of companies, or their successors, that jointly provided the previous opt-out notice.

(b) *Contents of renewal notice.* The renewal notice must be clear, conspicuous, and concise, and must accurately disclose:

(1) The name of the affiliate(s) providing the notice. If the notice is provided jointly by multiple affiliates and each affiliate shares a common name,

such as "ABC," then the notice may indicate that it is being provided by multiple companies with the ABC name or multiple companies in the ABC group or family of companies, for example, by stating that the notice is provided by "all of the ABC companies," "the ABC banking, credit card, insurance, and securities companies," or by listing the name of each affiliate providing the notice. But if the affiliates providing the joint notice do not all share a common name, then the notice must either separately identify each affiliate by name or identify each of the common names used by those affiliates, for example, by stating that the notice is provided by "all of the ABC and XYZ companies" or by "the ABC banking and credit card companies and the XYZ insurance companies;"

(2) A list of the affiliates or types of affiliates whose use of eligibility information is covered by the notice, which may include companies that become affiliates after the notice is provided to the consumer. If each affiliate covered by the notice shares a common name, such as "ABC," then the notice may indicate that it applies to multiple companies with the ABC name or multiple companies in the ABC group or family of companies, for example, by stating that the notice is provided by "all of the ABC companies," "the ABC banking, credit card, insurance, and securities companies," or by listing the name of each affiliate providing the notice. But if the affiliates covered by the notice do not all share a common name, then the notice must either separately identify each covered affiliate by name or identify each of the common names used by those affiliates, for example, by stating that the notice applies to "all of the ABC and XYZ companies" or to "the ABC banking and credit card companies and the XYZ insurance companies;"

(3) A general description of the types of eligibility information that may be used to make solicitations to the consumer;

(4) That the consumer previously elected to limit the use of certain information to make solicitations to the consumer;

(5) That the consumer's election has expired or is about to expire;

(6) That the consumer may elect to renew the consumer's previous election;

(7) If applicable, that the consumer's election to renew will apply for the specified period of time stated in the notice and that the consumer will be allowed to renew the election once that period expires; and

(8) A reasonable and simple method for the consumer to opt out.

(c) *Timing of the renewal notice*—(1) *In general.* A renewal notice may be provided to the consumer either—

(i) A reasonable period of time before the expiration of the opt-out period; or

(ii) Any time after the expiration of the opt-out period but before solicitations that would have been prohibited by the expired opt-out are made to the consumer.

(2) *Combination with annual privacy notice.* If you provide an annual privacy notice under the Gramm-Leach-Bliley Act, 15 U.S.C. 6801 *et seq.*, providing a renewal notice with the last annual privacy notice provided to the consumer before expiration of the opt-out period is a reasonable period of time before expiration of the opt-out in all cases.

(d) *No effect on opt-out period.* An opt-out period may not be shortened by sending a renewal notice to the consumer before expiration of the opt-out period, even if the consumer does not renew the opt-out.

§ 334.28 Effective date, compliance date, and prospective application.

(a) *Effective date.* This subpart is effective January 1, 2008.

(b) *Mandatory compliance date.* Compliance with this subpart is required not later than October 1, 2008.

(c) *Prospective application.* The provisions of this subpart shall not prohibit you from using eligibility information that you receive from an affiliate to make solicitations to a consumer if you receive such information prior to October 1, 2008. For purposes of this section, you are deemed to receive eligibility information when such information is placed into a common database and is accessible by you.

Subpart D—Medical Information

SOURCE: 70 FR 70664, Nov. 22, 2005, unless otherwise noted.

§ 334.30 Obtaining or using medical information in connection with a determination of eligibility for credit.

(a) *Scope.* This section applies to:

(1) Any of the following that participates as a creditor in a transaction:

(i) A State bank insured by the FDIC (other than members of the Federal Reserve System);

(ii) An insured State branch of a foreign bank; or

(2) Any other person that participates as a creditor in a transaction involving a person described in paragraph (a)(1) of this section.

(b) *General prohibition on obtaining or using medical information*—(1) *In general.* A creditor may not obtain or use medical information pertaining to a consumer in connection with any determination of the consumer's eligibility, or continued eligibility, for credit, except as provided in this section.

(2) *Definitions.* (i) *Credit* has the same meaning as in section 702 of the Equal Credit Opportunity Act, 15 U.S.C. 1691a.

(ii) *Creditor* has the same meaning as in section 702 of the Equal Credit Opportunity Act, 15 U.S.C. 1691a.

(iii) *Eligibility, or continued eligibility, for credit* means the consumer's qualification or fitness to receive, or continue to receive, credit, including the terms on which credit is offered. The term does not include:

(A) Any determination of the consumer's qualification or fitness for employment, insurance (other than a credit insurance product), or other non-credit products or services;

(B) Authorizing, processing, or documenting a payment or transaction on behalf of the consumer in a manner that does not involve a determination of the consumer's eligibility, or continued eligibility, for credit; or

(C) Maintaining or servicing the consumer's account in a manner that does not involve a determination of the consumer's eligibility, or continued eligibility, for credit.

(c) *Rule of construction for obtaining and using unsolicited medical information*—(1) *In general.* A creditor does not obtain medical information in violation of the prohibition if it receives medical information pertaining to a consumer in connection with any determination of the consumer's eligibility, or continued eligibility, for credit without specifically requesting medical information.

(2) *Use of unsolicited medical information.* A creditor that receives unsolicited medical information in the manner described in paragraph (c)(1) of this section may use that information in connection with any determination of the consumer's eligibility, or continued eligibility, for credit to the extent the creditor can rely on at least one of the exceptions in § 334.30(d) or (e).

(3) *Examples.* A creditor does not obtain medical information in violation of the prohibition if, for example:

(i) In response to a general question regarding a consumer's debts or expenses, the creditor receives information that the consumer owes a debt to a hospital.

(ii) In a conversation with the creditor's loan officer, the consumer informs the creditor that the consumer has a particular medical condition.

(iii) In connection with a consumer's application for an extension of credit, the creditor requests a consumer report from a consumer reporting agency and receives medical information in the consumer report furnished by the agency even though the creditor did not specifically request medical information from the consumer reporting agency.

(d) *Financial information exception for obtaining and using medical information*—(1) *In general.* A creditor may obtain and use medical information pertaining to a consumer in connection with any determination of the consumer's eligibility, or continued eligibility, for credit so long as:

(i) The information is the type of information routinely used in making credit eligibility determinations, such as information relating to debts, expenses, income, benefits, assets, collateral, or the purpose of the loan, including the use of proceeds;

(ii) The creditor uses the medical information in a manner and to an extent that is no less favorable than it would use comparable information that

Federal Deposit Insurance Corporation § 334.30

is not medical information in a credit transaction; and

(iii) The creditor does not take the consumer's physical, mental, or behavioral health, condition or history, type of treatment, or prognosis into account as part of any such determination.

(2) *Examples*—(i) *Examples of the types of information routinely used in making credit eligibility determinations.* Paragraph (d)(1)(i) of this section permits a creditor, for example, to obtain and use information about:

(A) The dollar amount, repayment terms, repayment history, and similar information regarding medical debts to calculate, measure, or verify the repayment ability of the consumer, the use of proceeds, or the terms for granting credit;

(B) The value, condition, and lien status of a medical device that may serve as collateral to secure a loan;

(C) The dollar amount and continued eligibility for disability income, workers' compensation income, or other benefits related to health or a medical condition that is relied on as a source of repayment; or

(D) The identity of creditors to whom outstanding medical debts are owed in connection with an application for credit, including but not limited to, a transaction involving the consolidation of medical debts.

(ii) *Examples of uses of medical information consistent with the exception.* (A) A consumer includes on an application for credit information about two $20,000 debts. One debt is to a hospital; the other debt is to a retailer. The creditor contacts the hospital and the retailer to verify the amount and payment status of the debts. The creditor learns that both debts are more than 90 days past due. Any two debts of this size that are more than 90 days past due would disqualify the consumer under the creditor's established underwriting criteria. The creditor denies the application on the basis that the consumer has a poor repayment history on outstanding debts. The creditor has used medical information in a manner and to an extent no less favorable than it would use comparable non-medical information.

(B) A consumer indicates on an application for a $200,000 mortgage loan that she receives $15,000 in long-term disability income each year from her former employer and has no other income. Annual income of $15,000, regardless of source, would not be sufficient to support the requested amount of credit. The creditor denies the application on the basis that the projected debt-to-income ratio of the consumer does not meet the creditor's underwriting criteria. The creditor has used medical information in a manner and to an extent that is no less favorable than it would use comparable non-medical information.

(C) A consumer includes on an application for a $10,000 home equity loan that he has a $50,000 debt to a medical facility that specializes in treating a potentially terminal disease. The creditor contacts the medical facility to verify the debt and obtain the repayment history and current status of the loan. The creditor learns that the debt is current. The applicant meets the income and other requirements of the creditor's underwriting guidelines. The creditor grants the application. The creditor has used medical information in accordance with the exception.

(iii) *Examples of uses of medical information inconsistent with the exception.* (A) A consumer applies for $25,000 of credit and includes on the application information about a $50,000 debt to a hospital. The creditor contacts the hospital to verify the amount and payment status of the debt, and learns that the debt is current and that the consumer has no delinquencies in her repayment history. If the existing debt were instead owed to a retail department store, the creditor would approve the application and extend credit based on the amount and repayment history of the outstanding debt. The creditor, however, denies the application because the consumer is indebted to a hospital. The creditor has used medical information, here the identity of the medical creditor, in a manner and to an extent that is less favorable than it would use comparable non-medical information.

(B) A consumer meets with a loan officer of a creditor to apply for a mortgage loan. While filling out the loan application, the consumer informs the

§ 334.30

loan officer orally that she has a potentially terminal disease. The consumer meets the creditor's established requirements for the requested mortgage loan. The loan officer recommends to the credit committee that the consumer be denied credit because the consumer has that disease. The credit committee follows the loan officer's recommendation and denies the application because the consumer has a potentially terminal disease. The creditor has used medical information in a manner inconsistent with the exception by taking into account the consumer's physical, mental, or behavioral health, condition, or history, type of treatment, or prognosis as part of a determination of eligibility or continued eligibility for credit.

(C) A consumer who has an apparent medical condition, such as a consumer who uses a wheelchair or an oxygen tank, meets with a loan officer to apply for a home equity loan. The consumer meets the creditor's established requirements for the requested home equity loan and the creditor typically does not require consumers to obtain a debt cancellation contract, debt suspension agreement, or credit insurance product in connection with such loans. However, based on the consumer's apparent medical condition, the loan officer recommends to the credit committee that credit be extended to the consumer only if the consumer obtains a debt cancellation contract, debt suspension agreement, or credit insurance product from a nonaffiliated third party. The credit committee agrees with the loan officer's recommendation. The loan officer informs the consumer that the consumer must obtain a debt cancellation contract, debt suspension agreement, or credit insurance product from a nonaffiliated third party to qualify for the loan. The consumer obtains one of these products and the creditor approves the loan. The creditor has used medical information in a manner inconsistent with the exception by taking into account the consumer's physical, mental, or behavioral health, condition, or history, type of treatment, or prognosis in setting conditions on the consumer's eligibility for credit.

(e) *Specific exceptions for obtaining and using medical information*—(1) *In general.* A creditor may obtain and use medical information pertaining to a consumer in connection with any determination of the consumer's eligibility, or continued eligibility, for credit:

(i) To determine whether the use of a power of attorney or legal representative that is triggered by a medical condition or event is necessary and appropriate or whether the consumer has the legal capacity to contract when a person seeks to exercise a power of attorney or act as legal representative for a consumer based on an asserted medical condition or event;

(ii) To comply with applicable requirements of local, state, or Federal laws;

(iii) To determine, at the consumer's request, whether the consumer qualifies for a legally permissible special credit program or credit-related assistance program that is:

(A) Designed to meet the special needs of consumers with medical conditions; and

(B) Established and administered pursuant to a written plan that:

(*1*) Identifies the class of persons that the program is designed to benefit; and

(*2*) Sets forth the procedures and standards for extending credit or providing other credit-related assistance under the program;

(iv) To the extent necessary for purposes of fraud prevention or detection;

(v) In the case of credit for the purpose of financing medical products or services, to determine and verify the medical purpose of a loan and the use of proceeds;

(vi) Consistent with safe and sound practices, if the consumer or the consumer's legal representative specifically requests that the creditor use medical information in determining the consumer's eligibility, or continued eligibility, for credit, to accommodate the consumer's particular circumstances, and such request is documented by the creditor;

(vii) Consistent with safe and sound practices, to determine whether the provisions of a forbearance practice or program that is triggered by a medical condition or event apply to a consumer;

Federal Deposit Insurance Corporation § 334.30

(viii) To determine the consumer's eligibility for, the triggering of, or the reactivation of a debt cancellation contract or debt suspension agreement if a medical condition or event is a triggering event for the provision of benefits under the contract or agreement; or

(ix) To determine the consumer's eligibility for, the triggering of, or the reactivation of a credit insurance product if a medical condition or event is a triggering event for the provision of benefits under the product.

(2) *Example of determining eligibility for a special credit program or credit assistance program.* A not-for-profit organization establishes a credit assistance program pursuant to a written plan that is designed to assist disabled veterans in purchasing homes by subsidizing the down payment for the home purchase mortgage loans of qualifying veterans. The organization works through mortgage lenders and requires mortgage lenders to obtain medical information about the disability of any consumer that seeks to qualify for the program, use that information to verify the consumer's eligibility for the program, and forward that information to the organization. A consumer who is a veteran applies to a creditor for a home purchase mortgage loan. The creditor informs the consumer about the credit assistance program for disabled veterans and the consumer seeks to qualify for the program. Assuming that the program complies with all applicable law, including applicable fair lending laws, the creditor may obtain and use medical information about the medical condition and disability, if any, of the consumer to determine whether the consumer qualifies for the credit assistance program.

(3) *Examples of verifying the medical purpose of the loan or the use of proceeds.* (i) If a consumer applies for $10,000 of credit for the purpose of financing vision correction surgery, the creditor may verify with the surgeon that the procedure will be performed. If the surgeon reports that surgery will not be performed on the consumer, the creditor may use that medical information to deny the consumer's application for credit, because the loan would not be used for the stated purpose.

(ii) If a consumer applies for $10,000 of credit for the purpose of financing cosmetic surgery, the creditor may confirm the cost of the procedure with the surgeon. If the surgeon reports that the cost of the procedure is $5,000, the creditor may use that medical information to offer the consumer only $5,000 of credit.

(iii) A creditor has an established medical loan program for financing particular elective surgical procedures. The creditor receives a loan application from a consumer requesting $10,000 of credit under the established loan program for an elective surgical procedure. The consumer indicates on the application that the purpose of the loan is to finance an elective surgical procedure not eligible for funding under the guidelines of the established loan program. The creditor may deny the consumer's application because the purpose of the loan is not for a particular procedure funded by the established loan program.

(4) *Examples of obtaining and using medical information at the request of the consumer.* (i) If a consumer applies for a loan and specifically requests that the creditor consider the consumer's medical disability at the relevant time as an explanation for adverse payment history information in his credit report, the creditor may consider such medical information in evaluating the consumer's willingness and ability to repay the requested loan to accommodate the consumer's particular circumstances, consistent with safe and sound practices. The creditor may also decline to consider such medical information to accommodate the consumer, but may evaluate the consumer's application in accordance with its otherwise applicable underwriting criteria. The creditor may not deny the consumer's application or otherwise treat the consumer less favorably because the consumer specifically requested a medical accommodation, if the creditor would have extended the credit or treated the consumer more favorably under the creditor's otherwise applicable underwriting criteria.

(ii) If a consumer applies for a loan by telephone and explains that his income has been and will continue to be interrupted on account of a medical

§ 334.31

condition and that he expects to repay the loan by liquidating assets, the creditor may, but is not required to, evaluate the application using the sale of assets as the primary source of repayment, consistent with safe and sound practices, provided that the creditor documents the consumer's request by recording the oral conversation or making a notation of the request in the consumer's file.

(iii) If a consumer applies for a loan and the application form provides a space where the consumer may provide any other information or special circumstances, whether medical or non-medical, that the consumer would like the creditor to consider in evaluating the consumer's application, the creditor may use medical information provided by the consumer in that space on that application to accommodate the consumer's application for credit, consistent with safe and sound practices, or may disregard that information.

(iv) If a consumer specifically requests that the creditor use medical information in determining the consumer's eligibility, or continued eligibility, for credit and provides the creditor with medical information for that purpose, and the creditor determines that it needs additional information regarding the consumer's circumstances, the creditor may request, obtain, and use additional medical information about the consumer as necessary to verify the information provided by the consumer or to determine whether to make an accommodation for the consumer. The consumer may decline to provide additional information, withdraw the request for an accommodation, and have the application considered under the creditor's otherwise applicable underwriting criteria.

(v) If a consumer completes and signs a credit application that is not for medical purpose credit and the application contains boilerplate language that routinely requests medical information from the consumer or that indicates that by applying for credit the consumer authorizes or consents to the creditor obtaining and using medical information in connection with a determination of the consumer's eligibility, or continued eligibility, for credit, the consumer has not specifically requested that the creditor obtain and use medical information to accommodate the consumer's particular circumstances.

(5) *Example of a forbearance practice or program.* After an appropriate safety and soundness review, a creditor institutes a program that allows consumers who are or will be hospitalized to defer payments as needed for up to three months, without penalty, if the credit account has been open for more than one year and has not previously been in default, and the consumer provides confirming documentation at an appropriate time. A consumer is hospitalized and does not pay her bill for a particular month. This consumer has had a credit account with the creditor for more than one year and has not previously been in default. The creditor attempts to contact the consumer and speaks with the consumer's adult child, who is not the consumer's legal representative. The adult child informs the creditor that the consumer is hospitalized and is unable to pay the bill at that time. The creditor defers payments for up to three months, without penalty, for the hospitalized consumer and sends the consumer a letter confirming this practice and the date on which the next payment will be due. The creditor has obtained and used medical information to determine whether the provisions of a medically-triggered forbearance practice or program apply to a consumer.

§ 334.31 Limits on redisclosure of information.

(a) *Scope.* This section applies to State banks insured by the FDIC (other than members of the Federal Reserve System) and insured State branches of foreign banks.

(b) *Limits on redisclosure.* If a person described in paragraph (a) of this section receives medical information about a consumer from a consumer reporting agency or its affiliate, the person must not disclose that information to any other person, except as necessary to carry out the purpose for which the information was initially disclosed, or as otherwise permitted by statute, regulation, or order.

Federal Deposit Insurance Corporation

§ 334.32 Sharing medical information with affiliates.

(a) *Scope.* This section applies to State banks insured by the FDIC (other than members of the Federal Reserve System) and insured State branches of foreign banks.

(b) *In general.* The exclusions from the term "consumer report" in section 603(d)(2) of the Act that allow the sharing of information with affiliates do not apply if a person described in paragraph (a) of this section communicates to an affiliate—

(1) Medical information;

(2) An individualized list or description based on the payment transactions of the consumer for medical products or services; or

(3) An aggregate list of identified consumers based on payment transactions for medical products or services.

(c) *Exceptions.* A person described in paragraph (a) of this section may rely on the exclusions from the term "consumer report" in section 603(d)(2) of the Act to communicate the information in paragraph (b) of this section to an affiliate—

(1) In connection with the business of insurance or annuities (including the activities described in section 18B of the model Privacy of Consumer Financial and Health Information Regulation issued by the National Association of Insurance Commissioners, as in effect on January 1, 2003);

(2) For any purpose permitted without authorization under the regulations promulgated by the Department of Health and Human Services pursuant to the Health Insurance Portability and Accountability Act of 1996 (HIPAA);

(3) For any purpose referred to in section 1179 of HIPAA;

(4) For any purpose described in section 502(e) of the Gramm-Leach-Bliley Act;

(5) In connection with a determination of the consumer's eligibility, or continued eligibility, for credit consistent with § 334.30; or

(6) As otherwise permitted by order of the FDIC.

Subpart E—Duties of Furnishers of Information

SOURCE: 74 FR 31517, July 1, 2009, unless otherwise noted.

§ 334.40 Scope.

This subpart applies to a financial institution or creditor that is an insured state nonmember bank, insured state licensed branch of a foreign bank, or a subsidiary of such entities (except dealers, persons providing insurance, investment companies, and investment advisers).

§ 334.41 Definitions.

For purposes of this subpart and Appendix E of this part, the following definitions apply:

(a) *Accuracy* means that information that a furnisher provides to a consumer reporting agency about an account or other relationship with the consumer correctly:

(1) Reflects the terms of and liability for the account or other relationship;

(2) Reflects the consumer's performance and other conduct with respect to the account or other relationship; and

(3) Identifies the appropriate consumer.

(b) *Direct dispute* means a dispute submitted directly to a furnisher (including a furnisher that is a debt collector) by a consumer concerning the accuracy of any information contained in a consumer report and pertaining to an account or other relationship that the furnisher has or had with the consumer.

(c) *Furnisher* means an entity that furnishes information relating to consumers to one or more consumer reporting agencies for inclusion in a consumer report. An entity is not a furnisher when it:

(1) Provides information to a consumer reporting agency solely to obtain a consumer report in accordance with sections 604(a) and (f) of the Fair Credit Reporting Act;

(2) Is acting as a "consumer reporting agency" as defined in section 603(f) of the Fair Credit Reporting Act;

(3) Is a consumer to whom the furnished information pertains; or

(4) Is a neighbor, friend, or associate of the consumer, or another individual

§ 334.42

with whom the consumer is acquainted or who may have knowledge about the consumer, and who provides information about the consumer's character, general reputation, personal characteristics, or mode of living in response to a specific request from a consumer reporting agency.

(d) *Identity theft* has the same meaning as in 16 CFR 603.2(a).

(e) *Integrity* means that information that a furnisher provides to a consumer reporting agency about an account or other relationship with the consumer:

(1) Is substantiated by the furnisher's records at the time it is furnished;

(2) Is furnished in a form and manner that is designed to minimize the likelihood that the information may be incorrectly reflected in a consumer report; and

(3) Includes the information in the furnisher's possession about the account or other relationship that the FDIC has:

(i) Determined that the absence of which would likely be materially misleading in evaluating a consumer's creditworthiness, credit standing, credit capacity, character, general reputation, personal characteristics, or mode of living; and

(ii) Listed in section I.(b)(2)(iii) of appendix E of this part.

§ 334.42 Reasonable policies and procedures concerning the accuracy and integrity of furnished information.

(a) *Policies and procedures.* Each furnisher must establish and implement reasonable written policies and procedures regarding the accuracy and integrity of the information relating to consumers that it furnishes to a consumer reporting agency. The policies and procedures must be appropriate to the nature, size, complexity, and scope of each furnisher's activities.

(b) *Guidelines.* Each furnisher must consider the guidelines in Appendix E of this part in developing its policies and procedures required by this section, and incorporate those guidelines that are appropriate.

(c) *Reviewing and updating policies and procedures.* Each furnisher must review its policies and procedures required by this section periodically and update

12 CFR Ch. III (1-1-12 Edition)

them as necessary to ensure their continued effectiveness.

§ 334.43 Direct disputes.

(a) *General rule.* Except as otherwise provided in this section, a furnisher must conduct a reasonable investigation of a direct dispute if it relates to:

(1) The consumer's liability for a credit account or other debt with the furnisher, such as direct disputes relating to whether there is or has been identity theft or fraud against the consumer, whether there is individual or joint liability on an account, or whether the consumer is an authorized user of a credit account;

(2) The terms of a credit account or other debt with the furnisher, such as direct disputes relating to the type of account, principal balance, scheduled payment amount on an account, or the amount of the credit limit on an open-end account;

(3) The consumer's performance or other conduct concerning an account or other relationship with the furnisher, such as direct disputes relating to the current payment status, high balance, date a payment was made, the amount of a payment made, or the date an account was opened or closed; or

(4) Any other information contained in a consumer report regarding an account or other relationship with the furnisher that bears on the consumer's creditworthiness, credit standing, credit capacity, character, general reputation, personal characteristics, or mode of living.

(b) *Exceptions.* The requirements of paragraph (a) of this section do not apply to a furnisher if:

(1) The direct dispute relates to:

(i) The consumer's identifying information (other than a direct dispute relating to a consumer's liability for a credit account or other debt with the furnisher, as provided in paragraph (a)(1) of this section) such as name(s), date of birth, Social Security number, telephone number(s), or address(es);

(ii) The identity of past or present employers;

(iii) Inquiries or requests for a consumer report;

(iv) Information derived from public records, such as judgments, bankruptcies, liens, and other legal matters

Federal Deposit Insurance Corporation § 334.43

(unless provided by a furnisher with an account or other relationship with the consumer);

(v) Information related to fraud alerts or active duty alerts; or

(vi) Information provided to a consumer reporting agency by another furnisher; or

(2) The furnisher has a reasonable belief that the direct dispute is submitted by, is prepared on behalf of the consumer by, or is submitted on a form supplied to the consumer by, a credit repair organization, as defined in 15 U.S.C. 1679a(3), or an entity that would be a credit repair organization, but for 15 U.S.C. 1679a(3)(B)(i).

(c) *Direct dispute address.* A furnisher is required to investigate a direct dispute only if a consumer submits a dispute notice to the furnisher at:

(1) The address of a furnisher provided by a furnisher and set forth on a consumer report relating to the consumer;

(2) An address clearly and conspicuously specified by the furnisher for submitting direct disputes that is provided to the consumer in writing or electronically (if the consumer has agreed to the electronic delivery of information from the furnisher); or

(3) Any business address of the furnisher if the furnisher has not so specified and provided an address for submitting direct disputes under paragraphs (c)(1) or (2) of this section.

(d) *Direct dispute notice contents.* A dispute notice must include:

(1) Sufficient information to identify the account or other relationship that is in dispute, such as an account number and the name, address, and telephone number of the consumer, if applicable;

(2) The specific information that the consumer is disputing and an explanation of the basis for the dispute; and

(3) All supporting documentation or other information reasonably required by the furnisher to substantiate the basis of the dispute. This documentation may include, for example: a copy of the relevant portion of the consumer report that contains the allegedly inaccurate information; a police report; a fraud or identity theft affidavit; a court order; or account statements.

(e) *Duty of furnisher after receiving a direct dispute notice.* After receiving a dispute notice from a consumer pursuant to paragraphs (c) and (d) of this section, the furnisher must:

(1) Conduct a reasonable investigation with respect to the disputed information;

(2) Review all relevant information provided by the consumer with the dispute notice;

(3) Complete its investigation of the dispute and report the results of the investigation to the consumer before the expiration of the period under section 611(a)(1) of the Fair Credit Reporting Act (15 U.S.C. 1681i(a)(1)) within which a consumer reporting agency would be required to complete its action if the consumer had elected to dispute the information under that section; and

(4) If the investigation finds that the information reported was inaccurate, promptly notify each consumer reporting agency to which the furnisher provided inaccurate information of that determination and provide to the consumer reporting agency any correction to that information that is necessary to make the information provided by the furnisher accurate.

(f) *Frivolous or irrelevant disputes.* (1) A furnisher is not required to investigate a direct dispute if the furnisher has reasonably determined that the dispute is frivolous or irrelevant. A dispute qualifies as frivolous or irrelevant if:

(i) The consumer did not provide sufficient information to investigate the disputed information as required by paragraph (d) of this section;

(ii) The direct dispute is substantially the same as a dispute previously submitted by or on behalf of the consumer, either directly to the furnisher or through a consumer reporting agency, with respect to which the furnisher has already satisfied the applicable requirements of the Act or this section; provided, however, that a direct dispute is not substantially the same as a dispute previously submitted if the dispute includes information listed in paragraph (d) of this section that had not previously been provided to the furnisher; or

(iii) The furnisher is not required to investigate the direct dispute because

§§ 334.80-334.81   12 CFR Ch. III (1-1-12 Edition)

one or more of the exceptions listed in paragraph (b) of this section applies.

(2) *Notice of determination.* Upon making a determination that a dispute is frivolous or irrelevant, the furnisher must notify the consumer of the determination not later than five business days after making the determination, by mail or, if authorized by the consumer for that purpose, by any other means available to the furnisher.

(3) *Contents of notice of determination that a dispute is frivolous or irrelevant.* A notice of determination that a dispute is frivolous or irrelevant must include the reasons for such determination and identify any information required to investigate the disputed information, which notice may consist of a standardized form describing the general nature of such information.

Subparts F-H [Reserved]

Subpart I—Duties of Users of Consumer Reports Regarding Address Discrepancies and Records Disposal

§§ 334.80-334.81 [Reserved]

§ 334.82 Duties of users regarding address discrepancies.

(a) *Scope.* This section applies to a user of consumer reports (user) that receives a notice of address discrepancy from a consumer reporting agency described in 15 U.S.C. 1681a(p) and that is an insured state nonmember bank, insured state licensed branch of a foreign bank, or a subsidiary of such entities (except brokers, dealers, persons providing insurance, investment companies, and investment advisers).

(b) *Definition.* For purposes of this section, a *notice of address discrepancy* means a notice sent to a user by a consumer reporting agency described in 15 U.S.C. 1681a(p) pursuant to 15 U.S.C. 1681c(h)(1), that informs the user of a substantial difference between the address for the consumer that the user provided to request the consumer report and the address(es) in the agency's file for the consumer.

(c) *Reasonable belief*—(1) *Requirement to form a reasonable belief.* A user must develop and implement reasonable policies and procedures designed to enable the user to form a reasonable belief that a consumer report relates to the consumer about whom it has requested the report, when the user receives a notice of address discrepancy.

(2) *Examples of reasonable policies and procedures.* (i) Comparing the information in the consumer report provided by the consumer reporting agency with information the user:

(A) Obtains and uses to verify the consumer's identity in accordance with the requirements of the Customer Identification Program (CIP) rules implementing 31 U.S.C. 5318(l) (31 CFR 1020.220);

(B) Maintains in its own records, such as applications, change of address notifications, other customer account records, or retained CIP documentation; or

(C) Obtains from third-party sources; or

(ii) Verifying the information in the consumer report provided by the consumer reporting agency with the consumer.

(d) *Consumer's address*—(1) *Requirement to furnish consumer's address to a consumer reporting agency.* A user must develop and implement reasonable policies and procedures for furnishing an address for the consumer that the user has reasonably confirmed is accurate to the consumer reporting agency described in 15 U.S.C. 1681a(p) from whom it received the notice of address discrepancy when the user:

(i) Can form a reasonable belief that the consumer report relates to the consumer about whom the user requested the report;

(ii) Establishes a continuing relationship with the consumer; and

(iii) Regularly and in the ordinary course of business furnishes information to the consumer reporting agency from which the notice of address discrepancy relating to the consumer was obtained.

(2) *Examples of confirmation methods.* The user may reasonably confirm an address is accurate by:

(i) Verifying the address with the consumer about whom it has requested the report;

(ii) Reviewing its own records to verify the address of the consumer;

Federal Deposit Insurance Corporation § 334.90

(iii) Verifying the address through third-party sources; or

(iv) Using other reasonable means.

(3) *Timing.* The policies and procedures developed in accordance with paragraph (d)(1) of this section must provide that the user will furnish the consumer's address that the user has reasonably confirmed is accurate to the consumer reporting agency described in 15 U.S.C. 1681a(p) as part of the information it regularly furnishes for the reporting period in which it establishes a relationship with the consumer.

[72 FR 63760, Nov. 9, 2007, as amended at 74 FR 22643, May 14, 2009; 76 FR 14794, Mar. 18, 2011]

§ 334.83 Disposal of consumer information.

(a) *In general.* You must properly dispose of any consumer information that you maintain or otherwise possess in accordance with the Interagency Guidelines Establishing Information Security Standards, as set forth in appendix B to part 364 of this chapter, prescribed pursuant to section 216 of the Fair and Accurate Credit Transactions Act of 2003 (15 U.S.C. 1681w) and section 501(b) of the Gramm-Leach-Bliley Act (15 U.S.C. 6801(b)), to the extent the Guidelines are applicable to you.

(b) *Rule of construction.* Nothing in this section shall be construed to:

(1) Require you to maintain or destroy any record pertaining to a consumer that is not imposed under any other law; or

(2) Alter or affect any requirement imposed under any other provision of law to maintain or destroy such a record.

Subpart J—Identity Theft Red Flags

SOURCE: 72 FR 63761, Nov. 9, 2007, unless otherwise noted.

§ 334.90 Duties regarding the detection, prevention, and mitigation of identity theft.

(a) *Scope.* This section applies to a financial institution or creditor that is an insured state nonmember bank, insured state licensed branch of a foreign bank, or a subsidiary of such entities (except brokers, dealers, persons providing insurance, investment companies, and investment advisers).

(b) *Definitions.* For purposes of this section and Appendix J, the following definitions apply:

(1) *Account* means a continuing relationship established by a person with a financial institution or creditor to obtain a product or service for personal, family, household or business purposes. Account includes:

(i) An extension of credit, such as the purchase of property or services involving a deferred payment; and

(ii) A deposit account.

(2) The term *board of directors* includes:

(i) In the case of a branch or agency of a foreign bank, the managing official in charge of the branch or agency; and

(ii) In the case of any other creditor that does not have a board of directors, a designated employee at the level of senior management.

(3) *Covered account* means:

(i) An account that a financial institution or creditor offers or maintains, primarily for personal, family, or household purposes, that involves or is designed to permit multiple payments or transactions, such as a credit card account, mortgage loan, automobile loan, margin account, cell phone account, utility account, checking account, or savings account; and

(ii) Any other account that the financial institution or creditor offers or maintains for which there is a reasonably foreseeable risk to customers or to the safety and soundness of the financial institution or creditor from identity theft, including financial, operational, compliance, reputation, or litigation risks.

(4) *Credit* has the same meaning as in 15 U.S.C. 1681a(r)(5).

(5) *Creditor* has the same meaning as in 15 U.S.C. 1681a(r)(5), and includes lenders such as banks, finance companies, automobile dealers, mortgage brokers, utility companies, and telecommunications companies.

(6) *Customer* means a person that has a covered account with a financial institution or creditor.

(7) *Financial institution* has the same meaning as in 15 U.S.C. 1681a(t).

(8) *Identity theft* has the same meaning as in 16 CFR 603.2(a).

(9) *Red Flag* means a pattern, practice, or specific activity that indicates the possible existence of identity theft.

(10) *Service provider* means a person that provides a service directly to the financial institution or creditor.

(c) *Periodic identification of covered accounts.* Each financial institution or creditor must periodically determine whether it offers or maintains covered accounts. As a part of this determination, a financial institution or creditor must conduct a risk assessment to determine whether it offers or maintains covered accounts described in paragraph (b)(3)(ii) of this section, taking into consideration:

(1) The methods it provides to open its accounts;

(2) The methods it provides to access its accounts; and

(3) Its previous experiences with identity theft.

(d) *Establishment of an Identity Theft Prevention Program*—(1) *Program requirement.* Each financial institution or creditor that offers or maintains one or more covered accounts must develop and implement a written Identity Theft Prevention Program (Program) that is designed to detect, prevent, and mitigate identity theft in connection with the opening of a covered account or any existing covered account. The Program must be appropriate to the size and complexity of the financial institution or creditor and the nature and scope of its activities.

(2) *Elements of the Program.* The Program must include reasonable policies and procedures to:

(i) Identify relevant Red Flags for the covered accounts that the financial institution or creditor offers or maintains, and incorporate those Red Flags into its Program;

(ii) Detect Red Flags that have been incorporated into the Program of the financial institution or creditor;

(iii) Respond appropriately to any Red Flags that are detected pursuant to paragraph (d)(2)(ii) of this section to prevent and mitigate identity theft; and

(iv) Ensure the Program (including the Red Flags determined to be relevant) is updated periodically, to reflect changes in risks to customers and to the safety and soundness of the financial institution or creditor from identity theft.

(e) *Administration of the Program.* Each financial institution or creditor that is required to implement a Program must provide for the continued administration of the Program and must:

(1) Obtain approval of the initial written Program from either its board of directors or an appropriate committee of the board of directors;

(2) Involve the board of directors, an appropriate committee thereof, or a designated employee at the level of senior management in the oversight, development, implementation and administration of the Program;

(3) Train staff, as necessary, to effectively implement the Program; and

(4) Exercise appropriate and effective oversight of service provider arrangements.

(f) *Guidelines.* Each financial institution or creditor that is required to implement a Program must consider the guidelines in Appendix J of this part and include in its Program those guidelines that are appropriate.

§ 334.91 Duties of card issuers regarding changes of address.

(a) *Scope.* This section applies to an issuer of a debit or credit card (card issuer) that is an insured state nonmember bank, insured state licensed branch of a foreign bank, or a subsidiary of such entities (except brokers, dealers, persons providing insurance, investment companies, and investment advisers).

(b) *Definitions.* For purposes of this section:

(1) *Cardholder* means a consumer who has been issued a credit or debit card.

(2) *Clear and conspicuous* means reasonably understandable and designed to call attention to the nature and significance of the information presented.

(c) *Address validation requirements.* A card issuer must establish and implement reasonable policies and procedures to assess the validity of a change of address if it receives notification of a change of address for a consumer's debit or credit card account and, within a short period of time afterwards

Federal Deposit Insurance Corporation

Pt. 334, App. C

(during at least the first 30 days after it receives such notification), the card issuer receives a request for an additional or replacement card for the same account. Under these circumstances, the card issuer may not issue an additional or replacement card, until, in accordance with its reasonable policies and procedures and for the purpose of assessing the validity of the change of address, the card issuer:

(1)(i) Notifies the cardholder of the request:

(A) At the cardholder's former address; or

(B) By any other means of communication that the card issuer and the cardholder have previously agreed to use; and

(ii) Provides to the cardholder a reasonable means of promptly reporting incorrect address changes; or

(2) Otherwise assesses the validity of the change of address in accordance with the policies and procedures the card issuer has established pursuant to § 334.90 of this part.

(d) *Alternative timing of address validation.* A card issuer may satisfy the requirements of paragraph (c) of this section if it validates an address pursuant to the methods in paragraph (c)(1) or (c)(2) of this section when it receives an address change notification, before it receives a request for an additional or replacement card.

(e) *Form of notice.* Any written or electronic notice that the card issuer provides under this paragraph must be clear and conspicuous and provided separately from its regular correspondence with the cardholder.

APPENDIXES A–B TO PART 334
[RESERVED]

APPENDIX C TO PART 334—MODEL FORMS FOR OPT-OUT NOTICES

a. Although use of the model forms is not required, use of the model forms in this Appendix (as applicable) complies with the requirement in section 624 of the Act for clear, conspicuous, and concise notices.

b. Certain changes may be made to the language or format of the model forms without losing the protection from liability afforded by use of the model forms. These changes may not be so extensive as to affect the substance, clarity, or meaningful sequence of the language in the model forms. Persons making such extensive revisions will lose the safe harbor that this Appendix provides. Acceptable changes include, for example:

1. Rearranging the order of the references to "your income," "your account history," and "your credit score."

2. Substituting other types of information for "income," "account history," or "credit score" for accuracy, such as "payment history," "credit history," "payoff status," or "claims history."

3. Substituting a clearer and more accurate description of the affiliates providing or covered by the notice for phrases such as "the [ABC] group of companies," including without limitation a statement that the entity providing the notice recently purchased the consumer's account.

4. Substituting other types of affiliates covered by the notice for "credit card," "insurance," or "securities" affiliates.

5. Omitting items that are not accurate or applicable. For example, if a person does not limit the duration of the opt-out period, the notice may omit information about the renewal notice.

6. Adding a statement informing consumers how much time they have to opt out before shared eligibility information may be used to make solicitations to them.

7. Adding a statement that the consumer may exercise the right to opt out at any time.

8. Adding the following statement, if accurate: "If you previously opted out, you do not need to do so again."

9. Providing a place on the form for the consumer to fill in identifying information, such as his or her name and address:

10. Adding disclosures regarding the treatment of opt-outs by joint consumers to comply with § 334.23(a)(2) of this part.

C–1 Model Form for Initial Opt-out Notice (Single-Affiliate Notice)

C–2 Model Form for Initial Opt-out Notice (Joint Notice)

C–3 Model Form for Renewal Notice (Single-Affiliate Notice)

C–4 Model Form for Renewal Notice (Joint Notice)

C–5 Model Form for Voluntary "No Marketing" Notice

C–1—Model Form for Initial Opt-out Notice (Single-Affiliate Notice)—[Your Choice To Limit Marketing]/[Marketing Opt-out]

• [Name of Affiliate] is providing this notice.

• [Optional: Federal law gives you the right to limit some but not all marketing from our affiliates. Federal law also requires us to give you this notice to tell you about your choice to limit marketing from our affiliates.]

• You may limit our affiliates in the [ABC] group of companies, such as our [credit card,

413

insurance, and securities] affiliates, from marketing their products or services to you based on your personal information that we collect and share with them. This information includes your [income], your [account history with us], and your [credit score].

• Your choice to limit marketing offers from our affiliates will apply [until you tell us to change your choice]/[for x years from when you tell us your choice]/[for at least 5 years from when you tell us your choice]. [Include if the opt-out period expires.] Once that period expires, you will receive a renewal notice that will allow you to continue to limit marketing offers from our affiliates for [another x years]/[at least another 5 years].

• [Include, if applicable, in a subsequent notice, including an annual notice, for consumers who may have previously opted out.] If you have already made a choice to limit marketing offers from our affiliates, you do not need to act again until you receive the renewal notice.

To limit marketing offers, contact us [include all that apply]:
• By telephone: 1-877-###-####
• On the Web: *www.---.com*
• By mail: Check the box and complete the form below, and send the form to:
[Company name]
[Company address]

__Do not allow your affiliates to use my personal information to market to me.

C-2—Model Form for Initial Opt-out Notice (Joint Notice)—[Your Choice To Limit Marketing]/[Marketing Opt-out]

• The [ABC group of companies] is providing this notice.

• [Optional: Federal law gives you the right to limit some but not all marketing from the [ABC] companies. Federal law also requires us to give you this notice to tell you about your choice to limit marketing from the [ABC] companies.]

• You may limit the [ABC] companies, such as the [ABC credit card, insurance, and securities] affiliates, from marketing their products or services to you based on your personal information that they receive from other [ABC] companies. This information includes your [income], your [account history], and your [credit score].

• Your choice to limit marketing offers from the [ABC] companies will apply [until you tell us to change your choice]/[for x years from when you tell us your choice]/[for at least 5 years from when you tell us your choice]. [Include if the opt-out period expires.] Once that period expires, you will receive a renewal notice that will allow you to continue to limit marketing offers from the [ABC] companies for [another x years]/[at least another 5 years].

• [Include, if applicable, in a subsequent notice, including an annual notice, for consumers who may have previously opted out.] If you have already made a choice to limit marketing offers from the [ABC] companies, you do not need to act again until you receive the renewal notice.

To limit marketing offers, contact us [include all that apply]:
• By telephone: 1-877-###-####
• On the Web: *www.---.com*
• By mail: Check the box and complete the form below, and send the form to:
[Company name]
[Company address]

__Do not allow any company [in the ABC group of companies] to use my personal information to market to me.

C-3—Model Form for Renewal Notice (Single-Affiliate Notice)—[Renewing Your Choice To Limit Marketing]/[Renewing Your Marketing Opt-out]

• [Name of Affiliate] is providing this notice.

• [Optional: Federal law gives you the right to limit some but not all marketing from our affiliates. Federal law also requires us to give you this notice to tell you about your choice to limit marketing from our affiliates.]

• You previously chose to limit our affiliates in the [ABC] group of companies, such as our [credit card, insurance, and securities] affiliates, from marketing their products or services to you based on your personal information that we share with them. This information includes your [income], your [account history with us], and your [credit score].

• Your choice has expired or is about to expire.

To renew your choice to limit marketing for [x] more years, contact us [include all that apply]:
• By telephone: 1-877-###-####
• On the Web: *www.---.com*
• By mail: Check the box and complete the form below, and send the form to:
[Company name]
[Company address]

__Renew my choice to limit marketing for [x] more years.

C-4—Model Form for Renewal Notice (Joint Notice)—[Renewing Your Choice To Limit Marketing]/[Renewing Your Marketing Opt-out]

• The [ABC group of companies] is providing this notice.

• [Optional: Federal law gives you the right to limit some but not all marketing from the [ABC] companies. Federal law also requires us to give you this notice to tell you about your choice to limit marketing from the [ABC] companies.]

Federal Deposit Insurance Corporation Pt. 334, App. E

- You previously chose to limit the [ABC] companies, such as the [ABC credit card, insurance, and securities] affiliates, from marketing their products or services to you based on your personal information that they receive from other ABC companies. This information includes your [income], your [account history], and your [credit score].
- Your choice has expired or is about to expire.

To renew your choice to limit marketing for [x] more years, contact us [include all that apply]:
- By telephone: 1–877–###–####
- On the Web: *www.---.com*
- By mail: Check the box and complete the form below, and send the form to:

[Company name]
[Company address]

___Renew my choice to limit marketing for [x] more years.

C–5—MODEL FORM FOR VOLUNTARY "NO MARKETING" NOTICE

YOUR CHOICE TO STOP MARKETING

- [Name of Affiliate] is providing this notice.
- You may choose to stop all marketing from us and our affiliates.
- [Your choice to stop marketing from us and our affiliates will apply until you tell us to change your choice.]

To stop all marketing, contact us [include all that apply]:
- By telephone: 1–877–###–####
- On the Web: www.—.com
- By mail: Check the box and complete the form below, and send the form to:

[Company name]
[Company address]
___Do not market to me.

[72 FR 62971, Nov. 7, 2007, as amended at 74 FR 22643, May 14, 2009]

APPENDIX D TO PART 334 [RESERVED]

APPENDIX E TO PART 334—INTERAGENCY GUIDELINES CONCERNING THE ACCURACY AND INTEGRITY OF INFORMATION FURNISHED TO CONSUMER REPORTING AGENCIES

The FDIC encourages voluntary furnishing of information to consumer reporting agencies. Section 334.42 of this part requires each furnisher to establish and implement reasonable written policies and procedures concerning the accuracy and integrity of the information it furnishes to consumer reporting agencies. Under §334.42(b), a furnisher must consider the guidelines set forth below in developing its policies and procedures. In establishing these policies and procedures, a furnisher may include any of its existing policies and procedures that are relevant and appropriate. Section 334.42(c) requires each furnisher to review its policies and procedures periodically and update them as necessary to ensure their continued effectiveness.

I. NATURE, SCOPE, AND OBJECTIVES OF POLICIES AND PROCEDURES

(a) *Nature and Scope.* Section 334.42(a) of this part requires that a furnisher's policies and procedures be appropriate to the nature, size, complexity, and scope of the furnisher's activities. In developing its policies and procedures, a furnisher should consider, for example:

(1) The types of business activities in which the furnisher engages;

(2) The nature and frequency of the information the furnisher provides to consumer reporting agencies; and

(3) The technology used by the furnisher to furnish information to consumer reporting agencies.

(b) *Objectives.* A furnisher's policies and procedures should be reasonably designed to promote the following objectives:

(1) To furnish information about accounts or other relationships with a consumer that is accurate, such that the furnished information:

(i) Identifies the appropriate consumer;

(ii) Reflects the terms of and liability for those accounts or other relationships; and

(iii) Reflects the consumer's performance and other conduct with respect to the account or other relationship;

(2) To furnish information about accounts or other relationships with a consumer that has integrity, such that the furnished information:

(i) Is substantiated by the furnisher's records at the time it is furnished;

(ii) Is furnished in a form and manner that is designed to minimize the likelihood that the information may be incorrectly reflected in a consumer report; thus, the furnished information should:

(A) Include appropriate identifying information about the consumer to whom it pertains; and

(B) Be furnished in a standardized and clearly understandable form and manner and with a date specifying the time period to which the information pertains; and

(iii) Includes the credit limit, if applicable and in the furnisher's possession;

(3) To conduct reasonable investigations of consumer disputes and take appropriate actions based on the outcome of such investigations; and

(4) To update the information it furnishes as necessary to reflect the current status of the consumer's account or other relationship, including, for example:

(i) Any transfer of an account (*e.g.*, by sale or assignment for collection) to a third party; and

(ii) Any cure of the consumer's failure to abide by the terms of the account or other relationship.

II. ESTABLISHING AND IMPLEMENTING POLICIES AND PROCEDURES

In establishing and implementing its policies and procedures, a furnisher should:

(a) Identify practices or activities of the furnisher that can compromise the accuracy or integrity of information furnished to consumer reporting agencies, such as by:

(1) Reviewing its existing practices and activities, including the technological means and other methods it uses to furnish information to consumer reporting agencies and the frequency and timing of its furnishing of information;

(2) Reviewing its historical records relating to accuracy or integrity or to disputes; reviewing other information relating to the accuracy or integrity of information provided by the furnisher to consumer reporting agencies; and considering the types of errors, omissions, or other problems that may have affected the accuracy or integrity of information it has furnished about consumers to consumer reporting agencies;

(3) Considering any feedback received from consumer reporting agencies, consumers, or other appropriate parties;

(4) Obtaining feedback from the furnisher's staff; and

(5) Considering the potential impact of the furnisher's policies and procedures on consumers.

(b) Evaluate the effectiveness of existing policies and procedures of the furnisher regarding the accuracy and integrity of information furnished to consumer reporting agencies; consider whether new, additional, or different policies and procedures are necessary; and consider whether implementation of existing policies and procedures should be modified to enhance the accuracy and integrity of information about consumers furnished to consumer reporting agencies.

(c) Evaluate the effectiveness of specific methods (including technological means) the furnisher uses to provide information to consumer reporting agencies; how those methods may affect the accuracy and integrity of the information it provides to consumer reporting agencies; and whether new, additional, or different methods (including technological means) should be used to provide information to consumer reporting agencies to enhance the accuracy and integrity of that information.

III. SPECIFIC COMPONENTS OF POLICIES AND PROCEDURES

In developing its policies and procedures, a furnisher should address the following, as appropriate:

(a) Establishing and implementing a system for furnishing information about consumers to consumer reporting agencies that is appropriate to the nature, size, complexity, and scope of the furnisher's business operations.

(b) Using standard data reporting formats and standard procedures for compiling and furnishing data, where feasible, such as the electronic transmission of information about consumers to consumer reporting agencies.

(c) Maintaining records for a reasonable period of time, not less than any applicable recordkeeping requirement, in order to substantiate the accuracy of any information about consumers it furnishes that is subject to a direct dispute.

(d) Establishing and implementing appropriate internal controls regarding the accuracy and integrity of information about consumers furnished to consumer reporting agencies, such as by implementing standard procedures and verifying random samples of information provided to consumer reporting agencies.

(e) Training staff that participates in activities related to the furnishing of information about consumers to consumer reporting agencies to implement the policies and procedures.

(f) Providing for appropriate and effective oversight of relevant service providers whose activities may affect the accuracy or integrity of information about consumers furnished to consumer reporting agencies to ensure compliance with the policies and procedures.

(g) Furnishing information about consumers to consumer reporting agencies following mergers, portfolio acquisitions or sales, or other acquisitions or transfers of accounts or other obligations in a manner that prevents re-aging of information, duplicative reporting, or other problems that may similarly affect the accuracy or integrity of the information furnished.

(h) Deleting, updating, and correcting information in the furnisher's records, as appropriate, to avoid furnishing inaccurate information.

(i) Conducting reasonable investigations of disputes.

(j) Designing technological and other means of communication with consumer reporting agencies to prevent duplicative reporting of accounts, erroneous association of information with the wrong consumer(s), and other occurrences that may compromise the accuracy or integrity of information provided to consumer reporting agencies.

Federal Deposit Insurance Corporation

Pt. 334, App. J

(k) Providing consumer reporting agencies with sufficient identifying information in the furnisher's possession about each consumer about whom information is furnished to enable the consumer reporting agency properly to identify the consumer.

(l) Conducting a periodic evaluation of its own practices, consumer reporting agency practices of which the furnisher is aware, investigations of disputed information, corrections of inaccurate information, means of communication, and other factors that may affect the accuracy or integrity of information furnished to consumer reporting agencies.

(m) Complying with applicable requirements under the Fair Credit Reporting Act and its implementing regulations.

[75 FR 31518, July 1, 2009]

APPENDICES F–I TO PART 334 [RESERVED]

APPENDIX J TO PART 334—INTERAGENCY GUIDELINES ON IDENTITY THEFT DETECTION, PREVENTION, AND MITIGATION

Section 334.90 of this part requires each financial institution and creditor that offers or maintains one or more covered accounts, as defined in §334.90(b)(3) of this part, to develop and provide for the continued administration of a written Program to detect, prevent, and mitigate identity theft in connection with the opening of a covered account or any existing covered account. These guidelines are intended to assist financial institutions and creditors in the formulation and maintenance of a Program that satisfies the requirements of §334.90 of this part.

I. The Program

In designing its Program, a financial institution or creditor may incorporate, as appropriate, its existing policies, procedures, and other arrangements that control reasonably foreseeable risks to customers or to the safety and soundness of the financial institution or creditor from identity theft.

II. Identifying Relevant Red Flags

(a) *Risk Factors.* A financial institution or creditor should consider the following factors in identifying relevant Red Flags for covered accounts, as appropriate:

(1) The types of covered accounts it offers or maintains;

(2) The methods it provides to open its covered accounts;

(3) The methods it provides to access its covered accounts; and

(4) Its previous experiences with identity theft.

(b) *Sources of Red Flags.* Financial institutions and creditors should incorporate relevant Red Flags from sources such as:

(1) Incidents of identity theft that the financial institution or creditor has experienced;

(2) Methods of identity theft that the financial institution or creditor has identified that reflect changes in identity theft risks; and

(3) Applicable supervisory guidance.

(c) *Categories of Red Flags.* The Program should include relevant Red Flags from the following categories, as appropriate. Examples of Red Flags from each of these categories are appended as Supplement A to this Appendix J.

(1) Alerts, notifications, or other warnings received from consumer reporting agencies or service providers, such as fraud detection services;

(2) The presentation of suspicious documents;

(3) The presentation of suspicious personal identifying information, such as a suspicious address change;

(4) The unusual use of, or other suspicious activity related to, a covered account; and

(5) Notice from customers, victims of identity theft, law enforcement authorities, or other persons regarding possible identity theft in connection with covered accounts held by the financial institution or creditor.

III. Detecting Red Flags.

The Program's policies and procedures should address the detection of Red Flags in connection with the opening of covered accounts and existing covered accounts, such as by:

(a) Obtaining identifying information about, and verifying the identity of, a person opening a covered account, for example, using the policies and procedures regarding identification and verification set forth in the Customer Identification Program rules implementing 31 U.S.C. 5318(l) (31 CFR 1020.220); and

(b) Authenticating customers, monitoring transactions, and verifying the validity of change of address requests, in the case of existing covered accounts.

IV. Preventing and Mitigating Identity Theft.

The Program's policies and procedures should provide for appropriate responses to the Red Flags the financial institution or creditor has detected that are commensurate with the degree of risk posed. In determining an appropriate response, a financial institution or creditor should consider aggravating factors that may heighten the risk of identity theft, such as a data security incident that results in unauthorized access to a customer's account records held by the financial

417

institution, creditor, or third party, or notice that a customer has provided information related to a covered account held by the financial institution or creditor to someone fraudulently claiming to represent the financial institution or creditor or to a fraudulent Web site. Appropriate responses may include the following:

(a) Monitoring a covered account for evidence of identity theft;

(b) Contacting the customer;

(c) Changing any passwords, security codes, or other security devices that permit access to a covered account;

(d) Reopening a covered account with a new account number;

(e) Not opening a new covered account;

(f) Closing an existing covered account;

(g) Not attempting to collect on a covered account or not selling a covered account to a debt collector;

(h) Notifying law enforcement; or

(i) Determining that no response is warranted under the particular circumstances.

V. *Updating the Program.*

Financial institutions and creditors should update the Program (including the Red Flags determined to be relevant) periodically, to reflect changes in risks to customers or to the safety and soundness of the financial institution or creditor from identity theft, based on factors such as:

(a) The experiences of the financial institution or creditor with identity theft;

(b) Changes in methods of identity theft;

(c) Changes in methods to detect, prevent, and mitigate identity theft;

(d) Changes in the types of accounts that the financial institution or creditor offers or maintains; and

(e) Changes in the business arrangements of the financial institution or creditor, including mergers, acquisitions, alliances, joint ventures, and service provider arrangements.

VI. Methods for Administering the Program

(a) *Oversight of Program.* Oversight by the board of directors, an appropriate committee of the board, or a designated employee at the level of senior management should include:

(1) Assigning specific responsibility for the Program's implementation;

(2) Reviewing reports prepared by staff regarding compliance by the financial institution or creditor with § 334.90 of this part; and

(3) Approving material changes to the Program as necessary to address changing identity theft risks.

(b) *Reports.* (1) *In general.* Staff of the financial institution or creditor responsible for development, implementation, and administration of its Program should report to the board of directors, an appropriate committee of the board, or a designated employee at the level of senior management, at least annually, on compliance by the financial institution or creditor with § 334.90 of this part.

(2) *Contents of report.* The report should address material matters related to the Program and evaluate issues such as: the effectiveness of the policies and procedures of the financial institution or creditor in addressing the risk of identity theft in connection with the opening of covered accounts and with respect to existing covered accounts; service provider arrangements; significant incidents involving identity theft and management's response; and recommendations for material changes to the Program.

(c) *Oversight of service provider arrangements.* Whenever a financial institution or creditor engages a service provider to perform an activity in connection with one or more covered accounts the financial institution or creditor should take steps to ensure that the activity of the service provider is conducted in accordance with reasonable policies and procedures designed to detect, prevent, and mitigate the risk of identity theft. For example, a financial institution or creditor could require the service provider by contract to have policies and procedures to detect relevant Red Flags that may arise in the performance of the service provider's activities, and either report the Red Flags to the financial institution or creditor, or to take appropriate steps to prevent or mitigate identity theft.

VII. Other Applicable Legal Requirements

Financial institutions and creditors should be mindful of other related legal requirements that may be applicable, such as:

(a) For financial institutions and creditors that are subject to 31 U.S.C. 5318(g), filing a Suspicious Activity Report in accordance with applicable law and regulation;

(b) Implementing any requirements under 15 U.S.C. 1681c–1(h) regarding the circumstances under which credit may be extended when the financial institution or creditor detects a fraud or active duty alert;

(c) Implementing any requirements for furnishers of information to consumer reporting agencies under 15 U.S.C. 1681s–2, for example, to correct or update inaccurate or incomplete information, and to not report information that the furnisher has reasonable cause to believe is inaccurate; and

(d) Complying with the prohibitions in 15 U.S.C. 1681m on the sale, transfer, and placement for collection of certain debts resulting from identity theft.

Supplement A to Appendix J

In addition to incorporating Red Flags from the sources recommended in section II.b. of the Guidelines in Appendix J of this part, each financial institution or creditor

Federal Deposit Insurance Corporation **Pt. 334, App. J**

may consider incorporating into its Program, whether singly or in combination, Red Flags from the following illustrative examples in connection with covered accounts:

Alerts, Notifications or Warnings from a Consumer Reporting Agency

1. A fraud or active duty alert is included with a consumer report.
2. A consumer reporting agency provides a notice of credit freeze in response to a request for a consumer report.
3. A consumer reporting agency provides a notice of address discrepancy, as defined in § 334.82(b) of this part.
4. A consumer report indicates a pattern of activity that is inconsistent with the history and usual pattern of activity of an applicant or customer, such as:
   a. A recent and significant increase in the volume of inquiries;
   b. An unusual number of recently established credit relationships;
   c. A material change in the use of credit, especially with respect to recently established credit relationships; or
   d. An account that was closed for cause or identified for abuse of account privileges by a financial institution or creditor.

Suspicious Documents

5. Documents provided for identification appear to have been altered or forged.
6. The photograph or physical description on the identification is not consistent with the appearance of the applicant or customer presenting the identification.
7. Other information on the identification is not consistent with information provided by the person opening a new covered account or customer presenting the identification.
8. Other information on the identification is not consistent with readily accessible information that is on file with the financial institution or creditor, such as a signature card or a recent check.
9. An application appears to have been altered or forged, or gives the appearance of having been destroyed and reassembled.

Suspicious Personal Identifying Information

10. Personal identifying information provided is inconsistent when compared against external information sources used by the financial institution or creditor. For example:
    a. The address does not match any address in the consumer report; or
    b. The Social Security Number (SSN) has not been issued, or is listed on the Social Security Administration's Death Master File.
11. Personal identifying information provided by the customer is not consistent with other personal identifying information provided by the customer. For example, there is a lack of correlation between the SSN range and date of birth.
12. Personal identifying information provided is associated with known fraudulent activity as indicated by internal or third-party sources used by the financial institution or creditor. For example:
    a. The address on an application is the same as the address provided on a fraudulent application; or
    b. The phone number on an application is the same as the number provided on a fraudulent application.
13. Personal identifying information provided is of a type commonly associated with fraudulent activity as indicated by internal or third-party sources used by the financial institution or creditor. For example:
    a. The address on an application is fictitious, a mail drop, or a prison; or
    b. The phone number is invalid, or is associated with a pager or answering service.
14. The SSN provided is the same as that submitted by other persons opening an account or other customers.
15. The address or telephone number provided is the same as or similar to the address or telephone number submitted by an unusually large number of other persons opening accounts or by other customers.
16. The person opening the covered account or the customer fails to provide all required personal identifying information on an application or in response to notification that the application is incomplete.
17. Personal identifying information provided is not consistent with personal identifying information that is on file with the financial institution or creditor.
18. For financial institutions and creditors that use challenge questions, the person opening the covered account or the customer cannot provide authenticating information beyond that which generally would be available from a wallet or consumer report.

Unusual Use of, or Suspicious Activity Related to, the Covered Account

19. Shortly following the notice of a change of address for a covered account, the institution or creditor receives a request for a new, additional, or replacement card or a cell phone, or for the addition of authorized users on the account.
20. A new revolving credit account is used in a manner commonly associated with known patterns of fraud. For example:
    a. The majority of available credit is used for cash advances or merchandise that is easily convertible to cash (e.g., electronics equipment or jewelry); or
    b. The customer fails to make the first payment or makes an initial payment but no subsequent payments.
21. A covered account is used in a manner that is not consistent with established patterns of activity on the account. There is, for example:

a. Nonpayment when there is no history of late or missed payments;
b. A material increase in the use of available credit;
c. A material change in purchasing or spending patterns;
d. A material change in electronic fund transfer patterns in connection with a deposit account; or
e. A material change in telephone call patterns in connection with a cellular phone account.

22. A covered account that has been inactive for a reasonably lengthy period of time is used (taking into consideration the type of account, the expected pattern of usage and other relevant factors).

23. Mail sent to the customer is returned repeatedly as undeliverable although transactions continue to be conducted in connection with the customer's covered account.

24. The financial institution or creditor is notified that the customer is not receiving paper account statements.

25. The financial institution or creditor is notified of unauthorized charges or transactions in connection with a customer's covered account.

Notice From Customers, Victims of Identity Theft, Law Enforcement Authorities, or Other Persons Regarding Possible Identity Theft in Connection With Covered Accounts Held by the Financial Institution or Creditor

26. The financial institution or creditor is notified by a customer, a victim of identity theft, a law enforcement authority, or any other person that it has opened a fraudulent account for a person engaged in identity theft.

[72 FR 63762, Nov. 9, 2007, as amended at 74 FR 22643, May 14, 2009; 76 FR 14794, Mar. 18, 2011]

PART 335—SECURITIES OF NONMEMBER INSURED BANKS

Sec.
335.101 Scope of part, authority and OMB control number.
335.111 Forms and schedules.
335.121 Listing standards related to audit committees.
335.201 Securities exempted from registration.
335.211 Registration and reporting.
335.221 Forms for registration of securities and cross reference to Regulation FD (Fair Disclosure).
335.231 Certification, suspension of trading, and removal from listing by exchanges.
335.241 Unlisted trading.
335.251 Forms for notification of action taken by national securities exchanges.
335.261 Exemptions; terminations; and definitions.
335.301 Reports of issuers of securities registered pursuant to section 12.
335.311 Forms for annual, quarterly, current, and other reports of issuers.
335.321 Maintenance of records and issuer's representations in connection with required reports.
335.331 Acquisition statements, acquisition of securities by issuers, and other matters.
335.401 Solicitations of proxies.
335.501 Tender offers.
335.601 Requirements of section 16 of the Securities Exchange Act of 1934.
335.611 Initial statements of beneficial ownership of securities (Form 3).
335.612 Statement of changes in beneficial ownership of securities (Form 4).
335.613 Annual statement of beneficial ownership of securities (Form 5).
335.701 Filing requirements, public reference, and confidentiality.
335.801 Inapplicable SEC regulations; FDIC substituted regulations; additional information.
335.901 Delegation of authority to act on matters with respect to disclosure laws and regulations.

AUTHORITY: 12 U.S.C. 1819; 15 U.S.C. 78l(i), 78m, 78n, 78p, 78w, 7241, 7242, 7243, 7244, 7261, 7262, 7264, and 7265.

SOURCE: 62 FR 6856, Feb. 14, 1997, unless otherwise noted.

§ 335.101 Scope of part, authority and OMB control number.

(a) This part is issued by the Federal Deposit Insurance Corporation (the FDIC) under section 12(i) of the Securities Exchange Act of 1934, as amended (15 U.S.C. 78) (the Exchange Act) and applies to all securities of FDIC insured banks (including foreign banks having an insured branch) which are neither a member of the Federal Reserve System nor a District bank (collectively referred to as nonmember banks) that are subject to the registration requirements of section 12(b) or section 12(g) of the Exchange Act (registered nonmember banks). The FDIC is vested with the powers, functions, and duties vested in the Securities and Exchange Commission (the Commission or SEC) to administer and enforce the provisions of sections 10A(m), 12, 13, 14(a), 14(c), 14(d), 14(f), and 16 of the Securities Exchange Act of 1934, as amended (the Exchange Act) (15 U.S.C. 78l, 78m, 78n(a), 78n(c), 78n(d), 78n(f),

Federal Deposit Insurance Corporation § 335.221

and 78(p)), and sections 302, 303, 304, 306, 401(b), 404, 406, and 407 of the Sarbanes-Oxley Act of 2002 (15 U.S.C. 7241, 7242, 7243, 7244, 7261, 7262, 7264, and 7265) regarding nonmember banks with one or more classes of securities subject to the registration provisions of sections 12(b) and 12(g) of the Exchange Act.

(b) Part 335 generally incorporates through cross reference the regulations of the SEC as these regulations are issued, revised, or updated from time to time under sections 10A(m), 12, 13, 14(a), 14(c), 14(d), 14(f), and 16 of the Exchange Act and sections 302, 303, 304, 306, 401(b), 404, 406, and 407 of the Sarbanes-Oxley Act of 2002 (Sarbanes-Oxley Act), except as provided at § 335.801 of this part. References to the Commission in the regulations of the SEC are deemed to refer to the FDIC unless the context otherwise requires.

[62 FR 6856, Feb. 14, 1997, as amended at 69 FR 19088, Apr. 12, 2004; 69 FR 59783, Oct. 6, 2004; 70 FR 16400, Mar. 31, 2005; 70 FR 44272, Aug. 2, 2005]

§ 335.111 Forms and schedules.

The Exchange Act regulations of the SEC, which are cross referenced under this part, require the filing of forms and schedules as applicable. Reference is made to SEC Exchange Act regulation 17 CFR part 249 regarding the availability of all applicable SEC Exchange Act forms. Required schedules are codified and are found within the context of the SEC's regulations. All forms and schedules shall be titled with the name of the FDIC in substitution for the name of the SEC. The filing of forms and schedules shall be made with the FDIC at the address in § 335.701 or may be filed electronically at FDIC*connect* at *https://www2.fdicconnect.gov/index.asp*. However, electronic filing of Beneficial Ownership Forms 3, 4 and 5 is required. Copies of Forms 3 (§ 335.611), 4 (§ 335.612) and 5 (§ 335.613) and the instructions thereto may be printed and downloaded from *https://www.fdic.gov/regulations/laws/forms*.

[75 FR 73949, Nov. 30, 2010]

§ 335.121 Listing standards related to audit committees.

The provisions of the applicable SEC regulation under section 10(A)(m) of the Exchange Act shall be followed as codified at 17 CFR part 240.

[75 FR 73949, Nov. 30, 2010]

§ 335.201 Securities exempted from registration.

Persons subject to registration requirements under Exchange Act section 12 and subject to this part shall follow the applicable and currently effective SEC regulations relative to exemptions from registration issued under sections 3 and 12 of the Exchange Act as codified at 17 CFR part 240.

[75 FR 73949, Nov. 30, 2010

§ 335.211 Registration and reporting.

Persons with securities subject to registration under Exchange Act sections 12(b) and 12(g), required to report under Exchange Act section 13, and subject to this part shall follow the applicable and currently effective SEC regulations issued under section 12(b) of the Exchange Act as codified at 17 CFR part 240.

[75 FR 73949, Nov. 30, 2010]

§ 335.221 Forms for registration of securities and cross reference to Regulation FD (Fair Disclosure).

(a) The applicable forms for registration of securities and similar matters are codified in 17 CFR part 249. All forms shall be filed with the FDIC as appropriate and shall be titled with the name of the FDIC instead of the SEC.

(b) The requirements for Financial Statements can generally be found in Regulation S–X (17 CFR part 210). Banks may also refer to the instructions for Federal Financial Institutions Examination Council (FFIEC) Consolidated Reports of Condition and Income when preparing unaudited interim statements. The requirements for Management's Discussion and Analysis of Financial Condition and Results of Operations can be found at 17 CFR part 229. Additional requirements are provided at Industry Guide 3, Statistical Disclosure by Bank Holding Companies, which is found at 17 CFR part 229.

(c) The provisions of the applicable and currently effective SEC regulation

§ 335.231

FD shall be followed as codified at 17 CFR part 243.

[75 FR 73949, Nov. 30, 2010]

§ 335.231 Certification, suspension of trading, and removal from listing by exchanges.

The provisions of the applicable and currently effective SEC regulations under section 12(d) of the Exchange Act shall be followed as codified at 17 part CFR 240.

[75 FR 73949, Nov. 30, 2010]

§ 335.241 Unlisted trading.

The provisions of the applicable and currently effective SEC regulations under section 12(f) of the Exchange Act shall be followed as codified at 17 CFR part 240.

[75 FR 73949, Nov. 30, 2010]

§ 335.251 Forms for notification of action taken by national securities exchanges.

The applicable forms for notification of action taken by national securities exchanges are codified in 17 CFR part 249. All forms shall be filed with the FDIC as appropriate and shall be titled with the name of the FDIC instead of the SEC.

[75 FR 73949, Nov. 30, 2010]

§ 335.261 Exemptions, terminations, and definitions.

The provisions of the applicable and currently effective SEC regulations under sections 12(g) and 12(h) of the Exchange Act shall be followed as codified in 17 CFR part 240.

[75 FR 73949, Nov. 30, 2010]

§ 335.301 Reports of issuers of securities registered pursuant to section 12.

The provisions of the applicable and currently effective SEC regulations under section 13(a) of the Exchange Act shall be followed as codified at 17 CFR part 240.

[75 FR 73949, Nov. 30, 2010]

§ 335.311 Forms for annual, quarterly, current, and other reports of issuers.

(a) The applicable forms for annual, quarterly, current, and other reports are codified in 17 CFR part 249. All forms shall be filed with the FDIC as appropriate and shall be titled with the name of the FDIC instead of the SEC.

(b) The requirements for Financial Statements can generally be found in Regulation S–X (17 CFR part 210). Banks may also refer to the instructions for FFIEC Consolidated Reports of Condition and Income when preparing unaudited interim reports. The requirements for Management's Discussion and Analysis of Financial Condition and Results of Operations can be found at 17 CFR part 229. Additional requirements are included in Industry Guide 3, Statistical Disclosure by Bank Holding Companies, which is found at 17 CFR part 229.

[75 FR 73949, Nov. 30, 2010]

§ 335.321 Maintenance of records and issuer's representations in connection with required reports.

The provisions of the applicable and currently effective SEC regulations under 13(b) of the Exchange Act shall be followed as codified at 17 CFR part 240.

[75 FR 73949, Nov. 30, 2010]

§ 335.331 Acquisition statements, acquisition of securities by issuers, and other matters.

The provisions of the applicable and currently effective SEC regulations under sections 13(d) and 13(e) of the Exchange Act shall be followed as codifed at 17 CFR part 240.

[75 FR 73949, Nov. 30, 2010]

§ 335.401 Solicitations of proxies.

The provisions of the applicable and currently effective SEC regulations under sections 14(a) and 14(c) of the Exchange Act shall be followed as codified at 17 CFR part 240.

[75 FR 73950, Nov. 30, 2010]

§ 335.501 Tender offers.

The provisions of the applicable and currently effective SEC regulations

Federal Deposit Insurance Corporation

§ 335.701

under sections 14(d), 14(e), and 14(f) of the Exchange Act shall be followed as codified at 17 CFR part 240.

[75 FR 73950, Nov. 30, 2010]

§ 335.601 Requirements of section 16 of the Securities Exchange Act of 1934.

Persons subject to section 16 of the Exchange Act with respect to securities registered under this part shall follow the applicable and currently effective SEC regulations issued under section 16 of the Exchange Act (17 CFR part 240), except that the forms described in § 335.611 (FDIC Form 3), § 335.612 (FDIC Form 4), and § 335.613 (FDIC Form 5) shall be used in lieu of SEC Form 3, Form 4, and Form 5, respectively. FDIC Forms 3, 4, and 5 shall be filed electronically on FDIC*connect* at *https://www2.fdicconnect.gov/index.asp*. Copies of FDIC Forms 3, 4, and 5 and the instructions thereto can be printed and downloaded at *https://www.fdic.gov/regulations/laws/forms*.

[75 FR 73950, Nov. 30, 2010]

§ 335.611 Initial statement of beneficial ownership of securities (Form 3).

This form shall be filed in lieu of SEC Form 3 pursuant to SEC rules for initial statements of beneficial ownership of securities. The FDIC is authorized to solicit the information required by this form pursuant to sections 16(a) and 23(a) of the Exchange Act (15 U.S.C. 78p and 78w) and the rules and regulations thereunder. SEC regulations referenced in this form are codified at 17 CFR part 240.

[75 FR 73950, Nov. 30, 2010]

§ 336.612 Statement of changes in beneficial ownership of securities (Form 4).

This form shall be filed in lieu of SEC Form 4 pursuant to SEC Rules for statements of changes in beneficial ownership of securities. The FDIC is authorized to solicit the information required by this form pursuant to sections 16(a) and 23(a) of the Exchange Act (15 U.S.C. 78p and 78w) and the rules and regulations thereunder. SEC regulations referenced in this form are codified at 17 CFR part 240.

[75 FR 73950, Nov. 30, 2010]

§ 336.613 Annual statement of beneficial ownership of securities (Form 5).

This form shall be filed in lieu of SEC Form 5 pursuant to SEC Rules for annual statements of beneficial ownership of securities. The FDIC is authorized to solicit the information required by this form pursuant to sections 16(a) and 23(a) of the Exchange Act (15 U.S.C. 78p and 78w) and the rules and regulations thereunder. SEC regulations referenced in this form are codified at 17 CFR part 240.

[75 FR 73950, Nov. 30, 2010]

§ 335.701 Filing requirements, public reference, and confidentiality.

(a) *Filing requirements.* Unless otherwise indicated in this part, one original and four conformed copies of all papers required to be filed with the FDIC under the Exchange Act or regulations thereunder shall be filed at its office in Washington, DC. Official filings may be filed electronically at *https://www2.fdicconnect.gov/index.asp*, except for FDIC Beneficial Ownership Forms 3, 4, and 5 for which electronic filing is mandatory as described in § 335.801(b). Paper filings should be submitted to the FDIC's office in Washington, DC, and should be addressed as follows: Accounting and Securities Disclosure Section, Division of Supervision and Consumer Protection, Federal Deposit Insurance Corporation, 550 17th Street, NW., Washington, DC 20429. Material may be filed by delivery to the FDIC through the mails or otherwise. The date on which paper filings are actually received by the designated FDIC office shall be the date of filing.

(b) *Inspection.* Except as provided in paragraph (c) of this section, all information filed regarding a security registered with the FDIC will be available for inspection at the Federal Deposit Insurance Corporation, Accounting and Securities Disclosure Section, Division of Supervision and Consumer Protection, 550 17th Street, NW., Washington, DC. Beneficial ownership report forms and other official filings that are electronically submitted to the FDIC are available for inspection on the FDIC's Web site at *http://www2.fdic.gov/efr/*.

(c) *Nondisclosure of certain information filed.* Any person filing any statement,

§ 335.701

report, or document with the FDIC under the Exchange Act may make a written objection to the public disclosure of any information contained therein in accordance with the procedure set forth in this paragraph (c) or the instructions provided for electronic filing available on the FDIC's Web site *https://www2.fdicconnect.gov/index.asp*.

(1) The person shall omit from the statement, report, or document, when it is filed, the portion thereof that it desires to keep undisclosed (hereinafter called the confidential portion). In lieu thereof, it shall indicate at the appropriate place in the statement, report, or document that the confidential portion has been so omitted and filed separately with the FDIC.

(2) The person shall file with the copies of the statement, report, or document filed with the FDIC:

(i) As many copies of the confidential portion, each clearly marked "Confidential Treatment," as there are copies of the statement, report, or document filed with the FDIC and with each exchange, if any. Each copy shall contain the complete text of the item and, notwithstanding that the confidential portion does not constitute the whole of the answer, the entire answer thereto; except that in the case where the confidential portion is part of a financial statement or schedule, only the particular financial statement or schedule need be included. All copies of the confidential portion shall be in the same form as the remainder of the statement, report, or document;

(ii) An application making objection to the disclosure of the confidential portion. Such application shall be on a sheet or sheets separate from the confidential portion and shall contain:

(A) An identification of the portion of the statement, report, or document that has been omitted;

(B) A statement of the grounds of the objection;

(C) Consent that the FDIC may determine the question of public disclosure upon the basis of the application, subject to proper judicial reviews;

(D) The name of each exchange, if any, with which the statement, report, or document is filed;

(iii) The copies of the confidential portion and the application filed in accordance with this paragraph shall be enclosed in a separate envelope marked "Confidential Treatment" and addressed to Executive Secretary, Federal Deposit Insurance Corporation, Washington, DC 20429.

(3) Pending the determination by the FDIC as to the objection filed in accordance with paragraph (c)(2)(ii) of this section, the confidential portion will not be disclosed by the FDIC.

(4) If the FDIC determines that the objection shall be sustained, a notation to that effect will be made at the appropriate place in the statement, report, or document.

(5) If the FDIC determines that disclosure of the confidential portion is in the public interest, a finding and determination to that effect will be entered and notice of the finding and determination will be sent by registered or certified mail to the person.

(6) The confidential portion shall be made available to the public:

(i) Upon the lapse of 15 days after the dispatch of notice by registered or certified mail of the finding and determination of the FDIC described in paragraph (c)(5) of this section, or the date of the electronic filing, if prior to the lapse of such 15 days the person shall not have filed a written statement that he intends in good faith to seek judicial review of the finding and determination;

(ii) Upon the lapse of 60 days after the dispatch of notice by registered or certified mail, or the date of the electronic filing, of the finding and determination of the FDIC, if the statement described in paragraph (c)(6)(i) of this section shall have been filed and if a petition for judicial review shall not have been filed within such 60 days; or

(iii) If such petition for judicial review shall have been filed within such 60 days upon final disposition, adverse to the person, of the judicial proceedings.

(7) If the confidential portion is made available to the public, a copy thereof shall be attached to each copy of the statement, report, or document filed with the FDIC and with each exchange concerned.

[75 FR 73950, Nov. 30, 2010]

Federal Deposit Insurance Corporation § 335.801

§ 335.801 **Inapplicable SEC regulations; FDIC substituted regulations; additional information.**

(a) *Filing fees.* Filing fees will not be charged relative to any filings or submissions of materials made with the FDIC pursuant to the cross reference to regulations of the SEC issued under sections 10A(m), 12, 13, 14, and 16 of the Securities Exchange Act of 1934 (15 U.S.C. 78), sections 302, 303, 304, 306, 401(b), 404, 406, and 407 of the Sarbanes-Oxley Act of 2002 (15 U.S.C. 7241, 7242, 7243, 7244, 7261, 7262, 7264, and 7265), and this part.

(b) *Electronic filings.* (1) The FDIC does not participate in the SEC's EDGAR (Electronic Data Gathering Analysis and Retrieval) electronic filing program (17 CFR part 232). The FDIC permits voluntary electronically transmitted filings and submissions of correspondence and other materials in electronic format to the FDIC, with the exception of Beneficial Ownership Reports (Forms 3, 4, and 5) for which electronic filing is mandatory. Beneficial Ownership Report filing requirements are provided in paragraph (b)(2) of this section.

(2) All reporting persons must electronically file Beneficial Ownership Reports (FDIC Forms 3, 4, and 5), including amendments and exhibits thereto, using the Internet-based interagency Beneficial Ownership Filings System, except that a reporting person that has obtained a continuing hardship exemption under these rules may file the forms with the FDIC in paper format. For electronic filing purposes, FDIC Forms 3, 4, and 5 are accessible at the Internet-based interagency Web site for Beneficial Ownership Filings at FDIC*connect* at *https://www2.fdicconnect.gov/index.asp*. These forms and the instructions thereto are available for printing and downloading at *http://www.fdic.gov/regulations/laws/forms*. A reporting person that has obtained a continuing hardship exemption under these rules may file the appropriate forms with the FDIC in paper format. Instructions for continuing hardship exemptions are provided in paragraph (b)(6) of this section.

(3) Electronic filings of FDIC beneficial ownership report Forms 3, 4, and 5 must be submitted to the FDIC through the interagency Beneficial Ownership Filings system. Beneficial ownership reports and any amendments are deemed filed with the FDIC upon electronic receipt on business days from 8 a.m. through 10 p.m., Eastern Standard Time or Eastern Daylight Saving Time, whichever is currently in effect (Eastern Time). Business days include each day, except Saturdays, Sundays and Federal holidays. All filings submitted electronically to the FDIC commencing after 10 p.m. Eastern Time on business days shall be deemed filed as of 8 a.m. on the following business day. All filings submitted electronically to the FDIC on non-business days shall be deemed filed as of 8 a.m. on the following business day.

(4) *Adjustment of the filing date.* If an electronic filer in good faith attempts to file a beneficial ownership report with the FDIC in a timely manner but the filing is delayed due to technical difficulties beyond the electronic filer's control, the electronic filer may request an adjustment of the filing date of such submission. The FDIC may grant the request if it appears that such adjustment is appropriate and consistent with the public interest and the protection of investors.

(5) *Exhibits.* (i) Exhibits to an electronic filing that have not previously been filed with the FDIC shall be filed in electronic format, absent a hardship exemption.

(ii) Previously filed exhibits, whether in paper or electronic format, may be incorporated by reference into an electronic filing to the extent permitted by applicable SEC rules under the Exchange Act. An electronic filer may, at its option, restate in electronic format an exhibit incorporated by reference that originally was filed in paper format.

(iii) Any document filed in paper format in violation of mandated electronic filing requirements shall not be incorporated by reference into an electronic filing.

(6) *Continuing Hardship Exemption.* The FDIC will not accept in paper format any beneficial ownership report filing required to be submitted electronically under this part unless the

filer satisfies the requirements for a continuing hardship exemption:

(i) A filer may apply in writing for a continuing hardship exemption if all or part of a filing or group of filings otherwise to be filed in electronic format cannot be so filed without undue burden or expense. Such written application shall be made at least ten business days prior to the required due date of the filing(s) or the proposed filing date, as appropriate, or within such shorter period as may be permitted. The written application shall be sent to the Accounting and Securities Disclosure Section, Division of Supervision and Consumer Protection, Federal Deposit Insurance Corporation, 550 17th Street NW., Washington, DC 20429, and shall contain the information set forth in paragraph (b)(6)(ii) of this section.

(A) The application shall not be deemed granted until the applicant is notified by the FDIC.

(B) If the FDIC denies the application for a continuing hardship exemption, the filer shall file the required document in electronic format on the required due date or the proposed filing date or such other date as may be permitted.

(C) If the FDIC determines that the grant of the exemption is appropriate and consistent with the public interest and the protection of investors and so notifies the applicant, the filer shall follow the procedures set forth in paragraph (b)(6)(iii) of this section.

(ii) The request for the continuing hardship exemption shall include, but not be limited to, the following:

(A) The reason(s) that the necessary hardware and software are not available without unreasonable burden and expense;

(B) The burden and expense involved to employ alternative means to make the electronic submission; and/or

(C) The reasons for not submitting electronically the document or group of documents, as well as justification for the requested time period for the exemption.

(iii) If the request for a continuing hardship exemption is granted, the electronic filer shall submit the document or group of documents for which the exemption is granted in paper format on the required due date specified in the applicable form, rule or regulation, or the proposed filing date, as appropriate. The paper format document(s) shall have placed at the top of page 1, or at the top of an attached cover page, a legend in capital letters: IN ACCORDANCE WITH 12 CFR 335.801(b), THIS (SPECIFY DOCUMENT) IS BEING FILED IN PAPER PURSUANT TO A CONTINUING HARDSHIP EXEMPTION.

(iv) Where a continuing hardship exemption is granted with respect to an exhibit only, the paper format exhibit shall be filed with the FDIC under Form SE (17 CFR part 249). The name of the FDIC shall be substituted for the name of the SEC on the form. Form SE shall be filed as a paper cover sheet to all exhibits to Beneficial Ownership Reports submitted to the FDIC in paper form pursuant to a hardship exemption.

(v) Form SE may be filed with the FDIC up to six business days prior to, or on the date of filing of, the electronic form to which it relates but shall not be filed after such filing date. If a paper exhibit is submitted in this manner, requirements that the exhibit be filed with, provided with, or accompany the electronic filing shall be satisfied. Any requirements as to delivery or furnishing the information to persons other than the FDIC shall not be affected by this section.

(7) *Signatures.* (i) Required signatures to, or within, any electronic submission must be in typed form. When used in connection with an electronic filing, the term "signature" means an electronic entry or other form of computer data compilation of any letters or series of letters or characters comprising a name, executed, adopted or authorized as a signature.

(ii) Each signatory to an electronic filing shall manually sign a signature page or other document authenticating, acknowledging or otherwise adopting his or her signature that appears in typed form within the electronic filing. Such document shall be executed before or at the time the electronic filing is made and shall be retained by the filer for a period of five years. Upon request, an electronic filer shall furnish to the FDIC a copy of any or all documents retained pursuant to this section.

Federal Deposit Insurance Corporation § 335.801

(iii) Where the FDIC's rules require a filer to furnish to a national securities exchange, a national securities association, or a bank, paper copies of a document filed with the FDIC in electronic format, signatures to such paper copies may be in typed form.

(c) *Legal proceedings.* Whenever this part or cross referenced provisions of the SEC regulations require disclosure of legal proceedings, administrative or judicial proceedings arising under section 8 of the Federal Deposit Insurance Act shall be deemed material and shall be described.

(d) *Indebtedness of management.* Whenever this part or cross referenced provisions of the SEC regulations require disclosure of indebtedness of management, extensions of credit to specified persons in excess of ten (10) percent of the equity capital accounts of the bank or $5 million, whichever is less, shall be deemed material and shall be disclosed in addition to any other required disclosure. The disclosure of this material indebtedness shall include the largest aggregate amount of indebtedness (in dollar amounts, and as a percentage of total equity capital accounts at the time), including extensions of credit or overdrafts, endorsements and guarantees outstanding at any time since the beginning of the bank's last fiscal year, and as of the latest practicable date.

(1) If aggregate extensions of credit to all specified persons as a group exceeded 20 percent of the equity capital accounts of the bank at any time since the beginning of the last fiscal year, the aggregate amount of such extensions of credit shall also be disclosed.

(2) Other loans are deemed material and shall be disclosed where:

(i) The extension(s) of credit was not made on substantially the same terms, including interest rates, collateral and repayment terms as those prevailing at the time for comparable transactions with other than the specified persons;

(ii) The extension(s) of credit was not made in the ordinary course of business; or

(iii) The extension(s) of credit has involved or presently involves more than a normal risk of collectibility or other unfavorable features including the restructuring of an extension of credit, or a delinquency as to payment of interest or principal.

(e) *Proxy material required to be filed.* (1) Three preliminary copies of each information statement, proxy statement, form of proxy, and other item of soliciting material to be furnished to security holders concurrently therewith, shall be filed with the FDIC by the bank or any other person making a solicitation subject to 12 CFR 335.401 at least ten calendar days (or 15 calendar days in the case of other than routine meetings, as defined in paragraph (e)(2) of this section) prior to the date such item is first sent or given to any security holders, or such shorter date as may be authorized.

(2) For the purposes of this paragraph (e), a routine meeting means:

(i) A meeting with respect to which no one is soliciting proxies subject to § 335.401 other than on behalf of the bank, and at which the bank intends to present no matters other than:

(A) The election of directors;

(B) The election, approval or ratification of accountants;

(C) A Security holder proposal included pursuant to SEC Rule 14(a)-8 (17 CFR 240.14a-8); and

(D) The approval or ratification of a plan as defined in paragraph (a)(7)(ii) of Item 402 of SEC Regulation S-K (17 CFR 229.402(a)(7)(ii)) or amendments to such a plan; and

(ii) The bank does not comment upon or refer to a solicitation in opposition (as defined in 17 CFR 240.14a-6) in connection with the meeting in its proxy material.

(3) Where preliminary copies of material are filed with the FDIC under this section, the printing of definitive copies for distribution to security holders should be deferred until the comments of the FDIC's staff have been received and considered.

(f) *Additional information; filing of other statements in certain cases.* (1) In addition to the information expressly required to be included in a statement, form, schedule or report, there shall be added such further material information, if any, as may be necessary to make the required statements, in light of the circumstances under which they are made, not misleading.

§ 335.901

(2) The FDIC may, upon the written request of the bank, and where consistent with the protection of investors, permit the omission of one or more of the statements or disclosures herein required, or the filing in substitution therefor of appropriate statements or disclosures of comparable character.

(3) The FDIC may also require the filing of other statements or disclosures in addition to, or in substitution for those herein required in any case where such statements are necessary or appropriate for an adequate presentation of the financial condition of any person whose financial statements are required, or disclosure about which is otherwise necessary for the protection of investors.

[62 FR 6856, Feb. 14, 1997, as amended at 69 FR 19088, Apr. 12, 2004; 69 FR 59783, Oct. 6, 2004; 70 FR 16400, Mar. 31, 2005; 70 FR 44273, Aug. 2, 2005; 75 FR 73951, Nov. 30, 2010]

§ 335.901 Delegation of authority to act on matters with respect to disclosure laws and regulations.

(a) Except as provided in paragraph (b) of this section, authority is delegated to the Director, Division of Supervision and Consumer Protection (DSC), and where confirmed in writing by the director, to a deputy director or an associate director, or to the appropriate regional director or deputy regional director or area director, to act on disclosure matters under and pursuant to sections 10A(m), 12, 13, 14(a), 14(c), 14(d), 14(f) and 16 of the Securities Exchange Act of 1934 (15 U.S.C. 78), sections 302, 303, 304, 306, 401(b), 404, 406, and 407 of the Sarbanes-Oxley Act of 2002 (15 U.S.C. 7241, 7242, 7243, 7244, 7261, 7262, 7264, and 7265), and this part.

(b) Authority to act on disclosure matters is retained by the FDIC Board of Directors when such matters involve:

(1) Exemption from disclosure requirements pursuant to section 12(h) of the Securities Exchange Act of 1934 (15 U.S.C. 78*l*(h)); or

(2) Exemption from tender offer requirements pursuant to section 14(d)(8) of the Securities Exchange Act of 1934 (15 U.S.C. 78n(d)(8)).

[62 FR 6856, Feb. 14, 1997, as amended at 70 FR 16400, Mar. 31, 2005; 70 FR 44273, Aug. 2, 2005]

PART 336—FDIC EMPLOYEES

Subpart A—Employee Responsibilities and Conduct

Sec.
336.1 Cross-reference to employee ethical conduct standards and financial disclosure regulations.

Subpart B—Minimum Standards of Fitness for Employment With the Federal Deposit Insurance Corporation

336.2 Authority, purpose and scope.
336.3 Definitions.
336.4 Minimum standards for appointment to a position with the FDIC.
336.5 Minimum standards for employment with the FDIC.
336.6 Verification of compliance.
336.7 Employee responsibility, counseling and distribution of regulation.
336.8 Sanctions and remedial actions.
336.9 Finality of determination.

Subpart C—One-Year Restriction on Post-Employment Activities of Senior Examiners

336.10 Purpose and scope.
336.11 Definitions.
336.12 One-year post-employment restriction.
336.13 Penalties.

SOURCE: 61 FR 28728, June 6, 1996, unless otherwise noted.

Subpart A—Employee Responsibilities and Conduct

AUTHORITY: 5 U.S.C. 7301; 12 U.S.C. 1819(a).

§ 336.1 Cross-reference to employee ethical conduct standards and financial disclosure regulations.

Employees of the Federal Deposit Insurance Corporation (Corporation) are subject to the Executive Branch-wide Standards of Ethical Conduct at 5 CFR part 2635, the Corporation regulation at 5 CFR part 3201 which supplements the Executive Branch-wide Standards, the Executive Branch-wide financial disclosure regulations at 5 CFR part 2634, and the Corporation regulation at 5 CFR part 3202, which supplements the

Federal Deposit Insurance Corporation § 336.3

Executive Branch-wide financial disclosure regulations.

Subpart B—Minimum Standards of Fitness for Employment With the Federal Deposit Insurance Corporation

AUTHORITY: 12 U.S.C. 1819 (Tenth), 1822(f).

§ 336.2 Authority, purpose and scope.

(a) *Authority.* This part is adopted pursuant to section 12(f) of the Federal Deposit Insurance Act, 12 U.S.C. 1822, and the rulemaking authority of the Federal Deposit Insurance Corporation (FDIC) found at 12 U.S.C. 1819. This part is in addition to, and not in lieu of, any other statutes or regulations which may apply to standards for ethical conduct or fitness for employment with the FDIC and is consistent with the goals and purposes of 18 U.S.C. 201, 203, 205, 208, and 209.

(b) *Purpose.* The purpose of this part is to state the minimum standards of fitness and integrity required of individuals who provide service to or on behalf of the FDIC and provide procedures for implementing these requirements.

(c) *Scope.* (1) This part applies to applicants for employment with the FDIC under title 5 of the U.S. Code appointing authority in either the excepted or competitive service, including Special Government Employees. This part applies to all appointments, regardless of tenure, including intermittent, temporary, time-limited and permanent appointments.

(2) In addition, this part applies to all employees of the FDIC who serve under an appointing authority under chapter 21 of title 5 of the U.S. Code.

(3) Further, this part applies to any individual who, pursuant to a contract or any other arrangement, performs functions or activities of the Corporation, under the direct supervision of an officer or employee of the Corporation.

§ 336.3 Definitions.

For the purposes of this part:

(a) *Company* means any corporation, firm, partnership, society, joint venture, business trust, association or similar organization, or any other trust unless by its terms it must terminate within twenty-five years or not later than twenty-one years and ten months after the death of individuals living on the effective date of the trust, or any other organization or institution, but shall not include any corporation the majority of the shares of which are owned by the United States, any state, or the District of Columbia.

(b) *Control* means the power to vote, directly or indirectly, 25 percent or more of any class of the voting stock of a company, the ability to direct in any manner the election of a majority of a company's directors or trustees, or the ability to exercise a controlling influence over the company's management and policies. For purposes of this definition, a general partner of a limited partnership is presumed to be in control of that partnership. For purposes of this part, an entity or individual shall be presumed to have control of a company if the entity or individual directly or indirectly, or acting in concert with one or more entities or individuals, or through one or more subsidiaries, owns or controls 25 percent or more of its equity, or otherwise controls or has power to control its management or policies.

(c) *Default on a material obligation* means a loan or advance from an insured depository institution which is or was delinquent for 90 or more days as to payment of principal or interest, or any combination thereof.

(d) *Employee* means any officer or employee, including a liquidation graded or temporary employee, providing service to or on behalf of the FDIC who has been appointed to a position under an authority contained in title 5 of the U.S. Code. This definition excludes those individuals designated by title 5 of the U.S. Code as officials in the Federal Executive Schedule.

(e) *Federal banking agency* means the Office of the Comptroller of the Currency, the Office of Thrift Supervision, the Board of Governors of the Federal Reserve System, or the Federal Deposit Insurance Corporation, or their successors.

(f) *Federal deposit insurance fund* means the Deposit Insurance Fund, the former Bank Insurance Fund, the former Savings Association Insurance

§ 336.4

Fund, the Federal Savings and Loan Insurance Corporation (FSLIC) Resolution Trust, or the funds formerly maintained by the Resolution Trust Corporation (RTC), or their successors, for the benefit of insured depositors.

(g) *FDIC* means the Federal Deposit Insurance Corporation, in its receivership and corporate capacities.

(h) *Insured depository institution* means any bank or savings association the deposits of which are insured by the FDIC.

(i) *Pattern or practice of defalcation regarding obligations* means:

(1) A history of financial irresponsibility with regard to debts owed to insured depository institutions which are in default in excess of $50,000 in the aggregate. Examples of such financial irresponsibility include, without limitation:

(i) Failure to pay a debt or debts totalling more than $50,000 secured by an uninsured property which is destroyed; or

(ii) Abuse of credit cards or incurring excessive debt well beyond the individual's ability to repay resulting in default(s) in excess of $50,000 in the aggregate.

(2) Wrongful refusal to fulfill duties and obligations to insured depository institutions. Examples of such wrongful refusal to fulfill duties and obligations include, without limitation:

(i) Any use of false financial statements;

(ii) Misrepresentation as to the individual's ability to repay debts;

(iii) Concealing assets from the insured depository institution;

(iv) Any instance of fraud, embezzlement or similar misconduct in connection with an obligation to the insured depository institution; and

(v) Any conduct described in any civil or criminal judgment against an individual for breach of any obligation, contractual or otherwise, or any duty of loyalty or care that the individual owed to an insured depository institution.

(3) Defaults shall not be considered a pattern or practice of defalcation where the defaults are caused by catastrophic events beyond the control of the employee such as death, disability, illness or loss of financial support.

(j) *Substantial loss to federal deposit insurance funds*—(1) *Substantial loss to federal deposit insurance funds* means:

(i) A loan or advance from an insured depository institution, which is now owed to the FDIC, RTC, FSLIC or their successors, or any federal deposit insurance fund, that is delinquent for ninety (90) or more days as to payment of principal, interest, or a combination thereof and on which there remains a legal obligation to pay an amount in excess of $50,000; or

(ii) A final judgment in excess of $50,000 in favor of any federal deposit insurance fund, the FDIC, RTC, FSLIC, or their successors regardless of whether it becomes forgiven in whole or in part in a bankruptcy proceeding.

(2) For purposes of computing the $50,000 ceiling in paragraphs (j)(1)(i) and (ii) of this section, all delinquent judgments, loans, or advances currently owed to the FDIC, RTC, FSLIC or their successors, or any federal deposit insurance fund, shall be aggregated. In no event shall delinquent loans or advances from different insured depository institutions be separately considered.

[61 FR 28728, June 6, 1996, as amended at 71 FR 20526, Apr. 21, 2006]

§ 336.4 Minimum standards for appointment to a position with the FDIC.

(a) No person shall become employed on or after June 18, 1994, by the FDIC or otherwise perform any service for or on behalf of the FDIC who has:

(1) Been convicted of any felony;

(2) Been removed from, or prohibited from participating in the affairs of, any insured depository institution pursuant to any final enforcement action by any appropriate federal banking agency;

(3) Demonstrated a pattern or practice of defalcation regarding obligations to insured depository institutions; or

(4) Caused a substantial loss to federal deposit insurance funds.

(b) Prior to an offer of employment, any person applying for employment with the FDIC shall sign a certification of compliance with the minimum standards listed in paragraphs (a) (1) through (4) of this section. In addition, any person applying for employment with the FDIC shall provide as an attachment to the certification any instance in which the applicant, or a company under the applicant's control, defaulted on a material obligation to an insured depository institution within the preceding five years.

(c) Incumbent employees who separate from the FDIC and are subsequently reappointed after a break in service of more than three days are subject to the minimum standards listed in paragraphs (a) (1) though (4) of this section. The former employee is required to submit a new certification statement including attachments, as provided in paragraph (b) of this section, prior to appointment to the new position.

§ 336.5 Minimum standards for employment with the FDIC.

(a) No person who is employed by the FDIC shall continue in employment in any manner whatsoever or perform any service for or on behalf of the FDIC who, beginning June 18, 1994 and thereafter:

(1) Is convicted of any felony;

(2) Is prohibited from participating in the affairs of any insured depository institution pursuant to any final enforcement action by any appropriate federal banking agency;

(3) Demonstrates a pattern or practice of defalcation regarding obligations to insured depository institution(s); or

(4) Causes a substantial loss to federal deposit insurance funds.

(b) Any noncompliance with the standards listed in paragraphs (a) (1) through (4) of this section is a basis for removal from employment with the FDIC.

§ 336.6 Verification of compliance.

The FDIC's Division of Administration shall order appropriate investigations as authorized by 12 U.S.C. 1819 and 1822 on newly appointed employees, either prior to or following appointment, to verify compliance with the minimum standards listed under § 336.4(a) (1) through (4).

§ 336.7 Employee responsibility, counseling and distribution of regulation.

(a) Each employee is responsible for being familiar with and complying with the provisions of this part.

(b) The Ethics Counselor shall provide a copy of this part to each new employee within 30 days of initial appointment.

(c) An employee who believes that he or she may not be in compliance with the minimum standards provided under § 336.5(a)(1) through (4), or who receives a demand letter from the FDIC for any reason, shall make a written report of all relevant facts to the Ethics Counselor within ten (10) business days after the employee discovers the possible noncompliance, or after the receipt of a demand letter from the FDIC.

(d) The Ethics Counselor shall provide guidance to employees regarding the appropriate statutes, regulations and corporate policies affecting employee's ethical responsibilities and conduct under this part.

(e) The Ethics Counselor shall provide the Personnel Services Branch with notice of an employee's noncompliance.

§ 336.8 Sanctions and remedial actions.

(a) Any employee found not in compliance with the minimum standards except as provided in paragraph (b) of this section below shall be terminated and prohibited from providing further service for or on behalf of the FDIC in any capacity. No other remedial action is authorized for sanctions for noncompliance.

(b) Any employee found not in compliance with the minimum standards under § 336.5(a)(3) based on financial irresponsibility as defined in § 336.3(i)(1) shall be terminated consistent with applicable procedures and prohibited from providing future services for or on behalf of the FDIC in any capacity, unless the employee brings him or herself into compliance with the minimum standards as provided in paragraphs (b) (1) and (2) of this section.

(1) Upon written notification by the Corporation of financial irresponsibility, the employee will be allowed a reasonable period of time to establish

§ 336.9

an agreement that satisfies the creditor and the FDIC as to resolution of outstanding indebtedness or otherwise resolves the matter to the satisfaction of the FDIC prior to the initiation of a termination action.

(2) As part of the agreement described in paragraph (b)(1) of this section, the employee shall provide authority to the creditor to report any violation by the employee of the terms of the agreement directly to the FDIC Ethics Counselor.

§ 336.9 Finality of determination.

Any determination made by the FDIC pursuant to this part shall be at the FDIC's sole discretion and shall not be subject to further review.

Subpart C—One-Year Restriction on Post-Employment Activities of Senior Examiners

SOURCE: 70 FR 69639, Nov. 17, 2005, unless otherwise noted.

AUTHORITY: 12 U.S.C. 1819 and 1820(k).

§ 336.10 Purpose and scope.

This subpart applies to officers or employees of the FDIC who are subject to the post-employment restrictions set forth in section 10(k) of the Federal Deposit Insurance Act, 12 U.S.C. 1820(k), and implements those restrictions as they apply to officers and employees of the FDIC.

§ 336.11 Definitions.

For purposes of this subpart:

(a) *Bank holding company* has the meaning given to such term in section 2 of the Bank Holding Company Act of 1956 (12 U.S.C. 1841(a)).

(b) A *consultant* for an insured depository institution or other company shall include only individuals who work directly on matters for, or on behalf of, such institution or other company.

(c) *Control* has the meaning given to such term in section 336.3(b), and a foreign bank shall be deemed to control any insured branch of the foreign bank.

(d) *Depository institution* means any bank or savings association, including a branch of a foreign bank, if such branch is located in the United States.

(e) *Foreign bank* means any bank or company described in section 8(a) of the International Banking Act of 1978 (12 U.S.C. 3106(a)).

(f) *Savings and loan holding company* has the meaning given to such term in section 10(a)(1)(D) of the Home Owners' Loan Act (12 U.S.C. 1467a(a)(1)(D)).

(g) A *senior examiner* for an insured depository institution means an officer or employee of the FDIC—

(1) who has been authorized by the FDIC to conduct examinations or inspections of insured depository institutions on behalf of the FDIC;

(2) who has been assigned continuing, broad, and lead responsibility for the examination or inspection of the institution;

(3) who routinely interacts with officers or employees of the institution or its affiliates; and

(4) whose responsibilities with respect to the institution represent a substantial portion of the FDIC officer or employee's overall responsibilities.

§ 336.12 One-year post-employment restriction.

(a) *Prohibition.* An officer or employee of the FDIC who serves as a senior examiner of an insured depository institution for at least 2 months during the last 12 months of that individual's employment with the FDIC may not, within 1 year after the termination date of his or her employment with the FDIC, knowingly accept compensation as an employee, officer, director, or consultant from—

(1) The insured depository institution; or

(2) Any company (including a bank holding company or savings and loan holding company) that controls such institution.

(b) *Waivers.* The post-employment restrictions in paragraph (a) of this section will not apply to a senior examiner if the FDIC Chairperson certifies in writing and on a case-by case basis that a waiver of the restrictions will not affect the integrity of the FDIC's supervisory program.

(c) *Effective Date.* The post-employment restrictions in paragraph (a) of this section will not apply to any officer or employee of the FDIC, or any former officer or employee of the FDIC,

Federal Deposit Insurance Corporation

who ceased to be an officer or employee of the FDIC before December 17, 2005.

§ 336.13 Penalties.

(a) *Penalties under section 10(k) of the FDI Act.* A senior examiner of the FDIC who violates the post-employment restrictions set forth in § 336.12 shall be subject to the following penalties—
   (1) An order—
   (i) Removing such person from office or prohibiting such person from further participation in the affairs of the relevant insured depository institution or company (including a bank holding company or savings and loan holding company) that controls such institution for a period of up to five years, and
   (ii) Prohibiting any further participation by such person, in any manner, in the affairs of any insured depository institution for a period of up to five years; or
   (2) A civil monetary penalty of not more than $250,000; or
   (3) Both.

(b) *Enforcement by appropriate Federal banking agency of hiring entity.* Violations of § 336.12 shall be enforced by the appropriate Federal banking agency of the depository institution, depository institution holding company, or other company at which the violation occurred, as determined under section 10(k)(6), which may be an agency other than the FDIC.

(c) *Scope of prohibition orders.* Any senior examiner who is subject to an order issued under paragraph (a)(1) of this section shall, as required by 12 U.S.C. 1820(k)(6)(B), be subject to paragraphs (6) and (7) of section 8(e) in the same manner and to the same extent as a person subject to an order issued under section 8(e).

(d) *Other penalties.* The penalties set forth in paragraph (a) of this section are not exclusive, and a senior examiner who violates the restrictions in § 336.12 may also be subject to other administrative, civil, or criminal remedies or penalties as provided by law.

PART 337—UNSAFE AND UNSOUND BANKING PRACTICES

Sec.
337.1 Scope.
337.2 Standby letters of credit.
337.3 Limits on extensions of credit to executive officers, directors, and principal shareholders of insured nonmember banks.
337.4 [Reserved]
337.5 Exemption.
337.6 Brokered deposits.
337.7–337.9 [Reserved]
337.10 Waiver.
337.11 Effect on other banking practices.
337.12 Frequency of examination.

AUTHORITY: 12 U.S.C. 375a(4), 375b, 1816, 1818(a), 1818(b), 1819, 1820(d)(10), 1821(f), 1828(j)(2), 1831.

SOURCE: 39 FR 29179, Aug. 14, 1974, unless otherwise noted.

§ 337.1 Scope.

The provisions of this part apply to certain banking practices which are likely to have adverse effects on the safety and soundness of insured State nonmember banks or which are likely to result in violations of law, rule, or regulation.

§ 337.2 Standby letters of credit.

(a) *Definition.* As used in this section, the term *standby letter of credit* means any letter of credit, or similar arrangement however named or described, which represents an obligation to the beneficiary on the part of the issuer: (1) To repay money borrowed by or advanced to or for the account of the account party, or (2) to make payment on account of any indebtedness undertaken by the account party, or (3) to make payment on account of any default (including any statement of default) by the account party in the performance of an obligation.[1] The term *similar arrangement* includes the creation of an acceptance or similar undertaking.

(b) *Restriction.* A standby letter of credit issued by an insured State nonmember bank shall be combined with all other standby letters of credit and all loans for purposes of applying any

---

[1] As defined in this paragraph (a), the term *standby letter of credit* would not include commercial letters of credit and similar instruments where the issuing bank expects the beneficiary to draw upon the issuer, which do not "guaranty" payment of a money obligation of the account party and which do not provide that payment is occasioned by default on the part of the account party.

§ 337.3

legal limitation on loans of the bank (including limitations on loans to any one borrower, on loans to affiliates of the bank, or on aggregate loans); *Provided, however,* That if such standby letter of credit is subject to separate limitation under applicable State or federal law, then the separate limitation shall apply in lieu of the loan limitation.[2]

(c) *Exceptions.* All standby letters of credit shall be subject to the provisions of paragraph (b) of this section except where:

(1) Prior to or at the time of issuance, the issuing bank is paid an amount equal to the bank's maximum liability under the standby letter of credit; or,

(2) Prior to or at the time of issuance, the issuing bank has set aside sufficient funds in a segregated deposit account, clearly earmarked for that purpose, to cover the bank's maximum liability under the standby letter of credit.

(d) *Disclosure.* Each insured State nonmember bank must maintain adequate control and subsidiary records of its standby letters of credit comparable to the records maintained in connection with the bank's direct loans so that at all times the bank's potential liability thereunder and the bank's compliance with this section may be readily determined. In addition, all such standby letters of credit must be adequately reflected on the bank's published financial statements.

§ 337.3 **Limits on extensions of credit to executive officers, directors, and principal shareholders of insured nonmember banks.**

(a) With the exception of 12 CFR 215.5(b), 215.5(c)(3), 215.5(c)(4), and 215.11, insured nonmember banks are subject to the restrictions contained in subpart A of Federal Reserve Board Regulation O (12 CFR part 215, subpart A) to the same extent and to the same manner as though they were member banks.

(b) For the purposes of compliance with § 215.4(b) of Federal Reserve Board Regulation O, no insured nonmember bank may extend credit or grant a line of credit to any of its executive officers, directors, or principal shareholders or to any related interest of any such person in an amount that, when aggregated with the amount of all other extensions of credit and lines of credit by the bank to that person and to all related interests of that person, exceeds the greater of $25,000 or five percent of the bank's capital and unimpaired surplus,[3] or $500,000 unless (1) the extension of credit or line of credit has been approved in advance by a majority of the entire board of directors of that bank and (2) the interested party has abstained from participating directly or indirectly in the voting.

(c)(1) No insured nonmember bank may extend credit in an aggregate amount greater than the amount permitted in paragraph (c)(2) of this section to a partnership in which one or more of the bank's executive officers are partners and, either individually or together, hold a majority interest. For the purposes of paragraph (c)(2) of this section, the total amount of credit extended by an insured nonmember bank to such partnership is considered to be extended to each executive officer of the insured nonmember bank who is a member of the partnership.

(2) An insured nonmember bank is authorized to extend credit to any executive officer of the bank for any other purpose not specified in § 215.5(c)(1) and (2) of Federal Reserve Board Regulation O (12 CFR 215.5(c)(1) and (2)) if the aggregate amount of such other extensions of credit does not exceed at any one time the higher of 2.5 percent of the bank's capital and unimpaired surplus or $25,000 but in no event more than $100,000, provided, however, that no such extension of credit shall be subject to this limit if the extension of credit is secured by:

(i) A perfected security interest in bonds, notes, certificates of indebtedness, or Treasury bills of the United

---

[2] Where the standby letter of credit is subject to a non-recourse participation agreement with another bank or other banks, this section shall apply to the issuer and each participant in the same manner as in the case of a participated loan.

[3] For the purposes of § 337.3, an insured nonmember bank's capital and unimpaired surplus shall have the same meaning as found in § 215.2(f) of Federal Reserve Board Regulation O (12 CFR 215.2(f)).

Federal Deposit Insurance Corporation § 337.6

States or in other such obligations fully guaranteed as to principal and interest by the United States;

(ii) Unconditional takeout commitments or guarantees of any department, agency, bureau, board, commission or establishment of the United States or any corporation wholly owned directly or indirectly by the United States; or

(iii) A perfected security interest in a segregated deposit account in the lending bank.

(3) Any extension of credit that was outstanding on May 28, 1992 and that would if made on or after that date violate paragraph (c)(1) or paragraph (c)(2) of this § 337.3 shall be reduced in amount by May 28, 1993 so that the extension of credit is in compliance with the lending limit set forth in paragraphs (c)(1) and (c)(2) of this section. Any renewal or extension of such an extension of credit on or after May 28, 1992 shall be made only on terms that will bring the extension of credit into compliance with the lending limit of paragraphs (c)(1) and (c)(2) of this section by May 28, 1993, however, any extension of credit made before May 28, 1992 that bears a specific maturity date of May 28, 1993 or later shall be repaid in accordance with its repayment schedule in existence on or before May 28, 1992.

(4) If an insured nonmember bank is unable to bring all extensions of credit outstanding as of May 28, 1992 into compliance as required by paragraph (c)(3) of this § 337.3, the bank may at the discretion of the appropriate FDIC regional director (Division of Supervision and Consumer Protection (DSC)) obtain, for good cause shown, not more than two additional one-year periods to come into compliance.

(5) For the purposes of paragraph (c) of this section, the definitions of the terms used in Federal Reserve Board Regulation O shall apply including the exclusion of executive officers of a bank's parent bank holding company and executive officers of any other subsidiary of that bank holding company from the definition of executive officer for the purposes of complying with the loan restrictions contained in section 22(g) of the Federal Reserve Act. For the purposes of complying with § 215.5(d) of Federal Reserve Board Regulation O, the reference to "the amount specified for a category of credit in paragraph (c) of this section" shall be understood to refer to the amount specified in paragraph (c)(2) of this § 337.3.

(Approved by the Office of Management and Budget under control number 3064-0108)

[47 FR 47003, Oct. 22, 1982, as amended at 48 FR 42971, Sept. 21, 1983; 57 FR 7649, Mar. 4, 1992; 57 FR 17850, Apr. 28, 1992; 57 FR 28457, June 25, 1992; 59 FR 66668, Dec. 28, 1994]

§ 337.4 [Reserved]

§ 337.5 Exemption.

Check guaranty card programs, customer-sponsored credit card programs, and similar arrangements in which a bank undertakes to guarantee the obligations of individuals who are its retail banking deposit customers are exempted from § 337.2: *Provided, however*, That the bank establishes the creditworthiness of the individual before undertaking to guarantee his/her obligations and that any such arrangement to which a bank's principal shareholders, directors, or executive officers are a party be in compliance with applicable provisions of Federal Reserve Regulation O (12 CFR part 215).

[50 FR 10495, Mar. 15, 1985]

§ 337.6 Brokered deposits.

(a) *Definitions*. For the purposes of this § 337.6, the following definitions apply:

(1) *Appropriate Federal banking agency* has the same meaning as provided under section 3(q) of the Federal Deposit Insurance Act (12 U.S.C. 1813(q)).

(2) *Brokered deposit* means any deposit that is obtained, directly or indirectly, from or through the mediation or assistance of a deposit broker.

(3) *Capital categories*. (i) For purposes of section 29 of the Federal Deposit Insurance Act and this § 337.6, the terms *well capitalized, adequately capitalized*, and *undercapitalized*,[11] shall have the

---

[11] The term *undercapitalized* includes any institution that is *significantly undercapitalized* or *critically undercapitalized* under regulations implementing section 38 of the Federal Deposit Insurance Act and issued by the
Continued

§ 337.6

same meaning as to each insured depository institution as provided under regulations implementing section 38 of the Federal Deposit Insurance Act issued by the appropriate federal banking agency for that institution.[12]

(ii) If the appropriate federal banking agency reclassifies a well capitalized insured depository institution as adequately capitalized pursuant to section 38 of the Federal Deposit Insurance Act, the institution so reclassified shall be subject to the provisions applicable to such lower capital category under this § 337.6.

(iii) An insured depository institution shall be deemed to be within a given capital category for purposes of this § 337.6 as of the date the institution is notified of, or is deemed to have notice of, its capital category, under regulations implementing section 38 of the Federal Deposit Insurance Act issued by the appropriate federal banking agency for that institution.[13]

(4) *Deposit* has the same meaning as provided under section 3(l) of the Federal Deposit Insurance Act (12 U.S.C. 1813(l)).

(5) *Deposit broker.* (i) The term *deposit broker* means:

(A) Any person engaged in the business of placing deposits, or facilitating the placement of deposits, of third parties with insured depository institutions, or the business of placing deposits with insured depository institutions for the purpose of selling interests in those deposits to third parties; and

(B) An agent or trustee who establishes a deposit account to facilitate a business arrangement with an insured depository institution to use the proceeds of the account to fund a prearranged loan.

(ii) The term *deposit broker* does not include:

(A) An insured depository institution, with respect to funds placed with that depository institution;

(B) An employee of an insured depository institution, with respect to funds placed with the employing depository institution;

(C) A trust department of an insured depository institution, if the trust or other fiduciary relationship in question has not been established for the primary purpose of placing funds with insured depository institutions;

(D) The trustee of a pension or other employee benefit plan, with respect to funds of the plan;

(E) A person acting as a plan administrator or an investment adviser in connection with a pension plan or other employee benefit plan provided that person is performing managerial functions with respect to the plan;

(F) The trustee of a testamentary account;

(G) The trustee of an irrevocable trust (other than one described in paragraph (a)(5)(i)(B) of this section), as long as the trust in question has not been established for the primary purpose of placing funds with insured depository institutions;

(H) A trustee or custodian of a pension or profit-sharing plan qualified under section 401(d) or 403(a) of the Internal Revenue Code of 1986 (26 U.S.C. 401(d) or 403(a));

(I) An agent or nominee whose primary purpose is not the placement of funds with depository institutions; or

---

appropriate federal banking agency for that institution.

[12] For the most part, the capital measure terms are defined in the following regulations: FDIC—12 CFR part 325, subpart B; Board of Governors of the Federal Reserve System—12 CFR part 208; Office of the Comptroller of the Currency—12 CFR part 6; Office of Thrift Supervision—12 CFR part 565.

[13] The regulations implementing section 38 of the Federal Deposit Insurance Act and issued by the federal banking agencies generally provide that an insured depository institution is deemed to have been notified of its capital levels and its capital category as of the most recent date: (1) A Consolidated Report of Condition and Income or Thrift Financial Report is required to be filed with the appropriate federal banking agency; (2) A final report of examination is delivered to the institution; or (3) Written notice is provided by the appropriate federal banking agency to the institution of its capital category for purposes of section 38 of the Federal Deposit Insurance Act and implementing regulations or that the institution's capital category has changed. Provisions specifying the effective date of determination of capital category are generally published in the following regulations: FDIC—12 CFR 325.102. Board of Governors of the Federal Reserve System—12 CFR 208.32. Office of the Comptroller of the Currency—12 CFR 6.3. Office of Thrift Supervision—12 CFR 565.3.

Federal Deposit Insurance Corporation § 337.6

(J) An insured depository institution acting as an intermediary or agent of a U.S. government department or agency for a government sponsored minority or women-owned depository institution deposit program.

(iii) Notwithstanding paragraph (a)(5)(ii) of this section, the term *deposit broker* includes any insured depository institution that is not well-capitalized, and any employee of any such insured depository institution, which engages, directly or indirectly, in the solicitation of deposits by offering rates of interest (with respect to such deposits) which are significantly higher than the prevailing rates of interest on deposits offered by other insured depository institutions in such depository institution's normal market area.

(6) *Employee* means any employee: (i) Who is employed exclusively by the insured depository institution;

(ii) Whose compensation is primarily in the form of a salary;

(iii) Who does not share such employee's compensation with a deposit broker; and

(iv) Whose office space or place of business is used exclusively for the benefit of the insured depository institution which employs such individual.

(7) *FDIC* means the Federal Deposit Insurance Corporation.

(8) *Insured depository institution* means any bank, savings association, or branch of a foreign bank insured under the provisions of the Federal Deposit Insurance Act (12 U.S.C. 1811 et seq.).

(b) *Solicitation and acceptance of brokered deposits by insured depository institutions.* (1) A well capitalized insured depository institution may solicit and accept, renew or roll over any brokered deposit without restriction by this section.

(2)(i) An adequately capitalized insured depository institution may not accept, renew or roll over any brokered deposit unless it has applied for and been granted a waiver of this prohibition by the FDIC in accordance with the provisions of this section.

(ii) Any adequately capitalized insured depository institution that has been granted a waiver to accept, renew or roll over a brokered deposit may not pay an effective yield on any such deposit which, at the time that such deposit is accepted, renewed or rolled over, exceeds by more than 75 basis points:

(A) The effective yield paid on deposits of comparable size and maturity in such institution's normal market area for deposits accepted from within its normal market area; or

(B) The national rate paid on deposits of comparable size and maturity for deposits accepted outside the institution's normal market area. For purposes of this paragraph (b)(2)(ii)(B), the national rate shall be a simple average of rates paid by all insured depository institutions and branches for which data are available. This rate shall be determined by the FDIC.

(3)(i) An undercapitalized insured depository institution may not accept, renew or roll over any brokered deposit.

(ii) An undercapitalized insured depository institution may not solicit deposits by offering an effective yield that exceeds by more than 75 basis points the prevailing effective yields on insured deposits of comparable maturity in such institution's normal market area or in the market area in which such deposits are being solicited.

(c) *Waiver.* The FDIC may, on a case-by-case basis and upon application by an adequately capitalized insured depository institution, waive the prohibition on the acceptance, renewal or rollover of brokered deposits upon a finding that such acceptance, renewal or rollover does not constitute an unsafe or unsound practice with respect to such institution. The FDIC may conclude that it is not unsafe or unsound and may grant a waiver when the acceptance, renewal or rollover of brokered deposits is determined to pose no undue risk to the institution. Any waiver granted may be revoked at any time by written notice to the institution. For filing requirements, consult 12 CFR 303.243.

(d) *Exclusion for institutions in FDIC conservatorship.* No insured depository institution for which the FDIC has been appointed conservator shall be subject to the prohibition on the acceptance, renewal or rollover of brokered deposits contained in this § 337.6

§§ 337.7–337.9

or section 29 of the Federal Deposit Insurance Act for 90 days after the date on which the institution was placed in conservatorship. During this 90-day period, the institution shall, nevertheless, be subject to the restriction on the payment of interest contained in paragraph (b)(2)(ii) of the section. After such 90-day period, the institution may not accept, renew or roll over any brokered deposit.

(e) A market is any readily defined geographical area in which the rates offered by any one insured depository institution soliciting deposits in that area may affect the rates offered by other insured depository institutions operating in the same area. The effective yield on a deposit with an odd maturity shall be determined by interpolating between the yields offered by other insured depository institutions on deposits of the next longer and shorter maturities offered in the market. For purposes of this § 337.6, a presumption shall exist that the prevailing rate or effective yield in the relevant market is the national rate as defined in paragraph (b)(2)(ii)(B) of this section unless the FDIC determines, in its sole discretion based on available evidence, that the effective yield in that market differs from the national rate. Evidence of the effective yield in a particular market may include (but is not limited to) the following:

(1) Evidence as to the rates paid by other insured depository institutions in the same State, county or metropolitan statistical area (though the FDIC shall not be obligated to recognize each State, county or metropolitan statistical area as a separate market area);

(2) Evidence as to the rates paid by credit unions in the same market area if the FDIC determines that the insured depository institution competes directly with these credit unions; and

(3) Evidence as to the different rates paid on different deposit products in the same market area (though the FDIC shall not be obligated to recognize all alleged distinctions among various deposit products). (*Example:* For a particular market, evidence exists that the rates on money market deposit accounts (MMDAs) differ from the rates on negotiable order of withdrawal (NOW) accounts. MMDAs are distinguishable from NOW accounts in that the two types of accounts are subject to different legal requirements. Under these circumstances, for this market, the FDIC could recognize that the prevailing rate on MMDAs is different than the prevailing rate on NOW accounts.)

[57 FR 23941, June 5, 1992, as amended at 58 FR 54935, Oct. 25, 1993; 60 FR 31384, June 15, 1995; 63 FR 44750, Aug. 20, 1998; 66 FR 17622, Apr. 3, 2001; 74 FR 27683, June 11, 2009]

§§ 337.7–337.9 [Reserved]

§ 337.10 Waiver.

An insured State nonmember bank has the right to petition the Board of Directors of the Corporation for a waiver of this part or any subpart thereof with respect to any particular transaction or series of similar transactions. A waiver may be granted at the discretion of the Board upon a showing of good cause. All such petitions should be filed with the Executive Secretary, Federal Deposit Insurance Corporation, 550 17th Street, NW., Washington, DC 20429.

[39 FR 29179, Aug. 14, 1974, as amended at 67 FR 71071, Nov. 29, 2002]

§ 337.11 Effect on other banking practices.

Nothing in this part shall be construed as restricting in any manner the Corporation's authority to deal with any banking practice which is deemed to be unsafe or unsound or otherwise not in accordance with law, rule, or regulation; or which violates any condition imposed in writing by the Corporation in connection with the granting of any application or other request by an insured State nonmember bank, or any written agreement entered into by such bank with the Corporation. Compliance with the provisions of this part shall not relieve an insured State nonmember bank from its duty to conduct its operations in a safe and sound manner nor prevent the Corporation from taking whatever action it deems necessary and desirable to deal with

Federal Deposit Insurance Corporation

specific acts or practices which, although they do not violate the provisions of this part, are considered detrimental to the safety and sound operation of the bank engaged therein.

§ 337.12 Frequency of examination.

(a) *General.* The Federal Deposit Insurance Corporation examines insured state nonmember banks pursuant to authority conferred by section 10 of the Federal Deposit Insurance Act (12 U.S.C. 1820). The FDIC is required to conduct a full-scope, on-site examination of every insured state nonmember bank at least once during each 12-month period.

(b) *18-month rule for certain small institutions.* The FDIC may conduct a full-scope, on-site examination of an insured state nonmember bank at least once during each 18-month period, rather than each 12-month period as provided in paragraph (a) of this section, if the following conditions are satisfied:

(1) The bank has total assets of less than $500 million;

(2) The bank is well capitalized as defined in § 325.103(b)(1) of this chapter;

(3) At the most recent FDIC or applicable State banking agency examination, the FDIC—

(i) Assigned the bank a rating of 1 or 2 for management as part of the bank's composite rating under the Uniform Financial Institutions Rating System (commonly referred to as CAMELS); and

(ii) Assigned the bank a composite rating of 1 or 2 under the Uniform Financial Institutions Rating System (copies of which are available at the addresses specified in § 309.4 of this chapter);

(4) The bank currently is not subject to a formal enforcement proceeding or order by the FDIC, OCC or the Federal Reserve and

(5) No person acquired control of the bank during the preceding 12-month period in which a full-scope, on-site examination would have been required but for this section.

(c) *Authority to conduct more frequent examinations.* This section does not limit the authority of the FDIC to examine any insured state nonmember bank as frequently as the agency deems necessary.

[63 FR 16381, Apr. 2, 1998, as amended at 72 FR 17803, Apr. 10, 2007]

PART 338—FAIR HOUSING

Subpart A—Advertising

Sec.
338.1 Purpose.
338.2 Definitions applicable to subpart A of this part.
338.3 Nondiscriminatory advertising.
338.4 Fair housing poster.

Subpart B—Recordkeeping

338.5 Purpose.
338.6 Definitions applicable to this subpart B.
338.7 Recordkeeping requirements.
338.8 Compilation of loan data in register format.
338.9 Mortgage lending of a controlled entity.

AUTHORITY: 12 U.S.C. 1817, 1818, 1819, 1820(b), 2801 *et seq.*; 15 U.S.C. 1691 *et seq.*; 42 U.S.C. 3605, 3608; 12 CFR parts 202, 203; 24 CFR part 110.

Subpart A—Advertising

§ 338.1 Purpose.

The purpose of this subpart A is to prohibit insured state nonmember banks from engaging in discriminatory advertising with regard to residential real estate-related transactions. This subpart A also requires insured state nonmember banks to publicly display either the Equal Housing Lender poster set forth in § 338.4(b) of the FDIC's regulations or the Equal Housing Opportunity poster prescribed by part 110 of the regulations of the United States Department of Housing and Urban Development (24 CFR part 110). This subpart A enforces section 805 of title VIII of the Civil Rights Act of 1968, 42 U.S.C. 3601–3619 (Fair Housing Act), as amended by the Fair Housing Amendments Act of 1988.

[62 FR 36204, July 7, 1997]

§ 338.2 Definitions applicable to subpart A of this part.

For purposes of subpart A of this part:

(a) *Bank* means an insured State nonmember bank as defined in section 3 of the Federal Deposit Insurance Act.

(b) *Dwelling* means any building, structure, or portion thereof which is occupied as, or designed or intended for occupancy as, a residence by one or more families, and any vacant land wihch is offered for sale or lease for the construction or location thereon of any such building, structure, portion thereof.

(c) *Handicap* means, with respect to a person:

(1) A physical or mental impairment which substantially limits one or more of such person's major life activities;

(2) A record of having such an impairment; or

(3) Being regarded as having such an impairment, but such term does not include current, illegal use of or addition to a controlled substance (as defined in section 102 of the Controlled Substances Act (21 U.S.C. 802)).

(d) *Familial status* means one or more individuals (who have not attained the age of 18 years) being domiciled with:

(1) A parent or another person having legal custody of such individual or individuals; or

(2) The designee of such parent or other person having such custody, with the written persmission of such parent or other person.

The protections afforded against discrimination on the basis of familial status shall apply to any person who is pregnant or is in the process of securing legal custody of any indivdual who has not attained the age of 18 years.

[56 FR 50039, Oct. 3, 1991]

§ 338.3 Nondiscriminatory advertising.

(a) Any bank which directly or through third parties engages in any form of advertising of any loan for the purpose of purchasing, constructing, improving, repairing, or maintaining a dwelling or any loan secured by a dwelling shall prominently indicate in such advertisement, in a manner appropriate to the advertising medium and format utilized, that the bank makes such loans without regard to race, color, religion, national origin, sex, handicap, or familial status.

(1) With respect to written and visual advertisements, this requirement may be satisfied by including in the advertisement a copy of the logotype with the Equal Housing Lender legend contained in the Equal Housing Lender poster prescribed in § 338.4(b) of the FDIC's regulations or a copy of the logotype with the Equal Housing Opportunity legend contained in thc Equal Housing Opportunity poster prescribed in § 110.25(a) of the United States Department of Housing and Urban Development's regulations (24 CFR 110.25(a)).

(2) With respect to oral advertisements, this requirement may be satisfied by a statement, in the spoken text of the advertisement, that the bank is an "Equal Housing Lender" or an "Equal Opportunity Lender."

(3) When an oral advertisement is used in conjunction with a written or visual advertisement, the use of either of the methods specified in paragraphs (a)(1) and (2) of this section will satisfy the requirements of this paragraph (a).

(b) No advertisement shall contain any words, symbols, models or other forms of communication which express, imply, or suggest a discriminatory preference or policy of exclusion in violation of the provisions of the Fair Housing Act or the Equal Credit Opportunity Act.

[43 FR 11563, Mar. 20, 1978, as amended at 54 FR 52930, Dec. 26, 1989. Redesignated and amended at 56 FR 50039, Oct. 3, 1991; 62 FR 36204, July 7, 1997]

§ 338.4 Fair housing poster.

(a) Each bank engaged in extending loans for the purpose of purchasing, constructing, improving, repairing, or maintaining a dwelling or any loan secured by a dwelling shall conspicuously display either the Equal Housing Lender poster set forth in paragraph (b) of this section or the Equal Housing Opportunity poster prescribed by § 110.25(a) of the United States Department of Housing and Urban Development's regulations (24 CFR 110.25(a)), in a central location within the bank where deposits are received or where such loans are made in a manner clearly visible to the general public entering the area, where the poster is displayed.

(b) The Equal Housing Lender Poster shall be at least 11 by 14 inches in size and have the following text:

Federal Deposit Insurance Corporation §338.4

EQUAL HOUSING LENDER

We Do Business in Accordance With Federal Fair Lending Laws

UNDER THE FEDERAL FAIR HOUSING ACT, IT IS ILLEGAL ON THE BASIS OF RACE, COLOR, NATIONAL ORIGIN, RELIGION, SEX, HANDICAP, OR FAMILIAL STATUS (HAVING CHILDREN UNDER THE AGE OF 18), TO:

- Deny a loan for the purpose of purchasing, constructing, improving, repairing, or maintaining a dwelling, or deny any loan secured by a dwelling; or
- Discriminate in fixing the amount, interest rate, duration, application procedure or other terms or conditions of such a loan, or in appraising property.

IF YOU BELIEVE YOU HAVE BEEN DISCRIMINATED AGAINST, YOU SHOULD SEND A COMPLAINT TO:

Assistant Secretary for Fair Housing and Equal Opportunity
Department of Housing & Urban Development
Washington, DC 20410
For processing under the Federal Fair Housing Act
and to:
FDIC Consumer Response Center
2345 Grand Boulevard, Suite 100
Kansas City, Missouri 64108
For processing under the FDIC Regulations

UNDER THE EQUAL CREDIT OPPORTUNITY ACT, IT IS ILLEGAL TO DISCRIMINATE IN ANY CREDIT TRANSACTION:

- On the basis of race, color, national origin, religion, sex, marital status, or age
- Because income is from public assistance, or
- Because a right was exercised under the Consumer Credit Protection Act

IF YOU BELIEVE YOU HAVE BEEN DISCRIMINATED AGAINST, YOU SHOULD SEND A COMPLAINT TO:

FDIC Consumer Response Center
2345 Grand Boulevard, Suite 100
Kansas City, Missouri 64108

P-6456-063-95

(c) The Equal Housing Lender Poster specified in this section was adopted under §110.25(b) of the United States Department of Housing and Urban Development's rules and regulations as an authorized substitution for the poster

§ 338.5

required in § 110.25(a) of those rules and regulations.

[54 FR 52930, Dec. 26, 1989. Redesignated at 56 FR 50039, Oct. 3, 1991, as amended by 59 FR 52667, Oct. 19, 1994; 62 FR 36204, July 7, 1997; 73 FR 45855, Aug. 7, 2008]

Subpart B—Recordkeeping

§ 338.5 Purpose.

The purpose of this subpart B is twofold. First, this subpart B notifies all insured state nonmember banks of their duty to collect and retain certain information about a home loan applicant's personal characteristics in accordance with Regulation B of the Board of Governors of the Federal Reserve System (12 CFR part 202) in order to monitor an institution's compliance with the Equal Credit Opportunity Act of 1974 (15 U.S.C. 1691 *et seq.*). Second, this subpart B notifies certain insured state nonmember banks of their duty to maintain, update and report a register of home loan applications in accordance with Regulation C of the Board of Governors of the Federal Reserve System (12 CFR part 203), which implements the Home Mortgage Disclosure Act (12 U.S.C. 2801 *et seq.*).

[62 FR 36204, July 7, 1997]

§ 338.6 Definitions applicable to this subpart B.

For purposes of this subpart B—

(a) *Bank* means an insured state nonmember bank as defined in section 3 of the Federal Deposit Insurance Act.

(b) *Controlled entity* means a corporation, partnership, association, or other business entity with respect to which a bank possesses, directly or indirectly, the power to direct or cause the direction of management and policies, whether through the ownership of voting securities, by contract, or otherwise.

[62 FR 36204, July 7, 1997]

§ 338.7 Recordkeeping requirements.

All banks that receive an application for credit primarily for the purchase or refinancing of a dwelling occupied or to be occupied by the applicant as a principal residence where the extension of credit will be secured by the dwelling shall request and retain the monitoring information required by Regulation B of the Board of Governors of the Federal Reserve System (12 CFR part 202).

[62 FR 36204, July 7, 1997]

§ 338.8 Compilation of loan data in register format.

Banks and other lenders required to file a Home Mortgage Disclosure Act loan application register (LAR) with the Federal Deposit Insurance Corporation shall maintain, update and report such LAR in accordance with Regulation C of the Board of Governors of the Federal Reserve System (12 CFR part 203).

[62 FR 36204, July 7, 1997]

§ 338.9 Mortgage lending of a controlled entity.

Any bank which refers any applicants to a controlled entity and which purchases any home purchase loans or home improvement loans as defined in Regulation C of the Board of Governors of the Federal Reserve Board (12 CFR part 203) originated by the controlled entity, as a condition to transacting any business with the controlled entity, shall require the controlled entity to enter into a written agreement with the bank. The written agreement shall provide that the entity shall:

(a) Comply with the requirements of §§ 338.3, 338.4 and 338.7, and, if otherwise subject to Regulation C of the Board of Governors of the Federal Reserve System (12 CFR part 203), § 338.8;

(b) Open its books and records to examination by the Federal Deposit Insurance Corporation; and

(c) Comply with all instructions and orders issued by the Federal Deposit Insurance Corporation with respect to its home loan practices.

[49 FR 35764, Sept. 12, 1984. Redesignated and amended at 56 FR 50039, Oct. 3, 1991; 62 FR 36204, July 7, 1997]

PART 339—LOANS IN AREAS HAVING SPECIAL FLOOD HAZARDS

Sec.
339.1 Authority, purpose, and scope.
339.2 Definitions.
339.3 Requirement to purchase flood insurance where available.
339.4 Exemptions.
339.5 Escrow requirement.

Federal Deposit Insurance Corporation § 339.3

339.6 Required use of standard flood hazard determination form.
339.7 Forced placement of flood insurance.
339.8 Determination fees.
339.9 Notice of special flood hazards and availability of Federal disaster relief assistance.
339.10 Notice of servicer's identity.

APPENDIX A TO PART 339—SAMPLE FORM OF NOTICE OF SPECIAL FLOOD HAZARDS AND AVAILABILITY OF FEDERAL DISASTER RELIEF ASSISTANCE

AUTHORITY: 42 U.S.C. 4012a, 4104a, 4104b, 4106, and 4128.

SOURCE: 61 FR 45706, Aug. 29, 1996, unless otherwise noted.

§ 339.1 Authority, purpose, and scope.

(a) *Authority.* This part is issued pursuant to 42 U.S.C. 4012a, 4104a, 4104b, 4106, and 4128.

(b) *Purpose.* The purpose of this part is to implement the requirements of the National Flood Insurance Act of 1968 and the Flood Disaster Protection Act of 1973, as amended (42 U.S.C. 4001–4129).

(c) *Scope.* This part, except for §§ 339.6 and 339.8, applies to loans secured by buildings or mobile homes located or to be located in areas determined by the Director of the Federal Emergency Management Agency to have special flood hazards. Sections 339.6 and 339.8 apply to loans secured by buildings or mobile homes, regardless of location.

§ 339.2 Definitions.

(a) *Act* means the National Flood Insurance Act of 1968, as amended (42 U.S.C. 4001–4129).

(b) *Bank* means an insured state nonmember bank and an insured state branch of a foreign bank or any subsidiary of an insured state nonmember bank.

(c) *Building* means a walled and roofed structure, other than a gas or liquid storage tank, that is principally above ground and affixed to a permanent site, and a walled and roofed structure while in the course of construction, alteration, or repair.

(d) *Community* means a State or a political subdivision of a State that has zoning and building code jurisdiction over a particular area having special flood hazards.

(e) *Designated loan* means a loan secured by a building or mobile home that is located or to be located in a special flood hazard area in which flood insurance is available under the Act.

(f) *Director of FEMA* means the Director of the Federal Emergency Management Agency.

(g) *Mobile home* means a structure, transportable in one or more sections, that is built on a permanent chassis and designed for use with or without a permanent foundation when attached to the required utilities. The term *mobile home* does not include a recreational vehicle. For purposes of this part, the term *mobile home* means a mobile home on a permanent foundation. The term *mobile home* includes a manufactured home as that term is used in the NFIP.

(h) *NFIP* means the National Flood Insurance Program authorized under the Act.

(i) *Residential improved real estate* means real estate upon which a home or other residential building is located or to be located.

(j) *Servicer* means the person responsible for:

(1) Receiving any scheduled, periodic payments from a borrower under the terms of a loan, including amounts for taxes, insurance premiums, and other charges with respect to the property securing the loan; and

(2) Making payments of principal and interest and any other payments from the amounts received from the borrower as may be required under the terms of the loan.

(k) *Special flood hazard area* means the land in the flood plain within a community having at least a one percent chance of flooding in any given year, as designated by the Director of FEMA.

(l) *Table funding* means a settlement at which a loan is funded by a contemporaneous advance of loan funds and an assignment of the loan to the person advancing the funds.

§ 339.3 Requirement to purchase flood insurance where available.

(a) *In general.* A bank shall not make, increase, extend, or renew any designated loan unless the building or mobile home and any personal property securing the loan is covered by flood insurance for the term of the loan. The

§ 339.4

amount of insurance must be at least equal to the lesser of the outstanding principal balance of the designated loan or the maximum limit of coverage available for the particular type of property under the Act. Flood insurance coverage under the Act is limited to the overall value of the property securing the designated loan minus the value of the land on which the property is located.

(b) *Table funded loans.* A bank that acquires a loan from a mortgage broker or other entity through table funding shall be considered to be making a loan for the purposes of this part.

§ 339.4 Exemptions.

The flood insurance requirement prescribed by § 339.3 does not apply with respect to:

(a) Any State-owned property covered under a policy of self-insurance satisfactory to the Director of FEMA, who publishes and periodically revises the list of States falling within this exemption; or

(b) Property securing any loan with an original principal balance of $5,000 or less and a repayment term of one year or less.

§ 339.5 Escrow requirement.

If a bank requires the escrow of taxes, insurance premiums, fees, or any other charges for a loan secured by *residential* improved real estate or a mobile home that is made, increased, extended, or renewed on or after October 1, 1996, the bank shall also require the escrow of all premiums and fees for any flood insurance required under § 339.3. The bank, or a servicer acting on behalf of the bank, shall deposit the flood insurance premiums on behalf of the borrower in an escrow account. This escrow account will be subject to escrow requirements adopted pursuant to section 10 of the Real Estate Settlement Procedures Act of 1974 (12 U.S.C. 2609) (RESPA), which generally limits the amount that may be maintained in escrow accounts for certain types of loans and requires escrow account statements for those accounts, only if the loan is otherwise subject to RESPA. Following receipt of a notice from the Director of FEMA or other provider of flood insurance that premiums are due, the bank, or a servicer acting on behalf of the bank, shall pay the amount owed to the insurance provider from the escrow account by the date when such premiums are due.

§ 339.6 Required use of standard flood hazard determination form.

(a) *Use of form.* A bank shall use the standard flood hazard determination form developed by the Director of FEMA when determining whether the building or mobile home offered as collateral security for a loan is or will be located in a special flood hazard area in which flood insurance is available under the Act. The standard flood hazard determination form may be used in a printed, computerized, or electronic manner. A non-member bank may obtain the standard flood hazard determination form by written request to FEMA, P.O. Box 2012, Jessup, MD 20794-2012.

(b) *Retention of form.* A bank shall retain a copy of the completed standard flood hazard determination form, in either hard copy or electronic form, for the period of time the bank owns the loan.

[61 FR 45706, Aug. 29, 1996, as amended at 64 FR 71274, Dec. 21, 1999]

§ 339.7 Forced placement of flood insurance.

If a bank, or a servicer acting on behalf of the bank, determines, at any time during the term of a designated loan, that the building or mobile home and any personal property securing the designated loan is not covered by flood insurance or is covered by flood insurance in an amount less than the amount required under § 339.3, then the bank or its servicer shall notify the borrower that the borrower should obtain flood insurance, at the borrower's expense, in an amount at least equal to the amount required under § 339.3, for the remaining term of the loan. If the borrower fails to obtain flood insurance within 45 days after notification, then the bank or its servicer shall purchase insurance on the borrower's behalf. The bank or its servicer may charge the borrower for the cost of premiums and fees incurred in purchasing the insurance.

Federal Deposit Insurance Corporation § 339.9

§ 339.8 Determination fees.

(a) *General.* Notwithstanding any Federal or State law other than the Flood Disaster Protection Act of 1973, as amended (42 U.S.C. 4001–4129), any bank, or a servicer acting on behalf of the bank, may charge a reasonable fee for determining whether the building or mobile home securing the loan is located or will be located in a special flood hazard area. A determination fee may also include, but is not limited to, a fee for life-of-loan monitoring.

(b) *Borrower fee.* The determination fee authorized by paragraph (a) of this section may be charged to the borrower if the determination:

(1) Is made in connection with a making, increasing, extending, or renewing of the loan that is initiated by the borrower;

(2) Reflects the Director of FEMA's revision or updating of floodplain areas or flood-risk zones;

(3) Reflects the Director of FEMA's publication of a notice or compendium that:

(i) Affects the area in which the building or mobile home securing the loan is located; or

(ii) By determination of the Director of FEMA, may reasonably require a determination whether the building or mobile home securing the loan is located in a special flood hazard area; or

(4) Results in the purchase of flood insurance coverage by the lender or its servicer on behalf of the borrower under § 339.7.

(c) *Purchaser or transferee fee.* The determination fee authorized by paragraph (a) of this section may be charged to the purchaser or transferee of a loan in the case of the sale or transfer of the loan.

§ 339.9 Notice of special flood hazards and availability of Federal disaster relief assistance.

(a) *Notice requirement.* When a bank makes, increases, extends, or renews a loan secured by a building or a mobile home located or to be located in a special flood hazard area, the bank shall mail or deliver a written notice to the borrower and to the servicer in all cases whether or not flood insurance is available under the Act for the collateral securing the loan.

(b) *Contents of notice.* The written notice must include the following information:

(1) A warning, in a form approved by the Director of FEMA, that the building or the mobile home is or will be located in a special flood hazard area;

(2) A description of the flood insurance purchase requirements set forth in section 102(b) of the Flood Disaster Protection Act of 1973, as amended (42 U.S.C. 4012a(b));

(3) A statement, where applicable, that flood insurance coverage is available under the NFIP and may also be available from private insurers; and

(4) A statement whether Federal disaster relief assistance may be available in the event of damage to the building or mobile home caused by flooding in a Federally-declared disaster.

(c) *Timing of notice.* The bank shall provide the notice required by paragraph (a) of this section to the borrower within a reasonable time before the completion of the transaction, and to the servicer as promptly as practicable after the bank provides notice to the borrower and in any event no later than the time the bank provides other similar notices to the servicer concerning hazard insurance and taxes. Notice to the servicer may be made electronically or may take the form of a copy of the notice to the borrower.

(d) *Record of receipt.* The bank shall retain a record of the receipt of the notices by the borrower and the servicer for the period of time the bank owns the loan.

(e) *Alternate method of notice.* Instead of providing the notice to the borrower required by paragraph (a) of this section, a bank may obtain satisfactory written assurance from a seller or lessor that, within a reasonable time before the completion of the sale or lease transaction, the seller or lessor has provided such notice to the purchaser or lessee. The bank shall retain a record of the written assurance from the seller or lessor for the period of time the bank owns the loan.

(f) *Use of prescribed form of notice.* A bank will be considered to be in compliance with the requirement for notice to the borrower of this section by providing written notice to the borrower containing the language presented in appendix A to this part within a reasonable time before the completion of the transaction. The notice presented in appendix A to this part satisfies the borrower notice requirements of the Act.

§ 339.10 Notice of servicer's identity.

(a) *Notice requirement.* When a bank makes, increases, extends, renews, sells, or transfers a loan secured by a building or mobile home located or to be located in a special flood hazard area, the bank shall notify the Director of FEMA (or the Director of FEMA's designee) in writing of the identity of the servicer of the loan. The Director of FEMA has designated the insurance provider to receive the bank's notice of the servicer's identity. This notice may be provided electronically if electronic transmission is satisfactory to the Director of FEMA's designee.

(b) *Transfer of servicing rights.* The bank shall notify the Director of FEMA (or the Director of FEMA's designee) of any change in the servicer of a loan described in paragraph (a) of this section within 60 days after the effective date of the change. This notice may be provided electronically if electronic transmission is satisfactory to the Director of FEMA's designee. Upon any change in the servicing of a loan described in paragraph (a) of this section, the duty to provide notice under this paragraph (b) shall transfer to the transferee servicer.

APPENDIX A TO PART 339—SAMPLE FORM OF NOTICE OF SPECIAL FLOOD HAZARDS AND AVAILABILITY OF FEDERAL DISASTER RELIEF ASSISTANCE

We are giving you this notice to inform you that:

The building or mobile home securing the loan for which you have applied is or will be located in an area with special flood hazards.

The area has been identified by the Director of the Federal Emergency Management Agency (FEMA) as a special flood hazard area using FEMA's *Flood Insurance Rate Map* or the *Flood Hazard Boundary Map* for the following community: _____. This area has at least a one percent (1%) chance of a flood equal to or exceeding the base flood elevation (a 100-year flood) in any given year. During the life of a 30-year mortgage loan, the risk of a 100-year flood in a special flood hazard area is 26 percent (26%).

Federal law allows a lender and borrower jointly to request the Director of FEMA to review the determination of whether the property securing the loan is located in a special flood hazard area. If you would like to make such a request, please contact us for further information.

_____. The community in which the property securing the loan is located participates in the National Flood Insurance Program (NFIP). Federal law will not allow us to make you the loan that you have applied for if you do not purchase flood insurance. The flood insurance must be maintained for the life of the loan. If you fail to purchase or renew flood insurance on the property, Federal law authorizes and requires us to purchase the flood insurance for you at your expense.

• Flood insurance coverage under the NFIP may be purchased through an insurance agent who will obtain the policy either directly through the NFIP or through an insurance company that participates in the NFIP. Flood insurance also may be available from private insurers that do not participate in the NFIP.

• At a minimum, flood insurance purchased must cover *the lesser of:*

(1) the outstanding principal balance of the loan; *or*

(2) the maximum amount of coverage allowed for the type of property under the NFIP.

Flood insurance coverage under the NFIP is limited to the overall value of the property securing the loan minus the value of the land on which the property is located.

• Federal disaster relief assistance (usually in the form of a low-interest loan) may be available for damages incurred in excess of your flood insurance if your community's participation in the NFIP is in accordance with NFIP requirements.

_____ Flood insurance coverage under the NFIP is not available for the property securing the loan because the community in which the property is located does not participate in the NFIP. In addition, if the nonparticipating community has been identified for at least one year as containing a special flood hazard area, properties located in the community will not be eligible for Federal disaster relief assistance in the event of a Federally-declared flood disaster.

PART 340—RESTRICTIONS ON SALE OF ASSETS BY THE FEDERAL DEPOSIT INSURANCE CORPORATION

Sec.

340.1 What is the statutory authority for the regulation, what are its purpose and

Federal Deposit Insurance Corporation

§ 340.2

scope, and can the FDIC have other policies on related topics?
340.2 Definitions.
340.3 What are the restrictions on the sale of assets by the FDIC if the buyer wants to finance the purchase with a loan from the FDIC?
340.4 What are the restrictions on the sale of assets by the FDIC regardless of the method of financing?
340.5 Can the FDIC deny a loan to a buyer who is not disqualified from purchasing assets using seller-financing under this regulation?
340.6 What is the effect of this part on transactions that were entered into before its effective date?
340.7 When is a certification required, and who does not have to provide a certification?
340.8 Does this part apply in the case of a workout, resolution, or settlement of obligations?

AUTHORITY: 12 U.S.C. 1819 (Tenth), 1821(p).

SOURCE: 65 FR 14818, Mar. 20, 2000, unless otherwise noted.

§ 340.1 What is the statutory authority for the regulation, what are its purpose and scope, and can the FDIC have other policies on related topics?

(a) *Authority.* The statutory authority for adopting this part is section 11(p) of the Federal Deposit Insurance Act (FDI Act), 12 U.S.C. 1821(p). Section 11(p) was added to the FDI Act by section 20 of the Resolution Trust Corporation Completion Act (Pub. L. 103–204, 107 Stat. 2369 (1993)).

(b) *Purpose.* The purpose of this part is to prohibit individuals or entities who profited or engaged in wrongdoing at the expense of an insured institution, or seriously mismanaged an insured institution, from buying assets of failed financial institutions from the FDIC.

(c) *Scope.* The restrictions of this part generally apply to assets of failed institutions owned or controlled by the FDIC in any capacity, even though the assets are not owned by the insured institution that the prospective purchaser injured. Unless we determine otherwise, this part does not apply to the sale of securities in connection with the investment of corporate and receivership funds pursuant to the Investment Policy for Liquidation Funds managed by the FDIC as it is in effect from time to time. In the case of a sale of securities backed by a pool of assets that may include assets of failed institutions by a trust or other entity, this part applies only to the sale of assets by the FDIC to an underwriter in an initial offering, and not to any other purchaser of the securities.

(d) *The FDIC retains the authority to establish other policies restricting asset sales.* Neither section 11(p) of the FDI Act nor this part in any way limits the authority of the FDIC to establish policies prohibiting the sale of assets to prospective purchasers who have injured any failed financial institution, or to other prospective purchasers, such as certain employees or contractors of the FDIC, or individuals who are not in compliance with the terms of any debt or duty owed to the FDIC. Any such policies may be independent of, in conjunction with, or in addition to the restrictions set forth in this part.

§ 340.2 Definitions.

(a) *Associated person* of an individual or entity means:

(1) With respect to an individual:

(i) The individual's spouse or dependent child or any member of his or her immediate household;

(ii) A partnership of which the individual is or was a general or limited partner; or

(iii) A corporation of which the individual is or was an officer or director;

(2) With respect to a partnership, a managing or general partner of the partnership; or

(3) With respect to any entity, an individual or entity who, acting individually or in concert with one or more individuals or entities, owns or controls 25 percent or more of the entity.

(b) *Default* means any failure to comply with the terms of an obligation to such an extent that:

(1) A judgment has been rendered in favor of the FDIC or a failed institution; or

(2) In the case of a secured obligation, the property securing such obligation is foreclosed on.

(c) *FDIC* means the Federal Deposit Insurance Corporation.

(d) *Failed institution* means any bank or savings association that has been

§ 340.3

under the conservatorship or receivership of the FDIC or RTC. For the purpose of this part, "failed institution" includes any entity owned and controlled by a failed institution.

(e) *Obligation* means any debt or duty to pay money owed to the FDIC or a failed institution, including any guarantee of any such debt or duty.

(f) *Person* means an individual, or an entity with a legally independent existence, including: a trustee; the beneficiary of at least a 25 percent share of the proceeds of a trust; a partnership; a corporation; an association; or other organization or society.

(g) *RTC* means the former Resolution Trust Corporation.

(h) *Substantial loss* means:

(1) An obligation that is delinquent for ninety (90) or more days and on which there remains an outstanding balance of more than $50,000;

(2) An unpaid final judgment in excess of $50,000 regardless of whether it becomes forgiven in whole or in part in a bankruptcy proceeding;

(3) A deficiency balance following a foreclosure of collateral in excess of $50,000, regardless of whether it becomes forgiven in whole or in part in a bankruptcy proceeding;

(4) Any loss in excess of $50,000 evidenced by an IRS Form 1099-C (Information Reporting for Discharge of Indebtedness).

§ 340.3 What are the restrictions on the sale of assets by the FDIC if the buyer wants to finance the purchase with a loan from the FDIC?

A person may not borrow money or accept credit from the FDIC in connection with the purchase of any assets from the FDIC or any failed institution if:

(a) There has been a default with respect to one or more obligations totaling in excess of $1,000,000 owed by that person or its associated person; and

(b) The person or its associated person made any fraudulent misrepresentations in connection with any such obligation(s).

§ 340.4 What are the restrictions on the sale of assets by the FDIC regardless of the method of financing?

(a) A person may not acquire any assets from the FDIC or from any failed institution if the person or its associated person:

(1) Has participated, as an officer or director of a failed institution or of an affiliate of a failed institution, in a material way in one or more transaction(s) that caused a substantial loss to that failed institution;

(2) Has been removed from, or prohibited from participating in the affairs of, a failed institution pursuant to any final enforcement action by the Office of the Comptroller of the Currency, the Office of Thrift Supervision, the Board of Governors of the Federal Reserve System, the FDIC, or any of their successors;

(3) Has demonstrated a pattern or practice of defalcation regarding obligations to any failed institution; or

(4) Has been convicted of committing or conspiring to commit any offense under 18 U.S.C. 215, 656, 657, 1005, 1006, 1007, 1014, 1032, 1341, 1343 or 1344 affecting any failed institution and there has been a default with respect to one or more obligations owed by that person or its associated person.

(b) For purposes of paragraph (a) of this section, a person has participated "in a material way in a transaction that caused a substantial loss to a failed institution" if, in connection with a substantial loss to a failed institution, the person has been found in a final determination by a court or administrative tribunal, or is alleged in a judicial or administrative action brought by the FDIC or by any component of the government of the United States or of any state:

(1) To have violated any law, regulation, or order issued by a federal or state banking agency, or breached or defaulted on a written agreement with a federal or state banking agency, or breached a written agreement with a failed institution;

(2) To have engaged in an unsafe or unsound practice in conducting the affairs of a failed institution; or

(3) To have breached a fiduciary duty owed to a failed institution.

Federal Deposit Insurance Corporation

(c) For purposes of paragraph (a) of this section, a person or its associated person has demonstrated a "pattern or practice of defalcation" regarding obligations to a failed institution if the person or associated person has:

(1) Engaged in more than one transaction that created an obligation on the part of such person or its associated person with intent to cause a loss to any financial institution insured by the FDIC or with reckless disregard for whether such transactions would cause a loss to any such insured financial institution; and

(2) The transactions, in the aggregate, caused a substantial loss to one or more failed institution(s).

§ 340.5 Can the FDIC deny a loan to a buyer who is not disqualified from purchasing assets using seller-financing under this regulation?

The FDIC still has the right to make an independent determination, based upon all relevant facts of a person's financial condition and history, of that person's eligibility to receive any loan or extension of credit from the FDIC, even if the person is not in any way disqualified from purchasing assets from the FDIC under the restrictions set forth in this part.

§ 340.6 What is the effect of this part on transactions that were entered into before its effective date?

This part does not affect the enforceability of a contract of sale and/or agreement for seller financing in effect prior to July 1, 2000.

§ 340.7 When is a certification required, and who does not have to provide a certification?

(a) Before any person may purchase any asset from the FDIC that person must certify, under penalty of perjury, that none of the restrictions contained in this part applies to the purchase. The FDIC may establish the form of the certification and may change the form from time to time.

(b) Notwithstanding paragraph (a) of this section, a state or political subdivision of a state, a federal agency or instrumentality such as the Government National Mortgage Association, or a federally-regulated, government-sponsored enterprise such as Fannie Mae or Freddie Mac does not have to give a certification before it can purchase assets from the FDIC, unless the Director of the FDIC's Division of Resolutions and Receiverships, or his designee, in his discretion, requires a certification of any such entity.

§ 340.8 Does this part apply in the case of a workout, resolution, or settlement of obligations?

The restrictions of §§ 340.3 and 340.4 do not apply if the sale or transfer of an asset resolves or settles, or is part of the resolution or settlement of, one or more obligations, regardless of the amount of such obligations.

PART 341—REGISTRATION OF SECURITIES TRANSFER AGENTS

Sec.
341.1 Scope.
341.2 Definitions.
341.3 Registration as securities transfer agent.
341.4 Amendments to registration.
341.5 Withdrawal from registration.
341.6 Reports.
341.7 Delegation of authority.

AUTHORITY: Secs. 2, 3, 17, 17A and 23(a), Securities Exchange Act of 1934, as amended (15 U.S.C. 78b, 78c, 78q, 78q–1 and 78w(a)).

SOURCE: 47 FR 38106, Aug. 30, 1982, unless otherwise noted.

§ 341.1 Scope.

This part is issued by the Federal Deposit Insurance Corporation (the *FDIC*) under sections 2, 3(a)(34)(B), 17, 17A and 23(a) of the Securities Exchange Act of 1934 (the *Act*), as amended (15 U.S.C. 78b, 78c(a)(34)(B), 78q, 78q–1 and 78w(a)) and applies to all insured nonmember banks, or subsidiaries of such banks, that act as transfer agents for securities registered under section 12 of the Act (15 U.S.C. 78*l*), or for securities exempt from registration under subsections (g)(2)(B) or (g)(2)(G) of section 12 (15 U.S.C. 78*l*(g)(2)(B) and (G)) (securities of investment companies, including mutual funds, and insurance companies). Such securities are *qualifying securities* for purposes of this part.

§ 341.2 Definitions.

For the purpose of this part, including all forms and instructions promulgated for use in connection herewith, unless the context otherwise requires:

(a) The term *transfer agent* means any person who engages on behalf of an issuer of qualifying securities or on behalf of itself as an issuer of qualifying securities in: (1) Countersigning such securities upon issuance;

(2) Monitoring the issuance of such securities with a view to preventing unauthorized issuance, a function commonly performed by a person called a registrar;

(3) Registering the transfer of such securities;

(4) Exchanging or converting such securities; or

(5) Transferring record ownership of securities by bookkeeping entry without physical issuance of such securities certificates. The term *transfer agent* includes any person who performs these functions as a co-transfer agent with respect to equity or debt issues, and any person who performs these functions as registrar or co-registrar with respect to debt issued by corporations.

NOTE: The following examples are illustrative of the kinds of activities engaged in by transfer agents under this part.

1. A transfer agent of stock or shares in a mutual fund maintains the records of shareholders and transfers stock from one shareholder to another by cancellation of the surrendered certificates and issuance of new certificates in the name of the new shareholder. A co-transfer agent also performs these functions.

2. A registrar of stock or shares in a mutual fund monitors the issuance of such securities to prevent over-issuance of shares, affixing its signature of each stock certificate issued to signify its authorized issuance. A co-registrar also performs these functions.

3. A registrar of corporate debt securities maintains the records of ownership of registered bonds; makes changes in such records; issues, transfers, and exchanges such certificates; and monitors the securities to prevent over-issuance of certificates. A co-registrar also performs these functions.

(b) The term *Act* means the Securities Exchange Act of 1934.

(c) The acronym *ARA* means the appropriate regulatory agency, as defined in section 3(a)(34)(B) of the Act.

(d) The phrase *Federal bank regulators* means the Office of the Comptroller of the Currency, the Board of Governors of the Federal Reserve System, and the Federal Deposit Insurance Corporation.

(e) The term *Form TA-1* means the form and any attachments to that form, whether filed as a registration or an amendment to a registration.

(f) The term *registrant* means the entity on whose behalf Form TA-1 is filed.

(g) The acronym *SEC* means the Securities and Exchange Commission.

(h) The term *insured nonmember bank* means a bank whose Deposits are insured by the Federal Deposit Insurance Corporation and that is not a member of the Federal Reserve System.

(i) The term *qualifying securities* means:

(1) Securities registered on a national securities exchange;

(2) Securities issued by a company or bank with 500 or more shareholders *and* $1 million or more in total assets, except for securities exempted from registration with the SEC by section 12(g)(2) (C, D, E, F and H) of the Act.

§ 341.3 Registration as securities transfer agent.

(a) *Requirement for registration.* Any insured nonmember bank which performs any of the functions of a transfer agent as described in § 341.2(a) with respect to qualifying securities shall register with the FDIC in the manner indicated in this section.

(b) *Application to register as transfer agent.* An application for registration under section 17A(c) of the Act, of a transfer agent for which the FDIC is the appropriate regulatory agency, as defined in section 3(a)(34)(B)(iii) of the Act, shall be filed with the FDIC at its Washington, DC headquarters on Form TA-1, in accordance with the instructions contained therein.

(c) *Effective date of registration.* Registration shall become effective 30 days after the date an application on Form

Federal Deposit Insurance Corporation

TA–1 is filed unless the FDIC accelerates, denies, or postpones such registration in accordance with section 17A(c) of the Act. The effective date of such registration may be postponed by order for a period not to exceed 15 days. Postponement of registration for more than 15 days shall be after notice and opportunity for hearing. Form TA–1 is available upon request from the Review Unit, Division of Supervision and Consumer Protection (DSC), FDIC, Washington, DC 20429.

[47 FR 38106, Aug. 30, 1982, as amended at 60 FR 31384, June 15, 1995]

§ 341.4 Amendments to registration.

(a) Within 60 calendar days following the date which any information reported on Form TA–1 becomes inaccurate, misleading, or incomplete, the registrant shall file an amendment on Form TA–1 correcting the inaccurate, misleading, or incomplete information.

(b) The filing of an amendment to an application for registration as a transfer agent under § 341.3, which registration has not become effective, shall postpone the effective date of the registration for 30 days following the date on which the amendment is filed unless the FDIC accelerates, denies, or postpones the registration in accordance with section 17A(c) of the Act.

[47 FR 38106, Aug. 30, 1982, as amended at 52 FR 1182, Jan. 12, 1987]

§ 341.5 Withdrawal from registration.

(a) *Notice of withdrawal from registration.* Any transfer agent registered under this part that ceases to engage in the functions of a transfer agent as defined in § 341.2(a) shall file a written notice of withdrawal from registration with the FDIC. A registered transfer agent that ceases to engage in one or more of the functions of transfer agent as defined in § 341.2(a), but continues to engage in another such function, shall not withdraw from registration.

(b) A notice of withdrawal shall be filed with the FDIC at its Washington, DC headquarters. Deregistration shall be effective upon receipt of notice of withdrawal by the FDIC. A Request for Deregistration form is available from the Review Unit, Division of Supervision and Consumer Protection (DSC), FDIC, Washington, DC 20429.

(c) If the FDIC finds that any registered transfer agent for which it is the ARA, is no longer in existence or has ceased to do business as a transfer agent, FDIC shall cancel or deny the registration by order of the Board of Directors.

(d) Registration of a transfer agent with another ARA shall cancel registration of the transfer agent with FDIC.

[47 FR 38106, Aug. 30, 1982, as amended at 60 FR 31384, June 15, 1995]

§ 341.6 Reports.

Every registration or amendment filed under this section shall constitute a *report* or *application* within the meaning or sections 17, 17A(c), and 32(a) of the Act.

§ 341.7 Delegation of authority.

(a) Except as provided in paragraph (b) of this section, authority is delegated to the Director and Deputy Director (DSC) and, where confirmed in writing by the Director, to an associate director and the appropriate regional director and deputy regional director, to act on disclosure matters under and pursuant to sections 17 and 17A of the Securities Exchange Act of 1934 (15 U.S.C. 78).

(b) Authority to act on disclosure matters is retained by the Board of Directors when such matters involve exemption from registration requirements pursuant to section 17A(c)(1) of the Securities Exchange Act of 1934 (15 U.S.C. 78q–1(c)(1)).

[63 FR 44750, Aug. 20, 1998]

PART 342 [RESERVED]

PART 343—CONSUMER PROTECTION IN SALES OF INSURANCE

Sec.
343.10　Purpose and scope.
343.20　Definitions.
343.30　Prohibited practices.
343.40　What you must disclose.
343.50　Where insurance activities may take place.
343.60　Qualification and licensing requirements for insurance sales personnel.

§ 343.10

12 CFR Ch. III (1–1–12 Edition)

APPENDIX A TO PART 343—CONSUMER GRIEVANCE PROCESS

AUTHORITY: 12 U.S.C. 1819 (Seventh and Tenth); 12 U.S.C. 1831x.

SOURCE: 65 FR 75843, Dec. 4, 2000, unless otherwise noted.

§ 343.10 Purpose and scope.

This part establishes consumer protections in connection with retail sales practices, solicitations, advertising, or offers of any insurance product or annuity to a consumer by:

(a) Any bank; or

(b) Any other person that is engaged in such activities at an office of the bank or on behalf of the bank.

§ 343.20 Definitions.

As used in this part:

(a) *Affiliate* means a company that controls, is controlled by, or is under common control with another company.

(b) *Bank* means an FDIC-insured, state-chartered commercial or savings bank that is not a member of the Federal Reserve System and for which the FDIC is the appropriate federal banking agency pursuant to section 3(q) of the Federal Deposit Insurance Act (12 U.S.C. 1813(q)).

(c) *Company* means any corporation, partnership, business trust, association or similar organization, or any other trust (unless by its terms the trust must terminate within twenty-five years or not later than twenty-one years and ten months after the death of individuals living on the effective date of the trust). It does not include any corporation the majority of the shares of which are owned by the United States or by any State, or a qualified family partnership, as defined in section 2(o)(10) of the Bank Holding Company Act of 1956, as amended (12 U.S.C. 1841(o)(10)).

(d) *Consumer* means an individual who purchases, applies to purchase, or is solicited to purchase from you insurance products or annuities primarily for personal, family, or household purposes.

(e) *Control* of a company has the same meaning as in section 3(w)(5) of the Federal Deposit Insurance Act (12 U.S.C. 1813(w)(5)).

(f) *Domestic violence* means the occurrence of one or more of the following acts by a current or former family member, household member, intimate partner, or caretaker:

(1) Attempting to cause or causing or threatening another person physical harm, severe emotional distress, psychological trauma, rape, or sexual assault;

(2) Engaging in a course of conduct or repeatedly committing acts toward another person, including following the person without proper authority, under circumstances that place the person in reasonable fear of bodily injury or physical harm;

(3) Subjecting another person to false imprisonment; or

(4) Attempting to cause or causing damage to property so as to intimidate or attempt to control the behavior of another person.

(g) *Electronic media* includes any means for transmitting messages electronically between you and a consumer in a format that allows visual text to be displayed on equipment, for example, a personal computer monitor.

(h) *Office* means the premises of a bank where retail deposits are accepted from the public.

(i) *Subsidiary* has the same meaning as in section 3(w)(4) of the Federal Deposit Insurance Act (12 U.S.C. 1813(w)(4)).

(j) (1) *You* means:

(i) A bank; or

(ii) Any other person only when the person sells, solicits, advertises, or offers an insurance product or annuity to a consumer at an office of the bank or on behalf of a bank.

(2) For purposes of this definition, activities on behalf of a bank include activities where a person, whether at an office of the bank or at another location sells, solicits, advertises, or offers an insurance product or annuity and at least one of the following applies:

(i) The person represents to a consumer that the sale, solicitation, advertisement, or offer of any insurance product or annuity is by or on behalf of the bank;

(ii) The bank refers a consumer to a seller of insurance products or annuities and the bank has a contractual arrangement to receive commissions or

452

Federal Deposit Insurance Corporation

fees derived from a sale of an insurance product or annuity resulting from that referral; or

(iii) Documents evidencing the sale, solicitation, advertising, or offer of an insurance product or annuity identify or refer to the bank.

§ 343.30 Prohibited practices.

(a) *Anticoercion and antitying rules.* You may not engage in any practice that would lead a consumer to believe that an extension of credit, in violation of section 106(b) of the Bank Holding Company Act Amendments of 1970 (12 U.S.C. 1972), is conditional upon either:

(1) The purchase of an insurance product or annuity from the bank or any of its affiliates; or

(2) An agreement by the consumer not to obtain, or a prohibition on the consumer from obtaining, an insurance product or annuity from an unaffiliated entity.

(b) *Prohibition on misrepresentations generally.* You may not engage in any practice or use any advertisement at any office of, or on behalf of, the bank or a subsidiary of the bank that could mislead any person or otherwise cause a reasonable person to reach an erroneous belief with respect to:

(1) The fact that an insurance product or annuity sold or offered for sale by you or any subsidiary of the bank is not backed by the Federal government or the bank, or the fact that the insurance product or annuity is not insured by the Federal Deposit Insurance Corporation;

(2) In the case of an insurance product or annuity that involves investment risk, the fact that there is an investment risk, including the potential that principal may be lost and that the product may decline in value; or

(3) In the case of a bank or subsidiary of the bank at which insurance products or annuities are sold or offered for sale, the fact that:

(i) The approval of an extension of credit to a consumer by the bank or subsidiary may not be conditioned on the purchase of an insurance product or annuity by the consumer from the bank or a subsidiary of the bank; and

(ii) The consumer is free to purchase the insurance product or annuity from another source.

(c) *Prohibition on domestic violence discrimination.* You may not sell or offer for sale, as principal, agent, or broker, any life or health insurance product if the status of the applicant or insured as a victim of domestic violence or as a provider of services to victims of domestic violence is considered as a criterion in any decision with regard to insurance underwriting, pricing, renewal, or scope of coverage of such product, or with regard to the payment of insurance claims on such product, except as required or expressly permitted under State law.

§ 343.40 What you must disclose.

(a) *Insurance disclosures.* In connection with the initial purchase of an insurance product or annuity by a consumer from you, you must disclose to the consumer, except to the extent the disclosure would not be accurate, that:

(1) The insurance product or annuity is not a deposit or other obligation of, or guaranteed by, the bank or an affiliate of the bank;

(2) The insurance product or annuity is not insured by the Federal Deposit Insurance Corporation (FDIC) or any other agency of the United States, the bank, or (if applicable) an affiliate of the bank; and

(3) In the case of an insurance product or annuity that involves an investment risk, there is investment risk associated with the product, including the possible loss of value.

(b) *Credit disclosure.* In the case of an application for credit in connection with which an insurance product or annuity is solicited, offered, or sold, you must disclose that the bank may not condition an extension of credit on either:

(1) The consumer's purchase of an insurance product or annuity from the bank or any of its affiliates; or

(2) The consumer's agreement not to obtain, or a prohibition on the consumer from obtaining, an insurance product or annuity from an unaffiliated entity.

(c) *Timing and method of disclosures*—(1) *In general.* The disclosures required by paragraph (a) of this section must be provided orally and in writing before the completion of the initial sale of an

§ 343.40

insurance product or annuity to a consumer. The disclosure required by paragraph (b) of this section must be made orally and in writing at the time the consumer applies for an extension of credit in connection with which an insurance product or annuity is solicited, offered, or sold.

(2) *Exception for transactions by mail.* If a sale of an insurance product or annuity is conducted by mail, you are not required to make the oral disclosures required by paragraph (a) of this section. If you take an application for credit by mail, you are not required to make the oral disclosure required by paragraph (b).

(3) *Exception for transactions by telephone.* If a sale of an insurance product or annuity is conducted by telephone, you may provide the written disclosures required by paragraph (a) of this section by mail within 3 business days beginning on the first business day after the sale, excluding Sundays and the legal public holidays specified in 5 U.S.C. 6103(a). If you take an application for credit by telephone, you may provide the written disclosure required by paragraph (b) of this section by mail, provided you mail it to the consumer within three days beginning the first business day after the application is taken, excluding Sundays and the legal public holidays specified in 5 U.S.C. 6103(a).

(4) *Electronic form of disclosures.* (i) Subject to the requirements of section 101(c) of the Electronic Signatures in Global and National Commerce Act (12 U.S.C. 7001(c)), you may provide the written disclosures required by paragraph (a) and (b) of this section through electronic media instead of on paper, if the consumer affirmatively consents to receiving the disclosures electronically and if the disclosures are provided in a format that the consumer may retain or obtain later, for example, by printing or storing electronically (such as by downloading).

(ii) Any disclosure required by paragraphs (a) or (b) of this section that is provided by electronic media is not required to be provided orally.

(5) *Disclosures must be readily understandable.* The disclosures provided shall be conspicuous, simple, direct, readily understandable, and designed to call attention to the nature and significance of the information provided. For instance, you may use the following disclosures in visual media, such as television broadcasting, ATM screens, billboards, signs, posters and written advertisements and promotional materials, as appropriate and consistent with paragraphs (a) and (b) of this section:

• NOT A DEPOSIT
• NOT FDIC-INSURED
• NOT INSURED BY ANY FEDERAL GOVERNMENT AGENCY
• NOT GUARANTEED BY THE BANK
• MAY GO DOWN IN VALUE

(6) *Disclosures must be meaningful.* (i) You must provide the disclosures required by paragraphs (a) and (b) of this section in a meaningful form. Examples of the types of methods that could call attention to the nature and significance of the information provided include:

(A) A plain-language heading to call attention to the disclosures;

(B) A typeface and type size that are easy to read;

(C) Wide margins and ample line spacing;

(D) Boldface or italics for key words; and

(E) Distinctive type size, style, and graphic devices, such as shading or sidebars, when the disclosures are combined with other information.

(ii) You have not provided the disclosures in a meaningful form if you merely state to the consumer that the required disclosures are available in printed material, but do not provide the printed material when required and do not orally disclose the information to the consumer when required.

(iii) With respect to those disclosures made through electronic media for which paper or oral disclosures are not required, the disclosures are not meaningfully provided if the consumer may bypass the visual text of the disclosures before purchasing an insurance product or annuity.

(7) *Consumer acknowledgment.* You must obtain from the consumer, at the time a consumer receives the disclosures required under paragraphs (a) or (b) of this section, or at the time of the initial purchase by the consumer of an

Federal Deposit Insurance Corporation § 344.1

insurance product or annuity, a written acknowledgment by the consumer that the consumer received the disclosures. You may permit a consumer to acknowledge receipt of the disclosures electronically or in paper form. If the disclosures required under paragraphs (a) or (b) of this section are provided in connection with a transaction that is conducted by telephone, you must:

(i) Obtain an oral acknowledgment of receipt of the disclosures and maintain sufficient documentation to show that the acknowledgment was given; and

(ii) Make reasonable efforts to obtain a written acknowledgment from the consumer.

(d) *Advertisements and other promotional material for insurance products or annuities.* The disclosures described in paragraph (a) of this section are required in advertisements and promotional material for insurance products or annuities unless the advertisements and promotional materials are of a general nature describing or listing the services or products offered by the bank.

§ 343.50 Where insurance activities may take place.

(a) *General rule.* A bank must, to the extent practicable, keep the area where the bank conducts transactions involving insurance products or annuities physically segregated from areas where retail deposits are routinely accepted from the general public, identify the areas where insurance product or annuity sales activities occur, and clearly delineate and distinguish those areas from the areas where the bank's retail deposit-taking activities occur.

(b) *Referrals.* Any person who accepts deposits from the public in an area where such transactions are routinely conducted in the bank may refer a consumer who seeks to purchase an insurance product or annuity to a qualified person who sells that product only if the person making the referral receives no more than a one-time, nominal fee of a fixed dollar amount for each referral that does not depend on whether the referral results in a transaction.

§ 343.60 Qualification and licensing requirements for insurance sales personnel.

A bank may not permit any person to sell or offer for sale any insurance product or annuity in any part of its office or on its behalf, unless the person is at all times appropriately qualified and licensed under applicable State insurance licensing standards with regard to the specific products being sold or recommended.

APPENDIX A TO PART 343—CONSUMER GRIEVANCE PROCESS

Any consumer who believes that any bank or any other person selling, soliciting, advertising, or offering insurance products or annuities to the consumer at an office of the bank or on behalf of the bank has violated the requirements of this part should contact the Division of Supervision and Consumer Protection (DSC), Federal Deposit Insurance Corporation, at the following address: 550 17th Street, NW., Washington, DC 20429, or telephone 202–942–3100 or 800–934–3342, or e-mail *dcainternet@fdic.gov.*

PART 344—RECORDKEEPING AND CONFIRMATION REQUIREMENTS FOR SECURITIES TRANSACTIONS

Sec.
344.1 Purpose and scope.
344.2 Exceptions.
344.3 Definitions.
344.4 Recordkeeping.
344.5 Content and time of notification.
344.6 Notification by agreement; alternative forms and times of notification.
344.7 Settlement of securities transactions.
344.8 Securities trading policies and procedures.
344.9 Personal securities trading reporting by bank officers and employees.
344.10 Waivers.

AUTHORITY: 12 U.S.C. 1817, 1818 and 1819.

SOURCE: 62 FR 9919, Mar. 5, 1997, unless otherwise noted.

§ 344.1 Purpose and scope.

(a) *Purpose.* The purpose of this part is to ensure that purchasers of securities in transactions effected by a state nonmember insured bank (except a District bank) or a foreign bank having an insured branch are provided adequate information regarding transactions. This part is also designed to ensure

§ 344.2

that banks subject to this part maintain adequate records and controls with respect to the securities transactions they effect.

(b) *Scope; general.* Any security transaction effected for a customer by a bank is subject to this part unless excepted by § 344.2. A bank effecting transactions in government securities is subject to the notification, recordkeeping, and policies and procedures requirements of this part. This part also applies to municipal securities transactions by a bank that is not registered as a "municipal securities dealer" with the Securities and Exchange Commission. See 15 U.S.C. 78c(a)(30) and 78o–4.

§ 344.2 Exceptions.

(a) A bank effecting securities transactions for customers is not subject to all or part of this part 344 to the extent that they qualify for one or more of the following exceptions:

(1) *Small number of transactions.* The requirements of §§ 344.4(a) (2) through (4) and 344.8(a) (1) through (3) do not apply to a bank effecting an average of fewer than 200 securities transactions per year for customers over the prior three calendar year period. The calculation of this average does not include transactions in government securities.

(2) *Government securities.* The recordkeeping requirements of § 344.4 do not apply to banks effecting fewer than 500 government securities brokerage transactions per year. This exemption does not apply to government securities dealer transactions by banks.

(3) *Municipal securities.* This part does not apply to transactions in municipal securities effected by a bank registered with the Securities and Exchange Commission as a "municipal securities dealer" as defined in title 15 U.S.C. 78c(a)(30). See 15 U.S.C. 78o–4.

(4) *Foreign branches.* Activities of foreign branches of a bank shall not be subject to the requirements of this part.

(5) *Transactions effected by registered broker/dealers.* (i) This part does not apply to securities transactions effected for a bank customer by a registered broker/dealer if:

(A) The broker/dealer is fully disclosed to the bank customer; and

(B) The bank customer has a direct contractual agreement with the broker/dealer.

(ii) This exemption extends to bank arrangements with broker/dealers which involve bank employees when acting as employees of, and subject to the supervision of, the registered broker/dealer when soliciting, recommending, or effecting securities transactions.

(b) *Safe and sound operations.* Notwithstanding this section, every bank effecting securities transactions for customers shall maintain, directly or indirectly, effective systems of records and controls regarding their customer securities transactions to ensure safe and sound operations. The records and systems maintained must clearly and accurately reflect the information required under this part and provide an adequate basis for an audit.

§ 344.3 Definitions.

(a) *Asset-backed security* means a security that is serviced primarily by the cash flows of a discrete pool of receivables or other financial assets, either fixed or revolving, that by their terms convert into cash within a finite time period plus any rights or other assets designed to assure the servicing or timely distribution of proceeds to the security holders.

(b) *Bank* means a state nonmember insured bank (except a District bank) or a foreign bank having an insured branch.

(c) *Cash management sweep account* means a prearranged, automatic transfer of funds above a certain dollar level from a deposit account to purchase a security or securities, or any prearranged, automatic redemption or sale of a security or securities when a deposit account drops below a certain level with the proceeds being transferred into a deposit account.

(d) *Collective investment fund* means funds held by a bank as fiduciary and, consistent with local law, invested collectively:

(1) In a common trust fund maintained by such bank exclusively for the collective investment and reinvestment of monies contributed thereto by

Federal Deposit Insurance Corporation § 344.3

the bank in its capacity as trustee, executor, administrator, guardian, or custodian under the Uniform Gifts to Minors Act; or

(2) In a fund consisting solely of assets of retirement, pension, profit sharing, stock bonus or similar trusts which are exempt from Federal income taxation under the Internal Revenue Code (26 U.S.C.).

(e) *Completion of the transaction* means:

(1) For purchase transactions, the time when the customer pays the bank any part of the purchase price (or the time when the bank makes the book-entry for any part of the purchase price, if applicable), however, if the customer pays for the security prior to the time payment is requested or becomes due, then the transaction shall be completed when the bank transfers the security into the account of the customer; and

(2) For sale transactions, the time when the bank transfers the security out of the account of the customer or, if the security is not in the bank's custody, then the time when the security is delivered to the bank, however, if the customer delivers the security to the bank prior to the time delivery is requested or becomes due then the transaction shall be completed when the bank makes payment into the account of the customer.

(f) *Crossing of buy and sell orders* means a security transaction in which the same bank acts as agent for both the buyer and the seller.

(g) *Customer* means any person or account, including any agency, trust, estate, guardianship, or other fiduciary account for which a bank effects or participates in effecting the purchase or sale of securities, but does not include a broker, dealer, bank acting as a broker or a dealer, issuer of the securities that are the subject of the transaction or a person or account having a direct, contractual agreement with a fully disclosed broker/dealer.

(h) *Debt security* means any security, such as a bond, debenture, note, or any other similar instrument that evidences a liability of the issuer (including any security of this type that is convertible into stock or a similar security) and fractional or participation interests in one or more of any of the foregoing; provided, however, that securities issued by an investment company registered under the Investment Company Act of 1940, 15 U.S.C. 80a-1 *et seq.*, shall not be included in this definition.

(i) *Government security* means:

(1) A security that is a direct obligation of, or obligation guaranteed as to principal and interest by, the United States;

(2) A security that is issued or guaranteed by a corporation in which the United States has a direct or indirect interest and which is designated by the Secretary of the Treasury for exemption as necessary or appropriate in the public interest or for the protection of investors;

(3) A security issued or guaranteed as to principal and interest by any corporation whose securities are designated, by statute specifically naming the corporation, to constitute exempt securities within the meaning of the laws administered by the Securities and Exchange Commission; or

(4) Any put, call, straddle, option, or privilege on a security described in paragraph (i) (1), (2), or (3) of this section other than a put, call, straddle, option, or privilege that is traded on one or more national securities exchanges, or for which quotations are disseminated through an automated quotation system operated by a registered securities association.

(j) *Investment discretion* means that, with respect to an account, a bank directly or indirectly:

(1) Is authorized to determine what securities or other property shall be purchased or sold by or for the account; or

(2) Makes decisions as to what securities or other property shall be purchased or sold by or for the account even though some other person may have responsibility for these investment decisions.

(k) *Municipal security* means a security which is a direct obligation of, or an obligation guaranteed as to principal or interest by, a State or any political subdivision, or any agency or instrumentality of a State or any political subdivision, or any municipal corporate instrumentality of one or more

457

§ 344.4

States or any security which is an industrial development bond (as defined in 26 U.S.C. 103(c)(2)) the interest on which is excludable from gross income under 26 U.S.C. 103(a)(1) if, by reason of the application of paragraph (4) or (6) of 26 U.S.C. 103(c) (determined as if paragraphs (4)(A), (5) and (7) were not included in 26 U.S.C. 103(c), paragraph (1) of 26 U.S.C. 103(c) does not apply to such security.

(1) *Periodic plan* means any written authorization for a bank to act as agent to purchase or sell for a customer a specific security or securities, in a specific amount (calculated in security units or dollars) or to the extent of dividends and funds available, at specific time intervals, and setting forth the commission or charges to be paid by the customer or the manner of calculating them. Periodic plans include dividend reinvestment plans, automatic investment plans, and employee stock purchase plans.

(m) *Security* means any note, stock, treasury stock, bond, debenture, certificate of interest or participation in any profit-sharing agreement or in any oil, gas, or other mineral royalty or lease, any collateral-trust certificate, preorganization certificate or subscription, transferable share, investment contract, voting-trust certificate, and any put, call, straddle, option, or privilege on any security or group or index of securities (including any interest therein or based on the value thereof), or, in general, any instrument commonly known as a "security"; or any certificate of interest or participation in, temporary or interim certificate for, receipt for, or warrant or right to subscribe to or purchase, any of the foregoing. The term security does not include:

(1) A deposit or share account in a federally or state insured depository institution;

(2) A loan participation;

(3) A letter of credit or other form of bank indebtedness incurred in the ordinary course of business;

(4) Currency;

(5) Any note, draft, bill of exchange, or bankers acceptance which has a maturity at the time of issuance of not exceeding nine months, exclusive of days of grace, or any renewal thereof the maturity of which is likewise limited;

(6) Units of a collective investment fund;

(7) Interests in a variable amount (master) note of a borrower of prime credit; or

(8) U.S. Savings Bonds.

§ 344.4 Recordkeeping.

(a) *General rule.* A bank effecting securities transactions for customers shall maintain the following records for at least three years:

(1) *Chronological records.* An itemized daily record of each purchase and sale of securities maintained in chronological order, and including:

(i) Account or customer name for which each transaction was effected;

(ii) Description of the securities;

(iii) Unit and aggregate purchase or sale price;

(iv) Trade date; and

(v) Name or other designation of the broker/dealer or other person from whom the securities were purchased or to whom the securities were sold;

(2) *Account records.* Account records for each customer, reflecting:

(i) Purchases and sales of securities;

(ii) Receipts and deliveries of securities;

(iii) Receipts and disbursements of cash; and

(iv) Other debits and credits pertaining to transactions in securities;

(3) *A separate memorandum (order ticket)* of each order to purchase or sell securities (whether executed or canceled), which shall include:

(i) The accounts for which the transaction was effected;

(ii) Whether the transaction was a market order, limit order, or subject to special instructions;

(iii) The time the order was received by the trader or other bank employee responsible for effecting the transaction;

(iv) The time the order was placed with the broker/dealer, or if there was no broker/dealer, time the order was executed or canceled;

(v) The price at which the order was executed; and

(vi) The broker/dealer utilized;

(4) *Record of broker/dealers.* A record of all broker/dealers selected by the

Federal Deposit Insurance Corporation § 344.5

bank to effect securities transactions and the amount of commissions paid or allocated to each broker during the calendar year; and

(5) *Notifications.* A copy of the written notification required by §§ 344.5 and 344.6.

(b) *Manner of maintenance.* Records may be maintained in whatever manner, form or format a bank deems appropriate, provided however, the records required by this section must clearly and accurately reflect the information required and provide an adequate basis for the audit of the information. Records may be maintained in hard copy, automated or electronic form provided the records are easily retrievable, readily available for inspection, and capable of being reproduced in a hard copy. A bank may contract with third party service providers, including broker/dealers, to maintain records required under this part.

§ 344.5 Content and time of notification.

Every bank effecting a securities transaction for a customer shall give or send, by mail, facsimile or other means of electronic transmission, to the customer at or before completion of the transaction one of the types of written notification identified below:

(a) *Broker/dealer's confirmations.* (1) A copy of the confirmation of a broker/dealer relating to the securities transaction. A bank may either have the broker/dealer send the confirmation directly to the bank's customer or send a copy of the broker/dealer's confirmation to the customer upon receipt of the confirmation by the bank. If a bank chooses to send a copy of the broker/dealer's confirmation, it must be sent within one business day from the bank's receipt of the broker/dealer's confirmation; and

(2) If the bank is to receive remuneration from the customer or any other source in connection with the transaction, a statement of the source and amount of any remuneration to be received if such would be required under paragraph (b)(6) of this section; or

(b) *Written notification.* A written notification disclosing:

(1) Name of the bank;

(2) Name of the customer;

(3) Whether the bank is acting as agent for such customer, as agent for both such customer and some other person, as principal for its own account, or in any other capacity;

(4) The date and time of execution, or the fact that the time of execution will be furnished within a reasonable time upon written request of the customer, and the identity, price, and number of shares or units (or principal amount in the case of debt securities) of the security purchased or sold by the customer;

(5) The amount of any remuneration received or to be received, directly or indirectly, by any broker/dealer from such customer in connection with the transaction;

(6)(i) The amount of any remuneration received or to be received by the bank from the customer, and the source and amount of any other remuneration received or to be received by the bank in connection with the transaction, unless:

(A) Remuneration is determined pursuant to a prior written agreement between the bank and the customer; or

(B) In the case of government securities and municipal securities, the bank received the remuneration in other than an agency transaction; or

(C) In the case of open end investment company securities, the bank has provided the customer with a current prospectus which discloses all current fees, loads and expenses at or before completion of the transaction;

(ii) If the bank elects not to disclose the source and amount of remuneration it has or will receive from a party other than the customer pursuant to paragraph (b)(6)(i) (A), (B), or (C) of this section, the written notification must disclose whether the bank has received or will receive remuneration from a party other than the customer, and that the bank will furnish within a reasonable time the source and amount of this remuneration upon written request of the customer. This election is not available, however, if, with respect to a purchase, the bank was participating in a distribution of that security; or, with respect to a sale, the bank was participating in a tender offer for that security;

459

§ 344.6

(7) Name of the broker/dealer utilized; or where there is no broker/dealer, the name of the person from whom the security was purchased or to whom the security was sold, or a statement that the bank will furnish this information within a reasonable time upon written request;

(8) In the case of a transaction in a debt security subject to redemption before maturity, a statement to the effect that the debt security may be redeemed in whole or in part before maturity, that the redemption could affect the yield represented and that additional information is available upon request;

(9) In the case of a transaction in a debt security effected exclusively on the basis of a dollar price:

(i) The dollar price at which the transaction was effected; and

(ii) The yield to maturity calculated from the dollar price, provided however, that this shall not apply to a transaction in a debt security that either has a maturity date that may be extended by the issuer thereof, with a variable interest payable thereon, or is an asset-backed security that represents an interest in or is secured by a pool of receivables or other financial assets that are subject continuously to prepayment;

(10) In the case of a transaction in a debt security effected on the basis of yield:

(i) The yield at which the transaction was effected, including the percentage amount and its characterization (e.g., current yield, yield to maturity, or yield to call) and if effected at yield to call, the type of call, the call date and call price;

(ii) The dollar price calculated from the yield at which the transaction was effected; and

(iii) If effected on a basis other than yield to maturity and the yield to maturity is lower than the represented yield, the yield to maturity as well as the represented yield; provided however, that this paragraph (b)(10) shall not apply to a transaction in a debt security that either has a maturity date that may be extended by the issuer with a variable interest rate payable thereon, or is an asset-backed security that represents an interest in or is secured by a pool of receivables or other financial assets that are subject continuously to prepayment;

(11) In the case of a transaction in a debt security that is an asset-backed security, which represents an interest in or is secured by a pool of receivables or other financial assets that are subject continuously to prepayment, a statement indicating that the actual yield of the asset-backed security may vary according to the rate at which the underlying receivables or other financial assets are prepaid and a statement of the fact that information concerning the factors that affect yield (including at a minimum estimated yield, weighted average life, and the prepayment assumptions underlying yield) will be furnished upon written request of the customer; and

(12) In the case of a transaction in a debt security, other than a government security, that the security is unrated by a nationally recognized statistical rating organization, if that is the case.

§ 344.6 **Notification by agreement; alternative forms and times of notification.**

A bank may elect to use the following alternative notification procedures if the transaction is effected for:

(a) *Notification by agreement.* Accounts (except periodic plans) where the bank does not exercise investment discretion and the bank and the customer agree in writing to a different arrangement as to the time and content of the written notification; provided however, that such agreement makes clear the customer's right to receive the written notification pursuant to § 344.5 (a) or (b) at no additional cost to the customer.

(b) *Trust accounts.* Accounts (except collective investment funds) where the bank exercises investment discretion in other than in an agency capacity, in which instance the bank shall, upon request of the person having the power to terminate the account or, if there is no such person, upon the request of any person holding a vested beneficial interest in such account, give or send to such person the written notification within a reasonable time. The bank may charge such person a reasonable fee for providing this information.

Federal Deposit Insurance Corporation

§ 344.7

(c) *Agency accounts.* Accounts where the bank exercises investment discretion in an agency capacity, in which instance:

(1) The bank shall give or send to each customer not less frequently than once every three months an itemized statement which shall specify the funds and securities in the custody or possession of the bank at the end of such period and all debits, credits and transactions in the customer's accounts during such period; and

(2) If requested by the customer, the bank shall give or send to each customer within a reasonable time the written notification described in § 344.5. The bank may charge a reasonable fee for providing the information described in § 344.5.

(d) *Cash management sweep accounts.* A bank effecting a securities transaction for a cash management sweep account shall give or send its customer a written statement, in the same form as required under paragraph (f) of this section, for each month in which a purchase or sale of a security takes place in the account and not less than once every three months if there are no securities transactions in the account. Notwithstanding the provisions of this paragraph (d), banks that retain custody of government securities that are the subject of a hold-in-custody repurchase agreement are subject to the requirements of 17 CFR 403.5(d).

(e) *Collective investment fund accounts.* The bank shall at least annually give or send to the customer a copy of a financial report of the fund, or provide notice that a copy of such report is available and will be furnished upon request to each person to whom a regular periodic accounting would ordinarily be rendered with respect to each participating account. This report shall be based upon an audit made by independent public accountants or internal auditors responsible only to the board of directors of the bank.

(f) *Periodic plan accounts.* The bank shall give or send to the customer not less than once every three months a written statement showing:

(1) The funds and securities in the custody or possession of the bank;

(2) All service charges and commissions paid by the customer in connection with the transaction; and

(3) All other debits and credits of the customer's account involved in the transaction; provided that upon written request of the customer, the bank shall give or send the information described in § 344.5, except that any such information relating to remuneration paid in connection with the transaction need not be provided to the customer when the remuneration is paid by a source other than the customer. The bank may charge a reasonable fee for providing information described in § 344.5.

§ 344.7 **Settlement of securities transactions.**

(a) A bank shall not effect or enter into a contract for the purchase or sale of a security (other than an exempted security as defined in 15 U.S.C. 78c(a)(12), government security, municipal security, commercial paper, bankers' acceptances, or commercial bills) that provides for payment of funds and delivery of securities later than the third business day after the date of the contract unless otherwise expressly agreed to by the parties at the time of the transaction.

(b) Paragraphs (a) and (c) of this section shall not apply to contracts:

(1) For the purchase or sale of limited partnership interests that are not listed on an exchange or for which quotations are not disseminated through an automated quotation system of a registered securities association; or

(2) For the purchase or sale of securities that the Securities and Exchange Commission (SEC) may from time to time, taking into account then existing market practices, exempt by order from the requirements of paragraph (a) of SEC Rule 15c6-1, 17 CFR 240.15c6-1(a), either unconditionally or on specified terms and conditions, if the SEC determines that an exemption is consistent with the public interest and the protection of investors.

(c) Paragraph (a) of this section shall not apply to contracts for the sale for cash of securities that are priced after 4:30 p.m. Eastern time on the date the securities are priced and that are sold

§ 344.8

by an issuer to an underwriter pursuant to a firm commitment underwritten offering registered under the Securities Act of 1933, 15 U.S.C. 77a *et seq.*, or sold to an initial purchaser by a bank participating in the offering. A bank shall not effect or enter into a contract for the purchase or sale of the securities that provides for payment of funds and delivery of securities later than the fourth business day after the date of the contract unless otherwise expressly agreed to by the parties at the time of the transaction.

(d) For purposes of paragraphs (a) and (c) of this section, the parties to a contract shall be deemed to have expressly agreed to an alternate date for payment of funds and delivery of securities at the time of the transaction for a contract for the sale for cash of securities pursuant to a firm commitment offering if the managing underwriter and the issuer have agreed to the date for all securities sold pursuant to the offering and the parties to the contract have not expressly agreed to another date for payment of funds and delivery of securities at the time of the transaction.

§ 344.8 Securities trading policies and procedures.

(a) *Policies and procedures.* Every bank effecting securities transactions for customers shall establish written policies and procedures providing:

(1) Assignment of responsibility for supervision of all officers or employees who:

(i) Transmit orders to or place orders with broker/dealers; or

(ii) Execute transactions in securities for customers;

(2) Assignment of responsibility for supervision and reporting, separate from those in paragraph (a)(1) of this section, with respect to all officers or employees who process orders for notification or settlement purposes, or perform other back office functions with respect to securities transactions effected for customers;

(3) For the fair and equitable allocation of securities and prices to accounts when orders for the same security are received at approximately the same time and are placed for execution either individually or in combination; and

(4) Where applicable, and where permissible under local law, for the crossing of buy and sell orders on a fair and equitable basis to the parties to the transaction.

§ 344.9 Personal securities trading reporting by bank officers and employees.

(a) *Officers and employees subject to reporting.* Bank officers and employees who:

(1) Make investment recommendations or decisions for the accounts of customers;

(2) Participate in the determination of such recommendations or decisions; or

(3) In connection with their duties, obtain information concerning which securities are being purchased or sold or recommend such action, must report to the bank, within 30-calendar days after the end of the calendar quarter, all transactions in securities made by them or on their behalf, either at the bank or elsewhere in which they have a beneficial interest. The report shall identify the securities purchased or sold and indicate the dates of the transactions and whether the transactions were purchases or sales.

(b) *Exempt transactions.* Excluded from this reporting requirement are:

(1) Transactions for the benefit of the officer or employee over which the officer or employee has no direct or indirect influence or control;

(2) Transactions in registered investment company shares;

(3) Transactions in government securities; and

(4) All transactions involving in the aggregate $10,000 or less during the calendar quarter.

(c) *Alternative report.* Where a bank acts as an investment adviser to an investment company registered under the Investment Company Act of 1940, the bank's officers and employees may fulfill their reporting requirement under paragraph (a) of this section by

Federal Deposit Insurance Corporation

filing with the bank the "access persons" personal securities trading report required by (SEC) Rule 17j–1, 17 CFR 270.17j–1.

[62 FR 9919, Mar. 5, 1997, as amended at 72 FR 60547, Oct. 25, 2007]

§ 344.10 Waivers.

The Board of Directors of the FDIC, in its discretion, may waive for good cause all or any part of this part 344.

PART 345—COMMUNITY REINVESTMENT

Subpart A—General

Sec.
345.11 Authority, purposes, and scope.
345.12 Definitions.

Subpart B—Standards for Assessing Performance

345.21 Performance tests, standards, and ratings, in general.
345.22 Lending test.
345.23 Investment test.
345.24 Service test.
345.25 Community development test for wholesale or limited purpose banks.
345.26 Small bank performance standards.
345.27 Strategic plan.
345.28 Assigned ratings.
345.29 Effect of CRA performance on applications.

Subpart C—Records, Reporting, and Disclosure Requirements

345.41 Assessment area delineation.
345.42 Data collection, reporting, and disclosure.
345.43 Content and availability of public file.
345.44 Public notice by banks.
345.45 Publication of planned examination schedule.

APPENDIX A TO PART 345—RATINGS
APPENDIX B TO PART 345—CRA NOTICE

AUTHORITY: 12 U.S.C. 1814–1817, 1819–1820, 1828, 1831u and 2901–2908, 3103–3104, and 3108(a).

SOURCE: 43 FR 47151, Oct. 12, 1978, unless otherwise noted.

Subpart A—General

SOURCE: 60 FR 22201, May 4, 1995, unless otherwise noted.

§ 345.11 Authority, purposes, and scope.

(a) *Authority and OMB control number*—(1) *Authority.* The authority for this part is 12 U.S.C. 1814–1817, 1819–1820, 1828, 1831u and 2901–2907, 3103–3104, and 3108(a).

(2) *OMB control number.* The information collection requirements contained in this part were approved by the Office of Management and Budget under the provisions of 44 U.S.C. 3501 *et seq.* and have been assigned OMB control number 3064–0092.

(b) *Purposes.* In enacting the Community Reinvestment Act (CRA), the Congress required each appropriate Federal financial supervisory agency to assess an institution's record of helping to meet the credit needs of the local communities in which the institution is chartered, consistent with the safe and sound operation of the institution, and to take this record into account in the agency's evaluation of an application for a deposit facility by the institution. This part is intended to carry out the purposes of the CRA by:

(1) Establishing the framework and criteria by which the Federal Deposit Insurance Corporation (FDIC) assesses a bank's record of helping to meet the credit needs of its entire community, including low- and moderate-income neighborhoods, consistent with the safe and sound operation of the bank; and

(2) Providing that the FDIC takes that record into account in considering certain applications.

(c) *Scope*—(1) *General.* Except for certain special purpose banks described in paragraph (c)(3) of this section, this part applies to all insured State nonmember banks, including insured State branches as described in paragraph (c)(2) and any uninsured State branch that results from an acquisition described in section 5(a)(8) of the International Banking Act of 1978 (12 U.S.C. 3103(a)(8)).

(2) *Insured State branches.* Insured State branches are branches of a foreign bank established and operating under the laws of any State, the deposits of which are insured in accordance with the provisions of the Federal Deposit Insurance Act. In the case of insured State branches, references in this part to *main office* mean the principal

§ 345.12

branch within the United States and the term *branch* or *branches* refers to any insured State branch or branches located within the United States. The *assessment area* of an insured State branch is the community or communities located within the United States served by the branch as described in § 345.41.

(3) *Certain special purpose banks.* This part does not apply to special purpose banks that do not perform commercial or retail banking services by granting credit to the public in the ordinary course of business, other than as incident to their specialized operations. These banks include banker's banks, as defined in 12 U.S.C. 24 (Seventh), and banks that engage only in one or more of the following activities: providing cash management controlled disbursement services or serving as correspondent banks, trust companies, or clearing agents.

§ 345.12 Definitions.

For purposes of this part, the following definitions apply:

(a) *Affiliate* means any company that controls, is controlled by, or is under common control with another company. The term *control* has the meaning given to that term in 12 U.S.C. 1841(a)(2), and a company is under common control with another company if both companies are directly or indirectly controlled by the same company.

(b) *Area median income* means:

(1) The median family income for the MSA, if a person or geography is located in an MSA, or for the metropolitan division, if a person or geography is located in an MSA that has been subdivided into metropolitan divisions; or

(2) The statewide nonmetropolitan median family income, if a person or geography is located outside an MSA.

(c) *Assessment area* means a geographic area delineated in accordance with § 345.41.

(d) *Remote Service Facility (RSF)* means an automated, unstaffed banking facility owned or operated by, or operated exclusively for, the bank, such as an automated teller machine, cash dispensing machine, point-of-sale terminal, or other remote electronic facility, at which deposits are received, cash dispersed, or money lent.

(e) *Bank* means a State nonmember bank, as that term is defined in section 3(e)(2) of the Federal Deposit Insurance Act, as amended (FDIA) (12 U.S.C. 1813(e)(2)), with Federally insured deposits, except as provided in § 345.11(c). The term bank also includes an insured State branch as defined in § 345.11(c).

(f) *Branch* means a staffed banking facility authorized as a branch, whether shared or unshared, including, for example, a mini-branch in a grocery store or a branch operated in conjunction with any other local business or nonprofit organization. The term "branch" only includes a "domestic branch" as that term is defined in section 3(o) of the FDIA (12 U.S.C. 1813(o)).

(g) *Community development* means:

(1) Affordable housing (including multifamily rental housing) for low- or moderate-income individuals;

(2) Community services targeted to low- or moderate-income individuals;

(3) Activities that promote economic development by financing businesses or farms that meet the size eligibility standards of the Small Business Administration's Development Company or Small Business Investment Company programs (13 CFR 121.301) or have gross annual revenues of $1 million or less;

(4) Activities that revitalize or stabilize—

(i) Low-or moderate-income geographies;

(ii) Designated disaster areas; or

(iii) Distressed or underserved nonmetropolitan middle-income geographies designated by the Board of Governors of the Federal Reserve System, FDIC, and Office of the Comptroller of the Currency, based on—

(A) Rates of poverty, unemployment, and population loss; or

(B) Population size, density, and dispersion. Activities revitalize and stabilize geographies designated based on population size, density, and dispersion if they help to meet essential community needs, including needs of low- and moderate-income individuals; or

(5) Loans, investments, and services that—

(i) Support, enable or facilitate projects or activities that meet the

Federal Deposit Insurance Corporation § 345.12

"eligible uses" criteria described in Section 2301(c) of the Housing and Economic Recovery Act of 2008 (HERA), Public Law 110–289, 122 Stat. 2654, as amended, and are conducted in designated target areas identified in plans approved by the United States Department of Housing and Urban Development in accordance with the Neighborhood Stabilization Program (NSP);

(ii) Are provided no later than two years after the last date funds appropriated for the NSP are required to be spent by grantees; and

(iii) Benefit low-, moderate-, and middle-income individuals and geographies in the bank's assessment area(s) or areas outside the bank's assessment area(s) provided the bank has adequately addressed the community development needs of its assessment area(s).

(h) *Community development loan* means a loan that:

(1) Has as its primary purpose community development; and

(2) Except in the case of a wholesale or limited purpose bank:

(i) Has not been reported or collected by the bank or an affiliate for consideration in the bank's assessment as a home mortgage, small business, small farm, or consumer loan, unless it is a multifamily dwelling loan (as described in Appendix A to Part 203 of this title); and

(ii) Benefits the bank's assessment area(s) or a broader statewide or regional area that includes the bank's assessment area(s).

(i) *Community development service* means a service that:

(1) Has as its primary purpose community development;

(2) Is related to the provision of financial services; and

(3) Has not been considered in the evaluation of the bank's retail banking services under § 345.24(d).

(j) *Consumer loan* means a loan to one or more individuals for household, family, or other personal expenditures. A consumer loan does not include a home mortgage, small business, or small farm loan. Consumer loans include the following categories of loans:

(1) *Motor vehicle loan*, which is a consumer loan extended for the purchase of and secured by a motor vehicle;

(2) *Credit card loan*, which is a line of credit for household, family, or other personal expenditures that is accessed by a borrower's use of a "credit card," as this term is defined in § 226.2 of this title;

(3) *Home equity loan*, which is a consumer loan secured by a residence of the borrower;

(4) *Other secured consumer loan*, which is a secured consumer loan that is not included in one of the other categories of consumer loans; and

(5) *Other unsecured consumer loan*, which is an unsecured consumer loan that is not included in one of the other categories of consumer loans.

(k) *Geography* means a census tract delineated by the United States Bureau of the Census in the most recent decennial census.

(l) *Home mortgage loan* means a "home improvement loan," "home purchase loan," or a "refinancing" as defined in § 203.2 of this title.

(m) *Income level* includes:

(1) *Low-income*, which means an individual income that is less than 50 percent of the area median income or a median family income that is less than 50 percent in the case of a geography.

(2) *Moderate-income*, which means an individual income that is at least 50 percent and less than 80 percent of the area median income or a median family income that is at least 50 and less than 80 percent in the case of a geography.

(3) *Middle-income*, which means an individual income that is at least 80 percent and less than 120 percent of the area median income or a median family income that is at least 80 and less than 120 percent in the case of a geography.

(4) *Upper-income*, which means an individual income that is 120 percent or more of the area median income or a median family income that is 120 percent or more in the case of a geography.

(n) *Limited purpose bank* means a bank that offers only a narrow product line (such as credit card or motor vehicle loans) to a regional or broader market and for which a designation as a limited purpose bank is in effect, in accordance with § 345.25(b).

§ 345.21

(o) *Loan location.* A loan is located as follows:

(1) A consumer loan is located in the geography where the borrower resides;

(2) A home mortgage loan is located in the geography where the property to which the loan relates is located; and

(3) A small business or small farm loan is located in the geography where the main business facility or farm is located or where the loan proceeds otherwise will be applied, as indicated by the borrower.

(p) *Loan production office* means a staffed facility, other than a branch, that is open to the public and that provides lending-related services, such as loan information and applications.

(q) *Metropolitan division* means a metropolitan division as defined by the Director of the Office of Management and Budget.

(r) *MSA* means a metropolitan statistical area as defined by the Director of the Office of Management and Budget.

(s) *Nonmetropolitan area* means any area that is not located in an MSA.

(t) *Qualified investment* means a lawful investment, deposit, membership share, or grant that has as its primary purpose community development.

(u) *Small bank*—(1) *Definition. Small bank* means a bank that, as of December 31 of either of the prior two calendar years, had assets of less than $1.160 billion. *Intermediate small bank* means a small bank with assets of at least $290 million as of December 31 of both of the prior two calendar years and less than $1.160 billion as of December 31 of either of the prior two calendar years.

(2) *Adjustment.* The dollar figures in paragraph (u)(1) of this section shall be adjusted annually and published by the FDIC, based on the year-to-year change in the average of the Consumer Price Index for Urban Wage Earners and Clerical Workers, not seasonally adjusted, for each twelve-month period ending in November, with rounding to the nearest million.

(v) *Small business loan* means a loan included in "loans to small businesses" as defined in the instructions for preparation of the Consolidated Report of Condition and Income.

(w) *Small farm loan* means a loan included in "loans to small farms" as defined in the instructions for preparation of the Consolidated Report of Condition and Income.

(x) *Wholesale bank* means a bank that is not in the business of extending home mortgage, small business, small farm, or consumer loans to retail customers, and for which a designation as a wholesale bank is in effect, in accordance with § 345.25(b).

[60 FR 22201, May 4, 1995, as amended at 60 FR 66050, Dec. 20, 1995; 61 FR 21364, May 10, 1996; 69 FR 41187, July 8, 2004; 70 FR 44269, Aug. 2, 2005; 71 FR 78337, Dec. 29, 2006; 72 FR 72573, Dec. 21, 2007; 73 FR 78155, Dec. 22, 2008; 74 FR 68664, Dec. 29, 2009; 75 FR 79286, Dec. 20, 2010; 75 FR 82219, Dec. 30, 2010; 76 FR 79531, Dec. 22, 2011]

Subpart B—Standards for Assessing Performance

SOURCE: 60 FR 22201, May 4, 1995, unless otherwise noted.

§ 345.21 Performance tests, standards, and ratings, in general.

(a) *Performance tests and standards.* The FDIC assesses the CRA performance of a bank in an examination as follows:

(1) *Lending, investment, and service tests.* The FDIC applies the lending, investment, and service tests, as provided in §§ 345.22 through 345.24, in evaluating the performance of a bank, except as provided in paragraphs (a)(2), (a)(3), and (a)(4) of this section.

(2) *Community development test for wholesale or limited purpose banks.* The FDIC applies the community development test for a wholesale or limited purpose bank, as provided in § 345.25, except as provided in paragraph (a)(4) of this section.

(3) *Small bank performance standards.* The FDIC applies the small bank performance standards as provided in § 345.26 in evaluating the performance of a small bank or a bank that was a small bank during the prior calendar year, unless the bank elects to be assessed as provided in paragraphs (a)(1), (a)(2), or (a)(4) of this section. The bank may elect to be assessed as provided in paragraph (a)(1) of this section only if it collects and reports the data required for other banks under § 345.42.

Federal Deposit Insurance Corporation § 345.21

(4) *Strategic plan.* The FDIC evaluates the performance of a bank under a strategic plan if the bank submits, and the FDIC approves, a strategic plan as provided in § 345.27.

(b) *Performance context.* The FDIC applies the tests and standards in paragraph (a) of this section and also considers whether to approve a proposed strategic plan in the context of:

(1) Demographic data on median income levels, distribution of household income, nature of housing stock, housing costs, and other relevant data pertaining to a bank's assessment area(s);

(2) Any information about lending, investment, and service opportunities in the bank's assessment area(s) maintained by the bank or obtained from community organizations, state, local, and tribal governments, economic development agencies, or other sources;

(3) The bank's product offerings and business strategy as determined from data provided by the bank;

(4) Institutional capacity and constraints, including the size and financial condition of the bank, the economic climate (national, regional, and local), safety and soundness limitations, and any other factors that significantly affect the bank's ability to provide lending, investments, or services in its assessment area(s);

(5) The bank's past performance and the performance of similarly situated lenders;

(6) The bank's public file, as described in § 345.43, and any written comments about the bank's CRA performance submitted to the bank or the FDIC; and

(7) Any other information deemed relevant by the FDIC.

(c) *Assigned ratings.* The FDIC assigns to a bank one of the following four ratings pursuant to § 345.28 and Appendix A of this part: "outstanding"; "satisfactory"; "needs to improve"; or "substantial noncompliance" as provided in 12 U.S.C. 2906(b)(2). The rating assigned by the FDIC reflects the bank's record of helping to meet the credit needs of its entire community, including low- and moderate-income neighborhoods, consistent with the safe and sound operation of the bank.

(d) *Safe and sound operations.* This part and the CRA do not require a bank to make loans or investments or to provide services that are inconsistent with safe and sound operations. To the contrary, the FDIC anticipates banks can meet the standards of this part with safe and sound loans, investments, and services on which the banks expect to make a profit. Banks are permitted and encouraged to develop and apply flexible underwriting standards for loans that benefit low- or moderate-income geographies or individuals, only if consistent with safe and sound operations.

(e) *Low-cost education loans provided to low-income borrowers.* In assessing and taking into account the record of a bank under this part, the FDIC considers, as a factor, low-cost education loans originated by the bank to borrowers, particularly in its assessment area(s), who have an individual income that is less than 50 percent of the area median income. For purposes of this paragraph, "low-cost education loans" means any education loan, as defined in section 140(a)(7) of the Truth in Lending Act (15 U.S.C. 1650(a)(7)) (including a loan under a state or local education loan program), originated by the bank for a student at an "institution of higher education," as that term is generally defined in sections 101 and 102 of the Higher Education Act of 1965 (20 U.S.C. 1001 and 1002) and the implementing regulations published by the U.S. Department of Education, with interest rates and fees no greater than those of comparable education loans offered directly by the U.S. Department of Education. Such rates and fees are specified in section 455 of the Higher Education Act of 1965 (20 U.S.C. 1087e).

(f) *Activities in cooperation with minority- or women-owned financial institutions and low-income credit unions.* In assessing and taking into account the record of a nonminority-owned and nonwomen-owned bank under this part, the FDIC considers as a factor capital investment, loan participation, and other ventures undertaken by the bank in cooperation with minority- and women-owned financial institutions and low-income credit unions. Such activities must help meet the credit needs of local communities in which

§ 345.22

the minority- and women-owned financial institutions and low-income credit unions are chartered. To be considered, such activities need not also benefit the bank's assessment area(s) or the broader statewide or regional area that includes the bank's assessment area(s).

[60 FR 22201, May 4, 1995, as amended at 75 FR 61045, Oct. 4, 2010]

§ 345.22 Lending test.

(a) *Scope of test.* (1) The lending test evaluates a bank's record of helping to meet the credit needs of its assessment area(s) through its lending activities by considering a bank's home mortgage, small business, small farm, and community development lending. If consumer lending constitutes a substantial majority of a bank's business, the FDIC will evaluate the bank's consumer lending in one or more of the following categories: motor vehicle, credit card, home equity, other secured, and other unsecured loans. In addition, at a bank's option, the FDIC will evaluate one or more categories of consumer lending, if the bank has collected and maintained, as required in § 345.42(c)(1), the data for each category that the bank elects to have the FDIC evaluate.

(2) The FDIC considers originations and purchases of loans. The FDIC will also consider any other loan data the bank may choose to provide, including data on loans outstanding, commitments and letters of credit.

(3) A bank may ask the FDIC to consider loans originated or purchased by consortia in which the bank participates or by third parties in which the bank has invested only if the loans meet the definition of community development loans and only in accordance with paragraph (d) of this section. The FDIC will not consider these loans under any criterion of the lending test except the community development lending criterion.

(b) *Performance criteria.* The FDIC evaluates a bank's lending performance pursuant to the following criteria:

(1) *Lending activity.* The number and amount of the bank's home mortgage, small business, small farm, and consumer loans, if applicable, in the bank's assessment area(s);

(2) *Geographic distribution.* The geographic distribution of the bank's home mortgage, small business, small farm, and consumer loans, if applicable, based on the loan location, including:

(i) The proportion of the bank's lending in the bank's assessment area(s);

(ii) The dispersion of lending in the bank's assessment area(s); and

(iii) The number and amount of loans in low-, moderate-, middle-, and upper-income geographies in the bank's assessment area(s);

(3) *Borrower characteristics.* The distribution, particularly in the bank's assessment area(s), of the bank's home mortgage, small business, small farm, and consumer loans, if applicable, based on borrower characteristics, including the number and amount of:

(i) Home mortgage loans to low-, moderate-, middle-, and upper-income individuals;

(ii) Small business and small farm loans to businesses and farms with gross annual revenues of $1 million or less;

(iii) Small business and small farm loans by loan amount at origination; and

(iv) Consumer loans, if applicable, to low-, moderate-, middle-, and upper-income individuals;

(4) *Community development lending.* The bank's community development lending, including the number and amount of community development loans, and their complexity and innovativeness; and

(5) *Innovative or flexible lending practices.* The bank's use of innovative or flexible lending practices in a safe and sound manner to address the credit needs of low- or moderate-income individuals or geographies.

(c) *Affiliate lending.* (1) At a bank's option, the FDIC will consider loans by an affiliate of the bank, if the bank provides data on the affiliate's loans pursuant to § 345.42.

(2) The FDIC considers affiliate lending subject to the following constraints:

(i) No affiliate may claim a loan origination or loan purchase if another institution claims the same loan origination or purchase; and

Federal Deposit Insurance Corporation § 345.24

(ii) If a bank elects to have the FDIC consider loans within a particular lending category made by one or more of the bank's affiliates in a particular assessment area, the bank shall elect to have the FDIC consider, in accordance with paragraph (c)(1) of this section, all the loans within that lending category in that particular assessment area made by all of the bank's affiliates.

(3) The FDIC does not consider affiliate lending in assessing a bank's performance under paragraph (b)(2)(i) of this section.

(d) *Lending by a consortium or a third party.* Community development loans originated or purchased by a consortium in which the bank participates or by a third party in which the bank has invested:

(1) Will be considered, at the bank's option, if the bank reports the data pertaining to these loans under § 345.42(b)(2); and

(2) May be allocated among participants or investors, as they choose, for purposes of the lending test, except that no participant or investor:

(i) May claim a loan origination or loan purchase if another participant or investor claims the same loan origination or purchase; or

(ii) May claim loans accounting for more than its percentage share (based on the level of its participation or investment) of the total loans originated by the consortium or third party.

(e) *Lending performance rating.* The FDIC rates a bank's lending performance as provided in Appendix A of this part.

§ 345.23 Investment test.

(a) *Scope of test.* The investment test evaluates a bank's record of helping to meet the credit needs of its assessment area(s) through qualified investments that benefit its assessment area(s) or a broader statewide or regional area that includes the bank's assessment area(s).

(b) *Exclusion.* Activities considered under the lending or service tests may not be considered under the investment test.

(c) *Affiliate investment.* At a bank's option, the FDIC will consider, in its assessment of a bank's investment performance, a qualified investment made by an affiliate of the bank, if the qualified investment is not claimed by any other institution.

(d) *Disposition of branch premises.* Donating, selling on favorable terms, or making available on a rent-free basis a branch of the bank that is located in a predominantly minority neighborhood to a minority depository institution or women's depository institution (as these terms are defined in 12 U.S.C. 2907(b)) will be considered as a qualified investment.

(e) *Performance criteria.* The FDIC evaluates the investment performance of a bank pursuant to the following criteria:

(1) The dollar amount of qualified investments;

(2) The innovativeness or complexity of qualified investments;

(3) The responsiveness of qualified investments to credit and community development needs; and

(4) The degree to which the qualified investments are not routinely provided by private investors.

(f) *Investment performance rating.* The FDIC rates a bank's investment performance as provided in Appendix A of this part.

§ 345.24 Service test.

(a) *Scope of test.* The service test evaluates a bank's record of helping to meet the credit needs of its assessment area(s) by analyzing both the availability and effectiveness of a bank's systems for delivering retail banking services and the extent and innovativeness of its community development services.

(b) *Area(s) benefited.* Community development services must benefit a bank's assessment area(s) or a broader statewide or regional area that includes the bank's assessment area(s).

(c) *Affiliate service.* At a bank's option, the FDIC will consider, in its assessment of a bank's service performance, a community development service provided by an affiliate of the bank, if the community development service is not claimed by any other institution.

(d) *Performance criteria—retail banking services.* The FDIC evaluates the availability and effectiveness of a bank's systems for delivering retail banking

§ 345.25

services, pursuant to the following criteria:

(1) The current distribution of the bank's branches among low-, moderate-, middle-, and upper-income geographies;

(2) In the context of its current distribution of the bank's branches, the bank's record of opening and closing branches, particularly branches located in low- or moderate-income geographies or primarily serving low- or moderate-income individuals;

(3) The availability and effectiveness of alternative systems for delivering retail banking services (*e.g.*, RSFs, RSFs not owned or operated by or exclusively for the bank, banking by telephone or computer, loan production offices, and bank-at-work or bank-by-mail programs) in low- and moderate-income geographies and to low- and moderate-income individuals; and

(4) The range of services provided in low-, moderate-, middle-, and upper-income geographies and the degree to which the services are tailored to meet the needs of those geographies.

(e) *Performance criteria—community development services.* The FDIC evaluates community development services pursuant to the following criteria:

(1) The extent to which the bank provides community development services; and

(2) The innovativeness and responsiveness of community development services.

(f) *Service performance rating.* The FDIC rates a bank's service performance as provided in Appendix A of this part.

§ 345.25 Community development test for wholesale or limited purpose banks.

(a) *Scope of test.* The FDIC assesses a wholesale or limited purpose bank's record of helping to meet the credit needs of its assessment area(s) under the community development test through its community development lending, qualified investments, or community development services.

(b) *Designation as a wholesale or limited purpose bank.* In order to receive a designation as a wholesale or limited purpose bank, a bank shall file a request, in writing, with the FDIC, at least three months prior to the proposed effective date of the designation. If the FDIC approves the designation, it remains in effect until the bank requests revocation of the designation or until one year after the FDIC notifies the bank that the FDIC has revoked the designation on its own initiative.

(c) *Performance criteria.* The FDIC evaluates the community development performance of a wholesale or limited purpose bank pursuant to the following criteria:

(1) The number and amount of community development loans (including originations and purchases of loans and other community development loan data provided by the bank, such as data on loans outstanding, commitments, and letters of credit), qualified investments, or community development services;

(2) The use of innovative or complex qualified investments, community development loans, or community development services and the extent to which the investments are not routinely provided by private investors; and

(3) The bank's responsiveness to credit and community development needs.

(d) *Indirect activities.* At a bank's option, the FDIC will consider in its community development performance assessment:

(1) Qualified investments or community development services provided by an affiliate of the bank, if the investments or services are not claimed by any other institution; and

(2) Community development lending by affiliates, consortia and third parties, subject to the requirements and limitations in § 345.22 (c) and (d).

(e) *Benefit to assessment area(s)*—(1) *Benefit inside assessment area(s).* The FDIC considers all qualified investments, community development loans, and community development services that benefit areas within the bank's assessment area(s) or a broader statewide or regional area that includes the bank's assessment area(s).

(2) *Benefit outside assessment area(s).* The FDIC considers the qualified investments, community development loans, and community development services that benefit areas outside the bank's assessment area(s), if the bank

Federal Deposit Insurance Corporation § 345.27

has adequately addressed the needs of its assessment area(s).

(f) *Community development performance rating.* The FDIC rates a bank's community development performance as provided in Appendix A of this part.

§ 345.26 Small bank performance standards.

(a) *Performance criteria*—(1) *Small banks that are not intermediate small banks.* The FDIC evaluates the record of a small bank that is not, or that was not during the prior calendar year, an intermediate small bank, of helping to meet the credit needs of its assessment area(s) pursuant to the criteria set forth in paragraph (b) of this section.

(2) *Intermediate small banks.* The FDIC evaluates the record of a small bank that is, or that was during the prior calendar year, an intermediate small bank, of helping to meet the credit needs of its assessment area(s) pursuant to the criteria set forth in paragraphs (b) and (c) of this section.

(b) *Lending test.* A small bank's lending performance is evaluated pursuant to the following criteria:

(1) The bank's loan-to-deposit ratio, adjusted for seasonal variation, and, as appropriate, other lending-related activities, such as loan originations for sale to the secondary markets, community development loans, or qualified investments;

(2) The percentage of loans and, as appropriate, other lending-related activities located in the bank's assessment area(s);

(3) The bank's record of lending to and, as appropriate, engaging in other lending-related activities for borrowers of different income levels and businesses and farms of different sizes;

(4) The geographic distribution of the bank's loans; and

(5) The bank's record of taking action, if warranted, in response to written complaints about its performance in helping to meet credit needs in its assessment area(s).

(c) *Community development test.* An intermediate small bank's community development performance also is evaluated pursuant to the following criteria:

(1) The number and amount of community development loans;

(2) The number and amount of qualified investments;

(3) The extent to which the bank provides community development services; and

(4) The bank's responsiveness through such activities to community development lending, investment, and services needs.

(d) *Small bank performance rating.* The FDIC rates the performance of a bank evaluated under this section as provided in appendix A of this part.

[70 FR 44269, Aug. 2, 2005, as amended at 71 FR 78337, Dec. 29, 2006; 72 FR 72573, Dec. 21, 2007]

§ 345.27 Strategic plan.

(a) *Alternative election.* The FDIC will assess a bank's record of helping to meet the credit needs of its assessment area(s) under a strategic plan if:

(1) The bank has submitted the plan to the FDIC as provided for in this section;

(2) The FDIC has approved the plan;

(3) The plan is in effect; and

(4) The bank has been operating under an approved plan for at least one year.

(b) *Data reporting.* The FDIC's approval of a plan does not affect the bank's obligation, if any, to report data as required by § 345.42.

(c) *Plans in general*—(1) *Term.* A plan may have a term of no more than five years, and any multi-year plan must include annual interim measurable goals under which the FDIC will evaluate the bank's performance.

(2) *Multiple assessment areas.* A bank with more than one assessment area may prepare a single plan for all of its assessment areas or one or more plans for one or more of its assessment areas.

(3) *Treatment of affiliates.* Affiliated institutions may prepare a joint plan if the plan provides measurable goals for each institution. Activities may be allocated among institutions at the institutions' option, provided that the same activities are not considered for more than one institution.

(d) *Public participation in plan development.* Before submitting a plan to the FDIC for approval, a bank shall:

§ 345.27

(1) Informally seek suggestions from members of the public in its assessment area(s) covered by the plan while developing the plan;

(2) Once the bank has developed a plan, formally solicit public comment on the plan for at least 30 days by publishing notice in at least one newspaper of general circulation in each assessment area covered by the plan; and

(3) During the period of formal public comment, make copies of the plan available for review by the public at no cost at all offices of the bank in any assessment area covered by the plan and provide copies of the plan upon request for a reasonable fee to cover copying and mailing, if applicable.

(e) *Submission of plan.* The bank shall submit its plan to the FDIC at least three months prior to the proposed effective date of the plan. The bank shall also submit with its plan a description of its informal efforts to seek suggestions from members of the public, any written public comment received, and, if the plan was revised in light of the comment received, the initial plan as released for public comment.

(f) *Plan content*—(1) *Measurable goals.* (i) A bank shall specify in its plan measurable goals for helping to meet the credit needs of each assessment area covered by the plan, particularly the needs of low- and moderate-income geographies and low- and moderate-income individuals, through lending, investment, and services, as appropriate.

(ii) A bank shall address in its plan all three performance categories and, unless the bank has been designated as a wholesale or limited purpose bank, shall emphasize lending and lending-related activities. Nevertheless, a different emphasis, including a focus on one or more performance categories, may be appropriate if responsive to the characteristics and credit needs of its assessment area(s), considering public comment and the bank's capacity and constraints, product offerings, and business strategy.

(2) *Confidential information.* A bank may submit additional information to the FDIC on a confidential basis, but the goals stated in the plan must be sufficiently specific to enable the public and the FDIC to judge the merits of the plan.

(3) *Satisfactory and outstanding goals.* A bank shall specify in its plan measurable goals that constitute "satisfactory" performance. A plan may specify measurable goals that constitute "outstanding" performance. If a bank submits, and the FDIC approves, both "satisfactory" and "outstanding" performance goals, the FDIC will consider the bank eligible for an "outstanding" performance rating.

(4) *Election if satisfactory goals not substantially met.* A bank may elect in its plan that, if the bank fails to meet substantially its plan goals for a satisfactory rating, the FDIC will evaluate the bank's performance under the lending, investment, and service tests, the community development test, or the small bank performance standards, as appropriate.

(g) *Plan approval*—(1) *Timing.* The FDIC will act upon a plan within 60 calendar days after the FDIC receives the complete plan and other material required under paragraph (e) of this section. If the FDIC fails to act within this time period, the plan shall be deemed approved unless the FDIC extends the review period for good cause.

(2) *Public participation.* In evaluating the plan's goals, the FDIC considers the public's involvement in formulating the plan, written public comment on the plan, and any response by the bank to public comment on the plan.

(3) *Criteria for evaluating plan.* The FDIC evaluates a plan's measurable goals using the following criteria, as appropriate:

(i) The extent and breadth of lending or lending-related activities, including, as appropriate, the distribution of loans among different geographies, businesses and farms of different sizes, and individuals of different income levels, the extent of community development lending, and the use of innovative or flexible lending practices to address credit needs;

(ii) The amount and innovativeness, complexity, and responsiveness of the bank's qualified investments; and

(iii) The availability and effectiveness of the bank's systems for delivering retail banking services and the extent and innovativeness of the

Federal Deposit Insurance Corporation

§ 345.29

bank's community development services.

(h) *Plan amendment.* During the term of a plan, a bank may request the FDIC to approve an amendment to the plan on grounds that there has been a material change in circumstances. The bank shall develop an amendment to a previously approved plan in accordance with the public participation requirements of paragraph (d) of this section.

(i) *Plan assessment.* The FDIC approves the goals and assesses performance under a plan as provided for in Appendix A of this part.

[60 FR 22201, May 4, 1995, as amended at 60 FR 66050, Dec. 20, 1995; 69 FR 41188, July 8, 2004]

§ 345.28 Assigned ratings.

(a) *Ratings in general.* Subject to paragraphs (b) and (c) of this section, the FDIC assigns to a bank a rating of "outstanding," "satisfactory," "needs to improve," or "substantial noncompliance" based on the bank's performance under the lending, investment and service tests, the community development test, the small bank performance standards, or an approved strategic plan, as applicable.

(b) *Lending, investment, and service tests.* The FDIC assigns a rating for a bank assessed under the lending, investment, and service tests in accordance with the following principles:

(1) A bank that receives an "outstanding" rating on the lending test receives an assigned rating of at least "satisfactory";

(2) A bank that receives an "outstanding" rating on both the service test and the investment test and a rating of at least "high satisfactory" on the lending test receives an assigned rating of "outstanding"; and

(3) No bank may receive an assigned rating of "satisfactory" or higher unless it receives a rating of at least "low satisfactory" on the lending test.

(c) *Effect of evidence of discriminatory or other illegal credit practices.* (1) The FDIC's evaluation of a bank's CRA performance is adversely affected by evidence of discriminatory or other illegal credit practices in any geography by the bank or in any assessment area by any affiliate whose loans have been considered as part of the bank's lending performance. In connection with any type of lending activity described in § 345.22(a), evidence of discriminatory or other credit practices that violate an applicable law, rule, or regulation includes, but is not limited to:

(i) Discrimination against applicants on a prohibited basis in violation, for example, of the Equal Credit Opportunity Act or the Fair Housing Act;

(ii) Violations of the Home Ownership and Equity Protection Act;

(iii) Violations of section 5 of the Federal Trade Commission Act;

(iv) Violations of section 8 of the Real Estate Settlement Procedures Act; and

(v) Violations of the Truth in Lending Act provisions regarding a consumer's right of rescission.

(2) In determining the effect of evidence of practices described in paragraph (c)(1) of this section on the bank's assigned rating, the FDIC considers the nature, extent, and strength of the evidence of the practices; the policies and procedures that the bank (or affiliate, as applicable) has in place to prevent the practices; any corrective action that the bank (or affiliate, as applicable) has taken or has committed to take, including voluntary corrective action resulting from self-assessment; and any other relevant information.

[60 FR 22201, May 4, 1995, as amended at 70 FR 44269, Aug. 2, 2005]

§ 345.29 Effect of CRA performance on applications.

(a) *CRA performance.* Among other factors, the FDIC takes into account the record of performance under the CRA of each applicant bank in considering an application for approval of:

(1) The establishment of a domestic branch or other facility with the ability to accept deposits;

(2) The relocation of the bank's main office or a branch;

(3) The merger, consolidation, acquisition of assets, or assumption of liabilities; and

(4) Deposit insurance for a newly chartered financial institution.

(b) *New financial institutions.* A newly chartered financial institution shall submit with its application for deposit insurance a description of how it will meet its CRA objectives. The FDIC

§ 345.41

takes the description into account in considering the application and may deny or condition approval on that basis.

(c) *Interested parties.* The FDIC takes into account any views expressed by interested parties that are submitted in accordance with the FDIC's procedures set forth in part 303 of this chapter in considering CRA performance in an application listed in paragraphs (a) and (b) of this section.

(d) *Denial or conditional approval of application.* A bank's record of performance may be the basis for denying or conditioning approval of an application listed in paragraph (a) of this section.

Subpart C—Records, Reporting, and Disclosure Requirements

SOURCE: 60 FR 22201, May 4, 1995, unless otherwise noted.

§ 345.41 Assessment area delineation.

(a) *In general.* A bank shall delineate one or more assessment areas within which the FDIC evaluates the bank's record of helping to meet the credit needs of its community. The FDIC does not evaluate the bank's delineation of its assessment area(s) as a separate performance criterion, but the FDIC reviews the delineation for compliance with the requirements of this section.

(b) *Geographic area(s) for wholesale or limited purpose banks.* The assessment area(s) for a wholesale or limited purpose bank must consist generally of one or more MSAs or metropolitan divisions (using the MSA or metropolitan division boundaries that were in effect as of January 1 of the calendar year in which the delineation is made) or one or more contiguous political subdivisions, such as counties, cities, or towns, in which the bank has its main office, branches, and deposit-taking ATMs.

(c) *Geographic area(s) for other banks.* The assessment area(s) for a bank other than a wholesale or limited purpose bank must:

(1) Consist generally of one or more MSAs or metropolitan divisions (using the MSA or metropolitan division boundaries that were in effect as of January 1 of the calendar year in which the delineation is made) or one or more contiguous political subdivisions, such as counties, cities, or towns; and

(2) Include the geographies in which the bank has its main office, its branches, and its deposit-taking RSFs, as well as the surrounding geographies in which the bank has originated or purchased a substantial portion of its loans (including home mortgage loans, small business and small farm loans, and any other loans the bank chooses, such as those consumer loans on which the bank elects to have its performance assessed).

(d) *Adjustments to geographic area(s).* A bank may adjust the boundaries of its assessment area(s) to include only the portion of a political subdivision that it reasonably can be expected to serve. An adjustment is particularly appropriate in the case of an assessment area that otherwise would be extremely large, of unusual configuration, or divided by significant geographic barriers.

(e) *Limitations on the delineation of an assessment area.* Each bank's assessment area(s):

(1) Must consist only of whole geographies;

(2) May not reflect illegal discrimination;

(3) May not arbitrarily exclude low- or moderate-income geographies, taking into account the bank's size and financial condition; and

(4) May not extend substantially beyond an MSA boundary or beyond a state boundary unless the assessment area is located in a multistate MSA. If a bank serves a geographic area that extends substantially beyond a state boundary, the bank shall delineate separate assessment areas for the areas in each state. If a bank serves a geographic area that extends substantially beyond an MSA boundary, the bank shall delineate separate assessment areas for the areas inside and outside the MSA.

(f) *Banks serving military personnel.* Notwithstanding the requirements of this section, a bank whose business predominantly consists of serving the needs of military personnel or their dependents who are not located within a defined geographic area may delineate

Federal Deposit Insurance Corporation § 345.42

its entire deposit customer base as its assessment area.

(g) *Use of assessment area(s).* The FDIC uses the assessment area(s) delineated by a bank in its evaluation of the bank's CRA performance unless the FDIC determines that the assessment area(s) do not comply with the requirements of this section.

[60 FR 22201, May 4, 1995, as amended at 69 FR 41188, July 8, 2004]

§ 345.42 Data collection, reporting, and disclosure.

(a) *Loan information required to be collected and maintained.* A bank, except a small bank, shall collect, and maintain in machine readable form (as prescribed by the FDIC) until the completion of its next CRA examination, the following data for each small business or small farm loan originated or purchased by the bank:

(1) A unique number or alpha-numeric symbol that can be used to identify the relevant loan file;

(2) The loan amount at origination;

(3) The loan location; and

(4) An indicator whether the loan was to a business or farm with gross annual revenues of $1 million or less.

(b) *Loan information required to be reported.* A bank, except a small bank or a bank that was a small bank during the prior calendar year, shall report annually by March 1 to the FDIC in machine readable form (as prescribed by the FDIC) the following data for the prior calendar year:

(1) *Small business and small farm loan data.* For each geography in which the bank originated or purchased a small business or small farm loan, the aggregate number and amount of loans:

(i) With an amount at origination of $100,000 or less;

(ii) With an amount at origination of more than $100,000 but less than or equal to $250,000;

(iii) With an amount at origination of more than $250,000; and

(iv) To businesses and farms with gross annual revenues of $1 million or less (using the revenues that the bank considered in making its credit decision);

(2) *Community development loan data.* The aggregate number and aggregate amount of community development loans originated or purchased; and

(3) *Home mortgage loans.* If the bank is subject to reporting under part 203 of this title, the location of each home mortgage loan application, origination, or purchase outside the MSAs in which the bank has a home or branch office (or outside any MSA) in accordance with the requirements of part 203 of this title.

(c) *Optional data collection and maintenance*—(1) *Consumer loans.* A bank may collect and maintain in machine readable form (as prescribed by the FDIC) data for consumer loans originated or purchased by the bank for consideration under the lending test. A bank may maintain data for one or more of the following categories of consumer loans: motor vehicle, credit card, home equity, other secured, and other unsecured. If the bank maintains data for loans in a certain category, it shall maintain data for all loans originated or purchased within that category. The bank shall maintain data separately for each category, including for each loan:

(i) A unique number or alpha-numeric symbol that can be used to identify the relevant loan file;

(ii) The loan amount at origination or purchase;

(iii) The loan location; and

(iv) The gross annual income of the borrower that the bank considered in making its credit decision.

(2) *Other loan data.* At its option, a bank may provide other information concerning its lending performance, including additional loan distribution data.

(d) *Data on affiliate lending.* A bank that elects to have the FDIC consider loans by an affiliate, for purposes of the lending or community development test or an approved strategic plan, shall collect, maintain, and report for those loans the data that the bank would have collected, maintained, and reported pursuant to paragraphs (a), (b), and (c) of this section had the loans been originated or purchased by the bank. For home mortgage loans, the bank shall also be prepared to identify the home mortgage loans reported under part 203 of this title by the affiliate.

§ 345.42

(e) *Data on lending by a consortium or a third party.* A bank that elects to have the FDIC consider community development loans by a consortium or third party, for purposes of the lending or community development tests or an approved strategic plan, shall report for those loans the data that the bank would have reported under paragraph (b)(2) of this section had the loans been originated or purchased by the bank.

(f) *Small banks electing evaluation under the lending, investment, and service tests.* A bank that qualifies for evaluation under the small bank performance standards but elects evaluation under the lending, investment, and service tests shall collect, maintain, and report the data required for other banks pursuant to paragraphs (a) and (b) of this section.

(g) *Assessment area data.* A bank, except a small bank or a bank that was a small bank during the prior calendar year, shall collect and report to the FDIC by March 1 of each year a list for each assessment area showing the geographies within the area.

(h) *CRA Disclosure Statement.* The FDIC prepares annually for each bank that reports data pursuant to this section a CRA Disclosure Statement that contains, on a state-by-state basis:

(1) For each county (and for each assessment area smaller than a county) with a population of 500,000 persons or fewer in which the bank reported a small business or small farm loan:

(i) The number and amount of small business and small farm loans reported as originated or purchased located in low-, moderate-, middle-, and upper-income geographies;

(ii) A list grouping each geography according to whether the geography is low-, moderate-, middle-, or upper-income;

(iii) A list showing each geography in which the bank reported a small business or small farm loan; and

(iv) The number and amount of small business and small farm loans to businesses and farms with gross annual revenues of $1 million or less;

(2) For each county (and for each assessment area smaller than a county) with a population in excess of 500,000 persons in which the bank reported a small business or small farm loan:

(i) The number and amount of small business and small farm loans reported as originated or purchased located in geographies with median income relative to the area median income of less than 10 percent, 10 or more but less than 20 percent, 20 or more but less than 30 percent, 30 or more but less than 40 percent, 40 or more but less than 50 percent, 50 or more but less than 60 percent, 60 or more but less than 70 percent, 70 or more but less than 80 percent, 80 or more but less than 90 percent, 90 or more but less than 100 percent, 100 or more but less than 110 percent, 110 or more but less than 120 percent, and 120 percent or more;

(ii) A list grouping each geography in the county or assessment area according to whether the median income in the geography relative to the area median income is less than 10 percent, 10 or more but less than 20 percent, 20 or more but less than 30 percent, 30 or more but less than 40 percent, 40 or more but less than 50 percent, 50 or more but less than 60 percent, 60 or more but less than 70 percent, 70 or more but less than 80 percent, 80 or more but less than 90 percent, 90 or more but less than 100 percent, 100 or more but less than 110 percent, 110 or more but less than 120 percent, and 120 percent or more;

(iii) A list showing each geography in which the bank reported a small business or small farm loan; and

(iv) The number and amount of small business and small farm loans to businesses and farms with gross annual revenues of $1 million or less;

(3) The number and amount of small business and small farm loans located inside each assessment area reported by the bank and the number and amount of small business and small farm loans located outside the assessment area(s) reported by the bank; and

(4) The number and amount of community development loans reported as originated or purchased.

(i) *Aggregate disclosure statements.* The FDIC, in conjunction with the Board of Governors of the Federal Reserve System, the Office of the Comptroller of the Currency, and the Office of Thrift Supervision, prepares annually, for

Federal Deposit Insurance Corporation

§ 345.43

each MSA or metropolitan division (including an MSA or metropolitan division that crosses a state boundary) and the nonmetropolitan portion of each state, an aggregate disclosure statement of small business and small farm lending by all institutions subject to reporting under this part or parts 25, 228, or 563e of this title. These disclosure statements indicate, for each geography, the number and amount of all small business and small farm loans originated or purchased by reporting institutions, except that the FDIC may adjust the form of the disclosure if necessary, because of special circumstances, to protect the privacy of a borrower or the competitive position of an institution.

(j) *Central data depositories.* The FDIC makes the aggregate disclosure statements, described in paragraph (i) of this section, and the individual bank CRA Disclosure Statements, described in paragraph (h) of this section, available to the public at central data depositories. The FDIC publishes a list of the depositories at which the statements are available.

[60 FR 22201, May 4, 1995, as amended at 69 FR 41188, July 8, 2004]

§ 345.43 Content and availability of public file.

(a) *Information available to the public.* A bank shall maintain a public file that includes the following information:

(1) All written comments received from the public for the current year and each of the prior two calendar years that specifically relate to the bank's performance in helping to meet community credit needs, and any response to the comments by the bank, if neither the comments nor the responses contain statements that reflect adversely on the good name or reputation of any persons other than the bank or publication of which would violate specific provisions of law;

(2) A copy of the public section of the bank's most recent CRA Performance Evaluation prepared by the FDIC. The bank shall place this copy in the public file within 30 business days after its receipt from the FDIC;

(3) A list of the bank's branches, their street addresses, and geographies;

(4) A list of branches opened or closed by the bank during the current year and each of the prior two calendar years, their street addresses, and geographies;

(5) A list of services (including hours of operation, available loan and deposit products, and transaction fees) generally offered at the bank's branches and descriptions of material differences in the availability or cost of services at particular branches, if any. At its option, a bank may include information regarding the availability of alternative systems for delivering retail banking services (*e.g.*, RSFs, RSFs not owned or operated by or exclusively for the bank, banking by telephone or computer, loan production offices, and bank-at-work or bank-by-mail programs);

(6) A map of each assessment area showing the boundaries of the area and identifying the geographies contained within the area, either on the map or in a separate list; and

(7) Any other information the bank chooses.

(b) *Additional information available to the public*—(1) *Banks other than small banks.* A bank, except a small bank or a bank that was a small bank during the prior calendar year, shall include in its public file the following information pertaining to the bank and its affiliates, if applicable, for each of the prior two calendar years:

(i) If the bank has elected to have one or more categories of its consumer loans considered under the lending test, for each of these categories, the number and amount of loans:

(A) To low-, moderate-, middle-, and upper-income individuals;

(B) Located in low-, moderate-, middle-, and upper-income census tracts; and

(C) Located inside the bank's assessment area(s) and outside the bank's assessment area(s); and

(ii) The bank's CRA Disclosure Statement. The bank shall place the statement in the public file within three business days of its receipt from the FDIC.

(2) *Banks required to report Home Mortgage Disclosure Act (HMDA) data.* A bank required to report home mortgage loan data pursuant part 203 of this title

§ 345.44

shall include in its public file a copy of the HMDA Disclosure Statement provided by the Federal Financial Institutions Examination Council pertaining to the bank for each of the prior two calendar years. In addition, a bank that elected to have the FDIC consider the mortgage lending of an affiliate for any of these years shall include in its public file the affiliate's HMDA Disclosure Statement for those years. The bank shall place the statement(s) in the public file within three business days after receipt.

(3) *Small banks.* A small bank or a bank that was a small bank during the prior calendar year shall include in its public file:

(i) The bank's loan-to-deposit ratio for each quarter of the prior calendar year and, at its option, additional data on its loan-to-deposit ratio; and

(ii) The information required for other banks by paragraph (b)(1) of this section, if the bank has elected to be evaluated under the lending, investment, and service tests.

(4) *Banks with strategic plans.* A bank that has been approved to be assessed under a strategic plan shall include in its public file a copy of that plan. A bank need not include information submitted to the FDIC on a confidential basis in conjunction with the plan.

(5) *Banks with less than satisfactory ratings.* A bank that received a less than satisfactory rating during its most recent examination shall include in its public file a description of its current efforts to improve its performance in helping to meet the credit needs of its entire community. The bank shall update the description quarterly.

(c) *Location of public information.* A bank shall make available to the public for inspection upon request and at no cost the information required in this section as follows:

(1) At the main office and, if an interstate bank, at one branch office in each state, all information in the public file; and

(2) At each branch:

(i) A copy of the public section of the bank's most recent CRA Performance Evaluation and a list of services provided by the branch; and

(ii) Within five calendar days of the request, all the information in the public file relating to the assessment area in which the branch is located.

(d) *Copies.* Upon request, a bank shall provide copies, either on paper or in another form acceptable to the person making the request, of the information in its public file. The bank may charge a reasonable fee not to exceed the cost of copying and mailing (if applicable).

(e) *Updating.* Except as otherwise provided in this section, a bank shall ensure that the information required by this section is current as of April 1 of each year.

§ 345.44 Public notice by banks.

A bank shall provide in the public lobby of its main office and each of its branches the appropriate public notice set forth in appendix B of this part. Only a branch of a bank having more than one assessment area shall include the bracketed material in the notice for branch offices. Only a bank that is an affiliate of a holding company shall include next to the last sentence of the notices. A bank shall include the last sentence of the notices only if it is an affiliate of a holding company that is not prevented by statute from acquiring additional banks.

§ 345.45 Publication of planned examination schedule.

The FDIC publishes at least 30 days in advance of the beginning of each calendar quarter a list of banks scheduled for CRA examinations in that quarter.

APPENDIX A TO PART 345—RATINGS

(a) *Ratings in general.* (1) In assigning a rating, the FDIC evaluates a bank's performance under the applicable performance criteria in this part, in accordance with §§ 345.21 and 345.28. This includes consideration of low-cost education loans provided to low-income borrowers and activities in cooperation with minority- or women-owned financial institutions and low-income credit unions, as well as adjustments on the basis of evidence of discriminatory or other illegal credit practices.

(2) A bank's performance need not fit each aspect of a particular rating profile in order to receive that rating, and exceptionally strong performance with respect to some aspects may compensate for weak performance in others. The bank's overall performance, however, must be consistent with safe and

Federal Deposit Insurance Corporation

sound banking practices and generally with the appropriate rating profile as follows.

(b) *Banks evaluated under the lending, investment, and service tests.*—(1) *Lending performance rating.* The FDIC assigns each bank's lending performance one of the five following ratings.

(i) *Outstanding.* The FDIC rates a bank's lending performance "outstanding" if, in general, it demonstrates:

(A) Excellent responsiveness to credit needs in its assessment area(s), taking into account the number and amount of home mortgage, small business, small farm, and consumer loans, if applicable, in its assessment area(s);

(B) A substantial majority of its loans are made in its assessment area(s);

(C) An excellent geographic distribution of loans in its assessment area(s);

(D) An excellent distribution, particularly in its assessment area(s), of loans among individuals of different income levels and businesses (including farms) of different sizes, given the product lines offered by the bank;

(E) An excellent record of serving the credit needs of highly economically disadvantaged areas in its assessment area(s), low-income individuals, or businesses (including farms) with gross annual revenues of $1 million or less, consistent with safe and sound operations;

(F) Extensive use of innovative or flexible lending practices in a safe and sound manner to address the credit needs of low- or moderate-income individuals or geographies; and

(G) It is a leader in making community development loans.

(ii) *High satisfactory.* The FDIC rates a bank's lending performance "high satisfactory" if, in general, it demonstrates:

(A) Good responsiveness to credit needs in its assessment area(s), taking into account the number and amount of home mortgage, small business, small farm, and consumer loans, if applicable, in its assessment area(s);

(B) A high percentage of its loans are made in its assessment area(s);

(C) A good geographic distribution of loans in its assessment area(s);

(D) A good distribution, particularly in its assessment area(s), of loans among individuals of different income levels and businesses (including farms) of different sizes, given the product lines offered by the bank;

(E) A good record of serving the credit needs of highly economically disadvantaged areas in its assessment area(s), low-income individuals, or businesses (including farms) with gross annual revenues of $1 million or less, consistent with safe and sound operations;

(F) Use of innovative or flexible lending practices in a safe and sound manner to address the credit needs of low- or moderate-income individuals or geographies; and

Pt. 345, App. A

(G) It has made a relatively high level of community development loans.

(iii) *Low satisfactory.* The FDIC rates a bank's lending performance "low satisfactory" if, in general, it demonstrates:

(A) Adequate responsiveness to credit needs in its assessment area(s), taking into account the number and amount of home mortgage, small business, small farm, and consumer loans, if applicable, in its assessment area(s);

(B) An adequate percentage of its loans are made in its assessment area(s);

(C) An adequate geographic distribution of loans in its assessment area(s);

(D) An adequate distribution, particularly in its assessment area(s), of loans among individuals of different income levels and businesses (including farms) of different sizes, given the product lines offered by the bank;

(E) An adequate record of serving the credit needs of highly economically disadvantaged areas in its assessment area(s), low-income individuals, or businesses (including farms) with gross annual revenues of $1 million or less, consistent with safe and sound operations;

(F) Limited use of innovative or flexible lending practices in a safe and sound manner to address the credit needs of low- or moderate-income individuals or geographies; and

(G) It has made an adequate level of community development loans.

(iv) *Needs to improve.* The FDIC rates a bank's lending performance "needs to improve" if, in general, it demonstrates:

(A) Poor responsiveness to credit needs in its assessment area(s), taking into account the number and amount of home mortgage, small business, small farm, and consumer loans, if applicable, in its assessment area(s);

(B) A small percentage of its loans are made in its assessment area(s);

(C) A poor geographic distribution of loans, particularly to low- or moderate-income geographies, in its assessment area(s);

(D) A poor distribution, particularly in its assessment area(s), of loans among individuals of different income levels and businesses (including farms) of different sizes, given the product lines offered by the bank;

(E) A poor record of serving the credit needs of highly economically disadvantaged areas in its assessment area(s), low-income individuals, or businesses (including farms) with gross annual revenues of $1 million or less, consistent with safe and sound operations;

(F) Little use of innovative or flexible lending practices in a safe and sound manner to address the credit needs of low- or moderate-income individuals or geographies; and

(G) It has made a low level of community development loans.

(v) *Substantial noncompliance.* The FDIC rates a bank's lending performance as being in "substantial noncompliance" if, in general, it demonstrates:

(A) A very poor responsiveness to credit needs in its assessment area(s), taking into account the number and amount of home mortgage, small business, small farm, and consumer loans, if applicable, in its assessment area(s);

(B) A very small percentage of its loans are made in its assessment area(s);

(C) A very poor geographic distribution of loans, particularly to low- or moderate-income geographies, in its assessment area(s);

(D) A very poor distribution, particularly in its assessment area(s), of loans among individuals of different income levels and businesses (including farms) of different sizes, given the product lines offered by the bank;

(E) A very poor record of serving the credit needs of highly economically disadvantaged areas in its assessment area(s), low-income individuals, or businesses (including farms) with gross annual revenues of $1 million or less, consistent with safe and sound operations;

(F) No use of innovative or flexible lending practices in a safe and sound manner to address the credit needs of low- or moderate-income individuals or geographies; and

(G) It has made few, if any, community development loans.

(2) *Investment performance rating.* The FDIC assigns each bank's investment performance one of the five following ratings.

(i) *Outstanding.* The FDIC rates a bank's investment performance "outstanding" if, in general, it demonstrates:

(A) An excellent level of qualified investments, particularly those that are not routinely provided by private investors, often in a leadership position;

(B) Extensive use of innovative or complex qualified investments; and

(C) Excellent responsiveness to credit and community development needs.

(ii) *High satisfactory.* The FDIC rates a bank's investment performance "high satisfactory" if, in general, it demonstrates:

(A) A significant level of qualified investments, particularly those that are not routinely provided by private investors, occasionally in a leadership position;

(B) Significant use of innovative or complex qualified investments; and

(C) Good responsiveness to credit and community development needs.

(iii) *Low satisfactory.* The FDIC rates a bank's investment performance "low satisfactory" if, in general, it demonstrates:

(A) An adequate level of qualified investments, particularly those that are not routinely provided by private investors, although rarely in a leadership position;

(B) Occasional use of innovative or complex qualified investments; and

(C) Adequate responsiveness to credit and community development needs.

(iv) *Needs to improve.* The FDIC rates a bank's investment performance "needs to improve" if, in general, it demonstrates:

(A) A poor level of qualified investments, particularly those that are not routinely provided by private investors;

(B) Rare use of innovative or complex qualified investments; and

(C) Poor responsiveness to credit and community development needs.

(v) *Substantial noncompliance.* The FDIC rates a bank's investment performance as being in "substantial noncompliance" if, in general, it demonstrates:

(A) Few, if any, qualified investments, particularly those that are not routinely provided by private investors;

(B) No use of innovative or complex qualified investments; and

(C) Very poor responsiveness to credit and community development needs.

(3) *Service performance rating.* The FDIC assigns each bank's service performance one of the five following ratings.

(i) *Outstanding.* The FDIC rates a bank's service performance "outstanding" if, in general, the bank demonstrates:

(A) Its service delivery systems are readily accessible to geographies and individuals of different income levels in its assessment area(s);

(B) To the extent changes have been made, its record of opening and closing branches has improved the accessibility of its delivery systems, particularly in low- or moderate-income geographies or to low- or moderate-income individuals;

(C) Its services (including, where appropriate, business hours) are tailored to the convenience and needs of its assessment area(s), particularly low- or moderate-income geographies or low- or moderate-income individuals; and

(D) It is a leader in providing community development services.

(ii) *High satisfactory.* The FDIC rates a bank's service performance "high satisfactory" if, in general, the bank demonstrates:

(A) Its service delivery systems are accessible to geographies and individuals of different income levels in its assessment area(s);

(B) To the extent changes have been made, its record of opening and closing branches has not adversely affected the accessibility of its delivery systems, particularly in low- and moderate-income geographies and to low- and moderate-income individuals;

(C) Its services (including, where appropriate, business hours) do not vary in a way that inconveniences its assessment area(s), particularly low- and moderate-income geographies and low- and moderate-income individuals; and

(D) It provides a relatively high level of community development services.

Federal Deposit Insurance Corporation

(iii) *Low satisfactory.* The FDIC rates a bank's service performance "low satisfactory" if, in general, the bank demonstrates:

(A) Its service delivery systems are reasonably accessible to geographies and individuals of different income levels in its assessment area(s);

(B) To the extent changes have been made, its record of opening and closing branches has generally not adversely affected the accessibility of its delivery systems, particularly in low- and moderate-income geographies and to low- and moderate-income individuals;

(C) Its services (including, where appropriate, business hours) do not vary in a way that inconveniences its assessment area(s), particularly low- and moderate-income geographies and low- and moderate-income individuals; and

(D) It provides an adequate level of community development services.

(iv) *Needs to improve.* The FDIC rates a bank's service performance "needs to improve" if, in general, the bank demonstrates:

(A) Its service delivery systems are unreasonably inaccessible to portions of its assessment area(s), particularly to low- or moderate-income geographies or to low- or moderate-income individuals;

(B) To the extent changes have been made, its record of opening and closing branches has adversely affected the accessibility its delivery systems, particularly in low- or moderate-income geographies or to low- or moderate-income individuals;

(C) Its services (including, where appropriate, business hours) vary in a way that inconveniences its assessment area(s), particularly low- or moderate-income geographies or low- or moderate-income individuals; and

(D) It provides a limited level of community development services.

(v) *Substantial noncompliance.* The FDIC rates a bank's service performance as being in "substantial noncompliance" if, in general, the bank demonstrates:

(A) Its service delivery systems are unreasonably inaccessible to significant portions of its assessment area(s), particularly to low- or moderate-income geographies or to low- or moderate-income individuals;

(B) To the extent changes have been made, its record of opening and closing branches has significantly adversely affected the accessibility of its delivery systems, particularly in low- or moderate-income geographies or to low- or moderate-income individuals;

(C) Its services (including, where appropriate, business hours) vary in a way that significantly inconveniences its assessment area(s), particularly low- or moderate-income geographies or low- or moderate-income individuals; and

(D) It provides few, if any, community development services.

(c) *Wholesale or limited purpose banks.* The FDIC assigns each wholesale or limited purpose bank's community development performance one of the four following ratings.

(1) *Outstanding.* The FDIC rates a wholesale or limited purpose bank's community development performance "outstanding" if, in general, it demonstrates:

(i) A high level of community development loans, community development services, or qualified investments, particularly investments that are not routinely provided by private investors;

(ii) Extensive use of innovative or complex qualified investments, community development loans, or community development services; and

(iii) Excellent responsiveness to credit and community development needs in its assessment area(s).

(2) *Satisfactory.* The FDIC rates a wholesale or limited purpose bank's community development performance "satisfactory" if, in general, it demonstrates:

(i) An adequate level of community development loans, community development services, or qualified investments, particularly investments that are not routinely provided by private investors;

(ii) Occasional use of innovative or complex qualified investments, community development loans, or community development services; and

(iii) Adequate responsiveness to credit and community development needs in its assessment area(s).

(3) *Needs to improve.* The FDIC rates a wholesale or limited purpose bank's community development performance as "needs to improve" if, in general, it demonstrates:

(i) A poor level of community development loans, community development services, or qualified investments, particularly investments that are not routinely provided by private investors;

(ii) Rare use of innovative or complex qualified investments, community development loans, or community development services; and

(iii) Poor responsiveness to credit and community development needs in its assessment area(s).

(4) *Substantial noncompliance.* The FDIC rates a wholesale or limited purpose bank's community development performance in "substantial noncompliance" if, in general, it demonstrates:

(i) Few, if any, community development loans, community development services, or qualified investments, particularly investments that are not routinely provided by private investors;

(ii) No use of innovative or complex qualified investments, community development loans, or community development services; and

(iii) Very poor responsiveness to credit and community development needs in its assessment area(s).

(d) *Banks evaluated under the small bank performance standards*—(1) *Lending test ratings*—(i) *Eligibility for a satisfactory lending test rating.* The FDIC rates a small bank's lending performance "satisfactory" if, in general, the bank demonstrates:

(A) A reasonable loan-to-deposit ratio (considering seasonal variations) given the bank's size, financial condition, the credit needs of its assessment area(s), and taking into account, as appropriate, other lending-related activities such as loan originations for sale to the secondary markets and community development loans and qualified investments;

(B) A majority of its loans and, as appropriate, other lending-related activities, are in its assessment area;

(C) A distribution of loans to and, as appropriate, other lending-related activities for individuals of different income levels (including low- and moderate-income individuals) and businesses and farms of different sizes that is reasonable given the demographics of the bank's assessment area(s);

(D) A record of taking appropriate action, when warranted, in response to written complaints, if any, about the bank's performance in helping to meet the credit needs of its assessment area(s); and

(E) A reasonable geographic distribution of loans given the bank's assessment area(s).

(ii) *Eligibility for an "outstanding" lending test rating.* A small bank that meets each of the standards for a "satisfactory" rating under this paragraph and exceeds some or all of those standards may warrant consideration for a lending test rating of "outstanding."

(iii) *Needs to improve or substantial noncompliance ratings.* A small bank may also receive a lending test rating of "needs to improve" or "substantial noncompliance" depending on the degree to which its performance has failed to meet the standard for a "satisfactory" rating.

(2) *Community development test ratings for intermediate small banks*—(i) *Eligibility for a satisfactory community development test rating.* The FDIC rates an intermediate small bank's community development performance "satisfactory" if the bank demonstrates adequate responsiveness to the community development needs of its assessment area(s) through community development loans, qualified investments, and community development services. The adequacy of the bank's response will depend on its capacity for such community development activities, its assessment area's need for such community development activities, and the availability of such opportunities for community development in the bank's assessment area(s).

(ii) *Eligibility for an outstanding community development test rating.* The FDIC rates an intermediate small bank's community development performance "outstanding" if the bank demonstrates excellent responsiveness to community development needs in its assessment area(s) through community development loans, qualified investments, and community development services, as appropriate, considering the bank's capacity and the need and availability of such opportunities for community development in the bank's assessment area(s).

(iii) *Needs to improve or substantial noncompliance ratings.* An intermediate small bank may also receive a community development test rating of "needs to improve" or "substantial noncompliance" depending on the degree to which its performance has failed to meet the standards for a "satisfactory" rating.

(3) *Overall rating*—(i) *Eligibility for a satisfactory overall rating.* No intermediate small bank may receive an assigned overall rating of "satisfactory" unless it receives a rating of at least "satisfactory" on both the lending test and the community development test.

(ii) *Eligibility for an outstanding overall rating.* (A) An intermediate small bank that receives an "outstanding" rating on one test and at least "satisfactory" on the other test may receive an assigned overall rating of "outstanding."

(B) A small bank that is not an intermediate small bank that meets each of the standards for a "satisfactory" rating under the lending test and exceeds some or all of those standards may warrant consideration for an overall rating of "outstanding." In assessing whether a bank's performance is "outstanding," the FDIC considers the extent to which the bank exceeds each of the performance standards for a "satisfactory" rating and its performance in making qualified investments and its performance in providing branches and other services and delivery systems that enhance credit availability in its assessment area(s).

(iii) *Needs to improve or substantial noncompliance overall ratings.* A small bank may also receive a rating of "needs to improve" or "substantial noncompliance" depending on the degree to which its performance has failed to meet the standards for a "satisfactory" rating.

(e) *Strategic plan assessment and rating*—(1) *Satisfactory goals.* The FDIC approves as "satisfactory" measurable goals that adequately help to meet the credit needs of the bank's assessment area(s).

(2) *Outstanding goals.* If the plan identifies a separate group of measurable goals that substantially exceed the levels approved as "satisfactory," the FDIC will approve those goals as "outstanding."

Federal Deposit Insurance Corporation

(3) *Rating.* The FDIC assesses the performance of a bank operating under an approved plan to determine if the bank has met its plan goals:

(i) If the bank substantially achieves its plan goals for a satisfactory rating, the FDIC will rate the bank's performance under the plan as "satisfactory."

(ii) If the bank exceeds its plan goals for a satisfactory rating and substantially achieves its plan goals for an outstanding rating, the FDIC will rate the bank's performance under the plan as "outstanding."

(iii) If the bank fails to meet substantially its plan goals for a satisfactory rating, the FDIC will rate the bank as either "needs to improve" or "substantial noncompliance," depending on the extent to which it falls short of its plan goals, unless the bank elected in its plan to be rated otherwise, as provided in § 345.27(f)(4).

[60 FR 22201, May 4, 1995, as amended at 70 FR 44270, Aug. 2, 2005; 75 FR 61045, Oct. 4, 2010]

APPENDIX B TO PART 345—CRA NOTICE

(a) *Notice for main offices and, if an interstate bank, one branch office in each state.*

COMMUNITY REINVESTMENT ACT NOTICE

Under the Federal Community Reinvestment Act (CRA), the Federal Deposit Insurance Corporation (FDIC) evaluates our record of helping to meet the credit needs of this community consistent with safe and sound operations. The FDIC also takes this record into account when deciding on certain applications submitted by us.

Your involvement is encouraged.

You are entitled to certain information about our operations and our performance under the CRA, including, for example, information about our branches, such as their location and services provided at them; the public section of our most recent CRA Performance Evaluation, prepared by the FDIC; and comments received from the public relating to our performance in helping to meet community credit needs, as well as our responses to those comments. You may review this information today.

At least 30 days before the beginning of each quarter, the FDIC publishes a nationwide list of the banks that are scheduled for CRA examination in that quarter. This list is available from the Regional Manager, Division of Supervision and Consumer Protection(DSC), FDIC (address). You may send written comments about our performance in helping to meet community credit needs to (name and address of official at bank) and FDIC Regional Manager. Your letter, together with any response by us, will be considered by the FDIC in evaluating our CRA performance and may be made public.

You may ask to look at any comments received by the FDIC Regional Manager. You may also request from the FDIC Regional Manager an announcement of our applications covered by the CRA filed with the FDIC. We are an affiliate of (name of holding company), a bank holding company. You may request from the (title of responsible official), Federal Reserve Bank of _____ (address) an announcement of applications covered by the CRA filed by bank holding companies.

(b) *Notice for branch offices.*

COMMUNITY REINVESTMENT ACT NOTICE

Under the Federal Community Reinvestment Act (CRA), the Federal Deposit Insurance Corporation (FDIC) evaluates our record of helping to meet the credit needs of this community consistent with safe and sound operations. The FDIC also takes this record into account when deciding on certain applications submitted by us.

Your involvement is encouraged.

You are entitled to certain information about our operations and our performance under the CRA. You may review today the public section of our most recent CRA evaluation, prepared by the FDIC, and a list of services provided at this branch. You may also have access to the following additional information, which we will make available to you at this branch within five calendar days after you make a request to us: (1) a map showing the assessment area containing this branch, which is the area in which the FDIC evaluates our CRA performance in this community; (2) information about our branches in this assessment area; (3) a list of services we provide at those locations; (4) data on our lending performance in this assessment area; and (5) copies of all written comments received by us that specifically relate to our CRA performance in this assessment area, and any responses we have made to those comments. If we are operating under an approved strategic plan, you may also have access to a copy of the plan.

[If you would like to review information about our CRA performance in other communities served by us, the public file for our entire bank is available at (name of office located in state), located at (address).]

At least 30 days before the beginning of each quarter, the FDIC publishes a nationwide list of the banks that are scheduled for CRA examination in that quarter. This list is available from the Regional Manager, Division of Supervision and Consumer Protection(DSC), FDIC (address). You may send written comments about our performance in helping to meet community credit needs to (name and address of official at bank) and the FDIC Regional Manager. Your letter, together with any response by us, will be considered by the FDIC in evaluating our CRA performance and may be made public.

You may ask to look at any comments received by the FDIC Regional Manager. You may also request from the FDIC Regional Manager an announcement of our applications covered by the CRA filed with the FDIC. We are an affiliate of (name of holding company), a bank holding company. You may request from the (title of responsible official), Federal Reserve Bank of _____ (address) an announcement of applications covered by the CRA filed by bank holding companies.

PART 346—DISCLOSURE AND REPORTING OF CRA-RELATED AGREEMENTS

Sec.
346.1 Purpose and scope of this part.
346.2 Definition of covered agreement.
346.3 CRA communications.
346.4 Fulfillment of the CRA.
346.5 Related agreements considered a single agreement.
346.6 Disclosure of covered agreements.
346.7 Annual reports.
346.8 Release of information under FOIA.
346.9 Compliance provisions.
346.10 Transition provisions.
346.11 Other definitions and rules of construction used in this part.

AUTHORITY: 12 U.S.C. 1831y.

SOURCE: 66 FR 2099, Jan. 10, 2001, unless otherwise noted.

§ 346.1 Purpose and scope of this part.

(a) *General.* This part implements section 711 of the Gramm-Leach-Bliley Act (12 U.S.C. 1831y). That section requires any nongovernmental entity or person, insured depository institution, or affiliate of an insured depository institution that enters into a covered agreement to—

(1) Make the covered agreement available to the public and the appropriate Federal banking agency; and

(2) File an annual report with the appropriate Federal banking agency concerning the covered agreement.

(b) *Scope of this part.* The provisions of this part apply to—

(1) State nonmember insured banks;

(2) Subsidiaries of state nonmember insured banks;

(3) Nongovernmental entities or persons that enter into covered agreements with any company listed in paragraph (b)(1) and (2) of this section.

(c) *Relation to Community Reinvestment Act.* This part does not affect in any way the Community Reinvestment Act of 1977 (12 U.S.C. 2901 *et seq.*) or the FDIC's Community Reinvestment regulation found at 12 CFR part 345, or the FDIC's interpretations or administration of that Act or regulation.

(d) *Examples.* (1) The examples in this part are not exclusive. Compliance with an example, to the extent applicable, constitutes compliance with this part.

(2) Examples in a paragraph illustrate only the issue described in the paragraph and do not illustrate any other issues that may arise in this part.

§ 346.2 Definition of covered agreement.

(a) *General definition of covered agreement.* A covered agreement is any contract, arrangement, or understanding that meets all of the following criteria—

(1) The agreement is in writing.

(2) The parties to the agreement include—

(i) One or more insured depository institutions or affiliates of an insured depository institution; and

(ii) One or more nongovernmental entities or persons (referred to hereafter as NGEPs).

(3) The agreement provides for the insured depository institution or any affiliate to—

(i) Provide to one or more individuals or entities (whether or not parties to the agreement) cash payments, grants, or other consideration (except loans) that have an aggregate value of more than $10,000 in any calendar year; or

(ii) Make to one or more individuals or entities (whether or not parties to the agreement) loans that have an aggregate principal amount of more than $50,000 in any calendar year.

(4) The agreement is made pursuant to, or in connection with, the fulfillment of the Community Reinvestment Act of 1977 (12 U.S.C. 2901 *et seq.*) (CRA), as defined in § 346.4.

(5) The agreement is with a NGEP that has had a CRA communication as

Federal Deposit Insurance Corporation

§ 346.2

described in § 346.3 prior to entering into the agreement.

(b) *Examples concerning written arrangements or understandings*—(1) *Example 1.* A NGEP meets with an insured depository institution and states that the institution needs to make more community development investments in the NGEP's community. The NGEP and insured depository institution do not reach an agreement concerning the community development investments the institution should make in the community, and the parties do not reach any mutual arrangement or understanding. Two weeks later, the institution unilaterally issues a press release announcing that it has established a general goal of making $100 million of community development grants in low- and moderate-income neighborhoods served by the insured depository institution over the next 5 years. The NGEP is not identified in the press release. The press release is not a written arrangement or understanding.

(2) *Example 2.* A NGEP meets with an insured depository institution and states that the institution needs to offer new loan programs in the NGEP's community. The NGEP and the insured depository institution reach a mutual arrangement or understanding that the institution will provide additional loans in the NGEP's community. The institution tells the NGEP that it will issue a press release announcing the program. Later, the insured depository institution issues a press release announcing the loan program. The press release incorporates the key terms of the understanding reached between the NGEP and the insured depository institution. The written press release reflects the mutual arrangement or understanding of the NGEP and the insured depository institution and is, therefore, a written arrangement or understanding.

(3) *Example 3.* An NGEP sends a letter to an insured depository institution requesting that the institution provide a $15,000 grant to the NGEP. The insured depository institution responds in writing and agrees to provide the grant in connection with its annual grant program. The exchange of letters constitutes a written arrangement or understanding.

(c) *Loan agreements that are not covered agreements.* A covered agreement does not include—

(1) Any individual loan that is secured by real estate; or

(2) Any specific contract or commitment for a loan or extension of credit to an individual, business, farm, or other entity, or group of such individuals or entities if—

(i) The funds are loaned at rates that are not substantially below market rates; and

(ii) The loan application or other loan documentation does not indicate that the borrower intends or is authorized to use the borrowed funds to make a loan or extension of credit to one or more third parties.

(d) *Examples concerning loan agreements*—(1) *Example 1.* An insured depository institution provides an organization with a $1 million loan that is documented in writing and is secured by real estate owned or to-be-acquired by the organization. The agreement is an individual mortgage loan and is exempt from coverage under paragraph (c)(1) of this section, regardless of the interest rate on the loan or whether the organization intends or is authorized to re-loan the funds to a third party.

(2) *Example 2.* An insured depository institution commits to provide a $500,000 line of credit to a small business that is documented by a written agreement. The loan is made at rates that are within the range of rates offered by the institution to similarly situated small businesses in the market and the loan documentation does not indicate that the small business intends or is authorized to re-lend the borrowed funds. The agreement is exempt from coverage under paragraph (c)(2) of this section.

(3) *Example 3.* An insured depository institution offers small business loans that are guaranteed by the Small Business Administration (SBA). A small business obtains a $75,000 loan, documented in writing, from the institution under the institution's SBA loan program. The loan documentation does not indicate that the borrower intends or is authorized to re-lend the funds.

§ 346.3

Although the rate charged on the loan is well below that charged by the institution on commercial loans, the rate is within the range of rates that the institution would charge a similarly situated small business for a similar loan under the SBA loan program. Accordingly, the loan is not made at substantially below market rates and is exempt from coverage under paragraph (c)(2) of this section.

(4) *Example 4.* A bank holding company enters into a written agreement with a community development organization that provides that insured depository institutions owned by the bank holding company will make $250 million in small business loans in the community over the next 5 years. The written agreement is not a specific contract or commitment for a loan or an extension of credit and, thus, is not exempt from coverage under paragraph (c)(2) of this section. Each small business loan made by the insured depository institution pursuant to this general commitment would, however, be exempt from coverage if the loan is made at rates that are not substantially below market rates and the loan documentation does not indicate that the borrower intended or was authorized to re-lend the funds.

(e) *Agreements that include exempt loan agreements.* If an agreement includes a loan, extension of credit or loan commitment that, if documented separately, would be exempt under paragraph (c) of this section, the exempt loan, extension of credit or loan commitment may be excluded for purposes of determining whether the agreement is a covered agreement.

(f) *Determining annual value of agreements that lack schedule of disbursements.* For purposes of paragraph (a)(3) of this section, a multi-year agreement that does not include a schedule for the disbursement of payments, grants, loans or other consideration by the insured depository institution or affiliate, is considered to have a value in the first year of the agreement equal to all payments, grants, loans and other consideration to be provided at any time under the agreement.

§ 346.3 CRA communications.

(a) *Definition of CRA communication.* A CRA communication is any of the following—

(1) Any written or oral comment or testimony provided to a Federal banking agency concerning the adequacy of the performance under the CRA of the insured depository institution, any affiliated insured depository institution, or any CRA affiliate.

(2) Any written comment submitted to the insured depository institution that discusses the adequacy of the performance under the CRA of the institution and must be included in the institution's CRA public file.

(3) Any discussion or other contact with the insured depository institution or any affiliate about—

(i) Providing (or refraining from providing) written or oral comments or testimony to any Federal banking agency concerning the adequacy of the performance under the CRA of the insured depository institution, any affiliated insured depository institution, or any CRA affiliate;

(ii) Providing (or refraining from providing) written comments to the insured depository institution that concern the adequacy of the institution's performance under the CRA and must be included in the institution's CRA public file; or

(iii) The adequacy of the performance under the CRA of the insured depository institution, any affiliated insured depository institution, or any CRA affiliate.

(b) *Discussions or contacts that are not CRA communications*—(1) *Timing of contacts with a Federal banking agency.* An oral or written communication with a Federal banking agency is not a CRA communication if it occurred more than 3 years before the parties entered into the agreement.

(2) *Timing of contacts with insured depository institutions and affiliates.* A communication with an insured depository institution or affiliate is not a CRA communication if the communication occurred—

(i) More than 3 years before the parties entered into the agreement, in the case of any written communication;

(ii) More than 3 years before the parties entered into the agreement, in the

Federal Deposit Insurance Corporation § 346.3

case of any oral communication in which the NGEP discusses providing (or refraining from providing) comments or testimony to a Federal banking agency or written comments that must be included in the institution's CRA public file in connection with a request to, or agreement by, the institution or affiliate to take (or refrain from taking) any action that is in fulfillment of the CRA; or

(iii) More than 1 year before the parties entered into the agreement, in the case of any other oral communication not described in paragraph (b)(2)(ii) of this section.

(3) *Knowledge of communication by insured depository institution or affiliate.* (i) A communication is only a CRA communication under paragraph (a) of this section if the insured depository institution or its affiliate has knowledge of the communication under this paragraph (b)(3)(ii) or (b)(3)(iii) of this section.

(ii) *Communication with insured depository institution or affiliate.* An insured depository institution or affiliate has knowledge of a communication by the NGEP to the institution or its affiliate under this paragraph only if one of the following representatives of the insured depository institution or any affiliate has knowledge of the communication—

(A) An employee who approves, directs, authorizes, or negotiates the agreement with the NGEP; or

(B) An employee designated with responsibility for compliance with the CRA or executive officer if the employee or executive officer knows that the institution or affiliate is negotiating, intends to negotiate, or has been informed by the NGEP that it expects to request that the institution or affiliate negotiate an agreement with the NGEP.

(iii) *Other communications.* An insured depository institution or affiliate is deemed to have knowledge of—

(A) Any testimony provided to a Federal banking agency at a public meeting or hearing;

(B) Any comment submitted to a Federal banking agency that is conveyed in writing by the agency to the insured depository institution or affiliate; and

(C) Any written comment submitted to the insured depository institution that must be and is included in the institution's CRA public file.

(4) *Communication where NGEP has knowledge.* A NGEP has a CRA communication with an insured depository institution or affiliate only if any of the following individuals has knowledge of the communication—

(i) A director, employee, or member of the NGEP who approves, directs, authorizes, or negotiates the agreement with the insured depository institution or affiliate;

(ii) A person who functions as an executive officer of the NGEP and who knows that the NGEP is negotiating or intends to negotiate an agreement with the insured depository institution or affiliate; or

(iii) Where the NGEP is an individual, the NGEP.

(c) *Examples of CRA communications—*(1) *Examples of actions that are CRA communications.* The following are examples of CRA communications. These examples are not exclusive and assume that the communication occurs within the relevant time period as described in paragraph (b)(1) or (b)(2) of this section and the appropriate representatives have knowledge of the communication as specified in paragraphs (b)(3) and (b)(4) of this section.

(i) *Example 1.* A NGEP files a written comment with a Federal banking agency that states than an insured depository institution successfully addresses the credit needs of its community. The written comment is in response to a general request from the agency for comments on an application of the insured depository institution to open a new branch and a copy of the comment is provided to the institution.

(ii) *Example 2.* A NGEP meets with an executive officer of an insured depository institution and states that the institution must improve its CRA performance.

(iii) *Example 3.* A NGEP meets with an executive officer of an insured depository institution and states that the institution needs to make more mortgage loans in low- and moderate-income neighborhoods in its community.

§ 346.3

(iv) *Example 4.* A bank holding company files an application with a Federal banking agency to acquire an insured depository institution. Two weeks later, the NGEP meets with an executive officer of the bank holding company to discuss the adequacy of the performance under the CRA of the target insured depository institution. The insured depository institution was an affiliate of the bank holding company at the time the NGEP met with the target institution. (See § 346.11(a).) Accordingly, the NGEP had a CRA communication with an affiliate of the bank holding company.

(2) *Examples of actions that are not CRA communications.* The following are examples of actions that are not by themselves CRA communications. These examples are not exclusive.

(i) *Example 1.* A NGEP provides to a Federal banking agency comments or testimony concerning an insured depository institution or affiliate in response to a direct request by the agency for comments or testimony from that NGEP. Direct requests for comments or testimony do not include a general invitation by a Federal banking agency for comments or testimony from the public in connection with a CRA performance evaluation of, or application for a deposit facility (as defined in section 803 of the CRA (12 U.S.C. 2902(3)) by, an insured depository institution or an application by a company to acquire an insured depository institution.

(ii) *Example 2.* A NGEP makes a statement concerning an insured depository institution or affiliate at a widely attended conference or seminar regarding a general topic. A public or private meeting, public hearing, or other meeting regarding one or more specific institutions, affiliates or transactions involving an application for a deposit facility is not considered a widely attended conference or seminar.

(iii) *Example 3.* A NGEP, such as a civil rights group, community group providing housing and other services in low- and moderate-income neighborhoods, veterans organization, community theater group, or youth organization, sends a fundraising letter to insured depository institutions and to other businesses in its community. The letter encourages all businesses in the community to meet their obligation to assist in making the local community a better place to live and work by supporting the fundraising efforts of the NGEP.

(iv) *Example 4.* A NGEP discusses with an insured depository institution or affiliate whether particular loans, services, investments, community development activities, or other activities are generally eligible for consideration by a Federal banking agency under the CRA. The NGEP and insured depository institution or affiliate do not discuss the adequacy of the CRA performance of the insured depository institution or affiliate.

(v) *Example 5.* A NGEP engaged in the sale or purchase of loans in the secondary market sends a general offering circular to financial institutions offering to sell or purchase a portfolio of loans. An insured depository institution that receives the offering circular discusses with the NGEP the types of loans included in the loan pool, whether such loans are generally eligible for consideration under the CRA, and which loans are made to borrowers in the institution's local community. The NGEP and insured depository institution do not discuss the adequacy of the institution's CRA performance.

(d) *Multiparty covered agreements.* (1) A NGEP that is a party to a covered agreement that involves multiple NGEPs is not required to comply with the requirements of this part if—

(i) The NGEP has not had a CRA communication; and

(ii) No representative of the NGEP identified in paragraph (b)(4) of this section has knowledge at the time of the agreement that another NGEP that is a party to the agreement has had a CRA communication.

(2) An insured depository institution or affiliate that is a party to a covered agreement that involves multiple insured depository institutions or affiliates is not required to comply with the disclosure and annual reporting requirements in §§ 346.6 and 346.7 if—

(i) No NGEP that is a party to the agreement has had a CRA communication concerning the insured depository institution or any affiliate; and

Federal Deposit Insurance Corporation § 346.5

(ii) No representative of the insured depository institution or any affiliate identified in paragraph (b)(3) of this section has knowledge at the time of the agreement that an NGEP that is a party to the agreement has had a CRA communication concerning any other insured depository institution or affiliate that is a party to the agreement.

§ 346.4 Fulfillment of the CRA.

(a) *List of factors that are in fulfillment of the CRA.* Fulfillment of the CRA, for purposes of this part, means the following list of factors—

(1) *Comments to a Federal banking agency or included in CRA public file.* Providing or refraining from providing written or oral comments or testimony to any Federal banking agency concerning the performance under the CRA of an insured depository institution or CRA affiliate that is a party to the agreement or an affiliate of a party to the agreement or written comments that are required to be included in the CRA public file of any such insured depository institution; or

(2) *Activities given favorable CRA consideration.* Performing any of the following activities if the activity is of the type that is likely to receive favorable consideration by a Federal banking agency in evaluating the performance under the CRA of the insured depository institution that is a party to the agreement or an affiliate of a party to the agreement—

(i) Home-purchase, home-improvement, small business, small farm, community development, and consumer lending, as described in 12 CFR 345.22, including loan purchases, loan commitments, and letters of credit;

(ii) Making investments, deposits, or grants, or acquiring membership shares, that have as their primary purpose community development, as described in 12 CFR 345.23;

(iii) Delivering retail banking services, as described in 12 CFR 345.24(d);

(iv) Providing community development services, as described in 12 CFR 345.24(e);

(v) In the case of a wholesale or limited-purpose insured depository institution, community development lending, including originating and purchasing loans and making loan commitments and letters of credit, making qualified investments, or providing community development services, as described in 12 CFR 345.25(c);

(vi) In the case of a small insured depository institution, any lending or other activity described in 12 CFR 345.26(a); or

(vii) In the case of an insured depository institution that is evaluated on the basis of a strategic plan, any element of the strategic plan, as described in 12 CFR 345.27(f).

(b) *Agreements relating to activities of CRA affiliates.* An insured depository institution or affiliate that is a party to a covered agreement that concerns any activity described in paragraph (a) of this section of a CRA affiliate must, prior to the time the agreement is entered into, notify each NGEP that is a party to the agreement that the agreement concerns a CRA affiliate.

§ 346.5 Related agreements considered a single agreement.

The following rules must be applied in determining whether an agreement is a covered agreement under § 346.2.

(a) *Agreements entered into by same parties.* All written agreements to which an insured depository institution or an affiliate of the insured depository institution is a party shall be considered to be a single agreement if the agreements—

(1) Are entered into with the same NGEP;

(2) Were entered into within the same 12-month period; and

(3) Are each in fulfillment of the CRA.

(b) *Substantively related contracts.* All written contracts to which an insured depository institution or an affiliate of the insured depository institution is a party shall be considered to be a single agreement, without regard to whether the other parties to the contracts are the same or whether each such contract is in fulfillment of the CRA, if the contracts were negotiated in a coordinated fashion and a NGEP is a party to each contract.

§ 346.6 Disclosure of covered agreements.

(a) *Applicability date.* This section applies only to covered agreements entered into after November 12, 1999.

(b) *Disclosure of covered agreements to the public*—(1) *Disclosure required.* Each NGEP and each insured depository institution or affiliate that enters into a covered agreement must promptly make a copy of the covered agreement available to any individual or entity upon request.

(2) *Nondisclosure of confidential and proprietary information permitted.* In responding to a request for a covered agreement from any individual or entity under paragraph (b)(1) of this section, a NGEP, insured depository institution, or affiliate may withhold from public disclosure confidential or proprietary information that the party believes the relevant supervisory agency could withhold from disclosure under the Freedom of Information Act (5 U.S.C. 552 et seq.) (FOIA).

(3) *Information that must be disclosed.* Notwithstanding paragraph (b)(2) of this section, a party must disclose any of the following information that is contained in a covered agreement—

(i) The names and addresses of the parties to the agreement;

(ii) The amount of any payments, fees, loans, or other consideration to be made or provided by any party to the agreement;

(iii) Any description of how the funds or other resources provided under the agreement are to be used;

(iv) The term of the agreement (if the agreement establishes a term); and

(v) Any other information that the relevant supervisory agency determines is not properly exempt from public disclosure.

(4) *Request for review of withheld information.* Any individual or entity may request that the relevant supervisory agency review whether any information in a covered agreement withheld by a party must be disclosed. Any requests for agency review of withheld information must be filed, and will be processed in accordance with, the relevant supervisory agency's rules concerning the availability of information (*see* the FDIC's rules regarding Disclosure of Information (12 CFR part 309)).

(5) *Duration of obligation.* The obligation to disclose a covered agreement to the public terminates 12 months after the end of the term of the agreement.

(6) *Reasonable copy and mailing fees.* Each NGEP and each insured depository institution or affiliate may charge an individual or entity that requests a copy of a covered agreement a reasonable fee not to exceed the cost of copying and mailing the agreement.

(7) *Use of CRA public file by insured depository institution or affiliate.* An insured depository institution and any affiliate of an insured depository institution may fulfill its obligation under this paragraph (b) by placing a copy of the covered agreement in the insured depository institution's CRA public file if the institution makes the agreement available in accordance with the procedures set forth in 12 CFR 345.43.

(c) *Disclosure by NGEPs of covered agreements to the relevant supervisory agency*—(1) Each NGEP that is a party to a covered agreement must provide the following within 30 days of receiving a request from the relevant supervisory agency—

(i) A complete copy of the agreement; and

(ii) In the event the NGEP proposes the withholding of any information contained in the agreement in accordance with paragraph (b)(2) of this section, a public version of the agreement that excludes such information and an explanation justifying the exclusions. Any public version must include the information described in paragraph (b)(3) of this section.

(2) The obligation of a NGEP to provide a covered agreement to the relevant supervisory agency terminates 12 months after the end of the term of the covered agreement.

(d) *Disclosure by insured depository institution or affiliate of covered agreements to the relevant supervisory agency*—(1) *In general.* Within 60 days of the end of each calendar quarter, each insured depository institution and affiliate must provide each relevant supervisory agency with—

(i)(A) A complete copy of each covered agreement entered into by the insured depository institution or affiliate during the calendar quarter; and

Federal Deposit Insurance Corporation § 346.7

(B) In the event the institution or affiliate proposes the withholding of any information contained in the agreement in accordance with paragraph (b)(2) of this section, a public version of the agreement that excludes such information (other than any information described in paragraph (b)(3) of this section) and an explanation justifying the exclusions; or

(ii) A list of all covered agreements entered into by the insured depository institution or affiliate during the calendar quarter that contains—

(A) The name and address of each insured depository institution or affiliate that is a party to the agreement;

(B) The name and address of each NGEP that is a party to the agreement;

(C) The date the agreement was entered into;

(D) The estimated total value of all payments, fees, loans and other consideration to be provided by the institution or any affiliate of the institution under the agreement; and

(E) The date the agreement terminates.

(2) *Prompt filing of covered agreements contained in list required.*—(i) If an insured depository institution or affiliate files a list of the covered agreements entered into by the institution or affiliate pursuant to paragraph (d)(1)(ii) of this section, the institution or affiliate must provide any relevant supervisory agency a complete copy and public version of any covered agreement referenced in the list within 7 calendar days of receiving a request from the agency for a copy of the agreement.

(ii) The obligation of an insured depository institution or affiliate to provide a covered agreement to the relevant supervisory agency under this paragraph (d)(2) terminates 36 months after the end of the term of the agreement.

(3) *Joint filings.* In the event that 2 or more insured depository institutions or affiliates are parties to a covered agreement, the insured depository institution(s) and affiliate(s) may jointly file the documents required by this paragraph (d). Any joint filing must identify the insured depository institution(s) and affiliate(s) for whom the filings are being made.

§ 346.7 **Annual reports.**

(a) *Applicability date.* This section applies only to covered agreements entered into on or after May 12, 2000.

(b) *Annual report required.* Each NGEP and each insured depository institution or affiliate that is a party to a covered agreement must file an annual report with each relevant supervisory agency concerning the disbursement, receipt, and uses of funds or other resources under the covered agreement.

(c) *Duration of reporting requirement—*(1) *NGEPs.* A NGEP must file an annual report for a covered agreement for any fiscal year in which the NGEP receives or uses funds or other resources under the agreement.

(2) *Insured depository institutions and affiliates.* An insured depository institution or affiliate must file an annual report for a covered agreement for any fiscal year in which the institution or affiliate—

(i) provides or receives any payments, fees, or loans under the covered agreement that must be reported under paragraphs (e)(1)(iii) and (iv) of this section; or

(ii) has data to report on loans, investments, and services provided by a party to the covered agreement under the covered agreement under paragraph (e)(1)(vi) of this section.

(d) *Annual reports filed by NGEP—*(1) *Contents of report.* The annual report filed by a NGEP under this section must include the following—

(i) The name and mailing address of the NGEP filing the report;

(ii) Information sufficient to identify the covered agreement for which the annual report is being filed, such as by providing the names of the parties to the agreement and the date the agreement was entered into or by providing a copy of the agreement;

(iii) The amount of funds or resources received under the covered agreement during the fiscal year; and

(iv) A detailed, itemized list of how any funds or resources received by the NGEP under the covered agreement were used during the fiscal year, including the total amount used for—

(A) Compensation of officers, directors, and employees;

(B) Administrative expenses;

§ 346.7

(C) Travel expenses;
(D) Entertainment expenses;
(E) Payment of consulting and professional fees; and
(F) Other expenses and uses (specify expense or use).

(2) *More detailed reporting of uses of funds or resources permitted*—(i) *In general.* If a NGEP allocated and used funds received under a covered agreement for a specific purpose, the NGEP may fulfill the requirements of paragraph (d)(1)(iv) of this section with respect to such funds by providing—

(A) A brief description of each specific purpose for which the funds or other resources were used; and
(B) The amount of funds or resources used during the fiscal year for each specific purpose.

(ii) *Specific purpose defined.* A NGEP allocates and uses funds for a specific purpose if the NGEP receives and uses the funds for a purpose that is more specific and limited than the categories listed in paragraph (d)(1)(iv) of this section.

(3) *Use of other reports.* The annual report filed by a NGEP may consist of or incorporate a report prepared for any other purpose, such as the Internal Revenue Service Return of Organization Exempt From Income Tax on Form 990, or any other Internal Revenue Service form, state tax form, report to members or shareholders, audited or unaudited financial statements, audit report, or other report, so long as the annual report filed by the NGEP contains all of the information required by this paragraph (d).

(4) *Consolidated reports permitted.* A NGEP that is a party to 2 or more covered agreements may file with each relevant supervisory agency a single consolidated annual report covering all the covered agreements. Any consolidated report must contain all the information required by this paragraph (d). The information reported under paragraphs (d)(1)(iv) and (d)(2) of this section may be reported on an aggregate basis for all covered agreements.

(5) *Examples of annual report requirements for NGEPs*—(i) *Example 1.* A NGEP receives an unrestricted grant of $15,000 under a covered agreement, includes the funds in its general operating budget, and uses the funds during its fiscal year. The NGEP's annual report for the fiscal year must provide the name and mailing address of the NGEP, information sufficient to identify the covered agreement, and state that the NGEP received $15,000 during the fiscal year. The report must also indicate the total expenditures made by the NGEP during the fiscal year for compensation, administrative expenses, travel expenses, entertainment expenses, consulting and professional fees, and other expenses and uses. The NGEP's annual report may provide this information by submitting an Internal Revenue Service Form 990 that includes the required information. If the Internal Revenue Service Form does not include information for all of the required categories listed in this part, the NGEP must report the total expenditures in the remaining categories either by providing that information directly or by providing another form or report that includes the required information.

(ii) *Example 2.* An organization receives $15,000 from an insured depository institution under a covered agreement and allocates and uses the $15,000 during the fiscal year to purchase computer equipment to support its functions. The organization's annual report must include the name and address of the organization, information sufficient to identify the agreement, and a statement that the organization received $15,000 during the year. In addition, since the organization allocated and used the funds for a specific purpose that is more narrow and limited than the categories of expenses included in the detailed, itemized list of expenses, the organization would have the option of providing either the total amount it used during the year for each category of expenses included in paragraph (d)(1)(iv) of this section, or a statement that it used the $15,000 to purchase computer equipment and a brief description of the equipment purchased.

(iii) *Example 3.* A community group receives $50,000 from an insured depository institution under a covered agreement. During its fiscal year, the community group specifically allocates and uses $5,000 of the funds to pay for a particular business trip and uses the remaining $45,000 for general operating

Federal Deposit Insurance Corporation

§ 346.7

expenses. The group's annual report for the fiscal year must include the name and address of the group, information sufficient to identify the agreement, and a statement that the group received $50,000. Because the group did not allocate and use all of the funds for a specific purpose, the group's annual report must provide the total amount of funds it used during the year for each category of expenses included in paragraph (d)(1)(iv) of this section. The group's annual report also could state that it used $5,000 for a particular business trip and include a brief description of the trip.

(iv) *Example 4.* A community development organization is a party to two separate covered agreements with two unaffiliated insured depository institutions. Under each agreement, the organization receives $15,000 during its fiscal year and uses the funds to support its activities during that year. If the organization elects to file a consolidated annual report, the consolidated report must identify the organization and the two covered agreements, state that the organization received $15,000 during the fiscal year under each agreement, and provide the total amount that the organization used during the year for each category of expenses included in paragraph (d)(1)(iv) of this section.

(e) *Annual report filed by insured depository institution or affiliate*—(1) *General.* The annual report filed by an insured depository institution or affiliate must include the following—

(i) The name and principal place of business of the insured depository institution or affiliate filing the report;

(ii) Information sufficient to identify the covered agreement for which the annual report is being filed, such as by providing the names of the parties to the agreement and the date the agreement was entered into or by providing a copy of the agreement;

(iii) The aggregate amount of payments, aggregate amount of fees, and aggregate amount of loans provided by the insured depository institution or affiliate under the covered agreement to any other party to the agreement during the fiscal year;

(iv) The aggregate amount of payments, aggregate amount of fees, and aggregate amount of loans received by the insured depository institution or affiliate under the covered agreement from any other party to the agreement during the fiscal year;

(v) A general description of the terms and conditions of any payments, fees, or loans reported under paragraphs (e)(1)(iii) and (iv) of this section, or, in the event such terms and conditions are set forth—

(A) In the covered agreement, a statement identifying the covered agreement and the date the agreement (or a list identifying the agreement) was filed with the relevant supervisory agency; or

(B) In a previous annual report filed by the insured depository institution or affiliate, a statement identifying the date the report was filed with the relevant supervisory agency; and

(vi) The aggregate amount and number of loans, aggregate amount and number of investments, and aggregate amount of services provided under the covered agreement to any individual or entity not a party to the agreement—

(A) By the insured depository institution or affiliate during its fiscal year; and

(B) By any other party to the agreement, unless such information is not known to the insured depository institution or affiliate filing the report or such information is or will be contained in the annual report filed by another party under this section.

(2) *Consolidated reports permitted*—(i) *Party to multiple agreements.* An insured depository institution or affiliate that is a party to 2 or more covered agreements may file a single consolidated annual report with each relevant supervisory agency concerning all the covered agreements.

(ii) *Affiliated entities party to the same agreement.* An insured depository institution and its affiliates that are parties to the same covered agreement may file a single consolidated annual report relating to the agreement with each relevant supervisory agency for the covered agreement.

(iii) *Content of report.* Any consolidated annual report must contain all the information required by this paragraph (e). The amounts and data required to be reported under paragraphs (e)(1)(iv) and (vi) of this section may be reported on an aggregate basis for all covered agreements.

(f) *Time and place of filing*—(1) *General.* Each party must file its annual report with each relevant supervisory agency for the covered agreement no later than six months following the end of the fiscal year covered by the report.

(2) *Alternative method of fulfilling annual reporting requirement for a NGEP.* (i) A NGEP may fulfill the filing requirements of this section by providing the following materials to an insured depository institution or affiliate that is a party to the agreement no later than six months following the end of the NGEP's fiscal year—

(A) A copy of the NGEP's annual report required under paragraph (d) of this section for the fiscal year; and

(B) Written instructions that the insured depository institution or affiliate promptly forward the annual report to the relevant supervisory agency or agencies on behalf of the NGEP.

(ii) An insured depository institution or affiliate that receives an annual report from a NGEP pursuant to paragraph (f)(2)(i) of this section must file the report with the relevant supervisory agency or agencies on behalf of the NGEP within 30 days.

§ 346.8 Release of information under FOIA.

The FDIC will make covered agreements and annual reports available to the public in accordance with the Freedom of Information Act (5 U.S.C. 552 *et seq.*) and the FDIC's rules regarding Disclosure of Information (12 CFR part 309). A party to a covered agreement may request confidential treatment of proprietary and confidential information in a covered agreement or an annual report under those procedures.

§ 346.9 Compliance provisions.

(a) *Willful failure to comply with disclosure and reporting obligations.* (1) If the FDIC determines that a NGEP has willfully failed to comply in a material way with §§ 346.6 or 346.7, the FDIC will notify the NGEP in writing of that determination and provide the NGEP a period of 90 days (or such longer period as the FDIC finds to be reasonable under the circumstances) to comply.

(2) If the NGEP does not comply within the time period established by the FDIC, the agreement shall thereafter be unenforceable by that NGEP by operation of section 48 of the Federal Deposit Insurance Act (12 U.S.C. 1831y).

(3) The FDIC may assist any insured depository institution or affiliate that is a party to a covered agreement that is unenforceable by a NGEP by operation of section 48 of the Federal Deposit Insurance Act (12 U.S.C. 1831y) in identifying a successor to assume the NGEP's responsibilities under the agreement.

(b) *Diversion of funds.* If a court or other body of competent jurisdiction determines that funds or resources received under a covered agreement have been diverted contrary to the purposes of the covered agreement for an individual's personal financial gain, the FDIC may take either or both of the following actions—

(1) Order the individual to disgorge the diverted funds or resources received under the agreement;

(2) Prohibit the individual from being a party to any covered agreement for a period not to exceed 10 years.

(c) *Notice and opportunity to respond.* Before making a determination under paragraph (a)(1) of this section, or taking any action under paragraph (b) of this section, the FDIC will provide written notice and an opportunity to present information to the FDIC concerning any relevant facts or circumstances relating to the matter.

(d) *Inadvertent or de minimis errors.* Inadvertent or de minimis errors in annual reports or other documents filed with the FDIC under §§ 346.6 or 346.7 will not subject the reporting party to any penalty.

(e) *Enforcement of provisions in covered agreements.* No provision of this part shall be construed as authorizing the FDIC to enforce the provisions of any covered agreement.

[66 FR 2099, Jan. 10, 2001, as amended at 66 FR 14071, Mar. 9, 2001]

§ 346.10 Transition provisions.

(a) *Disclosure of covered agreements entered into before the effective date of this part.* The following disclosure requirements apply to covered agreements

Federal Deposit Insurance Corporation § 346.11

that were entered into after November 12, 1999, and that terminated before April 1, 2001.

(1) *Disclosure to the public.* Each NGEP and each insured depository institution or affiliate that was a party to the agreement must make the agreement available to the public under § 346.6 until at least April 1, 2002.

(2) *Disclosure to the relevant supervisory agency.* (i) Each NGEP that was a party to the agreement must make the agreement available to the relevant supervisory agency under § 346.6 until at least April 1, 2002.

(ii) Each insured depository institution or affiliate that was a party to the agreement must, by June 30, 2001, provide each relevant supervisory agency either—

(A) A copy of the agreement under § 346.6(d)(1)(i); or

(B) The information described in § 346.6(d)(1)(ii) for each agreement.

(b) *Filing of annual reports that relate to fiscal years ending on or before December 31, 2000.* In the event that a NGEP, insured depository institution or affiliate has any information to report under § 346.7 for a fiscal year that ends on or before December 31, 2000, and that concerns a covered agreement entered into between May 12, 2000, and December 31, 2000, the annual report for that fiscal year must be provided no later than June 30, 2001, to—

(1) Each relevant supervisory agency; or

(2) In the case of a NGEP, to an insured depository institution or affiliate that is a party to the agreement in accordance with § 346.7(f)(2).

§ 346.11 Other definitions and rules of construction used in this part.

(a) *Affiliate.* "Affiliate" means—

(1) Any company that controls, is controlled by, or is under common control with another company; and

(2) For the purpose of determining whether an agreement is a covered agreement under § 346.2, an "affiliate" includes any company that would be under common control or merged with another company on consummation of any transaction pending before a Federal banking agency at the time—

(i) The parties enter into the agreement; and

(ii) The NGEP that is a party to the agreement makes a CRA communication, as described in § 346.3.

(b) *Control.* "Control" is defined in section 2(a) of the Bank Holding Company Act (12 U.S.C. 1841(a)).

(c) *CRA affiliate.* A "CRA affiliate" of an insured depository institution is any company that is an affiliate of an insured depository institution to the extent, and only to the extent, that the activities of the affiliate were considered by the appropriate Federal banking agency when evaluating the CRA performance of the institution at its most recent CRA examination prior to the agreement. An insured depository institution or affiliate also may designate any company as a CRA affiliate at any time prior to the time a covered agreement is entered into by informing the NGEP that is a party to the agreement of such designation.

(d) *CRA public file.* "CRA public file" means the public file maintained by an insured depository institution and described in 12 CFR 345.43.

(e) *Executive officer.* The term "executive officer" has the same meaning as in § 215.2(e)(1) of the Board of Governors of the Federal Reserve System's Regulation O (12 CFR 215.2(e)(1)).

(f) *Federal banking agency; appropriate Federal banking agency.* The terms "Federal banking agency" and "appropriate Federal banking agency" have the same meanings as in section 3 of the Federal Deposit Insurance Act (12 U.S.C. 1813).

(g) *Fiscal year.* (1) The fiscal year for a NGEP that does not have a fiscal year shall be the calendar year.

(2) Any NGEP, insured depository institution, or affiliate that has a fiscal year may elect to have the calendar year be its fiscal year for purposes of this part.

(h) *Insured depository institution.* "Insured depository institution" has the same meaning as in section 3 of the Federal Deposit Insurance Act (12 U.S.C. 1813).

(i) *NGEP.* "NGEP" means a nongovernmental entity or person.

(j) *Nongovernmental entity or person*—
(1) *General.* A "nongovernmental entity or person" is any partnership, association, trust, joint venture, joint stock company, corporation, limited liability

corporation, company, firm, society, other organization, or individual.

(2) *Exclusions.* A nongovernmental entity or person does not include—

(i) The United States government, a state government, a unit of local government (including a county, city, town, township, parish, village, or other general-purpose subdivision of a state) or an Indian tribe or tribal organization established under Federal, state or Indian tribal law (including the Department of Hawaiian Home Lands), or a department, agency, or instrumentality of any such entity;

(ii) A federally-chartered public corporation that receives Federal funds appropriated specifically for that corporation;

(iii) An insured depository institution or affiliate of an insured depository institution; or

(iv) An officer, director, employee, or representative (acting in his or her capacity as an officer, director, employee, or representative) of an entity listed in paragraphs (j)(2)(i) through (iii) of this section.

(k) *Party.* The term "party". The authority citation for part 405 continues to read as follows: with respect to a covered agreement means each NGEP and each insured depository institution or affiliate that entered into the agreement.

(l) *Relevant supervisory agency.* The "relevant supervisory agency" for a covered agreement means the appropriate Federal banking agency for—

(1) Each insured depository institution (or subsidiary thereof) that is a party to the covered agreement;

(2) Each insured depository institution (or subsidiary thereof) or CRA affiliate that makes payments or loans or provides services that are subject to the covered agreement; and

(3) Any company (other than an insured depository institution or subsidiary thereof) that is a party to the covered agreement.

(m) *Term of agreement.* An agreement that does not have a fixed termination date is considered to terminate on the last date on which any party to the agreement makes any payment or provides any loan or other resources under the agreement, unless the relevant supervisory agency for the agreement otherwise notifies each party in writing.

[66 FR 2099, Jan. 10, 2001, as amended at 66 FR 14071, Mar. 9, 2001]

PART 347—INTERNATIONAL BANKING

Subpart A—Foreign Banking and Investment by Insured State Nonmember Banks

Sec.
347.101　Authority, purpose, and scope.
347.102　Definitions.
347.103　Effect of state law on actions taken under this subpart.
347.104　Insured state nonmember bank investment in foreign organizations.
347.105　Permissible financial activities outside the United States.
347.106　Going concerns.
347.107　Joint ventures.
347.108　Portfolio investments.
347.109　Limitations on indirect investments in nonfinancial organizations.
347.110　Affiliate holdings.
347.111　Underwriting and dealing limits applicable to foreign organizations held by insured state nonmember banks.
347.112　Restrictions applicable to foreign organizations that act as futures commission merchants.
347.113　Restrictions applicable to activities by a foreign organization in the United States.
347.114　Extensions of credit to foreign organizations held by insured state nonmember banks; shares of foreign organizations held in connection with debts previously contracted.
347.115　Permissible activities for a foreign branch of an insured state nonmember bank.
347.116　Recordkeeping and supervision of the foreign activities of insured state nonmember banks.
347.117　General consent.
347.118　Expedited processing.
347.119　Specific consent.
347.120　Computation of investment amounts.
347.121　Requirements for insured state nonmember bank to close a foreign branch.
347.122　Limitations applicable to the authority provided in this subpart.

Subpart B—Foreign Banks

347.201　Authority, purpose, and scope.
347.202　Definitions.
347.203　Deposit insurance required for all branches of foreign banks engaged in domestic retail deposit activity in the same state.

Federal Deposit Insurance Corporation

§ 347.102

347.204 Commitment to be examined and provide information.
347.205 Record maintenance.
347.206 Domestic retail deposit activity requiring deposit insurance by U.S. branch of a foreign bank.
347.207 Disclosure of supervisory information to foreign supervisors.
347.208 Assessment base deductions by insured branch.
347.209 Pledge of assets.
347.210 Asset maintenance.
347.211 Examination of branches of foreign banks.
347.212 FDIC approval to conduct activities that are not permissible for federal branches.
347.213 Establishment or operation of non-insured foreign branch.
347.214 Branch established under section 5 of the International Banking Act.
347.215 Exemptions from deposit insurance requirement.
347.216 Depositor notification.

Subpart C—International Lending

347.301 Purpose, authority, and scope.
347.302 Definitions.
347.303 Allocated transfer risk reserve.
347.304 Accounting for fees on international loans.
347.305 Reporting and disclosure of international assets.

AUTHORITY: 12 U.S.C. 1813, 1815, 1817, 1819, 1820, 1828, 3103, 3104, 3105, 3108, 3109; Title IX, Pub. L. 98–181, 97 Stat. 1153.

SOURCE: 70 FR 17560, Apr. 6, 2005; 70 FR 20704, April 21, 2005, unless otherwise noted.

§ 347.101 Authority, purpose, and scope.

(a) This subpart is issued pursuant to section 18(d) and (*l*) of the Federal Deposit Insurance Act (12 U.S.C. 1828(d), 1828(*l*)).

(b) The rules in subpart A address the FDIC's requirements for insured state nonmember bank investments in foreign organizations, permissible foreign financial activities, loans or extensions of credit to or for the account of foreign organizations, and the FDIC's recordkeeping, supervision, and approval requirements. The rules also address the permissible activities for foreign branches of insured state nonmember banks, as well as the FDIC's requirements for establishing, operating, relocating and closing of branches in foreign countries.

§ 347.102 Definitions.

For the purposes of this subpart:

(a) An affiliate of an insured state nonmember bank means:

(1) Any entity of which the insured state nonmember bank is a direct or indirect subsidiary or which otherwise controls the insured state nonmember bank;

(2) Any organization which is a direct or indirect subsidiary of such entity or which is otherwise controlled by such entity; or

(3) Any other organization that is a direct or indirect subsidiary of the insured state nonmember bank or is otherwise controlled by the insured state nonmember bank.

(b) Control means the ability to control in any manner the election of a majority of an organization's directors or trustees; or the ability to exercise a controlling influence over the management and policies of an organization. An insured state nonmember bank is deemed to control an organization of which it is a general partner or its affiliate is a general partner.

(c) Domestic means United States.

(d) Eligible insured state nonmember bank means an eligible depository institution as defined in § 303.2(r) of this chapter.

(e) Equity interest means any ownership interest or rights in an organization, whether through an equity security, contribution to capital, general or limited partnership interest, debt or warrants convertible into ownership interests or rights, loans providing profit participation, binding commitments to acquire any such items, or some other form of business transaction.

(f) Equity security means voting or nonvoting shares, stock, investment contracts, or other interests representing ownership or participation in a company or similar enterprise, as well as any instrument convertible to any such interest at the option of the holder without payment of substantial additional consideration.

(g) FRB means the Board of Governors of the Federal Reserve System.

(h) Foreign bank means an organization that is organized under the laws of a foreign country, a territory of the United States, Puerto Rico, Guam,

American Samoa, or the Virgin Islands that:

(1) Is recognized as a bank by the bank supervisory or monetary authority of the country of its organization or the country in which its principal banking operations are located;

(2) Receives deposits to a substantial extent in the regular course of its business; and

(3) Has the power to accept demand deposits.

(i) *Foreign banking organization* means a foreign organization that is formed for the sole purpose of either holding shares of a foreign bank or performing nominee, fiduciary, or other banking services incidental to the activities of a foreign branch or foreign bank affiliate of the insured state nonmember bank.

(j) *Foreign branch* means an office or place of business located outside the United States, its territories, Puerto Rico, Guam, American Samoa, the Trust Territory of the Pacific Islands, or the Virgin Islands, at which banking operations are conducted, but does not include a representative office.

(k) *Foreign country* means any country other than the United States and includes any territory, dependency, or possession of any such country or of the United States.

(l) *Foreign organization* means an organization that is organized under the laws of a foreign country.

(m) *Insured state nonmember bank or bank* means a state bank, as defined by §3(a)(2) of the Federal Deposit Insurance Act (12 U.S.C. 1813(a)(2)), whose deposits are insured by the FDIC and that is not a member of the Federal Reserve System.

(n) *Indirectly* means investments held or activities conducted by a subsidiary of an organization.

(o) *Investment grade* means a security that is rated in one of the four highest categories by:

(1) Two or more NRSROs; or

(2) One NRSRO if the security is rated by only one NRSRO.

(p) *Loan or extension of credit* means all direct and indirect advances of funds to a person, government, or entity made on the basis of any obligation of that person, government, or entity to repay funds.

(q) *Organization or entity* means a corporation, partnership, association, bank, or other similar entity.

(r) *NRSRO* means a nationally recognized statistical rating organization as designated by the Securities and Exchange Commission.

(s) *Representative office* means an office that engages solely in representative functions such as soliciting new business for its home office or acting as liaison between the home office and local customers, but which has no authority to make business or contracting decisions other than those relating to the personnel and premises of the representative office.

(t) *Subsidiary* means any organization more than 50 percent of the voting equity interests of which are directly or indirectly held by another organization.

(u) *Tier 1 capital* means Tier 1 capital as defined in §325.2 of this chapter.

(v) *Well capitalized* means well capitalized as defined in §325.103 of this chapter.

§347.103 Effect of state law on actions taken under this subpart.

A bank may acquire and retain equity interests in a foreign organization or establish a foreign branch, subject to the requirements of this subpart, if it is authorized to do so by the law of the state in which the bank is chartered.

§347.104 Insured state nonmember bank investments in foreign organizations.

(a) *Investment in foreign banks or foreign banking organizations.* A bank may directly or indirectly acquire and retain equity interests in a foreign bank or foreign banking organization.

(b) *Investment in other foreign organizations.* A bank may only:

(1) acquire and retain equity interests in foreign organizations, other than foreign banks or foreign banking organizations in amounts of 50 percent or less of the foreign organization's voting equity interests, if the equity interest is held through a domestic or foreign subsidiary; and

(2) The bank meets its minimum capital requirements.

Federal Deposit Insurance Corporation § 347.105

§ 347.105 Permissible financial activities outside the United States.

(a) *Limitation on authorized activities.* A bank may not directly or indirectly acquire or hold equity interests in a foreign organization that will result in the bank and its affiliates:

(1) Holding more than 50 percent, in the aggregate, of the voting equity interest in such foreign organization; or

(2) Controlling such foreign organization, unless the activities of a foreign organization are limited to those authorized under paragraph (b) of this section.

(b) *Authorized activities.* The following financial activities are authorized outside the United States:

(1) Commercial and other banking activities.

(2) Financing, including commercial financing, consumer financing, mortgage banking, and factoring, subject to compliance with any attendant restrictions contained in 12 CFR 225.28(b).

(3) Leasing real or personal property, acting as agent, broker or advisor in leasing real or personal property, subject to compliance with any attendant restrictions in 12 CFR 225.28(b).

(4) Acting as a fiduciary, subject to compliance with any attendant restrictions in 12 CFR 225.28(b).

(5) Underwriting credit life, credit accident and credit health insurance.

(6) Performing services for other direct or indirect operations of a domestic banking organization, including representative functions, sale of long-term debt, name saving, liquidating assets acquired to prevent loss on a debt previously contracted in good faith, and other activities that are permissible for a bank holding company under sections 4(a)(2)(A) and 4(c)(1)(C) of the Bank Holding Company Act.

(7) Holding the premises of a branch of an Edge corporation or insured state nonmember bank or the premises of a direct or indirect subsidiary, or holding or leasing the residence of an officer or employee of a branch or a subsidiary.

(8) Providing investment, financial, or economic services, subject to compliance with any attendant restrictions in 12 CFR 225.28(b).

(9) General insurance agency and brokerage.

(10) Data processing.

(11) Organizing, sponsoring, and managing a mutual fund if the fund's shares are not sold or distributed in the United States or to U.S. residents and the fund does not exercise management control over the firms in which it invests.

(12) Performing management consulting services, provided that such services when rendered with respect to the domestic market must be restricted to the initial entry.

(13) Underwriting, distributing, and dealing in debt securities outside the United States.

(14) With the prior approval of the FDIC under section 347.119(d), underwriting, distributing, and dealing in equity securities outside the United States.

(15) Operating a travel agency in connection with financial services offered outside the United States by the bank or others.

(16) Providing futures commission merchant services, subject to compliance with any attendant restrictions in 12 CFR 225.28(b).

(17) Engaging in activities that the FRB has determined in Regulation Y (12 CFR 225.28(b)) are closely related to banking under section 4(c)(8) of the Bank Holding Company Act.

(18) Engaging in other activities, with the prior approval of the FDIC.

(c) *Limitation on activities authorized under Regulation Y.* If a bank relies solely on the cross-reference to Regulation Y contained in paragraph (b)(17) of this section as authority to engage in an activity, compliance with any attendant restrictions on the activity that are contained in 12 CFR 225.28(b) is required.

(d) *Approval of other activities.* Activities that are not specifically authorized by this section, but that are authorized by 12 CFR 211.10 or FRB interpretations of activities authorized by that section, may be authorized by specific consent of the FDIC on an individual basis and upon such terms and conditions as the FDIC may consider appropriate. Activities that will be engaged in as principal (defined by reference to section 362.1(b) of this chapter), and that are not authorized by 12 CFR 211.10 or FRB interpretations of

§ 347.106

activities authorized under that section, must satisfy the requirements of part 362 of this chapter and be approved by the FDIC under this part as well as part 362 of this chapter.

§ 347.106 Going concerns.

Going concerns. If a bank acquires an equity interest in a foreign organization that is a going concern, no more than 5 percent of either the consolidated assets or revenues of the foreign organization may be attributable to activities that are not permissible under § 347.105(b).

§ 347.107 Joint ventures.

(a) *Joint ventures.* If a bank, directly or indirectly, acquires or holds an equity interest in a foreign organization that is a joint venture, and the bank or its affiliates do not control the foreign organization, no more than 10 percent of either the consolidated assets or revenues of the foreign organization may be attributable to activities that are not permissible under § 347.105(b).

(b) *Joint venture defined.* For purposes of this section, the term "joint venture" means any organization in which 20 percent or more but not in excess of 50 percent of the voting equity interests, in the aggregate, are directly or indirectly held by a bank or its affiliates.

§ 347.108 Portfolio investments.

(a) *Portfolio investments.* If a bank, directly or indirectly, acquires or holds an equity interest in a foreign organization as a portfolio investment and the foreign organization is not controlled, directly or indirectly, by the bank or its affiliates:

(1) No more than 10 percent of either the consolidated assets or revenues of the foreign organization may be attributable to activities that are not permissible under § 347.105(b); and

(2) Any loans or extensions of credit made by the bank and its affiliates to the foreign organization must be on substantially the same terms, including interest rates and collateral, as those prevailing at the same time for comparable transactions between the bank or its affiliates and nonaffiliated organizations.

(b) *Portfolio investment defined.* For purposes of this section, the term "portfolio investment" means an investment in an organization in which less than 20 percent of the voting equity interests, in the aggregate, are directly or indirectly held by a bank or its affiliates.

§ 347.109 Limitations on indirect investments in nonfinancial foreign organizations.

(a) A bank may, through a subsidiary authorized by §§ 347.105 or 347.106, or an Edge corporation if also authorized by the FRB, acquire and hold equity interests in foreign organizations that are not foreign banks or foreign banking organizations and that engage generally in activities beyond those listed in § 347.105(b), subject to the following:

(1) The amount of the investment does not exceed 15 percent of the bank's Tier 1 capital;

(2) The aggregate holding of voting equity interests of one foreign organization by the bank and its affiliates must be less than:

(i) 20 percent of the foreign organization's voting equity interests; and

(ii) 40 percent of the foreign organization's voting and nonvoting equity interests;

(b) The bank or its affiliates must not otherwise control the foreign organization; and

(c) Loans or extensions of credit made by the bank and its affiliates to the foreign organization must be on substantially the same terms, including interest rates and collateral, as those prevailing at the same time for comparable transactions between the bank or its affiliates and nonaffiliated organizations.

§ 347.110 Affiliate holdings.

References in §§ 347.107, 347.108, and 347.109 to equity interests of foreign organizations held by an affiliate of a bank include equity interests held in connection with an underwriting or for distribution or dealing by an affiliate permitted to do so by §§ 362.8 or 362.18 of this chapter or section 4(c)(8) of the Bank Holding Company Act (12 U.S.C. 1843(c)(8)).

§ 347.111 Underwriting and dealing limits applicable to foreign organizations held by insured state nonmember banks.

A bank that holds an equity interest in one or more foreign organizations which underwrite, deal, or distribute equity securities outside the United States as authorized by § 347.105(b)(14) is subject to the following limitations:

(a) *Underwriting commitment limits.* (1) The aggregate underwriting commitments by the foreign organizations for the equity securities of a single entity, taken together with underwriting commitments by any affiliate of the bank under the authority of 12 CFR 211.10(b), may not exceed the lesser of $60 million or 25 percent of the bank's Tier 1 capital, except as otherwise provided in this paragraph.

(2) Underwriting commitments in excess of this limit must be either:

(i) Covered by binding commitments from subunderwriters or purchasers; or

(ii) Deducted from the capital of the bank, with at least 50 percent of the deduction being taken from Tier 1 capital, with the bank remaining well capitalized after this deduction.

(b) *Distribution and dealing limits.* The equity securities of any single entity held for distribution or dealing by the foreign organizations, taken together with equity securities held for distribution or dealing by any affiliate of the bank under the authority of 12 CFR 211.10:

(1) May not exceed the lesser of $30 million or 5 percent of the bank's Tier 1 capital, subject to the following:

(i) Any equity securities acquired pursuant to any underwriting commitment extending up to 90 days after the payment date for the underwriting may be excluded from this limit;

(ii) Any equity securities of the entity held under the authority of §§ 347.105 through 347.109 or 12 CFR 211.10 for purposes other than distribution or dealing must be included in this limit; and

(iii) Up to 75 percent of the position in an equity security may be reduced by netting long and short positions in the same security, or offsetting cash positions against derivative instruments referenced to the same security so long as the derivatives are part of a prudent hedging strategy; and

(2) Must be included in calculating the general consent limits under § 347.117(b)(3) if the bank relies on the general consent provisions as authority to acquire equity interests of the same foreign entity for investment or trading.

(c) *Additional distribution and dealing limits.* With the exception of equity securities acquired pursuant to any underwriting commitment extending up to 90 days after the payment date for the underwriting, equity securities of a single entity held for distribution or dealing by all affiliates of the bank (this includes shares held in connection with an underwriting or for distribution or dealing by an affiliate permitted to do so by §§ 362.8 or 362.18 of this chapter or section 4(c)(8) of the Bank Holding Company Act), combined with any equity interests held for investment or trading purposes by all affiliates of the bank, must conform to the limits of §§ 347.105 through 347.109.

(d) Combined limits. The aggregate of the following may not exceed 25 percent of the bank's Tier 1 capital:

(1) All equity interests of foreign organizations held for investment or trading under § 347.109 or by an affiliate of the bank under the corresponding paragraph of 12 CFR 211.10.

(2) All underwriting commitments under paragraph (a) of this section, taken together with all underwriting commitments by any affiliate of the bank under the authority of 12 CFR 211.10, after excluding the amount of any underwriting commitment:

(i) Covered by binding commitments from subunderwriters or purchasers under paragraph (a)(1) of this section or the comparable provision of 12 CFR 211.10; or

(ii) Already deducted from the bank's capital under paragraph (a)(2) of this section, or the appropriate affiliate's capital under the comparable provisions of 12 CFR 211.10; and

(3) All equity securities held for distribution or dealing under paragraph (b) of this section, taken together with all equity securities held for distribution or dealing by any affiliate of the bank under the authority of 12 CFR 211.10, after reducing by up to 75 percent the position in any equity security by netting and offset, as permitted

§ 347.112

by paragraph (b)(1)(iii) of this section or the comparable provision of 12 CFR 211.10.

§ 347.112 Restrictions applicable to foreign organizations that act as futures commission merchants.

(a) If a bank acquires or retains an equity interest in a foreign organization that acts as a futures commission merchant pursuant to § 347.105(b)(16), the foreign organization may not be a member of an exchange or clearing association that requires members to guarantee or otherwise contract to cover losses suffered by other members unless the:

(1) Foreign organization's liability does not exceed two percent of the bank's Tier 1 capital, or

(2) Bank has obtained the prior approval of the FDIC under § 347.120(d).

(b) [Reserved]

§ 347.113 Restrictions applicable to activities by a foreign organization in the United States.

(a) A bank, acting under the authority provided in this subpart, may not directly or indirectly hold:

(1) Equity interests of any foreign organization that engages in the general business of buying or selling goods, wares, merchandise, or commodities in the United States; or

(2) More than 5 percent of the equity interests of any foreign organization that engages in activities in the United States unless any activities in which the foreign organization engages in the United States are incidental to its international or foreign business.

(b) For purposes of this section:

(1) A foreign organization is not engaged in any business or activities in the United States unless it maintains an office in the United States other than a representative office.

(2) The following activities are incidental to international or foreign business:

(i) Activities that are permissible for an Edge corporation in the United States under 12 CFR 211.6; or

(ii) Other activities approved by the FDIC.

§ 347.114 Extensions of credit to foreign organizations held by insured state nonmember banks; shares of foreign organizations held in connection with debts previously contracted.

(a) *Loans or extensions of credit.* A bank that directly or indirectly holds equity interests in a foreign organization pursuant to the authority of this subpart may make loans or extensions of credit to or for the accounts of the organization without regard to the provisions of section 18(j) of the FDI Act (12 U.S.C. 1828(j)).

(b) *Debts previously contracted.* Equity interests acquired to prevent a loss upon a debt previously contracted in good faith are not subject to the limitations or procedures of this subpart; however, they must be disposed of promptly but in no event later than two years after their acquisition, unless the FDIC authorizes retention for a longer period.

§ 347.115 Permissible activities for a foreign branch of an insured state nonmember bank.

In addition to its general banking powers and if permitted by the law of the state in which the bank is chartered, a foreign branch of a bank may conduct the following activities to the extent that they are consistent with banking practices in a foreign country where the bank maintains a branch:

(a) *Guarantees.* Guarantee debts, or otherwise agree to make payments on the occurrence of readily ascertainable events including, without limitation, nonpayment of taxes, rentals, customs duties, or costs of transport and loss or nonconformance of shipping documents, if:

(1) The guarantee or agreement specifies a maximum monetary liability; and

(2) To the extent the guarantee or agreement is not subject to a separate amount limit under state or federal law, the amount of the guarantee or agreement is combined with loans and other obligations for purposes of applying any legal lending limits.

(b) *Government obligations.* Engage in the following types of transactions

Federal Deposit Insurance Corporation § 347.116

with respect to the obligations of foreign countries, so long as aggregate investments, securities held in connection with distribution and dealing, and underwriting commitments do not exceed ten percent of the bank's Tier 1 capital:

(1) Underwrite, distribute and deal, invest in, or trade obligations of:

(i) The national government of the country in which the branch is located or its political subdivisions; and

(ii) An agency or instrumentality of such national government if supported by the taxing authority, guarantee, or full faith and credit of the national government.

(2) Underwrite, distribute and deal, invest in or trade obligations[1] rated as investment grade of:

(i) The national government of any foreign country or its political subdivisions, to the extent permissible under the law of the issuing foreign country; and

(ii) An agency or instrumentality of the national government of any foreign country to the extent permissible under the law of the issuing foreign country, if supported by the taxing authority, guarantee, or full faith and credit of the national government.

(c) *Local investments.* (1) Acquire and hold local investments in:

(i) Equity securities of the central bank, clearinghouses, governmental entities, and government sponsored development banks of the country in which the branch is located;

(ii) Other debt securities eligible to meet local reserve or similar requirements; and

(iii) Shares of automated electronic payment networks, professional societies, schools, and similar entities necessary to the business of the branch.

(2) Aggregate local investments (other than those required by the law of the foreign country or permissible under section 5136 of the Revised Statutes (12 U.S.C. 24 (Seventh)) by all the bank's branches in a single foreign country must not exceed 1 percent of the total deposits in all the bank's branches in that country as reported in the preceding year-end Report of Income and Condition (Call Report):[2]

(d) *Insurance.* Act as an insurance agent or broker.

(e) *Employee benefits program.* Pay to an employee of a branch, as part of an employee benefits program, a greater rate of interest than that paid to other depositors of the branch.

(f) *Repurchase agreements.* Engage in repurchase agreements involving securities and commodities that are the functional equivalents of extensions of credit.

(g) *Other activities.* Engage in other activities, with the prior approval of the FDIC.

(h) *Approval of other activities.* Activities that are not specifically authorized by this section, but that are authorized by 12 CFR 211.4 or FRB interpretations of activities authorized by that section, may be authorized by specific consent of the FDIC on an individual basis and upon such terms and conditions as the FDIC may consider appropriate. Activities that will be engaged in as principal (defined by reference to section 362.1(b) of this chapter), and that are not authorized by 12 CFR 211.4 or FRB interpretations of activities authorized under that section, must satisfy the requirements of part 362 of this chapter and be approved by the FDIC under this part as well as part 362 of this chapter.

§ 347.116 **Recordkeeping and supervision of foreign activities of insured state nonmember banks.**

(a) *Records, controls and reports.* A bank with any foreign branch, any investment in a foreign organization of 20 percent or more of the organization's voting equity interests, or control of a foreign organization must maintain a system of records, controls and reports that, at minimum, provide for the following:

(1) *Risk assets.* To permit assessment of exposure to loss, information furnished or available to the main office should be sufficient to permit periodic

---

[1] If the obligation is an equity interest, it must be held through a subsidiary of the foreign branch and the insured state nonmember bank must meet its minimum capital requirements.

[2] If a branch has recently been acquired by the bank and the branch was not previously required to file a Call Report, branch deposits as of the acquisition date must be used.

§ 347.117

and systematic appraisals of the quality of risk assets, including loans and other extensions of credit. Coverage should extend to a substantial proportion of the risk assets in the branch or foreign organization, and include the status of all large credit lines and of credits to customers also borrowing from other offices or affiliates of the bank. Appropriate information on risk assets may include:

(i) A recent financial statement of the borrower or obligee and current information on the borrower's or obligee's financial condition;

(ii) Terms, conditions, and collateral;

(iii) Data on any guarantors;

(iv) Payment history; and

(v) Status of corrective measures employed.

(2) *Liquidity.* To enable assessment of local management's ability to meet its obligations from available resources, reports should identify the general sources and character of the deposits, borrowing, and other funding sources employed in the branch or foreign organization with special reference to their terms and volatility. Information should be available on sources of liquidity—cash, balances with banks, marketable securities, and repayment flows—such as will reveal their accessibility in time and any risk elements involved.

(3) *Contingencies.* Data on the volume and nature of contingent items such as loan commitments and guarantees or their equivalents that permit analysis of potential risk exposure and liquidity requirements.

(4) *Controls.* Reports on the internal and external audits of the branch or foreign organization in sufficient detail to permit determination of conformance to auditing guidelines. Appropriate audit reports may include coverage of:

(i) Verification and identification of entries on financial statements;

(ii) Income and expense accounts, including descriptions of significant chargeoffs and recoveries;

(iii) Operations and dual-control procedures and other internal controls;

(iv) Conformance to head office guidelines on loans, deposits, foreign exchange activities, accounting procedures in compliance with applicable accounting standards, and discretionary authority of local management;

(v) Compliance with local laws and regulations; and

(vi) Compliance with applicable U.S. laws and regulations.

(b) *Availability of information to examiners; reports.* (1) Information about foreign branches or foreign organizations must be made available to the FDIC by the bank for examination and other supervisory purposes.

(2) The FDIC may from time to time require a bank to make and submit such reports and information as may be necessary to implement and enforce the provisions of this subpart, and the bank shall submit an annual report of condition for each foreign branch pursuant to instructions provided by the FDIC.

§ 347.117 General consent.

(a) *General consent to establish or relocate a foreign branch.* General consent of the FDIC is granted, subject to the written notification requirement contained in section 303.182(a) and consistent with the requirements of this subpart, for an:

(1) Eligible bank to establish a foreign branch conducting activities authorized by section 347.115 of this section in any foreign country in which:

(i) The bank already operates one or more foreign branches or foreign bank subsidiaries;

(ii) The bank's holding company operates a foreign bank subsidiary; or

(iii) An affiliated bank or Edge or Agreement corporation operates one or more foreign branches or foreign bank subsidiaries.

(2) Insured state nonmember bank to relocate an existing foreign branch within a foreign country.

(b) *General consent to invest in a foreign organization.* General consent of the FDIC is granted, subject to the written notification requirement contained in section 303.183(a) (unless no notification is required because the investment is acquired for trading purposes) and consistent with the requirements of this subpart, for an eligible bank to make investments in foreign organizations, directly or indirectly, if:

(1) The bank operates at least one foreign bank subsidiary or foreign

Federal Deposit Insurance Corporation § 347.119

branch, an affiliated bank or Edge or Agreement corporation operates at least one foreign bank subsidiary or foreign branch, or the bank's holding company operates at least one foreign bank subsidiary in the country where the foreign organization will be located;

(2) In any instance where the bank and its affiliates will hold 20 percent or more of the foreign organization's voting equity interests or control the foreign organization, at least one state nonmember bank has a foreign bank subsidiary or foreign branch (other than a shell branch) in the country where the foreign organization will be located;[3] and

(3) The investment is within one of the following limits:

(i) The investment is acquired at net asset value from an affiliate;

(ii) The investment is a reinvestment of cash dividends received from the same foreign organization during the preceding 12 months; or

(iii) The total investment, directly or indirectly, in a single foreign organization in any transaction or series of transactions during a twelve-month period does not exceed 2 percent of the bank's Tier 1 capital, and such investments in all foreign organizations in the aggregate do not exceed:

(A) 5 percent of the bank's Tier 1 capital during a 12-month period; and

(B) Up to an additional 5 percent of the bank's Tier 1 capital if the investments are acquired for trading purposes.

§ 347.118 Expedited processing.

(a) *Expedited processing of branch applications.* An eligible bank may establish a foreign branch conducting activities authorized by § 347.115 in an additional foreign country, after complying with the expedited processing requirements contained in § 303.182(b) and (c)(1), if any of the following are located in two or more foreign countries:

(1) Foreign branches or foreign bank subsidiaries of the eligible bank;

(2) Foreign branches or foreign bank subsidiaries of banks and Edge or Agreement corporations affiliated with the eligible bank; and

(3) Foreign bank subsidiaries of the eligible bank's holding company.

(b) *Expedited processing of applications for investment in foreign organizations.* An investment that does not qualify for general consent but is otherwise in conformity with the limits and requirements of this subpart may be made 45 days after an eligible bank files a substantially complete application with the FDIC in compliance with the expedited processing requirements contained in § 303.183(b) and (c)(1), or within such earlier time as authorized by the FDIC.

§ 347.119 Specific consent.

General consent and expedited processing under this subpart do not apply in the following circumstances:

(a) *Limitation on access to supervisory information in foreign country.* (1) Applicable law or practice in the foreign country where the foreign organization or foreign branch would be located would limit the FDIC's access to information for supervisory purposes; and

(i) A bank would hold 20 percent or more of the voting equity interests of a foreign organization or control such organization as a result of a foreign investment; or

(ii) A bank would be establishing a foreign branch.

(b) *World Heritage site.* A foreign branch of a bank would be located on a site on the World Heritage List or on the foreign country's equivalent of the National Register of Historic Places, in accordance with section 403 of the National Historic Preservation Act Amendments of 1980 (16 U.S.C. 470a–2).

(c) *Modification or suspension of general consent or expedited processing.* The FDIC at any time notifies the bank that the FDIC is modifying or suspending its general consent or expedited processing procedure.

(d) *Specific consent.* Direct or indirect investments in or activities of foreign organizations by banks, the establishment of foreign branches or issues regarding the types or amounts of activity that can be engaged in by foreign branches, which are not authorized under §§ 347.117 or 347.118 require prior

---

[3] A list of these countries can be obtained from the FDIC's Internet Web Site at *http://www.fdic.gov*.

§ 347.120

review and specific consent of the FDIC.

§ 347.120 Computation of investment amounts.

In computing the amount that may be invested in any foreign organization under §§ 347.117 through 347.119, any investments held by an affiliate of a bank must be included.

§ 347.121 Requirements for insured state nonmember bank to close a foreign branch.

A bank must comply with the written notification requirement contained in § 303.182(d) when it closes a foreign branch.

§ 347.122 Limitations applicable to the authority provided in this subpart.

The FDIC may impose such conditions on authority granted in this subpart as it considers appropriate. If a bank is unable or fails to comply with the requirements of this subpart or any conditions imposed by the FDIC regarding transactions under this subpart, the FDIC may require termination of any activities or divestiture of investments permitted under this subpart after giving the bank notice and a reasonable opportunity to be heard on the matter.

Subpart B—Foreign Banks

§ 347.201 Authority, purpose, and scope.

(a) This subpart is issued pursuant to sections 5(c) and 10(b)(4) of the Federal Deposit Insurance Act (FDI Act)(12 U.S.C. 1815(c) and 1820(b)(4)) and sections 6, 7, and 15 of the International Banking Act of 1978 (IBA)(12 U.S.C. 3104, 3105, and 3109).

(b) This subpart implements the insured branch asset pledge and examination commitment requirement for foreign banks in the FDI Act. It also implements the deposit insurance, permissible activity, and cross-border cooperation provisions of the IBA regarding the FDIC. Sections 347.203–347.211 apply to state and federal branches whose deposits are insured. Sections 347.204 and 347.207 are applicable to depository institution subsidiaries of a foreign bank. Section 347.212 applies to insured state branches and §§ 347.213–347.216 apply to state branches whose deposits are not insured by the FDIC.

§ 347.202 Definitions.

For the purposes of this subpart:

(a) *Affiliate* means any entity that controls, is controlled by, or is under common control with another entity. An entity shall be deemed to "control" another entity if the entity directly or indirectly owns, controls, or has the power to vote 25 percent or more of any class of voting securities of the other entity or controls in any manner the election of a majority of the directors or trustees of the other entity.

(b) *Branch* means any office or place of business of a foreign bank located in any state of the United States at which deposits are received. The term does not include any office or place of business deemed by the state licensing authority or the Comptroller of the Currency to be an agency.

(c) *Deposit* has the same meaning as that term in section 3(l) of the Federal Deposit Insurance Act (12 U.S.C. 1813(l)).

(d) *Depository* means any insured state bank, national bank, or insured branch.

(e) *Domestic retail deposit activity* means the acceptance by a Federal or State branch of any initial deposit of less than an amount equal to the standard maximum deposit insurance amount ("SMDIA").

(f) *Federal branch* means a branch of a foreign bank established and operating under the provisions of section 4 of the International Banking Act of 1978 (12 U.S.C. 3102).

(g) *Foreign bank* means any company organized under the laws of a foreign country, any territory of the United States, Puerto Rico, Guam, American Samoa, the Northern Mariana Islands, or the Virgin Islands, which engages in the business of banking. The term includes foreign commercial banks, foreign merchant banks and other foreign institutions that engage in banking activities usual in connection with the business of banking in the countries where such foreign institutions are organized and operating. Except as otherwise specifically provided by the Federal Deposit Insurance Corporation,

Federal Deposit Insurance Corporation § 347.202

banks organized under the laws of a foreign country, any territory of the United States, Puerto Rico, Guam, American Samoa, the Northern Mariana Islands, or the Virgin Islands which are insured banks other than by reason of having an insured branch are not considered to be foreign banks for purposes of §§ 347.204, 347.205, 347.209, and 347.210.

(h) Foreign business means any entity including, but not limited to, a corporation, partnership, sole proprietorship, association, foundation or trust, which is organized under the laws of a foreign country or any United States entity which is owned or controlled by an entity which is organized under the laws of a foreign country or a foreign national.

(i) Foreign country means any country other than the United States and includes any colony, dependency or possession of any such country.

(j) FRB means the Board of Governors of the Federal Reserve System.

(k) Home state of a foreign bank means the state so determined by the election of the foreign bank, or in default of such election, by the Board of Governors of the Federal Reserve System.

(l) Immediate family member of a natural person means the spouse, father, mother, brother, sister, son or daughter of that natural person.

(m) Initial deposit means the first deposit transaction between a depositor and the branch where there is no existing deposit relationship. The initial deposit may be placed into different deposit accounts or into different kinds of deposit accounts, such as demand, savings or time. Deposit accounts that are held by a depositor in the same right and capacity may be added together for the purposes of determining the dollar amount of the initial deposit.

(n) Insured bank means any bank, including a foreign bank with an insured branch, the deposits of which are insured in accordance with the provisions of the Federal Deposit Insurance Act.

(o) Insured branch means a branch of a foreign bank any deposits of which branch are insured in accordance with the provisions of the Federal Deposit Insurance Act.

(p) Large United States business means any entity including, but not limited to, a corporation, partnership, sole proprietorship, association, foundation or trust which is organized under the laws of the United States or any state thereof, and:

(1) Whose securities are registered on a national securities exchange or quoted on the National Association of Securities Dealers Automated Quotation System; or

(2) Has annual gross revenues in excess of $1,000,000 for the fiscal year immediately preceding the initial deposit.

(q) A majority owned subsidiary means a company the voting stock of which is more than 50 percent owned or controlled by another company.

(r) Noninsured branch means a branch of a foreign bank deposits of which branch are not insured in accordance with the provisions of the Federal Deposit Insurance Act.

(s) OCC means the Office of the Comptroller of the Currency.

(t) Person means an individual, bank, corporation, partnership, trust, association, foundation, joint venture, pool, syndicate, sole proprietorship, unincorporated organization, or any other form of entity.

(u) Significant risk to the deposit insurance fund shall be understood to be present whenever there is a high probability that the Deposit Insurance Fund administered by the FDIC may suffer a loss.

(v) *Standard maximum deposit insurance amount,* referred to as the "SMDIA" hereafter, means $250,000 adjusted pursuant to subparagraph (F) of section 11(a)(1) of the FDI Act (12 U.S.C. 1821(a)(1)(F)).

(w) State means any state of the United States or the District of Columbia.

(x) State branch means a branch of a foreign bank established and operating under the laws of any state.

(y) Wholly owned subsidiary means a company the voting stock of which is 100 percent owned or controlled by another company except for a nominal number of directors' shares.

[70 FR 17560, Apr. 6, 2005; 70 FR 20704, April 21, 2005, as amended at 71 FR 20527, Apr. 21, 2006; 74 FR 47718, Sept. 17, 2009; 75 FR 49365, Aug. 13, 2010]

§ 347.203

§ 347.203 Deposit insurance required for all branches of foreign banks engaged in domestic retail deposit activity in the same State.

The FDIC will not insure deposits in any branch of a foreign bank unless the foreign bank agrees that every branch established or operated by the foreign bank in the same state that engages in domestic retail deposit activity will be an insured branch.

§ 347.204 Commitment to be examined and provide information.

(a) In connection with an application for deposit insurance for a U.S. branch or depository institution subsidiary of a foreign bank that has been determined to be subject to comprehensive consolidated supervision by the appropriate Federal banking agency, as defined in section 3(q) of the FDI Act (12 U.S.C. 1813(q)), the foreign bank shall provide binding written commitments (including a consent to U.S. jurisdiction and designation of agent for service, acceptable to the FDIC) to the following terms:

(1) The FDIC will be provided with any information about the foreign bank and its affiliates located outside of the United States that the FDIC requests to determine:

(i) The relationship between the U.S. branch or depository institution subsidiary and its affiliates; and

(ii) The effect of such relationship on such U.S. branch or depository institution subsidiary;

(2) The FDIC will be allowed to examine the affairs of any office, agency, branch or affiliate of the foreign bank located in the United States and will be provided any information requested to determine:

(i) The relationship between the U.S. branch or depository institution subsidiary and such offices, agencies, branches or affiliates; and

(ii) The effect of such relationship on such U.S. branch or depository institution subsidiary.

(3) The FDIC will not process a deposit insurance application for any U.S. branch or depository institution subsidiary of a foreign bank if the foreign bank fails to provide the written commitments, consent to U.S. jurisdiction, and designation of agent for service required by this section.

(b) The FDIC will consider the existence and extent of any prohibition or restrictions, if any, on its ability to utilize the commitments, consent to U.S. jurisdiction, and designation of agent for service required by this section, in determining whether to grant or deny a deposit insurance application for the U.S. branch or depository institution subsidiary of the foreign bank. In addition, the FDIC may consider any additional assurances or commitments provided by the foreign bank, including that it will cooperate and assist the FDIC, without limitation, by seeking to obtain waivers and exemptions from applicable confidentiality or secrecy restrictions or requirements to enable the foreign bank or its affiliates to make information about the foreign bank and its affiliates located outside of the United States available to the FDIC for review.

(c) The foreign bank's commitments, consent to U.S. jurisdiction, and designation of agent for service shall be signed by an officer of the foreign bank who has been so authorized by the foreign bank's board of directors and in all instances will be executed in a manner acceptable to the FDIC and shall be included with the branch or depository institution application for insurance. Any documents that are not in English shall be accompanied by an English translation.

§ 347.205 Record maintenance.

The records of each insured branch shall be kept as though it were a separate entity, with its assets and liabilities separate from the other operations of the head office, other branches or agencies of the foreign bank and its subsidiaries or affiliates. Each insured branch must keep a set of accounts and records in the words and figures of the English language that accurately reflects the business transactions of the insured branch on a daily basis. A foreign bank that has more than one insured branch in a state may treat such insured branches as one entity for record-keeping purposes and may designate one branch to maintain records for all the branches in the state.

Federal Deposit Insurance Corporation § 347.209

§ 347.206 Domestic retail deposit activity requiring deposit insurance by U.S. branch of a foreign bank.

(a) *Domestic retail deposit activity.* To initiate or conduct domestic retail deposit activity requiring deposit insurance protection in any state after December 19, 1991, a foreign bank must establish one or more insured U.S. bank subsidiaries for that purpose.

(b) *Exception.* Paragraph (a) of this section does not apply to any bank organized under the laws of any territory of the United States, Puerto Rico, Guam, American Samoa, or the Virgin Islands the deposits of which are insured by the FDIC pursuant to the Federal Deposit Insurance Act.

(c) *Grandfathered insured branches.* Domestic retail accounts with balances of less than an amount equal to the SMDIA that require deposit insurance protection may be accepted or maintained in an insured branch of a foreign bank only if such branch was an insured branch on December 19, 1991

(d) *Change in ownership of grandfathered insured branch.* The grandfathered status of an insured branch may not be transferred, except in certain merger and acquisition transactions that the FDIC determines are not designed, or motivated by the desire, to avoid compliance with section 6(d)(1) of the International Banking Act (12 U.S.C. 3104(d)(1)).

[70 FR 17560, Apr. 6, 2005, as amended at 74 FR 47718, Sept. 17, 2009]

§ 347.207 Disclosure of supervisory information to foreign supervisors.

(a) *Disclosure by the FDIC.* The FDIC may disclose information obtained in the course of exercising its supervisory or examination authority to a foreign bank regulatory or supervisory authority, if the FDIC determines that disclosure is appropriate for bank supervisory or regulatory purposes and will not prejudice the interests of the United States.

(b) *Confidentiality.* Before making any disclosure of information pursuant to paragraph (a) of this section, the FDIC will obtain, to the extent necessary, the agreement of the foreign bank regulatory or supervisory authority to maintain the confidentiality of such information to the extent possible under applicable law. The disclosure or transfer of information to a foreign bank regulatory or supervisory authority under this section will not waive any privilege applicable to the information that is disclosed or transferred.

§ 347.208 Assessment base deductions by insured branch.

Deposits in an insured branch to the credit of the foreign bank or any of its offices, branches, agencies, or wholly owned subsidiaries may be deducted from the assessment base of the insured branch.

§ 347.209 Pledge of assets.

(a) *Purpose.* A foreign bank that has an insured branch must pledge assets for the benefit of the FDIC or its designee(s). Whenever the FDIC is obligated under section 11(f) of the Federal Deposit Insurance Act (12 U.S.C. 1821(f)) to pay the insured deposits of an insured branch, the assets pledged under this section must become the property of the FDIC and be used to the extent necessary to protect the Deposit Insurance Fund.

(b) *Amount of assets to be pledged.* (1) For a newly insured branch, a foreign bank must pledge assets equal to at least 5 percent of the liabilities of the branch, based on the branch's projection of its liabilities at the end of each of the first three years of operations. For all other insured branches, a foreign bank must pledge assets equal to the appropriate percentage applicable to the insured branch, as determined by reference to the risk-based assessment schedule contained in this paragraph, of the insured branch's average liabilities for the last 30 days of the most recent calendar quarter.[4]

---

[4] This average must be computed by using the sum of the close of business figures for the 30 calendar days of the most recent calendar quarter, ending with and including the last day of the calendar quarter, divided by 30. For days on which the branch is closed, however, balances from the previous business day are to be used in determining its average liabilities. In determining its average liabilities, the insured branch may exclude liabilities to other offices, agencies, branches, and wholly owned subsidiaries of the foreign bank. The value of the pledged assets must

Continued

§ 347.209

(2) *Risk-based assessment schedule.* The risk-based asset pledge required by paragraph (b)(1) will be determined by utilizing the following risk-based assessment schedule:

Asset maintenance level	Supervisory risk subgroup		
	A (%)	B (%)	C (%)
Equal to or greater than 108%	2	3	4
Equal to or greater than 106%	4	5	6
Less than 106%	6	7	8

The appropriate asset pledge percentage will be determined based on the supervisory risk subgroup and asset maintenance level applicable to the insured branch.

(3) *Supervisory risk factors.* For purposes of this section, within each asset maintenance group, each institution will be assigned to one of three subgroups based on consideration by the FDIC of supervisory evaluations provided by the primary federal regulator for the insured branch. The supervisory evaluations include the results of examination findings by the primary federal regulator, as well as other information the primary federal regulator determines to be relevant. In addition, the FDIC will take into consideration such other information (such as state examination findings, if appropriate) as it determines to be relevant to the financial condition and the risk posed to the Deposit Insurance Fund. The three supervisory subgroups are:

(i) Subgroup "A". This subgroup consists of financially sound institutions with only a few minor weaknesses;

(ii) Subgroup "B". This subgroup consists of institutions that demonstrate weaknesses which, if not corrected, could result in significant deterioration of the institution and increased risk of loss to the deposit insurance fund; and

(iii) Subgroup "C". This subgroup consists of institutions that pose a substantial probability of loss to the deposit insurance fund.

(4) The FDIC may require a foreign bank to pledge additional assets or to compute its pledge on a daily basis whenever the FDIC determines that the condition of the foreign bank or the insured branch is such that the assets pledged under this section will not adequately protect the deposit insurance fund. In requiring a foreign bank to pledge additional assets, the FDIC will consult with the primary regulator for the insured branch. Among the factors to be considered in imposing these requirements are the concentration of risk to any one borrower or group of related borrowers, the concentration of transfer risk related to any one country, including the country in which the foreign bank's head office is located or any other factor the FDIC determines is relevant.

(5) Each insured branch must separately comply with the requirements of this section. A foreign bank which has more than one insured branch in a state may, however, treat all of its insured branches in the same state as one entity and will designate one insured branch to be responsible for compliance with this section.

(c) *Depository.* A foreign bank must place pledged assets for safekeeping at any depository which is located in any state. However, a depository may not be an affiliate of the foreign bank whose insured branch is seeking to use the depository. A foreign bank must obtain the FDIC's prior written approval of the depository selected, and such approval may be revoked and dismissal of the depository required whenever the depository does not fulfill any one of its obligations under the pledge agreement. A foreign bank shall appoint and constitute the depository as its attorney in fact for the sole purpose of transferring title to pledged assets

---

be computed based on the lesser of the principal amount (par value) or market value of such assets at the time of the original pledge and thereafter as of the last day of the most recent calendar quarter.

Federal Deposit Insurance Corporation § 347.209

to the FDIC as may be required to effectuate the provisions of paragraph (a) of this section.

(d) *Assets that may be pledged.* Subject to the right of the FDIC to require substitution, a foreign bank may pledge any of the kinds of assets listed in this paragraph (d); such assets must be denominated in United States dollars. A foreign bank shall be deemed to have pledged any such assets for the benefit of the FDIC or its designee at such time as any such asset is placed with the depository, as follows:

(1)(i) Negotiable certificates of deposit that are payable in the United States and that are issued by any state bank, national bank, state or federal savings association, or branch of a foreign bank which has executed a valid waiver of offset agreement or similar debt instruments that are payable in the United States and that are issued by any agency of a foreign bank which has executed a valid waiver of offset agreement; provided, that the maturity of any certificate or issuance is not greater than one year; and provided further, that the issuing branch or agency of a foreign bank is not an affiliate of the pledging bank or from the same country as the pledging bank's domicile;

(ii) Non-negotiable certificates of deposit, subject to the terms specified in paragraph (d)(1)(i) of this section other than the requirement of negotiability, that were pledged as collateral to the FDIC on March 18, 2005, until maturity according to the original terms of the existing deposit agreement.

(2) Treasury bills, interest bearing bonds, notes, debentures, or other direct obligations of or obligations fully guaranteed as to principal and interest by the United States or any agency or instrumentality thereof;

(3) Commercial paper that is rated P–1 or P–2, or their equivalent by a nationally recognized rating service; provided, that any conflict in a rating shall be resolved in favor of the lower rating;

(4) Banker's acceptances that are payable in the United States and that are issued by any state bank, national bank, state or federal savings association, or branch or agency of a foreign bank; provided, that the maturity of any acceptance is not greater than 180 days; and provided further, that the branch or agency issuing the acceptance is not an affiliate of the pledging bank or from the same country as the pledging bank's domicile;

(5) General obligations of any state of the United States, or any county or municipality of any state of the United States, or any agency, instrumentality, or political subdivision of the foregoing or any obligation guaranteed by a state of the United States or any county or municipality of any state of the United States; provided, that such obligations have a credit rating within the top two rating bands of a nationally recognized rating service (with any conflict in a rating resolved in favor of the lower rating);

(6) Obligations of the African Development Bank, Asian Development Bank, Inter-American Development Bank, and the International Bank for Reconstruction and Development;

(7) Notes issued by bank and thrift holding companies, banks, or savings associations organized under the laws of the United States or any state thereof or notes issued by United States branches or agencies of foreign banks, provided, that the notes have a credit rating within the top two rating bands of a nationally recognized rating service (with any conflict in a rating resolved in favor of the lower rating) and that they are payable in the United States, and provided further, that the issuer is not an affiliate of the foreign bank pledging the note; or

(8) Any other asset determined by the FDIC to be acceptable.

(e) *Pledge agreement.* A foreign bank shall not pledge any assets unless a pledge agreement in form and substance satisfactory to the FDIC has been executed by the foreign bank and the depository. The agreement, in addition to other terms not inconsistent with this paragraph (e), shall give effect to the following terms:

(1) *Original pledge.* The foreign bank shall place with the depository assets of the kind described in paragraph (d) of this section, having an aggregate value in the amount as required pursuant to paragraph (b) of this section.

(2) *Additional assets required to be pledged.* Whenever the foreign bank is

§ 347.209

required to pledge additional assets for the benefit of the FDIC or its designees pursuant to paragraph (b)(4) of this section, it shall deliver (within two business days after the last day of the most recent calendar quarter, unless otherwise ordered) additional assets of the kind described in paragraph (d) of this section, having an aggregate value in the amount required by the FDIC.

(3) *Substitution of assets.* The foreign bank, at any time, may substitute any assets for pledged assets, and, upon such substitution, the depository shall promptly release any such assets to the foreign bank; provided, that:

(i) The foreign bank pledges assets of the kind described in paragraph (d) of this section having an aggregate value not less than the value of the pledged assets for which they are substituted and certified as such by the foreign bank; and

(ii) The FDIC has not by written notification to the foreign bank, a copy of which shall be provided to the depository, suspended or terminated the foreign bank's right of substitution.

(4) *Delivery of other documents.* Concurrently with the pledge of any assets, the foreign bank will deliver to the depository all documents and instruments necessary or advisable to effectuate the transfer of title to any such assets and thereafter, from time to time, at the request of the FDIC, deliver to the depository any such additional documents or instruments. The foreign bank shall provide copies of all such documents described in this paragraph (e)(4) to the appropriate regional director concurrently with their delivery to the depository.

(5) *Acceptance and safekeeping responsibilities of the depository.* (i) The depository will accept and hold any assets pledged by the foreign bank pursuant to the pledge agreement for safekeeping free and clear of any lien, charge, right of offset, credit, or preference in connection with any claim the depository may assert against the foreign bank and shall designate any such assets as a special pledge for the benefit of the FDIC or its designee. The depository shall not accept the pledge of any such assets unless, concurrently with such pledge, the foreign bank delivers to the depository the documents and instruments necessary for the transfer of title thereto as provided in this part.

(ii) The depository shall hold any such assets separate from all other assets of the foreign bank or the depository. Such assets may be held in book-entry form but must at all times be segregated on the records of the depository and clearly identified as assets subject to the pledge agreement.

(6) *Reporting requirements of the insured branch and the depository—(i) Initial reports.* Upon the original pledge of assets as provided in paragraph (e)(1) of this section:

(A) The depository shall provide to the foreign bank and to the appropriate FDIC regional director a written report in the form of a receipt identifying each asset pledged and specifying in reasonable detail with respect to each such asset the complete title, interest rate, series, serial number (if any), principal amount (par value), maturity date and call date; and

(B) The foreign bank shall provide to the appropriate regional director a written report certified as correct by the foreign bank which sets forth the value of each pledged asset and the aggregate value of all such assets, and which states that the aggregate value of all such assets is at least equal to the amount required pursuant to paragraph (b) of this section and that all such assets are of the kind described in paragraph (d) of this section.

(ii) *Quarterly reports.* Within ten calendar days after the end of the most recent calendar quarter:

(A) The depository shall provide to the appropriate regional director a written report specifying in reasonable detail with respect to each asset currently pledged (including any asset pledged to satisfy the requirements of paragraph (b)(4) of this section and identified as such), as of two business days after the end of the most recent calendar quarter, the complete title, interest rate, series, serial number (if any), principal amount (par value), maturity date, and call date, provided, that if no substitution of any asset has occurred during the reporting period, the reporting need only specify that no substitution of assets has occurred; and

Federal Deposit Insurance Corporation § 347.209

(B) The foreign bank shall provide as of two business days after the end of the most recent calendar quarter to the appropriate regional director a written report certified as correct by the foreign bank which sets forth the value of each pledged asset and the aggregate value of all such assets, which states that the aggregate value of all such assets is at least equal to the amount required pursuant to paragraph (b) of this section and that all such assets are of the kind described in paragraph (d) of this section, and which states the average of the liabilities of each insured branch of the foreign bank computed in the manner and for the period prescribed in paragraph (b) of this section.

(iii) *Additional reports.* The foreign bank shall, from time to time, as may be required, provide to the appropriate regional director a written report in the form specified containing the information requested with respect to any asset then currently pledged.

(7) Access to assets. With respect to any asset pledged pursuant to the pledge agreement, the depository will provide representatives of the FDIC or the foreign bank with access (during regular business hours of the depository and at the location where any such asset is held, without other limitation or qualification) to all original instruments, documents, books, and records evidencing or pertaining to any such asset.

(8) Release upon the order of the FDIC. The depository shall release to the foreign bank any pledged assets, as specified in a written notification of the appropriate regional director, upon the terms and conditions provided in such notification, including without limitation the waiver of any requirement that any assets be pledged by the foreign bank in substitution of any released assets.

(9) *Release to the FDIC.* Whenever the FDIC is obligated under section 11(f) of the Federal Deposit Insurance Act to pay insured deposits of an insured branch, the FDIC by written certification shall so inform the depository; and the depository, upon receipt of such certification, shall thereupon promptly release and transfer title to any pledged assets to the FDIC or release such assets to the foreign bank, as specified in the certification. Upon release and transfer of title to all pledged assets specified in the certification, the depository shall be discharged from any further obligation under the pledge agreement.

(10) *Interest earned on assets.* The foreign bank may retain any interest earned with respect to the assets currently pledged unless the FDIC by written notice prohibits retention of interest by the foreign bank, in which case the notice shall specify the disposition of any such interest.

(11) *Expenses of agreement.* The FDIC shall not be required to pay any fees, costs, or expenses for services provided by the depository to the foreign bank pursuant to, or in connection with, the pledge agreement.

(12) *Substitution of depository.* The depository may resign, or the foreign bank may discharge the depository, from its duties and obligations under the pledge agreement by giving at least 60 days' written notice thereof to the other party and to the appropriate regional director. The FDIC, upon 30 days' written notice to the foreign bank and the depository, may require the foreign bank to dismiss the depository if the FDIC in its discretion determines that the depository is in breach of the pledge agreement. The depository shall continue to function as such until the appointment of a successor depository becomes effective and the depository has released to the successor depository the pledged assets and documents and instruments to effectuate transfer of title in accordance with the written instructions of the foreign bank as approved by the FDIC. The appointment by the foreign bank of a successor depository shall not be effective until:

(i) The FDIC has approved in writing the successor depository; and

(ii) A pledge agreement in form and substance satisfactory to the FDIC has been executed.

(13) *Waiver of terms.* The FDIC may by written order waive compliance by the foreign bank or the depository with

§ 347.210

any term or condition of the pledge agreement.

[70 FR 17560, Apr. 6, 2005; 70 FR 20704, April 21, 2005, as amended at 71 FR 20527, Apr. 21, 2006]

§ 347.210 Asset maintenance.

(a) An insured branch of a foreign bank shall maintain on a daily basis eligible assets in an amount not less than 106 percent of the preceding quarter's average book value of the insured branch's liabilities or, in the case of a newly-established insured branch, the estimated book value of its liabilities at the end of the first full quarter of operation, exclusive of liabilities due to the foreign bank's head office, other branches, agencies, offices, or wholly owned subsidiaries. The Director of the Division of Supervision and Consumer Protection or his designee may impose a computation of total liabilities on a daily basis in those instances where it is found necessary for supervisory purposes. The FDIC Board of Directors, after consulting with the insured branch's primary regulator, may require that a higher ratio of eligible assets be maintained if the financial condition of the insured branch warrants such action. Among the factors which will be considered in requiring a higher ratio of eligible assets are the concentration of risk to any one borrower or group of related borrowers, the concentration of transfer risk to any one country, including the country in which the foreign bank's head office is located or any other factor the FDIC determines is relevant. Eligible assets shall be payable in United States dollars.

(b) In determining eligible assets for the purposes of compliance with paragraph (a) of this section, the insured branch shall exclude the following:

(1) Any asset due from the foreign bank's head office, or its other branches, agencies, offices or affiliates;

(2) Any asset classified "Value Impaired," to the extent of the required Allocated Transfer Risk Reserves or equivalent write down, or "Loss" in the most recent state or federal examination report;

(3) Any deposit of the insured branch in a bank unless the bank has executed a valid waiver of offset agreement;

(4) Any asset not supported by sufficient credit information to allow a review of the asset's credit quality, as determined at the most recent state or federal examination, as follows:

(i) Whether an asset has sufficient credit information will be a function of the size of the borrower and the location within the foreign bank of the responsibility for authorizing and monitoring extensions of credit to the borrower. For large, well known companies, when credit responsibility is located in an office of the foreign bank outside the insured branch, the insured branch must have adequate documentation to show that the asset is of good quality and is being supervised adequately by the foreign bank. In such cases, copies of periodic memoranda that include an analysis of the borrower's recent financial statements and a report on recent developments in the borrower's operations and borrowing relationships with the foreign bank generally would constitute sufficient information. For other borrowers, periodic memoranda must be supplemented by information such as copies of recent financial statements, recent correspondence concerning the borrower's financial condition and repayment history, credit terms and collateral, data on any guarantors, and where necessary, the status of any corrective measures being employed;

(ii) Subsequent to the determination that an asset lacks sufficient credit information, an insured branch may not include the amount of that asset among eligible assets until the FDIC determines that sufficient documentation exists. Such a determination may be made either at the next federal examination, or upon request of the insured branch, by the appropriate regional director;

(5) Any asset not in the insured branch's actual possession unless the insured branch holds title to such asset and the insured branch maintains records sufficient to enable independent verification of the insured branch's ownership of the asset, as determined at the most recent state or federal examination;

(6) Any intangible asset;

(7) Any other asset not considered bankable by the FDIC.

Federal Deposit Insurance Corporation § 347.211

(c) A foreign bank which has more than one insured branch in a state may treat all of its insured branches in the same state as one entity for purposes of compliance with paragraph (a) of this section and shall designate one insured branch to be responsible for maintaining the records of the insured branches' compliance with this section.

(d) The average book value of the insured branch's liabilities for a quarter shall be, at the insured branch's option, either an average of the balances as of the close of business for each day of the quarter or an average of the balances as of the close of business on each Wednesday during the quarter. Quarters end on March 31, June 30, September 30, and December 31 of any given year. For days on which the insured branch is closed, balances from the previous business day are to be used. Calculations of the average book value of the insured branch's liabilities for a quarter shall be retained by the insured branch until the next federal examination.

§ 347.211 Examination of branches of foreign banks.

(a) *Frequency of on-site examination.* Each branch or agency of a foreign bank shall be examined on-site at least once during each 12-month period (beginning on the date the most recent examination of the office ended) by:

(1) The FRB;

(2) The FDIC, if an insured branch;

(3) The OCC, if the branch or agency of the foreign bank is licensed by the OCC; or

(4) The state supervisor, if the office of the foreign bank is licensed or chartered by the state.

(b) *18-month cycle for certain small institutions*—(1) *Mandatory standards.* The FDIC may conduct a full-scope, on-site examination at least once during each 18-month period, rather than each 12-month period as provided in paragraph (a) of this section, if the insured branch:

(i) Has total assets of less than $500 million;

(ii) Has received a composite ROCA supervisory rating (which rates risk management, operational controls, compliance, and asset quality) of 1 or 2 at its most recent examination;

(iii) Satisfies the requirement of either the following paragraph (b)(iii)(A) or (B):

(A) The foreign bank's most recently reported capital adequacy position consists of, or is equivalent to, Tier 1 and total risk-based capital ratios of at least 6 percent and 10 percent, respectively, on a consolidated basis; or

(B) The insured branch has maintained on a daily basis, over the past three quarters, eligible assets in an amount not less than 108 percent of the preceding quarter's average third party liabilities (determined consistent with applicable federal and state law) and sufficient liquidity is currently available to meet its obligations to third parties;

(iv) Is not subject to a formal enforcement action or order by the FRB, FDIC, or the OCC; and

(v) Has not experienced a change in control during the preceding 12-month period in which a full-scope, on-site examination would have been required but for this section.

(2) *Discretionary standards.* In determining whether an insured branch that meets the standards of paragraph (b)(1) of this section should not be eligible for an 18-month examination cycle pursuant to this paragraph (b), the FDIC may consider additional factors, including whether:

(i) Any of the individual components of the ROCA supervisory rating of an insured branch is rated "3" or worse;

(ii) The results of any off-site monitoring indicate a deterioration in the condition of the insured branch;

(iii) The size, relative importance, and role of a particular insured branch when reviewed in the context of the foreign bank's entire U.S. operations otherwise necessitate an annual examination; and

(iv) The condition of the parent foreign bank gives rise to such a need.

(c) *Authority to conduct more frequent examinations.* Nothing in paragraphs (a) and (b) of this section limits the authority of the FDIC to examine any insured branch as frequently as it deems necessary.

[70 FR 17560, Apr. 6, 2005; 70 FR 20704, April 21, 2005, as amended at 72 FR 17803, Apr. 10, 2007]

§ 347.212

§ 347.212 FDIC approval to conduct activities that are not permissible for federal branches.

(a) *Scope.* A foreign bank operating an insured state branch which desires to engage in or continue to engage in any type of activity that is not permissible for a federal branch, pursuant to the National Bank Act (12 U.S.C. 21 *et seq.*) or any other federal statute, regulation, official bulletin or circular, written order or interpretation, or decision of a court of competent jurisdiction, must file a written application for permission to conduct such activity with the FDIC.

(b) *Exceptions.* If the FDIC has already determined, pursuant to part 362 of this chapter, "Activities and Investment of Insured State Banks," that an activity does not present a significant risk to the Deposit Insurance Fund, no application is required under paragraph (a) of this section for a foreign bank operating an insured branch to engage or continue to engage in the same activity.

(c) *Agency activities.* A foreign bank operating an insured state branch is not required to submit an application pursuant to paragraph (a) of this section to engage in or continue engaging in an activity conducted as agent if the activity is:

(1) permissible agency activity for a state-chartered bank located in the state which the state-licensed insured branch of the foreign bank is located;

(2) permissible agency activity for a state-licensed branch of a foreign bank located in that state; and

(3) permissible pursuant to any other applicable federal law or regulation.

(d) *Conditions of approval.* (1) Approval of such an application required by paragraph (a) of this section may be conditioned on the agreement by the foreign bank and its insured state branch to conduct the activity subject to specific limitations, which may include pledging of assets in excess of the asset pledge and asset maintenance requirements contained in §§ 347.209 and 347.210.

(2) In the case of an application to initially engage in an activity, as opposed to an application to continue to conduct an activity, the insured state branch shall not commence the activity until it has been approved in writing by the FDIC pursuant to this part and the FRB, and any and all conditions imposed in such approvals have been satisfied.

(e) *Divestiture or cessation.* (1) If an application for permission to continue to conduct an activity is not approved by the FDIC or the FRB, the applicant shall submit a plan of divestiture or cessation of the activity to the appropriate regional director.

(2) A foreign bank operating an insured state branch which elects not to apply to the FDIC for permission to continue to conduct an activity which is rendered impermissible by any change in statute, regulation, official bulletin or circular, written order or interpretation, or decision of a court of competent jurisdiction shall submit a plan of divestiture or cessation to the appropriate regional director.

(3) All plans of divestitures or cessation required by this paragraph must be completed within one year from the date of the disapproval, or within such shorter period as the FDIC may direct.

(f) *Procedures.* Procedures for applications under this section are set out in section 303.187.

[70 FR 17560, Apr. 6, 2005; 70 FR 20704, April 21, 2005, as amended at 71 FR 20527, Apr. 21, 2006]

§ 347.213 Establishment or operation of noninsured foreign branch.

(a) A foreign bank may establish or operate a state branch, as provided by state law, without federal deposit insurance whenever:

(1) The branch only accepts initial deposits in an amount equal to the SMDIA or greater; or

(2) The branch meets the criteria set forth in § 347.214 or § 347.215.

(b) [Reserved]

[70 FR 17560, Apr. 6, 2005, as amended at 74 FR 47718, Sept. 17, 2009]

§ 347.214 Branch established under section 5 of the International Banking Act.

A foreign bank may operate any state branch as a noninsured branch whenever the foreign bank has entered into an agreement with the FRB to accept at that branch only those deposits

Federal Deposit Insurance Corporation § 347.215

as would be permissible for a corporation organized under section 25(a) of the Federal Reserve Act (12 U.S.C. 611 *et seq.*) and implementing rules and regulations administered by the FRB (12 CFR 211).

§ 347.215 Exemptions from deposit insurance requirement.

(a) *Deposit activities not requiring insurance.* A State branch will not be considered to be engaged in domestic retail deposit activity that requires the foreign bank parent to establish an insured U.S. bank subsidiary if the State branch accepts initial deposits only in an amount of less than an amount equal to the SMDIA that are derived solely from the following:

(1) Individuals who are not citizens or residents of the United States at the time of the initial deposit;

(2) Individuals who:

(i) Are not citizens of the United States;

(ii) Are residents of the United States; and

(iii) Are employed by a foreign bank, foreign business, foreign government, or recognized international organization;

(3) Persons (including immediate family members of natural persons) to whom the branch or foreign bank (including any affiliate thereof) has extended credit or provided other nondeposit banking services within the past twelve months or has entered into a written agreement to provide such services within the next twelve months;

(4) Foreign businesses, large United States businesses, and persons from whom an Edge or agreement corporation may accept deposits under 12 CFR 211.6(a)(1);

(5) Any governmental unit, including the United States government, any state government, any foreign government and any political subdivision or agency of any of the foregoing, and recognized international organizations;

(6) Persons who are depositing funds in connection with the issuance of a financial instrument by the branch for the transmission of funds or the transmission of such funds by any electronic means; and

(7) Any other depositor, but only if:

(i) The branch's average deposits under this paragraph (a)(7) do not exceed one percent of the branch's average total deposits, as calculated under paragraph (a)(7)(ii) if this section (*de minimis* exception).

(ii) For purposes of calculating this exception:

(A) The branch's average deposits under this paragraph and the average total deposits must be computed by summing the close of business figures for each of the last 30 calendar days, ending with and including the last day of the calendar quarter, and dividing the resulting sum by 30;

(B) For days on which the branch is closed, balances from the last previous business day are to be used;

(C) The branch may exclude deposits in the branch of other offices, branches, agencies or wholly owned subsidiaries of the bank to determine its average deposits;

(D) The branch must not solicit deposits from the general public by advertising, display of signs, or similar activity designed to attract the attention of the general public; and

(E) A foreign bank that has more than one state branch in the same state may aggregate deposits in such branches (excluding deposits of other branches, agencies or wholly owned subsidiaries of the bank) for the purpose of this paragraph (a)(7).

(b) *Application for an exemption.* (1) Whenever a foreign bank proposes to accept at a State branch initial deposits of less than an amount equal to the SMDIA and such deposits are not otherwise exempted under paragraph (a) of this section, the foreign bank may apply to the FDIC for consent to operate the branch as a noninsured branch. The Board of Directors may exempt the branch from the insurance requirement if the branch is not engaged in domestic retail deposit activities requiring insurance protection. The Board of Directors will consider the size and nature of depositors and deposit accounts, the importance of maintaining and improving the availability of credit to all sectors of the United States economy, including the international trade finance sector of the United

§ 347.216

States economy, whether the exemption would give the foreign bank an unfair competitive advantage over United States banking organizations, and any other relevant factors in making this determination.

(2) Procedures for applications under this section are set out in § 303.186.

(c) *Transition period.* A noninsured state branch may maintain a retail deposit lawfully accepted prior to April 1, 1996 pursuant to regulations in effect prior to July 1, 1998:

(1) If the deposit qualifies pursuant to paragraph (a) or (b) of this section; or

(2) If the deposit does not qualify pursuant to paragraph (a) or (b) of this section, in the case of a time deposit, no later than the first maturity date of the time deposit after April 1, 1996.

[70 FR 17560, Apr. 6, 2005, as amended at 74 FR 47718, Sept. 17, 2009]

§ 347.216   Depositor notification.

Any state branch that is exempt from the insurance requirement pursuant to § 347.215 shall:

(a) Display conspicuously at each window or place where deposits are usually accepted a sign stating that deposits are not insured by the FDIC; and

(b) Include in bold face conspicuous type on each signature card, passbook, and instrument evidencing a deposit the statement "This deposit is not insured by the FDIC"; or require each depositor to execute a statement which acknowledges that the initial deposit and all future deposits at the branch are not insured by the FDIC. This acknowledgment shall be retained by the branch so long as the depositor maintains any deposit with the branch. This provision applies to any negotiable certificates of deposit made in a branch on or after July 6, 1989, as well as to any renewals of such deposits which become effective on or after July 6, 1989.

Subpart C—International Lending

§ 347.301   Purpose, authority, and scope.

Under the International Lending Supervision Act of 1983 (Title IX, Pub. L. 98–181, 97 Stat. 1153) (12 U.S.C. 3901 *et seq.*) (ILSA), the Federal Deposit Insurance Corporation prescribes the regulations in this subpart relating to international lending activities of banks.

§ 347.302   Definitions.

For the purposes of this subpart:

(a) *Administrative cost* means those costs which are specifically identified with negotiating, processing and consummating the loan. These costs include, but are not necessarily limited to: legal fees; costs of preparing and processing loan documents; and an allocable portion of salaries and related benefits of employees engaged in the international lending function. No portion of supervisory and administrative expenses or other indirect expenses such as occupancy and other similar overhead costs shall be included.

(b) *Banking institution* means an insured state nonmember bank.

(c) *Federal banking agencies* means the Board of Governors of the Federal Reserve System, the Office of the Comptroller of the Currency, and the Federal Deposit Insurance Corporation.

(d) *International assets* means those assets required to be included in banking institutions' "Country Exposure Report" form (FFIEC No. 009).

(e) *International loan* means a loan as defined in the instructions to the "Report of Condition and Income" for the respective banking institution (FFIEC Nos. 031, 032, 033 and 034) and made to a foreign government, or to an individual, a corporation, or other entity not a citizen of, resident in, or organized or incorporated in the United States.

(f) *Restructured international loan* means a loan that meets the following criteria:

(1) The borrower is unable to service the existing loan according to its terms and is a resident of a foreign country in which there is a generalized inability of public and private sector obligors to meet their external debt obligations on a timely basis because of a lack of, or restraints on the availability of, needed foreign exchange in the country; and

(2) Either:

(i) The terms of the existing loan are amended to reduce stated interest or extend the schedule of payments; or

(ii) A new loan is made to, or for the benefit of, the borrower, enabling the

Federal Deposit Insurance Corporation § 347.303

borrower to service or refinance the existing debt.

(g) *Transfer risk* means the possibility that an asset cannot be serviced in the currency of payment because of a lack of, or restraints on the availability of, needed foreign exchange in the country of the obligor.

§ 347.303 Allocated transfer risk reserve.

(a) *Establishment of Allocated Transfer Risk Reserve.* A banking institution shall establish an allocated transfer risk reserve (ATRR) for specified international assets when required by the FDIC in accordance with this section.

(b) *Procedures and standards*—(1) *Joint agency determination.* At least annually, the federal banking agencies shall determine jointly, based on the standards set forth in paragraph (b)(2) of this section, the following:

(i) Which international assets subject to transfer risk warrant establishment of an ATRR;

(ii) The amount of the ATRR for the specified assets; and

(iii) Whether an ATRR established for specified assets may be reduced.

(2) *Standards for requiring ATRR*—(i) *Evaluation of assets.* The federal banking agencies shall apply the following criteria in determining whether an ATRR is required for particular international assets:

(A) Whether the quality of a banking institution's assets has been impaired by a protracted inability of public or private obligors in a foreign country to make payments on their external indebtedness as indicated by such factors, among others, as whether:

(1) Such obligors have failed to make full interest payments on external indebtedness; or

(2) Such obligors have failed to comply with the terms of any restructured indebtedness; or

(3) A foreign country has failed to comply with any International Monetary Fund or other suitable adjustment program; or

(B) Whether no definite prospects exist for the orderly restoration of debt service.

(ii) *Determination of amount of ATRR.*
(A) In determining the amount of the ATRR, the federal banking agencies shall consider:

(1) The length of time the quality of the asset has been impaired;

(2) Recent actions taken to restore debt service capability;

(3) Prospects for restored asset quality; and

(4) Such other factors as the federal banking agencies may consider relevant to the quality of the asset.

(B) The initial year's provision for the ATRR shall be ten percent of the principal amount of each specified international asset, or such greater or lesser percentage determined by the federal banking agencies. Additional provision, if any, for the ATRR in subsequent years shall be fifteen percent of the principal amount of each specified international asset, or such greater or lesser percentage determined by the federal banking agencies.

(3) *FDIC notification.* Based on the joint agency determinations under paragraph (b)(1) of this section, the FDIC shall notify each banking institution holding assets subject to an ATRR:

(i) Of the amount of the ATRR to be established by the institution for specified international assets; and

(ii) That an ATRR established for specified assets may be reduced.

(c) *Accounting treatment of ATRR*—(1) *Charge to current income.* A banking institution shall establish an ATRR by a charge to current income and the amounts so charged shall not be included in the banking institution's capital or surplus.

(2) *Separate accounting.* A banking institution shall account for an ATRR separately from the Allowance for Loan and Lease Losses, and shall deduct the ATRR from "gross loans and leases" to arrive at "net loans and leases." The ATRR must be established for each asset subject to the ATRR in the percentage amount specified.

(3) *Consolidation.* A banking institution shall establish an ATRR, as required, on a consolidated basis. For banks, consolidation should be in accordance with the procedures and tests of significance set forth in the instructions for preparation of Consolidated Reports of Condition and Income (FFIEC Nos. 031, 032, 033 and 034).

§ 347.304

(4) *Alternative accounting treatment.* A banking institution need not establish an ATRR if it writes down in the period in which the ATRR is required, or has written down in prior periods, the value of the specified international assets in the requisite amount for each such asset. For purposes of this paragraph (c)(4), international assets may be written down by a charge to the Allowance for Loan and Lease Losses or a reduction in the principal amount of the asset by application of interest payments or other collections on the asset; provided, that only those international assets that may be charged to the Allowance for Loan and Lease Losses pursuant to generally accepted accounting principles may be written down by a charge to the Allowance for Loan and Lease Losses. However, the Allowance for Loan and Lease Losses must be replenished in such amount necessary to restore it to a level which adequately provides for the estimated losses inherent in the banking institution's loan and lease portfolio.

(5) *Reduction of ATRR.* A banking institution may reduce an ATRR when notified by the FDIC or, at any time, by writing down such amount of the international asset for which the ATRR was established.

§ 347.304 Accounting for fees on international loans.

(a) *Restrictions on fees for restructured international loans.* No banking institution shall charge, in connection with the restructuring of an international loan, any fee exceeding the administrative cost of the restructuring unless it amortizes the amount of the fee exceeding the administrative cost over the effective life of the loan.

(b) *Accounting treatment.* Subject to paragraph (a) of this section, banking institutions shall account for fees on international loans in accordance with generally accepted accounting principles.

§ 347.305 Reporting and disclosure of international assets.

(a) *Requirements.* (1) Pursuant to section 907(a) of ILSA, a banking institution shall submit to the FDIC, at least quarterly, information regarding the amounts and composition of its holdings of international assets.

(2) Pursuant to section 907(b) of ILSA, a banking institution shall submit to the FDIC information regarding concentrations in its holdings of international assets that are material in relation to total assets and to capital of the institution, such information to be made publicly available by the FDIC on request.

(b) *Procedures.* The format, content and reporting and filing dates of the reports required under paragraph (a) of this section shall be determined jointly by the federal banking agencies. The requirements to be prescribed by the federal banking agencies may include changes to existing forms (such as revisions to the Country Exposure Report, Form FFIEC No. 009) or such other requirements as the federal banking agencies deem appropriate. The federal banking agencies also may determine to exempt from the requirements of paragraph (a) of this section banking institutions that, in the federal banking agencies' judgment, have *de minimis* holdings of international assets.

(c) *Reservation of Authority.* Nothing contained in this subpart shall preclude the FDIC from requiring from a banking institution such additional or more frequent information on the institution's holdings of international assets as the agency may consider necessary.

PART 348—MANAGEMENT OFFICIAL INTERLOCKS

Sec.
348.1 Authority, purpose, and scope.
348.2 Definitions.
348.3 Prohibitions.
348.4 Interlocking relationships permitted by statute.
348.5 Small market share exemption.
348.6 General exemption.
348.7 Change in circumstances.
348.8 Enforcement.

AUTHORITY: 12 U.S.C. 3207, 12 U.S.C. 1823(k).

SOURCE: 61 FR 40305, Aug. 2, 1996, unless otherwise noted.

§ 348.1 Authority, purpose, and scope.

(a) *Authority.* This part is issued under the provisions of the Depository Institution Management Interlocks

Federal Deposit Insurance Corporation § 348.2

Act (Interlocks Act) (12 U.S.C. 3201 *et seq.*), as amended.

(b) *Purpose.* The purpose of the Interlocks Act and this part is to foster competition by generally prohibiting a management official from serving two nonaffiliated depository organizations in situations where the management interlock likely would have an anticompetitive effect.

(c) *Scope.* This part applies to management officials of insured nonmember banks and their affiliates.

§ 348.2 Definitions.

For purposes of this part, the following definitions apply:

(a) *Affiliate.* (1) The term *affiliate* has the meaning given in section 202 of the Interlocks Act (12 U.S.C. 3201). For purposes of section 202, shares held by an individual include shares held by members of his or her immediate family. "Immediate family" means spouse, mother, father, child, grandchild, sister, brother or any of their spouses, whether or not any of their shares are held in trust.

(2) For purposes of section 202(3)(B) of the Interlocks Act (12 U.S.C. 3201(3)(B)), an affiliate relationship involving an insured nonmember bank based on common ownership does not exist if the FDIC determines, after giving the affected persons the opportunity to respond, that the asserted affiliation was established in order to avoid the prohibitions of the Interlocks Act and does not represent a true commonality of interest between the depository organizations. In making this determination, the FDIC considers, among other things, whether a person, including members of his or her immediate family whose shares are necessary to constitute the group, owns a nominal percentage of the shares of one of the organizations and the percentage is substantially disproportionate to that person's ownership of shares in the other organization.

(b) *Area median income* means:

(1) The median family income for the metropolitan statistical area (MSA), if a depository organization is located in an MSA; or

(2) The statewide nonmetropolitan median family income, if a depository organization is located outside an MSA.

(c) *Community* means a city, town, or village, and contiguous or adjacent cities, towns, or villages.

(d) *Contiguous or adjacent cities, towns, or villages* means cities, towns, or villages whose borders touch each other or whose borders are within 10 road miles of each other at their closest points. The property line of an office located in an unincorporated city, town, or village is the boundary line of that city, town, or village for the purpose of this definition.

(e) *Depository holding company* means a bank holding company or a savings and loan holding company (as more fully defined in section 202 of the Interlocks Act (12 U.S.C. 3201)) having its principal office located in the United States.

(f) *Depository institution* means a commercial bank (including a private bank), a savings bank, a trust company, a savings and loan association, a building and loan association, a homestead association, a cooperative bank, an industrial bank, or a credit union, chartered under the laws of the United States and having a principal office located in the United States. Additionally, a United States office, including a branch or agency, of a foreign commercial bank is a depository institution.

(g) *Depository institution affiliate* means a depository institution that is an affiliate of a depository organization.

(h) *Depository organization* means a depository institution or a depository holding company.

(i) *Low- and moderate-income areas* means census tracts (or, if an area is not in a census tract, block numbering areas delineated by the United States Bureau of the Census) where the median family income is less than 100 percent of the area median income.

(j) *Management official.* (1) The term *management official* means:

(i) A director;

(ii) An advisory or honorary director of a depository institution with total assets of $100 million or more;

(iii) A senior executive officer as that term is defined in 12 CFR 303.101(b).

(iv) A branch manager;

§ 348.3   12 CFR Ch. III (1-1-12 Edition)

(v) A trustee of a depository organization under the control of trustees; and

(vi) Any person who has a representative or nominee serving in any of the capacities in this paragraph (j)(1).

(2) The term *management official* does not include:

(i) A person whose management functions relate exclusively to the business of retail merchandising or manufacturing;

(ii) A person whose management functions relate principally to the business outside the United States of a foreign commercial bank; or

(iii) A person described in the provisos of section 202(4) of the Interlocks Act (12 U.S.C. 3201(4)) (referring to an officer of a State-chartered savings bank, cooperative bank, or trust company that neither makes real estate mortgage loans nor accepts savings).

(k) *Office* means a principal or branch office of a depository institution located in the United States. *Office* does not include a representative office of a foreign commercial bank, an electronic terminal, or a loan production office.

(l) *Person* means a natural person, corporation, or other business entity.

(m) *Relevant metropolitan statistical area (RMSA)* means an MSA, a primary MSA, or a consolidated MSA that is not comprised of designated Primary MSAs to the extent that these terms are defined and applied by the Office of Management and Budget.

(n) *Representative or nominee* means a natural person who serves as a management official and has an obligation to act on behalf of another person with respect to management responsibilities. The FDIC will find that a person has an obligation to act on behalf of another person only if the first person has an agreement, express or implied, to act on behalf of the second person with respect to management responsibilities. The FDIC will determine, after giving the affected persons an opportunity to respond, whether a person is a *representative or nominee*.

(o) *Total assets.* (1) The term *total assets* includes assets measured on a consolidated basis and reported in the most recent fiscal year-end Consolidated Report of Condition and Income.

(2) The term *total assets* does not include:

(i) Assets of a diversified savings and loan holding company as defined by section 10(a)(1)(F) of the Home Owners' Loan Act (12 U.S.C. 1467a(a)(1)(F)) other than the assets of its depository institution affiliate;

(ii) Assets of a bank holding company that are exempt from the prohibitions of section 4 of the Bank Holding Company Act of 1956 pursuant to an order issued under section 4(d) of that Act (12 U.S.C. 1843(d)) other than the assets of its depository institution affiliate; or

(iii) Assets of offices of a foreign commercial bank other than the assets of its United States branch or agency.

(p) *United States* means the United States of America, any State or territory of the United States of America, the District of Columbia, Puerto Rico, Guam, American Samoa, and the Virgin Islands.

[61 FR 40305, Aug. 2, 1996, as amended at 64 FR 51679, Sept. 24, 1999; 68 FR 50461, Aug. 21, 2003; 72 FR 1276, Jan. 11, 2007]

§ 348.3 Prohibitions.

(a) *Community.* A management official of a depository organization may not serve at the same time as a management official of an unaffiliated depository organization if the depository organizations in question (or a depository institution affiliate thereof) have offices in the same community.

(b) *RMSA.* A management official of a depository organization may not serve at the same time as a management official of an unaffiliated depository organization if the depository organizations in question (or a depository institution affiliate thereof) have offices in the same RMSA and each depository organization has total assets of $50 million or more.

(c) *Major assets.* A management official of a depository organization with total assets exceeding $2.5 billion (or any affiliate of such an organization) may not serve at the same time as a management official of an unaffiliated depository organization with total assets exceeding $1.5 billion (or any affiliate of such an organization), regardless of the location of the two depository organizations. The FDIC will adjust these thresholds, as necessary, based on the year-to-year change in the average of the Consumer Price Index for the Urban Wage Earners and Clerical Workers, not seasonally adjusted, with rounding to the nearest $100 million. The FDIC will announce the revised thresholds by publishing a final rule without notice and comment in the FEDERAL REGISTER.

[61 FR 40305, Aug. 2, 1996, as amended at 64 FR 51679, Sept. 24, 1999; 72 FR 1276, Jan. 11, 2007]

§ 348.4 Interlocking relationships permitted by statute.

The prohibitions of § 348.3 do not apply in the case of any one or more of the following organizations or to a subsidiary thereof:

(a) A depository organization that has been placed formally in liquidation, or which is in the hands of a receiver, conservator, or other official exercising a similar function;

(b) A corporation operating under section 25 or section 25A of the Federal Reserve Act (12 U.S.C. 601 et seq. and 12 U.S.C. 611 et seq., respectively) (Edge Corporations and Agreement Corporations);

(c) A credit union being served by a management official of another credit union;

(d) A depository organization that does not do business within the United States except as an incident to its activities outside the United States;

(e) A State-chartered savings and loan guaranty corporation;

(f) A Federal Home Loan bank or any other bank organized solely to serve depository institutions (a bankers' bank) or solely for the purpose of providing securities clearing services and services related thereto for depository institutions and securities companies;

(g) A depository organization that is closed or is in danger of closing as determined by the appropriate Federal depository institutions regulatory agency and is acquired by another depository organization. This exemption lasts for five years, beginning on the date the depository organization is acquired;

(h) A savings association whose acquisition has been authorized on an emergency basis in accordance with section 13(k) of the Federal Deposit Insurance Act (12 U.S.C. 1823(k)) with resulting dual service by a management official that would otherwise be prohibited under the Interlocks Act which may continue for up to 10 years from the date of the acquisition provided that the FDIC has given its approval for the continuation of such service; and

(i)(1) A diversified savings and loan holding company (as defined in section 10(a)(1)(F) of the Home Owners' Loan Act (12 U.S.C. 1467a(a)(1)(F)) with respect to the service of a director of such company who is also a director of an unaffiliated depository organization if:

(i) Both the diversified savings and loan holding company and the unaffiliated depository organization notify their appropriate Federal depository institutions regulatory agency at least 60 days before the dual service is proposed to begin; and

(ii) The appropriate regulatory agency does not disapprove the dual service before the end of the 60-day period.

(2) The FDIC may disapprove a notice of proposed service if it finds that:

(i) The service cannot be structured or limited so as to preclude an anticompetitive effect in financial services in any part of the United States;

(ii) The service would lead to substantial conflicts of interest or unsafe or unsound practices; or

(iii) The notificant failed to furnish all the information required by the FDIC.

(3) The FDIC may require that any interlock permitted under this paragraph (h) be terminated if a change in circumstances occurs with respect to one of the interlocked depository organizations that would have provided a basis for disapproval of the interlock during the notice period.

§ 348.5 Small market share exemption.

(a) *Exemption.* A management interlock that is prohibited by § 348.3 is permissible, if:

(1) The interlock is not prohibited by § 348.3(c); and

(2) The depository organizations (and their depository institution affiliates) hold, in the aggregate, no more than 20 percent of the deposits in each RMSA

§ 348.6

or community in which both depository organizations (or their depository institution affiliates) have offices. The amount of deposits shall be determined by reference to the most recent annual Summary of Deposits published by the FDIC for the RMSA or community.

(b) *Confirmation and records.* Each depository organization must maintain records sufficient to support its determination of eligibility for the exemption under paragraph (a) of this section, and must reconfirm that determination on an annual basis.

[64 FR 51680, Sept. 24, 1999]

§ 348.6 General exemption.

(a) *Exemption.* The FDIC may by agency order exempt an interlock from the prohibitions in § 348.3 if the FDIC finds that the interlock would not result in a monopoly or substantial lessening of competition and would not present safety and soundness concerns.

(b) *Presumptions.* In reviewing an application for an exemption under this section, the FDIC will apply a rebuttable presumption that an interlock will not result in a monopoly or substantial lessening of competition if the depository organization seeking to add a management official:

(1) Primarily serves low-and moderate-income areas;

(2) Is controlled or managed by persons who are members of a minority group, or women;

(3) Is a depository institution that has been chartered for less than two years; or

(4) Is deemed to be in "troubled condition" as defined in § 303.101(c).

(c) *Duration.* Unless a shorter expiration period is provided in the FDIC approval, an exemption permitted by paragraph (a) of this section may continue so long as it does not result in a monopoly or substantial lessening of competition, or is unsafe or unsound. If the FDIC grants an interlock exemption in reliance upon a presumption under paragraph (b) of this section, the interlock may continue for three years, unless otherwise provided by the FDIC in writing.

(d) *Procedures.* Procedures for applying for an exemption under this section are set forth in 12 CFR 303.249.

[64 FR 51680, Sept. 24, 1999, as amended at 71 FR 20527, Apr. 21, 2006]

§ 348.7 Change in circumstances.

(a) *Termination.* A management official shall terminate his or her service or apply for an exemption if a change in circumstances causes the service to become prohibited. A change in circumstances may include an increase in asset size of an organization, a change in the delineation of the RMSA or community, the establishment of an office, an increase in the aggregate deposits of the depository organization, or an acquisition, merger, consolidation, or reorganization of the ownership structure of a depository organization that causes a previously permissible interlock to become prohibited.

(b) *Transition period.* A management official described in paragraph (a) of this section may continue to serve the insured nonmember bank involved in the interlock for 15 months following the date of the change in circumstances. The FDIC may shorten this period under appropriate circumstances.

[61 FR 40305, Aug. 2, 1996, as amended at 64 FR 51680, Sept. 24, 1999]

§ 348.8 Enforcement.

Except as provided in this section, the FDIC administers and enforces the Interlocks Act with respect to insured nonmember banks and their affiliates and may refer any case of a prohibited interlocking relationship involving these entities to the Attorney General of the United States to enforce compliance with the Interlocks Act and this part. If an affiliate of an insured nonmember bank is subject to the primary regulation of another federal depository organization supervisory agency, then the FDIC does not administer and enforce the Interlocks Act with respect to that affiliate.

PART 349—RETAIL FOREIGN EXCHANGE TRANSACTIONS

Sec.
349.1 Authority, purpose, and scope.

Federal Deposit Insurance Corporation § 349.2

349.2 Definitions.
349.3 Prohibited transactions.
349.4 Filing procedures.
349.5 Application and closing out of offsetting long and short positions.
349.6 Disclosure.
349.7 Recordkeeping.
349.8 Capital requirements.
349.9 Margin requirements.
349.10 Required reporting to customers.
349.11 Unlawful representations.
349.12 Authorization to trade.
349.13 Trading and operational standards.
349.14 Supervision.
349.15 Notice of transfers.
349.16 Customer dispute resolution.

AUTHORITY: 12 U.S.C.1813(q), 1818, 1819, and 3108; 7 U.S.C. 2(c)(2)(E), 27 *et seq.*

SOURCE: 76 FR 40789, July 12, 2011, unless otherwise noted.

§ 349.1 Authority, purpose, and scope.

(a) *Authority.* An FDIC-supervised insured depository institution that engages in retail forex transactions shall comply with the requirements of this part.

(b) *Purpose.* This part establishes rules applicable to retail forex transactions engaged in by FDIC-supervised insured depository institutions and applies on or after the effective date.

(c) *Scope.* Except as provided in paragraph (d) of this section, this part applies to FDIC-supervised insured depository institutions.

(d) *International applicability.* Sections 349.3 and 349.5 to 349.16 do not apply to retail foreign exchange transactions between a foreign branch of an FDIC-supervised IDI and a non-U.S. customer. With respect to those transactions, an FDIC-supervised IDI must comply with any disclosure, recordkeeping, capital, margin, reporting, business conduct, documentation, and other requirements of applicable foreign law.

§ 349.2 Definitions.

For purposes of this part—

The following terms have the same meaning as in the Commodity Exchange Act: "Affiliated person of a futures commission merchant"; "Associated person"; "Contract of sale"; "Commodity"; "Eligible contract participant"; "Futures commission merchant"; "Security"; and "Security futures product".

Affiliate has the same meaning as in § 2(k) of the Bank Holding Company Act of 1956 (12 U.S.C. 1841(k)).

Commodity Exchange Act means the Commodity Exchange Act (7 U.S.C. 1 *et seq.*).

FDIC-supervised insured depository institution means any insured depository institution for which the Federal Deposit Insurance Corporation is the appropriate Federal banking agency pursuant to § 3(q) of the Federal Deposit Insurance Act, 12 U.S.C. 1813(q).

Forex means foreign exchange.

Institution-affiliated party or *IAP* has the same meaning as in 12 U.S.C. 1813(u)(1), (2), or (3).

Insured depository institution or *IDI* has the same meaning as in 12 U.S.C. 1813(c)(2).

Introducing broker means any person who solicits or accepts orders from a retail forex customer in connection with retail forex transactions.

Related person, when used in reference to a retail forex counterparty, means:

(1) Any general partner, officer, director, or owner of ten percent or more of the capital stock of the FDIC-supervised insured depository institution;

(2) An associated person or employee of the retail forex counterparty, if the retail forex counterparty is not an FDIC-supervised insured depository institution;

(3) An IAP, if the retail forex counterparty is an FDIC-supervised insured depository institution; and

(4) Any relative or spouse of any of the foregoing persons, or any relative of such spouse, who shares the same home as any of the foregoing persons.

Retail forex account means the account of a retail forex customer, established with an FDIC-supervised insured depository institution, in which retail forex transactions with the FDIC-supervised insured depository institution as counterparty are undertaken, or the account of a retail forex customer that is established in order to enter into such transactions.

Retail forex account agreement means the contractual agreement between an FDIC-supervised insured depository institution and a retail forex customer that contains the terms governing the customer's retail forex account with

§ 349.2

the FDIC-supervised insured depository institution.

Retail forex business means engaging in one or more retail forex transactions with the intent to derive income from those transactions, either directly or indirectly.

Retail forex counterparty includes, as appropriate:

(1) An FDIC-supervised insured depository institution;

(2) A retail foreign exchange dealer;

(3) A futures commission merchant; and

(4) An affiliated person of a futures commission merchant.

Retail forex customer means a customer that is not an eligible contract participant, acting on his, her, or its own behalf and engaging in retail forex transactions.

Retail forex obligations means obligations of a retail forex customer with respect to retail forex transactions, including, but not limited to, trading losses, fees, and commissions.

Retail forex proprietary account means: a retail forex account carried on the books of an FDIC-supervised insured depository institution for one of the following persons; a retail forex account of which 10 percent or more is owned by one of the following persons; or a retail forex account of which an aggregate of 10 percent or more of which is owned by more than one of the following persons:

(1) The FDIC-supervised insured depository institution;

(2) An officer, director or owner of ten percent or more of the capital stock of the FDIC-supervised insured depository institution; or

(3) An employee of the FDIC-supervised insured depository institution, whose duties include:

(i) The management of the FDIC-supervised insured depository institution's business;

(ii) The handling of the FDIC-supervised insured depository institution's retail forex transactions;

(iii) The keeping of records, including without limitation the software used to make or maintain those records, pertaining to the FDIC-supervised insured depository institution's retail forex transactions; or

(iv) The signing or co-signing of checks or drafts on behalf of the FDIC-supervised insured depository institution;

(4) A spouse or minor dependent living in the same household as of any of the foregoing persons; or

(5) An affiliate of the FDIC-supervised insured depository institution;

Retail forex transaction means an agreement, contract, or transaction in foreign currency, other than an identified banking product or a part of an identified banking product, that is offered or entered into by FDIC-supervised insured depository institution with a person that is not an eligible contract participant and that is:

(1) A contract of sale of a commodity for future delivery or an option on such a contract;

(2) An option, other than an option executed or traded on a national securities exchange registered pursuant to §6(a) of the Securities Exchange Act of 1934 (15 U.S.C. 78(f)(a)); or

(3) Offered or entered into on a leveraged or margined basis, or financed by an FDIC-supervised insured depository institution, its affiliate, or any person acting in concert with the FDIC-supervised insured depository institution or its affiliate on a similar basis, other than:

(i) A security that is not a security futures product as defined in § 1a(47) of the Commodity Exchange Act (7 U.S.C. 1a(47)); or

(ii) A contract of sale that—

(A) Results in actual delivery within two days; or

(B) Creates an enforceable obligation to deliver between a seller and buyer that have the ability to deliver and accept delivery, respectively, in connection with their line of business; or

(iii) An agreement, contract, or transaction that the FDIC determines is not functionally or economically similar to:

(A) A contract of sale of a commodity for future delivery or an option on such a contract; or

(B) An option, other than an option executed or traded on a national securities exchange registered pursuant to Section 6(a) of the Securities Exchange Act of 1934 (15 U.S.C. 78(f)(a)).

§ 349.3 Prohibited transactions.

(a) *Fraudulent conduct prohibited.* No FDIC-supervised insured depository institution or its IAPs may, directly or indirectly, in or in connection with any retail forex transaction:

(1) Cheat or defraud or attempt to cheat or defraud any person;

(2) Willfully make or cause to be made to any person any false report or statement or cause to be entered for any person any false record; or

(3) Willfully deceive or attempt to deceive any person by any means whatsoever.

(b) *Acting as counterparty and exercising discretion prohibited.* If an FDIC-supervised insured depository institution can cause retail forex transactions to be effected for a retail forex customer without the retail forex customer's specific authorization, then neither the FDIC-supervised insured depository institution nor its affiliates may act as the counterparty for any retail forex transaction with that retail forex customer.

§ 349.4 Filing procedures.

(a) *General.* Before commencing a retail forex business, an FDIC-supervised insured depository institution shall provide the FDIC prior written notice and obtain the FDIC's prior written consent.

(b) *Where to file.* A notice required by this section shall be submitted in writing to the appropriate FDIC office.

(c) *Contents of filing.* A complete letter notice shall include the following information:

(1) *Filings generally.* (i) A brief description of the FDIC-supervised institution's proposed retail forex business and the manner in which it will be conducted;

(ii) The amount of the institution's existing or proposed direct or indirect investment in the retail forex business as well as calculations sufficient to indicate compliance with all capital requirements in § 349.8 and all other applicable capital standards;

(iii) A copy of the FDIC-supervised insured depository institution's comprehensive business plan that includes a discussion of, among other things, how the operation of the retail forex business is consistent with the institution's overall strategy;

(iv) A description of the FDIC-supervised insured depository institution's target customers for its proposed retail forex business and related information, including without limitation credit evaluations, customer appropriateness, and "know your customer" documentation;

(v) A resolution by the FDIC-supervised insured depository institution's board of directors that the proposed retail forex business is an appropriate activity for the institution and that the institution's written policies, procedures, and risk measurement and management systems and controls address conducting retail forex business in a safe and sound manner and in compliance with this part;

(vi) Sample risk disclosures sufficient to demonstrate compliance with § 349.6.

(2) *Copy of application or notice filed with another agency.* If an FDIC-supervised insured depository institution has filed an application or notice with another regulatory authority which contains all of the information required by subparagraph (c)(1) of this part, the institution may submit a copy to the FDIC in lieu of a separate filing.

(3) *Additional information.* The FDIC may request additional information to complete the processing of the notification.

(d) *Treatment of Existing Retail Forex Business.* Any FDIC-supervised insured depository institution that is engaged in retail forex business on July 15, 2011 may continue to do so for up to six months, subject to an extension of time by the FDIC, provided that it notifies the FDIC of its retail forex business and requests the FDIC's written consent in accordance with paragraph (a) of this section.

(e) *Compliance with the Commodities Exchange Act.* Any FDIC-supervised insured depository institution that is engaged in retail forex business on July 15, 2011 shall be deemed, during the six-month period (including any extension) provided in paragraph (e) of this section, to be acting pursuant to a rule or regulation described in § 2(c)(2)(E)(ii)(I)

§ 349.5

of the Commodity Exchange Act (7 U.S.C. 2(c)(2)(E)(ii)(I)).

§ 349.5 Application and closing out of offsetting long and short positions.

(a) *Application of purchases and sales.* Any FDIC-supervised insured depository institution that—

(1) Engages in a retail forex transaction involving the purchase of any currency for the account of any retail forex customer when the account of such retail forex customer at the time of such purchase has an open retail forex transaction for the sale of the same currency;

(2) Engages in a retail forex transaction involving the sale of any currency for the account of any retail forex customer when the account of such retail forex customer at the time of such sale has an open retail forex transaction for the purchase of the same currency;

(3) Purchases a put or call option involving foreign currency for the account of any retail forex customer when the account of such retail forex customer at the time of such purchase has a short put or call option position with the same underlying currency, strike price, and expiration date as that purchased; or

(4) Sells a put or call option involving foreign currency for the account of any retail forex customer when the account of such retail forex customer at the time of such sale has a long put or call option position with the same underlying currency, strike price, and expiration date as that sold shall:

(i) Immediately apply such purchase or sale against such previously held opposite transaction; and

(ii) Promptly furnish such retail forex customer with a statement showing the financial result of the transactions involved and the name of any introducing broker to the account.

(b) *Close-out against oldest open position.* In all instances where the short or long position in a customer's retail forex account immediately prior to an offsetting purchase or sale is greater than the quantity purchased or sold, the FDIC-supervised insured depository institution shall apply such offsetting purchase or sale to the oldest portion of the previously held short or long position.

(c) *Transactions to be applied as directed by customer.* Notwithstanding paragraphs (a) and (b) of this section, the offsetting transaction shall be applied as directed by a retail forex customer's specific instructions. These instructions may not be made by the FDIC-supervised insured depository institution or an IAP.

§ 349.6 Disclosure.

(a) *Risk disclosure statement required.* No FDIC-supervised insured depository institution may open or maintain open an account that will engage in retail forex transactions for a retail forex customer unless the FDIC-supervised insured depository institution has furnished the retail forex customer with a separate written disclosure statement containing only the language set forth in paragraph (d) of this section and the disclosures required by paragraphs (e) and (f) of this section.

(b) *Acknowledgement of risk disclosure statement required.* The FDIC-supervised insured depository institution must receive from the retail forex customer a written acknowledgement signed and dated by the customer that the customer received and understood the written disclosure statement required by paragraph (a) of this section.

(c) *Placement of risk disclosure statement.* The disclosure statement may be attached to other documents as the initial page(s) of such documents and as the only material on such page(s).

(d) *Content of risk disclosure statement.* The language set forth in the written disclosure statement required by paragraph (a) of this section shall be as follows:

RISK DISCLOSURE STATEMENT

Retail forex transactions involve the leveraged trading of contracts denominated in foreign currency with an FDIC-supervised insured depository institution as your counterparty. Because of the leverage and the other risks disclosed here, you can rapidly lose all of the funds or property you give the FDIC-supervised insured depository institution as margin for such trading and you may lose more than you pledge as margin.

Your FDIC-supervised insured depository institution is prohibited from applying losses that you experience on retail forex transactions on any funds or property of yours

Federal Deposit Insurance Corporation

§ 349.6

other than funds or property that you have given or pledged as margin for retail forex transactions.

You should be aware of and carefully consider the following points before determining whether such trading is appropriate for you.

(1) Trading is a not on a regulated market or exchange—your FDIC-supervised insured depository institution is your trading counterparty and has conflicting interests. The retail forex transaction you are entering into is not conducted on an interbank market, nor is it conducted on a futures exchange subject to regulation as a designated contract market by the Commodity Futures Trading Commission. The foreign currency trades you transact are trades with your FDIC-supervised insured depository institution as the counterparty. When you sell, the FDIC-supervised insured depository institution is the buyer. When you buy, the FDIC-supervised insured depository institution is the seller. As a result, when you lose money trading, your FDIC-supervised insured depository institution is making money on such trades, in addition to any fees, commissions, or spreads the FDIC-supervised insured depository institution may charge.

(2) An electronic trading platform for retail foreign currency transactions is not an exchange. It is an electronic connection for accessing your FDIC-supervised insured depository institution. The terms of availability of such a platform are governed only by your contract with your FDIC-supervised insured depository institution. Any trading platform that you may use to enter into off-exchange foreign currency transactions is only connected to your FDIC-supervised insured depository institution. You are accessing that trading platform only to transact with your FDIC-supervised insured depository institution. You are not trading with any other entities or customers of the FDIC-supervised insured depository institution by accessing such platform. The availability and operation of any such platform, including the consequences of the unavailability of the trading platform for any reason, is governed only by the terms of your account agreement with the FDIC-supervised insured depository institution.

(3) You may be able to offset or liquidate any trading positions only through your banking entity because the transactions are not made on an exchange or regulated contract market, and your FDIC-supervised insured depository institution may set its own prices. Your ability to close your transactions or offset positions is limited to what your FDIC-supervised insured depository institution will offer to you, as there is no other market for these transactions. Your FDIC-supervised insured depository institution may offer any prices it wishes, including prices derived from outside sources or not in its discretion. Your FDIC-supervised insured depository institution may establish its prices by offering spreads from third party prices, but it is under no obligation to do so or to continue to do so. Your FDIC-supervised insured depository institution may offer different prices to different customers at any point in time on its own terms. The terms of your account agreement alone govern the obligations your FDIC-supervised insured depository institution has to you to offer prices and offer offset or liquidating transactions in your account and make any payments to you. The prices offered by your FDIC-supervised insured depository institution may or may not reflect prices available elsewhere at any exchange, interbank, or other market for foreign currency.

(4) Paid solicitors may have undisclosed conflicts. The FDIC-supervised insured depository institution may compensate introducing brokers for introducing your account in ways that are not disclosed to you. Such paid solicitors are not required to have, and may not have, any special expertise in trading, and may have conflicts of interest based on the method by which they are compensated. You should thoroughly investigate the manner in which all such solicitors are compensated and be very cautious in granting any person or entity authority to trade on your behalf. You should always consider obtaining dated written confirmation of any information you are relying on from your FDIC-supervised insured depository institution in making any trading or account decisions.

(5) Retail forex transactions are not insured by the Federal Deposit Insurance Corporation.

(6) Retail forex transactions are not a deposit in, or guaranteed by, an FDIC-supervised insured depository institution.

(7) Retail forex transactions are subject to investment risks, including possible loss of all amounts invested.

Finally, you should thoroughly investigate any statements by any FDIC-supervised insured depository institution that minimize the importance of, or contradict, any of the terms of this risk disclosure. These statements may indicate sales fraud.

This brief statement cannot, of course, disclose all the risks and other aspects of trading off-exchange foreign currency with an FDIC-supervised insured depository institution.

I hereby acknowledge that I have received and understood this risk disclosure statement.

lllllllllllllllllllllllll
Date
lllllllllllllllllllllllll
Signature of Customer

(e)(1) *Disclosure of profitable accounts ratio.* Immediately following the language set forth in paragraph (d) of this

529

§ 349.7

section, the statement required by paragraph (a) of this section shall include, for each of the most recent four calendar quarters during which the FDIC-supervised insured depository institution maintained retail forex customer accounts:

(i) The total number of retail forex customer accounts maintained by the FDIC-supervised insured depository institution over which the FDIC-supervised insured depository institution does not exercise investment discretion;

(ii) The percentage of such accounts that were profitable for retail forex customer accounts during the quarter; and

(iii) The percentage of such accounts that were not profitable for retail forex customer accounts during the quarter.

(2) The FDIC-supervised insured depository institution's statement of profitable trades shall include the following legend: "Past performance is not necessarily indicative of future results." Each FDIC-supervised insured depository institution shall provide, upon request, to any retail forex customer or prospective retail forex customer the total number of retail forex accounts maintained by the FDIC-supervised insured depository institution for which the FDIC-supervised insured depository institution does not exercise investment discretion, the percentage of such accounts that were profitable, and the percentage of such accounts that were not profitable for each calendar quarter during the most recent five-year period during which the FDIC-supervised insured depository institution maintained such accounts.

(f) *Disclosure of fees and other charges.* Immediately following the language required by paragraph (e) of this section, the statement required by paragraph (a) of this section shall include:

(1) The amount of any fee, charge, commission, or spreads that the FDIC-supervised insured depository institution may impose on the retail forex customer in connection with a retail forex account or retail forex transaction;

(2) An explanation of how the FDIC-supervised insured depository institution will determine the amount of such fees, charges, commissions, or spreads; and

(3) The circumstances under which the FDIC-supervised insured depository institution may impose such fees, charges, commissions, or spreads.

(g) *Future disclosure requirements.* If, with regard to a retail forex customer, the FDIC-supervised insured depository institution changes any fee, charge, commission or spreads required to be disclosed under paragraph (f) of this section, then the FDIC-supervised insured depository institution shall mail or deliver to the retail forex customer a notice of the changes at least 15 days prior to the effective date of the change.

(h) *Form of disclosure requirements.* The disclosures required by this section shall be clear and conspicuous and designed to call attention to the nature and significance of the information provided.

(i) *Other disclosure requirements unaffected.* This section does not relieve an FDIC-supervised insured depository institution from any other disclosure obligation it may have under applicable law.

§ 349.7 **Recordkeeping.**

(a) *General rule.* An FDIC-supervised insured depository institution engaging in retail forex transactions shall keep full, complete and systematic records, together with all pertinent data and memoranda, pertaining to its retail forex business, including:

(1) *Retail forex account records.* For each retail forex account:

(i) The name and address of the person for whom the account is carried or introduced and the principal occupation or business of the person.

(ii) The name of any other person guaranteeing the account or exercising trading control with respect to the account;

(iii) The establishment or termination of the account; and

(iv) A means to identify the person who has solicited and is responsible for the account or assign account numbers in such a manner as to identify that person.

(v) The funds in the account, net of any commissions and fees;

Federal Deposit Insurance Corporation

§ 349.7

(vi) The account's net profits and losses on open trades;

(vii) The funds in the account plus or minus the net profits and losses on open trades, adjusted for the net option value in the case of open options positions;

(viii) Financial ledger records that show separately for each retail forex customer all charges against and credits to such retail forex customer's account, including deposits, withdrawals, and transfers, and charges or credits resulting from losses or gains on closed transactions; and

(ix) A list of all retail forex transactions executed for the account, with the details specified in paragraph (a)(2) of this section;

(2) *Retail forex transaction records.* For each retail forex transaction:

(i) The price at which the FDIC-supervised insured depository institution placed the order, or, in the case of an option, the premium that the retail forex customer paid;

(ii) The customer account identification information;

(iii) The currency pair;

(iv) The size or quantity of the order;

(v) Whether the order was a buy or sell order;

(vi) The type of order, if the order was not a market order;

(vii) The size and price at which the order is executed, or in the case of an option, the amount of the premium paid for each option purchased, or the amount credited for each option sold;

(viii) For options, whether the option is a put or call, expiration date, quantity, underlying contract for future delivery or underlying physical, strike price, and details of the purchase price of the option, including premium, mark-up, commission, and fees; and

(ix) For futures, the delivery date; and

(x) If the order was made on a trading platform:

(A) The price quoted on the trading platform when the order was placed, or, in the case of an option, the premium quoted;

(B) The date and time the order was transmitted to the trading platform; and

(C) The date and time the order was executed;

(3) *Price changes on a trading platform.* If a trading platform is used, daily logs showing each price change on the platform, the time of the change to the nearest second, and the trading volume at that time and price;

(4) *Methods or algorithms.* Any method or algorithm used to determine the bid or asked price for any retail forex transaction or the prices at which customer orders are executed, including, but not limited to, any markups, fees, commissions or other items which affect the profitability or risk of loss of a retail forex customer's transaction;

(5) *Daily records* which show for each business day complete details of:

(i) All retail forex transactions that are futures transactions executed on that day, including the date, price, quantity, market, currency pair, delivery date, and the person for whom such transaction was made;

(ii) All retail forex transactions that are option transactions executed on that day, including the date, whether the transaction involved a put or call, the expiration date, quantity, currency pair, delivery date, strike price, details of the purchase price of the option, including premium, mark-up, commission and fees, and the person for whom the transaction was made;

(iii) All other retail forex transactions executed on that day for such account, including the date, price, quantity, currency and the person for whom such transaction was made; and

(6) *Other records.* Written acknowledgements of receipt of the risk disclosure statement required by section 349.6(b), records required under paragraph (b) through (f) of this section, trading cards, signature cards, street books, journals, ledgers, payment records, copies of statements of purchase, and all other records, data and memoranda that have been prepared in the course of the FDIC-supervised insured depository institution's retail forex business.

(b) *Ratio of profitable accounts.* (1) With respect to its active retail forex customer accounts over which it did not exercise investment discretion and that are not retail forex proprietary accounts open for any period of time during the quarter, an FDIC-supervised insured depository institution shall

531

prepare and maintain on a quarterly basis (calendar quarter):

(i) A calculation of the percentage of such accounts that were profitable;

(ii) A calculation of the percentage of such accounts that were not profitable; and

(iii) Data supporting the calculations described in paragraphs (b)(1)(i) and (b)(1)(ii) of this section.

(2) In calculating whether a retail forex account was profitable or not profitable during the quarter, the FDIC-supervised insured depository institution shall compute the realized and unrealized gains or losses on all retail forex transactions carried in the retail forex account at any time during the quarter, and subtract all fees, commissions, and any other charges posted to the retail forex account during the quarter, and add any interest income and other income or rebates credited to the retail forex account during the quarter. All deposits and withdrawals of funds made by the retail forex customer during the quarter must be excluded from the computation of whether the retail forex account was profitable or not profitable during the quarter. Computations that result in a zero or negative number shall be considered a retail forex account that was not profitable. Computations that result in a positive number shall be considered a retail forex account that was profitable.

(3) A retail forex account shall be considered "active" for purposes of paragraph (b)(1) of this section if and only if, for the relevant calendar quarter, a retail forex transaction was executed in that account or the retail forex account contained an open position resulting from a retail forex transaction.

(c) *Records related to possible violations of law.* An FDIC-supervised insured depository institution engaging in retail forex transactions shall make a record of all communications, including customer complaints, received by the FDIC-supervised insured depository institution or its IAPs concerning facts giving rise to possible violations of law related to the FDIC-supervised insured depository institution's retail forex business. The record shall contain: the name of the complainant, if provided; the date of the communication; the relevant agreement, contract, or transaction; the substance of the communication; the name of the person who received the communication, and the final disposition of the matter.

(d) *Records for noncash margin.* An FDIC-supervised insured depository institution shall maintain a record of all noncash margin collected pursuant to section 349.9. The record shall show separately for each retail forex customer:

(1) A description of the securities or property received;

(2) The name and address of such retail forex customer;

(3) The dates when the securities or property were received;

(4) The identity of the depositories or other places where such securities or property are segregated or held, if applicable;

(5) The dates in which the FDIC-supervised insured depository institution placed or removed such securities or property into or from such depositories; and

(6) The dates of return of such securities or property to such retail forex customer, or other disposition thereof, together with the facts and circumstances of such other disposition.

(e) *Order Tickets.* (1) Except as provided in paragraph (e)(2) of this section, immediately upon the receipt of a retail forex transaction order, an FDIC-supervised insured depository institution must prepare an order ticket for the order (whether unfulfilled, executed, or canceled). The order ticket must include:

(i) Account identification (account or customer name with which the retail forex transaction was effected);

(ii) Order number;

(iii) Type of order (market order, limit order, or subject to special instructions);

(iv) Date and time, to the nearest minute, the retail forex transaction order was received (as evidenced by timestamp or other timing device);

(v) Time, to the nearest minute, the retail forex transaction order was executed; and

(vi) Price at which the retail forex transaction was executed.

Federal Deposit Insurance Corporation § 349.9

(2) *Post-execution allocation of bunched orders.* Specific identifiers for retail forex accounts included in bunched orders need not be recorded at time of order placement or upon report of execution as required under paragraph (e)(1) of this section if the following requirements are met:

(i) The FDIC-supervised insured depository institution placing and directing the allocation of an order eligible for post-execution allocation has been granted written investment discretion with regard to participating customer accounts and makes the following information available to retail forex customers upon request:

(A) The general nature of the post-execution allocation methodology the FDIC-supervised insured depository institution will use;

(B) Whether the FDIC-supervised insured depository institution has any interest in accounts which may be included with customer accounts in bunched orders eligible for post-execution allocation; and

(C) Summary or composite data sufficient for that customer to compare its results with those of other comparable customers and, if applicable, any account in which the FDIC-supervised insured depository institution has an interest.

(ii) Post-execution allocations are made as soon as practicable after the entire transaction is executed;

(iii) Post-execution allocations are fair and equitable, with no account or group of accounts receiving consistently favorable or unfavorable treatment; and

(iv) The post-execution allocation methodology is sufficiently objective and specific to permit the FDIC to verify the fairness of the allocations using that methodology.

(f) *Record of monthly statements and confirmations.* An FDIC-supervised insured depository institution shall retain a copy of each monthly statement and confirmation required by section 349.10.

(g) *Manner of maintenance.* The records required by this section must clearly and accurately reflect the information required and provide an adequate basis for the audit of the information. Record maintenance may include the use of automated or electronic records provided that the records are easily retrievable, readily available for inspection, and capable of being reproduced in hard copy.

(h) *Length of maintenance.* An FDIC-supervised insured depository institution shall keep each record required by this section for at least five years from the date the record is created.

§ 349.8 **Capital requirements.**

An FDIC-supervised insured depository institution offering or entering into retail forex transactions must be well capitalized as defined by 12 CFR part 325, unless specifically exempted by the FDIC in writing.

§ 349.9 **Margin requirements.**

(a) *Margin required.* An FDIC-supervised insured depository institution engaging, or offering to engage, in retail forex transactions must collect from each retail forex customer an amount of margin not less than:

(1) Two percent of the notional value of the retail forex transaction for major currency pairs and 5 percent of the notional value of the retail forex transaction for all other currency pairs;

(2) For short options, 2 percent for major currency pairs and 5 percent for all other currency pairs of the notional value of the retail forex transaction, plus the premium received by the retail forex customer; or

(3) For long options, the full premium charged and received by the FDIC-supervised insured depository institution.

(b)(1) *Form of margin.* Margin collected under paragraph (a) of this section or pledged by a retail forex customer for retail forex transactions in excess of the requirements of paragraph (a) of this section must be in the form of cash or the following financial instruments:

(i) Obligations of the United States and obligations fully guaranteed as to principal and interest by the United States;

(ii) General obligations of any State or of any political subdivision thereof;

(iii) General obligations issued or guaranteed by any enterprise, as defined in 12 U.S.C. 4502(10);

533

§ 349.10

(iv) Certificates of deposit issued by an insured depository institution, as defined in § 3(c)(2) of the Federal Deposit Insurance Act (12 U.S.C. 1813(c)(2));

(v) Commercial paper;

(vi) Corporate notes or bonds;

(vii) General obligations of a sovereign nation;

(viii) Interests in money market mutual funds; and

(ix) Such other financial instruments as the FDIC deems appropriate.

(2) *Haircuts.* An FDIC-supervised insured depository institution shall establish written policies and procedures that include:

(i) Haircuts for noncash margin collected under this section; and

(ii) Annual evaluation, and, if appropriate, modification of the haircuts.

(c) *Separate margin account.* Margin collected by the FDIC-supervised insured depository institution from a retail forex customer for retail forex transactions or pledged by a retail forex customer for retail forex transactions shall be placed into a separate account containing only such margin.

(d) *Margin calls; liquidation of position.* For each retail forex customer, at least once per day, an FDIC-supervised insured depository institution shall:

(1) Mark the value of the retail forex customer's open retail forex positions to market;

(2) Mark the value of the margin collected under this section from the retail forex customer to market;

(3) Determine if, based on the marks in paragraphs (c)(1) and (2) of this section, the FDIC-supervised insured depository institution has collected margin from the retail forex customer sufficient to satisfy the requirements of this section; and

(4) Collect such margin from the retail forex customer as the FDIC-supervised insured depository institution may require to satisfy the requirements of this section, or liquidate the retail forex customer's retail forex transactions.

(e) *Set-off prohibited.* An FDIC-supervised insured depository institution may not:

(1) Apply a retail forex customer's retail forex obligations against any funds or other asset of the retail forex customer other than margin in the separate margin account described in paragraph (c) of this section;

(2) Apply a retail forex customer's retail forex obligations to increase the amount owed by the retail forex customer to the FDIC-supervised insured depository institution under any loan; or

(3) Collect the margin required under this section by use of any right of set-off.

§ 349.10 Required reporting to customers.

(a) *Monthly statements.* Each FDIC-supervised insured depository institution must promptly furnish to each retail forex customer, as of the close of the last business day of each month or as of any regular monthly date selected, except for accounts in which there are neither open positions at the end of the statement period nor any changes to the account balance since the prior statement period, but in any event not less frequently than once every three months, a statement that clearly shows:

(1) For each retail forex customer:

(i) The open retail forex transactions with prices at which acquired;

(ii) The net unrealized profits or losses in all open retail forex transactions marked to the market;

(iii) Any money, securities or other property in the separate margin account required by § 349.9(c); and

(iv) A detailed accounting of all financial charges and credits to the retail forex customer's retail forex accounts during the monthly reporting period, including: money, securities, or property received from or disbursed to such customer; realized profits and losses; and fees, charges, commissions, and spreads.

(2) For each retail forex customer engaging in retail forex transactions that are options:

(i) All such options purchased, sold, exercised, or expired during the monthly reporting period, identified by underlying retail forex transaction or underlying currency, strike price, transaction date, and expiration date;

(ii) The open option positions carried for such customer and arising as of the end of the monthly reporting period,

Federal Deposit Insurance Corporation § 349.11

identified by underlying retail forex transaction or underlying currency, strike price, transaction date, and expiration date;

(iii) All such option positions marked to the market and the amount each position is in the money, if any;

(iv) Any money, securities or other property in the separate margin account required by § 349.9(c); and

(v) A detailed accounting of all financial charges and credits to the retail forex customer's retail forex accounts during the monthly reporting period, including: money, securities, or property received from or disbursed to such customer; realized profits and losses; premiums and mark-ups; and fees, charges, and commissions.

(b) *Confirmation statement.* Each FDIC-supervised insured depository institution must, not later than the next business day after any retail forex transaction, send:

(1) To each retail forex customer, a written confirmation of each retail forex transaction caused to be executed by it for the customer, including offsetting transactions executed during the same business day and the rollover of an open retail forex transaction to the next business day;

(2) To each retail forex customer engaging in forex option transactions, a written confirmation of each forex option transaction, containing at least the following information:

(i) The retail forex customer's account identification number;

(ii) A separate listing of the actual amount of the premium, as well as each mark-up thereon, if applicable, and all other commissions, costs, fees and other charges incurred in connection with the forex option transaction;

(iii) The strike price;

(iv) The underlying retail forex transaction or underlying currency;

(v) The final exercise date of the forex option purchased or sold; and

(vi) The date the forex option transaction was executed.

(3) To each retail forex customer engaging in forex option transactions, upon the expiration or exercise of any option, a written confirmation statement thereof, which statement shall include the date of such occurrence, a description of the option involved, and, in the case of exercise, the details of the retail forex or physical currency position which resulted therefrom including, if applicable, the final trading date of the retail forex transaction underlying the option.

(c) Notwithstanding the provisions of paragraphs (b)(1) through (3) of this section, a retail forex transaction that is caused to be executed for a pooled investment vehicle that engages in retail forex transactions need be confirmed only to the operator of such pooled investment vehicle.

(d) *Controlled accounts.* With respect to any account controlled by any person other than the retail forex customer for whom such account is carried, each FDIC-supervised insured depository institution shall promptly furnish in writing to such other person the information required by paragraphs (a) and (b) of this section.

(e) *Introduced accounts.* Each statement provided pursuant to the provisions of this section must, if applicable, show that the account for which the FDIC-supervised insured depository institution was introduced by an introducing broker and the name of the introducing broker.

§ 349.11 **Unlawful representations.**

(a) *No implication or representation of limiting losses.* No FDIC-supervised insured depository institution engaged in retail foreign exchange transactions or its IAPs may imply or represent that it will, with respect to any retail customer forex account, for or on behalf of any person:

(1) Guarantee such person or account against loss;

(2) Limit the loss of such person or account; or

(3) Not call for or attempt to collect margin as established for retail forex customers.

(b) *No implication of representation of engaging in prohibited acts.* No FDIC-supervised insured depository institution or its IAPs may in any way imply or represent that it will engage in any of the acts or practices described in paragraph (a) of this section.

(c) *No Federal government endorsement.* No FDIC-supervised insured depository institution or its IAPs may represent or imply in any manner whatsoever

§ 349.12

that any retail forex transaction or retail forex product has been sponsored, recommended, or approved by the FDIC, the Federal government, or any agency thereof.

(d) *Assuming or sharing of liability from bank error.* This section shall not be construed to prevent an FDIC-supervised insured depository institution from assuming or sharing in the losses resulting from the FDIC-supervised insured depository institution's error or mishandling of a retail forex transaction.

(e) *Certain guaranties unaffected.* This section shall not affect any guarantee entered into prior to the effective date of this part, but this section shall apply to any extension, modification or renewal thereof entered into after such date.

§ 349.12 Authorization to trade.

(a) *Specific authorization required.* No FDIC-supervised insured depository institution may directly or indirectly effect a retail forex transaction for the account of any retail forex customer unless, before the transaction occurs, the retail forex customer specifically authorized the FDIC-supervised insured depository institution to effect the retail forex transaction.

(b) Requirements for specific authorization. A retail forex transaction is "specifically authorized" for purposes of this section if the retail forex customer specifies:

(1) The precise retail forex transaction to be effected;

(2) The exact amount of the foreign currency to be purchased or sold; and

(3) In the case of an option, the identity of the foreign currency or contract that underlies the option.

§ 349.13 Trading and operational standards.

(a) *Internal rules, procedures, and controls required.* An FDIC-supervised insured depository institution engaging in retail forex transactions shall establish and implement internal policies, procedures, and controls designed, at a minimum, to:

(1) Ensure, to the extent reasonable, that each order received from a retail forex transaction that is executable at or near the price that the FDIC-supervised insured depository institution has quoted to the retail forex customer is entered for execution before any order in any retail forex transaction for

(i) A any proprietary account;

(ii) An account in which a related person has an interest, or any account for which such a related person may originate orders without the prior specific consent of the account owner if the related person has gained knowledge of the retail forex customer's order prior to the transmission of an order for a proprietary account;

(iii) an account in which such a related person has an interest, if the related person has gained knowledge of the retail forex customer's order prior to the transmission of an order for a proprietary account; or

(iv) an account in which such a related person may originate orders without the prior specific consent of the account owner if the related person has gained knowledge of the retail forex customer's order prior to the transmission of an order for a proprietary account.

(2) Prevent FDIC-supervised insured depository institution related persons from placing orders, directly or indirectly, with another person in a manner designed to circumvent the provisions of paragraph (a)(1) of this section;

(3) Fairly and objectively establish settlement prices for retail forex transactions; and

(b) *Disclosure of retail forex transactions.* No FDIC-supervised insured depository institution engaging in retail forex transactions may disclose that an order of another person is being held by the FDIC-supervised insured depository institution, unless the disclosure is necessary to the effective execution of such order or the disclosure is made at the request of the FDIC.

(c) *Handling of retail forex accounts of related persons of retail forex counterparties.* No FDIC-supervised insured depository institution engaging in retail forex transactions may knowingly handle the retail forex account of an employee of another retail forex counterparty's retail forex business unless the FDIC-supervised insured depository institution:

Federal Deposit Insurance Corporation § 349.14

(1) Receives written authorization from a person designated by the other retail forex counterparty with responsibility for the surveillance over the account pursuant to paragraph (a)(2) of this section;

(2) Prepares immediately upon receipt of an order for the account a written record of the order, including the account identification and order number, and records thereon to the nearest minute, by time-stamp or other timing device, the date and time the order is received; and

(3) Transmits on a regular basis to the other retail forex counterparty copies of all statements for the account and of all written records prepared upon the receipt of orders for such account pursuant to paragraph (a)(2) of this section.

(d) *Related person of FDIC-supervised insured depository institution establishing account at another retail forex counterparty.* No related person of an FDIC-supervised insured depository institution working in the institution's retail forex business may have an account, directly or indirectly, with another retail forex counterparty unless the other retail forex counterparty:

(1) Receives written authorization to open and maintain the an account from a person designated by the FDIC-supervised insured depository institution of which it is a related person with responsibility for the surveillance over the account pursuant to paragraph (a)(2) of this section; and

(2) Transmits on a regular basis to the FDIC-supervised insured depository institution copies of all statements for such account and of all written records prepared by the other retail forex counterparty upon receipt of orders for the account pursuant to paragraph (c)(2) of this section are transmitted on a regular basis to the retail forex counterparty of which it is a related person.

(e) *Prohibited trading practices.* No FDIC-supervised insured depository institution engaging in retail forex transactions may:

(1) Enter into a retail forex transaction, to be executed pursuant to a market or limit order at a price that is not at or near the price at which other retail forex customers, during that same time period, have executed retail forex transactions with the FDIC-supervised insured depository institution;

(2) Adjust or alter prices for a retail forex transaction after the transaction has been confirmed to the retail forex customer;

(3) Provide a retail forex customer a new bid price for a retail forex transaction that is higher than its previous bid without providing a new asked price that is also higher than its previous asked price by a similar amount;

(4) Provide a retail forex customer a new bid price for a retail forex transaction that is lower than its previous bid without providing a new asked price that is also lower than its previous asked price by a similar amount; or

(5) Establish a new position for a retail forex customer (except one that offsets an existing position for that retail forex customer) where the FDIC-supervised insured depository institution holds outstanding orders of other retail forex customers for the same currency pair at a comparable price.

§ 349.14 Supervision.

(a) *Supervision by the FDIC-supervised insured depository institution.* An FDIC-supervised insured depository institution engaging in retail forex transactions shall diligently supervise the handling by its officers, employees, and agents (or persons occupying a similar status or performing a similar function) of all retail forex accounts carried, operated, or advised by at the FDIC-supervised insured depository institution and all activities of its officers, employees, and agents (or persons occupying a similar status or performing a similar function) relating to its retail forex business.

(b) *Supervision by officers, employees, or agents.* An officer, employee, or agent of an FDIC-supervised insured depository institution must diligently supervise his or her subordinates' handling of all retail forex accounts at the FDIC-supervised insured depository institution and all the subordinates' activities relating to the FDIC-supervised insured depository institution's retail forex business.

§ 349.15 Notice of transfers.

(a) *Prior notice generally required.* Except as provided in paragraph (b) of this section, an FDIC-supervised insured depository institution must provide a retail forex customer with 30 days' prior notice of any assignment of any position or transfer of any account of the retail forex customer. The notice must include a statement that the retail forex customer is not required to accept the proposed assignment or transfer and may direct the FDIC-supervised insured depository institution to liquidate the positions of the retail forex customer or transfer the account to a retail forex counterparty of the retail forex customer's selection.

(b) *Exceptions.* The requirements of paragraph (a) of this section shall not apply to transfers:

(1) Requested by the retail forex customer;

(2) Made by the Federal Deposit Insurance Corporation as receiver or conservator under the Federal Deposit Insurance Act; or

(3) Otherwise authorized by applicable law.

(c) *Obligations of transferee FDIC-supervised insured depository institution.* An FDIC-supervised insured depository institution to which retail forex accounts or positions are assigned or transferred under paragraph (a) of this section must provide to the affected retail forex customers the risk disclosure statements and forms of acknowledgment required by this part and receive the required signed acknowledgments within sixty days of such assignments or transfers. This requirement shall not apply if the FDIC-supervised insured depository institution has clear written evidence that the retail forex customer has received and acknowledged receipt of the required disclosure statements.

§ 349.16 Customer dispute resolution.

(a) *Voluntary submission of claims to dispute or settlement procedures.* No FDIC-supervised insured depository institution may enter into any agreement or understanding with a retail forex customer in which the customer agrees, prior to the time a claim or grievance arises, to submit such claim or grievance to any settlement procedure.

(b) *Election of forum.* (1) Within ten business days after receipt of notice from the retail forex customer that the customer intends to submit a claim to arbitration, the FDIC-supervised insured depository institution must provide the customer with a list of persons qualified in dispute resolution.

(2) The customer shall, within 45 days after receipt of such list, notify the FDIC-supervised insured depository institution of the person selected. The customer's failure to provide such notice shall give the FDIC-supervised insured depository institution the right to select a person from the list.

(c) *Enforceability.* A dispute settlement procedure may require parties using such procedure to agree, under applicable state law, submission agreement or otherwise, to be bound by an award rendered in the procedure, provided that the agreement to submit the claim or grievance to the voluntary procedure under paragraph (a) of this section or that agreement to submit the claim or grievance was made after the claim or grievance arose. Any award so rendered shall be enforceable in accordance with applicable law.

(d) *Time limits for submission of claims.* The dispute settlement procedure used by the parties shall not include any unreasonably short limitation period foreclosing submission of a customer's claims or grievances or counterclaims.

(e) *Counterclaims.* A procedure for the settlement of a retail forex customer's claims or grievances against an FDIC-supervised insured depository institution or employee thereof may permit the submission of a counterclaim in the procedure by a person against whom a claim or grievance is brought. Such a counterclaim may be permitted where it arises out of the transaction or occurrence that is the subject of the customer's claim or grievance and does not require for adjudication the presence of essential witnesses, parties, or third persons over which the settlement process lacks jurisdiction.

PART 350—DISCLOSURE OF FINANCIAL AND OTHER INFORMATION BY FDIC-INSURED STATE NONMEMBER BANKS

Sec.
350.1 Scope.
350.2 Definitions.
350.3 Requirement for annual disclosure statement.
350.4 Contents of annual disclosure statement.
350.5 Alternative annual disclosure statements.
350.6 Signature and attestation.
350.7 Notice and availability.
350.8 Delivery.
350.9 Disclosure of examination reports.
350.10 Prohibited conduct and penalties.
350.11 Safe harbor provision.
350.12 Disclosure required by applicable banking or securities law or regulations.

AUTHORITY: 12 U.S.C. 1817(a)(1), 1819 "Seventh" and "Tenth".

SOURCE: 52 FR 49379, Dec. 31, 1987, unless otherwise noted.

§ 350.1 Scope.

This part applies to FDIC-insured state-chartered banks that are not members of the Federal Reserve System, and to FDIC-Insured state-licensed branches of foreign banks.

§ 350.2 Definitions.

(a) *Bank.* For purposes of this part, the term *bank* means an FDIC-insured state-chartered organization that is not a member of the Federal Reserve System, and an FDIC-insured state-licensed branch of a foreign bank.

(b) *Call Report.* For purposes of this part, the term *Call Report* means the report filed by a bank pursuant to 12 U.S.C. 1817(a)(1).

§ 350.3 Requirement for annual disclosure statement.

(a) *Contents.* Each bank shall prepare as of December 31 and make available on request an annual disclosure statement. The statement shall contain information required by § 350.4(a) and (b) and may include other information that bank management believes appropriate, as provided in § 350.4(c).

(b) *Availability.* A bank shall make its annual disclosure statement available to the public beginning not later than the following March 31 or, if the bank mails an annual report to its shareholders, beginning not later than five days after the mailing of such reports, whichever occurs first. A bank shall make a disclosure statement available continuously until the disclosure statement for the succeeding year becomes available.

[62 FR 10200, Mar. 6, 1997]

§ 350.4 Contents of annual disclosure statement.

(a) *Financial reports.* The annual disclosure statement for any year shall reflect a fair presentation of the bank's financial condition at the end of that year and the preceding year and, except for state-licensed branches of foreign banks, the results of operations for each such year. The annual disclosure statement may, at the option of bank management, consist of the bank's entire Call Report, or applicable portions thereof, for the relevant dates and periods. At a minimum, the statement must contain information comparable to that provided in the following Call Report schedules:

(1) For insured state-chartered organizations that are not members of the Federal Reserve System:

(i) Schedule RC (Balance Sheet);

(ii) Schedule RC-N (Past Due and Nonaccrual, Loans, Leases, and Other Assets—column A covering financial instruments past due 30 through 89 days and still accruing and Memorandum item 1 need not be included);

(iii) Schedule RI (Income Statement);

(iv) Schedule RI-A (Changes in Equity Capital); and

(v) Schedule RI-B, Part II (Changes in Allowance for Loan and Lease Losses).

(2) For insured state-licensed branches of foreign banks:

(i) Schedule RAL (Assets and Liabilities);

(ii) Schedule E (Deposit Liabilities and Credit Balances); and

(iii) Schedule P (Other Borrowed Money).

(b) *Other required information.* The annual disclosure statement shall include such other information as the FDIC may require of a particular bank. This could include disclosure of enforcement actions where the FDIC deems it in the public interest to do so.

§ 350.5

(c) *Optional information.* A bank may, at its option, provide additional information that bank management considers important to an evaluation of the overall condition of the bank. This information could include, but is not limited to, a discussion of the financial data; information relating to mergers and acquisitions; the existence of and facts relating to regulatory enforcement actions; business plans; and material changes in balance sheet and income statement items.

(d) *Disclaimer.* The following legend shall be included in every annual disclosure statement to advise the public that the FDIC has not reviewed the information contained therein: "This statement has not been reviewed, or confirmed for accuracy or relevance, by the Federal Deposit Insurance Corporation."

[62 FR 10200, Mar. 6, 1997]

§ 350.5 Alternative annual disclosure statements.

The requirements of § 350.4(a) may be satisfied:

(a) *In the case of a bank having a class of securities registered pursuant to section 12 of the Securities Exchange Act of 1934,* by the bank's annual report to security holders for meetings at which directors are to be elected or the bank's annual report (see 12 CFR part 335);

(b) *In the case of a bank with independently audited financial statements,* by copies of the audited financial statements and the certificate or report of the independent accountant to the extent that such statements contain information comparable to that specified in § 350.4(a); and

(c) *In the case of a bank subsidiary of a one-bank holding company,* by an annual report of the one-bank holding company prepared in conformity with the regulations of the Securities and Exchange Commission or by sections in the holding company's consolidated financial statements on Form FR Y-9C pursuant to Regulation Y of the Federal Reserve Board (12 CFR part 225) that are comparable to the Call Report schedules enumerated in § 350.4(a)(1), provided that in either case not less than 95 percent of the holding company's consolidated total assets and total liabilities are assets and liabilities of the bank and the bank's consolidated subsidiaries.

(d) *In the case of a bank covered by 12 CFR part 363,* by an annual report prepared pursuant to 12 CFR 363.4. However, if the annual report is for a bank subsidiary of a holding company which provides only the consolidated financial statements of the holding company, this annual report may be used to satisfy the requirements of this part only if it is the report of a one-bank holding company and provided that not less than 95 percent of the holding company's consolidated total assets and total liabilities are assets and liabilities of the bank and the bank's consolidated subsidiaries.

[62 FR 10200, Mar. 6, 1997]

§ 350.6 Signature and attestation.

An authorized officer of the bank shall sign the annual disclosure statement. The officer shall also attest to the correctness of the information contained in the statement if the financial reports are not accompanied by a certificate or report of an independent accountant.

[62 FR 10200, Mar. 6, 1997]

§ 350.7 Notice and availability.

(a) *Shareholders.* If the bank provides written notice of the annual meeting of shareholders, the bank shall include with, or as part of, that notice an announcement that the bank's annual disclosure statement will be sent to the shareholder either automatically or upon request. For disclosure statements available on request, the announcement shall indicate at a minimum an address and telephone number to which requests may be directed. The first copy of the annual disclosure statement shall be provided to a shareholder without charge.

(b) *Customers and the general public.* In the lobby of its main office and each branch, the bank shall at all times display a notice that the annual disclosure statement may be obtained from the bank. The notice shall include at a minimum an address and telephone number of which requests should be directed. The first copy of the annual disclosure statement shall be provided to a requester free of charge.

Federal Deposit Insurance Corporation §352.1

§ 350.8 Delivery.

Each bank shall, after receiving a request for an annual disclosure statement, promptly mail or otherwise furnish a statement to the requester.

§ 350.9 Disclosure of examination reports.

Except as permitted under specific provisions of the FDIC's regulations (12 CFR part 309), a bank may not disclose any report of examination or report of supervisory activity or any portion thereof prepared by the FDIC. The bank also shall not make any representation concerning such report or the findings therein.

§ 350.10 Prohibited conduct and penalties.

(a) *Misrepresentations.* No officer, director, employee, agent, or other person participating in the affairs of a bank, shall, directly or indirectly:

(1) Disclose or cause to be disclosed false or misleading information in the annual disclosure statement, or omit or cause the omission of pertinent or required information in the annual disclosure statement; or

(2) Represent that the FDIC, or any employee thereof, has reviewed, or confirmed the accuracy or relevance of the disclosure statement.

(b) *Participating persons.* For purposes of this part, a person *participating in the affairs of a bank* shall include (but not be limited to) any person who provides information contained in, or directly or indirectly assists in the preparation of, the annual disclosure statement.

(c) *Enforcement actions.* Conduct that violates paragraph (a) of this section may constitute an unsafe or unsound banking practice or otherwise serve as a basis for an enforcement action by the FDIC.

§ 350.11 Safe harbor provision.

The provisions of § 350.10 shall not apply unless it is shown that the information disclosed was included without a reasonable basis or other than in good faith.

§ 350.12 Disclosure required by applicable banking or securities law or regulations.

The requirements of this part are not intended to replace or waive any disclosure required to be made under applicable banking or securities law or regulations.

[62 FR 10201, Mar. 6, 1997]

PART 351 [RESERVED]

PART 352—NONDISCRIMINATION ON THE BASIS OF DISABILITY

Sec.
352.1 Purpose.
352.2 Application.
352.3 Definitions.
352.4 Nondiscrimination in any program or activity conducted by the FDIC.
352.5 Accessibility to electronic and information technology.
352.6 Employment.
352.7 Accessibility of programs, and activities: Existing facilities.
352.8 Program accessibility: New construction and alterations.
352.9 Communications.
352.10 Compliance procedures.
352.11 Notice.

AUTHORITY: 12 U.S.C. 1819(a); 29 U.S.C. 794d.

SOURCE: 69 FR 26492, May 13, 2004, unless otherwise noted.

§ 352.1 Purpose.

(a) One purpose of this part is to implement the spirit of section 504 of the Rehabilitation Act of 1973 (the Rehabilitation Act) as amended by section 119 of the Rehabilitation, Comprehensive Services, and Developmental Disabilities Amendments of 1978 and the Workforce Investment Act of 1998. Section 504 prohibits discrimination on the basis of disability in programs and activities conducted by a federal executive agency. Although the FDIC does not believe that Congress contemplated coverage of non-appropriated, independent regulatory agencies such as the FDIC, the FDIC has chosen to promulgate this final regulation to ensure that, to the extent practicable, persons with disabilities are provided with equal access to FDIC programs and activities.

§ 352.2

(b) This part is also intended to implement section 508 of the Rehabilitation Act as amended. Section 508 requires each federal agency or department to ensure that the electronic and information technology they procure allows individuals with disabilities access to that technology comparable to the access of those who are not disabled, unless the agency would incur an undue burden.

§ 352.2 Application.

(a) This part applies to all programs, activities, and electronic and information technology developed, procured, maintained, used or conducted by the FDIC. The following programs and activities involve the direct provision of benefits and services to, or participation by, members of the public:

(1) Attending Board of Directors meetings open to the public and all other public meetings;

(2) Making inquiries or filing complaints at the FDIC Office of Legislative Affairs and Office of Public Affairs;

(3) Using the FDIC library in Washington, DC;

(4) Using the FDIC Web site on the Internet;

(5) Visiting an insured bank at which they conducted business (or an alternative liquidation site selected by the FDIC) and which has become insolvent, or been purchased by another bank under FDIC supervision, for the purpose of:

(i) Collecting FDIC checks for the insured amount of their deposits previously held in such bank; and/or

(ii) Discussing with FDIC representatives matters related to the repayment of debts which they previously owed to such bank, prior to its failure or purchase by another bank under FDIC supervision;

(6) Seeking employment with the FDIC;

(b) This regulation governs the conduct of FDIC personnel in their interaction with employees of insured banks and employees of other state or federal agencies while discharging the FDIC's statutory obligations as insurer and/or receiver of financial institutions. It does not apply to financial institutions insured by the FDIC.

(c) Although application for employment and employment with the FDIC are programs and activities of the FDIC for purposes of this regulation, they shall be governed only by the standards set forth in § 352.6 of this part.

§ 352.3 Definitions.

For purposes of this part, the term—

(a) "Auxiliary aids" means services or devices that enable persons with impaired sensory, manual, or speaking skills to have an equal opportunity to participate in, and enjoy the benefits of, the FDIC programs or activities, and Electronic and Information Technology set forth in § 352.2.

(b) "Electronic and Information Technology" ("EIT") has the same meaning as "information technology" except EIT also includes any equipment or interconnected system or subsystem of equipment that is used in the creation, conversion, or duplication of data or information. The term EIT includes, but is not limited to, telecommunication products (such as telephones), information kiosks and transaction machines, worldwide web sites, multimedia, and office equipment (such as copiers and fax machines).

(c) "Facility" means all or any portion of buildings, structures, equipment, roads, walks, parking lots and other real or personal property. As used in this definition, "personal property" means only furniture, carpeting and similar features not considered to be real property.

(d) "Individual with a disability" means any person who has a physical or mental impairment that substantially limits one or more major life activities, has a record of such an impairment, or is regarded as having such an impairment.

(e) "Qualified individual with a disability" means—

(1) With respect to any FDIC program or activity in which a person is required to perform services or to achieve a level of accomplishment, an individual with a disability who meets the essential eligibility requirements and can achieve the purpose of the program or activity without modifications in the program or activity that the FDIC can determine on the basis of a

Federal Deposit Insurance Corporation § 352.8

written record would result in a fundamental alteration in its nature;

(2) With respect to any other program or activity, an individual with a disability who meets the essential eligibility requirements for participation in, or receipt of benefits from, that program or activity;

(3) With respect to employment, an individual with a disability as defined in 29 CFR 1630.2(g), which is made applicable to this part by § 352.6.

(f) "Sections 504 and 508" mean sections 504 and 508 of the Rehabilitation Act of 1973 (Pub. L. 93–112, 87 Stat. 394 (29 U.S.C. 794 and 794d)), as amended by the Rehabilitation Act Amendments of 1974 (Pub. L. 93–516, 88 Stat. 1617), the Rehabilitation, Comprehensive Services, and Developmental Disabilities Amendments of 1978 (Pub. L. 95–602, 92 Stat. 2955), and the Workforce Investment Act of 1998 (Pub. L. 105–220, 112 Stat. 936). As used in this regulation, sections 504 and 508 shall be applied only to the programs, activities, and EIT conducted by the FDIC as set forth in §§ 352.2 and 352.3(b) of this regulation.

§ 352.4 Nondiscrimination in any program or activity conducted by the FDIC.

In accordance with section 504 of the Rehabilitation Act, no qualified individual with a disability shall, solely by reason of his or her disability, be excluded from participation in, be denied the benefits of, or be subjected to discrimination in any program or activity conducted by the FDIC.

§ 352.5 Accessibility to electronic and information technology.

(a) In accordance with section 508 of the Rehabilitation Act, the FDIC shall ensure, absent an undue burden, that the electronic and information technology the agency develops, procures, maintains or allows:

(1) Individuals with disabilities who are FDIC employees or applicants to have access to and use of information and data that is comparable to the access to and use of information and data by FDIC employees or applicants who are not individuals with disabilities; and

(2) Individuals with disabilities who are members of the public seeking information or services from the FDIC to have access to and use of information and data that is comparable to the access to and use of information and data by members of the public who are not individuals with disabilities.

(b) When development or procurement of electronic and information technology that meets the standards published by the Architectural and Transportation Barriers Compliance Board, 36 CFR 1194, would pose an undue burden, the FDIC shall provide individuals with disabilities covered by paragraph (a) of this section with the information and data by an alternative means of access that allows the individuals to use the information and data.

§ 352.6 Employment.

No qualified individual with a disability shall, on the basis of that disability, be subjected to discrimination in employment in any program or activity conducted by the FDIC. The definitions, requirements, and procedures (including those pertaining to employment discrimination complaints) of sections 501 of the Rehabilitation Act of 1973, as established in 29 CFR parts 1614 and 1630, shall apply to employment in the FDIC.

§ 352.7 Accessibility of programs and activities: Existing facilities.

The FDIC shall operate each of the programs or activities set forth in § 352.2 of this part so that when viewed in its entirety, the program or activity is readily accessible to and usable by individuals with disabilities.

§ 352.8 Program accessibility: New construction and alterations.

Each building or part of a building, whether newly constructed, or substantially altered, in which FDIC programs or activities will be conducted, shall be designed, constructed or altered so as to be readily accessible to, and usable by, individuals with disabilities.

§ 352.9 Communications.

(a) The FDIC shall take appropriate steps to ensure effective communication with participants in FDIC programs, activities and EIT.

(1) The FDIC shall furnish appropriate auxiliary aids where necessary to afford an individual with a disability an equal opportunity to participate in, and enjoy the benefits of, the FDIC programs or activities.

(i) In determining what type of auxiliary aid is necessary, the FDIC shall give primary consideration to any reasonable requests of the individual with a disability.

(ii) The FDIC need not provide individually prescribed devices, readers for personal use or study, or other devices of a personal nature.

(2) Where the FDIC communicates by telephone, it shall use telecommunications devices for deaf persons (TDD's) or equally effective telecommunication systems with hearing impaired participants and beneficiaries.

(b) The FDIC shall ensure that interested persons, including persons with impaired vision or hearing, can obtain information as to the existence and location of accessible services, activities, facilities and EIT. Interested persons may obtain such information by calling, writing or visiting the FDIC Office of Diversity and Economic Opportunity (ODEO), located at 3501 Fairfax Drive, Arlington, VA 22226. The FDIC telephone number is (877) 275–3342 or (703) 562–2473 (TTY).

(c) The FDIC shall provide information at a primary entrance to each of its facilities where programs or activities are conducted, directing users to a location at which they can obtain information about accessible facilities. The international symbol for accessibility shall be used at each primary entrance of an accessible facility.

[69 FR 26492, May 13, 2004, as amended at 73 FR 45857, Aug. 7, 2008]

§ 352.10 Compliance procedures.

(a) *Applicability.* Paragraph (b) of this section applies to employment complaints. The remaining sections concern complaints alleging disability discrimination in FDIC programs or activities and denial of technology access.

(b) *Employment complaints.* The FDIC shall process complaints alleging employment discrimination on the basis of disability according to the procedures established by the Equal Employment Opportunity Commission in 29 CFR parts 1614 and 1630 pursuant to section 501 of the Rehabilitation Act of 1973 (29 U.S.C. 791).

(c) *Informal process.* A complainant shall first exhaust informal administrative procedures before filing a formal complaint alleging disability discrimination in FDIC programs or activities, or a denial of technology access. The FDIC's Office of Diversity and Economic Opportunity shall be responsible for coordinating implementation of this section. An aggrieved individual initiates the process by filing an informal complaint with ODEO within 180 calendar days from the date of the alleged disability discrimination or denial of access to electronic information technology. An informal complaint with respect to any FDIC program or activity must include a written statement containing the individual's name and address which describes the FDIC's action in sufficient detail to inform the FDIC of the nature and date of the alleged violation of these regulations. An informal complaint for denial of technology access must clearly identify the individual and the manner in which the EIT was inaccessible. All informal complaints shall be signed by the complainant or one authorized to do so on his or her behalf. Informal complaints filed on behalf of third parties shall describe or identify (by name if possible) the alleged victim of discrimination or denial of technology access. During the informal resolution process, ODEO has 30 days to attempt a resolution of the matter. If the aggrieved individual elects to participate in mediation, the period for attempting informal resolution will be extended for an additional 60 calendar days. If the matter is not resolved informally, the individual will be provided written notice of the right to file a formal complaint. All complaints should be sent to the FDIC's Office of Diversity and Economic Opportunity, 3501 Fairfax Drive, Arlington, VA 22226.

Federal Deposit Insurance Corporation § 353.3

(d) If the FDIC receives a complaint over which it does not have jurisdiction, it shall promptly notify the complainant and shall make reasonable efforts to refer the complainant to the appropriate government entity.

(e) *Formal complaints.* The individual must file a written formal complaint within 15 calendar days after receiving the notice of a right to file a formal complaint. Formal complaints must be filed with the FDIC Chairman or the ODEO Director. Within 120 days of the receipt of such a complaint for which it has jurisdiction, the FDIC shall notify the complainant of the results of the investigation in a letter containing—

(1) A finding regarding the alleged violations;

(2) A description of a remedy for each violation found; and

(3) A notice of the right to appeal.

(f) Appeals of the findings or remedies must be filed by the complainant within 30 days of receipt from the FDIC of the letter required by § 352.10 (e). The FDIC may extend this time for good cause.

(g) Timely appeals shall be accepted and processed by the FDIC Chairman or ODEO Director.

(h) The FDIC Chairman or ODEO Director shall notify the complainant of the results of the appeal within 60 days of the receipt of the request. If the FDIC Chairman or ODEO Director determines that additional information is needed from the complainant, he or she shall have 60 days from the date of receipt of the additional information to make a determination on the appeal.

(i) The time limits set forth in (e) and (h) above may be extended for an individual case when the FDIC Chairman or ODEO Director determines that there is good cause, based on the particular circumstances of that case.

(j) The FDIC may delegate its authority for conducting complaint investigations to other federal agencies or independent contractors, except that the authority for making the final determination may not be delegated.

[69 FR 26492, May 13, 2004, as amended at 73 FR 45857, Aug. 7, 2008]

§ 352.11 Notice.

The FDIC shall make available to employees, applicants, participants, beneficiaries, and other interested persons such information regarding the provisions of this part and its applicability to the programs or activities conducted by the FDIC, and make such information available to them in such manner as the Chairman or designee finds necessary to apprise such persons of the protections against discrimination under section 504 or technology access provided under section 508 and this regulation.

PART 353—SUSPICIOUS ACTIVITY REPORTS

Sec.
353.1 Purpose and scope.
353.2 Definitions.
353.3 Reports and records.

AUTHORITY: 12 U.S.C. 1818, 1819; 31 U.S.C. 5318.

SOURCE: 61 FR 6099, Feb. 16, 1996, unless otherwise noted.

§ 353.1 Purpose and scope.

The purpose of this part is to ensure that an insured state nonmember bank files a Suspicious Activity Report when it detects a known or suspected criminal violation of federal law or a suspicious transaction related to a money laundering activity or a violation of the Bank Secrecy Act. This part applies to all insured state nonmember banks as well as any insured, state-licensed branches of foreign banks.

§ 353.2 Definitions.

For the purposes of this part:

(a) *FinCEN* means the Financial Crimes Enforcement Network of the Department of the Treasury.

(b) *Institution-affiliated party* means any institution-affiliated party as that term is defined in sections 3(u) and 8(b)(5) of the Federal Deposit Insurance Act (12 U.S.C. 1813(u) and 1818(b)(5)).

§ 353.3 Reports and records.

(a) *Suspicious activity reports required.* A bank shall file a suspicious activity report with the appropriate federal law enforcement agencies and the Department of the Treasury, in accordance

§ 353.3

with the form's instructions, by sending a completed suspicious activity report to FinCEN in the following circumstances:

(1) *Insider abuse involving any amount.* Whenever the bank detects any known or suspected federal criminal violation, or pattern of criminal violations, committed or attempted against the bank or involving a transaction or transactions conducted through the bank, where the bank believes it was either an actual or potential victim of a criminal violation, or series of criminal violations, or that the bank was used to facilitate a criminal transaction, and the bank has a substantial basis for identifying one of the bank's directors, officers, employees, agents, or other institution-affiliated parties as having committed or aided in the commission of the criminal violation, regardless of the amount involved in the violation;

(2) *Transactions aggregating $5,000 or more where a suspect can be identified.* Whenever the bank detects any known or suspected federal criminal violation, or pattern of criminal violations, committed or attempted against the bank or involving a transaction or transactions conducted through the bank, and involving or aggregating $5,000 or more in funds or other assets, where the bank believes it was either an actual or potential victim of a criminal violation, or series of criminal violations, or that the bank was used to facilitate a criminal transaction, and the bank has a substantial basis for identifying a possible suspect or group of suspects. If it is determined prior to filing this report that the identified suspect or group of suspects has used an "alias", then information regarding the true identity of the suspect or group of suspects, as well as alias identifiers, such as driver's license or social security numbers, addresses and telephone numbers, must be reported;

(3) *Transactions aggregating $25,000 or more regardless of potential suspects.* Whenever the bank detects any known or suspected federal criminal violation, or pattern of criminal violations, committed or attempted against the bank or involving a transaction or transactions conducted through the bank, involving or aggregating $25,000 or more in funds or other assets, where the bank believes it was either an actual or potential victim of a criminal violation, or series of criminal violations, or that the bank was used to facilitate a criminal transaction, even though the bank has no substantial basis for identifying a possible suspect or group of suspects; or

(4) *Transactions aggregating $5,000 or more that involve potential money laundering or violations of the Bank Secrecy Act.* Any transaction (which for purposes of this paragraph (a)(4) means a deposit, withdrawal, transfer between accounts, exchange of currency, loan, extension of credit, purchase or sale of any stock, bond, certificate of deposit, or other monetary instrument or investment security, or any other payment, transfer, or delivery by, through, or to a financial institution, by whatever means effected) conducted or attempted by, at or through the bank and involving or aggregating $5,000 or more in funds or other assets, if the bank knows, suspects, or has reason to suspect that:

(i) The transaction involves funds derived from illegal activities or is intended or conducted in order to hide or disguise funds or assets derived from illegal activities (including, without limitation, the ownership, nature, source, location, or control of such funds or assets) as part of a plan to violate or evade any federal law or regulation or to avoid any transaction reporting requirement under federal law;

(ii) The transaction is designed to evade any regulations promulgated under the Bank Secrecy Act; or

(iii) The transaction has no business or apparent lawful purpose or is not the sort of transaction in which the particular customer would normally be expected to engage, and the bank knows of no reasonable explanation for the transaction after examining the available facts, including the background and possible purpose of the transaction.

(b) *Time for reporting.* (1) A bank shall file the suspicious activity report no later than 30 calendar days after the date of initial detection of facts that may constitute a basis for filing a suspicious activity report. If no suspect was identified on the date of detection

Federal Deposit Insurance Corporation

§ 357.1

of the incident requiring the filing, a bank may delay filing a suspicious activity report for an additional 30 calendar days to identify a suspect. In no case shall reporting be delayed more than 60 calendar days after the date of initial detection of a reportable transaction.

(2) In situations involving violations requiring immediate attention, such as when a reportable violation is ongoing, the bank shall immediately notify, by telephone, an appropriate law enforcement authority and the appropriate FDIC regional office (Division of Supervision and Consumer Protection (DSC)) in addition to filing a timely report.

(c) *Reports to state and local authorities.* A bank is encouraged to file a copy of the suspicious activity report with state and local law enforcement agencies where appropriate.

(d) *Exemptions.* (1) A bank need not file a suspicious activity report for a robbery or burglary committed or attempted, that is reported to appropriate law enforcement authorities.

(2) A bank need not file a suspicious activity report for lost, missing, counterfeit, or stolen securities if it files a report pursuant to the reporting requirements of 17 CFR 240.17f–1.

(e) *Retention of records.* A bank shall maintain a copy of any suspicious activity report filed and the original or business record equivalent of any supporting documentation for a period of five years from the date of filing the suspicious activity report. Supporting documentation shall be identified and maintained by the bank as such, and shall be deemed to have been filed with the suspicious activity report. A bank must make all supporting documentation available to appropriate law enforcement authorities upon request.

(f) *Notification to board of directors.* The management of a bank shall promptly notify its board of directors, or a committee thereof, of any report filed pursuant to this section. The term "board of directors" includes the managing official of an insured state-licensed branch of a foreign bank for purposes of this part.

(g) *Confidentiality of suspicious activity reports.* Suspicious activity reports are confidential. Any bank subpoenaed or otherwise requested to disclose a suspicious activity report or the information contained in a suspicious activity report shall decline to produce the suspicious activity report or to provide any information that would disclose that a suspicious activity report has been prepared or filed citing this part, applicable law (*e.g.*, 31 U.S.C. 5318(g)), or both, and notify the appropriate FDIC regional office (Division of Supervision and Consumer Protection (DSC)).

(h) *Safe harbor.* The safe harbor provisions of 31 U.S.C. 5318(g), which exempts any bank that makes a disclosure of any possible violation of law or regulation from liability under any law or regulation of the United States, or any constitution, law or regulation of any state or political subdivision, cover all reports of suspected or known criminal violations and suspicious activities to law enforcement and financial institution supervisory authorities, including supporting documentation, regardless of whether such reports are filed pursuant to this part or are filed on a voluntary basis.

PART 357—DETERMINATION OF ECONOMICALLY DEPRESSED REGIONS

AUTHORITY: 12 U.S.C. 1819, 1823(k)(5).

§ 357.1 Economically depressed regions.

(a) *Purpose.* Section 13(k)(5) of the Federal Deposit Insurance Act (12 U.S.C. 1823(k)(5)) provides that the FDIC shall consider proposals for financial assistance for eligible insured savings associations before grounds exist for appointment of a conservator or receiver for such member. One of the criteria for eligibility is that an institution's offices are located in an economically depressed region as determined by the FDIC.

(b) *Economically depressed regions.* (1) For the purpose of determining "economically depressed regions", the FDIC will determine whether an institution qualifies as being located in an "economically depressed region" on a case-by-case basis. That determination will be based on four criteria:

(i) High unemployment rates;
(ii) Significant declines in non-farm employment;
(iii) High delinquency rates of real estate assets at insured depository institutions; and
(iv) Evidence indicating declining real estate values.

(2) In addition, the FDIC will also consider relevant information from institutions regarding their geographic market area, as well as information on whether that market is "economically depressed".

[55 FR 11161, Mar. 27, 1990, as amended at 63 FR 10295, Mar. 3, 1998; 71 FR 20527, Apr. 21, 2006]

PART 359—GOLDEN PARACHUTE AND INDEMNIFICATION PAYMENTS

Sec.
359.0 Scope.
359.1 Definitions.
359.2 Golden parachute payments prohibited.
359.3 Prohibited indemnification payments.
359.4 Permissible golden parachute payments.
359.5 Permissible indemnification payments.
359.6 Filing instructions.
359.7 Applicability in the event of receivership.

AUTHORITY: 12 U.S.C. 1828(k).

SOURCE: 61 FR 5930, Feb. 15, 1996, unless otherwise noted.

§ 359.0 Scope.

(a) This part limits and/or prohibits, in certain circumstances, the ability of insured depository institutions, their subsidiaries and affiliated depository institution holding companies to enter into contracts to pay and to make golden parachute and indemnification payments to institution-affiliated parties (IAPs).

(b) The limitations on golden parachute payments apply to troubled insured depository institutions which seek to enter into contracts to pay or to make golden parachute payments to their IAPs. The limitations also apply to depository institution holding companies which are troubled and seek to enter into contracts to pay or to make golden parachute payments to their IAPs as well as healthy holding companies which seek to enter into contracts to pay or to make golden parachute payments to IAPs of a troubled insured depository institution subsidiary. A "golden parachute payment" is generally considered to be any payment to an IAP which is contingent on the termination of that person's employment and is received when the insured depository institution making the payment is troubled or, if the payment is being made by an affiliated holding company, either the holding company itself or the insured depository institution employing the IAP, is troubled. The definition of golden parachute payment does not include payments pursuant to qualified retirement plans, non-qualified *bona fide* deferred compensation plans, nondiscriminatory severance pay plans, other types of common benefit plans, state statutes and death benefits. Certain limited exceptions to the golden parachute payment prohibition are provided for in cases involving the hiring of a white knight and unassisted changes in control. A procedure is also set forth whereby an institution or IAP can request permission to make what would otherwise be a prohibited golden parachute payment.

(c) The limitations on indemnification payments apply to all insured depository institutions, their subsidiaries and affiliated depository institution holding companies regardless of their financial health. Generally, this part prohibits insured depository institutions, their subsidiaries and affiliated holding companies from indemnifying an IAP for that portion of the costs sustained with regard to an administrative or civil enforcement action commenced by any federal banking agency which results in a final order or settlement pursuant to which the IAP is assessed a civil money penalty, removed from office, prohibited from participating in the affairs of an insured depository institution or required to cease and desist from or take an affirmative action described in section 8(b) (12 U.S.C. 1818(b)) of the Federal Deposit Insurance Act (FDI Act). However, there are exceptions to this general prohibition. First, an institution or holding company may purchase

Federal Deposit Insurance Corporation § 359.1

commercial insurance to cover such expenses, except judgments and penalties. Second, the institution or holding company may advance legal and other professional expenses to an IAP directly (except for judgments and penalties) if its board of directors makes certain specific findings and the IAP agrees in writing to reimburse the institution if it is ultimately determined that the IAP violated a law, regulation or other fiduciary duty.

§ 359.1 Definitions.

(a) *Act* means the Federal Deposit Insurance Act, as amended (12 U.S.C. 1811, *et seq.*).

(b) *Appropriate federal banking agency, bank holding company, depository institution holding company* and *savings and loan holding company* have the meanings given to such terms in section 3 of the Act.

(c) *Benefit plan* means any plan, contract, agreement or other arrangement which is an "employee welfare benefit plan" as that term is defined in section 3(1) of the Employee Retirement Income Security Act of 1974, as amended (29 U.S.C. 1002(1)), or other usual and customary plans such as dependent care, tuition reimbursement, group legal services or cafeteria plans; provided however, that such term shall not include any plan intended to be subject to paragraphs (f)(2) (iii) and (v) of this section.

(d) *Bona fide deferred compensation plan or arrangement* means any plan, contract, agreement or other arrangement whereby:

(1) An IAP voluntarily elects to defer all or a portion of the reasonable compensation, wages or fees paid for services rendered which otherwise would have been paid to such party at the time the services were rendered (including a plan that provides for the crediting of a reasonable investment return on such elective deferrals) and the insured depository institution or depository institution holding company either:

(i) Recognizes compensation expense and accrues a liability for the benefit payments according to generally accepted accounting principles (GAAP); or

(ii) Segregates or otherwise sets aside assets in a trust which may only be used to pay plan and other benefits, except that the assets of such trust may be available to satisfy claims of the institution's or holding company's creditors in the case of insolvency; or

(2) An insured depository institution or depository institution holding company establishes a nonqualified deferred compensation or supplemental retirement plan, other than an elective deferral plan described in paragraph (e)(1) of this section:

(i) Primarily for the purpose of providing benefits for certain IAPs in excess of the limitations on contributions and benefits imposed by sections 415, 401(a)(17), 402(g) or any other applicable provision of the Internal Revenue Code of 1986 (26 U.S.C. 415, 401(a)(17), 402(g)); or

(ii) Primarily for the purpose of providing supplemental retirement benefits or other deferred compensation for a select group of directors, management or highly compensated employees (excluding severance payments described in paragraph (f)(2)(v) of this section and permissible golden parachute payments described in § 359.4); and

(3) In the case of any nonqualified deferred compensation or supplemental retirement plans as described in paragraphs (d) (1) and (2) of this section, the following requirements shall apply:

(i) The plan was in effect at least one year prior to any of the events described in paragraph (f)(1)(ii) of this section;

(ii) Any payment made pursuant to such plan is made in accordance with the terms of the plan as in effect no later than one year prior to any of the events described in paragraph (f)(1)(ii) of this section and in accordance with any amendments to such plan during such one year period that do not increase the benefits payable thereunder;

(iii) The IAP has a vested right, as defined under the applicable plan document, at the time of termination of employment to payments under such plan;

(iv) Benefits under such plan are accrued each period only for current or prior service rendered to the employer (except that an allowance may be made

§ 359.1

for service with a predecessor employer);

(v) Any payment made pursuant to such plan is not based on any discretionary acceleration of vesting or accrual of benefits which occurs at any time later than one year prior to any of the events described in paragraph (f)(1)(ii) of this section;

(vi) The insured depository institution or depository institution holding company has previously recognized compensation expense and accrued a liability for the benefit payments according to GAAP or segregated or otherwise set aside assets in a trust which may only be used to pay plan benefits, except that the assets of such trust may be available to satisfy claims of the institution's or holding company's creditors in the case of insolvency; and

(vii) Payments pursuant to such plans shall not be in excess of the accrued liability computed in accordance with GAAP.

(e) *Corporation* means the Federal Deposit Insurance Corporation, in its corporate capacity.

(f) *Golden parachute payment.* (1) The term *golden parachute payment* means any payment (or any agreement to make any payment) in the nature of compensation by any insured depository institution or an affiliated depository institution holding company for the benefit of any current or former IAP pursuant to an obligation of such institution or holding company that:

(i) Is contingent on, or by its terms is payable on or after, the termination of such party's primary employment or affiliation with the institution or holding company; and

(ii) Is received on or after, or is made in contemplation of, any of the following events:

(A) The insolvency (or similar event) of the insured depository institution which is making the payment or bankruptcy or insolvency (or similar event) of the depository institution holding company which is making the payment; or

(B) The appointment of any conservator or receiver for such insured depository institution; or

(C) A determination by the insured depository institution's or depository institution holding company's appropriate federal banking agency, respectively, that the insured depository institution or depository institution holding company is in a troubled condition, as defined in the applicable regulations of the appropriate federal banking agency (§ 303.101(c) of this chapter); or

(D) The insured depository institution is assigned a composite rating of 4 or 5 by the appropriate federal banking agency or informed in writing by the Corporation that it is rated a 4 or 5 under the Uniform Financial Institutions Rating System of the Federal Financial Institutions Examination Council, or the depository institution holding company is assigned a composite rating of 4 or 5 or unsatisfactory by its appropriate federal banking agency; or

(E) The insured depository institution is subject to a proceeding to terminate or suspend deposit insurance for such institution; and

(iii)(A) Is payable to an IAP whose employment by or affiliation with an insured depository institution is terminated at a time when the insured depository institution by which the IAP is employed or with which the IAP is affiliated satisfies any of the conditions enumerated in paragraphs (f)(1)(ii) (A) through (E) of this section, or in contemplation of any of these conditions; or

(B) Is payable to an IAP whose employment by or affiliation with an insured depository institution holding company is terminated at a time when the insured depository institution holding company by which the IAP is employed or with which the IAP is affiliated satisfies any of the conditions enumerated in paragraphs (f)(1)(ii)(A), (C) or (D) of this section, or in contemplation of any of these conditions.

(2) *Exceptions.* The term *golden parachute payment* shall not include:

(i) Any payment made pursuant to a pension or retirement plan which is qualified (or is intended within a reasonable period of time to be qualified) under section 401 of the Internal Revenue Code of 1986 (26 U.S.C. 401) or pursuant to a pension or other retirement plan which is governed by the laws of any foreign country; or

Federal Deposit Insurance Corporation § 359.1

(ii) Any payment made pursuant to a benefit plan as that term is defined in paragraph (c) of this section; or

(iii) Any payment made pursuant to a *bona fide* deferred compensation plan or arrangement as defined in paragraph (d) of this section; or

(iv) Any payment made by reason of death or by reason of termination caused by the disability of an institution-affiliated party; or

(v) Any payment made pursuant to a nondiscriminatory severance pay plan or arrangement which provides for payment of severance benefits to all eligible employees upon involuntary termination other than for cause, voluntary resignation, or early retirement; *provided, however*, that no employee shall receive any such payment which exceeds the base compensation paid to such employee during the twelve months (or such longer period or greater benefit as the Corporation shall consent to) immediately preceding termination of employment, resignation or early retirement, and such severance pay plan or arrangement shall not have been adopted or modified to increase the amount or scope of severance benefits at a time when the insured depository institution or depository institution holding company was in a condition specified in paragraph (f)(1)(ii) of this section or in contemplation of such a condition without the prior written consent of the appropriate federal banking agency; or

(vi) Any severance or similar payment which is required to be made pursuant to a state statute or foreign law which is applicable to all employers within the appropriate jurisdiction (with the exception of employers that may be exempt due to their small number of employees or other similar criteria); or

(vii) Any other payment which the Corporation determines to be permissible in accordance with § 359.4.

(g) *Insured depository institution* means any bank or savings association the deposits of which are insured by the Corporation pursuant to the Act, or any subsidiary thereof.

(h) *Institution-affiliated party (IAP)* means:

(1) Any director, officer, employee, or controlling stockholder (other than a depository institution holding company) of, or agent for, an insured depository institution or depository institution holding company;

(2) Any other person who has filed or is required to file a change-in-control notice with the appropriate federal banking agency under section 7(j) of the Act (12 U.S.C. 1817(j));

(3) Any shareholder (other than a depository institution holding company), consultant, joint venture partner, and any other person as determined by the appropriate federal banking agency (by regulation or case-by-case) who participates in the conduct of the affairs of an insured depository institution or depository institution holding company; and

(4) Any independent contractor (including any attorney, appraiser, or accountant) who knowingly or recklessly participates in: Any violation of any law or regulation, any breach of fiduciary duty, or any unsafe or unsound practice, which caused or is likely to cause more than a minimal financial loss to, or a significant adverse effect on, the insured depository institution or depository institution holding company.

(i) *Liability or legal expense* means:

(1) Any legal or other professional fees and expenses incurred in connection with any claim, proceeding, or action;

(2) The amount of, and any cost incurred in connection with, any settlement of any claim, proceeding, or action; and

(3) The amount of, and any cost incurred in connection with, any judgment or penalty imposed with respect to any claim, proceeding, or action.

(j) *Nondiscriminatory* means that the plan, contract or arrangement in question applies to all employees of an insured depository institution or depository institution holding company who meet reasonable and customary eligibility requirements applicable to all employees, such as minimum length of service requirements. A nondiscriminatory plan, contract or arrangement may provide different benefits based only on objective criteria such as salary, total compensation, length of service, job grade or classification, which are applied on a proportionate

§ 359.2

basis (with a variance in severance benefits relating to any criterion of plus or minus ten percent) to groups of employees consisting of not less than the lesser of 33 percent of employees or 1,000 employees.

(k) *Payment* means:

(1) Any direct or indirect transfer of any funds or any asset;

(2) Any forgiveness of any debt or other obligation;

(3) The conferring of any benefit, including but not limited to stock options and stock appreciation rights; and

(4) Any segregation of any funds or assets, the establishment or funding of any trust or the purchase of or arrangement for any letter of credit or other instrument, for the purpose of making, or pursuant to any agreement to make, any payment on or after the date on which such funds or assets are segregated, or at the time of or after such trust is established or letter of credit or other instrument is made available, without regard to whether the obligation to make such payment is contingent on:

(i) The determination, after such date, of the liability for the payment of such amount; or

(ii) The liquidation, after such date, of the amount of such payment.

(l) *Prohibited indemnification payment.* (1) The term *prohibited indemnification payment* means any payment (or any agreement or arrangement to make any payment) by any insured depository institution or an affiliated depository institution holding company for the benefit of any person who is or was an IAP of such insured depository institution or holding company, to pay or reimburse such person for any civil money penalty or judgment resulting from any administrative or civil action instituted by any federal banking agency, or any other liability or legal expense with regard to any administrative proceeding or civil action instituted by any federal banking agency which results in a final order or settlement pursuant to which such person:

(i) Is assessed a civil money penalty;

(ii) Is removed from office or prohibited from participating in the conduct of the affairs of the insured depository institution; or

(iii) Is required to cease and desist from or take any affirmative action described in section 8(b) of the Act with respect to such institution.

(2) *Exceptions.* (i) The term *prohibited indemnification payment* shall not include any reasonable payment by an insured depository institution or depository institution holding company which is used to purchase any commercial insurance policy or fidelity bond, provided that such insurance policy or bond shall not be used to pay or reimburse an IAP for the cost of any judgment or civil money penalty assessed against such person in an administrative proceeding or civil action commenced by any federal banking agency, but may pay any legal or professional expenses incurred in connection with such proceeding or action or the amount of any restitution to the insured depository institution, depository institution holding company or receiver.

(ii) The term *prohibited indemnification payment* shall not include any reasonable payment by an insured depository institution or depository institution holding company that represents partial indemnification for legal or professional expenses specifically attributable to particular charges for which there has been a formal and final adjudication or finding in connection with a settlement that the IAP has not violated certain banking laws or regulations or has not engaged in certain unsafe or unsound banking practices or breaches of fiduciary duty, unless the administrative action or civil proceeding has resulted in a final prohibition order against the IAP.

[61 FR 5930, Feb. 15, 1996, as amended at 68 FR 50461, Aug. 21, 2003]

§ 359.2 Golden parachute payments prohibited.

No insured depository institution or depository institution holding company shall make or agree to make any golden parachute payment, except as provided in this part.

§ 359.3 Prohibited indemnification payments.

No insured depository institution or depository institution holding company shall make or agree to make any

Federal Deposit Insurance Corporation § 359.4

prohibited indemnification payment, except as provided in this part.

§ 359.4 Permissible golden parachute payments.

(a) An insured depository institution or depository institution holding company may agree to make or may make a golden parachute payment if and to the extent that:

(1) The appropriate federal banking agency, with the written concurrence of the Corporation, determines that such a payment or agreement is permissible; or

(2) Such an agreement is made in order to hire a person to become an IAP either at a time when the insured depository institution or depository institution holding company satisfies or in an effort to prevent it from imminently satisfying any of the criteria set forth in § 359.1(f)(1)(ii), and the institution's appropriate federal banking agency and the Corporation consent in writing to the amount and terms of the golden parachute payment. Such consent by the FDIC and the institution's appropriate federal banking agency shall not improve the IAP's position in the event of the insolvency of the institution since such consent can neither bind a receiver nor affect the provability of receivership claims. In the event that the institution is placed into receivership or conservatorship, the FDIC and/or the institution's appropriate federal banking agency shall not be obligated to pay the promised golden parachute and the IAP shall not be accorded preferential treatment on the basis of such prior approval; or

(3) Such a payment is made pursuant to an agreement which provides for a reasonable severance payment, not to exceed twelve months salary, to an IAP in the event of a change in control of the insured depository institution; *provided, however,* that an insured depository institution or depository institution holding company shall obtain the consent of the appropriate federal banking agency prior to making such a payment and this paragraph (a)(3) shall not apply to any change in control of an insured depository institution which results from an assisted transaction as described in section 13 of the Act (12 U.S.C. 1823) or the insured depository institution being placed into conservatorship or receivership; and

(4) An insured depository institution, depository institution holding company or IAP making a request pursuant to paragraphs (a)(1) through (3) of this section shall demonstrate that it does not possess and is not aware of any information, evidence, documents or other materials which would indicate that there is a reasonable basis to believe, at the time such payment is proposed to be made, that:

(i) The IAP has committed any fraudulent act or omission, breach of trust or fiduciary duty, or insider abuse with regard to the depository institution or depository institution holding company that has had or is likely to have a material adverse effect on the institution or holding company;

(ii) The IAP is substantially responsible for the insolvency of, the appointment of a conservator or receiver for, or the troubled condition, as defined by applicable regulations of the appropriate federal banking agency, of the insured depository institution, depository institution holding company or any insured depository institution subsidiary of such holding company;

(iii) The IAP has materially violated any applicable federal or state banking law or regulation that has had or is likely to have a material effect on the insured depository institution or depository institution holding company; and

(iv) The IAP has violated or conspired to violate section 215, 656, 657, 1005, 1006, 1007, 1014, 1032, or 1344 of title 18 of the United States Code, or section 1341 or 1343 of such title affecting a federally insured financial institution as defined in title 18 of the United States Code.

(b) In making a determination under paragraphs (a) (1) through (3) of this section, the appropriate federal banking agency and the Corporation may consider:

(1) Whether, and to what degree, the IAP was in a position of managerial or fiduciary responsibility;

(2) The length of time the IAP was affiliated with the insured depository institution or depository institution holding company, and the degree to which the proposed payment represents

§ 359.5

a reasonable payment for services rendered over the period of employment; and

(3) Any other factors or circumstances which would indicate that the proposed payment would be contrary to the intent of section 18(k) of the Act or this part.

§ 359.5 Permissible indemnification payments.

(a) An insured depository institution or depository institution holding company may make or agree to make reasonable indemnification payments to an IAP with respect to an administrative proceeding or civil action initiated by any federal banking agency if:

(1) The insured depository institution's or depository institution holding company's board of directors, in good faith, determines in writing after due investigation and consideration that the institution-affiliated party acted in good faith and in a manner he/she believed to be in the best interests of the institution;

(2) The insured depository institution's or depository institution holding company's board of directors, respectively, in good faith, determines in writing after due investigation and consideration that the payment of such expenses will not materially adversely affect the institution's or holding company's safety and soundness;

(3) The indemnification payments do not constitute prohibited indemnification payments as that term is defined in § 359.1(l); and

(4) The IAP agrees in writing to reimburse the insured depository institution or depository institution holding company, to the extent not covered by payments from insurance or bonds purchased pursuant to § 359.1(l)(2), for that portion of the advanced indemnification payments which subsequently become prohibited indemnification payments, as defined in § 359.1(l)

(b) An IAP requesting indemnification payments shall not participate in any way in the board's discussion and approval of such payments; *provided, however,* that such IAP may present his/her request to the board and respond to any inquiries from the board concerning his/her involvement in the circumstances giving rise to the administrative proceeding or civil action.

(c) In the event that a majority of the members of the board of directors are named as respondents in an administrative proceeding or civil action and request indemnification, the remaining members of the board may authorize independent legal counsel to review the indemnification request and provide the remaining members of the board with a written opinion of counsel as to whether the conditions delineated in paragraph (a) of this section have been met. If independent legal counsel opines that said conditions have been met, the remaining members of the board of directors may rely on such opinion in authorizing the requested indemnification.

(d) In the event that all of the members of the board of directors are named as respondents in an administrative proceeding or civil action and request indemnification, the board shall authorize independent legal counsel to review the indemnification request and provide the board with a written opinion of counsel as to whether the conditions delineated in paragraph (a) of this section have been met. If independent legal counsel opines that said conditions have been met, the board of directors may rely on such opinion in authorizing the requested indemnification.

§ 359.6 Filing instructions.

Requests to make excess nondiscriminatory severance plan payments pursuant to § 359.1(f)(2)(v) and golden parachute payments permitted by § 359.4 shall be submitted in writing to the appropriate regional director (DSC). For filing requirements, consult 12 CFR 303.244. In the event that the consent of the institution's primary federal regulator is required in addition to that of the FDIC, the requesting party shall submit a copy of its letter to the FDIC to the institution's primary federal regulator. In the case of national banks, such written requests shall be submitted to the OCC. In the case of state member banks and bank holding companies, such written requests shall be submitted to the Federal Reserve district bank where the institution or

Federal Deposit Insurance Corporation

holding company, respectively, is located. In the case of savings associations and savings association holding companies, such written requests shall be submitted to the OTS regional office where the institution or holding company, respectively, is located. In cases where only the prior consent of the institution's primary federal regulator is required and that agency is not the FDIC, a written request satisfying the requirements of this section shall be submitted to the primary federal regulator as described in this section.

[63 FR 44751, Aug. 20, 1998]

§ 359.7 Applicability in the event of receivership.

The provisions of this part, or any consent or approval granted under the provisions of this part by the FDIC (in its corporate capacity), shall not in any way bind any receiver of a failed insured depository institution. Any consent or approval granted under the provisions of this part by the FDIC or any other federal banking agency shall not in any way obligate such agency or receiver to pay any claim or obligation pursuant to any golden parachute, severance, indemnification or other agreement. Claims for employee welfare benefits or other benefits which are contingent, even if otherwise vested, when the FDIC is appointed as receiver for any depository institution, including any contingency for termination of employment, are not provable claims or actual, direct compensatory damage claims against such receiver. Nothing in this part may be construed to permit the payment of salary or any liability or legal expense of any IAP contrary to 12 U.S.C. 1828(k)(3).

PART 360—RESOLUTION AND RECEIVERSHIP RULES

Sec.
360.1 Least-cost resolution.
360.2 Federal Home Loan banks as secured creditors.
360.3 Priorities.
360.4 Administrative expenses.
360.5 Definition of qualified financial contracts.
360.6 Treatment of financial assets transferred in connection with a securitization or participation.
360.7 Post-insolvency interest.
360.8 Method for determining deposit and other liability account balances at a failed insured depository institution.
360.9 Large-bank deposit insurance determination modernization.
360.10 Resolution plans required for insured depository institutions with $50 billion or more in total assets.
APPENDIX A TO PART 360—NON-MONETARY TRANSACTION FILE STRUCTURE
APPENDIX B TO PART 360—DEBIT/CREDIT FILE STRUCTURE
APPENDIX C TO PART 360—DEPOSIT FILE STRUCTURE
APPENDIX D TO PART 360—SWEEP/AUTOMATED CREDIT ACCOUNT FILE STRUCTURE
APPENDIX E TO PART 360—HOLD FILE STRUCTURE
APPENDIX F TO PART 360—CUSTOMER FILE STRUCTURE
APPENDIX G TO PART 360—DEPOSIT-CUSTOMER JOIN FILE STRUCTURE
APPENDIX H TO PART 360—POSSIBLE FILE COMBINATIONS FOR DEPOSIT DATA

AUTHORITY: 12 U.S.C. 1817(b), 1818(a)(2), 1818(t), 1819(a) Seventh, Ninth and Tenth, 1820(b)(3), (4), 1821(d)(1), 1821(d)(10)(c), 1821(d)(11), 1821(e)(1), 1821(e)(8)(D)(i), 1823(c)(4), 1823(e)(2); Sec. 401(h), Pub. L. 101–73, 103 Stat. 357.

§ 360.1 Least-cost resolution.

(a) *General rule.* Except as provided in section 13(c)(4)(G) of the FDI Act (12 U.S.C. 1823 (c)(4)(G)), the FDIC shall not take any action, directly or indirectly, under sections 13(c), 13(d), 13(f), 13(h) or 13(k) of the FDI Act (12 U.S.C. 1823 (c), (d), (f), (h) or (k)) with respect to any insured depository institution that would have the effect of increasing losses to any insurance fund by protecting:

(1) Depositors for more than the insured portion of their deposits (determined without regard to whether such institution is liquidated); or

(2) Creditors other than depositors.

(b) *Purchase and assumption transactions.* Subject to the requirement of section 13(c)(4)(A) of the FDI Act (12 U.S.C. 1823(c)(4)(A)), paragraph (a) of this section shall not be construed as prohibiting the FDIC from allowing any person who acquires any assets or assumes any liabilities of any insured depository institution, for which the FDIC has been appointed conservator or receiver, to acquire uninsured deposit liabilities of such institution as long as the applicable insurance fund does not incur any loss with respect to such uninsured deposit liabilities in an amount greater than the loss which would have been incurred with respect to such liabilities if the institution had been liquidated.

[58 FR 67664, Dec. 22, 1993, as amended at 63 FR 37761, July 14, 1998]

§ 360.2 Federal Home Loan banks as secured creditors.

(a) Notwithstanding any other provisions of federal or state law or any other provisions of these regulations, the receiver of a borrower from a Federal Home Loan Bank shall recognize the priority of any security interest granted to a Federal Home Loan Bank by any member of any Federal Home Loan Bank or any affiliate of any such member, whether such security interest is in specifically designated assets or a blanket interest in all assets or categories of assets, over the claims and rights of any other party (including any receiver, conservator, trustee or similar party having rights of a lien creditor) other than claims and rights that

(1) Would be entitled to priority under otherwise applicable law; and

(2) Are held by actual bona fide purchasers for value or by actual secured parties that are secured by actual perfected security interests.

(b) If the receiver rather than the Bank shall have possession of any collateral consisting of notes, securities, other instruments, chattel paper or cash securing advances of the Bank, the receiver shall, upon request by the Bank, promptly deliver possession of such collateral to the Bank or its designee.

(c) In the event that a receiver is appointed for any member of a Federal Home Loan Bank, the following procedures shall apply:

(1) The receiver and the Bank shall immediately seek and develop a mutually agreeable plan for the payment of any advances made by the Bank to such borrower or for the servicing, foreclosure upon and liquidation of the collateral securing any such advances, taking into account the nature and amount of such collateral, the markets in which such collateral is normally traded or sold and other relevant factors.

(2) In the event that the receiver and the Bank shall not, in good faith, be able to develop such a mutually agreeable plan, or, in the interim, the Bank in good faith reasonably concludes that the value of such collateral is decreasing, because of interest rate or other market changes, at such a rate that to delay liquidation or other exercise of the Bank's rights as a secured party for the development of a mutually agreeable plan could reasonably cause the value of such collateral to decrease to an amount that is insufficient to satisfy the Bank's claim in full, the Bank may, at any time thereafter if permitted to do so by the terms of the advances or other security agreement with such borrower or otherwise by applicable law, proceed to foreclose upon, sell, lease or otherwise dispose of such collateral (or any portion thereof), or otherwise exercise its rights as a secured party, provided that the Bank acts in good faith and in a commercially reasonable manner and otherwise in accordance with applicable law.

(3) The foregoing provisions of this paragraph (c) shall not apply in the event that a purchase and assumption transaction is entered into regarding any such member.

(d) The Bank's rights pursuant to the second sentence of section 10(d) of the Federal Home Loan Bank Act shall not be affected or diminished by any provisions of state law that may be applicable to a security interest in property of the member.

(e) The receiver for a borrower from a Federal Home Loan Bank shall allow a claim for a prepayment fee by the Bank if, and only if:

(1) The claim is made pursuant to a written contract that provides for a prepayment fee, provided, however, that such prepayment fee allowed by the receiver shall not exceed the present value of the loss attributable to the difference between the contract rate of the secured borrowing and the reinvestment rate then available to the Bank; and

(2) The indebtedness owed to the Bank by such borrower is secured by sufficient collateral in which a perfected security interest in favor of the Bank exists or as to which the Bank's security interest is entitled to priority

Federal Deposit Insurance Corporation § 360.3

under section 306(d) of the Competitive Equality Banking Act of 1987 (CEBA) (12 U.S.C. 1430(e), footnote (1), or otherwise so that the aggregate of the outstanding principal on the advances secured by such collateral, the accrued but unpaid interest thereon and the prepayment fee applicable to such advances can be paid in full from the amounts realized from such collateral. For purposes of this paragraph (e)(2), the adequacy of such collateral shall be determined as of the date such prepayment fees shall be due and payable under the terms of the written contract providing therefor.

[54 FR 19156, May 4, 1989. Redesignated at 54 FR 42801, Oct. 18, 1989, and further redesignated at 55 FR 46496, Nov. 5, 1990. Redesignated at 58 FR 67664, Dec. 22, 1993, as amended at 63 FR 37761, July 14, 1998]

§ 360.3 Priorities.

(a) Unsecured claims against an association or the receiver that are proved to the satisfaction of the receiver shall have priority in the following order:

(1) Administrative expenses of the receiver, including the costs, expenses, and debts of the receiver;

(2) Administrative expenses of the association, *provided* that such expenses were incurred within thirty (30) days prior to the receiver's taking possession, and that such expenses shall be limited to reasonable expenses incurred for services actually provided by accountants, attorneys, appraisers, examiners, or management companies, or reasonable expenses incurred by employees which were authorized and reimbursable under a pre-existing expense reimbursement policy, that, in the opinion of the receiver, are of benefit to the receivership, and shall not include wages or salaries of employees of the association;

(3) Claims for wages and salaries, including vacation and sick leave pay and contributions to employee benefit plans, earned prior to the appointment of the receiver by an employee of the association whom the receiver determines it is in the best interests of the receivership to engage or retain for a reasonable period of time;

(4) If authorized by the receiver, claims for wages and salaries, including vacation and sick leave pay and contributions to employee benefits plans, earned prior to the appointment of the receiver, up to a maximum of three thousand dollars ($3,000) per person, by an employee of the association not engaged or retained pursuant to a determination by the receiver pursuant to the third category above;

(5) Claims of governmental units for unpaid taxes, other than Federal income taxes, except to the extent subordinated pursuant to applicable law; but no other claim of a governmental unit shall have a priority higher than that of a general creditor under paragraph (a)(6) of this section;

(6) Claims for withdrawable accounts, including those of the Corporation as subrogee or transferee, and all other claims which have accrued and become unconditionally fixed on or before the date of default, whether liquidated or unliquidated, except as provided in paragraphs (a)(1) through (a)(5) of this section, provided, however, that if the association is chartered and was operated under the laws of a state that provided a priority for holders of withdrawable accounts over such other claims or general creditors, such priority within this paragraph (a)(6) shall be observed by the receiver; and provided further, that if deposits of a Federal association are booked or registered at an office of such association that is located in a State that provides such priority with respect to State-chartered associations, such deposits in a Federal association shall have priority over such other claims or general creditors, which shall be observed by the receiver;

(7) Claims other than those that have accrued and become unconditionally fixed on or before the date of default, including claims for interest after the date of default on claims under paragraph (a)(6) of this section, *Provided* that any claim based on an agreement for accelerated, stipulated, or liquidated damages, which claim did not accrue prior to the date of default, shall be considered as not having accrued and become unconditionally fixed on or before the date of default;

(8) Claims of the United States for unpaid Federal income taxes;

(9) Claims that have been subordinated in whole or in part to general

§ 360.4

creditor claims, which shall be given the priority specified in the written instruments that evidence such claims; and

(10) Claims by holders of nonwithdrawable accounts, including stock, which shall have priority within this paragraph (a)(10) in accordance with the terms of the written instruments that evidence such claims.

(b) Interest after the date of default on claims under paragraph (a)(6) of this section shall be at a rate or rates adjusted monthly to reflect the average rate for U.S. Treasury bills with maturities of not more than ninety-one (91) days during the preceding three (3) months.

(c) [Reserved]

(d) All unsecured claims of any category or class or priority described in paragraphs (a)(1) through (a)(10) of this section shall be paid in full, or provision made for such payment, before any claims of lesser priority are paid. If there are insufficient funds to pay all claims of a category or class in full, distribution to claimants in such category or class shall be made pro rata. Notwithstanding anything to the contrary herein, the receiver may, at any time, and from time to time, prior to the payment in full of all claims of a category or class with higher priority, make such distributions to claimants in priority classes outlined in paragraphs (a)(1) through (a)(6) of this section as the receiver believes are reasonably necessary to conduct the receivership, *Provided* that the receiver determines that adequate funds exist or will be recovered during the receivership to pay in full all claims of any higher priority.

(e) If the association is in mutual form, and a surplus remains after making distribution in full of allowed claims as set forth in paragraphs (a) and (b) of this section, such surplus shall be distributed to the depositors in proportion to their accounts as of the date of default.

(f) Under the provisions of section 11(d)(11) of the Act (12 U.S.C. 1821(d)(11)), the provisions of this § 360.3 do not apply to any receivership established and liquidation or other resolution occurring after August 10, 1993.

[53 FR 25132, July 5, 1988, as amended at 53 FR 30667, Aug. 15, 1988. Redesignated and amended at 54 FR 42801, Oct. 18, 1989, and further redesignated and amended at 55 FR 46496, Nov. 5, 1990; 58 FR 43070, Aug. 13, 1993. Redesignated at 58 FR 67664, Dec. 22, 1993; 60 FR 35488, July 10, 1995]

§ 360.4 Administrative expenses.

The priority for *administrative expenses of the receiver*, as that term is used in section 11(d)(11) of the Act (12 U.S.C. 1821(d)(11), shall include those necessary expenses incurred by the receiver in liquidating or otherwise resolving the affairs of a failed insured depository institution. Such expenses shall include pre-failure and post-failure obligations that the receiver determines are necessary and appropriate to facilitate the smooth and orderly liquidation or other resolution of the institution.

[60 FR 35488, July 10, 1995]

§ 360.5 Definition of qualified financial contracts.

(a) *Authority and purpose.* Sections 11(e)(8) through (10) of the Federal Deposit Insurance Act, 12 U.S.C. 1821(e)(8) through (10), provide special rules for the treatment of qualified financial contracts of an insured depository institution for which the FDIC is appointed conservator or receiver, including rules describing the manner in which qualified financial contracts may be transferred or closed out. Section 11(e)(8)(D)(i) of the Federal Deposit Insurance Act, 12 U.S.C. 1821(e)(8)(D)(i), grants the Corporation authority to determine by regulation whether any agreement, other than those identified within section 11(e)(8)(D), should be recognized as qualified financial contracts under the statute. The purpose of this section is to identify additional agreements which the Corporation has determined to be qualified financial contracts.

(b) *Repurchase agreements.* The following agreements shall be deemed "repurchase agreements" under section 11(e)(8)(D)(v) of the Federal Deposit Insurance Act, as amended (12 U.S.C. 1821(e)(8)(D)(v)): A repurchase agreement on qualified foreign government

Federal Deposit Insurance Corporation

§ 360.6

securities is an agreement or combination of agreements (including master agreements) which provides for the transfer of securities that are direct obligations of, or that are fully guaranteed by, the central governments (as set forth at 12 CFR part 325, appendix A, section II.C, n. 17, as may be amended from time to time) of the OECD-based group of countries (as set forth at 12 CFR part 325, appendix A, section II.B.2., note 12 as may be amended from time to time) against the transfer of funds by the transferee of such securities with a simultaneous agreement by such transferee to transfer to the transferor thereof securities as described above, at a date certain not later than one year after such transfers or on demand, against the transfer of funds.

(c) *Swap agreements.* The following agreements shall be deemed "swap agreements" under section 11(e)(8)(D)(vi) of the Federal Deposit Insurance Act, as amended (12 U.S.C. 1821(e)(8)(D)(vi)): A spot foreign exchange agreement is any agreement providing for or effecting the purchase or sale of one currency in exchange for another currency (or a unit of account established by an intergovernmental organization such as the European Currency Unit) with a maturity date of two days or less after the agreement has been entered into, and includes short-dated transactions such as tomorrow/next day and same day/tomorrow transactions.

(d) Nothing in this section shall be construed as limiting or changing a party's obligation to comply with all reasonable trading practices and requirements, non-insolvency law requirements and any other requirements imposed by other provisions of the FDI Act. This section in no way limits the authority of the Corporation to take supervisory or enforcement actions, or to otherwise manage the affairs of a financial institution for which the Corporation has been appointed conservator or receiver.

[60 FR 66865, Dec. 27, 1995]

§ 360.6 Treatment of financial assets transferred in connection with a securitization or participation.

(a) *Definitions.*

(1) *Financial asset* means cash or a contract or instrument that conveys to one entity a contractual right to receive cash or another financial instrument from another entity.

(2) *Investor* means a person or entity that owns an obligation issued by an issuing entity.

(3) *Issuing entity* means an entity that owns a financial asset or financial assets transferred by the sponsor and issues obligations supported by such asset or assets. Issuing entities may include, but are not limited to, corporations, partnerships, trusts, and limited liability companies and are commonly referred to as special purpose vehicles or special purpose entities. To the extent a securitization is structured as a multi-step transfer, the term issuing entity would include both the issuer of the obligations and any intermediate entities that may be a transferee. Notwithstanding the foregoing, a Specified GSE or an entity established or guaranteed by a Specified GSE shall not constitute an issuing entity.

(4) *Monetary default* means a default in the payment of principal or interest when due following the expiration of any cure period.

(5) *Obligation* means a debt or equity (or mixed) beneficial interest or security that is primarily serviced by the cash flows of one or more financial assets or financial asset pools, either fixed or revolving, that by their terms convert into cash within a finite time period, or upon the disposition of the underlying financial assets, and by any rights or other assets designed to assure the servicing or timely distributions of proceeds to the security holders issued by an issuing entity. The term may include beneficial interests in a grantor trust, common law trust or similar issuing entity to the extent that such interests satisfy the criteria set forth in the preceding sentence, but does not include LLC interests, partnership interests, common or preferred equity, or similar instruments evidencing ownership of the issuing entity.

(6) *Participation* means the transfer or assignment of an undivided interest in all or part of a financial asset, that has all of the characteristics of a "participating interest," from a seller, known as the "lead," to a buyer, known as the

§ 360.6

"participant," without recourse to the lead, pursuant to an agreement between the lead and the participant. "Without recourse" means that the participation is not subject to any agreement that requires the lead to repurchase the participant's interest or to otherwise compensate the participant upon the borrower's default on the underlying obligation.

(7) *Securitization* means the issuance by an issuing entity of obligations for which the investors are relying on the cash flow or market value characteristics and the credit quality of transferred financial assets (together with any external credit support permitted by this section) to repay the obligations.

(8) *Servicer* means any entity responsible for the management or collection of some or all of the financial assets on behalf of the issuing entity or making allocations or distributions to holders of the obligations, including reporting on the overall cash flow and credit characteristics of the financial assets supporting the securitization to enable the issuing entity to make payments to investors on the obligations. The term "servicer" does not include a trustee for the issuing entity or the holders of obligations that makes allocations or distributions to holders of the obligations if the trustee receives such allocations or distributions from a servicer and the trustee does not otherwise perform the functions of a servicer.

(9) *Specified GSE* means each of the following:

(i) The Federal National Mortgage Association and any affiliate thereof;

(ii) Federal Home Loan Mortgage Corporation and any affiliate thereof;

(iii) The Government National Mortgage Association; and

(iv) Any federal or state sponsored mortgage finance agency.

(10) *Sponsor* means a person or entity that organizes and initiates a securitization by transferring financial assets, either directly or indirectly, including through an affiliate, to an issuing entity, whether or not such person owns an interest in the issuing entity or owns any of the obligations issued by the issuing entity.

(11) *Transfer* means:

12 CFR Ch. III (1–1–12 Edition)

(i) The conveyance of a financial asset or financial assets to an issuing entity or

(ii) The creation of a security interest in such asset or assets for the benefit of the issuing entity.

(b) *Coverage.* This section shall apply to securitizations that meet the following criteria:

(1) *Capital Structure and Financial Assets.* The documents creating the securitization must define the payment structure and capital structure of the transaction.

(i) *Requirements applicable to all securitizations:*

(A) The securitization shall not consist of re-securitizations of obligations or collateralized debt obligations unless the documents creating the securitization require that disclosures required in paragraph (b)(2) of this section are made available to investors for the underlying assets supporting the securitization at initiation and while obligations are outstanding; and

(B) The documents creating the securitization shall require that payment of principal and interest on the securitization obligation must be primarily based on the performance of financial assets that are transferred to the issuing entity and, except for interest rate or currency mismatches between the financial assets and the obligations, shall not be contingent on market or credit events that are independent of such financial assets. The securitization may not be an unfunded securitization or a synthetic transaction.

(ii) *Requirements applicable only to securitizations in which the financial assets include any residential mortgage loans:*

(A) The capital structure of the securitization shall be limited to no more than six credit tranches and cannot include "sub-tranches," grantor trusts or other structures. Notwithstanding the foregoing, the most senior credit tranche may include time-based sequential pay or planned amortization and companion sub-tranches; and

(B) The credit quality of the obligations cannot be enhanced at the issuing entity or pool level through external credit support or guarantees. However, the credit quality of the obligations

560

Federal Deposit Insurance Corporation

§ 360.6

may be enhanced by credit support or guarantees provided by Specified GSEs and the temporary payment of principal and/or interest may be supported by liquidity facilities, including facilities designed to permit the temporary payment of interest following appointment of the FDIC as conservator or receiver. Individual financial assets transferred into a securitization may be guaranteed, insured or otherwise benefit from credit support at the loan level through mortgage and similar insurance or guarantees, including by private companies, agencies or other governmental entities, or government-sponsored enterprises, and/or through co-signers or other guarantees.

(2) *Disclosures.* The documents shall require that the sponsor, issuing entity, and/or servicer, as appropriate, shall make available to investors, information describing the financial assets, obligations, capital structure, compensation of relevant parties, and relevant historical performance data set forth in paragraph (b)(2) of this section.

(i) *Requirements applicable to all securitizations:*

(A) The documents shall require that, on or prior to issuance of obligations and at the time of delivery of any periodic distribution report and, in any event, at least once per calendar quarter, while obligations are outstanding, information about the obligations and the securitized financial assets shall be disclosed to all potential investors at the financial asset or pool level, as appropriate for the financial assets, and security-level to enable evaluation and analysis of the credit risk and performance of the obligations and financial assets. The documents shall require that such information and its disclosure, at a minimum, shall comply with the requirements of Securities and Exchange Commission Regulation AB, 17 CFR 229.1100 through 1123 (to the extent then in effect) or any successor disclosure requirements for public issuances, even if the obligations are issued in a private placement or are not otherwise required to be registered. Information that is unknown or not available to the sponsor or the issuer after reasonable investigation may be omitted if the issuer includes a statement in the offering documents disclosing that the specific information is otherwise unavailable;

(B) The documents shall require that, on or prior to issuance of obligations, the structure of the securitization and the credit and payment performance of the obligations shall be disclosed, including the capital or tranche structure, the priority of payments and specific subordination features; representations and warranties made with respect to the financial assets, the remedies for and the time permitted for cure of any breach of representations and warranties, including the repurchase of financial assets, if applicable; liquidity facilities and any credit enhancements permitted by this rule, any waterfall triggers or priority of payment reversal features; and policies governing delinquencies, servicer advances, loss mitigation, and write-offs of financial assets;

(C) The documents shall require that while obligations are outstanding, the issuing entity shall provide to investors information with respect to the credit performance of the obligations and the financial assets, including periodic and cumulative financial asset performance data, delinquency and modification data for the financial assets, substitutions and removal of financial assets, servicer advances, as well as losses that were allocated to such tranche and remaining balance of financial assets supporting such tranche, if applicable, and the percentage of each tranche in relation to the securitization as a whole; and

(D) In connection with the issuance of obligations, the documents shall require that the nature and amount of compensation paid to the originator, sponsor, rating agency or third-party advisor, any mortgage or other broker, and the servicer(s), and the extent to which any risk of loss on the underlying assets is retained by any of them for such securitization be disclosed. The securitization documents shall require the issuer to provide to investors while obligations are outstanding any changes to such information and the amount and nature of payments of any deferred compensation or similar arrangements to any of the parties.

§ 360.6

(ii) *Requirements applicable only to securitizations in which the financial assets include any residential mortgage loans:*

(A) Prior to issuance of obligations, sponsors shall disclose loan level information about the financial assets including, but not limited to, loan type, loan structure (for example, fixed or adjustable, resets, interest rate caps, balloon payments, etc.), maturity, interest rate and/or Annual Percentage Rate, and location of property; and

(B) Prior to issuance of obligations, sponsors shall affirm compliance in all material respects with applicable statutory and regulatory standards for origination of mortgage loans, including that the mortgages are underwritten at the fully indexed rate relying on documented income, and comply with supervisory guidance governing the underwriting of residential mortgages, including the Interagency Guidance on Non-Traditional Mortgage Products, October 5, 2006, and the Interagency Statement on Subprime Mortgage Lending, July 10, 2007, and such other or additional guidance applicable at the time of loan origination. Sponsors shall disclose a third party due diligence report on compliance with such standards and the representations and warranties made with respect to the financial assets; and

(C) The documents shall require that prior to issuance of obligations and while obligations are outstanding, servicers shall disclose any ownership interest by the servicer or an affiliate of the servicer in other whole loans secured by the same real property that secures a loan included in the financial asset pool. The ownership of an obligation, as defined in this regulation, shall not constitute an ownership interest requiring disclosure.

(3) *Documentation and recordkeeping.* The documents creating the securitization must specify the respective contractual rights and responsibilities of all parties and include the requirements described in paragraph (b)(3) of this section and use as appropriate any available standardized documentation for each different asset class.

(i) *Requirements applicable to all securitizations.* The documents shall define the contractual rights and responsibilities of the parties, including but not limited to representations and warranties and ongoing disclosure requirements, and any measures to avoid conflicts of interest; and provide authority for the parties, including but not limited to the originator, sponsor, servicer, and investors, to fulfill their respective duties and exercise their rights under the contracts and clearly distinguish between any multiple roles performed by any party.

(ii) *Requirements applicable only to securitizations in which the financial assets include any residential mortgage loans:*

(A) Servicing and other agreements must provide servicers with authority, subject to contractual oversight by any master servicer or oversight advisor, if any, to mitigate losses on financial assets consistent with maximizing the net present value of the financial asset. Servicers shall have the authority to modify assets to address reasonably foreseeable default, and to take other action to maximize the value and minimize losses on the securitized financial assets. The documents shall require that the servicers apply industry best practices for asset management and servicing. The documents shall require the servicer to act for the benefit of all investors, and not for the benefit of any particular class of investors, that the servicer must commence action to mitigate losses no later than ninety (90) days after an asset first becomes delinquent unless all delinquencies on such asset have been cured, and that the servicer maintains records of its actions to permit full review by the trustee or other representative of the investors; and

(B) The servicing agreement shall not require a primary servicer to advance delinquent payments of principal and interest for more than three payment periods, unless financing or reimbursement facilities are available, which may include, but are not limited to, the obligations of the master servicer or issuing entity to fund or reimburse the primary servicer, or alternative reimbursement facilities. Such "financing or reimbursement facilities" under this paragraph shall not be dependent for repayment on foreclosure proceeds.

Federal Deposit Insurance Corporation § 360.6

(4) *Compensation.* The following requirements apply only to securitizations in which the financial assets include any residential mortgage loans. Compensation to parties involved in the securitization of such financial assets must be structured to provide incentives for sustainable credit and the long-term performance of the financial assets and securitization as follows:

(i) The documents shall require that any fees or other compensation for services payable to credit rating agencies or similar third-party evaluation companies shall be payable, in part, over the five (5) year period after the first issuance of the obligations based on the performance of surveillance services and the performance of the financial assets, with no more than sixty (60) percent of the total estimated compensation due at closing; and

(ii) The documents shall provide that compensation to servicers shall include incentives for servicing, including payment for loan restructuring or other loss mitigation activities, which maximizes the net present value of the financial assets. Such incentives may include payments for specific services, and actual expenses, to maximize the net present value or a structure of incentive fees to maximize the net present value, or any combination of the foregoing that provides such incentives.

(5) *Origination and retention requirements*—(i) *Requirements applicable to all securitizations.*

(A) Prior to the effective date of regulations required under new Section 15G of the Securities Exchange Act, 15 U.S.C. 78a *et seq.*, added by Section 941(b) of the Dodd-Frank Wall Street Reform and Consumer Protection Act, the documents shall require that the sponsor retain an economic interest in a material portion, defined as not less than five (5) percent, of the credit risk of the financial assets. This retained interest may be either in the form of an interest of not less than five (5) percent in each of the credit tranches sold or transferred to the investors or in a representative sample of the securitized financial assets equal to not less than five (5) percent of the principal amount of the financial assets at transfer. This retained interest may not be sold or pledged or hedged, except for the hedging of interest rate or currency risk, during the term of the securitization.

(B) Upon the effective date of regulations required under new Section 15G of the Securities Exchange Act, 15 U.S.C. 78a *et seq.*, added by Section 941(b) of the Dodd-Frank Wall Street Reform and Consumer Protection Act, such final regulations shall exclusively govern the requirement to retain an economic interest in a portion of the credit risk of the financial assets under this rule.

(ii) *Requirements applicable only to securitizations in which the financial assets include any residential mortgage loans:*

(A) The documents shall require the establishment of a reserve fund equal to at least five (5) percent of the cash proceeds of the securitization payable to the sponsor to cover the repurchase of any financial assets required for breach of representations and warranties. The balance of such fund, if any, shall be released to the sponsor one year after the date of issuance.

(B) The documents shall include a representation that the assets shall have been originated in all material respects in compliance with statutory, regulatory, and originator underwriting standards in effect at the time of origination. The documents shall include a representation that the mortgages included in the securitization were underwritten at the fully indexed rate, based upon the borrowers' ability to repay the mortgage according to its terms, and rely on documented income and comply with all existing supervisory guidance governing the underwriting of residential mortgages, including the Interagency Guidance on Non-Traditional Mortgage Products, October 5, 2006, and the Interagency Statement on Subprime Mortgage Lending, July 10, 2007, and such other or additional regulations or guidance applicable to insured depository institutions at the time of loan origination. Residential mortgages originated prior to the issuance of such guidance shall meet all supervisory guidance governing the underwriting of residential

§ 360.6　　　　　　　　　　　　　　　　　　　　　　　　　　　　　　12 CFR Ch. III (1–1–12 Edition)

mortgages then in effect at the time of loan origination.

(c) *Other requirements.* (1) The transaction should be an arms length, bona fide securitization transaction. The documents shall require that the obligations issued in a securitization shall not be predominantly sold to an affiliate (other than a wholly-owned subsidiary consolidated for accounting and capital purposes with the sponsor) or insider of the sponsor;

(2) The securitization agreements are in writing, approved by the board of directors of the bank or its loan committee (as reflected in the minutes of a meeting of the board of directors or committee), and have been, continuously, from the time of execution in the official record of the bank;

(3) The securitization was entered into in the ordinary course of business, not in contemplation of insolvency and with no intent to hinder, delay or defraud the bank or its creditors;

(4) The transfer was made for adequate consideration;

(5) The transfer and/or security interest was properly perfected under the UCC or applicable state law;

(6) The transfer and duties of the sponsor as transferor must be evidenced in a separate agreement from its duties, if any, as servicer, custodian, paying agent, credit support provider or in any capacity other than the transferor; and

(7) The documents shall require that the sponsor separately identify in its financial asset data bases the financial assets transferred into any securitization and maintain an electronic or paper copy of the closing documents for each securitization in a readily accessible form, a current list of all of its outstanding securitizations and issuing entities, and the most recent Form 10–K, if applicable, or other periodic financial report for each securitization and issuing entity. The documents shall provide that to the extent serving as servicer, custodian or paying agent for the securitization, the sponsor shall not comingle amounts received with respect to the financial assets with its own assets except for the time, not to exceed two business days, necessary to clear any payments received. The documents shall require that the sponsor shall make these records readily available for review by the FDIC promptly upon written request.

(d) *Safe harbor*—(1) *Participations.* With respect to transfers of financial assets made in connection with participations, the FDIC as conservator or receiver shall not, in the exercise of its statutory authority to disaffirm or repudiate contracts, reclaim, recover, or recharacterize as property of the institution or the receivership any such transferred financial assets, provided that such transfer satisfies the conditions for sale accounting treatment under generally accepted accounting principles, except for the "legal isolation" condition that is addressed by this section. The foregoing paragraph shall apply to a last-in, first-out participation, provided that the transfer of a portion of the financial asset satisfies the conditions for sale accounting treatment under generally accepted accounting principles that would have applied to such portion if it had met the definition of a "participating interest," except for the "legal isolation" condition that is addressed by this section.

(2) *Transition period safe harbor.* With respect to:

(i) Any participation or securitization for which transfers of financial assets were made on or before December 31, 2010 or

(ii) Any obligations of revolving trusts or master trusts, for which one or more obligations were issued as of the date of adoption of this rule, or

(iii) Any obligations issued under open commitments up to the maximum amount of such commitments as of the date of adoption of this rule if one or more obligations were issued under such commitments on or before December 31, 2010, the FDIC as conservator or receiver shall not, in the exercise of its statutory authority to disaffirm or repudiate contracts, reclaim, recover, or recharacterize as property of the institution or the receivership the transferred financial assets notwithstanding that the transfer of such financial assets does not satisfy all conditions for sale accounting treatment under generally accepted accounting principles as effective for reporting periods after

Federal Deposit Insurance Corporation

§ 360.6

November 15, 2009, provided that such transfer satisfied the conditions for sale accounting treatment under generally accepted accounting principles in effect for reporting periods before November 15, 2009, except for the "legal isolation" condition that is addressed by this paragraph and the transaction otherwise satisfied the provisions of § 360.6 in effect prior to the effective date of this regulation.

(3) *For securitizations meeting sale accounting requirements.* With respect to any securitization for which transfers of financial assets were made after December 31, 2010, or from a master trust or revolving trust established after adoption of this rule or from any open commitments that do not meet the requirements of paragraph (d)(2) of this section, and which complies with the requirements applicable to that securitization as set forth in paragraphs (b) and (c) of this section, the FDIC as conservator or receiver shall not, in the exercise of its statutory authority to disaffirm or repudiate contracts, reclaim, recover, or recharacterize as property of the institution or the receivership such transferred financial assets, provided that such transfer satisfies the conditions for sale accounting treatment under generally accepted accounting principles in effect for reporting periods after November 15, 2009, except for the "legal isolation" condition that is addressed by this paragraph (d)(3).

(4) *For securitization not meeting sale accounting requirements.* With respect to any securitization for which transfers of financial assets were made after December 31, 2010, or from a master trust or revolving trust established after adoption of this rule or from any open commitments that do not meet the requirements of paragraph (d)(2) or (d)(3) of this section, and which complies with the requirements applicable to that securitization as set forth in paragraphs (b) and (c) of this section, but where the transfer does not satisfy the conditions for sale accounting treatment set forth by generally accepted accounting principles in effect for reporting periods after November 15, 2009:

(i) *Monetary default.* If at any time after appointment, the FDIC as conservator or receiver is in a monetary default under a securitization due to its failure to pay or apply collections from the financial assets received by it in accordance with the securitization documents, whether as servicer or otherwise, and remains in monetary default for ten (10) business days after actual delivery of a written notice to the FDIC pursuant to paragraph (f) of this section requesting the exercise of contractual rights because of such monetary default, the FDIC hereby consents pursuant to 12 U.S.C. 1821(e)(13)(C) and 12 U.S.C. 1825(b)(2) to the exercise of any contractual rights in accordance with the documents governing such securitization, including but not limited to taking possession of the financial assets and exercising self-help remedies as a secured creditor under the transfer agreements, provided no involvement of the receiver or conservator is required other than such consents, waivers, or execution of transfer documents as may be reasonably requested in the ordinary course of business in order to facilitate the exercise of such contractual rights. Such consent shall not waive or otherwise deprive the FDIC or its assignees of any seller's interest or other obligation or interest issued by the issuing entity and held by the FDIC or its assignees, but shall serve as full satisfaction of the obligations of the insured depository institution in conservatorship or receivership and the FDIC as conservator or receiver for all amounts due.

(ii) *Repudiation.* If the FDIC as conservator or receiver provides a written notice of repudiation of the securitization agreement pursuant to which the financial assets were transferred, and the FDIC does not pay damages, defined in this paragraph, within ten (10) business days following the effective date of the notice, the FDIC hereby consents pursuant to 12 U.S.C. 1821(e)(13)(C) and 12 U.S.C. 1825(b)(2) to the exercise of any contractual rights in accordance with the documents governing such securitization, including but not limited to taking possession of the financial assets and exercising self-help remedies as a secured creditor under the transfer agreements, provided no involvement of the receiver or conservator is required other than such consents, waivers, or execution of

§ 360.6

transfer documents as may be reasonably requested in the ordinary course of business in order to facilitate the exercise of such contractual rights. For purposes of this paragraph, the damages due shall be in an amount equal to the par value of the obligations outstanding on the date of appointment of the conservator or receiver, less any payments of principal received by the investors through the date of repudiation, plus unpaid, accrued interest through the date of repudiation in accordance with the contract documents to the extent actually received through payments on the financial assets received through the date of repudiation. Upon payment of such repudiation damages, all liens or claims on the financial assets created pursuant to the securitization documents shall be released. Such consent shall not waive or otherwise deprive the FDIC or its assignees of any seller's interest or other obligation or interest issued by the issuing entity and held by the FDIC or its assignees, but shall serve as full satisfaction of the obligations of the insured depository institution in conservatorship or receivership and the FDIC as conservator or receiver for all amounts due.

(iii) *Effect of repudiation.* If the FDIC repudiates or disaffirms a securitization agreement, it shall not assert that any interest payments made to investors in accordance with the securitization documents before any such repudiation or disaffirmance remain the property of the conservatorship or receivership.

(e) *Consent to certain actions.* Prior to repudiation or, in the case of a monetary default referred to in paragraph (d)(4)(i) of this section, prior to the effectiveness of the consent referred to therein, the FDIC as conservator or receiver consents pursuant to 12 U.S.C. 1821(e)(13)(C) to the making of, or if serving as servicer, shall make, the payments to the investors to the extent actually received through payments on the financial assets (but in the case of repudiation, only to the extent supported by payments on the financial assets received through the date of the giving of notice of repudiation) in accordance with the securitization documents, and, subject to the FDIC's rights to repudiate such agreements, consents to any servicing activity required in furtherance of the securitization or, if acting as servicer the FDIC as receiver or conservator shall perform such servicing activities in accordance with the terms of the applicable servicing agreements, with respect to the financial assets included in securitizations that meet the requirements applicable to that securitization as set forth in paragraphs (b) and (c) of this section.

(f) *Notice for consent.* Any party requesting the FDIC's consent as conservator or receiver under 12 U.S.C. 1821(e)(13)(C) and 12 U.S.C. 1825(b)(2) pursuant to paragraph (d)(4)(i) of this section shall provide notice to the Deputy Director, Division of Resolutions and Receiverships, Federal Deposit Insurance Corporation, 550 17th Street, NW., F-7076, Washington, DC 20429-0002, and a statement of the basis upon which such request is made, and copies of all documentation supporting such request, including without limitation a copy of the applicable agreements and of any applicable notices under the contract.

(g) *Contemporaneous requirement.* The FDIC will not seek to avoid an otherwise legally enforceable agreement that is executed by an insured depository institution in connection with a securitization or in the form of a participation solely because the agreement does not meet the "contemporaneous" requirement of 12 U.S.C. 1821(d)(9), 1821(n)(4)(I), or 1823(e).

(h) *Limitations.* The consents set forth in this section do not act to waive or relinquish any rights granted to the FDIC in any capacity, pursuant to any other applicable law or any agreement or contract except as specifically set forth herein. Nothing contained in this section alters the claims priority of the securitized obligations.

(i) *No waiver.* Except as specifically set forth herein, this section does not authorize, and shall not be construed as authorizing the waiver of the prohibitions in 12 U.S.C. 1825(b)(2) against levy, attachment, garnishment, foreclosure, or sale of property of the FDIC, nor does it authorize nor shall it be construed as authorizing the attachment of any involuntary lien upon the

Federal Deposit Insurance Corporation § 360.8

property of the FDIC. Nor shall this section be construed as waiving, limiting or otherwise affecting the rights or powers of the FDIC to take any action or to exercise any power not specifically mentioned, including but not limited to any rights, powers or remedies of the FDIC regarding transfers or other conveyances taken in contemplation of the institution's insolvency or with the intent to hinder, delay or defraud the institution or the creditors of such institution, or that is a fraudulent transfer under applicable law.

(j) *No assignment.* The right to consent under 12 U.S.C. 1821(e)(13)(C) or 12 U.S.C. 1825(b)(2), may not be assigned or transferred to any purchaser of property from the FDIC, other than to a conservator or bridge bank.

(k) *Repeal.* This section may be repealed by the FDIC upon 30 days notice provided in the FEDERAL REGISTER, but any repeal shall not apply to any issuance made in accordance with this section before such repeal.

[75 FR 60297, Sept. 30, 2010]

§ 360.7 Post-insolvency interest.

(a) *Purpose and scope.* This section establishes rules governing the calculation and distribution of post-insolvency interest to creditors with proven claims in all FDIC-administered receiverships established after June 13, 2002.

(b) *Definitions*—(1) *Equityholder.* The owner of an equity interest in a failed depository institution, whether such ownership is represented by stock, membership in a mutual association, or otherwise.

(2) *Post-insolvency interest.* Interest calculated from the date the receivership is established on proven creditor claims in receiverships with surplus funds.

(3) *Post-insolvency interest rate.* For any calendar quarter, the coupon equivalent yield of the average discount rate set on the three-month Treasury bill at the last auction held by the United States Treasury Department during the preceding calendar quarter, and adjusted each quarter thereafter.

(4) *Principal amount.* The proven claim amount and any interest accrued thereon as of the date the receivership is established.

(5) *Proven claim.* A claim that is allowed by a receiver or upon which a final non-appealable judgment has been entered in favor of a claimant against a receivership by a court with jurisdiction to adjudicate the claim.

(c) *Post-insolvency interest distributions.* (1) Post-insolvency interest shall only be distributed following satisfaction by the receiver of the principal amount of all creditor claims.

(2) The receiver shall distribute post-insolvency interest at the post-insolvency interest rate prior to making any distribution to equityholders. Post-insolvency interest distributions shall be made in the order of priority set forth in section 11(d)(11)(A) of the Federal Deposit Insurance Act, 12 U.S.C. 1821(d)(11)(A).

(3) Post-insolvency interest distributions shall be made at such time as the receiver determines that such distributions are appropriate and only to the extent of funds available in the receivership estate. Post-insolvency interest shall be calculated on the outstanding balance of a proven claim, as reduced from time to time by any interim dividend distributions, from the date the receivership is established until the principal amount of a proven claim has been fully distributed but not thereafter. Post-insolvency interest shall be calculated on a contingent claim from the date such claim becomes proven.

(4) Post-insolvency interest shall be determined using a simple interest method of calculation.

[67 FR 34386, May 14, 2002]

§ 360.8 Method for determining deposit and other liability account balances at a failed insured depository institution.

(a) *Purpose.* The purpose of this section is to describe the process the FDIC will use to determine deposit and other liability account balances for insurance coverage and receivership purposes at a failed insured depository institution.

(b) *Definitions*—(1) The *FDIC Cutoff Point* means the point in time the FDIC establishes after it has been appointed receiver of a failed insured depository

§ 360.8

institution and takes control of the failed institution.

(2) The *Applicable Cutoff Time* for a specific type of deposit account transaction means the *earlier* of either the failed institution's normal cutoff time for that specific type of transaction or the *FDIC Cutoff Point*.

(3) *Close-of-Business Account Balance* means the closing end-of-day ledger balance of a deposit or other liability account on the day of failure of an insured depository institution determined by using the *Applicable Cutoff Times*. This balance may be adjusted to reflect steps taken by the receiver to ensure that funds are not received by or removed from the institution after the *FDIC Cutoff Point*.

(4) A *sweep account* is an account held pursuant to a contract between an insured depository institution and its customer involving the pre-arranged, automated transfer of funds from a deposit account to either another account or investment vehicle located within the depository institution (*internal sweep account*), or an investment vehicle located outside the depository institution (*external sweep account*).

(c) *Principles*—(1) In making deposit insurance determinations and in determining the value and nature of claims against the receivership on the institution's date of failure, the FDIC, as insurer and receiver, will treat deposits and other liabilities of the failed institution according to the ownership and nature of the underlying obligations based on end-of-day ledger balances for each account using, except as expressly provided otherwise in this section, the depository institution's normal posting procedures.

(2) In its role as receiver of a failed insured depository institution, in order to ensure the proper distribution of the failed institution's assets under the FDI Act (12 U.S.C. 1821(d)(11)) as of the FDIC Cutoff Point, the FDIC will use its best efforts to take all steps necessary to stop the generation, via transactions or transfers coming from or going outside the institution, of new liabilities or extinguishing existing liabilities for the depository institution.

(3) End-of-day ledger balances are subject to corrections for posted transactions that are inconsistent with the above principles.

(d) *Determining closing day balances*—(1) In determining account balances for insurance coverage and receivership purposes at a failed insured depository institution, the FDIC will use *Close-of-Business Account Balances*.

(2) A check posted to the *Close-of-Business Account Balance* but not collected by the depository institution will be included as part of the balance, subject to the correction of errors and omissions and adjustments for uncollectible items that the FDIC may make in its role as receiver of the failed depository institution.

(3) In determining *Close-of-Business Account Balances* involving sweep accounts:

(i) For internal sweep accounts, the FDIC will determine the ownership of the funds and the nature of the receivership claim based on the records established and maintained by the institution for that specific account or investment vehicle as of the closing day end-of-day ledger balance. (For example, if a sweep account entails the daily transfer of funds from a demand deposit account to a Eurodollar account at a foreign branch of the insured depository institution, if the institution should fail on that day, the FDIC would treat the funds swept to the Eurodollar account, as reflected on the institution's end-of-day records, as an unsecured general creditor's claim against the receivership.);

(ii) For external sweep accounts, the FDIC will treat swept funds consistent with their status in the end-of-day ledger balances of the depository institution and the external entity, as long as the transfer of funds is completed prior to the Applicable Cutoff Time. (For example, if funds held in connection with a money market sweep account are wired from a customer's deposit account at the insured depository institution to the mutual fund prior to the Applicable Cutoff Time, if the institution should fail on that day, the FDIC would recognize that sweep transaction as completed for claims and receivership purposes.);

(iii) For repurchase agreement sweep accounts, where, as a result of the

Federal Deposit Insurance Corporation § 360.9

sweep transaction, the customer becomes either the legal owner of identified assets subject to repurchase or obtains a perfected security interest in those assets, the FDIC will recognize, for receivership purposes, the customer's ownership interest or security interest in the assets.

(4) For deposit insurance and receivership purposes in connection with the failure of an insured depository institution, the FDIC will determine the rights of the depositor or other liability holder as of the point the *Close-of-Business Account Balance* is calculated.

(e) *Disclosure requirements.* Beginning July 1, 2009, in all new sweep account contracts, in renewals of existing sweep account contracts and within sixty days after July 1, 2009, and no less than annually thereafter, institutions must prominently disclose in writing to sweep account customers whether their swept funds are deposits within the meaning of 12 U.S.C. 1813(l). If the funds are not deposits, the institution must further disclose the status such funds would have if the institution failed—for example, general creditor status or secured creditor status. Such disclosures must be consistent with how the institution reports such funds on its quarterly Consolidated Reports of Condition and Income or Thrift Financial Reports. The disclosure requirements imposed under this provision do not apply to sweep accounts where: The transfers are within a single account, or a sub-account; or the sweep account involves only deposit-to-deposit sweeps, such as zero-balance accounts, unless the sweep results in a change in the customer's insurance coverage.

[74 FR 5806, Feb. 2, 2009]

§ 360.9 Large-bank deposit insurance determination modernization.

(a) *Purpose and scope.* This section is intended to allow the deposit and other operations of a large insured depository institution (defined as a "Covered Institution") to continue functioning on the day following failure. It also is intended to permit the FDIC to fulfill its legal mandates regarding the resolution of failed insured institutions to provide liquidity to depositors promptly, enhance market discipline, ensure equitable treatment of depositors at different institutions and reduce the FDIC's costs by preserving the franchise value of a failed institution.

(b) *Definitions.* (1) A *covered Institution* means an insured depository institution which, based on items as defined in Reports of Income and Condition or Thrift Financial Reports filed with the applicable federal regulator, has at least $2 billion in deposits and at least either:

(i) 250,000 deposit accounts; or

(ii) $20 billion in total assets, regardless of the number of deposit accounts.

(2) *Deposits, number of deposit accounts and total assets* are as defined in the instructions for the filing of Reports of Income and Condition and Thrift Financial Reports, as applicable to the insured depository institution for determining whether it qualifies as a covered institution. A foreign deposit means an uninsured deposit liability maintained in a foreign branch of an insured depository institution. An *international banking facility deposit* is as defined by the Board of Governors of the Federal Reserve System in Regulation D (12 CFR § 204.8(a)(2)). A *demand deposit account, NOW account, money market deposit account, savings deposit account and time deposit account* are as defined in the instructions for the filing of Reports of Income and Condition and Thrift Financial Reports.

(3) *Sweep account arrangements* consist of a deposit account linked to an interest-bearing investment vehicle whereby funds are swept to and from the deposit account according to prearranged rules, usually on a daily basis, where the sweep investment vehicle is not a deposit and is reflected on the books and records of the *Covered Institution.*

(4) *Automated credit account arrangements* consist of a deposit account into which funds are automatically credited from an interest-bearing investment vehicle where the funds in the interest-bearing investment vehicle were not invested by prearranged rules.

(5) *Non-covered institution* means an insured depository institution that does not meet the definition of a covered institution.

(6) *Provisional hold* means an effective restriction on access to some or all of

569

§ 360.9

a deposit or other liability account after the failure of an insured depository institution.

(c) *Posting and removing provisional holds.* (1) A covered institution shall have in place an automated process for implementing a provisional hold on deposit accounts, foreign deposit accounts and sweep and automated credit account arrangements immediately following the determination of the close-of-business account balances, as defined in § 360.8(b)(3), at the failed covered institution.

(2) The system requirements under paragraph (c)(1) must have the capability of placing the provisional holds prescribed under that provision no later than 9 a.m. local time the day following the FDIC cutoff point, as defined in § 360.8(b)(1).

(3) Pursuant to instructions to be provided by the FDIC, a covered institution must notify the FDIC of the person(s) responsible for producing the standard data download and administering provisional holds, both while the functionality is being constructed and on an on-going basis.

(4) For deposit accounts held in domestic offices of an insured depository institution, the provisional hold algorithm must be designed to exempt accounts below a specific account balance threshold, as determined by the FDIC. The account balance threshold could be any amount, including zero. For accounts above the account balance threshold determined by the FDIC, the algorithm must be designed to calculate and place a hold equal to the dollar amount of funds in excess of the account balance threshold multiplied by the provisional hold percentage determined by the FDIC. The provisional hold percentage could be any amount, from zero to one hundred percent. The account balance threshold as well as the provisional hold percentage could vary for the following four categories, as the covered institution customarily defines consumer accounts:

(i) Consumer demand deposit, NOW and money market deposit accounts;

(ii) Other consumer deposit accounts (time deposit and savings accounts, excluding NOW and money market deposit accounts);

(iii) Non-consumer demand deposit, NOW and money market deposit accounts; and

(iv) Other non-consumer deposit accounts (time deposit and savings accounts, excluding NOW and money market deposit accounts).

(5) For deposit accounts held in foreign offices of an insured depository institution, other than those connected to a sweep or automated credit arrangement, the provisional hold algorithm will apply a provisional hold percentage to the entire account balance. For deposit accounts held in foreign offices the provisional hold percentage may differ from that applied to deposit accounts. Also, the provisional hold percentage would not vary by account category (*i.e.*, consumer versus non-consumer and transaction versus non-transaction) as is the case with deposit accounts.

(6) For international banking facility deposits, other than those connected to a sweep or automated credit arrangements, the provisional hold algorithm will apply a provisional hold percentage to the entire account balance. For IBF deposits the provisional hold percentage may differ from that applied to deposit or foreign deposit accounts. Also, the provisional hold percentage would not vary by account category (*i.e.*, consumer versus non-consumer, and transaction versus non-transaction) as is the case with deposit accounts.

(7) For the interest-bearing investment vehicle of a sweep arrangement, the provisional hold algorithm must be designed with the capability to place a provisional hold on the interest-bearing investment vehicle with possibly a different account balance threshold and a different hold percentage according to the type of interest-bearing investment vehicle.

(8) For the interest-bearing investment vehicle of an automated credit account arrangement, the provisional hold algorithm must be designed with the capability to place a provisional hold on the interest-bearing investment vehicle with possibly a different account balance threshold and a different hold percentage according to the type of interest-bearing investment vehicle.

Federal Deposit Insurance Corporation § 360.9

(9) A covered institution may submit a request to the FDIC, using the address indicated in § 360.9(g): to develop a provisional hold process involving memo holds or alternative account mechanisms; or to exempt from the provisional hold requirements of this section those account systems servicing a relatively small number of accounts where the manual application of provisional holds is feasible. Such requests may be in the form of a letter and must include a justification for the request and address the relative effectiveness of the alternative for posting provisional holds in the event of failure. The FDIC will consider such requests on a case-by-case basis in light of the objectives of this section.

(10) The automated process for provisional holds required by paragraph (c)(1) of this section must include the capability of removing provisional holds in batch mode and, during the same processing cycle, applying debits, credits or additional holds on the deposit or other accounts from which the provisional holds were removed, as determined by the FDIC. The FDIC will provide files listing the accounts subject to: removal of provisional holds or additional holds (file format as specified in appendix A); application of debits or credits (file format as specified in appendix B); and application of additional holds (file format as specified in appendix A). In addition to the batch process used to remove provisional holds, the Covered Institution is required to have in place a mechanism for manual removal of provisional holds on a case-by-case basis.

(d) *Providing a standard data format for generating deposit account and customer data.* (1) A covered institution must have in place practices and procedures for providing the FDIC in a standard format upon the close of any day's business with required depositor and customer data for all deposit accounts held in domestic and foreign offices and interest-bearing investment accounts connected with sweep and automated credit arrangements. Such standard data files are to be created through a mapping of pre-existing data elements and internal institution codes into standard data formats. Deposit account and customer data provided must be current as of the close of business for that day.

(2) The requirements of paragraph (d)(1) of this section shall be provided in five separate files, as indicated in the appendices C through G to this part 360.

(3) Upon request by the FDIC, a covered institution must submit the data required by paragraph (d)(1) of this section to the FDIC, in a manner prescribed by the FDIC.

(4) In providing the data required under paragraph (d)(1) of this section to the FDIC, the *Covered Institution* must be able to reconcile the total deposit balances and the number of deposit accounts to the institution's subsidiary system control totals.

(e) *Implementation requirements.* (1) A covered institution must comply with the requirements of this section no later than February 18, 2010.

(2) An insured depository institution not within the definition of a covered institution on the effective date of this section must comply with the requirements of this section no later than eighteen months following the end of the second calendar quarter for which it meets the criteria for a covered institution.

(3) Upon the merger of two or more non-covered institutions, if the resulting institution meets the criteria for a covered institution, that covered institution must comply with the requirements of this section no later than eighteen months after the effective date of the merger.

(4) Upon the merger of two or more covered institutions, the merged institution must comply with the requirements of this section within eighteen months following the effective date of the merger. This provision, however, does not supplant any preexisting implementation date requirement, in place prior to the date of the merger, for the individual covered institution(s) involved in the merger.

(5) Upon the merger of one or more covered institutions with one or more non-covered institutions, the merged institution(s) must comply with the requirements of this section within eighteen months following the effective date of the merger. This provision,

§ 360.10

however, does not supplant any pre-existing implementation date requirement for the individual covered institution(s) involved in the merger.

(6) Notwithstanding the general requirements of this paragraph (e), on a case-by-case basis, the FDIC may accelerate, upon notice, the implementation timeframe of all or part of the requirements of this section for a covered institution that: Has a composite rating of 3, 4, or 5 under the Uniform Financial Institution's Rating System, or in the case of an insured branch of a foreign bank, an equivalent rating; is undercapitalized, as defined under the prompt corrective action provisions of 12 CFR part 325; or is determined by the appropriate Federal banking agency or the FDIC in consultation with the appropriate Federal banking agency to be experiencing a significant deterioration of capital or significant funding difficulties or liquidity stress, notwithstanding the composite rating of the institution by its appropriate Federal banking agency in its most recent report of examination. In implementing this paragraph (e)(6), the FDIC must consult with the covered institution's primary federal regulator and consider the: Complexity of the institution's deposit systems and operations, extent of the institution's asset quality difficulties, volatility of the institution's funding sources, expected near-term changes in the institution's capital levels, and other relevant factors appropriate for the FDIC to consider in its roles as insurer and possible receiver of the institution.

(7) Notwithstanding the general requirements of this paragraph (e), a covered institution may request, by letter, that the FDIC extend the deadline for complying with the requirements of this section. A request for such an extension is subject to the FDIC's rules of general applicability under 12 CFR. 303.251.

(f) A covered institution may apply to the FDIC for an exemption from the requirements of this § 360.9 if it has a high concentration of deposits incidental to credit card operations. The FDIC will consider such applications on a case-by-case basis in light of the objectives of this section.

(g) Requests for exemptions from the requirements of this section, for flexibility in the use of provisional holds or for extensions of the implementation requirements of this section and the submission of point-of-contact information should be submitted in writing to: Office of the Director, Division of Resolutions and Receiverships, Federal Deposit Insurance Corporation, 550 17th Street, NW., Washington, DC 20429–0002.

(h) *Testing requirements.* Covered institutions must provide appropriate assistance to the FDIC in its testing of the systems required by this section. The FDIC will provide testing details to covered institutions through the issuance of subsequent procedures and/or guidelines.

[73 FR 41195, July 17, 2008]

§ 360.10 **Resolution plans required for insured depository institutions with $50 billion or more in total assets.**

(a) *Scope and purpose.* This section requires each insured depository institution with $50 billion or more in total assets to submit periodically to the FDIC a plan for the resolution of such institution in the event of its failure. This section also establishes the rules and requirements regarding the submission and content of a resolution plan as well as procedures for review by the FDIC of a resolution plan. This section requires a covered insured depository institution to submit a resolution plan that should enable the FDIC, as receiver, to resolve the institution under Sections 11 and 13 of the Federal Deposit Insurance Act ("FDI Act"), 12 U.S.C. 1821 and 1823, in a manner that ensures that depositors receive access to their insured deposits within one business day of the institution's failure (two business days if the failure occurs on a day other than Friday), maximizes the net present value return from the sale or disposition of its assets and minimizes the amount of any loss realized by the creditors in the resolution. This rule is intended to ensure that the FDIC has access to all of the material information it needs to resolve efficiently a covered insured depository institution in the event of its failure.

Federal Deposit Insurance Corporation § 360.10

(b) *Definitions*—(1) *Affiliate* has the same meaning given such term in Section 3(w)(6) of the FDI Act, 12 U.S.C. 1813(w)(6).

(2) *Company* has the same meaning given such term in § 362.2(d) of the FDIC's Regulations, 12 CFR 362.2(d).

(3) *Core business lines* means those business lines of the covered insured depository institution ("CIDI"), including associated operations, services, functions and support, that, in the view of the CIDI, upon failure would result in a material loss of revenue, profit, or franchise value.

(4) *Covered insured depository institution ("CIDI")* means an insured depository institution with $50 billion or more in total assets, as determined based upon the average of the institution's four most recent Reports of Condition and Income or Thrift Financial Reports, as applicable to the insured depository institution.

(5) *Critical services* means services and operations of the CIDI, such as servicing, information technology support and operations, human resources and personnel that are necessary to continue the day-to-day operations of the CIDI.

(6) *Foreign-based company* means any company that is not incorporated or organized under the laws of the United States.

(7) *Insured depository institution* shall have the meaning given such term in Section 3(c)(2) of the FDI Act, 12 U.S.C. 1813(c)(2).

(8) *Material entity* means a company that is significant to the activities of a critical service or core business line.

(9) *Parent company* means the company that controls, directly or indirectly, an insured depository institution. In a multi-tiered holding company structure, parent company means the top-tier of the multi-tiered holding company only.

(10) *Parent company affiliate* means any affiliate of the parent company other than the CIDI and subsidiaries of the CIDI.

(11) *Resolution plan* means the plan described in paragraph (c) of this section for resolving the CIDI under Sections 11 and 13 of the FDI Act, 12 U.S.C. 1821 and 1823.

(12) *Subsidiary* has the same meaning given such term in Section 3(w)(4) of the FDI Act, 12 U.S.C. 1813(w)(4).

(13) *Total assets* are defined in the instructions for the filing of Reports of Condition and Income and Thrift Financial Reports, as applicable to the insured depository institution, for determining whether it qualifies as a CIDI.

(14) *United States* means the United States and includes any state of the United States, the District of Columbia, any territory of the United States, Puerto Rico, Guam, American Samoa and the Virgin Islands.

(c) *Resolution Plans to be submitted by CIDI to FDIC*—(1) *General*—(i) *Initial resolution plans required.* Each CIDI shall submit a resolution plan to the FDIC, Attention: Office of Complex Financial Institutions, 550 17th Street, NW., Washington, DC 20429, on or before the date set forth below ("Initial Submission Date"):

(A) July 1, 2012, with respect to a CIDI whose parent company, as of the effective date of this section, had $250 billion or more in total nonbank assets (or in the case of a parent company that is a foreign-based company, such company's total U.S. nonbank assets);

(B) July 1, 2013, with respect to any CIDI not described in paragraph (c)(1)(i)(A) of this section whose parent company, as of the effective date of this section, had $100 billion or more in total nonbank assets (or, in the case of a parent company that is a foreign-based company, such company's total U.S. nonbank assets); and

(C) December 31, 2013, with respect to any CIDI not described in paragraph (c)(1)(i)(A) or (B) of this section.

(ii) *Submission by new CIDIs.* An insured depository institution that becomes a CIDI after the effective date of this section shall submit its initial resolution plan no later than July 1 of the following calendar year.

(iii) After filing its initial Resolution Plan pursuant to paragraph (c)(1)(i) or (c)(1)(ii) of this section, each CIDI shall submit a Resolution Plan to the FDIC annually on or before each anniversary date of its Initial Submission Date.

(iv) Notwithstanding anything to the contrary in this paragraph (c)(1), the FDIC may determine that a CIDI shall

§ 360.10

file its initial or annual Resolution Plan by a date other than as provided in this paragraph (c). The FDIC shall provide a CIDI with written notice of a determination under this paragraph (c)(1)(iv) no later than 180 days prior to the date on which the FDIC determines to require the CIDI to submit its Resolution Plan.

(v) *Notice of material events.* (A) Each CIDI shall file with the FDIC a notice no later than 45 days after any event, occurrence, change in conditions or circumstances or other change that results in, or could reasonably be foreseen to have, a material effect on the resolution plan of the CIDI. Such notice shall describe the event, occurrence or change, describe any material effects that the event, occurrence or change may have on the resolution plan and summarize the changes that are required in the resolution plan. The CIDI shall address any event, occurrence or change with respect to which it has provided notice pursuant hereto in the following resolution plan submitted by the CIDI.

(B) A CIDI shall not be required to file a notice under paragraph (c)(1)(v)(A) of this section if the date on which the CIDI would be required to submit a notice under paragraph (c)(1)(v)(A) would be within 45 days prior to the date on which the CIDI is required to file an annual Resolution Plan under paragraph (c)(1)(iii) of this section.

(iv) *Incorporation of data and other information from a Dodd-Frank Act resolution plan.* The CIDI may incorporate data and other information from a resolution plan filed pursuant to Section 165(d) of the Dodd-Frank Wall Street Reform and Consumer Protection Act, 12 U.S.C. 5365(d), by its parent company.

(2) *Content of the resolution plan.* The resolution plan submitted should enable the FDIC, as receiver, to resolve the CIDI in the event of its insolvency under the FDI Act in a manner that ensures that depositors receive access to their insured deposits within one business day of the institution's failure (two business days if the failure occurs on a day other than Friday), maximizes the net present value return from the sale or disposition of its assets and minimizes the amount of any loss realized by the creditors in the resolution in accordance with Sections 11 and 13 of the FDI Act, 12 U.S.C. 1821 and 1823. The resolution plan strategies should take into account that failure of the CIDI may occur under the baseline, adverse and severely adverse economic conditions developed by the Board of Governors of the Federal Reserve System pursuant to 12 U.S.C. 5365(i)(1)(B); provided, however, a CIDI may submit its initial resolution plan assuming the baseline conditions only, or, if a baseline scenario is not then available, a reasonable substitute developed by the CIDI. At a minimum, the resolution plan shall:

(i) *Executive summary.* Include an executive summary describing the key elements of the CIDI's strategic plan for resolution under the FDI Act in the event of its insolvency. After the CIDI files its initial plan, each annual resolution plan shall also describe:

(A) Material events, such as acquisitions, sales, litigation and operational changes, since the most recently filed plan that may have a material effect on the plan;

(B) Material changes to the CIDI's resolution plan from its most recently filed plan; and

(C) Any actions taken by the CIDI since filing of the previous plan to improve the effectiveness of its resolution plan or remediate or otherwise mitigate any material weaknesses or impediments to the effective and timely execution of the resolution plan.

(ii) *Organizational structure: legal entities; core business lines and branches.* Provide the CIDI's, parent company's, and affiliates' legal and functional structures and identify core business lines. Provide a mapping of core business lines, including material asset holdings and liabilities related thereto, to material entities. Discuss the CIDI's overall deposit activities including, among other things, unique aspects of the deposit base or underlying systems that may create operational complexity for the FDIC, result in extraordinary resolution expenses in the event of failure and a description of the branch organization, both domestic and foreign. Identify key personnel tasked with managing core business

Federal Deposit Insurance Corporation § 360.10

lines and deposit activities and the CIDI's branch organization.

(iii) *Critical services.* Identify critical services and providers of critical services. Provide a mapping of critical services to material entities and core business lines. Describe the CIDI's strategy for continuing critical services in the event of the CIDI's failure. When critical services are provided by the parent company or a parent company affiliate, describe the CIDI's strategy for continuing critical services in the event of the parent company's or parent company affiliate's failure. Assess the ability of each parent company affiliate providing critical services to function on a standalone basis in the event of the parent company's failure.

(iv) *Interconnectedness to parent company's organization.* Identify the elements or aspects of the parent company's organizational structure, the interconnectedness of its legal entities, the structure of legal or contractual arrangements, or its overall business operations that would, in the event the CIDI were placed in receivership, diminish the CIDI's franchise value, obstruct its continued business operations or increase the operational complexity to the FDIC of resolution of the CIDI.

(v) *Strategy to separate from parent company's organization.* Provide a strategy to unwind or separate the CIDI and its subsidiaries from the organizational structure of its parent company in a cost-effective and timely fashion. Describe remediation or mitigating steps that could be taken to eliminate or mitigate obstacles to such separation.

(vi) *Strategy for the sale or disposition of deposit franchise, business lines and assets.* Provide a strategy for the sale or disposition of the deposit franchise, including branches, core business lines and major assets of the CIDI in a manner that ensures that depositors receive access to their insured deposits within one business day of the institution's failure (two business days if the failure occurs on a day other than Friday), maximizes the net present value return from the sale or disposition of such assets and minimizes the amount of any loss realized in the resolution of cases.

(vii) *Least costly resolution method.* Describe how the strategies for the separation of the CIDI and its subsidiaries from its parent company's organization and sale or disposition of deposit franchise, core business lines and major assets can be demonstrated to be the least costly to the Deposit Insurance Fund of all possible methods for resolving the CIDI.

(viii) *Asset valuation and sales.* Provide a detailed description of the processes the CIDI employs for:

(A) Determining the current market values and marketability of core business lines and material asset holdings;

(B) Assessing the feasibility of the CIDI's plans, under idiosyncratic and industry-wide stress scenarios (including timeframes), for executing any sales, divestitures, restructurings, recapitalizations, or similar actions contemplated in the CIDI's resolution plan; and

(C) Assessing the impact of any sales, divestitures, restructurings, recapitalizations, or other similar actions on the value, funding and operations of the CIDI and its core business lines.

(ix) *Major counterparties.* Identify the major counterparties of the CIDI and describe the interconnections, interdependencies and relationships with such major counterparties. Analyze whether the failure of each major counterparty would likely have an adverse impact on or result in the material financial distress or failure of the CIDI.

(x) *Off-balance-sheet exposures.* Describe any material off-balance-sheet exposures (including guarantees and contractual obligations) of the CIDI and map those exposures to core business lines.

(xi) *Collateral pledged.* Identify and describe processes used by the CIDI to:

(A) Determine to whom the CIDI has pledged collateral;

(B) Identify the person or entity that holds such collateral; and

(C) Identify the jurisdiction in which the collateral is located; and if different, the jurisdiction in which the security interest in the collateral is enforceable against the CIDI.

(xii) *Trading, derivatives and hedges.* Describe the practices of the CIDI and its core business lines related to the booking of trading and derivative activities. Identify each system on which the CIDI conducts a material number or value amount of trades. Map each trading system to the CIDI's legal entities and core business lines. Identify material hedges of the CIDI and its core business lines related to trading and derivative activities, including a mapping to legal entity. Describe hedging strategies of the CIDI.

(xiii) *Unconsolidated balance sheet of CIDI; material entity financial statements.* Provide an unconsolidated balance sheet for the CIDI and a consolidating schedule for all material entities that are subject to consolidation with the CIDI. Provide financial statements for material entities. When available, audited financial statements should be provided.

(xiv) *Payment, clearing and settlement systems.* Identify each payment, clearing and settlement system of which the CIDI, directly or indirectly, is a member. Map membership in each such system to the CIDI's legal entities and core business lines.

(xv) *Capital structure; funding sources.* Provide detailed descriptions of the funding, liquidity and capital needs of, and resources available to, the CIDI and its material entities, which shall be mapped to core business lines and critical services. Describe the material components of the liabilities of the CIDI and its material entities and identify types and amounts of short-term and long-term liabilities by type and term to maturity, secured and unsecured liabilities and subordinated liabilities.

(xvi) *Affiliate funding, transactions, accounts, exposures and concentrations.* Describe material affiliate funding relationships, accounts, and exposures, including terms, purpose, and duration, that the CIDI or any of its subsidiaries have with its parent or any parent company affiliate. Include in such description material affiliate financial exposures, claims or liens, lending or borrowing lines and relationships, guarantees, asset accounts, deposits, or derivatives transactions. Clearly identify the nature and extent to which parent company or parent company affiliates serve as a source of funding to the CIDI and its subsidiaries, the terms of any contractual arrangements, including any capital maintenance agreements, the location of related assets, funds or deposits and the mechanisms by which funds can be downstreamed from the parent company to the CIDI and its subsidiaries.

(xvii) *Systemically important functions.* Describe systemically important functions that the CIDI, its subsidiaries and affiliates provide, including the nature and extent of the institution's involvement in payment systems, custodial or clearing operations, large sweep programs, and capital markets operations in which it plays a dominant role. Discuss critical vulnerabilities, estimated exposure and potential losses, and why certain attributes of the businesses detailed in previous sections could pose a systemic risk to the broader economy.

(xviii) *Cross-border elements.* Describe individual components of the CIDI's structure that are based or located outside the United States, including foreign branches, subsidiaries and offices. Provide detail on the location and amount of foreign deposits and assets. Discuss the nature and extent of the CIDI's cross-border assets, operations, interrelationships and exposures and map to legal entities and core business lines.

(xix) *Management information systems; software licenses; intellectual property.* Provide a detailed inventory and description of the key management information systems and applications, including systems and applications for risk management, accounting, and financial and regulatory reporting, used by the CIDI and its subsidiaries. Identify the legal owner or licensor of the systems identified above; describe the use and function of the system or application, and provide a listing of service level agreements and any software and systems licenses or associated intellectual property related thereto. Identify and discuss any disaster recovery or other backup plans. Identify common or shared personnel, facilities, or systems. Describe the capabilities of the CIDI's processes and systems to collect, maintain, and report the information and other data underlying the resolution plan to management of the CIDI and, upon request to the FDIC.

Federal Deposit Insurance Corporation § 360.10

Describe any deficiencies, gaps or weaknesses in such capabilities and the actions the CIDI intends to take to promptly address such deficiencies, gaps, or weaknesses, and the time frame for implementing such actions.

(xx) *Corporate governance.* Include a detailed description of:

(A) How resolution planning is integrated into the corporate governance structure and processes of the CIDI;

(B) The CIDI's policies, procedures, and internal controls governing preparation and approval of the resolution plan; and

(C) The identity and position of the senior management official of the CIDI that is primarily responsible for overseeing the development, maintenance, implementation, and filing of the resolution plan and for the CIDI's compliance with this section.

(xxi) *Assessment of the resolution plan.* Describe the nature, extent, and results of any contingency planning or similar exercise conducted by the CIDI since the date of the most recently filed resolution plan to assess the viability of or improve the resolution plan.

(xxii) *Any other material factor.* Identify and discuss any other material factor that may impede the resolution of the CIDI.

(3) *Approval.* The CIDI's board of directors must approve the resolution plan. Such approval shall be noted in the Board minutes.

(4) *Review of resolution plan.* (i) Each resolution plan submitted shall be credible. A resolution plan is credible if its strategies for resolving the CIDI, and the detailed information required by this section, are well-founded and based on information and data related to the CIDI that are observable or otherwise verifiable and employ reasonable projections from current and historical conditions within the broader financial markets.

(ii) After receiving a resolution plan, the FDIC shall determine whether the submitted plan satisfies the minimum informational requirements of paragraph (c)(2) of this section; and either acknowledge acceptance of the plan for review or return the resolution plan if the FDIC determines that it is incomplete or that substantial additional information is required to facilitate review of the resolution plan.

(iii) If the FDIC determines that a resolution plan is informationally incomplete or that additional information is necessary to facilitate review of the plan, the FDIC shall inform the CIDI in writing of the area(s) in which the plan is informationally incomplete or with respect to which additional information is required.

(iv) The CIDI shall resubmit an informationally complete resolution plan or such additional information as requested to facilitate review of the resolution plan no later than 30 days after receiving the notice described in preceding paragraph, or such other time period as the FDIC may determine.

(v) Upon acceptance of a resolution plan as informationally complete, the FDIC will review the resolution plan in consultation with the appropriate Federal banking agency for the CIDI and its parent company. If the FDIC determines that the resolution plan of a CIDI submitted is not credible, the FDIC shall notify the CIDI in writing of such determination. Any notice provided under this paragraph shall identify the aspects of the resolution plan that the FDIC determines to be deficient.

(vi) Within 90 days of receiving a notice of deficiencies issued pursuant to paragraph (c)(4)(v) of this section, or such shorter or longer period as the FDIC may determine, a CIDI shall submit a revised resolution plan to the FDIC that addresses the deficiencies identified by the FDIC and discusses in detail the revisions made to address such deficiencies.

(vii) Upon its own initiative or a written request by a CIDI, the FDIC may extend any time period under this section. Each extension request shall be in writing and shall describe the basis and justification for the request.

(d) *Implementation matters.* (1) In order to allow evaluation of the resolution plan, each CIDI must provide the FDIC such information and access to such personnel of the CIDI as the FDIC determines is necessary to assess the credibility of the resolution plan and the ability of the CIDI to implement the resolution plan. The FDIC will rely to the fullest extent possible on examinations conducted by or on behalf of the appropriate Federal banking agency for the relevant company.

(2) Within a reasonable period of time, as determined by the FDIC, following its Initial Submission Date, the CIDI shall demonstrate its capability to produce promptly, in a format acceptable to the FDIC, the information and data underlying its resolution plan.

(3) Notwithstanding the general requirements of paragraph (c)(1) of this section, on a case-by-case basis, the FDIC may extend, on its own initiative or upon written request, the implementation and updating time frames for all or part of the requirements of this section.

(4) FDIC may, on its own initiative or upon written request, exempt a CIDI from one or more of the requirements of this section.

(e) *No limiting effect on FDIC.* No resolution plan provided pursuant to this section shall be binding on the FDIC as supervisor, deposit insurer or receiver for a CIDI or otherwise require the FDIC to act in conformance with such plan.

(f) *Form of resolution plans; confidential treatment of resolution plans.* (1) Each resolution plan of a CIDI shall be divided into a Public Section and a Confidential Section. Each CIDI shall segregate and separately identify the Public Section from the Confidential Section. The Public Section shall consist of an executive summary of the resolution plan that describes the business of the CIDI and includes, to the extent material to an understanding of the CIDI:

(i) The names of material entities;

(ii) A description of core business lines;

(iii) Consolidated financial information regarding assets, liabilities, capital and major funding sources;

(iv) A description of derivative activities and hedging activities;

(v) A list of memberships in material payment, clearing and settlement systems;

(vi) A description of foreign operations;

(vii) The identities of material supervisory authorities;

(viii) The identities of the principal officers;

(ix) A description of the corporate governance structure and processes related to resolution planning;

(x) A description of material management information systems; and

(xi) A description, at a high level, of the CIDI's resolution strategy, covering such items as the range of potential purchasers of the CIDI, its material entities and core business lines.

(2) The confidentiality of resolution plans shall be determined in accordance with applicable exemptions under the Freedom of Information Act (5 U.S.C. 552(b)) and the FDIC's Disclosure of Information Rules (12 CFR part 309).

(3) Any CIDI submitting a resolution plan or related materials pursuant to this section that desires confidential treatment of the information submitted pursuant to 5 U.S.C. 552(b)(4) and the FDIC's Disclosure of Information Rules (12 CFR part 309) and related policies may file a request for confidential treatment in accordance with those rules.

(4) To the extent permitted by law, information comprising the Confidential Section of a resolution plan will be treated as confidential.

(5) To the extent permitted by law, the submission of any nonpublicly available data or information under this section shall not constitute a waiver of, or otherwise affect, any privilege arising under Federal or state law (including the rules of any Federal or state court) to which the data or information is otherwise subject. Privileges that apply to resolution plans and related materials are protected pursuant to Section 18(x) of the FDI Act, 12 U.S.C. 1828(x).

[76 FR 58389, Sept. 21, 2011]

EDITORIAL NOTE: At 76 FR 58389, Sept. 21, 2011, §360.10 was added with two paragraphs (c)(1)(iv).

APPENDIX A TO PART 360—NON-MONETARY TRANSACTION FILE STRUCTURE

This is the structure of the data file the FDIC will provide to remove or add a FDIC hold for an individual account or sub-account. The file will be in a tab- or pipe-delimited ASCII format and provided through

Federal Deposit Insurance Corporation

FDICconnect or Direct Connect. The file will be encrypted using an FDIC-supplied algorithm.

Field name	Field description	Comments	Format
1. DP__Acct__Identifier	Account Identifier .... The primary field used to identify the account. This field may be the Account Number.	The Account Identifier may be composed of more than one physical data element. If multiple fields are required to identify the account, data should be placed in separate fields and the FDIC instructed how these fields are combined to uniquely identify the account.	Character (25).
2. DP__Acct__Identifier—2	Account Identifier—2 .... If necessary, the second element used to identify the account.		Character (25).
3. DP__Acct__Identifier—3	Account Identifier—3 .... If necessary, the third element used to identify the account.		Character (25).
4. DP__Acct__Identifier—4	Account Identifier—4 .... If necessary, the fourth element used to identify the account.		Character (25).
5. DP __Acct__Identifier—5	Account Identifier—5 .... If necessary, the fifth element used to identify the account.		Character (25).
6. DP__Sub__Acct__Identifier	Sub-Account Identifier .... If available, the Sub-Account identifier for the account.	The Sub-Account Identifier may identify separate deposits tied to this account where there are different processing parameters such as interest rates or maturity dates, but all owners are the same.	Character (25).
7. PH__Hold__Action	Hold Action·............................... The requested hold action to be taken for this account or sub-account. Possible values are: • R = Remove. • A = Add.		Character (1).
8. PH__Hold__Amt	Hold Amount .... Dollar amount of the FDIC hold to be removed or added.		Decimal (14,2).
9. PH__Hold__Desc	Hold Description .... FDIC hold to be removed or added.		Character (225).

[73 FR 41197, July 17, 2008]

APPENDIX B TO PART 360—DEBIT/CREDIT FILE STRUCTURE

This is the structure of the data file the FDIC will provide to apply debits and credits to an individual account or sub-account after the removal of FDIC holds. The file will be in a tab- or pipe-delimited ASCII format and provided through FDICconnect or Direct Connect. The file will be encrypted using an FDIC-supplied algorithm.

Field name	Field description	Comments	Format
1. DP__Acct__Identifier	Account Identifier .... The primary field used to identify the account. This field may the Account Number.	The Account Identifier may be composed of more than one physical data element. If multiple fields are required to identify the account, data should be placed in separate fields and the FDIC instructed how these fields are combined to uniquely identify the account.	Character (25).
2. DP __Acct__Identifier—2	Account Identifier—2 .... If necessary, the second element used to identify the account.		Character (25).
3. DP__Acct__Identifier—3	Account Identifier—3		Character (25).

Pt. 360, App. C   12 CFR Ch. III (1-1-12 Edition)

Field name	Field description	Comments	Format
4. DP__Acct__Identifier—4	If necessary, the third element used to identify the account. Account Identifier—4		Character (25).
5. DP__Acct__Identifier—5	If necessary, the fourth element used to identify the account. Account Identifier—5		Character (25).
6. DP__Sub__Acct__Identifier	If necessary, the fifth element used to identify the account. Sub-Account Identifier .... If available, the sub-account identifier for the account.	The Sub-Account Identifier may identify separate deposits tied to this account where there are different processing parameters such as interest rates or maturity dates, but all owners are the same.	Character (25).
7. DC__Debit__Amt	Debit Amount .... Dollar amount of the debit to be applied to the account or sub-account.		Decimal (14,2).
8. DC__Credit__Amt	Credit Amount .... Dollar amount of the credit to be applied to the account or sub-account.		Decimal (14,2).
9. DC__Transaction__Desc	Debit/Credit Description .... FDIC message associated with the debit or credit transaction.		Character (225).

[73 FR 41197, July 17, 2008]

APPENDIX C TO PART 360—DEPOSIT FILE STRUCTURE

This is the structure for the data file to provide deposit data to the FDIC. If data or information are not maintained or do not apply, a null value in the appropriate field should be indicated. The file will be in a tab- or pipe-delimited ASCII format. Each file name will contain the institution's FDIC Certificate Number, an indication that it is a deposit file type and the date of the extract. The files will be encrypted using an FDIC-supplied algorithm. The FDIC will transmit to the covered institution the encryption algorithm over FDIC*connect*.

The total deposit balances and the number of deposit accounts in each deposit file must be reconciled to the subsidiary system control totals.

The FDIC intends to fully utilize a covered institution's understanding of its customers and the data maintained around deposit accounts. Should additional information be available to the covered institution to help the FDIC more quickly complete its insurance determination process, it may add this information to the end of this data file. Should additional data elements be provided, a complete data dictionary for these elements must be supplied along with a description of how this information could be best used to establish account ownership or insurance category.

The deposit data elements provide information specific to deposit account balances and account data. The sequencing of these elements, their physical data structures and the field data format and field length must be provided to the FDIC along with the data structures identified below.

A header record will also be required at the beginning of this file. This record will contain the number of accounts to be included in this file, the maximum number of characters contained in largest account title field maintained within the deposit file and the maximum number of characters contained in largest address field maintained within the deposit file.

NOTE: Each record must contain the account title/name and current account statement mailing address. Fields 17-33 relate to the account name and address information. Some systems provide for separate fields for account title/name, street address, city, state, ZIP, and country, all of which are parsed out. Others systems may simply provide multiple lines for name, street address, city, state, ZIP, with no distinction. Populate fields that best fit the system's data, either fields 17-27 or fields 28-33.

Federal Deposit Insurance Corporation

Pt. 360, App. C

Field name	Field description	Comments	Format
1. DP__Acct__Identifier	Account Identifier. The primary field used to identify the account. This field may be the Account Number.	The Account Identifier may be composed of more than one physical data element. If multiple fields are required to identify the account, data should be placed in separate fields and the FDIC instructed how these fields are combined to uniquely identify the account.	Character (25).
2. DP__Acct__Identifier—2	Account Identifier—2. If necessary, the second element used to identify the account.		Character (25).
3. DP__Acct__Identifier—3	Account Identifier—3. If necessary, the third element used to identify the account.		Character (25).
4. DP__Acct__Identifier—4	Account Identifier—4. If necessary, the fourth element used to identify the account.		Character (25).
5. DP__Acct__Identifier—5	Account Identifier—5. If necessary, the fifth element used to identify the account.		Character (25).
6. DP__Sub__Acct__Identifier	Sub-Account Identifier. If available, the sub-account identifier for the account.	The Sub-Account Identifier may identify separate deposits tied to this account where there are different processing parameters such as interest rates or maturity dates, but all owners are the same.	Character (25).
7. DP__Bank__No	Bank Number. The bank number assigned to the deposit account.		Character (15).
8. DP__Tax__ID	Tax ID. The tax identification number maintained on the account.	For consumer accounts, typically, this would be the primary account holder's social security number ("SSN"). For business accounts it would be the federal tax identification number ("TIN"). Hyphens are optional in this field.	Character (15).
9. DP__Tax__Code	Tax ID Code. The type of the tax identification number. Possible values are: • S = Social Security Number. • T = Federal Tax Identification Number. • O = Other.	Generally deposit systems have flags or indicators set to indicate whether the number is an SSN or TIN.	Character (1).
10. DP__Branch	Branch Number. The branch or office associated with the account.	In lieu of a branch number this field may represent a specialty department or division.	Character (15).
11. DP__Cost__Center	Cost Center or G/L Code. The identifier used for organization reporting or ownership of the account. Insert null value if the cost center is not carried in the deposit record.	This field ties to the general ledger accounts.	Character (20).
12. DP__Dep__Type	Deposit Type Indicator. The type of deposit by office location. Possible values are: • D = Deposit (Domestic). • F = Foreign Deposit.	A deposit—also called a "domestic deposit"—includes only deposit liabilities payable in the United States, typically those deposits maintained in a domestic office of an insured depository institution, as defined in section 3(l) of the Federal Deposit Insurance Act (12 U.S.C. 1813(l)). A foreign deposit is a deposit liability in a foreign branch payable solely at a foreign branch or branches.	Character (1).
13. DP__Currency__Type	Currency Type. The ISO 4217 currency code.		Character (3).

581

Pt. 360, App. C — 12 CFR Ch. III (1-1-12 Edition)

Field name	Field description	Comments	Format
14. DP_Ownership_Ind	Customer Ownership Indicator ... The type of ownership at the account level. Possible values are: • S = Single. • J = Joint Account. • P = Partnership account. • C = Corporation. • B = Brokered Deposits. • I = IRA Accounts. • U = Unincorporated Association. • R = Revocable Trust. • IR = Irrevocable Trust. • G = Government Accounts. • E = Employee Benefit Plan Accounts. • O = Other.	*Single:* Accounts owned by an individual and those accounts held as Minor Accounts, Estate Accounts, Non-Minor Custodian/Guardian Accounts, Attorney in Fact Accounts and Sole Proprietorships. *Joint Account:* Accounts owned by two or more individuals, but does not include the ownership of a Payable on Death Account or Trust Account. *Partnership Account:* Accounts owned by a Partnership. *Corporation:* Accounts owned by a Corporation (e.g. Inc., L.L.C., or P.C.). *Brokered Deposits:* Accounts placed by a deposit broker who acts as an intermediary for the actual owner or sub-broker. *IRA Accounts:* Accounts for which the owner has the right to direct how the funds are invested including Keoghs and other Self-Directed Retirement Accounts. *Unincorporated Association:* An account owned by an association of two or more persons formed for some religious, educational, charitable, social or other non-commercial purpose. *Revocable Trusts:* Including PODs and formal revocable trusts (e.g. Living Trusts, Intervivos Trusts or Family Trusts). *Irrevocable Trusts:* Accounts held by a trust established by statute or written trust in which the grantor relinquishes all power to revoke the trust. *Government Accounts:* Accounts owned by a government entity (e.g. City, State, County or Federal government entities and their sub-divisions). *Employee Benefit Plan:* Accounts established by the administrator of an Employee Benefit Plan including defined contribution, defined benefit and employee welfare plans. *Other Accounts:* Accounts owned by an entity not described above.	Character (2).
15. DP_Prod_Cat	Product Category ... The product classification. Possible values are: • DDA = Non-Interest Bearing Checking accounts. • NOW = Interest Bearing Checking accounts. • MMA = Money Market Deposit Accounts. • SAV = Other savings accounts.	Product Category is sometimes referred to as "application type" or "system type".	Character (3).

582

Federal Deposit Insurance Corporation
Pt. 360, App. C

Field name	Field description	Comments	Format
	• CDS = Time Deposit accounts and Certificate of Deposit accounts, including any accounts with specified maturity dates that may or may not be renewable.		
16. DP_Stat_Code	Status Code .... Status or condition of the account. Possible values are: • O = Open. • D = Dormant. • I = Inactive. • E = Escheatment. • A = Abandoned. • C = Closing. • R = Restricted/Frozen/Blocked.		Character (1).
17. DP_Acct_Title—1	Account Title Line 1 .... Account styling or titling of the account.	These data will be used to identify the owners and beneficiaries of the account.	Character (100).
18. DP_Acct_Title—2	Account Title Line 2 .... If available, the second account title line.		Character (100).
19. DP_Acct_Title—3	Account Title Line 3 .... If available, the third account title line.		Character (100).
20. DP_Acct_Title—4	Account Title Line 4 .... If available, the fourth account title line.		Character (100).
21. DP_Street_Add_Ln—1	Street Address Line 1 .... The current account statement mailing address of record.		Character (100).
22. DP_Street_Add_Ln—2	Street Address Line 2 .... If available, the second mailing address line.		Character (100).
23. DP_Street_Add_Ln—3	Street Address Line 3 .... If available, the third mailing address line.		Character (100).
24. DP_City	City .... The city associated with the mailing address.		Character (50).
25. DP_State	State .... The state abbreviation associated with the mailing address.	Use a two-character state code (official U.S. Postal Service abbreviations).	Character (2).
26. DP_ZIP	ZIP .... The ZIP + 4 code associated with the mailing address.	If the "+4" code is not available provide only the 5-digit ZIP code. Hyphens are optional in this field.	Character (10).
27. DP_Country	Country .... The country associated with the mailing address.	Provide the country name or the standard IRS country code.	Character (10).
28. DP_NA_Line—1	Name/Address Line 1 .... Alternate name/address format for the current account statement mailing address of record, first line.	Fields 28–33 are to be used if address data are not parsed to populate Fields 17–27.	Character (100).
29. DP_NA_Line—2	Name/Address Line 2 .... Alternate name/address format, second line.		Character (100).
30. DP_NA_Line—3	Name/Address Line 3 .... Alternate name/address format, third line.		Character (100).
31. DP_NA_Line—4	Name/Address Line 4 .... Alternate name/address format, fourth line.		Character (100).
32. DP_NA_Line—5	Name/Address Line 5 .... Alternate name/address format, fifth line.		Character (100).
33. DP_NA_Line—6	Name/Address Line 6 .... Alternate name/address format, sixth line.		Character (100).

Pt. 360, App. C — 12 CFR Ch. III (1-1-12 Edition)

Field name	Field description	Comments	Format
34. DP_Cur_Bal	Current Balance. The current balance in the account at the end of business on the effective date of this file.	This balance should not be reduced by float or holds. For CDs and time deposits, the balance should reflect the principal balance plus any interest paid and available for withdrawal not already included in the principal (do not include accrued interest). The total of all current balances in this file should reconcile to the total deposit trial balance totals or other summary reconciliation of deposits performed by the institution.	Decimal (14,2).
35. DP_Int_Rate	Interest Rate. The current interest rate in effect for interest bearing accounts.	Interest rate should be expressed in decimal format, i.e., 2.0% should be represented as 0.020000000.	Decimal (10,9).
36. DP_Acc_Int	Accrued Interest. The amount of interest that has been earned but not yet paid to the account as of the date of the file.		Decimal (14,2).
37. DP_Lst_Int_Pd	Date Last Interest Paid. The date through which interest was last paid to the account.		Date (YYYYMMDD).
38. DP_Lst_Deposit	Date Last Deposit. The date of the last deposit transaction posted to the account.	For example, a deposit that included checks and/or cash.	Date (YYYYMMDD).
39. DP_Int_Term_No	Interest Term Number. The number of months in the current interest term.		Decimal (3,0).
40. DP_Nxt_Mat	Date of Next Maturity. For CD and time deposit accounts, the next date the account is to mature.	For non-renewing CDs that have matured and are waiting to be redeemed this date may be in the past.	Date (YYYYMMDD).
41. DP_Open_DT	Account Open Date. The date the account was opened.	If the account had previously been closed and re-opened, this should reflect the most recent re-opened date.	Date (YYYYMMDD).
42. DP_Sweep_Code	Sweep Code. Indicates if the account is a sweep account. Possible values are: • Y = Yes. • N = No.		Character (1).
43. DP_Hold_To_Post	Full Hold on the account: Indicator if all postings to this account are restricted. Possible values are: • Y = Yes. • N = No.		Character (1).
44. DP_Issue_Val_Amt	Issued Value Amount. The value of the current CD when issued.	For CDs only.	Decimal (14,2).
45. DP_Int_CD_Cde	Type of Interest for CD. Possible values are: • C = Rate Change Allowed. • N = Rate Change Not Allowed. • R = Change Rate to Default at Renewal. • T = Rate Change Allowed Only During the Term.	For CDs only.	Character (1).

Federal Deposit Insurance Corporation

Pt. 360, App. C

Field name	Field description	Comments	Format
46. DP__IRA__Cde	IRA Code .... The type of IRA. Possible values are: • C = Corporate Retirement • E = Educational IRA. • I = IRA Account. • K = Keogh Account. • R = Roth IRA Account. • S = SEP Account. • T = Transitional Roth IRA. • V = Versa Account. • H = Health Savings Account.	Optional code field to be used if available to help further identify the types of IRA accounts.	Character (1).
47. DP__Deposit__Class__Type	Deposit Class Type .... The deposit class. Possible values are: • RTL = Retail. • FED = Federal government. • STATE = State government. • COMM = Commercial. • CORP = Corporate. • BANK = Bank Owned. • DUE TO = Other Banks.	The institution may also use more or fewer class types.	Character (10).
48. DP__Product__Class__Cde	Deposit Class Codes .... The deposit class codes. Possible values are: RTL • 1 = Payable on Death. • 2 = Individual. • 3 = Living Trust—Intervivos or Family. • 4 = Irrevocable Trust (includes Educational IRAs). • 5 = Estate. • 6 = Attorney in Fact. • 7 = Minor—(includes all variations of Uniform Gifts to Minor Accounts). • 8 = Bankruptcy Personal. • 9 = Pre-Need Burial. • 10 = Escrow. • 11 = Representative Payee/Beneficiary. • 12 = Sole Proprietorship. • 13 = Joint. • 14 = Non-Minor Custodian/Guardian. • 15 = Other Retail.	These Product Class codes are used in conjunction with the Deposit Class Types in field 51. This field is to be used in concert with fields 12 and 13 identified above to enable the financial institution to capture more detailed information concerning account types. It is the intent of the FDIC to have the financial institution map its detailed account types to the codes identified in this field. The institution may also use additional codes, but in this event the institution must supply the detailed description and code value for each additional code used. If no additional account product type detail is available then this field should be left blank.	Character (2).

Field name	Field description	Comments	Format
	FED • 16 = FHA. • 17 = Federal Government. STATE • 18 = City. • 19 = State. • 20 = County, Clerk of Court. • 21 = Other State. COMMERCIAL • 22 = Business Escrow. • 23 = Bankruptcy. • 24 = Club. • 25 = Church. • 26 = Unincorporated Association. • 27 = Unincorporated Non-Profit. • • 28 = Other Commercial. CORPORATION • 29 = Business Trust. • 30 = Business Agent. • 31 = Business Guardian. • 32 = Incorporated Association. • 33 = Incorporated Non-Profit. • 33 = Incorporated Non-Profit. • 34 = Corporation. • 35 = Corporate Partnership. • 36 = Corporate Partnership Trust. • 37 = Corporate Agent. • 38 = Corporate Guardian. • 39 = Pre-Need Funeral Trust. • 40 = Limited Liability Incorporation. • 41 = LLC partnership. • 42 = Lawyer Trust. • 43 = Realtor Trust. • 44 = Other Corporation. BANK • 45 = Certified & Official Checks, Money Orders, Loan Disbursements Checks, and Expense Checks. • 46 = ATM Settlement. • 47 = Other Bank Owned Accounts. DUE TO (Other Banks) • 48 = Due to U.S. Banks. • 49 = Due to U.S. Branches of Foreign Banks. • 50 = Due to Other Depository Institutions. • 51 = Due to Foreign Banks. • 52 = Due to Foreign Branches of U.S. banks. • 53 = Due to Foreign Governments and Official Institutions.		

[73 FR 41197, July 17, 2008]

APPENDIX D TO PART 360—SWEEP/AUTOMATED CREDIT ACCOUNT FILE STRUCTURE

This is the structure of the data file to provide information to the FDIC on funds residing in investment vehicles linked to each non-closed deposit account or sub-account: (1) Involved in sweep activity where the sweep investment vehicle is not a deposit and is reflected on the books and records of the covered institution or (2) which accepts automated credits. A single record should be used for each instance where funds affiliated with the deposit account are held in an alternative investment vehicle. For any alternative investment vehicle, a separate account may or may not exist. If an account

Federal Deposit Insurance Corporation

Pt. 360, App. D

exists for the investment vehicle, it should be noted in the record. If no account exists, then a null value for the Sweep/Automated Credit Account Identifiers should be provided, but the remainder of the data fields defined below should be populated.

For data provided in the Sweep/Automated Credit Account File, the total account balances and the number of accounts must be reconciled to subsidiary system control totals. The file will be in a tab- or pipe-delimited ASCII format. The files will be encrypted using an FDIC-supplied algorithm. The FDIC will transmit the encryption algorithm over FDIC*connect*.

Field name	Field description	Comments	Format
1. DP_Acct_Identifier	Account Identifier .... The primary field used to identify the account from which funds are swept or debited. The field may be the Account number.	The Account Identifier may be composed of more than one physical data element. If multiple fields are required to identify the account, data should be placed in separate fields and the FDIC instructed how these fields are combined to uniquely identify the account.	Character (25).
2. DP_Acct_Identifier—2	Account Identifier—2 .... If necessary, the second element used to identify the account from which funds are swept or debited.	....	Character (25).
3. DP_Acct_Identifier—3	Account Identifier—3 .... If necessary, the third element used to identify the account from which funds are swept or debited.	....	Character (25).
4. DP_Acct_Identifier—4	Account Identifier—4 .... If necessary, the fourth element used to identify the account from which funds are swept or debited.	....	Character (25).
5. DP_Acct_Identifier—5	Account Identifier—5 .... If necessary, the fifth element used to identify the account from which funds are swept or debited.	....	Character (25).
6. DP_Sub_Acct_Identifier	Sub-Account Identifier .... If available, the sub-account identifier for the account.	The Sub-Account Identifier may identify separate deposits tied to this account where there are different processing parameters such as interest rates or maturity dates, but all owners are the same.	Character (25).
7. SW_Acct_Identifier	Sweep/Automated Credit Account Identifier. The primary field used to identify the account into which funds are swept or credited. This field may be the Account Number.	Funds may be swept into an investment vehicle not represented as an account. In this case this field should be a null value. The Sweep/Automated Credit Account Identifier may be composed of more than one physical data element. If multiple fields are required to identify the account, data should be placed in separate fields and the FDIC instructed how these fields are combined to uniquely identify the account.	Character (25).
8. SW_Acct_Identifier—2	Sweep/Automated Credit Account Identifier—2. If necessary, the second element of the account identifier used to identify the account into which funds are swept or credited.	....	Character (25).
9. SW_Acct_Identifier—3	Sweep/Automated Credit Account Identifier—3. If necessary, the third element of the account identifier used to identify the account into which funds are swept or credited.	....	Character (25).

Pt. 360, App. E

Field name	Field description	Comments	Format
10. SW_Acct_Identifier-4	Sweep/Automated Credit Account Identifier—4. If necessary, the fourth element of the account identifier used to identify the account into which funds are swept or credited.	....	Character (25).
11. SW_Acct_Identifier-5	Sweep/Automated Credit Account Identifier-5. If necessary, the fifth element of the account identifier used to identify the account into which funds are swept or credited.	....	Character (25).
12. SW_Sub_Acct_Identifier	Sweep/Automated Credit Sub-Account Identifier. If available, the sub-account identifier for the account.	....	Character (25).
13. SW_Type	Sweep/Automated Credit Type ...	The investment vehicle. Possible values are: • RE = Repurchase Agreement. • DD = Deposit Held in a Domestic Office. • DF = Deposit Held in a Foreign Office. • IBF = Deposit Held in an International Banking Facility. • AI = Deposit Held in an affiliated depository institution. • FF = Federal Funds. • CP = Commercial Paper. • OT = Other.	Character (3).
14. SW_Inv_Amount	Fund Balance in Sweep/Automated Credit Investment Vehicle. Dollar amount residing in the investment vehicle.	....	Decimal (14,2).
15. SW_Currency_Type	Currency Type .... The ISO 4217 currency code.	....	Character (3).
16. SW_Hold_Amount	FDIC Hold Amount .... Amount of FDIC hold on funds residing in the investment vehicle.	....	Decimal (14,2).
17. SW_Sweep_Interval	Sweep/Investment Frequency ..... The frequency with which the sweep or investment occurs. Possible values are: • D = Daily. • W = Weekly. • BW = Bi-Weekly. • M = Monthly. • BM = Bi-Monthly. • Q = Quarterly. • O = Other.	....	Character (2).

[73 FR 41197, July 17, 2008]

APPENDIX E TO PART 360—HOLD FILE STRUCTURE

This is the structure of the data file to provide information to the FDIC for each legal or collateral hold placed on a deposit account or sub-account. If data or information are not maintained or do not apply, a null value in the appropriate field should be indicated. The file will be in a tab-or pipe-delimited ASCII format. Each file name will contain the institution's FDIC Certificate Number, an indication that it is a hold data file type and the date of the extract. The files will be encrypted using an FDIC-supplied algorithm. The FDIC will transmit the encryption algorithm over FDIC*connect*.

Federal Deposit Insurance Corporation

Pt. 360, App. F

Field name	Field description	Comments	Format
1. DP__Acct__Identifier	Account Identifier .... The primary field used to identify the account. This field may be the Account Number.	The Account Identifier may be composed of more than one physical data element. If multiple fields are required to identify the account, data should be placed in separate fields and the FDIC instructed how these fields are combined to uniquely identify the account.	Character (25).
2. DP__Acct__Identifier—2	Account Identifier—2 .... If necessary, the second element used to identify the account.		Character (25).
3. DP__Acct__Identifier—3	Account Identifier—3 .... If necessary, the third element used to identify the account.		Character (25).
4. DP__Acct__Identifier—4	Account Identifier—4 .... If necessary, the fourth element used to identify the account.		Character (25).
5. DP __Acct__ Identifier—5	Account Identifier—5 .... If necessary, the fifth element used to identify the account.		Character (25).
6. DP__Sub__Acct__Identifier	Sub-Account Identifier .... If available, the sub-account identifier for the account.	The Sub-Account Identifier may identify separate deposits tied to this account where there are different processing parameters such as interest rates or maturity dates, but all owners are the same.	Character (25).
7. HD__Hold__Amt	Hold Amount .... Dollar amount of the hold.		Decimal (14,2).
8. HD__Hold__Reason	Hold Reason .... Reason for the hold. Possible values are: • LN = Loan Collateral Hold. • LG = Court Order Hold. • FD = FDIC hold. • OT = Other (do not include daily operational type holds).		Character (2).
9. HD__Hold__Desc	Hold Description .... Description of the hold available on the system.		Character (255).
10. HD__Hold__Start__Dt	Hold Start Date .... The date the hold was initiated.		Date (YYYYMMDD).
11. HD__Hold__Exp__Dt	Hold Expiration Date .... The date the hold is to expire.		Date (YYYYMMDD)

[73 FR 41197, July 17, 2008]

APPENDIX F TO PART 360—CUSTOMER FILE STRUCTURE

This is the structure of the data file to provide to the FDIC information related to each customer who has an account or sub-account reported in the deposit data or sweep/automated credit account file. If data or information are not maintained or do not apply, a null value in the appropriate field should be indicated. The file will be in a tab-or pipe-delimited ASCII format. Each file name will contain the institution's FDIC Certificate Number, an indication that it is a customer file type and the date of the extract. The files will be encrypted using an FDIC-supplied algorithm. The FDIC will transmit the encryption algorithm over FDIC*connect*.

NOTE: Each record must contain the customer's name and permanent legal address. Fields 4–12 relate to the customer name for individuals only. Fields 13–14 relate to the customer name for entities other than individuals. Some systems provide for separate fields for name, street address, city, state, ZIP, and country, all of which are parsed out. Others systems may simply provide multiple lines for name, street address, city, state, ZIP, with no distinction. In this case, certain name and address data elements must be parsed and provided in the appropriate fields.

Field name	Field description	Comments	Format
1. CS__Cust__Identifier	Customer Identifier	....	Character (25).

589

Pt. 360, App. F 12 CFR Ch. III (1-1-12 Edition)

Field name	Field description	Comments	Format
2. CS_Tax_ID	The unique field used by the institution to identify the customer. Customer Tax ID Number. The tax identification number on record for the customer.	Hyphens are optional in this field	Character (11).
3. CS_Tax_Code	Customer Tax ID Code. The type of the tax identification number of the customer. Possible values are: • S = Social Security Number. • T = Federal Tax Identification Number. • O = Other.		Character (1).
4. CS_Name_Line—1	Individual Customer Name Line 1. If available, the free-form name narrative of the customer, first line.		Character (100).
5. CS_Name_Line—2	Individual Customer Name Line 2. If available, the free-form name narrative of the customer, second line.		Character (100).
6. CS_Last_Name	Individual Customer Last Name. For individuals, the customer's last name.	This field is required if the data element is in the institution's records. If necessary, data should be parsed from fields 4 or 5 to obtain this element.	Character (50).
7. CS_First_Name	Individual Customer First Name. For individuals, the customer's first name.	This field is required if the data element is in the institution's records. If necessary, data should be parsed from fields 4 or 5 to obtain this element.	Character (50).
8. CS_Middle_Name	Individual Customer Middle Name. For individuals, the customer's middle name.	This field is required if the data element is in the institution's records. If necessary, data should be parsed from fields 4 or 5 to obtain this element.	Character (50).
9. CS_Suffix	Individual Professional Suffix. For individuals, the suffix designating customer's academic, professional or honorary status, such as Esq., Ph.D., M.D., and D.D.S.	This field is required if the data element is in the institution's records. If necessary, data should be parsed from fields 4 or 5 to obtain this element.	Character (20).
10. CS_Generation	Individual Generational Suffix. For individuals, the suffix designating the customer's generational status, such as Jr., Sr. or III.	This field is required if the data element is in the institution's records. If necessary, data should be parsed from fields 4 or 5 to obtain this element.	Character (10).
11. CS_Prefix	Individual Customer Prefix. For individuals, the prefix of the customer, such as Rev., Dr., Mrs., Mr. or Ms.	This field is required if the data element is in the institution's records. If necessary, data should be parsed from fields 4 or 5 to obtain this element.	Character (10).
12. CS_Birth_Dt	Individual Customer Birth Date. For individuals, the customer's birth date.		Date (YYYYMMDD).
13. CS_Ent_Name_Line—1.	Entity Name Line 1. For entities other than individuals, the free-form name narrative of the customer, first line.		Character (100).
14. CS_Ent_Name_Line—2.	Entity Name Line 2. If available for entities other than individuals, the free-form name narrative of the customer, second line.		Character (100).
15. CS_Nar_Addr_Line—1.	Customer Address Line 1. If available, the free-form permanent legal address narrative for the customer, line one.		Character (100).
16. CS_Nar_Addr_Line—2.	Customer Address Line 2. If available, the free-form permanent legal address narrative of the customer, line two.		Character (100).

Federal Deposit Insurance Corporation

Pt. 360, App. G

Field name	Field description	Comments	Format
17. CS_Nar_Addr_Line—3.	Customer Address Line 3 .... If available, the free-form permanent legal address narrative of the customer, line three.		Character (100).
18. CS_Street_Address—1	Street Address Line 1 .... The permanent legal address of the customer, line one.	This field is required. If necessary, data should be parsed from fields 16 or 17 to obtain this element.	Character (100).
19. CS_Street_Address—2	Street Address Line 2 .... The permanent legal address of the customer, line two.	This field is required. If necessary, data should be parsed from fields 16 or 17 to obtain this element.	Character (100).
20. CS_City	City .... The city associated with the permanent legal address.	This field is required. If necessary, data should be parsed from fields 16 or 17 to obtain this element.	Character (25).
21. CS_State	State .... The state abbreviation associated with the permanent legal address.	This field is required. If necessary, data should be parsed from fields 16 or 17 to obtain this element. Use a two-character state code (official U.S. Postal Service abbreviations).	Character (2).
22. CS_ZIP	ZIP .... The ZIP + 4 code associated with the permanent legal address.	This field is required. If necessary, data should be parsed from fields 16 or 17 to obtain this element. If the "+4" code is not available, provide only the 5-digit ZIP code. Hyphens are optional in this field.	Character (10).
23. CS_Country	Country .... The country associated with the permanent legal address.	This field is required. If necessary, data should be parsed from fields 16 or 17 to obtain this element. Provide the name of the country or the standard IRS country code.	Character (10).
24. CS_Telephone	Customer Telephone Number .... The telephone number on record for the customer.		Character (20).
25. CS_Email	Customer Email Address .... The e-mail address on record for the customer.		Character (150).

[73 FR 41197, July 17, 2008]

APPENDIX G TO PART 360—DEPOSIT-CUSTOMER JOIN FILE STRUCTURE

This is the structure of the data file to provide to the FDIC information necessary to link the records in the deposit and customer files. If data or information are not maintained or do not apply, a null value in the appropriate field should be indicated. The file will be in a tab- or pipe-delimited ASCII format. Each file name will contain the institution's FDIC Certificate Number, an indication that it is a join file type and the date of the extract. The files will be encrypted using an FDIC-supplied algorithm. The FDIC will transmit the encryption algorithm over FDIC*connect*.

The deposit-customer join file will have one or more records for each deposit account, depending on the number of relationships to each account. A simple individual account, for example, will be associated with only one record in the deposit-customer join file indicating the owner of the account. A joint account with two owners will be associated with two records in the deposit-customer join file, one for each owner. The deposit-customer join file will contain other records associated with a deposit account to designate, among other things, beneficiaries, custodians, trustees and agents. This methodology allows the FDIC to know all of the possible relationships for an individual account and also whether a single customer is involved in many accounts.

Field name	FDIC field description	Comments	Format
1. CS_Cust_Identifier	Customer Identifier		Character (25).

591

Field name	FDIC field description	Comments	Format
2. DP__Acct__Identifier	The unique field used by the institution to identify the customer. Account Identifier .... The primary field used to identify the account. This field may be the Account Number.	The Account Identifier may be composed of more than one physical data element. If multiple fields are required to identify the account, the data should be placed in separate fields and the FDIC instructed how these fields are combined to uniquely identify the account.	Character (25).
3. DP__Acct__Identifier—2	Account Identifier—2 .... If necessary, the second element used to identify the account.		Character (25).
4. DP__Acct__Identifier—3	Account Identifier—3 .... If necessary, the third element used to identify the account.		Character (25).
5. DP__Acct__Identifier—4	Account Identifier—4 .... If necessary, the fourth element used to identify the account.		Character (25).
6. DP__Acct__Identifier—5	Account Identifier—5 .... If necessary, the fifth element used to identify the account.		Character (25).
7. DP__Sub__Acct__Identifier	Sub-Account Identifier .... If available, the sub-account identifier for the account.	The Sub-Account Identifier may identify separate deposits tied to this account where there are different processing parameters such as interest rates or maturity dates, but all owners are the same.	Character (25).
8. CS__Rel__Code	Relationship Code .... The code indicating how the customer is related to the account. Possible values are: • ADM = Administrator. • AGT = Agent/Representative. • ATF = Attorney For. • AUT = Authorized Signer. • BNF = Beneficiary. • CSV = Conservator. • CUS = Custodian. • DBA = Doing Business As. • EXC = Executor. • GDN = Guardian. • MIN = Minor. • PRI = Primary Owner. • SEC = Secondary Owner(s). • TTE = Trustee.	Institutions must map their relationship codes to the codes in the list to the left. If the institution maintains more relationships they must supply the additional relationship codes being utilized along with the code definition.	Character (5).
9. CS__Bene__Code	Beneficiary Type Code .... If the customer is considered a beneficiary, the type of account associated with this customer. Possible values are: • I = IRA. • T = Trust—Irrevocable. • R = Trust—Revocable. • M = Uniform Gift to Minor. • P = Payable on Death. • O = Other.	This includes beneficiaries on retirement accounts, trust accounts, minor accounts, and payable-on-death accounts.	Character (1).

[73 FR 41197, July 17, 2008]

APPENDIX H TO PART 360—POSSIBLE FILE COMBINATIONS FOR DEPOSIT DATA

A covered institution must provide deposit data using separate deposit, sweep/automated credit, hold, customer, and deposit-customer join files. The simplest file structure involves providing one of each file. This basic file format is shown in Figure 1.

Federal Deposit Insurance Corporation   **Pt. 360, App. H**

Figure 1. Basic File Structure.

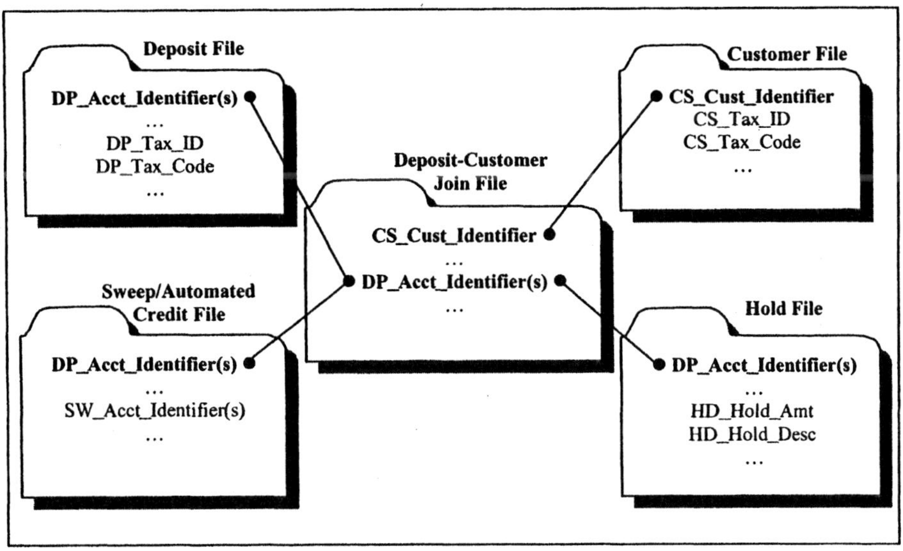

Deposit File
- DP_Acct_Identifier(s)
- ...
- DP_Tax_ID
- DP_Tax_Code
- ...

Customer File
- CS_Cust_Identifier
- CS_Tax_ID
- CS_Tax_Code
- ...

Deposit-Customer Join File
- CS_Cust_Identifier
- ...
- DP_Acct_Identifier(s)
- ...

Sweep/Automated Credit File
- DP_Acct_Identifier(s)
- ...
- SW_Acct_Identifier(s)
- ...

Hold File
- DP_Acct_Identifier(s)
- ...
- HD_Hold_Amt
- HD_Hold_Desc
- ...

Multiple combinations of deposit, sweep/automated credit, hold, customer, and deposit-customer join files are permissible, but only in the following circumstances:

1. Each separate deposit file must have companion sweep/automated credit and hold files covering the same deposit accounts.

2. A single customer file may be submitted covering customers affiliated with deposit accounts in one or more deposit files as long as the customer file contains information on all of the customers affiliated with the deposit files.

3. Several customer files may be submitted as long as each separate customer file contains information on all of the customers affiliated with the associated deposit files.

Figure 2 shows a permissible file configuration using a single Customer File affiliated with Deposit File A and Deposit File B. As required, Deposit File A has a companion Sweep/Automated Credit File A and Hold File A. The same is true for Deposit File B.

Another permissible combination of files is shown in Figure 3, which is a variation of the basic data file structure shown in Figure 1.

Pt. 360, App. H   12 CFR Ch. III (1-1-12 Edition)

Figure 2. Multiple Deposit Files, Single Customer File.

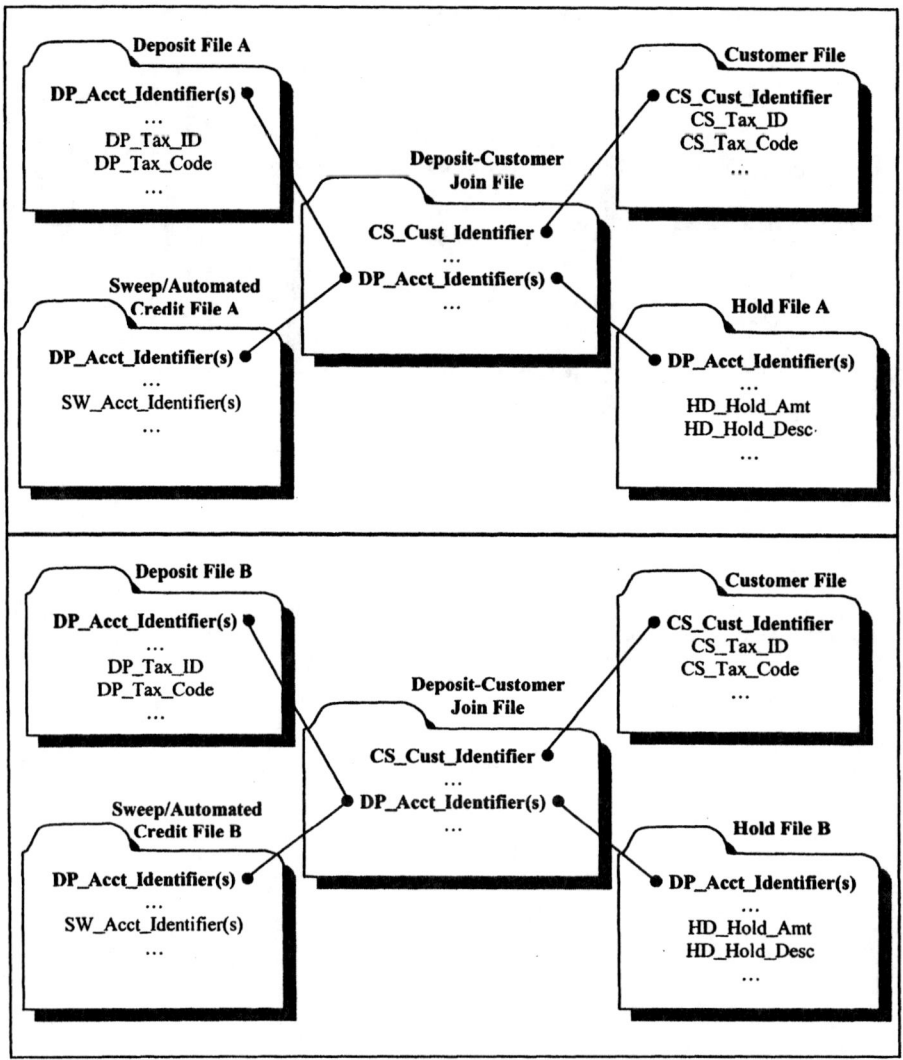

Federal Deposit Insurance Corporation   Pt. 361

Figure 3. Multiple File Sets.

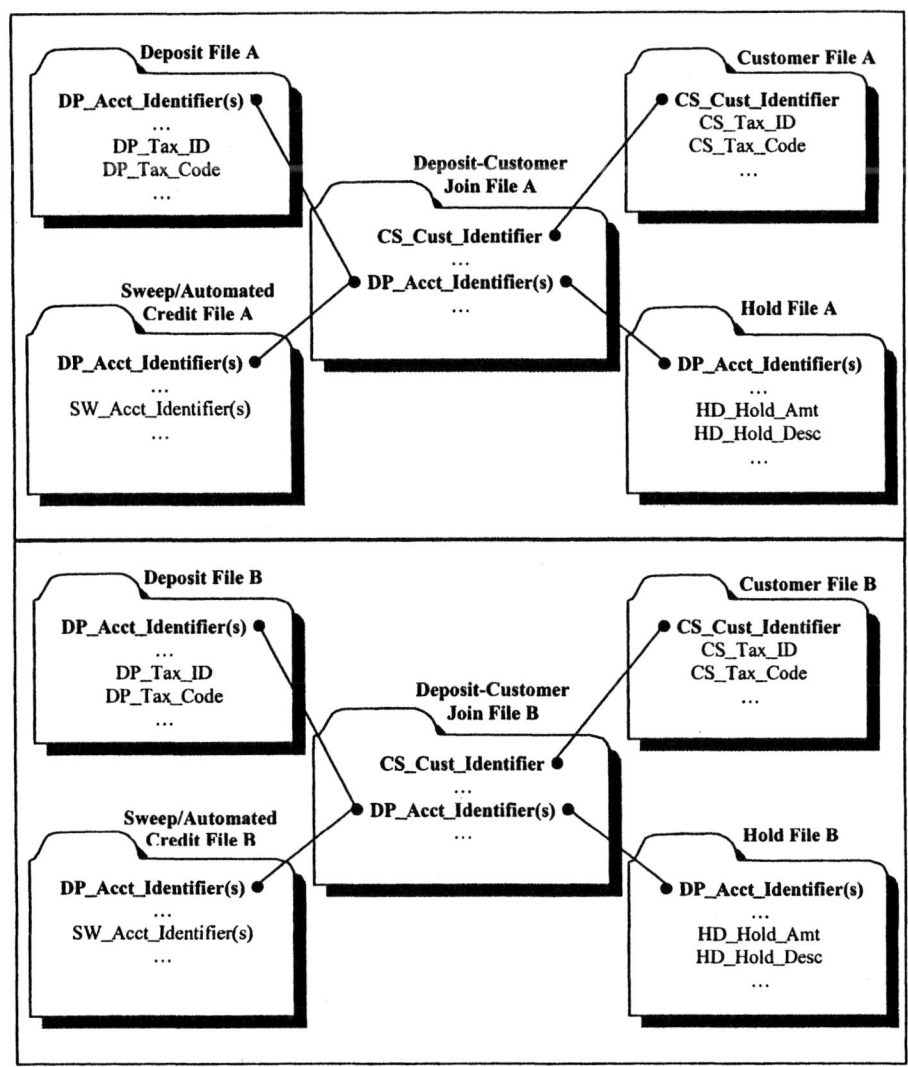

[73 FR 41197, July 17, 2008]

PART 361—MINORITY AND WOMEN OUTREACH PROGRAM CONTRACTING

Sec.
361.1 Why do minority- and women-owned businesses need this outreach regulation?
361.2 Why does the FDIC have this outreach program?
361.3 Who may participate in this outreach program?
361.4 What contracts are eligible for this outreach program?
361.5 What are the FDIC's oversight and monitoring responsibilities in administering this program?

595

§ 361.1

361.6 What outreach efforts are included in this program?

AUTHORITY: 12 U.S.C. 1833e.

SOURCE: 65 FR 31253, May 17, 2000, unless otherwise noted.

§ 361.1 Why do minority- and women-owned businesses need this outreach regulation?

The purpose of the FDIC Minority and Women Outreach Program (MWOP) is to ensure that minority- and women-owned businesses (MWOBs) are given the opportunity to participate fully in all contracts entered into by the FDIC.

§ 361.2 Why does the FDIC have this outreach program?

It is the policy of the FDIC that minorities and women, and businesses owned by them have the maximum practicable opportunity to participate in contracts awarded by the FDIC.

§ 361.3 Who may participate in this outreach program?

For purposes of this part:

(a) *Minority* has the same meaning as defined by the Small Business Administration at 13 CFR 124.103(b).

(b) *Legal Services* means all services provided by attorneys or law firms (including services of support staff).

§ 361.4 What contracts are eligible for this outreach program?

The FDIC outreach program applies to all contracts entered into by the FDIC. The outreach program is incorporated into FDIC policies and guidelines governing contracting and the retention of legal services.

§ 361.5 What are the FDIC's oversight and monitoring responsibilities in administering this program?

(a) The FDIC Office of Diversity and Economic Opportunity (ODEO) has overall responsibility for nationwide outreach oversight, which includes, but is not limited to, the monitoring, review and interpretation of relevant regulations. In addition, the ODEO is responsible for providing the FDIC with technical assistance and guidance to facilitate the identification, registration, and solicitation of MWOBs.

(b) Each FDIC office that performs contracting or outreach activities will submit information to the ODEO on a quarterly basis, or upon request. Quarterly submissions will include, at a minimum, statistical information on contract awards and solicitations by designated demographic categories.

§ 361.6 What outreach efforts are included in this program?

(a) Each office engaged in contracting with the private sector will designate one or more MWOP coordinators. The coordinators will perform outreach activities for MWOP and act as liaison between the FDIC and the public on MWOP issues. On a quarterly basis, or as requested by the ODEO, the coordinators will report to the ODEO on their implementation of the outreach program.

(b) Outreach includes the identification and registration of MWOBs who can provide goods and services utilized by the FDIC. This includes distributing information concerning the MWOP.

(c) The identification of MWOBs for the provision of legal and non-legal services will primarily be accomplished by:

(1) Obtaining various lists and directories of MWOBs maintained by other federal, state, and local governmental agencies;

(2) Participating in conventions, seminars and professional meetings comprised of, or attended predominately by, MWOBs;

(3) Conducting seminars, meetings, workshops and other various functions to promote the identification and registration of MWOBs;

(4) Placing MWOP promotional advertisements indicating opportunities with the FDIC in minority- and women-owned media; and

(5) Monitoring to assure that FDIC staff interfacing with the contracting community are knowledgeable of, and actively promoting, the MWOP.

PART 362—ACTIVITIES OF INSURED STATE BANKS AND INSURED SAVINGS ASSOCIATIONS

Subpart A—Activities of Insured State Banks

Sec.
362.1 Purpose and scope.

Federal Deposit Insurance Corporation

362.2 Definitions.
362.3 Activities of insured State banks.
362.4 Subsidiaries of insured State banks.
362.5 Approvals previously granted.

Subpart B—Safety and Soundness Rules Governing Insured State Nonmember Banks

362.6 Purpose and scope.
362.7 Definitions.
362.8 Restrictions on activities of insured State nonmember banks affiliated with certain securities companies.

Subpart C—Activities of Insured State Savings Associations

362.9 Purpose and scope.
362.10 Definitions.
362.11 Activities of insured State savings associations.
362.12 Service corporations of insured State savings associations.
362.13 Approvals previously granted.

Subpart D—Acquiring, Establishing, or Conducting New Activities Through a Subsidiary by an Insured Savings Association

362.14 Purpose and scope.
362.15 Acquiring or establishing a subsidiary; conducting new activities through a subsidiary.

Subpart E—Financial Subsidiaries of Insured State Nonmember Banks

362.16 Purpose and scope.
362.17 Definitions.
362.18 Financial subsidiaries of insured state nonmember banks.

AUTHORITY: 12 U.S.C. 1816, 1818, 1819(a)(Tenth), 1828(j), 1828(m), 1828a, 1831a, 1831e, 1831w, 1843(l).

SOURCE: 63 FR 66326, Dec. 1, 1998, unless otherwise noted.

Subpart A—Activities of Insured State Banks

§ 362.1 Purpose and scope.

(a) This subpart, along with the notice and application procedures in subpart G of part 303 of this chapter, implements the provisions of section 24 of the Federal Deposit Insurance Act (12 U.S.C. 1831a) that restrict and prohibit insured State banks and their subsidiaries from engaging in activities and investments that are not permissible for national banks and their subsidiaries. The phrase "activity permissible for a national bank" means any activity authorized for national banks under any statute including the National Bank Act (12 U.S.C. 21 *et seq.*), as well as activities recognized as permissible for a national bank in regulations, official circulars, bulletins, orders or written interpretations issued by the Office of the Comptroller of the Currency (OCC).

(b) This subpart does not cover the following activities:

(1) Activities conducted other than "as principal," defined for purposes of this subpart as activities conducted as agent for a customer, conducted in a brokerage, custodial, advisory, or administrative capacity, or conducted as trustee, or in any substantially similar capacity. For example, this subpart does not cover acting solely as agent for the sale of insurance, securities, real estate, or travel services; nor does it cover acting as trustee, providing personal financial planning advice, or safekeeping services;

(2) Interests in real estate in which the real property is used or intended in good faith to be used within a reasonable time by an insured State bank or its subsidiaries as offices or related facilities for the conduct of its business or future expansion of its business or used as public welfare investments of a type permissible for national banks; and

(3) Equity investments acquired in connection with debts previously contracted (DPC) if the insured State bank does not hold the property for speculation and takes only such actions as would be permissible for a national bank's DPC. The bank must dispose of the property within the shorter of the period set by Federal law for national banks or the period allowed under State law. For real estate, national banks may not hold DPC for more than 10 years. For equity securities, national banks must generally divest DPC as soon as possible consistent with obtaining a reasonable return.

(c) A subsidiary of an insured state bank may not engage in real estate investment activities that are not permissible for a subsidiary of a national bank unless the bank does so through a

§ 362.2

subsidiary of which the bank is a majority owner, is in compliance with applicable capital standards, and the FDIC has determined that the activity poses no significant risk to the appropriate deposit insurance fund. This subpart provides standards for majority-owned subsidiaries of insured state banks engaging in real estate investment activities that are not permissible for a subsidiary of a national bank.

(d) The FDIC intends to allow insured State banks and their subsidiaries to undertake only safe and sound activities and investments that do not present significant risks to the Deposit Insurance Fund and that are consistent with the purposes of Federal deposit insurance and other applicable law. This subpart does not authorize any insured State bank to make investments or to conduct activities that are not authorized or that are prohibited by either State or Federal law.

[63 FR 66326, Dec. 1, 1998, as amended at 66 FR 1028, Jan. 5, 2001; 71 FR 20527, Apr. 21, 2006]

§ 362.2 Definitions.

For the purposes of this subpart, the following definitions will apply:

(a) *Bank, State bank, savings association, State savings association, depository institution, insured depository institution, insured State bank, Federal savings association,* and *insured State nonmember bank* shall each have the same respective meaning contained in section 3 of the Federal Deposit Insurance Act (12 U.S.C. 1813).

(b) *Activity* means the conduct of business by a state-chartered depository institution, including acquiring or retaining an equity investment or other investment.

(c) *Change in control* means any transaction:

(1) By a State bank or its holding company for which a notice is required to be filed with the FDIC, or the Board of Governors of the Federal Reserve System (FRB), pursuant to section 7(j) of the Federal Deposit Insurance Act (12 U.S.C. 1817(j)) except a transaction that is presumed to be an acquisition of control under the FDIC's or FRB's regulations implementing section 7(j);

(2) As a result of which a State bank eligible for the exception described in § 362.3(a)(2)(iii) is acquired by or merged into a depository institution that is not eligible for the exception, or as a result of which its holding company is acquired by or merged into a holding company which controls one or more bank subsidiaries not eligible for the exception; or

(3) In which control of the State bank is acquired by a bank holding company in a transaction requiring FRB approval under section 3 of the Bank Holding Company Act (12 U.S.C. 1842), other than a one bank holding company formation in which all or substantially all of the shares of the holding company will be owned by persons who were shareholders of the bank.

(d) *Company* means any corporation, partnership, limited liability company, business trust, association, joint venture, pool, syndicate or other similar business organization.

(e) *Control* means the power to vote, directly or indirectly, 25 percent or more of any class of the voting securities of a company, the ability to control in any manner the election of a majority of a company's directors or trustees, or the ability to exercise a controlling influence over the management and policies of a company.

(f) *Convert its charter* means an insured State bank undergoes any transaction that causes the bank to operate under a different form of charter than it had as of December 19, 1991, except a change from mutual to stock form shall not be considered a charter conversion.

(g) *Equity investment* means an ownership interest in any company; any membership interest that includes a voting right in any company; any interest in real estate; any transaction which in substance falls into any of these categories even though it may be structured as some other form of business transaction; and includes an equity security. The term "equity investment" does not include any of the foregoing if the interest is taken as security for a loan.

(h) *Equity security* means any stock (other than adjustable rate preferred stock, money market (auction rate)

Federal Deposit Insurance Corporation § 362.3

preferred stock, or other newly developed instrument determined by the FDIC to have the character of debt securities), certificate of interest or participation in any profit-sharing agreement, collateral-trust certificate, preorganization certificate or subscription, transferable share, investment contract, or voting-trust certificate; any security immediately convertible at the option of the holder without payment of substantial additional consideration into such a security; any security carrying any warrant or right to subscribe to or purchase any such security; and any certificate of interest or participation in, temporary or interim certificate for, or receipt for any of the foregoing.

(i) *Extension of credit, executive officer, director, principal shareholder,* and *related interest* each has the same respective meaning as is applicable for the purposes of section 22(h) of the Federal Reserve Act (12 U.S.C. 375b) and § 337.3 of this chapter.

(j) *Institution* shall have the same meaning as "state-chartered depository institution."

(k) *Majority-owned subsidiary* means any corporation in which the parent insured State bank owns a majority of the outstanding voting stock.

(l) *National securities exchange* means a securities exchange that is registered as a national securities exchange by the Securities and Exchange Commission pursuant to section 6 of the Securities Exchange Act of 1934 (15 U.S.C. 78f) and the National Market System, i.e., the top tier of the National Association of Securities Dealers Automated Quotation System.

(m) *Real estate investment activity* means any interest in real estate (other than as security for a loan) held directly or indirectly that is not permissible for a national bank.

(n) *Residents of the state* includes individuals living in the State, individuals employed in the State, any person to whom the company provided insurance as principal without interruption since such person resided in or was employed in the State, and companies or partnerships incorporated in, organized under the laws of, licensed to do business in, or having an office in the State.

(o) *Security* has the same meaning as it has in part 344 of this chapter.

(p) *Significant risk to the Deposit Insurance Fund* shall be understood to be present whenever the FDIC determines there is a high probability that the Deposit Insurance Fund administered by the FDIC may suffer a loss. Such risk may be present either when an activity contributes or may contribute to the decline in condition of a particular state-chartered depository institution or when a type of activity is found by the FDIC to contribute or potentially contribute to the deterioration of the overall condition of the banking system.

(q) *State-chartered depository institution* means any State bank or State savings association insured by the FDIC.

(r) *Subsidiary* means any company that is owned or controlled directly or indirectly by one or more insured depository institutions.

(s) *Tier one capital* has the same meaning as set forth in part 325 of this chapter for an insured State nonmember bank. For other state-chartered depository institutions, the term "tier one capital" has the same meaning as set forth in the capital regulations adopted by the appropriate Federal banking agency.

(t) *Well-capitalized* has the same meaning set forth in part 325 of this chapter for an insured State nonmember bank. For other state-chartered depository institutions, the term "well-capitalized" has the same meaning as set forth in the capital regulations adopted by the appropriate Federal banking agency.

[63 FR 66326, Dec. 1, 1998, as amended at 66 FR 1028, Jan. 5, 2001; 71 FR 20527, Apr. 21, 2006]

§ 362.3 Activities of insured State banks.

(a) *Equity investments*—(1) *Prohibited equity investments.* No insured State bank may directly or indirectly acquire or retain as principal any equity investment of a type that is not permissible for a national bank unless one of the exceptions in paragraph (a)(2) of this section applies.

(2) *Exceptions*—(i) *Equity investment in majority-owned subsidiaries.* An insured

§ 362.3

State bank may acquire or retain an equity investment in a subsidiary of which the bank is a majority owner, provided that the subsidiary is engaging in activities that are allowed pursuant to the provisions of or by application under § 362.4(b).

(ii) *Investments in qualified housing projects.* An insured State bank may invest as a limited partner in a partnership, or as a noncontrolling interest holder of a limited liability company, the sole purpose of which is to invest in the acquisition, rehabilitation, or new construction of a qualified housing project, provided that the bank's aggregate investment (including legally binding commitments) does not exceed, when made, 2 percent of total assets as of the date of the bank's most recent consolidated report of condition prior to making the investment. For the purposes of this paragraph (a)(2)(ii), *Aggregate investment* means the total book value of the bank's investment in the real estate calculated in accordance with the instructions for the preparation of the consolidated report of condition. *Qualified housing project* means residential real estate intended to primarily benefit lower income persons throughout the period of the bank's investment including any project that has received an award of low income housing tax credits under section 42 of the Internal Revenue Code (26 U.S.C. 42) (such as a reservation or allocation of credits) from a State or local housing credit agency. A residential real estate project that does not qualify for the tax credit under section 42 of the Internal Revenue Code will qualify under this exception if 50 percent or more of the housing units are to be occupied by lower income persons. A project will be considered residential despite the fact that some portion of the total square footage of the project is utilized for commercial purposes, provided that such commercial use is not the primary purpose of the project. *Lower income* has the same meaning as "low income" and "moderate income" as defined for the purposes of § 345.12(n) (1) and (2) of this chapter.

(iii) *Grandfathered investments in common or preferred stock; shares of investment companies*—(A) *General.* An insured State bank that is located in a State which as of September 30, 1991, authorized investment in:

(*1*)(*i*) Common or preferred stock listed on a national securities exchange (listed stock); or

(*ii*) Shares of an investment company registered under the Investment Company Act of 1940 (15 U.S.C. 80a–1 *et seq.*) (registered shares); and

(*2*) Which during the period beginning on September 30, 1990, and ending on November 26, 1991, made or maintained an investment in listed stock or registered shares, may retain whatever lawfully acquired listed stock or registered shares it held and may continue to acquire listed stock and/or registered shares, provided that the bank files a notice in accordance with section 24(f)(6) of the Federal Deposit Insurance Act in compliance with § 303.121 of this chapter and the FDIC processes the notice without objection under § 303.122 of this chapter. Approval will be granted only if the FDIC determines that acquiring or retaining the stock or shares does not pose a significant risk to the Deposit Insurance Fund. Approval may be subject to whatever conditions or restrictions the FDIC determines are necessary or appropriate.

(B) *Loss of grandfather exception.* The exception for grandfathered investments under paragraph (a)(2)(iii)(A) of this section shall no longer apply if the bank converts its charter or the bank or its parent holding company undergoes a change in control. If any of these events occur, the bank may retain its existing investments unless directed by the FDIC or other applicable authority to divest the listed stock or registered shares.

(C) *Maximum permissible investment.* A bank's aggregate investment in listed stock and registered shares under paragraph (a)(2)(iii)(A) of this section shall in no event exceed, when made, 100 percent of the bank's tier one capital as measured on the bank's most recent consolidated report of condition (call report) prior to making any such investment. The lower of the bank's cost as determined in accordance with call report instructions or the market value of the listed stock and shares shall be used to determine compliance. The FDIC may determine when acting

Federal Deposit Insurance Corporation § 362.3

upon a notice filed in accordance with paragraph (a)(2)(iii)(A)(*2*) of this section that the permissible limit for any particular insured State bank is something less than 100 percent of tier one capital.

(iv) *Stock investment in insured depository institutions owned exclusively by other banks and savings associations.* An insured State bank may acquire or retain the stock of an insured depository institution if the insured depository institution engages only in activities permissible for national banks; the insured depository institution is subject to examination and regulation by a State bank supervisor; the voting stock is owned by 20 or more insured depository institutions, but no one institution owns more than 15 percent of the voting stock; and the insured depository institution's stock (other than directors' qualifying shares or shares held under or acquired through a plan established for the benefit of the officers and employees) is owned only by insured depository institutions.

(v) *Stock investment in insurance companies*—(A) *Stock of director and officer liability insurance company.* An insured State bank may acquire and retain up to 10 percent of the outstanding stock of a corporation that solely provides or reinsures directors', trustees', and officers' liability insurance coverage or bankers' blanket bond group insurance coverage for insured depository institutions.

(B) *Stock of savings bank life insurance company.* An insured State bank located in Massachusetts, New York, or Connecticut may own stock in a savings bank life insurance company, provided that the savings bank life insurance company provides written disclosures to purchasers or potential purchasers of life insurance policies, other insurance products, and annuities that are consistent with the disclosures described in the Interagency Statement on the Retail Sale of Nondeposit Investment Products (FIL–9–94,[1] February 17, 1994) or any successor requirement which indicates that the policies, products, and annuities are not FDIC insured deposits, are not guaranteed by the bank and are subject to investment risks, including possible loss of the principal amount invested.

(b) *Activities other than equity investments*—(1) *Prohibited activities.* An insured State bank may not directly or indirectly engage as principal in any activity, that is not an equity investment, and is of a type not permissible for a national bank unless one of the exceptions in paragraph (b)(2) of this section applies.

(2) *Exceptions*—(i) *Consent obtained through application.* An insured State bank that meets and continues to meet the applicable capital standards set by the appropriate Federal banking agency may conduct activities prohibited by paragraph (b)(1) of this section if the bank obtains the FDIC's prior written consent. Consent will be given only if the FDIC determines that the activity poses no significant risk to the Deposit Insurance Fund. Applications for consent should be filed in accordance with § 303.121 of this chapter and will be processed under § 303.122(b) of this chapter. Approvals granted under § 303.122(b) of this chapter may be made subject to any conditions or restrictions found by the FDIC to be necessary to protect the Deposit Insurance Fund from risk, to prevent unsafe or unsound banking practices, and/or to ensure that the activity is consistent with the purposes of Federal deposit insurance and other applicable law.

(ii) *Insurance underwriting*—(A) *Savings bank life insurance.* An insured State bank that is located in Massachusetts, New York or Connecticut may provide as principal savings bank life insurance through a department of the bank, provided that the department meets the core standards of paragraph (c) of this section or submits an application in compliance with § 303.121 of this chapter and the FDIC grants its consent under the procedures in § 303.122(b) of this chapter, and the department provides purchasers or potential purchasers of life insurance policies, other insurance products and annuities written disclosures that are consistent with the disclosures described in the Interagency Statement

---

[1] Financial institution letters (FILs) are available in the FDIC Public Information Center, room 100, 801 17th Street, N.W., Washington, D.C. 20429.

on the Retail Sale of Nondeposit Investment Products (FIL–9–94, February 17, 1994) and any successor requirement which indicates that the policies, products and annuities are not FDIC insured deposits, are not guaranteed by the bank, and are subject to investment risks, including the possible loss of the principal amount invested.

(B) *Federal crop insurance.* Any insured State bank that was providing insurance as principal on or before September 30, 1991, which was reinsured in whole or in part by the Federal Crop Insurance Corporation, may continue to do so.

(C) *Grandfathered insurance underwriting.* A well-capitalized insured State bank that on November 21, 1991, was lawfully providing insurance as principal through a department of the bank may continue to provide the same types of insurance as principal to the residents of the State or States in which the bank did so on such date provided that the bank's department meets the core standards of paragraph (c) of this section, or submits an application in compliance with §303.121 of this chapter and the FDIC grants its consent under the procedures in §303.122(b) of this chapter.

(iii) *Acquiring and retaining adjustable rate and money market preferred stock.* (A) An insured State bank's investment of up to 15 percent of the bank's tier one capital in adjustable rate preferred stock or money market (auction rate) preferred stock does not represent a significant risk to the Deposit Insurance Fund. An insured State bank may conduct this activity without first obtaining the FDIC's consent, provided that the bank meets and continues to meet the applicable capital standards as prescribed by the appropriate Federal banking agency. The fact that prior consent is not required by this subpart does not preclude the FDIC from taking any appropriate action with respect to the activities if the facts and circumstances warrant such action.

(B) An insured State bank may acquire or retain other instruments of a type determined by the FDIC to have the character of debt securities and not to represent a significant risk to the Deposit Insurance Fund. Such instruments shall be included in the 15 percent of tier one capital limit imposed in paragraph (b)(2)(iii)(A) of this section. An insured State bank may conduct this activity without first obtaining the FDIC's consent, provided that the bank meets and continues to meet the applicable capital standards as prescribed by the appropriate Federal banking agency. The fact that prior consent is not required by this subpart does not preclude the FDIC from taking any appropriate action with respect to the activities if the facts and circumstances warrant such action.

(c) *Core standards.* For any insured State bank to be eligible to conduct insurance activities listed in paragraph (b)(2)(ii)(A) or (C) of this section, the bank must conduct the activities in a department that meets the following core separation and operating standards:

(1) The department is physically distinct from the remainder of the bank;

(2) The department maintains separate accounting and other records;

(3) The department has assets, liabilities, obligations and expenses that are separate and distinct from those of the remainder of the bank;

(4) The department is subject to State statute that requires its obligations, liabilities and expenses be satisfied only with the assets of the department; and

(5) The department informs its customers that only the assets of the department may be used to satisfy the obligations of the department.

[63 FR 66326, Dec. 1, 1998, as amended at 71 FR 20527, Apr. 21, 2006]

§362.4 Subsidiaries of insured State banks.

(a) *Prohibition.* A subsidiary of an insured State bank may not engage as principal in any activity that is not of a type permissible for a subsidiary of a national bank, unless it meets one of the exceptions in paragraph (b) of this section.

(b) *Exceptions*—(1) *Consent obtained through application.* A subsidiary of an insured State bank may conduct otherwise prohibited activities if the bank obtains the FDIC's prior written consent and the insured State bank meets and continues to meet the applicable

Federal Deposit Insurance Corporation § 362.4

capital standards set by the appropriate Federal banking agency. Consent will be given only if the FDIC determines that the activity poses no significant risk to the Deposit Insurance Fund. Applications for consent should be filed in accordance with § 303.121 of this chapter and will be processed under § 303.122(b) of this chapter. Approvals granted under § 303.122(b) of this chapter may be made subject to any conditions or restrictions found by the FDIC to be necessary to protect the Deposit Insurance Fund from risk, to prevent unsafe or unsound banking practices, and/or to ensure that the activity is consistent with the purposes of Federal deposit insurance and other applicable law.

(2) *Grandfathered insurance underwriting subsidiaries.* A subsidiary of an insured State bank may:

(i) Engage in grandfathered insurance underwriting if the insured State bank or its subsidiary on November 21, 1991, was lawfully providing insurance as principal. The subsidiary may continue to provide the same types of insurance as principal to the residents of the State or states in which the bank or subsidiary did so on such date provided that:

(A)(*1*) The bank meets the capital requirements of paragraph (e) of this section; and

(*2*) The subsidiary is an "eligible subsidiary" as described in paragraph (c)(2) of this section; or

(B) The bank submits an application in compliance with § 303.121 of this chapter and the FDIC grants its consent under the procedures in § 303.122(b) of this chapter.

(ii) Continue to provide as principal title insurance, provided the bank was required before June 1, 1991, to provide title insurance as a condition of the bank's initial chartering under State law and neither the bank nor its parent holding company undergoes a change in control.

(iii) May continue to provide as principal insurance which is reinsured in whole or in part by the Federal Crop Insurance Corporation if the subsidiary was engaged in the activity on or before September 30, 1991.

(3) *Majority-owned subsidiaries' ownership of equity investments that represent a control interest in a company.* The FDIC has determined that investment in the following by a majority-owned subsidiary of an insured State bank does not represent a significant risk to the Deposit Insurance Fund:

(i) Equity investment in a company engaged in real estate or securities activities authorized in paragraph (b)(5) of this section if the bank complies with the following restrictions and files a notice in compliance with § 303.121 of this chapter and the FDIC processes the notice without objection under § 303.122(a) of this chapter. The FDIC is not precluded from taking any appropriate action or imposing additional requirements with respect to the activity if the facts and circumstances warrant such action. If changes to the management or business plan of the company at any time result in material changes to the nature of the company's business or the manner in which its business is conducted, the insured State bank shall advise the appropriate regional director (DSC) in writing within 10 business days after such change. Investment under this paragraph is authorized if:

(A) The majority-owned subsidiary controls the company;

(B) The bank meets the core eligibility criteria of paragraph (c)(1) of this section;

(C) The majority-owned subsidiary meets the core eligibility criteria of paragraph (c)(2) of this section (including any modifications thereof applicable under paragraph (b)(5)(i) of this section), or the company is a corporation meeting such criteria;

(D) The bank's transactions with the majority-owned subsidiary, and the bank's transactions with the company, comply with the investment and transaction limits of paragraph (d) of this section;

(E) The bank complies with the capital requirements of paragraph (e) of this section with respect to the majority-owned subsidiary and the company; and

(F) To the extent the company is engaged in securities activities authorized by paragraph (b)(5)(ii) of this section, the bank and the company comply with the additional requirements

§ 362.4

therein as if the company were a majority-owned subsidiary.

(ii) Equity securities of a company engaged in the following activities, if the majority-owned subsidiary controls the company or the company is controlled by insured depository institutions, and the bank meets and continues to meet the applicable capital standards as prescribed by the appropriate Federal banking agency. The FDIC consents that a majority-owned subsidiary may conduct such activity without first obtaining the FDIC's consent. The fact that prior consent is not required by this subpart does not preclude the FDIC from taking any appropriate action with respect to the activity if the facts and circumstances warrant such action:

(A) Any activity that is permissible for a national bank, including such permissible activities that may require the company to register as a securities broker;

(B) Acting as an insurance agency;

(C) Engaging in any activity permissible for an insured State bank under § 362.3(b)(2)(iii) to the same extent permissible for the insured bank thereunder, so long as instruments held under this paragraph (b)(3)(ii)(C), paragraph (b)(7) of this section, and § 362.3(b)(2)(iii) in the aggregate do not exceed the limit set by § 362.3(b)(2)(iii);

(D) Engaging in any activity permissible for a majority-owned subsidiary of an insured State bank under paragraph (b)(6) of this section to the same extent and manner permissible for the majority-owned subsidiary thereunder; and

(4) *Majority-owned subsidiary's ownership of certain securities that do not represent a control interest*—(i) *Grandfathered investments in common or preferred stock and shares of investment companies.* Any insured State bank that has received approval to invest in common or preferred stock or shares of an investment company pursuant to § 362.3(a)(2)(iii) may conduct the approved investment activities through a majority-owned subsidiary of the bank without any additional approval from the FDIC provided that any conditions or restrictions imposed with regard to the approval granted under § 362.3(a)(2)(iii) are met.

(ii) *Bank stock.* An insured State bank may indirectly through a majority-owned subsidiary organized for such purpose invest in up to ten percent of the outstanding stock of another insured bank.

(5) *Majority-owned subsidiaries conducting real estate investment activities and securities underwriting.* The FDIC has determined that the following activities do not represent a significant risk to the Deposit Insurance Fund, provided that the activities are conducted by a majority-owned subsidiary of an insured State bank in compliance with the core eligibility requirements listed in paragraph (c) of this section; any additional requirements listed in paragraph (b)(5) (i) or (ii) of this section; the bank complies with the investment and transaction limitations of paragraph (d) of this section; and the bank meets the capital requirements of paragraph (e) of this section. The FDIC consents that these listed activities may be conducted by a majority-owned subsidiary of an insured State bank if the bank files a notice in compliance with § 303.121 of this chapter and the FDIC processes the notice without objection under § 303.122(a) of this chapter. The FDIC is not precluded from taking any appropriate action or imposing additional requirements with respect to the activities if the facts and circumstances warrant such action. If changes to the management or business plan of the majority-owned subsidiary at any time result in material changes to the nature of the majority-owned subsidiary's business or the manner in which its business is conducted, the insured State bank shall advise the appropriate regional director (DSC) in writing within 10 business days after such change. Such a majority-owned subsidiary may:

(i) *Real estate investment activities.* Engage in real estate investment activities. However, the requirements of paragraph (c)(2) (ii), (v), (vi), and (xi) of this section need not be met if the bank's investment in the equity securities of the subsidiary does not exceed 2 percent of the bank's tier one capital; the bank has only one subsidiary engaging in real estate investment activities; and the bank's total investment in the subsidiary does not include

Federal Deposit Insurance Corporation

§ 362.4

any extensions of credit from the bank to the subsidiary, any debt instruments issued by the subsidiary, or any other transaction originated by the bank that is used to benefit the subsidiary.

(ii) *Securities activities.* Engage in the public sale, distribution or underwriting of securities that are not permissible for a national bank under section 16 of the Banking Act of 1933 (12 U.S.C. 24 Seventh), provided that the insured state nonmember bank lawfully controlled or acquired the subsidiary and had an approved notice or order from the FDIC prior to November 12, 1999 and provided that the following additional conditions are, and continue to be, met:

(A) The state-chartered depository institution adopts policies and procedures, including appropriate limits on exposure, to govern the institution's participation in financing transactions underwritten or arranged by an underwriting majority-owned subsidiary;

(B) The state-chartered depository institution may not express an opinion on the value or the advisability of the purchase or sale of securities underwritten or dealt in by a majority-owned subsidiary unless the state-chartered depository institution notifies the customer that the majority-owned subsidiary is underwriting or distributing the security;

(C) The majority-owned subsidiary is registered with the Securities and Exchange Commission, is a member in good standing with the appropriate self-regulatory organization, and promptly informs the appropriate regional director (DSC) in writing of any material actions taken against the majority-owned subsidiary or any of its employees by the State, the appropriate self-regulatory organizations or the Securities and Exchange Commission; and

(D) The state-chartered depository institution does not knowingly purchase as principal or fiduciary during the existence of any underwriting or selling syndicate any securities underwritten by the majority-owned subsidiary unless the purchase is approved by the state-chartered depository institution's board of directors before the securities are initially offered for sale to the public.

(6) *Real estate leasing.* A majority-owned subsidiary of an insured State bank acting as lessor under a real property lease which is the equivalent of a financing transaction, meeting the lease criteria of paragraph (b)(6)(i) of this section and the underlying real estate requirements of paragraph (b)(6)(ii) of this section, does not represent a significant risk to the Deposit Insurance Fund. A majority-owned subsidiary may conduct this activity without first obtaining the FDIC's consent, provided that the bank meets and continues to meet the applicable capital standards as prescribed by the appropriate Federal banking agency. The fact that prior consent is not required by this subpart does not preclude the FDIC from taking any appropriate action with respect to the activity if the facts and circumstances warrant such action.

(i) *Lease criteria*—(A) *Capital lease.* The lease must qualify as a capital lease as to the lessor under generally accepted accounting principles.

(B) *Nonoperating basis.* The bank and the majority-owned subsidiary shall not, directly or indirectly, provide or be obligated to provide servicing, repair, or maintenance to the property, except that the lease may include provisions permitting the subsidiary to protect the value of the leased property in the event of a change in circumstances that increases the subsidiary's exposure to loss, or the subsidiary may take reasonable and appropriate action to salvage or protect the value of the leased property in such circumstances.

(ii) *Underlying real property requirements*—(A) *Acquisition.* The majority-owned subsidiary may acquire specific real estate to be leased only after the subsidiary has entered into:

(*1*) A lease meeting the requirements of paragraph (b)(6)(i) of this section;

(*2*) A legally binding written commitment to enter into such a lease; or

(*3*) A legally binding written agreement that indemnifies the subsidiary against loss in connection with its acquisition of the property.

(B) *Improvements.* Any expenditures by the majority-owned subsidiary to

§ 362.4

make reasonable repairs, renovations, and improvements necessary to render the property suitable to the lessee shall not exceed 25 percent of the majority-owned subsidiary's full investment in the real estate.

(C) *Divestiture.* At the expiration of the initial lease (including any renewals or extensions thereof), the majority-owned subsidiary shall, as soon as practicable but in any event no less than two years, either:

(*1*) Re-lease the property under a lease meeting the requirement of paragraph (b)(6)(i)(B) of this section; or

(*2*) Divest itself of all interest in the property.

(7) *Acquiring and retaining adjustable rate and money market preferred stock and similar instruments.* The FDIC has determined it does not present a significant risk to the Deposit Insurance Fund for a majority-owned subsidiary of an insured State bank to engage in any activity permissible for an insured State bank under § 362.3(b)(2)(iii), so long as instruments held under this paragraph, paragraph (b)(3)(ii)(C) of this section, and § 362.3(b)(2)(iii) in the aggregate do not exceed the limit set by § 362.3(b)(2)(iii). A majority-owned subsidiary may conduct this activity without first obtaining the FDIC's consent, provided that the bank meets and continues to meet the applicable capital standards as prescribed by the appropriate Federal banking agency. The fact that prior consent is not required by this subpart does not preclude the FDIC from taking any appropriate action with respect to the activity if the facts and circumstances warrant such action.

(c) *Core eligibility requirements.* If specifically required by this part or by FDIC order, any state-chartered depository institution that wishes to be eligible and continue to be eligible to conduct as principal activities through a subsidiary that are not permissible for a subsidiary of a national bank must be an "eligible depository institution" and the subsidiary must be an "eligible subsidiary".

(1) A state-chartered depository institution is an "eligible depository institution" if it:

(i) Has been chartered and operating for three or more years, unless the appropriate regional director (DSC) finds that the state-chartered depository institution is owned by an established, well-capitalized, well-managed holding company or is managed by seasoned management;

(ii) Has an FDIC-assigned composite rating of 1 or 2 assigned under the Uniform Financial Institutions Rating System (UFIRS) (or such other comparable rating system as may be adopted in the future) as a result of its most recent Federal or State examination for which the FDIC assigned a rating;

(iii) Received a rating of 1 or 2 under the "management" component of the UFIRS as assigned by the institution's appropriate Federal banking agency;

(iv) Has a satisfactory or better Community Reinvestment Act rating at its most recent examination conducted by the institution's appropriate Federal banking agency;

(v) Has a compliance rating of 1 or 2 at its most recent examination conducted by the institution's appropriate Federal banking agency; and

(vi) Is not subject to a cease and desist order, consent order, prompt corrective action directive, formal or informal written agreement, or other administrative agreement with its appropriate Federal banking agency or chartering authority.

(2) A subsidiary of a state-chartered depository institution is an "eligible subsidiary" if it:

(i) Meets applicable statutory or regulatory capital requirements and has sufficient operating capital in light of the normal obligations that are reasonably foreseeable for a business of its size and character within the industry;

(ii) Is physically separate and distinct in its operations from the operations of the state-chartered depository institution, provided that this requirement shall not be construed to prohibit the state-chartered depository institution and its subsidiary from sharing the same facility if the area where the subsidiary conducts business with the public is clearly distinct from the area where customers of the state-chartered depository institution conduct business with the institution. The extent of the separation will vary according to the type and frequency of customer contact;

Federal Deposit Insurance Corporation § 362.4

(iii) Maintains separate accounting and other business records;

(iv) Observes separate business entity formalities such as separate board of directors' meetings;

(v) Has a chief executive officer of the subsidiary who is not an employee of the institution;

(vi) Has a majority of its board of directors who are neither directors nor executive officers of the state-chartered depository institution;

(vii) Conducts business pursuant to independent policies and procedures designed to inform customers and prospective customers of the subsidiary that the subsidiary is a separate organization from the state-chartered depository institution and that the state-chartered depository institution is not responsible for and does not guarantee the obligations of the subsidiary;

(viii) Has only one business purpose within the types described in paragraphs (b)(2) and (b)(5) of this section;

(ix) Has a current written business plan that is appropriate to the type and scope of business conducted by the subsidiary;

(x) Has qualified management and employees for the type of activity contemplated, including all required licenses and memberships, and complies with industry standards; and

(xi) Establishes policies and procedures to ensure adequate computer, audit and accounting systems, internal risk management controls, and has necessary operational and managerial infrastructure to implement the business plan.

(d) *Investment and transaction limits*—(1) *General.* If specifically required by this part or FDIC order, the following conditions and restrictions apply to an insured State bank and its subsidiaries that engage in and wish to continue to engage in activities which are not permissible for a national bank subsidiary.

(2) *Investment limits*—(i) *Aggregate investment in subsidiaries.* An insured state bank's aggregate investment in all subsidiaries conducting activities subject to this paragraph (d) shall not exceed 20 percent of the insured State bank's tier one capital.

(ii) *Definition of investment.* (A) For purposes of this paragraph (d), the term "investment" means:

(*1*) Any extension of credit to the subsidiary by the insured State bank;

(*2*) Any debt securities, as such term is defined in part 344 of this chapter, issued by the subsidiary held by the insured State bank;

(*3*) The acceptance by the insured State bank of securities issued by the subsidiary as collateral for an extension of credit to any person or company; and

(*4*) Any extensions of credit by the insured State bank to any third party for the purpose of making a direct investment in the subsidiary, making any investment in which the subsidiary has an interest, or which is used for the benefit of, or transferred to, the subsidiary.

(B) For the purposes of this paragraph (d), the term "investment" does not include:

(*1*) Extensions of credit by the insured State bank to finance sales of assets by the subsidiary which do not involve more than the normal degree of risk of repayment and are extended on terms that are substantially similar to those prevailing at the time for comparable transactions with or involving unaffiliated persons or companies;

(*2*) An extension of credit by the insured State bank to the subsidiary that is fully collateralized by government securities, as such term is defined in § 344.3 of this chapter; or

(*3*) An extension of credit by the insured State bank to the subsidiary that is fully collateralized by a segregated deposit in the insured State bank.

(3) *Transaction requirements*—(i) *Arm's length transaction requirement.* With the exception of giving the subsidiary immediate credit for uncollected items received in the ordinary course of business, an insured State bank may not carry out any of the following transactions with a subsidiary subject to this paragraph (d) unless the transaction is on terms and conditions that are substantially the same as those prevailing at the time for comparable transactions with unaffiliated parties:

(A) Make an investment in the subsidiary;

(B) Purchase from or sell to the subsidiary any assets (including securities);

(C) Enter into a contract, lease, or other type of agreement with the subsidiary;

(D) Pay compensation to a majority-owned subsidiary or any person or company who has an interest in the subsidiary; or

(E) Engage in any such transaction in which the proceeds thereof are used for the benefit of, or are transferred to, the subsidiary.

(ii) *Prohibition on purchase of low quality assets.* An insured State bank is prohibited from purchasing a low quality asset from a subsidiary subject to this paragraph (d). For purposes of this subsection, "low quality asset" means:

(A) An asset classified as "substandard", "doubtful", or "loss" or treated as "other assets especially mentioned" in the most recent report of examination of the bank;

(B) An asset in a nonaccrual status;

(C) An asset on which principal or interest payments are more than 30 days past due; or

(D) An asset whose terms have been renegotiated or compromised due to the deteriorating financial condition of the obligor.

(iii) *Insider transaction restriction.* Neither the insured State bank nor the subsidiary subject to this paragraph (d) may enter into any transaction (exclusive of those covered by § 337.3 of this chapter) with the bank's executive officers, directors, principal shareholders or related interests of such persons which relate to the subsidiary's activities unless:

(A) The transactions are on terms and conditions that are substantially the same as those prevailing at the time for comparable transactions with persons not affiliated with the insured State bank; or

(B) The transactions are pursuant to a benefit or compensation program that is widely available to employees of the bank, and that does not give preference to the bank's executive officers, directors, principal shareholders or related interests of such persons over other bank employees.

(iv) *Anti-tying restriction.* Neither the insured State bank nor the majority-owned subsidiary may require a customer to either buy any product or use any service from the other as a condition of entering into a transaction.

(4) *Collateralization requirements.* (i) An insured State bank is prohibited from making an investment in a subsidiary subject to this paragraph (d) unless such transaction is fully-collateralized at the time the transaction is entered into. No insured State bank may accept a low quality asset as collateral. An extension of credit is fully collateralized if it is secured at the time of the transaction by collateral having a market value equal to at least:

(A) 100 percent of the amount of the transaction if the collateral is composed of:

(*1*) Obligations of the United States or its agencies;

(*2*) Obligations fully guaranteed by the United States or its agencies as to principal and interest;

(*3*) Notes, drafts, bills of exchange or bankers acceptances that are eligible for rediscount or purchase by the Federal Reserve Bank; or

(*4*) A segregated, earmarked deposit account with the insured State bank;

(B) 110 percent of the amount of the transaction if the collateral is composed of obligations of any State or political subdivision of any State;

(C) 120 percent of the amount of the transaction if the collateral is composed of other debt instruments, including receivables; or

(D) 130 percent of the amount of the transaction if the collateral is composed of stock, leases, or other real or personal property.

(ii) An insured State bank may not release collateral prior to proportional payment of the extension of credit; however, collateral may be substituted if there is no diminution of collateral coverage.

(5) *Investment and transaction limits extended to insured State bank subsidiaries.* For purposes of applying paragraphs (d)(2) through (d)(4) of this section, any reference to "insured State bank" means the insured State bank and any subsidiaries of the insured State bank which are not themselves subject under this part or FDIC order

Federal Deposit Insurance Corporation § 362.5

to the restrictions of this paragraph (d).

(e) *Capital requirements.* If specifically required by this part or by FDIC order, any insured State bank that wishes to conduct or continue to conduct as principal activities through a subsidiary that are not permissible for a subsidiary of a national bank must:

(1) Be well-capitalized after deducting from its tier one capital the investment in equity securities of the subsidiary as well as the bank's pro rata share of any retained earnings of the subsidiary;

(2) Reflect this deduction on the appropriate schedule of the bank's consolidated report of income and condition; and

(3) Use such regulatory capital amount for the purposes of the bank's assessment risk classification under part 327 of this chapter and its categorization as a "well-capitalized", an "adequately capitalized", an "undercapitalized", or a "significantly undercapitalized" institution as defined in § 325.103(b) of this chapter, provided that the capital deduction shall not be used for purposes of determining whether the bank is "critically undercapitalized" under part 325 of this chapter.

[63 FR 66326, Dec. 1, 1998, as amended at 66 FR 1028, Jan. 5, 2001; 71 FR 20527, Apr. 21, 2006]

§ 362.5 Approvals previously granted.

(a) *FDIC consent by order or notice.* An insured State bank that previously filed an application or notice under part 362 in effect prior to January 1, 1999 (see 12 CFR part 362 revised as of January 1, 1998), and obtained the FDIC's consent to engage in an activity or to acquire or retain a majority-owned subsidiary engaging as principal in an activity or acquiring and retaining any investment that is prohibited under this subpart may continue that activity or retain that investment without seeking the FDIC's consent, provided that the insured State bank and its subsidiary, if applicable, continue to meet the conditions and restrictions of the approval. An insured State bank which was granted approval based on conditions which differ from the requirements of § 362.4(c)(2), (d) and (e) will be considered to meet the conditions and restrictions of the approval relating to being an eligible subsidiary, meeting investment and transactions limits, and meeting capital requirements if the insured State bank and subsidiary meet the requirements of § 362.4(c)(2), (d) and (e). If the majority-owned subsidiary is engaged in real estate investment activities not exceeding 2 percent of the tier one capital of a bank and meeting the other conditions of § 362.4(b)(5)(i), the majority-owned subsidiary's compliance with § 362.4(c)(2) under the preceding sentence may be pursuant to the modifications authorized by § 362.4(b)(5)(i). Once an insured State bank elects to comply with § 362.4 (c)(2), (d), and (e), it may not revert to the corresponding provisions of the approval order.

(b) *Approvals by regulation*—

(1)–(5) [Reserved]

(6) *Adjustable rate or money market preferred stock.* An insured State bank owning adjustable rate or money market (auction rate) preferred stock pursuant to § 362.4(c)(3)(v) in effect prior to January 1, 1999 (see 12 CFR part 362 revised as of January 1, 1998), in excess of the amount limit in § 362.3(b)(2)(iii) may continue to hold any overlimit shares of such stock acquired before January 1, 1999, until redeemed or repurchased by the issuer, but such stock shall be included as part of the amount limit in § 362.3(b)(2)(iii) when determining whether the bank may acquire new stock thereunder.

(c) *Charter conversions.* (1) An insured State bank that has converted its charter from an insured state savings association may continue activities through a majority-owned subsidiary that were permissible prior to the time it converted its charter only if the insured State bank receives the FDIC's consent. Except as provided in paragraph (c)(2) of this section, the insured State bank should apply under § 362.4(b)(1), submit any notice required under § 362.4(b) (4) or (5), or comply with the provisions of § 362.4(b) (3), (6), or (7) if applicable, to continue the activity.

(2) *Exception for prior consent.* If the FDIC had granted consent to the savings association under section 28 of the Federal Deposit Insurance Act (12

609

§ 362.6

U.S.C. 1831(e)) prior to the time the savings association converted its charter, the insured State bank may continue the activities without providing notice or making application to the FDIC, provided that the bank and its subsidiary as applicable are in compliance with:

(i) The terms of the FDIC approval order; and

(ii) The provisions of § 362.4(c)(2), (d), and (e) regarding operating as an "eligible subsidiary", "investment and transaction limits", and "capital requirements'.

(3) *Divestiture.* An insured State bank that does not receive FDIC consent shall divest of the nonconforming investment as soon as practical but in no event later than two years from the date of charter conversion.

[63 FR 66326, Dec. 1, 1998, as amended at 66 FR 1028, Jan. 5, 2001]

Subpart B—Safety and Soundness Rules Governing Insured State Nonmember Banks

§ 362.6 Purpose and scope.

This subpart, along with the notice and application procedures in subpart G of part 303 of this chapter apply to certain banking practices that may have adverse effects on the safety and soundness of insured state nonmember banks. This subpart contains the required prudential separations between certain securities underwriting affiliates and insured state nonmember banks. The standards only will apply to affiliates of insured state nonmember banks that are not controlled by an entity that is supervised by a federal banking agency.

[66 FR 1028, Jan. 5, 2001]

§ 362.7 Definitions.

For the purposes of this subpart, the following definitions apply:

(a) *Affiliate* has the same meaning contained in section 3 of the Federal Deposit Insurance Act (12 U.S.C. 1813).

(b) *Activity, company, control, equity security, insured state nonmember bank, security and subsidiary* have the same meaning as provided in subpart A of this part.

[63 FR 66326, Dec. 1, 1998, as amended at 66 FR 1028, Jan. 5, 2001]

§ 362.8 Restrictions on activities of insured state nonmember banks affiliated with certain securities companies.

(a) The FDIC has found that an unrestricted affiliation between an insured state nonmember bank and certain companies may have adverse effects on the safety and soundness of insured state nonmember banks.

(b) An insured state nonmember bank is prohibited from becoming or remaining affiliated with any securities underwriting affiliate company that directly engages in the public sale, distribution or underwriting of stocks, bonds, debentures, notes, or other securities activity, of a type not permissible for a national bank directly, unless the company is controlled by an entity that is supervised by a federal banking agency or the state nonmember bank submits an application in compliance with § 303.121 of this chapter and the FDIC grants its consent under the procedure in § 303.122(b) of this chapter, or the state nonmember bank and the securities underwriting affiliate company comply with the following requirements:

(1) The securities business of the affiliate is physically separate and distinct in its operations from the operations of the bank, provided that this requirement shall not be construed to prohibit the bank and its affiliate from sharing the same facility if the area where the affiliate conducts retail sales activity with the public is physically distinct from the routine deposit taking area of the bank;

(2) The affiliate conducts business pursuant to independent policies and procedures designed to inform customers and prospective customers of the affiliate that the affiliate is a separate organization from the bank and the state-chartered depository institution is not responsible for and does not guarantee the obligations of the affiliate;

(3) The bank adopts policies and procedures, including appropriate limits on exposure, to govern its participation

in financing transactions underwritten by an underwriting affiliate;

(4) The bank does not express an opinion on the value or the advisability of the purchase or sale of securities underwritten or dealt in by an affiliate unless it notifies the customer that the entity underwriting, making a market, distributing or dealing in the securities is an affiliate of the bank; and

(5) The bank complies with the investment and transaction limitations in sections 23A and 23B of the Federal Reserve Act (12 U.S.C. 371c and 371c-1) with respect to the affiliate.

[66 FR 1028, Jan. 5, 2001]

Subpart C—Activities of Insured State Savings Associations

§ 362.9 Purpose and scope.

(a) This subpart, along with the notice and application procedures in subpart H of part 303 of this chapter, implements the provisions of section 28 of the Federal Deposit Insurance Act (12 U.S.C. 1831e) that restrict and prohibit insured state savings associations and their service corporations from engaging in activities and investments of a type that are not permissible for Federal savings associations and their service corporations. The phrase "activity permissible for a Federal savings association" means any activity authorized for Federal savings associations under any statute including the Home Owners' Loan Act (HOLA, 12 U.S.C. 1464 *et seq.*), as well as activities recognized as permissible for a Federal savings association in regulations, official thrift bulletins, orders or written interpretations issued by the Office of Thrift Supervision (OTS), or its predecessor, the Federal Home Loan Bank Board.

(b) This subpart does not cover the following activities:

(1) Activities conducted by the insured state savings association other than "as principal", defined for purposes of this subpart as activities conducted as agent for a customer, conducted in a brokerage, custodial, advisory, or administrative capacity, or conducted as trustee, or in any substantially similar capacity. For example, this subpart does not cover acting solely as agent for the sale of insurance, securities, real estate, or travel services; nor does it cover acting as trustee, providing personal financial planning advice, or safekeeping services.

(2) Interests in real estate in which the real property is used or intended in good faith to be used within a reasonable time by an insured savings association or its service corporations as offices or related facilities for the conduct of its business or future expansion of its business or used as public welfare investments of a type and in an amount permissible for Federal savings associations.

(3) Equity investments acquired in connection with debts previously contracted (DPC) if the insured savings association or its service corporation takes only such actions as would be permissible for a Federal savings association's or its service corporation's DPC holdings.

(c) The FDIC intends to allow insured state savings associations and their service corporations to undertake only safe and sound activities and investments that do not present significant risks to the Deposit Insurance Fund and that are consistent with the purposes of Federal deposit insurance and other applicable law. This subpart does not authorize any insured state savings association to make investments or conduct activities that are not authorized or that are prohibited by either Federal or state law.

[63 FR 66326, Dec. 1, 1998, as amended at 71 FR 20527, Apr. 21, 2006]

§ 362.10 Definitions.

For the purposes of this subpart, the definitions provided in § 362.2 apply. Additionally, the following definitions apply to this subpart:

(a) *Affiliate* has the same meaning as provided in subpart B of this part.

(b) *Corporate debt securities not of investment grade* means any corporate debt security that when acquired was not rated among the four highest rating categories by at least one nationally recognized statistical rating organization. The term shall not include any obligation issued or guaranteed by a corporation that may be held by a Federal savings association without

§ 362.11

limitation as to percentage of assets under subparagraphs (D), (E), or (F) of section 5(c)(1) of HOLA (12 U.S.C. 1464(c)(1) (D), (E), (F)).

(c) *Insured state savings association* means any state-chartered savings association insured by the FDIC.

(d) *Qualified affiliate* means, in the case of a stock insured state savings association, an affiliate other than a subsidiary or an insured depository institution. In the case of a mutual savings association, "qualified affiliate" means a subsidiary other than an insured depository institution provided that all of the savings association's investments in, and extensions of credit to, the subsidiary are deducted from the savings association's capital.

(e) *Service corporation* means any corporation the capital stock of which is available for purchase by savings associations.

[63 FR 66326, Dec. 1, 1998, as amended at 66 FR 1029, Jan. 5, 2001]

§ 362.11 Activities of insured State savings associations.

(a) *Equity investments*—(1) *Prohibited investments.* No insured state savings association may directly acquire or retain as principal any equity investment of a type, or in an amount, that is not permissible for a Federal savings association unless the exception in paragraph (a)(2) of this section applies.

(2) *Exception: Equity investment in service corporations.* An insured state savings association that is and continues to be in compliance with the applicable capital standards as prescribed by the appropriate Federal banking agency may acquire or retain an equity investment in a service corporation:

(i) Not permissible for a Federal savings association to the extent the service corporation is engaging in activities that are allowed pursuant to the provisions of or an application under § 362.12(b); or

(ii) Of a type permissible for a Federal savings association, but in an amount exceeding the investment limits applicable to Federal savings associations, if the insured state savings association obtains the FDIC's prior consent. Consent will be given only if the FDIC determines that the amount of the investment in a service corpora-

tion engaged in such activities does not present a significant risk to the Deposit Insurance Fund. Applications should be filed in accordance with § 303.141 of this chapter and will be processed under § 303.142(b) of this chapter. Approvals granted under § 303.142(b) of this chapter may be made subject to any conditions or restrictions found by the FDIC to be necessary to protect the Deposit Insurance Fund from significant risk, to prevent unsafe or unsound practices, and/or to ensure that the activity is consistent with the purposes of Federal deposit insurance and other applicable law.

(b) *Activities other than equity investments*—(1) *Prohibited activities.* An insured state savings association may not directly engage as principal in any activity, that is not an equity investment, of a type not permissible for a Federal savings association, and an insured state savings association shall not make nonresidential real property loans in an amount exceeding that described in section 5(c)(2)(B) of HOLA (12 U.S.C. 1464(c)(2)(B)), unless one of the exceptions in paragraph (b)(2) of this section applies. This section shall not be read to require the divestiture of any asset (including a nonresidential real estate loan), if the asset was acquired prior to August 9, 1989; however, any activity conducted with such asset must be conducted in accordance with this subpart. After August 9, 1989, an insured state savings association directly or through a subsidiary (other than, in the case of a mutual savings association, a subsidiary that is a qualified affiliate), may not acquire or retain any corporate debt securities not of investment grade.

(2) *Exceptions*—(i) *Consent obtained through application.* An insured state savings association that meets and continues to meet the applicable capital standards set by the appropriate Federal banking agency may directly conduct activities prohibited by paragraph (b)(1) of this section if the savings association obtains the FDIC's prior consent. Consent will be given only if the FDIC determines that conducting the activity designated poses no significant risk to the Deposit Insurance Fund. Applications should be filed in accordance with § 303.141 of this

chapter and will be processed under § 303.142(b) of this chapter. Approvals granted under § 303.142(b) of this chapter may be made subject to any conditions or restrictions found by the FDIC to be necessary to protect the Deposit Insurance Fund from significant risk, to prevent unsafe or unsound practices, and/or to ensure that the activity is consistent with the purposes of Federal deposit insurance and other applicable law.

(ii) *Nonresidential realty loans permissible for a Federal savings association conducted in an amount not permissible.* An insured state savings association that meets and continues to meet the applicable capital standards set by the appropriate Federal banking agency may make nonresidential real property loans in an amount exceeding the amount described in section 5(c)(2)(B) of HOLA, if the savings association files a notice in compliance with § 303.141 of this chapter and the FDIC processes the notice without objection under § 303.142(a) of this chapter. Consent will be given only if the FDIC determines that engaging in such lending in the amount designated poses no significant risk to the Deposit Insurance Fund.

(iii) *Acquiring and retaining adjustable rate and money market preferred stock.* (A) An insured state savings association's investment of up to 15 percent of the association's tier one capital in adjustable rate preferred stock or money market (auction rate) preferred stock does not represent a significant risk to the Deposit Insurance Fund. An insured state savings association may conduct this activity without first obtaining the FDIC's consent, provided that the association meets and continues to meet the applicable capital standards as prescribed by the appropriate Federal banking agency. The fact that prior consent is not required by this subpart does not preclude the FDIC from taking any appropriate action with respect to the activities if the facts and circumstances warrant such action.

(B) An insured state savings association may acquire or retain other instruments of a type determined by the FDIC to have the character of debt securities and not to represent a significant risk to the Deposit Insurance Fund. Such instruments shall be included in the 15 percent of tier one capital limit imposed in paragraph (b)(2)(iii)(A) of this section. An insured state savings association may conduct this activity without first obtaining the FDIC's consent, provided that the association meets and continues to meet the applicable capital standards as prescribed by the appropriate Federal banking agency. The fact that prior consent is not required by this subpart does not preclude the FDIC from taking any appropriate action with respect to the activities if the facts and circumstances warrant such action.

(3) *Activities permissible for a Federal savings association conducted in an amount not permissible.* Except as provided in paragraph (b)(2)(ii) of this section, an insured state savings association may engage as principal in any activity, which is not an equity investment of a type permissible for a Federal savings association, in an amount in excess of that permissible for a Federal savings association, if the savings association meets and continues to meet the applicable capital standards set by the appropriate Federal banking agency, the institution has advised the appropriate regional director (DSC) under the procedure in § 303.142(c) of this chapter within thirty days before engaging in the activity, and the FDIC has not advised the insured state savings association that conducting the activity in the amount indicated poses a significant risk to the Deposit Insurance Fund. This section shall not be read to require the divestiture of any asset if the asset was acquired prior to August 9, 1989; however, any activity conducted with such asset must be conducted in accordance with this subpart.

[63 FR 66326, Dec. 1, 1998, as amended at 71 FR 20527, Apr. 21, 2006]

§ 362.12 Service corporations of insured State savings associations.

(a) *Prohibition.* A service corporation of an insured state savings association may not engage in any activity that is not permissible for a service corporation of a Federal savings association, unless it meets one of the exceptions in paragraph (b) of this section.

§ 362.12

(b) *Exceptions*—(1) *Consent obtained through application.* A service corporation of an insured state savings association may conduct activities prohibited by paragraph (a) of this section if the savings association obtains the FDIC's prior written consent and the insured state savings association meets and continues to meet the applicable capital standards set by the appropriate Federal banking agency. Consent will be given only if the FDIC determines that the activity poses no significant risk to the Deposit Insurance Fund. Applications for consent should be filed in accordance with § 303.141 of this chapter and will be processed under § 303.142(b) of this chapter. Approvals granted under § 303.142(b) of this chapter may be made subject to any conditions or restrictions found by the FDIC to be necessary to protect the Deposit Insurance Fund from risk, to prevent unsafe or unsound banking practices, and/or to ensure that the activity is consistent with the purposes of Federal deposit insurance and other applicable law. The activities covered by this paragraph may include, but are not limited to, acquiring and retaining equity securities of a company engaged in the public sale distribution or underwriting of securities.

(2) *Service corporations conducting unrestricted activities.* The FDIC has determined that the following activities do not represent a significant risk to the Deposit Insurance Fund:

(i) [Reserved]

(ii) A service corporation of an insured state savings association may acquire and retain equity securities of a company engaged in the following activities, if the service corporation controls the company or the company is controlled by insured depository institutions, and the association continues to meet the applicable capital standards as prescribed by the appropriate Federal banking agency. The FDIC consents that such activity may be conducted by a service corporation of an insured state savings association without first obtaining the FDIC's consent. The fact that prior consent is not required by this subpart does not preclude the FDIC from taking any appropriate action with respect to the activities if the facts and circumstances warrant such action.

(A) *Equity securities of a company that engages in permissible activities.* A service corporation may own the equity securities of a company that engages in any activity permissible for a Federal savings association.

(B) *Equity securities of a company that acquires and retains adjustable-rate and money market preferred stock.* A service corporation may own the equity securities of a company that engages in any activity permissible for an insured state savings association under § 362.11(b)(2)(iii) so long as instruments held under this paragraph (b)(2)(ii)(B), paragraph (b)(2)(iv) of this section, and § 362.11(b)(2)(iii) in the aggregate do not exceed the limit set by § 362.11(b)(2)(iii).

(C) *Equity securities of a company acting as an insurance agency.* A service corporation may own the equity securities of a company that acts as an insurance agency.

(iii) *Activities that are not conducted "as principal".* A service corporation controlled by the insured state savings association may engage in activities which are not conducted "as principal" such as acting as an agent for a customer, acting in a brokerage, custodial, advisory, or administrative capacity, or acting as trustee, or in any substantially similar capacity.

(iv) *Acquiring and retaining adjustable-rate and money market preferred stock.* A service corporation may engage in any activity permissible for an insured state savings association under § 362.11(b)(2)(iii) so long as instruments held under this paragraph (b)(2)(iv), paragraph (b)(2)(ii)(B) of this section, and § 362.11(b)(2)(iii) in the aggregate do not exceed the limit set by § 362.11(b)(2)(iii).

(3)–(4) [Reserved]

(c) *Investment and transaction limits.* The restrictions detailed in § 362.4(d) apply to transactions between an insured state savings association and any service corporation engaging in activities which are not permissible for a service corporation of a Federal savings association if specifically required by this part or FDIC order. For purposes of applying the investment limits in § 362.4(d)(2), the term "investment" includes only those items described in

§ 362.4(d)(2)(ii)(A) *(3)* and *(4).* For purposes of applying § 362.4(d) (2), (3), and (4) to this paragraph (c), references to the terms "insured State bank" and "subsidiary" in § 362.4(d)(2), (3), and (4), shall be deemed to refer, respectively, to the insured state savings association and the service corporation. For purposes of applying § 362.4(d)(5), references to the terms "insured State bank" and "subsidiary" in § 362.4(d)(5) shall be deemed to refer, respectively, to the insured state savings association and the service corporations or subsidiaries.

(d) *Capital requirements.* If specifically required by this part or by FDIC order, an insured state savings association that wishes to conduct as principal activities through a service corporation which are not permissible for a service corporation of a Federal savings association must:

(1) Be well-capitalized after deducting from its capital any investment in the service corporation, both equity and debt.

(2) Use such regulatory capital amount for the purposes of the insured state savings association's assessment risk classification under part 327 of this chapter.

[63 FR 66326, Dec. 1, 1998, as amended at 66 FR 1029, Jan. 5, 2001; 71 FR 20527, Apr. 21, 2006]]

§ 362.13 Approvals previously granted.

FDIC consent by order or notice. An insured state savings association that previously filed an application and obtained the FDIC's consent to engage in an activity or to acquire or retain an investment in a service corporation engaging as principal in an activity or acquiring and retaining any investment that is prohibited under this subpart may continue that activity or retain that investment without seeking the FDIC's consent, provided the insured state savings association and the service corporation, if applicable, continue to meet the conditions and restrictions of approval. An insured state savings association which was granted approval based on conditions which differ from the requirements of §§ 362.4(c)(2) and 362.12 (c) and (d) will be considered to meet the conditions and restrictions of the approval if the insured state savings association and any applicable service corporation meet the requirements of §§ 362.4(c)(2) and 362.12 (c) and (d). For the purposes of applying § 362.4(c)(2), references to the terms "eligible subsidiary" and "subsidiary" in § 362.4(c)(2) shall be deemed to refer, respectively, to the eligible service corporation and the service corporation.

Subpart D—Acquiring, Establishing, or Conducting New Activities Through a Subsidiary by an Insured Savings Association

§ 362.14 Purpose and scope.

This subpart implements section 18(m) of the Federal Deposit Insurance Act (12 U.S.C. 1828(m)) which requires that prior notice be given the FDIC when an insured savings association establishes or acquires a subsidiary or engages in any new activity in a subsidiary. For the purposes of this subpart, the term "subsidiary" does not include any insured depository institution as that term is defined in the Federal Deposit Insurance Act. Unless otherwise indicated, the definitions provided in § 362.2 apply to this subpart.

§ 362.15 Acquiring or establishing a subsidiary; conducting new activities through a subsidiary.

No state or Federal insured savings association may establish or acquire a subsidiary, or conduct any new activity through a subsidiary, unless it files a notice in compliance with § 303.142(c) of this chapter at least 30 days prior to establishment of the subsidiary or commencement of the activity and the FDIC does not object to the notice. This requirement does not apply to any Federal savings bank that was chartered prior to October 15, 1982, as a savings bank under State law or any savings association that acquired its principal assets from such an institution.

Subpart E—Financial Subsidiaries of Insured State Nonmember Banks

SOURCE: 66 FR 1029, Jan. 5, 2001, unless otherwise noted.

§ 362.16 Purpose and scope.

(a) This subpart, along with the notice and application procedures in subpart G of part 303 of this chapter, implements section 46 of the Federal Deposit Insurance Act (12 U.S.C. 1831w) and requires that an insured state nonmember bank certify certain facts and file a notice with the FDIC before the insured state nonmember bank may control or hold an interest in a financial subsidiary under section 46(a) of the Federal Deposit Insurance Act. This subpart also implements the statutory Community Reinvestment Act (CRA) (12 U.S.C. 2901 *et seq.*) requirement set forth in subsection (4)(l)(2) of the Bank Holding Company Act (12 U.S.C. 1843(l)(2)), which is applicable to state nonmember banks that commence new activities through a financial subsidiary or directly or indirectly acquire control of a company engaged in an activity under section 46(a).

(b) This subpart does not cover activities conducted other than "as principal". For purposes of this subpart, activities conducted other than "as principal" are defined as activities conducted as agent for a customer, conducted in a brokerage, custodial, advisory, or administrative capacity, or conducted as trustee, or in any substantially similar capacity. For example, this subpart does not cover acting solely as agent for the sale of insurance, securities, real estate, or travel services; nor does it cover acting as trustee, providing personal financial planning advice, or safekeeping services.

§ 362.17 Definitions.

For the purposes of this subpart, the following definitions will apply:

(a) *Activity, company, control, insured depository institution, insured state bank, insured state nonmember bank and subsidiary* have the same meaning as provided in subpart A of this part.

(b) *Affiliate* has the same meaning provided in subpart B of this part.

(c) *Financial subsidiary* means any company that is controlled by one or more insured depository institutions other than:

(1) A subsidiary that only engages in activities that the state nonmember bank is permitted to engage in directly and that are conducted on the same terms and conditions that govern the conduct of the activities by the state nonmember bank; or

(2) A subsidiary that the state nonmember bank is specifically authorized to control by the express terms of a federal statute (other than section 46(a) of the Federal Deposit Insurance Act (12 U.S.C. 1831w)), and not by implication or interpretation, such as the Bank Service Company Act (12 U.S.C. 1861 *et seq.*).

(d) *Tangible equity and Tier 2 capital* have the same meaning as set forth in part 325 of this chapter.

(e) *Well-managed* means:

(1) Unless otherwise determined in writing by the appropriate federal banking agency, the institution has received a composite rating of 1 or 2 under the Uniform Financial Institutions Rating System (or an equivalent rating under an equivalent rating system) in connection with the most recent state or federal examination or subsequent review of the depository institution and at least a rating of 2 for management, if such a rating is given; or

(2) In the case of any depository institution that has not been examined by its appropriate federal banking agency, the existence and use of managerial resources that the appropriate federal banking agency determines are satisfactory.

§ 362.18 Financial subsidiaries of insured state nonmember banks.

(a) *"As principal" activities.* An insured state nonmember bank may not obtain control of or hold an interest in a financial subsidiary that engages in activities as principal or commence any such new activity pursuant to section 46(a) of the Federal Deposit Insurance Act (12 U.S.C. 1831w) unless the insured state nonmember bank files a notice containing the information required in § 303.121(b) of this chapter and certifies that:

(1) The insured state nonmember bank is well-managed;

(2) The insured state nonmember bank and all of its insured depository

Federal Deposit Insurance Corporation § 362.18

institution affiliates are well-capitalized as defined in the appropriate capital regulation and guidance of each institution's primary federal regulator; and

(3) The insured state nonmember bank will deduct the aggregate amount of its outstanding equity investment, including retained earnings, in all financial subsidiaries that engage in activities as principal pursuant to section 46(a) of the Federal Deposit Insurance Act (12 U.S.C. 1831w), from the bank's total assets and tangible equity and deduct such investment from its total risk-based capital (this deduction shall be made equally from Tier 1 and Tier 2 capital).

(b) *Community Reinvestment Act (CRA).* An insured state nonmember bank may not commence any new activity subject to section 46(a) of the Federal Deposit Insurance Act (12 U.S.C. 1831w) or directly or indirectly acquire control of a company engaged in any such activity pursuant to § 362.18(a)(1), if the bank or any of its insured depository institution affiliates received a CRA rating of less than "satisfactory record of meeting community credit needs" in its most recent CRA examination.

(c) *Other requirements.* An insured state nonmember bank controlling or holding an interest in a financial subsidiary under section 46(a) of the Federal Deposit Insurance Act (12 U.S.C. 1831w) must meet and continue to meet the requirements set forth in paragraph (a) of this section as long as the insured state nonmember bank holds the financial subsidiary and:

(1) Disclose and continue to disclose the capital separation required in paragraph (a)(3) in any published financial statements;

(2) Comply and continue to comply with sections 23A and 23B of the Federal Reserve Act (12 U.S.C. 371c and 371c–1) as if the subsidiary were a financial subsidiary of a national bank; and

(3) Comply and continue to comply with the financial and operational standards provided by section 5136A(d) of the Revised Statutes of the United States (12 U.S.C. 24A(d)), unless otherwise determined by the FDIC.

(d) *Securities underwriting.* If the financial subsidiary of the insured state nonmember bank will engage in the public sale, distribution or underwriting of stocks, bonds, debentures, notes, or other securities activity of a type permissible for a national bank only through a financial subsidiary, then the state nonmember bank and the financial subsidiary also must comply and continue to comply with the following additional requirements:

(1) The securities business of the financial subsidiary must be physically separate and distinct in its operations from the operations of the bank, provided that this requirement shall not be construed to prohibit the bank and its financial subsidiary from sharing the same facility if the area where the financial subsidiary conducts securities business with the public is physically distinct from the routine deposit taking area of the bank;

(2) The financial subsidiary must conduct its securities business pursuant to independent policies and procedures designed to inform customers and prospective customers of the financial subsidiary that the financial subsidiary is a separate organization from the insured state nonmember bank and that the insured state nonmember bank is not responsible for and does not guarantee the obligations of the financial subsidiary;

(3) The bank must adopt policies and procedures, including appropriate limits on exposure, to govern its participation in financing transactions underwritten by its financial subsidiary; and

(4) The bank must not express an opinion on the value or the advisability of the purchase or sale of securities underwritten or dealt in by its financial subsidiary unless the bank notifies the customer that the entity underwriting, making a market, distributing or dealing in the securities is a financial subsidiary of the bank.

(e) *Applications for exceptions to certain requirements.* Any insured state nonmember bank that is unable to comply with the well-managed requirement of § 362.18(a)(1) and (c)(1), any state nonmember bank that has appropriate reasons for not meeting the financial and operational standards applicable to a financial subsidiary of a

§ 362.18

national bank conducting the same activities as provided in § 362.18(c)(3) or any state nonmember bank and its financial subsidiary subject to the securities underwriting activities requirements in § 362.18(d) that is unable to meet such requirements may submit an application in compliance with § 303.121 of this chapter to seek a waiver or modification of such requirements under the procedure in § 303.122(b) of this chapter. The FDIC may impose additional prudential safeguards as are necessary as a condition of its consent.

(f) *Failure to meet requirements*—(1) *Notification by FDIC.* The FDIC will notify the insured state nonmember bank in writing and identify the areas of noncompliance, if:

(i) The FDIC finds that an insured state nonmember bank or any of its insured depository institution affiliates is not in compliance with the CRA requirement of § 362.18(b) at the time any new activity is commenced or control of the financial subsidiary is acquired;

(ii) The FDIC finds that the facts to which an insured state nonmember bank certified under § 362.18(a) are not accurate in whole or in part; or

(iii) The FDIC finds that the insured state nonmember bank or any of its insured depository institution affiliates or the financial subsidiary fails to meet or continue to comply with the requirements of § 362.18(c) and (d), if applicable, and the FDIC has not granted an exception under the procedures set forth in § 362.18(e) and in § 303.122(b) of this chapter.

(2) *Notification by state nonmember bank.* An insured state nonmember bank that controls or holds an interest in a financial subsidiary must promptly notify the FDIC if the bank becomes aware that any depository institution affiliate of the bank has ceased to be well-capitalized.

(3) *Subsequent action by FDIC.* The FDIC may take any appropriate action or impose any limitations, including requiring that the insured state nonmember bank to divest control of any such financial subsidiary, on the conduct or activities of the insured state nonmember bank or any financial subsidiary of the insured state bank that fails to:

(i) Meet the requirements listed in § 362.18(a) and (b) at the time that any new section 46 activity is commenced or control of a financial subsidiary is acquired by an insured state nonmember bank; or

(ii) Meet and continue to meet the requirements listed in § 362.18(c) and (d), as applicable.

(g) *Coordination with section 24 of the Federal Deposit Insurance Act*—(1) *Continuing authority under section 24.* Notwithstanding § 362.18(a) through (f), an insured state bank may retain its interest in any subsidiary:

(i) That was conducting a financial activity with authorization in accordance with section 24 of the Federal Deposit Insurance Act (12 U.S.C. 1831a) and the applicable implementing regulation found in subpart A of this part 362 before the date on which any such activity became for the first time permissible for a financial subsidiary of a national bank; and

(ii) Which insured state nonmember bank and its subsidiary continue to meet the conditions and restrictions of the section 24 order or regulation approving the activity as well as other applicable law.

(2) *Continuing authority under section 24(f) of the Federal Deposit Insurance Act.* Notwithstanding § 362.18(a) through (f), an insured state bank with authority under section 24(f) of the Federal Deposit Insurance Act (12 U.S.C. 1831a(f)) to hold equity securities may continue to establish new subsidiaries to engage in that investment activity.

(3) *Relief from conditions.* Any state nonmember bank that meets the requirements of paragraph (g)(1) of this section or that is subject to section 46(b) of the Federal Deposit Insurance Act (12 U.S.C. 1831w(b)) may submit an application in compliance with § 303.121 of this chapter and seek the consent of the FDIC under the procedure in § 303.122(b) of this chapter for modification of any conditions or restrictions the FDIC previously imposed in connection with a section 24 order or regulation approving the activity.

(4) *New financial subsidiaries.* Notwithstanding subpart A of this part 362, an insured state bank may not, on or after November 12, 1999, acquire control of, or acquire an interest in, a financial

Federal Deposit Insurance Corporation § 363.1

subsidiary that engages in activities as principal or commences any new activity under section 46(a) of the Federal Deposit Insurance Act (12 U.S.C. 1831w) other than as provided in this section.

PART 363—ANNUAL INDEPENDENT AUDITS AND REPORTING REQUIREMENTS

Sec.
363.0 OMB control number.
363.1 Scope and definitions.
363.2 Annual reporting requirements.
363.3 Independent public accountant.
363.4 Filing and notice requirements.
363.5 Audit committees.
APPENDIX A TO PART 363—GUIDELINES AND INTERPRETATIONS
APPENDIX B TO PART 363—ILLUSTRATIVE MANAGEMENT REPORTS

AUTHORITY: 12 U.S.C. 1831m.

SOURCE: 74 FR 35745, July 20, 2009, unless otherwise noted.

§ 363.0 OMB control number.

The information collection requirements in this part have been approved by the Office of Management and Budget under OMB control number 3064–0113.

§ 363.1 Scope and definitions.

(a) *Applicability.* This part applies to any insured depository institution with respect to any fiscal year in which its consolidated total assets as of the beginning of such fiscal year are $500 million or more. The requirements specified in this part are in addition to any other statutory and regulatory requirements otherwise applicable to an insured depository institution.

(b) *Compliance by subsidiaries of holding companies.* (1) For an insured depository institution that is a subsidiary of a holding company, the audited financial statements requirement of § 363.2(a) may be satisfied:

(i) For fiscal years ending on or before June 14, 2010, by audited consolidated financial statements of the top-tier or any mid-tier holding company.

(ii) For fiscal years ending on or after June 15, 2010, by audited consolidated financial statements of the top-tier or any mid-tier holding company provided that the consolidated total assets of the insured depository institution (or the consolidated total assets of all of the holding company's insured depository institution subsidiaries, regardless of size, if the holding company owns or controls more than one insured depository institution) comprise 75 percent or more of the consolidated total assets of this top-tier or mid-tier holding company as of the beginning of its fiscal year.

(2) The other requirements of this part for an insured depository institution that is a subsidiary of a holding company may be satisfied by the top-tier or any mid-tier holding company if the insured depository institution meets the criterion specified in § 363.1(b)(1) and if:

(i) The services and functions comparable to those required of the insured depository institution by this part are provided at this top-tier or mid-tier holding company level; and

(ii) The insured depository institution has as of the beginning of its fiscal year:

(A) Total assets of less than $5 billion; or

(B) Total assets of $5 billion or more and a composite CAMELS rating of 1 or 2.

(3) The appropriate Federal banking agency may revoke the exception in paragraph (b)(2) of this section for any institution with total assets in excess of $9 billion for any period of time during which the appropriate Federal banking agency determines that the institution's exemption would create a significant risk to the Deposit Insurance Fund.

(c) *Financial reporting.* For purposes of the management report requirement of § 363.2(b) and the internal control reporting requirement of § 363.3(b), "financial reporting," at a minimum, includes both financial statements prepared in accordance with generally accepted accounting principles for the insured depository institution or its holding company and financial statements prepared for regulatory reporting purposes. For recognition and measurement purposes, financial statements prepared for regulatory reporting purposes shall conform to generally accepted accounting principles and section 37 of the Federal Deposit Insurance Act.

619

§ 363.2

(d) *Definitions.* For purposes of this part, the following definitions apply:

(1) *AICPA* means the American Institute of Certified Public Accountants.

(2) *GAAP* means generally accepted accounting principles.

(3) *PCAOB* means the Public Company Accounting Oversight Board.

(4) *Public company* means an insured depository institution or other company that has a class of securities registered with the U.S. Securities and Exchange Commission or the appropriate Federal banking agency under Section 12 of the Securities Exchange Act of 1934 and *nonpublic company* means an insured depository institution or other company that does not meet the definition of a *public company*.

(5) *SEC* means the U.S. Securities and Exchange Commission.

(6) *SOX* means the Sarbanes-Oxley Act of 2002.

§ 363.2 Annual reporting requirements.

(a) *Audited financial statements.* Each insured depository institution shall prepare annual financial statements in accordance with GAAP, which shall be audited by an independent public accountant. The annual financial statements must reflect all material correcting adjustments necessary to conform with GAAP that were identified by the independent public accountant.

(b) *Management report.* Each insured depository institution annually shall prepare, as of the end of the institution's most recent fiscal year, a management report that must contain the following:

(1) A statement of management's responsibilities for preparing the institution's annual financial statements, for establishing and maintaining an adequate internal control structure and procedures for financial reporting, and for complying with laws and regulations relating to safety and soundness that are designated by the FDIC and the appropriate Federal banking agency;

(2) An assessment by management of the insured depository institution's compliance with such laws and regulations during such fiscal year. The assessment must state management's conclusion as to whether the insured depository institution has complied with the designated safety and soundness laws and regulations during the fiscal year and disclose any noncompliance with these laws and regulations; and

(3) For an insured depository institution with consolidated total assets of $1 billion or more as of the beginning of such fiscal year, an assessment by management of the effectiveness of such internal control structure and procedures as of the end of such fiscal year that must include the following:

(i) A statement identifying the internal control framework [14] used by management to evaluate the effectiveness of the insured depository institution's internal control over financial reporting;

(ii) A statement that the assessment included controls over the preparation of regulatory financial statements in accordance with regulatory reporting instructions including identification of such regulatory reporting instructions; and

(iii) A statement expressing management's conclusion as to whether the insured depository institution's internal control over financial reporting is effective as of the end of its fiscal year. Management must disclose all material weaknesses in internal control over financial reporting, if any, that it has identified that have not been remediated prior to the insured depository institution's fiscal year-end. Management is precluded from concluding that the institution's internal control over financial reporting is effective if there are one or more material weaknesses.

(c) *Management report signatures.* Subject to the criteria specified in § 363.1(b):

(1) If the audited financial statements requirement specified in § 363.2(a) is satisfied at the insured depository institution level and the management report requirement specified in § 363.2(b) is satisfied in its entirety

---

[14] For example, in the United States, the Committee of Sponsoring Organizations (COSO) of the Treadway Commission has published *Internal Control—Integrated Framework,* including an addendum on safeguarding assets. Known as the COSO report, this publication provides a suitable and available framework for purposes of management's assessment.

Federal Deposit Insurance Corporation § 363.3

at the insured depository institution level, the management report must be signed by the chief executive officer and the chief accounting officer or chief financial officer of the insured depository institution;

(2) If the audited financial statements requirement specified in § 363.2(a) is satisfied at the holding company level and the management report requirement specified in § 363.2(b) is satisfied in its entirety at the holding company level, the management report must be signed by the chief executive officer and the chief accounting officer or chief financial officer of the holding company; and

(3) If the audited financial statements requirement specified in § 363.2(a) is satisfied at the holding company level and (i) the management report requirement specified in § 363.2(b) is satisfied in its entirety at the insured depository institution level or (ii) one or more of the components of the management report specified in § 363.2(b) is satisfied at the holding company level and the remaining components of the management report are satisfied at the insured depository institution level, the management report must be signed by the chief executive officers and the chief accounting officers or chief financial officers of both the holding company and the insured depository institution and the management report must clearly indicate the level (institution or holding company) at which each of its components is being satisfied.

§ 363.3 Independent public accountant.

(a) *Annual audit of financial statements.* Each insured depository institution shall engage an independent public accountant to audit and report on its annual financial statements in accordance with generally accepted auditing standards or the PCAOB's auditing standards, if applicable, and section 37 of the Federal Deposit Insurance Act (12 U.S.C. 1831n). The scope of the audit engagement shall be sufficient to permit such accountant to determine and report whether the financial statements are presented fairly and in accordance with GAAP.

(b) *Internal control over financial reporting.* For each insured depository institution with total assets of $1 billion or more at the beginning of the institution's fiscal year, the independent public accountant who audits the institution's financial statements shall examine, attest to, and report separately on the assertion of management concerning the effectiveness of the institution's internal control structure and procedures for financial reporting. The attestation and report shall be made in accordance with generally accepted standards for attestation engagements or the PCAOB's auditing standards, if applicable. The accountant's report must not be dated prior to the date of the management report and management's assessment of the effectiveness of internal control over financial reporting. Notwithstanding the requirements set forth in applicable professional standards, the accountant's report must include the following:

(1) A statement identifying the internal control framework used by the independent public accountant, which must be the same as the internal control framework used by management, to evaluate the effectiveness of the insured depository institution's internal control over financial reporting;

(2) A statement that the independent public accountant's evaluation included controls over the preparation of regulatory financial statements in accordance with regulatory reporting instructions including identification of such regulatory reporting instructions; and

(3) A statement expressing the independent public accountant's conclusion as to whether the insured depository institution's internal control over financial reporting is effective as of the end of its fiscal year. The report must disclose all material weaknesses in internal control over financial reporting that the independent public accountant has identified that have not been remediated prior to the insured depository institution's fiscal year-end. The independent public accountant is precluded from concluding that the insured depository institution's internal control over financial reporting is effective if there are one or more material weaknesses.

§ 363.4

(c) *Notice by accountant of termination of services.* An independent public accountant performing an audit under this part who ceases to be the accountant for an insured depository institution shall notify the FDIC, the appropriate Federal banking agency, and any appropriate State bank supervisor in writing of such termination within 15 days after the occurrence of such event, and set forth in reasonable detail the reasons for such termination. The written notice shall be filed at the place identified in § 363.4(f).

(d) *Communications with audit committee.* In addition to the requirements for communications with audit committees set forth in applicable professional standards, the independent public accountant must report the following on a timely basis to the audit committee:

(1) All critical accounting policies and practices to be used by the insured depository institution,

(2) All alternative accounting treatments within GAAP for policies and practices related to material items that the independent public accountant has discussed with management, including the ramifications of the use of such alternative disclosures and treatments, and the treatment preferred by the independent public accountant, and

(3) Other written communications the independent public accountant has provided to management, such as a management letter or schedule of unadjusted differences.

(e) *Retention of working papers.* The independent public accountant must retain the working papers related to the audit of the insured depository institution's financial statements and, if applicable, the evaluation of the institution's internal control over financial reporting for seven years from the report release date, unless a longer period of time is required by law.

(f) *Independence.* The independent public accountant must comply with the independence standards and interpretations of the AICPA, the SEC, and the PCAOB. To the extent that any of the rules within any one of these independence standards (AICPA, SEC, and PCAOB) is more or less restrictive than the corresponding rule in the other independence standards, the independent public accountant must comply with the more restrictive rule.

(g) *Peer reviews and inspection reports.* (1) Prior to commencing any services for an insured depository institution under this part, the independent public accountant must have received a peer review, or be enrolled in a peer review program, that meets acceptable guidelines. Acceptable peer reviews include peer reviews performed in accordance with the AICPA's Peer Review Standards and inspections conducted by the PCAOB.

(2) Within 15 days of receiving notification that a peer review has been accepted or a PCAOB inspection report has been issued, or before commencing any audit under this part, whichever is earlier, the independent public accountant must file two copies of the most recent peer review report and the public portion of the most recent PCAOB inspection report, if any, accompanied by any letters of comments, response, and acceptance, with the FDIC, Accounting and Securities Disclosure Section, 550 17th Street, NW., Washington, DC 20429, if the report has not already been filed. The peer review reports and the public portions of the PCAOB inspection reports will be made available for public inspection by the FDIC.

(3) Within 15 days of the PCAOB making public a previously nonpublic portion of an inspection report, the independent public accountant must file two copies of the previously nonpublic portion of the inspection report with the FDIC, Accounting and Securities Disclosure Section, 550 17th Street, NW., Washington, DC 20429. Such previously nonpublic portion of the PCAOB inspection report will be made available for public inspection by the FDIC.

§ 363.4 Filing and notice requirements.

(a) *Part 363 Annual Report.* (1) Each insured depository institution shall file with each of the FDIC, the appropriate Federal banking agency, and any appropriate State bank supervisor, two copies of its Part 363 Annual Report. A Part 363 Annual Report must contain audited comparative annual financial

Federal Deposit Insurance Corporation § 363.4

statements, the independent public accountant's report thereon, a management report, and, if applicable, the independent public accountant's attestation report on management's assessment concerning the institution's internal control structure and procedures for financial reporting as required by §§ 363.2(a), 363.3(a), 363.2(b), and 363.3(b), respectively.

(2) Subject to the criteria specified in § 363.1(b), each insured depository institution with consolidated total assets of less than $1 billion as of the beginning of its fiscal year that is required to file, or whose parent holding company is required to file, management's assessment of the effectiveness of internal control over financial reporting with the SEC or the appropriate Federal banking agency in accordance with section 404 of SOX must submit a copy of such assessment to the FDIC, the appropriate Federal banking agency, and any appropriate State bank supervisor with its Part 363 Annual Report as additional information. This assessment will not be considered part of the institution's Part 363 Annual Report.

(3)(i) Each insured depository institution that is neither a public company nor a subsidiary of a public company that meets the criterion specified in § 363.1(b)(1) shall file its Part 363 Annual Report within 120 days after the end of its fiscal year. (ii) Each insured depository institution that is a public company or a subsidiary of public company that meets the criterion specified in § 363.1(b)(1) shall file its Part 363 Annual Report within 90 days after the end of its fiscal year.

(b) *Public availability.* Except for the annual report in paragraph (a)(1) of this section and the peer reviews and inspection reports in § 363.3(g), which shall be available for public inspection, the FDIC has determined that all other reports and notifications required by this part are exempt from public disclosure by the FDIC.

(c) *Independent public accountant's letters and reports.* Except for the independent public accountant's reports that are included in its Part 363 Annual Report, each insured depository institution shall file with the FDIC, the appropriate Federal banking agency, and any appropriate State bank supervisor, a copy of any management letter or other report issued by its independent public accountant with respect to such institution and the services provided by such accountant pursuant to this part within 15 days after receipt. Such reports include, but are not limited to:

(1) Any written communication regarding matters that are required to be communicated to the audit committee (for example, critical accounting policies, alternative accounting treatments discussed with management, and any schedule of unadjusted differences);

(2) Any written communication of significant deficiencies and material weaknesses in internal control required by the AICPA's or the PCAOB's auditing standards;

(3) For institutions with total assets of less than $1 billion as of the beginning of their fiscal year that are public companies or subsidiaries of public companies that meet the criterion specified in § 363.1(b)(1), any independent public accountant's report on the audit of internal control over financial reporting required by section 404 of SOX and the PCAOB's auditing standards; and

(4) For all institutions that are public companies or subsidiaries of public companies that meet the criterion specified in § 363.1(b)(1), any independent public accountant's written communication of all deficiencies in internal control over financial reporting that are of a lesser magnitude than significant deficiencies required by the PCAOB's auditing standards.

(d) *Notice of engagement or change of accountants.* Each insured depository institution shall provide, within 15 days after the occurrence of any such event, written notice to the FDIC, the appropriate Federal banking agency, and any appropriate State bank supervisor of the engagement of an independent public accountant, or the resignation or dismissal of the independent public accountant previously engaged. The notice shall include a statement of the reasons for any such resignation or dismissal in reasonable detail.

(e) *Notification of late filing.* No extensions of time for filing reports required

§ 363.5

by § 363.4 shall be granted. An insured depository institution that is unable to timely file all or any portion of its Part 363 Annual Report or any other report or notice required by § 363.4 shall submit a written notice of late filing to the FDIC, the appropriate Federal banking agency, and any appropriate State bank supervisor. The notice shall disclose the institution's inability to timely file all or specified portions of its Part 363 Annual Report or any other report or notice and the reasons therefore in reasonable detail. The late filing notice shall also state the date by which the report or notice will be filed. The written notice shall be filed on or before the deadline for filing the Part 363 Annual Report or any other report or notice, as appropriate.

(f) *Place for filing.* The Part 363 Annual Report, any written notification of late filing, and any other report or notice required by § 363.4 should be filed as follows:

(1) *FDIC:* Appropriate FDIC Regional or Area Office (Division of Supervision and Consumer Protection), *i.e.,* the FDIC regional or area office in the FDIC region or area that is responsible for monitoring the institution or, in the case of a subsidiary institution of a holding company, the consolidated company. A filing made on behalf of several covered institutions owned by the same parent holding company should be accompanied by a transmittal letter identifying all of the institutions covered.

(2) *Office of the Comptroller of the Currency (OCC):* Appropriate OCC Supervisory Office.

(3) *Federal Reserve:* Appropriate Federal Reserve Bank.

(4) *Office of Thrift Supervision (OTS):* Appropriate OTS District Office.

(5) *State bank supervisor:* The filing office of the appropriate State bank supervisor.

§ 363.5 Audit committees.

(a) *Composition and duties.* Each insured depository institution shall establish an audit committee of its board of directors, the composition of which complies with paragraphs (a)(1), (2), and (3) of this section. The duties of the audit committee shall include the appointment, compensation, and oversight of the independent public accountant who performs services required under this part, and reviewing with management and the independent public accountant the basis for the reports issued under this part.

(1) Each insured depository institution with total assets of $1 billion or more as of the beginning of its fiscal year shall establish an independent audit committee of its board of directors, the members of which shall be outside directors who are independent of management of the institution.

(2) Each insured depository institution with total assets of $500 million or more but less than $1 billion as of the beginning of its fiscal year shall establish an audit committee of its board of directors, the members of which shall be outside directors, the majority of whom shall be independent of management of the institution. The appropriate Federal banking agency may, by order or regulation, permit the audit committee of such an insured depository institution to be made up of less than a majority of outside directors who are independent of management, if the agency determines that the institution has encountered hardships in retaining and recruiting a sufficient number of competent outside directors to serve on the audit committee of the institution.

(3) An outside director is a director who is not, and within the preceding fiscal year has not been, an officer or employee of the institution or any affiliate of the institution.

(b) *Committees of large institutions.* The audit committee of any insured depository institution with total assets of more than $3 billion as of the beginning of its fiscal year shall include members with banking or related financial management expertise, have access to its own outside counsel, and not include any large customers of the institution. If a large institution is a subsidiary of a holding company and relies on the audit committee of the holding company to comply with this rule, the holding company's audit committee shall not include any members who are large customers of the subsidiary institution.

(c) *Independent public accountant engagement letters.* (1) In performing its

Federal Deposit Insurance Corporation

duties with respect to the appointment of the institution's independent public accountant, the audit committee shall ensure that engagement letters and any related agreements with the independent public accountant for services to be performed under this part do not contain any limitation of liability provisions that:

(i) Indemnify the independent public accountant against claims made by third parties;

(ii) Hold harmless or release the independent public accountant from liability for claims or potential claims that might be asserted by the client insured depository institution, other than claims for punitive damages; or

(iii) Limit the remedies available to the client insured depository institution.

(2) Alternative dispute resolution agreements and jury trial waiver provisions are not precluded from engagement letters provided that they do not incorporate any limitation of liability provisions set forth in paragraph (c)(1) of this section.

APPENDIX A TO PART 363—GUIDELINES AND INTERPRETATIONS

TABLE OF CONTENTS

Introduction
Scope of Rule and Definitions (§ 363.1)
1. Measuring Total Assets
2. Insured Branches of Foreign Banks
3. Compliance by Holding Company Subsidiaries
4. Comparable Services and Functions
4A. Financial Reporting
Annual Reporting Requirements (§ 363.2)
5. Annual Financial Statements
5A. Institutions Merged out of Existence
6. Holding Company Statements
7. Insured Branches of Foreign Banks
7A. Compliance with Designated Laws and Regulations
8. Management Report
8A. Management's Reports on Internal Control over Financial Reporting under Part 363 and Section 404 of SOX
8B. Internal Control Reports and Part 363 Annual Reports for Acquired Businesses
8C. Management's Disclosure of Noncompliance with the Designated Laws and Regulations
9. Safeguarding of Assets
10. Standards for Internal Control
11. Service Organizations
12. Reserved
Role of Independent Public Accountant (§ 363.3)
13. General Qualifications
14. Reserved
15. Peer Review Guidelines
16. Reserved
17. Information to be Provided to the Independent Public Accountant
18. Attestation Report and Management Letters
18A. Internal Control Attestation Standards for Independent Auditors
19. Reviews with Audit Committee and Management
20. Notice of Termination
21. Reliance on Internal Auditors
Filing and Notice Requirements (§ 363.4)
22. Reserved
23. Notification of Late Filing
24. Public Availability
25. Reserved
26. Notices Concerning Accountants
Audit Committees (§ 363.5)
27. Composition
28. "Independent of Management" Considerations
29. Reserved
30. Holding Company Audit Committees
31. Duties
32. Banking or Related Financial Management Expertise
33. Large Customers
34. Access to Counsel
35. Transition Period for Forming and Restructuring Audit Committees
Other
36. Modifications of Guidelines

INTRODUCTION

Congress added section 36, "Early Identification of Needed Improvements in Financial Management" (section 36), to the Federal Deposit Insurance Act (FDI Act) in 1991.

The FDIC Board of Directors adopted 12 CFR part 363 of its rules and regulations (the Rule) to implement those provisions of section 36 that require rulemaking. The FDIC also approved these "Guidelines and Interpretations" (the Guidelines) and directed that they be published with the Rule to facilitate a better understanding of, and full compliance with, the provisions of section 36.

Although not contained in the Rule itself, some of the guidance offered restates or refers to statutory requirements of section 36 and is therefore mandatory. If that is the case, the statutory provision is cited.

Furthermore, upon adopting the Rule, the FDIC reiterated its belief that every insured depository institution, regardless of its size or charter, should have an annual audit of its financial statements performed by an independent public accountant, and should establish an audit committee comprised entirely of outside directors.

The following Guidelines reflect the views of the FDIC concerning the interpretation of

Pt. 363, App. A　　　　　　　　　　　　　　　　　　　　　　**12 CFR Ch. III (1-1-12 Edition)**

section 36. The Guidelines are intended to assist insured depository institutions (institutions), their boards of directors, and their advisors, including their independent public accountants and legal counsel, and to clarify section 36 and the Rule. It is recognized that reliance on the Guidelines may result in compliance with section 36 and the Rule which may vary from institution to institution. Terms which are not explained in the Guidelines have the meanings given them in the Rule, the FDI Act, or professional accounting and auditing literature.

SCOPE OF RULE AND DEFINITIONS (§ 363.1)

1. *Measuring Total Assets.* To determine whether this part applies, an institution should use total assets as reported on its most recent Report of Condition (Call Report) or Thrift Financial Report (TFR), the date of which coincides with the end of its preceding fiscal year. If its fiscal year ends on a date other than the end of a calendar quarter, it should use its Call Report or TFR for the quarter end immediately preceding the end of its fiscal year.

2. *Insured Branches of Foreign Banks.* Unlike other institutions, insured branches of foreign banks are not separately incorporated or capitalized. To determine whether this part applies, an insured branch should measure claims on non-related parties reported on its Report of Assets and Liabilities of U.S. Branches and Agencies of Foreign Banks (form FFIEC 002).

3. *Compliance by Holding Company Subsidiaries.* Audited consolidated financial statements and other reports or notices required by this part that are submitted by a holding company for any subsidiary institution should be accompanied by a cover letter identifying all subsidiary institutions subject to part 363 that are included in the holding company's submission. When submitting a Part 363 Annual Report, the cover letter should identify all subsidiary institutions subject to part 363 included in the consolidated financial statements and state whether the other annual report requirements (*i.e.*, management's statement of responsibilities, management's assessment of compliance with designated safety and soundness laws and regulations, and, if applicable, management's assessment of the effectiveness of internal control over financial reporting and the independent public accountant's attestation report on management's internal control assessment) are being satisfied for these institutions at the holding company level or at the institution level. An institution filing holding company consolidated financial statements as permitted by § 363.1(b)(1) also may report on changes in its independent public accountant on a holding company basis. An institution that does not meet the criteria in § 363.1(b)(2) must satisfy the remaining provisions of this part on an individual institution basis and maintain its own audit committee. Subject to the criteria in §§ 363.1(b)(1) and (2), a multi-tiered holding company may satisfy all of the requirements of this part at the top-tier or any mid-tier holding company level.

4. *Comparable Services and Functions.* Services and functions will be considered "comparable" to those required by this part if the holding company:

(a) Prepares reports used by the subsidiary institution to meet the requirements of this part;

(b) Has an audit committee that meets the requirements of this part appropriate to its largest subsidiary institution; and

(c) Prepares and submits management's assessment of compliance with the Designated Laws and Regulations defined in guideline 7A and, if applicable, management's assessment of the effectiveness of internal control over financial reporting based on information concerning the relevant activities and operations of those subsidiary institutions within the scope of the Rule.

4A. *Financial Statements Prepared for Regulatory Reporting Purposes.* (a) As set forth in § 363.3(c) of this part, "financial reporting," at a minimum, includes both financial statements prepared in accordance with generally accepted accounting principles for the insured depository institution or its holding company and financial statements prepared for regulatory reporting purposes. More specifically, financial statements prepared for regulatory reporting purposes include the schedules equivalent to the basic financial statements that are included in an insured depository institution's or its holding company's appropriate regulatory report (for example, Schedules RC, RI, and RI-A in the Consolidated Reports of Condition and Income (Call Report) for an insured bank; and Schedules SC and SO, and the Summary of Changes in Equity Capital section in Schedule SI in the Thrift Financial Report (TFR) for an insured thrift institution). For recognition and measurement purposes, financial statements prepared for regulatory reporting purposes shall conform to generally accepted accounting principles and section 37 of the Federal Deposit Insurance Act.

(b) Financial statements prepared for regulatory reporting purposes do not include regulatory reports prepared by a non-bank subsidiary of a holding company or an institution. For example, if a bank holding company or an insured depository institution owns an insurance subsidiary, financial statements prepared for regulatory reporting purposes would not include any regulatory reports that the insurance subsidiary is required to submit to its appropriate insurance regulatory agency.

Federal Deposit Insurance Corporation

ANNUAL REPORTING REQUIREMENTS (§ 363.2)

5. *Annual Financial Statements.* Each institution (other than an insured branch of a foreign bank) should prepare comparative annual consolidated financial statements (balance sheets and statements of income, changes in equity capital, and cash flows, with accompanying footnote disclosures) in accordance with GAAP for each of its two most recent fiscal years. Statements for the earlier year may be presented on an unaudited basis if the institution was not subject to this part for that year and audited statements were not prepared.

5A. *Institutions Merged Out of Existence.* An institution that is merged out of existence after the end of its fiscal year, but before the deadline for filing its Part 363 Annual Report (120 days after the end of its fiscal year for an institution that is neither a public company nor a subsidiary of a public company that meets the criterion specified in § 363.1(b)(1), and 90 days after the end of its fiscal year for an institution that is a public company or a subsidiary of a public company that meets the criterion specified in § 363.1(b)(1)), is not required to file a Part 363 Annual Report for the last fiscal year of its existence.

6. *Holding Company Statements.* Subject to the criterion specified in § 363.1(b)(1), subsidiary institutions may file copies of their holding company's audited financial statements filed with the SEC or prepared for their FR Y-6 Annual Report under the Bank Holding Company Act of 1956 to satisfy the audited financial statements requirement of § 363.2(a).

7. *Insured Branches of Foreign Banks.* An insured branch of a foreign bank should satisfy the financial statements requirement by filing one of the following for each of its two most recent fiscal years:

(a) Audited balance sheets, disclosing information about financial instruments with off-balance-sheet risk;

(b) Schedules RAL and L of form FFIEC 002, prepared and audited on the basis of the instructions for its preparation; or

(c) With written approval of the appropriate Federal banking agency, consolidated financial statements of the parent bank.

7A. *Compliance with Designated Laws and Regulations.* The designated laws and regulations are the Federal laws and regulations concerning loans to insiders and the Federal and, if applicable, State laws and regulations concerning dividend restrictions (the Designated Laws and Regulations). Table 1 to this Appendix A lists the designated Federal laws and regulations pertaining to insider loans and dividend restrictions (but not the State laws and regulations pertaining to dividend restrictions) that are applicable to each type of institution.

8. *Management Report.* Management should perform its own investigation and review of compliance with the Designated Laws and Regulations and, if required, the effectiveness of internal control over financial reporting. Management should maintain records of its determinations and assessments until the next Federal safety and soundness examination, or such later date as specified by the FDIC or the appropriate Federal banking agency. Management should provide in its assessment of the effectiveness of internal control over financial reporting, or supplementally, sufficient information to enable the accountant to report on its assertions. The management report of an insured branch of a foreign bank should be signed by the branch's managing official if the branch does not have a chief executive officer or a chief accounting or financial officer.

8A. *Management's Reports on Internal Control over Financial Reporting under Part 363 and Section 404 of SOX.* An institution with $1 billion or more in total assets as of the beginning of its fiscal year that is subject to both part 363 and the SEC's rules implementing section 404 of SOX (as well as a public holding company permitted under the holding company exception in § 363.1(b)(2) to file an internal control report on behalf of one or more subsidiary institutions with $1 billion or more in total assets) can choose either of the following two options for filing management's report on internal control over financial reporting.

(i) Management can prepare two separate reports on the institution's or the holding company's internal control over financial reporting to satisfy the FDIC's part 363 requirements and the SEC's section 404 requirements; or

(ii) Management can prepare a single report on internal control over financial reporting provided that it satisfies all of the FDIC's part 363 requirements and all of the SEC's section 404 requirements.

8B. *Internal Control Reports and Part 363 Annual Reports for Acquired Businesses.* Generally, the FDIC expects management's and the related independent public accountant's report on an institution's internal control over financial reporting to include controls at an institution in its entirety, including all of its consolidated entities. However, it may not always be possible for management to conduct an assessment of the internal control over financial reporting of an acquired business in the period between the consummation date of the acquisition and the due date of management's internal control assessment.

(a) In such instances, the acquired business's internal control structure and procedures for financial reporting may be excluded from management's assessment report and the accountant's attestation report on internal control over financial reporting.

However, the FDIC expects management's assessment report to identify the acquired business, state that the acquired business is excluded, and indicate the significance of this business to the institution's consolidated financial statements. Notwithstanding management's exclusion of the acquired business's internal control from its assessment, management should disclose any material change to the institution's internal control over financial reporting due to the acquisition of this business. Also, management may not omit the assessment of the acquired business's internal control from more than one annual part 363 assessment report on internal control over financial reporting. When the acquired business's internal control over financial reporting is excluded from management's assessment, the independent public accountant may likewise exclude this acquired business's internal control over financial reporting from the accountant's evaluation of internal control over financial reporting.

(b) If the acquired business is or has a consolidated subsidiary that is an insured depository institution subject to part 363 and the institution is not merged out of existence before the deadline for filing its Part 363 Annual Report (120 days after the end of its fiscal year for an institution that is neither a public company nor a subsidiary of a public company that meets the criterion specified in §363.1(b)(1), and 90 days after the end of its fiscal year for an institution that is a public company or a subsidiary of public company that meets the criterion specified in §363.1(b)(1)), the acquired institution must continue to comply with all of the applicable requirements of part 363, including filing its Part 363 Annual Report.

8C. *Management's Disclosure of Noncompliance with the Designated Laws and Regulations.* Management's disclosure of noncompliance, if any, with the Designated Laws and Regulations should separately indicate the number of instances or frequency of noncompliance with the Federal laws and regulations pertaining to insider loans and the Federal (and, if applicable, State) laws and regulations pertaining to dividend restrictions. The disclosure is not required to specifically identify by name the individuals (*e.g.*, officers or directors) who were responsible for or were the subject of any such noncompliance. However, the disclosure should include appropriate qualitative and quantitative information to describe the nature, type, and severity of the noncompliance and the dollar amount of the insider loan(s) or dividend(s) involved. Similar instances of noncompliance may be aggregated as to number of instances and quantified as to the dollar amounts or the range of dollar amounts of insider loans and/or dividends for which noncompliance occurred. Management may also wish to describe any corrective actions taken in response to the instances of noncompliance as well any controls or procedures that are being developed or that have been developed and implemented to prevent or detect and correct future instances of noncompliance on a timely basis.

9. *Safeguarding of Assets.* "Safeguarding of assets," as the term relates to internal control policies and procedures regarding financial reporting and which has precedent in accounting and auditing literature, should be encompassed in the management report and the independent public accountant's attestation discussed in guideline 18. Testing the existence of and compliance with internal controls on the management of assets, including loan underwriting and documentation, represents a reasonable implementation of section 36. The FDIC expects such internal controls to be encompassed by the assertion in the management report, but the term "safeguarding of assets" need not be specifically stated. The FDIC does not require the accountant to attest to the adequacy of safeguards, but does require the accountant to determine whether safeguarding policies exist.[15]

10. *Standards for Internal Control.* The management of each insured depository institution with $1 billion or more in total assets as of the beginning of its fiscal year should base its assessment of the effectiveness of the institution's internal control over financial reporting on a suitable, recognized control framework established by a body of experts that followed due-process procedures, including the broad distribution of the framework for public comment. In addition to being available to users of management's reports, a framework is suitable only when it:

• Is free from bias;

• Permits reasonably consistent qualitative and quantitative measurements of an institution's internal control over financial reporting;

• Is sufficiently complete so that those relevant factors that would alter a conclusion about the effectiveness of an institution's internal control over financial reporting are not omitted; and

• Is relevant to an evaluation of internal control over financial reporting.

In the United States, *Internal Control—Integrated Framework*, including its addendum on safeguarding assets, which was published by the Committee of Sponsoring Organizations of the Treadway Commission, and is known as the COSO report, provides a suitable and

---

[15] It is management's responsibility to establish policies concerning underwriting and asset management and to make credit decisions. The auditor's role is to test compliance with management's policies relating to financial reporting.

Federal Deposit Insurance Corporation

recognized framework for purposes of management's assessment. Other suitable frameworks have been published in other countries or may be developed in the future. Such other suitable frameworks may be used by management and the institution's independent public accountant in assessments, attestations, and audits of internal control over financial reporting.

11. *Service Organizations.* Although service organizations should be considered in determining if internal control over financial reporting is effective, an institution's independent public accountant, its management, and its audit committee should exercise independent judgment concerning that determination. Onsite reviews of service organizations may not be necessary to prepare the report required by the Rule, and the FDIC does not intend that the Rule establish any such requirement.

12. [Reserved]

ROLE OF INDEPENDENT PUBLIC ACCOUNTANT (§ 363.3)

13. *General Qualifications.* To provide audit and attest services to insured depository institutions, an independent public accountant should be registered or licensed to practice as a public accountant, and be in good standing, under the laws of the State or other political subdivision of the United States in which the home office of the institution (or the insured branch of a foreign bank) is located. As required by section 36(g)(3)(A)(i), the accountant must agree to provide copies of any working papers, policies, and procedures relating to services performed under this part.

14. [Reserved]

15. *Peer Review Guidelines.* The following peer review guidelines are acceptable:

(a) The external peer review should be conducted by an organization independent of the accountant or firm being reviewed, as frequently as is consistent with professional accounting practices;

(b) The peer review (other than a PCAOB inspection) should be generally consistent with AICPA Peer Review Standards; and

(c) The review should include, if available, at least one audit on an insured depository institution or consolidated depository institution holding company.

16. [Reserved]

17. *Information to be Provided to the Independent Public Accountant.* Attention is directed to section 36(h) which requires institutions to provide specified information to their accountants. An institution also should provide its accountant with copies of any notice that the institution's capital category is being changed or reclassified under section 38 of the FDI Act, and any correspondence from the appropriate Federal banking agency concerning compliance with this part.

18. *Attestation Report and Management Letters.* The independent public accountant should provide the institution with any management letter and, if applicable, an internal control attestation report (as required by section 36(c)(1)) at the conclusion of the audit. The independent public accountant's attestation report on internal control over financial reporting must specifically include a statement as to regulatory reporting. If a holding company subsidiary relies on its holding company's management report to satisfy the Part 363 Annual Report requirements, the accountant may attest to and report on the management's assertions in one report, without reporting separately on each subsidiary covered by the Rule. The FDIC has determined that management letters are exempt from public disclosure.

18A. *Internal Control Attestation Standards for Independent Auditors.* (a) § 363.3(b) provides that the independent public accountant's attestation and report on management's assertion concerning the effectiveness of an institution's internal control structure and procedures for financial reporting shall be made in accordance with generally accepted standards for attestation engagements or the PCAOB's auditing standards, if applicable. The standards that should be followed by the institution's independent public accountant concerning internal control over financial reporting for institutions with $1 billion or more in total assets can be summarized as follows:

(1) For an insured institution that is neither a public company nor a subsidiary of a public company, its independent public accountant need only follow the AICPA's attestation standards.

(2) For an insured institution that is a public company that is required to comply with the auditor attestation requirement of section 404 of SOX, its independent public accountant should follow the PCAOB's auditing standards.

(3) For an insured institution that is a public company but is not required to comply with the auditor attestation requirement of section 404 of SOX, its independent public accountant is not required to follow the PCAOB's auditing standards. In this case, the accountant need only follow the AICPA's attestation standards.

(4) For an insured institution that is a subsidiary of a public company that is required to comply with the auditor attestation requirement of section 404 of SOX, but is not itself a public company, the institution and its independent public accountant have flexibility in complying with the internal control requirements of part 363. If the conditions specified in § 363.1(b)(2) are met, management and the independent public accountant may choose to report on internal control over financial reporting at the consolidated holding

company level. In this situation, the independent public accountant's work would be performed for the public company in accordance with the PCAOB's auditing standards. Alternatively, the institution may choose to comply with the internal control reporting requirements of part 363 at the institution level and its independent public accountant could follow the AICPA's attestation standards.

(b) If an independent public accountant need only follow the AICPA's attestation standards, the accountant and the insured institution may instead agree to have the internal control attestation performed under the PCAOB's auditing standards.

19. *Reviews with Audit Committee and Management.* The independent public accountant should meet with the institution's audit committee to review the accountant's reports required by this part before they are filed. It also may be appropriate for the accountant to review its findings with the institution's board of directors and management.

20. *Notice of Termination.* The notice of termination required by §363.3(c) should state whether the independent public accountant agrees with the assertions contained in any notice filed by the institution under §363.4(d), and whether the institution's notice discloses all relevant reasons for the accountant's termination. Subject to the criterion specified in §363.1(b)(1) regarding compliance with the audited financial statements requirement at the holding company level, the independent public accountant for an insured depository institution that is a public company and files reports with its appropriate Federal banking agency, or is a subsidiary of a public company that files reports with the SEC, may submit the letter it furnished to management to be filed with the institution's or the holding company's current report (*e.g.,* SEC Form 8–K) concerning a change in accountant to satisfy the notice requirements of §363.3(c). Alternatively, if the independent public accountant confirms that management has filed a current report (*e.g.,* SEC Form 8–K) concerning a change in accountant that satisfies the notice requirements of §363.4(d) and includes an independent public accountant's letter that satisfies the requirements of §363.3(c), the independent public accountant may rely on the current report (*e.g.,* SEC Form 8–K) filed with the FDIC by management concerning a change in accountant to satisfy the notice requirements of §363.3(c).

21. *Reliance on Internal Auditors.* Nothing in this part or this Appendix is intended to preclude the ability of the independent public accountant to rely on the work of an institution's internal auditor.

FILING AND NOTICE REQUIREMENTS (§363.4)

22. [Reserved]

23. *Notification of Late Filing.* (a) An institution's submission of a written notice of late filing does not cure the requirement to timely file the Part 363 Annual Report or other reports or notices required by §363.4. An institution's failure to timely file is considered an apparent violation of part 363.

(b) If the late filing notice submitted pursuant to §363.4(e) relates only to a portion of a Part 363 Annual Report or any other report or notice, the insured depository institution should file the other components of the report or notice within the prescribed filing period together with a cover letter that indicates which components of its Part 363 Annual Report or other report or notice are omitted. An institution may combine the written late filing notice and the cover letter into a single notice that is submitted together with the other components of the report or notice that are being timely filed.

24. *Public Availability.* Each institution's Part 363 Annual Report should be available for public inspection at its main and branch offices no later than 15 days after it is filed with the FDIC. Alternatively, an institution may elect to mail one copy of its Part 363 Annual Report to any person who requests it. The Part 363 Annual Report should remain available to the public until the Part 363 Annual Report for the next year is available. An institution may use its Part 363 Annual Report under this part to meet the annual disclosure statement required by 12 CFR 350.3, if the institution satisfies all other requirements of 12 CFR Part 350.

25. [Reserved]

26. *Notices Concerning Accountants.* With respect to any selection, change, or termination of an independent public accountant, an institution's management and audit committee should be familiar with the notice requirements in §363.4(d) and guideline 20, and management should send a copy of any notice required under §363.4(d) to the independent public accountant when it is filed with the FDIC. An insured depository institution that is a public company and files reports required under the Federal securities laws with its appropriate Federal banking agency, or is a subsidiary of a public company that files such reports with the SEC, may use its current report (*e.g.,* SEC Form 8–K) concerning a change in accountant to satisfy the notice requirements of §363.4(d) subject to the criterion of §363.1(b)(1) regarding compliance with the audited financial statements requirement at the holding company level.

AUDIT COMMITTEES (§363.5)

27. *Composition.* The board of directors of each institution should determine whether each existing or potential audit committee member meets the requirements of section 36 and this part. To do so, the board of directors should maintain an approved set of written

Federal Deposit Insurance Corporation

Pt. 363, App. A

criteria for determining whether a director who is to serve on the audit committee is an outside director (as defined in § 363.5(a)(3)) and is independent of management. At least annually, the board of each institution should determine whether each existing or potential audit committee member is an outside director. In addition, at least annually, the board of an institution with $1 billion or more in total assets as of the beginning of its fiscal year should determine whether all existing and potential audit committee members are "independent of management of the institution" and the board of an institution with total assets of $500 million or more but less than $1 billion as of the beginning of its fiscal year should determine whether the majority of all existing and potential audit committee members are "independent of management of the institution." The minutes of the board of directors should contain the results of and the basis for its determinations with respect to each existing and potential audit committee member. Because an insured branch of a foreign bank does not have a separate board of directors, the FDIC will not apply the audit committee requirements to such branch. However, any such branch is encouraged to make a reasonable good faith effort to see that similar duties are performed by persons whose experience is generally consistent with the Rule's requirements for an institution the size of the insured branch.

28. *"Independent of Management" Considerations.* It is not possible to anticipate, or explicitly provide for, all circumstances that might signal potential conflicts of interest in, or that might bear on, an outside director's relationship to an insured depository institution and whether the outside director should be deemed "independent of management." When assessing an outside director's relationship with an institution, the board of directors should consider the issue not merely from the standpoint of the director himself or herself, but also from the standpoint of persons or organizations with which the director has an affiliation. These relationships can include, but are not limited to, commercial, banking, consulting, charitable, and family relationships. To assist boards of directors in fulfilling their responsibility to determine whether existing and potential members of the audit committee are "independent of management," paragraphs (a) through (d) of this guideline provide guidance for making this determination.

(a) If an outside director, either directly or indirectly, owns or controls, or has owned or controlled within the preceding fiscal year, 10 percent or more of any outstanding class of voting securities of the institution, the institution's board of directors should determine, and document its basis and rationale for such determination, whether such ownership of voting securities would interfere with the outside director's exercise of independent judgment in carrying out the responsibilities of an audit committee member, including the ability to evaluate objectively the propriety of management's accounting, internal control, and reporting policies and practices. Notwithstanding the criteria set forth in paragraphs (b), (c), and (d) of this guideline, if the board of directors determines that such ownership of voting securities would interfere with the outside director's exercise of independent judgment, the outside director will not be considered "independent of management."

(b) The following list sets forth additional criteria that, at a minimum, a board of directors should consider when determining whether an outside director is "independent of management." The board of directors may conclude that additional criteria are also relevant to this determination in light of the particular circumstances of its institution. Accordingly, an outside director will not be considered "independent of management" if:

(1) The director serves, or has served within the last three years, as a consultant, advisor, promoter, underwriter, legal counsel, or trustee of or to the institution or its affiliates.

(2) The director has been, within the last three years, an employee of the institution or any of its affiliates or an immediate family member is, or has been within the last three years, an executive officer of the institution or any of its affiliates.

(3) The director has participated in the preparation of the financial statements of the institution or any of its affiliates at any time during the last three years.

(4) The director has received, or has an immediate family member who has received, during any twelve-month period within the last three years, more than $100,000 in direct and indirect compensation from the institution, its subsidiaries, and its affiliates for consulting, advisory, or other services other than director and committee fees and pension or other forms of deferred compensation for prior service (provided such compensation is not contingent in any way on continued service). Direct compensation also would not include compensation received by the director for former service as an interim chairman or interim chief executive officer.

(5) The director or an immediate family member is a current partner of a firm that performs internal or external auditing services for the institution or any of its affiliates; the director is a current employee of such a firm; the director has an immediate family member who is a current employee of such a firm and who participates in the firm's audit, assurance, or tax compliance practice; or the director or an immediate family member was within the last three years (but no longer is) a partner or employee of such a firm and personally worked

on the audit of the insured depository institution or any of its affiliates within that time.

(6) The director or an immediate family member is, or has been within the last three years, employed as an executive officer of another entity where any of the present executive officers of the institution or any of its affiliates at the same time serves or served on that entity's compensation committee.

(7) The director is a current employee, or an immediate family member is a current executive officer, of an entity that has made payments to, or received payments from, the institution or any of its affiliates for property or services in an amount which, in any of the last three fiscal years, exceeds the greater of $200 thousand, or 5 percent of such entity's consolidated gross revenues. This would include payments made by the institution or any of its affiliates to not-for-profit entities where the director is an executive officer or where an immediate family member of the director is an executive officer.

(8) For purposes of paragraph (b) of this guideline:

(i) An "immediate family member" includes a person's spouse, parents, children, siblings, mothers- and fathers-in-law, sons- and daughters-in-law, brothers- and sisters-in-law, and anyone (other than domestic employees) who shares such person's home.

(ii) The term affiliate of, or a person affiliated with, a specified person, means a person or entity that directly, or indirectly through one or more intermediaries, controls, or is controlled by, or is under common control with, the person specified.

(iii) The term indirect compensation for consulting, advisory, or other services includes the acceptance of a fee for such services by a director's immediate family member or by an organization in which the director is a partner or principal that provides accounting, consulting, legal, investment banking, or financial advisory services to the institution, any of its subsidiaries, or any of its affiliates.

(iv) The terms direct and indirect compensation and payments do not include payments such as dividends arising solely from investments in the institution's equity securities, provided the same per share amounts are paid to all shareholders of that class; interest income from investments in the institution's deposit accounts and debt securities; loans from the institution that conform to all regulatory requirements applicable to such loans except that interest payments or other fees paid in association with such loans would be considered payments; and payments under non-discretionary charitable contribution matching programs.

(c) An insured depository institution that is a public company and a listed issuer (as defined in Rule 10A–3 of the Securities Exchange Act of 1934 (Exchange Act)), or is a subsidiary of a public company that meets the criterion specified in §363.1(b)(1) and is a listed issuer, may choose to use the definition of audit committee member independence set forth in the listing standards applicable to the public institution or its public company parent for purposes of determining whether an outside director is "independent of management."

(d) All other insured depository institutions may choose to use the definition of audit committee member independence set forth in the listing standards of a national securities exchange that is registered with the SEC pursuant to section 6 of the Exchange Act or a national securities association that is registered with the SEC pursuant to section 15A(a) of the Exchange Act for purposes of determining whether an outside director is "independent of management."

29. [Reserved]

30. *Holding Company Audit Committees.* (a) When an insured depository institution satisfies the requirements for the holding company exception specified in §§363.1(b)(1) and (2), the audit committee requirement of this part may be satisfied by the audit committee of the top-tier or any mid-tier holding company. Members of the audit committee of the holding company should meet all the membership requirements applicable to the largest subsidiary depository institution subject to part 363 and should perform all the duties of the audit committee of a subsidiary institution subject to part 363, even if the holding company directors are not directors of the institution.

(b) When an insured depository institution subsidiary with total assets of $1 billion or more as of the beginning of its fiscal year does not meet the requirements for the holding company exception specified in §§363.1(b)(1) and (2) or maintains its own separate audit committee to satisfy the requirements of this part, the members of the audit committee of the top-tier or any mid-tier holding company may serve on the audit committee of the subsidiary institution if they are otherwise independent of management of the subsidiary institution, and, if applicable, meet any other requirements for a large subsidiary institution covered by this part.

(c) When an insured depository institution with total assets of $500 million or more but less than $1 billion as of the beginning of its fiscal year does not meet the requirements for the holding company exception specified in §§363.1(b)(1) and (2) or maintains its own separate audit committee to satisfy the requirements of this part, the members of the audit committee of the top-tier or any mid-tier holding company may serve on the audit committee of the subsidiary institution provided a majority of the institution's audit

Federal Deposit Insurance Corporation

committee members are independent of management of the subsidiary institution.

(d) Officers and employees of a top-tier or any mid-tier holding company may not serve on the audit committee of a subsidiary institution subject to part 363.

31. *Duties.* The audit committee should perform all duties determined by the institution's board of directors and it should maintain minutes and other relevant records of its meetings and decisions. The duties of the audit committee should be appropriate to the size of the institution and the complexity of its operations, and, at a minimum, should include the appointment, compensation, and oversight of the independent public accountant; reviewing with management and the independent public accountant the basis for their respective reports issued under §§ 363.2(a) and (b) and §§ 363.3(a) and (b); reviewing and satisfying itself as to the independent public accountant's compliance with the required qualifications for independent public accountants set forth in §§ 363.3(f) and (g) and guidelines 13 through 16; ensuring that audit engagement letters comply with the provisions of § 363.5(c) before engaging an independent public accountant; being familiar with the notice requirements in § 363.4(d) and guideline 20 regarding the selection, change, or termination of an independent public accountant; and ensuring that management sends a copy of any notice required under § 363.4(d) to the independent public accountant when it is filed with the FDIC. Appropriate additional duties could include:

(a) Reviewing with management and the independent public accountant the scope of services required by the audit, significant accounting policies, and audit conclusions regarding significant accounting estimates;

(b) Reviewing with management and the accountant their assessments of the effectiveness of internal control over financial reporting, and the resolution of identified material weaknesses and significant deficiencies in internal control over financial reporting, including the prevention or detection of management override or compromise of the internal control system;

(c) Reviewing with management the institution's compliance with the Designated Laws and Regulations identified in guideline 7A;

(d) Discussing with management and the independent public accountant any significant disagreements between management and the independent public accountant; and

(e) Overseeing the internal audit function.

32. *Banking or Related Financial Management Expertise.* At least two members of the audit committee of a large institution shall have "banking or related financial management expertise" as required by section 36(g)(1)(C)(i). This determination is to be made by the board of directors of the insured depository institution. A person will be considered to have such required expertise if the person has significant executive, professional, educational, or regulatory experience in financial, auditing, accounting, or banking matters as determined by the board of directors. Significant experience as an officer or member of the board of directors or audit committee of a financial services company would satisfy these criteria. A person who has the attributes of an "audit committee financial expert" as set forth in the SEC's rules would also satisfy these criteria.

33. *Large Customers.* Any individual or entity (including a controlling person of any such entity) which, in the determination of the board of directors, has such significant direct or indirect credit or other relationships with the institution, the termination of which likely would materially and adversely affect the institution's financial condition or results of operations, should be considered a "large customer" for purposes of § 363.5(b).

34. *Access to Counsel.* The audit committee should be able to retain counsel at its discretion without prior permission of the institution's board of directors or its management. Section 36 does not preclude advice from the institution's internal counsel or regular outside counsel. It also does not require retaining or consulting counsel, but if the committee elects to do either, it also may elect to consider issues affecting the counsel's independence. Such issues would include whether to retain or consult only counsel not concurrently representing the institution or any affiliate, and whether to place limitations on any counsel representing the institution concerning matters in which such counsel previously participated personally and substantially as outside counsel to the committee.

35. *Transition Period for Forming and Restructuring Audit Committees.*

(a) When an insured depository institution's total assets as of the beginning of its fiscal year are $500 million or more for the first time and it thereby becomes subject to part 363, no regulatory action will be taken if the institution (1) develops and approves a set of written criteria for determining whether a director who is to serve on the audit committee is an outside director and is independent of management and (2) forms or restructures its audit committee to comply with § 363.5(a)(2) by the end of that fiscal year.

(b) When an insured depository institution's total assets as of the beginning of its fiscal year are $1 billion or more for the first time, no regulatory action will be taken if the institution forms or restructures its audit committee to comply with § 363.5(a)(1) by the end of that fiscal year, provided that the composition of its audit committee meets the requirements specified in

§ 363.5(a)(2) at the beginning of that fiscal year, if such requirements were applicable.

(c) When an insured depository institution's total assets as of the beginning of its fiscal year are $3 billion or more for the first time, no regulatory action will be taken if the institution forms or restructures its audit committee to comply with § 363.5(b) by the end of that fiscal year, provided that the composition of its audit committee meets the requirements specified in § 363.5(a)(1) at the beginning of that fiscal year, if such requirements were applicable.

OTHER

36. *Modifications of Guidelines.* The FDIC's Board of Directors has delegated to the Director of the FDIC's Division of Supervision and Consumer Protection authority to make and publish in the FEDERAL REGISTER minor technical amendments to the Guidelines in this Appendix and the guidance and illustrative reports in Appendix B, in consultation with the other appropriate Federal banking agencies, to reflect the practical experience gained from implementation of this part. It is not anticipated any such modification would be effective until affected institutions have been given reasonable advance notice of the modification. Any material modification or amendment will be subject to review and approval of the FDIC Board of Directors.

TABLE 1 TO APPENDIX A—DESIGNATED FEDERAL LAWS AND REGULATIONS APPLICABLE TO:

		National banks	State member banks	State non-member banks	Savings associations
Insider Loans—Parts and/or Sections of Title 12 of the United States Code
375a	Loans to Executive Officers of Banks	√	√	(A)	(A)
375b	Extensions of Credit to Executive Officers, Directors, and Principal Shareholders of Banks.	√	√	(A)	(A)
1468(b)	Extensions of Credit to Executive Officers, Directors, and Principal Shareholders.				√
1828(j)(2)	Extensions of Credit to Officers, Directors, and Principal Shareholders.			√	
1828(j)(3)(B)	Extensions of Credit to Officers, Directors, and Principal Shareholders.	(B)		(C)	
Parts and/or Sections of Title 12 of the Code of Federal Regulations
31	Extensions of Credit to Insiders	√			
32	Lending Limits	√			
215	Loans to Executive Officers, Directors, and Principal Shareholders of Member Banks.	√	√	(D)	(E)
337.3	Limits on Extensions of Credit to Executive Officers, Directors, and Principal Shareholders of Insured Nonmember Banks.			√	
563.43	Loans by Savings Associations to Their Executive Officers, Directors, and Principal Shareholders.				√
Dividend Restrictions—Parts and/or Sections of Title 12 of the United States Code
56	Prohibition on Withdrawal of Capital and Unearned Dividends.	√	√		
60	Dividends and Surplus Fund	√	√		
1467a(f)	Declaration of Dividend				√
1831o(d)(1)	Prompt Corrective Action—Capital Distributions Restricted.	√	√	√	√
Parts and/or Sections of Title 12 of the Code of Federal Regulations
5 Subpart E	Payment of Dividends	√			
6.6	Prompt Corrective Action—Restrictions on Undercapitalized Institutions.	√			
208.5	Dividends and Other Distributions		√		
208.45	Prompt Corrective Action—Restrictions on Undercapitalized Institutions.		√		

Federal Deposit Insurance Corporation   Pt. 363, App. B

TABLE 1 TO APPENDIX A—DESIGNATED FEDERAL LAWS AND REGULATIONS APPLICABLE TO:—Continued

		National banks	State member banks	State non-member banks	Savings associations
325.105	Prompt Corrective Action—Restrictions on Undercapitalized Institutions.			√	
563 Subpart E	Capital Distributions				√
565.6	Prompt Corrective Action—Restrictions on Undercapitalized Institutions.				√

A. Subsections (g) and (h) of section 22 of the Federal Reserve Act [12 U.S.C. 375a, 375b]
B. Applies only to insured Federal branches of foreign banks.
C. Applies only to insured State branches of foreign banks.
D. *See* 12 CFR 337.3.
E. *See* 12 CFR 563.43.

APPENDIX B TO PART 363—ILLUSTRATIVE MANAGEMENT REPORTS

TABLE OF CONTENTS

1. General
2. Reporting Scenarios for Institutions that are Holding Company Subsidiaries
3. Illustrative Statements of Management's Responsibilities
4. Illustrative Reports on Management's Assessment of Compliance with Designated Laws and Regulations
5. Illustrative Reports on Management's Assessment of Internal Control Over Financial Reporting
6. Illustrative Management Report—Combined Statement of Management's Responsibilities, Report on Management's Assessment of Compliance With Designated Laws and Regulations, and Report on Management's Assessment of Internal Control Over Financial Reporting
7. Illustrative Cover Letter—Compliance by Holding Company Subsidiaries

1. *General.* The reporting scenarios, illustrative management reports, and the cover letter (when complying at the holding company level) in Appendix B to part 363 are intended to assist managements of insured depository institutions in complying with the annual reporting requirements of § 363.2 and guideline 3, *Compliance by Holding Company Subsidiaries*, of Appendix A to part 363. However, use of the illustrative management reports and cover letter is not required. The managements of insured depository institutions are encouraged to tailor the wording of their management reports and cover letters to fit their particular circumstances, especially when reporting on material weaknesses in internal control over financial reporting or noncompliance with designated laws and regulations. Terms that are not explained in Appendix B have the meanings given them in part 363, the FDI Act, or professional accounting and auditing literature. Instructions to the preparer of the management reports are shown in brackets within the illustrative reports.

2. *Reporting Scenarios for Institutions that are Holding Company Subsidiaries.* (a) Subject to the criteria specified in § 363.1(b), an insured depository institution that is a subsidiary of a holding company has flexibility in satisfying the reporting requirements of part 363. When reporting at the holding company level, the management report, or the individual components thereof, should identify those subsidiary institutions that are subject to part 363 and the extent to which they are included in the scope of the management report or a component of the report. The following reporting scenarios reflect how an insured depository institution that meets the criteria set forth in § 363.1(b) could satisfy the annual reporting requirements of § 363.2. Other reporting scenarios are possible.

(i) An institution that is a subsidiary of a holding company may satisfy the requirements for audited financial statements; management's statement of responsibilities; management's assessment of the institution's compliance with the Federal laws and regulations pertaining to insider loans and the Federal and, if applicable, State laws and regulations pertaining to dividend restrictions; management's assessment of the effectiveness of internal control over financial reporting, if applicable; and the independent public accountant's attestation on management's assertion as to the effectiveness of internal control over financial reporting, if applicable, at the insured depository institution level.

(ii) An institution that is a subsidiary of a holding company may satisfy the requirements for audited financial statements; management's statement of responsibilities; management's assessment of the institution's compliance with the Federal laws and regulations pertaining to insider loans and the Federal and, if applicable, State laws and regulations pertaining to dividend restrictions; management's assessment of the effectiveness of internal control over financial reporting, if applicable; and the independent public accountant's attestation on management's assertion as to the effectiveness of internal control over financial reporting, if applicable, at the holding company level.

(iii) An institution that is a subsidiary of a holding company may satisfy the requirement for audited financial statements at the holding company level and may satisfy the requirements for management's statement of responsibilities; management's assessment of the institution's compliance with the Federal laws and regulations pertaining to insider loans and the Federal and, if applicable, State laws and regulations pertaining to dividend restrictions; management's assessment of the effectiveness of internal control over financial reporting, if applicable; and the independent public accountant's attestation on management's assertion as to the effectiveness of internal control over financial reporting, if applicable, at the insured depository institution level.

(iv) An institution that is a subsidiary of a holding company may satisfy the requirements for audited financial statements; management's statement of responsibilities; and management's assessment of the institution's compliance with the Federal laws and regulations pertaining to insider loans and the Federal and, if applicable, State laws and regulations pertaining to dividend restrictions at the insured depository institution level and may satisfy the requirements for the assessment by management of the effectiveness of internal control over financial reporting, if applicable; and the independent public accountant's attestation on management's assertion as to the effectiveness of internal control over financial reporting, if applicable, at the holding company level.

(b) For an institution with total assets of $1 billion or more as of the beginning of its fiscal year, the assessment by management of the effectiveness of internal control over financial reporting and the independent public accountant's attestation on management's assertion as to the effectiveness of internal control over financial reporting, if applicable, must both be performed at the same level, *i.e.*, either at the insured depository institution level or at the holding company level.

(c) Financial statements prepared for regulatory reporting purposes encompass the schedules equivalent to the basic financial statements in an institution's appropriate regulatory report, *e.g.*, the bank Consolidated Reports of Condition and Income (Call Report) and the Thrift Financial Report (TFR). Guideline 4A in Appendix A to part 363 identifies the schedules equivalent to the basic financial statements in the Call Report and TFR. When internal control assessments and attestations are performed at the holding company level, the FDIC believes that holding companies have flexibility in interpreting "financial reporting" as it relates to "regulatory reporting" and has not objected to several reporting approaches employed by holding companies to cover "regulatory reporting." Certain holding companies have had management's assessment and the accountant's attestation cover the schedules equivalent to the basic financial statements that are included in the appropriate regulatory report, *e.g.*, Call Report and the TFR, of each subsidiary institution subject to part 363. Other holding companies have had management's assessment and the accountant's attestation cover the schedules equivalent to the basic financial statements that are included in the holding company's year-end regulatory report (FR Y-9C report) to the Federal Reserve Board.

3. *Illustrative Statements of Management's Responsibilities.* The following illustrative statements of management's responsibilities satisfy the requirements of §363.2(b)(1).

(a) Statement Made at Insured Depository Institution Level

STATEMENT OF MANAGEMENT'S RESPONSIBILITIES

The management of ABC Depository Institution (the "Institution") is responsible for preparing the Institution's annual financial statements in accordance with generally accepted accounting principles; for establishing and maintaining an adequate internal control structure and procedures for financial reporting, including controls over the preparation of regulatory financial statements in accordance with the instructions for the [specify the regulatory report]; and for complying with the Federal laws and regulations pertaining to insider loans and the Federal and, if applicable, State laws and regulations pertaining to dividend restrictions.

ABC Depository Institution

John Doe, Chief Executive Officer
Date: _____

Jane Doe, Chief Financial Officer
Date: _____

(b) Statement Made at Holding Company Level

STATEMENT OF MANAGEMENT'S RESPONSIBILITIES

The management of BCD Holding Company (the "Company") is responsible for preparing the Company's annual financial statements in accordance with generally accepted accounting principles; for establishing and maintaining an adequate internal control

Federal Deposit Insurance Corporation

structure and procedures for financial reporting, including controls over the preparation of regulatory financial statements in accordance with the instructions for the [specify the regulatory report]; and for complying with the Federal laws and regulations pertaining to insider loans and the Federal and, if applicable, State laws and regulations pertaining to dividend restrictions. The following subsidiary institutions of the Company that are subject to Part 363 are included in this statement of management's responsibilities: [Identify the subsidiary institutions.]

BCD Holding Company

_____
John Doe, Chief Executive Officer
Date: _____

_____
Jane Doe, Chief Financial Officer
Date: _____

4. *Illustrative Reports on Management's Assessment of Compliance with Designated Laws and Regulations.* The following illustrative reports on management's assessment of compliance with Designated Laws and Regulations satisfy the requirements of § 363.2(b)(2).

(a) Statement Made at Insured Depository Institution Level—Compliance With Designated Laws and Regulations Pertaining to Insider Loans and Dividend Restrictions

MANAGEMENT'S ASSESSMENT OF COMPLIANCE WITH DESIGNATED LAWS AND REGULATIONS

The management of ABC Depository Institution (the "Institution") has assessed the Institution's compliance with the Federal laws and regulations pertaining to insider loans and the Federal and, if applicable, State laws and regulations pertaining to dividend restrictions during the fiscal year that ended on December 31, 20XX. Based upon its assessment, management has concluded that the Institution complied with the Federal laws and regulations pertaining to insider loans and the Federal and, if applicable, State laws and regulations pertaining to dividend restrictions during the fiscal year that ended on December 31, 20XX.

ABC Depository Institution

_____
John Doe, Chief Executive Officer
Date: _____

_____
Jane Doe, Chief Financial Officer
Date: _____

(b) Statement Made at Insured Depository Institution Level—Noncompliance With Designated Laws and Regulations Pertaining to Both Insider Loans and Dividend Restrictions

MANAGEMENT'S ASSESSMENT OF COMPLIANCE WITH DESIGNATED LAWS AND REGULATIONS

The management of ABC Depository Institution (the "Institution") has assessed the Institution's compliance with the Federal laws and regulations pertaining to insider loans and the Federal and, if applicable, State laws and regulations pertaining to dividend restrictions during the fiscal year that ended on December 31, 20XX. Based upon its assessment, management has determined that, because of the instance(s) of noncompliance noted below, the Institution did not comply with the Federal laws and regulations pertaining to insider loans and the Federal and, if applicable, State laws and regulations pertaining to dividend restrictions during the fiscal year that ended on December 31, 20XX.

[Identify and describe the instance or instances of noncompliance with the Federal laws and regulations pertaining to insider loans and the Federal and, if applicable, State laws and regulations pertaining to dividend restrictions, including appropriate qualitative and quantitative information to describe the nature, type, and severity of the noncompliance and the dollar amounts of the insider loan(s) and dividend(s) involved.]

ABC Depository Institution

_____
John Doe, Chief Executive Officer
Date: _____

_____
Jane Doe, Chief Financial Officer
Date: _____

(c) Statement Made at Insured Depository Institution Level—Compliance With Designated Laws and Regulations Pertaining to Insider Loans and Noncompliance With Designated Laws and Regulations Pertaining to Dividend Restrictions

MANAGEMENT'S ASSESSMENT OF COMPLIANCE WITH DESIGNATED LAWS AND REGULATIONS

The management of ABC Depository Institution (the "Institution") has assessed the Institution's compliance with the Federal laws and regulations pertaining to insider loans and the Federal and, if applicable, State laws and regulations pertaining to dividend restrictions during the fiscal year that ended on December 31, 20XX. Based upon its assessment, management has concluded that the Institution complied with the Federal laws and regulations pertaining to insider loans during the fiscal year that ended on

December 31, 20XX. Also, based upon its assessment, management has determined that, because of the instance(s) of noncompliance noted below, the Institution did not comply with the Federal and, if applicable, State laws and regulations pertaining to dividend restrictions during the fiscal year that ended on December 31, 20XX.

[Identify and describe the instance or instances of noncompliance with the Federal and, if applicable, State laws and regulations pertaining to dividend restrictions, including appropriate qualitative and quantitative information to describe the nature, type, and severity of the noncompliance and the dollar amount(s) of the dividend(s) involved.]

ABC Depository Institution

John Doe, Chief Executive Officer
Date: _____

Jane Doe, Chief Financial Officer
Date: _____

(d) Statement Made at Insured Depository Institution Level—Noncompliance With Designated Laws and Regulations Pertaining to Insider Loans and Compliance With Designated Laws and Regulations Pertaining to Dividend Restrictions

MANAGEMENT'S ASSESSMENT OF COMPLIANCE WITH DESIGNATED LAWS AND REGULATIONS

The management of ABC Depository Institution (the "Institution") has assessed the Institution's compliance with the Federal laws and regulations pertaining to insider loans and the Federal and, if applicable, State laws and regulations pertaining to dividend restrictions during the fiscal year that ended on December 31, 20XX. Based upon its assessment, management has determined that, because of the instance(s) of noncompliance noted below, the Institution did not comply with the Federal laws and regulations pertaining to insider loans during the fiscal year that ended on December 31, 20XX. Also, based upon its assessment, management has concluded that the Institution complied with the Federal and, if applicable, State laws and regulations pertaining to dividend restrictions during the fiscal year that ended on December 31, 20XX.

[Identify and describe the instance or instances of noncompliance with the Federal laws and regulations pertaining to insider loans, including appropriate qualitative and quantitative information to describe the nature, type, and severity of the noncompliance and the dollar amount(s) of the insider loan(s) involved.]

ABC Depository Institution

John Doe, Chief Executive Officer
Date: _____

Jane Doe, Chief Financial Officer
Date: _____

(e) Statement Made at Holding Company Level—Compliance With Designated Laws and Regulations Pertaining to Insider Loans and Dividend Restrictions

MANAGEMENT'S ASSESSMENT OF COMPLIANCE WITH DESIGNATED LAWS AND REGULATIONS

The management of BCD Holding Company (the "Company") has assessed the Company's compliance with the Federal laws and regulations pertaining to insider loans and the Federal and, if applicable, State laws and regulations pertaining to dividend restrictions during the fiscal year that ended on December 31, 20XX. Based upon its assessment, management has concluded that the Company complied with the Federal laws and regulations pertaining to insider loans and the Federal and, if applicable, State laws and regulations pertaining to dividend restrictions during the fiscal year that ended on December 31, 20XX. The following subsidiary institutions of the Company that are subject to Part 363 are included in this assessment of compliance with these designated laws and regulations: [Identify the subsidiary institutions.]

BCD Holding Company

John Doe, Chief Executive Officer
Date: _____

Jane Doe, Chief Financial Officer
Date: _____

(f) Statement Made at Holding Company Level—Noncompliance With Designated Laws and Regulations Pertaining to Both Insider Loans and Dividend Restrictions

MANAGEMENT'S ASSESSMENT OF COMPLIANCE WITH DESIGNATED LAWS AND REGULATIONS

The management of BCD Holding Company (the "Company") has assessed the Company's compliance with the Federal laws and regulations pertaining to insider loans and the Federal and, if applicable, State laws and regulations pertaining to dividend restrictions during the fiscal year that ended on December 31, 20XX. The following subsidiary institutions of the Company that are subject to Part 363 are included in this assessment of compliance with these designated laws and regulations: [Identify the subsidiary institutions.]

Based upon its assessment, management has determined that, because of the instance(s) of noncompliance noted below, the Company did not comply with the Federal

Federal Deposit Insurance Corporation

laws and regulations pertaining to insider loans and the Federal and, if applicable, State laws and regulations pertaining to dividend restrictions during the fiscal year that ended on December 31, 20XX.

[Identify and describe the instance or instances of noncompliance with the Federal laws and regulations pertaining to insider loans and the Federal and, if applicable, State laws and regulations pertaining to dividend restrictions, including appropriate qualitative and quantitative information to identify the subsidiary institutions of the Company that are subject to Part 363 that had instances of noncompliance and describe the nature, type, and severity of the noncompliance and the dollar amount(s) of the insider loan(s) and dividend(s) involved.]

BCD Holding Company

John Doe, Chief Executive Officer
Date: _____

Jane Doe, Chief Financial Officer
Date: _____

(g) Statement Made at Holding Company Level—Compliance With Designated Laws and Regulations Pertaining to Insider Loans and Noncompliance With Designated Laws and Regulations Pertaining to Dividend Restrictions

MANAGEMENT'S ASSESSMENT OF COMPLIANCE WITH DESIGNATED LAWS AND REGULATIONS

The management of BCD Holding Company (the "Company") has assessed the Company's compliance with the Federal laws and regulations pertaining to insider loans and the Federal and, if applicable, State laws and regulations pertaining to dividend restrictions during the fiscal year that ended on December 31, 20XX. The following subsidiary institutions of the Company that are subject to Part 363 are included in this assessment of compliance with these designated laws and regulations: [Identify the subsidiary institutions.]

Based upon its assessment, management has concluded that the Company complied with the Federal laws and regulations pertaining to insider loans during the fiscal year that ended on December 31, 20XX. Also, based upon its assessment, management has determined that, because of the instance(s) of noncompliance noted below, the Company did not comply with the Federal and, if applicable, State laws and regulations pertaining to dividend restrictions during the fiscal year that ended on December 31, 20XX.

[Identify and describe the instance or instances of noncompliance with the Federal and, if applicable, State laws and regulations pertaining to dividend restrictions, including appropriate qualitative and quantitative in-

Pt. 363, App. B

formation to identify the subsidiary institutions of the Company that are subject to Part 363 that had instances of noncompliance and describe the nature, type, and severity of the noncompliance and the dollar amount(s) of the dividend(s) involved.]

BCD Holding Company

John Doe, Chief Executive Officer
Date: _____

Jane Doe, Chief Financial Officer
Date: _____

(h) Statement Made at Holding Company Level—Noncompliance With Designated Laws and Regulations Pertaining to Insider Loans and Compliance With Designated Laws and Regulations Pertaining to Dividend Restrictions

MANAGEMENT'S ASSESSMENT OF COMPLIANCE WITH DESIGNATED LAWS AND REGULATIONS

The management of BCD Holding Company (the "Company") has assessed the Company's compliance with the Federal laws and regulations pertaining to insider loans and the Federal and, if applicable, State laws and regulations pertaining to dividend restrictions during the fiscal year that ended on December 31, 20XX. The following subsidiary institutions of the Company that are subject to Part 363 are included in this assessment of compliance with these designated laws and regulations: [Identify the subsidiary institutions.]

Based upon its assessment, management has determined that, because of the instance(s) of noncompliance noted below, the Company did not comply with the Federal laws and regulations pertaining to insider loans during the fiscal year that ended on December 31, 20XX. Also, based upon its assessment, management has concluded that the Company complied with the Federal and, if applicable, State laws and regulations pertaining to dividend restrictions during the fiscal year that ended on December 31, 20XX.

[Identify and describe the instance or instances of noncompliance with the Federal laws and regulations pertaining to insider loans, including appropriate qualitative and quantitative information to identify the subsidiary institutions of the Company that are subject to Part 363 that had instances of noncompliance and describe the nature, type, and severity of the noncompliance and the dollar amount(s) of the insider loan(s) involved.]

BCD Holding Company

John Doe, Chief Executive Officer
Date: _____

Pt. 363, App. B   **12 CFR Ch. III (1–1–12 Edition)**

Jane Doe, Chief Financial Officer
Date: _____

5. *Illustrative Reports on Management's Assessment of Internal Control Over Financial Reporting.* The following illustrative reports on management's assessment of internal control over financial reporting satisfy the requirements of § 363.2(b)(3).

(a) Statement Made at Insured Depository Institution Level—No Material Weaknesses

MANAGEMENT'S ASSESSMENT OF INTERNAL CONTROL OVER FINANCIAL REPORTING

ABC Depository Institution's (the "Institution") internal control over financial reporting is a process effected by those charged with governance, management, and other personnel, designed to provide reasonable assurance regarding the reliability of financial reporting and the preparation of reliable financial statements in accordance with accounting principles generally accepted in the United States of America and financial statements for regulatory reporting purposes, i.e., [specify the regulatory reports]. The Institution's internal control over financial reporting includes those policies and procedures that (1) pertain to the maintenance of records that, in reasonable detail, accurately and fairly reflect the transactions and dispositions of the assets of the Institution; (2) provide reasonable assurance that transactions are recorded as necessary to permit preparation of financial statements in accordance with accounting principles generally accepted in the United States of America and financial statements for regulatory reporting purposes, and that receipts and expenditures of the Institution are being made only in accordance with authorizations of management and directors of the Institution; and (3) provide reasonable assurance regarding prevention, or timely detection and correction of unauthorized acquisition, use, or disposition of the Institution's assets that could have a material effect on the financial statements.

Because of its inherent limitations, internal control over financial reporting may not prevent, or detect and correct misstatements. Also, projections of any evaluation of effectiveness to future periods are subject to the risk that controls may become inadequate because of changes in conditions, or that the degree of compliance with the policies and procedures may deteriorate.

Management is responsible for establishing and maintaining effective internal control over financial reporting including controls over the preparation of regulatory financial statements. Management assessed the effectiveness of the Institution's internal control over financial reporting, including controls over the preparation of regulatory financial statements in accordance with the instructions for the [specify the regulatory report], as of December 31, 20XX, based on the framework set forth by the Committee of Sponsoring Organizations of the Treadway Commission in *Internal Control—Integrated Framework*. Based upon its assessment, management has concluded that, as of December 31, 20XX, the Institution's internal control over financial reporting, including controls over the preparation of regulatory financial statements in accordance with the instructions for the [specify the regulatory report], is effective based on the criteria established in *Internal Control—Integrated Framework*.

Management's assessment of the effectiveness of internal control over financial reporting, including controls over the preparation of regulatory financial statements in accordance with the instructions for the [specify the regulatory report], as of December 31, 20XX, has been audited by [name of auditing firm], an independent public accounting firm, as stated in their report dated March XX, 20XY.

        ABC Depository Institution

John Doe, Chief Executive Officer
Date: _____

Jane Doe, Chief Financial Officer
Date: _____

(b) Statement Made at Insured Depository Institution Level—One or More Material Weaknesses

MANAGEMENT'S ASSESSMENT OF INTERNAL CONTROL OVER FINANCIAL REPORTING

ABC Depository Institution's (the "Institution") internal control over financial reporting is a process effected by those charged with governance, management, and other personnel, designed to provide reasonable assurance regarding the reliability of financial reporting and the preparation of reliable financial statements in accordance with accounting principles generally accepted in the United States of America and financial statements for regulatory reporting purposes, i.e., [specify the regulatory reports]. The Institution's internal control over financial reporting includes those policies and procedures that (1) pertain to the maintenance of records that, in reasonable detail, accurately and fairly reflect the transactions and dispositions of the assets of the Institution; (2) provide reasonable assurance that transactions are recorded as necessary to permit preparation of financial statements in accordance with accounting principles generally accepted in the United States of America and financial statements for regulatory reporting purposes, and that receipts

Federal Deposit Insurance Corporation

and expenditures of the Institution are being made only in accordance with authorizations of management and directors of the Institution; and (3) provide reasonable assurance regarding prevention, or timely detection and correction of unauthorized acquisition, use, or disposition of the Institution's assets that could have a material effect on the financial statements.

Because of its inherent limitations, internal control over financial reporting may not prevent, or detect and correct misstatements. Also, projections of any evaluation of effectiveness to future periods are subject to the risk that controls may become inadequate because of changes in conditions, or that the degree of compliance with the policies and procedures may deteriorate.

Management is responsible for establishing and maintaining effective internal control over financial reporting including controls over the preparation of regulatory financial statements. Management assessed the effectiveness of the Institution's internal control over financial reporting, including controls over the preparation of regulatory financial statements in accordance with the instructions for the [specify the regulatory report], as of December 31, 20XX, based on the framework set forth by the Committee of Sponsoring Organizations of the Treadway Commission in *Internal Control—Integrated Framework*. Because of the material weakness (or weaknesses) noted below, management determined that the Institution's internal control over financial reporting, including controls over the preparation of regulatory financial statements in accordance with the instructions for the [specify the regulatory report], was not effective as of December 31, 20XX.

[Identify and describe the material weakness or weaknesses.]

Management's assessment of the effectiveness of internal control over financial reporting, including controls over the preparation of regulatory financial statements in accordance with the instructions for the [specify the regulatory report], as of December 31, 20XX, has been audited by [name of auditing firm], an independent public accounting firm, as stated in their report dated March XX, 20XY.

ABC Depository Institution

John Doe, Chief Executive Officer
Date: _____

Jane Doe, Chief Financial Officer
Date: _____

Pt. 363, App. B

(c) Statement Made at Holding Company Level—No Material Weaknesses

MANAGEMENT'S ASSESSMENT OF INTERNAL CONTROL OVER FINANCIAL REPORTING

BCD Holding Company's (the "Company") internal control over financial reporting is a process designed and effected by those charged with governance, management, and other personnel, to provide reasonable assurance regarding the reliability of financial reporting and the preparation of reliable financial statements in accordance with accounting principles generally accepted in the United States of America and financial statements for regulatory reporting purposes, *i.e.*, [specify the regulatory reports]. The Company's internal control over financial reporting includes those policies and procedures that (1) pertain to the maintenance of records that, in reasonable detail, accurately and fairly reflect the transactions and dispositions of the assets of the Company; (2) provide reasonable assurance that transactions are recorded as necessary to permit preparation of financial statements in accordance with accounting principles generally accepted in the United States of America and financial statements for regulatory reporting purposes, and that receipts and expenditures of the Company are being made only in accordance with authorizations of management and directors of the Company; and (3) provide reasonable assurance regarding prevention, or timely detection and correction of unauthorized acquisition, use, or disposition of the Company's assets that could have a material effect on the financial statements.

Because of its inherent limitations, internal control over financial reporting may not prevent, or detect and correct misstatements. Also, projections of any evaluation of effectiveness to future periods are subject to the risk that controls may become inadequate because of changes in conditions, or that the degree of compliance with the policies and procedures may deteriorate.

Management is responsible for establishing and maintaining effective internal control over financial reporting including controls over the preparation of regulatory financial statements. Management assessed the effectiveness of the Company's internal control over financial reporting, including controls over the preparation of regulatory financial statements in accordance with the instructions for the [specify the regulatory report], as of December 31, 20XX, based on the framework set forth by the Committee of Sponsoring Organizations of the Treadway Commission in *Internal Control—Integrated Framework*. Based on that assessment, management concluded that, as of December 31, 20XX, the Company's internal control over financial reporting, including controls over the preparation of regulatory financial statements in accordance with the instructions for the [specify the regulatory report], is effective based on the criteria established in *Internal Control—Integrated Framework*. The following subsidiary institutions of the Company that are subject to Part 363 are included in this assessment of the effectiveness of internal control over financial reporting: [identify the subsidiary institutions.]

Management's assessment of the effectiveness of internal control over financial reporting, including controls over the preparation of regulatory financial statements in accordance with the instructions for the [specify the regulatory report], as of December 31, 20XX, has been audited by [name of auditing firm], an independent public accounting firm, as stated in their report dated March XX, 20XY.

BCD Holding Company

_____
John Doe, Chief Executive Officer
Date: _____

_____
Jane Doe, Chief Financial Officer
Date: _____

(d) Statement Made at Holding Company Level—One or More Material Weaknesses

MANAGEMENT'S ASSESSMENT OF INTERNAL CONTROL OVER FINANCIAL REPORTING

BCD Holding Company's (the "Company") internal control over financial reporting is a process effected by those charged with governance, management, and other personnel, designed to provide reasonable assurance regarding the reliability of financial reporting and the preparation of reliable financial statements in accordance with accounting principles generally accepted in the United States of America and financial statements for regulatory reporting purposes, i.e., [specify the regulatory reports]. The Company's internal control over financial reporting includes those policies and procedures that (1) pertain to the maintenance of records that, in reasonable detail, accurately and fairly reflect the transactions and dispositions of the assets of the Company; (2) provide reasonable assurance that transactions are recorded as necessary to permit preparation of financial statements in accordance with accounting principles generally accepted in the United States of America and financial statements for regulatory reporting purposes, and that receipts and expenditures of the Company are being made only in accordance with authorizations of management and directors of the Company; and (3) provide reasonable assurance regarding prevention, or timely detection and correction of unauthorized acquisition, use, or disposition of the Company's assets that could have a material effect on the financial statements.

Because of its inherent limitations, internal control over financial reporting may not prevent, or detect and correct misstatements. Also, projections of any evaluation of effectiveness to future periods are subject to the risk that controls may become inadequate because of changes in conditions, or that the degree of compliance with the policies and procedures may deteriorate.

Management is responsible for establishing and maintaining effective internal control over financial reporting including controls over the preparation of regulatory financial statements. Management assessed the effectiveness of the Company's internal control over financial reporting, including controls over the preparation of regulatory financial statements in accordance with the instructions for the [specify the regulatory report], as of December 31, 20XX, based on the framework set forth by the Committee of Sponsoring Organizations of the Treadway Commission in *Internal Control—Integrated Framework*. Because of the material weakness (or weaknesses) noted below, management determined that the Company's internal control over financial reporting, including controls over the preparation of regulatory financial statements in accordance with the instructions for the [specify the regulatory report], was not effective as of December 31, 20XX. The following subsidiary institutions of the Company that are subject to Part 363 are included in this assessment of the effectiveness of internal control over financial reporting: [Identify the subsidiary institutions.]

[Identify and describe the material weakness or weaknesses.]

Management's assessment of the effectiveness of internal control over financial reporting, including controls over the preparation of regulatory financial statements in accordance with the instructions for the [specify the regulatory report], as of December 31, 20XX, has been audited by [name of auditing firm], an independent public accounting firm, as stated in their report dated March XX, 20XY.

BCD Holding Company

_____
John Doe, Chief Executive Officer
Date: _____

_____
Jane Doe, Chief Financial Officer
Date: _____

6. *Illustrative Management Report—Combined Statement of Management's Responsibilities, Report on Management's Assessment of Compliance With Designated Laws and Regulations,*

Federal Deposit Insurance Corporation

Pt. 363, App. B

and *Report on Management's Assessment of Internal Control Over Financial Reporting*, if applicable. The following illustrative management reports satisfy the requirements of §§ 363.2(b)(1), (2), and (3).

(a) Management Report Made at Insured Depository Institution Level—Compliance With Designated Laws and Regulations Pertaining to Insider Loans and Dividend Restrictions and No Material Weaknesses in Internal Control Over Financial Reporting

MANAGEMENT REPORT

Statement of Management's Responsibilities

The management of ABC Depository Institution (the "Institution") is responsible for preparing the Institution's annual financial statements in accordance with generally accepted accounting principles; for establishing and maintaining an adequate internal control structure and procedures for financial reporting, including controls over the preparation of regulatory financial statements in accordance with the instructions for the [specify the regulatory report]; and for complying with the Federal laws and regulations pertaining to insider loans and the Federal and, if applicable, State laws and regulations pertaining to dividend restrictions.

Management's Assessment of Compliance With Designated Laws and Regulations

The management of the Institution has assessed the Institution's compliance with the Federal laws and regulations pertaining to insider loans and the Federal and, if applicable, State laws and regulations pertaining to dividend restrictions during the fiscal year that ended on December 31, 20XX. Based upon its assessment, management has concluded that the Institution complied with the Federal laws and regulations pertaining to insider loans and the Federal and, if applicable, State laws and regulations pertaining to dividend restrictions during the fiscal year that ended on December 31, 20XX.

Management's Assessment of Internal Control Over Financial Reporting

The Institution's internal control over financial reporting is a process effected by those charged with governance, management, and other personnel, designed to provide reasonable assurance regarding the reliability of financial reporting and the preparation of reliable financial statements in accordance with accounting principles generally accepted in the United States of America and financial statements for regulatory reporting purposes, *i.e.*, [specify the regulatory reports]. The Institution's internal control over financial reporting includes those policies and procedures that (1) pertain to the maintenance of records that, in reasonable detail, accurately and fairly reflect the transactions and dispositions of the assets of the Institution; (2) provide reasonable assurance that transactions are recorded as necessary to permit preparation of financial statements in accordance with accounting principles generally accepted in the United States of America and financial statements for regulatory reporting purposes, and that receipts and expenditures of the Institution are being made only in accordance with authorizations of management and directors of the Institution; and (3) provide reasonable assurance regarding prevention, or timely detection and correction of unauthorized acquisition, use, or disposition of the Institution's assets that could have a material effect on the financial statements.

Because of its inherent limitations, internal control over financial reporting may not prevent, or detect and correct misstatements. Also, projections of any evaluation of effectiveness to future periods are subject to the risk that controls may become inadequate because of changes in conditions, or that the degree of compliance with the policies and procedures may deteriorate.

Management assessed the effectiveness of the Institution's internal control over financial reporting, including controls over the preparation of regulatory financial statements in accordance with the instructions for the [specify the regulatory report], as of December 31, 20XX, based on the framework set forth by the Committee of Sponsoring Organizations of the Treadway Commission in *Internal Control—Integrated Framework*.

Based upon its assessment, management has concluded that, as of December 31, 20XX, the Institution's internal control over financial reporting, including controls over the preparation of regulatory financial statements in accordance with the instructions for the [specify the regulatory report], is effective based on the criteria established in *Internal Control—Integrated Framework*.

Management's assessment of the effectiveness of internal control over financial reporting, including controls over the preparation of regulatory financial statements in accordance with the instructions for the [specify the regulatory report], as of December 31, 20XX, has been audited by [name of auditing firm], an independent public accounting firm, as stated in their report dated March XX, 20XY.

ABC Depository Institution

John Doe, Chief Executive Officer
Date: _____

Jane Doe, Chief Financial Officer

Pt. 363, App. B

Date: _____

(b) Management Report Made at Holding Company Level—Compliance With Designated Laws and Regulations Pertaining to Insider Loans and Dividend Restrictions and No Material Weaknesses in Internal Control Over Financial Reporting

MANAGEMENT REPORT

[*Instruction*—The following illustrative introductory paragraph for the management report is applicable only if the same group of subsidiary institutions of the holding company that are subject to Part 363 are included in all three components of the management report required by Part 363: the statement of management's responsibilities, the report on management's assessment of compliance with the Designated Laws and Regulations pertaining to insider loans and dividend restrictions, and the report on management's assessment of internal control over financial reporting.]

In this management report, the following subsidiary institutions of the BCD Holding Company (the "Company") that are subject to Part 363 are included in the statement of management's responsibilities; the report on management's assessment of compliance with the Federal laws and regulations pertaining to insider loans and the Federal and, if applicable, State laws and regulations pertaining to dividend restrictions; and the report on management's assessment of internal control over financial reporting: [Identify the subsidiary institutions.]

[*Instruction*—The following illustrative introductory paragraph for the management report is applicable if the same group of subsidiary institutions of the holding company that are subject to Part 363 are included in the statement of management's responsibilities and management's assessment of compliance with the Designated Laws and Regulations pertaining to insider loans and dividend restrictions, but only some of the subsidiary institutions in the group are included in management's assessment of internal control over financial reporting.]

In this management report, the following subsidiary institutions of BCD Holding Company (the "Company") that are subject to Part 363 are included in the statement of management's responsibilities and the report on management's assessment of compliance with the Federal laws and regulations pertaining to insider loans and the Federal and, if applicable, State laws and regulations pertaining to dividend restrictions: [Identify the subsidiary institutions.] In addition, the following subsidiary institutions of the Company that are subject to Part 363 are included in the report on management's assessment of internal control over financial reporting: [Identify the subsidiary institutions.]

Statement of Management's Responsibilities

The management of the Company is responsible for preparing the Company's annual financial statements in accordance with generally accepted accounting principles; for establishing and maintaining an adequate internal control structure and procedures for financial reporting, including controls over the preparation of regulatory financial statements in accordance with the instructions for the [specify the regulatory report]; and for complying with the Federal laws and regulations pertaining to insider loans and the Federal and, if applicable, State laws and regulations pertaining to dividend restrictions.

Management's Assessment of Compliance With Designated Laws and Regulations

The management of the Company has assessed the Company's compliance with the Federal laws and regulations pertaining to insider loans and the Federal and, if applicable, State laws and regulations pertaining to dividend restrictions during the fiscal year that ended on December 31, 20XX. Based upon its assessment, management has concluded that the Company complied with the Federal laws and regulations pertaining to insider loans and the Federal and, if applicable, State laws and regulations pertaining to dividend restrictions during the fiscal year that ended on December 31, 20XX.

Management's Assessment of Internal Control Over Financial Reporting

The Company's internal control over financial reporting is a process effected by those charged with governance, management, and other personnel, designed to provide reasonable assurance regarding the reliability of financial reporting and the preparation of reliable financial statements in accordance with accounting principles generally accepted in the United States of America and financial statements for regulatory reporting purposes, *i.e.*, [specify the regulatory reports]. The Company's internal control over financial reporting includes those policies and procedures that (1) pertain to the maintenance of records that, in reasonable detail, accurately and fairly reflect the transactions and dispositions of the assets of the Company; (2) provide reasonable assurance that transactions are recorded as necessary to permit preparation of financial statements in accordance with accounting principles generally accepted in the United States of America and financial statements for regulatory reporting purposes, and that receipts and expenditures of the Company are being made only in accordance with authorizations

Federal Deposit Insurance Corporation

of management and directors of the Company; and (3) provide reasonable assurance regarding prevention, or timely detection and correction of unauthorized acquisition, use, or disposition of the Company's assets that could have a material effect on the financial statements.

Because of its inherent limitations, internal control over financial reporting may not prevent, or detect and correct misstatements. Also, projections of any evaluation of effectiveness to future periods are subject to the risk that controls may become inadequate because of changes in conditions, or that the degree of compliance with the policies and procedures may deteriorate.

Management assessed the effectiveness of the Company's internal control over financial reporting, including controls over the preparation of regulatory financial statements in accordance with the instructions for the [specify the regulatory report], as of December 31, 20XX, based on the framework set forth by the Committee of Sponsoring Organizations of the Treadway Commission in *Internal Control—Integrated Framework*. Based upon its assessment, management has concluded that, as of December 31, 20XX, the Company's internal control over financial reporting, including controls over the preparation of regulatory financial statements in accordance with the instructions for the [specify the regulatory report], is effective based on the criteria established in *Internal Control—Integrated Framework*.

Management's assessment of the effectiveness of internal control over financial reporting, including controls over the preparation of regulatory financial statements in accordance with the instructions for the [specify the regulatory report], as of December 31, 20XX, has been audited by [name of auditing firm], an independent public accounting firm, as stated in their report dated March XX, 20XY.

BCD Holding Company

_____
John Doe, Chief Executive Officer
Date: _____

_____
Jane Doe, Chief Financial Officer
Date: _____

7. *Illustrative Cover Letter—Compliance by Holding Company Subsidiaries.* The following illustrative cover letter satisfies the requirements of guideline 3, *Compliance by Holding Company Subsidiaries*, of Appendix A to part 363.

To: (Appropriate FDIC Regional or Area Office) Division of Supervision and Consumer Protection, FDIC, and (Appropriate District or Regional Office of the Primary Federal Regulator(s), if not the FDIC), and

(Appropriate State Bank Supervisor(s), if applicable)

Dear [Insert addressees]:

BCD Holding Company (the "Company") is filing two copies of the Part 363 Annual Report for the fiscal year ended December 31, 20XX, on behalf of its insured depository institution subsidiaries listed in the chart below that are subject to Part 363. The Part 363 Annual Report contains audited comparative annual financial statements, the independent public accountant's report on the audited financial statements, management's statement of responsibilities, management's assessment of compliance with the Designated Laws and Regulations pertaining to insider loans and dividend restrictions, and [if applicable] management's assessment of and the independent public accountant's attestation report on internal control over financial reporting. The chart below also indicates the level (institution or holding company) at which the requirements of Part 363 are being satisfied for each listed insured depository institution subsidiary. [If applicable] The Company's other insured depository institution subsidiaries that are subject to Part 363, which comply with all of the Part 363 annual reporting requirements at the institution level, have filed [or will file] their Part 363 Annual Reports separately.

Institutions subject to Part 363	Audited financial statements	Management's statement of responsibilities	Management's assessment of compliance with designated laws and regulations	Management's internal control assessment	Independent auditor's internal control attestation report
ABC Depository Institution.	Holding Company Level.	Holding Company Level.	Holding Company Level.	Holding Company Level.	Holding Company Level.
DEF Depository Institution.	Holding Company Level.	Institution Level	Institution Level	Institution Level	Institution Level.

If you have any questions regarding the annual report [or reports] of the Company's insured depository institution subsidiaries subject to Part 363 or if you need any further information, you may contact me at 987-654-3210.

BCD Holding Company

Date: _____
[Insert officer's name and title.]

PART 364—STANDARDS FOR SAFETY AND SOUNDNESS

Sec.
364.100 Purpose.
364.101 Standards for safety and soundness.
APPENDIX A TO PART 364—INTERAGENCY GUIDELINES ESTABLISHING STANDARDS FOR SAFETY AND SOUNDNESS
APPENDIX B TO PART 364—INTERAGENCY GUIDELINES ESTABLISHING INFORMATION SECURITY STANDARDS

AUTHORITY: 12 U.S.C. 1818 and 1819 (Tenth), 1831p–1; 15 U.S.C. 1681b, 1681s, 1681w, 6801(b), 6805(b)(1).

SOURCE: 60 FR 35685, July 10, 1995, unless outherwise noted.

§ 364.100 Purpose.

Section 39 of the Federal Deposit Insurance Act requires the Federal Deposit Insurance Corporation to establish safety and soundness standards. Pursuant to section 39, this part establishes safety and soundness standards by guideline.

§ 364.101 Standards for safety and soundness.

(a) *General standards.* The Interagency Guidelines Establishing Standards for Safety and Soundness prescribed pursuant to section 39 of the Federal Deposit Insurance Act (12 U.S.C. 1831p–1), as set forth as appendix A to this part, apply to all insured state nonmember banks and to state-licensed insured branches of foreign banks, that are subject to the provisions of section 39 of the Federal Deposit Insurance Act.

(b) *Interagency Guidelines Establishing Information Security Standards.* The Interagency Guidelines Establishing Information Security Standards prescribed pursuant to section 39 of the Federal Deposit Insurance Act (12 U.S.C. 1831p–1), and sections 501 and 505(b) of the Gramm-Leach-Bliley Act (15 U.S.C. 6801, 6805(b)), and with respect to the proper disposal of consumer information requirements pursuant to section 628 of the Fair Credit Reporting Act (15 U.S.C. 1681w), as set forth in appendix B to this part, apply to all insured state nonmember banks, insured state licensed branches of foreign banks, and any subsidiaries of such entities (except brokers, dealers, persons providing insurance, investment companies, and investment advisers). The interagency regulations and guidelines on identity theft detection, prevention, and mitigation prescribed pursuant to section 114 of the Fair and Accurate Credit Transactions Act of 2003, 15 U.S.C. 1681m(e), are set forth in §§ 334.90, 334.91, and appendix J of part 334.

[63 FR 55488, Oct. 15, 1998, as amended at 66 FR 8638, Feb. 1, 2001; 69 FR 77619, Dec. 28, 2004; 72 FR 63764, Nov. 9, 2007]

APPENDIX A TO PART 364—INTERAGENCY GUIDELINES ESTABLISHING STANDARDS FOR SAFETY AND SOUNDNESS

TABLE OF CONTENTS

I. Introduction

A. Preservation of existing authority.
B. Definitions.

II. Operational and Managerial Standards

A. Internal controls and information systems.
B. Internal audit system.
C. Loan documentation.
D. Credit underwriting.
E. Interest rate exposure.
F. Asset growth.
G. Asset quality.
H. Earnings.
I. Compensation, fees and benefits.

III. Prohibition on Compensation That Constitutes an Unsafe and Unsound Practice

A. Excessive compensation.
B. Compensation leading to material financial loss.

I. INTRODUCTION

i. Section 39 of the Federal Deposit Insurance Act[1] (FDI Act) requires each Federal banking agency (collectively, the agencies)

---

[1] Section 39 of the Federal Deposit Insurance Act (12 U.S.C. 1831p–1) was added by section 132 of the Federal Deposit Insurance Corporation Improvement Act of 1991 (FDICIA), Pub. L. 102–242, 105 Stat. 2236 (1991), and amended by section 956 of the Housing and Community Development Act of 1992, Pub. L. 102–550, 106 Stat. 3895 (1992) and section 318 of the Riegle Community Development and Regulatory Improvement Act of 1994, Pub. L. 103–325, 108 Stat. 2160 (1994).

Federal Deposit Insurance Corporation

to establish certain safety and soundness standards by regulation or by guideline for all insured depository institutions. Under section 39, the agencies must establish three types of standards: (1) Operational and managerial standards; (2) compensation standards; and (3) such standards relating to asset quality, earnings, and stock valuation as they determine to be appropriate.

ii. Section 39(a) requires the agencies to establish operational and managerial standards relating to: (1) Internal controls, information systems and internal audit systems, in accordance with section 36 of the FDI Act (12 U.S.C. 1831m); (2) loan documentation; (3) credit underwriting; (4) interest rate exposure; (5) asset growth; and (6) compensation, fees, and benefits, in accordance with subsection (c) of section 39. Section 39(b) requires the agencies to establish standards relating to asset quality, earnings, and stock valuation that the agencies determine to be appropriate.

iii. Section 39(c) requires the agencies to establish standards prohibiting as an unsafe and unsound practice any compensatory arrangement that would provide any executive officer, employee, director, or principal shareholder of the institution with excessive compensation, fees or benefits and any compensatory arrangement that could lead to material financial loss to an institution. Section 39(c) also requires that the agencies establish standards that specify when compensation is excessive.

iv. If an agency determines that an institution fails to meet any standard established by guideline under subsection (a) or (b) of section 39, the agency may require the institution to submit to the agency an acceptable plan to achieve compliance with the standard. In the event that an institution fails to submit an acceptable plan within the time allowed by the agency or fails in any material respect to implement an accepted plan, the agency must, by order, require the institution to correct the deficiency. The agency may, and in some cases must, take other supervisory actions until the deficiency has been corrected.

v. The agencies have adopted amendments to their rules and regulations to establish deadlines for submission and review of compliance plans.[2]

vi. The following Guidelines set out the safety and soundness standards that the agencies use to identify and address problems at insured depository institutions before capital becomes impaired. The agencies believe that the standards adopted in these Guidelines serve this end without dictating how institutions must be managed and operated. These standards are designed to identify potential safety and soundness concerns and ensure that action is taken to address those concerns before they pose a risk to the Deposit Insurance Fund.

A. *Preservation of Existing Authority*

Neither section 39 nor these Guidelines in any way limits the authority of the agencies to address unsafe or unsound practices, violations of law, unsafe or unsound conditions, or other practices. Action under section 39 and these Guidelines may be taken independently of, in conjunction with, or in addition to any other enforcement action available to the agencies. Nothing in these Guidelines limits the authority of the FDIC pursuant to section 38(i)(2)(F) of the FDI Act (12 U.S.C. 1831(o)) and Part 325 of Title 12 of the Code of Federal Regulations.

B. *Definitions*

1. *In general.* For purposes of these Guidelines, except as modified in the Guidelines or unless the context otherwise requires, the terms used have the same meanings as set forth in sections 3 and 39 of the FDI Act (12 U.S.C. 1813 and 1831p-1).

2. *Board of directors*, in the case of a state-licensed insured branch of a foreign bank and in the case of a federal branch of a foreign bank, means the managing official in charge of the insured foreign branch.

3. *Compensation* means all direct and indirect payments or benefits, both cash and non-cash, granted to or for the benefit of any executive officer, employee, director, or principal shareholder, including but not limited to payments or benefits derived from an employment contract, compensation or benefit agreement, fee arrangement, perquisite, stock option plan, postemployment benefit, or other compensatory arrangement.

4. *Director* shall have the meaning described in 12 CFR 215.2(c).[3]

5. *Executive officer* shall have the meaning described in 12 CFR 215.2(d).[4]

---

[2] For the Office of the Comptroller of the Currency, these regulations appear at 12 CFR Part 30; for the Board of Governors of the Federal Reserve System, these regulations appear at 12 CFR Part 263; for the Federal Deposit Insurance Corporation, these regulations appear at 12 CFR Part 308, subpart R, and for the Office of Thrift Supervision, these regulations appear at 12 CFR Part 570.

[3] In applying these definitions for savings associations, pursuant to 12 U.S.C. 1464, savings associations shall use the terms "savings association" and "insured savings association" in place of the terms "member bank" and "insured bank".

[4] See footnote 3 in section I.B.4. of this appendix.

6. *Principal shareholder* shall have the meaning described in 12 CFR 215.2(*l*).[5]

II. OPERATIONAL AND MANAGERIAL STANDARDS

A. *Internal controls and information systems.* An institution should have internal controls and information systems that are appropriate to the size of the institution and the nature, scope and risk of its activities and that provide for:

1. An organizational structure that establishes clear lines of authority and responsibility for monitoring adherence to established policies;
2. Effective risk assessment;
3. Timely and accurate financial, operational and regulatory reports;
4. Adequate procedures to safeguard and manage assets; and
5. Compliance with applicable laws and regulations.

B. *Internal audit system.* An institution should have an internal audit system that is appropriate to the size of the institution and the nature and scope of its activities and that provides for:

1. Adequate monitoring of the system of internal controls through an internal audit function. For an institution whose size, complexity or scope of operations does not warrant a full scale internal audit function, a system of independent reviews of key internal controls may be used;
2. Independence and objectivity;
3. Qualified persons;
4. Adequate testing and review of information systems;
5. Adequate documentation of tests and findings and any corrective actions;
6. Verification and review of management actions to address material weaknesses; and
7. Review by the institution's audit committee or board of directors of the effectiveness of the internal audit systems.

C. *Loan documentation.* An institution should establish and maintain loan documentation practices that:

1. Enable the institution to make an informed lending decision and to assess risk, as necessary, on an ongoing basis;
2. Identify the purpose of a loan and the source of repayment, and assess the ability of the borrower to repay the indebtedness in a timely manner;
3. Ensure that any claim against a borrower is legally enforceable;
4. Demonstrate appropriate administration and monitoring of a loan; and
5. Take account of the size and complexity of a loan.

D. *Credit underwriting.* An institution should establish and maintain prudent credit underwriting practices that:

1. Are commensurate with the types of loans the institution will make and consider the terms and conditions under which they will be made;
2. Consider the nature of the markets in which loans will be made;
3. Provide for consideration, prior to credit commitment, of the borrower's overall financial condition and resources, the financial responsibility of any guarantor, the nature and value of any underlying collateral, and the borrower's character and willingness to repay as agreed;
4. Establish a system of independent, ongoing credit review and appropriate communication to management and to the board of directors;
5. Take adequate account of concentration of credit risk; and
6. Are appropriate to the size of the institution and the nature and scope of its activities.

E. *Interest rate exposure.* An institution should:

1. Manage interest rate risk in a manner that is appropriate to the size of the institution and the complexity of its assets and liabilities; and
2. Provide for periodic reporting to management and the board of directors regarding interest rate risk with adequate information for management and the board of directors to assess the level of risk.

F. *Asset growth.* An institution's asset growth should be prudent and consider:

1. The source, volatility and use of the funds that support asset growth;
2. Any increase in credit risk or interest rate risk as a result of growth; and
3. The effect of growth on the institution's capital.

G. *Asset quality.* An insured depository institution should establish and maintain a system that is commensurate with the institution's size and the nature and scope of its operations to identify problem assets and prevent deterioration in those assets. The institution should:

1. Conduct periodic asset quality reviews to identify problem assets;
2. Estimate the inherent losses in those assets and establish reserves that are sufficient to absorb estimated losses;
3. Compare problem asset totals to capital;
4. Take appropriate corrective action to resolve problem assets;
5. Consider the size and potential risks of material asset concentrations; and
6. Provide periodic asset reports with adequate information for management and the board of directors to assess the level of asset risk.

H. *Earnings.* An insured depository institution should establish and maintain a system

---

[5] See footnote 3 in section I.B.4. of this appendix.

Federal Deposit Insurance Corporation

that is commensurate with the institution's size and the nature and scope of its operations to evaluate and monitor earnings and ensure that earnings are sufficient to maintain adequate capital and reserves. The institution should:

1. Compare recent earnings trends relative to equity, assets, or other commonly used benchmarks to the institution's historical results and those of its peers;

2. Evaluate the adequacy of earnings given the size, complexity, and risk profile of the institution's assets and operations;

3. Assess the source, volatility, and sustainability of earnings, including the effect of nonrecurring or extraordinary income or expense;

4. Take steps to ensure that earnings are sufficient to maintain adequate capital and reserves after considering the institution's asset quality and growth rate; and

5. Provide periodic earnings reports with adequate information for management and the board of directors to assess earnings performance.

I. *Compensation, fees and benefits.* An institution should maintain safeguards to prevent the payment of compensation, fees, and benefits that are excessive or that could lead to material financial loss to the institution.

III. PROHIBITION ON COMPENSATION THAT CONSTITUTES AN UNSAFE AND UNSOUND PRACTICE

A. Excessive Compensation

Excessive compensation is prohibited as an unsafe and unsound practice. Compensation shall be considered excessive when amounts paid are unreasonable or disproportionate to the services performed by an executive officer, employee, director, or principal shareholder, considering the following:

1. The combined value of all cash and non-cash benefits provided to the individual;

2. The compensation history of the individual and other individuals with comparable expertise at the institution;

3. The financial condition of the institution;

4. Comparable compensation practices at comparable institutions, based upon such factors as asset size, geographic location, and the complexity of the loan portfolio or other assets;

5. For postemployment benefits, the projected total cost and benefit to the institution;

6. Any connection between the individual and any fraudulent act or omission, breach of trust or fiduciary duty, or insider abuse with regard to the institution; and

7. Any other factors the agencies determines to be relevant.

B. Compensation Leading to Material Financial Loss

Compensation that could lead to material financial loss to an institution is prohibited as an unsafe and unsound practice.

[60 FR 35678, 35685, July 10, 1995; 61 FR 43951, Aug. 27, 1996, as amended at 71 FR 20527, Apr. 21, 2006]

APPENDIX B TO PART 364—INTERAGENCY GUIDELINES ESTABLISHING INFORMATION SECURITY STANDARDS

TABLE OF CONTENTS

I. Introduction
 A. Scope
 B. Preservation of Existing Authority
 C. Definitions
II. Standards for Safeguarding Customer Information
 A. Information Security Program
 B. Objectives
III. Development and Implementation of Customer Information Security Program
 A. Involve the Board of Directors
 B. Assess Risk
 C. Manage and Control Risk
 D. Oversee Service Provider Arrangements
 E. Adjust the Program
 F. Report to the Board
 G. Implement the Standards

I. INTRODUCTION

The Interagency Guidelines Establishing Information Security Standards (Guidelines) set forth standards pursuant to section 39 of the Federal Deposit Insurance Act, 12 U.S.C. 1831p–1, and sections 501 and 505(b), 15 U.S.C. 6801 and 6805(b), of the Gramm-Leach-Bliley Act. These Guidelines address standards for developing and implementing administrative, technical, and physical safeguards to protect the security, confidentiality, and integrity of customer information. These Guidelines also address standards with respect to the proper disposal of consumer information pursuant to sections 621 and 628 of the Fair Credit Reporting Act (15 U.S.C. 1681s and 1681w).

A. *Scope.* The Guidelines apply to customer information maintained by or on behalf of, and to the disposal of consumer information by or on behalf of, entities over which the Federal Deposit Insurance Corporation (FDIC) has authority. Such entities, referred to as "the bank" are banks insured by the FDIC (other than members of the Federal Reserve System), insured state branches of foreign banks, and any subsidiaries of such entities (except brokers, dealers, persons providing insurance, investment companies, and investment advisers).

B. *Preservation of Existing Authority.* Neither section 39 nor these Guidelines in any

Pt. 364, App. B

way limit the authority of the FDIC to address unsafe or unsound practices, violations of law, unsafe or unsound conditions, or other practices. The FDIC may take action under section 39 and these Guidelines independently of, in conjunction with, or in addition to, any other enforcement action available to the FDIC.

C. *Definitions.* 1. Except as modified in the Guidelines, or unless the context otherwise requires, the terms used in these Guidelines have the same meanings as set forth in sections 3 and 39 of the Federal Deposit Insurance Act (12 U.S.C. 1813 and 1831p–1).

2. For purposes of the Guidelines, the following definitions apply:

a. *Board of directors,* in the case of a branch or agency of a foreign bank, means the managing official in charge of the branch or agency.

b. *Consumer information* means any record about an individual, whether in paper, electronic, or other form, that is a consumer report or is derived from a consumer report and that is maintained or otherwise possessed by or on behalf of the bank for a business purpose. Consumer information also means a compilation of such records. The term does not include any record that does not personally identify an individual.

i. *Examples:*

(1) *Consumer information* includes:

(A) A consumer report that a bank obtains;

(B) information from a consumer report that the bank obtains from its affiliate after the consumer has been given a notice and has elected not to opt out of that sharing;

(C) information from a consumer report that the bank obtains about an individual who applies for but does not receive a loan, including any loan sought by an individual for a business purpose;

(D) information from a consumer report that the bank obtains about an individual who guarantees a loan (including a loan to a business entity); or

(E) information from a consumer report that the bank obtains about an employee or prospective employee.

(2) *Consumer information* does not include:

(A) aggregate information, such as the mean score, derived from a group of consumer reports; or

(B) blind data, such as payment history on accounts that are not personally identifiable, that may be used for developing credit scoring models or for other purposes.

c. *Consumer report* has the same meaning as set forth in the Fair Credit Reporting Act, 15 U.S.C. 1681a(d).

d. *Customer* means any customer of the bank as defined in §332.3(h) of this chapter.

e. *Customer information* means any record containing nonpublic personal information, as defined in §332.3(n) of this chapter, about a customer, whether in paper, electronic, or other form, that is maintained by or on behalf of the bank.

f. *Customer information systems* means any methods used to access, collect, store, use, transmit, protect, or dispose of customer information.

g. Service provider means any person or entity that maintains, processes, or otherwise is permitted access to customer information or consumer information through its provision of services directly to the bank.

II. STANDARDS FOR INFORMATION SECURITY

A. *Information Security Program.* Each bank shall implement a comprehensive written information security program that includes administrative, technical, and physical safeguards appropriate to the size and complexity of the bank and the nature and scope of its activities. While all parts of the bank are not required to implement a uniform set of policies, all elements of the information security program must be coordinated.

B. *Objectives.* A bank's information security program shall be designed to:

1. Ensure the security and confidentiality of customer information;

2. Protect against any anticipated threats or hazards to the security or integrity of such information;

3. Protect against unauthorized access to or use of such information that could result in substantial harm or inconvenience to any customer; and

4. Ensure the proper disposal of customer information and consumer information.

III. DEVELOPMENT AND IMPLEMENTATION OF INFORMATION SECURITY PROGRAM

A. *Involve the Board of Directors.* The board of directors or an appropriate committee of the board of each bank shall:

1. Approve the bank's written information security program; and

2. Oversee the development, implementation, and maintenance of the bank's information security program, including assigning specific responsibility for its implementation and reviewing reports from management.

B. *Assess Risk.*

Each bank shall:

1. Identify reasonably foreseeable internal and external threats that could result in unauthorized disclosure, misuse, alteration, or destruction of customer information or customer information systems.

2. Assess the likelihood and potential damage of these threats, taking into consideration the sensitivity of customer information.

3. Assess the sufficiency of policies, procedures, customer information systems, and other arrangements in place to control risks.

C. *Manage and Control Risk.* Each bank shall:

Federal Deposit Insurance Corporation

1. Design its information security program to control the identified risks, commensurate with the sensitivity of the information as well as the complexity and scope of the bank's activities. Each bank must consider whether the following security measures are appropriate for the bank and, if so, adopt those measures the bank concludes are appropriate:

a. Access controls on customer information systems, including controls to authenticate and permit access only to authorized individuals and controls to prevent employees from providing customer information to unauthorized individuals who may seek to obtain this information through fraudulent means.

b. Access restrictions at physical locations containing customer information, such as buildings, computer facilities, and records storage facilities to permit access only to authorized individuals;

c. Encryption of electronic customer information, including while in transit or in storage on networks or systems to which unauthorized individuals may have access;

d. Procedures designed to ensure that customer information system modifications are consistent with the bank's information security program;

e. Dual control procedures, segregation of duties, and employee background checks for employees with responsibilities for or access to customer information;

f. Monitoring systems and procedures to detect actual and attempted attacks on or intrusions into customer information systems;

g. Response programs that specify actions to be taken when the bank suspects or detects that unauthorized individuals have gained access to customer information systems, including appropriate reports to regulatory and law enforcement agencies; and

h. Measures to protect against destruction, loss, or damage of customer information due to potential environmental hazards, such as fire and water damage or technological failures.

2. Train staff to implement the bank's information security program.

3. Regularly test the key controls, systems and procedures of the information security program. The frequency and nature of such tests should be determined by the bank's risk assessment. Tests should be conducted or reviewed by independent third parties or staff independent of those that develop or maintain the security programs.

4. Develop, implement, and maintain, as part of its information security program, appropriate measures to properly dispose of customer information and consumer information in accordance with each of the requirements of this paragraph III.

D. *Oversee Service Provider Arrangements.* Each bank shall:

1. Exercise appropriate due diligence in selecting its service providers;

2. Require its service providers by contract to implement appropriate measures designed to meet the objectives of these Guidelines; and

3. Where indicated by the bank's risk assessment, monitor its service providers to confirm that they have satisfied their obligations as required by paragraph D.2. As part of this monitoring, a bank should review audits, summaries of test results, or other equivalent evaluations of its service providers.

E. *Adjust the Program.* Each bank shall monitor, evaluate, and adjust, as appropriate, the information security program in light of any relevant changes in technology, the sensitivity of its customer information, internal or external threats to information, and the bank's own changing business arrangements, such as mergers and acquisitions, alliances and joint ventures, outsourcing arrangements, and changes to customer information systems.

F. *Report to the Board.* Each bank shall report to its board or an appropriate committee of the board at least annually. This report should describe the overall status of the information security program and the bank's compliance with these Guidelines. The report, which will vary depending upon the complexity of each bank's program should discuss material matters related to its program, addressing issues such as: risk assessment; risk management and control decisions; service provider arrangements; results of testing; security breaches or violations, and management's responses; and recommendations for changes in the information security program.

G. *Implement the Standards.* 1. *Effective date.* Each bank must implement an information security program pursuant to these Guidelines by July 1, 2001.

2. *Two-year grandfathering of agreements with service providers.* Until July 1, 2003, a contract that a bank has entered into with a service provider to perform services for it or functions on its behalf, satisfies the provisions of paragraph III.D., even if the contract does not include a requirement that the servicer maintain the security and confidentiality of customer information as long as the bank entered into the contract on or before March 5, 2001.

3. *Effective date for measures relating to the disposal of consumer information.* Each bank must satisfy these Guidelines with respect to the proper disposal of consumer information by July 1, 2005.

4. *Exception for existing agreements with service providers relating to the disposal of consumer information.* Notwithstanding the requirement in paragraph III.G.3., a bank's contracts with its service providers that have access to consumer information and

that may dispose of consumer information, entered into before July 1, 2005, must comply with the provisions of the Guidelines relating to the proper disposal of consumer information by July 1, 2006.

SUPPLEMENT A TO APPENDIX B TO PART 364—INTERAGENCY GUIDANCE ON RESPONSE PROGRAMS FOR UNAUTHORIZED ACCESS TO CUSTOMER INFORMATION AND CUSTOMER NOTICE

I. BACKGROUND

This Guidance[1] interprets section 501(b) of the Gramm-Leach-Bliley Act ("GLBA") and the Interagency Guidelines Establishing Information Security Standards (the "Security Guidelines")[2] and describes response programs, including customer notification procedures, that a financial institution should develop and implement to address unauthorized access to or use of customer information that could result in substantial harm or inconvenience to a customer. The scope of, and definitions of terms used in, this Guidance are identical to those of the Security Guidelines. For example, the term "customer information" is the same term used in the Security Guidelines, and means any record containing nonpublic personal information about a customer, whether in paper, electronic, or other form, maintained by or on behalf of the institution.

A. Interagency Security Guidelines

Section 501(b) of the GLBA required the Agencies to establish appropriate standards for financial institutions subject to their jurisdiction that include administrative, technical, and physical safeguards, to protect the security and confidentiality of customer information. Accordingly, the Agencies issued Security Guidelines requiring every financial institution to have an information security program designed to:

1. Ensure the security and confidentiality of customer information;

2. Protect against any anticipated threats or hazards to the security or integrity of such information; and

3. Protect against unauthorized access to or use of such information that could result in substantial harm or inconvenience to any customer.

B. Risk Assessment and Controls

1. The Security Guidelines direct every financial institution to assess the following risks, among others, when developing its information security program:

a. Reasonably foreseeable internal and external threats that could result in unauthorized disclosure, misuse, alteration, or destruction of customer information or customer information systems;

b. The likelihood and potential damage of threats, taking into consideration the sensitivity of customer information; and

c. The sufficiency of policies, procedures, customer information systems, and other arrangements in place to control risks.[3]

2. Following the assessment of these risks, the Security Guidelines require a financial institution to design a program to address the identified risks. The particular security measures an institution should adopt will depend upon the risks presented by the complexity and scope of its business. At a minimum, the financial institution is required to consider the specific security measures enumerated in the Security Guidelines,[4] and adopt those that are appropriate for the institution, including:

a. Access controls on customer information systems, including controls to authenticate and permit access only to authorized individuals and controls to prevent employees from providing customer information to unauthorized individuals who may seek to obtain this information through fraudulent means;

b. Background checks for employees with responsibilities for access to customer information; and

c. Response programs that specify actions to be taken when the financial institution suspects or detects that unauthorized individuals have gained access to customer information systems, including appropriate reports to regulatory and law enforcement agencies.[5]

C. Service Providers

The Security Guidelines direct every financial institution to require its service providers by contract to implement appropriate measures designed to protect against unauthorized access to or use of customer information that could result in substantial harm or inconvenience to any customer.[6]

---

[1] This Guidance is being jointly issued by the Board of Governors of the Federal Reserve System (Board), the Federal Deposit Insurance Corporation (FDIC), the Office of the Comptroller of the Currency (OCC), and the Office of Thrift Supervision (OTS).

[2] 12 CFR part 30, app. B (OCC); 12 CFR part 208, app. D–2 and part 225, app. F (Board); 12 CFR part 364, app. B (FDIC); and 12 CFR part 570, app. B (OTS). The "Interagency Guidelines Establishing Information Security Standards" were formerly known as "The Interagency Guidelines Establishing Standards for Safeguarding Customer Information."

[3] *See* Security Guidelines, III.B.
[4] *See* Security Guidelines, III.C.
[5] *See* Security Guidelines, III.C.
[6] *See* Security Guidelines, II.B. and III.D. Further, the Agencies note that, in addition

Federal Deposit Insurance Corporation Pt. 364, App. B

II. RESPONSE PROGRAM

Millions of Americans, throughout the country, have been victims of identity theft.[7] Identity thieves misuse personal information they obtain from a number of sources, including financial institutions, to perpetrate identity theft. Therefore, financial institutions should take preventative measures to safeguard customer information against attempts to gain unauthorized access to the information. For example, financial institutions should place access controls on customer information systems and conduct background checks for employees who are authorized to access customer information.[8] However, every financial institution should also develop and implement a risk-based response program to address incidents of unauthorized access to customer information in customer information systems[9] that occur nonetheless. A response program should be a key part of an institution's information security program.[10] The program should be appropriate to the size and complexity of the institution and the nature and scope of its activities.

In addition, each institution should be able to address incidents of unauthorized access to customer information in customer information systems maintained by its domestic and foreign service providers. Therefore, consistent with the obligations in the Guidelines that relate to these arrangements, and with existing guidance on this topic issued by the Agencies,[11] an institution's contract with its service provider should require the service provider to take appropriate actions to address incidents of unauthorized access to the financial institution's customer information, including notification to the institution as soon as possible of any such incident, to enable the institution to expeditiously implement its response program.

A. Components of a Response Program

1. At a minimum, an institution's response program should contain procedures for the following:

a. Assessing the nature and scope of an incident, and identifying what customer information systems and types of customer information have been accessed or misused;

b. Notifying its primary Federal regulator as soon as possible when the institution becomes aware of an incident involving unauthorized access to or use of *sensitive* customer information, as defined below;

c. Consistent with the Agencies' Suspicious Activity Report ("SAR") regulations,[12] notifying appropriate law enforcement authorities, in addition to filing a timely SAR in

---

to contractual obligations to a financial institution, a service provider may be required to implement its own comprehensive information security program in accordance with the Safeguards Rule promulgated by the Federal Trade Commission ("FTC"), 16 CFR part 316.

[7] The FTC estimates that nearly 10 million Americans discovered they were victims of some form of identity theft in 2002. *See* The Federal Trade Commission, *Identity Theft Survey Report*, (September 2003), available at http://www.ftc.gov/os/2003/09/synovatereport.pdf.

[8] Institutions should also conduct background checks of employees to ensure that the institution does not violate 12 U.S.C. 1829, which prohibits an institution from hiring an individual convicted of certain criminal offenses or who is subject to a prohibition order under 12 U.S.C. 1818(e)(6).

[9] Under the Guidelines, an institution's *customer information systems* consist of all of the methods used to access, collect, store, use, transmit, protect, or dispose of customer information, including the systems maintained by its service providers. *See* Security Guidelines, I.C.2.d (I.C.2.c for OTS).

[10] *See* FFIEC Information Technology Examination Handbook, Information Security Booklet, Dec. 2002 available at http://www.ffiec.gov/ffiecinfobase/html_pages/infosec_book_frame.htm. Federal Reserve SR 97-32, Sound Practice Guidance for Information Security for Networks, Dec. 4, 1997; OCC Bulletin 2000-14, "Infrastructure Threats—Intrusion Risks" (May 15, 2000), for additional guidance on preventing, detecting, and responding to intrusions into financial institution computer systems.

[11] *See* Federal Reserve SR Ltr. 00-04, Outsourcing of Information and Transaction Processing, Feb. 9, 2000; OCC Bulletin 2001-47, "Third-Party Relationships Risk Management Principles," Nov. 1, 2001; FDIC FIL 68-99, Risk Assessment Tools and Practices for Information System Security, July 7, 1999; OTS Thrift Bulletin 82a, Third Party Arrangements, Sept. 1, 2004.

[12] An institution's obligation to file a SAR is set out in the Agencies' SAR regulations and Agency guidance. *See* 12 CFR 21.11 (national banks, Federal branches and agencies); 12 CFR 208.62 (State member banks); 12 CFR 211.5(k) (Edge and agreement corporations); 12 CFR 211.24(f) (uninsured State branches and agencies of foreign banks); 12 CFR 225.4(f) (bank holding companies and their nonbank subsidiaries); 12 CFR part 353 (State non-member banks); and 12 CFR 563.180 (savings associations). National banks must file SARs in connection with computer intrusions and other computer crimes. *See* OCC Bulletin 2000-14, "Infrastructure Threats—Intrusion Risks" (May 15, 2000); Advisory Letter 97-9, "Reporting Computer Related Crimes" (November 19, 1997) (general

Continued

situations involving Federal criminal violations requiring immediate attention, such as when a reportable violation is ongoing;

d. Taking appropriate steps to contain and control the incident to prevent further unauthorized access to or use of customer information, for example, by monitoring, freezing, or closing affected accounts, while preserving records and other evidence;[13] and

e. Notifying customers when warranted.

2. Where an incident of unauthorized access to customer information involves customer information systems maintained by an institution's service providers, it is the responsibility of the financial institution to notify the institution's customers and regulator. However, an institution may authorize or contract with its service provider to notify the institution's customers or regulator on its behalf.

III. CUSTOMER NOTICE

Financial institutions have an affirmative duty to protect their customers' information against unauthorized access or use. Notifying customers of a security incident involving the unauthorized access or use of the customer's information in accordance with the standard set forth below is a key part of that duty. Timely notification of customers is important to manage an institution's reputation risk. Effective notice also may reduce an institution's legal risk, assist in maintaining good customer relations, and enable the institution's customers to take steps to protect themselves against the consequences of identity theft. When customer notification is warranted, an institution may not forgo notifying its customers of an incident because the institution believes that it may be potentially embarrassed or inconvenienced by doing so.

---

guidance still applicable though instructions for new SAR form published in 65 FR 1229, 1230 (January 7, 2000)). *See also* Federal Reserve SR 01-11, Identity Theft and Pretext Calling, Apr. 26, 2001; SR 97-28, Guidance Concerning Reporting of Computer Related Crimes by Financial Institutions, Nov. 6, 1997; FDIC FIL 48-2000, Suspicious Activity Reports, July 14, 2000; FIL 47-97, Preparation of Suspicious Activity Reports, May 6, 1997; OTS CEO Memorandum 139, Identity Theft and Pretext Calling, May 4, 2001; CEO Memorandum 126, New Suspicious Activity Report Form, July 5, 2000; *http://www.ots.treas.gov/BSA* (for the latest SAR form and filing instructions required by OTS as of July 1, 2003).

[13] *See* FFIEC Information Technology Examination Handbook, Information Security Booklet, Dec. 2002, pp. 68–74.

A. *Standard for Providing Notice*

When a financial institution becomes aware of an incident of unauthorized access to sensitive customer information, the institution should conduct a reasonable investigation to promptly determine the likelihood that the information has been or will be misused. If the institution determines that misuse of its information about a customer has occurred or is reasonably possible, it should notify the affected customer as soon as possible. Customer notice may be delayed if an appropriate law enforcement agency determines that notification will interfere with a criminal investigation and provides the institution with a written request for the delay. However, the institution should notify its customers as soon as notification will no longer interfere with the investigation.

1. Sensitive Customer Information

Under the Guidelines, an institution must protect against unauthorized access to or use of customer information that could result in substantial harm or inconvenience to any customer. Substantial harm or inconvenience is most likely to result from improper access to *sensitive customer information* because this type of information is most likely to be misused, as in the commission of identity theft. For purposes of this Guidance, *sensitive customer information* means a customer's name, address, or telephone number, in conjunction with the customer's social security number, driver's license number, account number, credit or debit card number, or a personal identification number or password that would permit access to the customer's account. *Sensitive customer information* also includes any combination of components of customer information that would allow someone to log onto or access the customer's account, such as user name and password or password and account number.

2. Affected Customers

If a financial institution, based upon its investigation, can determine from its logs or other data precisely which customers' information has been improperly accessed, it may limit notification to those customers with regard to whom the institution determines that misuse of their information has occurred or is reasonably possible. However, there may be situations where the institution determines that a group of files has been accessed improperly, but is unable to identify which specific customers' information has been accessed. If the circumstances of the unauthorized access lead the institution to determine that misuse of the information is reasonably possible, it should notify all customers in the group.

Federal Deposit Insurance Corporation § 365.1

B. Content of Customer Notice

1. Customer notice should be given in a clear and conspicuous manner. The notice should describe the incident in general terms and the type of customer information that was the subject of unauthorized access or use. It also should generally describe what the institution has done to protect the customers' information from further unauthorized access. In addition, it should include a telephone number that customers can call for further information and assistance.[14] The notice also should remind customers of the need to remain vigilant over the next twelve to twenty-four months, and to promptly report incidents of suspected identity theft to the institution. The notice should include the following additional items, when appropriate:

a. A recommendation that the customer review account statements and immediately report any suspicious activity to the institution;

b. A description of fraud alerts and an explanation of how the customer may place a fraud alert in the customer's consumer reports to put the customer's creditors on notice that the customer may be a victim of fraud;

c. A recommendation that the customer periodically obtain credit reports from each nationwide credit reporting agency and have information relating to fraudulent transactions deleted;

d. An explanation of how the customer may obtain a credit report free of charge; and

e. Information about the availability of the FTC's online guidance regarding steps a consumer can take to protect against identity theft. The notice should encourage the customer to report any incidents of identity theft to the FTC, and should provide the FTC's Web site address and toll-free telephone number that customers may use to obtain the identity theft guidance and report suspected incidents of identity theft.[15]

2. The Agencies encourage financial institutions to notify the nationwide consumer reporting agencies prior to sending notices to a large number of customers that include contact information for the reporting agencies.

C. Delivery of Customer Notice

Customer notice should be delivered in any manner designed to ensure that a customer can reasonably be expected to receive it. For example, the institution may choose to contact all customers affected by telephone or by mail, or by electronic mail for those customers for whom it has a valid e-mail address and who have agreed to receive communications electronically.

[66 FR 8638, Feb. 1, 2001, as amended at 69 FR 77619, Dec. 28, 2004; 70 FR 15754, Mar. 29, 2005; 71 FR 5780, Feb. 3, 2006]

PART 365—REAL ESTATE LENDING STANDARDS

Subpart A—Real Estate Lending Standards

Sec.
365.1 Purpose and scope.
365.2 Real estate lending standards.
APPENDIX A TO SUBPART A OF PART 365—INTERAGENCY GUIDELINES FOR REAL ESTATE LENDING POLICIES

Subpart B—Registration of Residential Mortgage Loan Originators

365.101 Authority, purpose, and scope.
365.102 Definitions.
365.103 Registration of mortgage loan originators.
365.104 Policies and procedures.
365.105 Use of unique identifier.
APPENDIX A TO SUBPART B OF PART 365—EXAMPLES OF MORTGAGE LOAN ORIGINATOR ACTIVITIES

AUTHORITY: 12 U.S.C. 1828(o) and 5101 et seq.

SOURCE: 57 FR 62896, 62900, Dec. 31, 1992, unless otherwise noted.

Subpart A—Real Estate Lending Standards

§ 365.1 Purpose and scope.

This subpart, issued pursuant to section 304 of the Federal Deposit Insurance Corporation Improvement Act of 1991, 12 U.S.C. 1828(o), prescribes standards for real estate lending to be used by insured state nonmember banks (including state-licensed insured branches of foreign banks) in adopting internal real estate lending policies.

[57 FR 62896, 62900, Dec. 31, 1992, as amended at 75 FR 44692, July 28, 2010]

---

[14] The institution should, therefore, ensure that it has reasonable policies and procedures in place, including trained personnel, to respond appropriately to customer inquiries and requests for assistance.

[15] Currently, the FTC Web site for the ID Theft brochure and the FTC Hotline phone number are *http://www.consumer.gov/idtheft* and 1–877–IDTHEFT. The institution may also refer customers to any materials developed pursuant to section 151(b) of the FACT Act (educational materials developed by the FTC to teach the public how to prevent identity theft).

§ 365.2 Real estate lending standards.

(a) Each insured state nonmember bank shall adopt and maintain written policies that establish appropriate limits and standards for extensions of credit that are secured by liens on or interests in real estate, or that are made for the purpose of financing permanent improvements to real estate.

(b)(1) Real estate lending policies adopted pursuant to this section must:

(i) Be consistent with safe and sound banking practices;

(ii) Be appropriate to the size of the institution and the nature and scope of its operations; and

(iii) Be reviewed and approved by the bank's board of directors at least annually.

(2) The lending policies must establish:

(i) Loan portfolio diversification standards;

(ii) Prudent underwriting standards, including loan-to-value limits, that are clear and measurable;

(iii) Loan administration procedures for the bank's real estate portfolio; and

(iv) Documentation, approval, and reporting requirements to monitor compliance with the bank's real estate lending policies.

(c) Each insured state nonmember bank must monitor conditions in the real estate market in its lending area to ensure that its real estate lending policies continue to be appropriate for current market conditions.

(d) The real estate lending policies adopted pursuant to this section should reflect consideration of the Interagency Guidelines for Real Estate Lending Policies established by the Federal bank and thrift supervisory agencies.

APPENDIX A TO SUBPART A OF PART 365—INTERAGENCY GUIDELINES FOR REAL ESTATE LENDING POLICIES

The agencies' regulations require that each insured depository institution adopt and maintain a written policy that establishes appropriate limits and standards for all extensions of credit that are secured by liens on or interests in real estate or made for the purpose of financing the construction of a building or other improvements.[5] These guidelines are intended to assist institutions in the formulation and maintenance of a real estate lending policy that is appropriate to the size of the institution and the nature and scope of its individual operations, as well as satisfies the requirements of the regulation.

Each institution's policies must be comprehensive, and consistent with safe and sound lending practices, and must ensure that the institution operates within limits and according to standards that are reviewed and approved at least annually by the board of directors. Real estate lending is an integral part of many institutions' business plans and, when undertaken in a prudent manner, will not be subject to examiner criticism.

LOAN PORTFOLIO MANAGEMENT CONSIDERATIONS

The lending policy should contain a general outline of the scope and distribution of the institution's credit facilities and the manner in which real estate loans are made, serviced, and collected. In particular, the institution's policies on real estate lending should:

• Identify the geographic areas in which the institution will consider lending.

• Establish a loan portfolio diversification policy and set limits for real estate loans by type and geographic market (e.g., limits on higher risk loans).

• Identify appropriate terms and conditions by type of real estate loan.

• Establish loan origination and approval procedures, both generally and by size and type of loan.

• Establish prudent underwriting standards that are clear and measurable, including loan-to-value limits, that are consistent with these supervisory guidelines.

• Establish review and approval procedures for exception loans, including loans with loan-to-value percentages in excess of supervisory limits.

• Establish loan administration procedures, including documentation, disbursement, collateral inspection, collection, and loan review.

• Establish real estate appraisal and evaluation programs.

• Require that management monitor the loan portfolio and provide timely and adequate reports to the board of directors.

The institution should consider both internal and external factors in the formulation of its loan policies and strategic plan. Factors that should be considered include:

---

[5] The agencies have adopted a uniform rule on real estate lending. See 12 CFR part 365 (FDIC); 12 CFR part 208, subpart C (FRB); 12 CFR part 34, subpart D (OCC); and 12 CFR 563.100–101 (OTS).

Federal Deposit Insurance Corporation

- The size and financial condition of the institution.
- The expertise and size of the lending staff.
- The need to avoid undue concentrations of risk.
- Compliance with all real estate related laws and regulations, including the Community Reinvestment Act, anti-discrimination laws, and for savings associations, the Qualified Thrift Lender test.
- Market conditions.

The institution should monitor conditions in the real estate markets in its lending area so that it can react quickly to changes in market conditions that are relevant to its lending decisions. Market supply and demand factors that should be considered include:
- Demographic indicators, including population and employment trends.
- Zoning requirements.
- Current and projected vacancy, construction, and absorption rates.
- Current and projected lease terms, rental rates, and sales prices, including concessions.
- Current and projected operating expenses for different types of projects.
- Economic indicators, including trends and diversification of the lending area.
- Valuation trends, including discount and direct capitalization rates.

UNDERWRITING STANDARDS

Prudently underwritten real estate loans should reflect all relevant credit factors, including:
- The capacity of the borrower, or income from the underlying property, to adequately service the debt.
- The value of the mortgaged property.
- The overall creditworthiness of the borrower.
- The level of equity invested in the property.
- Any secondary sources of repayment.
- Any additional collateral or credit enhancements (such as guarantees, mortgage insurance or takeout commitments).

The lending policies should reflect the level of risk that is acceptable to the board of directors and provide clear and measurable underwriting standards that enable the institution's lending staff to evaluate these credit factors. The underwriting standards should address:
- The maximum loan amount by type of property.
- Maximum loan maturities by type of property.
- Amortization schedules.
- Pricing structure for different types of real estate loans.
- Loan-to-value limits by type of property.

For development and construction projects, and completed commercial properties, the policy should also establish, commensurate with the size and type of the project or property:
- Requirements for feasibility studies and sensitivity and risk analyses (*e.g.*, sensitivity of income projections to changes in economic variables such as interest rates, vacancy rates, or operating expenses).
- Minimum requirements for initial investment and maintenance of hard equity by the borrower (*e.g.*, cash or unencumbered investment in the underlying property).
- Minimum standards for net worth, cash flow, and debt service coverage of the borrower or underlying property.
- Standards for the acceptability of and limits on non-amortizing loans.
- Standards for the acceptability of and limits on the use of interest reserves.
- Pre-leasing and pre-sale requirements for income-producing property.
- Pre-sale and minimum unit release requirements for non-income-producing property loans.
- Limits on partial recourse or non-recourse loans and requirements for guarantor support.
- Requirements for takeout commitments.
- Minimum covenants for loan agreements.

LOAN ADMINISTRATION

The institution should also establish loan administration procedures for its real estate portfolio that address:
- Documentation, including:

    Type and frequency of financial statements, including requirements for verification of information provided by the borrower;
    Type and frequency of collateral evaluations (appraisals and other estimates of value).

- Loan closing and disbursement.
- Payment processing.
- Escrow administration.
- Collateral administration.
- Loan payoffs.
- Collections and foreclosure, including:

    Delinquency follow-up procedures;
    Foreclosure timing;
    Extensions and other forms of forbearance;
    Acceptance of deeds in lieu of foreclosure.

- Claims processing (*e.g.*, seeking recovery on a defaulted loan covered by a government guaranty or insurance program).
- Servicing and participation agreements.

SUPERVISORY LOAN-TO-VALUE LIMITS

Institutions should establish their own internal loan-to-value limits for real estate loans. These internal limits should not exceed the following supervisory limits:

Loan category	Loan-to-value limit (percent)
Raw land	65
Land development	75
Construction:	
Commercial, multifamily,[1] and other non-residential	80
1- to 4-family residential	85
Improved property	85
Owner-occupied 1- to 4-family and home equity	([2])

[1] Multifamily construction includes condominiums and cooperatives.

[2] A loan-to-value limit has not been established for permanent mortgage or home equity loans on owner-occupied, 1- to 4-family residential property. However, for any such loan with a loan-to-value ratio that equals or exceeds 90 percent at origination, an institution should require appropriate credit enhancement in the form of either mortgage insurance or readily marketable collateral.

The supervisory loan-to-value limits should be applied to the underlying property that collateralizes the loan. For loans that fund multiple phases of the same real estate project (e.g., a loan for both land development and construction of an office building), the appropriate loan-to-value limit is the limit applicable to the final phase of the project funded by the loan; however, loan disbursements should not exceed actual development or construction outlays. In situations where a loan is fully cross-collateralized by two or more properties or is secured by a collateral pool of two or more properties, the appropriate maximum loan amount under supervisory loan-to-value limits is the sum of the value of each property, less senior liens, multiplied by the appropriate loan-to-value limit for each property. To ensure that collateral margins remain within the supervisory limits, lenders should redetermine conformity whenever collateral substitutions are made to the collateral pool.

In establishing internal loan-to-value limits, each lender is expected to carefully consider the institution-specific and market factors listed under "Loan Portfolio Management Considerations," as well as any other relevant factors, such as the particular subcategory or type of loan. For any subcategory of loans that exhibits greater credit risk than the overall category, a lender should consider the establishment of an internal loan-to-value limit for that subcategory that is lower than the limit for the overall category.

The loan-to-value ratio is only one of several pertinent credit factors to be considered when underwriting a real estate loan. Other credit factors to be taken into account are highlighted in the "Underwriting Standards" section above. Because of these other factors, the establishment of these supervisory limits should not be interpreted to mean that loans at these levels will automatically be considered sound.

LOANS IN EXCESS OF THE SUPERVISORY LOAN-TO-VALUE LIMITS

The agencies recognize that appropriate loan-to-value limits vary not only among categories of real estate loans but also among individual loans. Therefore, it may be appropriate in individual cases to originate or purchase loans with loan-to-value ratios in excess of the supervisory loan-to-value limits, based on the support provided by other credit factors. Such loans should be identified in the institution's records, and their aggregate amount reported at least quarterly to the institution's board of directors. (See additional reporting requirements described under "Exceptions to the General Policy.")

The aggregate amount of all loans in excess of the supervisory loan-to-value limits should not exceed 100 percent of total capital.[2] Moreover, within the aggregate limit, total loans for all commercial, agricultural, multifamily or other non-1-to-4 family residential properties should not exceed 30 percent of total capital. An institution will come under increased supervisory scrutiny as the total of such loans approaches these levels.

EXCLUDED TRANSACTIONS

The agencies also recognize that there are a number of lending situations in which other factors significantly outweigh the need to apply the supervisory loan-to-value limits. These include:

• Loans guaranteed or insured by the U.S. government or its agencies, provided that the amount of the guaranty or insurance is

---

[2] For the state member banks, the term "total capital" means "total risk-based capital" as defined in appendix A to 12 CFR part 208. For insured state non-member banks, "total capital" refers to that term described in table I of appendix A to 12 CFR part 325. For national banks, the term "total capital" is defined at 12 CFR 3.2(e). For savings associations, the term "total capital" is defined at 12 CFR 567.5(c).

In determining the aggregate amount of such loans, institutions should: (a) Include all loans secured by the same property if any one of those loans exceeds the supervisory loan-to-value limits; and (b) include the recourse obligation of any such loan sold with recourse. Conversely, a loan should no longer be reported to the directors as part of aggregate totals when reduction in principal or senior liens, or additional contribution of collateral or equity (e.g., improvements to the real property securing the loan), bring the loan-to-value ratio into compliance with supervisory limits.

at least equal to the portion of the loan that exceeds the supervisory loan-to-value limit.
- Loans backed by the full faith and credit of a state government, provided that the amount of the assurance is at least equal to the portion of the loan that exceeds the supervisory loan-to-value limit.
- Loans guaranteed or insured by a state, municipal or local government, or an agency thereof, provided that the amount of the guaranty or insurance is at least equal to the portion of the loan that exceeds the supervisory loan-to-value limit, and provided that the lender has determined that the guarantor or insurer has the financial capacity and willingness to perform under the terms of the guaranty or insurance agreement.
- Loans that are to be sold promptly after origination, without recourse, to a financially responsible third party.
- Loans that are renewed, refinanced, or restructured without the advancement of new funds or an increase in the line of credit (except for reasonable closing costs), or loans that are renewed, refinanced, or restructured in connection with a workout situation, either with or without the advancement of new funds, where consistent with safe and sound banking practices and part of a clearly defined and well-documented program to achieve orderly liquidation of the debt, reduce risk of loss, or maximize recovery on the loan.
- Loans that facilitate the sale of real estate acquired by the lender in the ordinary course of collecting a debt previously contracted in good faith.
- Loans for which a lien on or interest in real property is taken as additional collateral through an abundance of caution by the lender (e.g., the institution takes a blanket lien on all or substantially all of the assets of the borrower, and the value of the real property is low relative to the aggregate value of all other collateral).
- Loans, such as working capital loans, where the lender does not rely principally on real estate as security and the extension of credit is not used to acquire, develop, or construct permanent improvements on real property.
- Loans for the purpose of financing permanent improvements to real property, but not secured by the property, if such security interest is not required by prudent underwriting practice.

EXCEPTIONS TO THE GENERAL LENDING POLICY

Some provision should be made for the consideration of loan requests from creditworthy borrowers whose credit needs do not fit within the institution's general lending policy. An institution may provide for prudently underwritten exceptions to its lending policies, including loan-to-value limits, on a loan-by-loan basis. However, any exceptions from the supervisory loan-to-value limits should conform to the aggregate limits on such loans discussed above.

The board of directors is responsible for establishing standards for the review and approval of exception loans. Each institution should establish an appropriate internal process for the review and approval of loans that do not conform to its own internal policy standards. The approval of any such loan should be supported by a written justification that clearly sets forth all of the relevant credit factors that support the underwriting decision. The justification and approval documents for such loans should be maintained as a part of the permanent loan file. Each institution should monitor compliance with its real estate lending policy and individually report exception loans of a significant size to its board of directors.

SUPERVISORY REVIEW OF REAL ESTATE LENDING POLICIES AND PRACTICES

The real estate lending policies of institutions will be evaluated by examiners during the course of their examinations to determine if the policies are consistent with safe and sound lending practices, these guidelines, and the requirements of the regulation. In evaluating the adequacy of the institution's real estate lending policies and practices, examiners will take into consideration the following factors:
- The nature and scope of the institution's real estate lending activities.
- The size and financial condition of the institution.
- The quality of the institution's management and internal controls.
- The expertise and size of the lending and loan administration staff.
- Market conditions.

Lending policy exception reports will also be reviewed by examiners during the course of their examinations to determine whether the institutions' exceptions are adequately documented and appropriate in light of all of the relevant credit considerations. An excessive volume of exceptions to an institution's real estate lending policy may signal a weakening of its underwriting practices, or may suggest a need to revise the loan policy.

DEFINITIONS

For the purposes of these Guidelines:
Construction loan means an extension of credit for the purpose of erecting or rehabilitating buildings or other structures, including any infrastructure necessary for development.
Extension of credit or *loan* means:
(1) The total amount of any loan, line of credit, or other legally binding lending commitment with respect to real property; and
(2) The total amount, based on the amount of consideration paid, of any loan, line of

§ 365.101

credit, or other legally binding lending commitment acquired by a lender by purchase, assignment, or otherwise.

Improved property loan means an extension of credit secured by one of the following types of real property:

(1) Farmland, ranchland or timberland committed to ongoing management and agricultural production;

(2) 1- to 4-family residential property that is not owner-occupied;

(3) Residential property containing five or more individual dwelling units;

(4) Completed commercial property; or

(5) Other income-producing property that has been completed and is available for occupancy and use, except income-producing owner-occupied 1- to 4-family residential property.

Land development loan means an extension of credit for the purpose of improving unimproved real property prior to the erection of structures. The improvement of unimproved real property may include the laying or placement of sewers, water pipes, utility cables, streets, and other infrastructure necessary for future development.

Loan origination means the time of inception of the obligation to extend credit (*i.e.*, when the last event or prerequisite, controllable by the lender, occurs causing the lender to become legally bound to fund an extension of credit).

Loan-to-value or *loan-to-value ratio* means the percentage or ratio that is derived at the time of loan origination by dividing an extension of credit by the total value of the property(ies) securing or being improved by the extension of credit plus the amount of any readily marketable collateral and other acceptable collateral that secures the extension of credit. The total amount of all senior liens on or interests in such property(ies) should be included in determining the loan-to-value ratio. When mortgage insurance or collateral is used in the calculation of the loan-to-value ratio, and such credit enhancement is later released or replaced, the loan-to-value ratio should be recalculated.

Other acceptable collateral means any collateral in which the lender has a perfected security interest, that has a quantifiable value, and is accepted by the lender in accordance with safe and sound lending practices. Other acceptable collateral should be appropriately discounted by the lender consistent with the lender's usual practices for making loans secured by such collateral. Other acceptable collateral includes, among other items, unconditional irrevocable standby letters of credit for the benefit of the lender.

Owner-occupied, when used in conjunction with the term *1- to 4-family residential property* means that the owner of the underlying real property occupies at least one unit of the real property as a principal residence of the owner.

Readily marketable collateral means insured deposits, financial instruments, and bullion in which the lender has a perfected interest. Financial instruments and bullion must be salable under ordinary circumstances with reasonable promptness at a fair market value determined by quotations based on actual transactions, on an auction or similarly available daily bid and ask price market. Readily marketable collateral should be appropriately discounted by the lender consistent with the lender's usual practices for making loans secured by such collateral.

Value means an opinion or estimate, set forth in an appraisal or evaluation, whichever may be appropriate, of the market value of real property, prepared in accordance with the agency's appraisal regulations and guidance. For loans to purchase an existing property, the term "value" means the lesser of the actual acquisition cost or the estimate of value.

1- to 4-family residential property means property containing fewer than five individual dwelling units, including manufactured homes permanently affixed to the underlying property (when deemed to be real property under state law).

[57 FR 62896, 62900, Dec. 31, 1992; 58 FR 4460, Jan. 14, 1993. Redesignated at 75 FR 44692, July 28, 2010]

Subpart B—Registration of Residential Mortgage Loan Originators

SOURCE: 75 FR 44692, July 28, 2010, unless otherwise noted.

§ 365.101 Authority, purpose, and scope.

(a) *Authority.* This subpart is issued pursuant to the Secure and Fair Enforcement for Mortgage Licensing Act of 2008, title V of the Housing and Economic Recovery Act of 2008 (S.A.F.E. Act) (Pub. L. 110–289, 122 Stat. 2654, 12 U.S.C. 5101 et seq.).

(b) *Purpose.* This subpart implements the S.A.F.E. Act's Federal registration requirement for mortgage loan originators. The S.A.F.E. Act provides that the objectives of this registration include aggregating and improving the flow of information to and between regulators; providing increased accountability and tracking of mortgage loan originators; enhancing consumer protections; supporting anti-fraud measures; and providing consumers with

Federal Deposit Insurance Corporation § 365.102

easily accessible information at no charge regarding the employment history of, and publicly adjudicated disciplinary and enforcement actions against, mortgage loan originators.

(c) *Scope*—(1) *In general.* This subpart applies to insured State nonmember banks (including State-licensed insured branches of foreign banks), their subsidiaries (except brokers, dealers, persons providing insurance, investment companies, and investment advisers) (collectively referred to in this subpart as insured State nonmember banks), and employees of such banks or subsidiaries who act as mortgage loan originators.

(2) *De minimis exception.* (i) This subpart and the requirements of 12 U.S.C. 5103(a)(1)(A) and (2) of the S.A.F.E. Act do not apply to any employee of an insured State nonmember bank who has never been registered or licensed through the Registry as a mortgage loan originator if during the past 12 months the employee acted as a mortgage loan originator for 5 or fewer residential mortgage loans.

(ii) Prior to engaging in mortgage loan origination activity that exceeds the exception limit in paragraph (c)(2)(i) of this section, an insured State nonmember bank employee must register with the Registry pursuant to this subpart.

(iii) *Evasion.* Insured State nonmember banks are prohibited from engaging in any act or practice to evade the limits of the *de minimis* exception set forth in paragraph (c)(2)(i) of this section.

§ 365.102 Definitions.

For purposes of this subpart, the following definitions apply:

(a) *Annual renewal period* means November 1 through December 31 of each year.

(b)(1) *Mortgage loan originator*[1] means an individual who:

(i) Takes a residential mortgage loan application; and

---

[1] Appendix A of this subpart provides examples of activities that would, and would not, cause an employee to fall within this definition of mortgage loan originator.

(ii) Offers or negotiates terms of a residential mortgage loan for compensation or gain.

(2) The term *mortgage loan originator* does not include:

(i) An individual who performs purely administrative or clerical tasks on behalf of an individual who is described in paragraph (b)(1) of this section;

(ii) An individual who only performs real estate brokerage activities (as defined in 12 U.S.C. 5102(3)(D)) and is licensed or registered as a real estate broker in accordance with applicable State law, unless the individual is compensated by a lender, a mortgage broker, or other mortgage loan originator or by any agent of such lender, mortgage broker, or other mortgage loan originator, and meets the definition of mortgage loan originator in paragraph (b)(1) of this section; or

(iii) An individual or entity solely involved in extensions of credit related to timeshare plans, as that term is defined in 11 U.S.C. 101(53D).

(3) *Administrative or clerical tasks* means the receipt, collection, and distribution of information common for the processing or underwriting of a loan in the residential mortgage industry and communication with a consumer to obtain information necessary for the processing or underwriting of a residential mortgage loan.

(c) *Nationwide Mortgage Licensing System and Registry* or *Registry* means the system developed and maintained by the Conference of State Bank Supervisors and the American Association of Residential Mortgage Regulators for the State licensing and registration of State-licensed mortgage loan originators and the registration of mortgage loan originators pursuant to 12 U.S.C. 5107.

(d) *Registered mortgage loan originator* or *registrant* means any individual who:

(1) Meets the definition of mortgage loan originator and is an employee of an insured State nonmember bank; and

(2) Is registered pursuant to this subpart with, and maintains a unique identifier through, the Registry.

(e) *Residential mortgage loan* means any loan primarily for personal, family, or household use that is secured by a mortgage, deed of trust, or other equivalent consensual security interest

§ 365.103

on a dwelling (as defined in section 103(v) of the Truth in Lending Act, 15 U.S.C. 1602(v)) or residential real estate upon which is constructed or intended to be constructed a dwelling, and includes refinancings, reverse mortgages, home equity lines of credit and other first and additional lien loans that meet the qualifications listed in this definition.

(f) *Unique identifier* means a number or other identifier that:

(1) Permanently identifies a registered mortgage loan originator;

(2) Is assigned by protocols established by the Nationwide Mortgage Licensing System and Registry, the Federal banking agencies, and the Farm Credit Administration to facilitate:

(i) Electronic tracking of mortgage loan originators; and

(ii) Uniform identification of, and public access to, the employment history of and the publicly adjudicated disciplinary and enforcement actions against mortgage loan originators; and

(3) Must not be used for purposes other than those set forth under the S.A.F.E. Act.

§ 365.103 Registration of mortgage loan originators.

(a) *Registration requirement*—(1) *Employee registration.* Each employee of an insured State nonmember bank who acts as a mortgage loan originator must register with the Registry, obtain a unique identifier, and maintain this registration in accordance with the requirements of this subpart. Any such employee who is not in compliance with the registration and unique identifier requirements set forth in this subpart is in violation of the S.A.F.E. Act and this subpart.

(2) *Insured State nonmember bank requirement*—(i) *In general.* An insured State nonmember bank that employs one or more individuals who act as a residential mortgage loan originator must require each such employee to register with the Registry, maintain this registration, and obtain a unique identifier in accordance with the requirements of this subpart.

(ii) *Prohibition.* An insured State nonmember bank must not permit an employee of the bank who is subject to the registration requirements of this subpart to act as a mortgage loan originator for the bank unless such employee is registered with the Registry pursuant to this subpart.

(3) *Implementation period for initial registration.* An employee of an insured State nonmember bank who is a mortgage loan originator must complete an initial registration with the Registry pursuant to this subpart within 180 days from the date that the FDIC provides in a public notice that the Registry is accepting registrations.

(4) *Employees previously registered or licensed through the Registry*—(i) *In general.* If an employee of an insured State nonmember bank was registered or licensed through, and obtained a unique identifier from, the Registry and has maintained this registration or license before the employee becomes subject to this subpart at this bank, then the registration requirements of the S.A.F.E. Act and this subpart are deemed to be met, provided that:

(A) The employment information in paragraphs (d)(1)(i)(C) and (d)(1)(ii) of this section is updated and the requirements of paragraph (d)(2) of this section are met;

(B) New fingerprints of the employee are submitted to the Registry for a background check, as required by paragraph (d)(1)(ix) of this section, unless the employee has fingerprints on file with the Registry that are less than 3 years old;

(C) The insured State nonmember bank information required in paragraphs (e)(1)(i) (to the extent the bank has not previously met these requirements) and (e)(2)(i) of this section is submitted to the Registry; and

(D) The registration is maintained pursuant to paragraphs (b) and (e)(1)(ii) of this section, as of the date that the employee becomes subject to this subpart.

(ii) *Rule for certain acquisitions, mergers, or reorganizations.* When registered or licensed mortgage loan originators become insured State nonmember bank employees as a result of an acquisition, merger, or reorganization, only the requirements of paragraphs (a)(4)(i)(A), (C), and (D) of this section must be met, and these requirements must be met within 60 days from the effective

Federal Deposit Insurance Corporation § 365.103

date of the acquisition, merger, or reorganization.

(b) *Maintaining registration.* (1) A mortgage loan originator who is registered with the Registry pursuant to paragraph (a) of this section must:

(i) Except as provided in paragraph (b)(3) of this section, renew the registration during the annual renewal period, confirming the responses set forth in paragraphs (d)(1)(i) through (viii) of this section remain accurate and complete, and updating this information, as appropriate; and

(ii) Update the registration within 30 days of any of the following events:

(A) A change in the name of the registrant;

(B) The registrant ceases to be an employee of the insured State nonmember bank; or

(C) The information required under paragraphs (d)(1)(iii) through (viii) of this section becomes inaccurate, incomplete, or out-of-date.

(2) A registered mortgage loan originator must maintain his or her registration, unless the individual is no longer engaged in the activity of a mortgage loan originator.

(3) The annual registration renewal requirement set forth in paragraph (b)(1) of this section does not apply to a registered mortgage loan originator who has completed his or her registration with the Registry pursuant to paragraph (a)(1) of this section less than 6 months prior to the end of the annual renewal period.

(c) *Effective dates*—(1) *Registration.* A registration pursuant to paragraph (a)(1) of this section is effective on the date the Registry transmits notification to the registrant that the registrant is registered.

(2) *Renewals or updates.* A renewal or update pursuant to paragraph (b) of this section is effective on the date the Registry transmits notification to the registrant that the registration has been renewed or updated.

(d) *Required employee information*—(1) *In general.* For purposes of the registration required by this section, an insured State nonmember bank must require each employee who is a mortgage loan originator to submit to the Registry, or must submit on behalf of the employee, the following categories of information to the extent this information is collected by the Registry:

(i) Identifying information, including the employee's:

(A) Name and any other names used;

(B) Home address and contact information;

(C) Principal business location address and business contact information;

(D) Social security number;

(E) Gender; and

(F) Date and place of birth;

(ii) Financial services-related employment history for the 10 years prior to the date of registration or renewal, including the date the employee became an employee of the bank;

(iii) Convictions of any criminal offense involving dishonesty, breach of trust, or money laundering against the employee or organizations controlled by the employee, or agreements to enter into a pretrial diversion or similar program in connection with the prosecution for such offense(s);

(iv) Civil judicial actions against the employee in connection with financial services-related activities, dismissals with settlements, or judicial findings that the employee violated financial services-related statutes or regulations, except for actions dismissed without a settlement agreement;

(v) Actions or orders by a State or Federal regulatory agency or foreign financial regulatory authority that:

(A) Found the employee to have made a false statement or omission or been dishonest, unfair or unethical; to have been involved in a violation of a financial services-related regulation or statute; or to have been a cause of a financial services-related business having its authorization to do business denied, suspended, revoked, or restricted;

(B) Are entered against the employee in connection with a financial services-related activity;

(C) Denied, suspended, or revoked the employee's registration or license to engage in a financial services-related activity; disciplined the employee or otherwise by order prevented the employee from associating with a financial services-related business or restricted the employee's activities; or

(D) Barred the employee from association with an entity or its officers

§ 365.103

regulated by the agency or authority or from engaging in a financial services-related business;

(vi) Final orders issued by a State or Federal regulatory agency or foreign financial regulatory authority based on violations of any law or regulation that prohibits fraudulent, manipulative, or deceptive conduct;

(vii) Revocation or suspension of the employee's authorization to act as an attorney, accountant, or State or Federal contractor;

(viii) Customer-initiated financial services-related arbitration or civil action against the employee that required action, including settlements, or which resulted in a judgment; and

(ix) Fingerprints of the employee, in digital form if practicable, and any appropriate identifying information for submission to the Federal Bureau of Investigation and any governmental agency or entity authorized to receive such information in connection with a State and national criminal history background check; however, fingerprints provided to the Registry that are less than 3 years old may be used to satisfy this requirement.

(2) *Employee authorizations and attestation.* An employee registering as a mortgage loan originator or renewing or updating his or her registration under this subpart, and not the employing insured State nonmember bank or other employees of the insured State nonmember bank, must:

(i) Authorize the Registry and the employing institution to obtain information related to sanctions or findings in any administrative, civil, or criminal action, to which the employee is a party, made by any governmental jurisdiction;

(ii) Attest to the correctness of all information required by paragraph (d) of this section, whether submitted by the employee or on behalf of the employee by the employing bank; and

(iii) Authorize the Registry to make available to the public information required by paragraphs (d)(1)(i)(A) and (C), and (d)(1)(ii) through (viii) of this section.

(3) *Submission of information.* An insured State nonmember bank may identify one or more employees of the bank who may submit the information required by paragraph (d)(1) of this section to the Registry on behalf of the bank's employees provided that this individual, and any employee delegated such authority, does not act as a mortgage loan originator, consistent with paragraph (e)(1)(i)(F) of this section. In addition, an insured State nonmember bank may submit to the Registry some or all of the information required by paragraphs (d)(1) and (e)(2) of this section for multiple employees in bulk through batch processing in a format to be specified by the Registry, to the extent such batch processing is made available by the Registry.

(e) *Required bank information.* An insured State nonmember bank must submit the following categories of information to the Registry:

(1) *Bank record.* (i) In connection with the registration of one or more mortgage loan originators:

(A) Name, main office address, and business contact information;

(B) Internal Revenue Service Employer Tax Identification Number (EIN);

(C) Research Statistics Supervision and Discount (RSSD) number, as issued by the Board of Governors of the Federal Reserve System;

(D) Identification of its primary Federal regulator;

(E) Name(s) and contact information of the individual(s) with authority to act as the bank's primary point of contact for the Registry;

(F) Name(s) and contact information of the individual(s) with authority to enter the information required by paragraphs (d)(1) and (e) of this section to the Registry and who may delegate this authority to other individuals. For the purpose of providing information required by paragraph (e) of this section, this individual and their delegates must not act as mortgage loan originators unless the bank has 10 or fewer full time or equivalent employees and is not a subsidiary; and

(G) If a subsidiary of an insured State nonmember bank, indication that it is a subsidiary and the RSSD number of the parent bank.

(ii) *Attestation.* The individual(s) identified in paragraphs (e)(1)(i)(E) and (F) of this section must comply with

Federal Deposit Insurance Corporation

§ 365.105

Registry protocols to verify their identity and must attest that they have the authority to enter data on behalf of the insured State nonmember bank, that the information provided to the Registry pursuant to this paragraph (e) is correct, and that the insured State nonmember bank will keep the information required by this paragraph (e) current and will file accurate supplementary information on a timely basis.

(iii) An insured State nonmember bank must update the information required by this paragraph (e) of this section within 30 days of the date that this information becomes inaccurate.

(iv) An insured State nonmember bank must renew the information required by paragraph (e) of this section on an annual basis.

(2) *Employee information.* In connection with the registration of each employee who acts as a mortgage loan originator:

(i) After the information required by paragraph (d) of this section has been submitted to the Registry, confirmation that it employs the registrant; and

(ii) Within 30 days of the date the registrant ceases to be an employee of the bank, notification that it no longer employs the registrant and the date the registrant ceased being an employee.

§ 365.104 Policies and procedures.

An insured State nonmember bank that employs one or more mortgage loan originators must adopt and follow written policies and procedures designed to assure compliance with this subpart. These policies and procedures must be appropriate to the nature, size, complexity, and scope of the mortgage lending activities of the bank, and apply only to those employees acting within the scope of their employment at the bank. At a minimum, these policies and procedures must:

(a) Establish a process for identifying which employees of the bank are required to be registered mortgage loan originators;

(b) Require that all employees of the insured State nonmember bank who are mortgage loan originators be informed of the registration requirements of the S.A.F.E. Act and this subpart and be instructed on how to comply with such requirements and procedures;

(c) Establish procedures to comply with the unique identifier requirements in § 365.105;

(d) Establish reasonable procedures for confirming the adequacy and accuracy of employee registrations, including updates and renewals, by comparisons with its own records;

(e) Establish reasonable procedures and tracking systems for monitoring compliance with registration and renewal requirements and procedures;

(f) Provide for independent testing for compliance with this subpart to be conducted at least annually by bank personnel or by an outside party;

(g) Provide for appropriate action in the case of any employee who fails to comply with the registration requirements of the S.A.F.E. Act, this subpart, or the bank's related policies and procedures, including prohibiting such employees from acting as mortgage loan originators or other appropriate disciplinary actions;

(h) Establish a process for reviewing employee criminal history background reports received pursuant to this subpart, taking appropriate action consistent with applicable Federal law, including section 19 of the Federal Deposit Insurance Act (12 U.S.C. 1829) and implementing regulations with respect to these reports, and maintaining records of these reports and actions taken with respect to applicable employees; and

(i) Establish procedures designed to ensure that any third party with which the bank has arrangements related to mortgage loan origination has policies and procedures to comply with the S.A.F.E. Act, including appropriate licensing and/or registration of individuals acting as mortgage loan originators.

§ 365.105 Use of unique identifier.

(a) The insured State nonmember bank shall make the unique identifier(s) of its registered mortgage loan originator(s) available to consumers in a manner and method practicable to the institution.

(b) A registered mortgage loan originator shall provide his or her unique identifier to a consumer:

(1) Upon request;

(2) Before acting as a mortgage loan originator; and

(3) Through the originator's initial written communication with a consumer, if any, whether on paper or electronically.

APPENDIX A TO SUBPART B OF PART 365—EXAMPLES OF MORTGAGE LOAN ORIGINATOR ACTIVITIES

This Appendix provides examples to aid in the understanding of activities that would cause an employee of an insured State nonmember bank to fall within or outside the definition of mortgage loan originator. The examples in this appendix are not all inclusive. They illustrate only the issue described and do not illustrate any other issues that may arise under this subpart. For purposes of the examples below, the term "loan" refers to a residential mortgage loan.

(a) *Taking a loan application.* The following examples illustrate when an employee takes, or does not take, a loan application.

(1) Taking an application includes: receiving information provided in connection with a request for a loan to be used to determine whether the consumer qualifies for a loan, even if the employee:

(i) Has received the consumer's information indirectly in order to make an offer or negotiate a loan;

(ii) Is not responsible for verifying information;

(iii) Is inputting information into an online application or other automated system on behalf of the consumer; or

(iv) Is not engaged in approval of the loan, including determining whether the consumer qualifies for the loan.

(2) Taking an application does not include any of the following activities performed solely or in combination:

(i) Contacting a consumer to verify the information in the loan application by obtaining documentation, such as tax returns or payroll receipts;

(ii) Receiving a loan application through the mail and forwarding it, without review, to loan approval personnel;

(iii) Assisting a consumer who is filling out an application by clarifying what type of information is necessary for the application or otherwise explaining the qualifications or criteria necessary to obtain a loan product;

(iv) Describing the steps that a consumer would need to take to provide information to be used to determine whether the consumer qualifies for a loan or otherwise explaining the loan application process;

(v) In response to an inquiry regarding a prequalified offer that a consumer has received from a bank, collecting only basic identifying information about the consumer and forwarding the consumer to a mortgage loan originator; or

(vi) Receiving information in connection with a modification to the terms of an existing loan to a borrower as part of the bank's loss mitigation efforts when the borrower is reasonably likely to default.

(b) *Offering or negotiating terms of a loan.* The following examples are designed to illustrate when an employee offers or negotiates terms of a loan, and conversely, what does not constitute offering or negotiating terms of a loan.

(1) Offering or negotiating the terms of a loan includes:

(i) Presenting a loan offer to a consumer for acceptance, either verbally or in writing, including, but not limited to, providing a disclosure of the loan terms after application under the Truth in Lending Act, even if:

(A) Further verification of information is necessary;

(B) The offer is conditional;

(C) Other individuals must complete the loan process; or

(D) Only the rate approved by the bank's loan approval mechanism function for a specific loan product is communicated without authority to negotiate the rate.

(ii) Responding to a consumer's request for a lower rate or lower points on a pending loan application by presenting to the consumer a revised loan offer, either verbally or in writing, that includes a lower interest rate or lower points than the original offer.

(2) Offering or negotiating terms of a loan does not include solely or in combination:

(i) Providing general explanations or descriptions in response to consumer queries regarding qualification for a specific loan product, such as explaining loan terminology (*i.e.*, debt-to-income ratio); lending policies (*i.e.*, the loan-to-value ratio policy of the insured State nonmember bank); or product-related services;

(ii) In response to a consumer's request, informing a consumer of the loan rates that are publicly available, such as on the insured State nonmember bank's Web site, for specific types of loan products without communicating to the consumer whether qualifications are met for that loan product;

(iii) Collecting information about a consumer in order to provide the consumer with information on loan products for which the consumer generally may qualify, without presenting a specific loan offer to the consumer for acceptance, either verbally or in writing;

(iv) Arranging the loan closing or other aspects of the loan process, including communicating with a consumer about those arrangements, provided that communication

Federal Deposit Insurance Corporation

with the consumer only verifies loan terms already offered or negotiated;

(v) Providing a consumer with information unrelated to loan terms, such as the best days of the month for scheduling loan closings at the bank;

(vi) Making an underwriting decision about whether the consumer qualifies for a loan;

(vii) Explaining or describing the steps or process that a consumer would need to take in order to obtain a loan offer, including qualifications or criteria that would need to be met without providing guidance specific to that consumer's circumstances; or

(viii) Communicating on behalf of a mortgage loan originator that a written offer, including disclosures provided pursuant to the Truth in Lending Act, has been sent to a consumer without providing any details of that offer.

(c) *Offering or negotiating a loan for compensation or gain.* The following examples illustrate when an employee does or does not offer or negotiate terms of a loan "for compensation or gain."

(1) Offering or negotiating terms of a loan for compensation or gain includes engaging in any of the activities in paragraph (b)(1) of this Appendix in the course of carrying out employment duties, even if the employee does not receive a referral fee or commission or other special compensation for the loan.

(2) Offering or negotiating terms of a loan for compensation or gain does not include engaging in a seller-financed transaction for the employee's personal property that does not involve the insured State nonmember bank.

PART 366—MINIMUM STANDARDS OF INTEGRITY AND FITNESS FOR AN FDIC CONTRACTOR

Sec.
366.0 Definitions.
366.1 What is the purpose of this part?
366.2 What is the scope of this part?
366.3 Who cannot perform contractual services for the FDIC?
366.4 When is there a pattern or practice of defalcation?
366.5 What causes a substantial loss to a federal deposit insurance fund?
366.6 How is my ownership or control determined?
366.7 Will the FDIC waive the prohibitions under §366.3?
366.8 Who can grant a waiver of a prohibition or conflict of interest?
366.9 What other requirements could prevent me from performing contractual services for the FDIC?
366.10 When would I have a conflict of interest?
366.11 Will the FDIC waive a conflict of interest?
366.12 What are the FDIC's minimum standards of ethical responsibility?
366.13 What is my obligation regarding confidential information?
366.14 What information must I provide the FDIC?
366.15 What advice or determinations will the FDIC provide me on the applicability of this part?
366.16 When may I seek a reconsideration or review of an FDIC determination?
366.17 What are the possible consequences for violating this part?

AUTHORITY: Section 9 (Tenth) of the Federal Deposit Insurance Act (FDI Act), 12 U.S.C. 1819 (Tenth); sections 12(f)(3) and (4) of the FDI Act, 12 U.S.C. 1822(f)(3) and (4); and section 19 of Pub. L. 103–204, 107 Stat. 2369.

SOURCE: 67 FR 69991, Nov. 20, 2002, unless otherwise noted.

§ 366.0 Definitions.

As used in this part:

(a) The word *person* refers to an individual, corporation, partnership, or other entity with a legally independent existence.

(b) The terms *we, our,* and *us* refer to the Federal Deposit Insurance Corporation (FDIC), except when acting as conservator or operator of a bridge bank.

(c) The terms *I, me, my, mine, you,* and *yourself* refer to a person who submits an offer to perform or performs, directly or indirectly, contractual services or functions on our behalf.

(d) The phrase *insured depository institution* refers to any bank or savings association whose deposits are insured by the FDIC.

§ 366.1 What is the purpose of this part?

This part establishes the minimum standards of integrity and fitness that contractors, subcontractors, and employees of contractors and subcontractors must meet if they perform any service or function on our behalf. This part includes regulations governing conflicts of interest, ethical responsibility, and use of confidential information in accordance with section 12(f)(3) of the FDI Act, 12 U.S.C. 1822(f)(3), and the prohibitions and the requirements for submission of information in accordance with section 12(f)(4) of the FDI Act, 12 U.S.C. 1822(f)(4)..

§ 366.2 What is the scope of this part?

(a) This part applies to a person who submits an offer to perform or performs, directly or indirectly, a contractual service or function on our behalf.

(b) This part does not apply to:

(1) An FDIC employee for the purposes of title 18, United States Code; or

(2) The FDIC when we operate an insured depository institution such as a bridge bank or conservatorship.

§ 366.3 Who cannot perform contractual services for the FDIC?

We will not enter into a contract with you to perform a service or function on our behalf, if you or any person that owns or controls you, or any entity you own or control:

(a) Has a felony conviction;

(b) Was removed from or is prohibited from participating in the affairs of an insured depository institution as a result of a federal banking agency final enforcement action;

(c) Has a pattern or practice of defalcation; or

(d) Is responsible for a substantial loss to the Deposit Insurance Fund (or any predecessor deposit insurance fund).

[67 FR 69991, Nov. 20, 2002, as amended at 71 FR 20527, Apr. 21, 2006]

§ 366.4 When is there a pattern or practice of defalcation?

(a) You have a pattern or practice of defalcation under § 366.3(c) when you, any person that owns or controls you, or any entity you own or control has a legal responsibility for the payment on at least two obligations that are:

(1) To one or more insured depository institutions;

(2) More than 90 days delinquent in the payment of principal, interest, or a combination thereof; and

(3) More than $50,000 each.

(b) The following are examples of when you have or do not have a pattern or practice of defalcation. These examples are not inclusive.

(1) You have five loans at insured depository institutions. Three of them are 90 days past due. Two of the three loans have outstanding balances of more than $50,000 each. You have a pattern or practice of defalcation.

(2) You have five loans at insured depository institutions. Two of them are 90 days past due. One of the two is with ABC Bank for $170,000. The other one is with XYZ bank for $60,000. You have a pattern or practice of defalcation.

(3) You have five loans at insured depository institutions. Three of them are 90 days past due. One of the three has an outstanding balance of more than $50,000. The other two have outstanding balances of less than $50,000. You do not have a pattern or practice of defalcation.

(4) You have five loans at insured depository institutions. Three of them have outstanding balances of more than $50,000. Two of those three were 90 days past due but are now current. You do not have a pattern or practice of defalcation.

§ 366.5 What causes a substantial loss to a federal deposit insurance fund?

You cause a substantial loss to the Deposit Insurance Fund (or any predecessor deposit insurance fund) under § 366.3(d) when you, or any person that owns or controls you, or any entity you own or control has:

(a) An obligation to us that is delinquent for 90 days or more and on which there is an outstanding balance of principal, interest, or a combination thereof of more than $50,000;

(b) An unpaid final judgment in our favor that is in excess of $50,000, regardless of whether it becomes discharged in whole or in part in a bankruptcy proceeding;

(c) A deficiency balance following foreclosure of collateral on an obligation owed to us that is in excess of $50,000, regardless of whether it becomes discharged in whole or in part in a bankruptcy proceeding; or

(d) A loss to us that is in excess of $50,000 that we report on IRS Form 1099–C, Information Reporting for Discharge of Indebtedness.

[67 FR 69991, Nov. 20, 2002, as amended at 71 FR 20527, Apr. 21, 2006]

§ 366.6 How is my ownership or control determined?

(a) Your ownership or control is determined on a case-by-case basis. Your ownership or control depends on the specific facts of your situation and the

Federal Deposit Insurance Corporation § 366.11

particular industry and legal entity involved. You must provide documentation to us to use in determining your ownership or control.

(b) The interest of a spouse or other family member in the same organization is imputed to you in determining your ownership or control.

(c) The following are examples of when your ownership or control may or may not exist. These examples are not inclusive.

(1) You have control if you are the president or chief executive officer of an organization.

(2) You have ownership or control if you are a partner in a small law firm. You might not have ownership or control if you are a partner in a large national law firm.

(3) You have control if you are a general partner of a limited partnership. You have ownership or control if you have a limited partnership interest of 25 percent or more.

(4) You have ownership or control if you have the:

(i) Power to vote, directly or indirectly, 25% or more interest of any class of voting stock of a company;

(ii) Ability to direct in any manner the election of a majority of a company's directors or trustees; or

(iii) Ability to exercise a controlling influence over the company's management and policies.

§ 366.7 Will the FDIC waive the prohibitions under § 366.3?

We may waive the prohibitions for entities other than individuals for good cause shown at our discretion when our need to contract for your services outweighs all relevant factors. The statute does not allow us to waive the prohibitions for individuals.

§ 366.8 Who can grant a waiver of a prohibition or conflict of interest?

The FDIC's Board of Directors delegates to the Chairman, or his designee, authority to issue waivers and implement procedures for part 366.

§ 366.9 What other requirements could prevent me from performing contractual services for the FDIC?

You must avoid a conflict of interest, be ethically responsible, and maintain confidential information as described in §§ 366.10 through 366.13. You must also provide us with the information we require in § 366.14. Failure to meet these requirements may prevent you from contracting with us.

§ 366.10 When would I have a conflict of interest?

(a) You have a conflict of interest when you, any person that owns or controls you, or any entity you own or control:

(1) Has a personal, business, or financial interest or relationship that relates to the services you perform under the contract;

(2) Is a party to litigation against us, or represents a party that is;

(3) Submits an offer to acquire an asset from us for which services were performed during the past three years, unless the contract allows for the acquisition; or

(4) Engages in an activity that would cause us to question the integrity of the service you provided, are providing or offer to provide us, or impairs your independence.

(b) The following are examples of a conflict of interest. These examples are not inclusive.

(1) You submit an offer to perform property management services for us and you own or manage a competing property.

(2) You audit a business under a contract with us and you or a partner in your firm has an ownership interest in that business.

(3) You perform loan services on a pool of loans we are selling, and you submit a bid to purchase one or more of the loans in the pool.

(4) You audit your own work or provide nonaudit services that are significant or material to the subject matter of the audit.

§ 366.11 Will the FDIC waive a conflict of interest?

(a) We may waive a conflict of interest for good cause shown at our discretion when our need to contract for your services outweighs all relevant factors.

(b) The following are examples of when we may grant you a waiver for a conflict of interest. These examples are not inclusive.

§ 366.12

(1) We may grant a waiver to an outside counsel who has a representational conflict. We will weigh all relevant facts and circumstances in making our determination.

(2) We may grant a waiver to allow a contractor to acquire an asset from us who is providing or has provided services on that asset. We will consider whether granting the waiver will adversely affect the fairness of the sale, the type of services provided, and other facts and circumstances relevant to the sale in making our determination.

§ 366.12 What are the FDIC's minimum standards of ethical responsibility?

(a) You and any person who performs services for us must not provide preferential treatment to any person in your dealings with the public on our behalf.

(b) You must ensure that any person you employ to perform services for us is informed about their responsibilities under this part.

(c) You must disclose to us waste, fraud, abuse or corruption. Contact the Inspector General at 1–800–964–FDIC or Ighotline@fdic.gov.

(d) You and any person who performs contract services to us must not:

(1) Accept or solicit for yourself or others any favor, gift, or other item of monetary value from any person who you reasonably believe is seeking an official action from you on our behalf, or has an interest that the performance or nonperformance of your duties to us may substantially affect;

(2) Use or allow the use of our property, except as specified in the contract;

(3) Make an unauthorized promise or commitment on our behalf; or

(4) Provide impermissible gifts or entertainment to an FDIC employee or other person providing services to us.

(e) The following are examples of when you are engaging in unethical behavior. These examples are not inclusive.

(1) Using government resources, including our Internet connection, to conduct any business that is unrelated to the performance of your contract with us.

(2) Submitting false invoices or claims, or making misleading or false statements.

(3) Committing us to forgive or restructure a debt or portion of a debt, unless we provide you with written authority to do so.

§ 366.13 What is my obligation regarding confidential information?

(a) Neither you nor any person who performs services on your behalf may use or disclose information obtained from us or a third party in connection with an FDIC contract, unless:

(1) The contract allows or we authorize the use or disclosure;

(2) The information is generally available to the general public; or

(3) We make the information available to the general public.

(b) The following are examples of when your use of confidential information is inappropriate. These examples are not inclusive.

(1) Disclosing information about an asset, such as internal asset valuations, appraisals or environmental reports, except as part of authorized due diligence materials, to a prospective asset purchaser.

(2) Disclosing a borrower's or guarantor's personal or financial information, such as a financial statement to an unauthorized party.

§ 366.14 What information must I provide the FDIC?

You must:

(a) Certify in writing that you can perform services for us under § 366.3 and have no conflict of interest under § 366.10(a).

(b) Submit a list and description of any instance during the preceding five years in which you, any person that owns or controls you, or any entity you own or control, defaulted on a material obligation to an insured depository institution. A default on a material obligation occurs when a loan or advance with an outstanding balance of more than $50,000 is or was delinquent for 90 days or more.

(c) Notify us within 10 business days after you become aware that you, or any person you employ to perform services for us, are not in compliance

Federal Deposit Insurance Corporation

with this part. Your notice must include a detailed description of the facts of the situation and how you intend to resolve the matter.

(d) Agree in writing that you will employ only persons who meet the requirements of this part to perform services on our behalf.

(e) Comply with any request from us for information.

(f) Retain any information you prepare or rely upon regarding the provisions of this part for a period of three years following termination or expiration and final payment of the related contract for services whichever occurs last.

§ 366.15 What advice or determinations will the FDIC provide me on the applicability of this part?

(a) We are available to you for consultation on those determinations you are responsible for making under this part, including those with respect to any person you employ or engage to perform services for us.

(b) We will determine if this part prohibits you from performing services for us prior to contract award, after contract award, and during the performance of a contract.

(c) We may determine what corrective action you must take.

(d) We may grant you a waiver for good cause shown where provided for under this part.

§ 366.16 When may I seek a reconsideration or review of an FDIC determination?

(a) You may seek reconsideration or review of our initial determination by sending a written request to the individual who issued you the initial decision.

(b) You must provide new information or explain a change in circumstances for our reconsideration of an initial decision. The individual who issued you the initial decision may either make a new determination or refer your request to a higher authority for review.

(c) You must provide an explanation of how you perceive that we misapplied this part that sets forth the legal or factual errors for our review of an initial decision.

§ 367.1

§ 366.17 What are the possible consequences for violating this part?

Depending on the circumstances, violations of this part may result in rescission or termination of a contract, as well as administrative, civil, or criminal sanctions.

PART 367—SUSPENSION AND EXCLUSION OF CONTRACTOR AND TERMINATION OF CONTRACTS

Sec.
367.1 Authority, purpose, scope and application.
367.2 Definitions.
367.3 Appropriate officials.
367.4 [Reserved]
367.5 Exclusions.
367.6 Causes for exclusion.
367.7 Suspensions.
367.8 Causes for suspension.
367.9 Imputation of causes.
367.10–67.11 [Reserved]
367.12 Procedures.
367.13 Notices.
367.14 Responses.
367.15 Additional proceedings as to disputed material facts.
367.16 Ethics Counselor decisions.
367.17 Duration of suspensions and exclusions.
367.18 Abrogation of contracts.
367.19 Exceptions to suspensions and exclusions.
367.20 Review and reconsideration of Ethics Counselor decisions.

AUTHORITY: 12 U.S.C. 1822(f) (4) and (5).

SOURCE: 61 FR 68560, Dec. 30, 1996, unless otherwise noted.

§ 367.1 Authority, purpose, scope and application.

(a) *Authority.* This part is adopted pursuant to section 12(f) (4) and (5) of the Federal Deposit Insurance Act, 12 U.S.C. 1822(f) (4) and (5), and the rulemaking authority of the Federal Deposit Insurance Corporation (FDIC) found at 12 U.S.C. 1819. Other regulations implementing these statutory directives appear at 12 CFR part 366.

(b) *Purpose.* This part is designed to inform contractors and subcontractors (including their affiliated business entities, key employees and management officials) regarding their rights to notice and an opportunity to be heard on FDIC actions involving suspension and exclusion from contracting and rescission of existing contracts. This part is

§ 367.2

in addition to, and not in lieu of, any other statute or regulation that may apply to such contractual activities.

(c) *Scope.* This part applies to:

(1) Contractors, other than attorneys or law firms providing legal services, submitting offers to provide services or entering into contracts to provide services to the FDIC acting in any capacity; and

(2) Subcontractors entering into contracts to perform services under a proposed or existing contract with the FDIC.

(d) *Application.* (1) This part will apply to entities that become contractors, as defined in § 367.2(f), on or after December 30, 1996. In addition, this part will apply to contractors as defined in § 367.2(f) that are performing contracts on December 30, 1996.

(2) This part will also apply to actions initiated on or after December 30, 1996 regardless of the date of the cause giving rise to the actions.

(3) Contracts entered into by the former Resolution Trust Corporation (RTC) that were transferred to the FDIC will be treated in the same manner as FDIC contracts under this part.

(4) RTC actions taken under the RTC regulations on or before December 31, 1995, will be honored as if taken by the FDIC. A contractor subject to an RTC exclusion or suspension will be precluded thereby from participation in the FDIC's contracting program unless that exclusion or suspension is modified or terminated under the provisions of this part.

§ 367.2 Definitions.

(a) *Adequate evidence* means information sufficient to support the reasonable belief that a particular act or omission has occurred.

(b) *Affiliated business entity* means a company that is under the control of the contractor, is in control of the contractor, or is under common control with the contractor.

(c) *Civil judgment* means a judgment of a civil offense or liability by any court of competent jurisdiction in the United States.

(d) *Company* means any corporation, firm, partnership, society, joint venture, business trust, association, consortium or similar organization.

(e) *Conflict of interest* means a situation in which:

(1) A contractor; any management officials or affiliated business entities of a contractor; or any employees, agents, or subcontractors of a contractor who will perform services under a proposed or existing contract with the FDIC:

(i) Has one or more personal, business, or financial interests or relationships which would cause a reasonable individual with knowledge of the relevant facts to question the integrity or impartiality of those who are or will be acting under a proposed or existing FDIC contract;

(ii) Is an adverse party to the FDIC, RTC, the former Federal Savings and Loan Insurance Corporation (FSLIC), or their successors in a lawsuit; or

(iii) Has ever been suspended, excluded, or debarred from contracting with a federal entity or has ever had a contract with the FDIC, RTC, FSLIC or their successors rescinded or terminated prior to the contract's completion and which rescission or termination involved issues of conflicts of interest or ethical responsibilities; or

(2) Any other facts exist which the FDIC, in its sole discretion, determines may, through performance of a proposed or existing FDIC contract, provide a contractor with an unfair competitive advantage which favors the interests of the contractor or any person with whom the contractor has or is likely to have a personal or business relationship.

(f) *Contractor* means a person or company which has submitted an offer to perform services for the FDIC or has a contractual arrangement with the FDIC to perform services. For purposes of this part, contractor also includes:

(1) A contractor's affiliated business entities, key employees, and management officials of the contractor;

(2) Any subcontractor performing services for the FDIC and the management officials and key employees of such subcontractors; and

(3) Any entity or organization seeking to perform services for the FDIC as a minority or woman-owned business (MWOB).

(g) *Contract(s)* means agreement(s) between FDIC and a contractor, including, but not limited to, agreements

Federal Deposit Insurance Corporation § 367.2

identified as "Task Orders", for a contractor to provide services to FDIC. Contracts also mean contracts between a contractor and its subcontractor.

(h) *Control* means the power to vote, directly or indirectly, 25 percent or more of any class of the voting stock of a company; the ability to direct in any manner the election of a majority of a company's directors or trustees; or the ability to exercise a controlling influence over the company's management and policies. For purposes of this definition, a general partner of a limited partnership is presumed to be in control of that partnership.

(i) *Conviction* means a judgment or conviction of a criminal offense by any court of competent jurisdiction, whether entered upon a verdict or plea, and includes pleas of nolo contendere.

(j) *FDIC* means the Federal Deposit Insurance Corporation acting in its receivership and corporate capacities, and FDIC officials or committees acting under delegated authority.

(k) *Indictment* shall include an information or other filing by a competent authority charging a criminal offense.

(l) *Key employee* means an individual who participates personally and substantially in the negotiation of, performance of, and/or monitoring for compliance under a contract with the FDIC. Such participation is made through, but is not limited to, decision, approval, disapproval, recommendation, or the rendering of advice under the contract.

(m) *Management official* means any shareholder, employee or partner who controls a company and any individual who directs the day-to-day operations of a company. With respect to a partnership, all partners are deemed to be management officials unless the partnership is governed by a management or executive committee with responsibility for the day-to-day operations. In partnerships with such committees, management official means only those partners who are a member of such a committee.

(n) *Material fact* means one that is necessary to determine the outcome of an issue or case and without which the case could not be supported.

(o) *Offer* means a proposal or other written or oral offer to provide services to FDIC.

(p) *Pattern or practice of defalcation regarding obligations* means two or more instances in which a loan or advance from an insured depository institution:

(1) Is in default for ninety (90) or more days as to payment of principal, interest, or a combination thereof, and there remains a legal obligation to pay an amount in excess of $50,000; or

(2) Where there has been a failure to comply with the terms of a loan or advance to such an extent that the collateral securing the loan or advance was foreclosed upon, resulting in a loss in excess of $50,000 to the insured depository institution.

(q) *Preponderance of the evidence* means proof by information that, compared with that opposing it, leads to the conclusion that the fact at issue is more probably true than not.

(r) *Subcontractor* means an entity or organization that enters into a contract with an FDIC contractor or another subcontractor to perform services under a proposed or existing contract with the FDIC.

(s) *Substantial loss to federal deposit insurance funds* means:

(1) A loan or advance from an insured depository institution, which is currently owed to the FDIC, RTC, FSLIC or their successors, or the former Bank Insurance Fund (BIF), the former Savings Association Insurance Fund (SAIF) or the Deposit Insurance Fund, the FSLIC Reserve Fund (FRF), or funds that were maintained by the RTC for the benefit of insured depositors, that is or has ever been delinquent for ninety (90) or more days as to payment of principal, interest, or a combination thereof and on which there remains a legal obligation to pay an amount in excess of $50,000;

(2) An obligation to pay an outstanding, unsatisfied, final judgment in excess of $50,000 in favor of the FDIC, RTC, FSLIC, or their successors, or the BIF, the SAIF, the FRF or the funds that were maintained by the RTC for the benefit of insured depositors; or

(3) A loan or advance from an insured depository institution which is currently owed to the FDIC, RTC, FSLIC or their successors, or the former BIF,

§ 367.3

the former SAIF, the Deposit Insurance Fund, the FRF or the funds that were maintained by the RTC for the benefit of insured depositors, where there has been a failure to comply with the terms to such an extent that the collateral securing the loan or advance was foreclosed upon, resulting in a loss in excess of $50,000.

[61 FR 68560, Dec. 30, 1996, as amended at 71 FR 20527, Apr. 21, 2006]

§ 367.3 Appropriate officials.

(a) The *Ethics Counselor* is the Executive Secretary of the FDIC. The Ethics Counselor shall act as the official responsible for rendering suspension and exclusion decisions under this part. In addition to taking suspension and/or exclusion action under this part, the Ethics Counselor has authority to terminate exclusion and suspension proceedings. As used in this part, "Ethics Counselor" includes any official designated by the Ethics Counselor to act on the Ethics Counselor's behalf.

(b) The *Corporation Ethics Committee* is the Committee appointed by the Chairman of the FDIC, or Chairman's designee, which provides review of any suspension or exclusion decision rendered by the Ethics Counselor that is appealed by a contractor who has been suspended and/or excluded from FDIC contracting.

(c) Information concerning the possible existence of any cause for suspension or exclusion shall be reported to the Office of the Executive Secretary (Ethics Section). This part does not modify the responsibility to report allegations of fraud, waste and abuse, including but not limited to criminal violations, to the Office of Inspector General.

§ 367.4 [Reserved]

§ 367.5 Exclusions.

(a) The Ethics Counselor may exclude a contractor from the FDIC contracting program for any of the causes set forth in § 367.6, using procedures established in this part.

(b) Exclusion is a serious action to be imposed when there exists a preponderance of the evidence that a contractor has violated one or more of the causes set forth in § 367.6. Contractors excluded from FDIC contracting programs are prohibited from entering into any new contracts with FDIC for the duration of the period of exclusion as determined pursuant to this part. The FDIC shall not solicit offers from, award contracts to, extend or modify existing contracts, award task orders under existing contracts, or consent to subcontracts with such contractors. Excluded contractors are also prohibited from conducting business with FDIC as agents or representatives of other contractors. *Provided however*, that these limitations do not become effective upon the notification of the contractor that there is a possible cause to exclude under § 367.13. Rather, they become effective only upon the Ethics Counselor's decision to exclude the contractor pursuant to § 367.16. *Provided further*, that the causes for exclusion set forth in § 367.6(a)(1) through (4) reflect statutorily established mandatory bars to contracting with the FDIC.

(c) Except when one or more of the statutorily established mandatory bars to contracting are shown to exist, the existence of a cause for exclusion does not necessarily require that the contractor be excluded; the seriousness of the contractor's acts or omissions and any mitigating or aggravating circumstances shall be considered in making any exclusion decision.

§ 367.6 Causes for exclusion.

The FDIC may exclude a contractor, in accordance with the procedures set forth in this part, upon a finding that:

(a) The contractor has been convicted of any felony;

(b) The contractor has been removed from, or prohibited from participating in the affairs of, any insured depository institution pursuant to any final enforcement action by the Office of the Comptroller of the Currency, the Office of Thrift Supervision, the Board of Governors of the Federal Reserve System, or the FDIC or their successors;

(c) The contractor has demonstrated a pattern or practice of defalcation;

(d) The contractor has caused a substantial loss to Deposit Insurance Fund (or any predecessor deposit insurance fund);

(e) The contractor has failed to disclose, pursuant to 12 CFR 366.6, a material fact to the FDIC;

(f) The contractor has failed to disclosed any material adverse change in the representations and certifications provided to FDIC under 12 CFR 366.6;

(g) The contractor has miscertified its status as a minority and/or woman owned business (MWOB);

(h) The contractor has a conflict of interest that was not waived by the Ethics Counselor or designee;

(i) The contractor has been subject to a final enforcement action by any federal financial institution regulatory agency, or has stipulated to such action;

(j) The contractor is debarred from participating in other federal programs;

(k) The contractor has been convicted of, or subject to a civil judgment for:

(1) Commission of fraud or a criminal offense in connection with obtaining, attempting to obtain, or performing a public or private agreement or transaction, or conspiracy to do the same;

(2) Violation of federal or state antitrust statutes, including those proscribing price fixing between competitors, allocation of customers between competitors, and bid rigging, or conspiracy to do the same;

(3) Commission of embezzlement, theft, forgery, bribery, falsification or destruction of records, making false statements, receiving stolen property, making false claims, obstructing of justice, or conspiracy to do the same;

(4) Commission of any other offense indicating a breach of trust, dishonesty or lack of integrity, or conspiracy to do the same;

(1) The contractor's performance under previous contract(s) with FDIC or RTC has resulted in:

(1) The FDIC or RTC declaring such contract(s) to be in default; or

(2) The termination of such contract(s) for poor performance; or

(3) A violation of the terms of a contract that would have resulted in a default or termination of the contract for poor performance if that violation had been discovered during the course of the contract; or

(m) The contractor has engaged in any conduct:

(1) Indicating a breach of trust, dishonesty, or lack of integrity that seriously and directly affects its ability to meet standards of present responsibility required of an FDIC contractor; or

(2) So serious or compelling in nature that it adversely affects the ability of a contractor to meet the minimum ethical standards required by 12 CFR part 366.

[61 FR 68560, Dec. 30, 1996, as amended at 71 FR 20528, Apr. 21, 2006]

§ 367.7 Suspensions.

(a) The Ethics Counselor may suspend a contractor for any of the causes in § 367.8 using the procedures established in this section.

(b) Suspension is an action to be imposed when there exists adequate evidence of one or more of the causes set out in § 367.8. This includes, but is not limited to, situations where immediate action is necessary to protect the integrity of the FDIC contracting program and/or the security of FDIC assets during the pendency of legal or investigative proceedings initiated by FDIC, any federal agency or any law enforcement authority.

(c) The duration of any suspension action shall be for a temporary period pending the completion of an investigation and such other legal proceedings as may ensue.

(d) A suspension shall become effective immediately upon issuance of the notice specified in § 367.13(b).

(e) Contractors suspended from FDIC contracting programs are prohibited from entering into any new contracts with the FDIC for the duration of the period of suspension. The FDIC shall not solicit offers from, award contracts to, extend or modify existing contracts, award task orders under existing contracts, or consent to subcontracts with such contractors. Suspended contractors are also prohibited from conducting business with FDIC as agents or representatives of other contractors.

§ 367.8 Causes for suspension.

(a) Suspension may be imposed under the procedures set forth in this section upon adequate evidence:

(1) Of suspension by another federal agency;

(2) That a cause for exclusion under § 367.6 may exist;

(3) Of the commission of any other offense indicating a breach of trust, dishonesty, or lack of integrity that seriously and directly affects the minimum ethical standards required of an FDIC contractor; or

(4) Of any other cause so serious or compelling in nature that it adversely affects the ability of a contractor to meet the minimal ethical standards required by 12 CFR part 366.

(b) Indictment for any offense described in § 367.6 is adequate evidence to suspend a contractor.

(c) In assessing the adequacy of the evidence, FDIC will consider how much information is available, how credible it is given the circumstances, whether or not important allegations are corroborated and what inferences can reasonably be drawn as a result.

§ 367.9 Imputation of causes.

(a) Where there is cause to suspend and/or exclude any affiliated business entity of the contractor, that conduct may be imputed to the contractor if the conduct occurred in connection with the affiliated business entity's performance of duties for or on behalf of the contractor, or with the contractor's knowledge, approval, or acquiescence. The contractor's acceptance of the benefits derived from the conduct shall be evidence of such knowledge, approval, or acquiescence.

(b) Where there is cause to suspend and/or exclude any contractor, that conduct may be imputed to any affiliated business entity, key employee, or management official of a contractor who participated in, knew of or had reason to know of the contractor's conduct.

(c) Where there is cause to suspend and/or exclude a key employee or management official of a contractor, that cause may be imputed to the contractor if the conduct occurred in connection with the key employee or management official's performance of duties for or on behalf of the contractor, or with the contractor's knowledge, approval, or acquiescence. The contractor's acceptance of the benefits derived from the conduct shall be evidence of such knowledge, approval, or acquiescence.

(d) Where there is cause to suspend and/or exclude one contractor participating in a joint venture or similar arrangement, that cause may be imputed to other participating contractors if the conduct occurred for or on behalf of the joint venture or similar arrangement, or with the knowledge, approval, or acquiescence of these contractors. Acceptance of the benefits derived from the conduct shall be evidence of such knowledge, approval, or acquiescence.

(e) Where there is cause to suspend and/or exclude a subcontractor, that cause may be imputed to the contractor for which the subcontractor performed services, if the conduct occurred for or on behalf of the contractor and with the contractor's knowledge, approval, or acquiescence. Acceptance of the benefits derived from the conduct shall be evidence of such knowledge, approval, or acquiescence.

§§ 367.10–367.11 [Reserved]

§ 367.12 Procedures.

(a) FDIC shall process suspension and exclusion actions as informally as practicable, consistent with its policy of providing contractors with adequate information on the grounds that give rise to the proposed action and affording contractors with a reasonable opportunity to respond.

(b) For purposes of determining filing dates for the pleadings required by this part, including responses, notices of appeal, appeals and requests for reconsideration, the provisions relating to the construction of time limits in 12 CFR 308.12 will control.

§ 367.13 Notices.

(a) *Exclusions.* Before excluding a contractor, the FDIC shall send it a written notice of possible cause to exclude. Such notice shall include:

Federal Deposit Insurance Corporation § 367.14

(1) Notification that exclusion for a specified period of time is being considered based on the specified cause(s) in § 367.6 to be relied upon;

(2) Identification of the event(s), circumstance(s), or condition(s) that indicates that there is cause to believe a cause for exclusion exists, described in sufficient detail to put the contractor on notice of the conduct or transaction(s) upon which an exclusion proceeding is based;

(3) Notification that the contractor is not prohibited from contracting with the FDIC unless and until it is either suspended from FDIC contracting or the FDIC Ethics Counselor issues a decision excluding the contractor, *provided however*, in any case where the possible cause for exclusion would also be an impediment to the contractor's eligibility pursuant to 12 CFR part 366, the contractor's eligibility for any contract will be determined under that part; and

(4) Notification of the regulatory provisions governing the exclusion proceeding and the potential effect of a final exclusion decision.

(b) *Suspensions.* Before suspending a contractor, the FDIC shall send it notice, including:

(1) Notice that a suspension is being imposed based on specified causes in § 367.8;

(2) Identification of the event(s), circumstance(s), or condition(s) that indicate that there is adequate evidence to believe a cause for suspension exists, described in sufficient detail to put the contractor on notice of the basis for the suspension, recognizing that the conduct of ongoing investigations and legal proceedings, including criminal proceedings, place limitations on the evidence that can be released;

(3) Notification that the suspension prohibits the contractor from contracting with the FDIC for a temporary period, pending the completion of an investigation or other legal proceedings; and

(4) Notification of the regulatory provisions governing the suspension proceeding.

(c) *Service of notices.* Notices will be sent to the contractor by first class mail, postage prepaid. For purposes of compliance with this section, notice shall be considered to have been received by the contractor if the notice is properly mailed to the last known address of such contractor. Whenever practical, a copy of the notice will also be transmitted to the contractor by facsimile. In the event the notice is not sent by facsimile, a copy will be sent by an overnight delivery service such as Express Mail or a commercial equivalent.

§ 367.14 Responses.

(a) The contractor will have 15 days from the date of the notice within which to respond.

(b) The response shall be in writing and may include: information and argument in opposition to the proposed exclusion and/or suspension, including any additional specific information pertaining to the possible causes for exclusion; and information and argument in mitigation of the proposed period of exclusion.

(c) The response may request a meeting with an FDIC official identified in the notice to permit the contractor to discuss issues of fact or law relating to the suspension and/or proposed exclusion or to otherwise resolve the pending matters.

(1) Any such meetings between a contractor and FDIC shall take such form as the FDIC deems appropriate.

(2) In cases of suspensions, no meeting will be held where a representative of the Department of Justice has advised in writing that the substantial interests of the Government would be prejudiced by such a meeting and the Ethics Counselor determines that a suspension is based on the same facts as pending or contemplated legal proceedings referenced by the representative of the Department of Justice.

(d) Failure to respond to the notice shall be deemed an admission of the existence of the cause(s) for suspension and/or exclusion set forth in the notice and an acceptance of the period of exclusion proposed therein. In such circumstances, the FDIC may proceed to a final decision without further proceedings.

(e) Where a contractor has received more than one notice, the FDIC may consolidate the pending proceedings,

§ 367.15

including the scheduling of any meetings, in accordance with this section.

§ 367.15 Additional proceedings as to disputed material facts.

(a) In actions not based upon a conviction or civil judgment, if the Ethics Counselor finds that the contractor's submission raises a genuine dispute over facts material to the proposed suspension and/or exclusion, the contractor shall be afforded an opportunity to appear (with counsel, if desired), submit documentary evidence, present witnesses, and confront any witnesses the FDIC presents.

(b) The Ethics Counselor may refer disputed material facts to another official for analysis and recommendation.

(c) If requested, a transcribed record of any additional proceedings shall be made available at cost to the contractor.

§ 367.16 Ethics Counselor decisions.

(a) Standard of proof:

(1) An exclusion must be based on a finding that the cause(s) for exclusion is established by a preponderance of the evidence in the administrative record of the case; and

(2) A suspension must be based on a finding that the cause(s) for suspension is established by adequate evidence in the administrative record of the case.

(b) The administrative record consists of the portion of any information, reports, documents or other evidence identified and relied upon in the Notice of Possible Cause to Exclude, the Notice of Suspension and/or supplemental notices, if any, together with any material portions of the contractor's response. When additional proceedings are necessary to determine disputed material facts, the Ethics Counselor shall base the decision on the facts as found, together with any information and argument submitted by the contractor and any other information in the administrative record.

(c) In actions based upon a conviction, judgment, a final enforcement action by a federal financial institution regulatory agency, or in which all facts and circumstances material to the exclusion action have been finally adjudicated in another forum, the Ethics Counselor may exclude a contractor without regard to the procedures set out in §§ 367.13 and 367.14. Any such decisions will be subject to the review and reconsideration provisions of § 367.20.

(d) *Notice of decisions.* Contractors shall be given prompt notice of the Ethics Counselor's decision in the manner described in § 367.13(c). If the Ethics Counselor suspends a contractor or imposes a period of exclusion, the decision shall:

(1) Set forth the cause(s) for suspension and/or exclusion included in the notice that were found by a preponderance of the evidence with reference to the administrative record support for that finding;

(2) Set forth the effect of the exclusion action and the effective dates of that action;

(3) Refer the contractor to its procedural rights of review and reconsideration under § 367.20; and

(4) Inform the contractor that a copy of the exclusion decision shall be placed in the FDIC Public Reading Room.

(e) If the FDIC Ethics Counselor decides that a period of exclusion is not warranted, the Notice of Possible Cause to Exclude may be withdrawn or the proceeding may be otherwise terminated. A decision to terminate an exclusion proceeding may include the imposition of appropriate conditions on the contractor in their future dealings with the FDIC.

§ 367.17 Duration of suspensions and exclusions.

(a) *Suspensions.* (1) Suspensions shall be for a temporary period pending the completion of an investigation or other legal or exclusion proceedings.

(2) If legal or administrative proceedings are not initiated within 12 months after the date of the suspension notice, the suspension shall be terminated unless a representative of the Department of Justice requests its extension in writing. In such cases, the suspension may be extended for an additional six months. In no event may a suspension be imposed for more than 18 months, unless such proceedings have been initiated within that period.

(3) FDIC shall notify the Department of Justice of an impending termination

Federal Deposit Insurance Corporation § 367.20

of a suspension at least 30 days before the 12-month period expires to give the Department of Justice an opportunity to request an extension.

(4) The time limitations for suspension in this section may be waived by the affected contractor.

(b) *Exclusions.* (1) Exclusions shall be for a period commensurate with the seriousness of the cause(s) after due consideration of mitigating evidence presented by the contractor.

(2) If a suspension precedes an exclusion, the suspension period shall be considered in determining the exclusion period.

(3) Exclusion for causes other than the mandatory bars in 12 CFR 366.4(a) generally should not exceed three years, but where circumstances warrant, a longer period of exclusion may be imposed.

(4) The Ethics Counselor may extend an existing exclusion for an additional period if the Ethics Counselor determines that an extension is necessary to protect the integrity of the FDIC contracting program and the public interest. However, an exclusion may not be extended solely on the basis of the facts and circumstances upon which the initial exclusion action was based. The standards and procedures in this part shall be applied in any proceeding to extend an exclusion.

§ 367.18 Abrogation of contracts.

(a) The FDIC may, in its discretion, rescind or terminate any contract in existence at the time a contractor is suspended or excluded.

(b) Any contract not rescinded or terminated shall continue in force in accordance with the terms thereof.

(c) The right to rescind or terminate a contract in existence is cumulative and in addition to any other remedies or rights the FDIC may have under the terms of the contract, at law, or otherwise.

§ 367.19 Exceptions to suspensions and exclusions.

(a) Exceptions to the effects of suspensions and exclusions may be available in unique circumstances, where there are compelling reasons to utilize a particular contractor for a specific task. Requests for such exceptions may be submitted only by the FDIC program office requesting the contract services.

(b) In the case of the modification or extension of an existing contract, the Ethics Counselor may except such a contracting action from the effects of suspension and/or exclusion upon a determination, in writing, that a compelling reason exists for utilization of the contractor in the particular instance. The Ethics Counselor's authority under this section shall not be delegated to any lower official.

(c) In the case of new contracts, the Corporation Ethics Committee may except a particular new contract from the effects of suspension and/or exclusion upon a determination in writing that a compelling reason exists for utilization of the contractor in the particular instance.

§ 367.20 Review and reconsideration of Ethics Counselor decisions.

(a) *Review.* (1) A suspended and/or excluded contractor may appeal the exclusion decision to the Corporation Ethics Committee.

(2) In order to avail itself of the right to appeal, a suspended and/or excluded contractor must file a written notice of intent to appeal within 5 days of the Ethics Counselor's decision.

(3) The appeal shall be filed in writing within 30 days of the decision.

(4) The Corporation Ethics Committee, at its discretion and after determining that it is in the best interests of the FDIC, may stay the effect of the suspension and/or exclusion pending conclusion of its review of the matter.

(b) *Reconsideration.* (1) A suspended and/or excluded contractor may submit a request to the Ethics Counselor to reconsider the suspension and/or exclusion decision, reduce the period of exclusion or terminate the suspension and/or exclusion.

(2) Such requests shall be in writing and supported by documentation that the requested action is justified by:

(i) Reversal of the conviction or civil judgment upon which the suspension and/or exclusion was based;

(ii) Newly discovered material evidence;

(iii) Bona fide change in ownership or management;

(iv) Elimination of other causes for which the suspension and/or exclusion was imposed; or

(v) Other reasons the FDIC Ethics Counselor deems appropriate.

(3) A request for reconsideration based on the reversal of the conviction or civil judgment may be filed at any time.

(4) Requests for reconsideration based on other grounds may only be filed during the period commencing 60 days after the Ethics Counselor's decision imposing the suspension and/or exclusion. Only one such request may be filed in any twelve month period.

(5) The Ethics Counselor's decision on a request for reconsideration is subject to the review procedure set forth in paragraph (a) of this section.

PART 368—GOVERNMENT SECURITIES SALES PRACTICES

Sec.
368.1 Scope.
368.2 Definitions.
368.3 Business conduct.
368.4 Recommendations to customers.
368.5 Customer information.
368.100 Obligations concerning institutional customers.

AUTHORITY: 15 U.S.C. 78o–5.

SOURCE: 62 FR 13287, Mar. 19, 1997, unless otherwise noted.

§ 368.1 Scope.

This part is applicable to state non-member banks and insured state branches of foreign banks that have filed notice as, or are required to file notice as, government securities brokers or dealers pursuant to section 15C of the Securities Exchange Act (15 U.S.C. 78o–5) and Department of the Treasury rules under section 15C (17 CFR 400.1(d) and part 401).

§ 368.2 Definitions.

(a) *Bank that is a government securities broker or dealer* means a state non-member bank or an insured state branch of a foreign bank that has filed notice, or is required to file notice, as a government securities broker or dealer pursuant to section 15C of the Securities Exchange Act (15 U.S.C. 78o–5) and Department of the Treasury rules under section 15C (17 CFR 400.1(d) and part 401).

(b) *Customer* does not include a broker or dealer or a government securities broker or dealer.

(c) *Government security* has the same meaning as this term has in section 3(a)(42) of the Securities Exchange Act of 1934 (15 U.S.C. 78c(a)(42)).

(d) *Non-institutional customer* means any customer other than:

(1) A bank, savings association, insurance company, or registered investment company;

(2) An investment adviser registered under section 203 of the Investment Advisers Act of 1940 (15 U.S.C. 80b–3); or

(3) Any entity (whether a natural person, corporation, partnership, trust, or otherwise) with total assets of at least $50 million.

§ 368.3 Business conduct.

A bank that is a government securities broker or dealer shall observe high standards of commercial honor and just and equitable principles of trade in the conduct of its business as a government securities broker or dealer.

§ 368.4 Recommendations to customers.

In recommending to a customer the purchase, sale or exchange of a government security, a bank that is a government securities broker or dealer shall have reasonable grounds for believing that the recommendation is suitable for the customer upon the basis of the facts, if any, disclosed by the customer as to the customer's other security holdings and as to the customer's financial situation and needs.

§ 368.5 Customer information.

Prior to the execution of a transaction recommended to a non-institutional customer, a bank that is a government securities broker or dealer shall make reasonable efforts to obtain information concerning:

(a) The customer's financial status;

(b) The customer's tax status;

(c) The customer's investment objectives; and

(d) Such other information used or considered to be reasonable by such

Federal Deposit Insurance Corporation § 368.100

bank in making recommendations to the customer.

§ 368.100 Obligations concerning institutional customers.

(a) As a result of broadened authority provided by the Government Securities Act Amendments of 1993 (15 U.S.C. 78o–3 and 78o–5), the FDIC is adopting sales practice rules for the government securities market, a market with a particularly broad institutional component. Accordingly, the FDIC believes it is appropriate to provide further guidance to banks on their suitability obligations when making recommendations to institutional customers.

(b) The FDIC's suitability rule (§ 368.4) is fundamental to fair dealing and is intended to promote ethical sales practices and high standards of professional conduct. Banks' responsibilities include having a reasonable basis for recommending a particular security or strategy, as well as having reasonable grounds for believing the recommendation is suitable for the customer to whom it is made. Banks are expected to meet the same high standards of competence, professionalism, and good faith regardless of the financial circumstances of the customer.

(c) In recommending to a customer the purchase, sale, or exchange of any government security, the bank shall have reasonable grounds for believing that the recommendation is suitable for the customer upon the basis of the facts, if any, disclosed by the customer as to the customer's other security holdings and financial situation and needs.

(d) The interpretation in this section concerns only the manner in which a bank determines that a recommendation is suitable for a particular institutional customer. The manner in which a bank fulfills this suitability obligation will vary, depending on the nature of the customer and the specific transaction. Accordingly, the interpretation in this section deals only with guidance regarding how a bank may fulfill customer-specific suitability obligations under § 368.4.[1]

(e) While it is difficult to define in advance the scope of a bank's suitability obligation with respect to a specific institutional customer transaction recommended by a bank, the FDIC has identified certain factors that may be relevant when considering compliance with § 368.4. These factors are not intended to be requirements or the only factors to be considered but are offered merely as guidance in determining the scope of a bank's suitability obligations.

(f) The two most important considerations in determining the scope of a bank's suitability obligations in making recommendations to an institutional customer are the customer's capability to evaluate investment risk independently and the extent to which the customer is exercising independent judgement in evaluating a bank's recommendation. A bank must determine, based on the information available to it, the customer's capability to evaluate investment risk. In some cases, the bank may conclude that the customer is not capable of making independent investment decisions in general. In other cases, the institutional customer may have general capability, but may not be able to understand a particular type of instrument or its risk. This is more likely to arise with relatively new types of instruments, or those with significantly different risk or volatility characteristics than other investments generally made by the institution. If a customer is either generally not capable of evaluating investment risk or lacks sufficient capability to evaluate the particular product, the scope of a bank's customer-specific obligations under § 368.4 would not be diminished by the fact that the bank was dealing with an institutional customer. On the other hand, the fact that a customer initially needed help understanding a potential investment need not necessarily imply that the customer did not ultimately develop an

---

[1] The interpretation in this section does not address the obligation related to suitability that requires that a bank have "* * * a 'reasonable basis' to believe that the recommendation could be suitable for at least some customers." *In the Matter of the Application of F.J. Kaufman and Company of Virginia and Frederick J. Kaufman, Jr.*, 50 SEC 164 (1989).

understanding and make an independent investment decision.

(g) A bank may conclude that a customer is exercising independent judgement if the customer's investment decision will be based on its own independent assessment of the opportunities and risks presented by a potential investment, market factors and other investment considerations. Where the bank has reasonable grounds for concluding that the institutional customer is making independent investment decisions and is capable of independently evaluating investment risk, then a bank's obligations under § 368.4 for a particular customer are fulfilled.[2] Where a customer has delegated decision-making authority to an agent, such as an investment advisor or a bank trust department, the interpretation in this section shall be applied to the agent.

(h) A determination of capability to evaluate investment risk independently will depend on an examination of the customer's capability to make its own investment decisions, including the resources available to the customer to make informed decisions. Relevant considerations could include:

(1) The use of one or more consultants, investment advisers, or bank trust departments;

(2) The general level of experience of the institutional customer in financial markets and specific experience with the type of instruments under consideration;

(3) The customer's ability to understand the economic features of the security involved;

(4) The customer's ability to independently evaluate how market developments would affect the security; and

(5) The complexity of the security or securities involved.

(i) A determination that a customer is making independent investment decisions will depend on the nature of the relationship that exists between the bank and the customer. Relevant considerations could include:

(1) Any written or oral understanding that exists between the bank and the customer regarding the nature of the relationship between the bank and the customer and the services to be rendered by the bank;

(2) The presence or absence of a pattern of acceptance of the bank's recommendations;

(3) The use by the customer of ideas, suggestions, market views and information obtained from other government securities brokers or dealers or market professionals, particularly those relating to the same type of securities; and

(4) The extent to which the bank has received from the customer current comprehensive portfolio information in connection with discussing recommended transactions or has not been provided important information regarding its portfolio or investment objectives.

(j) Banks are reminded that these factors are merely guidelines that will be utilized to determine whether a bank has fulfilled its suitability obligation with respect to a specific institutional customer transaction and that the inclusion or absence of any of these factors is not dispositive of the determination of suitability. Such a determination can only be made on a case-by-case basis taking into consideration all the facts and circumstances of a particular bank/customer relationship, assessed in the context of a particular transaction.

(k) For purposes of the interpretation in this section, an institutional customer shall be any entity other than a natural person. In determining the applicability of the interpretation in this section to an institutional customer, the FDIC will consider the dollar value of the securities that the institutional customer has in its portfolio and/or under management. While the interpretation in this section is potentially applicable to any institutional customer, the guidance contained in this section is more appropriately applied to an institutional customer with at least $10 million invested in securities in the aggregate in its portfolio and/or under management.

---

[2] See footnote 1 in paragraph (d) of this section.

PART 369—PROHIBITION AGAINST USE OF INTERSTATE BRANCHES PRIMARILY FOR DEPOSIT PRODUCTION

Sec.
369.1 Purpose and scope.
369.2 Definitions.
369.3 Loan-to-deposit ratio screen.
369.4 Credit needs determination.
369.5 Sanctions.

AUTHORITY: 12 U.S.C. 1819 (Tenth) and 1835a.

SOURCE: 62 FR 47737, Sept. 10, 1997, unless otherwise noted.

§ 369.1 Purpose and scope.

(a) *Purpose.* The purpose of this part is to implement section 109 (12 U.S.C. 1835a) of the Riegle-Neal Interstate Banking and Branching Efficiency Act of 1994 (Interstate Act).

(b) *Scope.* (1) This part applies to any State nonmember bank that has operated a covered interstate branch for a period of at least one year.

(2) This part describes the requirements imposed under 12 U.S.C. 1835a, which requires the appropriate Federal banking agencies (the FDIC, the Office of the Comptroller of the Currency, and the Board of Governors of the Federal Reserve System) to prescribe uniform rules that prohibit a bank from using any authority to engage in interstate branching pursuant to the Interstate Act, or any amendment made by the Interstate Act to any other provision of law, primarily for the purpose of deposit production.

§ 369.2 Definitions.

For purposes of this part, the following definitions apply:

(a) *Bank* means, unless the context indicates otherwise:

(1) A State nonmember bank; and

(2) A foreign bank as that term is defined in 12 U.S.C. 3101(7) and 12 CFR 346.1(a).

(b) *Covered interstate branch* means:

(1) Any branch of a State nonmember bank, and any insured branch of a foreign bank licensed by a State, that:

(i) Is established or acquired outside the bank's home State pursuant to the interstate branching authority granted by the Interstate Act or by any amendment made by the Interstate Act to any other provision of law; or

(ii) Could not have been established or acquired outside of the bank's home State but for the establishment or acquisition of a branch described in paragraph (b)(1)(i) of this section; and

(2) Any bank or branch of a bank controlled by an out-of-State bank holding company.

(c) *Home State* means:

(1) With respect to a State bank, the State that chartered the bank;

(2) With respect to a national bank, the State in which the main office of the bank is located;

(3) With respect to a bank holding company, the State in which the total deposits of all banking subsidiaries of such company are the largest on the later of:

(i) July 1, 1966; or

(ii) The date on which the company becomes a bank holding company under the Bank Holding Company Act;

(4) With respect to a foreign bank:

(i) For purposes of determining whether a U.S. branch of a foreign bank is a covered interstate branch, the home State of the foreign bank as determined in accordance with 12 U.S.C. 3103(c) and 12 CFR 347.202(j); and

(ii) For purposes of determining whether a branch of a U.S. bank controlled by a foreign bank is a covered interstate branch, the State in which the total deposits of all banking subsidiaries of such foreign bank are the largest on the later of:

(A) July 1, 1966; or

(B) The date on which the foreign bank becomes a bank holding company under the Bank Holding Company Act.

(d) *Host State* means a State in which a covered interstate branch is established or acquired.

(e) *Host state loan-to-deposit ratio* generally means, with respect to a particular host state, the ratio of total loans in the host state relative to total deposits from the host state for all banks (including institutions covered under the definition of "bank" in 12 U.S.C. 1813(a)(1)) that have that state as their home state, as determined and updated periodically by the appropriate Federal banking agencies and made available to the public.

§ 369.3

(f) *Out-of-State bank holding company* means, with respect to any State, a bank holding company whose home State is another State.

(g) *State* means state as that term is defined in 12 U.S.C. 1813(a)(3).

(h) *Statewide loan-to-deposit ratio* means, with respect to a bank, the ratio of the bank's loans to its deposits in a state in which the bank has one or more covered interstate branches, as determined by the FDIC.

[62 FR 47737, Sept. 10, 1997, as amended at 67 FR 38848, June 6, 2002]

§ 369.3 Loan-to-deposit ratio screen.

(a) *Application of screen.* Beginning no earlier than one year after a covered interstate branch is acquired or established, the FDIC will consider whether the bank's statewide loan-to-deposit ratio is less than 50 percent of the relevant host State loan-to-deposit ratio.

(b) *Results of screen.* (1) If the FDIC determines that the bank's statewide loan-to-deposit ratio is 50 percent or more of the host state loan-to-deposit ratio, no further consideration under this part is required.

(2) If the FDIC determines that the bank's statewide loan-to-deposit ratio is less than 50 percent of the host state loan-to-deposit ratio, or if reasonably available data are insufficient to calculate the bank's statewide loan-to-deposit ratio, the FDIC will make a credit needs determination for the bank as provided in § 369.4.

[62 FR 47737, Sept. 10, 1997, as amended at 67 FR 38848, June 6, 2002]

§ 369.4 Credit needs determination.

(a) *In general.* The FDIC will review the loan portfolio of the bank and determine whether the bank is reasonably helping to meet the credit needs of the communities in the host state that are served by the bank.

(b) *Guidelines.* The FDIC will use the following considerations as guidelines when making the determination pursuant to paragraph (a) of this section:

(1) Whether covered interstate branches were formerly part of a failed or failing depository institution;

(2) Whether covered interstate branches were acquired under circumstances where there was a low loan-to-deposit ratio because of the nature of the acquired institution's business or loan portfolio;

(3) Whether covered interstate branches have a high concentration of commercial or credit card lending, trust services, or other specialized activities, including the extent to which the covered interstate branches accept deposits in the host state;

(4) The Community Reinvestment Act (CRA) ratings received by the bank, if any, under 12 U.S.C. 2901 *et seq.*;

(5) Economic conditions, including the level of loan demand, within the communities served by the covered interstate branches;

(6) The safe and sound operation and condition of the bank; and

(7) The FDIC's Community Reinvestment regulations (12 CFR Part 345) and interpretations of those regulations.

§ 369.5 Sanctions.

(a) *In general.* If the FDIC determines that a bank is not reasonably helping to meet the credit needs of the communities served by the bank in the host state, and that the bank's statewide loan-to-deposit ratio is less than 50 percent of the host state loan-to-deposit ratio, the FDIC:

(1) May order that a bank's covered interstate branch or branches be closed unless the bank provides reasonable assurances to the satisfaction of the FDIC, after an opportunity for public comment, that the bank has an acceptable plan under which the bank will reasonably help to meet the credit needs of the communities served by the bank in the host state; and

(2) Will not permit the bank to open a new branch in the host state that would be considered to be a covered interstate branch unless the bank provides reasonable assurances to the satisfaction of the FDIC, after an opportunity for public comment, that the bank will reasonably help to meet the credit needs of the community that the new branch will serve.

(b) *Notice prior to closure of a covered interstate branch.* Before exercising the FDIC's authority to order the bank to close a covered interstate branch, the FDIC will issue to the bank a notice of the FDIC's intent to order the closure

Federal Deposit Insurance Corporation

§ 370.2

and will schedule a hearing within 60 days of issuing the notice.

(c) *Hearing.* The FDIC will conduct a hearing scheduled under paragraph (b) of this section in accordance with the provisions of 12 U.S.C. 1818(h) and 12 CFR part 308.

PART 370—TEMPORARY LIQUIDITY GUARANTEE PROGRAM

Sec.
370.1 Scope.
370.2 Definitions.
370.3 Debt Guarantee Program.
370.4 Transaction Account Guarantee Program.
370.5 Participation.
370.6 Assessments under the Debt Guarantee Program.
370.7 Assessments for the Transaction Account Guarantee Program.
370.8 Systemic risk emergency special assessment to recover loss.
370.9 Recordkeeping requirements.
370.10 Oversight.
370.11 Enforcement mechanisms.
370.12 Payment on the guarantee.

AUTHORITY: 12 U.S.C. U.S.C. 1813(l), 1813(m), 1817(i),1818, 1819(a)(Tenth); 1820(f), 1821(a); 1821(c); 1821(d); 1823(c)(4).

SOURCE: 73 FR 72266, Nov. 26, 2008, unless otherwise noted.

§ 370.1 Scope.

This part sets forth the eligibility criteria, limitations, procedures, requirements, and other provisions related to participation in the FDIC's temporary liquidity guarantee program.

§ 370.2 Definitions.

As used in this part, the terms listed in this section are defined as indicated below. Other terms used in this part that are defined in the Federal Deposit Insurance Act (FDI Act) have the meanings given them in the FDI Act except as otherwise provided herein.

(a) *Eligible entity.* (1) The term "eligible entity" means any of the following:

(i) An insured depository institution;

(ii) A U.S. bank holding company, provided that it controls, directly or indirectly, at least one subsidiary that is a chartered and operating insured depository institution;

(iii) A U.S. savings and loan holding company, provided that it controls, directly or indirectly, at least one subsidiary that is a chartered and operating insured depository institution; or

(iv) Any other affiliates of an insured depository institution that the FDIC, in its sole discretion and on a case-by-case basis, after written request and positive recommendation by the appropriate Federal banking agency, designates as an eligible entity; such affiliate, by seeking and obtaining such designation, also becomes a participating entity in the debt guarantee program.

(b) *Insured Depository Institution.* The term "insured depository institution" means an insured depository institution as defined in section 3(c)(2) of the FDI Act, 12 U.S.C. 1813(c)(2), except that it does not include an "insured branch" of a foreign bank as defined in section 3(s)(3) of the FDI Act, 12 U.S.C. 1813(s)(3), for purposes of the debt guarantee program.

(c) *U.S. Bank Holding Company.* The term "U.S. Bank Holding Company" means a "bank holding company" as defined in section 2(a) of the Bank Holding Company Act of 1956 ("BHCA"), 12 U.S.C. 1841(a), that is organized under the laws of any State or the District of Columbia.

(d) *U.S. Savings and Loan Holding Company.* The term "U.S. Savings and Loan Holding Company" means a "savings and loan holding company" as defined in section 10(a)(1)(D) of the Home Owners' Loan Act of 1933 ("HOLA"), 12 U.S.C. 1467a(a)(1)(D), that is organized under the laws of any State or the District of Columbia and either:

(1) Engages only in activities that are permissible for financial holding companies under section 4(k) of the BHCA, 12 U.S.C. 1843(k), or

(2) Has at least one insured depository institution subsidiary that is the subject of an application under section 4(c)(8) of the BHCA, 12 U.S.C. 1843(c)(8), that was pending on October 13, 2008.

(e) *Senior Unsecured Debt.* (1) The term "senior unsecured debt" means

(i) For the period from October 13, 2008 through December 5, 2008, unsecured borrowing that:

(A) Is evidenced by a written agreement or trade confirmation;

§ 370.2   12 CFR Ch. III (1-1-12 Edition)

(B) Has a specified and fixed principal amount;

(C) Is noncontingent and contains no embedded options, forwards, swaps, or other derivatives; and

(D) Is not, by its terms, subordinated to any other liability; and

(ii) After December 5, 2008, unsecured borrowing that satisfies the criteria listed in paragraphs (e)(1)(i)(A) through (e)(1)(i)(D) of this section and that has a stated maturity of more than 30 days.

(iii) After February 27, 2009, unsecured borrowing that satisfies the criteria listed in paragraphs (e)(1)(i)(A) through (e)(1)(i)(D) of this section, that has a stated maturity of more than 30 days, and that includes, without limitation, mandatory convertible debt.

(2) Senior unsecured debt may pay either a fixed or floating interest rate based on a commonly-used reference rate with a fixed amount of scheduled principal payments. The term "commonly-used reference rate" includes a single index of a Treasury bill rate, the prime rate, and LIBOR.

(3) Senior unsecured debt may include, for example, the following debt, provided it meets the requirements of paragraph (e)(1) of this section: mandatory convertible debt as described in paragraph (m) of this section, federal funds purchased, promissory notes, commercial paper, unsubordinated unsecured notes, including zero-coupon bonds, U.S. dollar denominated certificates of deposit owed to an insured depository institution, an insured credit union as defined in the Federal Credit Union Act, or a foreign bank, U.S. dollar denominated deposits in an international banking facility (IBF) of an insured depository institution owed to an insured depository institution or a foreign bank, and U.S. dollar denominated deposits on the books and records of foreign branches of U.S. insured depository institutions that are owed to an insured depository institution or a foreign bank. The term "foreign bank" does not include a foreign central bank or other similar foreign government entity that performs central bank functions or a quasi-governmental international financial institution such as the International Monetary Fund or the World Bank. References to debt owed to an insured depository institution, an insured credit union, or a foreign bank mean owed to the institution solely in its own capacity and not as agent.

(4) Senior unsecured debt, except deposits, may be denominated in foreign currency.

(5) Senior unsecured debt excludes, for example, any obligation that has a stated maturity of "one month"[1] obligations from guarantees or other contingent liabilities, derivatives, derivative-linked products, debts that are paired or bundled with other securities, convertible debt other than mandatory convertible debt described in paragraph (m) of this section, capital notes, the unsecured portion of otherwise secured debt, negotiable certificates of deposit, deposits denominated in a foreign currency or other foreign deposits (except as allowed under paragraph (e)(3) of this section), revolving credit agreements, structured notes, instruments that are used for trade credit, retail debt securities, and any funds regardless of form that are swept from individual, partnership, or corporate accounts held at depository institutions. Also excluded are loans from affiliates, including parents and subsidiaries, and institution-affiliated parties.

(f) *Newly issued senior unsecured debt.* (1) The term "newly issued senior unsecured debt" means:

(i) With respect to a participating entity that opted out of the debt guarantee program, senior unsecured debt that is issued on or after October 14, 2008, and on or before the date the entity opted out; and

(ii) With respect to a participating entity that has not opted out of the debt guarantee program, senior unsecured debt that is issued during the issuance period.

(2) The term "newly issued senior unsecured debt" includes, without limitation, senior unsecured debt

(i) That matures and is renewed during the issuance period; or

(ii) That is issued during such period pursuant to a shelf registration, regardless of the date of creation of the shelf registration.

―――――――――――
[1] This recognizes that certain instruments have stated maturities of "one month," but have a term of up to 35 days because of weekends, holidays, and calendar issues.

Federal Deposit Insurance Corporation § 370.2

(g) *Participating entity.* (1) Except as provided in paragraphs (g)(2) and (g)(3) of this section, the term "participating entity" means with respect to each of the debt guarantee program and the transaction account guarantee program,

(i) An eligible entity that became an eligible entity on or before December 5, 2008 and that has not opted out, or

(ii) An entity that becomes an eligible entity after December 5, 2008, and that the FDIC has allowed to participate in the program, except.

(2) A participating entity that opted out of the transaction account guarantee program in accordance with § 370.5(c)(2) ceased to be a participating entity in the transaction account guarantee program effective on January 1, 2010.

(3) A participating entity that opts out of the transaction account guarantee program in accordance with § 370.5(c)(23) ceases to be a participating entity in the transaction account guarantee program effective on July 1, 2010.

(h) *Noninterest-bearing transaction account.* (1) The term "noninterest-bearing transaction account" means a transaction account as defined in 12 CFR 204.2 that is

(i) Maintained at an insured depository institution;

(ii) With respect to which interest is neither accrued nor paid; and

(iii) On which the insured depository institution does not reserve the right to require advance notice of an intended withdrawal.

(2) A noninterest-bearing transaction account does not include, for example, an interest-bearing money market deposit account (MMDA) as those accounts are defined in 12 CFR 204.2.

(3) Notwithstanding paragraphs (h)(1) and (h)(2) of this section, for purposes of the transaction account guarantee program, a noninterest-bearing transaction account includes:

(i) Accounts commonly known as Interest on Lawyers Trust Accounts (IOLTAs) (or functionally equivalent accounts); and

(ii) Negotiable order of withdrawal accounts (NOW accounts) with interest rates:

(A) No higher than 0.50 percent through June 30, 2010, if the insured depository institution at which the account is held has committed to maintain the interest rate at or below 0.50 percent. through June 30, 2010; and

(B) No higher than 0.25 percent after June 30, 2010, if the insured depository institution at which the account is held has committed to maintain the interest rate at or below 0.25 percent after June 30, 2010 through the TAG expiration date.

(4) Notwithstanding paragraph (h)(3) of this section, a NOW account with an interest rate above 0.50 percent as of November 21, 2008, may be treated as a noninterest-bearing transaction account for purposes of this part:

(i) Through June 30, 2010, if the insured depository institution at which the account is held reduced the interest rate on that account to 0.50 percent or lower before January 1, 2009, and committed to maintain that interest rate at no more than 0.50 percent through June 30, 2010; and

(ii) After June 30, 2010 through the TAG expiration date, if the insured depository institution at which the account is held reduces the interest rate on that account to 0.25 percent or lower before July 1, 2010, and commits to maintain that interest rate at no more than 0.25 percent through the TAG expiration date.

(i) *FDIC-guaranteed debt.* The term "FDIC-guaranteed debt" means newly issued senior unsecured debt issued by a participating entity that meets the requirements of this part for debt that is guaranteed under the debt guarantee program, and is identified pursuant to § 370.5(h) as guaranteed by the FDIC.

(j) *Debt guarantee program.* The term "debt guarantee program" refers to the FDIC's guarantee program for newly issued senior unsecured debt as described in this part.

(k) *Transaction account guarantee program.* The term "transaction account guarantee program" refers to the FDIC's guarantee program for funds in noninterest-bearing transaction accounts as described in this part.

(l) *Temporary liquidity guarantee program.* The term "temporary liquidity guarantee program" includes both the debt guarantee program and the transaction account guarantee program.

§ 370.3

(m) *Mandatory convertible debt.* The term "mandatory convertible debt" means senior unsecured debt that is required by the terms of the debt instrument to convert into common shares of the issuing entity on a fixed and specified date, on or before the expiration of the guarantee, unless the issuing entity:

(1) Fails to timely make any payment required under the debt instrument, or

(2) Merges or consolidates with any other entity and is not the surviving or resulting entity.

(n) *Issuance period.* (1) Except as provided in paragraph (n)(2) of this section, the term "issuance period" means

(i) With respect to the issuance, by a participating entity that is either an insured depository institution, an entity that has issued FDIC-guaranteed debt before April 1, 2009, or an entity that has been approved pursuant to § 370.3(h) to issue FDIC-guaranteed debt after June 30, 2009, and on or before October 31, 2009, of:

(A) Mandatory convertible debt, the period from February 27, 2009, to and including October 31, 2009, and

(B) All other senior unsecured debt, the period from October 14, 2008, to and including October 31, 2009; and

(ii) With respect to the issuance, by any other participating entity, of

(A) Mandatory convertible debt, the period from February 27, 2009, to and including June 30, 2009, and

(B) All other senior unsecured debt, the period from October 14, 2008, to and including June 30, 2009.

(2) The "issuance period" for a participating entity that has been approved to issue FDIC-guaranteed debt pursuant to § 370.3(k) of this part is the period after October 31, 2009, and on or before April 30, 2010.

(o) *TAG expiration date.* The term "TAG expiration date" means December 31, 2010 unless the Board of Directors of the FDIC (the "Board"), for good cause, extends the transaction account guarantee program beyond December 31, 2010 for an additional period of time not to exceed one year, in which case the term "TAG expiration date" means the last day of such additional period of time. Good cause exists if the Board finds that the economic conditions and circumstances that led to the establishment of the transaction account guarantee program are likely to continue beyond December 31, 2010 and that extending the transaction account guarantee program for an additional period of time will help mitigate or resolve those conditions and circumstances. If the Board decides to extend the transaction account guarantee program beyond December 31, 2010 for an additional period of time, it will do so without further rulemaking; however, the FDIC will publish notice of any extension no later than October 29, 2010. Participating entities must update the disclosures required by § 370.5(h)(5), as necessary, to reflect the current TAG expiration date, including any extension of such date.

[73 FR 72266, Nov. 26, 2008, as amended at 74 FR 9524, Mar. 4, 2009; 74 FR 12082, Mar. 23, 2009; 74 FR 45098, Sept. 1, 2009; 74 FR 54747, Oct. 23, 2009; 75 FR 20263, Apr. 19, 2010; 75 FR 36510, June 28, 2010]

§ 370.3 Debt Guarantee Program.

(a) Upon the uncured failure of a participating entity to make a timely payment of principal or interest as required under an FDIC-guaranteed debt instrument, the FDIC will pay the unpaid principal and/or interest, in accordance with § 370.12 and subject to the other provisions of this part.

(b) *Debt guarantee limit.* (1) Except as provided in paragraphs (b)(2) through (b)(6) of this section, the maximum amount of outstanding debt that is guaranteed under the debt guarantee program for each participating entity at any time is limited to 125 percent of the par value of the participating entity's senior unsecured debt, as that term is defined in § 370.2(e)(1)(i) (excluding mandatory convertible debt), that was outstanding as of the close of business September 30, 2008 and that was scheduled to mature on or before June 30, 2009.

(2) If a participating entity that is an insured depository institution had either no senior unsecured debt as that term is defined in § 370.2(e)(1)(i), or only had federal funds purchased, outstanding on September 30, 2008, its debt guarantee limit is two percent of its consolidated total liabilities as of September 30, 2008. For the purposes of this

Federal Deposit Insurance Corporation § 370.3

paragraph (b)(2) of this section, the term "federal funds purchased" means:

(i) For insured depository institutions that file Reports of Condition and Income, unsecured "federal funds purchased" as that term is used in defining "Federal Funds Transactions" in the Glossary of the FFIEC Reports of Condition and Income Instructions, and

(ii) For insured depository institutions that file Thrift Financial Reports, "Federal Funds" as that term is defined in the Glossary of the 2008 Thrift Financial Report Instruction Manual.

(3) If a participating entity, other than an insured depository institution, had no senior unsecured debt as that term is defined in § 370.2(e)(1)(i) outstanding on September 30, 2008, the entity may seek to have some amount of debt covered by the debt guarantee program. The FDIC, after consultation with the appropriate Federal banking agency, will decide, on a case-by-case basis, whether such a request will be granted and, if granted, what the entity's debt guarantee limit will be.

(4) If an entity becomes an eligible entity after October 13, 2008, the FDIC will establish the entity's debt guarantee limit at the time of such designation.

(5) If an affiliate of a participating entity is designated as an eligible entity by the FDIC after a written request and positive recommendation by the appropriate Federal banking agency (or if the affiliate has no appropriate Federal banking agency, a written request and positive recommendation by the appropriate Federal banking agency of the affiliated insured depository institution), the FDIC will establish the entity's debt guarantee limit at the time of such designation.

(6) The FDIC may make exceptions to an entity's debt guarantee limit. For example, the FDIC may allow a participating entity to exceed the limit determined in paragraph (b)(1) or (b)(2) of this section, reduce the limit below the amount determined in paragraph (b)(1) or (b)(2) of this section, and/or impose other limits or requirements after consultation with the entity's appropriate Federal banking agency.

(7) If a participating entity issues debt identified as guaranteed under the debt guarantee program that exceeds its debt guarantee limit, it will be subject to assessment increases and enforcement action as provided in § 370.6(e).

(8) A participating entity that is both an insured depository institution and a direct or indirect subsidiary of a parent participating entity may, absent direction by the FDIC to the contrary, increase its debt guarantee limit above the limit determined in accordance with paragraphs (b)(1) through (b)(6) of this section, provided that:

(i) The amount of the increase does not exceed the debt guarantee limit(s) of one or more of its parent participating entities;

(ii) The insured depository institution provides prior written notice to the FDIC and to each such parent participating entity of the amount of the increase, the name of each contributing parent participating entity, and the starting and ending dates of the increase; and

(iii) For so long as the institution's debt guarantee limit is increased by such amount, the debt guarantee limit of each contributing parent participating entity is reduced by an amount corresponding to the amount of its contribution to the amount of the increase.

(9) The debt guarantee limit of the surviving entity of a merger between or among eligible entities is equal to the sum of the debt guarantee limits of the merging eligible entities calculated on a pro forma basis as of the close of business September 30, 2008, absent action by the FDIC after consultation with the surviving entity and its appropriate Federal banking agency.

(10) For purposes of determining the amount of guaranteed debt outstanding under paragraph (b)(1) of this section, debt issued in a foreign currency will be converted into U.S. dollars using the exchange rate in effect on the date that the debt is funded.

(c) *Calculation and reporting responsibility.* Participating entities are responsible for calculating and reporting to the FDIC the amount of senior unsecured debt as defined in § 370.2(e)(1)(i) as of September 30, 2008.

§ 370.3

(1) Each participating entity shall calculate the amount of its senior unsecured debt outstanding as of the close of business September 30, 2008, that was scheduled to mature on or before June 30, 2009.

(2) Each participating entity shall report the calculated amount to the FDIC, even if such amount is zero, in an approved format via FDICconnect no later than December 5, 2008.

(3) In each subsequent report to the FDIC concerning debt issuances or balances outstanding, each participating entity shall state whether it has issued debt identified as FDIC-guaranteed debt that exceeded its debt guarantee limit at any time since the previous reporting period.

(4) The Chief Financial Officer (CFO) or equivalent of each participating entity shall certify the accuracy of the information reported in each report submitted pursuant to this section.

(d) *Expiration of Guarantee.* (1) With respect to debt that is issued before April 1, 2009 by any participating entity, the guarantee expires on the earliest of the mandatory conversion date for mandatory convertible debt, the maturity date of the debt, or June 30, 2012.

(2) With respect to debt that is issued on or after April 1, 2009, by a participating entity that is either an insured depository institution, a participating entity that has issued guaranteed debt before April 1, 2009, a participating entity that has been approved pursuant to § 370.3(h) to issue guaranteed debt after June 30, 2009, and on or before October 31, 2009, or a participating entity that has been approved pursuant to § 370.3(k) to issue guaranteed debt after October 31, 2009, the guarantee expires on the earliest of the mandatory conversion date (for mandatory convertible debt), the maturity date of the debt, or December 31, 2012.

(3) With respect to guaranteed debt that is issued on or after April 1, 2009 by a participating entity other than an entity described in paragraph (d)(2) of this section, the guarantee expires on the earliest of the mandatory conversion date for mandatory convertible debt, the maturity date of the debt, or on June 30, 2012.

(e) Debt cannot be issued and identified as guaranteed by the FDIC if:

(1) The proceeds are used to prepay debt that is not FDIC-guaranteed;

(2) The issuing entity has previously opted out of the debt guarantee program, except as provided in § 370.5(d);

(3) The issuing entity has had its participation in the debt guarantee program terminated by the FDIC or is not a participating entity;

(4) The issuing entity has exceeded its debt guarantee limit for issuing guaranteed debt as specified in paragraph (b) of this section,

(5) The debt is owed to an affiliate, an institution-affiliated party, insider of the participating entity, or an insider of an affiliate or

(6) The debt does not otherwise meet the requirements of this part for FDIC guaranteed debt.

(f) The FDIC's agreement to include a participating entity's senior unsecured debt in the debt guarantee program does not exempt the entity from complying with any applicable law including, without limitation, Securities and Exchange Commission registration or disclosure requirements.

(g) *Long term non-guaranteed debt option.* On or before 11:59 p.m., Eastern Standard Time, December 5, 2008, a participating entity may also notify the FDIC that it has elected to issue senior unsecured non-guaranteed debt with maturities beyond June 30, 2012, at any time, in any amount, and without regard to the guarantee limit. By making this election the participating entity agrees to pay to the FDIC the nonrefundable fee as provided in § 370.6(f).

(h) *Applications for exceptions, eligibility, and issuance of certain debt.* (1) The following requests require written application to the FDIC and the appropriate Federal banking agency of the entity or the entity's lead affiliated insured depository institution:

(i) A request by a participating entity to establish, increase, or decrease its debt guarantee limit,

(ii) A request by an entity that becomes an eligible entity after October 13, 2008, for an increase in its presumptive debt guarantee limit of zero,

Federal Deposit Insurance Corporation § 370.3

(iii) A request by a non-participating surviving entity in a merger transaction to opt in to either the debt guarantee program or the transaction account guarantee program,

(iv) A request by an affiliate of an insured depository institution to participate in the debt guarantee program,

(v) A request by a participating entity to issue FDIC-guaranteed mandatory convertible debt,

(vi) A request by a participating entity that is neither an insured depository institution nor an entity that has issued FDIC-guaranteed debt before April 1, 2009, to issue FDIC-guaranteed debt after June 30, 2009, and on or before October 31, 2009,

(vii) A request by a participating entity to issue senior unsecured non-guaranteed debt after June 30, 2009, and

(viii) A request by a participating entity to issue FDIC-guaranteed debt after October 31, 2009 under the Emergency Guarantee Facility pursuant to paragraph (k) of this section.

(2) Each letter application must describe the details of the request, provide a summary of the applicant's strategic operating plan, describe the proposed use of the debt proceeds, and

(i) With respect to an application for approval of the issuance of mandatory convertible debt, must also include:

(A) The proposed date of issuance,

(B) The total amount of the mandatory convertible debt to be issued,

(C) The mandatory conversion date,

(D) The conversion rate (*i.e.*, the total number of shares of common stock that will result from the conversion divided by the total dollar amount of the mandatory convertible debt to be issued),

(E) Confirmation that all applications and all notices required under the Bank Holding Company Act of 1956, as amended, the Home Owners' Loan Act, as amended, or the Change in Bank Control Act, as amended, have been submitted to the applicant's appropriate Federal banking agency in connection with the proposed issuance, and

(F) Any other relevant information that the FDIC deems appropriate;

(ii) With respect to an application pursuant to paragraph (h)(1)(vi) of this section to extend the period for issuance of FDIC-guaranteed debt to and including October 31, 2009, the entity's plans for the retirement of the guaranteed debt, a description of the entity's financial history, current condition, and future prospects, and any other relevant information that the FDIC deems appropriate;

(iii) With respect to an application pursuant to paragraph (h)(1)(vii) of this section to issue senior unsecured non-guaranteed debt, a summary of the applicant's strategic operating plan and the entity's plans for the retirement of any guaranteed debt; and

(iv) With respect to an application pursuant to paragraph (h)(1)(viii) of this section to issue FDIC-guaranteed debt under the Emergency Guarantee Facility, a projection of the sources and uses of funds through December 31, 2012, a summary of the entity's contingency plans, a description of the collateral that an entity can make available to secure the entity's obligation to reimburse the FDIC for any payments made pursuant to the guarantee, a description of the plans for retirement of the FDIC-guaranteed debt, a description of the market disruptions or other circumstances beyond the entity's control that prevent the entity from replacing maturing debt with non-guaranteed debt, a description of management's efforts to mitigate the effects of such disruptions or circumstances, conclusive evidence that demonstrates an entity's inability to issue non-guaranteed debt, and any other relevant information.

(3) In addition to any other relevant factors that the FDIC deems appropriate, the FDIC will consider the following factors in evaluating applications filed pursuant to paragraph (h) of this section:

(i) For applications pursuant to paragraphs (h)(1)(i), (h)(1)(ii), (h)(1)(iii), and (h)(1)(v) of this section: The proposed use of the proceeds; the financial condition and supervisory history of the eligible/surviving entity;

(ii) For applications pursuant to paragraph (h)(1)(iv) of this section: The proposed use of the proceeds; the extent of the financial activity of the entities within the holding company structure; the strength, from a ratings

§ 370.3

perspective of the issuer of the obligations that will be guaranteed; the size and extent of the activities of the organization;

(iii) For applications pursuant to paragraph (h)(1)(vi) of this section: The proposed use of the proceeds; the entity's plans for the retirement of the guaranteed debt, the entity's financial history, current condition, future prospects, capital, management, and the risk presented to the FDIC;

(iv) For applications pursuant to paragraph (h)(1)(vii) of this section: The entity's plans for the retirement of the guaranteed debt; and

(v) For applications pursuant to paragraph (h)(1)(viii) of this section, the applicant's strategic operating plan, the proposed use of the debt proceeds, the entity's plans for the retirement of the FDIC-guaranteed debt, the entity's contingency plans, the nature and extent of the market disruptions or other circumstances beyond the entity's control that prevent the entity from replacing maturing debt with non-guaranteed debt, the collateral that an entity can make available to secure the entity's obligation to reimburse the FDIC for any payments made pursuant to the guarantee, management's efforts to mitigate the effects of such conditions or circumstances, the evidence that demonstrates an entity's inability to issue non-guaranteed debt, and the risk presented to the FDIC.

(4) Applications required under this part must be in letter form and addressed to the Director, Division of Supervision and Consumer Protection, Federal Deposit Insurance Corporation, 550 17th Street, NW., Washington, DC 20429.

(5) The filing deadlines for certain applications are:

(i) At the same time the merger application is filed with the appropriate Federal banking agency, for an application pursuant to paragraph (h)(1)(iii) of this section (which must include a copy of the merger application);

(ii) October 31, 2009, for an application pursuant to paragraph (h)(1)(v) of this section that is filed by a participating entity that is either an insured depository institution, an entity that has issued FDIC-guaranteed debt before April 1, 2009, or an entity that has been

12 CFR Ch. III (1–1–12 Edition)

approved pursuant to paragraph (h) of this section to issue FDIC-guaranteed debt after June 30, 2009, and on or before October 31, 2009;

(iii) June 30, 2009, for an application pursuant to paragraph (h)(1)(v) of this section that is filed by a participating entity other than an entity described in paragraph (h)(5)(ii) of this section;

(iv) June 30, 2009, for an application pursuant to paragraph (h)(1)(vi); and

(v) April 30, 2010, for applications pursuant to paragraph (h)(1)(viii).

(6) In granting its approval of an application filed pursuant to paragraph (h) of this section the FDIC may impose any conditions it deems appropriate, including without limitation, requirements that the issuer

(i) Hedge any foreign currency risk, or

(ii) Pledge collateral to secure the issuer's obligation to reimburse the FDIC for any payments made pursuant to the guarantee.

(iii) Limit executive compensation and bonuses, and/or

(iv) Limit or refrain from the payment of dividends.

(i) *Time limits on issuance of guaranteed debt.* (1) A participating entity that is either an insured depository institution, an entity that has issued FDIC-guaranteed debt before April 1, 2009, or an entity that has been approved pursuant to paragraph (h) of this section to issue FDIC-guaranteed debt after June 30, 2009 and on or before October 31, 2009, may issue FDIC-guaranteed debt under the debt guarantee program through and including October 31, 2009.

(2) A participating entity other than an entity described in paragraph (i)(1) of this section may issue FDIC-guaranteed debt under the debt guarantee program through and including June 30, 2009.

(j) *Issuance of non-guaranteed debt after June 30, 2009.* (1) After obtaining the FDIC's prior written approval to issue non-guaranteed debt pursuant to paragraph (h)(1) of this section, any participating entity that has elected pursuant to paragraph (g) of this section to issue senior unsecured non-guaranteed debt with maturities after June 30, 2012 and that has paid the fee provided in § 370.6(f), may issue after

Federal Deposit Insurance Corporation

§ 370.5

June 30, 2009 senior unsecured non-guaranteed debt in any amount with maturities on or before June 30, 2012. A participating entity that has both made the election provided by paragraph (g) of this section and paid the fee provided by § 370.6(f) does not need the FDIC's approval to issue senior unsecured non guaranteed debt that matures after June 30, 2012.

(2) After obtaining the FDIC's prior written approval to issue non-guaranteed debt pursuant to paragraph (h)(1) of this section, any participating entity, other than an entity described in paragraph (j)(1) of this section, may issue after June 30, 2009 senior unsecured non-guaranteed debt in any amount with any maturity.

(k) Emergency Guarantee Facility. In the event that a participating entity that is either an insured depository institution or an entity that has issued FDIC-guaranteed debt on or before September 9, 2009 is unable, after October 31, 2009, to issue non-guaranteed debt to replace maturing senior unsecured debt as a result of market disruptions or other circumstances beyond the entity's control, the participating entity may, with the FDIC's prior approval under paragraph (h) of this section, issue FDIC-guaranteed debt after October 31, 2009, and on or before April 30, 2010. Any such issuance is subject to all of the terms and conditions imposed by the FDIC in its approval decision as well as all of the provisions of this part, including without limitation, the payment of the applicable assessment and compliance with the disclosure requirements.

[73 FR 72266, Nov. 26, 2008, as amended at 74 FR 9524, Mar. 4, 2009; 74 FR 12083, Mar. 23, 2009; 74 FR 54747, Oct. 23, 2009]

§ 370.4 Transaction Account Guarantee Program.

(a) In addition to the coverage afforded to depositors under 12 CFR Part 330, a depositor's funds in a non-interest-bearing transaction account maintained at a participating entity that is an insured depository institution are guaranteed in full (irrespective of the standard maximum deposit insurance amount defined in 12 CFR 330.1(n)) from October 14, 2008 through:

(1) The date of opt-out, in the case of an entity that opted out prior to December 5, 2008;

(2) December 31, 2009, in the case of an entity that opted out effective on January 1, 2010; or

(3) June 30, 2010, in the case of an entity that opts out of the transaction account guarantee program effective on July 1, 2010; or

(4) The TAG expiration date, in the case of an entity that does not opt out.

(b) In determining whether funds are in a noninterest-bearing transaction account for purposes of this section, the FDIC will apply its normal rules and procedures under § 360.8 (12 CFR 360.8) for determining account balances at a failed insured depository institution. Under these procedures, funds may be swept or transferred from a noninterest-bearing transaction account to another type of deposit or nondeposit account. Unless the funds are in a noninterest-bearing transaction account after the completion of a sweep under § 360.8, the funds will not be guaranteed under the transaction account guarantee program.

(c) Notwithstanding paragraph (b) of this section, in the case of funds swept from a noninterest-bearing transaction account to a noninterest-bearing savings deposit account, the FDIC will treat the swept funds as being in a noninterest-bearing transaction account. As a result of this treatment, the funds swept from a noninterest-bearing transaction account to a noninterest-bearing savings account, as defined in 12 CFR 204.2(d), will be guaranteed under the transaction account guarantee program.

[73 FR 72266, Nov. 26, 2008, as amended at 74 FR 45098, Sept. 1, 2009; 75 FR 20264, Apr. 19, 2010]

§ 370.5 Participation.

(a) *Initial period.* All eligible entities are covered under the temporary liquidity guarantee program for the period from October 14, 2008, through December 5, 2008, unless they opt out on or before 11:59 p.m., Eastern Standard Time, December 5, 2008, in which case the coverage ends on the date of the opt-out.

(b) The issuance of FDIC-guaranteed debt subject to the protections of the

§ 370.5

debt guarantee program is an affirmative action by a participating entity that constitutes its agreement to be:

(1) Bound by the terms and conditions of the program, including without limitation, assessments and the terms of the Master Agreement as set forth on the FDIC's Web site;

(2) Subject to, and to comply with, any FDIC request to provide information relevant to participation in the debt guarantee program and to be subject to FDIC on-site reviews as needed, after consultation with the appropriate Federal banking agency, to determine compliance with the terms and requirements of the debt guarantee program; and

(3) Bound by the FDIC's decisions, in consultation with the appropriate Federal banking agency, regarding the management of the temporary liquidity guarantee program.

(c) *Opt-out and opt-in options.* (1) From October 14, 2008 through December 5, 2008, each eligible entity is a participating entity in both the debt guarantee program and the transaction account guarantee program, unless the entity opts out. No later than 11:59 p.m., Eastern Standard Time, December 5, 2008, each eligible entity must inform the FDIC if it desires to opt out of the debt guarantee program or the transaction account guarantee program, or both. Failure to opt out by 11:59 p.m., Eastern Standard Time, December 5, 2008 constitutes a decision to continue in the program after that date. Prior to December 5, 2008 an eligible entity may opt in to either or both programs by informing the FDIC that it will not opt out of either or both programs.

(2) Any insured depository institution that is participating in the transaction account guarantee program may elect to opt out of such program effective on January 1, 2010. Any such election to opt-out must be made in accordance with the procedures set forth in paragraph (g)(2) of this section. An election to opt out once made is irrevocable.

(3) Any insured depository institution that is participating in the transaction account guarantee program may request authorization to opt out of such program effective on July 1, 2010.

Any such election to opt-out must be made in accordance with the procedures set forth in paragraph (g)(3) of this section. If the FDIC grants the request, the opt out is irrevocable.

(d) An eligible entity may elect to opt out of either the debt guarantee program or the transaction account guarantee program or both. The choice to opt out, once made, is irrevocable, except that, in the case of a merger between two eligible entities, the resulting institution will have a one-time option to revoke a prior decision to opt-out. This option must be requested by application to the FDIC in accordance with § 370.3(h). Similarly, the choice to affirmatively opt in, as provided in paragraph (c) of this section, once made, is irrevocable.

(e) All eligible entities that are affiliates of a U.S. bank holding company or that are affiliates of an eligible entity that is a U.S. savings and loan holding company must make the same decision regarding continued participation in each guarantee program; failure to do so constitutes an opt out by all members of the group.

(f) Except as provided in paragraphs (g), (j), and (k) of § 370.3, participating entities are not permitted to select which newly issued senior unsecured debt is guaranteed debt; all senior unsecured debt issued by a participating entity up to its debt guarantee limit must be issued and identified as FDIC-guaranteed debt as and when issued.

(g) *Procedures for opting out.* (1) Except as provided in paragraphs (g)(2) and (g)(3) of this section, the FDIC will provide procedures for opting out and for making an affirmative decision to opt in using FDIC's secure e-business Web site, FDICconnect. Entities that are not insured depository institutions will select and solely use an affiliated insured depository institution to submit their opt-out election or their affirmative decision to opt in.

(2) Pursuant to paragraph (c)(2) of this section a participating entity may opt out of the transaction account guarantee program effective on January 1, 2010 by submitting to the FDIC on or before 11:59 p.m., Eastern Standard Time, on November 2, 2009 an email conveying the entity's election to opt out. The subject line of the email must

Federal Deposit Insurance Corporation § 370.5

include: "TLGP Election to Opt Out—Cert. No. _____." The email must be addressed to *dcas@fdic.gov* and must include the following:
 (i) Institution Name;
 (ii) FDIC Certificate number;
 (iii) City, State, ZIP;
 (iv) Name, Telephone Number and Email Address of a Contact Person;
 (v) A statement that the institution is opting out of the transaction account guarantee program effective January 1, 2010; and
 (vi) Confirmation that no later than November 16, 2009 the institution will post a prominent notice in the lobby of its main office and each domestic branch and, if it offers Internet deposit services, on its website clearly indicating that after December 31, 2009, funds held in noninterest-bearing transaction accounts will no longer be guaranteed in full under the Transaction Account Guarantee Program, but will be insured up to $250,000 under the FDIC's general deposit insurance rules.

(3) Pursuant to paragraph (c)(3) of this section a participating entity may request authorization to opt out of the transaction account guarantee program effective on July 1, 2010 by submitting to the FDIC on or before 11:59 p.m., Eastern Daylight Saving Time, on April 30, 2010 an e-mail conveying the entity's request to opt out. The subject line of the e-mail must include: "TLGP Request to Opt Out—Cert. No. _____." The e-mail must be addressed to *optout@fdic.gov* and must include the following:
 (i) Institution Name;
 (ii) FDIC Certificate number;
 (iii) City, State, ZIP;
 (iv) Name, Telephone Number and Email Address of a Contact Person;
 (v) A statement that the institution is requesting authorization to opt out of the transaction account guarantee program effective July 1, 2010; and
 (vi) Confirmation that no later than May 20, 2010 the institution will post a prominent notice in the lobby of its main office and each domestic branch and, if it offers Internet deposit services, on its Web site clearly indicating that after June 30, 2010, funds held in noninterest-bearing transaction accounts will no longer be guaranteed in full under the Transaction Account Guarantee Program, but will be insured up to $250,000 under the FDIC's general deposit insurance rules.

(h) *Disclosures regarding participation in the temporary liquidity guarantee program.* (1) The FDIC will publish on its Web site:
 (i) A list of the eligible entities that have opted out of the debt guarantee program, and
 (ii) A list of the eligible entities that have opted out of the transaction account guarantee program.

(2) Each participating entity that is either an insured depository institution, an entity that has issued FDIC-guaranteed debt before April 1, 2009, an entity that has been approved pursuant to § 370.3(h) to issue FDIC-guaranteed debt after June 30, 2009, and on or before October 31, 2009, or a participating entity that has been approved pursuant to § 370.3(k) to issue FDIC-guaranteed debt after October 31, 2009, must include the following disclosure statement in all written materials provided to lenders or creditors regarding any senior unsecured debt that is issued by it during the applicable issuance period and that is guaranteed under the debt guarantee program:

This debt is guaranteed under the Federal Deposit Insurance Corporation's Temporary Liquidity Guarantee Program and is backed by the full faith and credit of the United States. The details of the FDIC guarantee are provided in the FDIC's regulations, 12 CFR Part 370, and at the FDIC's Web site, http://www.fdic.gov/tlgp. [If the debt being issued is mandatory convertible debt, add: *The expiration date of the FDIC's guarantee is the earlier of the mandatory conversion date or December 31, 2012*]. [If the debt being issued is any other senior unsecured debt, add: *The expiration date of the FDIC's guarantee is the earlier of the maturity date of the debt or December 31, 2012.*]

(3) Each participating entity other than an entity described in paragraph (h)(2) of this section must include the following disclosure statement in all written materials provided to lenders or creditors regarding any senior unsecured debt that is issued by it during the applicable issuance period and that is guaranteed under the debt guarantee program:

This debt is guaranteed under the Federal Deposit Insurance Corporation's Temporary Liquidity Guarantee Program and is backed by

§ 370.5

the full faith and credit of the United States. The details of the FDIC guarantee are provided in the FDIC's regulations, 12 CFR Part 370, and at the FDIC's Web site, http://www.fdic.gov/tlgp. [If the debt being issued is mandatory convertible debt, add: *The expiration date of the FDIC's guarantee is the earlier of the mandatory conversion date or June 30, 2012.* [If the debt being issued is any other senior unsecured debt, add: *The expiration date of the FDIC's guarantee is the earlier of the maturity date of the debt or June 30, 2012.*]

(4) Each participating entity must include the following disclosure statement in all written materials provided to lenders or creditors regarding any senior unsecured debt issued by it during the applicable issuance period that is not guaranteed under the debt guarantee program:

This debt is not guaranteed under the Federal Deposit Insurance Corporation's Temporary Liquidity Guarantee Program.

(5) Each insured depository institution that offers noninterest-bearing transaction accounts must post a prominent notice in the lobby of its main office, each domestic branch and, if it offers Internet deposit services, on its Web site clearly indicating whether the institution is participating in the transaction account guarantee program. If the institution is participating in the transaction account guarantee program, the notice must state that funds held in noninterest-bearing transactions accounts at the entity are guaranteed in full by the FDIC. Participating entities must update their disclosures to reflect the current TAG expiration date, including any extension pursuant to § 370.2(o) or, if applicable, any decision to opt-out.

(i) These disclosures must be provided in simple, readily understandable text. Sample disclosures are as follows:

For Participating Institutions

[Institution Name] is participating in the FDIC's Transaction Account Guarantee Program. Under that program, through [June 30, 2010, December 31, 2010, or such other date established by the Board as the TAG expiration date pursuant to § 370.2(o), whichever is applicable], all noninterest-bearing transaction accounts are fully guaranteed by the FDIC for the entire amount in the account. Coverage under the Transaction Account Guarantee Program is in addition to and separate from the coverage available under the FDIC's general deposit insurance rules.

For Participating Institutions That Elect To Opt-Out of the Extended Transaction Account Guaranty Program Effective on July 1, 2010

Beginning July 1, 2010 [Institution Name] will no longer participate in the FDIC's Transaction Account Guarantee Program. Thus, after June 30, 2010, funds held in noninterest-bearing transaction accounts will no longer be guaranteed in full under the Transaction Account Guarantee Program, but will be insured up to $250,000 under the FDIC's general deposit insurance rules.

For Non-Participating Institutions

[Institution Name] has chosen not to participate in the FDIC's Transaction Account Guarantee Program. Customers of [Institution Name] with noninterest-bearing transaction accounts will continue to be insured for up to $250,000 under the FDIC's general deposit insurance rules.

(ii) If the institution uses sweep arrangements or takes other actions that result in funds being transferred or reclassified to an account that is not guaranteed under the transaction account guarantee program, for example, an interest-bearing account, the institution must disclose those actions to the affected customers and clearly advise them, in writing, that such actions will void the FDIC's guarantee with respect to the swept, transferred, or reclassified funds.

(i) *Participation By New Eligible Entities And Continued Eligibility.* The FDIC will determine eligibility in consultation with the eligible entity's appropriate Federal banking agency.

(1) Participation by an entity that is organized after October 13, 2008 or that becomes an entity described § 370.2(a) after October 13, 2008 will be: with respect to the transaction account guarantee program, effective on the date of the entity's opt-in as described in § 370.2(g)(2), and with respect to the debt guarantee program, considered by the FDIC on a case-by-case basis in consultation with the entity's appropriate Federal banking agency.

(2) An eligible entity that is not an insured depository institution will cease to be eligible to participate in the debt guarantee program once it is no longer affiliated with a chartered and operating insured depository institution.

Federal Deposit Insurance Corporation § 370.6

(j) No mandatory convertible debt may be issued without obtaining the FDIC's prior written approval.

[73 FR 72266, Nov. 26, 2008, as amended at 74 FR 9525, Mar. 4, 2009; 74 FR 12084, Mar. 23, 2009; 74 FR 45099, Sept. 1, 2009; 74 FR 54749, Oct. 23, 2009; 75 FR 20264, Apr. 19, 2010; 75 FR 36510, June 28, 2010]

§ 370.6 Assessments under the Debt Guarantee Program.

(a) *Waiver of assessment for certain initial periods.* No eligible entity shall pay any assessment associated with the debt guarantee program for the period from October 14, 2008 through November 12, 2008. An eligible entity that opts out of the program on or before December 5, 2008 will not pay any assessment under the program.

(b) *Notice to the FDIC.* No guaranteed debt shall be issued by a participating entity under the FDIC's debt guarantee program unless notice of the issuance of such debt and payment of associated assessments is provided to the FDIC as required by this section and, for guaranteed debt issued after November 21, 2008, the participating entity agrees to be bound by the terms of the Master Agreement, as set forth on the FDIC's Web site.

(1) Any eligible entity that does not opt out of the debt guarantee program on or before December 5, 2008, as provided in § 370.5, and that issues any guaranteed debt during the period from October 14, 2008 through December 5, 2008 which is still outstanding on December 5, 2008, shall notify the FDIC of that issuance via the FDIC's e-business Web site FDIC*connect* on or before December 19, 2008, and the entity's Chief Financial Officer or equivalent shall certify that the issuances identified as FDIC-guaranteed debt outstanding at each point of time did not exceed the debt guarantee limit as set forth in § 370.3

(2) Each participating entity that issues guaranteed debt after December 5, 2008, shall notify the FDIC of that issuance via the FDIC's e-business Web site FDIC*connect* within the time period specified by the FDIC. The eligible entity's Chief Financial Officer or equivalent shall certify that the issuance of guaranteed debt does not exceed the debt guarantee limit as set forth in § 370.3.

(3) The FDIC will provide procedures governing notice to the FDIC and certification of guaranteed amount limits for purposes of this section.

(c) *Initiation of assessments.* Assessments, calculated in accordance with paragraph (d) of this section, will accrue, with respect to each eligible entity that does not opt out of the debt guarantee program on or before December 5, 2008:

(1) Beginning on November 13, 2008, on all senior unsecured debt, as defined in § 370.2(e)(1)(i) (except for overnight debt), issued by it on or after October 14, 2008, and on or before December 5, 2008, that is still outstanding on December 5, 2008; and

(2) Beginning on December 6, 2008, on all senior unsecured debt, as defined in paragraphs (e)(1)(ii) or (e)(1)(iii) of § 370.2, issued by it on or after December 6, 2008.

(d) *Amount of assessments for debt within the debt guarantee limit.* (1) *Calculation of assessment.* Subject to paragraphs (d)(3) and (h) of this section, and except as provided in paragraph (i) of this section, the amount of assessment will be determined by multiplying the amount of FDIC-guaranteed debt times the term of the debt or, in the case of mandatory convertible debt, the time period from issuance to the mandatory conversion date, times an annualized assessment rate determined in accordance with the following table.

For debt with a maturity or time period to conversion date of—	The annualized assessment rate (in basis points) is—
180 days or less (excluding overnight debt)	50
181–364 days	75
365 days or greater	100

(2) If the debt being issued has a maturity date that occurs after the expiration date of the guarantee, the expiration date of the guarantee instead of the maturity date will be used to calculate the assessment.

697

§ 370.6   12 CFR Ch. III (1-1-12 Edition)

(3) The amount of assessment for a participating entity, other than an insured depository institution, that controls, directly or indirectly, or is otherwise affiliated with, at least one insured depository institution will be determined by multiplying the amount of FDIC-guaranteed debt times the term of the debt or, in the case of mandatory convertible debt, the time period from issuance to the mandatory conversion date, times an annualized assessment rate determined in accordance with the rates set forth in the table in paragraph (d)(1) of this section, except that each such rate shall be increased by 10 basis points, if the combined assets of all insured depository institutions affiliated with such entity constitute less than 50 percent of consolidated holding company assets. The comparison of assets for purposes of this paragraph shall be determined as of September 30, 2008, except that in the case of an entity that becomes an eligible entity after October 13, 2008, the comparison of assets shall be determined as of the date that it becomes an eligible entity.

(4) *Assessment Invoicing.* As soon as the participating entity provides notice as required in paragraph (b) of this section, the invoice for the appropriate fee will be automatically generated and posted on *FDICconnect* for the account associated with the participating entity, and the time limits for providing payment in paragraph (g) of this section will apply.

(5) *No assessment reduction for early retirement of guaranteed debt.* A participating entity's assessment shall not be reduced if guaranteed debt is retired prior to its scheduled maturity date or conversion date.

(e) *Increased assessments for debt exceeding the debt guarantee limit.* Any participating entity that issues guaranteed debt represented as being guaranteed by the FDIC exceeding its debt guarantee limit as set forth in § 370.3(b) shall have its applicable assessment rate(s) for all outstanding guaranteed debt increased by 100 percent for purposes of the calculations in paragraph (d)(1) of this section. The FDIC may reduce the assessments under this paragraph upon a showing of good cause by the entity. In addition, any entity making such a misrepresentation may also be subject to enforcement action under 12 U.S.C. 1818, as further described in § 370.11.

(f) *Long term non-guaranteed debt fee.* Each participating entity that elects to issue long term non-guaranteed debt pursuant to § 370.3(g) must pay the FDIC a nonrefundable fee equal to 37.5 basis points times the amount of the entity's senior unsecured debt, as defined in § 370.2(e)(1)(i), that had a maturity date on or before June 30, 2009, and was outstanding as of September 30, 2008. If the entity had no such debt outstanding as of September 30, 2008, the fee will equal 37.5 basis points times the amount of the entity's debt guarantee limit established under § 370.3(b).

(1) The nonrefundable fee will be collected in six equal monthly installments.

(2) An entity electing the nonrefundable fee option will also be billed as it issues guaranteed debt under the debt guarantee program, and the amounts paid as a nonrefundable fee under this paragraph will be applied to offset these bills until the nonrefundable fee is exhausted.

(3) Thereafter, the institution will have to pay additional assessments on guaranteed debt as it issues the debt, as otherwise required by this section.

(g) *Collection of assessments—ACH Debit.* (1) Each participating entity shall take all actions necessary to allow the Corporation to debit assessments from the participating entity's designated deposit account as provided for in § 327.3(a)(2). The assessment payments of a participating entity that is not an insured depository institution shall be debited from the designated account of the affiliated insured depository institution it selected for *FDICconnect* access under § 370.5(g).

(2) Each participating entity shall ensure that funds in an amount at least equal to the amount of the assessment are available in the designated account for direct debit by the Corporation on the first business day after posting of the invoice on *FDICconnect*. A participating entity that is not an insured depository institution shall provide the necessary funds for payment of its assessments.

698

Federal Deposit Insurance Corporation §370.7

(3) Failure to take all necessary action or to provide funding to allow the Corporation to debit assessments shall be deemed to constitute nonpayment of the assessment, and such failure by any participating entity will be subject to the penalties for failure to timely pay assessments as provided for at §308.132(c)(3)(v).

(4) For purposes of this paragraph (g) of this section, assessments shall include all applicable surcharges imposed pursuant to paragraph (h) of this section.

(h) *Surcharges on assessments.* (1) For FDIC-guaranteed debt that has a time period to conversion (in the case of mandatory convertible debt) or a maturity of one year or more, that is issued on or after April 1, 2009 and on or before June 30, 2009, and that matures or converts on or before June 30, 2012, the assessment rate provided in the table in paragraph (d)(1) of this section shall be increased by:

(i) 10 basis points for such debt that is issued by a participating entity that is an insured depository institution, and

(ii) 20 basis points for such debt that is issued by any other participating entity.

(2) For FDIC-guaranteed debt that has a time period to conversion (in the case of mandatory convertible debt) or a maturity of one year or more, and that is either issued on or after April 1, 2009 with a maturity or conversion date after June 30, 2012, or issued after June 30, 2009, the assessment rate provided in the table in paragraph (d)(1) of this section shall be increased by

(i) 25 basis points for such debt that is issued by a participating entity that is an insured depository institution, and

(ii) 50 basis points for such debt that is issued by any other participating entity.

(i) *Assessment for debt issued under the Emergency Guarantee Facility.* The amount of the assessment for FDIC-guaranteed debt issued pursuant to §370.3(k) of this part is equal to the amount of the debt times the term of the debt (or in the case of mandatory convertible debt, the time period to conversion) times an annualized assessment rate of 300 basis points, or such greater rate as the FDIC may determine in its decision approving such issuance.

[73 FR 72266, Nov. 26, 2008, as amended at 74 FR 9525, Mar. 4, 2009; 74 FR 12085, Mar. 23, 2009; 74 FR 54749, Oct. 23, 2009]

§370.7 Assessment for the Transaction Account Guarantee Program.

(a) *Waiver of assessment for certain initial periods.* No eligible entity shall pay any assessment associated with the transaction account guarantee program for the period from October 14, 2008, through November 12, 2008. An eligible entity that opts out of the program on or before December 5, 2008 will not pay any assessment under the program.

(b) *Initiation of assessments.* Beginning on November 13, 2008 each eligible entity that does not opt out of the transaction account guarantee program on or before December 5, 2008 will be required to pay the FDIC assessments on all deposit amounts in noninterest-bearing transaction accounts calculated in accordance with paragraph (c) of this section.

(c) *Amount of assessment.* (1) Except as provided in paragraphs (c)(2) and (c)(3) of this section any eligible entity that does not opt out of the transaction account guarantee program shall pay quarterly an annualized 10 basis point assessment on any deposit amounts exceeding the existing deposit insurance limit of $250,000, as reported on its quarterly Consolidated Reports of Condition and Income, Thrift Financial Report, or Report of Assets and Liabilities of U.S. Branches and Agencies of Foreign Banks (each, a "Call Report") in any noninterest-bearing transaction accounts (as defined in §370.2(h)), including any such amounts swept from a noninterest-bearing transaction account into an noninterest-bearing savings deposit account as provided in §370.4(c).

(2) For the period after December 31, 2009 through and including June 30, 2010, each participating entity that does not opt out of the transaction account guarantee program in accordance with §370.5(c)(2) shall pay quarterly a fee based upon its Risk Category rating. The amount of the fee for each such entity is equal to the

§ 370.8

annualized, TAG assessment rate for the entity multiplied by the amount of the deposits held in noninterest-bearing transaction accounts (as defined in § 370.2(h) and including any amounts swept from a noninterest- bearing transaction account into an non-interest-bearing savings deposit account as provided in § 370.4(c)) that exceed the existing deposit insurance limit of $250,000, as reported on the entity's most recent quarterly Call Report.

(3) Beginning on July 1, 2010, each participating entity that does not opt out of the transaction account guarantee program shall pay quarterly a fee based upon its Risk Category rating. The amount of the fee for each such entity is equal to the annualized, TAG assessment rate for the entity multiplied by the aggregate amount of the deposits held in noninterest-bearing transaction accounts (as defined in § 370.2(h) and including any amounts swept from a noninterest-bearing transaction account into an noninterest-bearing savings deposit account as provided in § 370.4(c)) that exceed the existing deposit insurance limit of $250,000, calculated based upon the average daily balances in such accounts as reported on the entity's most recent quarterly Call Report.

(4) The annualized TAG assessment rates are as follows:

(i) 15 basis points, for the portion of each quarter in which the entity is assigned to Risk Category I;

(ii) 20 basis points, for the portion of each quarter in which the entity is assigned to Risk Category II; and

(iii) 25 basis points, for the portion of each quarter in which the entity is assigned to either Risk Category III or Risk Category IV.

(5) The amount to be reported for each noninterest-bearing transaction account as the average daily balance is the total dollar amount held in such account that exceeds $250,000 for each calendar day during the quarter divided by the number of calendar days in the quarter. For those days that an office of the reporting institution is closed (e.g., Saturdays, Sundays, or holidays), the amounts outstanding from the previous business day should be used. The total number of accounts to be reported should be calculated on the same basis. Documentation supporting the amounts used in the calculation of the average daily balance amounts must be retained and be readily available upon request by the FDIC or the institution's primary Federal regulator. In addition, all institutions that do not opt of the transaction account guarantee program must establish procedures to gather the necessary daily data beginning July 1, 2010.

(6) An entity's Risk Category is determined in accordance with the FDIC's risk-based premium system described in 12 CFR part 327. The assessments provided in this paragraph (c) shall be in addition to an institution's risk-based assessment imposed under Part 327.

(d) *Collection of assessment.* Assessments for the transaction account guarantee program shall be collected along with a participating entity's quarterly deposit insurance payment as provided in § 327.3, and subject to penalties for failure to timely pay assessments as referenced in § 308.132(c)(3)(v).

[73 FR 72266, Nov. 26, 2008, as amended at 74 FR 45099, Sept. 1, 2009; 75 FR 20265, Apr. 19, 2010]

§ 370.8 Systemic risk emergency special assessment to recover loss.

To the extent that the assessments provided under § 370.6 or § 370.7, other than the surcharges provided in § 370.6(h), are insufficient to cover any loss or expenses arising from the temporary liquidity guarantee program, the Corporation shall impose an emergency special assessment on insured depository institutions as provided under 12 U.S.C. 1823(c)(4)(G)(ii) of the FDI Act.

[74 FR 12085, Mar. 23, 2009]

§ 370.9 Recordkeeping requirements.

The FDIC will establish procedures, require reports, and require participating entities to provide and preserve any information needed for the operation and supervision of this program.

[74 FR 12085, Mar. 23, 2009]

Federal Deposit Insurance Corporation

§ 370.12

§ 370.10 Oversight.

(a) Participating entities are subject to the FDIC's oversight regarding compliance with the terms of the temporary liquidity guarantee program.

(b) A participating entity's default in the payment of any debt may be considered an unsafe or unsound practice and may result in enforcement action as described in § 370.11.

(c) In general, with respect to a participating entity that is an insured depository institution, the FDIC shall consider the existence of conditions which rise to an obligation to pay on its guarantee as providing grounds for the appointment of the FDIC as conservator or receiver under Section 11(c)(5)(C) and (F) of the Federal Deposit Insurance Act, 12 U.S.C. 1821(c)(5)(C) and (F).

(d) By issuing guaranteed debt, all participating entities agree, for the duration of the temporary liquidity guarantee program, to be subject to the FDIC's authority to determine compliance with the provisions and requirements of the program.

§ 370.11 Enforcement mechanisms.

(a) *Termination of Participation.* If the FDIC, in its discretion, after consultation with the participating entity's appropriate Federal banking agency, determines that the participating entity should no longer be permitted to continue to participate in the temporary liquidity guarantee program, the FDIC will inform the entity that it will no longer be provided the protections of the temporary liquidity guarantee program.

(1) Termination of participation in the temporary liquidity guarantee program will solely have prospective effect. All previously issued guaranteed debt will continue to be guaranteed as set forth in this part.

(2) The FDIC will work with the participating entity and its appropriate Federal banking agency to assure that the entity notifies its counterparties or creditors that subsequent debt issuances are not covered by the temporary liquidity guarantee program.

(b) *Enforcement Actions.* Violating any provision of the temporary liquidity guarantee program constitutes a violation of a regulation and may subject the participating entity and its institution-affiliated parties to enforcement actions under Section 8 of the FDI Act (12 U.S.C. 1818), including, for example, assessment of civil money penalties under section 8(i) of the FDI Act (12 U.S.C. 1818(i)), removal and prohibition orders under section 8(e) of the FDI Act (12 U.S.C. 1818(e)), and cease and desist orders under section 8(b) of the FDI Act (12 U.S.C. 1818(b)). The violation of any provision of the program by an insured depository institution also constitutes grounds for terminating the institution's deposit insurance under section 8(a)(2) of the FDI Act (12 U.S.C. 1818(a)(2)). The appropriate Federal banking agency for the participating entity will consult with the FDIC in enforcing the provisions of this part. The appropriate Federal banking agency and the FDIC also have enforcement authority under section 18(a)(4)(C) of the FDI Act (12 U.S.C. 1828(a)(4)(C)) to pursue an enforcement action if a person knowingly misrepresents that any deposit liability, obligation, certificate, or share is insured when it is not in fact insured.

§ 370.12 Payment on the guarantee.

(a) *Claims for Deposits in Noninterest-bearing Transaction Accounts.* (1) *In general.* The FDIC will pay the guaranteed claims of depositors for funds in a noninterest-bearing transaction account in an insured depository institution that is a participating entity as soon as possible upon the failure of the entity. Unless otherwise provided for in this paragraph (a), the guaranteed claims of depositors who hold noninterest-bearing transaction deposit accounts in such entities will be paid in accordance with 12 U.S.C. 1821(f) and 12 CFR parts 330 and 370.

(2) *Subrogation rights of FDIC.* Upon payment of such claims, the FDIC will be subrogated to the claims of depositors in accordance with 12 U.S.C. 1821(g).

(3) *Review of final determination.* The final determination of the amount guaranteed shall be considered a final agency action of the FDIC reviewable in accordance with Chapter 7 of Title 5, by the United States district court for the federal judicial district where the

§ 370.12

principal place of business of the depository institution is located. Any request for review of the final determination shall be filed with the appropriate district court not later than sixty (60) days of the date on which the final determination is issued.

(b) *Payments on Guaranteed Debt of participating entities in default*—(1) *In general.* The FDIC's obligation to pay holders of FDIC-guaranteed debt issued by a participating entity shall arise upon the uncured failure of such entity to make a timely payment of principal or interest as required under the debt instrument (a "payment default").

(2) *Method of payment.* Upon the occurrence of a payment default, the FDIC shall satisfy its guarantee obligation by making scheduled payments of principal and interest pursuant to the terms of the debt instrument through maturity, or in the case of mandatory convertible debt, through the mandatory conversion date (without regard to default or penalty provisions). Any principal payment on mandatory convertible debt shall be limited to amounts paid by holders under the issuance. The FDIC may in its discretion, at any time after the expiration of the guarantee period, elect to make a final payment of all outstanding principal and interest due under a guaranteed debt instrument whose maturity extends beyond that date. In such case, the FDIC shall not be liable for any prepayment penalty.

(3) *Demand for payment; proofs of claim*—(i) *Payment through authorized representative.* Except as provided in paragraph (b)(3)(ii) of this section, a demand for payment on the guaranteed amount shall be made on behalf of all holders of debt subject to a payment default that is made by a duly authorized representative of such debtholders if the issuer shall have elected to provide for one in the Master Agreement submitted pursuant to § 370.6(b). Such demand must be accompanied by a proof of claim, which shall include evidence, to the extent not previously provided in the Master Agreement, in form and content satisfactory to the FDIC, of: the representative's financial and organizational capacity to act as representative; the representative's exclusive authority to act on behalf each and every debtholder and its fiduciary responsibility to the debtholder when acting as such, as established by the terms of the debt instrument; the occurrence of a payment default; and the authority to make an assignment of each debtholder's right, title, and interest in the FDIC-guaranteed debt to the FDIC and to effect the transfer to the FDIC of each debtholder's claim in any insolvency proceeding. This assignment shall include the right of the FDIC to receive any and all distributions on the debt from the proceeds of the receivership or bankruptcy estate. If any holder of the FDIC-guaranteed debt has received any distribution from the receivership or bankruptcy estate prior to the FDIC's payment under the guarantee, the guaranteed amount paid by the FDIC shall be reduced by the amount the holder has received in the distribution from the receivership or bankruptcy estate. All such demands must be made within 60 days of the occurrence of the payment default upon which the demand is based. Upon receipt of a conforming proof of claim, if timely filed, the FDIC will make a payment of the amount guaranteed.

(ii) *Individual debtholders:* Individual debtholders who are not represented by an authorized representative provided for in a Master Agreement submitted pursuant to § 370.6(b), or who elect not to be represented by such authorized representative, may make demand for payment of the guaranteed amount upon the FDIC. The FDIC may reject a demand made by a person who the FDIC determines has not opted out of representation by an authorized representative. In order to be considered for payment, such demand must be accompanied by a proof of claim, which shall include evidence in form and content satisfactory to the FDIC of: the occurrence of a payment default; and the claimant's ownership of the FDIC-guaranteed debt obligation. The demand also must be accompanied by an assignment, in form and content satisfactory to the FDIC, of the debtholder's rights, title, and interest in the FDIC-guaranteed debt to the FDIC and the transfer to the FDIC of the debtholder's claim in any insolvency proceeding. This assignment shall include the right of the FDIC to receive any and all distributions on the debt from the proceeds of the receivership or bankruptcy estate. If any holder of the FDIC-guaranteed debt has received any distribution from the receivership or bankruptcy estate prior to the FDIC's payment under the guarantee, the guaranteed amount paid by the FDIC shall be reduced by the amount the holder has received in the distribution from the receivership or bankruptcy estate. All such demands must be made within 60 days of the occurrence of the payment default upon which the demand is based. Upon receipt of a conforming proof of claim, if timely filed, the FDIC will make a payment of the amount guaranteed.

(iii) Any demand under this subsection shall be made in writing and directed to the Director, Division of Resolutions and Receiverships, Federal Deposit Insurance Corporation, Washington, DC., and must include all supporting evidence as set forth in the previous subsections, and shall certify to the accuracy thereof

(iv) *Demand period.* Failure of the holder of the FDIC-guaranteed debt or an authorized representative to make demand for payment within sixty (60) days of the occurrence of payment default will deprive the holder of the FDIC-guaranteed debt of all further rights and remedies with respect to the guarantee claim.

(4) *Subrogation.* Upon payment under either method under paragraph (b)(2) of this section, the FDIC will be subrogated to the rights of any debtholder against the issuer, including in respect of any insolvency proceeding, to the extent of the payments made under the guarantee.

(5) *Release and satisfaction.* Payment under paragraph (b)(2) of this section shall constitute, to the extent of payments made, satisfaction of all FDIC obligations under the debt guarantee program with respect to that debtholder or holders. Acceptance of any such payments shall constitute a release of any liability of the FDIC under the debt guarantee program with respect to those payments. Each participating entity agrees and acknowledges that it shall be indebted to the FDIC for any payments made under these provisions (including amounts paid to a participating entity in return for its assumption of a guaranteed debt issuance) and shall honor immediately a demand by the FDIC for reimbursement therefore. A participating entity's undertakings in this regard shall be evidenced and governed by the "Master Agreement" it shall execute and submit, in connection with its election pursuant to §370.6(b) to participate in the Debt Guarantee Program.

(6) *Final determination; review of final determination.* The FDIC's determination under this paragraph shall be a final administrative determination subject to judicial review. The holder of FDIC-guaranteed debt shall have the right to seek judicial review of the FDIC's final determination in the United States District Court for the District of Columbia or the United States District Court for the federal district where the issuer's principal place of business was located. Failure of the holder of the FDIC-guaranteed debt to seek such judicial review within sixty (60) days of the date of the rendering of the final determination will deprive the holder of the FDIC-guaranteed debt of all further rights and remedies with respect to the guarantee claim.

[73 FR 72266, Nov. 26, 2008, as amended at 74 FR 9525, Mar. 4, 2009; 74 FR 12085, Mar. 23, 2009; 74 FR 26945, June 5, 2009]

PART 371—RECORDKEEPING REQUIREMENTS FOR QUALIFIED FINANCIAL CONTRACTS

Sec.
371.1 Scope, purpose and applicability.
371.2 Definitions.
371.3 Form, availability and maintenance of records.
371.4 Content of records.
371.5 Enforcement actions.

APPENDIX A TO PART 371—FILE STRUCTURE FOR QUALIFIED FINANCIAL CONTRACT (QFC) RECORDS

AUTHORITY: 12 U.S.C. 1819(a)(Tenth); 1820(g); 1821(e)(8)(D) and (H); 1831g; 1831i, and 1831s.

SOURCE: 73 FR 78170, Dec. 22, 2008 unless otherwise noted.

§371.1 Scope, purpose and applicability.

(a) *Scope.* This part applies to insured depository institutions that are in a troubled condition as defined in §371.2(f).

(b) *Purpose.* This part establishes recordkeeping requirements with respect to qualified financial contracts for insured depository institutions that are in a troubled condition.

(c) *Applicability.* An insured depository institution shall comply with this part within 60 days after written notification by the institution's appropriate Federal banking agency or the FDIC that it is in a troubled condition under §371.2(f). The FDIC may, at its discretion, grant one or more extensions of time for compliance with this part. No single extension shall be for a period of more than 30 days. An insured depository institution may request an extension of time by submitting a written request to the FDIC at least 15 days prior to the deadline for its compliance with the requirements of this part. The written request for an extension must contain a statement of the reasons why the institution cannot comply by the deadline for compliance.

§371.2 Definitions.

For purposes of this part:

(a) *Affiliate* means any company that controls, is controlled by, or is under common control with another company.

(b) *Appropriate Federal banking agency* means the agency or agencies designated under 12 U.S.C. 1813(q).

(c) *Insured depository institution* means any bank or savings association, as defined in 12 U.S.C. 1813, the deposits of which are insured by the FDIC.

(d) *Position* means the rights and obligations of a person or entity as a party to an individual transaction under a QFC.

(e) *Qualified financial contracts* (QFCs) mean those qualified financial contracts that are defined in 12 U.S.C. 1821(e)(8)(D) to include securities contracts, commodity contracts, forward contracts, repurchase agreements, and swap agreements and any other contract determined by the FDIC to be a QFC as defined in that section.

(f) *Troubled condition* means for purposes of this part, any insured depository institution that:

(1) Has a composite rating, as determined by its appropriate Federal banking agency in its most recent report of examination, of 3 (only for insured depository institutions with total consolidated assets of ten billion dollars or greater), 4, or 5 under the Uniform Financial Institution Rating System, or in the case of an insured branch of a foreign bank, an equivalent rating;

(2) Is subject to a proceeding initiated by the FDIC for termination or suspension of deposit insurance;

(3) Is subject to a cease-and-desist order or written agreement issued by the appropriate Federal banking agency, as defined in 12 U.S.C. 1813(q), that requires action to improve the financial condition of the insured depository institution or is subject to a proceeding initiated by the appropriate Federal banking agency which contemplates the issuance of an order that requires action to improve the financial condition of the insured depository institution, unless otherwise informed in writing by the appropriate Federal banking agency;

(4) Is informed in writing by the insured depository institution's appropriate Federal banking agency that it is in troubled condition for purposes of 12 U.S.C. 1831i on the basis of the institution's most recent report of condition or report of examination, or other information available to the institution's appropriate Federal banking agency; or

(5) Is determined by the appropriate Federal banking agency or the FDIC in consultation with the appropriate Federal banking agency to be experiencing a significant deterioration of capital or significant funding difficulties or liquidity stress, notwithstanding the composite rating of the institution by its appropriate Federal banking agency in its most recent report of examination.

§371.3 Form, availability and maintenance of records.

(a) *Form and availability.* The records required to be maintained by an insured depository institution for QFCs under this part—

(1) Except for records that must be maintained through electronic files under appendix A of this part, may be maintained in any form, including in an electronic file, provided that the records are updated at least daily;

(2) If the records are not maintained in written form, will be capable of being reproduced or printed in written form; and

(3) Will be made available upon written request by the FDIC immediately at the close of processing of the institution's business day, for a period provided in that written request.

(b) *Maintenance of records after the institution is no longer in a troubled condition.* Insured depository institutions that are in a troubled condition as defined in § 371.2(f) shall continue to maintain the capacity to produce records required under this part on a daily basis for a period of one year after the date that the appropriate Federal banking agency notifies the institution that it is no longer in a troubled condition as defined in § 371.2(f).

(c) *Maintenance of records after an acquisition of an institution that is in a troubled condition.* If an insured depository institution that has been determined by the appropriate Federal banking agency to be in a troubled condition ceases to exist as an insured depository institution as a result of a merger or a similar transaction into an insured depository institution that is not in a troubled condition immediately following the acquisition, the obligation to maintain records under this part on a daily basis will terminate when the institution in a troubled condition ceases to exist as a separately insured depository institution.

§ 371.4 Content of records.

For each QFC for which an insured depository institution is a party or is subject to a master netting agreement involving the QFC, that institution must maintain records as listed under appendix A of this part.

§ 371.5 Enforcement actions.

Violating the terms or requirements of the recordkeeping requirements set forth in this part constitutes a violation of a regulation and subjects the participating entity to enforcement actions under Section 8 of the FDI Act (12 U.S.C. 1818).

APPENDIX A TO PART 371—FILE STRUCTURE FOR QUALIFIED FINANCIAL CONTRACT (QFC) RECORDS

QFC RECORDKEEPING REQUIREMENTS

A. Electronic Files To Be Maintained for QFCs

Any insured depository institution that is subject to this part ("institution") must produce and maintain, in an electronic file in a format acceptable to the FDIC, the position level data found in Table A1 for all open positions in QFCs entered into by that institution or for which the institution is subject. To fulfill this requirement, not later than three business days after the institution's receipt of the written notification from the FDIC under § 371.1(c) of this part, the institution must provide the FDIC with (i) a directory of the electronic files that will be used by the institution to maintain the position level data found in Table A1 and (ii) a point of contact at the institution should the FDIC have follow-up questions concerning this information. In addition, for such data, the institution must produce at the close of processing of the institution's business day a report in a format acceptable to the FDIC that aggregates the current market value and the amount of QFCs by each of the fields in Table A1. The institution must produce the report within 60 days of a written notification by the FDIC for the period specified in the notification. Notwithstanding the above requirements, for institutions in a troubled condition with less than twenty open QFC positions upon receipt of the written notification from the FDIC or the institution's appropriate Federal banking agency under part 371 and this appendix, the data required in Table A1 are not required to be recorded and maintained in electronic form as would otherwise be required by this part, so long as all required information is capable of being updated on a daily basis. If at any time after receiving such notification an institution has twenty or more open QFC positions at any point in time, it must within 60 days after that first occurs, comply with all provisions of part 371.

Pt. 371, App. A

12 CFR Ch. III (1–1–12 Edition)

TABLE A1—POSITION-LEVEL DATA

Field	Example	Data application
Unique position identifier and CUSIP, if available	999999999AU	Information needed to readily track and distinguish positions; unique trade confirmation number if available.
Portfolio location identifier (to identify the headquarters or branch where the position is booked).	XY12Z	Information needed to determine the headquarters or branch where the position is booked (see section B.1 of this Appendix).
Type of position (including the general nature of the reference asset or interest rate).	Interest rate swap, credit default swap, equity swap, foreign exchange forward, securities repurchase agreement, loan repurchase agreement.	Information needed to determine the extent to which the institution is involved in any particular QFC market.
Purpose of the position (if the purpose consists of hedging strategies, include the general category of the item(s) hedged).	Trading, hedging mortgage servicing, hedging certificates of deposit.	Information needed to determine the role of the QFC in the institution's business strategy.
Termination date (date the position terminates or is expected to terminate, expire, mature, or when final performance is required).	3/31/2010	Information needed to determine when the institution's rights and obligations regarding the position are expected to end.
Next call, put, or cancellation date	9/30/08	Information needed to determine when a call, put, or cancellation may occur with respect to a position.
Next payment date	9/30/08	Information needed to anticipate potential upcoming obligations.
Current market value of the position (as of the date of the file).	$995,000	Information needed to determine if the institution is in or out-of-the money with the counterparty.
Unique counterparty identifier	AB999C	Information needed to aggregate positions by counterparty.
Notional or principal amount of the position (this is the notional amount, where applicable).	$1,000,000	Information needed to help evaluate the position.
Documentation status of position	Affirmed, confirmed, or neither affirmed nor confirmed.	Information needed to determine reliability of a booked position and its legal status.

Also, the institution must maintain, in an electronic file in a format acceptable to the FDIC, the counterparty-level data found in Table A2 for all open positions in QFCs entered into by that institution. In addition, the institution must, at the FDIC's written request, produce immediately at the close of processing of the institution's business day, for a period provided in that written request, a report in a format acceptable to the FDIC that (i) itemizes, by each counterparty and by each of its affiliates, the data required in each field in Table A2, and (ii) aggregates by field, for each counterparty and its affiliates, the data required in each field in Table A2. Notwithstanding the above requirements, for institutions in a troubled condition with less than twenty open QFC positions upon receipt of the written notification from the FDIC or the institution's appropriate Federal banking agency under part 371 and this Appendix, the data required in Table A2 is not required to be recorded in electronic form as would otherwise be required by this part, so long as all required information is maintained and is capable of being updated on a daily basis. If at any time after receiving such notification an institution has twenty or more open QFC positions at any point in time, it must within 60 days after that first occurs, comply with all provisions of part 371.

TABLE A2—COUNTERPARTY-LEVEL DATA

Field	Example	Data Application
Unique counterparty identifier	AB999C	Information needed to aggregate positions by counterparty.
Current market value of all positions, as aggregated and, to the extent permitted under each applicable agreement, netted[29] (as of the date of the file).	($1,000,000)	Information needed to help evaluate the positions.
Current market value of all collateral and the type of collateral, if any, that the institution has posted against all positions with each counterparty.	$950,000; U.S. treasuries.	Information needed to determine the extent to which the institution has provided collateral.

TABLE A2—COUNTERPARTY-LEVEL DATA—Continued

Field	Example	Data Application
Current market value of all collateral and the type of collateral, if any, that the counterparty has posted against all positions.	$50,000; U.S. treasuries	Information needed to determine the extent to which the counterparty has provided collateral.
Institution's collateral excess or deficiency with respect to all of the institution's positions, as determined under each applicable agreement including thresholds and haircuts where applicable [30].	($25,000)	Information needed to determine the extent to which the institution has satisfied collateral requirements under each applicable agreement.
Counterparty's collateral excess or deficiency with respect to all of the institution's positions with each counterparty, as determined under each applicable agreement including thresholds and haircuts where applicable.	$50,000	Information needed to determine the extent to which the counterparty has satisfied collateral requirements under each applicable agreement.
The institution's collateral excess or deficiency with respect to all the positions, based on the aggregate market value of the positions (after netting to the extent permitted under each applicable agreement) and the aggregate market value of all collateral posted by the institution against the positions, in whole or in part.	($50,000)	Information needed to determine the extent to which the institution's obligations regarding the positions may be unsecured.

[29] If one or more positions cannot be netted against others, they should be maintained as separate entries.
[30] If all positions are not secured by the same collateral, then separate entries should be maintained for each position or set of positions secured by the same collateral.

B. Other Files (in Written or Electronic Form) To Be Maintained for QFCs

Within 60 days after the written notification by the FDIC, the institution must, produce the following files at the close of processing of the institution's business day, for a period provided in that written notification.

1. Each institution must maintain the following files in written or electronic form:

• A list of counterparty identifiers, with the associated counterparties and contact information;

• A list of the affiliates of the counterparties that are also counterparties to QFC transactions with the institution or its affiliates, and the specific master netting agreements, if any, under which they are counterparties;

• A list of affiliates of the institution that are counterparties to QFC transactions where such transactions are subject to a master agreement that also governs QFC transactions entered into by the institution. Such list must specify (i) which affiliates are direct or indirect subsidiaries of the institution and (ii) the specific master agreements under which those affiliates are counterparties to QFC transactions; and

• A list of portfolio identifiers (see Table A1), with the associated booking locations.

2. For each QFC, the institution must maintain in a readily-accessible format all of the following documents:

• Agreements (including master agreements and annexes, supplements or other modifications with respect to the agreements) between the institution and its counterparties that govern the QFC transactions;

• Documents related to and affirming the position;

• Active or "open" confirmations, if the position has been confirmed;

• Credit support documents; and

• Assignment documents, if applicable, including documents that confirm that all required consents, approvals, or other conditions precedent for such assignment(s) have been obtained or satisfied.

3. The institution must maintain:

• A legal-entity organizational chart, showing the institution, its corporate parent and all other affiliates, if any; and

• An organizational chart, including names and position titles, of all personnel significantly involved in QFC-related activities at the institution, its parent and its affiliates;

• Contact information for the primary contact person for purposes of compliance with this part by the institution.

4. The institution must maintain a list of vendors supporting the QFC-related activities and their contact information.

PART 380—ORDERLY LIQUIDATION AUTHORITY

Subpart A—General and Miscellaneous Provisions

Sec.
380.1 Definitions.
380.2 [Reserved]
380.3 Treatment of personal service agreements.
380.4 [Reserved]

§ 380.1

380.5 Treatment of covered financial companies that are subsidiaries of insurance companies.
380.6 Limitation on liens on assets of covered financial companies that are insurance companies or covered subsidiaries of insurance companies.
380.7 Recoupment of compensation from senior executives and directors.
380.8 [Reserved]
380.9 Treatment of fraudulent and preferential transfers.
380.10–380.19 [Reserved]

Subpart B—Priorities

380.20 [Reserved]
380.21 Priorities.
380.22 Administrative expenses of the receiver.
380.23 Amounts owed to the United States.
380.24 Priority of claims arising out of loss of setoff rights.
380.25 Post-insolvency interest.
380.26 Effect of transfer of assets and obligations to a bridge financial company.
380.27 Treatment of similarly situated claimants.
380.28–380.29 [Reserved]

Subpart C—Receivership Administrative Claims Process

380.30 Receivership administrative claims process.
380.31 Scope.
380.32 Claims bar date.
380.33 Notice requirements.
380.34 Procedures for filing claim.
380.35 Determination of claims.
380.36 Decision period.
380.37 Notification of determination.
380.38 Procedures for seeking judicial determination of disallowed claim.
380.39 Contingent claims.
380.40–380.49 [Reserved]
380.50 Determination of secured claims.
380.51 Consent to certain actions.
380.52 Adequate protection.
380.53 Repudiation of secured contract.

AUTHORITY: 12 U.S.C. 5389; 12 U.S.C. 5390(s)(3); 12 U.S.C. 5390(b)(1)(C); 12 U.S.C. 5390(a)(7)(D).

SOURCE: 76 FR 4215, January 25, 2011, unless otherwise noted.

Subpart A—General and Miscellaneous Provisions

§ 380.1 Definitions.

For purposes of this part, the following terms are defined as follows:

Allowed claim. The term "allowed claim" means a claim against the covered financial company or receiver that is allowed by the Corporation as receiver or upon which a final non-appealable judgment has been entered in favor of a claimant against a receivership by a court with jurisdiction to adjudicate the claim.

Board of Governors. The term "Board of Governors" means the Board of Governors of the Federal Reserve System.

Bridge financial company. The term "bridge financial company" means a new financial company organized by the Corporation in accordance with 12 U.S.C. 5390(h) for the purpose of resolving a covered financial company.

Claim. The term "claim" means any right to payment from either the covered financial company or the Corporation as receiver, whether or not such right is reduced to judgment, liquidated, unliquidated, fixed, contingent, matured, unmatured, disputed, undisputed, legal, equitable, secured, or unsecured.

Compensation. The term "compensation" means any direct or indirect financial remuneration received from the covered financial company, including, but not limited to, salary; bonuses; incentives; benefits; severance pay; deferred compensation; golden parachute benefits; benefits derived from an employment contract, or other compensation or benefit arrangement; perquisites; stock option plans; post-employment benefits; profits realized from a sale of securities in the covered financial company; or any cash or noncash payments or benefits granted to or for the benefit of the senior executive or director.

Corporation. The term "Corporation" means the Federal Deposit Insurance Corporation.

Covered financial company. The term "covered financial company" means (a) a financial company for which a determination has been made under 12 U.S.C. 5383(b) and (b) does not include an insured depository institution.

Covered subsidiary. The term "covered subsidiary" means a subsidiary of a covered financial company other than:
(1) An insured depository institution;
(2) An insurance company; or
(3) A covered broker or dealer.

Creditor. The term "creditor" means a person asserting a claim.

Federal Deposit Insurance Corporation § 380.3

Director. The term "director" means a member of the board of directors of a company or of a board or committee performing a similar function to a board of directors with authority to vote on matters before the board or committee.

Dodd-Frank Act. The term "Dodd-Frank Act" shall mean the Dodd-Frank Wall Street Reform and Consumer Protection Act, Public Law 111–203, 12 U.S.C. 5301 et seq. (2010).

Employee benefit plan. The term "employee benefit plan" has the meaning set forth in the Employee Retirement Income Security Act, 29 U.S.C. 1002(3).

Insurance company. The term "insurance company" means any entity that is:

(1) Engaged in the business of insurance,

(2) Subject to regulation by a State insurance regulator, and

(3) Covered by a State law that is designed to specifically deal with the rehabilitation, liquidation or insolvency of an insurance company.

Senior executive. The term "senior executive" means any person who participates or has authority to participate (other than in the capacity of a director) in major policymaking functions of the company, whether or not: The person has an official title; the title designates the officer an assistant; or the person is serving without salary or other compensation. The chairman of the board, the president, every vice president, the secretary, and the treasurer or chief financial officer, general partner and manager of a company are considered senior executives, unless the person is excluded, by resolution of the board of directors, the bylaws, the operating agreement or the partnership agreement of the company, from participation (other than in the capacity of a director) in major policymaking functions of the company, and the person does not actually participate therein.

[76 FR 41639, July 15, 2011]

§ 380.2 [Reserved]

§ 380.3 Treatment of personal service agreements.

(a) For the purposes of this section, the term "personal service agreement" means a written agreement between an employee and a covered financial company or a bridge financial company setting forth the terms of employment. This term also includes an agreement between any group or class of employees and a covered financial company, or a bridge financial company, including, without limitation, a collective bargaining agreement.

(b)(1) If before repudiation or disaffirmance of a personal service agreement, the Corporation as receiver of a covered financial company, or a bridge financial company accepts performance of services rendered under such agreement, then:

(i) The terms and conditions of such agreement shall apply to the performance of such services; and

(ii) Any payments for the services accepted by the Corporation as receiver shall be treated as an administrative expense of the receiver.

(2) If a bridge financial company accepts performance of services rendered under such agreement, then the terms and conditions of such agreement shall apply to the performance of such services.

(c) No party acquiring a covered financial company or any operational unit, subsidiary or assets thereof from the Corporation as receiver or from any bridge financial company shall be bound by a personal service agreement unless the acquiring party expressly assumes the personal service agreement.

(d) The acceptance by the Corporation as receiver for a covered financial company, or by any bridge financial company or the Corporation as receiver for a bridge financial company of services subject to a personal service agreement shall not limit or impair the authority of the receiver to disaffirm or repudiate any personal service agreement in the manner provided for the disaffirmance or repudiation of any agreement under 12 U.S.C. 5390(c).

(e) Paragraph (b) of this section shall not apply to any personal service agreement with any senior executive or director of the covered financial company or covered subsidiary, nor shall it in any way limit or impair the ability

§ 380.4

of the receiver to recover compensation from any senior executive or director of a covered financial company under 12 U.S.C. 5390 and the regulations promulgated thereunder.

[76 FR 41640, July 15, 2011]

§ 380.4 [Reserved]

§ 380.5 Treatment of covered financial companies that are subsidiaries of insurance companies.

The Corporation as receiver shall distribute the value realized from the liquidation, transfer, sale or other disposition of the direct or indirect subsidiaries of an insurance company, that are not themselves insurance companies, solely in accordance with the order of priorities set forth in 12 U.S.C. 5390(b)(1) and the regulations promulgated thereunder.

[76 FR 41640, July 15, 2011]

§ 380.6 Limitation on liens on assets of covered financial companies that are insurance companies or covered subsidiaries of insurance companies.

(a) In the event that the Corporation makes funds available to a covered financial company that is an insurance company or to any covered subsidiary of an insurance company, or enters into any other transaction with respect to such covered entity under 12 U.S.C. 5384(d), the Corporation will exercise its right to take liens on any or all assets of the covered entities receiving such funds to secure repayment of any such transactions only when the Corporation, in its sole discretion, determines that:

(1) Taking such lien is necessary for the orderly liquidation of the entity; and

(2) Taking such lien will not either unduly impede or delay the liquidation or rehabilitation of such insurance company, or the recovery by its policyholders.

(b) This section shall not be construed to restrict or impair the ability of the Corporation to take a lien on any or all of the assets of any covered financial company or covered subsidiary in order to secure financing provided by the Corporation or the receiver in connection with the sale or transfer of the covered financial company or covered subsidiary or any or all of the assets of such covered entity.

[76 FR 41640, July 15, 2011]

§ 380.7 Recoupment of compensation from senior executives and directors.

(a) *Substantially responsible.* The Corporation, as receiver of a covered financial company, may file an action to recover from any current or former senior executive or director substantially responsible for the failed condition of the covered financial company any compensation received during the 2-year period preceding the date on which the Corporation was appointed as the receiver of the covered financial company, except that, in the case of fraud, no time limit shall apply. A senior executive or director shall be deemed to be substantially responsible for the failed condition of a covered financial company that is placed into receivership under the orderly liquidation authority of the Dodd-Frank Act if he or she:

(1) Failed to conduct his or her responsibilities with the degree of skill and care an ordinarily prudent person in a like position would exercise under similar circumstances, and

(2) As a result, individually or collectively, caused a loss to the covered financial company that materially contributed to the failure of the covered financial company under the facts and circumstances.

(b) *Presumptions.* The following presumptions shall apply for purposes of assessing whether a senior executive or director is substantially responsible for the failed condition of a covered financial company:

(1) It shall be presumed that a senior executive or director is substantially responsible for the failed condition of a covered financial company that is placed into receivership under the orderly liquidation authority of the Dodd-Frank Act under any of the following circumstances:

(i) The senior executive or director served as the chairman of the board of directors, chief executive officer, president, chief financial officer, or in any other similar role regardless of his or

Federal Deposit Insurance Corporation

§ 380.9

her title if in this role he or she had responsibility for the strategic, policy-making, or company-wide operational decisions of the covered financial company prior to the date that it was placed into receivership under the orderly liquidation authority of the Dodd-Frank Act;

(ii) The senior executive or director is adjudged liable by a court or tribunal of competent jurisdiction for having breached his or her duty of loyalty to the covered financial company;

(iii) The senior executive was removed from the management of the covered financial company under 12 U.S.C. 5386(4); or

(iv) The director was removed from the board of directors of the covered financial company under 12 U.S.C. 5386(5).

(2) The presumption under paragraph (b)(1)(i) of this section may be rebutted by evidence that the senior executive or director conducted his or her responsibilities with the degree of skill and care an ordinarily prudent person in a like position would exercise under similar circumstances. The presumptions under paragraphs (b)(1)(ii), (b)(1)(iii) and (b)(1)(iv) of this section may be rebutted by evidence that the senior executive or director did not cause a loss to the covered financial company that materially contributed to the failure of the covered financial company under the facts and circumstances.

(3) The presumptions do not apply to:

(i) A senior executive hired by the covered financial company during the two years prior to the Corporation's appointment as receiver to assist in preventing further deterioration of the financial condition of the covered financial company; or

(ii) A director who joined the board of directors of the covered financial company during the two years prior to the Corporation's appointment as receiver under an agreement or resolution to assist in preventing further deterioration of the financial condition of the covered financial company.

(4) Notwithstanding that the presumption does not apply under paragraphs (b)(3)(i) and (ii) of this section, the Corporation as receiver still may pursue recoupment of compensation from a senior executive or director in paragraphs (b)(3)(i) or (ii) if they are substantially responsible for the failed condition of the covered financial company.

(c) *Savings Clause.* Nothing in this section shall limit or impair any rights of the Corporation as receiver under other applicable law, including any rights under Title II of the Dodd-Frank Act to pursue any other claims or causes of action it may have against senior executives and directors of the covered financial company for losses they cause to the covered financial company in the same or separate actions.

[76 FR 41640, July 15, 2011]

§ 380.8 [Reserved]

§ 380.9 Treatment of fraudulent and preferential transfers.

(a) *Coverage.* This section shall apply to all receiverships in which the FDIC is appointed as receiver under 12 U.S.C. 5382(a) or 5390(a)(1)(E) of a covered financial company or a covered subsidiary, respectively, as defined in 12 U.S.C. 5381(a)(8) and (9).

(b) *Avoidance standard for transfer of property.* (1) In applying 12 U.S.C. 5390(a)(11)(H)(i)(II) to a transfer of property for purposes of 12 U.S.C. 5390(a)(11)(A), the Corporation, as receiver of a covered financial company or a covered subsidiary, which is thereafter deemed to be a covered financial company pursuant to 12 U.S.C. 5390(a)(1)(E)(ii), shall determine whether the transfer has been perfected such that a *bona fide* purchaser from such covered financial company or such covered subsidiary, as applicable, against whom applicable law permits such transfer to be perfected cannot acquire an interest in the property transferred that is superior to the interest in such property of the transferee.

(2) In applying 12 U.S.C. 5390(a)(11)(H)(i)(II) to a transfer of real property, other than fixtures, but including the interest of a seller or purchaser under a contract for the sale of real property, for purposes of 12 U.S.C. 5390(a)(11)(B), the Corporation, as receiver of a covered financial company or a covered subsidiary, which is thereafter deemed to be a covered financial

§ 380.9

company pursuant to 12 U.S.C. 5390(a)(1)(E)(ii), shall determine whether the transfer has been perfected such that a *bona fide* purchaser from such covered financial company or such covered subsidiary, as applicable, against whom applicable law permits such transfer to be perfected cannot acquire an interest in the property transferred that is superior to the interest in such property of the transferee. For purposes of this section, the term fixture shall be interpreted in accordance with U.S. Federal bankruptcy law.

(3) In applying 12 U.S.C. 5390(a)(11)(H)(i)(II) to a transfer of a fixture or property, other than real property, for purposes of 12 U.S.C. 5390(a)(11)(B), the Corporation, as receiver of a covered financial company or a covered subsidiary which is thereafter deemed to be a covered financial company pursuant to 12 U.S.C. 5390(a)(1)(E)(ii), shall determine whether the transfer has been perfected such that a creditor on a simple contract cannot acquire a judicial lien that is superior to the interest of the transferee, and the standard of whether the transfer is perfected such that a bona fide purchaser cannot acquire an interest in the property transferred that is superior to the interest in such property of the transferee of such property shall not apply to any such transfer under this paragraph (b)(3).

(c) *Grace period for perfection.* In determining when a transfer occurs for purposes of 12 U.S.C. 5390(a)(11)(B), the Corporation, as receiver of a covered financial company or a covered subsidiary, which is thereafter deemed to be a covered financial company pursuant to 12 U.S.C. 5390(a)(1)(E)(ii), shall apply the following standard:

(1) Except as provided in paragraph (c)(2) of this section, a transfer shall be deemed to have been made

(i) At the time such transfer takes effect between the transferor and the transferee, if such transfer is perfected at, or within 30 days after, such time, except as provided in paragraph (c)(1)(ii) of this section;

(ii) At the time such transfer takes effect between the transferor and the transferee, with respect to a transfer of an interest of the transferor in property that creates a security interest in property acquired by the transferor:

(A) To the extent such security interest secures new value that was:

(1) Given at or after the signing of a security agreement that contains a description of such property as collateral;

(2) Given by or on behalf of the secured party under such agreement;

(3) Given to enable the transferor to acquire such property; and

(4) In fact used by the transferor to acquire such property; and

(B) That is perfected on or before 30 days after the transferor receives possession of such property;

(iii) At the time such transfer is perfected, if such transfer is perfected after the 30-day period described in paragraph (c)(1)(i) or (ii) of this section, as applicable; or

(iv) Immediately before the appointment of the Corporation as receiver of a covered financial company or a covered subsidiary which is thereafter deemed to be a covered financial company pursuant to 12 U.S.C. 5390(a)(1)(E)(ii), if such transfer is not perfected at the later of—

(A) The earlier of

(1) The date of the filing, if any, of a petition by or against the transferor under Title 11 of the United States Code; and

(2) The date of the appointment of the Corporation as receiver of such covered financial company or such covered subsidiary; or

(B) Thirty days after such transfer takes effect between the transferor and the transferee.

(2) For the purposes of this paragraph (c), a transfer is not made until the covered financial company or a covered subsidiary, which is thereafter deemed to be a covered financial company pursuant to 12 U.S.C. 5390(a)(1)(E)(ii), has acquired rights in the property transferred.

(d) *Limitations.* The provisions of this section do not act to waive, relinquish, limit or otherwise affect any rights or powers of the Corporation in any capacity, whether pursuant to applicable law or any agreement or contract.

[76 FR 41641, July 15, 2011]

Federal Deposit Insurance Corporation

§ 380.21

§ 380.10–380.19 [Reserved]

Subpart B—Priorities

SOURCE: 76 FR 41642, July 15, 2011, unless otherwise noted.

§ 380.20 [Reserved]

§ 380.21 Priorities.

(a) The unsecured amount of allowed claims shall be paid in the following order of priority:

(1) Repayment of debt incurred by or credit obtained by the Corporation as receiver for a covered financial company, provided that the receiver has determined that it is otherwise unable to obtain unsecured credit for the covered financial company from commercial sources.

(2) Administrative expenses of the receiver, as defined in § 380.22, other than those described in paragraph (a)(1) of this section.

(3) Any amounts owed to the United States, as defined in § 380.23 (which is not an obligation described in paragraphs (a)(1) or (2) of this section).

(4) Wages, salaries, or commissions, including vacation, severance, and sick leave pay earned by an individual (other than an individual described in paragraph (a)(9) of this section), but only to the extent of $11,725 for each individual (as adjusted for inflation in accordance with paragraph (b) of this section) earned within 180 days before the date of appointment of the receiver.

(5) Contributions owed to employee benefit plans arising from services rendered within 180 days before the date of appointment of the receiver, to the extent of the number of employees covered by each such plan multiplied by $11,725 (as adjusted for inflation in accordance with paragraph (b) of this section); less the sum of (i) the aggregate amount paid to such employees under paragraph (a)(4) of this section, plus (ii) the aggregate amount paid by the Corporation as receiver on behalf of such employees to any other employee benefit plan.

(6) Any amounts due to creditors who have an allowed claim for loss of setoff rights as described in § 380.24.

(7) Any other general or senior liability of the covered financial company (which is not a liability described under paragraphs (a)(8), (9) or (11) of this section).

(8) Any obligation subordinated to general creditors (which is not an obligation described under paragraphs (a)(9) or (11) of this section).

(9) Any wages, salaries, or commissions, including vacation, severance, and sick leave pay earned, that is owed to senior executives and directors of the covered financial company.

(10) Post-insolvency interest in accordance with § 380.25, provided that interest shall be paid on allowed claims in the order of priority of the claims set forth in paragraphs (a)(1) through (9) of this section.

(11) Any amount remaining shall be distributed to shareholders, members, general partners, limited partners, or other persons with interests in the equity of the covered financial company arising as a result of their status as shareholders, members, general partners, limited partners, or other persons with interests in the equity of the covered financial company, in proportion to their relative equity interests.

(b) All payments under paragraphs (a)(4) and (a)(5) of this section shall be adjusted for inflation in the same manner that claims under 11 U.S.C. 507(a)(1)(4) are adjusted for inflation by the Judicial Conference of the United States pursuant to 11 U.S.C. 104.

(c) All unsecured claims of any category or priority described in paragraphs (a)(1) through (a)(10) of this section shall be paid in full or provision made for such payment before any claims of lesser priority are paid. If there are insufficient funds to pay all claims of a particular category or priority of claims in full, then distributions to creditors in such category or priority shall be made *pro rata*. A subordination agreement is enforceable with respect to the priority of payment of allowed claims within any creditor class or among creditor classes to the extent that such agreement is enforceable under applicable non-insolvency law.

§ 380.22 Administrative expenses of the receiver.

(a) The term "administrative expenses of the receiver" includes those actual and necessary pre- and post-failure costs and expenses incurred by the Corporation in connection with its role as receiver in liquidating the covered financial company; together with any obligations that the receiver for the covered financial company determines to be necessary and appropriate to facilitate the smooth and orderly liquidation of the covered financial company. Administrative expenses of the Corporation as receiver for a covered financial company include:

(1) Contractual rent pursuant to an existing lease or rental agreement accruing from the date of the appointment of the Corporation as receiver until the later of

(i) The date a notice of the disaffirmance or repudiation of such lease or rental agreement is mailed, or

(ii) The date such disaffirmance or repudiation becomes effective; provided that the lesser of such lease is not in default or breach of the terms of the lease.

(2) Amounts owed pursuant to the terms of a contract for services performed and accepted by the receiver after the date of appointment of the receiver up to the date the receiver repudiates, terminates, cancels or otherwise discontinues such contract or notifies the counterparty that it no longer accepts performance of such services;

(3) Amounts owed under the terms of a contract or agreement executed in writing and entered into by the Corporation as receiver for the covered financial company after the date of appointment, or any contract or agreement entered into by the covered financial company before the date of appointment of the receiver that has been expressly approved in writing by the receiver after the date of appointment; and

(4) Expenses of the Inspector General of the Corporation incurred in carrying out its responsibilities under 12 U.S.C. 5391(d).

(b) Obligations to repay any extension of credit obtained by the Corporation as receiver through enforcement of any contract to extend credit to the covered financial company that was in existence prior to appointment of the receiver pursuant to 12 U.S.C. 5390(c)(13)(D) shall be treated as administrative expenses of the receiver. Other unsecured credit extended to the receivership shall be treated as administrative expenses except with respect to debt incurred by, or credit obtained by, the Corporation as receiver for a covered financial company as described in § 380.21(a)(1).

§ 380.23 Amounts owed to the United States.

(a) The term "amounts owed to the United States" as used in § 380.21(a)(3) includes all unsecured amounts owed to the United States, other than expenses included in the definition of administrative expenses of the receiver under § 380.22 that are related to funds provided for the orderly liquidation of a covered financial company, funds provided to avoid or mitigate adverse effects on the financial stability of the United States or unsecured amounts owed to the U.S. Treasury on account of tax liabilities of the covered financial company, without regard for whether such amounts are included as debt or capital on the books and records of the covered financial company. Such amounts shall include obligations incurred before and after the appointment of the Corporation as receiver. Without limitation, "amounts owed to the United States" include all of the following, which all shall have equal priority under § 380.21(a)(3):

(1) Unsecured amounts owed to the Corporation for any extension of credit by the Corporation, including any amounts made available under 12 U.S.C. 5384(d);

(2) Unsecured amounts owed to the U.S. Treasury on account of unsecured tax liabilities of the covered financial company;

(3) Unsecured amounts paid or payable by the Corporation pursuant to its guarantee of any debt issued by the covered financial company under the Temporary Liquidity Guaranty Program, 12 CFR part 370, any widely available debt guarantee program authorized under 12 U.S.C. 5612, or any other debt or obligation of any kind or

Federal Deposit Insurance Corporation § 380.25

nature that is guaranteed by the Corporation;

(4) The unsecured amount of any debt owed to a Federal reserve bank including loans made through programs or facilities authorized under the Federal Reserve Act, 12 U.S.C. 221 et seq.; and

(5) Any unsecured amount expressly designated in writing in a form acceptable to the Corporation by the appropriate United States department, agency or instrumentality that shall specify the particular debt, obligation or amount to be included as an "amount owed to the United States" for the purpose of this rule at the time of such advance, guaranty or other transaction.

(b) Other than those amounts included in paragraph (a) of this section, unsecured amounts owed to a department, agency or instrumentality of the United States that are obligations incurred in the ordinary course of the business of the covered financial company prior to the appointment of the receiver generally will not be in the class of claims designated as "amounts owed to the United States" under section 380.21(a)(3), including, but not limited to:

(1) Unsecured amounts owed to government sponsored entities including, without limitation, the Federal Home Loan Mortgage Corporation and the Federal National Mortgage Corporation;

(2) Unsecured amounts owed to Federal Home Loan Banks; and

(3) Unsecured amounts owed as satisfaction of filing, registration or permit fees due to any government department, agency or instrumentality.

(c) The United States may, in its sole discretion, consent to subordinate the repayment of any amount owed to the United States to any other obligation of the covered financial company provided that such consent is provided in writing in a form acceptable to the Corporation by the appropriate department, agency or instrumentality and shall specify the particular debt, obligation or other amount to be subordinated including the amount thereof and shall reference this paragraph (c) or 12 U.S.C. 5390(b)(1); and provided further that unsecured claims of the United States shall, at a minimum, have a higher priority than liabilities of the covered financial company that count as regulatory capital on the books and records of the covered financial company.

§ 380.24 **Priority of claims arising out of loss of setoff rights.**

(a) Notwithstanding any right of any creditor to offset a mutual debt owed by such creditor to any covered financial company that arose before the date of appointment of the receiver against a claim by such creditor against the covered financial company, the Corporation as receiver may sell or transfer any assets of the covered financial company to a bridge financial company or to a third party free and clear of any such rights of setoff.

(b) If the Corporation as receiver sells or transfers any asset free and clear of the setoff rights of any party, such party shall have a claim against the receiver in the amount of the value of such setoff established as of the date of the sale or transfer of such assets, provided that the setoff rights meet all of the criteria established under 12 U.S.C. 3590(a)(12).

(c) Any allowed claim pursuant to 12 U.S.C. 5390(a)(12) shall be paid prior to any other general or senior liability of the covered financial company described in section 380.21(a)(7). In the event that the setoff amount is less than the amount of the allowed claim, the balance of the allowed claim shall be paid at the otherwise applicable level of priority for such category of claim under § 380.21.

(d) Nothing in this section shall modify in any way the treatment of qualified financial contracts under Title II of the Dodd-Frank Wall Street Reform and Consumer Protection Act.

§ 380.25 **Post-insolvency interest.**

(a) *Date of accrual.* Post-insolvency interest shall be paid at the post-insolvency interest rate calculated on the principal amount of an allowed claim from the later of (i) the date of the appointment of the Corporation as receiver for the covered financial company; or (ii) in the case of a claim arising or becoming fixed and certain after the date of the appointment of the receiver, the date such claim arises or becomes fixed and certain.

§ 380.26

(b) *Interest rate.* Post-insolvency interest rate shall equal, for any calendar quarter, the coupon equivalent yield of the average discount rate set on the three-month U.S. Treasury bill at the last auction held by the United States Treasury Department during the preceding calendar quarter. Post-insolvency interest shall be computed quarterly and shall be computed using a simple interest method of calculation.

(c) *Principal amount.* The principal amount of an allowed claim shall be the full allowed claim amount, including any interest that may have accrued to the extent such interest is included in the allowed claim.

(d) *Post-insolvency interest distributions.* (1) Post-insolvency interest shall only be distributed following satisfaction of the principal amount of all creditor claims set forth in § 380.21(a)(1) through 380.21(a)(9) and prior to any distribution pursuant to § 380.21(a)(11).

(2) Post-insolvency interest distributions shall be made at such time as the Corporation as receiver determines that such distributions are appropriate and only to the extent of funds available in the receivership estate. Post-insolvency interest shall be calculated on the outstanding principal amount of an allowed claim, as reduced from time to time by any interim distributions on account of such claim by the receiver.

§ 380.26 Effect of transfer of assets and obligations to a bridge financial company.

(a) The purchase of any asset or assumption of any asset or liability of a covered financial company by a bridge financial company, through the express agreement of such bridge financial company, constitutes assumption of any contract or agreement giving rise to such asset or liability. Such contracts or agreements, together with any contract the bridge financial company may through its express agreement enter into with any other party, shall become the obligation of the bridge financial company from and after the effective date of the purchase, assumption or agreement, and the bridge financial company shall have the right and obligation to observe, perform and enforce their terms and provisions. In the event that the Corporation shall act as receiver of the bridge financial company any allowed claim arising out of any breach of such contract or agreement by the bridge financial company shall be paid as an administrative expense of the receiver of the bridge financial company.

(b) In the event that the Corporation as receiver of a bridge financial company shall act to dissolve the bridge financial company, it shall wind up the affairs of the bridge financial company in conformity with the laws, rules and regulations relating to the liquidation of covered financial companies, including the laws, rules and regulations governing priorities of claims, subject however to the authority of the Corporation to authorize the bridge financial company to obtain unsecured credit or issue unsecured debt with priority over any or all of the other unsecured obligations of the bridge financial company, provided that unsecured debt is not otherwise generally available to the bridge financial company.

(c) Upon the final dissolution or termination of the bridge financial company whether following a merger or consolidation, a stock sale, a sale of assets, or dissolution and liquidation at the end of the term of existence of such bridge financial company, any proceeds that remain after payment of all administrative expenses of the bridge financial company and all other claims against such bridge financial company will be distributed to the receiver for the related covered financial company.

§ 380.27 Treatment of similarly situated claimants.

(a) For the purposes of this section, the term "long-term senior debt" means senior debt issued by the covered financial company to bondholders or other creditors that has a term of more than 360 days. It does not include partially funded, revolving or other open lines of credit that are necessary to continuing operations essential to the receivership or any bridge financial company, nor to any contracts to extend credit enforced by the receiver under 12 U.S.C. 5390(c)(13)(D).

(b) In applying any provision of the Dodd-Frank Wall Street Reform and Consumer Protection Act permitting the Corporation as receiver to exercise its discretion, upon appropriate determination, to make payments or credit amounts, pursuant to 12 U.S.C. 5390(b)(4), (d)(4), or (h)(5)(E) to or for some creditors but not others similarly situated at the same level of payment priority, the receiver shall not exercise such authority in a manner that would result in the following recovering more than the amount established and due under 12 U.S.C. 5390(b)(1), or other priorities of payment specified by law:

(1) Holders of long-term senior debt who have a claim entitled to priority of payment at the level set out under 12 U.S.C. 5390(b)(1)(E);

(2) Holders of subordinated debt who have a claim entitled to priority of payment at the level set out under 12 U.S.C. 5390(b)(1)(F);

(3) Shareholders, members, general partners, limited partners, or other persons who have a claim entitled to priority of payment at the level set out under 12 U.S.C. 5390 (b)(1)(H); or

(4) Other holders of claims entitled to priority of payment at the level set out under 12 U.S.C. 5390(b)(1)(E) unless the Corporation, through the affirmative vote of a majority the members of the Board of Directors then serving, and in its sole discretion, specifically determines that additional payments or credit amounts to such holders are necessary and meet all of the requirements under 12 U.S.C. 5390(b)(4), (d)(4), or (h)(5)(E), as applicable. The authority of the Board to make the foregoing determination cannot be delegated.

§§ 380.28–380.29 [Reserved]

Subpart C—Receivership Administrative Claims Process

SOURCE: 76 FR 41644, July 15, 2011, unless otherwise noted.

§ 380.30 Receivership administrative claims process.

The Corporation as receiver of a covered financial company shall determine claims against the covered financial company and the receiver of the covered financial company in accordance with the procedures set forth in 12 U.S.C. 5390(a)(2)–(5) and the regulations promulgated by the Corporation.

§ 380.31 Scope.

Nothing in this subpart C shall apply to any liability or obligation of a bridge financial company or its assets or liabilities, or to any extension of credit from a Federal reserve bank or the Corporation to a covered financial company.

§ 380.32 Claims bar date.

Upon its appointment as receiver for a covered financial company, the Corporation as receiver shall establish a claims bar date by which date creditors of the covered financial company shall present their claims, together with proof, to the receiver. The claims bar date shall be not less than 90 days after the date on which the notice to creditors to file claims is first published under § 380.33(a).

§ 380.33 Notice requirements.

(a) *Notice by publication.* Promptly after its appointment as receiver for a covered financial company, the Corporation as receiver shall publish a notice to the creditors of the covered financial company to file their claims with the receiver no later than the claims bar date. The Corporation as receiver shall republish such notice 1 month and 2 months, respectively, after the date the notice is first published. The notice to creditors shall be published in one or more newspapers of general circulation where the covered financial company has its principal place or places of business. In addition to such publication in a newspaper, the Corporation as receiver may post the notice on the FDIC's Web site at *www.fdic.gov.*

(b) *Notice by mailing.* At the time of the first publication of the notice to creditors, the Corporation as receiver shall mail a notice to present claims no later than the claims bar date to any creditor shown in the books and records of the covered financial company. Such notice shall be sent to the last known address of the creditor appearing in the books and records or appearing in any claim found in the records of the covered financial company.

(c) *Notice by electronic media.* After publishing and mailing notice as required by paragraphs (a) and (b) of this

§ 380.34

section, the Corporation as receiver may communicate by electronic media with any claimant who expressly agrees to such form of communication.

(d) *Discovered claimants.* Upon discovery of the name and address of a claimant not appearing in the books and records of the covered financial company, the Corporation as receiver shall, not later than 30 days after the discovery of such name and address, mail a notice to such claimant to file a claim no later than the claims bar date. Any claimant not appearing on the books and records that is discovered before the claims bar date shall be required to file a claim before the claims bar date, subject to the exception of § 380.35(b)(2). If a claimant not appearing on the books and records is discovered after the claims bar date, the Corporation as receiver shall notify the claimant to file a claim by a date not later than 90 days from the date appearing on the notice that is mailed to such creditor. Any claim filed after such date shall be disallowed, and such disallowance shall be final.

§ 380.34 Procedures for filing claim.

(a) *In general.* The Corporation as receiver shall provide, in a reasonably practicable manner, instructions for filing a claim, including by the following means:

(1) Providing contact information in the publication notice;

(2) Including in the mailed notice a proof of claim form that has filing instructions; or

(3) Posting filing instructions on the Corporation's public Web site at *www.fdic.gov.*

(b) *When claim is deemed filed.* A claim that is mailed to the receiver in accordance with the instructions established under paragraph (a) of this section shall be deemed to be filed as of the date of postmark. A claim that is sent to the receiver by electronic media or fax in accordance with the instructions established under paragraph (a) shall be deemed to be filed as of the date of transmission by the claimant.

(c) *Class claimants.* If a claimant is a member of a class for purposes of a class action lawsuit, whether or not the class has been certified by a court,

each claimant must file its claim with the Corporation as receiver separately.

(d) *Indenture trustee.* A trustee appointed under an indenture or other applicable trust document related to investments or other financial activities may file a claim on behalf of the persons who appointed the trustee.

(e) *Legal effect of filing.* (1) Pursuant to 12 U.S.C. 5390(a)(3)(E)(i), the filing of a claim with the receiver shall constitute a commencement of an action for purposes of any applicable statute of limitations.

(2) *No prejudice to continuation of action.* Pursuant to 12 U.S.C. 5390(a)(3)(E)(ii) and subject to 12 U.S.C. 5390(a)(8), the filing of a claim with the receiver shall not prejudice any right of the claimant to continue, after the receiver's determination of the claim, any action which was filed before the date of appointment of the receiver for the covered financial company.

§ 380.35 Determination of claims.

(a) *In general.* The Corporation as receiver shall allow any claim received by the receiver on or before the claims bar date if such claim is proved to the satisfaction of the receiver. Except as provided in 12 U.S.C. 5390(a)(3)(D)(iii), the Corporation as receiver may disallow any portion of any claim by a creditor or claim of a security, preference, setoff, or priority which is not proved to the satisfaction of the receiver.

(b) *Disallowance of claims filed after the claims bar date.* (1) Except as otherwise provided in this section, any claim filed after the claims bar date shall be disallowed, and such disallowance shall be final, as provided by 12 U.S.C. 5390(a)(3)(C)(i).

(2) *Certain exceptions.* Paragraph (b)(1) of this section shall not apply with respect to any claim filed by a claimant after the claims bar date and such claim shall be considered by the receiver if:

(i) The claimant did not receive notice of the appointment of the receiver in time to file such claim before the claims bar date, or the claim is based upon an act or omission of the Corporation as receiver that occurs after the claims bar date has passed, and

Federal Deposit Insurance Corporation § 380.38

(ii) The claim is filed in time to permit payment. A claim is "filed in time to permit payment" when it is filed before a final distribution is made by the receiver.

§ 380.36 Decision period.

(a) *In general.* Prior to the 180th day after the date on which a claim against a covered financial company or the Corporation as receiver is filed with the receiver, the receiver shall notify the claimant whether it allows or disallows the claim.

(b) *Extension of time.* The 180-day period described in paragraph (a) of this section may be extended by a written agreement between the claimant and the Corporation as receiver executed not later than 180 days after the date on which the claim against the covered financial company or the receiver is filed with the receiver. If an extension is agreed to, the Corporation as receiver shall notify the claimant whether it allows or disallows the claim prior to the end of the extended claims determination period.

§ 380.37 Notification of determination.

(a) *In general.* The Corporation as receiver shall notify the claimant by mail of the decision to allow or disallow the claim. Notice shall be mailed to the address of the claimant as it last appears on the books, records, or both of the covered financial company; in the claim filed by the claimant with the Corporation as receiver; or in documents submitted in the proof of the claim. If the claimant has filed the claim electronically, the receiver may notify the claimant of the determination by electronic means.

(b) *Contents of notice of disallowance.* If the Corporation as receiver disallows a claim, the notice to the claimant shall contain a statement of each reason for the disallowance, and the procedures required to file or continue an action in court.

(c) *Failure to notify deemed to be disallowance.* If the Corporation as receiver does not notify the claimant before the end of the 180-day claims determination period, or before the end of any extended claims determination period, the claim shall be deemed to be disallowed, and the claimant may file or continue an action in court pursuant to 12 U.S.C. 5390(a)(4)(A).

§ 380.38 Procedures for seeking judicial determination of disallowed claim.

(a) *In general.* In order to seek a judicial determination of a claim that has been disallowed, in whole or in part, by the Corporation as receiver, the claimant, pursuant to 12 U.S.C. 5390(a)(4)(A), may either:

(1) File suit on such claim in the district or territorial court of the United States for the district within which the principal place of business of the covered financial company is located; or

(2) Continue an action commenced before the date of appointment of the receiver, in the court in which the action was pending.

(b) *Timing.* Pursuant to 12 U.S.C. 5390(a)(4)(B), a claimant who seeks a judicial determination of a claim disallowed by the Corporation as receiver must file suit on such claim before the end of the 60-day period beginning on the earlier of:

(1) The date of any notice of disallowance of such claim;

(2) The end of the 180-day claims determination period; or

(3) If the claims determination period was extended with respect to such claim under § 380.36(b), the end of such extended claims determination period.

(c) *Statute of limitations.* Pursuant to 12 U.S.C. 5390(a)(4)(C), if any claimant fails to file suit on such claim (or to continue an action on such claim commenced before the date of appointment of the Corporation as receiver) prior to the end of the 60-day period described in 12 U.S.C. 5390(a)(4)(B), the claim shall be deemed to be disallowed (other than any portion of such claim which was allowed by the receiver) as of the end of such period, such disallowance shall be final, and the claimant shall have no further rights or remedies with respect to such claim.

(d) *Jurisdiction.* Pursuant to 12 U.S.C. 5390(a)(9)(D), unless the claimant has first exhausted its administrative remedies by obtaining a determination from the receiver regarding a claim filed with the receiver, no court shall have jurisdiction over:

§ 380.39

(1) Any claim or action for payment from, or any action seeking a determination of rights with respect to, the assets of any covered financial company for which the Corporation has been appointed receiver, including any assets which the Corporation may acquire from itself as such receiver; or

(2) Any claim relating to any act or omission of such covered financial company or the Corporation as receiver.

§ 380.39 Contingent claims.

(a) The Corporation as receiver shall not disallow a claim based on an obligation of the covered financial company solely because the obligation is contingent. To the extent the obligation is contingent, the receiver shall estimate the value of the claim, as such value is measured based upon the likelihood that such contingent obligation would become fixed and the probable magnitude thereof.

(b) If the receiver repudiates a contingent obligation of a covered financial company consisting of a guarantee, letter of credit, loan commitment, or similar credit obligation, the actual direct compensatory damages for repudiation shall be no less than the estimated value of the claim as of the date the Corporation was appointed receiver of the covered financial company, as such value is measured based upon the likelihood that such contingent claim would become fixed and the probable magnitude thereof.

(c) The Corporation as receiver shall estimate the value of a claim under paragraphs (a) or (b) of this section no later than 180 days after the claim is filed, unless such period is extended by a written agreement between the claimant and the receiver.

(d) Except for a contingent claim that becomes absolute and fixed prior to the receiver's determination of the estimated value, such estimated value of a contingent claim shall be recognized as the allowed amount of the claim for purposes of distribution.

(e) The estimated value of a contingent claim shall constitute the receiver's determination of the claim for purposes of § 380.38(d) and 12 U.S.C. 5390(a)(9)(D).

§§ 380.40–380.49 [Reserved]

§ 380.50 Determination of secured claims.

(a) In the case of a claim against a covered financial company that is secured by any property of the covered financial company, the Corporation as receiver shall determine the amount of the claim, whether the claimant's security interest is legally enforceable and perfected, the priority of the claimant's security interest, and the fair market value of the property that is subject to the security interest. The Corporation as receiver may treat the portion of the claim which exceeds an amount equal to the fair market value of such property as an unsecured claim.

(b) The fair market value of any property of a covered financial company that secures a claim shall be determined in light of the purpose of the valuation and of the proposed disposition or use of such property and at the time of such proposed disposition or use.

(c) The Corporation as receiver may recover from any property of a covered financial company that secures a claim the reasonable and necessary costs and expenses of preserving or disposing of such property to the extent of any benefit to the claimant, including the payment of all ad valorem property taxes with respect to such property.

(d) To the extent that a claim is secured by property of a covered financial company and the value of such property, after any recovery under paragraph (c) of this section, is greater than the amount of such claim, there shall be allowed to the claimant a secured claim for interest on such claim and any reasonable fees, costs, or charges provided for under the agreement or State statute under which the claim arose to the extent of the value of such property.

§ 380.51 Consent to certain actions.

(a) *In general.* Any claimant alleging a legally valid and enforceable or perfected security interest in property of a covered financial company or control of any legally valid and enforceable security entitlement in respect of any asset held by the covered financial company for which the Corporation has

Federal Deposit Insurance Corporation

§ 380.52

been appointed receiver may seek the consent of the receiver for relief from the provisions of 12 U.S.C. 5390(c)(13)(C).

(b) *Contents of request.* A request for consent of the Corporation as receiver for relief from the provisions of 12 U.S.C. 5390(c)(13)(C) shall be in writing and contain the following information:

(1) The amount of the claim, with supporting documentation;

(2) A description of the property that secures the claim, with supporting documentation of the claimant's interest in the property;

(3) The value of the property, as established by an appraisal or other supporting documentation; and

(4) The proposed disposition of the property by the claimant, including the expected date of such disposition.

(c) *Determination by receiver.* The Corporation as receiver shall grant its consent to a request for relief from the provisions of 12 U.S.C. 5390(c)(13)(C) if it determines that the claimant has a legally valid and enforceable or perfected security interest or other lien against the property of a covered financial company and the receiver will not use, sell, or lease the property. If the Corporation as receiver determines that it will use, sell, or lease such property and that adequate protection is necessary and appropriate, the receiver may provide adequate protection instead of granting consent.

(d) *Consent deemed granted.* If the Corporation as receiver has not notified the claimant of the determination whether to grant or withhold consent under this section within 30 days after a request for consent has been submitted, consent shall be deemed to be granted.

(e) *Expiration by operation of law.* Notwithstanding any determination by the Corporation as receiver to withhold consent under this section, the prohibitions described in 12 U.S.C. 5390(c)(13)(C)(i) are no longer applicable 90 days after the appointment of the receiver.

(f) *Limitations.* Any consent granted by the Corporation as receiver under this section shall not act to waive or relinquish any rights granted to the Corporation in any capacity, pursuant to any other applicable law or any agreement or contract, and shall not be construed as waiving, limiting or otherwise affecting the rights or powers of the Corporation as receiver to take any action or to exercise any power not specifically mentioned, including but not limited to any rights, powers or remedies of the receiver regarding transfers taken in contemplation of the covered financial company's insolvency or with the intent to hinder, delay or defraud the covered financial company or the creditors of such company, or that is a fraudulent transfer under applicable law.

(g) *Exceptions.* (1) This section shall not apply in the case of a contract that is repudiated or disaffirmed by the Corporation as receiver.

(2) This section shall not apply to a director or officer liability insurance contract, a financial institution bond, the rights of parties to certain qualified financial contracts pursuant to 12 U.S.C. 5390(c)(8), the rights of parties to netting contracts pursuant to 12 U.S.C. 4401 et seq., or any extension of credit from any Federal reserve bank or the Corporation to any covered financial company or any security interest in the assets of a covered financial company securing any such extension of credit.

§ 380.52 Adequate protection.

(a) If the Corporation as receiver determines that it will use, sell, or lease or grant a security interest or other lien against property of the covered financial company that is subject to a security interest of a claimant, the receiver shall provide adequate protection by any of the following means:

(1) Making a cash payment or periodic cash payments to the claimant to the extent that the sale, use, or lease of the property or the grant of a security interest or other lien against the property by the Corporation as receiver results in a decrease in the value of such claimant's security interest in the property;

(2) Providing to the claimant an additional or replacement lien to the extent that the sale, use, or lease of the

§ 380.53

property or the grant of a security interest against the property by the Corporation as receiver results in a decrease in the value of the claimant's security interest in the property; or

(3) Providing any other relief that will result in the realization by the claimant of the indubitable equivalent of the claimant's security interest in the property.

(b) Adequate protection of the claimant's security interest will be presumed if the value of the property is not depreciating or is sufficiently greater than the amount of the claim so that the claimant's security interest is not impaired.

§ 380.53 Repudiation of secured contract.

To the extent that a contract to which a covered financial company is a party is secured by property of the covered financial company, the repudiation of the contract by the Corporation as receiver shall not be construed as permitting the avoidance of any legally enforceable and perfected security interest in the property, and the security interest shall secure any claim for repudiation damages.

PART 381—RESOLUTION PLANS

Sec.
381.1 Authority and scope.
381.2 Definitions.
381.3 Resolution plan required.
381.4 Informational content of a resolution plan.
381.5 Review of resolution plans; resubmission of deficient resolution plans.
381.6 Failure to cure deficiencies on resubmission of a resolution plan.
381.7 Consultation.
381.8 No limiting effect or private right of action; confidentiality of resolution plans.
381.9 Enforcement.

AUTHORITY: 12 U.S.C. 5365(d).

SOURCE: 76 FR 67334, Nov. 1, 2011, unless otherwise noted.

§ 381.1 Authority and scope.

(a) *Authority*. This part is issued pursuant to section 165(d)(8) of the Dodd-Frank Wall Street Reform and Consumer Protection Act (the *Dodd-Frank Act*) (Pub. L. 111–203, 124 Stat. 1376, 1426–1427), 12 U.S.C. 5365(d)(8), which requires the Board of Governors of the Federal Reserve System (*Board*) and the Federal Deposit Insurance Corporation (*Corporation*) to jointly issue rules implementing the provisions of section 165(d) of the Dodd-Frank Act.

(b) *Scope*. This part applies to each covered company and establishes rules and requirements regarding the submission and content of a resolution plan, as well as procedures for review by the Board and Corporation of a resolution plan.

§ 381.2 Definitions.

For purposes of this part:

(a) *Bankruptcy Code* means Title 11 of the United States Code.

(b) *Company* means a corporation, partnership, limited liability company, depository institution, business trust, special purpose entity, association, or similar organization, but does not include any organization, the majority of the voting securities of which are owned by the United States.

(c) *Control*. A company controls another company when the first company, directly or indirectly, owns, or holds with power to vote, 25 percent or more of any class of the second company's outstanding voting securities.

(d) *Core business lines* means those business lines of the covered company, including associated operations, services, functions and support, that, in the view of the covered company, upon failure would result in a material loss of revenue, profit, or franchise value.

(e) *Council* means the Financial Stability Oversight Council established by section 111 of the Dodd-Frank Act (12 U.S.C. 5321).

(f) *Covered company*—(1) *In general*. A "covered company" means:

(i) Any nonbank financial company supervised by the Board;

(ii) Any bank holding company, as that term is defined in section 2 of the Bank Holding Company Act, as amended (12 U.S.C. 1841), and the Board's Regulation Y (12 CFR part 225), that has $50 billion or more in total consolidated assets, as determined based on the average of the company's four most recent Consolidated Financial Statements for Bank Holding Companies as reported on the Federal Reserve's Form FR Y–9C ("FR Y–9C"); and

Federal Deposit Insurance Corporation § 381.2

(iii) Any foreign bank or company that is a bank holding company or is treated as a bank holding company under section 8(a) of the International Banking Act of 1978 (12 U.S.C. 3106(a)), and that has $50 billion or more in total consolidated assets, as determined based on the foreign bank's or company's most recent annual or, as applicable, the average of the four most recent quarterly Capital and Asset Reports for Foreign Banking Organizations as reported on the Federal Reserve's Form FR Y-7Q ("FR Y-7Q").

(2) Once a covered company meets the requirements described in paragraph (f)(1)(ii) or (iii) of this section, the company shall remain a covered company for purposes of this part unless and until the company has less than $45 billion in total consolidated assets, as determined based on the—

(i) Average total consolidated assets as reported on the company's four most recent FR Y-9Cs, in the case of a covered company described in paragraph (f)(1)(ii) of this section; or

(ii) Total consolidated assets as reported on the company's most recent annual FR Y-7Q, or, as applicable, average total consolidated assets as reported on the company's four most recent quarterly FR Y-7Qs, in the case of a covered company described in paragraph (f)(1)(iii) of this section. Nothing in this paragraph (f)(2) shall preclude a company from becoming a covered company pursuant to paragraph (f)(1) of this section.

(3) *Multi-tiered holding company.* In a multi-tiered holding company structure, covered company means the top-tier of the multi-tiered holding company only.

(4) *Asset threshold for bank holding companies and foreign banking organizations.* The Board may, pursuant to a recommendation of the Council, raise any asset threshold specified in paragraph (f)(1)(ii) or (iii) of this section.

(5) *Exclusion.* A bridge financial company chartered pursuant to 12 U.S.C. 5390(h) shall not be deemed to be a covered company hereunder.

(g) *Critical operations* means those operations of the covered company, including associated services, functions and support, the failure or discontinuance of which, in the view of the covered company or as jointly directed by the Board and the Corporation, would pose a threat to the financial stability of the United States.

(h) *Depository institution* has the same meaning as in section 3(c)(1) of the Federal Deposit Insurance Act (12 U.S.C. 1813(c)(1)) and includes a state-licensed uninsured branch, agency, or commercial lending subsidiary of a foreign bank.

(i) *Foreign banking organization* means—

(1) A foreign bank, as defined in section 1(b)(7) of the International Banking Act of 1978 (12 U.S.C. 3101(7)), that:

(i) Operates a branch, agency, or commercial lending company subsidiary in the United States;

(ii) Controls a bank in the United States; or

(iii) Controls an Edge corporation acquired after March 5, 1987; and

(2) Any company of which the foreign bank is a subsidiary.

(j) *Foreign-based company* means any covered company that is not incorporated or organized under the laws of the United States.

(k) *Functionally regulated subsidiary* has the same meaning as in section 5(c)(5) of the Bank Holding Company Act, as amended (12 U.S.C. 1844(c)(5)).

(l) *Material entity* means a subsidiary or foreign office of the covered company that is significant to the activities of a critical operation or core business line (as defined in this part).

(m) *Material financial distress* with regard to a covered company means that:

(1) The covered company has incurred, or is likely to incur, losses that will deplete all or substantially all of its capital, and there is no reasonable prospect for the company to avoid such depletion;

(2) The assets of the covered company are, or are likely to be, less than its obligations to creditors and others; or

(3) The covered company is, or is likely to be, unable to pay its obligations (other than those subject to a bona fide dispute) in the normal course of business.

(n) *Nonbank financial company supervised by the Board* means a nonbank financial company or other company that the Council has determined under section 113 of the Dodd-Frank Act (12

§ 381.3

U.S.C. 5323) shall be supervised by the Board and for which such determination is still in effect.

(o) *Rapid and orderly resolution* means a reorganization or liquidation of the covered company (or, in the case of a covered company that is incorporated or organized in a jurisdiction other than the United States, the subsidiaries and operations of such foreign company that are domiciled in the United States) under the Bankruptcy Code that can be accomplished within a reasonable period of time and in a manner that substantially mitigates the risk that the failure of the covered company would have serious adverse effects on financial stability in the United States.

(p) *Subsidiary* means a company that is controlled by another company, and an indirect subsidiary is a company that is controlled by a subsidiary of a company.

(q) *United States* means the United States and includes any state of the United States, the District of Columbia, any territory of the United States, Puerto Rico, Guam, American Samoa, and the Virgin Islands.

§ 381.3 Resolution plan required.

(a) *Initial and annual resolution plans required.* (1) Each covered company shall submit its initial resolution plan to the Board and the Corporation on or before the date set forth below ("Initial Submission Date"):

(i) July 1, 2012, with respect to any covered company that, as of the effective date of this part, had $250 billion or more in total nonbank assets (or, in the case of a covered company that is a foreign-based company, in total U.S. nonbank assets);

(ii) July 1, 2013, with respect to any covered company that is not described in paragraph (a)(1)(i) of this section, and that, as of the effective date of this part had $100 billion or more in total nonbank assets (or, in the case of a covered company that is a foreign-based company, in total U.S. nonbank assets); and

(iii) December 31, 2013, with respect to any other covered company that is a covered company as of the effective date of this part but that is not described in paragraph (a)(1)(i) or (ii) of this section.

(2) A company that becomes a covered company after the effective date of this part shall submit its initial resolution plan no later than the next July 1 following the date the company becomes a covered company, provided such date occurs no earlier than 270 days after the date on which the company became a covered company.

(3) After filing its initial resolution plan pursuant to paragraph (a)(1) or (2) of this section, each covered company shall annually submit a resolution plan to the Board and the Corporation on or before each anniversary date of its Initial Submission Date.

(4) Notwithstanding anything to the contrary in this paragraph (a), the Board and Corporation may jointly determine that a covered company shall file its initial or annual resolution plan by a date other than as provided in this paragraph (a). The Board and the Corporation shall provide a covered company with written notice of a determination under this paragraph (a)(4) no later than 180 days prior to the date on which the Board and Corporation jointly determined to require the covered company to submit its resolution plan.

(b) *Authority to require interim updates and notice of material events*—(1) *In general.* The Board and the Corporation may jointly require that a covered company file an update to a resolution plan submitted under paragraph (a) of this section, within a reasonable amount of time, as jointly determined by the Board and Corporation. The Board and the Corporation shall make a request pursuant to this paragraph (b)(1) in writing, and shall specify the portions or aspects of the resolution plan the covered company shall update.

(2) *Notice of material events.* Each covered company shall provide the Board and the Corporation with a notice no later than 45 days after any event, occurrence, change in conditions or circumstances, or other change that results in, or could reasonably be foreseen to have, a material effect on the resolution plan of the covered company. Such notice should describe the event, occurrence or change and explain why the event, occurrence or

Federal Deposit Insurance Corporation § 381.4

change may require changes to the resolution plan. The covered company shall address any event, occurrence or change with respect to which it has provided notice pursuant to this paragraph (b)(2) in the following resolution plan submitted by the covered company.

(3) *Exception.* A covered company shall not be required to file a notice under paragraph (b)(2) of this section if the date on which the covered company would be required to submit the notice under paragraph (b)(2) would be within 90 days prior to the date on which the covered company is required to file an annual resolution plan under paragraph (a) of this section.

(c) *Authority to require more frequent submissions or extend time period.* The Board and Corporation may jointly:

(1) Require that a covered company submit a resolution plan more frequently than required pursuant to paragraph (a) of this section; and

(2) Extend the time period that a covered company has to submit a resolution plan or a notice following material events under paragraphs (a) and (b) of this section.

(d) *Access to information.* In order to allow evaluation of the resolution plan, each covered company must provide the Board and the Corporation such information and access to personnel of the covered company as the Board and the Corporation jointly determine during the period for reviewing the resolution plan is necessary to assess the credibility of the resolution plan and the ability of the covered company to implement the resolution plan. The Board and the Corporation will rely to the fullest extent possible on examinations conducted by or on behalf of the appropriate Federal banking agency for the relevant company.

(e) *Board of directors approval of resolution plan.* Prior to submission of a resolution plan under paragraph (a) of this section, the resolution plan of a covered company shall be approved by:

(1) The board of directors of the covered company and noted in the minutes; or

(2) In the case of a foreign-based covered company only, a delegee acting under the express authority of the board of directors of the covered company to approve the resolution plan.

(f) *Resolution plans provided to the Council.* The Board shall make the resolution plans and updates submitted by the covered company pursuant to this section available to the Council upon request.

§ 381.4 **Informational content of a resolution plan.**

(a) *In general*—(1) *Domestic covered companies.* Except as otherwise provided in paragraph (a)(3) of this section, the resolution plan of a covered company that is organized or incorporated in the United States shall include the information specified in paragraphs (b) through (i) of this section with respect to the subsidiaries and operations that are domiciled in the United States as well as the foreign subsidiaries, offices, and operations of the covered company.

(2) *Foreign-based covered companies.* Except as otherwise provided in paragraph (a)(3) of the section, the resolution plan of a covered company that is organized or incorporated in a jurisdiction other than the United States (other than a bank holding company) or that is a foreign banking organization shall include:

(i) The information specified in paragraphs (b) through (i) of this section with respect to the subsidiaries, branches and agencies, and critical operations and core business lines, as applicable, that are domiciled in the United States or conducted in whole or material part in the United States. With respect to the information specified in paragraph (g) of this section, the resolution plan of a foreign-based covered company shall also identify, describe in detail, and map to legal entity the interconnections and interdependencies among the U.S. subsidiaries, branches and agencies, and critical operations and core business lines of the foreign-based covered company and any foreign-based affiliate; and

(ii) A detailed explanation of how resolution planning for the subsidiaries, branches and agencies, and critical operations and core business lines of the foreign-based covered company that are domiciled in the United States or conducted in whole or material part

725

§ 381.4

in the United States is integrated into the foreign-based covered company's overall resolution or other contingency planning process.

(3) *Tailored resolution plan*—(i) *Eligible covered company.* Paragraph (a)(3)(ii) of this section applies to any covered company that as of December 31 of the calendar year prior to the date its resolution plan is required to be submitted under this part—

(A) Has less than $100 billion in total nonbank assets (or, in the case of a covered company that is a foreign-based company, in total U.S. nonbank assets); and

(B) The total insured depository institution assets of which comprise 85 percent or more of the covered company's total consolidated assets (or, in the case of a covered company that is a foreign-based company, the assets of the U.S. insured depository institution operations, branches, and agencies of which comprise 85 percent or more of such covered company's U.S. total consolidated assets).

(ii) *Tailored resolution plan elements.* A covered company described in paragraph (a)(3)(i) of this section may file a resolution plan that is limited to the following items—

(A) An executive summary, as specified in paragraph (b) of this section;

(B) The information specified in paragraphs (c) through (f) and paragraph (h) of this section, but only with respect to the covered company and its nonbanking material entities and operations;

(C) The information specified in paragraphs (g) and (i) of this section with respect to the covered company and all of its insured depository institutions (or, in the case of a covered company that is a foreign-based company, the U.S. insured depository institutions, branches, and agencies) and nonbank material entities and operations. The interconnections and interdependencies identified pursuant to (g) of this section shall be included in the analysis provided pursuant to paragraph (c) of this section.

(iii) *Notice.* A covered company that meets the requirements of paragraph (a)(3)(i) of this section and that intends to submit a resolution plan pursuant to this paragraph (a)(3), shall provide the Board and Corporation with written notice of such intent and its eligibility under paragraph (a)(3)(i) no later than 270 days prior to the date on which the covered company is required to submit its resolution plan. Within 90 of receiving such notice, the Board and Corporation may jointly determine that the covered company must submit a resolution plan that meets some or all of the requirements as set forth in paragraph (a)(1) or (2) of this section, as applicable.

(4) *Required and prohibited assumptions.* In preparing its plan for rapid and orderly resolution in the event of material financial distress or failure required by this part, a covered company shall:

(i) Take into account that such material financial distress or failure of the covered company may occur under the baseline, adverse and severely adverse economic conditions provided to the covered company by the Board pursuant to 12 U.S.C. 5365(i)(1)(B); provided, however, a covered company may submit its initial resolution plan assuming the baseline conditions only, or, if a baseline scenario is not then available, a reasonable substitute developed by the covered company; and

(ii) Not rely on the provision of extraordinary support by the United States or any other government to the covered company or its subsidiaries to prevent the failure of the covered company.

(b) *Executive summary.* Each resolution plan of a covered company shall include an executive summary describing:

(1) The key elements of the covered company's strategic plan for rapid and orderly resolution in the event of material financial distress at or failure of the covered company.

(2) Material changes to the covered company's resolution plan from the company's most recently filed resolution plan (including any notices following a material event or updates to the resolution plan).

(3) Any actions taken by the covered company since filing of the previous resolution plan to improve the effectiveness of the covered company's resolution plan or remediate or otherwise mitigate any material weaknesses or

Federal Deposit Insurance Corporation § 381.4

impediments to effective and timely execution of the resolution plan.

(c) *Strategic analysis.* Each resolution plan shall include a strategic analysis describing the covered company's plan for rapid and orderly resolution in the event of material financial distress or failure of the covered company. Such analysis shall—

(1) Include detailed descriptions of the—

(i) Key assumptions and supporting analysis underlying the covered company's resolution plan, including any assumptions made concerning the economic or financial conditions that would be present at the time the covered company sought to implement such plan;

(ii) Range of specific actions to be taken by the covered company to facilitate a rapid and orderly resolution of the covered company, its material entities, and its critical operations and core business lines in the event of material financial distress or failure of the covered company;

(iii) Funding, liquidity and capital needs of, and resources available to, the covered company and its material entities, which shall be mapped to its critical operations and core business lines, in the ordinary course of business and in the event of material financial distress at or failure of the covered company;

(iv) Covered company's strategy for maintaining operations of, and funding for, the covered company and its material entities, which shall be mapped to its critical operations and core business lines;

(v) Covered company's strategy in the event of a failure or discontinuation of a material entity, core business line or critical operation, and the actions that will be taken by the covered company to prevent or mitigate any adverse effects of such failure or discontinuation on the financial stability of the United States; provided, however, if any such material entity is subject to an insolvency regime other than the Bankruptcy Code, a covered company may exclude that entity from its strategic analysis unless that entity either has $50 billion or more in total assets or conducts a critical operation; and

(vi) Covered company's strategy for ensuring that any insured depository institution subsidiary of the covered company will be adequately protected from risks arising from the activities of any nonbank subsidiaries of the covered company (other than those that are subsidiaries of an insured depository institution);

(2) Identify the time period(s) the covered company expects would be needed for the covered company to successfully execute each material aspect and step of the covered company's plan;

(3) Identify and describe any potential material weaknesses or impediments to effective and timely execution of the covered company's plan;

(4) Discuss the actions and steps the covered company has taken or proposes to take to remediate or otherwise mitigate the weaknesses or impediments identified by the covered company, including a timeline for the remedial or other mitigatory action; and

(5) Provide a detailed description of the processes the covered company employs for:

(i) Determining the current market values and marketability of the core business lines, critical operations, and material asset holdings of the covered company;

(ii) Assessing the feasibility of the covered company's plans (including timeframes) for executing any sales, divestitures, restructurings, recapitalizations, or other similar actions contemplated in the covered company's resolution plan; and

(iii) Assessing the impact of any sales, divestitures, restructurings, recapitalizations, or other similar actions on the value, funding, and operations of the covered company, its material entities, critical operations and core business lines.

(d) *Corporate governance relating to resolution planning.* Each resolution plan shall:

(1) Include a detailed description of:

(i) How resolution planning is integrated into the corporate governance structure and processes of the covered company;

§ 381.4

(ii) The covered company's policies, procedures, and internal controls governing preparation and approval of the covered company's resolution plan;

(iii) The identity and position of the senior management official(s) of the covered company that is primarily responsible for overseeing the development, maintenance, implementation, and filing of the covered company's resolution plan and for the covered company's compliance with this part; and

(iv) The nature, extent, and frequency of reporting to senior executive officers and the board of directors of the covered company regarding the development, maintenance, and implementation of the covered company's resolution plan;

(2) Describe the nature, extent, and results of any contingency planning or similar exercise conducted by the covered company since the date of the covered company's most recently filed resolution plan to assess the viability of or improve the resolution plan of the covered company; and

(3) Identify and describe the relevant risk measures used by the covered company to report credit risk exposures both internally to its senior management and board of directors, as well as any relevant risk measures reported externally to investors or to the covered company's appropriate Federal regulator.

(e) *Organizational structure and related information.* Each resolution plan shall—

(1) Provide a detailed description of the covered company's organizational structure, including:

(i) A hierarchical list of all material entities within the covered company's organization (including legal entities that directly or indirectly hold such material entities) that:

(A) Identifies the direct holder and the percentage of voting and nonvoting equity of each legal entity and foreign office listed; and

(B) The location, jurisdiction of incorporation, licensing, and key management associated with each material legal entity and foreign office identified;

(ii) A mapping of the covered company's critical operations and core business lines, including material asset holdings and liabilities related to such critical operations and core business lines, to material entities;

(2) Provide an unconsolidated balance sheet for the covered company and a consolidating schedule for all material entities that are subject to consolidation by the covered company;

(3) Include a description of the material components of the liabilities of the covered company, its material entities, critical operations and core business lines that, at a minimum, separately identifies types and amounts of the short-term and long-term liabilities, the secured and unsecured liabilities, and subordinated liabilities;

(4) Identify and describe the processes used by the covered company to:

(i) Determine to whom the covered company has pledged collateral;

(ii) Identify the person or entity that holds such collateral; and

(iii) Identify the jurisdiction in which the collateral is located, and, if different, the jurisdiction in which the security interest in the collateral is enforceable against the covered company;

(5) Describe any material off-balance sheet exposures (including guarantees and contractual obligations) of the covered company and its material entities, including a mapping to its critical operations and core business lines;

(6) Describe the practices of the covered company, its material entities and its core business lines related to the booking of trading and derivatives activities;

(7) Identify material hedges of the covered company, its material entities, and its core business lines related to trading and derivative activities, including a mapping to legal entity;

(8) Describe the hedging strategies of the covered company;

(9) Describe the process undertaken by the covered company to establish exposure limits;

(10) Identify the major counterparties of the covered company and describe the interconnections, interdependencies and relationships with such major counterparties;

(11) Analyze whether the failure of each major counterparty would likely have an adverse impact on or result in

Federal Deposit Insurance Corporation § 381.4

the material financial distress or failure of the covered company; and

(12) Identify each trading, payment, clearing, or settlement system of which the covered company, directly or indirectly, is a member and on which the covered company conducts a material number or value amount of trades or transactions. Map membership in each such system to the covered company's material entities, critical operations and core business lines.

(f) *Management information systems.* (1) Each resolution plan shall include—

(i) A detailed inventory and description of the key management information systems and applications, including systems and applications for risk management, accounting, and financial and regulatory reporting, used by the covered company and its material entities. The description of each system or application provided shall identify the legal owner or licensor, the use or function of the system or application, service level agreements related thereto, any software and system licenses, and any intellectual property associated therewith;

(ii) A mapping of the key management information systems and applications to the material entities, critical operations and core business lines of the covered company that use or rely on such systems and applications;

(iii) An identification of the scope, content, and frequency of the key internal reports that senior management of the covered company, its material entities, critical operations and core business lines use to monitor the financial health, risks, and operation of the covered company, its material entities, critical operations and core business lines; and

(iv) A description of the process for the appropriate supervisory or regulatory agencies to access the management information systems and applications identified in paragraph (f) of this section; and

(v) A description and analysis of—

(A) The capabilities of the covered company's management information systems to collect, maintain, and report, in a timely manner to management of the covered company, and to the Board, the information and data underlying the resolution plan; and

(B) Any deficiencies, gaps or weaknesses in such capabilities, and a description of the actions the covered company intends to take to promptly address such deficiencies, gaps, or weaknesses, and the time frame for implementing such actions.

(2) The Board will use its examination authority to review the demonstrated capabilities of each covered company to satisfy the requirements of paragraph (f)(1)(v) of this section. The Board will share with the Corporation information regarding the capabilities of the covered company to collect, maintain, and report in a timely manner information and data underlying the resolution plan.

(g) *Interconnections and interdependencies.* To the extent not elsewhere provided, identify and map to the material entities the interconnections and interdependencies among the covered company and its material entities, and among the critical operations and core business lines of the covered company that, if disrupted, would materially affect the funding or operations of the covered company, its material entities, or its critical operations or core business lines. Such interconnections and interdependencies may include:

(1) Common or shared personnel, facilities, or systems (including information technology platforms, management information systems, risk management systems, and accounting and recordkeeping systems);

(2) Capital, funding, or liquidity arrangements;

(3) Existing or contingent credit exposures;

(4) Cross-guarantee arrangements, cross-collateral arrangements, cross-default provisions, and cross-affiliate netting agreements;

(5) Risk transfers; and

(6) Service level agreements.

(h) *Supervisory and regulatory information.* Each resolution plan shall—

(1) Identify any:

(i) Federal, state, or foreign agency or authority (other than a Federal banking agency) with supervisory authority or responsibility for ensuring the safety and soundness of the covered company, its material entities, critical operations and core business lines; and

§ 381.5

(ii) Other Federal, state, or foreign agency or authority (other than a Federal banking agency) with significant supervisory or regulatory authority over the covered company, and its material entities and critical operations and core business lines.

(2) Identify any foreign agency or authority responsible for resolving a foreign-based material entity and critical operations or core business lines of the covered company; and

(3) Include contact information for each agency identified in paragraphs (h)(1) and (2) of this section.

(i) *Contact information.* Each resolution plan shall identify a senior management official at the covered company responsible for serving as a point of contact regarding the resolution plan of the covered company, and include contact information (including phone number, email address, and physical address) for a senior management official of the material entities of the covered company.

(j) *Inclusion of previously submitted resolution plan informational elements by reference.* An annual submission of or update to a resolution plan submitted by a covered company may include by reference informational elements (but not strategic analysis or executive summary elements) from a resolution plan previously submitted by the covered company to the Board and the Corporation, provided that:

(1) The resolution plan seeking to include informational elements by reference clearly indicates:

(i) The informational element the covered company is including by reference; and

(ii) Which of the covered company's previously submitted resolution plan(s) originally contained the information the covered company is including by reference; and

(2) The covered company certifies that the information the covered company is including by reference remains accurate.

(k) *Exemptions.* The Board and the Corporation may jointly exempt a covered company from one or more of the requirements of this section.

§ 381.5 Review of resolution plans; resubmission of deficient resolution plans.

(a) *Acceptance of submission and review.* (1) The Board and Corporation shall review a resolution plan submitted under section this subpart within 60 days.

(2) If the Board and Corporation jointly determine within the time described in paragraph (a)(1) of this section that a resolution plan is informationally incomplete or that substantial additional information is necessary to facilitate review of the resolution plan:

(i) The Board and Corporation shall jointly inform the covered company in writing of the area(s) in which the resolution plan is informationally incomplete or with respect to which additional information is required; and

(ii) The covered company shall resubmit an informationally complete resolution plan or such additional information as jointly requested to facilitate review of the resolution plan no later than 30 days after receiving the notice described in paragraph (a)(2)(i) of this section, or such other time period as the Board and Corporation may jointly determine.

(b) *Joint determination regarding deficient resolution plans.* If the Board and Corporation jointly determine that the resolution plan of a covered company submitted under § 381.3(a) is not credible or would not facilitate an orderly resolution of the covered company under the Bankruptcy Code, the Board and Corporation shall jointly notify the covered company in writing of such determination. Any joint notice provided under this paragraph shall identify the aspects of the resolution plan that the Board and Corporation jointly determined to be deficient.

(c) *Resubmission of a resolution plan.* Within 90 days of receiving a notice of deficiencies issued pursuant to paragraph (b) of this section, or such shorter or longer period as the Board and Corporation may jointly determine, a covered company shall submit a revised resolution plan to the Board and Corporation that addresses the deficiencies jointly identified by the Board and Corporation, and that discusses in detail:

(1) The revisions made by the covered company to address the deficiencies jointly identified by the Board and the Corporation;

(2) Any changes to the covered company's business operations and corporate structure that the covered company proposes to undertake to facilitate implementation of the revised resolution plan (including a timeline for the execution of such planned changes); and

(3) Why the covered company believes that the revised resolution plan is credible and would result in an orderly resolution of the covered company under the Bankruptcy Code.

(d) *Extensions of time.* Upon their own initiative or a written request by a covered company, the Board and Corporation may jointly extend any time period under this section. Each extension request shall be supported by a written statement of the covered company describing the basis and justification for the request.

§ 381.6 **Failure to cure deficiencies on resubmission of a resolution plan.**

(a) *In general.* The Board and Corporation may jointly determine that a covered company or any subsidiary of a covered company shall be subject to more stringent capital, leverage, or liquidity requirements, or restrictions on the growth, activities, or operations of the covered company or the subsidiary if:

(1) The covered company fails to submit a revised resolution plan under § 381.5(c) within the required time period; or

(2) The Board and the Corporation jointly determine that a revised resolution plan submitted under § 381.5(c) does not adequately remedy the deficiencies jointly identified by the Board and the Corporation under § 381.5(b).

(b) *Duration of requirements or restrictions.* Any requirements or restrictions imposed on a covered company or a subsidiary thereof pursuant to paragraph (a) of this section shall cease to apply to the covered company or subsidiary, respectively, on the date that the Board and the Corporation jointly determine the covered company has submitted a revised resolution plan that adequately remedies the deficiencies jointly identified by the Board and the Corporation under § 381.5(b).

(c) *Divestiture.* The Board and Corporation, in consultation with the Council, may jointly, by order, direct the covered company to divest such assets or operations as are jointly identified by the Board and Corporation if:

(1) The Board and Corporation have jointly determined that the covered company or a subsidiary thereof shall be subject to requirements or restrictions pursuant to paragraph (a) of this section; and

(2) The covered company has failed, within the 2-year period beginning on the date on which the determination to impose such requirements or restrictions under paragraph (a) of this section was made, to submit a revised resolution plan that adequately remedies the deficiencies jointly identified by the Board and the Corporation under § 381.5(b); and

(3) The Board and Corporation jointly determine that the divestiture of such assets or operations is necessary to facilitate an orderly resolution of the covered company under the Bankruptcy Code in the event the company was to fail.

§ 381.7 **Consultation.**

Prior to issuing any notice of deficiencies under § 381.5(b), determining to impose requirements or restrictions under § 381.6(a), or issuing a divestiture order pursuant to § 381.6(c) with respect to a covered company that is likely to have a significant impact on a functionally regulated subsidiary or a depository institution subsidiary of the covered company, the Board—

(a) Shall consult with each Council member that primarily supervises any such subsidiary; and

(b) May consult with any other Federal, state, or foreign supervisor as the Board considers appropriate.

§ 381.8 **No limiting effect or private right of action; confidentiality of resolution plans.**

(a) *No limiting effect on bankruptcy or other resolution proceedings.* A resolution plan submitted pursuant to this part shall not have any binding effect on:

(1) A court or trustee in a proceeding commenced under the Bankruptcy Code;

(2) A receiver appointed under Title II of the Dodd-Frank Act (12 U.S.C. 5381 et seq.);

(3) A bridge financial company chartered pursuant to 12 U.S.C. 5390(h); or

(4) Any other authority that is authorized or required to resolve a covered company (including any subsidiary or affiliate thereof) under any other provision of Federal, state, or foreign law.

(b) *No private right of action.* Nothing in this part creates or is intended to create a private right of action based on a resolution plan prepared or submitted under this part or based on any action taken by the Board or the Corporation with respect to any resolution plan submitted under this part.

(c) *Form of resolution plans.* Each resolution plan of a covered company shall be divided into a public section and a confidential section. Each covered company shall segregate and separately identify the public section from the confidential section. The public section shall consist of an executive summary of the resolution plan that describes the business of the covered company and includes, to the extent material to an understanding of the covered company:

(1) The names of material entities;

(2) A description of core business lines;

(3) Consolidated or segment financial information regarding assets, liabilities, capital and major funding sources;

(4) A description of derivative activities and hedging activities;

(5) A list of memberships in material payment, clearing and settlement systems;

(6) A description of foreign operations;

(7) The identities of material supervisory authorities;

(8) The identities of the principal officers;

(9) A description of the corporate governance structure and processes related to resolution planning;

(10) A description of material management information systems; and

(11) A description, at a high level, of the covered company's resolution strategy, covering such items as the range of potential purchasers of the covered company, its material entities and core business lines.

(d) *Confidential treatment of resolution plans.* (1) The confidentiality of resolution plans and related materials shall be determined in accordance with applicable exemptions under the Freedom of Information Act (5 U.S.C. 552(b)) and the Board's Rules Regarding Availability of Information (12 CFR part 261), and the Corporation's Disclosure of Information Rules (12 CFR part 309).

(2) Any covered company submitting a resolution plan or related materials pursuant to this part that desires confidential treatment of the information under 5 U.S.C. 552(b)(4), the Board's Rules Regarding Availability of Information (12 CFR part 261), and the Corporation's Disclosure of Information Rules (12 CFR part 309) may file a request for confidential treatment in accordance with those rules.

(3) To the extent permitted by law, information comprising the Confidential Section of a resolution plan will be treated as confidential.

(4) To the extent permitted by law, the submission of any nonpublic data or information under this part shall not constitute a waiver of, or otherwise affect, any privilege arising under Federal or state law (including the rules of any Federal or state court) to which the data or information is otherwise subject. Privileges that apply to resolution plans and related materials are protected pursuant to Section 18(x) of the FDI Act, 12 U.S.C. 1828(x).

§ 381.9 **Enforcement.**

The Board and Corporation may jointly enforce an order jointly issued by the Board and Corporation under § 381.6(a) or 381.6(c) of this part. The Board, in consultation with the Corporation, may take any action to address any violation of this part by a covered company under section 8 of the Federal Deposit Insurance Act (12 U.S.C. 1818).

Federal Deposit Insurance Corporation

PART 390—REGULATIONS TRANSFERRED FROM THE OFFICE OF THRIFT SUPERVISION

Subpart A—Restrictions on Post-Employment Activities of Senior Examiners

Sec.
390.1 What does this subpart do?
390.2 Who is a senior examiner?
390.3 What post-employment restrictions apply to senior examiners?
390.4 When will the FDIC waive the post-employment restrictions?
390.5 What are the penalties for violating the post-employment restrictions?

Subpart B—Removals, Suspensions, and Prohibitions Where a Crime Is Charged or Proven

390.10 Scope.
390.11 Definitions.
390.12 Issuance of Notice or Order.
390.13 Contents and service of the Notice or Order.
390.14 Petition for hearing.
390.15 Initiation of hearing.
390.16 Conduct of hearings.
390.17 Default.
390.18 Rules of evidence.
390.19 Burden of persuasion.
390.20 Relevant considerations.
390.21 Proposed findings and conclusions and recommended decision.
390.22 Decision of the FDIC Board of Directors.
390.23 Miscellaneous.

Subpart C—Rules of Practice and Procedure in Adjudicatory Proceedings

390.30 Scope.
390.31 Rules of construction.
390.32 Definitions.
390.33 Authority of the Board of Directors.
390.34 Authority of the administrative law judge.
390.35 Appearance and practice in adjudicatory proceedings.
390.36 Good faith certification.
390.37 Conflicts of interest.
390.38 Ex parte communications.
390.39 Filing of papers.
390.40 Service of papers.
390.41 Construction of time limits.
390.42 Change of time limits.
390.43 Witness fees and expenses.
390.44 Opportunity for informal settlement.
390.45 The FDIC's right to conduct examination.
390.46 Collateral attacks on adjudicatory proceeding.
390.47 Commencement of proceeding and contents of notice.
390.48 Answer.
390.49 Amended pleadings.
390.50 Failure to appear.
390.51 Consolidation and severance of actions.
390.52 Motions.
390.53 Scope of document discovery.
390.54 Request for document discovery from parties.
390.55 Document subpoenas to nonparties.
390.56 Deposition of witness unavailable for hearing.
390.57 Interlocutory review.
390.58 Summary disposition.
390.59 Partial summary disposition.
390.60 Scheduling and prehearing conferences.
390.61 Prehearing submissions.
390.62 Public hearings.
390.63 Hearing subpoenas.
390.64 Conduct of hearings.
390.65 Evidence.
390.66 Post-hearing filings.
390.67 Recommended decision and filing of record.
390.68 Exceptions to recommended decision.
390.69 Review by the Board of Directors.
390.70 Stays pending judicial review.
390.71 Scope.
390.72 Appointment of Office of Financial Institution Adjudication.
390.73 Discovery.
390.74 Civil money penalties.
390.75 Additional procedures.

Subpart D—Rules for Investigative Proceedings and Formal Examination Proceedings

390.80 Scope of subpart.
390.81 Definitions.
390.82 Confidentiality of proceedings.
390.83 Transcripts.
390.84 Rights of witnesses.
390.85 Obstruction of the proceedings.
390.86 Subpoenas.

Subpart E—Practice Before the FDIC

390.90 Scope of subpart.
390.91 Definitions.
390.92 Who may practice.
390.93 Suspension and debarment.
390.94 Reinstatement.
390.95 Duty to file information concerning adverse judicial or administrative action.
390.96 Proceeding under this subpart.
390.97 Removal, suspension, or debarment of independent public accountants and accounting firms performing audit services.

Subpart F—Application Processing Procedures

390.100 What does this subpart do?
390.101 Do the same procedures apply to all applications under this subpart?

390.102 How does the FDIC compute time periods under this subpart?
390.103 Must I meet with the FDIC before I file my application?
390.104 What information must I include in my draft business plan?
390.105 What type of application must I file?
390.106 What information must I provide with my application?
390.107 May I keep portions of my application confidential?
390.108 Where do I file my application?
390.109 What is the filing date of my application?
390.110 How do I amend or supplement my application?
390.111 Who must publish a public notice of an application?
390.112 What information must I include in my public notice?
390.113 When must I publish the public notice?
390.114 Where must I publish the public notice?
390.115 What language must I use in my publication?
390.116 Comment procedures.
390.117 Who may submit a written comment?
390.118 What information should a comment include?
390.119 Where are comments filed?
390.120 How long is the comment period?
390.121 Meeting procedures.
390.122 When will the FDIC conduct a meeting on an application?
390.123 What procedures govern the conduct of the meeting?
390.124 Will the FDIC approve or disapprove an application at a meeting?
390.125 Will a meeting affect application processing time frames?
390.126 If I file a notice under expedited treatment, when may I engage in the proposed activities?
390.127 What will the FDIC do after I file my application?
390.128 If the FDIC requests additional information to complete my application, how will it process my application?
390.129 Will the FDIC conduct an eligibility examination?
390.130 What may the FDIC require me to do after my application is deemed complete?
390.131 Will the FDIC require me to publish a new public notice?
390.132 May the FDIC suspend processing of my application?
390.133 How long is the FDIC review period?
390.134 How will I know if my application has been approved?
390.135 What will happen if the FDIC does not approve or disapprove my application within two calendar years after the filing date?

Subpart G—Nondiscrimination Requirements

390.140 Definitions.
390.141 Supplementary guidelines.
390.142 Nondiscrimination in lending and other services.
390.143 Nondiscriminatory appraisal and underwriting.
390.144 Nondiscrimination in applications.
390.145 Nondiscriminatory advertising.
390.146 Equal Housing Lender Poster.
390.147 Loan application register.
390.148 Nondiscrimination in employment.
390.149 Complaints.
390.150 Guidelines relating to nondiscrimination in lending.

Subpart H—Disclosure and Reporting of CRA-Related Agreements

390.160 Purpose and scope of this subpart.
390.161 Definition of covered agreement.
390.162 CRA communications.
390.163 Fulfillment of the CRA.
390.164 Related agreements considered a single agreement.
390.165 Disclosure of covered agreements.
390.166 Annual reports.
390.167 Release of information under FOIA.
390.168 Compliance provisions.
390.169 [Reserved]
390.170 Other definitions and rules of construction used in this subpart.

Subpart I—Consumer Protection in Sales of Insurance

390.180 Purpose and scope.
390.181 Definitions.
390.182 Prohibited practices.
390.183 What you must disclose.
390.184 Where insurance activities may take place.
390.185 Qualification and licensing requirements for insurance sales personnel.
APPENDIX A TO SUBPART I OF PART 390—CONSUMER GRIEVANCE PROCESS

Subpart J—Fiduciary Powers of State Savings Associations

390.190 What regulations govern the fiduciary operations of State savings associations?

Subpart K—Recordkeeping and Confirmation Requirements for Securities Transactions

390.200 What does this subpart do?
390.201 Must I comply with this subpart?
390.202 What requirements apply to all transactions?
390.203 What definitions apply to this subpart?

Federal Deposit Insurance Corporation Pt. 390

390.204 What records must I maintain for securities transactions?
390.205 How must I maintain my records?
390.206 What type of notice must I provide when I effect a securities transaction for a customer?
390.207 How do I provide a registered broker-dealer confirmation?
390.208 How do I provide a written notice?
390.209 What are the alternate notice requirements?
390.210 May I provide a notice electronically?
390.211 May I charge a fee for a notice?
390.212 When must I settle a securities transaction?
390.213 What policies and procedures must I maintain and follow for securities transactions?
390.214 How do my officers and employees file reports of personal securities trading transactions?

Subpart L—Electronic Operations

390.220 What does this subpart do?
390.221 Must I inform the FDIC before I use electronic means or facilities?
390.222 How do I notify the FDIC?

Subpart M—Deposits

390.230 What does this subpart do?
390.231 What records should I maintain on deposit activities?

Subpart N—Possession by Conservators and Receivers for Federal and State Savings Associations

390.240 Procedure upon taking possession.
390.241 Notice of appointment.

Subpart O—Subordinate Organizations

390.250 What does this subpart cover?
390.251 Definitions.
390.252 How must separate corporate identities be maintained?
390.253 What notices are required to establish or acquire a new subsidiary or engage in new activities through an existing subsidiary?
390.254 How may a subsidiary of a State savings association issue securities?
390.255 How may a State savings association exercise its salvage power in connection with a service corporation or lower-tier entities?

Subpart P—Lending and Investment

390.260 General.
390.261 [Reserved]
390.262 Definitions.
390.263 [Reserved]
390.264 Real estate lending standards; purpose and scope.
390.265 Real estate lending standards.
390.266 [Reserved]
390.267 Letters of credit and other independent undertakings to pay against documents.
390.268 Investment in State housing corporations.
390.269 Prohibition on loan procurement fees.
390.270 Asset classification.
390.271 Records for lending transactions.
390.272 Re-evaluation of real estate owned.

Subpart Q—Definitions for Regulations Affecting All State Savings Associations

390.280 When do the definitions in this subpart apply?
390.281 Account.
390.282 Accountholder.
390.283 Affiliate.
390.284 Affiliated person.
390.285 Audit period.
390.286 Certificate account.
390.287 Consumer credit.
390.288 Controlling person.
390.289 Corporation.
390.290 Demand accounts.
390.291 Director.
390.292 Financial institution.
390.293 Immediate family.
390.294 Land loan.
390.295 Low-rent housing.
390.296 Money Market Deposit Accounts.
390.297 Negotiable Order of Withdrawal Accounts.
390.298 Nonresidential construction loan.
390.299 Nonwithdrawable account.
390.300 Note account.
390.301 [Reserved]
390.302 Officer.
390.303 Parent company; subsidiary.
390.304 Political subdivision.
390.305 Principal office.
390.306 Public unit.
390.307 Savings account.
390.308 State savings association.
390.309 Security.
390.310 Service corporation.
390.311 State.
390.312 Subordinated debt security.
390.313 Tax and loan account.
390.314 United States Treasury General Account.
390.315 United States Treasury Time Deposit Open Account.
390.316 With recourse.

Subpart R—Regulatory Reporting Standards

390.320 Regulatory reporting requirements.
390.321 Regulatory reports.
390.322 Audit of State savings associations.

Subpart S—State Savings Associations—Operations

390.330 Chartering documents.

Pt. 390

390.331 Securities: Statement of non-insurance.
390.332 Merger, consolidation, purchase or sale of assets, or assumption of liabilities.
390.333 Advertising.
390.334 Directors, officers, and employees.
390.335 Tying restriction exception.
390.336 Employment contracts.
390.337 Transactions with affiliates.
390.338 Loans by State savings associations to their executive officers, directors, and principal shareholders.
390.339 Pension plans.
390.340 Offers and sales of securities at an office of a State savings association.
390.341 Inclusion of subordinated debt securities and mandatorily redeemable preferred stock as supplementary capital.
390.342 Capital distributions by State savings associations.
390.343 What is a capital distribution?
390.344 Definitions applicable to capital distributions.
390.345 Must I file with the FDIC?
390.346 How do I file with the FDIC?
390.347 May I combine my notice or application with other notices or applications?
390.348 Will the FDIC permit my capital distribution?
390.349 Management and financial policies.
390.350 Examinations and audits; appraisals; establishment and maintenance of records.
390.351 Frequency of safety and soundness examination.
390.352 Financial derivatives.
390.353 Interest-rate-risk-management procedures.
390.354 Procedures for monitoring Bank Secrecy Act (BSA) compliance.
390.355 Suspicious Activity Reports and other reports and statements.
390.356 Bonds for directors, officers, employees, and agents; form of and amount of bonds.
390.357 Bonds for agents.
390.358 Conflicts of interest.
390.359 Corporate opportunity.
390.360 Change of director or senior executive officer.
390.361 Applicable definitions.
390.362 Who must give prior notice?
390.363 What procedures govern the filing of my notice?
390.364 What information must I include in my notice?
390.365 What procedures govern the FDIC's review of my notice for completeness?
390.366 What standards and procedures will govern the FDIC review of the substance of my notice?
390.367 When may a proposed director or senior executive officer begin service?
390.368 When will the FDIC waive the prior notice requirement?

12 CFR Ch. III (1-1-12 Edition)

Subpart T—Accounting Requirements

390.380 Form and content of financial statements.
390.381 Definitions.
390.382 Qualification of public accountant.
390.383 Condensed financial information [Parent only].
390.384 Financial statements for conversions, SEC filings, and offering circulars.

Subpart U—Securities of State Savings Associations

390.390 Requirements under certain sections of the Securities Exchange Act of 1934.
390.391 [Reserved]
390.392 Liability for certain statements by State savings associations.
390.393 Form and content of financial statements.
390.394 Interpretations related to SEC filings.
390.395 Description of business.

Subpart V—Management Official Interlocks

390.400 Authority, purpose, and scope.
390.401 Definitions.
390.402 Prohibitions.
390.403 Interlocking relationships permitted by statute.
390.404 Small market share exemption.
390.405 General exemption.
390.406 Change in circumstances.
390.407 Enforcement.
390.408 Interlocking relationships permitted pursuant to Federal Deposit Insurance Act.

Subpart W—Securities Offerings

390.410 Definitions.
390.411 Offering circular requirement.
390.412 Exemptions.
390.413 Non-public offering.
390.414 Filing and signature requirements.
390.415 Effective date.
390.416 Form, content, and accounting.
390.417 Use of the offering circular.
390.418 Escrow requirement.
390.419 Unsafe or unsound practices.
390.420 Withdrawal or abandonment.
390.421 Securities sale report.
390.422 Public disclosure and confidential treatment.
390.423 Waiver.
390.424 Requests for interpretive advice or waiver.
390.425 Delayed or continuous offering and sale of securities.
390.426 Sales of securities at an office of a State savings association.
390.427 Current and periodic reports.
390.428 Approval of the security.
390.429 Form for securities sale report.

Federal Deposit Insurance Corporation

Pt. 390

390.430 Filing of copies of offering circulars in certain exempt offerings.

Subpart X—Appraisals

390.440 Authority, purpose, and scope.
390.441 Definitions.
390.442 Appraisals required; transactions requiring a State certified or licensed appraiser.
390.443 Minimum appraisal standards.
390.444 Appraiser independence.
390.445 Professional association membership; competency.
390.446 Enforcement.
390.447 Appraisal policies and practices of State savings associations and subsidiaries.

Subpart Y—Prompt Corrective Action

390.450 Authority, purpose, scope, other supervisory authority, and disclosure of capital categories.
390.451 Definitions.
390.452 Notice of capital category.
390.453 Capital measures and capital category definitions.
390.454 Capital restoration plans.
390.455 Mandatory and discretionary supervisory actions under section 38.
390.456 Directives to take prompt corrective action.
390.457 Procedures for reclassifying a State savings association based on criteria other than capital.
390.458 Order to dismiss a director or senior executive officer.
390.459 Enforcement of directives.

Subpart Z—Capital

390.460 Scope.
390.461 Definitions.
390.462 Minimum regulatory capital requirement.
390.463 Individual minimum capital requirements.
390.464 Capital directives.
390.465 Components of capital.
390.466 Risk-based capital credit risk-weight categories.
390.467 Leverage ratio.
390.468 Tangible capital requirement.
390.469 Consequences of failure to meet capital requirements.
390.470 Reservation of authority.
390.471 Purchased credit card relationships, servicing assets, intangible assets (other than purchased credit card relationships and servicing assets), credit-enhancing interest-only strips, and deferred tax assets.

APPENDIX A TO SUBPART Z OF PART 390—RISK-BASED CAPITAL REQUIREMENTS—INTERNAL-RATINGS-BASED AND ADVANCED MEASUREMENT APPROACHES

AUTHORITY: 12 U.S.C. 1819.

Subpart A also issued under 12 U.S.C. 1820.
Subpart B also issued under 12 U.S.C. 1818.
Subpart C also issued under 5 U.S.C. 504; 554–557; 12 U.S.C. 1464; 1467; 1468; 1817; 1818; 1820; 1829; 3349, 4717; 15 U.S.C. 78l; 78o–5; 78u–2; 28 U.S.C. 2461 note; 31 U.S.C. 5321; 42 U.S.C. 4012a.
Subpart D also issued under 12 U.S.C. 1817; 1818; 1820; 15 U.S.C. 78l.
Subpart E also issued under 12 U.S.C. 1813; 1831m; 15 U.S.C. 78.
Subpart F also issued under 5 U.S.C. 552; 559; 12 U.S.C. 2901 et seq.
Subpart G also issued under 12 U.S.C. 2810 et seq., 2901 et seq.; 15 U.S.C. 1691; 42 U.S.C. 1981, 1982, 3601–3619.
Subpart H also issued under 12 U.S.C. 1464; 1831y.
Subpart I also issued under 12 U.S.C. 1831x.
Subpart J also issued under 12 U.S.C. 1831p–1.
Subpart K also issued under 12 U.S.C. 1817; 1818; 15 U.S.C. 78c; 78l.
Subpart L also issued under 12 U.S.C. 1831p–1.
Subpart M also issued under 12 U.S.C. 1818.
Subpart N also issued under 12 U.S.C. 1821.
Subpart O also issued under 12 U.S.C. 1828.
Subpart P also issued under 12 U.S.C. 1470; 1831e; 1831n; 1831p–1; 3339.
Subpart Q also issued under 12 U.S.C. 1462; 1462a; 1463; 1464.
Subpart R also issued under 12 U.S.C. 1463; 1464; 1831m; 1831n; 1831p–1.
Subpart S also issued under 12 U.S.C. 1462; 1462a; 1463; 1464; 1468a; 1817; 1820; 1828; 1831e; 1831o; 1831p–1; 1881–1884; 3207; 3339; 15 U.S.C. 78b; 78l; 78m; 78n; 78p; 78q; 78w; 31 U.S.C. 5318; 42 U.S.C. 4106.
Subpart T also issued under 12 U.S.C. 1462a; 1463; 1464; 15 U.S.C. 78c; 78l; 78m; 78n; 78w.
Subpart U also issued under 12 U.S.C. 1462a; 1463; 1464; 15 U.S.C. 78c; 78l; 78m; 78n; 78p; 78w; 78d–1; 7241; 7242; 7243; 7244; 7261; 7264; 7265.
Subpart V also issued under 12 U.S.C. 3201–3208.
Subpart W also issued under 12 U.S.C. 1462a; 1463; 1464; 15 U.S.C. 78c; 78l; 78m; 78n; 78p; 78w.
Subpart X also issued under 12 U.S.C. 1462a; 1463; 1464; 1828; 3331 et seq.
Subpart Y also issued under 12 U.S.C.1831o.
Subpart Z also issued under 12 U.S.C. 1462a; 1463; 1464; 1828 (note).

SOURCE: 76 FR 47655, Aug. 5, 2011, unless otherwise noted.

Subpart A—Restrictions on Post-Employment Activities of Senior Examiners

§ 390.1 What does this subpart do?

This subpart implements section 10(k) of the Federal Deposit Insurance Act (FDIA), (12 U.S.C. 1820(k)), which prohibits senior examiners from accepting compensation from certain companies following the termination of their employment. Except where otherwise provided, the terms used in this subpart have the meanings given in section 3 of the FDIA (12 U.S.C. 1813).

§ 390.2 Who is a senior examiner?

An individual is a senior examiner for a particular savings association or savings and loan holding company if—

(a) The individual was an officer or employee of the Office of Thrift Supervision (OTS) (including a special government employee) who was authorized by the OTS to conduct examinations or inspections of savings associations or savings and loan holding companies;

(b) The individual was assigned continuing, broad and lead responsibility for the examination or inspection of that savings association or savings and loan holding company; and

(c) The individual's responsibilities for examining, inspecting, or supervising that savings association or savings and loan holding company:

(1) Represented a substantial portion of the individual's assigned responsibilities at the OTS; and

(2) Required the individual to interact on a routine basis with officers and employees of the savings association, savings and loan holding company, or its affiliates.

§ 390.3 What post-employment restrictions apply to senior examiners?

(a) *Prohibition*—(1) *Senior examiner of savings association.* An individual who served as a senior examiner of a savings association for two or more of the last 12 months of his or her employment with OTS may not, within one year after the termination date of his or her employment with OTS, knowingly accept compensation as an employee, officer, director, or consultant from—

(i) The savings association; or

(ii) A savings and loan holding company, bank holding company, or any other company that controls the savings association.

(2) *Senior examiner of a savings and loan holding company.* An individual who served as a senior examiner of a savings and loan holding company for two or more of the last 12 months of his or her employment with OTS may not, within one year after the termination date of his or her employment with OTS, knowingly accept compensation as an employee, officer, director, or consultant from—

(i) The savings and loan holding company; or

(ii) Any depository institution that is controlled by the savings and loan holding company.

(b) [Reserved]

(c) *Definitions.* For the purposes of this section—

Consultant. An individual acts as a consultant for a savings association or other company only if he or she directly works on matters for, or on behalf of, the savings association or company.

Control. Control has the same meaning given in 12 CFR part 391, subpart E.

§ 390.4 When will the FDIC waive the post-employment restrictions?

The post-employment restriction in § 390.3 will not apply to a senior examiner if the Chairperson, or his or her designee, certifies in writing and on a case-by-case basis that a waiver of the restriction will not affect the integrity of the FDIC's supervisory program.

§ 390.5 What are the penalties for violating the post-employment restrictions?

(a) *Penalties.* A senior examiner who violates § 390.3 shall, in accordance with 12 U.S.C. 1820(k)(6), be subject to one or both of the following penalties:

(1) An order—

(i) Removing the person from office or prohibiting the person from further participating in the conduct of the affairs of the relevant depository institution, savings and loan holding company, bank holding company or other company for up to five years, and

(ii) Prohibiting the person from participating in the affairs of any insured

Federal Deposit Insurance Corporation

§ 390.12

depository institution for up to five years.

(2) A civil money penalty not to exceed $250,000.

(b) *Scope of prohibition orders.* Any senior examiner who is subject to an order issued under paragraph (a)(1) of this section shall be subject to 12 U.S.C. 1818(e)(6) and (7) in the same manner and to the same extent as a person subject to an order issued under 12 U.S.C. 1818(e).

(c) *Procedures.* 12 U.S.C. 1820(k) describes the procedures that are applicable to actions under paragraph (a) of this section and the appropriate Federal banking agency authorized to take the action, which may be an agency other than the FDIC. Where the FDIC is the appropriate Federal banking agency, it will conduct administrative proceedings under subpart C of this part.

(d) *Other penalties.* The penalties under this section are not exclusive. A senior examiner who violates the restriction in § 390.3 may also be subject to other administrative, civil, or criminal remedy or penalty as provided by law.

Subpart B—Removals, Suspensions, and Prohibitions Where a Crime Is Charged or Proven

§ 390.10 Scope.

The rules in this subpart apply to hearings, which are exempt from the adjudicative provisions of the Administrative Procedure Act, afforded to any officer, director, or other person participating in the conduct of the affairs of a State savings association, where such person has been suspended or removed from office or prohibited from further participation in the conduct of the affairs of the State savings association by a Notice or Order served by the Board of Directors upon the grounds set forth in section 8(g) of the Federal Deposit Insurance Act (FDIA), (12 U.S.C. 1818(g)).

§ 390.11 Definitions.

As used in this subpart—

(a) The term *Board of Directors* means the Board of Directors of the FDIC or its designee.

(b) The term *Notice* means a Notice of Suspension or Notice of Prohibition issued by the Board of Directors pursuant to section 8(g) of the FDIA.

(c) The term *Order* means an Order of Removal or Order of Prohibition issued by the Board of Directors pursuant to section 8(g) of the FDIA.

(d) The term *association* means a State savings association within the meaning of section 3(b)(3) of the FDIA, (12 U.S.C. 1813(b)(3)).

(e) The term *subject individual* means a person served with a Notice or Order.

(f) The term *petitioner* means a subject individual who has filed a petition for informal hearing under this part.

§ 390.12 Issuance of Notice or Order.

(a) The Board of Directors may issue and serve a Notice upon an officer, director, or other person participating in the conduct of the affairs of an association, where the individual is charged in any information, indictment, or complaint with the commission of or participation in a crime involving dishonesty or breach of trust that is punishable by imprisonment for a term exceeding one year under State or Federal law, if the Board of Directors, upon due deliberation, determines that continued service or participation by the individual may pose a threat to the interests of the association's depositors or may threaten to impair public confidence in the association. The Notice shall remain in effect until the information, indictment, or complaint is finally disposed of or until terminated by the Board of Directors.

(b) The Board of Directors may issue and serve an Order upon a subject individual against whom a judgment of conviction, or an agreement to enter a pretrial diversion or other similar program has been rendered, where such judgment is not subject to further appellate review, and the Board of Directors, upon the deliberation, has determined that continued service or participation by the subject individual may pose a threat to the interests of the association's depositors or may threaten to impair public confidence in the association.

§ 390.13 Contents and service of the Notice or Order.

(a) The Notice or Order shall set forth the basis and facts in support of the Board of Directors' issuance of such Notice or Order, and shall inform the subject individual of his right to a hearing, in accordance with this part, for the purpose of determining whether the Notice or Order should be continued, terminated, or otherwise modified.

(b) The Executive Secretary shall serve a copy of the Notice or Order upon the subject individual and the related association in the manner set forth in § 390.40.

(c) Upon receipt of the Notice or Order, the subject individual shall immediately comply with the requirements thereof.

§ 390.14 Petition for hearing.

(a) To obtain a hearing, the subject individual must file two copies of a petition with the Executive Secretary within 30 days of being served with the Notice or Order.

(b) The petition filed under this section shall admit or deny specifically each allegation in the Notice or Order, unless the petitioner is without knowledge or information, in which case the petition shall so state and the statement shall have the effect of a denial. Any allegation not denied shall be deemed to be admitted. When a petitioner intends in good faith to deny only a part of or to qualify an allegation, he shall specify so much of it as is true and shall deny only the remainder.

(c) The petition shall state whether the petitioner is requesting termination or modification of the Notice or Order, and shall state with particularity how the petitioner intends to show that his continued service to or participation in the conduct of the affairs of the association would not, or is not likely to, pose a threat to the interests of the association's depositors or to impair public confidence in the association.

§ 390.15 Initiation of hearing.

(a) Within 10 days of the filing of a petition for hearing, the Board of Directors shall notify the petitioner of the time and place fixed for hearing, and it shall designate one or more Board of Directors employees to serve as presiding officer.

(b) The hearing shall be scheduled to be held no later than 30 days from the date the petition was filed, unless the time is extended at the request of the petitioner.

(c) A petitioner may appear personally or through counsel, but if represented by counsel, said counsel is required to comply with § 390.35.

(d) A representative(s) of the FDIC enforcement staff also may attend the hearing and participate therein as a party.

§ 390.16 Conduct of hearings.

(a) Hearings provided by this section are not subject to the adjudicative provisions of the Administrative Procedure Act (5 U.S.C. 554–557). The presiding officer is, however, authorized to exercise all of the powers enumerated in § 390.34.

(b) Witnesses may be presented, within time limits specified by the presiding officer, provided that at least 10 days prior to the hearing date, the party presenting the witnesses furnishes the presiding officer and the opposing party with a list of such witnesses and a summary of the proposed testimony. However, the requirement for furnishing such a witness list and summary of testimony shall not apply to the presentation of rebuttal witnesses. The presiding officer may ask questions of any witness, and each party shall have an opportunity to cross-examine any witness presented by an opposing party.

(c) Upon the request of either the petitioner or a representative of the FDIC enforcement staff, the record shall remain open for a period of 5 business days following the hearing, during which time the parties may make any additional submissions for the record. Thereafter, the record shall be closed.

(d) Following the introduction of all evidence, the petitioner and the representative of the FDIC enforcement staff shall have an opportunity for oral argument; however, the parties may jointly waive the right to oral argument, and, in lieu thereof, elect to submit written argument.

(e) All oral testimony and oral argument shall be recorded, and transcripts made available to the petitioner upon payment of the cost thereof. A copy of the transcript shall be sent directly to the presiding officer, who shall have authority to correct the record *sua sponte* or upon the motion of any party.

(f) The parties may, in writing, jointly waive an oral hearing and instead elect a hearing upon a written record in which all evidence and argument would be submitted to the presiding officer in documentary form and statements of individuals would be made by affidavit.

§ 390.17 Default.

If the subject individual fails to file a petition for a hearing, or fails to appear at a hearing, either in person or by attorney, or fails to submit a written argument where oral argument has been waived pursuant to § 390.16(d) or (f), the Notice shall remain in effect until the information, indictment, or complaint is finally disposed of and the Order shall remain in effect until terminated by the Board of Directors.

§ 390.18 Rules of evidence.

(a) Formal rules of evidence shall not apply to a hearing, but the presiding officer may limit the introduction of irrelevant, immaterial, or unduly repetitious evidence.

(b) All matters officially noticed by the presiding officer shall appear on the record.

§ 390.19 Burden of persuasion.

The petitioner has the burden of showing, by a preponderance of the evidence, that his or her continued service to or participation in the conduct of the affairs of the association does not, or is not likely to, pose a threat to the interests of the association's depositors or threaten to impair public confidence in the association.

§ 390.20 Relevant considerations.

(a) In determining whether the petitioner has shown that his or her continued service to or participation in the conduct of the affairs of the association would not, or is not likely to, pose a threat to the interests of the association's depositors or threaten to impair public confidence in the association, in order to decide whether the Notice or Order should be continued, terminated, or otherwise modified, the Board of Directors will consider:

(1) The nature and extent of the petitioner's participation in the affairs of the association;

(2) The nature of the offense with which the petitioner has been charged;

(3) The extent of the publicity accorded the indictment and trial; and

(4) Such other relevant factors as may be entered on the record.

(b) When considering a request for the termination or modification of a Notice, the Board of Directors will not consider the ultimate guilt or innocence of the petitioner with respect to the criminal charge that is outstanding.

(c) When considering a request for the termination or modification of an Order which has been issued following a final judgment of conviction against a subject individual, the Board of Directors will not collaterally review such final judgment of conviction.

§ 390.21 Proposed findings and conclusions and recommended decision.

(a) Within 30 days after completion of oral argument or the submission of written argument where oral argument has been waived, the presiding officer shall file with the Executive Secretary and certify to the Board of Directors for decision the entire record of the hearing, which shall include a recommended decision, the Notice or Order, and all other documents filed in connection with the hearing.

(b) The recommended decision shall contain:

(1) A statement of the issue(s) presented,

(2) A statement of findings and conclusions, and the reasons or basis therefor, on all material issues of fact, law, or discretion presented on the record, and

(3) An appropriate recommendation as to whether the suspension, removal, or prohibition should be continued, modified, or terminated.

§ 390.22 Decision of the FDIC Board of Directors.

(a) Within 30 days after the recommended decision has been certified to the Board of Directors, the Board of Directors shall issue a final decision.

(b) The Board of Director's final decision shall contain a statement of the basis therefor. The Board of Directors may satisfy this requirement where it adopts the recommended decision of the presiding officer upon finding that the recommended decision satisfies the requirements of § 390.67.

(c) The Executive Secretary shall serve upon the petitioner and the representative of the FDIC enforcement staff a copy of the Board of Director's final decision and the related recommended decision.

§ 390.23 Miscellaneous.

The provisions of §§ 390.39–390.41 shall apply to proceedings under this subpart.

Subpart C—Rules of Practice and Procedure in Adjudicatory Proceedings

§ 390.30 Scope.

Sections 390.30–390.70 prescribe Uniform Rules of practice and procedure applicable to adjudicatory proceedings as to which hearings on the record are provided for by the following statutory provisions:

(a) Cease-and-desist proceedings under section 8(b) of the Federal Deposit Insurance Act (FDIA) (12 U.S.C. 1818(b));

(b) Removal and prohibition proceedings under section 8(e) of the FDIA (12 U.S.C. 1818(e));

(c) Change-in-control proceedings under section 7(j)(4) of the FDIA (12 U.S.C. 1817(j)(4)) to determine whether the FDIC should issue an order to approve or disapprove a person's proposed acquisition of an institution and/or institution holding company;

(d) Proceedings under section 15C(c)(2) of the Securities Exchange Act of 1934 (Exchange Act) (15 U.S.C. 78o–5), to impose sanctions upon any government securities broker or dealer or upon any person associated or seeking to become associated with a government securities broker or dealer for which the FDIC is the appropriate regulatory agency;

(e) Assessment of civil money penalties by the FDIC against institutions, institution-affiliated parties, and certain other persons for which it is the appropriate regulatory agency for any violation of:

(1) Section 5 of the Home Owners' Loan Act (HOLA) or any regulation or order issued thereunder, pursuant to 12 U.S.C. 1464(d), (s) and (v);

(2) Section 9 of the HOLA or any regulation or order issued thereunder, pursuant to 12 U.S.C. 1467(d);

(3) Section 10 of HOLA, pursuant to 12 U.S.C. 1467a(i) and (r);

(4) Any provisions of the Change in Bank Control Act, any regulation or order issued thereunder or certain unsafe or unsound practices or breaches of fiduciary duty, pursuant to 12 U.S.C. 1817(j)(16);

(5) Sections 22(h) and 23 of the Federal Reserve Act, or any regulation issued thereunder or certain unsafe or unsound practices or breaches of fiduciary duty, pursuant to 12 U.S.C. 1468;

(6) Certain provisions of the Exchange Act, pursuant to section 21B of the Exchange Act (15 U.S.C. 78u–2);

(7) Section 1120 of Financial Institutions Reform, Recovery and Enforcement Act of 1989 (12 U.S.C. 3349), or any order or regulation issued thereunder;

(8) The terms of any final or temporary order issued or enforceable pursuant to section 8 of the FDIA or of any written agreement executed by the FDIC, the terms of any conditions imposed in writing by the FDIC in connection with the grant of an application or request, certain unsafe or unsound practices or breaches of fiduciary duty, or any law or regulation not otherwise provided herein pursuant to 12 U.S.C. 1818(i)(2);

(9) Any provision of law referenced in section 102 of the Flood Disaster Protection Act of 1973 (42 U.S.C. 4012a(f)) or any order or regulation issued thereunder; and

(10) Any provision of law referenced in 31 U.S.C. 5321 or any order or regulation issued thereunder;

(f) Remedial action under section 102 of the Flood Disaster Protection Act of 1973 (42 U.S.C. 4012a(g));

Federal Deposit Insurance Corporation

§ 390.32

(g) Proceedings under section 10(k) of the FDIA (12 U.S.C. 1820(k)) to impose penalties on senior examiners for violation of post-employment prohibitions; and

(h) Sections 390.30 through 390.70 of this part also apply to all other adjudications required by statute to be determined on the record after opportunity for an agency hearing, unless otherwise specifically provided for in the Local Rules.

§ 390.31 Rules of construction.

For purposes of §§ 390.30 through 390.70 of this part:

(a) Any term in the singular includes the plural, and the plural includes the singular, if such use would be appropriate;

(b) Any use of a masculine, feminine, or neuter gender encompasses all three, if such use would be appropriate;

(c) The term *counsel* includes a non-attorney representative; and

(d) Unless the context requires otherwise, a party's counsel of record, if any, may, on behalf of that party, take any action required to be taken by the party.

§ 390.32 Definitions.

For purposes of §§ 390.30 through 390.70 of this part, unless explicitly stated to the contrary:

Adjudicatory proceeding means a proceeding conducted pursuant to these rules and leading to the formulation of a final order other than a regulation.

Administrative law judge means one who presides at an administrative hearing under authority set forth at 5 U.S.C. 556.

Board of Directors means the Board of Directors of the Federal Deposit Insurance Corporation or its designee.

Decisional employee means any member of the FDIC's or administrative law judge's staff who has not engaged in an investigative or prosecutorial role in a proceeding and who may assist the Board of Directors or the administrative law judge, respectively, in preparing orders, recommended decisions, decisions, and other documents under the Uniform Rules.

Enforcement Counsel means any individual who files a notice of appearance as counsel on behalf of the FDIC in an adjudicatory proceeding.

FDIC means the Federal Deposit Insurance Corporation.

Final order means an order issued by the FDIC with or without the consent of the affected institution or the institution-affiliated party, that has become final, without regard to the pendency of any petition for reconsideration or review.

Institution includes any State savings association as that term is defined in section 3(b) of the FDIA, (12 U.S.C. 1813(b)), any savings and loan holding company or any subsidiary thereof whether wholly or partly owned (other than a bank) as those terms are defined in section 10(a) of the HOLA, (12 U.S.C. 1467(a)).

Institution-affiliated party means any institution-affiliated party as that term is defined in section 3(u) of the FDIA, (12 U.S.C. 1813(u)).

Local Rules means those rules found in §§ 390.71 through 390.75 of this part.

Office of Financial Institution Adjudication or *OFIA* means the executive body charged with overseeing the administration of administrative enforcement proceedings for the Office of the Comptroller of the Currency, the Board of Governors of the Federal Reserve Board, the National Credit Union Administration, and the FDIC.

Party means the FDIC and any person named as a party in any notice.

Person means an individual, sole proprietor, partnership, corporation, unincorporated association, trust, joint venture, pool, syndicate, agency or other entity or organization, including an institution as defined in paragraph (g) of this section.

Respondent means any party other than the FDIC.

Uniform Rules means those rules in §§ 390.30 through 390.70 of this part.

Violation includes any action (alone or with another or others) for or toward causing, bringing about, participating in, counseling, or aiding or abetting a violation.

§ 390.33 Authority of the Board of Directors.

The Board of Directors may, at any time during the pendency of a proceeding perform, direct the performance of, or waive performance of, any act which could be done or ordered by the administrative law judge.

§ 390.34 Authority of the administrative law judge.

(a) *General rule.* All proceedings governed by this part shall be conducted in accordance with the provisions of chapter 5 of title 5 of the United States Code. The administrative law judge shall have all powers necessary to conduct a proceeding in a fair and impartial manner and to avoid unnecessary delay.

(b) *Powers.* The administrative law judge shall have all powers necessary to conduct the proceeding in accordance with paragraph (a) of this section, including the following powers:

(1) To administer oaths and affirmations;

(2) To issue subpoenas, subpoenas *duces tecum*, and protective orders, as authorized by this part, and to quash or modify any such subpoenas and orders;

(3) To receive relevant evidence and to rule upon the admission of evidence and offers of proof;

(4) To take or cause depositions to be taken as authorized by this subpart;

(5) To regulate the course of the hearing and the conduct of the parties and their counsel;

(6) To hold scheduling and/or prehearing conferences as set forth in § 390.60;

(7) To consider and rule upon all procedural and other motions appropriate in an adjudicatory proceeding, provided that only the Board of Directors shall have the power to grant any motion to dismiss the proceeding or to decide any other motion that results in a final determination of the merits of the proceeding;

(8) To prepare and present to the Board of Directors a recommended decision as provided herein;

(9) To recuse himself or herself by motion made by a party or on his or her own motion;

(10) To establish time, place and manner limitations on the attendance of the public and the media for any public hearing; and

(11) To do all other things necessary and appropriate to discharge the duties of a presiding officer.

§ 390.35 Appearance and practice in adjudicatory proceedings.

(a) *Appearance before an FDIC or an administrative law judge*—(1) *By attorneys.* Any member in good standing of the bar of the highest court of any state, commonwealth, possession, territory of the United States, or the District of Columbia may represent others before the FDIC if such attorney is not currently suspended or debarred from practice before the FDIC.

(2) *By non-attorneys.* An individual may appear on his or her own behalf; a member of a partnership may represent the partnership; a duly authorized officer, director, or employee of any government unit, agency, institution, corporation or authority may represent that unit, agency, institution, corporation or authority if such officer, director, or employee is not currently suspended or debarred from practice before the FDIC.

(3) *Notice of appearance.* Any individual acting as counsel on behalf of a party, including the FDIC, shall file a notice of appearance with OFIA at or before the time that individual submits papers or otherwise appears on behalf of a party in the adjudicatory proceeding. The notice of appearance must include a written declaration that the individual is currently qualified as provided in paragraph (a)(1) or (2) of this section and is authorized to represent the particular party. By filing a notice of appearance on behalf of a party in an adjudicatory proceeding, the counsel agrees and represents that he or she is authorized to accept service on behalf of the represented party and that, in the event of withdrawal from representation, he or she will, if required by the administrative law judge, continue to accept service until new counsel has filed a notice of appearance or until the represented party indicates that he or she will proceed on a *pro se* basis.

(b) *Sanctions.* Dilatory, obstructionist, egregious, contemptuous or

Federal Deposit Insurance Corporation

contumacious conduct at any phase of any adjudicatory proceeding may be grounds for exclusion or suspension of counsel from the proceeding.

§ 390.36 Good faith certification.

(a) *General requirement.* Every filing or submission of record following the issuance of a notice shall be signed by at least one counsel of record in his or her individual name and shall state that counsel's address and telephone number. A party who acts as his or her own counsel shall sign his or her individual name and state his or her address and telephone number on every filing or submission of record.

(b) *Effect of signature.* (1) The signature of counsel or a party shall constitute a certification that: the counsel or party has read the filing or submission of record; to the best of his or her knowledge, information, and belief formed after reasonable inquiry, the filing or submission of record is well-grounded in fact and is warranted by existing law or a good faith argument for the extension, modification, or reversal of existing law; and the filing or submission of record is not made for any improper purpose, such as to harass or to cause unnecessary delay or needless increase in the cost of litigation.

(2) If a filing or submission of record is not signed, the administrative law judge shall strike the filing or submission of record, unless it is signed promptly after the omission is called to the attention of the pleader or movant.

(c) *Effect of making oral motion or argument.* The act of making any oral motion or oral argument by any counsel or party constitutes a certification that to the best of his or her knowledge, information, and belief formed after reasonable inquiry, his or her statements are well-grounded in fact and are warranted by existing law or a good faith argument for the extension, modification, or reversal of existing law, and are not made for any improper purpose, such as to harass or to cause unnecessary delay or needless increase in the cost of litigation.

§ 390.37 Conflicts of interest.

(a) *Conflict of interest in representation.* No person shall appear as counsel for another person in an adjudicatory proceeding if it reasonably appears that such representation may be materially limited by that counsel's responsibilities to a third person or by the counsel's own interests. The administrative law judge may take corrective measures at any stage of a proceeding to cure a conflict of interest in representation, including the issuance of an order limiting the scope of representation or disqualifying an individual from appearing in a representative capacity for the duration of the proceeding.

(b) *Certification and waiver.* If any person appearing as counsel represents two or more parties to an adjudicatory proceeding or also represents a non-party on a matter relevant to an issue in the proceeding, counsel must certify in writing at the time of filing the notice of appearance required by § 390.35(a):

(1) That the counsel has personally and fully discussed the possibility of conflicts of interest with each such party and non-party; and

(2) That each such party and non-party waives any right it might otherwise have had to assert any known conflicts of interest or to assert any nonmaterial conflicts of interest during the course of the proceeding.

§ 390.38 Ex parte communications.

(a) *Definition*—(1) *Ex parte communication* means any material oral or written communication relevant to the merits of an adjudicatory proceeding that was neither on the record nor on reasonable prior notice to all parties that takes place between:

(i) An interested person outside the FDIC (including such person's counsel); and

(ii) The administrative law judge handling that proceeding, the Board of Directors, or a decisional employee.

(2) *Exception.* A request for status of the proceeding does not constitute an *ex parte* communication.

(b) *Prohibition of ex parte communications.* From the time the notice is issued by the Board of Directors until the date that the Board of Directors

§ 390.39

issues the final decision pursuant to § 390.69(c):

(1) No interested person outside the FDIC shall make or knowingly cause to be made an *ex parte* communication to the Board of Directors, the administrative law judge, or a decisional employee; and

(2) The Board of Directors, administrative law judge, or decisional employee shall not make or knowingly cause to be made to any interested person outside the FDIC any *ex parte* communication.

(c) *Procedure upon occurrence of ex parte communication.* If an *ex parte* communication is received by the administrative law judge, the Board of Directors or other person identified in paragraph (a) of this section, that person shall cause all such written communications (or, if the communication is oral, a memorandum stating the substance of the communication) to be placed on the record of the proceeding and served on all parties. All other parties to the proceeding shall have an opportunity, within ten days of receipt of service of the *ex parte* communication to file responses thereto and to recommend any sanctions, in accordance with paragraph (d) of this section, that they believe to be appropriate under the circumstances.

(d) *Sanctions.* Any party or his or her counsel who makes a prohibited *ex parte* communication, or who encourages or solicits another to make any such communication, may be subject to any appropriate sanction or sanctions imposed by the Board of Directors or the administrative law judge including, but not limited to, exclusion from the proceedings and an adverse ruling on the issue which is the subject of the prohibited communication.

(e) *Separation-of-functions.* Except to the extent required for the disposition of *ex parte* matters as authorized by law, the administrative law judge may not consult a person or party on any matter relevant to the merits of the adjudication, unless on notice and opportunity for all parties to participate. An employee or agent engaged in the performance of investigative or prosecuting functions for the FDIC in a case may not, in that or a factually related case, participate or advise in the decision, recommended decision, or agency review of the recommended decision under § 390.69, except as witness or counsel in public proceedings.

§ 390.39 Filing of papers.

(a) *Filing.* Any papers required to be filed, excluding documents produced in response to a discovery request pursuant to §§ 390.54 and 390.55, shall be filed with the OFIA, except as otherwise provided.

(b) *Manner of filing.* Unless otherwise specified by the Board of Directors or the administrative law judge, filing may be accomplished by:

(1) Personal service;

(2) Delivering the papers to a reliable commercial courier service, overnight delivery service, or to the U.S. Post Office for Express Mail delivery;

(3) Mailing the papers by first class, registered, or certified mail; or

(4) Transmission by electronic media, only if expressly authorized, and upon any conditions specified, by the Board of Directors or the administrative law judge. All papers filed by electronic media shall also concurrently be filed in accordance with paragraph (c) of this section as to form.

(c) *Formal requirements as to papers filed*—(1) *Form.* All papers filed must set forth the name, address, and telephone number of the counsel or party making the filing and must be accompanied by a certification setting forth when and how service has been made on all other parties. All papers filed must be double-spaced and printed or typewritten on 8½ x 11 inch paper, and must be clear and legible.

(2) *Signature.* All papers must be dated and signed as provided in § 390.36.

(3) *Caption.* All papers filed must include at the head thereof, or on a title page, the name of the FDIC and of the filing party, the title and docket number of the proceeding, and the subject of the particular paper.

(4) *Number of copies.* Unless otherwise specified by the Board of Directors, or the administrative law judge, an original and one copy of all documents and papers shall be filed, except that only one copy of transcripts of testimony and exhibits shall be filed.

Federal Deposit Insurance Corporation § 390.41

§ 390.40 Service of papers.

(a) *By the parties.* Except as otherwise provided, a party filing papers shall serve a copy upon the counsel of record for all other parties to the proceeding so represented, and upon any party not so represented.

(b) *Method of service.* Except as provided in paragraphs (c)(2) and (d) of this section, a serving party shall use one or more of the following methods of service:

(1) Personal service;

(2) Delivering the papers to a reliable commercial courier service, overnight delivery service, or to the U.S. Post Office for Express Mail delivery;

(3) Mailing the papers by first class, registered, or certified mail; or

(4) Transmission by electronic media, only if the parties mutually agree. Any papers served by electronic media shall also concurrently be served in accordance with the requirements of § 390.39(c) as to form.

(c) *By the Board of Directors or the administrative law judge.* (1) All papers required to be served by the Board of Directors or the administrative law judge upon a party who has appeared in the proceeding through a counsel of record, shall be served by any means specified in paragraph (b) of this section.

(2) If a party has not appeared in the proceeding in accordance with § 390.35, the Board of Directors or the administrative law judge shall make service by any of the following methods:

(i) By personal service;

(ii) If the person to be served is an individual, by delivery to a person of suitable age and discretion at the physical location where the individual resides or works;

(iii) If the person to be served is a corporation or other association, by delivery to an officer, managing or general agent, or to any other agent authorized by appointment or by law to receive service and, if the agent is one authorized by statute to receive service and the statute so requires, by also mailing a copy to the party;

(iv) By registered or certified mail addressed to the person's last known address; or

(v) By any other method reasonably calculated to give actual notice.

(d) *Subpoenas.* Service of a subpoena may be made:

(1) By personal service;

(2) If the person to be served is an individual, by delivery to a person of suitable age and discretion at the physical location where the individual resides or works;

(3) By delivery to an agent, which in the case of a corporation or other association, is delivery to an officer, managing or general agent, or to any other agent authorized by appointment or by law to receive service and, if the agent is one authorized by statute to receive service and the statute so requires, by also mailing a copy to the party;

(4) By registered or certified mail addressed to the person's last known address; or

(5) By any other method reasonably calculated to give actual notice.

(e) *Area of service.* Service in any state, territory, possession of the United States, or the District of Columbia, on any person or company doing business in any state, territory, possession of the United States, or the District of Columbia, or on any person as otherwise provided by law, is effective without regard to the place where the hearing is held, provided that if service is made on a foreign bank in connection with an action or proceeding involving one or more of its branches or agencies located in any state, territory, possession of the United States, or the District of Columbia, service shall be made on at least one branch or agency so involved.

§ 390.41 Construction of time limits.

(a) *General rule.* In computing any period of time prescribed by this subpart, the date of the act or event that commences the designated period of time is not included. The last day so computed is included unless it is a Saturday, Sunday, or Federal holiday. When the last day is a Saturday, Sunday, or Federal holiday, the period runs until the end of the next day that is not a Saturday, Sunday, or Federal holiday. Intermediate Saturdays, Sundays, and Federal holidays are included in the computation of time. However, when the time period within which an act is to be performed is ten days or less, not including any additional time allowed for

§ 390.42

in paragraph (c) of this section, intermediate Saturdays, Sundays, and Federal holidays are not included.

(b) *When papers are deemed to be filed or served.* (1) Filing and service are deemed to be effective:

(i) In the case of personal service or same day commercial courier delivery, upon actual service;

(ii) In the case of overnight commercial delivery service, U.S. Express mail delivery, or first class, registered, or certified mail, upon deposit in or delivery to an appropriate point of collection; or

(iii) In the case of transmission by electronic media, as specified by the authority receiving the filing, in the case of filing, and as agreed among the parties, in the case of service.

(2) The effective filing and service dates specified in paragraph (b)(1) of this section may be modified by the Board of Directors or administrative law judge in the case of filing or by agreement of the parties in the case of service.

(c) *Calculation of time for service and filing of responsive papers.* Whenever a time limit is measured by a prescribed period from the service of any notice or paper, the applicable time limits are calculated as follows:

(1) If service is made by first class, registered, or certified mail, add three calendar days to the prescribed period;

(2) If service is made by express mail or overnight delivery service, add one calendar day to the prescribed period; or

(3) If service is made by electronic media transmission, add one calendar day to the prescribed period, unless otherwise determined by the Board of Directors or the administrative law judge in the case of filing, or by agreement among the parties in the case of service.

§ 390.42 Change of time limits.

Except as otherwise provided by law, the administrative law judge may, for good cause shown, extend the time limits prescribed by the Uniform Rules or any notice or order issued in the proceedings. After the referral of the case to the Board of Directors pursuant to § 390.67, the Board of Directors may grant extensions of the time limits for good cause shown. Extensions may be granted at the motion of a party or on the Board of Director's or the administrative law judge's own motion after notice and opportunity to respond is afforded all non-moving parties.

§ 390.43 Witness fees and expenses.

Witnesses subpoenaed for testimony or deposition shall be paid the same fees for attendance and mileage as are paid in the United States district courts in proceedings in which the United States is a party, provided that, in the case of a discovery subpoena addressed to a party, no witness fees or mileage need be paid. Fees for witnesses shall be tendered in advance by the party requesting the subpoena, except that fees and mileage need not be tendered in advance where the FDIC is the party requesting the subpoena. The FDIC shall not be required to pay any fees to, or expenses of, any witness not subpoenaed by the FDIC.

§ 390.44 Opportunity for informal settlement.

Any respondent may, at any time in the proceeding, unilaterally submit to Enforcement Counsel written offers or proposals for settlement of a proceeding, without prejudice to the rights of any of the parties. No such offer or proposal shall be made to any FDIC representative other than Enforcement Counsel. Submission of a written settlement offer does not provide a basis for adjourning or otherwise delaying all or any portion of a proceeding under this part. No settlement offer or proposal, or any subsequent negotiation or resolution, is admissible as evidence in any proceeding.

§ 390.45 The FDIC's right to conduct examination.

Nothing contained in this subpart limits in any manner the right of the FDIC to conduct any examination, inspection, or visitation of any institution or institution-affiliated party, or the right of the FDIC to conduct or continue any form of investigation authorized by law.

Federal Deposit Insurance Corporation § 390.48

§ 390.46 Collateral attacks on adjudicatory proceeding.

If an interlocutory appeal or collateral attack is brought in any court concerning all or any part of an adjudicatory proceeding, the challenged adjudicatory proceeding shall continue without regard to the pendency of that court proceeding. No default or other failure to act as directed in the adjudicatory proceeding within the times prescribed in this subpart shall be excused based on the pendency before any court of any interlocutory appeal or collateral attack.

§ 390.47 Commencement of proceeding and contents of notice.

(a) *Commencement of proceeding.* (1)(i) Except for change-in-control proceedings under section 7(j)(4) of the FDIA (12 U.S.C. 1817(j)(4)), a proceeding governed by this subpart is commenced by issuance of a notice by the FDIC.

(ii) The notice must be served by the Executive Secretary upon the respondent and given to any other appropriate financial institution supervisory authority where required by law.

(iii) The notice must be filed with the OFIA.

(2) Change-in control proceedings under section 7(j)(4) of the FDIA (12 U.S.C. 1817(j)(4)) commence with the issuance of an order by the Board of Directors.

(b) *Contents of notice.* The notice must set forth:

(1) The legal authority for the proceeding and for the FDIC's jurisdiction over the proceeding;

(2) A statement of the matters of fact or law showing that the FDIC is entitled to relief;

(3) A proposed order or prayer for an order granting the requested relief;

(4) The time, place, and nature of the hearing as required by law or regulation;

(5) The time within which to file an answer as required by law or regulation;

(6) The time within which to request a hearing as required by law or regulation; and

(7) The answer and/or request for a hearing shall be filed with OFIA.

§ 390.48 Answer.

(a) *When.* Within 20 days of service of the notice, respondent shall file an answer as designated in the notice. In a civil money penalty proceeding, respondent shall also file a request for a hearing within 20 days of service of the notice.

(b) *Content of answer.* An answer must specifically respond to each paragraph or allegation of fact contained in the notice and must admit, deny, or state that the party lacks sufficient information to admit or deny each allegation of fact. A statement of lack of information has the effect of a denial. Denials must fairly meet the substance of each allegation of fact denied; general denials are not permitted. When a respondent denies part of an allegation, that part must be denied and the remainder specifically admitted. Any allegation of fact in the notice which is not denied in the answer must be deemed admitted for purposes of the proceeding. A respondent is not required to respond to the portion of a notice that constitutes the prayer for relief or proposed order. The answer must set forth affirmative defenses, if any, asserted by the respondent.

(c) *Default*—(1) *Effect of failure to answer.* Failure of a respondent to file an answer required by this section within the time provided constitutes a waiver of his or her right to appear and contest the allegations in the notice. If no timely answer is filed, Enforcement Counsel may file a motion for entry of an order of default. Upon a finding that no good cause has been shown for the failure to file a timely answer, the administrative law judge shall file with the Board of Directors a recommended decision containing the findings and the relief sought in the notice. Any final order issued by the Board of Directors based upon a respondent's failure to answer is deemed to be an order issued upon consent.

(2) *Effect of failure to request a hearing in civil money penalty proceedings.* If respondent fails to request a hearing as required by law within the time provided, the notice of assessment constitutes a final and unappealable order.

§ 390.49 Amended pleadings.

(a) *Amendments.* The notice or answer may be amended or supplemented at any stage of the proceeding. The respondent must answer an amended notice within the time remaining for the respondent's answer to the original notice, or within ten days after service of the amended notice, whichever period is longer, unless the Board of Directors or administrative law judge orders otherwise for good cause.

(b) *Amendments to conform to the evidence.* When issues not raised in the notice or answer are tried at the hearing by express or implied consent of the parties, they will be treated in all respects as if they had been raised in the notice or answer, and no formal amendments are required. If evidence is objected to at the hearing on the ground that it is not within the issues raised by the notice or answer, the administrative law judge may admit the evidence when admission is likely to assist in adjudicating the merits of the action and the objecting party fails to satisfy the administrative law judge that the admission of such evidence would unfairly prejudice that party's action or defense upon the merits. The administrative law judge may grant a continuance to enable the objecting party to meet such evidence.

§ 390.50 Failure to appear.

Failure of a respondent to appear in person at the hearing or by a duly authorized counsel constitutes a waiver of respondent's right to a hearing and is deemed an admission of the facts as alleged and consent to the relief sought in the notice. Without further proceedings or notice to the respondent, the administrative law judge shall file with the Board of Directors a recommended decision containing the findings and the relief sought in the notice.

§ 390.51 Consolidation and severance of actions.

(a) *Consolidation.* (1) On the motion of any party, or on the administrative law judge's own motion, the administrative law judge may consolidate, for some or all purposes, any two or more proceedings, if each such proceeding involves or arises out of the same transaction, occurrence or series of transactions or occurrences, or involves at least one common respondent or a material common question of law or fact, unless such consolidation would cause unreasonable delay or injustice.

(2) In the event of consolidation under paragraph (a)(1) of this section, appropriate adjustment to the prehearing schedule must be made to avoid unnecessary expense, inconvenience, or delay.

(b) *Severance.* The administrative law judge may, upon the motion of any party, sever the proceeding for separate resolution of the matter as to any respondent only if the administrative law judge finds that:

(1) Undue prejudice or injustice to the moving party would result from not severing the proceeding; and

(2) Such undue prejudice or injustice would outweigh the interests of judicial economy and expedition in the complete and final resolution of the proceeding.

§ 390.52 Motions.

(a) *In writing.* (1) Except as otherwise provided herein, an application or request for an order or ruling must be made by written motion.

(2) All written motions must state with particularity the relief sought and must be accompanied by a proposed order.

(3) No oral argument may be held on written motions except as otherwise directed by the administrative law judge. Written memoranda, briefs, affidavits or other relevant material or documents may be filed in support of or in opposition to a motion.

(b) *Oral motions.* A motion may be made orally on the record unless the administrative law judge directs that such motion be reduced to writing.

(c) *Filing of motions.* Motions must be filed with the administrative law judge, but upon the filing of the recommended decision, motions must be filed with the Executive Secretary for disposition by the Board of Directors.

(d) *Responses.* (1) Except as otherwise provided herein, within ten days after service of any written motion, or within such other period of time as may be established by the administrative law judge or the Executive Secretary, any

Federal Deposit Insurance Corporation

§ 390.54

party may file a written response to a motion. The administrative law judge shall not rule on any oral or written motion before each party has had an opportunity to file a response.

(2) The failure of a party to oppose a written motion or an oral motion made on the record is deemed a consent by that party to the entry of an order substantially in the form of the order accompanying the motion.

(e) *Dilatory motions.* Frivolous, dilatory or repetitive motions are prohibited. The filing of such motions may form the basis for sanctions.

(f) *Dispositive motions.* Dispositive motions are governed by §§ 390.58 and 390.59.

§ 390.53 Scope of document discovery.

(a) *Limits on discovery.* (1) Subject to the limitations set out in paragraphs (b), (c), and (d) of this section, a party to a proceeding under this subpart may obtain document discovery by serving a written request to produce documents. For purposes of a request to produce documents, the term "documents" may be defined to include drawings, graphs, charts, photographs, recordings, data stored in electronic form, and other data compilations from which information can be obtained, or translated, if necessary, by the parties through detection devices into reasonably usable form, as well as written material of all kinds.

(2) Discovery by use of deposition is governed by § 390.73.

(3) Discovery by use of interrogatories is not permitted.

(b) *Relevance.* A party may obtain document discovery regarding any matter, not privileged, that has material relevance to the merits of the pending action. Any request to produce documents that calls for irrelevant material, that is unreasonable, oppressive, excessive in scope, unduly burdensome, or repetitive of previous requests, or that seeks to obtain privileged documents will be denied or modified. A request is unreasonable, oppressive, excessive in scope or unduly burdensome if, among other things, it fails to include justifiable limitations on the time period covered and the geographic locations to be searched, the time provided to respond in the request is inadequate, or the request calls for copies of documents to be delivered to the requesting party and fails to include the requestor's written agreement to pay in advance for the copying, in accordance with § 390.54.

(c) *Privileged matter.* Privileged documents are not discoverable. Privileges include the attorney-client privilege, work-product privilege, any government's or government agency's deliberative-process privilege, and any other privileges the Constitution, any applicable act of Congress, or the principles of common law provide.

(d) *Time limits.* All discovery, including all responses to discovery requests, shall be completed at least 20 days prior to the date scheduled for the commencement of the hearing, except as provided in the Local Rules. No exceptions to this time limit shall be permitted, unless the administrative law judge finds on the record that good cause exists for waiving the requirements of this paragraph (d).

§ 390.54 Request for document discovery from parties.

(a) *General rule.* Any party may serve on any other party a request to produce for inspection any discoverable documents that are in the possession, custody, or control of the party upon whom the request is served. The request must identify the documents to be produced either by individual item or by category, and must describe each item and category with reasonable particularity. Documents must be produced as they are kept in the usual course of business or must be organized to correspond with the categories in the request.

(b) *Production or copying.* The request must specify a reasonable time, place, and manner for production and performing any related acts. In lieu of inspecting the documents, the requesting party may specify that all or some of the responsive documents be copied and the copies delivered to the requesting party. If copying of fewer than 250 pages is requested, the party to whom the request is addressed shall bear the cost of copying and shipping charges. If a party requests 250 pages or more of copying, the requesting party shall pay for the copying and shipping charges.

751

§ 390.54

Copying charges are the current per-page copying rate imposed under part 309 for requests under the Freedom of Information Act (5 U.S.C. 552). The party to whom the request is addressed may require payment in advance before producing the documents.

(c) *Obligation to update responses.* A party who has responded to a discovery request with a response that was complete when made is not required to supplement the response to include documents thereafter acquired, unless the responding party learns that:

(1) The response was materially incorrect when made; or

(2) The response, though correct when made, is no longer true and a failure to amend the response is, in substance, a knowing concealment.

(d) *Motions to limit discovery.* (1) Any party that objects to a discovery request may, within ten days of being served with such request, file a motion in accordance with the provisions of § 390.52 to revoke or otherwise limit the request. If an objection is made to only a portion of an item or category in a request, the portion objected to shall be specified. Any objections not made in accordance with this paragraph and § 390.52 are waived.

(2) The party who served the request that is the subject of a motion to revoke or limit may file a written response within five days of service of the motion. No other party may file a response.

(e) *Privilege.* At the time other documents are produced, the producing party must reasonably identify all documents withheld on the grounds of privilege and must produce a statement of the basis for the assertion of privilege. When similar documents that are protected by deliberative process, attorney-work-product, or attorney-client privilege are voluminous, these documents may be identified by category instead of by individual document. The administrative law judge retains discretion to determine when the identification by category is insufficient.

(f) *Motions to compel production.* (1) If a party withholds any documents as privileged or fails to comply fully with a discovery request, the requesting party may, within ten days of the assertion of privilege or of the time the failure to comply becomes known to the requesting party, file a motion in accordance with the provisions of § 390.52 for the issuance of a subpoena compelling production.

(2) The party who asserted the privilege or failed to comply with the request may file a written response to a motion to compel within five days of service of the motion. No other party may file a response.

(g) *Ruling on motions.* After the time for filing responses pursuant to this section has expired, the administrative law judge shall rule promptly on all motions filed pursuant to this section. If the administrative law judge determines that a discovery request, or any of its terms, calls for irrelevant material, is unreasonable, oppressive, excessive in scope, unduly burdensome, or repetitive of previous requests, or seeks to obtain privileged documents, he or she may deny or modify the request, and may issue appropriate protective orders, upon such conditions as justice may require. The pendency of a motion to strike or limit discovery or to compel production is not a basis for staying or continuing the proceeding, unless otherwise ordered by the administrative law judge. Notwithstanding any other provision in this subpart, the administrative law judge may not release, or order a party to produce, documents withheld on grounds of privilege if the party has stated to the administrative law judge its intention to file a timely motion for interlocutory review of the administrative law judge's order to produce the documents, and until the motion for interlocutory review has been decided.

(h) *Enforcing discovery subpoenas.* If the administrative law judge issues a subpoena compelling production of documents by a party, the subpoenaing party may, in the event of noncompliance and to the extent authorized by applicable law, apply to any appropriate United States district court for an order requiring compliance with the subpoena. A party's right to seek court enforcement of a subpoena shall not in any manner limit the sanctions that may be imposed by the administrative law judge against a party who fails to produce subpoenaed documents.

§ 390.55 Document subpoenas to nonparties.

(a) *General rules.* (1) Any party may apply to the administrative law judge for the issuance of a document discovery subpoena addressed to any person who is not a party to the proceeding. The application must contain a proposed document subpoena and a brief statement showing the general relevance and reasonableness of the scope of documents sought. The subpoenaing party shall specify a reasonable time, place, and manner for making production in response to the document subpoena.

(2) A party shall only apply for a document subpoena under this section within the time period during which such party could serve a discovery request under § 390.53(d). The party obtaining the document subpoena is responsible for serving it on the subpoenaed person and for serving copies on all parties. Document subpoenas may be served in any state, territory, or possession of the United States, the District of Columbia, or as otherwise provided by law.

(3) The administrative law judge shall promptly issue any document subpoena requested pursuant to this section. If the administrative law judge determines that the application does not set forth a valid basis for the issuance of the subpoena, or that any of its terms are unreasonable, oppressive, excessive in scope, or unduly burdensome, he or she may refuse to issue the subpoena or may issue it in a modified form upon such conditions as may be consistent with the Uniform Rules.

(b) *Motion to quash or modify.* (1) Any person to whom a document subpoena is directed may file a motion to quash or modify such subpoena, accompanied by a statement of the basis for quashing or modifying the subpoena. The movant shall serve the motion on all parties, and any party may respond to such motion within ten days of service of the motion.

(2) Any motion to quash or modify a document subpoena must be filed on the same basis, including the assertion of privilege, upon which a party could object to a discovery request under § 390.54(d), and during the same time limits during which such an objection could be filed.

(c) *Enforcing document subpoenas.* If a subpoenaed person fails to comply with any subpoena issued pursuant to this section or any order of the administrative law judge which directs compliance with all or any portion of a document subpoena, the subpoenaing party or any other aggrieved party may, to the extent authorized by applicable law, apply to an appropriate United States district court for an order requiring compliance with so much of the document subpoena as the administrative law judge has not quashed or modified. A party's right to seek court enforcement of a document subpoena shall in no way limit the sanctions that may be imposed by the administrative law judge on a party who induces a failure to comply with subpoenas issued under this section.

§ 390.56 Deposition of witness unavailable for hearing.

(a) *General rules.* (1) If a witness will not be available for the hearing, a party may apply in accordance with the procedures set forth in paragraph (a)(2) of this section, to the administrative law judge for the issuance of a subpoena, including a subpoena *duces tecum,* requiring the attendance of the witness at a deposition. The administrative law judge may issue a deposition subpoena under this section upon showing that:

(i) The witness will be unable to attend or may be prevented from attending the hearing because of age, sickness or infirmity, or will otherwise be unavailable;

(ii) The witness' unavailability was not procured or caused by the subpoenaing party;

(iii) The testimony is reasonably expected to be material; and

(iv) Taking the deposition will not result in any undue burden to any other party and will not cause undue delay of the proceeding.

(2) The application must contain a proposed deposition subpoena and a brief statement of the reasons for the issuance of the subpoena. The subpoena must name the witness whose deposition is to be taken and specify the time and place for taking the deposition. A

deposition subpoena may require the witness to be deposed at any place within the country in which that witness resides or has a regular place of employment or such other convenient place as the administrative law judge shall fix.

(3) Any requested subpoena that sets forth a valid basis for its issuance must be promptly issued, unless the administrative law judge on his or her own motion, requires a written response or requires attendance at a conference concerning whether the requested subpoena should be issued.

(4) The party obtaining a deposition subpoena is responsible for serving it on the witness and for serving copies on all parties. Unless the administrative law judge orders otherwise, no deposition under this section shall be taken on fewer than ten days' notice to the witness and all parties. Deposition subpoenas may be served in any state, territory, possession of the United States, or the District of Columbia, on any person or company doing business in any state, territory, possession of the United States, or the District of Columbia, or as otherwise permitted by law.

(b) *Objections to deposition subpoenas.* (1) The witness and any party who has not had an opportunity to oppose a deposition subpoena issued under this section may file a motion with the administrative law judge to quash or modify the subpoena prior to the time for compliance specified in the subpoena, but not more than ten days after service of the subpoena.

(2) A statement of the basis for the motion to quash or modify a subpoena issued under this section must accompany the motion. The motion must be served on all parties.

(c) *Procedure upon deposition.* (1) Each witness testifying pursuant to a deposition subpoena must be duly sworn, and each party shall have the right to examine the witness. Objections to questions or documents must be in short form, stating the grounds for the objection. Failure to object to questions or documents is not deemed a waiver except where the ground for the objection might have been avoided if the objection had been timely presented. All questions, answers, and objections must be recorded.

(2) Any party may move before the administrative law judge for an order compelling the witness to answer any questions the witness has refused to answer or submit any evidence the witness has refused to submit during the deposition.

(3) The deposition must be subscribed by the witness, unless the parties and the witness, by stipulation, have waived the signing, or the witness is ill, cannot be found, or has refused to sign. If the deposition is not subscribed by the witness, the court reporter taking the deposition shall certify that the transcript is a true and complete transcript of the deposition.

(d) *Enforcing subpoenas.* If a subpoenaed person fails to comply with any order of the administrative law judge which directs compliance with all or any portion of a deposition subpoena under paragraph (b) or (c)(2) of this section, the subpoenaing party or other aggrieved party may, to the extent authorized by applicable law, apply to an appropriate United States district court for an order requiring compliance with the portions of the subpoena that the administrative law judge has ordered enforced. A party's right to seek court enforcement of a deposition subpoena in no way limits the sanctions that may be imposed by the administrative law judge on a party who fails to comply with or procures a failure to comply with, a subpoena issued under this section.

§ 390.57 Interlocutory review.

(a) *General rule.* The Board of Directors may review a ruling of the administrative law judge prior to the certification of the record to the Board of Directors only in accordance with the procedures set forth in this section and § 390.52.

(b) *Scope of review.* The Board of Directors may exercise interlocutory review of a ruling of the administrative law judge if the Board of Directors finds that:

(1) The ruling involves a controlling question of law or policy as to which substantial grounds exist for a difference of opinion;

Federal Deposit Insurance Corporation

§ 390.59

(2) Immediate review of the ruling may materially advance the ultimate termination of the proceeding;

(3) Subsequent modification of the ruling at the conclusion of the proceeding would be an inadequate remedy; or

(4) Subsequent modification of the ruling would cause unusual delay or expense.

(c) *Procedure.* Any request for interlocutory review shall be filed by a party with the administrative law judge within ten days of his or her ruling and shall otherwise comply with § 390.52. Any party may file a response to a request for interlocutory review in accordance with § 390.52(d). Upon the expiration of the time for filing all responses, the administrative law judge shall refer the matter to the Board of Directors for final disposition.

(d) *Suspension of proceeding.* Neither a request for interlocutory review nor any disposition of such a request by the Board of Directors under this section suspends or stays the proceeding unless otherwise ordered by the administrative law judge or the Board of Directors.

§ 390.58 Summary disposition.

(a) *In general.* The administrative law judge shall recommend that the Board of Directors issue a final order granting a motion for summary disposition if the undisputed pleaded facts, admissions, affidavits, stipulations, documentary evidence, matters as to which official notice may be taken, and any other evidentiary materials properly submitted in connection with a motion for summary disposition show that:

(1) There is no genuine issue as to any material fact; and

(2) The moving party is entitled to a decision in its favor as a matter of law.

(b) *Filing of motions and responses.* (1) Any party who believes that there is no genuine issue of material fact to be determined and that he or she is entitled to a decision as a matter of law may move at any time for summary disposition in its favor of all or any part of the proceeding. Any party, within 20 days after service of such a motion, or within such time period as allowed by the administrative law judge, may file a response to such motion.

(2) A motion for summary disposition must be accompanied by a statement of the material facts as to which the moving party contends there is no genuine issue. Such motion must be supported by documentary evidence, which may take the form of admissions in pleadings, stipulations, depositions, investigatory depositions, transcripts, affidavits and any other evidentiary materials that the moving party contends support his or her position. The motion must also be accompanied by a brief containing the points and authorities in support of the contention of the moving party. Any party opposing a motion for summary disposition must file a statement setting forth those material facts as to which he or she contends a genuine dispute exists. Such opposition must be supported by evidence of the same type as that submitted with the motion for summary disposition and a brief containing the points and authorities in support of the contention that summary disposition would be inappropriate.

(c) *Hearing on motion.* At the request of any party or on his or her own motion, the administrative law judge may hear oral argument on the motion for summary disposition.

(d) *Decision on motion.* Following receipt of a motion for summary disposition and all responses thereto, the administrative law judge shall determine whether the moving party is entitled to summary disposition. If the administrative law judge determines that summary disposition is warranted, the administrative law judge shall submit a recommended decision to that effect to the Board of Directors. If the administrative law judge finds that no party is entitled to summary disposition, he or she shall make a ruling denying the motion.

§ 390.59 Partial summary disposition.

If the administrative law judge determines that a party is entitled to summary disposition as to certain claims only, he or she shall defer submitting a recommended decision as to those claims. A hearing on the remaining issues must be ordered. Those claims for which the administrative law judge has determined that summary disposition is warranted will be addressed in

§ 390.60

the recommended decision filed at the conclusion of the hearing.

§ 390.60 Scheduling and prehearing conferences.

(a) *Scheduling conference.* Within 30 days of service of the notice or order commencing a proceeding or such other time as parties may agree, the administrative law judge shall direct counsel for all parties to meet with him or her in person at a specified time and place prior to the hearing or to confer by telephone for the purpose of scheduling the course and conduct of the proceeding. This meeting or telephone conference is called a "scheduling conference." The identification of potential witnesses, the time for and manner of discovery, and the exchange of any prehearing materials including witness lists, statements of issues, stipulations, exhibits and any other materials may also be determined at the scheduling conference.

(b) *Prehearing conferences.* The administrative law judge may, in addition to the scheduling conference, on his or her own motion or at the request of any party, direct counsel for the parties to meet with him or her (in person or by telephone) at a prehearing conference to address any or all of the following:

(1) Simplification and clarification of the issues;

(2) Stipulations, admissions of fact, and the contents, authenticity and admissibility into evidence of documents;

(3) Matters of which official notice may be taken;

(4) Limitation of the number of witnesses;

(5) Summary disposition of any or all issues;

(6) Resolution of discovery issues or disputes;

(7) Amendments to pleadings; and

(8) Such other matters as may aid in the orderly disposition of the proceeding.

(c) *Transcript.* The administrative law judge, in his or her discretion, may require that a scheduling or prehearing conference be recorded by a court reporter. A transcript of the conference and any materials filed, including orders, becomes part of the record of the proceeding. A party may obtain a copy of the transcript at its expense.

(d) *Scheduling or prehearing orders.* At or within a reasonable time following the conclusion of the scheduling conference or any prehearing conference, the administrative law judge shall serve on each party an order setting forth any agreements reached and any procedural determinations made.

§ 390.61 Prehearing submissions.

(a) Within the time set by the administrative law judge, but in no case later than 14 days before the start of the hearing, each party shall serve on every other party, his or her:

(1) Prehearing statement;

(2) Final list of witnesses to be called to testify at the hearing, including name and address of each witness and a short summary of the expected testimony of each witness;

(3) List of the exhibits to be introduced at the hearing along with a copy of each exhibit; and

(4) Stipulations of fact, if any.

(b) *Effect of failure to comply.* No witness may testify and no exhibits may be introduced at the hearing if such witness or exhibit is not listed in the prehearing submissions pursuant to paragraph (a) of this section, except for good cause shown.

§ 390.62 Public hearings.

(a) *General rule.* All hearings shall be open to the public, unless the FDIC, in its discretion, determines that holding an open hearing would be contrary to the public interest. Within 20 days of service of the notice or, in the case of change-in-control proceedings under section 7(j)(4) of the FDIA (12 U.S.C. 1817(j)(4)), within 20 days from service of the hearing order, any respondent may file with the Executive Secretary a request for a private hearing, and any party may file a reply to such a request. A party must serve on the administrative law judge a copy of any request or reply the party files with the Executive Secretary. The form of, and procedure for, these requests and replies are governed by § 390.52. A party's failure to file a request or a reply constitutes a waiver of any objections regarding whether the hearing will be public or private.

Federal Deposit Insurance Corporation § 390.64

(b) *Filing document under seal.* Enforcement Counsel, in his or her discretion, may file any document or part of a document under seal if disclosure of the document would be contrary to the public interest. The administrative law judge shall take all appropriate steps to preserve the confidentiality of such documents or parts thereof, including closing portions of the hearing to the public.

§ 390.63 Hearing subpoenas.

(a) *Issuance.* (1) Upon application of a party showing general relevance and reasonableness of scope of the testimony or other evidence sought, the administrative law judge may issue a subpoena or a subpoena *duces tecum* requiring the attendance of a witness at the hearing or the production of documentary or physical evidence at the hearing. The application for a hearing subpoena must also contain a proposed subpoena specifying the attendance of a witness or the production of evidence from any state, territory, or possession of the United States, the District of Columbia, or as otherwise provided by law at any designated place where the hearing is being conducted. The party making the application shall serve a copy of the application and the proposed subpoena on every other party.

(2) A party may apply for a hearing subpoena at any time before the commencement of a hearing. During a hearing, a party may make an application for a subpoena orally on the record before the administrative law judge.

(3) The administrative law judge shall promptly issue any hearing subpoena requested pursuant to this section. If the administrative law judge determines that the application does not set forth a valid basis for the issuance of the subpoena, or that any of its terms are unreasonable, oppressive, excessive in scope, or unduly burdensome, he or she may refuse to issue the subpoena or may issue it in a modified form upon any conditions consistent with this subpart. Upon issuance by the administrative law judge, the party making the application shall serve the subpoena on the person named in the subpoena and on each party.

(b) *Motion to quash or modify.* (1) Any person to whom a hearing subpoena is directed or any party may file a motion to quash or modify the subpoena, accompanied by a statement of the basis for quashing or modifying the subpoena. The movant must serve the motion on each party and on the person named in the subpoena. Any party may respond to the motion within ten days of service of the motion.

(2) Any motion to quash or modify a hearing subpoena must be filed prior to the time specified in the subpoena for compliance, but not more than ten days after the date of service of the subpoena upon the movant.

(c) *Enforcing subpoenas.* If a subpoenaed person fails to comply with any subpoena issued pursuant to this section or any order of the administrative law judge which directs compliance with all or any portion of a document subpoena, the subpoenaing party or any other aggrieved party may seek enforcement of the subpoena pursuant to section § 390.55(c).

§ 390.64 Conduct of hearings.

(a) *General rules.* (1) Hearings shall be conducted so as to provide a fair and expeditious presentation of the relevant disputed issues. Each party has the right to present its case or defense by oral and documentary evidence and to conduct such cross examination as may be required for full disclosure of the facts.

(2) *Order of hearing.* Enforcement Counsel shall present its case-in-chief first, unless otherwise ordered by the administrative law judge, or unless otherwise expressly specified by law or regulation. Enforcement Counsel shall be the first party to present an opening statement and a closing statement, and may make a rebuttal statement after the respondent's closing statement. If there are multiple respondents, respondents may agree among themselves as to their order of presentation of their cases, but if they do not agree the administrative law judge shall fix the order.

(3) *Examination of witnesses.* Only one counsel for each party may conduct an examination of a witness, except that in the case of extensive direct examination, the administrative law judge

§ 390.65

may permit more than one counsel for the party presenting the witness to conduct the examination. A party may have one counsel conduct the direct examination and another counsel conduct re-direct examination of a witness, or may have one counsel conduct the cross examination of a witness and another counsel conduct the re-cross examination of a witness.

(4) *Stipulations.* Unless the administrative law judge directs otherwise, all stipulations of fact and law previously agreed upon by the parties, and all documents, the admissibility of which have been previously stipulated, will be admitted into evidence upon commencement of the hearing.

(b) *Transcript.* The hearing must be recorded and transcribed. The reporter will make the transcript available to any party upon payment by that party to the reporter of the cost of the transcript. The administrative law judge may order the record corrected, either upon motion to correct, upon stipulation of the parties, or following notice to the parties upon the administrative law judge's own motion.

§ 390.65 Evidence.

(a) *Admissibility.* (1) Except as is otherwise set forth in this section, relevant, material, and reliable evidence that is not unduly repetitive is admissible to the fullest extent authorized by the Administrative Procedure Act and other applicable law.

(2) Evidence that would be admissible under the Federal Rules of Evidence is admissible in a proceeding conducted pursuant to this subpart.

(3) Evidence that would be inadmissible under the Federal Rules of Evidence may not deemed or ruled to be inadmissible in a proceeding conducted pursuant to this subpart if such evidence is relevant, material, reliable and not unduly repetitive.

(b) *Official notice.* (1) Official notice may be taken of any material fact which may be judicially noticed by a United States district court and any material information in the official public records of any Federal or state government agency.

(2) All matters officially noticed by the administrative law judge or Board of Directors shall appear on the record.

(3) If official notice is requested or taken of any material fact, the parties, upon timely request, shall be afforded an opportunity to object.

(c) *Documents.* (1) A duplicate copy of a document is admissible to the same extent as the original, unless a genuine issue is raised as to whether the copy is in some material respect not a true and legible copy of the original.

(2) Subject to the requirements of paragraph (a) of this section, any document, including a report of examination, supervisory activity, inspection or visitation, prepared by the appropriate Federal financial institution regulatory agency or state regulatory agency, is admissible either with or without a sponsoring witness.

(3) Witnesses may use existing or newly created charts, exhibits, calendars, calculations, outlines or other graphic material to summarize, illustrate, or simplify the presentation of testimony. Such materials may, subject to the administrative law judge's discretion, be used with or without being admitted into evidence.

(d) *Objections.* (1) Objections to the admissibility of evidence must be timely made and rulings on all objections must appear on the record.

(2) When an objection to a question or line of questioning propounded to a witness is sustained, the examining counsel may make a specific proffer on the record of what he or she expected to prove by the expected testimony of the witness, either by representation of counsel or by direct interrogation of the witness.

(3) The administrative law judge shall retain rejected exhibits, adequately marked for identification, for the record, and transmit such exhibits to the Board of Directors.

(4) Failure to object to admission of evidence or to any ruling constitutes a waiver of the objection.

(e) *Stipulations.* The parties may stipulate as to any relevant matters of fact or the authentication of any relevant documents. Such stipulations must be received in evidence at a hearing, and are binding on the parties with respect to the matters therein stipulated.

(f) *Depositions of unavailable witnesses.* (1) If a witness is unavailable to testify

Federal Deposit Insurance Corporation §390.67

at a hearing, and that witness has testified in a deposition to which all parties in a proceeding had notice and an opportunity to participate, a party may offer as evidence all or any part of the transcript of the deposition, including deposition exhibits, if any.

(2) Such deposition transcript is admissible to the same extent that testimony would have been admissible had that person testified at the hearing, provided that if a witness refused to answer proper questions during the depositions, the administrative law judge may, on that basis, limit the admissibility of the deposition in any manner that justice requires.

(3) Only those portions of a deposition received in evidence at the hearing constitute a part of the record.

§ 390.66 Post-hearing filings.

(a) *Proposed findings and conclusions and supporting briefs.* (1) Using the same method of service for each party, the administrative law judge shall serve notice upon each party, that the certified transcript, together with all hearing exhibits and exhibits introduced but not admitted into evidence at the hearing, has been filed. Any party may file with the administrative law judge proposed findings of fact, proposed conclusions of law, and a proposed order within 30 days following service of this notice by the administrative law judge or within such longer period as may be ordered by the administrative law judge.

(2) Proposed findings and conclusions must be supported by citation to any relevant authorities and by page references to any relevant portions of the record. A post-hearing brief may be filed in support of proposed findings and conclusions, either as part of the same document or in a separate document. Any party who fails to file timely with the administrative law judge any proposed finding or conclusion is deemed to have waived the right to raise in any subsequent filing or submission any issue not addressed in such party's proposed finding or conclusion.

(b) *Reply briefs.* Reply briefs may be filed within 15 days after the date on which the parties' proposed findings, conclusions, and order are due. Reply briefs must be strictly limited to responding to new matters, issues, or arguments raised in another party's papers. A party who has not filed proposed findings of fact and conclusions of law or a post-hearing brief may not file a reply brief.

(c) *Simultaneous filing required.* The administrative law judge shall not order the filing by any party of any brief or reply brief in advance of the other party's filing of its brief.

§ 390.67 Recommended decision and filing of record.

(a) *Filing of recommended decision and record.* Within 45 days after expiration of the time allowed for filing reply briefs under §390.66(b), the administrative law judge shall file with and certify to the Executive Secretary, for decision, the record of the proceeding. The record must include the administrative law judge's recommended decision, recommended findings of fact, recommended conclusions of law, and proposed order; all prehearing and hearing transcripts, exhibits, and rulings; and the motions, briefs, memoranda, and other supporting papers filed in connection with the hearing. The administrative law judge shall serve upon each party the recommended decision, findings, conclusions, and proposed order.

(b) *Filing of index.* At the same time the administrative law judge files with and certifies to the Board of Directors for final determination the record of the proceeding, the administrative law judge shall furnish to the Executive Secretary a certified index of the entire record of the proceeding. The certified index shall include, at a minimum, an entry for each paper, document or motion filed with the administrative law judge in the proceeding, the date of the filing, and the identity of the filer. The certified index shall also include an exhibit index containing, at a minimum, an entry consisting of exhibit number and title or description for: Each exhibit introduced and admitted into evidence at the hearing; each exhibit introduced but not admitted into evidence at the hearing; each exhibit introduced and admitted into evidence after the completion of the hearing; and each exhibit introduced but

§ 390.68

not admitted into evidence after the completion of the hearing.

§ 390.68 Exceptions to recommended decision.

(a) *Filing exceptions.* Within 30 days after service of the recommended decision, findings, conclusions, and proposed order under § 390.67, a party may file with the Executive Secretary written exceptions to the administrative law judge's recommended decision, findings, conclusions or proposed order, to the admission or exclusion of evidence, or to the failure of the administrative law judge to make a ruling proposed by a party. A supporting brief may be filed at the time the exceptions are filed, either as part of the same document or in a separate document.

(b) *Effect of failure to file or raise exceptions.* (1) Failure of a party to file exceptions to those matters specified in paragraph (a) of this section within the time prescribed is deemed a waiver of objection thereto.

(2) No exception need be considered by the Board of Directors if the party taking exception had an opportunity to raise the same objection, issue, or argument before the administrative law judge and failed to do so.

(c) *Contents.* (1) All exceptions and briefs in support of such exceptions must be confined to the particular matters in, or omissions from, the administrative law judge's recommendations to which that party takes exception.

(2) All exceptions and briefs in support of exceptions must set forth page or paragraph references to the specific parts of the administrative law judge's recommendations to which exception is taken, the page or paragraph references to those portions of the record relied upon to support each exception, and the legal authority relied upon to support each exception.

§ 390.69 Review by the Board of Directors.

(a) *Notice of submission to the Board of Directors.* When the Executive Secretary determines that the record in the proceeding is complete, the Board of Directors shall serve notice upon the parties that the proceeding has been submitted to the Board of Directors for final decision.

(b) *Oral argument before the Board of Directors.* Upon the initiative of the Board of Directors or on the written request of any party filed with the Executive Secretary within the time for filing exceptions, the Board of Directors may order and hear oral argument on the recommended findings, conclusions, decision, and order of the administrative law judge. A written request by a party must show good cause for oral argument and state reasons why arguments cannot be presented adequately in writing. A denial of a request for oral argument may be set forth in the Board of Director's final decision. Oral argument before the Board of Directors must be on the record.

(c) *Board of Director's final decision.* (1) Decisional employees may advise and assist the Board of Directors in the consideration and disposition of the case. The final decision of the Board of Directors will be based upon review of the entire record of the proceeding, except that the director may limit the issues to be reviewed to those findings and conclusions to which opposing arguments or exceptions have been filed by the parties.

(2) The Board of Directors shall render a final decision within 90 days after notification of the parties that the case has been submitted for final decision, or 90 days after oral argument, whichever is later, unless the Board of Directors orders that the action or any aspect thereof be remanded to the administrative law judge for further proceedings. Copies of the final decision and order of the Board of Directors shall be served upon each party to the proceeding, upon other persons required by statute, and, if directed by the Board of Directors or required by statute, upon any appropriate state or Federal supervisory authority.

§ 390.70 Stays pending judicial review.

The commencement of proceedings for judicial review of a final decision and order of the FDIC may not, unless specifically ordered by the Board of Directors or a reviewing court, operate as a stay of any order issued by the Board of Directors. The Board of Directors

Federal Deposit Insurance Corporation § 390.73

may, in its discretion, and on such terms as it finds just, stay the effectiveness of all or any part of its order pending a final decision on a petition for review of the order.

§ 390.71 Scope.

The rules and procedures in §§ 390.71 through 390.75 shall apply to those proceedings covered by §§ 390.30 through 390.70. In addition, §§ 390.30 through 390.75 shall apply to adjudicatory proceedings for which hearings on the record are provided for by the following statutory provisions:

(a) Proceedings under section 10(a)(2)(D) of the HOLA (12 U.S.C. 1467a(a)(2)(D)) to determine whether any person directly or indirectly exercises a controlling influence over the management or policies of a State savings association or any other company;

(b) [Reserved]; and

(c) Proceedings under section 15(c)(4) of the Securities and Exchange Act of 1934 (15 U.S.C. 78o(c)(4)) (Exchange Act) to determine whether any association or person subject to the jurisdiction of the FDIC pursuant to section 12(i) of the Exchange Act (15 U.S.C. 78*l*(i)) has failed to comply with the provisions of sections 12, 13, 14(a), 14(c), 14(d) or 14(f) of the Exchange Act.

§ 390.72 Appointment of Office of Financial Institution Adjudication.

Unless otherwise directed by the FDIC, all hearings under sections 390.30–390.75 shall be conducted by administrative law judges under the direction of the Office of Financial Institution Adjudication, 1700 G Street, NW., Washington, DC 20552.

§ 390.73 Discovery.

(a) *In general.* A party may take the deposition of an expert, or of a person, including another party, who has direct knowledge of matters that are non-privileged, relevant and material to the proceeding and where there is a need for the deposition. The deposition of experts shall be limited to those experts who are expected to testify at the hearing.

(b) *Notice.* A party desiring to take a deposition shall give reasonable notice in writing to the deponent and to every other party to the proceeding. The notice must state the time and place for taking the deposition and the name and address of the person to be deposed.

(c) *Time limits.* A party may take depositions at any time after the commencement of the proceeding, but no later than ten days before the scheduled hearing date, except with permission of the administrative law judge for good cause shown.

(d) *Conduct of the deposition.* The witness must be duly sworn, and each party shall have the right to examine the witness with respect to all non-privileged, relevant and material matters of which the witness has factual, direct and personal knowledge. Objections to questions or exhibits shall be in short form, stating the grounds for objection. Failure to object to questions or exhibits is not a waiver except where the grounds for the objection might have been avoided if the objection had been timely presented. The court reporter shall transcribe or otherwise record the witness's testimony, as agreed among the parties.

(e) *Protective orders.* At any time after notice of a deposition has been given, a party may file a motion for the issuance of a protective order. Such protective order may prohibit, terminate, or limit the scope or manner of the taking of a deposition. The administrative law judge shall grant such protective order upon a showing of sufficient grounds, including that the deposition:

(1) Is unreasonable, oppressive, excessive in scope, or unduly burdensome;

(2) Involves privileged, investigative, trial preparation, irrelevant or immaterial matters; or

(3) Is being conducted in bad faith or in such manner as to unreasonably annoy, embarrass, or oppress the deponent.

(f) *Fees.* Deposition witnesses, including expert witnesses, shall be paid the same expenses in the same manner as are paid witnesses in the district courts of the United States in proceedings in which the United States Government is a party. Expenses in accordance with this paragraph shall be paid by the party seeking to take the deposition.

§ 390.74

(g) *Deposition subpoenas.* (1) *Issuance.* At the request of a party, the administrative law judge shall issue a subpoena requiring the attendance of a witness at a deposition. The attendance of a witness may be required from any place in any state or territory that is subject to the jurisdiction of the United States or as otherwise permitted by law.

(2) *Service.* The party requesting the subpoena must serve it on the person named therein or upon that person's counsel, by any of the methods identified in § 390.40(d). The party serving the subpoena must file proof of service with the administrative law judge.

(3) *Motion to quash.* A person named in the subpoena or a party may file a motion to quash or modify the subpoena. A statement of the reasons for the motion must accompany it and a copy of the motion must be served on the party that requested the subpoena. The motion must be made prior to the time for compliance specified in the subpoena and not more than ten days after the date of service of the subpoena, or if the subpoena is served within 15 days of the hearing, within five days after the date of service.

(4) *Enforcement of deposition subpoena.* Enforcement of a deposition subpoena shall be in accordance with the procedures of § 390.56(d).

§ 390.74 Civil money penalties.

(a) *Assessment.* In the event of consent, or if upon the record developed at the hearing the Board of Directors finds that any of the grounds specified in the notice issued pursuant to § 390.47 have been established, the Executive Secretary may serve an order of assessment of civil money penalty upon the party concerned. The assessment order shall be effective immediately upon service or upon such other date as may be specified therein and shall remain effective and enforceable until it is stayed, modified, terminated, or set aside by the Board of Directors or by a reviewing court.

(b) *Payment.* (1) Civil penalties assessed pursuant to §§ 390.30 through 390.75 are payable and to be collected within 60 days after the issuance of the notice of assessment, unless the Board of Directors fixes a different time for payment where it determines that the purpose of the civil money penalty would be better served thereby; however, if a party has made a timely request for a hearing to challenge the assessment of the penalty, the party may not be required to pay such penalty until the Board of Directors has issued a final order of assessment following the hearing. In such instances, the penalty shall be paid within 60 days of service of such order unless the Board of Directors fixes a different time for payment. Notwithstanding the foregoing, the FDIC may seek to attach the party's assets or to have a receiver appointed to secure payment of the potential civil money penalty or other obligation in advance of the hearing in accordance with section 8(i)(4) of the FDIA (12 U.S.C. 1818(i)(4)).

(2) [Reserved]

(c) *Inflation adjustment.* Under the Federal Civil Monetary Penalties Inflation Adjustment Act of 1990 (28 U.S.C. 2461 note), FDIC must adjust for inflation the civil money penalties in statutes that it administers. The following chart displays the adjusted civil money penalties. The amounts in this chart apply to violations that occur after October 27, 2008:

U.S. Code citation	CMP description	New maximum amount
12 U.S.C. 1464(v)(4)	Reports of Condition—1st Tier	$2,200
12 U.S.C. 1464(v)(5)	Reports of Condition—2nd Tier	32,500
12 U.S.C. 1464(v)(6)	Reports of Condition—3rd Tier	1,375,000
12 U.S.C. 1467(d)	Refusal to Cooperate in Exam	7,500
12 U.S.C. 1467a(i)(2)	Holding Company Act Violation	32,500
12 U.S.C. 1467a(i)(3)	Holding Company Act Violation	32,500
12 U.S.C. 1467a(r)(1)	Late/Inaccurate Reports—1st Tier	2,200
12 U.S.C. 1467a(r)(2)	Late/Inaccurate Reports—2nd Tier	32,500
12 U.S.C. 1467a(r)(3)	Late/Inaccurate Reports—3rd Tier	1,375,000
12 U.S.C. 1817(j)(16)(A)	Change in Control—1st Tier	7,500
12 U.S.C. 1817(j)(16)(B)	Change in Control—2nd Tier	37,500
12 U.S.C. 1817(j)(16)(C)	Change in Control—3rd Tier	1,375,000
12 U.S.C. 1818(i)(2)(A)	Violation of Law or Unsafe or Unsound Practice—1st Tier	7,500

Federal Deposit Insurance Corporation § 390.75

U.S. Code citation	CMP description	New maximum amount
12 U.S.C. 1818(i)(2)(B)	Violation of Law or Unsafe or Unsound Practice—2nd Tier	37,500
12 U.S.C. 1818(i)(2)(C)	Violation of Law or Unsafe or Unsound Practice—3rd Tier	1,375,000
12 U.S.C. 1820(k)(6)(A)(ii)	Violation of Post Employment Restrictions	275,000
12 U.S.C. 1884	Violation of Security Rules	110
12 U.S.C. 3349(b)	Appraisals Violation—1st Tier	7,500
12 U.S.C. 3349(b)	Appraisals Violation—2nd Tier	37,500
12 U.S.C. 3349(b)	Appraisals Violation—3rd Tier	1,375,000
42 U.S.C. 4012a(f)	Flood Insurance	[1] 385
		[2] 135,000

[1] Per day.
[2] Per year.

§ 390.75 Additional procedures.

(a) *Replies to exceptions.* Replies to written exceptions to the administrative law judge's recommended decision, findings, conclusions or proposed order pursuant to § 390.68 shall be filed within 10 days of the date such written exceptions were required to be filed.

(b) *Motions.* All motions shall be filed with the administrative law judge and an additional copy shall be filed with the Executive Secretary, who receives adjudicatory filings; provided, however, that once the administrative law judge has certified the record to the Executive Secretary pursuant to § 390.67, all motions must be filed with the Board of Directors, to the attention of the Executive Secretary, within the 10-day period following the filing of exceptions allowed for the filing of replies to exceptions. Responses to such motions filed in a timely manner with the Board of Directors, other than motions for oral argument before the Board of Directors, shall be allowed pursuant to the procedures at § 390.52(d). No response is required for the Board of Directors to make a determination on a motion for oral argument.

(c) *Authority of administrative law judge.* In addition to the powers listed in § 390.34, the administrative law judge shall have the authority to deny any dispositive motion and shall follow the procedures set forth for motions for summary disposition at § 390.58 and partial summary disposition at § 390.59 in making determinations on such motions.

(d) *Notification of submission of proceeding to the Board of Directors.* Upon the expiration of the time for filing any exceptions, any replies to such exceptions or any motions and any ruling thereon, and after receipt of certified record, the Executive Secretary shall notify the parties within ten days of the submission of the proceeding to the Board of Directors for final determination.

(e) *Extensions of time for final determination.* The Board of Directors may, *sua sponte,* extend the time for final determination by signing an order of extension of time within the 90 day time period and notifying the parties of such extension thereafter.

(f) *Service upon the FDIC.* Service of any document upon the FDIC shall be made by filing with the Executive Secretary, in addition to the individuals and/or offices designated by the FDIC in its Notice issued pursuant to § 390.47, or such other means reasonably suited to provide notice of the person and/or office designated to receive filings.

(g) *Filings with the Board of Directors.* An additional copy of all materials required or permitted to be filed with or referred to the administrative law judge pursuant to this subpart shall be filed with the Executive Secretary. This rule shall not apply to the transcript of testimony and exhibits adduced at the hearing or to proposed exhibits submitted in advance of the hearing pursuant to an order of the administrative law judge under § 390.61. Materials required or permitted to be filed with or referred to the Board of Directors pursuant to this part shall be filed with the Executive Secretary, to the attention of the Board of Directors.

(h) *Presence of cameras and other recording devices.* The use of cameras and other recording devices, other than those used by the court reporter, shall be prohibited and excluded from the proceedings.

Subpart D—Rules for Investigative Proceedings and Formal Examination Proceedings

§ 390.80 Scope of subpart.

This subpart prescribes rules of practice and procedure applicable to the conduct of investigative proceedings under section 7(j)(15) of the Federal Deposit Insurance Act, as amended, 12 U.S.C. 1817(j)(15) ("FDIA"), section 8(n) of the FDIA, 12 U.S.C. 1818(n), or section 10(c) of the FDIA, 12 U.S.C. 1820(c). This subpart does not apply to adjudicatory proceedings as to which hearings are required by statute, the rules for which are contained in subpart C.

§ 390.81 Definitions.

As used in this subpart:

Board of Directors means the Board of Directors of the Federal Deposit Insurance Corporation or its designee;

Designated representative means the person or persons empowered by the Board of Directors to conduct an investigative proceeding or a formal examination proceeding;

FDIC means the Federal Deposit Insurance Corporation;

Formal examination proceeding means the administration of oaths and affirmations, taking and preserving of testimony, requiring the production of books, papers, correspondence, memoranda, and all other records, the issuance of subpoenas, and all related activities in connection with examination of State savings associations and their affiliates conducted pursuant to section 7(j)(15) of the FDIA, section 8(n) of the FDIA or section 10(c) of the FDIA;

General Counsel means the General Counsel of the Federal Deposit Insurance Corporation; and

Investigative proceeding means an investigation conducted under section 10(c) of the FDIA.

§ 390.82 Confidentiality of proceedings.

All formal examination proceedings shall be private and, unless otherwise ordered by the FDIC, all investigative proceedings shall also be private. Unless otherwise ordered or permitted by the FDIC, or required by law, and except as provided in §§ 390.83 and 390.84, the entire record of any investigative proceeding or formal examination proceeding, including the order initiating the proceeding, the transcript of such proceeding, and all documents and information obtained by the designated representative(s) during the course of said proceedings shall be confidential.

§ 390.83 Transcripts.

Transcripts or other recordings, if any, of investigative proceedings or formal examination proceedings shall be prepared solely by an official reporter or by any other person or means authorized by the designated representative. A person who has submitted documentary evidence or given testimony in an investigative proceeding or formal examination proceeding may procure a copy of his own documentary evidence or transcript of his own testimony upon payment of the cost thereof; *provided,* that a person seeking a transcript of his own testimony must file a written request with the designated representative stating the reason he desires to procure such transcript, and said persons may for good cause deny such request. In any event, any witness (or his counsel) shall have the right to inspect the transcript of the witness' own testimony.

§ 390.84 Rights of witnesses.

(a) Any person who is compelled or requested to furnish documentary evidence or give testimony at an investigative proceeding or formal examination proceeding shall have the right to examine, upon request, the order authorizing such proceeding. Copies of such resolution shall be furnished, for their retention, to such persons only with the written approval of the designated representative.

(b) Any witness at an investigative proceeding or formal examination proceeding may be accompanied and advised by an attorney personally representing that witness.

(1) Such attorney shall be a member in good standing of the bar of the highest court of any state, Commonwealth, possession, territory, or the District of Columbia, who has not been suspended or debarred from practice by the bar of any such political entity or before the FDIC in accordance with the provisions

Federal Deposit Insurance Corporation § 390.86

of subpart E and has not been excluded from the particular investigative proceeding or formal examination proceeding in accordance with paragraph (b)(3) of this section.

(2) Such attorney may advise the witness before, during, and after the taking of his testimony and may briefly question the witness, on the record, at the conclusion of his testimony, for the sole purpose of clarifying any of the answers the witness has given. During the taking of the testimony of a witness, such attorney may make summary notes solely for his use in representing his client. All witnesses shall be sequestered, and, unless permitted in the discretion of the designated representative, no witness or accompanying attorney may be permitted to be present during the taking of testimony of any other witness called in such proceeding. Neither attorney(s) for the association(s) that are the subjects of the investigative proceedings or formal examination proceedings, nor attorneys for any other interested persons, shall have any right to be present during the testimony of any witness not personally being represented by such attorney.

(3) The Board of Directors, for good cause, may exclude a particular attorney from further participation in any investigation in which the Board of Directors has found the attorney to have engaged in dilatory, obstructionist, egregious, contemptuous or contumacious conduct. The person conducting an investigation may report to the Board of Directors instances of apparently dilatory, obstructionist, egregious, contemptuous or contumacious conduct on the part of an attorney. After due notice to the attorney, the FDIC may take such action as the circumstances warrant based upon a written record evidencing the conduct of the attorney in that investigation or such other or additional written or oral presentation as the Board of Directors may permit or direct.

§ 390.85 Obstruction of the proceedings.

The designated representative shall report to the Board of Directors any instances where any witness or counsel has engaged in dilatory, obstructionist, or contumacious conduct or has otherwise violated any provision of this part during the course of an investigative proceeding or formal examination proceeding; and the Board of Directors may take such action as the circumstances warrant, including the exclusion of counsel from further participation in such proceeding.

§ 390.86 Subpoenas.

(a) *Service.* Service of a subpoena in connection with any investigative proceeding or formal examination proceeding shall be effected in the following manner:

(1) *Service upon a natural person.* Service of a subpoena upon a natural person may be effected by handing it to such person; by leaving it at his office with the person in charge thereof, or, if there is no one in charge, by leaving it in a conspicuous place therein; by leaving it at his dwelling place or usual place of abode with some person of suitable age and discretion then residing therein; by mailing it to him by registered or certified mail or by an express delivery service at his last known address; or by any method whereby actual notice is given to him.

(2) *Service upon other persons.* When the person to be served is not a natural person, service of the subpoena may be effected by handing the subpoena to a registered agent for service, or to any officer, director, or agent in charge of any office of such person; by mailing it to any such representative by registered or certified mail or by an express delivery service at his last known address; or by any method whereby actual notice is given to such person.

(b) *Motions to quash.* Any person to whom a subpoena is directed may, prior to the time specified therein for compliance, but in no event more than 10 days after the date of service of such subpoena, apply to the General Counsel or his designee to quash or modify such subpoena, accompanying such application with a statement of the reasons therefor. The General Counsel or his designee, as appropriate, may:

(1) Deny the application;

(2) Quash or revoke the subpoena;

(3) Modify the subpoena; or

(4) Condition the granting of the application on such terms as the General

§ 390.90

Counsel or his designee determines to be just, reasonable, and proper.

(c) *Attendance of witnesses.* Subpoenas issued in connection with an investigative proceeding or formal examination proceeding may require the attendance and/or testimony of witnesses from any State or territory of the United States and the production by such witnesses of documentary or other tangible evidence at any designated place where the proceeding is being (or is to be) conducted. Foreign nationals are subject to such subpoenas if such service is made upon a duly authorized agent located in the United States.

(d) *Witness fees and mileage.* Witnesses summoned in any proceeding under this part shall be paid the same fees and mileage that are paid witnesses in the district courts of the United States. Such fees and mileage need not be tendered when the subpoena is issued on behalf of the FDIC by any of its designated representatives.

Subpart E—Practice Before the FDIC

§ 390.90 Scope of subpart.

This subpart prescribes rules with regard to general practice before the FDIC on one's own behalf or in a representative capacity and prescribes rules describing the circumstances under which attorneys, accountants, appraisers, or other persons may be suspended or debarred, either temporarily or permanently, from practicing before the FDIC. In connection with any particular matter, reference also should be made to any special requirements of procedure and practice that may be contained in the particular statute involved or the rules and forms adopted by the FDIC thereunder, which special requirements are controlling. In addition to any suspension hereunder, a person may be excluded from further participation under parts 390 and 391 from an adjudicatory proceeding in accordance with § 390.35(a)(1), from a removal hearing in accordance with § 390.12, or from an investigatory proceeding in accordance with § 390.84(b)(2). Furthermore, no person who has been suspended or debarred from practice before the FDIC in accordance with the provisions of this subpart may submit to the FDIC, either directly or on behalf of an interested party, any written documents or petitions otherwise permitted under the Administrative Procedure Act.

§ 390.91 Definitions.

As used in this subpart:

Attorney means any person who is a member in good standing of the bar of the highest court of any State, possession, territory, Commonwealth or the District of Columbia;

Executive Secretary means the Executive Secretary of the FDIC;

FDIC means the Federal Deposit Insurance Corporation;

OTS means the Office of Thrift Supervision;

Practice means transacting any business with the FDIC, including:

(1) The representation of another person at any adjudicatory, investigatory, removal or rulemaking proceeding conducted before the FDIC, a presiding officer or the FDIC's staff, including those proceedings covered in subparts B, C, and D;

(2) The preparation of any statement, opinion, financial statement, appraisal report, audit report, or other document or report by any attorney, accountant, appraiser or other licensed expert which is filed with or submitted to the FDIC, with such expert's consent or knowledge in connection with any application or other filing with the FDIC;

(3) A presentation to the FDIC, a presiding officer or the FDIC's staff at a conference or meeting relating to an association's or other person's rights, privileges or liabilities under the laws administered by the FDIC and rules and regulations promulgated thereunder;

(4) Any business correspondence or communication with the FDIC, a presiding officer or the FDIC's staff;

(5) The transaction of any other formal business with the FDIC on behalf of another, in the capacity of an attorney, accountant, appraiser or other licensed expert; and

Presiding officer includes the Board of Directors or an administrative law judge appointed under section 3105 or detailed pursuant to section 3344 of title 5 of the U.S. Code and, as used in this subpart, the term shall be construed to refer to whichever of the above-identified individuals presides at a hearing or other proceeding, except as otherwise specified in the text.

§ 390.92 **Who may practice.**

(a) *By non-attorneys.* (1) An individual may appear on his own behalf (*pro se*); a member of a partnership may represent the partnership; a bona fide and duly authorized officer of a corporation, trust or association may represent the corporation, trust or association; and an officer or employee of a commission, department or political subdivision may represent that commission, department or political subdivision before the FDIC.

(2) Any accountant, appraiser or other licensed expert may practice before the FDIC in a professional capacity.

(b) *By attorneys.* Any association or other person may be represented in any proceeding or other matter before the FDIC by an attorney.

(c) *Authority to act as representative.* Any licensed expert or professional transacting business with the FDIC in a representative capacity may be required to show his authority to act in such capacity.

§ 390.93 **Suspension and debarment.**

(a) The FDIC may censure any person practicing before it or may deny, temporarily or permanently, the privilege of any person to practice before it if such person is found by the FDIC, after notice of and opportunity for hearing in the matter,

(1) Not to possess the requisite qualifications to represent others,

(2) To be lacking in character or professional integrity,

(3) To have engaged in any dilatory, obstructionist, egregious, contemptuous, contumacious or other unethical or improper professional conduct before the OTS or FDIC, or

(4) To have willfully violated, or willfully aided and abetted the violation of, any provision of the laws administered by the OTS or FDIC or the rules and regulations promulgated thereunder.

(b) *Automatic suspension.* (1) Any person who, after being licensed as a professional or expert by any competent authority, has been convicted of a felony, or of a misdemeanor involving moral turpitude, personal dishonesty or breach of trust, shall be suspended forthwith from practicing before the FDIC.

(2) Any accountant, appraiser or other licensed expert whose license to practice has been revoked in any State, possession, territory, Commonwealth or the District of Columbia, shall be suspended forthwith from practice before the FDIC.

(3) Any attorney who has been suspended or disbarred by a court of the United States or in any State, possession, territory, Commonwealth or the District of Columbia, shall be suspended forthwith from practicing before the FDIC.

(4) A conviction (including a judgment or order on a plea of *nolo contendere*), revocation, suspension or disbarment under paragraphs (b)(1), (b)(2) and (b)(3) of this section shall be deemed to have occurred when the convicting, revoking, suspending or disbarring agency or tribunal enters its judgment or order, regardless of whether an appeal is pending or could be taken.

(5) For purposes of this part, it shall be irrelevant that any attorney, accountant, appraiser or other licensed expert who has been suspended, disbarred or otherwise disqualified from practice before a court or in a jurisdiction continues in professional good standing before other courts or in other jurisdictions.

(c) *Temporary suspension.* (1) The FDIC, with due regard to the public interest and without preliminary hearing, by order, may temporarily suspend any person from appearing or practicing before it who, by name, has been:

(i) Permanently enjoined (whether by consent, default or summary judgment or after trial) by any court of competent jurisdiction or by the OTS or FDIC itself in a final administrative order, by reason of his misconduct in any action brought by the OTS or FDIC based upon violations of, or aiding and abetting the violation of, the Home Owners' Loan Act of 1933, as amended, 12 U.S.C. 1461 *et seq.*, the Federal Deposit Insurance Act, as amended, 12

§ 390.94

U.S.C. 1811 et seq. or any provision of the Securities Exchange Act of 1934, as amended, 15 U.S.C. 78a, et seq., which is administered by the FDIC, or of any rule or regulation promulgated thereunder; or

(ii) Found by any court of competent jurisdiction (whether by consent, default, or summary judgment, or after trial) in any action brought by the OTS or FDIC to which he is a party or found by the OTS or FDIC (whether by consent, default, upon summary judgment or after hearing) in any administrative proceeding in which the OTS or FDIC is a complainant and he is a party, to have willfully committed, caused or aided or abetted a violation of any provision of the Home Owners' Loan Act of 1933, as amended, 12 U.S.C. 1461 et seq., the Federal Deposit Insurance Act, as amended, 12 U.S.C. 1811 et seq. or any provision of the Securities Exchange Act of 1934, as amended, 15 U.S.C. 78a, et seq., which is administered by the OTS or FDIC, or of any rule or regulation promulgated thereunder.

(2) An order of temporary suspension shall become effective when served by certified or registered mail directed to the last known business or residential address of the person involved. No order of temporary suspension shall be entered by the FDIC pursuant to paragraph (c)(1) of this section more than three months after the final judgment or order entered in a judicial or administrative proceeding described in paragraphs (c)(1)(i) or (ii) of this section has become effective and all review or appeal procedures have been completed or are no longer available.

(3) Any person temporarily suspended from appearing and practicing before the OTS or FDIC in accordance with paragraph (c)(1) of this section may, within 30 days after service upon him of the order of temporary suspension, petition the FDIC to lift such suspension. If no petition is received by the FDIC within those 30 days, the suspension shall become permanent.

(4) Within 30 days after the filing of a petition in accordance with paragraph (c)(3) of this section, the FDIC shall either lift the temporary suspension or set the matter down for hearing at a time and place to be designated by the FDIC, or both. After opportunity for hearing, the FDIC may censure the petitioner or may suspend the petitioner from appearing or practicing before the FDIC temporarily or permanently. In every case in which the temporary suspension has not been lifted, the hearing and any other action taken pursuant to this paragraph (c)(4) shall be expedited by the FDIC in order to ensure the petitioner's right to address the allegations against him.

(5) In any hearing held on a petition filed in accordance with paragraph (c)(3) of this section, a showing that the petitioner has been enjoined or has been found to have committed, caused or aided or abetted violations as described in paragraph (c)(1) of this section, without more, may be a basis for suspension or debarment; that showing having been made, the burden shall then be on the petitioner to show why he should not be censured or be temporarily or permanently suspended or debarred. A petitioner will not be permitted to contest any findings against him or any admissions made by him in the judicial or administrative proceedings upon which the proposed censure, suspension or debarment is based. A petitioner who has consented to the entry of a permanent injunction or order as described in paragraph (c)(1)(i) of this section, without admitting the facts set forth in the complaint, shall nevertheless be presumed for all purposes under this section to have been enjoined or ordered by reason of the misconduct alleged in the complaint.

§ 390.94 Reinstatement.

(a) Any person who is suspended from practicing before the OTS or FDIC under § 390.93(a) or (c) of may file an application for reinstatement at any time. Denial of the privilege of practicing before the FDIC shall continue unless and until the applicant has been reinstated by order of the FDIC for good cause shown.

(b) Any person suspended under paragraph § 390.93(b) shall be reinstated by the FDIC, upon appropriate application, if all of the grounds for application of the provisions of § 390.93(b) subsequently are removed by a reversal of the conviction or termination of the suspension, disbarment or revocation.

Federal Deposit Insurance Corporation

An application for reinstatement on any other grounds by any person suspended under § 390.93(b) may be filed at any time. Such application shall state with particularity the relief desired and the grounds therefor and shall include supporting evidence, when available. The applicant shall be accorded an opportunity for an informal hearing in the matter, unless the applicant has waived a hearing in the application and, instead, has elected to have the matter determined on the basis of written submissions. Such hearing shall utilize the procedures established in §§ 390.12 and 390.16(a). However, such suspension shall continue unless and until the applicant has been reinstated by order of the FDIC for good cause shown.

§ 390.95 Duty to file information concerning adverse judicial or administrative action.

Any person appearing or practicing before the FDIC who has been or is the subject of a conviction, suspension, debarment, license revocation, injunction or other finding of the kind described in § 390.93(b) or (c) in an action not instituted by the OTS or FDIC shall promptly file a copy of the relevant order, judgment or decree with the Executive Secretary together with any related opinion or statement of the agency or tribunal involved. Any person who fails to so file a copy of the order, judgment or decree within 30 days after the entry of the order, judgment or decree, or the date such person initiates practice before the FDIC, for that reason alone may be disqualified from practicing before the FDIC until such time as the appropriate filing shall be made, but neither the filing of these documents nor the failure of a person to file them shall in any way impair the operation of any other provision of this subpart.

§ 390.96 Proceeding under this subpart.

(a) All hearings required or permitted to be held under § 390.93(a) and (c) of this subpart shall be held before a presiding officer utilizing the procedures established in the rules of practice and procedure in adjudicatory proceedings under subpart C of this part.

(b) All hearings held under this subpart shall be closed to the public unless the FDIC on its own motion or upon the request of a party otherwise directs.

(c) Any proceeding brought under any section of this subpart shall not preclude a proceeding under any other section of this subpart or any other part of the FDIC's regulations.

§ 390.97 Removal, suspension, or debarment of independent public accountants and accounting firms performing audit services.

(a) *Scope.* This subpart, which implements section 36(g)(4) of the Federal Deposit Insurance Act (FDIA), (12 U.S.C. 1831m(g)(4)), provides rules and procedures for the removal, suspension, or debarment of independent public accountants and their accounting firms from performing independent audit and attestation services required by section 36 of the FDIA for insured State savings associations.

(b) *Definitions.* As used in this section, the following terms have the meaning given below unless the context requires otherwise:

Accounting firm. The term *accounting firm* means a corporation, proprietorship, partnership, or other business firm providing audit services.

Audit services. The term *audit services* means any service required to be performed by an independent public accountant by section 36 of the FDIA and part 363, including attestation services. Audit services include any service performed with respect to a savings and loan holding company of a State savings association that is used to satisfy requirements imposed by section 36 of the FDIA or part 363 on that State savings association.

Independent public accountant. The term *independent public accountant* means any individual who performs or participates in providing audit services.

(c) *Removal, suspension, or debarment of independent public accountants.* The FDIC may remove, suspend, or debar an independent public accountant from performing audit services for State savings associations that are subject to section 36 of the FDIA if, after service

§ 390.97

of a notice of intention and opportunity for hearing in the matter, the FDIC finds that the independent public accountant:

(1) Lacks the requisite qualifications to perform audit services;

(2) Has knowingly or recklessly engaged in conduct that results in a violation of applicable professional standards, including those standards and conflicts of interest provisions applicable to independent public accountants through the Sarbanes-Oxley Act of 2002, Public Law 107–204, 116 Stat. 745 (2002) (Sarbanes-Oxley Act), and developed by the Public Company Accounting Oversight Board and the Securities and Exchange Commission;

(3) Has engaged in negligent conduct in the form of:

(i) A single instance of highly unreasonable conduct that results in a violation of applicable professional standards in circumstances in which an independent public accountant knows, or should know, that heightened scrutiny is warranted; or

(ii) Repeated instances of unreasonable conduct, each resulting in a violation of applicable professional standards, that indicate a lack of competence to perform audit services;

(4) Has knowingly or recklessly given false or misleading information or knowingly or recklessly participated in any way in the giving of false or misleading information to the FDIC or any officer or employee of the FDIC;

(5) Has engaged in, or aided and abetted, a material and knowing or reckless violation of any provision of the Federal banking or securities laws or the rules and regulations thereunder, or any other law;

(6) Has been removed, suspended, or debarred from practice before any federal or state agency regulating the banking, insurance, or securities industries, other than by action listed in paragraph (j) of this section, on grounds relevant to the provision of audit services; or

(7) Is suspended or debarred for cause from practice as an accountant by any duly constituted licensing authority of any state, possession, commonwealth, or the District of Columbia.

(d) *Removal, suspension or debarment of an accounting firm.* If the FDIC determines that there is good cause for the removal, suspension, or debarment of a member or employee of an accounting firm under paragraph (c) of this section, the FDIC also may remove, suspend, or debar such firm or one or more offices of such firm. In considering whether to remove, suspend, or debar an accounting firm or office thereof, and the term of any sanction against an accounting firm under this section, the FDIC may consider, for example:

(1) The gravity, scope, or repetition of the act or failure to act that constitutes good cause for the removal, suspension, or debarment;

(2) The adequacy of, and adherence to, applicable policies, practices, or procedures for the accounting firm's conduct of its business and the performance of audit services;

(3) The selection, training, supervision, and conduct of members or employees of the accounting firm involved in the performance of audit services;

(4) The extent to which managing partners or senior officers of the accounting firm have participated, directly or indirectly through oversight or review, in the act or failure to act; and

(5) The extent to which the accounting firm has, since the occurrence of the act or failure to act, implemented corrective internal controls to prevent its recurrence.

(e) *Remedies.* The remedies provided in this section are in addition to any other remedies the FDIC may have under any other applicable provisions of law, rule, or regulation.

(f) *Proceedings to remove, suspend, or debar.* (1) The FDIC may initiate a proceeding to remove, suspend, or debar an independent public accountant or accounting firm from performing audit services by issuing a written notice of intention to take such action that names the individual or firm as a respondent and describes the nature of the conduct that constitutes good cause for such action.

(2) An independent public accountant or accounting firm named as a respondent in the notice issued under paragraph (f)(1) of this section may request a hearing on the allegations in the notice. Hearings conducted under this paragraph shall be conducted in the

Federal Deposit Insurance Corporation § 390.97

same manner as other hearings under the Uniform Rules of Practice and Procedure contained in subpart C.

(g) *Immediate suspension from performing audit services.* (1) If the FDIC serves written notice of intention to remove, suspend, or debar an independent public accountant or accounting firm from performing audit services, the FDIC may, with due regard for the public interest and without preliminary hearing, immediately suspend an independent public accountant or accounting firm from performing audit services for savings associations, if the FDIC:

(i) Has a reasonable basis to believe that the independent public accountant or accounting firm engaged in conduct (specified in the notice served upon the independent public accountant or accounting firm under paragraph (f) of this section) that would constitute grounds for removal, suspension, or debarment under paragraph (c) or (d) of this section;

(ii) Determines that immediate suspension is necessary to avoid immediate harm to an insured depository institution or its depositors or to the depository system as a whole; and

(iii) Serves such independent public accountant or accounting firm with written notice of the immediate suspension.

(2) An immediate suspension notice issued under this paragraph will become effective upon service. Such suspension will remain in effect until the date the FDIC dismisses the charges contained in the notice of intention, or the effective date of a final order of removal, suspension, or debarment issued by the FDIC to the independent public accountant or accounting firm.

(h) *Petition to stay.* (1) Any independent public accountant or accounting firm immediately suspended from performing audit services in accordance with paragraph (g) of this section may, within 10 calendar days after service of the notice of immediate suspension, file a petition with the FDIC for a stay of such suspension. If no petition is filed within 10 calendar days, the immediate suspension shall remain in effect.

(2) Upon receipt of a stay petition, the FDIC will designate a presiding officer who shall fix a place and time (not more than 10 calendar days after receipt of such petition, unless extended at the request of the petitioner), at which the immediately suspended party may appear, personally or through counsel, to submit written materials and oral argument. Any FDIC employee engaged in investigative or prosecuting functions for the FDIC in a case may not, in that or a factually related case, serve as a presiding officer or participate or advise in the decision of the presiding officer or of the FDIC, except as witness or counsel in the proceeding. In the sole discretion of the presiding officer, upon a specific showing of compelling need, oral testimony of witnesses may also be presented. In hearings held pursuant to this paragraph, there will be no discovery and the provisions of §§ 390.35 through 390.41, 390.45, and 390.50 of the Uniform Rules will apply.

(3) Within 30 calendar days after the hearing, the presiding officer shall issue a decision. The presiding officer will grant a stay upon a demonstration that a substantial likelihood exists of the respondent's success on the issues raised by the notice of intention and that, absent such relief, the respondent will suffer immediate and irreparable injury, loss, or damage. In the absence of such a demonstration, the presiding officer will notify the parties that the immediate suspension will be continued pending the completion of the administrative proceedings pursuant to the notice.

(4) The parties may seek review of the presiding officer's decision by filing a petition for review with the presiding officer within 10 calendar days after service of the decision. Replies must be filed within 10 calendar days after the petition filing date. Upon receipt of a petition for review and any reply, the presiding officer must promptly certify the entire record to the Board of Directors. Within 60 calendar days of the presiding officer's certification, the Board of Directors shall issue an order notifying the affected party whether or not the immediate suspension should be continued or reinstated. The order shall state the basis of the Board of Director's decision.

§ 390.97

(i) *Scope of any order of removal, suspension, or debarment.* (1) Except as provided in paragraph (i)(2) of this section, any independent public accountant or accounting firm that has been removed, suspended (including an immediate suspension), or debarred from performing audit services by the FDIC may not, while such order is in effect, perform audit services for any State savings association.

(2) An order of removal, suspension (including an immediate suspension), or debarment may, at the discretion of the FDIC, be made applicable to a limited number of State savings associations. (limited scope order).

(j) *Automatic removal, suspension, and debarment.* (1) An independent public accountant or accounting firm may not perform audit services for a State savings association if the independent public accountant or accounting firm:

(i) Is subject to a final order of removal, suspension, or debarment (other than a limited scope order) issued by the Board of Governors of the Federal Reserve System, the Comptroller of the Currency, or the FDIC under section 36 of the FDIA;

(ii) Is subject to a temporary suspension or permanent revocation of registration or a temporary or permanent suspension or bar from further association with any registered public accounting firm issued by the Public Company Accounting Oversight Board or the Securities and Exchange Commission under sections 105(c)(4)(A) or (B) of the Sarbanes-Oxley Act (15 U.S.C. 7215(c)(4)(A) or (B)); or

(iii) Is subject to an order of suspension or denial of the privilege of appearing or practicing before the Securities and Exchange Commission.

(2) Upon written request, the FDIC, for good cause shown, may grant written permission to an independent public accountant or accounting firm to perform audit services for State savings associations. The request must contain a concise statement of action requested. The FDIC may require the applicant to submit additional information.

(k) *Notice of removal, suspension, or debarment.* (1) Upon issuance of a final order for removal, suspension, or debarment of an independent public accountant or accounting firm from providing audit services, the FDIC shall make the order publicly available and provide notice of the order to the other Federal banking agencies.

(2) An independent public accountant or accounting firm that provides audit services to a State savings association must provide the FDIC with written notice of:

(i) Any currently effective order or other action described in paragraphs (c)(6) through (c)(7) or paragraphs (j)(1)(ii) through (iii) of this section; and

(ii) Any currently effective action by the Public Company Accounting Oversight Board under sections 105(c)(4)(C) or (G) of the Sarbanes-Oxley Act (15 U.S.C. 7215(c)(4)(C) or (G)).

(3) Written notice required by this paragraph shall be given no later than 15 calendar days following the effective date of an order or action or 15 calendar days before an independent public accountant or accounting firm accepts an engagement to provide audit services, whichever date is earlier.

(l) *Application for reinstatement.* (1) Unless otherwise ordered by the FDIC, an independent public accountant, accounting firm, or office of a firm that was removed, suspended or debarred under this section may apply for reinstatement in writing at any time. The request shall contain a concise statement of action requested. The FDIC may require the applicant to submit additional information.

(2) An applicant for reinstatement under paragraph (l)(1) of this section may, in the FDIC's sole discretion, be afforded a hearing. The independent public accountant or accounting firm shall bear the burden of going forward with an application and the burden of proving the grounds supporting the application. The FDIC may, in its sole discretion, direct that any reinstatement proceeding be limited to written submissions. The removal, suspension, or debarment shall continue until the FDIC, for good cause shown, has reinstated the applicant or until, in the case of a suspension, the suspension period has expired. The filing of a petition for reinstatement shall not stay

Federal Deposit Insurance Corporation § 390.101

the effectiveness of the removal, suspension, or debarment of an independent public accountant or accounting firm.

Subpart F—Application Processing Procedures

§ 390.100 What does this subpart do?

(a) This subpart explains the FDIC's procedures for processing applications, notices, or filings (applications) under parts 390 and 391 for State savings associations. Except as provided in paragraph (b) of this section, §§ 390.103 through 390.110 and §§ 390.126 through 390.135 apply whenever an FDIC regulation requires any person (you) to file an application with the FDIC. Sections 390.111 through 390.125, however, only apply when a FDIC regulation incorporates the procedures in those sections or where otherwise required by the FDIC.

(b) This subpart does not apply to any of the following:

(1) An application related to a transaction under section 13(c) or (k) of the Federal Deposit Insurance Act, 12 U.S.C. 1823(c) or (k).

(2) A request for reconsideration, modification, or appeal of a final FDIC action.

(3) A request related to litigation, an enforcement proceeding, a supervisory directive or supervisory agreement. Such requests include a request seeking approval under, modification of, or termination of an order issued under subparts C or D, a supervisory agreement, a supervisory directive, a consent merger agreement or a document negotiated in settlement of an enforcement matter or other litigation, unless an applicable FDIC regulation specifically requires an application under this subpart.

(4) An application filed under a FDIC regulation that prescribes other application processing procedures and time frames for the approval of applications.

(c) If a FDIC regulation for a specific type of application prescribes some application processing procedures, or time frames, the FDIC will apply this subpart to the extent necessary to process the application. For example, if a FDIC regulation for a specific type of application does not identify time periods for the processing of an application, the time periods in this subpart apply.

§ 390.101 Do the same procedures apply to all applications under this subpart?

The FDIC processes applications for State savings associations under this subpart using two procedures, expedited treatment and standard treatment. To determine which treatment applies, you may use the following chart:

If . . .	Then the FDIC will process your application under . . .
(a) The applicable regulation does not specifically state that expedited treatment is available	Standard treatment.
(b) You are not a State savings association	Standard treatment.
(c) Your composite rating is 3, 4, or 5. The composite rating is the composite numeric rating that the FDIC or the other federal banking regulator assigned to you under the Uniform Financial Institutions Rating System or under a comparable rating system. The composite rating refers to the rating assigned and provided to you, in writing, as a result of the most recent examination.	Standard treatment.
(d) Your Community Reinvestment Act (CRA) rating is Needs to Improve or Substantial Noncompliance. The CRA rating is the Community Reinvestment Act performance rating that the FDIC or the other federal banking regulator assigned and provided to you, in writing, as a result of the most recent compliance examination. See, for example, 12 CFR 195.28.	Standard treatment.
(e) Your compliance rating is 3, 4, or 5. The compliance rating is the numeric rating that the FDIC or the other federal banking regulator assigned to you under the FDIC compliance rating system, or a comparable rating system used by the other federal banking regulator. The compliance rating refers to the rating assigned and provided to you, in writing, as a result of the most recent compliance examination.	Standard treatment.
(f) You fail any one of your capital requirements under subpart Z	Standard treatment.
(g) The FDIC has notified you that you are an association in troubled condition	Standard treatment.
(h) Neither the FDIC nor any other federal banking regulator has assigned you a composite rating, a CRA rating or a compliance rating.	Standard treatment.
(i) You do not meet any of the criteria listed in paragraphs (a) through (h) of this section	Expedited treatment.

773

§ 390.102 How does the FDIC compute time periods under this subpart?

In computing time periods under this subpart, the FDIC does not include the day of the act or event that commences the time period. When the last day of a time period is a Saturday, Sunday, or Federal holiday, the time period runs until the end of the next day that is not a Saturday, Sunday, or Federal holiday.

§ 390.103 Must I meet with the FDIC before I file my application?

(a) *Chart.* To determine whether you must attend a pre-filing meeting before you file an application, please consult the following chart:

If you file . . .	Then . . .
An application to acquire control of a State savings association.	The FDIC may require you to meet with the FDIC before filing your application and may require you to submit a draft business plan or other relevant information before this meeting.

(b) *Contacting the appropriate FDIC region.* (1) You must contact the appropriate FDIC region a reasonable time before you file an application described in paragraph (a) of this section. Unless paragraph (a) already requires a pre-filing meeting or a draft business plan, the appropriate FDIC region will determine whether it will require a pre-filing meeting, and whether you must submit a business plan or other relevant information before the meeting. The appropriate FDIC region will also establish a schedule for any meeting and the submission of any information.

(2) All other applicants are encouraged to contact the appropriate FDIC region to determine whether a pre-filing meeting or the submission of a draft business plan or other relevant information would expedite the application review process.

§ 390.104 What information must I include in my draft business plan?

If you are required to submit a draft business plan under § 309.103, your plan must:

(a) Clearly and completely describe the State savings association's projected operations and activities;

(b) Describe the risks associated with the transaction and the impact of this transaction on any existing activities and operations of the State savings association, including financial projections for a minimum of three years;

(c) Identify the majority of the proposed board of directors and the key senior executive officers (as defined in § 390.361) of the State savings association and demonstrate that these individuals have the expertise to prudently manage the activities and operations described in the savings association's draft business plan; and

(d) Demonstrate how applicable requirements regarding serving the credit and lending needs in the market areas served by the State savings association will be met.

§ 390.105 What type of application must I file?

(a) *Expedited treatment.* If you are eligible for expedited treatment under § 390.101, you may file your application in the form of a notice that includes all information required by the applicable substantive regulation. If the FDIC has designated a form for your notice, you must file that form. Your notice is an application for the purposes of all statutory and regulatory references to "applications."

(b) *Standard treatment.* If you are subject to standard treatment under § 390.101, you must file your application following all applicable substantive regulations and guidelines governing the filing of applications. If the FDIC has a designated form for your application, you must file that form.

(c) *Waiver requests.* If you want the FDIC to waive a requirement that you provide certain information with the notice or application, you must include a written waiver request:

(1) Describing the requirement to be waived and

(2) Explaining why the information is not needed to enable the FDIC to evaluate your notice or application under applicable standards.

Federal Deposit Insurance Corporation

§ 390.108

§ 390.106 What information must I provide with my application?

(a) *Required information.* You may obtain information about required certifications, other regulations and guidelines affecting particular notices and applications, appropriate forms, and instructions from the appropriate FDIC region.

(b) *Captions and exhibits.* You must caption the original application and required copies with the type of filing, and must include all exhibits and other pertinent documents with the original application and all required copies. You are not required to include original signatures on copies if you include a copy of the signed signature page or the copy otherwise indicates that the original was signed.

§ 390.107 May I keep portions of my application confidential?

(a) *Confidentiality.* The FDIC makes submissions under this subpart available to the public, but may keep portions of your application confidential based on the rules in this section.

(b) *Confidentiality request.* (1) You may request the FDIC to keep portions of your application confidential. You must submit your request in writing with your application and must explain in detail how your request is consistent with the standards under the Freedom of Information Act (5 U.S.C. 552) and part 309 of this chapter. For example, you should explain how you will be substantially harmed by public disclosure of the information. You must separately bind and mark the portions of the application you consider confidential and the portions you consider nonconfidential.

(2) The FDIC will not treat as confidential the portion of your application describing how you plan to meet your Community Reinvestment Act (CRA) objectives. The FDIC will make information in your CRA plan, including any information incorporated by reference from other parts of your application, available to the public upon request.

(c) *FDIC determination on confidentiality.* The FDIC will determine whether information that you designate as confidential may be withheld from the public under the Freedom of Information Act (5 U.S.C. 552) and part 309 of this chapter. The FDIC will advise you before it makes information you designate as confidential available to the public.

§ 390.108 Where do I file my application?

(a) *Appropriate FDIC region.* (1) You must file the original application and the number of copies indicated on the applicable form with the appropriate FDIC region. The appropriate FDIC region addresses are listed in paragraph (a)(2) of this section. If the form does not indicate the number of copies you must file or if FDIC has not prescribed a form for your application, you must file the original application and two copies.

(2) The addresses of appropriate FDIC region and the states covered by each office are:

Region	Office address	States served
New York	350 Fifth Avenue, Suite 1200, New York, NY 10118.	Connecticut, Delaware, District of Columbia, Maine, Maryland, Massachusetts, New Hampshire, New Jersey, New York, Pennsylvania, Puerto Rico, Rhode Island, Vermont, Virgin Islands.
Atlanta	10 Tenth Street, NE., Suite 800, Atlanta, GA 30309–3906.	Alabama, Florida, Georgia, North Carolina, South Carolina, Virginia, West Virginia.
Chicago	300 South Riverside Plaza, Suite 1700, Chicago, Illinois 60606.	Illinois, Indiana, Kentucky, Ohio, Michigan, Wisconsin.
Kansas	1100 Walnut St., Suite 2100, Kansas City, MO 64106.	Iowa, Kansas, Minnesota, Missouri, Nebraska, North Dakota, South Dakota.
Dallas	1601 Bryan Street, Dallas, TX 75201	Arkansas, Colorado, Louisiana, Mississippi, New Mexico, Oklahoma, Tennessee, Texas.
San Francisco	25 Jessie Street at Ecker Square, Suite 2300, San Francisco, CA 94105–2780.	Alaska, Arizona, California, Guam, Hawaii, Idaho, Montana, Nevada, Northern Mariana Islands, Oregon, Utah, Washington, Wyoming.

§ 390.109

(b) *Additional filings with FDIC headquarters.* (1) In addition to filing in the appropriate FDIC region, if your application involves a significant issue of law or policy or if an applicable regulation or form directs you to file with FDIC Headquarters, you must also file copies of your application with the Risk Management and Applications Section at FDIC headquarters, 550 17th Street, NW., Washington, DC 20429. You must file the number of copies indicated on the applicable form. If the form does not indicate the number of copies you must file or if FDIC has not prescribed a form for your application, you must file three copies.

(2)(i) You may request a list of applications involving significant issues of law or policy by contacting appropriate FDIC region.

(ii) The FDIC reserves the right to identify significant issues of law or policy in a particular application. The FDIC will advise you, in writing, if it makes this determination.

§ 390.109 What is the filing date of my application?

(a) Your application's filing date is the date that you complete all of the following requirements.

(1) You attend a pre-filing meeting and submit a draft business plan or relevant information, if the FDIC requires you to do so under § 390.103.

(2) You file your application and all required copies with the FDIC, as described under § 390.108.

(i) If you are required to file with an appropriate FDIC region and with the FDIC headquarters, you have not filed with the FDIC until you file with both offices.

(ii) You have not filed with the appropriate FDIC region or the FDIC headquarters until you file the application and the required number of copies with that office.

(iii) If you file after the close of business established by appropriate FDIC region or the FDIC headquarters, you have filed with that office on the next business day.

(3) [Reserved]

(b) The FDIC may notify you that it has adjusted your application filing date if you fail to meet any applicable publication requirements.

(c) If, after you properly file your application with the appropriate FDIC region, the FDIC determines that a significant issue of law or policy exists under § 390.108(b)(2)(ii), the filing date of your application is the day you filed with the appropriate FDIC region. The 30-day review period under § 390.126 or § 390.127 will restart in its entirety when the appropriate FDIC region forwards the appropriate number of copies of your application to the FDIC headquarters.

§ 390.110 How do I amend or supplement my application?

To amend or supplement your application, you must file the amendment or supplemental information at the appropriate FDIC region along with the number of copies required under § 390.108. Your amendment or supplemental information also must meet the caption and exhibit requirements at § 390.106(b).

§ 390.111 Who must publish a public notice of an application?

Sections 390.111 through 390.115 apply whenever a FDIC regulation requires an applicant ("you") to follow the public notice procedures in this subpart.

§ 390.112 What information must I include in my public notice?

Your public notice must include the following:

(a) Your name and address.

(b) The type of application.

(c) The name of the depository institution(s) that is the subject matter of the application.

(d) A statement indicating that the public may submit comments to the appropriate FDIC region.

(e) The address of the appropriate FDIC region where the public may submit comments.

(f) The date that the comment period closes.

(g) A statement indicating that the nonconfidential portions of the application are on file in the appropriate FDIC region, and are available for public inspection during regular business hours.

(h) Any other information that the FDIC requires you to publish. You may find the format for various publication

Federal Deposit Insurance Corporation

§ 390.120

notices in the appendix to the FDIC application processing handbook.

§ 390.113 When must I publish the public notice?

You must publish a public notice of the application no earlier than seven days before and no later than the date of filing of the application.

§ 390.114 Where must I publish the public notice?

You must publish the notice in a newspaper having a general circulation in the communities indicated in the following chart:

If you file . . .	You must publish in the following communities . . .
(a) Bank Merger Act application under 390.332(a), or an application for a mutual to stock conversion under 12 CFR part 192.	The community in which your home office is located.
(b) A change of control notice under part 391, subpart E.	The community in which the home office of the State savings association whose stock is to be acquired is located and, if applicable, the community in which the home office of the acquiror's largest subsidiary State savings association is located.

§ 390.115 What language must I use in my publication?

(a) *English.* You must publish the notice in a newspaper printed in the English language.

(b) *Other than English.* If the FDIC determines that the primary language of a significant number of adult residents of the community is a language other than English, the FDIC may require that you simultaneously publish additional notice(s) in the community in the appropriate language(s).

§ 390.116 Comment procedures.

Sections 390.116 though 390.120 contain the procedures governing the submission of public comments on certain types of applications or notices ("applications") pending before the FDIC. It applies whenever a regulation incorporates the procedures in §§ 390.116 through 390.120, or where otherwise required by the FDIC.

§ 390.117 Who may submit a written comment?

Any person may submit a written comment supporting or opposing an application.

§ 390.118 What information should a comment include?

(a) A comment should recite relevant facts, including any demographic, economic, or financial data, supporting the commenter's position. A comment opposing an application should also:

(1) Address at least one of the reasons why the FDIC may deny the application under the relevant statute or regulation;

(2) Recite any relevant facts and supporting data addressing these reasons; and

(3) Address how the approval of the application could harm the commenter or any community.

(b) A commenter must include any request for a meeting under § 390.122 in its comment. The commenter must describe the nature of the issues or facts to be discussed and the reasons why written submissions are insufficient to adequately address these facts or issues.

§ 390.119 Where are comments filed?

A commenter must file with the appropriate FDIC region (See table at § 390.108(a)(2)). The commenter must simultaneously send a copy of the comment to the applicant.

§ 390.120 How long is the comment period?

(a) *General.* Except as provided in paragraph (b) of this section, a commenter must file a written comment with the FDIC within 30 calendar days after the date of publication of the initial public notice.

(b) *Late-filed comments.* The FDIC may consider late-filed comments if the FDIC determines that the comment will assist in the disposition of the application.

§ 390.121 Meeting procedures.

Sections 390.121 through 390.125 contain meeting procedures. They apply whenever a regulation incorporates the procedures in §§ 390.121 through 390.125, or when otherwise required by the FDIC.

§ 390.122 When will the FDIC conduct a meeting on an application?

(a) The FDIC will grant a meeting request or conduct a meeting on its own initiative, if it finds that written submissions are insufficient to address facts or issues raised in an application, or otherwise determines that a meeting will benefit the decision-making process. The FDIC may limit the issues considered at the meeting to issues that the FDIC decides are relevant or material.

(b) The FDIC will inform the applicant and all commenters requesting a meeting of its decision to grant or deny a meeting request, or of its decision to conduct a meeting on its own initiative.

(c) If the FDIC decides to conduct a meeting, the FDIC will invite the applicant and any commenters requesting a meeting and raising an issue that FDIC intends to consider at the meeting. The FDIC may also invite other interested persons to attend. The FDIC will inform the participants of the date, time, location, issues to be considered, and format for the meeting a reasonable time before the meeting.

§ 390.123 What procedures govern the conduct of the meeting?

(a) The FDIC may conduct meetings in any format including, but not limited to, a telephone conference, a face-to-face meeting, or a more formal meeting.

(b) The Administrative Procedure Act (5 U.S.C. 551 *et seq.*), the Federal Rules of Evidence (28 U.S.C. Appendix), the Federal Rules of Civil Procedure (28 U.S.C. Rule 1 *et seq.*) 'and the FDIC Rules of Practice and Procedure in Adjudicatory Proceedings (subpart C) do not apply to meetings under this section.

§ 390.124 Will FDIC approve or disapprove an application at a meeting?

The FDIC will not approve or deny an application at a meeting under §§ 390.121 through 390.125.

§ 390.125 Will a meeting affect application processing time frames?

If the FDIC decides to conduct a meeting, it may suspend applicable application processing time frames, including the time frames for deeming an application complete and the applicable approval time frames in §§ 390.126 through 390.135. If the FDIC suspends applicable application processing time frames, the time period will resume when the FDIC determines that a record has been developed that sufficiently supports a determination on the issues considered at the meeting.

§ 390.126 If I file a notice under expedited treatment, when may I engage in the proposed activities?

If you are eligible for expedited treatment and you have appropriately filed your notice with the FDIC, you may engage in the proposed activities upon the expiration of 30 days after the filing date of your notice, unless the FDIC takes one of the following actions before the expiration of that time period:

(a) The FDIC notifies you in writing that you must file additional information supplementing your notice. If you are required to file additional information, you may engage in the proposed activities upon the expiration of 30 calendar days after the date you file the additional information, unless the FDIC takes one of the actions described in paragraphs (b) through (d) of this section before the expiration of that time period;

(b) The FDIC notifies you in writing that your notice is subject to standard treatment under §§ 390.126 through 390.135. The FDIC will subject your notice to standard treatment if it raises a supervisory concern, raises a significant issue of law or policy, or requires significant additional information;

(c) The FDIC notifies you in writing that it is suspending the applicable time frames under § 390.125; or

Federal Deposit Insurance Corporation §390.128

(d) The FDIC notifies you that it disapproves your notice.

§390.127 What will the FDIC do after I file my application?

(a) *FDIC action.* Within 30 calendar days after the filing date of your application, the FDIC will take one of the following actions:

If the FDIC . . .	Then . . .
(1) Notifies you, in writing, that your application is complete * * *.	The applicable review period will begin on the date that the FDIC deems your application complete.
(2) Notifies you, in writing, that you must submit addition information to complete your application * * *.	You must submit the required additional information under §390.128.
(3) Notifies you, in writing, that your application is materially deficient * * *.	The FDIC will not process your application.
(4) Takes no action * * *	Your application is deemed complete. The applicable review period will begin on the day the 30-day time period expires.

(b) *Waiver requests.* If your application includes a request for waiver of an information requirement under §390.105(b), and the FDIC has not notified you that you must submit additional information under paragraph (a)(2) of this section, your request for waiver is granted.

§390.128 If the FDIC requests additional information to complete my application, how will it process my application?

(a) You may use the following chart to determine the procedure that applies to your submission of additional information under §390.127(a)(1):

If, within 30 calendar days after the date of FDIC's request for additional information . . .	Then, FDIC may . . .	And . . .
(1) You file a response to all information requests * * *.	(i) Notify you in writing within 15 days after the filing date of your response that your application is complete * * * applicable to all response that your application is complete * * *.	The applicable review period will begin on the date that the FDIC deems your application complete.
	(ii) Notify you in writing within 15 calendar days after the filing date of your response that you must submit additional information regarding matters derived from or prompted by information already furnished or any additional information necessary to resolve the issues presented in your application * * *.	You must respond to the additional information request within the time period required by the FDIC. The FDIC will review your response under the procedures described in this section.
	(iii) Notify you in writing within 15 calendar days after the filing date of your response that your application is materially deficient * * *.	The FDIC will not process your application.
	(iv) Take no action within 15 calendar days after the filing date of your response * * *.	Your application is deemed complete. The applicable review period will begin on the day that the 15-day time period expires.
(2) You request an extension of time to file additional information * * *.	(i) Grant an extension, in writing, specifying the number of days for the extension * * *.	You must fully respond within the extended time period specified by the FDIC. The FDIC will review your response under the procedures described under this section.
	(ii) Notify you in writing that your extension request is disapproved * * *.	The FDIC will not process your application further. You may resubmit the application for processing as a new filing under the applicable regulation.
(3) You fail to respond completely * * *.	(i) Notify you in writing that your application is deemed withdrawn * * *.	The FDIC will not process your application further. You may resubmit the application for processing as a new filing under the applicable regulation.
	(ii) Notify you, in writing, that your response is incomplete and extend the response period, specifying the number of days for the respond extension * * *.	You must fully respond within the extended time period specified by the FDIC. The FDIC will review your response under the procedures described under this section.

§ 390.129

(b) The FDIC may extend the 15-day period referenced in paragraph (a)(1) of this section by up to 15 calendar days, if the FDIC requires the additional time to review your response. The FDIC will notify you that it has extended the period before the end of the initial 15-day period and will briefly explain why the extension is necessary.

(c) If your response filed under paragraph (a)(1) of this section includes a request for a waiver of an informational requirement, your request for a waiver is granted if the FDIC fails to act on it within 15 calendar days after the filing of your response, unless the FDIC extends the review period under paragraph (b) of this section. If the FDIC extends the review period under paragraph (b), your request is granted if the FDIC fails to act on it by the end of the extended review period.

§ 390.129 Will the FDIC conduct an eligibility examination?

(a) *Eligibility examination.* The FDIC may notify you at any time before it deems your application complete that it will conduct an eligibility examination. If the FDIC decides to conduct an eligibility examination, it will not deem your application complete until it concludes the examination.

(b) *Additional information.* The FDIC may, as a result of the eligibility examination, notify you that you must submit additional information to complete your application. If so, you must respond to the additional information request within the time period required by the FDIC. The FDIC will review your response under the procedures described in § 390.128.

§ 390.130 What may the FDIC require me to do after my application is deemed complete?

After your application is deemed complete, but before the end of the applicable review period,

(a) The FDIC may require you to provide additional information if the information is necessary to resolve or clarify the issues presented by your application.

(b) The FDIC may determine that a major issue of law or a change in circumstances arose after you filed your application, and that the issue or changed circumstances will substantially effect your application. If the FDIC identifies such an issue or changed circumstances, it may:

(1) Notify you, in writing, that your application is now incomplete and require you to submit additional information to complete the application under the procedures described at § 390.128; and

(2) Require you to publish a new public notice of your application under § 390.131.

§ 390.131 Will the FDIC require me to publish a new public notice?

(a) If your application was subject to a publication requirement, the FDIC may require you to publish a new public notice of your application if:

(1) You submitted a revision to the application, you submitted new or additional information, or a major issue of law or a change in circumstances arose after the filing of your application; and

(2) The FDIC determines that additional comment on these matters is appropriate because of the significance of the new information or circumstances.

(b) The FDIC will notify you in writing if you must publish a new public notice of your revised application.

(c) If you are required to publish a new public notice of your revised application, you must notify the FDIC after you publish the new public notice.

§ 390.132 May the FDIC suspend processing of my application?

(a) *Suspension.* The FDIC may, at any time, indefinitely suspend processing of your application if:

(1) The FDIC, another governmental entity, or a self-regulatory trade or professional organization initiates an investigation, examination, or administrative proceeding that is relevant to the FDIC's evaluation of your application;

(2) You request the suspension or there are other extraordinary circumstances that have a significant impact on the processing of your application.

(b) *Notice.* The FDIC will promptly notify you, in writing, if it suspends your application.

§ 390.133 How long is the FDIC review period?

(a) *General.* The applicable FDIC review period is 60 calendar days after the date that your application is deemed complete, unless an applicable FDIC regulation specifies a different review period.

(b) *Multiple applications.* If you submit more than one application in connection with a proposed action or if two or more applicants submit related applications, the applicable review period for all applications is the review period for the application with the longest review period, subject to statutory review periods.

(c) *Extensions.* (1) The FDIC may extend the review period for up to 30 calendar days beyond the period described in paragraph (a) or (b) of this section. The FDIC must notify you in writing of the extension and the duration of the extension. The FDIC must issue the written extension before the end of the review period.

(2) The FDIC may also extend the review period as needed until it acts on the application, if the application presents a significant issue of law or policy that requires additional time to resolve. The FDIC must notify you in writing of the extension and the general reasons for the extension. The FDIC must issue the written extension before the end of the review period, including any extension of that period under paragraph (c)(1) of this section.

§ 390.134 How will I know if my application has been approved?

(a) *FDIC approval or denial.* (1) The FDIC will approve or deny your application before the expiration of the applicable review period, including any extensions of the review period.

(2) The FDIC will promptly notify you in writing of its decision to approve or deny your application.

(b) *No FDIC action.* If the FDIC fails to act under paragraph (a)(1) of this section, your application is approved.

§ 390.135 What will happen if the FDIC does not approve or disapprove my application within two calendar years after the filing date?

(a) *Withdrawal.* If the FDIC has not approved or denied your pending application within two calendar years after the filing date under § 390.109, the FDIC will notify you, in writing, that your application is deemed withdrawn unless the FDIC determines that you are actively pursuing a final FDIC determination on your application. You are not actively pursuing a final FDIC determination if you have failed to timely take an action required under this part, including filing required additional information, or the FDIC has suspended processing of your application under § 390.132 based on circumstances that are, in whole or in part, within your control and you have failed to take reasonable steps to resolve these circumstances.

(b) [Reserved]

Subpart G—Nondiscrimination Requirements

§ 390.140 Definitions.

As used in this subpart—

Application. For purposes of this part, an application for a loan or other service is as defined in Regulation C, 12 CFR 203.2(b).

Dwelling. The term "dwelling" means a residential structure (whether or not it is attached to real property) located in a state of the United States of America, the District of Colombia, or the Commonwealth of Puerto Rico. The term includes an individual condominium unit, cooperative unit, or mobile or manufactured home.

State savings association. The term "State savings association" means any State savings association as defined in 12 U.S.C. 1813(b).

§ 390.141 Supplementary guidelines.

The FDIC's policy statement found at 12 CFR 390.150 supplements this subpart and should be read together with this subpart. Refer also to the HUD Fair Housing regulations at 24 CFR parts 100 *et seq.*, Federal Reserve Regulation B at 12 CFR part 202, and Federal Reserve Regulation C at 12 CFR part 203.

§ 390.142 Nondiscrimination in lending and other services.

(a) No State savings association may deny a loan or other service, or discriminate in the purchase of loans or securities or discriminate in fixing the amount, interest rate, duration, application procedures, collection or enforcement procedures, or other terms or conditions of such loan or other service on the basis of the age or location of the dwelling, or on the basis of the race, color, religion, sex, handicap, familial status (having one or more children under the age of 18), marital status, age (provided the person has the capacity to contract) or national origin of:

(1) An applicant or joint applicant;

(2) Any person associated with an applicant or joint applicant regarding such loan or other service, or with the purposes of such loan or other service;

(3) The present or prospective owners, lessees, tenants, or occupants of the dwelling(s) for which such loan or other service is to be made or given;

(4) The present or prospective owners, lessees, tenants, or occupants of other dwellings in the vicinity of the dwelling(s) for which such loan or other service is to be made or given.

(b) A State savings association shall consider without prejudice the combined income of joint applicants for a loan or other service.

(c) No State savings association may discriminate against an applicant for a loan or other service on any prohibited basis (as defined in 12 CFR 202.2(z) and 24 CFR part 100).

§ 390.143 Nondiscriminatory appraisal and underwriting.

(a) *Appraisal.* No State savings association may use or rely upon an appraisal of a dwelling which the State savings association knows, or reasonably should know, is discriminatory on the basis of the age or location of the dwelling, or is discriminatory per se or in effect under the Fair Housing Act of 1968 or the Equal Credit Opportunity Act.

(b) *Underwriting.* Each State savings association shall have clearly written, non-discriminatory loan underwriting standards, available to the public upon request, at each of its offices. Each association shall, at least annually, review its standards, and business practices implementing them, to ensure equal opportunity in lending.

§ 390.144 Nondiscrimination in applications.

(a) No State savings association may discourage, or refuse to allow, receive, or consider, any application, request, or inquiry regarding a loan or other service, or discriminate in imposing conditions upon, or in processing, any such application, request, or inquiry on the basis of the age or location of the dwelling, or on the basis of the race, color, religion, sex, handicap, familial status (having one or more children under the age of 18), marital status, age (provided the person has the capacity to contract), national origin, or other characteristics prohibited from consideration in § 390.142(c), of the prospective borrower or other person, who:

(1) Makes application for any such loan or other service;

(2) Requests forms or papers to be used to make application for any such loan or other service; or

(3) Inquires about the availability of such loan or other service.

(b) A State savings association shall inform each inquirer of his or her right to file a written loan application, and to receive a copy of the association's underwriting standards.

§ 390.145 Nondiscriminatory advertising.

No State savings association may directly or indirectly engage in any form of advertising that implies or suggests a policy of discrimination or exclusion in violation of title VIII of the Civil Rights Acts of 1968, the Equal Credit Opportunity Act, or this subpart. Advertisements for any loan for the purpose of purchasing, constructing, improving, repairing, or maintaining a dwelling or any loan secured by a dwelling shall include a facsimile of the following logotype and legend:

Federal Deposit Insurance Corporation § 390.147

§ 390.146 Equal Housing Lender Poster.

(a) Each State savings association shall post and maintain one or more Equal Housing Lender Posters, the text of which is prescribed in paragraph (b) of this section, in the lobby of each of its offices in a prominent place or places readily apparent to all persons seeking loans. The poster shall be at least 11 by 14 inches in size, and the text shall be easily legible. It is recommended that savings associations post a Spanish language version of the poster in offices serving areas with a substantial Spanish-speaking population.

(b) The text of the Equal Housing Lender Poster shall be as follows:

We Do Business In Accordance With Federal Fair Lending Laws.

UNDER THE FEDERAL FAIR HOUSING ACT, IT IS ILLEGAL, ON THE BASIS OF RACE, COLOR, NATIONAL ORIGIN, RELIGION, SEX, HANDICAP, OR FAMILIAL STATUS (HAVING CHILDREN UNDER THE AGE OF 18) TO:

[ ] Deny a loan for the purpose of purchasing, constructing, improving, repairing or maintaining a dwelling or to deny any loan secured by a dwelling; or

[ ] Discriminate in fixing the amount, interest rate, duration, application procedures, or other terms or conditions of such a loan or in appraising property.

IF YOU BELIEVE YOU HAVE BEEN DISCRIMINATED AGAINST, YOU SHOULD:

SEND A COMPLAINT TO:

Assistant Secretary for Fair Housing and Equal Opportunity, Department of Housing and Urban Development, Washington, DC 20410.

For processing under the Federal Fair Housing Act

AND TO:

Federal Deposit Insurance Corporation, Consumer Response Center, 1100 Walnut St, Box #11, Kansas City, MO 64106

For processing under FDIC Regulations.

UNDER THE EQUAL CREDIT OPPORTUNITY ACT, IT IS ILLEGAL TO DISCRIMINATE IN ANY CREDIT TRANSACTION:

[ ] On the basis of race, color, national origin, religion, sex, marital status, or age;

[ ] Because income is from public assistance; or

[ ] Because a right has been exercised under the Consumer Credit Protection Act.

IF YOU BELIEVE YOU HAVE BEEN DISCRIMINATED AGAINST, YOU SHOULD SEND A COMPLAINT TO:

Federal Deposit Insurance Corporation, Consumer Response Center, 1100 Walnut St, Box #11, Kansas City, MO 64106

§ 390.147 Loan application register.

State savings associations and other lenders required to file Home Mortgage

§ 390.148

Disclosure Act Loan Application Registers with the FDIC in accordance with 12 CFR part 203 must enter the reason for denial, using the codes provided in 12 CFR part 203, with respect to all loan denials.

§ 390.148 Nondiscrimination in employment.

(a) No State savings association shall, because of an individual's race, color, religion, sex, or national origin:

(1) Fail or refuse to hire such individual;

(2) Discharge such individual;

(3) Otherwise discriminate against such individual with respect to such individual's compensation, promotion, or the terms, conditions, or privileges of such individual's employment; or

(4) Discriminate in admission to, or employment in, any program of apprenticeship, training, or retraining, including on-the-job training.

(b) No State savings association shall limit, segregate, or classify its employees in any way which would deprive or tend to deprive any individual of employment opportunities or otherwise adversely affect such individual's status as an employee because of such individual's race, color, religion, sex, or national origin.

(c) No State savings association shall discriminate against any employee or applicant for employment because such employee or applicant has opposed any employment practice made unlawful by Federal, State, or local law or regulation or because he has in good faith made a charge of such practice or testified, assisted, or participated in any manner in an investigation, proceeding, or hearing of such practice by any lawfully constituted authority.

(d) No State savings association shall print or publish or cause to be printed or published any notice or advertisement relating to employment by such savings association indicating any preference, limitation, specification, or discrimination based on race, color, religion, sex, or national origin.

(e) This regulation shall not apply in any case in which the Federal Equal Employment Opportunities law is made inapplicable by the provisions of section 2000e-1 or sections 2000e-2 (e) through (j) of title 42, United States Code.

(f) Any violation of the following laws or regulations by a State savings association shall be deemed to be a violation of this subpart:

(1) The Equal Employment Opportunity Act, as amended, 42 U.S.C. 2000e-2000h-2, and Equal Employment Opportunity Commission (EEOC) regulations at 29 CFR part 1600;

(2) The Age Discrimination in Employment Act, 29 U.S.C. 621-633, and EEOC and Department of Labor regulations;

(3) Department of the Treasury regulations at 31 CFR part 12 and Office of Federal Contract Compliance Programs (OFCCP) regulations at 41 CFR part 60;

(4) The Veterans Employment and Readjustment Act of 1972, 38 U.S.C. 2011-2012, and the Vietnam Era Veterans Readjustment Adjustment Assistance Act of 1974, 38 U.S.C. 2021-2026;

(5) The Rehabilitation Act of 1973, 29 U.S.C. 701 *et al.*; and

(6) The Immigration and Nationality Act, 8 U.S.C. 1324b, and INS regulations at 8 CFR part 274a.

§ 390.149 Complaints.

Complaints regarding discrimination in lending by a State savings association shall be referred to the Assistant Secretary for Fair Housing and Equal Opportunity, U.S. Department of Housing and Urban Development, Washington, DC 20410 for processing under the Fair Housing Act, and to the Director, Division of Depositor and Consumer Protection, Federal Deposit Insurance Corporation, 550 17th Street, NW., Washington, DC 20249 for processing under FDIC regulations. Complaints regarding discrimination in employment by a State savings association should be referred to the Equal Employment Opportunity Commission, Washington, DC 20506 and a copy, for information only, sent to the Director, Division of Depositor and Consumer Protection, Federal Deposit Insurance Corporation, 550 17th Street, NW., Washington, DC 20249.

§ 390.150 Guidelines relating to nondiscrimination in lending.

(a) *General.* Fair housing and equal opportunity in home financing is a policy of the United States established by Federal statutes and Presidential orders and proclamations. In furtherance of the Federal civil rights laws and the economical home financing purposes of the statutes administered by the FDIC, the FDIC has adopted, in this subpart, nondiscrimination regulations that, among other things, prohibit arbitrary refusals to consider loan applications on the basis of the age or location of a dwelling, and prohibit discrimination based on race, color, religion, sex, handicap, familial status (having one or more children under the age of 18), marital status, age (provided the person has the capacity to contract), or national origin in fixing the amount, interest rate, duration, application procedures, collection or enforcement procedures, or other terms or conditions of housing related loans. Such discrimination is also prohibited in the purchase of loans and securities. This section provides supplementary guidelines to aid savings associations in developing and implementing nondiscriminatory lending policies. Each State savings association should reexamine its underwriting standards at least annually in order to ensure equal opportunity.

(b) *Loan underwriting standards.* The basic purpose of the FDIC's nondiscrimination regulations is to require that every applicant be given an equal opportunity to obtain a loan. Each loan applicant's creditworthiness should be evaluated on an individual basis without reference to presumed characteristics of a group. The use of lending standards which have no economic basis and which are discriminatory in effect is a violation of law even in the absence of an actual intent to discriminate. However, a standard which has a discriminatory effect is not necessarily improper if its use achieves a genuine business need which cannot be achieved by means which are not discriminatory in effect or less discriminatory in effect.

(c) *Discriminatory practices*—(1) *Discrimination on the basis of sex or marital status.* The Civil Rights Act of 1968 and the National Housing Act prohibit discrimination in lending on the basis of sex. The Equal Credit Opportunity Act, in addition to this prohibition, forbids discrimination on the basis of marital status. Refusing to lend to, requiring higher standards of creditworthiness of, or imposing different requirements on, members of one sex or individuals of one marital status, is discrimination based on sex or marital status. Loan underwriting decisions must be based on an applicant's credit history and present and reasonably foreseeable economic prospects, rather than on the basis of assumptions regarding comparative differences in creditworthiness between married and unmarried individuals, or between men and women.

(2) *Discrimination on the basis of language.* Requiring fluency in the English language as a prerequisite for obtaining a loan may be a discriminatory practice based on national origin.

(3) *Income of husbands and wives.* A practice of discounting all or part of either spouse's income where spouses apply jointly is a violation of section 527 of the National Housing Act. As with other income, when spouses apply jointly for a loan, the determination as to whether a spouse's income qualifies for credit purposes should depend upon a reasonable evaluation of his or her past, present, and reasonably foreseeable economic circumstances. Information relating to child-bearing intentions of a couple or an individual may not be requested.

(4) *Supplementary income.* Lending standards which consider as effective only the non-overtime income of the primary wage-earner may result in discrimination because they do not take account of variations in employment patterns among individuals and families. The FDIC favors loan underwriting which reasonably evaluates the credit worthiness of each applicant based on a realistic appraisal of his or her own past, present, and foreseeable economic circumstances. The determination as to whether primary income or additional income qualifies as effective for credit purposes should depend upon whether such income may reasonably be expected to continue

§ 390.150

through the early period of the mortgage risk. Automatically discounting other income from bonuses, overtime, or part-time employment, will cause some applicants to be denied financing without a realistic analysis of their credit worthiness. Since statistics show that minority group members and low- and moderate-income families rely more often on such supplemental income, the practice may be racially discriminatory in effect, as well as artificially restrictive of opportunities for home financing.

(5) *Applicant's prior history.* Loan decisions should be based upon a realistic evaluation of all pertinent factors respecting an individual's creditworthiness, without giving undue weight to any one factor. The State savings association should, among other things, take into consideration that:

(i) In some instances, past credit difficulties may have resulted from discriminatory practices;

(ii) A policy favoring applicants who previously owned homes may perpetuate prior discrimination;

(iii) A current, stable earnings record may be the most reliable indicator of credit-worthiness, and entitled to more weight than factors such as educational level attained;

(iv) Job or residential changes may indicate upward mobility; and

(v) Preferring applicants who have done business with the lender can perpetuate previous discriminatory policies.

(6) *Income level or racial composition of area.* Refusing to lend or lending on less favorable terms in particular areas because of their racial composition is unlawful. Refusing to lend, or offering less favorable terms (such as interest rate, downpayment, or maturity) to applicants because of the income level in an area can discriminate against minority group persons.

(7) *Age and location factors.* Sections 390.142–390.144 prohibit loan denials based upon the age or location of a dwelling. These restrictions are intended to prohibit use of unfounded or unsubstantiated assumptions regarding the effect upon loan risk of the age of a dwelling or the physical or economic characteristics of an area. Loan decisions should be based on the present market value of the property offered as security (including consideration of specific improvements to be made by the borrower) and the likelihood that the property will retain an adequate value over the term of the loan. Specific factors which may negatively affect its short-range future value (up to 3–5 years) should be clearly documented. Factors which in some cases may cause the market value of a property to decline are recent zoning changes or a significant number of abandoned homes in the immediate vicinity of the property. However, not all zoning changes will cause a decline in property values, and proximity to abandoned buildings may not affect the market value of a property because of rehabilitation programs or affirmative lending programs, or because the cause of abandonment is unrelated to high risk. Proper underwriting considerations include the condition and utility of the improvements, and various physical factors such as street conditions, amenities such as parks and recreation areas, availability of public utilities and municipal services, and exposure to flooding and land faults. However, arbitrary decisions based on age or location are prohibited, since many older, soundly constructed homes provide housing opportunities which may be precluded by an arbitrary lending policy.

(8) *Fair Housing Act (title VIII, Civil Rights Act of 1968, as amended).* State savings associations, must comply with all regulations promulgated by the Department of Housing and Urban Development to implement the Fair Housing Act, found at 24 CFR part 100 *et seq.*, except that they shall use the Equal Housing Lender logo and poster prescribed by FDIC regulations at §§ 390.145 and 390.146 rather than the Equal Housing Opportunity logo and poster required by 24 CFR parts 109 and 110.

(d) *Marketing practices.* State savings associations should review their advertising and marketing practices to ensure that their services are available without discrimination to the community they serve. Discrimination in lending is not limited to loan decisions and underwriting standards; a State savings association does not meet its

Federal Deposit Insurance Corporation § 390.161

obligations to the community or implement its equal lending responsibility if its marketing practices and business relationships with developers and real estate brokers improperly restrict its clientele to segments of the community. A review of marketing practices could begin with an examination of an association's loan portfolio and applications to ascertain whether, in view of the demographic characteristics and credit demands of the community in which the institution is located, it is adequately serving the community on a nondiscriminatory basis. The FDIC will systematically review marketing practices where evidence of discrimination in lending is discovered.

Subpart H—Disclosure and Reporting of CRA-Related Agreements

§ 390.160 Purpose and scope of this subpart.

(a) *General.* This subpart implements section 711 of the Gramm-Leach-Bliley Act (12 U.S.C. 1831y). That section requires any nongovernmental entity or person (NGEP), insured depository institution, or affiliate of an insured depository institution that enters into a covered agreement to—

(1) Make the covered agreement available to the public and the appropriate Federal banking agency; and

(2) File an annual report with the appropriate Federal banking agency concerning the covered agreement.

(b) *Scope of this subpart.* The provisions of this subpart apply to—

(1) State savings associations, as defined in section 3(b) of the Federal Deposit Insurance Act (FDIA), (12 U.S.C. 1813(b)) and their subsidiaries;

(2) [Reserved]

(3) Affiliates of State savings associations and savings and loan holding companies, other than bank holding companies, banks, and subsidiaries of bank holding companies and banks; and

(4) NGEPs that enter into covered agreements with any company listed in paragraphs (b)(1) through (b)(3) of this section.

(c) *Relation to Community Reinvestment Act.* This subpart does not affect in any way the Community Reinvestment Act of 1977 (CRA) (12 U.S.C. 2901 *et seq.*), 12 CFR Part 345, 12 CFR part 195 issued by the Office of the Comptroller of the Currency and applicable to State savings associations, or FDIC's interpretations or administration of the CRA or Community Reinvestment rule.

(d) *Examples.* (1) The examples in this subpart are not exclusive. Compliance with an example, to the extent applicable, constitutes compliance with this subpart.

(2) Examples in a paragraph illustrate only the issue described in the paragraph and do not illustrate any other issues that may arise in this subpart.

§ 390.161 Definition of covered agreement.

(a) *General definition of covered agreement.* A covered agreement is any contract, arrangement, or understanding that meets all of the following criteria—

(1) The agreement is in writing.

(2) The parties to the agreement include—

(i) One or more insured depository institutions or affiliates of an insured depository institution; and

(ii) One or more NGEPs.

(3) The agreement provides for the insured depository institution or any affiliate to—

(i) Provide to one or more individuals or entities (whether or not parties to the agreement) cash payments, grants, or other consideration (except loans) that have an aggregate value of more than $10,000 in any calendar year; or

(ii) Make to one or more individuals or entities (whether or not parties to the agreement) loans that have an aggregate principal amount of more than $50,000 in any calendar year.

(4) The agreement is made pursuant to, or in connection with, the fulfillment of the CRA, as defined in § 390.163.

(5) The agreement is with a NGEP that has had a CRA communication as described in § 390.162 prior to entering into the agreement.

(b) *Examples concerning written arrangements or understandings*—(1) *Example 1.* A NGEP meets with an insured depository institution and states that the institution needs to make more

§ 390.161

community development investments in the NGEP's community. The NGEP and insured depository institution do not reach an agreement concerning the community development investments the institution should make in the community, and the parties do not reach any mutual arrangement or understanding. Two weeks later, the institution unilaterally issues a press release announcing that it has established a general goal of making $100 million of community development grants in low- and moderate-income neighborhoods served by the insured depository institution over the next 5 years. The NGEP is not identified in the press release. The press release is not a written arrangement or understanding.

(2) *Example 2.* A NGEP meets with an insured depository institution and states that the institution needs to offer new loan programs in the NGEP's community. The NGEP and the insured depository institution reach a mutual arrangement or understanding that the institution will provide additional loans in the NGEP's community. The institution tells the NGEP that it will issue a press release announcing the program. Later, the insured depository institution issues a press release announcing the loan program. The press release incorporates the key terms of the understanding reached between the NGEP and the insured depository institution. The written press release reflects the mutual arrangement or understanding of the NGEP and the insured depository institution and is, therefore, a written arrangement or understanding.

(3) *Example 3.* An NGEP sends a letter to an insured depository institution requesting that the institution provide a $15,000 grant to the NGEP. The insured depository institution responds in writing and agrees to provide the grant in connection with its annual grant program. The exchange of letters constitutes a written arrangement or understanding.

(c) *Loan agreements that are not covered agreements.* A covered agreement does not include—

(1) Any individual loan that is secured by real estate; or

(2) Any specific contract or commitment for a loan or extension of credit to an individual, business, farm, or other entity, or group of such individuals or entities, if—

(i) The funds are loaned at rates that are not substantially below market rates; and

(ii) The loan application or other loan documentation does not indicate that the borrower intends or is authorized to use the borrowed funds to make a loan or extension of credit to one or more third parties.

(d) *Examples concerning loan agreements*—(1) *Example 1.* An insured depository institution provides an organization with a $1 million loan that is documented in writing and is secured by real estate owned or to-be-acquired by the organization. The agreement is an individual mortgage loan and is exempt from coverage under paragraph (c)(1) of this section, regardless of the interest rate on the loan or whether the organization intends or is authorized to re-loan the funds to a third party.

(2) *Example 2.* An insured depository institution commits to provide a $500,000 line of credit to a small business that is documented by a written agreement. The loan is made at rates that are within the range of rates offered by the institution to similarly situated small businesses in the market and the loan documentation does not indicate that the small business intends or is authorized to re-lend the borrowed funds. The agreement is exempt from coverage under paragraph (c)(2) of this section.

(3) *Example 3.* An insured depository institution offers small business loans that are guaranteed by the Small Business Administration (SBA). A small business obtains a $75,000 loan, documented in writing, from the institution under the institution's SBA loan program. The loan documentation does not indicate that the borrower intends or is authorized to re-lend the funds. Although the rate charged on the loan is well below that charged by the institution on commercial loans, the rate is within the range of rates that the institution would charge a similarly situated small business for a similar loan

Federal Deposit Insurance Corporation § 390.162

under the SBA loan program. Accordingly, the loan is not made at substantially below market rates and is exempt from coverage under paragraph (c)(2) of this section.

(4) *Example 4.* A bank holding company enters into a written agreement with a community development organization that provides that insured depository institutions owned by the bank holding company will make $250 million in small business loans in the community over the next 5 years. The written agreement is not a specific contract or commitment for a loan or an extension of credit and, thus, is not exempt from coverage under paragraph (c)(2) of this section. Each small business loan made by the insured depository institution pursuant to this general commitment would, however, be exempt from coverage if the loan is made at rates that are not substantially below market rates and the loan documentation does not indicate that the borrower intended or was authorized to re-lend the funds.

(e) *Agreements that include exempt loan agreements.* If an agreement includes a loan, extension of credit or loan commitment that, if documented separately, would be exempt under paragraph (c) of this section, the exempt loan, extension of credit or loan commitment may be excluded for purposes of determining whether the agreement is a covered agreement.

(f) *Determining annual value of agreements that lack schedule of disbursements.* For purposes of paragraph (a)(3) of this section, a multi-year agreement that does not include a schedule for the disbursement of payments, grants, loans or other consideration by the insured depository institution or affiliate, is considered to have a value in the first year of the agreement equal to all payments, grants, loans and other consideration to be provided at any time under the agreement.

§ 390.162 CRA communications.

(a) *Definition of CRA communication.* A CRA communication is any of the following—

(1) Any written or oral comment or testimony provided to a Federal banking agency concerning the adequacy of the performance under the CRA of the insured depository institution, any affiliated insured depository institution, or any CRA affiliate.

(2) Any written comment submitted to the insured depository institution that discusses the adequacy of the performance under the CRA of the institution and must be included in the institution's CRA public file.

(3) Any discussion or other contact with the insured depository institution or any affiliate about—

(i) Providing (or refraining from providing) written or oral comments or testimony to any Federal banking agency concerning the adequacy of the performance under the CRA of the insured depository institution, any affiliated insured depository institution, or any CRA affiliate;

(ii) Providing (or refraining from providing) written comments to the insured depository institution that concern the adequacy of the institution's performance under the CRA and must be included in the institution's CRA public file; or

(iii) The adequacy of the performance under the CRA of the insured depository institution, any affiliated insured depository institution, or any CRA affiliate.

(b) *Discussions or contacts that are not CRA communications*—(1) *Timing of contacts with a Federal banking agency.* An oral or written communication with a Federal banking agency is not a CRA communication if it occurred more than 3 years before the parties entered into the agreement.

(2) *Timing of contacts with insured depository institutions and affiliates.* A communication with an insured depository institution or affiliate is not a CRA communication if the communication occurred—

(i) More than 3 years before the parties entered into the agreement, in the case of any written communication;

(ii) More than 3 years before the parties entered into the agreement, in the case of any oral communication in which the NGEP discusses providing (or refraining from providing) comments or testimony to a Federal banking agency or written comments that must be included in the institution's CRA public file in connection with a request to, or agreement by, the institution or affiliate to take (or refrain from taking) any action that is in fulfillment of the CRA; or

(iii) More than 1 year before the parties entered into the agreement, in the case of any other oral communication not described in paragraph (b)(2)(ii) of this section.

(3) *Knowledge of communication by insured depository institution or affiliate.* (i) A communication is only a CRA communication under paragraph (a) of this section if the insured depository institution or its affiliate has knowledge of the communication under paragraph (b)(3)(ii) or (iii) of this section.

(ii) *Communication with insured depository institution or affiliate.* An insured depository institution or affiliate has knowledge of a communication by the NGEP to the institution or its affiliate under this paragraph only if one of the following representatives of the insured depository institution or any affiliate has knowledge of the communication—

(A) An employee who approves, directs, authorizes, or negotiates the agreement with the NGEP; or

(B) An employee designated with responsibility for compliance with the CRA or executive officer if the employee or executive officer knows that the institution or affiliate is negotiating, intends to negotiate, or has been informed by the NGEP that it expects to request that the institution or affiliate negotiate an agreement with the NGEP.

(iii) *Other communications.* An insured depository institution or affiliate is deemed to have knowledge of—

(A) Any testimony provided to a Federal banking agency at a public meeting or hearing;

(B) Any comment submitted to a Federal banking agency that is conveyed in writing by the agency to the insured depository institution or affiliate; and

(C) Any written comment submitted to the insured depository institution that must be and is included in the institution's CRA public file.

(4) *Communication where NGEP has knowledge.* A NGEP has a CRA communication with an insured depository institution or affiliate only if any of the following individuals has knowledge of the communication—

(i) A director, employee, or member of the NGEP who approves, directs, authorizes, or negotiates the agreement with the insured depository institution or affiliate;

(ii) A person who functions as an executive officer of the NGEP and who knows that the NGEP is negotiating or intends to negotiate an agreement with the insured depository institution or affiliate; or

(iii) Where the NGEP is an individual, the NGEP.

(c) *Examples of CRA communications—* (1) *Examples of actions that are CRA communications.* The following are examples of CRA communications. These examples are not exclusive and assume that the communication occurs within the relevant time period as described in paragraph (b)(1) or (2) of this section and the appropriate representatives have knowledge of the communication as specified in paragraphs (b)(3) and (4) of this section.

(i) *Example 1.* A NGEP files a written comment with a Federal banking agency that states than an insured depository institution successfully addresses the credit needs of its community. The written comment is in response to a general request from the agency for comments on an application of the insured depository institution to open a new branch and a copy of the comment is provided to the institution.

(ii) *Example 2.* A NGEP meets with an executive officer of an insured depository institution and states that the institution must improve its CRA performance.

(iii) *Example 3.* A NGEP meets with an executive officer of an insured depository institution and states that the institution needs to make more mortgage loans in low- and moderate-income neighborhoods in its community.

(iv) *Example 4.* A bank holding company files an application with a Federal banking agency to acquire an insured depository institution. Two weeks later, the NGEP meets with an executive officer of the bank holding company to discuss the adequacy of the performance under the CRA of the target insured depository institution. The insured depository institution was an

Federal Deposit Insurance Corporation § 390.162

affiliate of the bank holding company at the time the NGEP met with the target institution. (*See* § 390.170(a)) Accordingly, the NGEP had a CRA communication with an affiliate of the bank holding company.

(2) *Examples of actions that are not CRA communications.* The following are examples of actions that are not by themselves CRA communications. These examples are not exclusive.

(i) *Example 1.* A NGEP provides to a Federal banking agency comments or testimony concerning an insured depository institution or affiliate in response to a direct request by the agency for comments or testimony from that NGEP. Direct requests for comments or testimony do not include a general invitation by a Federal banking agency for comments or testimony from the public in connection with a CRA performance evaluation of, or application for a deposit facility (as defined in section 803 of the CRA (12 U.S.C. 2902(3)) by, an insured depository institution or an application by a company to acquire an insured depository institution.

(ii) *Example 2.* A NGEP makes a statement concerning an insured depository institution or affiliate at a widely attended conference or seminar regarding a general topic. A public or private meeting, public hearing, or other meeting regarding one or more specific institutions, affiliates or transactions involving an application for a deposit facility is not considered a widely attended conference or seminar.

(iii) *Example 3.* A NGEP, such as a civil rights group, community group providing housing and other services in low- and moderate-income neighborhoods, veterans organization, community theater group, or youth organization, sends a fundraising letter to insured depository institutions and to other businesses in its community. The letter encourages all businesses in the community to meet their obligation to assist in making the local community a better place to live and work by supporting the fundraising efforts of the NGEP.

(iv) *Example 4.* A NGEP discusses with an insured depository institution or affiliate whether particular loans, services, investments, community development activities, or other activities are generally eligible for consideration by a Federal banking agency under the CRA. The NGEP and insured depository institution or affiliate do not discuss the adequacy of the CRA performance of the insured depository institution or affiliate.

(v) *Example 5.* A NGEP engaged in the sale or purchase of loans in the secondary market sends a general offering circular to financial institutions offering to sell or purchase a portfolio of loans. An insured depository institution that receives the offering circular discusses with the NGEP the types of loans included in the loan pool, whether such loans are generally eligible for consideration under the CRA, and which loans are made to borrowers in the institution's local community. The NGEP and insured depository institution do not discuss the adequacy of the institution's CRA performance.

(d) *Multiparty covered agreements.* (1) A NGEP that is a party to a covered agreement that involves multiple NGEPs is not required to comply with the requirements of this part if—

(i) The NGEP has not had a CRA communication; and

(ii) No representative of the NGEP identified in paragraph (b)(4) of this section has knowledge at the time of the agreement that another NGEP that is a party to the agreement has had a CRA communication.

(2) An insured depository institution or affiliate that is a party to a covered agreement that involves multiple insured depository institutions or affiliates is not required to comply with the requirements in §§ 390.165 and 390.166 if—

(i) No NGEP that is a party to the agreement has had a CRA communication concerning the insured depository institution or any affiliate; and

(ii) No representative of the insured depository institution or any affiliate identified in paragraph (b)(3) of this section has knowledge at the time of the agreement that an NGEP that is a party to the agreement has had a CRA communication concerning any other insured depository institution or affiliate that is a party to the agreement.

§ 390.163 Fulfillment of the CRA.

(a) *List of factors that are in fulfillment of the CRA.* Fulfillment of the CRA, for purposes of this subpart, means the following list of factors—

(1) *Comments to a Federal banking agency or included in CRA public file.* Providing or refraining from providing written or oral comments or testimony to any Federal banking agency concerning the performance under the CRA of an insured depository institution or CRA affiliate that is a party to the agreement or an affiliate of a party to the agreement or written comments that are required to be included in the CRA public file of any such insured depository institution; or

(2) *Activities given favorable CRA consideration.* Performing any of the following activities if the activity is of the type that is likely to receive favorable consideration by a Federal banking agency in evaluating the performance under the CRA of the insured depository institution that is a party to the agreement or an affiliate of a party to the agreement—

(i) Home-purchase, home-improvement, small business, small farm, community development, and consumer lending, as described in 12 CFR 195.22, including loan purchases, loan commitments, and letters of credit;

(ii) Making investments, deposits, or grants, or acquiring membership shares, that have as their primary purpose community development, as described in 12 CFR 195.23;

(iii) Delivering retail banking services, as described in 12 CFR 195.24(d);

(iv) Providing community development services, as described in 12 CFR 195.24(e);

(v) In the case of a wholesale or limited-purpose insured depository institution, community development lending, including originating and purchasing loans and making loan commitments and letters of credit, making qualified investments, or providing community development services, as described in 12 CFR 195.25(c);

(vi) In the case of a small insured depository institution, any lending or other activity described in 12 CFR 195.26(a); or

(vii) In the case of an insured depository institution that is evaluated on the basis of a strategic plan, any element of the strategic plan, as described in 12 CFR 195.27(f).

(b) *Agreements relating to activities of CRA affiliates.* An insured depository institution or affiliate that is a party to a covered agreement that concerns any activity described in paragraph (a) of this section of a CRA affiliate must, prior to the time the agreement is entered into, notify each NGEP that is a party to the agreement that the agreement concerns a CRA affiliate.

§ 390.164 Related agreements considered a single agreement.

The following rules must be applied in determining whether an agreement is a covered agreement under § 390.161.

(a) *Agreements entered into by same parties.* All written agreements to which an insured depository institution or an affiliate of the insured depository institution is a party shall be considered to be a single agreement if the agreements—

(1) Are entered into with the same NGEP;

(2) Were entered into within the same 12-month period; and

(3) Are each in fulfillment of the CRA.

(b) *Substantively related contracts.* All written contracts to which an insured depository institution or an affiliate of the insured depository institution is a party shall be considered to be a single agreement, without regard to whether the other parties to the contracts are the same or whether each such contract is in fulfillment of the CRA, if the contracts were negotiated in a coordinated fashion and a NGEP is a party to each contract.

§ 390.165 Disclosure of covered agreements.

(a) *Applicability date.* This section applies only to covered agreements entered into after November 12, 1999.

(b) *Disclosure of covered agreements to the public*—(1) *Disclosure required.* Each NGEP and each insured depository institution or affiliate that enters into a covered agreement must make a copy of the covered agreement available to any individual or entity upon request.

Federal Deposit Insurance Corporation § 390.165

(2) *Nondisclosure of confidential and proprietary information permitted.* In responding to a request for a covered agreement from any individual or entity under paragraph (b)(1) of this section, a NGEP, insured depository institution, or affiliate may withhold from public disclosure confidential or proprietary information that the party believes the relevant supervisory agency could withhold from disclosure under the Freedom of Information Act (5 U.S.C. 552 et seq.) (FOIA).

(3) *Information that must be disclosed.* Notwithstanding paragraph (b)(2) of this section, a party must disclose any of the following information that is contained in a covered agreement—

(i) The names and addresses of the parties to the agreement;

(ii) The amount of any payments, fees, loans, or other consideration to be made or provided by any party to the agreement;

(iii) Any description of how the funds or other resources provided under the agreement are to be used;

(iv) The term of the agreement (if the agreement establishes a term); and

(v) Any other information that the relevant supervisory agency determines is not properly exempt from public disclosure.

(4) *Request for review of withheld information.* Any individual or entity may request that the relevant supervisory agency review whether any information in a covered agreement withheld by a party must be disclosed. Any requests for agency review of withheld information must be filed, and will be processed in accordance with, the relevant supervisory agency's rules concerning the availability of information (see part 309).

(5) *Duration of obligation.* The obligation to disclose a covered agreement to the public terminates 12 months after the end of the term of the agreement.

(6) *Reasonable copy and mailing fees.* Each NGEP and each insured depository institution or affiliate may charge an individual or entity that requests a copy of a covered agreement a reasonable fee not to exceed the cost of copying and mailing the agreement.

(7) *Use of CRA public file by insured depository institution or affiliate.* An insured depository institution and any affiliate of an insured depository institution may fulfill its obligation under this paragraph (b) by placing a copy of the covered agreement in the insured depository institution's CRA public file if the institution makes the agreement available in accordance with the procedures set forth in 12 CFR 195.43.

(c) *Disclosure by NGEPs of covered agreements to the relevant supervisory agency.* (1) Each NGEP that is a party to a covered agreement must provide the following within 30 days of receiving a request from the relevant supervisory agency—

(i) A complete copy of the agreement; and

(ii) In the event the NGEP proposes the withholding of any information contained in the agreement in accordance with paragraph (b)(2) of this section, a public version of the agreement that excludes such information and an explanation justifying the exclusions. Any public version must include the information described in paragraph (b)(3) of this section.

(2) The obligation to provide a covered agreement to the relevant supervisory agency terminates 12 months after the end of the term of the covered agreement.

(d) *Disclosure by insured depository institution or affiliate of covered agreements to the relevant supervisory agency*—(1) *In general.* Within 60 days of the end of each calendar quarter, each insured depository institution and affiliate must provide each relevant supervisory agency with—

(i)(A) A complete copy of each covered agreement entered into by the insured depository institution or affiliate during the calendar quarter; and

(B) In the event the institution or affiliate proposes the withholding of any information contained in the agreement in accordance with paragraph (b)(2) of this section, a public version of the agreement that excludes such information (other than any information described in paragraph (b)(3) of this section) and an explanation justifying the exclusions; or

(ii) A list of all covered agreements entered into by the insured depository institution or affiliate during the calendar quarter that contains—

793

(A) The name and address of each insured depository institution or affiliate that is a party to the agreement;

(B) The name and address of each NGEP that is a party to the agreement;

(C) The date the agreement was entered into;

(D) The estimated total value of all payments, fees, loans and other consideration to be provided by the institution or any affiliate of the institution under the agreement; and

(E) The date the agreement terminates.

(2) *Prompt filing of covered agreements contained in list required.* (i) If an insured depository institution or affiliate files a list of the covered agreements entered into by the institution or affiliate pursuant to paragraph (d)(1)(ii) of this section, the institution or affiliate must provide any relevant supervisory agency a complete copy and public version of any covered agreement referenced in the list within 7 calendar days of receiving a request from the agency for a copy of the agreement.

(ii) The obligation of an insured depository institution or affiliate to provide a covered agreement to the relevant supervisory agency under this paragraph (d)(2) terminates 36 months after the end of the term of the covered agreement.

(3) *Joint filings.* In the event that 2 or more insured depository institutions or affiliates are parties to a covered agreement, the insured depository institution(s) and affiliate(s) may jointly file the documents required by this paragraph (d) of this section. Any joint filing must identify the insured depository institution(s) and affiliate(s) for whom the filings are being made.

§ 390.166 Annual reports.

(a) *Applicability date.* This section applies only to covered agreements entered into on or after May 12, 2000.

(b) *Annual report required.* Each NGEP and each insured depository institution or affiliate that is a party to a covered agreement must file an annual report with each relevant supervisory agency concerning the disbursement, receipt, and uses of funds or other resources under the covered agreement.

(c) *Duration of reporting requirement*— (1) *NGEPs.* A NGEP must file an annual report for a covered agreement for any fiscal year in which the NGEP receives or uses funds or other resources under the agreement.

(2) *Insured depository institutions and affiliates.* An insured depository institution or affiliate must file an annual report for a covered agreement for any fiscal year in which the institution or affiliate—

(i) Provides or receives any payments, fees, or loans under the covered agreement that must be reported under paragraphs (e)(1)(iii) and (iv) of this section; or

(ii) Has data to report on loans, investments, and services provided by a party to the covered agreement under the covered agreement under paragraph (e)(1)(vi) of this section.

(d) *Annual reports filed by NGEP.*—(1) *Contents of report.* The annual report filed by a NGEP under this section must include the following—

(i) The name and mailing address of the NGEP filing the report;

(ii) Information sufficient to identify the covered agreement for which the annual report is being filed, such as by providing the names of the parties to the agreement and the date the agreement was entered into or by providing a copy of the agreement;

(iii) The amount of funds or resources received under the covered agreement during the fiscal year; and

(iv) A detailed, itemized list of how the funds or resources received by the NGEP under the covered agreement were used during the fiscal year, including the total amount used for—

(A) Compensation of officers, directors, and employees;

(B) Administrative expenses;

(C) Travel expenses;

(D) Entertainment expenses;

(E) Payment of consulting and professional fees; and

(F) Other expenses and uses (specify expense or use).

(2) *More detailed reporting of uses of funds or resources permitted*—(i) *In general.* If a NGEP allocated and used funds received under a covered agreement for a specific purpose, the NGEP

Federal Deposit Insurance Corporation § 390.166

may fulfill the requirements of paragraph (d)(1)(iv) of this section with respect to such funds by providing—

(A) A brief description of each specific purpose for which the funds or other resources were used; and

(B) The amount of funds or resources used during the fiscal year for each specific purpose.

(ii) *Specific purpose defined.* A NGEP allocates and uses funds for a specific purpose if the NGEP receives and uses the funds for a purpose that is more specific and limited than the categories listed in paragraph (d)(1)(iv) of this section.

(3) *Use of other reports.* The annual report filed by a NGEP may consist of or incorporate a report prepared for any other purpose, such as the Internal Revenue Service Return of Organization Exempt From Income Tax on Form 990, or any other Internal Revenue Service form, state tax form, report to members or shareholders, audited or unaudited financial statements, audit report, or other report, so long as the annual report filed by the NGEP contains all of the information required by this paragraph (d).

(4) *Consolidated reports permitted.* A NGEP that is a party to 2 or more covered agreements may file with each relevant supervisory agency a single consolidated annual report covering all the covered agreements. Any consolidated report must contain all the information required by this paragraph (d). The information reported under paragraphs (d)(1)(iv) and (d)(2) of this section may be reported on an aggregate basis for all covered agreements.

(5) *Examples of annual report requirements for NGEPs*—(i) *Example 1.* A NGEP receives an unrestricted grant of $15,000 under a covered agreement, includes the funds in its general operating budget and uses the funds during its fiscal year. The NGEP's annual report for the fiscal year must provide the name and mailing address of the NGEP, information sufficient to identify the covered agreement, and state that the NGEP received $15,000 during the fiscal year. The report must also indicate the total expenditures made by the NGEP during the fiscal year for compensation, administrative expenses, travel expenses, entertainment expenses, consulting and professional fees, and other expenses and uses. The NGEP's annual report may provide this information by submitting an Internal Revenue Service Form 990 that includes the required information. If the Internal Revenue Service Form does not include information for all of the required categories listed in this part, the NGEP must report the total expenditures in the remaining categories either by providing that information directly or by providing another form or report that includes the required information.

(ii) *Example 2.* An organization receives $15,000 from an insured depository institution under a covered agreement and allocates and uses the $15,000 during the fiscal year to purchase computer equipment to support its functions. The organization's annual report must include the name and address of the organization, information sufficient to identify the agreement, and a statement that the organization received $15,000 during the year. In addition, since the organization allocated and used the funds for a specific purpose that is more narrow and limited than the categories of expenses included in the detailed, itemized list of expenses, the organization would have the option of providing either the total amount it used during the year for each category of expenses included in paragraph (d)(1)(iv) of this section, or a statement that it used the $15,000 to purchase computer equipment and a brief description of the equipment purchased.

(iii) *Example 3.* A community group receives $50,000 from an insured depository institution under a covered agreement. During its fiscal year, the community group specifically allocates and uses $5,000 of the funds to pay for a particular business trip and uses the remaining $45,000 for general operating expenses. The group's annual report for the fiscal year must include the name and address of the group, information sufficient to identify the agreement, and a statement that the group received $50,000. Because the group did not allocate and use all of the funds for a specific purpose, the group's annual report must provide the total amount of funds it used during the year for each category of expenses included in

795

§ 390.166

paragraph (d)(1)(iv) of this section. The group's annual report also could state that it used $5,000 for a particular business trip and include a brief description of the trip.

(iv) *Example 4.* A community development organization is a party to two separate covered agreements with two unaffiliated insured depository institutions. Under each agreement, the organization receives $15,000 during its fiscal year and uses the funds to support its activities during that year. If the organization elects to file a consolidated annual report, the consolidated report must identify the organization and the two covered agreements, state that the organization received $15,000 during the fiscal year under each agreement, and provide the total amount that the organization used during the year for each category of expenses included in paragraph (d)(1)(iv) of this section.

(e) *Annual report filed by insured depository institution or affiliate*—(1) *General.* The annual report filed by an insured depository institution or affiliate must include the following—

(i) The name and principal place of business of the insured depository institution or affiliate filing the report;

(ii) Information sufficient to identify the covered agreement for which the annual report is being filed, such as by providing the names of the parties to the agreement and the date the agreement was entered into or by providing a copy of the agreement;

(iii) The aggregate amount of payments, aggregate amount of fees, and aggregate amount of loans provided by the insured depository institution or affiliate under the covered agreement to any other party to the agreement during the fiscal year;

(iv) The aggregate amount of payments, aggregate amount of fees, and aggregate amount of loans received by the insured depository institution or affiliate under the covered agreement from any other party to the agreement during the fiscal year;

(v) A general description of the terms and conditions of any payments, fees, or loans reported under paragraphs (e)(1)(iii) and (iv) of this section, or, in the event such terms and conditions are set forth—

(A) In the covered agreement, a statement identifying the covered agreement and the date the agreement (or a list identifying the agreement) was filed with the relevant supervisory agency; or

(B) In a previous annual report filed by the insured depository institution or affiliate, a statement identifying the date the report was filed with the relevant supervisory agency; and

(vi) The aggregate amount and number of loans, aggregate amount and number of investments, and aggregate amount of services provided under the covered agreement to any individual or entity not a party to the agreement—

(A) By the insured depository institution or affiliate during its fiscal year; and

(B) By any other party to the agreement, unless such information is not known to the insured depository institution or affiliate filing the report or such information is or will be contained in the annual report filed by another party under this section.

(2) *Consolidated reports permitted*—(i) *Party to multiple agreements.* An insured depository institution or affiliate that is a party to 2 or more covered agreements may file a single consolidated annual report with each relevant supervisory agency concerning all the covered agreements.

(ii) *Affiliated entities party to the same agreement.* An insured depository institution and its affiliates that are parties to the same covered agreement may file a single consolidated annual report relating to the agreement with each relevant supervisory agency for the covered agreement.

(iii) *Content of report.* Any consolidated annual report must contain all the information required by this paragraph (e). The amounts and data required to be reported under paragraphs (e)(1)(iv) and (vi) of this section may be reported on an aggregate basis for all covered agreements.

(f) *Time and place of filing*—(1) *General.* Each party must file its annual report with each relevant supervisory agency for the covered agreement no later than six months following the end of the fiscal year covered by the report.

(2) *Alternative method of fulfilling annual reporting requirement for a NGEP.*

Federal Deposit Insurance Corporation § 390.170

(i) A NGEP may fulfill the filing requirements of this section by providing the following materials to an insured depository institution or affiliate that is a party to the agreement no later than six months following the end of the NGEP's fiscal year—

(A) A copy of the NGEP's annual report required under paragraph (d) of this section for the fiscal year; and

(B) Written instructions that the insured depository institution or affiliate promptly forward the annual report to the relevant supervisory agency or agencies on behalf of the NGEP.

(ii) An insured depository institution or affiliate that receives an annual report from a NGEP pursuant to paragraph (f)(2)(i) of this section must file the report with the relevant supervisory agency or agencies on behalf of the NGEP within 30 days.

§ 390.167 Release of information under FOIA.

FDIC will make covered agreements and annual reports available to the public in accordance with the Freedom of Information Act (5 U.S.C. 552 et seq.) and the FDIC's rules (part 309). A party to a covered agreement may request confidential treatment of proprietary and confidential information in a covered agreement or an annual report under those procedures.

§ 390.168 Compliance provisions.

(a) *Willful failure to comply with disclosure and reporting obligations.* (1) If FDIC determines that a NGEP has willfully failed to comply in a material way with § 390.165 or § 390.166, FDIC will notify the NGEP in writing of that determination and provide the NGEP a period of 90 days (or such longer period as FDIC finds to be reasonable under the circumstances) to comply.

(2) If the NGEP does not comply within the time period established by FDIC, the agreement shall thereafter be unenforceable by that NGEP by operation of section 48 of the Federal Deposit Insurance Act (12 U.S.C. 1831y).

(3) FDIC may assist any insured depository institution or affiliate that is a party to a covered agreement that is unenforceable by a NGEP by operation of section 48 of the Federal Deposit Insurance Act (12 U.S.C. 1831y) in identifying a successor to assume the NGEP's responsibilities under the agreement.

(b) *Diversion of funds.* If a court or other body of competent jurisdiction determines that funds or resources received under a covered agreement have been diverted contrary to the purposes of the covered agreement for an individual's personal financial gain, FDIC may take either or both of the following actions—

(1) Order the individual to disgorge the diverted funds or resources received under the agreement;

(2) Prohibit the individual from being a party to any covered agreement for a period not to exceed 10 years.

(c) *Notice and opportunity to respond.* Before making a determination under paragraph (a)(1) of this section, or taking any action under paragraph (b) of this section, FDIC will provide written notice and an opportunity to present information to FDIC concerning any relevant facts or circumstances relating to the matter.

(d) *Inadvertent or de minimis errors.* Inadvertent or *de minimis* errors in annual reports or other documents filed with FDIC under §§ 390.165 or 390.166 will not subject the reporting party to any penalty.

(e) *Enforcement of provisions in covered agreements.* No provision of this subpart shall be construed as authorizing FDIC to enforce the provisions of any covered agreement.

§ 390.169 [Reserved]

§ 390.170 Other definitions and rules of construction used in this subpart.

(a) *Affiliate. Affiliate* means—

(1) Any company that controls, is controlled by, or is under common control with another company; and

(2) For the purpose of determining whether an agreement is a covered agreement under § 390.161, an *affiliate* includes any company that would be under common control or merged with another company on consummation of any transaction pending before a Federal banking agency at the time—

(i) The parties enter into the agreement; and

(ii) The NGEP that is a party to the agreement makes a CRA communication, as described in § 390.162.

797

§ 390.170

(b) *Control.* Control is defined in section 2(a) of the Bank Holding Company Act (12 U.S.C. 1841(a)).

(c) *CRA affiliate.* A *CRA affiliate* of an insured depository institution is any company that is an affiliate of an insured depository institution to the extent, and only to the extent, that the activities of the affiliate were considered by the appropriate Federal banking agency when evaluating the CRA performance of the institution at its most recent CRA examination prior to the agreement. An insured depository institution or affiliate also may designate any company as a CRA affiliate at any time prior to the time a covered agreement is entered into by informing the NGEP that is a party to the agreement of such designation.

(d) *CRA public file. CRA public file* means the public file maintained by an insured depository institution and described in 12 CFR 195.43.

(e) *Executive officer.* The term *executive officer* has the same meaning as in § 215.2(e)(1) of the Board of Governors of the Federal Reserve's Regulation O (12 CFR 215.2(e)(1)). In applying this definition under this subpart, the term *State savings association* shall be used in place of the term *bank.*

(f) *Federal banking agency; appropriate Federal banking agency.* The terms *Federal banking agency* and *appropriate Federal banking agency* have the same meanings as in section 3 of the Federal Deposit Insurance Act (12 U.S.C. 1813).

(g) *Fiscal year.* (1) The fiscal year for a NGEP that does not have a fiscal year shall be the calendar year.

(2) Any NGEP, insured depository institution, or affiliate that has a fiscal year may elect to have the calendar year be its fiscal year for purposes of this part.

(h) *Insured depository institution. Insured depository institution* has the same meaning as in section 3 of the Federal Deposit Insurance Act (12 U.S.C. 1813).

(i) *Nongovernmental entity or person* or *NGEP*—(1) *General.* A *nongovernmental entity or person* or *NGEP* is any partnership, association, trust, joint venture, joint stock company, corporation, limited liability company, company, firm, society, other organization, or individual.

(2) *Exclusions.* A nongovernmental entity or person does not include—

(i) The United States government, a state government, a unit of local government (including a county, city, town, township, parish, village, or other general-purpose subdivision of a state) or an Indian tribe or tribal organization established under Federal, state or Indian tribal law (including the Department of Hawaiian Home Lands), or a department, agency, or instrumentality of any such entity;

(ii) A federally-chartered public corporation that receives Federal funds appropriated specifically for that corporation;

(iii) An insured depository institution or affiliate of an insured depository institution; or

(iv) An officer, director, employee, or representative (acting in his or her capacity as an officer, director, employee, or representative) of an entity listed in paragraphs (i)(2)(i), (ii), or (iii) of this section.

(j) *Party.* The term *party* with respect to a covered agreement means each NGEP and each insured depository institution or affiliate that entered into the agreement.

(k) *Relevant supervisory agency.* The *relevant supervisory agency* for a covered agreement means the appropriate Federal banking agency for—

(1) Each insured depository institution (or subsidiary thereof) that is a party to the covered agreement;

(2) Each insured depository institution (or subsidiary thereof) or CRA affiliate that makes payments or loans or provides services that are subject to the covered agreement; and

(3) Any company (other than an insured depository institution or subsidiary thereof) that is a party to the covered agreement.

(l) *Term of agreement.* An agreement that does not have a fixed termination date is considered to terminate on the last date on which any party to the agreement makes any payment or provides any loan or other resources under the agreement, unless the relevant supervisory agency for the agreement otherwise notifies each party in writing.

Federal Deposit Insurance Corporation § 390.181

Subpart I—Consumer Protection in Sales of Insurance

§ 390.180 Purpose and scope.

(a) *General rule.* This subpart establishes consumer protections in connection with retail sales practices, solicitations, advertising, or offers of any insurance product or annuity to a consumer by:

(1) Any State savings association, as defined in section 3 of the Federal Deposit Insurance Act (FDIA), (12 U.S.C. 1813(b)); or

(2) Any other person that is engaged in such activities at an office of a State savings association or on behalf of a State savings association.

(b) *Application to subsidiaries.* A subsidiary is subject to this subpart only to the extent that it sells, solicits, advertises, or offers insurance products or annuities at an office of a State savings association or on behalf of a State savings association.

§ 390.181 Definitions.

As used in this subpart:

Affiliate means a company that controls, is controlled by, or is under common control with another company.

Company means any corporation, partnership, business trust, association or similar organization, or any other trust (unless by its terms the trust must terminate within twenty-five years or not later than twenty-one years and ten months after the death of individuals living on the effective date of the trust). It does not include any corporation the majority of the shares of which are owned by the United States or by any State, or a qualified family partnership, as defined in section 2(o)(10) of the Bank Holding Company Act of 1956, as amended (12 U.S.C. 1841(o)(10)).

Consumer means an individual who purchases, applies to purchase, or is solicited to purchase from a covered person insurance products or annuities primarily for personal, family, or household purposes.

Control of a company has the same meaning as in section 3(w)(5) of the FDIA, (12 U.S.C. 1813(w)(5)).

Domestic violence means the occurrence of one or more of the following acts by a current or former family member, household member, intimate partner, or caretaker:

(1) Attempting to cause or causing or threatening another person physical harm, severe emotional distress, psychological trauma, rape, or sexual assault;

(2) Engaging in a course of conduct or repeatedly committing acts toward another person, including following the person without proper authority, under circumstances that place the person in reasonable fear of bodily injury or physical harm;

(3) Subjecting another person to false imprisonment; or

(4) Attempting to cause or causing damage to property so as to intimidate or attempt to control the behavior of another person.

Electronic media includes any means for transmitting messages electronically between a covered person and a consumer in a format that allows visual text to be displayed on equipment, for example, a personal computer monitor.

Office means the premises of a State savings association where retail deposits are accepted from the public.

Subsidiary has the same meaning as in section 3(w)(4) of the FDIA, (12 U.S.C. 1813(w)(4)).

You means:

(1) A State savings association, as defined in § 390.308; or

(2) Any other person only when the person sells, solicits, advertises, or offers an insurance product or annuity to a consumer at an office of a State savings association, or on behalf of a State savings association. For purposes of this definition, activities on behalf of a State savings association include activities where a person, whether at an office of the State savings association or at another location, sells, solicits, advertises, or offers an insurance product or annuity and at least one of the following applies:

(i) The person represents to a consumer that the sale, solicitation, advertisement, or offer of any insurance product or annuity is by or on behalf of the State savings association;

(ii) The State savings association refers a consumer to a seller of insurance products and annuities and the State savings association has a contractual

§ 390.182

arrangement to receive commissions or fees derived from a sale of an insurance product or annuity resulting from that referral; or

(iii) Documents evidencing the sale, solicitation, advertising, or offer of an insurance product or annuity identify or refer to the State savings association.

§ 390.182 Prohibited practices.

(a) *Anti-coercion and anti-tying rules.* You may not engage in any practice that would lead a consumer to believe that an extension of credit, in violation of section 5(q) of the Home Owners' Loan Act (12 U.S.C. 1464(q)), is conditional upon either:

(1) The purchase of an insurance product or annuity from a State savings association or any of its affiliates; or

(2) An agreement by the consumer not to obtain, or a prohibition on the consumer from obtaining, an insurance product or annuity from an unaffiliated entity.

(b) *Prohibition on misrepresentations generally.* You may not engage in any practice or use any advertisement at any office of, or on behalf of, a State savings association or a subsidiary of a State savings association that could mislead any person or otherwise cause a reasonable person to reach an erroneous belief with respect to:

(1) The fact that an insurance product or annuity you or any subsidiary of a State savings association sell or offer for sale is not backed by the Federal government or a State savings association, or the fact that the insurance product or annuity is not insured by the Federal Deposit Insurance Corporation;

(2) In the case of an insurance product or annuity that involves investment risk, the fact that there is an investment risk, including the potential that principal may be lost and that the product may decline in value; or

(3) In the case of a State savings association or subsidiary of a State savings association at which insurance products or annuities are sold or offered for sale, the fact that:

(i) The approval of an extension of credit to a consumer by the State savings association or subsidiary may not be conditioned on the purchase of an insurance product or annuity by the consumer from the State savings association or a subsidiary of a State savings association; and

(ii) The consumer is free to purchase the insurance product or annuity from another source.

(c) *Prohibition on domestic violence discrimination.* You may not sell or offer for sale, as principal, agent, or broker, any life or health insurance product if the status of the applicant or insured as a victim of domestic violence or as a provider of services to victims of domestic violence is considered as a criterion in any decision with regard to insurance underwriting, pricing, renewal, or scope of coverage of such product, or with regard to the payment of insurance claims on such product, except as required or expressly permitted under State law.

§ 390.183 What you must disclose.

(a) *Insurance disclosures.* In connection with the initial purchase of an insurance product or annuity by a consumer from you, you must disclose to the consumer, except to the extent the disclosure would not be accurate, that:

(1) The insurance product or annuity is not a deposit or other obligation of, or guaranteed by, a State savings association or an affiliate of a State savings association;

(2) The insurance product or annuity is not insured by the Federal Deposit Insurance Corporation (FDIC) or any other agency of the United States, a State savings association, or (if applicable) an affiliate of a State savings association; and

(3) In the case of an insurance product or annuity that involves an investment risk, there is investment risk associated with the product, including the possible loss of value.

(b) *Credit disclosures.* In the case of an application for credit in connection with which an insurance product or annuity is solicited, offered, or sold, you must disclose that a State savings association may not condition an extension of credit on either:

(1) The consumer's purchase of an insurance product or annuity from the State savings association or any of its affiliates; or

(2) The consumer's agreement not to obtain, or a prohibition on the consumer from obtaining, an insurance product or annuity from an unaffiliated entity.

(c) *Timing and method of disclosures*— (1) *In general.* The disclosures required by paragraph (a) of this section must be provided orally and in writing before the completion of the initial sale of an insurance product or annuity to a consumer. The disclosure required by paragraph (b) of this section must be made orally and in writing at the time the consumer applies for an extension of credit in connection with which an insurance product or annuity is solicited, offered, or sold.

(2) *Exception for transactions by mail.* If you conduct an insurance product or annuity sale by mail, you are not required to make the oral disclosures required by paragraph (a) of this section. If you take an application for credit by mail, you are not required to make the oral disclosure required by paragraph (b) of this section.

(3) *Exception for transactions by telephone.* If a sale of an insurance product or annuity is conducted by telephone, you may provide the written disclosures required by paragraph (a) of this section by mail within 3 business days beginning on the first business day after the sale, solicitation, or offer, excluding Sundays and the legal public holidays specified in 5 U.S.C. 6103(a). If you take an application for credit by telephone, you may provide the written disclosure required by paragraph (b) of this section by mail, provided you mail it to the consumer within three days beginning the first business day after the application is taken, excluding Sundays and the legal public holidays specified in 5 U.S.C. 6103(a).

(4) *Electronic form of disclosures.* (i) Subject to the requirements of section 101(c) of the Electronic Signatures in Global and National Commerce Act (12 U.S.C. 7001(c)), you may provide the written disclosures required by paragraph (a) and (b) of this section through electronic media instead of on paper, if the consumer affirmatively consents to receiving the disclosures electronically and if the disclosures are provided in a format that the consumer may retain or obtain later, for example, by printing or storing electronically (such as by downloading).

(ii) You are not required to provide orally any disclosures required by paragraphs (a) or (b) of this section that you provide by electronic media.

(5) *Disclosures must be readily understandable.* The disclosures provided shall be conspicuous, simple, direct, readily understandable, and designed to call attention to the nature and significance of the information provided. For instance, you may use the following disclosures in visual media, such as television broadcasting, ATM screens, billboards, signs, posters and written advertisements and promotional materials, as appropriate and consistent with paragraphs (a) and (b) of this section:
• NOT A DEPOSIT
• NOT FDIC-INSURED
• NOT INSURED BY ANY FEDERAL GOVERNMENT AGENCY
• NOT GUARANTEED BY THE STATE SAVINGS ASSOCIATION
• MAY GO DOWN IN VALUE

(6) *Disclosures must be meaningful.* (i) You must provide the disclosures required by paragraphs (a) and (b) of this section in a meaningful form. Examples of the types of methods that could call attention to the nature and significance of the information provided include:

(A) A plain-language heading to call attention to the disclosures;

(B) A typeface and type size that are easy to read;

(C) Wide margins and ample line spacing;

(D) Boldface or italics for key words; and

(E) Distinctive type size, style, and graphic devices, such as shading or sidebars, when the disclosures are combined with other information.

(ii) You have not provided the disclosures in a meaningful form if you merely state to the consumer that the required disclosures are available in printed material, but do not provide the printed material when required and do not orally disclose the information to the consumer when required.

(iii) With respect to those disclosures made through electronic media for which paper or oral disclosures are not required, the disclosures are not meaningfully provided if the consumer may

§ 390.184

bypass the visual text of the disclosures before purchasing an insurance product or annuity.

(7) *Consumer acknowledgment.* You must obtain from the consumer, at the time a consumer receives the disclosures required under paragraphs (a) or (b) of this section, or at the time of the initial purchase by the consumer of an insurance product or annuity, a written acknowledgment by the consumer that the consumer received the disclosures. You may permit a consumer to acknowledge receipt of the disclosures electronically or in paper form. If the disclosures required under paragraphs (a) or (b) of this section are provided in connection with a transaction that is conducted by telephone, you must:

(i) Obtain an oral acknowledgment of receipt of the disclosures and maintain sufficient documentation to show that the acknowledgment was given; and

(ii) Make reasonable efforts to obtain a written acknowledgment from the consumer.

(d) *Advertisements and other promotional material for insurance products or annuities.* The disclosures described in paragraph (a) of this section are required in advertisements and promotional material for insurance products or annuities unless the advertisements and promotional material are of a general nature describing or listing the services or products offered by a State savings association.

§ 390.184 Where insurance activities may take place.

(a) *General rule.* A State savings association must, to the extent practicable:

(1) Keep the area where the State savings association conducts transactions involving insurance products or annuities physically segregated from areas where retail deposits are routinely accepted from the general public;

(2) Identify the areas where insurance product or annuity sales activities occur; and

(3) Clearly delineate and distinguish those areas from the areas where the State savings association's retail deposit-taking activities occur.

(b) *Referrals.* Any person who accepts deposits from the public in an area where such transactions are routinely conducted in a State savings association may refer a consumer who seeks to purchase an insurance product or annuity to a qualified person who sells that product only if the person making the referral receives no more than a one-time, nominal fee of a fixed dollar amount for each referral that does not depend on whether the referral results in a transaction.

§ 390.185 Qualification and licensing requirements for insurance sales personnel.

A State savings association may not permit any person to sell or offer for sale any insurance product or annuity in any part of the State savings association's office or on its behalf, unless the person is at all times appropriately qualified and licensed under applicable State insurance licensing standards with regard to the specific products being sold or recommended.

APPENDIX A TO SUBPART I OF PART 390—CONSUMER GRIEVANCE PROCESS

Any consumer who believes that any State savings association or any other person selling, soliciting, advertising, or offering insurance products or annuities to the consumer at an office of the State savings association or on behalf of the State savings association has violated the requirements of this subpart should contact the FDIC at the following address: Federal Deposit Insurance Corporation, Consumer Response Center, 1100 Walnut St, Box #11, Kansas City, MO 64106, or telephone 1-877-275-3342 (1-877-ASK FDIC), or e-mail *http://www.fdic.gov/consumers/consumer/ccc/contact.html.*

Subpart J—Fiduciary Powers of State Savings Associations

§ 390.190 What regulations govern the fiduciary operations of State savings associations?

A State savings association must conduct its fiduciary operations in accordance with applicable State law, and must exercise its fiduciary powers in a safe and sound manner.

Subpart K—Recordkeeping and Confirmation Requirements for Securities Transactions

§ 390.200 What does this subpart do?

This subpart establishes recordkeeping and confirmation requirements that apply when a State savings association ("you") effects certain securities transactions for customers.

§ 390.201 Must I comply with this subpart?

(a) *General.* Except as provided under paragraph (b) of this section, you must comply with this subpart when:

(1) You effect a securities transaction for a customer.

(2) You effect a transaction in government securities.

(3) You effect a transaction in municipal securities and are not registered as a municipal securities dealer with the SEC.

(4) You effect a securities transaction as fiduciary. If you are a State savings association, you must comply with applicable law when you effect such a transaction.

(b) *Exceptions*—(1) *Small number of transactions.* You are not required to comply with § 390.204(b) through (d) (recordkeeping) and § 390.213(a) through (c) (policies and procedures), if you effected an average of fewer than 500 securities transactions per year for customers over the three prior calendar years. You may exclude transactions in government securities when you calculate this average.

(2) *Government securities.* If you effect fewer than 500 government securities brokerage transactions per year, you are not required to comply with § 390.204 (recordkeeping) for those transactions. This exception does not apply to government securities dealer transactions. See 17 CFR 404.4(a).

(3) *Municipal securities.* If you are registered with the SEC as a "municipal securities dealer," as defined in 15 U.S.C. 78c(a)(30) (see 15 U.S.C. 78o–4), you are not required to comply with this subpart when you conduct municipal securities transactions.

(4) *Foreign branches.* You are not required to comply with this subpart when you conduct a transaction at your foreign branch.

(5) *Transactions by registered broker-dealers.* You are not required to comply with this subpart for securities transactions effected by a registered broker-dealer, if the registered broker-dealer directly provides the customer with a confirmation. These transactions include a transaction effected by your employee who also acts as an employee of a registered broker-dealer ("dual employee").

§ 390.202 What requirements apply to all transactions?

You must effect all transactions, including transactions excepted under § 390.201, in a safe and sound manner. You must maintain effective systems of records and controls regarding your customers' securities transactions. These systems must clearly and accurately reflect all appropriate information and provide an adequate basis for an audit.

§ 390.203 What definitions apply to this subpart?

Asset-backed security means a security that is primarily serviced by the cash flows of a discrete pool of receivables or other financial assets, either fixed or revolving, that by their terms convert into cash within a finite time period. *Asset-backed security* includes any rights or other assets designed to ensure the servicing or timely distribution of proceeds to the security holders.

Common or collective investment fund means with respect to a fiduciary account, a fund established and administered by you in compliance with 12 CFR 9.18 or any fund established under 12 CFR 9.18.

Completion of the transaction means:

(1) If the customer purchases a security through or from you, except as provided in paragraph (2) of this definition, the time the customer pays you any part of the purchase price. If payment is made by a bookkeeping entry, the time you make the bookkeeping entry for any part of the purchase price.

(2) If the customer purchases a security through or from you and pays for the security before you request payment or notify the customer that payment is due, the time you deliver the

803

security to or into the account of the customer.

(3) If the customer sells a security through or to you, except as provided in paragraph (4) of this definition, the time the customer delivers the security to you. If you have custody of the security at the time of sale, the time you transfer the security from the customer's account.

(4) If the customer sells a security through or to you and delivers the security to you before you request delivery or notify the customer that delivery is due, the time you pay the customer or pay into the customer's account.

Customer means a person or account, including an agency, trust, estate, guardianship, or other fiduciary account for which you effect a securities transaction. *Customer* does not include a broker or dealer, or you when you: act as a broker or dealer; act as a fiduciary with investment discretion over an account; are a trustee that acts as the shareholder of record for the purchase or sale of securities; or are the issuer of securities that are the subject of the transaction.

Debt security means any security, such as a bond, debenture, note, or any other similar instrument that evidences a liability of the issuer (including any security of this type that is convertible into stock or a similar security). *Debt security* also includes a fractional or participation interest in these debt securities. *Debt security* does not include securities issued by an investment company registered under the Investment Company Act of 1940, 15 U.S.C. 80a–1, *et seq.*

Government security means:

(1) A security that is a direct obligation of, or an obligation that is guaranteed as to principal and interest by, the United States;

(2) A security that is issued or guaranteed by a corporation in which the United States has a direct or indirect interest if the Secretary of the Treasury has designated the security for exemption as necessary or appropriate in the public interest or for the protection of investors;

(3) A security issued or guaranteed as to principal and interest by a corporation if a statute specifically designates, by name, the corporation's securities as exempt securities within the meaning of the laws administered by the SEC; or

(4) Any put, call, straddle, option, or privilege on a government security described in this definition, other than a put, call, straddle, option, or privilege:

(i) That is traded on one or more national securities exchanges; or

(ii) For which quotations are disseminated through an automated quotation system operated by a registered securities association.

Investment company plan means any plan under which:

(1) A customer purchases securities issued by an open-end investment company or unit investment trust registered under the Investment Company Act of 1940, making the payments directly to, or made payable to, the registered investment company, or the principal underwriter, custodian, trustee, or other designated agent of the registered investment company; or

(2) A customer sells securities issued by an open-end investment company or unit investment trust registered under the Investment Company Act of 1940 under:

(i) An individual retirement or individual pension plan qualified under the Internal Revenue Code; or

(ii) A contractual or systematic agreement under which the customer purchases at the applicable public offering price, or redeems at the applicable redemption price, securities in specified amounts (calculated in security units or dollars) at specified time intervals, and stating the commissions or charges (or the means of calculating them) that the customer will pay in connection with the purchase.

Investment discretion means with respect to a fiduciary account, the sole or shared authority to determine what securities or other assets to purchase or sell on behalf of the account, regardless of whether this authority has been exercised.

Municipal security means:

(1) A security that is a direct obligation of, or an obligation guaranteed as to principal or interest by, a State or any political subdivision, or any agency or instrumentality of a State or any political subdivision.

Federal Deposit Insurance Corporation § 390.204

(2) A security that is a direct obligation of, or an obligation guaranteed as to principal or interest by, any municipal corporate instrumentality of one or more States; or

(3) A security that is an industrial development bond, the interest on which is excludable from gross income under section 103(a) of the Code (26 U.S.C. 103(a)).

Periodic plan means a written document that authorizes you to act as agent to purchase or sell for a customer a specific security or securities (other than securities issued by an open end investment company or unit investment trust registered under the Investment Company Act of 1940). The written document must authorize you to purchase or sell in specific amounts (calculated in security units or dollars) or to the extent of dividends and funds available, at specific time intervals, and must set forth the commission or charges to be paid by the customer or the manner of calculating them.

SEC means the Securities and Exchange Commission.

Security means any note, stock, treasury stock, bond, debenture, certificate of interest or participation in any profit-sharing agreement or in any oil, gas, or other mineral royalty or lease, any collateral-trust certificate, preorganization certificate or subscription, transferable share, investment contract, voting-trust certificate, and any put, call, straddle, option, or privilege on any security or group or index of securities (including any interest therein or based on the value thereof), or, in general, any instrument commonly known as a "security"; or any certificate of interest or participation in, temporary or interim certificate for, receipt for, or warrant or right to subscribe to or purchase, any of the foregoing. *Security* does not include currency; any note, draft, bill of exchange, or banker's acceptance which has a maturity at the time of issuance of less than nine months, exclusive of days of grace, or any renewal thereof, the maturity of which is likewise limited; a deposit or share account in a Federal or State chartered depository institution; a loan participation; a letter of credit or other form of bank indebtedness incurred in the ordinary course of business; units of a collective investment fund; interests in a variable amount (master) note of a borrower of prime credit; U.S. Savings Bonds; or any other instrument FDIC determines does not constitute a security for purposes of this subpart.

Sweep account means any prearranged, automatic transfer or sweep of funds above a certain dollar level from a deposit account to purchase a security or securities, or any prearranged, automatic redemption or sale of a security or securities when a deposit account drops below a certain level with the proceeds being transferred into a deposit account.

§ 390.204 What records must I maintain for securities transactions?

If you effect securities transactions for customers, you must maintain all of the following records for at least three years:

(a) *Chronological records.* You must maintain an itemized daily record of each purchase and sale of securities in chronological order, including:

(1) The account or customer name for which you effected each transaction;

(2) The name and amount of the securities;

(3) The unit and aggregate purchase or sale price;

(4) The trade date; and

(5) The name or other designation of the registered broker-dealer or other person from whom you purchased the securities or to whom you sold the securities.

(b) *Account records.* You must maintain account records for each customer reflecting:

(1) Purchases and sales of securities;

(2) Receipts and deliveries of securities;

(3) Receipts and disbursements of cash; and

(4) Other debits and credits pertaining to transactions in securities.

(c) *Memorandum (order ticket).* You must make and keep current a memorandum (order ticket) of each order or any other instruction given or received for the purchase or sale of securities (whether executed or not), including:

(1) The account or customer name for which you effected each transaction;

§ 390.205

(2) Whether the transaction was a market order, limit order, or subject to special instructions;

(3) The time the trader received the order;

(4) The time the trader placed the order with the registered broker-dealer, or if there was no registered broker-dealer, the time the trader executed or cancelled the order;

(5) The price at which the trader executed the order;

(6) The name of the registered broker-dealer you used.

(d) *Record of registered broker-dealers.* You must maintain a record of all registered broker-dealers that you selected to effect securities transactions and the amount of commissions that you paid or allocated to each registered broker-dealer during each calendar year.

(e) *Notices.* You must maintain a copy of the written notice required under sections 390.206–390.211.

§ 390.205 How must I maintain my records?

(a) You may maintain the records required under § 390.204 in any manner, form, or format that you deem appropriate. However, your records must clearly and accurately reflect the required information and provide an adequate basis for an audit of the information.

(b) You, or the person that maintains and preserves records on your behalf, must:

(1) Arrange and index the records in a way that permits easy location, access, and retrieval of a particular record;

(2) Separately store, for the time required for preservation of the original record, a duplicate copy of the record on any medium allowed by this section;

(3) Provide promptly any of the following that FDIC examiners or your directors may request:

(i) A legible, true, and complete copy of the record in the medium and format in which it is stored;

(ii) A legible, true, and complete printout of the record; and

(iii) Means to access, view, and print the records.

(4) In the case of records on electronic storage media, you, or the person that maintains and preserves records for you, must establish procedures:

(i) To maintain, preserve, and reasonably safeguard the records from loss, alteration, or destruction;

(ii) To limit access to the records to properly authorized personnel, your directors, and FDIC examiners; and

(iii) To reasonably ensure that any reproduction of a non-electronic original record on electronic storage media is complete, true, and legible when retrieved.

(c) You may contract with third party service providers to maintain the records.

§ 390.206 What type of notice must I provide when I effect a securities transaction for a customer?

If you effect a securities transaction for a customer, you must give or send the customer the registered broker-dealer confirmation described at § 390.207, or the written notice described at § 390.208. For certain types of transactions, you may elect to provide the alternate notices described in § 390.209.

§ 390.207 How do I provide a registered broker-dealer confirmation?

(a) If you elect to satisfy § 390.206 by providing the customer with a registered broker-dealer confirmation, you must provide the confirmation by having the registered broker-dealer send the confirmation directly to the customer or by sending a copy of the registered broker-dealer's confirmation to the customer within one business day after you receive it.

(b) If you have received or will receive remuneration from any source, including the customer, in connection with the transaction, you must provide a statement of the source and amount of the remuneration in addition to the registered broker-dealer confirmation described in paragraph (a) of this section.

§ 390.208 How do I provide a written notice?

If you elect to satisfy § 390.206 by providing the customer a written notice, you must give or send the written notice at or before the completion of the

Federal Deposit Insurance Corporation § 390.208

securities transaction. You must include all of the following information in a written notice:

(a) Your name and the customer's name.

(b) The capacity in which you acted (for example, as agent).

(c) The date and time of execution of the securities transaction (or a statement that you will furnish this information within a reasonable time after the customer's written request), and the identity, price, and number of shares or units (or principal amount in the case of debt securities) of the security the customer purchased or sold.

(d) The name of the person from whom you purchased or to whom you sold the security, or a statement that you will furnish this information within a reasonable time after the customer's written request.

(e) The amount of any remuneration that you have received or will receive from the customer in connection with the transaction unless the remuneration paid by the customer is determined under a written agreement, other than on a transaction basis.

(f) The source and amount of any other remuneration you have received or will receive in connection with the transaction. If, in the case of a purchase, you were not participating in a distribution, or in the case of a sale, were not participating in a tender offer, the written notice may state whether you have or will receive any other remuneration and state that you will furnish the source and amount of the other remuneration within a reasonable time after the customer's written request.

(g) That you are not a member of the Securities Investor Protection Corporation, if that is the case. This does not apply to a transaction in shares of a registered open-end investment company or unit investment trust if the customer sends funds or securities directly to, or receives funds or securities directly from, the registered open-end investment company or unit investment trust, its transfer agent, its custodian, or a designated broker or dealer who sends the customer either a confirmation or the written notice in this section.

(h) *Additional disclosures.* You must provide all of the additional disclosures described in the following chart for transactions involving certain debt securities:

If you effect a transaction involving . . .	You must provide the following additional information in your written notice . . .
(1) A debt security subject to redemption before maturity	A statement that the issuer may redeem the debt security in whole or in part before maturity, that the redemption could affect the represented yield, and that additional redemption information is available upon request.

(2) A debt security that you effected exclusively on the basis of a dollar price.	(i) The dollar price at which you effected the transaction; and
	(ii) The yield to maturity calculated from the dollar price. You do not have to disclose the yield to maturity if:
	   (A) The issuer may extend the maturity date of the security with a variable interest rate; or
	   (B) The security is an asset-backed security that represents an interest in, or is secured by, a pool of receivables or other financial assets that are subject continuously to prepayment.

(3) A debt security that you effected on basis of yield	(i) The yield at which the transaction, including the percentage amount and its characterization (e.g., current yield, yield to maturity, or yield to call). If you effected the transaction at yield to call, you must indicate the type of call, the call date, and the call price;
	(ii) The dollar price calculated from that yield; and
	(iii) The yield to maturity and the represented yield, if you effected the transaction on a basis other than yield to maturity and the yield to maturity is lower than the represented yield. You are not required to disclose this information if:
	   (A) The issuer may extend the maturity date of the security with a variable interest rate; or
	   (B) The security is an asset-backed security that represents an interest in, or is secured by, a pool of receivables or other financial assets that are subject continuously to prepayment.

§ 390.209

If you effect a transaction involving . . .	You must provide the following additional information in your written notice . . .
(4) A debt security that is an asset-backed security that represents an interest in, or is secured by, a pool of receivables or other financial assets that are subject continuously to prepayment.	(i) A statement that the actual yield of the asset-backed security may vary according to the rate at which the underlying receivables or other financial assets are prepaid; and (ii) A statement that you will furnish information concerning the factors that affect yield (including at a minimum estimated yield, weighted average life, and the prepayment assumptions underlying yield) upon the customer's written request.
(5) A debt security, other than a government security	A statement that the security is unrated by a nationally recognized statistical rating organization, if that is the case.

§ 390.209 What are the alternate notice requirements?

You may elect to satisfy § 390.206 by providing the alternate notices described in the following chart for certain types of transactions.

If you effect a securities transaction . . .	Then you may elect to . . .
(a) For or with the account of a customer under a periodic plan, sweep account, or investment company plan.	Give or send to the customer within five business days after the end of each quarterly period a written statement disclosing: (1) Each purchase and redemption that you effected for or with, and each dividend or distribution that you credited to or reinvested for, the customer's account during the period; (2) The date of each transaction; (3) The identity, number, and price of any securities that the customer purchased or redeemed in each transaction; (4) The total number of shares of the securities in the customer's account; (5) Any remuneration that you received or will receive in connection with the transaction; and (6) That you will give or send the registered broker-dealer confirmation described in § 390.207 or the written notice described in § 390.208 within a reasonable time after the customer's written request.
(b) For or with the account of a customer in shares of an open-ended management company registered under the Investment Company Act of 1940 that holds itself out as a money market fund and attempts to maintain a stable net asset value per share.	Give or send to the customer the written statement described at paragraph (a) of this section on a monthly basis. You may not use the alternate notice, however, if you deduct sales loads upon the purchase or redemption of shares in the money market fund.
(c) For an account for which you do not exercise investment discretion, and for which you and the customer have agreed in writing to an arrangement concerning the time and content of the written notice.	Give or send to the customer a written notice at the agreed-upon time and with the agreed-upon content, and include a statement that you will furnish the registered broker-dealer confirmation described in § 390.207 or the written notice described in § 390.208 within a reasonable time after the customer's written request.
(d) For an account for which you exercise investment discretion other than in an agency capacity, excluding common or collective investment funds.	Give or send the registered broker-dealer confirmation described in § 390.207 or the written notice described in § 390.208 within a reasonable time after a written request by the person with the power to terminate the account or, if there is no such person, any person holding a vested beneficial interest in the account.
(e) For an account in which you exercise investment discretion in an agency capacity.	Give or send each customer a written itemized statement specifying the funds and securities in your custody or possession and all debits, credits, and transactions in the customer's account. You must provide this information to the customer not less than once every three months. You must give or send the registered broker-dealer confirmation described in § 390.207 or the written notice described in § 390.208 within a reasonable time after a customer's written request.
(f) For a common or collective investment fund	(1) Give or send to a customer who invests in the fund a copy of the annual financial report of the fund, or

Federal Deposit Insurance Corporation § 390.213

If you effect a securities transaction . . .	Then you may elect to . . .
	(2) Notify the customer that a copy of the report is available and that you will furnish the report within a reasonable time after a written request by a person to whom a regular periodic accounting would ordinarily be rendered with respect to each participating account.

§ 390.210 May I provide a notice electronically?

You may provide any written notice required under §§ 390.206 through 390.211 electronically. If a customer has a facsimile machine, you may send the notice by facsimile transmission. You may use other electronic communications if:

(a) The parties agree to use electronic instead of hard copy notices;
(b) The parties are able to print or download the notice;
(c) Your electronic communications system cannot automatically delete the electronic notice; and
(d) Both parties are able to receive electronic messages.

§ 390.211 May I charge a fee for a notice?

You may not charge a fee for providing a notice required under §§ 390.206 through 390.211, except that you may charge a reasonable fee for the notices provided under § 390.209(a), (d), and (e).

§ 390.212 When must I settle a securities transaction?

(a) You may not effect or enter into a contract for the purchase or sale of a security that provides for payment of funds and delivery of securities later than the latest of:

(1) The third business day after the date of the contract. This deadline is no later than the fourth business day after the contract for contracts involving the sale for cash of securities that are priced after 4:30 p.m. Eastern Standard Time on the date the securities are priced and are sold by an issuer to an underwriter under a firm commitment underwritten offering registered under the Securities Act of 1933, 15 U.S.C. 77a, *et seq.*, or are sold by you to an initial purchaser participating in the offering;

(2) Such other time as the SEC specifies by rule (*see* SEC Rule 15c6–1, 17 CFR 240.15c6–1); or

(3) Such time as the parties expressly agree at the time of the transaction. The parties to a contract are deemed to have expressly agreed to an alternate date for payment of funds and delivery of securities at the time of the transaction for a contract for the sale for cash of securities under a firm commitment offering, if the managing underwriter and the issuer have agreed to the date for all securities sold under the offering and the parties to the contract have not expressly agreed to another date for payment of funds and delivery of securities at the time of the transaction.

(b) The deadlines in paragraph (a) of this section do not apply to the purchase or sale of limited partnership interests that are not listed on an exchange or for which quotations are not disseminated through an automated quotation system of a registered securities association.

§ 390.213 What policies and procedures must I maintain and follow for securities transactions?

If you effect securities transactions for customers, you must maintain and follow policies and procedures that meet all of the following requirements:

(a) Your policies and procedures must assign responsibility for the supervision of all officers or employees who:

(1) Transmit orders to, or place orders with, registered broker-dealers;

(2) Execute transactions in securities for customers; or

(3) Process orders for notice or settlement purposes, or perform other back office functions for securities transactions that you effect for customers. Policies and procedures for personnel described in this paragraph (a)(3) must provide supervision and reporting lines that are separate from supervision and reporting lines for personnel described in paragraphs (a)(1) and (2) of this section.

§ 390.214

(b) Your policies and procedures must provide for the fair and equitable allocation of securities and prices to accounts when you receive orders for the same security at approximately the same time and you place the orders for execution either individually or in combination.

(c) Your policies and procedures must provide for securities transactions in which you act as agent for the buyer and seller (crossing of buy and sell orders) on a fair and equitable basis to the parties to the transaction, where permissible under applicable law.

(d) Your policies and procedures must require your officers and employees to file the personal securities trading reports described at § 390.214, if the officer or employee:

(1) Makes investment recommendations or decisions for the accounts of customers;

(2) Participates in the determination of these recommendations or decisions; or

(3) In connection with their duties, obtains information concerning which securities you intend to purchase, sell, or recommend for purchase or sale.

§ 390.214 How do my officers and employees file reports of personal securities trading transactions?

An officer or employee described in § 390.213(d) must report all personal transactions in securities made by or on behalf of the officer or employee if he or she has a beneficial interest in the security.

(a) *Contents and filing of report.* The officer or employee must file the report with you no later than 30 calendar days after the end of each calendar quarter. The report must include the following information:

(1) The date of each transaction, the title and number of shares, the interest rate and maturity date (if applicable), and the principal amount of each security involved.

(2) The nature of each transaction (*i.e.*, purchase, sale, or other type of acquisition or disposition).

(3) The price at which each transaction was effected.

(4) The name of the broker, dealer, or other intermediary effecting the transaction.

(5) The date the officer or employee submitted the report.

(b) *Report not required for certain transactions.* Your officer or employee is not required to report a transaction if:

(1) He or she has no direct or indirect influence or control over the account for which the transaction was effected or over the securities held in that account;

(2) The transaction was in shares issued by an open-end investment company registered under the Investment Company Act of 1940;

(3) The transaction was in direct obligations of the government of the United States;

(4) The transaction was in bankers' acceptances, bank certificates of deposit, commercial paper or high quality short term debt instruments, including repurchase agreements; or

(5) The officer or employee had an aggregate amount of purchases and sales of $10,000 or less during the calendar quarter.

(c) *Alternate report.* When you act as an investment adviser to an investment company registered under the Investment Company Act of 1940, an officer or employee that is an "access person" may fulfill his or her reporting requirements under this section by filing with you the "access person" personal securities trading report required by SEC Rule 17j–1(d), 17 CFR 270.17j–1(d).

Subpart L—Electronic Operations

§ 390.220 What does this subpart do?

This subpart addresses notification of the FDIC by State savings associations who intend to establish a transactional Web site.

§ 390.221 Must I inform FDIC before I use electronic means or facilities?

(a) *General.* A State savings association ("you") are not required to inform FDIC before you use electronic means or facilities, except as provided in paragraphs (b) and (c) of this section. However, FDIC encourages you to consult with your appropriate FDIC region before you engage in any activities using electronic means or facilities.

Federal Deposit Insurance Corporation

(b) *Activities requiring advance notice.* You must file a written notice as described in § 390.222 before you establish a transactional Web site. A transactional Web site is an Internet site that enables users to conduct financial transactions such as accessing an account, obtaining an account balance, transferring funds, processing bill payments, opening an account, applying for or obtaining a loan, or purchasing other authorized products or services.

(c) *Other procedures.* If the appropriate FDIC region informs you of any supervisory or compliance concerns that may affect your use of electronic means or facilities, you must follow any procedures it imposes in writing.

§ 390.222 How do I notify FDIC?

(a) *Notice requirement.* You must file a written notice with the appropriate FDIC region at least 30 days before you establish a transactional Web site. The notice must do three things:

(1) Describe the transactional Web site.

(2) Indicate the date the transactional Web site will become operational.

(3) List a contact familiar with the deployment, operation, and security of the transactional Web site.

(b) [Reserved]

Subpart M—Deposits

§ 390.230 What does this subpart do?

This subpart applies to the deposit activities of State savings associations.

§ 390.231 What records should I maintain on deposit activities?

All State savings associations ("you") should establish and maintain deposit documentation practices and records that demonstrate that you appropriately administer and monitor deposit-related activities. Your records should adequately evidence ownership, balances, and all transactions involving each account. You may maintain records on deposit activities in any format that is consistent with standard business practices.

Subpart N—Possession by Conservators and Receivers for Federal and State Savings Associations

§ 390.240 Procedure upon taking possession.

(a) The conservator or receiver for a Federal or State savings association shall take possession of the savings association by taking possession of the principal office of the Federal or State savings association in accordance with the terms of the OCC's or State bank supervisor's, as appropriate, appointment.

(b) Upon taking possession, the conservator or receiver shall immediately:

(1) Take possession of the savings association's books, records and assets.

(2) Notify in writing, served personally or by registered mail or telegraph, all persons and entities that the conservator or receiver knows to be holding or in possession of assets of the savings association, that the conservator or receiver has succeeded to all rights, titles, powers and privileges of the savings associations.

(3) File with the Executive Secretary a statement that possession was taken, including the time of the taking, which statement shall be conclusive evidence thereof.

(4) Post a notice on the door of the principal and other offices of the savings association in the form, if any, prescribed by the OCC or State bank supervisor, as appropriate.

(5) By operation of law and without any conveyance or other instrument, act or deed, succeed to the rights, titles, powers and privileges of the savings association, and to the rights, powers, and privileges of its stockholders, members, accountholders, depositors, officers, and directors. No stockholder, member, accountholder, depositor, officer or director shall thereafter have or exercise any right, power, or privilege, or act in connection with any of the savings association's assets or property.

§ 390.241 Notice of appointment.

(a) When the OCC or State bank supervisor, as appropriate, issues an

§ 390.250

order for the appointment of a conservator or receiver, the FDIC will designate the persons or entities whose employees or agents must, before the conservator or receiver takes possession of the savings association:

(1) Give notice of the appointment to any officer or employee who is present in and appears to be in charge at the principal office of the savings association as determined by the FDIC.

(2) Serve a copy of the order for the appointment upon the savings association or upon the conservator by:

(i) Leaving a certified copy of the order of appointment at the principal office of the savings association as determined by the FDIC; or

(ii) Handing a certified copy of the order of appointment to the previous conservator of the savings association, or to the officer or employee of the savings association, or to the previous conservator who is present in and appears to be in charge at the principal office of the savings association as determined by the FDIC.

(3) File with the Executive Secretary of the FDIC a statement that includes the date and time that notice of the appointment was given and service of the order of appointment was made.

(b) If the OCC or State bank supervisor, as appropriate, appoints a conservator or receiver under this subpart, the FDIC will immediately file a notice of the appointment for publication in the FEDERAL REGISTER.

Subpart O—Subordinate Organizations

§ 390.250 What does this subpart cover?

(a) The FDIC is issuing this subpart O pursuant to its general rulemaking and supervisory authority under the Federal Deposit Insurance Act, 12 U.S.C. 1811 *et seq.*, and its specific authority under section 18(m) of the Federal Deposit Insurance Act, 12 U.S.C. 1828(m). This subpart applies to subordinate organizations of State savings associations. The FDIC may, at any time, limit a State savings association's investment in any of these entities, or may limit or refuse to permit any activities of any of these entities for supervisory, legal, or safety and soundness reasons.

(b) Notices under this subpart are applications for purposes of statutory and regulatory references to "applications." Any conditions that the FDIC imposes in approving any application are enforceable as a condition imposed in writing by the FDIC in connection with the granting of a request by a State savings association within the meaning of 12 U.S.C. 1818(b) or 1818(i).

§ 390.251 Definitions.

For purposes of this subpart:

Control has the same meaning as in part 391, subpart E.

GAAP-consolidated subsidiary means an entity in which a State savings association has a direct or indirect ownership interest and whose assets are consolidated with those of the savings association for purposes of reporting under Generally Accepted Accounting Principles (GAAP). Generally, these are entities in which a State savings association has a majority ownership interest.

Lower-tier entity includes any company in which a subsidiary has a direct or indirect ownership interest.

Ownership interest means any equity interest in a business organization, including stock, limited or general partnership interests, or shares in a limited liability company.

Subordinate organization means any corporation, partnership, business trust, association, joint venture, pool, syndicate, or other similar business organization in which a State savings association has a direct or indirect ownership interest, unless that ownership interest qualifies as a pass-through investment and is so designated by the investing State savings association.

Subsidiary means any subordinate organization directly or indirectly controlled by a State savings association.

§ 390.252 How must separate corporate identities be maintained?

(a) Each State savings association and subordinate organization thereof must be operated in a manner that demonstrates to the public that each maintains a separate corporate existence. Each must operate so that:

(1) Their respective business transactions, accounts, and records are not intermingled;
(2) Each observes the formalities of their separate corporate procedures;
(3) Each is adequately financed as a separate unit in light of normal obligations reasonably foreseeable in a business of its size and character;
(4) Each is held out to the public as a separate enterprise; and
(5) Unless the parent State savings association has guaranteed a loan to the subordinate organization, all borrowings by the subordinate organization indicate that the parent is not liable.

(b) The FDIC regulations that apply both to State savings associations and subordinate organizations shall not be construed as requiring a State savings association and its subordinate organizations to operate as a single entity.

§ 390.253 What notices are required to establish or acquire a new subsidiary or engage in new activities through an existing subsidiary?

When required by section 18(m) of the Federal Deposit Insurance Act, a State savings association ("you") must file a notice ("Notice") with the FDIC before establishing or acquiring a subsidiary or engaging in new activities in a subsidiary. The Notice must contain all of the information the required under 12 CFR 362.15. If the FDIC notifies you within 30 days that the Notice presents supervisory concerns, or raises significant issues of law or policy, you must apply for and receive the FDIC's prior written approval before establishing or acquiring the subsidiary or engaging in new activities in the subsidiary.

§ 390.254 How may a subsidiary of a State savings association issue securities?

(a) A subsidiary may issue, either directly or through a third party intermediary, any securities that its parent State savings association ("you") may issue. The subsidiary must not state or imply that the securities it issues are covered by federal deposit insurance. A subsidiary may not issue any security the payment, maturity, or redemption of which may be accelerated upon the condition that you are insolvent or have been placed into receivership.

(b) You must file a notice with the FDIC in accordance with § 390.253 at least 30 days before your first issuance of any securities through an existing subsidiary or in conjunction with establishing or acquiring a new subsidiary. If the FDIC notifies you within 30 days that the notice presents supervisory concerns or raises significant issues of law or policy, you must receive the FDIC's prior written approval before issuing securities through your subsidiary.

(c) For as long as any securities are outstanding, you must maintain all records generated through each securities issuance in the ordinary course of business, including a copy of any prospectus, offering circular, or similar document concerning such issuance, and make such records available for examination by the FDIC. Such records must include, but are not limited to:

(1) The amount of your assets or liabilities (including any guarantees you make with respect to the securities issuance) that have been transferred or made available to the subsidiary; the percentage that such amount represents of the current book value of your assets on an unconsolidated basis; and the current book value of all such assets of the subsidiary;

(2) The terms of any guarantee(s) issued by you or any third party;

(3) A description of the securities the subsidiary issued;

(4) The net proceeds from the issuance of securities (or the pro rata portion of the net proceeds from securities issued through a jointly owned subsidiary); the gross proceeds of the securities issuance; and the market value of assets collateralizing the securities issuance (any assets of the subsidiary, including any guarantees of its securities issuance you have made);

(5) The interest or dividend rates and yields, or the range thereof, and the frequency of payments on the subsidiary's securities;

(6) The minimum denomination of the subsidiary's securities; and

(7) Where the subsidiary marketed or intends to market the securities.

§ 390.255 How may a State savings association exercise its salvage power in connection with a service corporation or lower-tier entities?

(a) In accordance with this section, a State savings association ("you") may exercise your salvage power to make a contribution or a loan (including a guarantee of a loan made by any other person) to a lower-tier entity ("salvage investment") that exceeds the maximum amount otherwise permitted under law or regulation. You must notify the FDIC at least 30 days before making such a salvage investment. This notice must demonstrate that:

(1) The salvage investment protects your interest in the lower-tier entity;

(2) The salvage investment is consistent with safety and soundness; and

(3) You considered alternatives to the salvage investment and determined that such alternatives would not adequately satisfy paragraphs (a)(1) and (2) of this section.

(b) If the FDIC notifies you within 30 days that the Notice presents supervisory concerns, or raises significant issues of law or policy, you must apply for and receive the FDIC's prior written approval before making a salvage investment.

(c) If your lower-tier entity is a GAAP-consolidated subsidiary, your salvage investment under this section will be considered an investment in a subsidiary for purposes of subpart Z.

Subpart P—Lending and Investment

§ 390.260 General.

(a) *Authority and scope.* This subpart is being issued by the FDIC under its general rulemaking and supervisory authority under the Federal Deposit Insurance Act (FDIA), 12 U.S.C. 1811 *et seq.* Sections 390.264, 390.265, and 390.267 through 390.272 contain safety-and-soundness based lending and investment provisions applicable to State savings associations.

(b) *General lending standards.* Each State savings association is expected to conduct its lending and investment activities prudently. Each State savings association should use lending and investment standards that are consistent with safety and soundness, ensure adequate portfolio diversification and are appropriate for the size and condition of the institution, the nature and scope of its operations, and conditions in its lending market. Each State savings association should adequately monitor the condition of its portfolio and the adequacy of any collateral securing its loans.

§ 390.261 [Reserved]

§ 390.262 Definitions.

For purposes of this subpart:

Consumer loans include loans for personal, family, or household purposes and loans reasonably incident thereto, and may be made as either open-end or closed-end consumer credit (as defined at 12 CFR 226.2(a)(10) and (20)). Consumer loans do not include credit extended in connection with credit card loans, bona fide overdraft loans, and other loans that the State savings association has designated as made under investment or lending authority other than section 5(c)(2)(D) of the HOLA.

Credit card is any card, plate, coupon book, or other single credit device that may be used from time to time to obtain credit.

Credit card account is a credit account established in conjunction with the issuance of, or the extension of credit through, a credit card. This term includes loans made to consolidate credit card debt, including credit card debt held by other lenders, and participation certificates, securities and similar instruments secured by credit card receivables.

Home loans include any loans made on the security of a home (including a dwelling unit in a multi-family residential property such as a condominium or a cooperative), combinations of homes and business property (*i.e.*, a home used in part for business), farm residences, and combinations of farm residences and commercial farm real estate.

Loan commitment includes a loan in process, a letter of credit, or any other commitment to extend credit.

Real estate loan is a loan for which the State savings association substantially relies upon a security interest in real estate given by the borrower as a

Federal Deposit Insurance Corporation § 390.265

condition of making the loan. A loan is made on the security of real estate if:

(1) The security property is real estate pursuant to the law of the state in which the property is located;

(2) The security interest of the State savings association may be enforced as a real estate mortgage or its equivalent pursuant to the law of the state in which the property is located;

(3) The security property is capable of separate appraisal; and

(4) With regard to a security property that is a leasehold or other interest for a period of years, the term of the interest extends, or is subject to extension or renewal at the option of the State savings association for a term of at least five years following the maturity of the loan.

Small business includes a small business concern or entity as defined by section 3(a) of the Small Business Act, 15 U.S.C. 632(a), and implemented by the regulations of the Small Business Administration at 13 CFR part 121.

Small business loans and *loans to small businesses* include any loan to a small business as defined in this section; or a loan that does not exceed $2 million (including a group of loans to one borrower) and is for commercial, corporate, business, or agricultural purposes.

§ 390.263 [Reserved]

§ 390.264 Real estate lending standards; purpose and scope.

This section, and § 390.265, issued pursuant to section 18(o) of the Federal Deposit Insurance Act, (12 U.S.C. 1828(o)), prescribe standards for real estate lending to be used by State savings associations and all their includable subsidiaries, as defined in § 390.461, over which the State savings associations exercise control, in adopting internal real estate lending policies.

§ 390.265 Real estate lending standards.

(a) Each State savings association shall adopt and maintain written policies that establish appropriate limits and standards for extensions of credit that are secured by liens on or interests in real estate, or that are made for the purpose of financing permanent improvements to real estate.

(b)(1) Real estate lending policies adopted pursuant to this section must:

(i) Be consistent with safe and sound banking practices;

(ii) Be appropriate to the size of the institution and the nature and scope of its operations; and

(iii) Be reviewed and approved by the State savings association's board of directors at least annually.

(2) The lending policies must establish:

(i) Loan portfolio diversification standards;

(ii) Prudent underwriting standards, including loan-to-value limits, that are clear and measurable;

(iii) Loan administration procedures for the State savings association's real estate portfolio; and

(iv) Documentation, approval, and reporting requirements to monitor compliance with the State savings association's real estate lending policies.

(c) Each State savings association must monitor conditions in the real estate market in its lending area to ensure that its real estate lending policies continue to be appropriate for current market conditions.

(d) The real estate lending policies adopted pursuant to this section should reflect consideration of the Interagency Guidelines for Real Estate Lending Policies established by the Federal banking agencies.

APPENDIX TO § 390.265—INTERAGENCY GUIDELINES FOR REAL ESTATE LENDING POLICIES

The agencies' regulations require that each insured depository institution adopt and maintain a written policy that establishes appropriate limits and standards for all extensions of credit that are secured by liens on or interests in real estate or made for the purpose of financing the construction of a building or other improvements.[1] These guidelines are intended to assist institutions in the formulation and maintenance of a real estate lending policy that is appropriate to the size of the institution and the nature and scope of its individual operations, as well as satisfies the requirements of the regulation.

---

[1] The agencies have adopted a uniform rule on real estate lending. See 12 CFR part 365 and §§ 390.264–390.265 (FDIC); 12 CFR part 208, subpart C (FRB); and 12 CFR part 34, subpart D (OCC).

Each institution's policies must be comprehensive, and consistent with safe and sound lending practices, and must ensure that the institution operates within limits and according to standards that are reviewed and approved at least annually by the board of directors. Real estate lending is an integral part of many institutions' business plans and, when undertaken in a prudent manner, will not be subject to examiner criticism.

Loan Portfolio Management Considerations

The lending policy should contain a general outline of the scope and distribution of the institution's credit facilities and the manner in which real estate loans are made, serviced, and collected. In particular, the institution's policies on real estate lending should:

• Identify the geographic areas in which the institution will consider lending.
• Establish a loan portfolio diversification policy and set limits for real estate loans by type and geographic market (e.g., limits on higher risk loans).
• Identify appropriate terms and conditions by type of real estate loan.
• Establish loan origination and approval procedures, both generally and by size and type of loan.
• Establish prudent underwriting standards that are clear and measurable, including loan-to-value limits, that are consistent with these supervisory guidelines.
• Establish review and approval procedures for exception loans, including loans with loan-to-value percentages in excess of supervisory limits.
• Establish loan administration procedures, including documentation, disbursement, collateral inspection, collection, and loan review.
• Establish real estate appraisal and evaluation programs.
• Require that management monitor the loan portfolio and provide timely and adequate reports to the board of directors.

The institution should consider both internal and external factors in the formulation of its loan policies and strategic plan. Factors that should be considered include:

• The size and financial condition of the institution.
• The expertise and size of the lending staff.
• The need to avoid undue concentrations of risk.
• Compliance with all real estate related laws and regulations, including the Community Reinvestment Act, anti-discrimination laws, and for State savings associations, the Qualified Thrift Lender test.
• Market conditions.

The institution should monitor conditions in the real estate markets in its lending area so that it can react quickly to changes in market conditions that are relevant to its lending decisions. Market supply and demand factors that should be considered include:

• Demographic indicators, including population and employment trends.
• Zoning requirements.
• Current and projected vacancy, construction, and absorption rates.
• Current and projected lease terms, rental rates, and sales prices, including concessions.
• Current and projected operating expenses for different types of projects.
• Economic indicators, including trends and diversification of the lending area.
• Valuation trends, including discount and direct capitalization rates.

Underwriting Standards

Prudently underwritten real estate loans should reflect all relevant credit factors, including:

• The capacity of the borrower, or income from the underlying property, to adequately service the debt.
• The value of the mortgaged property.
• The overall creditworthiness of the borrower.
• The level of equity invested in the property.
• Any secondary sources of repayment.
• Any additional collateral or credit enhancements (such as guarantees, mortgage insurance or takeout commitments).

The lending policies should reflect the level of risk that is acceptable to the board of directors and provide clear and measurable underwriting standards that enable the institution's lending staff to evaluate these credit factors. The underwriting standards should address:

• The maximum loan amount by type of property.
• Maximum loan maturities by type of property.
• Amortization schedules.
• Pricing structure for different types of real estate loans.
• Loan-to-value limits by type of property.

For development and construction projects, and completed commercial properties, the policy should also establish, commensurate with the size and type of the project or property:

• Requirements for feasibility studies and sensitivity and risk analyses (e.g., sensitivity of income projections to changes in economic variables such as interest rates, vacancy rates, or operating expenses).
• Minimum requirements for initial investment and maintenance of hard equity by the borrower (e.g., cash or unencumbered investment in the underlying property).

Federal Deposit Insurance Corporation § 390.265

- Minimum standards for net worth, cash flow, and debt service coverage of the borrower or underlying property.
- Standards for the acceptability of and limits on non-amortizing loans.
- Standards for the acceptability of and limits on the use of interest reserves.
- Pre-leasing and pre-sale requirements for income-producing property.
- Pre-sale and minimum unit release requirements for non-income-producing property loans.
- Limits on partial recourse or non-recourse loans and requirements for guarantor support.
- Requirements for takeout commitments.
- Minimum covenants for loan agreements.

LOAN ADMINISTRATION

The institution should also establish loan administration procedures for its real estate portfolio that address:
- Documentation, including:
Type and frequency of financial statements, including requirements for verification of information provided by the borrower;
Type and frequency of collateral evaluations (appraisals and other estimates of value).
- Loan closing and disbursement.
- Payment processing.
- Escrow administration.
- Collateral administration.
- Loan payoffs.
- Collections and foreclosure, including: Delinquency follow-up procedures; Foreclosure timing; Extensions and other forms of forbearance; Acceptance of deeds in lieu of foreclosure.
- Claims processing (e.g., seeking recovery on a defaulted loan covered by a government guaranty or insurance program).
- Servicing and participation agreements.

SUPERVISORY LOAN-TO-VALUE LIMITS

Institutions should establish their own internal loan-to-value limits for real estate loans. These internal limits should not exceed the following supervisory limits:

Loan category	Loan-to-value limit (percent)
Raw land	65
Land development	75
Construction:	
Commercial, multifamily,[2] and other non-residential	80
1- to 4-family residential	85
Improved property	85
Owner-occupied 1- to 4-family and home equity	([3])

[2] Multifamily construction includes condominiums and cooperatives.

The supervisory loan-to-value limits should be applied to the underlying property that collateralizes the loan. For loans that fund multiple phases of the same real estate project (e.g., a loan for both land development and construction of an office building), the appropriate loan-to-value limit is the limit applicable to the final phase of the project funded by the loan; however, loan disbursements should not exceed actual development or construction outlays. In situations where a loan is fully cross-collateralized by two or more properties or is secured by a collateral pool of two or more properties, the appropriate maximum loan amount under supervisory loan-to-value limits is the sum of the value of each property, less senior liens, multiplied by the appropriate loan-to-value limit for each property. To ensure that collateral margins remain within the supervisory limits, lenders should redetermine conformity whenever collateral substitutions are made to the collateral pool.

In establishing internal loan-to-value limits, each lender is expected to carefully consider the institution-specific and market factors listed under "Loan Portfolio Management Considerations," as well as any other relevant factors, such as the particular subcategory or type of loan. For any subcategory of loans that exhibits greater credit risk than the overall category, a lender should consider the establishment of an internal loan-to-value limit for that subcategory that is lower than the limit for the overall category.

The loan-to-value ratio is only one of several pertinent credit factors to be considered when underwriting a real estate loan. Other credit factors to be taken into account are highlighted in the "Underwriting Standards" section above. Because of these other factors, the establishment of these supervisory limits should not be interpreted to mean that loans at these levels will automatically be considered sound.

LOANS IN EXCESS OF THE SUPERVISORY LOAN-TO-VALUE LIMITS

The agencies recognize that appropriate loan-to-value limits vary not only among categories of real estate loans but also among individual loans. Therefore, it may be appropriate in individual cases to originate or purchase loans with loan-to-value ratios

[3] A loan-to-value limit has not been established for permanent mortgage or home equity loans on owner-occupied, 1- to 4-family residential property. However, for any such loan with a loan-to-value ratio that equals or exceeds 90 percent at origination, an institution should require appropriate credit enhancement in the form of either mortgage insurance or readily marketable collateral.

§ 390.265

12 CFR Ch. III (1–1–12 Edition)

in excess of the supervisory loan-to-value limits, based on the support provided by other credit factors. Such loans should be identified in the institutions' records, and their aggregate amount reported at least quarterly to the institution's board of directors. (See additional reporting requirements described under "Exceptions to the General Policy.") The aggregate amount of all loans in excess of the supervisory loan-to-value limits should not exceed 100 percent of total capital.[4] Moreover, within the aggregate limit, total loans for all commercial, agricultural, multifamily or other non-1- to 4-family residential properties should not exceed 30 percent of total capital. An institution will come under increased supervisory scrutiny as the total of such loans approaches these levels.

In determining the aggregate amount of such loans, institutions should: (a) Include all loans secured by the same property if any one of those loans exceeds the supervisory loan-to-value limits; and (b) include the recourse obligation of any such loan sold with recourse. Conversely, a loan should no longer be reported to the directors as part of aggregate totals when reduction in principal or senior liens, or additional contribution of collateral or equity (e.g., improvements to the real property securing the loan), bring the loan-to-value ratio into compliance with supervisory limits.

EXCLUDED TRANSACTIONS

The agencies also recognize that there are a number of lending situations in which other factors significantly outweigh the need to apply the supervisory loan-to-value limits.

These include:
• Loans guaranteed or insured by the U.S. government or its agencies, provided that the amount of the guaranty or insurance is at least equal to the portion of the loan that exceeds the supervisory loan-to-value limit.
• Loans backed by the full faith and credit of a state government, provided that the amount of the assurance is at least equal to the portion of the loan that exceeds the supervisory loan-to-value limit.
• Loans guaranteed or insured by a state, municipal or local government, or an agency thereof, provided that the amount of the guaranty or insurance is at least equal to

the portion of the loan that exceeds the supervisory loan-to-value limit, and provided that the lender has determined that the guarantor or insurer has the financial capacity and willingness to perform under the terms of the guaranty or insurance agreement.
• Loans that are to be sold promptly after origination, without recourse, to a financially responsible third party.
• Loans that are renewed, refinanced, or restructured without the advancement of new funds or an increase in the line of credit (except for reasonable closing costs), or loans that are renewed, refinanced, or restructured in connection with a workout situation, either with or without the advancement of new funds, where consistent with safe and sound banking practices and part of a clearly defined and well-documented program to achieve orderly liquidation of the debt, reduce risk of loss, or maximize recovery on the loan.
• Loans that facilitate the sale of real estate acquired by the lender in the ordinary course of collecting a debt previously contracted in good faith.
• Loans for which a lien on or interest in real property is taken as additional collateral through an abundance of caution by the lender (e.g., the institution takes a blanket lien on all or substantially all of the assets of the borrower, and the value of the real property is low relative to the aggregate value of all other collateral).
• Loans, such as working capital loans, where the lender does not rely principally on real estate as security and the extension of credit is not used to acquire, develop, or construct permanent improvements on real property.
• Loans for the purpose of financing permanent improvements to real property, but not secured by the property, if such security interest is not required by prudent underwriting practice.

EXCEPTIONS TO THE GENERAL LENDING POLICY

Some provision should be made for the consideration of loan requests from creditworthy borrowers whose credit needs do not fit within the institution's general lending policy. An institution may provide for prudently underwritten exceptions to its lending policies, including loan-to-value limits, on a loan-by-loan basis. However, any exceptions from the supervisory loan-to-value limits should conform to the aggregate limits on such loans discussed above.

The board of directors is responsible for establishing standards for the review and approval of exception loans. Each institution should establish an appropriate internal process for the review and approval of loans that do not conform to its own internal policy standards. The approval of any such loan

---

[4] For the state member banks, the term "total capital" means "total risk-based capital" as defined in appendix A to 12 CFR part 208. For insured state non-member banks, "total capital" refers to that term described in table I of appendix A to 12 CFR part 325. For national banks, the term "total capital" is defined at 12 CFR 3.2(e). For State savings associations, the term "total capital" refers to the term as described in subpart Z.

Federal Deposit Insurance Corporation § 390.265

should be supported by a written justification that clearly sets forth all of the relevant credit factors that support the underwriting decision. The justification and approval documents for such loans should be maintained as a part of the permanent loan file. Each institution should monitor compliance with its real estate lending policy and individually report exception loans of a significant size to its board of directors.

SUPERVISORY REVIEW OF REAL ESTATE LENDING POLICIES AND PRACTICES

The real estate lending policies of institutions will be evaluated by examiners during the course of their examinations to determine if the policies are consistent with safe and sound lending practices, these guidelines, and the requirements of the regulation. In evaluating the adequacy of the institution's real estate lending policies and practices, examiners will take into consideration the following factors:

• The nature and scope of the institution's real estate lending activities.
• The size and financial condition of the institution.
• The quality of the institution's management and internal controls.
• The expertise and size of the lending and loan administration staff.
• Market conditions.

Lending policy exception reports will also be reviewed by examiners during the course of their examinations to determine whether the institutions' exceptions are adequately documented and appropriate in light of all of the relevant credit considerations. An excessive volume of exceptions to an institution's real estate lending policy may signal a weakening of its underwriting practices, or may suggest a need to revise the loan policy.

DEFINITIONS

For the purposes of these Guidelines:

Construction loan means an extension of credit for the purpose of erecting or rehabilitating buildings or other structures, including any infrastructure necessary for development.

Extension of credit or loan means:

(1) The total amount of any loan, line of credit, or other legally binding lending commitment with respect to real property; and

(2) The total amount, based on the amount of consideration paid, of any loan, line of credit, or other legally binding lending commitment acquired by a lender by purchase, assignment, or otherwise.

Improved property loan means an extension of credit secured by one of the following types of real property:

(1) Farmland, ranchland or timberland committed to ongoing management and agricultural production;

(2) 1- to 4-family residential property that is not owner-occupied;

(3) Residential property containing five or more individual dwelling units;

(4) Completed commercial property; or

(5) Other income-producing property that has been completed and is available for occupancy and use, except income-producing owner-occupied 1- to 4-family residential property.

Land development loan means an extension of credit for the purpose of improving unimproved real property prior to the erection of structures. The improvement of unimproved real property may include the laying or placement of sewers, water pipes, utility cables, streets, and other infrastructure necessary for future development.

Loan origination means the time of inception of the obligation to extend credit (*i.e.*, when the last event or prerequisite, controllable by the lender, occurs causing the lender to become legally bound to fund an extension of credit).

Loan-to-value or *loan-to-value ratio* means the percentage or ratio that is derived at the time of loan origination by dividing an extension of credit by the total value of the property(ies) securing or being improved by the extension of credit plus the amount of any readily marketable collateral and other acceptable collateral that secures the extension of credit. The total amount of all senior liens on or interests in such property(ies) should be included in determining the loan-to-value ratio. When mortgage insurance or collateral is used in the calculation of the loan-to-value ratio, and such credit enhancement is later released or replaced, the loan-to-value ratio should be recalculated.

Other acceptable collateral means any collateral in which the lender has a perfected security interest, that has a quantifiable value, and is accepted by the lender in accordance with safe and sound lending practices. Other acceptable collateral should be appropriately discounted by the lender consistent with the lender's usual practices for making loans secured by such collateral. Other acceptable collateral includes, among other items, unconditional irrevocable standby letters of credit for the benefit of the lender.

Owner-occupied, when used in conjunction with the term *1- to 4-family residential property* means that the owner of the underlying real property occupies at least one unit of the real property as a principal residence of the owner.

Readily marketable collateral means insured deposits, financial instruments, and bullion in which the lender has a perfected interest. Financial instruments and bullion must be salable under ordinary circumstances with reasonable promptness at a fair market value determined by quotations based on actual transactions, on an auction or similarly

§ 390.266

available daily bid and ask price market. Readily marketable collateral should be appropriately discounted by the lender consistent with the lender's usual practices for making loans secured by such collateral.

Value means an opinion or estimate, set forth in an appraisal or evaluation, whichever may be appropriate, of the market value of real property, prepared in accordance with the agency's appraisal regulations and guidance. For loans to purchase an existing property, the term "value" means the lesser of the actual acquisition cost or the estimate of value.

1- to 4-family residential property means property containing fewer than five individual dwelling units, including manufactured homes permanently affixed to the underlying property (when deemed to be real property under state law).

§ 390.266 [Reserved]

§ 390.267 Letters of credit and other independent undertakings to pay against documents.

(a) *General authority.* A State savings association may issue and commit to issue letters of credit within the scope of applicable laws or rules of practice recognized by law. It may also issue other independent undertakings within the scope of such laws or rules of practice recognized by law, that have been approved by the FDIC (approved undertaking).[1] Under such letters of credit and approved undertakings, the State savings association's obligation to honor depends upon the presentation of specified documents and not upon nondocumentary conditions or resolution of questions of fact or law at issue between the account party and the beneficiary. A State savings association may also confirm or otherwise undertake to honor or purchase specified documents upon their presentation under another person's independent undertaking within the scope of such laws or rules.

(b) *Safety and soundness considerations*—(1) *Terms.* As a matter of safe and sound banking practice, State savings associations that issue letters of credit or approved undertakings should not be exposed to undue risk. At a minimum, State savings associations should consider the following:

(i) The independent character of the letter of credit or approved undertaking should be apparent from its terms (such as terms that subject it to laws or rules providing for its independent character);

(ii) The letter of credit or approved undertaking should be limited in amount;

(iii) The letter of credit or approved undertaking should:

(A) Be limited in duration; or

(B) Permit the State savings association to terminate the letter of credit or approved undertaking, either on a periodic basis (consistent with the State savings association's ability to make any necessary credit assessments) or at will upon either notice or payment to the beneficiary; or

(C) Entitle the State savings association to cash collateral from the account party on demand (with a right to accelerate the customer's obligations, as appropriate); and

(iv) The State savings association either should be fully collateralized or have a post-honor right of reimbursement from its customer or from another issuer of a letter of credit or an independent undertaking. Alternatively, if the State savings association's undertaking is to purchase documents of title, securities, or other valuable documents, it should obtain a first priority right to realize on the documents if the State savings association is not otherwise to be reimbursed.

(2) *Additional considerations in special circumstances.* Certain letters of credit

---

[1] Samples of laws or rules of practice applicable to letters of credit and other independent undertakings include, but are not limited to: the applicable version of Article 5 of the Uniform Commercial Code (UCC) (1962, as amended 1990) or revised Article 5 of the UCC (as amended 1995) (available from West Publishing Co., 1/800/328–4880); the Uniform Customs and Practice for Documentary Credits (International Chamber of Commerce (ICC) Publication No. 500) (available from ICC Publishing, Inc., 212/206–1150; the United Nations Convention on Independent Guarantees and Standby Letters of Credit (adopted by the U.N. General Assembly in 1995 and signed by the U.S. in 1997) (available from the U.N. Commission on International Trade Law, 212/963–5353); and the Uniform Rules for Bank-to-Bank Reimbursements Under Documentary Credits (ICC Publication No. 525) (available from ICC Publishing, Inc., 212/206–1150).

Federal Deposit Insurance Corporation

§ 390.270

and approved undertakings require particular protections against credit, operational, and market risk:

(i) In the event that the undertaking is to honor by delivery of an item of value other than money, the State savings association should ensure that market fluctuations that affect the value of the item will not cause the State savings association to assume undue market risk;

(ii) In the event that the undertaking provides for automatic renewal, the terms for renewal should allow the State savings association to make any necessary credit assessment prior to renewal;

(iii) In the event that a State savings association issues an undertaking for its own account, the underlying transaction for which it is issued must be within the State savings association's authority and comply with any safety and soundness requirements applicable to that transaction.

(3) *Operational expertise.* The State savings association should possess operational expertise that is commensurate with the sophistication of its letter of credit or independent undertaking activities.

(4) *Documentation.* The State savings association must accurately reflect its letters of credit or approved undertakings in its records, including any acceptance or deferred payment or other absolute obligation arising out of its contingent undertaking.

§ 390.268 Investment in State housing corporations.

(a) Any State savings association to the extent it has legal authority to do so, may make investments in, commitments to invest in, loans to, or commitments to lend to any state housing corporation; provided, that such obligations or loans are secured directly, or indirectly through a fiduciary, by a first lien on improved real estate which is insured under the National Housing Act, as amended, and that in the event of default, the holder of such obligations or loans has the right directly, or indirectly through a fiduciary, to subject to the satisfaction of such obligations or loans the real estate described in the first lien, or the insurance proceeds.

(b) Any State savings association that is adequately capitalized may, to the extent it has legal authority to do so, invest in obligations (including loans) of, or issued by, any state housing corporation incorporated in the state in which such State savings association has its home or a branch office; provided (except with respect to loans), that:

(1) The obligations are rated in one of the four highest grades as shown by the most recently published rating made of such obligations by a nationally recognized rating service; or

(2) The obligations, if not rated, are approved by the FDIC. The aggregate outstanding direct investment in obligations under paragraph (b) of this section shall not exceed the amount of the State savings association's total capital.

(c) Each state housing corporation in which a State savings association invests under the authority of paragraph (b) of this section shall agree, before accepting any such investment (including any loan or loan commitment), to make available at any time to the FDIC such information as the FDIC may consider to be necessary to ensure that investments are properly made under this section.

§ 390.269 Prohibition on loan procurement fees.

If you are a director, officer, or other natural person having the power to direct the management or policies of a State savings association, you must not receive, directly or indirectly, any commission, fee, or other compensation in connection with the procurement of any loan made by the State savings association or a subsidiary of the State savings association.

§ 390.270 Asset classification.

(a)(1) Each State savings association must evaluate and classify its assets on a regular basis in a manner consistent with, or reconcilable to, the asset classification system used by the FDIC.

(2) In connection with the examination of a State savings association or its affiliates, the FDIC examiners may identify problem assets and classify them, if appropriate. The association

§ 390.271

must recognize such examiner classifications in its subsequent reports to the FDIC.

(b) Based on the evaluation and classification of its assets, each State savings association shall establish adequate valuation allowances or charge-offs, as appropriate, consistent with generally accepted accounting principles and the practices of the federal banking agencies.

§ 390.271 Records for lending transactions.

In establishing and maintaining its records pursuant to § 390.350, each State savings association should establish and maintain loan documentation practices that:

(a) Ensure that the institution can make an informed lending decision and can assess risk on an ongoing basis;

(b) Identify the purpose and all sources of repayment for each loan, and assess the ability of the borrower(s) and any guarantor(s) to repay the indebtedness in a timely manner;

(c) Ensure that any claims against a borrower, guarantor, security holders, and collateral are legally enforceable;

(d) Demonstrate appropriate administration and monitoring of its loans; and

(e) Take into account the size and complexity of its loans.

§ 390.272 Re-evaluation of real estate owned.

A State savings association shall appraise each parcel of real estate owned at the earlier of in-substance foreclosure or at the time of the State savings association's acquisition of such property, and at such times thereafter as dictated by prudent management policy; such appraisals shall be consistent with the requirements of subpart X of this part. The appropriate regional director or his or her designee may require subsequent appraisals if, in his or her discretion, such subsequent appraisal is necessary under the particular circumstances. The foregoing requirement shall not apply to any parcel of real estate that is sold and reacquired less than 12 months subsequent to the most recent appraisal made pursuant to this subpart. A dated, signed copy of each report of appraisal made pursuant to any provisions of this subpart shall be retained in the State savings association's records.

Subpart Q—Definitions for Regulations Affecting All State Savings Associations

§ 390.280 When do the definitions in this subpart apply?

The definitions in this subpart apply throughout parts 390 and 391, unless another definition is specifically provided.

§ 390.281 Account.

The term *account* means any savings account, demand account, certificate account, tax and loan account, note account, United States Treasury general account or United States Treasury time deposit-open account, whether in the form of a deposit or a share, held by an accountholder in a State savings association.

§ 390.282 Accountholder.

The term *accountholder* means the holder of an account or accounts in a State savings association insured by the Deposit Insurance Fund. The term does not include the holder of any subordinated debt security or any mortgage-backed bond issued by the State savings association.

§ 390.283 Affiliate.

The term *affiliate* of a State savings association, unless otherwise defined, means any corporation, business trust, association, or other similar organization:

(a) Of which a State savings association, directly or indirectly, owns or controls either a majority of the voting shares or more than 50 per centum of the number of shares voted for the election of its directors, trustees, or other persons exercising similar functions at the preceding election, or controls in any manner the election of a majority of its directors, trustees, or other persons exercising similar functions; or

(b) Of which control is held, directly or indirectly through stock ownership or in any other manner, by the shareholders of a State savings association who own or control either a majority of the shares of such State savings association or more than 50 per centum of the number of shares voted for the election of directors of such State savings association at the preceding election, or by trustees for the benefit of the shareholders of any such State savings association; or

(c) Of which a majority of its directors, trustees, or other persons exercising similar functions are directors of any one State savings association.

§ 390.284 Affiliated person.

The term *affiliated person* of a State savings association means the following:

(a) A director, officer, or controlling person of such association;

(b) A spouse of a director, officer, or controlling person of such association;

(c) A member of the immediate family of a director, officer, or controlling person of such association, who has the same home as such person or who is a director or officer of any subsidiary of such association or of any holding company affiliate of such association;

(d) Any corporation or organization (other than the State savings association or a corporation or organization through which the State savings association operates) of which a director, officer or the controlling person of such association:

(1) Is chief executive officer, chief financial officer, or a person performing similar functions;

(2) Is a general partner;

(3) Is a limited partner who, directly or indirectly either alone or with his or her spouse and the members of his or her immediate family who are also affiliated persons of the association, owns an interest of 10 percent or more in the partnership (based on the value of his or her contribution) or who, directly or indirectly with other directors, officers, and controlling persons of such association and their spouses and their immediate family members who are also affiliated persons of the association, owns an interest of 25 percent or more in the partnership; or

(4) Directly or indirectly either alone or with his or her spouse and the members of his or her immediate family who are also affiliated persons of the association, owns or controls 10 percent or more of any class of equity securities or owns or controls, with other directors, officers, and controlling persons of such association and their spouses and their immediate family members who are also affiliated persons of the association, 25 percent or more of any class of equity securities; and

(5) Any trust or other estate in which a director, officer, or controlling person of such association or the spouse of such person has a substantial beneficial interest or as to which such person or his or her spouse serves as trustee or in a similar fiduciary capacity.

§ 390.285 Audit period.

The *audit period* of a State savings association means the twelve month period (or other period in the case of a change in audit period) covered by the annual audit conducted to satisfy § 390.350.

§ 390.286 Certificate account.

The term *certificate account* means a savings account evidenced by a certificate that must be held for a fixed or minimum term.

§ 390.287 Consumer credit.

The term *consumer credit* means credit extended to a natural person for personal, family, or household purposes, including loans secured by liens on real estate and chattel liens secured by mobile homes and leases of personal property to consumers that may be considered the functional equivalent of loans on personal security: *Provided,* the State savings association relies substantially upon other factors, such as the general credit standing of the borrower, guaranties, or security other than the real estate or mobile home, as the primary security for the loan. Appropriate evidence to demonstrate justification for such reliance should be retained in a State savings association's files. Among the types of credit included within this term are consumer loans; educational loans; unsecured

§ 390.288

loans for real property alteration, repair or improvement, or for the equipping of real property; loans in the nature of overdraft protection; and credit extended in connection with credit cards.

§ 390.288 Controlling person.

The term *controlling person* of a State savings association means any person or entity which, either directly or indirectly, or acting in concert with one or more other persons or entities, owns, controls, or holds with power to vote, or holds proxies representing, ten percent or more of the voting shares or rights of such State savings association; or controls in any manner the election or appointment of a majority of the directors of such State savings association. However, a director of a State savings association will not be deemed to be a controlling person of such State savings association based upon his or her voting, or acting in concert with other directors in voting, proxies:

(a) Obtained in connection with an annual solicitation of proxies, or

(b) Obtained from savings account holders and borrowers if such proxies are voted as directed by a majority vote of the entire board of directors of such association, or of a committee of such directors if such committee's composition and authority are controlled by a majority vote of the entire board and if its authority is revocable by such a majority.

§ 390.289 Corporation.

The terms *Corporation* and *FDIC* mean the Federal Deposit Insurance Corporation.

§ 390.290 Demand accounts.

The term *demand accounts* means non-interest-bearing demand deposits that are subject to check or to withdrawal or transfer on negotiable or transferable order to the State savings association and that are permitted to be issued by statute, regulation, or otherwise and are payable on demand.

§ 390.291 Director.

The term *director* means any director, trustee, or other person performing similar functions with respect to any organization whether incorporated or unincorporated. Such term does not include an advisory director, honorary director, director emeritus, or similar person, unless the person is otherwise performing functions similar to those of a director.

§ 390.292 Financial institution.

The term *financial institution* has the same meaning as the term *depository institution* set forth in 12 U.S.C. 1813(c)(1).

§ 390.293 Immediate family.

The term *immediate family* of any natural person means the following (whether by the full or half blood or by adoption):

(a) Such person's spouse, father, mother, children, brothers, sisters, and grandchildren;

(b) The father, mother, brothers, and sisters of such person's spouse; and

(c) The spouse of a child, brother, or sister of such person.

§ 390.294 Land loan.

The term *land loan* means a loan:

(a) Secured by real estate upon which all facilities and improvements have been completely installed, as required by local regulations and practices, so that it is entirely prepared for the erection of structures;

(b) To finance the purchase of land and the accomplishment of all improvements required to convert it to developed building lots; or

(c) Secured by land upon which there is no structure.

§ 390.295 Low-rent housing.

The term *low-rent housing* means real estate which is, or which is being constructed, remodeled, rehabilitated, modernized, or renovated to be, the subject of an annual contributions contract for low-rent housing under the provisions of the United States Housing Act of 1937, as amended.

§ 390.296 Money Market Deposit Accounts.

(a) *Money Market Deposit Accounts* (*MMDAs*) offered by State savings associations in accordance with applicable state law are savings accounts on

Federal Deposit Insurance Corporation § 390.300

which interest may be paid if issued subject to the following limitations:

(1) The State savings association shall reserve the right to require at least seven days' notice prior to withdrawal or transfer of any funds in the account; and

(2)(i) The depositor is authorized by the State savings association to make no more than six transfers per calendar month or statement cycle (or similar period) of at least four weeks by means of preauthorized, automatic, telephonic, or data transmission agreement, order, or instruction to another account of the depositor at the same State savings association to the State savings association itself, or to a third party.

(ii) State savings associations may permit holders of MMDAs to make unlimited transfers for the purpose of repaying loans (except overdraft loans on the depositor's demand account) and associated expenses at the same State savings association (as originator or servicer), to make unlimited transfers of funds from this account to another account of the same depositor at the same State savings association or to make unlimited payments directly to the depositor from the account when such transfers or payments are made by mail, messenger, automated teller machine, or in person, or when such payments are made by telephone (via check mailed to the depositor).

(3) In order to ensure that no more than the number of transfers specified in paragraph (a)(2)(i) of this section are made, a State savings association must either:

(i) Prevent transfers of funds in excess of the limitations; or

(ii) Adopt procedures to monitor those transfers on an after-the-fact basis and contact customers who exceed the limits on more than an occasional basis. For customers who continue to violate those limits after being contacted by the depository State savings association the depository State savings association must either place funds in another account that the depositor is eligible to maintain or take away the account's transfer and draft capacities.

(iii) Insured State savings associations at their option, may use on a consistent basis either the date on a check or the date it is paid in determining whether the transfer limitations within the specified interval are exceeded.

(b) State savings associations may offer MMDAs to any depositor not inconsistent with applicable state law.

§ 390.297 Negotiable Order of Withdrawal Accounts.

(a) *Negotiable Order of Withdrawal (NOW)* accounts are savings accounts authorized by 12 U.S.C. 1832 on which the State savings association reserves the right to require at least seven days' notice prior to withdrawal or transfer of any funds in the account.

(b) For purposes of 12 U.S.C. 1832:

(1) An organization shall be deemed "operated primarily for religious, philanthropic, charitable, educational, or other similar purposes and * * * not * * * for profit" if it is described in sections 501(c)(3) through (13), 501(c)(19), or 528 of the Internal Revenue Code; and

(2) The funds of a sole proprietorship or unincorporated business owned by a husband and wife shall be deemed beneficially owned by "one or more individuals."

§ 390.298 Nonresidential construction loan.

The term *nonresidential construction loan* means a loan for construction of other than one or more dwelling units.

§ 390.299 Nonwithdrawable account.

The term *nonwithdrawable account* means an account which by the terms of the contract of the accountholder with the State savings association or by provisions of state law cannot be paid to the accountholder until all liabilities, including other classes of share liability of the State savings association have been fully liquidated and paid upon the winding up of the State savings association is referred to as a *nonwithdrawable account.*

§ 390.300 Note account.

The term *note account* means a note, subject to the right of immediate call, evidencing funds held by depositories electing the note option under applicable United States Treasury Department regulations. Note accounts are

§ 390.301

not savings accounts or savings deposits.

§ 390.301 [Reserved]

§ 390.302 Officer.

The term *Officer* means the president, any vice-president (but not an assistant vice-president, second vice-president, or other vice president having authority similar to an assistant or second vice-president), the secretary, the treasurer, the comptroller, and any other person performing similar functions with respect to any organization whether incorporated or unincorporated. The term *officer* also includes the chairman of the board of directors if the chairman is authorized by the charter or by-laws of the organization to participate in its operating management or if the chairman in fact participates in such management.

§ 390.303 Parent company; subsidiary.

The term *parent company* means any company which directly or indirectly controls any other company or companies. The term *subsidiary* means any company which is owned or controlled directly or indirectly by a person, and includes a subsidiary owned in whole or in part by a State savings association, or a subsidiary of that subsidiary.

§ 390.304 Political subdivision.

The term *political subdivision* includes any subdivision of a public unit, any principal department of such public unit:

(a) The creation of which subdivision or department has been expressly authorized by state statute,

(b) To which some functions of government have been delegated by state statute, and

(c) To which funds have been allocated by statute or ordinance for its exclusive use and control. It also includes drainage, irrigation, navigation, improvement, levee, sanitary, school or power districts and bridge or port authorities and other special districts created by state statute or compacts between the states. Excluded from the term are subordinate or nonautonomous divisions, agencies or boards within principal departments.

§ 390.305 Principal office.

The term *principal office* means the home office of a State savings association established as such in conformity with the laws under which the State savings association is organized.

§ 390.306 Public unit.

The term *public unit* means the United States, any state of the United States, the District of Columbia, any territory of the United States, Puerto Rico, the Virgin Islands, any county, any municipality or any political subdivision thereof.

§ 390.307 Savings account.

The term *savings account* means any withdrawable account, except a demand account as defined in § 390.290, a tax and loan account, a note account, a United States Treasury general account, or a United States Treasury time deposit-open account.

§ 390.308 State savings association.

The term *State savings association* means a State savings association as defined in section 3 of the Federal Deposit Insurance Act, the deposits of which are insured by the Corporation. It includes a building and loan, savings and loan, or homestead association, or a cooperative bank (other than a cooperative bank which is a State bank as defined in section 3(a)(2) of the Federal Deposit Insurance Act) organized and operating according to the laws of the State in which it is chartered or organized, or a corporation (other than a bank as defined in section 3(a)(1) of the Federal Deposit Insurance Act) that the Board of Directors of the Federal Deposit Insurance Corporation determine to be operating substantially in the same manner as a State savings association.

§ 390.309 Security.

The term *security* means any non-withdrawable account, note, stock, treasury stock, bond, debenture, evidence of indebtedness, certificate of interest or participation in any profit-sharing agreement, collateral-trust certificate, preorganization certificate or subscription, transferable share, investment contract, voting-trust certificate, or, in general, any interest or instrument commonly known as a *security*, or any certificate of interest or participation in, temporary or interim certificate for, receipt for, guarantee of, or warrant or right to subscribe to or purchase, any of the foregoing, except that a *security* shall not include an account or deposit insured by the Federal Deposit Insurance Corporation.

§ 390.310 Service corporation.

The term *service corporation* means any corporation, the majority of the capital stock of which is owned by one or more savings associations and which engages, directly or indirectly, in any activities similar to activities which may be engaged in by a service corporation in which a Federal savings association may invest.

§ 390.311 State.

The term *State* means a State, the District of Columbia, Guam, Puerto Rico, and the Virgin Islands of the United States.

§ 390.312 Subordinated debt security.

The term *subordinated debt security* means any unsecured note, debenture, or other debt security issued by a State savings association and subordinated on liquidation to all claims having the same priority as account holders or any higher priority.

§ 390.313 Tax and loan account.

The term *tax and loan account* means an account, the balance of which is subject to the right of immediate withdrawal, established for receipt of payments of Federal taxes and certain United States obligations. Such accounts are not savings accounts or savings deposits.

§ 390.314 United States Treasury General Account.

The term *United States Treasury General Account* means an account maintained in the name of the United States Treasury the balance of which is subject to the right of immediate withdrawal, except in the case of the closure of the member, and in which a zero balance may be maintained. Such accounts are not savings accounts or savings deposits.

§ 390.315 United States Treasury Time Deposit Open Account.

The term *United States Treasury Time Deposit Open Account* means a non-interest-bearing account maintained in the name of the United States Treasury which may not be withdrawn prior to the expiration of 30 days' written notice from the United States Treasury, or such other period of notice as the Treasury may require. Such accounts are not savings accounts or savings deposits.

§ 390.316 With recourse.

(a) The term *with recourse* means, in connection with the sale of a loan or a participation interest in a loan, an agreement or arrangement under which the purchaser is to be entitled to receive from the seller a sum of money or thing of value, whether tangible or intangible (including any substitution), upon default in payment of any loan involved or any part thereof or to withhold or to have withheld from the seller a sum of money or anything of value by way of security against default. The recourse liability resulting from a sale with recourse shall be the total book value of any loan sold with recourse less:

(1) The amount of any insurance or guarantee against loss in the event of default provided by a third party,

(2) The amount of any loss to be borne by the purchaser in the event of default, and

(3) The amount of any loss resulting from a recourse obligation entered on the books and records of the State savings association.

(b) The term *with recourse* does not include loans or interests therein where the agreement of sale provides for the State savings association directly or indirectly

(1) To hold or retain a subordinate interest in a specified percentage of the loans or interests; or

(2) To guarantee against loss up to a specified percentage of the loans or interests, which specified percentage shall not exceed ten percent of the outstanding balance of the loans or interests at the time of sale: *Provided*, that

§ 390.320

the State savings association designates adequate reserves for the subordinate interest or guarantee.

(c) This definition does not apply for purposes of determining the capital adequacy requirements under subpart Z.

Subpart R—Regulatory Reporting Standards

§ 390.320 Regulatory reporting requirements.

(a) *Authority and scope.* This subpart is issued by the FDIC pursuant to 12 U.S.C. sections 1831m; 1831n(a)(2); 1831p–1;1464(v)(1). It applies to all State savings associations regulated by the FDIC.

(b) *Records and reports—general—*(1) *Records.* Each State savings association and its affiliates shall maintain accurate and complete records of all business transactions. Such records shall support and be readily reconcilable to any regulatory reports submitted to the FDIC and financial reports prepared in accordance with GAAP. The records shall be maintained in the United States and be readily accessible for examination and other supervisory purposes within 5 business days upon request by the FDIC, at a location acceptable to the FDIC.

(2) *Reports.* For purposes of examination by and regulatory reports to the FDIC and compliance with this section, all State savings associations shall use such forms and follow such regulatory reporting requirements as the FDIC may require by regulation or otherwise.

§ 390.321 Regulatory reports.

(a) *Definition and scope.* This section applies to all regulatory reports, as defined herein. A regulatory report is any report that the FDIC prepares, or is submitted to, or is used by the FDIC, to determine compliance with its rules and regulations, and to evaluate the safe and sound condition and operation of State savings associations. Regulatory reports are regulatory documents, not accounting documents.

(b) *Regulatory reporting requirements*—(1) *General.* The instructions to regulatory reports are referred to as "regulatory reporting requirements." Regulatory reporting requirements include, but are not limited to, the accounting instructions, guidance contained in FDIC regulations, financial institution letters, manuals, bulletins, examination handbooks, and safe and sound practices. Regulatory reporting requirements are not limited to the minimum requirements under generally accepted accounting principles (GAAP) because of the special supervisory, regulatory, and economic policy needs served by such reports. Regulatory reporting by State savings associations that purports to comply with GAAP shall incorporate the GAAP that best reflects the underlying economic substance of the transaction at issue. Regulatory reporting requirements shall, at a minimum:

(i) Incorporate GAAP whenever GAAP is the referenced accounting instruction for regulatory reports to the Federal banking agencies;

(ii) Incorporate safe and sound practices contained in FDIC regulations, financial institution letters, bulletins, examination handbooks, manuals, and instructions to regulatory reports; and

(iii) Incorporate additional safety and soundness requirements more stringent than GAAP, as the FDIC may prescribe.

(2) *Exceptions.* Regulatory reporting requirements that are not consistent with GAAP, if any, are not required to be reflected in audited financial statements, including financial statements contained in securities filings submitted to the FDIC pursuant to the Securities and Exchange Act of 1934 or subparts U and W and 12 CFR part 192.

(3) *Compliance.* When the FDIC determines that a State savings association's regulatory reports did not conform to regulatory reporting requirements in previous reporting periods, the association shall correct its regulatory reports in accordance with the directions of the FDIC.

§ 390.322 Audit of State savings associations.

(a) *General.* The FDIC may require, at any time, an independent audit of the financial statements of, or the application of procedures agreed upon by the FDIC to a State savings association, by

Federal Deposit Insurance Corporation § 390.332

qualified independent public accountants when needed for any safety and soundness reason identified by the FDIC.

(b) *Audits required for safety and soundness purposes.* The FDIC requires an independent audit for safety and soundness purposes:

(1) If a State savings association has received a composite rating of 3, 4 or 5, as defined at § 390.101(c).

(2) [Reserved]

(c) *Procedures.* (1) When the FDIC requires an independent audit because such an audit is needed for safety and soundness purposes, the FDIC shall determine whether the audit was conducted and filed in a manner satisfactory to the FDIC.

(2) The FDIC may waive the independent audit requirement described at paragraph (b)(1) of this section, if the FDIC determines that an audit would not provide further information on safety and soundness issues relevant to the examination rating.

(3) When the FDIC requires the application of procedures agreed upon by the FDIC for safety and soundness purposes, the FDIC shall identify the procedures to be performed. The FDIC shall also determine whether the agreed upon procedures were conducted and filed in a manner satisfactory to the FDIC.

(d) *Qualifications for independent public accountants.* The audit shall be conducted by an independent public accountant who:

(1) Is registered or licensed to practice as a public accountant, and is in good standing, under the laws of the state or other political subdivision of the United States in which the State savings association's or holding company's principal office is located;

(2) Agrees in the engagement letter to provide the FDIC with access to and copies of any work papers, policies, and procedures relating to the services performed;

(3)(i) Is in compliance with the American Institute of Certified Public Accountants' (AICPA) Code of Professional Conduct; and

(ii) Meets the independence requirements and interpretations of the Securities and Exchange Commission and its staff; and

(4) Has received, or is enrolled in, a peer review program that meets guidelines acceptable to the FDIC.

(e) *Voluntary audits.* When a State savings association obtains an independent audit voluntarily, it must be performed by an independent public accountant who satisfies the requirements of paragraphs (d)(1), (2), and (3)(i) of this section.

Subpart S—State Savings Associations—Operations

§ 390.330 Chartering documents.

(a) *Submission for approval.* Any de novo State savings association prior to commencing operations shall file its charter and bylaws with the FDIC for approval, together with a certification that such charter and bylaws are permissible under all applicable laws, rules and regulations.

(b) *Availability of chartering documents.* Each State savings association shall cause a true copy of its charter and bylaws and all amendments thereto to be available to accountholders at all times in each office of the State savings association, and shall upon request deliver to any accountholders a copy of such charter and bylaws or amendments thereto.

§ 390.331 Securities: Statement of non-insurance.

Every security issued by a State savings association must include in its provisions a clear statement that the security is not insured by the Federal Deposit Insurance Corporation.

§ 390.332 Merger, consolidation, purchase or sale of assets, or assumption of liabilities.

(a) No State savings association may, without application to and approval by the FDIC:

(1) Combine with any insured depository institution, if the acquiring or resulting institution is to be a State savings association; or

(2) Assume liability to pay any deposit made in, any insured depository institution.

(b)(1) No State savings association may, without notifying the FDIC, as provided in paragraph (h)(1) of this section:

§ 390.332

(i) Combine with another insured depository institution where a State savings association is not the resulting institution; or

(ii) In the case of a State savings association that meets the conditions for expedited treatment under § 390.101, convert, directly or indirectly, to a national or state bank.

(2) A State savings association that does not meet the conditions for expedited treatment under § 390.101 may not, directly or indirectly, convert to a national or state bank without prior application to and approval of FDIC, as provided in paragraph (h)(2)(ii) of this section.

(c) No State savings association may make any transfer (excluding transfers subject to paragraphs (a) or (b) of this section) without notice or application to the FDIC, as provided in paragraph (h)(2) of this section. For purposes of this paragraph, the term "transfer" means purchases or sales of assets or liabilities in bulk not made in the ordinary course of business including, but not limited to, transfers of assets or savings account liabilities, purchases of assets, and assumptions of deposit accounts or other liabilities, and combinations with a depository institution other than an insured depository institution.

(d)(1) In determining whether to confer approval for a transaction under paragraphs (a), (b)(2), or (c) of this section, the FDIC shall take into account the following:

(i) The capital level of any resulting State savings association;

(ii) The financial and managerial resources of the constituent institutions;

(iii) The future prospects of the constituent institutions;

(iv) The convenience and needs of the communities to be served;

(v) The conformity of the transaction to applicable law, regulation, and supervisory policies;

(vi) Factors relating to the fairness of and disclosure concerning the transaction, including, but not limited to:

(A) *Equitable treatment.* The transaction should be equitable to all concerned—savings account holders, borrowers, creditors and stockholders (if any) of each State savings association—giving proper recognition of and protection to their respective legal rights and interests. The transaction will be closely reviewed for fairness where the transaction does not appear to be the result of arms' length bargaining or, in the case of a stock State savings association, where controlling stockholders are receiving different consideration from other stockholders. No finder's or similar fee should be paid to any officer, director, or controlling person of a State savings association which is a party to the transaction.

(B) *Full disclosure.* The filing should make full disclosure of all written or oral agreements or understandings by which any person or company will receive, directly or indirectly, any money, property, service, release of pledges made, or other thing of value, whether tangible or intangible, in connection with the transaction.

(C) *Compensation to officers.* Compensation, including deferred compensation, to officers, directors and controlling persons of the disappearing State savings association by the resulting institution or an affiliate thereof should not be in excess of a reasonable amount, and should be commensurate with their duties and responsibilities. The filing should fully justify the compensation to be paid to such persons. The transaction will be particularly scrutinized where any of such persons is to receive a material increase in compensation above that paid by the disappearing State savings association prior to the commencement of negotiations regarding the proposed transaction. An increase in compensation in excess of the greater of 15% or $10,000 gives rise to presumptions of unreasonableness and sale of control. In the case of such an increase, evidence sufficient to rebut such presumptions should be submitted.

(D) *Advisory boards.* Advisory board members should be elected for a term not exceeding one year. No advisory board fees should be paid to salaried officers or employees of the resulting State savings association. The filing should describe and justify the duties and responsibilities and any compensation paid to any advisory board of the resulting State savings association that consists of officers, directors or

Federal Deposit Insurance Corporation § 390.332

controlling persons of the disappearing institution, particularly if the disappearing institution experienced significant supervisory problems prior to the transaction. No advisory board fees should exceed the director fees paid by the resulting State savings association. Advisory board fees that are in excess of 115 percent of the director fees paid by the disappearing State savings association prior to commencement of negotiations regarding the transaction give rise to presumptions of unreasonableness and sale of control unless sufficient evidence to rebut such presumptions is submitted. Rebuttal evidence is not required if:

(*1*) The advisory board fees do not exceed the fee that advisory board members of the resulting institution receive for each monthly meeting attended or $150, whichever is greater; or

(*2*) The advisory board fees do not exceed $100 per meeting attended for disappearing State savings associations with assets greater than $10,000,000 or $50 per meeting attended for disappearing State savings associations with assets of $10,000,000 or less, based on a schedule of 12 meetings per year.

(E) The accounting and tax treatment of the transaction; and

(F) Fees paid and professional services rendered in connection with the transaction.

(2) In conferring approval of a transaction under paragraph (a) of this section, the FDIC also will consider the competitive impact of the transaction, including whether:

(i) The transaction would result in a monopoly, or would be in furtherance of any monopoly or conspiracy to monopolize or to attempt to monopolize the State savings association business in any part of the United States; or

(ii) The effect of the transaction on any section of the country may be substantially to lessen competition, or tend to create a monopoly, or in any other manner would be in restraint of trade, unless the FDIC finds that the anticompetitive effects of the proposed transaction are clearly outweighed in the public interest by the probable effect of the transaction in meeting the convenience and needs of the communities to be served.

(3) Applications and notices filed under this section shall be upon forms prescribed by the FDIC.

(4) Applications filed under paragraph (a) of this section must be processed in accordance with the time frames set forth in §§ 390.127 through 390.135, provided that the period for review may be extended only if the FDIC determines that the applicant has failed to furnish all requested information or that the information submitted is substantially inaccurate, in which case the review period may be extended for up to 30 days.

(e)(1) The following procedures apply to applications described in paragraph (a) of this section, unless the FDIC finds that it must act immediately to prevent the probable default of one of the depository institutions involved:

(i) The applicant must publish a public notice of the application in accordance with the procedures in §§ 390.111 through 390.115. In addition to the initial publication, the applicant must also publish on a weekly basis during the public comment period.

(ii) Commenters may submit comments on an application in accordance with the procedures in §§ 390.116 through 390.120. The public comment period is 30 calendar days after the date of publication of the initial public notice. However, if the FDIC has advised the Attorney General that an emergency exists requiring expeditious action, the public comment period is 10 calendar days after the date of publication of the initial public notice.

(iii) The FDIC may arrange a meeting in accordance with the procedures in §§ 390.121 through 390.125.

(iv) The FDIC will request the Attorney General, the Office of the Comptroller of the Currency, and the Board of Governors of the Federal Reserve System to provide reports on the competitive impacts involved in the transaction.

(v) The FDIC will immediately notify the Attorney General of the approval of the transaction. The applicant may not consummate the transaction before the date established under 12 U.S.C. 1828(c)(6).

§ 390.332

(2) For applications described in § 390.332, certain State savings associations described below must provide affected accountholders with a notice of a proposed account transfer and an option of retaining the account in the transferring State savings association. The notice must allow affected accountholders at least 30 days to consider whether to retain their accounts in the transferring State savings association. The following State savings associations must provide the notices:

(i) A State savings association transferring account liabilities to an institution the accounts of which are not insured by the Deposit Insurance Fund or the National Credit Union Share Insurance Fund; and

(ii) Any mutual State savings association transferring account liabilities to a stock form depository institution.

(f) *Automatic approvals by the FDIC.* Applications filed pursuant to paragraph (a) of this section shall be deemed to be approved automatically by the FDIC 30 calendar days after the FDIC sends written notice to the applicant that the application is complete, unless:

(1) The acquiring State savings association does not meet the criteria for expedited treatment under § 390.101;

(2) The FDIC recommends the imposition of non-standard conditions prior to approving the application;

(3) The FDIC suspends the applicable processing time frames under § 390.125;

(4) The FDIC raises objections to the transaction;

(5) The resulting State savings association would be one of the 3 largest depository institutions competing in the relevant geographic area where before the transaction there were 5 or fewer depository institutions, the resulting State savings association would have 25 percent or more of the total deposits held by depository institutions in the relevant geographic area, and the share of total deposits would have increased by 5 percent or more;

(6) The resulting State savings association would be one of the 2 largest depository institutions competing in the relevant geographic area where before the transaction there were 6 to 11 depository institutions the resulting State savings association would have 30 percent or more of the total deposits held by depositing institutions in the relevant geographic area, and the share of total deposits would have increased by 10 percent or more;

(7) The resulting State savings association would be one of the 2 largest depository institutions competing in the relevant geographic area where before the transaction there were 12 or more depository institutions, the resulting State savings association would have 35 percent or more of the total deposits held by the depository institutions in the relevant geographic area, and the share of total deposits would have increased by 15 percent or more;

(8) The Herfindahl-Hirschman Index (HHI) in the relevant geographic area was more than 1800 before the transaction, and the increase in the HHI used by the transaction would be 50 or more;

(9) In a transaction involving potential competition, the FDIC determines that the acquiring State savings association is one of three or fewer potential entrants into the relevant geographic area;

(10) The acquiring State savings association has assets of $1 billion or more and proposes to acquire assets of $1 billion or more;

(11) The State savings association that will be the resulting State savings association in the transaction has a composite Community Reinvestment Act rating of less than satisfactory, or is otherwise seriously deficient with respect to the FDIC's nondiscrimination regulations and the deficiencies have not been resolved to the satisfaction of the FDIC;

(12) The transaction involves any supervisory or assistance agreement with the FDIC;

(13) The transaction is part of a conversion under 12 CFR part 192;

(14) The transaction raises a significant issue of law or policy; or

(15) The transaction is opposed by any constituent institution or contested by a competing acquiror.

(g) *Definitions.* (1) The terms used in this subpart shall have the same meaning as set forth in 12 CFR 152.13(b).

(2) *Insured depository institution. Insured depository institution* has the same

meaning as defined in section 3(c)(2) of the Federal Deposit Insurance Act.

(3) With regard to paragraph (f) of this section, the term *relevant geographic area* is used as a substitute for *relevant geographic market*, which means the area within which the competitive effects of a merger or other combination may be evaluated. The relevant geographic area shall be delineated as a county or similar political subdivision, an area smaller than a county, or an aggregation of counties within which the merging or combining insured depository institutions compete. In addition, the FDIC may consider commuting patterns, newspaper and other advertising activities, or other factors as the FDIC deems relevant.

(h) *Special requirements and procedures for transactions under paragraphs (b) and (c) of this section*—(1)(i) *Certain transactions with no surviving State savings association.* The FDIC must be notified of any transaction under paragraph (b)(1) of this section. Such notification must be submitted to the appropriate FDIC region, as defined in §303.2 of this chapter, at least 30 days prior to the effective date of the transaction, but not later than the date on which an application relating to the proposed transaction is filed with the primary regulator of the resulting institution; the FDIC may, upon request or on its own initiative, shorten the 30-day prior notification requirement. Notifications under this paragraph must demonstrate compliance with applicable stockholder or accountholder approval requirements. Where the State savings association submitting the notification maintains a liquidation account established pursuant to 12 CFR part 192, the notification must state that the resulting institution will assume such liquidation account.

(ii) The notification may be in the form of either a letter describing the material features of the transaction or a copy of a filing made with another Federal or state regulatory agency seeking approval from that agency for the transaction under the Bank Merger Act or other applicable statute. If the action contemplated by the notification is not completed within one year after the FDIC's receipt of the notification, a new notification must be submitted to the FDIC.

(2) *Other transfer transactions*—(i) *Expedited treatment.* A notice in conformity with §390.105(a) may be submitted to the appropriate FDIC region, as defined in §303.2 of this chapter, under §390.108 for any transaction under paragraph (c) of this section, provided all constituent State savings associations meet the conditions for expedited treatment under §390.101. Notices submitted under this paragraph must be deemed approved automatically by the FDIC 30 days after receipt, unless the FDIC advises the applicant in writing prior to the expiration of such period that the proposed transaction may not be consummated without the FDIC's approval of an application under paragraphs (h)(2)(ii) or (h)(2)(iii) of this section.

(ii) *Standard treatment.* An application in conformity with §390.105(b) and paragraph (d) of this section must be submitted to the appropriate FDIC region, as defined in §303.2 of this chapter, under §390.108 by each State savings association participating in a transaction under paragraph (b)(2) or (c) of this section, where any constituent State savings association does not meet the conditions for expedited treatment under §390.101. Applications under this paragraph must be processed in accordance with §§390.103 through 390.110 and §§390.126 through 390.135.

§ 390.333 Advertising.

No State savings association shall use advertising (which includes print or broadcast media, displays or signs, stationery, and all other promotional materials), or make any representation which is inaccurate in any particular or which in any way misrepresents its services, contracts, investments, or financial condition.

§ 390.334 Directors, officers, and employees.

(a) *Directors*—(1) *Requirements.* The composition of the board of directors of a State savings association must be in accordance with the following requirements:

(i) A majority of the directors must not be salaried officers or employees of the State savings association or of any subsidiary or (except in the case of a State savings association having 80% or more of any class of voting shares owned by a holding company) any holding company affiliate thereof.

(ii) Not more than two of the directors may be members of the same immediate family.

(iii) Not more than one director may be an attorney with a particular law firm.

(2) *Prospective application.* In the case of an association whose board of directors does not conform with any requirement set forth in paragraph (a)(1) of this section as of October 5, 1983, this paragraph (a) shall not prohibit the uninterrupted service, including re-election and re-appointment, of any person serving on the board of directors at that date.

(b) [Reserved]

§ 390.335 **Tying restriction exception.**

For applicable rules, see the regulations issued by the Board of Governors of the Federal Reserve System.

§ 390.336 **Employment contracts.**

(a) *General.* A State savings association may enter into an employment contract with its officers and other employees only in accordance with the requirements of this section. All employment contracts shall be in writing and shall be approved specifically by a State savings association's board of directors. A State savings association shall not enter into an employment contract with any of its officers or other employees if such contract would constitute an unsafe or unsound practice. The making of such an employment contract would be an unsafe or unsound practice if such contract could lead to material financial loss or damage to the State savings association or could interfere materially with the exercise by the members of its board of directors of their duty or discretion provided by law, charter, bylaw or regulation as to the employment or termination of employment of an officer or employee of the State savings association. This may occur, depending upon the circumstances of the case, where an employment contract provides for an excessive term.

(b) *Required provisions.* Each employment contract shall provide that:

(1) The State savings association's board of directors may terminate the officer or employee's employment at any time, but any termination by the State savings association's board of directors other than termination for cause, shall not prejudice the officer or employee's right to compensation or other benefits under the contract. The officer or employee shall have no right to receive compensation or other benefits for any period after termination for cause. Termination for cause shall include termination because of the officer or employee's personal dishonesty, incompetence, willful misconduct, breach of fiduciary duty involving personal profit, intentional failure to perform stated duties, willful violation of any law, rule, or regulation (other than traffic violations or similar offenses) or final cease-and-desist order, or material breach of any provision of the contract.

(2) If the officer or employee is suspended and/or temporarily prohibited from participating in the conduct of the State savings association's affairs by a notice served under section 8(e)(3) or (g)(1) of Federal Deposit Insurance Act (12 U.S.C. 1818(e)(3) and (g)(1)), the State savings association's obligations under the contract shall be suspended as of the date of service unless stayed by appropriate proceedings. If the charges in the notice are dismissed, the State savings association may in its discretion:

(i) Pay the officer or employee all or part of the compensation withheld while its contract obligations were suspended; and

(ii) Reinstate (in whole or in part) any of its obligations which were suspended.

(3) If the officer or employee is removed and/or permanently prohibited from participating in the conduct of the State savings association's affairs by an order issued under section 8 (e)(4) or (g)(1) of the Federal Deposit Insurance Act (12 U.S.C. 1818 (e)(4) or (g)(1)), all obligations of the State savings association under the contract shall terminate as of the effective date of the order, but vested rights of the contracting parties shall not be affected.

Federal Deposit Insurance Corporation § 390.339

(4) If the State savings association is in default (as defined in section 3(x)(1) of the Federal Deposit Insurance Act), all obligations under the contract shall terminate as of the date of default, but this paragraph (b)(4) shall not affect any vested rights of the contracting parties: *Provided*, that this paragraph (b)(4) need not be included in an employment contract if prior written approval is secured from the FDIC.

(5)(i) All obligations under the contract shall be terminated, except to the extent determined that continuation of the contract is necessary of the continued operation of the State savings association

(A) By the FDIC, at the time the FDIC enters into an agreement to provide assistance to or on behalf of the State savings association under the authority contained in 13(c) of the Federal Deposit Insurance Act; or

(B) By the FDIC, at the time the FDIC approves a supervisory merger to resolve problems related to operation of the State savings association or when the State savings association is determined by the FDIC to be in an unsafe or unsound condition.

(ii) Any rights of the parties that have already vested, however, shall not be affected by such action.

§ 390.337 Transactions with affiliates.

For applicable rules, see the regulations issued by the Board of Governors of the Federal Reserve System.

§ 390.338 Loans by State savings associations to their executive officers, directors, and principal shareholders.

For applicable rules, see the regulations issued by the Board of Governors of the Federal Reserve System.

§ 390.339 Pension plans.

(a) *General.* No State savings association shall sponsor an employee pension plan which, because of unreasonable costs or any other reason, could lead to material financial loss or damage to the sponsor. For purposes of this section, an employee pension plan is defined in section 3(2) of the Employee Retirement Income Security Act of 1974, as amended. The prospective obligation or liability of a plan sponsor to each plan participant shall be stated in or determinable from the plan, and, for a defined benefit plan, shall also be based upon an actuarial estimate of future experience under the plan.

(b) *Funding.* Actuarial cost methods permitted under the Employee Retirement Income Security Act of 1974 and the Internal Revenue Code of 1954, as amended, shall be used to determine plan funding.

(c) *Plan amendment.* A plan may be amended to provide reasonable annual cost-of-living increases to retired participants: *Provided*, That

(1) Any such increase shall be for a period and amount determined by the sponsor's board of directors, but in no event shall it exceed the annual increase in the Consumer Price Index published by the Bureau of Labor Statistics; and

(2) No increase shall be granted unless:

(i) Anticipated charges to net income for future periods have first been found by such board of directors to be reasonable and are documented by appropriate resolution and supporting analysis; and

(ii) The increase will not reduce the State savings association's regulatory capital below its regulatory capital requirement.

(d) *Termination.* The plan shall permit the sponsor's board of directors and its successors to terminate such plan. Notice of intent to terminate shall be filed with the FDIC at least 60 days prior to the proposed termination date.

(e) *Records.* Each State savings association maintaining a plan not subject to recordkeeping and reporting requirements of the Employee Retirement Income Security Act of 1974, and the Internal Revenue Code of 1954, as amended, shall establish and maintain records containing the following:

(1) Plan description;

(2) Schedule of participants and beneficiaries;

(3) Schedule of participants and beneficiaries' rights and obligations;

(4) Plan's financial statements; and

(5) Except for defined contribution plans, an opinion signed by an enrolled actuary (as defined by the Employee Retirement Income Security Act of

§ 390.340

1974) affirming that actuarial assumptions in the aggregate are reasonable, take into account the plan's experience and expectations, and represent the actuary's best estimate of the plan's projected experiences.

§ 390.340 Offers and sales of securities at an office of a State savings association.

(a) A State saving association may not offer or sell debt or equity securities issued by the State savings association or an affiliate of the State savings association at an office of the State savings association; except that equity securities issued by the State savings association or an affiliate in connection with the State savings association's conversion from the mutual to stock form of organization in a conversion approved pursuant to 12 CFR part 192 may be offered and sold at the State savings association's offices: *Provided*, That:

(1) The FDIC does not object on supervisory grounds that the offer and sale of the securities at the offices of the State savings association;

(2) No commissions, bonuses, or comparable payments are paid to any employee of the State savings association or its affiliates or to any other person in connection with the sale of securities at an office of a State savings association; except that compensation and commissions consistent with industry norms may be paid to securities personnel of registered broker-dealers;

(3) No offers or sales are made by tellers or at the teller counter, or by comparable persons at comparable locations;

(4) Sales activity is conducted in a segregated or separately identifiable area of the State savings association's offices apart from the area accessible to the general public for the purposes of making or withdrawing deposits;

(5) Offers and sales are made only by regular, full-time employees of the State savings association or by securities personnel who are subject to supervision by a registered broker-dealer;

(6) An acknowledgment, in the form set forth in paragraph (c) of this section, is signed by any customer to whom the security is sold in the State savings association's offices prior to the sale of any such securities;

(7) A legend that the security is not a deposit or account and is not federally insured or guaranteed appears conspicuously on the security and in all offering documents and advertisements for the securities; the legend must state in bold or other prominent type at least as large as other textual type in the document that "This security is not a deposit or account and is not federally insured or guaranteed"; and

(8) The State savings association will be in compliance with its current capital requirements upon completion of the conversion stock offering.

(b) Securities sales practices, advertisements, and other sales literature used in connection with offers and sales of securities by State savings associations shall be subject to § 390.419.

(c) Offers and sales of securities of a State savings association or its affiliates in any office of the State savings association must use a one-page, unambiguous, certification in substantially the following form:

FORM OF CERTIFICATION

I ACKNOWLEDGE THAT THIS SECURITY IS NOT A DEPOSIT OR ACCOUNT AND IS NOT FEDERALLY INSURED, AND IS NOT GUARANTEED BY [*insert name of State savings association*] OR BY THE FEDERAL GOVERNMENT.

If anyone asserts that this security is federally insured or guaranteed, or is as safe as an insured deposit, I should call the FDIC's appropriate regional director [*insert name and telephone number with area code of the appropriate regional director, as defined in section 303.2 of this chapter*].

I further certify that, before purchasing the [*description of security being offered*] of [*name of issuer, name of State savings association and affiliation to issuer (if different)*], I received an offering circular.

The offering circular that I received contains disclosure concerning the nature of the security being offered and describes the risks involved in the investment, including:

[*List briefly the principal risks involved and cross reference certain specified pages of the offering circular where a more complete description of the risks is made.*]

Signature: _____

Date: _____

(d) For purposes of this section, an "office" of a State savings association means any premises used by the State savings association that are identified

Federal Deposit Insurance Corporation § 390.341

to the public through advertising or signage using the State savings association's name, trade name, or logo.

§ 390.341 Inclusion of subordinated debt securities and mandatorily redeemable preferred stock as supplementary capital.

(a) *Scope.* A State savings association must comply with this section in order to include subordinated debt securities or mandatorily redeemable preferred stock ("covered securities") in supplementary capital (tier 2 capital) under subpart Z. If a State savings association does not include covered securities in supplementary capital, it is not required to comply with this section.

(b) *Application and notice procedures.* (1) A State savings association must file an application or notice under §§ 390.103 through 390.110 seeking FDIC approval of, or non-objection to, the inclusion of covered securities in supplementary capital. The State savings association may file its application or notice before or after it issues covered securities, but may not include covered securities in supplementary capital until the FDIC approves the application or does not object to the notice.

(2) A State savings association must also comply with the securities offering rules at subpart W by filing an offering circular for a proposed issuance of covered securities, unless the offering qualifies for an exemption under that subpart.

(c) *Securities requirements.* To be included in supplementary capital, covered securities must meet the following requirements:

(1) *Form.* (i) Each certificate evidencing a covered security must:

(A) Bear the following legend on its face, in bold type: "This security is *not* a savings account or deposit and it is *not* insured by the United States or any agency or fund of the United States;"

(B) State that the security is subordinated on liquidation, as to principal, interest, and premium, to all claims against the State savings association that have the same priority as savings accounts or a higher priority;

(C) State that the security is not secured by the State savings association's assets or the assets of any affiliate of the State savings association. For purposes of this subpart, the term *affiliate* means any person or company which controls, is controlled by, or is under common control with such State savings association.

(D) State that the security is not eligible collateral for a loan by the State savings association;

(E) State the prohibition on the payment of dividends or interest at 12 U.S.C. 1828(b) and, in the case of subordinated debt securities, state the prohibition on the payment of principal and interest at 12 U.S.C. 1831o(h);

(F) For subordinated debt securities, state or refer to a document stating the terms under which the State savings association may prepay the obligation; and

(G) State or refer to a document stating that the State savings association must obtain FDIC approval before the voluntarily prepayment of principal on subordinated debt securities, the acceleration of payment of principal on subordinated debt securities, or the voluntarily redemption of mandatorily redeemable preferred stock (other than scheduled redemptions), if the State savings association is undercapitalized, significantly undercapitalized, or critically undercapitalized as described in § 390.453(4)(b), fails to meet the regulatory capital requirements at subpart Z, or would fail to meet any of these standards following the payment.

(ii) A State savings association must include such additional statements as the FDIC may prescribe for certificates, purchase agreements, indentures, and other related documents.

(2) *Maturity requirements.* Covered securities must have an original weighted average maturity or original weighted average period to required redemption of at least five years.

(3) *Mandatory prepayment.* Subordinated debt securities and related documents may not provide events of default or contain other provisions that could result in a mandatory prepayment of principal, other than events of default that:

(i) Arise from the State savings association's failure to make timely payment of interest or principal;

(ii) Arise from its failure to comply with reasonable financial, operating, and maintenance covenants of a type

§ 390.341

that are customarily included in indentures for publicly offered debt securities; or

(iii) Relate to bankruptcy, insolvency, receivership, or similar events.

(4) *Indenture.* (i) Except as provided in paragraph (c)(4)(ii) of this section, a State savings association must use an indenture for subordinated debt securities. If the aggregate amount of subordinated debt securities publicly offered (excluding sales in a non-public offering as defined in § 390.413 and sold in any consecutive 12-month or 36-month period exceeds $5,000,000 or $10,000,000 respectively (or such lesser amount that the Securities and Exchange Commission shall establish by rule or regulation under 15 U.S.C. 77ddd), the indenture must provide for the appointment of a trustee other than the State savings association or an affiliate of the State savings association (as defined at § 390.283) and for collective enforcement of the security holders' rights and remedies.

(ii) A State savings association is not required to use an indenture if the subordinated debt securities are sold only to accredited investors, as that term is defined in 15 U.S.C. 77d(6). A State savings association must have an indenture that meets the requirements of paragraph (c)(4)(i) of this section in place before any debt securities for which an exemption from the indenture requirement is claimed, are transferred to any non-accredited investor. If a State savings association relies on this exemption from the indenture requirement, it must place a legend on the debt securities indicating that an indenture must be in place before the debt securities are transferred to any non-accredited investor.

(d) *FDIC review.* (1) The FDIC will review notices and applications under §§ 390.126 through 390.135.

(2) In reviewing notices and applications under this section, the FDIC will consider whether:

(i) The issuance of the covered securities is authorized under applicable laws and regulations and is consistent with the State savings association's charter and bylaws.

(ii) The State savings association is at least adequately capitalized under § 390.453(4)(b) and meets the regulatory capital requirements at subpart Z.

(iii) The State savings association is or will be able to service the covered securities.

(iv) The covered securities are consistent with the requirements of this section.

(v) The covered securities and related transactions sufficiently transfer risk from the Deposit Insurance Fund.

(vi) The FDIC has no objection to the issuance based on the State savings association's overall policies, condition, and operations.

(3) The FDIC approval or non-objection is conditioned upon no material changes to the information disclosed in the application or notice submitted to the FDIC. The FDIC may impose such additional requirements or conditions as it may deem necessary to protect purchasers, the State savings association, or the Deposit Insurance Fund.

(e) *Amendments.* If a State savings association amends the covered securities or related documents following the completion of the FDIC's review, it must obtain the FDIC's approval or non-objection under this section before it may include the amended securities in supplementary capital.

(f) *Sale of covered securities.* The State savings association must complete the sale of covered securities within one year after the FDIC's approval or non-objection under this section. A State savings association may request an extension of the offering period by filing a written request with the FDIC. The State savings association must demonstrate good cause for the extension and file the request at least 30 days before the expiration of the offering period or any extension of the offering period.

(g) *Reports.* A State savings association must file the following information with the FDIC within 30 days after the State savings association completes the sale of covered securities includable as supplementary capital. If the State savings association filed its application or notice following the completion of the sale, it must submit this information with its application or notice:

(1) A written report indicating the number of purchasers, the total dollar

Federal Deposit Insurance Corporation § 390.345

amount of securities sold, the net proceeds received by the State savings association from the issuance, and the amount of covered securities, net of all expenses, to be included as supplementary capital;

(2) Three copies of an executed form of the securities and a copy of any related documents governing the issuance or administration of the securities; and

(3) A certification by the appropriate executive officer indicating that the State savings association complied with all applicable laws and regulations in connection with the offering, issuance, and sale of the securities.

§ 390.342 Capital distributions by State savings associations.

Sections 390.342 through 390.348 apply to all capital distributions by a State savings association ("you").

§ 390.343 What is a capital distribution?

A capital distribution is:

(a) A distribution of cash or other property to your owners made on account of their ownership, but excludes:

(1) Any dividend consisting only of your shares or rights to purchase your shares; or

(2) If you are a mutual State savings association, any payment that you are required to make under the terms of a deposit instrument and any other amount paid on deposits that the FDIC determines is not a distribution for the purposes of this section;

(b) Your payment to repurchase, redeem, retire or otherwise acquire any of your shares or other ownership interests, any payment to repurchase, redeem, retire, or otherwise acquire debt instruments included in your total capital under subpart Z, and any extension of credit to finance an affiliate's acquisition of your shares or interests;

(c) Any direct or indirect payment of cash or other property to owners or affiliates made in connection with a corporate restructuring. This includes your payment of cash or property to shareholders of another savings association or to shareholders of its holding company to acquire ownership in that savings association, other than by a distribution of shares;

(d) Any other distribution charged against your capital accounts if you would not be well capitalized, as set forth in § 390.453(b)(1), following the distribution; and

(e) Any transaction that the FDIC determines, by order or regulation, to be in substance a distribution of capital.

§ 390.344 Definitions applicable to capital distributions.

The following definitions apply to sections 390.342 through 390.348:

Affiliate means an affiliate, as defined in regulations governing transactions with affiliates as issued by the Board of Governors of the Federal Reserve System.

Capital means total capital, as computed under subpart Z.

Net income means your net income computed in accordance with generally accepted accounting principles.

Retained net income means your net income for a specified period less total capital distributions declared in that period.

Shares means common and preferred stock, and any options, warrants, or other rights for the acquisition of such stock. The term "share" also includes convertible securities upon their conversion into common or preferred stock. The term does not include convertible debt securities prior to their conversion into common or preferred stock or other securities that are not equity securities at the time of a capital distribution.

§ 390.345 Must I file with the FDIC?

Whether and what you must file with the FDIC depends on whether you and your proposed capital distribution fall within certain criteria.

(a) *Application required.*

If:	Then you:
(1) You are not eligible for expedited treatment under § 390.101	Must file an application with the FDIC.

839

§ 390.346

If:	Then you:
(2) The total amount of all of your capital distributions (including the proposed capital distribution) for the applicable calendar year exceeds your net income for that year to date plus your retained net income for the preceding two years.	Must file an application with the FDIC.
(3) You would not be at least adequately capitalized, as set forth in § 390.453(b)(2), following the distribution.	Must file an application with the FDIC.
(4) Your proposed capital distribution would violate a prohibition contained in any applicable statute, regulation, or agreement between you and the FDIC, or violate a condition imposed on you in an FDIC-approved application or notice.	Must file an application with the FDIC.

(b) *Notice required.*

If you are not required to file an application under paragraph (a) of this section, but:	Then you:
(1) You would not be well capitalized, as set forth under § 390.453(b)(1), following the distribution.	Must file a notice with the FDIC.
(2) Your proposed capital distribution would reduce the amount of or retire any part of your common or preferred stock or retire any part of debt instruments such as notes or debentures included in capital under subpart Z (other than regular payments required under a debt instrument approved under § 390.341).	Must file a notice with the FDIC.

(c) *No prior notice required.*

If neither you nor your proposed capital distribution meet any of the criteria listed in paragraphs (a) and (b) of this section.	Then you do not need to file a notice or an application with the FDIC before making a capital distribution.

§ 390.346 How do I file with the FDIC?

(a) *Contents.* Your notice or application must:

(1) Be in narrative form.

(2) Include all relevant information concerning the proposed capital distribution, including the amount, timing, and type of distribution.

(3) Demonstrate compliance with § 390.348.

(b) *Schedules.* Your notice or application may include a schedule proposing capital distributions over a specified period, not to exceed 12 months.

(c) *Timing.* You must file your notice or application at least 30 days before the proposed declaration of dividend or approval of the proposed capital distribution by your board of directors.

§ 390.347 May I combine my notice or application with other notices or applications?

You may combine the notice or application required under § 390.345 with any other notice or application, if the capital distribution is a part of, or is proposed in connection with, another transaction requiring a notice or application under Parts 390 and 391. If you submit a combined filing, you must:

(a) State that the related notice or application is intended to serve as a notice or application under §§ 390.342 through 390.348; and

(b) Submit the notice or application in a timely manner.

§ 390.348 Will the FDIC permit my capital distribution?

The FDIC will review your notice or application under the review procedures in §§ 390.126 through 390.135. The FDIC may disapprove your notice or deny your application filed under § 390.345 in whole or in part, if the FDIC makes any of the following determinations.

(a) You will be undercapitalized, significantly undercapitalized, or critically undercapitalized as set forth in § 390.453(b), following the capital distribution. If so, the FDIC will determine if your capital distribution is permitted under 12 U.S.C. 1831o(d)(1)(B).

(b) Your proposed capital distribution raises safety or soundness concerns.

Federal Deposit Insurance Corporation § 390.350

(c) Your proposed capital distribution violates a prohibition contained in any statute, regulation, agreement between you and the FDIC or a condition imposed on you in an FDIC-approved application or notice. If so, the FDIC will determine whether it may permit your capital distribution notwithstanding the prohibition or condition.

§ 390.349 Management and financial policies.

(a)(1) For the protection of depositors and other State savings associations, each State savings association must be well managed and operate safely and soundly. Each also must pursue financial policies that are safe and consistent with economical home financing and the purposes of State savings associations.

(2) As part of meeting its requirements under paragraph (a)(1) of this section, each State savings association must maintain sufficient liquidity to ensure its safe and sound operation.

(b) Compensation to officers, directors, and employees of each State savings association shall not be in excess of that which is reasonable and commensurate with their duties and responsibilities. Former officers, directors, and employees of State savings association who regularly perform services therefor under consulting contracts are employees thereof for purposes of this paragraph (b).

§ 390.350 Examinations and audits; appraisals; establishment and maintenance of records.

(a) *Examinations and audits.* Each State savings association and affiliate thereof shall be examined periodically, and may be examined at any time, by the FDIC, with appraisals when deemed advisable, in accordance with general policies from time to time established by the FDIC.

(b) *Appraisals.* (1) Unless otherwise ordered by the FDIC, appraisal of real estate by the FDIC in connection with any examination or audit of a State savings association or its affiliate shall be made by an appraiser, or by appraisers, selected by the appropriate FDIC region, as that term is defined in § 303.2 of this chapter, in which such State savings association is located. The cost of such appraisal shall promptly be paid by such State savings association or its affiliate direct to such appraiser or appraisers upon receipt by the State savings association or its affiliate of a statement of such cost as approved by the appropriate regional director. A copy of the report of each appraisal made by the FDIC pursuant to any of the foregoing provisions of this section shall be furnished to the State savings association or its affiliate, as appropriate within a reasonable time, not to exceed 90 days, following the completion of such appraisals and the filing of a report thereof by the appraiser, or appraisers, with the appropriate FDIC office.

(2) The FDIC may obtain at any time, at its expense, such appraisals of any of the assets, including the security therefor, of a State savings association or its affiliate as the FDIC deems appropriate.

(c) *Establishment and maintenance of records.* To enable the FDIC to examine State savings associations and affiliates and audit State savings associations and its affiliates, pursuant to the provisions of paragraph (a) of this section, each State savings association, and its affiliate shall establish and maintain such accounting and other records as will provide an accurate and complete record of all business it transacts. This includes, without limitation, establishing and maintaining such other records as are required by statute or any other regulation to which the State savings association and its affiliate is subject. The documents, files, and other material or property comprising said records shall at all times be available for such examination and audit wherever any of said records, documents, files, material, or property may be.

(d) *Change in location of records.* A State savings association shall not transfer the location of any of its general accounting or control records, or the maintenance thereof, from its home office to a branch or service office, or from a branch or service office to its home office or to another branch or service office unless prior to the date of transfer its board of directors has:

§ 390.351

(1) By resolution authorized the transfer or maintenance and;

(2) Sent a certified copy of the resolution to the appropriate regional director for the region in which the principal office of the State savings association is located.

(e) *Use of data processing services for maintenance of records.* A State savings association which determines to maintain any of its records by means of data processing services shall so notify the appropriate regional director for the region in which the principal office of such State savings association is located, in writing, at least 90 days prior to the date on which such maintenance of records will begin. Such notification shall include identification of the records to be maintained by data processing services and a statement as to the location at which such records will be maintained. Any contract, agreement, or arrangement made by a State savings association pursuant to which data processing services are to be performed for such State savings association shall be in writing and shall expressly provide that the records to be maintained by such services shall at all times be available for examination and audit.

§ 390.351 **Frequency of safety and soundness examination.**

(a) *General.* The FDIC examines State savings associations pursuant to authority conferred by 12 U.S.C. 1463 and the requirements of 12 U.S.C. 1820(d). The FDIC is required to conduct a full-scope, on-site examination of every State savings association at least once during each 12-month period.

(b) *18-month rule for certain small institutions.* The FDIC may conduct a full-scope, on-site examination of a State savings association at least once during each 18-month period, rather than each 12-month period as provided in paragraph (a) of this section, if the following conditions are satisfied:

(1) The State savings association has total assets of less than $500 million;

(2) The State savings association is well capitalized as defined in § 390.453;

(3) At its most recent examination, the FDIC—

(i) Assigned the State savings association a rating of 1 or 2 for manage-

12 CFR Ch. III (1–1–12 Edition)

ment as part of the State savings association's composite rating under the Uniform Financial Institutions Rating System (commonly referred to as CAMELS), and

(ii) Determined that the State savings association was in outstanding or good condition, that is, it received a composite rating, as defined in § 390.101(c), of 1 or 2;

(4) The State savings association currently is not subject to a formal enforcement proceeding or order by the FDIC; and

(5) No person acquired control of the State savings association during the preceding 12-month period in which a full-scope, on-site examination would have been required but for this section.

(c) *Authority to conduct more frequent examinations.* This section does not limit the authority of the FDIC to examine any State savings association as frequently as the agency deems necessary.

§ 390.352 **Financial derivatives.**

(a) *What is a financial derivative?* A financial derivative is a financial contract whose value depends on the value of one or more underlying assets, indices, or reference rates. The most common types of financial derivatives are futures, forward commitments, options, and swaps. A mortgage derivative security, such as a collateralized mortgage obligation or a real estate mortgage investment conduit, is not a financial derivative under this section.

(b) *May I engage in transactions involving financial derivatives?* (1) [Reserved]

(2) If you are a State savings association, you may engage in a transaction involving a financial derivative if your charter or applicable State law authorizes you to engage in such transactions, the transaction is safe and sound, and you otherwise meet the requirements in this section.

(3) In general, if you engage in a transaction involving a financial derivative, you should do so to reduce your risk exposure.

(c) *What are my board of directors' responsibilities with respect to financial derivatives?* (1) Your board of directors is responsible for effective oversight of financial derivatives activities.

842

Federal Deposit Insurance Corporation

§ 390.354

(2) Before you may engage in any transaction involving a financial derivative, your board of directors must establish written policies and procedures governing authorized financial derivatives. Your board of directors should review Thrift Bulletin 13a, "Management of Interest Rate Risk, Investment Securities, and Derivatives Activities," and other applicable agency guidance on establishing a sound risk management program.

(3) Your board of directors must periodically review:

(i) Compliance with the policies and procedures established under paragraph (c)(2) of this section; and

(ii) The adequacy of these policies and procedures to ensure that they continue to be appropriate to the nature and scope of your operations and existing market conditions.

(4) Your board of directors must ensure that management establishes an adequate system of internal controls for transactions involving financial derivatives.

(d) *What are management's responsibilities with respect to financial derivatives?* (1) Management is responsible for daily oversight and management of financial derivatives activities. Management must implement the policies and procedures established by the board of directors and must establish a system of internal controls. This system of internal controls should, at a minimum, provide for periodic reporting to the board of directors and management, segregation of duties, and internal review procedures.

(2) Management must ensure that financial derivatives activities are conducted in a safe and sound manner and should review Thrift Bulletin 13a, "Management of Interest Rate Risk, Investment Securities, and Derivatives Activities," and other applicable agency guidance on implementing a sound risk management program.

(e) *What records must I keep on financial derivative transactions?* You must maintain records adequate to demonstrate compliance with this section and with your board of directors' policies and procedures on financial derivatives.

§ 390.353 Interest-rate-risk-management procedures.

State savings associations shall take the following actions:

(a) The board of directors or a committee thereof shall review the State savings association's interest-rate-risk exposure and devise a policy for the State savings association's management of that risk.

(b) The board of directors shall formerly adopt a policy for the management of interest-rate risk. The management of the State savings association shall establish guidelines and procedures to ensure that the board's policy is successfully implemented.

(c) The management of the State savings association shall periodically report to the board of directors regarding implementation of the State savings association's policy for interest-rate-risk management and shall make that information available upon request to the FDIC.

(d) The State savings association's board of directors shall review the results of operations at least quarterly and shall make such adjustments as it considers necessary and appropriate to the policy for interest-rate-risk management, including adjustments to the authorized acceptable level of interest-rate risk.

§ 390.354 Procedures for monitoring Bank Secrecy Act (BSA) compliance.

(a) *Purpose.* The purpose of this regulation is to require State savings associations (as defined by § 390.308 to establish and maintain procedures reasonably designed to assure and monitor compliance with the requirements of subchapter II of chapter 53 of title 31, United States Code, and the implementing regulations promulgated thereunder by the U.S. Department of Treasury, 31 CFR part 103.

(b) *Establishment of a BSA compliance program*—(1) *Program requirement.* Each State savings association shall develop and provide for the continued administration of a program reasonably designed to assure and monitor compliance with the recordkeeping and reporting requirements set forth in subchapter II of chapter 53 of title 31,

§ 390.355

United States Code and the implementing regulations issued by the Department of the Treasury at 31 CFR part 103. The compliance program must be written, approved by the State savings association's board of directors, and reflected in the minutes of the State savings association.

(2) *Customer identification program.* Each State savings association is subject to the requirements of 31 U.S.C. 5318(1) and the implementing regulation promulgated at 31 CFR 103.121, which require a customer identification program to be implemented as part of the BSA compliance program required under this section.

(c) *Contents of compliance program.* The compliance program shall, at a minimum:

(1) Provide for a system of internal controls to assure ongoing compliance;

(2) Provide for independent testing for compliance to be conducted by a savings association's in-house personnel or by an outside party;

(3) Designate individual(s) responsible for coordinating and monitoring day-to-day compliance; and

(4) Provide training for appropriate personnel.

§ 390.355 Suspicious Activity Reports and other reports and statements.

(a) *Periodic reports.* Each State savings association shall make such periodic or other reports of its affairs in such manner and on such forms as the FDIC may prescribe. The FDIC may provide that reports filed by State savings associations to meet the requirements of other regulations also satisfy requirements imposed under this section.

(b) *False or misleading statements or omissions.* No State savings association or director, officer, agent, employee, affiliated person, or other person participating in the conduct of the affairs of such State savings association nor any person filing or seeking approval of any application shall knowingly:

(1) Make any written or oral statement to the FDIC or to an agent, representative or employee of the FDIC that is false or misleading with respect to any material fact or omits to state a material fact concerning any matter within the jurisdiction of the FDIC; or

(2) Make any such statement or omission to a person or organization auditing a State savings association or otherwise preparing or reviewing its financial statements concerning the accounts, assets, management condition, ownership, safety, or soundness, or other affairs of the State savings association.

(c) *Notifications of loss and reports of increase in deductible amount of bond.* A State savings association maintaining bond coverage as required by § 390.356 shall promptly notify its bond company and file a proof of loss under the procedures provided by its bond, concerning any covered losses greater than twice the deductible amount.

(d) *Suspicious Activity Reports*—(1) *Purpose and scope.* This paragraph (d) ensures that State savings associations and service corporations file a Suspicious Activity Report when they detect a known or suspected violation of Federal law or a suspicious transaction related to a money laundering activity or a violation of the Bank Secrecy Act.

(2) *Definitions.* For the purposes of this paragraph (d):

(i) *FinCEN* means the Financial Crimes Enforcement Network of the Department of the Treasury.

(ii) *Institution-affiliated party* means any institution-affiliated party as that term is defined in sections 3(u) and 8(b)(9) of the Federal Deposit Insurance Act (12 U.S.C. 1813(u) and 1818(b)(9)).

(iii) *SAR* means a Suspicious Activity Report on the form prescribed by the FDIC.

(3) *SARs required.* A State savings association shall file a SAR with the appropriate Federal law enforcement agencies and the Department of the Treasury in accordance with the form's instructions, by sending a completed SAR to FinCEN in the following circumstances:

(i) *Insider abuse involving any amount.* Whenever the State savings association detects any known or suspected Federal criminal violation, or pattern of criminal violations, committed or attempted against the State savings association or involving a transaction or transactions conducted through the State savings association where the State savings association believes that

Federal Deposit Insurance Corporation § 390.355

it was either an actual or potential victim of a criminal violation, or series of criminal violations, or that it was used to facilitate a criminal transaction, and it has a substantial basis for identifying one of its directors, officers, employees, agents or other institution-affiliated parties as having committed or aided in the commission of a criminal act, regardless of the amount involved in the violation.

(ii) *Violations aggregating $5,000 or more where a suspect can be identified.* Whenever the State savings association detects any known or suspected Federal criminal violation, or pattern of criminal violations, committed or attempted against the State savings association involving a transaction or transactions conducted through the State savings association and involving or aggregating $5,000 or more in funds or other assets, where the State savings association believes that it was either an actual or potential victim of a criminal violation or series of criminal violations, or that it was used to facilitate a criminal transaction, and it has a substantial basis for identifying a possible suspect or group of suspects. If it is determined prior to filing this report that the identified suspect or group of suspects has used an alias, then information regarding the true identity of the suspect or group of suspects, as well as alias identifiers, such as drivers' license or social security numbers, addresses and telephone numbers, must be reported.

(iii) *Violations aggregating $25,000 or more regardless of potential suspects.* Whenever the State savings association detects any known or suspected Federal criminal violation, or pattern of criminal violations, committed or attempted against the State savings association involving a transaction or transactions conducted through the State savings association and involving or aggregating $25,000 or more in funds or other assets, where the State savings association believes that it was either an actual or potential victim of a criminal violation or series of criminal violations, or that it was used to facilitate a criminal transaction, even though there is no substantial basis for identifying a possible suspect or group of suspects.

(iv) *Transactions aggregating $5,000 or more that involve potential money laundering or violations of the Bank Secrecy Act.* Any transaction (which for purposes of this paragraph (d)(3)(iv) means a deposit, withdrawal, transfer between accounts, exchange of currency, loan, extension of credit, purchase or sale of any stock, bond, certificate of deposit, or other monetary instrument or investment security, or any other payment, transfer, or delivery by, through, or to a financial institution, by whatever means effected) conducted or attempted by, at or through the State savings association involving or aggregating $5,000 or more in funds or other assets, if the State savings association knows, suspects, or has reason to suspect that:

(A) The transaction involves funds derived from illegal activities or is intended or conducted in order to hide or disguise funds or assets derived from illegal activities (including, without limitation, the ownership, nature, source, location, or control of such funds or assets) as part of a plan to violate or evade any law or regulation or to avoid any transaction reporting requirement under Federal law;

(B) The transaction is designed to evade any regulations promulgated under the Bank Secrecy Act; or

(C) The transaction has no business or apparent lawful purpose or is not the sort in which the particular customer would normally be expected to engage, and the institution knows of no reasonable explanation for the transaction after examining the available facts, including the background and possible purpose of the transaction.

(4) [Reserved]

(5) *Time for reporting.* A State savings association is required to file a SAR no later than 30 calendar days after the date of initial detection of facts that may constitute a basis for filing a SAR. If no suspect was identified on the date of detection of the incident requiring the filing, a State savings association may delay filing a SAR for an additional 30 calendar days to identify a suspect. In no case shall reporting be delayed more than 60 calendar days after the date of initial detection of a reportable transaction. In situations

§ 390.355

involving violations requiring immediate attention, such as when a reportable violation is ongoing, the State savings association shall immediately notify, by telephone, an appropriate law enforcement authority and the FDIC in addition to filing a timely SAR.

(6) *Reports to state and local authorities.* A State savings association is encouraged to file a copy of the SAR with state and local law enforcement agencies where appropriate.

(7) *Exception.* A State savings association need not file a SAR for a robbery or burglary committed or attempted that is reported to appropriate law enforcement authorities.

(8) *Retention of records.* A State savings association shall maintain a copy of any SAR filed and the original or business record equivalent of any supporting documentation for a period of five years from the date of the filing of the SAR. Supporting documentation shall be identified and maintained by the State savings association as such, and shall be deemed to have been filed with the SAR. A State savings association shall make all supporting documentation available to appropriate law enforcement agencies upon request.

(9) *Notification to board of directors*—(i) *Generally.* Whenever a State savings association files a SAR pursuant to this paragraph (d), the management of the State savings association shall promptly notify its board of directors, or a committee of directors or executive officers designated by the board of directors to receive notice.

(ii) *Suspect is a director or executive officer.* If the State savings association files a SAR pursuant to this paragraph (d) and the suspect is a director or executive officer, the State savings association may not notify the suspect, pursuant to 31 U.S.C. 5318(g)(2), but shall notify all directors who are not suspects.

(10) *Compliance.* Failure to file a SAR in accordance with this section and the instructions may subject the State savings association, its directors, officers, employees, agents, or other institution-affiliated parties to supervisory action.

(11) *Obtaining SARs.* A State savings association may obtain SARs and the instructions from the appropriate FDIC region as defined in § 303.2 of this chapter.

(12) *Confidentiality of SARs.* SARs are confidential. Any institution or person subpoenaed or otherwise requested to disclose a SAR or the information contained in a SAR shall decline to produce the SAR or to provide any information that would disclose that a SAR has been prepared or filed, citing this paragraph (d), applicable law (*e.g.,* 31 U.S.C. 5318(g)), or both, and shall notify the FDIC.

(13) *Safe harbor.* The safe harbor provision of 31 U.S.C. 5318(g), which exempts any financial institution that makes a disclosure of any possible violation of law or regulation from liability under any law or regulation of the United States, or any constitution, law or regulation of any state or political subdivision, covers all reports of suspected or known criminal violations and suspicious activities to law enforcement and financial institution supervisory authorities, including supporting documentation, regardless of whether such reports are filed pursuant to this paragraph (d), or are filed on a voluntary basis.

(e) *Adjustable-rate mortgage indices*—(1) *Reporting obligation.* Upon the request of a Federal Home Loan Bank, all State savings associations within the jurisdiction of that Federal Home Loan Bank shall report the data items set forth in paragraph (e)(2) of this section for the Federal Home Loan Bank to use in calculating and publishing an adjustable-rate mortgage index.

(2) *Data to be reported.* For purposes of paragraph (e)(1) of this section, the term "data items" means the data items previously collected from the monthly Thrift Financial Report or Consolidated Reports of Condition or Income ("Call Report"), as applicable, and such data items as may be altered, amended, or substituted by the requesting Federal Home Loan Bank.

(3) *Applicable indices.* For the purpose of this reporting requirement, the term "adjustable-rate mortgage index" means any of the adjustable-rate mortgage indices calculated and published by a Federal Home Loan Bank or the Federal Home Loan Bank Board on or before August 9, 1989.

Federal Deposit Insurance Corporation § 390.359

§ 390.356 Bonds for directors, officers, employees, and agents; form of and amount of bonds.

(a) Each State savings association shall maintain fidelity bond coverage. The bond shall cover each director, officer, employee, and agent who has control over or access to cash, securities, or other property of the State savings association.

(b) The amount of coverage to be required for each State savings association shall be determined by the association's management, based on its assessment of the level that would be safe and sound in view of the association's potential exposure to risk; provided, such determination shall be subject to approval by the association's board of directors.

(c) Each State savings association may maintain bond coverage in addition to that provided by the insurance underwriter industry's standard forms, through the use of endorsements, riders, or other forms of supplemental coverage, if, in the judgment of the State savings association's board of directors, additional coverage is warranted.

(d) The board of directors of each State savings association shall formally approve the State savings association's bond coverage. In deciding whether to approve the bond coverage, the board shall review the adequacy of the standard coverage and the need for supplemental coverage. Documentation of the board's approval shall be included as a part of the minutes of the meeting at which the board approves coverage. Additionally, the board of directors shall review the State savings association's bond coverage at least annually to assess the continuing adequacy of coverage.

§ 390.357 Bonds for agents.

In lieu of the bond provided in § 390.356 in the case of agents appointed by a State savings association, a fidelity bond may be provided in an amount at least twice the average monthly collections of such agents, provided such agents shall be required to make settlement with the State savings association at least monthly, and provided such bond is approved by the board of directors of the State savings association. No bond need be obtained for any agent that is a financial institution insured by the FDIC.

§ 390.358 Conflicts of interest.

If you are a director, officer, or employee of a State savings association, or have the power to direct its management or policies, or otherwise owe a fiduciary duty to a State savings association:

(a) You must not advance your own personal or business interests, or those of others with whom you have a personal or business relationship, at the expense of the State savings association; and

(b) You must, if you have an interest in a matter or transaction before the board of directors:

(1) Disclose to the board all material nonprivileged information relevant to the board's decision on the matter or transaction, including:

(i) The existence, nature and extent of your interests; and

(ii) The facts known to you as to the matter or transaction under consideration;

(2) Refrain from participating in the board's discussion of the matter or transaction; and

(3) Recuse yourself from voting on the matter or transaction (if you are a director).

§ 390.359 Corporate opportunity.

(a) If you are a director or officer of a State savings association, or have the power to direct its management or policies, or otherwise owe a fiduciary duty to a State savings association, you must not take advantage of corporate opportunities belonging to the State savings association.

(b) A corporate opportunity belongs to a State savings association if:

(1) The opportunity is within the corporate powers of the State savings association or a subsidiary of the State savings association; and

(2) The opportunity is of present or potential practical advantage to the State savings association, either directly or through its subsidiary.

(c) The FDIC will not deem you to have taken advantage of a corporate opportunity belonging to the State savings association if a disinterested

§ 390.360

and independent majority of the State savings association's board of directors, after receiving a full and fair presentation of the matter, rejected the opportunity as a matter of sound business judgment.

§ 390.360 Change of director or senior executive officer.

Sections 390.360 through 390.368 implement 12 U.S.C. 1831i, which requires certain State savings associations to notify the FDIC before appointing or employing directors and senior executive officers.

§ 390.361 Applicable definitions.

The following definitions apply to §§ 390.360 through 390.368:

Director means an individual who serves on the board of directors of a State savings association. This term does not include an advisory director who:

(1) Is not elected by the shareholders;

(2) Is not authorized to vote on any matters before the board of directors or any committee of the board of directors;

(3) Provides only general policy advice to the board of directors or any committee of the board of directors; and

(4) Has not been identified by the FDIC in writing as an individual who performs the functions of a director, or who exercises significant influence over, or participates in, major policymaking decisions of the board of directors.

Senior executive officer means an individual who holds the title or performs the function of one or more of the following positions (without regard to title, salary, or compensation): president, chief executive officer, chief operating officer, chief financial officer, chief lending officer, or chief investment officer. *Senior executive officer* also includes any other person identified by the FDIC in writing as an individual who exercises significant influence over, or participates in, major policymaking decisions, whether or not hired as an employee.

Troubled condition means:

(1) A State savings association that has a composite rating of 4 or 5, as composite rating is defined in § 390.101(c).

(2) [Reserved]

(3) A State savings association that is subject to a capital directive, a cease-and-desist order, a consent order, a formal written agreement, or a prompt corrective action directive relating to the safety and soundness or financial viability of the State savings association, unless otherwise informed in writing by the FDIC; or

(4) A State savings association that is informed in writing by the FDIC that it is in troubled condition based on information available to the FDIC.

§ 390.362 Who must give prior notice?

(a) *State savings association.* Except as provided under § 390.368, you must notify the FDIC at least 30 days before adding or replacing any member of your board of directors, employing any person as a senior executive officer, or changing the responsibilities of any senior executive officer so that the person would assume a different senior executive position if:

(1) You are a State savings association and at least one of the following circumstances apply:

(i) You do not comply with all minimum capital requirements under subpart Z;

(ii) You are in troubled condition; or

(iii) The FDIC has notified you, in connection with its review of a capital restoration plan required under section 38 of the Federal Deposit Insurance Act or subpart Y or otherwise, that a notice is required under §§ 390.360 through 390.368; or

(2) [Reserved]

(b) *Notice by individual.* If you are an individual seeking election to the board of directors of a State savings association described in paragraph (a) of this section, and have not been nominated by management, you must either provide the prior notice required under paragraph (a) of this section or follow the process under § 390.368(b).

§ 390.363 What procedures govern the filing of my notice?

The procedures found in §§ 390.103 through 390.110 govern the filing of your notice under § 390.362.

§ 390.364 What information must I include in my notice?

(a) *Content requirements.* Your notice must include:

(1) The information required under 12 U.S.C. 1817(j)(6)(A), and the information prescribed in the Interagency Notice of Change in Director or Senior Executive Officer and the Interagency Biographical and Financial Report which are available from the appropriate FDIC regions as defined in § 303.2 of this chapter;

(2) Legible fingerprints of the proposed director or senior executive officer. You are not required to file fingerprints if, within three years prior to the date of submission of the notice, the proposed director or senior executive officer provided legible fingerprints as part of a notice filed with the FDIC under 12 U.S.C. 1831i; and

(3) Such other information required by the FDIC.

(b) *Modification of content requirements.* The FDIC may require or accept other information in place of the content requirements in paragraph (a) of this section.

§ 390.365 What procedures govern the FDIC's review of my notice for completeness?

The FDIC will first review your notice to determine whether it is complete.

(a) If your notice is complete, the FDIC will notify you in writing of the date that the FDIC received the complete notice.

(b) If your notice is not complete, the FDIC will notify you in writing what additional information you need to submit, why we need the information, and when you must submit it. You must, within the specified time period, provide additional information or request that the FDIC suspend processing of the notice. If you fail to act within the specified time period, the FDIC may treat the notice as withdrawn or may review the application based on the information provided.

§ 390.366 What standards and procedures will govern the FDIC review of the substance of my notice?

The FDIC will disapprove a notice if, pursuant to the standard set forth in 12 U.S.C. 1831i(e), the FDIC finds that the competence, experience, character, or integrity of the proposed FDIC or senior executive officer indicates that it would not be in the best interests of the depositors of the State savings association or of the public to permit the individual to be employed by, or associated with, the State savings association. If the FDIC disapproves a notice, it will issue a written notice that explains why the FDIC disapproved the notice. The FDIC will send the notice to the State savings association and the individual.

§ 390.367 When may a proposed director or senior executive officer begin service?

(a) A proposed director or senior executive officer may begin service 30 days after the date the FDIC receives all required information, unless:

(1) The FDIC notifies you that it has disapproved the notice; or

(2) The FDIC extends the 30-day period for an additional period not to exceed 60 days. If the FDIC extends the 30-day period, it will notify you in writing that the period has been extended, and will state the reason for the extension. The proposed director or senior executive officer may begin service upon expiration of the extended period, unless the FDIC notifies you that it has disapproved the notice during the extended period.

(b) Notwithstanding paragraph (a) of this section, a proposed or senior executive officer may begin service after the FDIC notifies you, in writing, of its intention not to disapprove the notice.

§ 390.368 When will the FDIC waive the prior notice requirement?

(a) *Waiver request.* (1) An individual may serve as a director or senior executive officer before filing a notice as described in §§ 390.360 through 390.368 if the FDIC issues a written finding that:

(i) Delay would threaten the safety or soundness of the State savings association;

(ii) Delay would not be in the public interest; or

(iii) Other extraordinary circumstances exist that justify waiver of prior notice.

§ 390.380

(2) If the FDIC grants a waiver, you must file a notice as described in §§ 390.360–390.368 within the time period specified by the FDIC.

(b) *Automatic waiver.* An individual may serve as a director before filing a notice as described in §§ 390.360 through 390.368, if the individual was not nominated by management and the individual submits a notice as described in §§ 390.360 through 390.368 within seven days after election as a director.

(c) *Subsequent FDIC action.* The FDIC may disapprove a notice within 30 days after the FDIC issues a waiver under paragraph (a) of this section or within 30 days after the election of an individual who has filed a notice and is serving pursuant to an automatic waiver under paragraph (b) of this section.

Subpart T—Accounting Requirements

§ 390.380 Form and content of financial statements.

(a) This section states the requirements as to form and content of financial statements included by a State savings association in the following documents. However, the FDIC's regulations governing the applicable documents specify the actual financial statements that are to be included in that document.

(1) Any proxy statement or offering circular required to be used in connection with a conversion under 12 CFR part 192.

(2) Any offering circular or nonpublic offering materials required to be used in connection with an offer or sale of securities under subpart W.

(3) Any filing under the Securities Exchange Act of 1934, 15 U.S.C. 78a *et seq.*, made pursuant to the requirements of subpart U.

(b) Except as otherwise provided by the FDIC by rule, regulation, or order made specifically applicable to financial statements governed by this section, financial statements shall:

(1) Be prepared and presented in accordance with generally accepted accounting principles;

(2) Comply with § 390.384;

(3) Consistent with the provisions of this subpart, comply with articles 1, 2, 3, 4, 10, and 11 of Regulation S–X adopted by the Securities and Exchange Commission (17 CFR 210.1 through 210.4, 210.10, and 210.11).

(4) Be audited, when required, by an independent auditor in accordance with the standards imposed by the American Institute of Certified Public Accountants.

(c) The term "financial statements" includes all notes to the statements and related schedules.

§ 390.381 Definitions.

(See also 17 CFR 210.1–02.)

(a) *Registrant.* The term "registrant" means an applicant, a State savings association, or any other person required to prepare financial statements in accordance with this subpart.

(b) *Significant subsidiary.* The term "significant subsidiary" means a subsidiary, including its subsidiaries, which meets any of the following conditions:

(1) The State savings association's and its other subsidiaries' investments in and advances to the subsidiary exceed 10 percent of the total assets of the association and its subsidiaries consolidated as of the end of the most recently completed fiscal year (for purposes of determining whether financial statements of a business acquired or to be acquired in a business combination accounted for as a pooling of interests are required pursuant to 17 CFR 210.3–05, this condition is also met when the number of common shares exchanged by the State savings association exceeds 10 percent of its total common shares outstanding at the date the combination is initiated); or

(2) The State savings association's and its other subsidiaries' proportionate share of the total assets (after intercompany eliminations) of the subsidiary exceeds 10 percent of the total assets of the State savings association and its subsidiaries consolidated as of the end of the most recently completed fiscal year; or

(3) The State savings association's and its other subsidiaries' equity in the income from continuing operations before income taxes, extraordinary items, and cumulative effect of a change in accounting principle of the subsidiary exceeds 10 percent of such income of the State savings association and its

Federal Deposit Insurance Corporation § 390.384

subsidiaries consolidated for the most recently completed fiscal year.

(4) Computational note: For purposes of making the prescribed income test the following guidance should be applied:

(i) When a loss has been incurred by either the parent or its consolidated subsidiaries or the tested subsidiary, but not both, the equity in the income or loss of the tested subsidiary should be excluded from the income of the State savings association and its subsidiaries consolidated for purposes of the computation.

(ii) If income of the State savings association and its subsidiaries consolidated for the most recent fiscal year is at least 10 percent lower than the average of the income for the last five fiscal years, such average income should be substituted for purposes of the computation. Any loss years should be omitted for purposes of computing average income.

§ 390.382 Qualification of public accountant.

(See also 17 CFR 210.2-01.) The term "qualified public accountant" means a certified public accountant or licensed public accountant certified or licensed by a regulatory authority of a State or other political subdivision of the United States who is in good standing as such under the laws of the jurisdiction where the home office of the registrant to be audited is located. Any person or firm who is suspended from practice before the Securities and Exchange Commission or other governmental agency is not a "qualified public accountant" for purposes of this section.

§ 390.383 Condensed financial information [Parent only].

(a) The information prescribed by Schedule III required by section IV of the appendix to § 390.384 shall be presented in a note to the financial statements when the restricted net assets (17 CFR 210.4-08(e)(3)) of consolidated subsidiaries exceed 25 percent of consolidated net assets as of the end of the most recently completed fiscal year. The investment in and indebtedness of and to State savings association subsidiaries shall be stated separately in the condensed balance sheet from amounts for other subsidiaries; and the amount of cash dividends paid to the parent State savings association for each of the last three years by the State savings association subsidiaries shall be stated separately in the condensed income statement from amounts for other subsidiaries.

(b) For purposes of the above test, restricted net assets of consolidated subsidiaries shall mean that amount of the State savings association's proportionate share of net assets of consolidated subsidiaries (after intercompany eliminations) which as of the end of the most recent year may not be transferred to the parent company by subsidiaries in the form of loans, advances, or cash dividends without the consent of a third party (*i.e.*, lender, regulatory agency, foreign government, *etc.*).

(c) Where restrictions on the amount of funds which may be loaned or advanced differ from the amount restricted as to transfer in the form of cash dividends, the amount least restrictive to the subsidiary shall be used. Redeemable preferred stocks (See item I (22) in the appendix to § 390.384) and minority interest (See item I (21) in the appendix to § 390.384) shall be deducted in computing net assets for purposes of this test.

§ 390.384 Financial statements for conversions, SEC filings, and offering circulars.

This section and its appendix pertain to the form and content of financial statements included as part of:

(a) A conversion application under 12 CFR part 192 including financial statements in proxy statements and offering circulars,

(b) A filing under the Securities Exchange Act of 1934, 15 U.S.C. 78a *et seq.*, and

(c) Any offering circular required to be used in connection with the issuance of mutual capital certificates under 12 CFR 163.74 and debt securities under § 390.341.

APPENDIX TO § 390.384—FINANCIAL STATEMENT PRESENTATION.

This appendix specifies the various line items which should appear on the face of the financial statements governed by § 390.384 and additional disclosures which should be

§ 390.384

included with the financial statements in related notes.

I. BALANCE SHEET

Balance sheets shall comply with the following provisions:

Assets

1. *Cash and amounts due from depository institutions.* (a) The amounts in this caption should include noninterest-bearing deposits with depository institutions.

(b) State in a note the amount and terms of any deposits in depository institutions held as compensating balances against long- or short-term borrowing arrangements. This disclosure should include the provisions of any restrictions as to withdrawal or usage. Restrictions may include legally restricted deposits held as compensating balances against short-term borrowing arrangements, contracts entered into with others, or company statements of intention with regard to particular deposits; however, time deposits and short-term certificates of deposits are not generally included in legally restricted deposits. In cases where compensating balance arrangements exist but are not agreements which legally restrict the use of cash amounts shown on the balance sheet, describe in the notes to the financial statements these arrangements and the amount involved, if determinable, for the most recent audited balance sheet required and for any subsequent unaudited balance sheet required. Compensating balances that are maintained under an agreement to ensure future credit availability shall be disclosed in the notes to the financial statements along with the amount and terms of the agreement.

(c) Checks outstanding in excess of an applicant's book balance in a demand deposit account shall be shown as a liability.

2. *Interest-bearing deposits in other banks.*

3. *Federal funds sold and securities purchased under resale agreements or similar arrangements.* These amounts should be presented, i.e., gross and not netted against Federal funds purchased and securities sold under agreement to repurchase, as reported in caption 15.

4. *Trading account assets.* Include securities considered to be held for trading purposes.

5. *Other short-term investments.*

6. *Investment securities.* (a) Include securities considered to be held for investment purposes. Disclose the aggregate book value of investment securities as the line item on the balance sheet; and also show on the face of the balance sheet the aggregate market value at the balance sheet date. The aggregate amounts should include securities pledged, loaned, or sold under repurchase agreements and similar arrangements. Borrowed securities and securities purchased under resale agreements or similar arrangements should be excluded.

(b) Disclose in a note the carrying value and market value of securities of (i) the U.S. Treasury and other U.S. Government agencies and corporations; (ii) states of the U.S. and political subdivisions thereof; and (iii) other securities.

7. *Assets held for sale.* Investments in assets considered to be held for sale purposes should be reported separately in the statement of financial condition.

8. *Loans.* (a) Disclose separately: (i) Total loans (including financing type leases), (ii) allowance for loan losses, (iii) unearned income on installment loans, (iv) discount on loans purchased, and (v) loans in process.

(b) State on the balance sheet or in a note the amount of loans in each of the following categories: (i) Real estate mortgage; (ii) real estate construction; (iii) installment; and (iv) commercial, financial, and agricultural.

(c)(i) Include under the real estate mortgage category loans payable in monthly, quarterly, or other periodic installments and secured by developed income property and/or personal residences.

(ii) Include under the real estate construction category loans secured by real estate which are made for the purpose of financing construction of real estate and land development projects.

(iii) Include under the installment category loans to individuals generally repayable in monthly installments. This category shall include, but not be limited to, credit card and related activities, individual automobile loans, other installment loans, mobile home loans, and residential repair and modernization loans.

(iv) Include under the commercial, financial, and agricultural category all loans not included in another category. This category shall include, but not be limited to, loans to real estate investment trusts, mortgage companies, banks, and other financial institutions; loans for carrying securities; and loans for agricultural purposes. Do not include loans secured primarily by developed real estate.

(d) State separately any other loan category regardless of relative size if necessary to reflect any unusual risk concentration.

(e) Unearned income on installment loans shall be shown and deducted separately from total loans.

(f) Unamortized discounts on purchased loans shall be deducted separately from total loans.

(g) Loans in process shall be deducted separately from total loans.

(h) A series of categories other than those specified in item (b) of paragraph 8. may be used to present details of loans if considered a more appropriate presentation. The categories specified in item (b) of paragraph 8.

Federal Deposit Insurance Corporation § 390.384

should be considered the minimum categories that may be presented.

(i) For each period for which an income statement is presented, disclose in a note the total dollar amount of loans being serviced by the State savings association for the benefit of others.

(j)(i)(A) As of each balance sheet date, disclose in a note the aggregate dollar amount of loans (exclusive of loans to any such persons which in the aggregate do not exceed $60,000 during the last year) made by the State savings association or any of its subsidiaries to directors, executive officers, or principal holders of equity securities (17 CFR 210.1–02) of the State savings association or any of its significant subsidiaries (17 CFR 210.1–02) or to any associate of such persons. For the latest fiscal year, an analysis of activity with respect to such aggregate loans to related parties should be provided. The analysis should include at the beginning of the period new loans, repayments, and other changes. (Other changes, if significant, should be explained.)

(B) This disclosure need not be furnished when the aggregate amount of such loans at the balance sheet date (or with respect to the latest fiscal year, the maximum amount outstanding during the period) does not exceed 5 percent of stockholders' equity at the balance sheet date.

(ii) If a significant portion of the aggregate amount of loans outstanding at the end of the fiscal year disclosed pursuant to item (i)(A) of this paragraph (j) relates to non-accrual, past due, restructured, and potential problem loans (see Securities and Exchange Commission's Securities Act Industry Guide 3, section III.C.), so state and disclose the aggregate amount of such loans along with such other information necessary to an understanding of the effects of the transactions on the financial statements.

(iii) Notwithstanding the aggregate disclosure called for by paragraph (j)(i) of this balance sheet caption 8, if any loans were not made in the ordinary course of business during any period for which an income statement is required to be filed, provide an appropriate description of each such loan (see 17 CFR 210.9–03.7(e)(3)).

(iv) For purposes only of Balance Sheet item 8(j), the following definitions shall apply:

(A) *Associate* used to indicate a relationship with any person means (1) any corporation, venture, or organization of which such person is a general partner or is, directly or indirectly, the beneficial owner of 10 percent or more of any class of equity securities; (2) any trust or other estate in which such person has a substantial beneficial interest or for which such person serves as trustee or in a similar capacity; and (3) any member of the immediate family of any of the foregoing persons.

(B) *Executive officer* means the president, any vice president in charge of a principal business unit, division, or function (such as loans, investments, operations, administration, or finance), and any other officer or person who performs similar policy-making functions.

(C) *Immediate family* with regard to a person means such person's spouse, parents, children, siblings, mother- and father-in-law, sons- and daughters-in-law, and brothers- and sisters-in-law.

(D) *Ordinary course of business* with regard to loans means those loans which were made on substantially the same terms, including interest rate and collateral, as those prevailing at the same time for comparable transactions with unrelated persons and did not involve more than the normal risk of collectibility or present other unfavorable features.

(k) For each period for which an income statement is presented, furnish in a note a statement of changes in the allowance for loan losses, showing balances at beginning and end of the period, provision charged to income, recoveries of amounts previously charged off, and losses charged to the allowance.

9. *Premises and equipment.*

10. *Real estate owned.* State, parenthetically or otherwise:

(a) The amount of real estate owned by class as described in item (b) of paragraph 10. and the basis for determining that amount; and

(b) A description of each class of real estate owned (i) acquired by foreclosure or by deed in lieu of foreclosure, (ii) in judgment and subject to redemption, or (iii) acquired for development or resale. Show separately any accumulated depreciation or valuation allowances. Disclose the policies regarding, and amounts of, capitalized costs, including interest.

11. *Investment in joint ventures.* In a note, present summarized aggregate financial statements for investments in real estate or other joint ventures which individually (a) are 20 percent or more owned by the State savings association or any of its subsidiaries, or (b) have liabilities (including contingent liabilities) to the parent exceeding 10 percent of the parent's regulatory capital. If an allowance for real estate losses subsequent to acquisition is maintained, the amount shall be disclosed, deducted from the other real estate owned, and a statement of changes in the allowance showing balances at beginning and end of period should be included. Provision charged to income and losses charged to the allowance account shall be furnished for each period for which an income statement is filed.

12. *Other assets.* (a) Disclose separately on the balance sheet or in a note thereto any of the following assets or any other asset the

§ 390.384

amount of which exceeds 30 percent of stockholders' equity. The remaining assets may be shown as one amount.

(i) *Accrued interest receivable.* State separately those amounts relating to loans and those amounts relating to investments.

(ii) Excess of cost over assets acquired (net of amortization).

(h) State in a note (i) amounts representing investments in affiliates and investments in other persons which are accounted for by the equity method, and (ii) indebtedness of affiliates and other persons, the investments in which are accounted for by the equity method. State the basis of determining the amounts reported under paragraph (b)(i).

13. *Total assets.*

Liabilities, and Stockholders' Equity

14. *Deposits.* (a) Disclose separately on the balance sheet or in a note the amounts in the following categories of interest-bearing and noninterest-bearing deposits: (i) NOW account and MMDA deposits, (ii) savings deposits, and (iii) time deposits.

(b) Include under the savings-deposits category interest-bearing deposits without specified maturity or contractual provisions requiring advance notice of intention to withdraw funds. Include deposits for which a State savings association may require at its option written notice of intended withdrawal not less than 14 days in advance.

(c) Include under the time-deposits category deposits subject to provisions specifying maturity or other withdrawal conditions such as time certificates of deposits, open account time deposits, and deposits accumulated for the payment of personal loans.

(d) Include accrued interest or dividends, if appropriate.

15. *Short-term borrowings.* (a) State separately, here or in a note, the amounts payable for (i) Federal funds purchased and securities sold under agreements to repurchase, (ii) commercial paper, and (iii) other short-term borrowings.

(b) Federal funds purchased and sales of securities under repurchase agreements shall be reported gross and not netted against sales of Federal funds and purchase of securities under resale agreements.

(c) Include as securities sold under agreements to repurchase all transactions of this type regardless of (i) whether they are called simultaneous purchases and sales, buybacks, turnarounds, overnight transactions, delayed deliveries, or other terms signifying the same substantive transaction, and (ii) whether the transactions are with the same or different institutions, if the purpose of the transactions is to repurchase identical or similar securities.

(d) The amount and terms (including commitment fees and the conditions under which lines may be withdrawn) of unused lines of credit for short-term financing shall be disclosed, if significant, in the notes to the financial statements. The amount of these lines of credit which support a commercial paper borrowing arrangement or similar arrangements shall be separately identified.

16. *Advance payments by borrowers for taxes and insurance.*

17. *Other liabilities.* Disclose separately on the balance sheet or in a note any of the following liabilities or any other items which are individually in excess of 30 percent of stockholders' equity (except that amounts in excess of 5 percent of stockholders' equity should be disclosed with respect to item (d)). The remaining items may be shown as one amount.

(a) Income taxes payable.

(b) Deferred income taxes.

(c) Indebtedness to affiliate and other persons the investment in which is accounted for by the equity method.

(d) Indebtedness to directors, executive officers, and principal holders of equity securities of the registrant or any of its significant subsidiaries. (The guidance in balance sheet caption "8(j)" shall be used to identify related parties for purposes of this disclosure.)

18. *Bonds, mortgages, and similar debt.* (a) Include bonds, Federal Home Loan Bank advances, capital notes, debentures, mortgages, and similar debt.

(b) For each issue or type of obligation state in a note:

(i) The general character of each type of debt, including: (A) The rate of interest, (B) the date of maturity, or, if maturing serially, a brief indication of the serial maturities, such as "maturing serially from 1980 to 1990," (C) if the payment of principal or interest is contingent, an appropriate indication of such contingency, (D) a brief indication of priority, and (E) if convertible, the basis. For amounts owed to related parties see 17 CFR 210.4–08(k).

(ii) The amount and terms (including commitment fees and the conditions under which commitments may be withdrawn) of unused commitments for long-term financing arrangements that, if used, would be disclosed under this caption shall be disclosed in the notes to the financial statements, if significant.

(c) State in the notes with appropriate explanations (i) the title and amount of each issue of debt of a subsidiary included in item (a) of paragraph 18 which has not been assumed or guaranteed by the State savings association, and (ii) any liens on premises of a subsidiary or its consolidated subsidiaries which have not been assumed by the subsidiary or its consolidated subsidiaries.

19. *Deferred credits.* State separately those items which exceed 30 percent of stockholders' equity.

Federal Deposit Insurance Corporation § 390.384

20. *Commitments and contingent liabilities.* Total commitments to fund loans should be disclosed. The dollar amounts and terms of other than floating market-rate commitments should also be disclosed.

21. *Minority interest in consolidated subsidiaries.*

22. *Preferred stock subject to mandatory redemption requirements or the redemption of which is outside the control of the issuer.* (a) Include under this caption amounts applicable to any class of stock which has any of the following characteristics: (i) It is redeemable at a fixed or determinable price on a fixed or determinable date or dates, whether by operation of a sinking fund or otherwise; (ii) it is redeemable at the option of the holder; or (iii) it has conditions for redemption which are not solely within the control of the issuer, such as stock which must be redeemed out of future earnings. Amounts attributable to preferred stock which is not redeemable or is redeemable solely at the option of the issuer shall be included under caption 23 unless it meets one or more of the above criteria.

(b) State on the face of the balance sheet the title, carrying amount, and redemption amount of each issue. (If there is more than one issue, these amounts may be aggregated on the face of the balance sheet and details concerning each issue may be presented in the note required by item (c) of paragraph 22.) Show also the dollar amount of any shares subscribed for but unissued, and show the deduction of subscriptions receivable therefrom. If the carrying value is different from the redemption amount, describe the accounting treatment for such difference in the note required by item (c) of paragraph 22. Also state in this note or on the face of the balance sheet, for each issue, the number of shares authorized and the number of shares issued or outstanding, as appropriate. (See 17 CFR 210.4-07.)

(c) State in a separate note captioned "Redeemable Preferred Stock" (i) a general description of each issue, including its redemption features (e.g., sinking fund, at option of holders, out of future earnings) and the rights, if any, of holders in the event of default, including the effect, if any, on junior securities in the event a required dividend, sinking fund, or other redemption payment(s) is not made, (ii) the combined aggregate amount of redemption requirements for all issues each year for the five years following the date of the latest balance sheet, and (iii) the changes in each issue for each period for which an income statement is required to be presented. (See also 17 CFR 210.4-08(d).)

(d) Securities reported under this caption are not to be included under a general heading "stockholders' equity" or combined in a total with items described in captions 23, 24 or 25, which follow.

23. *Preferred stock which is not redeemable or is redeemed solely at the option of the issuer.* State on the face of the balance sheet, or, if more than one issue is outstanding, state in a note, the title of each issue and the dollar amount thereof. Show also the dollar amount of any shares subscribed for but unissued, and show the deduction of subscriptions receivable. State on the face of the balance sheet or in a note, for each issue, the number of shares authorized and the number of shares issued or outstanding, as appropriate. (See 17 CFR 210.4-07.) Show in a note or separate statement the changes in each class of preferred shares reported under this caption for each period for which an income statement is required to be presented. (See also 17 CFR 210.4-08(d).)

24. *Common stock.* For each class of common shares state, on the face of the balance sheet, the number of shares issued or outstanding, as appropriate (see 17 CFR 210.4-07), and the dollar amount thereof. If convertible, this fact should be indicated on the face of the balance sheet. For each class of common stock state, on the face of the balance sheet or in a note, the title of the issue, the number of shares authorized, and, if convertible, the basis for conversion (see also 17 CFR 210.4-08(d).) Show also the dollar amount of any common stock subscribed for but unissued, and show the deduction of subscriptions receivable. Show in a note or statement the changes in each class of common stock for each period for which an income statement is required to be presented.

25. *Other stockholders' equity.* (a) Separate captions shall be shown on the face of the balance sheet for (i) additional paid-in capital, (ii) other additional capital, and (iii) retained earnings, both (A) restricted and (B) unrestricted. (See 17 CFR 210.4-08(e).) Additional paid-in capital and other additional capital may be combined with the stock caption to which it applies, if appropriate. State whether or not the State savings association is in compliance with the Federal regulatory capital requirements (and state requirements where applicable). Also include the dollar amount of those regulatory capital requirements and the amount by which the State savings association exceeds or fails to meet those requirements.

(b) For a period of at least 10 years subsequent to the effective date of a quasi-reorganization, any description of retained earnings shall indicate the point in time from which the new retained earnings dates, and for a period of at least three years shall indicate, on the face of the balance sheet, the total amount of the deficit eliminated.

(c) Changes in stockholders' equity shall be disclosed in accordance with the requirements of 17 CFR 210.3-04.

26. *Total liabilities and stockholders' equity.*

II. INCOME STATEMENT

Income statements shall comply with the following provisions:

1. *Interest and fees on loans.* (a) Include interest, service charges, and fees which are related to or are an adjustment of the loan interest yield.

(b) Current amortization of premiums on mortgages or other loans shall be deducted from interest on loans, and current accretion of discount on such items shall be added to interest on loans.

(c) Discounts and other deferred amounts which are related to or are an adjustment of the loan interest yield shall be amortized into income using the interest (level yield) method.

2. *Interest and dividends on investment securities.* Include accretion of discount on securities and deduct amortization of premiums on securities.

3. *Trading account interest.* Include interest from securities carried in a dealer trading account or accounts that are held principally for resale to customers.

4. *Other interest income.* Include interest on short-term investments (Federal funds sold and securities purchased under agreements to resell) and interest on bank deposits.

5. *Total interest income.*

6. *Interest on deposits.* Include interest on all deposits. On the income statement or in a note, state separately, in the same categories as those specified for deposits at balance sheet caption 14(a), the interest on those deposits. Early withdrawal penalties should be netted against interest on deposits and, if material, disclosed on the income statement.

7. *Interest on short-term borrowings.* Include interest on borrowed funds, including Federal funds purchased, securities sold under agreements to repurchase, commercial paper, and other short-term borrowings.

8. *Interest on long-term borrowings.* Include interest on bonds, capital notes, debentures, mortgages on State savings association premises, capitalized leases, and similar debt.

9. *Total interest expense.*
10. *Net interest income.*
11. *Provision for loan losses.*
12. *Net interest income after provision for loan losses.*
13. *Other income.* Disclose separately any of the following amounts, or any other item of other income, which exceeds 1 percent of the aggregate of total interest income and other income. The remaining amount may be shown as one amount, except for investment securities gains or losses which shall be shown separately regardless of size.

(a) Commissions and fees from fiduciary activities.

(b) Fees for other services to customers.

(c) Commissions, fees, and markups on securities underwriting and other securities activities.

(d) Profit or loss on transactions in investment securities.

(e) Equity in earnings of unconsolidated subsidiaries and 50-percent- or less-owned persons.

(f) Gains or losses on disposition of investments in securities of subsidiaries and 50-percent- or less-owned persons.

(g) Profit or loss from real estate operations.

(h) Other fees related to loan originations or commitments not included in income statement caption 1.

The remaining other income may be shown in one amount.

(i) Investment securities gains or losses. The method followed in determining the cost of investments sold (*e.g.*, "average cost," "first-in, first-out," or "identified certificate") and related income taxes shall be disclosed.

14. *Other expenses.* Disclose separately any of the following amounts, or any other item of other expense, which exceeds 1 percent of the aggregate of total interest income and other income. The remaining amounts may be shown as one amount.

(a) Salaries and employee benefits.

(b) Net occupancy expense of premises.

(c) Net cost of operations of other real estate (including provisions for real estate losses, rental income, and gains and losses on sales of real estate).

(d) Minority interest in income of consolidated subsidiaries.

(e) Goodwill amortization.

15. *Other income and expenses.* State separately material events or transactions that are unusual in nature or occur infrequently, but not both, and therefore do not meet both criteria for classification as an extraordinary item. Examples of items which would be reported separately are gain or loss from the sale of premises and equipment, provision for loss on real estate owned, or provision for gain or loss on the sale of loans.

16. *Income or losses before income tax expense.*

17. *Income tax expense.* The information required by 17 CFR 210.4–08(h) should be disclosed.

18. *Income or loss before extraordinary items effects of changes in accounting principles.*

19. *Extraordinary items, less applicable tax.*

20. *Cumulative effects of changes in accounting principles.*

21. *Net income or loss.*

22. *Earnings-per-share data.*

23. *Conversion footnote.* If the State savings association is an applicant for conversion from a mutual to a stock association or has converted within the last three years, describe in a note the general terms of the conversion and restrictions on the operations of the State savings association imposed by the

Federal Deposit Insurance Corporation § 390.384

conversion. Also, state the amount of net proceeds received from the conversion and costs associated with the conversion.

24. *Mergers and acquisitions.* For the period in which a business combination occurs and is accounted for by the purchase method of accounting, in addition to those disclosures required by Accounting Principles Board Opinion No. 16, the State savings association shall make those disclosures as noted below for all combinations involving significant acquisitions. (A significant acquisition is defined for this purpose to be one in which the assets of the acquired State savings association, or group of State savings associations, exceed 10 percent of the assets of the consolidated State savings association at the end of the most recent period being reported upon).

(a) Amounts and descriptions of discounts and premiums related to recording the aggregate interest-bearing assets and liabilities at their fair market value. The disclosure should also include the methods of amortization or accretion and the estimated remaining lives.

(b) The net effect on net income before taxes of the amortization and accretion of discounts, premiums, and intangible assets related to the purchase accounting transaction(s). For subsequent periods, the State savings association shall disclose the remaining total unamortized or unaccreted amounts of discounts, premiums, and intangible assets as of the date of the most recent balance sheet presented. In addition, the State savings association shall disclose the net effect on net income before taxes of the amortization and accretion of discounts, premiums, and intangible assets related to prior business combinations accounted for by the purchase method of accounting. Such disclosures need not be made if the total amounts of discounts, premiums, or intangible assets do not exceed 30 percent of stockholders' equity as of the date of the most recent balance sheet presented.

III. STATEMENT OF CASH FLOWS

The amounts shown in this statement should be those items which materially enhance the reader's understanding of the State savings association's business. For example, gains from sales of loans should be segregated from sales of mortgage-backed securities and other securities, if material, proceeds from principal repayments and maturities from loans and mortgage-backed securities should be segregated from proceeds from sales of loans and mortgage-backed securities, purchases of loans, mortgage-backed securities and other securities should be segregated, if material. Additional guidance may be found in the FASB's Statement of Financial Accounting Standards No. 95 Statement of Cash Flows.

IV. SCHEDULES REQUIRED TO BE FILED

The following schedules, which should be examined by an independent accountant, shall be filed unless the required information is not applicable or is presented in the related financial statements:

(1) *Schedule I—Indebtedness of and to related parties—Not Current.* For each period for which an income statement is required, the following schedule should be filed in support of the amounts required to be reported by balance sheet items 8(j) and 17(c) unless such aggregate amount does not exceed 5 percent of stockholders' equity at either the beginning or the end of the period:

INDEBTEDNESS OF AND TO RELATED PARTIES—NOT CURRENT

Name of person [1]	Indebtedness of—			
	Balance at beginning	Additions [2]	Deductions [3]	Balance at end
A	B	C	D	E

INDEBTEDNESS OF AND TO RELATED PARTIES—NOT CURRENT

Name of person [1]	Indebtedness to—			
	Balance at beginning	Additions [2]	Deductions [3]	Balance at end
A	F	G	H	I

(2) *Schedule II—Guarantees of securities of other issuers.* The following schedule should be filed as of the date of the most recently audited balance sheet with respect to any guarantees of securities of other issuers by the person for which the statements are being filed:

---

[1] The persons named shall be grouped as in the related schedule required for investments in related parties. The information called for shall be shown separately for any
Continued

857

§ 390.390

GUARANTEES OF SECURITIES OF OTHER ISSUERS [4]

Col. A. Name of issuer of securities guaranteed by person for which statement is filed	Col. B. Title of issue of each class of securities guaranteed	Col. C. Total amount guaranteed and outstanding [5]	Col. D. Amount owned by person or persons for which statement is filed

GUARANTEES OF SECURITIES OF OTHER ISSUERS [4]

Col. A. Name of issuer of securities guaranteed by person for which statement is filed	Col. E. Amount in treasury of issuer of securities guaranteed	Col. F. Nature of guarantee [6]	Col. G. Nature of any default by issue of securities guaranteed in principal, interest, sinking fund or redemption provisions, or payment of dividends [7]

(3) *Schedule III—Condensed financial information.* The following schedule shall be filed as of the dates and for the periods specified in the schedule.

Condensed Financial Information

[Parent only]

[The State savings association may determine disclosure based on information provided in footnotes below]

(a) Provide condensed financial information as to financial position, changes in financial position, and results of operations of the State savings association as of the same dates and for the same periods for which audited consolidated financial statements are required. The financial information required need not be presented in greater detail than is required for condensed statement by 17 CFR 210.10–01(a) (2), (3), (4). Detailed footnote disclosure which would normally be included with complete financial statements may be omitted with the exception of disclosure regarding material contingencies, long-term obligations, and guarantees. Description of significant provisions of the state savings association's long-term obligations, mandatory dividend, or redemption requirements of redeemable stocks, and guarantees of the State savings association shall be provided along with a 5-year schedule of maturities of debt. If the material contingencies, long-term obligations, redeemable stock requirements, and guarantees of the State savings association have been separately disclosed in the consolidated statements, they need not be repeated in this schedule.

(b) Disclose separately the amount of cash dividends paid to the State savings association for each of the last three fiscal years by consolidated subsidiaries, unconsolidated subsidiaries, and 50-percent- or less-owned persons accounted for by the equity method, respectively.

Subpart U—Securities of State Savings Associations

§ 390.390 **Requirements under certain sections of the Securities Exchange Act of 1934.**

In respect to any securities issued by State savings associations, the powers, functions, and duties vested in the Securities and Exchange Commission (the "Commission") to administer and enforce sections 10A(m), 12, 13, 14(a), 14(c),

---

persons whose investments were shown separately in such related schedule.

[2] For each person named in column A, explain in a note the nature and purpose of any increase during the period that is in excess of 10 percent of the related balance at either the beginning or end of the period.

[3] If deduction was other than a receipt or disbursement of cash, explain.

[4] Indicate in a note to the most recent schedule being filed for a particular person or group any significant changes since the date of the related balance sheet. If this schedule is filed in support of consolidated or combined statements, there shall be set forth guarantees by any person included in the consolidation or combination, except that such guarantees of securities which are included in the consolidated or combined balance sheet need not be set forth.

[5] Indicate any amounts included in column C which are included also in column D or E.

[6] There need be made only a brief statement of the nature of the guarantee, such as "Guarantee of principal and interest," or "Guarantee of dividends." If the guarantee is of interest or dividends, state the annual aggregate amount of interest or dividends so guaranteed.

[7] Only a brief statement as to any such defaults need be made.

Federal Deposit Insurance Corporation § 390.392

14(d), 14(f), and 16 of the Securities Exchange Act of 1934, as amended (the "Act") (15 U.S.C. 78*l*, 78m, 78n(a), 78n(c), 78n(d), 78n(f), and 78p), and sections 302, 303, 304, 306, 401(b), 404, 406, and 407 of the Sarbanes-Oxley Act of 2002 (15 U.S.C. 7241, 7242, 7243, 7244, 7261, 7262, 7264, and 7265) are vested in the FDIC. The rules, regulations and forms prescribed by the Commission pursuant to those sections or applicable in connection with obligations imposed by those sections, shall apply to securities issued by State savings associations, except as otherwise provided. The term "Commission" as used in those rules and regulations shall, with respect to securities issued by State savings associations, be deemed to refer to the FDIC unless the context otherwise requires. All filings with respect to securities issued by State savings associations required by those rules and regulations to be made with the Commission shall be made with the FDIC, ATTN: Accounting and Securities Disclosure Section, 550 17th Street, NW, Washington, DC 20429, by submitting such filings to the above address, except as noted in § 390.391.

§ 390.391 [Reserved]

§ 390.392 Liability for certain statements by State savings associations.

This section replaces adherence to 17 CFR 240.3b–6 and applies as follows:

(a) A statement within the coverage of paragraph (b) of this section which is made by or on behalf of an issuer or by an outside reviewer retained by the issuer shall be deemed not to be a fraudulent statement (as defined in paragraph (d) of this section), unless it is shown that such statement was made or reaffirmed without a reasonable basis or was disclosed other than in good faith.

(b) This section applies to the following statements:

(1) A forward-looking statement (as defined in paragraph (c) of this section) made in a proxy statement or offering circular filed with the OCC under 12 CFR part 192; in a registration statement filed with the FDIC under the Act on Form 10 (17 CFR 249.210); in part I of a quarterly report filed with the FDIC on Form 10–Q (17 CFR 249.308a); in an annual report to shareholders meeting the requirements of § 390.390, particularly 17 CFR 240.14a–3(b) and (c) or 17 CFR 240.14c–3(a) and (b) under the Act; in a statement reaffirming such forward-looking statement subsequent to the date the document was filed or the annual report was made publicly available; or a forward-looking statement made prior to the date the document was filed or the date the annual report was made publicly available if such statement is reaffirmed in a filed document or annual report made publicly available within a reasonable time after the making of such forward-looking statement: *Provided*, that

(i) At the time such statements are made or reaffirmed, either:

(A) The issuer is subject to the reporting requirements of section 13(a) or 15(d) of the Act and has complied with the requirements of 17 CFR 240.13a–1 or 240.15d–1 thereunder, if applicable, to file its most recent annual report on Form 10–K; or

(B) If the issuer is not subject to the reporting requirements of section 13(a) or 15(d) of the Act, the statements are made either in a registration statement filed under the Securities Act of 1933 or pursuant to section 12(b) or (g) of the Act, or in a proxy statement or offering circular filed with the OCC under 12 CFR part 192 if such statements are reaffirmed in a registration statement under the Act on Form 10, filed with the FDIC within 180 days of the State savings association's conversion, and

(ii) The statements are not made by or on behalf of an issuer that is an investment company registered under the Investment Company Act of 1940;

(2) Information—

(i) Relating to the effects of changing prices on the business enterprise presented voluntarily or pursuant to item 303 of Regulation S–K (17 CFR 229.303), management's discussion and analysis of financial condition and results of operations, or item 302 of Regulation S–K (17 CFR 229.302), supplementary financial information; and

(ii) Disclosed in a document filed with the FDIC or in an annual report to shareholders meeting the requirements of 17 CFR 240.14a–3(b) and (c) or 17 CFR 240.14c–3(a) and (b) under the

859

§ 390.393

Act: *Provided*, that such information included in a proxy statement or offering circular filed pursuant to 12 CFR part 192 shall be reaffirmed in a registration statement under the Act on Form 10 filed with the OCC within 180 days of the association's conversion.

(c) For purposes of this section, the term "forward-looking statement" shall mean and shall be limited to:

(1) A statement containing a projection of revenues, income (loss), earnings (loss) per share, capital expenditures, dividends, capital structure, or other financial items;

(2) A statement of management's plans and objectives for future operations;

(3) A statement of future economic performance contained in management's discussion and analysis of financial condition and results of operations pursuant to item 303 of Regulation S-K; or

(4) A statement of the assumptions underlying or relating to any of the statements described in paragraph (c)(1), (2), or (3) of this section.

(d) For purposes of this section, the term "fraudulent statement" shall mean a statement which is an untrue statement of a material fact, a statement false or misleading with respect to any material fact, an omission to state a material fact necessary to make a statement not misleading, or which constitutes the employment of a manipulative, deceptive, or fraudulent device, contrivance, scheme, transaction, act, practice, course of business, or an artifice to defraud, as those terms are used in the Securities Act of 1933 or the rules or regulations promulgated thereunder.

§ 390.393 Form and content of financial statements.

The financial statements required to be contained in filings with the FDIC under the Act are as set out in the applicable form and Regulation S-X, 17 CFR part 210. Those financial statements, however, shall conform as to form and content to the requirements of § 390.380.

§ 390.394 Interpretations related to SEC filings.

Sections 390.394 and 390.395 contain interpretations pertaining to the requirements of the Act and the rules and regulations thereunder as applied to State savings associations by the FDIC.

§ 390.395 Description of business.

(a) This section applies to the description-of-business portion of:

(1) Registration statements filed on Form 10 (item 1) (17 CFR 249.210),

(2) Proxy and information statements relating to mergers, consolidations, acquisitions, and similar matters (item 14 of Schedule 14A and item 1 of Schedule 14C) (17 CFR 240.14a–101 and 240.14c–101), and

(3) Annual reports filed on Form 10–K (item 7) (17 CFR 249.310).

(b) The description of business should conform to the description of business required by item 7 of Form PS under 12 CFR part 192.

(c) No repetitive disclosure is required by virtue of similar requirements in item 7 of Form PS and items 301 and 303 of Regulation S–K (17 CFR 229.301, 303). However, there should be included appropriate disclosure which arises by virtue of the registrant being a State savings association that is organized in stock form. For example, the table regarding return on equity and assets, item 7(d)(5), should include a line item for "dividend payout ratio (dividends declared per share divided by net income per share)."

Subpart V—Management Official Interlocks

§ 390.400 Authority, purpose, and scope.

(a) *Authority.* This subpart is issued under the provisions of the Federal Deposit Insurance Act, 12 U.S.C. 1819 (Tenth) and the Depository Institution Management Interlocks Act (Interlocks Act) (12 U.S.C. 3201 *et seq.*), as amended.

(b) *Purpose.* The purpose of the Interlocks Act and this subpart is to foster competition by generally prohibiting a management official from serving two nonaffiliated depository organizations

Federal Deposit Insurance Corporation § 390.401

in situations where the management interlock likely would have an anticompetitive effect.

(c) *Scope.* This part applies to management officials of State savings associations and their affiliates.

§ 390.401 Definitions.

For purposes of this subpart, the following definitions apply:

(a) *Affiliate.* (1) The term *affiliate* has the meaning given in section 202 of the Interlocks Act (12 U.S.C. 3201). For purposes of that section 202, shares held by an individual include shares held by members of his or her immediate family. "Immediate family" means spouse, mother, father, child, grandchild, sister, brother, or any of their spouses, whether or not any of their shares are held in trust.

(2) For purposes of section 202(3)(B) of the Interlocks Act (12 U.S.C. 3201(3)(B)), an affiliate relationship involving a State savings association based on common ownership does not exist if the FDIC determines, after giving the affected persons the opportunity to respond, that the asserted affiliation was established in order to avoid the prohibitions of the Interlocks Act and does not represent a true commonality of interest between the depository organizations. In making this determination, the FDIC considers, among other things, whether a person, including members of his or her immediate family, whose shares are necessary to constitute the group owns a nominal percentage of the shares of one of the organizations and the percentage is substantially disproportionate to that person's ownership of shares in the other organization.

(b) *Area median income* means:

(1) The median family income for the metropolitan statistical area (MSA), if a depository organization is located in an MSA; or

(2) The statewide nonmetropolitan median family income, if a depository organization is located outside an MSA.

(c) *Community* means a city, town, or village, and contiguous or adjacent cities, towns, or villages.

(d) *Contiguous or adjacent cities, towns, or villages* means cities, towns, or villages whose borders touch each other or whose borders are within 10 road miles of each other at their closest points. The property line of an office located in an unincorporated city, town, or village is the boundary line of that city, town, or village for the purpose of this definition.

(e) *Depository holding company* means a bank holding company or a savings and loan holding company (as more fully defined in section 202 of the Interlocks Act (12 U.S.C. 3201)) having its principal office located in the United States.

(f) *Depository institution* means a commercial bank (including a private bank), a savings bank, a trust company, a State savings association, a building and loan association, a homestead association, a cooperative bank, an industrial bank, or a credit union, chartered under the laws of the United States and having a principal office located in the United States. Additionally, a United States office, including a branch or agency, of a foreign commercial bank is a depository institution.

(g) *Depository institution affiliate* means a depository institution that is an affiliate of a depository organization.

(h) *Depository organization* means a depository institution or a depository holding company.

(i) *Low- and moderate-income areas* means census tracts (or, if an area is not in a census tract, block numbering areas delineated by the United States Bureau of the Census) where the median family income is less than 100 percent of the area median income.

(j) *Management official.* (1) The term *management official* means:

(i) A director;

(ii) An advisory or honorary director of a depository institution with total assets of $100 million or more;

(iii) A senior executive officer as that term is defined in § 390.361;

(iv) A branch manager;

(v) A trustee of a depository organization under the control of trustees; and

(vi) Any person who has a representative or nominee serving in any of the capacities in this paragraph (j)(1).

(2) The term *management official* does not include:

861

(i) A person whose management functions relate exclusively to the business of retail merchandising or manufacturing;

(ii) A person whose management functions relate principally to the business outside the United States of a foreign commercial bank; or

(iii) A person described in the provisos of section 202(4) of the Interlocks Act (12 U.S.C. 3201(4)) (referring to an officer of a State-chartered savings bank, cooperative bank, or trust company that neither makes real estate mortgage loans nor accepts savings).

(k) *Office* means a principal or branch office of a depository institution located in the United States. *Office* does not include a representative office of a foreign commercial bank, an electronic terminal, or a loan production office.

(l) *Person* means a natural person, corporation, or other business entity.

(m) *Relevant metropolitan statistical area (RMSA)* means an MSA, a primary MSA, or a consolidated MSA that is not comprised of designated Primary MSAs to the extent that these terms are defined and applied by the Office of Management and Budget.

(n) *Representative or nominee* means a natural person who serves as a management official and has an obligation to act on behalf of another person with respect to management responsibilities. The FDIC will find that a person has an obligation to act on behalf of another person only if the first person has an agreement, express or implied, to act on behalf of the second person with respect to management responsibilities. The FDIC will determine, after giving the affected persons an opportunity to respond, whether a person is a *representative or nominee*.

(o) *State savings association* means:

(1) [Reserved]

(2) Any State savings association (as defined in section 3(b)(3) of the Federal Deposit Insurance Act (12 U.S.C. 1813(b)(3)) the deposits of which are insured by the Federal Deposit Insurance Corporation; and

(3) Any corporation (other than a bank as defined in section 3(a)(1) of the Federal Deposit Insurance Act (12 U.S.C. 1813(a)(1)) the deposits of which are insured by the Federal Deposit Insurance Corporation, that the Board of Directors of the Federal Deposit Insurance Corporation determines to be operating in substantially the same manner as a State savings association.

(p) *Total assets.* (1) The term *total assets* means assets measured on a consolidated basis and reported in the most recent fiscal year-end Consolidated Report of Condition and Income.

(2) The term *total assets* does not include:

(i) Assets of a diversified savings and loan holding company as defined by section 10(a)(1)(F) of the Home Owners' Loan Act (12 U.S.C. 1467a(a)(1)(F)) other than the assets of its depository institution affiliate;

(ii) Assets of a bank holding company that is exempt from the prohibitions of section 4 of the Bank Holding Company Act of 1956 pursuant to an order issued under section 4(d) of that Act (12 U.S.C. 1843(d)) other than the assets of its depository institution affiliate; or

(iii) Assets of offices of a foreign commercial bank other than the assets of its United States branch or agency.

(q) *United States* means the United States of America, any State or territory of the United States of America, the District of Columbia, Puerto Rico, Guam, American Samoa, and the Virgin Islands.

§ 390.402 Prohibitions.

(a) *Community.* A management official of a depository organization may not serve at the same time as a management official of an unaffiliated depository organization if the depository organizations in question (or a depository institution affiliate thereof) have offices in the same community.

(b) *RMSA.* A management official of a depository organization may not serve at the same time as a management official of an unaffiliated depository organization if the depository organizations in question (or a depository institution affiliate thereof) have offices in the same RMSA and each depository organization has total assets of $50 million or more.

(c) *Major assets.* A management official of a depository organization with total assets exceeding $2.5 billion (or any affiliate of such an organization) may not serve at the same time as a management official of an unaffiliated

Federal Deposit Insurance Corporation

§ 390.403

depository organization with total assets exceeding $1.5 billion (or any affiliate of such an organization), regardless of the location of the two depository organizations. The FDIC will adjust these thresholds, as necessary, based on the year-to-year change in the average of the Consumer Price Index for the Urban Wage Earners and Clerical Workers, not seasonally adjusted, with rounding to the nearest $100 million. The FDIC will announce the revised thresholds by publishing a final rule without notice and comment in the FEDERAL REGISTER.

§ 390.403 Interlocking relationships permitted by statute.

The prohibitions of § 390.402 do not apply in the case of any one or more of the following organizations or to a subsidiary thereof:

(a) A depository organization that has been placed formally in liquidation, or which is in the hands of a receiver, conservator, or other official exercising a similar function;

(b) A corporation operating under section 25 or section 25A of the Federal Reserve Act (12 U.S.C. 601 *et seq.* and 12 U.S.C. 611 *et seq.*, respectively) (Edge Corporations and Agreement Corporations);

(c) A credit union being served by a management official of another credit union;

(d) A depository organization that does not do business within the United States except as an incident to its activities outside the United States;

(e) A State-chartered savings and loan guaranty corporation;

(f) A Federal Home Loan Bank or any other bank organized solely to serve depository institutions (a bankers' bank) or solely for the purpose of providing securities clearing services and services related thereto for depository institutions and securities companies;

(g) A depository organization that is closed or is in danger of closing as determined by the appropriate Federal depository institutions regulatory agency and is acquired by another depository organization. This exemption lasts for five years, beginning on the date the depository organization is acquired;

(h)(1) A diversified savings and loan holding company (as defined in section 10(a)(1)(F) of the Home Owners' Loan Act (12 U.S.C. 1467a(a)(1)(F)) with respect to the service of a director of such company who also is a director of an unaffiliated depository organization if:

(i) Both the diversified savings and loan holding company and the unaffiliated depository organization notify their appropriate Federal depository institutions regulatory agency at least 60 days before the dual service is proposed to begin; and

(ii) The appropriate regulatory agency does not disapprove the dual service before the end of the 60-day period.

(2) The FDIC may disapprove a notice of proposed service if it finds that:

(i) The service cannot be structured or limited so as to preclude an anticompetitive effect in financial services in any part of the United States;

(ii) The service would lead to substantial conflicts of interest or unsafe or unsound practices; or

(iii) The notificant failed to furnish all the information required by the FDIC.

(3) The FDIC may require that any interlock permitted under this paragraph (h) be terminated if a change in circumstances occurs with respect to one of the interlocked depository organizations that would have provided a basis for disapproval of the interlock during the notice period; and

(i) Any State savings association which has issued stock in connection with a qualified stock issuance pursuant to section 10(q) of the Home Owners' Loan Act, except that this paragraph (i) shall apply only with regard to service as a single management official of such State savings association or any subsidiary of such State savings association by a single management official of a savings and loan holding company which purchased the stock issued in connection with such qualified stock issuance, and shall apply only when the FDIC has determined that such service is consistent with the purposes of the Interlocks Act and the Home Owners' Loan Act.

§ 390.404 Small market share exemption.

(a) *Exemption.* A management interlock that is prohibited by § 390.402 is permissible, if:

(1) The interlock is not prohibited by § 390.402(c); and

(2) The depository organizations (and their depository institution affiliates) hold, in the aggregate, no more than 20 percent of the deposits in each RMSA or community in which both depository organizations (or their depository institution affiliates) have offices. The amount of deposits shall be determined by reference to the most recent annual Summary of Deposits published by the FDIC for the RMSA or community.

(b) *Confirmation and records.* Each depository organization must maintain records sufficient to support its determination of eligibility for the exemption under paragraph (a) of this section, and must reconfirm that determination on an annual basis.

§ 390.405 General exemption.

(a) *Exemption.* The FDIC may exempt an interlock from the prohibitions in § 390.402 if the FDIC finds that the interlock would not result in a monopoly or substantial lessening of competition and would not present safety and soundness concerns. A depository organization may apply to FDIC for an exemption under §§ 390.126 through 390.135.

(b) *Presumptions.* In reviewing an application for an exemption under this section, the FDIC will apply a rebuttable presumption that an interlock will not result in a monopoly or substantial lessening of competition if the depository organization seeking to add a management official:

(1) Primarily serves low- and moderate-income areas;

(2) Is controlled or managed by persons who are members of a minority group, or women;

(3) Is a depository institution that or has been chartered for less than two years; or

(4) Is deemed to be in "troubled condition" as defined in § 390.361.

(c) *Duration.* Unless a shorter expiration period is provided in the FDIC approval, an exemption permitted by paragraph (a) of this section may continue so long as it does not result in a monopoly or substantial lessening of competition, or is unsafe or unsound. If the FDIC grants an interlock exemption in reliance upon a presumption under paragraph (b) of this section, the interlock may continue for three years, unless otherwise provided by the FDIC in writing.

§ 390.406 Change in circumstances.

(a) *Termination.* A management official shall terminate his or her service or apply for an exemption if a change in circumstances causes the service to become prohibited. A change in circumstances may include an increase in asset size of an organization, a change in the delineation of the RMSA or community, the establishment of an office, an increase in the aggregate deposits of the depository organization, or an acquisition, merger, consolidation, or reorganization of the ownership structure of a depository organization that causes a previously permissible interlock to become prohibited.

(b) *Transition period.* A management official described in paragraph (a) of this section may continue to serve the depository organization involved in the interlock for 15 months following the date of the change in circumstances. The FDIC may shorten this period under appropriate circumstances.

§ 390.407 Enforcement.

Except as provided in this section, the FDIC administers and enforces the Interlocks Act with respect to State savings associations and its affiliates, and may refer any case of a prohibited interlocking relationship involving these entities to the Attorney General of the United States to enforce compliance with the Interlocks Act and this subpart. If an affiliate of a State savings association is subject to the primary regulation of another Federal depository organization supervisory agency, then the FDIC does not administer and enforce the Interlocks Act with respect to that affiliate.

§ 390.408 Interlocking relationships permitted pursuant to Federal Deposit Insurance Act.

A management official or prospective management official of a depository organization may enter into an otherwise

Federal Deposit Insurance Corporation § 390.410

prohibited interlocking relationship with another depository organization for a period of up to 10 years if such relationship is approved by the Federal Deposit Insurance Corporation pursuant to section 13(k)(1)(A)(v) of the Federal Deposit Insurance Act, as amended (12 U.S.C. 1823(k)(1)(A)(v)).

Subpart W—Securities Offerings

§ 390.410 Definitions.

(a) For purposes of this subpart, the following definitions apply:

(1) *Accredited investor* means the same as in Commission Rule 501(a) (17 CFR 230.501(a)) under the Securities Act, and includes any State savings association.

(2) *Commission* means the Securities and Exchange Commission.

(3) *Dividend or interest reinvestment plan* means a plan which is offered solely to existing security holders of the State savings association which allows such persons to reinvest dividends or interest paid to them on securities issued by the State savings association, and which also may allow additional cash amounts to be contributed by the participants in the plan, provided that the securities to be issued are newly issued, or are purchased for the account of plan participants, at prices not in excess of current market prices at the time of purchase, or at prices not in excess of an amount determined in accordance with a pricing formula specified in the plan and based upon average or current market prices at the time of purchase.

(4) *Employee benefit plan* means any purchase, savings, option, rights, bonus, ownership, appreciation, profit sharing, thrift, incentive, pension or similar plan solely for officers, directors or employees.

(5) *Exchange Act* means the Securities Exchange Act of 1934 (15 U.S.C. 78a–78jj).

(6) *Filing date* means the date on which a document is actually received during business hours, 9 a.m. to 5 p.m. Eastern Standard Time, by the FDIC, 550 17th Street, NW., Washington, DC 20429. However if the last date on which a document can be accepted falls on a Saturday, Sunday, or holiday, such document may be filed on the next business day.

(7) *Issuer* means a State savings association which issues or proposes to issue any security.

(8) *Offer; Sale* or *sell*. For purposes of this subpart, the term *offer, offer to sell,* or *offer for sale* shall include every attempt or offer to dispose of, or solicitation of an offer to buy, a security or interest in a security, for value. However, these terms shall not include preliminary negotiations or agreements between an issuer and any underwriter or among underwriters who are or are to be in privity of contract with the issuer. *Sale* and *sell* includes every contract to sell or otherwise dispose of a security or interest in a security for value. Every offer or sale of a warrant or right to purchase or subscribe to another security of the same or another issuer, as well as every sale or offer of a security which gives the holder a present or future right or privilege to convert the security into another security of the same or another issuer, includes an offer and sale of the other security only at the time of the offer or sale of the warrant or right or convertible security; but neither the exercise of the right to purchase or subscribe or to convert nor the issuance of securities pursuant thereto is an offer or sale.

(9) *Person* means the same as in 12 CFR 192.25, and includes a State savings association.

(10) *Purchase* and *buy* mean the same as in 12 CFR 192.25.

(11) *State savings association* means the same as in section 3(b) of the Federal Deposit Insurance Act (12 U.S.C. 1813(b)), and includes a state-chartered savings association in organization which is granted conditional approval of insurance of accounts by the Federal Deposit Insurance Corporation. In addition, for purposes of § 390.411, *State savings association* includes any underwriter participating in the distribution of securities of a State savings association.

(12) *Securities Act* means the Securities Act of 1933 (15 U.S.C. 77a–77aa).

(13) *Security* means any non-withdrawable account, note, stock,

§ 390.410

treasury stock, bond, debenture, evidence of indebtedness, certificate of interest or participation in any profit-sharing agreement, collateral-trust certificate, preorganization or subscription, transferable share, investment contract, voting trust certificate or, in general, any interest or instrument commonly known as a *security*, or any certificate of interest or participation in, temporary or interim certificate for, receipt for, guarantee of, or warrant or right to subscribe to or purchase any of the foregoing, except that a *security* shall not include an account insured, in whole or in part, by the Federal Deposit Insurance Corporation.

(14) *Underwriter* means any person who has purchased from an issuer with a view to, or offers or sells for an issuer in connection with, the distribution of any security, or participates or has a participation in the direct or indirect underwriting of any such undertaking; but such term shall not include a person whose interest is limited to a commission from an underwriter or dealer not in excess of the usual and customary distributors' or sellers' commission and such term shall also not include any person who has continually held the securities being transferred for a period of two (2) consecutive years provided that the securities sold in any one (1) transaction shall be less than ten percent (10%) of the issued and outstanding securities of the same class. The following shall apply for the purpose of determining the period securities have been held:

(i) *Stock dividends, splits and recapitalizations.* Securities acquired from the issuer as a dividend or pursuant to a stock split, reverse split or recapitalization shall be deemed to have been acquired at the same time as the securities on which the dividend or, if more than one, the initial dividend was paid, the securities involved in the split or reverse split, or the securities surrendered in connection with the recapitalization.

(ii) *Conversions.* If the securities sold were acquired from the issuer for consideration consisting solely of other securities of the same issuer surrendered for conversion, the securities so acquired shall be deemed to have been acquired at the same time as the securities surrendered for conversion.

(iii) *Contingent issuance of securities.* Securities acquired as a contingent payment of the purchase price of an equity interest in a business, or the assets of a business, sold to the issuer or an affiliate of the issuer shall be deemed to have been acquired at the time of such sale if the issuer was then committed to issue the securities subject only to conditions other than the payment of further consideration for such securities. An agreement entered into in connection with any such purchase to remain in the employment of, or not to compete with, the issuer or affiliate or the rendering of services pursuant to such agreement shall not be deemed to be the payment of further consideration for such securities.

(iv) *Pledged securities.* Securities which are *bona fide* pledged by any person other than the issuer when sold by the pledgee, or by a purchaser, after a default in the obligation secured by the pledge, shall be deemed to have been acquired when they were acquired by the pledgor, except that if the securities were pledged without recourse they shall be deemed to have been acquired by the pledgee at the time of the pledge or by the purchaser at the time of purchase.

(v) *Gifts of securities.* Securities acquired from any person, other than the issuer, by gift shall be deemed to have been acquired by the donee when they were acquired by the donor.

(vi) *Trusts.* Securities acquired from the settler of a trust by the trust or acquired from the trust by the beneficiaries thereof shall be deemed to have been acquired when they were acquired by the settler.

(vii) *Estates.* Securities held by the estate of a deceased person or acquired from such an estate by the beneficiaries thereof shall be deemed to have been acquired when they were acquired by the deceased person, except that no holding period is required if the estate is not an affiliate of the issuer or if the securities are sold by a beneficiary of the estate who is not such an affiliate.

(viii) *Exchange transactions.* A person receiving securities in a transaction involving an exchange of the securities of

Federal Deposit Insurance Corporation

§ 390.412

one issuer for securities of another issuer shall be deemed to have acquired the securities received when such person acquired the securities exchanged.

(b) A term not defined in this subpart but defined elsewhere in this part, when used in subpart, shall have the meanings given elsewhere in this part, unless the context otherwise requires.

(c) When used in the rules, regulations, or forms of the Commission referred to in this subpart, the term *Commission* shall be deemed to refer to the FDIC, the term *registrant* shall be deemed to refer to an issuer defined in this subpart, and the term *registration statement* or *prospectus* shall be deemed to refer to an offering circular filed under this subpart, unless the context otherwise requires.

§ 390.411 Offering circular requirement.

(a) *General.* No State savings association shall offer or sell, directly or indirectly, any security issued by it unless:

(1) The offer or sale is accompanied or preceded by an offering circular which includes the information required by this subpart and which has been filed and declared effective pursuant to this subpart; or

(2) An exemption is available under this subpart.

(b) *Communications not deemed an offer.* The following communications shall not be deemed an offer under this subpart:

(1) Prior to filing an offering circular, any notice of a proposed offering which satisfies the requirements of Commission Rule 135 (17 CFR 230.135) under the Securities Act;

(2) Subsequent to filing an offering circular, any notice circular, advertisement, letter, or other communication published or transmitted to any person which satisfies the requirements of Commission Rule 134 (17 CFR 230.134) under the Securities Act; and

(3) Oral offers of securities covered by an offering circular made after filing the offering circular with the FDIC.

(c) *Preliminary offering circular.* Notwithstanding paragraph (a) of this section, a preliminary offering circular may be used for an offer of any security prior to the effective date of the offering circular if:

(1) The preliminary offering circular has been filed pursuant to this subpart;

(2) The preliminary offering circular includes the information required by this subpart, except for the omission of information relating to offering price, discounts or commissions, amount of proceeds, conversion rates, call prices, or other matters dependent on the offering price; and

(3) The offering circular declared effective by the FDIC is furnished to the purchaser prior to, or simultaneously with, the sale of any such security.

§ 390.412 Exemptions.

The offering circular requirement of § 390.411 shall not apply to an issuer's offer or sale of securities:

(a) [Reserved]

(b) Exempt from registration under either section 3(a) or section 4 of the Securities Act, but only by reason of an exemption other than section 3(a)(5) (for regulated State savings associations), and section 3(a)(11) (for intrastate offerings) of the Securities Act;

(c) In a conversion from the mutual to the stock form of organization pursuant to 12 CFR part 192, except for a supervisory conversion undertaken pursuant to subpart C of 12 CFR part 192;

(d) In a non-public offering which satisfies the requirements of § 390.413;

(e) That are debt securities issued in denominations of $100,000 or more, which are fully collateralized by cash, any security issued, or guaranteed as to principal and interest, by the United States, the Federal Home Loan Mortgage Corporation, Federal National Mortgage Association, Government National Mortgage Association or by interests in mortgage notes secured by real property;

(f) Distributed exclusively abroad to foreign nationals: *Provided,* That—

(1) The offering is made subject to safeguards reasonably designed to preclude distribution or redistribution of the securities within, or to nationals of, the United States; and

(2) Such safeguards include, without limitation, measures that would be sufficient to ensure that registration of the securities would not be required if the securities were not exempt under the Securities Act; or

867

(g) To its officers, directors or employees pursuant to an employee benefit plan or a dividend or interest reinvestment plan, and provided that any such plan has been approved by the majority of shareholders present in person or by proxy at an annual or special meeting of the shareholders of the State savings association.

§ 390.413 Non-public offering.

Offers and sales of securities by an issuer that satisfy the conditions of paragraph (a) or (b) of this section and the requirements of paragraphs (c) and (d) of this section shall be deemed to be transactions not involving any public offering within the meaning of section 4(2) of the Securities Act and §§ 390.412(b) and 390.412(d). However, an issuer shall not be deemed to be not in compliance with the provisions of this subpart solely by reason of making an untimely filing of the notice required to be filed by paragraph (c) of this section so long as the notice is actually filed and all other conditions and requirements of this subpart are satisfied.

(a) *Regulation D.* The offer and sale of all securities in the transaction satisfies the Commission's Regulation D (17 CFR 230.501–230.506), except for the notice requirements of Commission Rule 503 (17 CFR 230.503) and the limitations on resale in Commission Rule 502(d) (17 CFR 230.502(d)).

(b) *Sales to 35 persons.* The offer and sale of all securities in the transaction satisfies each of the following conditions:

(1) Sales of the security are not made to more than 35 persons during the offering period, as determined under the integration provisions of Commission Rule 502(a) (17 CFR 230.502(a)). The number of purchasers referred to above is exclusive of any accredited investor, officer, director or affiliate of the issuer. For purposes of paragraph (b) of this section, a husband and wife (together with any custodian or trustee acting for the account of their minor children) are counted as one person and a partnership, corporation or other organization which was not specifically formed for the purpose of purchasing the security offered in reliance upon this exemption, is counted as one person.

(2) All purchasers either have a pre-existing personal or business relationship with the issuer or any of its officers, directors or controlling persons, or by reason of their business or financial experience or the business or financial experience of their professional advisors who are unaffiliated with and who are not compensated by the issuer or any affiliate or selling agent of the issuer, directly or indirectly, could reasonably be assumed to have the capacity to protect their own interests in connection with the transaction.

(3) Each purchaser represents that the purchaser is purchasing for the purchaser's own account (or a trust account if the purchaser is a trustee) and not with a view to or for sale in connection with any distribution of the security.

(4) The offer and sale of the security is not accomplished by the publication of any advertisement.

(c) *Filing of notice of sales.* Within 30 days after the first sale of the securities, every six months after the first sale of the securities and not later than 30 days after the last sale of securities in an offering pursuant to this subpart, the issuer, shall file with the FDIC a report describing the results of the sale of securities as required by § 390.421(b).

(d) *Limitation on resale.* The issuer shall exercise reasonable care to assure that the purchasers of the securities are not underwriters within the meaning of § 390.410(a)(14), which reasonable care shall include, but not be limited to, the following:

(1) Reasonable inquiry to determine if the purchaser is acquiring the securities for the purchaser or for other persons;

(2) Written disclosure to each purchaser prior to the sale that the securities are not offered by an offering circular filed with, and declared effective by, the FDIC pursuant to § 390.411, but instead are being sold in reliance upon the exemption from the offering circular requirement provided for by this subpart; and

(3) Placement of a legend on the certificate, or other document evidencing

Federal Deposit Insurance Corporation § 390.415

the securities, indicating that the securities have not been offered by an offering circular filed with, and declared effective by, the FDIC and that due care should be taken to ensure that the seller of the securities is not an underwriter within the meaning of § 390.410(a)(14).

§ 390.414 Filing and signature requirements.

(a) *Procedures.* An offering circular, amendment, notice, report, or other document required by this subpart shall, unless otherwise indicated, be filed in accordance with the requirements of 12 CFR 192.115(a), 192.150(a)(6), 192.155, 192.180(b), and Form AC, General Instruction B, of this subpart.

(b) *Number of copies.* (1) Unless otherwise required, any filing under this subpart shall include nine copies of the document to be filed with the FDIC, as follows:

(i) Seven copies, which shall include one manually signed copy with exhibits, three conformed copies with exhibits, and three conformed copies without exhibits, to the FDIC, ATTN: Accounting and Securities Disclosure Section, 550 17th Street NW, Washington, DC 20429; and

(ii) Two copies, which shall include one manually signed copy with exhibits and one conformed copy, without exhibits, to the appropriate regional director.

(2) Within five days after the effective date of an offering circular or the commencement of a public offering after the effective date, whichever occurs later, nine copies of the offering circular used shall be filed with the FDIC as follows: Seven copies to the FDIC, 550 17th Street NW., ATTN: Accounting and Securities Disclosure Section, Washington, DC, and two copies to the appropriate Regional Director.

(3) After the effective date of an offering circular, an offering circular which varies from the form previously filed shall not be used, unless it includes only non-material supplemental or additional information and until 10 copies have been filed with the FDIC in the manner required.

(c) *Signature.* (1) Any offering circular, amendment, or consent filed with the FDIC pursuant to this subpart shall include an attached manually signed signature page which authorizes the filing and has been signed by:

(i) The issuer, by its duly authorized representative;

(ii) The issuer's principal executive officer;

(iii) The issuer's principal financial officer;

(iv) The issuer's principal accounting officer; and

(v) At least a majority of the issuer's directors.

(2) Any other document filed pursuant to this subpart shall be signed by a person authorized to do so.

(3) At least *one copy* of every document filed pursuant to this subpart shall be manually signed, and every copy of a document filed shall:

(i) Have the name of each person who signs typed or printed beneath the signature;

(ii) State the capacity or capacities in which the signature is provided;

(iii) Provide the name of each director of the issuer, if a majority of directors is required to sign the document; and

(iv) With regard to any copies not manually signed, bear typed or printed signatures.

§ 390.415 Effective date.

(a) Except as provided for in paragraph (d) of this section, an offering circular filed by a State savings association shall be deemed to be automatically declared effective by the FDIC on the twentieth day after filing or on such earlier date as the FDIC may determine for good cause shown.

(b) If any amendment is filed prior to the effective date, the offering circular shall be deemed to have been filed when such amendment was filed.

(c) The period until automatic effectiveness under this subpart shall be stated at the bottom of the facing page of the Form OC or any amendment.

(d) The effectiveness will be delayed if a duly authorized amendment, telegram confirmed in writing, or letter states that the effective date is delayed until a further amendment is filed specifically stating that the offering circular will become effective in accordance with this subpart.

§ 390.416

(e) An amendment filed after the effective date of the offering circular shall become effective on such date as the FDIC may determine.

(f) If it appears to the FDIC at any time that the offering circular includes any untrue statement of a material fact or omits to state any material fact required to be stated therein or necessary to make the statements therein not misleading, then the FDIC may pursue any remedy it is authorized to pursue under section 8 of the Federal Deposit Insurance Act, as amended (12 U.S.C. 1818), including, but not limited to, institution of cease-and-desist proceedings.

§ 390.416 Form, content, and accounting.

(a) *Form and content.* Any offering circular or amendment filed pursuant to this subpart shall:

(1) Be filed under cover of Form OC, which is under 12 CFR part 192;

(2) Comply with the requirements of Items 3 and 4 of Form OC and the requirements of all items of the form for registration (17 CFR part 239) that the issuer would be eligible to use were it required to register the securities under the Securities Act;

(3) Comply with all item requirements of the Form S-1 (17 CFR part 239) for registration under the Securities Act, if the association issuing the securities is not in compliance with the FDIC's regulatory capital requirements during the time the offering is made;

(4) Where a form specifies that the information required by an item in the Commission's Regulation S-K (17 CFR part 229) should be furnished, include such information and all of the information required by Item 7 of Form PS, which is under 12 CFR part 192;

(5) Include after the facing page of the Form OC a cross-reference sheet listing each item requirement of the form for registration under the Securities Act and indicate for each item the applicable heading or subheading in the offering circular under which the required information is disclosed;

(6) Include in part II of the Form OC the applicable undertakings required by the form for registration under the Securities Act;

(7) If the issuer has not previously been required to file reports pursuant to section 13(a) of the Exchange Act or § 390.427, include in part II of Form OC the following undertaking: "The issuer hereby undertakes, in connection with any distribution of the offering circular, to have a preliminary or effective offering circular including the information required by this subpart distributed to all persons expected to be mailed confirmations of sale not less than 48 hours prior to the time such confirmations are expected to be mailed;"

(8) In offerings involving the issuance of options, warrants, subscription rights or conversion rights within the meaning of § 390.410(a)(8), include in part II of Form OC an undertaking to provide a copy of the issuer's most recent audited financial statements to persons exercising such options, warrants or rights promptly upon receiving written notification of the exercise thereof;

(9) Include as supplemental information and not as part of the Form OC and only with respect to *de novo* offerings, a copy of the application for insurance of accounts as submitted to the Federal Deposit Insurance Corporation for state-chartered savings associations; and

(10) In addition to the information expressly required to be included by this subpart, there shall be added such further material information, if any, as may be necessary to make the required statements, in light of the circumstances under which they are made, not misleading.

(b) *Accounting requirements.* To be declared effective an offering circular or amendment shall satisfy the accounting requirements in subpart T.

§ 390.417 Use of the offering circular.

(a) An offering circular or amendment declared effective by the FDIC shall not be used more than nine months after the effective date, unless the information contained therein is as of a date not more than 16 months prior to such use.

Federal Deposit Insurance Corporation § 390.421

(b) An offering circular filed under § 390.414(b)(3) shall not extend the period for which an effective offering circular or amendment may be used under paragraph (c) of this section.

(c) If any event arises, or change in fact occurs, after the effective date and such event or change in fact, individually or in the aggregate, results in the offering circular containing any untrue statement of material fact, or omitting to state a material fact necessary in order to make statements made in the offering circular not misleading under the circumstances, then no offering circular, which has been declared effective under this subpart, shall be used until an amendment reflecting such event or change in fact has been filed with, and declared effective by, the FDIC.

§ 390.418 Escrow requirement.

(a) Any funds received in an offering which is offered and sold on a best efforts all-or-none condition or with a minimum-maximum amount to be sold shall be held in an escrow or similar separate account until such time as all of the securities are sold with respect to a best efforts all-or-none offering or the stated minimum amount of securities are sold in a minimum-maximum offering.

(b) If the amount of securities required to be sold under escrow conditions in paragraph (a) of this section are not sold within the time period for the offering as disclosed in the offering circular, all funds in the escrow account shall be promptly refunded unless the FDIC otherwise approves an extension of the offering period upon a showing of good cause and provided that the extension is consistent with the public interest and the protection of investors.

§ 390.419 Unsafe or unsound practices.

(a) No person shall directly or indirectly,

(1) Employ any device, scheme or artifice to defraud,

(2) Make any untrue statement of a material fact or omit to state a material fact necessary in order to make statements made, in light of the circumstances under which they were made, not misleading, or

(3) Engage in any act, practice, or course of business which operates as a fraud or deceit upon any person, in connection with the purchase or sale of any security of a State savings association.

(b) Violations of this subpart shall constitute an unsafe or unsound practice within the meaning of section 8 of the Federal Deposit Insurance Act, as amended, 12 U.S.C. 1818.

(c) Nothing in this subpart shall be construed as a limitation on the applicability of section 10(b) of the Exchange Act (15 U.S.C. 78j(b)) or Rule 10b-5 promulgated thereunder (17 CFR 240.10b-5).

§ 390.420 Withdrawal or abandonment.

(a) Any offering circular, amendment, or exhibit may be withdrawn prior to the effective date. A withdrawal shall be signed and state the grounds upon which it is made. Any document withdrawn will not be removed from the files of the FDIC, but will be marked "Withdrawn upon the request of the issuer on (date)."

(b) When an offering circular or amendment has been on file with the FDIC for a period of nine months and has not become effective, the FDIC may, in its discretion, determine whether the filing has been abandoned, after notifying the issuer that the filing is out of date and must either be amended to comply with the applicable requirements of this subpart or be withdrawn within 30 days after the date of such notice. When a filing is abandoned, the filing will not be removed from the files of the FDIC, but will be marked "Declared abandoned by the FDIC on (date)."

§ 390.421 Securities sale report.

(a) Within 30 days after the first sale of the securities, every six months after such 30 day period and not later than 30 days after the later of the last sale of securities in an offering pursuant to § 390.411 or the application of the proceeds therefrom, the issuer shall file with the FDIC a report describing the results of the sale of the securities and the application of the proceeds, which shall include all of the information required by Form G-12 set forth at

§ 390.429 and shall also include the following:

(1) The name, address, and docket number of the issuer;

(2) The title, number, aggregate and per-unit offering price of the securities sold;

(3) The aggregate and per-unit dollar amounts of actual itemized expenses, discounts or commissions, and other fees;

(4) The aggregate and per-unit dollar amounts of the net proceeds raised, and the use of proceeds therefrom; and

(5) The number of purchasers of each class of securities sold and the number of owners of record of each class of the issuer's equity securities after the issuance of the securities or termination of the offer.

(b) Within 30 days after the first sale of the securities, every six months after the first sale of the securities and not later than 30 days after the last sale of securities in an offering pursuant to § 390.413, the issuer shall file with the FDIC a report describing the results of the sale of securities, which shall include all of the information required by Form G-12 set forth at § 390.429, and shall also include the following:

(1) All of the information required by paragraph (a) of this section; and

(2) A detailed statement of the factual and legal grounds for the exemption claimed.

§ 390.422 Public disclosure and confidential treatment.

(a) Any offering circular, amendment, exhibit, notice, or report filed pursuant to this subpart will be publicly available. Any other related documents will be treated in accordance with the provisions of the Freedom of Information Act (5 U.S.C. 552), the Privacy Act of 1974 (5 U.S.C. 552a), and parts 309 and 310 of this chapter.

(b) Any requests for confidential treatment of information in a document required to be filed under this subpart shall be made as required under Commission Rule 24b-2 (17 CFR 240.24b-2) under the Exchange Act.

§ 390.423 Waiver.

(a) The FDIC may waive any requirement of this subpart, or any required information:

(1) Determined to be unnecessary by the FDIC;

(2) In connection with a transaction approved by the FDIC for supervisory reasons, or

(3) Where a provision of this subpart conflicts with a requirement of applicable state law.

(b) Any condition, stipulation or provision binding any person acquiring a security issued by a State savings association which seeks to waive compliance with any provision of this subpart shall be void, unless approved by the FDIC.

§ 390.424 Requests for interpretive advice or waiver.

Any requests to the FDIC for interpretive advice or a waiver with respect to any provision of this subpart shall satisfy the following requirements:

(a) A copy of the request, including any attachments, shall be filed with the FDIC;

(b) The provisions of this subpart to which the request relates, the participants in the proposed transaction, and the reasons for the request, shall be specifically identified or described; and

(c) The request shall include a legal opinion as to each legal issue raised and an accounting opinion as to each accounting issue raised.

§ 390.425 Delayed or continuous offering and sale of securities.

Any offer or sale of securities under § 390.411 may be made on a continuous or delayed basis in the future, if:

(a) The securities would satisfy all of the eligibility requirements of the Commission's Rule 415, 17 CFR 230.415; and

(b) The association issuing the securities is in compliance with the FDIC's regulatory capital requirements during the time the offering is made.

§ 390.426 Sales of securities at an office of a State savings association.

Sales of securities of a State savings association or its affiliates at an office of a State savings association may

Federal Deposit Insurance Corporation

§ 390.429

only be made in accordance with the provisions of § 390.340.

§ 390.427 Current and periodic reports.

(a) Each State savings association which files an offering circular which becomes effective pursuant to this subpart, after such effective date, shall file with the FDIC periodic and current reports on Forms 8–K, 10–Q and 10–K as may be required by section 13 of the Exchange Act (15 U.S.C. 78m) as if the securities sold by such offering circular were securities registered pursuant to section 12 of the Exchange Act (15 U.S.C. 78l). The duty to file periodic and current reports under this subpart shall be automatically suspended if and so long as any issue of securities of the State savings association is registered pursuant to section 12 of the Exchange Act (15 U.S.C. 78l). The duty to file under this subpart shall also be automatically suspended as to any fiscal year, other than the fiscal year within which such offering circular became effective, if, at the beginning of such fiscal year, the securities of each class to which the offering circular relates are held of record by less than three hundred persons and upon the filing of a Form 15.

(b) For purposes of registering securities under section 12(b) or 12(g) of the Exchange Act, an issuer subject to the reporting requirements of paragraph (a) of this section may use the Commission's registration statement on Form 10 or Form 8–A or 8–B as applicable.

§ 390.428 Approval of the security.

Any securities of a State savings association which are not exempt under this subpart and are offered or sold pursuant to an offering circular which becomes effective under this subpart, are deemed to be approved as to form and terms for purposes of this subpart.

§ 390.429 Form for securities sale report.

FDIC, 550 17th Street, NW., Washington, DC 20429

[Form G–12]

Securities Sale Report Pursuant to § 390.12

FDIC No. _____
Issuer's Name: _____

Address: _____

If in organization, state the date of FDIC certification of insurance of accounts: ____

State the title, number, aggregate and per-unit offering price of the securities sold: _____

State the aggregate and per-unit dollar amounts of actual itemized offering expenses, discounts, commissions, and other fees: _____

State the aggregate and per-unit dollar amounts of the net proceeds raised: _____

Describe the use of proceeds. If unknown, provide reasonable estimates of the dollar amount allocated to each purpose for which the proceeds will be used: _____

State the number of purchasers of each class of securities sold and the number of owners of record of each class of the issuer's equity securities at the close or termination of the offering: _____

For a non-public offering, also state the factual and legal grounds for the exemption claimed (attach additional pages if necessary): _____

For a non-public offering, all offering materials used should be listed: _____

Person to Contact: _____
Telephone No.: _____

This issuer has duly caused this securities sale report to be signed on its behalf by the undersigned person.

Date of securities sale report _____
Issuer: _____
Signature: _____
Name: _____
Title: _____

Instruction: Print the name and title of the signing representative under his or her signature. Ten copies of the securities sale report should be filed, including one copy manually signed, as required under 12 CFR 390.414.

Attention

Intentional misstatements or omissions of fact constitute violations of Federal law (See 18 U.S.C. 1001 and § 390.355(b)).

§ 390.430 Filing of copies of offering circulars in certain exempt offerings.

A copy of the offering circular, or similar document, if any, used in connection with an offering exempt from the offering circular requirement of § 390.411 by reason of § 390.412(e) or § 390.413 shall be mailed to the FDIC within 30 days after the first sale of such securities. Such copy of the offering circular, or similar document, is solely for the information of the FDIC and shall not be deemed to be "filed" with the FDIC pursuant to § 390.411. The mailing to the FDIC of such offering circular, or similar document, shall not be a pre-condition of the applicable exemption from the offering circular requirements of § 390.411.

Subpart X—Appraisals

§ 390.440 Authority, purpose, and scope.

(a) *Authority.* This subpart is issued by the FDIC under title XI of the Financial Institutions Reform, Recovery, and Enforcement Act of 1989 ("FIRREA") (Pub. L. 101–73, 103 Stat. 183, 511 (1989)), 12 U.S.C. 3301 *et seq.*, and portions of the Home Owners' Loan Act ("HOLA"), 12 U.S.C. 1461 *et seq.*, as amended by FIRREA.

(b) *Purpose and scope.* (1) Title XI provides protection for federal financial and public policy interests in real estate related transactions by requiring real estate appraisals used in connection with federally related transactions to be performed in writing, in accordance with uniform standards, by appraisers whose competency has been demonstrated and whose professional conduct will be subject to effective supervision. This subpart implements the requirements of title XI and applies to all federally related transactions entered into by the FDIC or by institutions regulated by the FDIC ("regulated institutions").

(2) This subpart:

(i) Identifies which real estate related financial transactions require the services of an appraiser;

(ii) Prescribes which categories of federally related transactions shall be appraised by a State certified appraiser and which by a State licensed appraiser; and

(iii) Prescribes minimum standards for the performance of real estate appraisals in connection with federally related transactions under the jurisdiction of the FDIC.

§ 390.441 Definitions.

Appraisal means a written statement independently and impartially prepared by a qualified appraiser setting forth an opinion as to the market value of an adequately described property as of a specific date(s), supported by the presentation and analysis of relevant market information.

Appraisal Foundation means the Appraisal Foundation established on November 30, 1987, as a not-for-profit corporation under the laws of Illinois.

Appraisal Subcommittee means the Appraisal Subcommittee of the Federal Financial Institution Examination Council.

Business loan means a loan or extension of credit to any corporation, general or limited partnership, business trust, joint venture, pool, syndicate, sole proprietorship, or other business entity.

Complex 1-to-4 family residential property appraisal means one in which the property to be appraised, the form of ownership, or market conditions are atypical.

Federally related transaction means any real estate-related financial transaction entered into on or after August 9, 1990, that:

(1) The FDIC or any regulated institution engages in or contracts for; and

(2) Requires the services of an appraiser.

Market value means the most probable price which a property should bring in a competitive and open market under all conditions requisite to a fair sale, the buyer and seller each acting prudently and knowledgeably, and assuming the price is not affected by undue stimulus. Implicit in this definition is the consummation of a sale as of a specified date and the passing of title from seller to buyer under conditions whereby:

(1) Buyer and seller are typically motivated;

Federal Deposit Insurance Corporation § 390.442

(2) Both parties are well informed or well advised, and acting in what they consider their own best interests;

(3) A reasonable time is allowed for exposure in the open market;

(4) Payment is made in terms of cash in U.S. dollars or in terms of financial arrangements comparable thereto; and

(5) The price represents the normal consideration for the property sold unaffected by special or creative financing or sales concessions granted by anyone associated with the sale.

Real estate or *real property* means an identified parcel or tract of land, with improvements, and includes easements, rights of way, undivided or future interests, or similar rights in a tract of land, but does not include mineral rights, timber rights, growing crops, water rights, or similar interests severable from the land when the transaction does not involve the associated parcel or tract of land.

Real estate-related financial transaction means any transaction involving:

(1) The sale, lease, purchase, investment in or exchange of real property, including interests in property, or the financing thereof; or

(2) The refinancing of real property or interests in real property; or

(3) The use of real property or interests in property as security for a loan or investment, including mortgage-backed securities.

State certified appraiser means any individual who has satisfied the requirements for certification in a State or territory whose criteria for certification as a real estate appraiser currently meet the minimum criteria for certification issued by the Appraiser Qualifications Board of the Appraisal Foundation. No individual shall be a State certified appraiser unless such individual has achieved a passing grade upon a suitable examination administered by a State or territory that is consistent with and equivalent to the Uniform State Certification Examination issued or endorsed by the Appraiser Qualifications Board of the National Foundation. In addition, the Appraisal Subcommittee must not have issued a finding that the policies, practices, or procedures of the State or territory are inconsistent with title XI of FIRREA. The FDIC may, from time to time, impose additional qualification criteria for certified appraisers performing appraisals in connection with federally related transactions within its jurisdiction.

State licensed appraiser means any individual who has satisfied the requirements for licensing in a State or territory where the licensing procedures comply with title XI of FIRREA and where the Appraisal Subcommittee has not issued a finding that the policies, practices, or procedures of the State or territory are inconsistent with title XI. The FDIC may, from time to time, impose additional qualification criteria for licensed appraisers performing appraisals in connection with federally related transactions within its jurisdiction.

Tract development means a project of five units or more that is constructed or is to be constructed as a single development.

Transaction value means:

(1) For loans or other extensions of credit, the amount of the loan or extension of credit;

(2) For sales, leases, purchases, and investments in or exchanges of real property, the market value of the real property interest involved; and

(3) For the pooling of loans or interests in real property for resale or purchase, the amount of the loan or market value of the real property calculated with respect to each such loan or interest in real property.

§ 390.442 Appraisals required; transactions requiring a State certified or licensed appraiser.

(a) *Appraisals required.* An appraisal performed by a State certified or licensed appraiser is required for all real estate-related financial transactions except those in which:

(1) The transaction value is $250,000 or less;

(2) A lien on real estate has been taken as collateral in an abundance of caution;

(3) The transaction is not secured by real estate;

(4) A lien on real estate has been taken for purposes other than the real estate's value;

(5) The transaction is a business loan that:

§ 390.442

(i) Has a transaction value of $1 million or less; and

(ii) Is not dependent on the sale of, or rental income derived from, real estate as the primary source of repayment;

(6) A lease of real estate is entered into, unless the lease is the economic equivalent of a purchase or sale of the leased real estate;

(7) The transaction involves an existing extension of credit at the lending institution, provided that:

(i) There has been no obvious and material change in market conditions or physical aspects of the property that threatens the adequacy of the institution's real estate collateral protection after the transaction, even with the advancement of new monies; or

(ii) There is no advancement of new monies, other than funds necessary to cover reasonable closing costs;

(8) The transaction involves the purchase, sale, investment in, exchange of, or extension of credit secured by, a loan or interest in a loan, pooled loans, or interests in real property, including mortgaged-backed securities, and each loan or interest in a loan, pooled loan, or real property interest met the FDIC's regulatory requirements for appraisals at the time of origination;

(9) The transaction is wholly or partially insured or guaranteed by a United States government agency or United States government sponsored agency;

(10) The transaction either:

(i) Qualifies for sale to a United States government agency or United States government sponsored agency; or

(ii) Involves a residential real estate transaction in which the appraisal conforms to the Federal National Mortgage Association or Federal Home Loan Mortgage Corporation appraisal standards applicable to that category of real estate;

(11) The regulated institution is acting in a fiduciary capacity and is not required to obtain an appraisal under other law; or

(12) The FDIC determines that the services of an appraiser are not necessary in order to protect Federal financial and public policy interests in real estate-related financial transactions or to protect the safety and soundness of the institution.

(b) *Evaluations required.* For a transaction that does not require the services of a State certified or licensed appraiser under paragraph (a)(1), (5), or (7) of this section, the institution shall obtain an appropriate evaluation of real property collateral that is consistent with safe and sound banking practices.

(c) *Appraisals to address safety and soundness concerns.* The FDIC reserves the right to require an appraisal under this subpart whenever the agency believes it is necessary to address safety and soundness concerns.

(d) *Transactions requiring a State certified appraiser*—(1) *All transactions of $1,000,000 or more.* All federally related transactions having a transaction value of $1,000,000 or more shall require an appraisal prepared by a State certified appraiser.

(2) *Nonresidential and residential (other than 1-to-4 family) transactions of $250,000 or more.* All federally related transactions having a transaction value of $250,000 or more, other than those involving appraisals of 1-to-4 family residential properties, shall require an appraisal prepared by a State certified appraiser.

(3) *Complex residential transactions of $250,000 or more.* All complex 1-to-4 family residential property appraisals rendered in connection with federally related transactions shall require a State certified appraiser if the transaction value is $250,000 or more. A regulated institution may presume that appraisals of 1-to-4 family residential properties are not complex, unless the institution has readily available information that a given appraisal will be complex. The regulated institution shall be responsible for making the final determination of whether the appraisal is complex. If during the course of the appraisal a licensed appraiser identifies factors that would result in the property, form of ownership, or market conditions being considered atypical, then either:

(i) The regulated institution may ask the licensed appraiser to complete the appraisal and have a certified appraiser approve and co-sign the appraisal; or

Federal Deposit Insurance Corporation

(ii) The institution may engage a certified appraiser to complete the appraisal.

(e) *Transactions requiring either a State certified or licensed appraiser.* All appraisals for federally related transactions not requiring the services of a State certified appraiser shall be prepared by either a State certified appraiser or a State licensed appraiser.

(f) *Effective date.* State savings associations are required to use State certified or licensed appraisers as set forth in this subpart no later than December 31, 1992.

§ 390.443 Minimum appraisal standards.

For federally related transactions, all appraisals shall, at a minimum:

(a) Conform to generally accepted appraisal standards as evidenced by the Uniform Standards of Professional Appraisal Practice (USPAP) promulgated by the Appraisal Standards Board of the Appraisal Foundation, 1029 Vermont Ave., NW., Washington, DC 20005, unless principles of safe and sound banking require compliance with stricter standards;

(b) Be written and contain sufficient information and analysis to support the institution's decision to engage in the transaction;

(c) Analyze and report appropriate deductions and discounts for proposed construction or renovation, partially leased buildings, non-market lease terms, and tract developments with unsold units;

(d) Be based upon the definition of market value as set forth in this subpart; and

(e) Be performed by State licensed or certified appraisers in accordance with requirements set forth in this subpart.

§ 390.444 Appraiser independence.

(a) *Staff appraisers.* If an appraisal is prepared by a staff appraiser, that appraiser must be independent of the lending, investment, and collection functions and not involved, except as an appraiser, in the federally related transaction, and have no direct or indirect interest, financial or otherwise, in the property. If the only qualified persons available to perform an appraisal are involved in the lending, investment, or collection functions of the regulated institution, the regulated institution shall take appropriate steps to ensure that the appraisers exercise independent judgment and that the appraisal is adequate. Such steps include, but are not limited to, prohibiting an individual from performing an appraisal in connection with federally related transactions in which the appraiser is otherwise involved and prohibiting directors and officers from participating in any vote or approval involving assets on which they performed an appraisal.

(b) *Fee appraisers.* (1) If an appraisal is prepared by a fee appraiser, the appraiser shall be engaged directly by the regulated institution or its agent, and have no direct or indirect interest, financial or otherwise, in the property or the transaction.

(2) A regulated institution also may accept an appraisal that was prepared by an appraiser engaged directly by another financial services institution, if:

(i) The appraiser has no direct or indirect interest, financial or otherwise, in the property or the transaction; and

(ii) The regulated institution determines that the appraisal conforms to the requirements of this subpart and is otherwise acceptable.

§ 390.445 Professional association membership; competency.

(a) *Membership in appraisal organizations.* A State certified appraiser or a State licensed appraiser may not be excluded from consideration for an assignment for a federally related transaction solely by virtue of membership or lack of membership in any particular appraisal organization.

(b) *Competency.* All staff and fee appraisers performing appraisals in connection with federally related transactions must be State certified or licensed, as appropriate. However, a State certified or licensed appraiser may not be considered competent solely by virtue of being certified or licensed. Any determination of competency shall be based upon the individual's experience and educational background as they relate to the particular appraisal assignment for which he or she is being considered.

§ 390.446 Enforcement.

Institutions and institution-affiliated parties, including staff appraisers and fee appraisers, who violate this subpart may be subject to removal and/or prohibition orders, cease and desist orders, and the imposition of civil money penalties pursuant to the Federal Deposit Insurance Act, 12 U.S.C. 1811 *et seq.*, as amended, or other applicable law.

§ 390.447 Appraisal policies and practices of State savings associations and subsidiaries.

(a) *Introduction.* The soundness of a State savings association's mortgage loans and real estate investments, and those of its subsidiary(ies), depends to a great extent upon the adequacy of the loan underwriting used to support these transactions. An appraisal standard is one of several critical components of a sound underwriting policy because appraisal reports contain estimates of the value of collateral held or assets owned. This section sets forth the responsibilities of management to develop, implement, and maintain appraisal standards in determining compliance with the appraisal requirements of § 390.350.

(b) *Definition.* For purposes of this section, management means: the directors and officers of a State savings association or subsidiary(ies) of such State savings association as those terms are defined in §§ 390.291 and 390.302, respectively.

(c) *Responsibilities of management.* An appraisal is a critical component of the loan underwriting or real estate investment decision. Therefore, management shall develop, implement, and maintain appraisal policies to ensure that appraisals reflect professional competence and to facilitate the reporting of estimates of market value upon which State savings associations may rely to make lending decisions. To achieve these results:

(1) Management shall develop written appraisal policies, subject to formal adoption by the State savings association's board of directors, that it shall implement in consultation with other appropriate personnel. These policies shall ensure that adequate appraisals are obtained and proper appraisal procedures are followed consistent with the requirements of this subpart.

(2) Management shall develop and adopt guidelines and institute procedures pertaining to the hiring of appraisers to perform appraisal services for the State savings association consistent with the requirements of this subpart. These guidelines shall set forth specific factors to be considered by management including, but not limited to, an appraiser's State certification or licensing, professional education, and type of experience. An appraiser's membership in professional appraisal organizations may be considered consistent with the requirements of subpart X.

(3) Management shall review on an annual basis the performance of all approved appraisers used within the preceding 12-month period for compliance with:

(i) The State savings association's appraisal policies and procedures; and

(ii) The reasonableness of the value estimates reported.

(d) *Exemptions.* The requirements of § 390.443(b) through (d) shall not apply with respect to appraisals on nonresidential properties prepared on form reports approved by the FDIC and completed in accordance with the applicable instructional booklet.

Subpart Y—Prompt Corrective Action

§ 390.450 Authority, purpose, scope, other supervisory authority, and disclosure of capital categories.

(a) *Authority.* This subpart is issued by the FDIC pursuant to section 38 of the Federal Deposit Insurance Act (FDI Act) as added by section 131 of the Federal Deposit Insurance Corporation Improvement Act of 1991 (Pub. L. 102–242, 105 Stat. 2236 (1991)) (12 U.S.C. 1831o).

(b) *Purpose.* Section 38 of the FDI Act establishes a framework of supervisory actions for insured depository institutions that are not adequately capitalized. The principal purpose of this subpart is to define, for State savings associations, the capital measures and capital levels that are used for determining the supervisory actions authorized under section 38 of the FDI Act.

This subpart also establishes procedures for submission and review of capital restoration plans and for issuance and review of directives and orders pursuant to section 38.

(c) *Scope.* This subpart implements the provisions of section 38 of the FDI Act as they apply to State savings associations. Certain of these provisions also apply to officers, directors and employees of State savings associations.

(d) *Other supervisory authority.* Neither section 38 nor this subpart in any way limits the authority of the FDIC under any other provision of law to take supervisory actions to address unsafe or unsound practices, deficient capital levels, violations of law, unsafe or unsound conditions, or other practices. Action under section 38 of the FDI Act and this subpart may be taken independently of, in conjunction with, or in addition to any other enforcement action available to the FDIC, including issuance of cease and desist orders, capital directives, approval or denial of applications or notices, assessment of civil money penalties, or any other actions authorized by law.

(e) *Disclosure of capital categories.* The assignment of a State savings association under this subpart within a particular capital category is for purposes of implementing and applying the provisions of section 38. Unless permitted by the FDIC or otherwise required by law, no State savings association may state in any advertisement or promotional material its capital category under this subpart or that the FDIC or any other federal banking agency has assigned the State savings association to a particular category.

§ 390.451 Definitions.

For purposes of this subpart, except as modified in this section or unless the context otherwise requires, the terms used in this subpart have the same meanings as set forth in sections 38 and 3 of the FDI Act.

(a)(1) *Control* has the same meaning assigned to it in section 2 of the Bank Holding Company Act (12 U.S.C. 1841), and the term "controlled" shall be construed consistently with the term "control."

(2) *Exclusion for fiduciary ownership.* No insured depository institution or company controls another insured depository institution or company by virtue of its ownership or control of shares in a fiduciary capacity. Shares shall not be deemed to have been acquired in a fiduciary capacity if the acquiring insured depository institution or company has sole discretionary authority to exercise voting rights with respect thereto.

(3) *Exclusion for debts previously contracted.* No insured depository institution or company controls another insured depository institution or company by virtue of its ownership or control of shares acquired in securing or collecting a debt previously contracted in good faith, until two years after the date of acquisition. The two-year period may be extended at the discretion of the appropriate federal banking agency for up to three one-year periods.

(b) *Controlling person* means any person having control of an insured depository institution and any company controlled by that person.

(c) *Leverage ratio* means the ratio of Tier 1 capital to adjusted total assets, as calculated in accordance with subpart Z.

(d) *Management fee* means any payment of money or provision of any other thing of value to a company or individual for the provision of management services or advice to the State savings association or related overhead expenses, including payments related to supervisory, executive, managerial or policymaking functions, other than compensation to an individual in the individual's capacity as an officer or employee of the State savings association.

(e) *Risk-weighted assets* means total risk-weighted assets, as calculated in accordance with subpart Z.

(f) *Tangible equity* means the amount of a State savings association's core capital as computed in subpart Z plus the amount of its outstanding cumulative perpetual preferred stock (including related surplus), minus intangible assets as defined in § 390.461, except mortgage servicing assets to the extent they are includable under § 390.471. Non-mortgage servicing assets that have not been previously deducted

§ 390.452

in calculating core capital are deducted.

(g) *Tier 1 capital* means the amount of core capital as defined in subpart Z.

(h) *Tier 1 risk-based capital ratio* means the ratio of Tier 1 capital to risk-weighted assets, as calculated in accordance with subpart Z.

(i) *Total assets*, for purposes of § 390.453(b)(5), means adjusted total assets as calculated in accordance with subpart Z, minus intangible assets as provided in the definition of tangible equity.

(j) *Total risk-based capital ratio* means the ratio of total capital to risk-weighted assets, as calculated in accordance with subpart Z.

§ 390.452 Notice of capital category.

(a) *Effective date of determination of capital category.* A State savings association shall be deemed to be within a given capital category for purposes of section 38 of the FDI Act and this subpart as of the date the State savings association is notified of, or is deemed to have notice of, its capital category, pursuant to paragraph (b) of this section.

(b) *Notice of capital category.* A State savings association shall be deemed to have been notified of its capital levels and its capital category as of the most recent date:

(1) A Thrift Financial Report (TFR) or Consolidated Reports of Condition or Income ("Call Report"), as applicable, is required to be filed with the FDIC;

(2) A final report of examination is delivered to the State savings association; or

(3) Written notice is provided by the FDIC to the State savings association of its capital category for purposes of section 38 of the FDI Act and this subpart or that the State savings association's capital category has changed as provided in paragraph (c) of this section or § 390.453(c).

(c) *Adjustments to reported capital levels and category* —(1) *Notice of adjustment by State savings association.* A State savings association shall provide the FDIC with written notice that an adjustment to the State savings association's capital category may have occurred no later than 15 calendar days following the date that any material event has occurred that would cause the State savings association to be placed in a lower capital category from the category assigned to the State savings association for purposes of section 38 and this section on the basis of the State savings association's most recent report of examination.

(2) *Determination by the FDIC to change capital category.* After receiving notice pursuant to paragraph (c)(1) of this section, the FDIC shall determine whether to change the capital category of the State savings association and shall notify the State savings association of the FDIC's determination.

§ 390.453 Capital measures and capital category definitions.

(a) *Capital measures.* For purposes of section 38 and this subpart, the relevant capital measures shall be:

(1) The total risk-based capital ratio;

(2) The Tier 1 risk-based capital ratio; and

(3) The leverage ratio.

(b) *Capital categories.* For purposes of section 38 and this subpart, a State savings association shall be deemed to be:

(1) *Well capitalized* if the State savings association:

(i) Has a total risk-based capital ratio of 10.0 percent or greater; and

(ii) Has a Tier 1 risk-based capital ratio of 6.0 percent or greater; and

(iii) Has a leverage ratio of 5.0 percent or greater; and

(iv) Is not subject to any written agreement, order, capital directive, or prompt corrective action directive issued by FDIC under section 8 of the FDI Act, the International Lending Supervision Act of 1983 (12 U.S.C. 3907), the Home Owners' Loan Act (12 U.S.C. 1464(t)(6)), or section 38 of the FDI Act, or any regulation thereunder, to meet and maintain a specific capital level for any capital measure.

(2) *Adequately capitalized* if the State savings association:

(i) Has a total risk-based capital ratio of 8.0 percent or greater; and

(ii) Has a Tier 1 risk-based capital ratio of 4.0 percent or greater; and

(iii) Has:

(A) A leverage ratio of 4.0 percent or greater; or

Federal Deposit Insurance Corporation § 390.454

(B) A leverage ratio of 3.0 percent or greater if the State savings association is assigned a composite rating of 1, as composite rating is defined in § 390.101(c); and

(iv) Does not meet the definition of a *well capitalized* State savings association.

(3) *Undercapitalized* if the State savings association:

(i) Has a total risk-based capital ratio that is less than 8.0 percent; or

(ii) Has a Tier 1 risk-based capital ratio that is less than 4.0 percent; or

(iii) (A) Except as provided in paragraph (b)(3)(iii)(B) of this section, has a leverage ratio that is less than 4.0 percent; or

(B) Has a leverage ratio that is less than 3.0 percent if the State savings association is assigned a composite rating of 1, as composite rating is defined in § 390.101(c).

(4) *Significantly undercapitalized* if the State savings association has:

(i) A total risk-based capital ratio that is less than 6.0 percent; or

(ii) A Tier 1 risk-based capital ratio that is less than 3.0 percent; or

(iii) A leverage ratio that is less than 3.0 percent.

(5) *Critically undercapitalized* if the State savings association has a ratio of tangible equity to total assets that is equal to or less than 2.0 percent.

(c) *Reclassification based on supervisory criteria other than capital.* The FDIC may reclassify a well capitalized State savings association as adequately capitalized and may require an adequately capitalized or undercapitalized State savings association to comply with certain mandatory or discretionary supervisory actions as if the State savings association were in the next lower capital category (except that the FDIC may not reclassify a significantly undercapitalized State savings association as critically undercapitalized) (each of these actions are hereinafter referred to generally as "reclassifications") in the following circumstances:

(1) *Unsafe or unsound condition.* The FDIC has determined, after notice and opportunity for hearing pursuant to § 390.457(a), that the State savings association is in an unsafe or unsound condition; or

(2) *Unsafe or unsound practice.* The FDIC has determined, after notice and an opportunity for hearing pursuant to § 390.457(a) that the State savings association received a less-than-satisfactory rating for any rating category (other than in a rating category specifically addressing capital adequacy) under the Uniform Financial Institutions Rating System,[1] or an equivalent rating under a comparable rating system adopted by the FDIC; and has not corrected the conditions that served as the basis for the less than satisfactory rating. Ratings under this paragraph (c)(2) refer to the most recent ratings (as determined either on-site or off-site by the most recent examination) of which the State savings association has been notified in writing.

§ 390.454 **Capital restoration plans.**

(a) *Schedule for filing plan*—(1) *In general.* A State savings association shall file a written capital restoration plan with the appropriate Regional Office within 45 days of the date that the State savings association receives notice or is deemed to have notice that the State savings association is undercapitalized, significantly undercapitalized, or critically undercapitalized, unless the FDIC notifies the State savings association in writing that the plan is to be filed within a different period. An adequately capitalized State savings association that has been required pursuant to § 390.453(c) to comply with supervisory actions as if the State savings association were undercapitalized is not required to submit a capital restoration plan solely by virtue of the reclassification.

(2) *Additional capital restoration plans.* Notwithstanding paragraph (a)(1) of this section, a State savings association that has already submitted and is operating under a capital restoration plan approved under section 38 and this subpart is not required to submit an additional capital restoration plan based on a revised calculation of its capital measures or a reclassification of the institution under § 390.453(c) unless the FDIC notifies the State savings association that it must submit a

---

[1] Copies are available at the address specified in § 390.108.

§ 390.454

new or revised capital plan. A State savings association that is notified that it must submit a new or revised capital restoration plan shall file the plan in writing with the appropriate Regional Office within 45 days of receiving such notice, unless the FDIC notifies the State savings association in writing that the plan is to be filed within a different period.

(b) *Contents of plan.* All financial data submitted in connection with a capital restoration plan shall be prepared in accordance with the instructions provided on the TFR, or Consolidated Reports of Condition or Income ("Call Report"), as applicable, unless the FDIC instructs otherwise. The capital restoration plan shall include all of the information required to be filed under section 38(e)(2) of the FDI Act. A State savings association that is required to submit a capital restoration plan as the result of a reclassification of the State savings association pursuant to § 390.453(c) shall include a description of the steps the State savings association will take to correct the unsafe or unsound condition or practice. No plan shall be accepted unless it includes any performance guarantee described in section 38(e)(2)(C) of the FDI Act by each company that controls the State savings association.

(c) *Review of capital restoration plans.* Within 60 days after receiving a capital restoration plan under this subpart, the FDIC shall provide written notice to the State savings association of whether the plan has been approved. The FDIC may extend the time within which notice regarding approval of a plan shall be provided.

(d) *Disapproval of capital plan.* If a capital restoration plan is not approved by the FDIC, the State savings association shall submit a revised capital restoration plan, when directed to do so, within the time specified by the FDIC. Upon receiving notice that its capital restoration plan has not been approved, any undercapitalized State savings association (as defined in § 390.453(b)(3)) shall be subject to all of the provisions of section 38 and this section applicable to significantly undercapitalized institutions. These provisions shall be applicable until such time as a new or revised capital restoration plan submitted by the State savings association has been approved by the FDIC.

(e) *Failure to submit a capital restoration plan.* A State savings association that is undercapitalized (as defined in § 390.453(b)(3)) and that fails to submit a written capital restoration plan within the period provided in this section shall, upon the expiration of that period, be subject to all of the provisions of section 38 and this subpart applicable to significantly undercapitalized institutions.

(f) *Failure to implement a capital restoration plan.* Any undercapitalized State savings association that fails in any material respect to implement a capital restoration plan shall be subject to all of the provisions of section 38 and this subpart applicable to significantly undercapitalized institutions.

(g) *Amendment of capital plan.* A State savings association that has filed an approved capital restoration plan may, after prior written notice to and approval by the FDIC, amend the plan to reflect a change in circumstance. Until such time as a proposed amendment has been approved, the State savings association shall implement the capital restoration plan as approved prior to the proposed amendment.

(h) [Reserved]

(i) *Performance guarantee by companies that control a State savings association—* (1) *Limitation on liability—*(i) *Amount limitation.* The aggregate liability under the guarantee provided under section 38 and this subpart for all companies that control a specific State savings association that is required to submit a capital restoration plan under this subpart shall be limited to the lesser of:

(A) An amount equal to 5.0 percent of the State savings association's total assets at the time the State savings association was notified or deemed to have notice that the State savings association was undercapitalized; or

(B) The amount necessary to restore the relevant capital measures of the State savings association to the levels required for the State savings association to be classified as adequately capitalized, as those capital measures and levels are defined at the time that the

State savings association initially fails to comply with a capital restoration plan under this subpart.

(ii) *Limit on duration.* The guarantee and limit of liability under section 38 and this subpart shall expire after the FDIC notifies the State savings association that it has remained adequately capitalized for each of four consecutive calendar quarters. The expiration or fulfillment by a company of a guarantee of a capital restoration plan shall not limit the liability of the company under any guarantee required or provided in connection with any capital restoration plan filed by the same State savings association after expiration of the first guarantee.

(iii) *Collection on guarantee.* Each company that controls a given State savings association shall be jointly and severally liable for the guarantee for such State savings association as required under section 38 and this subpart, and the FDIC may require and collect payment of the full amount of that guarantee from any or all of the companies issuing the guarantee.

(2) *Failure to provide guarantee.* In the event that a State savings association that is controlled by any company submits a capital restoration plan that does not contain the guarantee required under section 38(e)(2) of the FDI Act, the State savings association shall, upon submission of the plan, be subject to the provisions of section 38 and this subpart are applicable to State savings associations that have not submitted an acceptable capital restoration plan.

(3) *Failure to perform guarantee.* Failure by any company that controls a State savings association to perform fully its guarantee of any capital plan shall constitute a material failure to implement the plan for purposes of section 38(f) of the FDI Act. Upon such failure, the State savings association shall be subject to the provisions of section 38 and this subpart that are applicable to State savings associations that have failed in a material respect to implement a capital restoration plan.

§ 390.455 **Mandatory and discretionary supervisory actions under section 38.**

(a) *Mandatory supervisory actions*—(1) *Provisions applicable to all State savings associations.* All State savings associations are subject to the restrictions contained in section 38(d) of the FDI Act on payment of capital distributions and management fees.

(2) *Provisions applicable to undercapitalized, significantly undercapitalized, and critically undercapitalized State savings associations.* Immediately upon receiving notice or being deemed to have notice, as provided in § 390.452 or § 390.454, that the State savings association is undercapitalized, significantly undercapitalized, or critically undercapitalized, the State savings association shall become subject to the provisions of section 38 of the FDI Act:

(i) Restricting payment of capital distributions and management fees (section 38(d));

(ii) Requiring that the FDIC monitor the condition of the State savings association (section 38(e)(1));

(iii) Requiring submission of a capital restoration plan within the schedule established in this subpart (section 38(e)(2));

(iv) Restricting the growth of the State savings association's assets (section 38(e)(3)); and

(v) Requiring prior approval of certain expansion proposals (section 38(e)(4)).

(3) *Additional provisions applicable to significantly undercapitalized, and critically undercapitalized State savings associations.* In addition to the provisions of section 38 of the FDI Act described in paragraph (a)(2) of this section, immediately upon receiving notice or being deemed to have notice, as provided in § 390.452 or § 390.454, that the State savings association is significantly undercapitalized, or critically undercapitalized, or that the State savings association is subject to the provisions applicable to institutions that are significantly undercapitalized because the State savings association failed to submit or implement in any material respect an acceptable capital restoration plan, the State savings association shall become subject to the provisions

§ 390.456

of section 38 of the FDI Act that restrict compensation paid to senior executive officers of the institution (section 38(f)(4)).

(4) *Additional provisions applicable to critically undercapitalized State savings associations.* In addition to the provisions of section 38 of the FDI Act described in paragraphs (a)(2) and (a)(3) of this section, immediately upon receiving notice or being deemed to have notice, as provided in § 390.452 that the State savings association is critically undercapitalized, the State savings association shall become subject to the provisions of section 38 of the FDI Act:

(i) Restricting the activities of the State savings association (section 38(h)(1)); and

(ii) Restricting payments on subordinated debt of the State savings association (section 38(h)(2)).

(b) *Discretionary supervisory actions.* In taking any action under section 38 that is within the FDIC's discretion to take in connection with: A State savings association that is deemed to be undercapitalized, significantly undercapitalized or critically undercapitalized, or has been reclassified as undercapitalized, or significantly undercapitalized; an officer or director of such State savings association; or a company that controls such State savings association, the FDIC shall follow the procedures for issuing directives under §§ 390.456 and 390.458 unless otherwise provided in section 38 or this subpart.

§ 390.456 Directives to take prompt corrective action.

(a) *Notice of intent to issue a directive*—(1) *In general.* The FDIC shall provide an undercapitalized, significantly undercapitalized, or critically undercapitalized State savings association or, where appropriate, any company that controls the State savings association, prior written notice of the FDIC's intention to issue a directive requiring such State savings association or company to take actions or to follow proscriptions described in section 38 of the FDI Act that are within the FDIC's discretion to require or impose under section 38 of the FDI Act, including sections 38(e)(5), (f)(2), (f)(3), or (f)(5). The State savings association shall have such time to respond to a proposed directive as provided by the FDIC under paragraph (c) of this section.

(2) *Immediate issuance of final directive.* If the FDIC finds it necessary in order to carry out the purposes of section 38 of the FDI Act, the FDIC may, without providing the notice prescribed in paragraph (a)(1) of this section, issue a directive requiring a State savings association or any company that controls a State savings association immediately to take actions or to follow proscriptions described in section 38 that are within the FDIC's discretion to require or impose under section 38 of the FDI Act, including section 38(e)(5), (f)(2), (f)(3), or (f)(5). A State savings association or company that is subject to such an immediately effective directive may submit a written appeal of the directive to the FDIC. Such an appeal must be received by the FDIC within 14 calendar days of the issuance of the directive, unless the FDIC permits a longer period. The FDIC shall consider any such appeal, if filed in a timely matter, within 60 days of receiving the appeal. During such period of review, the directive shall remain in effect unless the FDIC, in its sole discretion, stays the effectiveness of the directive.

(b) *Contents of notice.* A notice of intention to issue a directive shall include:

(1) A statement of the State savings association's capital measures and capital levels;

(2) A description of the restrictions, prohibitions or affirmative actions that the FDIC proposes to impose or require;

(3) The proposed date when such restrictions or prohibitions would be effective or the proposed date for completion of such affirmative actions; and

(4) The date by which the State savings association or company subject to the directive may file with the FDIC a written response to the notice.

(c) *Response to notice*—(1) *Time for response.* A State savings association or company may file a written response to a notice of intent to issue a directive within the time period set by the FDIC. The date shall be at least 14 calendar days from the date of the notice unless

Federal Deposit Insurance Corporation § 390.457

the FDIC determines that a shorter period is appropriate in light of the financial condition of the State savings association or other relevant circumstances.

(2) *Content of response.* The response should include:

(i) An explanation why the action proposed by the FDIC is not an appropriate exercise of discretion under section 38;

(ii) Any recommended modification of the proposed directive; and

(iii) Any other relevant information, mitigating circumstances, documentation, or other evidence in support of the position of the State savings association or company regarding the proposed directive.

(d) *FDIC consideration of response.* After considering the response, the FDIC may:

(1) Issue the directive as proposed or in modified form;

(2) Determine not to issue the directive and so notify the State savings association or company; or

(3) Seek additional information or clarification of the response from the State savings association or company, or any other relevant source.

(e) *Failure to file response.* Failure by a State savings association or company to file with the FDIC, within the specified time period, a written response to a proposed directive shall constitute a waiver of the opportunity to respond and shall constitute consent to the issuance of the directive.

(f) *Request for modification or rescission of directive.* Any State savings association or company that is subject to a directive under this subpart, upon a change in circumstances, request in writing that the FDIC reconsider the terms of the directive, and may propose that the directive be rescinded or modified. Unless otherwise ordered by the FDIC, the directive shall continue in place while such request is pending before the FDIC.

§ 390.457 Procedures for reclassifying a State savings association based on criteria other than capital.

(a) *Reclassification based on unsafe or unsound condition or practice*—(1) *Issuance of notice of proposed reclassification*—(i) *Grounds for reclassification.*

(A) Pursuant to § 390.453(c), the FDIC may reclassify a well capitalized State savings association as adequately capitalized or subject an adequately capitalized or undercapitalized institution to the supervisory actions applicable to the next lower capital category if:

(1) The FDIC determines that the State savings association is in unsafe or unsound condition; or

(2) The FDIC deems the State savings association to be engaged in an unsafe or unsound practice and not to have corrected the deficiency.

(B) Any action pursuant to this paragraph (a)(1)(i) shall hereinafter be referred to as "reclassification."

(ii) *Prior notice to institution.* Prior to taking action pursuant to § 390.453(c)(1), the FDIC shall issue and serve on the State savings association a written notice of the FDIC's intention to reclassify the State savings association.

(2) *Contents of notice.* A notice of intention to reclassify a State savings association based on unsafe or unsound condition shall include:

(i) A statement of the State savings association's capital measures and capital levels and the category to which the State savings association would be reclassified;

(ii) The reasons for reclassification of the State savings association;

(iii) The date by which the State savings association subject to the notice of reclassification may file with the FDIC a written appeal of the proposed reclassification and a request for a hearing, which shall be at least 14 calendar days from the date of service of the notice unless the FDIC determines that a shorter period is appropriate in light of the financial condition of the State savings association or other relevant circumstances.

(3) *Response to notice of proposed reclassification.* A State savings association may file a written response to a notice of proposed reclassification within the time period set by the FDIC. The response should include:

(i) An explanation of why the State savings association is not in unsafe or unsound condition or otherwise should not be reclassified; and

(ii) Any other relevant information, mitigating circumstances, documentation, or other evidence in support of

§ 390.458

the position of the State savings association or company regarding the reclassification.

(4) *Failure to file response.* Failure by a State savings association to file, within the specified time period, a written response with the FDIC to a notice of proposed reclassification shall constitute a waiver of the opportunity to respond and shall constitute consent to the reclassification.

(5) *Request for hearing and presentation of oral testimony or witnesses.* The response may include a request for an informal hearing before the FDIC or its designee under this section. If the State savings association desires to present oral testimony or witnesses at the hearing, the State savings association shall include a request to do so with the request for an informal hearing. A request to present oral testimony or witnesses shall specify the names of the witnesses and the general nature of their expected testimony. Failure to request a hearing shall constitute a waiver of any right to a hearing, and failure to request the opportunity to present oral testimony or witnesses shall constitute a waiver of any right to present oral testimony or witnesses.

(6) *Order for informal hearing.* Upon receipt of a timely written request that includes a request for a hearing, the FDIC shall issue an order directing an informal hearing to commence no later than 30 days after receipt of the request, unless the FDIC allows further time at the request of the State savings association. The hearing shall be held in Washington, DC or at such other place as may be designated by the FDIC, before a presiding officer(s) designated by the FDIC to conduct the hearing.

(7) *Hearing procedures.* (i) The State savings association shall have the right to introduce relevant written materials and to present oral argument at the hearing. The State savings association may introduce oral testimony and present witnesses only if expressly authorized by the FDIC or the presiding officer(s). Neither the provisions of the Administrative Procedure Act (5 U.S.C. 554–557) governing adjudications required by statute to be determined on the record nor subpart C apply to an informal hearing under this section unless the FDIC orders that such procedures shall apply.

(ii) The informal hearing shall be recorded and a transcript furnished to the State savings association upon request and payment of the cost thereof. Witnesses need not be sworn, unless specifically requested by a party or the presiding officer(s). The presiding officer(s) may ask questions of any witness.

(iii) The presiding officer(s) may order that the hearing be continued for a reasonable period (normally five business days) following completion of oral testimony or argument to allow additional written submissions to the hearing record.

(8) *Recommendation of presiding officers.* Within 20 calendar days following the date the hearing and the record on the proceeding are closed, the presiding officer(s) shall make a recommendation to the FDIC on the reclassification.

(9) *Time for decision.* Not later than 60 calendar days after the date the record is closed or the date of the response in a case where no hearing was requested, the FDIC will decide whether to reclassify the State savings association and notify the State savings association of the FDIC's decision.

(b) *Request for rescission of reclassification.* Any State savings association that has been reclassified under this section, may, upon a change in circumstances, request in writing that the FDIC reconsider the reclassification, and may propose that the reclassification be rescinded and that any directives issued in connection with the reclassification be modified, rescinded, or removed. Unless otherwise ordered by the FDIC, the State savings association shall remain subject to the reclassification and to any directives issued in connection with that reclassification while such request is pending before the FDIC.

§ 390.458 **Order to dismiss a director or senior executive officer.**

(a) *Service of notice.* When the FDIC issues and serves a directive on a State savings association pursuant to § 390.456 requiring the State savings association

Federal Deposit Insurance Corporation § 390.458

to dismiss any director or senior executive officer under section 38(f)(2)(F)(ii) of the FDI Act, the FDIC shall also serve a copy of the directive, or the relevant portions of the directive where appropriate, upon the person to be dismissed.

(b) *Response to directive*—(1) *Request for reinstatement.* A director or senior executive officer who has been served with a directive under paragraph (a) of this section (Respondent) may file a written request for reinstatement. The request for reinstatement shall be filed within 10 calendar days of the receipt of the directive by the Respondent, unless further time is allowed by the FDIC at the request of the Respondent.

(2) *Contents of request; informal hearing.* The request for reinstatement should include reasons why the Respondent should be reinstated, and may include a request for an informal hearing before the FDIC or its designee under this section. If the Respondent desires to present oral testimony or witnesses at the hearing, the Respondent shall include a request to do so with the request for an informal hearing. The request to present oral testimony or witnesses shall specify the names of the witnesses and the general nature of their expected testimony. Failure to request a hearing shall constitute a waiver of any right to a hearing and failure to request the opportunity to present oral testimony or witnesses shall constitute a waiver of any right or opportunity to present oral testimony or witnesses.

(3) *Effective date.* Unless otherwise ordered by the FDIC, the dismissal shall remain in effect while a request for reinstatement is pending.

(c) *Order for informal hearing.* Upon receipt of a timely written request from a Respondent for an informal hearing on the portion of a directive requiring a State savings association to dismiss from office any director or senior executive officer, the FDIC shall issue an order directing an informal hearing to commence no later than 30 days after receipt of the request, unless the Respondent requests a later date. The hearing shall be held in Washington, DC, or at such other place as may be designated by the FDIC, before a presiding officer(s) designated by the FDIC to conduct the hearing.

(d) *Hearing procedures.* (1) A Respondent may appear at the hearing personally or through counsel. A Respondent shall have the right to introduce relevant written materials and to present oral argument. A Respondent may introduce oral testimony and present witnesses only if expressly authorized by the FDIC or the presiding officer(s). Neither the provisions of the Administrative Procedure Act governing adjudications required by statute to be determined on the record nor subpart C apply to an informal hearing under this section unless the FDIC orders that such procedures shall apply.

(2) The informal hearing shall be recorded and a transcript furnished to the Respondent upon request and payment of the cost thereof. Witnesses need not be sworn, unless specifically requested by a party or the presiding officer(s). The presiding officer(s) may ask questions of any witness.

(3) The presiding officer(s) may order that the hearing be continued for a reasonable period (normally five business days) following completion of oral testimony or argument to allow additional written submissions to the hearing record.

(e) *Standard for review.* A Respondent shall bear the burden of demonstrating that his or her continued employment by or service with the State savings association would materially strengthen the State savings association's ability:

(1) To become adequately capitalized, to the extent that the directive was issued as a result of the State savings association's capital level or failure to submit or implement a capital restoration plan; and

(2) To correct the unsafe or unsound condition or unsafe or unsound practice, to the extent that the directive was issued as a result of classification of the State savings association based on supervisory criteria other than capital, pursuant to section 38(g) of the FDI Act.

(f) *Recommendation of presiding officers.* Within 20 calendar days following the date the hearing and the record on the proceeding are closed, the presiding

§ 390.459

officer(s) shall make a recommendation to the FDIC concerning the Respondent's request for reinstatement with the State savings association.

(g) *Time for decision.* Not later than 60 calendar days after the date the record is closed or the date of the response in a case where no hearing has been requested, the FDIC shall grant or deny the request for reinstatement and notify the Respondent of the FDIC's decision. If the FDIC denies the request for reinstatement, the FDIC shall set forth in the notification the reasons for the FDIC's action.

§ 390.459 Enforcement of directives.

(a) *Judicial remedies.* Whenever a State savings association or company that controls a State savings association fails to comply with a directive issued under section 38, the FDIC may seek enforcement of the directive in the appropriate United States district court pursuant to section 8(i)(1) of the FDI Act.

(b) *Administrative remedies*—(1) *Failure to comply with directive.* Pursuant to section 8(i)(2)(A) of the FDI Act, the FDIC may assess a civil money penalty against any State savings association or company that controls a State savings association that violates or otherwise fails to comply with any final directive issued under section 38 and against any institution-affiliated party who participates in such violation or noncompliance.

(2) *Failure to implement capital restoration plan.* The failure of a State savings association to implement a capital restoration plan required under section 38, or this subpart, or the failure of a company having control of a State savings association to fulfill a guarantee of a capital restoration plan made pursuant to section 38(e)(2) of the FDI Act shall subject the State savings association or company to the assessment of civil money penalties pursuant to section 8(i)(2)(A) of the FDI Act.

(c) *Other enforcement action.* In addition to the actions described in paragraphs (a) and (b) of this section, the FDIC may seek enforcement of the provisions of section 38 or this subpart through any other judicial or administrative proceeding authorized by law.

Subpart Z—Capital

§ 390.460 Scope.

(a) This subpart prescribes the minimum regulatory capital requirements for State savings associations. The subpart applies to State savings associations, except as described in paragraph (b) of this section.

(b)(1) A State savings association that uses appendix A must comply with the minimum qualifying criteria for internal risk measurement and management processes for calculating risk-based capital requirements, utilize the methodologies for calculating risk-based capital requirements, and make the required disclosures described in that appendix.

(2) Sections 390.461 through 390.471 do not apply to the computation of risk-based capital requirements by a State savings association that uses appendix A of this subpart. However, these State savings associations:

(i) Must compute the components of capital under § 390.465, subject to the modifications in sections 11 and 12 of appendix A of this subpart.

(ii) Must meet the leverage ratio requirement at §§ 390.462(a)(2) and 390.467 with tier 1 capital, as computed under sections 11 and 12 of appendix A of this subpart.

(iii) Must meet the tangible capital requirement described at §§ 390.462(a)(3) and 390.468.

(iv) Are subject to §§ 390.463 (individual minimum capital requirement), 390.464 (capital directives); and 390.469 (consequences of failure to meet capital requirements).

(v) Are subject to the reservations of authority at § 390.470, which supplement the reservations of authority at section 1 of appendix A of this subpart.

§ 390.461 Definitions.

For the purposes of this subpart:

Adjusted total assets. The term *adjusted total assets* means:

(1) A State savings association's total assets as that term is defined in this section;

(2) Plus

(i) The prorated assets of any includable subsidiary in which the State savings association has a minority ownership interest that is not consolidated

Federal Deposit Insurance Corporation § 390.461

under generally accepted accounting principles; and

(ii) The remaining goodwill (FSLIC Capital Contributions) resulting from prior regulatory accounting practices as provided in the definition of *qualifying supervisory goodwill* in this section;

(3) Minus

(i) Assets not included in the applicable capital standard except for those subject to paragraphs (3)(ii) and (3)(iii) of this definition;

(ii) Investments in any includable subsidiary in which a State savings association has a minority interest;

(iii) Investments in any subsidiary subject to consolidation under paragraph (2)(ii) of this definition; and

(iv) For purposes of determining core capital, qualifying supervisory goodwill.

Asset-backed commercial paper program. The term *asset-backed commercial paper program* (ABCP program) means a program that primarily issues commercial paper that has received a credit rating from an NRSRO and that is backed by assets or other exposures held in a bankruptcy-remote special purpose entity. The term *sponsor* of an ABCP program means a State savings association that:

(1) Establishes an ABCP program;

(2) Approves the sellers permitted to participate in an ABCP program;

(3) Approves the asset pools to be purchased by an ABCP program; or

(4) Administers the ABCP program by monitoring the assets, arranging for debt placement, compiling monthly reports, or ensuring compliance with the program documents and with the program's credit and investment policy.

Cash items in the process of collection. The term *cash items in the process of collection* means checks or drafts in the process of collection that are drawn on another depository institution, including a central bank, and that are payable immediately upon presentation; U.S. Government checks that are drawn on the United States Treasury or any other U.S. Government or Government-sponsored agency and that are payable immediately upon presentation; broker's security drafts and commodity or bill-of-lading drafts payable immediately upon presentation; and unposted debits.

Commitment. The term *commitment* means any arrangement that obligates a State savings association to:

(1) Purchase loans or securities;

(2) Extend credit in the form of loans or leases, participations in loans or leases, overdraft facilities, revolving credit facilities, home equity lines of credit, eligible ABCP liquidity facilities, or similar transactions.

Common stockholders' equity. The term *common stockholders' equity* means common stock, common stock surplus, retained earnings, and adjustments for the cumulative effect of foreign currency translation, less net unrealized losses on available-for-sale equity securities with readily determinable fair values.

Conditional guarantee. The term *conditional guarantee* means a contingent obligation of the United States Government or its agencies, the validity of which to the beneficiary is dependent upon some affirmative action—*e.g.*, servicing requirements—on the part of the beneficiary of the guarantee or a third party.

Credit derivative. The term *credit derivative* means a contract that allows one party (the protection purchaser) to transfer the credit risk of an asset or off-balance sheet credit exposure to another party (the protection provider). The value of a credit derivative is dependent, at least in part, on the credit performance of a "referenced asset."

Credit-enhancing interest-only strip. (1) The term *credit-enhancing interest-only strip* means an on-balance sheet asset that, in form or in substance:

(i) Represents the contractual right to receive some or all of the interest due on transferred assets; and

(ii) Exposes the State savings association to credit risk directly or indirectly associated with the transferred assets that exceeds its *pro rata* share of the State savings association's claim on the assets whether through subordination provisions or other credit enhancement techniques.

(2) The FDIC reserves the right to identify other cash flows or related interests as a credit-enhancing interest-only strip. In determining whether a particular interest cash flow functions

889

as a credit-enhancing interest-only strip, the FDIC will consider the economic substance of the transaction.

Credit-enhancing representations and warranties. (1) The term *credit-enhancing representations and warranties* means representations and warranties that are made or assumed in connection with a transfer of assets (including loan servicing assets) and that obligate a State savings association to protect investors from losses arising from credit risk in the assets transferred or loans serviced.

(2) Credit-enhancing representations and warranties include promises to protect a party from losses resulting from the default or nonperformance of another party or from an insufficiency in the value of the collateral.

(3) Credit-enhancing representations and warranties do not include:

(i) Early-default clauses and similar warranties that permit the return of, or premium refund clauses covering, qualifying mortgage loans for a period not to exceed 120 days from the date of transfer. These warranties may cover only those loans that were originated within one year of the date of the transfer;

(ii) Premium refund clauses covering assets guaranteed, in whole or in part, by the United States government, a United States government agency, or a United States government-sponsored enterprise, provided the premium refund clause is for a period not to exceed 120 days from the date of transfer; or

(iii) Warranties that permit the return of assets in instances of fraud, misrepresentation or incomplete documentation.

Depository institution. The term *domestic depository institution* means a financial institution that engages in the business of banking; that is recognized as a bank by the bank supervisory or monetary authorities of the country of its incorporation and the country of its principal banking operations; that receives deposits to a substantial extent in the regular course of business; and that has the power to accept demand deposits. In the United States, this definition encompasses all federally insured offices of commercial banks, mutual and stock savings banks, savings or building and loan associations (stock and mutual), cooperative banks, credit unions, and international banking facilities of domestic depository institutions. Bank holding companies and savings and loan holding companies are excluded from this definition. For the purposes of assigning risk weights, the differentiation between OECD depository institutions and non-OECD depository institutions is based on the country of incorporation. Claims on branches and agencies of foreign banks located in the United States are to be categorized on the basis of the parent bank's country of incorporation.

Direct credit substitute. The term *direct credit substitute* means an arrangement in which a State savings association assumes, in form or in substance, credit risk associated with an on- or off-balance sheet asset or exposure that was not previously owned by the State savings association (third-party asset) and the risk assumed by the State savings association exceeds the *pro rata* share of the State savings association's interest in the third-party asset. If a State savings association has no claim on the third-party asset, then the State savings association's assumption of any credit risk is a direct credit substitute. Direct credit substitutes include:

(1) Financial standby letters of credit that support financial claims on a third party that exceed a State savings association's *pro rata* share in the financial claim;

(2) Guarantees, surety arrangements, credit derivatives, and similar instruments backing financial claims that exceed a State savings association's *pro rata* share in the financial claim;

(3) Purchased subordinated interests that absorb more than their *pro rata* share of losses from the underlying assets;

(4) Credit derivative contracts under which the State savings association assumes more than its *pro rata* share of credit risk on a third-party asset or exposure;

(5) Loans or lines of credit that provide credit enhancement for the financial obligations of a third party;

(6) Purchased loan servicing assets if the servicer is responsible for credit

Federal Deposit Insurance Corporation § 390.461

losses or if the servicer makes or assumes credit-enhancing representations and warranties with respect to the loans serviced. Servicer cash advances as defined in this section are not direct credit substitutes;

(7) Clean-up calls on third party assets. However, clean-up calls that are 10 percent or less of the original pool balance and that are exercisable at the option of the State savings association are not direct credit substitutes; and

(8) Liquidity facilities that provide support to asset-backed commercial paper (other than eligible ABCP liquidity facilities).

Eligible ABCP liquidity facility. The term *eligible ABCP liquidity facility* means a liquidity facility that supports asset-backed commercial paper, in form or in substance, and that meets the following criteria:

(1)(i) At the time of the draw, the liquidity facility must be subject to an asset quality test that precludes funding against assets that are 90 days or more past due or in default; and

(ii) If the assets that the liquidity facility is required to fund against are assets or exposures that have received a credit rating by a NRSRO at the time the inception of the facility, the facility can be used to fund only those assets or exposures that are rated investment grade by an NRSRO at the time of funding; or

(2) If the assets that are funded under the liquidity facility do not meet the criteria described in paragraph (1) of this definition, the assets must be guaranteed, conditionally or unconditionally, by the United States Government, its agencies, or the central government of an OECD country.

Eligible State savings association. (1) The term *eligible State savings association* means a State savings association with respect to which the FDIC has determined, on the basis of information available at the time, that:

(i) The State savings association's management appears to be competent;

(ii) The State savings association, as certified by its Board of Directors, is in substantial compliance with all applicable statutes, regulations, orders and written agreements and directives; and

(iii) The State savings association's management, as certified by its Board of Directors, has not engaged in insider dealing, speculative practices, or any other activities that have or may jeopardize the association's safety and soundness or contributed to impairing the association's capital.

(2) State savings associations, for purposes of this paragraph, will be deemed to be eligible unless the FDIC makes a determination otherwise or notifies the State savings association of its intent to conduct either an informal or formal examination to determine eligibility and provides written notification thereof to the State savings association.

Equity investments. (1) The term *equity investments* includes investments in equity securities and real property that would be considered an equity investment under generally accepted accounting principles.

(2)(i) The term *equity securities* means any:

(A) Stock, certificate of interest of participation in any profit-sharing agreement, collateral trust certificate or subscription, preorganization certificate or subscription, transferable share, investment contract, or voting trust certificate; or

(B) In general, any interest or instrument commonly known as an equity security; or

(C) Loans having profit sharing features which generally accepted accounting principles would reclassify as equity securities; or

(D) Any security immediately convertible at the option of the holder without payment of substantial additional consideration into such a security; or

(E) Any security carrying any warrant or right to subscribe to or purchase such a security; or

(F) Any certificate of interest or participation in, temporary or Interim certificate for, or receipt for any of the foregoing or any partnership interest; or

(G) Investments in equity securities and loans or advances to and guarantees issued on behalf of partnerships or joint ventures in which a State savings association holds an interest in real property under generally accepted accounting principles.

§ 390.461

(ii) The term *equity securities* does not include investments in a subsidiary as that term is defined in this section, equity investments that are permissible for national banks, ownership interests in pools of assets that are risk-weighted in accordance with § 390.466(a)(1)(vi), or the stock of Federal Home Loan Banks or Federal Reserve Banks.

(3) For purposes of this subpart, the term *equity investments in real property* does not include interests in real property that are primarily used or intended to be used by the State savings association, its subsidiaries, or its affiliates as offices or related facilities for the conduct of its business.

(4) In addition, for purposes of this part, the term *equity investments in real property* does not include interests in real property that are acquired in satisfaction of a debt previously contracted in good faith or acquired in sales under judgments, decrees, or mortgages held by the State savings association, provided that the property is not intended to be held for real estate investment purposes but is expected to be disposed of within five years or a longer period approved by the FDIC.

Exchange rate contracts. The term *exchange rate contracts* includes cross-currency interest rate swaps; forward foreign exchange rate contracts; currency options purchased; and any similar instrument that, in the opinion of the FDIC, may give rise to similar risks.

Face amount. The term *face amount* means the notational principal, or face value, amount of an off-balance sheet item or the amortized cost of an on-balance sheet asset.

Financial asset. The term *financial asset* means cash or other monetary instrument, evidence of debt, evidence of an ownership interest in an entity, or a contract that conveys a right to receive or exchange cash or another financial instrument from another party.

Financial standby letter of credit. The term *financial standby letter of credit* means a letter of credit or similar arrangement that represents an irrevocable obligation to a third-party beneficiary:

(1) To repay money borrowed by, or advanced to, or for the account of, a second party (the account party); or

(2) To make payment on behalf of the account party, in the event that the account party fails to fulfill its obligation to the beneficiary.

Includable subsidiary. The term *includable subsidiary* means a subsidiary of a State savings association that is:

(1) Engaged solely in activities not impermissible for a national bank;

(2) Engaged in activities not permissible for a national bank, but only if acting solely as agent for its customers and such agency position is clearly documented in the State savings association's files;

(3) Engaged solely in mortgage-banking activities;

(4)(i) Itself an insured depository institution or a company the sole investment of which is an insured depository institution, and

(ii) Was acquired by the parent State savings association prior to May 1, 1989; or

(5) A subsidiary of any Federal savings association existing as a Federal savings association on August 9, 1989 that

(i) Was chartered prior to October 15, 1982, as a savings bank or a cooperative bank under State law, or

(ii) Acquired its principal assets from an association that was chartered prior to October 15, 1982, as a savings bank or a cooperative bank under State law.

Intangible assets. The term *intangible assets* means assets considered to be intangible assets under generally accepted accounting principles. These assets include, but are not limited to, goodwill, core deposit premiums, purchased credit card relationships, favorable leaseholds, and servicing assets (mortgage and non-mortgage). Interest-only strips receivable and other nonsecurity financial instruments are not intangible assets under this definition.

Interest-rate contracts. The term *interest-rate contracts* includes single currency interest-rate swaps; basis swaps; forward rate agreements; interest-rate options purchased; forward deposits accepted; and any other instrument that, in the opinion of the FDIC, may give rise to similar risks, including when-issued securities.

Federal Deposit Insurance Corporation § 390.461

Liquidity facility. The term *liquidity facility* means a legally binding commitment to provide liquidity support to asset-backed commercial paper by lending to, or purchasing assets from any structure, program or conduit in the event that funds are required to repay maturing asset-backed commercial paper.

Mortgage-related securities. The term *mortgage-related securities* means any mortgage-related qualifying securities under section 3(a)(41) of the Securities Exchange Act of 1934, 15 U.S.C. 78c(a)(41), *Provided,* That the rating requirements of that section shall not be considered for purposes of this definition.

Nationally recognized statistical rating organization (NRSRO). The term *nationally recognized statistical rating organization* means an entity recognized by the Division of Market Regulation of the Securities and Exchange Commission (Commission) as a nationally recognized statistical rating organization for various purposes, including the Commission's uniform net capital requirements for brokers and dealers.

OECD-based country. The term *OECD-based country* means a member of that grouping of countries that are full members of the Organization for Economic Cooperation and Development (OECD) plus countries that have concluded special lending arrangements with the International Monetary Fund (IMF) associated with the IMF's General Arrangements to Borrow. This term excludes any country that has rescheduled its external sovereign debt within the previous five years. A rescheduling of external sovereign debt generally would include any renegotiation of terms arising from a country's inability or unwillingness to meet its external debt service obligations, but generally would not include renegotiations of debt in the normal course of business, such as a renegotiation to allow the borrower to take advantage of a decline in interest rates or other change in market conditions.

Original maturity. The term *original maturity* means, with respect to a commitment, the earliest date after a commitment is made on which the commitment is scheduled to expire (*i.e.,* it will reach its stated maturity and cease to be binding on either party), *Provided,* That either:

(i) The commitment is not subject to extension or renewal and will actually expire on its stated expiration date; or

(ii) If the commitment is subject to extension or renewal beyond its stated expiration date, the stated expiration date will be deemed the original maturity only if the extension or renewal must be based upon terms and conditions independently negotiated in good faith with the customer at the time of the extension or renewal and upon a new, *bona fide* credit analysis utilizing current information on financial condition and trends.

Performance-based standby letter of credit. The term *performance-based standby letter of credit* means any letter of credit, or similar arrangement, however named or described, which represents an irrevocable obligation to the beneficiary on the part of the issuer to make payment on account of any default by a third party in the performance of a nonfinancial or commercial obligation. Such letters of credit include arrangements backing subcontractors' and suppliers' performance, labor and materials contracts, and construction bids.

Perpetual preferred stock. The term *perpetual preferred stock* means preferred stock without a fixed maturity date that cannot be redeemed at the option of the holder, and that has no other provisions that will require future redemption of the issue. For purposes of these instruments, preferred stock that can be redeemed at the option of the holder is deemed to have an "original maturity" of the earliest possible date on which it may be so redeemed. Cumulative perpetual preferred stock is preferred stock where the dividends accumulate from one period to the next. Noncumulative perpetual preferred stock is preferred stock where the unpaid dividends are not carried over to subsequent dividend periods.

Problem institution. The term *problem institution* means a State savings association that, at the time of its acquisition, merger, purchase of assets or other business combination with or by another State savings association:

§ 390.461

(1) Was subject to special regulatory controls by its primary Federal or state regulatory authority;

(2) Posed particular supervisory concerns to its primary Federal or state regulatory authority; or

(3) Failed to meet its regulatory capital requirement immediately before the transaction.

Prorated assets. The term *prorated assets* means the total assets (as determined in the most recently available GAAP report but in no event more than one year old) of a subsidiary (including those subsidiaries where the State savings association has a minority interest) multiplied by the State savings association's percentage of ownership of that subsidiary.

Qualifying mortgage loan. (1) The term *qualifying mortgage loan* means a loan that:

(i) Is fully secured by a first lien on a one-to four-family residential property;

(ii) Is underwritten in accordance with prudent underwriting standards, including standards relating the ratio of the loan amount to the value of the property (LTV ratio). See Appendix to 12 CFR 390.265. A nonqualifying mortgage loan that is paid down to an appropriate LTV ratio (calculated using value at origination) may become a qualifying loan if it meets all other requirements of this definition;

(iii) Maintains an appropriate LTV ratio based on the amortized principal balance of the loan; and

(iv) Is performing and is not more than 90 days past due.

(2) If a State savings association holds the first and junior lien(s) on a residential property and no other party holds an intervening lien, the transaction is treated as a single loan secured by a first lien for the purposes of determining the LTV ratio and the appropriate risk weight under § 390.466(a).

(3) A loan to an individual borrower for the construction of the borrower's home may be included as a qualifying mortgage loan.

(4) A loan that meets the requirements of this section prior to modification on a permanent or trial basis under the U.S. Department of Treasury's Home Affordable Mortgage Program may be included as a *qualifying mortgage loan,* so long as the loan is not 90 days or more past due.

Qualifying multifamily mortgage loan. (1) The term *qualifying multifamily mortgage loan* means a loan secured by a first lien on multifamily residential properties consisting of 5 or more dwelling units, provided that:

(i) The amortization of principal and interest occurs over a period of not more than 30 years;

(ii) The original minimum maturity for repayment of principal on the loan is not less than seven years;

(iii) When considering the loan for placement in a lower risk-weight category, all principal and interest payments have been made on a timely basis in accordance with its terms for the preceding year;

(iv) The loan is performing and not 90 days or more past due;

(v) The loan is made by the State savings association in accordance with prudent underwriting standards; and

(vi) If the interest rate on the loan does not change over the term of the loan:

(A) The current loan balance amount does not exceed 80 percent of the value of the property securing the loan; and

(B) For the property's most recent fiscal year, the ratio of annual net operating income generated by the property (before payment of any debt service on the loan) to annual debt service on the loan is not less than 120 percent, or in the case of cooperative or other not-for-profit housing projects, the property generates sufficient cash flows to provide comparable protection to the institution; or

(vii) If the interest rate on the loan changes over the term of the loan:

(A) The current loan balance amount does not exceed 75 percent of the value of the property securing the loan; and

(B) For the property's most recent fiscal year, the ratio of annual net operating income generated by the property (before payment of any debt service on the loan) to annual debt service on the loan is not less than 115 percent, or in the case of cooperative or other not-for-profit housing projects, the property generates sufficient cash flows to provide comparable protection to the institution.

Federal Deposit Insurance Corporation § 390.461

(2) The term *qualifying multifamily mortgage loan* also includes a multifamily mortgage loan that on March 18, 1994 was a first mortgage loan on an existing property consisting of 5–36 dwelling units with an initial loan-to-value ratio of not more than 80% where an average annual occupancy rate of 80% or more of total units had existed for at least one year, and continues to meet these criteria.

(3) For purposes of paragraphs (1)(vi) and (vii) of this definition, the term *value of the property* means, at origination of a loan to purchase a multifamily property: the lower of the purchase price or the amount of the initial appraisal, or if appropriate, the initial evaluation. In cases not involving the purchase of a multifamily loan, the *value of the property* is determined by the most current appraisal, or if appropriate, the most current evaluation.

(4) In cases where a borrower refinances a loan on an existing property, as an alternative to paragraphs (1)(iii), (vi), and (vii) of this definition:

(i) All principal and interest payments on the loan being refinanced have been made on a timely basis in accordance with the terms of that loan for the preceding year; and

(ii) The net income on the property for the preceding year would support timely principal and interest payments on the new loan in accordance with the applicable debt service requirement.

Qualifying residential construction loan. (1) The term *qualifying residential construction loan*, also referred to as a residential bridge loan, means a loan made in accordance with sound lending principles satisfying the following criteria:

(i) The builder must have substantial project equity in the home construction project;

(ii) The residence being constructed must be a 1–4 family residence sold to a home purchaser;

(iii) The lending State savings association must obtain sufficient documentation from a permanent lender (which may be the construction lender) demonstrating that:

(A) The home buyer intends to purchase the residence; and

(B) Has the ability to obtain a permanent qualifying mortgage loan sufficient to purchase the residence;

(iv) The home purchaser must have made a substantial earnest money deposit;

(v) The construction loan must not exceed 80 percent of the sales price of the residence;

(vi) The construction loan must be secured by a first lien on the lot, residence under construction, and other improvements;

(vii) The lending State savings association must retain sufficient undisbursed loan funds throughout the construction period to ensure project completion;

(viii) The builder must incur a significant percentage of direct costs (*i.e.*, the actual costs of land, labor, and material) before any drawdown on the loan;

(ix) If at any time during the life of the construction loan any of the criteria of this rule are no longer satisfied, the State savings association must immediately recategorize the loan at a 100 percent risk-weight and must accurately report the loan in the State savings association's next quarterly Thrift Financial Report or Consolidated Reports of Condition or Income ("Call Report"), as applicable;

(x) The home purchaser must intend that the home will be owner-occupied;

(xi) The home purchaser(s) must be an individual(s), not a partnership, joint venture, trust corporation, or any other entity (including an entity acting as a sole proprietorship) that is purchasing the home(s) for speculative purposes; and

(xii) The loan must be performing and not more than 90 days past due.

(2) The documentation for each loan and home sale must be sufficient to demonstrate compliance with the criteria in paragraph (1) of this definition. The FDIC retains the discretion to determine that any loans not meeting sound lending principles must be placed in a higher risk-weight category. The FDIC also reserves the discretion to modify these criteria on a case-by-case basis provided that any such modifications are not inconsistent with the safety and soundness objectives of this definition.

§ 390.461

Qualifying securities firm. The term *qualifying securities firm* means:

(1) A securities firm incorporated in the United States that is a broker-dealer that is registered with the Securities and Exchange Commission (SEC) and that complies with the SEC's net capital regulations (17 CFR 240.15c3(1)); and

(2) A securities firm incorporated in any other OECD-based country, if the State savings association is able to demonstrate that the securities firm is subject to consolidated supervision and regulation (covering its subsidiaries, but not necessarily its parent organizations) comparable to that imposed on depository institutions in OECD countries. Such regulation must include risk-based capital requirements comparable to those imposed on depository institutions under the Accord on International Convergence of Capital Measurement and Capital Standards (1988, as amended in 1998).

Reciprocal holdings of depository institution instruments. The term *reciprocal holdings of depository institution instruments* means cross-holdings or other formal or informal arrangements in which two or more depository institutions swap, exchange, or otherwise agree to hold each other's capital instruments. This definition does not include holdings of capital instruments issued by other depository institutions that were taken in satisfaction of debts previously contracted, provided that the reporting State savings association has not held such instruments for more than five years or a longer period approved by the FDIC.

Recourse. The term *recourse* means a State savings association's retention, in form or in substance, of any credit risk directly or indirectly associated with an asset it has sold (in accordance with generally accepted accounting principles) that exceeds a *pro rata* share of that State savings association's claim on the asset. If a State savings association has no claim on an asset it has sold, then the retention of any credit risk is recourse. A recourse obligation typically arises when a State savings association transfers assets in a sale and retains an explicit obligation to repurchase assets or to absorb losses due to a default on the payment of principal or interest or any other deficiency in the performance of the underlying obligor or some other party. Recourse may also exist implicitly if a State savings association provides credit enhancement beyond any contractual obligation to support assets it has sold. Recourse obligations include:

(1) Credit-enhancing representations and warranties made on transferred assets;

(2) Loan servicing assets retained pursuant to an agreement under which the State savings association will be responsible for losses associated with the loans serviced. Servicer cash advances as defined in this section are not recourse obligations;

(3) Retained subordinated interests that absorb more than their *pro rata* share of losses from the underlying assets;

(4) Assets sold under an agreement to repurchase, if the assets are not already included on the balance sheet;

(5) Loan strips sold without contractual recourse where the maturity of the transferred portion of the loan is shorter than the maturity of the commitment under which the loan is drawn;

(6) Credit derivatives that absorb more than the State savings association's pro rata share of losses from the transferred assets;

(7) Clean-up calls on assets the State savings association has sold. However, clean-up calls that are 10 percent or less of the original pool balance and that are exercisable at the option of the State savings association are not recourse arrangements; and

(8) Liquidity facilities that provide support to asset-backed commercial paper (other than eligible ABCP liquidity facilities).

Replacement cost. The term *replacement cost* means, with respect to interest rate and exchange-rate contracts, the loss that would be incurred in the event of a counterparty default, as measured by the net cost of replacing the contract at the current market value. If default would result in a theoretical profit, the replacement value is considered to be zero. This mark-to-market process must incorporate

Federal Deposit Insurance Corporation § 390.461

changes in both interest rates and counterparty credit quality.

Residential properties. The term *residential properties* means houses, condominiums, cooperative units, and manufactured homes. This definition does not include boats or motor homes, even if used as a primary residence, or timeshare properties.

Residual characteristics. The term *residual characteristics* means interests similar to a multi-class pay-through obligation representing the excess cash flow generated from mortgage collateral over the amount required for the issue's debt service and ongoing administrative expenses or interests presenting similar degrees of interest-rate/prepayment risk and principal loss risks.

Residual interest. (1) The term *residual interest* means any on-balance sheet asset that:

(i) Represents an interest (including a beneficial interest) created by a transfer that qualifies as a sale (in accordance with generally accepted accounting principles) of financial assets, whether through a securitization or otherwise; and

(ii) Exposes a State savings association to credit risk directly or indirectly associated with the transferred asset that exceeds a *pro rata* share of that State savings association's claim on the asset, whether through subordination provisions or other credit enhancement techniques.

(2) Residual interests generally include credit-enhancing interest-only strips, spread accounts, cash collateral accounts, retained subordinated interests (and other forms of overcollateralization), and similar assets that function as a credit enhancement.

(3) Residual interests further include those exposures that, in substance, cause the State savings association to retain the credit risk of an asset or exposure that had qualified as a residual interest before it was sold.

(4) Residual interests generally do not include assets purchased from a third party. However, a credit-enhancing interest-only strip that is acquired in any asset transfer is a residual interest.

Risk participation. The term *risk participation* means a participation in which the originating party remains liable to the beneficiary for the full amount of an obligation (*e.g.*, a direct credit substitute), notwithstanding that another party has acquired a participation in that obligation.

Risk-weighted assets. The term *risk-weighted assets* means the sum total of risk-weighted on-balance sheet assets and the total of risk-weighted off-balance sheet credit equivalent amounts. These assets are calculated in accordance with § 390.466.

Securitization. The term *securitization* means the pooling and repackaging by a special purpose entity of assets or other credit exposures that can be sold to investors. *Securitization* includes transactions that create stratified credit risk positions whose performance is dependent upon an underlying pool of credit exposures, including loans and commitments.

Servicer cash advance. The term *servicer cash advance* means funds that a residential mortgage servicer advances to ensure an uninterrupted flow of payments, including advances made to cover foreclosure costs or other expenses to facilitate the timely collection of the loan. A servicer cash advance is not a recourse obligation or a direct credit substitute if:

(1) The servicer is entitled to full reimbursement and this right is not subordinated to other claims on the cash flows from the underlying asset pool; or

(2) For any one loan, the servicer's obligation to make nonreimbursable advances is contractually limited to an insignificant amount of the outstanding principal amount on that loan.

State. The term *State* means any one of the several states of the United States of America, the District of Columbia, Puerto Rico, and the territories and possessions of the United States.

Structured financing program. The term *structured financing program* means a program where receivable interests and asset- or mortgage-backed

§ 390.462

securities issued by multiple participants are purchased by a special purpose entity that repackages those exposures into securities that can be sold to investors. Structured financing programs allocate credit risk, generally, between the participants and credit enhancement provided to the program.

Subsidiary. The term *subsidiary* means any corporation, partnership, business trust, joint venture, association or similar organization in which a State savings association directly or indirectly holds an ownership interest and the assets of which are consolidated with those of the State savings association for purposes of reporting under Generally Accepted Accounting Principles (GAAP). Generally, these are majority-owned subsidiaries.[1] This definition does not include ownership interests that were taken in satisfaction of debts previously contracted, provided that the reporting State savings association has not held the interest for more than five years or a longer period approved by the FDIC.

Tier 1 capital. The term *Tier 1 capital* means core capital as computed in accordance with § 390.465(a).

Tier 2 capital. The term *Tier 2 capital* means supplementary capital as computed in accordance with § 390.465.

Total assets. The term *total assets* means total assets as would be required to be reported for consolidated entities on period-end reports filed with the FDIC in accordance with generally accepted accounting principles.

Traded position. The term *traded position* means a position retained, assumed, or issued in connection with a securitization that is rated by a NRSRO, where there is a reasonable expectation that, in the near future, the rating will be relied upon by:

(1) Unaffiliated investors to purchase the security; or

(2) An unaffiliated third party to enter into a transaction involving the position, such as a purchase, loan, or repurchase agreement.

Unconditionally cancelable. The term *unconditionally cancelable* means, with respect to a commitment-type lending arrangement, that the State savings association may, at any time, with or without cause, refuse to advance funds or extend credit under the facility. In the case of home equity lines of credit, the State savings association is deemed able to unconditionally cancel the commitment if it can, at its option, prohibit additional extensions of credit, reduce the line, and terminate the commitment to the full extent permitted by relevant Federal law.

United States Government or its agencies. The term *United States Government or its agencies* means an instrumentality of the U.S. Government whose debt obligations are fully and explicitly guaranteed as to the timely payment of principal and interest by the full faith and credit of the United States Government.

United States Government-sponsored agency or corporation. The term *United States Government-sponsored agency or corporation* means an agency or corporation originally established or chartered to serve public purposes specified by the United States Congress but whose obligations are not explicitly guaranteed by the full faith and credit of the United States Government.

§ 390.462 Minimum regulatory capital requirement.

(a) To meet its regulatory capital requirement a State savings association must satisfy each of the following capital standards:

(1) *Risk-based capital requirement.* (i) A State savings association's minimum risk-based capital requirement shall be an amount equal to 8% of its risk-weighted assets as measured under § 390.466.

(ii) A State savings association may not use supplementary capital to satisfy this requirement in an amount greater than 100% of its core capital as defined in § 390.465.

(2) *Leverage ratio requirement.* (i) A State savings association's minimum leverage ratio requirement shall be the amount set forth in § 390.467.

---

[1] The FDIC reserves the right to review a State savings association's investment in a subsidiary on a case-by-case basis. If the FDIC determines that such investment is more appropriately treated as an equity security or an ownership interest in a subsidiary, it will make such determination regardless of the percentage of ownership held by the State savings association.

Federal Deposit Insurance Corporation § 390.463

(ii) A State savings association must satisfy this requirement with core capital as defined in § 390.465(a).

(3) *Tangible capital requirement.* (i) A State savings association's minimum tangible capital requirement shall be the amount set forth in § 390.468.

(ii) A State savings association must satisfy this requirement with tangible capital as defined in § 390.468 in an amount not less than 1.5% of its adjusted total assets.

(b) [Reserved]

(c) State savings associations are expected to maintain compliance with all of these standards at all times.

§ 390.463 Individual minimum capital requirements.

(a) *Purpose and scope.* The rules and procedures specified in this section apply to the establishment of an individual minimum capital requirement for a State savings association that varies from the risk-based capital requirement, the leverage ratio requirement or the tangible capital requirement that would otherwise apply to the State savings association under this subpart.

(b) *Appropriate considerations for establishing individual minimum capital requirements.* Minimum capital levels higher than the risk-based capital requirement, the leverage ratio requirement or the tangible capital requirement required under this subpart may be appropriate for individual State savings associations. Increased individual minimum capital requirements may be established upon a determination that the State savings association's capital is or may become inadequate in view of its circumstances. For example, higher capital levels may be appropriate for:

(1) A State savings association receiving special supervisory attention;

(2) A State savings association that has or is expected to have losses resulting in capital inadequacy;

(3) A State savings association that has a high degree of exposure to interest rate risk, prepayment risk, credit risk, concentration of credit risk, certain risks arising from nontraditional activities, or similar risks; or a high proportion of off-balance sheet risk, especially standby letters of credit;

(4) A State savings association that has poor liquidity or cash flow;

(5) A State savings association growing, either internally or through acquisitions, at such a rate that supervisory problems are presented that are not dealt with adequately by other FDIC regulations or other guidance;

(6) A State savings association that may be adversely affected by the activities or condition of its holding company, affiliate(s), subsidiaries, or other persons or State savings associations with which it has significant business relationships, including concentrations of credit;

(7) A State savings association with a portfolio reflecting weak credit quality or a significant likelihood of financial loss, or that has loans in nonperforming status or on which borrowers fail to comply with repayment terms;

(8) A State savings association that has inadequate underwriting policies, standards, or procedures for its loans and investments; or

(9) A State savings association that has a record of operational losses that exceeds the average of other, similarly situated State savings associations; has management deficiencies, including failure to adequately monitor and control financial and operating risks, particularly the risks presented by concentrations of credit and nontraditional activities; or has a poor record of supervisory compliance.

(c) *Standards for determination of appropriate individual minimum capital requirements.* The appropriate minimum capital level for an individual State savings association cannot be determined solely through the application of a rigid mathematical formula or wholly objective criteria. The decision is necessarily based, in part, on subjective judgment grounded in agency expertise. The factors to be considered in the determination will vary in each case and may include, for example:

(1) The conditions or circumstances leading to the determination that a higher minimum capital requirement is appropriate or necessary for the State savings association;

(2) The exigency of those circumstances or potential problems;

(3) The overall condition, management strength, and future prospects of

§ 390.463

the State savings association and, if applicable, its holding company, subsidiaries, and affiliates;

(4) The State savings association's liquidity, capital and other indicators of financial stability, particularly as compared with those of similarly situated State savings associations; and

(5) The policies and practices of the State savings association's directors, officers, and senior management as well as the internal control and internal audit systems for implementation of such adopted policies and practices.

(d) *Procedures*—(1) *Notification.* When the FDIC determines that a minimum capital requirement is necessary or appropriate for a particular State savings association, it shall notify the State savings association in writing of its proposed individual minimum capital requirement; the schedule for compliance with the new requirement; and the specific causes for determining that the higher individual minimum capital requirement is necessary or appropriate for the State savings association. The FDIC shall forward the notifying letter to the appropriate state supervisor if a state-chartered savings association would be subject to an individual minimum capital requirement.

(2) *Response.* (i) The response shall include any information that the State savings association wants the FDIC to consider in deciding whether to establish or to amend an individual minimum capital requirement for the State savings association, what the individual capital requirement should be, and, if applicable, what compliance schedule is appropriate for achieving the required capital level. The responses of the State savings association and appropriate state supervisor must be in writing and must be delivered to the FDIC within 30 days after the date on which the notification was received. Such response must be filed in accordance with §§ 390.106 and 390.108. The FDIC may extend the time period for good cause. The time period for response by the insured State savings association may be shortened for good cause:

(A) When, in the opinion of the FDIC, the condition of the State savings association so requires, and the FDIC informs the State savings association of the shortened response period in the notice;

(B) With the consent of the State savings association; or

(C) When the State savings association already has advised the FDIC that it cannot or will not achieve its applicable minimum capital requirement.

(ii) Failure to respond within 30 days, or such other time period as may be specified by the FDIC, may constitute a waiver of any objections to the proposed individual minimum capital requirement or to the schedule for complying with it, unless the FDIC has provided an extension of the response period for good cause.

(3) *Decision.* After expiration of the response period, the FDIC shall decide whether or not it believes the proposed individual minimum capital requirement should be established for the State savings association, or whether that proposed requirement should be adopted in modified form, based on a review of the State savings association's response and other relevant information. The FDIC's decision shall address comments received within the response period from the State savings association and the appropriate state supervisor and shall state the level of capital required, the schedule for compliance with this requirement, and any specific remedial action the State savings association could take to eliminate the need for continued applicability of the individual minimum capital requirement. The FDIC shall provide the State savings association and the appropriate state supervisor with a written decision on the individual minimum capital requirement, addressing the substantive comments made by the State savings association and setting forth the decision and the basis for that decision. Upon receipt of this decision by the State savings association, the individual minimum capital requirement becomes effective and binding upon the State savings association. This decision represents final agency action.

(4) *Failure to comply.* Failure to satisfy an individual minimum capital requirement, or to meet any required incremental additions to capital under a schedule for compliance with such an

Federal Deposit Insurance Corporation　§ 390.464

individual minimum capital requirement, shall constitute a legal basis for issuing a capital directive pursuant to § 390.464.

(5) *Change in circumstances.* If, after a decision is made under paragraph (d)(3) of this section, there is a change in the circumstances affecting the State savings association's capital adequacy or its ability to reach its required minimum capital level by the specified date, FDIC may amend the individual minimum capital requirement or the State savings association's schedule for such compliance. The FDIC may decline to consider a State savings association's request for such changes that are not based on a significant change in circumstances or that are repetitive or frivolous. Pending the FDIC's reexamination of the original decision, that original decision and any compliance schedule established thereunder shall continue in full force and effect.

§ 390.464 Capital directives.

(a) *Issuance of a Capital Directive*—(1) *Purpose.* In addition to any other action authorized by law, the FDIC, may issue a capital directive to a State savings association that does not have an amount of capital satisfying its minimum capital requirement. Issuance of such a capital directive may be based on a State savings association's noncompliance with the risk-based capital requirement, the leverage ratio requirement, the tangible capital requirement, or individual minimum capital requirement established under this subpart, by a written agreement under 12 U.S.C. 1464(s), or as a condition for approval of an application. A capital directive may order a State savings association to:

(i) Achieve its minimum capital requirement by a specified date;

(ii) Adhere to the compliance schedule for achieving its individual minimum capital requirement;

(iii) Submit and adhere to a capital plan acceptable to the FDIC describing the means and a time schedule by which the State savings association shall reach its required capital level;

(iv) Take other action, including but not limited to, reducing the State savings association's assets or its rate of liability growth, or imposing restrictions on the State savings association's payment of dividends, in order to cause the State savings association to reach its required capital level;

(v) Take any action authorized under § 390.469(e); or

(vi) Take a combination of any of these actions.

(2) *Enforcement of capital directive.* A capital directive issued under this section, including a plan submitted pursuant to a capital directive, is enforceable under 12 U.S.C. 1818 in the same manner and to the same extent as an effective and outstanding cease and desist order which has become final under 12 U.S.C. 1818.

(3) *Notice of intent to issue capital directive.* The FDIC will determine whether to initiate the process of issuing a capital directive. The FDIC will notify a State savings association in writing by registered mail of its intention to issue a capital directive. Since a state-chartered savings association is involved, the FDIC will also notify and solicit comment from the appropriate state supervisor. The notice will state:

(i) The reasons for issuance of the capital directive and

(ii) The proposed contents of the capital directive.

(3) *Response to notice of intent.* (i) A State savings association may respond to the notice of intent by submitting its own compliance plan, or may propose an alternative plan. The response should also include any information that the State savings association wishes the FDIC to consider in deciding whether to issue a capital directive. The appropriate state supervisor may also submit a response. These responses must be in writing and be delivered within 30 days after the receipt of the notices. Such responses must be filed in accordance with §§ 390.106 and 390.108. In its discretion, the FDIC may extend the time period for the response for good cause. The FDIC may, for good cause, shorten the 30-day time period for response by the insured State savings association:

(A) When, in the opinion of the FDIC, the condition of the State savings association so requires, and the FDIC informs the State savings association of

§ 390.465

the shortened response period in the notice;

(B) With the consent of the State savings association; or

(C) When the State savings association already has advised the FDIC that it cannot or will not achieve its applicable minimum capital requirement.

(ii) Failure to respond within 30 days of receipt, or such other time period as may be specified by the FDIC, may constitute a waiver of any objections to the capital directive unless the FDIC grants an extension of the time period for good cause.

(4) *Decision.* After the closing date of the State savings association's response period, or upon receipt of the State savings association's response, if earlier, the FDIC shall consider the State savings association's response and may seek additional information or clarification of the response. Thereafter, the FDIC will determine whether or not to issue a capital directive and, if one is to be issued, whether it should be as originally proposed or in modified form.

(5) *Service and effectiveness.* (i) Upon issuance, a capital directive will be served upon the State savings association. It will include or be accompanied by a statement of reasons for its issuance and shall address the responses received during the response period.

(ii) A capital directive shall become effective upon the expiration of 30 days after service upon the State savings association, unless the FDIC determines that a shorter effective period is necessary either on account of the public interest or in order to achieve the capital directive's purpose. If the State savings association has consented to issuance of the capital directive, it may become effective immediately. A capital directive shall remain in effect and enforceable unless, and then only to the extent that, it is stayed, modified, or terminated by the FDIC.

(6) *Change in circumstances.* Upon a change in circumstances, a State savings association may submit a request to the FDIC to reconsider the terms of the capital directive or consider changes in the State savings association's capital plan issued under a directive for the State savings association to achieve its minimum capital requirement. If the FDIC believes such a change is warranted, the FDIC may modify the State savings association's capital requirement or may refuse to make such modification if it determines that there are not significant changes in circumstances. Pending a decision on reconsideration, the capital directive and capital plan shall continue in full force and effect.

(b) *Relation to other administrative actions.* The FDIC—

(1) May consider a State savings association's progress in adhering to any capital plan required under this section whenever such State savings association or any affiliate of such State savings association seeks approval for any proposal that would have the effect of diverting earnings, diminishing capital, or otherwise impeding such State savings association's progress in meeting its minimum capital requirement; and

(2) May disapprove any proposal referred to in paragraph (b)(1) of this section if the FDIC determines that the proposal would adversely affect the ability of the State savings association on a current or pro forma basis to satisfy its capital requirement.

§ 390.465 Components of capital.

(a) *Core Capital.* (1) The following elements,[1] less the amount of any deductions pursuant to paragraph (a)(2) of this section, comprise a State savings association's core capital:

(i) Common stockholders' equity (including retained earnings);

(ii) Noncumulative perpetual preferred stock and related surplus;[2]

---

[1] Stock issues where the dividend is reset periodically based on current market conditions and the State savings association's current credit rating, including but not limited to, auction rate, money market or remarketable preferred stock, are assigned to supplementary capital, regardless of cumulative or noncumulative characteristics.

[2] Stock issued by subsidiaries that may not be counted by the parent State savings association on the Thrift Financial Report or Consolidated Reports of Condition or Income ("Call Report"), as applicable, likewise shall not be considered in calculating capital. For example, preferred stock issued by a State savings association or a subsidiary that is, in effect, collateralized by assets of the State

Federal Deposit Insurance Corporation § 390.465

(iii) Minority interests in the equity accounts of the subsidiaries that are fully consolidated.

(iv) Nonwithdrawable accounts and pledged deposits of mutual State savings associations (excluding any treasury shares held by the State savings association) meeting the criteria of regulations and memoranda of the FDIC to the extent that such accounts or deposits have no fixed maturity date, cannot be withdrawn at the option of the accountholder, and do not earn interest that carries over to subsequent periods;

(2) *Deductions from core capital.* (i) Intangible assets, as defined in § 390.461, are deducted from assets and capital in computing core capital, except as otherwise provided by § 390.471.

(ii) Servicing assets that are not includable in core capital pursuant to § 390.471 are deducted from assets and capital in computing core capital.

(iii) Credit-enhancing interest-only strips that are not includable in core capital under § 390.471 are deducted from assets and capital in computing core capital.

(iv) Investments, both equity and debt, in subsidiaries that are not includable subsidiaries (including those subsidiaries where the State savings association has a minority ownership interest) are deducted from assets and, thus core capital except as provided in paragraphs (a)(2)(v) and (vi) of this section.

(v) If a State savings association has any investments (both debt and equity) in one or more subsidiaries engaged in any activity that would not fall within the scope of activities in which includable subsidiaries may engage, it must deduct such investments from assets and, thus, core capital in accordance with this paragraph (a)(2)(v). The State savings association must first deduct from assets and, thus, core capital the amount by which any investments in such subsidiary(ies) exceed the amount of such investments held by the State savings association as of April 12, 1989. Next the State savings association must deduct from assets and, thus, core capital, the State savings association's investments in and extensions of credit to the subsidiary on the date as of which the State savings association's capital is being determined.

(vi) If a State savings association holds a subsidiary (either directly or through a subsidiary) that is itself a domestic depository institution, the FDIC may, in its sole discretion upon determining that the amount of core capital that would be required would be higher if the assets and liabilities of such subsidiary were consolidated with those of the parent State savings association than the amount that would be required if the parent State savings association's investment were deducted pursuant to paragraphs (a)(2)(iv) and (v) of this section, consolidate the assets and liabilities of that subsidiary with those of the parent State savings association in calculating the capital adequacy of the parent State savings association, regardless of whether the subsidiary would otherwise be an includable subsidiary as defined in § 390.461.

(vii) Deferred tax assets that are not includable in core capital pursuant to § 390.471 are deducted from assets and capital in computing core capital.

(b) *Supplementary Capital.* Supplementary capital counts towards a State savings association's total capital up to a maximum of 100% of the State savings association's core capital. The following elements comprise a State savings association's supplementary capital:

(1) *Permanent Capital Instruments.* (i) Cumulative perpetual preferred stock and other perpetual preferred stock[3] issued pursuant to regulations and memoranda of the FDIC;

(ii) [Reserved]

---

savings association or one of its subsidiaries shall not be included in capital. Similarly, common stock with mandatorily redeemable provisions is not includable in core capital.

[3] Preferred stock issued by subsidiaries that may not be counted by the parent State savings association on the Thrift Financial Report or Consolidated Reports of Condition or Income ("Call Report"), as applicable, likewise may not be considered in calculating capital. Preferred stock issued by a State savings association or a subsidiary that is, in effect, collateralized by assets of the State savings association or one of its subsidiaries may not be included in capital.

(iii) Nonwithdrawable accounts and pledged deposits (excluding any treasury shares held by the State savings association) meeting the criteria of 12 CFR 390.307 to the extent that such instruments are not included in core capital under paragraph (a) of this section;

(iv) Perpetual subordinated debt issued pursuant to regulations and memoranda of the FDIC; and

(v) Mandatory convertible subordinated debt (capital notes) issued pursuant to regulations and memoranda of the FDIC.

(2) *Maturing Capital Instruments.* (i) Subordinated debt issued pursuant to regulations and memoranda of the FDIC;

(ii) Intermediate-term preferred stock issued pursuant to regulations and memoranda of the FDIC and any related surplus;

(iii) Mandatory convertible subordinated debt (commitment notes) issued pursuant to regulations and memoranda of the FDIC; and

(iv) Mandatorily redeemable preferred stock that was issued before July 23, 1985 or issued pursuant to regulations and memoranda of the Office of Thrift Supervision and approved in writing by the FSLIC for inclusion as regulatory capital before or after issuance.

(3) *Transition rules for maturing capital instruments*—A State savings association may include maturing capital instruments issued on or before November 7, 1989, in supplementary capital in accordance with the treatment set forth in paragraph (b)(3)(ii) of this section.

(A) At the beginning of each of the last five years of the life of the maturing capital instrument, the amount that is eligible to be included as supplementary capital is reduced by 20% of the original amount of that instrument (net of redemptions).[4]

(B) Only the aggregate amount of maturing capital instruments that mature in any one year during the seven years immediately prior to an instrument's maturity that does not exceed 20% of an institution's capital will qualify as supplementary capital.

(C) Once a State savings association selects either paragraph (b)(3)(ii)(A) or (B) of this section for the issuance of a maturing capital instrument, it must continue to elect that option for all subsequent issuances of maturing capital instruments for as long as there is a balance outstanding of such post-November 7, 1989, issuances. Only when such issuances have all been repaid and the State savings association has no balance of such issuances outstanding may the State savings association elect the other option.

(4) *Allowance for loan and lease losses.* Allowance for loan and lease losses established under FDIC regulations and memoranda to a maximum of 1.25 percent of risk-weighted assets.[5]

(5) *Unrealized gains on equity securities.* Up to 45 percent of unrealized gains on available-for-sale equity securities with readily determinable fair values may be included in supplementary capital. Unrealized gains are unrealized holding gains, net of unrealized holding losses, before income taxes, calculated as the amount, if any, by which fair value exceeds historical cost. The FDIC may disallow such inclusion in the calculation of supplementary capital if the FDIC determines that the equity securities are not prudently valued.

---

[4] Capital instruments may be redeemed prior to maturity and without the prior approval of the FDIC, as long as the instruments are redeemed with the proceeds of, or replaced by, a like amount of a similar or higher quality capital instrument. However, the FDIC must be notified in writing at least 30 days in advance of such redemption.

[5] The amount of the allowance for loan and lease losses that may be included in capital is based on a percentage of risk-weighted assets. The gross sum of risk-weighted assets used in this calculation includes all risk-weighted assets, with the exception of assets required to be deducted under § 390.466 in establishing risk-weighted assets. "Excess reserves for loan and lease losses" is defined as assets required to be deducted from capital under § 390.465(a)(2). A State savings association may deduct excess reserves for loan and lease losses from the gross sum of risk-weighted assets (*i.e.,* risk-weighted assets including allowance for loan and lease losses) in computing the denominator of the risk-based capital standard. Thus, a State savings association will exclude the same amount of excess allowance for loan and lease losses from both the numerator and the denominator of the risk-based capital ratio.

Federal Deposit Insurance Corporation § 390.466

(c) *Total capital.* (1) A State savings association's total capital equals the sum of its core capital and supplementary capital (to the extent that such supplementary capital does not exceed 100% of its core capital).

(2) The following assets, in addition to assets required to be deducted elsewhere in calculating core capital, are deducted from assets for purposes of determining total capital:

(i) Reciprocal holdings of depository institution capital instruments; and

(ii) All equity investments.

§ 390.466 Risk-based capital credit risk-weight categories.

(a) *Risk-weighted assets.* Risk-weighted assets equal risk-weighted on-balance sheet assets (computed under paragraph (a)(1) of this section), plus risk-weighted off-balance sheet activities (computed under paragraph (a)(2) of this section), plus risk-weighted recourse obligations, direct credit substitutes, and certain other positions (computed under paragraph (b) of this section). Assets not included (*i.e.*, deducted from capital) for purposes of calculating capital under § 390.465 are not included in calculating risk-weighted assets.

(1) *On-balance sheet assets.* Except as provided in paragraph (b) of this section, risk-weighted on-balance sheet assets are computed by multiplying the on-balance sheet asset amounts times the appropriate risk-weight categories. The risk-weight categories are:

(i) *Zero percent Risk Weight (Category 1).* (A) Cash, including domestic and foreign currency owned and held in all offices of a State savings association or in transit. Any foreign currency held by a State savings association must be converted into U.S. dollar equivalents;

(B) Securities issued by and other direct claims on the U.S. Government or its agencies (to the extent such securities or claims are unconditionally backed by the full faith and credit of the United States Government) or the central government of an OECD country;

(C) Notes and obligations issued by either the Federal Savings and Loan Insurance Corporation or the Federal Deposit Insurance Corporation and backed by the full faith and credit of the United States Government;

(D) Deposit reserves at, claims on, and balances due from Federal Reserve Banks;

(E) The book value of paid-in Federal Reserve Bank stock;

(F) That portion of assets that is fully covered against capital loss and/or yield maintenance agreements by the Federal Savings and Loan Insurance Corporation or any successor agency;

(G) That portion of assets directly and unconditionally guaranteed by the United States Government or its agencies, or the central government of an OECD country;

(H) Claims on, and claims guaranteed by, a qualifying securities firm that are collateralized by cash on deposit in the State savings association or by securities issued or guaranteed by the United States Government or its agencies, or the central government of an OECD country. To be eligible for this risk weight, the State savings association must maintain a positive margin of collateral on the claim on a daily basis, taking into account any change in a State savings association's exposure to the obligor or counterparty under the claim in relation to the market value of the collateral held in support of the claim.

(ii) *20 percent Risk Weight (Category 2).* (A) Cash items in the process of collection;

(B) That portion of assets collateralized by the current market value of securities issued or guaranteed by the United States government or its agencies, or the central government of an OECD country;

(C) That portion of assets conditionally guaranteed by the United States Government or its agencies, or the central government of an OECD country;

(D) Securities (not including equity securities) issued by and other claims on the U.S. Government or its agencies which are not backed by the full faith and credit of the United States Government;

(E) Securities (not including equity securities) issued by, or other direct claims on, United States Government-sponsored agencies;

§ 390.466

(F) That portion of assets guaranteed by United States Government-sponsored agencies;

(G) That portion of assets collateralized by the current market value of securities issued or guaranteed by United States Government-sponsored agencies;

(H) Claims on, and claims guaranteed by, a qualifying securities firm, subject to the following conditions:

(*1*) A qualifying securities firm must have a long-term issuer credit rating, or a rating on at least one issue of long-term unsecured debt, from a NRSRO. The rating must be in one of the three highest investment grade categories used by the NRSRO. If two or more NRSROs assign ratings to the qualifying securities firm, the State savings association must use the lowest rating to determine whether the rating requirement of this paragraph is met. A qualifying securities firm may rely on the rating of its parent consolidated company, if the parent consolidated company guarantees the claim.

(*2*) A collateralized claim on a qualifying securities firm does not have to comply with the rating requirements under paragraph (a)(1)(ii)(H)(*1*) of this section if the claim arises under a contract that:

(*i*) Is a reverse repurchase/repurchase agreement or securities lending/borrowing transaction executed using standard industry documentation;

(*ii*) Is collateralized by debt or equity securities that are liquid and readily marketable;

(*iii*) Is marked-to-market daily;

(*iv*) Is subject to a daily margin maintenance requirement under the standard industry documentation; and

(*v*) Can be liquidated, terminated or accelerated immediately in bankruptcy or similar proceeding, and the security or collateral agreement will not be stayed or avoided under applicable law of the relevant jurisdiction. For example, a claim is exempt from the automatic stay in bankruptcy in the United States if it arises under a securities contract or a repurchase agreement subject to section 555 or 559 of the Bankruptcy Code (11 U.S.C. 555 or 559), a qualified financial contract under section 11(e)(8) of the Federal Deposit Insurance Act (12 U.S.C. 1821(e)(8)), or a netting contract between or among financial institutions under sections 401–407 of the Federal Deposit Insurance Corporation Improvement Act of 1991 (12 U.S.C. 4401–4407), or Regulation EE (12 CFR part 231).

(*3*) If the securities firm uses the claim to satisfy its applicable capital requirements, the claim is not eligible for a risk weight under this paragraph (a)(1)(ii)(H);

(I) Claims representing general obligations of any public-sector entity in an OECD country, and that portion of any claims guaranteed by any such public-sector entity;

(J) Bonds issued by the Financing Corporation or the Resolution Funding Corporation;

(K) Balances due from and all claims on domestic depository institutions. This includes demand deposits and other transaction accounts, savings deposits and time certificates of deposit, federal funds sold, loans to other depository institutions, including overdrafts and term federal funds, holdings of the State savings association's own discounted acceptances for which the account party is a depository institution, holdings of bankers acceptances of other institutions and securities issued by depository institutions, except those that qualify as capital;

(L) The book value of paid-in Federal Home Loan Bank stock;

(M) Deposit reserves at, claims on and balances due from the Federal Home Loan Banks;

(N) Assets collateralized by cash held in a segregated deposit account by the reporting State savings association;

(O) Claims on, or guaranteed by, official multilateral lending institutions or regional development institutions in which the United States Government is a shareholder or contributing member;[1]

(P) That portion of assets collateralized by the current market value of securities issued by official

---

[1] These institutions include, but are not limited to, the International Bank for Reconstruction and Development (World Bank), the Inter-American Development Bank, the Asian Development Bank, the African Development Bank, the European Investments Bank, the International Monetary Fund and the Bank for International Settlements.

Federal Deposit Insurance Corporation § 390.466

multilateral lending institutions or regional development institutions in which the United States Government is a shareholder or contributing member;

(Q) All claims on depository institutions incorporated in an OECD country, and all assets backed by the full faith and credit of depository institutions incorporated in an OECD country. This includes the credit equivalent amount of participations in commitments and standby letters of credit sold to other depository institutions incorporated in an OECD country, but only if the originating bank remains liable to the customer or beneficiary for the full amount of the commitment or standby letter of credit. Also included in this category are the credit equivalent amounts of risk participations in bankers' acceptances conveyed to other depository institutions incorporated in an OECD country. However, bank-issued securities that qualify as capital of the issuing bank are not included in this risk category;

(R) Claims on, or guaranteed by depository institutions other than the central bank, incorporated in a non-OECD country, with a remaining maturity of one year or less;

(S) That portion of local currency claims conditionally guaranteed by central governments of non-OECD countries, to the extent the State savings association has local currency liabilities in that country.

(iii) *50 percent Risk Weight (Category 3)*. (A) Revenue bonds issued by any public-sector entity in an OECD country for which the underlying obligor is a public-sector entity, but which are repayable solely from the revenues generated from the project financed through the issuance of the obligations;

(B) Qualifying mortgage loans and qualifying multifamily mortgage loans;

(C) Privately-issued mortgage-backed securities (*i.e.*, those that do not carry the guarantee of a government or government sponsored entity) representing an interest in qualifying mortgage loans or qualifying multifamily mortgage loans. If the security is backed by qualifying multifamily mortgage loans, the State savings association must receive timely payments of principal and interest in accordance with the terms of the security. Payments will generally be considered timely if they are not 30 days past due;

(D) Qualifying residential construction loans as defined in § 390.461.

(iv) *100 percent Risk Weight (Category 4)*. All assets not specified above or deducted from calculations of capital pursuant to § 390.465, including, but not limited to:

(A) Consumer loans;
(B) Commercial loans;
(C) Home equity loans;
(D) Non-qualifying mortgage loans;
(E) Non-qualifying multifamily mortgage loans;
(F) Residential construction loans;
(G) Land loans;
(H) Nonresidential construction loans;
(I) Obligations issued by any state or any political subdivision thereof for the benefit of a private party or enterprise where that party or enterprise, rather than the issuing state or political subdivision, is responsible for the timely payment of principal and interest on the obligations, *e.g.*, industrial development bonds;
(J) Debt securities not otherwise described in this section;
(K) Investments in fixed assets and premises;
(L) Certain nonsecurity financial instruments including servicing assets and intangible assets includable in core capital under § 390.471;
(M) Interest-only strips receivable, other than credit-enhancing interest-only strips;
(N)–(O) [Reserved]
(P) That portion of equity investments not deducted pursuant to § 390.465;
(Q) The prorated assets of subsidiaries (except for the assets of includable, fully consolidated subsidiaries) to the extent such assets are included in adjusted total assets;
(R) All repossessed assets or assets that are more than 90 days past due; and
(S) Equity investments that the FDIC determines have the same risk characteristics as foreclosed real estate by the State savings association;
(T) Equity investments permissible for a national bank.

§ 390.466

(v) [Reserved]

(vi) *Indirect ownership interests in pools of assets.* Assets representing an indirect holding of a pool of assets, *e.g.,* mutual funds, are assigned to risk-weight categories under this section based upon the risk weight that would be assigned to the assets in the portfolio of the pool. An investment in shares of a mutual fund whose portfolio consists primarily of various securities or money market instruments that, if held separately, would be assigned to different risk-weight categories, generally is assigned to the risk-weight category appropriate to the highest risk-weighted asset that the fund is permitted to hold in accordance with the investment objectives set forth in its prospectus. The State savings association may, at its option, assign the investment on a pro rata basis to different risk-weight categories according to the investment limits in its prospectus. In no case will an investment in shares in any such fund be assigned to a total risk weight less than 20 percent. If the State savings association chooses to assign investments on a pro rata basis, and the sum of the investment limits of assets in the fund's prospectus exceeds 100 percent, the State savings association must assign the highest pro rata amounts of its total investment to the higher risk categories. If, in order to maintain a necessary degree of short-term liquidity, a fund is permitted to hold an insignificant amount of its assets in short-term, highly liquid securities of superior credit quality that do not qualify for a preferential risk weight, such securities will generally be disregarded in determining the risk-weight category into which the State savings association's holding in the overall fund should be assigned. The prudent use of hedging instruments by a mutual fund to reduce the risk of its assets will not increase the risk weighting of the mutual fund investment. For example, the use of hedging instruments by a mutual fund to reduce the interest rate risk of its government bond portfolio will not increase the risk weight of that fund above the 20 percent category. Nonetheless, if the fund engages in any activities that appear speculative in nature or has any other characteristics that are inconsistent with the preferential risk-weighting assigned to the fund's assets, holdings in the fund will be assigned to the 100 percent risk-weight category.

(2) *Off-balance sheet items.* Except as provided in paragraph (b) of this section, risk-weighted off-balance sheet items are determined by the following two-step process. First, the face amount of the off-balance sheet item must be multiplied by the appropriate credit conversion factor listed in this paragraph (a)(2). This calculation translates the face amount of an off-balance sheet exposure into an on-balance sheet credit-equivalent amount. Second, the credit-equivalent amount must be assigned to the appropriate risk-weight category using the criteria regarding obligors, guarantors, and collateral listed in paragraph (a)(1) of this section, *provided* that the maximum risk weight assigned to the credit-equivalent amount of an interest-rate or exchange-rate contract is 50 percent. The following are the credit conversion factors and the off-balance sheet items to which they apply.

(i) *100 percent credit conversion factor (Group A).*

(A) [Reserved]

(B) Risk participations purchased in bankers' acceptances;

(C) [Reserved]

(D) Forward agreements and other contingent obligations with a certain draw down, *e.g.,* legally binding agreements to purchase assets at a specified future date. On the date an institution enters into a forward agreement or similar obligation, it should convert the principal amount of the assets to be purchased at 100 percent as of that date and then assign this amount to the risk-weight category appropriate to the obligor or guarantor of the item, or the nature of the collateral;

(E) Indemnification of customers whose securities the State savings association has lent as agent. If the customer is not indemnified against loss by the State savings association, the transaction is excluded from the risk-based capital calculation. When a State savings association lends its own securities, the transaction is treated as

Federal Deposit Insurance Corporation § 390.466

a loan. When a State savings association lends its own securities or is acting as agent, agrees to indemnify a customer, the transaction is assigned to the risk weight appropriate to the obligor or collateral that is delivered to the lending or indemnifying institution or to an independent custodian acting on their behalf.

(ii) *50 percent credit conversion factor (Group B)*. (A) Transaction-related contingencies, including, among other things, performance bonds and performance-based standby letters of credit related to a particular transaction;

(B) Unused portions of commitments (including home equity lines of credit and eligible ABCP liquidity facilities) with an original maturity exceeding one year except those listed in paragraph (a)(2)(v) of this section. For eligible ABCP liquidity facilities, the resulting credit equivalent amount is assigned to the risk category appropriate to the assets to be funded by the liquidity facility based on the assets or the obligor, after considering any collateral or guarantees, or external credit ratings under paragraph (b)(3) of this section, if applicable; and

(C) Revolving underwriting facilities, note issuance facilities, and similar arrangements pursuant to which the State savings association's customer can issue short-term debt obligations in its own name, but for which the State savings association has a legally binding commitment to either:

(*1*) Purchase the obligations the customer is unable to sell by a stated date; or

(*2*) Advance funds to its customer, if the obligations cannot be sold.

(iii) *20 percent credit conversion factor (Group C)*. Trade-related contingencies, *i.e.*, short-term, self-liquidating instruments used to finance the movement of goods and collateralized by the underlying shipment. A commercial letter of credit is an example of such an instrument.

(iv) *10 percent credit conversion factor (Group D)*. Unused portions of eligible ABCP liquidity facilities with an original maturity of one year or less. The resulting credit equivalent amount is assigned to the risk category appropriate to the assets to be funded by the liquidity facility based on the assets or the obligor, after considering any collateral or guarantees, or external credit ratings under paragraph (b)(3) of this section, if applicable;

(v) *Zero percent credit conversion factor (Group E)*. (A) Unused portions of commitments with an original maturity of one year or less, except for eligible ABCP liquidity facilities;

(B) Unused commitments with an original maturity greater than one year, if they are unconditionally cancelable at any time at the option of the State savings association and the State savings association has the contractual right to make, and in fact does make, either:

(*1*) A separate credit decision based upon the borrower's current financial condition before each drawing under the lending facility; or

(*2*) An annual (or more frequent) credit review based upon the borrower's current financial condition to determine whether or not the lending facility should be continued; and

(C) The unused portion of retail credit card lines or other related plans that are unconditionally cancelable by the State savings association in accordance with applicable law.

(vi) *Off-balance sheet contracts; interest-rate and foreign exchange rate contracts (Group F)*—(A) *Calculation of credit equivalent amounts.* The credit equivalent amount of an off-balance sheet interest rate or foreign exchange rate contract that is not subject to a qualifying bilateral netting contract in accordance with paragraph (a)(2)(vi)(B) of this section is equal to the sum of the current credit exposure, *i.e.*, the replacement cost of the contract, and the potential future credit exposure of the off-balance sheet rate contract. The calculation of credit equivalent amounts is measured in U.S. dollars, regardless of the currency or currencies specified in the off-balance sheet rate contract.

(*1*) *Current credit exposure.* The current credit exposure of an off-balance sheet rate contract is determined by the mark-to-market value of the contract. If the mark-to-market value is positive, then the current credit exposure equals that mark-to-market value. If the mark-to-market value is zero or negative, then the current exposure is zero. In determining its current credit exposure for multiple off-balance sheet rate contracts executed with a single counterparty, a State savings association may net positive and negative mark-to-market values of off-balance sheet rate contracts if subject to a bilateral netting contract as provided in paragraph (a)(2)(vi)(B) of this section.

(2) *Potential future credit exposure.* The potential future credit exposure of an off-balance sheet rate contract, including a contract with a negative mark-to-market value, is estimated by multiplying the notional principal[2] by a credit conversion factor. State savings associations, subject to examiner review, should use the effective rather than the apparent or stated notional amount in this calculation. The conversion factors are:[3]

Remaining maturity	Interest rate contracts (percents)	Foreign exchange rate contracts (percents)
One year or less	0.0	1.0
Over one year	0.5	5.0

(B) *Off-balance sheet rate contracts subject to bilateral netting contracts.* In determining its current credit exposure for multiple off-balance sheet rate contracts executed with a single counterparty, a State savings association may net off-balance sheet rate contracts subject to a bilateral netting contract by offsetting positive and negative mark-to-market values, provided that:

(*1*) The bilateral netting contract is in writing;

(*2*) The bilateral netting contract creates a single legal obligation for all individual off-balance sheet rate contracts covered by the bilateral netting contract. In effect, the bilateral netting contract provides that the State savings association has a single claim or obligation either to receive or pay only the net amount of the sum of the positive and negative mark-to-market values on the individual off-balance sheet rate contracts covered by the bilateral netting contract. The single legal obligation for the net amount is operative in the event that a counterparty, or a counterparty to whom the bilateral netting contract has been validly assigned, fails to perform due to any of the following events: default, insolvency, bankruptcy, or other similar circumstances;

(*3*) The State savings association obtains a written and reasoned legal opinion(s) representing, with a high degree of certainty, that in the event of a legal challenge, including one resulting from default, insolvency, bankruptcy or similar circumstances, the relevant court and administrative authorities would find the State savings association's exposure to be the net amount under:

(*i*) The law of the jurisdiction in which the counterparty is chartered or the equivalent location in the case of noncorporate entities, and if a branch of the counterparty is involved, then also under the law of the jurisdiction in which the branch is located;

(*ii*) The law that governs the individual off-balance sheet rate contracts covered by the bilateral netting contract; and

(*iii*) The law that governs the bilateral netting contract;

(*4*) The State savings association establishes and maintains procedures to monitor possible changes in relevant law and to ensure that the bilateral netting contract continues to satisfy the requirements of this section; and

(*5*) The State savings association maintains in its files documentation adequate to support the netting of an off-balance sheet rate contract.[4]

---

[2] For purposes of calculating potential future credit exposure for foreign exchange contracts and other similar contracts, in which notional principal is equivalent to cash flows, total notional principal is defined as the net receipts to each party falling due on each value date in each currency.

[3] No potential future credit exposure is calculated for single currency interest rate swaps in which payments are made based upon two floating rate indices, so-called floating/floating or basis swaps; the credit equivalent amount is measured solely on the basis of the current credit exposure.

[4] By netting individual off-balance sheet rate contracts for the purpose of calculating its credit equivalent amount, a State savings association represents that documentation

Federal Deposit Insurance Corporation § 390.466

(C) *Walkaway clause.* A bilateral netting contract that contains a walkaway clause is not eligible for netting for purposes of calculating the current credit exposure amount. The term "walkaway clause" means a provision in a bilateral netting contract that permits a nondefaulting counterparty to make a lower payment than it would make otherwise under the bilateral netting contract, or no payment at all, to a defaulter or the estate of a defaulter, even if the defaulter or the estate of the defaulter is a net creditor under the bilateral netting contract.

(D) *Risk weighting.* Once the State savings association determines the credit equivalent amount for an off-balance sheet rate contract, that amount is assigned to the risk-weight category appropriate to the counterparty, or, if relevant, to the nature of any collateral or guarantee. Collateral held against a netting contract is not recognized for capital purposes unless it is legally available for all contracts included in the netting contract. However, the maximum risk weight for the credit equivalent amount of such off-balance sheet rate contracts is 50 percent.

(E) *Exceptions.* The following off-balance sheet rate contracts are not subject to the above calculation, and therefore, are not part of the denominator of a State savings association's risk-based capital ratio:

(*1*) A foreign exchange rate contract with an original maturity of 14 calendar days or less; and

(*2*) Any interest rate or foreign exchange rate contract that is traded on an exchange requiring the daily payment of any variations in the market value of the contract.

---

adequate to support the netting of an off-balance sheet rate contract is in the State savings association's files and available for inspection by the FDIC. Upon determination by the FDIC that a State savings association's files are inadequate or that a bilateral netting contract may not be legally enforceable under any one of the bodies of law described in paragraphs (a)(2)(vi)(B)(3) (i) through (iii) of this section, the underlying individual off-balance sheet rate contracts may not be netted for the purposes of this section.

(*3*) If a State savings association has multiple overlapping exposures (such as a program-wide credit enhancement and a liquidity facility) to an ABCP program that is not consolidated for risk-based capital purposes, the State savings association is not required to hold duplicative risk-based capital under this subpart against the overlapping position. Instead, the State savings association should apply to the overlapping position the applicable risk-based capital treatment that results in the highest capital charge.

(b) *Recourse obligations, direct credit substitutes, and certain other positions*— (1) *In general.* Except as otherwise permitted in this paragraph (b), to determine the risk-weighted asset amount for a recourse obligation or a direct credit substitute (but not a residual interest):

(i) Multiply the full amount of the credit-enhanced assets for which the State savings association directly or indirectly retains or assumes credit risk by a 100 percent conversion factor. (For a direct credit substitute that is an on-balance sheet asset (*e.g.*, a purchased subordinated security), a State savings association must use the amount of the direct credit substitute and the full amount of the asset its supports, *i.e.*, all the more senior positions in the structure); and

(ii) Assign this credit equivalent amount to the risk-weight category appropriate to the obligor in the underlying transaction, after considering any associated guarantees or collateral. Paragraph (a)(1) of this section lists the risk-weight categories.

(2) *Residual interests.* Except as otherwise permitted under this paragraph (b), a State savings association must maintain risk-based capital for residual interests as follows:

(i) *Credit-enhancing interest-only strips.* After applying the concentration limit under § 390.471(e)(2), a state saving association must maintain risk-based capital for a credit-enhancing interest-only strip equal to the remaining amount of the strip (net of any existing associated deferred tax liability), even if the amount of risk-based capital that must be maintained exceeds the full risk-based capital requirement for the assets transferred. Transactions that,

911

§ 390.466

in substance, result in the retention of credit risk associated with a transferred credit-enhancing interest-only strip are treated as if the strip was retained by the State savings association and was not transferred.

(ii) *Other residual interests.* A state saving association must maintain risk-based capital for a residual interest (excluding a credit-enhancing interest-only strip) equal to the face amount of the residual interest (net of any existing associated deferred tax liability), even if the amount of risk-based capital that must be maintained exceeds the full risk-based capital requirement for the assets transferred. Transactions that, in substance, result in the retention of credit risk associated with a transferred residual interest are treated as if the residual interest was retained by the State savings association and was not transferred.

(iii) *Residual interests and other recourse obligations.* Where a State savings association holds a residual interest (including a credit-enhancing interest-only strip) and another recourse obligation in connection with the same transfer of assets, the State savings association must maintain risk-based capital equal to the greater of:

(A) The risk-based capital requirement for the residual interest as calculated under paragraph (b)(2)(i) and (ii) of this section; or

(B) The full risk-based capital requirement for the assets transferred, subject to the low-level recourse rules under paragraph (b)(7) of this section.

(3) *Ratings-based approach*—(i) *Calculation.* A State savings association may calculate the risk-weighted asset amount for an eligible position described in paragraph (b)(3)(ii) of this section by multiplying the face amount of the position by the appropriate risk weight determined in accordance with Table A or B of this section.

NOTE: Stripped mortgage-backed securities or other similar instruments, such as interest-only and principal-only strips, that are not credit enhancing must be assigned to the 100% risk-weight category.

TABLE A TO § 390.466

Long term rating category	Risk weight (in percent)
Highest or second highest investment grade	20

TABLE A TO § 390.466—Continued

Long term rating category	Risk weight (in percent)
Third highest investment grade	50
Lowest investment grade	100
One category below investment grade	200

TABLE B TO § 390.466

Short term rating category	Risk weight (in percent)
Highest investment grade	20
Second highest investment grade	50
Lowest investment grade	100

(ii) *Eligibility*—(A) *Traded positions.* A position is eligible for the treatment described in paragraph (b)(3)(i) of this section, if:

(*1*) The position is a recourse obligation, direct credit substitute, residual interest, or asset- or mortgage-backed security and is not a credit-enhancing interest-only strip;

(*2*) The position is a traded position; and

(*3*) The NRSRO has rated a long term position as one grade below investment grade or better or a short term position as investment grade. If two or more NRSROs assign ratings to a traded position, the State savings association must use the lowest rating to determine the appropriate risk-weight category under paragraph (b)(3)(i) of this section.

(B) *Non-traded positions.* A position that is not traded is eligible for the treatment described in paragraph (b)(3)(i) of this section if:

(*1*) The position is a recourse obligation, direct credit substitute, residual interest, or asset- or mortgage-backed security extended in connection with a securitization and is not a credit-enhancing interest-only strip;

(*2*) More than one NRSRO rate the position;

(*3*) All of the NRSROs that provide a rating rate a long term position as one grade below investment grade or better or a short term position as investment grade. If the NRSROs assign different ratings to the position, the State savings association must use the lowest rating to determine the appropriate risk-weight category under paragraph (b)(3)(i) of this section;

(*4*) The NRSROs base their ratings on the same criteria that they use to rate

Federal Deposit Insurance Corporation § 390.466

securities that are traded positions; and

(5) The ratings are publicly available.

(C) *Unrated senior positions.* If a recourse obligation, direct credit substitute, residual interest, or asset- or mortgage-backed security is not rated by an NRSRO, but is senior or preferred in all features to a traded position (including collateralization and maturity), the State savings association may risk-weight the face amount of the senior position under paragraph (b)(3)(i) of this section, based on the rating of the traded position, subject to supervisory guidance. The State savings association must satisfy FDIC that this treatment is appropriate. This paragraph (b)(3)(i)(C) applies only if the traded position provides substantive credit support to the unrated position until the unrated position matures.

(4) *Certain positions that are not rated by NRSROs*—(i) *Calculation.* A State savings association may calculate the risk-weighted asset amount for eligible position described in paragraph (b)(4)(ii) of this section based on the State savings association's determination of the credit rating of the position. To risk-weight the asset, the State savings association must multiply the face amount of the position by the appropriate risk weight determined in accordance with Table C of this section.

TABLE C TO § 390.466

Rating category	Risk weight (in percent)
Investment grade	100
One category below investment grade	200

(ii) *Eligibility.* A position extended in connection with a securitization is eligible for the treatment described in paragraph (b)(4)(i) of this section if it is not rated by an NRSRO, is not a residual interest, and meets one of the three alternative standards described in paragraph (b)(4)(ii)(A), (B), or (C) of this section:

(A) *Position rated internally.* A direct credit substitute, but not a purchased credit-enhancing interest-only strip, is eligible for the treatment described under paragraph (b)(4)(i) of this section, if the position is assumed in connection with an asset-backed commercial paper program sponsored by the State savings association. Before it may rely on an internal credit risk rating system, the state saving association must demonstrate to FDIC's satisfaction that the system is adequate. Adequate internal credit risk rating systems typically:

(1) Are an integral part of the State savings association's risk management system that explicitly incorporates the full range of risks arising from the State savings association's participation in securitization activities;

(2) Link internal credit ratings to measurable outcomes, such as the probability that the position will experience any loss, the expected loss on the position in the event of default, and the degree of variance in losses in the event of default on that position;

(3) Separately consider the risk associated with the underlying loans or borrowers, and the risk associated with the structure of the particular securitization transaction;

(4) Identify gradations of risk among "pass" assets and other risk positions;

(5) Use clear, explicit criteria to classify assets into each internal rating grade, including subjective factors;

(6) Employ independent credit risk management or loan review personnel to assign or review the credit risk ratings;

(7) Include an internal audit procedure to periodically verify that internal risk ratings are assigned in accordance with the State savings association's established criteria;

(8) Monitor the performance of the assigned internal credit risk ratings over time to determine the appropriateness of the initial credit risk rating assignment, and adjust individual credit risk ratings or the overall internal credit risk rating system, as needed; and

(9) Make credit risk rating assumptions that are consistent with, or more conservative than, the credit risk rating assumptions and methodologies of NRSROs.

(B) *Program ratings.* (1) A recourse obligation or direct credit substitute, but not a residual interest, is eligible for the treatment described in paragraph (b)(4)(i) of this section, if the position

§ 390.466

is retained or assumed in connection with a structured finance program and an NRSRO has reviewed the terms of the program and stated a rating for positions associated with the program. If the program has options for different combinations of assets, standards, internal or external credit enhancements and other relevant factors, and the NRSRO specifies ranges of rating categories to them, the State savings association may apply the rating category applicable to the option that corresponds to the State savings association's position.

(2) To rely on a program rating, the State savings association must demonstrate to FDIC's satisfaction that the credit risk rating assigned to the program meets the same standards generally used by NRSROs for rating traded positions. The State savings association must also demonstrate to FDIC's satisfaction that the criteria underlying the assignments for the program are satisfied by the particular position.

(3) If a State savings association participates in a securitization sponsored by another party, FDIC may authorize the State savings association to use this approach based on a program rating obtained by the sponsor of the program.

(C) *Computer program.* A recourse obligation or direct credit substitute, but not a residual interest, is eligible for the treatment described in paragraph (b)(4)(i) of this section, if the position is extended in connection with a structured financing program and the State savings association uses an acceptable credit assessment computer program to determine the rating of the position. An NRSRO must have developed the computer program and the State savings association must demonstrate to FDIC's satisfaction that the ratings under the program correspond credibly and reliably with the rating of traded positions.

(5) *Alternative capital computation for small business obligations*—(i) *Definitions.* For the purposes of this paragraph (b)(5):

(A) *Qualified State savings association* means a State savings association that:

(*1*) Is well capitalized as defined in § 390.453 without applying the capital treatment described in this paragraph (b)(5); or

(*2*) Is adequately capitalized as defined in § 390.453 without applying the capital treatment described in this paragraph (b)(5) and has received written permission from the FDIC to apply that capital treatment.

(B) *Small business* means a business that meets the criteria for a small business concern established by the Small Business Administration in 13 CFR 121 pursuant to 15 U.S.C. 632.

(ii) *Capital requirement.* Notwithstanding any other provision of this paragraph (b), with respect to a transfer of a small business loan or lease of personal property with recourse that is a sale under generally accepted accounting principles, a qualified State savings association may elect to include only the amount of its recourse in its risk-weighted assets. To qualify for this election, the State savings association must establish and maintain a reserve under generally accepted accounting principles sufficient to meet the reasonable estimated liability of the State savings association under the recourse obligation.

(iii) *Aggregate amount of recourse.* The total outstanding amount of recourse retained by a qualified State savings association with respect to transfers of small business loans and leases of personal property and included in the risk-weighted assets of the State savings association as described in paragraph (b)(5)(ii) of this section, may not exceed 15 percent of the association's total capital computed under § 390.465(c).

(iv) *State savings association that ceases to be a qualified State savings association or that exceeds aggregate limits.* If a State savings association ceases to be a qualified State savings association or exceeds the aggregate limit described in paragraph (b)(5)(iii) of this section, the State savings association may continue to apply the capital treatment described in paragraph (b)(5)(ii) of this section to transfers of small business loans and leases of personal property that occurred when the association was a qualified State savings association and did not exceed the limit.

Federal Deposit Insurance Corporation § 390.466

(v) *Prompt corrective action not affected.* (A) A State savings association shall compute its capital without regard to this paragraph (b)(5) of this section for purposes of prompt corrective action (12 U.S.C. 1831o), unless the State savings association is adequately or well capitalized without applying the capital treatment described in this paragraph (b)(5) and would be well capitalized after applying that capital treatment.

(B) A State savings association shall compute its capital requirement without regard to this paragraph (b)(5) for the purposes of applying 12 U.S.C. 1831o(g), regardless of the association's capital level.

(6) *Risk participations and syndications of direct credit substitutes.* A State savings association must calculate the risk-weighted asset amount for a risk participation in, or syndication of, a direct credit substitute as follows:

(i) If a State savings association conveys a risk participation in a direct credit substitute, the State savings association must convert the full amount of the assets that are supported by the direct credit substitute to a credit equivalent amount using a 100 percent conversion factor. The State savings association must assign the *pro rata* share of the credit equivalent amount that was conveyed through the risk participation to the lower of: The risk-weight category appropriate to the obligor in the underlying transaction, after considering any associated guarantees or collateral; or the risk-weight category appropriate to the party acquiring the participation. The State savings association must assign the *pro rata* share of the credit equivalent amount that was not participated out to the risk-weight category appropriate to the obligor, after considering any associated guarantees or collateral.

(ii) If a State savings association acquires a risk participation in a direct credit substitute, the State savings association must multiply its *pro rata* share of the direct credit substitute by the full amount of the assets that are supported by the direct credit substitute, and convert this amount to a credit equivalent amount using a 100 percent conversion factor. The State savings association must assign the resulting credit equivalent amount to the risk-weight category appropriate to the obligor in the underlying transaction, after considering any associated guarantees or collateral.

(iii) If the State savings association holds a direct credit substitute in the form of a syndication where each State savings association or other participant is obligated only for its *pro rata* share of the risk and there is no recourse to the originating party, the State savings association must calculate the credit equivalent amount by multiplying only its *pro rata* share of the assets supported by the direct credit substitute by a 100 percent conversion factor. The State savings association must assign the resulting credit equivalent amount to the risk-weight category appropriate to the obligor in the underlying transaction after considering any associated guarantees or collateral.

(7) *Limitations on risk-based capital requirements*—(i) *Low-level exposure rule.* If the maximum contractual exposure to loss retained or assumed by a State savings association is less than the effective risk-based capital requirement, as determined in accordance with this paragraph (b), for the assets supported by the State savings association's position, the risk-based capital requirement is limited to the State savings association's contractual exposure less any recourse liability account established in accordance with generally accepted accounting principles. This limitation does not apply when a State savings association provides credit enhancement beyond any contractual obligation to support assets it has sold.

(ii) *Mortgage-related securities or participation certificates retained in a mortgage loan swap.* If a State savings association holds a mortgage-related security or a participation certificate as a result of a mortgage loan swap with recourse, it must hold risk-based capital to support the recourse obligation and that percentage of the mortgage-related security or participation certificate that is not covered by the recourse obligation. The total amount of risk-based capital required for the security (or certificate) and the recourse obligation is limited to the risk-based

915

capital requirement for the underlying loans, calculated as if the State savings association continued to hold these loans as an on-balance sheet asset.

(iii) *Related on-balance sheet assets.* If an asset is included in the calculation of the risk-based capital requirement under this paragraph (b) and also appears as an asset on the State savings association's balance sheet, the State savings association must risk-weight the asset only under this paragraph (b), except in the case of loan servicing assets and similar arrangements with embedded recourse obligations or direct credit substitutes. In that case, the State savings association must separately risk-weight the on-balance sheet servicing asset and the related recourse obligations and direct credit substitutes under this section, and incorporate these amounts into the risk-based capital calculation.

(8) *Obligations of subsidiaries.* If a State savings association retains a recourse obligation or assumes a direct credit substitute on the obligation of a subsidiary that is not an includable subsidiary, and the recourse obligation or direct credit substitute is an equity or debt investment in that subsidiary under generally accepted accounting principles, the face amount of the recourse obligation or direct credit substitute is deducted for capital under §§ 390.465(a)(2) and 390.468(c). All other recourse obligations and direct credit substitutes retained or assumed by a State savings association on the obligations of an entity in which the State savings association has an equity investment are risk-weighted in accordance with this paragraph (b).

§ 390.467 Leverage ratio.

(a) The minimum leverage capital requirement for a State savings association assigned a composite rating of 1, as defined in this subpart, shall consist of a ratio of core capital to adjusted total assets of 3 percent. These generally are strong State savings associations that are not anticipating or experiencing significant growth and have well-diversified risks, including no undue interest rate risk exposure, excellent asset quality, high liquidity, and good earnings.

(b) For all State savings associations not meeting the conditions set forth in paragraph (a) of this section, the minimum leverage capital requirement shall consist of a ratio of core capital to adjusted total assets of 4 percent. Higher capital ratios may be required if warranted by the particular circumstances or risk profiles of an individual State savings association. In all cases, State savings associations should hold capital commensurate with the level and nature of all risks, including the volume and severity of problem loans, to which they are exposed.

§ 390.468 Tangible capital requirement.

(a) State savings associations shall have and maintain tangible capital in an amount equal to at least 1.5% of adjusted total assets.

(b) The following elements, less the amount of any deductions pursuant to paragraph (c) of this section, comprise a State savings association's tangible capital:

(1) Common stockholders' equity (including retained earnings);

(2) Noncumulative perpetual preferred stock and related earnings;

(3) Nonwithdrawable accounts and pledged deposits that would qualify as core capital under § 390.465; and

(4) Minority interests in the equity accounts of fully consolidated subsidiaries.

(c) *Deductions from tangible capital.* In calculating tangible capital, a State savings association must deduct from assets, and, thus, from capital:

(1) Intangible assets (as defined in § 390.461) except for mortgage servicing assets to the extent they are includable in tangible capital under § 390.471, and credit enhancing interest-only strips and deferred tax assets not includable in tangible capital under § 390.471.

(2) Investments, both equity and debt, in subsidiaries that are not includable subsidiaries (including those subsidiaries where the State savings association has a minority ownership interest), except as provided in paragraphs (c)(3) and (4) of this section.

(3) If a State savings association has any investments (both debt and equity) in one or more subsidiary(ies) engaged

Federal Deposit Insurance Corporation § 390.469

as of April 12, 1989, and continuing to be engaged in any activity that would not fall within the scope of activities in which includable subsidiaries may engage, it must deduct such investments from assets and, thus, tangible capital in accordance with this paragraph (c)(3). The State savings association must first deduct from assets and, thus, capital the amount by which any investments in such a subsidiary(ies) exceed the amount of such investments held by the State savings association as of April 12, 1989. Next, the State savings association must deduct from assets and, thus, tangible capital the lesser of:

(i) The State savings association's investments in and extensions of credit to the subsidiary as of April 12, 1989; or

(ii) The State savings association's investments in and extensions of credit to the subsidiary on the date as of which the State savings association's capital is being determined.

(4) If a State savings association holds a subsidiary (either directly or through a subsidiary) that is itself a domestic depository institution the FDIC may, in its sole discretion upon determining that the amount of tangible capital that would be required would be higher if the assets and liabilities of such subsidiary were consolidated with those of the parent State savings association than the amount that would be required if the parent State savings association's investment were deducted pursuant to paragraphs (c)(2) and (3) of this section, consolidate the assets and liabilities of that subsidiary with those of the parent State savings association in calculating the capital adequacy of the parent State savings association, regardless of whether the subsidiary would otherwise be an includable subsidiary as defined in § 390.461.

§ 390.469 Consequences of failure to meet capital requirements.

(a) *Capital plans.* (1) [Reserved]

(2) The FDIC shall require any State savings association not in compliance with capital standards to submit a capital plan that:

(i) Addresses the State savings association's need for increased capital;

(ii) Describes the manner in which the State savings association will increase capital so as to achieve compliance with capital standards;

(iii) Specifies types and levels of activities in which the State savings association will engage;

(iv) Requires any increase in assets to be accompanied by increase in tangible capital not less in percentage amount than the leverage limit then applicable;

(v) Requires any increase in assets to be accompanied by an increase in capital not less in percentage amount than required under the risk-based capital standard then applicable; and

(vi) Is acceptable to the FDIC.

(3) To be acceptable to the FDIC under this section, a plan must, in addition to satisfying all of the requirements set forth in paragraphs (a)(2)(i) through (v) of this section, contain a certification that while the plan is under review by the FDIC, the State savings association will not, without the prior written approval of the appropriate Regional Director:

(i) Grow beyond net interest credited;

(ii) Make any capital distributions; or

(iii) Act inconsistently with any other limitations on activities established by statute, regulation or by the FDIC in supervisory guidance for State savings associations not meeting capital standards.

(4) If the plan submitted to the FDIC under paragraph (a)(2) of this section is not approved by the FDIC, the State savings association shall immediately and without any further action, be subject to the following restrictions:

(i) It may not increase its assets beyond the amount held on the day it receives written notice of the FDIC's disapproval of the plan; and

(ii) It must comply with any other restrictions or limitations set forth in the written notice of the FDIC's disapproval of the plan.

(b) On or after January 1, 1991, the FDIC shall:

(1) Prohibit any asset growth by any State savings association not in compliance with capital standards, *except* as provided in paragraph (d) of this section; and

§ 390.470

(2) Require any State savings association not in compliance with capital standards to comply with a capital directive issued by the FDIC which may include the restrictions contained in paragraph (e) of this section and any other restrictions the FDIC determines appropriate.

(c) A State savings association that wishes to obtain an exemption from the sanctions provided in paragraph (b)(2) of this section must file a request for exemption with the appropriate Regional Director. Such request must include a capital plan that satisfies the requirements of paragraph (a)(2) of this section.

(d) The FDIC may permit any State savings association that is subject to paragraph (b) of this section to increase its assets in an amount not exceeding the amount of net interest credited to the State savings association's deposit liabilities, if:

(1) The State savings association obtains the FDIC's prior approval;

(2) Any increase in assets is accompanied by an increase in tangible capital in an amount not less than 3% of the increase in assets;

(3) Any increase in assets is accompanied by an increase in capital not less in percentage amount than required under the risk-based capital standards then applicable;

(4) Any increase in assets is invested in low-risk assets; and

(5) The State savings association's ratio of core capital to total assets is not less than the ratio existing on January 1, 1991.

(e) If a State savings association fails to meet the risk-based capital requirement, the leverage ratio requirement, or the tangible capital requirement established under this subpart, the FDIC may, through enforcement proceedings or otherwise, require such State savings association to take one or more of the following corrective actions:

(1) Increase the amount of its regulatory capital to a specified level or levels;

(2) Convene a meeting or meetings with the FDIC for the purpose of accomplishing the objectives of this section;

(3) Reduce the rate of earnings that may be paid on savings accounts;

(4) Limit the receipt of deposits to those made to existing accounts;

(5) Cease or limit the issuance of new accounts of any or all classes or categories, except in exchange for existing accounts;

(6) Cease or limit lending or the making of a particular type or category of loan;

(7) Cease or limit the purchase of loans or the making of specified other investments;

(8) Limit operational expenditures to specified levels;

(9) Increase liquid assets and maintain such increased liquidity at specified levels; or

(10) Take such other action or actions as the FDIC may deem necessary or appropriate for the safety and soundness of the State savings association, or depositors or investors in the State savings association.

(f) The FDIC shall treat as an unsafe and unsound practice any material failure by a State savings association to comply with any plan, regulation, written agreement undertaken under this section or order or directive issued to comply with the requirements of this subpart.

§ 390.470 Reservation of authority.

(a) *Transactions for purposes of evasion.* The FDIC may disregard any transaction entered into primarily for the purpose of reducing the minimum required amount of regulatory capital or otherwise evading the requirements of this subpart.

(b) *Average versus period-end figures.* The FDIC reserves the right to require a State savings association to compute its capital ratios on the basis of average, rather than period-end, assets when the FDIC determines appropriate to carry out the purposes of this subpart.

(c)(1) *Reservation of authority.* Notwithstanding the definitions of core and supplementary capital in § 390.465, the FDIC may find that a particular type of purchased intangible asset or capital instrument constitutes or may constitute core or supplementary capital, and may permit one or more State savings associations to include all or a portion of such intangible asset or

Federal Deposit Insurance Corporation

§ 390.471

funds obtained through such capital instrument as core or supplementary capital, permanently or on a temporary basis, for the purposes of compliance with this subpart or for any other purposes. Similarly, the FDIC may find that a particular asset or core or supplementary capital component has characteristics or terms that diminish its contribution to a State savings association's ability to absorb losses, and the FDIC may require the discounting or deduction of such asset or component from the computation of core, supplementary, or total capital.

(2) Notwithstanding §390.466, the FDIC will look to the substance of a transaction and may find that the assigned risk weight for any asset, or credit equivalent amount or credit conversion factor for any off-balance sheet item does not appropriately reflect the risks imposed on the State savings association. The FDIC may require the State savings association to apply another risk-weight, credit equivalent amount, or credit conversion factor that the FDIC deems appropriate.

(3) The FDIC may find that the capital treatment for an exposure to a transaction not subject to consolidation on the State savings association's balance sheet does not appropriately reflect the risks imposed on the State savings association. Accordingly, the FDIC may require the State savings association to treat the transaction as if it were consolidated on the State savings association's balance sheet. The FDIC will look to the substance of and risk associated with the transaction as well as other relevant factors in determining whether to require such treatment and in calculating risk based capital as the FDIC deems appropriate.

(4) If this subpart does not specifically assign a risk weight, credit equivalent amount, or credit conversion factor, the FDIC may assign any risk weight, credit equivalent amount, or credit conversion factor that it deems appropriate. In making this determination, the FDIC will consider the risks associated with the asset or off-balance sheet item as well as other relevant factors.

(d) In making a determination under this paragraph (c) of this section, the FDIC will notify the State savings association of the determination and solicit a response from the State savings association. After review of the response by the State savings association, the FDIC shall issue a final supervisory decision regarding the determination made under paragraph (c) of this section.

§ 390.471 Purchased credit card relationships, servicing assets, intangible assets (other than purchased credit card relationships and servicing assets), credit-enhancing interest-only strips, and deferred tax assets.

(a) *Scope.* This section prescribes the maximum amount of purchased credit card relationships, serving assets, intangible assets (other than purchased credit card relationships and servicing assets), credit-enhancing interest-only strips, and deferred tax assets that State savings associations may include in calculating tangible and core capital.

(b) *Computation of core and tangible capital.* (1) Purchased credit card relationships may be included (that is, not deducted) in computing core capital in accordance with the restrictions in this section, but must be deducted in computing tangible capital.

(2) In accordance with the restrictions in this section, mortgage servicing assets may be included in computing core and tangible capital and nonmortgage servicing assets may be included in core capital.

(3) Intangible assets, as defined in § 390.461, other than purchased credit card relationships described in paragraph (b)(1) of this section, servicing assets described in paragraph (b)(2) of this section, and core deposit intangibles described in paragraph (g)(3) of this section, are deducted in computing tangible and core capital, subject to paragraph (e)(3)(ii) of this section.

(4) Credit-enhancing interest-only strips may be included (that is not deducted) in computing core capital subject to the restrictions of this section, and may be included in tangible capital in the same amount.

§ 390.471

(5) *Deferred tax assets* may be included (that is not deducted) in computing core capital subject to the restrictions of paragraph (h) of this section, and may be included in tangible capital in the same amount.

(c) *Market valuations.* The FDIC reserves the authority to require any State savings association to perform an independent market valuation of assets subject to this section on a case-by-case basis or through the issuance of policy guidance. An independent market valuation, if required, shall be conducted in accordance with any policy guidance issued by the FDIC. A required valuation shall include adjustments for any significant changes in original valuation assumptions, including changes in prepayment estimates or attrition rates. The valuation shall determine the current fair value of assets subject to this section. This independent market valuation may be conducted by an independent valuation expert evaluating the reasonableness of the internal calculations and assumptions used by the State savings association in conducting its internal analysis. The State savings association shall calculate an estimated fair value for assets subject to this section at least quarterly regardless of whether an independent valuation expert is required to perform an independent market valuation.

(d) *Value limitation.* For purposes of calculating core capital under this subpart (but not for financial statement purposes), purchased credit card relationships and servicing assets must be valued at the lesser of:

(1) Ninety (90) percent of their fair value determined in accordance with paragraph (c) of this section; or

(2) One hundred (100) percent of their remaining unamortized book value determined in accordance with the instructions for the Thrift Financial Report or Consolidated Reports of Condition or Income ("Call Report."), as applicable.

(e) *Core capital limitations*—(1) *Servicing assets and purchased credit card relationships.* (i) The maximum aggregate amount of servicing assets and purchased credit card relationships that may be included in core capital is limited to the lesser of:

(A) 100 percent of the amount of core capital; or

(B) The amount of servicing assets and purchased credit card relationships determined in accordance with paragraph (d) of this section.

(ii) In addition to the aggregate limitation in paragraph (e)(1)(i) of this section, a sublimit applies to purchased credit card relationships and non mortgage-related serving assets. The maximum allowable amount of these two types of assets combined is limited to the lesser of:

(A) 25 percent the amount of core capital; and

(B) The amount of purchased credit card relationships and non mortgage-related servicing assets determined in accordance with paragraph (d) of this section.

(2) *Credit-enhancing interest-only strips.* The maximum aggregate amount of credit-enhancing interest-only strips that may be included in core capital is limited to 25 percent of the amount of core capital. Purchased and retained credit-enhancing interest-only strips, on a non-tax adjusted basis, are included in the total amount that is used for purposes of determining whether a State savings association exceeds the core capital limit.

(3) *Computation.* (i) For purposes of computing the limits and sublimits in paragraphs (e) and (h) of this section, core capital is computed before the deduction of disallowed servicing assets, disallowed purchased credit card relationships, disallowed credit-enhancing interest-only strips (purchased and retained), and disallowed deferred tax assets.

(ii) A State savings association may elect to deduct the following items on a basis net of deferred tax liabilities:

(A) Disallowed servicing assets;

(B) Goodwill such that only the net amount must be deducted from Tier 1 capital;

(C) Disallowed credit-enhancing interest-only strips (both purchased and retained); and

(D) Other intangible assets arising from non-taxable business combinations. A deferred tax liability that is specifically related to an intangible asset (other than purchased credit card

Federal Deposit Insurance Corporation § 390.471

relationships) arising from a nontaxable business combination may be netted against this intangible asset. The net amount of the intangible asset must be deducted from Tier 1 capital.

(iii) Deferred tax liabilities that are netted in accordance with paragraph (e)(3)(ii) of this section cannot also be netted against deferred tax assets when determining the amount of deferred tax assets that are dependent upon future taxable income.

(f) *Tangible capital limitation.* The maximum amount of mortgage servicing assets that may be included in tangible capital shall be the same amount includable in core capital in accordance with the limitations set by paragraph (e) of this section. All non-mortgage servicing assets are deducted in computing tangible capital.

(g) *Exemption for certain subsidiaries*— (1) *Exemption standard.* A State savings association holding purchased mortgage servicing rights in separately capitalized, non-includable subsidiaries may submit an application for approval by the FDIC for an exemption from the deductions and limitations set forth in this section. The deductions and limitations will apply to such purchased mortgage servicing rights, however, if the FDIC determines that:

(i) The State savings association and subsidiary are not conducting activities on an arm's length basis; or

(ii) The exemption is not consistent with the State savings association's safe and sound operation.

(2) *Applicable requirements.* If the FDIC determines to grant or to permit the continuation of an exemption under paragraph (h)(1) of this section, the State savings association receiving the exemption must ensure the following:

(i) The State savings association's investments in, and extensions of credit to, the subsidiary are deducted from capital when calculating capital under this subpart;

(ii) Extensions of credit and other transactions with the subsidiary are conducted in compliance with the rules for covered transactions with affiliates set forth in sections 23A and 23B of the Federal Reserve Act, as applied to State savings associations; and

(iii) Any contracts entered into by the subsidiary include a written disclosure indicating that the subsidiary is not a bank or State savings association; the subsidiary is an organization separate and apart from any bank or State savings association; and the obligations of the subsidiary are not backed or guaranteed by any bank or State savings association and are not insured by the FDIC.

(h) *Treatment of deferred tax assets.* For purposes of calculating Tier 1 capital under this subpart (but not for financial statement purposes) deferred tax assets are subject to the conditions, limitations, and restrictions described in this section.

(1) *Tier 1 capital limitations.* (i) The maximum allowable amount of deferred tax assets net of any valuation allowance that are dependent upon future taxable income will be limited to the lesser of:

(A) The amount of deferred tax assets that are dependent upon future taxable income that is expected to be realized within one year of the calendar quarter-end date, based on a projected future taxable income for that year; or

(B) Ten percent of the amount of Tier 1 capital that exists before the deduction of any disallowed servicing assets, any disallowed purchased credit card relationships, any disallowed credit-enhancing interest-only strips, and any disallowed deferred tax assets.

(ii) For purposes of this limitation, all existing temporary differences should be assumed to fully reverse at the calendar quarter-end date. The recorded amount of deferred tax assets that are dependent upon future taxable income, net of any valuation allowance for deferred tax assets, in excess of this limitation will be deducted from assets and from equity capital for purposes of determining Tier 1 capital under this subpart. The amount of deferred tax assets that can be realized from taxes paid in prior carryback years and from the reversal of existing taxable temporary differences generally would not be deducted from assets and from equity capital.

(iii) Notwithstanding paragraph (h)(1)(B)(ii) of this section, the amount of carryback potential that may be considered in calculating the amount of deferred tax assets that a State savings association that is part of a consolidated group (for tax purposes) may include in Tier 1 capital may not exceed the amount which the association could reasonably expect to have refunded by its parent.

(2) *Projected future taxable income.* Projected future taxable income should not include net operating loss carryforwards to be used within one year of the most recent calendar quarter-end date or the amount of existing temporary differences expected to reverse within that year. Projected future taxable income should include the estimated effect of tax planning strategies that are expected to be implemented to realize tax carryforwards that will otherwise expire during that year. Future taxable income projections for the current fiscal year (adjusted for any significant changes that have occurred or are expected to occur) may be used when applying the capital limit at an interim calendar quarter-end date rather than preparing a new projection each quarter.

(3) *Unrealized holding gains and losses on available-for-sale debt securities.* The deferred tax effects of any unrealized holding gains and losses on available-for-sale debt securities may be excluded from the determination of the amount of deferred tax assets that are dependent upon future taxable income and the calculation of the maximum allowable amount of such assets. If these deferred tax effects are excluded, this treatment must be followed consistently over time.

APPENDIX A TO SUBPART Z OF PART 390—RISK-BASED CAPITAL REQUIREMENTS—INTERNAL-RATINGS-BASED AND ADVANCED MEASUREMENT APPROACHES

Part I General Provisions
Section 1 Purpose, Applicability, Reservation of Authority, and Principle of Conservatism
Section 2 Definitions
Section 3 Minimum Risk-Based Capital Requirements
Part II Qualifying Capital
Section 11 Additional Deductions
Section 12 Deductions and Limitations Not Required
Section 13 Eligible Credit Reserves
Part III Qualification
Section 21 Qualification Process
Section 22 Qualification Requirements
Section 23 Ongoing Qualification
Section 24 Merger and Acquisition Transitional Arrangements
Part IV Risk-Weighted Assets for General Credit Risk
Section 31 Mechanics for Calculating Total Wholesale and Retail Risk-Weighted Assets
Section 32 Counterparty Credit Risk of Repo-Style Transactions, Eligible Margin Loans, and OTC Derivative Contracts
Section 33 Guarantees and Credit Derivatives: PD Substitution and LGD Adjustment Approaches
Section 34 Guarantees and Credit Derivatives: Double Default Treatment
Section 35 Risk-Based Capital Requirement for Unsettled Transactions.
Part V Risk-Weighted Assets for Securitization Exposures
Section 41 Operational Criteria for Recognizing the Transfer of Risk
Section 42 Risk-Based Capital Requirement for Securitization Exposures
Section 43 Ratings-Based Approach (RBA)
Section 44 Internal Assessment Approach (IAA)
Section 45 Supervisory Formula Approach (SFA)
Section 46 Recognition of Credit Risk Mitigants for Securitization Exposures
Section 47 Risk-Based Capital Requirement for Early Amortization Provisions
Part VI Risk-Weighted Assets for Equity Exposures
Section 51 Introduction and Exposure Measurement
Section 52 Simple Risk Weight Approach (SRWA)
Section 53 Internal Models Approach (IMA)
Section 54 Equity Exposures to Investment Funds
Section 55 Equity Derivative Contracts
Part VII Risk-Weighted Assets for Operational Risk
Section 61 Qualification Requirements for Incorporation of Operational Risk Mitigants
Section 62 Mechanics of Risk-Weighted Asset Calculation
Part VIII Disclosure
Section 71 Disclosure Requirements
Part IX Transition Provisions
Section 81 Optional Transition Provisions Related to the Implementation of Consolidation Requirements Under FAS 167

PART I. GENERAL PROVISIONS

Section 1. Purpose, Applicability, Reservation of Authority, and Principle of Conservatism

(a) *Purpose.* This appendix establishes:
(1) Minimum qualifying criteria for State savings associations using State savings association-specific internal risk measurement

Federal Deposit Insurance Corporation

Pt. 390, Subpt. Z, App. A

and management processes for calculating risk-based capital requirements;

(2) Methodologies for such State savings associations to calculate their risk-based capital requirements; and

(3) Public disclosure requirements for such State savings associations.

(b) *Applicability.* (1) This appendix applies to a State savings association that:

(i) Has consolidated assets, as reported on the most recent year-end Thrift Financial Report (TFR) or Consolidated Reports of Condition or Income ("Call Report"), as applicable, equal to $250 billion or more;

(ii) Has consolidated total on-balance sheet foreign exposure at the most recent year-end equal to $10 billion or more (where total on-balance sheet foreign exposure equals total cross-border claims less claims with head office or guarantor located in another country plus redistributed guaranteed amounts to the country of head office or guarantor plus local country claims on local residents plus revaluation gains on foreign exchange and derivative products, calculated in accordance with the Federal Financial Institutions Examination Council (FFIEC) 009 Country Exposure Report);

(iii) Is a subsidiary of a depository institution that uses 12 CFR part 3, appendix C, 12 CFR part 208, appendix F, 12 CFR part 325, appendix D, or 12 CFR subpart Z of part 390, appendix A, to calculate its risk-based capital requirements; or

(iv) Is a subsidiary of a bank holding company that uses 12 CFR part 225, appendix G, to calculate its risk-based capital requirements.

(2) Any State savings association may elect to use this appendix to calculate its risk-based capital requirements.

(3) A State savings association that is subject to this appendix must use this appendix unless the FDIC determines in writing that application of this appendix is not appropriate in light of the State savings association's asset size, level of complexity, risk profile, or scope of operations. In making a determination under this paragraph, the FDIC will apply notice and response procedures in the same manner and to the same extent as the notice and response procedures in § 390.463(d).

(c) *Reservation of authority*—(1) *Additional capital in the aggregate.* The FDIC may require a State savings association to hold an amount of capital greater than otherwise required under this appendix if the FDIC determines that the State savings association's risk-based capital requirement under this appendix is not commensurate with the State savings association's credit, market, operational, or other risks. In making a determination under this paragraph, the FDIC will apply notice and response procedures in the same manner and to the same extent as the notice and response procedures in § 390.463(d).

(2) *Specific risk-weighted asset amounts.* (i) If the FDIC determines that the risk-weighted asset amount calculated under this appendix by the State savings association for one or more exposures is not commensurate with the risks associated with those exposures, the FDIC may require the State savings association to assign a different risk-weighted asset amount to the exposures, to assign different risk parameters to the exposures (if the exposures are wholesale or retail exposures), or to use different model assumptions for the exposures (if relevant), all as specified by the FDIC.

(ii) If the FDIC determines that the risk-weighted asset amount for operational risk produced by the State savings association under this appendix is not commensurate with the operational risks of the State savings association, the FDIC may require the State savings association to assign a different risk-weighted asset amount for operational risk, to change elements of its operational risk analytical framework, including distributional and dependence assumptions, or to make other changes to the State savings association's operational risk management processes, data and assessment systems, or quantification systems, all as specified by the FDIC.

(3) *Regulatory capital treatment of unconsolidated entities.* The FDIC may find that the capital treatment for an exposure to a transaction not subject to consolidation on the State savings association's balance sheet does not appropriately reflect the risks imposed on the State savings association. Accordingly, the FDIC may require the State savings association to treat the transaction as if it were consolidated on the State savings association's balance sheet. The FDIC will look to the substance of and risk associated with the transaction as well as other relevant factors in determining whether to require such treatment and in calculating risk-based capital as the FDIC deems appropriate.

(4) *Other supervisory authority.* Nothing in this appendix limits the authority of the FDIC under any other provision of law or regulation to take supervisory or enforcement action, including action to address unsafe or unsound practices or conditions, deficient capital levels, or violations of law.

(d) *Principle of conservatism.* Notwithstanding the requirements of this appendix, a State savings association may choose not to apply a provision of this appendix to one or more exposures, provided that:

(1) The State savings association can demonstrate on an ongoing basis to the satisfaction of the FDIC that not applying the provision would, in all circumstances, unambiguously generate a risk-based capital requirement for each such exposure greater than

that which would otherwise be required under this appendix;

(2) The State savings association appropriately manages the risk of each such exposure;

(3) The State savings association notifies the FDIC in writing prior to applying this principle to each such exposure; and

(4) The exposures to which the State savings association applies this principle are not, in the aggregate, material to the State savings association.

Section 2. Definitions

Advanced internal ratings-based (IRB) systems means a State savings association's internal risk rating and segmentation system; risk parameter quantification system; data management and maintenance system; and control, oversight, and validation system for credit risk of wholesale and retail exposures.

Advanced systems means a State savings association's advanced IRB systems, operational risk management processes, operational risk data and assessment systems, operational risk quantification systems, and, to the extent the State savings association uses the following systems, the internal models methodology, double default excessive correlation detection process, IMA for equity exposures, and IAA for securitization exposures to ABCP programs.

Affiliate with respect to a company means any company that controls, is controlled by, or is under common control with, the company.

Applicable external rating means:

(1) With respect to an exposure that has multiple external ratings assigned by NRSROs, the lowest solicited external rating assigned to the exposure by any NRSRO; and

(2) With respect to an exposure that has a single external rating assigned by an NRSRO, the external rating assigned to the exposure by the NRSRO.

Applicable inferred rating means:

(1) With respect to an exposure that has multiple inferred ratings, the lowest inferred rating based on a solicited external rating; and

(2) With respect to an exposure that has a single inferred rating, the inferred rating.

Asset-backed commercial paper (ABCP) program means a program that primarily issues commercial paper that:

(1) Has an external rating; and

(2) Is backed by underlying exposures held in a bankruptcy-remote SPE.

Asset-backed commercial paper (ABCP) program sponsor means a State savings association that:

(1) Establishes an ABCP program;

(2) Approves the sellers permitted to participate in an ABCP program;

(3) Approves the exposures to be purchased by an ABCP program; or

(4) Administers the ABCP program by monitoring the underlying exposures, underwriting or otherwise arranging for the placement of debt or other obligations issued by the program, compiling monthly reports, or ensuring compliance with the program documents and with the program's credit and investment policy.

Backtesting means the comparison of a State savings association's internal estimates with actual outcomes during a sample period not used in model development. In this context, backtesting is one form of out-of-sample testing.

Bank holding company is defined in section 2 of the Bank Holding Company Act (12 U.S.C. 1841).

Benchmarking means the comparison of a State savings association's internal estimates with relevant internal and external data or with estimates based on other estimation techniques.

Business environment and internal control factors means the indicators of a State savings association's operational risk profile that reflect a current and forward-looking assessment of the State savings association's underlying business risk factors and internal control environment.

Carrying value means, with respect to an asset, the value of the asset on the balance sheet of the State savings association, determined in accordance with GAAP.

Clean-up call means a contractual provision that permits an originating State savings association or servicer to call securitization exposures before their stated maturity or call date. See also *eligible clean-up call*.

Commodity derivative contract means a commodity-linked swap, purchased commodity-linked option, forward commodity-linked contract, or any other instrument linked to commodities that gives rise to similar counterparty credit risks.

Company means a corporation, partnership, limited liability company, depository institution, business trust, special purpose entity, association, or similar organization.

Control. A person or company *controls* a company if it:

(1) Owns, controls, or holds with power to vote 25 percent or more of a class of voting securities of the company; or

(2) Consolidates the company for financial reporting purposes.

Controlled early amortization provision means an early amortization provision that meets all the following conditions:

(1) The originating State savings association has appropriate policies and procedures to ensure that it has sufficient capital and liquidity available in the event of an early amortization;

Federal Deposit Insurance Corporation

Pt. 390, Subpt. Z, App. A

(2) Throughout the duration of the securitization (including the early amortization period), there is the same pro rata sharing of interest, principal, expenses, losses, fees, recoveries, and other cash flows from the underlying exposures based on the originating State savings association's and the investors' relative shares of the underlying exposures outstanding measured on a consistent monthly basis;

(3) The amortization period is sufficient for at least 90 percent of the total underlying exposures outstanding at the beginning of the early amortization period to be repaid or recognized as in default; and

(4) The schedule for repayment of investor principal is not more rapid than would be allowed by straight-line amortization over an 18-month period.

Credit derivative means a financial contract executed under standard industry credit derivative documentation that allows one party (the protection purchaser) to transfer the credit risk of one or more exposures (reference exposure) to another party (the protection provider). See also *eligible credit derivative.*

Credit-enhancing interest-only strip (CEIO) means an on-balance sheet asset that, in form or in substance:

(1) Represents a contractual right to receive some or all of the interest and no more than a minimal amount of principal due on the underlying exposures of a securitization; and

(2) Exposes the holder to credit risk directly or indirectly associated with the underlying exposures that exceeds a pro rata share of the holder's claim on the underlying exposures, whether through subordination provisions or other credit-enhancement techniques.

Credit-enhancing representations and warranties means representations and warranties that are made or assumed in connection with a transfer of underlying exposures (including loan servicing assets) and that obligate a State savings association to protect another party from losses arising from the credit risk of the underlying exposures. Credit-enhancing representations and warranties include provisions to protect a party from losses resulting from the default or nonperformance of the obligors of the underlying exposures or from an insufficiency in the value of the collateral backing the underlying exposures. Credit-enhancing representations and warranties do not include:

(1) Early default clauses and similar warranties that permit the return of, or premium refund clauses that cover, first-lien residential mortgage exposures for a period not to exceed 120 days from the date of transfer, provided that the date of transfer is within one year of origination of the residential mortgage exposure;

(2) Premium refund clauses that cover underlying exposures guaranteed, in whole or in part, by the U.S. government, a U.S. government agency, or a U.S. government sponsored enterprise, provided that the clauses are for a period not to exceed 120 days from the date of transfer; or

(3) Warranties that permit the return of underlying exposures in instances of misrepresentation, fraud, or incomplete documentation.

Credit risk mitigant means collateral, a credit derivative, or a guarantee.

Credit-risk-weighted assets means 1.06 multiplied by the sum of:

(1) Total wholesale and retail risk-weighted assets;

(2) Risk-weighted assets for securitization exposures; and

(3) Risk-weighted assets for equity exposures.

Current exposure means, with respect to a netting set, the larger of zero or the market value of a transaction or portfolio of transactions within the netting set that would be lost upon default of the counterparty, assuming no recovery on the value of the transactions. Current exposure is also called replacement cost.

Default—(1) *Retail.* (i) A retail exposure of a State savings association is in default if:

(A) The exposure is 180 days past due, in the case of a residential mortgage exposure or revolving exposure;

(B) The exposure is 120 days past due, in the case of all other retail exposures; or

(C) The State savings association has taken a full or partial charge-off, write-down of principal, or material negative fair value adjustment of principal on the exposure for credit-related reasons.

(ii) Notwithstanding paragraph (1)(i) of this definition, for a retail exposure held by a non-U.S. subsidiary of the State savings association that is subject to an internal ratings-based approach to capital adequacy consistent with the Basel Committee on Banking Supervision's "International Convergence of Capital Measurement and Capital Standards: A Revised Framework" in a non-U.S. jurisdiction, the State savings association may elect to use the definition of default that is used in that jurisdiction, provided that the State savings association has obtained prior approval from the FDIC to use the definition of default in that jurisdiction.

(iii) A retail exposure in default remains in default until the State savings association has reasonable assurance of repayment and performance for all contractual principal and interest payments on the exposure.

(2) *Wholesale.* (i) A State savings association's wholesale obligor is in default if:

(A) The State savings association determines that the obligor is unlikely to pay its credit obligations to the State savings association in full, without recourse by the State

925

savings association to actions such as realizing collateral (if held); or

(B) The obligor is past due more than 90 days on any material credit obligation(s) to the State savings association.[1]

(ii) An obligor in default remains in default until the State savings association has reasonable assurance of repayment and performance for all contractual principal and interest payments on all exposures of the State savings association to the obligor (other than exposures that have been fully written-down or charged-off).

Dependence means a measure of the association among operational losses across and within units of measure.

Depository institution is defined in section 3 of the Federal Deposit Insurance Act (12 U.S.C. 1813).

Derivative contract means a financial contract whose value is derived from the values of one or more underlying assets, reference rates, or indices of asset values or reference rates. Derivative contracts include interest rate derivative contracts, exchange rate derivative contracts, equity derivative contracts, commodity derivative contracts, credit derivatives, and any other instrument that poses similar counterparty credit risks. Derivative contracts also include unsettled securities, commodities, and foreign exchange transactions with a contractual settlement or delivery lag that is longer than the lesser of the market standard for the particular instrument or five business days.

Early amortization provision means a provision in the documentation governing a securitization that, when triggered, causes investors in the securitization exposures to be repaid before the original stated maturity of the securitization exposures, unless the provision:

(1) Is triggered solely by events not directly related to the performance of the underlying exposures or the originating State savings association (such as material changes in tax laws or regulations); or

(2) Leaves investors fully exposed to future draws by obligors on the underlying exposures even after the provision is triggered.

Economic downturn conditions means, with respect to an exposure held by the State savings association, those conditions in which the aggregate default rates for that exposure's wholesale or retail exposure subcategory (or subdivision of such subcategory selected by the State savings association) in the exposure's national jurisdiction (or subdivision of such jurisdiction selected by the State savings association) are significantly higher than average.

---

[1] Overdrafts are past due once the obligor has breached an advised limit or been advised of a limit smaller than the current outstanding balance.

Effective maturity (M) of a wholesale exposure means:

(1) For wholesale exposures other than repo-style transactions, eligible margin loans, and OTC derivative contracts described in paragraph (2) or (3) of this definition:

(i) The weighted-average remaining maturity (measured in years, whole or fractional) of the expected contractual cash flows from the exposure, using the undiscounted amounts of the cash flows as weights; or

(ii) The nominal remaining maturity (measured in years, whole or fractional) of the exposure.

(2) For repo-style transactions, eligible margin loans, and OTC derivative contracts subject to a qualifying master netting agreement for which the State savings association does not apply the internal models approach in paragraph (d) of section 32 of this appendix, the weighted-average remaining maturity (measured in years, whole or fractional) of the individual transactions subject to the qualifying master netting agreement, with the weight of each individual transaction set equal to the notional amount of the transaction.

(3) For repo-style transactions, eligible margin loans, and OTC derivative contracts for which the State savings association applies the internal models approach in paragraph (d) of section 32 of this appendix, the value determined in paragraph (d)(4) of section 32 of this appendix.

Effective notional amount means, for an eligible guarantee or eligible credit derivative, the lesser of the contractual notional amount of the credit risk mitigant and the EAD of the hedged exposure, multiplied by the percentage coverage of the credit risk mitigant. For example, the effective notional amount of an eligible guarantee that covers, on a pro rata basis, 40 percent of any losses on a $100 bond would be $40.

Eligible clean-up call means a clean-up call that:

(1) Is exercisable solely at the discretion of the originating State savings association or servicer;

(2) Is not structured to avoid allocating losses to securitization exposures held by investors or otherwise structured to provide credit enhancement to the securitization; and

(3)(i) For a traditional securitization, is only exercisable when 10 percent or less of the principal amount of the underlying exposures or securitization exposures (determined as of the inception of the securitization) is outstanding; or

(ii) For a synthetic securitization, is only exercisable when 10 percent or less of the principal amount of the reference portfolio of underlying exposures (determined as of the inception of the securitization) is outstanding.

Federal Deposit Insurance Corporation   Pt. 390, Subpt. Z, App. A

Eligible credit derivative means a credit derivative in the form of a credit default swap, nth-to-default swap, total return swap, or any other form of credit derivative approved by the FDIC, provided that:

(1) The contract meets the requirements of an eligible guarantee and has been confirmed by the protection purchaser and the protection provider;

(2) Any assignment of the contract has been confirmed by all relevant parties;

(3) If the credit derivative is a credit default swap or nth-to-default swap, the contract includes the following credit events:

(i) Failure to pay any amount due under the terms of the reference exposure, subject to any applicable minimal payment threshold that is consistent with standard market practice and with a grace period that is closely in line with the grace period of the reference exposure; and

(ii) Bankruptcy, insolvency, or inability of the obligor on the reference exposure to pay its debts, or its failure or admission in writing of its inability generally to pay its debts as they become due, and similar events;

(4) The terms and conditions dictating the manner in which the contract is to be settled are incorporated into the contract;

(5) If the contract allows for cash settlement, the contract incorporates a robust valuation process to estimate loss reliably and specifies a reasonable period for obtaining post-credit event valuations of the reference exposure;

(6) If the contract requires the protection purchaser to transfer an exposure to the protection provider at settlement, the terms of at least one of the exposures that is permitted to be transferred under the contract provides that any required consent to transfer may not be unreasonably withheld;

(7) If the credit derivative is a credit default swap or nth-to-default swap, the contract clearly identifies the parties responsible for determining whether a credit event has occurred, specifies that this determination is not the sole responsibility of the protection provider, and gives the protection purchaser the right to notify the protection provider of the occurrence of a credit event; and

(8) If the credit derivative is a total return swap and the State savings association records net payments received on the swap as net income, the State savings association records offsetting deterioration in the value of the hedged exposure (either through reductions in fair value or by an addition to reserves).

Eligible credit reserves means all general allowances that have been established through a charge against earnings to absorb credit losses associated with on- or off-balance sheet wholesale and retail exposures, including the allowance for loan and lease losses (ALLL) associated with such exposures but excluding specific reserves created against recognized losses.

Eligible double default guarantor, with respect to a guarantee or credit derivative obtained by a State savings association, means:

(1) *U.S.-based entities.* A depository institution, a bank holding company, a savings and loan holding company (as defined in 12 U.S.C. 1467a) provided all or substantially all of the holding company's activities are permissible for a financial holding company under 12 U.S.C. 1843(k), a securities broker or dealer registered with the SEC under the Securities Exchange Act of 1934 (15 U.S.C. 78o *et seq.*), or an insurance company in the business of providing credit protection (such as a monoline bond insurer or re-insurer) that is subject to supervision by a State insurance regulator, if:

(i) At the time the guarantor issued the guarantee or credit derivative or at any time thereafter, the State savings association assigned a PD to the guarantor's rating grade that was equal to or lower than the PD associated with a long-term external rating in the third-highest investment-grade rating category; and

(ii) The State savings association currently assigns a PD to the guarantor's rating grade that is equal to or lower than the PD associated with a long-term external rating in the lowest investment-grade rating category; or

(2) *Non-U.S.-based entities.* A foreign bank (as defined in §211.2 of the Federal Reserve Board's Regulation K (12 CFR 211.2)), a non-U.S.-based securities firm, or a non-U.S.-based insurance company in the business of providing credit protection, if:

(i) The State savings association demonstrates that the guarantor is subject to consolidated supervision and regulation comparable to that imposed on U.S. depository institutions, securities broker-dealers, or insurance companies (as the case may be), or has issued and outstanding an unsecured long-term debt security without credit enhancement that has a long-term applicable external rating of at least investment grade;

(ii) At the time the guarantor issued the guarantee or credit derivative or at any time thereafter, the State savings association assigned a PD to the guarantor's rating grade that was equal to or lower than the PD associated with a long-term external rating in the third-highest investment-grade rating category; and

(iii) The State savings association currently assigns a PD to the guarantor's rating grade that is equal to or lower than the PD associated with a long-term external rating in the lowest investment-grade rating category.

Eligible guarantee means a guarantee that:
(1) Is written and unconditional;

(2) Covers all or a pro rata portion of all contractual payments of the obligor on the reference exposure;

(3) Gives the beneficiary a direct claim against the protection provider;

(4) Is not unilaterally cancelable by the protection provider for reasons other than the breach of the contract by the beneficiary;

(5) Is legally enforceable against the protection provider in a jurisdiction where the protection provider has sufficient assets against which a judgment may be attached and enforced;

(6) Requires the protection provider to make payment to the beneficiary on the occurrence of a default (as defined in the guarantee) of the obligor on the reference exposure in a timely manner without the beneficiary first having to take legal actions to pursue the obligor for payment;

(7) Does not increase the beneficiary's cost of credit protection on the guarantee in response to deterioration in the credit quality of the reference exposure; and

(8) Is not provided by an affiliate of the State savings association, unless the affiliate is an insured depository institution, bank, securities broker or dealer, or insurance company that:

(i) Does not control the State savings association; and

(ii) Is subject to consolidated supervision and regulation comparable to that imposed on U.S. depository institutions, securities broker-dealers, or insurance companies (as the case may be).

Eligible margin loan means an extension of credit where:

(1) The extension of credit is collateralized exclusively by liquid and readily marketable debt or equity securities, gold, or conforming residential mortgages;

(2) The collateral is marked to market daily, and the transaction is subject to daily margin maintenance requirements;

(3) The extension of credit is conducted under an agreement that provides the State savings association the right to accelerate and terminate the extension of credit and to liquidate or set off collateral promptly upon an event of default (including upon an event of bankruptcy, insolvency, or similar proceeding) of the counterparty, provided that, in any such case, any exercise of rights under the agreement will not be stayed or avoided under applicable law in the relevant jurisdictions; [2] and

---

[2] This requirement is met where all transactions under the agreement are (i) executed under U.S. law and (ii) constitute "securities contracts" under section 555 of the Bankruptcy Code (11 U.S.C. 555), qualified financial contracts under section 11(e)(8) of the Federal Deposit Insurance Act (12 U.S.C. 1821(e)(8)), or netting contracts between or among financial institutions under sections 401–407 of the Federal Deposit Insurance Corporation Improvement Act of 1991 (12 U.S.C. 4401–4407) or the Federal Reserve Board's Regulation EE (12 CFR part 231).

(4) The State savings association has conducted sufficient legal review to conclude with a well-founded basis (and maintains sufficient written documentation of that legal review) that the agreement meets the requirements of paragraph (3) of this definition and is legal, valid, binding, and enforceable under applicable law in the relevant jurisdictions.

Eligible operational risk offsets means amounts, not to exceed expected operational loss, that:

(1) Are generated by internal business practices to absorb highly predictable and reasonably stable operational losses, including reserves calculated consistent with GAAP; and

(2) Are available to cover expected operational losses with a high degree of certainty over a one-year horizon.

Eligible purchased wholesale exposure means a purchased wholesale exposure that:

(1) The State savings association or securitization SPE purchased from an unaffiliated seller and did not directly or indirectly originate;

(2) Was generated on an arm's-length basis between the seller and the obligor (intercompany accounts receivable and receivables subject to contra-accounts between firms that buy and sell to each other do not satisfy this criterion);

(3) Provides the State savings association or securitization SPE with a claim on all proceeds from the exposure or a pro rata interest in the proceeds from the exposure;

(4) Has an M of less than one year; and

(5) When consolidated by obligor, does not represent a concentrated exposure relative to the portfolio of purchased wholesale exposures.

Eligible securitization guarantor means:

(1) A sovereign entity, the Bank for International Settlements, the International Monetary Fund, the European Central Bank, the European Commission, a Federal Home Loan Bank, Federal Agricultural Mortgage Corporation (Farmer Mac), a multilateral development bank, a depository institution, a bank holding company, a savings and loan holding company (as defined in 12 U.S.C. 1467a) provided all or substantially all of the holding company's activities are permissible for a financial holding company under 12 U.S.C. 1843(k), a foreign bank (as defined in §211.2 of the Federal Reserve Board's Regulation K (12 CFR 211.2)), or a securities firm;

Federal Deposit Insurance Corporation

(2) Any other entity (other than a securitization SPE) that has issued and outstanding an unsecured long-term debt security without credit enhancement that has a long-term applicable external rating in one of the three highest investment-grade rating categories; or

(3) Any other entity (other than a securitization SPE) that has a PD assigned by the State savings association that is lower than or equal to the PD associated with a long-term external rating in the third highest investment-grade rating category.

Eligible servicer cash advance facility means a servicer cash advance facility in which:

(1) The servicer is entitled to full reimbursement of advances, except that a servicer may be obligated to make non-reimbursable advances for a particular underlying exposure if any such advance is contractually limited to an insignificant amount of the outstanding principal balance of that exposure;

(2) The servicer's right to reimbursement is senior in right of payment to all other claims on the cash flows from the underlying exposures of the securitization; and

(3) The servicer has no legal obligation to, and does not, make advances to the securitization if the servicer concludes that the advances are unlikely to be repaid.

Equity derivative contract means an equity-linked swap, purchased equity-linked option, forward equity-linked contract, or any other instrument linked to equities that gives rise to similar counterparty credit risks.

Equity exposure means:

(1) A security or instrument (whether voting or non-voting) that represents a direct or indirect ownership interest in, and is a residual claim on, the assets and income of a company, unless:

(i) The issuing company is consolidated with the State savings association under GAAP;

(ii) The State savings association is required to deduct the ownership interest from tier 1 or tier 2 capital under this appendix;

(iii) The ownership interest incorporates a payment or other similar obligation on the part of the issuing company (such as an obligation to make periodic payments); or

(iv) The ownership interest is a securitization exposure;

(2) A security or instrument that is mandatorily convertible into a security or instrument described in paragraph (1) of this definition;

(3) An option or warrant that is exercisable for a security or instrument described in paragraph (1) of this definition; or

(4) Any other security or instrument (other than a securitization exposure) to the extent the return on the security or instrument is based on the performance of a security or instrument described in paragraph (1) of this definition.

Pt. 390, Subpt. Z, App. A

Excess spread for a period means:

(1) Gross finance charge collections and other income received by a securitization SPE (including market interchange fees) over a period minus interest paid to the holders of the securitization exposures, servicing fees, charge-offs, and other senior trust or similar expenses of the SPE over the period; divided by

(2) The principal balance of the underlying exposures at the end of the period.

Exchange rate derivative contract means a cross-currency interest rate swap, forward foreign-exchange contract, currency option purchased, or any other instrument linked to exchange rates that gives rise to similar counterparty credit risks.

Excluded mortgage exposure means any one- to four-family residential pre-sold construction loan for a residence for which the purchase contract is cancelled that would receive a 100 percent risk weight under section 618(a)(2) of the Resolution Trust Corporation Refinancing, Restructuring, and Improvement Act and under 12 CFR 390.461 (definition of "qualifying residential construction loan") and 12 CFR 390.466(a)(1)(iv).

Expected credit loss (ECL) means:

(1) For a wholesale exposure to a non-defaulted obligor or segment of non-defaulted retail exposures that is carried at fair value with gains and losses flowing through earnings or that is classified as held-for-sale and is carried at the lower of cost or fair value with losses flowing through earnings, zero.

(2) For all other wholesale exposures to non-defaulted obligors or segments of non-defaulted retail exposures, the product of PD times LGD times EAD for the exposure or segment.

(3) For a wholesale exposure to a defaulted obligor or segment of defaulted retail exposures, the State savings association's impairment estimate for allowance purposes for the exposure or segment.

(4) Total ECL is the sum of expected credit losses for all wholesale and retail exposures other than exposures for which the State savings association has applied the double default treatment in section 34 of this appendix.

Expected exposure (EE) means the expected value of the probability distribution of non-negative credit risk exposures to a counterparty at any specified future date before the maturity date of the longest term transaction in the netting set. Any negative market values in the probability distribution of market values to a counterparty at a specified future date are set to zero to convert the probability distribution of market values to the probability distribution of credit risk exposures.

Expected operational loss (EOL) means the expected value of the distribution of potential aggregate operational losses, as generated by the State savings association's

929

operational risk quantification system using a one-year horizon.

Expected positive exposure (EPE) means the weighted average over time of expected (nonnegative) exposures to a counterparty where the weights are the proportion of the time interval that an individual expected exposure represents. When calculating risk-based capital requirements, the average is taken over a one-year horizon.

Exposure at default (EAD). (1) For the on-balance sheet component of a wholesale exposure or segment of retail exposures (other than an OTC derivative contract, or a repo-style transaction, or eligible margin loan for which the State savings association determines EAD under section 32 of this appendix), EAD means:

(i) If the exposure or segment is a security classified as available-for-sale, the State savings association's carrying value (including net accrued but unpaid interest and fees) for the exposure or segment less any unrealized gains on the exposure or segment and plus any unrealized losses on the exposure or segment; or

(ii) If the exposure or segment is not a security classified as available-for-sale, the State savings association's carrying value (including net accrued but unpaid interest and fees) for the exposure or segment.

(2) For the off-balance sheet component of a wholesale exposure or segment of retail exposures (other than an OTC derivative contract, or a repo-style transaction or eligible margin loan for which the State savings association determines EAD under section 32 of this appendix) in the form of a loan commitment, line of credit, trade-related letter of credit, or transaction-related contingency, EAD means the State savings association's best estimate of net additions to the outstanding amount owed the State savings association, including estimated future additional draws of principal and accrued but unpaid interest and fees, that are likely to occur over a one-year horizon assuming the wholesale exposure or the retail exposures in the segment were to go into default. This estimate of net additions must reflect what would be expected during economic downturn conditions. Trade-related letters of credit are short-term, self-liquidating instruments that are used to finance the movement of goods and are collateralized by the underlying goods. Transaction-related contingencies relate to a particular transaction and include, among other things, performance bonds and performance-based letters of credit.

(3) For the off-balance sheet component of a wholesale exposure or segment of retail exposures (other than an OTC derivative contract, or a repo-style transaction or eligible margin loan for which the State savings association determines EAD under section 32 of this appendix) in the form of anything other than a loan commitment, line of credit, trade-related letter of credit, or transaction-related contingency, EAD means the notional amount of the exposure or segment.

(4) EAD for OTC derivative contracts is calculated as described in section 32 of this appendix. A State savings association also may determine EAD for repo-style transactions and eligible margin loans as described in section 32 of this appendix.

(5) For wholesale or retail exposures in which only the drawn balance has been securitized, the State savings association must reflect its share of the exposures' undrawn balances in EAD. Undrawn balances of revolving exposures for which the drawn balances have been securitized must be allocated between the seller's and investors' interests on a pro rata basis, based on the proportions of the seller's and investors' shares of the securitized drawn balances.

Exposure category means any of the wholesale, retail, securitization, or equity exposure categories.

External operational loss event data means, with respect to a State savings association, gross operational loss amounts, dates, recoveries, and relevant causal information for operational loss events occurring at organizations other than the State savings association.

External rating means a credit rating that is assigned by an NRSRO to an exposure, provided:

(1) The credit rating fully reflects the entire amount of credit risk with regard to all payments owed to the holder of the exposure. If a holder is owed principal and interest on an exposure, the credit rating must fully reflect the credit risk associated with timely repayment of principal and interest. If a holder is owed only principal on an exposure, the credit rating must fully reflect only the credit risk associated with timely repayment of principal; and

(2) The credit rating is published in an accessible form and is or will be included in the transition matrices made publicly available by the NRSRO that summarize the historical performance of positions rated by the NRSRO.

Financial collateral means collateral:

(1) In the form of:

(i) Cash on deposit with the State savings association (including cash held for the State savings association by a third-party custodian or trustee);

(ii) Gold bullion;

(iii) Long-term debt securities that have an applicable external rating of one category below investment grade or higher;

(iv) Short-term debt instruments that have an applicable external rating of at least investment grade;

(v) Equity securities that are publicly traded;

(vi) Convertible bonds that are publicly traded;

(vii) Money market mutual fund shares and other mutual fund shares if a price for the shares is publicly quoted daily; or

(viii) Conforming residential mortgages; and

(2) In which the State savings association has a perfected, first priority security interest or, outside of the United States, the legal equivalent thereof (with the exception of cash on deposit and notwithstanding the prior security interest of any custodial agent).

GAAP means generally accepted accounting principles as used in the United States.

Gain-on-sale means an increase in the equity capital (as reported on Schedule SC of the Thrift Financial Report or in the Consolidated Reports of Condition or Income ("Call Report"), as applicable, of a State savings association that results from a securitization (other than an increase in equity capital that results from the State savings association's receipt of cash in connection with the securitization).

Guarantee means a financial guarantee, letter of credit, insurance, or other similar financial instrument (other than a credit derivative) that allows one party (beneficiary) to transfer the credit risk of one or more specific exposures (reference exposure) to another party (protection provider). See also *eligible guarantee*.

High volatility commercial real estate (HVCRE) exposure means a credit facility that finances or has financed the acquisition, development, or construction (ADC) of real property, unless the facility finances:

(1) One- to four-family residential properties; or

(2) Commercial real estate projects in which:

(i) The loan-to-value ratio is less than or equal to the applicable maximum supervisory loan-to-value ratio in the FDIC's real estate lending standards at 12 CFR 390.264–390.265;

(ii) The borrower has contributed capital to the project in the form of cash or unencumbered readily marketable assets (or has paid development expenses out-of-pocket) of at least 15 percent of the real estate's appraised "as completed" value; and

(iii) The borrower contributed the amount of capital required by paragraph (2)(ii) of this definition before the State savings association advances funds under the credit facility, and the capital contributed by the borrower, or internally generated by the project, is contractually required to remain in the project throughout the life of the project. The life of a project concludes only when the credit facility is converted to permanent financing or is sold or paid in full. Permanent financing may be provided by the State savings association that provided the ADC facility as long as the permanent financing is subject to the State savings association's underwriting criteria for long-term mortgage loans.

Inferred rating. A securitization exposure has an *inferred rating* equal to the external rating referenced in paragraph (2)(i) of this definition if:

(1) The securitization exposure does not have an external rating; and

(2) Another securitization exposure issued by the same issuer and secured by the same underlying exposures:

(i) Has an external rating;

(ii) Is subordinated in all respects to the unrated securitization exposure;

(iii) Does not benefit from any credit enhancement that is not available to the unrated securitization exposure; and

(iv) Has an effective remaining maturity that is equal to or longer than that of the unrated securitization exposure.

Interest rate derivative contract means a single-currency interest rate swap, basis swap, forward rate agreement, purchased interest rate option, when-issued securities, or any other instrument linked to interest rates that gives rise to similar counterparty credit risks.

Internal operational loss event data means, with respect to a State savings association, gross operational loss amounts, dates, recoveries, and relevant causal information for operational loss events occurring at the State savings association.

Investing State savings association means, with respect to a securitization, a State savings association that assumes the credit risk of a securitization exposure (other than an originating State savings association of the securitization). In the typical synthetic securitization, the investing State savings association sells credit protection on a pool of underlying exposures to the originating State savings association.

Investment fund means a company:

(1) All or substantially all of the assets of which are financial assets; and

(2) That has no material liabilities.

Investors' interest EAD means, with respect to a securitization, the EAD of the underlying exposures multiplied by the ratio of:

(1) The total amount of securitization exposures issued by the securitization SPE to investors; divided by

(2) The outstanding principal amount of underlying exposures.

Loss given default (LGD) means:

(1) For a wholesale exposure, the greatest of:

(i) Zero;

(ii) The State savings association's empirically based best estimate of the long-run default-weighted average economic loss, per dollar of EAD, the State savings association would expect to incur if the obligor (or a typical obligor in the loss severity grade assigned by the State savings association to the exposure) were to default within a one-year horizon over a mix of economic conditions, including economic downturn conditions; or

(iii) The State savings association's empirically based best estimate of the economic loss, per dollar of EAD, the State savings association would expect to incur if the obligor (or a typical obligor in the loss severity grade assigned by the State savings association to the exposure) were to default within a one-year horizon during economic downturn conditions.

(2) For a segment of retail exposures, the greatest of:

(i) Zero;

(ii) The State savings association's empirically based best estimate of the long-run default-weighted average economic loss, per dollar of EAD, the State savings association would expect to incur if the exposures in the segment were to default within a one-year horizon over a mix of economic conditions, including economic downturn conditions; or

(iii) The State savings association's empirically based best estimate of the economic loss, per dollar of EAD, the State savings association would expect to incur if the exposures in the segment were to default within a one-year horizon during economic downturn conditions.

(3) The economic loss on an exposure in the event of default is all material credit-related losses on the exposure (including accrued but unpaid interest or fees, losses on the sale of collateral, direct workout costs, and an appropriate allocation of indirect workout costs). Where positive or negative cash flows on a wholesale exposure to a defaulted obligor or a defaulted retail exposure (including proceeds from the sale of collateral, workout costs, additional extensions of credit to facilitate repayment of the exposure, and draw-downs of unused credit lines) occur after the date of default, the economic loss must reflect the net present value of cash flows as of the default date using a discount rate appropriate to the risk of the defaulted exposure.

Main index means the Standard & Poor's 500 Index, the FTSE All-World Index, and any other index for which the State savings association can demonstrate to the satisfaction of the FDIC that the equities represented in the index have comparable liquidity, depth of market, and size of bid-ask spreads as equities in the Standard & Poor's 500 Index and FTSE All-World Index.

Multilateral development bank means the International Bank for Reconstruction and Development, the International Finance Corporation, the Inter-American Development Bank, the Asian Development Bank, the African Development Bank, the European Bank for Reconstruction and Development, the European Investment Bank, the European Investment Fund, the Nordic Investment Bank, the Caribbean Development Bank, the Islamic Development Bank, the Council of Europe Development Bank, and any other multilateral lending institution or regional development bank in which the U.S. government is a shareholder or contributing member or which the FDIC determines poses comparable credit risk.

Nationally recognized statistical rating organization (NRSRO) means an entity registered with the SEC as a nationally recognized statistical rating organization under section 15E of the Securities Exchange Act of 1934 (15 U.S.C. 78o–7).

Netting set means a group of transactions with a single counterparty that are subject to a qualifying master netting agreement or qualifying cross-product master netting agreement. For purposes of the internal models methodology in paragraph (d) of section 32 of this appendix, each transaction that is not subject to such a master netting agreement is its own netting set.

Nth-to-default credit derivative means a credit derivative that provides credit protection only for the nth-defaulting reference exposure in a group of reference exposures.

Obligor means the legal entity or natural person contractually obligated on a wholesale exposure, except that a State savings association may treat the following exposures as having separate obligors:

(1) Exposures to the same legal entity or natural person denominated in different currencies;

(2)(i) An income-producing real estate exposure for which all or substantially all of the repayment of the exposure is reliant on the cash flows of the real estate serving as collateral for the exposure; the State savings association, in economic substance, does not have recourse to the borrower beyond the real estate collateral; and no cross-default or cross-acceleration clauses are in place other than clauses obtained solely out of an abundance of caution; and

(ii) Other credit exposures to the same legal entity or natural person; and

(3) (i) A wholesale exposure authorized under section 364 of the U.S. Bankruptcy Code (11 U.S.C. 364) to a legal entity or natural person who is a debtor-in-possession for purposes of Chapter 11 of the Bankruptcy Code; and

(ii) Other credit exposures to the same legal entity or natural person.

Operational loss means a loss (excluding insurance or tax effects) resulting from an operational loss event. Operational loss includes all expenses associated with an operational loss event except for opportunity costs, forgone revenue, and costs related to risk management and control enhancements

Federal Deposit Insurance Corporation

implemented to prevent future operational losses.

Operational loss event means an event that results in loss and is associated with any of the following seven operational loss event type categories:

(1) Internal fraud, which means the operational loss event type category that comprises operational losses resulting from an act involving at least one internal party of a type intended to defraud, misappropriate property, or circumvent regulations, the law, or company policy, excluding diversity- and discrimination-type events.

(2) External fraud, which means the operational loss event type category that comprises operational losses resulting from an act by a third party of a type intended to defraud, misappropriate property, or circumvent the law. Retail credit card losses arising from non-contractual, third-party initiated fraud (for example, identity theft) are external fraud operational losses. All other third-party initiated credit losses are to be treated as credit risk losses.

(3) Employment practices and workplace safety, which means the operational loss event type category that comprises operational losses resulting from an act inconsistent with employment, health, or safety laws or agreements, payment of personal injury claims, or payment arising from diversity- and discrimination-type events.

(4) Clients, products, and business practices, which means the operational loss event type category that comprises operational losses resulting from the nature or design of a product or from an unintentional or negligent failure to meet a professional obligation to specific clients (including fiduciary and suitability requirements).

(5) Damage to physical assets, which means the operational loss event type category that comprises operational losses resulting from the loss of or damage to physical assets from natural disaster or other events.

(6) Business disruption and system failures, which means the operational loss event type category that comprises operational losses resulting from disruption of business or system failures.

(7) Execution, delivery, and process management, which means the operational loss event type category that comprises operational losses resulting from failed transaction processing or process management or losses arising from relations with trade counterparties and vendors.

Operational risk means the risk of loss resulting from inadequate or failed internal processes, people, and systems or from external events (including legal risk but excluding strategic and reputational risk).

Operational risk exposure means the 99.9th percentile of the distribution of potential aggregate operational losses, as generated by the State savings association's operational risk quantification system over a one-year horizon (and not incorporating eligible operational risk offsets or qualifying operational risk mitigants).

Originating State savings association, with respect to a securitization, means a State savings association that:

(1) Directly or indirectly originated or securitized the underlying exposures included in the securitization; or

(2) Serves as an ABCP program sponsor to the securitization.

Other retail exposure means an exposure (other than a securitization exposure, an equity exposure, a residential mortgage exposure, an excluded mortgage exposure, a qualifying revolving exposure, or the residual value portion of a lease exposure) that is managed as part of a segment of exposures with homogeneous risk characteristics, not on an individual-exposure basis, and is either:

(1) An exposure to an individual for non-business purposes; or

(2) An exposure to an individual or company for business purposes if the State savings association's consolidated business credit exposure to the individual or company is $1 million or less.

Over-the-counter (OTC) derivative contract means a derivative contract that is not traded on an exchange that requires the daily receipt and payment of cash-variation margin.

Probability of default (PD) means:

(1) For a wholesale exposure to a non-defaulted obligor, the State savings association's empirically based best estimate of the long-run average one-year default rate for the rating grade assigned by the State savings association to the obligor, capturing the average default experience for obligors in the rating grade over a mix of economic conditions (including economic downturn conditions) sufficient to provide a reasonable estimate of the average one-year default rate over the economic cycle for the rating grade.

(2) For a segment of non-defaulted retail exposures, the State savings association's empirically based best estimate of the long-run average one-year default rate for the exposures in the segment, capturing the average default experience for exposures in the segment over a mix of economic conditions (including economic downturn conditions) sufficient to provide a reasonable estimate of the average one-year default rate over the economic cycle for the segment and adjusted upward as appropriate for segments for which seasoning effects are material. For purposes of this definition, a segment for which seasoning effects are material is a segment where there is a material relationship between the time since origination of exposures within the segment and the State savings association's best estimate of the long-

run average one-year default rate for the exposures in the segment.

(3) For a wholesale exposure to a defaulted obligor or segment of defaulted retail exposures, 100 percent.

Protection amount (P) means, with respect to an exposure hedged by an eligible guarantee or eligible credit derivative, the effective notional amount of the guarantee or credit derivative, reduced to reflect any currency mismatch, maturity mismatch, or lack of restructuring coverage (as provided in section 33 of this appendix).

Publicly traded means traded on:

(1) Any exchange registered with the SEC as a national securities exchange under section 6 of the Securities Exchange Act of 1934 (15 U.S.C. 78f); or

(2) Any non-U.S.-based securities exchange that:

(i) Is registered with, or approved by, a national securities regulatory authority; and

(ii) Provides a liquid, two-way market for the instrument in question, meaning that there are enough independent bona fide offers to buy and sell so that a sales price reasonably related to the last sales price or current bona fide competitive bid and offer quotations can be determined promptly and a trade can be settled at such a price within five business days.

Qualifying central counterparty means a counterparty (for example, a clearinghouse) that:

(1) Facilitates trades between counterparties in one or more financial markets by either guaranteeing trades or novating contracts;

(2) Requires all participants in its arrangements to be fully collateralized on a daily basis; and

(3) The State savings association demonstrates to the satisfaction of the FDIC is in sound financial condition and is subject to effective oversight by a national supervisory authority.

Qualifying cross-product master netting agreement means a qualifying master netting agreement that provides for termination and close-out netting across multiple types of financial transactions or qualifying master netting agreements in the event of a counterparty's default, provided that:

(1) The underlying financial transactions are OTC derivative contracts, eligible margin loans, or repo-style transactions; and

(2) The State savings association obtains a written legal opinion verifying the validity and enforceability of the agreement under applicable law of the relevant jurisdictions if the counterparty fails to perform upon an event of default, including upon an event of bankruptcy, insolvency, or similar proceeding.

Qualifying master netting agreement means any written, legally enforceable bilateral agreement, provided that:

(1) The agreement creates a single legal obligation for all individual transactions covered by the agreement upon an event of default, including bankruptcy, insolvency, or similar proceeding, of the counterparty;

(2) The agreement provides the State savings association the right to accelerate, terminate, and close-out on a net basis all transactions under the agreement and to liquidate or set off collateral promptly upon an event of default, including upon an event of bankruptcy, insolvency, or similar proceeding, of the counterparty, provided that, in any such case, any exercise of rights under the agreement will not be stayed or avoided under applicable law in the relevant jurisdictions;

(3) The State savings association has conducted sufficient legal review to conclude with a well-founded basis (and maintains sufficient written documentation of that legal review) that:

(i) The agreement meets the requirements of paragraph (2) of this definition; and

(ii) In the event of a legal challenge (including one resulting from default or from bankruptcy, insolvency, or similar proceeding) the relevant court and administrative authorities would find the agreement to be legal, valid, binding, and enforceable under the law of the relevant jurisdictions;

(4) The State savings association establishes and maintains procedures to monitor possible changes in relevant law and to ensure that the agreement continues to satisfy the requirements of this definition; and

(5) The agreement does not contain a walkaway clause (that is, a provision that permits a non-defaulting counterparty to make a lower payment than it would make otherwise under the agreement, or no payment at all, to a defaulter or the estate of a defaulter, even if the defaulter or the estate of the defaulter is a net creditor under the agreement).

Qualifying revolving exposure (QRE) means an exposure (other than a securitization exposure or equity exposure) to an individual that is managed as part of a segment of exposures with homogeneous risk characteristics, not on an individual-exposure basis, and:

(1) Is revolving (that is, the amount outstanding fluctuates, determined largely by the borrower's decision to borrow and repay, up to a pre-established maximum amount);

(2) Is unsecured and unconditionally cancelable by the State savings association to the fullest extent permitted by Federal law; and

(3) Has a maximum exposure amount (drawn plus undrawn) of up to $100,000.

Repo-style transaction means a repurchase or reverse repurchase transaction, or a securities borrowing or securities lending transaction, including a transaction in which the State savings association acts as agent for a customer and indemnifies the customer against loss, provided that:

(1) The transaction is based solely on liquid and readily marketable securities, cash, gold, or conforming residential mortgages;

(2) The transaction is marked-to-market daily and subject to daily margin maintenance requirements;

(3)(i) The transaction is a "securities contract" or "repurchase agreement" under section 555 or 559, respectively, of the Bankruptcy Code (11 U.S.C. 555 or 559), a qualified financial contract under section 11(e)(8) of the Federal Deposit Insurance Act (12 U.S.C. 1821(e)(8)), or a netting contract between or among financial institutions under sections 401–407 of the Federal Deposit Insurance Corporation Improvement Act of 1991 (12 U.S.C. 4401–4407) or the Federal Reserve Board's Regulation EE (12 CFR part 231); or

(ii) If the transaction does not meet the criteria set forth in paragraph (3)(i) of this definition, then either:

(A) The transaction is executed under an agreement that provides the State savings association the right to accelerate, terminate, and close-out the transaction on a net basis and to liquidate or set off collateral promptly upon an event of default (including upon an event of bankruptcy, insolvency, or similar proceeding) of the counterparty, provided that, in any such case, any exercise of rights under the agreement will not be stayed or avoided under applicable law in the relevant jurisdictions; or

(B) The transaction is:

(1) Either overnight or unconditionally cancelable at any time by the State savings association; and

(2) Executed under an agreement that provides the State savings association the right to accelerate, terminate, and close-out the transaction on a net basis and to liquidate or set off collateral promptly upon an event of counterparty default; and

(4) The State savings association has conducted sufficient legal review to conclude with a well-founded basis (and maintains sufficient written documentation of that legal review) that the agreement meets the requirements of paragraph (3) of this definition and is legal, valid, binding, and enforceable under applicable law in the relevant jurisdictions.

Residential mortgage exposure means an exposure (other than a securitization exposure, equity exposure, or excluded mortgage exposure) that is managed as part of a segment of exposures with homogeneous risk characteristics, not on an individual-exposure basis, and is:

(1) An exposure that is primarily secured by a first or subsequent lien on one- to four-family residential property; or

(2) An exposure with an original and outstanding amount of $1 million or less that is primarily secured by a first or subsequent lien on residential property that is not one to four family.

Retail exposure means a residential mortgage exposure, a qualifying revolving exposure, or another retail exposure.

Retail exposure subcategory means the residential mortgage exposure, qualifying revolving exposure, or other retail exposure subcategory.

Risk parameter means a variable used in determining risk-based capital requirements for wholesale and retail exposures, specifically probability of default (PD), loss given default (LGD), exposure at default (EAD), or effective maturity (M).

Scenario analysis means a systematic process of obtaining expert opinions from business managers and risk management experts to derive reasoned assessments of the likelihood and loss impact of plausible high-severity operational losses. Scenario analysis may include the well-reasoned evaluation and use of external operational loss event data, adjusted as appropriate to ensure relevance to a State savings association's operational risk profile and control structure.

SEC means the U.S. Securities and Exchange Commission.

Securitization means a traditional securitization or a synthetic securitization.

Securitization exposure means an on-balance sheet or off-balance sheet credit exposure that arises from a traditional or synthetic securitization (including credit-enhancing representations and warranties).

Securitization special purpose entity (securitization SPE) means a corporation, trust, or other entity organized for the specific purpose of holding underlying exposures of a securitization, the activities of which are limited to those appropriate to accomplish this purpose, and the structure of which is intended to isolate the underlying exposures held by the entity from the credit risk of the seller of the underlying exposures to the entity.

Senior securitization exposure means a securitization exposure that has a first priority claim on the cash flows from the underlying exposures. When determining whether a securitization exposure has a first priority claim on the cash flows from the underlying exposures, a State savings association is not required to consider amounts due under interest rate or currency derivative contracts, fees due, or other similar payments. Both the most senior commercial paper issued by an ABCP program and a liquidity facility that supports the ABCP program may be senior securitization exposures if the liquidity facility provider's right to reimbursement of the drawn amounts is senior to all claims on the cash flows from the underlying exposures except amounts due under interest rate or currency derivative contracts, fees due, or other similar payments.

Servicer cash advance facility means a facility under which the servicer of the underlying exposures of a securitization may advance cash to ensure an uninterrupted flow of payments to investors in the securitization, including advances made to cover foreclosure costs or other expenses to facilitate the timely collection of the underlying exposures. See also *eligible servicer cash advance facility*.

Sovereign entity means a central government (including the U.S. government) or an agency, department, ministry, or central bank of a central government.

Sovereign exposure means:

(1) A direct exposure to a sovereign entity; or

(2) An exposure directly and unconditionally backed by the full faith and credit of a sovereign entity.

Subsidiary means, with respect to a company, a company controlled by that company.

Synthetic securitization means a transaction in which:

(1) All or a portion of the credit risk of one or more underlying exposures is transferred to one or more third parties through the use of one or more credit derivatives or guarantees (other than a guarantee that transfers only the credit risk of an individual retail exposure);

(2) The credit risk associated with the underlying exposures has been separated into at least two tranches reflecting different levels of seniority;

(3) Performance of the securitization exposures depends upon the performance of the underlying exposures; and

(4) All or substantially all of the underlying exposures are financial exposures (such as loans, commitments, credit derivatives, guarantees, receivables, asset-backed securities, mortgage-backed securities, other debt securities, or equity securities).

Tier 1 capital is defined in §§ 390.461–390.471, as modified in part II of this appendix.

Tier 2 capital is defined in §§ 390.461–390.471, as modified in part II of this appendix.

Total qualifying capital means the sum of tier 1 capital and tier 2 capital, after all deductions required in this appendix.

Total risk-weighted assets means:

(1) The sum of:

(i) Credit risk-weighted assets; and

(ii) Risk-weighted assets for operational risk; minus

(2) Excess eligible credit reserves not included in tier 2 capital.

Total wholesale and retail risk-weighted assets means the sum of risk-weighted assets for wholesale exposures to non-defaulted obligors and segments of non-defaulted retail exposures; risk-weighted assets for wholesale exposures to defaulted obligors and segments of defaulted retail exposures; risk-weighted assets for assets not defined by an exposure category; and risk-weighted assets for nonmaterial portfolios of exposures (all as determined in section 31 of this appendix) and risk-weighted assets for unsettled transactions (as determined in section 35 of this appendix) minus the amounts deducted from capital pursuant to §§ 390.461–390.471 (excluding those deductions reversed in section 12 of this appendix).

Traditional securitization means a transaction in which:

(1) All or a portion of the credit risk of one or more underlying exposures is transferred to one or more third parties other than through the use of credit derivatives or guarantees;

(2) The credit risk associated with the underlying exposures has been separated into at least two tranches reflecting different levels of seniority;

(3) Performance of the securitization exposures depends upon the performance of the underlying exposures;

(4) All or substantially all of the underlying exposures are financial exposures (such as loans, commitments, credit derivatives, guarantees, receivables, asset-backed securities, mortgage-backed securities, other debt securities, or equity securities);

(5) The underlying exposures are not owned by an operating company;

(6) The underlying exposures are not owned by a small business investment company described in section 302 of the Small Business Investment Act of 1958 (15 U.S.C. 682); and

(7) The underlying exposures are not owned by a firm an investment in which is designed primarily to promote community welfare, including the welfare of low- and moderate-income communities or families, such as by providing services or jobs.

(8) The FDIC may determine that a transaction in which the underlying exposures are owned by an investment firm that exercises substantially unfettered control over the size and composition of its assets, liabilities, and off-balance sheet exposures is not a traditional securitization based on the transaction's leverage, risk profile, or economic substance.

(9) The FDIC may deem a transaction that meets the definition of a traditional securitization, notwithstanding paragraph (5), (6), or (7) of this definition, to be a traditional securitization based on the transaction's leverage, risk profile, or economic substance.

Tranche means all securitization exposures associated with a securitization that have the same seniority level.

Underlying exposures means one or more exposures that have been securitized in a securitization transaction.

Unexpected operational loss (UOL) means the difference between the State savings association's operational risk exposure and the

Federal Deposit Insurance Corporation

State savings association's expected operational loss.

Unit of measure means the level (for example, organizational unit or operational loss event type) at which the State savings association's operational risk quantification system generates a separate distribution of potential operational losses.

Value-at-Risk (VaR) means the estimate of the maximum amount that the value of one or more exposures could decline due to market price or rate movements during a fixed holding period within a stated confidence interval.

Wholesale exposure means a credit exposure to a company, natural person, sovereign entity, or governmental entity (other than a securitization exposure, retail exposure, excluded mortgage exposure, or equity exposure). Examples of a wholesale exposure include:

(1) A non-tranched guarantee issued by a State savings association on behalf of a company;

(2) A repo-style transaction entered into by a State savings association with a company and any other transaction in which a State savings association posts collateral to a company and faces counterparty credit risk;

(3) An exposure that a State savings association treats as a covered position under any applicable market risk rule for which there is a counterparty credit risk capital requirement;

(4) A sale of corporate loans by a State savings association to a third party in which the State savings association retains full recourse;

(5) An OTC derivative contract entered into by a State savings association with a company;

(6) An exposure to an individual that is not managed by a State savings association as part of a segment of exposures with homogeneous risk characteristics; and

(7) A commercial lease.

Wholesale exposure subcategory means the HVCRE or non-HVCRE wholesale exposure subcategory.

Section 3. Minimum Risk-Based Capital Requirements

(a) Except as modified by paragraph (c) of this section or by section 23 of this appendix, each State savings association must meet a minimum ratio of:

(1) Total qualifying capital to total risk-weighted assets of 8.0 percent; and

(2) Tier 1 capital to total risk-weighted assets of 4.0 percent.

(b) Each State savings association must hold capital commensurate with the level and nature of all risks to which the State savings association is exposed.

(c) When a State savings association subject to any applicable market risk rule calculates its risk-based capital requirements

Pt. 390, Subpt. Z, App. A

under this appendix, the State savings association must also refer to any applicable market risk rule for supplemental rules to calculate risk-based capital requirements adjusted for market risk.

PART II. QUALIFYING CAPITAL

Section 11. Additional Deductions

(a) *General.* A State savings association that uses this appendix must make the same deductions from its tier 1 capital and tier 2 capital required in §§ 390.461–390.471 except that:

(1) A State savings association is not required to deduct certain equity investments and CEIOs (as provided in section 12 of this appendix); and

(2) A State savings association also must make the deductions from capital required by paragraphs (b) and (c) of this section.

(b) *Deductions from tier 1 capital.* A State savings association must deduct from tier 1 capital any gain-on-sale associated with a securitization exposure as provided in paragraph (a) of section 41 and paragraphs (a)(1), (c), (g)(1), and (h)(1) of section 42 of this appendix.

(c) *Deductions from tier 1 and tier 2 capital.* A State savings association must deduct the exposures specified in paragraphs (c)(1) through (c)(7) in this section 50 percent from tier 1 capital and 50 percent from tier 2 capital. If the amount deductible from tier 2 capital exceeds the State savings association's actual tier 2 capital, however, the State savings association must deduct the excess from tier 1 capital.

(1) *Credit-enhancing interest-only strips (CEIOs).* In accordance with paragraphs (a)(1) and (c) of section 42 of this appendix, any CEIO that does not constitute gain-on-sale.

(2) *Non-qualifying securitization exposures.* In accordance with paragraphs (a)(4) and (c) of section 42 of this appendix, any securitization exposure that does not qualify for the Ratings-Based Approach, the Internal Assessment Approach, or the Supervisory Formula Approach under sections 43, 44, and 45 of this appendix, respectively.

(3) *Securitizations of non-IRB exposures.* In accordance with paragraphs (c) and (g)(4) of section 42 of this appendix, certain exposures to a securitization any underlying exposure of which is not a wholesale exposure, retail exposure, securitization exposure, or equity exposure.

(4) *Low-rated securitization exposures.* In accordance with section 43 and paragraph (c) of section 42 of this appendix, any securitization exposure that qualifies for and must be deducted under the Ratings-Based Approach.

(5) *High-risk securitization exposures subject to the Supervisory Formula Approach.* In accordance with paragraphs (b) and (c) of section 45 of this appendix and paragraph (c) of

section 42 of this appendix, certain high-risk securitization exposures (or portions thereof) that qualify for the Supervisory Formula Approach.

(6) *Eligible credit reserves shortfall.* In accordance with paragraph (a)(1) of section 13 of this appendix, any eligible credit reserves shortfall.

(7) *Certain failed capital markets transactions.* In accordance with paragraph (e)(3) of section 35 of this appendix, the State savings association's exposure on certain failed capital markets transactions.

Section 12. Deductions and Limitations Not Required

(a) *Deduction of CEIOs.* A State savings association is not required to make the deduction from capital for CEIOs in 12 CFR 390.465(a)(2)(iii) and 390.471(e).

(b) *Deduction for certain equity investments.* A State savings association is not required to deduct equity securities from capital under 12 CFR 390.465(c)(2)(ii). However, it must continue to deduct equity investments in real estate under that section. *See* 12 CFR 390.461, which defines equity investments, including equity securities and equity investments in real estate.

Section 13. Eligible Credit Reserves

(a) *Comparison of eligible credit reserves to expected credit losses*—(1) *Shortfall of eligible credit reserves.* If a State savings association's eligible credit reserves are less than the State savings association's total expected credit losses, the State savings association must deduct the shortfall amount 50 percent from tier 1 capital and 50 percent from tier 2 capital. If the amount deductible from tier 2 capital exceeds the State savings association's actual tier 2 capital, the State savings association must deduct the excess amount from tier 1 capital.

(2) *Excess eligible credit reserves.* If a State savings association's eligible credit reserves exceed the State savings association's total expected credit losses, the State savings association may include the excess amount in tier 2 capital to the extent that the excess amount does not exceed 0.6 percent of the State savings association's credit-risk-weighted assets.

(b) *Treatment of allowance for loan and lease losses.* Regardless of any provision in §§ 390.461 through 390.471, the ALLL is included in tier 2 capital only to the extent provided in paragraph (a)(2) of this section and in section 24 of this appendix.

PART III. QUALIFICATION

Section 21. Qualification Process

(a) *Timing.* (1) A State savings association that is described in paragraph (b)(1) of section 1 of this appendix must adopt a written implementation plan no later than six months after the later of April 1, 2008, or the date the State savings association meets a criterion in that section. The implementation plan must incorporate an explicit first floor period start date no later than 36 months after the later of April 1, 2008, or the date the State savings association meets at least one criterion under paragraph (b)(1) of section 1 of this appendix. The FDIC may extend the first floor period start date.

(2) A State savings association that elects to be subject to this appendix under paragraph (b)(2) of section 1 of this appendix must adopt a written implementation plan.

(b) *Implementation plan.* (1) The State savings association's implementation plan must address in detail how the State savings association complies, or plans to comply, with the qualification requirements in section 22 of this appendix. The State savings association also must maintain a comprehensive and sound planning and governance process to oversee the implementation efforts described in the plan. At a minimum, the plan must:

(i) Comprehensively address the qualification requirements in section 22 of this appendix for the State savings association and each consolidated subsidiary (U.S. and foreign-based) of the State savings association with respect to all portfolios and exposures of the State savings association and each of its consolidated subsidiaries;

(ii) Justify and support any proposed temporary or permanent exclusion of business lines, portfolios, or exposures from application of the advanced approaches in this appendix (which business lines, portfolios, and exposures must be, in the aggregate, immaterial to the State savings association);

(iii) Include the State savings association's self-assessment of:

(A) The State savings association's current status in meeting the qualification requirements in section 22 of this appendix; and

(B) The consistency of the State savings association's current practices with the FDIC's supervisory guidance on the qualification requirements;

(iv) Based on the State savings association's self-assessment, identify and describe the areas in which the State savings association proposes to undertake additional work to comply with the qualification requirements in section 22 of this appendix or to improve the consistency of the State savings association's current practices with the FDIC's supervisory guidance on the qualification requirements (gap analysis);

(v) Describe what specific actions the State savings association will take to address the areas identified in the gap analysis required by paragraph (b)(1)(iv) of this section;

(vi) Identify objective, measurable milestones, including delivery dates and a date when the State savings association's implementation of the methodologies described in this appendix will be fully operational;

(vii) Describe resources that have been budgeted and are available to implement the plan; and

(viii) Receive approval of the State savings association's board of directors.

(2) The State savings association must submit the implementation plan, together with a copy of the minutes of the board of directors' approval, to the FDIC at least 60 days before the State savings association proposes to begin its parallel run, unless the FDIC waives prior notice.

(c) *Parallel run.* Before determining its risk-based capital requirements under this appendix and following adoption of the implementation plan, the State savings association must conduct a satisfactory parallel run. A satisfactory parallel run is a period of no less than four consecutive calendar quarters during which the State savings association complies with the qualification requirements in section 22 of this appendix to the satisfaction of the FDIC. During the parallel run, the State savings association must report to the FDIC on a calendar quarterly basis its risk-based capital ratios using §§ 390.461 through 390.471 and the risk-based capital requirements described in this appendix. During this period, the State savings association is subject to §§ 390.461 through 390.471.

(d) *Approval to calculate risk-based capital requirements under this appendix.* The FDIC will notify the State savings association of the date that the State savings association may begin its first floor period if the FDIC determines that:

(1) The State savings association fully complies with all the qualification requirements in section 22 of this appendix;

(2) The State savings association has conducted a satisfactory parallel run under paragraph (c) of this section; and

(3) The State savings association has an adequate process to ensure ongoing compliance with the qualification requirements in section 22 of this appendix.

(e) *Transitional floor periods.* Following a satisfactory parallel run, a State savings association is subject to three transitional floor periods.

(1) *Risk-based capital ratios during the transitional floor periods*—(i) *Tier 1 risk-based capital ratio.* During a State savings association's transitional floor periods, the State savings association's tier 1 risk-based capital ratio is equal to the lower of:

(A) The State savings association's floor-adjusted tier 1 risk-based capital ratio; or

(B) The State savings association's advanced approaches tier 1 risk-based capital ratio.

(ii) *Total risk-based capital ratio.* During a State savings association's transitional floor periods, the State savings association's total risk-based capital ratio is equal to the lower of:

(A) The State savings association's floor-adjusted total risk-based capital ratio; or

(B) The State savings association's advanced approaches total risk-based capital ratio.

(2) *Floor-adjusted risk-based capital ratios.* (i) A State savings association's floor-adjusted tier 1 risk-based capital ratio during a transitional floor period is equal to the State savings association's tier 1 capital as calculated under §§ 390.461–390.471, divided by the product of:

(A) The State savings association's total risk-weighted assets as calculated under §§ 390.461 through 390.471; and

(B) The appropriate transitional floor percentage in Table 1.

(ii) A State savings association's floor-adjusted total risk-based capital ratio during a transitional floor period is equal to the sum of the State savings association's tier 1 and tier 2 capital as calculated under §§ 390.461 through 390.471, divided by the product of:

(A) The State savings association's total risk-weighted assets as calculated under §§ 390.461 through 390.471; and

(B) The appropriate transitional floor percentage in Table 1.

(iii) A State savings association that meets the criteria in paragraph (b)(1) or (b)(2) of section 1 of this appendix as of April 1, 2008, must use §§ 390.461 through 390.471 during the parallel run and as the basis for its transitional floors.

TABLE 1—TRANSITIONAL FLOORS

Transitional floor period	Transitional floor percentage
First floor period	95
Second floor period	90
Third floor period	85

(3) *Advanced approaches risk-based capital ratios.* (i) A State savings association's advanced approaches tier 1 risk-based capital ratio equals the State savings association's tier 1 risk-based capital ratio as calculated under this appendix (other than this section on transitional floor periods).

(ii) A State savings association's advanced approaches total risk-based capital ratio equals the State savings association's total risk-based capital ratio as calculated under this appendix (other than this section on transitional floor periods).

(4) *Reporting.* During the transitional floor periods, a State savings association must report to the FDIC on a calendar quarterly basis both floor-adjusted risk-based capital ratios and both advanced approaches risk-based capital ratios.

(5) *Exiting a transitional floor period.* A State savings association may not exit a transitional floor period until the State savings association has spent a minimum of four consecutive calendar quarters in the period and the FDIC has determined that the State savings association may exit the floor period. The FDIC's determination will be based on an assessment of the State savings association's ongoing compliance with the qualification requirements in section 22 of this appendix.

(6) *Interagency study.* After the end of the second transition year (2010), the Federal banking agencies will publish a study that evaluates the advanced approaches to determine if there are any material deficiencies. For any primary Federal supervisor to authorize any institution to exit the third transitional floor period, the study must determine that there are no such material deficiencies that cannot be addressed by then-existing tools, or, if such deficiencies are found, they are first remedied by changes to this appendix. Notwithstanding the preceding sentence, a primary Federal supervisor that disagrees with the finding of material deficiency may not authorize any institution under its jurisdiction to exit the third transitional floor period unless it provides a public report explaining its reasoning.

Section 22. Qualification Requirements

(a) *Process and systems requirements.* (1) A State savings association must have a rigorous process for assessing its overall capital adequacy in relation to its risk profile and a comprehensive strategy for maintaining an appropriate level of capital.

(2) The systems and processes used by a State savings association for risk-based capital purposes under this appendix must be consistent with the State savings association's internal risk management processes and management information reporting systems.

(3) Each State savings association must have an appropriate infrastructure with risk measurement and management processes that meet the qualification requirements of this section and are appropriate given the State savings association's size and level of complexity. Regardless of whether the systems and models that generate the risk parameters necessary for calculating a State savings association's risk-based capital requirements are located at any affiliate of the State savings association, the State savings association itself must ensure that the risk parameters and reference data used to determine its risk-based capital requirements are representative of its own credit risk and operational risk exposures.

(b) *Risk rating and segmentation systems for wholesale and retail exposures.* (1) A State savings association must have an internal risk rating and segmentation system that accurately and reliably differentiates among degrees of credit risk for the State savings association's wholesale and retail exposures.

(2) For wholesale exposures:

(i) A State savings association must have an internal risk rating system that accurately and reliably assigns each obligor to a single rating grade (reflecting the obligor's likelihood of default). A State savings association may elect, however, not to assign to a rating grade an obligor to whom the State savings association extends credit based solely on the financial strength of a guarantor, provided that all of the State savings association's exposures to the obligor are fully covered by eligible guarantees, the State savings association applies the PD substitution approach in paragraph (c)(1) of section 33 of this appendix to all exposures to that obligor, and the State savings association immediately assigns the obligor to a rating grade if a guarantee can no longer be recognized under this appendix. The State savings association's wholesale obligor rating system must have at least seven discrete rating grades for non-defaulted obligors and at least one rating grade for defaulted obligors.

(ii) Unless the State savings association has chosen to directly assign LGD estimates to each wholesale exposure, the State savings association must have an internal risk rating system that accurately and reliably assigns each wholesale exposure to a loss severity rating grade (reflecting the State savings association's estimate of the LGD of the exposure). A State savings association employing loss severity rating grades must have a sufficiently granular loss severity grading system to avoid grouping together exposures with widely ranging LGDs.

(3) For retail exposures, a State savings association must have an internal system that groups retail exposures into the appropriate retail exposure subcategory, groups the retail exposures in each retail exposure subcategory into separate segments with homogeneous risk characteristics, and assigns accurate and reliable PD and LGD estimates for each segment on a consistent basis. The State savings association's system must identify and group in separate segments by subcategories exposures identified in paragraphs (c)(2)(ii) and (iii) of section 31 of this appendix.

(4) The State savings association's internal risk rating policy for wholesale exposures must describe the State savings association's rating philosophy (that is, must describe how wholesale obligor rating assignments are affected by the State savings association's choice of the range of economic, business, and industry conditions that are considered in the obligor rating process).

(5) The State savings association's internal risk rating system for wholesale exposures

Federal Deposit Insurance Corporation

must provide for the review and update (as appropriate) of each obligor rating and (if applicable) each loss severity rating whenever the State savings association receives new material information, but no less frequently than annually. The State savings association's retail exposure segmentation system must provide for the review and update (as appropriate) of assignments of retail exposures to segments whenever the State savings association receives new material information, but generally no less frequently than quarterly.

(c) *Quantification of risk parameters for wholesale and retail exposures.* (1) The State savings association must have a comprehensive risk parameter quantification process that produces accurate, timely, and reliable estimates of the risk parameters for the State savings association's wholesale and retail exposures.

(2) Data used to estimate the risk parameters must be relevant to the State savings association's actual wholesale and retail exposures, and of sufficient quality to support the determination of risk-based capital requirements for the exposures.

(3) The State savings association's risk parameter quantification process must produce appropriately conservative risk parameter estimates where the State savings association has limited relevant data, and any adjustments that are part of the quantification process must not result in a pattern of bias toward lower risk parameter estimates.

(4) The State savings association's risk parameter estimation process should not rely on the possibility of U.S. government financial assistance, except for the financial assistance that the U.S. government has a legally binding commitment to provide.

(5) Where the State savings association's quantifications of LGD directly or indirectly incorporate estimates of the effectiveness of its credit risk management practices in reducing its exposure to troubled obligors prior to default, the State savings association must support such estimates with empirical analysis showing that the estimates are consistent with its historical experience in dealing with such exposures during economic downturn conditions.

(6) PD estimates for wholesale obligors and retail segments must be based on at least five years of default data. LGD estimates for wholesale exposures must be based on at least seven years of loss severity data, and LGD estimates for retail segments must be based on at least five years of loss severity data. EAD estimates for wholesale exposures must be based on at least seven years of exposure amount data, and EAD estimates for retail segments must be based on at least five years of exposure amount data.

(7) Default, loss severity, and exposure amount data must include periods of economic downturn conditions, or the State savings association must adjust its estimates of risk parameters to compensate for the lack of data from periods of economic downturn conditions.

(8) The State savings association's PD, LGD, and EAD estimates must be based on the definition of default in this appendix.

(9) The State savings association must review and update (as appropriate) its risk parameters and its risk parameter quantification process at least annually.

(10) The State savings association must at least annually conduct a comprehensive review and analysis of reference data to determine relevance of reference data to the State savings association's exposures, quality of reference data to support PD, LGD, and EAD estimates, and consistency of reference data to the definition of default contained in this appendix.

(d) *Counterparty credit risk model.* A State savings association must obtain the prior written approval of the FDIC under section 32 of this appendix to use the internal models methodology for counterparty credit risk.

(e) *Double default treatment.* A State savings association must obtain the prior written approval of the FDIC under section 34 of this appendix to use the double default treatment.

(f) *Securitization exposures.* A State savings association must obtain the prior written approval of the FDIC under section 44 of this appendix to use the Internal Assessment Approach for securitization exposures to ABCP programs.

(g) *Equity exposures model.* A State savings association must obtain the prior written approval of the FDIC under section 53 of this appendix to use the Internal Models Approach for equity exposures.

(h) *Operational risk*—(1) *Operational risk management processes.* A State savings association must:

(i) Have an operational risk management function that:

(A) Is independent of business line management; and

(B) Is responsible for designing, implementing, and overseeing the State savings association's operational risk data and assessment systems, operational risk quantification systems, and related processes;

(ii) Have and document a process (which must capture business environment and internal control factors affecting the State savings association's operational risk profile) to identify, measure, monitor, and control operational risk in State savings association products, activities, processes, and systems; and

(iii) Report operational risk exposures, operational loss events, and other relevant operational risk information to business unit management, senior management, and the board of directors (or a designated committee of the board).

(2) *Operational risk data and assessment systems.* A State savings association must have operational risk data and assessment systems that capture operational risks to which the State savings association is exposed. The State savings association's operational risk data and assessment systems must:
(i) Be structured in a manner consistent with the State savings association's current business activities, risk profile, technological processes, and risk management processes; and
(ii) Include credible, transparent, systematic, and verifiable processes that incorporate the following elements on an ongoing basis:
(A) *Internal operational loss event data.* The State savings association must have a systematic process for capturing and using internal operational loss event data in its operational risk data and assessment systems.
(1) The State savings association's operational risk data and assessment systems must include a historical observation period of at least five years for internal operational loss event data (or such shorter period approved by the FDIC to address transitional situations, such as integrating a new business line).
(2) The State savings association must be able to map its internal operational loss event data into the seven operational loss event type categories.
(3) The State savings association may refrain from collecting internal operational loss event data for individual operational losses below established dollar threshold amounts if the State savings association can demonstrate to the satisfaction of the FDIC that the thresholds are reasonable, do not exclude important internal operational loss event data, and permit the State savings association to capture substantially all the dollar value of the State savings association's operational losses.
(B) *External operational loss event data.* The State savings association must have a systematic process for determining its methodologies for incorporating external operational loss event data into its operational risk data and assessment systems.
(C) *Scenario analysis.* The State savings association must have a systematic process for determining its methodologies for incorporating scenario analysis into its operational risk data and assessment systems.
(D) *Business environment and internal control factors.* The State savings association must incorporate business environment and internal control factors into its operational risk data and assessment systems. The State savings association must also periodically compare the results of its prior business environment and internal control factor assessments against its actual operational losses incurred in the intervening period.

(3) *Operational risk quantification systems.* (i) The State savings association's operational risk quantification systems:
(A) Must generate estimates of the State savings association's operational risk exposure using its operational risk data and assessment systems;
(B) Must employ a unit of measure that is appropriate for the State savings association's range of business activities and the variety of operational loss events to which it is exposed, and that does not combine business activities or operational loss events with demonstrably different risk profiles within the same loss distribution;
(C) Must include a credible, transparent, systematic, and verifiable approach for weighting each of the four elements, described in paragraph (h)(2)(ii) of this section, that a State savings association is required to incorporate into its operational risk data and assessment systems;
(D) May use internal estimates of dependence among operational losses across and within units of measure if the State savings association can demonstrate to the satisfaction of the FDIC that its process for estimating dependence is sound, robust to a variety of scenarios, and implemented with integrity, and allows for the uncertainty surrounding the estimates. If the State savings association has not made such a demonstration, it must sum operational risk exposure estimates across units of measure to calculate its total operational risk exposure; and
(E) Must be reviewed and updated (as appropriate) whenever the State savings association becomes aware of information that may have a material effect on the State savings association's estimate of operational risk exposure, but the review and update must occur no less frequently than annually.
(ii) With the prior written approval of the FDIC, a State savings association may generate an estimate of its operational risk exposure using an alternative approach to that specified in paragraph (h)(3)(i) of this section. A State savings association proposing to use such an alternative operational risk quantification system must submit a proposal to the FDIC. In determining whether to approve a State savings association's proposal to use an alternative operational risk quantification system, the FDIC will consider the following principles:
(A) Use of the alternative operational risk quantification system will be allowed only on an exception basis, considering the size, complexity, and risk profile of the State savings association;
(B) The State savings association must demonstrate that its estimate of its operational risk exposure generated under the alternative operational risk quantification system is appropriate and can be supported empirically; and

Federal Deposit Insurance Corporation

Pt. 390, Subpt. Z, App. A

(C) A State savings association must not use an allocation of operational risk capital requirements that includes entities other than depository institutions or the benefits of diversification across entities.

(i) *Data management and maintenance.* (1) A State savings association must have data management and maintenance systems that adequately support all aspects of its advanced systems and the timely and accurate reporting of risk-based capital requirements.

(2) A State savings association must retain data using an electronic format that allows timely retrieval of data for analysis, validation, reporting, and disclosure purposes.

(3) A State savings association must retain sufficient data elements related to key risk drivers to permit adequate monitoring, validation, and refinement of its advanced systems.

(j) *Control, oversight, and validation mechanisms.* (1) The State savings association's senior management must ensure that all components of the State savings association's advanced systems function effectively and comply with the qualification requirements in this section.

(2) The State savings association's board of directors (or a designated committee of the board) must at least annually review the effectiveness of, and approve, the State savings association's advanced systems.

(3) A State savings association must have an effective system of controls and oversight that:

(i) Ensures ongoing compliance with the qualification requirements in this section;

(ii) Maintains the integrity, reliability, and accuracy of the State savings association's advanced systems; and

(iii) Includes adequate governance and project management processes.

(4) The State savings association must validate, on an ongoing basis, its advanced systems. The State savings association's validation process must be independent of the advanced systems' development, implementation, and operation, or the validation process must be subjected to an independent review of its adequacy and effectiveness. Validation must include:

(i) An evaluation of the conceptual soundness of (including developmental evidence supporting) the advanced systems;

(ii) An ongoing monitoring process that includes verification of processes and benchmarking; and

(iii) An outcomes analysis process that includes back-testing.

(5) The State savings association must have an internal audit function independent of business-line management that at least annually assesses the effectiveness of the controls supporting the State savings association's advanced systems and reports its findings to the State savings association's board of directors (or a committee thereof).

(6) The State savings association must periodically stress test its advanced systems. The stress testing must include a consideration of how economic cycles, especially downturns, affect risk-based capital requirements (including migration across rating grades and segments and the credit risk mitigation benefits of double default treatment).

(k) *Documentation.* The State savings association must adequately document all material aspects of its advanced systems.

Section 23. Ongoing Qualification

(a) *Changes to advanced systems.* A State savings association must meet all the qualification requirements in section 22 of this appendix on an ongoing basis. A State savings association must notify the FDIC when the State savings association makes any change to an advanced system that would result in a material change in the State savings association's risk-weighted asset amount for an exposure type, or when the State savings association makes any significant change to its modeling assumptions.

(b) *Failure to comply with qualification requirements.* (1) If the FDIC determines that a State savings association that uses this appendix and has conducted a satisfactory parallel run fails to comply with the qualification requirements in section 22 of this appendix, the FDIC will notify the State savings association in writing of the State savings association's failure to comply.

(2) The State savings association must establish and submit a plan satisfactory to the FDIC to return to compliance with the qualification requirements.

(3) In addition, if the FDIC determines that the State savings association's risk-based capital requirements are not commensurate with the State savings association's credit, market, operational, or other risks, the FDIC may require such a State savings association to calculate its risk-based capital requirements:

(i) Under §§ 390.461 through 390.471; or

(ii) Under this appendix with any modifications provided by the FDIC.

Section 24. Merger and Acquisition Transitional Arrangements

(a) *Mergers and acquisitions of companies without advanced systems.* If a State savings association merges with or acquires a company that does not calculate its risk-based capital requirements using advanced systems, the State savings association may use §§ 390.461 through 390.471 to determine the risk-weighted asset amounts for, and deductions from capital associated with, the merged or acquired company's exposures for up to 24 months after the calendar quarter

943

during which the merger or acquisition consummates. The FDIC may extend this transition period for up to an additional 12 months. Within 90 days of consummating the merger or acquisition, the State savings association must submit to the FDIC an implementation plan for using its advanced systems for the acquired company. During the period when §390.460 applies to the merged or acquired company, any ALLL associated with the merged or acquired company's exposures may be included in the State savings association's tier 2 capital up to 1.25 percent of the acquired company's risk-weighted assets. All general allowances of the merged or acquired company must be excluded from the State savings association's eligible credit reserves. In addition, the risk-weighted assets of the merged or acquired company are not included in the State savings association's credit-risk-weighted assets but are included in total risk-weighted assets. If a State savings association relies on this paragraph, the State savings association must disclose publicly the amounts of risk-weighted assets and qualifying capital calculated under this appendix for the acquiring State savings association and under §§ 390.461 through 390.471 for the acquired company.

(b) *Mergers and acquisitions of companies with advanced systems*—(1) If a State savings association merges with or acquires a company that calculates its risk-based capital requirements using advanced systems, the State savings association may use the acquired company's advanced systems to determine the risk-weighted asset amounts for, and deductions from capital associated with, the merged or acquired company's exposures for up to 24 months after the calendar quarter during which the acquisition or merger consummates. The FDIC may extend this transition period for up to an additional 12 months. Within 90 days of consummating the merger or acquisition, the State savings association must submit to the FDIC an implementation plan for using its advanced systems for the merged or acquired company.

(2) If the acquiring State savings association is not subject to the advanced approaches in this appendix at the time of acquisition or merger, during the period when §§ 390.461 through 390.471 apply to the acquiring State savings association, the ALLL associated with the exposures of the merged or acquired company may not be directly included in tier 2 capital. Rather, any excess eligible credit reserves associated with the merged or acquired company's exposures may be included in the State savings association's tier 2 capital up to 0.6 percent of the credit-risk-weighted assets associated with those exposures.

PART IV. RISK-WEIGHTED ASSETS FOR GENERAL CREDIT RISK

Section 31. Mechanics for Calculating Total Wholesale and Retail Risk-Weighted Assets

(a) *Overview.* A State savings association must calculate its total wholesale and retail risk-weighted asset amount in four distinct phases:

(1) Phase 1—categorization of exposures;
(2) Phase 2—assignment of wholesale obligors and exposures to rating grades and segmentation of retail exposures;
(3) Phase 3—assignment of risk parameters to wholesale exposures and segments of retail exposures; and
(4) Phase 4—calculation of risk-weighted asset amounts.

(b) *Phase 1—Categorization.* The State savings association must determine which of its exposures are wholesale exposures, retail exposures, securitization exposures, or equity exposures. The State savings association must categorize each retail exposure as a residential mortgage exposure, a QRE, or an other retail exposure. The State savings association must identify which wholesale exposures are HVCRE exposures, sovereign exposures, OTC derivative contracts, repo-style transactions, eligible margin loans, eligible purchased wholesale exposures, unsettled transactions to which section 35 of this appendix applies, and eligible guarantees or eligible credit derivatives that are used as credit risk mitigants. The State savings association must identify any on-balance sheet asset that does not meet the definition of a wholesale, retail, equity, or securitization exposure, as well as any non-material portfolio of exposures described in paragraph (e)(4) of this section.

(c) *Phase 2—Assignment of wholesale obligors and exposures to rating grades and retail exposures to segments*—(1) *Assignment of wholesale obligors and exposures to rating grades.*

(i) The State savings association must assign each obligor of a wholesale exposure to a single obligor rating grade and must assign each wholesale exposure to which it does not directly assign an LGD estimate to a loss severity rating grade.

(ii) The State savings association must identify which of its wholesale obligors are in default.

(2) *Segmentation of retail exposures.* (i) The State savings association must group the retail exposures in each retail subcategory into segments that have homogeneous risk characteristics.

(ii) The State savings association must identify which of its retail exposures are in default. The State savings association must segment defaulted retail exposures separately from non-defaulted retail exposures.

(iii) If the State savings association determines the EAD for eligible margin loans

Federal Deposit Insurance Corporation

Pt. 390, Subpt. Z, App. A

using the approach in paragraph (b) of section 32 of this appendix, the State savings association must identify which of its retail exposures are eligible margin loans for which the State savings association uses this EAD approach and must segment such eligible margin loans separately from other retail exposures.

(3) *Eligible purchased wholesale exposures.* A State savings association may group its eligible purchased wholesale exposures into segments that have homogeneous risk characteristics. A State savings association must use the wholesale exposure formula in Table 2 in this section to determine the risk-based capital requirement for each segment of eligible purchased wholesale exposures.

(d) *Phase 3—Assignment of risk parameters to wholesale exposures and segments of retail exposures—*(1) *Quantification process.* Subject to the limitations in this paragraph (d), the State savings association must:

(i) Associate a PD with each wholesale obligor rating grade;

(ii) Associate an LGD with each wholesale loss severity rating grade or assign an LGD to each wholesale exposure;

(iii) Assign an EAD and M to each wholesale exposure; and

(iv) Assign a PD, LGD, and EAD to each segment of retail exposures.

(2) *Floor on PD assignment.* The PD for each wholesale obligor or retail segment may not be less than 0.03 percent, except for exposures to or directly and unconditionally guaranteed by a sovereign entity, the Bank for International Settlements, the International Monetary Fund, the European Commission, the European Central Bank, or a multilateral development bank, to which the State savings association assigns a rating grade associated with a PD of less than 0.03 percent.

(3) *Floor on LGD estimation.* The LGD for each segment of residential mortgage exposures (other than segments of residential mortgage exposures for which all or substantially all of the principal of each exposure is directly and unconditionally guaranteed by the full faith and credit of a sovereign entity) may not be less than 10 percent.

(4) *Eligible purchased wholesale exposures.* A State savings association must assign a PD, LGD, EAD, and M to each segment of eligible purchased wholesale exposures. If the State savings association can estimate ECL (but not PD or LGD) for a segment of eligible purchased wholesale exposures, the State savings association must assume that the LGD of the segment equals 100 percent and that the PD of the segment equals ECL divided by EAD. The estimated ECL must be calculated for the exposures without regard to any assumption of recourse or guarantees from the seller or other parties.

(5) *Credit risk mitigation—credit derivatives, guarantees, and collateral.* (i) A State savings association may take into account the risk reducing effects of eligible guarantees and eligible credit derivatives in support of a wholesale exposure by applying the PD substitution or LGD adjustment treatment to the exposure as provided in section 33 of this appendix or, if applicable, applying double default treatment to the exposure as provided in section 34 of this appendix. A State savings association may decide separately for each wholesale exposure that qualifies for the double default treatment under section 34 of this appendix whether to apply the double default treatment or to use the PD substitution or LGD adjustment treatment without recognizing double default effects.

(ii) A State savings association may take into account the risk reducing effects of guarantees and credit derivatives in support of retail exposures in a segment when quantifying the PD and LGD of the segment.

(iii) Except as provided in paragraph (d)(6) of this section, a State savings association may take into account the risk reducing effects of collateral in support of a wholesale exposure when quantifying the LGD of the exposure and may take into account the risk reducing effects of collateral in support of retail exposures when quantifying the PD and LGD of the segment.

(6) *EAD for OTC derivative contracts, repo-style transactions, and eligible margin loans.* (i) A State savings association must calculate its EAD for an OTC derivative contract as provided in paragraphs (c) and (d) of section 32 of this appendix. A State savings association may take into account the risk-reducing effects of financial collateral in support of a repo-style transaction or eligible margin loan and of any collateral in support of a repo-style transaction that is included in the State savings association's VaR-based measure under any applicable market risk rule through an adjustment to EAD as provided in paragraphs (b) and (d) of section 32 of this appendix. A State savings association that takes collateral into account through such an adjustment to EAD under section 32 of this appendix may not reflect such collateral in LGD.

(ii) A State savings association may attribute an EAD of zero to:

(A) Derivative contracts that are publicly traded on an exchange that requires the daily receipt and payment of cash-variation margin;

(B) Derivative contracts and repo-style transactions that are outstanding with a qualifying central counterparty (but not for those transactions that a qualifying central counterparty has rejected); and

(C) Credit risk exposures to a qualifying central counterparty in the form of clearing deposits and posted collateral that arise from transactions described in paragraph (d)(6)(ii)(B) of this section.

945

Pt. 390, Subpt. Z, App. A

(7) *Effective maturity.* An exposure's M must be no greater than five years and no less than one year, except that an exposure's M must be no less than one day if the exposure has an original maturity of less than one year and is not part of a State savings association's ongoing financing of the obligor. An exposure is not part of a State savings association's ongoing financing of the obligor if the State savings association:

(i) Has a legal and practical ability not to renew or roll over the exposure in the event of credit deterioration of the obligor;

(ii) Makes an independent credit decision at the inception of the exposure and at every renewal or roll over; and

(iii) Has no substantial commercial incentive to continue its credit relationship with the obligor in the event of credit deterioration of the obligor.

(e) *Phase 4—Calculation of risk-weighted assets*—(1) *Non-defaulted exposures.* (i) A State savings association must calculate the dollar risk-based capital requirement for each of its wholesale exposures to a non-defaulted obligor (except eligible guarantees and eligible credit derivatives that hedge another wholesale exposure and exposures to which the State savings association applies the double default treatment in section 34 of this appendix) and segments of non-defaulted retail exposures by inserting the assigned risk parameters for the wholesale obligor and exposure or retail segment into the appropriate risk-based capital formula specified in Table 2 and multiplying the output of the formula (K) by the EAD of the exposure or segment. Alternatively, a State savings association may apply a 300 percent risk weight to the EAD of an eligible margin loan if the State savings association is not able to meet the agencies' requirements for estimation of PD and LGD for the margin loan.

Table 2 – IRB Risk-Based Capital Formulas for Wholesale Exposures to Non-Defaulted Obligors and Segments of Non-Defaulted Retail Exposures[1]

Retail	Capital Requirement (K) Non-Defaulted Exposures	$K = \left[LGD \times N\left(\dfrac{N^{-1}(PD) + \sqrt{R} \times N^{-1}(0.999)}{\sqrt{1-R}} \right) - (LGD \times PD) \right]$
	Correlation Factor (R)	For residential mortgage exposures: $R = 0.15$
		For qualifying revolving exposures: $R = 0.04$
		For other retail exposures: $R = 0.03 + 0.13 \times e^{-35 \times PD}$
Wholesale	Capital Requirement (K) Non-Defaulted Exposures	$K = \left[LGD \times N\left(\dfrac{N^{-1}(PD) + \sqrt{R} \times N^{-1}(0.999)}{\sqrt{1-R}} \right) - (LGD \times PD) \right] \times \left(\dfrac{1 + (M - 2.5) \times b}{1 - 1.5 \times b} \right)$
	Correlation Factor (R)	For HVCRE exposures: $R = 0.12 + 0.18 \times e^{-50 \times PD}$
		For wholesale exposures other than HVCRE exposures: $R = 0.12 + 0.12 \times e^{-50 \times PD}$
	Maturity Adjustment (b)	$b = (0.11852 - 0.05478 \times \ln(PD))^2$

[1] N(.) means the cumulative distribution function for a standard normal random variable. N^{-1}(.) means the inverse cumulative distribution function for a standard normal random variable. The symbol e refers to the base of the natural logarithms, and the function ln(.) refers to the natural logarithm of the expression within parentheses. The formulas apply when PD is greater than zero. If PD equals zero, the capital requirement K is set equal to zero.

(ii) The sum of all the dollar risk-based capital requirements for each wholesale exposure to a non-defaulted obligor and segment of non-defaulted retail exposures calculated in paragraph (e)(1)(i) of this section and in paragraph (e) of section 34 of this appendix equals the total dollar risk-based capital requirement for those exposures and segments.

(iii) The aggregate risk-weighted asset amount for wholesale exposures to non-defaulted obligors and segments of non-defaulted retail exposures equals the total dollar risk-based capital requirement calculated in paragraph (e)(1)(ii) of this section multiplied by 12.5.

(2) *Wholesale exposures to defaulted obligors and segments of defaulted retail exposures.* (i) The dollar risk-based capital requirement for each wholesale exposure to a defaulted obligor equals 0.08 multiplied by the EAD of the exposure.

(ii) The dollar risk-based capital requirement for a segment of defaulted retail exposures equals 0.08 multiplied by the EAD of the segment.

(iii) The sum of all the dollar risk-based capital requirements for each wholesale exposure to a defaulted obligor calculated in paragraph (e)(2)(i) of this section plus the dollar risk-based capital requirements for each segment of defaulted retail exposures calculated in paragraph (e)(2)(ii) of this section equals the total dollar risk-based capital requirement for those exposures and segments.

(iv) The aggregate risk-weighted asset amount for wholesale exposures to defaulted obligors and segments of defaulted retail exposures equals the total dollar risk-based capital requirement calculated in paragraph (e)(2)(iii) of this section multiplied by 12.5.

(3) *Assets not included in a defined exposure category.* (i) A State savings association may assign a risk-weighted asset amount of zero to cash owned and held in all offices of the State savings association or in transit and for gold bullion held in the State savings association's own vaults, or held in another State savings association's vaults on an allocated basis, to the extent the gold bullion assets are offset by gold bullion liabilities.

(ii) The risk-weighted asset amount for the residual value of a retail lease exposure equals such residual value.

(iii) The risk-weighted asset amount for any other on-balance-sheet asset that does not meet the definition of a wholesale, retail, securitization, or equity exposure equals the carrying value of the asset.

(4) *Non-material portfolios of exposures.* The risk-weighted asset amount of a portfolio of exposures for which the State savings association has demonstrated to the FDIC's satisfaction that the portfolio (when combined with all other portfolios of exposures that the State savings association seeks to treat under this paragraph) is not material to the sum of the carrying values of on-balance sheet exposures plus the notional amounts of off-balance sheet exposures in the portfolio. For purposes of this paragraph (e)(4), the notional amount of an OTC derivative contract that is not a credit derivative is the EAD of the derivative as calculated in section 32 of this appendix.

Section 32. Counterparty Credit Risk of Repo-Style Transactions, Eligible Margin Loans, and OTC Derivative Contracts

(a) *In General.* (1) This section describes two methodologies—a collateral haircut approach and an internal models methodology—that a State savings association may use instead of an LGD estimation methodology to recognize the benefits of financial collateral in mitigating the counterparty credit risk of repo-style transactions, eligible margin loans, collateralized OTC derivative contracts, and single product netting sets of such transactions and to recognize the benefits of any collateral in mitigating the counterparty credit risk of repo-style transactions that are included in a State savings association's VaR-based measure under any applicable market risk rule. A third methodology, the simple VaR methodology, is available for single product netting sets of repo-style transactions and eligible margin loans.

(2) This section also describes the methodology for calculating EAD for an OTC derivative contract or a set of OTC derivative contracts subject to a qualifying master netting agreement. A State savings association also may use the internal models methodology to estimate EAD for qualifying cross-product master netting agreements.

(3) A State savings association may only use the standard supervisory haircut approach with a minimum 10-business-day holding period to recognize in EAD the benefits of conforming residential mortgage collateral that secures repo-style transactions (other than repo-style transactions included in the State savings association's VaR-based measure under any applicable market risk rule), eligible margin loans, and OTC derivative contracts.

(4) A State savings association may use any combination of the three methodologies for collateral recognition; however, it must use the same methodology for similar exposures.

(b) *EAD for eligible margin loans and repo-style transactions*—(1) *General.* A State savings association may recognize the credit risk mitigation benefits of financial collateral that secures an eligible margin loan, repo-style transaction, or single-product netting set of such transactions by factoring the collateral into its LGD estimates for the exposure. Alternatively, a State savings association may estimate an unsecured LGD for the exposure, as well as for any repo-style transaction that is included in the State savings association's VaR-based measure under any applicable market risk rule, and determine the EAD of the exposure using:

(i) The collateral haircut approach described in paragraph (b)(2) of this section;

(ii) For netting sets only, the simple VaR methodology described in paragraph (b)(3) of this section; or

(iii) The internal models methodology described in paragraph (d) of this section.

(2) *Collateral haircut approach*—(i) *EAD equation.* A State savings association may determine EAD for an eligible margin loan, repo-style transaction, or netting set by setting EAD equal to max {0, [(ΣE−ΣC) + Σ(Es × Hs) + Σ(Efx × Hfx)]}, where:

(A) ΣE equals the value of the exposure (the sum of the current market values of all instruments, gold, and cash the State savings association has lent, sold subject to repurchase, or posted as collateral to the counterparty under the transaction (or netting set));

(B) ΣC equals the value of the collateral (the sum of the current market values of all instruments, gold, and cash the State savings association has borrowed, purchased subject to resale, or taken as collateral from the counterparty under the transaction (or netting set));

(C) Es equals the absolute value of the net position in a given instrument or in gold (where the net position in a given instrument or in gold equals the sum of the current market values of the instrument or gold the State savings association has lent, sold subject to repurchase, or posted as collateral to the counterparty minus the sum of the current market values of that same instrument or gold the State savings association has borrowed, purchased subject to resale, or taken as collateral from the counterparty);

(D) Hs equals the market price volatility haircut appropriate to the instrument or gold referenced in Es;

(E) Efx equals the absolute value of the net position of instruments and cash in a currency that is different from the settlement currency (where the net position in a given currency equals the sum of the current market values of any instruments or cash in the currency the State savings association has lent, sold subject to repurchase, or posted as collateral to the counterparty minus the sum of the current market values of any instruments or cash in the currency the State savings association has borrowed, purchased subject to resale, or taken as collateral from the counterparty); and

(F) Hfx equals the haircut appropriate to the mismatch between the currency referenced in Efx and the settlement currency.

(ii) *Standard supervisory haircuts.* (A) Under the standard supervisory haircuts approach:

(1) A State savings association must use the haircuts for market price volatility (Hs) in Table 3, as adjusted in certain circumstances as provided in paragraph (b)(2)(ii)(A)(3) and (4) of this section;

TABLE 3—STANDARD SUPERVISORY MARKET PRICE VOLATILITY HAIRCUTS [3]

Applicable external rating grade category for debt securities	Residual maturity for debt securities	Issuers exempt from the 3 basis point floor	Other issuers
Two highest investment-grade rating categories for long-term ratings/highest investment-grade rating category for short-term ratings.	≤ 1 year	0.005	0.01
	>1 year, ≤ 5 years	0.02	0.04
	> 5 years	0.04	0.08
Two lowest investment-grade rating categories for both short- and long-term ratings.	≤ 1 year	0.01	0.02
	> 1 year, ≤ 5 years	0.03	0.06
	> 5 years	0.06	0.12
One rating category below investment grade	All	0.15	0.25
Main index equities (including convertible bonds) and gold		0.15	
Other publicly traded equities (including convertible bonds), conforming residential mortgages, and nonfinancial collateral.		0.25	
Mutual funds		Highest haircut applicable to any security in which the fund can invest.	
Cash on deposit with the State savings association (including a certificate of deposit issued by the State savings association).		0	

(2) For currency mismatches, a State savings association must use a haircut for foreign exchange rate volatility (Hfx) of 8 percent, as adjusted in certain circumstances as provided in paragraph (b)(2)(ii)(A)(3) and (4) of this section.

(3) For repo-style transactions, a State savings association may multiply the supervisory haircuts provided in paragraphs (b)(2)(ii)(A)(1) and (2) of this section by the square root of ½ (which equals 0.707107).

(4) A State savings association must adjust the supervisory haircuts upward on the basis of a holding period longer than ten business days (for eligible margin loans) or five business days (for repo-style transactions) where and as appropriate to take into account the illiquidity of an instrument.

---

[3] The market price volatility haircuts in Table 3 are based on a ten-business-day holding period.

(iii) *Own internal estimates for haircuts.* With the prior written approval of the FDIC, a State savings association may calculate haircuts (Hs and Hfx) using its own internal estimates of the volatilities of market prices and foreign exchange rates.

(A) To receive FDIC approval to use its own internal estimates, a State savings association must satisfy the following minimum quantitative standards:

(1) A State savings association must use a 99th percentile one-tailed confidence interval.

(2) The minimum holding period for a repo-style transaction is five business days and for an eligible margin loan is ten business days. When a State savings association calculates an own-estimates haircut on a T_N-day holding period, which is different from the minimum holding period for the transaction type, the applicable haircut (H_M) is calculated using the following square root of time formula:

949

$$H_M = H_N \sqrt{\frac{T_M}{T_N}}, \text{ where}$$

(i) T_M equals 5 for repo-style transactions and 10 for eligible margin loans;
(ii) T_N equals the holding period used by the State savings association to derive H_N; and
(iii) H_N equals the haircut based on the holding period T_N.

(3) A State savings association must adjust holding periods upwards where and as appropriate to take into account the illiquidity of an instrument.

(4) The historical observation period must be at least one year.

(5) A State savings association must update its data sets and recompute haircuts no less frequently than quarterly and must also reassess data sets and haircuts whenever market prices change materially.

(B) With respect to debt securities that have an applicable external rating of investment grade, a State savings association may calculate haircuts for categories of securities. For a category of securities, the State savings association must calculate the haircut on the basis of internal volatility estimates for securities in that category that are representative of the securities in that category that the State savings association has lent, sold subject to repurchase, posted as collateral, borrowed, purchased subject to resale, or taken as collateral. In determining relevant categories, the State savings association must at a minimum take into account:

(1) The type of issuer of the security;
(2) The applicable external rating of the security;
(3) The maturity of the security; and
(4) The interest rate sensitivity of the security.

(C) With respect to debt securities that have an applicable external rating of below investment grade and equity securities, a State savings association must calculate a separate haircut for each individual security.

(D) Where an exposure or collateral (whether in the form of cash or securities) is denominated in a currency that differs from the settlement currency, the State savings association must calculate a separate currency mismatch haircut for its net position in each mismatched currency based on estimated volatilities of foreign exchange rates between the mismatched currency and the settlement currency.

(E) A State savings association's own estimates of market price and foreign exchange rate volatilities may not take into account the correlations among securities and foreign exchange rates on either the exposure or collateral side of a transaction (or netting set) or the correlations among securities and foreign exchange rates between the exposure and collateral sides of the transaction (or netting set).

(3) *Simple VaR methodology.* With the prior written approval of the FDIC, a State savings association may estimate EAD for a netting set using a VaR model that meets the requirements in paragraph (b)(3)(iii) of this section. In such event, the State savings association must set EAD equal to max {0, [(ΣE−ΣC) + PFE]}, where:

(i) ΣE equals the value of the exposure (the sum of the current market values of all instruments, gold, and cash the State savings association has lent, sold subject to repurchase, or posted as collateral to the counterparty under the netting set);
(ii) ΣC equals the value of the collateral (the sum of the current market values of all instruments, gold, and cash the State savings association has borrowed, purchased subject to resale, or taken as collateral from the counterparty under the netting set); and
(iii) PFE (potential future exposure) equals the State savings association's empirically based best estimate of the 99th percentile, one-tailed confidence interval for an increase in the value of (ΣE−ΣC) over a five-business-day holding period for repo-style transactions or over a ten-business-day holding period for eligible margin loans using a minimum one-year historical observation period of price data representing the instruments that the State savings association has lent, sold subject to repurchase, posted as collateral, borrowed, purchased subject to resale, or taken as collateral. The State savings association must validate its VaR model, including by establishing and maintaining a rigorous and regular back-testing regime.

(c) *EAD for OTC derivative contracts.* (1) A State savings association must determine the EAD for an OTC derivative contract that is not subject to a qualifying master netting agreement using the current exposure methodology in paragraph (c)(5) of this section or using the internal models methodology described in paragraph (d) of this section.

(2) A State savings association must determine the EAD for multiple OTC derivative contracts that are subject to a qualifying master netting agreement using the current exposure methodology in paragraph (c)(6) of this section or using the internal models methodology described in paragraph (d) of this section.

(3) *Counterparty credit risk for credit derivatives.* Notwithstanding the above, (i) a State savings association that purchases a credit derivative that is recognized under section 33 or 34 of this appendix as a credit risk mitigant for an exposure that is not a covered position under any applicable market

risk rule need not compute a separate counterparty credit risk capital requirement under this section so long as the State savings association does so consistently for all such credit derivatives and either includes all or excludes all such credit derivatives that are subject to a master netting agreement from any measure used to determine counterparty credit risk exposure to all relevant counterparties for risk-based capital purposes.

(ii) A State savings association that is the protection provider in a credit derivative must treat the credit derivative as a wholesale exposure to the reference obligor and need not compute a counterparty credit risk capital requirement for the credit derivative under this section, so long as it does so consistently for all such credit derivatives and either includes all or excludes all such credit derivatives that are subject to a master netting agreement from any measure used to determine counterparty credit risk exposure to all relevant counterparties for risk-based capital purposes (unless the State savings association is treating the credit derivative as a covered position under any applicable market risk rule, in which case the State savings association must compute a supplemental counterparty credit risk capital requirement under this section).

(4) *Counterparty credit risk for equity derivatives.* A State savings association must treat an equity derivative contract as an equity exposure and compute a risk-weighted asset amount for the equity derivative contract under part VI (unless the State savings association is treating the contract as a covered position under any applicable market risk rule). In addition, if the State savings association is treating the contract as a covered position under any applicable market risk rule and in certain other cases described in section 55 of this appendix, the State savings association must also calculate a risk-based capital requirement for the counterparty credit risk of an equity derivative contract under this subpart.

(5) *Single OTC derivative contract.* Except as modified by paragraph (c)(7) of this section, the EAD for a single OTC derivative contract that is not subject to a qualifying master netting agreement is equal to the sum of the State savings association's current credit exposure and potential future credit exposure (PFE) on the derivative contract.

(i) *Current credit exposure.* The current credit exposure for a single OTC derivative contract is the greater of the mark-to-market value of the derivative contract or zero.

(ii) *PFE.* The PFE for a single OTC derivative contract, including an OTC derivative contract with a negative mark-to-market value, is calculated by multiplying the notional principal amount of the derivative contract by the appropriate conversion factor in Table 4. For purposes of calculating either the PFE under this paragraph or the gross PFE under paragraph (c)(6) of this section for exchange rate contracts and other similar contracts in which the notional principal amount is equivalent to the cash flows, notional principal amount is the net receipts to each party falling due on each value date in each currency. For any OTC derivative contract that does not fall within one of the specified categories in Table 4, the PFE must be calculated using the "other" conversion factors. A State savings association must use an OTC derivative contract's effective notional principal amount (that is, its apparent or stated notional principal amount multiplied by any multiplier in the OTC derivative contract) rather than its apparent or stated notional principal amount in calculating PFE. PFE of the protection provider of a credit derivative is capped at the net present value of the amount of unpaid premiums.

TABLE 4—CONVERSION FACTOR MATRIX FOR OTC DERIVATIVE CONTRACTS [4]

Remaining maturity [5]	Interest rate	Foreign exchange rate and gold	Credit (investment-grade reference obligor) [6]	Credit (non-investment-grade reference obligor)	Equity	Precious metals (except gold)	Other
One year or less	0.00	0.01	0.05	0.10	0.06	0.07	0.10
Over one to five years	0.005	0.05	0.05	0.10	0.08	0.07	0.12
Over five years	0.015	0.075	0.05	0.10	0.10	0.08	0.15

(6) *Multiple OTC derivative contracts subject to a qualifying master netting agreement.* Except as modified by paragraph (c)(7) of this

---

[4] For an OTC derivative contract with multiple exchanges of principal, the conversion factor is multiplied by the number of remaining payments in the derivative contract.

[5] For an OTC derivative contract that is structured such that on specified dates any outstanding exposure is settled and the terms are reset so that the market value of the contract is zero, the remaining maturity equals the time until the next reset date. For an interest rate derivative contract with

Continued

section, the EAD for multiple OTC derivative contracts subject to a qualifying master netting agreement is equal to the sum of the net current credit exposure and the adjusted sum of the PFE exposure for all OTC derivative contracts subject to the qualifying master netting agreement.

(i) *Net current credit exposure.* The net current credit exposure is the greater of:

(A) The net sum of all positive and negative mark-to-market values of the individual OTC derivative contracts subject to the qualifying master netting agreement; or

(B) zero.

(ii) *Adjusted sum of the PFE.* The adjusted sum of the PFE, Anet, is calculated as Anet = (0.4×Agross)+(0.6×NGR×Agross), where:

(A) Agross = the gross PFE (that is, the sum of the PFE amounts (as determined under paragraph (c)(5)(ii) of this section) for each individual OTC derivative contract subject to the qualifying master netting agreement); and

(B) NGR = the net to gross ratio (that is, the ratio of the net current credit exposure to the gross current credit exposure). In calculating the NGR, the gross current credit exposure equals the sum of the positive current credit exposures (as determined under paragraph (c)(5)(i) of this section) of all individual OTC derivative contracts subject to the qualifying master netting agreement.

(7) *Collateralized OTC derivative contracts.* A State savings association may recognize the credit risk mitigation benefits of financial collateral that secures an OTC derivative contract or single-product netting set of OTC derivatives by factoring the collateral into its LGD estimates for the contract or netting set. Alternatively, a State savings association may recognize the credit risk mitigation benefits of financial collateral that secures such a contract or netting set that is marked to market on a daily basis and subject to a daily margin maintenance requirement by estimating an unsecured LGD for the contract or netting set and adjusting the EAD calculated under paragraph (c)(5) or (c)(6) of this section using the collateral haircut approach in paragraph (b)(2) of this section. The State savings association must substitute the EAD calculated under paragraph (c)(5) or (c)(6) of this section for ΣE in the equation in paragraph (b)(2)(i) of this section and must use a ten-business-day minimum holding period (T_M= 10).

(d) *Internal models methodology.* (1) With prior written approval from the FDIC, a State savings association may use the internal models methodology in this paragraph (d) to determine EAD for counterparty credit risk for OTC derivative contracts (collateralized or uncollateralized) and single-product netting sets thereof, for eligible margin loans and single-product netting sets thereof, and for repo-style transactions and single-product netting sets thereof. A State savings association that uses the internal models methodology for a particular transaction type (OTC derivative contracts, eligible margin loans, or repo-style transactions) must use the internal models methodology for all transactions of that transaction type. A State savings association may choose to use the internal models methodology for one or two of these three types of exposures and not the other types. A State savings association may also use the internal models methodology for OTC derivative contracts, eligible margin loans, and repo-style transactions subject to a qualifying cross-product netting agreement if:

(i) The State savings association effectively integrates the risk mitigating effects of cross-product netting into its risk management and other information technology systems; and

(ii) The State savings association obtains the prior written approval of the FDIC. A State savings association that uses the internal models methodology for a transaction type must receive approval from the FDIC to cease using the methodology for that transaction type or to make a material change to its internal model.

(2) Under the internal models methodology, a State savings association uses an internal model to estimate the expected exposure (EE) for a netting set and then calculates EAD based on that EE.

(i) The State savings association must use its internal model's probability distribution for changes in the market value of a netting set that are attributable to changes in market variables to determine EE.

(ii) Under the internal models methodology, EAD = α x effective EPE, or, subject to FDIC approval as provided in paragraph (d)(7), a more conservative measure of EAD.

---

a remaining maturity of greater than one year that meets these criteria, the minimum conversion factor is 0.005.

[6] A State savings association must use the column labeled "Credit (investment-grade reference obligor)" for a credit derivative whose reference obligor has an outstanding unsecured long-term debt security without credit enhancement that has a long-term applicable external rating of at least investment grade. A State savings association must use the column labeled "Credit (non-investment-grade reference obligor)" for all other credit derivatives.

Federal Deposit Insurance Corporation

$$(A)\ \text{Effective EPE}_{t_k} = \sum_{i=1}^{n} \text{Effective EE}_{t_k} \times \Delta t_k$$

(that is, effective EPE is the time-weighted average of effective EE where the weights are the proportion that an individual effective EE represents in a one-year time interval) where:

(1) Effective EE$_t$k= max (Effective EE$_t$k−1, EE$_t$k) (that is, for a specific date$_t$k, effective EE is the greater of EE at that date or the effective EE at the previous date); and

(2)$_t$k represents the kth future time period in the model and there are n time periods represented in the model over the first year; and

(B) α = 1.4 except as provided in paragraph (d)(6), or when the FDIC has determined that the State savings association must set α higher based on the State savings association's specific characteristics of counterparty credit risk.

(iii) A State savings association may include financial collateral currently posted by the counterparty as collateral (but may not include other forms of collateral) when calculating EE.

(iv) If a State savings association hedges some or all of the counterparty credit risk associated with a netting set using an eligible credit derivative, the State savings association may take the reduction in exposure to the counterparty into account when estimating EE. If the State savings association recognizes this reduction in exposure to the counterparty in its estimate of EE, it must also use its internal model to estimate a separate EAD for the State savings association's exposure to the protection provider of the credit derivative.

(3) To obtain the FDIC's approval to calculate the distributions of exposures upon which the EAD calculation is based, the State savings association must demonstrate to the satisfaction of the FDIC that it has been using for at least one year an internal model that broadly meets the following minimum standards, with which the State savings association must maintain compliance:

(i) The model must have the systems capability to estimate the expected exposure to the counterparty on a daily basis (but is not expected to estimate or report expected exposure on a daily basis).

(ii) The model must estimate expected exposure at enough future dates to reflect accurately all the future cash flows of contracts in the netting set.

(iii) The model must account for the possible non-normality of the exposure distribution, where appropriate.

(iv) The State savings association must measure, monitor, and control current counterparty exposure and the exposure to the counterparty over the whole life of all contracts in the netting set.

(v) The State savings association must be able to measure and manage current exposures gross and net of collateral held, where appropriate. The State savings association must estimate expected exposures for OTC derivative contracts both with and without the effect of collateral agreements.

(vi) The State savings association must have procedures to identify, monitor, and control specific wrong-way risk throughout the life of an exposure. Wrong-way risk in this context is the risk that future exposure to a counterparty will be high when the counterparty's probability of default is also high.

(vii) The model must use current market data to compute current exposures. When estimating model parameters based on historical data, at least three years of historical data that cover a wide range of economic conditions must be used and must be updated quarterly or more frequently if market conditions warrant. The State savings association should consider using model parameters based on forward-looking measures, where appropriate.

(viii) A State savings association must subject its internal model to an initial validation and annual model review process. The model review should consider whether the inputs and risk factors, as well as the model outputs, are appropriate.

(4) *Maturity.* (i) If the remaining maturity of the exposure or the longest-dated contract in the netting set is greater than one year, the State savings association must set M for the exposure or netting set equal to the lower of five years or M(EPE),[7] where:

---

[7] Alternatively, a State savings association that uses an internal model to calculate a one-sided credit valuation adjustment may use the effective credit duration estimated by the model as M(EPE) in place of the formula in paragraph (d)(4).

$$\text{(A)} \quad M(EPE) = 1 + \frac{\sum_{t_k > 1\,year}^{maturity} EE_k \times \Delta t_k \times df_k}{\sum_{k=1}^{t_k \leq 1\,year} \text{effective} EE_k \times \Delta t_k \times df_k}$$

(B) df_k is the risk-free discount factor for future time period t_k; and

(C) $\Delta t_k = t_k - t_{k-1}$.

(ii) If the remaining maturity of the exposure or the longest-dated contract in the netting set is one year or less, the State savings association must set M for the exposure or netting set equal to one year, except as provided in paragraph (d)(7) of section 31 of this appendix.

(5) *Collateral agreements.* A State savings association may capture the effect on EAD of a collateral agreement that requires receipt of collateral when exposure to the counterparty increases but may not capture the effect on EAD of a collateral agreement that requires receipt of collateral when counterparty credit quality deteriorates. For this purpose, a collateral agreement means a legal contract that specifies the time when, and circumstances under which, the counterparty is required to pledge collateral to the State savings association for a single financial contract or for all financial contracts in a netting set and confers upon the State savings association a perfected, first priority security interest (notwithstanding the prior security interest of any custodial agent), or the legal equivalent thereof, in the collateral posted by the counterparty under the agreement. This security interest must provide the State savings association with a right to close out the financial positions and liquidate the collateral upon an event of default of, or failure to perform by, the counterparty under the collateral agreement. A contract would not satisfy this requirement if the State savings association's exercise of rights under the agreement may be stayed or avoided under applicable law in the relevant jurisdictions. Two methods are available to capture the effect of a collateral agreement:

(i) With prior written approval from the FDIC, a State savings association may include the effect of a collateral agreement within its internal model used to calculate EAD. The State savings association may set EAD equal to the expected exposure at the end of the margin period of risk. The margin period of risk means, with respect to a netting set subject to a collateral agreement, the time period from the most recent exchange of collateral with a counterparty until the next required exchange of collateral plus the period of time required to sell and realize the proceeds of the least liquid collateral that can be delivered under the terms of the collateral agreement and, where applicable, the period of time required to re-hedge the resulting market risk, upon the default of the counterparty. The minimum margin period of risk is five business days for repo-style transactions and ten business days for other transactions when liquid financial collateral is posted under a daily margin maintenance requirement. This period should be extended to cover any additional time between margin calls; any potential closeout difficulties; any delays in selling collateral, particularly if the collateral is illiquid; and any impediments to prompt re-hedging of any market risk.

(ii) A State savings association that can model EPE without collateral agreements but cannot achieve the higher level of modeling sophistication to model EPE with collateral agreements can set effective EPE for a collateralized netting set equal to the lesser of:

(A) The threshold, defined as the exposure amount at which the counterparty is required to post collateral under the collateral agreement, if the threshold is positive, plus an add-on that reflects the potential increase in exposure of the netting set over the margin period of risk. The add-on is computed as the expected increase in the netting set's exposure beginning from current exposure of zero over the margin period of risk. The margin period of risk must be at least five business days for netting sets consisting only of repo-style transactions subject to daily re-margining and daily marking-to-market, and ten business days for all other netting sets; or

(B) Effective EPE without a collateral agreement.

(6) *Own estimate of alpha.* With prior written approval of the FDIC, a State savings association may calculate alpha as the ratio of economic capital from a full simulation of counterparty exposure across counterparties that incorporates a joint simulation of market and credit risk factors (numerator) and economic capital based on EPE (denominator), subject to a floor of 1.2. For purposes of this calculation, economic capital is the unexpected losses for all counterparty credit risks measured at a 99.9 percent confidence level over a one-year horizon. To receive approval, the State savings association must meet the following minimum standards to the satisfaction of the FDIC:

Federal Deposit Insurance Corporation

(i) The State savings association's own estimate of alpha must capture in the numerator the effects of:

(A) The material sources of stochastic dependency of distributions of market values of transactions or portfolios of transactions across counterparties;

(B) Volatilities and correlations of market risk factors used in the joint simulation, which must be related to the credit risk factor used in the simulation to reflect potential increases in volatility or correlation in an economic downturn, where appropriate; and

(C) The granularity of exposures (that is, the effect of a concentration in the proportion of each counterparty's exposure that is driven by a particular risk factor).

(ii) The State savings association must assess the potential model uncertainty in its estimates of alpha.

(iii) The State savings association must calculate the numerator and denominator of alpha in a consistent fashion with respect to modeling methodology, parameter specifications, and portfolio composition.

(iv) The State savings association must review and adjust as appropriate its estimates of the numerator and denominator of alpha on at least a quarterly basis and more frequently when the composition of the portfolio varies over time.

(7) *Other measures of counterparty exposure.* With prior written approval of the FDIC, a State savings association may set EAD equal to a measure of counterparty credit risk exposure, such as peak EAD, that is more conservative than an alpha of 1.4 (or higher under the terms of paragraph (d)(2)(ii)(B) of this section) times EPE for every counterparty whose EAD will be measured under the alternative measure of counterparty exposure. The State savings association must demonstrate the conservatism of the measure of counterparty credit risk exposure used for EAD. For material portfolios of new OTC derivative products, the State savings association may assume that the current exposure methodology in paragraphs (c)(5) and (c)(6) of this section meets the conservatism requirement of this paragraph for a period not to exceed 180 days. For immaterial portfolios of OTC derivative contracts, the State savings association generally may assume that the current exposure methodology in paragraphs (c)(5) and (c)(6) of this section meets the conservatism requirement of this paragraph.

Section 33. Guarantees and Credit Derivatives: PD Substitution and LGD Adjustment Approaches

(a) *Scope.* (1) This section applies to wholesale exposures for which:

(i) Credit risk is fully covered by an eligible guarantee or eligible credit derivative; or

Pt. 390, Subpt. Z, App. A

(ii) Credit risk is covered on a pro rata basis (that is, on a basis in which the State savings association and the protection provider share losses proportionately) by an eligible guarantee or eligible credit derivative.

(2) Wholesale exposures on which there is a tranching of credit risk (reflecting at least two different levels of seniority) are securitization exposures subject to the securitization framework in part V.

(3) A State savings association may elect to recognize the credit risk mitigation benefits of an eligible guarantee or eligible credit derivative covering an exposure described in paragraph (a)(1) of this section by using the PD substitution approach or the LGD adjustment approach in paragraph (c) of this section or, if the transaction qualifies, using the double default treatment in section 34 of this appendix. A State savings association's PD and LGD for the hedged exposure may not be lower than the PD and LGD floors described in paragraphs (d)(2) and (d)(3) of section 31 of this appendix.

(4) If multiple eligible guarantees or eligible credit derivatives cover a single exposure described in paragraph (a)(1) of this section, a State savings association may treat the hedged exposure as multiple separate exposures each covered by a single eligible guarantee or eligible credit derivative and may calculate a separate risk-based capital requirement for each separate exposure as described in paragraph (a)(3) of this section.

(5) If a single eligible guarantee or eligible credit derivative covers multiple hedged wholesale exposures described in paragraph (a)(1) of this section, a State savings association must treat each hedged exposure as covered by a separate eligible guarantee or eligible credit derivative and must calculate a separate risk-based capital requirement for each exposure as described in paragraph (a)(3) of this section.

(6) A State savings association must use the same risk parameters for calculating ECL as it uses for calculating the risk-based capital requirement for the exposure.

(b) *Rules of recognition.* (1) A State savings association may only recognize the credit risk mitigation benefits of eligible guarantees and eligible credit derivatives.

(2) A State savings association may only recognize the credit risk mitigation benefits of an eligible credit derivative to hedge an exposure that is different from the credit derivative's reference exposure used for determining the derivative's cash settlement value, deliverable obligation, or occurrence of a credit event if:

(i) The reference exposure ranks *pari passu* (that is, equally) with or is junior to the hedged exposure; and

(ii) The reference exposure and the hedged exposure are exposures to the same legal entity, and legally enforceable cross-default or cross-acceleration clauses are in place to assure payments under the credit derivative are triggered when the obligor fails to pay under the terms of the hedged exposure.

(c) *Risk parameters for hedged exposures*—(1) *PD substitution approach*—(i) *Full coverage.* If an eligible guarantee or eligible credit derivative meets the conditions in paragraphs (a) and (b) of this section and the protection amount (P) of the guarantee or credit derivative is greater than or equal to the EAD of the hedged exposure, a State savings association may recognize the guarantee or credit derivative in determining the State savings association's risk-based capital requirement for the hedged exposure by substituting the PD associated with the rating grade of the protection provider for the PD associated with the rating grade of the obligor in the risk-based capital formula applicable to the guarantee or credit derivative in Table 2 and using the appropriate LGD as described in paragraph (c)(1)(iii) of this section. If the State savings association determines that full substitution of the protection provider's PD leads to an inappropriate degree of risk mitigation, the State savings association may substitute a higher PD than that of the protection provider.

(ii) *Partial coverage.* If an eligible guarantee or eligible credit derivative meets the conditions in paragraphs (a) and (b) of this section and the protection amount (P) of the guarantee or credit derivative is less than the EAD of the hedged exposure, the State savings association must treat the hedged exposure as two separate exposures (protected and unprotected) in order to recognize the credit risk mitigation benefit of the guarantee or credit derivative.

(A) The State savings association must calculate its risk-based capital requirement for the protected exposure under section 31 of this appendix, where PD is the protection provider's PD, LGD is determined under paragraph (c)(1)(iii) of this section, and EAD is P. If the State savings association determines that full substitution leads to an inappropriate degree of risk mitigation, the State savings association may use a higher PD than that of the protection provider.

(B) The State savings association must calculate its risk-based capital requirement for the unprotected exposure under section 31 of this appendix, where PD is the obligor's PD, LGD is the hedged exposure's LGD (not adjusted to reflect the guarantee or credit derivative), and EAD is the EAD of the original hedged exposure minus P.

(C) The treatment in this paragraph (c)(1)(ii) is applicable when the credit risk of a wholesale exposure is covered on a partial pro rata basis or when an adjustment is made to the effective notional amount of the guarantee or credit derivative under paragraph (d), (e), or (f) of this section.

(iii) *LGD of hedged exposures.* The LGD of a hedged exposure under the PD substitution approach is equal to:

(A) The lower of the LGD of the hedged exposure (not adjusted to reflect the guarantee or credit derivative) and the LGD of the guarantee or credit derivative, if the guarantee or credit derivative provides the State savings association with the option to receive immediate payout upon triggering the protection; or

(B) The LGD of the guarantee or credit derivative, if the guarantee or credit derivative does not provide the State savings association with the option to receive immediate payout upon triggering the protection.

(2) *LGD adjustment approach*—(i) *Full coverage.* If an eligible guarantee or eligible credit derivative meets the conditions in paragraphs (a) and (b) of this section and the protection amount (P) of the guarantee or credit derivative is greater than or equal to the EAD of the hedged exposure, the State savings association's risk-based capital requirement for the hedged exposure is the greater of:

(A) The risk-based capital requirement for the exposure as calculated under section 31 of this appendix, with the LGD of the exposure adjusted to reflect the guarantee or credit derivative; or

(B) The risk-based capital requirement for a direct exposure to the protection provider as calculated under section 31 of this appendix, using the PD for the protection provider, the LGD for the guarantee or credit derivative, and an EAD equal to the EAD of the hedged exposure.

(ii) *Partial coverage.* If an eligible guarantee or eligible credit derivative meets the conditions in paragraphs (a) and (b) of this section and the protection amount (P) of the guarantee or credit derivative is less than the EAD of the hedged exposure, the State savings association must treat the hedged exposure as two separate exposures (protected and unprotected) in order to recognize the credit risk mitigation benefit of the guarantee or credit derivative.

(A) The State savings association's risk-based capital requirement for the protected exposure would be the greater of:

(1) The risk-based capital requirement for the protected exposure as calculated under section 31 of this appendix, with the LGD of the exposure adjusted to reflect the guarantee or credit derivative and EAD set equal to P; or

(2) The risk-based capital requirement for a direct exposure to the guarantor as calculated under section 31 of this appendix, using the PD for the protection provider, the LGD for the guarantee or credit derivative, and an EAD set equal to P.

(B) The State savings association must calculate its risk-based capital requirement for the unprotected exposure under section 31 of this appendix, where PD is the obligor's PD, LGD is the hedged exposure's LGD (not adjusted to reflect the guarantee or credit derivative), and EAD is the EAD of the original hedged exposure minus P.

(3) *M of hedged exposures.* The M of the hedged exposure is the same as the M of the exposure if it were unhedged.

(d) *Maturity mismatch.* (1) A State savings association that recognizes an eligible guarantee or eligible credit derivative in determining its risk-based capital requirement for a hedged exposure must adjust the effective notional amount of the credit risk mitigant to reflect any maturity mismatch between the hedged exposure and the credit risk mitigant.

(2) A maturity mismatch occurs when the residual maturity of a credit risk mitigant is less than that of the hedged exposure(s).

(3) The residual maturity of a hedged exposure is the longest possible remaining time before the obligor is scheduled to fulfill its obligation on the exposure. If a credit risk mitigant has embedded options that may reduce its term, the State savings association (protection purchaser) must use the shortest possible residual maturity for the credit risk mitigant. If a call is at the discretion of the protection provider, the residual maturity of the credit risk mitigant is at the first call date. If the call is at the discretion of the State savings association (protection purchaser), but the terms of the arrangement at origination of the credit risk mitigant contain a positive incentive for the State savings association to call the transaction before contractual maturity, the remaining time to the first call date is the residual maturity of the credit risk mitigant. For example, where there is a step-up in cost in conjunction with a call feature or where the effective cost of protection increases over time even if credit quality remains the same or improves, the residual maturity of the credit risk mitigant will be the remaining time to the first call.

(4) A credit risk mitigant with a maturity mismatch may be recognized only if its original maturity is greater than or equal to one year and its residual maturity is greater than three months.

(5) When a maturity mismatch exists, the State savings association must apply the following adjustment to the effective notional amount of the credit risk mitigant: $Pm = E \times (t-0.25)/(T-0.25)$, where:

(i) Pm = effective notional amount of the credit risk mitigant, adjusted for maturity mismatch;

(ii) E = effective notional amount of the credit risk mitigant;

(iii) t = the lesser of T or the residual maturity of the credit risk mitigant, expressed in years; and

(iv) T = the lesser of five or the residual maturity of the hedged exposure, expressed in years.

(e) *Credit derivatives without restructuring as a credit event.* If a State savings association recognizes an eligible credit derivative that does not include as a credit event a restructuring of the hedged exposure involving forgiveness or postponement of principal, interest, or fees that results in a credit loss event (that is, a charge-off, specific provision, or other similar debit to the profit and loss account), the State savings association must apply the following adjustment to the effective notional amount of the credit derivative: $Pr = Pm \times 0.60$, where:

(1) Pr = effective notional amount of the credit risk mitigant, adjusted for lack of restructuring event (and maturity mismatch, if applicable); and

(2) Pm = effective notional amount of the credit risk mitigant adjusted for maturity mismatch (if applicable).

(f) *Currency mismatch.* (1) If a State savings association recognizes an eligible guarantee or eligible credit derivative that is denominated in a currency different from that in which the hedged exposure is denominated, the State savings association must apply the following formula to the effective notional amount of the guarantee or credit derivative: $Pc = Pr \times (1 - H_{FX})$, where:

(i) Pc = effective notional amount of the credit risk mitigant, adjusted for currency mismatch (and maturity mismatch and lack of restructuring event, if applicable);

(ii) Pr = effective notional amount of the credit risk mitigant (adjusted for maturity mismatch and lack of restructuring event, if applicable); and

(iii) H_{FX} = haircut appropriate for the currency mismatch between the credit risk mitigant and the hedged exposure.

(2) A State savings association must set H_{FX} equal to 8 percent unless it qualifies for the use of and uses its own internal estimates of foreign exchange volatility based on a ten-business-day holding period and daily marking-to-market and remargining. A State savings association qualifies for the use of its own internal estimates of foreign exchange volatility if it qualifies for:

(i) The own-estimates haircuts in paragraph (b)(2)(iii) of section 32 of this appendix;

(ii) The simple VaR methodology in paragraph (b)(3) of section 32 of this appendix; or

(iii) The internal models methodology in paragraph (d) of section 32 of this appendix.

(3) A State savings association must adjust H_{FX} calculated in paragraph (f)(2) of this section upward if the State savings association revalues the guarantee or credit derivative less frequently than once every ten business days using the square root of time formula provided in paragraph (b)(2)(iii)(A)(2) of section 32 of this appendix.

Section 34. Guarantees and Credit Derivatives: Double Default Treatment

(a) *Eligibility and operational criteria for double default treatment.* A State savings association may recognize the credit risk mitigation benefits of a guarantee or credit derivative covering an exposure described in paragraph (a)(1) of section 33 of this appendix by applying the double default treatment in this section if all the following criteria are satisfied.

(1) The hedged exposure is fully covered or covered on a pro rata basis by:

(i) An eligible guarantee issued by an eligible double default guarantor; or

(ii) An eligible credit derivative that meets the requirements of paragraph (b)(2) of section 33 of this appendix and is issued by an eligible double default guarantor.

(2) The guarantee or credit derivative is:

(i) An uncollateralized guarantee or uncollateralized credit derivative (for example, a credit default swap) that provides protection with respect to a single reference obligor; or

(ii) An nth-to-default credit derivative (subject to the requirements of paragraph (m) of section 42 of this appendix).

(3) The hedged exposure is a wholesale exposure (other than a sovereign exposure).

(4) The obligor of the hedged exposure is not:

(i) An eligible double default guarantor or an affiliate of an eligible double default guarantor; or

(ii) An affiliate of the guarantor.

(5) The State savings association does not recognize any credit risk mitigation benefits of the guarantee or credit derivative for the hedged exposure other than through application of the double default treatment as provided in this section.

(6) The State savings association has implemented a process (which has received the prior, written approval of the FDIC) to detect excessive correlation between the creditworthiness of the obligor of the hedged exposure and the protection provider. If excessive correlation is present, the State savings association may not use the double default treatment for the hedged exposure.

(b) *Full coverage.* If the transaction meets the criteria in paragraph (a) of this section and the protection amount (P) of the guarantee or credit derivative is at least equal to the EAD of the hedged exposure, the State savings association may determine its risk-weighted asset amount for the hedged exposure under paragraph (e) of this section.

(c) *Partial coverage.* If the transaction meets the criteria in paragraph (a) of this section and the protection amount (P) of the guarantee or credit derivative is less than the EAD of the hedged exposure, the State savings association must treat the hedged exposure as two separate exposures (protected and unprotected) in order to recognize double default treatment on the protected portion of the exposure.

(1) For the protected exposure, the State savings association must set EAD equal to P and calculate its risk-weighted asset amount as provided in paragraph (e) of this section.

(2) For the unprotected exposure, the State savings association must set EAD equal to the EAD of the original exposure minus P and then calculate its risk-weighted asset amount as provided in section 31 of this appendix.

(d) *Mismatches.* For any hedged exposure to which a State savings association applies double default treatment, the State savings association must make applicable adjustments to the protection amount as required in paragraphs (d), (e), and (f) of section 33 of this appendix.

(e) *The double default dollar risk-based capital requirement.* The dollar risk-based capital requirement for a hedged exposure to which a State savings association has applied double default treatment is K_{DD} multiplied by the EAD of the exposure. K_{DD} is calculated according to the following formula: $K_{DD}= K_o \times (0.15 + 160 \times PD_g)$,

Where:

(1)

$$K_O = LGD_g \times \left[N\left(\frac{N^{-1}(PD_o) + N^{-1}(0.999)\sqrt{\rho_{os}}}{\sqrt{1-\rho_{os}}} \right) - PD_o \right] \times \left[\frac{1+(M-2.5)\times b}{1-1.5\times b} \right]$$

(2) PD_g = PD of the protection provider.

(3) PD_o = PD of the obligor of the hedged exposure.

(4) LGD_g = (i) The lower of the LGD of the hedged exposure (not adjusted to reflect the guarantee or credit derivative) and the LGD of the guarantee or credit derivative, if the guarantee or credit derivative provides the State savings association with the option to receive immediate payout on triggering the protection; or

(ii) The LGD of the guarantee or credit derivative, if the guarantee or credit derivative does not provide the State savings association with the option to receive immediate payout on triggering the protection.

(5) ρ$_{os}$(asset value correlation of the obligor) is calculated according to the appropriate formula for (R) provided in Table 2 in section 31 of this appendix, with PD equal to PD$_o$.

(6) b (maturity adjustment coefficient) is calculated according to the formula for b provided in Table 2 in section 31 of this appendix, with PD equal to the lesser of PD$_o$ and PD$_g$.

(7) M (maturity) is the effective maturity of the guarantee or credit derivative, which may not be less than one year or greater than five years.

Section 35. Risk-Based Capital Requirement for Unsettled Transactions

(a) *Definitions.* For purposes of this section:

(1) *Delivery-versus-payment (DvP) transaction* means a securities or commodities transaction in which the buyer is obligated to make payment only if the seller has made delivery of the securities or commodities and the seller is obligated to deliver the securities or commodities only if the buyer has made payment.

(2) *Payment-versus-payment (PvP) transaction* means a foreign exchange transaction in which each counterparty is obligated to make a final transfer of one or more currencies only if the other counterparty has made a final transfer of one or more currencies.

(3) *Normal settlement period.* A transaction has a *normal settlement period* if the contractual settlement period for the transaction is equal to or less than the market standard for the instrument underlying the transaction and equal to or less than five business days.

(4) *Positive current exposure.* The positive current exposure of a State savings association for a transaction is the difference between the transaction value at the agreed settlement price and the current market price of the transaction, if the difference results in a credit exposure of the State savings association to the counterparty.

(b) *Scope.* This section applies to all transactions involving securities, foreign exchange instruments, and commodities that have a risk of delayed settlement or delivery. This section does not apply to:

(1) Transactions accepted by a qualifying central counterparty that are subject to daily marking-to-market and daily receipt and payment of variation margin;

(2) Repo-style transactions, including unsettled repo-style transactions (which are addressed in sections 31 and 32 of this appendix);

(3) One-way cash payments on OTC derivative contracts (which are addressed in sections 31 and 32 of this appendix); or

(4) Transactions with a contractual settlement period that is longer than the normal settlement period (which are treated as OTC derivative contracts and addressed in sections 31 and 32 of this appendix).

(c) *System-wide failures.* In the case of a system-wide failure of a settlement or clearing system, the FDIC may waive risk-based capital requirements for unsettled and failed transactions until the situation is rectified.

(d) *Delivery-versus-payment (DvP) and payment-versus-payment (PvP) transactions.* A State savings association must hold risk-based capital against any DvP or PvP transaction with a normal settlement period if the State savings association's counterparty has not made delivery or payment within five business days after the settlement date. The State savings association must determine its risk-weighted asset amount for such a transaction by multiplying the positive current exposure of the transaction for the State savings association by the appropriate risk weight in Table 5.

TABLE 5—RISK WEIGHTS FOR UNSETTLED DvP AND PvP TRANSACTIONS

Number of business days after contractual settlement date	Risk weight to be applied to positive current exposure (percent)
From 5 to 15	100
From 16 to 30	625
From 31 to 45	937.5
46 or more	1,250

(e) *Non-DvP/non-PvP (non-delivery-versus-payment/non-payment-versus-payment) transactions.* (1) A State savings association must hold risk-based capital against any non-DvP/non-PvP transaction with a normal settlement period if the State savings association has delivered cash, securities, commodities, or currencies to its counterparty but has not received its corresponding deliverables by the end of the same business day. The State savings association must continue to hold risk-based capital against the transaction until the State savings association has received its corresponding deliverables.

(2) From the business day after the State savings association has made its delivery until five business days after the counterparty delivery is due, the State savings association must calculate its risk-based capital requirement for the transaction by treating the current market value of the deliverables owed to the State savings association as a wholesale exposure.

(i) A State savings association may assign an obligor rating to a counterparty for which it is not otherwise required under this appendix to assign an obligor rating on the basis of the applicable external rating of any outstanding unsecured long-term debt security without credit enhancement issued by the counterparty.

(ii) A State savings association may use a 45 percent LGD for the transaction rather than estimating LGD for the transaction provided the State savings association uses the 45 percent LGD for all transactions described in paragraphs (e)(1) and (e)(2) of this section.

(iii) A State savings association may use a 100 percent risk weight for the transaction provided the State savings association uses this risk weight for all transactions described in paragraphs (e)(1) and (e)(2) of this section.

(3) If the State savings association has not received its deliverables by the fifth business day after the counterparty delivery was due, the State savings association must deduct the current market value of the deliverables owed to the State savings association 50 percent from tier 1 capital and 50 percent from tier 2 capital.

(f) *Total risk-weighted assets for unsettled transactions.* Total risk-weighted assets for unsettled transactions is the sum of the risk-weighted asset amounts of all DvP, PvP, and non-DvP/non-PvP transactions.

PART V. RISK-WEIGHTED ASSETS FOR SECURITIZATION EXPOSURES

Section 41. Operational Criteria for Recognizing the Transfer of Risk

(a) *Operational criteria for traditional securitizations.* A State savings association that transfers exposures it has originated or purchased to a securitization SPE or other third party in connection with a traditional securitization may exclude the exposures from the calculation of its risk-weighted assets only if each of the conditions in this paragraph (a) is satisfied. A State savings association that meets these conditions must hold risk-based capital against any securitization exposures it retains in connection with the securitization. A State savings association that fails to meet these conditions must hold risk-based capital against the transferred exposures as if they had not been securitized and must deduct from tier 1 capital any after-tax gain-on-sale resulting from the transaction. The conditions are:

(1) The transfer is considered a sale under GAAP;

(2) The State savings association has transferred to third parties credit risk associated with the underlying exposures; and

(3) Any clean-up calls relating to the securitization are eligible clean-up calls.

(b) *Operational criteria for synthetic securitizations.* For synthetic securitizations, a State savings association may recognize for risk-based capital purposes the use of a credit risk mitigant to hedge underlying exposures only if each of the conditions in this paragraph (b) is satisfied. A State savings association that fails to meet these conditions must hold risk-based capital against the underlying exposures as if they had not been synthetically securitized. The conditions are:

(1) The credit risk mitigant is financial collateral, an eligible credit derivative from an eligible securitization guarantor or an eligible guarantee from an eligible securitization guarantor;

(2) The State savings association transfers credit risk associated with the underlying exposures to third parties, and the terms and conditions in the credit risk mitigants employed do not include provisions that:

(i) Allow for the termination of the credit protection due to deterioration in the credit quality of the underlying exposures;

(ii) Require the State savings association to alter or replace the underlying exposures to improve the credit quality of the pool of underlying exposures;

(iii) Increase the State savings association's cost of credit protection in response to deterioration in the credit quality of the underlying exposures;

(iv) Increase the yield payable to parties other than the State savings association in response to a deterioration in the credit quality of the underlying exposures; or

(v) Provide for increases in a retained first loss position or credit enhancement provided by the State savings association after the inception of the securitization;

(3) The State savings association obtains a well-reasoned opinion from legal counsel that confirms the enforceability of the credit risk mitigant in all relevant jurisdictions; and

(4) Any clean-up calls relating to the securitization are eligible clean-up calls.

Section 42. Risk-Based Capital Requirement for Securitization Exposures

(a) *Hierarchy of approaches.* Except as provided elsewhere in this section:

(1) A State savings association must deduct from tier 1 capital any after-tax gain-on-sale resulting from a securitization and must deduct from total capital in accordance with paragraph (c) of this section the portion of any CEIO that does not constitute gain-on-sale.

(2) If a securitization exposure does not require deduction under paragraph (a)(1) of this section and qualifies for the Ratings-Based Approach in section 43 of this appendix, a State savings association must apply the Ratings-Based Approach to the exposure.

(3) If a securitization exposure does not require deduction under paragraph (a)(1) of this section and does not qualify for the Ratings-Based Approach, the State savings association may either apply the Internal Assessment Approach in section 44 of this appendix to the exposure (if the State savings association, the exposure, and the relevant ABCP program qualify for the Internal Assessment

Federal Deposit Insurance Corporation

Approach) or the Supervisory Formula Approach in section 45 of this appendix to the exposure (if the State savings association and the exposure qualify for the Supervisory Formula Approach).

(4) If a securitization exposure does not require deduction under paragraph (a)(1) of this section and does not qualify for the Ratings-Based Approach, the Internal Assessment Approach, or the Supervisory Formula Approach, the State savings association must deduct the exposure from total capital in accordance with paragraph (c) of this section.

(5) If a securitization exposure is an OTC derivative contract (other than a credit derivative) that has a first priority claim on the cash flows from the underlying exposures (notwithstanding amounts due under interest rate or currency derivative contracts, fees due, or other similar payments), with approval of the FDIC, a State savings association may choose to set the risk-weighted asset amount of the exposure equal to the amount of the exposure as determined in paragraph (e) of this section rather than apply the hierarchy of approaches described in paragraphs (a)(1) through (4) of this section.

(b) *Total risk-weighted assets for securitization exposures.* A State savings association's total risk-weighted assets for securitization exposures is equal to the sum of its risk-weighted assets calculated using the Ratings-Based Approach in section 43 of this appendix, the Internal Assessment Approach in section 44 of this appendix, and the Supervisory Formula Approach in section 45 of this appendix, and its risk-weighted assets amount for early amortization provisions calculated in section 47 of this appendix.

(c) *Deductions.* (1) If a State savings association must deduct a securitization exposure from total capital, the State savings association must take the deduction 50 percent from tier 1 capital and 50 percent from tier 2 capital. If the amount deductible from tier 2 capital exceeds the State savings association's tier 2 capital, the State savings association must deduct the excess from tier 1 capital.

(2) A State savings association may calculate any deduction from tier 1 capital and tier 2 capital for a securitization exposure net of any deferred tax liabilities associated with the securitization exposure.

(d) *Maximum risk-based capital requirement.* Regardless of any other provisions of this subpart, unless one or more underlying exposures does not meet the definition of a wholesale, retail, securitization, or equity exposure, the total risk-based capital requirement for all securitization exposures held by a single State savings association associated with a single securitization (including any risk-based capital requirements that relate to an early amortization provision of

Pt. 390, Subpt. Z, App. A

the securitization but excluding any risk-based capital requirements that relate to the State savings association's gain-on-sale or CEIOs associated with the securitization) may not exceed the sum of:

(1) The State savings association's total risk-based capital requirement for the underlying exposures as if the State savings association directly held the underlying exposures; and

(2) The total ECL of the underlying exposures.

(e) *Amount of a securitization exposure.* (1) The amount of an on-balance sheet securitization exposure that is not a repo-style transaction, eligible margin loan, or OTC derivative contract (other than a credit derivative) is:

(i) The State savings association's carrying value minus any unrealized gains and plus any unrealized losses on the exposure, if the exposure is a security classified as available-for-sale; or

(ii) The State savings association's carrying value, if the exposure is not a security classified as available-for-sale.

(2) The amount of an off-balance sheet securitization exposure that is not an OTC derivative contract (other than a credit derivative) is the notional amount of the exposure. For an off-balance-sheet securitization exposure to an ABCP program, such as a liquidity facility, the notional amount may be reduced to the maximum potential amount that the State savings association could be required to fund given the ABCP program's current underlying assets (calculated without regard to the current credit quality of those assets).

(3) The amount of a securitization exposure that is a repo-style transaction, eligible margin loan, or OTC derivative contract (other than a credit derivative) is the EAD of the exposure as calculated in section 32 of this appendix.

(f) *Overlapping exposures.* If a State savings association has multiple securitization exposures that provide duplicative coverage of the underlying exposures of a securitization (such as when a State savings association provides a program-wide credit enhancement and multiple pool-specific liquidity facilities to an ABCP program), the State savings association is not required to hold duplicative risk-based capital against the overlapping position. Instead, the State savings association may apply to the overlapping position the applicable risk-based capital treatment that results in the highest risk-based capital requirement.

(g) *Securitizations of non-IRB exposures.* If a State savings association has a securitization exposure where any underlying exposure is not a wholesale exposure, retail exposure, securitization exposure, or equity exposure, the State savings association must:

961

(1) If the State savings association is an originating State savings association, deduct from tier 1 capital any after-tax gain-on-sale resulting from the securitization and deduct from total capital in accordance with paragraph (c) of this section the portion of any CEIO that does not constitute gain-on-sale;

(2) If the securitization exposure does not require deduction under paragraph (g)(1), apply the RBA in section 43 of this appendix to the securitization exposure if the exposure qualifies for the RBA;

(3) If the securitization exposure does not require deduction under paragraph (g)(1) and does not qualify for the RBA, apply the IAA in section 44 of this appendix to the exposure (if the State savings association, the exposure, and the relevant ABCP program qualify for the IAA); and

(4) If the securitization exposure does not require deduction under paragraph (g)(1) and does not qualify for the RBA or the IAA, deduct the exposure from total capital in accordance with paragraph (c) of this section.

(h) *Implicit support.* If a State savings association provides support to a securitization in excess of the State savings association's contractual obligation to provide credit support to the securitization (implicit support):

(1) The State savings association must hold regulatory capital against all of the underlying exposures associated with the securitization as if the exposures had not been securitized and must deduct from tier 1 capital any after-tax gain-on-sale resulting from the securitization; and

(2) The State savings association must disclose publicly:

(i) That it has provided implicit support to the securitization; and

(ii) The regulatory capital impact to the State savings association of providing such implicit support.

(i) *Eligible servicer cash advance facilities.* Regardless of any other provisions of this part, a State savings association is not required to hold risk-based capital against the undrawn portion of an eligible servicer cash advance facility.

(j) *Interest-only mortgage-backed securities.* Regardless of any other provisions of this part, the risk weight for a non-credit-enhancing interest-only mortgage-backed security may not be less than 100 percent.

(k) *Small-business loans and leases on personal property transferred with recourse.* (1) Regardless of any other provisions of this part, a State savings association that has transferred small-business loans and leases on personal property (small-business obligations) with recourse must include in risk-weighted assets only the contractual amount of retained recourse if all the following conditions are met:

(i) The transaction is a sale under GAAP.

(ii) The State savings association establishes and maintains, pursuant to GAAP, a non-capital reserve sufficient to meet the State savings association's reasonably estimated liability under the recourse arrangement.

(iii) The loans and leases are to businesses that meet the criteria for a small-business concern established by the Small Business Administration under section 3(a) of the Small Business Act (15 U.S.C. 632).

(iv) The State savings association is well capitalized, as defined in the FDIC's prompt corrective action regulation at Subpart Y of Part 390. For purposes of determining whether a State savings association is well capitalized for purposes of this paragraph, the State savings association's capital ratios must be calculated without regard to the capital treatment for transfers of small-business obligations with recourse specified in paragraph (k)(1) of this section.

(2) The total outstanding amount of recourse retained by a State savings association on transfers of small-business obligations receiving the capital treatment specified in paragraph (k)(1) of this section cannot exceed 15 percent of the State savings association's total qualifying capital.

(3) If a State savings association ceases to be well capitalized or exceeds the 15 percent capital limitation, the preferential capital treatment specified in paragraph (k)(1) of this section will continue to apply to any transfers of small-business obligations with recourse that occurred during the time that the State savings association was well capitalized and did not exceed the capital limit.

(4) The risk-based capital ratios of the State savings association must be calculated without regard to the capital treatment for transfers of small-business obligations with recourse specified in paragraph (k)(1) of this section as provided in 12 CFR 390.466(b)(5)(v).

(l) *Nth-to-default credit derivatives*—(1) *First-to-default credit derivatives*—(i) *Protection purchaser.* A State savings association that obtains credit protection on a group of underlying exposures through a first-to-default credit derivative must determine its risk-based capital requirement for the underlying exposures as if the State savings association synthetically securitized the underlying exposure with the lowest risk-based capital requirement and had obtained no credit risk mitigant on the other underlying exposures.

(ii) *Protection provider.* A State savings association that provides credit protection on a group of underlying exposures through a first-to-default credit derivative must determine its risk-weighted asset amount for the derivative by applying the RBA in section 43 of this appendix (if the derivative qualifies for the RBA) or, if the derivative does not qualify for the RBA, by setting its risk-weighted asset amount for the derivative equal to the product of:

(A) The protection amount of the derivative;

(B) 12.5; and
(C) The sum of the risk-based capital requirements of the individual underlying exposures, up to a maximum of 100 percent.

(2) *Second-or-subsequent-to-default credit derivatives*—(i) *Protection purchaser.* (A) A State savings association that obtains credit protection on a group of underlying exposures through a nth-to-default credit derivative (other than a first-to-default credit derivative) may recognize the credit risk mitigation benefits of the derivative only if:

(1) The State savings association also has obtained credit protection on the same underlying exposures in the form of first-through-(n-1)-to-default credit derivatives; or

(2) If n-1 of the underlying exposures have already defaulted.

(B) If a State savings association satisfies the requirements of paragraph (m)(2)(i)(A) of this section, the State savings association must determine its risk-based capital requirement for the underlying exposures as if the State savings association had only synthetically securitized the underlying exposure with the nth-lowest risk-based capital requirement and had obtained no credit risk mitigant on the other underlying exposures.

(ii) *Protection provider.* A State savings association that provides credit protection on a group of underlying exposures through a nth-to-default credit derivative (other than a first-to-default credit derivative) must determine its risk-weighted asset amount for the derivative by applying the RBA in section 43 of this appendix (if the derivative qualifies for the RBA) or, if the derivative does not qualify for the RBA, by setting its risk-weighted asset amount for the derivative equal to the product of:

(A) The protection amount of the derivative;
(B) 12.5; and
(C) The sum of the risk-based capital requirements of the individual underlying exposures (excluding the n-1 underlying exposures with the lowest risk-based capital requirements), up to a maximum of 100 percent.

Section 43. Ratings-Based Approach (RBA)

(a) *Eligibility requirements for use of the RBA*—(1) *Originating State savings association.* An originating State savings association must use the RBA to calculate its risk-based capital requirement for a securitization exposure if the exposure has two or more external ratings or inferred ratings (and may not use the RBA if the exposure has fewer than two external ratings or inferred ratings).

(2) *Investing State savings association.* An investing State savings association must use the RBA to calculate its risk-based capital requirement for a securitization exposure if the exposure has one or more external or inferred ratings (and may not use the RBA if the exposure has no external or inferred rating).

(b) *Ratings-based approach.* (1) A State savings association must determine the risk-weighted asset amount for a securitization exposure by multiplying the amount of the exposure (as defined in paragraph (e) of section 42 of this appendix) by the appropriate risk weight provided in Table 6 and Table 7.

(2) A State savings association must apply the risk weights in Table 6 when the securitization exposure's applicable external or applicable inferred rating represents a long-term credit rating, and must apply the risk weights in Table 7 when the securitization exposure's applicable external or applicable inferred rating represents a short-term credit rating.

(i) A State savings association must apply the risk weights in column 1 of Table 6 or Table 7 to the securitization exposure if:

(A) N (as calculated under paragraph (e)(6) of section 45 of this appendix) is six or more (for purposes of this section only, if the notional number of underlying exposures is 25 or more or if all of the underlying exposures are retail exposures, a State savings association may assume that N is six or more unless the State savings association knows or has reason to know that N is less than six); and

(B) The securitization exposure is a senior securitization exposure.

(ii) A State savings association must apply the risk weights in column 3 of Table 6 or Table 7 to the securitization exposure if N is less than six, regardless of the seniority of the securitization exposure.

(iii) Otherwise, a State savings association must apply the risk weights in column 2 of Table 6 or Table 7.

TABLE 6—LONG-TERM CREDIT RATING RISK WEIGHTS UNDER RBA AND IAA

Applicable external or inferred rating (Illustrative rating example)	Column 1 Risk weights for senior securitization exposures backed by granular pools (percent)	Column 2 Risk weights for non-senior securitization exposures backed by granular pools (percent)	Column 3 Risk weights for securitization exposures backed by non-granular pools (percent)
Highest investment grade (for example, AAA)	7	12	20
Second highest investment grade (for example, AA)	8	15	25

TABLE 6—LONG-TERM CREDIT RATING RISK WEIGHTS UNDER RBA AND IAA—Continued

Applicable external or inferred rating (Illustrative rating example)	Column 1 Risk weights for senior securitization exposures backed by granular pools (percent)	Column 2 Risk weights for non-senior securitization exposures backed by granular pools (percent)	Column 3 Risk weights for securitization exposures backed by non-granular pools (percent)
Third-highest investment grade—positive designation (for example, A+)	10	18	35
Third-highest investment grade (for example, A)	12	20	
Third-highest investment grade—negative designation (for example, A−)	20	35	
Lowest investment grade—positive designation (for example, BBB+)	35	50	50
Lowest investment grade (for example, BBB)	60	75	75
Lowest investment grade—negative designation (for example, BBB−)		100	
One category below investment grade—positive designation (for example, BB+)		250	
One category below investment grade (for example, BB)		425	
One category below investment grade—negative designation (for example, BB−)		650	
More than one category below investment grade	Deduction from tier 1 and tier 2 capital.		

TABLE 7—SHORT-TERM CREDIT RATING RISK WEIGHTS UNDER RBA AND IAA

Applicable external or inferred rating (Illustrative rating example)	Column 1 Risk weights for senior securitization exposures backed by granular pools (percent)	Column 2 Risk weights for non-senior securitization exposures backed by granular pools (percent)	Column 3 Risk weights for securitization exposures backed by non-granular pools (percent)
Highest investment grade (for example, A1)	7	12	20
Second highest investment grade (for example, A2)	12	20	35
Third highest investment grade (for example, A3)	60	75	75
All other ratings	Deduction from tier 1 and tier 2 capital.		

Section 44. Internal Assessment Approach (IAA)

(a) *Eligibility requirements.* A State savings association may apply the IAA to calculate the risk-weighted asset amount for a securitization exposure that the State savings association has to an ABCP program (such as a liquidity facility or credit enhancement) if the State savings association, the ABCP program, and the exposure qualify for use of the IAA.

(1) *State savings association qualification criteria.* A State savings association qualifies for use of the IAA if the State savings association has received the prior written approval of the FDIC. To receive such approval, the State savings association must demonstrate to the FDIC's satisfaction that the State savings association's internal assessment process meets the following criteria:

(i) The State savings association's internal credit assessments of securitization exposures must be based on publicly available rating criteria used by an NRSRO.

(ii) The State savings association's internal credit assessments of securitization exposures used for risk-based capital purposes must be consistent with those used in the State savings association's internal risk management process, management information reporting systems, and capital adequacy assessment process.

(iii) The State savings association's internal credit assessment process must have sufficient granularity to identify gradations of risk. Each of the State savings association's internal credit assessment categories must correspond to an external rating of an NRSRO.

(iv) The State savings association's internal credit assessment process, particularly the stress test factors for determining credit enhancement requirements, must be at least as conservative as the most conservative of the publicly available rating criteria of the NRSROs that have provided external ratings to the commercial paper issued by the ABCP program.

Federal Deposit Insurance Corporation

(A) Where the commercial paper issued by an ABCP program has an external rating from two or more NRSROs and the different NRSROs' benchmark stress factors require different levels of credit enhancement to achieve the same external rating equivalent, the State savings association must apply the NRSRO stress factor that requires the highest level of credit enhancement.

(B) If any NRSRO that provides an external rating to the ABCP program's commercial paper changes its methodology (including stress factors), the State savings association must evaluate whether to revise its internal assessment process.

(v) The State savings association must have an effective system of controls and oversight that ensures compliance with these operational requirements and maintains the integrity and accuracy of the internal credit assessments. The State savings association must have an internal audit function independent from the ABCP program business line and internal credit assessment process that assesses at least annually whether the controls over the internal credit assessment process function as intended.

(vi) The State savings association must review and update each internal credit assessment whenever new material information is available, but no less frequently than annually.

(vii) The State savings association must validate its internal credit assessment process on an ongoing basis and at least annually.

(2) *ABCP-program qualification criteria.* An ABCP program qualifies for use of the IAA if all commercial paper issued by the ABCP program has an external rating.

(3) *Exposure qualification criteria.* A securitization exposure qualifies for use of the IAA if the exposure meets the following criteria:

(i) The State savings association initially rated the exposure at least the equivalent of investment grade.

(ii) The ABCP program has robust credit and investment guidelines (that is, underwriting standards) for the exposures underlying the securitization exposure.

(iii) The ABCP program performs a detailed credit analysis of the sellers of the exposures underlying the securitization exposure.

(iv) The ABCP program's underwriting policy for the exposures underlying the securitization exposure establishes minimum asset eligibility criteria that include the prohibition of the purchase of assets that are significantly past due or of assets that are defaulted (that is, assets that have been charged off or written down by the seller prior to being placed into the ABCP program or assets that would be charged off or written down under the program's governing contracts), as well as limitations on concentration to individual obligors or geographic areas and the tenor of the assets to be purchased.

(v) The aggregate estimate of loss on the exposures underlying the securitization exposure considers all sources of potential risk, such as credit and dilution risk.

(vi) Where relevant, the ABCP program incorporates structural features into each purchase of exposures underlying the securitization exposure to mitigate potential credit deterioration of the underlying exposures. Such features may include wind-down triggers specific to a pool of underlying exposures.

(b) *Mechanics.* A State savings association that elects to use the IAA to calculate the risk-based capital requirement for any securitization exposure must use the IAA to calculate the risk-based capital requirements for all securitization exposures that qualify for the IAA approach. Under the IAA, a State savings association must map its internal assessment of such a securitization exposure to an equivalent external rating from an NRSRO. Under the IAA, a State savings association must determine the risk-weighted asset amount for such a securitization exposure by multiplying the amount of the exposure (as defined in paragraph (e) of section 42 of this appendix) by the appropriate risk weight in Table 6 and Table 7 in paragraph (b) of section 43 of this appendix.

Section 45. Supervisory Formula Approach (SFA)

(a) *Eligibility requirements.* A State savings association may use the SFA to determine its risk-based capital requirement for a securitization exposure only if the State savings association can calculate on an ongoing basis each of the SFA parameters in paragraph (e) of this section.

(b) *Mechanics.* Under the SFA, a securitization exposure incurs a deduction from total capital (as described in paragraph (c) of section 42 of this appendix) and/or an SFA risk-based capital requirement, as determined in paragraph (c) of this section. The risk-weighted asset amount for the securitization exposure equals the SFA risk-based capital requirement for the exposure multiplied by 12.5.

(c) *The SFA risk-based capital requirement.* (1) If K_{IRB} is greater than or equal to $L + T$, the entire exposure must be deducted from total capital.

(2) If K_{IRB} is less than or equal to L, the exposure's SFA risk-based capital requirement is UE multiplied by TP multiplied by the greater of:

(i) $0.0056 * T$; or

(ii) $S[L + T] - S[L]$.

(3) If K_{IRB} is greater than L and less than $L + T$, the State savings association must deduct from total capital an amount equal to

UE *TP * (K_{IRB} − L), and the exposure's SFA risk-based capital requirement is UE multiplied by TP multiplied by the greater of:

(i) 0.0056 * (T − (K_{IRB} − L)); or
(ii) S[L + T] − S[K_{IRB}].

(d) *The supervisory formula:*

(1) $$S[Y] = \begin{cases} Y & \text{when } Y \leq K_{IRB} \\ K_{IRB} + K[Y] - K[K_{IRB}] + \dfrac{d \cdot K_{IRB}}{20}(1 - e^{\frac{20(K_{IRB}-Y)}{K_{IRB}}}) & \text{when } Y > K_{IRB} \end{cases}$$

(2) $$K[Y] = (1-h) \cdot \left[(1 - \beta[Y; a, b]) \cdot Y + \beta[Y; a+1, b] \cdot c\right]$$

(3) $$h = \left(1 - \frac{K_{IRB}}{EWALGD}\right)^N$$

(4) $a = g \cdot c$

(5) $b = g \cdot (1 - c)$

(6) $$c = \frac{K_{IRB}}{1 - h}$$

(7) $$g = \frac{(1-c) \cdot c}{f} - 1$$

(8) $$f = \frac{v + K_{IRB}^2}{1 - h} - c^2 + \frac{(1 - K_{IRB}) \cdot K_{IRB} - v}{(1 - h) \cdot 1000}$$

(9) $$v = K_{IRB} \cdot \frac{(EWALGD - K_{IRB}) + .25 \cdot (1 - EWALGD)}{N}$$

(10) $d = 1 - (1 - h) \cdot (1 - \beta[K_{IRB}; a, b])$.

(11) In these expressions, β[Y; a, b] refers to the cumulative beta distribution with parameters a and b evaluated at Y. In the case where N = 1 and EWALGD = 100 percent, S[Y] in formula (1) must be calculated with K[Y] set equal to the product of K_{IRB} and Y, and d set equal to 1 − K_{IRB}.

(e) *SFA parameters*—(1) *Amount of the underlying exposures (UE).* UE is the EAD of any underlying exposures that are wholesale and retail exposures (including the amount of any funded spread accounts, cash collateral accounts, and other similar funded credit enhancements) plus the amount of any underlying exposures that are securitization exposures (as defined in paragraph (e) of section 42 of this appendix) plus the adjusted carrying value of any underlying exposures that are equity exposures (as defined in paragraph (b) of section 51 of this appendix).

(2) *Tranche percentage (TP).* TP is the ratio of the amount of the State savings association's securitization exposure to the amount of the tranche that contains the securitization exposure.

(3) *Capital requirement on underlying exposures (K_{IRB}).* (i) K_{IRB} is the ratio of:

(A) The sum of the risk-based capital requirements for the underlying exposures plus the expected credit losses of the underlying exposures (as determined under this appendix as if the underlying exposures were directly held by the State savings association); to

(B) UE.

(ii) The calculation of K_{IRB} must reflect the effects of any credit risk mitigant applied to the underlying exposures (either to an individual underlying exposure, to a group of underlying exposures, or to the entire pool of underlying exposures).

(iii) All assets related to the securitization are treated as underlying exposures, including assets in a reserve account (such as a cash collateral account).

(4) *Credit enhancement level (L).* (i) L is the ratio of:

(A) The amount of all securitization exposures subordinated to the tranche that contains the State savings association's securitization exposure; to

(B) UE.

(ii) A State savings association must determine L before considering the effects of any tranche-specific credit enhancements.

(iii) Any gain-on-sale or CEIO associated with the securitization may not be included in L.

(iv) Any reserve account funded by accumulated cash flows from the underlying exposures that is subordinated to the tranche that contains the State savings association's securitization exposure may be included in the numerator and denominator of L to the extent cash has accumulated in the account. Unfunded reserve accounts (that is, reserve accounts that are to be funded from future cash flows from the underlying exposures) may not be included in the calculation of L.

(v) In some cases, the purchase price of receivables will reflect a discount that provides credit enhancement (for example, first loss protection) for all or certain tranches of the securitization. When this arises, L should be calculated inclusive of this discount if the discount provides credit enhancement for the securitization exposure.

(5) *Thickness of tranche (T).* T is the ratio of:

(i) The amount of the tranche that contains the State savings association's securitization exposure; to

(ii) UE.

(6) *Effective number of exposures (N).* (i) Unless the State savings association elects to use the formula provided in paragraph (f) of this section,

$$N = \frac{(\sum_i EAD_i)^2}{\sum_i EAD_i^2}$$

where EAD_i represents the EAD associated with the ith instrument in the pool of underlying exposures.

(ii) Multiple exposures to one obligor must be treated as a single underlying exposure.

(iii) In the case of a re-securitization (that is, a securitization in which some or all of the underlying exposures are themselves securitization exposures), the State savings association must treat each underlying exposure as a single underlying exposure and must not look through to the originally securitized underlying exposures.

(7) *Exposure-weighted average loss given default (EWALGD).* EWALGD is calculated as:

$$EWALGD = \frac{\sum_i LGD_i \cdot EAD_i}{\sum_i EAD_i}$$

where LGD_i represents the average LGD associated with all exposures to the ith obligor. In the case of a re-securitization, an LGD of 100 percent must be assumed for the underlying exposures that are themselves securitization exposures.

(f) *Simplified method for computing N and EWALGD.* (1) If all underlying exposures of a securitization are retail exposures, a State savings association may apply the SFA using the following simplifications:

(i) h = 0; and

(ii) v = 0.

(2) Under the conditions in paragraphs (f)(3) and (f)(4) of this section, a State savings association may employ a simplified method for calculating N and EWALGD.

(3) If C_1 is no more than 0.03, a State savings association may set EWALGD = 0.50 if none of the underlying exposures is a securitization exposure or EWALGD = 1 if one or more of the underlying exposures is a securitization exposure, and may set N equal to the following amount:

$$N = \frac{1}{C_1 C_m + \left(\frac{C_m - C_1}{m-1}\right) \max(1 - mC_1, 0)}$$

Where:

(i) C_m is the ratio of the sum of the amounts of the 'm' largest underlying exposures to UE; and

(ii) The level of m is to be selected by the State savings association.

(4) Alternatively, if only C_1 is available and C_1 is no more than 0.03, the State savings association may set EWALGD = 0.50 if none of the underlying exposures is a securitization exposure or EWALGD = 1 if one or more of the underlying exposures is a securitization exposure and may set N = 1/C_1.

Section 46. Recognition of Credit Risk Mitigants for Securitization Exposures

(a) *General.* An originating State savings association that has obtained a credit risk mitigant to hedge its securitization exposure to a synthetic or traditional securitization that satisfies the operational criteria in section 41 of this appendix may recognize the credit risk mitigant, but only as provided in this section. An investing State savings association that has obtained a credit risk mitigant to hedge a securitization exposure may recognize the credit risk mitigant, but only as provided in this section. A State savings association that has used the RBA in section 43 of this appendix or the IAA in section 44 of this appendix to calculate its risk-based capital requirement for a securitization exposure whose external or inferred rating (or equivalent internal rating under the IAA) reflects the benefits of a credit risk mitigant provided to the associated securitization or that supports some or all of the underlying exposures may not use the credit risk mitigation rules in this section to further reduce its risk-based capital requirement for the exposure to reflect that credit risk mitigant.

(b) *Collateral*—(1) *Rules of recognition.* A State savings association may recognize financial collateral in determining the State savings association's risk-based capital requirement for a securitization exposure (other than a repo-style transaction, an eligible margin loan, or an OTC derivative contract for which the State savings association has reflected collateral in its determination of exposure amount under section 32 of this appendix) as follows. The State savings association's risk-based capital requirement for the collateralized securitization exposure is equal to the risk-based capital requirement for the securitization exposure as calculated under the RBA in section 43 of this appendix or under the SFA in section 45 of this appendix multiplied by the ratio of adjusted exposure amount (SE*) to original exposure amount (SE),

where:

(i) SE* = max {0, [SE—C x (1 − Hs − Hfx)]};
(ii) SE = the amount of the securitization exposure calculated under paragraph (e) of section 42 of this appendix;
(iii) C = the current market value of the collateral;
(iv) Hs = the haircut appropriate to the collateral type; and
(v) Hfx = the haircut appropriate for any currency mismatch between the collateral and the exposure.

(2) *Mixed collateral.* Where the collateral is a basket of different asset types or a basket of assets denominated in different currencies, the haircut on the basket will be

$$H = \sum_i a_i H_i,$$

where a_i is the current market value of the asset in the basket divided by the current market value of all assets in the basket and H_i is the haircut applicable to that asset.

(3) *Standard supervisory haircuts.* Unless a State savings association qualifies for use of and uses own-estimates haircuts in paragraph (b)(4) of this section:

(i) A State savings association must use the collateral type haircuts (Hs) in Table 3;
(ii) A State savings association must use a currency mismatch haircut (Hfx) of 8 percent if the exposure and the collateral are denominated in different currencies;
(iii) A State savings association must multiply the supervisory haircuts obtained in paragraphs (b)(3)(i) and (ii) by the square root of 6.5 (which equals 2.549510); and
(iv) A State savings association must adjust the supervisory haircuts upward on the basis of a holding period longer than 65 business days where and as appropriate to take into account the illiquidity of the collateral.

(4) *Own estimates for haircuts.* With the prior written approval of the FDIC, a State savings association may calculate haircuts using its own internal estimates of market price volatility and foreign exchange volatility, subject to paragraph (b)(2)(iii) of section 32 of this appendix. The minimum holding period (TM) for securitization exposures is 65 business days.

(c) *Guarantees and credit derivatives*—(1) *Limitations on recognition.* A State savings association may only recognize an eligible guarantee or eligible credit derivative provided by an eligible securitization guarantor in determining the State savings association's risk-based capital requirement for a securitization exposure.

(2) *ECL for securitization exposures.* When a State savings association recognizes an eligible guarantee or eligible credit derivative provided by an eligible securitization guarantor in determining the State savings association's risk-based capital requirement for a securitization exposure, the State savings association must also:

(i) Calculate ECL for the protected portion of the exposure using the same risk parameters that it uses for calculating the risk-weighted asset amount of the exposure as described in paragraph (c)(3) of this section; and
(ii) Add the exposure's ECL to the State savings association's total ECL.

(3) *Rules of recognition.* A State savings association may recognize an eligible guarantee or eligible credit derivative provided by an eligible securitization guarantor in determining the State savings association's risk-based capital requirement for the securitization exposure as follows:

(i) *Full coverage.* If the protection amount of the eligible guarantee or eligible credit derivative equals or exceeds the amount of the securitization exposure, the State savings association may set the risk-weighted asset amount for the securitization exposure equal to the risk-weighted asset amount for a direct exposure to the eligible securitization guarantor (as determined in the wholesale risk weight function described in section 31 of this appendix), using the

State savings association's PD for the guarantor, the State savings association's LGD for the guarantee or credit derivative, and an EAD equal to the amount of the securitization exposure (as determined in paragraph (e) of section 42 of this appendix).

(ii) *Partial coverage.* If the protection amount of the eligible guarantee or eligible credit derivative is less than the amount of the securitization exposure, the State savings association may set the risk-weighted asset amount for the securitization exposure equal to the sum of:

(A) *Covered portion.* The risk-weighted asset amount for a direct exposure to the eligible securitization guarantor (as determined in the wholesale risk weight function described in section 31 of this appendix), using the State savings association's PD for the guarantor, the State savings association's LGD for the guarantee or credit derivative, and an EAD equal to the protection amount of the credit risk mitigant; and

(B) *Uncovered portion.* (1) 1.0 minus the ratio of the protection amount of the eligible guarantee or eligible credit derivative to the amount of the securitization exposure); multiplied by

(2) The risk-weighted asset amount for the securitization exposure without the credit risk mitigant (as determined in sections 42 through 45 of this appendix).

(4) *Mismatches.* The State savings association must make applicable adjustments to the protection amount as required in paragraphs (d), (e), and (f) of section 33 of this appendix for any hedged securitization exposure and any more senior securitization exposure that benefits from the hedge. In the context of a synthetic securitization, when an eligible guarantee or eligible credit derivative covers multiple hedged exposures that have different residual maturities, the State savings association must use the longest residual maturity of any of the hedged exposures as the residual maturity of all the hedged exposures.

Section 47. Risk-Based Capital Requirement for Early Amortization Provisions

(a) *General.* (1) An originating State savings association must hold risk-based capital against the sum of the originating State savings association's interest and the investors' interest in a securitization that:

(i) Includes one or more underlying exposures in which the borrower is permitted to vary the drawn amount within an agreed limit under a line of credit; and

(ii) Contains an early amortization provision.

(2) For securitizations described in paragraph (a)(1) of this section, an originating State savings association must calculate the risk-based capital requirement for the originating State savings association's interest under sections 42 through 45 of this appendix, and the risk-based capital requirement for the investors' interest under paragraph (b) of this section.

(b) *Risk-weighted asset amount for investors' interest.* The originating State savings association's risk-weighted asset amount for the investors' interest in the securitization is equal to the product of the following 5 quantities:

(1) The investors' interest EAD;

(2) The appropriate conversion factor in paragraph (c) of this section;

(3) K_{IRB} (as defined in paragraph (e)(3) of section 45 of this appendix);

(4) 12.5; and

(5) The proportion of the underlying exposures in which the borrower is permitted to vary the drawn amount within an agreed limit under a line of credit.

(c) *Conversion factor.* (1)(i) Except as provided in paragraph (c)(2) of this section, to calculate the appropriate conversion factor, a State savings association must use Table 8 for a securitization that contains a controlled early amortization provision and must use Table 9 for a securitization that contains a non-controlled early amortization provision. In circumstances where a securitization contains a mix of retail and nonretail exposures or a mix of committed and uncommitted exposures, a State savings association may take a pro rata approach to determining the conversion factor for the securitization's early amortization provision. If a pro rata approach is not feasible, a State savings association must treat the mixed securitization as a securitization of nonretail exposures if a single underlying exposure is a nonretail exposure and must treat the mixed securitization as a securitization of committed exposures if a single underlying exposure is a committed exposure.

(ii) To find the appropriate conversion factor in the tables, a State savings association must divide the three-month average annualized excess spread of the securitization by the excess spread trapping point in the securitization structure. In securitizations that do not require excess spread to be trapped, or that specify trapping points based primarily on performance measures other than the three-month average annualized excess spread, the excess spread trapping point is 4.5 percent.

TABLE 8—CONTROLLED EARLY AMORTIZATION PROVISIONS

	Uncommitted	Committed
Retail Credit Lines	Three-month average annualized excess spread Conversion Factor (CF)	90% CF.

TABLE 8—CONTROLLED EARLY AMORTIZATION PROVISIONS—Continued

	Uncommitted	Committed
Non-retail Credit Lines	133.33% of trapping point or more, 0% CF. less than 133.33% to 100% of trapping point, 1% CF. less than 100% to 75% of trapping point, 2% CF. less than 75% to 50% of trapping point, 10% CF. less than 50% to 25% of trapping point, 20% CF. less than 25% of trapping point, 40% CF. 90% CF	90% CF.

TABLE 9—NON-CONTROLLED EARLY AMORTIZATION PROVISIONS

	Uncommitted	Committed
Retail Credit Lines	Three-month average annualized excess spread Conversion Factor (CF) .... 133.33% of trapping point or more, 0% CF. less than 133.33% to 100% of trapping point, 5% CF. less than 100% to 75% of trapping point, 15% CF. less than 75% to 50% of trapping point, 50% CF. less than 50% of trapping point, 100% CF.	100% CF.
Non-retail Credit Lines	100% CF	100% CF.

(2) For a securitization for which all or substantially all of the underlying exposures are residential mortgage exposures, a State savings association may calculate the appropriate conversion factor using paragraph (c)(1) of this section or may use a conversion factor of 10 percent. If the State savings association chooses to use a conversion factor of 10 percent, it must use that conversion factor for all securitizations for which all or substantially all of the underlying exposures are residential mortgage exposures.

PART VI. RISK-WEIGHTED ASSETS FOR EQUITY EXPOSURES

Section 51. Introduction and Exposure Measurement

(a) *General.* To calculate its risk-weighted asset amounts for equity exposures that are not equity exposures to investment funds, a State savings association may apply either the Simple Risk Weight Approach (SRWA) in section 52 of this appendix or, if it qualifies to do so, the Internal Models Approach (IMA) in section 53 of this appendix. A State savings association must use the look-through approaches in section 54 of this appendix to calculate its risk-weighted asset amounts for equity exposures to investment funds.

(b) *Adjusted carrying value.* For purposes of this part, the adjusted carrying value of an equity exposure is:

(1) For the on-balance sheet component of an equity exposure, the State savings association's carrying value of the exposure reduced by any unrealized gains on the exposure that are reflected in such carrying value but excluded from the State savings association's tier 1 and tier 2 capital; and

(2) For the off-balance sheet component of an equity exposure, the effective notional principal amount of the exposure, the size of which is equivalent to a hypothetical on-balance sheet position in the underlying equity instrument that would evidence the same change in fair value (measured in dollars) for a given small change in the price of the underlying equity instrument, minus the adjusted carrying value of the on-balance sheet component of the exposure as calculated in paragraph (b)(1) of this section. For unfunded equity commitments that are unconditional, the effective notional principal amount is the notional amount of the commitment. For unfunded equity commitments that are conditional, the effective notional principal amount is the State savings association's best estimate of the amount that would be funded under economic downturn conditions.

Section 52. Simple Risk Weight Approach (SRWA)

(a) *General.* Under the SRWA, a State savings association's aggregate risk-weighted asset amount for its equity exposures is equal to the sum of the risk-weighted asset amounts for each of the State savings association's individual equity exposures (other than equity exposures to an investment fund) as determined in this section and the risk-weighted asset amounts for each of the State savings association's individual equity exposures to an investment fund as determined in section 54 of this appendix.

(b) *SRWA computation for individual equity exposures.* A State savings association must determine the risk-weighted asset amount for an individual equity exposure (other than an equity exposure to an investment fund) by multiplying the adjusted carrying value of the equity exposure or the effective portion and ineffective portion of a hedge pair (as defined in paragraph (c) of this section)

Federal Deposit Insurance Corporation Pt. 390, Subpt. Z, App. A

by the lowest applicable risk weight in this paragraph (b).

(1) *0 percent risk weight equity exposures.* An equity exposure to an entity whose credit exposures are exempt from the 0.03 percent PD floor in paragraph (d)(2) of section 31 of this appendix is assigned a 0 percent risk weight.

(2) *20 percent risk weight equity exposures.* An equity exposure to a Federal Home Loan Bank or Farmer Mac is assigned a 20 percent risk weight.

(3) *100 percent risk weight equity exposures.* The following equity exposures are assigned a 100 percent risk weight:

(i) An equity exposure that is designed primarily to promote community welfare, including the welfare of low- and moderate-income communities or families, such as by providing services or jobs, excluding equity exposures to an unconsolidated small business investment company and equity exposures held through a consolidated small business investment company described in section 302 of the Small Business Investment Act of 1958 (15 U.S.C. 682).

(ii) *Effective portion of hedge pairs.* The effective portion of a hedge pair.

(iii) *Non-significant equity exposures.* Equity exposures, excluding exposures to an investment firm that would meet the definition of a traditional securitization were it not for the FDIC's application of paragraph (8) of that definition and has greater than immaterial leverage, to the extent that the aggregate adjusted carrying value of the exposures does not exceed 10 percent of the State savings association's tier 1 capital plus tier 2 capital.

(A) To compute the aggregate adjusted carrying value of a State savings association's equity exposures for purposes of this paragraph (b)(3)(iii), the State savings association may exclude equity exposures described in paragraphs (b)(1), (b)(2), (b)(3)(i), and (b)(3)(ii) of this section, the equity exposure in a hedge pair with the smaller adjusted carrying value, and a proportion of each equity exposure to an investment fund equal to the proportion of the assets of the investment fund that are not equity exposures or that meet the criterion of paragraph (b)(3)(i) of this section. If a State savings association does not know the actual holdings of the investment fund, the State savings association may calculate the proportion of the assets of the fund that are not equity exposures based on the terms of the prospectus, partnership agreement, or similar contract that defines the fund's permissible investments. If the sum of the investment limits for all exposure classes within the fund exceeds 100 percent, the State savings association must assume for purposes of this paragraph (b)(3)(iii) that the investment fund invests to the maximum extent possible in equity exposures.

(B) When determining which of a State savings association's equity exposures qualify for a 100 percent risk weight under this paragraph, a State savings association first must include equity exposures to unconsolidated small business investment companies or held through consolidated small business investment companies described in section 302 of the Small Business Investment Act of 1958 (15 U.S.C. 682), then must include publicly traded equity exposures (including those held indirectly through investment funds), and then must include non-publicly traded equity exposures (including those held indirectly through investment funds).

(4) *300 percent risk weight equity exposures.* A publicly traded equity exposure (other than an equity exposure described in paragraph (b)(6) of this section and including the ineffective portion of a hedge·pair) is assigned a 300 percent risk weight.

(5) *400 percent risk weight equity exposures.* An equity exposure (other than an equity exposure described in paragraph (b)(6) of this section) that is not publicly traded is assigned a 400 percent risk weight.

(6) *600 percent risk weight equity exposures.* An equity exposure to an investment firm that:

(i) Would meet the definition of a traditional securitization were it not for the FDIC's application of paragraph (8) of that definition; and

(ii) Has greater than immaterial leverage is assigned a 600 percent risk weight.

(c) *Hedge transactions* —(1) *Hedge pair.* A hedge pair is two equity exposures that form an effective hedge so long as each equity exposure is publicly traded or has a return that is primarily based on a publicly traded equity exposure.

(2) *Effective hedge.* Two equity exposures form an effective hedge if the exposures either have the same remaining maturity or each has a remaining maturity of at least three months; the hedge relationship is formally documented in a prospective manner (that is, before the State savings association acquires at least one of the equity exposures); the documentation specifies the measure of effectiveness (E) the State savings association will use for the hedge relationship throughout the life of the transaction; and the hedge relationship has an E greater than or equal to 0.8. A State savings association must measure E at least quarterly and must use one of three alternative measures of E:

(i) Under the dollar-offset method of measuring effectiveness, the State savings association must determine the ratio of value change (RVC). The RVC is the ratio of the cumulative sum of the periodic changes in value of one equity exposure to the cumulative sum of the periodic changes in the value of the other equity exposure. If RVC is positive, the hedge is not effective and E equals 0. If RVC is negative and greater than or equal to −1 (that is, between zero and

−1), then E equals the absolute value of RVC. If RVC is negative and less than −1, then E equals 2 plus RVC.

(ii) Under the variability-reduction method of measuring effectiveness:

$$E = 1 - \frac{\sum_{t=1}^{T}(X_t - X_{t-1})^2}{\sum_{t=1}^{T}(A_t - A_{t-1})^2}, \text{ where}$$

(A) $X_t = A_t - B_t$;
(B) A_t = the value at time t of one exposure in a hedge pair; and
(C) B_t = the value at time t of the other exposure in a hedge pair.

(iii) Under the regression method of measuring effectiveness, E equals the coefficient of determination of a regression in which the change in value of one exposure in a hedge pair is the dependent variable and the change in value of the other exposure in a hedge pair is the independent variable. However, if the estimated regression coefficient is positive, then the value of E is zero.

(3) The effective portion of a hedge pair is E multiplied by the greater of the adjusted carrying values of the equity exposures forming a hedge pair.

(4) The ineffective portion of a hedge pair is (1−E) multiplied by the greater of the adjusted carrying values of the equity exposures forming a hedge pair.

Section 53. Internal Models Approach (IMA)

(a) *General.* A State savings association may calculate its risk-weighted asset amount for equity exposures using the IMA by modeling publicly traded and non-publicly traded equity exposures (in accordance with paragraph (c) of this section) or by modeling only publicly traded equity exposures (in accordance with paragraph (d) of this section).

(b) *Qualifying criteria.* To qualify to use the IMA to calculate risk-based capital requirements for equity exposures, a State savings association must receive prior written approval from the FDIC. To receive such approval, the State savings association must demonstrate to the FDIC's satisfaction that the State savings association meets the following criteria:

(1) The State savings association must have one or more models that:

(i) Assess the potential decline in value of its modeled equity exposures;

(ii) Are commensurate with the size, complexity, and composition of the State savings association's modeled equity exposures; and

(iii) Adequately capture both general market risk and idiosyncratic risk.

(2) The State savings association's model must produce an estimate of potential losses for its modeled equity exposures that is no less than the estimate of potential losses produced by a VaR methodology employing a 99.0 percent, one-tailed confidence interval of the distribution of quarterly returns for a benchmark portfolio of equity exposures comparable to the State savings association's modeled equity exposures using a long-term sample period.

(3) The number of risk factors and exposures in the sample and the data period used for quantification in the State savings association's model and benchmarking exercise must be sufficient to provide confidence in the accuracy and robustness of the State savings association's estimates.

(4) The State savings association's model and benchmarking process must incorporate data that are relevant in representing the risk profile of the State savings association's modeled equity exposures, and must include data from at least one equity market cycle containing adverse market movements relevant to the risk profile of the State savings association's modeled equity exposures. In addition, the State savings association's benchmarking exercise must be based on daily market prices for the benchmark portfolio. If the State savings association's model uses a scenario methodology, the State savings association must demonstrate that the model produces a conservative estimate of potential losses on the State savings association's modeled equity exposures over a relevant long-term market cycle. If the State savings association employs risk factor models, the State savings association must demonstrate through empirical analysis the appropriateness of the risk factors used.

(5) The State savings association must be able to demonstrate, using theoretical arguments and empirical evidence, that any proxies used in the modeling process are comparable to the State savings association's modeled equity exposures and that the State savings association has made appropriate adjustments for differences. The State savings association must derive any proxies for its modeled equity exposures and benchmark portfolio using historical market data

Federal Deposit Insurance Corporation

that are relevant to the State savings association's modeled equity exposures and benchmark portfolio (or, where not, must use appropriately adjusted data), and such proxies must be robust estimates of the risk of the State savings association's modeled equity exposures.

(c) *Risk-weighted assets calculation for a State savings association modeling publicly traded and non-publicly traded equity exposures.* If a State savings association models publicly traded and non-publicly traded equity exposures, the State savings association's aggregate risk-weighted asset amount for its equity exposures is equal to the sum of:

(1) The risk-weighted asset amount of each equity exposure that qualifies for a 0 percent, 20 percent, or 100 percent risk weight under paragraphs (b)(1) through (b)(3)(i) of section 52 (as determined under section 52 of this appendix) and each equity exposure to an investment fund (as determined under section 54 of this appendix); and

(2) The greater of:

(i) The estimate of potential losses on the State savings association's equity exposures (other than equity exposures referenced in paragraph (c)(1) of this section) generated by the State savings association's internal equity exposure model multiplied by 12.5; or

(ii) The sum of:

(A) 200 percent multiplied by the aggregate adjusted carrying value of the State savings association's publicly traded equity exposures that do not belong to a hedge pair, do not qualify for a 0 percent, 20 percent, or 100 percent risk weight under paragraphs (b)(1) through (b)(3)(i) of section 52 of this appendix, and are not equity exposures to an investment fund;

(B) 200 percent multiplied by the aggregate ineffective portion of all hedge pairs; and

(C) 300 percent multiplied by the aggregate adjusted carrying value of the State savings association's equity exposures that are not publicly traded, do not qualify for a 0 percent, 20 percent, or 100 percent risk weight under paragraphs (b)(1) through (b)(3)(i) of section 52 of this appendix, and are not equity exposures to an investment fund.

(d) *Risk-weighted assets calculation for a State savings association using the IMA only for publicly traded equity exposures.* If a State savings association models only publicly traded equity exposures, the State savings association's aggregate risk-weighted asset amount for its equity exposures is equal to the sum of:

(1) The risk-weighted asset amount of each equity exposure that qualifies for a 0 percent, 20 percent, or 100 percent risk weight under paragraphs (b)(1) through (b)(3)(i) of section 52 (as determined under section 52 of this appendix), each equity exposure that qualifies for a 400 percent risk weight under paragraph (b)(5) of section 52 or a 600 percent

Pt. 390, Subpt. Z, App. A

risk weight under paragraph (b)(6) of section 52 (as determined under section 52 of this appendix), and each equity exposure to an investment fund (as determined under section 54 of this appendix); and

(2) The greater of:

(i) The estimate of potential losses on the State savings association's equity exposures (other than equity exposures referenced in paragraph (d)(1) of this section) generated by the State savings association's internal equity exposure model multiplied by 12.5; or

(ii) The sum of:

(A) 200 percent multiplied by the aggregate adjusted carrying value of the State savings association's publicly traded equity exposures that do not belong to a hedge pair, do not qualify for a 0 percent, 20 percent, or 100 percent risk weight under paragraphs (b)(1) through (b)(3)(i) of section 52 of this appendix, and are not equity exposures to an investment fund; and

(B) 200 percent multiplied by the aggregate ineffective portion of all hedge pairs.

Section 54. Equity Exposures to Investment Funds

(a) *Available approaches.* (1) Unless the exposure meets the requirements for a community development equity exposure in paragraph (b)(3)(i) of section 52 of this appendix, a State savings association must determine the risk-weighted asset amount of an equity exposure to an investment fund under the Full Look-Through Approach in paragraph (b) of this section, the Simple Modified Look-Through Approach in paragraph (c) of this section, the Alternative Modified Look-Through Approach in paragraph (d) of this section, or, if the investment fund qualifies for the Money Market Fund Approach, the Money Market Fund Approach in paragraph (e) of this section.

(2) The risk-weighted asset amount of an equity exposure to an investment fund that meets the requirements for a community development equity exposure in paragraph (b)(3)(i) of section 52 of this appendix is its adjusted carrying value.

(3) If an equity exposure to an investment fund is part of a hedge pair and the State savings association does not use the Full Look-Through Approach, the State savings association may use the ineffective portion of the hedge pair as determined under paragraph (c) of section 52 of this appendix as the adjusted carrying value for the equity exposure to the investment fund. The risk-weighted asset amount of the effective portion of the hedge pair is equal to its adjusted carrying value.

(b) *Full Look-Through Approach.* A State savings association that is able to calculate a risk-weighted asset amount for its proportional ownership share of each exposure held by the investment fund (as calculated under this appendix as if the proportional ownership share of each exposure were held directly by the State savings association) may either:

(1) Set the risk-weighted asset amount of the State savings association's exposure to the fund equal to the product of:

(i) The aggregate risk-weighted asset amounts of the exposures held by the fund as if they were held directly by the State savings association; and

(ii) The State savings association's proportional ownership share of the fund; or

(2) Include the State savings association's proportional ownership share of each exposure held by the fund in the State savings association's IMA.

(c) *Simple Modified Look-Through Approach.* Under this approach, the risk-weighted asset amount for a State savings association's equity exposure to an investment fund equals the adjusted carrying value of the equity exposure multiplied by the highest risk weight in Table 10 that applies to any exposure the fund is permitted to hold under its prospectus, partnership agreement, or similar contract that defines the fund's permissible investments (excluding derivative contracts that are used for hedging rather than speculative purposes and that do not constitute a material portion of the fund's exposures).

TABLE 10—MODIFIED LOOK-THROUGH APPROACHES FOR EQUITY EXPOSURES TO INVESTMENT FUNDS

Risk weight	Exposure class
0 percent	Sovereign exposures with a long-term applicable external rating in the highest investment-grade rating category and sovereign exposures of the United States.
20 percent	Non-sovereign exposures with a long-term applicable external rating in the highest or second-highest investment-grade rating category; exposures with a short-term applicable external rating in the highest investment-grade rating category; and exposures to, or guaranteed by, depository institutions, foreign banks (as defined in 12 CFR 211.2), or securities firms subject to consolidated supervision and regulation comparable to that imposed on U.S. securities broker-dealers that are repo-style transactions or bankers' acceptances.
50 percent	Exposures with a long-term applicable external rating in the third-highest investment-grade rating category or a short-term applicable external rating in the second-highest investment-grade rating category.
100 percent	Exposures with a long-term or short-term applicable external rating in the lowest investment-grade rating category.
200 percent	Exposures with a long-term applicable external rating one rating category below investment grade.
300 percent	Publicly traded equity exposures.
400 percent	Non-publicly traded equity exposures; exposures with a long-term applicable external rating two rating categories or more below investment grade; and exposures without an external rating (excluding publicly traded equity exposures).
1,250 percent	OTC derivative contracts and exposures that must be deducted from regulatory capital or receive a risk weight greater than 400 percent under this appendix.

(d) *Alternative Modified Look-Through Approach.* Under this approach, a State savings association may assign the adjusted carrying value of an equity exposure to an investment fund on a pro rata basis to different risk weight categories in Table 10 based on the investment limits in the fund's prospectus, partnership agreement, or similar contract that defines the fund's permissible investments. The risk-weighted asset amount for the State savings association's equity exposure to the investment fund equals the sum of each portion of the adjusted carrying value assigned to an exposure class multiplied by the applicable risk weight. If the sum of the investment limits for exposure classes within the fund exceeds 100 percent, the State savings association must assume that the fund invests to the maximum extent permitted under its investment limits in the exposure class with the highest risk weight under Table 10, and continues to make investments in order of the exposure class with the next highest risk weight under Table 10 until the maximum total investment level is reached. If more than one exposure class applies to an exposure, the State savings association must use the highest applicable risk weight. A State savings association may exclude derivative contracts held by the fund that are used for hedging rather than for speculative purposes and do not constitute a material portion of the fund's exposures.

(e) *Money Market Fund Approach.* The risk-weighted asset amount for a State savings association's equity exposure to an investment fund that is a money market fund subject to 17 CFR 270.2a–7 and that has an applicable external rating in the highest investment-grade rating category equals the adjusted carrying value of the equity exposure multiplied by 7 percent.

Section 55. Equity Derivative Contracts

Under the IMA, in addition to holding risk-based capital against an equity derivative contract under this part, a State savings association must hold risk-based capital against the counterparty credit risk in the equity derivative contract by also treating the equity derivative contract as a wholesale

Federal Deposit Insurance Corporation

exposure and computing a supplemental risk-weighted asset amount for the contract under part IV. Under the SRWA, a State savings association may choose not to hold risk-based capital against the counterparty credit risk of equity derivative contracts, as long as it does so for all such contracts. Where the equity derivative contracts are subject to a qualified master netting agreement, a State savings association using the SRWA must either include all or exclude all of the contracts from any measure used to determine counterparty credit risk exposure.

PART VII. RISK-WEIGHTED ASSETS FOR OPERATIONAL RISK

Section 61. Qualification Requirements for Incorporation of Operational Risk Mitigants

(a) *Qualification to use operational risk mitigants.* A State savings association may adjust its estimate of operational risk exposure to reflect qualifying operational risk mitigants if:

(1) The State savings association's operational risk quantification system is able to generate an estimate of the State savings association's operational risk exposure (which does not incorporate qualifying operational risk mitigants) and an estimate of the State savings association's operational risk exposure adjusted to incorporate qualifying operational risk mitigants; and

(2) The State savings association's methodology for incorporating the effects of insurance, if the State savings association uses insurance as an operational risk mitigant, captures through appropriate discounts to the amount of risk mitigation:

(i) The residual term of the policy, where less than one year;

(ii) The cancellation terms of the policy, where less than one year;

(iii) The policy's timeliness of payment;

(iv) The uncertainty of payment by the provider of the policy; and

(v) Mismatches in coverage between the policy and the hedged operational loss event.

(b) *Qualifying operational risk mitigants.* Qualifying operational risk mitigants are:

(1) Insurance that:

(i) Is provided by an unaffiliated company that has a claims payment ability that is rated in one of the three highest rating categories by a NRSRO;

(ii) Has an initial term of at least one year and a residual term of more than 90 days;

(iii) Has a minimum notice period for cancellation by the provider of 90 days;

(iv) Has no exclusions or limitations based upon regulatory action or for the receiver or liquidator of a failed depository institution; and

(v) Is explicitly mapped to a potential operational loss event; and

(2) Operational risk mitigants other than insurance for which the FDIC has given prior written approval. In evaluating an operational risk mitigant other than insurance, the FDIC will consider whether the operational risk mitigant covers potential operational losses in a manner equivalent to holding regulatory capital.

Section 62. Mechanics of Risk-Weighted Asset Calculation

(a) If a State savings association does not qualify to use or does not have qualifying operational risk mitigants, the State savings association's dollar risk-based capital requirement for operational risk is its operational risk exposure minus eligible operational risk offsets (if any).

(b) If a State savings association qualifies to use operational risk mitigants and has qualifying operational risk mitigants, the State savings association's dollar risk-based capital requirement for operational risk is the greater of:

(1) The State savings association's operational risk exposure adjusted for qualifying operational risk mitigants minus eligible operational risk offsets (if any); or

(2) 0.8 multiplied by the difference between:

(i) The State savings association's operational risk exposure; and

(ii) Eligible operational risk offsets (if any).

(c) The State savings association's risk-weighted asset amount for operational risk equals the State savings association's dollar risk-based capital requirement for operational risk determined under paragraph (a) or (b) of this section multiplied by 12.5.

PART VIII. DISCLOSURE

Section 71. Disclosure Requirements

(a) Each State savings association must publicly disclose each quarter its total and tier 1 risk-based capital ratios and their components (that is, tier 1 capital, tier 2 capital, total qualifying capital, and total risk-weighted assets).[8]

(b) A State savings association must comply with paragraph (c) of section 71 of this appendix unless it is a consolidated subsidiary of a depository institution or bank holding company that is subject to these requirements.

(c)(1) Each consolidated State savings association described in paragraph (b) of this section that is not a subsidiary of a non-U.S. banking organization that is subject to comparable public disclosure requirements in its home jurisdiction and has successfully completed its parallel run must provide timely

---

[8] Other public disclosure requirements continue to apply—for example, Federal securities law and regulatory reporting requirements.

public disclosures each calendar quarter of the information in tables 11.1 through 11.11 of this appendix. If a significant change occurs, such that the most recent reported amounts are no longer reflective of the State savings association's capital adequacy and risk profile, then a brief discussion of this change and its likely impact must be provided as soon as practicable thereafter. Qualitative disclosures that typically do not change each quarter (for example, a general summary of the State savings association's risk management objectives and policies, reporting system, and definitions) may be disclosed annually, provided any significant changes to these are disclosed in the interim. Management is encouraged to provide all of the disclosures required by this appendix in one place on the State savings association's public Web site.[9] The State savings association must make these disclosures publicly available for each of the last three years (twelve quarters) or such shorter period since it began its first floor period.

(2) Each State savings association is required to have a formal disclosure policy approved by the board of directors that addresses its approach for determining the disclosures it makes. The policy must address the associated internal controls and disclosure controls and procedures. The board of directors and senior management are responsible for establishing and maintaining an effective internal control structure over financial reporting, including the disclosures required by this appendix, and must ensure that appropriate review of the disclosures takes place. One or more senior officers of the State savings association must attest that the disclosures required by this appendix meet the requirements of this appendix.

(3) If a State savings association believes that disclosure of specific commercial or financial information would prejudice seriously its position by making public information that is either proprietary or confidential in nature, the State savings association need not disclose those specific items, but must disclose more general information about the subject matter of the requirement, together with the fact that, and the reason why, the specific items of information have not been disclosed.

---

[9] Alternatively, a State savings association may provide the disclosures in more than one place, as some of them may be included in public financial reports (for example, in Management's Discussion and Analysis included in SEC filings) or other regulatory reports. The State savings association must provide a summary table on its public Web site that specifically indicates where all the disclosures may be found (for example, regulatory report schedules, page numbers in annual reports).

Federal Deposit Insurance Corporation Pt. 390, Subpt. Z, App. A

TABLE 11.1—SCOPE OF APPLICATION

Qualitative Disclosures	(a) The name of the top corporate entity in the group to which the appendix applies.
	(b) An outline of differences in the basis of consolidation for accounting and regulatory purposes, with a brief description of the entities [10] within the group that are fully consolidated; that are deconsolidated and deducted; for which the regulatory capital requirement is deducted; and that are neither consolidated nor deducted (for example, where the investment is risk-weighted).
	(c) Any restrictions, or other major impediments, on transfer of funds or regulatory capital within the group.
Quantitative Disclosures	(d) The aggregate amount of surplus capital of insurance subsidiaries (whether deducted or subjected to an alternative method) included in the regulatory capital of the consolidated group.
	(e) The aggregate amount by which actual regulatory capital is less than the minimum regulatory capital requirement in all subsidiaries with regulatory capital requirements and the name(s) of the subsidiaries with such deficiencies.

---

[10] Entities include securities, insurance and other financial subsidiaries, commercial subsidiaries (where permitted), and significant minority equity investments in insurance, financial and commercial entities.

Pt. 390, Subpt. Z, App. A 12 CFR Ch. III (1-1-12 Edition)

TABLE 11.2—CAPITAL STRUCTURE

Qualitative Disclosures	(a) Summary information on the terms and conditions of the main features of all capital instruments, especially in the case of innovative, complex or hybrid capital instruments.
Quantitative Disclosures	(b) The amount of tier 1 capital, with separate disclosure of: • Common stock/surplus; • Retained earnings; • Minority interests in the equity of subsidiaries; • Regulatory calculation differences deducted from tier 1 capital;[11] and • Other amounts deducted from tier 1 capital, including goodwill and certain intangibles. (c) The total amount of tier 2 capital. (d) Other deductions from capital.[12] (e) Total eligible capital.

TABLE 11.3—CAPITAL ADEQUACY

Qualitative Disclosures	(a) A summary discussion of the State savings association's approach to assessing the adequacy of its capital to support current and future activities.
Quantitative Disclosures	(b) Risk-weighted assets for credit risk from: • Wholesale exposures; • Residential mortgage exposures; • Qualifying revolving exposures; • Other retail exposures; • Securitization exposures; • Equity exposures; • Equity exposures subject to the simple risk weight approach; and • Equity exposures subject to the internal models approach. (c) Risk-weighted assets for market risk as calculated under any applicable market risk rule:[13] • Standardized approach for specific risk; and • Internal models approach for specific risk. (d) Risk-weighted assets for operational risk. (e) Total and tier 1 risk-based capital ratios:[14] • For the top consolidated group; and • For each DI subsidiary.

General Qualitative Disclosure Requirement

For each separate risk area described in tables 11.4 through 11.11, the State savings association must describe its risk management objectives and policies, including:

• Strategies and processes;
• The structure and organization of the relevant risk management function;
• The scope and nature of risk reporting and/or measurement systems;

---

[11] Representing 50 percent of the amount, if any, by which total expected credit losses as calculated within the IRB approach exceed eligible credit reserves, which must be deducted from tier 1 capital.

[12] Including 50 percent of the amount, if any, by which total expected credit losses as calculated within the IRB approach exceed eligible credit reserves, which must be deducted from tier 2 capital.

[13] Risk-weighted assets determined under any applicable market risk rule are to be disclosed only for the approaches used.

[14] Total risk-weighted assets should also be disclosed.

978

Federal Deposit Insurance Corporation

Pt. 390, Subpt. Z, App. A

- Policies for hedging and/or mitigating risk and strategies and processes for monitoring the continuing effectiveness of hedges/mitigants.

TABLE 11.4 [15]—CREDIT RISK: GENERAL DISCLOSURES

Qualitative Disclosures	(a) The general qualitative disclosure requirement with respect to credit risk (excluding counterparty credit risk disclosed in accordance with Table 11.6), including: • Definitions of past due and impaired (for accounting purposes); • Description of approaches followed for allowances, including statistical methods used where applicable; and • Discussion of the State savings association's credit risk management policy.
Quantitative Disclosures	(b) Total credit risk exposures and average credit risk exposures, after accounting offsets in accordance with GAAP,[16] and without taking into account the effects of credit risk mitigation techniques (for example, collateral and netting), over the period broken down by major types of credit exposure.[17] (c) Geographic [18] distribution of exposures, broken down in significant areas by major types of credit exposure. (d) Industry or counterparty type distribution of exposures, broken down by major types of credit exposure. (e) Remaining contractual maturity breakdown (for example, one year or less) of the whole portfolio, broken down by major types of credit exposure. (f) By major industry or counterparty type: • Amount of impaired loans; • Amount of past due loans; [19] • Allowances; and • Charge-offs during the period. (g) Amount of impaired loans and, if available, the amount of past due loans broken down by significant geographic areas including, if practical, the amounts of allowances related to each geographical area.[20] (h) Reconciliation of changes in the allowance for loan and lease losses.[21]

Such a breakdown might, for instance, be (a) loans, off-balance sheet commitments, and other non-derivative off-balance sheet exposures, (b) debt securities, and (c) OTC derivatives.

---

[15] Table 4 does not include equity exposures.

[16] For example, FASB Interpretations 39 and 41.

[17] For example, State savings associations could apply a breakdown similar to that used for accounting purposes.

[18] Geographical areas may comprise individual countries, groups of countries, or regions within countries.

[19] A State savings association is encouraged also to provide an analysis of the aging of past-due loans.

[20] The portion of general allowance that is not allocated to a geographical area should be disclosed separately.

A State savings association might choose to define the geographical areas based on the way the company's portfolio is geographically managed. The criteria used to allocate the loans to geographical areas must be specified.

---

[21] The reconciliation should include the following: a description of the allowance; the opening balance of the allowance; charge-offs taken against the allowance during the period; amounts provided (or reversed) for estimated probable loan losses during the period; any other adjustments (for example, exchange rate differences, business combinations, acquisitions and disposals of subsidiaries), including transfers between allowances; and the closing balance of the allowance. Charge-offs and recoveries that have been recorded directly to the income statement should be disclosed separately.

TABLE 11.5—CREDIT RISK: DISCLOSURES FOR PORTFOLIOS SUBJECT TO IRB RISK-BASED CAPITAL FORMULAS

Qualitative Disclosures	(a) Explanation and review of the: • Structure of internal rating systems and relation between internal and external ratings; • Use of risk parameter estimates other than for regulatory capital purposes; • Process for managing and recognizing credit risk mitigation (see table 11.7); and • Control mechanisms for the rating system, including discussion of independence, accountability, and rating systems review. (b) Description of the internal ratings process, provided separately for the following: • Wholesale category; • Retail subcategories; • Residential mortgage exposures; • Qualifying revolving exposures; and • Other retail exposures. For each category and subcategory the description should include: • The types of exposure included in the category/subcategories; and • The definitions, methods and data for estimation and validation of PD, LGD, and EAD, including assumptions employed in the derivation of these variables.[22]
Quantitative Disclosures: Risk assessment.	(c) For wholesale exposures, present the following information across a sufficient number of PD grades (including default) to allow for a meaningful differentiation of credit risk:[23] • Total EAD;[24] • Exposure-weighted average LGD (percentage); • Exposure-weighted average risk weight; and • Amount of undrawn commitments and exposure-weighted average EAD for wholesale exposures. For each retail subcategory, present the disclosures outlined above across a sufficient number of segments to allow for a meaningful differentiation of credit risk.
Quantitative Disclosures: Historical results.	(d) Actual losses in the preceding period for each category and subcategory and how this differs from past experience. A discussion of the factors that impacted the loss experience in the preceding period—for example, has the State savings association experienced higher than average default rates, loss rates or EADs.

---

[22] This disclosure does not require a detailed description of the model in full—it should provide the reader with a broad overview of the model approach, describing definitions of the variables and methods for estimating and validating those variables set out in the quantitative risk disclosures below. This should be done for each of the four category/subcategories. The State savings association should disclose any significant differences in approach to estimating these variables within each category/subcategories.

[23] The PD, LGD and EAD disclosures in Table 11.5(c) should reflect the effects of collateral, qualifying master netting agreements, eligible guarantees and eligible credit derivatives as defined in part I. Disclosure of each PD grade should include the exposure-weighted average PD for each grade. Where a State savings association aggregates PD grades for the purposes of disclosure, this should be a representative breakdown of the distribution of PD grades used for regulatory capital purposes.

[24] Outstanding loans and EAD on undrawn commitments can be presented on a combined basis for these disclosures.

Federal Deposit Insurance Corporation Pt. 390, Subpt. Z, App. A

TABLE 11.5—CREDIT RISK: DISCLOSURES FOR PORTFOLIOS SUBJECT TO IRB RISK-BASED CAPITAL FORMULAS—Continued

	(e) State savings association's estimates compared against actual outcomes over a longer period.[25] At a minimum, this should include information on estimates of losses against actual losses in the wholesale category and each retail subcategory over a period sufficient to allow for a meaningful assessment of the performance of the internal rating processes for each category/subcategory.[26] Where appropriate, the State savings association should further decompose this to provide analysis of PD, LGD, and EAD outcomes against estimates provided in the quantitative risk assessment disclosures above.[27]

TABLE 11.6—GENERAL DISCLOSURE FOR COUNTERPARTY CREDIT RISK OF OTC DERIVATIVE CONTRACTS, REPO-STYLE TRANSACTIONS, AND ELIGIBLE MARGIN LOANS

Qualitative Disclosures	(a) The general qualitative disclosure requirement with respect to OTC derivatives, eligible margin loans, and repo-style transactions, including: • Discussion of methodology used to assign economic capital and credit limits for counterparty credit exposures; • Discussion of policies for securing collateral, valuing and managing collateral, and establishing credit reserves; • Discussion of the primary types of collateral taken; • Discussion of policies with respect to wrong-way risk exposures; and • Discussion of the impact of the amount of collateral the State savings association would have to provide if the State savings association were to receive a credit rating downgrade.
Quantitative Disclosures	(b) Gross positive fair value of contracts, netting benefits, netted current credit exposure, collateral held (including type, for example, cash, government securities), and net unsecured credit exposure.[28] Also report measures for EAD used for regulatory capital for these transactions, the notional value of credit derivative hedges purchased for counterparty credit risk protection, and, for State savings associations not using the internal models methodology in section 32(d) of this appendix, the distribution of current credit exposure by types of credit exposure.[29]

---

[25] These disclosures are a way of further informing the reader about the reliability of the information provided in the "quantitative disclosures: risk assessment" over the long run. The disclosures are requirements from year-end 2010; in the meantime, early adoption is encouraged. The phased implementation is to allow a State savings association sufficient time to build up a longer run of data that will make these disclosures meaningful.

[26] This regulation is not prescriptive about the period used for this assessment. Upon implementation, it might be expected that a State savings association would provide these disclosures for as long a run of data as possible—for example, if a State savings association has 10 years of data, it might choose to disclose the average default rates for each PD grade over that 10-year period. Annual amounts need not be disclosed.

[27] A State savings association should provide this further decomposition where it will allow users greater insight into the reliability of the estimates provided in the "quantitative disclosures: risk assessment." In particular, it should provide this information where there are material differences between its estimates of PD, LGD or EAD compared to actual outcomes over the long run. The State savings association should also provide explanations for such differences.

[28] Net unsecured credit exposure is the credit exposure after considering the benefits from legally enforceable netting agreements and collateral arrangements, without taking into account haircuts for price volatility, liquidity, etc.

[29] This may include interest rate derivative contracts, foreign exchange derivative contracts, equity derivative contracts, credit derivatives, commodity or other derivative contracts, repo-style transactions, and eligible margin loans.

Pt. 390, Subpt. Z, App. A 12 CFR Ch. III (1-1-12 Edition)

TABLE 11.6—GENERAL DISCLOSURE FOR COUNTERPARTY CREDIT RISK OF OTC DERIVATIVE CONTRACTS, REPO-STYLE TRANSACTIONS, AND ELIGIBLE MARGIN LOANS—Continued

	(c) Notional amount of purchased and sold credit derivatives, segregated between use for the State savings association's own credit portfolio and for its intermediation activities, including the distribution of the credit derivative products used, broken down further by protection bought and sold within each product group.
	(d) The estimate of alpha if the State savings association has received supervisory approval to estimate alpha.

TABLE 11.7—CREDIT RISK MITIGATION [30] [31] [32]

Qualitative Disclosures	(a) The general qualitative disclosure requirement with respect to credit risk mitigation including: • Policies and processes for, and an indication of the extent to which the State savings association uses, on- and off-balance sheet netting; • Policies and processes for collateral valuation and management; • A description of the main types of collateral taken by the State savings association; • The main types of guarantors/credit derivative counterparties and their creditworthiness; and • Information about (market or credit) risk concentrations within the mitigation taken.
Quantitative Disclosures	(b) For each separately disclosed portfolio, the total exposure (after, where applicable, on-or off-balance sheet netting) that is covered by guarantees/credit derivatives.

TABLE 11.8—SECURITIZATION

Qualitative Disclosures	(a) The general qualitative disclosure requirement with respect to securitization (including synthetics), including a discussion of: • The State savings association's objectives relating to securitization activity, including the extent to which these activities transfer credit risk of the underlying exposures away from the State savings association to other entities; • The roles played by the State savings association in the securitization process [33] and an indication of the extent of the State savings association's involvement in each of them; and • The regulatory capital approaches (for example, RBA, IAA and SFA) that the State savings association follows for its securitization activities.

---

[30] At a minimum, a State savings association must provide the disclosures in Table 11.7 in relation to credit risk mitigation that has been recognized for the purposes of reducing capital requirements under this appendix. Where relevant, State savings associations are encouraged to give further information about mitigants that have not been recognized for that purpose.

[31] Credit derivatives that are treated, for the purposes of this appendix, as synthetic securitization exposures should be excluded from the credit risk mitigation disclosures and included within those relating to securitization.

[32] Counterparty credit risk-related exposures disclosed pursuant to Table 11.6 should be excluded from the credit risk mitigation disclosures in Table 11.7.

[33] For example: originator, investor, servicer, provider of credit enhancement, sponsor of asset backed commercial paper facility, liquidity provider, or swap provider.

Federal Deposit Insurance Corporation
Pt. 390, Subpt. Z, App. A

TABLE 11.8—SECURITIZATION—Continued

Quantitative Disclosures	(b) Summary of the State savings association's accounting policies for securitization activities, including: • Whether the transactions are treated as sales or financings; • Recognition of gain-on-sale; • Key assumptions for valuing retained interests, including any significant changes since the last reporting period and the impact of such changes; and • Treatment of synthetic securitizations. (c) Names of NRSROs used for securitizations and the types of securitization exposure for which each agency is used. (d) The total outstanding exposures securitized by the State savings association in securitizations that meet the operational criteria in section 41 of this appendix (broken down into traditional/synthetic), by underlying exposure type.[34][35][36] (e) For exposures securitized by the State savings association in securitizations that meet the operational criteria in Section 41 of this appendix: • Amount of securitized assets that are impaired/past due; and • Losses recognized by the State savings association during the current period[37] broken down by exposure type. (f) Aggregate amount of securitization exposures broken down by underlying exposure type. (g) Aggregate amount of securitization exposures and the associated IRB capital requirements for these exposures broken down into a meaningful number of risk weight bands. Exposures that have been deducted from capital should be disclosed separately by type of underlying asset. (h) For securitizations subject to the early amortization treatment, the following items by underlying asset type for securitized facilities: • The aggregate drawn exposures attributed to the seller's and investors' interests; and • The aggregate IRB capital charges incurred by the State savings association against the investors' shares of drawn balances and undrawn lines. (i) Summary of current year's securitization activity, including the amount of exposures securitized (by exposure type), and recognized gain or loss on sale by asset type.

TABLE 11.9—OPERATIONAL RISK

Qualitative Disclosures	(a) The general qualitative disclosure requirement for operational risk. (b) Description of the AMA, including a discussion of relevant internal and external factors considered in the State savings association's measurement approach.

---

[34] Underlying exposure types may include, for example, one- to four-family residential loans, home equity lines, credit card receivables, and auto loans.

[35] Securitization transactions in which the originating State savings association does not retain any securitization exposure should be shown separately but need only be reported for the year of inception.

[36] Where relevant, a State savings association is encouraged to differentiate between exposures resulting from activities in which they act only as sponsors, and exposures that result from all other State savings association securitization activities.

[37] For example, charge-offs/allowances (if the assets remain on the State savings association's balance sheet) or write-downs of I/O strips and other residual interests.

TABLE 11.9—OPERATIONAL RISK—Continued

	(c) A description of the use of insurance for the purpose of mitigating operational risk.

TABLE 11.10—EQUITIES NOT SUBJECT TO MARKET RISK RULE

Qualitative Disclosures	(a) The general qualitative disclosure requirement with respect to equity risk, including: • Differentiation between holdings on which capital gains are expected and those held for other objectives, including for relationship and strategic reasons; and • Discussion of important policies covering the valuation of and accounting for equity holdings in the banking book. This includes the accounting techniques and valuation methodologies used, including key assumptions and practices affecting valuation as well as significant changes in these practices.
Quantitative Disclosures	(b) Value disclosed in the balance sheet of investments, as well as the fair value of those investments; for quoted securities, a comparison to publicly-quoted share values where the share price is materially different from fair value. (c) The types and nature of investments, including the amount that is: • Publicly traded; and • Non-publicly traded. (d) The cumulative realized gains (losses) arising from sales and liquidations in the reporting period. (e) • Total unrealized gains (losses) [38] • Total latent revaluation gains (losses) [39] • Any amounts of the above included in tier 1 and/or tier 2 capital. (f) Capital requirements broken down by appropriate equity groupings, consistent with the State savings association's methodology, as well as the aggregate amounts and the type of equity investments subject to any supervisory transition regarding regulatory capital requirements.[40]

TABLE 11.11—INTEREST RATE RISK FOR NON-TRADING ACTIVITIES

Qualitative Disclosures	(a) The general qualitative disclosure requirement, including the nature of interest rate risk for non-trading activities and key assumptions, including assumptions regarding loan prepayments and behavior of non-maturity deposits, and frequency of measurement of interest rate risk for non-trading activities.
Quantitative Disclosures	(b) The increase (decline) in earnings or economic value (or relevant measure used by management) for upward and downward rate shocks according to management's method for measuring interest rate risk for non-trading activities, broken down by currency (as appropriate).

---

[38] Unrealized gains (losses) recognized in the balance sheet but not through earnings.

[39] Unrealized gains (losses) not recognized either in the balance sheet or through earnings.

[40] This disclosure should include a breakdown of equities that are subject to the 0 percent, 20 percent, 100 percent, 300 percent, 400 percent, and 600 percent risk weights, as applicable.

PART IX—TRANSITION PROVISIONS

Section 81. Optional Transition Provisions Related to the Implementation of Consolidation Requirements Under FAS 167

(a) *Scope, applicability, and purpose.* This section 81 provides optional transition provisions for a State savings association that is required for financial and regulatory reporting purposes, as a result of its implementation of Statement of Financial Accounting Standards No. 167, *Amendments to FASB Interpretation No. 46(R)* (FAS 167), to consolidate certain variable interest entities (VIEs) as defined under GAAP. These transition provisions apply through the end of the fourth quarter following the date of a State savings association's implementation of FAS 167 (implementation date).

(b) *Exclusion period.*

(1) *Exclusion of risk-weighted assets for the first and second quarters.* For the first two quarters after the implementation date (exclusion period), including for the two calendar quarter-end regulatory report dates within those quarters, a State savings association may exclude from risk-weighted assets:

(i) Subject to the limitations in paragraph (d) of section 81, assets held by a VIE, provided that the following conditions are met:

(A) The VIE existed prior to the implementation date,

(B) The State savings association did not consolidate the VIE on its balance sheet for calendar quarter-end regulatory report dates prior to the implementation date,

(C) The State savings association must consolidate the VIE on its balance sheet beginning as of the implementation date as a result of its implementation of FAS 167, and

(D) The State savings association excludes all assets held by VIEs described in paragraphs (b)(1)(i)(A) through (C) of this section 81; and

(ii) Subject to the limitations in paragraph (d) of this section 81, assets held by a VIE that is a consolidated ABCP program, provided that the following conditions are met:

(A) The State savings association is the sponsor of the ABCP program,

(B) Prior to the implementation date, the State savings association consolidated the VIE onto its balance sheet under GAAP and excluded the VIE's assets from the State savings association's risk-weighted assets, and

(C) The State savings association chooses to exclude all assets held by ABCP program VIEs described in paragraphs (b)(1)(ii)(A) and (B) of this section 81.

(2) *Risk-weighted assets during exclusion period.* During the exclusion period, including for the two calendar quarter-end regulatory report dates within the exclusion period, a State savings association adopting the optional provisions in paragraph (b) of this section must calculate risk-weighted assets for its contractual exposures to the VIEs referenced in paragraph (b)(1) of this section 81 on the implementation date and include this calculated amount in risk-weighted assets. Such contractual exposures may include direct-credit substitutes, recourse obligations, residual interests, liquidity facilities, and loans.

(3) *Inclusion of ALLL in tier 2 capital for the first and second quarters.* During the exclusion period, including for the two calendar quarter-end regulatory report dates within the exclusion period, a State savings association that excludes VIE assets from risk-weighted assets pursuant to paragraph (b)(1) of this section 81 may include in tier 2 capital the full amount of the ALLL calculated as of the implementation date that is attributable to the assets it excludes pursuant to paragraph (b)(1) of this section 81 (inclusion amount). The amount of ALLL includable in tier 2 capital in accordance with this paragraph shall not be subject to the limitations set forth in section 13(A)(2) and 13(b) of this Appendix.

(c) *Phase-in period.*

(1) *Exclusion amount.* For purposes of this paragraph (c), exclusion amount is defined as the amount of risk-weighted assets excluded in paragraph (b)(1) of this section as of the implementation date.

(2) *Risk-weighted assets for the third and fourth quarters.* A State savings association that excludes assets of consolidated VIEs from risk-weighted assets pursuant to paragraph (b)(1) of this section may, for the third and fourth quarters after the implementation date (phase-in period), including for the two calendar quarter-end regulatory report dates within those quarters, exclude from risk-weighted assets 50 percent of the exclusion amount, provided that the State savings association may not include in risk-weighted assets pursuant to this paragraph an amount less than the aggregate risk-weighted assets calculated pursuant to paragraph (b)(2) of this section 81.

(3) *Inclusion of ALLL in tier 2 capital for the third and fourth quarters.* A State savings association that excludes assets of consolidated VIEs from risk-weighted assets pursuant to paragraph (c)(2) of this section may, for the phase-in period, include in tier 2 capital 50 percent of the inclusion amount it included in tier 2 capital, during the exclusion period, notwithstanding the limit on including ALLL in tier 2 capital in section 13(a)(2) and 13(b) of this Appendix.

(d) *Implicit recourse limitation.* Notwithstanding any other provision in this section 81, assets held by a VIE to which the State savings association has provided recourse through credit enhancement beyond any contractual obligation to support assets it has sold may not be excluded from risk-weighted assets.

PART 391—FORMER OFFICE OF THRIFT SUPERVISION REGULATIONS

Subpart A—Security Procedures

Sec.
391.1　Authority, purpose, and scope.
391.2　Designation of security officer.
391.3　Security program.
391.4　Report.
391.5　Protection of customer information.

Subpart B—Safety and Soundness Guidelines and Compliance Procedures

391.10　Authority, purpose, scope, and preservation of existing authority.
391.11　Determination and notification of failure to meet safety and soundness standards and request for compliance plan.
391.12　Filing of safety and soundness compliance plan.
391.13　Issuance of orders to correct deficiencies and to take or refrain from taking other actions.
391.14　Enforcement of orders.
APPENDIX A TO SUBPART B OF PART 391—INTERAGENCY GUIDELINES ESTABLISHING STANDARDS FOR SAFETY AND SOUNDNESS
APPENDIX B TO SUBPART B OF PART 391—INTERAGENCY GUIDELINES ESTABLISHING INFORMATION SECURITY STANDARDS

Subpart C—Fair Credit Reporting

391.20　Examples.
391.21　Disposal of consumer information.
391.22　Duties regarding the detection, prevention, and mitigation of identity theft.
391.23　Duties of card issuers regarding changes of address.
APPENDIX TO SUBPART C OF PART 391—INTERAGENCY GUIDELINES ON IDENTITY THEFT DETECTION, PREVENTION, AND MITIGATION

Subpart D—Loans in Areas Having Special Flood Hazards

391.30　Authority, purpose, and scope.
391.31　Definitions.
391.32　Requirement to purchase flood insurance where available.
391.33　Exemptions.
391.34　Escrow requirement.
391.35　Required use of standard flood hazard determination form.
391.36　Forced placement of flood insurance.
391.37　Determination fees.
391.38　Notice of special flood hazards and availability of Federal disaster relief assistance.
391.39　Notice of servicer's identity.
APPENDIX TO SUBPART D OF PART 391—SAMPLE FORM OF NOTICE OF SPECIAL FLOOD HAZARDS AND AVAILABILITY OF FEDERAL DISASTER RELIEF ASSISTANCE

Subpart E—Acquisition of Control of State Savings Associations

391.40　Scope of subpart.
391.41　Definitions.
391.42　Acquisition of control of State savings associations.
391.43　Control.
391.44　Certifications of ownership.
391.45　Procedural requirements.
391.46　Determination by the FDIC.
391.47　[Reserved]
391.48　Rebuttal of control agreement.

AUTHORITY: 12 U.S.C. 1819 (Tenth).

Subpart A also issued under 12 U.S.C. 1462a; 1463; 1464; 1828; 1831p–1; 1881–1884; 15 U.S.C. 1681w; 15 U.S.C. 6801; 6805.

Subpart B also issued under 12 U.S.C. 1462a; 1463; 1464; 1828; 1831p–1; 1881–1884; 15 U.S.C.1681w; 15 U.S.C. 6801; 6805.

Subpart C also issued under 12 U.S.C. 1462a; 1463; 1464; 1828; 1831p–1; and 1881–1884; 15 U.S.C. 1681m; 1681w.

Subpart D also issued under 12 U.S.C. 1462; 1462a; 1463; 1464; 42 U.S.C. 4012a; 4104a; 4104b; 4106; 4128.

Subpart E also issued under 12 U.S.C. 1467a; 1468; 1817; 1831i.

SOURCE: 76 FR 47811, Aug. 5, 2011, unless otherwise noted.

Subpart A—Security Procedures

§ 391.1 Authority, purpose, and scope.

(a) This subpart is issued by the Federal Deposit Insurance Corporation (FDIC) under section 3 of the Bank Protection Act of 1968 (12 U.S.C 1828), and sections 501 and 505(b)(1) of the Gramm-Leach-Bliley Act (15 U.S.C. 6801 and 6805(b)(1)), and section 628 of the Fair Credit Reporting Act (15 U.S.C. 1681w). This subpart is applicable to State savings associations. It requires each State savings association to adopt appropriate security procedures to discourage robberies, burglaries, and larcenies and to assist in the identification and prosecution of persons who commit such acts. Section 391.5 is applicable to State savings associations and their subsidiaries (except brokers, dealers, persons providing insurance, investment companies, and investment advisers). Section 391.5 requires covered institutions to establish and implement appropriate administrative, technical, and physical safeguards to protect the security, confidentiality, and integrity of customer information.

(b) It is the responsibility of a State savings association's board of directors to comply with this regulation and ensure that a written security program for the State savings association's main office and branches is developed and implemented.

§ 391.2 Designation of security officer.

Within 30 days after the effective date of insurance of accounts, the board of directors of each State savings association shall designate a security officer who shall have the authority, subject to the approval of the board of directors, to develop, within a reasonable time but no later than 180 days, and to administer a written security program for each of the State savings association's offices.

§ 391.3 Security program.

(a) *Contents of security program.* The security program shall:

(1) Establish procedures for opening and closing for business and for the safekeeping of all currency, negotiable securities, and similar valuables at all times;

(2) Establish procedures that will assist in identifying persons committing crimes against the State savings association and that will preserve evidence that may aid in their identification and prosecution. Such procedures may include, but are not limited to:

(i) Maintaining a camera that records activity in the office;

(ii) Using identification devices, such as prerecorded serial-numbered bills, or chemical and electronic devices; and

(iii) Retaining a record of any robbery, burglary, or larceny committed against the State savings association;

(3) Provide for initial and periodic training of officers and employees in their responsibilities under the security program and in proper employee conduct during and after a burglary, robbery, or larceny; and

(4) Provide for selecting, testing, operating and maintaining appropriate security devices, as specified in paragraph (b) of this section.

(b) *Security devices.* Each State savings association shall have, at a minimum, the following security devices:

(1) A means of protecting cash and other liquid assets, such as a vault, safe, or other secure space;

(2) A lighting system for illuminating, during the hours of darkness, the area around the vault, if the vault is visible from outside the office;

(3) Tamper-resistant locks on exterior doors and exterior windows that may be opened;

(4) An alarm system or other appropriate device for promptly notifying the nearest responsible law enforcement officers of an attempted or perpetrated robbery or burglary; and

(5) Such other devices as the security officer determines to be appropriate, taking into consideration:

(i) The incidence of crimes against financial institutions in the area;

(ii) The amount of currency and other valuables exposed to robbery, burglary, or larceny;

(iii) The distance of the office from the nearest responsible law enforcement officers;

(iv) The cost of the security devices;

(v) Other security measures in effect at the office; and

(vi) The physical characteristics of the structure of the office and its surroundings.

§ 391.4 Report.

The security officer for each State savings association shall report at least annually to the State savings association's board of directors on the implementation, administration, and effectiveness of the security program.

§ 391.5 Protection of customer information.

State savings associations and their subsidiaries (except brokers, dealers, persons providing insurance, investment companies, and investment advisers) must comply with the Interagency Guidelines Establishing Information Security Standards set forth in appendix B to subpart B. Supplement A to appendix B to subpart B provides interpretive guidance.

Subpart B—Safety and Soundness Guidelines and Compliance Procedures

§ 391.10 Authority, purpose, scope, and preservation of existing authority.

(a) *Authority.* This subpart and the Guidelines in appendices A and B to this subpart are issued by the FDIC under section 39 (section 39) of the Federal Deposit Insurance Act (FDI Act) (12 U.S.C. 1831p–1) as added by section 132 of the Federal Deposit Insurance Corporation Improvement Act of 1991 (FDICIA) (Pub. L. 102–242, 105 Stat. 2236 (1991)), and as amended by section 956 of the Housing and Community Development Act of 1992 (Pub. L. 102–550, 106 Stat. 3895 (1992)), and as amended by section 318 of the Community Development Banking Act of 1994 (Pub. L. 103–325, 108 Stat. 2160 (1994)). Appendix B to this subpart is further issued under sections 501(b) and 505 of the Gramm-Leach-Bliley Act (Pub. L. 106–102, 113 Stat. 1338 (1999)).

(b) *Purpose.* Section 39 of the FDI Act requires the FDIC to establish safety and soundness standards. Pursuant to section 39, a State savings association may be required to submit a compliance plan if it is not in compliance with a safety and soundness standard established by guideline under section 39(a) or (b). An enforceable order under section 8 of the FDI Act may be issued if, after being notified that it is in violation of a safety and soundness standard prescribed under section 39, the State savings association fails to submit an acceptable compliance plan or fails in any material respect to implement an accepted plan. This subpart establishes procedures for submission and review of safety and soundness compliance plans and for issuance and review of orders pursuant to section 39. Interagency Guidelines Establishing Standards for Safety and Soundness pursuant to section 39 of the FDI Act are set forth in appendix A to this subpart. Interagency Guidelines Establishing Information Security Standards are set forth in appendix B to this subpart.

(c) *Scope.* This subpart and the Interagency Guidelines Establishing Standards for Safety and Soundness as set forth at appendix A to this subpart and the Interagency Guidelines Establishing Information Security Standards at appendix B to this subpart implement the provisions of section 39 of the FDI Act as they apply to State savings associations.

(d) *Preservation of existing authority.* Neither section 39 of the FDI Act nor this subpart in any way limits the authority of the FDIC under any other provision of law to take supervisory actions to address unsafe or unsound practices, violations of law, unsafe or unsound conditions, or other practices. Action under section 39 and this subpart may be taken independently of, in conjunction with, or in addition to any other enforcement action available to the FDIC.

§ 391.11 Determination and notification of failure to meet safety and soundness standards and request for compliance plan.

(a) *Determination.* The FDIC may, based upon an examination, inspection, or any other information that becomes available to the FDIC, determine that a State savings association has failed to satisfy the safety and soundness standards contained in the Interagency Guidelines Establishing Standards for Safety and Soundness as set forth in appendix A to this subpart or the Interagency Guidelines Establishing Information Security Standards as set forth in appendix B to this subpart.

(b) *Request for compliance plan.* If the FDIC determines that a State savings association has failed to meet a safety and soundness standard pursuant to paragraph (a) of this section, the FDIC may request by letter or through a report of examination, the submission of a compliance plan. The State savings association shall be deemed to have notice of the request three days after mailing or delivery of the letter or report of examination by the FDIC.

§ 391.12 Filing of safety and soundness compliance plan.

(a) *Schedule for filing compliance plan*—(1) *In general.* A State savings association shall file a written safety and soundness compliance plan with the FDIC within 30 days of receiving a request for a compliance plan pursuant to § 391.11(b), unless the FDIC notifies

Federal Deposit Insurance Corporation

§ 391.13

the State savings association in writing that the plan is to be filed within a different period.

(2) *Other plans.* If a State savings association is obligated to file, or is currently operating under, a capital restoration plan submitted pursuant to section 38 of the FDI Act (12 U.S.C. 1831o), a cease-and-desist order entered into pursuant to section 8 of the FDI Act, a formal or informal agreement, or a response to a report of examination, it may, with the permission of the FDIC, submit a compliance plan under this section as part of that plan, order, agreement, or response, subject to the deadline provided in paragraph (a)(1) of this section.

(b) *Contents of plan.* The compliance plan shall include a description of the steps the State savings association will take to correct the deficiency and the time within which those steps will be taken.

(c) *Review of safety and soundness compliance plans.* Within 30 days after receiving a safety and soundness compliance plan under this subpart, the FDIC shall provide written notice to the State savings association of whether the plan has been approved or seek additional information from the State savings association regarding the plan. The FDIC may extend the time within which notice regarding approval of a plan will be provided.

(d) *Failure to submit or implement a compliance plan.* If a State savings association fails to submit an acceptable plan within the time specified by the FDIC or fails in any material respect to implement a compliance plan, then the FDIC shall, by order, require the State savings association to correct the deficiency and may take further actions provided in section 39(e)(2)(B) of the FDI Act. Pursuant to section 39(e)(3), the FDIC may be required to take certain actions if the State savings association commenced operations or experienced a change in control within the previous 24-month period, or the State savings association experienced extraordinary growth during the previous 18-month period.

(e) *Amendment of compliance plan.* A State savings association that has filed an approved compliance plan may, after prior written notice to and approval by the FDIC, amend the plan to reflect a change in circumstance. Until such time as a proposed amendment has been approved, the State savings association shall implement the compliance plan as previously approved.

§ 391.13 Issuance of orders to correct deficiencies and to take or refrain from taking other actions.

(a) *Notice of intent to issue order*—(1) *In general.* The FDIC shall provide a State savings association prior written notice of the FDIC's intention to issue an order requiring the State savings association to correct a safety and soundness deficiency or to take or refrain from taking other actions pursuant to section 39 of the FDI Act. The State savings association shall have such time to respond to a proposed order as provided by the FDIC under paragraph (c) of this section.

(2) *Immediate issuance of final order.* If the FDIC finds it necessary in order to carry out the purposes of section 39 of the FDI Act, the FDIC may, without providing the notice prescribed in paragraph (a)(1) of this section, issue an order requiring a State savings association immediately to take actions to correct a safety and soundness deficiency or to take or refrain from taking other actions pursuant to section 39. A State savings association that is subject to such an immediately effective order may submit a written appeal of the order to the FDIC. Such an appeal must be received by the FDIC within 14 calendar days of the issuance of the order, unless the FDIC permits a longer period. The FDIC shall consider any such appeal, if filed in a timely manner, within 60 days of receiving the appeal. During such period of review, the order shall remain in effect unless the FDIC, in its sole discretion, stays the effectiveness of the order.

(b) *Contents of notice.* A notice of intent to issue an order shall include:

(1) A statement of the safety and soundness deficiency or deficiencies that have been identified at the State savings association;

(2) A description of any restrictions, prohibitions, or affirmative actions that the FDIC proposes to impose or require;

§ 391.14

(3) The proposed date when such restrictions or prohibitions would be effective or the proposed date for completion of any required action; and

(4) The date by which the State savings association subject to the order may file with the FDIC a written response to the notice.

(c) *Response to notice*—(1) *Time for response.* A State savings association may file a written response to a notice of intent to issue an order within the time period set by the FDIC. Such a response must be received by the FDIC within 14 calendar days from the date of the notice unless the FDIC determines that a different period is appropriate in light of the safety and soundness of the State savings association or other relevant circumstances.

(2) *Contents of response.* The response should include:

(i) An explanation why the action proposed by the FDIC is not an appropriate exercise of discretion under section 39 of the FDI Act;

(ii) Any recommended modification of the proposed order; and

(iii) Any other relevant information, mitigating circumstances, documentation, or other evidence in support of the position of the State savings association regarding the proposed order.

(d) *The FDIC's consideration of response.* After considering the response, the FDIC may:

(1) Issue the order as proposed or in modified form;

(2) Determine not to issue the order and so notify the State savings association; or

(3) Seek additional information or clarification of the response from the State savings association, or any other relevant source.

(e) *Failure to file response.* Failure by a State savings association to file with the FDIC, within the specified time period, a written response to a proposed order shall constitute a waiver of the opportunity to respond and shall constitute consent to the issuance of the order.

(f) *Request for modification or rescission of order.* Any State savings association that is subject to an order under this subpart may, upon a change in circumstances, request in writing that the FDIC reconsider the terms of the order, and may propose that the order be rescinded or modified. Unless otherwise ordered by the FDIC, the order shall continue in place while such request is pending before the FDIC.

§ 391.14 Enforcement of orders.

(a) *Judicial remedies.* Whenever a State savings association fails to comply with an order issued under section 39 of the FDI Act, the FDIC may seek enforcement of the order in the appropriate United States district court pursuant to section 8(i)(1) of the FDI Act.

(b) *Administrative remedies.* Pursuant to section 8(i)(2)(A) of the FDI Act, the FDIC may assess a civil money penalty against any State savings association that violates or otherwise fails to comply with any final order issued under section 39 and against any State savings association-affiliated party who participates in such violation or noncompliance.

(c) *Other enforcement action.* In addition to the actions described in paragraphs (a) and (b) of this section, the FDIC may seek enforcement of the provisions of section 39 of the FDI Act or this part through any other judicial or administrative proceeding authorized by law.

APPENDIX A TO SUBPART B OF PART 391—INTERAGENCY GUIDELINES ESTABLISHING STANDARDS FOR SAFETY AND SOUNDNESS

I. Introduction
  A. Preservation of existing authority.
  B. Definitions.
II. Operational and Managerial Standards
  A. Internal controls and information systems.
  B. Internal audit system.
  C. Loan documentation.
  D. Credit underwriting.
  E. Interest rate exposure.
  F. Asset growth.
  G. Asset quality.
  H. Earnings.
  I. Compensation, fees and benefits.
III. Prohibition on Compensation That Constitutes an Unsafe and Unsound Practice
  A. Excessive compensation.
  B. Compensation leading to material financial loss.

I. INTRODUCTION

i. Section 39 of the Federal Deposit Insurance Act[1] (FDI Act) requires each Federal banking agency (collectively, the agencies) to establish certain safety and soundness standards by regulation or by guideline for all insured depository institutions. Under section 39, the agencies must establish three types of standards: (1) Operational and managerial standards; (2) compensation standards; and (3) such standards relating to asset quality, earnings, and stock valuation as they determine to be appropriate.

ii. Section 39(a) requires the agencies to establish operational and managerial standards relating to: (1) Internal controls, information systems and internal audit systems, in accordance with section 36 of the FDI Act (12 U.S.C. 1831m); (2) loan documentation; (3) credit underwriting; (4) interest rate exposure; (5) asset growth; and (6) compensation, fees, and benefits, in accordance with subsection (c) of section 39. Section 39(b) requires the agencies to establish standards relating to asset quality, earnings, and stock valuation that the agencies determine to be appropriate.

iii. Section 39(c) requires the agencies to establish standards prohibiting as an unsafe and unsound practice any compensatory arrangement that would provide any executive officer, employee, director, or principal shareholder of the institution with excessive compensation, fees or benefits and any compensatory arrangement that could lead to material financial loss to an institution. Section 39(c) also requires that the agencies establish standards that specify when compensation is excessive.

iv. If an agency determines that an institution fails to meet any standard established by guideline under subsection (a) or (b) of section 39, the agency may require the institution to submit to the agency an acceptable plan to achieve compliance with the standard. In the event that an institution fails to submit an acceptable plan within the time allowed by the agency or fails in any material respect to implement an accepted plan, the agency must, by order, require the institution to correct the deficiency. The agency may, and in some cases must, take other supervisory actions until the deficiency has been corrected.

v. The agencies have adopted amendments to their rules and regulations to establish deadlines for submission and review of compliance plans.[2]

vi. The following Guidelines set out the safety and soundness standards that the agencies use to identify and address problems at insured depository institutions before capital becomes impaired. The agencies believe that the standards adopted in these Guidelines serve this end without dictating how institutions must be managed and operated. These standards are designed to identify potential safety and soundness concerns and ensure that action is taken to address those concerns before they pose a risk to the Deposit Insurance Fund.

A. Preservation of Existing Authority

Neither section 39 nor these Guidelines in any way limits the authority of the agencies to address unsafe or unsound practices, violations of law, unsafe or unsound conditions, or other practices. Action under section 39 and these Guidelines may be taken independently of, in conjunction with, or in addition to any other enforcement action available to the agencies. Nothing in these Guidelines limits the authority of the FDIC pursuant to section 38(i)(2)(F) of the FDI Act (12 U.S.C. 1831(o)) and Part 325 of Title 12 of the Code of Federal Regulations.

B. Definitions

1. *In general.* For purposes of these Guidelines, except as modified in the Guidelines or unless the context otherwise requires, the terms used have the same meanings as set forth in sections 3 and 39 of the FDI Act (12 U.S.C. 1813 and 1831p–1).

2. *Board of directors,* in the case of a state-licensed insured branch of a foreign bank and in the case of a federal branch of a foreign bank, means the managing official in charge of the insured foreign branch.

3. *Compensation* means all direct and indirect payments or benefits, both cash and non-cash, granted to or for the benefit of any executive officer, employee, director, or principal shareholder, including but not limited to payments or benefits derived from an employment contract, compensation or benefit agreement, fee arrangement, perquisite, stock option plan, postemployment benefit, or other compensatory arrangement.

---

[1] Section 39 of the Federal Deposit Insurance Act (12 U.S.C. 1831p–1) was added by section 132 of the Federal Deposit Insurance Corporation Improvement Act of 1991 (FDICIA), Public Law 102–242, 105 Stat. 2236 (1991), and amended by section 956 of the Housing and Community Development Act of 1992, Public Law 102–550, 106 Stat. 3895 (1992) and section 318 of the Riegle Community Development and Regulatory Improvement Act of 1994, Public Law 103–325, 108 Stat. 2160 (1994).

[2] For the Office of the Comptroller of the Currency, these regulations appear at 12 CFR part 30; for the Board of Governors of the Federal Reserve System, these regulations appear at 12 CFR part 263; for the Federal Deposit Insurance Corporation, these regulations appear at 12 CFR part 308, subpart R, and subpart B of part 391.

4. *Director* shall have the meaning described in 12 CFR 215.2(d).[3]
5. *Executive officer* shall have the meaning described in 12 CFR 215.2(e).[4]
6. *Principal shareholder* shall have the meaning described in 12 CFR 215.2(m).[5]

II. OPERATIONAL AND MANAGERIAL STANDARDS

A. *Internal controls and information systems.* An institution should have internal controls and information systems that are appropriate to the size of the institution and the nature, scope and risk of its activities and that provide for:
1. An organizational structure that establishes clear lines of authority and responsibility for monitoring adherence to established policies;
2. Effective risk assessment;
3. Timely and accurate financial, operational and regulatory reports;
4. Adequate procedures to safeguard and manage assets; and
5. Compliance with applicable laws and regulations.

B. *Internal audit system.* An institution should have an internal audit system that is appropriate to the size of the institution and the nature and scope of its activities and that provides for:
1. Adequate monitoring of the system of internal controls through an internal audit function. For an institution whose size, complexity or scope of operations does not warrant a full scale internal audit function, a system of independent reviews of key internal controls may be used;
2. Independence and objectivity;
3. Qualified persons;
4. Adequate testing and review of information systems;
5. Adequate documentation of tests and findings and any corrective actions;
6. Verification and review of management actions to address material weaknesses; and
7. Review by the institution's audit committee or board of directors of the effectiveness of the internal audit systems.

C. *Loan documentation.* An institution should establish and maintain loan documentation practices that:
1. Enable the institution to make an informed lending decision and to assess risk, as necessary, on an ongoing basis;
2. Identify the purpose of a loan and the source of repayment, and assess the ability of the borrower to repay the indebtedness in a timely manner;
3. Ensure that any claim against a borrower is legally enforceable;
4. Demonstrate appropriate administration and monitoring of a loan; and
5. Take account of the size and complexity of a loan.

D. *Credit underwriting.* An institution should establish and maintain prudent credit underwriting practices that:
1. Are commensurate with the types of loans the institution will make and consider the terms and conditions under which they will be made;
2. Consider the nature of the markets in which loans will be made;
3. Provide for consideration, prior to credit commitment, of the borrower's overall financial condition and resources, the financial responsibility of any guarantor, the nature and value of any underlying collateral, and the borrower's character and willingness to repay as agreed;
4. Establish a system of independent, ongoing credit review and appropriate communication to management and to the board of directors;
5. Take adequate account of concentration of credit risk; and
6. Are appropriate to the size of the institution and the nature and scope of its activities.

E. *Interest rate exposure.* An institution should:
1. Manage interest rate risk in a manner that is appropriate to the size of the institution and the complexity of its assets and liabilities; and
2. Provide for periodic reporting to management and the board of directors regarding interest rate risk with adequate information for management and the board of directors to assess the level of risk.

F. *Asset growth.* An institution's asset growth should be prudent and consider:
1. The source, volatility and use of the funds that support asset growth;
2. Any increase in credit risk or interest rate risk as a result of growth; and
3. The effect of growth on the institution's capital.

G. *Asset quality.* An insured depository institution should establish and maintain a system that is commensurate with the institution's size and the nature and scope of its operations to identify problem assets and prevent deterioration in those assets. The institution should:
1. Conduct periodic asset quality reviews to identify problem assets;
2. Estimate the inherent losses in those assets and establish reserves that are sufficient to absorb estimated losses;
3. Compare problem asset totals to capital;

---

[3] In applying these definitions for State savings associations, State savings associations shall use the terms "State savings association" and "insured State savings association" in place of the terms "member bank" and "insured bank."

[4] See footnote 3 in section I.B.4. of this appendix.

[5] See footnote 3 in section I.B.4. of this appendix.

4. Take appropriate corrective action to resolve problem assets;

5. Consider the size and potential risks of material asset concentrations; and

6. Provide periodic asset reports with adequate information for management and the board of directors to assess the level of asset risk.

H. *Earnings.* An insured depository institution should establish and maintain a system that is commensurate with the institution's size and the nature and scope of its operations to evaluate and monitor earnings and ensure that earnings are sufficient to maintain adequate capital and reserves. The institution should:

1. Compare recent earnings trends relative to equity, assets, or other commonly used benchmarks to the institution's historical results and those of its peers;

2. Evaluate the adequacy of earnings given the size, complexity, and risk profile of the institution's assets and operations;

3. Assess the source, volatility, and sustainability of earnings, including the effect of nonrecurring or extraordinary income or expense;

4. Take steps to ensure that earnings are sufficient to maintain adequate capital and reserves after considering the institution's asset quality and growth rate; and

5. Provide periodic earnings reports with adequate information for management and the board of directors to assess earnings performance.

I. *Compensation, fees and benefits.* An institution should maintain safeguards to prevent the payment of compensation, fees, and benefits that are excessive or that could lead to material financial loss to the institution.

III. PROHIBITION ON COMPENSATION THAT CONSTITUTES AN UNSAFE AND UNSOUND PRACTICE

A. *Excessive Compensation*

Excessive compensation is prohibited as an unsafe and unsound practice. Compensation shall be considered excessive when amounts paid are unreasonable or disproportionate to the services performed by an executive officer, employee, director, or principal shareholder, considering the following:

1. The combined value of all cash and noncash benefits provided to the individual;

2. The compensation history of the individual and other individuals with comparable expertise at the institution;

3. The financial condition of the institution;

4. Comparable compensation practices at comparable institutions, based upon such factors as asset size, geographic location, and the complexity of the loan portfolio or other assets;

5. For postemployment benefits, the projected total cost and benefit to the institution;

6. Any connection between the individual and any fraudulent act or omission, breach of trust or fiduciary duty, or insider abuse with regard to the institution; and

7. Any other factors the agencies determines to be relevant.

B. *Compensation Leading to Material Financial Loss*

Compensation that could lead to material financial loss to an institution is prohibited as an unsafe and unsound practice.

APPENDIX B TO SUBPART B OF PART 391—INTERAGENCY GUIDELINES ESTABLISHING INFORMATION SECURITY STANDARDS

TABLE OF CONTENTS

I. Introduction
 A. Scope
 B. Preservation of Existing Authority
 C. Definitions
II. Standards for Safeguarding Customer Information
 A. Information Security Program
 B. Objectives
III. Development and Implementation of Customer Information Security Program
 A. Involve the Board of Directors
 B. Assess Risk
 C. Manage and Control Risk
 D. Oversee Service Provider Arrangements
 E. Adjust the Program
 F. Report to the Board
 G. Implement the Standards

I. INTRODUCTION

The Interagency Guidelines Establishing Information Security Standards (Guidelines) set forth standards pursuant to section 39(a) of the Federal Deposit Insurance Act (12 U.S.C. 1831p–1), and sections 501 and 505(b) of the Gramm-Leach-Bliley Act (15 U.S.C. 6801 and 6805(b)). These Guidelines address standards for developing and implementing administrative, technical, and physical safeguards to protect the security, confidentiality, and integrity of customer information. These Guidelines also address standards with respect to the proper disposal of consumer information, pursuant to section 628 of the Fair Credit Reporting Act (15 U.S.C. 1681w).

A. *Scope.* The Guidelines apply to customer information maintained by or on behalf of entities over which FDIC has authority. For purposes of this appendix, these entities are State savings associations whose deposits are FDIC-insured and any subsidiaries of such State savings associations, except brokers, dealers, persons providing insurance, investment companies, and investment advisers. This appendix refers to such entities

Pt. 391, Subpt. B, App. A

as "you". These Guidelines also apply to the proper disposal of consumer information by or on behalf of such entities.

B. *Preservation of Existing Authority.* Neither section 39 nor these Guidelines in any way limit FDIC's authority to address unsafe or unsound practices, violations of law, unsafe or unsound conditions, or other practices. FDIC may take action under section 39 and these Guidelines independently of, in conjunction with, or in addition to, any other enforcement action available to FDIC.

C. *Definitions.* 1. Except as modified in the Guidelines, or unless the context otherwise requires, the terms used in these Guidelines have the same meanings as set forth in sections 3 and 39 of the Federal Deposit Insurance Act (12 U.S.C. 1813 and 1831p–1).

2. For purposes of the Guidelines, the following definitions apply:

a. *Consumer information* means any record about an individual, whether in paper, electronic, or other form, that is a consumer report or is derived from a consumer report and that is maintained or otherwise possessed by you or on your behalf for a business purpose. Consumer information also means a compilation of such records. The term does not include any record that does not identify an individual.

i. *Examples.* (1) *Consumer information* includes:

(A) A consumer report that a State savings association obtains;

(B) Information from a consumer report that you obtain from your affiliate after the consumer has been given a notice and has elected not to opt out of that sharing;

(C) Information from a consumer report that you obtain about an individual who applies for but does not receive a loan, including any loan sought by an individual for a business purpose;

(D) Information from a consumer report that you obtain about an individual who guarantees a loan (including a loan to a business entity); or

(E) Information from a consumer report that you obtain about an employee or prospective employee.

(2) *Consumer information* does not include:

(A) Aggregate information, such as the mean credit score, derived from a group of consumer reports; or

(B) Blind data, such as payment history on accounts that are not personally identifiable, that may be used for developing credit scoring models or for other purposes.

b. *Consumer report* has the same meaning as set forth in the Fair Credit Reporting Act, 15 U.S.C. 1681a(d).

c. *Customer* means any consumer who has a customer relationship with you.

d. *Customer information* means any record containing nonpublic personal information about a customer, whether in paper, electronic, or other form, that you maintain or that is maintained on your behalf.

e. *Customer information systems* means any methods used to access, collect, store, use, transmit, protect, or dispose of customer information.

f. *Service provider* means any person or entity that maintains, processes, or otherwise is permitted access to customer information or consumer information, through its provision of services directly to you.

II. STANDARDS FOR INFORMATION SECURITY

A. *Information Security Program.* You shall implement a comprehensive written information security program that includes administrative, technical, and physical safeguards appropriate to your size and complexity and the nature and scope of your activities. While all parts of your organization are not required to implement a uniform set of policies, all elements of your information security program must be coordinated.

B. *Objectives.* Your information security program shall be designed to:

1. Ensure the security and confidentiality of customer information;

2. Protect against any anticipated threats or hazards to the security or integrity of such information;

3. Protect against unauthorized access to or use of such information that could result in substantial harm or inconvenience to any customer; and

4. Ensure the proper disposal of customer information and consumer information.

III. DEVELOPMENT AND IMPLEMENTATION OF INFORMATION SECURITY PROGRAM

A. *Involve the Board of Directors.* Your board of directors or an appropriate committee of the board shall:

1. Approve your written information security program; and

2. Oversee the development, implementation, and maintenance of your information security program, including assigning specific responsibility for its implementation and reviewing reports from management.

B. *Assess Risk.* You shall:

1. Identify reasonably foreseeable internal and external threats that could result in unauthorized disclosure, misuse, alteration, or destruction of customer information or customer information systems.

2. Assess the likelihood and potential damage of these threats, taking into consideration the sensitivity of customer information.

3. Assess the sufficiency of policies, procedures, customer information systems, and other arrangements in place to control risks.

C. *Manage and Control Risk.* You shall:

Federal Deposit Insurance Corporation

1. Design your information security program to control the identified risks, commensurate with the sensitivity of the information as well as the complexity and scope of your activities. You must consider whether the following security measures are appropriate for you and, if so, adopt those measures you conclude are appropriate:

a. Access controls on customer information systems, including controls to authenticate and permit access only to authorized individuals and controls to prevent employees from providing customer information to unauthorized individuals who may seek to obtain this information through fraudulent means.

b. Access restrictions at physical locations containing customer information, such as buildings, computer facilities, and records storage facilities to permit access only to authorized individuals;

c. Encryption of electronic customer information, including while in transit or in storage on networks or systems to which unauthorized individuals may have access;

d. Procedures designed to ensure that customer information system modifications are consistent with your information security program;

e. Dual control procedures, segregation of duties, and employee background checks for employees with responsibilities for or access to customer information;

f. Monitoring systems and procedures to detect actual and attempted attacks on or intrusions into customer information systems;

g. Response programs that specify actions for you to take when you suspect or detect that unauthorized individuals have gained access to customer information systems, including appropriate reports to regulatory and law enforcement agencies; and

h. Measures to protect against destruction, loss, or damage of customer information due to potential environmental hazards, such as fire and water damage or technological failures.

2. Train staff to implement your information security program.

3. Regularly test the key controls, systems and procedures of the information security program. The frequency and nature of such tests should be determined by your risk assessment. Tests should be conducted or reviewed by independent third parties or staff independent of those that develop or maintain the security programs.

4. Develop, implement, and maintain, as part of your information security program, appropriate measures to properly dispose of customer information and consumer information in accordance with each of the requirements in this paragraph III.

D. *Oversee Service Provider Arrangements.* You shall:

1. Exercise appropriate due diligence in selecting your service providers;

2. Require your service providers by contract to implement appropriate measures designed to meet the objectives of these Guidelines; and

3. Where indicated by your risk assessment, monitor your service providers to confirm that they have satisfied their obligations as required by paragraph D.2. As part of this monitoring, you should review audits, summaries of test results, or other equivalent evaluations of your service providers.

E. *Adjust the Program.* You shall monitor, evaluate, and adjust, as appropriate, the information security program in light of any relevant changes in technology, the sensitivity of your customer information, internal or external threats to information, and your own changing business arrangements, such as mergers and acquisitions, alliances and joint ventures, outsourcing arrangements, and changes to customer information systems.

F. *Report to the Board.* You shall report to your board or an appropriate committee of the board at least annually. This report should describe the overall status of the information security program and your compliance with these Guidelines. The reports should discuss material matters related to your program, addressing issues such as: risk assessment; risk management and control decisions; service provider arrangements; results of testing; security breaches or violations and management's responses; and recommendations for changes in the information security program.

G. *Implement the Standards.* 1. *Effective date.* You must implement an information security program pursuant to these Guidelines by July 1, 2001.

2. *Two-year grandfathering of agreements with service providers.* Until July 1, 2003, a contract that you have entered into with a service provider to perform services for you or functions on your behalf satisfies the provisions of paragraph III.D., even if the contract does not include a requirement that the servicer maintain the security and confidentiality of customer information, as long as you entered into the contract on or before March 5, 2001.

3. *Effective date for measures relating to the disposal of consumer information.* You must satisfy these Guidelines with respect to the proper disposal of consumer information by July 1, 2005.

4. *Exception for existing agreements with service providers relating to the disposal of consumer information.* Notwithstanding the requirement in paragraph III.G.3., your contracts with service providers that have access to consumer information and that may dispose of consumer information, entered into before July 1, 2005, must comply with the provisions of the Guidelines relating to

the proper disposal of consumer information by July 1, 2006.

Supplement to Appendix B of Part 391— Interagency Guidance on Response Programs for Unauthorized Access to Customer Information and Customer Notice

I. BACKGROUND

This Guidance[1] interprets section 501(b) of the Gramm-Leach-Bliley Act ("GLBA") and the Interagency Guidelines Establishing Information Security Standards (the "Security Guidelines")[2] and describes response programs, including customer notification procedures, that a financial institution should develop and implement to address unauthorized access to or use of customer information that could result in substantial harm or inconvenience to a customer. The scope of, and definitions of terms used in, this Guidance are identical to those of the Security Guidelines. For example, the term "customer information" is the same term used in the Security Guidelines, and means any record containing nonpublic personal information about a customer, whether in paper, electronic, or other form, maintained by or on behalf of the institution.

A. Interagency Security Guidelines

Section 501(b) of the GLBA required the Agencies to establish appropriate standards for financial institutions subject to their jurisdiction that include administrative, technical, and physical safeguards, to protect the security and confidentiality of customer information.

Accordingly, the Agencies issued Security Guidelines requiring every financial institution to have an information security program designed to:

1. Ensure the security and confidentiality of customer information;
2. Protect against any anticipated threats or hazards to the security or integrity of such information; and
3. Protect against unauthorized access to or use of such information that could result in substantial harm or inconvenience to any customer.

B. Risk Assessment and Controls

1. The Security Guidelines direct every financial institution to assess the following risks, among others, when developing its information security program:

a. Reasonably foreseeable internal and external threats that could result in unauthorized disclosure, misuse, alteration, or destruction of customer information or customer information systems;

b. The likelihood and potential damage of threats, taking into consideration the sensitivity of customer information; and

c. The sufficiency of policies, procedures, customer information systems, and other arrangements in place to control risks.[3]

2. Following the assessment of these risks, the Security Guidelines require a financial institution to design a program to address the identified risks. The particular security measures an institution should adopt will depend upon the risks presented by the complexity and scope of its business. At a minimum, the financial institution is required to consider the specific security measures enumerated in the Security Guidelines,[4] and adopt those that are appropriate for the institution, including:

a. Access controls on customer information systems, including controls to authenticate and permit access only to authorized individuals and controls to prevent employees from providing customer information to unauthorized individuals who may seek to obtain this information through fraudulent means;

b. Background checks for employees with responsibilities for access to customer information; and

c. Response programs that specify actions to be taken when the financial institution suspects or detects that unauthorized individuals have gained access to customer information systems, including appropriate reports to regulatory and law enforcement agencies.[5]

C. Service Providers

The Security Guidelines direct every financial institution to require its service providers by contract to implement appropriate measures designed to protect against unauthorized access to or use of customer information that could result in substantial harm or inconvenience to any customer.[6]

---

[1] This Guidance is being jointly issued by the Board of Governors of the Federal Reserve System (Board), the Federal Deposit Insurance Corporation (FDIC), and the Office of the Comptroller of the Currency (OCC).

[2] 12 CFR part 30, app. B (OCC); 12 CFR part 208, app. D–2 and part 225, app. F (Board); 12 CFR part 364, app. A and app. B of Subpart B of Part 391 (FDIC). The "Interagency Guidelines Establishing Information Security Standards" were formerly known as "The Interagency Guidelines Establishing Standards for Safeguarding Customer Information."

[3] See Security Guidelines, III.B.
[4] See Security Guidelines, III.C.
[5] See Security Guidelines, III.C.
[6] See Security Guidelines, II.B. and III.D. Further, the Agencies note that, in addition

Federal Deposit Insurance Corporation

II. RESPONSE PROGRAM

Millions of Americans, throughout the country, have been victims of identity theft.[7] Identity thieves misuse personal information they obtain from a number of sources, including financial institutions, to perpetrate identity theft. Therefore, financial institutions should take preventative measures to safeguard customer information against attempts to gain unauthorized access to the information. For example, financial institutions should place access controls on customer information systems and conduct background checks for employees who are authorized to access customer information.[8] However, every financial institution should also develop and implement a risk-based response program to address incidents of unauthorized access to customer information in customer information systems[9] that occur nonetheless. A response program should be a key part of an institution's information security program.[10] The program should be appropriate to the size and complexity of the institution and the nature and scope of its activities.

In addition, each institution should be able to address incidents of unauthorized access to customer information in customer information systems maintained by its domestic and foreign service providers. Therefore, consistent with the obligations in the Guidelines that relate to these arrangements, and with existing guidance on this topic issued by the Agencies,[11] an institution's contract with its service provider should require the service provider to take appropriate actions to address incidents of unauthorized access to the financial institution's customer information, including notification to the institution as soon as possible of any such incident, to enable the institution to expeditiously implement its response program.

A. Components of a Response Program

1. At a minimum, an institution's response program should contain procedures for the following:

a. Assessing the nature and scope of an incident, and identifying what customer information systems and types of customer information have been accessed or misused;

b. Notifying its primary Federal regulator as soon as possible when the institution becomes aware of an incident involving unauthorized access to or use of *sensitive* customer information, as defined below;

c. Consistent with the Agencies' Suspicious Activity Report ("SAR") regulations,[12] notifying appropriate law enforcement authorities, in addition to filing a timely SAR in

---

to contractual obligations to a financial institution, a service provider may be required to implement its own comprehensive information security program in accordance with the Safeguards Rule promulgated by the Federal Trade Commission ("FTC"), 16 CFR part 314.

[7] The FTC estimates that nearly 10 million Americans discovered they were victims of some form of identity theft in 2002. See The Federal Trade Commission, Identity Theft Survey Report, (September 2003), available at http://www.ftc.gov/os/2003/09/synovatereport.pdf.

[8] Institutions should also conduct background checks of employees to ensure that the institution does not violate 12 U.S.C. 1829, which prohibits an institution from hiring an individual convicted of certain criminal offenses or who is subject to a prohibition order under 12 U.S.C. 1818(e)(6).

[9] Under the Guidelines, an institution's customer information systems consist of all of the methods used to access, collect, store, use, transmit, protect, or dispose of customer information, including the systems maintained by its service providers. See Security Guidelines, I.C.2.d (I.C.2.c for FDIC).

[10] See FFIEC Information Technology Examination Handbook, Information Security Booklet, Dec. 2002 available at http://www.ffiec.gov/ffiecinfobase/html_pages/infosec_book_frame.htm. Federal Reserve SR 97–32, Sound Practice Guidance for Information Security for Networks, Dec. 4, 1997; OCC Bulletin 2000–14, "Infrastructure Threats—Intrusion Risks" (May 15, 2000), for additional guidance on preventing, detecting, and responding to intrusions into financial institution computer systems.

[11] See Federal Reserve SR Ltr. 00–04, Outsourcing of Information and Transaction Processing, Feb. 9, 2000; OCC Bulletin 2001–47, "Third-Party Relationships Risk Management Principles," Nov. 1, 2001; FDIC FIL 68–99, Risk Assessment Tools and Practices for Information System Security, July 7, 1999; Thrift Bulletin 82a, Third Party Arrangements, Sept. 1, 2004.

[12] An institution's obligation to file a SAR is set out in the Agencies' SAR regulations and Agency guidance. See 12 CFR 21.11 (national banks, Federal branches and agencies); 12 CFR 208.62 (State member banks); 12 CFR 211.5(k) (Edge and agreement corporations); 12 CFR 211.24(f) (uninsured State branches and agencies of foreign banks); 12 CFR 225.4(f) (bank holding companies and their nonbank subsidiaries); 12 CFR part 353 (State non-member banks); and 390.355 (State savings associations). National banks must file SARs in connection with computer intrusions and other computer crimes. See OCC Bulletin 2000–14, "Infrastructure Threats—Intrusion Risks" (May 15, 2000); Advisory Letter 97–9, "Reporting Computer Related Crimes" (November 19, 1997) (general guidance still applicable though instructions

Continued

situations involving Federal criminal violations requiring immediate attention, such as when a reportable violation is ongoing;

d. Taking appropriate steps to contain and control the incident to prevent further unauthorized access to or use of customer information, for example, by monitoring, freezing, or closing affected accounts, while preserving records and other evidence;[13] and

e. Notifying customers when warranted.

2. Where an incident of unauthorized access to customer information involves customer information systems maintained by an institution's service providers, it is the responsibility of the financial institution to notify the institution's customers and regulator. However, an institution may authorize or contract with its service provider to notify the institution's customers or regulator on its behalf.

III. CUSTOMER NOTICE

Financial institutions have an affirmative duty to protect their customers' information against unauthorized access or use. Notifying customers of a security incident involving the unauthorized access or use of the customer's information in accordance with the standard set forth below is a key part of that duty. Timely notification of customers is important to manage an institution's reputation risk. Effective notice also may reduce an institution's legal risk, assist in maintaining good customer relations, and enable the institution's customers to take steps to protect themselves against the consequences of identity theft. When customer notification is warranted, an institution may not forgo notifying its customers of an incident because the institution believes that it may be potentially embarrassed or inconvenienced by doing so.

A. Standard for Providing Notice

When a financial institution becomes aware of an incident of unauthorized access to sensitive customer information, the institution should conduct a reasonable investigation to promptly determine the likelihood that the information has been or will be misused. If the institution determines that misuse of its information about a customer has occurred or is reasonably possible, it should notify the affected customer as soon as possible. Customer notice may be delayed if an appropriate law enforcement agency determines that notification will interfere with a criminal investigation and provides the institution with a written request for the delay. However, the institution should notify its customers as soon as notification will no longer interfere with the investigation.

1. Sensitive Customer Information

Under the Guidelines, an institution must protect against unauthorized access to or use of customer information that could result in substantial harm or inconvenience to any customer. Substantial harm or inconvenience is most likely to result from improper access to *sensitive customer information* because this type of information is most likely to be misused, as in the commission of identity theft. For purposes of this Guidance, *sensitive customer information* means a customer's name, address, or telephone number, in conjunction with the customer's social security number, driver's license number, account number, credit or debit card number, or a personal identification number or password that would permit access to the customer's account. *Sensitive customer information* also includes any combination of components of customer information that would allow someone to log onto or access the customer's account, such as user name and password or password and account number.

2. Affected Customers

If a financial institution, based upon its investigation, can determine from its logs or other data precisely which customers' information has been improperly accessed, it may limit notification to those customers with regard to whom the institution determines that misuse of their information has occurred or is reasonably possible. However, there may be situations where the institution determines that a group of files has been accessed improperly, but is unable to identify which specific customers' information has been accessed. If the circumstances of the unauthorized access lead the institution to determine that misuse of the information is reasonably possible, it should notify all customers in the group.

B. Content of Customer Notice

1. Customer notice should be given in a clear and conspicuous manner. The notice should describe the incident in general terms and the type of customer information that was the subject of unauthorized access or use. It also should generally describe what

---

for new SAR form published in 65 FR 1229, 1230 (January 7, 2000)). See also Federal Reserve SR 01–11, Identity Theft and Pretext Calling, Apr. 26, 2001; SR 97–28, Guidance Concerning Reporting of Computer Related Crimes by Financial Institutions, Nov. 6, 1997; FDIC FIL 48–2000, Suspicious Activity Reports, July 14, 2000; FIL 47–97, Preparation of Suspicious Activity Reports, May 6, 1997; CEO Memorandum 139, Identity Theft and Pretext Calling, May 4, 2001; CEO Memorandum 126, New Suspicious Activity Report Form, July 5, 2000.

[13] See FFIEC Information Technology Examination Handbook, Information Security Booklet, Dec. 2002, pp. 68–74.

Federal Deposit Insurance Corporation § 391.22

the institution has done to protect the customers' information from further unauthorized access. In addition, it should include a telephone number that customers can call for further information and assistance.[14] The notice also should remind customers of the need to remain vigilant over the next twelve to twenty-four months, and to promptly report incidents of suspected identity theft to the institution. The notice should include the following additional items, when appropriate:

a. A recommendation that the customer review account statements and immediately report any suspicious activity to the institution;

b. A description of fraud alerts and an explanation of how the customer may place a fraud alert in the customer's consumer reports to put the customer's creditors on notice that the customer may be a victim of fraud;

c. A recommendation that the customer periodically obtain credit reports from each nationwide credit reporting agency and have information relating to fraudulent transactions deleted;

d. An explanation of how the customer may obtain a credit report free of charge; and

e. Information about the availability of the FTC's online guidance regarding steps a consumer can take to protect against identity theft. The notice should encourage the customer to report any incidents of identity theft to the FTC, and should provide the FTC's Web site address and toll-free telephone number that customers may use to obtain the identity theft guidance and report suspected incidents of identity theft.[15]

2. The Agencies encourage financial institutions to notify the nationwide consumer reporting agencies prior to sending notices to a large number of customers that include contact information for the reporting agencies.

C. Delivery of Customer Notice

Customer notice should be delivered in any manner designed to ensure that a customer can reasonably be expected to receive it. For example, the institution may choose to contact all customers affected by telephone or by mail, or by electronic mail for those customers for whom it has a valid e-mail address and who have agreed to receive communications electronically.

Subpart C—Fair Credit Reporting

§ 391.20 Examples.

The examples in this subpart are not exclusive. Compliance with an example, to the extent applicable, constitutes compliance with this subpart. Examples in a section illustrate only the issue described in the section and do not illustrate any other issue that may arise in this subpart.

§ 391.21 Disposal of consumer information.

(a) *Scope.* This section applies to State savings associations whose deposits are insured by the Federal Deposit Insurance Corporation (defined as "you").

(b) *In general.* You must properly dispose of any consumer information that you maintain or otherwise possess in accordance with the Interagency Guidelines Establishing Information Security Standards, to the extent that you are covered by the scope of the Guidelines.

(c) *Rule of construction.* Nothing in this section shall be construed to:

(1) Require you to maintain or destroy any record pertaining to a consumer that is not imposed under any other law; or

(2) Alter or affect any requirement imposed under any other provision of law to maintain or destroy such a record.

§ 391.22 Duties regarding the detection, prevention, and mitigation of identity theft.

(a) *Scope.* This section applies to a financial institution or creditor that is a State savings association whose deposits are insured by the Federal Deposit Insurance Corporation.

(b) *Definitions.* For purposes of this section and the appendix to subpart C of part 391, the following definitions apply:

(1) *Account* means a continuing relationship established by a person with a

---

[14] The institution should, therefore, ensure that it has reasonable policies and procedures in place, including trained personnel, to respond appropriately to customer inquiries and requests for assistance.

[15] Currently, the FTC Web site for the ID Theft brochure and the FTC Hotline phone number are *http://www.consumer.gov/idtheft* and 1-877-IDTHEFT. The institution may also refer customers to any materials developed pursuant to section 151(b) of the FACT Act (educational materials developed by the FTC to teach the public how to prevent identity theft).

§ 391.22

financial institution or creditor to obtain a product or service for personal, family, household or business purposes. Account includes:

(i) An extension of credit, such as the purchase of property or services involving a deferred payment; and

(ii) A deposit account.

(2) The term *board of directors* includes:

(i) In the case of a branch or agency of a foreign bank, the managing official in charge of the branch or agency; and

(ii) In the case of any other creditor that does not have a board of directors, a designated employee at the level of senior management.

(3) *Covered account* means:

(i) An account that a financial institution or creditor offers or maintains, primarily for personal, family, or household purposes, that involves or is designed to permit multiple payments or transactions, such as a credit card account, mortgage loan, automobile loan, margin account, cell phone account, utility account, checking account, or savings account; and

(ii) Any other account that the financial institution or creditor offers or maintains for which there is a reasonably foreseeable risk to customers or to the safety and soundness of the financial institution or creditor from identity theft, including financial, operational, compliance, reputation, or litigation risks.

(4) *Credit* has the same meaning as in 15 U.S.C. 1681a(r)(5).

(5) *Creditor* has the same meaning as in 15 U.S.C. 1681a(r)(5), and includes lenders such as banks, finance companies, automobile dealers, mortgage brokers, utility companies, and telecommunications companies.

(6) *Customer* means a person that has a covered account with a financial institution or creditor.

(7) *Financial institution* has the same meaning as in 15 U.S.C. 1681a(t).

(8) *Identity theft* has the same meaning as in 16 CFR 603.2(a).

(9) *Red Flag* means a pattern, practice, or specific activity that indicates the possible existence of identity theft.

(10) *Service provider* means a person that provides a service directly to the financial institution or creditor.

(c) *Periodic identification of covered accounts.* Each financial institution or creditor must periodically determine whether it offers or maintains covered accounts. As a part of this determination, a financial institution or creditor must conduct a risk assessment to determine whether it offers or maintains covered accounts described in paragraph (b)(3)(ii) of this section, taking into consideration:

(1) The methods it provides to open its accounts;

(2) The methods it provides to access its accounts; and

(3) Its previous experiences with identity theft.

(d) *Establishment of an Identity Theft Prevention Program*—(1) *Program requirement.* Each financial institution or creditor that offers or maintains one or more covered accounts must develop and implement a written Identity Theft Prevention Program (Program) that is designed to detect, prevent, and mitigate identity theft in connection with the opening of a covered account or any existing covered account. The Program must be appropriate to the size and complexity of the financial institution or creditor and the nature and scope of its activities.

(2) *Elements of the Program.* The Program must include reasonable policies and procedures to:

(i) Identify relevant Red Flags for the covered accounts that the financial institution or creditor offers or maintains, and incorporate those Red Flags into its Program;

(ii) Detect Red Flags that have been incorporated into the Program of the financial institution or creditor;

(iii) Respond appropriately to any Red Flags that are detected pursuant to paragraph (d)(2)(ii) of this section to prevent and mitigate identity theft; and

(iv) Ensure the Program (including the Red Flags determined to be relevant) is updated periodically, to reflect changes in risks to customers and to the safety and soundness of the financial institution or creditor from identity theft.

(e) *Administration of the Program.* Each financial institution or creditor that is required to implement a Program must provide for the continued administration of the Program and must:

(1) Obtain approval of the initial written Program from either its board of directors or an appropriate committee of the board of directors;

(2) Involve the board of directors, an appropriate committee thereof, or a designated employee at the level of senior management in the oversight, development, implementation and administration of the Program;

(3) Train staff, as necessary, to effectively implement the Program; and

(4) Exercise appropriate and effective oversight of service provider arrangements.

(f) *Guidelines.* Each financial institution or creditor that is required to implement a Program must consider the guidelines in the appendix to this subpart and include in its Program those guidelines that are appropriate.

§ 391.23 Duties of card issuers regarding changes of address.

(a) *Scope.* This section applies to an issuer of a debit or credit card (card issuer) that is a State savings association whose deposits are insured by the Federal Deposit Insurance Corporation.

(b) *Definitions.* For purposes of this section:

(1) *Cardholder* means a consumer who has been issued a credit or debit card.

(2) *Clear and conspicuous* means reasonably understandable and designed to call attention to the nature and significance of the information presented.

(c) *Address validation requirements.* A card issuer must establish and implement reasonable policies and procedures to assess the validity of a change of address if it receives notification of a change of address for a consumer's debit or credit card account and, within a short period of time afterwards (during at least the first 30 days after it receives such notification), the card issuer receives a request for an additional or replacement card for the same account. Under these circumstances, the card issuer may not issue an additional or replacement card, until, in accordance with its reasonable policies and procedures and for the purpose of assessing the validity of the change of address, the card issuer:

(1)(i) Notifies the cardholder of the request:

(A) At the cardholder's former address; or

(B) By any other means of communication that the card issuer and the cardholder have previously agreed to use; and

(ii) Provides to the cardholder a reasonable means of promptly reporting incorrect address changes; or

(2) Otherwise assesses the validity of the change of address in accordance with the policies and procedures the card issuer has established pursuant to § 391.22.

(d) *Alternative timing of address validation.* A card issuer may satisfy the requirements of paragraph (c) of this section if it validates an address pursuant to the methods in paragraph (c)(1) or (c)(2) of this section when it receives an address change notification, before it receives a request for an additional or replacement card.

(e) *Form of notice.* Any written or electronic notice that the card issuer provides under this paragraph must be clear and conspicuous and provided separately from its regular correspondence with the cardholder.

APPENDIX TO SUBPART C OF PART 391—INTERAGENCY GUIDELINES ON IDENTITY THEFT DETECTION, PREVENTION, AND MITIGATION

Section 391.22 requires each financial institution and creditor that offers or maintains one or more covered accounts, as defined in § 391.22(b)(3), to develop and provide for the continued administration of a written Program to detect, prevent, and mitigate identity theft in connection with the opening of a covered account or any existing covered account. These guidelines are intended to assist financial institutions and creditors in the formulation and maintenance of a Program that satisfies the requirements of § 391.22.

I. THE PROGRAM

In designing its Program, a financial institution or creditor may incorporate, as appropriate, its existing policies, procedures, and other arrangements that control reasonably foreseeable risks to customers or to the safety and soundness of the financial institution or creditor from identity theft.

II. IDENTIFYING RELEVANT RED FLAGS

(a) *Risk Factors.* A financial institution or creditor should consider the following factors in identifying relevant Red Flags for covered accounts, as appropriate:

(1) The types of covered accounts it offers or maintains;

(2) The methods it provides to open its covered accounts;

(3) The methods it provides to access its covered accounts; and

(4) Its previous experiences with identity theft.

(b) *Sources of Red Flags.* Financial institutions and creditors should incorporate relevant Red Flags from sources such as:

(1) Incidents of identity theft that the financial institution or creditor has experienced;

(2) Methods of identity theft that the financial institution or creditor has identified that reflect changes in identity theft risks; and

(3) Applicable supervisory guidance.

(c) *Categories of Red Flags.* The Program should include relevant Red Flags from the following categories, as appropriate. Examples of Red Flags from each of these categories are appended as Supplement A to this Appendix.

(1) Alerts, notifications, or other warnings received from consumer reporting agencies or service providers, such as fraud detection services;

(2) The presentation of suspicious documents;

(3) The presentation of suspicious personal identifying information, such as a suspicious address change;

(4) The unusual use of, or other suspicious activity related to, a covered account; and

(5) Notice from customers, victims of identity theft, law enforcement authorities, or other persons regarding possible identity theft in connection with covered accounts held by the financial institution or creditor.

III. DETECTING RED FLAGS

The Program's policies and procedures should address the detection of Red Flags in connection with the opening of covered accounts and existing covered accounts, such as by:

(a) Obtaining identifying information about, and verifying the identity of, a person opening a covered account, for example, using the policies and procedures regarding identification and verification set forth in the Customer Identification Program rules implementing 31 U.S.C. 5318(l) (31 CFR 103.121); and

(b) Authenticating customers, monitoring transactions, and verifying the validity of change of address requests, in the case of existing covered accounts.

IV. PREVENTING AND MITIGATING IDENTITY THEFT

The Program's policies and procedures should provide for appropriate responses to the Red Flags the financial institution or creditor has detected that are commensurate with the degree of risk posed. In determining an appropriate response, a financial institution or creditor should consider aggravating factors that may heighten the risk of identity theft, such as a data security incident that results in unauthorized access to a customer's account records held by the financial institution, creditor, or third party, or notice that a customer has provided information related to a covered account held by the financial institution or creditor to someone fraudulently claiming to represent the financial institution or creditor or to a fraudulent Web site. Appropriate responses may include the following:

(a) Monitoring a covered account for evidence of identity theft;

(b) Contacting the customer;

(c) Changing any passwords, security codes, or other security devices that permit access to a covered account;

(d) Reopening a covered account with a new account number;

(e) Not opening a new covered account;

(f) Closing an existing covered account;

(g) Not attempting to collect on a covered account or not selling a covered account to a debt collector;

(h) Notifying law enforcement; or

(i) Determining that no response is warranted under the particular circumstances.

V. UPDATING THE PROGRAM

Financial institutions and creditors should update the Program (including the Red Flags determined to be relevant) periodically, to reflect changes in risks to customers or to the safety and soundness of the financial institution or creditor from identity theft, based on factors such as:

(a) The experiences of the financial institution or creditor with identity theft;

(b) Changes in methods of identity theft;

(c) Changes in methods to detect, prevent, and mitigate identity theft;

(d) Changes in the types of accounts that the financial institution or creditor offers or maintains; and

(e) Changes in the business arrangements of the financial institution or creditor, including mergers, acquisitions, alliances, joint ventures, and service provider arrangements.

VI. METHODS FOR ADMINISTERING THE PROGRAM

(a) *Oversight of Program.* Oversight by the board of directors, an appropriate committee of the board, or a designated employee at the level of senior management should include:

Federal Deposit Insurance Corporation

(1) Assigning specific responsibility for the Program's implementation;

(2) Reviewing reports prepared by staff regarding compliance by the financial institution or creditor with §391.22; and

(3) Approving material changes to the Program as necessary to address changing identity theft risks.

(b) *Reports.* (1) *In general.* Staff of the financial institution or creditor responsible for development, implementation, and administration of its Program should report to the board of directors, an appropriate committee of the board, or a designated employee at the level of senior management, at least annually, on compliance by the financial institution or creditor with §391.22.

(2) *Contents of report.* The report should address material matters related to the Program and evaluate issues such as: The effectiveness of the policies and procedures of the financial institution or creditor in addressing the risk of identity theft in connection with the opening of covered accounts and with respect to existing covered accounts; service provider arrangements; significant incidents involving identity theft and management's response; and recommendations for material changes to the Program.

(c) *Oversight of service provider arrangements.* Whenever a financial institution or creditor engages a service provider to perform an activity in connection with one or more covered accounts the financial institution or creditor should take steps to ensure that the activity of the service provider is conducted in accordance with reasonable policies and procedures designed to detect, prevent, and mitigate the risk of identity theft. For example, a financial institution or creditor could require the service provider by contract to have policies and procedures to detect relevant Red Flags that may arise in the performance of the service provider's activities, and either report the Red Flags to the financial institution or creditor, or to take appropriate steps to prevent or mitigate identity theft.

VII. OTHER APPLICABLE LEGAL REQUIREMENTS

Financial institutions and creditors should be mindful of other related legal requirements that may be applicable, such as:

(a) For financial institutions and creditors that are subject to 31 U.S.C. 5318(g), filing a Suspicious Activity Report in accordance with applicable law and regulation;

(b) Implementing any requirements under 15 U.S.C. 1681c–1(h) regarding the circumstances under which credit may be extended when the financial institution or creditor detects a fraud or active duty alert;

(c) Implementing any requirements for furnishers of information to consumer reporting agencies under 15 U.S.C. 1681s–2, for example, to correct or update inaccurate or incomplete information, and to not report information that the furnisher has reasonable cause to believe is inaccurate; and

(d) Complying with the prohibitions in 15 U.S.C. 1681m on the sale, transfer, and placement for collection of certain debts resulting from identity theft.

Supplement A to Appendix to Subpart C of Part 391

In addition to incorporating Red Flags from the sources recommended in section II.b. of the Guidelines in this Appendix, each financial institution or creditor may consider incorporating into its Program, whether singly or in combination, Red Flags from the following illustrative examples in connection with covered accounts:

Alerts, Notifications or Warnings from a Consumer Reporting Agency

1. A fraud or active duty alert is included with a consumer report.

2. A consumer reporting agency provides a notice of credit freeze in response to a request for a consumer report.

3. A consumer reporting agency provides a notice of address discrepancy;

4. A consumer report indicates a pattern of activity that is inconsistent with the history and usual pattern of activity of an applicant or customer, such as:

a. A recent and significant increase in the volume of inquiries;

b. An unusual number of recently established credit relationships;

c. A material change in the use of credit, especially with respect to recently established credit relationships; or

d. An account that was closed for cause or identified for abuse of account privileges by a financial institution or creditor.

Suspicious Documents

5. Documents provided for identification appear to have been altered or forged.

6. The photograph or physical description on the identification is not consistent with the appearance of the applicant or customer presenting the identification.

7. Other information on the identification is not consistent with information provided by the person opening a new covered account or customer presenting the identification.

8. Other information on the identification is not consistent with readily accessible information that is on file with the financial institution or creditor, such as a signature card or a recent check.

9. An application appears to have been altered or forged, or gives the appearance of having been destroyed and reassembled.

Suspicious Personal Identifying Information

10. Personal identifying information provided is inconsistent when compared against

external information sources used by the financial institution or creditor. For example:

a. The address does not match any address in the consumer report; or

b. The Social Security Number (SSN) has not been issued, or is listed on the Social Security Administration's Death Master File.

11. Personal identifying information provided by the customer is not consistent with other personal identifying information provided by the customer. For example, there is a lack of correlation between the SSN range and date of birth.

12. Personal identifying information provided is associated with known fraudulent activity as indicated by internal or third-party sources used by the financial institution or creditor. For example:

a. The address on an application is the same as the address provided on a fraudulent application; or

b. The phone number on an application is the same as the number provided on a fraudulent application.

13. Personal identifying information provided is of a type commonly associated with fraudulent activity as indicated by internal or third-party sources used by the financial institution or creditor. For example:

a. The address on an application is fictitious, a mail drop, or a prison; or

b. The phone number is invalid, or is associated with a pager or answering service.

14. The SSN provided is the same as that submitted by other persons opening an account or other customers.

15. The address or telephone number provided is the same as or similar to the address or telephone number submitted by an unusually large number of other persons opening accounts or by other customers.

16. The person opening the covered account or the customer fails to provide all required personal identifying information on an application or in response to notification that the application is incomplete.

17. Personal identifying information provided is not consistent with personal identifying information that is on file with the financial institution or creditor.

18. For financial institutions and creditors that use challenge questions, the person opening the covered account or the customer cannot provide authenticating information beyond that which generally would be available from a wallet or consumer report.

Unusual Use of, or Suspicious Activity Related to, the Covered Account

19. Shortly following the notice of a change of address for a covered account, the institution or creditor receives a request for a new, additional, or replacement card or a cell phone, or for the addition of authorized users on the account.

20. A new revolving credit account is used in a manner commonly associated with known patterns of fraud. For example:

a. The majority of available credit is used for cash advances or merchandise that is easily convertible to cash (*e.g.*, electronics equipment or jewelry); or

b. The customer fails to make the first payment or makes an initial payment but no subsequent payments.

21. A covered account is used in a manner that is not consistent with established patterns of activity on the account. There is, for example:

a. Nonpayment when there is no history of late or missed payments;

b. A material increase in the use of available credit;

c. A material change in purchasing or spending patterns;

d. A material change in electronic fund transfer patterns in connection with a deposit account; or

e. A material change in telephone call patterns in connection with a cellular phone account.

22. A covered account that has been inactive for a reasonably lengthy period of time is used (taking into consideration the type of account, the expected pattern of usage and other relevant factors).

23. Mail sent to the customer is returned repeatedly as undeliverable although transactions continue to be conducted in connection with the customer's covered account.

24. The financial institution or creditor is notified that the customer is not receiving paper account statements.

25. The financial institution or creditor is notified of unauthorized charges or transactions in connection with a customer's covered account.

Notice from Customers, Victims of Identity Theft, Law Enforcement Authorities, or Other Persons Regarding Possible Identity Theft in Connection With Covered Accounts Held by the Financial Institution or Creditor

26. The financial institution or creditor is notified by a customer, a victim of identity theft, a law enforcement authority, or any other person that it has opened a fraudulent account for a person engaged in identity theft.

Subpart D—Loans in Areas Having Special Flood Hazards

§ 391.30 Authority, purpose, and scope.

(a) *Authority.* This subpart is issued pursuant to 12 U.S.C. 1462, 1462a, 1463, 1464, 1819 (Tenth) and 42 U.S.C. 4012a, 4104a, 4104b, 4106, 4128.

Federal Deposit Insurance Corporation § 391.32

(b) *Purpose.* The purpose of this subpart is to implement the requirements of the National Flood Insurance Act of 1968 and the Flood Disaster Protection Act of 1973, as amended (42 U.S.C. 4001–4129).

(c) *Scope.* This subpart, except for §§ 391.35 and 391.37, applies to loans secured by buildings or mobile homes located or to be located in areas determined by the Director of the Federal Emergency Management Agency to have special flood hazards. Sections 391.35 and 391.37 apply to loans secured by buildings or mobile homes, regardless of location.

§ 391.31 Definitions.

(a) *Act* means the National Flood Insurance Act of 1968, as amended (42 U.S.C. 4001–4129).

(b) *State savings association* means, for purposes of this subpart, a State savings association as that term is defined in 12 U.S.C. 1813(b)(3) and any subsidiaries thereof.

(c) *Building* means a walled and roofed structure, other than a gas or liquid storage tank, that is principally above ground and affixed to a permanent site, and a walled and roofed structure while in the course of construction, alteration, or repair.

(d) *Community* means a State or a political subdivision of a State that has zoning and building code jurisdiction over a particular area having special flood hazards.

(e) *Designated loan* means a loan secured by a building or mobile home that is located or to be located in a special flood hazard area in which flood insurance is available under the Act.

(f) *Director of FEMA* means the Director of the Federal Emergency Management Agency.

(g) *Mobile home* means a structure, transportable in one or more sections, that is built on a permanent chassis and designed for use with or without a permanent foundation when attached to the required utilities. The term *mobile home* does not include a recreational vehicle. For purposes of this subpart, the term *mobile home* means a mobile home on a permanent foundation. The term *mobile home* includes a manufactured home as that term is used in the NFIP.

(h) *NFIP* means the National Flood Insurance Program authorized under the Act.

(i) *Residential improved real estate* means real estate upon which a home or other residential building is located or to be located.

(j) *Servicer* means the person responsible for:

(1) Receiving any scheduled, periodic payments from a borrower under the terms of a loan, including amounts for taxes, insurance premiums, and other charges with respect to the property securing the loan; and

(2) Making payments of principal and interest and any other payments from the amounts received from the borrower as may be required under the terms of the loan.

(k) *Special flood hazard area* means the land in the flood plain within a community having at least a one percent chance of flooding in any given year, as designated by the Director of FEMA.

(l) *Table funding* means a settlement at which a loan is funded by a contemporaneous advance of loan funds and an assignment of the loan to the person advancing the funds.

§ 391.32 Requirement to purchase flood insurance where available.

(a) *In general.* A State savings association shall not make, increase, extend, or renew any designated loan unless the building or mobile home and any personal property securing the loan is covered by flood insurance for the term of the loan. The amount of insurance must be at least equal to the lesser of the outstanding principal balance of the designated loan or the maximum limit of coverage available for the particular type of property under the Act. Flood insurance coverage under the Act is limited to the overall value of the property securing the designated loan minus the value of the land on which the property is located.

(b) *Table funded loans.* A State savings association that acquires a loan from a mortgage broker or other entity through table funding shall be considered to be making a loan for the purposes of this subpart.

§ 391.33 Exemptions.

The flood insurance requirement prescribed by § 391.32 does not apply with respect to:

(a) Any State-owned property covered under a policy of self-insurance satisfactory to the Director of FEMA, who publishes and periodically revises the list of States falling within this exemption; or

(b) Property securing any loan with an original principal balance of $5,000 or less and a repayment term of one year or less.

§ 391.34 Escrow requirement.

If a State savings association requires the escrow of taxes, insurance premiums, fees, or any other charges for a loan secured by *residential* improved real estate or a mobile home that is made, increased, extended, or renewed on or after October 1, 1996, the State savings association shall also require the escrow of all premiums and fees for any flood insurance required under § 391.32. The State savings association, or a servicer acting on behalf of the State savings association, shall deposit the flood insurance premiums on behalf of the borrower in an escrow account. This escrow account will be subject to escrow requirements adopted pursuant to section 10 of the Real Estate Settlement Procedures Act of 1974 (12 U.S.C. 2609) (RESPA), which generally limits the amount that may be maintained in escrow accounts for certain types of loans and requires escrow account statements for those accounts, only if the loan is otherwise subject to RESPA. Following receipt of a notice from the Director of FEMA or other provider of flood insurance that premiums are due, the State savings association, or a servicer acting on behalf of the State savings association, shall pay the amount owed to the insurance provider from the escrow account by the date when such premiums are due.

§ 391.35 Required use of standard flood hazard determination form.

(a) *Use of form.* A State savings association shall use the standard flood hazard determination form developed by the Director of FEMA when determining whether the building or mobile home offered as collateral security for a loan is or will be located in a special flood hazard area in which flood insurance is available under the Act. The standard flood hazard determination form may be used in a printed, computerized, or electronic manner. A State savings association may obtain the standard flood hazard determination form from FEMA, P.O. Box 2012, Jessup, MD 20794–2012.

(b) *Retention of form.* A State savings association shall retain a copy of the completed standard flood hazard determination form, in either hard copy or electronic form, for the period of time the State savings association owns the loan.

§ 391.36 Forced placement of flood insurance.

If a State savings association, or a servicer acting on behalf of the State savings association, determines at any time during the term of a designated loan that the building or mobile home and any personal property securing the designated loan is not covered by flood insurance or is covered by flood insurance in an amount less than the amount required under § 391.32, then the State savings association or its servicer shall notify the borrower that the borrower should obtain flood insurance, at the borrower's expense, in an amount at least equal to the amount required under § 391.32, for the remaining term of the loan. If the borrower fails to obtain flood insurance within 45 days after notification, then the State savings association or its servicer shall purchase insurance on the borrower's behalf. The State savings association or its servicer may charge the borrower for the cost of premiums and fees incurred in purchasing the insurance.

§ 391.37 Determination fees.

(a) *General.* Notwithstanding any Federal or State law other than the Flood Disaster Protection Act of 1973, as amended (42 U.S.C. 4001–4129), any State savings association, or a servicer acting on behalf of the State savings association, may charge a reasonable fee for determining whether the building or mobile home securing the loan is located or will be located in a special flood hazard area. A determination fee

Federal Deposit Insurance Corporation § 391.38

may also include, but is not limited to, a fee for life-of-loan monitoring.

(b) *Borrower fee.* The determination fee authorized by paragraph (a) of this section may be charged to the borrower if the determination:

(1) Is made in connection with a making, increasing, extending, or renewing of the loan that is initiated by the borrower;

(2) Reflects the Director of FEMA's revision or updating of floodplain areas or flood-risk zones;

(3) Reflects the Director of FEMA's publication of a notice or compendium that:

(i) Affects the area in which the building or mobile home securing the loan is located; or

(ii) By determination of the Director of FEMA, may reasonably require a determination whether the building or mobile home securing the loan is located in a special flood hazard area; or

(4) Results in the purchase of flood insurance coverage by the lender or its servicer on behalf of the borrower under § 391.36.

(c) *Purchaser or transferee fee.* The determination fee authorized by paragraph (a) of this section may be charged to the purchaser or transferee of a loan in the case of the sale or transfer of the loan.

§ 391.38 Notice of special flood hazards and availability of Federal disaster relief assistance.

(a) *Notice requirement.* When a State savings association makes, increases, extends, or renews a loan secured by a building or a mobile home located or to be located in a special flood hazard area, the State savings association shall mail or deliver a written notice to the borrower and to the servicer in all cases whether or not flood insurance is available under the Act for the collateral securing the loan.

(b) *Contents of notice.* The written notice must include the following information:

(1) A warning, in a form approved by the Director of FEMA, that the building or the mobile home is or will be located in a special flood hazard area;

(2) A description of the flood insurance purchase requirements set forth in section 102(b) of the Flood Disaster Protection Act of 1973, as amended (42 U.S.C. 4012a(b));

(3) A statement, where applicable, that flood insurance coverage is available under the NFIP and may also be available from private insurers; and

(4) A statement whether Federal disaster relief assistance may be available in the event of damage to the building or mobile home caused by flooding in a Federally-declared disaster.

(c) *Timing of notice.* The State savings association shall provide the notice required by paragraph (a) of this section to the borrower within a reasonable time before the completion of the transaction, and to the servicer as promptly as practicable after the State savings association provides notice to the borrower and in any event no later than the State savings association provides other similar notices to the servicer concerning hazard insurance and taxes. Notice to the servicer may be made electronically or may take the form of a copy of the notice to the borrower.

(d) *Record of receipt.* The State savings association shall retain a record of the receipt of the notices by the borrower and the servicer for the period of time the State savings association owns the loan.

(e) *Alternate method of notice.* Instead of providing the notice to the borrower required by paragraph (a) of this section, a State savings association may obtain satisfactory written assurance from a seller or lessor that, within a reasonable time before the completion of the sale or lease transaction, the seller or lessor has provided such notice to the purchaser or lessee. The State savings association shall retain a record of the written assurance from the seller or lessor for the period of time the State savings association owns the loan.

(f) *Use of prescribed form of notice.* A State savings association will be considered to be in compliance with the requirement for notice to the borrower of this section by providing written notice to the borrower containing the language presented in appendix A to this subpart within a reasonable time

§ 391.39

before the completion of the transaction. The notice presented in appendix A to this subpart satisfies the borrower notice requirements of the Act.

§ 391.39 Notice of servicer's identity.

(a) *Notice requirement.* When a State savings association makes, increases, extends, renews, sells, or transfers a loan secured by a building or mobile home located or to be located in a special flood hazard area, the State savings association shall notify the Director of FEMA (or the Director's designee) in writing of the identity of the servicer of the loan. The Director of FEMA has designated the insurance provider to receive the State savings association's notice of the servicer's identity. This notice may be provided electronically if electronic transmission is satisfactory to the Director of FEMA's designee.

(b) *Transfer of servicing rights.* The State savings association shall notify the Director of FEMA (or the Director's designee) of any change in the servicer of a loan described in paragraph (a) of this section within 60 days after the effective date of the change. This notice may be provided electronically if electronic transmission is satisfactory to the Director of FEMA's designee. Upon any change in the servicing of a loan described in paragraph (a) of this section, the duty to provide notice under this paragraph (b) shall transfer to the transferee servicer.

APPENDIX TO SUBPART D OF PART 391—SAMPLE FORM OF NOTICE OF SPECIAL FLOOD HAZARDS AND AVAILABILITY OF FEDERAL DISASTER RELIEF ASSISTANCE

We are giving you this notice to inform you that:

(a) The building or mobile home securing the loan for which you have applied is or will be located in an area with special flood hazards.

(b) The area has been identified by the Director of the Federal Emergency Management Agency (FEMA) as a special flood hazard area using FEMA's *Flood Insurance Rate Map* or the *Flood Hazard Boundary Map* for the following community: ____. This area has at least a one percent (1%) chance of a flood equal to or exceeding the base flood elevation (a 100-year flood) in any given year. During the life of a 30-year mortgage loan the risk of a 100-year flood in a special flood hazard area is 26 percent (26%).

(c) Federal law allows a lender and borrower jointly to request the Director of FEMA to review the determination of whether the property securing the loan is located in a special flood hazard area. If you would like to make such a request, please contact us for further information.

(d) The community in which the property securing the loan is located participates in the National Flood Insurance Program (NFIP). Federal law will not allow us to make you the loan that you have applied for if you do not purchase flood insurance. The flood insurance must be maintained for the life of the loan. If you fail to purchase or renew flood insurance on the property, Federal law authorizes and requires us to purchase the flood insurance for you at your expense.

• Flood insurance coverage under the NFIP may be purchased through an insurance agent who will obtain the policy either directly through the NFIP or through an insurance company that participates in the NFIP. Flood insurance also may be available from private insurers that do not participate in the NFIP.

• At a minimum, flood insurance purchased must cover *the lesser of:*

(1) The outstanding principal balance of the loan; or

(2) The maximum amount of coverage allowed for the type of property under the NFIP.

(e) Flood insurance coverage under the NFIP is limited to the overall value of the property securing the loan minus the value of the land on which the property is located.

• Federal disaster relief assistance (usually in the form of a low-interest loan) may be available for damages incurred in excess of your flood insurance if your community's participation in the NFIP is in accordance with NFIP requirements.

(f) Flood insurance coverage under the NFIP is not available for the property securing the loan because the community in which the property is located does not participate in the NFIP. In addition, if the non-participating community has been identified for at least one year as containing a special flood hazard area, properties located in the community will not be eligible for Federal disaster relief assistance in the event of a Federally-declared flood disaster.

Subpart E—Acquisition of Control of State Savings Associations

§ 391.40 Scope of subpart.

The purpose of this subpart is to implement the provisions of the Change in Bank Control Act, 12 U.S.C. 1817 (j)

Federal Deposit Insurance Corporation

§ 391.41

("Control Act"), relating to acquisitions and changes in control of State savings associations that are organized in stock form.

§ 391.41 Definitions.

As used in this subpart and in the forms under this subpart, the following definitions apply, unless the context otherwise requires:

Acquire when used in connection with the acquisition of stock of a State savings association means obtaining ownership, control, power to vote, or sole power of disposition of stock, directly or indirectly or through one or more transactions or subsidiaries, through purchase, assignment, transfer, exchange, succession, or other means, including:

(1) An increase in percentage ownership resulting from a redemption, repurchase, reverse stock split or a similar transaction involving other securities of the same class, and

(2) The acquisition of stock by a group of persons and/or companies acting in concert which shall be deemed to occur upon formation of such group: *Provided,* That an investment advisor shall not be deemed to acquire the voting stock of its advisee if the advisor:

(i) Votes the stock only upon instruction from the beneficial owner, and

(ii) Does not provide the beneficial owner with advice concerning the voting of such stock.

Acquiror means a person or company.

Acting in concert means:

(1) Knowing participation in a joint activity or interdependent conscious parallel action towards a common goal whether or not pursuant to an express agreement, or

(2) A combination or pooling of voting or other interests in the securities of an issuer for a common purpose pursuant to any contract, understanding, relationship, agreement or other arrangement, whether written or otherwise.

(3) A person or company which acts in concert with another person or company ("other party") shall also be deemed to be acting in concert with any person or company who is also acting in concert with that other party, except that any tax-qualified employee stock benefit plan as defined in 12 CFR 192.25 will not be deemed to be acting in concert with its trustee or a person who serves in a similar capacity solely for the purpose of determining whether stock held by the trustee and stock held by the plan will be aggregated.

Affiliate means any person or company which controls, is controlled by or is under common control with a person, State savings association, or company.

Company means any corporation, partnership, trust, association, joint venture, pool, syndicate, unincorporated organization, joint-stock company or similar organization, as defined in the definition of *similar organization* in this section; but a company does not include:

(1) The FDIC or any Federal Home Loan Bank, or

(2) Any company the majority of shares of which is owned by:

(i) The United States or any State;

(ii) An officer of the United States or any State in his or her official capacity;

(iii) An instrumentality of the United States or any State; or

(iv) A savings and loan holding company registered under section 10(b) of the Home Owners' Loan Act.

Controlling shareholder means any person who directly or indirectly or acting in concert with one or more persons or companies, or together with members of his or her immediate family, owns, controls, or holds with power to vote 10 percent or more of the voting stock of a company or controls in any manner the election or appointment of a majority of the company's board of directors.

Immediate family means a person's spouse, father, mother, children, brothers, sisters and grandchildren; the father, mother, brothers, and sisters of the person's spouse; and the spouse of the person's child, brother or sister.

Management official means any president, chief executive officer, chief operating officer, vice president, director, partner, or trustee, or any other person who performs or has a representative or nominee performing similar policymaking functions, including executive officers of principal business units or divisions or subsidiaries who perform policymaking functions, for a State

§ 391.41

savings association or a company, whether or not incorporated.

Person means an individual or a group of individuals acting in concert who do not constitute a *company* as defined in this section.

Repealed Control Act means the Change in Savings and Loan Control Act, 12 U.S.C. 1730(q), as in effect immediately prior to its repeal by the Financial Institutions Reform, Recovery, and Enforcement Act of 1989.

Similar organization for purposes *company* as defined in this section means a combination of parties with the potential for or practical likelihood of continuing rather than temporary existence, where the parties thereto have knowingly and voluntarily associated for a common purpose pursuant to identifiable and binding relationships which govern the parties with respect to either:

(1) The transferability and voting of any stock or other indicia of participation in another entity, or

(2) Achievement of a common or shared objective, such as to collectively manage or control another entity.

State savings association means a state-chartered savings association, building and loan, savings and loan or homestead association or a cooperative bank (other than a cooperative bank described in 12 U.S.C. 1813(a)(2)) the deposits of which are insured by the FDIC, and any corporation (other than a bank) the deposits of which are insured by the FDIC that the FDIC determines to be operating in substantially the same manner as a State savings association.

Stock means common or preferred stock, general or limited partnership shares or interests, or similar interests.

Uninsured institution means any financial institution the deposits of which are not insured by the FDIC.

Voting stock means:

(1) Common or preferred stock, general or limited partnership shares or interests, or similar interests if the shares or interests, by statute, charter or in any manner, entitle the holder:

(i) To vote for or to select directors, trustees, or partners (or persons exercising similar functions of the issuing State savings association or company); or

(ii) To vote or to direct the conduct of the operations or other significant policies of the issuer.

(2) Notwithstanding anything in this definition, preferred stock, limited partnership shares or interests, or similar interests are not *voting stock* if:

(i) Voting rights associated with the stock, shares or interests are limited solely to the type customarily provided by statute with regard to matters that would significantly and adversely affect the rights or preference of the stock, security or other interest, such as the issuance of additional amounts or classes of senior securities, the modification of the terms of the stock, security or interest, the dissolution of the issuer, or the payment of dividends by the issuer when preferred dividends are in arrears;

(ii) The stock, shares or interests represent an essentially passive investment or financing device and do not otherwise provide the holder with control over the issuer; and

(iii) The stock, shares or interests do not at the time entitle the holder, by statute, charter, or otherwise, to select or to vote for the selection of directors, trustees, or partners (or persons exercising similar functions) of the issuer;

(3) Notwithstanding anything in this definition, *voting stock* shall be deemed to include stock and other securities that, upon transfer or otherwise, are convertible into voting stock or exercisable to acquire voting stock where the holder of the stock, convertible security or right to acquire voting stock has the preponderant economic risk in the underlying voting stock. Securities immediately convertible into voting stock at the option of the holder without payment of additional consideration shall be deemed to constitute the voting stock into which they are convertible; other convertible securities and rights to acquire voting stock shall not be deemed to vest the holder with the preponderant economic risk in the underlying voting stock if the holder has paid less than 50 percent of the consideration required to directly acquire the voting stock and has no other economic interest in the underlying

Federal Deposit Insurance Corporation

§ 391.42

voting stock. For purposes of calculating the percentage of voting stock held by a particular acquiror, stock or other securities convertible into voting stock or exercisable to acquire voting stock which are deemed voting stock under this paragraph (3) shall be included in calculating the amount of voting stock held by the acquiror and the total amount of stock outstanding only to the extent of the voting stock obtainable by such acquiror by such conversion or exercise of rights.

§ 391.42 Acquisition of control of State savings associations.

(a) [Reserved]

(b) *Acquisition by a person or company.* Unless a transaction is exempt from prior notice under paragraph (d) of this section, no person or company (other than certain persons affiliated with a savings and loan holding company who are subject to § 10(e)(4) of the Home Owners' Loan Act), shall acquire control, as defined in § 391.43 (a) and (b), of a State savings association until written notice has been provided to the FDIC and (1) the FDIC indicates in writing its intent not to disapprove the proposed acquisition or (2) 60 days (or such period of time as the FDIC may specify if the review period has been extended under § 391.45(c)(3)) have passed since receipt of a notice deemed sufficient under § 391.45(c)(2). Notwithstanding the forgoing, acquisitions by persons or companies by means of a merger with an interim association are not subject to this subpart, but shall be subject to approval under § 390.332, and either 12 CFR 152.13 or applicable state law.

(c) *Exempt transactions.* (1) [Reserved]

(2) The following transactions are exempt from the notice requirements of paragraph (b) of this section:

(i)(A) Control of a State savings association acquired by a bank holding company that is registered under and subject to, the Bank Holding Company Act of 1956, or any company controlled by such bank holding company;

(B) Control of a State savings association acquired solely as a result of a pledge or hypothecation of stock to secure a loan contracted for in good faith or the liquidation of a loan contracted for in good faith, in either case where such loan was made in the ordinary course of the business of the lender: *Provided, further,* That acquisition of control pursuant to such pledge, hypothecation or liquidation is reported to the FDIC within 30 days, and *Provided, further,* That the acquiror shall not retain such control for more than one year from the date on which such control was acquired; however, the FDIC may, upon application by an acquiror, extend such one-year period from year to year, for an additional period of time not exceeding three years, if the FDIC finds such extension is warranted and would not be detrimental to the public interest;

(C) Control of a State savings association acquired through a percentage increase in stock ownership following a *pro rata* stock dividend or stock split, if the proportional interests of the recipients remain substantially the same;

(D) Acquisition of additional stock after a non-disapproval under § 391.46, or any predecessor provision, has been received: *Provided,* That such acquisition is consistent with any conditions imposed in connection with such approval and with the representations made by the acquirer in its application;

(E) Acquisitions of up to twenty-five percent (25%) of a class of stock by a tax-qualified employee stock benefit plan as defined in 12 CFR 192.25; and

(ii) Transactions for which approval is required under the Home Owners' Loan Act;

(iii) Transactions for which approval is required under 12 CFR 152.13 and 390.332;

(iv) Transactions for which a change of control notice must be submitted to the Board of Governors of the Federal Reserve System pursuant to the Change in Bank Control Act, 12 U.S.C. 1817(j);

(v) Acquisition of additional stock of a State savings association by any person who:

(A) Has held power to vote 25 percent or more of any class of voting stock in such association continuously since March 9, 1979; or

(B) Has maintained control of the State savings association continuously since acquiring control in compliance with the Control Act (or the Repealed

§ 391.43

Control Act) and the regulations thereunder then in effect: *Provided,* That such acquisition is consistent with any conditions imposed in connection with such acquisition of control and with the representations made by the acquiror in its notice; and

(vi) [Reserved]

(3) An acquiror that would be considered to be in control of a State savings association pursuant to § 391.43 on December 26, 1985, shall not be subject to this § 391.42 unless the acquiror acquires additional stock of the State savings association or obtains a control factor with respect to such association after December 26, 1985: *Provided,* That an acquiror shall not be deemed to have acquired control of a State savings association on the basis of actions taken prior to December 26, 1985, or on the basis of actions taken after December 26, 1985, if such actions are pursuant to and consistent with a materially complete application under the Holding Company Act or notice under the Repealed Control Act filed prior to December 26, 1985, if such acquisition is made pursuant to an application approved under the Holding Company Act or a notice under the Repealed Control Act that was not disapproved.

(d) *Transactions exempt from prior approval or notice.* (1) Subject to the conditions set forth in paragraph (d)(2) of this section, the following transactions are exempt from prior approval and prior notice under § 391.42: *Provided,* That the timing of the transaction was not within the control of the acquiror.

(i) Control of a State savings association acquired through *bona fide* gift;

(ii) Control of a State savings association acquired through liquidation of a loan contracted in good faith where the loan was not made in the ordinary course of business of the lender;

(iii) Control of a State savings association acquired through a percentage increase in ownership following a stock split or redemption that was not *pro rata;*

(iv) Control determined pursuant to § 391.43 (a) or (b) as a result of actions by third parties that are not within the control of the acquiror;

(v) Control of a State savings association acquired through testate or intestate succession: *Provided,* That the acquiror transmits written notification of the acquisition to the FDIC within 60 days of the acquisition and provides such additional information as the FDIC may specifically request.

(2) The exemptions provided by paragraphs (d)(1)(i) through (d)(1)(iv) of this section are subject to the following conditions:

(i) The acquiror shall file a notice or rebuttal, as appropriate, with the FDIC within 90 days of acquisition of control;

(ii) The acquiror shall not take any action to direct the management or policies of the State savings association or which are designed to effect a change in the business plan of the State savings association other than voting on matters that may be presented to stockholders by management of the State savings association until the FDIC has acted favorably upon the acquiror's notice or rebuttal, and the FDIC may require that the acquiror take such steps as the FDIC deems necessary to insure that control is not exercised; and

(iii) If the FDIC disapproves the acquiror's notice or rebuttal, the acquiror shall divest such portion of the stock held by the acquiror so as to cause the acquiror not to be determined to be in control of the State savings association under § 391.43, within one year or such shorter period of time and in the manner that the FDIC may order.

§ 391.43 Control.

(a) *Conclusive control.* (1) An acquiror shall be deemed to have acquired control of a State savings association, other than a savings and loan holding company, if the acquiror directly or indirectly, through one or more subsidiaries or transactions or acting in concert with one or more persons or companies:

(i) Acquires 25 percent or more of any class of voting stock of the State savings association; or

(ii) Acquires irrevocable proxies representing 25 percent or more of any class of voting stock of the State savings association; or

(iii) Acquires any combination of voting stock and irrevocable proxies representing 25 percent or more of any

1012

Federal Deposit Insurance Corporation § 391.43

class of voting stock of a State savings association; or

(iv) [Reserved]

(2)—(3) [Reserved]

(4) A person or company shall be deemed to control a State savings association if the FDIC determines that such person has the power to direct the management or policies of the State savings association.

(b) *Rebuttable control determinations.* (1) An acquiror shall be determined, subject to rebuttal, to have acquired control of a State savings association, if the acquiror directly or indirectly, or through one or more subsidiaries or transactions or acting in concert with one or more persons or companies:

(i) Acquires more than 10 percent of any class of voting stock of the State savings association and is subject to any control factor, as defined in paragraph (c) of this section;

(ii) Acquires 25 percent or more of any class of stock of the State savings association and is subject to any control factor, as defined in paragraph (c) of this section.

(2) An acquiror shall be determined, subject to rebuttal, to have acquired control of a State savings association, if the acquiror directly or indirectly, or through one or more subsidiaries or transactions or acting in concert with one or more persons or companies, holds any combination of voting stock and revocable and/or irrevocable proxies, representing 25 percent or more of any class of voting stock of a State savings association, excluding such proxies held in connection with a solicitation by, or in opposition to, a solicitation on behalf of management of the State savings association, but including a solicitation in connection with an election of directors, and such proxies would enable the acquiror to:

(i) Elect one-third or more of the State savings association's board of directors, including nominees or representatives of the acquiror currently serving on such board;

(ii) Cause the State savings association's stockholders to approve the acquisition or corporate reorganization of the State savings association; or

(iii) Exert a continuing influence on a material aspect of the business operations of the State savings association.

(c) *Control factors.* For purposes of paragraph (b)(1) of this section, the following constitute control factors. References to the acquiror include actions taken directly or indirectly, or through one or more subsidiaries or transactions or acting in concert with one or more persons or companies:

(1) The acquiror would be one of the two largest holders of any class of voting stock of the State savings association.

(2) The acquiror would hold 25 percent or more of the total stockholders' equity of the State savings association.

(3) The acquiror would hold more than 35 percent of the combined debt securities and stockholders' equity of the State savings association.

(4) The acquiror is party to any agreement:

(i) Pursuant to which the acquiror possesses a material economic stake in the State savings association resulting from a profit-sharing arrangement, use of common names, facilities or personnel, or the provision of essential services to the State savings association; or

(ii) That enables the acquiror to influence a material aspect of the management or policies of the State savings association, other than agreements to which the State savings association is a party where the restrictions are customary under the circumstances and in the case of an acquisition agreement, which apply only during the period when the acquiror is seeking the FDIC's approval to acquire the State savings association, the agreement prohibits transactions between the acquiror and the State savings association and their respective affiliates without approval by the appropriate Regional Director during the pendency of the notice process, and the agreement contains no material forfeiture provisions applicable to the State savings association in the event the acquisition is not approved or not approved by a specified date.

(5) The acquiror would have the ability, other than through the holding of revocable proxies, to direct the votes of 25 percent or more of a class of the State savings association's voting stock or to vote 25 percent or more of

1013

§ 391.43

a class of the State savings association's voting stock in the future upon the occurrence of a future event.

(6) The acquiror would have the power to direct the disposition of 25 percent or more of a class of the State savings association's voting stock in a manner other than a widely dispersed or public offering.

(7) The acquiror and/or the acquiror's representatives or nominees would constitute more than one member of the State savings association's board of directors.

(8) The acquiror or a nominee or management official of the acquiror would serve as the chairman of the board of directors, chairman of the executive committee, chief executive officer, chief operating officer, chief financial officer or in any position with similar policymaking authority in the State savings association.

(d) *Rebuttable presumptions of concerted action.* An acquiror will be presumed to be acting in concert with the following persons and companies:

(1) A company will be presumed to be acting in concert with a controlling shareholder, partner, trustee or management official of such company with respect to the acquisition of stock of a State savings association, if

(i) Both the company and the person own stock in the State savings association,

(ii) The company provides credit to the person to purchase the State savings association's stock, or

(iii) The company pledges its assets or otherwise is instrumental in obtaining financing for the person to acquire stock of the State savings association;

(2) A person will be presumed to be acting in concert with members of the person's immediate family;

(3) Persons will be presumed to be acting in concert with each other where

(i) Both own stock in a State savings association and both are also management officials, controlling shareholders, partners, or trustees of another company, or

(ii) One person provides credit to another person or is instrumental in obtaining financing for another person to purchase stock of the State savings association;

(4) A company controlling or controlled by another company and companies under common control will be presumed to be acting in concert;

(5) Persons or companies will be presumed to be acting in concert where they constitute a group under the beneficial ownership reporting rules under section 13 or the proxy rules under section 14 of the Securities Exchange Act of 1934, promulgated by the Securities and Exchange Commission.

(6) A person or company will be presumed to be acting in concert with any trust for which such person or company serves as trustee, except that a tax-qualified employee stock benefit plan as defined in 12 CFR 192.25 shall not be presumed to be acting in concert with its trustee or person acting in a similar fiduciary capacity solely for the purposes of determining whether to combine the holdings of a plan and its trustee or fiduciary.

(7) Persons or companies will be presumed to be acting in concert with each other and with any other person or company with which they also are presumed to act in concert.

(e) *Procedures for rebuttal*—(1) *Rebuttal of control determination.* An acquiror attempting to rebut a determination of control that would arise under paragraph (b) of this section shall file a submission with the FDIC setting forth the facts and circumstances which support the acquiror's contention that no control relationship would exist if the acquiror acquires stock or obtains a control factor with respect to a State savings association. The rebuttal must be filed and accepted in accordance with this section before the acquiror acquires such stock or control factor.

(i) An acquiror seeking to rebut the determination of control arising under paragraph (b)(1) of this section shall submit to the FDIC an executed agreement materially conforming to the agreement set forth at § 391.48. Unless agreed to by the FDIC in writing, no other agreement or filing shall be deemed to rebut the determination of control arising under paragraph (b)(1) of this section. If accepted by the FDIC the acquiror shall furnish a copy of the executed agreement to the association to which the rebuttal pertains.

Federal Deposit Insurance Corporation

§ 391.43

(ii) An acquiror seeking to rebut the determination of control with respect to holding of proxies arising under paragraph (b)(2) of this section shall be subject to the requirements of paragraph (e)(1) of this section, except that in the case of a rebuttal of the presumption of control arising under paragraph (b)(2) of this section, the FDIC may require the acquiror to furnish information in response to a specific request for information and depending upon the particular facts and circumstances, to provide an executed rebuttal agreement materially conforming to the agreement set forth at § 391.48, with any modifications deemed necessary by the FDIC.

(2) *Presumptions of concerted action.* An acquiror attempting to rebut the presumption of concerted action arising under paragraph (d) of this section shall file a submission with the FDIC setting forth facts and circumstances which clearly and convincingly demonstrate the acquiror's contention that no action in concert exists. Such a statement must be accompanied by an affidavit, in form and content satisfactory to the FDIC, executed by each person or company presumed to be acting in concert, stating that such person or company does not and shall not, without having made necessary filings and obtained approval or clearance thereof under the Holding Company Act or the Control Act, as applicable, have any agreements or understandings, written or tacit, with respect to the exercise of control, directly or indirectly, over the management or policies of the State savings association, including agreements relating to voting, acquisition or disposition of the State savings association's stock. The affidavit shall also recite that the signatory is aware that the filing of a false affidavit may subject the person or company to criminal sanctions, would constitute a violation of the FDIC's regulations at § 390.355(b) and would be considered a "presumptive disqualifier" under 12 CFR 391.46(g)(1)(v).

(3) *Determination.* A rebuttal filed pursuant to paragraph (e) of this section shall not be deemed sufficient unless it includes all the information, agreements, and affidavits required by the FDIC and this subpart, as well as any additional relevant information as the FDIC may require by written request to the acquiror. Within 20 calendar days after proper filing of a rebuttal submission, the FDIC will provide written notification of its determination to accept or reject the submission; request additional information in connection with the submission; or return the submission to the acquiror as materially deficient. Within 15 calendar days after proper filing of any additional information furnished in response to a specific request by the FDIC, the FDIC shall notify the acquiror in writing as to whether the rebuttal is thereby deemed to be sufficient. If the FDIC fails to notify an acquiror within such time, the rebuttal shall be deemed to be accepted. The FDIC may reject any rebuttal which is inconsistent with facts and circumstances known to it or where the rebuttal does not clearly and convincingly refute the rebuttable determination of control or presumption of action in concert, and may determine to reject a submission solely on such bases.

(f) *Safe harbor.* Notwithstanding any other provision of this section, where an acquiror has no intention to participate in or to seek to exercise control over a State savings association's management or policies, the acquiror may seek to qualify for a safe harbor with respect to its ownership of stock of a State savings association.

(1) In order to qualify for the safe harbor, an acquiror must submit a certification to the FDIC that shall be signed by the acquiror or an authorized representative thereof and shall read as follows:

The undersigned makes this submission pursuant to § 391.43(f) with respect to [name of State savings association] and hereby certifies to the FDIC the following:

The undersigned is not in control of [name of State savings association] under § 391.43(a);

The undersigned is not subject to any control factor as enumerated in § 391.43(c) with respect to the [name of State savings association];

The undersigned will not solicit proxies relating to the voting stock of [name of State savings association];

Before any change in status occurs that would bring the undersigned within the scope of § 391.43(a) or (b), the undersigned will

1015

§ 391.44

file and obtain approval of a rebuttal, or non-disapproval of a notice, or holding company application, as appropriate.

The undersigned has not acquired stock of [name of State savings association] for the purpose or effect of changing or influencing the control of [name of State savings association] or in connection with or as a participant in any transaction having such purpose or effect.

(2) An acquiror claiming safe-harbor status may vote freely and dissent with respect to its own stock. Certifications provided for in this paragraph must be filed with FDIC in accordance with §§ 390.106 and 390.108.

§ 391.44 Certifications of ownership.

(a) *Acquisition of stock.* (1) Upon the acquisition of beneficial ownership that exceeds, in the aggregate, 10 percent of any class of stock of a State savings association or additional stock above 10 percent of the stock of a State savings association occurring after December 26, 1985, an acquiror shall file with the FDIC a certification as described in this section.

(2) The certification filed pursuant to this section shall be signed by the acquiror or an authorized representative thereof and shall read as follows:

The undersigned is the beneficial owner of 10 percent or more of a class of stock of [name of State savings association]. The undersigned is not in control of such association, as defined in 12 CFR 391.43(a), and is not subject to a rebuttable determination of control under § 391.43(b), and will take no action that would result in a determination of control or a rebuttable determination of control without first filing and obtaining approval of an application under the Savings and Loan Holding Company Act, 12 U.S.C. 1467a, or a notice under the Change in Bank Control Act, 12 U.S.C. 1817(j), or filing and obtaining acceptance by the FDIC of a rebuttal of the rebuttable determination of control.

(3) Notwithstanding anything contained in this paragraph (a), an acquiror is not required to file a certification if—

(i) The FDIC has issued a notice of non-disapproval of the acquisition of the State savings association; or

(ii) The acquiror has filed a materially complete notice pursuant to § 391.42.

(b) *Privacy.* All certifications filed under this § 391.44 shall be for the information of the FDIC in connection with its examination functions and shall be provided confidential treatment by the FDIC.

§ 391.45 Procedural requirements.

(a) *Form of application or notice.* A notice required by § 391.42 shall be filed on the form indicated below. An acquiror may request confidential treatment of portions of a notice only by complying with the requirements of paragraph (f) of this section.

(a)(1)—(5) [Reserved]

(6) *Notice Form 1393, parts A and B.* This form shall be used for all notices filed under § 391.42(b) regarding the acquisition of control of a State savings association by any person or persons not constituting a company.

(b) *Filing requirements*—(1) *Notices and rebuttals.* (i) Complete copies including exhibits and all other pertinent documents of notices, and rebuttal submissions shall be filed with the appropriate Regional Director in the region in which the State savings association or associations involved in the transaction have their home office or offices. Unsigned copies shall be conformed. Each copy shall include a summary of the proposed transaction.

(ii) Any person or company may amend a notice or rebuttal submission, or file additional information, upon request of the FDIC or, in the case of the party filing a notice or rebuttal, upon such party's own initiative.

(2) [Reserved]

(c) *Sufficiency and waiver.* (1) Except as provided in § 391.45(c)(5), a notice filed pursuant to § 391.42(b) shall not be deemed sufficient unless it includes all of the information required by the form prescribed by the FDIC and this section, including a complete description of the acquiror's proposed plan for acquisition of control whether pursuant to one or more transactions, and any additional relevant information as the FDIC may require by written request to the acquiror. Unless a notice specifically indicates otherwise, the notice shall be considered to pertain to acquisition of 100 percent of a State savings association's voting stock. Where a notice pertains to a lesser amount of stock, the FDIC may condition its non-disapproval to apply only to such amount, in which case additional acquisitions may be made only

Federal Deposit Insurance Corporation

§ 391.45

by amendment to the acquiror's notice and the FDIC's approval or non-disapproval thereof. Failure by an applicant to respond completely to a written request by the FDIC for additional information within 30 calendar days of the date of such request may be deemed to constitute withdrawal of the notice or rebuttal filing or may be treated as grounds for issuance of a notice of disapproval of a notice or rejection of a rebuttal.

(2) The period for the FDIC's review of any proposed acquisition will commence upon receipt by the FDIC of a notice deemed sufficient under paragraph (c)(1) of this section. The FDIC shall notify an acquiror in writing within 30 calendar days after proper filing of a notice as to whether the notice—

(i) Is sufficient;

(ii) Is insufficient, and what additional information is requested in order to render the application or notice sufficient; or

(iii) Is materially deficient and will not be processed. The FDIC shall also notify an acquiror in writing within 15 calendar days after proper filing of any additional information furnished in response to a specific request by the FDIC as to whether the notice is thereby deemed to be sufficient. If the FDIC fails to so notify an acquiror within such time, the application or notice shall be deemed to be sufficient as of the expiration of the applicable period.

(3) After additional information has been requested and supplied, the FDIC may request additional information only with respect to matters derived from or prompted by information already furnished, or information of a material nature that was not reasonably available from the acquiror, was concealed, or pertains to developments subsequent to the time of the FDIC's initial request for additional information. With regard to information of a material nature that was not reasonably available from the acquiror or was concealed at the time a notice was deemed to be sufficient or which pertains to developments subsequent to the time a notice was deemed to be sufficient, the FDIC, at its option, may request such additional information as it considers necessary, or may deem the notice not to be sufficient until such additional information is furnished and cause the review period to commence again in its entirety upon receipt of such additional information.

(i) The 60-day period for the FDIC's review of a notice deemed to be sufficient also may be extended by the FDIC for up to an additional 30 days.

(ii) The period for the FDIC's review of a notice may be further extended not to exceed two additional times for not more than 45 days each time if—

(A) The FDIC determines that any acquiring party has not furnished all the information required under this subpart;

(B) In the FDIC's judgment, any material information submitted is substantially inaccurate;

(C) The FDIC has been unable to complete an investigation of each acquiror because of any delay caused by, or the inadequate cooperation of, such acquiror; or

(D) The FDIC determines that additional time is needed to investigate and determine that no acquiring party has a record of failing to comply with the requirements of subchapter II of chapter 53 of title 31 of the United States Code.

(4) [Reserved]

(5) The FDIC may waive any requirements of this paragraph (c) determined to be unnecessary by the FDIC, upon its own initiative, upon the written request of an acquiring person, or in a supervisory case.

(d) *Public notice.* (1) The acquiror must publish a public notice of a notice under § 391.42(b), in accordance with the procedures in §§ 390.111 through 390.115. Promptly after publication, the acquiror must transmit copies of the public notice and the publisher's affidavit to FDIC.

(2) The acquiror must provide a copy of the public notice to the State savings association whose stock is sought to be acquired, and may provide a copy of the public notice to any other person who may have an interest in the notice.

(3) The FDIC will notify the appropriate state supervisor and will notify persons whose requests for announcements, as described in 12 CFR 163e, appendix B, have been received in time

§ 391.45

for the notification. The FDIC may also notify any other persons who may have an interest in the notice.

(e) *Submission of comments.* Commenters may submit comments on the notice in accordance with the procedures in §§ 390.116 through 390.120.

(f) *Disclosure.* (1) Any notice, other filings, public comment, or portion thereof, made pursuant to this subpart for which confidential treatment is not requested in accordance with this paragraph (f), shall be immediately available to the public and not subject to the procedures set forth herein. Public disclosure shall be made of other portions of a notice, other filing or public comment in accordance with paragraph (f)(2) of this section, the provisions of the Freedom of Information Act (5 U.S.C. 552a) and parts 309 and 310. Applicants and other submitters should provide confidential and non-confidential versions of their filings, as described in § 391.45(f)(2) and (3) in order to facilitate this process.

(2) Any person who submits any information or causes or permits any information to be submitted to the FDIC pursuant to this subpart may request that the FDIC afford confidential treatment under the Freedom of Information Act to such information for reasons of personal privacy or business confidentiality, which shall include such information that would be deemed to result in the commencement of a tender offer under § 240.14d–2 of title 17 of the Code of Federal Regulations, or for any other reason permitted by Federal law. Such request for confidentiality must be made and justified in accordance with paragraph (f)(5) of this section at the time of filing, and must, to the extent practicable, identify with specificity the information for which confidential treatment may be available and not merely indicate portions of documents or entire documents in which such information is contained. Failure to specifically identify information for which confidential treatment is requested, failure to specifically justify the bases upon which confidentiality is claimed in accordance with paragraph (f)(5) of this section, or overbroad and indiscriminate claims for confidential treatment, may be bases for denial of the request. In addition, the filing party should take all steps reasonably necessary to ensure, as nearly as practicable, that at the time the information is first received by the FDIC it is supplied segregated from information for which confidential treatment is not being requested, it is appropriately marked as confidential, and it is accompanied by a written request for confidential treatment which identifies with specificity the information as to which confidential treatment is requested. Any such request must be substantiated in accordance with paragraph (f)(5) of this section.

(3) All documents which contain information for which a request for confidential treatment is made or the appropriate segregable portions thereof shall be marked by the person submitting the records with a prominent stamp, typed legend, or other suitable form of notice on each page or segregable portion of each page, stating "Confidential Treatment Requested by [name]." If such marking is impracticable under the circumstances, a cover sheet prominently marked "Confidential Treatment Requested by [name]" should be securely attached to each group of records submitted for which confidential treatment is requested. Each of the records transmitted in this manner should be individually marked with an identifying number and code so that they are separately identifiable.

(4) A determination as to the validity of any request for confidential treatment may be made when a request for disclosure of the information under the Freedom of Information Act is received, or at any time prior thereto. If the FDIC receives a request for the information under the Freedom of Information Act, FDIC will advise the filing party before it discloses material for which confidential treatment has been requested.

(5) Substantiation of a request for confidential treatment shall consist of a statement setting forth, to the extent appropriate or necessary for the determination of the request for confidential treatment, the following information regarding the request:

(i) The reasons, concisely stated and referring to specific exemptive provisions of the Freedom of Information

Federal Deposit Insurance Corporation § 391.46

Act, why the information should be withheld from access under the Freedom of Information Act;

(ii) The applicability of any specific statutory or regulatory provisions which govern or may govern the treatment of the information;

(iii) The existence and applicability of any prior determination by the FDIC, other Federal agencies, or a court, concerning confidential treatment of the information;

(iv) The adverse consequences to a business enterprise, financial or otherwise, that would result from disclosure of confidential commercial or financial information, including any adverse effect on the business' competitive position;

(v) The measures taken by the business to protect the confidentiality of the commercial or financial information in question and of similar information, prior to, and after, its submission to the FDIC;

(vi) The ease or difficulty of a competitor's obtaining or compiling the commercial or financial information;

(vii) Whether commercial or financial information was voluntarily submitted to the FDIC, and, if so, whether and how disclosure of the information would tend to impede the availability of similar information to the FDIC;

(viii) The extent, if any, to which portions of the substantiation of the request for confidential treatment should be afforded confidential treatment;

(ix) The amount of time after the consummation of the proposed acquisition for which the information should remain confidential and a justification thereof;

(x) Such additional facts and such legal and other authorities as the requesting person may consider appropriate.

(6) Any person requesting access to a notice, other filing, or public comment made pursuant to this subpart for purposes of commenting on a pending submission may prominently label such request: "Request for Disclosure of Filing(s) Made Under Subpart E of Part 391/Priority Treatment Requested."

(g) *Supervisory cases.* The provisions of paragraphs (d), (e), and (f) of this section may be waived by the FDIC in connection with a transaction approved by the FDIC for supervisory reasons.

(h) *Notification of State supervisor.* Upon receiving a notice relating to an acquisition of control of a State savings association, the FDIC shall forward a copy of the notice to the appropriate state savings and loan association supervisory agency, and shall allow 30 days within which the views and recommendations of such state supervisory agency may be submitted. The FDIC shall give due consideration to the views and recommendations of such state agency in determining whether to disapprove any proposed acquisition. Notwithstanding the provisions of this paragraph (h), if the FDIC determines that it must act immediately upon any notice of a proposed acquisition in order to prevent the default of the association involved in the proposed acquisition, the FDIC may dispense with the requirement of this paragraph (h) or, if a copy of the notice is forwarded to the state supervisory agency, the FDIC may request that the views and recommendations of such state supervisory agency be submitted immediately in any form or by any means acceptable to the FDIC.

(i) *Additional procedures for acquisitions involving mergers.* Acquisitions of control involving mergers (including mergers with an interim association) shall also be subject to the procedures set forth in § 390.332 to the extent applicable, except as provided in paragraph (a) of this section.

(j) *Additional procedures for acquisitions of recently converted State savings associations.* Notices and rebuttals involving acquisitions of the stock of a recently converted State savings association under 12 CFR 192.3(i)(3) shall also address the criteria for approval set forth at 12 CFR 192.3(i)(5).

§ 391.46 Determination by the FDIC.

(a)—(c) [Reserved]

(d) *Notice criteria.* In making its determination whether to disapprove a notice, the FDIC may disapprove any proposed acquisition, if the FDIC determines that:

(1) The proposed acquisition of control would result in a monopoly or

§ 391.46

would be in furtherance of any combination or conspiracy to monopolize or to attempt to monopolize the banking business in any part of the United States;

(2) The effect of the proposed acquisition of control in any section of the country may be substantially to lessen competition or to tend to create a monopoly or the proposed acquisition of control would in any other manner be in restraint of trade, and the anticompetitive effects of the proposed acquisition of control are not clearly outweighed in the public interest by the probable effect of the transaction in meeting the convenience and needs of the community to be served;

(3) The financial condition of the acquiring person is such as might jeopardize the financial stability of the association or prejudice the interests of the depositors of the State savings association;

(4) The competence, experience, or integrity of the acquiring person or any of the proposed management personnel indicates that it would not be in the interests of the depositors of the State savings association, the FDIC, or the public to permit such person to control the State savings association;

(5) The acquiring person fails or refuses to furnish information requested by the FDIC; or

(6) The FDIC determines that the proposed acquisition would have an adverse effect on the Deposit Insurance Fund.

(e) *Failure to disapprove a notice.* If, upon expiration of the 60-day review period of any notice deemed to be sufficient filed pursuant to § 391.45(c), or extension thereof, the FDIC has failed to disapprove such notice, the proposed acquisition may take place: *Provided,* That it is consummated within one year and in accordance with the terms and representations in the notice and that there is no material change in circumstances prior to the acquisition.

(f) [Reserved]

(g) *Presumptive disqualifiers* —(1) *Integrity factors.* The following factors shall give rise to a rebuttable presumption that an acquiror may fail to satisfy the integrity test of paragraph (d)(4) of this section:

(i) During the 10-year period immediately preceding filing the notice, criminal, civil or administrative judgments, consents or orders, and any indictments, formal investigations, examinations, or civil or administrative proceedings (excluding routine or customary audits, inspections and investigations) that terminated in any agreements, undertakings, consents or orders, issued against, entered into by, or involving the acquiror or affiliates of the acquiror by any federal or state court, any department, agency, or commission of the U.S. Government, any state or municipality, any Federal Home Loan Bank, any self-regulatory trade or professional organization, or any foreign government or governmental entity, which involve:

(A) Fraud, moral turpitude, dishonesty, breach of trust or fiduciary duties, organized crime or racketeering;

(B) Violation of securities or commodities laws or regulations;

(C) Violation of depository institution laws or regulations;

(D) Violation of housing authority laws or regulations; or

(E) Violation of the rules, regulations, codes of conduct or ethics of a self-regulatory trade or professional organization;

(ii) Denial, or withdrawal after receipt of formal or informal notice of an intent to deny, by the acquiror or affiliates of the acquiror, of

(A) Any application relating to the organization of a financial institution,

(B) An application to acquire any financial institution or holding company thereof under the Holding Company Act or the Bank Holding Company Act or otherwise,

(C) A notice relating to a change in control of any of the foregoing under the Control Act or the Repealed Control Act; or

(D) An application or notice under a state holding company or change in control statute;

(iii) The acquiror or affiliates of the acquiror were placed in receivership or conservatorship during the preceding 10 years, or any management official of the acquiror was a management official or director (other than an official or director serving at the request of the FDIC, the former Resolution Trust

Federal Deposit Insurance Corporation § 391.48

Corporation, or the former Federal Savings and Loan Insurance Corporation) or controlling shareholder of a company or savings association that was placed into receivership, conservatorship, or a management consignment program, or was liquidated during his or her tenure or control or within two years thereafter;

(iv) Felony conviction of the acquiror, an affiliate of the acquiror or a management official of the acquiror or an affiliate of the acquiror;

(v) Knowingly making any written or oral statement to the FDIC or any predecessor agency (or its delegate) in connection with a notice or other filing under this subpart that is false or misleading with respect to a material fact or omits to state a material fact with respect to information furnished or requested in connection with such notice or other filing;

(vi) Acquisition and retention at the time of submission of a notice, of stock in the State savings association by the acquiror in violation of § 391.42 or its predecessor sections.

(2) *Financial factors.* The following shall give rise to a rebuttable presumption that an acquiror may fail to satisfy the financial condition test of paragraph (d)(3) of this section:

(i) Liability for amounts of debt which, in the opinion of the FDIC, create excessive risks of default and pressure on the State savings association to be acquired; or

(ii) Failure to furnish a business plan or furnishing a business plan projecting activities which are inconsistent with economical home financing.

§ 391.47 [Reserved]

§ 391.48 Rebuttal of control agreement.

Agreement
Rebuttal of Rebuttable Determination Of Control Under Subpart A

I. WHEREAS

A. [ ] is the owner of [ ] shares (the "Shares") of the [ ] stock (the "Stock") of [name and address of State savings association], which Shares represent [ ] percent of a class of "voting stock" of [ ] as defined under the Acquisition of Control Regulations ("Regulations") of the FDIC, Subpart A of Part 391 ("Voting Stock");

B. [ ] is a "State savings association" within the meaning of the Regulations;

C. [ ] seeks to acquire additional shares of stock of [ ] ("Additional Shares"), such that [ ]'s ownership thereof will represent 10 percent or more of a class of Voting Stock but will not represent 25 percent or more of any class of Voting Stock of [ ]; [and/or] [ ] seeks to [ ], which would constitute the acquisition of a "control factor" as defined in the Regulations ("Control Factor");

D. [ ] does not seek to acquire the [Additional Shares or Control Factor] for the purpose or effect of changing the control of [ ] or in connection with or as a participant in any transaction having such purpose or effect;

E. The Regulations require a company or a person who intends to hold 10 percent or more but not 25 percent or more of any class of Voting Stock of a State savings association or holding company thereof and that also would possess any of the Control Factors specified in the Regulations, to file and obtain clearance of a notice ("Notice") under the Change in Control Act ("Control Act"), 12 U.S.C. 1817(j), prior to acquiring such amount of stock and a Control Factor unless the rebuttable determination of control has been rebutted.

F. Under the Regulations, [ ] would be determined to be in control, subject to rebuttal, of [ ] upon acquisition of the [Additional Shares or Control Factor];

G. [ ] has no intention to manage or control, directly or indirectly, [ ];

H. [ ] has filed on [ ], a written statement seeking to rebut the determination of control, attached hereto and incorporated by reference herein, (this submission referred to as the "Rebuttal");

I. In order to rebut the rebuttable determination of control, [ ] agrees to offer this Agreement as evidence that the acquisition of the [Additional Shares or Control Factor] as proposed would not constitute an acquisition of control under the Regulations.

II. The FDIC has determined, and hereby agrees, to act favorably on the Rebuttal, and in consideration of such a determination and agreement by the FDIC to act favorably on the Rebuttal, [ ] and any other existing, resulting or successor entities of [ ] agree with the FDIC that:

A. Unless [ ] shall have filed a Notice under the Control Act, or an Application under the Holding Company Act, as appropriate, and shall have obtained clearance of the Notice in accordance with the Regulations, [ ] will not, except as expressly permitted otherwise herein or pursuant to an amendment to this Rebuttal Agreement:

1. Seek or accept representation of more than one member of the board of directors of [insert name of State savings association and any holding company thereof];

2. Have or seek to have any representative serve as the chairman of the board of directors, or chairman of an executive or similar

1021

§ 391.48

committee of [insert name of State savings association and any holding company thereof]'s board of directors or as president or chief executive officer of [insert name of State savings association and any holding company thereof];

3. Engage in any intercompany transaction with [ ] or [ ]'s affiliates;

4. Propose a director in opposition to nominees proposed by the management of [insert name of State savings association and any holding company thereof] for the board of directors of [insert name of State savings association and any holding company thereof] other than as permitted in paragraph A–1;

5. Solicit proxies or participate in any solicitation of proxies with respect to any matter presented to the stockholders [ ] other than in support of, or in opposition to, a solicitation conducted on behalf of management of [ ];

6. Do any of the following, except as necessary solely in connection with [ ]'s performance of duties as a member of [ ]'s board of directors:

(a) Influence or attempt to influence in any respect the loan and credit decisions or policies of [ ], the pricing of services, any personnel decisions, the location of any offices, branching, the hours of operation or similar activities of [ ];

(b) Influence or attempt to influence the dividend policies and practices of [ ] or any decisions or policies of [ ] as to the offering or exchange of any securities;

(c) Seek to amend, or otherwise take action to change, the bylaws, articles of incorporation, or charter of [ ];

(d) Exercise, or attempt to exercise, directly or indirectly, control or a controlling influence over the management, policies or business operations of [ ]; or

(e) Seek or accept access to any non-public information concerning [ ].

B. [ ] is not a party to any agreement with [ ].

C. [ ]shall not assist, aid or abet any of [ ]'s affiliates or associates that are not parties to this Agreement to act, or act in concert with any person or company, in a manner which is inconsistent with the terms hereof or which constitutes an attempt to evade the requirements of this Agreement.

D. Any amendment to this Agreement shall only be proposed in connection with an amended rebuttal filed by [ ] with the FDIC for its determination;

E. Prior to acquisition of any shares of "Voting Stock" of [ ] as defined in the Regulations in excess of the Additional Shares, any required filing will be made by [ ] under the Control Act or the Holding Company Act and either approval of the acquisition under the Holding Company Act shall be obtained or any Notice filed under the Control Act shall be cleared in accordance with the Regulations;

F. At any time during which 10 percent or more of any class of Voting Stock of [ ] is owned or controlled by [ ], no action which is inconsistent with the provisions of this Agreement shall be taken by [ ] until [ ] files and either obtains from the FDIC a favorable determination with respect to either an amended rebuttal or clearance of a Notice under the Control Act, in accordance with the Regulations;

G. Where any amended rebuttal filed by[ ] is denied or disapproved, [ ] shall take no action which is inconsistent with the terms of this Agreement, except after either (1) reducing the amount of shares of Voting Stock of [ ] owned or controlled by [ ] to an amount under 10 percent of a class of Voting Stock, or immediately ceasing any other actions that give rise to a conclusive or rebuttable determination of control under the Regulations; or (2) filing a Notice under the Control Act, or an Application under the Holding Company Act, as appropriate, and either obtaining approval of the Application or clearance of the Notice, in accordance with the Regulations;

H. Where any Notice filed by [ ] is disapproved, [ ] shall take no action which is inconsistent with the terms of this Agreement, except after reducing the amount of shares of Voting Stock of [ ] owned or controlled by [ ] to an amount under 10 percent of any class of Voting Stock, or immediately ceasing any other actions that give rise to a conclusive or rebuttable determination of control under the Regulations;

I. Should circumstances beyond [ ]'s control result in [ ] being placed in a position to direct the management or policies of [ ], then [ ] shall either (1) promptly file a Notice under the Control Act or an Application under the Holding Company Act, as appropriate, and take no affirmative steps to enlarge that control pending either a final determination with respect to the Application or Notice, or (2) promptly reduce the amount of shares of [ ] Voting Stock owned or controlled by [ ] to an amount under 10 percent of any class of Voting Stock or immediately cease any actions that give rise to a conclusive or rebuttable determination of control under the Regulations;

J. By entering into this Agreement and by offering it for reliance in reaching a decision on the request to rebut the presumption of control under the Regulations, as long as 10 percent or more of any class of Voting Stock of [ ] is owned or controlled, directly or indirectly, by [ ], and [ ] possesses any Control Factor as defined in the Regulations, [ ] will submit to the jurisdiction of the Regulations, including (1) the filing of an amended rebuttal or Notice for any proposed action which is prohibited by this Agreement, and (2) the provisions relating to a penalty for any person who willfully violates or with

Federal Deposit Insurance Corporation

§ 391.48

reckless disregard for the safety or soundness of a State savings association participates in a violation of the Control Act and the Regulations thereunder, and any regulation or order issued by the FDIC.

K. Any violation of this Agreement shall be deemed to be a violation of the [Control Act or Holding Company Act] and the Regulations, and shall be subject to such remedies and procedures as are provided in the [Control Act or Holding Company Act] and the Regulations for a violation thereunder and in addition shall be subject to any such additional remedies and procedures as are provided under any other applicable statutes or regulations for a violation, willful or otherwise, of any agreement entered into with the FDIC.

III. This Agreement may be executed in one or more counterparts, each of which shall be deemed an original but all of which counterparts collectively shall constitute one instrument representing the Agreement among the parties thereto. It shall not be necessary that any one counterpart be signed by all of the parties hereto as long as each of the parties has signed at least one counterpart.

IV. This Agreement shall be interpreted in a manner consistent with the provisions of the Rules and Regulations of the FDIC.

V. This Agreement shall terminate upon (i) clearance by the FDIC of [ ]'s Notice under the Control Act to acquire [ ], and consummation of the transaction as described in Notice, (ii) in the disposition by [ ] of a sufficient number of shares of [ ], or (iii) the taking of such other action that thereafter [ ] is not in control and would not be determined to be in control of [ ] under the Control Act or the Regulations of the FDIC as in effect at that time.

VI. *In Witness Thereof*, the parties thereto have executed this Agreement by their duly authorized officer.

[Acquiror]

Federal Deposit Insurance Corporation.

CHAPTER IV—EXPORT-IMPORT BANK OF THE UNITED STATES

Part		Page
400	Employee financial disclosure and ethical conduct standards regulations	1025
403	Classification, declassification, and safeguarding of national security information	1025
404	Information disclosure	1036
405	[Reserved]	
407	Regulations governing public observation of Eximbank meetings	1052
408	Procedures for compliance with the National Environmental Policy Act	1056
410	Enforcement of nondiscrimination on the basis of handicap in programs or activities conducted by Export-Import Bank of the United States	1058
411	New restrictions on lobbying	1064
412	Acceptance of payment from a non-Federal source for travel expenses	1075
414	Conference and other fees	1077
415–499	[Reserved]	

PART 400—EMPLOYEE FINANCIAL DISCLOSURE AND ETHICAL CONDUCT STANDARDS REGULATIONS

AUTHORITY: 5 U.S.C. 7301.

§ 400.101 Cross-reference to employee financial disclosure and ethical conduct standards regulations.

Employees of the Export-Import Bank of the United States (Bank) should refer to:
(a) The executive branch-wide financial disclosure regulations at 5 CFR part 2634;
(b) The executive branch-wide Standards of Ethical Conduct at 5 CFR part 2635; and
(c) The Bank regulations at 5 CFR part 6201 which supplement the executive branch-wide standards.

[60 FR 17628, Apr. 7, 1995]

PART 403—CLASSIFICATION, DECLASSIFICATION, AND SAFEGUARDING OF NATIONAL SECURITY INFORMATION

Sec.
403.1 General policies and definitions.
403.2 Responsibilities.
403.3 Classification principles and authority.
403.4 Derivative classification.
403.5 Declassification and downgrading.
403.6 Systematic review for declassification.
403.7 Mandatory review for declassification.
403.8 Appeals.
403.9 Fees.
403.10 Safeguarding.
403.11 Enforcement and investigation procedures.

AUTHORITY: E.O. 12356, National Security Information, April 2, 1982 (3 CFR, 1982 Comp. p. 166) (hereafter referred to as the *Order*), Information Security Oversight Directive No. 1, June 25, 1982 (32 CFR part 2001) (hereafter referred to as the *Directive*), and National Security Decision Directive 84, "Safeguarding National SecurityInformation," signed by the President on March 11, 1983 (hereafter referred to as *NSDD 84*).

SOURCE: 50 FR 27215, July 2, 1985, unless otherwise noted.

§ 403.1 General policies and definitions.

(a) This regulation of the Export-Import Bank (the Bank) implements executive orders which govern the classification, declassification, and safeguarding of national security information and material of the United States. This regulation is based on Executive Order 12356, National Security Information, April 2, 1982 (3 CFR, 1982 Comp. p. 166) (hereafter referred to as the *Order*), Information Security Oversight Directive No. 1, June 25, 1982 (32 CFR part 2001) (hereafter referred to as the *Directive*), and National Security Decision Directive 84, "Safeguarding National Security Information," signed by the President on March 11, 1983 (hereafter referred to as *NSDD 84*). Violation of the provisions of part 403 may result in the imposition of administrative penalties, and civil and criminal penalties under applicable law. Executive Order 12356 prescribes a uniform system for classifying, declassifying, and safeguarding national security information. It recognizes that it is essential that the public be informed concerning the activities of the Government, but that the interests of the United States and its citizens require that certain information concerning the national defense and foreign relations be protected against unauthorized disclosure. Information may not be classified under the Order unless its disclosure reasonably could be expected to cause damage to the national security.

(b) For the purposes of the Order, the Directive and these guidelines, the following terms shall have the meanings specified below:

(1) *Information* means any information or material, regardless of its physical form or characteristics, that is owned by, produced by or for, or is under the control of the United States Government.

(2) *National security information* means information that has been determined pursuant to this Order or any predecessor order to require protection against unauthorized disclosure and that is so designated.

(3) *Foreign government information* means: (i) Information provided by a foreign government or governments, an international organization of governments, or any element thereof with the expectation, expressed or implied, that

the information, the source of the information, or both, are to be held in confidence; or

(ii) Information produced by the United States pursuant to or as a result of a joint arrangement with a foreign government or governments or an international organization of governments, or any element thereof, requiring that the information, the arrangement, or both, are to be held in confidence.

(4) *National security* means the national defense or foreign relations of the United States.

(5) *Confidential source* means any individual or organization that has provided, or that may reasonably be expected to provide, information to the United States on matters pertaining to the national security with the expectation, expressed or implied, that the information or relationship, or both, be held in confidence.

(6) *Original classification* means an initial determination that information requires, in the interest of national security, protection against unauthorized disclosure, together with a classification designation signifying the level of protection required.

§ 403.2 Responsibilities.

In the carrying out of security procedures, responsibility falls on all personnel generally and on certain personnel in a more particular manner.

(a) *Individual.* Each employee of the Bank having access to classified material has an individual responsibility to protect such information. Classified information should be secured in approved equipment or facilities whenever it is not under the direct control of the employee.

(b) *Office and Division Heads.* These officials have the additional responsibility of a continuing review for ascertaining that security procedures are properly observed by the personnel comprising their respective offices.

(c) *Security Officer.* (1) The Security Officer has the responsibility for developing, inspecting, and advising on procedures and controls for safeguarding classified material originating in, received by, in transit through, or in custody of the Bank; the training and orientation of employees; the carrying out of inspections; and the destruction of obsolete and non-record material.

(2) The Security Officer shall be responsible for disseminating written material and conducting oral briefings to inform Bank personnel of the Order, Directive, and regulations. An explanation of the practical application of these procedures and the underlying policy objectives thereof shall be emphasized.

(d) *Security Committee.* (1) This Committee consists of the General Counsel, as Chairperson, the Security Officer, and other Bank employees, as designated by the President and Chairman (hereinafter referred to as the *Chairman*) and is responsible for the implementation and enforcement of the Order and the Directive. This Committee will act on all matters with respect to the Bank's administration of these regulations.

(2) All suggestions and complaints regarding the Bank's Information Security Program, including those regarding over-classification, failure to declassify, or delay in declassifying, not otherwise provided for herein, shall be referred to the Security Committee for review.

(3) The Security Committee shall have responsibility for recommending to the Chairman appropriate administrative action to correct abuse or violation of these regulations or of any provision of the Order or Directive thereunder, including but not limited to notification by warning letter, formal suspension without pay, and removal. Upon receipt of such a recommendation, the Chairman shall make a decision and advise the Security Committee of this action.

§ 403.3 Classification principles and authority.

(a) *Classification Principles.* (1) Except as provided in the Atomic Energy Act of 1954, as amended, the Order provides the only basis for classifying national security information. Information held by the Bank will be made available to the public to the extent possible consistent with the need to protect the national defense or foreign relations, as required by the interests of the United

Export-Import Bank of the U.S. § 403.3

States and its citizens. Accordingly, security classification shall be applied only to protect the national security.

(2) Before a classification determination is made, each item of information that may require protection shall be identified exactly. This requires identification of that specific information, disclosure of which could affect the national security. When there is reasonable doubt about the need to classify, the information should be safeguarded as if it were confidential until a final determination is made by an authorized classifier as to its classification. The final determination must be made within thirty (30) days.

(b) *Classification Designations.* Information which requires protection against unauthorized disclosure in the interest of national security (*classified information*) shall be classified at one of the following three levels:

(1) TOP SECRET shall be applied only to information, the unauthorized disclosure of which reasonably could be expected to cause exceptionally grave damage to the national security.

(2) SECRET shall be applied only to information, the unauthorized disclosure of which reasonably could be expected to cause serious damage to the national security.

(3) CONFIDENTIAL shall be applied to information, the unauthorized disclosure of which reasonably could be expected to cause damage to the national security.

Except as provided by statute, no other terms, such as *SENSITIVE, OFFICIAL BUSINESS ONLY, AGENCY, BUSINESS, ADMINISTRATIVELY,* etc., shall be used within the Bank in conjunction with any of the three classification levels defined above.

(c) *Original Classification Authority and Criteria.* (1) The Bank's authority to assign original classification to any document is limited as follows and is nondelegable:

Classification	Classifier
CONFIDENTIAL.	President and Chairman. First Vice President and Vice Chairman. General Counsel. Senior Vice Presidents. Security Officer.

(2) A determination to classify information shall be made by an original classification authority when the information concerns one or more of categories (i) through (x) of this paragraph, and when the unauthorized disclosure of the information, either by itself or in the context of other information, reasonably could be expected to cause damage to the national security. Information shall be considered for classification if it concerns:

(i) Military plans, weapons, or operations;

(ii) The vulnerabilities or capabilities of systems, installations, projects, or plans relating to the national security;

(iii) Foreign government information;

(iv) Intelligence activities (including special activities), or intelligence sources or methods;

(v) Foreign relations or foreign activities of the United States;

(vi) Scientific, technological, or economic matters relating to the national security;

(vii) United States Government programs for safeguarding nuclear materials or facilities;

(viii) Cryptology;

(ix) A confidential source; or

(x) Other categories of information that are related to the national security and that require protection against unauthorized disclosure as determined by the President of the United States, by the Chairman or by other officials who have been delegated original classification authority by the President. Recommendations concerning the need to designate additional categories of information that may be considered for classification shall be forwarded through the Security Officer to the Chairman for determination. Such a determination shall be reported to the Director of the Information Security Oversight Office.

(3) Information that is determined to concern one or more of the above categories shall be classified when an original classification authority also determines that its unauthorized disclosure, either by itself or in the context of other information, reasonably could be expected to cause damage to

§ 403.3

the national security. Accordingly, certain information which would otherwise be unclassified may require classification when associated with other unclassified or classified information. Classification on this basis shall be supported by a written explanation that, at a minimum, shall be maintained with the file or reference on the recent copy of the information.

(4) Unauthorized disclosure of foreign government information, the identity of a confidential foreign source, or disclosure of intelligence sources or methods is presumed to cause damage to the national security.

(5) Information classified in accordance with the above classification categories shall not be declassified automatically as a result of any unofficial publication or inadvertent or unauthorized disclosure in the United States or abroad of identical or similar information.

(d) *Duration of Original Classification.* (1) Information shall be classified as long as required by national security considerations. When it can be determined, a specific date or event for declassification shall be set by the original classification authority at the time the information is originally classified. If the date or event for declassification cannot be determined at the time of classification, the standard notation "Originating Agency's Determination Required", or its abbreviation "OADR", should be entered on the "Declassify on" line.

(2) Automatic declassification determinations under predecessor orders shall remain valid unless the classification is extended by an authorized declassification authority. These extensions may be by individual documents or categories of information, provided, however, that any extension of classification on other than an individual document basis shall be reported to the Director of the Information Security Oversight Office. The declassification authority shall be responsible for notifying holders of the information of such extensions.

(3) Information classified under predecessor orders and marked for declassification review shall remain classified until reviewed for declassification under the provisions of the Order.

(e) *Marking and Identification.* (1) Classified information must be marked, or otherwise identified, to inform and warn the holder of the information of its sensitivity. The classifier is responsible for ensuring that proper classification markings are applied. At the time of classification, the following information shall be shown on the face of all classified documents, or clearly associated with other forms of classified information in a manner appropriate to the medium involved, unless this information itself would reveal a confidential source or relationship not otherwise evident in the document or information:

(i) One of the three classification levels defined in § 403.3(b); "(TS)" for Top Secret, "(S)" for Secret, "(C)" for Confidential, and "(U)" for Unclassified; with each page marked at top and bottom according to the highest level of classified information on each page.

(ii) The identity of the original classification authority if other than the person whose name appears as the approving or signing official;

(iii) The agency and office of origin; and

(iv) The date or event for declassification, or the notation "Originating Agency's Determination Required."

(2) Each classified document shall, by marking or other means, indicate which portions are classified, with the applicable classification level, and which portions are not classified. The Chairman may, for good cause, grant and revoke waivers of this requirement for specified classes of documents or information. The Director of the Information Security Oversight Office shall be notified of any waivers.

(3) Marking designations implementing the provisions of the Order, including abbreviations, shall conform to the standards prescribed in implementing directives issued by the Information Security Oversight Office. All authorized classifiers shall be issued a uniform stamp that has a "Classified by" line and a "Declassify on" line.

(4) Documents that contain foreign government information shall include either the marking, "FOREIGN GOVERNMENT INFORMATION", or a marking that otherwise indicates that the information is foreign government

information. If that fact must be concealed, the document will be marked as if it were of U.S. origin. Foreign government information shall either retain its original classification or be assigned a United States classification that shall ensure a degree of protection at least equivalent to that required by the entity that furnished the information.

(5) Documents that contain information relating to intelligence sources or methods shall include the following marking unless proscribed by the Director of the Central Intelligence; WARNING NOTICE—INTELLIGENCE SOURCES OR METHODS INVOLVED.

(6) Information assigned a level of classification under predecessor orders shall be considered as classified at that level of classification despite the omission of other required markings. Omitted markings may be inserted on a document by the General Counsel or the Security Officer.

(f) *Limitations on Classification.* (1) In no case shall information be classified in order to conceal violations of law, inefficiency, or administrative error; to prevent embarrassment to a person, organization, or agency; to restrain competition; or to prevent or delay the release of information that does not require protection in the interest of national security.

(2) Basic scientific research information not clearly related to the national security may not be classified.

(3) The Chairman or other authorized original classifiers may reclassify information previously declassified and disclosed if it is determined in writing that—

(i) The information requires protection in the interest of national security, and

(ii) The information may reasonably be recovered.

In making such determination, the Chairman or any other authorized original classifier shall consider the following factors: The lapse of time following disclosure; the nature and extent of disclosure; the ability to bring the fact of reclassification to the attention of persons to whom the information was disclosed; the ability to prevent further disclosure; and the ability to retrieve the information voluntarily from persons not authorized access to its reclassified state. These reclassification actions shall be reported promptly to the Director of the Information Security Oversight Office.

(4) Information may be classified or reclassified after an agency has received a request for it under the Freedom of Information Act (5 U.S.C. 552) or the Privacy Act of 1974 (5 U.S.C. 552a), or the mandatory review provisions of the Order and these regulations, if such classification meets the requirements of the Order and is accomplished personally and on a document-by-document basis by the Chairman, the Vice Chairman, or the Security Officer.

§ 403.4 Derivative classification.

(a) *Use of derivative classification.* (1) Unlike original classification which is an initial determination, derivative classification is an incorporation, paraphrasing, restatement, or generation in new form of information that is already classified. Derivative classification is the responsibility of those who only reproduce, extract, or summarize classified information, or who only apply classification markings derived from source material or as directed by a classification guide. Original classification authority is not required for derivative classification.

(2) Persons who apply such derivative classification markings shall:

(i) Respect original classification decisions;

(ii) Verify the information's current level of classification so far as practicable before applying the markings; and

(iii) Carry forward to any newly created documents the assigned dates or events for declassification or review. The latest date for declassification should be entered in the case of multiple source documents.

(b) *New Material.* (1) New material that derives its classification from information classified on or after the effective date of the Order, April 2, 1982, shall be marked with the declassification date or event, or the date for review, as assigned to the source information.

§ 403.5

(2) New material that derives its classification under prior orders shall be treated as follows:

(i) If the source material bears a classification date or event 20 years or less from the date or origin, that date or event shall be carried forward on the new material.

(ii) If the source material bears no declassification date or event or is marked for declassification beyond 20 years, the new material shall be marked with a date for review for declassification at 20 years from the date of original classification of the source material.

(iii) If the source material is foreign government information bearing no date or event for declassification or is marked for declassification beyond 30 years, the new material shall be marked for review for declassification at 30 years from the date of original classification of the source materials.

(iv) A copy of the source document or documents should be maintained with the file copy of the new document or documents which have been derivatively classified.

§ 403.5 Declassification and downgrading.

(a) *Authority and policy for declassification and downgrading.* Information that continues to meet the classification requirements prescribed in § 403.3(c) despite the passage of time will continue to be safeguarded. However, information which is properly classified at the time it is developed may not necessarily require protection indefinitely. National security information over which the Bank exercises final classification jurisdiction shall be declassified or downgraded as soon as national security considerations permit. Information shall be declassified or downgraded by:

(1) The official who authorized the original classification, if that official is still serving in the same position, by a successor, or by a supervisory official of either; or

(2) Officials specifically delegated this authority in writing by the Chairman or by the Security Officer. A list of those who may be so delegated shall be maintained by the Security Officer.

(3) If the Director of the Information Security Oversight Office determines that information is unlawfully classified, the Director may require the Export-Import Bank to declassify it. Any such decision by the Director may be appealed to the National Security Council. The information shall remain classified until the appeal is decided.

(b) *Declassification Procedure.* Information marked with a specific declassification date or event shall be declassified on that date or upon occurrence of that event. The overall classification markings shall be lined through a statement placed on the cover or first page to indicate the declassification authority, by name and title, and the date of declassification. If practicable, the classification markings on each page shall be cancelled; otherwise, the statement on the cover or first page shall indicate that the declassification applies to the entire document.

(c) *Notification to Holders.* When classified information has been properly marked with specific dates or events for declassification it is not necessary to issue notices of declassification to any holders. However, when declassification action is taken earlier than originally scheduled, or the duration of classification is extended, the authority making such changes shall promptly notify all holders to whom the information was originally transmitted. This notification shall include the marking action to be taken, the authority for the change (name and title), and the effective date of the change. Upon receipt of notification, recipients shall make the proper changes and shall notify holders to whom they have transmitted the classified information.

(d) *Downgrading.* Information designated a particular level of classification may be assigned a lower classification level by the original classifier or by an official authorized to declassify the same information. Prompt notice of such downgrading shall be provided to known holders of the information. Classified information marked for automatic downgrading under previous Executive Orders shall be reviewed to determine that it no longer continues to meet classification requirements despite the passage of time.

Export-Import Bank of the U.S. § 403.7

(e) *Transferred Information.* Classified information transferred from one agency to another in conjunction with a transfer of functions, and not merely for storage purposes, shall be considered under the control of the receiving agency for purposes of downgrading and declassification, subject to consultation with any other agency that has an interest in the subject matter of the information. Prior to forwarding classified information to an approved storage facility of the Bank, to a Federal records center, or to the National Archives for permanent preservation, the information shall be reviewed for downgrading or declassification.

§ 403.6 Systematic review for declassification.

Classified information determined by the Archivist of the United States to be of sufficient value to warrant permanent retention will be subject to systematic declassification review by the Archivist in accordance with guidelines provided by the Bank, as originator of the information. These guidelines shall be developed by the Security Officer who is designated by the Bank to assist the Archivist in the review process. The guidelines shall be reviewed every five years or as requested by the Archivist of the United States.

§ 403.7 Mandatory review for declassification.

(a) Classified information under the jurisdiction of the Bank shall be reviewed for declassification upon receipt of a request by a United States citizen or permanent resident alien, a Federal agency, or a State or local government. A request for mandatory review of classified information shall be submitted in writing and describe the information with sufficient particularity to locate it with a reasonable amount of effort. Requests may be addressed to the:

General Counsel, Export-Import Bank of the U.S., 811 Vermont Avenue, NW., Washington, DC 20571

(b) The Bank's response to mandatory review requests will be governed by the amount of search and review time required to process the request. The Bank will acknowledge receipt of all requests, and will inform the requester if additional time is needed to process the request. Except in unusual circumstances, the Bank will make a final determination within one year from the date of receipt of the request.

(c) When information cannot be declassified in its entirety, the Bank will make a reasonable effort to release, consistent with other applicable laws, those declassified portions that constitute a coherent segment.

(d) The bank shall determine whether information under the classification jurisdiction of the Bank or any reasonably segregable portion of it no longer requires protection. If so, the General Counsel shall promptly make such information available to the requester, and shall inform the requester of any fees due before releasing the document. If the information may not be released, in whole or in part, the General Counsel shall give the requester a brief statement of the reasons, and a notice, mailed with return receipt requested, of the right to appeal the determination within 60 days of the denial letter's receipt.

(e) The agency that initially received or classified records containing foreign government information shall be responsible for making a declassification determination on review requests for classified records which contain such foreign government information. Such requests shall be referred to the appropriate agency for action.

(f) When the Bank receives a mandatory declassification review request for records in its possession that were originated by another agency, it shall forward the request to that agency. The Bank may request notification of the declassification determination.

(g) Information originated by a President, the White House staff, by committees, commissions, or boards appointed by the President, or other specifically providing advice and counsel to a President or acting on behalf of a President is exempted from the provisions of mandatory review for declassification, except as consistent with applicable laws that pertain to presidential papers or records.

(h) The bank shall process requests for declassification that are submitted under the provisions of the Freedom of Information Act, as amended, or the

1033

§ 403.8

Privacy Act of 1974, in accordance with the provisions of those acts. (*See*, 12 CFR part 404 and 12 CFR part 405, respectively.) In any case, however, exemptions under the Freedom of Information Act or other exemptions under applicable law may be invoked by the Bank to deny material on grounds other than classification.

(i) The Bank shall refuse to confirm or deny the existence or non-existence of requested information whenever the fact of its existence or non-existence is itself classifiable under the Order.

§ 403.8 Appeals.

(a) The Vice Chairman is designated to receive appeals on requests for declassification which have been denied by the Bank. Such appeals shall be addressed to:

First Vice President & Vice Chairman, Export-Import Bank of the United States, 811 Vermont Avenue NW., Washington, DC 20571

The appeal must be received within 60 days after receipt by appellant of the denial letter. Appeals shall be decided within 30 days of their receipt by the Vice Chairman.

(1) If the decision is to declassify the materials in their entirety, the Vice Chairman shall promptly make such information available to the requester, and inform the requester of any fees due before releasing the documents.

(2) If the decision is to deny declassification of a portion of the material, the Vice Chairman shall promptly make the part which was declassified available to the requester, and shall advise the requester, in writing, of the reasons for the partial denial of declassification.

(3) If the decision is to deny declassification of all the material, the Vice Chairman shall promptly advise the requester, in writing, of the reasons for such denial.

§ 403.9 Fees.

The following specific fees shall be applicable with respect to services rendered to members of the public under these regulations, by the Bank, except that the search fee will normally be waived when the search involves less than one-half hour of clerical time.

(a) Search for records, per hour or fraction thereof:
(i) Professional $11.00
(ii) Clerical 6.00
(b) Computer service charges per second for actual use of computer central processing unit .... .25
(c) Copies made by photostat or otherwise (per page); maximum of 5 copies will be provided .... .10
(d) Certification of each record as a true copy 1.00
(e) Certification of each record as a true copy under official seal 1.50
(f) Duplication of architectural photographs and drawings 2.00

Fees must be paid in full prior to issuance of requested copies. Remittances shall be in the form either of a personal check or bank draft drawn on a bank in the United States, or postal money order. Remittances shall be made payable to the order of the Export-Import Bank of the United States, and mailed to:

General Counsel, Export-Import Bank of the United States, 811 Vermont Avenue NW., Washington, DC 20571

§ 403.10 Safeguarding.

(a) *General Access Requirements.* Except as provided in § 403.10(c), access to classified information shall be granted in accordance with the following:

(1) *Determination of Trustworthiness.* No person shall be given access to classified information or material unless a favorable determination has been made as to his trustworthiness. The determination of eligibility, refered to as a security clearance, shall be based on such investigations as the Bank may require in accordance with the standards and criteria of applicable law and Executive orders.

(2) *Determination of Need to Know.* In addition to a security clearance, a person must have a need for access to the particular classified information or material sought in connection with the performance of official duties or contractual obligations. The determination of that need shall be made by officials having responsibility for the classified information or material.

(b) *Classified Information Nondisclosure Agreement.* All persons with authorized access to classified information shall be required to sign a nondisclosure agreement, Standard Form 189, as a

Export-Import Bank of the U.S. § 403.10

condition of access. This form shall be retained in the security file of the individual for 50 years.

(c) *Access by Historical Researchers and Former Presidential Appointees.* The Bank shall obtain written agreements from requesters to safeguard the information to which they are given access as permitted by the Order and written consent to the Bank's review of their notes and manuscripts for the purpose of determining that no classified information is contained therein. A determination of trustworthiness is a precondition to a requester's access. If the access requested by historical researchers and former Presidential Appointees requires the rendering of services for which fair and equitable fees may be charged pursuant to Title 5 of the Independent Offices Appropriations Act, 65 Stat. 290, 31 U.S.C. 483a (1976), the requester shall be so notified and the fees may be imposed.

(d) *Media Contacts.* All contacts by members of the media which concern classified information shall be directed to the attention of the Security Officer, Room 1031, Export-Import Bank of the United States, 811 Vermont Avenue NW., Washington, DC 20571.

(e) *Dissemination.* Except as otherwise provided by directives issued by the President through the National Security Council, classified information originating in another agency and in the possession of the Bank may not be disseminated outside the Bank without the consent of the originating agency.

(f) *Accountability Procedures.* Dissemination of various levels of classified information or material shall be within the control and responsibility of designated control officers. Particularly stringent controls shall be placed on information and material classified as TOP SECRET.

(1) *TOP SECRET.* Designated as TOP SECRET control officers are the Chairman, Vice Chairman and the Security Officer who alone have authority to receive TOP SECRET information for the Bank. Other personnel authorized in writing by the Chairman or Security Officer also may receive TOP SECRET information for the Bank. It shall be the responsibility of these individuals with respect to all TOP SECRET information:

(i) To receive the material for the Bank;

(ii) To maintain registers which will reflect the routing of the material and the return thereof in a reasonable length of time for security storage;

(iii) To dispatch and make record of material disseminated to authorize persons outside the Bank;

(iv) To make a physical inventory of all material at least annually; and

(v) To maintain current access records.

(2) *SECRET.* Designated as SECRET control officers are the Security Officer and the Analysis, Records & Communications Manager, who have the responsibility with respect to all information classified in this category:

(i) To receive the material for the Bank;

(ii) To maintain registers which will reflect the routing of the material and the return thereof in a reasonable length of time for security storage;

(iii) To dispatch and make record of material disseminated to authorized persons outside the Bank;

(iv) To maintain current access records.

(3) *CONFIDENTIAL.* Designated as CONFIDENTIAL control officers are the Security Officer and the Analysis, Records & Communications Manager who have responsibility with respect to all information classified in this category:

(i) To review material for the Bank;

(ii) To route the material to proper Bank offices;

(iii) To dispatch and make record of material disseminated to authorized persons outside the Bank;

(iv) To maintain current access records.

(g) *Storage.* Classified information shall be stored only in facilities or under conditions adequate to prevent unauthorized persons from gaining access to it and in accordance with the Directive as well as General Services Administration standards and specifications. Reference may be made to 32 CFR 2001.41, 2001.43 for preliminary guidance regarding these standards and specifications.

(h) *Coversheets.* Department of State (DSC) classified incoming cables are to

§ 403.10

be logged in and routed to the appropriate offices in double envelopes. When these cables are being used in various offices, classified coversheets must be used to protect the documents. This practice eliminates the possibility of inadvertently mixing classified with non-classified material, and promotes security awareness. Coversheets are obtainable from the Office of the Security Director.

(i) *Transmittal.* (1) To be transmitted outside the Bank, all classified documents must be sent through the Security Office and have attached EIB Form 71-2, approved by one of the following: the President and Chairman, First Vice President and Vice Chairman, a Senior Vice President, General Counsel, Vice President or Security Officer.

(2) *Preparation and Receipting.* Classified information shall be enclosed in opaque inner and outer covers before transmitting. The inner cover shall be a sealed wrapper or envelope plainly marked with the assigned classification and addresses of both sender and addressee. Transmittal documents shall indicate on their face the highest level of any information transmitted, and must clearly state whether or not the transmittal document itself is classified after removal of enclosures and attachments. The outer cover shall be sealed and addressed with no identification of the classification of its contents. A receipt shall be attached to or enclosed in the inner cover, except that CONFIDENTIAL information shall require a receipt only if the sender deems it necessary. The receipt shall identify the sender, addressee, and the document but shall contain no classified information. It shall be immediately signed by the recipient and returned to the sender. Any of these wrapping and receipting requirements may be waived by agency heads under conditions that will provide adequate protection and prevent access by unauthorized persons.

(3) *Transmittal of CONFIDENTIAL information.* CONFIDENTIAL information shall be transmitted within and between the fifty States, the District of Columbia, the Commonwealth of Puerto Rico, and U.S. territories or possessions by one of the means established for higher classifications, or by United States Postal Service, certified first class, or express mail service, when prescribed by an agency head. Outside these areas, CONFIDENTIAL information shall be transmitted only as is authorized for higher classification levels.

(4) Transmittal of TOP SECRET and SECRET information shall be in accordance with the Directive. Reference may be made to 32 CFR 2001.44 for preliminary guidance.

(j) *Destruction.* Classified information no longer needed in working files or for record or reference purposes shall be processed for appropriate disposition in accordance with Chapters 21 and 33 of title 44 U.S.C., when govern disposition of Federal Records. All classified information approved for destruction must be torn and placed in containers designated as burnbags which are available through the Office Services Section of the Bank. Destruction of such information will be carried out by the Security Officer or a designee by use of a disintegrator or by burning. The method of destruction selected must preclude recognition or reconstruction of the classified information or material. Records of destruction will be maintained by the Security Office for TOP SECRET information and material with serialized markings or material for which there is a special need to record its destruction.

(k) *Reproduction controls.* (1) Reproduction of classified documents is prohibited, except by personnel authorized in writing by the Chairman or Security Officer.

(2) TOP SECRET documents may not be reproduced without the consent of the originating agency unless otherwise marked by the originating office.

(3) Reproduction of SECRET and CONFIDENTIAL documents may be restricted by the originating agency.

(4) Reproduced copies of classified documents are subject to the same accountability and controls as the original documents.

(5) Records shall be maintained by the Security Officer to show the number and distribution or reproduced copies of all TOP SECRET documents, of all documents covered by special access programs distributed outside the

Export-Import Bank of the U.S. § 403.11

originating agency, and all SECRET and all CONFIDENTIAL documents which are marked with special dissemination and reproduction limitations.

§ 403.11 Enforcement and investigation procedures.

(a) *Loss or Possible Compromise.* Any person who has knowledge of the loss or possible compromise of classified information shall immediately report the circumstances to the Security Officer of the Bank. In turn, the originating agency shall be notified about the loss or compromise in order that a damage assessment may be conducted and appropriate measures taken to negate or minimize any adverse effect, and prevent further such loss or compromise. An immediate inquiry shall be initiated by the Bank for the purposes: (1) Of determining cause and responsibility and (2) taking corrective measures and appropriate administrative, disciplinary, or legal action.

(b) *Reporting and Investigating Unauthorized Disclosures.* (1) Employees who have reason to believe that an unauthorized disclosure of classified information has occurred shall report the disclosure to their supervisor, who shall inform the Security Officer.

(2) The Bank shall promptly notify the Information Security Oversight Office at the General Services Administration, Washington, DC 20405, of all unauthorized disclosures of classified information.

(3) If the Bank believes that it is the source of an unauthorized disclosure of classified information that it originated, it shall evaluate the disclosure under paragraph (b)(7) of this section. If the disclosure is serious, the Bank shall report the disclosure and the results of the evaluation to the Department of Justice together with notification that it is conducting an internal investigation.

(4) If the Bank believes that it is the source of an unauthorized disclosure of classified information that it handled but did not originate, it shall report the disclosure to the Department of Justice and to the originating agency(ies) or department(s) for evaluation under paragraph (b)(7) of this section. If the Bank cannot determine the identity of the originating agency(ies) or department(s), it shall report the disclosure to the Department of Justice together with any information or reasonable inferences as to the identity of the originating agency(ies) or department(s).

(5) If the Bank receives a request for an evaluation of information it originated, it shall, if the evaluation shows the disclosure was serious, inform the agency(ies) or department(s) from which the disclosure occurred of this conclusion and request that the agency(ies) or department(s) conduct an internal investigation.

(6) If the Bank determines that an unauthorized disclosure of classified information has occurred but that it neither originated, handled nor disclosed the information, it shall report the disclosure to the likely originating agency(ies) or department(s).

(7) In determining whether a disclosure is sufficiently serious to warrant reporting to the Department of Justice, the Bank, if it is the originating agency, shall ascertain the nature of the disclosed information, determine the extent to which it disseminated the information and evaluate the disclosure to determine whether it seriously damages its mission and responsibilities. In evaluating the damage caused by the disclosure, the Bank shall consider such matters as whether the disclosure jeopardizes an ongoing project, operation or source of information and to what extent the policy goals underlying the project or operation must be altered.

(8) In any instance where the Bank is determined to be the source of an unauthorized disclosure and an evaluation by the Bank or the originating agency(ies) or department(s) determines the disclosure to be of a serious nature, an internal investigation will be initiated and an investigation report, containing such information as may be required by the Department of Justice, will be submitted to the Department of Justice within 15 days after notification from the originating agency or Department of Justice, but in any case no later than 30 days. If the investigation report is not completed within 15 days, the Bank shall submit as much of the required information as is available at that time and furnish

additional information as it is developed.

(9) Whenever the Bank determines during the course of an investigation that it is necessary to compel or induce the cooperation of an employee, the Bank shall first consult with the Department of Justice. The Department of Justice will coordinate with the Bank to determine the procedures the Bank may use to compel an employee's participation without foreclosing possible criminal proceedings.

(10) The Bank shall maintain records of all disclosures that have been reported or investigated.

(11) All employees shall cooperate fully with officials of the Bank or other agencies who are conducting investigations of unauthorized disclosures of classified information.

(12) Employees determined by the Bank to have knowingly participated in an unauthorized disclosure of classified information or who have refused to cooperate with an investigation of such a disclosure shall be denied further access to classified information and shall be subject to other appropriate administrative sanctions. Prior to taking action against an employee in connection with the unauthorized disclosure or classified information, the Bank shall consult with the Department of Justice, National Security Division.

[50 FR 27215, July 2, 1985, as amended at 72 FR 66043, Nov. 27, 2007]

PART 404—INFORMATION DISCLOSURE

Subpart A—Procedures for Disclosure of Records Under the Freedom of Information Act.

Sec.
404.1 General provisions.
404.2 Definitions.
404.3 Public reference facilities.
404.4 Request requirements.
404.5 Time for processing.
404.6 Release of records under the Freedom of Information Act.
404.7 Confidential business information.
404.8 Initial determination.
404.9 Schedule of fees.
404.10 Fee waivers or reductions.
404.11 Administrative appeal.

Subpart B—Protection of Privacy and Access to Records Under the Privacy Act of 1974

404.12 General provisions.
404.13 Definitions.
404.14 Requirements of request for access.
404.15 Initial determination.
404.16 Schedule of fees.
404.17 Appeal of denials of access.
404.18 Requests for correction of records.
404.19 Request for accounting of record disclosures.
404.20 Notice of court-ordered and emergency disclosures.
404.21 Submission of social security and passport numbers.
404.22 Government contracts.
404.23 Other rights and services.

Subpart C—Demands for Testimony of Current and Former Ex-Im Bank Personnel and for Production of Ex-Im Bank Records

404.24 General provisions.
404.25 Applicability.
404.26 Definitions.
404.27 Demand requirements.
404.28 Notification of General Counsel required.
404.29 Restrictions on testimony and production of records.
404.30 Factors General Counsel may consider in determining whether to authorize testimony and/or the production of records.
404.31 Procedure for declining to testify and/or produce records.
404.32 Procedure in the event a decision concerning a demand is not made prior to the time a response to the demand is required.
404.33 Procedure in the event of an adverse ruling.
404.34 Procedure for demands for testimony or production of documents regarding confidential information.
404.35 Procedure for requests for Ex-Im Bank employees to provide expert or opinion testimony.
404.36 No private right of action.

Subparts D–E [Reserved]

AUTHORITY: 5 U.S.C. 552 and 552a.
Section 404.7 also issued under E.O. 12600, 52 FR 23781, 3 CFR, 1987 Comp., p. 235.
Section 404.21 also issued under 5 U.S.C. 552a note.
Subpart C also issued under 5 U.S.C. 301, 12 U.S.C. 635.

SOURCE: 64 FR 14374, Mar. 25, 1999, unless otherwise noted.

Export-Import Bank of the U.S. § 404.2

Subpart A—Procedures for Disclosure of Records Under the Freedom of Information Act.

§ 404.1 General provisions.

(a) *Purpose.* This subpart establishes policy, procedures, requirements, and responsibilities for administration of the Freedom of Information Act (FOIA), 5 U.S.C. 552, at the Export-Import Bank of the United States (Ex-Im Bank).

(b) *Policy.* It is Ex-Im Bank's policy to honor all requests for the disclosure of its records, provided that disclosure would not adversely affect a legitimate public or private interest and would not impose an unreasonable burden on Ex-Im Bank. However, this subpart also recognizes that the soundness of many Ex-Im Bank programs depends upon the receipt of reliable commercial, technical, financial, and business information relating to applicants for Ex-Im Bank assistance and that receipt of such information depends on Ex-Im Bank's ability to hold such information in confidence. Consequently, except as provided by applicable law and this regulation, information provided to Ex-Im Bank in confidence will not be disclosed without the submitter's consent.

(c) *Scope.* All record requests made to Ex-Im Bank shall be processed under this subpart, except that information customarily furnished to the public in the regular course of the performance of official duties may continue to be furnished to the public without complying with this subpart. Requests made by individuals under the Privacy Act of 1974 which are processed under subpart B of this part also shall be processed under this subpart A.

(d) *Ex-Im Bank Internet site.* Ex-Im Bank maintains an Internet site at *http://www.exim.gov.* The site contains information on Ex-Im Bank functions, activities, programs, and transactions. Web site visitors have access to Board of Directors and Loan Committee meeting minutes, country information, and Ex-Im Bank press releases, among other information. Ex-Im Bank encourages all prospective FOIA requesters to visit the site prior to submission of a FOIA request.

(e) *Delegation.* Any action or determination in this subpart which is the responsibility of a specific Ex-Im Bank employee, may be delegated to a duly designated alternate.

(f) *Ex-Im Bank address.* The Export-Import Bank of the United States is located at 811 Vermont Avenue, NW, Washington, DC 20571.

§ 404.2 Definitions.

For purposes of this subpart, the following definitions shall apply:

All other requesters—Requesters other than commercial use requesters, educational and non-commercial scientific requesters, or representatives of the news media.

Appeal—A written request to the Ex-Im Bank Assistant General Counsel for Administration for reversal of an adverse initial determination.

Business information—Potentially confidential commercial or financial information that is provided to Ex-Im Bank.

Business submitter—Any person who provides business information to Ex-Im Bank.

Commercial use request—A request for a use or purpose that furthers the commercial, trade or profit interest of the requester.

Direct costs—Expenditures incurred in the search, review, and duplication of records in response to a FOIA request.

Educational institution—A preschool, a public or private elementary or secondary school, an institution of undergraduate or graduate higher education, or an institution of professional or vocational education.

Final determination—The written decision by the Assistant General Counsel for Administration on an appeal.

Initial determination—The initial written determination by Ex-Im Bank regarding disclosure of requested records.

Non-commercial scientific institution—An institution that is operated for the purpose of conducting scientific research the results of which are not intended to promote any particular product or industry and that is not operated solely for purposes of furthering a business, trade or profit interest.

§ 404.3

Person—An individual, partnership, corporation, association or organization other than a federal government agency.

Record—All papers, memoranda or other documentary material, or copies thereof, regardless of physical form or characteristics, created or received by Ex-Im Bank and preserved as evidence of the activities of Ex-Im Bank. "Record" does not include publications which are available to the public through the FEDERAL REGISTER, sale or free distribution.

Redaction—The process of removing non-disclosable material from a record so that the remainder may be released.

Representative of the news media—A person actively gathering information on behalf of an entity organized and operated to publish or broadcast news to the public. Freelance journalists shall qualify as representatives of the news media when they can demonstrate that a request is reasonably likely to lead to publication.

Request—Any record request made to Ex-Im Bank under the FOIA.

Requester—Any person making a request.

Review—The process of examining a record to determine whether any portion is required to be withheld. It includes redaction, duplication, and any other preparation for release. Review does not include time spent resolving general legal and policy issues regarding the application of exemptions.

Search—The process of identifying and collecting records pursuant to a request.

Trade secrets—All forms and types of financial, business, scientific, technical, economic or engineering information, including, but not limited to, patterns, plans, compilations, program devices, formulas, designs, prototypes, methods, techniques, processes, procedures, programs or codes.

Unusual circumstances—The need to search for and collect requested records from facilities that are separate from Ex-Im Bank headquarters; the need to search for, collect, and appropriately examine a voluminous amount of separate and distinct records which are demanded in a single request; or the need for consultation with another agency a person that has a substantial interest in the determination of the request.

Working days—All calendar days excluding Saturdays, Sundays, and Federal Government holidays.

§ 404.3 Public reference facilities.

Ex-Im Bank maintains a public reading room which contains the Ex-Im Bank records that the FOIA requires to be made available for public inspection and copying. The records available under this section include copies of records released pursuant to the FOIA that Ex-Im Bank determines have, or are likely to, become the subject of subsequent requests for substantially the same records. Requesters shall be responsible for the cost of duplicating such material in accordance with the provisions of § 404.9(e). Persons desiring to use the reading room should contact the Ex-Im Bank Freedom of Information and Privacy Office, either in writing at the address at § 404.1(f) or by telephone at (202) 565–3946 or (800) 565–3946, to arrange a time to inspect the available records.

§ 404.4 Request requirements.

(a) *Form.* Requests must be made in writing and must be signed by, or on behalf of, the requester. Requests should be addressed to the Freedom of Information and Privacy Office at the address in § 404.1(f) and should contain both the return address and telephone number of the requester.

(b) *Description of records requested.* Each request must describe the records sought in sufficient detail so as to enable a professional employee of Ex-Im Bank familiar with the subject matter of the request to locate the record with a reasonable amount of effort. A request shall not be deemed to have been received until such time as the request adequately identifies the records sought. To the extent practicable, a description should include relevant dates, format, subject matter, and the name of any person to whom the record is known to relate. A general request for records with no accompanying date restriction, either express or implied, shall be deemed to be a request for records created within the preceding twelve months.

Export-Import Bank of the U.S. § 404.6

(c) *Fee statement.* The request must contain a statement expressing willingness to pay fees for the requested records or a request for a fee waiver (see § 404.10) before the request shall be deemed to have been received. A fee statement may specify the maximum amount a requester is willing to pay for processing the request.

(1) Whenever a requester submits a FOIA request that does not contain a fee statement or a request for a fee waiver, Ex-Im Bank shall advise the requester of the requirements of this paragraph. If the requester fails to respond within ten working days of such notification, then the Freedom of Information and Privacy Office shall notify the requester, in writing, that Ex-Im Bank will not process the request.

(2) A general statement by the requester expressing willingness to pay all applicable fees under § 404.9 shall be deemed an agreement to pay up to $50.00. If Ex-Im Bank estimates that the fees for a request will exceed $50.00, then Ex-Im Bank shall offer the requester the opportunity to agree, in writing, either to pay a greater fee or to modify the request as a means of limiting the cost.

(d) *Written notice of amendment.* The requester should provide any amendment to the original request in writing to Ex-Im Bank.

(e) *Requester assistance.* Ex-Im Bank shall make reasonable efforts to assist a requester in complying with the requirements of this section.

§ 404.5 Time for processing.

(a) *General.* Ex-Im Bank shall respond to requests within twenty working days of the date of receipt of the request unless unusual circumstances exist. Ex-Im Bank shall provide written notice to the requester whenever such unusual circumstances necessitate an extension. If the extension is expected to exceed ten working days, then Ex-Im Bank shall offer the requester the opportunity to:

(1) Alter the request so that it may be processed within the time limit; or

(2) Propose an alternative, feasible time frame for processing the request.

(b) *Date of receipt.* A request shall be deemed to have been received on the date that the request is received in the Freedom of Information and Privacy Office, provided that the requester has met all the requirements of § 404.4. Ex-Im Bank shall notify the requester of the date on which a request was officially received.

(c) *Order of processing.* Ex-Im Bank ordinarily shall process requests according to their order of receipt.

(d) *Expedited processing.* A request for expedited processing must be included in the original request for records and may be granted at the discretion of Ex-Im Bank based upon the requester's demonstration of:

(1) An imminent threat to the life or physical safety of an individual; or

(2) In the case of a requester who is a representative of the news media, an urgency to inform the public concerning actual or alleged Federal Government activity. Ex-Im Bank shall provide notice of its determination on expedited processing to the requester. A requester may file an administrative appeal, as set forth at § 404.11, based on a denial of a request for expedited processing. Ex-Im Bank shall grant expeditious consideration to any such appeal.

§ 404.6 Release of records under the Freedom of Information Act.

(a) *Creation of records.* A reasonable request for material not in existence may be honored at Ex-Im Bank's discretion when tabulation or compilation will not significantly burden Ex-Im Bank, its programs or its activities.

(b) *Discretionary release.* Consistent with federal government policy, material technically qualifying for exemption from disclosure under 5 U.S.C. 552(b)(5) may be made available when disclosure would not adversely affect legitimate public or private interests, violate law or impose an unreasonable burden on Ex-Im Bank. This policy does not, however, create any right enforceable in a court of law.

(c) *Segregable records.* Whenever it is determined that a portion of a record is exempt from disclosure, any reasonably segregable portion of the record shall be provided to the requester after redaction of the exempt material. If segregation would render the document meaningless, Ex-Im Bank shall withhold the entire record.

§ 404.7

(d) *Date for determining responsive records.* Only those records within Ex-Im Bank's possession and control as of the date of receipt of a request shall be deemed to be responsive to a request.

§ 404.7 Confidential business information.

(a) *Scope.* This section applies to all business information, as defined in § 404.2. Such information shall only be disclosed pursuant to a FOIA request in accordance with this section.

(b) *Submitter designation.* All business submitters should designate, by appropriate markings, either at the time of submission or at a reasonable time thereafter, any portion of any submission that they consider to be exempt from disclosure under 5 U.S.C. 552(b)(4).

(c) *Pre-disclosure notice to the business submitter.* Whenever Ex-Im Bank receives a FOIA request seeking disclosure of business information, Ex-Im Bank shall provide prompt written notice to the submitter of such information. This notice shall include a description or a copy of the records containing the business information. Such notice shall not be required, however, if:

(1) Ex-Im Bank determines that the records shall not be disclosed;

(2) The records have been published or otherwise made available to the public; or

(3) disclosure of the records is required by law.

(d) *Opportunity to object to disclosure.* The business submitter shall have ten working days from and including the date of the notification letter to provide Ex-Im Bank with a detailed statement of any objection to disclosure of the records. A submitter located outside the United States shall have twenty working days to object to disclosure. Ex-Im Bank may extend the time for objection upon timely request from the submitter and for good cause shown. A statement of objection must specify all grounds under the FOIA for withholding the information.

(e) *Notice to the requester.* The Freedom of Information and Privacy Office shall notify the requester in writing whenever a business submitter is afforded the opportunity to object to disclosure of records pursuant to paragraph (c) of this section.

(f) *Disclosure of confidential business information.* Ex-Im Bank shall consider any objections raised by the business submitter prior to making its disclosure decision.

(g) *Notice of intent to disclose.* Whenever Ex-Im Bank determines to disclose business information over the objection of a business submitter, Ex-Im Bank shall notify the business submitter, in writing, of such determination, the reasons for the decision, and the expected disclosure date. This notification—which shall be provided at least ten days prior to the planned disclosure date and which shall include a copy or description of the records at issue—is intended to afford the submitter the opportunity to seek judicial review.

(h) *Notice to requester of disclosure date.* If Ex-Im Bank determines to disclose records over a business submitter's objection, then Ex-Im Bank shall notify the requester of the expected disclosure date.

(i) *Appeal.* Whenever Ex-Im Bank determines to disclose, pursuant to an administrative appeal, business information that initially was withheld from disclosure under 5 U.S.C. 552(b)(4), Ex-Im Bank shall notify the business submitter. Such notice shall be in writing and shall be provided ten working days prior to the proposed disclosure date. It shall include a copy or description of the records at issue and a statement of Ex-Im Bank's reasons for disclosure.

(j) *Notice of FOIA lawsuit.* Ex-Im Bank shall promptly notify the submitter whenever a requester brings suit against Ex-Im Bank seeking to compel the release of business information covered by this section. Ex-Im Bank shall promptly notify the requester when a submitter brings suit against Ex-Im seeking to restrict the release of business information that is covered by this section.

(k) *Exception.* Notwithstanding the foregoing provisions of this part, Ex-Im Bank may, upon request or on its own initiative, publicly disclose the parties to transactions for which Ex-Im Bank approves support, the amount of such

Export-Import Bank of the U.S. § 404.9

support, the identity of any participants involved, a general description of the related U.S. exports, and the country to which such exports are destined.

§ 404.8 Initial determination.

(a) *Authority to grant or deny requests.* The Freedom of Information and Privacy Office shall be responsible for search, review, and the initial determination.

(b) *Referrals to other government agencies.* A requested record in Ex-Im Bank's possession that was created or classified by another Federal agency shall be referred to such agency for direct response to the requester. The Freedom of Information and Privacy Office shall notify the requester of any such referral, the number of documents so referred, and the name and address of each agency to which the request has been referred.

(c) *Notification of Ex-Im Bank action.* The Freedom of Information and Privacy Office shall notify the requester in writing of its decision to grant or deny the request.

(1) If the decision is made to grant a request, then Ex-Im Bank shall promptly disclose the requested records and shall inform the requester of any fee payable under § 404.9.

(2) A denial is a determination to withhold any requested record in whole or in part, a determination that a requested record does not exist or cannot be located or a determination that what has been requested is not a record subject to the FOIA. Whenever Ex-Im Bank withholds information, such notice shall include:

(i) The name, title, and signature of the person responsible for the determination;

(ii) The statutory basis for non-disclosure; and

(iii) A statement that any denial may be appealed under § 404.11 and a brief description of the requirements of that section.

(d) *Material withheld.* Ex-Im Bank shall make reasonable efforts to inform the requester of the volume of material withheld pursuant to a full or partial denial and the extent of any redaction. Ex-Im Bank shall not, however, indicate the extent of any denial when doing so could harm an interest protected by an applicable exemption.

§ 404.9 Schedule of fees.

(a) *General.* Ex-Im Bank shall charge fees to recover the full allowable direct costs it incurs in processing requests. Ex-Im Bank shall attempt to conduct searches in the most efficient manner to minimize costs for both Ex-Im Bank and the requester.

(b) *Categories of requesters.* Fees shall be assessed according to the status of the requester. The specific schedule of fees for each requester category (each as defined in § 404.2) is prescribed as follows:

(1) *Commercial use requesters.* Ex-Im Bank shall charge the full costs for search, review, and duplication.

(2) *Educational and non-commercial scientific institution requesters.* Ex-Im Bank shall charge only for the cost of duplication in excess of 100 pages. No fee will be charged for search or review.

(3) *Representatives of the news media.* Ex-Im Bank shall charge only for the cost of duplication in excess of 100 pages. No fee will be charged for search or review.

(4) *All other requesters.* Ex-Im Bank shall charge for the cost of search, review, and duplication, except that 100 pages of duplication and two hours of professional search time shall be furnished without charge.

(c) *Search and review fees.* Ex-Im Bank shall charge the following fees for search and review:

(1) *Clerical.* Hourly rate—$16.00.

(2) *Professional.* Hourly rate—$32.00.

(3) *Computer Searches.* Hourly rate—based upon the salary of the employee performing the work and the cost of operating any equipment.

(d) *Administrative appeals.* Ex-Im Bank shall not charge for administrative review of an exemption applied in an initial determination. Ex-Im Bank shall charge, however, for search and review pursuant to an administrative appeal if the appeal is based on a claim other than the application of an exemption in the initial determination.

(e) *Duplication.* Ex-Im Bank shall charge $.10 per page for paper copy duplication. Ex-Im Bank shall charge the actual or estimated cost of copies prepared by computer, such as tape or

§ 404.10

printouts, or for other methods of duplication. When duplication charges are expected to exceed $50.00, Ex-Im Bank shall seek the requester's consent to be responsible for the estimated charges unless a requester has already expressed a willingness to pay duplication fees in excess of $50.00. Ex-Im Bank shall also offer the requester the opportunity to alter the request in order to reduce duplication costs.

(f) *Fees for searches that produce no records.* Fees shall be payable as provided in this section even though searches and review do not generate any disclosable records.

(g) *Aggregating requests.* A requester, or a group of requesters acting in concert, shall not file multiple requests, seeking portions of a record or similar or related records, in order to avoid payment of fees. Ex-Im Bank shall aggregate any such requests and charge as if the requests were a single request.

(h) *Special services charges.* Complying with requests for special services such as those listed in this paragraph is entirely at the discretion of Ex-Im Bank. Ex-Im Bank shall recover the full costs of providing such services to the extent that it elects to provide them.

(1) *Certifications.* Ex-Im Bank shall charge $25.00 to certify the authenticity of any Ex-Im Bank record or any copy of such record.

(2) *Special shipping.* Ex-Im Bank may ship by special means (e.g., express mail) if the requester so desires, provided that the requester has paid or has expressly undertaken to pay all costs of such special services. Ex-Im Bank shall not charge for ordinary packaging and mailing.

(i) *Minimum fee.* Ex-Im Bank shall waive a final fee of $5.00 or less.

(j) *Advance payment.* Whenever Ex-Im Bank estimates that the fees are likely to exceed $250.00, Ex-Im Bank shall notify the requester of the likely cost and shall require an advance payment of an amount up to the full estimated charges.

(k) *Failure to pay fee.* Ex-Im Bank shall not process a request by a requester who has failed to pay a fee for a previous request unless and until such a requester had paid the full amount owed and also has paid, in advance, the total estimated charges for the new request. The administrative time limits for the new request—set forth in § 404.5—shall begin to run only after Ex-Im Bank has received the payments described in this section.

§ 404.10 **Fee waivers or reductions.**

(a) *General.* Upon request, Ex-Im Bank shall consider a discretionary fee waiver or reduction of the fees chargeable under § 404.9.

(b) *Form of request for fee waiver.* Ex-Im Bank shall deny a request for a waiver or reduction of fees that does not clearly address each of the following:

(1) The proposed use of the records and whether the requester will derive income or other benefit from such use;

(2) An explanation of the reasons why the public will benefit from such use; and

(3) If specialized use of the records is contemplated, a statement of the requester's qualifications that are relevant to the specialized use.

(d) *Burden of proof.* In all cases, the requester has the burden of presenting sufficient evidence or information to justify the fee waiver or reduction. The requester may use the procedures set forth in § 404.11 to appeal a denial of a fee waiver request.

(e) *Employee requests.* Fees of less than $50.00 shall be waived in connection with any request by an employee, former employee, or applicant for employment, related to a grievance or complaint of discrimination against Ex-Im Bank.

§ 404.11 **Administrative appeal.**

(a) *General.* Whenever a request for records, a fee waiver or expedited processing has been denied, the requester may appeal the denial within thirty days of the date of Ex-Im Bank's issuance of notice of such action. Any denial under this subpart must be appealed according to this section before a requester is eligible to seek judicial review.

(b) *Form.* Appeals must be made in writing and must be signed by the appellant. Appeals should be addressed to the Assistant General Counsel for Administration at the address at § 404.1(f). Both the envelope and the appeal letter should be clearly marked in capital letters: "FREEDOM OF INFORMATION ACT APPEAL." Failure to properly mark or address the appeal may slow its processing. The letter should include:

(1) A copy of the denied request or a description of the records requested;

(2) The name and title of the Ex-Im Bank employee who denied the request;

(3) The date on which the request was denied;

(4) The Ex-Im Bank identification number assigned to the request; and

(5) The return address and telephone number of the appellant.

(c) *Processing schedule.* Appeals shall not be deemed to have been received until the Assistant General Counsel for Administration receives the appeal. Ex-Im Bank shall notify the requester of the date on which an appeal was officially received. The disposition of an appeal shall be made in writing within twenty working days after the date of receipt of an appeal. The Assistant General Counsel for Administration may extend the time for response an additional ten working days if unusual circumstances exist, provided that the Assistant General Counsel for Administration notifies the requester in writing.

(d) *Ex-Im Bank decision.* A final determination which affirms an adverse initial determination shall set forth the reasons for affirming the denial and shall advise the requester of the right to seek judicial review. If the initial determination is reversed on appeal, the request shall be remanded to the Freedom of Information and Privacy Office to be processed promptly in accordance with the decision on appeal, subject to § 404.7(i).

Subpart B—Access to Records Under the Privacy Act of 1974

§ 404.12 General provisions.

(a) *Purpose.* This subpart establishes policies, procedures, requirements, and responsibilities for administration of the Privacy Act of 1974, 5 U.S.C. 552a, at the Export-Import Bank of the United States (Ex-Im Bank).

(b) *Relationship to the Freedom of Information Act.* The Privacy Act applies to records contained in a systems of records, as defined in § 404.13. If an individual submits a request for access to records and cites the Privacy Act, but the records sought are not contained in a Privacy Act system of records, then the request shall be processed only under subpart A of this part, Procedures for Disclosure of Records Under the Freedom of Information Act. All requests properly processed under this subpart B shall also be processed under subpart A of this part.

(c) *Appellate authority.* The Ex-Im Bank Assistant General Counsel for Administration is the appellate authority for all Privacy Act requests.

(d) *Delegation.* Any action or determination in this subpart which is the responsibility of a specific Ex-Im Bank employee may be delegated to a duly designated alternate.

(e) *Ex-Im Bank address.* The Export-Import Bank of the United States is located at 811 Vermont Avenue, NW, Washington, DC 20571.

§ 404.13 Definitions.

For purposes of this subpart, the following definitions shall apply:

Appeal—A written request to the Ex-Im Bank Assistant General Counsel for Administration for reversal of an adverse initial determination.

Final determination—The written decision by the Assistant General Counsel for Administration on an appeal.

Individual—A citizen of the United States or an alien lawfully admitted for permanent residence.

Initial determination—The initial written determination in response to a Privacy Act request.

Record—Any item, collection or grouping of information about an individual that is maintained within a system of records and that contains the individual's name or an identifying number, symbol or other identifying particular assigned to the individual.

Redaction—The process of removing non-disclosable material from a record so that the remainder may be released.

Request for access—A request to view a record.

Request for accounting—A request for a list of all disclosures of a record.

Request for correction—A request to modify a record.

§ 404.14

Requester—An individual who makes a request under the Privacy Act.

Review—The process of examining a record to determine whether any portion is required to be withheld.

Search—The process of identifying and collecting records pursuant to a request.

System of records—A group of any records under the control of an agency from which information is retrieved by the name of the individual or some identifying number, symbol or other identifying particular assigned to the individual.

Working days—All calendar days excluding Saturdays, Sundays, and Federal Government holidays.

§ 404.14 Requirements of request for access.

(a) *Form.* Requests for access must be made in writing and must be signed by the requester. Requests should be addressed to the Freedom of Information and Privacy Office at the address in § 404.12(e) and should contain both the return address and telephone number of the requester.

(b) *Description of records sought.* A request for access must describe the records sought in sufficient detail so as to enable Ex-Im Bank personnel to locate the system of records containing the records with a reasonable amount of effort. To the extent practicable, such description should include the nature of the record sought, the date of the record or the period in which the record was compiled, and the name or identifying number of the system of records in which the requester believes the record is kept. A requester may include his or her social security number in the request in order to facilitate the identification and location of the requested records.

(c) *Fee statement.* The request must contain a statement expressing willingness to pay fees for processing the request or a request for a fee waiver (see § 404.16(d)).

(1) Whenever a requester submits a request for access that does not contain a fee statement or a request for a fee waiver, Ex-Im Bank shall advise the requester of the requirements of this section. If the requester fails to respond within ten working days of such notification, then the Freedom of Information and Privacy Office shall notify the requester, in writing, that Ex-Im Bank will not process the request.

(2) A general statement by the requester expressing willingness to pay all applicable fees shall be deemed an agreement to pay up to $25.00. If Ex-Im Bank estimates that the fees for a request will exceed $25.00, then Ex-Im Bank shall notify the requester. Ex-Im Bank shall offer the requester the opportunity to agree, in writing, either to pay a greater fee or to modify the request as a means of limiting the cost.

(3) Whenever the estimated fee chargeable under this section exceeds $25.00, Ex-Im Bank reserves the right to require a requester to make an advance payment prior to processing the request.

(4) Ex-Im Bank shall not process a request by a requester who has failed to pay a fee for a previous request unless and until such requester had paid the full amount owed and also has paid, in advance, the total estimated charges for the new request.

(d) *Verification of identity.* An individual who submits a request for access must verify his or her identity. The request must include the requesters full name, current address, and date and place of birth. In addition, such requester must provide a notarized statement attesting to his or her identity.

(e) *Verification of guardianship.* When a parent or guardian of a minor or the guardian of a person judicially determined to be incompetent submits a request for access to records that relate to the minor or incompetent, such parent or guardian must establish:

(1) His or her own identity and the identity of the subject of the record in accordance with paragraph (d) of this section; and

(2) Parentage or guardianship of the subject of the record, either by providing a copy of the subject's birth certificate showing parentage or by providing a court order establishing guardianship.

(f) *Written notice of amendment.* The requester must provide any amendment to the original request in writing to Ex-Im Bank.

(g) *Requester assistance.* Ex-Im Bank shall make reasonable efforts to assist a requester in complying with the requirements of this section.

(h) *Date of receipt.* Requests for access shall be deemed to have been received on the date that the request is received by the Freedom of Information and Privacy Office, provided that all the requirements of this section have been met. Ex-Im Bank shall notify the requester of the date on which it officially received a request.

§ 404.15 Initial determination.

(a) *Time for processing.* The Freedom of Information and Privacy Office shall respond to valid requests for access within twenty working days of the date of receipt of the request letter. The time for response may be extended an additional ten working days for good cause, provided that the Freedom of Information and Privacy Office notifies the requester in writing.

(b) *Notice regarding request for access.* The Freedom of Information and Privacy Office shall notify the requester in writing of its decision to grant or deny a request for access.

(1) If the request is granted, then the notice shall either include the requested records, in releasable form, or shall describe the manner in which access to the record will be granted. The notice also shall inform the requester of any processing fee.

(2) A denial is a determination to withhold any requested record in whole or in part or a determination that the requested record does not exist or cannot be located. If the request is denied, then the denial notice shall state:

(i) The name, signature, and title or position of the person responsible for the denial;

(ii) The reasons for the denial; and

(iii) The procedure for appeal of the denial under § 404.17 and a brief description of the requirements of that section.

(c) *Form of record disclosure.* Ex-Im Bank shall grant access to the requested records either by providing the requester with a copy of the record or, at the requester's option, by making the record available for inspection at a reasonable time and place. If Ex-Im Bank makes the record available for inspection, such inspection shall not unreasonably disrupt Ex-Im Bank operations. In addition, the requester must provide a form of official photographic identification—such as a passport, driver's license or identification badge—and any other form of identification bearing his or her name and address prior to inspection of the requested records. Records may be inspected by the requester in the presence of another individual, provided that the requester signs a form stating that Ex-Im Bank is authorized to disclose the record in the presence of both individuals.

§ 404.16 Schedule of fees.

(a) *Search and review.* Ex-Im Bank shall not charge for search and review.

(b) *Duplication.* Ex-Im Bank shall charge $.10 per page for paper copy duplication. Ex-Im Bank shall charge the actual or estimated cost of copies prepared by computer, such as tape or printouts, or for other methods of reproduction or duplication.

(c) *Minimum fee.* Ex-Im Bank shall waive final fees of $5.00 or less.

(d) *Fee waivers.* Ex-Im Bank may waive fees whenever it is determined to be in the public interest. Fees of less than $50.00 shall be waived in connection with any request by an employee, former employee or applicant for employment, related to a grievance or complaint of discrimination against Ex-Im Bank.

(e) *Special services charges.* Complying with requests for special services such as those listed in this paragraph is entirely at the discretion of Ex-Im Bank. Ex-Im Bank shall recover the full costs of providing such services to the extent that it elects to provide them.

(1) *Certifications.* Ex-Im Bank shall charge $25.00 to certify the authenticity of any Ex-Im Bank record or any copy of such record.

(2) *Special shipping.* Ex-Im Bank may ship by special means (e.g., express mail) if the requester so desires, provided that the requester has paid or has expressly undertaken to pay all costs of such special services. Ex-Im Bank shall not charge for ordinary packaging and mailing.

§ 404.17 Appeal of denials of access.

(a) *Appeals to the Assistant General Counsel for Administration.* Whenever

Ex-Im Bank denies a request for access or for waiver or reduction of fees, the requester may appeal the denial to the Assistant General Counsel for Administration within 30 working days of the date of Ex-Im Bank's issuance of notice of such action. Appeals must be made in writing and must be signed by the appellant. Appeals should be addressed to the Assistant General Counsel for Administration at the address in §404.12(e). Both the envelope and the appeal letter should be clearly marked in capital letters: "PRIVACY ACT APPEAL." Failure to properly mark or address the appeal may slow its processing. An appeal shall not be deemed to have been received by Ex-Im Bank until the Assistant General Counsel for Administration receives the appeal letter. The letter should include:

(1) A copy of the denied request or a description of the records requested;

(2) The name and title of the Ex-Im Bank employee who denied the request;

(3) The date on which the request was denied; and

(4) The Ex-Im Bank identification number assigned to the request.

(b) *Final determination.* The disposition of an access appeal shall be made in writing within twenty working days after the date of receipt of the appeal. The Assistant General Counsel for Administration may extend the time for response an additional ten working days for good cause, provided that the requester is notified in writing. A decision affirming the denial of a request for access shall include a brief statement of the reasons for affirming the denial and shall advise the requester of the right to seek judicial review. If the initial determination is reversed, then the request shall be remanded to the Freedom of Information and Privacy Office to be processed in accordance with the decision on appeal.

§ 404.18 Requests for correction of records.

(a) *Form.* Requests for correction must be made in writing and must be signed by the requester. Requests should be addressed to the Freedom of Information and Privacy Office at the address in § 404.12(e) and should contain both the return address and telephone number of the requester. The request must identify the particular record in question, state the correction sought, and set forth the justification for the correction. The requester also must verify his or her identity in accordance with the procedures set forth at § 404.14(d) and (e). Both the envelope and the request for correction itself should be clearly marked in capital letters: "PRIVACY ACT CORRECTION REQUEST."

(b) *Initial determination.* The Freedom of Information and Privacy Office shall respond to valid correction requests within ten working days of receipt of the request letter. If Ex-Im Bank grants the request for correction, then the Freedom of Information and Privacy Office shall advise the requester of his or her right to obtain a copy, in releasable form, of the corrected record. A denial notice shall state the reasons for the denial and shall advise the requester of the right to appeal. Ex-Im Bank shall not charge for processing requests for correction.

(c) *Appeal of denial of request for correction.* Whenever Ex-Im Bank denies a request for correction, the requester may appeal the denial to the Assistant General Counsel for Administration within thirty working days of Ex-Im Bank's issuance of notice of such action. Appeals must be made in writing and must be signed by the appellant. Appeals should be addressed to the Assistant General Counsel for Administration at the address set forth in § 404.12(e). Both the envelope and the appeal letter should be clearly marked in capital letters: "PRIVACY ACT CORRECTION APPEAL." Failure to properly mark or address the appeal may slow its processing. An appeal shall not be deemed to have been received by Ex-Im Bank until the Assistant General Counsel for Administration receives the appeal letter. The letter must include:

(1) A copy of the denied request or a description of the correction sought;

(2) The name and title of the Ex-Im Bank employee who denied the request;

(3) The date on which the request was denied;

(4) The Ex-Im Bank identification number assigned to the request; and

(5) Any information said to justify the correction.

Export-Import Bank of the U.S. § 404.19

(d) *Final determination on correction appeal.* (1) The disposition of an appeal shall be made in writing within twenty working days after the date of receipt of an appeal. The Assistant General Counsel for Administration may extend the time for response an additional ten working days for good cause, provided that the requester is notified in writing.

(2) A decision affirming the denial of a request for access shall advise the appellant of the:

(i) Reasons for affirming the denial;

(ii) Right to seek judicial review; and

(iii) Right to file a statement of disagreement, as provided in paragraph (e) of this section.

(3) If the initial determination is reversed, then the request shall be remanded to the Freedom of Information and Privacy Office to be processed in accordance with the decision on appeal.

(e) *Statement of disagreement.* Upon denial of a correction appeal, the appellant shall have the right to file a statement of disagreement with Ex-Im Bank, setting forth his or her reasons for disagreeing with the Agency's action. The statement should be addressed to the Freedom of Information and Privacy Office at the address in § 404.12(e) and must be received within thirty working days of Ex-Im Bank's issuance of the denial notice. A statement of disagreement must not exceed one typed page per fact disputed. Statements exceeding this limit shall be returned to the requester for editing. Upon receipt of a statement of disagreement under this section, the Freedom of Information and Privacy Office shall have the statement included in the system of records in which the disputed record is maintained and shall have the disputed record marked so as to indicate that a Statement of Disagreement has been filed. Ex-Im Bank may also append to the disputed record a written statement regarding Ex-Im Bank's reasons for denying the request to correct the record.

(f) *Notices of correction or disagreement.* In any disclosure of a record for which Ex-Im Bank has received a statement of disagreement, Ex-Im Bank shall clearly note any portion of the record which is disputed and shall provide a copy of the statement of disagreement. Ex-Im Bank also may provide its own statement regarding the disputed record. In addition, whenever Ex-Im Bank corrects a record or receives a statement of disagreement, Ex-Im Bank shall, as is reasonable under the circumstances, advise any person or agency to which it previously disclosed such record of the correction or statement, provided that an accounting of such disclosure exists.

§ 404.19 **Request for accounting of record disclosures.**

(a) *Required information.* With respect to each system of records under Ex-Im Bank control, Ex-Im Bank shall maintain an accurate accounting of the date, nature, and purpose of each external disclosure of a record and the name and address of all persons, organizations, and agencies to which disclosure has been made. Ex-Im Bank shall retain this accounting for at least five years or the life of the record, whichever is longer.

(b) *Form.* An individual may obtain an accounting of all disclosures of a record, provided that such individual establishes his or her identity as the subject of such record in accordance with the procedures set forth at § 404.14(d) and (e). A request for an accounting must be made in writing and must be signed by the requester. The request should be addressed to the Freedom of Information and Privacy Office at the address in § 404.12(e) and should contain both the return address and telephone number of the requester. Both the envelope and the request itself should be clearly be marked in capital letters: "PRIVACY ACT ACCOUNTING REQUEST." Failure to properly mark or address the request may slow its processing. The request shall not be deemed to have been received by Ex-Im Bank until the Freedom of Information and Privacy Office receives the request. The letter must clearly identify the particular record for which the accounting is requested.

(c) *Initial determination.* The Freedom of Information and Privacy Office shall notify the requester whether the request will be granted or denied within ten working days of receipt of a valid request for an accounting. Ex-Im Bank

§ 404.20

shall not charge for processing such a request.

(d) *Exceptions.* Ex-Im Bank shall not be required to provide an accounting to an individual when the accounting relates to a disclosure made:

(1) To an employee within the agency;

(2) Under the FOIA; or

(3) To a law enforcement agency for an authorized law enforcement activity in response to a written request from such agency which specified the law enforcement activity for which the disclosure was sought.

§ 404.20 Notice of court-ordered and emergency disclosures.

(a) *Court-ordered disclosures.* When a record pertaining to an individual is required to be disclosed by a court order, the Assistant General Counsel for Administration shall make reasonable efforts to provide notice to the subject individual. Notice shall be given within a reasonable time after Ex-Im Bank's receipt of the order, except that in a case in which the order is not a matter of public record, notice shall be given only after the order becomes public. Such notice shall be mailed to the individual's last known address and shall contain a copy of the order and a description of the information disclosed.

(b) *Emergency disclosures.* If a record has been disclosed by Ex-Im Bank under compelling circumstances affecting the health or safety of any person, then, within ten working days, the Assistant General Counsel for Administration shall notify the subject individual of the disclosure at his or her last known address. The notice of such disclosure shall be in writing and shall state the:

(1) Nature of the information disclosed;

(2) Person, organization or agency to which it was disclosed;

(3) Date of disclosure; and

(4) Compelling circumstances justifying the disclosure.

§ 404.21 Submission of social security and passport numbers.

(a) *Policy.* Ex-Im Bank recognizes the importance of assessing, to the extent reasonably possible, the risks associated with transactions supported by Ex-Im Bank. It is often difficult to assess risks related to individuals and non-publicly trade entities. Therefore, when an individual or a non-publicly traded entity applies for participation in an Ex-Im Bank program or is proposed as a guarantor for an Ex-Im Bank transaction, Ex-Im Bank may request social security and/or U.S. passport numbers from such individual or from the principals of such entity. Ex-Im Bank shall not require submission of this information, and unwillingness or inability to provide a social security or passport number shall not affect Ex-Im Bank's decision on an application for Ex-Im Bank assistance.

(b) *Use.* Ex-Im Bank shall use social security and passport numbers to assess the creditworthiness of Ex-Im Bank program participants and as a mechanism for enforcing agreements with Ex-Im Bank. Such information shall not be disclosed, except as warranted by law and regulation.

(c) *Notice.* Whenever Ex-Im Bank requests a social security or passport number, Ex-Im Bank shall place an appropriate Privacy Act notification on the form used to collect the information.

§ 404.22 Government contracts.

(a) *Approval by Assistant General Counsel for Administration.* Ex-Im Bank shall not contract for the operation of a system of records or for an activity that requires access to a system of records without the express, written approval of the Assistant General Counsel for Administration.

(b) *Contract clauses.* Any contract authorized under paragraph (a) of this section shall contain the standard contract clauses required by the Federal Acquisition Regulation (48 CFR 24.104) to ensure compliance with the requirements imposed by the Privacy Act. The division within Ex-Im Bank that is responsible for technical supervision of the contract shall be responsible for ensuring that the contractor complies with the Privacy Act contract requirements.

(c) *Contractor status.* Any contractor that operates an Ex-Im Bank system of records or engages in an activity that requires access to an Ex-Im Bank system of records shall be considered an

Ex-Im Bank employee for purposes of this subpart. Ex-Im Bank shall supply any such contractor with a copy of the regulations in this subpart upon entering into a contract with Ex-Im Bank.

§ 404.23 Other rights and services.

Nothing in this subpart shall be construed to entitle any person to any service or to the disclosure of any record to which such person is not entitled under the Privacy Act.

Subpart C—Demands for Testimony of Current and Former Ex-Im Bank Personnel and for Production of Ex-Im Bank Records

SOURCE: 71 FR 14361, Mar. 22, 2006, unless otherwise noted.

§ 404.24 General provisions.

(a) *Purpose.* This subpart establishes policy, assigns responsibilities and prescribes procedures with respect to:

(1) The production or disclosure of official information or records of Ex-Im Bank in all legal proceedings to which Ex-Im Bank is not a party;

(2) Demands for testimony of Ex-Im Bank personnel related to information acquired as a result of performance of their official duties, or by virtue of their official status, in all legal proceedings where Ex-Im Bank is not a party; and

(3) The offer of expert or opinion testimony by Ex-Im Bank personnel regarding matters related to the performance of their official duties.

(b) *Policy.* Ex-Im Bank seeks to further the following goals in enacting this subpart:

(1) Conservation of agency resources for official business;

(2) Minimization of agency involvement in controversial issues unrelated to its mission;

(3) Maintenance of the agency's impartiality amongst private litigants;

(4) Protection of confidential and/or sensitive information; and

(5) Maintenance of the integrity of the agency's deliberative processes.

§ 404.25 Applicability.

This subpart applies exclusively to demands for testimony and/or production of records issued to Ex-Im Bank personnel, in connection with legal proceedings to which Ex-Im Bank is not a party, regarding information acquired in the course of the performance of official duties or due to their official status. Nothing in this subpart shall be construed to waive the sovereign immunity of the United States. This subpart shall not apply to the following:

(a) Demands for testimony and/or production of records pursuant to a legal proceeding to which Ex-Im Bank is a party;

(b) Demands for testimony and/or production of records in those instances in which Ex-Im Bank personnel are asked to disclose information wholly unrelated to their official duties; and

(c) Congressional demands and requests for testimony or records.

§ 404.26 Definitions.

For purposes of this subpart, the following definitions shall apply—

Demand—includes an order, subpoena, or other compulsory process issued by a party in litigation or a court of competent jurisdiction, requiring the production or release of Ex-Im Bank information or records, or requiring the testimony of Ex-Im Bank personnel.

Ex-Im Bank personnel—includes any current or former officer or employee of Ex-Im Bank, including all individuals who have been appointed by, or subject to, the official supervision, jurisdiction, or control of any Ex-Im Bank employees. This definition encompasses all individuals hired through contractual agreements with Ex-Im Bank, such as: consultants, contractors, sub-contractors, and their employees.

Legal proceeding—a case or controversy pending before any federal, state, or local court, including a grand jury proceeding; a proceeding before a federal, state, or local administrative judge, board, or other similar body with adjudicative powers; or a legislative proceeding before a state or local legislative body.

§ 404.27

Records—all documentary materials that Ex-Im Bank creates or receives in connection with the transaction of official business, including any materials classified as "Federal records" under 44 U.S.C. 3301 and its implementing regulations.

Testimony—written or oral statements, including, but not limited to, depositions, answers to interrogatories, affidavits, declarations, and any other statements made in a legal proceeding, including any expert or opinion testimony.

§ 404.27 Demand requirements.

A party's demand for testimony and/or production of records by Ex-Im Bank personnel regarding information acquired in the course of their performance of official duties or due to their official status shall be set forth in, or accompanied by, a signed affidavit or other written statement. Such affidavit or written statement must be submitted at least 30 days prior to the date such testimony and/or production of records is requested to be taken and/or produced. A copy of the affidavit or written statement shall be served on the other parties to the legal proceeding. The affidavit or written statement must:

(a) Be addressed to the Export-Import Bank of the United States, Office of the General Counsel, 811 Vermont Ave., NW., Washington, DC 20571;

(b) State the nature of the legal proceeding, including any docket number, title of the case, and the name of the administrative or adjudicative body before which the proceedings are to be heard;

(c) State the nature of the testimony or records sought;

(d) State the relevance of the information sought to the legal proceedings;

(e) State why such information can only be obtained through testimony or production of records by Ex-Im Bank personnel; and

(f) Comply with all procedures governing valid service of process.

§ 404.28 Notification of General Counsel required.

Ex-Im Bank personnel receiving a demand for testimony and/or production of records regarding information acquired in the course of their performance of official duties, or due to their official status, shall immediately notify the General Counsel of Ex-Im Bank ("General Counsel") upon receipt of such demand. The General Counsel maintains the exclusive authority to waive the requirements of any or all sections of this subpart and reserves the right to delegate his or her authority under this subpart to other appropriate Ex-Im Bank personnel.

§ 404.29 Restrictions on testimony and production of records.

Ex-Im Bank personnel may not provide testimony and/or produce records regarding information acquired in the course of their performance of official duties, or due to their official status, in connection with any legal proceeding to which this subpart applies, without authorization by the General Counsel. Such authorization must be in writing, unless the General Counsel determines that circumstances warrant an oral authorization, and such oral authorization is subsequently documented.

§ 404.30 Factors General Counsel may consider in determining whether to authorize testimony and/or the production of records.

In determining whether to authorize Ex-Im Bank personnel to provide testimony and/or produce records regarding information acquired in the course of their performance of official duties, or due to their official status, the General Counsel may consider factors including, but not limited to, the following:

(a) Efficiency—the conservation of the time and resources of Ex-Im Bank personnel for the conduct of official business;

(b) Undue burden—whether the demand creates an undue burden upon Ex-Im Bank or is otherwise inappropriate under any applicable administrative or court rules;

(c) Appearance of bias—whether the testimony and/or production of records could result in the public perception that Ex-Im Bank is favoring one party over another, or advocating the position of a party to the proceeding;

Export-Import Bank of the U.S. § 404.33

(d) Furtherance of agency policy—whether the testimony and/or production of records is consistent with the policy and mission of the Ex-Im Bank;

(e) Prevention of fraud or injustice—whether the disclosure of the information requested is necessary to prevent the perpetration of fraud or injustice;

(f) Relevance to litigation—whether the testimony and/or production of records sought is relevant to the subject litigation;

(g) Necessity—whether the testimony and/or production of records, including a release of such *in camera*, is appropriate or necessary as determined by either the procedural rules governing the legal proceeding, or according to the relevant laws concerning privilege;

(h) Availability from another source—whether the information sought through testimony or production of records is available from another source;

(i) Violations of laws or regulations—whether the testimony and/or production of records would violate a statute, regulation, executive order, or other official directive;

(j) Classified information—whether the testimony and/or production of records would improperly reveal information classified pursuant to applicable statute or Executive Order; and

(k) Compromise of rights and interests—whether the testimony and/or production of records would compromise any of the following: law enforcement interests, constitutional rights, national security interests, foreign policy interests, or the confidentiality of commercial and/or financial information.

§ 404.31 Procedure for declining to testify and/or produce records.

Ex-Im Bank personnel receiving a demand to provide testimony and/or produce records regarding information acquired in the course of their performance of official duties, or due to their official status, and who have not received written authorization from the General Counsel to provide such information, shall:

(a) Respectfully decline to answer or appear for examination on the grounds that such testimony is forbidden by this subpart;

(b) Request the opportunity to consult with the General Counsel;

(c) Explain that only upon consultation may they be granted approval to provide such testimony;

(d) Explain that providing such testimony or records absent approval may subject the individual to criminal liability under 18 U.S.C. 641, as well as other applicable laws, and other disciplinary action; and

(e) Request a stay of the request or demand pending a determination by the General Counsel.

§ 404.32 Procedure in the event a decision concerning a demand is not made prior to the time a response to the demand is required.

If response to a demand is required before a determination has been rendered by the General Counsel, the U.S. Attorney or such other attorney as may be designated for the purpose will appear with the Ex-Im Bank personnel upon whom the demand has been made, and will furnish the court or other authority with a copy of the regulations contained in this subpart and inform the court or other authority that the demand has been or is being, as the case may be, referred for prompt consideration of the General Counsel. The court or other authority shall be requested respectfully to stay the demand pending determination by the General Counsel.

§ 404.33 Procedure in the event of an adverse ruling.

If the court or other authority declines to stay the effect of the demand in response to a request made in accordance with § 404.32 pending a determination by the General Counsel, or if the court or other authority rules that the demand must be complied with irrespective of the instructions from the General Counsel not to produce the material or disclose the information sought, the Ex-Im Bank personnel upon whom the demand has been made shall respectfully decline to comply with the demand (*United States ex rel. Touhy* v. *Ragen*, 340 U.S. 462).

§ 404.34 Procedure for demands for testimony or production of documents regarding confidential information.

In addition to compliance with the requirements of this subpart, demands to provide testimony and/or produce records that concern information protected by the Privacy Act, 5 U.S.C. 552a, or any other authority mandating confidentiality of certain classes of records or information, must also satisfy the requirements for disclosure imposed by such authority before records may be produced or testimony given.

§ 404.35 Procedures for requests for Ex-Im Bank employees to provide expert or opinion testimony.

No Ex-Im Bank personnel may, unless specifically authorized by the General Counsel, testify in any legal proceeding as an expert or opinion witness as to any matter related to his or her duties or the functions of the Ex-Im Bank, including the meaning of Ex-Im Bank documents. Any demand for expert or opinion testimony shall comply with the policies and procedures outlined in this subpart.

§ 404.36 No private right of action.

Nothing in this subpart shall be construed as creating any right, substantive or procedural, enforceable at law or equity by a party against Ex-Im Bank or the United States.

Subparts D-E [Reserved]

PART 405 [RESERVED]

PART 407—REGULATIONS GOVERNING PUBLIC OBSERVATION OF EX-IMBANK MEETINGS

Sec.
407.1 Purpose, scope and definitions.
407.2 Closing meetings.
407.3 Procedures applicable to regularly scheduled meetings.
407.4 Procedures applicable to other meetings.
407.5 Certification by General Counsel.
407.6 Transcripts, recordings and minutes of closed meetings.
407.7 Relationship to Freedom of Information Act.

AUTHORITY: Sec. (g) Government in the Sunshine Act, 5 U.S.C. 552b(g); secs. (b) through (f), 5 U.S.C. 552b.

SOURCE: 42 FR 12417, Mar. 4, 1977, unless otherwise noted.

§ 407.1 Purpose, scope and definitions.

(a) Consistent with the principles that: (1) The public is entitled to the fullest practicable information regarding the decision-making processes of the Federal Government, and (2) the rights of individuals and the ability of the Export-Import Bank of the United States to carry out its statutory responsibilities should be protected, this part is promulgated pursuant to the directive of section (g) of the Government in the Sunshine Act, 5 U.S.C. 552b(g), and specifically implements sections (b) through (f) of said Act, 5 U.S.C. 552b (b) through (f).

(b) The term *meeting* means any meeting of the Board of Directors of Eximbank at which a quorum is present and where deliberations determine or result in the joint conduct or disposition of official Eximbank business.

(c) The term *regularly scheduled meeting* means meetings of the Board of Directors or the Executive Committee which are held at 9:30 a.m. on Thursday of each week.

(d) The term *General Counsel* means the General Counsel and his or her designees.

[42 FR 12417, Mar. 4, 1977, as amended at 47 FR 12136, Mar. 22, 1982; 49 FR 41237, Oct. 22, 1984; 72 FR 66043, Nov. 27, 2007]

§ 407.2 Closing meetings.

(a) Except where Eximbank finds that the public interest requires otherwise, a meeting, or any portion thereof, may be closed to the public, where the Board of Directors determines that such meetings, or any portion thereof, or information pertaining to such meeting, or any portion thereof, is likely to:

(1) Disclose matters that are: (i) Specifically authorized under criteria established by an Executive order to be kept secret in the interests of national defense or foreign policy and (ii) in fact properly classified pursuant to such Executive order;

Export-Import Bank of the U.S. § 407.2

(2) Relate solely to the internal personnel rules and practices of Eximbank or any other agency;

(3) Disclose matters specifically exempted from disclosure by statute (other than section 552 of title 5 U.S.C.), provided that such statute: (i) Requires that the matters be withheld from the public in such a manner as to leave no discretion on the issue, or (ii) establishes particular criteria for withholding or refers to particular types of matters to be withheld;

(4) Disclose trade secrets and commercial or financial information obtained from a person and privileged or confidential;

(5) Involve accusing any person of a crime, or formally censuring any person;

(6) Disclose information of a personal nature where disclosure would constitute a clearly unwarranted invasion of personal privacy;

(7) Disclose investigatory records compiled for law enforcement purposes, or information which if written would be contained in such records, but only to the extent that the production of such records or information would:

(i) Interfere with enforcement proceedings,

(ii) Deprive a person of a right to a fair trial or an impartial adjudication,

(iii) Constitute an unwarranted invasion of personal privacy,

(iv) Disclose the identity of a confidential source and, in the case of a record compiled by a criminal law enforcement authority in the course of a criminal investigation, or by an agency conducting a lawful national security intelligence investigation, confidential information funished only by the confidential source,

(v) Disclose investigative techniques and procedures, or

(vi) Endanger the life or physical safety of law enforcement personnel;

(8) Disclose information contained in or related to examination, operating, or condition reports prepared by, on behalf of, or for the use of an agency responsible for the regulation or supervision of financial institutions;

(9) Disclose information the premature disclosure of which would:

(i) In the case of an agency which regulates currencies, securities, commodities, or financial institutions, be likely to: (A) Lead to significant financial speculation in currencies, securities, or commodities, or (B) significantly endanger the stability of any financial institution; or

(ii) In the case of Eximbank or any other agency, be likely to significantly frustrate implementation of a proposed agency action;

except that paragraph (a)(9)(ii) of this section shall not apply in any instance where the agency has already disclosed to the public the content or nature of its proposed action, or where the agency is required by law to make such disclosure on its own initiative prior to taking final agency on such proposal; or

(10) Specifically concern Eximbank's issuance of a subpoena, or Eximbank's participation in a civil action or proceeding, an action in a foreign court or international tribunal, or an arbitration.

(b) Inasmuch as opening any regularly scheduled meeting, or any portion thereof, to public observation will be likely to result in the disclosure of the kind of information set forth in paragraph (a) (4), (8), (9)(i) or (a)(10) of this section, or any combination thereof, of paragraph (a) of this section, the Board of Directors expects to close all regularly scheduled meetings to the public.

(c) Any other meeting of Eximbank, or any portion thereof, will be open to public observation except where the Board of Directors determines that such meeting, or any portion thereof, is likely to disclose information of the kind set forth in any paragraph of §407.2(a). In the event that the Board of Directors closes such meeting, or any portion thereof, by virtue of paragraph (a)(4), (8), (9)(i)(A) or (a)(10) of this section, or any combination thereof, the procedure set forth in §407.3 below will apply, and in the event that the Board of Directors closes such meeting, or any portion thereof, by virtue of any of the remaining paragraphs of §407.2(a), or any combination thereof, the procedures set forth in §407.4 will apply.

[42 FR 12417, Mar. 4, 1977, as amended at 72 FR 66043, Nov. 27, 2007]

§ 407.3 Procedures applicable to regularly scheduled meetings.

(a) *Announcements.* Regularly scheduled meetings of the Board of Directors will be held at 9:30 a.m. every Thursday in the Board Room (Room 1141) of the Bank's headquarters. In the event that a regularly scheduled meeting is rescheduled, public announcement of the time, date and place of such meeting will be made at the earliest practicable time in the form of a notice posted in the Office of the Secretary. An agenda setting forth the subject matter of each regularly scheduled meeting will be made available in the Office of the Secretary (Room 935), telephone number (202) (566–8871) at the earliest practicable time, *Provided,* That individual items may be added to or deleted from any agenda at any time. Inquiries from the public regarding any regularly scheduled meeting shall be directed to the Office of the Secretary.

(b) *Voting.* At the beginning of each regularly scheduled meeting, the Board of Directors will vote by recorded vote on whether to close such meeting. No proxy vote will be permitted. A record of such vote indicating the vote of each Director will be posted in the Office of the Secretary immediately following the conclusion of such meeting.

[42 FR 12417, Mar. 4, 1977, as amended at 47 FR 12136, Mar. 22, 1982; 49 FR 9560, Mar. 14, 1984; 49 FR 41237, Oct. 22, 1984; 50 FR 8606, Mar. 4, 1985; 72 FR 66043, Nov. 27, 2007]

§ 407.4 Procedures applicable to other meetings.

(a) *Amendments.* (1) For every meeting which is to be open to public observation or which is to be closed pursuant to any paragraph of § 407.2(a) other than paragraphs (a) (4), (8), (9)(i) or (10), or any combination thereof, public announcement will be made at least one week before the meeting of the time, place, and the agenda setting forth the subject matter of such meeting, and whether the meeting, or any portion thereof, is to be open or closed to the public.

(2) Inquiries from the public regarding any such meeting shall be directed to the Office of the Secretary.

(3) The one-week period for the announcement required by paragraph (a)(1) of this section may be reduced if the Board of Directors determines by a recorded vote that Eximbank business requires such meeting to be called at an earlier date. Public announcement of the time, place, and subject matter of such meeting, and whether open or closed to the public, will be made at the earliest practicable time.

(4) The time or place of a meeting may be changed following the announcement required by paragraph (a)(1) of this section only if public announcement is made of such change at the earliest practicable time.

(5) The subject matter of a meeting or the determination of the Board of Directors to open or close a meeting, or any portion thereof, to the public, may be changed following the announcement required by paragraph (a) of this section only if:

(i) A majority of the entire voting membership of the Board of Directors determines by a recorded vote that Eximbank business so requires and that no earlier announcement of the change was possible; and

(ii) The Board of Directors announces such change and the vote of each Director upon such change at the earliest practicable time.

(6) Individual items may be added to or deleted from any agenda at any time.

(7) The announcements required pursuant to this section shall be made in the form of a notice posted in the Office of the Secretary. In addition, immediately following each announcement required by this section, notice of: (i) The time, place and subject matter of a meeting which is to be open to public observation or which is to be closed pursuant to any section of § 407.2(a) other than paragraphs (a) (4), (8), (9)(i) or (10), or any combination thereof, (ii) the decision to open or close such meeting, or any portion thereof, or (iii) any change in any announcement previously made shall be submitted for publication in the FEDERAL REGISTER.

(8) The information required by this subsection shall be disclosed except to the extent that it is exempt from disclosure under any section of § 407.2(a).

(b) *Voting.* (1) Action to close a meeting, or any portion thereof, pursuant to any section of § 407.2(a), other than

Export-Import Bank of the U.S. § 407.6

paragraphs (a) (4), (8), (9)(i), or (10), or any combination thereof, shall be taken only when a majority of the entire voting membership of the Board of Directors votes to take such action.

(2) A separate vote of the Board of Directors shall be taken with respect to each meeting, or any portion thereof, which is proposed to be closed to the public pursuant to any section of § 407.2(a) other than paragraphs (a) (4), (8), (9)(i) or (10), or any combination thereof, or with respect to any information which is proposed to be withheld under any section of § 407.2(a), other than paragraphs (a) (4), (8), (9)(i) or (10), or any combination thereof.

(3) A single vote of the Board of Directors may be taken with respect to a series of meetings, or any portion thereof, which are proposed to be closed to the public pursuant to any paragraph of § 407.2(a), other than paragraphs (a) (4), (8), (9)(i) or (10), or combination thereof, or with respect to any information concerning such series of meetings, so long as each meeting in such series involves the same particular matters and is scheduled to be held no more than 30 days after the initial meeting in such series.

(4) Whenever any person whose interests may be directly affected by any portion of a meeting which is to be open to public observation submits a request in writing to the Office of the Secretary that the Board of Directors close such portion to the public under paragraph (a) (5), (6) or (7) of § 407.2, the Board of Directors, shall vote by recorded vote on whether to close such portion.

(5) No proxy vote will be permitted for any vote required under this section.

(6) A record of each vote indicating the vote of each Director pursuant to paragraphs (b) (1), (2), (3) or (4) of this section will be posted in the Office of the Secretary within one day after it has been taken, *Provided*, That if a meeting or portion thereof is to be closed, such record shall be accompanied by: (i) A full written explanation of the reasons for closing such meeting or portion thereof and (ii) a list of all persons expected to attend such meeting or portion thereof and their affiliation.

[42 FR 12417, Mar. 4, 1977, as amended at 72 FR 66043, Nov. 27, 2007]

§ 407.5 Certification by General Counsel.

For every meeting closed pursuant to any paragraph of § 407.2(a), the General Counsel of Eximbank will be asked to certify prior to such meeting that in his or her opinion such meeting may properly be closed to the public, and to state which of the exemptions set forth in § 407.2(a) he or she has relied upon. A copy of such certification will be posted in the Office of the Secretary. The original certification together with a statement from the presiding officer of such meeting setting forth the time, date and place of such meeting and the persons present will be retained by Eximbank as part of the transcript, recording or minutes of such meeting described below.

§ 407.6 Transcripts, recordings and minutes of closed meetings.

Eximbank will maintain a complete transcript or electronic recording of the proceedings of every meeting or portion thereof closed to the public, *Provided, however*, That if any meeting or portion thereof is closed pursuant to paragraphs (8), (9)(i) or (10) of § 407.2(a), Eximbank may maintain a set of detailed minutes for such meetings in lieu of a transcript or electronic recording. The entire transcript, electronic recording or set of minutes of a meeting will be made promptly available to the public for inspection and copying in the Office of the Secretary. Copies of such transcript or minutes, as well as copies of the transcription of such recording disclosing the identity of each speaker, will be furnished to any person at the actual cost of duplication or transcription. However, Eximbank will not make available for inspection or copying the transcript, electronic recording or minutes of the discussions of any item on the agenda of such meeting which contains information of the kind described in § 407.2(a). Requests to inspect or to have copies made of any transcript, electronic recording or set of minutes of any meeting or item(s) on the agenda, thereof should be made in writing to the General Counsel and if possible, identify the time, date and place of such meeting and briefly describe the item(s) being sought. Eximbank will maintain a complete verbatim copy of the transcript, a complete electronic recording or a complete copy of the minutes of each meeting, or portion thereof, closed to the public for two years after such meeting or one year from the date of final action of the Board of Directors on all items on the agenda of such meeting, whichever occurs later.

[42 FR 12417, Mar. 4, 1977, as amended at 72 FR 66143, Nov. 27, 2007]

§ 407.7 Relationship to Freedom of Information Act.

Nothing in this part expands or limits the present rights of any person under part 404, except that the exemptions contained in § 407.2 shall govern in the case of any request made pursuant to part 404 to copy or inspect the transcripts, recordings or minutes described in § 407.6.

PART 408—PROCEDURES FOR COMPLIANCE WITH THE NATIONAL ENVIRONMENTAL POLICY ACT

Subpart A—General

Sec.
408.1 Background.
408.2 Purpose.
408.3 Applicability.

Subpart B—Eximbank Implementing Procedures

408.4 Early involvement in foreign activities for which Eximbank financing may be requested.
408.5 Ensuring environmental documents are actually considered in Agency decision-making.
408.6 Typical classes of action.
408.7 Environmental information.

AUTHORITY: National Environmental Policy Act of 1969; 42 U.S.C. 4321 et seq.

SOURCE: 44 FR 50811, Aug. 30, 1979, unless otherwise noted.

Subpart A—General

§ 408.1 Background.

(a) The National Environmental Policy Act (NEPA) of 1969 (42 U.S.C. 4321 et seq.) establishes national policies and goals for the protection of the environment. Section 102(2) of NEPA contains certain procedural requirements directed toward the attainment of such goals. In particular, all Federal agencies are required to give appropriate consideration to the environmental effects of their proposed actions in their decision-making and to prepare detailed environmental statements on recommendations or reports on proposals for legislation and other major Federal Actions significantly affecting the quality of the human environment.

(b) Executive Order 11991 of May 24, 1977, directed the Council on Environmental Quality (CEQ) to issue regulations to implement the procedural provisions of NEPA (NEPA Regulations). Accordingly, CEQ issued final NEPA Regulations which are binding on all Federal agencies as of July 30, 1979 (40 CFR parts 1500 through 1508) on November 29, 1979. These Regulations provide that each Federal agency shall as necessary adopt implementing procedures to supplement the NEPA Regulations. Section 1507.3(b) of the NEPA Regulations identifies those sections of the NEPA Regulations which must be addressed in agency procedures.

§ 408.2 Purpose.

The purpose of this part is to establish procedures which supplement the NEPA Regulations and provide for the implementation of those provisions identified in § 1507.3(b) of the NEPA Regulations.

§ 408.3 Applicability.

Historically, virtually all financing provided by Eximbank has been in aid of U.S. exports which involve no effects on the quality of the environment within the United States, its territories or possessions. Eximbank has separate procedures for conducting environmental reviews where such reviews are required by E.O. 12114 (January 4, 1979) because of potential effects on the environment of global commons areas or on the environment of foreign

Export-Import Bank of the U.S. § 408.5

nations. The procedures set forth in this part apply to the relatively rare cases where Eximbank financing of U.S. exports may affect environmental quality in the United States, its territories or possessions.

Subpart B—Eximbank Implementing Procedures

§ 408.4 Early involvement in foreign activities for which Eximbank financing may be requested.

(a) Section 1501.2(d) of the NEPA Regulations requires agencies to provide for early involvement in actions which, while planned by private applicants or other non-Federal entities, require some form of Federal approval. Pursuant to the Export-Import Bank Act of 1945, as amended, Eximbank is asked to provide financing for transactions involving exports of U.S. goods and services for projects in foreign countries which are planned by non-U.S. entities (Transactions).

(b) To implement the requirements of § 1501.2(d) with respect to these Transactions, Eximbank:

(1) Will provide on a project-by-project basis to applicant seeking financing from Eximbank guidance as to the scope and level of environmental information to be used in evaluating a proposed Transaction where: (i) The proposed Eximbank financing would be a major action and (ii) a Transaction may significantly affect the quality of the human environment in the United States, its territories or possessions.

(2) Upon receipt of an application for Eximbank financing or notification that an application will be filed, will consult as required with other appropriate parties to initiate and coordinate the necessary environmental analyses.

These responsibilities will be performed by the General Counsel and the Engineers of Eximbank.

(c) To facilitate Eximbank review of Transactions for which positive determinations have been made under paragraphs (b)(1)(i) and (ii) of this section, applicants should:

(1) Consult with the Engineer as early as possible in the planning process for guidance on the scope and level of environmental information required to be submitted in support of their application;

(2) Conduct any studies which are deemed necessary and appropriate by Eximbank to determine the impact of the proposed action on the quality of the human environment;

(3) Consult with appropriate U.S. (Federal, regional, State and local) agencies and other potentially interested parties during preliminary planning stages to ensure that all environmental factors are identified;

(4) Submit applications for all U.S. (Federal, regional, State and local) approvals as early as possible in the planning process;

(5) Notify Eximbank as early as possible of all other applicable legal requirements for project completion so that all applicable Federal environmental reviews may be coordinated; and

(6) Notify Eximbank of all known parties potentially affected by or interested in the proposed action.

§ 408.5 Ensuring environmental documents are actually considered in Agency decision-making.

Section 1505.1 of the NEPA Regulations contains requirements to ensure adequate consideration of environmental documents in agency decision-making. To implement these requirements, Eximbank officials will:

(a) Consider all relevant environmental documents in evaluating applications for Eximbank financing;

(b) Ensure that all relevant environmental documents, comments and responses accompany the application through Eximbank's review processes;

(c) Consider only those alternatives encompassed by the range of alternatives discussed in the relevant environmental documents when evaluating an application which is the subject of an EIS.

§ 408.6

Eximbank actions	Start of NEPA process	Completion of NEPA process	Key officials or offices required to consider environmental documents
Issuance of Preliminary Commitment (P.C.).	When application is received.	When the Board of Directors meets to consider application. The Board may notify applicant that environmental effects will be considered when final commitment is requested and request information on environmental matters.	Under § 408.4(b)(1) (i) and (ii), General Counsel to determine whether requested Eximbank financing is a major action and Engineer to determine whether proposed Transaction may significantly affect the quality of the human environment in the United States, its territories or possessions.
Issuance of Final Commitment.	When application is received.	When the Board of Directors meets to consider application.	(If no P.C. has been issued, key offices will make determinations mentioned above.) Engineer to collect, prepare or arrange for preparation of all environmental documents.

§ 408.6 Typical classes of action.

(a) Section 1507.3(c)(2) of the NEPA Regulations in conjunction with § 1508.4 thereof requires agencies to establish three typical classes of action for similar treatment under NEPA. These typical classes of action are set forth below:

Actions normally requiring EIS's	Actions normally requiring assessments but not necessarily EIS's	Actions normally not requiring assessments or EIS's
None	Applications for Eximbank financing under the direct lending program in support of transactions for which determinations under § 408.4(b)(1) (i) and (ii) above may be affirmative.	Applications for Eximbank financing in the form of insurance or guarantees.

(b) Eximbank will independently determine whether an EIS or an environmental assessment is required where:

(1) A proposal for agency action is not covered by one of the typical classes of action above; or

(2) For actions which are covered, the presence of extraordinary circumstances indicates that some other level of environmental review may be appropriate.

§ 408.7 Environmental information.

Interested persons may contact the General Counsel regarding Eximbank's compliance with NEPA.

PART 410—ENFORCEMENT OF NONDISCRIMINATION ON THE BASIS OF HANDICAP IN PROGRAMS OR ACTIVITIES CONDUCTED BY EXPORT-IMPORT BANK OF THE UNITED STATES

Sec.
410.101 Purpose.
410.102 Application.
410.103 Definitions.
410.104–410.109 [Reserved]
410.110 Self-evaluation.
410.111 Notice.
410.112–410.129 [Reserved]
410.130 General prohibitions against discrimination.
410.131–410.139 [Reserved]
410.140 Employment.
410.141–410.148 [Reserved]
410.149 Program accessibility: Discrimination prohibited.
410.150 Program accessibility: Existing facilities.
410.151 Program accessibility: New construction and alterations.
410.152–410.159 [Reserved]
410.160 Communications.
410.161–410.169 [Reserved]
410.170 Compliance procedures.
410.171–410.999 [Reserved]

AUTHORITY: 29 U.S.C. 794.

SOURCE: 51 FR 4575, 4579, Feb. 5, 1986, unless otherwise noted.

§ 410.101 Purpose.

This part effectuates section 119 of the Rehabilitation, Comprehensive Services, and Developmental Disabilities Amendments of 1978, which amended section 504 of the Rehabilitation Act of 1973 to prohibit discrimination on the basis of handicap in programs or activities conducted by Executive agencies or the United States Postal Service.

Export-Import Bank of the U.S. § 410.103

§ 410.102 Application.

This part applies to all programs or activities conducted by the agency.

§ 410.103 Definitions.

For purposes of this part, the term—

Assistant Attorney General means the Assistant Attorney General, Civil Rights Division, United States Department of Justice.

Auxiliary aids means services or devices that enable persons with impaired sensory, manual, or speaking skills to have an equal opportunity to participate in, and enjoy the benefits of, programs or activities conducted by the agency. For example, auxiliary aids useful for persons with impaired vision include readers, Brailled materials, audio recordings, telecommunications devices and other similar services and devices. Auxiliary aids useful for persons with impaired hearing include telephone handset amplifiers, telephones compatible with hearing aids, telecommunication devices for deaf persons (TDD's), interpreters, notetakers, written materials, and other similar services and devices.

Complete complaint means a written statement that contains the complainant's name and address and describes the agency's alleged discriminatory action in sufficient detail to inform the agency of the nature and date of the alleged violation of section 504. It shall be signed by the complainant or by someone authorized to do so on his or her behalf. Complaints filed on behalf of classes or third parties shall describe or identify (by name, if possible) the alleged victims of discrimination.

Facility means all or any portion of buildings, structures, equipment, roads, walks, parking lots, rolling stock or other conveyances, or other real or personal property.

Handicapped person means any person who has a physical or mental impairment that substantially limits one or more major life activities, has a record of such an impairment, or is regarded as having such an impairment.

As used in this definition, the phrase:

(1) *Physical or mental impairment* includes—

(i) Any physiological disorder or condition, cosmetic disfigurement, or anatomical loss affecting one or more of the following body systems: Neurological; musculoskeletal; special sense organs; respiratory, including speech organs; cardiovascular; reproductive; digestive; genitourinary; hemic and lymphatic; skin; and endocrine; or

(ii) Any mental or psychological disorder, such as mental retardation, organic brain syndrome, emotional or mental illness, and specific learning disabilities. The term *physical or mental impairment* includes, but is not limited to, such diseases and conditions as orthopedic, visual, speech, and hearing impairments, cerebral palsy, epilepsy, muscular dystrophy, multiple sclerosis, cancer, heart disease, diabetes, mental retardation, emotional illness, and drug addition and alcholism.

(2) *Major life activities* includes functions such as caring for one's self, performing manual tasks, walking, seeing, hearing, speaking, breathing, learning, and working.

(3) *Has a record of such an impairment* means has a history of, or has been misclassified as having, a mental or physical impairment that substantially limits one or more major life activities.

(4) *Is regarded as having an impairment* means—

(i) Has a physical or mental impairment that does not substantially limit major life activities but is treated by the agency as constituting such a limitation;

(ii) Has a physical or mental impairment that substantially limits major life activities only as a result of the attitudes of others toward such impairment; or

(iii) Has none of the impairments defined in paragraph (1) of this definition but is treated by the agency as having such an impairment.

Qualified handicapped person means—

(1) With respect to any agency program or activity under which a person is required to perform services or to achieve a level of accomplishment, a handicapped person who meets the essential eligibility requirements and who can achieve the purpose of the program or activity without modifications in the program or activity that the agency can demonstrate would result in a fundamental alteration in its nature; or

(2) With respect to any other program or activity, a handicapped person who meets the essential eligibility requirements for participation in, or receipt of benefits from, that program or activity.

(3) *Qualified handicapped person* is defined for purposes of employment in 29 CFR 1613.702(f), which is made applicable to this part by § 410.140.

Section 504 means section 504 of the Rehabilitation Act of 1973 (Pub. L. 93–112, 87 Stat. 394 (29 U.S.C. 794)), as amended by the Rehabilitation Act Amendments of 1974 (Pub. L. 93–516, 88 Stat. 1617), and the Rehabilitation, Comprehensive Services, and Developmental Disabilities Amendments of 1978 (Pub. L. 95–602, 92 Stat. 2955). As used in this part, section 504 applies only to programs or activities conducted by Executive agencies and not to federally assisted programs.

[51 FR 4575, 4579, Feb. 5, 1986; 51 FR 7543, Mar. 5, 1986]

§§ 410.104–410.109 [Reserved]

§ 410.110 Self-evaluation.

(a) The agency shall, by April 9, 1987, evaluate its current policies and practices, and the effects thereof, that do not or may not meet the requirements of this part, and, to the extent modification of any such policies and practices is required, the agency shall proceed to make the necessary modifications.

(b) The agency shall provide an opportunity to interested persons, including handicapped persons or organizations representing handicapped persons, to participate in the self-evaluation process by submitting comments (both oral and written).

(c) The agency shall, until three years following the completion of the self-evaluation, maintain on file and make available for public inspections:

(1) A description of areas examined and any problems identified, and

(2) A description of any modifications made.

§ 410.111 Notice.

The agency shall make available to employees, applicants, participants, beneficiaries, and other interested persons such information regarding the provisions of this part and its applicability to the programs or activities conducted by the agency, and make such information available to them in such manner as the head of the agency finds necessary to apprise such persons of the protections against discrimination assured them by section 504 and this regulation.

§§ 410.112–410.129 [Reserved]

§ 410.130 General prohibitions against discrimination.

(a) No qualified handicapped person shall, on the basis of handicap, be excluded from participation in, be denied the benefits of, or otherwise be subjected to discrimination under any program or activity conducted by the agency.

(b)(1) The agency, in providing any aid, benefit, or service, may not, directly or through contractual, licensing, or other arrangements, on the basis of handicap—

(i) Deny a qualified handicapped person the opportunity to participate in or benefit from the aid, benefit, or service;

(ii) Afford a qualfied handicapped person an opportunity to participate in or benefit from the aid, benefit, or service that is not equal to that afforded others;

(iii) Provide a qualified handicapped person with an aid, benefit, or service that is not as effective in affording equal opportunity to obtain the same result, to gain the same benefit, or to reach the same level of achievement as that provided to others;

(iv) Provide different or separate aid, benefits, or services to handicapped persons or to any class of handicapped persons than is provided to others unless such action is necessary to provide qualified handicapped persons with aid, benefits, or services that are as effective as those provided to others;

(v) Deny a qualified handicapped person the opportunity to participate as a member of planning or advisory boards; or

(vi) Otherwise limit a qualified handicapped person in the enjoyment of any right, privilege, advantage, or opportunity enjoyed by others receiving the aid, benefit, or service.

Export-Import Bank of the U.S. § 410.150

(2) The agency may not deny a qualified handicapped person the opportunity to participate in programs or activities that are not separate or different, despite the existence of permissibly separate or different programs or activities.

(3) The agency may not, directly or through contractual or other arrangements, utilize criteria or methods of administration the purpose or effect of which would—

(i) Subject qualified handicapped persons to discrimination on the basis of handicap; or

(ii) Defeat or substantially impair accomplishment of the objectives of a program or activity with respect to handicapped persons.

(4) The agency may not, in determining the site or location of a facility, make selections the purpose or effect of which would—

(i) Exclude handicapped persons from, deny them the benefits of, or otherwise subject them to discrimination under any program or activity conducted by the agency; or

(ii) Defeat or substantially impair the accomplishment of the objectives of a program or activity with respect to handicapped persons.

(5) The agency, in the selection of procurement contractors, may not use criteria that subject qualified handicapped persons to discrimination on the basis of handicap.

(c) The exclusion of nonhandicapped persons from the benefits of a program limited by Federal statute or Executive order to handicapped persons or the exclusion of a specific class of handicapped persons from a program limited by Federal statute or Executive order to a different class of handicapped persons is not prohibited by this part.

(d) The agency shall administer programs and activities in the most integrated setting appropriate to the needs of qualified handicapped persons.

§§ 410.131–410.139 [Reserved]

§ 410.140 Employment.

No qualified handicapped person shall, on the basis of handicap, be subjected to discrimination in employment under any program or activity conducted by the agency. The definitions, requirements, and procedures of section 501 of the Rehabilitation Act of 1973 (29 U.S.C. 791), as established by the Equal Employment Opportunity Commission in 29 CFR part 1613, shall apply to employment in federally conducted programs or activities.

§§ 410.141–410.148 [Reserved]

§ 410.149 Program accessibility: Discrimination prohibited.

Except as otherwise provided in § 410.150, no qualified handicapped person shall, because the agency's facilities are inaccessible to or unusable by handicapped persons, be denied the benefits of, be excluded from participation in, or otherwise be subjected to discrimination under any program or activity conducted by the agency.

§ 410.150 Program accessibility: Existing facilities.

(a) *General.* The agency shall operate each program or activity so that the program or activity, when viewed in its entirety, is readily accessible to and usable by handicapped persons. This paragraph does not—

(1) Necessarily require the agency to make each of its existing facilities accessible to and usable by handicapped persons; or

(2) Require the agency to take any action that it can demonstrate would result in a fundamental alteration in the nature of a program or activity or in undue financial and administrative burdens. In those circumstances where agency personnel believe that the proposed action would fundamentally alter the program or activity or would result in undue financial and administrative burdens, the agency has the burden of proving that compliance with § 410.150(a) would result in such alteration or burdens. The decision that compliance would result in such alteration or burdens must be made by the agency head or his or her designee after considering all agency resources available for use in the funding and operation of the conducted program or activity, and must be accompanied by a written statement of the reasons for reaching that conclusion. If an action would result in such an alteration or

such burdens, the agency shall take any other action that would not result in such an alteration or such burdens but would nevertheless ensure that handicapped persons receive the benefits and services of the program or activity.

(b) *Methods.* The agency may comply with the requirements of this section through such means as redesign of equipment, reassignment of services to accessible buildings, assignment of aides to beneficiaries, home visits, delivery of services at alternate accessible sites, alteration of existing facilities and construction of new facilities, use of accessible rolling stock, or any other methods that result in making its programs or activities readily accessible to and usable by handicapped persons. The agency is nor required to make structural changes in existing facilities where other methods are effective in achieving compliance with this section. The agency, in making alterations to existing buildings, shall meet accessibility requirements to the extent compelled by the Architectural Barriers Act of 1968, as amended (42 U.S.C. 4151 through 4157), and any regulations implementing it. In choosing among available methods for meeting the requirements of this section, the agency shall give priority to those methods that offer programs and activities to qualified handicapped persons in the most integrated setting appropriate.

(c) *Time period for compliance.* The agency shall comply with the obligations established under this section by June 6, 1986, except that where structural changes in facilities are undertaken, such changes shall be made by April 7, 1989, but in any event as expeditiously as possible.

(d) *Transition plan.* In the event that structural changes to facilities will be undertaken to achieve program accessibility, the agency shall develop, by October 7, 1986, a transition plan setting forth the steps necessary to complete such changes. The agency shall provide an opportunity to interested persons, including handicapped persons or organizations representing handicapped persons, to participate in the development of the transition plan by submitting comments (both oral and written). A copy of the transition plan shall be made available for public inspection. The plan shall, at a minimum—

(1) Identify physical obstacles in the agency's facilities that limit the accessibility of its programs or activities to handicapped persons;

(2) Describe in detail the methods that will be used to make the facilities accessible;

(3) Specify the schedule for taking the steps necessary to achieve compliance with this section and, if the time period of the transition plan is longer than one year, identify steps that will be taken during each year of the transition period; and

(4) Indicate the official responsible for implementation of the plan.

[51 FR 4575, 4579, Feb. 5, 1986; 51 FR 7543, Mar. 5, 1986]

§ 410.151 **Program accessibility: New construction and alterations.**

Each building or part of a building that is constructed or altered by, on behalf of, or for the use of the agency shall be designed, constructed, or altered so as to be readily accessible to and usable by handicapped persons. The definitions, requirements, and standards of the Architectural Barriers Act (42 U.S.C. 4151 through 4157), as established in 41 CFR 101–19.600 to 101–19.607, apply to buildings covered by this section.

§§ 410.152–410.159 **[Reserved]**

§ 410.160 **Communications.**

(a) The agency shall take appropriate steps to ensure effective communication with applicants, participants, personnel of other Federal entities, and members of the public.

(1) The agency shall furnish appropriate auxiliary aids where necessary to afford a handicapped person an equal opportunity to participate in, and enjoy the benefits of, a program or activity conducted by the agency.

(i) In determining what type of auxiliary aid is necessary, the agency shall give primary consideration to the requests of the handicapped person.

(ii) The agency need not provide individually prescribed devices, readers for personal use or study, or other devices of a personal nature.

(2) Where the agency communicates with applicants and beneficiaries by telephone, telecommunication devices for deaf persons (TDD's) or equally effective telecommunication systems shall be used.

(b) The agency shall ensure that interested persons, including persons with impaired vision or hearing, can obtain information as to the existence and location of accessible services, activities, and facilities.

(c) The agency shall provide signage at a primary entrance to each of its inaccessible facilities, directing users to a location at which they can obtain information about accessible facilities. The international symbol for accessibility shall be used at each primary entrance of an accessible facility.

(d) This section does not require the agency to take any action that it can demonstrate would result in a fundamental alteration in the nature of a program or activity or in undue financial and administrative burdens. In those circumstances where agency personnel believe that the proposed action would fundamentally alter the program or activity or would result in undue financial and administrative burdens, the agency has the burden of proving that compliance with § 410.160 would result in such alteration or burdens. The decision that compliance would result in such alteration or burdens must be made by the agency head or his or her designee after considering all agency resources available for use in the funding and operation of the conducted program or activity, and must be accompanied by a written statement of the reasons for reaching that conclusion. If an action required to comply with this section would result in such an alteration or such burdens, the agency shall take any other action that would not result in such an alteration or such burdens but would nevertheless ensure that, to the maximum extent possible, handicapped persons receive the benefits and services of the program or activity.

§§ 410.161–410.169 [Reserved]

§ 410.170 Compliance procedures.

(a) Except as provided in paragraph (b) of this section, this section applies to all allegations of discrimination on the basis of handicap in programs or activities conducted by the agency.

(b) The agency shall process complaints alleging violations of section 504 with respect to employment according to the procedures established by the Equal Employment Opportunity Commission in 29 CFR part 1613 pursuant to section 501 of the Rehabilitation Act of 1973 (29 U.S.C. 791).

(c) General Counsel, Export-Import Bank of the United States shall be responsible for coordinating implementation of this section. Complaints may be sent to General Counsel, Export-Import Bank of the United States, 811 Vermont Avenue, NW., Room 947, Washington, DC 20571.

(d) The agency shall accept and investigate all complete complaints for which it has jurisdiction. All complete complaints must be filed within 180 days of the alleged act of discrimination. The agency may extend this time period for good cause.

(e) If the agency receives a complaint over which it does not have jurisdiction, it shall promptly notify the complainant and shall make reasonable efforts to refer the complaint to the appropriate government entity.

(f) The agency shall notify the Architectural and Transportation Barriers Compliance Board upon receipt of any complaint alleging that a building or facility that is subject to the Architectural Barriers Act of 1968, as amended (42 U.S.C. 4151 through 4157), or section 502 of the Rehabilitation Act of 1973, as amended (29 U.S.C. 792), is not readily accessible to and usable by handicapped persons.

(g) Within 180 days of the receipt of a complete complaint for which it has jurisdiction, the agency shall notify the complainant of the results of the investigation in a letter containing—

(1) Findings of fact and conclusions of law;

(2) A description of a remedy for each violation found;

(3) A notice of the right to appeal.

(h) Appeals of the findings of fact and conclusions of law or remedies must be filed by the complainant within 90 days of receipt from the agency of the letter required by § 410.170(g). The agency may extend this time for good cause.

(i) Timely appeals shall be accepted and processed by the head of the agency.

(j) The head of the agency shall notify the complainant of the results of the appeal within 60 days of the receipt of the request. If the head of the agency determines that additional information is needed from the complainant, he or she shall have 60 days from the date of receipt of the additional information to make his or her determination on the appeal.

(k) The time limits cited in paragraphs (g) and (j) of this section may be extended with the permission of the Assistant Attorney General.

(l) The agency may delegate its authority for conducting complaint investigations to other Federal agencies, except that the authority for making the final determination may not be delegated to another agency.

[51 FR 4575, 4579, Feb. 5, 1986, as amended at 51 FR 7543, Mar. 5, 1986]

§§ 410.171–410.999 [Reserved]

PART 411—NEW RESTRICTIONS ON LOBBYING

Subpart A—General

Sec.
411.100 Conditions on use of funds.
411.105 Definitions.
411.110 Certification and disclosure.

Subpart B—Activities by Own Employees

411.200 Agency and legislative liaison.
411.205 Professional and technical services.
411.210 Reporting.

Subpart C—Activities by Other Than Own Employees

411.300 Professional and technical services.

Subpart D—Penalties and Enforcement

411.400 Penalties.
411.405 Penalty procedures.
411.410 Enforcement.

Subpart E—Exemptions

411.500 Secretary of Defense.

Subpart F—Agency Reports

411.600 Semi-annual compilation.
411.605 Inspector General report.

Appendix A to Part 411—Certification Regarding Lobbying
Appendix B to Part 411—Disclosure Form To Report Lobbying

Authority: Sec. 319, Pub. L. 101–121 (31 U.S.C. 1352); 5 U.S.C. 552a.

Source: 55 FR 6737, 6747, Feb. 26, 1990, unless otherwise noted.

Cross Reference: See also Office of Management and Budget notice published at 54 FR 52306, Dec. 20, 1989.

Subpart A—General

§ 411.100 Conditions on use of funds.

(a) No appropriated funds may be expended by the recipient of a Federal contract, grant, loan, or cooperative ageement to pay any person for influencing or attempting to influence an officer or employee of any agency, a Member of Congress, an officer or employee of Congress, or an employee of a Member of Congress in connection with any of the following covered Federal actions: the awarding of any Federal contract, the making of any Federal grant, the making of any Federal loan, the entering into of any cooperative agreement, and the extension, continuation, renewal, amendment, or modification of any Federal contract, grant, loan, or cooperative agreement.

(b) Each person who requests or receives from an agency a Federal contract, grant, loan, or cooperative agreement shall file with that agency a certification, set forth in appendix A, that the person has not made, and will not make, any payment prohibited by paragraph (a) of this section.

(c) Each person who requests or receives from an agency a Federal contract, grant, loan, or a cooperative agreement shall file with that agency a disclosure form, set forth in appendix B, if such person has made or has agreed to make any payment using nonappropriated funds (to include profits from any covered Federal action),

Export-Import Bank of the U.S.

§ 411.105

which would be prohibited under paragraph (a) of this section if paid for with appropriated funds.

(d) Each person who requests or receives from an agency a commitment providing for the United States to insure or guarantee a loan shall file with that agency a statement, set forth in appendix A, whether that person has made or has agreed to make any payment to influence or attempt to influence an officer or employee of any agency, a Member of Congress, an officer or employee of Congress, or an employee of a Member of Congress in connection with that loan insurance or guarantee.

(e) Each person who requests or receives from an agency a commitment providing for the United States to insure or guarantee a loan shall file with that agency a disclosure form, set forth in appendix B, if that person has made or has agreed to make any payment to influence or attempt to influence an officer or employee of any agency, a Member of Congress, an officer or employee of Congress, or an employee of a Member of Congress in connection with that loan insurance or guarantee.

§ 411.105 Definitions.

For purposes of this part:

(a) *Agency*, as defined in 5 U.S.C. 552(f), includes Federal executive departments and agencies as well as independent regulatory commissions and Government corporations, as defined in 31 U.S.C. 9101(1).

(b) *Covered Federal action* means any of the following Federal actions:

(1) The awarding of any Federal contract;

(2) The making of any Federal grant;

(3) The making of any Federal loan;

(4) The entering into of any cooperative agreement; and,

(5) The extension, continuation, renewal, amendment, or modification of any Federal contract, grant, loan, or cooperative agreement.

Covered Federal action does not include receiving from an agency a commitment providing for the United States to insure or guarantee a loan. Loan guarantees and loan insurance are addressed independently within this part.

(c) *Federal contract* means an acquisition contract awarded by an agency, including those subject to the Federal Acquisition Regulation (FAR), and any other acquisition contract for real or personal property or services not subject to the FAR.

(d) *Federal cooperative agreement* means a cooperative agreement entered into by an agency.

(e) *Federal grant* means an award of financial assistance in the form of money, or property in lieu of money, by the Federal Government or a direct appropriation made by law to any person. The term does not include technical assistance which provides services instead of money, or other assistance in the form of revenue sharing, loans, loan guarantees, loan insurance, interest subsidies, insurance, or direct United States cash assistance to an individual.

(f) *Federal loan* means a loan made by an agency. The term does not include loan guarantee or loan insurance.

(g) *Indian tribe* and *tribal organization* have the meaning provided in section 4 of the Indian Self-Determination and Education Assistance Act (25 U.S.C. 450B). Alaskan Natives are included under the definitions of Indian tribes in that Act.

(h) *Influencing or attempting to influence* means making, with the intent to influence, any communication to or appearance before an officer or employee or any agency, a Member of Congress, an officer or employee of Congress, or an employee of a Member of Congress in connection with any covered Federal action.

(i) *Loan guarantee* and *loan insurance* means an agency's guarantee or insurance of a loan made by a person.

(j) *Local government* means a unit of government in a State and, if chartered, established, or otherwise recognized by a State for the performance of a governmental duty, including a local public authority, a special district, an intrastate district, a council of governments, a sponsor group representative organization, and any other instrumentality of a local government.

(k) *Officer or employee of an agency* includes the following individuals who are employed by an agency:

1067

§ 411.110

(1) An individual who is appointed to a position in the Government under title 5, U.S. Code, including a position under a temporary appointment;

(2) A member of the uniformed services as defined in section 101(3), title 37, U.S. Code;

(3) A special Government employee as defined in section 202, title 18, U.S. Code; and,

(4) An individual who is a member of a Federal advisory committee, as defined by the Federal Advisory Committee Act, title 5, U.S. Code appendix 2.

(l) *Person* means an individual, corporation, company, association, authority, firm, partnership, society, State, and local government, regardless of whether such entity is operated for profit or not for profit. This term excludes an Indian tribe, tribal organization, or any other Indian organization with respect to expenditures specifically permitted by other Federal law.

(m) *Reasonable compensation* means, with respect to a regularly employed officer or employee of any person, compensation that is consistent with the normal compensation for such officer or employee for work that is not furnished to, not funded by, or not furnished in cooperation with the Federal Government.

(n) *Reasonable payment* means, with respect to perfessional and other technical services, a payment in an amount that is consistent with the amount normally paid for such services in the private sector.

(o) *Recipient* includes all contractors, subcontractors at any tier, and subgrantees at any tier of the recipient of funds received in connection with a Federal contract, grant, loan, or cooperative agreement. The term excludes an Indian tribe, tribal organization, or any other Indian organization with respect to expenditures specifically permitted by other Federal law.

(p) *Regularly employed* means, with respect to an officer or employee of a person requesting or receiving a Federal contract, grant, loan, or cooperative agreement or a commitment providing for the United States to insure or guarantee a loan, an officer or employee who is employed by such person for at least 130 working days within one year immediately preceding the date of the submission that initiates agency consideration of such person for receipt of such contract, grant, loan, cooperative agreement, loan insurance commitment, or loan guarantee commitment. An officer or employee who is employed by such person for less than 130 working days within one year immediately preceding the date of the submission that initiates agency consideration of such person shall be considered to be regularly employed as soon as he or she is employed by such person for 130 working days.

(q) *State* means a State of the United States, the District of Columbia, the Commonwealth of Puerto Rico, a territory or possession of the United States, an agency or instrumentality of a State, and a multi-State, regional, or interstate entity having governmental duties and powers.

§ 411.110 Certification and disclosure.

(a) Each person shall file a certification, and a disclosure form, if required, with each submission that initiates agency consideration of such person for:

(1) Award of a Federal contract, grant, or cooperative agreement exceeding $100,000; or

(2) An award of a Federal loan or a commitment providing for the United States to insure or guarantee a loan exceeding $150,000.

(b) Each person shall file a certification, and a disclosure form, if required, upon receipt by such person of:

(1) A Federal contract, grant, or cooperative agreement exceeding $100,000; or

(2) A Federal loan or a commitment providing for the United States to insure or guarantee a loan exceeding $150,000,

Unless such person previously filed a certification, and a disclosure form, if required, under paragraph (a) of this section.

(c) Each person shall file a disclosure form at the end of each calendar quarter in which there occurs any event that requires disclosure or that materially affects the accuracy of the information contained in any disclosure form previously filed by such person under paragraph (a) or (b) of this section. An event that materially affects the accuracy of the information reported includes:

(1) A cumulative increase of $25,000 or more in the amount paid or expected to be paid for influencing or attempting to influence a covered Federal action; or

(2) A change in the person(s) or individual(s) influencing or attempting to influence a covered Federal action; or,

(3) A change in the officer(s), employee(s), or Member(s) contacted to influence or attempt to influence a covered Federal action.

(d) Any person who requests or receives from a person referred to in paragraph (a) or (b) of this section:

(1) A subcontract exceeding $100,000 at any tier under a Federal contract;

(2) A subgrant, contract, or subcontract exceeding $100,000 at any tier under a Federal grant;

(3) A contract or subcontract exceeding $100,000 at any tier under a Federal loan exceeding $150,000; or,

(4) A contract or subcontract exceeding $100,000 at any tier under a Federal cooperative agreement,

Shall file a certification, and a disclosure form, if required, to the next tier above.

(e) All disclosure forms, but not certifications, shall be forwarded from tier to tier until received by the person referred to in paragraph (a) or (b) of this section. That person shall forward all disclosure forms to the agency.

(f) Any certification or disclosure form filed under paragraph (e) of this section shall be treated as a material representation of fact upon which all receiving tiers shall rely. All liability arising from an erroneous representation shall be borne solely by the tier filing that representation and shall not be shared by any tier to which the erroneous representation is forwarded. Submitting an erroneous certification or disclosure constitutes a failure to file the required certification or disclosure, respectively. If a person fails to file a required certification or disclosure, the United States may pursue all available remedies, including those authorized by section 1352, title 31, U.S. Code.

(g) For awards and commitments in process prior to December 23, 1989, but not made before that date, certifications shall be required at award or commitment, covering activities occurring between December 23, 1989, and the date of award or commitment. However, for awards and commitments in process prior to the December 23, 1989 effective date of these provisions, but not made before December 23, 1989, disclosure forms shall not be required at time of award or commitment but shall be filed within 30 days.

(h) No reporting is required for an activity paid for with appropriated funds if that activity is allowable under either subpart B or C.

Subpart B—Activities by Own Employees

§ 411.200 Agency and legislative liaison.

(a) The prohibition on the use of appropriated funds, in § 411.100 (a), does not apply in the case of a payment of reasonable compensation made to an officer or employee of a person requesting or receiving a Federal contract, grant, loan, or cooperative agreement if the payment is for agency and legislative liaison activities not directly related to a covered Federal action.

(b) For purposes of paragraph (a) of this section, providing any information specifically requested by an agency or Congress is allowable at any time.

(c) For purposes of paragraph (a) of this section, the following agency and legislative liaison activities are allowable at any time only where they are not related to a specific solicitation for any covered Federal action:

(1) Discussing with an agency (including individual demonstrations) the qualities and characteristics of the person's products or services, conditions or terms of sale, and service capabilities; and,

(2) Technical discussions and other activities regarding the application or adaptation of the person's products or services for an agency's use.

(d) For purposes of paragraph (a) of this section, the following agencies and

§411.205

legislative liaison activities are allowable only where they are prior to formal solicitation of any covered Federal action:

(1) Providing any information not specifically requested but necessary for an agency to make an informed decision about initiation of a covered Federal action;

(2) Technical discussions regarding the preparation of an unsolicited proposal prior to its official submission; and,

(3) Capability presentations by persons seeking awards from an agency pursuant to the provisions of the Small Business Act, as amended by Pub. L. 95–507 and other subsequent amendments.

(e) Only those activities expressly authorized by this section are allowable under this section.

§411.205 Professional and technical services.

(a) The prohibition on the use of appropriated funds, in §411.100 (a), does not apply in the case of a payment of reasonable compensation made to an officer or employee of a person requesting or receiving a Federal contract, grant, loan, or cooperative agreement or an extension, continuation, renewal, amendment, or modification of a Federal contract, grant, loan, or cooperative agreement if payment is for professional or technical services rendered directly in the preparation, submission, or negotiation of any bid, proposal, or application for that Federal contract, grant, loan, or cooperative agreement or for meeting requirements imposed by or pursuant to law as a condition for receiving that Federal contract, grant, loan, or cooperative agreement.

(b) For purposes of paragraph (a) of this section, *professional and technical services* shall be limited to advice and analysis directly applying any professional or technical discipline. For example, drafting of a legal document accompanying a bid or proposal by a lawyer is allowable. Similarly, technical advice provided by an engineer on the performance or operational capability of a piece of equipment rendered directly in the negotiation of a contract is allowable. However, communications with the intent to influence made by a professional (such as a licensed lawyer) or a technical person (such as a licensed accountant) are not allowable under this section unless they provide advice and analysis directly applying their professional or technical expertise and unless the advice or analysis is rendered directly and solely in the preparation, submission or negotiation of a covered Federal action. Thus, for example, communications with the intent to influence made by a lawyer that do not provide legal advice or analysis directly and solely related to the legal aspects of his or her client's proposal, but generally advocate one proposal over another are not allowable under this section because the lawyer is not providing professional legal services. Similarly, communications with the intent to influence made by an engineer providing an engineering analysis prior to the preparation or submission of a bid or proposal are not allowable under this section since the engineer is providing technical services but not directly in the preparation, submission or negotiation of a covered Federal action.

(c) Requirements imposed by or pursuant to law as a condition for receiving a covered Federal award include those required by law or regulation, or reasonably expected to be required by law or regulation, and any other requirements in the actual award documents.

(d) Only those services expressly authorized by this section are allowable under this section.

§411.210 Reporting.

No reporting is required with respect to payments of reasonable compensation made to regularly employed officers or employees of a person.

Subpart C—Activities by Other Than Own Employees

§411.300 Professional and technical services.

(a) The prohibition on the use of appropriated funds, in §411.100 (a), does not apply in the case of any reasonable payment to a person, other than an officer or employee of a person requesting or receiving a covered Federal action, if the payment is for professional or technical services rendered directly in the preparation, submission, or negotiation of any bid, proposal, or application for that Federal contract, grant, loan, or cooperative agreement or for meeting requirements imposed by or pursuant to law as a condition for receiving that Federal contract, grant, loan, or cooperative agreement.

(b) The reporting requirements in § 411.110 (a) and (b) regarding filing a disclosure form by each person, if required, shall not apply with respect to professional or technical services rendered directly in the preparation, submission, or negotiation of any commitment providing for the United States to insure or guarantee a loan.

(c) For purposes of paragraph (a) of this section, *professional and technical services* shall be limited to advice and analysis directly applying any professional or technical discipline. For example, drafting or a legal document accompanying a bid or proposal by a lawyer is allowable. Similarly, technical advice provided by an engineer on the performance or operational capability of a piece of equipment rendered directly in the negotiation of a contract is allowable. However, communications with the intent to influence made by a professional (such as a licensed lawyer) or a technical person (such as a licensed accountant) are not allowable under this section unless they provide advice and analysis directly applying their professional or technical expertise and unless the advice or analysis is rendered directly and solely in the preparation, submission or negotiation of a covered Federal action. Thus, for example, communications with the intent to influence made by a lawyer that do not provide legal advice or analysis directly and solely related to the legal aspects of his or her client's proposal, but generally advocate one proposal over another are not allowable under this section because the lawyer is not providing professional legal services. Similarly, communications with the intent to influence made by an engineer providing an engineering analysis prior to the preparation or submission of a bid or proposal are not allowable under this section since the engineer is providing technical services but not directly in the preparation, submission or negotiation of a covered Federal action.

(d) Requirements imposed by or pursuant to law as a condition for receiving a covered Federal award include those required by law or regulation, or reasonably expected to be required by law or regulation, and any other requirements in the actual award documents.

(e) Persons other than officers or employees of a person requesting or receiving a covered Federal action include consultants and trade associations.

(f) Only those services expressly authorized by this section are allowable under this section.

Subpart D—Penalties and Enforcement

§ 411.400 Penalties.

(a) Any person who makes an expenditure prohibited herein shall be subject to a civil penalty of not less than $10,000 and not more than $100,000 for each such expenditure.

(b) Any person who fails to file or amend the disclosure form (see appendix B) to be filed or amended if required herein, shall be subject to a civil penalty of not less than $10,000 and not more than $100,000 for each such failure.

(c) A filing or amended filing on or after the date on which an administrative action for the imposition of a civil penalty is commenced does not prevent the imposition of such civil penalty for a failure occurring before that date. An administrative action is commenced with respect to a failure when an investigating official determines in writing to commence an investigation of an allegation of such failure.

(d) In determining whether to impose a civil penalty, and the amount of any such penalty, by reason of a violation by any person, the agency shall consider the nature, circumstances, extent, and gravity of the violation, the effect on the ability of such person to continue in business, any prior violations by such person, the degree of culpability of such person, the ability of the person to pay the penalty, and such other matters as may be appropriate.

(e) First offenders under paragraph (a) or (b) of this section shall be subject to a civil penalty of $10,000, absent aggravating circumstances. Second and subsequent offenses by persons shall be subject to an appropriate civil penalty between $10,000 and $100,000, as determined by the agency head or his or her designee.

(f) An imposition of a civil penalty under this section does not prevent the United States from seeking any other remedy that may apply to the same conduct that is the basis for the imposition of such civil penalty.

§ 411.405 Penalty procedures.

Agencies shall impose and collect civil penalties pursuant to the provisions of the Program Fraud and Civil Remedies Act, 31 U.S.C. sections 3803 (except subsection (c)), 3804, 3805, 3806, 3807, 3808, and 3812, insofar as these provisions are not inconsistent with the requirements herein.

§ 411.410 Enforcement.

The head of each agency shall take such actions as are necessary to ensure that the provisions herein are vigorously implemented and enforced in that agency.

Subpart E—Exemptions

§ 411.500 Secretary of Defense.

(a) The Secretary of Defense may exempt, on a case-by-case basis, a covered Federal action from the prohibition whenever the Secretary determines, in writing, that such an exemption is in the national interest. The Secretary shall transmit a copy of each such written exemption to Congress immediately after making such a determination.

(b) The Department of Defense may issue supplemental regulations to implement paragraph (a) of this section.

Subpart F—Agency Reports

§ 411.600 Semi-annual compilation.

(a) The head of each agency shall collect and compile the disclosure reports (see appendix B) and, on May 31 and November 30 of each year, submit to the Secretary of the Senate and the Clerk of the House of Representatives a report containing a compilation of the information contained in the disclosure reports received during the six-month period ending on March 31 or September 30, respectively, of that year.

(b) The report, including the compilation, shall be available for public inspection 30 days after receipt of the report by the Secretary and the Clerk.

(c) Information that involves intelligence matters shall be reported only to the Select Committee on Intelligence of the Senate, the Permanent Select Committee on Intelligence of the House of Representatives, and the Committees on Appropriations of the Senate and the House of Representatives in accordance with procedures agreed to by such committees. Such information shall not be available for public inspection.

(d) Information that is classified under Executive Order 12356 or any successor order shall be reported only to the Committee on Foreign Relations of the Senate and the Committee on Foreign Affairs of the House of Representatives or the Committees on Armed Services of the Senate and the House of Representatives (whichever such committees have jurisdiction of matters involving such information) and to the Committees on Appropriations of the Senate and the House of Representatives in accordance with procedures agreed to by such committees. Such information shall not be available for public inspection.

(e) The first semi-annual compilation shall be submitted on May 31, 1990, and shall contain a compilation of the disclosure reports received from December 23, 1989 to March 31, 1990.

(f) Major agencies, designated by the Office of Management and Budget (OMB), are required to provide machine-readable compilations to the Secretary of the Senate and the Clerk of the House of Representatives no

Export-Import Bank of the U.S.

later than with the compilations due on May 31, 1991. OMB shall provide detailed specifications in a memorandum to these agencies.

(g) Non-major agencies are requested to provide machine-readable compilations to the Secretary of the Senate and the Clerk of the House of Representatives.

(h) Agencies shall keep the originals of all disclosure reports in the official files of the agency.

§ 411.605 Inspector General report.

(a) The Inspector General, or other official as specified in paragraph (b) of this section, of each agency shall prepare and submit to Congress each year, commencing with submission of the President's Budget in 1991, an evaluation of the compliance of that agency with, and the effectiveness of, the requirements herein. The evaluation may include any recommended changes that may be necessary to strengthen or improve the requirements.

(b) In the case of an agency that does not have an Inspector General, the agency official comparable to an Inspector General shall prepare and submit the annual report, or, if there is no such comparable official, the head of the agency shall prepare and submit the annual report.

(c) The annual report shall be submitted at the same time the agency submits its annual budget justifications to Congress.

(d) The annual report shall include the following: All alleged violations relating to the agency's covered Federal actions during the year covered by the report, the actions taken by the head of the agency in the year covered by the report with respect to those alleged violations and alleged violations in previous years, and the amounts of civil penalties imposed by the agency in the year covered by the report.

APPENDIX A TO PART 411—
CERTIFICATION REGARDING LOBBYING

Certification for Contracts, Grants, Loans, and Cooperative Agreements

The undersigned certifies, to the best of his or her knowledge and belief, that:

(1) No Federal appropriated funds have been paid or will be paid, by or on behalf of the undersigned, to any person for influencing or attempting to influence an officer or employee of an agency, a Member of Congress, an officer or employee of Congress, or an employee of a Member of Congress in connection with the awarding of any Federal contract, the making of any Federal grant, the making of any Federal loan, the entering into of any cooperative agreement, and the extension, continuation, renewal, amendment, or modification of any Federal contract, grant, loan, or cooperative agreement.

(2) If any funds other than Federal appropriated funds have been paid or will be paid to any person for influencing or attempting to influence an officer or employee of any agency, a Member of Congress, an officer or employee of Congress, or an employee of a Member of Congress in connection with this Federal contract, grant, loan, or cooperative agreement, the undersigned shall complete and submit Standard Form-LLL, "Disclosure Form to Report Lobbying," in accordance with its instructions.

(3) The undersigned shall require that the language of this certification be included in the award documents for all subawards at all tiers (including subcontracts, subgrants, and contracts under grants, loans, and cooperative agreements) and that all subrecipients shall certify and disclose accordingly.

This certification is a material representation of fact upon which reliance was placed when this transaction was made or entered into. Submission of this certification is a prerequisite for making or entering into this transaction imposed by section 1352, title 31, U.S. Code. Any person who fails to file the required certification shall be subject to a civil penalty of not less than $10,000 and not more than $100,000 for each such failure.

Statement for Loan Guarantees and Loan Insurance

The undersigned states, to the best of his or her knowledge and belief, that:

If any funds have been paid or will be paid to any person for influencing or attempting to influence an officer or employee of any agency, a Member of Congress, an officer or employee of Congress, or an employee of a Member of Congress in connection with this commitment providing for the United States to insure or guarantee a loan, the undersigned shall complete and submit Standard Form-LLL, "Disclosure Form to Report Lobbying," in accordance with its instructions.

Submission of this statement is a prerequisite for making or entering into this transaction imposed by section 1352, title 31, U.S. Code. Any person who fails to file the required statement shall be subject to a civil penalty of not less than $10,000 and not more than $100,000 for each such failure.

Pt. 411, App. B   **12 CFR Ch. IV (1-1-12 Edition)**

APPENDIX B TO PART 411—DISCLOSURE FORM TO REPORT LOBBYING

DISCLOSURE OF LOBBYING ACTIVITIES

Complete this form to disclose lobbying activities pursuant to 31 U.S.C. 1352
(See reverse for public burden disclosure.)

Approved by OMB
0348-0046

1. Type of Federal Action:	2. Status of Federal Action:	3. Report Type:
☐ a. contract b. grant c. cooperative agreement d. loan e. loan guarantee f. loan insurance	☐ a. bid/offer/application b. initial award c. post-award	☐ a. initial filing b. material change For Material Change Only: year _____ quarter _____ date of last report _____

4. Name and Address of Reporting Entity: ☐ Prime ☐ Subawardee Tier _____, if known: Congressional District, if known:	5. If Reporting Entity in No. 4 is Subawardee, Enter Name and Address of Prime: Congressional District, if known:
6. Federal Department/Agency:	**7.** Federal Program Name/Description: CFDA Number, if applicable: _____
8. Federal Action Number, if known:	**9.** Award Amount, if known: $
10. a. Name and Address of Lobbying Entity (if individual, last name, first name, MI):	**b.** Individuals Performing Services (including address if different from No. 10a) (last name, first name, MI):

(attach Continuation Sheet(s) SF-LLL-A, if necessary)

11. Amount of Payment (check all that apply): $ _____ ☐ actual ☐ planned 12. Form of Payment (check all that apply): ☐ a. cash ☐ b. in-kind; specify: nature _____ value _____	13. Type of Payment (check all that apply): ☐ a. retainer ☐ b. one-time fee ☐ c. commission ☐ d. contingent fee ☐ e. deferred ☐ f. other; specify: _____

14. Brief Description of Services Performed or to be Performed and Date(s) of Service, including officer(s), employee(s), or Member(s) contacted, for Payment Indicated in Item 11:

(attach Continuation Sheet(s) SF-LLL-A, if necessary)

15. Continuation Sheet(s) SF-LLL-A attached: ☐ Yes   ☐ No

16. Information requested through this form is authorized by title 31 U.S.C. section 1352. This disclosure of lobbying activities is a material representation of fact upon which reliance was placed by the tier above when this transaction was made or entered into. This disclosure is required pursuant to 31 U.S.C. 1352. This information will be reported to the Congress semi-annually and will be available for public inspection. Any person who fails to file the required disclosure shall be subject to a civil penalty of not less than $10,000 and not more than $100,000 for each such failure.

Signature: _____
Print Name: _____
Title: _____
Telephone No.: _____ Date: _____

Federal Use Only: Authorized for Local Reproduction
                                                                   Standard Form - LLL

Export-Import Bank of the U.S. Pt. 411, App. B

INSTRUCTIONS FOR COMPLETION OF SF-LLL, DISCLOSURE OF LOBBYING ACTIVITIES

This disclosure form shall be completed by the reporting entity, whether subawardee or prime Federal recipient, at the initiation or receipt of a covered Federal action, or a material change to a previous filing, pursuant to title 31 U.S.C. section 1352. The filing of a form is required for each payment or agreement to make payment to any lobbying entity for influencing or attempting to influence an officer or employee of any agency, a Member of Congress, an officer or employee of Congress, or an employee of a Member of Congress in connection with a covered Federal action. Use the SF-LLL-A Continuation Sheet for additional information if the space on the form is inadequate. Complete all items that apply for both the initial filing and material change report. Refer to the implementing guidance published by the Office of Management and Budget for additional information.

1. Identify the type of covered Federal action for which lobbying activity is and/or has been secured to influence the outcome of a covered Federal action.

2. Identify the status of the covered Federal action.

3. Identify the appropriate classification of this report. If this is a followup report caused by a material change to the information previously reported, enter the year and quarter in which the change occurred. Enter the date of the last previously submitted report by this reporting entity for this covered Federal action.

4. Enter the full name, address, city, state and zip code of the reporting entity. Include Congressional District, if known. Check the appropriate classification of the reporting entity that designates if it is, or expects to be, a prime or subaward recipient. Identify the tier of the subawardee, e.g., the first subawardee of the prime is the 1st tier. Subawards include but are not limited to subcontracts, subgrants and contract awards under grants.

5. If the organization filing the report in item 4 checks "Subawardee", then enter the full name, address, city, state and zip code of the prime Federal recipient. Include Congressional District, if known.

6. Enter the name of the Federal agency making the award or loan commitment. Include at least one organizational level below agency name, if known. For example, Department of Transportation, United States Coast Guard.

7. Enter the Federal program name or description for the covered Federal action (item 1). If known, enter the full Catalog of Federal Domestic Assistance (CFDA) number for grants, cooperative agreements, loans, and loan commitments.

8. Enter the most appropriate Federal identifying number available for the Federal action identified in item 1 (e.g., Request for Proposal (RFP) number; Invitation for Bid (IFB) number; grant announcement number; the contract, grant, or loan award number; the application/proposal control number assigned by the Federal agency). Include prefixes, e.g., "RFP-DE-90-001."

9. For a covered Federal action where there has been an award or loan commitment by the Federal agency, enter the Federal amount of the award/loan commitment for the prime entity identified in item 4 or 5.

10. (a) Enter the full name, address, city, state and zip code of the lobbying entity engaged by the reporting entity identified in item 4 to influence the covered Federal action.

    (b) Enter the full names of the individual(s) performing services, and include full address if different from 10 (a). Enter Last Name, First Name, and Middle Initial (MI).

11. Enter the amount of compensation paid or reasonably expected to be paid by the reporting entity (item 4) to the lobbying entity (item 10). Indicate whether the payment has been made (actual) or will be made (planned). Check all boxes that apply. If this is a material change report, enter the cumulative amount of payment made or planned to be made.

12. Check the appropriate box(es). Check all boxes that apply. If payment is made through an in-kind contribution, specify the nature and value of the in-kind payment.

13. Check the appropriate box(es). Check all boxes that apply. If other, specify nature.

14. Provide a specific and detailed description of the services that the lobbyist has performed, or will be expected to perform, and the date(s) of any services rendered. Include all preparatory and related activity, not just time spent in actual contact with Federal officials. Identify the Federal official(s) or employee(s) contacted or the officer(s), employee(s), or Member(s) of Congress that were contacted.

15. Check whether or not a SF-LLL-A Continuation Sheet(s) is attached.

16. The certifying official shall sign and date the form, print his/her name, title, and telephone number.

Public reporting burden for this collection of information is estimated to average 30 mintues per response, including time for reviewing instructions, searching existing data sources, gathering and maintaining the data needed, and completing and reviewing the collection of information. Send comments regarding the burden estimate or any other aspect of this collection of information, including suggestions for reducing this burden, to the Office of Management and Budget, Paperwork Reduction Project (0348-0046), Washington, D.C. 20503.

DISCLOSURE OF LOBBYING ACTIVITIES
CONTINUATION SHEET

Approved by OMB
0348-0046

Reporting Entity: _____   Page _____ of _____

Authorized for Local Reproduction
Standard Form - LLL-A

PART 412—ACCEPTANCE OF PAYMENT FROM A NON-FEDERAL SOURCE FOR TRAVEL EXPENSES

Sec.
412.1 Authority.
412.3 General.
412.5 Policy.
412.7 Conditions for acceptance.
412.9 Conflict of interest analysis.
412.11 Payment guidelines.
412.13 Limitations and penalties.

AUTHORITY: 5 U.S.C. 5701–5709; 12 U.S.C. 635(2)(a)(1).

SOURCE: 59 FR 31136, June 17, 1994, unless otherwise noted.

§ 412.1 Authority.

This part is issued under the authority of 5 U.S.C. 553, 5 U.S.C. 5701–5709 and 12 U.S.C. 635(2)(a)(1).

§ 412.3 General.

(a) *Applicability.* This part applies to acceptance by the Export-Import Bank of the United States (Eximbank) of payment from a non-Federal source for travel, subsistence, and related expenses with respect to the attendance of an employee in a travel status at any meeting or similar event relating to the official duties of the employee, other than those described in 41 CFR 304–1.2. This part does not authorize acceptance of such payments by an employee in his/her personal capacity.

(b) *Solicitation prohibited.* An employee shall not solicit payment for travel, subsistence and related expenses from a non-Federal source. However, after receipt of an invitation from a non-Federal source to attend a meeting or similar event, Eximbank or the employee may inform the non-Federal source of this authority.

(c) *Definitions.* As used in this part, the following definitions apply:

(1) *Conflicting non-Federal source.* Conflicting non-Federal source means any person who, or entity other than the Government of the United States which, has interests that may be substantially affected by the performance or nonperformance of the employee's duties.

(2) *Employee. Employee* means any director, officer or other employee of Eximbank.

(3) *Meeting or similar event. Meeting or similar event* means a meeting, formal gathering, site visit, negotiation session or similar event that takes place away from the employee's official station and which is directly related to the mission of Eximbank. This term does not include any meeting or similar function described in 41 CFR 304–1.2 or sponsored by Eximbank. A meeting or similar event need not be widely attended for purposes of this definition.

(4) *Non-Federal source. Non-Federal source* means any person or entity other than the Government of the United States. The term includes any individual, private or commercial entity, nonprofit organization or association, state, local, or foreign government, or international or multinational organization.

(5) *Payment. Payment* means funds paid or reimbursed to Eximbank by a non-Federal source for travel, subsistence, and related expenses by check or similar instrument, or payment in kind.

(6) *Payment in kind. Payment in kind* means goods, services or other benefits provided by a non-Federal source for travel, subsistence, and related expenses in lieu of funds paid to Eximbank by check or similar instrument for the same purpose.

(7) *Travel, subsistence and related expenses. Travel, subsistence and related expenses* means the same types of expenses payable under 41 CFR chapter 301.

§ 412.5 Policy.

As provided in this part, Eximbank may accept payment from a non-Federal source (or authorize an employee to receive such payment on its behalf) with respect to attendance of the employee at a meeting or similar event which the employee has been authorized to attend in an official capacity on behalf of Eximbank. The employee's immediate supervisor and Eximbank's designated agency ethics official or his/her designee (DAEO) must approve any offer and acceptance of payment under this part in accordance with the procedures described below. If the employee is a member of Eximbank's Board of Directors, only the DAEO's approval is required. Any employee authorized to

§ 412.7

travel in accordance with this part is subject to the maximum per diem or actual subsistence expense rates and transportation class of service limitations prescribed in 41 CFR chapter 301.

§ 412.7 Conditions for acceptance.

(a) Eximbank may accept payment for employee travel from a non-Federal source when a written authorization to accept payment is issued in advance of the travel following a determination by the employee's supervisor (except in the case of Board members) and the DAEO that the payment is:

(1) For travel relating to an employee's official duties under an official travel authorization issued to the employee;

(2) For attendance at a meeting or similar event as defined in § 412.3(c)(3):

(i) In which the employee's participation is necessary in order to further the mission of Eximbank;

(ii) Which cannot be held at the offices of Eximbank for justifiable business reasons in light of the location and number of participants and the purpose of the meeting or similar event; and

(iii) Which is taking place at a location and for a period of time that is appropriate for the purpose of the meeting or similar event;

(3) From a non-Federal source that is not a conflicting non-Federal source or from a conflicting non-Federal source that has been approved under § 412.9; and

(4) In an amount which does not exceed the maximum per diem or actual subsistence expense rates and transportation class of service limitations prescribed in 41 CFR chapter 301.

(b) An employee requesting approval of payment of travel expenses by a non-Federal source under this part shall submit to the employee's supervisor (except in the case of Board members) and the DAEO a written description of the following: the nature of the meeting or similar event and the reason that it cannot be held at Eximbank, the date(s) and location of the meeting or similar event, the identities of all participants in the meeting or similar event, the name of the non-Federal source offering to make the payment, the amount and method of the proposed payment, and the nature of the expenses.

(c) Payments may be accepted from multiple sources under paragraph (a) of this section.

§ 412.9 Conflict of interest analysis.

Eximbank may accept payment from a conflicting non-Federal source if the conditions of § 412.7 are met and the employee's supervisor (except in the case of Board members) and the DAEO determine that Eximbank's interest in the employee's attendance at or participation in the meeting or similar event outweighs concern that acceptance of the payment by Eximbank may cause a reasonable person to question the integrity of Eximbank's programs and operations. In determining whether to accept payment, Eximbank shall consider all relevant factors, including the purpose of the meeting or similar event, the importance of the travel for Eximbank, the nature and sensitivity of any pending matter affecting the interests of the conflicting non-Federal source, the significance of the employee's role in any such matter, the identity of other expected participants, and the location and duration of the meeting or similar event.

§ 412.11 Payment guidelines.

(a) Payments from a non-Federal source, other than payments in kind, shall be by check or similar instrument made payable to Eximbank. Payments from a non-Federal source, including payments in kind, are subject to the maximum per diem or actual subsistence expense rates and transportation class of service limitations prescribed in 41 CFR chapter 301.

(b) If Eximbank determines in advance of the travel that a payment covers some but not all of the per diem costs to be incurred by the employee, Eximbank shall authorize a reduced per diem rate, in accordance with 41 CFR part 301–7.12.

§ 412.13 Limitations and penalties.

(a) This part is in addition to and not in place of any other authority under which Eximbank may accept payment from a non-Federal source or authorize an employee to accept such payment on behalf of Eximbank. This part shall

Export-Import Bank of the U.S. § 414.1

not be applied in connection with the acceptance by Eximbank of payment for travel, subsistence, and related expenses incurred by an employee to attend a meeting or similar function described in and authorized by 41 CFR part 304-1.

(b) An employee who accepts any payment in violation of this part is subject to the following:

(1) The employee may be required, in addition to any penalty provided by law and applicable regulations, to repay for deposit to the general fund of the Treasury, an amount equal to the amount of the payment so accepted; and

(2) When repayment is required under paragraph (b)(1) of this section, the employee shall not be entitled to any payment or reimbursement from Eximbank for such expenses.

PART 414—CONFERENCE AND OTHER FEES

AUTHORITY: 12 U.S.C. 635(a)(1), 5 U.S.C. 553.

§ 414.1 Collection of conference and other fees.

Ex-Im Bank may impose and collect reasonable fees to cover the costs of conferences and seminars sponsored by, and publications provided by Ex-Im Bank. Amounts received under the preceding sentence shall be credited to the fund which initially paid for such activities and shall be offset against the expenses of Ex-Im Bank for such activities.

[72 FR 66043, Nov. 27, 2007]

PARTS 415–499 [RESERVED]

FINDING AIDS

A list of CFR titles, subtitles, chapters, subchapters and parts and an alphabetical list of agencies publishing in the CFR are included in the CFR Index and Finding Aids volume to the Code of Federal Regulations which is published separately and revised annually.

Table of CFR Titles and Chapters
Alphabetical List of Agencies Appearing in the CFR
List of CFR Sections Affected

Table of CFR Titles and Chapters
(Revised as of January 1, 2012)

Title 1—General Provisions

I   Administrative Committee of the Federal Register (Parts 1—49)
II Office of the Federal Register (Parts 50—299)
III Administrative Conference of the United States (Parts 300—399)
IV Miscellaneous Agencies (Parts 400—500)

Title 2—Grants and Agreements

SUBTITLE A—OFFICE OF MANAGEMENT AND BUDGET GUIDANCE FOR GRANTS AND AGREEMENTS

I   Office of Management and Budget Governmentwide Guidance for Grants and Agreements (Parts 2—199)
II Office of Management and Budget Circulars and Guidance (200—299)

SUBTITLE B—FEDERAL AGENCY REGULATIONS FOR GRANTS AND AGREEMENTS

III   Department of Health and Human Services (Parts 300—399)
IV   Department of Agriculture (Parts 400—499)
VI   Department of State (Parts 600—699)
VII   Agency for International Development (Parts 700—799)
VIII   Department of Veterans Affairs (Parts 800—899)
IX   Department of Energy (Parts 900—999)
XI   Department of Defense (Parts 1100—1199)
XII   Department of Transportation (Parts 1200—1299)
XIII   Department of Commerce (Parts 1300—1399)
XIV   Department of the Interior (Parts 1400—1499)
XV   Environmental Protection Agency (Parts 1500—1599)
XVIII National Aeronautics and Space Administration (Parts 1800—1899)
XX   United States Nuclear Regulatory Commission (Parts 2000—2099)
XXII   Corporation for National and Community Service (Parts 2200—2299)
XXIII Social Security Administration (Parts 2300—2399)
XXIV   Housing and Urban Development (Parts 2400—2499)
XXV   National Science Foundation (Parts 2500—2599)
XXVI   National Archives and Records Administration (Parts 2600—2699)
XXVII Small Business Administration (Parts 2700—2799)
XXVIII Department of Justice (Parts 2800—2899)

Title 2—Grants and Agreements—Continued

Chap.	
XXX	Department of Homeland Security (Parts 3000—3099)
XXXI	Institute of Museum and Library Services (Parts 3100—3199)
XXXII	National Endowment for the Arts (Parts 3200—3299)
XXXIII	National Endowment for the Humanities (Parts 3300—3399)
XXXV	Export-Import Bank of the United States (Parts 3500—3599)
XXXVII	Peace Corps (Parts 3700—3799)
LVIII	Election Assistance Commission (Parts 5800—5899)

Title 3—The President

I	Executive Office of the President (Parts 100—199)

Title 4—Accounts

I	Government Accountability Office (Parts 1—99)
II	Recovery Accountability and Transparency Board (Parts 200—299)

Title 5—Administrative Personnel

I	Office of Personnel Management (Parts 1—1199)
II	Merit Systems Protection Board (Parts 1200—1299)
III	Office of Management and Budget (Parts 1300—1399)
V	The International Organizations Employees Loyalty Board (Parts 1500—1599)
VI	Federal Retirement Thrift Investment Board (Parts 1600—1699)
VIII	Office of Special Counsel (Parts 1800—1899)
IX	Appalachian Regional Commission (Parts 1900—1999)
XI	Armed Forces Retirement Home (Parts 2100—2199)
XIV	Federal Labor Relations Authority, General Counsel of the Federal Labor Relations Authority and Federal Service Impasses Panel (Parts 2400—2499)
XV	Office of Administration, Executive Office of the President (Parts 2500—2599)
XVI	Office of Government Ethics (Parts 2600—2699)
XXI	Department of the Treasury (Parts 3100—3199)
XXII	Federal Deposit Insurance Corporation (Parts 3200—3299)
XXIII	Department of Energy (Parts 3300—3399)
XXIV	Federal Energy Regulatory Commission (Parts 3400—3499)
XXV	Department of the Interior (Parts 3500—3599)
XXVI	Department of Defense (Parts 3600—3699)
XXVIII	Department of Justice (Parts 3800—3899)
XXIX	Federal Communications Commission (Parts 3900—3999)
XXX	Farm Credit System Insurance Corporation (Parts 4000—4099)
XXXI	Farm Credit Administration (Parts 4100—4199)
XXXIII	Overseas Private Investment Corporation (Parts 4300—4399)

Title 5—Administrative Personnel—Continued

Chap.	
XXXIV	Securities and Exchange Commission (Parts 4400—4499)
XXXV	Office of Personnel Management (Parts 4500—4599)
XXXVII	Federal Election Commission (Parts 4700—4799)
XL	Interstate Commerce Commission (Parts 5000—5099)
XLI	Commodity Futures Trading Commission (Parts 5100—5199)
XLII	Department of Labor (Parts 5200—5299)
XLIII	National Science Foundation (Parts 5300—5399)
XLV	Department of Health and Human Services (Parts 5500—5599)
XLVI	Postal Rate Commission (Parts 5600—5699)
XLVII	Federal Trade Commission (Parts 5700—5799)
XLVIII	Nuclear Regulatory Commission (Parts 5800—5899)
XLIX	Federal Labor Relations Authority (Parts 5900—5999)
L	Department of Transportation (Parts 6000—6099)
LII	Export-Import Bank of the United States (Parts 6200—6299)
LIII	Department of Education (Parts 6300—6399)
LIV	Environmental Protection Agency (Parts 6400—6499)
LV	National Endowment for the Arts (Parts 6500—6599)
LVI	National Endowment for the Humanities (Parts 6600—6699)
LVII	General Services Administration (Parts 6700—6799)
LVIII	Board of Governors of the Federal Reserve System (Parts 6800—6899)
LIX	National Aeronautics and Space Administration (Parts 6900—6999)
LX	United States Postal Service (Parts 7000—7099)
LXI	National Labor Relations Board (Parts 7100—7199)
LXII	Equal Employment Opportunity Commission (Parts 7200—7299)
LXIII	Inter-American Foundation (Parts 7300—7399)
LXIV	Merit Systems Protection Board (Parts 7400—7499)
LXV	Department of Housing and Urban Development (Parts 7500—7599)
LXVI	National Archives and Records Administration (Parts 7600—7699)
LXVII	Institute of Museum and Library Services (Parts 7700—7799)
LXVIII	Commission on Civil Rights (Parts 7800—7899)
LXIX	Tennessee Valley Authority (Parts 7900—7999)
LXX	Court Services and Offender Supervision Agency for the District of Columbia (Parts 8000—8099)
LXXI	Consumer Product Safety Commission (Parts 8100—8199)
LXXIII	Department of Agriculture (Parts 8300—8399)
LXXIV	Federal Mine Safety and Health Review Commission (Parts 8400—8499)
LXXVI	Federal Retirement Thrift Investment Board (Parts 8600—8699)
LXXVII	Office of Management and Budget (Parts 8700—8799)
LXXX	Federal Housing Finance Agency (Parts 9000—9099)
LXXXII	Special Inspector General for Iraq Reconstruction (Parts 9200—9299)

Chap.
Title 5—Administrative Personnel—Continued

XCVII Department of Homeland Security Human Resources Management System (Department of Homeland Security—Office of Personnel Management) (Parts 9700—9799)

Title 6—Domestic Security

I Department of Homeland Security, Office of the Secretary (Parts 1—99)

Title 7—Agriculture

SUBTITLE A—OFFICE OF THE SECRETARY OF AGRICULTURE (PARTS 0—26)

SUBTITLE B—REGULATIONS OF THE DEPARTMENT OF AGRICULTURE

I Agricultural Marketing Service (Standards, Inspections, Marketing Practices), Department of Agriculture (Parts 27—209)

II Food and Nutrition Service, Department of Agriculture (Parts 210—299)

III Animal and Plant Health Inspection Service, Department of Agriculture (Parts 300—399)

IV Federal Crop Insurance Corporation, Department of Agriculture (Parts 400—499)

V Agricultural Research Service, Department of Agriculture (Parts 500—599)

VI Natural Resources Conservation Service, Department of Agriculture (Parts 600—699)

VII Farm Service Agency, Department of Agriculture (Parts 700—799)

VIII Grain Inspection, Packers and Stockyards Administration (Federal Grain Inspection Service), Department of Agriculture (Parts 800—899)

IX Agricultural Marketing Service (Marketing Agreements and Orders; Fruits, Vegetables, Nuts), Department of Agriculture (Parts 900—999)

X Agricultural Marketing Service (Marketing Agreements and Orders; Milk), Department of Agriculture (Parts 1000—1199)

XI Agricultural Marketing Service (Marketing Agreements and Orders; Miscellaneous Commodities), Department of Agriculture (Parts 1200—1299)

XIV Commodity Credit Corporation, Department of Agriculture (Parts 1400—1499)

XV Foreign Agricultural Service, Department of Agriculture (Parts 1500—1599)

XVI Rural Telephone Bank, Department of Agriculture (Parts 1600—1699)

XVII Rural Utilities Service, Department of Agriculture (Parts 1700—1799)

XVIII Rural Housing Service, Rural Business-Cooperative Service, Rural Utilities Service, and Farm Service Agency, Department of Agriculture (Parts 1800—2099)

XX Local Television Loan Guarantee Board (Parts 2200—2299)

Title 7—Agriculture—Continued

Chap.

XXV	Office of Advocacy and Outreach, Department of Agriculture (Parts 2500—2599)
XXVI	Office of Inspector General, Department of Agriculture (Parts 2600—2699)
XXVII	Office of Information Resources Management, Department of Agriculture (Parts 2700—2799)
XXVIII	Office of Operations, Department of Agriculture (Parts 2800—2899)
XXIX	Office of Energy Policy and New Uses, Department of Agriculture (Parts 2900—2999)
XXX	Office of the Chief Financial Officer, Department of Agriculture (Parts 3000—3099)
XXXI	Office of Environmental Quality, Department of Agriculture (Parts 3100—3199)
XXXII	Office of Procurement and Property Management, Department of Agriculture (Parts 3200—3299)
XXXIII	Office of Transportation, Department of Agriculture (Parts 3300—3399)
XXXIV	National Institute of Food and Agriculture (Parts 3400—3499)
XXXV	Rural Housing Service, Department of Agriculture (Parts 3500—3599)
XXXVI	National Agricultural Statistics Service, Department of Agriculture (Parts 3600—3699)
XXXVII	Economic Research Service, Department of Agriculture (Parts 3700—3799)
XXXVIII	World Agricultural Outlook Board, Department of Agriculture (Parts 3800—3899)
XLI	[Reserved]
XLII	Rural Business-Cooperative Service and Rural Utilities Service, Department of Agriculture (Parts 4200—4299)

Title 8—Aliens and Nationality

I	Department of Homeland Security (Immigration and Naturalization) (Parts 1—499)
V	Executive Office for Immigration Review, Department of Justice (Parts 1000—1399)

Title 9—Animals and Animal Products

I	Animal and Plant Health Inspection Service, Department of Agriculture (Parts 1—199)
II	Grain Inspection, Packers and Stockyards Administration (Packers and Stockyards Programs), Department of Agriculture (Parts 200—299)
III	Food Safety and Inspection Service, Department of Agriculture (Parts 300—599)

Title 10—Energy

Chap.
- I Nuclear Regulatory Commission (Parts 0—199)
- II Department of Energy (Parts 200—699)
- III Department of Energy (Parts 700—999)
- X Department of Energy (General Provisions) (Parts 1000—1099)
- XIII Nuclear Waste Technical Review Board (Parts 1300—1399)
- XVII Defense Nuclear Facilities Safety Board (Parts 1700—1799)
- XVIII Northeast Interstate Low-Level Radioactive Waste Commission (Parts 1800—1899)

Title 11—Federal Elections

- I Federal Election Commission (Parts 1—9099)
- II Election Assistance Commission (Parts 9400—9499)

Title 12—Banks and Banking

- I Comptroller of the Currency, Department of the Treasury (Parts 1—199)
- II Federal Reserve System (Parts 200—299)
- III Federal Deposit Insurance Corporation (Parts 300—399)
- IV Export-Import Bank of the United States (Parts 400—499)
- V Office of Thrift Supervision, Department of the Treasury (Parts 500—599)
- VI Farm Credit Administration (Parts 600—699)
- VII National Credit Union Administration (Parts 700—799)
- VIII Federal Financing Bank (Parts 800—899)
- IX Federal Housing Finance Board (Parts 900—999)
- X Bureau of Consumer Financial Protection (Parts 1000—1099)
- XI Federal Financial Institutions Examination Council (Parts 1100—1199)
- XII Federal Housing Finance Agency (Parts 1200—1299)
- XIII Financial Stability Oversight Council (Parts 1300—1399)
- XIV Farm Credit System Insurance Corporation (Parts 1400—1499)
- XV Department of the Treasury (Parts 1500—1599)
- XVI Office of Financial Research (Parts 1600—1699)
- XVII Office of Federal Housing Enterprise Oversight, Department of Housing and Urban Development (Parts 1700—1799)
- XVIII Community Development Financial Institutions Fund, Department of the Treasury (Parts 1800—1899)

Title 13—Business Credit and Assistance

- I Small Business Administration (Parts 1—199)
- III Economic Development Administration, Department of Commerce (Parts 300—399)
- IV Emergency Steel Guarantee Loan Board (Parts 400—499)
- V Emergency Oil and Gas Guaranteed Loan Board (Parts 500—599)

Title 14—Aeronautics and Space

Chap.

I Federal Aviation Administration, Department of Transportation (Parts 1—199)

II Office of the Secretary, Department of Transportation (Aviation Proceedings) (Parts 200—399)

III Commercial Space Transportation, Federal Aviation Administration, Department of Transportation (Parts 400—1199)

V National Aeronautics and Space Administration (Parts 1200—1299)

VI Air Transportation System Stabilization (Parts 1300—1399)

Title 15—Commerce and Foreign Trade

SUBTITLE A—OFFICE OF THE SECRETARY OF COMMERCE (PARTS 0—29)

SUBTITLE B—REGULATIONS RELATING TO COMMERCE AND FOREIGN TRADE

I Bureau of the Census, Department of Commerce (Parts 30—199)

II National Institute of Standards and Technology, Department of Commerce (Parts 200—299)

III International Trade Administration, Department of Commerce (Parts 300—399)

IV Foreign-Trade Zones Board, Department of Commerce (Parts 400—499)

VII Bureau of Industry and Security, Department of Commerce (Parts 700—799)

VIII Bureau of Economic Analysis, Department of Commerce (Parts 800—899)

IX National Oceanic and Atmospheric Administration, Department of Commerce (Parts 900—999)

XI Technology Administration, Department of Commerce (Parts 1100—1199)

XIII East-West Foreign Trade Board (Parts 1300—1399)

XIV Minority Business Development Agency (Parts 1400—1499)

SUBTITLE C—REGULATIONS RELATING TO FOREIGN TRADE AGREEMENTS

XX Office of the United States Trade Representative (Parts 2000—2099)

SUBTITLE D—REGULATIONS RELATING TO TELECOMMUNICATIONS AND INFORMATION

XXIII National Telecommunications and Information Administration, Department of Commerce (Parts 2300—2399)

Title 16—Commercial Practices

I Federal Trade Commission (Parts 0—999)

II Consumer Product Safety Commission (Parts 1000—1799)

Title 17—Commodity and Securities Exchanges

Chap.
- I Commodity Futures Trading Commission (Parts 1—199)
- II Securities and Exchange Commission (Parts 200—399)
- IV Department of the Treasury (Parts 400—499)

Title 18—Conservation of Power and Water Resources

- I Federal Energy Regulatory Commission, Department of Energy (Parts 1—399)
- III Delaware River Basin Commission (Parts 400—499)
- VI Water Resources Council (Parts 700—799)
- VIII Susquehanna River Basin Commission (Parts 800—899)
- XIII Tennessee Valley Authority (Parts 1300—1399)

Title 19—Customs Duties

- I U.S. Customs and Border Protection, Department of Homeland Security; Department of the Treasury (Parts 0—199)
- II United States International Trade Commission (Parts 200—299)
- III International Trade Administration, Department of Commerce (Parts 300—399)
- IV U.S. Immigration and Customs Enforcement, Department of Homeland Security (Parts 400—599)

Title 20—Employees' Benefits

- I Office of Workers' Compensation Programs, Department of Labor (Parts 1—199)
- II Railroad Retirement Board (Parts 200—399)
- III Social Security Administration (Parts 400—499)
- IV Employees' Compensation Appeals Board, Department of Labor (Parts 500—599)
- V Employment and Training Administration, Department of Labor (Parts 600—699)
- VI Office of Workers' Compensation Programs, Department of Labor (Parts 700—799)
- VII Benefits Review Board, Department of Labor (Parts 800—899)
- VIII Joint Board for the Enrollment of Actuaries (Parts 900—999)
- IX Office of the Assistant Secretary for Veterans' Employment and Training Service, Department of Labor (Parts 1000—1099)

Title 21—Food and Drugs

- I Food and Drug Administration, Department of Health and Human Services (Parts 1—1299)
- II Drug Enforcement Administration, Department of Justice (Parts 1300—1399)
- III Office of National Drug Control Policy (Parts 1400—1499)

Title 22—Foreign Relations

Chap.	
I	Department of State (Parts 1—199)
II	Agency for International Development (Parts 200—299)
III	Peace Corps (Parts 300—399)
IV	International Joint Commission, United States and Canada (Parts 400—499)
V	Broadcasting Board of Governors (Parts 500—599)
VII	Overseas Private Investment Corporation (Parts 700—799)
IX	Foreign Service Grievance Board (Parts 900—999)
X	Inter-American Foundation (Parts 1000—1099)
XI	International Boundary and Water Commission, United States and Mexico, United States Section (Parts 1100—1199)
XII	United States International Development Cooperation Agency (Parts 1200—1299)
XIII	Millennium Challenge Corporation (Parts 1300—1399)
XIV	Foreign Service Labor Relations Board; Federal Labor Relations Authority; General Counsel of the Federal Labor Relations Authority; and the Foreign Service Impasse Disputes Panel (Parts 1400—1499)
XV	African Development Foundation (Parts 1500—1599)
XVI	Japan-United States Friendship Commission (Parts 1600—1699)
XVII	United States Institute of Peace (Parts 1700—1799)

Title 23—Highways

I	Federal Highway Administration, Department of Transportation (Parts 1—999)
II	National Highway Traffic Safety Administration and Federal Highway Administration, Department of Transportation (Parts 1200—1299)
III	National Highway Traffic Safety Administration, Department of Transportation (Parts 1300—1399)

Title 24—Housing and Urban Development

SUBTITLE A—OFFICE OF THE SECRETARY, DEPARTMENT OF HOUSING AND URBAN DEVELOPMENT (PARTS 0—99)

SUBTITLE B—REGULATIONS RELATING TO HOUSING AND URBAN DEVELOPMENT

I	Office of Assistant Secretary for Equal Opportunity, Department of Housing and Urban Development (Parts 100—199)
II	Office of Assistant Secretary for Housing-Federal Housing Commissioner, Department of Housing and Urban Development (Parts 200—299)
III	Government National Mortgage Association, Department of Housing and Urban Development (Parts 300—399)
IV	Office of Housing and Office of Multifamily Housing Assistance Restructuring, Department of Housing and Urban Development (Parts 400—499)

Title 24—Housing and Urban Development—Continued

Chap.

V   Office of Assistant Secretary for Community Planning and Development, Department of Housing and Urban Development (Parts 500—599)

VI   Office of Assistant Secretary for Community Planning and Development, Department of Housing and Urban Development (Parts 600—699) [Reserved]

VII   Office of the Secretary, Department of Housing and Urban Development (Housing Assistance Programs and Public and Indian Housing Programs) (Parts 700—799)

VIII   Office of the Assistant Secretary for Housing—Federal Housing Commissioner, Department of Housing and Urban Development (Section 8 Housing Assistance Programs, Section 202 Direct Loan Program, Section 202 Supportive Housing for the Elderly Program and Section 811 Supportive Housing for Persons With Disabilities Program) (Parts 800—899)

IX   Office of Assistant Secretary for Public and Indian Housing, Department of Housing and Urban Development (Parts 900—1699)

X   Office of Assistant Secretary for Housing—Federal Housing Commissioner, Department of Housing and Urban Development (Interstate Land Sales Registration Program) (Parts 1700—1799)

XII   Office of Inspector General, Department of Housing and Urban Development (Parts 2000—2099)

XV   Emergency Mortgage Insurance and Loan Programs, Department of Housing and Urban Development (Parts 2700—2799)

XX   Office of Assistant Secretary for Housing—Federal Housing Commissioner, Department of Housing and Urban Development (Parts 3200—3899)

XXIV   Board of Directors of the HOPE for Homeowners Program (Parts 4000—4099)

XXV   Neighborhood Reinvestment Corporation (Parts 4100—4199)

Title 25—Indians

I   Bureau of Indian Affairs, Department of the Interior (Parts 1—299)

II   Indian Arts and Crafts Board, Department of the Interior (Parts 300—399)

III   National Indian Gaming Commission, Department of the Interior (Parts 500—599)

IV   Office of Navajo and Hopi Indian Relocation (Parts 700—799)

V   Bureau of Indian Affairs, Department of the Interior, and Indian Health Service, Department of Health and Human Services (Part 900)

VI   Office of the Assistant Secretary-Indian Affairs, Department of the Interior (Parts 1000—1199)

VII   Office of the Special Trustee for American Indians, Department of the Interior (Parts 1200—1299)

Chap.
Title 26—Internal Revenue

I Internal Revenue Service, Department of the Treasury (Parts 1—End)

Title 27—Alcohol, Tobacco Products and Firearms

I Alcohol and Tobacco Tax and Trade Bureau, Department of the Treasury (Parts 1—399)
II Bureau of Alcohol, Tobacco, Firearms, and Explosives, Department of Justice (Parts 400—699)

Title 28—Judicial Administration

I Department of Justice (Parts 0—299)
III Federal Prison Industries, Inc., Department of Justice (Parts 300—399)
V Bureau of Prisons, Department of Justice (Parts 500—599)
VI Offices of Independent Counsel, Department of Justice (Parts 600—699)
VII Office of Independent Counsel (Parts 700—799)
VIII Court Services and Offender Supervision Agency for the District of Columbia (Parts 800—899)
IX National Crime Prevention and Privacy Compact Council (Parts 900—999)
XI Department of Justice and Department of State (Parts 1100—1199)

Title 29—Labor

SUBTITLE A—OFFICE OF THE SECRETARY OF LABOR (PARTS 0—99)
SUBTITLE B—REGULATIONS RELATING TO LABOR
I National Labor Relations Board (Parts 100—199)
II Office of Labor-Management Standards, Department of Labor (Parts 200—299)
III National Railroad Adjustment Board (Parts 300—399)
IV Office of Labor-Management Standards, Department of Labor (Parts 400—499)
V Wage and Hour Division, Department of Labor (Parts 500—899)
IX Construction Industry Collective Bargaining Commission (Parts 900—999)
X National Mediation Board (Parts 1200—1299)
XII Federal Mediation and Conciliation Service (Parts 1400—1499)
XIV Equal Employment Opportunity Commission (Parts 1600—1699)
XVII Occupational Safety and Health Administration, Department of Labor (Parts 1900—1999)
XX Occupational Safety and Health Review Commission (Parts 2200—2499)
XXV Employee Benefits Security Administration, Department of Labor (Parts 2500—2599)

Chap.

Title 29—Labor—Continued

XXVII   Federal Mine Safety and Health Review Commission (Parts 2700—2799)
XL   Pension Benefit Guaranty Corporation (Parts 4000—4999)

Title 30—Mineral Resources

I   Mine Safety and Health Administration, Department of Labor (Parts 1—199)
II   Bureau of Safety and Environmental Enforcement, Department of the Interior (Parts 200—299)
IV   Geological Survey, Department of the Interior (Parts 400—499)
V   Bureau of Ocean Energy Management, Department of the Interior (Parts 500—599)
VII   Office of Surface Mining Reclamation and Enforcement, Department of the Interior (Parts 700—999)
XII   Office of Natural Resources Revenue, Department of the Interior (Parts 1200—1299)

Title 31—Money and Finance: Treasury

SUBTITLE A—OFFICE OF THE SECRETARY OF THE TREASURY (PARTS 0—50)

SUBTITLE B—REGULATIONS RELATING TO MONEY AND FINANCE

I   Monetary Offices, Department of the Treasury (Parts 51—199)
II   Fiscal Service, Department of the Treasury (Parts 200—399)
IV   Secret Service, Department of the Treasury (Parts 400—499)
V   Office of Foreign Assets Control, Department of the Treasury (Parts 500—599)
VI   Bureau of Engraving and Printing, Department of the Treasury (Parts 600—699)
VII   Federal Law Enforcement Training Center, Department of the Treasury (Parts 700—799)
VIII   Office of International Investment, Department of the Treasury (Parts 800—899)
IX   Federal Claims Collection Standards (Department of the Treasury—Department of Justice) (Parts 900—999)
X   Financial Crimes Enforcement Network, Department of the Treasury (Parts 1000—1099)

Title 32—National Defense

SUBTITLE A—DEPARTMENT OF DEFENSE

I   Office of the Secretary of Defense (Parts 1—399)
V   Department of the Army (Parts 400—699)
VI   Department of the Navy (Parts 700—799)
VII   Department of the Air Force (Parts 800—1099)

SUBTITLE B—OTHER REGULATIONS RELATING TO NATIONAL DEFENSE

1094

Title 32—National Defense—Continued

Chap.

XII	Defense Logistics Agency (Parts 1200—1299)
XVI	Selective Service System (Parts 1600—1699)
XVII	Office of the Director of National Intelligence (Parts 1700—1799)
XVIII	National Counterintelligence Center (Parts 1800—1899)
XIX	Central Intelligence Agency (Parts 1900—1999)
XX	Information Security Oversight Office, National Archives and Records Administration (Parts 2000—2099)
XXI	National Security Council (Parts 2100—2199)
XXIV	Office of Science and Technology Policy (Parts 2400—2499)
XXVII	Office for Micronesian Status Negotiations (Parts 2700—2799)
XXVIII	Office of the Vice President of the United States (Parts 2800—2899)

Title 33—Navigation and Navigable Waters

I	Coast Guard, Department of Homeland Security (Parts 1—199)
II	Corps of Engineers, Department of the Army (Parts 200—399)
IV	Saint Lawrence Seaway Development Corporation, Department of Transportation (Parts 400—499)

Title 34—Education

SUBTITLE A—OFFICE OF THE SECRETARY, DEPARTMENT OF EDUCATION (PARTS 1—99)

SUBTITLE B—REGULATIONS OF THE OFFICES OF THE DEPARTMENT OF EDUCATION

I	Office for Civil Rights, Department of Education (Parts 100—199)
II	Office of Elementary and Secondary Education, Department of Education (Parts 200—299)
III	Office of Special Education and Rehabilitative Services, Department of Education (Parts 300—399)
IV	Office of Vocational and Adult Education, Department of Education (Parts 400—499)
V	Office of Bilingual Education and Minority Languages Affairs, Department of Education (Parts 500—599)
VI	Office of Postsecondary Education, Department of Education (Parts 600—699)
VII	Office of Educational Research and Improvement, Department of Education [Reserved]
XI	National Institute for Literacy (Parts 1100—1199)

SUBTITLE C—REGULATIONS RELATING TO EDUCATION

XII	National Council on Disability (Parts 1200—1299)

Title 35 [Reserved]

Title 36—Parks, Forests, and Public Property

I	National Park Service, Department of the Interior (Parts 1—199)

Title 36—Parks, Forests, and Public Property—Continued

Chap.
- II   Forest Service, Department of Agriculture (Parts 200—299)
- III   Corps of Engineers, Department of the Army (Parts 300—399)
- IV   American Battle Monuments Commission (Parts 400—499)
- V   Smithsonian Institution (Parts 500—599)
- VI   [Reserved]
- VII   Library of Congress (Parts 700—799)
- VIII   Advisory Council on Historic Preservation (Parts 800—899)
- IX   Pennsylvania Avenue Development Corporation (Parts 900—999)
- X   Presidio Trust (Parts 1000—1099)
- XI   Architectural and Transportation Barriers Compliance Board (Parts 1100—1199)
- XII   National Archives and Records Administration (Parts 1200—1299)
- XV   Oklahoma City National Memorial Trust (Parts 1500—1599)
- XVI   Morris K. Udall Scholarship and Excellence in National Environmental Policy Foundation (Parts 1600—1699)

Title 37—Patents, Trademarks, and Copyrights

- I   United States Patent and Trademark Office, Department of Commerce (Parts 1—199)
- II   Copyright Office, Library of Congress (Parts 200—299)
- III   Copyright Royalty Board, Library of Congress (Parts 300—399)
- IV   Assistant Secretary for Technology Policy, Department of Commerce (Parts 400—499)
- V   Under Secretary for Technology, Department of Commerce (Parts 500—599)

Title 38—Pensions, Bonuses, and Veterans' Relief

- I   Department of Veterans Affairs (Parts 0—99)
- II   Armed Forces Retirement Home (Parts 200—299)

Title 39—Postal Service

- I   United States Postal Service (Parts 1—999)
- III   Postal Regulatory Commission (Parts 3000—3099)

Title 40—Protection of Environment

- I   Environmental Protection Agency (Parts 1—1099)
- IV   Environmental Protection Agency and Department of Justice (Parts 1400—1499)
- V   Council on Environmental Quality (Parts 1500—1599)
- VI   Chemical Safety and Hazard Investigation Board (Parts 1600—1699)
- VII   Environmental Protection Agency and Department of Defense; Uniform National Discharge Standards for Vessels of the Armed Forces (Parts 1700—1799)

Title 41—Public Contracts and Property Management

Chap.

SUBTITLE A—FEDERAL PROCUREMENT REGULATIONS SYSTEM [NOTE]

SUBTITLE B—OTHER PROVISIONS RELATING TO PUBLIC CONTRACTS

50 Public Contracts, Department of Labor (Parts 50–1—50–999)
51 Committee for Purchase From People Who Are Blind or Severely Disabled (Parts 51–1—51–99)
60 Office of Federal Contract Compliance Programs, Equal Employment Opportunity, Department of Labor (Parts 60–1—60–999)
61 Office of the Assistant Secretary for Veterans' Employment and Training Service, Department of Labor (Parts 61–1—61–999)
62—100 [Reserved]

SUBTITLE C—FEDERAL PROPERTY MANAGEMENT REGULATIONS SYSTEM

101 Federal Property Management Regulations (Parts 101–1—101–99)
102 Federal Management Regulation (Parts 102–1—102–299)
103—104 [Reserved]
105 General Services Administration (Parts 105–1—105–999)
109 Department of Energy Property Management Regulations (Parts 109–1—109–99)
114 Department of the Interior (Parts 114–1—114–99)
115 Environmental Protection Agency (Parts 115–1—115–99)
128 Department of Justice (Parts 128–1—128–99)
129—200 [Reserved]

SUBTITLE D—OTHER PROVISIONS RELATING TO PROPERTY MANAGEMENT [RESERVED]

SUBTITLE E—FEDERAL INFORMATION RESOURCES MANAGEMENT REGULATIONS SYSTEM [RESERVED]

SUBTITLE F—FEDERAL TRAVEL REGULATION SYSTEM

300 General (Parts 300–1—300–99)
301 Temporary Duty (TDY) Travel Allowances (Parts 301–1—301–99)
302 Relocation Allowances (Parts 302–1—302–99)
303 Payment of Expenses Connected with the Death of Certain Employees (Part 303–1—303–99)
304 Payment of Travel Expenses from a Non-Federal Source (Parts 304–1—304–99)

Title 42—Public Health

I Public Health Service, Department of Health and Human Services (Parts 1—199)
IV Centers for Medicare & Medicaid Services, Department of Health and Human Services (Parts 400—599)
V Office of Inspector General-Health Care, Department of Health and Human Services (Parts 1000—1999)

Title 43—Public Lands: Interior

Chap.

SUBTITLE A—OFFICE OF THE SECRETARY OF THE INTERIOR (PARTS 1—199)

SUBTITLE B—REGULATIONS RELATING TO PUBLIC LANDS

I   Bureau of Reclamation, Department of the Interior (Parts 200—599)

II   Bureau of Land Management, Department of the Interior (Parts 1000—9999)

III   Utah Reclamation Mitigation and Conservation Commission (Parts 10000—10099)

Title 44—Emergency Management and Assistance

I   Federal Emergency Management Agency, Department of Homeland Security (Parts 0—399)

IV   Department of Commerce and Department of Transportation (Parts 400—499)

Title 45—Public Welfare

SUBTITLE A—DEPARTMENT OF HEALTH AND HUMAN SERVICES (PARTS 1—199)

SUBTITLE B—REGULATIONS RELATING TO PUBLIC WELFARE

II   Office of Family Assistance (Assistance Programs), Administration for Children and Families, Department of Health and Human Services (Parts 200—299)

III   Office of Child Support Enforcement (Child Support Enforcement Program), Administration for Children and Families, Department of Health and Human Services (Parts 300—399)

IV   Office of Refugee Resettlement, Administration for Children and Families, Department of Health and Human Services (Parts 400—499)

V   Foreign Claims Settlement Commission of the United States, Department of Justice (Parts 500—599)

VI   National Science Foundation (Parts 600—699)

VII   Commission on Civil Rights (Parts 700—799)

VIII   Office of Personnel Management (Parts 800—899) [Reserved]

X   Office of Community Services, Administration for Children and Families, Department of Health and Human Services (Parts 1000—1099)

XI   National Foundation on the Arts and the Humanities (Parts 1100—1199)

XII   Corporation for National and Community Service (Parts 1200—1299)

XIII   Office of Human Development Services, Department of Health and Human Services (Parts 1300—1399)

XVI   Legal Services Corporation (Parts 1600—1699)

XVII   National Commission on Libraries and Information Science (Parts 1700—1799)

XVIII   Harry S. Truman Scholarship Foundation (Parts 1800—1899)

XXI   Commission on Fine Arts (Parts 2100—2199)

Title 45—Public Welfare—Continued

Chap.

XXIII Arctic Research Commission (Part 2301)

XXIV James Madison Memorial Fellowship Foundation (Parts 2400–2499)

XXV Corporation for National and Community Service (Parts 2500–2599)

Title 46—Shipping

I Coast Guard, Department of Homeland Security (Parts 1—199)

II Maritime Administration, Department of Transportation (Parts 200—399)

III Coast Guard (Great Lakes Pilotage), Department of Homeland Security (Parts 400—499)

IV Federal Maritime Commission (Parts 500—599)

Title 47—Telecommunication

I Federal Communications Commission (Parts 0—199)

II Office of Science and Technology Policy and National Security Council (Parts 200—299)

III National Telecommunications and Information Administration, Department of Commerce (Parts 300—399)

IV National Telecommunications and Information Administration, Department of Commerce, and National Highway Traffic Safety Administration, Department of Transportation (Parts 400—499)

Title 48—Federal Acquisition Regulations System

1 Federal Acquisition Regulation (Parts 1—99)

2 Defense Acquisition Regulations System, Department of Defense (Parts 200—299)

3 Health and Human Services (Parts 300—399)

4 Department of Agriculture (Parts 400—499)

5 General Services Administration (Parts 500—599)

6 Department of State (Parts 600—699)

7 Agency for International Development (Parts 700—799)

8 Department of Veterans Affairs (Parts 800—899)

9 Department of Energy (Parts 900—999)

10 Department of the Treasury (Parts 1000—1099)

12 Department of Transportation (Parts 1200—1299)

13 Department of Commerce (Parts 1300—1399)

14 Department of the Interior (Parts 1400—1499)

15 Environmental Protection Agency (Parts 1500—1599)

16 Office of Personnel Management, Federal Employees Health Benefits Acquisition Regulation (Parts 1600—1699)

17 Office of Personnel Management (Parts 1700—1799)

Title 48—Federal Acquisition Regulations System—Continued

Chap.

18	National Aeronautics and Space Administration (Parts 1800—1899)
19	Broadcasting Board of Governors (Parts 1900—1999)
20	Nuclear Regulatory Commission (Parts 2000—2099)
21	Office of Personnel Management, Federal Employees Group Life Insurance Federal Acquisition Regulation (Parts 2100—2199)
23	Social Security Administration (Parts 2300—2399)
24	Department of Housing and Urban Development (Parts 2400—2499)
25	National Science Foundation (Parts 2500—2599)
28	Department of Justice (Parts 2800—2899)
29	Department of Labor (Parts 2900—2999)
30	Department of Homeland Security, Homeland Security Acquisition Regulation (HSAR) (Parts 3000—3099)
34	Department of Education Acquisition Regulation (Parts 3400—3499)
51	Department of the Army Acquisition Regulations (Parts 5100—5199)
52	Department of the Navy Acquisition Regulations (Parts 5200—5299)
53	Department of the Air Force Federal Acquisition Regulation Supplement [Reserved]
54	Defense Logistics Agency, Department of Defense (Parts 5400—5499)
57	African Development Foundation (Parts 5700—5799)
61	Civilian Board of Contract Appeals, General Services Administration (Parts 6100—6199)
63	Department of Transportation Board of Contract Appeals (Parts 6300—6399)
99	Cost Accounting Standards Board, Office of Federal Procurement Policy, Office of Management and Budget (Parts 9900—9999)

Title 49—Transportation

SUBTITLE A—OFFICE OF THE SECRETARY OF TRANSPORTATION (PARTS 1—99)

SUBTITLE B—OTHER REGULATIONS RELATING TO TRANSPORTATION

I	Pipeline and Hazardous Materials Safety Administration, Department of Transportation (Parts 100—199)
II	Federal Railroad Administration, Department of Transportation (Parts 200—299)
III	Federal Motor Carrier Safety Administration, Department of Transportation (Parts 300—399)
IV	Coast Guard, Department of Homeland Security (Parts 400—499)
V	National Highway Traffic Safety Administration, Department of Transportation (Parts 500—599)
VI	Federal Transit Administration, Department of Transportation (Parts 600—699)

Title 49—Transportation—Continued

Chap.

VII National Railroad Passenger Corporation (AMTRAK) (Parts 700—799)
VIII National Transportation Safety Board (Parts 800—999)
X Surface Transportation Board, Department of Transportation (Parts 1000—1399)
XI Research and Innovative Technology Administration, Department of Transportation [Reserved]
XII Transportation Security Administration, Department of Homeland Security (Parts 1500—1699)

Title 50—Wildlife and Fisheries

I United States Fish and Wildlife Service, Department of the Interior (Parts 1—199)
II National Marine Fisheries Service, National Oceanic and Atmospheric Administration, Department of Commerce (Parts 200—299)
III International Fishing and Related Activities (Parts 300—399)
IV Joint Regulations (United States Fish and Wildlife Service, Department of the Interior and National Marine Fisheries Service, National Oceanic and Atmospheric Administration, Department of Commerce); Endangered Species Committee Regulations (Parts 400—499)
V Marine Mammal Commission (Parts 500—599)
VI Fishery Conservation and Management, National Oceanic and Atmospheric Administration, Department of Commerce (Parts 600—699)

CFR Index and Finding Aids

Subject/Agency Index
List of Agency Prepared Indexes
Parallel Tables of Statutory Authorities and Rules
List of CFR Titles, Chapters, Subchapters, and Parts
Alphabetical List of Agencies Appearing in the CFR

Alphabetical List of Agencies Appearing in the CFR
(Revised as of January 1, 2012)

Agency	CFR Title, Subtitle or Chapter
Administrative Committee of the Federal Register	1, I
Administrative Conference of the United States	1, III
Advisory Council on Historic Preservation	36, VIII
Advocacy and Outreach, Office of	7, XXV
African Development Foundation	22, XV
Federal Acquisition Regulation	48, 57
Agency for International Development	2, VII; 22, II
Federal Acquisition Regulation	48, 7
Agricultural Marketing Service	7, I, IX, X, XI
Agricultural Research Service	7, V
Agriculture Department	2, IV; 5, LXXIII
Advocacy and Outreach, Office of	7, XXV
Agricultural Marketing Service	7, I, IX, X, XI
Agricultural Research Service	7, V
Animal and Plant Health Inspection Service	7, III; 9, I
Chief Financial Officer, Office of	7, XXX
Commodity Credit Corporation	7, XIV
Economic Research Service	7, XXXVII
Energy Policy and New Uses, Office of	2, IX; 7, XXIX
Environmental Quality, Office of	7, XXXI
Farm Service Agency	7, VII, XVIII
Federal Acquisition Regulation	48, 4
Federal Crop Insurance Corporation	7, IV
Food and Nutrition Service	7, II
Food Safety and Inspection Service	9, III
Foreign Agricultural Service	7, XV
Forest Service	36, II
Grain Inspection, Packers and Stockyards Administration	7, VIII; 9, II
Information Resources Management, Office of	7, XXVII
Inspector General, Office of	7, XXVI
National Agricultural Library	7, XLI
National Agricultural Statistics Service	7, XXXVI
National Institute of Food and Agriculture	7, XXXIV
Natural Resources Conservation Service	7, VI
Operations, Office of	7, XXVIII
Procurement and Property Management, Office of	7, XXXII
Rural Business-Cooperative Service	7, XVIII, XLII, L
Rural Development Administration	7, XLII
Rural Housing Service	7, XVIII, XXXV, L
Rural Telephone Bank	7, XVI
Rural Utilities Service	7, XVII, XVIII, XLII, L
Secretary of Agriculture, Office of	7, Subtitle A
Transportation, Office of	7, XXXIII
World Agricultural Outlook Board	7, XXXVIII
Air Force Department	32, VII
Federal Acquisition Regulation Supplement	48, 53
Air Transportation Stabilization Board	14, VI
Alcohol and Tobacco Tax and Trade Bureau	27, I
Alcohol, Tobacco, Firearms, and Explosives, Bureau of	27, II
AMTRAK	49, VII
American Battle Monuments Commission	36, IV
American Indians, Office of the Special Trustee	25, VII
Animal and Plant Health Inspection Service	7, III; 9, I

Agency	CFR Title, Subtitle or Chapter
Appalachian Regional Commission	5, IX
Architectural and Transportation Barriers Compliance Board	36, XI
Arctic Research Commission	45, XXIII
Armed Forces Retirement Home	5, XI
Army Department	32, V
Engineers, Corps of	33, II; 36, III
Federal Acquisition Regulation	48, 51
Bilingual Education and Minority Languages Affairs, Office of	34, V
Blind or Severely Disabled, Committee for Purchase from People Who Are	41, 51
Broadcasting Board of Governors	22, V
Federal Acquisition Regulation	48, 19
Bureau of Ocean Energy Management, Regulation, and Enforcement	30, II
Census Bureau	15, I
Centers for Medicare & Medicaid Services	42, IV
Central Intelligence Agency	32, XIX
Chemical Safety and Hazardous Investigation Board	40, VI
Chief Financial Officer, Office of	7, XXX
Child Support Enforcement, Office of	45, III
Children and Families, Administration for	45, II, III, IV, X
Civil Rights, Commission on	5, LXVIII; 45, VII
Civil Rights, Office for	34, I
Court Services and Offender Supervision Agency for the District of Columbia	5, LXX
Coast Guard	33, I; 46, I; 49, IV
Coast Guard (Great Lakes Pilotage)	46, III
Commerce Department	2, XIII; 44, IV; 50, VI
Census Bureau	15, I
Economic Affairs, Under Secretary	37, V
Economic Analysis, Bureau of	15, VIII
Economic Development Administration	13, III
Emergency Management and Assistance	44, IV
Federal Acquisition Regulation	48, 13
Foreign-Trade Zones Board	15, IV
Industry and Security, Bureau of	15, VII
International Trade Administration	15, III; 19, III
National Institute of Standards and Technology	15, II
National Marine Fisheries Service	50, II, IV
National Oceanic and Atmospheric Administration	15, IX; 50, II, III, IV, VI
National Telecommunications and Information Administration	15, XXIII; 47, III, IV
National Weather Service	15, IX
Patent and Trademark Office, United States	37, I
Productivity, Technology and Innovation, Assistant Secretary for	37, IV
Secretary of Commerce, Office of	15, Subtitle A
Technology, Under Secretary for	37, V
Technology Administration	15, XI
Technology Policy, Assistant Secretary for	37, IV
Commercial Space Transportation	14, III
Commodity Credit Corporation	7, XIV
Commodity Futures Trading Commission	5, XLI; 17, I
Community Planning and Development, Office of Assistant Secretary for	24, V, VI
Community Services, Office of	45, X
Comptroller of the Currency	12, I
Construction Industry Collective Bargaining Commission	29, IX
Consumer Financial Protection Bureau	12, X
Consumer Product Safety Commission	5, LXXI; 16, II
Copyright Office	37, II
Copyright Royalty Board	37, III
Corporation for National and Community Service	2, XXII; 45, XII, XXV
Cost Accounting Standards Board	48, 99
Council on Environmental Quality	40, V
Court Services and Offender Supervision Agency for the District of Columbia	5, LXX; 28, VIII

Agency	CFR Title, Subtitle or Chapter
Customs and Border Protection	19, I
Defense Contract Audit Agency	32, I
Defense Department	2, XI; 5, XXVI; 32, Subtitle A; 40, VII
Advanced Research Projects Agency	32, I
Air Force Department	32, VII
Army Department	32, V; 33, II; 36, III; 48, 51
Defense Acquisition Regulations System	48, 2
Defense Intelligence Agency	32, I
Defense Logistics Agency	32, I, XII; 48, 54
Engineers, Corps of	33, II; 36, III
National Imagery and Mapping Agency	32, I
Navy Department	32, VI; 48, 52
Secretary of Defense, Office of	2, XI; 32, I
Defense Contract Audit Agency	32, I
Defense Intelligence Agency	32, I
Defense Logistics Agency	32, XII; 48, 54
Defense Nuclear Facilities Safety Board	10, XVII
Delaware River Basin Commission	18, III
District of Columbia, Court Services and Offender Supervision Agency for the	5, LXX; 28, VIII
Drug Enforcement Administration	21, II
East-West Foreign Trade Board	15, XIII
Economic Affairs, Under Secretary	37, V
Economic Analysis, Bureau of	15, VIII
Economic Development Administration	13, III
Economic Research Service	7, XXXVII
Education, Department of	5, LIII
Bilingual Education and Minority Languages Affairs, Office of	34, V
Civil Rights, Office for	34, I
Educational Research and Improvement, Office of	34, VII
Elementary and Secondary Education, Office of	34, II
Federal Acquisition Regulation	48, 34
Postsecondary Education, Office of	34, VI
Secretary of Education, Office of	34, Subtitle A
Special Education and Rehabilitative Services, Office of	34, III
Vocational and Adult Education, Office of	34, IV
Educational Research and Improvement, Office of	34, VII
Election Assistance Commission	2, LVIII; 11, II
Elementary and Secondary Education, Office of	34, II
Emergency Oil and Gas Guaranteed Loan Board	13, V
Emergency Steel Guarantee Loan Board	13, IV
Employee Benefits Security Administration	29, XXV
Employees' Compensation Appeals Board	20, IV
Employees Loyalty Board	5, V
Employment and Training Administration	20, V
Employment Standards Administration	20, VI
Endangered Species Committee	50, IV
Energy, Department of	2, IX; 5, XXIII; 10, II, III, X
Federal Acquisition Regulation	48, 9
Federal Energy Regulatory Commission	5, XXIV; 18, I
Property Management Regulations	41, 109
Energy, Office of	7, XXIX
Engineers, Corps of	33, II; 36, III
Engraving and Printing, Bureau of	31, VI
Environmental Protection Agency	2, XV; 5, LIV; 40, I, IV, VII
Federal Acquisition Regulation	48, 15
Property Management Regulations	41, 115
Environmental Quality, Office of	7, XXXI
Equal Employment Opportunity Commission	5, LXII; 29, XIV
Equal Opportunity, Office of Assistant Secretary for	24, I
Executive Office of the President	3, I
Administration, Office of	5, XV

Agency	CFR Title, Subtitle or Chapter
Environmental Quality, Council on	40, V
Management and Budget, Office of	2, Subtitle A; 5, III, LXXVII; 14, VI; 48, 99
National Drug Control Policy, Office of	21, III
National Security Council	32, XXI; 47, 2
Presidential Documents	3
Science and Technology Policy, Office of	32, XXIV; 47, II
Trade Representative, Office of the United States	15, XX
Export-Import Bank of the United States	2, XXXV; 5, LII; 12, IV
Family Assistance, Office of	45, II
Farm Credit Administration	5, XXXI; 12, VI
Farm Credit System Insurance Corporation	5, XXX; 12, XIV
Farm Service Agency	7, VII, XVIII
Federal Acquisition Regulation	48, 1
Federal Aviation Administration	14, I
Commercial Space Transportation	14, III
Federal Claims Collection Standards	31, IX
Federal Communications Commission	5, XXIX; 47, I
Federal Contract Compliance Programs, Office of	41, 60
Federal Crop Insurance Corporation	7, IV
Federal Deposit Insurance Corporation	5, XXII; 12, III
Federal Election Commission	5, XXXVII; 11, I
Federal Emergency Management Agency	44, I
Federal Employees Group Life Insurance Federal Acquisition Regulation	48, 21
Federal Employees Health Benefits Acquisition Regulation	48, 16
Federal Energy Regulatory Commission	5, XXIV; 18, I
Federal Financial Institutions Examination Council	12, XI
Federal Financing Bank	12, VIII
Federal Highway Administration	23, I, II
Federal Home Loan Mortgage Corporation	1, IV
Federal Housing Enterprise Oversight Office	12, XVII
Federal Housing Finance Agency	5, LXXX; 12, XII
Federal Housing Finance Board	12, IX
Federal Labor Relations Authority	5, XIV, XLIX; 22, XIV
Federal Law Enforcement Training Center	31, VII
Federal Management Regulation	41, 102
Federal Maritime Commission	46, IV
Federal Mediation and Conciliation Service	29, XII
Federal Mine Safety and Health Review Commission	5, LXXIV; 29, XXVII
Federal Motor Carrier Safety Administration	49, III
Federal Prison Industries, Inc.	28, III
Federal Procurement Policy Office	48, 99
Federal Property Management Regulations	41, 101
Federal Railroad Administration	49, II
Federal Register, Administrative Committee of	1, I
Federal Register, Office of	1, II
Federal Reserve System	12, II
Board of Governors	5, LVIII
Federal Retirement Thrift Investment Board	5, VI, LXXVI
Federal Service Impasses Panel	5, XIV
Federal Trade Commission	5, XLVII; 16, I
Federal Transit Administration	49, VI
Federal Travel Regulation System	41, Subtitle F
Financial Crimes Enforcement Network	31, X
Financial Research Office	12, XVI
Financial Stability Oversight Council	12, XIII
Fine Arts, Commission on	45, XXI
Fiscal Service	31, II
Fish and Wildlife Service, United States	50, I, IV
Food and Drug Administration	21, I
Food and Nutrition Service	7, II
Food Safety and Inspection Service	9, III
Foreign Agricultural Service	7, XV
Foreign Assets Control, Office of	31, V
Foreign Claims Settlement Commission of the United States	45, V
Foreign Service Grievance Board	22, IX

Agency	CFR Title, Subtitle or Chapter
Foreign Service Impasse Disputes Panel	22, XIV
Foreign Service Labor Relations Board	22, XIV
Foreign-Trade Zones Board	15, IV
Forest Service	36, II
General Services Administration	5, LVII; 41, 105
Contract Appeals, Board of	48, 61
Federal Acquisition Regulation	48, 5
Federal Management Regulation	41, 102
Federal Property Management Regulations	41, 101
Federal Travel Regulation System	41, Subtitle F
General	41, 300
Payment From a Non-Federal Source for Travel Expenses	41, 304
Payment of Expenses Connected With the Death of Certain Employees	41, 303
Relocation Allowances	41, 302
Temporary Duty (TDY) Travel Allowances	41, 301
Geological Survey	30, IV
Government Accountability Office	4, I
Government Ethics, Office of	5, XVI
Government National Mortgage Association	24, III
Grain Inspection, Packers and Stockyards Administration	7, VIII; 9, II
Harry S. Truman Scholarship Foundation	45, XVIII
Health and Human Services, Department of	2, III; 5, XLV; 45, Subtitle A,
Centers for Medicare & Medicaid Services	42, IV
Child Support Enforcement, Office of	45, III
Children and Families, Administration for	45, II, III, IV, X
Community Services, Office of	45, X
Family Assistance, Office of	45, II
Federal Acquisition Regulation	48, 3
Food and Drug Administration	21, I
Human Development Services, Office of	45, XIII
Indian Health Service	25, V
Inspector General (Health Care), Office of	42, V
Public Health Service	42, I
Refugee Resettlement, Office of	45, IV
Homeland Security, Department of	2, XXX; 6, I
Coast Guard	33, I; 46, I; 49, IV
Coast Guard (Great Lakes Pilotage)	46, III
Customs and Border Protection	19, I
Federal Emergency Management Agency	44, I
Human Resources Management and Labor Relations Systems	5, XCVII
Immigration and Customs Enforcement Bureau	19, IV
Immigration and Naturalization	8, I
Transportation Security Administration	49, XII
HOPE for Homeowners Program, Board of Directors of	24, XXIV
Housing and Urban Development, Department of	2, XXIV; 5, LXV; 24, Subtitle B
Community Planning and Development, Office of Assistant Secretary for	24, V, VI
Equal Opportunity, Office of Assistant Secretary for	24, I
Federal Acquisition Regulation	48, 24
Federal Housing Enterprise Oversight, Office of	12, XVII
Government National Mortgage Association	24, III
Housing—Federal Housing Commissioner, Office of Assistant Secretary for	24, II, VIII, X, XX
Housing, Office of, and Multifamily Housing Assistance Restructuring, Office of	24, IV
Inspector General, Office of	24, XII
Public and Indian Housing, Office of Assistant Secretary for	24, IX
Secretary, Office of	24, Subtitle A, VII
Housing—Federal Housing Commissioner, Office of Assistant Secretary for	24, II, VIII, X, XX
Housing, Office of, and Multifamily Housing Assistance Restructuring, Office of	24, IV
Human Development Services, Office of	45, XIII

Agency	CFR Title, Subtitle or Chapter
Immigration and Customs Enforcement Bureau	19, IV
Immigration and Naturalization	8, I
Immigration Review, Executive Office for	8, V
Independent Counsel, Office of	28, VII
Indian Affairs, Bureau of	25, I, V
Indian Affairs, Office of the Assistant Secretary	25, VI
Indian Arts and Crafts Board	25, II
Indian Health Service	25, V
Industry and Security, Bureau of	15, VII
Information Resources Management, Office of	7, XXVII
Information Security Oversight Office, National Archives and Records Administration	32, XX
Inspector General	
Agriculture Department	7, XXVI
Health and Human Services Department	42, V
Housing and Urban Development Department	24, XII, XV
Institute of Peace, United States	22, XVII
Inter-American Foundation	5, LXIII; 22, X
Interior Department	2, XIV
American Indians, Office of the Special Trustee	25, VII
Bureau of Ocean Energy Management, Regulation, and Enforcement	30, II
Endangered Species Committee	50, IV
Federal Acquisition Regulation	48, 14
Federal Property Management Regulations System	41, 114
Fish and Wildlife Service, United States	50, I, IV
Geological Survey	30, IV
Indian Affairs, Bureau of	25, I, V
Indian Affairs, Office of the Assistant Secretary	25, VI
Indian Arts and Crafts Board	25, II
Land Management, Bureau of	43, II
National Indian Gaming Commission	25, III
National Park Service	36, I
Natural Resource Revenue, Office of	30, XII
Ocean Energy Management, Bureau of	30, V
Reclamation, Bureau of	43, I
Secretary of the Interior, Office of	2, XIV; 43, Subtitle A
Surface Mining Reclamation and Enforcement, Office of	30, VII
Internal Revenue Service	26, I
International Boundary and Water Commission, United States and Mexico, United States Section	22, XI
International Development, United States Agency for	22, II
Federal Acquisition Regulation	48, 7
International Development Cooperation Agency, United States	22, XII
International Joint Commission, United States and Canada	22, IV
International Organizations Employees Loyalty Board	5, V
International Trade Administration	15, III; 19, III
International Trade Commission, United States	19, II
Interstate Commerce Commission	5, XL
Investment Security, Office of	31, VIII
James Madison Memorial Fellowship Foundation	45, XXIV
Japan–United States Friendship Commission	22, XVI
Joint Board for the Enrollment of Actuaries	20, VIII
Justice Department	2, XXVIII; 5, XXVIII; 28, I, XI; 40, IV
Alcohol, Tobacco, Firearms, and Explosives, Bureau of	27, II
Drug Enforcement Administration	21, II
Federal Acquisition Regulation	48, 28
Federal Claims Collection Standards	31, IX
Federal Prison Industries, Inc.	28, III
Foreign Claims Settlement Commission of the United States	45, V
Immigration Review, Executive Office for	8, V
Offices of Independent Counsel	28, VI
Prisons, Bureau of	28, V
Property Management Regulations	41, 128

Agency	CFR Title, Subtitle or Chapter
Labor Department	5, XLII
Employee Benefits Security Administration	29, XXV
Employees' Compensation Appeals Board	20, IV
Employment and Training Administration	20, V
Employment Standards Administration	20, VI
Federal Acquisition Regulation	48, 29
Federal Contract Compliance Programs, Office of	41, 60
Federal Procurement Regulations System	41, 50
Labor-Management Standards, Office of	29, II, IV
Mine Safety and Health Administration	30, I
Occupational Safety and Health Administration	29, XVII
Office of Workers' Compensation Programs	20, VII
Public Contracts	41, 50
Secretary of Labor, Office of	29, Subtitle A
Veterans' Employment and Training Service, Office of the Assistant Secretary for	41, 61; 20, IX
Wage and Hour Division	29, V
Workers' Compensation Programs, Office of	20, I
Labor-Management Standards, Office of	29, II, IV
Land Management, Bureau of	43, II
Legal Services Corporation	45, XVI
Library of Congress	36, VII
Copyright Office	37, II
Copyright Royalty Board	37, III
Local Television Loan Guarantee Board	7, XX
Management and Budget, Office of	5, III, LXXVII; 14, VI; 48, 99
Marine Mammal Commission	50, V
Maritime Administration	46, II
Merit Systems Protection Board	5, II, LXIV
Micronesian Status Negotiations, Office for	32, XXVII
Millennium Challenge Corporation	22, XIII
Mine Safety and Health Administration	30, I
Minority Business Development Agency	15, XIV
Miscellaneous Agencies	1, IV
Monetary Offices	31, I
Morris K. Udall Scholarship and Excellence in National Environmental Policy Foundation	36, XVI
Museum and Library Services, Institute of	2, XXXI
National Aeronautics and Space Administration	2, XVIII; 5, LIX; 14, V
Federal Acquisition Regulation	48, 18
National Agricultural Library	7, XLI
National Agricultural Statistics Service	7, XXXVI
National and Community Service, Corporation for	2, XXII; 45, XII, XXV
National Archives and Records Administration	2, XXVI; 5, LXVI; 36, XII
Information Security Oversight Office	32, XX
National Capital Planning Commission	1, IV
National Commission for Employment Policy	1, IV
National Commission on Libraries and Information Science	45, XVII
National Council on Disability	34, XII
National Counterintelligence Center	32, XVIII
National Credit Union Administration	12, VII
National Crime Prevention and Privacy Compact Council	28, IX
National Drug Control Policy, Office of	21, III
National Endowment for the Arts	2, XXXII
National Endowment for the Humanities	2, XXXIII
National Foundation on the Arts and the Humanities	45, XI
National Highway Traffic Safety Administration	23, II, III; 47, VI; 49, V
National Imagery and Mapping Agency	32, I
National Indian Gaming Commission	25, III
National Institute for Literacy	34, XI
National Institute of Food and Agriculture	7, XXXIV
National Institute of Standards and Technology	15, II
National Intelligence, Office of Director of	32, XVII
National Labor Relations Board	5, LXI; 29, I
National Marine Fisheries Service	50, II, IV

Agency	CFR Title, Subtitle or Chapter
National Mediation Board	29, X
National Oceanic and Atmospheric Administration	15, IX; 50, II, III, IV, VI
National Park Service	36, I
National Railroad Adjustment Board	29, III
National Railroad Passenger Corporation (AMTRAK)	49, VII
National Science Foundation	2, XXV; 5, XLIII; 45, VI
Federal Acquisition Regulation	48, 25
National Security Council	32, XXI
National Security Council and Office of Science and Technology Policy	47, II
National Telecommunications and Information Administration	15, XXIII; 47, III, IV
National Transportation Safety Board	49, VIII
Natural Resources Conservation Service	7, VI
Natural Resource Revenue, Office of	30, XII
Navajo and Hopi Indian Relocation, Office of	25, IV
Navy Department	32, VI
Federal Acquisition Regulation	48, 52
Neighborhood Reinvestment Corporation	24, XXV
Northeast Interstate Low-Level Radioactive Waste Commission	10, XVIII
Nuclear Regulatory Commission	2, XX; 5, XLVIII; 10, I
Federal Acquisition Regulation	48, 20
Occupational Safety and Health Administration	29, XVII
Occupational Safety and Health Review Commission	29, XX
Ocean Energy Management, Bureau of	30, V
Offices of Independent Counsel	28, VI
Office of Workers' Compensation Programs	20, VII
Oklahoma City National Memorial Trust	36, XV
Operations Office	7, XXVIII
Overseas Private Investment Corporation	5, XXXIII; 22, VII
Patent and Trademark Office, United States	37, I
Payment From a Non-Federal Source for Travel Expenses	41, 304
Payment of Expenses Connected With the Death of Certain Employees	41, 303
Peace Corps	2, XXXVII; 22, III
Pennsylvania Avenue Development Corporation	36, IX
Pension Benefit Guaranty Corporation	29, XL
Personnel Management, Office of	5, I, XXXV; 45, VIII
Human Resources Management and Labor Relations Systems, Department of Homeland Security	5, XCVII
Federal Acquisition Regulation	48, 17
Federal Employees Group Life Insurance Federal Acquisition Regulation	48, 21
Federal Employees Health Benefits Acquisition Regulation	48, 16
Pipeline and Hazardous Materials Safety Administration	49, I
Postal Regulatory Commission	5, XLVI; 39, III
Postal Service, United States	5, LX; 39, I
Postsecondary Education, Office of	34, VI
President's Commission on White House Fellowships	1, IV
Presidential Documents	3
Presidio Trust	36, X
Prisons, Bureau of	28, V
Procurement and Property Management, Office of	7, XXXII
Productivity, Technology and Innovation, Assistant Secretary	37, IV
Public Contracts, Department of Labor	41, 50
Public and Indian Housing, Office of Assistant Secretary for	24, IX
Public Health Service	42, I
Railroad Retirement Board	20, II
Reclamation, Bureau of	43, I
Recovery Accountability and Transparency Board	4, II
Refugee Resettlement, Office of	45, IV
Relocation Allowances	41, 302
Research and Innovative Technology Administration	49, XI
Rural Business-Cooperative Service	7, XVIII, XLII, L
Rural Development Administration	7, XLII

Agency	CFR Title, Subtitle or Chapter
Rural Housing Service	7, XVIII, XXXV, L
Rural Telephone Bank	7, XVI
Rural Utilities Service	7, XVII, XVIII, XLII, L
Saint Lawrence Seaway Development Corporation	33, IV
Science and Technology Policy, Office of	32, XXIV
Science and Technology Policy, Office of, and National Security Council	47, II
Secret Service	31, IV
Securities and Exchange Commission	5, XXXIV; 17, II
Selective Service System	32, XVI
Small Business Administration	2, XXVII; 13, I
Smithsonian Institution	36, V
Social Security Administration	2, XXIII; 20, III; 48, 23
Soldiers' and Airmen's Home, United States	5, XI
Special Counsel, Office of	5, VIII
Special Education and Rehabilitative Services, Office of	34, III
Special Inspector General for Iraq Reconstruction	5, LXXXVII
State Department	2, VI; 22, I; 28, XI
Federal Acquisition Regulation	48, 6
Surface Mining Reclamation and Enforcement, Office of	30, VII
Surface Transportation Board	49, X
Susquehanna River Basin Commission	18, VIII
Technology Administration	15, XI
Technology Policy, Assistant Secretary for	37, IV
Technology, Under Secretary for	37, V
Tennessee Valley Authority	5, LXIX; 18, XIII
Thrift Supervision Office, Department of the Treasury	12, V
Trade Representative, United States, Office of	15, XX
Transportation, Department of	2, XII; 5, L
Commercial Space Transportation	14, III
Contract Appeals, Board of	48, 63
Emergency Management and Assistance	44, IV
Federal Acquisition Regulation	48, 12
Federal Aviation Administration	14, I
Federal Highway Administration	23, I, II
Federal Motor Carrier Safety Administration	49, III
Federal Railroad Administration	49, II
Federal Transit Administration	49, VI
Maritime Administration	46, II
National Highway Traffic Safety Administration	23, II, III; 47, IV; 49, V
Pipeline and Hazardous Materials Safety Administration	49, I
Saint Lawrence Seaway Development Corporation	33, IV
Secretary of Transportation, Office of	14, II; 49, Subtitle A
Surface Transportation Board	49, X
Transportation Statistics Bureau	49, XI
Transportation, Office of	7, XXXIII
Transportation Security Administration	49, XII
Transportation Statistics Bureau	49, XI
Travel Allowances, Temporary Duty (TDY)	41, 301
Treasury Department	5, XXI; 12, XV; 17, IV; 31, IX
Alcohol and Tobacco Tax and Trade Bureau	27, I
Community Development Financial Institutions Fund	12, XVIII
Comptroller of the Currency	12, I
Customs and Border Protection	19, I
Engraving and Printing, Bureau of	31, VI
Federal Acquisition Regulation	48, 10
Federal Claims Collection Standards	31, IX
Federal Law Enforcement Training Center	31, VII
Financial Crimes Enforcement Network	31, X
Fiscal Service	31, II
Foreign Assets Control, Office of	31, V
Internal Revenue Service	26, I
Investment Security, Office of	31, VIII
Monetary Offices	31, I
Secret Service	31, IV
Secretary of the Treasury, Office of	31, Subtitle A

Agency	CFR Title, Subtitle or Chapter
Thrift Supervision, Office of	12, V
Truman, Harry S. Scholarship Foundation	45, XVIII
United States and Canada, International Joint Commission	22, IV
United States and Mexico, International Boundary and Water Commission, United States Section	22, XI
Utah Reclamation Mitigation and Conservation Commission	43, III
Veterans Affairs Department	2, VIII; 38, I
Federal Acquisition Regulation	48, 8
Veterans' Employment and Training Service, Office of the Assistant Secretary for	41, 61; 20, IX
Vice President of the United States, Office of	32, XXVIII
Vocational and Adult Education, Office of	34, IV
Wage and Hour Division	29, V
Water Resources Council	18, VI
Workers' Compensation Programs, Office of	20, I
World Agricultural Outlook Board	7, XXXVIII

List of CFR Sections Affected

All changes in this volume of the Code of Federal Regulations that were made by documents published in the FEDERAL REGISTER since January 1, 2001, are enumerated in the following list. Entries indicate the nature of the changes effected. Page numbers refer to FEDERAL REGISTER pages. The user should consult the entries for chapters and parts as well as sections for revisions.

For the period before January 1, 2001, see the "List of CFR Sections Affected, 1949–1963, 1964–1972, 1973–1985, and 1986–2000" published in 11 separate volumes.

2001

12 CFR   66 FR Page

Chapter III
- 303.14 Added 54650
- 303.120 Regulation at 65 FR 15529 confirmed; revised 1027
- 303.121 Regulation at 65 FR 15529 confirmed 1027
- 303.122 Regulation at 65 FR 15530 confirmed; (a) and (b) amended 1027
- 303.123 Regulation at 65 FR 15530 confirmed 1027
- 303.141 (b)(1)(ii) revised 1028
- 303.142 (a), (b) and (c) amended 1028
- 308 Authority citation revised 8638, 9189
- 308.101 (b) revised 9189
- 308.132 (c)(3)(xv) revised 9189
- 308.302 (a) revised 8638
- 308.500—308.546 (Subpart T) Added 9189
- 325.2 (g) through (x) redesignated as (i) through (z); new (g) and (h) added; new (v) and (x) revised 59652
- 325.3 (b)(1) amended 59652
- 325.5 (f) and (g)(2) revised 59652
- 325.103 (b) amended 59653
- 325 Appendix A amended 59653
- Appendix B amended 59661
- 337.4 Removed 1028
- 337.6 (e) removed 17622
- 343 Regulation at 65 FR 75843 eff. date delayed 15348
- 346 Added 2099
- 346.9 (a)(1) corrected 14071
- 346.11 (j)(2)(iv) corrected 14071

12 CFR—Continued   66 FR Page

Chapter III—Continued
- 362 Authority citation revised 1028
- 362.1 (c) revised 1028
- 362.2 (r) revised 1028
- 362.4 (b)(5)(ii) introductory text and (c)(2)(vi) revised 1028
- 362.5 (b)(1), (2) and (3) removed 1028
- 362.6 Revised 1028
- 362.7 (a) and (b) revised 1028
- 362.8 Revised 1028
- 362.10 (a) revised 1029
- 362.12 (b)(2)(i) and (4) removed; (c) heading and (b)(1) amended 1029
- 362.16—362.18 (Subpart E) Regulation at 65 FR 15530 confirmed; revised 1029
- 364 Authority citation revised 8638
- 364.101 (b) revised 8638
- 364 Appendix B revised 8638

2002

12 CFR   67 FR Page

Chapter III
- Chapter III Nomenclature change 44351
- 303 Revised 79247
- 304 Revised 18794
- 308.102 (b)(2) amended 71070
- 309.5 (b)(1), (ii), (iii), (d)(1), (2)(i), (ii), (f)(1)(x), (4)(ii) and (h)(1) amended 71071
- 309.6 (b) amended 71071
- 309.7 (a) and (b) amended 71071
- 310.3 (b) amended 71071
- 310.4 (a) amended 71071
- 310.5 (b) and (c) amended 71071

1113

12 CFR—Continued

Chapter III—Continued — 67 FR Page

310.7 Amended	71071
310.8 (a) amended	71071
310.9 (a) amended	71071
311.4 (e) amended	71071
311.5 (b)(2) amended	71071
311.8 (d)(1) and (2) amended	71071
313 Added	48527
325.2 (v) and (x) revised	3804
325.5 (f)(3), (4) and (g)(2)(i) revised	3804
325 Appendix A amended	3804, 16978
Appendix A corrected	34991
337.10 Amended	71071
360 Authority citation revised	34386
360.7 Added	34386
366 Revised	69991
366 Revised; interim	34596
369.2 (b), (c) and (d) revised; (f) and (g) redesignated as (g) and (h); new (f) added	38848
369.3 (a) revised	38849

2003

12 CFR — 68 FR Page

Chapter III

303.2 Amended	50459
303.4 Amended	50459
303.11 (g)(3)(ii) revised	50459
303.12 Added	50459
303.15 Added	7308
303.22 (a)(1) amended	50459
303.80 Revised	50459
303.81 Revised	50459
303.82 (a) through (d) revised	50460
303.83 (a)(1), (2), (6) and (7), (b)(1) and (2) revised; (a)(8) added	50460
303.85 (a) and (b) revised	50460
303.86 (c) revised	50461
303.244 (c)(4) and (5) revised; (c)(6) added	50461
308 Authority citation revised	48269
308.109 (b)(3) amended	48270
308.600—308.605 (Subpart U) Added	48270
325 Appendix A amended; interim	56536
326 Authority citation revised	25112
326.8 (b) revised	25112
333.4 (a) and (c) amended	50461
347.108 (f) revised	50461
348.2 (j)(1)(iii) revised	50461
359.1 (f)(1)(ii)(C) amended	50461

Chapter IV

413 Added; interim	66544, 66569

12 CFR—Continued

Chapter IV—Continued — 68 FR Page

413.440 Added; interim	66570

2004

12 CFR — 69 FR Page

Chapter III

308.116 (b)(4) introductory text, (i), (ii), (iii)(A) and (B) amended	61305
308.132 (c)(2)(ii), (iii)(B), (C), (3) introductory text, (i), (ii), (iii), (ix), (xiv), (xv) and (xvi) amended	61305
325 Appendix A amended; interim	22385
Appendix A amended	44921
Appendix C amended	44924
327.2 Revised; eff. 3-1-05	68073
330.10 (f) revised	2829
334 Added; eff. 7-1-05	77618
335.101 (a) amended; interim	19088
(a) amended	59783
335.111 Amended; interim	19088
Amended	59783
Form F-7 amended	59784
Form F-8 amended	59786
Form F-8A amended	59787
335.601 Revised; interim	19088
Revised	59783
335.611 Heading revised; interim	19088
Heading revised	59783
Form F-7 amended	59784
335.612 Heading revised; interim	19088
Heading revised	59783
Form F-8 amended	59786
335.613 Heading revised; interim	19088
Heading revised	59783
Form F-8A amended	59787
335.701 (a) and (b) revised; interim	19088
(a) and (b) revised	59783
335.801 (b) revised; interim	19088
(b) revised	59783
345.12 (g) removed; (h) through (q) and (s) through (w) redesignated as (g) through (p) and (t) through (x); new (q) and (s) added; (b)(1), new (k), (l) and (r) revised; interim	41187
345.27 (g)(1) amended; interim	41188
345.41 (b), (c)(1) and (e)(4) revised; interim	41188
345.42 (i) revised; interim	41188

List of CFR Sections Affected

12 CFR—Continued

69 FR Page

Chapter III—Continued
352 Revised.....................................26492
364 Authority citation revised......77619
364.101 (b) revised; eff. 7-1-05..........77619
364 Appendix B amended; eff. 7-1-05...77619

2005

12 CFR

70 FR Page

Chapter III
303 Authority citation revised......17558
303.182 Revised............................17558
303.183 Heading, (a), (b)(1) and (c)(1) revised............................17558
303.184 (b)(1) revised; (e) added.......17559
303.186 Heading and (a)(1) revised...17559
303.187 Heading, (a)(1), (2)(iv) and (b)(1) revised............................17559
308.1 (f) amended; (g) redesignated as (h); new (g) added.........69639
323 Policy statement....................59987
325.103 (c) revised........................17559
327.4 (a)(1)(i)(B)(*1*), (2), (ii)(B)(*1*) and (2) revised..............................17559
330.11 (a)(2) revised; interim..........33692
(a)(2) revised................................62059
333.101 (b) revised........................60422
334 Authority citation revised.....33985, 70685
334.1—334.3 (Subpart A) Added; interim; eff. 3-7-06......................33985
Regulation at 70 FR 33985 eff. date delayed to 4-1-06................70664
Added; eff. 4-1-06..........................70685
Correctly revised..........................75931
334.30—334.32 (Subpart D) Added; interim; eff. 3-7-06......................33986
Regulation at 70 FR 33986 eff. date delayed to 4-1-06................70664
Added; eff. 4-1-06..........................70686
Correctly revised..........................75931
335 Authority citation revised......16400
335.101 (b) revised; interim............16400
(b) revised......................................44272
335.121 Revised; interim................16400
Revised...44272
335.201 Revised; interim................16400
Revised...44272
335.211 Revised; interim................16400
Revised...44272
335.221 (d) added; interim.............16400
Heading and (d) revised................44272
335.261 Revised; interim................16400
Revised...44272
335.331 Revised; interim................16400

12 CFR—Continued

70 FR Page

Chapter III—Continued
Revised...44272
335.801 (a) revised; interim............16400
(a) revised.....................................44273
335.901 Heading and (a) revised; interim......................................16400
Heading and (a) revised................44273
336.10—336.13 (Subpart C) Added..69639
345.12 Regulation at 69 FR 41187 confirmed....................................15574
(g)(4) and (u) revised...................44269
345.26 Revised..............................44269
345.27 Regulation at 69 FR 41188 confirmed....................................15574
345.28 (c) revised..........................44269
345.41 Regulation at 69 FR 41188 confirmed....................................15574
345.42 Regulation at 69 FR 41188 confirmed....................................15574
345 Appendix A amended..............44270
347 Revised...................................17560
347.301—347.305 (Subpart C) Correctly added............................20704
363.1 (b)(2)(ii)(B) revised...............71232
363.2 (b)(2) revised; (b)(3) added......71232
363.3 (b) revised............................71232
363.5 (a) revised............................71232
363 Appendix A amended..............71232
364 Authority citation revised......15754
364 Appendix B amended..............15754

2006

12 CFR

71 FR Page

Chapter III
303.61 (d) removed; (e) redesignated as (d)...............................20526
303.62 (b)(3) removed; (b)(4), (5) and (6) redesignated as (b)(3), (4) and (5).................................20526
303.162 (b) amended....................20526
303.187 (a)(2)(vi) amended............20526
303.245 (a) amended....................20526
303.246 Removed; redesignated from 303.247...............................20526
303.247 Redesignated as 303.246; redesignated from 303.248..........20526
303.248 Redesignated as 303.247; redesignated from 303.249..........20526
303.249 Redesignated as 303.248; redesignated from 303.250..........20526
303.250 Redesignated as 303.249; redesignated from 303.251..........20526
303.251 Redesignated as 303.250; redesignated from 303.252..........20526
303.252 Redesignated as 303.251......20526

12 CFR—Continued

71 FR Page

Chapter III—Continued
- 307 Revised 8791
- 308.111 (f) amended 20526
- 308.132 (c)(3)(v) revised 65713
- 312 Removed 20526
- 313 Authority citation revised 75661
- 313.1 (c) revised 75661
- 313.3 (n) through (v) redesignated as (o) through (w); new (n) added; (d), (h), (j) and new (r) revised 75661
- 313.4 Introductory text revised 75661
- 313.125 Redesignated as 313.126; new 313.125 added 75661
- 313.126 Redesignated as 313.127; new 313.126 redesignated from 313.125 75661
- 313.127 Redesignated as 313.128; new 313.127 redesignated from 313.126 75661
- 313.128 Redesignated from 313.127 75661
- 325 Appendix C amended 8937
- 327 Authority citation revised 69277
- 327.1 Revised 69277
- 327.2 Revised 69277
- 327.3 Revised 69277
- 327.4 Revised 69277
- (g) added 69326
- 327.5 Revised 69277
- 327.6 Revised 69277
- 327.7 Revised 69277
- 327.8 Revised 69277
- 327.9 Revised 69309
- 327.10 Revised 69309
- 327.1—327.10 (Subpart A) Appendices A, B and C added 69313
- 327.30—327.36 (Subpart B) Revised 61383
- 327.50—327.55 (Subpart C) Added 61389
- 328 Revised; eff. 11–13–07 66102
- 330.1 (n), (o) and (p) redesignated as (o), (p) and (q); new (n) added; interim 14631
- 330.6 (a) through (d) amended; interim 14631
- 330.7 (e) amended; interim 14631
- 330.8 (a) amended; interim 14631
- 330.9 (a) and (b) amended; interim 14631
- 330.10 (a), (c), (d) and (f)(3) amended; interim 14631
- 330.11 Amended; interim 14631
- 330.12 (a) and (b)(1) amended; interim 14631
- 330.13 Amended; interim 14631

12 CFR—Continued

71 FR Page

Chapter III—Continued
- 330.14 (b) and (h) removed; (c) through (g) redesignated as (b) through (f); new (c)(3), (d) and (e) amended; (a) and new (b)(2) revised; interim 14631
- (b)(2)(A), (B) and (C) redesignated as (b)(2)(i), (ii) and (iii); (a) and new (b)(2)(ii) revised 53550
- 330.15 Amended; interim 14631
- 330.16 Removed; interim 14631
- 336.3 (f) revised 20526
- 345.12 (u)(1) revised 78337
- 345.26 (d) added 78337
- 347.202 (u) amended 20527
- 347.209 (a) and (b)(3) amended 20527
- 347.212 (b) amended 20527
- 348.6 (d) amended 20527
- 349 Removed 78338
- 357.1 (a) amended 20527
- 362.1 (d) amended 20527
- 362.2 (p) amended 20527
- 362.3 (a)(2)(iii)(A)(2), (b)(2)(i), (iii)(A) and (B) amended 20527
- 362.4 (b)(1), (3), (5), (6) and (7) amended 20527
- 362.9 (c) amended 20527
- 362.11 Amended 20527
- 362.12 Amended 20527
- 363.1 (b)(3) amended 20527
- 364 Appendix B correctly amended 5780
- Appendix A amended 20527
- 366.3 (d) amended 20527
- 366.5 Introductory text amended 20527
- 367.2 (s)(1) and (3) amended 20527
- 367.6 (d) amended 20528

Chapter IV
- 404 Authority citation revised 14361
- 404.24—404.36 (Subpart C) Added 14361

2007

12 CFR

72 FR Page

Chapter III
- 308 Authority citation revised 67235
- 308.127 (a) revised 67235
- 308.161—308.164 (Subpart N) Revised 67235
- 325 Appendix D added and amended; eff. 4–1–08 69437
- 334 Authority citation revised 62963, 63760
- 334.1 Added 62963

List of CFR Sections Affected

12 CFR—Continued
72 FR Page

Chapter III—Continued
334.3 Introductory text revised 63760
334.20—334.28 (Subpart C) Added 62963
334.80—334.83 (Subpart I) Heading revised 63760
334.82 Added 63760
334.90—334.91 (Subpart J) Added 63760
334 Appendices A, B and C added... 62971
Appendix J added 63762
337 Authority citation revised 17803
337.12 (b) revised; interim.............. 17803
Regulation at 72 FR 17803 confirmed...................................... 54349
344.9 (a)(3) revised........................ 60547
345.12 (u)(1) correctly revised 72573
345.26 (a)(1) heading correctly revised.. 72573
347.211 (b)(1)(i) revised; interim...................................... 17803
Regulation at 72 FR 17803 confirmed...................................... 54349
348.2 (j)(1)(vi) amended; interim 1276
Regulation at 72 FR 1276 confirmed.. 38755
348.3 (b) amended; interim.............. 1276
Regulation at 72 FR 1276 confirmed.. 38755
364 Authority citation revised 63764
364.101 (b) amended 63764
Chapter IV
403.11 (b)(12) amended 66043
407.1 (b) revised; (c) amended.......... 66043
407.2 (a) introductory text amended..................................... 66043
407.3 (a) and (b) amended 66043
407.4 Amended 66043
407.6 Amended 66043
413 Removed.................................. 30244
414 Added 66043

2008

12 CFR
73 FR Page

Chapter III
303 Authority citation revised........ 2145
Regulation at 73 FR 2145 confirmed...................................... 55434
Comment resubmission opportunity.. 63338
303.20 Amended; interim 2145
Regulation at 73 FR 2145 confirmed...................................... 55434

12 CFR—Continued
73 FR Page

Chapter III—Continued
303.41 (a) introductory text revised; interim 35338
(a) revised 55432
303.46 Added; interim 35338
Added 55432
303.61 (b) revised; interim 2145
Regulation at 73 FR 2145 confirmed...................................... 55434
303.63 (d) removed; interim............. 2145
Regulation at 73 FR 2145 confirmed...................................... 55434
308.111 (c) revised; interim.............. 2145
Regulation at 73 FR 2145 confirmed...................................... 55434
308.116 (b)(4) introductory text, (i), (ii), (iii)(A) and (B) correctly amended......................... 73157
308.132 (c)(2)(i) introductory text, (A), (B), (ii), (iii)(B), (C), (3) introductory text, (i) introductory text, (ii), (iii), (vi), (ix), (xiv), (xv) and (xvi) correctly amended; (c)(3)(xvii) correctly added... 73157
309.6 (b)(3) amended; interim 2146
Regulation at 73 FR 2146 confirmed...................................... 55434
325 Technical correction............... 21690
Policy statement 44620
325.5 (g)(5) revised; eff. 1-29-09 79606
327.10 (d) added 78161
327.50—327.54 (Subpart C) Revised.. 73162
330.1 (n) revised; interim 61660
330.7 (d) revised; interim 61660
330.10 Revised; interim 56711
338.4 (b) amended 45855
345.12 (u)(1) revised 78155
352.9 (b) amended 45857
352.10 (c) amended......................... 45857
360.8 Added; interim; eff. in part 7-1-09... 41179
360.9 Added 41195
360 Appendices A through H added... 41197
370 Added; interim........................ 64186
Revised....................................... 72266
370.2 (f) and (g) amended; interim...................................... 66163
370.3 (b) and (f) amended; interim...................................... 66163
370.5 (a), (c), (f), (h) and (j) amended; interim............................... 66163
370.6 (a), (b)(1), (2) and (c) revised; interim....................................... 66163

12 CFR—Continued

73 FR Page

Chapter III—Continued
370.7 (a) and (b) revised; interim 66163
371 Added; eff. 1-21-09 78170

2009

12 CFR

74 FR Page

Chapter III
308 Technical correction 40478
308.604 (c) revised 32245
   (c) correctly revised 35745
325 Appendix A amended; interim 31166
   Appendix A amended 60143
327.3 (a)(1) revised 9550
327.6 (b)(1) revised 9551
327.8 (g), (h), (i), (l) and (m) revised; (o) through (s) added 9551
327.9 Revised 9552
327.10 Revised 9556
327.12 Added 59065
327.1—327.10 (Subpart A) Appendix A revised 9557
   Appendix B revised 9559
   Appendix C revised 9560
327.11 Added 25644
327.15 Added; interim 9341
329.1 (b)(3) revised 47051
329.102 Introductory text revised 47052
330.1 (n) revised 47716
330.7 (d) revised 47716
330.9 (b) revised 47716
330.10 Revised 47716
332.2 Revised 62935
332.6 (b) and (f) revised; (g) added; (g) removed eff. 1-1-12 62935
332.7 (i) added 62936
332 Appendix A redesignated as Appendix B; new Appendix A added 62936
   Appendix B amended; Appendix B removed eff. 1-1-12 62945
334 Authority citation revised 31517
334.40—334.43 (Subpart E) Added 31517
334.82 (a), (b), (c)(2)(i)(A), (d)(1) and (3) amended 22643
334 Appendices C and J amended 22643
   Appendix E added 31518
337 Revised 26520
337.6 (b)(2)(ii)(B) revised; (b)(4) removed; (e) added 26520
   Regulation at 74 FR 26520 withdrawn 27683

12 CFR—Continued

74 FR Page

Chapter III—Continued
   (b)(2)(ii)(B) revised; (b)(4) removed; (e) added 27683
345.12 (u)(1) revised 68664
347.202 (e) revised; (v), (w) and (x) redesignated as (w), (x) and (y); new (v) added 47718
347.206 (c) revised 47718
347.213 (a)(1) revised 47718
347.215 (a) introductory text and (b) revised 47718
360.6 (b) redesignated as (b)(1); (b)(2) added; interim 59068
360.8 Revised 5806
360 Appendices C and F corrected; CFR correction 68499
363 Revised 32245
   Correctly revised 35745
   Technical correction 40478
370.2 (e)(1)(iii) and (m) added; (e)(3) and (5) amended; interim 9524
   (f) and (m) introductory text revised; (n) added; interim 12082
   Regulation at 74 FR 12082 confirmed 26525
   Regulation at 74 FR 9524 confirmed 26945
   (g) and (h)(4) revised 45098
   (n) revised 54747
370.3 (b)(1), (d), (h) heading and (2) revised; (h)(1)(v) added; (h)(3) and (4) amended; interim 9524
   (c) introductory text, (d), (e)(3), (h)(1)(i), (v), (2) through (5) and (i) revised; (h)(1)(vi), (vii), (6) and (j) added; interim 12083
   Regulation at 74 FR 12083 confirmed 26525
   Regulation at 74 FR 9524 confirmed 26945
   (d)(2), (h)(1), (2), (3), (5) and (6) revised; (k) added 54747
370.4 (a) revised 45098
370.5 (h)(2) amended; (j) added; interim 9525
   (b)(1), (f) and (h)(2) through (5) revised; interim 12084
   Regulation at 74 FR 12084 confirmed 26525
   Regulation at 74 FR 9525 confirmed 26945
   (c), (g) and (h)(5) revised 45099
   (f) and (h)(2) revised 54749
370.6 (d)(1) and (5) revised; (d)(3) amended; interim 9525

List of CFR Sections Affected

12 CFR—Continued

74 FR Page

Chapter III—Continued
(c)(2), (d)(1) introductory text, (2) and (4) revised; (d)(3) amended; (g)(4) and (h) added; interim.......12085
Regulation at 74 FR 12085 confirmed......................................26525
Regulation at 74 FR 9524 confirmed......................................26945
(d)(1) revised; (i) added.................54749
370.7 (c) revised............................45099
370.8 Revised; interim...................12085
Regulation at 74 FR 12085 confirmed......................................26525
370.9 Revised; interim...................12085
Regulation at 74 FR 12085 confirmed......................................26525
370.12 (b)(2) amended; interim.........9525
(b)(2) revised; interim...................12085
Regulation at 74 FR 12085 confirmed......................................26525
Regulation at 74 FR 9524 confirmed; (b)(2) revised.................26945

2010

12 CFR

75 FR Page

Chapter III
325 Appendix A amended.........4650, 4651
Appendix D amended.....................4651
327 Authority citation revised.......79293
327.4 (g) revised...............................79293
328.1 (a) amended..........................49365
330.1 (n) revised..............................49365
(r) added....................................69583
330.16 Added..................................69583
335.111 Revised; interim................73949
335.121 Revised; interim................73949
335.201 Revised; interim................73949
335.211 Revised; interim................73949
335.221 Revised; interim................73949
335.231 Revised; interim................73949
335.241 Revised; interim................73949
335.251 Revised; interim................73949
335.261 Revised; interim................73949
335.301 Revised; interim................73949
335.311 Revised; interim................73949
335.321 Revised; interim................73949
335.331 Revised; interim................73949
335.401 Revised; interim................73950
335.501 Revised; interim................73950
335.601 Revised; interim................73950
335.611 Revised; interim................73950
335.612 Revised; interim................73950
335.613 Revised; interim................73950
335.701 Revised; interim................73950
335.801 (b)(1), (2), (6)(iv) and (v) revised; interim............................73951

12 CFR—Continued

75 FR Page

Chapter III—Continued
345 Authority citation revised......61045
345.12 (g)(3) and (4)(iii)(B) amended; (g)(5) added; eff. 1–19–11........79286
(u)(1) revised...............................82219
345.21 (e) and (f) added..................61045
345 Appendix A amended...............61045
347.202 (v) revised..........................49365
360.6 Regulation at 74 FR 59068 confirmed; (b)(2) revised...........12965
Technical correction....................14331
Revised..60297
365 Authority citation revised......44692
Technical correction....................51623
365.1—365.2 (Subpart A) Heading added for new Subpart A............44692
365.1 Moved under new Subpart A; amended.....................................44692
365.2 Moved under new Subpart A 44692
365.1—365.2 (Subpart A) Appendix redesignated from Part 365 Appendix A 44692
365.101—365.105 (Subpart B) Added.......................................44692
365 Appendix A redesignated as Appendix A to new Subpart A; heading revised..........................44692
370.2 (g), (h)(3) and (4) revised; (o) added; interim..........................20263
(o) revised...................................36510
370.4 (a) revised; interim...............20264
370.5 (c)(3) and (g)(3) added; (g)(1) and (h)(5) revised; interim.........20264
(h)(5) revised..............................36510
370.7 (b) and (c) revised; interim...20265
Chapter IV
400 Regulation at 60 FR 17628 confirmed....................................55942

2011

12 CFR

76 FR Page

Chapter III
Chapter III OTS regulations list..39246
309.1 Revised; interim...................35965
309.4 (b) revised; interim...............35965
309.5 (b)(1)(ii), (iii), (f)(4)(ii) and (h)(1) revised; interim...............35965
(b)(1)(ii) amended........................63818
309.6 (b)(3) and (5) introductory text revised; interim................35965
310.1 Revised; interim...................35965
310.3 (b) revised; interim...............35965

1119

12 CFR—Continued

76 FR Page

Chapter III—Continued

Section	Change	Page
310.4	(a) revised; interim	35966
310.7	Revised; interim	35966
310.8	(a) revised; interim	35966
310.9	(a) revised; interim	35966
325	Appendices A and D amended	37629
326.8	Revised	14793
327.4	(c) and (f) revised	10704
327.5	Revised	10704
327.6	Revised	10706
327.8	(e) and (f) removed; (g) through (s) redesignated as new (e) through (q); new (e), (f), (g) and (k) through (p) revised; new (r) through (u) added	10707
327.9	Revised	10708
327.10	Revised	10717
327.1—327.15	(Subpart A) Appendices A, B and C revised	10720
	Appendix D added	10724
	Appendix A correctly amended	17521
327.50	Revised	10725
327.51	Removed	10725
327.52	Removed	10725
327.53	Removed	10725
327.54	Removed	10725
329	Removed	41394
330.1	(r) revised	4816
	(k) through (r) redesignated as (l) through (s); new (k) added	41395
330.6	(b) amended	41395
330.9	(c)(1) amended	41395
330.12	(a) and (b)(1) amended	41395
330.13	(a) amended	41395
330.16	(c)(1) and (2) revised	4816
	(a) amended	41395
330.101	Added	41395
334.82	(c)(2)(i)(A) revised	14794
334	Appendix J amended	14794
335.111	Regulation at 75 FR 73949 confirmed	28169
335.121	Regulation at 75 FR 73949 confirmed	28169
335.201	Regulation at 75 FR 73949 confirmed	28169
335.211	Regulation at 75 FR 73949 confirmed	28169
335.221	Regulation at 75 FR 73949 confirmed	28169

12 CFR—Continued

76 FR Page

Chapter III—Continued

Section	Change	Page
335.231	Regulation at 75 FR 73949 confirmed	28169
335.241	Regulation at 75 FR 73949 confirmed	28169
335.251	Regulation at 75 FR 73949 confirmed	28169
335.261	Regulation at 75 FR 73949 confirmed	28169
335.301	Regulation at 75 FR 73949 confirmed	28169
335.311	Regulation at 75 FR 73949 confirmed	28169
335.321	Regulation at 75 FR 73949 confirmed	28169
335.331	Regulation at 75 FR 73949 confirmed	28169
335.401	Regulation at 75 FR 73950 confirmed	28169
335.501	Regulation at 75 FR 73950 confirmed	28169
335.601	Regulation at 75 FR 73950 confirmed	28169
335.611	Regulation at 75 FR 73950 confirmed	28169
335.612	Regulation at 75 FR 73950 confirmed	28169
335.613	Regulation at 75 FR 73950 confirmed	28169
335.701	Regulation at 75 FR 73950 confirmed	28169
335.801	Regulation at 75 FR 73951 confirmed	28169
345.12	(u)(1) revised	79531
	(u)(1) correctly revised; CFR correction	81789
349	Added	40789
360	Authority citation revised	58389
360.10	Added; interim	58389
380	Added; interim	4215
	Authority citation revised	41639
380.1—380.9	(Subpart A) Designated as Subpart A; heading added	41639
380.1	Revised	41639
380.2	Removed	41640
380.3	Revised	41640
380.4	Removed	41640
380.5	Revised	41640
380.6	Revised	41640
380.7	Added	41640
380.9	Added	41641

List of CFR Sections Affected

12 CFR—Continued

76 FR Page

Chapter III—Continued
380.20—380.29 (Subpart B)
　　Added 41642
380.30—380.53 (Subpart C)
　　Added 41644

12 CFR—Continued

76 FR Page

Chapter III—Continued
381　Added 67340
390　Added 47665
391　Added 47665